Common Law Library



# Chitty on Contracts

**VOLUMES IN THE COMMON LAW LIBRARY**

Arlidge, Eady & Smith on Contempt
Benjamin's Sale of Goods
Bowstead & Reynolds on Agency
Bullen & Leake & Jacob's Precedents of Pleadings
Charlesworth & Percy on Negligence
Chitty on Contracts
Clerk & Lindsell on Torts
Gatley on Libel and Slander
Goff & Jones, The Law of Restitution
Jackson & Powell on Professional Negligence
McGregor on Damages
Phipson on Evidence

COMMON LAW LIBRARY

# CHITTY ON CONTRACTS

SECOND CUMULATIVE SUPPLEMENT TO THE THIRTY-THIRD EDITION

Up-to-date with material available by July 31, 2020

SWEET & MAXWELL

THOMSON REUTERS

Published in 2020 by Thomson Reuters,
trading as Sweet & Maxwell. Thomson Reuters is registered in England & Wales, Company No. 1679046.
Registered office and address for service: 5 Canada Square, Canary Wharf, London E14 5AQ.

For further information on our products and services, visit *http://www.sweetandmaxwell.co.uk*.

Computerset by Sweet & Maxwell.
Printed and bound by CPI Group (UK) Ltd Croydon, CR0 4YY.
No natural forests were destroyed to make this product; only farmed timber was used and re-planted.
A CIP catalogue record of this book is available from the British Library.

ISBN Main Work (full set): 9780414065130

ISBN Supplement (print): 9780414081512

ISBN Supplement (e-book): 9780414081598

ISBN Supplement (print and e-book): 9780414081581

*GENERAL EDITOR*

H. G. Beale, Q.C. (Hon.), B.A., F.B.A.
*Honorary Bencher of Lincoln's Inn; Emeritus Professor of Law, University of Warwick; Senior Research Fellow of Harris Manchester College and Visiting Professor, University of Oxford*

*EDITORS*

JEREMIAS F.B.B. ADAMS-PRASSL, M.A., D.Phil (Oxon), LL.M. (Harvard)
*Fellow of Magdalen College and Professor of Law, University of Oxford*

MINDY CHEN-WISHART, BA (Hons), LL.B., LL.M. (Otago), MA (Oxon)
*Fellow of Merton College, Professor of the Law of Contract, and Dean of the Faculty of Law, University of Oxford*

PAUL S. DAVIES, M.A., Ph.D. (Cantab.)
*of Lincoln's Inn, Barrister; Professor of Commercial Law, University College London*

M. R. FREEDLAND, Q.C. (Hon.), LL.B., M.A., D.Phil., F.B.A.
*Bencher of Gray's Inn; Emeritus Research Fellow of St John's College and Emeritus Professor of Employment Law, University of Oxford*

R. J. A. HOOLEY, M.A. (Cantab.)
*of the Middle Temple, Barrister; Fellow of Fitzwilliam College and University Lecturer, University of Cambridge*

EVA LOMNICKA, Q.C. (Hon), M.A. (Cantab.), LL.B. (Cantab.)
*Bencher of the Middle Temple; Professor of Law, King's College London*

DAVID McCLEAN, C.B.E., Q.C. (Hon.), D.C.L., Hon.Litt.D., F.B.A.
*Bencher of Gray's Inn; Emeritus Professor of Law, University of Sheffield*

P. J. S. MACDONALD EGGERS, Q.C., LL.B. (Syd.), LL.M. (Cantab.)
*of the Middle Temple, Barrister; Visiting Professor, University College London*

E. G. McKENDRICK, Q.C. (Hon.), LL.B., B.C.L., M.A.
*Bencher of Gray's Inn; Fellow of Lady Margaret Hall, Professor of English Private Law, University of Oxford*

L. MERRETT, M.A., Ph.D. (Cantab.)
*of Gray's Inn, Barrister; Fellow of Trinity College and Reader in International Commercial Law, University of Cambridge*

P. P. MITCHELL, B.A., D.Phil. (Oxon)
*Professor of Laws, University College London*

VINCENT MORAN, Q.C., M.A. (Cantab.)
*Bencher of Gray's Inn, Barrister*

MATTHEW O'REGAN, LL.B. (Nottingham), LL.M. (Amsterdam)
*of the Middle Temple, Barrister*

D. D. PRENTICE, LL.B., J.D., M.A.
*of Lincoln's Inn, Barrister; Emeritus Fellow of Pembroke College and formerly Allen & Overy Professor of Corporate Law, University of Oxford*

F. M. B. REYNOLDS, Q.C. (Hon.), D.C.L., F.B.A.
*Barrister and Honorary Bencher of the Inner Temple; Emeritus Fellow of Worcester College and Professor of Law Emeritus, University of Oxford*

G. J. VIRGO, Q.C. (Hon.), M.A. (Cantab.), B.C.L. (Oxon)
*Bencher of Lincoln's Inn; Fellow of Downing College, Senior Pro-Vice-Chancellor (Education) and Professor of English Private Law, University of Cambridge*

WILLIAM WEBB, B.A. (Cantab.), LL.M. (Virginia), B.C.L. (Oxon)
*of Lincoln's Inn, Barrister*

SIMON WHITTAKER, D.Phil., D.C.L. (Oxon)
*of Lincoln's Inn, Barrister; Fellow of St John's College and Professor of European Comparative Law, University of Oxford*

# HOW TO USE THIS SUPPLEMENT

This is the Second Cumulative Supplement to the Thirty-third Edition of *Chitty on Contracts*, and has been compiled according to the structure of the main work.

At the beginning of each chapter of this Supplement, a mini table of contents of the sections in the main volume has been included. Where a heading in this table of contents has been marked with a square pointer, this indicates that there is relevant information in this Supplement to which the reader should refer. Material that is new to the Cumulative Supplement is indicated by the symbol ■. Material that has been included from the previous supplement is indicated by the symbol □.

Within each chapter, updating information is referenced to the relevant paragraph in the main volume.

It should be noted that for this Supplement there is no material for Chapter 41.

The original text of Chapters 4, 18 and 41 was prepared by the late Professor Sir Guenter Treitel; Chapters 4 and 18 have been supplemented by Paul S. Davies. The original text of Chapter 8 was prepared by Hugh Beale and supplemented by Mindy Chen-Wishart. The original text of Chapters 17, 19 and 28 were prepared by Andrew Burrows and supplemented by Hugh Beale. The original text of Chapter 43 was prepared by Richard Whish and supplemented by Matthew O'Regan.

Please note that in this supplement we have included included a vertical side-line to indicate new material or changes to the text of a paragraph or a footnote in the Main Work.

# TABLE OF CONTENTS

VOLUME 1

# TABLE OF STATUTES

Where a reference indicates significant discussion of the statute in the text, it is in **bold**. Where a reference is to a footnote, it is *italic*.

# TABLE OF STATUTORY INSTRUMENTS

Where a reference indicates significant discussion of the statute in the text, it is in **bold**. Where a reference is to a footnote, it is *italic*.

# TABLE OF EUROPEAN UNION LEGISLATION

Where a reference indicates significant discussion of the legislation in the text, it is in **bold**. Where a reference is to a footnote, it is *italic*.

**REGULATIONS**

**DIRECTIVES**

# TABLE OF INTERNATIONAL STATUTORY MATERIAL

Where a reference indicates significant discussion of the statute in the text, it is in **bold**. Where a reference is to a footnote, it is *italic*.

# TABLE OF CASES

*Where a reference indicates significant discussion of the case in the text, it is in* **bold**. *Where a reference is to a footnote, it is* italic

# TABLE OF EU CASES

Where a reference indicates significant discussion of the case in the text, it is in **bold**. Where a reference is to a footnote, it is *italic*.

Chapter 1

# INTRODUCTORY

## 1. SOURCES OF ENGLISH CONTRACT LAW

### The different sources of contract law

*Replace paragraph with:*

**1-002** English contract law in this usual sense possesses four legal sources: common law, statute, international convention and (at least historically) EU law.[3]

[3] On the sources of English law more generally see J. Bell, "The Sources of Law" in A. Burrows (ed.) *English Private Law*, 2nd edn (2007), Ch.1. In the case of EU law, its importance is as a source of English contract law while the UK was a Member State of the EU and also during the transitional ("implementation") period put in place by the Withdrawal Agreement between the UK and the EU. On this see below, paras 1-014 et seq.

## (b) Statute

### Consumer contracts

*Replace paragraph with:*

**1-008** Consumer contracts have long been the object of legislative intervention, with special rules governing exemption clauses,[38] unfair contract terms more generally[39] and aspects of particular types of consumer contract (such as consumer credit,[40] sale of goods,[41] package holiday contracts[42] or timeshare contracts[43]). There have also been information requirements for contracts concluded in certain circumstances (notably "doorstep selling"[44] and "distance contracts"[45]), with accompanying short-lived rights of cancellation for the consumer. Earlier legislation was scattered across a series of legislative instruments (some primary legislation, some secondary) and formed part of and/or overlapped with protective rules which could apply other than for the benefit of consumers.[46] Moreover, the key definitions of the person protected (the consumer) and the other party to the contract (the party acting in the course of business) differed between the various legislative instruments.[47] However, over the last decade legislation has sought to address the problems of inconsistency between consumer protection legislative instruments and has also sought to mark a clear separation between legislation governing consumer contracts and legislation governing contracts more generally. The central pillar of this recast legislative framework is the Consumer Rights Act 2015, whose most important provisions provide for a set of statutory terms governing consumer "goods contracts", "digital content contracts" and "services contracts" (with sets of special remedies for their breach) and which also provide for the control of unfair terms.[48] At the same time, the 2015 Act amended earlier, more general, statutes (notably the Misrepresentation Act 1967, the Unfair Contract Terms Act 1977 and the Sale of Goods Act 1979) so that their provisions do not apply where the provisions of the 2015 Act apply.[49] Moreover, other legislation has reshaped and extended earlier legislative controls so as to place *most* of the information duties on traders in a single set of statutory regulations[50] and to create new rights to redress for certain unfair commercial practices committed by a trader.[51] The overall result is the creation of a distinct and distinctive body of statutory law governing "consumer contracts" paralleling (but separated from) the law applicable more generally, whether statutory or common law.[52] Having said that, however, this body of consumer contract law by no means provides a complete legislative regime governing consumer contracts. First, a good deal of legislation specifically governing consumer contracts remains outside the four main relevant legislative instruments,[53] including the very important Consumer Credit Act 1974[54] and legislation governing consumer insurance contracts.[55] Secondly, even for those types of contract where the Consumer Rights Act 2015 provides discrete rules (notably governing sales of goods to consumers), wider general legislation still applies to issues *not* regulated by those discrete rules.[56] And, thirdly, many issues arising between parties to a consumer contract (or a would-be consumer contract) are not governed by legislation at all and where this is the case the common law rules (whether applicable to contracts generally or to specific types of contract) apply. These relatively recent patterns of legislation governing consumer contracts are the subject of Ch.38 in Vol.II of the present work.[57]

[38] Unfair Contract Terms Act 1977 ss.3–5, 6(2) and 7(2), 12 (as enacted) on which see below, paras 15-062 et seq.

[39] Unfair Terms in Consumer Contracts Regulations 1999 (SI 1999/2083) on which see Vol.II, paras 38-220 et seq.

[40] See Consumer Credit Act 1974 and Vol.II, Ch.39.

[41] See notably, Sale of Goods Act 1979 Pt 5A as inserted by Sale and Supply of Goods to Consumers Regulations 2002 (SI 2002/3045) on which see Vol.II, paras 38-439 et seq.

[42] Package Travel, Package Holidays and Package Tours Regulations 1992 (SI 1992/3288) replaced by the Package Travel and Linked Travel Arrangements Regulations 2018 (SI 2018/634) (in force July 1, 2018) on which see Vol.II, paras 38-137—38-141.

[43] Timeshare, Holiday Products, Resale and Exchange Contracts Regulations 2010 (SI 2010/2960) (replacing earlier provisions) on which see Vol.II, paras 38-148—38-154.

[44] Consumer Protection (Cancellation of Contracts Concluded Away from Business Premises) Regulations 1987 (SI 1987/2117).

[45] Consumer Protection (Distance Selling) Regulations 2000 (SI 2000/2334); Financial Services (Distance Marketing) Regulations 2004 (SI 2004/2095) (on which see Vol.II, para.38-136).

[46] This was notably the case as regards the Misrepresentation Act 1967 and the Unfair Contract Terms Act 1977.

[47] A key example was the definition of a person "dealing as consumer" within the meaning of the Unfair Contract Terms Act 1977 and "consumer" within the meaning of the Unfair Terms in Consumer Contracts Regulations 1999: see below, paras 15-073—15-079 and Vol.II, paras 38-030 et seq.

[48] See Vol.II, paras 38-365—38-426, 38-432—38-587. The Consumer Rights Act 2015 Pts 1 and 2 came into force generally on October 1, 2015: see Vol.II, paras 38-216 and 38-366.

[49] For the details see below, paras 15-064 et seq. and Vol.II, paras 38-367—38-375 and 38-470—38-476.

[50] Consumer Contracts (Information, Cancellation and Additional Charges) Regulations 2013 (SI 2013/3134) on which see Vol.II, paras 38-059 et seq.

[51] Consumer Protection (Amendment) Regulations 2014 (SI 2014/870) inserting, notably, new Pt 4A Consumers' Rights to Redress in Consumer Protection from Unfair Trading Regulations 2008 (SI 2008/1277), on which see Vol.II, paras 38-157 et seq.

[52] On the distinctive features of modern consumer contract law see Whittaker (2017) 133 L.Q.R. 47.

[53] Consumer Protection from Unfair Trading Regulations 2008; Consumer Contracts (Information, Cancellation and Additional Charges) Regulations 2013; Consumer Rights Act 2015.

[54] See Vol.II, Ch.39.

[55] Consumer Insurance (Disclosure and Representations) Act 2012; Insurance Act 2015 and see Vol.II, paras 42-046 et seq.

[56] See Vol. II, paras 38-471—38-476.

[57] Vol.II, Ch.38.

## (d) EU Law

### *(i) The Current Position*

*The title of sub-section (i) should be changed to:*

The Development of a "European Contract Law" and its Historical Importance for English law

**EU law governing contracts: the Union acquis**

*Replace paragraph with:*

**1-011** Various elements of EU law have affected the conclusion and the regulation of contracts by English law. As regards the Treaties themselves, one prominent area is the law of competition, which has both a general impact on the environment within which contracts are made and which holds certain categories of contract or contract term unlawful.[63] EU legislation (principally in the form of directives) has also regulated aspects of a number of types of contract. Consumer contracts have been an important object of attention, with directives requiring rules controlling the fairness of most of their standard terms, rules governing aspects of contracts made in certain circumstances (as with "distance contracts" or "off-premises contracts") and of certain types (sale of goods, consumer credit, time-share and package holidays).[64] Outside the consumer context, directives have required rules governing commercial agency contracts[65] and particular aspects of commercial contracts in general (notably, as regards late payment of commercial debts).[66] The public procurement directives have had a major impact on the process of public contracting[67]; and a series of employment directives have created or reshaped rights of employees in a number of ways.[68] EU law instruments have also an important impact on international jurisdiction and applicable law in the area of contract law.[69] This catalogue illustrates, however, that EU legislation harmonising contract law has been piecemeal, targeting particular situations or particular aspects of the rules governing contracts.

[63] Notably, as being an "agreement between undertakings ... which may affect trade between Member States and which [has] as [its] object or effect the prevention, restriction or distortion of competition within the internal market": art.101 TFEU (ex art.81 EC). On this law, see generally Vol.II, Ch.43, especially paras 43-004 et seq.

[64] Directive 93/13/EEC of April 5, 1993 on unfair terms in consumer contracts [1993] O.J. L95/29 (see Vol.II, paras 38-218—38-219); Directive 97/7/EC on the protection of consumers in respect of distance

contracts [1997] O.J. L144/19; Directive 85/577/EEC to protect the consumer in respect of contracts negotiated away from business premises [1985] O.J. L372/31 (the latter two of which were revoked and replaced by Directive 2011/83/EU on consumer rights [2011] O.J. L304/64) (see Vol.II, paras 38-060—38-065); Directive 99/44/EC on certain aspects of the sale of consumer goods and associated guarantees [1999] O.J. L171/7 (see Vol.II, paras 38-433—38-435 though repealed and replaced by Directive (EU) 2019/770 of the European Parliament and of the Council of 20 May 2019 [2019] O.J. L.136/1 (to be implemented by January 1, 2022, on which see Vol.II, para.38-436); Directive 2002/65/EC concerning the distance marketing of consumer financial services [2002] O.J. L271/16 (see Vol.II, para.38-136); Directive 2005/29/EC concerning unfair business-to-consumer commercial practices in the internal market [2005] O.J. L149/22 (see Vol.II, paras 38-159—38-164); Directive 2008/48/EC on credit agreements for consumers and repealing Council Directive 87/102/EEC [2008] O.J. L133/66 below, Vol.II, para.39-011; Directive 2008/122/EC on the protection of consumers in respect of certain aspects of timeshare, long-term holiday product, resale and exchange contracts [2009] O.J. L33/30 (see Vol.II, para.38-148); Directive 90/314/EEC of June 13, 1990 on package travel, package holidays and package tours [1990] O.J. L158/59 itself repealed and replaced by Directive 2015/2302/EU on package travel and linked travel arrangements [2015] O.J. L326/1 as from July 1, 2018 (arts 28 and 29) (see Vol.II, paras 38-137 et seq.); Regulation (EC) 261/2004 establishing common rules on compensation and assistance to passengers in the event of denied boarding and of cancellation or long delay of flights [2004] O.J. L46/1 (see Vol.II, paras 35–071—35–073); Directive 2014/17/EU on credit agreements for consumers relating to residential immovable property [2014] O.J. L2014/34 on which see Vol.II, paras 39-003 and 39-531.

65 Council Directive 86/653/EEC on the coordination of the laws of the Member States relating to self-employed commercial agents [1986] O.J. L382/17: see Vol.II, paras 31-017—31-020.

66 Directive 2011/7/EU on combating late payment in commercial transactions [2011] O.J. L48/1 (replacing Directive 2000/35/EC on combating late payment in commercial transactions). The 2011 Directive is implemented in UK law by the Late Payment of Commercial Debts (Interest) Act 1998 as amended by SI 2013/395, SI 2015/1336 and SI 2018/117 on which see below, paras 26-277—26-280.

67 In 2004 these were placed into the "Legislative package": Directive 2004/18/EC of the European Parliament and of the Council of March 31, 2004 on the co-ordination of procedures for the award of public works contracts, public supply contracts and public service contracts [2004] O.J. L134/114; Directive 2004/17/EC of the European Parliament and of the Council of March 31, 2004 co-ordinating the procurement procedures of entities operating in the water, energy, transport and postal services sectors [2004] O.J. L134/1. As from April 18, 2016, the two 2004 directives were repealed and replaced by Directive 2014/24/EU on public procurement and repealing Directive 2004/18/EC [2014] O.J. L94/65 (see esp. art.91) and Directive 2014/25/EU on procurement by entities operating in the water, energy, transport and postal services sectors and repealing Directive 2004/17/EC [2014] O.J. L94/243 (see esp. art.107), which were supplemented by Directive 2014/23/EU on the award of concession contracts [2014] O.J. L94/1. On these see below, paras 11-052—11-053.

68 See Vol.II, Ch.40 especially paras 40-039, 40-112, 40-136, 40-156, 40-157, 40-173, 40-180 and 40-246.

69 Regulation 44/2001 on jurisdiction and the recognition and enforcement of judgments in civil and commercial matters [2001] O.J. L12/1 (the "Brussels I Regulation"), especially arts 5(1) (special jurisdiction in "matters relating to a contract"), 8–14 (matters relating to insurance), 15–17 (jurisdiction over consumer contracts), 18–21 (jurisdiction over individual contracts of employment), 23 (jurisdiction agreements). The Brussels I Regulation was itself replaced as from January 10, 2015 by Regulation (EU) 1215/2012 of December 12, 2012 on jurisdiction and the recognition and enforcement of judgments in civil and commercial matters (recast) ("the Brussels Ibis Regulation"). See also Regulation 593/2008 on the law applicable to contractual obligations ("Rome I") [2008] O.J. L177/6, on which see below, paras 30-018 et seq. For the effect of the UK's leaving the EU on "exit day" on these private international law instruments see below, para.1-016C.

## The Proposed Common European Sales Law (CESL)

*Replace footnote 89 with:*

89 European Commission, Annex 2 to the *Commission Work Programme 2015* COM(2014) 910 final, p.12. See also the Communication from the Commission, *A Digital Single Market Strategy for Europe* 2015 COM(2015) 192 final, pp.4–5. One expression of this strategy may be found in the enactment of Directive (EU) 2019/771 on certain aspects concerning contracts for the sale of goods etc of the European Parliament and of the Council of 20 May 2019 [2019] O.J. L136/28 and Directive (EU) 2019/770 on certain aspects concerning contracts for the supply of digital content and digital services of the European Parliament and of the Council of 20 May 2019 [2019] O.J. L136/1, on which see Vol.II, para.38-436. **1-013**

### (ii) *United Kingdom's Exit from the EU ("Brexit")*

1-014 *Change title of paragraph:*

**Background**

*Replace paragraph with:*

1-014 After a national referendum held on June 23, 2016 at which a majority voted in favour of the UK leaving the EU, the UK Conservative Government formed on July 16, 2016 declared its intention to end the UK's membership of the EU ("Brexit") and on March 29, 2017 the then Prime Minister, the Right Hon. Mrs Theresa May MP, set in motion the process of doing so under art.50 of the Treaty of the European Union (TEU).[94] The Conservative Government set out its intentions as to the position of existing EU law in the UK in two white papers, *The United Kingdom's exit from and new partnership with the European Union*[95] and *Legislating for the United Kingdom's withdrawal from the European Union*.[96]

[94] The Prime Minister's authority to do so was given by the European Union (Notification of Withdrawal) Act 2017 s.1.

[95] Department for Exiting the European Union, Cm.9417 (February 2017).

[96] Department for Exiting the European Union, Cm.9446 (March 2017).

**European Union (Withdrawal) Act 2018**

*Replace paragraph with:*

1-015 After a general election held on June 8, 2017, the Conservative Government formed by Mrs May remained in office. On June 26, 2018 the European Union (Withdrawal) Act 2018 ("2018 Act") received Royal Assent. The 2018 Act made provision for repeal of the European Communities Act 1972 and further provision in connection with the withdrawal of the UK from the EU.[97] The Act was accompanied by Explanatory Notes ("Explanatory Notes to the 2018 Act"). The Act made detailed provision for the coming into force of its own provisions,[98] but the intention at the time was that the UK would leave the EU on March 29, 2019 ("exit day").[98a] Mrs May's government made an agreement with the EU Council on November 25, 2018 relating to the withdrawal of the UK from the EU, but this agreement was not approved by the UK Parliament. The UK and the European Council therefore agreed a first extension (until April 12, 2019 at the latest)[98b] and then a second, flexible extension with a cut-off of October 31, 2019. The 2018 Act was therefore amended so as to redefine "exit day" as October 31, 2019 at 11pm.[98c] On May 24, 2019 Mrs May announced her resignation as Prime Minister and on July 24, 2019 the Right Hon. Mr Boris Johnson MP became Prime Minister.

[97] 2018 Act s.25 makes detailed provision for the coming into force of its own provisions.

[98] See 2018 Act s.25.

[98a] 2018 Act s.20(1) "exit day".

[98b] Put into effect in the UK by the European Union (Withdrawal) Act (Exit Day) (Amendment) Regulations 2019 (SI 2019/718).

[98c] European Union (Withdrawal) Act 2018 (Exit Day) (Amendment) (No. 2) Regulations 2019 (SI 2019/859) reg.2(2).

*Add new paragraphs:*

**The Withdrawal Agreement between the UK and the EU and the European Union (Withdrawal Agreement) Act 2020** The UK Government formed by Mr Johnson agreed a further extension of the withdrawal period with the European Council until 11.00pm on January 31, 2020.[98d] The UK Government then concluded a Withdrawal Agreement with the EU under which the UK left the EU from 11.00pm on January 31, 2020 ("exit day").[98e] It was further agreed between the UK and the EU that there would be a transition period running from exit day until 11pm on December 31, 2020[98f] under which EU law would still apply in the UK (with certain exceptions)[98g] and 1-015A

> "shall produce in respect of and in the United Kingdom the same legal effects as those which it produces within the Union and its Member States, and shall be interpreted and applied in accordance with the same methods and general principles as those applicable within the Union."[98h]

This effect was achieved as a matter of UK law by the amendment of the 2018 Act by the European Union (Withdrawal Agreement) Act 2020 ("2020 Act"), which refers to the transition period as the "implementation period" ("IP") and the date on which it expires as "IP completion day".[98i]

As a result, the 2020 Act postponed the effect of the 2018 Act until the end of the implementation period (December 31, 2020).[98j] During that period, therefore, EU law still has effect in the UK.[98k] In particular, the European Communities Act 1972 is "saved" for the implementation period[98l]; and both directly applicable EU law and EU-derived domestic legislation which "has effect in the UK as it has effect in domestic law immediately before exit day, continues to have effect in domestic law on and after exit day".[98m] Moreover, this means that the EU-derived legislation which is brought across to form part of UK domestic law as "retained EU law" after the end of the implementation period (as will be explained below[98n]) refers to that legislation which is operative immediately before the end of the implementation period (IP completion day) rather than immediately before exit day.[98o] On the other hand, this also means that in principle directly applicable EU law coming into force *after* IP completion day will not form part of "retained EU law"; nor as presently provided is the UK under any obligation to implement any EU Directive which requires Member States to adopt measures to implement it *after* IP completion day.[98p] The latter includes, for example, the EU Directive of 2019 governing certain aspects of the law governing consumer contracts for the sale of goods (and repealing the Consumer Sales Directive 1999[98q]) which is not due to be implemented until July 1, 2021[98r] and the EU Directive of 2019 on the better enforcement of consumer protection rules which is not due to be implemented until November 28, 2021.[98s] However, this position could change if the date of IP completion day were to be put back or if these matters were included within any agreement made between the UK and the EU as to their future relationship. And it would of course remain open to the UK legislator itself to choose to amend its domestic law (whether or not that law forms part of "retained EU law") in a way or in a similar way as is required by an EU directive.

[98d] The request by the UK for an extension was mandated by the European Union (Withdrawal) (No. 2) Act 2019.

98e Agreement on the Withdrawal of the United Kingdom of Great Britain and Northern Ireland from the European Union and the European Atomic Energy Community (January 24, 2020) (the "Withdrawal Agreement 2020") art.185.

98f Under the Withdrawal Agreement 2020 art.132, this period may be extended for one or two years if agreed by a "Joint Committee" by July 1, 2020, but as a matter of UK law, the European Union (Withdrawal) Act 2018 s.15A as inserted by the European Union (Withdrawal Agreement) Act 2020 s.33 prohibits UK ministers agreeing such an extension. No such extension had been agreed by July 1, 2020.

98g Withdrawal Agreement 2020 art.127(1).

98h Withdrawal Agreement 2020 art.127(3).

98i 2018 Act s.1A(6) (as inserted by the 2020 Act s.1) referring for "IP completion day" to the 2020 Act s.39(1)–(5).

98j On the earlier possibility of changing this date, see note, above in this paragraph.

98k See, e.g. the guidance from the Competition and Markets Authority in CMA, *UK exit from the EU, Guidance on the functions of the CMA under the Withdrawal Agreement* (CMA113, January 28, 2020) ("CMA Guidance 2020"), paras 2.15–2.21.

98l 2018 Act s.1A (as inserted by 2020 Act s.1) (as in force January 31, 2020). The remainder of s.1A explains and qualifies this general position. On IP completion day (i.e. December 31, 2020), s.1A is subject to further amendment by which s.1A(1)–(4) are repealed.

98m 2018 Act s.1B(2) (as inserted by 2020 Act s.2) (in force January 31, 2020). The remainder of s.1B explains and qualifies this general position.

98n Below, paras 1-016 et seq.

98o CMA Guidance 2020, para.2.19.

98p This follows from the Withdrawal Agreement itself, as art.127(3) states that the EU law which generally applies to the UK during the transition "shall produce in respect of and in the United Kingdom the same legal effects as those which it produces within the Union and its Member States".

98q Directive 1999/44/EC on certain aspects of the sale of consumer goods and associated guarantees [1999] O.J. L171/12, on which see Vol.II, paras 38-433—38-435.

98r Directive (EU) 2019/771 of the European Parliament and of the Council of 20 May 2019 on certain aspects concerning contracts for the sale of goods, etc [2019] O.J. L136/28, art.24.

98s Directive (EU) 2019/2161 of the European Parliament and of the Council of 27 November 2019 amending Council Directive 93/13/EEC and Directives 98/6/EC, 2005/29/EC and 2011/83/EU of the European Parliament and of the Council as regards the better enforcement and modernisation of Union consumer protection rules [2019] O.J. L328/7.

1-015B **English contract law after the end of the implementation period** In terms of the impact of the UK leaving the EU on English contract law after the end of the transition (or implementation) period on IP completion day, there are two sets of legislative sources which should be considered. First, there are the terms of the 2018 Act itself (as amended or to be amended by the 2020 Act where this applies) which seeks to give effect to a general policy of the preservation of the UK's EU legislative acquis while making provision for the amendment and, where necessary, replacement of certain legislative instruments or particular legislative provisions in the light of the UK's leaving the EU.[98t] Secondly, there are a considerable number of statutory instruments made under the 2018 Act, many of these being made at a time when it was unclear whether the UK would leave the EU with or without an agreement. The following paragraphs (as updated in July 2020) will note the general approach of the 2018 Act (as amended or to be amended[98u]) to the EU legislative acquis and provide examples of the changes foreseen by statutory instruments made under the 2018 Act affecting the UK legislation.

98t The powers to make these amendments are contained in the 2018 Act s.8.

98u Some of the amendments to the 2018 Act foreseen by the 2020 Act are not yet brought into force.

*Change title of paragraph:* 1-016

**The general preservation of the UK's EU legislative acquis on "IP completion day"**

*Replace paragraph with:*

At the end of the implementation period ("IP completion day", set as December 31, 2020[99]), the saving provisions introduced by the 2020 Act will themselves be repealed with the effect, inter alia, that the repeal of the European Communities Act 1972 which took place on "exit day" will take effect.[100] However, despite this fully effective repeal of the 1972 Act, the 2018 Act will in principle retain the EU legislative acquis as part of UK law after IP completion day. Taken together the resulting body of laws is referred to by the 2018 Act as "retained EU law".[101] There are, however, two types of qualifications on this position. First, the 2018 Act itself sets out certain exceptions for this purpose.[102] Secondly, the 2018 Act provides for the amendment or repeal of legislation (primary or secondary) whose source is in EU legislation, distinguishing for this purpose between "retained direct principal EU legislation" and "retained direct minor EU legislation".[103] In the course of 2018 and 2019 a considerable body of subordinate legislation was made under the 2018 Act as enacted for this purpose, and in the context of contracts these instruments have in common that their operative provisions were generally expressed as due to come into force on "exit day".[104] As earlier noted, the definition of "exit day" changed and is now set as January 31, 2020, but the text of these earlier subordinate instruments has not been changed. Instead, the 2020 Act states that any subordinate legislation made under the 2018 Act or any other enactment 1-016

> "which provides, by reference to exit day (however expressed), for all or part of that or any other subordinate legislation to come into force immediately before exit day, on exit day or at any time after exit day is to be read instead as providing for the subordinate legislation or (as the case may be) the part to come into force immediately before IP completion day, on IP completion day or (as the case may be) at the time concerned after IP completion day."[105]

Subordinate legislation made under the 2018 Act after EU exit day is sometimes expressed directly as coming into force by reference to IP completion day.[106] What remains unclear at the time of writing is whether any of these statutory instruments amending retained EU law will be affected by any agreement between the UK and the EU as to their future relationship.

[99] 2018 Act s.1A(6) (as inserted by the 2020 Act s.1) referring for "IP completion day" to s.39(1)–(5) of the 2020 Act. For the possibility of this changing see above, para.1-015A, note.

[100] 2018 Act s.1 states that "[t]he European Communities Act 1972 is repealed on exit day"; the operative provisions saving the 1972 Act in s.1A(1)–(4) are repealed on IP completion day: s.1A(5).

[101] 2018 Act s.6(7) (as amended by the 2020 Act s.26(1)(a), in force for this purpose on January 31, 2020) defines "retained EU law" by reference to "anything which, on or after IP completion day, continues to be, or forms part of, domestic law by virtue of" ss.2, 3, 4 or 6(3) or (6) of the Act, "as that body of law is added to or otherwise modified by or under the Act or by other domestic law from time to time".

[102] 2018 Act s.5 (exceptions provided by the Act itself, e.g. s.5(4) states that "the Charter of Fundamental Rights is not part of domestic law on or after exit day"). As in force at the time of writing (August 4, 2020), s.5 refers to "exit day", but these references are due to be amended by the 2020 Act to "IP completion day" on a day to be appointed: 2020 Act s.25(4)(a).

[103] 2018 Act ss.7 and 8 (with amendments made and pending under the 2020 Act). Section 7(6) defines "retained direct principal EU legislation" and "retained direct minor EU legislation" for this purpose,

"retained direct EU legislation" being defined by s.20(1) as any direct EU legislation which forms part of domestic law by virtue of s.3 (as modified) and s.7(1)–(5) provides for the modification of these two categories of retained direct legislation itself and by reference to other powers in the Act.

104 Where appropriate, the amending secondary legislation provides that relevant provisions leave unaffected contracts entered into before "exit day". For example, the Consumer Protection (Amendment etc.) (EU Exit) Regulations 2018 (SI 2018/1326) reg.1(3) provides that most of its Parts come into effect on "exit day" (which must be read to refer to IP completion day: 2020 Act s.39(1), Sch.5 para.1). The 2018 Regulations reg.11 later provides that "nothing in regulation 3 [which amends the Consumer Rights Act 2015] or regulation 6(2) [which amends the Consumer Protection from Unfair Trading Regulations 2008] applies to a contract entered into before exit day" (the reference to "exit day" is due to be replaced by "IP completion day"; Consumer Protection (Enforcement) (Amendment etc.) (EU Exit) Regulations 2020 (Draft) Pt 3 reg.4(8)). On these amendments see below, Vol.II, paras 38-465 (note) and 38-165 (note) respectively.

105 2020 Act s.39(1), Sch.5 para.1. Schedule 5 makes further provision regarding, in particular, exceptions to be made to this general position.

106 e.g. the Draft Alternative Dispute Resolution for Consumer Disputes (Extension of Time Limits for Legal Proceedings) (Amendment etc.) (EU Exit) Regulations 2020 reg.1(2) providing that the Regulations generally come into force on IP completion day.

*Add new paragraphs:*

1-016A **Examples from the law governing contracts** The 2018 Act distinguishes three categories of legislation which forms part of or which is derived from EU law.[107]

107 2018 Act ss.2 and 3 (as prospectively amended by the 2020 Act and coming into force on a day to be appointed: 2018 Act s.25(4)).

1-016B First, in principle "EU-derived domestic legislation, as it has effect in domestic law immediately before IP completion day, continues to have effect in domestic law on and after IP completion day".[108] This provision in principle preserves important UK consumer protection legislation affecting, for example, consumer contracts enacted as secondary legislation under the European Communities Act 1972,[109] as in the case of the Consumer Contracts (Information, Cancellation and Additional Charges) Regulations 2013[110] and the Consumer Protection from Unfair Trading Regulations 2008.[111] This preservation also applies to UK primary legislation enacted for the purpose of implementing EU obligations (such as is contained in the Consumer Rights Act 2015 Pts 1 and 2,[112] which are due to be subject to some amendment[113]).[114]

108 2018 Act s.2(1) (as prospectively amended by the 2020 Act and coming into force on a day to be appointed: 2018 Act s.25(4)). Section 1B(7) (in force, as inserted by the 2020 Act s.2) defines "EU-derived domestic legislation" for the purposes of the 2018 Act to include, in particular, any enactment made under s.2(2) of the European Communities Act 1972. The exceptions to this general position are set out by s.5 and Sch.1 (as amended and prospectively amended).

109 Secondary legislation with the same purpose of implementing any EU obligation but made under statutory powers other than those contained in s.2(2) of the 1972 Act is also retained: 2018 Act s.2(2)(b) and see Explanatory Notes to 2018 Act para.77, which gives as an example domestic health and safety law implementing EU obligations made under powers in the Health and Safety at Work etc. Act 1974 rather than the European Communities Act 1972.

110 SI 2013/3134 implementing Directive 2011/83/EU on consumer rights [2011] O.J. L304/64 on which see Vol.II, paras 38-061 et seq. The 2013 Regulations are to be amended on IP completion day by the Consumer Protection (Amendment etc.) (EU Exit) Regulations 2018 (SI 2018/1326) reg.8 (making modest and merely technical amendments) (the reference to "exit day" in reg.1(3) must be read as referring to IP completion day: 2020 Act Sch.5 para.1 and see above, para.1-015A).

111 The 2008 Regulations (on which see Vol.II, paras 38-157 et seq.) are amended on "exit day" by the Consumer Protection (Amendment etc.) (EU Exit) Regulations 2018 (SI 2018/1326) reg.6 (making modest amendments): reg.1(3), but the reference to exit day must be read as referring to IP completion day: 2020 Act Sch.5 para.1 and see above, para.1-015A.

[112] The 2015 Act implements Directive 1999/44/EC on certain aspects of the sale of consumer goods and associated guarantees [1999] O.J. L171/12 (principally in Pt 1 Ch.2 of the Act); Directive 93/13/EEC of April 5, 1993 on unfair terms in consumer contracts [1993] O.J. L95/29 (principally in Pt 2 of the Act) and certain aspects of Directive 2011/83/EU on consumer rights [2011] O.J. L304/64 (ss.11(4)–(6), 12; ss.36(3)–(4) and 37; and s.50(3)–(4) of the Act). On this see Vol.II, paras 38-365 et seq. and paras 38-465 et seq.

[113] Consumer Protection (Amendment etc.) (EU Exit) Regulations 2018 (SI 2018/1326) reg.3 (the reference in reg.1(3) to the coming into force of Pt 3 (which consists of reg.3) on exit day must be read as referring to IP completion day: 2020 Act Sch.5 para.1 and see above, para.1-015A). The most significant of these amendments concern the 2015 Act ss.32 and 74 at present governing contracts applying the law of a non-EEA State and, as amended, governing "contracts applying law of a country other than the UK".

[114] This follows from the definition of "EU-derived domestic legislation" in the 2018 Act s.1B(7) as including "any enactment so far as ... passed or made, or operating, for a purpose mentioned in section 2(2)(a) or (b) of [the 1972] Act".

Secondly, "[d]irect EU legislation, so far as operative immediately before IP completion day, forms part of domestic law on or after IP completion day".[115] Such direct EU legislation in principle includes EU regulations[115a] and therefore concerns such instruments as the Brussels Ibis Regulation on international jurisdiction and the recognition of judgments[115b] and, more directly affecting contracts, the Rome I Regulation on the law applicable to contractual obligations[115c] in the area of private international law, and the Denied Boarding Regulation in the area of consumer protection.[115d] As presently foreseen, the fate of these three EU Regulations is set to differ considerably. In the case of the Brussels Ibis Regulation,[115e] whose provisions on international jurisdiction and enforcement of judgments rest on the EU legal principle of mutual recognition, UK regulations have been made (which will come into force on IP completion day) which would revoke the Brussels Ibis Regulation, and would make significant consequential amendment to the UK primary legislation (notably the Civil Jurisdiction and Judgments Act 1982) and UK secondary legislation.[115f] Other EU regulations which are discussed later in this work and which put in place various mechanisms of intra-EU co-operation (such as the Regulation on cooperation in the area of consumer protection[115g]) or co-ordination (for example, the Regulation on consumer ODR[115h]) are set not to be retained on IP completion day. **1-016C**

[115] 2018 Act s.3(1) (as prospectively amended by the 2020 Act and coming into force on a day to be appointed: 2018 Act s.25(4)).

[115a] 2018 Act s.3(2).

[115b] Regulation (EU) 1215/2012 of December 12, 2012 on jurisdiction and the recognition and enforcement of judgments in civil and commercial matters (recast) [2012] O.J. L351/1.

[115c] Regulation 593/2008 on the law applicable to contractual obligations ("Rome I") [2008] O.J. L177/6, on which see below, paras 30-018 et seq.

[115d] Regulation (EC) 261/2004 establishing common rules on compensation and assistance to passengers in the event of denied boarding and of cancellation or long delay of flights [2004] O.J. L46/1 on which see Vol.II, paras 35-045—35-059.

[115e] Civil Jurisdiction and Judgments (Amendment) (EU Exit) Regulations 2019 (SI 2019/479) ("SI 2019/479") reg.84 (the reference in reg.1(1) to their coming into force on "exit day" must be read as referring to IP completion day: 2020 Act Sch.5 para.1 and see above, para.1-015A).

[115f] SI 2019/479 Pts 2 and 3 (the reference in the Regulations reg.1(1) to their coming into force on "exit day" must be read as referring to IP completion day: 2020 Act Sch.5 para.1. The amendments to the 1982 Act include the insertion of new provisions modelled on the consumer contract and employment contract provisions in the Brussels Ibis Regulation though with revisions consequential on the UK's exit from the EU: SI 2019/479 reg.26 creating new ss.15A–15C, and 15E of the 1982 Act. Special provision for the transition period was made by the Withdrawal Agreement 2020 art.67.

[115g] The earlier Regulation (EC) 2006/2004 on cooperation between national authorities responsible for the enforcement of the consumer protection law [2004] O.J. L364/1 was revoked and replaced on January 17, 2020 by Regulation (EU) 2017/2394 on cooperation between national authorities responsible for the enforcement of consumer protection laws and repealing Regulation (EC) 2006/2004 [2017] O.J. L345/1 (on which see Vol.II, paras 38-133—38-134). The "retained UK" 2006 EC Regulation was to be revoked by the Consumer Protection (Enforcement) Amendment etc.) (EU Exit) Regulations 2019 (SI 2019/203) reg.8 and it would appear that the 2017 Regulation will also be revoked on IP completion day. The CMA has advised that, after IP completion day, "businesses based in the UK or elsewhere that trade with UK consumers must comply with UK consumer protection laws" and that, although the CMA will seek "to continue to develop relationships and work with all our international counterparts", "the exact nature of consumer protection law enforcement cooperation to be agreed with the EU as part of the Future Relationship is not known": CMA, *UK exit from the EU, Guidance on the functions of the CMA under the Withdrawal Agreement* (CMA113, January 28, 2020) paras 5.19–5.21.

[115h] Regulation (EU) 524/2013 of the European Parliament and of the Council of 21 May 2013 on online dispute resolution for consumer disputes etc (Regulation on consumer ODR) on which see Vol.II, para.38-155) is to be revoked on IP completion day by the Consumer Protection (Amendment etc.) (EU Exit) Regulations 2018 (SI 2018/1326) reg.10 (the reference in the 2018 Regulations reg.1(3) to reg.10's coming into force on exit day must be read as referring to IP completion day: 2020 Act Sch.5 para.1 and see above, para.1-015A).

**1-017** *Change title of paragraph:*

**The recognition of remaining EU rights and obligations**

*Replace paragraph with:*

**1-017** The 2018 Act makes provision to ensure that any remaining EU rights and obligations which are not preserved in the way just explained[116] continue to be recognised and available in domestic law after IP completion day[116a]; these include directly effective rights contained in the European Treaties themselves.[117]

[116] Above, paras 1-016A–1-016C.

[116a] On IP completion day, see above, para.1-015A.

[117] 2018 Act s.4 (as prospectively amended by the 2020 Act and coming into force on a day to be appointed: 2018 Act s.25(4)).

*Add new paragraphs:*

**1-017A** **The status of the "principle of the supremacy of EU law"** The 2018 Act provides that "the principle of the supremacy of EU law does not apply to any enactment or rule of law passed or made on or after IP completion day",[118] although it still applies "so far as relevant to the interpretation, disapplication or quashing of any enactment or rule of law passed or made before IP completion day". As this recognises, as a matter of EU law, the principle of supremacy has been held to mean that a national court may have an obligation to "disapply" a clear national legal rule where it is incompatible with EU law.[118a]

[118] 2018 Act s.5(1) and (2) (as prospectively amended by the 2020 Act and coming into force on a day to be appointed: 2018 Act s.25(4)).

[118a] On this see famously, *The Queen v Secretary of State for Transport Ex p. Factortame Ltd (C-213/89)* [1990] I-2433 and generally Craig and de Búrca, *EU Law, Text, Cases & Materials* (6th edn) 2015, Ch.9.

**1-017B** **Interpretation of UK legislation whose source is EU law** Provision is made by the 2018 Act (as amended by the 2020 Act) for the future authoritative interpretation after IP completion day of the UK legislation whose source is EU law.[119] For this purpose a broad distinction is drawn between the case law of, or principles laid down by, UK courts in relation to EU law ("retained domestic case law") and the Court of Justice of the EU ("retained EU case law") as they have effect *before* and *on or after* IP completion day.

As regards case law and principles laid down before IP completion day, "retained EU law"[120] is in principle to be interpreted "in accordance with any retained case law [domestic or EU[120a] ] and any retained general principles of EU law,[121] and, having regard (among other things) to the limits, immediately before IP completion day, of EU competences".[122] The European Union (Withdrawal) Act 2018 then makes an exception to this position in that "the Supreme Court is not bound by any retained EU case law",[123] the Act providing that "[i]n deciding whether to depart from any retained EU case law, the Supreme Court ... must apply the same test as it would apply in deciding whether to depart from its own case law".[124] This therefore treats "retained EU case law" as "normally binding" but it would allow the Supreme Court to depart from it "when it appears right to do so".[125] Moreover, the European Union (Withdrawal Agreement) Act 2020 provided for a second category of exception to the general position by providing that a Minister may determine by regulation that other UK courts or tribunals are not bound by any retained EU case law so far as is provided for by regulations.[126]

As regards the position of EU case law and principles laid down after the UK's leaving the EU is brought into full effect on IP completion day, the 2018 Act provides that "[a] court or tribunal ... is not bound by any principles laid down, or any decisions made, on or after IP completion day by the European Court",[127] but in principle it "*may* have regard to anything done on or after IP completion day by the European Court, another EU entity or the EU so far as it is relevant to any matter before the court or tribunal".[128] This means that UK courts will not be required even to *consider* case law of the Court of Justice laid down after IP completion day, though they may do so if they think it appropriate.[129] In this respect, the position will differ from the duty of UK courts under the Human Rights Act 1998, s.2(1) of which provides that in determining a question which has arisen in connection with a right under the European Convention on Human Rights a court "must take into account any ... judgment, decision, declaration or advisory opinion of the European Court of Human Rights".

119 On IP completion day, it will cease to be possible for a UK court or tribunal to refer any matter to the European Court: 2018 Act s.6(1).

120 See above, para.1-015A.

120a 2018 Act s.6(7) "retained case law" (as amended by 2020 Act and in force on January 30, 2020).

121 Defined in terms of temporal origin by the 2018 Act s.6(7) as those which are made or laid down as they have effect immediately before IP completion day (as amended by the 2020 Act and in force January 30, 2020). An example of "retained EU general principle" may be found in the principle of effectiveness which has been relied on by the CJEU in the context of consumer protection see Vol.II, paras 38-020, 38-333, 38-344 and 38-333. A further important example may be found in the principle of conforming interpretation according to which national courts must interpret national law (including national implementing legislation) "so far as possible, in the light of the wording and purpose of the directive in order to achieve an outcome consistent with the objective pursued by the directive": *Schulte v Deutsche Bausparkasse Badenia AG* (C-350/03) EU:C:2005:637, [2005] E.C.R. I-9215 at [71] and see also *Marleasing SA v La Comercial Internacionale de Alimentacion SA* (C-106/89) EU:C:1990:395 and see Vol.II, para.38-014.

122 2018 Act s.6(3) (as amended by the 2020 Act and coming into force on a day to be appointed: 2018 Act s.25(4)).

123 2018 Act s.6(4)(a) (in force on a day to be appointed (except where already in force for the purposes of s.6(7)): 2018 Act s.25(4)). Further provision is made as regards the (Scottish) High Court of Justiciary.

124 2018 Act s.6(5) (into force on a day to be appointed (except where already in force for the purposes of s.6(7)): 2018 Act s.25(4)).

125 Department for Exiting the European Union, Cm.9446 (March 2017) para.2.16 quoting the House

of Lords Practice Statement (Judicial Precedent) of 1966, [1966] 1 W.L.R. 1234; and see also Explanatory Notes to 2018 Act as enacted, paras 113 and 115.

126 2018 Act s.6(4)(ba); s.6(5A)–(5D) (as inserted into 2018 Act s.6 by the 2020 Act s.26(1)(d); in force on May 19, 2020 (European Union (Withdrawal Agreement) Act 2020 (Commencement No. 3) Regulations (SI 2020/518) reg.2). At the time of writing (August 4, 2020), the Ministry of Justice is consulting on the exercise of the powers in the s.6(5A)–(5D) in relation to two options, i.e. (as regards England and Wales): (i) the extension of the power to depart from retained EU case law to the Court of Appeal and the Court Martial Appeal Court; or (ii) in addition to this extension, a further extension of this power to the High Court of Justice. The Ministry is also consulting on the test or tests to be applied by these courts in departing from retained EU case law and the considerations which are to be relevant to them in so doing: Ministry of Justice, *Retained EU Case Law, Consultation on the departure from retained EU case law by UK courts and tribunals* (July 2020), pp.17 et seq. These powers must be exercised (if at all) by December 31, 2020: 2018 Act s.6(5D) (as inserted by 2020 Act s.26(1)(d)) referring to IP completion day).

127 2018 Act s.6(1)(a) (as amended by the 2020 Act s.26(1)(a) and coming into force on a day to be appointed (except where already in force for the purposes of s.6(7)): 2018 Act s.25(4)).

128 2018 Act s.6(2) (as amended by the 2020 Act s.26(1)(a) and coming into force on a day to be appointed (except where already in force for the purposes of s.6(7)): 2018 Act s.25(4)) (emphasis added).

129 Explanatory Notes to 2018 Act, para.110.

**1-018** *Change title of paragraph:*

### Position until IP completion day

*Replace paragraph with:*

**1-018** As has earlier been noted, until the end of the transition period on IP completion day, EU law has been preserved in the UK despite its having left the EU.[130] This work therefore remains written on this basis thereby treating EU law and UK legislation implementing EU law as though the UK were still a Member State. However, it will note, where relevant and practicable, the principal particular changes to UK law presently foreseen to take effect on IP completion day by the relevant amending regulations made under the 2018 Act.[130a] It should be borne in mind, however, that these may themselves be changed, in particular if the subject-matter of the legislation forms part of any agreement between the UK and the EU regarding their future relationship. More generally, given what has been said about the changing significance of principles and caselaw laid down by the Court of Justice of the EU *before* and *after* IP completion day, the timing of its judgments will acquire a very considerable importance.[130b]

130 Above, paras 1-016A–1-016C.

130a Above, para.1-016.

130b cf. above, para.1-017B.

## 2. DEFINITIONS OF CONTRACT

### Difficulties with "contract as agreement"

*Replace footnote 150 with:*

**1-021** 150 Peel (ed.), *Treitel on The Law of Contract*, 15th edn (2020), para.3–172. cf. Burrows, *A Restatement of the English Law of Contract* (2016), paras 2 and 8(1), commentary on pp.63–64, which includes agreements supported by a deed within its definition of contract, but distinguishes deeds which contain agreements and those which do not (deeds poll).

## EU law definitions of contract

*Replace paragraph with:*

The definitions which we have so far discussed have been those which have arisen from analysis of the common law, equitable and statutory material native to English law or the legal systems which have developed from it. However, as earlier noted,[182] legislation of the EU has had a very considerable effect on the law governing English contracts. In these areas, the relevant EU legislation often makes the application of legislation contingent on the existence of a contract, but, in the absence of an express definition of "contract" in the legislation itself,[183] the question arises whether this notion should be interpreted according to the understanding of the various Member State laws or instead on the basis of an "autonomous" definition to be formulated by the Court of Justice of the EU. It is submitted that there is not likely to be any single answer to be given to this question and that different answers may be given according to the context of the legislation in question, these turning on a variety of considerations, but particularly on the degree of juristic integration which the Court of Justice thinks desirable and practicable in that context. However, where the Court of Justice considers it right to take an autonomous view of "contract" for the purposes of EU legislation, it may well take as its starting-point the definition of contract set out in the Proposed Regulation on a Common European Sales Law, which defines "contract" as "an agreement intended to give rise to obligations or other legal effects".[184] It is to be noticed, in particular, that this definition makes no requirement of reciprocity or provision of value such as is found in the doctrine of consideration with the result that, in principle, purely gratuitous agreements could fall within its scope.[185] The following paragraphs consider the approach to definitions of "contract" following existing case law of the European Court. **1-025**

[182] Above, para.1-011.

[183] cf. Amended Proposal for a Directive of the European Parliament and of the Council on certain aspects concerning contracts for the online and other distance sales of goods COM(2017) 637 final, art.2(g) and a Proposal for a Directive of the European Parliament and of the Council on certain aspects concerning contracts for the supply of digital content COM(2015) 634 art.2(7), where "contract" is defined for the purposes of the proposed directives as "an agreement intended to give rise to obligations or other legal effects". However, these definitions of "contract" were not retained in the directives as enacted: Directive (EU) 2019/771 of the European Parliament and of the Council of 20 May 2019 on certain aspects concerning contracts for the sale of goods, etc. [2019] O.J. L136/28 and Directive (EU) 2019/770 of the European Parliament and of the Council of 20 May 2019 on certain aspects concerning contracts for the supply of digital content and digital services [2019] O.J. L136/1, but they do provide that they "shall not affect the freedom of Member States to regulate aspects of general contract law, such as rules on the formation, validity, nullity or effects of contracts, including the consequences of the termination of a contract, in so far as they are not regulated [by the directives], or the right to damages": Directive (EU) 2019/771 art.3(9) and Directive (EU) 2019/770 art.3(10). These features suggest that the definition of contract is left for national contract laws: Sein and Spindler (2019) 15 E.R.C.L. 257 at 260–261 (arguing from the omission of the definition in proposal of Directive (EU) 2019/770).

[184] Proposal for a Regulation of the European Parliament and of the Council on a Common European Sales, Law COM(2011) 635 final art.2(a). On the Proposal, see above, para.1-013. As noted above, this definition was adopted by recent proposals for directives in the areas of contracts of sales of goods and for the supply of digital content, but in the directives as enacted.

[185] cf. the inclusion within those contracts for which the Common European Sales Law would have been available of "contracts for the supply of digital content ... irrespective of whether the digital content is supplied in exchange for the payment of a price": Proposal COM(2011) 635 final, art.5(b). However, Directive (EU) 2019/770 of the European Parliament and of the Council of 20 May 2019 on certain aspects concerning contracts for the supply of digital content and digital services [2019] O.J. L136/1

art.3(1) first sentence restricts the scope of the directive generally to "any contract where the trader supplies or undertakes to supply digital content or a digital service to the consumer and the consumer pays or undertakes to pay a price" (defining "price" (art.2(7) as "money or a digital representation of value that is due in exchange for the supply of digital content or a digital service"), but then adds that it also applies "where the trader supplies or undertakes to supply digital content or a digital service to the consumer, and the consumer provides or undertakes to provide personal data to the trader" (with certain exceptions).

## EU private international law

*Replace paragraph with:*

**1-026** The Court of Justice itself has had occasion to hold that a European and "autonomous" view should be taken of the understanding of what constitutes a contractual as opposed to an non-contractual matter for the purposes of jurisdictional rules under the Brussels Convention ( later brought within EU law as the Brussels Ibis Regulation),[186] and this has meant that an action classified in one Member State (France) as contractual has been held extra-contractual for these purposes.[187] The European Court decided that:

> "... the phrase 'matters relating to a contract' within the meaning of Article 5(1) of the Convention should not be understood to cover a situation where there is no obligation freely entered into by one party to another. Where a sub-buyer of goods which are bought from an intermediate seller brings an action against a manufacturer for damages on the sole ground that the goods are not in conformity, it is important to observe that there is no contractual link between the sub-buyer and the manufacturer because the latter has not undertaken a contractual obligation of any kind to the former."[188]

As regards the EU instruments governing applicable law, the Rome II Regulation on the law applicable to non-contractual obligations specifies that "the concept of non-contractual obligation" must be understood as an "autonomous concept"[189] and includes certain areas of law (notably, "product liability" and pre-contractual liability ("culpa in contrahendo")) which in some national laws fall within contract and in others outside it.[190] The scope of the Rome I Regulation (replacing the earlier Rome Convention) on the law applicable to *contractual* obligations is to be interpreted in a way consistent with the earlier Rome II Regulation.[191] For this purpose, the Court of Justice of the EU has held that "the concept of 'contractual obligation' [under the Rome I Regulation] designates a legal obligation freely consented to by one person towards another".[192]

[186] *Kalfelis v Schröder* (189/87) EU:C:1988:459, [1988] E.C.R. 5565 especially at 5577 (A.G. Darmon), 5585; *ÖFAB, Östergötlands Fastigheter AB v Koot* (C-147/12) EU:C:2013:490, July 18, 2013 at para.33; *Brogsitter v Fabrication de Montres Normandes EURL* (C-548/12) EU:C:2014:148, March 13, 2014 at para.18; *ERGO Insurance SE v If P&C Insurance AS* (Joined Cases C-359/14 and C-475/14) EU:C:2016:40, January 21, 2016 at para.43; *Kolassa v Barclays Bank Plc* (C-375/13) EU:C:2015:37, January 28, 2015 at para.43; *Granarolo SpA v Ambrosi Emmi France SA* (C-196/15) EU:C:2016:559, July 14, 2016 at para.19; *flightright GmbH v Air Nostrum* (Joined cases C-274/16, C-447/16 and C-448/16) of March 7, 2018 EU:C:2017:787 at [58]–[65]. The Brussels Convention was replaced as from March 1, 2002 by the Council Regulation 44/2001 on jurisdiction and the recognition and enforcement of judgments in civil and commercial matters [2001] O.J. L012/1 ("Brussels I Regulation"), which was in turn replaced as from January 10, 2015 by Regulation (EU) 1215/2012 of 12 December 2012 on jurisdiction and the recognition and enforcement of judgments in civil and commercial matters (recast) ("the Brussels Ibis Regulation"). And see below, para.1-209. On the effect of the Brussels I Regulation on IP completion day, see above, para.1-016C.

[187] *Jakob Handte & Co GmbH v Société Traitements Mécano-chimiques des Surfaces (TMCS)* (C-26/91) EU:C:1992:268, [1993] I.L.Pr. 5 and see below, para.1-209.

[188] [1993] I.L.Pr. 5 at 22.

189 Regulation 864/2007 of the European Parliament and of the Council law applicable to non-contractual obligations ("Rome II Regulation") [2007] O.J. L199/40 recital 11. On IP completion day, the Rome II Regulation is due to form part of "retained EU law" as amended: see above, para.1-016C.

190 Rome II Regulation arts 5 and 12 respectively.

191 Regulation (EC) 593/2008 on the law applicable to contractual obligations ("Rome I") [2008] O.J. L177/6 recital 7. On IP completion day, the Rome I Regulation is due to form part of "retained EU law" as amended: see above, para.1-016C. See below, Ch.30 and especially para.30-018.

192 *ERGO Insurance SE v If P&C Insurance AS* (Joined Cases C-359/14 and C-475/14) EU:C:2016:40, January 21, 2016 para.44; *Verein für Konsumenteninformation v Amazon EU Sàrl* (C-191/15) EU:C:2016:612, July 28, 2016 esp. at para.60 (action for cessation of use of unfair contract terms falls under Rome II as concerning a non-contractual obligation, though the assessment of the terms falls under Rome I as concerning a contractual obligation following the nature of these terms whether this arises in an action for cessation or in an individual action between a trader and a consumer); *Committeri v Club Mediterranee SA* [2016] EWHC 1510 (QB) at [45]–[48]; *Pan Oceanic Inc v UNIPEC UK Co Ltd* [2016] EWHC 2774 (Comm), [2017] 2 All E.R. (Comm) 196 at [153]–[163].

### "Consumer contract"

*Replace paragraph with:*

Finally, while it is clear that certain aspects of the notion of "consumer contract" for the purposes of the Directive on Unfair Terms in Consumer Contracts 1993[196] are to be interpreted "autonomously", it is less clear whether the notion of "contract" itself will also be so interpreted by the Court of Justice of the EU or will instead fall to be governed by the legislation or case law of the Member States.[197] If it were interpreted autonomously, then the significance of "contract" may well differ from that given by English law, notably as regards the latter's requirement of consideration, a requirement which is not shared by the other Member States except the Republic of Ireland. Furthermore, in coming to a view as to what constitutes "a contract" for this purpose, the Court of Justice is likely to be inspired by the definition already noted in the Proposal for a Regulation on a common European sales law.[196] **1-028**

196 See Vol.II, paras 38-218—38-219.

197 Whittaker (2000) 116 L.Q.R. 95 and see Vol.II, paras 38-015, 38-229—38-230. cf. the position under the Consumer Rights Directive 2011 art.6(5), on which see Vol.II, paras 38-063—38-065. However, in *KH v Sparkasse Sudholstein* (C-639/18) of March 12, 2020 at paras 45–51 A.G. Sharpston advised that the notion of a "contract concerning financial services" in art.2(a) of Directive 2002/65/EC concerning the distance marketing of consumer financial services [2002] O.J. L271/16 should be given an autonomous interpretation and that for this purpose "a key element for a 'contract' to exist within the meaning of Article 2(a) is that there should be an agreement between the parties, that is to say a meeting of minds" (para.51) (the decision of the CJEU of June 18, 2020 did not express a view on this issue). On this directive and its implementation in UK law by the Financial Services (Distance Marketing) Regulations 2004 (SI 2004/2095) see Vol.II, para.38-136.

196 Above, para.1-025.

## 3. Fundamental Principles of Contract Law

## (a) Freedom of Contract

### (iii) Restricted freedom as to terms

*Replace footnote 266 with:*

266 While *le contrat d'adhésion* did not appear in the French Civil Code as promulgated in 1804, it was introduced there on the reform of French contract law in 2016 (and subsequently amended on ratification of *Ordonnance* No.2016/131 of February 10, 2016 by the French Parliament by *Loi* No.2018/287 of April 20, 2018): see arts 1110 and 1171 C.civ. On this law see further Whittaker (2019) 39 O.J.L.S. 404. **1-039**

### (iv) Regulation of the contractual environment

*Replace paragraph with:*

**1-040** Other statutory techniques for the regulation of contracts are less direct. For example, one aim of modern competition law is to help ensure that no "undertaking" is able to impose what terms it likes on those with whom it deals because of its "dominant position" in the market.[281] Moreover, if, after market investigation, the Competition and Markets Authority (CMA) considers that "any feature or combination of features" of a market prevent, restrict or distort competition in the UK or part of it, it has a duty to remedy these adverse effects,[281a] a prominent example of this being the regulation of the market for the supply of retail groceries by the Groceries Supply Code of Practice.[281b] These bodies of law can be seen either as an intervention in the market (and therefore as interfering with the principle of freedom of contract[282]) or as a mechanism for ensuring that the market functions properly (and therefore as promoting freedom of contract). Another modern technique is for legislation to set up a system of regulation for a particular type of business. For example, under the Financial Services and Markets Act 2000, there is a general prohibition on the carrying on without authorisation or exemption of a regulated investment activity,[283] and doing so may constitute an offence and give rise to civil liability.[284] The Act gives to the Financial Conduct Authority very considerable rule-making powers for the conduct of investment business,[285] and breach of a rule so made is actionable at the suit of a private person who suffers loss as a result, though it will not constitute a criminal offence.[286] Clearly, this system of regulation affects the way in which contracts relating to investment business are concluded, even though breach of the rules does not affect the validity of any such contract.[287] A further example of the regulation of contractual behaviour is to be found in the Unfair Commercial Practices Directive 2005, implemented in UK law by the Consumer Protection from Unfair Trading Regulations 2008.[288] The Directive sets a very broad standard of commercial behaviour in relation to consumers in a "general clause" which prohibits practices which contrary to "professional diligence", "materially distort the economic behaviour" of an average consumer.[289] This general standard frames particular protections given to consumers by existing EU directives and is fleshed out by the 2005 Directive itself by the setting of two main examples of unfair commercial practices: misleading actions and omissions and aggressive commercial practices.[290] The Directive also provides a black list of particular commercial practices which "are in all circumstances [to be] considered unfair".[291] On the other hand, the concern of the Directive is to prohibit unfair commercial practices, and it explicitly provides that it is "without prejudice to contract law and, in particular, to the rules on the validity, formation or effect of a contract"[292] and the UK's initial implementing regulations reflected this feature and provided explicitly that "an agreement shall not be void or unenforceable by reason only of a breach of these regulations"[293] though they said no more as to the wider lack of effect of the Regulations on the "law of contract", apparently on the basis that they set out the consequences of the new controls and do not need to set out other non-consequences. However, in 2014 the 2008 Regulations were amended so as to create a series of "rights to redress" for consumers against traders in respect of *some* categories of unfair commercial practices.[294]

[281] See art.101 TFEU (ex 81 EC), art.102 TFEU (ex 82 EC); Vol.II, Ch.43, especially paras 43-004 et seq.

281a Enterprise Act 2002 ss.131, 134, 138 and 161; and see Whish and Bailey, *Competition Law*, 9th edn (OUP, 2018) Ch.11.

281b Competition Commission, Groceries (Supply Chain Practices) Market Investigation Order 2009 arts 4 and 5 and Sch.1; Groceries Code Adjudicator Act 2013 (creating the office of Groceries Code Adjudicator). And see Whittaker (2019) 39 O.J.L.S. at 427–431.

282 See, e.g. *European Commission v Alrosa Co Ltd* (C-441/07) EU:C:2010:377, [2010] 5 C.M.L.R. 11 at para.225.

283 Financial Services and Markets Act 2000 s.19(1). "Regulated activities" are defined by s.22.

284 ss.23, 20(3), respectively.

285 Financial Services and Markets Act 2000 Pt IXA.

286 Financial Services and Markets Act 2000 ss.138D(2), 138E(1).

287 Financial Services and Markets Act 2000 s.138E(2).

288 Consumer Protection from Unfair Trading Regulations 2008 (SI 2008/1277) implementing Directive 2005/29 concerning unfair business-to-consumer commercial practices in the internal market, on which see Vol.II, paras 38-157 et seq.

289 Unfair Commercial Practices Directive art.5; Consumer Protection from Unfair Trading Regulations 2008 reg.3(3).

290 Unfair Commercial Practices Directive arts 6 and 7; Consumer Protection from Unfair Trading Regulations 2008 regs 5, 6 and 7.

291 Unfair Commercial Practices Directive art.5(5) referring to Annex I; Consumer Protection from Unfair Trading Regulations 2008 reg.3(4)(d), Sch.1.

292 Unfair Commercial Practices Directive art.3(2) on which see Whittaker in Weatherill and Bernitz at Ch.8.

293 2008 Regulations reg.29.

294 Consumer Protection (Amendment) Regulations 2014 (SI 2014/870) on which see Vol.II, paras 38-172 et seq.

## (b) The Binding Force of Contract

### General significance

*In line 8, page [36], after "of profits" on", replace "breach based on the principle of unjustified enrichment." with:*

breach. **1-041**

### Limits on binding force of contracts

*To the end of paragraph, after "into account for this purpose.[335]", add:*

**1-043** Finally, legislation has recently been enacted which invalidates contract terms which prohibit the assignment of a receivable (defined as a right to be paid any amount under a contract for the supply of goods, services or intangible assets) where the supplier of goods etc. is *not* a "large enterprise" or a "special purpose vehicle".[335a]

335a Business Contract Terms (Assignment of Receivables) Regulations 2018 (SI 2018/1254), esp. regs 1(3) ("receivable"), 2 (rendering the terms of "no effect"), 3 (exception for large enterprises and special purpose vehicles) and 4 (further exceptions, including for consumer contracts (reg.4(c)). The 2018 Regulations were made under the Small Business, Enterprise and Employment Act 2015 ss.1 and 161. On the 2018 Regulations see below, para.19-047A; Day (2019) 135 L.Q.R. 205.

## (c) A Principle of Good Faith or of Contractual Fairness?

### No general principle of good faith

*Replace footnote 341 with:*

1-044 [341] Bridge (1984) 9 Can. Bus. L.J. 385; Collins, *The Law of Contract*, 4th edn (2003), Chs 13 and 15; Finn in Finn (ed.), *Essays on Contract Law* (1987), p.104; Lücke in Finn (ed.), *Essays on Contract Law*, p.155; Steyn (1991) Denning L.J. 131; Carter and Furmston (1994) 8 J.C.L. 1; Brownsword (1994) 7 J.C.L. 197; Staughton (1994) 7 J.C.L. 193; Beatson and Friedmann (eds), *Good Faith and Fault in Contract Law* (1995), especially the essays by Beatson and Friedmann, p.3; Cohen, p.25; McKendrick, p.305; Friedmann, p.399; Brownsword in Deakin and Michie (eds), *Contracts, Co-operation and Competition* (1997), p.255; Stein (1997) 113 L.Q.R. 433; Teubner (1998) 6 M.L.R. 11; Brownsword [1997] C.L.P. 111; McKendrick, *Contract Law*, 7th edn (2016), Ch.15; Smith, *Atiyah's Introduction to the Law of Contract*, 6th edn (2006), pp.164–166; Campbell (2014) 77 M.L.R. 475; Tan (2015) J.B.L. 420; Foxton (2017) L.M.C.L.Q. 360; Campbell (2017) Edinburgh L.R. 376; Cheung (2017) 34 International Construction L.R. 242; Saintier (2017) J.B.L. 441; Bridge (2017) Uniform L.R. 98; Bridge (2019) 135 L.Q.R. 227; Leggatt (2019) J.B.L. 104. Burrows, *A Restatement of the English Law of Contract* (2016) considers that it remains clear that there is no freestanding rule imposing a duty to perform in good faith in English law, though notes that English law sometimes comes to the same result by implying a term: commentary to s.5, p.50; commentary to ss.15(3)–(4), p.93.

### "Good faith" and "good faith and fair dealing" in EU law

*Replace footnote 390 with:*

1-048 [390] Directive (EU) 2019/771 on certain aspects concerning contracts for the sale of goods etc of the European Parliament and of the Council of 20 May 2019 [2019] O.J. L136/28 and Directive (EU) 2019/770 on certain aspects concerning contracts for the supply of digital content and digital services of the European Parliament and of the Council of 20 May 2019 [2019] O.J. L136/1.

### (i) Duties to consider other party's interest

*Replace footnote 396 with:*

1-050 [396] *Downsview Ltd v First City Corp Ltd* [1993] A.C. 295, 312 and see also *Albany Home Loans Ltd v Massey* [1997] 2 All E.R. 609, 612–613; *Alpstream AG v PK Airfinance Sarl* [2015] EWCA Civ 1318, [2016] 2 P. & C.R. 2 at [115]. In *UBS AG v Rose Capital Ventures Ltd* [2018] EWHC 3137 (Ch) at [36] it was noted that the duty of good faith between the mortgagee and the mortgagor "does not arise by contractual implication but by virtue of the creation of a mortgage", referring to *Socimer International Bank Ltd v Standard Bank London Ltd (No.2)* [2008] EWCA Civ 116, [2008] 1 Lloyd's Rep. 558 at [148]–[150] where Lloyd L.J. noted that the origin of the mortgagee's obligations go back to the early intervention of equity in mortgages.

### (ii) Express terms as to good faith or fairness

*Replace paragraph with:*

1-051 Sometimes, the express terms of a contract require one or both of the parties to act fairly or in good faith towards the other in a particular context or respect, or more generally.[401a] The contract may also stipulate expressly that its terms are to be interpreted according to good faith.[401b]

[401a] Below, paras 1-052—1-054A.

[401b] Below, para.1-054B.

### Express terms to act in good faith

*Replace footnote 427 with:*

1-054 [427] [2013] EWCA Civ 200 at [106] per Jackson L.J., with whom Lewison and Beatson L.JJ. agreed. See similarly *Portsmouth City Council v Ensign Highways Ltd* [2015] EWHC 1969 (TCC) at [92]–[96]. However, the HC accepted (at [110]–[112]) that the exercise of a party's decision-making power under the contract which affected the other party's rights was subject to an implied term that it would be exercised honestly, on proper grounds and not in a manner that is arbitrary, irrational or capricious, on which cf. below, paras 1-059—1-060. See also *BP Gas Marketing Ltd v La Societe Sonatrach* [2016] EWHC 2461 (Comm), 169 Con. L.R. 141 (express term requiring one party to act in good faith while performing its contractual obligations requires other party to identify one or more such obligations and their breach by not acting in good faith in a particular way at a particular time or times; there was no "free-standing obligation of good faith" (at [403] per Simon Bryan Q.C.); and on the facts no such breach was established: at [409]); *VR Global Partners LP v Exotix Partners LLP* [2017] EWHC 2620 (Comm) (express terms "to act in good faith in relation to any unwinding" of the transaction not breached on the facts). In *Unwin v Bond* [2020] EWHC 1768 (Comm) at [215] et seq. the HC emphasised the importance of context in interpreting the requirements of an express duty of good faith, but it identified five "minimum standards" which the party contractually bound to act in good faith must observe: "i) they must act honestly; ii) they must be faithful to the parties' agreed common purpose as derived from their agreement; iii) they must not use their powers for an ulterior purpose; iv) when acting they must deal fairly and openly with the claimant; v) they can consider and take into account their own interests but they must also have regard to the claimant's interest": [2020] EWHC 1768 (Comm) at [230] per H.H. Judge Klein. The case itself concerned an express duty of good faith in a shareholders' agreement, one of the shareholders claiming that another had not acted in good faith in dismissing him from employment in a subsidiary company. The court held that, as a matter of construction, this duty did apply to the defendant's decision to terminate the claimant's employment and that, while not acting dishonestly nor with an ulterior motive, the defendant had breached this duty in that he had not dealt fairly and openly with the claimant and did not have regard to his interests: [2020] EWHC 1768 (Comm) at [241] and [246]. See similarly *Re Audas Group Ltd* [2019] EWHC 2304 (Ch) at [109]–[111] and [120] (unfair prejudice petition by minority shareholder).

*Add new paragraph:*

**Express term requiring interpretation of the contract in good faith** In *Kabab-Ji SAL (Lebanon) v Kout Food Group (Kuwait)*[442a] the Court of Appeal considered the effect of an express contract term in an international franchise development agreement ("FDA") requiring that: 1-054B

> "The provisions of the Agreement, as well as any statements made by the Parties in connection therewith, shall be interpreted in good faith."[442b]

One of the issues before the court was whether this term pointed towards the application to the parties' *arbitration* agreement of a law other than English law (which was chosen by an express choice of law for the FDA). The Court of Appeal held that it did not, as it "tells one nothing about the governing law of the arbitration agreement".[442c] Moreover, according to Flaux L.J.:

> "In any event, the fact that the [contractual] provisions are to be interpreted in good faith cannot justify an interpretation which goes beyond what has been agreed or which seeks to rewrite the Agreement."[442d]

And, on its proper construction, the express term choosing English law applied not merely to the FDA itself but also to the arbitration agreement.[442e] For the same reason the express term requiring good faith in interpretation "cannot enable the [party] to override the No Oral Modification clauses on broader grounds than laid down in *Rock Advertising*".[442f]

[442a] [2020] EWCA Civ 6.

[442b] [2020] EWCA Civ 6 (art.2). The term also required the parties to act in accordance with good faith and fair dealing in carrying out their obligations. The idea of interpretation of a contract in good faith is explicitly adopted by the German Civil Code (BGB) para.157 ("Contracts are to be interpreted as required by good faith, taking customary practice into consideration" (Official translation by German Ministry of Justice available at *https://www.gesetze-im-internet.de/englisch_bgb/englisch_bgb.html#p0406* (consulted August 8, 2020)).

[442c] [2020] EWCA Civ 6 at [65] per Flaux L.J. (giving the judgment of the court).

[442d] [2020] EWCA Civ 6 at [65] referring to *R. v Immigration Officer at Prague Airport* [2004] UKHL 55, [2005] 2 A.C. 1 at [19] per Lord Bingham of Cornhill. Flaux L.J. noted that this dictum was "in the context of the interpretation of international treaties in good faith" but he saw (at [77]) the analogy of

interpretation of treaties as an "apt one". The *Prague Airport* case concerned the proper interpretation of the Geneva Convention Relating to the Status of Refugees 1951 (and its protocols), the claimants arguing, inter alia, that, although the Convention art.1A(2) provided that a person is a "refugee" only if they are "outside the country of his nationality", a particular UK government immigration policy which took effect at Prague Airport "frustrated the Convention's central purpose and was contrary to the United Kingdom's obligation to perform its treaty obligations in good faith": [2005] 2 A.C. 1 at 7. The Vienna Convention on the Law of Treaties art.26 requires that "every treaty in force is binding upon the parties to it and must be performed by them in good faith" and art.31(1) provides that: "[a] treaty shall be interpreted in good faith in accordance with the ordinary meaning to be given to the terms of the treaty in their context and in the light of its object and purpose". According to Lord Bingham, "[t]aken together, these rules call for good faith in the interpretation and performance of a treaty, and neither rule is open to question. But there is no want of good faith if a state interprets a treaty as meaning what it says and declines to do anything significantly greater than or different from what it agreed to do": at [19]. Baroness Hale of Richmond and Lord Carswell agreed with Lord Bingham on this issue (at [72] and [106] respectively) and Lord Steyn and Lord Hope of Craighead gave speeches to similar effect (at [43] and [57]–[64] respectively).

442e [2020] EWCA Civ 6 at [62].

442f [2020] EWCA Civ 6 at [77], referring to *Rock Advertising Ltd v MWB Business Exchange Centres Ltd* [2018] UKSC 24, [2019] A.C. 119 at [16] where Lord Sumption J.S.C. accepted that the effect of a no oral modification clause could be qualified by "various doctrines of estoppel" in English law, these being the equivalent of recourse to good faith or the abuse of rights in some legal systems and to the qualification in the Unidroit, *Principles of International Commercial Contracts*, Article 2.1.18 (2nd sentence) that "a party may be precluded by its conduct from asserting [a clause requiring modification by agreement of a written contract to be in a particular form] to the extent that the other party has reasonably acted in reliance on that conduct". (On effect of the *Rock Advertising* case on no oral modification clauses, see below, para.22-045.) In *Kabab-Ji* the appellant had argued that the contract had been varied (by making another company party to it) by the respondent's inconsistent behaviour, "extensive conduct" and "unequivocal performance": [2020] EWCA Civ 6 at [43] and [71]. See similarly [2020] EWCA Civ 6 at [77], where Flaux L.J. gave as an additional reason that the contract term requiring interpretation of the contract in good faith could not override the no oral modification clauses in circumstances not foreseen by Lord Sumption J.S.C. in *Rock Advertising Ltd* as this would contradict the strict wording of another express term of the FDA. The CA also held that the express term requiring the parties to perform their contractual obligations in accordance with good faith and fair dealing "cannot be used to make someone a party to the [contract] who would not otherwise be a party as a matter of English law, assuming that there was no estoppel precluding reliance on the Oral Modification clauses": [2020] EWCA Civ 6 at [77].

### (iv) Implied terms

*Replace footnote 459 with:*

1-057 459 [1992] 1 A.C. 294; *James-Bowen v Commissioner of Police of the Metropolis* [2018] UKSC 40, [2018] 1 W.L.R. 4021 at [19]. cf. *University of Nottingham v Eyett* [1999] 1 W.L.R. 594.

#### A general implied term to perform in good faith?

*Replace paragraph with:*

1-058 In *Yam Seng Pte Ltd v International Trade Corp Ltd*[468] Leggatt J. considered, obiter, that a contract for a licence to distribute and for the supply of branded goods contained an implied term of good faith in its performance which had the significance in the context of not *knowingly* providing false information on which the other party was likely to rely.[469] While this decision may be fitted easily into established case-law on the implication of terms of good faith in particular circumstances or as regards particular types of contract,[470] in the course of a lengthy discussion of implied terms as to good faith, Leggatt J. appeared on occasion to go further and argue in favour of the implication of a term requiring good faith in performance not merely in what he referred to as "relational contracts"[471] but in most, if not all, commercial contracts on the ground of the expectations of their parties.[472] In his view, for this purpose, while good faith may have the significance of honesty, "not all bad faith conduct would necessarily be described as dishonest. Other epithets which might be used to describe such conduct include 'improper', 'commercially unacceptable' or 'unconscionable'".[473] With respect, the implication of such an implied term applicable generally (or even widely) to commercial contracts would undermine to an unjustified extent English law's general position rejecting a general legal requirement of good faith.[474] Subsequent judicial comments on Leggatt J.'s discussion have suggested that it should not be seen as establishing a principle of general application to all commercial contracts, but rather as recognising a particular example of a type of contract where a term as to good faith (requiring honesty and sometimes commercially acceptable behaviour[474a]) should be implied.[474b] In particular, in *Mid Essex Hospital Services NHS Trust v Compass Group UK and Ireland Ltd (t/a Medirest)* Jackson L.J. noted that, while there is no general doctrine of "good faith" in English contract law, a duty of good faith may be implied by law as an incident of certain categories of contract, citing *Yam Seng Pte Ltd* as an example.[475] Similarly, in *Greenclose Ltd v National Westminster Bank Plc* Andrews J. observed that:

> "... there is no general doctrine of good faith in English contract law and such a term is unlikely to arise by way of necessary implication in a contract between two sophisticated commercial parties negotiating at arms' length."[476]

In Andrew J.'s view, *Yam Seng Pte Ltd* is not to be regarded as laying down any general principle applicable to all commercial contracts, but rather "the implication of an obligation of good faith is heavily dependent on the context," as Leggatt J. had expressly recognised.[477] Moreover, the approach of the Supreme Court to the implication of terms in *Marks & Spencer Plc v BNP Paribas Securities Services Trust Co (Jersey) Ltd*[478] may lead to a greater reluctance in the courts to imply terms requiring good faith in at least some commercial contracts: as Lord Neuberger of Abbotsbury there observed, "a term should not be implied into a detailed commercial contract merely because it appears fair".[479] Finally, as earlier noted, any implied term of good faith must be consistent with the express terms of the contract as properly construed[479a] and some judges have expressed the view that any implied term as to good faith should not qualify a right provided by an express term of the contract.[479b] This reflects a similar concern to the one expressed by Moore-Bick L.J. in *MSC Mediterranean Shipping Co SA v Cottonex Anstaldt* quoted above in relation to a "general principle of good faith".[479c]

[468] [2013] EWHC 111 (QB), [2013] Lloyd's Rep. 526; Whittaker (2013) 129 L.Q.R. 463; Campbell (2014) 77 M.L.R. 475.

[469] [2013] EWHC 111 (QB) at [156]. See for the acceptance (by the parties and the court) of a similar implied term of honesty and integrity *D&G Cars Ltd v Essex Police Authority* [2015] EWHC 226 (QB), at [174]–[176] (contract under which contractor dealt over a relatively lengthy period with the recovered property of members of the public acting on behalf of the police authority); *Wales (t/a Selective Investment Services) v CBRE Managed Services Ltd* [2020] EWHC 16 (Comm) at [66] (contract for the provision of pension advice to company). cf. *Bhasin v Hrynew* 2014 SCC 71, [2014] 3 S.C.R. 495 (above, para.1-046) where the Supreme Court of Canada held that there is a common law duty which applies to all contracts to act honestly in the performance of contractual obligations.

[470] See the cases noted above, para.1-057.

[471] [2013] EWHC 111 (QB) at [143]. Leggatt J. saw as examples of this category of contract joint venture agreements, franchise agreements and long-term distributorship agreements, on which cf. above, para.1-057.

[472] [2013] EWHC 111 (QB) at [132], [135]–[136].

[473] [2013] EWHC 111 (QB) at [138].

[474] The general position is set out above, paras 1-044—1-045. In particular, it is difficult to see that Leggatt J.'s statement ([2013] EWHC 111 (QB) at [138]) that "[i]n addition to honesty, there are other standards of commercial dealing which are so generally accepted that the contracting parties would

reasonably be understood to take them as read without explicitly stating them in their contractual document", if intended to apply to commercial contracts in general, is compatible with the general position there set out. See also Whittaker (2013) 129 L.Q.R. 463. Cf. *Bates v Post Office Ltd (No.3: Common Issues)* [2019] EWHC 606 (QB) at [710] (Fraser J.).

474a *Wales (t/a Selective Investment Services) v CBRE Managed Services Ltd* [2020] EWHC 16 (Comm) at [66], [72]–[80] provides an example where it was said to be rightly conceded that a contract for the provision of services relating to a company pension contained an implied term requiring honesty but where it was held that it did *not* contain one requiring good faith in the sense of "fair and open dealing".

474b *TSG Building Services Plc v South Anglia Housing Ltd* [2013] EWHC 1151 (TCC), esp. at [46] (no principle of general application to commercial contracts to be drawn from the judgment in *Yam Seng*); *Hamsard 3147 Ltd (t/a Mini Mode Childrenswear) v Boots UK Ltd* [2013] EWHC 3251 (Pat) at [83]–[84] (no implied term requiring good faith in the implicit contract, brought about by force of circumstance, as an interim arrangement subsequent to a contract of joint venture containing an express term requiring good faith in relation to the operation of the contract; but, if there were, it would only have imposed on the parties "a duty to deal with one another on an open and collaborative basis" and not an "obligation to maximise profit" (at [87]), and it would not qualify a party's implied right of termination on reasonable notice by limiting it to exercise only in "good faith" (at [89]) or its contractual right to set prices (at [90]); the relevant party would still be free to exercise its contractual rights honestly in its own commercial interests (at [92])); *Bristol Groundschool Ltd v Whittingham* [2014] EWHC 2145 (Ch) at [196] (contract which combined joint venture and product distribution agreement held to be a "relational contract" and to contain an implied term requiring honesty, judged in terms of behaviour "'commercially unacceptable' by reasonable and honest people in the particular context involved", and the action of the party concerned was found not to "accord with the normally accepted standards of honest conduct"); *Acer Investment Management Ltd v Mansion Group Ltd* [2014] EWHC 3011 (QB) at [101]–[109] (no implied term of good faith in contract for the distribution of financial products as it was not a "relational contract"); *Globe Motors Inc v TRW Lucas Varity Electric Steering Ltd* [2016] EWCA Civ 396, [2017] 1 All E.R. (Comm) 601 at [67] (courts may be more willing to find duties of co-operation or good faith in certain categories of long-term contracts); *Monde Petroleum SA v WesternZagros Ltd* [2016] EWHC 1472 (Comm), [2017] 1 All E.R. (Comm) 1009 at [249]–[275] (mere fact that contract is a long-term or relational contract is not, of itself, sufficient to justify implied term of good faith and no term to be implied so as to qualify express contractual right of termination); *Apollo Window Blinds Ltd v McNeil* [2016] EWHC 2307 (QB) (no implied term in contract of franchise requiring one party (the franchisor) to inform the other (the franchisee) of its contractual rights); *National Private Air Transport Services Co (National Air Services) Ltd v Creditrade LLP* [2016] EWHC 2144 (Comm) at [132]–[136] (no implied term in aircraft lease, as not a "relational" contract and lessor was entitled to redelivery in compliance with contract terms (obiter)); *Property Alliance Group Ltd v Royal Bank of Scotland Plc* [2016] EWHC 3342 (Ch) at [250] and [275]–[276] (no implied term requiring good faith and fair dealing in "swap agreement" between sophisticated commercial parties negotiating at arm's length) (affirmed in relation to other issues [2018] EWCA Civ 355, [2018] 1 W.L.R. 3529); *TAQA Bratani Ltd v Rockrose UKCS8 LLC* [2020] EWHC 58 (Comm), 188 Con. L.R. 141 at [55]–[56] (even if a "relational contract", no implied term as to good faith so as to qualify an express contractual power construed as absolute); *New Balance Athletics Inc v Liverpool Football Club and Athletic Grounds Ltd* [2019] EWHC 2837 (Comm) (parties agreed that express term allowing party to match third party offer for renewal of a sponsorship contract with a football club was subject to a duty of good faith; it was held that this duty could be "breached not only by dishonesty but also by conduct which lacks fidelity to the parties' bargain" bearing in mind "the nature of the bargain, the terms of the contract and the context in which the matter arises", but that there was no breach on the facts; at [44] and [68]–[70] respectively (Teare J.); *Essex CC v UBB Waste (Essex) Ltd* [2020] EWHC 1581 (TCC) at [114]–[116] (duty of good faith requires asking whether a party's conduct would be regarded as "commercially unacceptable" by reasonable and honest people, but (at [282]) such a duty does not require a party to renegotiate key aspects of the contract or to give up its right to hold the other party to its bargain); *Cathay Pacific Airways Ltd v Lufthansa Technik Ag* [2020] EWHC 1789 (Ch) at [185]–[183] esp. at [197] (strictly speaking, *Yam Seng* decided no principle of law but rather found an implied term requiring good faith in both parties as a matter of fact). In *Astor Management AG v Atalaya Mining Plc* [2017] EWHC 425 (Comm), [2017] 1 Lloyd's Rep. 476 Leggatt J. observed (at [98]) that "[a] duty to act in good faith, where it exists, is a modest requirement. It does no more than reflect the expectation that a contracting party will act honestly towards the other party and will not conduct itself in a way which is calculated to frustrate the purpose of the contract or which would be regarded as commercially unacceptable by reasonable and honest people", considering it therefore a "lesser duty" than an express contractual "positive obligation to use all reasonable endeavours to achieve a specified result"; *Al Nehayan v Kent* [2018] EWHC 333 (Comm) at [167]–[176] (Leggatt L.J. sitting in the HC holding that a contract of joint venture contained an implied term requiring good faith on the basis that it was a "relational contract" based on "trust that the other party will act with integrity and in a spirit of cooperation" (at [167]), whether this term was implied in fact or in law (at [174])). See also *Bates v Post Office Ltd (No.3: Common Issues)* [2019] EWHC 606 (QB), below.

475 [2013] EWCA Civ 200, [2013] B.L.R. 265 at [105] and see also at [150]. Cf. *UBS AG v Rose Capital Ventures Ltd* [2018] EWHC 3137 (Ch) at [36] where it was noted that the duty of good faith between

mortgagee and mortgagor "does not arise by contractual implication but by virtue of the creation of a mortgage" and distinguishing the implied terms of good faith in relation to "business contracts").

476 [2014] EWHC 1156 (Ch), [2014] 2 Lloyd's Rep. 169 at [150]; *Property Alliance Group Ltd v Royal Bank of Scotland Plc* [2016] EWHC 3342 (Ch) at [250] and [276].

477 [2014] EWHC 1156 (Ch) at [150], referring to [2013] EWHC 111 (QB) at [147]. cf. *Hockin v Royal Bank of Scotland* [2016] EWHC 925 (Ch) at [44]–[47] (no strike out of claim for breach of implied term as to the exercise of a right/discretion under a contract in the absence of factual matrix to be established at trial).

478 [2015] UKSC 72, [2015] 3 W.L.R. 1843.

479 [2015] UKSC 72 at [21] and see for an example of this approach being adopted in the context of good faith: *Hockin v Royal Bank of Scotland* [2016] EWHC 925 (Ch) at [46] (high threshold for the implication of a term in a standard commercial contract). On the decision of the SC in *Marks & Spencers Plc* generally, see below, paras 14-011—14-012.

479a *Globe Motors Inc v TRW Lucas Varity Electric Steering Ltd* [2016] EWCA Civ 396, [2017] 1 All E.R. (Comm) 601 at [68] per Beatson L.J. ("an implication of a duty of good faith will only be possible where the language of the contract, viewed against its context, permits it"); *Monde Petroleum SA v WesternZagros Ltd* [2016] EWHC 1472 (Comm), [2017] 1 All E.R. (Comm) at [250]. See also *Trustees of Edward Higgs Charity v SISU Capital Ltd* [2014] EWHC 1194 (QB) at [27]–[28], where Leggatt J. held that it was impossible to imply a longer duty to negotiate in good faith than the period set by an express term to this effect. And see above, para.1-057.

479b *TSG Building Services Plc v South Anglia Housing Ltd* [2013] EWHC 1151 (TCC) at [51] (rejecting the existence of an implied term by analogy with the term of trust and confidence in employment, but observing that "[e]ven if there was some implied term of good faith, it would not and could not circumscribe or restrict what the parties had expressly agreed in [an express term of the contract], which was in effect that either of them for no, good or bad reason could terminate at any time before the term of four years was completed", though putting aside the case of "material fraud or dishonesty" which was not present on the facts (per Akenhead J.); *Property Alliance Group Ltd v Royal Bank of Scotland Plc* [2016] EWHC 3342 (Ch) at [250] and [275]–[276] (no implied term requiring good faith and fair dealing in "swap agreement" between sophisticated commercial parties in part as it would have been inconsistent with express terms excluding equitable or fiduciary duties) (affirmed in relation to other issues [2018] EWCA Civ 355, [2018] 1 W.L.R. 3529); *Chambers v Rushmon Ltd* [2017] EWHC 124 (Ch) at [6] (no implied term as to good faith where inconsistent with express terms).

479c [2016] EWCA Civ 789, [2016] 2 Lloyd's Rep. 494 at [45], above, para.1-044.

*Add new paragraph:*

Nonetheless, in *Bates v Post Office Ltd*[479d] the High Court took a more expansive view of the implication of terms requiring good faith in the context. Fraser J. held that the contracts between the Post Office and sub-postmasters before him were "relational contracts",[479e] holding this to be an established concept in the case-law[479f] and setting out criteria for the identification of this category of contract.[479g] The learned judge concluded that the contracts therefore included an implied term requiring good faith,[479h] and that this had as its consequence a series of more particular implied terms,[479i] including ones which concerned the Post Office suspending the sub-postmaster, terminating the contract, exercising its discretion not arbitrarily, irrationally or capriciously, and exercising its contractual or other powers "honestly and in good faith for the purpose for which [they were] conferred".[479j] The effect of the latter two of these implied terms was held to apply to the exercise of all the Post Office's contractual powers and discretions under the contract.[479k] In this respect, the decision in *Bates* combines elements of the approach to the implication of terms of good faith in *Yam Seng Pte Ltd* with the qualification of contractual powers by implied term associated with the decision of the Supreme Court in *Braganza v BP Shipping Ltd*,[479l] as noted in the following paragraph. **1-058A**

479d *Bates v Post Office Ltd (No.3: Common Issues)* [2019] EWHC 606 (QB) (Fraser J.). This decision is one of several made in complex litigation under a Group Litigation Order (GLO).

479e [2019] EWHC 606 (QB) at [702] et seq.

479f [2019] EWHC 606 (QB) at [705]–[720].

479g [2019] EWHC 606 (QB) at [721]–[737] and esp. at [725]. Fraser J. held that there were no express terms in the contract preventing such a duty of good faith being implied, considering that, if there were, the contracts could not be "relational contracts": at [737]. In *Wales (t/a Selective Investment Services) v CBRE Managed Services Ltd* [2020] EWHC 16 (Comm) at [72]–[80] H.H. Judge Halliwell considered the discussion in *Bates* on "relational contracts" in holding that a contract for the provision of professional advisory services on pensions to a company did not contain an implied term requiring good faith to the recipient of these services as its legal incident given the particular features of the relationship created by the contract nor was such an implied term "necessary"; it had, however, been rightly conceded that the contract contained an implied term to deal honestly: [2020] EWHC 16 (Comm) at [66]. See also *Essex CC v UBB Waste (Essex) Ltd* [2020] EWHC 1581 (TCC) at [99]–[113] (25 year PFI contract for the design, construction and operation of a biological waste treatment plant held to be "a paradigm example of a relational contract in which the law implies a duty of good faith" (per Pepperall J. at [113]) but there was no breach of this duty ([2020] EWHC 1581 (TCC) at [452.7]). Cf. *Cathay Pacific Airways Ltd v Lufthansa Technik Ag* [2020] EWHC 1789 (Ch) at [185]–[241] (no term requiring good faith should be implied as a matter of law in a long-term aircraft engine maintenance contract as it was not a "relational contract"; nor should such a term be implied as a matter of fact under the test of necessity); *Morley (t/a Morley Estates) v Royal Bank of Scotland* [2020] EWHC 88 (Ch) at [159] (contract not "relational" as it was an "ordinary loan facility agreement").

479h [2019] EWHC 606 (QB) at [727]–[728] and [738].

479i [2019] EWHC 606 (QB) at [743] et seq. Fraser J. considered (at [743] et seq.) each of the 21 distinct implied terms alleged by the claimants both in terms of whether they were consequential on his finding that the contracts were "relational" and also, if they were not so consequential, in terms of whether they were necessary to give business efficacy to the contracts, that is, on the basis of the test for the first category of implied terms recognised by Baroness Hale of Richmond J.S.C. in *Geys v Société Générale* [2013] UKSC 63, [2013] 1 A.C. 523 at [55] (on which see below, paras 14-005 et seq.). In Fraser J.'s judgment, the 17 particular implied terms which he held consequential on the implied term of good faith are identified (at [746]) by reference to their paragraphs in "Common Issue 2" (set out at [45] but in two cases as amended by Fraser J.). Three terms were held to be implied under the business efficacy test even though they were not held to be consequential on the implied term of good faith (at [749] and [750]–[752]) and one alleged implied term was rejected on either basis (at [753]–[754]).

479j [2019] EWHC 606 (QB) at [755]. In respect of these four implied terms, Fraser J. further held that if his findings that the contracts were "relational" and/or that these terms were consequential on this finding were wrong, these terms would implied in any event as being necessary to give efficacy to the contracts: at [757]–[761]. Other implied terms were also found to be both the consequence of the implied term of good faith and necessary in this way: [762] et seq.

479k [2019] EWHC 606 (QB) at [768] (two further implied terms also had this effect).

479l [2015] UKSC 17, [2015] 1 W.L.R. 1661. See also Bridge (2019) 135 L.Q.R. 277 (written before the decision in *Bates*) drawing attention to the relationship between implied terms of good faith and on the qualification of express contractual powers as explained in para.15-059 below.

## Implied restrictions on broad contractual powers

*Replace footnote 480 with:*

**1-059** 480 See, in particular, Morgan (2015) L.M.C.L.Q. 483; Chan (2019) 135 L.Q.R. 88; Bridge (2019) 135 L.Q.R. 227. Cf. *Johnstone v Bloomsbury Health Authority* [1992] Q.B. 333 (express discretionary power in employer read subject to duty not to harm employee's health), below, para.1-189.

*Replace footnote 496 with:*

**1-059** 496 [2013] EWCA Civ 200, [2013] B.L.R. 265. For other cases discussing similar qualifications on the exercise of a broad contractual discretion see *JML Direct Ltd v Freesat UK Ltd* [2010] EWCA Civ 34 at [14] (satellite television service contracting to supply a provider of television shopping channels with two shopping channels on its platform and having discretion under the contract in the allocation of logical channel numbers); *Mckay v Centurion Credit Resources LLC* [2012] EWCA Civ 1941, especially at [17], [21]–[22] (term for advance of funds on demand of borrower); *WestLB AG v Nomura Bank International Plc* [2012] EWCA Civ 495, especially at [30], [32] (discretion as to valuation of fund); *TSG Building Services Plc v South Anglia Housing Ltd* [2013] EWHC 1151 (TCC) (no implied term of good faith restricting the exercise of an apparently unfettered right in party to terminate contract); *Brogden v Investec Bank Plc* [2014] EWHC 2785 (Comm), [2014] I.R.L.R. 924 at [91], [95]–[102] (term in employment contract for payment of bonus); *Greenclose Ltd National Westminster Bank Plc* [2014] EWHC 1156 (Ch), [2014] 1 C.L.C. 562 at [144]–[151] (no implied qualifications on express "unqualified right" to extend the term of an interest rate hedging transaction); *Myers v Kestrels Acquisitions Ltd* [2015] EWHC 916 (Ch) at [40]–[41], [50]–[63] (no implied term that a power in a loan-note instrument to modify its terms had to be exercised in good faith); *Portsmouth City Council v Ensign Highways*

*Ltd* [2015] EWHC 1969 (TCC) at [110]–[112]; *Monde Petroleum SA v WesternZagros Ltd* [2016] EWHC 1472 (Comm), [2017] 1 All E.R. (Comm) 1009 at [261]–[275] (affirmed on other grounds [2018] EWCA Civ 25); *Multiplex Construction Europe Ltd v R&F One (UK) Ltd* [2019] EWHC 3464 (TCC) at [27]–[28] (not "arbitrary or capricious" to exercise a contractual discretion to suspend performance on the ground of failure to provide payment security as stipulated as to do so "would be exercising its discretion consistently with the contractual purpose of the right to suspend"); *Everwarm Ltd v BN Rendering Ltd* [2019] EWHC 3060 (TCC) at [122]–[123], [129]–[131] (express term entitling the employer of a building contractor to assess the value of work done and what it therefore owed and, as relevant, to recover the difference from what it had paid was subject to an implied term that it would not be undertaken in an arbitrary, capricious or irrational manner; it was held that the assessments had not been undertaken in accordance with the regime set out in the express term nor with the implied term, in particular, as the method of valuation was arbitrary); *Essex CC v UBB Waste (Essex) Ltd* [2020] EWHC 1581 (TCC) at [96]–[98], [149], [271] and [278] (no breach of implied term to act rationally, not capriciously). In *British Telecommunications Plc v Telefónica O2 UK Ltd* [2014] UKSC 42, [2014] 4 All E.R. 907 at [37] Lord Sumption observed that, although the matter remains a matter of construction, it is "well established that in the absence of very clear language to the contrary, a contractual discretion must be exercised in good faith and not arbitrarily or capriciously". See also *Braganza v BP Shipping Ltd* [2015] UKSC 17, [2015] 1 W.L.R. 1661, below, para.1-060.

*Replace paragraph with:*

In some cases it may not be straightforward to draw the line between a contractual discretionary power of the type which attracts the application of the qualifying implied term foreseen by *Socimer*[511] and *Braganza*[512] and "a simple decision whether or not to exercise an absolute contractual right"[513] which does not.[514] In *Property Alliance Group Ltd v Royal Bank of Scotland Plc*[515] a contract under which a bank provided a financial facility to a property investment business (the borrower) contained express authority (by a "valuation clause") for the bank to obtain a professional valuation of the premises charged as security for the funding provided at the cost of the borrower. The borrower claimed, inter alia, that the bank's power to obtain such a valuation was subject to an implied term that the bank must act reasonably, in a commercially acceptable or rational way, in good faith, not capriciously nor arbitrarily and for the purpose for which the power was conferred and that, on the facts, a purported exercise by the bank of this power was "pointless, without good or rational reason" and so in breach of this implied term.[516] At first instance, Asplin J. observed that a discretion "requires the contracting party to make some kind of assessment or to choose from a range of options" and held that "no element of discretion, assessment, or formulation of opinion arises" arose in relation to the exercise of the power in the valuation clause and that instead the bank had an "absolute right to call for the valuation" so as to preclude the application of the *Socimer* implied term.[517] On this point, however, the Court of Appeal disagreed, holding that the bank's power under the valuation clause was "not wholly unfettered".[518] While the clause was indeed inserted for the benefit of the bank which must have been "free to act in its own interests" and "was under no duty to attempt to balance its interests against those of [the borrower]", nevertheless, it could be inferred: **1-061**

> "… that the parties intend the power granted by [the valuation clause] to be exercised in pursuit of legitimate commercial aims rather than, say, to vex [the borrower] maliciously."[519]

Accordingly, the bank was not entitled to commission a valuation "for a purpose unrelated to its legitimate commercial interests or if doing so could not rationally be thought to advance them".[520] However, the facts did not justify a finding that such an implied term had been broken so that the decision below holding that the bank was entitled to commission the valuation and to recover its cost was affirmed.[521]

[511] *Socimer International Bank Ltd v Standard Bank London Ltd (No.2)* [2008] EWCA Civ 116, [2008] 1 Lloyd's Rep. 558, above, para.1-059.

[512] *Braganza v BP Shipping Ltd* [2015] UKSC 17, [2015] 1 W.L.R. 1661.

[513] *Mid Essex Hospital Services NHS Trust v Compass Group UK and Ireland Ltd (t/a Medirest)* [2013] EWCA Civ 200, [2013] B.L.R. 265 at [83], per Jackson L.J., above, para.1-059.

[514] See also *Watson v Watchfinder.co.uk Ltd* [2017] EWHC 1275 (Comm), [2017] Bus. L.R. 1309 which concerned a contractual option to purchase shares in a company which formed part of a wider commercial relationship between the parties and which was contingent on the consent of that company's board. The HC held that the company board had a discretion as to the consent which must be exercised in a way which was not arbitrary, capricious or irrational, following the SC's decision in *Braganza* [2015] UKSC 17 at [102]–[103] and [116] et seq. See similarly *B.H.L. v Leumi ABL Ltd* [2017] EWHC 1871 (QB), [2017] 2 Lloyd's Rep. 237 at [36]–[41] (contractual power to set an additional percentage fee for collection of receivables must be exercised in a way which is not arbitrary, capricious or irrational in a public law sense) but cf. *Shurbanova v Forex Capital Markets Ltd* [2017] EHWC 2133 (QB) (contractual power to revoke trades made by a customer on an online foreign exchange and commodities facility were held not to be of a type to attract the qualification recognised in *Braganza* but was instead an "absolute contractual right" (at [93]–[95]), though a contractual power to revoke trades on the ground that they were based on "manifest error" would have been subject to such a qualification absent an express contractual duty to act fairly (at [81]); *UBS AG v Rose Capital Ventures Ltd* [2018] EWHC 3137 (Ch) at [49]–[57] (a lender's power under an express term in a commercial loan secured by mortgage to call in the loan "in its absolute discretion" was not qualified by "a Braganza term" as it was a power that is always exercised solely for the benefit of the mortgagee, though it was noted that the mortgagor retained the protection of the equitable duty of good faith as between mortgagor and mortgagee); *Cathay Pacific Airways Ltd v Lufthansa Technik Ag* [2020] EWHC 1789 (Ch) at [150]–[183] (no *Braganza*-type restriction on the exercise of an express option in one party to a long-term aircraft engine maintenance contract); *Morley (t/a Morley Estates) v Royal Bank of Scotland* [2020] EWHC 88 (Ch) at [160] (Kerr J.) (bank's decision to call in a loan made under a loan facility agreement was an absolute contractual right and not a discretion, but its powers to obtain a revaluation of the charged assets and to charge a default interest rate were both discretions which "had to be exercised for purposes rationally connected to the bank's commercial interests and not so as to vex the [borrower] maliciously"; but there was no breach as "all the bank's actions were rationally connected to its commercial interests": at [191].

[515] [2016] EWHC 3342 (Ch); [2018] EWCA Civ 355, [2018] 1 W.L.R. 3529.

[516] [2018] EWCA Civ 355 at [162].

[517] [2016] EWHC 3342 (Ch) at [278] per Asplin J.

[518] [2018] EWCA Civ 355 at [169] (approved judgment of Sir Terence Etherton M.R., Longmore and Newey L.JJ.).

[519] [2018] EWCA Civ 355 at [169].

[520] [2018] EWCA Civ 355 at [169].

[521] [2018] EWCA Civ 355 at [174]–[175].

*Add new paragraphs:*

**1-061A** In *Equitas Insurance Ltd v Municipal Mutual Insurance Ltd*,[521a] the Court of Appeal considered the significance of the *Braganza* implied term in the context of an aspect of the reinsurance implications of the special rules governing causation in claims for mesothelioma resulting from exposure of employees to asbestos (the so-called "*Fairchild* enclave").[521b] Under these rules, "any employer who has exposed a victim to asbestos in breach of duty, for however short a period, is liable in full to a victim of mesothelioma, while any [employers liability] insurer of such an employer is liable in full to indemnify the employer, again regardless of the period for which it has provided insurance and received premium".[521c] The Court of Appeal considered whether an insurer which had so indemnified an employer could then claim an indemnity against its reinsurer "for its full loss under whichever annual reinsurance policy within this period [of exposure to asbestos] it chooses in order to maximise its reinsurance recovery, or whether it is limited to claiming under each annual reinsurance policy a pro rata share of the settlement sum".[521d] In addressing this question, Males L.J. (with whom Patten L.J. agreed) considered that it was desirable to correct the anomalies created by the *Fairchild* enclave once its objective of ensuring victim protection had been achieved by returning to common law principles by which liability should be apportioned by reference to contribution to the risk.[521e] In this respect, he considered whether the insurer's "contractual right to present its reinsurance claims to the policy year of its choice"[521f] was qualified in a way suggested by the line of cases associated with *Braganza*.[521g] For this purpose, Males L.J. noted Jackson L.J.'s distinction in the *Mid Essex* case between discretions involving "an assessment or choosing from a range of options, taking into account the interests of both parties" and "those involving a simple decision whether or not to exercise an absolute contractual",[521h] observing that

> "although the *Mid Essex* case uses the expression 'absolute contractual right' that is the result of a process of construction which takes account of the characteristics of the parties, the terms of the contract as a whole and the contractual context, not a starting point intrinsic to the term itself. It is only possible to say whether a term conferring a contractual choice on one party represents an absolute contractual right after that process of construction has been undertaken."[521i]

521a [2019] EWCA Civ 718, [2020] 1 Q.B. 418.

521b *Fairchild v Glenhaven Funeral Services Ltd* [2002] UKHL 22, [2003] 1 A.C. 32; Compensation Act 2006 s.3 and see [2019] EWCA Civ 718 at [24] et seq.

521c [2019] EWCA Civ 718 at [5].

521d [2019] EWCA Civ 718 at [4].

521e [2019] EWCA Civ 718 at [91]–[93].

521f [2019] EWCA Civ 718 at [102].

521g [2019] EWCA Civ 718 at [106]. Males L.J. considered that as a matter of authority the post-contractual duty of an insurer to act in good faith did not extend to this situation: [2019] EWCA Civ 718 at [104].

521h [2019] EWCA Civ 718 at [111]; *Mid Essex Hospital Services NHS Trust v Compass Group UK and Ireland Ltd (t/a Medirest)* [2013] EWCA Civ 200, [2013] B.L.R. 265 at [83] per Jackson L.J. quoted above, para.1-059.

521i [2019] EWCA Civ 718 at [113].

Males L.J. saw "powerful reasons" to support the implication of a term requiring the exercise of the insurer's contractual choice as to the year of presentation of its reinsurance claims "in a manner which is not arbitrary, irrational or capricious" in the very specific reinsurance context existing within the *Fairchild* enclave[521j] and held that, in this context, "rationality requires that [the insurer's claims] be presented by reference to each year's contribution to the risk, which will normally be measured by reference to time on risk unless in the particular circumstances there is a good reason ... for some other basis of presentation" as allowing the insurer to choose which year within the period of exposure in which to claim "is inconsistent with the presumed intentions and reasonable expectations of the parties at the time when the contracts were concluded".[521k] While such an implied term may be described conveniently as requiring "good faith" this is merely a label as its content and rationale is particular to the context as Males L.J. had set out.[521l] **1-061B**

521j [2019] EWCA Civ 718 at [114].

521k [2019] EWCA Civ 718 at [114].

521l [2019] EWCA Civ 718 at [116].

Leggatt L.J. (with whom Patten L.J. also agreed) concurred with Males L.J. and noted the development of **1-061C**

> "the readiness of courts to imply a term as to the manner in which contractual power may be exercised so as to ensure that the power is not abused and is exercised in good faith. The doctrine of good faith in this context requires a contractual power to be exercised in a way which is consistent with the justified expectations of the parties arising from their agreement, construed in its relevant context."[521m]

Leggatt L.J. saw the basis of such an implied term of good faith as proceeding from the construction of the express terms and founded on the test of necessity,[521n] it being, in the words of Lord Steyn, "essential to give effect to the reasonable expectations of the parties".[521o] For this purpose, "the courts recognise that, where the contract permits a party to make a choice or requires it to make an evaluative judgment, it is for that party and not the court to make the relevant choice or evaluation"[521p] and this is the reason why the courts have had recourse to a standard of review similar to the review of administrative action, though "[w]hat is honest and reasonable is judged by reference to the purpose(s) which the contract requires or permits the party exercising the relevant power to pursue".[521q] On the other hand, Leggatt L.J. recognised that there are also occasions in which a contractual power is not fettered by an implied term in this way, this also being a matter of construction.[521r] In the particular case before the court, he held that it was "necessary to imply a term which restricts the exercise of the reinsured's power to select how it will present its claim as between policy years" so as to "make the contracts work as consistently as is possible with the parties' presumed intention and reasonable expectations".[521s] Such an implied term prevents the insurer from abusing its contractual power to allocate loss among policy years.[521t]

[521m] [2019] EWCA Civ 718 at [148].

[521n] [2019] EWCA Civ 718 at [149]–[150]. On the test of necessity see below, paras 14-011 et seq.

[521o] *Equitable Life Assurance Society v Hyman* [2002] 1 A.C. 408, 459 quoted [2019] EWCA Civ 718 at [149].

[521p] [2019] EWCA Civ 718 at [151].

[521q] [2019] EWCA Civ 718 at [151].

[521r] [2019] EWCA Civ 718 at [155] citing *Compass Group UK and Ireland Ltd (trading as Medirest) v Mid Essex Hospital Services NHS Trust* [2013] B.L.R. 265 (on which see above, para.1-059) where "the only discretion which the trust had was to decide whether or not to exercise an absolute contractual right": [2019] EWCA Civ 718 at [156].

[521s] [2019] EWCA Civ 718 at [158].

[521t] [2019] EWCA Civ 718 at [162].

**1-061D** By contrast, in *TAQA Bratani Ltd v Rockrose UKCS8 LLC*[521u] in a very different commercial and legal context, the High Court held that a contractual power in a professionally drafted joint operation agreement relating to North Sea oil fields to terminate the status as "operator" of the fields of one of its participants was as a matter of its construction "an absolute right to discharge", unqualified apart from its express conditions as to the required participants of the deciding body and as to the giving of minimum notice.[521v] In these circumstances, no term should be implied that qualifies the manner in which it may be exercised as in *Socimer International Bank Ltd*[521w] or *Braganza*[521x] as this would not be necessary (as required under the general law of implied terms), would be inconsistent with the express terms of the contract and also with established authority to the effect "that unqualified termination provisions take effect in accordance with their terms".[521y] In this respect, the contrast with the *Equitas* decision of the Court of Appeal underlines the observation of H.H. Judge Pelling Q.C. in *TAQA Bratani Ltd* that:

> "The case law[521z] ... emphasises time and again the importance of context in deciding the scope of any term implied either under the *Braganza* doctrine or by reference to the Relational Contracts case law."[521za]

[521u] [2020] EWHC 58 (Comm), 188 Con. L.R. 141. See also *Cathay Pacific Airways Ltd v Lufthansa Technik Ag* [2020] EWHC 1789 (Ch) at [183].

[521v] [2020] EWHC 58 (Comm) at [34]–[37] and [44].

[521w] *Socimer International Bank Ltd v Standard Bank London Ltd* [2008] EWCA Civ 116, [2008] 1 Lloyd's Rep. 558, and see above, para.1-059.

[521x] *Braganza v BP Shipping Ltd* [2015] UKSC 17, [2015] 1 W.L.R. 1661, and see above, para.1-060.

[521y] [2020] EWHC 58 (Comm) at [47] per H.H. Judge Pelling Q.C. and see also at [47]–[49].

[521z] The learned judge had referred, inter alia, to *Yam Seng Pte v International Trade Corp* [2013] EWHC 111 (QB), [2013] 1 All E.R. (Comm) 132; *British Telecommunications Plc v Telefonica O2UK Ltd* [2014] UKSC 42, [2014] 4 All E.R. 907; *Equitas Insurance Ltd v Municipal Insurance Ltd* [2019] EWCA Civ 718; *Mid Essex Hospital Services NHS Trust v Compass Group UK* [2013] EWCA Civ 200 as well as *Socimer* and *Braganza*.

[521za] [2020] EWHC 58 (Comm) at [64].

*Add new paragraphs:*

**(vii) Good faith as the principle justifying rectification of contractual document** In *FSHC Group Holdings Ltd v GLAS Trust Corp Ltd*, Leggatt L.J. (with whom Rose and Flaux L.JJ. joined) explained that the doctrine of rectification "to give effect to a 'common continuing intention' not amounting to a legally enforceable contract" should be seen as being based on an "equitable principle of good faith".[532a] This development is discussed below.[532b] **1-063A**

[532a] *FSHC Group Holdings Ltd v GLAS Trust Corporation Ltd* [2019] EWCA Civ 1361 at [142] and see also at [54]–[55] and [146]–[147].

[532b] Below, para.3-081B.

**Government guidance on responsible contractual behaviour in response to Covid-19 epidemic** In May 2020, the UK Government (and specifically the Cabinet Office) issued a note, *Guidance on responsible contractual behaviour in the performance and enforcement of contracts impacted by the Covid-19 emergency*.[532c] As its title suggests, the note "sets out guidance and recommendations for parties to contracts, in both the public and private sectors, where the performance of contracts (including an obligation to make payment) is materially impacted by the Covid-19 emergency".[532d] The problem which the Cabinet Office Guidance identifies is that "parties to some contracts may find it difficult or impossible to perform those contracts in accordance with their agreed terms as a result of the impact of Covid-19".[532e] Accordingly, **1-063B**

> "the Government is strongly encouraging all individuals, businesses (including funders) and public authorities to act responsibly and fairly in the national interest in performing and enforcing their contracts, to support the response to Covid-19 and to protect jobs and the economy."[532f]

For this purpose, the Cabinet Office Guidance explains responsible and fair contractual behaviour in general terms:

> "This includes being reasonable and proportionate in responding to performance issues and enforcing contracts (including dealing with any disputes), acting in a spirit of cooperation and aiming to achieve practical, just and equitable contractual outcomes having regard

to the impact on the other party (or parties), the availability of financial resources, the protection of public health and the national interest."[532g]

It then lists 15 particular contexts in which fair and responsible contractual behaviour is encouraged, including, notably, requesting, and giving, relief for impaired performance; making, and responding, to claims for, force majeure or frustration or requests for contract changes and variations; making claims for payment, damages, or termination; and making and responding to court procedures and alternative dispute resolution.[532h] The Guidance also strongly encourages the use of "negotiation, mediation or other alternative or fast-track dispute resolution" to settle contractual disputes.[532i]

1-063C However, as the Cabinet Office Guidance itself makes clear, it sets out merely "guidance and recommendations for parties to contracts",[532j] it is "non-statutory"[532k] and it is expressed in the language of "strong encouragement" rather than the imposition of any new duty or duties on contracting parties. Moreover, it states that, in particular, it does not override specific guidance or procurement policy notes issued by the Government (or any public or regulatory authority); any specific support or relief available in the relevant contract, or in law, custom or practice (including any equitable relief), or from the Government in response to the Covid-19 emergency.[532l] Nor does it override "any other legal duties or obligations with which a party to a contract is bound to comply and any national security interests".[532m] Given these restrictions (and especially the restriction as to the parties' legal duties or obligations), it would appear that the Cabinet Office Guidance explicitly disavows any intention of affecting the legal rights or duties of parties to contracts.[532n] It remains unclear whether the courts themselves will nevertheless take it into account in their decision-making, for example, in relation to the exercise of a discretion (for instance, in relation to the remedies of specific performance or injunction), or in the assessment of the significance of reasonableness or good faith in the broader sense of commercially acceptable behaviour[532o] in the context of Covid-19 where these are required as a matter of law or under the particular contract.

[532c] Cabinet Office (May 7, 2020) ("Cabinet Office Guidance (2020)") available at *https://www.gov.uk/government/publications/guidance-on-responsible-contractual-behaviour-in-the-performance-and-enforcement-of-contracts-impacted-by-the-covid-19-emergency*.

[532d] Cabinet Office Guidance (2020), para.6.

[532e] Cabinet Office Guidance (2020), para.12.

[532f] Cabinet Office Guidance (2020), para.3.

[532g] Cabinet Office Guidance (2020), para.14.

[532h] Cabinet Office Guidance (2020), para.15.

[532i] Cabinet Office Guidance (2020), para.17.

[532j] Cabinet Office Guidance (2020), para.17.

[532k] Cabinet Office Guidance (2020), para.6.

[532l] Cabinet Office Guidance (2020), para.7(a) and (b).

[532m] Cabinet Office Guidance (2020), para.7(c).

[532n] The note indicates that further measures could be taken, including the introduction of legislation: Cabinet Office Guidance (2020), para.23.

[532o] See above, para.1-058.

## 4. THE HUMAN RIGHTS ACT 1998 AND CONTRACTS

## (a) Contracts made before October 2, 2000

### *(ii) Contracts made by "Public Authorities"*

**Effect of any unlawful performance by a public authority**

*Replace footnote 574 with:*

[574] cf. Peel (ed.), *Treitel on The Law of Contract*, 15th edn (2020), paras 19-052—19-053 and see below, paras 23-066—23-069. **1-070**

## (b) Contracts made on or after October 2, 2000

### *(i) The Construction and Review of Legislation Governing Contracts*

**Unenforceable contractual rights and engaging art.1 of the First Protocol**

*Replace footnote 589 with:*

[589] [2003] UKHL 40, [2003] 3 W.L.R. 568 at [39]. This view may be supported from the Strasbourg case law, e.g. *Stran Greek Refineries & Stratis Andreadis v Greece* (1995) 19 E.H.R.R. 293 at [60]–[62] (right under arbitration award); *Stretch v UK* (2004) 38 E.H.R.R. 12 especially at [32] (option to renew lease later considered void as ultra vires the public authority lessor's power). For discussion as to which contractual rights can constitute "possessions" for the purposes of art.1 of the First Protocol see *Murungaru v Secretary of State for the Home Department* [2008] EWCA Civ 1015, [2009] I.N.L.R. 180 at [30]–[32], [43]–[58] ("touchstone ... is whether the rights and interests can be regarded as constituting 'assets'": at [47] per Lewison J.); *Breyer Group Plc v Department of Energy and Climate Change* [2015] EWCA Civ 408, [2015] 1 W.L.R. 455 at [22]–[23], [28]–[46] and [49]; *Solaria Energy UK Ltd v Department for Business Energy and Industrial Strategy* [2019] EWHC 2188 (TCC) at [35]–[66] and esp. at [52] (the key question is whether or not the contractual rights of claimant under the contract had "a monetary value which could be marketed for consideration") (appeal pending). **1-074**

### *(iv) Contractual Confidentiality and s.12 of the 1998 Act*

**The impact of s.12 on duties of confidentiality**

*Replace footnote 763 with:*

[763] *Douglas v Hello! Ltd (No.1)* [2001] Q.B. 967; *A v B Plc* [2002] EWCA Civ 337, [2003] Q.B. 195; *London Regional Transport v Mayor of London* [2001] EWCA Civ 1491, [2003] E.M.L.R. 4; *Douglas v Hello! Ltd (No.6)* [2003] EWHC 786, (2003) 153 N.L.J. 595; *Lady Archer v Williams* [2003] EWHC 1670, [2003] E.M.L.R. 38; *Campbell v MGN Ltd* [2004] UKHL 22, [2004] 2 A.C. 457; *Douglas v Hello! Ltd (No.3)* [2005] EWCA Civ 595, [2006] Q.B. 125; *McKennitt v Ash* [2006] EWCA Civ 1714, [2007] 3 W.L.R. 194; *Ntuli v Donald* [2010] EWCA Civ 1276, [2011] 1 W.L.R. 294; *PJS v News Group Newspapers Ltd* [2016] UKSC 26, [2016] A.C. 1081. **1-101**

## 5. CLASSIFICATION OF CONTRACTS

## (c) Classification of Contracts According to their Form or Means of Formation

**Formal and informal contracts**

*Replace footnote 812 with:*

[812] *Rann v Hughes* (1778) 7 T.R. 350n. See also *Blue v Ashley* [2017] EWHC 1928 (Comm) at [49]. **1-110**

## 6. CONTRACTS CONTAINED IN DEEDS

## (a) General

### General abolition of the requirement of sealing

*Replace paragraph with:*

1-121 In 1989, legislation was enacted which abolished the ancient requirement of sealing for the execution of the deeds in many situations.[854] As regards deeds executed by an individual, s.1 of the Law of Property (Miscellaneous Provisions) Act 1989 (the "1989 Act") replaced the requirement of sealing with requirements that the intention of the party making a deed should make this intention clear on its face, of signature by that party[855] and of attestation.[856] As regards companies incorporated under the Companies Acts ("companies"), the requirement of sealing for the execution of *documents*[857] was supplemented by an alternative method of execution of a document which required signature by a director and the secretary of the company or by two directors and the expression "in whatever form of words" that it was executed by the company; and it was further provided that where a document made clear on its face that it was intended to be a *deed*, it should take effect on delivery as a deed, delivery being rebuttably presumed where it was so executed.[858] Similar provisions were enacted in 1993 to govern the position of charities incorporated under the Charities Act 1993, later replaced by the Charities Act 2011.[859] In the case of deeds executed by other persons (including other corporations aggregate[860] and corporations sole[861]), the common law requirement of sealing was left unaffected.

[854] On the ancient requirement see Sheppard's *Touchstone of Common Assurances*, 7th edn (1820), p.56. The recognition of "electronic seals" by Regulation (EU) 910/2014 of 23 July 2014 on electronic identification and trust services for electronic transactions in the internal market and repealing Directive 1999/93/EC [2014] O.J. L257/73 (the "eIDAS Regulation"), see esp. arts 2(25), 35–40, does not affect the law described in the text, as art.2(3) provides that the Regulation does not affect national or Union law related to the conclusion and validity of contracts or other legal or procedural obligations relating to form: see further below, para.5-008, which also notes the effect of the UK's leaving the EU on this law.

[855] This requirement had been imposed by the Law of Property Act 1925 s.73.

[856] Law of Property (Miscellaneous Provisions) Act 1989 s.1. See also Law Commission, *Electronic execution of documents* (August 21, 2018) (Consultation Paper) Ch.4; Law Commission, *Electronic execution of documents*, Law Com. No.386 (Report) (September 3, 2019) Chs 5 and 6, the latter recommending a general review of the law of deeds to see whether the concept remains fit for purpose and outline the issues to be addressed by such a review.

[857] Companies Act 1985 s.36A(2) (as inserted by the Companies Act 1989 (c.40) ss.130(2), 213(2)). This provision has been superseded as explained at para.1-135 below.

[858] Companies Act 1985 s.36A(4) and (5) (as inserted by the Companies Act 1989 (c.40) ss.130(2), 213(2)). This provision has been superseded as explained at para.1-135 below.

[859] Charities Act 1993 ss.50 and 60; Charities Act 2011 ss.252 and 260–261.

[860] A corporation aggregate may be defined as consisting of: "[A] body of persons which is recognised by the law as having a personality which is distinct from the separate personalities of the members of the body or the personality of the individual holder of the office in question for the time being": Law Com. No.253 para.4.1, n.1 referring to *Halsbury's Laws of England*, 4th edn (reissue, 1998), Vol.9(2), para.1005.

[861] A corporation sole may be defined as consisting of: "[O]ne person and his or her successors in some particular office or status, who are incorporated in law in order to give them certain legal capacities and advantages which they would not have in their natural person": Law Com. No.253 para.4.23 referring to *Halsbury's Laws of England*, 4th edn, Vol.9(2), para.1007 and giving as examples a government minister or Church of England bishop.

*Replace footnote 866 with the following:*

## Electronic documents and deeds[866]

[866] "Electronic documents and deeds" for the purposes of the Land Registration Act 2002 (which are the subject of the present paragraph) are to be distinguished from "electronic seals" recognised by Regulation (EU) 910/2014 of 23 July 2014 on electronic identification and trust services for electronic transactions in the internal market and repealing Directive 1999/93/EC [2014] O.J. L257/73 (the "eIDAS Regulation"), see below, para.5-008. On the question whether a deed can be executed using electronic means see Law Commission, *Electronic execution of documents*, Consultation Paper No.237 (August 21, 2018), Ch.4. **1-123**

*Replace paragraph with:*

Following the recommendations of the Law Commission,[867] the Land Registration Act 2002 made provision for the creation of a framework in which it will be possible to transfer and create interests in registered land by electronic means through a network controlled by the Land Registry ("e-conveyancing"). In order to permit this, Pt 8 of the Act makes provision for the fulfilment of formality requirements by the transactions in question. Accordingly, by s.91(4) and (5) of the 2002 Act: **1-123**

> "... a document to which this section applies is to be regarded as: (a) in writing; and (b) signed by each individual, and sealed by each corporation, whose electronic signature it has. [And such a document] is to be regarded for the purposes of any enactment as a deed."[868]

Section 91 applies to "documents in electronic form" of certain types dealing with registered interests in land[869] as long as: (a) the document makes provision for the time and date when it takes effect; (b) the document has the electronic signature of each person by whom it purports to be authenticated; (c) each electronic signature is certified; and (d) such other conditions as rules may provide are met. This provision does not, therefore, create a new type of deed capable of being made electronically; rather it assimilates certain qualifying electronic documents to deeds for the purposes of any enactment requiring the dispositions to which those documents relate to use a deed.[870] A further stage in e-conveyancing would bring into force s.93 of the 2002 Act and would involve the compulsory use of electronic conveyancing; without electronic creation, there would be no proprietary interest nor even a contractual or other personal right.[871] At the time of writing, these new systems have not yet been brought into operation.[872]

[867] Law Commission, *Land Registration for the Twenty-First Century* (2001) Law Com. No.271.

[868] Land Registration Act 2002 (Commencement No.4) Order 2003 (SI 2003/1725) brought this provision into force on October 13, 2003.

[869] The relevant dispositions are specified by the Land Registration Act 2002 s.91(2).

[870] Land Registration Act 2002 s.91(3).

[871] Land Registration Act 2002 s.93(2) and see Smith, *Property Law*, 9th edn (2017), 115–116.

[872] See Smith, *Property Law*, 9th edn (2017), pp.113–115 discussing the Land Registration Act 2002 and noting that in 2011 the Land Registry halted the e-conveyancing project: Land Registry Annual Report and Accounts 2010–2011, p.26; Megarry and Wade, *The Law of Real Property* 8th edn (2012) by Harpum, Bridge and Dixon, paras 7-157—7-163. See further Law Commission, *Updating the Land Registration Act 2002*, Law Com No.380 (July 2018), Ch.20, noting (at paras 20.2 and 20.9) that, though progress has been made, the electronic system envisaged by the 2002 Act had not been developed, and making recommendations on three specific issues: the requirement for simultaneous completion and registration, the powers to "switch on" electronic conveyancing and to "switch off" paper-based conveyancing, and the ability to overreach an interest under a trust if a single conveyancer has signed a deed on behalf of multiple trustees. See also Department of Housing, Communities and Local Govern-

ment, *Improving the home buying and selling process, Summary of responses to the Call for Evidence and government response* (April 2018); *Emmet & Farrand on Title* (2019), para. 9-003.

## (b) Intention, Form and Delivery

### *(i) Deeds Executed on or after July 31, 1989 and before or on September 14, 2005*

#### Deeds executed by an individual

*Replace paragraph with:*

1-125 The law introduced by the Law of Property (Miscellaneous Provisions) Act 1989 s.1 requires that for an instrument made by an individual to be a deed, it must make:

> "... clear on its face that it is intended to be a deed by the person making it or, as the case may be, by the parties to it (whether by describing itself as a deed or expressing itself to be executed or signed as a deed or otherwise)."[874]

It has been observed that:

> "... the Act provides that documents can be deeds without using the word 'deed'; but ... that a document is only to be held to be a deed if it is clear from the wording of the document itself ('on its face') that it was intended to be a deed."[875]

As a result, words which indicate an intention by the parties that a document should be legally binding are not enough: "what is needed is something showing that the parties intended the document to have the extra status of being a deed".[876] The 1989 Act also introduced other requirements for the execution of a deed by an individual and preserved an existing one. For an instrument to be validly executed as a deed, it must be:

> "... signed (i) by him in the presence of a witness who attests the signature; or (ii) at his direction and in his presence and the presence of two witnesses who each attest the signature."[877]

"Signature" is defined later in the section to include making one's mark.[878] The Act specifically preserved the common law requirement that for an instrument to be validly executed as a deed it must be "delivered" as a deed by him or a person authorised to do so on his behalf.[879]

[874] s.1(2)(a). Section 1(11) of the 1989 Act provided that "nothing in this section applies in relation to instruments *delivered* as deeds before this section comes into force" i.e. July 31, 1989. This appears to mean that an *instrument* made before this date but delivered after it remains governed by the earlier law.

[875] *HSBC Trust Co v Quinn* [2007] EWHC 1543 (Ch), [2007] All E.R. (D) 125 (Jul) at [50], per Christopher Nugee Q.C. followed *Katara Hospitality v Guez* [2018] EWHC 3063 (Comm). Cf. *Johnsey Estates (1900) Ltd v Newport Marketworld Ltd* Unreported May 10, 1996 (noted and criticised by Law Com. No.253, paras 2.17–2.18) where it was held that the mere fact that a document was made under seal is sufficient to make it clear that it was executed as a deed.

[876] [2007] EWHC 1543 (Ch) at [51]; *Katara Hospitality v Guez* [2018] EWHC 3063 (Comm) at [50].

[877] Law of Property (Miscellaneous Provisions) Act 1989 s.1(3) (as enacted). It has been said that the signature and attestation must form part of the same physical document which constitutes the deed: *R. (on the application of Mercury Tax Group Ltd) v Revenue and Customs Commissioners* [2008] EWHC 2721 (Admin), [2009] S.T.C. 743 at [40]. While the Law Commission has seen this proposition as obiter, it has endorsed the suggestions of the Law Society as to practical arrangements for "virtual signings" by which the requirement stated in *Mercury Tax Group* can be satisfied: *Electronic execution of documents*, Law Com. No.386 (September 3, 2019) (Report) at paras 5.45–5.55 referring to The Law Society Company

Law Committee and the City of London Law Society Company Law and Financial Law Committees, "Note on execution of documents at a virtual signing or closing" (May 2009, with amendments February 2010). The Law Commission considered that a person may witness an electronic signature as "what they can see is the signatory purporting to add their signature to a document on the screen" (para.5.20) but considered that it is not clear that the requirement that the witness is present can be satisfied other than by being physically present, which puts in doubt witnessing by remote means such as by video link: paras 5.21–5.37 esp. at paras 5.30 and 5.35. On the other hand, it has been held that there is no requirement that the witness must sign in the presence of the person signing the deed: *Wood v Commercial First Business Ltd* [2019] EWHC 2205 (Ch), [2020] C.T.L.C. 1 at [42]–[48] (appeal pending).

[878] Law of Property (Miscellaneous Provisions) Act 1989 s.1(4). The question whether the requirement of signature may be satisfied other than by a party writing his or her name or mark with his or her own hand remains unclear. There is authority for the purposes of s.2 of the 1989 Act that appears to require such writing (*Firstpost Homes Ltd v Johnson* [1995] 1 W.L.R. 1567 though on this see below, paras 5-037–5-037D), but a more liberal position has been taken for the purposes of the (less demanding) formalities of s.4 of the Statute of Frauds: *J Pereira Fernandes SA v Mehta* [2006] EWHC 813 (Ch), [2006] 2 All E.R. 881 at [31]; *Golden Ocean Group Ltd v Salgaocar Mining Industries Pvt Ltd* [2012] EWCA Civ 265, [2012] 1 Lloyd's Rep. 542 at [32] (on which see Vol.II, para.45-057). In *Ramsay v Love* [2015] EWHC 65 (Ch) at [7], Morgan J. observed (in the context of s.1(3) of the 1989 Act, obiter) that the position in *Firstpost Homes Ltd v Johnson* ( which appears to require signature by an executing party with a pen in his own hand) was not designed to distinguish between signing in such a way and by use of a signature writing machine. For further discussion of the significance of "signature" see Law Commission, *Electronic execution of documents*, Law Com. No.386 (September 3, 2019) Ch.3 and para.5.9 (taking the view that an electronic signature can satisfy the statutory requirement of a signature for the purposes of the 1989 Act s.1); *Emmet & Farrand on Title* (2019) paras 2–041—2–041.06. For the possibility that an "electronic signature" may satisfy this requirement by way of s.7 of the Electronic Communications Act 2000 see below, para.5-008.

[879] 1989 Act s.1(3)(b).

### Delivery

*Replace footnote 895 with:*

[895] *Xenos v Wickham* (1863) 14 C.B.(N.S.) 435, 473; *Termes de la Ley*, s.v. Fait; Co Litt. 171b; Law of Property (Miscellaneous Provisions) Act 1989 s.1(3)(b). See also the Law Commission, *Electronic execution of documents*, Consultation Paper No.237 (August 21, 2018), paras 4.58–4.87. **1-128**

## *(ii) Documents Executed on or after September 15, 2005*

### The new general requirements for deeds after the 2005 Order

*To the end of paragraph, after "of "valid execution").", add new footnote 914a:*

[914a] See also Law Commission, *Electronic execution of documents*, Consultation Paper No.237 (August 21, 2018), Ch.4; Law Commission, *Electronic execution of documents*, Law Com. No.386 (September 3, 2019) Ch.5 as to how electronic deeds may be possible under the current law. **1-131**

### "Valid execution": individuals

*Replace paragraph with:*

After amendment by the 2005 Order, the 1989 Act provides that for an instrument to be validly executed as a deed by an individual, it must be: **1-134**

> "... signed
>
> (i) by him in the presence of a witness who attests the signature; or
> (ii) at his direction and in his presence and the presence of two witnesses who each attest the signature."[924]

"Signature" is defined later in the section to include making one's mark.[925] The 2005 Order preserved the further common law requirement that for an instrument to be validly executed as a deed it must be "delivered" as a deed.[926]

[924] Law of Property (Miscellaneous Provisions) Act 1989 s.1(3) (as amended by 2005 Order art.7(3)). The signature and attestation must form part of the same physical document which constitutes the deed: *R. (on the application of Mercury Tax Group Ltd) v Revenue and Customs Commissioners* at [2008] EWHC 2721 (Admin), [2009] S.T.C. 743 at [40]. See, however, the discussion of how these formal requirements may be satisfied using electronic means in Law Commission, *Electronic execution of documents*, Law Com. No.386 (September 3, 2019) (Report) at paras 5.45–5.55 where the proposition in *Mercury Tax Group Ltd* is seen as obiter: see further above, para.1-125. A signature of an unidentified individual added later cannot constitute attestation for these purposes: *Darjan Estate Co Plc v Hurley* [2012] EWHC 189 (Ch), [2012] 1 W.L.R. 1782 at [11]–[12].

[925] Law of Property (Miscellaneous Provisions) Act 1989 s.1(4)(b) as amended by the 2005 Order Sch.1 para.14.

[926] Law of Property (Miscellaneous Provisions) Act 1989 s.1(3)(b).

### *(iii) Common Aspects*

*Add new paragraph:*

1-138A **Effect of failure to comply with formal requirements** The wording of s.1 of the 1989 Act makes clear that a failure to satisfy the formal requirements which it sets out leads to the invalidity of the instrument as a deed. Section 1(2) provides that:

> "[a]n instrument *shall not be a deed unless*
>
> (a) it makes it clear on its face that it is intended to be a deed by the person making it or, as the case may be, by the parties to it (whether by describing itself as a deed or expressing itself to be executed or signed as a deed or otherwise); and
>
> (b) it is validly executed as a deed."[940a]

And s.2(3) specifies that an "instrument is validly executed as a deed by an individual if, and only if" it is signed (as then detailed) and delivered as a deed. On the other hand, this does not prevent an agreement which is contained in a deed invalid for want of formality from being enforced as a simple contract as long as it is supported by consideration and unless the particular type of contract has to be made by deed.[940b]

[940a] (emphasis added). See above, paras 1-125–1-126, 1-131, 1-134–1-135 for these requirements and the related requirements applicable to companies.

[940b] *Signature Living Hotel Ltd v Sulyok* [2020] EWHC 257 (Ch), [2020] Bus. L.R. 588 at [29]–[34] (in the context of the requirements for the valid execution of a document by a company in the Companies Act 2006 s.44), approving the position adopted by Andrews & Millett, *Law of Guarantees*, 7th edn (2015), para.2-021 (which cites *Lloyds TSB Bank Plc v The Dye House Ltd* [2005] EWHC 1998 (Comm) as an example) and the Law Commission, *Execution of Deeds and Documents by or on behalf of Bodies Corporate* (1998) (Law Com No.253) (Cm.4026), para.2.45 and not following a possible reading to the contrary of a passage of Underhill J. in *R. (on the application of Mercury Tax Group Ltd) v Revenue and Customs Commissioners* [2008] EWHC 2721 (Admin), [2009] S.T.C. 743 at [40].

**Delivery of deed as an escrow**

*Replace footnote 950 with:*

1-140 [950] It may be difficult to distinguish between a deed which has not been delivered at all and one which has been delivered as an escrow: Peel (ed.), *Treitel on The Law of Contract*, 15th edn (2020), para.3–175; *Vincent v Primo Enterprises (Voucher Sales) Ltd* [1969] 2 Q.B. 609, 620; *Kingston v American Investments Ltd* [1975] 1 W.L.R. 161; *Windsor Refrigerator Co Ltd v Branch Nominees Ltd* [1961] Ch. 88 at 102 (reversed on other grounds [1961] Ch. 375); *Silver Queen Maritime Ltd v Persia Petroleum Services Ltd* [2010] EWHC 2867 (QB).

## (d) Other Aspects

### Period of limitation

*Replace footnote 1008 with:*

1008 Limitation Act 1980 s.8(1) (but subject to s.8(2)). Section 8 refers to an "action on a specialty" and in *Liberty Partnership Ltd v Tancred* [2018] EWHC 2707 (Comm), [2019] 2 W.L.R. 923 at [52]–[64] it was held as a preliminary issue that an instrument which was a "deed" within s.1 of the 1989 Act was a "speciality" for the purposes of s.8 of the 1980 Act even in the absence of a seal by one or more of its parties. See, e.g. *Aiken v Stewart Wrightson Members Agency Ltd* [1995] 1 W.L.R. 1281, 1292. See below, paras 28-002, 28-003. **1-151**

## 7. The Relationship between Contract and Tort

## (b) Differences of Substance between Contract and Tort

### General

*Replace footnote 1052 with:*

1052 Peel (ed.), *Treitel on The Law of Contract*, 15th edn (2020), para.20–024. **1-155**

### Other differences

*Replace paragraph with:*

**1-160** A contractual right, for example, to a certain sum due under a contract, can generally be assigned, but a right of action in tort generally cannot.[1088] The rules of the conflict of laws governing both jurisdiction[1089] and applicable law are different in matters relating to tort and to contract.[1090] The law governing the capacity of parties may be different: so, for example, a minor is in principle liable for his torts, but only to a limited extent on his contracts.[1091] Statutory provisions sometimes distinguish according to rights arising out of a contract, and other rights (which would include tort) though this appears to be a diminishing practice.[1092]

1088 See below, para.19-050.

1089 Regulation (EU) 1215/2012 on jurisdiction and the recognition and enforcement of judgments in civil and commercial matters (recast) ("the Brussels Ibis Regulation") [2012] O.J. L351/1 arts 7(1) and 7(2) replacing Regulation (EC) 44/2001 of 2001 on jurisdiction and the recognition and enforcement of judgments in civil and commercial matters ("Brussels I Regulation) art.5(1) ("matters relating to a contract") and (3) ("matters relating to tort, delict or quasi-delict") which itself replaced the Convention on Jurisdiction and the Enforcement of Judgments in Civil and Commercial Matters 1968 (the "Brussels Convention"). On the effect of the UK's leaving the EU on the Brussels I Regulation, see above, para.1-016C.

1090 See in particular Regulation (EC) 593/2008 on the law applicable to contractual obligations ("Rome I") [2008] O.J. L177/6; Regulation (EC) 864/2007 applicable to non-contractual obligations ("Rome II Regulation") [2007] O.J. L199/40 and generally *Dicey, Morris and Collins on the Conflict of Laws*, 15th edn (2014), Chs 32–35. On IP completion day, the Rome I and Rome II Regulations are due to form part of "retained EU law" as amended: see above, para.1-016C. On the Rome I Regulation, see below, paras 30-019 et seq.

1091 See below, paras 9-053—9-054. See also below, para.10-081 (trade unions).

1092 An example may be found in Companies Act 2006 ss.81 and 83 (replacing ss.4 and 5 of the Business Names Act 1985). The former distinction in the Bankruptcy Act 1914 s.30(1) between demands arising by reason of contract which were provable in bankruptcy and others which were not normally so provable, is not found in the provisions which replaced it in the Insolvency Act 1985 (ss.163, 211(1), (2) and (3)).

## (c) Concurrence of Actions in Contract and Tort

### (i) Pre-contractual Liability

#### Damages for misrepresentation

*Replace paragraph with:*

**1-168** Finally, although there are considerable differences between damages in tort and for breach of contract,[1122] not all of these are significant in the context of pre-contractual statements. In general, an injured party can claim damages for the loss of an expectation or performance interest in contract but not in tort, and in the context of pre-contractual representation the latter rule means that a claimant can recover damages for misrepresentation in tort only so as to put him in a position as though the representation (and, therefore, it is assumed, the contract) had not been made and not damages as though the representation had been true.[1123] By contrast, if a court finds that a party made a contractual promise or warranty that his pre-contractual statement was true, then he can recover damages for breach of contract to put him in the position as thought the statement had been true.[1124] On the other hand, in some cases where a claim is based on breach of a term which has resulted from the incorporation of a pre-contractual statement,[1125] there will be no difference on this ground between the contractual and tortious measures of damages. In *Esso Petroleum Co Ltd v Mardon*,[1126] the Court of Appeal accepted that a representation of "throughput" of petrol of a garage by Esso which later proved false, was incorporated into the contract as a warranty. However, the ability of the representee to claim for breach of contract did not affect the damages which he could recover, in particular it did not allow him to claim for the loss of profits he expected to make from taking a lease of the garage with the throughput represented, despite such claims for lost profits being typical of contract. This refusal resulted from the court's decision as to the *content* of the warranty: it was construed not as a promise that the throughput would be a certain amount, but rather that Esso had taken reasonable care in making the estimate of throughput.[1127] A claim in contract can indeed put an injured party in the position as though the contract had been performed, but if Esso had performed this contractual warranty, and as a result Mardon had been given a true estimate of the throughput of the garage, then Mardon would not have entered into the contract.[1128] In this way, damages in contract and in tort[1129] are based on the same measure, viz to put the claimant in the position as though the contract had not been made.[1130] On the other hand, while it has been stated that a claimant will not recover more damages in tort than he would in contract,[1131] it is clear that a claimant may indeed recover more damages where his claim is based on fraud or for negligent misrepresentation under the 1967 Act,[1132] as the test of remoteness of damage applicable to these claims is more generous than the test which applies to claims for breach of contract.[1133] Furthermore, it is possible (if unlikely) that someone suing for fraud may be able to recover punitive damages,[1134] whereas these are not available for claims for breach of contract.[1135]

[1122] See above, paras 1-157—1-158.

[1123] *Doyle v Olby (Ironmongers) Ltd* [1969] 2 Q.B. 158; *André & Cie SA v Ets Michel Blanc et Fils* [1977] 2 Lloyd's Rep. 166; *East v Maurer* [1991] 1 W.L.R. 461; *Clef Aquitaine SARL v Laporte Materials (Barrow) Ltd* [2001] Q.B. 488; *OMV Petrom SA v Glencore International AG* [2016] EWCA Civ 778, [2017] 3 All E.R. 157 and see below, paras 7-059—7-079.

[1124] Cartwright, *Misrepresentation, Mistake, and Non-disclosure*, 4th edn (2017), paras 8–22—8–24.

[1125] Peel (ed.), *Treitel on The Law of Contract*, 15th edn (2020), paras 9–056—9–064 and Atiyah, *Essays on Contract* (1986), Essay 10.

[1126] [1976] 1 Q.B. 801.

[1127] [1976] 1 Q.B. 801 at 818, 823–824.

[1128] [1976] 1 Q.B. 801 at 820 (Lord Denning M.R.) and [834] (Shaw L.J.). This reasoning is based on two assumptions: first, that if Esso had taken reasonable care in making its statement as to throughput it would have made an accurate estimate and, secondly, that if Mardon had been given an accurate estimate he would not have entered the contract or perhaps, would not have entered it on the same terms. Ormrod L.J. expressed no view on the claim for loss of profits as it was "virtually incapable of proof": at 829.

[1129] The Court of Appeal based its decision in tort on *Hedley Byrne & Co Ltd v Heller & Partners Ltd* [1964] A.C. 465.

[1130] The Court of Appeal did allow Mardon damages for loss of his "general expectations", i.e. what he would have expected to have earned if he had not spent his time running the garage: [1976] 1 Q.B. 801, 821.

[1131] *Chinery v Viall* (1860) 5 H. & N. 28, 29 L.J. Ex. 180; *Johnson v Stear* (1863) 33 L.J. C.P. 130 (both conversion).

[1132] *Royscott Trust Ltd v Rogerson* [1991] 2 Q.B. 297, in which the Court of Appeal rejected the proposition that a claim for damages under s.2(1) of the Misrepresentation Act 1967 possesses the same test of remoteness of damage as applies generally to claims in the tort of negligence; and see below, para.7-080.

[1133] See below, paras 26-126—26-128. It is also more generous than the test for remoteness of damage applicable to a claim for damages by a consumer under the Consumer Protection from Unfair Trading Regulations 2008 Pt 4A and especially reg.27J(4), which applies a requirement that the loss was "reasonably foreseeable at the time of the prohibited practice": see Vol.II, para.38-201.

[1134] *Mafo v Adams* [1970] 1 Q.B. 548; *Cassell & Co Ltd v Broome* [1972] A.C. 1027, 1076; *Archer v Brown* [1985] 1 Q.B. 401, 418–421 and see below, para.7-072.

[1135] See below, para.26-048.

### Liability for non-disclosure

*Replace footnote 1137 with:*

[1137] *Rust v Abbey Life Assurance Co Ltd* [1978] 2 Lloyd's Rep. 386; *Cornish v Midland Bank Plc* [1985] 3 All E.R. 513, 522–523; *Al-Kandari v J.R. Brown & Co* [1988] Q.B. 665, 672; *Banque Keyser Ullmann SA v Skandia (UK) Co Insurance Ltd* [1990] 1 Q.B. 665, 794. cf. *Argy Trading Developments Ltd v Lapid Developments Ltd* [1977] 1 W.L.R. 444, 461; *Barclays Bank Plc v Khaira* [1992] 1 W.L.R. 623; *Ashmore v Corp of Lloyd's* [1992] 2 Lloyd's Rep. 1, 5 (and see [1992] 2 Lloyd's Rep. 620). See also Cartwright, *Misrepresentation, Mistake, and Non-disclosure*, 4th edn (2017), para.17–44. 1-169

## *(ii) Torts Committed in the Course of Performance of a Contract*

### Contractual silence and "assumption of responsibility"

*In line 51, after "care in contract.", add new footnote 1315a:*

[1315a] See, e.g. *Barness v Ingenious Media Ltd* [2019] EWHC 3299 (Ch) at [49], [61]–[67] where it was held that there was no implied term relating to the suitability of a tax-avoidance scheme for which the defendant bank had made loans to the claimants, but the court nevertheless considered whether the defendant had communicated with the claimants so as to assume responsibility to advise and whether the latter had relied on that assumption so as to found a claim in the tort of negligence, finding that they had not. 1-197

### Relationship between the scope of duty in tort and the scope of contractual implied term

*In line 28, page [158], after "closely similar.[1332] According to", delete "the".* 1-198

*Add new paragraphs:*

However, in *James-Bowen v Commissioner of Police of the Metropolis* the 1-198A

Supreme Court considered the proper relationship between the implication of a term in a standardised contract of employment and the recognition of a duty of care in a novel situation.[1336a] In that case, police officers claimed damages against their Police Commissioner (who was treated as their employer for these purposes[1336b]) on the ground that the Commissioner owed a duty of care to them in the conduct of the defence of civil proceedings brought against her as vicariously liable for their actions, this duty requiring her to act "as effectively as possible" in order to protect the officers from economic or reputational harm.[1336c] Lord Lloyd-Jones J.S.C.[1336d] noted that, if approached on the basis of implied contract terms, the issue whether such a duty of care could be extracted from the recognised implied term of trust and confidence in employment contracts had not been decided before and doing so "would be to move substantially beyond the specific derivative duties established to date".[1336e] Lord Lloyd-Jones added that he had:

> difficulty in understanding how this principal argument [based on an implied contract term] on behalf of the officers can circumvent the requirement adverted to by Lord Bridge in *Caparo Industries Plc v Dickman*[1336f] that the imposition of the duty must be fair, just and reasonable. In order to establish such a duty of care, the officers rely here upon a class of implied terms which are implied in law as a necessary incident of a particular class of contractual relationship.[1336g]

In deciding whether to imply a term as a necessary incident of a particular class of contractual relationship, the court should look to considerations of reasonableness, fairness and the balancing of competing policy considerations[1336h] and "[s]uch an implied term could not … be wider in scope than the duty imposed by the law of tort".[1336i] Accordingly, "the battlefield on which the conflicting contentions as to the existence of such a duty must be fought out is the scope of the duty of care in tort".[1336j] As the claim was clearly novel, the law should develop incrementally and taking into account considerations of legal policy and having regard both to the achievement of justice and the coherent development of the law.[1336k] The Supreme Court concluded that no such duty of care should be imposed on the grounds that it would create a conflict between the Commissioner's own interests (as employer) and the interests (reputational and economic) of the officers (as employees),[1336l] that her public duty in respect of the conduct of the Metropolitan Police would be "totally inconsistent" with duties of care of this sort to the officers,[1336m] and on other grounds of public policy relating to the conduct of litigation.[1336n] Given its earlier view as to the relationship between duty of care in tort and in contract, the Supreme Court's decision rejecting the novel duty of care in the tort of negligence as relied on by the claimants also determined the question whether a term could be implied as an incident of this standardised contract.[1336o]

[1336a] [2018] UKSC 40, [2018] 1 W.L.R. 4021. See similarly *Elite Property Holdings Ltd v Barclays Bank Plc* [2018] EWCA Civ1688, [2019] Bus. L.R. 129 [27], [62]–[68] (reasons against the existence of a duty of care in tort in the circumstances recognised by earlier authority militate strongly against recognition of a contractual obligation to the same effect in the absence of a clear expression of intention by the defendant to assume such an obligation).

[1336b] This was the case even though it was acknowledged that the officers as constables were not employees; [2018] UKSC 40 at [15].

[1336c] [2018] UKSC 40 at [13] (this was the sole remaining allegation before the SC, though other allegations had been put earlier).

[1336d] With whom Baroness Hale of Richmond, Lord Kerr of Tonaghmore, Lord Wilson and Lord Mance agreed.

[1336e] [2018] UKSC 40 at [17].

[1336f] [1990] 2 A.C. 605.

[1336g] [2018] UKSC 40 at [21].

[1336h] [2018] UKSC 40 at [21] quoting with approval to this effect Dyson L.J. in *Crossley v Faithful & Gould Holdings Ltd* [2004] I.C.R. 1615 at [36].

[1336i] [2018] UKSC 40 at [21].

[1336j] [2018] UKSC 40 at [21].

[1336k] [2018] UKSC 40 at [23].

[1336l] [2018] UKSC 40 at [31]–[32].

[1336m] [2018] UKSC 40 at [33].

[1336n] [2018] UKSC 40 at [34]–[38] and [47].

[1336o] See above in this paragraph, referring to [2018] UKSC 40 at [21].

**Scope of duty in tort affecting claim for breach of express contract term** 1-198B

Shortly after the decision of the Supreme Court in *James-Bowen* noted in the previous paragraph, though without reference to it,[1336p] in *ARB v IVF Hammersmith Ltd* the Court of Appeal adopted a similar approach to a claim for "wrongful life" on the basis of breach of an express term of contract.[1336q] There, the father claimed damages representing his financial loss in respect of the upbringing of a child born using his gametes without his consent as required by an express term of the contract which he had concluded with the defendant's clinic. In these circumstances, the Court of Appeal held that the legal policy considerations which precluded an action for damages in the tort of negligence for financial losses flowing from the birth of a healthy child, namely the impossibility of calculating this loss given the benefits and burdens of bringing up such a child,[1336r] applied equally to claims founded upon breach of an express contract term imposing a strict obligation,[1336s] in the absence of the parties having sought to quantify the damages in the event of breach, for example, by a liquidated damages clause.[1336t]

[1336p] *James-Bowen v Commissioner of Police of the Metropolis* [2018] UKSC 40, [2018] 1 W.L.R. 4021, above, para.1-098A.

[1336q] [2019] 2 W.L.R. 1094.

[1336r] *McFarlane v Tayside Health Board* [2000] 2 A.C. 59 and *Rees v Darlington Memorial Hospital NHS Trust* [2003] UKHL 52, [2004] 1 A.C. 309.

[1336s] [2018] EWCA Civ 2803 at [49].

[1336t] [2018] EWCA Civ 2803 at [32]–[36] and [39].

## Wellesley Partners LLP v Withers LLP

*Replace footnote 1405 with:*

[1405] Peel (ed.), *Treitel on The Law of Contract*, 15th edn (2020), para.20–133 and see similarly *McGregor on Damages* 20th edn (2017), para.24–009. 1-205

## The conflict of laws: jurisdiction

*Replace footnote 1423 with:*

[1423] [2014] O.J. L351/1 arts 7(1) and 7(2) (in force on January 10, 2015) replacing Regulation 44/2001 on jurisdiction and the enforcement of judgments in civil and commercial matters ("Brussels I Regulation") arts 5(1) and 5(3), which itself replaced the Brussels Convention on Jurisdiction and the Enforcement of Judgments in Civil and Commercial Matters 1968. For the law under the Brussels I Regulation see *Dicey, Morris and Collins on the Conflict of Laws*, 15th edn (updated to 2017), Ch.11. On the effect of the UK's leaving the EU on the Brussels I Regulation, see above, para.1-016C. 1-209

### Conflict of laws: applicable law

*Replace paragraph with:*

1-210 Under the Rome Convention on the Law Applicable to Contractual Obligations[1434] it was held that there is nothing to prevent a party to a contract from framing his claim in tort so as to attract the choice of law rules applicable to that basis of liability, rather than in contract whose applicable law would be determined by that Convention.[1435] However, after the enactment of the Regulation (EC) 864/2007 on the law applicable to non-contractual obligations ("Rome II Regulation")[1436] and the replacement for most purposes of the Rome Convention by Regulation (EC) 593/2008 on the law applicable to contractual obligations ("Rome I"),[1437] it is highly unlikely that a claimant will have the option as to how to frame his or her claim given that the two EU regulations will classify claims within their scope autonomously as being "contractual" or "non-contractual" for these purposes and these classifications are likely to be held mutually exclusive.[1438]

[1434] Introduced into English law by the Contracts (Applicable Law) Act 1990 and see generally, below, paras 30-018 et seq.

[1435] *Base Metal Trading Ltd v Shamurin* [2004] EWCA Civ 1316, [2005] 1 W.L.R. 1157 especially at [33].

[1436] Regulation 864/2007 [2007] O.J. L199/40 and see *Dicey, Morris and Collins on the Conflict of Laws* 15th edn (2014), Ch.35. On IP completion day, the Rome II Regulation is due to form part of "retained EU law" as amended: see above, para.1-016C.

[1437] [2008] O.J. L177/6. On which see below, paras 30-019 et seq. and *Dicey, Morris and Collins on the Conflict of Laws*, 15th edn (2014) paras 32-012 et seq. On IP completion day, the Rome I Regulation is due to form part of "retained EU law" as amended: see above, para.1-016C.

[1438] Below, para.30-041 and see *ERGO Insurance SE v If P&C Insurance AS* (Joined Cases C-359/14 and C-475/14) EU:C:2016:40, January 21, 2016 paras 43–45; *Verein für Konsumenteninformation v Amazon EU Sàrl* (C-191/15) EU:C:2016:612, July 28, 2016, paras 36–53 and 58 and *Committeri v Club Mediterranee SA* [2016] EWHC 1510 (QB) at [49]–[53].

## (d) The Influence of Contract on Tort Beyond Privity

### Subsequent cases

*Replace footnote 1530 with:*

1-225 [1530] These include *Siddell v Smith Cooper & Partners* [1999] P.N.L.R. 511; *Barex Brothers Ltd v Morris Dean & Co* [1999] P.N.L.R. 344, 349; *A.J. Fabrication (Batley) Ltd v Grant Thornton* [1999] B.C.C. 807; *Electra Private Equity Partners v KPMG Peat Marwick* [1999] 1 Lloyd's Rep. P.N. 670; *Connolly-Martin v Davis, The Times*, June 8, 1999; *Yorkshire Bank Plc v Lloyds Bank Plc* [1999] 2 All E.R. (Comm.) 153; *Hamble Fisheries Ltd v L. Gardner and Sons Ltd* [1999] 2 Lloyd's Rep. 1; *Gorham v British Telecommunications Plc* [2000] 1 W.L.R. 2129; *B.D.G. Roof-Bond v Douglas* [2000] 1 B.C.L.C. 401; *European Gas Turbines Ltd v MSAS Cargo International Inc* [2002] C.L.C. 880; *Killick v PricewaterhouseCoopers (A Firm)* [2001] 1 B.C.L.C. 65; *Merrett v Babb* [2001] 3 W.L.R. 1; *Weldon v GRE Linked Life Assurance Ltd* [2000] 2 All E.R. (Comm.) 914; *Dean v Allin and Watts* [2001] EWCA Civ 758, [2001] 2 Lloyd's Rep. 249; *Niru Battery Manufacturing Co v Milestone Trading Ltd* [2002] EWHC 1425 (Comm.), [2002] All E.R. (D) 206; *European International Reinsurance Co Ltd v Curzon Insurance Ltd* [2003] EWCA Civ 1074, [2003] Lloyd's Rep. I.R. 793; *BP Plc v Aon Ltd* [2006] EWHC 424 (Comm), [2006] 1 All E.R. (Comm.) 789; *Riyad Bank Plc v Ahli United Bank Plc* [2006] EWCA Civ 780, [2006] 2 Lloyd's Rep. 292; *Galliford Try Infrastructure Ltd v Mott MacDonald Ltd* [2008] EWHC 1570 (TCC), [2009] P.N.L.R. 9; *Scullion v Bank of Scotland* [2011] EWCA Civ 693, [2011] 1 W.L.R. 3212; *Argos Ltd v Leather Trade House Ltd* [2012] EWHC 1348 (QB), [2012] E.C.C. 34 at [42]; *Hunt v Optima (Cambridge) Ltd* [2014] EWCA Civ 714, [2015] 1 W.L.R. 1346; *Swynson Ltd v Lowick Rose LLP* [2014] EWHC 2085, [2014] P.N.L.R. 27; *Summit Advances Ltd v Bush* [2015] EWHC 665 (QB), [2015] P.N.L.R. 18; *Golden Belt 1 Sukuk Co BSC(c) v BNP Paribas* [2017] EWHC 3182 (Comm) esp. at [162]–[208]; *CGL Group Ltd v The Royal Bank of Scotland* [2017] EWCA Civ 1073, [2017] C.T.L.C. 97 at [62]–[105]; *P & P Property Ltd v Owen White & Caitlin LLP* [2018] EWCA Civ 1082, [2019] Ch. 273 at [75]–[82] and [122]–[124].

*Replace footnote 1545 with:* 1-225A

1545 [2018] UKSC 43, [2018] 1 W.L.R. 4041; Grower (2019) 135 L.Q.R. 177.

CHAPTER 2

# THE AGREEMENT

## 2. THE OFFER

### Offer defined

*Replace paragraph with:*

2-003 An offer is an expression of willingness to contract on specified terms made with the intention that it is to become binding as soon as it is accepted by the person to whom it is addressed.[10] Under the objective test of agreement,[11] an apparent intention to be bound may suffice, i.e. the alleged offeror (A) may be bound if his words or conduct[12] are such as to induce a reasonable offeree to believe that he intends to be bound, even though in fact he has no such intention. This was, for example, held to be the case where a university had made an offer of a place to an intending student as a result of a clerical error[13]; and where a solicitor, who had been instructed by his client to settle a claim for $155,000, by mistake offered to settle it for the higher sum of £150,000.[14] Similarly, if A offers to sell a book to B for £10 and B accepts the offer, A cannot escape liability merely by showing that his actual intention was to offer the book to B for £20, or that he intended the offer to relate to a book other than that specified in the offer.[15]

[10] *Air Transworld Ltd v Bombardier Inc* [2012] EWHC 243 (Comm), [2012] 1 Lloyd's Rep. 349 at [75]; e.g. *Storer v Manchester City Council* [1974] 1 W.L.R. 1403; *First Energy (UK) Ltd v Hungarian International Bank Ltd* [1993] 2 Lloyd's Rep. 195, 201; *Glencore Energy UK Ltd v Cirrus Oil Services Ltd* [2014] EWHC 87 (Comm), [2014] 1 All E.R. (Comm) 513, where a communication was held to be an offer as it was "intended to be capable of acceptance with a binding contract being thereby concluded" ([at 59]; cf. at [67]); *Crest Nicholson (Londinium) Ltd v Akaria Investments Ltd* [2010] EWCA Civ 1331 at [226]. Contrast *André & Cie v Cook Industries Inc* [1987] 2 Lloyd's Rep. 463; *Schuldenfrei v Hilton (Inspector of Taxes)* [1998] S.T.C. 404 (statement that something *had* been done, not an offer). For other illustrations of statements held not to amount to offers, see *Destiny 1 Ltd v Lloyd's TSB Bank Plc* [2010] EWHC 1233 (proposal forming part of a negotiating "package"); *Global 5000 Ltd v Wadhawan* [2011] EWHC 853 (Comm), [2011] 2 All E.R. (Comm) at [55] (applying the objective test: at [46]); [2012] EWCA Civ 13, [2012] 2 All E.R. (Comm) 18 at [65], appeal dismissed on the different ground that there was "no serious issue to be tried as to the existence of [the alleged] contract …"; *UK Learning Academy Ltd v Secretary of State for Education* [2018] EWHC 2915 (Comm) at [241], [245].

[11] Above, para.2-002; *Ignazio Messina & Co v Polskie Linie Oceaniczne* [1995] 2 Lloyd's Rep. 566, 571; *Bowerman v ABTA Ltd* [1995] N.L.J. 1815; *Covington Marine Corp v Xiamen Shipbuilding Industry Co Ltd* [2005] EWHC 2912 (Comm), [2006] 1 Lloyd's Rep. 748 at [43].

[12] For offers made by conduct, see below, para.2-005; *The Aramis* [1989] 1 Lloyd's Rep. 213 (where the objective test was not satisfied); *G. Percy Trentham Ltd v Archital Luxfer Ltd* [1993] 1 Lloyd's Rep. 25, 27.

[13] *Moran v University College Salford (No.2), The Times,* November 23, 1993; cf. *UK Learning Academy Ltd v Secretary of State for Education* [2018] EWHC 2915 (Comm) at [280]–[283] (offer posted in error had been accepted by post).

[14] *O.T. Africa Line Ltd v Vickers Plc* [1996] 1 Lloyd's Rep. 700.

[15] cf. *Centrovincial Estates Plc v Merchant Investors Assurance Co Ltd* [1983] Com. L.R. 158; cited with approval in *Whittaker v Campbell* [1984] Q.B. 318, 327, in *Food Corp of India v Antclizo Shipping Corp (The Antclizo)* [1987] 2 Lloyd's Rep. 130, 146, affirmed [1988] 1 W.L.R. 603 and in *O.T. Africa Line Ltd v Vickers Plc* [1996] 1 Lloyd's Rep. 700, 702.

### State of mind of alleged offeree

*Replace paragraph with:*

2-004 Whether A is actually bound by an acceptance of his apparent offer depends on the state of mind of the alleged offeree (B); to this extent, the test of agreement can be said to be not "wholly objective".[16] If B actually and reasonably believes that A has the requisite intention, the objective test is satisfied so that B can hold A to his apparent offer even though A did not, subjectively, have the requisite intention.[17] However, if B knows that, in spite of the objective appearance, A does not have the requisite intention, A is not bound; the objective test does not apply in favour of B as he knows the truth about A's actual intention.[18] There are other permutations. If B does not know, but ought to have known that A does not have the requisite intention, English law gives no clear answer.[19] However, there are suggestions that B will not be able to hold A to his apparent offer.[20] It is also possible, although highly unlikely, that A and B, unknown to each other, both have the same requisite intention but a reasonable third party would not have thought they did, or would have thought that they had the requisite intention in respect of a different term. There is no authority on such a case, but it is submitted that where A and B reach agreement on term X but the unexpressed intention of both is that this means Y, the parties should be held to a valid contract for Y although a third party's objective interpretation is that the agreement is for X.[21] Lastly, B may have simply formed no view on the question of A's intention, so that B neither believes that A has the requisite intention nor knows that A does not have this intention. This situation has given rise to a conflict of judicial opinion. One view is that A is not bound: in other words, the objective test is satisfied only if A's conduct is such as to induce a reasonable person to believe that A had the requisite intention *and* if B actually held that belief.[22] The opposing view is that A is bound: in other words, the objective test is satisfied if A's words or conduct would induce a reasonable person to believe that A had the requisite intention, so long as B does not actually know that A does *not* have any such intention.[23] However, it is hard to see why B should be protected in this situation. Where B has no positive belief in A's (apparent) intention to be bound, he cannot be prejudiced by acting in reliance on it. It is therefore submitted that the objective test should not apply to the last situation. For this purpose, it should make no difference whether B's state of mind amounts to ignorance of, or merely to indifference to, the truth.

16 *Paal Wilson & Co A/S v Partenreederei Hannah Blumenthal (The Hannah Blumenthal)* [1983] 1 A.C. 854, 924.

17 *André & Cie SA v Marine Transocean Ltd (The Splendid Sun)* [1981] 1 Q.B. 694, as explained in *The Hannah Blumenthal*, above; *Challoner v Bower* (1984) 269 E.G. 725; *Tankrederei Ahrenkeil GmbH v Frahuil SA (The Multibank Holsatia)* 2 Lloyd's Rep. 486, 493 ("subjective understanding").

18 *Ignazio Messina & Co v Polskie Linie Oceaniczne* [1995] 2 Lloyd's Rep. 566, 571; *O.T. Africa Line Ltd v Vickers Plc* [1996] 1 Lloyd's Rep. 700, 703; *Covington Marine Corp v Xiamen Shipbuilding Industry Co Ltd* [2005] EWHC 2912 (Comm), [2006] 1 Lloyd's Rep. 748 at [45] ("Subject only to actual knowledge on the part of the buyer [the offeree] that no offer was intended"); *HSBC Bank Plc v 5th Avenue Partners Ltd* [2007] EWHC 2819 (Comm) at [117] (objective principle "not engaged" where absence of any intention to vary an existing contract was known to both parties, affirmed on other issues [2009] EWCA Civ 296); and see the authorities cited in n.23, below. The passage of the text ending with n.18 is evidently that in the 30th edition of this book to which approving reference is made in *Attrill v Dresdner Kleinwort Ltd* [2012] EWHC 1189 (QB) at [130], [154], affirmed: [2013] EWCA Civ 394, [86]. See also *Maple Leaf Macro Volatility Master Fund v Rouvroy* [2009] EWHC 257 (Comm) at [229], though doubted in the CA: [2009] EWCA Civ 1334 at [17]; *Novus Aviation Ltd v Alubaf Arab International Bank BSC(c)* [2016] EWHC 1575 (Comm) at [54]–[57]; *Blue v Ashley* [2017] EWHC 1928 (Comm) at [64]. See further on the mistake of term known to the other party at paras 3-018, 3-022, 3-035, and rectification for unilateral mistake as to terms at paras 3-069—3-076.

19 In *Merrill Lynch International v Amorim Partners Ltd* [2014] EWHC 74 (QB) at [54] Hamblen J. said that a mistake will only give rise to relief if it was known to the other party, but the point does not appear to have been argued and the mistake was in any event not as to the terms of the contract, see below, para.3-023.

20 See *Centrovincial Estates Plc v Merchant Investors Assurance Co Ltd* [1983] Com. L.R. 158; *O.T. Africa Line Ltd v Vickers Plc* [1996] 1 Lloyd's Rep. 700 at 703, where Mance J. said that the objective principle would be displaced if a party knew or ought to have known of the mistake.

21 See below, paras 3-065 and 3-086.

22 *The Hannah Blumenthal*, above, as interpreted in *Allied Marine Transport v Vale de Rio Doce Navegaceo SA (The Leonidas D.)* [1985] 1 W.L.R. 925; Beatson (1986) 102 L.Q.R. 1; Atiyah (1986)

102 L.Q.R. 363; *Gebr. van Weelde Scheepvaart Kantoor BV v Homeric Marine Services (The Agrabele)* [1987] 2 Lloyd's Rep. 223, especially at 235; cf. *Cie Française d'Importation, etc., SA v Deutsche Continental Handelsgesellschaft* [1985] 2 Lloyd's Rep. 592, 597; *Amherst v James Walker Goldsmith and Silversmith Ltd* [1983] Ch. 305. The view that, in the third of the situations described in the text above, there is no contract is referred to with approval by Andrew Smith J. in *Maple Leaf Volatility Master Fund v Rouvroy* [2009] EWHC 257 (Comm), [2009] 1 Lloyd's Rep. 475 at [228], affirmed [2009] EWCA Civ 1134, [2010] 2 All E.R. (Comm) 788 where Longmore L.J. at [22] paid "tribute to the careful and thorough judgment of Andrew Smith J" but nonetheless (at [17]) doubted that subjective intentions are ever relevant.

[23] *Excomm Ltd v Guan Guan Shipping (Pte) Ltd (The Golden Bear)* [1987] 1 Lloyd's Rep. 330, 341 (doubted on another point in para.2-070 n.368 below, and see para.2-006 n.32); this view was approved in *The Antclizo* [1987] 2 Lloyd's Rep. 130, 143 but doubted at 147 (affirmed [1988] 1 W.L.R. 603 without reference to the point); and semble in *Floating Dock Ltd v Hong Kong and Shanghai Bank Ltd* [1986] 1 Lloyd's Rep. 65, 77; *The Multibank Holsatia* [1988] 2 Lloyd's Rep. 486, 492 ("at least did not conflict with [B's] subjective understanding"); *Thai-Europe Tapioca Service Ltd v Seine Navigation Inc (The Maritime Winner)* [1989] 2 Lloyd's Rep. 506, 515 (using similar language). A dictum in *Furness Withy (Australia) Pty Ltd v Metal Distribution (UK) Ltd (The Amazonia)* [1990] 1 Lloyd's Rep. 236, 242 goes even further in suggesting that there may be a contract even though "*neither* [party] intended to make a contract".

## Offer and invitation to treat

*Replace footnote 37 with:*

2-007 [37] [1979] 1 W.L.R. 294 and see *Kyte v Revenue and Customs Commissioners* [2018] EWHC 1146 (Ch); [2018] B.T.C. 20 at [57] where no offer, but only an invitation to treat was found because the suggestion that there was a "settlement opportunity" used language which was a "considerable distance from the type of language which could be described as 'promissory language' or the language of commitment". cf. *Michael Gerson (Leasing) Ltd v Wilkinson* [2000] Q.B. 514 at 540 ("I am willing to make an outright sale [of specified machinery] for £319,000 ...") not an offer and, even if it was, it had not been accepted: below, para.2-026. Contrast *Basso v Wadhwani* [2019] EWHC 3212 (QB) at [52] (in the circumstances, proposal that certain amounts paid "could be deducted" from the final calculation amounted to an offer).

## Other displays

*Replace paragraph with:*

2-013 The principles stated in paras 2-011 and 2-012 above can also apply to other displays. Thus, where a menu is displayed outside a restaurant, or handed to a customer, it seems that the proprietor only makes an invitation to treat,[69] the offer coming from the customer. On the other hand, a notice at the entrance to an automatic car park may be an offer which can be accepted by driving in[70]; a notice on a car park ticketing machine that overpaid sums would be accepted with no change given was held to be an offer to provide parking for whatever sum, equal to or over the stipulated sum, that the customer put into the machine[70a]; and a display of deck-chairs for *hire* has been held to be an offer.[71] There is no perfectly general answer to the question whether such displays are offers or invitations to treat; the answer depends in each case on the intention with which the display was made.[72] In *University of Edinburgh v Onifade*[73] a notice displayed by a landowner on its land stated that any persons parking their cars there without permit would be liable to a "fine" of £30 per day. A motorist who had so parked his car was held liable for the specified amount as his conduct amounted to an acceptance[74]; so that it must have been assumed that the notice was an offer. However, with respect, it is open to question whether the landowner had any objective intention to enter into a contract with persons parking without permit. Rather, the landowner's intention seems to have been to deter unauthorised parking. The point could be significant if an action had been brought against the landowner, e.g. in respect of loss of or damage to the car.

[69] cf. *Guildford v Lockyer* [1975] Crim. L.R. 235.

[70] *Thornton v Shoe Lane Parking Ltd* [1971] 2 Q.B. 163, 169.

[70a] *National Car Parks Ltd v Revenue and Customs Commissioners* [2019] EWCA Civ 854, [2019] 3 All E.R. 590 at [18].

[71] *Chapelton v Barry UDC* [1940] 1 K.B. 532.

[72] cf. the cases discussed below, para.2-018.

[73] 2005 S.L.T. (Sh Ct) 63.

[74] See below, paras 2-026, 2-029.

## 3. The Acceptance

### (a) Definition

#### Negotiation after apparent agreement

*Replace paragraph with:*

Businessmen do not, any more than the courts, find it easy to say precisely when they have reached agreement, and may continue to negotiate after they appear to have agreed to the same terms. The court will then look at the entire course of negotiations to decide whether an apparently unqualified acceptance did in fact conclude the agreement.[153] If it did, the fact that the parties continued negotiations after this point does not affect the existence of the contract between them[154]: for example, in one such case the subsequent negotiations showed "only that the parties wished to discuss the *implementation* of the agreement[155] and that [one of them] wished to improve the terms that *had been agreed*". The position would, of course, be different if the continued negotiations could be construed[156] as an agreement to rescind the contract. A fortiori, the binding force of an oral contract is not affected or altered merely by the fact that, after its conclusion, one party sends to the other a document containing terms significantly different from those which had been orally agreed.[157] **2-028**

[153] *Hussey v Horne-Payne* (1878) 4 App. Cas. 311; *Bristol, Cardiff & Swansea Aerated Bread Co v Maggs* (1890) 44 Ch. D. 616; *British Guiana Credit Corp v Da Silva* [1965] 1 W.L.R. 248; *Container Transport International Inc v Oceanus Mutual, etc., Association* [1984] 1 Lloyd's Rep. 476; *Asty Maritime Co Ltd v Rocco Guiseppe & Figli (The Astyanax)* [1985] 2 Lloyd's Rep. 109, 112; *Hofflinghouse & Co Ltd v C. Trade SA (The Intra Transporter)* [1986] 2 Lloyd's Rep. 132; *Pagnan SpA v Granaria BV* [1986] 2 Lloyd's Rep. 547; *Pagnan SpA v Feed Products Ltd* [1987] 2 Lloyd's Rep. 601, 619; *Ignazio Messina & Co v Polskie Linie Oceaniczne* [1995] 2 Lloyd's Rep. 566 (no contract); *Frota Oceanica Brasilieira SA v Steamship Mutual Underwriting Association (The Frotanorte)* [1996] 2 Lloyd's Rep. 461 (no contract as matters of substance remained unresolved); *Cockett Marine DMCC v ING Bank NV* [2019] EWHC 1533 (Comm) (no contact as the claimant's purported acceptance included additional terms and a request for a copy of the defendant's terms and conditions). The same principle has been applied in the context of the question whether a contract had been rescinded: *Drake Insurance Plc v Provident Insurance Plc* [2003] EWCA Civ 1834, [2004] Q.B. 601 at [100]. See also *Tryggingarfelagio Foroyar P/F v CPT Empresas Maritimas SA (The Athena)* [2011] EWHC 589 (Admlty) at [44], citing the above text with apparent approval.

[154] *Perry v Suffields Ltd* [1916] 2 Ch. 187; *Davies v Sweet* [1962] 2 Q.B. 300; *Cranleigh Precision Engineering Ltd v Bryant* [1965] 1 W.L.R. 1293; *Harmony Shipping Co SA v Saudi-Europe Line Ltd (The Good Helmsman)* [1981] 1 Lloyd's Rep. 377, 409, 416. Contrast *Global Asset Capital Inc v Aabar Block Sarl* [2017] EWCA Civ 37, where no contract was found because acceptance of an offer letter that was "subject to contract" would not remove the subject to contract condition, and subsequent communications by both parties were materially inconsistent with the existence of a contract.

[155] cf. para.2-123 below.

[156] *Maple Leaf Macro Volatility Master Fund v Rouvroy* [2009] EWHC 257 (Comm), [2009] 1 Lloyd's Rep. 475 at [230], affirmed [2009] EWCA Civ 1334, [2010] 2 All E.R. (Comm) 786 without reference to this point, but see above, para.2-004 n.22.

[157] *Jayaar Impex Ltd v Toaken Group Ltd* [1996] 2 Lloyd's Rep. 437. Cf. *Cockett Marine DMCC v ING Bank NV* [2019] EWHC 1533 (Comm).

## Acceptance by conduct

*Replace paragraph with:*

**2-029** An offer may be accepted by conduct. For example, an offer to buy goods can be accepted by supplying them[159]; an offer to sell goods made by sending them to the offeree, can be accepted by using them[160]; an offer contained in a request for services can be accepted by beginning to render them[161]; an offer of services may be accepted by the offeree's conduct in arranging an appointment in certain circumstances[162]; where a customer of a bank draws a cheque which will, if honoured, cause his account to be overdrawn, the bank, by deciding to honour the cheque, impliedly accepts the customer's implied request for an overdraft on the bank's usual terms[163]; and when a car park ticketing machine displays a notice that overpaid sums would be accepted with no change given, the offer is accepted by the customer paying the stipulated sum or more, and pressing a green button to obtain a ticket.[163a] But conduct will only amount to acceptance if it is clear that the offeree's alleged act of acceptance was done with the intention (ascertained in accordance with the objective principle[164]) of accepting the offer. Thus, a buyer's taking delivery of goods after the conclusion of an oral contract of sale will not amount to his acceptance of written terms which differ significantly from those orally agreed, and which are sent to him by the seller after the oral contract was made but before taking delivery.[165] That conduct is then referable to the oral contract rather than to the later attempted variation. Nor is a company's offer to insure a car accepted by taking the car out on the road, if there is evidence that the driver intended to insure with another company.[166] Nor is a managing director's proposal of an employment contract accepted by the company paying him at the stated rate, if there is doubt over whether the company accepted the other terms.[167] Nor is there acceptance by conduct simply because a professional adviser who made an offer was subsequently invited to a management conference and a site visit (which were part of the "services" offered) since the invitation was "not necessarily or unequivocally referable to the acceptance of any offer made".[167a] Furthermore, in the absence of an express offer, a failure to object to the claimant's alleged offer by conduct does not amount to an acceptance of that offer by conduct.[167b] Moreover, since "it is possible to make a payment without entering into a contract … it necessarily follows that proof of a payment cannot, in and of itself, prove the existence of a contract".[167c] It may be "explicable for some other reason which does not involve a contract having been entered into".[167d] A fortiori, there is no acceptance where the offeree's conduct clearly indicates an intention to reject the offer. This was the position in a Scottish case where a notice on a package containing computer software stated that opening the package would indicate acceptance of the terms on which the supply was made, and the customer returned the package unopened.[168]

[159] *Harvey v Johnson* (1848) 6 C.B. 305; cf. *Steven v Bromley & Son* [1919] 2 K.B. 722, 728; *Greenmast Shipping Co SA v Jean Lion et Cie (The Saronikos)* [1986] 2 Lloyd's Rep. 277; cf. *Interfoto Picture Library Ltd v Stiletto Visual Programmes Ltd* [1989] Q.B. 433, 436; *Re Charge Card Services* [1989] Ch. 497 (above, para.2-011); *Carlyle Finance Ltd v Pallas Industrial Finance Ltd* [1999] 1 All E.R. (Comm) 659 at 670; and see below, para.2-075; *Photolibrary Group Ltd v Burda Senator Verlag GmbH* [2008] EWHC 1343 (QB), [2008] 2 All E.R. (Comm) 811; *Finmoon Ltd v Baltic Reefers Management Ltd* [2012] EWHC 920 (Comm), [2012] 2 Lloyd's Rep. 388, where para.2-030 of the 30th edition of the Main Work is cited at [22] with apparent approval; *Hamad M Aldrees & Partners v Rotex Europe Ltd* [2019] EWHC 574 (TCC), 184 C.L.R. 145; contrast *Capital Finance Co Ltd v Bray* [1964] 1 W.L.R. 323. As to counter-offers, see below, paras 2-098, 2-100.

[160] *Weatherby v Bonham* (1832) 5 C. & P. 228; *Brogden v Metropolitan Ry* (1877) 2 App. Cas. 666, below, para.2-030 at n.172; cf. *Hart v Mills* (1846) 15 L.J. Ex. 200; *Confetti Records v Warner Music*

*UK Ltd* [2003] EWHC 1274, *The Times,* June 12, 2003. It is assumed that the goods are not "unsolicited" within the legislation against "inertia selling" (above, para.2-005).

[161] *Smit International Singapore Pte Ltd v Kurnia Dewi Shipping SA (The Kurnia Dewi)* [1997] 1 Lloyd's Rep. 553; cf. *Datec Electronics Holdings Ltd v United Parcels Ltd* [2007] UKHL 23, [2007] 1 W.L.R. 1325 at [23], discussed in para.2-009 above.

[162] *Aroca Seiquer & Asociados v Adams* [2018] EWCA Civ 1589 at [35]–[37]. And see *Anchor 2020 Ltd v Midas Construction Ltd* [2019] EWHC 435 (TCC), [2019] 1 All E.R. (Comm) 421 at [113] (continued performance of the agreement indicated the parties' intention to create legal relations).

[163] *Lloyds Bank v Voller* [2000] 2 All E.R. (Comm) 978.

[163a] *National Car Parks Ltd v Revenue and Customs Commissioners* [2019] EWCA Civ 854, [2019] 3 All E.R. 590.

[164] Above, paras 2-002, 2-003. For the application of the objective principle to an acceptance by conduct, see *University of Edinburgh v Onifade* 2005 S.L.T. (Sh Ct) 63, above para.2-026 n.143.

[165] *Jayaar Impex Ltd v Toaken Group Ltd* [1996] 2 Lloyd's Rep. 437.

[166] *Taylor v Allon* [1966] 1 Q.B. 304. The objective principle (above, paras 2-002, 2-003) could not apply in this case, as the conduct alleged to constitute the acceptance had never come to the notice of the offeror. cf. *Picardi v Cuniberti* [2002] EWHC 2933, (2003) 19 Const. L.J. 350: payments made under another contract held not to amount to acceptance of an offer to enter into the alleged new contract; and see, in another context, *Re Leyland Daf Ltd* [1994] 4 All E.R. 300, affirmed sub nom. *Powdrill v Watson* [1995] 2 A.C. 394.

[167] *Arley Homes North West Ltd v Cosgrave* Unreported April 14, 2016, EAT.

[167a] *Moorgate Capital (Corporate Finance) Ltd v Sun European Partners LLP* [2020] EWHC 593 (Comm) at [116].

[167b] *Atlas Residential Solutions Management UK Ltd* [2020] EWHC 366 (Comm) at [90]–[93].

[167c] *Avonwick Holdings Ltd v Azitio Holdings Ltd* [2020] EWHC 1844 (Comm) at [681], quoting Lord Pollock M.R. in *Chillingworth v Esche* [1924] 1 Ch. 97, 110.

[167d] *Avonwick Holdings Ltd v Azitio Holdings Ltd* [2020] EWHC 1844 (Comm) at [703].

[168] *Beta Computers (Europe) v Adobe Systems (Europe)* 1996 S.L.T. 604; even opening the package would not necessarily be an acceptance so as to incorporate the printed terms: see Tapper in (ed. Rose) *Consensus ad Idem, Essays in the Law of Contract in Honour of Guenter Treitel*, 287–288.

## Establishing the terms of contracts made by conduct

*Replace footnote 173 with:*

[173] Contrast *Jayaar Impex Ltd v Toaken Group Ltd* [1996] 2 Lloyd's Rep. 437, where the conduct of the buyer was referable, not to the draft sent by the seller, but to the earlier oral agreement (above at n.165) between the parties; and *UK Safety Group Ltd v Heane* [1998] 2 B.C.L.C. 208 (company director not bound by terms of a draft agreement which was under the company's Articles required to be, but had not been, authorised by the board). This paragraph was approved in *Ghosh v Hanover Gate Mansions Ltd* [2019] UKUT 290 (LC) at [24], and see [21]–[22], where the Upper Tribunal interpreted *Brogden v Metropolitan Ry* as authority for the proposition that a contract comes into effect upon performance in accordance with the terms of the agreement and not only when the goods or services are paid for. **2-030**

## Correspondence between acceptance and offer

*Replace footnote 175 with:*

[175] *North West Leicestershire DC v East Midlands Housing Association* [1981] 1 W.L.R. 1396. And see *China Export and Credit Insurance Corp v Emerald Energy Resources Ltd* [2018] EWHC 1503 (Comm), [2018] 2 Lloyd's Rep. 179 at [39], where the claimant's letters stated that "interest continues to accrue but it may consider waiving this interest", while the defendant's letters stated that "no additional interest will be due". **2-031**

## One party's "usual conditions"

*Replace footnote 189 with:*

[189] Below, paras 13-008—13-018. If the test of reasonable notice or signature is satisfied, the contract will be on B's conditions. See *Cockett Marine DMCC v ING Bank NV* [2019] EWHC 1533 (Comm) **2-034**

(B's communication constituted a counter-offer, which was accepted by A accepting the goods; B's terms and conditions formed part of the contract).

### Each party refers to own conditions

*Replace footnote 191 with:*

2-035 [191] *A E Yates Trenchless Solutions v Black & Veatch Ltd* [2008] EWHC 3183 (TCC), 124 Con. L.R. 188 at [60]; cf. *Claxton Engineering Services Ltd v TXM Olaj-és Gázkutató Kft* [2010] EWHC 2567 (Comm), [2011] 2 All E.R. 38, where general conditions in an order form sent by the buyer to the seller contained a Hungarian arbitration and choice of law clause, while the seller in an email message to the buyer proposed a variation containing an English choice of law and exclusion jurisdiction clause; the latter was held to be a counter-offer, which the buyer accepted by "performance", i.e. presumably by taking delivery of the goods (for further proceedings in this case, see [2011] EWHC 345, [2011] 2 All E.R. (Comm) 128); *Hamad M Aldrees & Partners v Rotex Europe Ltd* [2019] EWHC 574 (TCC), 184 Con. L.R. 145 at [173] (the defendant provided a quotation and the claimant buyer made a purchase order in response, which contained provisions that conflicted with those of the quotation; the order was held to be a counter-offer, which the defendant accepted by supplying the products ordered).

## (b) Communication of Acceptance

### General requirement of communication

*Replace footnote 241 with:*

2-044 [241] *Best's Case* (1865) 2 D.J. & S. 650; cf. *Gunn's Case* (1867) L.R. 3 Ch. App. 40. And see *UK Learning Academy Ltd v Secretary of State for Education* [2018] EWHC 2915 (Comm) (no contract as the defendant had not communicated acceptance, and the claimant had not waived the requirement of communication).

## (d) Prescribed Mode of Acceptance

### Method must generally be complied with

*Replace footnote 340 with:*

2-064 [340] There is no "prescribed" mode of acceptance in the sense under consideration here merely because "the agreement envisages a signature [by each party] and leaves a space for these signatures": *Maple Leaf Macro Volatility Master Fund v Rouvroy* [2009] EWCA Civ 1334, [2010] 2 All E.R. (Comm) 788 at [16]. Even if the offer expressly refers to a method of acceptance (such as signature by the offeree) that method need only be complied with if, on the true construction of the offer, it is intended to be the *only* method of acceptance: *Mulcaire v News Group Newspapers Ltd* [2011] EWHC 3469 (Ch), [2012] Ch. 435 at [11]. And see *Re Carluccio's Ltd (In Administration)* [2020] EWHC 886 (Ch) at [51] (variation offer letter expressly required employees to positively respond, thus consent could not be inferred from silence).

## (e) Silence

### Offeree generally not bound

*In line 3, after "accepted by silence.", add new footnote 356a:*

2-069 [356a] Contrast *Re Carluccio's Ltd (In Administration)* [2020] EWHC 886 (Ch) at [51] (offer "expressly required employees to respond positively in order to agree the variation, and warned that a failure to respond could lead to them being considered for redundancy. These terms did not suggest that a failure to respond would be taken as consent to be furloughed, but suggested precisely the opposite").

### Silence and conduct

*Replace footnote 412 with:*

2-076 [412] *Yona International Ltd v La Réunion Française, etc.* [1996] 2 Lloyd's Rep. 84, 110 (where no inference of assent was drawn from silence); *Atlas Residential Solutions Management UK Ltd* [2020] EWHC 366 (Comm) at [93] (acceptance of the principle but not applicable on the facts).

## 4. TERMINATION OF THE OFFER

## (b) Rejection

### Inquiries and requests for information

*To the end of paragraph, after "is "merely exploratory".[523]", add:*

In another case,[523a] the defendant's submission of a Risk Register to be included as part of the contract documents did not to amount to a counter-offer because the evidence was "not clear as to [the Risk Register's] importance and ... appeared, objectively, simply to suggest that it would be included for the sake of completeness". 2-100

[523a] *Anchor 2020 Ltd v Midas Construction Ltd* [2019] EWHC 435 (TCC) at [94].

## (g) Supervening Corporate Incapacity

### Company as offeror

*Replace footnote 574 with:*

[574] For a discussion of policy considerations which should govern the outcome in such cases, see Treitel, *The Law of Contract*, 15th edn (2020), para.12–084. 2-115

## 6. INCOMPLETE AGREEMENT

### Agreement in principle only

*Replace paragraph with:*

Parties may reach agreement on essential matters of principle, but leave important points unsettled so that their agreement is incomplete.[602] It has, for example, been held that there was no contract where an agreement for a lease failed to specify the date on which the term was to commence[603]; that an agreement "in principle" for the redevelopment and disposal of residential property, which specified core terms but left important matters, such as the timing of the project, for future discussion was an "incomplete agreement" and so did not amount to a binding contract[604]; that an agreement for sale of land by instalments was not a binding contract where it provided for conveyance of "a proportionate part" as each instalment of the price was paid, but failed to specify which part is to be conveyed on each payment[605]; that where, though agreement had been reached "covering some significant matters",[606] there was no contract because "many fundamental matters remained to be resolved",[607] that an agreement to transfer money and property conditional on the transferee's retraction of comments in an affidavit, an undertaking of confidentiality and the transferor's satisfaction, was not intended to be binding until the conditions were fulfilled, the conditions being, anyway, too uncertain,[608] that any agreement reached by the parties was not binding as it failed to cover "significant" and "essential" issues such as the division of profits and the distribution of the risk of litigation between parties,[609] that a memorandum of understanding was not binding because the fact that it was "followed by other drafts makes it impossible to conclude that the parties had already entered into a final and binding agreement"[610] (there was also a lack of clarity on a number of terms[610a]), and that an agreement to design a racing car was not binding as it failed to deal with numerous matters of considerable commercial importance, including who would have 2-120 ownership over the relevant intellectual property rights.[610b] An agreement is also incomplete if it expressly provides that it is "subject to" specified points; there is no contract in such a case until either those points are resolved or the parties agree that their resolution is no longer necessary for the agreement to enter into contractual force.[611]

602 Referred to with apparent approval in *Western Broadcasting Services v Seaga* [2007] UKPC 19, [2007] E.M.L.R. 18 at [19].

603 *Harvey v Pratt* [1965] 1 W.L.R. 1025; and see *Re Day's Will Trusts* [1962] 1 W.L.R. 1419; *Kyte v Revenue and Customs Commissioners* [2018] EWHC 1146 (Ch); [2018] B.T.C. 20 at [60] where a date for settling tax liabilities was missing.

604 *Cobbe v Yeoman's Row Management Ltd* [2008] UKHL 55, [2008] 1 W.L.R. 1752 at [15]; see also at [7], [88].

605 *Bushwall Properties Ltd v Vortex Properties* [1976] 1 W.L.R. 591; cf. *Hillreed Land v Beautridge* [1994] E.G.C.S. 55; *Avintar v Avill* 1995 S.C.L.R. 1012; *Hadley v Kemp* [1999] E.M.L.R. 589 at 628; *London & Regional Development v TBI Plc* [2002] EWCA Civ 355; *Spectra International Plc v Tiscali Ltd* [2002] EWHC 2084 (Comm); [2002] All E.R. (D) 2009 (Oct); *Morgan Grenfell Development v Arrows Autosport Ltd* [2003] EWHC 333 (Ch); [2003] All E.R. (D) 417 (Feb); *Jordan Grand Prix Ltd v Vodafone Group Plc* [2003] EWHC 1956 (Comm); [2003] 2 All E.R. (Comm) 864; *Compagnie Noga D'Importation et D'Exportation SA v Abacha* [2003] EWCA Civ 1100; [2003] 2 All E.R. (Comm) 915. It may sometimes be possible to resolve uncertainty as to the subject-matter of the contract by extrinsic evidence, as in *Westville Properties Ltd v Dow Properties Ltd* [2010] EWHC 30 (Ch), [2010] 2 P & C.R. 19.

606 *Bols Distilleries BV v Superior Yacht Services Ltd* [2006] UKPC 45, [2007] 1 W.L.R. 12 at [32].

607 *Bols Distilleries BV v Superior Yacht Services Ltd* [2006] UKPC 45 at [35]. cf. *Whittle Movers Ltd v Hollywood Express Ltd* [2009] EWCA Civ 1189 at [14] (no express contract as important terms were still being negotiated; nor, for reasons given in para.2-170 below could any contract be implied); *Haden Young Ltd v Laing O'Rourke Midlands Ltd* [2008] EWHC 1016 (TCC) at [87], [116] and [138] (no contract between the relevant parties as essential terms had not been agreed); *Barbudev v Eurocom Cable Management Bulgaria EOOD* [2012] EWCA Civ 548 at [52] (no enforceable contract where essential terms had not been agreed).

608 *Harb v Aziz* [2018] EWHC 508 (Ch) at [192], [197]–[199], [211].

609 *Rotam Agrochemical Co Ltd v GAT Microencapsulation GmbH (formerly GAT Microencapsulation AG)* [2018] EWHC 2765 (Comm) at [154].

610 *Avonwick Holdings Ltd v Azitio Holdings Ltd* [2020] EWHC 1844 (Comm) at [660].

610a *Avonwick Holdings Ltd v Azitio Holdings Ltd* [2020] EWHC 1844 (Comm) at [673].

610b *CRS GT Ltd v McLaren Automotive Ltd* [2018] EWHC 3209 (Comm) at [135].

611 *Electrosteel Castings Ltd v Scan-Trans Shipping & Chartering Co* [2002] EWHC 1993 (Comm); [2002] 2 All E.R. (Comm) 1064 at [24].

## Agreement complete despite lack of detail

*Replace paragraph with:*

**2-121** On the other hand, an agreement may be complete although it is not worked out in meticulous detail.[612] Thus an agreement for the sale of goods may be complete as soon as the parties have agreed to buy and sell, where the remaining details can be determined by the standard of reasonableness or by law.[613] Even failure to agree the price is not necessarily fatal in such a case. Section 8(2) of the Sale of Goods Act 1979 provides that, if no price is determined by the contract, a reasonable price must be paid. Under s.15(1) of the Supply of Goods and Services Act 1982, a reasonable sum must similarly be paid where a contract for the supply of services fails to fix the remuneration to be paid for them.[614] These statutory provisions assume that the agreement amounts to a contract in spite of its failure to fix the price or remuneration. The very fact that the parties have not reached agreement on this vital point may indicate that there is *no* contract, e.g. because the price or remuneration is to be fixed by further agreement.[615] In such a case, the statutory provisions for payment of a reasonable sum do not apply. The same applies to the date of delivery left to be mutually agreed where the inclusion of a "best efforts" clause implicitly recognised that both sides could have regard to their own interests and so precludes fixing a delivery date by reference to what would be "reasonable".[616] There may, however, be a claim for payment of such a sum at common law: for example, where work is done in the belief that there was a contract or in the expectation that the negotiations between the parties would result in the conclusion of a contract.[617] Such liability is based on the need to deprive the recipient of the services of unjust enrichment that may result from his having benefited from the services without being required to pay for them[618]; and it arises in spite of the fact that there was *no* contract.[619] It follows that the party doing the work, though he is entitled to a reasonable sum, is not liable in damages, e.g. for failing to do the work within a reasonable time.[620] If the claim arose under a contract by virtue of s.15(1) of the 1982 Act, the party doing the work would be both entitled and liable.

612 *First Energy (UK) Ltd v Hungarian International Bank Ltd* [1993] 2 Lloyd's Rep. 195, 205; cf. *de Jongh Weill v Mean Fiddler Holdings Ltd* [2003] EWCA Civ 1058; *RTS Flexible Systems Ltd v Molkerei Alois Müller GmbH & Co KG (UK Production)* [2010] UKSC 14, [2010] 1 W.L.R. 753 at [48]; *Attrill v Dresdner Kleinwort Ltd* [2011] EWCA Civ 229, [2011] I.R.L.R. 613 at [29] at [28], [31] (promise by employer to employees to establish a minimum bonus pool held legally binding through an individual employee could not point to any specific amount payable to him out of the pool). On appeal in the *Attrill* case, see [2012] EWHC 1189 (QB), the Court of Appeal affirming the decision, rejected the argument that the agreement was too uncertain to be enforced, even though "there were some loose ends": [2013] EWCA Civ 394 at [60]. And see *Proton Energy Group SA v Orten Lietuva* [2013] EWHC 2872 (Comm), [2014] 1 Lloyd's Rep. 100 at [39]: "This was a classic spot deal where the speed of the market requires that the parties agree the main terms and leave the details, some of which may be important, to be agreed later." Accordingly, a contract was held to have been made as soon as each party regarded itself as committed to the other even though the agreement stated that "other contractual terms not indicated in the offer shall be discussed and mutually agreed between the parties upon contract negotiations" (at [17]). See also *Singh v Redford* [2018] EWHC 2390 (Ch) at [71], [72] and [77]; *Anchor 2020 Ltd v Midas Construction Ltd* [2019] EWHC 435 (TCC) at [93]–[108]; and *Abberley v Abberley* [2019] EWHC 1564 (Ch).

613 See *Bear Stearns Bank Plc v Forum Global Equity Ltd* [2007] EWHC (below, para.2-122), where the fact that no settlement date had been agreed did not prevent the conclusion of a contract since, in the absence of express agreement on this point, there was "an implied term of the agreement that the parties would execute it within a reasonable time" (at [164]; cf. at [169]); *SK Properties (Midlands) Ltd v Byrne* [2018] UKUT 394 (LC), where an agreement for the sale of property was not void for uncertainty, despite not stipulating a time limit for the completion of relevant formalities. The court held that there was an implied term to complete the formalities "as soon as reasonably possible", which is "necessary to give business efficacy to the contract and ... represents the obvious but unexpressed common intention of the parties" (at [43]).

614 cf. at common law, *Way v Latilla* [1937] 3 All E.R. 759; *Furmans Electrical Contractors Ltd v Elecref Ltd* [2009] EWCA Civ 170 at [32], where the claim was described as "not strictly a quantum meruit claim", presumably because it arose *under* a contract and not (as in the situations discussed at nn.617–619 below) in spite of the absence of one; and see, as to agents' commissions, *British Bank of Foreign Trade v Novinex* [1949] 1 K.B. 623; *Powell v Braun* [1954] 1 W.L.R. 401.

615 e.g. *May & Butcher v R.* [1934] 2 K.B. 17, below, para.2-134; *Courtney & Fairbairn Ltd v Tolaini Bros (Hotels) Ltd* [1975] 1 W.L.R. 297; Dugdale and Lowe [1976] J.B.L. 312; *Chamberlain v Boodle & King* [1982] 1 W.L.R. 1443; *Pagnan SpA v Granaria BV* [1986] 2 Lloyd's Rep. 547; *Russell Bros. (Paddington) Ltd v John Elliott Management Ltd* (1995) 11 Const. L.J. 377; *Southwark LBC v Logan* (1996) 8 Admin. L.R. 315.

616 *Teekay Tankers Ltd v STX Offshore and Shipbuilding Co Ltd* [2017] EWHC 253 at [175]–[210].

617 Below, paras 2-222, 29-071 and 29-072. For the availability of a restitutionary remedy where no contract was concluded, see also *Whittle Movers Ltd v Hollywood Express Ltd* [2009] EWCA Civ 1189 at [48] (where, for reasons given in paras 2-120 above and 2-124 and 2-170 below, the negotiations did not lead to the conclusion of a contract).

618 *Cobbe v Yeoman's Row Management Ltd* [2008] UKHL 55, [2008] 1 W.L.R. 1752 at [40]–[45], [93]. In *Hughes v Pendragon Sabre Ltd (t/a Porche Centre Bolton)* [2016] EWCA Civ 18 the Court of Appeal held that a customer had entered into a binding contract with a car dealership to buy a limited edition Porsche, even though the contract did not stipulate the price, specification or delivery date of the vehicle. These could be resolved by reference to the Sale of Goods Act 1979.

619 For the distinction between cases in which a claim for a reasonable sum arises *under* a contract in spite of failure to agree on details and cases in which such a claim arises on restitutionary principles in spite of the fact that *no* contract was formed because of the parties' failure to reach a sufficient measure of agreement, see *Benourad v Compass Group Plc* [2010] EWHC 1182 (QB) at [106(g) to (l)]. In that case, Beatson J. concluded that, while in principle such a restitutionary claim might be available, there was no evidence on which he could determine its amount (see at [132], [134] and [135]). Contrast *Haden Young v Laing O'Rourke Midlands Ltd* [2008] EWHC 1016 (TCC), allowing a restitutionary claim of the kind here described where work had been done in anticipation of a contract which, for reasons given in paras 2-120 above and 2-124 below, never came into existence.

620 *B.S.C. v Cleveland Bridge & Engineering Co Ltd* [1984] 1 All E.R. 504.

*Replace paragraph with:*

**2-122** Even an agreement for sale of land dealing only with the barest essentials may be regarded as complete if that was the clear intention of the parties. Thus, in *Perry v Suffields Ltd*[621] an offer to sell a public house with vacant possession for £7,000 was accepted without qualification. It was held that there was a binding contract even though many important points, e.g. the date for completion[622] and the question of paying a deposit, were left open. Lord Cozens-Hardy M.R. stated that:

> "Mere arrangements which in the ordinary course of business are left to the legal advisers to settle, such as the date for completion, are subsequent matters which do not prevent the two letters constituting a concluded agreement."[623]

In another case[624] a buyer and seller of corn feed pellets had reached agreement on the "cardinal terms of the deal: product, price, quantity, period of shipment, range of loading ports and governing contract terms".[625] The agreement was held to have contractual force even though the parties had not yet reached agreement on a number of other important points, such as the loading port,[626] the rate of loading and certain payments (other than the price) which might in certain events become payable under the contract. The gaps can be filled by implications of reasonableness and commercial practice.[627] Where an estate agent and a seller reached an oral agreement without specifying the event which would trigger the agent's entitlement to a commission, the agreement was binding as "a reasonable person would understand that the parties intended the commission to be payable on completion and from the proceeds of sale".[627a] Where parties had, in negotiations for the manufacture by the claimants of machinery to be delivered to the defendants, reached agreement on "all essential terms"[628] and "substantial works were then carried out",[629] a contract between them was held to have been concluded even though some points had been left unresolved[630]; and even though those points were of "economic or other significance".[631] In another case, "the essentials of each of the heads of terms were set out in the signed document with sufficient certainty to be capable of amounting to a binding contract" although technical difficulties meant that the agreement was handwritten by the mediator, the division of farmland referred to differently coloured portions but was recorded only by pencil, and the parties subsequently attempted to negotiate details and submit documentation.[631a] An even more striking illustration of this approach is provided by a case[632] in which parties had reached an oral agreement by telephone for the sale of notes evidencing "distressed debt" of a company which was in liquidation. The agreement identified the subject-matter and specified the price; and it was held to be contractually binding even though it did not specify the settlement date and left many other important points to be resolved by further agreement. In all these cases, the courts took the view that the parties intended to be bound at once in spite of the fact that further significant terms were to be agreed later and that even their failure to reach such agreement would not invalidate the contract unless without such agreement it was unworkable or too uncertain[633] to be enforced. Moreover, the Supreme Court has stated, in obiter, that an incomplete bargain can be turned into a binding one by adding implied terms to expressly agreed terms: "it is possible to imply something that is so obvious that it goes without saying into anything, including something the law regards as no more than an offer. If the offer is accepted, the contract is made on the terms of the words used and what those words imply".[633a]

[621] [1916] 2 Ch. 187; cf. *Elias v George Sahely & Co (Barbados) Ltd* [1982] 3 All E.R. 801.

[622] cf. *Storer v Manchester City Council* [1974] 1 W.L.R. 1403.

[623] [1916] 2 Ch. 187 at 191.

[624] *Pagnan SpA v Feed Products Ltd* [1987] 2 Lloyd's Rep. 601.

[625] *Pagnan SpA v Feed Products Ltd* [1987] 2 Lloyd's Rep. 601 at 611.

[626] cf. below, para.2-151.

[627] *Pagnan SpA v Feed Products Ltd* [1987] 2 Lloyd's Rep. 601 at [164] and [166].

[627a] *Wells v Devani* [2019] UKSC 4, [2019] 2 W.L.R. 617.

[628] *RTS Flexible Systems Ltd v Molkerei Alois Müller GmbH & Co KG (UK Production)* [2010] UKSC 14, [2010] 1 W.L.R. 753 (before [70]); and at [61]. And see *Malcolm Charles Contracts Ltd v Crispin* [2014] EWHC 3898 at [55]–[59], [67]–[74]; *Bieber v Teathers Ltd (In Liquidation)* [2014] EWHC 4205 at [50]–[58].

[629] [2010] UKSC 14, [2010] 1 W.L.R. 753 at [61]

[630] The further argument that no contract had come into existence because a requirement for the execution of formal contractual documents had not been complied with was also rejected: see below, para.2-124.

[631] *RTS* case [2010] UKSC 14 at [61]; *Benourad v Compass Group Plc* [2010] EWHC 1882 (QB) at [106(f)].

[631a] *Abberley v Abberley* [2019] EWHC 1564 (Ch) at [54].

[632] *Bear Stearns Bank Plc v Forum Global Equity Ltd* [2007] EWHC 1576.

[633] Below, paras 2-138, 2-139, 2-148.

[633a] *Wells v Devani* [2019] UKSC 4, [2019] 2 W.L.R. 617 at [30].

### Stipulation for the execution of a formal document

*Replace paragraph with:*

The effect of a stipulation that an agreement is to be embodied in a formal written document[637] depends on its purpose.[638] One possibility is that the agreement is regarded by the parties as incomplete, or as not intended to be legally binding,[639] until the terms of the formal document are agreed and the document is duly executed in accordance with the terms of the preliminary agreement (e.g. by signature).[640] This is generally the position where "solicitors are involved on both sides, formal written agreements are to be produced and arrangements are made for their execution".[641] Moreover: **2-124**

> "… [t]he more complicated the subject matter, the more likely the parties are to want to enshrine their contract in a written document, thereby enabling them to review all the terms before being committed to any of them."[642]

The normal inference will then be that "the parties are not bound unless and until both of them sign the agreement".[643] A second possibility is that such a document is intended only as a solemn record of an already complete and binding agreement.[644] This was the conclusion[645] where the terms of the agreement strongly indicated the parties' intention to become legally bound; the terms set out were not vague or uncertain and included terms specifying which law would govern the agreement and which courts would have jurisdiction; there was nothing on the face of those provisions to indicate that any further agreement was required before they became enforceable; and the parties' conduct and email correspondence before and after the date originally set for the execution of the contractual document showed that they did not regard it as determining the bindingness of their agreement. Likewise, an agreement was legally binding despite certain parts of it being left incomplete, and its stipulation that the parties would "agree a formal contract 'within 90 days of commencement'" of the relationship; the parties intended to create legal relations since the agreement was formally executed, it was the product of lengthy negotiations, and the parties had acted in reliance on the agreement.[645a] Yet a third possibility is that the main agreement lacks contractual force for want of execution of the formal document but that, nevertheless, a separate preliminary contract comes into existence at an earlier stage, e.g. when one party begins to render services requested by the other, so that under this contract the former party will be entitled to a reasonable[646] or agreed[647] remuneration for those services. This may even take the form of a letter of intent,[648] so long as the words "subject to contract" are absent.[649] The fourth possibility is that an agreement that originally lacked contractual force for want of execution of the formal document may acquire such force by reason of supervening events. This could, for example, be the position where "it can be objectively ascertained that the continuing intention [sc. not to be bound until execution of the document] has changed or ... subsequent events have occurred whereby the non-executing party is estopped from relying on his non-execution"[650]; or where the party resisting the enforcement of the contract had "waive[d] ... [the] requirement" of "a formal written contract".[651] An oral agreement for the sale of land was enforceable in equity under a constructive trust despite not being in writing where both parties had considered it to be immediately binding upon them, and where the prospective buyer had then acted to his detriment in reliance upon it.[652] Where an agreement for the joint acquisition of property lacks contractual force for want of execution of a formal document and one of the parties then acquires the property for himself, he may also be liable to hold a share of that property for the other party by virtue of a constructive trust.[653] These possibilities are further illustrated in the following paragraphs.

[637] The mere fact that a document about the terms of which the parties had negotiated contained spaces for their signatures does not amount to a stipulation for its execution by signature: *Maple Leaf Volatility Master Fund v Rouvroy* [2009] EWCA 1334, [2010] 2 All E.R. (Comm) 788.

[638] *Von Hatzfeldt-Wildenburg v Alexander* [1912] 1 Ch. 284, 288–289.

[639] *B.S.C. v Cleveland Bridge & Engineering Co Ltd* [1984] 1 All E.R. 504; *Manatee Towing Co v Oceanbulk Maritime SA (The Bay Ridge)* [1999] 2 All E.R. (Comm) 306 at 329 ("no intention to create legal relations"); *Eurodata Systems Plc v Michael Gershon (Finance) Plc, The Times,* March 25, 2003; *Emcor Drake & Scull Ltd v Sir Robert McAlpine Ltd* [2004] EWCA Civ 1733, 98 Con. L.R. 1; *Haden Young Ltd v O'Rourke Midlands Ltd* [2008] EWHC 1016 (TCC) at [115]; *JD Cleverly Ltd v Family Finance Ltd* [2010] EWCA Civ 1477, [2011] R.T.R. 22; *Goodwood Investments Holdings Inc v Thyssenkrupp Industrial Solutions AG* [2018] EWHC 1056 (Comm) at [32]–[33]; cf. the wording of the "Total Price Box" in *Smith Glaziers (Dunfermline) v Customs & Excise Commissioners* [2003] UKHL 7, [2003] 1 W.L.R. 656.

[640] *Okura & Co Ltd v Navara Shipping Corp SA* [1982] 2 Lloyd's Rep. 537; cf. *R. v Sevenoaks DC Ex p. Terry* [1985] 3 All E.R. 226; *Samos Shipping Enterprises Ltd v Eckhart & Co KG (The Nissos Samos)* [1985] 1 Lloyd's Rep. 378; *Hofflinghouse & Co Ltd v C-Trade SA (The Intra Transporter)* [1985] 2 Lloyd's Rep. 158, 163; affirmed [1986] 2 Lloyd's Rep. 132; Debattista [1985] L.M.C.L.Q. 241; *Star Steamship Society v Beogradska Plovidba (The Junior K.)* [1988] 2 Lloyd's Rep. 583; Debattista [1988] L.M.C.L.Q. 441; *Atlantic Marine Transport Corp v Coscol Petroleum Corp (The Pina)* [1992] 2 Lloyd's Rep. 103, 107; *New England Reinsurance Corp v Messaghios Insurance Co SA* [1992] 2 Lloyd's Rep. 251; *CPC Consolidated Pool Carriers GmbH v CTM Cia Transmediterranea SA (The CPC Gallia)*

[1994] 1 Lloyd's Rep. 68; *Ignazio Messina & Co v Polskie Linie Oceaniczne* [1995] 2 Lloyd's Rep. 566; *Drake Scull Engineering Ltd v Higgs & Hill (Northern) Ltd* (1995) 11 Const. L.J. 214; *Regalian Properties Plc v London Dockland Development Corp* [1995] 1 W.L.R. 212; *Enfield LBC v Arajah* [1995] E.G.C.S. 164; *Galliard Homes Ltd v Jarvis Interiors Ltd* [2000] C.L.C. 411; *Britvic Soft Drinks Ltd v Messer UK Ltd* [2001] 1 Lloyd's Rep. 20 at [64]; affirmed on other grounds [2002] EWCA Civ 548, [2002] 2 All E.R. (Comm) 321; *Sun Life Assurance Co of Canada v CX Reinsurance Co Ltd* [2003] EWCA Civ 283; *Thoreson & Co (Bangkok) Ltd v Fathom Marine Co* [2004] EWHC 167 (Comm), [2004] 1 All E.R. (Comm) 935 (agreement for sale of ship "sub details" not a binding contract); *Petromec Inc v Petroleo Brasileiro SA Petrobas* [2005] EWCA Civ 891, [2006] 1 Lloyd's Rep. 121 at [74]–[77] (MOA to be governed by later Transaction Documents not a binding contract; for further proceedings, see [2006] EWHC 1443 (Comm), [2007] 1 Lloyd's Rep. 629); *Oceonografia SA de CV v DSND Subsea AS (The Botnica)* [2006] EWHC 1300 (Comm), [2007] 1 All E.R. (Comm) 28 (charter "subject to the signing of mutually agreeable terms and condition" not a binding contract); *Service Power Asia Pacific Pty Ltd v Service Power Business Solutions Ltd* [2009] EWCH 179 (Ch), [2010] 1 All E.R. (Comm) 238 at [20] (stipulation for outcome of negotiations to be reduced to writing containing detailed terms); *Whittle Movers Ltd v Hollywood Express Ltd* [2009] EWCA Civ 1189 (tender process "subject to contract" and contemplating execution of formal contract); *Benourad v Compass Group Plc* [2010] EWHC 1882 at [110] (draft providing that it would become effective from signature); *CRS GT Ltd v McLaren Automotive Ltd* [2018] EWHC 3209 (Comm) at [135] (the agreement, which expressly provided for the preparation and signing of a formal contract, was not binding); cf. *Prudential Assurance Co Ltd v Mount Eden Land Co Ltd* [1997] 1 E.G.L.R. 37 (consent to alterations given by landlord "subject to licence" held effective as the consent was a unilateral act, so that no question of agreement arose). For a borderline case, see *Grant v Bragg* [2009] EWCA Civ 1228, [2010] 1 All E.R. (Comm) 1166, where Lord Neuberger concluded that, "contrary to ... [his] initial impression", there was to be no contract before formal signature of the draft (at [32]). The sentence (in the 30th edition of this book) ending with what is now n.644 is cited with apparent approval in *Investec Bank (UK) Ltd v Zulman* [2010] EWCA Civ 536 at [16], where failure to execute a formal document negatived contractual intention even though the words "subject to contract" (below, para.2-126), or words to the same effect, were not used; see also *Benourad v Compass Group Plc* [2010] EWHC 1882 (QB) at [106(a)]; *Datasat Communications Ltd v Swindon Town Football Club Ltd* [2009] EWHC 859 (Comm) at [87]; *Wright v Rowland* [2017] EWHC 2478 (Comm) at [74]; *IMS SA v Capital Oil and Gas Industries Ltd* [2018] EWHC 894 (Comm) at [58]–[61]; *Rosalina Investments Ltd v New Balance Athletic Shoes (UK) Ltd* [2018] EWHC 1014 (QB) at [42]; *AMP Advisory and Management Partners AG v Force India Formula One Team Ltd (In Liquidation)* [2019] EWHC 2426 (Comm) at [88] (repeated insistence by the claimant for a signature supported inference that the parties had not waived the requirement for a signature).

[641] *Cheverny Consulting Ltd v Whitehead Mann Ltd* [2006] EWCA Civ 1303; [2007] 1 All E.R. (Comm) 124 at [45], per Sir Andrew Morritt C.; the above statement was accepted at [81] by Carnwath L.J., who dissented in the result. And see *Rotam Agrochemical Co Ltd v GAT Microencapsulation GmbH (formerly GAT Microencapsulation AG)* [2018] EWHC 2765 (Comm) at [148], where "it was implicit in the discussions ... that to the extent that matters were the subject of agreement between those present, they would be embodied in the formal agreement which was being negotiated, so that the parties could then review all the terms before being committed to any of them".

[642] *Paul David Allen (Trustee in Bankruptcy of Michelle Danique Young) v Michelle Danique Young* [2017] B.P.I.R. 1116 at [77]. And see *Cheverny Consulting Ltd v Whitehead Mann Ltd* [2006] EWCA Civ 1303; *Benourad v Compass Group Plc* [2010] EWHC 1882 (QB) at [106(a)]; *Elleray v Bourne* [2018] UKUT 3 (LC) at [69]–[71]; *Rotam Agrochemical Co Ltd v GAT Microencapsulation GmbH (formerly GAT Microencapsulation AG)* [2018] EWHC 2765 (Comm) at [148].

[643] *Cheverny Consulting Ltd v Whitehead Mann Ltd* [2006] EWCA Civ 1303 at [45]; *Kyte v Revenue and Customs Commissioners* [2018] EWHC 1146 (Ch); [2018] B.T.C. 20 at [64]; *Rotam Agrochemical Co Ltd v GAT Microencapsulation GmbH (formerly GAT Microencapsulation AG)* [2018] EWHC 2765 (Comm) at [176] and [179]; *Broomhead v National Westminster Bank Plc* [2018] EWHC 1574 (Ch) at [282]; cf. *Crossco No.4 Unlimited v Jolan Ltd, Note* [2011] EWCA Civ 1619, [2012] 2 All E.R. 754 at [106], where similar reasoning was said at [108] to be "fatal to the claim to a constructive trust", even though there was *no* stipulation for the execution of a formal document.

[644] *Rossiter v Miller* (1878) 3 App. Cas. 1124 (below, para.2-131); *Filby v Hounsell* [1896] 2 Ch. 737; *Branca v Cobarro* [1947] K.B. 854 (below, para.2-131); *E.R. Ives Investments Ltd v High* [1967] 2 Q.B. 379; *Elias v George Sahely & Co (Barbados) Ltd* [1982] 3 All E.R. 801; *Damon Cie Naviera SA v Hapag-Lloyd International SA (The Blankenstein)* [1985] 1 W.L.R. 435; *Clipper Maritime Ltd v Shirlstar Container Transport Ltd (The Anemone)* [1987] 1 Lloyd's Rep. 547; *Malcolm v Chancellor, Masters and Scholars of the University of Oxford, The Times*, December 19, 1990; *Ateni Maritime Corp v Great Marine Ltd (The Great Marine) (No.2)* [1990] 2 Lloyd's Rep. 250; affirmed (without reference to this point) [1991] 1 Lloyd's Rep. 421; *Jayaar Impex Ltd v Toaken Group Ltd* [1996] 2 Lloyd's Rep. 437; *The Kurnia Dewi* [1997] 1 Lloyd's Rep. 553 at 559; *Harvey Shopfitters Ltd v ADI Ltd* [2004] EWCA Civ 1752, [2004] 2 All E.R. 982; *Bryen & Langley Ltd v Boston* [2005] EWCA Civ 973, [2005] B.L.R. 508; *Fitzpatrick Contractors Ltd v Tyco Fire and Integrated Solutions (UK) Ltd* [2008] EWHC 1301 (TCC), 119 Con. L.R. 155 at [55], [56]; *Whitney v Monster Worldwide Ltd* [2010] EWCA Civ 1312,

[2011] Pens. L.R. 1; *Immingham Storage Co Ltd v Clear Plc* [2011] EWCA Civ 89 at [18]; *Tryggingarfelagio Foroyar P/F v CPT Empresas Maritimas SA (The Athena)* [2011] EWHC 589 (Admlty) at [45]; *Air Studios (Lyndhurst) Ltd v Lombard North Central Plc* [2012] EWHC 3162 (QB), [2013] 1 Lloyd's Rep. 63 at [70]; and *Golden Ocean Group Ltd v Salgaocar Mining Industries PVT Ltd* [2012] EWCA Civ 265, [2012] 1 Lloyd's Rep. 542 at [30], where the actual decision turned on the question whether the formal requirement of signature imposed by Statute of Frauds 1677 s.4 had been satisfied; cf. *Crowden v Aldridge* [1993] 1 W.L.R. 433, applying the same principle to a document which was not a contract but a direction by beneficiaries to executors; *Crabbe v Townsend* [2016] EWHC 2450 (Ch) at [12]; *Ely v Robson* [2016] EWCA Civ 774 at [41]; *Paul David Allen (Trustee in Bankruptcy of Michelle Danique Young) v Michelle Danique Young* [2017] B.P.I.R. 1116 at [30]; *Mena Energy DMCC v Hascol Petroleum Ltd* [2017] EWHC 262 (Comm) at [169]; *Harvil Roofing Ltd v Lakehouse Contracts Ltd* [2017] EWHC 3310 (TCC) at [36]–[37]; *Edge Tools and Equipment Ltd v Greatstar Europe Ltd* [2018] EWHC 170 (QB) at [20].

645 *Edge Tools and Equipment Ltd v Greatstar Europe Ltd* [2018] EWHC 170 (QB) at [40]–[46]. See also *RTS Flexible Systems Ltd v Molkerei Alois Müller GmbH & Co KG (UK Production)* [2010] UKSC 14, [2010] 1 W.L.R. 753, see below, para.2-126; *Anchor 2020 Ltd v Midas Construction Ltd* [2019] EWHC 435 (TCC), 184 Con. L.R. 215 at [94], where the court found that the parties' agreement to enter into a novation agreement was not a condition precedent to the contract coming into force.

645a *Green Deal Marketing Southern Ltd v Economy Energy Trading Ltd* [2019] EWHC 507 (Ch), [2019] 2 All E.R. (Comm) 191 at [98].

646 *Smit International Singapore Pte Ltd v Kurnia Dewi Shipping SA (The Kurnia Dewi)* [1997] 1 Lloyd's Rep. 553; *Galliard Homes Ltd v Jarvis Interiors Ltd* [2000] C.L.C. 411, where an incomplete agreement expressly provided for a reasonable remuneration to be paid in the events which happened. The "third possibility" described in the text above (para.2-117 in the 30th edition of this book) is referred to with apparent approval by Beatson J. in *Benourad v Compass Group Plc* [2010] EWHC 1882 (QB) at [106(f)]. For the possible availability of a restitutionary remedy where *no* contract was concluded, see above, para.2-121; on the facts of the *Benourad* case, no such remedy was available: see above, para.2-121 n.619.

647 *Arcadis Consulting (UK) Ltd (formerly Hyder Consulting (UK) Ltd) v AMEC (BCS) Ltd (formerly CV Buchan Ltd)* [2016] EWHC 2509 (TCC).

648 See below, para.2-133.

649 *Arcadis Consulting (UK) Ltd (formerly Hyder Consulting (UK) Ltd) v AMEC (BCS) Ltd (formerly CV Buchan Ltd)* [2016] EWHC 2509 (TCC) at [53] and [56]. And see *Harvil Roofing Ltd v Lakehouse Contracts Ltd* [2017] EWHC 3310 (TCC) at [34]–[38] where the agreement did not provide that it would have no legal effect until signed.

650 *Cheverny Consulting Ltd v Whitehead Mann Ltd* [2006] EWCA Civ 1303, [2007] 1 All E.R. (Comm) 124 at [46]; *Benourad v Compass Group Plc* [2010] EWHC 1882 at [106(b)]. These dicta envisage that the non-executing party may be *bound* by the "estoppel". *The Botnica* [2006] EWHC 1300 (Comm), [2007] 1 All E.R. (Comm) 28 envisages the further possibility that the non-executing party may, by "waiver" or "a kind of election" (at [90]) *acquire rights* under the unexecuted document. For this possibility, see further para.4-082 below.

651 *RTS Flexible Systems Ltd v Molkerei Alois Müller GmbH & Co KG (UK Production)* [2010] UKSC 14, [2010] 1 W.L.R. 753 at [86]; for the facts of this case, see below paras 2-124 and 2-132; *Reveille Independent LLC v Anotech International (UK) Ltd* [2016] EWCA Civ 443, where the respondent had clearly and unequivocally represented by its conduct that it was bound by the deal memorandum and had waived the requirement to sign; *Singh v Redford* [2018] EWHC 2390 (Ch) at [70], where the parties' initial agreement for the sale of a business was not binding due to lack of formal documentation, but it became binding when the seller handed over running of the business to the buyer evidencing their intention to be bound. Contrast *JD Cleverly Ltd v Family Finance Ltd* [2010] EWCA Civ 1477, [2011] R.T.R. 22, when there was no conduct from which a waiver could be inferred (at [26]).

652 *Matchmove Ltd v Dowding* [2016] EWCA Civ 1233; see below, paras 4-142 and 5-040.

653 *Banner Homes Group Plc v Luff Developments Ltd* [2000] Ch. 372; contrast *London & Regional Investments Ltd v TBI Plc* [2000] EWCA Civ 355, where the joint venture agreement was expressly "subject to contract" (below, para.2-126), thus reserving a right to withdraw. In *Crossco No.4 Unlimited v Jolan Ltd Note* [2011] EWCA Civ 1619, [2012] 2 All E.R. 754 Arden and Mcfarlane L.JJ. took the view that the decision in the *Banner Homes* case was based on constructive trust (at [129], [119], [124]) while Etherton L.J. took the view that it rested on breach of fiduciary duty (at [88], [93]). This difference of judicial opinion did not affect the outcome of the *Crossco* case and further discussion of it is beyond the scope of this chapter.

## Agreement "subject to contract"

*Replace paragraph with:*

Agreements for the sale of land by private treaty are usually[656] made "subject to contract". Such agreements are normally[657] regarded as incomplete until the terms of a formal contract have been settled and approved by the parties. Thus, in *Winn v Bull*[658] an agreement to take a lease of a house for a specified time at a stated rent, "subject to the preparation and approval of a formal contract" was held not to have given rise to an enforceable contract. Jessell M.R. said that, "where you have a proposal or agreement made in writing expressed to be subject to a formal contract being prepared, it means what it says; it is subject to and is dependent upon a formal contract being prepared".[659] The same principle has been applied to an agreement to purchase freehold land "subject to a proper contract to be prepared by the vendor's solicitors"[660]; to an agreement to take a flat "subject to suitable agreements being arranged between your solicitors and mine"[661]; to an agreement to grant a lease "subject to the terms of a lease" (because this meant "subject to the terms to be contained in a lease executed by the lessor"[662]); and to an agreement to purchase a house "subject to formal contract to be prepared by the vendors' solicitors if the vendors shall so require."[663] In each of these cases the court held that the agreement gave rise to no legal liability.[664] The principle that agreements "subject to contract" are not legally binding, though most frequently applied to contracts for the sale of land, is not restricted to such contracts. It has, for example, been held that an agreement to pay a fee to an estate agent was not legally binding where it was expressed to be "subject to contract".[665] In *Goodwood Investments Holdings Inc v Thyssenkrupp Industrial Solutions AG*[666] the court found that the arbitration claim under a shipbuilding contract had not been settled in without prejudice correspondence between the parties' solicitors because of terms requiring board approval and the use of the language "subject to contract". By a process of further analogous extension, the same reasoning has been applied to an agreement which was neither one for the sale of land nor one which was expressly "subject to contract". In *RTS Flexible Systems Ltd v Molkerei Alois Müller GmbH & Co KG (UK Production)*[667] the principle was discussed in connection with a draft contract for the supply of goods, clause 48 of which provided that the proposed contract "shall not become effective until each party has executed a counterpart and exchanged it with the other". This was described[668] as "the subject to contract clause;" and, if matters had rested there, the draft would not have had any contractual force. But the actual decision was that, in view of the parties' subsequent conduct, the objective interpretation of the parties' words and conduct at formation,[669] the fact that substantial works were then carried out[670] and thereafter, the basis for the work done varied, failure to comply with the requirements of clause 48 did not prevent the formation of a binding contract. **2-126**

[656] Not always: see *Storer v Manchester City Council* [1974] 1 W.L.R. 1403; *Tweddell v Henderson* [1975] 1 W.L.R. 1496, 1501–1502; *Elias v Group Sahely & Co (Barbados) Ltd* [1982] 3 All E.R. 801.

[657] See the qualifications discussed in paras 2-128—2-132, below.

[658] (1877) 7 Ch. D. 29. See also *Santa Fé Land Co v Forestal Land Co* (1910) 26 T.L.R. 534.

[659] (1877) 7 Ch. D. 29, 32.

[660] *Chillingworth v Esche* [1924] 1 Ch. 97.

[661] *Lockett v Norman-Wright* [1925] Ch. 56.

[662] *Raingold v Bromley* [1931] 2 Ch. 307. See also *Berry Ltd v Brighton and Sussex Building Society* [1939] 3 All E.R. 217.

663 *Riley v Troll* [1953] 1 All E.R. 966.

664 See also *Kingston-upon-Hull (Governors) v Petch* (1854) 10 Ex. 610; *Chinnock v Marchioness of Ely* (1865) 4 De G.J. & S. 638; *Harvey v Barnard's Inn* (1881) 50 L.J. Ch. 750; *May v Thomson* (1882) 20 Ch. D. 705; *Hawkesworth v Chaffey* (1886) 55 L.J. Ch. 335; *Von Hatzfeldt-Wildenburg v Alexander* [1912] 1 Ch. 284 (disapproving *North v Percival* [1898] 2 Ch. 128); *Rossdale v Denny* [1921] 1 Ch. 57; *Looker v Law Union Insurance Co Ltd* [1928] 1 K.B. 554; *Brilliant v Michaels* [1945] 1 All E.R. 121; *Lowis v Wilson* [1949] Ir.R. 347; *Graham & Scott (Southgate) Ltd v Oxlade* [1950] 2 K.B. 257; *Bennett, Walden & Co v Wood* [1950] 2 All E.R. 134; *Christie, Owen and Davies Ltd v Stockton* [1953] 1 W.L.R. 1353.

665 *Ronald Preston & Partners v Markheath Securities* [1988] 2 E.G.L.R. 23; *Farrar v Rylatt* [2019] EWCA Civ 1864 at [79] (profit sharing agreement "subject to contract" not enforceable). For the potential applicability of the principle that an agreement "subject to contract" is not legally binding to an offer "subject to contract" to buy *goods*, see *Air Studios (Lyndhurst) Ltd v Lombard North Central Plc* [2012] EWHC 3162 (QB), [2013] 1 Lloyd's Rep. 63 at [70], quoted in para.2-118 at n.588. And see *Elleray v Bourne* [2018] UKUT 3 (LC) regarding the sale of a mobile home.

666 [2018] EWHC 1056 (Comm) at [32]–[33].

667 *RTS Flexible Systems Ltd v Molkerei Alois Müller GmbH & Co KG (UK Production)* [2010] UKSC 14, [2010] 1 W.L.R. 753 at [48].

668 [2010] UKSC 14 at [86].

669 [2010] UKSC 14 at [45]–[48]: "The parties agreed to bind themselves to agreed terms, leaving certain subsidiary and legally inessential terms to be decided later."

670 [2010] UKSC 14 at [61], and see below at para.2-132. Cf. *Farrar v Rylatt* [2019] EWCA Civ 1864 at [68] and [84], where the agreement "subject to contract" was held not to be binding because there was no subsequent performance in relation to the disputed profit share agreement.

## Letters of intent; letters of comfort

*Replace paragraph with:*

**2-133** Issues of contractual intention have arisen in a number of cases concerned with the legal effects of the commercial practice whereby parties to a transaction issue or exchange "letters of intent" on which they act pending the preparation of formal contracts. One possibility is that such letters may, by their express terms or on their true construction, negative contractual intention.[710] There is, similarly, judicial support for the view that "a letter of comfort, properly so called," is "one that does not give rise to contractual liability".[711] This position is illustrated by a case[712] in which a company issued a "letter of comfort" to a lender in respect of a loan to one of the company's subsidiaries. The letter stated that "it is our policy that [the subsidiary] is at all times in a position to meet its liabilities". This was held to be no more than a statement of the present policy of the company: it was not an undertaking that the policy would not be changed since the parties had not intended it to take effect as a contractually binding promise. On the other hand, "[t]he label used by the parties is not necessarily determinative",[713] so that "sometimes a legal obligation may arise as a matter of construction, notwithstanding the rubric of a letter of comfort".[714] Hence where the language of such a document, or of a letter of intent, does not negative contractual intention, it is open to the courts to hold the parties bound by the document.[715] They will, in particular, be inclined to do so where the parties have acted on the document for a long period of time or have expended considerable sums of money in reliance on it.[716] The fact that the parties envisage that the letter is to be superseded by a later, more formal, contractual document does not, of itself, prevent the letter from taking effect as a contract.[717] The final possibility is that a letter of intent may be so worded that one part of it has, while the rest of it does not, have, contractual force. In *Shaker v VistaJet Group Holding SA*,[718] one of the terms of a letter of intent (LOI) began with the words:

"Non-binding: other than the provisions relating to the application, payment and refund of the Deposit and the confidentiality provisions hereunder, it is specifically understood as agreed that this letter of intent does not constitute a binding agreement upon the Guarantor, Seller and Buyer to enter into the Transaction Documents."

On this basis, it was held that the claimant buyer was contractually entitled to enforce the provisions of the LOI relating to the return of his deposit,[719] even though other parts of the LOI, in particular, the buyer's undertaking to negotiate in good faith, had no contractual force, because of the express terms of the LOI quoted above. In any case, an undertaking to negotiate in good faith is not binding in law.[720] The binding force of the provisions as to the repayment would not be impaired even if they were subject to a condition precedent[721] that the buyer should negotiate in good faith, since such a *condition* could not, any more than an *undertaking* to negotiate in good faith, be enforced in law.[722] In another case,[723] a "letter of intent" was held to be binding since "where works have been carried out, it will usually be implausible to argue that there was no contract". However, none of the three sets of competing contractual terms and conditions proposed between the parties purporting to limit liability were incorporated into the contract as they had been continually amended and were never finally agreed.

[710] Below, para.2-195; cf. *Snelling v John G. Snelling Ltd* [1973] 1 Q.B. 87.

[711] *Associated British Ports v Ferryways* [2008] EWCA Civ 189, [2009] 1 Lloyd's Rep. 595 at [24], per Maurice Kay L.J.; *Barbudev v Eurocom Cable Management Bulgaria EOOD* [2011] EWHC 1560 (Comm), [2011] 2 All E.R. (Comm) 951, where it was said at [93] that the relevant document was "not expressed to be a 'letter of comfort', though that is not conclusive", and was held "as a matter of construction ... not intended to be legally binding" (at [96]); *Avonwick Holdings Ltd v Azitio Holdings Ltd* [2020] EWHC 1844 (Comm) at [597]–[702] (memorandum of understanding not binding, they were merely "records of ongoing negotiations" which were subject to continual revision and amendment: at [630]), and see para.2-195 below.

[712] *Kleinwort Benson Ltd v Malaysian Mining Corp* [1989] 1 All E.R. 785; Reynolds 104 L.Q.R. 353 (1988); Davenport [1988] L.M.C.L.Q. 290; Prentice (1989) 105 L.Q.R. 346; Ayres and Moore [1989] L.M.C.L.Q. 281; Tyree (1989) 2 J.C.L. 279, cf. *Chemco Leasing SpA v Rediffusion* [1987] 1 F.T.L.R. 201 (where such a letter was held to be an offer but to have lapsed before acceptance); *Monk Construction v Norwich Union Life Insurance Society* (1992) 62 B.L.R. 107.

[713] *Associated British Ports v Ferryways* [2008] EWCA Civ 189 at [24].

[714] *Associated British Ports v Ferryways* [2008] EWCA Civ 189 at [27]. See also *Twintec Ltd v Volkerfitzpatrick Ltd* [2014] EWHC 10, [2014] B.L.R. 150, where a building contractor issued a letter of intent (LOI) to a flooring sub-contractor and the parties accepted that the LOI constituted a binding contract (at [23]) but disagreed as to which terms of the contemplated later formal contract were intended to be incorporated into the LOI agreement.

[715] In *Associated British Ports v Ferryways* [2008] EWCA Civ 189, a "letter of comfort" was held to be a legally binding guarantee, though this had been discharged by a later agreement.

[716] cf. *Turriff Construction Ltd v Regalia Knitting Mills* (1971) 22 E.G. 169 (letter of intent held to be a collateral contract for preliminary work); *Wilson Smithett & Cape (Sugar) Ltd v Bangladesh Sugar Industries Ltd* [1986] 1 Lloyd's Rep. 378 (LOI held to be an acceptance); *Chemco Leasing SpA v Rediffusion* [1987] 1 F.T.L.R. 201 (LOI held to be an offer but to have lapsed before acceptance); *Spartafield Ltd v Penten Group Ltd* [2016] EWHC 2295 (TCC); 168 Con. L.R. 221 (LOI displaced by contract when the key principles for the contract were agreed; the contemplated execution of a formal contract was not a precondition to the existence of the contract); *Arcadis Consulting (UK) Ltd (formerly Hyder Consulting (UK) Ltd) v AMEC (BCS) Ltd (formerly CV Buchan Ltd)* [2018] EWCA Civ 2222, [2019] 1 All E.R. (Comm) 421 (LOI held to be an offer, which was accepted by letters of response and subsequent conduct). Contrast *Volumatic Ltd v Ideas for Life Ltd* [2019] EWHC 2273 (IPEC) at [25] (signed document expressing the parties intention not binding because, inter alia, of parties' lack of reliance on it for over 11 years).

[717] Above, para.2-124. For a combination of the factors described in the text above at nn.715 and 716, see Diamond Build Ltd v Clapham Park Homes Ltd [2008] EWHC 1439 (TCC), 119 Con. L.R. 33 where a LOI was held to have contractual force even though its provisions indicated that a formal contract was to be executed but the parties acted on the letter without executing any such contract; see also *Arcadis Consulting (UK) Ltd (formerly Hyder Consulting (UK) Ltd) v AMEC (BCS) Ltd (formerly CV Buchan Ltd)* [2016] EWHC 2509 (TCC).

718 [2012] EWHC 1329 (Comm), [2012] 2 Lloyd's Rep. 93.

719 [2012] EWHC 1329 (Comm) at [8].

720 [2012] EWHC 1329 (Comm) at [7]; see below paras 2-144, 2-195.

721 The existence of such a condition was doubted in [2012] EWHC 1329 (Comm) at [9].

722 [2012] EWHC 1329 (Comm) at [12].

723 *Arcadis Consulting (UK) Ltd (formerly Hyder Consulting (UK) Ltd) v AMEC (BCS) Ltd (formerly CV Buchan Ltd)* [2016] EWHC 2509 (TCC) at [51].

### Terms "to be agreed"

*Replace footnote 729 with:*

**2-134** 729 *Metal Scrap Trade Corp v Kate Shipping Co Ltd (The Gladys)* [1994] 2 Lloyd's Rep. 402; *Ignazio Messina & Co v Polskie Linie Oceaniczne* [1995] 2 Lloyd's Rep. 566. Cf. *Green Deal Marketing Southern Ltd v Economy Energy Trading Ltd* [2019] EWHC 507 (Ch), [2019] 2 All E.R. (Comm) 191 at [98], see below para.2-137.

### Agreement not incomplete merely because further agreement is required

*Replace paragraph with:*

**2-137** Thus an agreement is not incomplete *merely* because it calls for some further agreement between the parties. The parties' later failure to agree on the matters left outstanding may then vitiate the contract only if it makes it "unworkable or void for uncertainty".[749] Often, the failure will not have this effect, for it may be possible to resolve the uncertainty in one of the ways already discussed, e.g. by applying the standard of reasonableness[750]; or the matter to be negotiated may be of such subsidiary importance[751] as not to negative the intention of the parties to be bound by the more significant terms to which they have agreed. Thus in *Neilson v Stewart*[752] a contract for the sale of shares provided that part of the price payable by the buyer was to be lent back to him and to a third party on repayment terms to be negotiated after one year. The House of Lords held that there was nevertheless a binding contract for the sale of the shares as the parties had not intended the validity of this contract to depend on the outcome of the negotiations as to the repayment of the loan. In *Green Deal Marketing Southern Ltd v Economy Energy Trading Ltd*,[752a] the parties' agreement was held to be legally binding despite certain parts of it being left incomplete and despite its stipulation that the parties would "agree a formal contract 'within 90 days of commencement'" of the relationship. Judge Keyser QC said[752b]:

> "An intention to create legal relations is not negatived by the mere fact that the Heads of Terms makes clear at various points that matters remain to be agreed. ... The Heads of Terms makes expressly clear that a formal contract was contemplated; there is no reason why it should not contain indications of what would go in the formal contract but had not yet been agreed. That does not mean that the matters which had been agreed were not to have immediate contractual effect."

In *RTS Flexible Systems Ltd v Molkerei Alois Müller GmbH & Co KG (UK Production)*[753] the Supreme Court held that a contract had come into existence when "essentially all the terms were agreed between the parties",[754] even though other terms were still the subject of further negotiations between them.[755] In *Toptip Holding Pte Ltd v Mercuria energy Trading Pte Ltd (The "Pan Gold")*[756] a binding contract was found despite the offer being made "Subject to review" of the charterer's pro forma charterparty "with logical amendment" because all essential terms were agreed, the context indicated that the clause was not intended to prevent a binding contract from arising and the parties' conduct indicated the existence of a binding contract. The clause should be regarded merely as a condition subsequent.[757] There can be no doubt as to the commercial convenience of the judicial approach described in this paragraph. Commercial agreements are often intended to be binding in principle even though the parties are not at the time able or willing to settle all the details. For example, contracts of insurance may be made "at a premium to be arranged" when immediate cover is required but there is no time to go into all the details at once: such agreements are perfectly valid and a reasonable premium must be paid.[758] All this is not to say that the courts will hold parties bound when they have not yet reached substantial agreement,[759] but once they have reached such agreement it is not fatal that some points (even important ones) remain to be settled by further negotiation.[760]

[749] *Pagnan SpA v Feed Products Ltd* [1987] 2 Lloyd's Rep. 601, 619.

[750] Above, para.2-121; below, para.2-151; or by imposing on one party the duty to resolve the uncertainty: below, para.2-152; *Pagnan SpA v Feed Products Ltd* [1987] 2 Lloyd's Rep. 601.

[751] Though this point is not decisive: see above, para.2-134 at n.729.

[752] (1991) S.L.T. 523.

[752a] *Green Deal Marketing Southern Ltd v Economy Energy Trading Ltd* [2019] EWHC 507 (Ch), [2019] 2 All E.R. (Comm) 191 at [98].

[752b] *Green Deal Marketing Southern Ltd v Economy Energy Trading Ltd* [2019] EWHC 507 (Ch), [2019] 2 All E.R. (Comm) 191 at [98]. Contrast *Farrar v Rylatt* [2019] EWCA Civ 1864 at [85] ("Heads of Terms" expressly subject to contract not binding as the parties made eight attempts to "finalise" the profit share agreement).

[753] [2010] UKSC 14, [2010] 1 W.L.R. 753.

[754] [2010] UKSC 14 at [61].

[755] [2010] UKSC 14 at [61]. And see *MRI Trading AG v Erdenet Mining Corp LLC* [2013] EWCA Civ 156, [2013] 1 Lloyd's Rep. 638. In that case a "Settlement Agreement" left a number of issues (such as shipping schedules, treatment charges (TC) and refining charges (RC)) "to be agreed" between the parties. Tomlinson L.J. held the settlement to be enforceable since "the language used by the parties" showed that "they did not intend that" "they should remain free to agree or disagree" about the points which were "to be agreed"; rather, a term was "to be implied that the TC/RC and shipping schedule shall be reasonable, and that in the event of any dispute ... [the matter was] to be determined by arbitration" (at [19]). At [20]–[22] Tomlinson L.J. expressed his agreement with Eder J. who had, in the court below [2012] EWHC 1988, [2012] 2 Lloyd's Rep. 638 at [30] and [31] relied on the mandatory language and other expressions used by the parties to show that the parties intended the agreements in question to be legally binding. For the application of the standard of reasonableness, cf. para.2-136 at n.742. See also *Glencore Energy UK Ltd v Cirrus Oil Services Ltd* [2014] EWHC 87 (Comm), [2014] 1 All E.R. (Comm) 513 at [61], [64], where acceptance of an offer (see paras 2-003, 2-027) was held to have concluded a contract even though the acceptance envisaged further "fine tuning" of detailed terms.

[756] [2017] SGCA 64, [2018] 1 Lloyd's Rep. 316 at [41]–[57], [61].

[757] See below para.2-159.

[758] *Gliksten & Son Ltd v State Assurance Co* (1922) 10 Ll.L. Rep. 604; cf. Marine Insurance Act 1906 s.31(2); and *American Airline Inc v Hope* [1973] 1 Lloyd's Rep. 233; affirmed [1974] 2 Lloyd's Rep. 301 ("at an additional premium *and geographical area* to be agreed").

[759] e.g. *Shakleford's Case* (1866) L.R. 1 Ch. App. 567; *Bertel v Neveux* (1878) 39 L.T. 257; *Loftus v Roberts* (1902) 18 T.L.R. 532; *Hofflinghouse SpA v C-Trade SA (The Intra Transporter)* [1986] 2 Lloyd's Rep. 132; *Pagnan SpA v Granaria BV* [1986] 2 Lloyd's Rep. 547; *Alfred McAlpine Construction Ltd v Panatown Ltd* [2001] EWCA Civ 485, (2001) 76 Con. L.R. 224 at [35]; *Midgulf International Ltd v Groupe Chimiche Tunisien* [2010] EWCA Civ 66 at [40] ("It is not commercially sensible to suppose that the parties can have intended to enter into a contract of this size for sulphur of indeterminate quantity, to be delivered over an indeterminate period and with no provision as to payment." At a later stage an agreement not open to this objection was reached: see at [48]).

[760] *Voest Alpine Intertrading GmbH v Chevron International Oil Co Ltd* [1987] 2 Lloyd's Rep. 547; *Maple Leaf Volatility Master Fund v Rouvroy* [2009] EWHC 257 (Comm), [2009] 1 Lloyd's Rep. 475 at [223]; affirmed without further reference to this point [2009] EWCA Civ 1334, [2010] 2 All E.R. (Comm) 788 (for this case, see also above, para.2-004 n.22); *Mahmood v The Big Bus Co* [2017] EWHC 3582 (QB) at [30] where Laing J. held that the claimant had a real prospect of showing that a "Head of

Agreement" comprised of both terms dealing with the shape of the parties' future joint venture agreement, *and* other clauses that "govern and are intended to govern in a binding way" the parties' relationship, which "would continue to exist unless and until the joint venture agreement had been entered into".

### Agreement to negotiate

*In line 8, after "in good faith.", add new footnote 803a:*

2-144 [803a] Cf. *Basso v Wadhwani* [2019] EWHC 3212 (QB) at [59] (agreement to set-off future payments against sums owed under a prior contract enforceable although the parties had yet to agree the amount owed as this could be determined with certainty either by agreement or by court ruling).

## 7. CERTAINTY OF TERMS

### Requirement of certainty

*Replace paragraph with:*

2-148 An agreement may lack contractual force because it is so vague or uncertain that no definite meaning can be given to it without adding further terms. For example, in *G. Scammell & Nephew Ltd v Ouston*,[827] the House of Lords held that an agreement to acquire goods "on hire-purchase" was too vague to be enforced since there were many kinds of hire-purchase agreements in widely different terms, so that it was impossible to specify the terms on which the parties had agreed. In *Blue v Ashley*[828] the court denied the existence of an enforceable contract because, inter alia, the alleged agreement to pay £15 million if the claimant raised the company share price to £8 failed to stipulate the period for achieving this. There was no objective standard the court could invoke to imply that the obligation would be performed within a reasonable period.[829] In *Kyte v Revenue and Customs Commissioners*[830] the alleged contract was held to be "insufficiently precise" to be a binding settlement of the claimant's tax liabilities, given that the "claimant's tax liabilities were plainly complex", the claimant sought a "settlement deed", and the reference to the "the claimant's tax affairs being 'brought up to date' [being] far too general to be of assistance". In *George v Revenue and Customs Commissioners*,[830a] an oral agreement for the enfranchisement of a party's shares in a company was held to be insufficiently certain, as it did not specify, inter alia, the classes of shares to be enfranchised, and this could not be implied due to uncertainty. In *Broomhead v National Westminster Bank Plc*,[830b] a bank's alleged promise to renew overdraft facilities to if, inter alia, the customer "didn't do anything silly" was too vague to have contractual effect. Similar reasoning may be applied where the agreement is expressed to be subject to a condition that depends on the satisfaction of one of the parties[831]; the problems arising from such provisions are discussed in para.2-164, below.

[827] [1941] A.C. 251, described as "a rare case of uncertainty" in *Scammell v Dicker* [2005] EWCA Civ 405, [2005] 3 All E.R. 838 at [41]. See also *Davies v Davies* (1887) 36 Ch. D. 359; *Kingsley & Keith Ltd v Glynn Bros. (Chemicals) Ltd* [1953] 1 Lloyd's Rep. 211; *Judge v Crown Leisure Ltd* [2005] EWCA Civ 571, [2005] I.R.L.R. 823 at [23]; *Landmark Brickwork Ltd v Sutcliffe* [2011] EWHC 1239 at [39]; and below, para.2-150 at n.835.

[828] [2017] EWHC 1928 (Comm). And see *MacInnes v Gross* [2017] EWHC 46 (QB).

[829] [2017] EWHC 1928 (Comm) at [136]. And see *Landmark Brickwork Ltd v Sutcliffe* [2011] EWHC 1239 at [39] where a covenant in a contract of employment restricting competition in two named counties and in others "to the south" of them was too uncertain to be enforced.

[830] [2018] EWHC 1146 (Ch); [2018] B.T.C. 20 at [62]–[63].

[830a] [2018] UKFTT 509 (TC) at [82] and [84]. And see *Avonwick Holdings Ltd v Azitio Holdings Ltd* [2020] EWHC 1844 (Comm) at [699] ("The parties did not agree on essential terms" because, inter alia, the parties had not agreed on the precise assets to be transferred).

[830b] [2018] EWHC 1574 (Ch). It was also unclear over what period the loan would be automatically renewed.

[831] e.g. *Montreal Gas Co v Vasey* [1900] A.C. 595; *Hofflinghouse & Co Ltd v C. Trade SA (The Intra Transporter)* [1986] 2 Lloyd's Rep. 132; *Shipping Enterprises Ltd v Eckhart & Co K G (The Nissos Samos)* [1985] 1 Lloyd's Rep. 378, 385; *Stabilad Ltd v Stephens & Carter Ltd (No.2)* [1999] 2 All E.R. (Comm) 651, 659 ("void for uncertainty").

*To the end of title, add new footnote 831a:*

**Qualifications of the requirement of certainty**[831a]

[831a] This paragraph was cited with approval in *SK Properties (Midlands) Ltd v Byrne* [2018] UKUT 394 (LC) at [24]. **2-149**

*Replace paragraph with:*

The courts do not expect commercial documents to be drafted with strict legal precision. The cases provide many examples of judicial awareness of the danger that too strict an application of the requirement of certainty could result in the striking down of agreements intended by the parties to have binding force. The courts are reluctant to reach such a conclusion, particularly where the parties have acted on the agreement.[832] As Lord Wright said in *Hillas & Co Ltd v Arcos Ltd*[833]: **2-149**

> "Businessmen often record the most important agreements in crude and summary fashion; modes of expression sufficient and clear to them in the course of their business may appear to those unfamiliar with the business far from complete or precise. It is accordingly the duty of the court to construe such documents fairly and broadly, without being too astute or subtle in finding defects; but, on the contrary, the court should seek to apply the old maxim of English law, *verba ita sunt intelligenda ut res magis valeat quam pereat.* That maxim, however, does not mean that the court is to make a contract for the parties, or to go outside the words they have used, except in so far as they are appropriate implications of law."

In addition, so long as there is no "conceptual uncertainty", it is no bar to finding a binding agreement that the matter may be difficult "to resolve in practice"; the latter is "a matter for interpretation".[834] Rix L.J. said[835]:

> "... it is simply a non sequitur to argue from a disagreement about the meaning and effect of a contract to its legal uncertainty ... For that to occur—and it very rarely occurs—it has to be legally or practically impossible to give to the parties' agreement any sensible content ... that is certain which can be rendered certain ..."

In accordance with these principles, the courts have developed a number of qualifications to the requirement of certainty; these qualifications are stated in paras 2-150—2-155, below.

[832] *Brown v Gould* [1977] Ch. 53, 57–58; *Tito v Waddell (No.2)* [1977] Ch. 106, 314; *Sudbrook Trading Estate Ltd v Eggleton* [1983] 1 A.C. 444; *Anangel Atlas Compania Anangel Atlas Compania Naviera SA v Ishikawajima-Harima Heavy Industries Co (No.2)* [1990] 2 Lloyd's Rep. 526, 545–6; *Clement v Gibbs* [1996] C.L.Y. 1209; *Hanjin Shipping Co Ltd v Zenith Chartering Corp (The Mercedes Envoy)* [1995] 2 Lloyd's Rep. 559, 564; *Hackney LBC v Thompson* [2001] L. & T. Rep. 7; *Alstom Signalling Ltd v Jarvis Facilities Ltd* [2004] EWHC 1232, 95 Con. L.R. 55; *Whitecap v John H Rundle* [2008] EWCA Civ 429 at [22]; *Maple Leaf Volatility Master Fund v Rouvroy* [2009] EWHC 257 (Comm), [2009] 1 Lloyd's Rep. 257 at [235], approved on appeal [2010] EWCA Civ 1334, [2010] 2 All E.R. (Comm) 788, especially at [22]; *Barbudev v Eurocom Cable Management Bulgaria EOOD* [2012] EWCA Civ 548 at [32]; *Benourad v Compass Plc* [2010] EWHC 1882 (QB) at [106(d)]; and cf. *TTMI SARL v Statoil SA (The Sibohelle)* [2011] EWHC 1150 (Comm), [2011] 2 Lloyd's Rep. 222 at [43], [47] (where the reason why the express negotiations had failed to give rise to a contract was not want of certainty but mistake, and the conduct of the parties in performing the transaction nevertheless supported the inference that a contract had been concluded); *Dhananiv Crasnianski* [2011] EWHC 926 (Comm), [2011] 2 All E.R. (Comm) 799 at [70] (fact that work has been done under the contract a

"relevant factor" but not a decisive one, so that in that case no contract had been concluded: below, para.2-195); *Vinci Construction UK Ltd v Beumer Group UK Ltd* [2017] EWHC 2196 (TCC); *Openwork Ltd v Forte* [2018] EWCA Civ 783; *Abberley v Abberley* [2019] EWHC 1564 (Ch) (there was sufficient certainty for a binding contract although technical difficulties resulted in the agreement being handwritten by the mediator, reference to coloured portions of land were recorded by pencil only, and subsequently, the parties attempted to agree further details). The reluctance referred to in the text above may account for the lack of "enthusiasm" with which Dyson L.J. and Sir Robin Auld in *Schweppe v Harper* [2008] EWCA Civ 442 at [75] and [82] concluded that the agreement in that case was too uncertain to be enforced; and for Ward L.J.'s dissent in that case.

833 (1932) 147 L.T. 503, 514; cf. *Rahcassi Shipping Co v Blue Star Line* [1969] 1 Q.B. 173 (agreement for arbitration "by commercial men and not lawyers" upheld); *Nea Agrex SA v Baltic Shipping Co Ltd* [1976] Q.B. 933; *Tropwood AG of Zug v Jade Enterprises Inc (The Tropwind)* [1981] 1 Lloyd's Rep. 232; *Deutsche Schachtbau und Tiefbohrgesellschaft mbH v Ras Al Khaimah National Oil Co* [1990] 1 A.C. 295, 306; reversed on other grounds, at 329 et seq.; *Grace Shipping Inc v C.F. Sharpe (Malaysia) Pte* [1987] 1 Lloyd's Rep. 207; *Didymi Corp v Atlantic Lines & Navigation Co Inc* [1987] 2 Lloyd's Rep. 166; affirmed [1988] 2 Lloyd's Rep. 108 (above, para.2-138); *Anangel Atlas Compania Naviera SA v Ishikawajima Harima Heavy Industries Corp (No.2)* [1990] 2 Lloyd's Rep. 526, 546; *Star Shipping AS v China National Foreign Trade Transportation Corp (The Star Texas)* [1993] 2 Lloyd's Rep. 445, 455; *Scammell v Dicker* [2005] EWCA Civ 405, [2005] 3 All E.R. 838 at [31]; *Halpern v Halpern* [2006] EWHC 603 (Comm), [2006] 2 Lloyd's Rep. 83 at [115], affirmed on this point [2007] EWCA Civ 291, [2007] 3 All E.R. 478 at [50]; *Durham Tees Valley Airport Ltd v Bmibaby Ltd* [2010] EWCA Civ 485, [2011] 1 Lloyd's Rep. 68 at [54], [88] (paras 2-123 above and 2-152 below); *Astra Zeneca UK Ltd v Albemarle International Corp* [2011] EWHC 1574 (Comm) at [31]; *Trebor Bassett Holdings Ltd v ADT Fire & Security Plc* [2011] EWHC 1936 (TCC), [2011] B.L.R. 661 at [150]; *Re Lehman Brothers International (Europe) (In Administration)* [2012] EWHC 2997 (Ch) at [193]–[196]; *Chaggar v Chaggar* [2018] EWHC 1203 (QB) at [186]–[198] Morris J. set out the general principles for a binding agreement. See also Fridman (1960) 76 L.Q.R. 521.

834 *Re Lehman Brothers International (Europe) (In Administration)* [2012] EWHC 2997 (Ch) at [197]–[198]. And see *GLC v Connolly* [1970] 2 Q.B. 100, 108, 110; *Chaggar v Chaggar* [2018] EWHC 1203 (QB) at [187].

835 *Scammell v Dicker* [2005] EWCA Civ 405 at [30] and [39]. And see *Volumatic Ltd v Ideas for Life Ltd* [2019] EWHC 2273 (IPEC) at [31] (agreement sufficiently certain and could have been given meaning although it was contained in the minutes of a meeting, had there been intention to be bound).

## 8. CONDITIONAL AGREEMENTS

## (a) Classification

### Conditions precedent and subsequent

*To the end of paragraph, after "a condition subsequent.", add:*

2-159 Whether a condition precedent or subsequent exists is a matter of interpretation.[870a]

870a See *Peacock v Imagine Property Developments Ltd* [2018] EWHC 1113 (TCC) where payment of the deposit was found not to be a condition precedent to the valid exercise of an option to purchase, but merely payable "on" such exercise.

## (b) Degrees of Obligation

### Waiver of condition

*Replace footnote 915 with:*

2-167 915 *Wood Preservation Ltd v Prior* [1969] 1 W.L.R. 1077; cf. *Heron Garages Properties Ltd v Moss* [1974] 1 W.L.R. 148. And see *Anchor 2020 Ltd v Midas Construction Ltd* [2019] EWHC 435 (TCC) at [94].

## 9. CONTRACTUAL INTENTION

*To the end of title, add new footnote 917a:*

### General[917a]

917a Paras 2-168—2-174, 2-193 were cited by Judge Klein with approval in *Broomhead v National Westminster Bank Plc* [2018] EWHC 1574 (Ch). 2-168

### Burden of proof: agreements inferred from conduct

*Replace paragraph with:*

The rule as to burden of proof stated in para.2-168 above applies where the parties had entered into an express agreement, whether written or oral.[926] Claims or defences are, however, sometimes based on the allegation that parties between whom there was no express agreement had so conducted themselves in relation to each other that an *implied* contract was to be inferred from their conduct; and in a number of cases of this kind the allegation has been rejected on the ground that there was no contractual intention.[927] Such cases illustrate the judicial attitude that "contracts are not lightly to be implied" and that the courts must (in cases of this kind) be able "to conclude with confidence that ... the parties intended to create contractual relations".[928] Thus, the burden of proof on this issue appears, in cases of implied contracts, to be on the proponent of the contract, contrary to the rule which applies to express agreements regulating commercial relationships. In *Modahl v British Athletics Federation*,[929] the burden was held to have been discharged so that a contract came into existence between an athlete and the Federation, under whose rules the athlete had for a long time competed. The rules of the Federation had contractual force by reason of the "continuous long-term relationship based on a programme and rules couched in language of a contractual character and purporting to impose mutual rights and obligations".[930] Likewise, in *Re MF Global UK Ltd (In Special Administration)*[931] the court implied a contract between two companies in administration, pursuant to which one company paid the expenses of staff seconded to a second company within the same group. The established relationship between the companies was only explicable in the particular circumstances on the basis that it had a contractual foundation. In *Glencore Energy UK Ltd v OMV Supply & Trading Ltd*[932] the court implied a contract from one party's request that the second party move the vessel carrying the oil to wait offshore until a berth was available, the latter accepted this by conduct and was entitled to remuneration for the time the vessel spent waiting. This was "necessary for an implied contract to this effect 'to give business reality to a transaction to create enforceable obligations between parties who are dealing with one another in circumstances in which one would expect that business reality and those enforceable obligations to exist'".[933] In contrast, the burden of proof was not discharged where, following a serious oil spill from an insured ship, the insurer asserted a contract with an international fund, set up to compensate for damage caused by oil pollution, to indemnify the insurer in respect of aspects of its liability.[934] On the facts, it was impossible to construe the international fund's communications as making the offer alleged expressly or impliedly, let alone clearly and unequivocally.[935] Likewise, no implied contract for arbitration collateral to the main express contract was found where there was "no necessity to imply the alleged contract"[936]; and no implied contract was found between the claimant volunteer children's water polo instructor at a club and the defendant national governing body when the club 2-170 suspended the former for safeguarding concerns, because there was no intention to create legal relations: "there is a deliberate two-tier structure whereby any obligations in respect of [the defendant's] rules are owed to the Club and any benefits in terms of participation in [the defendant's] events are derived through membership of the Club",[936a] there was thus, no necessity for implying a contract, and unlike *Modahl v British Athletics Federation*,[936b] the defendant's rules in the present dispute were not of a contractual flavour, and there was no long-standing relationship found between the present parties.

[926] *Bottrill v Harling* [2015] EWCA Civ 564 at [14]–[16], [19]–[21], the Court of Appeal held that in deciding whether an oral agreement was made it is entirely acceptable to consider how the parties conducted themselves.

[927] *Hispanica de Petroleos SA v Vencedora Oceana Navegaceon SA (The Kapetan Markos N.L.) (No.2)* [1987] 2 Lloyd's Rep. 321; *The Aramis* [1989] 1 Lloyd's Rep. 213; *Mitsui & Co Ltd v Novorossiysk Shipping Co (The Gudermes)* [1993] 1 Lloyd's Rep. 311; in some of these cases rights and liabilities under the shipping documents would now arise by virtue of Carriage of Goods by Sea Act 1992 ss.2 and 3. Part of the ground covered by these sections of the 1992 Act will, if the Rotterdam Rules (below, para.18-036) are given the force of law in the United Kingdom, be covered by arts 57 and 58 of those Rules, so that it is likely that the 1992 Act will, in that event, have to be amended. The scope of arts 57 and 58 is significantly narrower than that of ss.2 and 3 of the 1992 Act: see, for example, para.18-054 below.

[928] *Blackpool and Fylde Aero Club v Blackpool BC* [1990] 1 W.L.R. 1195, 1202; cf. *Baird Textile Holdings Ltd v Marks & Spencer Plc* [2001] EWCA Civ 274, [2002] 1 All E.R. (Comm) 737 at [20], [21], [30], [62] where the argument that there was an implied contract was rejected for the reasons given in para.2-173 below. The argument was likewise rejected in *West Bromwich Albion Football Club v El Safty* [2006] EWCA Civ 1299, (2006) 92 B.M.L.R. 179 at [43], [48] (below, para.18-004) and *Cairns v Visteon UK Ltd* [2007] I.R.L.R. 175 at [18], [23] on the ground that in these two cases there was no "necessity" for any such implication; and see below, para.18-005. For other cases in which it was held that it was not "necessary" to imply a contract, see *Whittle Movers Ltd v Hollywood Express Ltd* [2009] EWCA Civ 1189 at [17]; *Commissioners for Her Majesty's Revenue and Customs v Benchdollar Ltd* [2009] EWHC 1310 (Ch) at [38], where there was no such "necessity" because both parties believed (though mistakenly: see below, para.4-036 n.234) that their arrangement was binding as an acknowledgement within Limitation Act 1980 s.29(5); *Classic Maritime Inc v Lion Diversified Holdings Berhad* [2009] EWHC 1142 (Comm), [2010] 1 Lloyd's Rep. 69 at [9]; cf. *CN Associates v Holbeton Ltd* [2011] EWHC 43 (TCC), [2011] B.L.R. 261; *Tod v Swim Wales* [2018] EWHC 665 (QB) at [94] and [100], where there was no implied contract as there was no contractual intention and no necessity to imply a contract; *Bot v Barnick* [2018] EWHC 3132 (QB) at [20], there was no implied contract between doctors and the partners of patients due to conflicts of interest, and the potentially large scope of liability that such a contract would have imposed, see below para.2-173. Contrast *Goshaw Dedicated Ltd v Tyser & Co Ltd* [2006] EWCA Civ 54, [2006] 1 All E.R. (Comm) 501 at [66], apparently rejecting the argument that there was no implied contract.

[929] [2001] EWCA Civ 1447, [2002] 1 W.L.R. 1192; cf. recognition of the distinction, for the purpose of burden of proof, between express and implied agreements, drawn in paras 2-169 and 2-170 above, in *Baird Textile Holdings Ltd v Marks & Spencer Plc* [2001] EWCA Civ 274, [2002] 1 All E.R. (Comm) 737 at [61]; and *JD Cleverly Ltd v Family Finance Ltd* [2010] EWCA Civ 1477, [2011] R.T.R. 22 at [28]–[32], where the proponent of the contract failed to discharge the burden as the conduct in question was not "consistent only" (at [36]) with an intention to enter into contractual relations; see also the *CN Associates* case [2011] EWHC 43 (TCC) at [36] and the *Classic Maritime* case [2009] EWHC 1142 (Comm) at [9] and [14]. And see *Re MF Global UK Ltd (In Special Administration)* [2015] EWHC 883 (Ch); [2015] Pens. L.R. 405 at [56]–[58] where an implied contract was found between companies in a group; one employed staff and seconded them to another which paid the associated costs, notwithstanding the absence of any express agreement between them as to the provision of staff.

[930] [2001] EWCA Civ 1447 at [109], cf. at [52]. Jonathan Parker L.J. dissented on this point. For discussion of factors which led to the conclusion that the requirement of contractual intention had been satisfied in *Attrill v Dresdner Kleinwort Ltd* [2012] EWHC 1189 (QB), see that case [134] et seq., [2013] EWCA Civ 394 at [89], n.937. The case was one of express agreement, not one of agreement inferred from conduct.

[931] [2016] EWCA Civ 569.

[932] [2018] EWHC 895 (Comm).

[933] [2018] EWHC 895 (Comm) at [51] citing *The Aramis* [1989] 1 Lloyd's Rep 213, 224 per Bingham L.J. approving May L.J. in *The Elli 2* [1985] 1 Lloyd's Rep 107, 115.

[934] *Assuranceforeningen Gard Gjensidig v International Oil Pollution Compensation Fund* [2014] EWHC 3369 (Comm).

[935] [2014] EWHC 3369 at [102], [110], [114] and [123].

[936] *Bony v Kacou* [2017] EWHC 2146 (Ch) at [47]–[48], citing *Baird Textiles Holdings Ltd v Marks & Spencer* [2001] EWCA Civ 274, [2002] 1 All E.R. (Comm) 737 at [18].

[936a] *Tod v Swim Wales* [2018] EWHC 665 (QB), which distinguished *Modahl v BAF* [2001] EWCA Civ 1447 at [94]. This outcome is "not surprising" as "if that were not the case, the result would be that [the defendant] would owe contractual obligations to many thousands of club members (many of whom will be minors and therefore lacking in any capacity to contract) across the land" (at [97]).

[936b] [2001] EWCA Civ 1447, [2002] 1 W.L.R. 1192.

## Intention judged objectively

*Replace first paragraph with:*

In deciding issues of contractual intention, the courts normally apply an objective test[937]: for example, where the sale of a house is *not* "subject to contract",[938] both parties are likely to be bound even though one of them subjectively believed that he would not be bound until the usual exchange of contracts had taken place.[939] In *Edmonds v Lawson*,[940] the Court of Appeal similarly applied the objective test to hold that the requirement of contractual intention was satisfied where a pupil barrister accepted an offer of pupillage with a set of chambers. The resulting contract[941] was between the pupil and all the members of the chambers—not between the pupil and the individual members of the chambers who acted as her pupil masters. In *New Media Holding Co LLC v Kuznetsov*[942] the court found an intention to create legal relations in respect of a "Term Sheet" signed by both parties. On the one hand: the language of the document was brief and did not mention consideration; the document was prepared in a casual and informal way; further formalities were required; and the rights transferred were not capable of immediate enforcement. On the other hand: the parties were experienced and sophisticated businessmen; the document contained clear express terms; the language was consistent with a legally binding agreement; and the "Term Sheet" was consistent with an intention that this be part of a package agreement (with other terms, including the consideration, to be dealt with elsewhere) and with the parties' pre-existing relationship, which itself raised a strong presumption that the parties intended to be legally bound. In *Dacy Building Services Ltd v IDM Properties Ltd*[942a] it was held that the claimant builder had not made its oral agreement with the main contractor, but rather with the employer's agent. This was based on an assessment of witness evidence, which made complete business and common sense, and because it would be "verging on the commercially suicidal" for the claimant to enter a contract with the main contractor since the latter already owed the claimant substantial sums. Where there has been substantial performance, courts are especially reluctant to reach the unrealistic conclusion that the parties lacked intention to be legally bound.[943] The objective test is, however, here (as elsewhere)[944] subject to the limitation that it does not apply in favour of a party who knows the truth. Thus, in the house sale example given above, the party who did not intend to be bound would not be bound if his state of mind was actually known to the other party.[945] Nor could a party who did not in fact intend to be bound invoke the objective test so as to bind the other party to the contract[946]: to permit this would pervert the purpose of the objective test, which is to protect a party who has relied on the objective appearance of consent from the prejudice which he would suffer if the other party could escape liability on the ground that he had no real intention to be bound. The objective test, moreover, merely prevents a party from relying on his *uncommunicated* belief as to the binding force of the agreement. The test therefore does not apply where the parties have **2-171** expressed their actual intention in the document alleged to constitute the contract: the question whether they intended the document to have contractual force then becomes one "of construction of the documents as a whole what effect is to be given to such a statement"[947]; and the general rule in cases of this kind is that a party who has signed the document is then bound by its terms, as so construed.[948]

937 See *Carlill v Carbolic Smoke Ball Co* [1893] 1 Q.B. 256; *Ignazio Messina & Co v Polskie Linie Oceaniczne* [1995] 2 Lloyd's Rep. 566, 579; *Bowerman v Association of British Travel Agents* [1995] N.L.J. 1815; *Manatee Towing Co v Oceanbulk Maritime SA (The Bay Ridge)* [1999] 2 All E.R. (Comm) 306 at 327; *London Baggage (Charing Cross) Ltd v Railtrack Plc* [2000] E.G.C.S. 57; *Baird Textile Holdings Ltd v Marks & Spencer Plc* [2001] EWCA Civ 274, [2002] 1 All E.R. (Comm) 737; *Maple Leaf Volatility Master Fund v Rouvroy* [2009] EWHC 257 (Comm), 1 Lloyd's Rep. 475 at [223], [224] and [2009] EWCA Civ 1334, [2010] 2 All E.R. (Comm) 788 at [17] (affirming the decision below); *RTS Flexible Systems Ltd v Molkerei Alois Müller GmbH & Co KG (UK Production)* [2010] UKSC 14, [2010] 1 W.L.R. 753 at [45], [46]; *Benourad v Compass Group Plc* [2010] EWHC 1882 (QB) at [106(b)]; *Dhanani v Crasnianski* [2011] EWHC 926 (Comm), [2011] 2 All E.R. (Comm) 799 at [80], [88] ("objectively assessed"); *Barbudev v Eurocom Cable Management Bulgaria EOOD* [2011] EWHC 1560 (Comm), [2011] 2 All E.R. (Comm) 951 at [92]–[94], affirmed [2012] EWCA Civ 548, where the objective test is stated at [30]. For a statement of the objective test of contractual intention, see also *Bear Stearns Bank Plc v Forum Global Equity Ltd* [2007] EWHC 1576, above para.2-122, where an oral acceptance of a "firm" offer (also made orally) was held to give rise to a contract although at the stage of that acceptance many important points remained unresolved; this was also the position in the *RTS* case, above: see at [61]; *Chaggar v Chaggar* [2018] EWHC 1203 (QB) at [186]–[198] Morris J. set out the general principles for a binding agreement; cf. the *Benourad* case above, at [106(f)] and above, para.2-122 at n.632. And see *Attrill v Dresdner Kleinwort Ltd* [2013] EWCA Civ 394 at [61]: the Court of Appeal enforced the employer's promise to their employees to maintain a "guaranteed minimum bonus pool" from which discretionary bonuses payable under the contracts of employment were to be distributed "no matter what" (at [22]). The Court relied, in particular, on the facts that it was made "in the context of a pre-existing legal relationship" (i.e. of employer and employee); that the promise was originally that of the employer's Chief Executive Officer; that it was made as "part of a vitally important strategy to retain staff"; that it "related to pay, the most fundamental obligation under the employment contract"; and that by its terms "the promise assured staff that the fund was guaranteed come what may" (at [89]). cf. *Crowden v Aldridge* [1993] 1 W.L.R. 433, applying the objective test of intention to produce legal consequences to a noncontractual direction to executors in favour of a third party. Quaere whether, in the absence of reliance on the direction, the policy which justifies the objective test in a contractual context extends to the situation which arose in this case.

938 Above, para.2-126.

939 *Tweddell v Henderson* [1975] 1 W.L.R. 1496; *Storer v Manchester City Council* [1974] 1 W.L.R. 1403, 1408.

940 [2000] Q.B. 501.

941 For the consideration moving from the pupil, see below, para.4-039.

942 [2016] EWHC 360 (QB).

942a [2018] EWHC 178 (TCC) at [54].

943 *Purton (t/a Richwood Interiors) v Kilker Projects Ltd* [2015] EWHC 2624 (TCC) at [7]; *Anchor 2020 Ltd v Midas Construction Ltd* [2019] EWHC 435 (TCC) at [113]. Cf. *CRS GT Ltd v McLaren Automotive Ltd* [2018] EWHC 3209 (Comm) (although work had been carried out, the agreement was fundamentally incomplete, its language was casual and vague, the agreement provided for formal execution, and subsequent communication between the parties showed that neither understood a binding contract had come into force). And see *Volumatic Ltd v Ideas for Life Ltd* [2019] EWHC 2273 (IPEC) (no intention to be bound by assignment agreement although the parties continued to trade for 11 years).

944 Above, para.2-004. In contrast, no intention to be bound was concluded in *Price v Euro Car Parks Ltd* [2015] EWHC 3253 (QB) where the claimant put a business proposal and sent an "In Principle Heads of Agreement" that neither signed, to the defendant. The defendant never accepted any offer made by the claimant; it merely allowed the claimant to go ahead (at his own risk) to research his business proposal. Moreover, the "In Principle Heads of Agreement" was too indefinite. Nor was there intention to be bound in *Burgess v Lejonvarn* [2016] EWHC 40 (TCC), [2016] T.C.L.R. 3, where an architect, for no fee, had found a contractor to landscape her friends' garden with a view to her providing subsequent design input for consideration. There was no contract to project manage the landscaping because the written discussions were simply too inchoate, there was no intention to be legally bound and there had been no consideration.

945 *Pateman v Pay* (1974) 263 E.G. 467; *Attrill v Dresdner Kleinwort Ltd* [2013] EWCA Civ 394 at [86] where the requirement of contractual intention was satisfied: see n.929.

946 *Lark v Outhwaite* [1991] 2 Lloyd's Rep. 132, 141.

947 *R. v Lord Chancellor's Department Ex p. Nangle* [1991] I.C.R. 743, 751.

948 See *L'Estrange v F Graucob Ltd* [1934] 2 K.B. 394; below, para.13-002. Contrast *Volumatic Ltd v Ideas for Life Ltd* [2019] EWHC 2273 (IPEC) at [24] (signatures on the document did not reflect an intention to be bound by its contents merely signified agreement as to what was discussed).

## Intention impliedly negatived

*Replace paragraph with:*

In *Baird Textile Holdings Ltd v Marks & Spencer Plc*[969] the claimants had for some 30 years been a principal supplier of clothing to the defendants, a leading retail chain. When the defendants terminated the arrangement with effect from the end of the then current production season, the claimants sought damages, basing their claim on, inter alia,[970] an alleged implied contract not to terminate the arrangement except on reasonable notice of three years. The claim was rejected because of "the absence of any intention to create legal relations".[971] One factor[972] on which this conclusion was based was that the defendants had (as the claimants themselves had alleged in their points of claim)[973] deliberately abstained from entering into a long-term contractual relationship with the claimants in order to maintain the flexibility of the de facto long-term commercial relationship between the parties.[974] It followed that the claimants must be taken to have accepted the risk inherent in such a relationship "without specific contractual protection".[975] Contractual retention was, again, impliedly negatived in *Cobbe v Yeoman's Row Management Ltd*[976] where an agreement "in principle" for the redevelopment and disposal of residential property left other aspects of the scheme to be settled by further negotiations between the parties. It was held that the agreement "in principle" lacked contractual force since, until those outstanding matters had been settled and embodied in a formal agreement between the parties, each regarded the other as bound in honour only.[977] There was no implied contract between a doctor and his patient's partner in relation to the provision of accurate information about the patient's condition in *Bot v Barnick*.[977a] There were "strong reasons for concluding the necessity of [not implying a contract]", as there would be a "risk of conflict" between the duty owed to the patient and the alleged duty owed to the partner. Such a contract would have a "potentially large scope" of liability which "the defendant would have declined to assume", even if the partner had offered a fee. Implying such a contract would "go against common sense and business efficacy".[977b] In *Dieno George v Revenue and Customs Commissioners*,[977c] the tribunal held that the parties did not intend to create legal relations. Not only was the agreement uncertain, but also it was made in the context of a "wide-ranging" discussion, where "many issues" were discussed. It was implausible that the parties intended the conclusions on the other issues discussed to be legally binding and there was no segregation or distinction made between those matters and the agreement reached. Accordingly, there was no legally enforceable contract. Likewise, no intention to be bound was found by the court in respect of an oral exchange over a social lunch where discussion of business was not expected; the proposal was being put forward on behalf of someone not known for the work being proposed, "let alone a deal of this scale",[977d] and the claimant subsequently sent a draft agreement which it repeatedly called for the defendant to sign.[977e] The same conclusion was reached in respect of an agreement, reached by a telephone conversation, to pay £1 million for advice, because it was unlikely a contract of the type alleged and for the substantial fee claimed would have been 2-173 concluded in a brief telephone conversation and in a manner which was at odds with market practice.[977f]

[969] [2001] EWCA Civ 274, [2002] 1 All E.R. (Comm) 737.

[970] For the alternative basis of the claim on the ground of estoppel, see below, para.4-099.

[971] *Baird* case [2001] EWCA Civ 274 at [30], [47], [69].

[972] For another such factor, see below, para.2-195.

[973] *Baird* case [2001] EWCA Civ 274 at [10], [46], [73].

[974] *Baird* case [2001] EWCA Civ 274 at [30], [47], [73], [74]; cf. *Alstom Transport v Tilson* [2010] EWCA Civ 1308, [2010] I.R.L.R. 169 at [50] (no implied contract where one party had actually refused to enter into an express contract with the other).

[975] *Baird* case [2001] EWCA Civ 274 at [76]. For somewhat similar reasoning, see *Raiffeisen Zentralbank Osterreich AG v Royal Bank of Scotland Plc* [2010] EWHC 1392, [2011] 1 Lloyd's Rep. 123 (oral assurances given by borrower to lender held not to be legally binding since to give them contractual force would have defeated their commercial objective, which made it "important that they should *not* have legal effect" (at [143])).

[976] [2008] UKHL 55, [2008] 1 W.L.R. 1752.

[977] [2008] UKHL 55 at [7], [71].

[977a] [2018] EWHC 3132 (QB).

[977b] [2018] EWHC 3132 (QB) at [20].

[977c] [2018] UKFTT 509 (TC) at [96] and [99].

[977d] *AMP Advisory and Management Partners AG v Force India Formula One Team Ltd (In Liquidation)* [2019] EWHC 2426 (Comm) at [69].

[977e] *AMP Advisory and Management Partners AG v Force India Formula One Team Ltd (In Liquidation)* [2019] EWHC 2426 (Comm) at [71].

[977f] *Moorgate Capital (Corporate Finance) Ltd v Sun European Partners LLP* [2020] EWHC 593 (Comm) at [89], [92].

### Statements inducing a contract

*In line 8, after "his product was", replace "“foolproof ”" with:*

2-174 “foolproof”

### Social agreements

*Replace paragraph with:*

2-178 Many social arrangements do not amount to contracts because they are not intended to be legally binding. “The ordinary example is where two parties agree to take a walk together, or where there is an offer and an acceptance of hospitality.”[995] Similarly it has been held that the winner of a competition held by a golf club could not sue for his prize where:

> “... no one concerned with that competition ever intended that there should be any legal results flowing from the conditions posted and the acceptance by the competitor of those conditions”[996]

that the rules of a competition organised by a “jalopy club” for charitable purposes did not have contractual force[997]; that “car pool” and similar arrangements between friends or neighbours did not amount to contracts even though one party contributed to the running costs of the other’s vehicle[998]; that an agreement between members of a group of friends relating to musical performances by the group was not intended to have contractual effect[999]; that the provision of free residential accommodation for close friends did not amount to a contract as it was an act of bounty, done without any intention to enter into legal relations[1000]; that an oral exchange over a social lunch was not intended to be legally binding because the defendant had not expected to discuss business, particularly of the type and scale proposed[1000a]; and that a statement made during an informal meeting in a pub by the majority owner of a company that he would pay a consultant £15 million if he raised the company's share price to £8 would not reasonably have been understood as a serious offer capable of creating a legally binding contract.[1001] In the latter case, the Judge took into account[1002] the informal setting,[1003] the social purpose of the occasion, the nature and tone of the conversation, the lack of commercial sense of the alleged agreement, the vagueness of the "offer", perceptions of the witness, the claimant's inconsistent subsequent conduct, and the lack of certainty on a vital term. On the other hand, contractual intention was found in an agreement between an employer and employee to play the lottery and share any winnings.[1004]

995 *Balfour v Balfour* [1919] 2 K.B. 571, 578; *Rose & Frank Co v J.R. Crompton & Bros Ltd* [1923] 2 K.B. 261, 293; *Wyatt v Kreglinger & Fernau* [1933] 1 K.B. 793, 806.

996 *Lens v Devonshire Club, The Times,* December 4, 1914; referred to in *Wyatt's* case [1933] 1 K.B. 793 from which the quotation in the text is taken.

997 *White v Blackmore* [1972] 2 Q.B. 651.

998 *Coward v M.I.B.* [1963] 1 Q.B. 259; overruled, but not on the issue of contractual intention, in *Albert v M.I.B.* [1972] A.C. 301; *Buckpitt v Oates* [1968] 1 All E.R. 1145, criticised on this point by Karsten (1969) 32 M.L.R. 88. The actual decisions are obsolete by reason of Road Traffic Act 1988 ss.145, 149; cf. also s.150; but an issue of contractual intention might still arise if one party to such an arrangement simply failed to turn up at the agreed time. For another context in which sharing of expenses did not give rise to an inference of contractual intention, see *Monmouth BC v Marlog, The Times,* May 4, 1994.

999 *Hadley v Kemp* [1999] E.M.L.R. 589; *McPhail v Bourne* [2008] EWHC 1235.

1000 *Heslop v Burns* [1974] 1 W.L.R. 1241; cf. *Horrocks v Forray* [1976] 1 W.L.R. 230.

1000a *AMP Advisory and Management Partners AG v Force India Formula One Team Ltd (In Liquidation)* [2019] EWHC 2426 (Comm) at [69].

1001 *Blue v Ashley* [2017] EWHC 1928 (Comm), citing paras 2-177, 2-194 and 2-195 in *Chitty on Contracts*, 32nd edn (2015).

1002 [2017] EWHC 1928 (Comm) at [80]–[112]. And see *MacInnes v Gross* [2017] EWHC 46 (QB).

1003 In *MacInnes v Gross* [2017] EWHC 46 (QB) Coulson J. said that the fact that discussions took place over dinner in a restaurant did not preclude a binding contract from coming into existence; however, the highly informal setting meant that the court should closely scrutinise whether there was an intention to create legal relations.

1004 *Kucukkoylu v Ozcan* [2014] EWHC 1972.

## Vague agreements

*Replace paragraph with:*

Another factor relevant to the issue of contractual intention is the degree of precision with which the agreement is expressed. It has been held that a husband's promise to let his deserted wife stay in the matrimonial home had no contractual force because it was not "intended by him, or understood by her, to have any contractual basis or effect".[1097] The promise was too vague: it did not state for how long or on what terms the wife could stay in the house.[1098] So, too, the use of deliberately vague language was held to negative contractual intention where a property developer reached an "understanding" with a firm of solicitors to employ them in connection with a proposed development, but neither side entered into a definite commitment.[1099] For the same reason, "letters of intent"[1100] or "letters of comfort"[1101] may lack the force of legally binding contracts[1102]; and likewise a memorandum of understanding.[1102a] The assumption in all these cases was that the parties had reached agreement, but lack of contractual intention prevented that **2-195** agreement from having legal effect. Vagueness may also be a ground for concluding that the parties had never reached agreement at all.[1103] This is a separate issue from that of contractual intention, which strictly speaking concerns only the *effect* of an agreement which is first shown to exist.[1104] On the one hand, the parties may agree on terms that are sufficiently certain but deprive that agreement of contractual force by express words, as in the "subject to contract" cases discussed earlier in this chapter.[1105] On the other hand, an agreement may satisfy the requirement of contractual intention, yet be too vague to enforce. An example, of the latter situation is *Dhanani v Crasnianski*.[1106] There, Ramsay J. held that an agreement to set up a private equity fund satisfied the requirement of contractual intention[1107] but nevertheless lacked contractual force because it was "in essence an agreement to agree"[1108] on terms which were "essential for such an agreement to be enforced"[1109] and "[w]ithout such further agreement the fund could not be set up",[1110] there being "no objective criteria"[1111] by which the outstanding points could be resolved. The view that contractual intention and certainty are separate requirements is further supported by the reasoning of *Barbudev v Eurocom Cable Management Bulgaria Eood*,[1112] where the issue was whether a "side letter" to a contract for the acquisition of shares in a company, gave the claimant (a major shareholder in the company) the right to acquire shares in the purchase company on terms to be agreed. The Court of Appeal held that the side letter was intended to create legal relations,[1113] but that it did not give rise to a legally binding contract entitling the claimant to acquire the shares in the purchaser company since it was no more than an agreement to agree,[1114] and *also* since many of the essential terms of the alleged contract had not been agreed.[1115] While the issues of contractual intention and vagueness are conceptually distinct, they may overlap in borderline cases[1116]; the question whether an agreement exists will depend on the degree of vagueness or on whether the vagueness can be resolved, e.g. by applying the standard of reasonableness. In one case "the absence of any intention to create legal relations"[1117] was said to have been a ground for holding that no agreement ever came into existence. Thus, contractual intention may be negatived on the ground of vagueness where the claim is based, not on an express agreement, but on one alleged to be implied from conduct.[1118]

[1097] *Vaughan v Vaughan* [1953] 1 Q.B. 762, 765; cf. *Booker v Palmer* [1942] 2 All E.R. 674; *Horrocks v Forray* [1976] 1 W.L.R. 230; *Windeler v Whitehall* [1990] 2 F.L.R. 505.

[1098] cf. *Jones v Padavatton* [1969] 1 W.L.R. 328; and see *Gould v Gould* [1970] 1 Q.B. 275; *Layton v Morris, The Times,* December 11, 1985.

[1099] *J.H. Milner & Son v Percy Bilton Ltd* [1966] 1 W.L.R. 1582. See also *Wright v Rowland* [2017] EWHC 2478 (Comm) at [73] and [74]. In *MacInnes v Gross* [2017] EWHC 46 (QB) at [77] where this paragraph was cited with approval.

[1100] Above, para.2-133.

[1101] *Kleinwort Benson Ltd v Malaysian Mining Corp* [1989] 1 W.L.R. 379; see also *Associated British Ports v Ferryways NV* [2009] EWCA Civ 189, [2009] 1 Lloyd's Rep. 595, above para.2-133 (where a "letter of comfort" was held to have given rise to a legally binding contract, though that contract had later been discharged).

[1102] cf. *Snelling v John G. Snelling Ltd* [1973] 1 Q.B. 87, 93; *Montreal Gas Co v Vasey* [1900] A.C. 595; *B.S.C. v Cleveland Bridge & Engineering Co Ltd* [1984] 1 All E.R. 504; cf. *Turriff Construction Ltd v Regalia Knitting Mills* (1971) 222 E.G. 169 (letter of intent held to be a collateral contract to pay for preliminary work); *Diamond Build Ltd v Clapham Park Homes Ltd* [2008] EWHC 1439 (TCC), 119 Con. L.R. 32 (binding letter of intent: above, para.2-132). *Wilson Smithett & Cope (Sugar) Ltd v Bangladesh Sugar Industries Ltd* [1986] 1 Lloyd's Rep. 378 (letter of intent held to be an acceptance).

[1102a] *Avonwick Holdings Ltd v Azitio Holdings Ltd* [2020] EWHC 1844 (Comm) at [673] (the precise assets to be transferred unclear) and at [558], citing the first part of this sentence with approval.

[1103] Above, para.2-148.

1104 See *Re Goodchild* [1997] 1 W.L.R. 1216 where it is said at 1226 that one of the parties to alleged mutual wills "regarded the arrangement as irrevocable, but ... [the other] did not"; cf. *Taylor v Dickens* [1998] 1 F.L.R. 806 (the reasoning of this case is doubted, but not on the issue of contractual intention, in *Gillett v Holt* [2001] Ch. 210). See also *Judge v Crown Leisure Ltd* [2005] EWCA Civ 571, [2005] I.R.L.R. 823 (above, para.2-148) at [23], distinguishing between the two issues; and *Bear Stearns Bank Plc v Forum Global Equity Ltd* [2007] EWHC 1576 at [152], [170] and [171], where certainty and intention to create legal relations were treated as separate requirements, both of which were satisfied. See also below at n.1116.

1105 Above, paras 2-126, 2-172. The terms of such agreements may be elaborated in considerable detail, but contractual intention is generally negatived until the requirement of "exchange of contracts" (above, para.2-126) is satisfied.

1106 *Dhanani v Crasnianski* [2011] EWHC 926 (Comm), [2011] 2 All E.R. (Comm) 799.

1107 At [75], [80], [81], [89].

1108 [2011] EWHC 926 (Comm) at [95]; see above para.2-144 for such agreements.

1109 [2011] EWHC 926 (Comm) at [105].

1110 [2011] EWHC 926 (Comm) at [94].

1111 [2011] EWHC 926 (Comm) at [104]; for similar reasoning, see *Shaker v VistaJet Group Holding SA* [2012] EWHC 1329 (Comm), [2012] 2 Lloyd's Rep. 93 at [7], where an "agreement to use reasonable endeavours to agree" was held to be unenforceable because there were "no objective criteria by which the court can decide whether a party has acted unreasonably" (i.e. in relation to those endeavours); for such criteria, cf. above, paras 2-126, 2-136, 2-151.

1112 [2012] EWCA Civ 548.

1113 [2012] EWCA Civ 548 at [37].

1114 [2012] EWCA Civ 548 at [44].

1115 [2012] EWCA Civ 548 at [52].

1116 This view is supported by passages in *Judge v Crown Leisure Ltd* [2005] EWCA Civ 571 at [9] and [24]. For another borderline case, see *Monovan Construction Ltd v Davenport* [2006] EWHC 1094, 108 Con. L.R. 15 where an agreement to do building work for a "provisional guide price" of £100,000 failed to specify the exact scope of the work and was said not to be legally enforceable as it was not intended to have contractual effect (at [17]). And see *Wright v Rowland* [2017] EWHC 2478 (Comm) at [73] and [74].

1117 *Baird Textile Holdings Ltd v Marks & Spencer Plc* [2001] EWCA Civ 274, [2002] 1 All E.R. (Comm) 737 at [30]; and see above, paras 2-151, 2-173.

1118 As in the *Baird* case [2001] EWCA Civ 274.

## 10. LIABILITY WHEN NEGOTIATIONS DO NOT PRODUCE A CONTRACT

## (c) Negotiations Broken Off without Preliminary Agreements

### Quantum meruit

*Replace footnote 1230 with:*

1230 See below, para.29-077. In *Dowman Imports Ltd v 2 Toobz Ltd* [2020] EWHC 291 (Comm) at [51], the court discussed unconscionability in terms of the defendant's part "in increasing the level of risk of one [a contract] not being concluded beyond that which the claimant can be taken to have assumed when he began to provide the relevant services". The question is "whether the defendant at some stage changed 'the rules of the game' ... by moving the goalposts at which the claimant thought he had been aiming". 2-222

*Add new paragraph:*

**Restitution for failure of consideration** Where money has been paid in anticipation of a contract that does not eventuate, the payor may be able to recover the sums paid for failure of consideration.[1234] In *Sharma v Simposh Ltd* Toulson L.J. said[1235]: 2-223

> "The agreement between the parties lacked formal validity and so had no contractual effect. It was no more than a mutual declaration of intent. An important part of the law

of restitution is concerned with money paid or benefits conferred in respect of legally ineffective transactions. Goff & Jones' textbook on the Law of Restitution 7th. Ed. 2007, [states at paras 19-001 and 19-002]:

> 'Transactions may be or become ineffective for a variety of reasons. But the reason the courts will award restitution is in each case fundamentally the same, namely, that the plaintiff's expectations have not been fulfilled. '
>
> ...
>
> 'If money has been paid under a contract which is or becomes ineffective, the recipient is evidently enriched. It is a distinct question whether that enrichment is an unjust enrichment ... In most of the situations, however, the ground of recovery is that the expected return for the payment, or consideration, as it is confusingly called, has failed. '"

[1234] See below, Ch.29, section 2(f) on Failure of basis.

[1235] [2011] EWCA Civ 1383, [2012] 3 W.L.R. 503 at [21]–[22]. And see *Rotam Agrochemical Co Ltd v GAT Microencapsulation GmbH (formerly GAT Microencpasulation AG)* [2018] EWHC 2765 (Comm), at [185]–[197]; *AMP Advisory and Management Partners AG v Force India Formula One Team Ltd (In Liquidation)* [2019] EWHC 2426 (Comm) at [199].

Chapter 3

# MISTAKES AS TO THE TERMS OR AS TO IDENTITY



*Replace footnote 1 with:*

[1] See generally Cheshire (1944) 60 L.Q.R. 175; Tylor (1948) 11 M.L.R. 257; Slade (1954) 70 L.Q.R. 385; Stoljar (1965) 28 M.L.R. 265; Stoljar, *Mistake and Misrepresentation: A Study in Contractual Principles* (1968); Smith (1994) 110 L.Q.R. 400; Friedmann (2003) 19 L.Q.R. 68; Cartwright, *Misrepresentation, Mistake and Non-disclosure*, 5th edn (2019); Macmillan, *Mistakes in Contract Law* (2010).

## 1. Introduction to Mistake

### Types of mistake

*Replace footnote 6 with:*

[6] The 29th and earlier editions of this work used the phrase "mutual mistake", following the terminology used by Lord Atkin in *Bell v Lever Bros* [1932] A.C. 161, and until recently some other works adhered to this usage: e.g. Beatson, *Anson's Law of Contract*, 28th edn (2002), Ch.8. It is now more common to refer to this type of mistake as "common mistake" (e.g. Beatson, Burrows and Cartwright (eds) *Anson's Law of Contract*, 31st edn (2020), Ch.8; Cheshire, Fifoot and Furmston, *Law of Contract*, 17th edn (2017), Ch.8). The courts have also referred to common mistake: e.g. *Great Peace Shipping Ltd v Tsavliris Salvage (International) Ltd (The Great Peace)* [2002] EWCA Civ 1407, [2003] Q.B. 679. One reason for using the phrase "common mistake" is to reduce the risk of confusion with what is termed here "mutual misunderstanding" (where the parties are at cross-purposes as to the terms of the contract): see below, para.3-019. 3-001

### Mistakes as to terms and mistakes as to facts

*Replace footnote 12 with:*

3-002 [12] Beatson, Burrows and Cartwright (eds), *Anson's Law of Contract*, 31st edn (2020), p.296.

### "Mistake" implies a positive belief

*Replace footnote 20 with:*

3-007 [20] cf. Cartwright, *Misrepresentation, Mistake and Non-disclosure*, 5th edn (2019), para.12-03. In *Pitt v Holt* [2013] UKSC 26, [2013] 2 W.L.R. 1200, a case of a mistake affecting a voluntary settlement, Lord Walker said (at [108]–[109]) that a mistake is different from ignorance, inadvertence and misprediction as to the future. A mistake encompasses two states of mind, namely an incorrect conscious belief or an incorrect tacit assumption as to a present matter of fact or law, but does not encompass mere causative ignorance but for which the claimant would not have acted as he did. The nature of the mistake that must be shown for a settlor to obtain rectification of a voluntary settlement was discussed extensively: see below, para.29-052.

### Mistakes that are not legally relevant

*Replace footnote 26 with:*

3-008 [26] Compare Anson's famous "Dresden china" example: *Anson's Law of Contract*, 28th edn, p.324 (second scenario). The example is omitted from the 31st edition by Beatson, Burrows and Cartwright (eds) ( 2020) but it is explained that a unilateral mistake of fact or law does not render the contract void or give rise to an equitable jurisdiction to set aside the contract: p.296. Friedmann (2003) 119 L.Q.R. 68, 79–81 argues that in such a case relief should be given, by analogy of cases of innocent misrepresentation.

## 2. MISTAKES AS TO TERMS OR IDENTITY

## (a) Underlying Principles

### Lack of agreement or agreement ambiguous

*Replace paragraph with:*

3-014 No contract can be formed if there is no correspondence between the offer and the acceptance,[53] or if the agreement is not sufficiently certain.[54] The starting point must be whether the parties have reached an agreement that there is a contract between them on the same terms, so that subjectively they are agreed on the same thing. If so there will be a contract on the agreed terms.[55] If, however, one party claims that he did not intend to contract at all, or did not intend to contract on the terms which the other party claims were agreed, then the question is whether there is a contract (or, as it is often put, whether or not the "contract is void"). The intention of the parties is, as a general rule, to be construed objectively: the language used by one party, whatever his real intention may be, is to be construed in the sense in which it was reasonably understood by the other.[56] Thus:

> "... if one party (O) so acts that his conduct, objectively considered, constitutes an offer, and the other party (A), believing that the conduct of O represents his actual intention, accepts O's offer, then a contract will come into existence, and on those facts it will make no difference if O did not in fact intend to make an offer, or if he misunderstood A's acceptance, so that O's state of mind is, in such circumstances, irrelevant."[57]

Nevertheless cases may occur in which the terms of the offer and acceptance do not match or suffer from such latent ambiguity that it is impossible reasonably to impute any agreement between the parties. For example, if it was reasonable for A to interpret the words of O's offer as meaning *x* when O in fact meant *y*, but it was equally reasonable for O to interpret A's reply as an acceptance of the offer as O intended it (i.e. as meaning *y*), there is no agreement even on an objective basis.[58] Thus "mutual misunderstanding" may prevent the formation of a contract,[59] and arguably this is no more than an application of the requirements of offer and acceptance and certainty.[59a]

[53] See above, para.2-031.

[54] See above, para.2-148.

[55] Cartwright, *Misrepresentation, Mistake and Non-disclosure*, 5th edn (2019), para.13-10, citing Glanville Williams (1954) 17 M.L.R. 154–155; Stoljar, *Mistake and Misrepresentation: A Study in Contractual Principles* (1968), p.11; Vorster (1987) 104 L.Q.R. 274, 286; Lord Macnaghten in *Falcke v Williams* [1900] A.C. 176 at 178–179, PC; and Blackburn J. in *Smith v Hughes* (1871) L.R. 6 Q.B. 597, 607, who clearly assumes that the objective test need be used only if there was no subjective agreement. Cartwright rightly points out that some decisions, such as *Paal Wilson & Co A/S v Partenreederi Hannah Blumenthal (The Hannah Blumenthal)* [1983] 1 A.C. 854, discuss the objective test without mentioning the subjective test. Each party must, of course, have signalled willingness to contract to the other, or there will be no agreement which a contract can be based (see above, para.2-001; and the need for some "outward accord" in rectification cases, below, para.3-064). For an example in German law, see RG 8 Jun 1920 II (Ziv), RGZ 99, 147, in which both parties thought that the Norwegian word *Haakjöringsköd* meant whale meat when in fact it means shark meat. It was held that the contract was for whale meat. (The case is translated in Beale, Fauvarque-Cosson, Rutgers, Tallon and Vogenauer *Ius Commune Casebooks for the Common Law of Europe: Cases, Materials and Text on Contract Law*, 3rd edn (2019), 502.) The importance of the parties' sharing subjective intentions will be when they both intend the contract to mean something other than its apparent meaning, when the communications are unclear, or where there is evidently an agreement but it is not clear what its terms are. For the possibility that a written agreement can be rectified to match what the parties were subjectively agreed on, see below, para.3-065.

[56] *Cornish v Abington* (1859) 4 H. & N. 549, 556; *Fowkes v Manchester and London Assurance Association* (1863) 3 B. & S. 917, 929; *Smith v Hughes* (1871) L.R. 6 Q.B. 597, 607; *Woodhouse A.C. Israel Cocoa Ltd SA v Nigerian Products Marketing Co Ltd* [1972] A.C. 741; *McInerny v Lloyds Bank* [1974] 1 Lloyd's Rep. 246. Compare the effect of a mistake in a contractual notice. In *Mannai Investment Co Ltd v Eagle Star Life Assurance Co Ltd* [1997] A.C. 749 (below, para.13-054) the House of Lords held that a contractual notice to determine a lease was effective although it did not comply exactly with the break clause in the contract, provided that the notice given would convey the lessee's intention to exercise its rights under the clause unambiguously to a reasonable recipient.

[57] Goff L.J. in *Allied Marine Transport Ltd v Vale do Rio Navegacao SA, The Leonidas D* [1985] 1 W.L.R. 925, summarising the approach of Lord Brightman in *Paal Wilson & Co A/S v Partenreederi Hannah Blumenthal, The Hannah Blumenthal* [1983] 1 A.C. 854, 924. The Court of Appeal in *The Leonidas D* preferred Lord Brightman's formulation of the objective principle to those of Lords Brandon and Diplock ([1985] 1 W.L.R. 925, 936). See above, para.2-004.

[58] Cartwright, *Misrepresentation, Mistake and Non-disclosure*, 5th edn (2019), para.13-18.

[59] See below, para.3-019.

[59a] It may be that a similar result will follow if a "mistake" over the terms renders the contract legally impossible in the sense of being unworkable, as was suggested in *Lehman Brothers International (Europe) (In Administration) v Exotix Partners LLP* [2019] EWHC 2380 (Ch), [2020] 1 All E.R. (Comm) 635 (though the case was discussed as one of a common mistake of the kind that normally relates to the facts not the terms: see below, para.6-038). If that were the case the contract might again be void, but on the facts the court implied a term to make the contract workable.

## Older "subjective" notions

*Replace footnote 63 with:*

[63] See Beatson, Burrows and Cartwright, *Anson's Law of Contract*, 31st edn (2020), pp.265–266. 3-017

*Replace footnote 65 with:*

## Test not wholly objective[65]

[65] The points in the paragraph are particularly well made in Cartwright, *Misrepresentation, Mistake and Non-disclosure*, 5th edn (2019), paras 13-07—13-19. Cartwright's summary of the law was adopted in *DNA Production (Europe) Ltd v Manoukian* [2008] EWHC 943 (Ch) at [47], [50]. 3-018

## (c) Unilateral Mistake as to Terms

### (i) *When Mistake will Affect Contract*

**Mistake known to the other party**

*Replace footnote 83 with:*

3-022 [83] The question is strictly speaking not one of whether either party was at fault, but of whether one knew (or possibly ought to have known; see next paragraph) of the other's intention: see Cartwright, *Misrepresentation, Mistake and Non-disclosure*, 5th edn (2019), paras 13-24—13-26. Contrast *LCC v Henry Boot & Sons Ltd* [1959] 1 W.L.R. 1069, criticised by Goodhart (1960) 76 L.Q.R. 32.

**Mistakes which ought to have been apparent**

*Replace footnote 92 with:*

3-023 [92] [1983] Com. L.R. 158. In this case it was said that if the other party did not know and had no reason to know of the mistake, he is entitled to hold the mistaken party to the terms of the contract in their objective sense; it is immaterial that he has not changed his position or relied upon the contract. This appears to be consistent with the objective test of liability, see Cartwright, *Misrepresentation, Mistake and Non-disclosure*, 5th edn (2019), para.13-22.

**Mistake as to the terms of the contract**

*Replace paragraph with:*

3-025 It is not sufficient that one party knows the other has entered the contract under a mistake of some kind. The mistake must relate to the terms of the contract.[99] If it relates, for example, to what is the subject matter that is being bought and sold (i.e. as to its contractual description), the mistake is to the terms and may prevent there being a contract; but if the mistake is merely to the quality or the substance of the thing contracted for, it will be a mistake as to the facts (or "an error in motive") and it is well established that an error in motive will not avoid a contract.[100] In *Smith v Hughes*[101] the defendant purchased from the plaintiff a quantity of oats in the belief that they were old oats, whereas in fact they were new oats and quite unsuitable for the purpose for which he wanted them. On discovering his mistake, he refused to accept them and was sued by the plaintiff for the price. The judge asked the jury whether the plaintiff believed the defendant to believe, or to be under the impression, that he was contracting for the purchase of old oats. If so, they were to return a verdict for the defendant. On a motion for a new trial, the Court of Queen's Bench considered that this direction would not sufficiently distinguish between a mistake on the part of the defendant that the oats were old oats, and a mistake that they were being offered to him as old oats. In the former case, the contract would be valid, as the error would be one of motive; in the latter, the mistake would be as to the terms of the contract, and, if known to the plaintiff, would provide a defence to the action. A new trial was ordered. It is not clear whether the defendant would, on the latter hypothesis, have been free from liability on the ground that the contract was void, or on the ground that the seller was in breach by delivering new oats.[102] As the buyer had been given a sample of the oats it is difficult to see how, on similar facts occurring today, any sort of a defence could be made out. In a more recent case, the parties had reached a compromise over the amount of demurrage due. One party had made an offer, basing its calculations on a mistaken assumption as to the date the ship had completed its unloading. The mistaken party was not entitled to relief even though the other party was aware of the mistake when it accepted the offer and decided to say nothing.[103] It was not a term of the contract that discharge was completed on the date the claimant supposed.[104] There is no equitable jurisdiction to set the contract aside where one party has made a unilateral mistake as to a fact or state of affairs which is the basis upon which the terms of the contract are agreed, but that assumption does not become a term of the contract.[105]

[99] Or, where the mistake is over one party's identity, must prevent effective offer and acceptance: above, para.3-002 and below, paras 3-036 et seq.

[100] *Balfour v Sea Fire and Life Assurance Co* (1857) 3 C.B.(N.S.) 300; *Scrivener v Pask* (1866) L.R. 1 C.P. 715; *Pope v Buenos Ayres New Gas Co* (1892) 8 T.L.R. 758; cf. *Gill v M'Dowell* [1903] 2 Ir.Rep. 463. In *G & S Fashions v B&Q Plc* [1995] 1 W.L.R. 1088 it was held that, if a landlord purports to forfeit a lease in the mistaken belief that the tenant is in breach of covenant, the fact that the tenant knows of the landlord's mistake does not prevent it accepting the forfeiture. See also *Bank of Credit and Commerce International SA (In Liquidation) v Ali* [1999] 2 All E.R. 1005, 1019. See further above, para.3-002. A contract will not be invalidated by a unilateral mistake over a separate document that was itself of no legal effect: *Donegal International Ltd v Zambia* [2007] EWHC 197, [2007] 1 Lloyd's Rep. 397 at [471], referring to this paragraph.

[101] (1871) L.R. 6 Q.B. 597.

[102] cf. *Roberts & Co Ltd v Leicestershire CC* [1961] Ch. 555 (rectification in case of unilateral mistake); see below, para.3-069.

[103] *Statoil ASA v Louis Dreyfus Energy Services LP (The Harriette N)* [2008] EWHC 2257 (Comm), [2008] 2 Lloyd's Rep. 685; followed in *UTB LLC v Sheffield United Ltd* [2019] EWHC 2322 (Ch) at [280].

[104] [2008] EWHC 2257 (Comm) at [91]. See also *Merrill Lynch International v Amorim Partners Ltd* [2014] EWHC 74 (QB) at [55].

[105] [2008] EWHC 2257 (Comm) at [105], refusing to follow in this respect suggestions made by the judge at first instance (and not discussed by the Court of Appeal, [2003] EWCA Civ 1104) in *Huyton SA v Distribuidora Internacional de Productos Agricolas SA* [2002] EWHC 2088 (Comm) at [455], both reported in [2003] 2 Lloyd's Rep. 780. See also *UTB LLC v Sheffield United Ltd* [2019] EWHC 2322 (Ch) at [280]–[285], where it is pointed out that in the *Statoil* case the judge did not address the different question whether a mistake that was not about the terms of the contract might lead the court to refuse specific performance (on which see below, para.3-026). In Canada relief has been given when the claimant has made a "calculation error" which has led to its bid being underpriced, even though the mistake was not in the terms of the offer itself: see McCamus (2008) 87 Can. B.R. 1, 6 (compare *The Harriette N*, where relief was refused because the mistake was not as to a term of the offer, see text above).

### Refusal of specific performance for unilateral mistakes not known to the other party or not as to terms

*Replace paragraph with:*

Even though a mistake by one party has no effect at common law, for example because the other party neither knew nor had reason to know of it,[106] or because it is not a mistake as to the terms of the contract,[107] it may be a ground on which the court will refuse to order specific performance when it would otherwise have done so. In *Barrow v Scammell*[108] Bacon V.C. said: **3-026**

> "It cannot be disputed that courts of equity have at all times relieved against honest mistakes in contracts, where the literal effect and the specific performance of them would be to impose a burden not contemplated, and which it would be against all reason and justice to fix, upon the person who, without the imputation of fraud, has inadvertently committed an accidental mistake; and also where not to correct the mistake would be to give an unconscionable advantage to the other party."

It has been held that specific performance may be refused if it would cause the defendant "a hardship amounting to injustice"[109] although he may still be liable to an action for damages at law.[110] It has also been held that mistake may also be a defence if the plaintiff has in some way contributed, even unwittingly, to the mistake.[111] But a mistake which is entirely the product of the defendant's own carelessness will afford no ground for relief[112] unless (perhaps) the case is one of considerable harshness or hardship.[113] Most of the cases are ones in which one party made a mistake about the terms and the other party did not know of the mistake,[114] but there is no reason in principle why the mistake might not have been one as to the surrounding facts rather than the terms of the contract and at least one case involved that.[115] However, most of the cases on refusal of specific performance are old. It is not clear whether the modern tendency to cut down defences of unilateral mistake as grounds for rectifying a contract, or refusing rescission as an alternative,[116] will extend also to cases where the defendant seeks to be excused from specific performance.

106 See above, para.3-008.

107 See previous paragraph.

108 (1881) 19 Ch. D. 175, 182. See also *Preston v Luck* (1884) 27 Ch. D. 497, 506; *Stewart v Kennedy* (1890) 15 App. Cas. 75, 105; *UTB LLC v Sheffield United Ltd* [2019] EWHC 2322 (Ch) at [280], [284].

109 *Tamplin v James* (1880) 15 Ch. D. 215, 221.

110 *Webster v Cecil* (1861) 30 Beav. 62, 64.

111 *Baskomb v Beckwith* (1869) L.R. 8 Eq. 100; *Denny v Hancock* (1870) L.R. 6 Ch. App. 1; *Wilding v Sanderson* [1897] 2 Ch. 534.

112 *Tamplin v James* (1880) 15 Ch. D. 215.

113 *Manser v Back* (1848) 6 Hare 443; *Malins v Freeman* (1837) 2 Keen 25; *Van Praagh v Everidge* [1903] 1 Ch. 434.

114 If the other party did know of the mistake, it would have the effects described below: see para.3-029.

115 *Jones v Rimmer* (1880) 14 Ch. D. 588 (though the omission of any mention of the ground rent in otherwise very detailed particulars makes the case very close to one of misrepresentation by a misleading half-truth: see below, para.7-021). See also *Heath v Heath* [2009] EWHC 1908 (Ch), [2009] 2 P. & C.R. DG21 at [26] ("specific performance is a discretionary remedy and mistake may ... still be a relevant factor in refusing equitable relief, at all events where the mistake has been induced by the words or conduct of the person seeking specific performance. In such a case ... the mistake may also amount to, or be practically indistinguishable from, a misrepresentation"). In *UTB LLC v Sheffield United Ltd* [2019] EWHC 2322 (Ch) at [280], [284] the court accepted that specific performance might be refused if the claimant was seeking to take advantage of a mistake by the defendant that was not one as to the terms of the contract, but on the facts the defendant was not disadvantaged (see at [496]).

116 See below, paras 3-073—3-075.

### *(ii) Effect on Contract*

#### **Effect of mistake as to terms: mistaken party's intention known to other**

*Replace footnote 125 with:*

**3-029** 125 See also Beatson, Burrows and Cartwright (eds), *Anson's Law of Contract*, 31st edn (2020), p.274; contrast Peel (ed.), *Treitel on The Law of Contract*, 15th edn (2020), para.8-057 (possibly seller could have held buyer to contract on the *stated* terms had he wished to do so). Contra, Cartwright, *Misrepresentation, Mistake and Non-disclosure*, 5th edn (2019), para.13-28 ("there can be no contract for the simple reason that though the defendant may have intended the contract to be on a different set of terms, there is no external evidence by which he can say that the claimant in fact agreed to it"). See also McLauchlan (2008) 124 L.Q.R. 608, 613. However, if the claimant purported to accept the defendant's offer, there does seem to be such evidence, whether the contract was oral or written, unless it was not reasonable for the claimant to think that the defendant was accepting the claimant's offer as he intended it. For example, on facts like those in *Chwee Kin Keong v Digilandmall.com Pte Ltd* [2005] SGCA 2, [2005] 1 S.L.R. 502, in which buyers tried to take advantage of an offer on the internet to sell goods at a mistakenly low price and ordered large quantities of them, even if the buyers knew what the correct price should be, it would not reasonable for the seller to assume that a buyer was agreeing to buy large quantities of the goods at the correct price.

## (d) Mistaken Identity

### Offer to B cannot be accepted by C

*Replace footnote 148 with:*

[148] Beatson, Burrows and Cartwright (eds), *Anson's Law of Contract*, 31st edn (2020), p.286; see *Shogun Finance Ltd v Hudson* [2003] UKHL 62, [2004] 1 A.C. 919 at [63], [125] and [184]. **3-038**

### Identity and attributes

*Replace footnote 194 with:*

[194] See Peel (ed.), *Treitel on The Law of Contract*, 15th edn (2020), para.8-038. **3-045**

## 3. NON EST FACTUM

### Definition

*Replace footnote 205 with:*

[205] *Yedina v Yedin* [2017] EWHC 3319 (Ch) at [262] (Mann J.). In *Kerr v Jamison* [2019] NICh 4, in which this paragraph was cited with the omission of (c), an elderly person who could not read the document she signed was held to be entitled to rely on the doctrine. The document had not been explained to her and she believed that it would entitle her to £40,000 for the land when in fact it was a gratuitous transfer. **3-049**

## 4. RECTIFICATION OF WRITTEN AGREEMENTS

*Replace footnote 233 with:* **3-057**

[233] Hodge, *Rectification*, 2nd edn (2016); A Burrows, "Construction and Rectification" in A. Burrows and E. Peel (eds), *Contract Terms* (2007), 77; Cartwright, *Misrepresentation, Mistake and Non-disclosure*, 5th edn (2019), paras 13-38—13-54; McLauchlan (2008) 124 L.Q.R. 608, (2010) 126 L.Q.R. 8 and (2014) 130 L.Q.R. 83. N. Patten, "Does the law need to be rectified? Chartbrook revisited", *Chancery Bar Association Annual Lecture* 2013, available at *http://www.chba.org.uk/for-members/library/annual-lectures/does-the-law-need-to-be-rectified-chartbrook-revisited*; R. Toulson, "Does Rectification Require Rectifying?", *TECBar Lecture* 2013, available at *https://www.supremecourt.uk/docs/speech-131031.pdf*; T. Etherton, "Contract and the Fog of Rectification" (2015) 68 *Current Legal Problems* 367.

## (a) Introduction

### Rectification of document to match agreement

*Replace paragraph with:*

Rectification only applies to contracts which have been reduced to writing. It is a process by which the document is made to conform to what was actually agreed between the parties, or what the law, applying the objective principle, treats as being their agreement. **3-057**

> "... the remedy of rectification is one permitted by the Court, not for the purpose of altering the terms of an agreement entered into between two or more parties, but for that of correcting a written instrument which, by a mistake in verbal expression, does not accurately reflect their true agreement."[234]

It has become customary to divide rectification cases into two types. Most of the cases involve what has been agreed by the parties having been wrongly recorded in the document without either party being aware of the mistake. These cases involve what may be termed rectification to correct a common mistake; the document is rectified to bring it into line with the prior agreement. Rectification may also be available when, whether or not the parties had reached a prior agreement, one party signed a written document which did not record his intentions correctly, and the other party knew of the first party's intentions.[235] In this case the court may rectify the document so that it reflects the first party's intentions. This may be termed a case of rectification to correct a unilateral mistake. But in the case of *Chartbrook Ltd v Persimmon Homes Ltd*[236] the House of Lords seemed to create an extended version of rectification based on a common mistake, or perhaps a third category of rectification case. It said that rectification can also[236a] be ordered if the parties were not in actual agreement on the content or effect of their prior agreement but, under the objective approach, the prior agreement has a content or effect that differs from the content or effect of the document: again the document can be rectified to bring it into line with the prior agreement as objectively ascertained. This extended version of common mistake has proven to be controversial. It stretches the natural meaning of the phrase "common mistake"[236b] and it seems to cut across the distinction between "common mistake" and "unilateral mistake" rectification in such a way as to make that distinction of doubtful utility. The Court of Appeal, however, has recently said that rectification of the document is available to bring the final document into line with the objective meaning of the prior agreement only when the prior agreement amounted to a concluded contract that was replaced by the final document; if the prior agreement did not amount to a concluded contract, rectification should be granted only if the written document did not conform to the common subjective intentions of the parties and these intentions had been outwardly expressed in communications that "crossed the line".[236c] In this section we will consider first "traditional" common mistake rectification, then unilateral mistake rectification and then the extended version before considering some general principles which apply in all situations.[237]

[234] *Agip SpA v Navigazione Alta Italia SpA (The Nai Genova and the Nai Superba)* [1984] 1 Lloyd's Rep. 353, 359. For further discussion of what "the parties' agreement" is, see below, paras 3-064 et seq.

[235] And possibly also if the other party should have known of the first party's intentions: see below, para.3-076.

[236] [2009] UKHL 38, [2009] 1 A.C. 1101. See further below, para.3-077.

[236a] It is not thought that Lord Hoffmann intended to exclude rectification in cases in which the parties shared the same intention and had expressed this to each other in communications that had crossed the line: see below, para.3-081B.

[236b] See below, para.3-081.

[236c] *FSHC Group Holdings Ltd v GLAS Trust Corp Ltd* [2019] EWCA Civ 1361, [2020] Ch. 365 esp. at [176]; see below, paras 3-081B et seq.

[237] See below, paras 3-089 et seq.

## (b) Common Mistake

### Mistake in recording of terms or as to legal effect

*Replace footnote 248 with:*

3-059 [248] *Ashcroft v Barnsdale* [2010] EWHC 1948 (Ch), [2010] S.T.C. 2544 at [17]; *Kennedy v Kennedy* [2014] EWHC 4129 (Ch) at [43] (voluntary settlement). See also Hodge, *Rectification*, 2nd edn (2016), paras 4-63 et seq. In *AMP (UK) Plc v Barker* [2001] Pens. L.R. 77 Lawrence Collins J. suggested that the distinction "is simply a formula designed to ensure that the policy involved in equitable relief is effectuated to keep it within reasonable bounds and to ensure that it is not used simply when parties are mistaken about the commercial effects of their transactions or have second thoughts about them", but in that case it was conceded that the mistake was as to the effect of the words, not their consequences (at [70]). The distinction may not be easy to draw: *FSHC Group Holdings Ltd v Barclays Bank Plc* [2018] EWHC 1558 (Ch) at [18], but it was re-affirmed by the Court of Appeal in that case, [2019] EWCA Civ 1361, [2020] Ch. 365 at [179]–[182].

## Conditions for rectification on the ground of common mistake

*Replace paragraph with:*

In *Chartbrook Ltd v Persimmon Homes Ltd* Lord Hoffmann said[271] that the requirements for rectification had been "succinctly summarised" by Peter Gibson L.J. in *Swainland Builders Ltd v Freehold Properties Ltd*[272]: **3-062**

> "The party seeking rectification must show that: (1) the parties had a common continuing intention, whether or not amounting to an agreement, in respect of a particular matter in the instrument to be rectified; (2) there was an outward expression of accord; (3) the intention continued at the time of the execution of the instrument sought to be rectified; (4) by mistake, the instrument did not reflect that common intention."

The conditions for rectification on the ground of common mistake will be discussed more fully in the paragraphs that follow.

[271] [2009] UKHL 38, [2009] 1 A.C. 1101 at [48]. Lord Hoffmann's statements on rectification were obiter, as the case was decided on a question of construction (see para.3-060), but appear to have been supported by the other members of the Judicial Committee (see [2009] UKHL 38 at [1], [71], [97] and [101]). See, however, below, para.3-081.

[272] [2002] 2 E.G.L.R. 71 at 74, para.33. Compare the statement by Leggatt L.J. in *FSHC Group Holdings Ltd v GLAS Trust Corp Ltd* [2019] EWCA Civ 1361 at [176], below, para.3-081B.

*Change title of paragraph:* **3-063**

## Concluded prior contract not required

*To the end of paragraph, after "the written contract.", add:*

However the Court of Appeal has now said that where the prior agreement did not amount to a concluded contract, the test for common mistake rectification is whether the written document matches the common subjective intentions of the parties, as outwardly expressed; whereas if the prior agreement amounted to a concluded contract, its meaning must be assessed on the normal objective basis and the final document may be rectified if it does not match the objective meaning of the prior contract.[277a] **3-063**

[277a] *FSHC Group Holdings Ltd v GLAS Trust Corp Ltd* [2019] EWCA Civ 1361; see further below, paras 3-081A et seq.

## Outward expression of accord

*Replace paragraph with:*

Although it is unnecessary to show that there was a binding agreement prior to the execution of the written document, in *Joscelyne v Nissen* it was said that there must have been an "outward expression of accord".[278] The Court of Appeal cited with approval its previous decision, *Lovell and Christmas Ltd v Wall*[279] and, in particular, the following passage from the judgment of Buckley L.J.: **3-064**

> "In ordering rectification the court does not rectify contracts, but what it rectifies is the erroneous expression of contracts in documents. For rectification it is not enough to set about to find out what one or even both of the parties to the contract intended. What you have got to find out is what intention was communicated by one side to the other, and with what common intention and common agreement they made their bargain."

It is not necessary that the parties had formulated their intention into words at the time provided they had a common intention as to the substance, but there must have been some outward agreement.[280] The requirement of an "outward expression of accord" had been said not to be an absolute one, but one of evidence that the parties shared a common intention even if they had not put it into words. The requirement of outward accord was first relaxed in a series of cases involving pension schemes[281] but in *Munt v Beasley*, which involved rectification of a lease, Mummery L.J., with whom the other members of the court agreed, said:

> "I would also accept ... that the recorder was wrong to treat 'an outward expression of accord' as a strict legal requirement for rectification in a case such as this, where the party resisting rectification has in fact admitted ... that his true state of belief when he entered into the transaction was the same as that of the other party and there was therefore a continuing common intention which, by mistake, was not given effect in the relevant legal document. I agree with the trend in recent cases to treat the expression 'outward expression of accord' more as an evidential factor rather than a strict legal requirement in all cases of rectification."[282]

However, in *FSHC Group Holdings Ltd v GLAS Trust Corp Ltd*[282a] the Court of Appeal said that the authorities relied on in *Munt v Beasley* did not justify this conclusion, as they involved the rectification of pension schemes, which do not depend on mutual agreement[282b]; for rectification of a contract on the ground of common mistake, an outward expression of accord is an absolute requirement.[282c] The Court of Appeal said that the agreement might be "tacit", and accepted the formulation that "the accord may include understandings that the parties thought so obvious as to go without saying, or that were reached without being spelled out in so many words",[283] "[p]rovided that it is understood that on a claim for rectification the court is concerned with what the parties actually communicated to each other, and not with identifying their presumed intention by means of an officious bystander test".[283a]

278 [1970] 2 Q.B. 86, 98. Use of this phrase is criticised by Bromley in (1971) 87 L.Q.R. 532; but compare Smith (2007) 123 L.Q.R. 116.

279 (1911) 104 L.T. 85.

280 *Grand Metropolitan Plc v William Hill Group Ltd* [1997] 1 B.C.L.C. 390. In *Mangistaumunaigaz Oil Production Association v United World Trading Inc* [1995] 1 Lloyd's Rep. 617 no prior agreement was shown and rectification was refused. In *Mace v Rutland House Textiles Ltd (In Administrative Receivership), The Times,* January 11, 2000 rectification was permitted when the text of the agreement had been prepared by a person instructed by both parties and did not represent their common intention although that had not been expressed in a settled form of words. In *Prowting 1968 Trustee One Ltd v Amos-Yeo* [2015] EWHC 2480 (Ch), [2015] B.T.C. 33 rectification was ordered when an agreement did not reflect the parties' intention to transfer enough shares to entitle the claimants to tax relief, although the parties had left the number to be determined by a trustee, who had miscalculated the number (see at [37]–[38]).

281 In particular *AMP v Barker* [2001] P.L.R. 77 and *Gallaher v Gallaher Pensions Ltd* [2005] EWHC 42 (Ch), [2005] All E.R. (D) 177 (Jan).

282 [2006] EWCA Civ 370, [2006] All E.R. (D) 29 (Apr), at [36].

282a [2019] EWCA Civ 1361, [2020] Ch. 365.

282b See [2019] EWCA Civ 1361 at [78]–[79].

282c [2019] EWCA Civ 1361 at [77]. The *FSHC* case was applied in *Gwynt y Mor OFTO Plc v Gwynt y Mor Offshore Wind Farm Ltd* [2020] EWHC 850 (Comm).

283 As it was put in the 33rd edn of this work (though at this paragraph, rather than at the paragraph indicated in the CA's judgment). The authorities cited by Chitty are Carnwath L.J. in *JIS (1974) Ltd v MCP Investment Nominees Ltd* [2003] EWCA Civ 721 at [33]–[34]; see also *Cambridge Antibody Technology v Abbott Biotechnology Ltd* [2004] EWHC 2974 (Pat), [2005] F.S.R. 27 at [105]–[112].

"Whilst it must be shown what was the common intention, the exact form of words in which the common intention is to be expressed is immaterial if in substance and in detail the common intention can be ascertained": *Co-operative Insurance Society Ltd v Centremoor Ltd* [1983] 2 E.G.L.R. 52 at 54, cited in *Swainland Builders Ltd v Freehold Properties Ltd* [2002] EWCA Civ 560 at [34]. The sentence quoted in the text was accepted as correct in *DS-Rendite-Fonds Nr.106 VLCC Titan Glory GmbH & Co Tankschiff KG v Titan Maritime SA* [2013] EWHC 3492 (Comm) (at [47]). The party claiming rectification must be able "to articulate with precision the form the agreement should take when rectified": *Musst Holdings Ltd v Astra Asset Management UK Ltd* [2020] EWHC 337 (Ch) at [34].

283a [2019] EWCA Civ 1361 at [87].

## Unexpressed but shared intentions

*Replace paragraph with:*

Despite the insistence by the Court of Appeal in *FSHC Group Holdings Ltd v GLAS Trust Corp Ltd*[283b] that an outward expression of accord is an absolute requirement (which on the facts of the case was satisfied), it remains unclear that it would never be proper to grant rectification based on intentions that were never expressed to the other party in any form, if the unexpressed intentions of each party in fact coincide. One argument is that unexpressed and unknown subjective intentions are irrelevant.[284] Rectification is to make the document conform to the agreement and in English law some outward manifestation is required for there to be an agreement. However, it has been argued that if the parties appear to have contracted, even if neither party has expressed his true intentions and neither party's intention coincides with the apparent agreement, if in fact their intentions coincide there may be a contract on the terms subjectively intended by both. If the apparent agreement is in writing, it might then be possible to rectify the written agreement to accord with the parties' subjective agreement.[285] If this were not the case, the parties would end up being bound by a written agreement that represented neither party's intentions. But it is conceded that modern authority requires, as Leggatt L.J. put it in *FSHC Group Holdings Ltd v GLAS Trust Corp Ltd*: **3-065**

> "an 'outward expression of accord' – meaning that, as a result of communication between them, the parties understood each other to share that intention."[285a]

283b [2019] EWCA Civ 1361, [2020] Ch. 365.

284 cf. Smith (2007) 123 L.Q.R. 116; *Tartsinis v Navona Management Co* [2015] EWHC 57 (Comm) at [88]–[89]. Similarly, it has been said that in establishing what the prior understanding was, "the court is not concerned with what the parties *thought* they had agreed or what they *thought* their agreement meant—a subjective inquiry. What it is concerned with is what the parties said and did, and what that would convey to a reasonable person in their position—an objective question": *PT Berlian Laju Tanker TBK v Nuse Shipping Ltd (The Aktor)* [2008] EWHC 1330 (Comm), [2008] 2 Lloyd's Rep. 246 at [38]. Christopher Clarke J. added that it was immaterial that both parties, although agreeing "X", thought that "X" meant something that, objectively, it does not mean. He added (at [41]) that "a continuing common intention is not sufficient unless it has found expression in outward agreement". See also *Chartbrook Ltd v Persimmon Homes Ltd* [2009] UKHL 38, [2009] 1 A.C. 1101 at [57]; and the lectures by Lord Justice Patten and Sir Terence Etherton, above, para.3-057. However, it is submitted that if each party understands "X" to mean "Y" and believes that the other has the same understanding (though the other has not expressed it), the actual agreement is on "Y" (see above, para.3-014). If this is correct, possibly the written document can be rectified accordingly. But cases in which it can be shown that the parties in fact intended the same thing but never expressed this outwardly to each other will be very rare.

285 Cartwright, *Misrepresentation, Mistake and Non-disclosure*, 5th edn (2019), para.13-40. Compare Hodge, *Rectification*, 2nd edn (2016), paras 3-51–3-52. Bromley (1971) 87 L.Q.R. 532 argued that an outward expression of accord is not necessary.

285a [2019] EWCA Civ 1361 at [176].

## Continuing intention

*Replace paragraph with:*

3-066 Where it is sought to rectify a document in accordance with a prior agreement between the parties, it must be shown that the intention of the parties continued unaltered up to the time of the execution of the document.[286] If A prepares a draft of the written agreement, and the draft differs from the prior agreement, but B approves and signs the written agreement without noticing the change, can A resist rectification on the grounds that B knew or should have known that A had changed its mind? It cannot be that a difference between the prior agreement and the draft always prevents there being a continuing common intention or no rectification plea would ever succeed.[287] If A's intention is unchanged, and the difference between the prior agreement and the version that is signed is merely a slip, then there is a continuing intention and rectification can properly be granted.[288] But what if though the parties originally shared the same intention, A subsequently changed its mind and prepared the draft on the basis of its new intention without informing B of the change? In most cases, A will know that the draft does not reflect B's intentions and B will be entitled to rectification on the basis of unilateral mistake, as will be explained in the next section. However, there may be cases in which A does not know that B still has its original intention, for example because A believes that B will have spotted and accepted the change. This can happen whether or not the prior agreement amounted to a "concluded contract".

[286] *Fowler v Fowler* (1859) 4 De G. & J. 250; *Swainland Builders Ltd v Freehold Properties Ltd* [2002] 2 E.G.L.R. 71 at 74, para.33, cited with approval in *Chartbrook Ltd v Persimmon Homes Ltd* [2009] UKHL 38 at [48]; see above, para.3-062. It has been said that the word "continuing" in Peter Gibson L.J.'s first requirement in the *Swainland Builders* case seems to be superfluous; it is more accurate to say that there needs to be a common intention (requirement 1) which was continuing at the time that the contract was executed (requirement 3): *Milton Keynes BC v Viridor (Community Recycling MK) Ltd* [2017] EWHC 239 (TCC), [2017] B.L.R. 216 at [48] (Coulson J.). If the parties have altered their agreement extensively before the document was executed, rectification will not be appropriate because their initial intention on the point at issue may well have changed also (as in *Pindos Shipping Corp v Raven ("The Mata Hari")* [1983] 2 Lloyd's Rep. 449), but the fact that there have been minor changes to other aspects of the agreement does not prevent rectification: [2017] EWHC 239 (TCC), [2017] B.L.R. 216 at [62]–[63], citing *Dunlop Haywards Ltd v Erinaceous Insurance Services Ltd* [2009] EWCA Civ 354 at [82].

[287] *Daventry District Council v Daventry and District Housing Ltd* [2011] EWCA Civ 1153, [2012] 1 W.L.R. 1333 at [59], per Toulson L.J., and at [211], per Lord Neuberger M.R. Compare below, para.3-094.

[288] The absence of any discussion of a change may be evidence that the parties did not intend one, but it all depends on the circumstances: *FSHC Group Holdings Ltd v Barclays Bank Plc* [2018] EWHC 1558 (Ch) at [47].

*Add new paragraph:*

3-066A In *Daventry District Council v Daventry and District Housing Ltd*,[289] where the prior agreement did not amount to a concluded contract,[289a] there was a difference of opinion over the correct test to apply, and also on its application to the facts.[290] The case involved a prior, non-binding agreement which the parties had understood in different ways but which, as properly interpreted, placed an obligation on Daventry and District Housing (DDH) to pay a pension deficit. DDH made a deliberate change in the draft contract, so that it no longer represented what had been the prior agreement (as properly interpreted[291]): it contained a term requiring Daventry and District Council (DDC) to pay the deficit, so making explicit DDH's understanding of the prior agreement. However, DDC did not appreciate the effect of the draft and continued to think that the agreement was in the terms of the prior agreement as DDC had (reasonably) understood it. (The same issue would arise when the draft prepared by A was different to the prior agreement because A had changed its mind.) Though the members of the Court of Appeal agreed that the question whether there was a continuing intention must be answered on an objective test,[291a] they took different approaches to what the test should be. Toulson L.J. asked "whether on a fair view there was a renegotiation of the prior agreement or a mistake"[292] and concluded that there was no attempt to renegotiate, as there was nothing to show that DDC had changed its mind.[293] For Etherton L.J. the test was "whether objectively, prior to the execution of the contract, DDH communicated to DCC that it intended to contract on a different basis" than the payment provided for in the prior agreement.[294] The Master of the Rolls pointed out that Toulson L.J.'s approach would require an assessment of DDC's reaction to the draft, which he considered unnecessary: as the prior accord was not legally binding, "there was no need for DDC to agree to DDH's resiling from the prior accord before that resiling could be effective". He therefore preferred Etherton L.J.'s approach.[295] However, Etherton L.J. and the Master of the Rolls reached different conclusions on the facts. The Master of the Rolls held that "the hypothetical observer would not have concluded that DDH was signalling a departure from the prior accord: the observer would have believed that DDH was making a mistake"[296] and therefore there was a continuing intention. Etherton L.J., dissenting, held that the trial judge[297] had been right to find that DDH had objectively, prior to the execution of the contract, communicated to DDC that it intended to contract on a different basis, and therefore the appeal should be dismissed.[298] In a postscript to his judgment Etherton L.J. explained why he considers the Master of the Rolls' finding that the reasonable observer would have concluded that DDH was "making a mistake" to have been an incorrect application of the objective test, given that the wording inserted in the draft clearly placed the obligation to pay the deficit on DDC.[299] In the light of these disagreements, it is difficult to extract a clear ratio on how "continuing intention" is to be assessed from the *Daventry* case.[300]

[289] [2011] EWCA Civ 1153, [2012] 1 W.L.R. 133. See McLauchlan (2014) 131 L.Q.R. 83; and the very full account of the *Daventry* case and the commentary on it in Hodge, *Rectification*, 2nd edn (2016), paras 3-61 et seq.

[289a] Where the prior agreement was not binding, the Court of Appeal has said that the document can only be rectified if it does not reflect the subjective intentions of the parties (as outwardly expressed): *FSHC Group Holdings Ltd v GLAS Trust Corp Ltd* [2019] EWCA Civ 1361, [2020] Ch. 365. See below, paras 3-081A et seq.

[290] See the summary of the differences in the postscript to Etherton L.J.'s judgment at [104]–[105].

[291] In other words, the case was one within the "extended" notion of common mistake: see below, para.3-077.

[291a] See *AML Global Ltd v ExxonMobil Petroleum and Chemical BVBA* [2018] EWHC 3321 (TCC) at [39]. However the Court of Appeal has now declined to apply the objective approach in cases in which the prior agreement was not binding: *FSHC Group Holdings Ltd v GLAS Trust Corp Ltd* [2019] EWCA Civ 1361. See below, paras 3-081A et seq.

[292] [2011] EWCA Civ 1153 at [160].

[293] [2011] EWCA Civ 1153 at [170].

[294] [2011] EWCA Civ 1153 at [91].

[295] [2011] EWCA Civ 1153 at [207]. In *AML Global Ltd v ExxonMobil Petroleum and Chemical BVBA* [2018] EWHC 3321 (TCC) at [41] Waksman J. doubted whether Toulson L.J's approach led to a different result; if it did, the judge preferred Etherton L.J's approach.

[296] [2011] EWCA Civ 1153 at [213].

[297] [2010] EWHC 1935 (Ch).

[298] [2011] EWCA Civ 1153 at [91]–[92].

299 [2011] EWCA Civ 1153 at [106]–[115], esp. at [110]–[112]. In *FSHC Group Holdings Ltd v GLAS Trust Corp Ltd* [2019] EWCA Civ 1361 the appellants argued that the reasonable observer would conclude from the documents sent for signature, which not only had the effect that the respondents provided the security that had mistakenly been omitted from previous arrangements between the parties but also imposed "Additional Obligations" on the respondents, that the intentions of the parties assessed objectively, was that the respondents were undertaking the Additional Obligations. Although it was not necessary to decide what was the objectively-ascertained common intention (as the parties' shared and outwardly manifested subjective intentions were that the respondents should only provide the security; see at [177] and [183]), given the factual matrix of the new agreement and the earlier communications between the parties, the Court of Appeal upheld the finding of the trial judge that the objective observer would have understood that the accession deeds were not intended to do more than fill the gap in the security (at [183]–[193]).

300 *Daventry District Council v Daventry and District Housing Ltd* [2011] EWCA Civ 1153, [2012] 1 W.L.R. 1333.

*Replace paragraph with:*

**3-067** It is submitted that when A submits to B a draft which differs from the parties' earlier agreement, and it appears that A no longer shares the previously common intention, the correct approach in principle is to ask whether B realised or should reasonably have realised that the draft agreement was intended to differ from the prior agreement rather than to implement the prior accord.[301] That B did not realise this is evidence of what it was reasonable for B to understand but no more. Though in the context of rectification the question is slightly different, this approach is consistent with the normal approach to the interpretation of contractual intention. In the case of a statement of intention such as an offer, the question is how should B as a reasonable person in the circumstances, have understood A's offer[302]; in the context of ascertaining whether or not there was a continuing common intention for the purposes of rectification, it is how B should reasonably have understood the draft, as merely to set down what was previously agreed, or as a new proposal (or perhaps a deliberate assertion that A did not accept the "objective" meaning of the prior agreement).[303] However, the practical application of the test suggested may vary according to whether or not the prior agreement was "a concluded contract". If the parties had reached a concluded contract, but later signed a document that does not match the prior agreement as objectively interpreted, either party is entitled to have the document rectified unless it is clear that this was not the result of a mistake but of the parties agreeing to vary their earlier agreement. It is submitted that unless one party clearly indicates a wish to vary the prior agreement and the other acts in such a way as to indicate its assent to the change, the court will assume that there has been a mistake. In contrast, where no concluded contract had yet been reached; as we will see below,[303a] the courts seem to give much greater weight to the final document—in effect, they expect B to check the concluding draft.[303b]

301 However, in *Liberty Mercian Ltd v Cuddy Civil Engineering Ltd* [2013] EWHC 2688 (TCC) the court applied the test of whether a hypothetical observer would have concluded that the draft agreement contained a mistake or that the intention of the parties had changed, and held that the hypothetical observer would have concluded the latter (at [123]–[129]).

302 cf. above, para.3-022.

303 cf. below, para.3-071.

303a See para.3-083.

303b Cf. Davies (2016) 75 C.L.J. 62, 75.

## (c) Unilateral Mistake

### Unilateral mistake

*Replace paragraph with:*

In this section we deal with cases in which one party makes a mistake over the terms of the contract and the other party does not intend to contract on the terms intended by the first party. If Lord Hoffmann's approach to rectification for common mistake in *Chartbrook Ltd v Persimmon Homes Ltd*[306] were followed, rectification for unilateral mistake would be less important than hitherto[306a]; but that approach has been rejected by the Court of Appeal in *FSHC Group Holdings Ltd v GLAS Trust Corp Ltd*.[306b] In any event it rectification on the basis of a unilateral mistake will remain important in cases in which there was no agreement (concluded contract or not) prior to the document being signed but the defendant knows that the document does not express the claimant's intention correctly. In this type of case rectification cannot be given on the ground of common mistake.[307] Where the mistake is unilateral, that is of one party only, it was formerly thought that rectification would not be granted unless a case of fraud or misrepresentation,[308] or unfair dealing,[309] or perhaps sharp practice, could be shown. In *Roberts & Co Ltd v Leicestershire CC*[310] it was said that the doctrine might be based on either fraud or estoppel, when: 3-069

> "... it is not an essential ingredient of the right of action to establish any particular degree of obliquity to be attributed to the defendants in such circumstances."[311]

In *Thomas Bates Son v Wyndhams Ltd* the Court of Appeal rejected these limits on the availability of the remedy of rectification.[312] Where one party is mistaken as to the incorporation of the agreement in the document, and the other knows of the mistake, and does not draw it to the attention of the first party, it suffices that it would be inequitable to allow the second party to insist on the binding force of the document, either because this would benefit him or because it would be detrimental to the mistaken party. Buckley L.J. said:

> "For this doctrine—that is to say the doctrine of *A. Roberts & Co. Ltd. v. Leicestershire County Council*—to apply I think it must be shown: first, that one party A erroneously believed that the document sought to be rectified contained a particular term or provision, or possibly did not contain a particular term or provision which, mistakenly, it did contain; secondly, that the other party B was aware of the omission or the inclusion and that it was due to a mistake on the part of A; thirdly, that B has omitted to draw the mistake to the notice of A. And I think there must be a fourth element[313] involved, namely, that the mistake must be one calculated to benefit B. If these requirements are satisfied, the court may regard it as inequitable to allow B to resist rectification to give effect to A's intention on the ground that the mistake was not, at the time of execution of the document, a mutual mistake."[314]

There are at least two issues which require discussion: the degree of knowledge required and the "fourth element", which Buckley L.J. put as whether, in addition to knowing of the mistake, the defendant must be guilty of some inequity.[315]

[306] [2009] UKHL 38, [2009] 1 A.C. 1101; see below, para.3-077.

[306a] See the discussion of *FSHC Group Holdings Ltd v GLAS Trust Corp Ltd* [2019] EWCA Civ 1361, [2020] Ch. 365, below, paras 3-081A et seq.

[306b] [2019] EWCA Civ 1361, [2020] Ch. 365.

[307] cf. paras 3-058 et seq.; but compare *Ulster Bank Ltd v Lambe* [2012] NIQB 31, cited in para.3-060, where it was held that D must have known of the mistake of euros for pounds in P's offer when accepting it and that the contract meant what P intended.

[308] *Wood v Scarth* (1855) 2 K. & J. 33, 41; *May v Platt* [1900] 1 Ch. 616.

[309] *McCausland v Young* [1949] N.I. 49.

[310] *Roberts & Co Ltd v Leicestershire CC* [1961] Ch. 555.

[311] Pennycuick J. at 570.

[312] *Thomas Bates & Son v Wyndhams Ltd* [1981] 1 W.L.R. 505.

[313] Differing views were expressed by the members of the Court of Appeal in *Thomas Bates & Son v Wyndhams Ltd* [1981] 1 W.L.R. 505 on this fourth element. See below, para.3-072.

[314] [1981] 1 W.L.R. 505, 516. In unilateral mistake cases, it may be said that rectification can be granted without there having been an antecedent agreement between the parties: *Littman v Aspen Oil (Broking) Ltd* [2005] EWCA Civ 1579, [2006] 2 P. & C.R. 2; but as Jacobs L.J. noted at [24], a party who accepts a clause knowing full well what the other party (mistakenly) thinks it means or says is in effect agreeing to the other party's version.

[315] See below, para.3-072.

### Mistake that ought to have been known to the defendant

*In line 1, after "The", replace "requirement" with:*

**3-076** requirements

## (d) The Extended Notion of Common Mistake

### Subjective agreement not required

*Replace paragraph with:*

**3-077** In *Chartbrook Ltd v Persimmon Homes Ltd*[367] Lord Hoffmann said that if there was an outward expression of common intention such that on an objective view the parties appeared to be in agreement, but the document signed did not reflect the objective meaning of that agreement, rectification is available on the basis of common mistake, whether or not the prior agreement was itself binding. It is not wholly clear whether Lord Hoffmann meant that that it not sufficient for rectification that the parties were subjectively agreed on the same terms, or merely that it was not necessary—in other words, that rectification could also be given on the basis of shared (and outwardly expressed) subjective intentions.[367a] In *FSHC Group Holdings Ltd v GLAS Trust Corp Ltd* it was argued that rectification could only be granted on the basis of a difference between the objective meaning of the prior agreement and the document signed.[367b] The Court of Appeal expressed the unanimous view that, though where the prior agreement amounted to a binding contract, the question is whether the document reflects the objective meaning of the prior agreement, where the prior agreement is not binding rectification is available only if the final document differs from the shared (and outwardly expressed) subjective intentions of the parties.[367c]

[367] [2009] UKHL 38, [2009] 1 A.C. 1101. The point on rectification did not have to be decided but it had been fully argued. The other members of the Judicial Committee agreed with Lord Hoffmann, see above, para.3-062.

[367a] In practice, if the parties shared a common intention and each had each expressed their intention outwardly, that will normally be the objective meaning of the prior agreement.

[367b] [2019] EWCA Civ 1361, [2020] Ch. 365 at [47]–[48].

[367c] As there was no challenge to the trial judge's findings that the parties subjectively intended that the agreement would only provide for the respondent to give security and did not intend to impose on the respondent the additional obligations in fact contained in the document signed, and that they had

expressed their intentions outwardly, it seems that the CA's view that, where the prior agreement is not binding, rectification cannot be given on the "objective" basis is technically obiter.

*Add new paragraph:*

**The Chartbrook case** It has been said in the House of Lords that it is not necessary for rectification on the basis of common mistake that the parties were subjectively agreed on the same terms; it suffices for there to be an outward expression of common intention that on an objective view the parties appeared to be in agreement. In *Chartbrook Ltd v Persimmon Homes Ltd*[367d] Lord Hoffmann said that for rectification for common mistake, the document must differ from what the parties had agreed, objectively determined. He said[368]: 3-077A

> "Now that it has been established that rectification is also available when there was no binding antecedent agreement but the parties had a common continuing intention in respect of a particular matter in the instrument to be rectified, it would be anomalous if the 'common continuing intention' were to be an objective fact if it amounted to an enforceable contract but a subjective belief if it did not. On the contrary, the authorities suggest that in both cases the question is what an objective observer would have thought the intentions of the parties to be. Perhaps the clearest statement is by Denning L.J. in *Frederick E Rose (London) Ltd v William H Pim Jnr & Co Ltd*[369]:
>
> > 'Rectification is concerned with contracts and documents, not with intentions. In order to get rectification it is necessary to show that the parties were in complete agreement on the terms of their contract, but by an error wrote them down wrongly; and in this regard, in order to ascertain the terms of their contract, you do not look into the inner minds of the parties—into their intentions any more than you do in the formation of any other contract. You look at their outward acts, that is, at what they said or wrote to one another in coming to their agreement, and then compare it with the document which they have signed. If you can predicate with certainty what their contract was, and that it is, by a common mistake, wrongly expressed in the document, then you rectify the document; but nothing less will suffice. '"

What one or other party believed they had agreed was not the issue.[370] Lord Hoffmann said that evidence of what a party believed should not be excluded, "but that is not inconsistent with an objective approach to what the terms of the prior consensus were".[371]

[367d] [2009] UKHL 38, [2009] 1 A.C. 1101.

[368] [2009] UKHL 38 at [60].

[369] [1953] 2 Q.B. 450, 461.

[370] [2009] UKHL 38 at [59].

[371] [2009] UKHL 38 at [64]–[65].

### The Daventry case

*In line 8, after "the Chartbrook principle", add:*

(the correctness of which was not challenged in the *Daventry* case) 3-079

### Criticism of the Chartbrook decision

*Replace paragraph with:*

This extended notion of rectification for common mistake adopted by the House of Lords in *Chartbrook Ltd v Persimmon Homes Ltd*[376] has been criticised by both academic commentators and judges. Thus it has been said: 3-081

"It is difficult to accept that Chartbrook was mistaken, at least in any usual sense of the word. The company intended the contract to provide the benefits that [on the assumption that the written agreement did provide for super overage] it did provide for."[377]

In the *Daventry*[378] case Toulson L.J. doubted the correctness of the *Chartbrook* principle but was prepared to apply it since its correctness had not been argued before the court and because it would cause no injustice, as it was arguable that because the defendant's employee knew of the Council's intention, the Council would be entitled to rectification on the basis of a unilateral mistake.[379] The Master of the Rolls also considered that the *Chartbrook* principle "may have to be reconsidered or at least refined"[380] but agreed with Toulson's L.J's approach.[381] Etherton L.J. did not share the doubt about the *Chartbrook* principle[382] but dissented for other reasons, discussed above.[383] In *Tartsinis v Navona Management Co*[384] Leggatt J. said that in *Britoil Plc v Hunt Overseas Oil Inc*[385] the Court of Appeal had held that rectification for common mistake is available only where it is proved that both parties were in fact mistaken about the effect of the final document, and that was not the case in *Chartbrook*.[386] He also said that he found it

"... difficult to see the equity of imposing the view that a hypothetical reasonable observer would have formed of what had been agreed on a party who did not have that understanding of what had been agreed and whose understanding is reflected in the proper interpretation of the final document",[387]

unless the party against whom rectification is sought knew that the party seeking it was mistaken, so that the requirements of rectification for unilateral mistake were satisfied.[388]

[376] [2009] UKHL 38, [2009] 1 A.C. 1101. The point on rectification did not have to be decided but it had been fully argued. The other members of the Judicial Committee agreed with Lord Hoffmann see above, para.3-062.

[377] McLauchlan (2010) 126 L.Q.R. 8, 13.

[378] *Daventry District Council v Daventry and District Housing Ltd* [2011] EWCA Civ 1153, [2012] 1 W.L.R. 1333. See McLauchlan (2014) 131 L.Q.R. 83. See also Lord Toulson's lecture, above, para.3-057 and the very full account of the *Daventry* case and the commentary on it in Hodge, *Rectification*, 2nd edn (2016), paras 3-61 et seq.

[379] [2011] EWCA Civ 1153 at [178]–[185]. Etherton L.J (at [97]–[98]) held that rectification could not be granted on the basis of unilateral mistake as the trial judge held the Council had not proved that the Housing Association knew of the Council's mistake, and had found that the Housing Association's representative was not guilty of dishonesty. The Master of the Rolls found it unnecessary to decide whether rectification should be granted on the ground of unilateral mistake (at [226]).

[380] [2011] EWCA Civ 1153 at [19]. In *NHS Commissioning Board v Silovsky* [2015] EWHC 3141 (Comm), Leggatt J. respectfully agreed with Lord Neuberger M.R. but held that he was bound to apply Lord Hoffmann's "strong" objective approach: at [31]. The case was affirmed without reference to this point, [2017] EWCA Civ 1389. See also *Magellan Spirit ApS v Vitol SA (The Magellan Spirit)* [2016] EWHC 454 (Comm), [2016] 2 Lloyd's Rep. 1 at [42].

[381] [2011] EWCA Civ 1153 at [196]–[202].

[382] [2011] EWCA Civ 1153 at [104].

[383] See above, para. 3-066A.

[384] [2015] EWHC 57 (Comm).

[385] [1994] C.L.C. 561.

[386] [2015] EWHC 57 (Comm) at [91].

[387] [2015] EWHC 57 (Comm) at [92].

[388] [2015] EWHC 57 (Comm) at [93]. See also *AML Global Ltd v ExxonMobil Petroleum and Chemical BVBA* [2018] EWHC 3321 (TCC) at [43].

*Add new paragraphs:*

**Prior agreement not a concluded contract** Some commentators accept that where the prior agreement amounted to a concluded contract and the final document does not match the objective meaning of the prior agreement, then rectification on the basis of a common mistake should be possible without showing that the parties subjectively meant (and had outwardly expressed) the same thing,[388a] but argue that this should not be possible where there was no concluded contract.[388b] In the latter case it should be available only on the basis of either a subjective common intention or unilateral mistake. It is argued that to allow it on the basis of the objective meaning of incomplete negotiations would favour, in the words of Hobhouse L.J. in *Britoil Plc v Hunt Overseas Oil Inc*,[388c] "less formal, less considered and less carefully drafted earlier documents" over the carefully considered final version. This was the approach adopted unanimously by the Court of Appeal in *FSHC Group Holdings Ltd v GLAS Trust Corp Ltd*.[388d] 3-081A

388a Hodge, *Rectification*, 2nd edn (2016), paras 3-53 et seq. and 3-107, points out that even this should not be permitted where the objective meaning of the prior agreement was not consistent with what the claimant subjectively intended at the time.

388b Ruddell [2014] L.M.C.L.Q. 48; Hodge, *Rectification*, 2nd edn (2016), paras 3-92 et seq. and 3-107 (with which Waksman J. agreed, obiter, in *AML Global Ltd v ExxonMobil Petroleum and Chemical BVBA* [2018] EWHC 3321 (TCC) at [44]); and see the lecture by Lord Justice Patten, above, para.3-057.

388c [1994] C.L.C. 561.

388d [2019] EWCA Civ 1361, [2020] Ch. 365.

**The FSHC Group case** In *FSHC Group Holdings Ltd v GLAS Trust Corp Ltd*,[388e] as part of a corporate acquisition in 2012, the parent company (the respondent) had undertaken to provide the appellant's predecessors (Barclays Bank) with security in the form of an assignment of the benefit of a shareholder loan, but it seems that this had been overlooked. The parties then agreed that the respondents should provide the missing security; and the mechanism chosen was that the respondents should accede to two pre-existing security agreements. Neither party realised that these agreements contained clauses imposing additional obligations on the respondent. The trial judge concluded that it was both "objectively" and "subjectively" the common intention of the parties to execute a document which satisfied the parent company's obligation to grant security over the shareholder loan and which did no more than this; and granted rectification.[388f] Barclays Bank's replacement as security agent, GLAS Trust Corp Ltd, appealed, arguing first that rectification could only be granted on the basis of a difference between the objective meaning of the prior agreement and the document signed, the test being "purely objective"; and, secondly, that the reasonable observer would conclude from the documents sent for signature, which not only had the effect that the respondents provided the security that had mistakenly been omitted but also imposed the additional obligations on the respondents, that the intentions of the parties, assessed objectively, was that the respondents were undertaking the additional obligations.[388g] Leggatt L.J., delivering the judgment of the Court of Appeal as a whole, held that the Court of Appeal was not bound to follow the *Daventry* case, as the case had been decided on the basis that Lord Hoffmann's obiter dicta were correct without that proposition being challenged and two members of the court had expressed doubt as to is correctness.[388h] Leggatt L.J. refused to follow Lord Hoffmann's approach. Where the prior agreement amounted to a binding contract, the question is whether 3-081B the document reflects the objective meaning of the prior agreement.[388i] But, Leggatt L.J. said, where the prior agreement is not binding, rectification is available only if the final document differs from the shared (and outwardly expressed) subjective intentions of the parties. Both parties must make the same mistake, that the document differs from their shared intention.[388j] This was established by the judgment of the majority in *Britoil Plc v Hunt Overseas Oil Inc*.[388k] Only then would it be inconsistent with good faith for a party to take advantage of the mistake.[388l] Thus if the prior agreement is not itself binding and the subjective intentions of the parties (which must be outwardly expressed) do not coincide and differ from what is in the document, rectification cannot be given. Leggatt L.J. summarised the position thus:

> "[B]efore a written contract may be rectified on the basis of a common mistake, it is necessary to show either (1) that the document fails to give effect to a prior concluded contract or (2) that, when they executed the document, the parties had a common intention in respect of a particular matter which, by mistake, the document did not accurately record. In the latter case it is necessary to show not only that each party to the contract had the same actual intention with regard to the relevant matter, but also that there was an 'outward expression of accord' – meaning that, as a result of communication between them, the parties understood each other to share that intention."[388m]

However, as the trial judge's findings in the *FSHC* case showed that the parties had a shared intention, derived from communications with each other, that the respondents should grant security over the shareholder loan and no more, the appeal failed.

[388e] [2019] EWCA Civ 1361, [2020] Ch. 365; Beale and Beale [2020] L.M.C.L.Q. 1; Davies (2020) 79 C.L.J. 8; Peel (2020) 136 L.Q.R. 205.

[388f] *FSHC Group Holdings Ltd v Barclays Bank Plc* [2018] EWHC 1558 (Ch).

[388g] [2019] EWCA Civ 1361 at [5] and [184].

[388h] [2019] EWCA Civ 1361 at [134]. (Nor was the *Chartbrook* principle questioned in *Persimmon Homes Ltd v Hillier* [2019] EWCA Civ 800, which was not cited in the *FSHC* case.)

[388i] As Leggatt L.J. pointed out, this has sometimes been seen as analogous to granting specific performance of the prior agreement: [2019] EWCA Civ 1361 at [93] and [141], referring to *Lovell and Christmas Ltd v Wall* (1911) 104 L.T. 85, 88.

[388j] [2019] EWCA Civ 1361 at [122].

[388k] [2019] EWCA Civ 1361 at [162], referring to [1994] C.L.C. 5561, esp. at 573. In *Chartbrook Ltd v Persimmon Homes Ltd* [2009] UKHL 38, [2009] 1 A.C. 1101 Lord Hoffmann had explained the *Britoil* decision as resting on the fact that the prior agreement was too uncertain for the court to be able to predicate what that agreement was: at [63].

[388l] At [142] and [147]. It seems that Leggatt L.J. is referring to a lack of good faith in the sense of dishonesty; compare the somewhat stronger versions (e.g. "commercially unacceptable") that have been advocated in other contexts, see above, paras 1-058 et seq.

[388m] *FSHC Group Holdings Ltd v GLAS Trust Corp Ltd* [2019] EWCA Civ 1361 at [176].

### Evaluation of the "extended approach"

*Replace paragraph with:*

**3-082** It is submitted that, despite the strictures of the Court of Appeal in *FSHC Group Holdings Ltd v GLAS Trust Corp Ltd*,[388n] Lord Hoffmann's approach can be justified, but that much depends on the circumstances, in particular the degree of agreement that the parties believed they had reached at the "prior accord" stage and the purpose of the parties in drawing up a final document. Further, the "objective approach to what the terms of the prior consensus were" must be treated with care.

Determining the agreement between the parties is more complex than applying a simple objective test, as will be explained in the paragraphs that follow.

[388n] [2019] EWCA Civ 1361, [2020] Ch. 365 at [155]–[163].

*Change title of paragraph:* **3-083**

## Subjective accord may not be necessary

*Replace paragraph with:*

It is submitted that much depends on the extent to which the parties regarded themselves as having "concluded" an agreement. Although in *Britoil Plc v Hunt Overseas Oil Inc*[389] Hobhouse L.J. does seem to have considered that the parties must have expressed the same intention, another reason that the Court of Appeal refused rectification in the *Britoil* case was that, in the view of the majority, the "heads of agreement" did not constitute the final version: it was in some respects unclear and a witness conceded that part of the point of drawing up a final version was to eliminate any ambiguities. It is not surprising therefore that Hobhouse L.J said that to base rectification on going "back to successively less formal, less considered and less carefully drafted earlier documents ... cannot be right".[390] But if the parties had thought that their prior agreement was complete, even if not binding on them, and had merely instructed lawyers to incorporate it into a final document that they both signed without careful study, it is not inappropriate to rectify any discrepancy between the objective meaning of the prior agreement and the final document even without proof that the parties shared, or still shared, the same subjective intention. In the *Britoil* case Hoffmann L.J. dissented precisely because: **3-083**

> "... there was no further negotiation or discussion between the parties and that the common intention was that the definitive agreement should reflect the meaning of the heads of agreement, whatever that might be."[391-394]

[389] [1994] C.L.C. 561.

[390] [1994] C.L.C. 561, 573.

[391-394] [1994] C.L.C. 561, 577.

*In line 1, after "This suggests that,", replace "at least where there is a concluded prior agreement, rectification should be given" with:*

even where there is no concluded prior contract, it may sometimes be appropriate to grant rectification **3-084**

*Add new paragraph:*

It may be added that when in "common mistake" cases in the past the courts have determined the terms of the prior agreement, it is not clear that they have always looked for actual subjective agreement. It is only subjective intentions that have been outwardly expressed or "crossed the line" that matter. So typically in rectification cases the court looks at the outward expression to determine what the agreement was. Though evidence of what a party intended or thought the words meant is admissible and may be relevant, at least when the prior agreement is in writing the court determines its meaning in the usual way. Thus in *Britoil Plc v Hunt Overseas Oil Inc*[396a] the court considered the meaning of the prior "heads of agreement" document without asking what each party actually meant.[396b] Hobhouse L.J. referred[396c] to an earlier summary of the law by Mustill J., where the latter said: **3-084A**

"3. The prior transaction may consist either of a concluded agreement or of a continuing common intention. In the latter event, the intention must be objectively manifested. It is the words and acts of the parties demonstrating their intention, not the inward thoughts of the parties, which matter."[396d]

In *FSHC Group Holdings Ltd v GLAS Trust Corp Ltd*[396e] Leggatt L.J. explained Mustill J.'s statement as being merely a reference to the requirement of an outward expression of accord, but with respect it is not wholly clear that Mustill J. thought that shared subjective intentions must also be proved. If during their negotiations A has manifested a particular intention to B, who shares that intention, and A has never subsequently gone back on what he indicated, should A really be able to resist rectification on the ground that his subjective intention was not in fact what he outwardly expressed?[396f]

396a [1994] C.L.C. 561.

396b See also Ruddell [2014] L.M.C.L.Q. 48, 58.

396c [1994] C.L.C. 561, 569.

396d *Etablissements Levy v Adderley Navigation Co Panama SA (The Olympic Pride)* [1980] 2 Lloyd's Rep. 67, 72–73.

396e [2019] EWCA Civ 1361, [2020] Ch. 365 at [159].

396f If A was aware that B had a different understanding of what was agreed, then rectification may be available on the basis of a unilateral mistake.

*Replace title and paragraph with:*

**3-085** It is submitted, therefore, that for this purpose no absolute distinction should be drawn between concluded prior contracts and partially negotiated agreements. First, while it may be the case that while negotiations on any aspect continue, the parties will regard the whole transaction as still open, this will not always be so. The parties may regard some issues as completely settled (not realising that their intentions on the point differ) and therefore not examine the relevant parts of the final document with care, so that they fail spot the difference between it and the final document. Although neither party is acting dishonestly, there seems no reason why this situation must necessarily be treated differently from that of the concluded prior agreement. It is a matter of degree, of the extent to which the parties regarded the matter as "settled" and of whether the party against whom rectification is claimed had indicated that it was proposing a change or at least a clarification.[397–400] Secondly, even when no concluded contract has been reached, it seems appropriate to allow each party to rely on what the other has "outwardly manifested", rather than insist on proof of each party's subjective intention.

397–400 See above, para.3-067.

### "Objective" meaning known not to be party's intention

*Replace paragraph with:*

**3-086** It is submitted, however, that even when the parties had concluded a prior agreement, and (if the arguments in the preceding paragraphs are accepted) in cases in which there was no conclude agreement but the parties regarded their negotiations on the relevant issue as complete, and the final document does not reflect accurately the seemingly "objective" meaning of the prior agreement, it would not always be right to rectify the document to match that objective meaning. Lord Hoffmann's dictum in *Chartbrook Ltd v Persimmon Homes Ltd*[401] quoted earlier,[402] like the statement he quotes from Denning L.J., appears to look only at the evidence of prior agreement in a purely objective way,[403] from the view point of "the reasonable fly on the wall".[404] The test normally used in English contract law to determine the content or meaning of a contract is not wholly objective in this sense.[405] First, as submitted earlier, if the parties were in fact in subjective agreement as the meaning of their words, it is at least arguable that their subjective intentions should govern.[406] Secondly, if there is no subjective agreement, the question is how A understood B's words and whether A's interpretation was reasonable, and vice versa.[407] Normally it will be reasonable to understand the words of the prior agreement on their "purely objective" sense.[407a] However, if A knew B's intention to be different from the "purely objective" meaning of the words of the prior agreement, A cannot hold B to that meaning.[408] If the subsequent written agreement provides what B had intended, A should not be entitled to rectification, even if the result is that A is bound by a contract that he did not intend to make. If the written agreement were in the same terms as the prior agreement, but to A's knowledge B still intended it mean something different, B would be entitled to have it rectified on the basis of a unilateral mistake.[409] It is submitted that even if it cannot be shown that A had actual knowledge that B was still mistaken at the stage of the final draft, B should still be entitled to have the final draft rectified to match the intention that A knew that B had at the earlier stage, unless again B should reasonably have understood the draft as not merely setting down what was previously agreed, but as a new proposal (or perhaps a deliberate assertion that A did not accept the "objective" meaning of the prior agreement).[410] The aim of rectification should be "to ensure the written agreement reflects the true bargain between the parties as determined by ordinary principles of contract formation".[411]

[401] [2009] UKHL 38, [2009] 1 A.C. 1101 at [60].

[402] Above, para. 3-077A.

[403] Cartwright, *Misrepresentation, Mistake and Non-disclosure*, 5th edn (2019), para.13-40.

[404] Spencer [1973] C.L.J. 104, 108.

[405] See above, para.2-004.

[406] See above, paras 3-014 and 3-065.

[407] See above, para.3-014.

[407a] In *Scottish Widows Fund and Life Assurance Society v BGC International* [2012] EWCA Civ 607 Arden L.J. pointed out that Lord Hoffmann's test is not fully objective as the meaning of any words is taken to be that which the meaning would convey to a reasonable person having all the background knowledge which would have been available to the parties in the situation in which the parties were at the time of their agreement (at [46]).

[408] No more than A can accept an apparent offer from B which A knows does not represent B's true intention: see *Hartog v Colin and Shields* [1939] 3 All E.R. 566, above, para.3-022. See also para.2-004; *Maple Leaf Macro Volatility Master Fund v Rouvroy* [2009] EWHC 257 (Comm) at [228], though doubted in the CA: [2009] EWCA Civ 1334 at [17]; *Novus Aviation Ltd v Alubaf Arab International Bank BSC(c)* [2016] EWHC 1575 (Comm) at [54]–[57]; *Blue v Ashley* [2017] EWHC 1928 (Comm) at [64].

[409] *Daventry District Council v Daventry and District Housing Ltd* [2011] EWCA Civ 1153 at [177], per Toulson L.J. at [178]. For rectification on the basis of unilateral mistake see above, paras 3-069 et seq.

[410] See above, para.3-067.

[411] McLauchlan (2008) 124 L.Q.R. 608, 640.

## A "unilateral mistake" approach

*Replace paragraph with:*

The examples discussed in the two previous paragraphs raise the issue of whether **3-088** in cases in which the parties were not in subjective agreement over the "prior accord", it is more appropriate to consider rectification for unilateral mistake than to use rectification for common mistake.[415] Unilateral mistake focuses on the intentions and understandings of the parties at the stage of signature of the document, rather than on the meaning of the prior agreement and whether there was a continuing common intention. On the authorities as they stand at present, rectification can be given on the ground of unilateral mistake only if the defendant knew that the document signed did not represent the claimant's intention, or deliberately caused the mistake.[416] It is submitted that this might leave some deserving claimants without a remedy. Suppose in the prior negotiations, A intends *x* and B intends *y*. The "objective meaning" of the agreement is *x*. That must be because this is what the words used would mean to the reasonable person in the circumstances (and that A did not know of B's actual intention). The parties then draft a document into which B, without any intent to deceive, has inserted a clause providing for *y*. A may reasonably assume that the document merely represents what was previously agreed and sign without noticing the slip.[417] It is submitted that A should be able to obtain rectification, provided that A reasonably understood the draft as merely setting down what was previously agreed, rather than as a new proposal (or perhaps a deliberate assertion that B did not accept the "objective" meaning of the prior agreement). But in this case rectification could not be given either on the basis of a subjective common intention, nor on the basis of unilateral mistake, as the law is currently understood,[418] as B did not know of A's mistake. If the doctrine of relief for unilateral mistake were to be extended in the fashion suggested in the preceding paragraph, it might deal adequately with cases like the one envisaged in this paragraph. It could be argued that B should have known, from the "purely objective" meaning of the prior agreement and the fact that he has not flagged up a change, that the final document did not represent A's intentions. A could then at least seek to have the document cancelled. However, such an extension of relief has yet to be made and is likely to be controversial. Unless and until it is made, it is submitted that rectification to bring the agreement into line with the objective meaning of the prior agreement (concluded or not) is a useful supplement to rectification when the final document is different to the subjective understanding of one of the parties and rectification for unilateral mistake is not available.

[415] McLauchlan (2010) 126 L.Q.R. 8, 13 argues that if Chartbrook knew of Persimmon's mistake, there would be a claim based on unilateral mistake, on which see above, para.3-069. As they did not know, the writer concludes that the only proper basis for rectification would be if Chartbrook ought to have known that Persimmon did not intend super overage to be payable, when there might also be a claim based on unilateral mistake or the contract might be void, see above, para.3-076.

[416] See above, paras 3-070—3-071.

[417] See above, para.3-066.

[418] See above, para.3-076.

## (e) General Principles

### Proof of mistake

*Replace footnote 427 with:*

3-089 [427] *Tartsinis v Navona Management Co* [2015] EWHC 57 (Comm) at [85]. See also *Price v Saundry* [2019] EWHC 496 (Ch) at [15]. The evidential weight to be given to the document will vary according to the circumstances, for example whether it was prepared after long negotiations with the help of legal advisers, how clearly the document is drafted and whether the drafters were working in their first language: [2015] EWHC 57 (Comm) at [86]).

## Mistake as to terms

*Replace paragraph with:*

There must be a disparity between the terms of the prior agreement and those of the document which it is sought to rectify. In *Frederick E. Rose (London) Ltd v William H. Pim Junior & Co Ltd*,[431] the parties entered into an oral agreement for the purchase of horsebeans, in the belief that they were the same as "feveroles", and a subsequent written agreement embodied the same terms. Denning L.J. said: 3-090

> "Rectification is concerned with contracts and documents, not with intentions. In order to get rectification it is necessary to show that the parties were in complete agreement on the terms of their contract, but by an error wrote them down wrongly. ... in order to ascertain the terms of their contract, you do not look into the inner minds of the parties—into their intentions any more than you do in the formation of any other contract. You look at their outward acts ..."

Insofar as this dictum seems to say that the subjective intentions of the parties, even if expressed outwardly as in that case, has given rise to some difficulties of interpretation.[431a] However, it is submitted that the case is readily explicable on a simpler basis, which was in fact the basis on which the other members of Court of Appeal decided it. Rectification was refused because both the oral and written contracts were for horse-beans; the mistake was not about the terms of the contract but one of fact, namely that the parties both thought that feveroles and horsebeans were the same, so that horsebeans would fulfil the buyers' requirements. In contrast, in *London Weekend Television v Paris and Griffith*[432] Megaw J. held that, where two persons expressly agree with one another what is the meaning of a particular phrase used in a written contract, the contract can be rectified to make it clear that the phrase bears the meaning agreed.[433]

431 [1953] 2 Q.B. 450, 461. Compare above, para.3-025.

431a See the discussion of the case at [2019] EWCA Civ 1361 at [63]–[66] and [69]–[71].

432 (1969) 113 S.J. 222. Thus "rectification is available where the words of the document were purposely used but it was mistakenly considered that they bore a different meaning from their correct meaning as a matter of construction": *Re Butlin's Settlement Trusts* [1976] Ch. 251, 260 (a case involving a voluntary settlement); applied to rectification of a contract in *Phillips Petroleum Co UK Ltd v Snamprogetti Ltd* (2001) 79 Con. L.R. 80 at [39] (affirmed on other grounds [2001] EWCA Civ 889). And see above, para.3-059. However, in the case of a voluntary settlement it seems that the test is not whether the mistake was as to the legal effect of the instrument or its consequences, as was said by Millett J. in *Gibbon v Mitchell* [1990] 1 W.L.R. 1304, 1309, but a broader one of whether the mistake was of sufficient gravity: see *Pitt v Holt* [2013] UKSC 26, [2013] 2 A.C. 108 at [122], where Lord Walker added: the test will normally be satisfied only when there is a mistake either as to the legal character or nature of a transaction, or as to some matter of fact or law which is basic to the transaction. This was, applied in *Payne v Tyler* [2019] EWHC 2347 (Ch) at [23]; but compare *Rogge v Rogge* [2019] EWHC 1949 (Ch) at [119]–[120] (some mistakes as to matters too far removed from transaction).

433 See also above, para.3-059.

## Live issue required

*Replace footnote 434 with:*

434 *Whiteside v Whiteside* [1950] Ch. 65; cf. *Re Colebrook's Conveyances* [1972] 1 W.L.R. 1397; *Etablissements Georges et Paul Levy v Adderley Navigation Co SA* [1980] 2 Lloyd's Rep. 67. Provided that there is an issue capable of being contested by the parties it is no bar to rectification that both sides wish the document to be rectified so as to reduce one party's tax liability: *Lake v Lake* [1989] S.T.C. 865; *Racal Group Services Ltd v Ashmore* [1995] S.T.C. 1151. However, where the parties have resolved the issue (as to who was a party to the contract) between themselves by means of a deed of rectification, and rectification of the document would merely bring a tax advantage to one of the parties, rectification will be refused unless there was a specific shared intention to bring about that tax consequence: *MV Promotions Ltd v Telegraph Media Group Ltd* [2020] EWHC 1357 (Ch). 3-091

## Other instances of rectification

*Replace paragraph with:*

3-101 The court has rectified a bill of exchange,[453] a marine insurance policy,[454] a transfer of shares wrongly numbered,[455] a bill of quantities,[456] and bought and sold notes by inserting therein a clause customary in a particular trade,[457] a disclosure letter that had the effect of qualifying contractual warranties given by a seller[457a] and very frequently conveyances of land.[458] A charge registered at the Land Registry pursuant to the Land Registration Act 2002 may be rectified.[459]

[453] *Druiff v Lord Parker* (1868) L.R. 5 Eq. 131.

[454] *Spalding v Crocker* (1897) 2 Com. Cas. 189.

[455] *Re International Contract Co* (1872) L.R. 7 Ch. App. 485.

[456] *Neill v Midland Ry* (1869) 17 W.R. 871.

[457] *Caraman Rowley & May v Aperghis* (1923) 40 T.L.R. 124.

[457a] *Persimmon Homes Ltd v Hillier* [2019] EWCA Civ 800, [2020] 1 All E.R. (Comm) 475.

[458] *Beale v Kyte* [1907] 1 Ch. 564; *Craddock Bros v Hunt* [1923] 2 Ch. 136. In *Lee v Lee* [2018] EWHC 149 (Ch) a notice of severance was rectified.

[459] See *Cherry Tree Investments Ltd v Landmain Ltd* [2012] EWCA Civ 736, [2013] Ch. 305.

## Voluntary settlements

*Replace footnote 466 with:*

3-104 [466] *Re Butlin's Settlement Trusts* [1976] Ch. 251. It is the subjective intention of the settlor, rather than the intention of an agent of the settlor, which is relevant: see *Day v Day* [2013] EWCA Civ 280, [2013] 2 P. & C.R. DG1. The burden of proof of the kind of transaction involved is on the party seeking rectification, and whether the transaction is voluntary or one for value is to be judged by the unrectified document, not by what it would be if rectified: *Price v Saundry* [2019] EWHC 496 (Ch) at [19].

CHAPTER 4

# CONSIDERATION

## 2. DEFINITIONS

### Invented consideration

*Replace footnote 50 with:*

4-010 [50] Atiyah, *Consideration in Contracts: A Fundamental Restatement* (1971), accused the previous editor of this chapter (Sir Guenter Treitel) of having "invented the concept of invented consideration". The editor's response (in earlier versions of this footnote) was that all the editor could claim to have invented was a phrase for describing what the courts sometimes actually do. The phrase did not imply approval of the practice; see below. Nor did the phrase necessarily imply inconsistency between decisions, as Atiyah suggests; courts could *consistently* hold that an act or forbearance was consideration although it was not the promisor's object to secure it. In fact, the decisions on the point are not perfectly consistent with each other: see at the end of this paragraph; but that is hardly unusual in a common law system.

## 3. ADEQUACY OF CONSIDERATION

### Courts generally will not judge adequacy

*In line 11, after "payment was irrationally generous.", add new footnote 74a:*

4-014 [74a] *National Car Parks Ltd v Revenue and Customs Commissioners* [2019] EWCA Civ 854 concerned the analogous situation where motorists pay more than the specified tariff for parking when inserting coins into "pay and display" machines which do not give change. The court found that the consideration for the parking was the amount of money paid into the machine, including the overpayment. Consideration should be assessed objectively (at [18]).

## 4. THE CONCEPT OF "VALUABLE" CONSIDERATION

### "Value in the eye of the law"

*Replace footnote 138 with:*

4-022 [138] *Bret v J.S.* (1600) Cro. Eliz. 755; *Tweddle v Atkinson* (1861) 1 B. & S. 393, disapproving of *Dutton v Poole* (1677) 2 Lev. 210; cf. *Horrocks v Forray* [1976] 1 W.L.R. 230; *Mansukhani v Sharkey* [1992] 2 E.G.L.R. 125; *Kerr v Jamison* [2019] NICh 4.

## 5. PAST CONSIDERATION

### Past act done at promisor's request

*Replace footnote 200 with:*

4-030 [200] *Re Casey's Patents* [1892] 1 Ch. 104, 115–116; cf. *Lampleigh v Brathwait* (1615) Hob. 105. For further discussion in the context of guarantees, see Vol.II, para.45-022, recently considered in *Longulf Trading (UK) Ltd v Niyazi Onen Gida Sanayi AS* [2019] EWHC 1573 (Comm) at [11].

## 6. CONSIDERATION MUST MOVE FROM THE PROMISEE

### Promisee must provide consideration

*Replace footnote 236 with:*

4-037 [236] *Barber v Fox* (1669) 2 Saund. 134, n.(e); *Thomas v Thomas* (1842) 2 Q.B. 851, 859; *Tweddle v Atkinson* (1861) 1 B. & S. 393, 399; *Pollway v Abdullah* [1974] 1 W.L.R. 493, 497; cf. *Dickinson v Abel* [1969] 1 W.L.R. 295, and (for VAT purposes) *Customs and Excise Commissioners v Telemed* [1992] S.T.C. 89. In *Revenue and Customs Commissioners v Aimia Coalition Loyalty UK Ltd* [2013] UKSC 15, [2013] 2 All E.R. 719 (the facts of which are stated in para.18-009 below) the judgments of the Supreme Court contain many references to "third party consideration" (see at [12] and passim). This phrase simply reflects the words of art.11 of the relevant EC Council Directive (95/7 of 10 April 1995) which defines the taxable amount for VAT purposes as "the *consideration* which has been obtained by the supplier from the purchaser or a *third party* for such supplies" (italics supplied). The phrase carries no implication to the effect that the "third party consideration" gives any promise to the force of a binding contract. For criticism of a possibly contrary dictum, see below, para.4-045. See too *Dixons Carphone Plc v Revenue and Customs Commissioners* [2018] UKFTT 557 (TC).

## 7. COMPROMISE AND FORBEARANCE TO SUE

### (b) Invalid or Doubtful Claims

#### Claims which are doubtful in law

*To the end of paragraph, after "a valid contract".[299]", add:*

And in *Simantob v Shavleyan* the Court of Appeal held that giving up an argument that a clause to pay $1,000 per day in interest was a penalty clause did constitute good consideration, even though that argument had previously been rejected in an application for summary judgment.[299a] 4-052

[299a] [2019] EWCA Civ 1105, citing this paragraph at [53].

## 8. EXISTING DUTIES AS CONSIDERATION

### (b) Duty Imposed by Contract with Promisor

#### Factual benefit to promisor

*Replace third paragraph with:*

In the *Williams* case, *Stilk v Myrick* was not overruled; indeed Purchas L.J. described it as a "pillarstone of the law of contract".[382] But he added that the case might be differently decided today[383]; while Glidewell L.J. said that the present decision did not "contravene" but did "refine and limit"[384] the principle of the earlier case; and Russell L.J. said that the "rigid approach" to consideration in *Stilk v Myrick* was "no longer necessary or desirable".[385] However, in a more recent case in which the Court of Appeal had applied the same approach to a promise to allow the debtor an extended period in which to pay,[386] the Supreme Court, obiter, expressed reservations as to whether the decision in the *Williams* case can stand with the decision of the House of Lords in *Foakes v Beer*.[387] Lord Sumption, with whom Lady Hale, Lord Wilson and Lord Lloyd-Jones agreed, said that it was unnecessary to decide the point, but continued[388]: 4-070

> "It is also, I think, undesirable to do so. The issue is a difficult one. The only consideration which can be said to have been given for accepting a less advantageous schedule of payments was (i) the prospect that the payments were more likely to be made if they were loaded onto the back end of the contract term, and (ii) the fact that MWB would be less likely to have the premises left vacant on its hands while it sought a new licensee. These were both expectations of practical value, but neither was a contractual entitlement. In *Williams v Roffey Bros & Nicholls (Contractors) Ltd*, the Court of Appeal held that an expectation of commercial advantage was good consideration. The problem about this was that practical expectation of benefit was the very thing which the House of Lords held not to be adequate consideration in *Foakes v Beer*: see in particular … per Lord Blackburn.[389] There are arguable points of distinction, although the arguments are somewhat forced … The reality is that any decision on this point is likely to involve a re-examination of the decision in *Foakes v Beer*. It is probably ripe for re-examination. But if it is to be overruled or its effect substantially modified, it should be before an enlarged panel of the court and in a case where the decision would be more than obiter dictum."

Thus whether a factual benefit to B in securing A's performance of the earlier contract normally suffices to constitute consideration is now in doubt. But so too is the rule in *Foakes v Beer* and, it seems to follow, the rule in *Stilk v Myrick*. Unless and until the *Williams* case is overruled, however, it appears to be binding on lower courts.[390]

382 [1991] 1 Q.B. 1, 20.

383 [1991] 1 Q.B. 1, 21. But he was not prepared to accept the American case of *Watkins v Carrig* 21 A. 2d 591 (1941), where a contractor who had agreed to do excavating work unexpectedly struck hard rock and was held entitled to enforce a promise to pay nine times the originally agreed sum. The case was said not to represent English law in *North Ocean Shipping Co Ltd v Hyundai Construction Co Ltd (The Atlantic Baron)* [1979] Q.B. 705, 714. It was cited with apparent approval in *Compagnie Noga D'Importation et D'Exportation SA v Abacha* [2003] EWCA Civ 1100; [2003] 2 All E.R. (Comm) 915 at [54] but on the point that the requirement of consideration was satisfied by rescission of the original contract, followed by the making of a new one: below, paras 4-072, 4-080. No mention was made in the *Compagnie Noga* case, above, of the more sceptical references to *Watkins v Carrig* in the *Williams* case and in *The Atlantic Baron*, cited earlier in this note.

384 [1991] 1 Q.B. 1, 16.

385 [1991] 1 Q.B. 1, 18.

386 *MWB Business Exchange Centres Ltd v Rock Advertising Ltd* [2016] EWCA Civ 553, [2017] Q.B. 604. In *Re Selectmove Ltd* [1995] 1 W.L.R. 474 a differently constituted Court of Appeal had declined to apply the *Williams v Roffey* principle *to* an obligation to make payment on the ground that it "would in effect leave the principle in *Foakes v Beer* without any application" ([1995] 1 W.L.R. 474, 481).

387 (1884) 9 App. Cas. 605.

388 *MWB Business Exchange Centres Ltd v Rock Advertising Ltd* [2018] UKSC 24, [2019] A.C. 119 at [18]. Lord Briggs, who gave a separate judgment, agreed (at [20]) that it would not be desirable for the court to address the issue of consideration, for the reasons which Lord Sumption gives.

389 Quoted in para. 4-069 above.

390 See *Simantob v Shavleyan* [2018] EWHC 2005 (QB) at [127] (upheld without discussing the point: [2019] EWCA Civ 1105).

## 9. DISCHARGE AND VARIATION OF CONTRACTUAL DUTIES

## (b) Variation

### *(iii) Equitable Mitigations*

#### The promise or representation must be "clear" or "unequivocal"

*Replace footnote 488 with:*

**4-091** 488 *B.P. Exploration Co (Libya) Ltd v Hunt (No.2)* [1979] 1 W.L.R. 783, 812 (affirmed without reference to this point [1983] 2 A.C. 352.); *Spence v Shell* (1980) 256 E.G. 55, 63; *James v Heim Galleries* (1980) 256 E.G. 819, 821; *Société Italo-Belge pour le Commerce et l'Industrie v Palm & Vegetable Oils (Malaysia) Sdn Bhd (The Post Chaser)* [1981] 2 Lloyd's Rep. 695, 700; *Goldsworthy v Brickell* [1987] Ch. 378, 410; *Hiscox v Outhwaite (No.3)* [1991] 2 Lloyd's Rep. 523, 524, 535; *Rowan Companies Inc v Lambert Eggink Offshore Transport Consultants* [1999] 2 Lloyd's Rep. 443 at 448, *Thameside MBC v Barlow Securities Group Services Ltd* [2001] EWCA Civ 1; [2001] B.L.R. 113 and *Evans v Amicus Healthcare Ltd* [2003] EWHC 2161 (Fam), [2003] 4 All E.R. 903 at [303]–[306] (where this requirement was not satisfied), affirmed on other grounds [2004] EWCA Civ 727; [2005] Fam. 1 (see above, para.4-089); for the requirement of an "unequivocal representation in a case of "waiver ... by estoppel", see *Warren v Burns* [2014] EWHC 3671 (QB) at [17] (where this requirement was not satisfied: at [20]); *MWB Business Exchange Centres Ltd v Rock Advertising Ltd* [2016] EWCA Civ 553 [2017] Q.B. 604 at [51], [52] and passim; as the promise in this case was held to be supported by consideration (see below, para.4-119) it was not strictly necessary to decide the estoppel issue: see at [50]. (The *MWB* case was reversed on other grounds without reference to estoppel, [2018] UKSC 24, [2018] 2 W.L.R. 1603, see below, paras 4-119 and 22-045.) See too *Greenhouse v Paysafe Financial Services Ltd* [2018] EWHC 3296 (Comm) at [17] where paras 4-091–4-093 were cited with apparent approval.

## Analogy with waiver

*Replace footnote 611 with:*

611 e.g. *Bremer Handelsgesellschaft mbH v Westzucker GmbH* [1981] 1 Lloyd's Rep. 207, 212–213; *Peacock v Imagine Property Developments Ltd* [2018] EWHC 1113 (TCC) at [61]–[72]. **4-105**

## Distinguished from estoppel by convention

*Replace paragraph with:*

Estoppel by convention may arise where both[631] parties to a transaction "act on assumed state of facts[632] or law,[633] the assumption being either shared by both or made by one and acquiesced in by the other".[634] The parties are then precluded from denying the truth of that assumption, if it would be unjust or unconscionable[635] (typically because the party claiming the benefit has been "materially influenced"[636] by the common assumption)[637] to allow them (or one of them) to go back on it.[638] Such an estoppel differs from estoppel by representation and from promissory estoppel[639] in that it does not depend on any representation or promise.[640] It can arise by virtue of a common assumption which was not induced by the party alleged to be estopped but which was based on a mistake spontaneously made by the party relying on it and acquiesced in by the other party.[641] It seems, however, that the assumption resembles the representation required to give rise to other forms of estoppel to the extent that it must be "unambiguous and unequivocal"[642]; and this common feature can make it hard to distinguish between these two forms of estoppel.[643] Estoppel by convention has also been said to arise out of an express agreement by which the parties had compromised a disputed claim[644]; but where such a compromise is supported by consideration (in accordance with the principles discussed earlier in this Chapter[645]) it is binding as a contract,[646] so that there is, it is submitted, no need to rely on estoppel by convention.[647] **4-108**

631 There can be no such estoppel where one party is not yet in existence: see *Rover International Ltd v Cannon Film Sales Ltd* (1987) 3 B.C.C. 369, reversed in part on other grounds [1989] 1 W.L.R. 912 (company not yet formed).

632 In *ING Bank NV v Ros Roca SA* [2011] EWCA Civ 353, [2012] 1 W.L.R. 472 it was argued at [63] that "fact" here referred to "present fact", but Carnwath L.J. said that the "understanding" giving rise to the estoppel could "relate to the factual or legal basis on which a current transaction is proceeding, even if that understanding includes reference to events in the future" (at [64(i)]). This view is indirectly supported by Rix L.J. who adopted Carnwath L.J.'s "solution in terms of estoppel by convention" even though his preference was for the view that the estoppel arose from a "promissory representation" so that it could give rise to a promissory estoppel (at [85]–[86]).

633 See below, para.4-111.

634 *Republic of India v India Steamship Co (The Indian Endurance) (No.2)* [1998] A.C. 878, 913; and see *Norwegian American Cruises A/S v Paul Mundy Ltd (The Vistafjord)* [1988] 2 Lloyd's Rep. 343, 351; *Shearson Lehman Hutton Inc v Maclaine Watson & Co Ltd* [1989] 2 Lloyd's Rep. 570, 596; see also *Blindley Heath Investments v Bass* [2014] EWHC 1366 (Ch) at [127] to [134], where the requirements of estoppel by convention were satisfied, and para.3-107 of the 31st edition of this book (para.4-108 of this edition) was cited with apparent approval; *Phillip Collins Ltd v Davis* [2000] 3 All E.R. 808 at 823 (where there was no common assumption or acquiescence): *Thor Navigation Inc v Ingosstrakh Insurance* [2005] EWHC 19 (Comm), [2005] 1 Lloyd's Rep. 547 at [66], [70]; *Triodos Bank NV v Dobbs* [2005] EWCA Civ 630, [2005] 2 Lloyd's Rep. 588 at [2]; *Canmer International Insurance v UK Mutual Assurance* [2005] EWHC 1694, [2005] 2 Lloyd's Rep. 479 at [41], where there was no common assumption and hence no estoppel by convention; *Tamil Nadu Electricity Board v ST-CMS Electricity Company Private Ltd* [2007] EWHC 1713 (Comm), [2007] 2 All E.R. (Comm) 701 at [104], where again there was no evidence of the alleged shared assumption (at [115]); *Kosmar Villa Holidays Plc v Trustees of Syndicate 1243* [2007] EWHC 458 (Comm), [2007] 2 All E.R. (Comm) 215 at [53], where reliance on estoppel by convention failed on the same ground. On appeal this aspect of the decision at first instance in the *Kosmar* case was affirmed ([2008] EWCA Civ 147, [2008] 2 All E.R. (Comm) 14 at [85]) even though the actual decision was reversed on the ground that the principle of "estoppel by election" (cf. below para.24-003) did not there apply; or, if it did apply, the requirement of an "unequivocal com-

munication" (at [71]) needed to give rise to such an estoppel had not been satisfied (at [79]). For other cases in which the requirements of estoppel by convention were discussed but not satisfied (usually for want of the requisite common assumption) see *Haden Young Ltd v Laing O'Rourke Midlands Ltd* [2008] EWHC 1016 (TCC) at [187]–[192]; *The W D Fairway (No.3)* [2009] EWHC 1782 (Admlty), [2009] 2 Lloyd's Rep. 420 at [22]; *Republic of Serbia v ImageSut International NV* [2009] EWHC 2853 (Comm), [2010] 1 Lloyd's Rep. 325 at [68], [69]; *Pindell v Airasia Berhad* [2010] EWHC 2516 (Comm), [2011] 1 All E.R. (Comm) 396 at [55]; *Khan v Tyne and Wear Passenger Transport Executive* [2015] UKUT 43 at [41], where the requirement stated in para.4-110 below was also said not to have been satisfied and *Crossco No.4 Unlimited v Jolan Ltd* [2011] EWHC 803, where paras 3-107—3-114 of the 30th edition of this book (paras 4-108—4-115 in this edition) are referred to with apparent approval; *Mears Ltd v Shoreline Housing Partnership Ltd* [2015] EWHC 1396 (TCC), where the requirements and effects of estoppel by convention are fully discussed at [43]–[50] and summarised at [57]. The decision in the *Crossco* case (above) was affirmed on appeal ([2011] EWCA Civ 1619, [2012] 2 All E.R. 754) without further discussion of the requirements of estoppel by convention. So far as the claim was based on this kind of estoppel, it failed on the findings of fact in the court below: see [2011] EWCA Civ 1619 at [115]. The requirements of estoppel by convention are again summarised in *Spliethoff's Bevrachtingskantoor BV v Bank of China* [2015] EWHC 999 (Comm), [2015] 2 Lloyd's Rep. 123 at [159], citing "paras 3-107 [of the 31st edition of this book] and following" (paras 4-108 and following in the present edition) with apparent approval. Carr J. would have held those requirements to have been satisfied but it was "strictly unnecessary" (at [154]) to decide the point since his "primary conclusion" (at [170]) was that the facts which the claimant sought to estop the defendant from denying had been established by the evidence (see at [147]–[154]). See also *F G Wilson (Engineering) Ltd v John Holt & Co (Liverpool) Ltd* [2012] EWHC 2477 (Comm), [2012] 2 Lloyd's Rep. 479, where the argument that there was an estoppel by convention was rejected on the facts as there "was no relevant communicated assumption which was shared by [the parties] ... or in which [the party alleged to be estopped] ... acquiesced" (at [73]); reversed, sub nom. *Caterpillar (NJ) Ltd v John Holt & Co (Liverpool) Ltd* [2013] EWCA Civ 1232, [2014] 1 All E.R. 785, without further reference to estoppel. The Court of Appeal's decision was doubted in *PST Energy 7 Shipping LLC v O W Bunker Malta Ltd (The Res Cogitans)* [2016] UKSC 23, [1916] 2 W.L.R. 1193, but not on the estoppel point for which it is cited in this footnote. See also *Crabbe v Townsend* [2016] EWHC 2450 (Ch), [2017] W.T.L.R. 13 where an agreement between the claimant and the defendant (her brother) was held to have contractual force (see above, para.2-124) and the defendant further argued that the claimant was estopped by convention from enforcing that agreement. The requirements of this form of estoppel were stated at [2016] EWHC 2450 (Ch) at [7] but were held not to have been satisfied on the ground that the parties had not made any "common assumption" (at [18]) and on the further grounds that there had been no reliance on any such assumption (at [19]), nor would it have been "unjust or unconscionable" (at [20]) for the claimant to enforce the agreement, so that the requirement of "unjust or unconscionable" stated below would also not have been satisfied, since no detriment had been suffered by the defendant nor any benefit obtained by the claimant (at [20]). Contrast *Stevensdrake Ltd v Hunt* [2017] EWCA Civ 1173, [2017] 4 Costs L.R. 781, where the requirements of estoppel by convention are stated at [60], quoting para.4-108 of the 32nd edition of this book (para.4-108 of the present edition) with apparent approval and where the requirements of this form of estoppel were held (at [90] to [97]) to have been satisfied, though Briggs L.J. (at [100]) found this point "more difficult". See tooDawson (1989) L.S. 16.

635 *Crédit Suisse v Borough Council of Allerdale* [1995] 2 Lloyd's Rep. 315, 367–370 (where this requirement was not satisfied); affirmed on other grounds [1997] Q.B. 362; *Gloyne v Richardson* [2001] EWCA Civ 716, [2001] 2 B.C.L.C. 669 at [41] (below, para.4-110); *Thor Navigation* case [2005] EWHC 19 (Comm) at [66] and *Ease Faith Ltd v Leonis Marine Management* [2006] EWHC 232 (Comm), [2006] 1 Lloyd's Rep. 673 at [171] and *Durham v BAI (Run Off) Ltd* [2008] EWHC 2692 (QB), [2009] 4 All E.R. 26, at [277], [278], where the requirements of estoppel by convention were not satisfied; for the appeals in the *Durham* case, see above, para.4-100. cf. *Townsend v Persistence Holdings* [2013] UKPC 12, where vendors of a property terminated the contract under a term entitling them to do so if a licence requisite for its lawful performance were not granted within 12 months. It was held that acts done by the purchaser in relation to the property did not estop the vendor from terminating, apparently because "what happened was precisely what the contract envisaged would, or at least could, happen" (at [38]).

636 See the *Stevensdrake* case [2017] EWCA Civ 1173, approving the above phrase at [61] and [96].

637 *Mears Ltd v Shoreline Housing Partnership Ltd* [2015] EWHC 1396 (TCC) at [51], relying on Robert Goff J. in *Amalgamated Investment and Property Co Ltd v Texas Commerce Bank International Ltd* [1982] Q.B. 84 at 104 F–G (the reference to p."34" in para.[44] of the Official Transcript of the *Mears* case appears to be a misprint).

638 *Norwegian American Cruises A/S v Paul Mundy Ltd (The Vistafjord)* [1988] 2 Lloyd's Rep. 343, 352; *Hiscox v Outhwaite (No.1)* [1992] 1 A.C. 562, affirmed on other grounds at 585; *The Indian Endurance (No.2)* [1998] A.C. 878, 913; *Mitchell v Watkinson* [2014] EWCA Civ 1472, [2015] L. & T.R. 22 at [51], where para.3-107 of the 31st edition of this book (para.4-108 of the present edition) is cited with apparent approval; in that case the defence of estoppel by convention failed for want of a common assumption (at [60]—but the appeal was dismissed on other grounds, at [95]; *Musst Holdings Ltd v Astra Asset Management UK Ltd* [2020] EWHC 337 (Ch), [39] (citing this paragraph); cf. *Edray Ltd v Can-*

*ning* [2015] EWHC 2744 where the two requirements of estoppel by convention stated above (that there must be a common assumption and that it must be unjust to allow the party alleged to be estopped to resile from that assumption (at [38]) were held to have been satisfied (at [48]); and *Roundlistic Ltd v Jones* [2016] UKUT 325 where the requirements of this kind of estoppel are stated at [47] and [48] and no such estoppel was held to have arisen as the parties had not made any "common assumption" (at [50] and [56]; *Preedy v Dunne* [2016] EWCA Civ 805, [2016] C.P. Rep. 44, where, after the claim based on proprietary estoppel had been rejected at first instance, an alternative claim was made on appeal that the facts gave rise to an estoppel by convention. This claim, too, was rejected on the grounds that the parties had not made any "common assumption" ([2016] EWCA Civ 805 at [64]) and that, even if there had been such an assumption, there had been no reliance on it by the party claiming the benefit of the estoppel ([2016] EWCA Civ 805 at [64]). For the difficulties of applying estoppel by convention so as to bind members of a company pension scheme, see *Trustee Solutions v Dubery* [2006] EWHC 1426 (Ch), [2007] I.C.R. 412. They arise mainly from the need to show that "the general body of members" (at [50]) had all put the same interpretation on the scheme and had acted on the assumption. Here "the evidence was simply too exiguous" to support such a conclusion. The decision was reversed on other grounds: [2007] EWCA Civ 771, [2008] I.C.R. 101; there was no appeal on the estoppel point: see [2007] EWCA Civ 771 at [12]. For the requirements of estoppel by convention "arising out of non-contractual dealings", see *Revenue and Customs Commissioners v Benchdollar Ltd* [2009] EWHC 1310 (Ch) at [52], cited in *Grieveson v Grieveson* [2011] EWHC 1367 (Ch) at [27] and *First National Trustco (UK) Ltd v Page* [2019] EWHC 1187 (Ch) at [99]–[135].

639 cf. the discussion of the distinction between various kinds of estoppel in para.4-104, above.

640 *Amalgamated Investment & Property Co Ltd v Texas Commerce International Bank Ltd* [1982] Q.B. 84, 131–132 below, para.4-109; *Republic of Serbia v ImageSat International NV* [2008] EWHC 2853 (Comm), [2010] 1 Lloyd's Rep. 235 at [71]: "no requirement of an unequivocal *representation*" (italics supplied), as opposed to an "unambiguous and unequivocal" *assumption* (see below); *Dixon v Blindley Heath Investments Ltd* [2015] EWCA Civ 1023, [2016] 4 All E.R. 490 at [73] (not founded on a unilateral representation"); *Monde Petroleum SA v Western Zagros Ltd* [2016] EWHC 1472 (Comm), [2016] 2 Lloyd's Rep. 229 at [227] ("does not depend on any representation or promise"); *Process Components Ltd v Kason Kek-Gardner Ltd* [2016] EWHC 2198 (Ch) at [116], [117], distinguishing between estoppel by convention and estoppel by representation (in this case the requirements of both these forms of estoppel were satisfied: see at [135]). See also *Costain Ltd v Tarmac Holdings Ltd* [2017] EWHC 319 (TCC), [2017] 1 Lloyd's Rep. 333 at [101], where the statement that "Estoppel by convention depends on a shared assumption, not a representation ..." forms part of Coulson J.'s discussion of the "ingredients of estoppel by convention". In that case the attempt to invoke estoppel by convention failed on the ground that there was no "common understanding" (at [111]), no "sharp practice" (at [113]) by the party alleged to be estopped, nor any detriment suffered by the other party (at [118]) so that it would not be unconscionable for the former party to act inconsistently with any assumption, had it been made (see above).

641 The passage running from the words "the assumption being ..." to this point (then in para.3-107 of the 31st edition) was quoted with apparent approval by the Court of Appeal in *Dixon v Blindley Heath Investments Ltd* [2015] EWCA Civ 1023, [2016] 4 All E.R. 490 at [74], in turn quoting from the judgment of the Court below [2014] EWHC 1366 (Ch). In the *Dixon* case, it was further held that such an estoppel was not "confined to cases of mistake" but could extend to cases in which the common assumption of the parties had arisen simply because they had forgotten the true facts since "a mistaken recollection [was] not ... legally different from a state of forgetfulness" (at [79]). In this case the erroneous common assumption of parties to a share transfer arose because they had forgotten that valid rights of pre-emption existed in relation to the shares.

642 *Smithkline Beecham Plc v Apotex Europe Ltd* [2006] EWCA Civ 658, [2007] Ch. 71 at [102], where this point was "not disputed" and the concession was evidently approved by the Court; cf. *Commercial Union Assurance Plc v Sun Alliance Group Plc* [1992] 1 Lloyd's Rep. 475, 481 where the argument based on estoppel by convention failed as the evidence did not "clearly and unequivocally establish the agreement of the parties ... on the conventional interpretation". A passage from *Troop v Gibson* [1986] 1 E.G.L.R. 1 cited in *Baird Textile Holdings Ltd v Marks & Spencer Plc* [2001] EWCA Civ 274, [2002] 1 All E.R. (Comm) 734 at [84] must be read as denying the requirement of a representation rather than the quality of clarity of the common assumption: see the reference there to "sufficient clarity and certainty of the common assumption"; cf. *Baird Textile Holdings Ltd v Marks & Spencer Plc* at [38]; cf. the *Republic of Serbia* case [2008] EWHC 2853 (Comm) at [71] ("clarity and certainty necessary for a conventional agreement") and [81] ("with clarity"). The present requirement was doubted in *ING Bank NV v Ros Roca SA* [2011] EWCA Civ 353, [2012] 1 W.L.R. 472 at [64(iii)] but, as only one of the authorities cited in this note (viz *Troop v Gibson*) was, in this context, drawn to the attention of the Court of Appeal in the *ING* case, the doubt there expressed may call for further consideration. In *Aras v National Bank of Greece SA* [2018] EWHC 1389 (Comm) at [115] it was said that what is required "is clarity over what comprises the common assumption (if there is such a common assumption) as determined by the Court and not by the parties".

643 See *Menolly Investments 3 SARL v Cemp SARL* [2009] EWHC 516 (Ch), 125 Con. L.R. 75 where the estoppel was said to have been based on the fact that the party allegedly estopped had "represented

... that practical completion [of building works] had been achieved" (at [153(g)]) or on both parties having "conducted themselves on a common understanding or convention" to that effect (at [153h]); see also [184], where "[154]" seems to be a misprint for "[153]". The further reference to "promissory" estoppel at [154] is puzzling since, insofar as the estoppel was based on a representation, that representation (as quoted above) was one of existing fact rather than one amounting to a promise (see above, para.4-104). The further point that the estoppel was said to arise from failure to perform "a duty to speak out" (at [184]) can be explained that the case fell within one of the "exceptional circumstances" in which estoppel by representation can arise from non-disclosure, as opposed to a positive representation (below, para.7-104).

644 *Colchester BC v Smith* [1992] Ch. 421, 434.

645 Above, paras 4-048 et seq.

646 *Colchester BC v Smith*, above, at 435.

647 *Briggs v Gleeds (Head Office)* [2014] EWHC 1178 (Ch), [2015] 1 All E.R. 553 at [179]. cf. *Finmoon Ltd v Baltic Reefers Management Ltd* [2012] EWHC 920 (Comm), [2012] 2 Lloyd's Rep. 388 where, as a "contract by conduct" had come into existence (see above, para.2-029) it was "not necessary to determine" an issue relating to estoppel by convention: see at [21], [37]. In *Dixon v Blindley Heath Investments Ltd* [2015] EWCA Civ 1023, [2016] 4 All E.R. 490 the Court of Appeal did "not think that there must be expression of accord" and that the common assumption could be "inferred from conduct, or even silence ..." (at [92]), though this view did not dispense with the requirement, discussed in para.4-110 below, that "something must be shown to have 'crossed the line' to manifest an assent to the assumption" (at [92]). "Silence", could it seems, only satisfy this requirement in cases where the party alleged to be estopped was under a "duty to speak", as, for example in *Process Components Ltd v Kason Kek-Gardner Ltd* [2016] EWHC 2198 (Ch): see at [129]–[132].

## "Communication" passing "across the line"

*Replace paragraph with:*

**4-110** To give rise to an estoppel by convention, the mistaken assumption of the party claiming the benefit of the estoppel must, however, have been shared or acquiesced in by the party alleged to be estopped; and both parties must have conducted themselves on the basis of such a shared assumption[655]: the estoppel "requires communications to pass across the line between the parties. It is not enough that each of two parties acts on an assumption not communicated to the other".[656] Such communication may be effected by the conduct of one party, known to the other.[657] But no estoppel by convention arose where each party spontaneously made a different mistake and there was no subsequent conduct by the party alleged to be estopped from which any acquiescence in the other party's mistaken assumption could be inferred.[658] An estoppel by convention likewise cannot arise where neither party was aware of the facts on which the alleged common assumption is said to have been based[659]; or where the conduct alleged to have given rise to the estoppel can with equal or greater plausibility, be explained on grounds other than that the party alleged to be estopped shared an assumption made by the other party or as amounting to a communication by the former to the latter party.[660] Nor can a party (A) invoke such an estoppel to prevent the other (B) from denying facts alleged to have been agreed between A and B if A has later withdrawn from that agreement; for in the light of A's withdrawal it is no longer unjust to allow B to rely on the true state of affairs.[661]

655 *Empresa Lineas Maritimas Argentinas v The Oceanus Mutual Underwriting Association (Bermuda) Ltd* [1984] 2 Lloyd's Rep. 517 (where neither of these requirements was satisfied); *Astilleros Canarios SA v Cape Hatteras Shipping Co SA* [1982] 1 Lloyd's Rep. 518, 527; *Heinrich Hanno & Co B.V. v Fairlight Shipping Co (The Kostas K.)* [1985] 1 Lloyd's Rep. 231, 237; *The Vistafjord* [1988] 2 Lloyd's Rep. 343; *Thor Navigation Inc v Ingosstrakh Insurance* [2005] EWHC 19 (Comm), [2005] 1 Lloyd's Rep. 547 at [66]; *Fortisbank SA v Trenwick International* [2005] EWHC 399 (Comm), [2005] Lloyd's Rep. I.R. 464 at [43], where the present requirement was not satisfied; *Tamil Nadu Electricity Board v ST-CMS Electricity Company Private Ltd* [2007] EWHC 1713 (Comm), [2007] 2 All E.R. (Comm) 701 at [125], where again this requirement was not satisfied; *Bear Stearns Plc v Forum Global Equities Ltd* [2007] EWHC 1576 at [192], where again the present requirement was not satisfied but the actual decision was that the communications between the parties had given rise to a contract: see above, para.2-

122; *Briggs v Gleeds (Head Office)* [2014] EWHC 1178 (Ch), [2015] 1 All E.R. 533 at [209], where this requirement was not satisfied: see at [185], and see similarly *Yuchai Dongte Special Purpose Automobile Co Ltd v Suisse Credit Capital (2009) Ltd* [2018] EWHC 2580 (Comm), [2019] 1 Lloyd's Rep. 457 at [95].

656 *Compania Portorafti Commerciale SA v Ultramar Panama Inc (The Captain Gregos) (No.2)* [1990] 2 Lloyd's Rep. 395, 405, following *K. Lokumal & Sons (London) Ltd v Lotte Shipping Co Pty Ltd (The August P. Leonhardt)* [1985] 2 Lloyd's Rep. 28, 35; *Hiscox v Outhwaite (No.3)* [1991] 2 Lloyd's Rep. 524, 533; *The Indian Endurance* [1998] A.C. 878, 913; *Republic of Serbia v ImageSat International NV* [2009] EWHC 2853, [2010] 1 Lloyd's Rep. 325 at [69].

657 As in *The Vistafjord* [1988] 2 Lloyd's Rep. 343, 351 ("very clear conduct crossing the line ... of which the other party was fully cognisant"). An even stricter requirement was stated in *Bank Leumi (UK) Plc v Phillip Robert Akrill* [2014] EWCA Civ 909, where it was said that there was no estoppel by convention because the assumption in question had not been "*expressly* communicated" (at [55], italics supplied) between the parties, though there is also judicial support for the view that the common assumption could be inferred from conduct (see below) or even from "silence": see *Dixon v Blindley Heath Investments Ltd* [2015] EWCA Civ 1023, [2016] 4 All E.R. 490 at [92], quoted above, para.4-109.

658 *K. Lokumal & Sons (London) Ltd v Lotte Shipping Co Pty Ltd (The August P. Leonhardt)* [1985] 2 Lloyd's Rep. 28, reversing [1984] 1 Lloyd's Rep. 332, which had been followed in *The Leila*, above n.635. The present status of *The Leila* therefore remains in some doubt but the two cases can be reconciled on the ground that in *The Leila* there was, while in *The August P. Leonhardt* there was not, conduct by the party alleged to be estopped from which acquiescence in the other party's mistaken belief could be inferred.

659 *HIH Casualty & General Insurance v Axa Corporate Solutions* [2002] EWCA Civ 1253; [2002] 2 All E.R. (Comm) 1053 at [32].

660 *Blankley v Central Manchester etc. NHS Trust* [2014] EWHC 168 (QB), [2014] 2 All E.R. 1104 where the actual decision was that the state of facts which the defendant was alleged to be estopped from denying actually existed (at [59]). But it was also said (at [60]) that, if that had not been the case, the alleged estoppel would not have arisen since no inference of any shared assumption by, or communication from, the defendant could be drawn from the latter's conduct as this conduct was more readily explicable on other grounds. See too *Musst Holdings Ltd v Astra Asset Management UK Ltd* [2020] EWHC 337 (Ch) at [40] (citing this paragraph).

661 *Gloyne v Richardson* [2001] EWCA Civ 716; [2001] 2 B.C.L.C. 669 at [41]; *Zvi Construction Co LLC v Notre Dame University (USA) in England* [2016] EWHC 1924 (TCC), [2016] B.L.R. 604 where it was said at [64] that the estoppel which operated in relation to the dispute before the Court did not apply to any future disputes, presumably because by the time they arose the truth would have been revealed in the instant proceedings. But where the common assumption was that intellectual property was vested in one of the parties sharing that assumption it was held that the other party was "permanently (like a tenant or bailee) estopped from denying" that the property was so vested and that a licence agreement relating to it had been terminated: *Process Components Ltd v Kason Kek-Gardner Ltd* [2016] EWHC 2198 (Ch) at [136], apparently cross referring to [128].

## Effect of estoppel by convention

*Replace footnote 681 with:*

681 e.g. (apparently) *Troop v Gibson* [1986] 1 E.G.L.R. 1. This paragraph, and the preceding four paragraphs, were cited with approval in *Yuchai Dongte Special Purpose Automobile Co Ltd v Suisse Credit Capital (2009) Ltd* [2018] EWHC 2580 (Comm), [2019] 1 Lloyd's Rep. 457 at [83]. **4-112**

## Whether estoppel by convention creates new rights

*Replace footnote 696 with:*

696 [1988] 2 Lloyd's Rep. 343; above, para.4-109. In *Shearson Lehman Hutton Inc v Maclaine Watson & Co Ltd* [1989] 2 Lloyd's Rep. 570, the estoppel would likewise (if supported on the facts) have operated defensively; cf. also *Mitsui Babcock Energy Ltd v John Brown Energy Ltd* (1996) 51 Con. L.R. 129, 185–186 where the effect of the estoppel would (if the contract in question had not existed) again have been to *restrict* the plaintiff's rights by reference to the terms of the (in that event non-existent) contract; see too *Cargill International Trading Pte Ltd v Uttam Galva Steels Ltd* Unreported February 28, 2019 (Commercial Court) at [30]. **4-114**

### "Contractual estoppel"

*Replace footnote 719 with:*

4-116 [719] *Peekay Intermark Ltd v Australia & New Zealand Banking Group Ltd* [2006] EWCA Civ 386, [2006] 2 Lloyd's Rep. 511 at [57]; *Springwell Navigation Corp v J P Morgan Chase Bank* [2010] EWCA Civ 1221 at [157]–[170]; *Raiffeisen Zentralbank Osterreich AG v Royal Bank of Scotland Plc* [2010] EWHC 1392 (Comm), [2011] 1 Lloyd's Rep. 123 at [230]; *Cassa Di Risparmio della Republica di San Marino SpA v Barclays Bank Ltd* [2011] EWHC 484 (Comm) at [466]; *Shaker v VistaJet Group Holding SA* [2012] EWHC 1329 (Comm), heading before [18] where "contractual estoppel" is mentioned but is not the ground of decision; *First Tower Trustees Ltd v CDS (Superstores International) Ltd* [2018] EWCA Civ 1396, [2019] 1 W.L.R. 637 at [47]–[48] and [91]–[95]. See also the reference in *NRAM v McAdam* [2014] EWHC 4174 (Comm), [2015] 1 All E.R. (Comm) 1239 at [14] and [29] to "estoppel by convention and/or contractual estoppel". The phrase (at [14(iii)(a)]) "if *either* can be established" (italics supplied) appears to treat these two concepts as distinct, but it is less clear whether they are likewise treated as distinct at [29]. If the nature of "contractual estoppel" is correctly stated in the text above after the present note, then there seems in principle to be no reason why such an "estoppel" should not be used as a sword even if estoppel by convention cannot be so used (see above, para.4-114); and a hint to the contrary at [14](iii)(a)] in the *NRAM* case above is, with respect, open to question. It has been said that a statement need not be one "as to a *past* state of affairs" in order to give rise to a "contractual estoppel": *Crédit Suisse International v Sticthing Vestia Groep* [2014] EWHC 3103 (Comm) at [307]–[309]. In allowing an appeal from the decision in the *NARH* case (above) the Court of Appeal referred to "estoppel by convention and/or contractual estoppel": [2015] EWCA Civ 751, [2016] 2 All E.R. (Comm) 333 at [52] and [56]. Neither of these passages refers to any requirement that the statement or common assumption must relate to a "past" state of affairs to be capable of giving rise (in cases of alleged "contractual" estoppel) to a cause of action.

## 10. PART PAYMENT OF A DEBT

## (a) General Rule

### Effects of the rule

*Replace footnote 762 with:*

4-119 [762] See *Simantob v Shavleyan* [2018] EWHC 2005 (QB) at [127], though on the facts of the case the debtor provided consideration by agreeing not to raise various possible defences to the claim (see at [141]–[142], and upheld on this basis at [2019] EWCA Civ 1105).

## (b) Limitations at Common Law

### Disputed claims

*Replace footnote 764 with:*

4-120 [764] *Cooper v Parker* (1855) 15 C.B. 822; *Re Warren* (1884) 53 L.J. Ch. 1016; *Anangel Atlas Compania Naviera SA v Ishikawajima Harima Heavy Industries Co Ltd (No.2)* [1990] 2 Lloyd's Rep. 526, 544; for other consideration in this case, see *Anangel Atlas Compania Naviera SA v Ishikawajima Harima Heavy Industries Co Ltd (No.2)* at 545 and below, para.4-125; *Huyton SA v Peter Cremer GmbH* [1999] 1 Lloyd's Rep. 620 at 629; *Simantob v Shavleyan* [2019] EWCA Civ 1105.

## (c) Limitations in Equity

### Extinctive effects in exceptional cases

*In line 23, page [511], after "(b) the debtor's making the stipulated part payment.", add new footnote 845a:*

4-134 [845a] See too *MWB Business Exchange Centres Ltd v Rock Advertising Ltd* [2016] EWCA Civ 553, [2017] Q.B. 604 at [61]–[63] and [92] (reversed on other grounds: [2018] UKSC 24, [2018] 2 W.L.R. 1603, see below, para.22-045).

## 11. PROPRIETARY ESTOPPEL

## (c) Conditions Giving Rise to Liability

### Main elements of proprietary estoppel

*Replace footnote 934 with:*

934 *Thorner v Major* [2009] UKHL 18, [2009] 1 W.L.R. 776 at [15], [29], [42]; *Crossco No.4 Unlimited v Jolan Ltd, Note* [2011] EWCA Civ 1629, [2012] 2 All E.R. 754 at [114]; *Burton v Liden* [2016] EWCA Civ 275, [2017] 1 F.L.R. 310 at [16]; *Davies v Davies* [2014] EWCA Civ 565 at [29], also making the point that such "main elements" could not "be treated as subdivided into three or four watertight compartments" (at [30], quoting Walker L.J. in *Gillett v Holt* [2001] Ch. 210 at 232) and illustrating ways in which these elements relate to or overlap with each other; see also *Davies v Davies* [2016] EWCA Civ 463, [2016] 2 P. & C.R. 10 restating the main elements of proprietary estoppel and repeating the point that they could not be divided into "watertight compartments" (at [38]); this was followed in *Moore v Moore* [2018] EWCA Civ 2669, [2019] 1 F.L.R. 1277 at [24]–[25]. See too *Suggitt v Suggitt* [2012] EWCA Civ 1140, [2012] W.T.L.R. 1607 at [19], where Arden L.J. states the above three requirements and adds a fourth: "the relief granted by the court". As appears from these words, this fourth requirement is concerned with the legal effects of, or remedies for, proprietary estoppel, to be discussed in paras 4-168—4-180 below. The first three requirements, by contrast, are those which have to be satisfied before a proprietary estoppel can arise. In *Davies v Davies*, above, the requirements of reliance and detriment were held to have been satisfied, but the scope of the remedy was left over to be determined in later proceedings (see at [57] and [26]). See also *Thompson v Thompson* [2018] EWHC 1338 (Ch). For a case in which a daughter's claim against her mother's estate, based on proprietary estoppel, was rejected because none of the three requirements stated in the text above had been satisfied, see *Wright v Waters* [2014] EWHC 3614, [2015] W.T.L.R. 353. See also *MWB Business Exchange Centres Ltd v Rock Advertising Ltd* [2016] EWCA Civ 553, [2017] Q.B. 604 (reversed on other grounds [2018] UKSC 24, [2018] 2 W.L.R. 1603, see below, para.22-045) where the "three main elements" of proprietary estoppel are stated ([2016] EWCA Civ 553 at [65]) but it was held that no such estoppel arose because (1) the right claimed by the person relying on the estoppel was not "a proprietary right" and (2) that person had not "suffered any detriment". **4-146**

### Detrimental reliance by promisee

*Replace footnote 1022 with:*

1022 *Gillett v Holt* [2001] Ch. 210 at 232, a dictum cited with approval by Lord Neuberger in *Fisher v Brooker* [2009] UKHL 41, [2009] 1 W.L.R. 1764 at [63], stating the requirement of detriment to be "part of a broad enquiry into unconscionability". In that case the requirement was not satisfied: see at [63], [71] and [11]; *Jennings v Rice* [2002] EWCA Civ 159; [2002] W.T.L.R. 367 at [21], [42]; *Kinane v Mackie-Conteh* [2005] EWCA Civ 45, [2005] W.T.L.R. 345 at [29]; *Hopper v Hopper* [2008] EWHC 228 (CL), [2008] I F.C.R 557 at [111]. In *Habberfield v Habberfield* [2019] EWCA Civ 890 the Court of Appeal held that it would have been unconscionable for the promisor to resile from a promise to transfer the running of the farm to the promisee on the promisor's retirement (and that the promisee would inherit the farm upon the promisor's death), even though the promisee later rejected an offer to run the farm in partnership with the promisee: the partnership offer would not have fulfilled the promisee's expectation (at [30]) and was not presented as a final offer (at [44]). **4-158**

### Relationship between the Cobbe and Thorner cases

*Replace footnote 1091 with:*

1091 [2009] UKHL 18 at [97]. For the "distinction between domestic and commercial cases" in the present context, see also *Crossco No.4 Unlimited v Jolan Ltd, Note* [2011] EWCA Civ 1619, [2012] 2 All E.R. 754 at [80], [121]; *Sahota v Prior* [2019] EWHC 1418 (Ch) at [32]–[33]. **4-166**

## (d) Effects of the Doctrine

### Operation of a proprietary estoppel

*Delete footnote 1116.* **4-169**

## Estoppel may operate conditionally

*Replace footnote 1140 with:*

4-172 [1140] *Thorner v Major* [2009] UKHL 18 at [48]; cf. *Bradbury v Taylor* [2012] EWCA Civ 1208, [2013] W.T.L.R. 29 at [52], affirming the trial judge's conclusion that there was a proprietary estoppel in favour of the promisees "subject to their paying the inheritance tax attributable to" the property. See too *Moore v Moore* [2018] EWCA Civ 2669, [2019] 1 F.L.R. 1277 at [89]–[99]. See also *Malik v Kalyan* [2010] EWCA Civ 113, where the Court of Appeal (at [31] to [33]) in principle approved the trial judge's method of satisfying the "equity" by awarding ownership of the disputed property to the person claiming the benefit of the estoppel, subject to his paying half of the pecuniary legacies left by the will of the former owner of the property. The actual decision was to order a limited retrial on a point not here relevant.

## Remedy: principled discretion

*Replace paragraph with:*

4-173 The remedy in cases of proprietary estoppel is "extremely flexible", its object being "to do what is equitable in all the circumstances".[1143] Although the court thus has a considerable discretion with regard to the remedy in cases of proprietary estoppel, that discretion is not a "completely unfettered"[1144] one and a "principled approach"[1145] must be taken to its exercise. In giving effect to the "equity"[1146] account must be taken, not only of the claimant's expectations "but also of the extent of his detrimental reliance"[1147]; and there must also be "proportionality between the expectation and the detriment".[1148] For the purpose of achieving such "proportionality" regard must be had to the degree of precision of the promise giving rise to the expectation. Where this amounts to an assurance that an interest in specific property will be transferred in return for specified acts, then an order for the specific enforcement of that promise (once the acts have been done) may be the appropriate remedy.[1149] Where, on the other hand, the terms of the promise are less precise, amounting only to an assurance that some indeterminate benefit will be conferred on the promisee, so that the expectations reasonably arising from it are, at least objectively, uncertain, then the court will not give effect in full to expectations which the promisee may in fact have formed if they are "uncertain or extravagant or out of all proportion to the detriment which the claimant has suffered".[1150] In such cases, compensation in money is likely to be the more appropriate remedy. That compensation must be proportionate to the detriment, but need not be its precise equivalent[1151]: the fact that the detriment was incurred in response to a promise indicating (though in vague terms) some higher level of recompense is also to be taken into account. In *Habberfield v Habberfield* Lewison L.J. said:

> "Looking back from the moment when assurances are repudiated, the nearer the overall outcome comes to the expected reciprocal performance of requested acts in return for the assurance, the stronger will be the case for an award based on or approximating to the expectation interest created by the assurance. That does no more than to recognise party autonomy to decide for themselves what a proportionate reward would be for the contemplated detriment."[1151a]

[1143] *Roebuck v Mungovin* [1994] 2 A.C. 224 at 235; *Henry v Henry* [2010] UKPC 3, [2010] 1 All E.R. 998 at [52] ("wide discretion"); cf. the remedy granted in *Gillett v Holt* [2001] Ch. 210, below, para.4-178. Gardner, (1999) 115 L.Q.R. 348. For the flexibility of the remedy in cases of proprietary estoppel, see also *Moore v Moore* [2018] EWCA Civ 2669, [2019] 1 F.L.R. 1277; *Clark v Clark* [2006] EWHC 725, [2006] 1 F.C.R. 421, above, para.4-170; *Thorner v Curtis* [2007] EWHC 2422 (Ch), [2008] W.T.L.R. 155; *Hopper v Hopper* [2008] EWHC 228 (Ch), [2008] I F.C.R. 557; *Kim v Chasewood Park Residents Ltd* [2013] EWCA Civ 239, [2013] H.L.R. 24 (above, para.4-090) at [45]; the actual decision was that, for the reason given in para.4-146 above, no proprietary estoppel had arisen.

[1144] *Jennings v Rice* [2002] EWCA Civ 159; [2002] W.T.L.R. 367 at [43].

1145 *Jennings v Rice* [2002] EWCA Civ 159; [2002] W.T.L.R. 367 at [43].

1146 See above, para.4-170.

1147 *Jennings v Rice* [2002] EWCA Civ 159 at [49].

1148 *Jennings v Rice* [2002] EWCA Civ 159 at [36], cf. at [56] ("proportionality between remedy and detriment"); *Henry v Henry* [2010] UKPC 3 at [66] ("Proportionality lies at the heart of proprietary estoppel"); *Fischer v Brooker* [2009] UKHL 41, [2009] 1 W.L.R. 1761 at [11], where the estoppel claim failed for want of proof of detrimental reliance: above, para.4-158; for the importance of "proportionality" in assessing the amount of monetary relief available to the promise, see also *Davies v Davies* [2016] EWCA Civ 463, [2016] 2 P. & C.R. 10 at [38], quoting from the Court below; *Guest v Guest* [2020] EWCA Civ 387. See also *Suggitt v Suggitt* [2012] EWCA Civ 1140, [2012] W.T.L.R. 1607, where it is not altogether clear whether the proportionality of the remedy must be with (i) the detriment suffered by the promisee in reliance on the promise (at [44]) or (ii) the promisee's reasonable expectations generated by the promise (at [45]). The distinction between the two views is not clear cut since the terms of the promise form the starting point of both. But in *Suggitt v Suggitt* itself the considerable value of the property (see at [50]) seems to have exceeded the promisee's detriment but was nevertheless awarded (see at [27], [52] as "the values only reflect the assurances" at [50]), thus supporting the second of the above views; and *Gee v Gee* [2018] EWHC 1393 (Ch). For criticism of *Suggitt v Suggitt*, and strong support for the view that there must be proportionality between remedy and detriment, see *Habberfield v Habberfield* [2019] EWCA Civ 890 at [57]. For the relevance of the promisor's conduct *after* the facts giving rise to the estoppel, see below, para.4-176.

1149 *Jennings v Rice* [2002] EWCA Civ 159 at [45]. cf. *Joyce v Epsom and Ewell Borough Council* [2012] EWCA Civ 1398, [2013] 1 E.G.L.R. 24, where the remedy was by way of a declaration that the party relying on the estoppel was entitled to the grant of the promised right of way (for the scope of which see above, para.4-170).

1150 *Jennings v Rice* [2002] EWCA Civ 159 at [50].

1151 *Jennings v Rice* [2002] EWCA Civ 159; [2002] W.T.L.R. 367 at [43] at [51].

1151a [2019] EWCA Civ 890 at [68]. In that case, the judge had been correct to "scale down" the remedy, even though the claimant had fulfilled her side of the bargain: the remedy is flexible, and it will not generally be equitable to award the claimant more than her expectation (at [70]).

CHAPTER 5

# FORM



## 1. IN GENERAL

### Types of formal requirement

*Replace footnote 12 with:*

[12] e.g. Landlord and Tenant Act 1985 s.4; Employment Rights Act 1996 ss.1–2, 4–6 (as amended); Estate Agents Act 1979 s.18. **5-002**

### Effect of non-compliance

*Replace paragraph with:*

**5-004** Non-compliance with statutory requirements of form may produce various effects. It may make the contract void,[20] or unenforceable,[21] or unenforceable by one party[22] or enforceable only on an order of the court.[23] It may simply deprive the transaction of certain effects which it would have had, if the formal requirement had been observed, without generally impairing its validity or enforceability; this would be the case, for example, if a lease for more than three years were not made by deed[24]; if an assignment of a chose in action were made orally[25]; or if the sort of promise which is normally contained in a bill of exchange or promissory note were made orally. In some cases, a failure to satisfy a statutory requirement of form may have no effect on the validity of the contract, while in others cases it may do so in the light of the purposes of the requirement and the evidence on the facts.[25a] Failure to comply with formal requirements may also be a criminal offence, and in some cases this is the sole consequence of failure which is actually specified in the relevant statute.[26] The civil consequences of failure to comply with a statutory requirement of form in such a case would presumably depend on the court's view of the objects which the legislature sought to achieve in imposing the requirement.[26a] If the requirement was imposed to protect one of the parties to a contract, that party would probably be able to enforce the contract notwithstanding the formal defect;

whether the other party could enforce it would depend on the law's general approach to illegality discussed elsewhere in this book.[27]

[20] Bills of Sale Act (1878) Amendment Act 1882 s.9; Law of Property (Miscellaneous Provisions) Act 1989 s.2.

[21] e.g. Law of Property Act 1925 s.40 subsequently repealed and replaced by s.2 of the Law of Property (Miscellaneous Provisions) Act 1989 see above, paras 1-115, 1-119 and below, para.5-039.

[22] Timeshare, Holiday Products, Resale and Exchange Contracts Regulations 2010 (SI 2010/2960) regs 20–24 ("right of withdrawal").

[23] Consumer Credit Act 1974 ss.65 and 127.

[24] Law of Property Act 1925 s.52(1) ("void for the purpose of conveying or creating a legal estate"); and see s.54, as amended by the Law of Property (Miscellaneous Provisions) Act 1989 s.1 and Sch.1 para.2.

[25] Below, paras 19-007, 19-016, 19-037.

[25a] e.g. *David Roberts Art Foundation Ltd v Riedweg* [2019] EWHC 1358 (Ch), [2019] W.T.L.R. 741 (Chief Master Marsh), which concerned an exception to the general requirement that dispositions in land by charitable trustees can be made only on the order of the Charities Commission or the court: Charities Act 2011 Pt 7 and esp. s.117(1) and (2). The exception (contained in s.117(2)(b) of the Act) imposed certain requirements (set out in s.119) of advertising and the obtaining of a professional survey; s.122(2) imposed a further requirement of the making of a statement in the contract for the disposition of land including to the effect that the vendor is a charity and whether or not it is an exempt charity. In considering the validity of an (unexecuted) contract of sale of land by a charity, the HC distinguished between a failure by a charity to make the requisite statutory statement, which does not lead to the invalidity of the contract ("whether by being void, voidable or unenforceable") as such "an outcome would be disproportionate to the role played by the statement in the statutory regime" (at [89]). On the other hand, the requirement as to advertising "ought to be interpreted in light of the overriding test that emerges from section 119(1)(c) namely that the terms of the disposition are the best that can reasonably be obtained for the charity"; equally, if the court is satisfied that the disposal achieves the best price reasonably obtainable, the transaction would not be unenforceable because a surveyor's report was obtained later than envisaged by the statute. In both respects, however, the charity had failed to provide cogent evidence and so summary judgment was refused: at [101].

[26] e.g. Landlord and Tenant Act 1962 s.1, repealed and replaced by Landlord and Tenant Act 1985 s.4; *Shaw v Groom* [1970] 2 Q.B. 504.

[26a] cf. the approach of the court in *David Roberts Art Foundation Ltd v Riedweg* [2019] EWHC 1358 (Ch) noted above in this paragraph.

[27] See below, paras 16-175 et seq.

### Impact on formality requirements

*Replace paragraph with:*

**5-007** At first sight, art.9 of this Directive might appear to have required the United Kingdom to revise a good deal of its law of contractual formalities, much of which requires a contract to be contained or evidenced in writing and/or signed, neither of these appearing to be able to be achieved by electronic means. However, the Law Commission advised the Government that in general requirements of "writing" and of "signature" can be fulfilled via some electronic means without any changes being made to the law.[39] So, as to "writing" this requirement can be fulfilled by electronic mail and website trading, but not by electronic data interchange as this does not involve any visible text so as to satisfy s.5 of the Interpretation Act 1978's definition of writing.[40] Its view was that "writing" does not need any "physical memorial", such as paper.[41] Secondly, the Law Commission's view was that requirements of signature can generally be interpreted in a functional way, by asking whether or not the conduct of a would-be signatory indicates an authenticating intention to a reasonable person, though each requirement must be considered in its own statutory context.[42] Following this approach, a requirement of signature can be fulfilled in a number of ways: by "electronic signature" using a dual-key encryption system and a certification authority[43]; by use of a manuscript signature scanned into a computer and incorporated into an email or other document; by a person typing their name or initials or by setting up a system by which this occurs automatically[44]; and even by a purchaser on a website "clicking" a button after entering onto the web details of the goods that they wish to purchase, confirming payment and personal details.[45] The Law Commission concluded that:

> "... there is no need for general legislative reform, because we consider that legislation is not only unnecessary but also risky. It is difficult to envisage a simple global reform that would be effective in all eventualities ... [So], it is only in very rare cases that the statute book will conflict with Article 9 of the Electronic Commerce Directive."[46]

Where legislative change is needed, it can be effected by exercise of the power contained in s.8 of the Electronic Communications Act 2000. One particular context in which this may need to be the case is s.2 of the Law of Property (Miscellaneous) Provisions Act 1989. For, as will be explained, in this context it has been said that "signature" must be given its ordinary linguistic meaning, so as to require each of the parties to contracts for the sale or other disposition of an interest in land to write their names with their own hands upon the document.[47] However, some or all of the contracts contained within this category may come within one of the exceptions to art.9 of the EU Directive so as to allow English law to retain a formal requirement which is inconsistent with the effectiveness of a contract made by electronic means.[48] Moreover, the courts may well consider that in some other statutory contexts (for example, contracts of guarantee under s.4 of the Statute of Frauds) either "writing" or "signature" should not be interpreted as broadly as the Law Commission generally propose, in the interests of the protection of the person to be bound thereby.[49] Here, without legislative intervention, a conflict may arise between the interpretation of the English courts and the requirements of art.9 of the Electronic Commerce Directive, which does allow a Member State to make an exception for contracts of suretyship but only where undertaken by persons "acting outside their trade, business or profession".[50]

39 Law Commission, *Electronic Commerce: Formal Requirements in Commercial Transactions* (2001), available in full at *http://lawcommission.justice.gov.uk* and see a shorter version in Beale and Griffiths (2002) L.M.C.L.Q. 467 to which the following references will relate. The Law Commission has recently confirmed its view to this effect for signatures required for documents generally, while acknowledging "that there are situations in which the law is more prescriptive as to the form or type of signature required": *Electronic execution of documents*, Law Com. No.386 (September 3, 2019) Ch.3 esp. para.3.4.

40 Beale and Griffiths (2002) L.M.C.L.Q. 467, 471–472. The Interpretation Act 1978 s.5 states that: "'Writing' includes typing, printing, lithography, photography and other modes of representing or reproducing words in a visible form, and expressions referring to writing are construed accordingly."

41 Beale and Griffiths (2002) L.M.C.L.Q. 467, 472.

42 Beale and Griffiths (2002) L.M.C.L.Q. 467, 473.

43 And see below, para.5-008.

44 In *J Pereira Fernandes SA v Mehta* [2006] EWHC 813 (Ch), [2006] 2 All E.R. 881 at [25]–[30], it was held that the automatic insertion of an email address in a message by an internet service provider did not constitute a signature by the writer of the message as it did not represent any intention to authenticate the message by the writer. However, Judge Pelling Q.C. accepted that: "[I]f a party or a party's agent sending an e-mail types his or her or his or her principal's name to the extent required or permitted by existing case law in the body of an e-mail, then ... that would be sufficient signature for the purposes of section 4 [of the Statute of Frauds]" (at [31]), the learned judge noting the position of the Law Commission to this effect. In *Golden Ocean Group Ltd v Salgaocar Mining Industries Pvt Ltd* [2012] EWCA Civ 265, [2012] 1 Lloyd's Rep. 542 at [32] it was common ground before (and accepted by) the CA that an electronic signature is sufficient for the purposes of s.4 of the Statute of Frauds and that a first name, initials or perhaps a nickname will suffice, as long as it was done in a manner which indicates that it is intended to authenticate the document. And in *Bassano v Toft* [2014] EWHC 377 (QB),

[2014] E.C.C. 14 at [42]–[44] it was held that clicking an electronic "I accept" button and thereby generating a document sent to the other party bearing the "signatory's" typed name constituted signature for the purposes of s.61 of the Consumer Credit Act 1974: see Vol.II, para.39-083. The Law Commission has recently reaffirmed its general view as to the ways in which an electronic signature can be established: *Electronic execution of documents*, Law Com. No.386 (September 3, 2019) paras 3.42 et seq., discussing cases where a disputed electronic or non-handwritten signature has been held not to have satisfied a statutory requirement for a signature.

[45] Beale and Griffiths (2002) L.M.C.L.Q. 467, 473–474.

[46] Beale and Griffiths (2002) L.M.C.L.Q. 467, 473.

[47] *Firstpost Homes Ltd v Johnson* [1995] 1 W.L.R. 1567, 1574–1577 and see below, paras 5-037—5-037C discussing more recent authority on the point.

[48] Directive 2000/31 art.9(2)(a), above, para.5-006.

[49] cf. *J Pereira Fernandes SA v Mehta* [2006] EWHC 813 (Ch), [2006] 2 All E.R. 881 at [31], where the Law Commission's broad approach was approved.

[50] Directive 2000/31 art.9(2)(d), above, para.5-006.

*To the end of title, add new footnote 50a:*

**Electronic signatures**[50a]

5-008 [50a] See also Law Commission, *Electronic execution of documents*, Law Com. No.386 (September 3, 2019), esp. Ch.3.

*Replace paragraph with:*

5-008 In 1999, the EU legislator enacted the Electronic Signatures Directive,[51] the purposes of which were to facilitate the use of "electronic signatures" and to contribute to their legal recognition, and to establish a legal framework for electronic signatures and certain certification services. It expressly did not cover aspects relating to the conclusion or validity of contracts or other legal obligations where there are requirements as regards form imposed by national or Community law, nor the rules and limits governing the use of documents.[52] An "electronic signature" was defined by the Directive as:

> "... data in electronic form which are attached to or logically associated with other electronic data and which serve as a method of authentication."[53]

The United Kingdom implemented the Electronic Signatures Directive 1999 by two instruments. First, s.7 of the Electronic Communications Act 2000 provided for the admissibility in evidence of electronic signatures and certification by any person of such a signature:

> "in relation to any question as to the authenticity of the communication or data or as to the integrity of the communication or data"

and followed for this purpose the definition of "electronic signature" in the Directive.[54] On its terms, this provision was broad enough to include evidence for the purposes of formal requirements of a contract (such as s.2 of the Law of Property (Miscellaneous Provisions) Act 1989[55]), but, if it were so interpreted, it would go beyond the scope of the requirements of the 1999 Directive. Secondly, the Electronic Signatures Regulations 2002 provided for the supervision and liability of "certification-service providers" (i.e. persons who issue certificates or provide other services related to electronic signatures) and for consequential matters relating to data protection.[56] However, the Electronic Signatures Directive 1999 was repealed and replaced by the EU Electronic Identification and Electronic Trust Services Regulation 2014 (the "eIDAS Regulation", applicable in general from July

1, 2016),[57] which lays down the conditions under which Member States mutually recognise "electronic identification means of natural persons and legal persons falling under a notified electronic identification scheme of another Member State",[57a] and "rules for trust services, in particular for electronic transactions"; and which establishes:

> "... a legal framework for electronic signatures, electronic seals, electronic time stamps, electronic documents, electronic registered delivery services and certificate services for website authentication."[58]

Article 25(1) of the eIDAS Regulation provides that:

> "An electronic signature shall not be denied legal effect and admissibility as evidence in legal proceedings solely on the grounds that it is in an electronic form or that it does not meet the requirements for qualified electronic signatures."[58a]

However, following the pattern of the 1999 Directive, the eIDAS Regulation also provides expressly that it:

> "... does not affect national or Union law related to the conclusion and validity of contracts or other legal or procedural obligations relating to form."[59]

Instead, its main purpose is to ensure that businesses and individuals can use their own national electronic identification schemes (eIDs) to access public services in other EU countries where electronic identification schemes are available. It also aims to create a European internal market for electronic trust services—electronic signatures, electronic seals, time stamps, etc.—by ensuring that they will work across borders and have the same legal status as traditional paper-based processes.[60] By way of implementation of some aspects of the eIDAS Regulation, the United Kingdom revoked and replaced the Electronic Signature Regulations 2002 by the Electronic Identification and Trust Services for Electronic Transactions Regulations 2016, which came into force on July 22, 2016.[61] The 2016 Regulations also amended s.7 of the Electronic Communications Act 2000 so as to follow the simplified definition of "electronic signature" in the eIDAS Regulation as:

> "... so much of anything in electronic form as—
>
> (a) is incorporated into or otherwise logically associated with any electronic communication or electronic data; and
> (b) purports to be used by the individual creating it to sign."[62]

The main import of s.7 remains the same, viz to make general provision for the recognition of electronic signatures as evidence in legal proceedings.[63] The 2016 Regulations also made new provision for electronic seals and related certificates, electronic time stamps and related certificates, electronic documents and related certificates, and electronic registered delivery service and related certificates.[64] However, the eIDAS Regulation itself (as earlier noted[65]) does not affect the law governing the definitions of signature for the purposes of formal requirements of English contract law[66]; nor does its provision for "electronic seals" affect the common law or statutory requirements for the execution of a deed.[67] It is submitted that the uncertainty as to the impact of s.7 of the Electronic Communications Act 2000 in relation to these same formalities remains after its amendment by the 2016 Regulations.[68]

[51] Directive 1999/93 on a Community framework for electronic signatures [2000] O.J. L13/12.

[52] Directive 1999/93 art.1.

[53] Directive 1999/93 art.2(1).

[54] Electronic Communications Act 2000 s.7(2) (as enacted).

[55] On which see below, paras 5-010 et seq.

[56] SI 2002/318.

[57] Regulation (EU) 910/2014 of 23 July 2014 on electronic identification and trust services for electronic transactions in the internal market and repealing Directive 1999/93/EC [2014] O.J. L 257/73 art.52(2) (with the exceptions there noted). On IP completion day (on which generally see above, paras 1-014 et seq.), the eIDAS Regulation is due to remain part of UK law as "retained EU law" but subject to considerable amendment: see the Electronic Identification and Trust Services for Electronic Transactions (Amendment etc.) (EU Exit) Regulations 2019 (SI 2019/89) ("SI 2019/89") reg.2 and Sch. (the reference in reg.1(2) to these regulations coming into force on "exit day" must be read as referring to IP completion day: European Union (Withdrawal Agreement) Act 2020 s.39(1), Sch.5 para.1). Apart from its refocusing on the UK, the amendments are due to remove Ch.II's provisions (arts 6–12) on electronic identification.

[57a] On IP completion day (on which see the previous note), these words in art.1(a) are due to be deleted: SI 2019/89 reg.2(1)(a) and Sch. para.2.

[58] Regulation (EU) 910/2014 art.1 (amendments due on IP completion day: SI 2019/89 reg.2(1)(a) and Sch. para.2).

[58a] See also eIDAS Regulation recital 21.

[59] Regulation (EU) 910/2014 art.2(3) (on IP completion day, the reference to "national or Union law" is due to be replaced with "the law": SI 2019/89 reg.2(1)(a) and Sch. para.3) and see alsorecital 21.

[60] See EU Commission, *https://ec.europa.eu/digital-single-market/en/trust-services-and-eid.*

[61] SI 2016/696. On IP completion day, the 2016 Regulations are due to be subject to minor amendment: SI 2019/89 reg.2(1)(d), Sch. para.60.

[62] 2000 Act s.7(2) as amended by SI 2016/696 reg.5, Sch.3 para.1(2). The definition of certification of such an electronic signature was amended to similar effect: 2000 Act s.7(3) as amended by SI 2016/696 reg.5, Sch.3 para.1(3).

[63] Electronic Communications Act 2000 s.7(1). See also Law Commission, *Electronic execution of documents*, Law Com. No.386 (September 3, 2019) para.3.19 where it is also noted that there are opposing views as to whether s.7 is relevant to the question as to the extent to which existing statutory signature requirements are capable of being satisfied electronically.

[64] Electronic Communications Act 2000 ss.7A–7D (as inserted by SI 2016/696 reg.5, Sch.3 para.1(4)).

[65] Regulation (EU) 910/2014 art.2(3). Later general statements in the Regulation, such as the statement in art.25(2) that "[a] qualified electronic signature shall have the equivalent legal effect of a handwritten signature" must be read subject to the general definition of the scope of the Regulation in art.2(3).

[66] This position is taken by the Law Commission, *Electronic execution of documents*, Law Com. No.386 (September 3, 2019) paras 3.32–3.34 noting art.2(3) of the eIDAS Regulation and giving by way of examples of a contractual formality in the situations where the law requires a signature to be witnessed or to be "in a specified form (such as being handwritten)". "Signature" is relevant to the formal requirements imposed, inter alia, by the Law of Property (Miscellaneous Provisions) Act 1989 s.1 in relation to deeds (on which see above, para.1-125); by s.2 of the same Act in relation to contracts for the sale or other disposition of an interest in land (on which see below, paras 5-010 et seq. and esp. paras 5-037—5-037D); and by the Statute of Frauds s.4 in relation to contracts of guarantee (on which see Vol.II, paras 45-042 et seq. and esp. para.45-057). The position as regards the so-called rule in *L'Estrange v F Graucob Ltd* [1934] 2 K.B. 394 which governs the incorporation of written terms by signature (on which see below, para.13-002) is more arguable as it is not clear that the incorporation of contract terms relates to the "conclusion and validity of contracts or other legal or procedural obligations relating to form" within the meaning of the exclusion from the scope of the eIDAS Regulation reg.2(3).

[67] See above, paras 1-120 et seq.

[68] For further discussion of "signature" and electronic communications see *Emmet & Farrand on Title* (2019), paras 2-041—2-041.06.

### Electronic documents and deeds

*Replace paragraph with:*

Following the recommendations of the Law Commission,[69] the Land Registration Act 2002 made provision for the creation of a framework in which it will be possible to transfer and create interests in registered land by electronic means through a network controlled by the Land Registry.[70] In order to permit this, Pt 8 of the Act makes provision for the fulfilment electronically of formality requirements by the transactions in question, doing so by assimilating certain qualifying electronic documents to deeds for the purposes of any enactment requiring the dispositions to which those documents relate to use a deed. However, the system of electronic conveyancing which these legislation provisions envisaged has not been brought into being and the Law Commission has made recommendations that would enable a modified scheme to be brought into effect.[71] **5-009**

[69] Law Commission, *Land Registration for the Twenty-First Century, A Conveyancing Revolution* (2001), Law Com. No.271 and see above, para.1-123.

[70] See Smith, *Property Law*, 9th edn (2017), pp.113–115 discussing the Land Registration Act 2002 and noting that in 2011 the Land Registry halted the e-conveyancing project: *Land Registry Annual Report and Accounts* 2010–2011, p.26; Megarry and Wade, *The Law of Real Property*, 8th edn (2012) by Harpum, Bridge and Dixon, paras 7-160—7-166; *Emmet & Farrand on Title* (2019), paras 9-003–9-005.

[71] See further Law Commission, *Updating the Land Registration Act 2002*, Law Com. No.380 (July 2018) Ch.20, noting (at paras 20.2 and 20.9) that, though progress has been made, the electronic system envisaged by the 2002 Act had not been developed, and making recommendations on three specific issues: the requirement for simultaneous completion and registration, the power to "switch on" electronic conveyancing and the power to "switch off" paper-based conveyancing, and the ability to overreach an interest under a trust if a single conveyancer has signed a deed on behalf of multiple trustees. See also Department of Housing, Communities and Local Government, *Improving the home buying and selling process: summary of responses to the call for evidence and government response* (April 2018). According to *Emmet & Farrand on Title* (2019), para.9-003, "a revival [of the move to electronic conveyancing] may be under way" by virtue of the Land Registration (Amendment) Rules 2018 (SI 2018/70) (in force April 6, 2018), r.6 of which revoked the Land Registration (Electronic Conveyancing) Rules 2008 (SI 2008/1750). *Emmet & Farrand* quotes the explanatory memorandum to the 2018 Rules, para.7.3 which states that: "HM Land Registry is building a new digital mortgage service and will build other digital services in the future. The principal rules will specify that all transactions of registered land that have to be registered can be carried out using electronic documents with electronic signatures, once the registrar is satisfied that adequate arrangements are in place, and publishes a notice to that effect". The memorandum refers to the Land Registration Rules 2003 (SI 2003/1417) rr.54A–54D entitled "Electronic dispositions" (as inserted by the 2018 Rules Sch.1 para.11).

## 2. Contracts for the Sale or Other Disposition of an Interest in Land

## (a) Contracts within s.2 of the Law of Property (Miscellaneous Provisions) Act 1989

### Section 2 and "executory" or "contingent" agreements

*Replace footnote 100 with:*

[100] *Singh v Beggs* (1996) 71 P. & C.R. 120; *Kahrmann v Harrison-Morgan* [2019] EWCA Civ 2094 at [106] (CA prepared to accept this proposition on the "rather slender authority" of *Singh v Beggs*). cf. *McManus v Cooke* (1887) L.R. 35 Ch. D 681 (executory contract within s.4 of the Statute of Frauds 1677). **5-016**

### Variations

*Replace footnote 115 with:*

[115] *Glen Courtney v Corp Ltd* [2006] EWCA Civ 518 at [12]–[14] applied *Oakley v Harper McKay Developments Ltd* [2018] EWHC 3405 (Ch) at [73]–[79]. See also *Ladywalk LLP v Revenue and* **5-018**

*Customs Commissioners* [2020] UKFTT 207 (TC) at [253]–[257] (agreement was "a further contractual arrangement that operates by reference to, and takes its meaning from" the earlier contract for the sale of land but did not vary it: at [257]).

## Options and rights of pre-emption

*Replace paragraph with:*

5-020 In *Spiro v Glencrown Properties Ltd*[127] the question arose whether an option granted by a vendor of land is a "contract for the sale or other disposition of an interest in land" within the meaning of s.2(1) of the 1989 Act.[128] Hoffmann J. held that it was, but that the notice by which the option was exercised was not: the section

> "... was intended to prevent disputes over whether the parties had entered into a binding agreement or over what terms they had agreed. It prescribes the formalities for recording their mutual consent. But only the grant of the option depends upon consent. The exercise of the option is a unilateral act. It would destroy the very purpose of the option if the purchaser had to obtain the vendor's countersignature to the notice by which it was exercised."[129]

As Scott L.J. observed in a later case, the alternative view which Hoffmann J. rejected, and according to which the exercise of options is subject to the section's formal requirements, would mean that it "had by an unintended side wind destroyed the enforceability of options".[130] The approach of Hoffmann J. has been held to apply equally to a "put option" in a lease (i.e. one where it is the potential grantor or lessor who is to exercise it), as well as to a "call option" (as in *Spiro v Glencrown Properties Ltd*,[131] where it is the potential grantee or purchaser who can exercise the option).[132] On the other hand, the position of a right of pre-emption (under which a person holding an interest grants another person a right to acquire it if he chooses to sell) is less clear.[133] As regards registered land, a right of pre-emption is deemed by statute to have effect "from the time of creation as an interest capable of binding successors in title" and this strongly suggests that it should be regarded as an "interest in land" for the purposes of s.2[134]; but as regards unregistered land a right of pre-emption has been held to confer:

> "... no immediate right upon the prospective purchaser. It imposes a negative obligation on the possible vendor requiring him to refrain from selling the land to any other person without giving to the holder of the right of first refusal the opportunity of purchasing in preference to any other buyer."[135]

For this reason, the 1989 Act is thought not to apply to any contract which creates a right of pre-emption over unregistered land.[136] However, this leaves the question as to the application of s.2 to any subsequent agreement arising from the right of pre-emption. In *Bircham & Co, Nominees Ltd v Worrell Holdings Ltd*,[137] a clause in a lease was held to have created a mere right of pre-emption (as opposed to an option) in a landlord in respect of its tenant's interest in the land and the tenant notified the landlord of the circumstances giving rise to the latter's opportunity to acquire this interest in exercise of this right. In these circumstances, the Court of Appeal held that any "acceptance" by the landlord of this offer by the tenant in its notice could take effect only by contract and had therefore to conform to the formal requirements of s.2 of the 1989 Act.

[127] [1991] Ch. 537; and see Jenkins [1993] Conv. 13.

[128] As Scott L.J. remarked in a later case "[i]t is evident that the draftsman of this section did not take account of options": *Trustees of the Chippenham Golf Club v North Wiltshire DC* (1991) 64 P. & C.R. 527, 530.

[129] [1991] Ch. 537, 541, per Hoffmann J.; *Bircham & Co, Nominees Ltd v Worrell Holdings Ltd* [2001] EWCA Civ 775, (2001) 82 P. & C.R. 34 at [39]–[45].

[130] *Trustees of the Chippenham Golf Club v North Wiltshire DC* (1991) 64 P. & C.R. 527, 530; and see further *Tootal Clothing Ltd v Guinea Properties Ltd* (1991) 64 P. & C.R. 452, 455.

[131] [1991] Ch. 537. See also *Sharma v Simposh Ltd* [2011] EWCA Civ 1383, [2012] 1 P. & C.R. 12 at [11].

[132] *Active Estates Ltd v Parness* [2002] EWHC 893, [2002] B.P.I.R. 865.

[133] Smith, *Property Law*, 9th edn (2017), pp.103–104; *Emmet & Farrand on Title* (2020), paras 2.085–2.089.

[134] Land Registration Act 2002 s.115; Smith, *Property Law*, 9th edn (2017), p.104. cf. *Emmet & Farrand on Title* (2020), para.2.089.

[135] *Mackay v Wilson* (1947) 47 S.R. (NSW) 315, 325, per Street J. quoted with approval by Goff and Stephenson L.JJ. in *Pritchard v Briggs* [1980] Ch. 338, 390 and 423 respectively.

[136] Smith, *Property Law*, 9th edn (2017) p.104, but see the discussion in *Emmet & Farrand on Title* (2020), para.2.086; Megarry and Wade, *The Law of Real Property*, 8th edn (2012) by Harpum, Bridge and Dixon, para.15-018.

[137] [2001] EWCA Civ 775, (2001) 82 P. & C.R. 34.

### Partnerships

*Replace footnote 180 with:*

[180] [2004] EWHC 2547 at [203], per Lewison J. Cf. *Bennett v Bennett* [2018] EWHC 1931 (Ch) at [295]–[296] where it was held, obiter, that s.2 does not apply to a contract of partnership formed for the purpose of buying and conducting business on land owned by a stranger to the partnership. **5-028**

## (b) Formal Requirements

### "All the terms which the parties have expressly agreed in one document": generally

*Replace paragraph with:*

At first sight, the omission of an express term of an oral agreement would seem to have the effect of rendering the whole contract a nullity as one can "only be made ... by incorporating all the terms ... expressly agreed".[212] However, s.2(4) of the Act recognises the power of the court to order the rectification of a written document so as to conform with the express terms of the oral agreement which it records and provides that where a written document relating to the sale of land has been so rectified, "the contract shall come into being, or be deemed to have come into being, at such a time as may be specified in the order". In *Firstpost Homes Ltd v Johnson*,[213] the Court of Appeal explained what is meant by the requirement that the contract be made in one document. There, an owner of certain farm property had agreed orally with a director of a company to sell the property to it at a cost of £1,000 per acre. The director had then typed a letter purporting to come from the owner agreeing to sell the land at this price, with a place for her signature and with an enclosed plan, which showed the land in question outlined in colour and which was signed by the director. The Court of Appeal held that, on these facts, the requirements of s.2 of the 1989 Act had not been fulfilled, as the letter and the plan constituted two documents (the former referring to the latter as being enclosed with it), but the letter (which allegedly contained the contract) had not been signed by the director on behalf of the company as was required.[214] This decision was ap- **5-033** plied in *Francis v F Berndes Ltd*,[215] where the document allegedly recording the agreement "was in form no more than a counter-signed offer, and ... did not set out in writing the obligation to purchase" by the claimants.[216] While:

> "... this is a highly technical distinction, and one which may be productive of injustice in cases where the nature of the 'missing' term is obvious once the document is construed in its factual context, ... one of the main purposes of the 1989 Act was to produce certainty in relation to contracts for the sale of land, and to reduce as far as possible the need for extrinsic evidence to establish the terms of the contract."[217]

In this respect, Lord Sumption has recently drawn attention to the useful role of entire agreement clauses which usually provide that the document sets out "the entire agreement between the parties and supersede[s] all proposals and prior agreements, arrangements and understandings between the parties".[218] In the context of contracts for the sale of land, such a clause can serve the important function of ensuring that a contract is not avoided under s.2 of the 1989 Act on the ground that the terms are not all contained in one document.[219]

*Shelford v Revenue and Customs Commissioners* illustrates the impact of s.2's requirement that all the terms agreed by the parties must be contained in one document in a very different context.[219a] In that case, the First-tier Tribunal (Tax Chamber) considered four arrangements made by the deceased (D) with a view to removing the value of his home from his estate: (i) a trust deed by which D transferred the property to trustees (D and his solicitor), with D retaining a life interest in possession in the property; (ii) a sale by D of his life interest to the trustees for a price (its current value) on standard terms (which included an entire agreement clause); (iii) a loan agreement under which D loaned the trustees the same sum as the price; and (iv) a deed of assignment by D of the benefit of the loan agreement to his children. In these circumstances, the tribunal held that the sale of the house and the loan in fact formed part of a composite agreement: the true effect of the documents was that D agreed to sell the house to the trustees with completion to occur (and the price paid) on notice following his death.[219b] This being the case, it held the sale agreement void under the s.2 of the 1989 Act in that it did not incorporate all the terms of the contract of sale of the freehold, the tribunal rejecting the arguments that the loan formed a collateral agreement or that, on its terms, the sale agreement incorporated the loan agreement by reference.[219c] The entire agreement clause did not affect this decision.[219d] Moreover, the fact that the two agreements did not reflect the true agreement of the parties meant that, even if read together, they could not satisfy the requirement of s.2 as to the incorporation of all the terms of the sale.[219e]

212 Law of Property (Miscellaneous Provisions) Act 1989 s.2(1). Section 2 does not affect the court's approach to the construction of the contract, so that the usual principles apply, including as to the relevance of background facts where appropriate and the correction of mistakes: *Westvilla Properties v Dow Properties Ltd* [2010] EWHC 30 (Ch), [2010] 2 P. & C.R. 19 at [19]–[20]; *Rabiu v Marlbray Ltd* [2013] EWHC 3272 (Ch) at [14] and [91] (one of several joined cases reversed on other grounds sub nom. *Marlbray Ltd v Laditi* [2016] EWCA Civ 476) and see on construction generally below paras 13-041 et seq. The questions discussed in this paragraph are to be distinguished from the question as to whether and, if so, how s.2 applies to composite transactions, that is, where the parties have chosen to structure their agreement so that the land contract is separated from the rest of the transaction, on which see above, para.5-029.

213 [1995] 1 W.L.R. 1567.

214 See below, paras 5-036—5-038.

215 [2011] EWHC 3377 (Ch), [2012] 1 All E.R. (Comm) 735.

[216] [2011] EWHC 3377 (Ch) at [26].

[217] [2011] EWHC 3377 (Ch) at [27], per Henderson J. Cf. *Kuznetsov v Camden LBC* [2019] EWHC 805 (Ch) at [50] and [56] (a letter signed by one party and returned signed by the other party which incorporated all terms essential to the contract and omitted no other terms can satisfy the requirements of s.2 (appeal from striking out)).

[218] *Rock Advertising Ltd v MWB Business Exchange Centres Ltd* [2018] UKSC 24, [2018] 2 W.L.R. 1603 at [14].

[219] *Rock Advertising Ltd v MWB Business Exchange Centres Ltd* [2018] UKSC 24 at [14] referring to *McGrath v Shah* (1898) 57 P & C.R. 451, 459 where a similar point was made in relation to the earlier formal requirements in the Law of Property Act 1925 s.40(1). On "entire agreement clauses" more generally, see above, para.13-117.

[219a] [2020] UKFTT 53 (TC).

[219b] [2020] UKFTT 53 (TC) at [71].

[219c] [2020] UKFTT 53 (TC) at [77]–[84]. As a result, the tribunal held the deed of assignment void on the ground of common fundamental mistake as there were no sale proceeds on which the deed could "bite": at [85]. The result was that the house formed part of D's estate for tax purposes.

[219d] [2020] UKFTT 53 (TC) at [79]. The entire agreement clause incorporated by reference from the Standard Conditions of Sale (3rd Edition) stated that "This Agreement constitutes the entire contract between the Seller and the Buyer and may only be varied or modified (whether by way of collateral contract or otherwise) in writing under the hands of the Seller and the Buyer or their respective Solicitors" (quoted, [2020] UKFTT 53 (TC) at [20]) but the aspect of the entire agreement clause argued before the tribunal was that it permitted no oral variation, whereas the tribunal held that the loan agreement did not constitute a collateral agreement to the sale agreement and therefore did not directly address the significance of the "entire contract" aspect of the clause.

[219e] [2020] UKFTT 53 (TC) at [83].

## "Exchange of contracts"

*Replace footnote 231 with:*

[231] The Court of Appeal distinguished its earlier unreported decision in *Hooper v Sherman* November 30, 1994 which took a different position adding that it had been made on the basis of a wrong concession by counsel: [1995] Ch. 259, 289, 295. Cf. *Kuznetsov v Camden LBC* [2019] EWHC 805 (Ch) at [49]–[59] (*Commission for the New Towns v Cooper (Great Britain) Ltd* does not establish that a letter which was signed by one party and returned signed by the other party (and in this sense "exchanged") cannot satisfy the requirements of s.2 as it may be "made in writing … incorporating all the terms which the parties have expressly agreed" (appeal from striking out)). **5-035**

## Meaning of "signature"

*Replace paragraph with:*

What is required for a party to be held to have signed a document for the purposes of s.2 of the 1989 Act has been the subject of some controversy. In *Firstpost Homes Ltd v Johnson*[238] the director of the claimant company (the purchaser) agreed orally with the defendant (the seller) to buy some land and he prepared a letter for her to sign addressed to himself. She signed the letter, but he did not do so, signing only the enclosed plan of the property. First, the Court of Appeal in *Firstpost Homes Ltd* held that the letter and the plan could not form a single document so as to comply with s.2's requirements of signature; instead, the letter was one document which incorporated the terms in the plan (a second document) by reference, and the plan had not been signed by the purchaser.[239] In these circumstances, the Court of Appeal held that the requirements of s.2 had not been satisfied. For this purpose, the Court considered what is required for a document to be "signed" and, in particular, whether this requires a manuscript signature and, secondly, it made clear the need for the signature to authenticate the whole document. **5-037**

[238] [1995] 1 W.L.R. 1567.

[239] [1995] 1 W.L.R. 1567 at 1573 (Peter Gibson L.J., with whom Hutchinson L.J. agreed; Balcombe L.J. gave a separate judgment agreeing with Peter Gibson L.J.).

*Add new paragraphs:*

**5-037A** Having held that the letter and the plan could not form a single document so as to comply with s.2's requirements of signature, Peter Gibson L.J. considered whether, if the letter was itself a contract, the name and address of the purchaser as addressee of the letter could constitute the purchaser's signature. He held that it could not and observed that "it is an artificial use of language to describe the printing or the typing of the name of an addressee in the letter as the signature by the addressee when he has printed or typed that document" and quoted with approval a dictum of Denning L.J. in *Goodman v J. Eban Ltd* according to which "[i]n modern English usage, when a document is required to be 'signed by' someone, that means that he must write his name with his own hand upon it".[240] In doing so, Peter Gibson L.J. expressly rejected the "liberal interpretation" of the statutory formalities in earlier authorities[241] given the "new and different philosophy" of the requirements of s.2 of the 1989 Act[242] and he rejected recourse to this "ancient baggage, particularly when it does not leave the "signed" with a meaning which the ordinary man would understand it to have" though he added that "[t]his decision is of course limited to a case where the party whose signature is said to appear on a contract is only named as the addressee of a letter prepared by him. No doubt other considerations will apply in other circumstances".[243] Despite this qualification, the Court of Appeal in *Firstpost Homes Ltd* clearly considered that a "signature" for the purposes of s.2 required that the party "write his name with his own hand upon [the document]".[244]

[240] [1995] 1 W.L.R. 1567 at 1575 quoting Denning L.J. (dissenting) in *Goodman v J. Eban Ltd* [1954] 1 Q.B. 550 at 561. However, while he expressed some sympathy for the view that a manuscript signature should be required (at 555), Sir Raymond Evershed M.R. (with whom Romer L.J. agreed at 563) held that, following the established approach in the authorities, "the essential requirement of signing is the affixing in some way, whether by writing with a pen or pencil or by otherwise impressing upon the document, one's name or 'signature' so as personally to authenticate the document" (at 557) and so a rubber stamp of the signed name of a firm of solicitors *could* satisfy the requirement of signature by the solicitor of a bill of costs under Solicitors Act 1932 s.65: at 557–559.

[241] [1995] 1 W.L.R. 1567 at 1574–1575, discussing in particular *Evans v Hoare* [1892] 1 Q.B. 593 decided in the context of the Statute of Frauds 1677 s.4.

[242] [1995] 1 W.L.R. 1567 at 1576.

[243] [1995] 1 W.L.R. 1567 at 1576 and see similarly at 1577 (Balcombe L.J.).

[244] [1995] 1 W.L.R. 1567 at 1575 quoting Denning L.J. as noted above. This view of the CA's position is also taken by *Emmet & Farrand on Title*, para.2-041.01.

**5-037B** However, this view as to what is required for signature has been the subject of increasing criticism.[245] In particular, the Law Commission has noted that the decision in *Firstpost Homes Ltd* "focused on the fact that the alleged signature of the buyer was of the buyer as addressee of the letter, rather than on the fact that it was not handwritten" and has argued that it should be confined to its facts.[245a] In its view, *Firstpost Homes Ltd* "reiterated the principle that a signature must demonstrate an intention of the party to authenticate the document", and it noted that the High Court in *Re Stealth Construction Ltd*[245b] "has subsequently said that, in principle, a string of emails, containing the typed signatures of the parties, could create a contract satisfying the requirements of section 2".[245c] The Law Commission's conclusion was that the "case law has developed to accommodate increasingly frequent use of technology".[245d] This approach has recently been approved by the High Court in *Neocleous v Rees*, which concerned a claim for specific performance of an alleged contract of compromise which involved a disposition of an interest in land contained in an exchange of emails.[245e] The claimants argued that "the typed name of the sender at the foot of an email, whether entered by the sender or generated by the software used to manage emails, renders the document "signed" within the meaning of s.2(1) so long as the inclusion of the name was for the purpose of giving authenticity to the document"[245f]; the defendants countered that s.2 requires a handwritten name or at least a facsimile of a handwritten name, relying on Firstpost Homes as authority that the proper test is "whether an 'ordinary man' would understand it to have been signed".[245g] In their submission, the defendant's solicitor's name in type at the end of an email is not enough, in particular where automatically generated.[245h] In this respect, H.H. Judge Pearce considered what such an "ordinary person" would consider to be a signature *at the time of his decision*, rather than at the time of the Court of Appeal's decision in *Goodman* (in 1954)[245i] and concluded that:

> "Many an 'ordinary person' would consider that what is produced when one stores a name in the Microsoft Outlook "Signature" function with the intent that it is automatically posted on the bottom of every email is indeed a 'signature'."[245j]

Accordingly, Judge Pearce was able to *apply* the approach of the Court of Appeal in *Firstpost Homes Ltd* (which he considered binding on him) on the basis that it requires recourse to the test of the ordinary person rather than a particular view of what such a person would have understood by signature at some point in the past.[245k] He therefore held that words which include the sender's name automatically added at the end of an email are *capable* of constituting the sender's signature, the proper test being "whether the name was applied with authenticating intent".[245l] For this purpose, no distinction should be drawn between a manually typed name at the end of an email and an "automatically" generated name as the latter "involved the conscious action at some stage of a person entering the relevant information and settings" in the email software.[245m] In both situations, "the presence of the name indicates a clear intention to associate oneself with the email—to authenticate it or to sign it".[245n] In this way, and with respect, the approach taken by the court in *Neocleous v Rees* manages to uphold the proper authority of the Court of Appeal in *Firstpost Homes Ltd*, while allowing the law to reflect the practical changes to transactional practice of the electronic age.

[245] See in particular *Emmet & Farrand on Title*, para.2-041.01 which criticises Peter Gibson L.J.'s treatment of *Goodman v J. Eban Ltd* [1954] 1 Q.B. 550 and argues that "there is nothing in the Law Commission's Report, the Parliamentary debates or the [1989] statute itself to indicate any intention to depart from the established meaning of 'signed'". Even so, *Emmet & Farrand* concludes that, taking account in particular the decision of the CA in Firstpost Homes Ltd "conveyancers should be as cautious as practicable and prefer in practice 'wet ink' signatures for contracts for the sale of land": *Emmet & Farrand on Title* at para.2.041.04, not following the view expressed by the Law Society in its practice note, *Execution of documents at virtual signings or closings* (February 16, 2010, available at *http://www.lawsociety.org.uk*).

[245a] Law Com. No.386, para.3.51 citing Smith, *Internet Law and Regulation*, 4th edn (2007), para.10-113, n.79. See also Law Commission, *Electronic execution of documents*, Consultation Paper No.237 (August 21, 2018) Ch.3 esp. para.3.57.

[245b] *Re Stealth Construction Ltd; Green (Liquidator of Stealth Construction Ltd) v Ireland* [2011] EWHC 1305 (Ch), [2012] 1 B.C.L.C. 297 at [44]–[45] (the point had apparently been conceded). See also *Ramsay v Love* [2015] EWHC 65 (Ch) at [7], where Morgan J. observed (obiter and in the context of s.1(3) rather than s.2 of the 1989 Act) that the statements in *Firstpost Homes Ltd v Johnson* which require signature by an executing party to be made with a pen in his own hand were not designed to distinguish between signing in such a way and by the use of a signature writing machine. cf. *Butts Park Ventures (Coventry) Ltd v Bryant Homes Central Ltd* [2003] EWHC 2487 (Ch), [2004] B.C.C. 207 at

[9]–[10] (dispute as to whether a photocopied signature would qualify as a "signature" for the purposes of s.2).

245c Law Com. No.386, para.3.53.

245d Law Com. No.386, para.3.53. Nevertheless, the Law Commission has suggested that the government should consider whether a more general legislative statement should be introduced in the interests of clarification of the position: Ch.4.

245e [2019] EWHC 2462 (Ch), [2020] 2 P. & C.R. 4 (Chancery Division District Registry (Manchester), H.H. Judge Pearce).

245f [2019] EWHC 2462 (Ch) at [30].

245g [2019] EWHC 2462 (Ch) at [44].

245h [2019] EWHC 2462 (Ch) at [45].

245i [2019] EWHC 2462 (Ch) at [51].

245j [2019] EWHC 2462 (Ch) at [51].

245k [2019] EWHC 2462 (Ch) at [52].

245l [2019] EWHC 2462 (Ch) at [53], adopting the approach in *J Pereira Fernandes SA v Mehta* [2006] EWHC 813 (Ch), [2006] 2 All E.R. 881 for the purposes of the Statute of Frauds s.4.

245m [2019] EWHC 2462 (Ch) at [54].

245n [2019] EWHC 2462 (Ch) at [55]. The insertion of "Many thanks" after the text of the email and the automatic signature was seen as showing an intention to connect the name with its contents: at [57].

**5-037C** **Use of initials** While Peter Gibson L.J. in *Firstpost Homes Ltd* referred to a party writing his *name* on the document,[245o] it has been held that a party can sign a document by writing only his initials, provided that it is clear that he intended to authenticate the full terms of the document.[245p]

245o [1995] 1 W.L.R. 1567 at 1575 and see above, para.5-038A.

245p *Newell v Tarrant* [2004] EWHC 772, (2004) 148 S.J.L.B. 509 at [47].

**5-037D** **Authentification of the whole instrument** In *Firstpost Homes Ltd*, Peter Gibson L.J. accepted that the principle laid down by the House of Lords in *Caton v Caton*[245q] in relation to the Statute of Frauds 1677 to the effect that the party's signature must be inserted in such a way as to authenticate the whole instrument applies equally to the requirement of signature made by s.2 of the 1989 Act. Thus, where a letter in which A agrees to sell a piece of land to B refers to a plan of the land in question and the court considers that the letter and the plans constitute a single document, B's signature of the plan may well not constitute authentication of the whole.[245r] Similarly, while a manuscript initialling of a document may constitute its "signature", the mere initialling of corrections at the margins of a document does not constitute its signing for the purposes of s.2 of the 1989 Act, as it does not evidence assent to the whole document.[245s]

245q (1867) L.R. 2 H.L. 127.

245r *Firstpost Homes Ltd v Johnson* [1995] 1 W.L.R. 1567, 1573 (though on the facts the Court of Appeal held that the letter and plan before them constituted *two* documents: see above, para.5-033).

245s *Newell v Tarrant* [2004] EWHC 772, (2004) 148 S.J.L.B. 509 at [48].

## Signature by agent

*Replace footnote 248 with:*

**5-038** 248 *Emmet and Farrand on Title* (2020), para.2.042.

## (c) The Effect of Failure to Comply with the Formal Requirements

### Constructive trust

*Replace paragraph with:*

Section 2(5) of the Law of Property (Miscellaneous Provisions) Act 1989 specifically precludes that section's requirements from affecting "the creation or operation of ... constructive trusts". In *Yaxley v Gotts*[272] Robert Walker L.J. considered that the relevant "species of constructive" trust for this purpose is one based on "common intention" and is to be found where, in the words of Lord Bridge in *Lloyds Bank Plc v Rosset*[273] there is an: **5-040**

> "'... agreement, arrangement or understanding' actually reached between the parties, and relied on and acted on by the claimant ... Equity enforces it because it would be unconscionable for the other party to disregard the claimant's rights."[274]

In *Yaxley v Gotts* itself, A made an oral agreement to give B the ground floor of a house which he (A) was proposing to buy in exchange for B's supplying labour and materials to convert the house into flats and managing the letting of the property. The house was purchased in the name of A's son, C, who subsequently refused to grant B any interest in the property and B, believing A to be the owner, performed his side of the bargain, supplying labour, materials and management services. At first instance, it was held that C had adopted the oral agreement between A and B and that C was bound by proprietary estoppel to grant a 99-year lease of the ground floor to B. The Court of Appeal upheld this result, rejecting A and C's argument based on s.2 of the 1989 Act, but preferring to rely on the ground of constructive trust rather than proprietary estoppel, though seeing these as running together on the facts.[275] While the oral agreement between A and B was void by reason of the 1989 Act, which had abolished the doctrine of part performance and required all contracts for the sale or disposal of land to be in writing, the agreement could be enforced on the basis of a constructive trust in circumstances where, previously, the doctrine of part performance might have been relied upon.[276] Similarly, in *Kinane v Mackie-Conteh*[277] the claimant had loaned money to a company of which one of the defendants was managing director, this loan being intended to be secured by a charge on a house in the form of a "security agreement" signed by himself and his wife. The Court of Appeal held that, while the security agreement fell under the formal requirements found in s.2 of the 1989 Act, on the facts "a proprietary estoppel overlapping with a constructive trust" was established so as to come within the exception found in s.2(5) of the 1989 Act, in that the defendants had encouraged the claimant in his erroneous belief that the agreement created an enforceable obligation.[278] A further illustration of the way in which a constructive trust may avoid the formal requirements imposed by s.2 of the 1989 Act may be found in the application of the so-called *Pallant v Morgan* equity.[279] Where A and B agree that A will acquire some specific property for the joint benefit of A and B, and B, in reliance on A's agreement, refrains from attempting to acquire the property, then equity will not permit A, when he acquires the property, to keep it for his own benefit, to the exclusion of B. It has been said that because this equity is in the nature of a constructive trust, it is unaffected by s.2(1) the 1989 Act.[280]

[272] [2000] Ch. 162.

[273] [1991] 1 A.C. 107, 132.

[274] [2000] Ch. 162 at 180. See similarly *David Vincent S v Susan Ann S (now M)* [2006] EWHC 2892

(Fam), [2007] 1 F.L.R. 1123 at [56]; *Ely v Robson* [2016] EWCA Civ 774, [2017] 1 P. & C.R. DG1; *Kahrmann v Harrison-Morgan* [2019] EWCA Civ 2094 at [107]–[111]. See also *Dowding v Matchmove Ltd* [2016] EWCA Civ 1233, [2017] 1 W.L.R. 749 esp. at [35]–[36] (oral agreement complete in all essential terms intended by both parties to be binding immediately, relied upon by claimants to their detriment). It has been held that where an agreement for the disposition of an interest in land is made subject to a condition, then no constructive trust can arise until the condition is fulfilled so as to allow the "beneficiary" under the would-be trust (the would-be transferee) to require the would-be "trustee" (the would-be transferor) to transfer the beneficial interest (the interest in land in question): *Representative Body of the Church in Wales v Newton* [2005] EWHC 631 (QB), [2005] All E.R. (D) 163 (Apr) especially at [64].

[275] [2000] Ch. 162 at 180, 181 and 193.

[276] *Yaxley v Gotts* [2000] Ch. 162 at 179–181.

[277] [2005] EWCA Civ 45, [2005] W.T.L.R. 345.

[278] [2005] EWCA Civ 45 at [28]–[32]. cf. *McGuane v Welch* [2008] EWCA Civ 785, [2008] 2 P. & C.R. 24 where the CA held on the facts that "[a] constructive trust could not be properly inferred or imposed by the court as, to do so, was inconsistent with the express agreement of the parties that the Lease would be held by [the appellant] on an express trust for [the respondent] for a period of three years after which the deed of transfer of the Lease to [the respondent] would take effect": [2008] EWCA Civ 785 at [35], per Mummery L.J.

[279] *Pallant v Morgan* [1953] Ch. 43; *Banner Homes Group Plc v Luff Developments Ltd* [2000] Ch. 372; *Crossco No.4 Unlimited v Jolan Ltd* [2011] EWCA Civ 1619, [2012] 2 All E.R. 754; *Farrar v Miller* [2018] EWCA Civ 172, [2018] 2 P. & C.R. DG3.

[280] *Kilcarne Holdings Ltd v Targetfollow (Birmingham) Ltd* [2004] EWHC 2547 at [219] (where it was held inapplicable on the facts); *Farrar v Miller* [2018] EWCA Civ 172, [2018] 2 P. & C.R. DG3 esp. at [43] and [49].

## Earlier cases on use of proprietary estoppel

*Replace footnote 307 with:*

**5-045** [307] [2000] Ch. 162 at 180; *McGuane v Welch* [2008] EWCA Civ 785, [2008] 2 P. & C.R. 24 at [37], per Mummery L.J. cf. Lord Walker's "lesser enthusiasm" for the complete assimilation of "common intention" constructive trust and proprietary estoppel in *Stack v Dowden* [2007] UKHL 17, [2007] 2 A.C. 432 at [37]. See further *Kahrmann v Harrison-Morgan* [2019] EWCA Civ 2094 at [107]–[111].

## Herbert v Doyle

*Replace footnote 320 with:*

**5-048** [320] [2010] EWCA Civ 1095, [2010] N.P.C. 100. See also *Kinnear v Whittaker* [2011] EWHC 1479 (QB), [2011] All E.R. (D) 78 (Jun) (allowing the possibility of proprietary estoppel and preferring the approach of the CA in *Yaxley v Gotts* [2000] Ch. 162 (above, para.5-040) to the approach found in Lord Scott's speech in *Cobbe*, quoted above, para.5-046; *Ghazaani v Rowshan* [2015] EWHC 1922 (Ch) at [192] and [197] (allowing the possibility of proprietary estoppel/constructive trust in the "exceptional circumstances" of the case); *Muhammad v ARY Properties Ltd* [2016] EWHC 1698 (Ch) at [32]–[50] and *Pinisetty v Manikonda* [2017] EWHC 838 (QB), [2017] 5 Costs L.O. 565 at [39]–[42] (agreement not sufficiently certain to be enforced); *Farrar v Miller* [2018] EWCA Civ 172, [2018] 2 P. & C.R. DG3 at [50]–[63] (where Kitchin L.J., with whom Floyd and Patten L.J. agreed (at [84] and [85]), expressed the view that a claim for proprietary estoppel is not barred by s.2 of the 1989 Act, though he left the determination of the issue to trial); *Raza v Chaudhary* [2019] EWHC 1720 (Ch) at [40] (conditions for proprietary estoppel not established on the facts); *Sahota v Prior* [2019] EWHC 1418 (Ch) at [19]–[35] (proprietary estoppel established in a "domestic case", although it concerned estoppel relating to a disposition of land rather than a contract for its disposition (at [29]); *Kensington Mortgage v Mallon* [2019] EWHC 2512 (Ch) at [37], [65], [141]–[151]; *Wills v Souvray* [2020] EWHC 939 (Ch) at [251]–[256] (allowing a claim for proprietary estoppel "irrespective of the fact that there is no agreement in writing for the purpose" of s.2 of the 1989 Act (at [256]).

## Restitution: recovery of money paid by purchaser under a mistake of law

*Replace footnote 350 with:*

**5-054** [350] (1991) 64 P. & C.R. 452, 455. cf. *Keay v Morris Homes (West Midlands) Ltd* [2012] EWCA Civ 900, [2012] 1 W.L.R. 2855 at [42] where Rimer L.J. interpreted this passage as saying "no more than that the fact that any agreed land transaction may not be compliant with section 2 does not prevent the parties proceeding to its practical completion (for example, in the most conventional case, by an assurance of the land interest against payment of the price)". In *Kuznetsov v Camden LBC* [2019] EWHC 805 (Ch) at [45] (the observation in *Tootal Clothing* applies only where the contract has been completed and not, therefore, where an alleged party has entered possession under a compulsory purchase order (appeal from striking out)).

Chapter 6

# COMMON MISTAKE



*Replace footnote 1 with:*

[1] See generally Cheshire (1944) 60 L.Q.R. 175; Tylor (1948) 11 M.L.R. 257; Slade (1954) 70 L.Q.R. 385; Stoljar (1965) 28 M.L.R. 265; Stoljar, *Mistake and Misrepresentation: A Study in Contractual Principles* (1968); Smith (1994) 110 L.Q.R. 400; Friedmann (2003) 119 L.Q.R. 68; Cartwright, *Misrepresentation, Mistake and Non-disclosure*, 5th edn (2019); Macmillan (2003) 119 L.Q.R. 625; Macmillan, *Mistakes in Contract Law* (2010).

## 1. Introduction to Mistake

### Types of mistake

*Replace footnote 6 with:*

6-001 [6] The 29th and earlier editions of this work used the phrase "mutual mistake", following the terminology used by Lord Atkin in *Bell v Lever Bros* [1932] A.C. 161, and until recently some other works adhered to this usage: e.g. Beatson, *Anson's Law of Contract*, 28th edn (2002), Ch.8. It is now more common to refer to this type of mistake as "common mistake" (e.g. Beatson, Burrows and Cartwright (eds), *Anson's Law of Contract*, 31st edn (2020), Ch.8; Cheshire, Fifoot and Furmston, *Law of Contract*, 17th edn (2017), Ch.8). The courts have also referred to common mistake: e.g. *Great Peace Shipping Ltd v Tsavliris Salvage (International) Ltd (The Great Peace)* [2002] EWCA Civ 1407, [2003] Q.B. 679. One reason for using the phrase "common mistake" is to reduce the risk of confusion with what is termed here "mutual misunderstanding" (where the parties are at cross-purposes as to the terms of the contract): see above, para.3-019.

### Mistakes as to facts and mistakes as to terms

*Replace paragraph with:*

6-002 In other words, the distinction between the two situations drawn in the previous paragraph is one between mistakes as to the terms and mistakes as to the facts or law.[7] It is common to categorise the situations in which the doctrine of mistake affects a contract[8] into cases of "common mistake", "unilateral mistake" or "mutual misunderstanding".[9] This is useful, but it highlights only one of the distinctions between the cases. For the purposes of the law, there is a second and vital distinction between common mistake on the one hand and unilateral mistake or mutual misunderstanding on the other. The doctrine of mistake takes account of a mistake as to the factual circumstances in which the contract is made only if the mistake was common, i.e. both parties made substantially the same mistake—for example, when an agreement was made to rent a room overlooking the route of a coronation procession, that both parties believed that the procession was scheduled to take place on the date concerned when in fact it had been cancelled.[10] Common mistake cases are ones in which:

> "both parties make the same mistake of fact or law relating to the subject-matter or the facts surrounding the formation of the contract."[11]

(As will be seen, the mistake must also be fundamental.[12]) In contrast, where only one of the parties is mistaken as to the facts—a "unilateral" mistake as to the facts—there is no basis for relief under the doctrine of mistake.[13] A unilateral mistake or a mutual misunderstanding will only operate where the mistake or misunderstanding is about the terms of the contract—for example, the price or the contractual description of what is being sold,[14] and in cases of mistaken identity.[15]

[7] As to mistake of law, see below, para.6-052.

[8] Compare those cases in which the mistake is not legally relevant, below, para.6-005.

[9] Above, para.6-001.

[10] *Griffith v Brymer* (1903) 19 T.L.R. 434.

[11] Beatson, Burrows and Cartwright (eds), *Anson's Law of Contract*, 31st edn (2020), p.296.

[12] Below, para.6-015.

[13] *Smith v Hughes* (1871) L.R. 6 Q.B. 597; *Statoil ASA v Louis Dreyfus Energy Services LP (The Hariette N)* [2008] EWHC 2257 (Comm), [2008] 2 Lloyd's Rep. 685; *UTB LLC v Sheffield United Ltd* [2019] EWHC 2322 (Ch) at [280]–[285].

[14] See above, para.3-025.

[15] See above, paras 3-036 et seq.

## "Mistake" implies a positive belief

*Replace footnote 17 with:*

6-004 [17] cf. Cartwright, *Misrepresentation, Mistake and Non-disclosure*, 5th edn (2019), para.12-03. In *Pitt v Holt* [2013] UKSC 26, [2013] 2 A.C. 108, a case of a mistake affecting a voluntary settlement, Lord Walker said (at [108]–[109]) that a mistake is different from ignorance, inadvertence and misprediction as to the future. A mistake encompasses two states of mind, namely an incorrect conscious belief or an incorrect tacit assumption as to a present matter of fact or law, but does not encompass mere causative ignorance but for which the claimant would not have acted as he did. See also *Co-operative Bank Plc v Hayes Freehold Ltd* [2017] EWHC 1820 (Ch) at [143(i)], citing this paragraph; and *Triple Seven MSN 27251 Ltd v Azman Air Services Ltd* [2018] EWHC 1348 (Comm), [2018] 4 W.L.R. 97 at [87].

## Mistakes that are not legally relevant

*Replace footnote 22 with:*

6-005 [22] Compare Anson's famous "Dresden china" example: *Anson's Law of Contract*, 28th edn, p.324 (second scenario). The example is omitted from the 31st edition by Beatson, Burrows and Cartwright (eds) (2020) but it is explained that a unilateral mistake of fact or law does not render the contract void or give rise to an equitable jurisdiction to set aside the contract: p.296. Friedmann (2003) 119 L.Q.R.

68, 79–81 argues that in such a case relief should be given, by analogy of cases of innocent misrepresentation.

## Underlying policy

*Replace footnote 30 with:*

6-006

[30] For French and German Law see Beale, Fauvarque-Cosson, Rutgers, Tallon and Vogenauer (eds), *Casebooks on the Common Law of Europe: Contract Law*, 3rd edn (2018), Ch.14, section 3; for a broader survey of the European legal systems, Sefton-Green, *Mistake, Fraud and Duties to Inform in European Contract Law*, 2nd edn (2009) and Cartwright, *Misrepresentation, Mistake and Non-disclosure*, 5th edn (2019), para.15-35. See also Friedmann (2003) 119 L.Q.R. 68, who demonstrates the links between the English doctrine of mistake and the "objective" principle in contract (on which see above, para.2-003); H. Beale, *Mistake and Non-disclosure of Facts: Models for English Contract Law* (2012).

## Common mistake and construction of the contract

*Replace paragraph with:*

6-014

The question of the effect of common mistake in the law of contract is basically one of the allocation of risk as to the facts being as assumed.[64] In most situations one or other of the parties will be considered to have assumed the risk of the ordinary uncertainties which exist when an agreement is concluded.[65] Where contracts of sale of goods are concerned, for example, the seller will normally be held to have assumed the risk that the goods do not correspond to their description, or, if the seller sells in the course of a business, that they may be defective, under express or implied terms, except insofar as the usual conditions are validly excluded, or may in the particular circumstances be inapplicable.[66] The risk that for other reasons the goods will be less useful than the parties envisaged will be borne by the buyer. Thus it has been said that one must first determine whether the contract itself, by express or implied condition (promissory or non-promissory) or otherwise, provides who bears the risk of the relevant mistake. Only if the contract is silent on the point is there scope for invoking the rules or "doctrine" of mistake.[67] It has been pointed out that if the enquiry whether the construction of the contract is only as to:

> "whether either party has given an undertaking as to the matter at issue (i.e. if that is what is meant by a provision as to 'who bears the risk of the relevant mistake'), and the answer is that neither has"

that does not preclude a second enquiry as to the effect of the mistake; but if it includes asking whether, if neither bears the risk, the contract is as a matter of construction subject to an implied condition precedent that the facts assumed existed, there seems to be no scope for asking whether the contract is void for mistake.[68] In other words, if it does include asking whether the contract is subject to such a condition, there is no room for an independent doctrine of common mistake.[69] Although the courts have held that there is a separate doctrine of mistake,[70] this is a formidable argument. It will be submitted that it can really be met only by admitting that, in cases which involve the kind of facts to which the doctrine of common mistake might apply, the process of construction and the application of the rules of mistake are really merely alternative ways of formulating the same thing and reaching the same result.[71] We will see later, however, that sometimes courts have held a contract to be ineffective because as a matter of construction it was subject to an implied condition which has not been fulfilled, in circumstances in which the requirements of common mistake do not seem to have been met.[72]

[64] *Amalgamated Investment & Property Co Ltd v John Walker & Sons Ltd* [1977] 1 W.L.R. 164; McTurnan, An Introduction to Common Mistake in English Law (1963) 41 Can. Bar Rev. 1; Swan, "The Allocation of Risk in the Analysis of Mistake and Frustration" in Reiter and Swan, *Studies in Contract Law* (1980); American Law Institute's *Restatement of Contracts* (2d), para.152.

[65] *Co-operative Bank Plc v Hayes Freehold Ltd* [2017] EWHC 1820 (Ch) at [143(ii)], citing this sentence of the paragraph.

[66] e.g. *Gloucestershire CC v Richardson* [1969] 1 A.C. 480 (normal implied term did not apply when contractor had no right to object to supplier nominated by employer and supplier would contract only on limited liability terms).

[67] *Associated Japanese Bank International Ltd v Credit du Nord SA* [1989] 1 W.L.R. 255, 268; *Great Peace Shipping Ltd v Tsavliris Salvage (International) Ltd (The Great Peace)* [2002] EWCA Civ 1407, [2003] Q.B. 679 at [74]–[75]; *Butters v BBC Worldwide Ltd* [2009] EWHC 1954 (Ch) at [68]–[69], referring to this paragraph. See also *William Sindall Plc v Cambridgeshire CC* [1994] 1 W.L.R. 1016, 1035; *Grains & Fourriers SA v Huyton* [1997] 1 Lloyd's Rep. 628. Thus, in *Kalsep Ltd v X-Flow BV, The Times,* May 3, 2001 it was held that the risk of the mistake which had been made was allocated to one party by an express clause of the agreement. In *Standard Chartered Bank v Banque Marocaine De Commerce Exterieur* [2006] EWHC 413 (Comm), [2006] All E.R. (D) 213 (Feb) the contract was held to be binding on the alternative grounds that the mistake did not make the agreement essentially different and that the risk was clearly allocated to one party. In *Natixis SA v Marex Financial* [2019] EWHC 2549 (Comm), [2019] 2 Lloyd's Rep. 431 it was held that the sellers were obliged to deliver "objectively genuine" warehouse receipts (at [174]); this precluded an argument that the contract was void for common mistake when it turned out that the receipts were forgeries (at [181]).

[68] Smith (1994) 110 L.Q.R. 400, 407. See also Morgan (2018) 77 C.L.J. 559, discussing recent cases.

[69] Smith (1994) 110 L.Q.R. 400, 419. The court might conclude that the contract has not allocated the risk to either party, but the conditions for common mistake are not fulfilled (e.g. because the mistake is not sufficiently fundamental), so that the loss lies where it falls. But this does not demonstrate that there is a separate doctrine of mistake, as the same might occur on a "construction" approach.

[70] *Great Peace Shipping Ltd v Tsavliris Salvage (International) Ltd (The Great Peace)* [2002] EWCA Civ 1407, [2003] Q.B. 679 at [73] and [82], discussed below, para.6-034.

[71] See below, paras 6-029 and 6-062—6-063.

[72] See *Graves v Graves* [2007] EWCA Civ 660, [2007] 3 F.C.R. 26, discussed below, para.6-063.

## 3. DIFFERENT APPROACHES BEFORE BELL V LEVER BROS

### Kennedy's case

*Replace footnote 91 with:*

**6-020** [91] Although when a contract is void for common mistake either party will be able to obtain restitution (see, e.g. Peel (ed.), *Treitel on The Law of Contract*, 15th edn (2020), para.22-021), there is some uncertainty as to the basis of the restitutionary remedy. One possibility is that restitution is permitted simply because the contract is void: Treitel at paras 22-022—22-023. When a contract is void for mistake there will usually be a total failure of consideration, as was held to be the case in *Strickland v Turner* (1852) 7 Ex. 208, but it has been argued that this does not necessarily follow from the fact that the contract is void, as it might nonetheless have been completely executed: Burrows, *Law of Restitution*, 3rd edn (2011), p.386. But even in such a case it seems that either party would be able to recover on the basis that he had performed under a mistake: see Treitel at para. 22-024. Mistake appears to have been the basis of recovery in *Pritchard v Merchant's and Tradesman's Mutual Life Assurance Society* (1858) 3 C.B.(N.S.) 622, 645. See Burrows at pp.387–388.

## 4. MISTAKE AT COMMON LAW

## (b) The Modern Doctrine

### *(ii) Conditions for Common Mistake to Render Contract Void*

**Risk not allocated to either party**

*Replace footnote 156 with:*

[156] In *Standard Chartered Bank v Banque Marocaine De Commerce Exterieur* [2006] EWHC 413 (Comm), [2006] All E.R. (D) 213 (Feb) the contract was held to be binding on the alternative grounds that the mistake did not make the agreement essentially different and that the risk was clearly allocated to one party. See also *Butters v BBC Worldwide Ltd* [2009] EWHC 1954 (Ch) at [68]–[69]; *Dana Gas PJSC v Dana Gas SUKUK Ltd* [2017] EWHC 2928 (Comm), [2018] 1 Lloyd's Rep. 177 at [66]–[78]. In *Natixis SA v Marex Financial* [2019] EWHC 2549 (Comm), [2019] 2 Lloyd's Rep. 431 it was held that the sellers were obliged to deliver "objectively genuine" warehouse receipts (at [174]); this precluded an argument that the contract was void for common mistake when it turned out that the receipts were forgeries (at [181]). **6-037**

**Non-existence of the state of affairs must not be attributable to the fault of either party**

*Replace paragraph with:*

**6-038** The most obvious meaning of this is that the contract will not be void if one party should have known the truth, since he could have prevented the parties from making the mistake they did.[159] The rule that a party who should have known the truth cannot rely on common mistake at common law was first stated by Steyn J. in the *Associated Japanese Bank* case[160]: he derived it from *McRae's* case, in which the High Court of Australia had said that a party cannot rely on a mistake consisting:

> "of a belief which is entertained without any reasonable ground, and ... deliberately induced by him in the mind of the other party."[161]

Steyn J. also referred to a similar requirement stated in *Solle v Butcher*,[162] one of the "equitable mistake cases which is no longer treated as good law".[163] It has been pointed out that Steyn J.'s principle goes further than what is stated in *McRae's* case, since the latter refers only to cases in which one party should have known the truth and (by a promise or representation) induced the other party to share the same mistaken belief.[164] In those circumstances the party who induced the other's belief will almost invariably have committed at least a negligent misstatement if not (as in *McRae's* case) a breach of warranty, and he should not be permitted to avoid liability by arguing that the resulting contract was void. But it is submitted that relief on the ground of mistake should be denied in at least two further cases.[165]

[159] In *Natixis SA v Marex Financial* [2019] EWHC 2549 (Comm), [2019] 2 Lloyd's Rep. 431 at [211] it was said that on this point the boundaries of the doctrine are uncertain. It is possible that there is an exception to the meaning suggested in the text when s.6 of the Sale of Goods Act 1979 applies, since that section seems at first sight to state an absolute rule that the contract is void: but it will be submitted that this is not the correct interpretation of the section, which should be interpreted as stating the prima facie position. See below, para.6-045. In *National Private Air Transport Co v Kaki* [2017] EWHC 1496 (Comm) the state of affairs was attributable to the claimant's fault because it resulted from the claimant's non-performance of another contract (see at [25(ii)]). However, it has been said that where the mistake means that the contract is legally impossible to perform (not in the sense that it would be illegal but simply that it is not workable), it will be void and there will be a failure of consideration without the need to enquire whether the mistake was more the fault of one party rather than another: *Lehman Brothers International (Europe) (In Administration) v Exotix Partners LLP* [2019] EWHC 2380 (Ch) at [202]–[203]. But in this case the mistake was over the terms of the agreement and it seems more

appropriate to analyse the case as one in which the parties never reached an effective agreement: see above, para.3-014.

160 *Associated Japanese Bank (International) Ltd v Crédit du Nord* [1989] 1 W.L.R. 255, 268. Steyn L.J.'s dictum was applied in *National Private Air Transport Co v Kaki* [2017] EWHC 1496 (Comm) at [25(i)].

161 (1951) 84 C.L.R. 377, 408.

162 [1950] 1 K.B. 671, 693. Steyn J. also noted that the civilian doctrine of error in substantia is qualified by the principles governing culpa in contrahendo: [1989] 1 W.L.R 255, 269.

163 See below, para.6-058.

164 Cartwright, *Misrepresentation, Mistake and Non-disclosure*, 5th edn (2019), para.15-22; Peel (ed.), *Treitel on The Law of Contract*, 15th edn (2020), para.8-005.

165 The second is considered in para.6-040.

## Section 6 cases

*Replace paragraph with:*

**6-045** Where, however, the case is one of the sale of goods which have perished before the contract was made, s.6 of the Sale of Goods Act 1979 may preclude such a result, since it provides that the contract will be void.[179] It is possible that the parties are unable to vary this rule by contrary agreement.[180] In the light of *McRae*'s case and the fact that under s.6 a seller who knows that the goods no longer exist may nonetheless commit himself to deliver, it seems unlikely that a modern court would accept that s.6 necessarily has the effect that a seller who ought to have known that the goods no longer exist will escape liability. It is submitted that even though s.6 is not expressly stated to apply only if the parties have not agreed otherwise, it is a statement of the "default position" which will apply unless in the circumstances the contract should be construed otherwise.[181]

179 cf. Atiyah (1957) 83 L.Q.R. 340, 348; Sale of Goods Act 1979 s.55. An extensive discussion of the meaning of "perish", in the context of the New Zealand equivalent of s.7, can be found in *Oldfields Asphalts v Govedale Coolstores (1994) Ltd* [1998] 3 N.Z.L.R. 479.

180 See Peel (ed.), *Treitel on The Law of Contract*, 15th edn (2020), para.8-010.

181 cf. Twigg-Flessner, Canavan and MacQueen (eds), *Atiyah and Adams' Sale of Goods*, 13th edn (2016), p.80; *Benjamin's Sale of Goods*, 10th edn (2017), para.1-132. Alternatively, it might be held that the seller was liable for breach of a collateral warranty (see below, para.13-004, though there might be problems over consideration, see Peel (ed.), *Treitel on The Law of Contract*, 15th edn (2020), para.8-010) or in tort for damages for negligent misstatement, if such should exist, under the principle stated in *Hedley Byrne & Co v Heller & Partners* [1964] A.C. 465. It is doubtful whether he could be liable under Misrepresentation Act 1967 s.2(1), as that subsection applies "where a person has entered a contract" and thus may not apply when the contract is void for mistake.

## What mistakes may frustrate contractual venture?

*Replace paragraph with:*

**6-051** Clearly a contract which turns out to be literally impossible to perform may be void for mistake, provided the other conditions set out above are met. But what other kinds of case may fall within the phrase, "frustration of the contractual venture"—or, for that matter, following Lord Atkin's formulation, make the subject matter "essentially different from the thing it was believed to be"?[201] The cases give examples: a contract for "a room with a view" when in fact there was no procession to look at[202]; a guarantee of a lease of machines when in fact no machines existed[203]; possibly the sale of a life insurance policy on someone the parties did not know was already dead.[204] Beyond this it is not easy to generalise. However it has been argued that an appropriate test for determining whether a mistake is fundamental is to ask the parties "what are you contracting about"? If they would both identify the subject matter in terms that are correct (e.g. in *Bell v Lever Bros* they would have answered, "[w]e are contracting about a service agreement") the mistake is not fundamental. If they would identify the subject matter in terms that in fact are not correct, the mistake is fundamental.[205] This argument is attractive but it presupposes that the correct test is one of the identity of the subject matter. That fits Lord Atkin's analysis[206] but not necessarily that in *The Great Peace*. In *Triple Seven MSN 27251 Ltd v Azman Air Services Ltd*, Peter MacDonald Eggers Q.C., sitting as a deputy High Court judge, suggested that

> "the test determining the application of the doctrine of common mistake is best applied by (a) assessing the fundamental nature of the shared assumption to the contract, and (b) comparing the disparity between the assumed state of affairs and the actual state of affairs and analysing whether that disparity is sufficiently fundamental or essential or radical."[207]

201 See above, para.6-048.

202 *Griffiths v Brymer* (1903) 19 T.L.R. 434, above, para.6-023.

203 *Associated Japanese Bank (International) Ltd v Crédit du Nord* [1989] 1 W.L.R. 255, cited with apparent approval in *The Great Peace* [2002] EWCA Civ 1407 at [93].

204 *Scott v Coulson* [1903] 2 Ch. 249. In *The Great Peace* [2002] EWCA Civ 1407 the Court seems to have had some difficulty in explaining this decision but did not say it was wrong (at [87]–[88]).

205 Peel (ed.), *Treitel on The Law of Contract*, 15th edn (2020), para.8-020.

206 But not his example of the picture thought to be an Old Master, where the parties would presumably have said they were buying and selling "a Rembrandt" rather than just "a picture": see Peel (ed.), *Treitel on The Law of Contract*, 15th edn (2020), para.8-021.

207 [2018] EWHC 1348 (Comm), [2018] 4 W.L.R. 97 at [66]. The judge added that it is not sufficient if both parties would not have entered into the contract had they known of the true state of affairs; it is necessary that the mistaken assumption induced the contract, but that is not sufficient (at [70]–[72]). On the facts the mistake was not sufficiently fundamental to render the agreements void, see at [87].

## 5. MISTAKES OF LAW

### Mistake of law and compromise agreements

*To the end of paragraph, after "treated as taking the risk.[230]", add:*

In *Elston v King*[230a] Marcus Smith J. accepted that a mistake of law might sometimes render a contract void[230b] but held that it is important to distinguish a mistake from a misprediction of what a court will decide on a point of law that is known to be doubtful.[230c] The judge said that it is not quite clear how the requirement of impossibility applies in compromise cases but accepted that the mistake must at least render the subject matter of the contract radically different from what the parties agreed.[230d] **6-053**

230a [2020] EWHC 55 (Ch).

230b The judge was not asked to consider whether compromises are exempt from the rules on common mistake as a matter of public policy: see at [23]–[25].

230c [2020] EWHC 55 (Ch) at [27]–[30].

230d [2020] EWHC 55 (Ch) at [38], accepting the formulation of George H.H.J. at first instance.

## 6. NO SEPARATE RULE IN EQUITY

### No separate doctrine of common mistake in equity

*Replace footnote 237 with:*

6-055 [237] *Pitt v Holt* [2013] UKSC 26, [2013] 2 A.C. 108 at [115]. The case involved rectification of a voluntary settlement.

### Refusal of specific performance

*Replace footnote 281 with:*

6-061 [281] "It would be dangerous to attempt an exhaustive definition of the cases in which the court will refuse specific performance": Brett L.J. in *Tamplin v James* (1879) 15 Ch. D. 215, 221. For a recent case, in which it appears that both parties were mistaken as to the facts, see *Heath v Heath* [2009] EWHC 1908 (Ch), [2009] 2 P. & C.R. DG21 at [26] ("specific performance is a discretionary remedy and mistake may ... still be a relevant factor in refusing equitable relief, at all events where the mistake has been induced by the words or conduct of the person seeking specific performance. In such a case ... the mistake may also amount to, or be practically indistinguishable from, a misrepresentation"). In *UTB LLC v Sheffield United Ltd* [2019] EWHC 2322 (Ch) at [280], [284] the court accepted that specific performance might be refused if the claimant was seeking to take advantage of a mistake by the defendant that was not one as to the terms of the contract, but on the facts the defendant was not disadvantaged (see at [496]).

## 7. MISTAKE AND CONSTRUCTION

### Contract void as a matter of construction where no common mistake

*Replace footnote 287 with:*

6-063 [287] Peel (ed.), *Treitel on The Law of Contract*, 15 edn (2020), para.2-067.

CHAPTER 7

# MISREPRESENTATION



*Replace footnote 1 with:*

[1] See Allen, *Misrepresentation* (1988); Cartwright, *Unequal Bargaining* (1991), Ch.3; Cartwright, *Misrepresentation, Mistake and Non-disclosure*, 5th edn (2019); Spencer Bower and Handley, *Actionable Misrepresentation*, 5th edn (2014).

## 1. IN GENERAL

### Preliminary

*In line 6, page [650], after "amounted to a", replace "tehaywardrm" with:*
term 7-001

## 2. WHAT CONSTITUTES EFFECTIVE MISREPRESENTATION

7-006 *To the end of title, add new footnote 19a:*

[19a] The general requirements for misrepresentation (in the context of an action for damages for fraud) were set out by Jacobs J. in *Vald Nielsen Holding A/S v Baldorino* [2019] EWHC 1926 (Comm) at [130]–[159].

### (a) False Statement of Fact

#### Statements of fact

*Replace footnote 31 with:*

7-007 [31] *IFE Fund SA v Goldman Sachs International* [2006] EWHC 2887 (Comm), [2007] 1 Lloyd's Rep. 264, per Toulson J. at [50] (affirmed without comment on this point [2007] EWCA Civ 811, [2007] 2 Lloyd's Rep. 449). Toulson J.'s statement was adopted by the Court of Appeal in *Webster v Liddington* [2014] EWCA Civ 560 at [40]. See also the dictum of Mance J. in *Bankers Trust International v PT Dharmala Sakti Sejahtera* [1996] C.L.C. 518 at 531, referring to "the potential relevance of the parties' relationship and the surrounding circumstances to a decision whether any and if so what representation was made in the particular case. The meaning and effect of words never falls to be viewed in a vacuum. It is shaped by the context of their communication, including the parties' respective positions, knowledge and experience. A description or commendation which may obviously be irrelevant or may even serve as a warning to one recipient, because of its generality, superficiality or laudatory nature, or because of the recipient's own knowledge and experience, may constitute a material representation if made to another less informed or sophisticated receiver". See also (in the context of materiality: below, para.7-042) *MCI WorldCom International Inc v Primus Telecommunications Inc* [2004] EWCA Civ 957 ("judged objectively according to the impact that whatever is said may be expected to have on a reasonable representee in the position and with the known characteristics of the actual representee": per Mance L.J., at [30]); *Raiffeisen Zentralbank Osterreich AG v Royal Bank of Scotland Plc* [2010] EWHC 1392 (Comm) at [90]; *Mabanga v Ophir Energy Plc* [2012] EWHC 1589 (QB) at [26]–[27]. As Christopher Clarke J. pointed out in *Raiffeisen Zentralbank Osterreich AG v Royal Bank of Scotland Plc* [2010] EWHC 1392 (Comm) at [87], the claimant must show that he understood the statement in the sense (so far as material) which the court ascribes to it and that, having that understanding, he relied on it. See further Cartwright, *Misrepresentation, Mistake and Non-disclosure*, 5th edn (2019), para.3-06.

#### Statement of opinion amounts to statement of fact if not honestly held

*Replace footnote 36 with:*

7-009 [36] *Connolly Ltd v Bellway Homes Ltd* [2007] EWHC 895, [2007] All E.R. (D) 182 (Apr). The sentences in this paragraph were cited with approval in *Economides v Commercial Union Assurance Co Plc* [1998] Q.B. 587, by Simon Brown L.J. at 598 (who considered that *Brown v Raphael* [1958] Ch. 636, below, para.7-010, fell into a different category) and Sir Iain Glidewell (who considered that the statement summarised that case accurately also), 608–609. Another way to put the same point is that if a person states that he holds an opinion that in fact he does not hold, or that he has an intention that in fact he does not have, he makes a false statement of fact. See Cartwright, *Misrepresentation, Mistake and Non-disclosure*, 5th edn (2019), para.3-18.

#### Statement of opinion may carry implication that grounds for belief

*Replace paragraph with:*

7-010 In *Brown v Raphael*,[38] the purchaser of an absolute reversion in a trust fund expectant on the death of an annuitant was likewise held entitled to rescind: the particulars of sale stated that estate duty would be payable on the death of the annuitant, "who is believed to have no aggregable estate"; the vendor's solicitors honestly believed this to be true but had no reasonable grounds for this belief. The Court of Appeal held that as the vendor was in a far stronger position than the purchaser to ascertain the facts, there must be implied a further representation that the former had reasonable grounds for his belief.[39] If, on the other hand, it is clear that the person who expressed the opinion had no real way of knowing whether or not it was correct, no such implication can be made.[40] In *Economides v Com-*

*mercial Union Assurance Co Plc*[41] it was held that a statement by an insured, a private person with no specialist knowledge, of the value of the contents of a flat which contained his parents' belongings as well as his own, did not carry an implication that he had an objectively reasonable basis for the value stated. Thus a statement of the value which the insured made honestly was not a misrepresentation even though it was inaccurate. Equally, propositions put forward by parties engaged in negotiating the settlement of a dispute are likely to be treated as mere statements of opinion and, at least when the negotiations are conducted by experienced professionals in good faith, are unlikely to be treated as including a representation that they are based on reasonable grounds.[42] The fact that there was a relationship between the parties is not enough, as a matter of law, to create an implied representation that there is a reasonable basis for the opinion.[43] Subject to the principle illustrated by *Brown v Raphael*,[44] an opinion expressed in good faith is not to be held to be a misrepresentation merely because it turns out to be incorrect.[45] But a statement of opinion which is published as if it were a fact may be regarded as a statement of fact.[46]

[38] [1958] Ch. 636; *Crédit Lyonnais Bank Nederland v Export Credit Guarantee Department* [1996] 1 Lloyd's Rep. 200 (bank's statement that a management was "respectable and trustworthy" a misrepresentation as it was contrary to the bank's actual experience of the management). See also *Patterson v Landsberg & Son* (1905) 7 F. 675.

[39] It is possible that *Smith v Land House Property Corp* (1889) 28 Ch. D. 7 was also decided on the basis that the vendor was impliedly representing that he had reasonable grounds for his belief, or at least that he knew of nothing which might be inconsistent with it: Bennett (1998) 61 M.L.R. 886, 888. See also *Highland Insurance Co v Continental Insurance Co* [1987] 1 Lloyd's Rep. 109; *Crédit Lyonnais Bank Nederland v Export Credit Guarantee Department* [1996] 1 Lloyd's Rep. 200; *Barings Plc (In Liquidation) v Coopers & Lybrand* [2002] EWHC 461 (Ch), [2002] 2 B.C.L.C. 410 at [50]–[51]. A party who merely gives a contractual warranty does not necessarily represent that the fact warranted is true (see *Sycamore Bidco Ltd v Breslin* [2012] EWHC 3443 (Ch) at [203]–[209] and *Idemitsu Kosan Co Ltd v Sumitomo Corp* [2016] EWHC 1909 (Comm), [2016] 2 C.L.C. 297, declining to follow the unreported decision in *Invertec Ltd v De Mol Holding BV* [2009] EWHC 2471 (Ch)). Merely offering for signature a document containing the warranty is not a representation of the truth of the facts warranted: [2016] EWHC 1909 (Comm) at [28]–[30]. If there was a previous representation, followed by a warranty, the fact of the warranty does tend to imply that the party giving the warranty has reasonable grounds for believing the facts warranted: *Avrora Fine Arts Investment Ltd v Christie, Manson & Woods Ltd* [2012] EWHC 2198 (Ch) at [133].

[40] *Bisset v Wilkinson* [1927] A.C. 177; *Hummingbird Motors Ltd v Hobbs* [1986] R.T.R. 276. Further, there is no implication that the party giving the opinion has reasonable grounds for it if the facts justifying the opinion were stated: *Wilson and Sharp Investments Ltd v Falmouth Property Investments Ltd* Unreported January 21, 2019, Master Davison at [23]. Permission to appeal on this point was refused, see [2019] EWHC 2108 (QB) at [34] (Soole J.).

[41] [1998] Q.B. 587. Simon Brown and Peter Gibson L.JJ. expressed the view that under the Marine Insurance Act 1906 s.20(5), which stated that a representation as to a matter of expectation or belief is true if it be made in good faith, there is no room for such an implication, doubting a dictum to the contrary by Steyn J. in *Highlands Insurance Co v Continental Insurance Co* [1987] 1 Lloyd's Rep. 109, 112–113. Sir Iain Glidewell preferred to leave the matter open. But see Bennett (1998) 61 M.L.R. 886; Cartwright, *Misrepresentation, Mistake and Non-disclosure*, 5th edn (2019), para.3-17. See further below, paras 7-013 and 42-038. Section 20 was repealed when the Insurance Act 2015 came into force (see below, para.7-162): s.21(2).

[42] *Kyle Bay Ltd (trading as Astons Nightclub) v Underwriters subscribing under policy 019057/08/01* [2006] EWHC 607 (Comm), [2006] All E.R. (D) 433 (Mar), Jonathan Hirst Q.C. at [45]–[47], [52]–[54]. On appeal, this was accepted as the correct approach in principle: [2007] EWCA Civ 57, [2007] 1 C.L.C. 164 at [31]; see below, para.7-011. Likewise, when a party had expressly stated that it was giving no representation as to the accuracy of the information provided, there was no implication that it had no further information suggesting that what was stated might not be correct. The question is what would the reasonable person in the context have inferred was being implicitly represented: *IFE Fund SA v Goldman Sachs International* [2006] EWHC 2887 (Comm), [2007] 1 Lloyd's Rep. 264 at [50]; affirmed [2007] EWCA Civ 811, [2007] 2 Lloyd's Rep. 449. There might be an implied representation that the information was supplied in good faith, but not one that the party knew of nothing that might possibly cast doubt on it: [2006] EWHC 2887 (Comm) at [60].

[43] *Springwell Navigation Corp v JP Morgan Chase Bank* [2010] EWCA Civ 1221, [2010] 2 C.L.C. 705 at [121].

[44] [1958] Ch. 636.

[45] *New Brunswick and Canada Ry and Land Co v Conybeare* (1862) 9 H.L. Cas. 711; *Anderson v Pacific Insurance Co* (1872) L.R. 7 C.P. 65; *Bisset v Wilkinson* [1927] A.C. 177; *Sanders v Gall* [1952] Current Property Law 343.

[46] See *Reese River Silver Mining Co Ltd v Smith* (1869) L.R. 4 H.L. 64.

## Statement of intention not honestly held

*Replace footnote 53 with:*

7-013 [53] See *Edgington v Fitzmaurice* (1885) 29 Ch. D. 459; *Angus v Clifford* [1891] 2 Ch. 449, 470; *Goff v Gauthier* (1991) P. & C.R. 388; *C21 London Estates Ltd v Maurice Macneill Iona Ltd* [2017] EWHC 998 (Ch) at [44] and *Inter Export Llc v Townley* [2018] EWCA Civ 2068, applying this paragraph in the 32nd edition (but in the *London Estates* case it was not shown that the representation was false). cf. *Lewin v Barratt Homes Ltd* [2000] Crim. L.R. 323 (a case under Property Misdescriptions Act 1991 s.1). As David Richards J. said in *Abbar v Saudi Economic & Development Co (SEDCO) Real Estate Ltd* [2013] EWHC 1414 (Ch) at [197], it is difficult to see how a party could negligently, as opposed to fraudulently, misrepresent his own intentions. Nonetheless, the judge could see the possibility that a party might state its current intention yet negligently omit to reveal that his intention was qualified in that he had considered reviewing it at a later date: at [207].

## Statement as to future may carry implication of fact

*Replace footnote 57 with:*

7-014 [57] See *Spice Girls Ltd v Aprilia World Service BV* [2002] E.M.L.R. 27, 29; *Fitzroy Robinson Ltd v Mentmore Towers Ltd* [2009] EWHC 1552 (TCC) at [160]; *FoodCo UK LLP (t/a Muffin Break) v Henry Boot Developments Ltd* [2010] EWHC 358 (Ch) at [198]; *Inter Export Llc v Townley* [2018] EWCA Civ 2068, applying this paragraph in the 32nd edition.

## Implied representations

*Replace footnote 65 with:*

7-015 [65] *Property Alliance Group Ltd v Royal Bank of Scotland Plc* [2018] EWCA Civ 355, [2018] 1 W.L.R. 3529 at [126]. "A Court will not (or is very unlikely to) imply a representation from conduct in terms which are vague, uncertain, imprecise or elastic": *Marme Inversiones 2007 SL v Natwest Markets Plc* [2019] EWHC 366 (Comm) at [120] and [123]. Passive conduct may sometimes give rise to an implied representation but "the broader and more complex the alleged representations, the more active and specific the conduct must be to give rise to the implication": [2019] EWHC 366 (Comm) at [157].

## Liability in tort for incorrect opinions and forecasts

*Replace footnote 73 with:*

7-016 [73] See Cartwright, *Misrepresentation, Mistake and Non-disclosure*, 5th edn (2019), para.6-12.

## Statements of law

*Replace paragraph with:*

7-017 It used commonly to be said that a statement of law cannot be treated as a misrepresentation.[75] But the proposition was always in need of qualification and it is now more accurate to say that a statement of law will amount to a misrepresentation unless, in the circumstances, it reasonably appeared that the statement was put forward as nothing more than an opinion on which it would not be reasonable to rely. First, a statement of law may be regarded as a statement of opinion, but just as a statement of opinion may be a representation of fact, so too a statement of law may amount to a representation, or misrepresentation, as the case may be. So a wilful misstatement of law would always amount to a misrepresentation[76] and even an innocent misstatement of law may do so where it carries an implication of fact which is itself untrue. Secondly, the question whether a statement is one of law or fact gives rise to no small difficulty,[77] especially as statements of law and of fact are so frequently intermingled. It has been said that the dichotomy between statements of fact and statements of law is too neat, and is apt to mislead.[78] It seems that the courts tend to regard statements of mixed law and fact, and statements capable of having either meaning, as statements of fact,[79] and therefore as representations; that they also regard statements as to the purport, effect and objects of documents as representations[80]; and in *Cooper v Phibbs*,[81] a statement as to private rights, as distinct from the general law, was regarded as a statement of fact.[82] So a representation that planning permission exists for a particular use is a representation of fact, and not of law[83]; similarly with a representation by a landlord that he accepts liability for repairs under a lease.[84] On the other hand a statement of law made separately from a statement of fact was held not to be a misrepresentation.[85] This seems to rest on a distinction between a statement of an abstract proposition of law, which was not regarded as a misrepresentation, and a statement applying the law to the facts of a particular situation which, at least in some circumstances, may constitute a misrepresentation.[86] But thirdly, in the law of restitution the distinction between a payment made under a mistake of fact and one made under a mistake of law has been held by the House of Lords not to be part of English law,[87] and, in the light of this, it was held in *Pankhania v Hackney LBC*[88] that the "misrepresentation of law" rule is no longer good law. Thus, for the purposes of the law of misrepresentation, the distinction between statements of law and statements of fact is no longer maintainable and that even an incorrect statement of an abstract proposition of law may amount to a misrepresentation unless it is apparent that all that is being offered is an opinion without implication that the speaker has reasonable grounds for that opinion.[89] It is submitted that the underlying principle here is the same as that suggested in the previous paragraph, viz that even a statement as to the law may be a misrepresentation if it was reasonable, in all the circumstances, for the representee to rely upon it.[90] In any event a statement of foreign law is here (as elsewhere in the law) treated as a statement of fact.[91]

[75] *Beattie v Ebury* (1872) L.R. 7 Ch. App. 777, 802; *Beesly v Hallwood Estates Ltd* [1960] 1 W.L.R. 549, 560.

[76] *West London Commercial Bank v Kitson* (1884) 13 Q.B.D. 360, 362–363; *Oudaille v Lawson* [1922] N.Z.L.R. 259.

[77] See *Solle v Butcher* [1950] 1 K.B. 671.

[78] *Brikom Investments Ltd v Seaford* [1981] 1 W.L.R. 863.

[79] *Reynell v Sprye* (1852) 1 De G.M. & G. 660; *West London Commercial Bank v Kitson* (1884) 13 Q.B.D. 360; *Hughes v Liverpool Victoria Legal Friendly Society* [1916] 2 K.B. 482.

[80] *Hirshfeld v L.B. & S.C. Ry* (1876) 2 Q.B.D. 1; *De Tchihatchef v Salerni Coupling Ltd* [1932] 1 Ch. 330; *Curtis v Chemical Cleaning & Dyeing Co* [1951] 1 K.B. 805.

[81] (1867) L.R. 2 H.L. 149.

[82] (1867) L.R. 2 H.L. 149 at 170.

[83] *Laurence v Lexcourt Holdings Ltd* [1977] 1 W.L.R. 1128.

[84] *Brikom Investments Ltd v Seaford* [1981] 1 W.L.R. 863. But cf. *China Pacific SA v Food Corp of India* [1981] Q.B. 403, 429 (reversed on different grounds [1982] A.C. 939) where an admission of liability was said to be a representation of law.

[85] *Rashdall v Ford* (1866) L.R. 2 Eq. 750; *Harse v Pearl Life Assurance Co* [1904] 1 K.B. 558.

[86] See also, below, paras 29-044—29-049.

[87] *Kleinwort Benson Ltd v Lincoln City Council* [1999] 2 A.C. 349. See below, para.29-046.

[88] [2002] EWHC 2441(Ch). See also above, para.6-052.

[89] cf. above, para.7-011. It has rightly been remarked that the reasons often given for refusing relief on the grounds of a mistake of law—for example, that it would be easy to claim a mistaken belief in the law and hard to disprove it—have much less weight when the mistake was the result of a misrepresentation by the other party: Cartwright, *Misrepresentation, Mistake and Non-disclosure*, 5th edn (2019), para.3-31.

[90] See Cartwright, *Misrepresentation, Mistake and Non-disclosure*, 5th edn (2019), para.3-40.

[91] *André & Cie SA v Ets Michel Blanc & Fils* [1977] 2 Lloyd's Rep. 166.

## Non-disclosure

*Replace footnote 95 with:*

7-018 [95] See *Keates v Cadogan* (1851) 10 C.B. 591; *New Brunswick and Canada Ry and Land Co v Conybeare* (1862) 9 H.L. Cas. 711; *Smith v Hughes* (1871) L.R. 6 Q.B. 597; *Turner v Green* [1895] 2 Ch. 205; see also *Jewson & Son Ltd v Arcos Ltd* (1933) 39 Com. Cas. 59; *Wales v Wadham* [1977] 1 W.L.R. 199. This sentence of the text was cited with approval in *Donegal International Ltd v Zambia* [2007] EWHC 197 (Comm), [2007] 1 Lloyd's Rep. 397 at [465] and in *ING Bank NV v Ros Roca* [2011] EWCA Civ 353, [2012] 1 W.L.R. 472 at [92].

## Partial non-disclosure

7-021 *In line 15, after "be a misrepresentation.[118]", delete ".".*

## Continuity of representations

*Replace paragraph with:*

7-023 Representations are treated for many purposes as continuing in their effect until the contract between the parties is actually concluded.[121a] This is one reason why a statement which is true when made, but which ceases to be true to the knowledge of the representor before the contract is concluded, is treated as a misrepresentation unless the representor informs the representee of the change in circumstances.[122] This principle may have other effects as well. First, as we have just seen, if a representation is made innocently but falsely, and facts later come to the knowledge of the representor which show that the statement was false, a failure to inform the representee of the truth may convert what was originally an innocent misrepresentation into a fraudulent one.[123] Again, if a man truthfully states that he intends to do something but changes his mind at a later stage he may come under a duty to disclose that change.[124] The principle is also recognised by s.2(1) of the Misrepresentation Act which extends the right to damages for negligent misrepresentation,[125] for a misrepresentation falls within this subsection unless the representor had reasonable grounds to believe and did believe *up to the time the contract was made* that the facts represented were true.[126] Another consequence of the principle that representations are continuous in their effect is that if a representation is made by an agent who is acting without authority, and he subsequently obtains the authority of his principal to continue the negotiations, the principal will become responsible for the representations previously made by the agent.[127] Conversely, if the contract is ultimately concluded not between the representor and the original representee but between the representor and a third person (on the facts of the case, a company formed for the purpose only after the original representation had been made), the representation may be treated as being made to the third party.[128] On the facts of the case the original representee continued to act as agent of the third person, so the representation could be regarded as continuing to be made to him, though in a different capacity. It is submitted that this is not a necessary condition, at least if the representor knows that the statement made earlier is likely to be passed on to the third person and does nothing to withdraw it or to indicate that there should be a fresh start to the negotiations, so that "the earlier misrepresentation is to be regarded as water under the bridge".[129] There are some circumstances in which a contract may be treated as commercially binding before it becomes legally binding, and in such a case it seems that the principle of continuity of representations does not operate beyond the time when the contract becomes commercially binding. So, for instance, an insured was held not to be obliged (despite the general duty of disclosure in insurance contracts)[130] to disclose facts coming to his notice after the insurer had initialled a slip indicating that he was at risk, although there was no binding legal contract until a policy was issued later.[131]

121a See *Cramaso LLP v Viscount Reidhaven's Trustees* [2014] UKSC 9, [2014] A.C. 1093 at [16]–[23]; *Inter Export LLC v Townley* [2018] EWCA Civ 2068 at [30]–[31].

122 Above, para.7-022.

123 *Davies v London Provincial Marine Insurance Co* (1878) 8 Ch. D. 469.

124 *Ray v Sempers* [1974] A.C. 370. But contrast *Wales v Wadham* [1977] 1 W.L.R. 199, 211 (wife not obliged to reveal change of intention not to marry; overruled on another ground but apparent approval given to the decision on this point, *Livesey v Jenkins* [1985] A.C. 424, 439); see Cartwright, *Unequal Bargaining*, pp.84–88.

125 This is dealt with fully below, paras 7-077 et seq.

126 *Corner v Munday* [1987] C.L.Y. 479.

127 *Briess v Woolley* [1954] A.C. 333.

128 *Cramaso LLP v Viscount Reidhaven's Trustees* [2014] UKSC 9, [2014] A.C. 1093.

129 [2014] UKSC 9 at [56].

130 Below, paras 7-160 et seq.

131 *Cory v Patton* (1872) L.R. 7 Q.B. 304; cf. *Berger and Light Diffusers Pty Ltd v Pollock* [1973] 2 Lloyd's Rep. 442, 460–461.

### Withdrawals and corrections

*Replace footnote 132 with:*

132 *Cramaso LLP v Viscount Reidhaven's Trustees* [2014] UKSC 9, [2014] A.C. 1093 at [20]. On inducement see paras 7-036 et seq. 7-024

## (c) Other Requirements

### Intention

*Replace paragraph with:*

It is also sometimes said that a misrepresentation will not be effective to create liability for deceit unless it was intended to be acted on by the representee.[178] If this means no more than that the representee cannot complain unless the misrepresentation was addressed to him, or to a class of persons to whom he was one, the statement is doubtless correct. This point has been dealt with earlier.[179] But if the statement that the representor must have intended the representee to act on the representation means that the representor will not be liable if he did not intend that the person to whom he was deliberately giving the false information should act on it at all, or not in the way he did, the proposition must be treated with some caution. First, it seems that any requirement of intention applies only to cases of fraud[180] and perhaps (because of the "fiction of fraud") to cases in which it is claimed that the misrepresentor is liable in damages under Misrepresentation Act 1967 s.2(1).[181] In cases of liability in tort for negligence, the test is one of reasonable foreseeability.[182] It is submitted in cases in which the claimant seeks to rescind on the grounds of a 7-034 non-fraudulent misrepresentation it will suffice that the misrepresentor should have realised that the misrepresentee might, not unreasonably, act on the representation, as then the statement will be one on which the misrepresentee was entitled to rely.[183] Secondly, even in fraud cases the authorities are not clear on whether it suffices that it must have been obvious that the claimant or someone in his position might rely on the statement. In *Cullen v Thomson*[184] three company directors were responsible for reading a report to a shareholders' meeting which contained a completely fraudulent account of the company's financial condition. It seems probable that the report was merely intended to conceal the company's financial condition from the shareholders, but the plaintiff, himself a shareholder, purchased additional shares in reliance on this report. It was held that the directors were liable for their fraudulent misrepresentations if they were made:

> "... with the real intent to cause the [representee] to act on that representation, or under such circumstances as they must have supposed would probably induce a person in the situation of the [representee] to act upon it."[185]

In *Tackey v McBain*[186] it was held that a manager of a company who said that he had no information to a broker about an important find of oil when in fact he did was not liable to a party who as a result sold his shares at a low price, whether or not the plaintiff was within the class to whom the statement was addressed, because the manager did not intend anyone to act as the plaintiff did and therefore had no fraudulent intent.[187] The likelihood of reliance was not discussed.

[178] Cartwright, *Misrepresentation, Mistake and Non-disclosure*, 5th edn (2019), para.5-19; Compare *Clerk & Lindsell on Torts*, 22nd edn (2017), para.18-30.

[179] See above, para.7-032.

[180] Cartwright, *Misrepresentation, Mistake and Non-disclosure*, 5th edn (2019), para.3-50. In a case of fraud it is necessary only that the representor intended the representation to be acted on: *Goose v Wilson Sandford (No.2)* [2000] All E.R. (D) 324 at [48]; *Mead v Babington (formerly t/a Babington Estate Agents)* [2007] EWCA Civ 518 at [16].

[181] See below, para.7-080; *Banque Keyser Ullman SA v Skandia (UK) Insurance Ltd* [1990] 1 Q.B. 665, 790 (affirmed on other grounds [1991] 2 A.C. 249).

[182] See above, para.7-033.

[183] See above, para.7-007.

[184] (1862) 6 L.T. 870.

[185] (1862) 6 L.T. 870, 874.

[186] [1912] A.C. 186, PC.

[187] See also *Banque Keyser Ullman SA v Skandia (UK) Insurance Ltd* [1990] 1 Q.B. 665, 790 (affirmed on other grounds [1991] 2 A.C. 249). In *Gabriel v Little* [2013] EWCA Civ 1513 it was held that "whilst the motive of the representor is irrelevant, an intention to influence the mind of the representee must be shown if the requisite dishonest intention is to be established" (at [33]).

## Inducement

*Replace footnote 193 with:*

7-036 [193] Cited with approval, *Brown v InnovatorOne Plc* [2012] EWHC 1321 (Comm) at [883]. Where the representation is implied, the claimant must prove that it understood the representation to have been made: [2012] EWHC 1321 (Comm) at [906]. It has been said that the claimant must have given conscious thought to the representation, even if not to the precise formulation that the court later decides the representation comprised: *Marme Inversiones 2007 SL v Natwest Markets Plc* [2019] EWHC 366 (Comm) at [286]. If it would have been unreasonable of the representee to rely upon the representation, that may go to show that the representee did not in fact rely on it: *Monde Petroleum SA v WesternZagros Ltd* [2016] EWHC 1472 (Comm), [2016] 2 Lloyd's Rep. 229 at [219].

## Burden of proof

*Replace paragraph with:*

The burden of proving that the claimant's decision to enter the contract was not induced by a misrepresentation normally lies on the defendant. In previous editions of this work it was stated that: **7-037**

> "The burden of proving that the claimant had actual knowledge of the truth, and therefore was not deceived by the misrepresentation, lies on the defendant; if established, knowledge on the part of the representee is a complete defence, because he is then unable to show that he was misled by the misrepresentation."[203]

This statement was cited in *Hayward v Zurich Insurance Co Plc*.[204] The Supreme Court did not accept that knowledge of the falsity was always a defence: its decision shows that the question is whether the claimant's decision was induced by the misrepresentation, not necessarily whether the claimant suspected or possibly even knew the statement to be untrue.[205] The Court did not comment explicitly on the burden of proof but it referred to "rebutting" the presumption of inducement that arises (as a matter of fact) once it has been shown that the false statement was material.[206] On the other hand Lord Clarke said that even in a case in which the claimant knows that the representation was a lie, it "may be able to establish inducement on the facts".[207] This suggests that the question of the burden of proof is an evidential one, not a rule of law; and this has been confirmed by the Court of Appeal.[207a]

[203] 32nd edn (2015), para.7-036, citing *Dyer v Hargrave* (1805) 10 Ves. 505; *Attwood v Small* (1838) 6 Cl. & F. 232; *Vigers v Pike* (1842) 8 Cl. & F. 562, 650.

[204] [2016] UKSC 48, [2017] A.C. 142.

[205] See above, para.7-036.

[206] [2016] UKSC 48 at [34], [36]. On the presumption of inducement see below, para.7-041. The representee has no duty to be careful, suspicious or diligent in research: *Playboy Club London Ltd v Banca Nazionale del Lavoro SpA* [2018] UKSC 43, [2018] 1 W.L.R. 4041 at [39].

[207] At [45].

[207a] *BV Nederlandse Industrie Van Eiprodukten v Rembrandt Enterprises Inc* [2019] EWCA Civ 596, [2020] Q.B. 551, see at [32] and [44].

## Need not be sole inducement

*Replace paragraph with:*

It is not necessary that the misrepresentation should be the sole cause which induced the representee to make the contract. It is sufficient if it can be shown to have been one of the inducing causes.[208] Thus in *Edgington v Fitzmaurice*[209] the plaintiff was induced to take debentures in a company partly because of a misrepresentation in the prospectus, but also because of a mistaken belief of his own that the debentures conferred a charge on the company's property. He was held to be entitled to have the contract rescinded, and Cotton L.J. said, "[i]t is not necessary to show that the misstatement was the sole cause of his acting as he did".[210] The plaintiff appears to have agreed to take the debentures because of a combination of the misrepresentation and his own mistake.[211] What is required is that the misrepresentee would not have entered the contract but for the misrepresentation.[212] **7-038**

[208] *Western Bank of Scotland v Addie* (1867) L.R. 1 Sc. & Div. 145, 158; *Geest Plc v Fyffes Plc* [1999] 1 All E.R. (Comm) 672; *Brown v InnovatorOne Plc* [2012] EWHC 1321 (Comm) at [883]; *Taberna Europe CDO II Plc v Selskabet* [2015] EWHC 871 (Comm) at [153], citing this paragraph (reversed on

other grounds [2016] EWCA Civ 1262, [2017] Q.B. 633); *Hayward v Zurich Insurance Co Plc* [2016] UKSC 48, [2017] A.C. 142 at [33], also citing this paragraph.

209 (1885) 29 Ch. D. 459.

210 (1885) 29 Ch. D. 459, 481. See also *BV Nederlandse Industrie Van Eiprodukten v Rembrandt Enterprises Inc* [2019] EWCA Civ 596.

211 See the judgment of Fry L.J. at 483. Bowen L.J. seems to have applied a slightly different test, whether the representation was "actively present to his mind" so that it might have influenced his decision, though in *Marme Inversiones 2007 SL v Natwest Markets Plc* [2019] EWHC 366 (Comm) at [307] Picken J. said he read Bowen L.J. as also addressing only the question whether it is sufficient if the fraudulent statement was one of several causes. See further para.7-040 below.

212 See next paragraph.

### "But for" causation normally required

*Replace footnote 214 with:*

7-039 214 *Assicurazioni Generali SpA v Arab Insurance Group* [2003] 1 All E.R. (Comm) 140; *Taberna Europe CDO II Plc v Selskabet* [2015] EWHC 871 (Comm) at [153], citing this paragraph in the 31st edition (reversed on other grounds [2016] EWCA Civ 1262); *BV Nederlandse Industrie Van Eiprodukten v Rembrandt Enterprises Inc* [2019] EWCA Civ 596, [2020] Q.B. 551, also citing this paragraph. This is consistent with the decision of the House of Lords in *Pan Atlantic Insurance Co Ltd v Pine Top Insurance Co Ltd* [1995] 1 A.C. 501 (see below) and *Raiffeisen Zentralbank Osterreich AG v Royal Bank of Scotland Plc* [2010] EWHC 1392 (Comm), [2011] 1 Lloyd's Rep. 123 at [163]–[173]. See also *Cassa di Risparmio della Repubblica di San Marino SpA v Barclays Bank Ltd* [2011] EWHC 484 (Comm) at [232]; *Leni Gas and Oil Investments Ltd v Malta Oil Pty Ltd* [2014] EWHC 893 (Comm) at [17]; *Marme Inversiones 2007 SL v Natwest Markets Plc* [2019] EWHC 366 (Comm) at [304] and [317]. The test is whether the misrepresentee would have entered the contract had the representation not been made, rather than what he would have done had he known the truth: [2010] EWHC 1392 (Comm) at [174]–[191]; *Cassa di Risparmio della Repubblica di San Marino SpA v Barclays Bank Ltd* [2011] EWHC 484 (Comm) at [232]; *Leni Gas and Oil Investments Ltd v Malta Oil Pty Ltd* [2014] EWHC 893 (Comm) at [17]; *Marme Inversiones 2007 SL v Natwest Markets Plc* [2019] EWHC 366 (Comm) at [298].

### "But for" causation not required for rescission for fraud

*Replace paragraph with:*

7-040 In cases of fraud, in contrast, if the representee seeks to rescind, it is no defence for the representor to show that if the misrepresentation had not been made, the misrepresentee might still have made the contract.[217] It is sufficient if there is evidence to show that he was materially influenced by the misrepresentation merely in the sense that it had some impact on his thinking, "was actively present to his mind".[218] As Lord Cross put it in a case of duress to the person[219]:

> "... [i]n this field the court does not allow an examination into the relative importance of contributory causes.
>
> > 'Once make out that there has been anything like deception, and no contract resting in any degree on that foundation can stand':
>
> per Lord Cranworth L.J. in *Reynell v Sprye*."[220]

The Privy Council applied this "fraud rule" when B had entered a contract with A after A had made threats against B's life. It held that B was entitled to relief even though he might well have entered into the contract if A had uttered no threats. It was only if it were shown that B did not allow the threat to affect his judgment at all that relief would be denied.[221] The Court of Appeal has held that this is not a reversal of the usual burden of proof,[221a] but it seems still to suffice that the false statement was "actively present to [the representee's mind]", even if he might still have entered the contract anyway—in other words, a special rule that in fraud cases that, provided the misrepresentation had some influence, it is no defence that the misrepresentee would have entered the contract even if the statement had not been made.[222] The rule is intended to deter fraud.[223] The same approach has been applied by the Court of Appeal in a case of "actual" undue influence,[224] which is seen as a "species of fraud".[225] The rule applies only to fraud,[226] and only when the remedy sought is rescission. The victim of fraud cannot recover damages unless the loss for which damages are claimed would not have been suffered but for the fraud.[227]

[217] See *Re London & Leeds Bank* (1887) 56 L.J. Ch. 321.

[218] Bowen L.J. in *Edgington v Fitzmaurice* (1885) 29 Ch. D. 459, 483; *Brown v InnovatorOne Plc* [2012] EWHC 1321 (Comm) at [883]. Bowen L.J. seems to have applied this test to a claim for damages for fraud, but he seems to have been in the minority; see above, para.7-038. In *Marme Inversiones 2007 SL v Natwest Markets Plc* [2019] EWHC 366 (Comm) at [296] Picken J. emphasised "the ... distinction between the question of whether a misrepresentation has induced a claimant to act in a certain way and the separate question of whether loss has been caused to the claimant as a result of the representation", referring to MacDonald Eggers, *Vitiation of Contractual Consent*, 1st edn (2016) at pp.646–647; and (at [317]) considered that the but for test should apply to claims for damages for fraud. However, in *BV Nederlandse Industrie Van Eiprodukten v Rembrandt Enterprises Inc* [2019] EWCA Civ 596, [2020] Q.B. 551 Longmore L.J. (with whom the other members of the Court agreed) stated the "actively present to his mind" test as being applicable also to the tort of deceit, see at [32].

[219] *Barton v Armstrong* [1976] A.C. 104, PC at 118–119. In *Hayward v Zurich Insurance Co Plc* [2016] UKSC 48, [2017] A.C. 142 at [33] Lord Clarke quoted the first sentence of Lord Cross's statement but did not address the question of whether but for causation is required. On the facts of the *Hayward* case, any "but-for" requirement was satisfied.

[220] (1852) 1 De G.M. & G. 660, 708. See also *Arnison v Smith* (1889) 41 Ch. D. 348, 369, where Lord Halsbury L.C. said, "[y]ou cannot weight the elements by ounces".

[221] [1976] A.C. 104, PC at 118–119.

[221a] In *BV Nederlandse Industrie Van Eiprodukten v Rembrandt Enterprises Inc* [2019] EWCA Civ 596 Longmore L.J. (with whom the other members of the Court of Appeal agreed) emphasised that the representee must still prove inducement, albeit with the assistance of a presumption that "will be very difficult to rebut", so that a court that "cannot make up its mind on inducement" should not give the representee the benefit of the doubt as a matter of law: at [45].

[222] The rule is usefully discussed in Burrows, *Law of Restitution*, 3rd edn (2011), pp.94–95.

[223] cf. below, para.7-066.

[224] *UCB Corporate Services Ltd v Williams* [2002] EWCA Civ 555 at [86].

[225] See below, para.8-074.

[226] *Ross River Ltd v Cambridge City Football Club Ltd* [2007] EWHC 2115 (Ch), [2008] 1 All E.R. 1004 at [202], referring to this paragraph in an earlier edition; *Raiffeisen Zentralbank Osterreich AG v Royal Bank of Scotland Plc* [2010] EWHC 1392 (Comm) at [198]. The but for test is said to apply to non-disclosure where there is a duty to disclose: *Assicurazioni Generali SpA v Arab Insurance Group* [2003] 1 All E.R. (Comm) 140 at [59], [187], but note the doubts of Ward L.J. at [218].

[227] See above, para.7-039.

## Materiality

*Replace footnote 231 with:*

[231] Peel (ed.), *Treitel on The Law of Contract*, 15th edn (2020), paras 9-023–9-024 (but noting that exceptions mean the requirement will seldom not be met). 7-042

## Unforeseeable reliance

*Replace footnote 239 with:*

[239] It is submitted that this was the question in *Goff v Gauthier* (1991) 62 P. & C.R. 388, although the court referred to an earlier version of the previous paragraph of this work. It was also the question in *Museprime Properties Ltd v Adhill Properties Ltd* [1990] 2 E.G.L.R. 196 (representee did not take opportunity to check accuracy.) cf. Peel (ed.), *Treitel on The Law of Contract*, 15th edn (2020), para.9-023. 7-043

### Representee could have discovered truth: rescission

*Replace footnote 245 with:*

7-044 [245] Peel (ed.), *Treitel on The Law of Contract*, 14th edn (2015), para.9-028; the suggestion is not repeated in the 15th edn (2020), para.9-033, which instead suggests that the principle stated in the first sentence of this paragraph applies only once it is clear that a misrepresentation has been made.

## 3. DAMAGES FOR MISREPRESENTATION

## (a) Fraudulent Misrepresentation

### Claims for damages for fraud

*Replace footnote 262 with:*

7-048 [262] *Archer v Brown* [1985] Q.B. 401. The rules relating to liability for damages for fraud are set out in some detail in *Vald Nielsen Holding A/S v Baldorino* [2019] EWHC 1926 (Comm) at [130]–[159].

### Absence of honest belief

*Replace footnote 273 with:*

7-050 [273] (1889) 14 App. Cas. 337, 379. The decisions in *Barlow Clowes International Ltd v Eurotrust International Ltd* [2005] UKPC 37, [2006] 1 W.L.R. 1476 and *Ivey v Genting Casinos UK Ltd* [2017] UKSC 67, [2018] A.C. 391 have not rendered the test of dishonesty an objective one, and only if the representor has been shown to not to have believed the truth of the statement can the question arise whether his conduct was honest or dishonest by the (objective) standards of ordinary people: *Glossop Cartons and Print Ltd v Contact (Print and Packaging) Ltd* [2019] EWHC 2314 (Ch) at [49].

### Motive irrelevant

*Replace paragraph with:*

7-052 Further, it is not necessary to establish that the defendant's motive was dishonest.[276] However, it must be shown that the representor intended the representee to act on the representation.[277] In the case of an implied representation, if the representor intended what he said to be relied on by the representee in deciding whether to contract, he must be taken to have intended that the representee should rely on the objective meaning of what he said.[277a]

[276] See *Polhill v Walter* (1832) 3 B. & Ad. 114; *Denton v G.N. Ry* (1856) 5 El. & Bl. 860; *Brown Jenkinson & Co Ltd v Percy Dalton (London) Ltd* [1957] 2 Q.B. 621; *Standard Chartered Bank v Pakistan National Shipping Corp* [1995] 2 Lloyd's Rep. 365; *Standard Chartered Bank v Pakistan National Shipping Corp (No.2)* [2000] 1 Lloyd's Rep. 218, 224 (reversed in part on other grounds, [2002] UKHL 43, [2003] 1 A.C. 959); *Gabriel v Little* [2013] EWCA Civ 1513 at [32]. See also *Morrell v Stewart* [2015] EWHC 962 (Ch) (fraud if vendors said no work done on property knowing work had been done but believing it had cured any problem). The definition of criminal fraud under the Fraud Act 2006 is different. Section 2 requires both dishonesty and an intention, by making the representation, either to make a gain for oneself or to cause loss to another or to expose another to the risk of loss. "It is not necessary that the maker of the statement was 'dishonest' as that word is used in the criminal law ... What is required is dishonest knowledge, in the sense of an absence of belief in truth": *Vald Nielsen Holding A/S v Baldorino* [2019] EWHC 1926 (Comm) at [147]; *Glossop Cartons and Print Ltd v Contact (Print and Packaging) Ltd* [2019] EWHC 2314 (Ch) at [49].

[277] *Gabriel v Little* [2013] EWCA Civ 1513 at [33]. That paragraph refers to "a dishonest intention", but it has been held that there is no separate requirement of an intention to deceive: *Eco3 Capital Ltd v Ludsin Overseas Ltd* [2013] EWCA Civ 413 at [78]; *Marme Inversiones 2007 SL v Natwest Markets Plc* [2019] EWHC 366 (Comm) at [254].

[277a] *Raiffeisen Zentralbank Osterreich AG v Royal Bank of Scotland Plc* [2010] EWHC 1392 (Comm) at [222]; *Marme Inversiones 2007 SL v Natwest Markets Plc* [2019] EWHC 366 (Comm) at [261]. Similarly, the representor may be taken to know that the statement would be acted on: see *Marme Inversiones 2007 SL v Natwest Markets Plc* [2019] EWHC 366 (Comm) at [263]–[264].

## Ambiguity

*Replace footnote 281 with:*

281 *Gross v Lewis Hillman Ltd* [1970] Ch. 445; *Goose v Wilson Sandford (No.2)* [2000] All E.R. (D) 324 at [41]; *Cassa di Risparmio della Repubblica di San Marino SpA v Barclays Bank Ltd* [2011] EWHC 484 (Comm), [2011] 1 C.L.C. 701 at [221]; *Vald Nielsen Holding A/S v Baldorino* [2019] EWHC 1926 (Comm) at [140]–[141]. **7-053**

## Principal and agent

*Replace footnote 285 with:*

285 *Ludgater v Love* (1881) 44 L.T. 694; *Occidental Worldwide Investment Corp v Skibs A/S Avanti* [1976] 1 Lloyd's Rep. 293, 320–321 and *UBS AG v Kommunale Wasserwerke Leipzig GmbH* [2014] EWHC 3615 (Comm) at [755] (in both cases this sentence in the text was cited with approval). See also *GG 132 Ltd v Hampson Industries Plc* [2011] EWHC 1137 (Comm) at [42]. **7-054**

## Causation in damages for fraud

*Replace paragraph with:*

As stated earlier,[286] when the claimant seeks damages for fraud as opposed to rescission, the normal "but for" rule of causation seems to apply. Thus if the claimant would have entered the contract on the same terms even if the misrepresentation had not been made, his claim for damages will fail.[287] The court is not required to speculate as to what the misrepresentee would have done had he known the truth,[287a] and the defendant will not be permitted to argue that the misrepresentee might have entered the contract on the same terms anyway.[288] But if the misrepresentor can be definitively show that this is what the misrepresentee would have done, it will be very difficult for the misrepresentee to argue that it was induced by the fraudulent misrepresentation.[289] **7-055**

286 Above, para.7-039.

287 See above, para.7-039; *Clerk & Lindsell on Torts*, 22nd edn (2017), para.18-34; see *Templeton Insurance Ltd v Motorcare Warranties Ltd* [2010] EWHC 3113 (Comm) at [168] (need not be sole cause; sufficient that substantially contributed to deceiving the claimant). The action will fail if the claimant would have done the same thing even if no representation had been made but the defendant will not normally be permitted to argue that the claimant might have done the same thing had he known the truth.

287a See *Leni Gas and Oil Investments Ltd v Malta Oil Pty Ltd* [2014] EWHC 893 (Comm) at [17]; *Marme Inversiones 2007 SL v Natwest Markets Plc* [2019] EWHC 366 (Comm) at [298].

288 *Downs v Chappell* [1997] 1 W.L.R. 426 at 433; see also *Smith New Court Securities Ltd v Scrimgeour Vickers (Asset Management) Ltd* [1997] A.C. 254, 283. This principle cannot prevent *the claimant* from giving evidence that it would not have acted as it did if it had known the true position, as demonstrating inducement by the fraudulent misrepresentation: *Parabola Investments Ltd v Browallia Cal Ltd* [2009] EWHC 901 (Comm), [2009] 2 All E.R. (Comm) 589 at [105], per Flaux J. (affirmed without reference to this point, [2010] EWCA Civ 486, [2011] Q.B. 477).

289 *Dadourian Group International Inc v Simms* [2009] EWCA Civ 169, [2009] 1 Lloyd's Rep. 601 at [107]. This dictum is criticised by Handley (2015) 131 L.Q.R. 275, 283. However, it is consistent with what appears to be the case if it can be shown that, if the misrepresentation had not occurred and the misrepresentee would not have entered the contract, nonetheless he would have entered another losing contract. See below, para.7-068.

## Lost opportunity

*Replace footnote 293 with:*

293 [1991] 1 W.L.R. 461. See also *Clef Aquitaine SARL v Laporte Materials (Barrow) Ltd* [2001] Q.B. 488 (claimants had agreed to buy goods from defendants at prices which defendants had fraudulently stated to be those charged to the defendants' UK customers. Although claimants had been able to resell the goods profitably, they were still entitled to the difference between the prices they had paid and those they would probably have been able to negotiate had the misrepresentation not been made). Similar damages for wasted expenditure and loss of other opportunities were awarded in *Esso Petroleum Ltd v* **7-058**

*Mardon* [1976] Q.B. 801. But cf. *Davis v Churchward* Unreported May 6, 1993 noted in (1994) 110 L.Q.R. 35. See also *Smith Kline & French Laboratories Ltd v Long* [1989] 1 W.L.R. 1, in which sellers, who had been tricked into supplying goods to a buyer who was unable to pay, recovered the normal wholesale price of the goods, not just the cost of producing them. It has been argued persuasively that the decision in *Smith Kline* on this point was wrong, as it had not been shown that the plaintiff had lost an opportunity to sell the goods to someone else: Burrows, *Remedies for Torts, Breach of Contract and Equitable Wrongs*, 4th edn (2019), pp.224–225. The point was left open by the House of Lords in *Smith New Court Securities Ltd v Scrimgeour Vickers (Asset Management) Ltd* [1997] A.C. 254, 283 and the *Smith Kline* case remains binding on the Court of Appeal: *Inter Export LLC v Townley* [2018] EWCA Civ 2068, though it was said that "[t]here may ... be special rules which apply to matters surrounding the measurement of loss in the case of deceit which do not apply in the case of a negligent misstatement" (at [66]). There is no suggestion in the *Smith New Court* case, however, that damages for fraud should put the claimant into the position it would have been in had the statement been true. In the *Inter Export* case itself, *Smith Kline* was not applicable. A seller of goods who had been tricked into supplying them to a company by a false representation by a director that the company was able to pay for them, which it was not able to do, was entitled to recover the market value of the goods at the moment when it relied on the representation by allowing the goods to be delivered, rather than a measure of its loss at the earlier date when the representation was first made (at [67]).

## Assessing damages for fraud

*To the end of point (2), after "caused by the transaction", add new footnote 300a:*

7-061 [300a] Thus it should not include potential losses which [the representee] had fully appreciated and factored into the purchase price: *Glossop Cartons and Print Ltd v Contact (Print and Packaging) Ltd* [2019] EWHC 2314 (Ch) at [103], and see the further proceedings in the same case [2020] EWHC 1377 (Ch).

## Subsequent falls in value of property

*Replace footnote 306 with:*

7-063 [306] See the speech of Lord Steyn in *Smith New Court Securities Ltd v Scrimgeour Vickers (Asset Management) Ltd* [1997] A.C. 254, 284; *Great Future International Ltd v Sealand Housing Corp* [2002] All E.R. (D) 28; *McGregor on Damages*, 20th edn (2017), para.49-011.

## "Already flawed assets"

*Replace footnote 310 with:*

7-064 [310] [1997] A.C. 254. See also *Glossop Cartons and Print Ltd v Contact (Print and Packaging) Ltd* [2019] EWHC 2314 (Ch) at [46] and [61].

## Claimant would have entered another losing transaction

*In line 5, page [691], after "would have entered another losing transaction.", add new footnote 331a:*

7-068 [331a] This might be because even if the false representation (an alleged implied representation that interest rates were not being manipulated) had not been made, the claimant would not have discovered the truth (*Marme Inversiones 2007 SL v Natwest Markets Plc* [2019] EWHC 366 (Comm) at [360]) or, as in that case, the claimants would have entered a similar transaction even without the representation and could not show that, had the truth been known. The transaction would have been on better terms (at [510]).

## Exemplary damages

*Replace paragraph with:*

7-072 It is not yet wholly clear if exemplary damages can be awarded for fraud.[340] Until recently it seemed very unlikely. Even if fraud could be brought within the first or second of Lord Devlin's three categories in *Rookes v Barnard*,[341] namely, first, oppressive, arbitrary or unconstitutional action by the servants of government or, secondly, cases in which the defendant's conduct has been calculated to make a profit for himself which may well exceed the compensation payable to the plaintiff,[342] the interpretation of those categories by the House of Lords in *Cassell & Co Ltd v Broome*[343] and by the Court of Appeal in *AB v South West Water Services Ltd*[344] required that for exemplary damages to be awarded the tort must be one in respect of which such an award had been made prior to 1964, and deceit is not such a tort.[345] However in *Kuddus v Chief Constable of Leicestershire Constabulary*[346] the House of Lords held that the power to award exemplary damages is not limited to those cases in which such awards had been made before 1964. *AB v South West Water Services Ltd* was overruled. This seems to open the way for awards of exemplary damages in cases of deceit which fall into Lord Devlin's first two categories. Although both Lord Nicholls[347] and Lord Scott[348] remarked that the growth of remedies for unjust enrichment may make Lord Devlin's second category of less importance as the defendant's profit may be removed without an award of exemplary damages,[349] exemplary damages were awarded in a case involving fraudulent insurance claims where the anticipated profit would have exceeded the loss.[350] The argument (made in previous editions of this work) that it would be wrong to award exemplary where the defendant has already been convicted and imprisoned for the same fraud, because would infringe the basic principle that a person should not be punished twice for the same offence,[351] has been rejected.[352]

[340] See *Mafo v Adams* [1970] 1 Q.B. 548; *Cassell & Co Ltd v Broome* [1972] A.C. 1027 and *Archer v Brown* [1985] 1 Q.B. 401, 418–421.

[341] [1964] A.C. 1129.

[342] *Rookes v Barnard* [1964] A.C. 1129, 1225–1226.

[343] *Cassell Co Ltd v Broome* [1972] A.C. 1027, *Mafo v Adams* [1970] 1 Q.B. 548 was criticised.

[344] [1993] Q.B. 507.

[345] *Cassell & Co Ltd v Broome* [1972] A.C. 1027, 1076, per Lord Hailsham L.C. See also Law Commission, *Aggravated, Exemplary and Restitutionary Damages* (Report No.247, 1997), para.4.25. In *Parabola Investments Ltd v Browallia Cal Ltd* [2009] EWHC 901 (Comm) Flaux J. said that his own research had shown that "exemplary damages have been awarded in cases of deceit, primarily in the case of fraudulent insurance claims by insureds dealt with in the county courts. This is no doubt because such cases do fall into that category, as the insurer's remedy is rejection of the claim coupled with avoidance and retention of the premium and it would not expect any compensation as such" (at [205]). However, he declined to make an award when the defendant's responsibility was only vicarious (see at [206]–[208]). The Court of Appeal ([2010] EWCA Civ 486, [2011] Q.B. 477) did not refer to this question.

[346] [2001] UKHL 29, [2002] 2 A.C. 122.

[347] [2001] UKHL 29 at [67]. Lord Nicholls considered that Lord Devlin's second category should be expanded to include cases in which the defendant had acted with a malicious motive.

[348] [2001] UKHL 29 at [109]. Lord Scott thought that if exemplary damages were to be retained (which he personally regretted), deceit practised by a government or local authority official, or by a police officer, would be a suitable case for their award (at [122]).

[349] See above, para.7-069 and below, para.26-055. The Law Commission, in its Report on *Aggravated, Exemplary and Restitutionary Damages* (No.247, 1997) had recommended that punitive damages be available when, in committing a wrong or in subsequent conduct, the defendant deliberately disregarded the claimant's rights: see above, para.7-071.

[350] *AXA Insurance UK Plc v Financial Claims Solutions Ltd* [2018] EWCA Civ 1330, [2019] R.T.R. 1.

[351] Suggested in *Archer v Brown* [1985] Q.B. 401, 426.

[352] *AXA Insurance UK Plc v Financial Claims Solutions Ltd* [2018] EWCA Civ 1330 at [33], applying *Borders (UK) Ltd v Commissioner of Police of the Metropolis* [2005] EWCA Civ 197.

### Compound interest

*Replace footnote 357 with:*

7-074 [357] The categories given by Lord Brandon in *President of India v LaPintada Compania Navigacion SA* [1985] A.C. 104 at 116A. This was the view of the majority in *Westdeutsche Landesbank Girozentrale v Islington LBC* [1996] A.C. 669. For a case in which a party that had obtained money from a trust by deceit was held to be a constructive trustee and liable to pay compound interest, see *Glenn v Watson* [2018] EWHC 2483 (Ch).

## (b) Negligent Misrepresentation

### Not strictly speaking liability for negligence

*Replace footnote 372 with:*

7-078 [372] An action under s.2(1) is not an action for negligence within the meaning of the Limitation Act 1980 s.14A, since it is not necessary for the claimant to aver any negligent act or omission: *Laws v Society of Lloyd's* [2003] EWCA Civ 1887, *The Times,* January 23, 2004 at [91] (whether it is an action in tort was left open, see at [92]); *Thomas v Taylor Wimpey Developments Ltd* [2019] EWHC 1134 (TCC), [2019] B.L.R. 382 at [41].

### Application of rules on damages for fraud

*Replace paragraph with:*

7-080 It has been shown that damages for fraud are governed by somewhat different rules to damages for negligent misrepresentation at common law: losses may be recoverable even though they were not of a foreseeable kind[379] and, in some circumstances, consequential losses may include compensation for falls in the value of the property acquired which were unrelated to the fraudulent statement.[380] It is not clear whether these rules, which appear to be justified by considerations of morality and deterrence,[381] are applicable to damages claimed under s.2(1). In the 26th edn of this work it was suggested[382] that the first rule did not apply, but this was rejected by the Court of Appeal in *Royscot Trust Ltd v Rogerson*[383] on the ground that this interpretation "is to ignore the plain words of the subsection".[384] In *Smith New Court Securities Ltd v Scrimgeour Vickers (Asset Management) Ltd*[385] both Lords Browne-Wilkinson and Steyn declined to comment on the correctness of the *Royscot* case. If the interpretation of s.2(1) taken in *Royscot* is correct, however, it would presumably follow that damages under s.2(1) can also include compensation for loss of value caused by a fall in the market, at least where the claimant has acquired an "already flawed asset",[386] and that contributory negligence will not necessarily be a defence or lead to a reduction in the claimant's damages.[387] Whether it is necessary to interpret s.2(1) in this way may, with respect, be doubted.[388] It does not seem appropriate to apply the special rules governing damages for fraud, which are justified by considerations of morality and deterrence,[389] to cases in which there was, by definition, no fraud.[390]

[379] Above, para.7-057.

[380] Above, paras 7-063—7-068. In *Young v Hamilton* [2012] NICh 4 damages for distress were awarded (cf. above, para.7-070) under s.2(1) without referring to the fiction of fraud.

[381] See the words of Lord Steyn in *Smith New Court Securities Ltd v Scrimgeour Vickers (Asset Management) Ltd* [1997] A.C. 254, 280, referred to earlier, para.7-066.

[382] *Chitty*, 26th edn, Ch.6, para.439, referring to Treitel, *The Law of Contract*, 7th edn, p.278.

[383] [1991] 2 Q.B. 297. See the criticisms of that case in (1991) 107 L.Q.R. 547.

[384] [1991] 2 Q.B. 297 at 307 and 309.

385 [1997] A.C. 254 at 267 and 283. In *Avon Insurance v Swire* [2000] 1 All E.R. (Comm) 573 the defendants reserved the right to argue the correctness of the *Royscot* case in a higher court. See also *Cheltenham BC v Laird* [2009] I.R.L.R. 621 at [524]; *Cassa di Risparmio della Repubblica di San Marino SpA v Barclays Bank Ltd* [2011] EWHC 484 (Comm), [2011] 1 C.L.C. 701 at [223]. But see *Forest International Gaskets Ltd v Fosters Marketing Ltd* [2005] EWCA Civ 700 at [15]–[16]. The Singapore Court of Appeal doubted the correctness of the *Royscot* case in *RBC Properties v Defu Furniture Pte Ltd* [2014] SGCA 62, [2015] 1 S.L.R. 997; see Liau [2015] L.M.C.L.Q. 464.

386 Above, paras 7-063—7-068. See *Yam Seng Pte Ltd v International Trade Corp Ltd* [2013] EWHC 111 (QB), [2013] 1 Lloyd's Rep. 526 at [207].

387 See above, para.7-073 and below, para.7-084. Lord Tenterden's Act may also apply: see above, para.7-047.

388 In *Yam Seng Pte Ltd v International Trade Corp Ltd* [2013] EWHC 111 (QB), [2013] 1 Lloyd's Rep. 526 Leggatt J. said (at [206]) that "It is possible to construe the words 'and as a result thereof has suffered loss' as requiring the claimant to show that he has suffered loss as a reasonably foreseeable result of a misrepresentation having been made to him, and to treat the following words as imposing an additional requirement (that the defendant would be liable to damages had the misrepresentation been made fraudulently) which must also be satisfied", but held that unless and until *Royscot Trust* is over-ruled he was bound to apply it.

389 See above, para.7-066.

390 cf. *McGregor on Damages*, 20th edn (2017), para.49-056; Peel (ed.), *Treitel on The Law of Contract*, 15th edn (2020), para.9-082.

### Liability for negligence at common law

*Replace footnote 418 with:*

418 For a full account see *Clerk & Lindsell on Torts*, 22nd edn (2017), paras 8-97—8-131 and especially 8-120—8-126; Cartwright, *Misrepresentation, Mistake and Non-disclosure*, 5th edn (2019), Ch.6. **7-088**

### Special relationship between parties negotiating contract

*Replace footnote 455 with:*

455 [1977] 1 W.L.R. 444. Similarly, in *Property Alliance Group Ltd v Royal Bank of Scotland Plc* [2018] EWCA Civ 355, [2018] 1 W.L.R. 3529 it was common ground that a bank selling a swap to a customer had a duty not to mis-state (at [68]); but it was held that the bank had no duty to disclose information about possible "break costs" (at [78]). **7-095**

### Other legislative provisions creating liability for negligent misrepresentations: financial services

*Replace paragraph with:*

There are a number of legislative provisions that in effect create liability for negligent misrepresentation in particular circumstances.[475] For example, Financial Services and Markets Act 2000 Pt VI imposes stringent duties on persons responsible for listing particulars of securities for admission to the Official List, and prospectuses.[476] The legislation makes the person responsible liable to pay compensation to a person who has acquired securities to which the legislation applies,[477] and who has suffered loss as the result of any untrue or misleading statement in the prospectus or, in the case of listing particulars, the particulars.[478] It then provides a number of exceptions, one of which is that liability for the loss will not be incurred if the person responsible satisfies the court that, at the time when the particulars were submitted to the relevant authority or delivered for registration, he reasonably believed that the statement was true and not misleading.[479] There is also liability for failure to publish a supplementary prospectus when necessary.[480] **7-100**

475 Financial Services Act 2012 ss.89–92 impose criminal liability for knowingly or recklessly making false or misleading statements in relation to financial services, impressions as to the market in or the price or value of any relevant investments or false or misleading statements in relation to benchmarks;

but it does not appear that there will be civil liability. These sections replace Financial Services and Markets Act 2000 s.397, that section replacing Financial Services Act 1986 s.47, which was held not to confer any right to damages or other civil remedy: *Norwich Union Life Insurance Society v Qureshi* [1999] 2 All E.R. (Comm) 707, CA. See further Cartwright, *Misrepresentation, Mistake and Non-disclosure*, 5th edn (2019), paras 7-77–7-80. For the possibility of a restitution order on the basis that the conduct may constitute market abuse within the Market Abuse Regulation (Regulation (EU) 596/2014) see Gower and Davies, *Principles of Modern Company Law*, 10th edn (2016), paras 30-51 and 30-55, and cf. *Securities and Investments Board Ltd v Pantell SA (No.2)* [1993] Ch. 256, decided under the Financial Services Act 1986.

[476] See generally, Gower and Davies, *Principles of Modern Company Law*, 10th edn (2016), paras 25–10 et seq.; Cartwright, *Misrepresentation, Mistake and Non-disclosure*, 5th edn (2019), paras 7-49 et seq. For the duties of disclosure imposed by these provisions see below, para.7-172.

[477] Thus investors who have bought on the market after dealing has commenced are now protected.

[478] Financial Services and Markets Act 2000 ss.85, 90(1). Note that s.90 is without prejudice to any liability which may be incurred apart from the section or regulation: s.90(6). These provisions stem ultimately from the Directors Liability Act 1890, which was passed to reverse the effect of *Derry v Peek* (1889) 14 App. Cas. 337, so far as it applied to prospectuses.

[479] Financial Services and Markets Act 2000 Sch.10 para.1(2). For the possible application of the *Hedley Byrne* principle (above, para.7-091) and of Misrepresentation Act 1967 to misstatements in prospectuses and particulars, see Gower and Davies, *Principles of Modern Company Law*, 10th edn (2016), paras 25-36—25-39.

[480] See further below, para.7-172.

### Package travel, etc.

*Replace footnote 488 with:*

7-102 [488] Cartwright, *Misrepresentation, Mistake and Non-disclosure*, 4th edn (2017), para.7-68; the 1992 Regulations are not discussed in the 5th edn (2019), see para.7-77.

## (c) Innocent Misrepresentation

### Section 2(2) and consequential loss

*Replace footnote 522 with:*

7-109 [522] In favour of this alternative is the literal interpretation given to s.2(1) by the Court of Appeal in *Royscot Trust Ltd v Rogerson* [1991] 2 Q.B. 297. Against it is the analogy of damages under Lord Cairns' Act 1858 *in lieu* of an award of specific performance where (it was said) the damages are to be assessed as at common law, and not in accordance with some special measure: *Johnson v Agnew* [1980] A.C. 367, 400. But subsequently this has been interpreted as referring primarily to the date of assessment; it should not be taken to imply that the measure of damages must be the same as for damages at common law for breach of contract: *Morris-Garner v One Step (Support) Ltd* [2018] UKSC 20, [2019] A.C. 649 at [47]; see below, para.26-005.

## 4. RESCISSION FOR MISREPRESENTATION

## (a) General

### Misrepresentation as defence to proceedings

*Replace paragraph with:*

7-118 There is no doubt that a misrepresentation which would justify rescission of a contract may also be used as a defence to an action brought by the representor against the representee. The use of misrepresentation as a defence has sometimes been distinguished from its use as a ground for rescission,[556] and it is possible that the principles governing the two situations are not in all respects identical[557] but generally speaking they appear to be the same. Indeed, the courts have sometimes treated the setting up of a misrepresentation as a defence as though this were in itself one way of rescinding the contract.[558] Accordingly, it is thought that although s.2(2) of the 1967 Act speaks of rescission, its provisions would apply equally to a case in which the misrepresentation is set up by way of defence. However, fraud may be used as a defence to a claim for specific performance (which is a discretionary remedy[559]) even where the right to rescind has been lost (save by affirmation, when the inconsistency of affirming and then resisting specific performance would be unconscionable).[560] It was said that impossibility of restoring the parties to their original position will not necessarily prevent the use of fraud as a defence; it will depend on the impact that enforcement would have on the representee, and especially on whether it would cause hardship, whether on the facts any estoppel had arisen and the importance of the term to be enforced and the breach of it. The fact that there would be a claim for damages for deceit should be taken into account.[561]

556 Peel (ed.), *Treitel on The Law of Contract*, 15th edn (2020), para.9-098.

557 *Treitel* (15th edn (2020), para.9-106) points to the rule that an insurer who uses fraud as a defence could repudiate liability and keep the premiums: see below, Vol.II, para.42-076. Further, *Treitel* suggests that in cases of criminal fraud a representee who sets the fraud up by way of defence need not return money received under the contract (*Berg v Sadler & Moore* [1937] 2 K.B. 158), whereas if he sues for rescission he must do so (*Spence v Crawford* [1939] 3 All E.R. 271). *Berg v Sadler Moore* is contrary to dicta of the Exchequer Chamber in *Clough v L. & N.W. Ry* (1871) L.R. 7 Ex. 26, 37 which do not seem to have been cited, and the refusal of the claim for return of the money may be better explained on the basis of illegality.

558 *Clough v L. & N.W. Ry* (1871) L.R. 7 Ex. 26; *Academy of Health and Fitness Pty Ltd v Power* [1973] V.R. 254.

559 See below, para.27-046.

560 *Geest Plc v Fyffes Plc* [1999] 1 All E.R. (Comm) 627, 694 et seq.

561 *Geest Plc v Fyffes Plc* [1999] 1 All E.R. (Comm) 627. On the facts of the case, restitutio was impossible. To refuse specific performance altogether of the undertaking to provide security for an indemnity that the defendant had given the plaintiff would expose the plaintiff to very different risks. Specific performance would be granted but limited to the excess of the claim over any counterclaim for damages.

## Effect of rescission

*Replace paragraph with:*

When a contract is rescinded it has the effect of revesting any property transferred in the transferor, so far as no formal steps are required for the retransfer.[571] Thus property in goods will revest in the victim of fraud without more.[572] If land has been conveyed, rescission will have the effect that the representor holds the title on constructive trust for the representee.[573] Although the contract is avoided retrospectively, some clauses that are regarded as "separable" may continue to have effect. Thus unless otherwise agreed an arbitration agreement is unaffected by the invalidity of the substantive contract of which it forms part[574]; and an exclusive jurisdiction clause will survive rescission.[575] In contrast, a "no set-off" clause, even if it is reasonable under Misrepresentation Act 1967 s.3,[575a] may not survive rescission for fraud.[575b] **7-123**

571 Until the contract is rescinded, the accepted view is that the misrepresentee has no proprietary right in the property transferred but only a "mere equity": below, para.7-141.

572 *Car & Universal Finance Co Ltd v Caldwell* [1961] 1 Q.B. 525. But note that the fact that the contract has been rescinded does not prevent Sale of Goods Act s.25 (sale by buyer in possession) from applying. See below, Vol.II, para.44-221.

573 Megarry & Wade, *The Law of Real Property*, 9th edn (2019), para.10-023. Note that completion of the contract is no longer a bar to rescission: Misrepresentation Act 1967 s.1(b), below, para.7-144.

574 Arbitration Act 1996 s.7; Vol.II, para.32-028.

575 *FAI General Insurance Co Ltd v Ocean Marine Mutual Protection and Indemnity Association* [1998] L.R.L.R. 24, 28; Vol.II, para.32-028.

575a See below, para.7-155.

575b See *Ahuja Investments Ltd v Victorygame Ltd* [2020] EWHC 1153 (Ch) at [89].

## (b) Restitutio in Integrum

### Partial rescission not allowed

*Replace footnote 601 with:*

7-127 601 [2002] 1 Lloyd's Rep. 271 at [6.9]. See also *Marme Inversiones 2007 SL v Natwest Markets Plc* [2019] EWHC 366 (Comm) at [332]–[349]. This paragraph in the 31st edition was cited with approval in *NGM Sustainable Developments Ltd v Wallis* [2015] EWHC 2089 (Ch) at [226].

## (c) Other Bars to Remedy of Rescission

### A "mere equity"

*Replace footnote 657 with:*

7-141 657 *Clough v L. & N.W. Ry* (1871) L.R. 7 Ex. 26, 32, 34; *Bristol and West Building Society v Mothew* [1998] Ch. 1, 22; *Barclays Bank Plc v Boulter* [1999] 1 W.L.R. 1919, HL, at 1925; *Twinsectra Ltd v Yardley* [1999] Lloyd's Rep. Bank. 438, CA at [461]–[462]; *Shalson v Russo* [2003] EWHC 1637 (Ch), *The Times*, September 3, 2003, Ch D (defendant did not hold property on constructive trust before rescission). For a full discussion see Cartwright, *Misrepresentation, Mistake and Non-disclosure*, 5th edn (2019), para.4-10, and Worthington [2002] R.L.R. 28.

## 5. EXCLUSION OF LIABILITY FOR MISREPRESENTATION

### Position at common law

*Replace paragraph with:*

7-145 At common law a person could not contract out of liability for fraud inducing the making of a contract with him, at least where the fraud was his own.[666] It is, however, possible that he could do so where the fraud was that of his employees[667] or agents[668] and there seems no doubt that it was possible, by a provision of the contract itself, to exclude or modify the normal consequences of innocent or negligent misrepresentation.[669] Such clauses were, however, subject to the normal principles of construction common to all exemption clauses.[670] Any exclusion of liability for misrepresentation must be clearly stated.[671] Thus a clause containing a statement by one party that "we are acting for our own account and have made our own independent decisions" would not exclude liability for misrepresentations in investment advice or recommendations[672]; and a clause stating that "this Agreement shall supersede any prior promises, agreements, representations, undertakings or implications whether made orally or in writing between you and us relating to the subject matter of this Agreement" was not only held not to exclude or supersede misrepresentations as to matters that were not the subject of the terms of the Agreement[673] but also to be dealing only with whether representations had become terms of the contract and not with liability for misrepresentation.[674]

666 *S. Pearson & Son Ltd v Dublin Corp* [1907] A.C. 351; *HIH Casualty and General Insurance Ltd v Chase Manhattan Bank* [2003] UKHL 6, [2003] 2 Lloyd's Rep. 61 at [16], [76], [121]. This will include, in a case where there is a duty of disclosure (see below, paras 7-158 et seq.), fraudulent non-disclosure: *HIH Casualty and General Insurance Ltd v Chase Manhattan Bank* [2003] UKHL 6 at [21], [72].

667 See *John Carter (Fine Worsteds) Ltd v Hanson Haulage (Leeds) Ltd* [1965] 2 Q.B. 495.

[668] This question was left open by the House of Lords in *HIH Casualty and General Insurance Ltd v Chase Manhattan Bank* [2003] UKHL 6, [2003] 2 Lloyd's Rep. 61, see at [16], [76]–[82]. In that case the clause was not in sufficiently clear and unmistakable terms to exclude remedies for alleged fraud on the part of the agent.

[669] *Boyd and Forrest v Glasgow Ry* (1915) S.C.(H.L.) 20, 36. A properly worded clause which excludes a right of avoidance will be effective (assuming it is not affected by Misrepresentation Act 1967 s.3; see para.7-148) notwithstanding a purported rescission of the contract as a whole by the misrepresentee: *Toomey v Eagle Star Insurance Co Ltd (No.2)* [1995] 2 Lloyd's Rep. 88.

[670] Below, paras 15-007—15-022. Thus a clause stating that a contract of reinsurance was "neither cancellable nor voidable by either party" was held to apply only to cases of innocent misrepresentation or non-disclosure, and not to alleged negligence, nor to exclude the right to damages under Misrepresentation Act 1967 s.2(1): *Toomey v Eagle Star Insurance Co Ltd (No.2)* [1995] 2 Lloyd's Rep. 88. A disclaimer "without responsibility" does not prevent rescission on the ground of misrepresentation: *Crédit Lyonnais Bank Nederland v Export Credit Guarantee Department* [1996] 1 Lloyd's Rep. 1. However, a clause applying to "rights, obligations and liabilities arising ... in connection with this contract" may apply to a claim for misrepresentation: *Strachan & Henshaw Ltd v Stein Industrie (UK) Ltd (No.2)* (1997) 87 B.L.R. 52; but in *First Tower Trustees Ltd, Intertrust Trustees Ltd v CDS (Superstores International) Ltd* [2018] EWCA Civ 1396, [2019] 1 W.L.R. 637 a clause protecting trustees from personal contractual liability was held not to apply to their liability under s.2(1) of the Misrepresentation Act 1967 (at [80]–[87]).

[671] *AXA Sun Life Services Plc v Campbell Martin Ltd* [2011] EWCA Civ 133, [2011] 2 Lloyd's Rep. 1 at [94]; see also *NF Football Investments Ltd v NFFC Group Holdings Ltd* [2018] EWHC 1346 (Ch) at [25]. No particular form is required, [2018] EWHC 1346 (Ch) at [27].

[672] *Cassa di Risparmio della Repubblica di San Marino SpA v Barclays Bank Ltd* [2011] EWHC 484 (Comm), [2011] 1 C.L.C. 701 at [513]. However, the next sentence of the same clause, stating that "We are not relying on any communication (written or oral) from you as investment advice or as a recommendation" was effective under the principle to be discussed in the next paragraph.

[673] *AXA Sun Life Services Plc v Campbell Martin Ltd* [2011] EWCA Civ 133, [2011] 2 Lloyd's Rep. 1 at [36]; *Al-Hasawi v Nottingham Forest Football Club Ltd* [2018] EWHC 2884 (Ch). The *AXA* decision is criticised by A. Trukhtanov (2011) 127 L.Q.R. 345. In *Mears Ltd v Shoreline Housing Partnership Ltd* [2013] EWCA Civ 639 the entire agreement clause did not exclude liability for misrepresentation: see at [16]. However, in *Bikam OOD v Adria Cable Sarl* [2012] EWHC 621 (Comm), where in one clause of the contract the seller acknowledged the buyer's reliance on specified warranties by the seller, it was held that the effect of an "entire agreement" clause was that, subject to the exception of fraud, the parties' rights were confined to those arising under the agreement, and rights in respect of warranties and representations not expressly set out in the agreement were waived (at [45]).

[674] [2011] EWCA Civ 133 at [81], applying the approach of Ramsay J. in *BSkyB Ltd v HP Enterprise Services UK Ltd* [2010] EWHC 86 (TCC), (2010) 129 Con. L.R. 147. Rix L.J. pointed out that the word "representations" was "completely sandwiched between words of contractual import" (at [80]) and that "supersede" is "a word of agreement rather than exclusion" (at [81]). A simple "entire agreement clause" is not apt to exclude liability for misrepresentation: *Thomas Witter Ltd v T.B.P. Industries Ltd* [1996] 2 All E.R. 573; *Deepak Fertilisers and Petrochemicals Corp v ICI* [1999] 1 Lloyd's Rep. 387, 395; *Mears Ltd v Shoreline Housing Partnership Ltd* [2013] EWCA Civ 639 at [16]. However, there may be a separate clause waiving rights in respect of warranties and representations not expressly set out in the agreement, as in *Trident Turboprop (Dublin) Ltd v First Flight Couriers Ltd* [2009] EWCA Civ 290, [2010] Q.B. 86 at [37]; see also *Bikam OOD v Adria Cable Sarl* [2012] EWHC 621 (Comm) (at [45]).

## "No reliance" clauses

*Replace footnote 675 with:*

[675] In *First Tower Trustees Ltd, Intertrust Trustees Ltd v CDS (Superstores International) Ltd* [2018] EWCA Civ 1396, [2019] 1 W.L.R. 637 Leggatt L.J. said that in this context, "basis" merely means only that the parties have agreed to assume that the relevant state of affairs is true, and suggested it would be better to avoid use of the phrase "basis clause" (at [95]). **7-146**

## Section 3 and no reliance clauses

*Replace paragraph with:*

Whether s.3 applies to clauses under which one party acknowledges that it has not relied on any statement made to it[701] has been the subject of apparently conflicting views.[702] In *Raiffeisen Zentralbank Osterreich AG v Royal Bank of Scotland Plc* Christopher Clarke J. said: **7-152**

"... the essential question is whether the clause in question goes to whether the alleged representation was made (or, I would add, was intended to be understood and acted on as a representation), or whether it excludes or restricts liability in respect of representations made, intended to be acted on and in fact acted on; and that question is one of substance not form.[703]

In this respect the key question, as it seems to me, is whether the clause attempts to rewrite history or parts company with reality. If sophisticated commercial parties agree, in terms of which they are both aware, to regulate their future relationship by prescribing the basis on which they will be dealing with each other and what representations they are or are not making, a suitably drafted clause may properly be regarded as establishing that no representations (or none other than honest belief) are being made or are intended to be relied on. Such parties are capable of distinguishing between statements which are to be treated as representations on which the recipient is entitled to rely, and statements which do not have that character, and should be allowed to agree among themselves into which category any given statement may fall.

Per contra, to tell the man in the street that the car you are selling him is perfect and then agree that the basis of your contract is that no representations have been made or relied on, may be nothing more than an attempt retrospectively to alter the character and effect of what has gone before, and in substance an attempt to exclude or restrict liability."[704]

In *Springwell Navigation Corp v JP Morgan Chase Bank*[705] the Court of Appeal held that statements by one party that it had made its decision to contract independently, without relying on the other party, and that it was fully familiar with the risks, created a contractual estoppel to the effect that any statement by other would amount to merely one of opinion[706] and were not within s.3.[707] In contrast, a sentence in the same paragraph of the document which stated that the other party would not be liable for any loss suffered by the first party unless the loss was caused by gross negligence or wilful misconduct was within s.3, though in the circumstances it was reasonable and therefore effective.[708] Aikens L.J., delivering the only full judgment, said that a statement that "... no representation or warranty, express or implied, is or will be made" by the relevant party "is more difficult to classify"; but he was inclined to treat it as falling within s.3 following because it "may be nothing more than an attempt retrospectively to alter the character and effect of what has gone before".[709] Aikens L.J. held that the same was true of a non-reliance clause in the agreement.[710] In *First Tower Trustees Ltd v CDS (Superstores International) Ltd*[711] the Court of Appeal rejected suggestions that the question is not one of whether the clause attempts to re-write history but to determine whether, as a matter of construction, the terms define the basis on which the parties were transacting business.[712] The Court agreed expressly with Christopher Clarke J.'s statement in the *Raiffeisen* case that the question is one of fact: if in fact there has been reliance on what the person to whom it was made would reasonably understand to be a representation, the clause will be an attempt to exclude liability and thus will fall within s.3.

"The situation might be different in the unlikely scenario that before he contracts the buyer sees the clause and, eyes wide open, agrees that he is not relying on what he may have been told."[713]

701 See above, para.7-146.

702 Compare *Cremdean v Nash* (1977) 241 E.G. 837, CA, *Zanzibar v British Aerospace (Lancaster House) Ltd* [2000] 1 W.L.R. 2333, 2347 and *FoodCo UK LLP (t/a Muffin Break) v Henry Boot Developments Ltd* [2010] EWHC 358 (Ch) on the one hand to, on the other, *William Sindall Plc v Cambridgeshire CC* [1994] 1 W.L.R. 1016 at 1034 and *Watford Electronics Ltd v Sanderson CFL Ltd* [2001] EWCA

Civ 317, [2001] Build. L.R. 142 at [40]. In *First Tower Trustees Ltd v CDS (Superstores International) Ltd* [2018] EWCA Civ 1396, [2019] 1 W.L.R. 637 Leggatt L.J. suggested that in any event a mere acknowledgement of non-reliance should not suffice: "If what the parties wish to agree is that A will not assert in any future dispute that it relied on a representation made by B even if A did in fact rely on such a representation, then it seems to me that this is what the clause ought to say"; but he accepted that in *Springwell Navigation Corp v JP Morgan Chase Bank* (see below; at [170]) the Court of Appeal had taken a different view.

703 *Raiffeisen Zentralbank Osterreich AG v Royal Bank of Scotland Plc* [2010] EWHC 1392 (Comm), [2011] 1 Lloyd's Rep. 123 at [310]. See also *Morgan v Pooley* [2010] EWHC 2447 (QB) at [114]; *Welven Ltd v Soar Group* [2011] EWHC 3240 (Comm) at [111].

704 [2010] EWHC 1392 (Comm) at [314]–[315]. Christopher Clarke J. referred to a passage in *IFE Fund SA v Goldman Sachs International* [2006] EWHC 2887 (Comm), [2007] 1 Lloyd's Rep. 264 (affirmed without comment on this point [2007] EWCA Civ 811, [2007] 2 Lloyd's Rep. 449), where Toulson J. said (at [68]–[69]): "If a seller of a car said to a buyer 'I have serviced the car since it was new, it has had only one owner and the clock reading is accurate', those statements would be representations, and they would still have that character even if the seller added the words 'but those statements are not representations on which you can rely' ... If, however, the seller of the car said 'The clock reading is 20,000 miles, but I have no knowledge whether the reading is true or false', the position would be different, because the qualifying words could not fairly be regarded as an attempt to exclude liability for a false representation arising from the first half of the sentence." (Toulson J. held that on the facts no representation had been made, see above, para.7-008). Christopher Clarke J.'s words were seemingly accepted as correct by the Court of Appeal in *First Tower Trustees Ltd v CDS (Superstores International) Ltd* save that Leggatt L.J. said (at [101]–[103]) that what matters is not the status of the parties (commercially sophisticated or "man in the street") but whether the clause was to govern their future relationship or was looking back towards what had already happened.

705 [2010] EWCA Civ 1221, [2010] 2 C.L.C. 705. See McMeel [2011] L.M.C.L.Q. 185.

706 [2010] EWCA Civ 1221 at [173]; see above, para.7-147.

707 [2010] EWCA Civ 1221 at [181]. See also *Cassa di Risparmio della Repubblica di San Marino SpA v Barclays Bank Ltd* [2011] EWHC 484 (Comm), [2011] 1 C.L.C. 701 at [514]. *Camerata Property Inc v Credit Suisse Securities (Europe) Ltd* [2011] EWHC 479 (Comm), [2011] 1 C.L.C. 627 at [186]; *Standard Chartered Bank v Ceylon Petroleum Corp* [2011] EWHC 1785 (Comm) at [568].

708 [2010] EWCA Civ 1221 at [181]. On reasonableness see below, para.7-155.

709 [2010] EWCA Civ 1221 at [181], referring to [2010] EWHC 1392 (Comm) at [315], quoted above; applied in *Avrora Fine Arts Investment Ltd v Christie, Manson & Woods Ltd* [2012] EWHC 2198 (Ch) at [144]–[145].

710 [2010] EWCA Civ 1221 at [182].

711 [2018] EWCA Civ 1396, [2019] 1 W.L.R. 637 at [50]–[66], [99] ("No rational legislator could have intended that the need for a contract term to satisfy a test of reasonableness could be avoided simply by felicity in drafting the contract term": Leggatt L.J.) and [113].

712 See *Thornbridge Ltd v Barclays Bank Plc* [2015] EWHC 3430 (QB) at [97]–[121], in particular at [105]; *Sears v Minco Plc* [2016] EWHC 433 (Ch) at [80]. This approach had been rejected by the judge at first instance in the *First Tower* case, Michael Brindle Q.C. [2017] EWHC 891 (Ch), [2017] 4 W.L.R. 73 at [32]. See also *Carney v NM Rothschild and Sons Ltd* [2018] EWHC 958 (Comm).

713 [2018] EWCA Civ 1396 at [58]–[59] approving Christopher Clarke J.'s statements in [2010] EWHC 1392 (Comm) at [286] and [308]–[310].

## Timing of notice of the clause

*Replace footnote 716 with:*

716 [2018] EWCA Civ 1396, [2019] 1 W.L.R. 637. **7-153**

## Reasonableness

*Replace paragraph with:*

Reasonableness under the Act is discussed below (paras 15-101—15-111) and only selected points will be considered here.[722] It seems that the court must consider the reasonableness of the provision as a whole.[723] A clause may be invalid because, taken as a whole, it is too wide, even though it would not necessarily be unreasonable to exclude or restrict liability on the facts which have occurred. Thus it has **7-155** been held that a clause which purports to exclude liability for misrepresentation of any kind will be unreasonable, since it is not reasonable to exclude liability for fraud, and the clause as a whole will be invalid.[724] However, this decision must be considered in the light of other cases that have held that an exclusion or restriction of one form of liability will not necessarily be unreasonable under the Unfair Contract Terms Act 1977 merely because the clause purports also to exclude another liability which under the Act cannot be excluded: the necessarily invalid part of the clause may be excised.[725] In any event, the court should not, however, hold a clause unreasonable because it might extend to some situation which is unlikely to occur.[726] But if the clause is too wide, the court cannot rewrite the clause in a reasonable fashion and, as the test under s.11(1) of the Unfair Contract Terms Act 1977 is whether the term was "a fair and reasonable one to be included", the court cannot allow the misrepresentor to rely on it so far as seems reasonable.[727] Thus it cannot uphold a provision in so far as it would bar rescission, but reject it in so far as it would bar a claim for damages. However, it is possible that a clause which is in distinct parts might be severed and the reasonable parts upheld. It has been said in the Court of Appeal that there are at least two good reasons why the courts should not refuse to give effect to an exclusion of remedies for misrepresentation in a commercial contract between experienced parties of equal bargaining power—a fortiori, where those parties have the benefit of professional advice. First, it is reasonable to assume that the parties desire commercial certainty; and secondly, it is reasonable to assume that the price to be paid reflects the commercial risk which each party—or, more usually, the purchaser—is willing to accept.[728]

[722] It has been held that condition 17 of the National Conditions of Sale (19th edn) was invalid as unreasonable under s.3 of the Misrepresentation Act: *Walker v Boyle* [1982] 1 W.L.R. 495. Condition 17 stated that replies to questions by the vendor or his agents do not obviate the need for the buyer to make his own inquiries and inspections, and are not to be treated as representations. See also *Southwestern General Property Co Ltd v Marton* (1982) 263 E.G. 1090; *White Cross Equipment Ltd v Farrell* (1982) 2 Tr.L.R. 21; *Cooper v Tamms* [1988] 1 E.G.L.R. 257; *Goff v Gauthier* [1991] 62 P. & C.R. 388; *Cleaver v Schyde Investments Ltd* [2011] EWCA Civ 929, [2011] 2 P. & C.R. 21. In *Lloyd v Browning* [2013] EWCA Civ 1637, [2014] 1 P. & C.R. 11 it was held that a special condition, commonly used within the area, stating that the buyer entered into the contract solely as a result of his inspection of the property and that no statement by the seller, other than written statements made in reply to enquiries, had induced him to enter into the contract, was a reasonable one to be included in the particular contract. Thus where a "no-reliance" clause is subject to the Act (see above, para.7-152) it is likely to be reasonable if it expressly permits reliance on any reply given by the landlord's or vendor's solicitors to the tenant's or purchaser's solicitors, whereas one that seeks to prevent the landlord or vendor from incurring any liability for misrepresentation other than for fraud is unlikely to be reasonable: see *FoodCo UK LLP (t/a Muffin Break) v Henry Boot Developments Ltd* [2010] EWHC 358 (Ch) at [177]; *Lloyd v Browning* [2013] EWCA Civ 1637 at [34]; *First Tower Trustees Ltd v CDS (Superstores International) Ltd* [2017] EWHC 891 (Ch), [2017] 4 W.L.R. 73 at [36]–[38] ("not a reasonable clause to put into the lease, even if the parties are of equal bargaining power and act on legal advice, because its effect would render the whole exercise of making inquiries and relying on answers thereto all but nugatory" (at [39]–[40]); upheld on appeal, [2018] EWCA Civ 1396, [2019] 1 W.L.R. 637 at [75]). In *Djurberg (t/a Hampton Riviera) v Small* Unreported September 1, 2017, Ch D it was said that if the clause in that case (seemingly an entire agreement clause) applied to misrepresentations, it would be unreasonable as the buyers (a couple who were buying a houseboat from a trader) were in a weak bargaining position and there had been no negotiation about the terms. See further below, para.15-104.

[723] See below, para.15-112.

[724] *Thomas Witter Ltd v TBP Industries Ltd* [1992] All E.R. 573. cf. *Stewart Gill Ltd v Horatio Myer & Co Ltd* [1992] Q.B. 600; below, para.15-112. In *Skipskredittforeningen v Emperor Navigation* [1998] 1 Lloyd's Rep. 66 it was held not to be unreasonable to include in a loan agreement a no-set off clause which might apply even in cases of fraud; but see *Ahuja Investments Ltd v Victorygame Ltd* [2020] EWHC 1153 (Ch) at [72]–[84].

[725] See *Goodlife Foods Ltd v Hall Fire Protection Ltd* [2017] EWHC 767 (TCC), [2017] B.L.R. 389 at [66]–[70], discussed below, para.15-114.

[726] *Skipskredittforeningen v Emperor Navigation* [1998] 1 Lloyd's Rep. 66, 75–76.

[727] Compare the formulation used by the original version of s.3 before amendment by the 1977 Act: "[T]hat provision shall be of no effect except to the extent that ... the court or arbitrator may allow reliance on it as being fair and reasonable in the circumstances of the case". But see the doubts expressed by Mance J. in *Skipskredittforeningen v Emperor Navigation* [1998] 1 Lloyd's Rep. 66, 75; and also *Bacardi-Martini Beverages Ltd v Thomas Hardy Packaging Ltd* [2002] EWCA Civ 549, [2002] 2 Lloyd's Rep. 379 at [26].

[728] See *National Westminster Bank Plc v Utrecht-America Finance Co* [2001] EWCA Civ 658, [2001] 3 All E.R. 733 at [60]–[61], citing an unreported judgment of Chadwick L.J. in *E A Grimstead & Son Ltd v McGarrigan* Unreported October 27, 1999; *Watford Electronics Ltd v Sanderson CFL Ltd* [2001] EWCA Civ 317, [2001] Build. L.R. 143 at [39]. See also *FoodCo UK LLP (t/a Muffin Break) v Henry Boot Developments Ltd* [2010] EWHC 358 (Ch), at [177]; *Raiffeisen Zentralbank Osterreich AG v Royal Bank of Scotland Plc* [2010] EWHC 1392 (Comm), [2011] 1 Lloyd's Rep. 123 at [319]–[327]. In *Springwell Navigation Corp v JP Morgan Chase Bank* [2010] EWCA Civ 1221, [2010] 2 C.L.C. 705, at [183]–[184] the Court of Appeal agreed with the trial judge (see [2008] EWHC 1186 (Comm)) that clauses restricting liability towards a sophisticated investor who was aware of the risks were reasonable. See also *Camerata Property Inc v Credit Suisse Securities (Europe) Ltd* [2011] EWHC 479 (Comm) at [187]; *AXA Sun Life Services Plc v Campbell Martin Ltd* [2011] EWCA Civ 133, [2011] 2 Lloyd's Rep. 1 at [48]–[75]; *Standard Chartered Bank v Ceylon Petroleum Corp* [2011] EWHC 1785 (Comm) at [569]–[572]; *Welven Ltd v Soar Group* [2011] EWHC 3240 (Comm) at [115].

### Clauses covering breach

*Replace paragraph with:*

The section does not seem to apply to a provision which excludes or restricts liability arising solely from breach of a contractual term, whether the term is a promise or a representation of fact. Read literally, the section might appear to apply to a provision which excludes or restricts liabilities or remedies arising both from misrepresentations as such and from misrepresentations as contractual terms,[729] but it seems more likely that it will be interpreted as affecting only any remedies arising from the misrepresentation.[730] What is less clear is the position if a single term of the contract purports to exclude or limit liability for both misrepresentation and breach, and the clause is held to not to be reasonable. Again read literally, s.3 appears to invalidate the term as a whole.[731] Again it is suggested that the section should be interpreted as invalidating the term only so far as remedies for misrepresentation are concerned. **7-156**

[729] As already seen (above, para.7-114) s.1(a) of the 1967 Act provides that a misrepresentation continues to be effective as such even if it becomes a term of the contract. See also below, para.15-130.

[730] Peel (ed.), *Treitel on The Law of Contract*, 15th edn (2020), para.9-145.

[731] Peel (ed.), *Treitel on The Law of Contract*, 15th edn (2020), para.9-146.

## 6. CONTRACTS WHERE A DUTY OF DISCLOSURE

### Non-disclosure

*Replace footnote 742 with:*

[742] See also Cartwright, *Misrepresentation, Mistake and Non-disclosure*, 5th edn (2019), para.17-03. **7-158**

### Rescission but not damages

*Replace footnote 758 with:*

[758] Liability in damages for fraudulent non-disclosure had been mooted as a possibility by Rix L.J. in *HIH Casualty & General Insurance Ltd v Chase Manhattan Bank* [2001] EWCA Civ 1250, [2001] 2 Lloyd's Rep. 483 at [48], [164] and [168] but the point was neither argued nor decided. In the House of Lords, Lord Bingham did say that the deliberate withholding of information which the person knows or believes to be material, if done dishonestly or recklessly, may amount to a fraudulent misrepresentation: [2003] UKHL 6, [2003] 2 Lloyd's Rep. 61 at [21]. However this appears to refer to cases where in the circumstances a failure to disclose amounts to a positive misrepresentation, and it is **7-159**

not clear that Lord Bingham thought this included every case of a duty to disclose. Lord Hoffmann said that "nondisclosure (whether dishonest or otherwise) does not as such give rise to a claim in damages" (at [75]); he referred to the judgments in *Banque Keyser Ullmann SA v Skandia (UK) Insurance Co Ltd* [1990] 1 Q.B. 665, 777–781 and 788 ("without a misrepresentation there can be no fraud in the sense of giving rise to a claim for damages in tort") and [1991] 2 A.C. 249 at 280 (per Lord Templeman) and at 281 (per Lord Jauncey of Tullichettle). Moreover, in *Manifest Shipping Co v Uni-Polaris Insurance Co, The Star Sea* [2001] UKHL 1, [2003] 1 A.C. 469 at [46], Lord Hobhouse regarded the *Banque Keyser Ullman* case as deciding authoritatively that a breach of duty to disclose does not give rise to damages. Damages may be recovered in tort for deceit but even deliberate non-disclosure does not give rise to an action for deceit. See *Clerk & Lindsell on Torts*, 22nd edn (2017), para.18-09; Cartwright, *Misrepresentation, Mistake and Non-disclosure*, 5th edn (2019), para.17-37.

## (a) Insurance

### Duty on insurer abolished

*Replace footnote 794 with:*

7-167 [794] Marine Insurance Act 1906 s.18(1), now repealed. On the interpretation of this section see *PCW Syndicates v PCW Reinsurers* [1996] 1 W.L.R. 1136.

### Burden of proof

*Replace footnote 812 with:*

7-170 [812] Consumer Insurance (Disclosure and Representations) Act 2012 s.2(2).

## (b) Contracts to Take Shares in Companies

### Companies

*Replace footnote 817 with:*

7-172 [817] See generally, Gower and Davies *Principles of Modern Company Law*, 10th edn (2016), paras 25-8—25-43; Cartwright, *Misrepresentation, Mistake and Non-disclosure*, 5th edn (2019), para.17-53 et seq.

CHAPTER 8

# DURESS AND UNDUE INFLUENCE



## 2 DURESS

### (a) Introduction

*Change title of paragraph:* **8-003**

**Introductory remarks** |

## (c) Types of Illegitimate Pressure

### Types of illegitimate pressure

*Replace paragraph with:*

**8-011** Duress is a form of constraint on the victim's choice, and it is normally assumed that the constraint involves a threat by the other party to harm the victim in some way.[61] Certainly nearly all the cases, particularly of economic duress, have involved threats. However, in *Borrelli v Ting*[62] liquidators urgently needed to conclude a settlement agreement, and agreed to the defendant's terms when as the result of delays caused by the defendant "opposing the scheme for no good reason and in using forgery and false evidence in support of that opposition, all in order to prevent the Liquidators from investigating his conduct ... or making claims against him arising out of that conduct", they could wait no longer. The Privy Council held that the agreement could be avoided on the ground of economic duress. Duress was defined as "the obtaining of agreement or consent by illegitimate means".[63] Lord Saville described the defendant's conduct as unconscionable.[64] This decision suggests not only that a constraint caused by actual illegitimate conduct, as opposed to threatened conduct, may amount to duress,[65] but also that the doctrines of duress and of unconscionable conduct[66] may not be clearly separable. Cases of actual undue influence[66a] based on the relationship between the contract parties may also overlap with that of economic duress or duress by threatening a lawful act.[66b] Indeed, David Richards L.J. has observed that[66c]:

> "The equitable doctrines of unconscionable transactions (or undue pressure, as it is called in some jurisdictions such as Australia) and undue influence are particularly relevant in the context of economic duress. Both involve the possibility of the court setting aside a contract made in circumstances which may involve pressure being put on a party to enter into the contract."

However, traditionally, relief on the ground of unconscionability or undue influence does not depend on the defendant having done anything that is otherwise unlawful or illegitimate.

[61] e.g. Burrows, *Law of Restitution*, 3rd edn (2011), p.255 ("pressurised ... by illegitimate threats"); see also Goff and Jones, *Law of Restitution*, 7th edn (2007), paras 10-004 et seq., in which the examples seemed to involve threats in one form or another; compare Goff and Jones, *Law of Unjust Enrichment*, 9th edn (2016), para.10-02. It is usually said that duress to the person may result from actual physical violence (see below, para.8-012) but it is presumably the threat of repetition which constitutes the constraint.

[62] [2010] UKPC 21, noted [2011] L.M.C.L.Q. 333.

[63] [2010] UKPC 21 at [34].

[64] [2010] UKPC 21 at [32].

[65] See also *Carter v Carter* (1829) 5 Bing. 406, 130 E.R. 1118, cited by Goff and Jones, *Law of Unjust Enrichment*, 9th edn (2016), para.10-02.

[66] See below, paras 8-132 et seq.

[66a] See below paras 8-056 et seq.

[66b] See below para.8-046.

[66c] *Times Travel (UK) Ltd v Pakistan International Airlines Corp* [2019] EWCA Civ 828, [2019] 2 Lloyd's Rep. 89 at [40].

*Add new paragraph:*

**Illegitimate pressure against a state** Certain acts of one state against another, such as trade restrictive measures, threatened use of force, military aggression by invasion and supporting military action, are capable of constituting duress under English law such as to raise a defence against a contractual action.[66d] The Court of Appeal in *Ukraine v Law Debenture Trust Corp Plc* state that[66e]: 8-011A

> "Although moral and social standards are more attenuated in the relations between states on the international plane than is the case in a purely domestic commercial context, international law sets out reasonably determinate standards of conduct applicable between states on the international plane. In our view, there is no reason why the law of duress should not treat these as providing an appropriate test of illegitimate pressure."

66d *Ukraine v Law Debenture Trust Corp Plc* [2018] EWCA Civ 2026, [2019] 2 W.L.R. 655, allowing an appeal against summary judgment in respect of a claim for $3 billion, and applying the public policy exception to the act of foreign state doctrine which would otherwise make such acts non-justiciable.

66e [2018] EWCA Civ 2026 at [160] (Gloster, Sales and David Richards L.JJ.).

## *(i) Duress of the Person*

### Form of duress to the person

*Replace paragraph with:*

Duress of the person may consist in violence to the person, or threats of violence, or in imprisonment whether actual or threatened.[67] The threat of violence need not be directed at the claimant[68]: a threat of violence against the claimant's spouse or near relation suffices[69] and a threat against the claimant's employees has been held to constitute duress.[70] It is suggested that a threat against even a stranger should be enough if the claimant genuinely believed that submission was the only way to prevent the stranger from being injured or worse.[71] 8-012

67 For modern examples, see *Friedeberg-Seeley v Klass* (1957) 101 S.J. 275; *Barton v Armstrong* [1976] A.C. 104; *Singh v Redford* [2018] EWHC 2390 (Ch). But compare *R. v HM Att-Gen for England and Wales* [2003] UKPC 22 (threat to return member of armed forces to his unit lawful). Threats of armed force between states are non-justiciable and cannot give rise to a defence of duress in English law: *Law Debenture Trust Corp Plc v Ukraine* [2017] EWHC 655 (Comm), [2017] Q.B. 1249 at [308].

68 See further below, para.8-052.

69 *Kaufman v Gerson* [1904] 1 K.B. 591; *Singh v Redford* [2018] EWHC 2390 (Ch) (threats of violence to the claimant and his family); cf. *Williams v Bayley* (1866) L.R. 1 H.L. 200 (threat to prosecute relation); and see below, para.8-052. See Goff and Jones, *Law of Unjust Enrichment*, 9th edn (2016), para.10-15.

70 *Royal Boskalis Westminster NV v Mountain* [1999] Q.B. 674 (threat to use employees as human shield); *Gulf Azov Shipping Co Ltd v Chief Idisi (No.2)* [2001] EWCA Civ 505, [2001] 1 Lloyd's Rep. 727 (detention of ship and crew).

71 See further below, para.8-052.

## *(iii) Economic Duress*

### Recognition of economic duress

*Replace footnote 92 with:*

92 *B. & S. Contracts & Design Ltd v Victor Green Publications Ltd* [1984] I.C.R. 419; *Atlas Express Ltd v Kafco (Importers and Distributors) Ltd* [1989] Q.B. 833 (carrier refused to perform without extra payment after miscalculating number of cartons it could carry per load); *The Alev* [1989] 1 Lloyd's Rep. 138 (owner demanded "financial assistance" from consignee before it would deliver goods under freight pre-paid bills when charterer had failed to pay hire); *Carillion Construction Ltd v Felix (UK) Ltd* [2001] B.L.R. 1 (sub-contractor threatened to withhold performance if main contractor did not settle contested account); *Cantor Index Ltd v Shortall* [2002] All E.R. (D) (Nov) (payment made under threat to close 8-019

customer's bets); *Kolmar Group AG v Traxpo Enterprises Pvt Ltd* [2010] EWHC 113 (Comm); *Borrelli v Ting* [2010] UKPC 21 (a case of illegitimate pressure which did not take the form of a threat: above, para.8-011); *Progress Bulk Carriers Ltd v Tube City IMS LLC (The Cenk Kaptanoglu)* [2012] EWHC 273 (Comm), [2012] 1 Lloyd's Rep. 501. See also *Alec Lobb Ltd v Total Oil G.B. Ltd* [1983] 1 W.L.R. 87 (varied on other points, [1985] 1 W.L.R. 173); *Dimskal Shipping Co Ltd v I.T.W.F.* [1992] 2 A.C. 152; *CTN Cash and Carry Ltd v Gallaher Ltd* [1994] 4 All E.R. 714 (below, para.8-047); *Sapporo Breweries Ltd v Lupofresh Ltd* [2012] EWHC 2013 (QB) (at [55]); *Finance Ltd v Bank of New Zealand* (1993) 32 N.S.W.L.R. 50 (NSWCA); *Morley (t/a Morley Estates) v Royal Bank of Scotland Plc* [2020] EWHC 88 (Ch).

## Relationship between doctrine of consideration and economic duress

*Add new paragraph:*

**8-020A** The separation of the issues of consideration and economic duress is reinforced by the Court of Appeal decision in *MWB Business Exchange Centres Ltd v Rock Advertising Ltd.*[100a] Rock was a licensee in office space operated and managed by MWB. Rock incurred arrears of licence fees and other charges, whereupon the parties agreed an oral variation to reschedule the debt. Rock paid £3,500 on the same day in accordance with the revised payment schedule. The Court of Appeal upheld the variation on the basis that the acceptance of *Williams v Roffey* of "practical benefit" as good consideration for promises to pay more for the performance of existing obligations logically applies to promises to relieve from existing obligations.[100b] This was held not to contradict *Foakes v Beer*[100c] and *Re Selectmove*[100d] (in which the Court of Appeal had rejected "practical benefit" as a valid form of consideration in promises to accept part payment) by emphasising the practical benefit to MWB of "avoiding the void" in the sense of avoiding "unoccupied and therefore unproductive property, which may cause loss in the form of loss of rent and in other ways".[100e] The Supreme Court reversed the decision on a different issue.[100f] However, in dicta, Lord Sumption recognised the difficulty of reconciling the notion of practical benefit with *Foakes v Beer* while accepting the need to re-examine that decision.[100g] For now, therefore, *Re Selectmove*[100h] remains the law,[100i] but the Court of Appeal's pronouncement on consideration in the *MWB* case remains pertinent.

[100a] *MWB Business Exchange Centres Ltd v Rock Advertising Ltd* [2016] EWCA Civ 553, [2017] Q.B. 604.

[100b] [2016] EWCA Civ 553 at [79]. The Supreme Court of New South Wales had already accepted this in *Musumeci v Winadell Pty Ltd* (1994) 34 N.S.W.L.R. 72.

[100c] *Foakes v Beer* (1884) 9 App. Cas. 605 (HL).

[100d] *Re Selectmove Ltd* [1995] 1 W.L.R. 474 (CA).

[100e] *MWB Business Exchange Centres Ltd v Rock Advertising Ltd* [2016] EWCA Civ 553, [2017] Q.B. 604 at [72], see also [73] and [75], and see Kitchen L.J. at [47]–[48].

[100f] *MWB Business Exchange Centres Ltd v Rock Advertising Ltd* [2018] UKSC 24, [2019] A.C. 119. The Supreme Court held that the contract variation was unenforceable because the original contract contained an enforceable "no oral variation" clause.

[100g] [2018] UKSC 24 at [18].

[100h] *Re Selectmove Ltd* [1995] 1 W.L.R. 474 (CA).

[100i] *Simantob v Shavleyan* [2018] EWHC 2005 (QB) at [128].

## Non-contractual payments

*Replace footnote 101 with:*

**8-021** [101] *CTN Cash and Carry Ltd v Gallaher Ltd* [1994] 4 All E.R. 714, 717. Although see Burrows, *The Law of Restitution*, 3rd edn (2011), at pp.277–280, where he suggests that a wider scope for economic duress may be warranted in a non-contractual context.

## (d) Causation

### Causation in duress to the person

*Replace paragraph with:*

In *Barton v Armstrong*[106] the Privy Council, relying on the analogy of fraud,[107] held that it was sufficient that the threat was a reason for the victim entering the contract: not only did it not have to be the predominant reason, but the victim was entitled to relief even if he had not shown that he would not have entered the contract without the threat (i.e. even if he would have entered the contract without the threat). The burden of proof is reversed such that it would be up to the party who made the threat to show that it had not influenced the victim in any way.[108] 8-026

[106] [1976] A.C. 104. And see *Singh v Redford* [2018] EWHC 2390 (Ch) at [87]: "It is enough that duress be a contributory cause of the transfer of a benefit by a claimant to a defendant, without it being the sole or operative cause".

[107] cf. above, para.7-040.

[108] [1976] A.C. 104, 120, 121.

### Causation in economic duress: "but for"

*Replace footnote 121 with:*

[121] See also Goff and Jones, *Law of Unjust Enrichment*, 9th edn (2016), paras 10-73—10-74. 8-028

### "Predominant cause" not required

*In line 6, after "dictum quoted above,", add:*

[128a] suggests that the combination of threat and other pressures need not be overwhelming, or 8-031

[128a] Above, para.8-028.

### Reasonable alternative

*Replace paragraph with:*

It is certainly relevant whether or not the victim had a reasonable alternative. The victim's lack of choice was emphasised by Lord Scarman in the *Pao On*[129] and *Universe Sentinel*[130] cases and has clearly been an important factor in those cases in which relief has been given.[131] It is not clear whether this is a prerequisite or merely evidential[132]; but it seems that if the victim had a reasonable alternative to submitting to the other party's demand, he will seldom obtain relief.[133] This is sometimes explicable on causal grounds. Thus a refusal, in breach of contract, to supply goods unless some extra consideration is supplied by the buyer, may lack genuine coercive force where alternative supplies are available in the market. Similarly, where the party claiming relief had adequate time to claim redress at law, and there is no reason to think that this would not protect or compensate him, submission to the threat may simply reflect that party's belief that his best interests would be served by such submission rather than by resort to the courts. The existence of a reasonable alternative may have been relevant in the *Pao On*[134] decision itself: Lord Scarman referred in general terms to American case law stressing the importance of examining the alternatives available to the party claiming relief.[135] But it is possible to argue that the existence of a reasonable alternative is not just a matter of proving causation. Cases can be imagined in which the illegitimate demand was the factor which "tipped the balance" and led to the victim agreeing 8-032 to the demand even though he had an alternative. It is not clear that relief would be available even though "but for" causation was satisfied. It has been said that "economic duress can only provide a basis for avoiding a contract if there was no real alternative".[136] This suggests that a plea of duress would fail if a reasonable person would have thought that an alternative was practical, even if the actual victim did not and it is shown that he would not have entered the contract but for the threat.

[129] *Pao On v Lau Liu Long* [1980] A.C. 614, 635. See also Halson (1991) 107 L.Q.R. 649.

[130] "The classic case of duress is, however, not the lack of will to submit but the victim's intentional submission arising from the realisation that there is no practical choice open to him": [1983] 1 A.C. 366, 400.

[131] e.g. *North Ocean Shipping Co Ltd v Hyundai Construction Co Ltd* [1979] Q.B. 705; *B. & S. Contracts & Design Ltd v Victor Green Publications Ltd* [1984] I.C.R. 419; *The Alev* [1989] 1 Lloyd's Rep. 138. cf. *Adam Opel GmbH v Mitras Automotive UK Ltd* [2007] EWHC 3252 (QB), [2007] All E.R. (D) 272 (Dec) (in the circumstances, an injunction was not an adequate alternative to nullify pressure caused by threat to refuse to deliver supplies: at [33]); *Kolmar Group AG v Traxpo Enterprises Pvt Ltd* [2010] EWHC 113 (Comm), [2010] 2 Lloyd's Rep. 653 (if did not perform, the victim would face having very large claims which were unsecured: see at [94]).

[132] See Beatson *The Use and Abuse of Unjust Enrichment* (1991), pp.122–126.

[133] *Huyton SA v Peter Cremer GmbH* [1999] 1 Lloyd's Rep. 620, 638; *Morley (t/a Morley Estates) v Royal Bank of Scotland Plc* [2020] EWHC 88 (Ch) at [270]–[271] (no economic duress because the claimant "retained the choice to resist the threat" initially by not signing the agreement and later by choosing not to litigate).

[134] [1980] A.C. 614.

[135] For examples, see *Tristate Roofing Co of Uniontown v Simon* (1958) A.2d. 333, 335; *Gallagher Switchboard Corp v Heckler Electric Co* (1962) 229 N.Y.S. 2d. 623, 630.

[136] Sir John Donaldson M.R. in *Hennessy v Craigmyle & Co Ltd* [1986] I.C.R. 461, 468.

### Reasonable alternative: a matter of evidence

*Replace paragraph with:*

**8-033** Mance J. has said that even though it is clear that the innocent party would never have acted as he did but for the threat, relief may be denied if he had "an alternative remedy which any and possibly some other reasonable persons would have pursued", so that he could have resisted the pressure.[137] He said where the threatened party had such an alternative, relief will seldom be appropriate. However, the judge also remarked that absence of a reasonable alternative was not "an inflexible third ingredient" (in addition to illegitimate pressure and causation).[138] David Richards L.J. has expressed the same view[138a]: that whether the victim had any realistic alternative goes to the question of causation. It is submitted that absence of a reasonable alternative is not an absolute requirement but rather very strong evidence of whether the victim was in fact influenced by the threat.[139]

[137] *Huyton SA v Peter Cremer GmbH & Co* [1999] 1 Lloyd's Rep. 620, 638. The objective approach to whether there was a reasonable alternative is criticised in Goff and Jones, *Law of Unjust Enrichment*, 9th edn (2016), para.10-55; and the authors point out that in fact the courts seem quite ready to accept that the victim had no real alternative: Goff and Jones, paras 10-75 and 10-77.

[138] *Huyton SA v Peter Cremer GmbH & Co* [1999] 1 Lloyd's Rep. 620, 638. In *DSND Subsea Ltd v Petroleum Geo-services ASA* [2000] B.L.R. 530, para.638, Dyson J. said "compulsion on, or lack of practical choice for, the victim" was one of "the ingredients of actionable duress"; but it is suggested that he did not mean lack of practical alternative to be an absolute requirement, since (also at [31]) he listed "whether the victim had any realistic practical alternative but to submit to the pressure" as one a range of factors to be taken into account: see below, para.8-045.

[138a] *Times Travel (UK) Ltd v Pakistan International Airlines Corp* [2019] EWCA Civ 828, [2019] 2 Lloyd's Rep. 89 at [65], in reference to the range of factors set out by Dyson J. in *DSND Subsea Ltd v Petroleum Geo Services ASA* [2000] B.L.R. 530 at [131].

[139] This was accepted in *Kolmar Group AG v Traxpo Enterprises Pvt Ltd* [2010] EWHC 113 (Comm) at [92]. In *Chaggar v Chaggar* [2018] EWHC 1203 (QB) it was pointed out (at [233]) that it may make little difference where in the analysis the absence of a reasonable alternative falls.

### Protest

*Replace paragraph with:*

In the *Pao On* case[142] it was said that it was relevant whether or not the victim **8-035** protested. This again seems to be a question of evidence as to whether or not the threat had a coercive effect. It has been accepted for many years that when a payment is made in order to avoid the wrongful seizure of goods, protest "affords some evidence ... that the payment was not voluntarily made",[143] but that the fact that the payment was made without protest does not necessarily mean that the payment was voluntary.[144] The victim may not protest because he sees no point in it or he may not wish to antagonise the coercing party whose performance he needs.

[142] *Pao On v Lau Yiu Long* [1980] A.C. 614.

[143] *Maskell v Horner* [1915] 3 K.B. 106, 120.

[144] See below, para.29-117.

### Independent advice

*In lines 5–6, after "had an alternative", replace "remedy and what the practical implications of following it would be are" with:*

remedy, and the practical implications of following it, would be **8-036**

## (e) Legitimacy of the Demand

### Threat to commit an unlawful act

*Replace footnote 151 with:*

[151] In *Dimskal Shipping Co SA v ITWF, The Evia Luck* [1992] 2 A.C. 152 the House of Lords held that **8-038** the question of whether economic pressure amounted to duress was prima facie a matter for the proper law of the contract, so that whether the conduct was lawful or not fell to be determined by the proper law of the contract rather than by that of the place where the threat was made. In *Royal Boskalis Westminster NV v Mountain* [1999] Q.B. 674, 689, 730 it was said that, nonetheless, counsel had been correct to concede, in the light of *Kaufman v Gerson* [1904] 1 K.B. 591, that some forms of duress are so shocking that English law would not enforce a contract made under such duress irrespective of whether the threat would be acceptable, and the contract valid, under the governing law. See below, para.30-293. And see *Morley (t/a Morley Estates) v Royal Bank of Scotland Plc* [2020] EWHC 88 (Ch) at [262], [267]–[268], where it was held that absent bad faith, duress requires an unlawful threat vis-à-vis the claimant. This did not occur because the defendant's breach of a mortgagee's duties in the circumstances could not cause the claimant any loss. The defendant's "threat flirted with illegality but did not inexorably commit to it". It was not "unequivocally" unlawful. The defendant "stayed, just, the right side of the line. ... I should categorise [defendant's] threat as part of what Dyson J. in the *DSND Subsea Ltd* [*v Petroleum Geo Services ASA* [2000] B.L.R. 530 at [131]] case called 'the rough and tumble of the pressures of normal commercial bargaining'".

## (f) Threats of Actions not in Themselves Wrongful

*To the end of title, add new footnote 191a:*

### Threat to commit otherwise lawful act[191a]

[191a] This paragraph of the 33rd edition was discussed and cited with approval in *Times Travel (UK) Ltd v Pakistan International Airlines Corp* [2019] EWCA Civ 828, [2019] 2 Lloyd's Rep. 89 at [91]–[93]. **8-046**

*Replace paragraph with:*

Threatening to carry out something perfectly within one's rights will not normally **8-046** amount to duress; for instance, a party who relies on his existing contractual rights to drive a hard bargain is not, on that ground alone, guilty of economic duress.[192] But there can be no doubt that even a threat to commit what would otherwise be a perfectly lawful act may be improper if the threat is coupled with a demand which goes substantially beyond what is normal or legitimate in commercial arrangements.[192a] It was at one time suggested that it could not be unlawful to threaten to exercise one's legal rights, no matter what the motive.[193] But such a principle is too widely stated. There are, for example, many cases where a man who has a "right", in the sense of a liberty or capacity to do an act which is not unlawful, but which is calculated seriously to injure another, will be liable to a charge of blackmail if he demands money from that other as the price of abstaining, e.g. from disclosing discreditable incidents in the victim's life.[194] Although it is, in general, true to say that a contract is not rendered voidable by reason of the fact that pressure has been lawfully applied so as to compel the promisor to accept its terms,[195] it is unlikely that a court would refuse to entertain an action at the suit of one who had paid money under a threat amounting to blackmail, or to set aside any agreement entered into as the result of such a threat.[196] In American law there are many illustrations of other threats to commit acts lawful in themselves which have been held to amount to duress when coupled with unreasonable demands.[197] For instance, a threat (lawfully) to dismiss an injured employee unless he accepted a manifestly low settlement for his injuries has been held to be unlawful duress.[198] It seems probable that a similar decision would be reached on such facts by an English court, but such a threat would be unlawful as a threatened unfair dismissal in this jurisdiction, and the settlement may also be voidable for undue influence or as an unconscionable bargain.[198a] On the other hand, care must be taken in treating threats lawful in themselves as amounting to duress, for otherwise threats commonly used in business (e.g. of lawful strikes[199]) would fall into the category of economic duress.

[192] *Alec Lobb Ltd v Total Oil G.B. Ltd* [1983] 1 W.L.R. 87 (varied on other points, [1985] 1 W.L.R. 173).

[192a] Doubt was cast on this sentence as applicable "in a purely commercial context" in the New Zealand decision of *Dold v Murphy* [2020] NZCA 313 at [73].

[193] *Allen v Flood* [1898] A.C. 1; *Ware and De Freville v Motor Trade Association* [1921] 3 K.B. 40; *Hardie and Lane Ltd v Chilton* [1928] 2 K.B. 306; *Chapman v Honig* [1963] 2 Q.B. 502; cf. *Quinn v Leathem* [1901] A.C. 495.

[194] *Thorne v Motor Trade Association* [1937] A.C. 797, 822; *Universe Tankships of Monrovia Inc v I.T.W.F.* [1983] 1 A.C. 366, 401.

[195] *Hardie and Lane Ltd v Chilton* [1928] 2 K.B. 306; *Eric Gnapp Ltd v Petroleum Board* [1949] 1 All E.R. 980.

[196] *Norreys v Zeffert* [1939] 2 All E.R. 187; *United Australia Ltd v Barclays Bank Ltd* [1941] A.C. 1, 29; *Universe Tankships of Monrovia Inc v I.T.W.F.* [1983] A.C. 366, 401.

[197] See *Restatement of Contracts*, para.176(2).

[198] *Mitchell v C.C. Sanitation Co* (1968) 430 S.W. 2d. 933; cf. the somewhat similar facts in *Arrale v Costain Engineering Ltd* [1976] 2 Lloyd's Rep. 98, though there was no real duress in this case.

[198a] See *Times Travel (UK) Ltd v Pakistan International Airlines Corp* [2019] EWCA Civ 828 at [92].

[199] Threats of unlawful strikes are usually protected by the statutory immunities governing acts done in the course of furtherance of a trade dispute: see Trade Union and Labour Relations Consolidation Act 1992. But coercive threats falling outside these immunities will often constitute unlawful duress, see, e.g. *Universe Tankships of Monrovia Inc v I.T.W.F.* [1983] A.C. 366, above, para.8-018.

*Replace paragraph with:*

**8-047** In *CTN Cash and Carry Ltd v Gallaher Ltd*[200] the plaintiffs had ordered goods from the defendants, who delivered them by mistake to the wrong warehouse, from which they were stolen. The defendants, honestly but wrongly believing that the goods were at the plaintiffs' risk, invoiced them. The plaintiffs initially refused to pay but did so after the defendants threatened to withdraw the plaintiffs' credit facilities, which, it was said, would seriously jeopardise the plaintiffs' business. The defendants had the right to withdraw credit facilities at any time. The plaintiffs later sought repayment. The Court of Appeal upheld the trial judge's decision that no case of economic duress had been made out. Steyn L.J., with whom the other members of the Court agreed, said that the combination of the facts that: (i) the defendants were entitled to refuse to enter into any future contracts with the plaintiffs for any reason; and (ii), critically, that the defendants bona fide thought that the plaintiffs owed the sum in question, was sufficient to distinguish cases in which a plea of economic duress had succeeded. The fact that the defendants were in a sense in a monopoly position was irrelevant, the control of monopolies being as matter for Parliament. Although there are cases in which the courts have accepted that a threat of a lawful action coupled with a demand for payment may be illegitimate,[201] it would be a relatively rare case in which "lawful act duress" could be established in a commercial context.[202] In *R. v Attorney-General for England and Wales*[203] the Privy Council held that a confidentiality agreement signed by a member of the SAS under threat of being returned to his original unit if he did not sign was not voidable for duress: the threat was not unlawful, as the Crown had the right to transfer any member of the SAS to another unit, and the demand could be justified on the ground that the Ministry of Defence was reasonably entitled to regard anyone unwilling to accept the obligation of confidentiality as unsuitable for the SAS.[204] In *Times Travel (UK) Ltd v Pakistan International Airlines Corp*,[204a] David Richards L.J., giving the leading judgment, rejected Leggatt L.J.'s obiter observations in *Al Nehayan v Kent*, which supported a broader doctrine of lawful act duress by determining the legitimacy of the demand by reference to "basic minimum standards of acceptable behaviour".[204b] David Richards L.J. concluded that the doctrine of lawful act duress did not extend to the use of lawful pressure to make a demand that the party exerting the pressure believed itself, in good faith to be entitled. This seems uncontroversial.[204c] But, the case makes clear that this position holds "whether or not, objectively speaking, it has reasonable grounds for that belief".[204d] There is no authority to require objective reasonableness of the demand; to do so would be unjustified and would compromise the certainty of the law.[204e] This is reinforced by the fact that the common law does not recognise any general doctrine of abuse of rights,[204f] and has rejected a doctrine of inequality of bargaining power, and the use of monopoly position as a ground for setting aside contracts.[204g] Nevertheless, as his Lordship concedes, as a matter of fact finding, the more objectively unreasonable the ground for a party's belief, the less likely it is that a court will accept that belief to be in good faith.[204h]

200 [1994] 4 All E.R. 715; *Marsden v Barclays Bank Plc* [2016] EWHC 1601 (QB), [2016] 2 Lloyd's Rep. 420. Compare *Progress Bulk Carriers Ltd v Tube City IMS LLC (The Cenk Kaptanoglu)* [2012] EWHC 273 (Comm), [2012] 1 Lloyd's Rep. 501, where the owners had earlier broken the charter by failing to provide the chartered ship; they then refused to provide a replacement vessel unless the charterers waived any claim for damages. It was held that the agreement to waive claims voidable for economic duress. It is submitted that despite the discussion of conduct which is not itself unlawful at [36], this is a case in which not only had the owner's committed a wrongful act already but their threat to provide a replacement only if the charterers gave up their rights to damages was itself a threat of a wrongful act, i.e. refusing to provide the charterers with a full remedy for the initial breach.

201 e.g. *Thorne v Motor Trade Association* [1937] A.C. 797.

202 *Marsden v Barclays Bank Plc* [2016] EWHC 1601 (QB), [2016] 2 Lloyd's Rep. 420 at [35]. The threat, if not wrongful, must at least be immoral or unconscionable. There is nothing unconscionable

in the owner of goods let on hire purchase threatening to repossess them when the hirer is in default and has not applied for relief against forfeiture: *Alf Vaughan & Co Ltd v Royscot Trust Ltd* [1999] 1 All E.R. (Comm) 856. Nor is there duress if a party who is entitled under the terms of the contract to stop performing until it has been paid makes an illegitimate threat when it refuses to go on unless the other party gives a guarantee of payment: *Flying Music Co Ltd v Theater Entertainment SA* [2017] EWHC 3192 (QB) at [87]. See also *Holyoake v Candy* [2017] EWHC 3397 (Ch) at [236] and [441].

203 [2003] UKPC 22.

204 [2003] UKPC 22 at [17]–[18].

204a *Times Travel (UK) Ltd v Pakistan International Airlines Corp* [2019] EWCA Civ 828, [2019] 2 Lloyd's Rep. 89 at [38]–[56], [62], [70]–[76], [84]–[90], [100]–[104]. An appeal to the Supreme Court is outstanding.

204b In *Al Nehayan v Kent* [2018] EWHC 333 (Comm) at [185].

204c See above paras 4-053 and 4-054; applied in *Morley (t/a Morley Estates) v Royal Bank of Scotland Plc* [2020] EWHC 88 (Ch) at [236]–[237] ("'lawful act' duress cannot exist in the absence of bad faith on the part of the person applying the pressure", and rejecting "Steyn LJ's less stringent standard of conduct which is morally or socially unacceptable". Moreover, "[a]ggression and unpleasantness is not the same thing as bad faith").

204d *Times Travel (UK) Ltd v Pakistan International Airlines Corp* [2019] EWCA Civ 828 at [105] (emphasis added).

204e [2019] EWCA Civ 828 at [106]. It is "very unclear why or on what basis the common law should hold that a party with a private law right, whose exercise is not subject to any overriding duty, cannot use it to achieve a purpose which is both lawful and advanced in good faith".

204f [2019] EWCA Civ 828 at [41] and [97].

204g [2019] EWCA Civ 828 at [103].

204h [2019] EWCA Civ 828 at [106].

## Threat not to contract

*Replace paragraph with:*

8-048 It is not clear whether a threat not to enter into a contract unless the threatener's terms are met could ever amount to improper pressure, for example where the threatener's terms are extortionate. There are a number of salvage cases in which extortionate demands have been made to rescue a vessel (or those on board) and the contracts so entered into have been set aside, or refused enforcement.[205] But these cases may rest upon the principle of maritime law that a duty to rescue human life is imposed on putative rescuers, so that the threat not to rescue may be unlawful. Otherwise, a party that is under no duty to enter into a contract with another is entitled to set its own terms, even though these may seem extortionate and the other party may have little choice but to comply.[206] In *Times Travel (UK) Ltd v Pakistan International Airlines Corp*[207] an existing agreement between the parties had been terminated by notice and a new agreement entered under which the claimant travel agents would receive lower commissions and give up their claim to commissions payable under the old agreement. It was held that the new agreement could not be avoided on the ground of duress; even though the defendant was effectively in a monopoly position, its threat not to contract with the claimant was lawful and its demand was made in good faith. There was no duress although, on the facts, the defendant's demand was unreasonable, at least in part, and although the defendant had not established its good faith. The latter was irrelevant since it was for the claimant to establish the defendant's bad faith and this had not been done.[207a]

205 See *Akerblom v Price* (1881) 7 Q.B.D. 129; *The Rialto* [1891] P.175; *The Port Caledonia and the Anna* [1903] P.184; *The Crusader* [1907] P.196. See now Merchant Shipping Act 1995 s.224, which provides for the Salvage Convention 1989 (contained in Sch.11 to the Act) to have the force of law. The Convention provides in art.7:

"*Annulment and modification of contracts*
A contract or any terms thereof may be annulled or modified if—

(a) the contract has been entered into under undue influence or the influence of danger and its terms are inequitable; or
(b) the payment under the contract is in an excessive degree too large or too small for the services actually rendered."

Art.13 sets out criteria for fixing the proper reward.

[206] See, e.g. *Smith v William Charlick Ltd* (1924) 34 C.L.R. 38; *Morton Construction v City of Hamilton* (1961) 31 D.L.R. (2d) 323; *Dold v Murphy* [2020] NZCA 313, [75], [76], [79]. See Goff and Jones, *Law of Unjust Enrichment*, 9th edn (2016), paras 10-71—10-72.

[207] *Times Travel (UK) Ltd v Pakistan International Airlines Corp* [2019] EWCA Civ 828.

[207a] [2019] EWCA Civ 828 at [41], [110]–[112].

## (h) General Effect of Duress

### Contract under duress is voidable

*Replace footnote 241 with:*

[241] As in *North Ocean Shipping Co Ltd v Hyundai Construction Ltd* [1979] Q.B. 705, in which this passage was cited. See further below, para.8-103. In *Royal Boskalis Westminster NV v Mountain* [1999] Q.B. 674, 730, Phillips L.J. expressed some difficulty in saying that a contract has been avoided on the grounds of duress if it is governed by a foreign law which would afford no right of avoidance, even where the duress was so unconscionable that English law would override the proper law of the contract (see above, para.8-038). However, he considered that English law would not recognise the effects of the contract (at 731). See also *Morley (t/a Morley Estates) v Royal Bank of Scotland Plc* [2020] EWHC 88 (Ch) at [218], where para.8-054 was cited with approval; the claimant had affirmed the agreements by failing to take any steps over five years to set them aside (at [272]). **8-054**

## 3. UNDUE INFLUENCE

## (b) Direct Proof of Undue Influence

### Coercion or actual pressure

*Replace paragraph with:*

Undue influence may be proved by showing that there was coercion by the donee. **8-068** This does not necessarily involve a pre-existing relationship between the parties.[337] However, these cases are probably now better viewed as cases of illegitimate pressure[338] and, accordingly, they were treated in the previous section.[339] Although there are few modern cases on the point, it seems that undue influence may be proved by showing that the defendant used his relationship with the claimant to put pressure on the claimant.[340] Many of the old cases on this point have concerned spiritual "advisers", who have used their expert knowledge of the next world to obtain advantages in this.[341] In *Morley v Loughnan*[342] executors recovered from the defendant large sums of money obtained by him from their testator during the last seven years of his life, on the ground that they had been obtained by undue influence in the guise of religion, it being held unnecessary to decide whether there was a fiduciary or confidential relationship between the defendant and the testator.[343] There have also been cases where an employee obtained complete control over an employer of weak understanding,[344] and where an older man acquired a strong influence over a younger one, inducing him to execute securities for debts contracted by them in their career of mutual dissipation.[345] The transactions were set aside. In *CIBC Mortgages Plc v Pitt* there was a finding of actual undue influence which seems to have rested largely on the pressure that the husband placed upon the wife.[346] But there may have been some change in what pressure wives are expected to have to withstand. In *Royal Bank of Scotland v Etridge (No.2)* Lord Nicholls said:

> "Statements or conduct by a husband which do not pass beyond the bounds of what may be expected of a reasonable husband in the circumstances should not, without more, be castigated as undue influence."[347]

[337] See *Royal Bank of Scotland v Etridge (No.2)* [2001] UKHL 44, [2002] 2 A.C. 773 at [103] (Lord Hobhouse); *Libyan Investment Authority v Goldman Sachs* [2016] EWHC 2530 (Ch) at [136]–[137] (Rose J.).

[338] Birks and Chin in *Good Faith and Fault in Contract Law*, pp.63–65; Capper (1998) 114 L.Q.R. 479, 484, 493. An example of actual undue influence that seems to have amounted to illegitimate pressure is *Drew v Daniel* [2005] EWCA Civ 507, [2005] 2 F.C.R. 365. Ward L.J. pointed out that in all cases of undue influence, "the critical question is whether or not the influence has invaded the free volition of the donor to accept or reject the persuasion or withstand the influence" (at [36]).

[339] In *Royal Bank of Scotland v Etridge (No.2)* [2001] UKHL 44, [2002] 2 A.C. 773 at [8], Lord Nicholls said that overt acts of improper pressure or coercion, such as unlawful threats, might amount to undue influence but continued: "Today there is much overlap with the principle of duress as this principle has subsequently developed." In *Holyoake v Candy* [2017] EWHC 3397 (Ch) Nugee J. said that he could not see what a plea of actual undue influence of this kind adds to a plea of duress, or how it could succeed if a plea of duress fails on the facts: at [407]. Compare *De Sena v Notaro* [2020] EWHC 1031 (Ch) at [216], where H.H. Judge Paul Matthews (sitting as a Judge of the High Court) held that actual undue influence "involves pleading and proving 'overt acts of improper pressure or coercion such as unlawful threats', and that this overlaps with the principle of duress at common law".

[340] An example seems to be *Coldunell Ltd v Gallon* [1986] Q.B. 1184; see at 1196. Compare *De Sena v Notaro* [2020] EWHC 1031 (Ch) at [217]–[218] (commercial pressure which cannot be regarded as improper or illegitimate is insufficient, "I do not say that the first defendant did not put any pressure on the first claimant. I accept that his business style could be self-centred, brusque and occasionally abrasive. He was every inch a businessman, who looked out for the interests of his company… [and of] himself. That is not wrong. To put pressure on another person to do a deal that you would like to do is not without more wrong." Since the claimant "was an experienced businesswoman" the first defendant's conduct cannot "properly be regarded as acts of improper or illegitimate pressure or coercion. This was a case of a hard negotiation by experienced business people in a commercial transaction, and nothing more").

[341] *Norton v Relly* (1764) 2 Eden 286; *Nottidge v Prince* (1860) 2 Giff. 246; *Lyon v Home* (1868) L.R. 6 Eq. 655.

[342] [1893] 1 Ch. 736.

[343] It is such cases that Lord Nicholls may have had in mind when he said that undue influence includes "cases where a vulnerable person has been exploited": *Royal Bank of Scotland v Etridge (No.2)* [2001] UKHL 44, [2002] 2 A.C. 773 at [11].

[344] *Bridgeman v Green* (1755) 2 Ves. Sen. 627; *Re Craig* [1971] Ch. 95. Whether there was actual influence depends on the individual involved, not on whether a normal person would be influenced: *Re Brocklehurst's Estate* [1978] Ch. 14, 40.

[345] *Smith v Kay* (1859) 7 H.L. Cas. 750. The position in relation to a will alleged to have been procured by undue influence is different: see *Edwards v Edwards* [2007] W.T.L.R. 1387; *Hubbard v Scott* [2011] EWHC 2750 (Ch); *Wharton v Bancroft* [2011] EWHC 3250 (Ch).

[346] See the finding of the trial judge recounted in the Court of Appeal (1993) 66 P.&C.R. 179, 182 (affirmed [1994] 1 A.C. 200).

[347] *Royal Bank of Scotland v Etridge (No.2)* [2001] UKHL 44, [2002] 2 A.C. 773 at [32]. cf. *Hurley v Darjan Estate Co Plc* [2012] EWHC 189 (Ch), [2012] 1 W.L.R. 1782 at [40] (fact that wife signed in the heat of the moment to keep the husband happy did not mean her consent was not free and informed; cf. the claim of undue influence made in *Barclays Bank v O'Brien*, which failed before the Court of Appeal and was not pursued: [1993] Q.B. 109, 113–117).

### Independent and informed judgment

*Replace paragraph with:*

**8-069** However, "importunity and pressure … [are] neither always necessary nor sufficient".[348] On the one hand, actual undue influence may be denied although pressure was applied by the defendant where a claimant "was not a timid housewife, inexperienced in business ... she was an experienced businesswoman, used to dealing with professional advisers in relation both to the corporate business and to her personal affairs ... This was a case of a hard negotiation by experienced business people in a commercial transaction, and nothing more".[348a] On the other hand, undue influence may be shown without proof of pressure by showing that the stronger party exercised such a degree of domination or control over the mind of the weaker party that the latter's independence of decision was substantially undermined.[349] The critical question is whether the complainant was allowed to exercise an independent and informed judgment.[350] In *Bank of Montreal v Stuart* the wife succeeded in establishing undue influence even though the husband had put no pressure on her because none was needed, as "she had no will of her own ... she was ready to sign and do anything he told her to do".[351] In *Bank of Credit and Commerce International SA v Aboody*,[352] the wife trusted her husband in business matters and signed documents he put before her without question. Although there was also evidence that he bullied her and that she signed because she wanted peace, the Court of Appeal did not rely on these facts; it considered that if the husband had intentionally exploited her trust to get the wife to sign manifestly disadvantageous documents without explaining them to her, that would constitute undue influence.[353] As now in cases where undue influence is actually proved it is not necessary to prove that the transaction was manifestly disadvantageous in order to obtain relief,[354] it seems that a party who is shown to have exploited another's trust to get them to enter the transaction in question without proper consideration or explanation will be held to be exercising undue influence, without more; the influenced party's mind is still "a mere channel through which the will of [the influencing party] operates".[355] As Lord Nicholls put it:

> "In cases of this ... nature the influence one person has over another provides scope for misuse without any specific acts of persuasion. The relationship between two individuals may be such that, without more, one of them is disposed to agree to a course of action proposed by the other. Typically this occurs when one person places trust in another to look after his affairs and interests, and the latter betrays this trust by preferring his own interests."[356]

There is a close parallel between these cases of "actual" undue influence and cases in which undue influence may be presumed. In each case the capacity to influence the complainant exists because of the trust and confidence that the complainant had in the other party, at least in relation to the transaction in question. The fact that the confidence has been abused may be *presumed* from the fact that the complainant has entered a transaction that is not readily explicable by the relationship of the parties[357]; but if it is shown that the particular transaction was the result of the complainant simply following the other party's suggestions, and the latter did not allow the complainant to exercise his or her own free and informed judgment but furthered his own interests,[358] that will amount[359] to actual undue influence.[360] Manifest disadvantage is merely powerful evidence that undue influence has been exercised.[361]

[348] *Royal Bank of Scotland v Etridge (No.2)* [1998] 4 All E.R. 705, 712. See also *Dunbar Bank Plc v Nadeem* [1998] 3 All E.R. 876, 883.

[348a] *De Sena v Notaro* [2020] EWHC 1031 (Ch) at [218].

[349] *Bank of Montreal v Stuart* [1911] A.C. 120.

[350] "The donor may be led but she must not be driven; and her will must be the offspring of her own volition, not a record of someone else's": *Thompson v Foy* [2009] EWHC 1076 (Ch), [2010] 1 P. & C.R. 16 at [101].

[351] [1911] A.C. 120, 136–137. In *Royal Bank of Scotland v Etridge (No.2)* [1998] 4 All E.R. 705, 712, Stuart-Smith L.J. said that this would today be more readily classed as a Class 2B case. If there is a sufficient relationship for Class 2B (below, para.8-085) and also a transaction calling for explanation, it will be in the weaker party's interest to plead the case as Class 2B as it then is up to the other party to rebut the presumption of undue influence; but actual undue influence remains an attractive alternative if there is doubt about the nature of the relationship or the need for an explanation of the transaction.

[352] [1990] 1 Q.B. 923, 967.

[353] The court held that manifest disadvantage was essential to a plea of actual undue influence. As on the facts it did not consider the transactions to be manifestly disadvantageous, it refused relief.

[354] *CIBC Mortgages Plc v Pitt* [1994] 1 A.C. 200, overruling *Bank of Credit & Commerce International SA v Aboody* [1990] 1 Q.B. 923.

[355] *Bank of Credit and Commerce International SA v Aboody* [1990] 1 Q.B. 923, 969, referring to the observations of Jenkins and Morris L.JJ. in *Tufton v Sperni* [1952] 2 T.L.R. 516, 530, 532.

[356] *Royal Bank of Scotland v Etridge (No.2)* [2001] UKHL 44, [2002] 2 A.C. 773 at [9]. See the discussion in *McGregor v Michael Taylor & Co* [2002] 2 Lloyd's Rep. 468, where at [24]–[27] these are described as "trust me" cases.

[357] *McGregor v Michael Taylor & Co* [2002] 2 Lloyd's Rep. 468, at [21]; see further below, para.8-092.

[358] See above, para.8-061 and below, para.8-072.

[359] Subject to the point to be discussed in paras 8-072—8-073.

[360] *Royal Bank of Scotland v Etridge (No.2)* [2001] UKHL 44, [2002] 2 A.C. 773 at [17]: "such a plaintiff may succeed even where this presumption was not available to him; for instance where the impugned transaction was not one which called for an explanation."

[361] *Royal Bank of Scotland v Etridge (No.2)* [1998] 4 All E.R. 705, 713; cf. [2001] UKHL 44, [2002] 2 A.C. at [104].

## Misrepresentation and non-disclosure as forms of undue influence

*Replace footnote 365 with:*

**8-070** [365] [2010] EWHC 105 (Ch) at [131]; see also at [140]. In *Syndicate Bank v Dansingani* [2019] EWHC 3439 (Ch) at [217] the husband and brother of the wife misled her as to the basis of the mortgage and this amounted to undue influence. In *Hewett v First Plus Financial Plc* [2010] EWCA Civ 312 a husband's concealment from his wife of an affair with another woman amounted to undue influence. Compare *Davies v AIB Group (UK) Plc* [2012] EWHC 2178 (Ch) (held at [113]–[114] that no undue influence: husband made full disclosure of the entire transaction and all of the relevant documents so as to put wife's solicitor in the position to tender full and informed advice to her). A question is whether knowledge of the surety's solicitor should be imputed to her. The general rule is that, subject to any statutory variation, a solicitor's knowledge is treated as that of his client (see *AIB v Martin and Gold* Unreported March 15, 1999, Jacob J.), but in *Davies v AIB Group (UK) Plc* [2012] EWHC 2178 (Ch) at [116], without deciding the issue, Norris J. thought that some caution might be required in the context of undue influence arguments: "A principle of attributing the knowledge of an agent to the principal does not really assist in identifying how an intention to enter a transaction was produced—freely or under undue influence."

## Causation

*Replace paragraph with:*

**8-074** As in cases of fraud, the fraud must have induced the contract, so actual undue influence must have influenced the contract.[383] However, the analogies with fraud and duress suggest that the undue influence need only be "a significant reason" for the complainant entering the contract,[384] rather than, for instance, the principal reason. What was less clear until recently was whether, as has been held in some fraud cases,[385] provided that the undue influence had some effect, it does not matter that the complainant would have entered the contract in any event. In *Bank of Credit and Commerce International SA v Aboody*[386] it was said that it would not be appropriate for the court to exercise its jurisdiction to set aside the contract "where the evidence establishes that on the balance of probabilities the complainant would have entered the contract in any event". But in *UCB Corporate Services Ltd v Williams*[387] the Court of Appeal held that, as undue influence is a species of fraud, it is no answer that the person influenced would have entered the transaction anyway: it is the fact that she has been deprived of the opportunity to make a free choice that founds her equity to set aside the transaction. The proposition in *Aboody's* case was said to be:

> "... flatly inconsistent with Lord Browne-Wilkinson's statement of principle[388] ... that a victim of undue influence is entitled to have the transaction set aside 'as of right'. The words 'as of right' seem ... to admit of only one meaning; viz., regardless of other considerations."[389]

The matter was put even more strongly in *Syndicate Bank v Dansingani*[389a] H.H. Judge Dight said:

> "I ... reject the ... argument that there has to be a causal link between the alleged undue influence and execution of the challenged document in the sense that ... [the claimant] has to show that had she been fully informed she would not have entered into the transaction. Causation in that sense is not part of the principles relating to undue influence which concerns the free will of the complainant at the point of entry into the transaction, to which an understanding is, of course, relevant, but is not the only or indeed main factor. If she did not enter into the transaction of her own free will she did not consent to it and she has a right in principle to set the transaction aside."

Presumably it would follow also that the same presumption applies as in fraud, so that it will be for the stronger party to show that the undue influence had no impact at all on the complainant's decision.[390]

[383] See above, para.7-036.

[384] See above, paras 7-038 and 8-027—8-028.

[385] See above, paras 7-040 and 8-026.

[386] [1990] 1 Q.B. 923, 971.

[387] [2002] EWCA Civ 555 at [86].

[388] *CIBC Mortgages Plc v Pitt* [1994] 1 A.C. 200, 209.

[389] [2002] EWCA Civ 555 at [91].

[389a] *Syndicate Bank v Dansingani* [2019] EWHC 3439 (Ch) at [96].

[390] This is the rule suggested by the statement in *Bank of Credit and Commerce International SA v Aboody* [1990] 1 Q.B. 923, 971, quoted in this paragraph. For the rule in fraud cases see above, para.7-040.

## (c) Presumed Undue Influence

### *(ii) Confidential Relationship Shown on Facts in Earlier Decisions*

**Confidential relationship shown on facts: a separate class?**

*In line 10, after "a wife shows that in respect", add:*

of **8-087**

### Examples

*Replace paragraph with:*

8-089 Where a young man in financial difficulties sought the advice of a more experienced relative, who himself purchased the young man's property at a third of its proper price,[467] where a young woman granted a mining lease to her uncle and to the son of her father's executor, being advised to do so by the executor in whom she placed "the greatest confidence",[468] and where a member of a committee set up to establish a Moslem cultural centre in London was induced by a fellow member to buy the latter's house from him for the purpose at a price which greatly exceeded its market value,[469] the transactions were set aside on the ground that the defendants had failed to rebut the presumption of undue influence.

[467] *Tate v Williamson* (1866) L.R. 2 Ch. App. 55.

[468] *Grosvenor v Sherratt* (1860) 28 Beav. 659.

[469] *Tufton v Sperni* [1952] 2 T.L.R. 516.

*Replace paragraph with:*

8-090 **Relationship may arise from transaction** It has been held that a confidential relationship may arise from the circumstances of the very transaction in question, e.g. if the defendant has advised and assisted the claimant over it and the claimant has relied on the defendant for that.[470]

[470] *Turkey v Awadh* [2005] EWCA Civ 382, [2005] 2 F.C.R. 7, referring to *Macklin v Dowsett* [2004] EWCA Civ 904, [2004] All E.R. (D) 95 (Jun). In that case the defendant, who was impecunious, had made an arrangement to give up his rights to land for a small sum unless he completed building a bungalow on the land within three years, which he was very unlikely to be able to do. Cf. *Perwaz v Perwaz* [2018] UKUT 325 (TCC) (Elizabeth Cooke J.): to benefit from the evidential presumption, the relationship of trust and confidence must precede the transaction calling for an explanation. This case is pending appeal.

*Add new paragraphs:*

8-090A **Relationship of trust and confidence may be inferred** The existence of a relationship of trust and confidence may be inferred from the fact that one party has entered an excessively onerous transaction at the request of the other (in the case in question, a junior employee with no stake in the business had at her employer's request given a second charge over her flat and an unlimited all monies guarantee of the employer's business debts).[471] In *Malik (Deceased) v Shiekh* Fancourt J. stated that:

> "the true nature and effect of the transaction is a matter that is capable of affecting the assessment of whether or not a relationship of influence is shown to exist. A transaction that is seriously and inexplicably detrimental to a disponor is plainly likely to lead to a conclusion that it can only have been the result of a relationship of trust and confidence on the one side and influence on the other side. ... [T]here is a connection between the two separate factual assessments, which themselves are aspects of undue influence generally, such that the more disadvantageous and inexplicable the transaction the more easily a relationship of influence will be established to exist."[472]

Further, in *Paull v Paull*[472a] it was held that:

> "where, or if, it is demonstrated that following a transfer, or transaction, there is evidence of a relationship of trust and confidence, it is, unless there is other conflicting evidence,

a perfectly proper and permissible inference that that state of affairs also existed at the date of the transaction in question."

In that case, the complainant, a vulnerable and eccentric 67-year-old man with limited means transferred his home where he lived with his disabled partner, to his son for no consideration. Following the transfer, the son's address became the registered address for the complainant's banking and pension documentation and the son was authorised to open them.

[471] *Crèdit Lyonnais Bank Nederland NV v Burch* [1997] 1 All E.R. 144, especially at 154 and 158. See Chen-Wishart [1997] C.L.J. 60, 65–66. In such an extreme case the plaintiff may be able to set aside the transaction on the basis of unconscionability, see below, para.8-134.

[472] *Malik (Deceased) v Shiekh* [2018] EWHC 973 (Ch), [2018] 4 W.L.R. 86 at [45].

[472a] *Paull v Paull* [2018] EWHC 2520 (Ch) at [16] and see [36].

**Relationship may arise from vulnerability** In *Thompson v Foy*[472b] Lewison J. said that although in *Etridge*[472c] Lord Nicholls of Birkenhead described the paradigm case of a relationship where influence is presumed as being one in which the complainant reposed trust and confidence in the other party in relation to the management of the complainant's *financial* affairs, he did not consider that this description was intended to be exhaustive. In *Malik (Deceased) v Shiekh* Fancourt J. held: 8-090B

> "the principle is not confined to cases where trust and confidence is reposed, either financially or generally, but extends to cases where there is evidence of dependence or vulnerability..."[472d]

In that case, an elderly woman who was infirm, immobile, with impending mental degeneration and unable to understand English, transferred, for no consideration, her two properties to herself and the respondent as equal tenants in common, for the benefit of her sons and their company. Fancourt J. concluded that the woman was in a relationship of influence with her sons (with whom she lived and on whom she depended for information) who procured her consent to the contract as the respondent's agents. It should be noted that in this case, the complainant evidently had a pre-existing relationship with her sons. If the scope of a confidential relationship were to be found simply on the basis of "vulnerability", then it would be difficult to maintain a clear distinction between undue influence and the unconscionable bargains doctrine.

[472b] [2009] EWHC 1076 (Ch) at [100].

[472c] [2001] UKHL 44 at [14].

[472d] *Malik (Deceased) v Shiekh* [2018] EWHC 973 (Ch), [2018] 4 W.L.R. 86 at [50], citing *Beech v Birmingham City Council* [2014] EWCA Civ 830 at [59], per Sir Terence Etherton C., referring to *Etridge* at [11]. This was applied in *Paull v Paull* [2018] EWHC 2520 (Ch) at [8] and [17].

## Husband and wife

*Replace footnote 475 with:*

[475] See *Syndicate Bank v Dansingani* [2019] EWHC 3439 (Ch) at [60], where the court found the husband to be entirely in control of his wife's finances; the wife placed trust and confidence in him and played no independent role. Compare *Society of Lloyd's v Khan* [1998] 3 F.C.R. 93. 8-091

### *(iii) A Transaction Not Explicable by Ordinary Motives*

**Transaction not explicable by ordinary motives**

*In line 11, after "influence was used,", add new footnote 481a:*

8-092 [481a] *Malik (Deceased) v Shiekh* [2018] EWHC 973 (Ch), [2018] 4 W.L.R. 86, Fancourt J. at [42]: "The nature of the transaction tends to suggest that there might have been abuse of trust and confidence or the exertion of some influence" to induce the complainant to enter the transaction; and see at [46].

## (d) Rebutting the Presumption

**Rebutting the presumption**

*Replace paragraph with:*

8-099 In order to rebut the presumption of undue influence, evidence must be adduced to satisfy the court "that the donor was acting independently of any influence from the donee and with the full appreciation of what he was doing".[508] The most usual, though not the only, way of rebutting the presumption is to prove that the claimant had competent and independent advice,[509] and the position of the defendant is stronger if the claimant's action was taken in accordance with, than if it was taken in spite of, such advice. Sometimes to show that the complainant had independent advice will be the only way of rebutting the inference of undue influence,[510] but circumstances may establish the fact that the claimant's will was freely exercised although no independent advice was given or although such advice was disregarded.[511] Conversely, proof of outside advice does not necessarily show that there was no undue influence: it is a question of fact to be decided on the evidence.[512] As Master Bowles explained in *Paull v Paull*:

> "whether the intervention of a solicitor, or the advice given by a solicitor, is sufficient to rebut the presumption is dependent not upon some formulaic, or mechanistic approach, whereby certain advice given in certain circumstances inevitably, or automatically, rebuts the presumption. The question, rather, is whether, in the particular circumstances of the case, the court can be affirmatively satisfied that the consequence of the advice given has been to procure the emancipation of the donor, or benefactor, from the influence exercised by the donee, or beneficiary."[512a]

Moreover, "[t]he greater the trust reposed ... the greater the clarity that will be required before the court can be satisfied that the influence emanating from that trust has been negated".[512b] In the context of *Paull v Paull*, the complainant "would have had to be so informed in circumstances whereby [the defendant] ... was neither present when that information was imparted, nor sufficiently close by for his presence, nearby, to impact upon, or affect" the complainant.[512c]

[508] *Inche Noriah v Shaik Allie Bin Omar* [1929] A.C. 127, 135. In order to rebut the presumption it is not sufficient to show that C understood what he or she was doing and intended to do it: *Curtis v Pulbrook* [2009] EWHC 782 (Ch) at [143], citing *Snell's Equity*, 31st edn (2005), para.8-30. At this stage, whether or not there was manifest disadvantage is irrelevant: *Smith v Cooper* [2010] EWCA Civ 722, [2010] 2 F.C.R. 551 at [65].

[509] *Morley v Loughnan* [1893] 1 Ch. 736, 752; *Re Coomber* [1911] 1 Ch. 723; *Inche Noriah v Shaik Allie Bin Omar* [1929] A.C. 127.

[510] *Inche Noriah v Shaik Allie Bin Omar* [1929] A.C. 127, PC.

[511] [1929] A.C. 127, 135; *Re Estate of Brocklehurst* [1978] Ch. 14.

[512] *Royal Bank of Scotland v Etridge (No.2)* [2001] UKHL 44, [2002] 2 A.C. 773 at [20]. The Court of Appeal should interfere with the trial judge's findings on this point only if the judge went wrong in principle: *Curtis v Curtis* [2011] EWCA Civ 1602 at [14].

[512a] *Paull v Paull* [2018] EWHC 2520 (Ch) at [14].

[512b] *Paull v Paull* [2018] EWHC 2520 (Ch) at [112].

[512c] *Paull v Paull* [2018] EWHC 2520 (Ch) at [115].

### Adequacy of advice

*In line 5, after "presumption will not be rebutted.", add new footnote 521a:*

[521a] See *Paull v Paull* [2018] EWHC 2520 (Ch) at [117] where the defendant's misrepresentation meant that the solicitor could not adequately advise the complainant on the implications and effect of the transaction. The transaction was set aside even though the complainant was also party to the misrepresentation. **8-102**

## (e) Remedies for Undue Influence

### Affirmation

*Replace paragraph with:*

A transaction entered into as the result of undue influence is voidable and not void. The right to rescind on the ground of undue influence may be lost either by express affirmation of the transaction by the victim,[526] by estoppel or by delay amounting to proof of acquiescence.[527] Although there can normally be no affirmation until the party knows he has the right to rescind, it has been doubted whether this is a hard and fast rule: "the whole of the circumstances must be looked at to see whether it is just that the complaining beneficiary should succeed".[528] Estoppel requires a clear and unequivocal representation that the claimant would not seek to set the agreement aside, intended to be acted on and in fact acted on by the other party to his detriment or in such a way that it would be inequitable to allow the claimant to go back on his representation.[529] In either case, to be of any value, the affirmation must take place after the influence has ceased: **8-103**

> "The right to property acquired by such means cannot be confirmed in this court unless there be full knowledge of all the facts, full knowledge of the equitable rights arising out of those facts, and an absolute release from the undue influence by means of which the frauds were practised."[530]

Lapse of time in itself does not seem to constitute a bar to relief,[531] but it will provide evidence of acquiescence if the victim fails to take any steps to set aside the transaction within a reasonable time after he is freed from the undue influence.[532] And where he has himself failed to commence proceedings in this way during his lifetime, his personal representatives cannot do so after his death.[533]

[526] *Mitchell v Homfray* (1881) 8 Q.B.D. 587; *Morse v Royal* (1806) 12 Ves. Jr. 355.

[527] *Allcard v Skinner* (1887) 36 Ch. D. 145; *Turner v Collins* (1871) L.R. 7 Ch. App. 329. See below, paras 28-137—28-143.

[528] *Goldsworthy v Brickell* [1987] Ch. 378, 412 (Nourse L.J.) and 416 (Parker L.J.). Nourse L.J. considered that the defence might have succeeded on the basis that by the time of the alleged act of affirmation, the complainant had consulted solicitors. cf. *Lloyds Bank Plc v Lucken*, heard with the *Etridge* case, [1998] 4 All E.R. 705, 738, 751; *De Sena v Notaro* [2020] EWHC 1031 (Ch) at [231] (noted obiter dictum that the claimant had affirmed by selling part of the subject matter of the contract after having acquired knowledge of all facts necessary for its claim).

[529] *Goldsworthy v Brickell* [1987] Ch. 378, 410–411. In *Habib Bank Ltd v Tufail* [2006] EWCA Civ 374, [2006] All E.R. (D) 92 (Apr) Lloyd L.J. drew a distinction between affirmation, which requires knowledge of the right to rescind (at [19]) and acquiescence. Acquiescence can operate rather like promissory estoppel, though in *Goldsworthy v Brickell* [1987] Ch. 378 at 409, Nourse L.J. had pointed out that promissory estoppel is normally concerned with the giving up of rights under a contract whose validity is not in dispute, and its requirements are more formalised than those of acquiescence. Thus if

before she seeks to avoid the contract the victim of undue influence or misrepresentation indicates that she will perform it, and the other party acts on that representation to its detriment, the victim will lose the right to avoid the contract, at least if the representation was made after she knew of the facts giving her the right to avoid (at [22]; Lloyd L.J. doubted whether the supposed further requirement that her representation be intended to be acted on added anything). If, as on the facts of the case, the other party cannot show that the representation (on the facts, that solicitors had been instructed to sell the mortgaged property) led it to act differently, it cannot rely on acquiescence (at [25]) and the victim may still be entitled to avoid the contract. The case was one in which a mortgage to a bank had been entered into as the result of misrepresentation by a third party of which the bank had constructive notice (see below, paras 8-111 et seq.) but the same principle applies in a two-party case like *Goldsworthy v Brickell.*

530 *Moxon v Payne* (1873) L.R. 8 Ch. App. 881, 885.

531 *Hatch v Hatch* (1804) 9 Ves. 292; *Re Pauling's Settlement Trusts* [1964] Ch. 303.

532 *Allcard v Skinner* (1887) L.R. 36 Ch. D. 145; cf. *Bullock v Lloyds Bank Ltd* [1955] Ch. 317; *De Sena v Notaro* [2020] EWHC 1031 (Ch) at [233] (a delay of almost six years triggered the doctrine of laches).

533 *Wright v Vanderplank* (1855) 2 Kay. & J. 1; *Mitchell v Homfray* (1881) 8 Q.B.D. 587.

### Equitable compensation

*Replace footnote 540 with:*

8-107 540 [1996] 3 All E.R. 61. Compare *De Sena v Notaro* [2020] EWHC 1031 (Ch) at [230], where the court held that restitutio in integrum would be impossible but left open the possibility that "some other remedy could be awarded, such as equitable compensation".

## (f) Undue Influence by a Third Party

### Undue influence over a surety

*Replace footnote 553 with:*

8-111 553 e.g. *CIBC Mortgages Plc v Pitt* [1994] 1 A.C. 200; *Syndicate Bank v Dansingani* [2019] EWHC 3439 (Ch).

### Constructive notice: Barclays Bank v O'Brien

*Replace paragraph with:*

8-114 The creditor with the relevant knowledge[563] should explain to the surety the amount of her potential liability and of the risks involved, and advise her to seek independent legal advice before entering the guarantee[564]; and this should be done in a personal interview, as written warnings are often not read and are sometimes intercepted by the debtor.[565] The interview should not be attended by the husband. As in *O'Brien*'s case the bank's clerk, in disregard of her instructions, had not warned the wife of the risks involved nor recommended her to take legal advice before getting her to sign the documents charging the matrimonial home, the bank could not enforce the charge. If the bank has notice of facts rendering misrepresentation or undue influence not just possible but probable, it must insist that the wife actually is separately advised.[566]

563 See above, para.8-113.

564 This much is required for "guarantees for personal and micro-enterprise lending" by the Lending Code, 2nd edn (2011, rev. October 2014 and September 2015), paras 67–75. (This replaces the Banking Code, which was first adopted by banks and building societies (as the Code of Banking Practice) in March 1992.) The code also provides that unlimited guarantees or security should not be taken from an individual (other than to support a customer's liabilities under a merchant agreement): para.71. On July 21, 2016, the Lending Standards Board published a new Standards of Lending Practice, which come into force on October 1, 2016. The Standards of Lending Practice replaced the Lending Code. The Standards of Lending Practice apply to personal customers and cover loans, credit cards and current account overdrafts. The new Standards represent a move away from the Lending Code, which was focused more on compliance with provisions than customer outcomes. New Standards of Lending Practice for Busi-

ness Customers were published on March 28, 2017 and became effective on July 1, 2017 (a revised version of the Standards of Lending Practice for Business Customers will come into operation on November 1, 2019 ("the 2019 Standards")). They replace the micro-enterprise provisions of the Lending Code. See further below, para.34-219. Until July 2017, the existing protections of the Lending Code continued to apply to micro-enterprises (Standards of Lending Practice, p.3). The issue of guarantees provided by individuals is dealt with in a separate document issued by the Lending Standards Board, The Standards of Lending Practice for Personal Customers: Account Maintenance and Servicing (September 2016), Pt 8.

565 [1994] 1 A.C. 180, 198.

566 [1994] 1 A.C. 180, 197.

## Relationships giving rise to notice

*Replace footnote 581 with:*

581 *Etridge*'s case [2001] UKHL 44 at [84]. See also *Barclays Bank Plc v O'Brien* [1994] 1 A.C. 180, at 198; *Avon Finance Co Ltd v Bridger* (1979) [1985] 2 All E.R. 281 (vulnerable elderly parents providing security for the debts of their adult son); *Santander UK Plc v Fletcher* [2018] EWHC 2778 (Ch), [2019] P. & C.R. 4 (son took advantage of relationship with mother when she was emotionally vulnerable to induce her by undue influence and fraud to mortgage her home to secure a loan to him). **8-118**

## Transaction not on its face to the advantage of the surety

*Replace paragraph with:*

The bank is put on inquiry whenever a wife offers to stand surety for her husband's debts.[584] The bank is not put on inquiry if the money is advanced jointly to the couple, unless the bank is aware that the loan is being made for the husband's purposes.[585] Thus in *CIBC Mortgages Plc v Pitt*,[586] which was heard with *O'Brien*'s case, the loan appeared on its face to be a normal one for the joint benefit of husband and wife and therefore the creditor was not fixed with constructive notice of the undue influence used by the husband to secure the wife's agreement.[587] But if one party becomes surety for a company whose shares are held by both, the bank is put on inquiry, even if they have equal shareholdings or if the surety is also a director or secretary of the company.[588] This applies in the: **8-119**

> "commonly found situation where a wife has an interest in a debtor company (whose debts are intended to be secured by the wife) but no involvement, understanding or control in respect of the company and that the business has been structured by the husband so as to give the appearance of joint ownership and control because it suited his purposes. The risk that the wife may be persuaded (in ignorance of the risks involved) to give security for a business which is really the husband's vehicle is just as great as in the cases where she has no such interest ... [L]enders may know full well that the wife is an owner of a shareholding and an officer of the company in name only and it would be contrary to common sense to treat them as believing that the wife was fully involved and up to speed with the company business and financial situation."[588a]

584 [2001] UKHL 44 at [44].

585 [2001] UKHL 44 at [48]; cf. *Allied Irish Bank Plc v Byrne* [1995] 2 F.L.R. 325. Similarly, the third party is unlikely to be put on constructive notice when the agreement will confer a joint tenancy on the wife: *Darjan Estate Co Plc v Hurley* [2012] EWHC 189 (Ch), [2012] 1 W.L.R. 1782 at [34]; where the claimant gets the direct benefit in the form of an interest in land, the creditor will assume that she has an interest in the business (at [36]).

586 [1994] 1 A.C. 200.

587 And see *Society of Lloyds v Khan* [1998] 3 F.C.R. 93 (Lloyds not put on notice when wife agreed to be a Name, which enabled her to undertake a risk in return for reward); *Mortgage Agency Services Number Two Ltd v Chater* [2003] EWCA Civ 490, [2004] 1 P. & C.R. 4 (joint loan to mother and son).

588 *Etridge*'s case [2001] UKHL 44 at [49]. See also *Mahon v FBN Bank (UK) Ltd* [2011] EWHC 1432 (Ch) at [51] ("where the wife's interest and/or involvement is substantive rather than titular, if she is an

active participant in managing the company's affairs and is rewarded by remuneration for her work and/or dividends or interest for her investment, the loan may well be equated with a joint loan; but ... where the financial arrangements with the bank are negotiated by the husband and the wife plays no part in those negotiations but is asked to become surety for the debts of her husband or the business, the bank should be aware of the vulnerability of the wife and of the risk that her agreement might be procured by undue influence or misrepresentation on the part of the husband, and is 'put on inquiry'"). Nor is a bank excused from making enquiry when the wife is the husband's partner in the business, especially if there is a change in the nature or scale of the lending: *O'Neill v Ulster Bank Ltd* [2015] NICA 64 at [17]. See also *Syndicate Bank v Dansingani* [2019] EWHC 3439 (Ch) at [27] (the bank was fixed with the relevant knowledge even though the wife was a director of the company and a shareholder of equal shares).

[588a] *Syndicate Bank v Dansingani* [2019] EWHC 3439 (Ch) at [27], per H.H. Judge Dight.

## Reasonable steps

*Replace footnote 589 with:*

**8-120** [589] [2001] UKHL 44 at [50], referring to the steps described by Lord Browne-Wilkinson in *O'Brien*'s case [1994] 1 A.C. 180, 196–197 and referred to above, para.8-114. In *Royal Bank of Scotland Plc v Chandra* [2010] EWHC 105 (Ch), [2010] 1 Lloyd's Rep. 677 (affirmed [2011] EWCA Civ 192) the "past transaction" rule was applied to a contract which was in train when the *Etridge* case was decided and was completed a few weeks later (see at [175]). And see *Syndicate Bank v Dansingani* [2019] EWHC 3439 (Ch) at [95]–[98] (faxed letter signed by the wife, stating that she fully understood the implications of the guarantee and that she did not require an independent solicitor, failed to discharge the claimant bank of its obligations to bring home to the wife the risk she was taking).

## Jointly-owned homes

*Replace footnote 613 with:*

**8-129** [613] See *First National Bank Plc v Achampong* [2003] EWCA Civ 487, [2004] 1 F.C.R. 18, noted by Thompson [2003] Conv. 314. And see *Santander UK Plc v Fletcher* [2018] EWHC 2778 (Ch), [2019] 2 P. & C.R. 4 (son fraudulently induced his mother into mortgage after transferring her property into their joint names; the bank acquired an equitable charge over his beneficial interest, although the mortgage was avoided for undue influence).

## Other cases

*Replace footnote 616 with:*

**8-130** [616] [1985] Q.B. 428. See also *Malik (Deceased) v Shiekh* [2018] EWHC 973 (Ch), [2018] 4 W.L.R. 86 where the complainant's sons, who were in a confidential relationships with the complainant, acted as the respondent's agents, to procure transactions that were beneficial to the sons and the respondent.

# 4. Unconscionable Bargains and Inequality of Bargaining Power

## Equitable relief against unconscionable bargains

*Replace footnote 622 with:*

**8-132** [622] See in particular the Unfair Contract Terms Act 1977, below, paras 15-062 et seq., Unfair Terms in Consumer Contracts Regulations 1999 or Consumer Rights Act 2015 Pt 2, below Ch.38, and Consumer Credit Act 1974 ss.140A–140C (inserted by ss.19–22 of the Consumer Credit Act 2006; the provisions on extortionate credit bargains, former ss.137–140, have been repealed by s.70 and Sch.4 of the 2006 Act): see Vol.II, para.39-212. The Unconscionable Conduct in Commerce Bill [HL] 2019 proposes a new criminal offence of unconscionable conduct in trade or commerce that is punishable by imprisonment or fine or both. Relevant factors detailed in s.2(1) include: "... (b) a system of conduct or pattern of behaviour ...; (c) consideration of the terms of a contract; (d) the manner in which and the extent to which a contract is carried out ...; (e) the relative strengths of the bargaining positions ...; (f) whether ... [the] customer was required to comply with conditions that were not reasonably necessary for the protection of the legitimate interests of the supplier; (g) whether any undue influence or pressure was exerted on or any unfair tactics were used against a customer ... including imposition of unrealistic timescales having regard to circumstances and the reasonable capacity of the customer; (h) whether a customer was able to understand any documents ...; (i) the amount for which, and the circumstances under which, the customer could have acquired identical or equivalent goods or services from a person other than the supplier; ... (k) the requirements of any applicable industry code; ... (m) the extent to which a supplier unreasonably failed to disclose to the customer ... any risks to the customer arising from the supplier's intended conduct (being risks that the supplier should have foreseen would not be apparent to the customer); ... (o) whether the supplier has a contractual right to vary unilaterally a term or condition of a contract between the supplier and the customer for the supply of the goods or services; (p) the extent to which the supplier and the customer acted in good faith".

## Unconscionable bargains with poor and ignorant persons

*Replace footnote 630 with:*

[630] e.g. *Aylesford v Morris* (1872-73) L.R. 8 Ch. App. 484. See Treitel in Peel (ed.), *The Law of Contract*, 15th edn (2020), para.10-047; Burrows, *Law of Restitution*, 3rd edn (2011), 302. **8-134**

## Scope of the doctrine

*Replace footnote 639 with:*

[639] In *Irvani v Irvani* [2000] 1 Lloyd's Rep. 412, 424, Buxton L.J., delivering the only full judgment in the Court of Appeal, said that this paragraph (in the 28th edition of this work) accurately sets out the limitations on the doctrine of unconscionability. The doctrine is quite distinct from that of undue influence, which: "is concerned with the prior relationship between the contracting parties, and whether that was the motivation or reason for which the bargain was entered into". (In Australia it seems that the courts may be abandoning this distinction: see *Bridgewater v Leahy* [1998] HCA 66, [1998] 158 A.L.R 66, High Ct.) In *Bank of Credit and Commerce International SA v Ali (No.1)* [2000] I.R.L.R. 398 the Court of Appeal (Buxton L.J. dubitante) held that equity can give relief against a release of a claim on the ground of unconscionability where the release was procured by the other party's deliberate concealment of facts, if that party knew or believed that the party giving the release could not discover the facts and the releasing party had not in fact known of them. In the House of Lords ([2001] UKHL 8, [2002] 1 A.C. 251), the case was decided upon other grounds, but there is a suggestion by Lord Nicholls (at [32]–[33]) that in extreme cases, unconscionability might have a part to play within a principle of "sharp practice": see above, paras 6-007 and 7-183; and see *Yukos Hydrocarbons Investments (into which Fair Oaks Trade and Invest Ltd has merged) v Georgiades* [2020] EWHC 173 (Comm) [223]–[229], where Moulder J. explored the implications of Lord Nicholls' principle of "sharp practice" and held that it did not apply to a settlement negotiated by sophisticated commercial parties of equal bargaining strength. **8-135**

## The complainant's circumstances

*Replace footnote 656 with:*

[656] *Alec Lobb Ltd v Total Oil (Great Britain) Ltd* [1983] 1 W.L.R. 87, 94–95, per Peter Millett Q.C. sitting as a Deputy High Court Judge (reversed in part [1985] 1 W.L.R. 173) (emphasis supplied). In *Barclays Bank Plc v Schwartz, The Times*, August 2, 1995 Millett L.J. observed that a person whose illiteracy or inability to speak English is taken advantage of may, in an appropriate case, be able to have the contract set aside on the grounds of unconscionability. It is arguable that relief may be given when the claimant's "bargaining weakness" took the form of not knowing of a clause in the contract he was signing, or not appreciating its possible effect: relief can then be given if the result is that the deal is worth a great deal less to the claimant than he thought, and if the other party deliberately took advantage of the claimant's ignorance or lack of understanding. This form of bargaining weakness seems to fall within Fullagar J.'s words in *Blomley v Ryan* (1956) 99 C.L.R. 362, 405, quoted in the text of the paragraph, which included "lack of assistance or explanation where assistance or explanation is necessary": see Beale, "Undue Influence and Unconscionability" in Dyson, Goudkamp and Wilmot-Smith (eds), *Defences in Contract* (2017), Ch.5. In *Nosworthy v Instinctif Partners Ltd* Unreported February 28, 2019 (EAT) at [49], relief was denied since there was no "poverty, or ignorance or lack of advice or otherwise leaving the individual vulnerable to unfair disadvantage". **8-137**

## Commonwealth and American developments

*Replace footnote 674 with:*

[674] See, e.g. *Black v Wilcox* (1976) 30 D.L.R. (3d) 192; *Paris v Machnik* (1972) 30 D.L.R. (3d) 723; *Morrison v Coast Finance* (1965) 55 D.L.R. (2d) 710; and other cases cited in Waddams, *Law of Contracts*, 6th edn (2010), para.518 and Enman (1987) 16 Anglo-Am.L.R. 191. And see *Uber Technologies Inc v Heller* 2020 SCC 16. **8-142**

CHAPTER 9

# PERSONAL INCAPACITY

## 2. MINORS

### (b) Contracts Binding on a Minor

#### (i) Liability for Necessaries

**Meaning of necessaries**

*Replace footnote 46 with:*

9-011 [46] *Nash v Inman* [1908] 2 K.B. 1, 5, per Cozens-Hardy M.R., *Maddox v Miller* (1813) 1 M. & s.738; *Harrison v Fane* (1840) 1 M. & G. 550; *Brooker v Scott* (1843) 11 M. & W. 67; *Ryder v Wombwell* (1869) L.R. 4 Ex. 32. As was noted in *Take-Two Interactive Software Inc v James* [2020] EWHC 179 (Pat) at [32], this dictum (and in particular its reference to suitability of goods to a minors "actual requirements at the time") may be limited to the context of sale of goods (as distinct, notably, from contracts for services) as the latter part of its wording echoes the Sale of Goods Act 1893 s.2 (a wording which was retained by the Sale of Goods Act 1979 s.3(3)). Cf. the unified treatment of the definition of necessary goods and services under the Mental Capacity Act 2005 s.7(2), which provides that "'Necessary' means suitable to a person's condition in life and to his actual requirements at the time when the goods or services are supplied", on which see below, para.9-097.

**Executory contracts for necessary goods**

*Replace footnote 59 with:*

9-014 [59] Peel (ed.), *Treitel on The Law of Contract*, 15th edn (2020), para.12-010.

**Goods necessary when delivered, but not when sold, and vice versa**

*Replace footnote 66 with:*

9-015 [66] It is, however, arguable that the words of s.3 of the Sale of Goods Act "at the time of the sale and delivery" appear to contemplate one time only. See also Peel (ed.), *Treitel on The Law of Contract*, 15th edn (2020), para.12-010. If a minor is liable on an executory contract it would have to be decided whether the goods must be necessary when sold, or at the time when they ought to have been delivered, or perhaps even when the minor refuses to take delivery.

**Necessary services**

*In line 1, after "as goods may be necessaries.", add new footnote 66a:*

9-016 [66a] In *Take-Two Interactive Software Inc v James* [2020] EWHC 179 (Pat) at [32] it was said that the test of necessary services may differ from that applicable to necessary goods: cf. above, para.9-014 (note).

**Examples**

*To the end of paragraph, after "second-hand sports car.[96]", add:*

9-019 Finally, the possibility that the supply of game software to a minor was for a necessary service was considered sufficient to deny the supplier summary judgment against the minor for breach of the contract of supply.[96a]

[96a] *Take-Two Interactive Software Inc v James* [2020] EWHC 179 (Pat) at [32] (summary judgment granted on other grounds).

### (ii) *Apprenticeship, Employment and Other Beneficial Contracts*

**Statutory "apprenticeship agreements"**

*Replace footnote 136 with:*

136 Apprenticeships, Skills, Children and Learning Act 2009, esp. Ch.A1 as inserted by the Deregulation Act 2015 Sch.1 para.1 and as amended by the Technical and Further Education Act 2017. **9-029**

## (c) Contracts Binding on a Minor Unless Repudiated

**Contracts for an interest of a permanent nature**

*Replace paragraph with:*

Despite this explanation there does not seem to be any general principle to the effect that *any* contract conferring an interest in a subject matter of a permanent nature is valid until repudiated.[178a] There appear to be four types of case which fall within this category though it is not clear whether these are exhaustive. These are contracts to lease or purchase land, marriage settlements, contracts to subscribe for or to purchase shares, and partnerships. On the other hand, a contract of hire or of hire-purchase entered into by a minor as hirer is either valid (if for necessaries) or unenforceable against the minor without a need for repudiation.[179] **9-037**

178a The discussion in this paragraph was cited by the court in the context of an application for summary judgment in *Take-Two Interactive Software Inc v James* [2020] EWHC 179 (Pat) at [28]–[30], where Falk J. was not prepared to accept without argument either that a contract of license of a computer game to a minor conferred an interest in that minor of a permanent nature, or that, for this purpose, it did not need to fall within one of the established categories noted in the text.

179 See *Mercantile Union Guarantee Corp v Ball* [1937] 2 K.B. 498. For criticism see Peel (ed.), *Treitel on The Law of Contract*, 15th edn (2020), para.12-027.

**Minors as successors to secured or statutory tenants**

*Replace "Kingston upon Thames BC v Prince" with:*
*Kingston upon Thames RBC v Prince* **9-042**

**Partnerships**

*Replace footnote 216 with:*

216 *Goode v Harrison* (1821) 5 B. Ald. 147. Peel (ed.), *Treitel on The Law of Contract*, 15th edn (2020), para.12-022, n.87 suggests that the same rules appear to apply to the relations between persons who become members of a limited liability partnership if one or more of them is a minor, noting that ss.4 and 5 of the Limited Liability Partnerships Act 2000 make no mention of minority. Such a minor's liability to contribute to the assets of the partnership would seem to be governed by the rules governing a minor who subscribes for shares in a company: above, para.9-045. **9-046**

## (f) Liability of Minor in Tort and Contract

**Torts independent of the contract**

*Replace paragraph with:*

On the other hand, if the tort may properly be considered as arising independently of the contract or outside its ambit altogether, the minor can be made liable. So a minor who hired a mare "merely for a ride" and was warned at the hiring that she was unfit for jumping, having lent her to a friend who killed her by that act, was held to be guilty of a bare trespass, not within the object of the hiring, and to be consequently liable.[263] A minor who embezzled money belonging to his employer **9-054** was held liable in an action for money had and received because he would have been liable in trover[264]; and one who hired a microphone and improperly parted with it to a friend was held liable in an action of detinue.[265] It is generally assumed that a minor who buys non-necessary goods cannot be sued in conversion even where he fails to pay the price and keeps the goods.[266] But it has been held that a bailee underage who refuses to return goods delivered to him by the bailor may be sued in detinue,[267] and that non-necessary goods sold to a minor can be recovered, when he refuses to pay for them, though the minor is not liable to damages for conversion.[268] It is more likely, however, that a court will exercise its discretion under s.3 of the Minors' Contracts Act 1987 to require a minor to transfer to the claimant any property acquired by the defendant under the contract, or any property representing it.[269]

[263] *Burnard v Haggis* (1863) 14 C.B.(N.S.) 45. See also *Walley v Holt* (1876) 35 L.T. 631.

[264] *Bristow v Eastman* (1794) 1 Esp. 172; *Re Seager* (1889) 60 L.T. 665. cf. *Cowern v Nield* [1912] 2 K.B. 419.

[265] *Ballett v Mingay* [1943] K.B. 281. In *Take-Two Interactive Software Inc v James* [2020] EWHC 179 (Pat) a minor had entered a contract allowing him to use a computer game (the contract being treated as for the provision of services and a license to use copyright material). It was held in the context of an application for summary judgment that while a claim against him for breach of the contract terms of the license in selling "cheat" software to other players might fail on the ground of his minority, he could nevertheless be liable for infringement of copyright and in the tort of inducing breach of contract as "the rules governing whether contracts are binding on a minor ... have no application to the tort of inducing breach of contract or in relation to the copyright infringement claim": per Falk J. at [33].

[266] Atiyah (1959) 22 M.L.R. 273, 281. The view that the minor is not liable is supported by the generally accepted opinion that property in non-necessary goods may pass to the minor: *Stocks v Wilson* [1913] 2 K.B. 235, 246 and see Peel (ed.), *Treitel on The Law of Contract*, 15th edn (2020), para.12-032. cf. Minors' Contracts Act 1987 s.3(1) which refers to "property acquired" by the minor and to the power of the court to order him to "transfer" such property.

[267] *Mills v Graham* (1804) 1 B. & P.N.R. 140 (minor refusing to return skins delivered for finishing). Detinue was abolished by s.2(1) of the Torts (Interference with Goods) Act 1977, and replaced by liability in conversion. See also *R. v McDonald* (1885) 15 Q.B.D. 323; *Robinson's Motor Vehicles Ltd v Graham* [1956] N.Z.L.R. 545.

[268] *Re Henderson* (1916) 12 Tas. L.R. 40; cf. *Hall v Wells* [1962] Tas. S.R. 122, 128–129.

[269] See below, paras 9-061 et seq.

## (g) Liability of Minor to Make Restitution

### Restoration of gains

*Replace footnote 289 with:*

**9-058** [289] Beatson, Burrows and Cartwright, *Anson's Law of Contract*, 30th edn (2016), pp.263–264; Peel (ed.), *Treitel on The Law of Contract*, 15th edn (2020), para.12-047. cf. Burrows, *The Law of Restitution*, 3rd edn (2012), pp.701–702.

### Minors' Contracts Act 1987 s.3

*Replace footnote 297 with:*

**9-061** [297] See above, para.9-057. In support of the view that the discretion in s.3 of the 1987 Act does not require fraud in the minor see Peel (ed.), *Treitel on The Law of Contract*, 15th edn (2020), para.12-042 referring to *Law Commission Report* (1984) No.134, para.4.21.

### "Property"

*Replace footnote 301 with:*

**9-062** [301] Peel (ed.), *Treitel on The Law of Contract*, 15th edn (2020), para.12-042.

### "Any property representing it"

*Replace footnote 305 with:*

305 Peel (ed.), *Treitel on The Law of Contract*, 15th edn (2020), para.12-043. **9-063**

## (h) Agency and Membership of Societies

### Membership of societies

*Replace footnote 315 with:*

315 Explicit provision to this effect was formerly found in the Trade Union Act Amendment Act 1876 s.9 but this Act was repealed by the Industrial Relations Act 1971 and the right of a minor to be a member of a trade union seems now to depend on inference. **9-067**

## (j) Procedure in Actions

### Procedure

*Replace footnote 322 with:*

322 CPR r.21.2(2). **9-069**

## 3. PERSONS LACKING MENTAL CAPACITY

## (a) The Rule in Imperial Loan Co Ltd v Stone

### *(ii) Constructive Knowledge of a Party's Mental Incapacity*

### The Supreme Court's view in Dunhill v Burgin

*Replace paragraph with:*

In *Imperial Loan Co Ltd* the Court of Appeal expressed the rule allowing a mentally incapable person to avoid a contract as subject to a condition that the other party *knew* of the incapacity[354] and this is the way in which the rule was expressed by earlier editions of the present work,[355] and by other works on English contract law.[356] However, in 2014 in *Dunhill v Burgin*, Baroness Hale of Richmond, with whom the other members of the Supreme Court agreed,[357] expressed the rule in *Imperial Loan Co Ltd v Stone*[358] in distinctly different terms from the way in which it was expressed both in the judgments of the Court of Appeal in *Imperial Loan Co Ltd* itself, and more generally, observing that it is now generally accepted that a person may avoid a contract which he or she has concluded without the requisite mental capacity where the other party to the contract either knew or *ought to have known* of this incapacity (the latter being referred to for convenience in the present discussion as constructive knowledge).[359] This observation was made in the context of holding that a settlement of a claim by a mentally incapable person is valid only with the approval of the court, this result being held to follow from the terms of the CPR.[360] Given this interpretation of the CPR, the Supreme Court held that the normal rule applicable to contracts made by a mentally incapable person which it had described does not apply to settlements of claims and, therefore, did not apply to the case before it.[361] This means that the Supreme Court's observations on the content of the normal rule applicable to contracts generally were expressly obiter. They have, nevertheless, been accepted by the High Court as an accurate statement of English law.[362] **9-078**

[354] Above, para.9-076.

[355] See the 31st edition (2012), para.8-070.

[356] Notably, Beatson, Burrows and Cartwright, *Anson's Law of Contract*, 29th edn (2010), p.247; Peel (ed.), *Treitel on The Law of Contract*, 13th edn (2011), para.12-055; McKendrick, *Contract Law*, 9th edn (2011), p.291; Goff and Jones, *The Law of Unjust Enrichment*, 8th edn (2012), para.24-09 (observing that the rule is "arguably harsh"); Burrows, *A Restatement of the English Law of Unjust Enrichment*, (2012), p.85. cf. Watts, *Bowstead & Reynolds on Agency*, 20th edn (2010), para.2-009 and n.28 (referring to the situation where a party "knew, or ought to have known, of the incapacity", without citation of explicit authority justifying "ought to have known").

[357] [2014] UKSC 18, [2014] 1 W.L.R. 933. Lord Kerr, Lord Dyson, Lord Wilson and Lord Reed agreed without further comment.

[358] [2014] UKSC 18 at [1].

[359] [2014] UKSC 18 at [1] and [25]. The Supreme Court did not specify the source of its formulation of the rule so as to include cases where the other party ought to have known of the incapacity, but it may have come from *Bowstead & Reynolds on Agency*, 20th edn (2010) by Watts, para.2-009, which takes this position and which was cited by the defendant's counsel in relation to the question of the effect of a principal's incapacity on a contract of agency, a question on which the Supreme Court did not find it necessary to form a view: [2014] UKSC 18 at [31].

[360] CPR r.21.10(1). On this decision, see below, para.9-098.

[361] [2014] UKSC 18 at [25]–[30].

[362] *Josife v Summertrot Holdings Ltd* [2014] EWHC 996 (Ch), (2014) B.P.I.R. 1250 at [19] and [20] (Norris J.) (holding that the correct test was to consider whether it would have been obvious to the other party that the person lacked capacity and holding that there was no real prospect of showing that that it would have been); *Mackay v Wesley* [2020] EWHC 1215 (Ch) at [125]–[128].

## Comments

*Replace footnote 363 with:*

9-079 [363] For comments on Baroness Hale's reformulation of the test see Peel (ed.), *Treitel on The Law of Contract*, 15th edn (2020), para.12-056 (*Imperial Loan* and other decisions require actual knowledge, describing Baroness Hale's comment as obiter dictum and noting the decision on the position of a compromise made in the absence of a "litigation friend"); Beatson, Burrows and Cartwright, *Anson's Law of Contract*, 31st edn (2020), p.262 at n.194 (stating the rule as being that the other party needs to have been aware of the incapacity, though noting Baroness Hale's view that constructive knowledge is sufficient); Burrows, *A Restatement of the English Law of Contract* (2016), s.43(3) (stating the rule as being that "a contract is voidable where an individual enters into it while lacking mental capacity ... provided the other party knew of that lack of mental capacity ..." and commenting (at p.219) on Baroness Hale's obiter dictum that "caution may here be needed so as not to water down what has traditionally been a clear and certain test to one of mere negligence (which would seem insufficient)"). cf. Varney 37 L.S. (2017) 494 esp. at 511–515 (arguing for acceptance of constructive knowledge of mental incapacity as sufficient to invalidate the contract as this better takes into account social factors, such as the protection of human dignity).

## Mental incapacity apparent

*In line 18, after "was intended by", replace "Lady" with:*

9-081 Baroness

### *(iii) The Nature of Mental Capacity and Establishing Incapacity*

## Relevance of advice?

*Replace footnote 435 with:*

9-090 [435] *Fehily v Atkinson* [2016] EWHC 3069 (Ch), [2017] Bus. L.R. 695 at [86]. Cf. the significance of legal advice in helping a person to make decisions for the purposes of the Mental Capacity Act 2005: *PBM v TGT* [2019] EWCOP 6 at [32] (pre-nuptial agreement).

### Relationship of common law and statutory tests of mental capacity

*Replace footnote 450 with:*

[450] See above, para.9-089. The statutory test does apply to the statutory liability of a person lacking capacity for necessaries: below, para.9-097. Moreover, the test has been applied to the questions whether a person has the capacity to marry and to enter a pre-nuptial agreement: *Mundell v (Name 1)* [2019] EWCOP 50, [2019] 4 W.L.R. 139 at [9]–[17], [27] and [31]; *PBM v TGT* [2019] EWCOP 6 at [28]–[30] and [32]. **9-093**

## (b) Liability for Necessaries

### Liability for necessaries: the new law

*Replace footnote 476 with:*

[476] Peel (ed.), *Treitel on The Law of Contract*, 15th edn (2020), para.12-054. **9-097**

## (d) Property and Affairs Under the Control of the Court

### Position under the Mental Capacity Act 2005

*Replace footnote 497 with:*

[497] Peel (ed.), *Treitel on The Law of Contract*, 15th edn (2020) at paras 12-057—12-058. **9-100**

CHAPTER 10

# CORPORATIONS AND UNINCORPORATED ASSOCIATIONS



## 1. CORPORATIONS

## (a) Kinds of Corporations

### Kinds of corporations

*To the end of paragraph, after "trading or non-trading.[2]", add:*

Statute creates distinctions between various types of corporation for various purposes.[2a] **10-001**

[2a] e.g. Insolvency Act 1986 s.A2 and Sch.ZA1, inserted by Corporate Insolvency and Governance Act 2020 s.1, exempts certain types of financial institutions from the moratorium introduced by the 2020 Act.

## (d) Registered Companies

### *(i) Contracts between Companies and Third Parties*

*Replace footnote 229 with:*

### Registration of charges[229]

[229] For details, see Beale, Bridge, Gullifer and Lomnicka, *The Law of Security and Title-based Finance*, 3rd edn (2018), Ch.10. **10-046**

*Replace paragraph with:*

**10-046** A contract entered into by a company before April 6, 2013 which involved a charge on its assets often required registration with the registrar of companies under Pt 25 of the Companies Act 2006.[230] Charges created since that date may require registration under the Companies Act 2006 Pt 25 Ch.A1.[231] When a company creates a charge,[232] particulars of it and a certified copy of any charge instrument[233] must be delivered for registration within 21 days of the creation of the charge, unless the charge is exempt from registration either under the Companies Act 2006 itself[233a] or other legislation.[233b] The new regime permits registration of charges online. The registrar must register the documents if they are delivered by either the company or by any person interested in the charge[233c] (typically, the secured creditor) within 21 days of the charge being created. Both the particulars and the charge document are placed on the register. If the documents are not delivered within the period, the charge will be void against a liquidator or administrator of the company and against any creditor of the company.[233d] There is provision for late registration by permission of the court. Where a company acquires property that is already subject to a charge, the charge may also be registered but there is no sanction for non-registration.[233e] There is also provision for entries showing that the debt for which the charge was given has been satisfied or that part of the property has been released.[233f] The provisions of the 2006 Act apply to companies registered in the United Kingdom.[233g]

[230] On the registration of charges created before April 6, 2013 see Beale, et al., *The Law of Security and Title-based Finance* (2018), para.10.02.

[231] Companies Act 2006 ss.859A–859Q, as inserted by the Companies Act 2006 (Amendment of Part 25) Regulations 2013 (SI 2013/600) with effect from April 6, 2013. On the registration of charges created before April 6, 2013, see Beale, et al., *The Law of Security and Title-based Finance* (2018), para.10.02.

[232] Including mortgages: Companies Act 2006 s.859A(7)(a). It should be noted that this includes many charges that may also be registrable in a specialist asset register such as for mortgages over land, ships and aircraft.

[233] Companies Act 2006 s.859A(3).

[233a] Companies Act 2006 s.859A(6)(a) (charges on cash deposits taken as security for leases of land) and (b) (charges created by members of Lloyd's).

[233b] Companies Act 2006 s.859A(6)(c): the principal exceptions are for financial collateral and for charges over aircraft objects (i.e. airframes, aircraft engines, or helicopters) that are international interests.

[233c] Companies Act 2006 s.859A(2).

[233d] Companies Act 2006 s.859H.

[233e] Companies Act 2006 s.859C.

[233f] Companies Act 2006 s.859L.

[233g] Companies Act 2006 s.859A(7). Compare Companies Act 1985 s.395.

CHAPTER 11

# THE CROWN, PUBLIC AUTHORITIES AND THE EUROPEAN UNION



## 1. INTRODUCTION

### The European Union

*Add new paragraph:*

The provisions of the Treaty were made directly applicable in English law by the European Communities Act 1972 s.2(1). Under the legislative provisions governing Brexit the 1972 Act is repealed.[4a] However, the European Union (Withdrawal) Act 2018 s.4[4b] provides that "rights" and "powers" created by European Communities Act 1972 s.2(1) shall "continue on and after IP completion day to be recognised and available in domestic law". 11-002A

[4a] See above, paras 1-014 et seq.

[4b] As amended by European Union (Withdrawal Agreement) Act 2020 s.25(3)(a).

## 2. CROWN CONTRACTS

### (b) Fettering of Discretion

#### Express terms fettering the Crown's discretion

*In line 20, page [951], after "should not be followed[53]", add:*

11-009 ; and the Court of Appeal of New South Wales, describing the Amphitrite rule as "Perhaps the most extreme and unqualified articulation of the Fettering Doctrine", has favoured a different approach, in which specific performance and injunctions are denied, but damages are generally recoverable against the executive for breach of contract.[53a]

[53a] *Searle v Commonwealth of Australia* [2019] NSWCA 127 at [101].

### (c) Agency

#### Whether servant or agent of the Crown

*Replace paragraph with:*

11-011 Since Crown contracts are subject to certain special rules, both substantive[64] and procedural,[65] it may be crucial to determine whether the contracting party has entered the contract as a servant or agent of the Crown. The starting point is the list of "authorised departments" published pursuant to the Crown Proceedings Act 1947 s.17.[66] These departments may institute "civil proceedings by the Crown",[67] and may be sued in "civil proceedings against the Crown"[68]; it can therefore be assumed that they are Crown servants or agents.[69] However, the list is not exhaustive. For contracting parties not on the list a common law test must be applied which balances a range of factors. The main factor to consider is the degree of control which the Crown is entitled to exercise over the party who is alleged to have made the contract on its behalf.[70] If that party has wide powers, which can be exercised independently of the Crown, that will strongly suggest that the contracting party is not a Crown servant.[71] Conversely, if the Crown has the right to exercise a close degree of control over the party's activities, that will suggest that the contracting party is a Crown servant or agent (a right to control the appointment of board members or directors is insufficient[71a]). It may even be possible, where a contracting party exercises several functions, to distinguish between functions in respect of which the Crown is entitled to exercise control, and those in respect of which it is not. The contracting party would be a Crown servant for contracts relating to the former functions, but not for contracts relating to the latter.[72] It should emphasised that, in ascertaining the degree of control, the statutory provisions setting out the contracting party's rights and duties are "highly important"[73]; whether, as a matter of fact, the Crown exerted its right of control is irrelevant.[74] It also seems that the statutory definition of rights and duties prevails over other statutory indications. Thus, in *Hills (Patents) Ltd v University College Hospital Board of Governors*[75] the question was whether the defendants occupied hospital premises as agents for the Minister of Health. Despite the statement in the National Health Service Act 1946 s.13 that hospital boards managed hospitals "on behalf of" the Minister, it was held that the Board's statutory duties to manage, control and maintain the hospital, and appoint its staff, meant that the board occupied as a principal, not as the Minister's agent. A second factor to consider in determining whether a contracting party is a servant or agent of the Crown is whether the contracting party is performing a function linked to an existing Crown prerogative. Thus, for instance, in *Bank voor Handel en Scheepvaart NV v Administrator of Hungarian Property*[76] both Lord Tucker and Lord Asquith were influenced in their decision that the Custodian of Hungarian Property was a Crown servant by the fact that his functions were linked to the Crown prerogative to wage war.[77] Similarly, in *Gilbert v The Corp of Trinity House*[78] it was held that the defendants' remoteness from the scope of the Crown's prerogative powers indicated that they were not Crown servants. It is submitted that the relationship between the contracting party's functions and the Crown's prerogative powers deserves only little weight. As has been powerfully pointed out, to emphasise the importance of the prerogative powers is, in effect, to confine the sphere of potential Crown servants to activities which, historically, were seen as the Crown's responsibility: it freezes the law in a condition which will inevitably fail to reflect contemporary understandings of the Crown's role.[79] Other relevant factors suggesting that a party is not a Crown servant are financial independence,[80] liability of property to be levied,[81] and incorporation.[82]

[64] See above, paras 11-005—11-009.

[65] Particularly under the Crown Proceedings Act 1947. For further discussion see below, paras 11-016—11-020.

[66] CPR Practice Direction 66, Annex 2.

[67] Crown Proceedings Act 1947 s.17(2).

[68] Crown Proceedings Act 1947 s.17(3).

[69] Griffith (1951–1952) 9 *University of Toronto Law Journal* 169, 169; Treitel [1957] P.L. 321, 328.

[70] *Bank voor Handel en Scheepvaart NV v Administrator of Hungarian Property* [1954] A.C. 584; *Intraline Resources Sdn Bhd v Owners of the Ship or Vessel "Hua Tian Long"* [2010] HKCFI 361 at [50]–[52]; Treitel [1957] P.L. 321, 327 (describing this criterion as "entitled, if not to exclusive recognition, at any rate to pre-eminence").

[71] *Metropolitan Meat Industry Board v Sheedy* [1927] A.C. 899.

[71a] *Tamlin v Hannaford* [1950] 1 K.B. 18; *Royal Brompton & Harefield Hospitals Charity v Roupell* [2018] EWHC 1873 (Ch), [2019] 1 P. & C.R. 10.

[72] *Intraline Resources Sdn Bhd v Owners of the Ship or Vessel "Hua Tian Long"* [2010] HKCFI 361 at [52].

[73] *Bank voor Handel en Scheepvaart NV v Administrator of Hungarian Property* [1954] A.C. 584, 616, per Lord Reid.

[74] [1954] A.C. 584, 617.

[75] [1956] 1 Q.B. 90.

[76] [1954] A.C. 584.

[77] *Bank voor Handel en Scheepvaart NV v Administrator of Hungarian Property* [1954] A.C. 584, 628, per Lord Tucker, 632, per Lord Asquith. See also *BBC v Johns (Inspector of Taxes)* [1965] 1 Ch. 32 (broadcasting outside province of government).

[78] (1886) 17 Q.B.D. 795. The test of whether the body in question is an "emanation" of the Crown, used in this case, has subsequently been disapproved: *Tamlin v Hannaford* [1950] 1 K.B. 18; *BBC v Johns (Inspector of Taxes)* [1965] 1 Ch. 32.

[79] Friedmann (1948) 22 A.L.J. 7; Friedmann (1950) 24 A.L.J. 275; Griffith (1951–1952) 9 *University of Toronto Law Journal* 169.

[80] *Metropolitan Meat Industry Board v Sheedy* [1927] A.C. 899.

[81] *Tamlin v Hannaford* [1950] 1 K.B. 18. Crown property cannot be levied: Crown Proceedings Act 1947 s.25(4).

[82] *Tamlin v Hannaford* [1950] 1 K.B. 18; *Hills (Patents) Ltd v University College Hospital Board of Governors* [1956] 1 Q.B. 90; cf. *Metropolitan Meat Industry Board v Sheedy* [1927] A.C. 899, 905: "[t]hat they were not incorporated does not matter." For a powerful argument that incorporation should be decisive against being a Crown servant or agent see Friedmann (1948) 22 A.L.J. 7; (1950) 24 A.L.J. 275.

**11-012** *Change title of paragraph:*

**Contracts not expressly authorised**

*Replace paragraph with:*

**11-012** Although Lord Denning put forward the view that all contracts should bind the Crown where government officers or departments took it upon themselves to assume authority,[83] that view was rejected by dicta in the House of Lords,[84] and criticised persuasively in the literature.[85] The better view, it is submitted, is that the general principles of the law of agency apply to the Crown: hence, where there is no actual express authority for entering the contract, the analysis should proceed to consider whether there is actual implied authority (such as usual authority), or, failing that, ostensible (or apparent) authority.[86]

[83] *Robertson v Minister of Pensions* [1949] 1 K.B. 227; *Falmouth Boat Construction Co Ltd v Howell* [1950] 2 K.B. 16.

[84] *Howell v Falmouth Boat Construction Co Ltd* [1951] A.C. 837.

[85] Treitel [1957] P.L. 321, 335–337.

[86] See Ch.31 of this work for the general principles of agency. For an illustrative example of the principles of usual and ostensible authority being applied to a transaction entered by a government minister, see *Law Debenture Trust Corp Plc v Ukraine* [2018] EWCA Civ 206, [2019] 2 W.L.R. 655.

*Add new paragraph:*

**11-012A** **Actual implied authority and usual authority** Implied authority, being "inferred from the conduct of the parties and the circumstances of the case",[87] will sometimes be a highly fact-sensitive question. The doctrine of usual authority, however, recognises that there are certain stereotypical situations in which an agency relationship with a conventional scope of authority is taken to have arisen without the parties expressly saying so. This "usual authority" is typically found where an agent occupies a position which involves the conduct of a particular trade or business, or where an agent's occupation involves certain ways of acting (for instance, as a solicitor, or auctioneer). In such situations, the agent has authority to do whatever is usually done in such circumstances.[88] The doctrine has been recognised as applicable to finance ministers, in respect of whom an assessment must be made of their role in their particular State, and the particular transaction entered.[88a] When applying the doctrine of usual authority to Crown contracts, it has long been recognised that any statutory restrictions on the scope of authority are crucial. As the Privy Council observed in *Att-Gen for Ceylon v Silva*, holding the Crown bound by a contract entered in excess of a statutorily defined authority would, in effect, be:

> "... to hold that public officers had dispensing powers because they then could by unauthorized acts nullify or extend the provisions of the [statute]."[88b]

The Court of Appeal's analysis in *Law Debenture Trust Corp Plc v Ukraine*[88c] provides a valuable explanation of why, as a matter of orthodox agency principles, such statutory (and other) restrictions on authority are decisive, and also illustrates how questions of usual authority should be analysed in Crown contracts. Ukraine, acting through its Minister of Finance (who was acting on the instructions of the Cabinet of Ministers of Ukraine) had issued Eurobond notes, which had been subscribed by the Russian Ministry of Finance. The date for payment passed, but Ukraine denied liability arguing, inter alia, that the Minister had lacked authority to issue the notes. The Court of Appeal held that "usual authority" was best seen as a species of implied actual authority,[88d] and turned on what could be inferred from the conduct of the principal and agent.[88e] It followed that, where the scope of authority had been expressly limited, as it had been on the facts of the case by legislation, it was impossible to invoke some broader "usual" authority for the transaction. In such circumstances, the only viable argument for the transaction being authorised was that it had been made under ostensible authority.

[87] *Hely-Hutchinson v Brayhead Ltd* [1968] 1 Q.B. 549, 583.

[88] See further below, Vol.II, para.31-047.

[88a] *Law Debenture Trust Corp Plc v Ukraine* [2017] EWHC 655 (Comm), [2017] Q.B. 1249 at [160]. This point was not challenged on appeal: [2018] EWCA Civ 206 at [82].

[88b] *Att-Gen for Ceylon v Silva* [1953] A.C. 461, 481.

[88c] [2018] EWCA Civ 2026, [2019] 2 W.L.R. 655. An appeal to the Supreme Court was heard in December 2019.

[88d] [2018] EWCA Civ 2026 at [79].

[88e] [2018] EWCA Civ 2026 at [80], quoting with approval from *Hely-Hutchinson v Brayhead Ltd* [1968] 1 Q.B. 549.

**Ostensible authority**

*Replace paragraph with:*

In order to establish ostensible authority it must be shown that the principal, or someone authorised to act for him, represented to a third party that the agent has authority, and the third party acted on that representation; a representation by the agent as to the extent of his own authority is insufficient.[89] In *Att-Gen for Ceylon v Silva*[90] the Privy Council indicated that the requirement of a representation by either the principal or someone authorised to act for him limited the potential application of ostensible authority to the Crown: **11-013**

> "No public officer, unless he possesses some special power, can hold out on behalf of the Crown that he or some other public officer has the right to enter into a contract in respect of the Crown when in fact no such right exists."[91]

Such a special power will be rare, although not impossible to find.[92] Ostensible authority will not be found where the third party knows, or could be expected to know, that such authority conflicts with a constitutional restriction.[93] Although ostensible authority is a form of estoppel,[94] it is treated as an exception to the general principle that estoppel cannot be relied upon to rehabilitate a transaction entered in excess of powers.[95]

[89] See below, Vol.II, para.31-056.

[90] [1953] A.C. 461.

[91] *Att-Gen for Ceylon v Silva* [1953] A.C. 461, 479. See also *Bowstead and Reynolds on Agency*, 21st edn (2017), para.8-042; para.8-044 of the 17th edn (containing the text now in para.8-042) was quoted with approval in *Marubeni Hong Kong and South China Ltd v Government of Mongolia* [2004] EWHC 472 (Comm), [2004] 2 Lloyd's Rep. 198 at [124].

[92] Treitel [1957] P.L. 321, 338 n.4 suggests that it might exist where the holding out was done by the "directing mind" of the relevant government department. cf. Turpin, *Government Contracts* (1972), p.35, where it is suggested that the "special power" would exist wherever an officer had actual authority to do the act that he was holding out the agent as having authority to do. In *Marubeni Hong Kong and South China Ltd v Government of Mongolia* [2004] EWHC 472 (Comm), [2004] 2 Lloyd's Rep. 198 it was held that the Mongolian Ministry of Justice had such a power in respect of the Minister of Finance's authority to sign a guarantee. (This aspect of the decision was not challenged on appeal: [2005] EWCA Civ 395, [2005] 1 W.L.R. 2497 at [6].) See also *Law Debenture Trust Corp Plc v Ukraine* [2018] EWCA

Civ 2026, [2019] 2 W.L.R. 655 (ostensible authority of Minister of Finance of Ukraine to issue Eurobond debt notes).

[93] *Donegal International Ltd v Zambia* [2007] EWHC 197 (Comm), [2007] 1 Lloyd's Rep. 397 at [451]; *Law Debenture Trust Corp Plc v Ukraine* [2018] EWCA Civ 2026, [2019] 2 W.L.R. 655 at [111].

[94] *Marubeni Hong Kong and South China Ltd v Government of Mongolia* [2004] EWHC 472 (Comm), [2004] 2 Lloyd's Rep. 198 at [124].

[95] For the general principle see below, para.11-047.

### (d) Crown Proceedings Act 1947

**Interim remedies**

*Replace footnote 124 with:*

11-018 [124] CPR r.25.1; see *Intertrade Wholesale Ltd v Revenue and Customs Commissioners* [2018] EWHC 3476 (QB) at [64].

## 3. PUBLIC AUTHORITIES

### (a) The Scope of Statutory Powers

#### *(i) Express Powers*

**Construction of statutory language**

*Replace paragraph with:*

11-022 In ascertaining whether the contract or promise in question is within the scope of the authority's statutory powers, the statute must be construed. There is no typical form of words for the conferment of powers to contract, and the range of bodies on whom such powers are conferred has led to an equally diverse array of statutory language. No special rules of construction apply[145]—the aim is to identify a "reasonable" interpretation of the words.[146] Where the power is said to be contained in a rate-levying provision, that provision "must not be strained to cover purposes which are not fairly within it".[146a]

[145] *Att-Gen v London CC* [1901] 1 Ch. 781, 788; *Att-Gen v Manchester Corp* [1906] 1 Ch. 643, 653.

[146] *Att-Gen v London CC* [1901] 1 Ch. 781, 788.

[146a] *Mexico Infrastructure Finance LLC v Corporation of Hamilton* [2019] UKPC 2 at [51].

*Add new paragraph (formerly part of para.11-022):*

11-022A **Examples of express powers to contract** The power to contract may be narrowly set out, as it is in the Police Act 1996 s.25(1), which limits the power to charge for policing to "special police services" provided "at the request of any person". As the Court of Appeal has observed, this subsection envisages a contract between the parties, in the sense that a request must have been accepted by the chief constable.[147] However, the power may also be expressed more broadly, and need not refer specifically to contracts. For instance, s.2 of the Local Government Act 2000 (which now applies only in Wales)[148] confers a power on local authorities to do "anything which they consider is likely to achieve" the "promotion or improvement" of the "economic", "social", or "environmental well-being of their area". In *Brent London BC v Risk Management Partners Ltd*[149] the Court of Appeal held that, although the section should be construed broadly, it did not authorise entering transactions solely for the purpose of improving the authority's financial position;

some "reasonably well defined outcome which [the authority] considers will promote or improve the well-being of its area" was required.[150] The Localism Act 2011 s.1(1) supersedes the broad power set out in the Local Government Act 2000, by providing that "A local authority has power to do anything that individuals generally may do".[151] The breadth of this statutory language is such that, where a contract falls under the Act, no recourse to implied powers of contracting will be required to justify it. However, the Act does not eliminate all restrictions on local authorities' powers, since pre-existing restrictions are preserved, the power to charge for services is limited, and things may only be done for a commercial purpose if they could also be legitimately done for a non-commercial purpose under the general power.[152] The effect of the Act is, therefore, to alter the focus of legal analysis from whether an authority's activity is permitted to whether there are any restrictions on it.[153]

147 *West Yorkshire Police Authority v Reading Festival Ltd* [2006] EWCA Civ 524, [2006] 1 W.L.R. 2005 at [21] and [50]. See further *Glasbrook Brothers Ltd v Glamorgan County Council* [1925] A.C. 270; *Harris v Sheffield United Football Club Ltd* [1988] 1 Q.B. 77; *Leeds United Football Club Ltd v Chief Constable of West Yorkshire Police* [2013] EWCA Civ 115, [2014] Q.B. 168; *Ipswich Town Football Club Co Ltd v Chief Constable of Suffolk* [2017] EWCA Civ 1484, [2017] 4 W.L.R. 195 and discussion at para.4-064 above. The statutory provision may implicitly exclude a claim for unjust enrichment where no request for police services is shown: *Chief Constable of the Greater Manchester Police v Wigan Athletic AFC Ltd* [2008] EWCA Civ 1449, [2009] 1 W.L.R. 1580 at [51].

148 Localism Act 2011 Sch.1 para.3.

149 [2009] EWCA Civ 490, [2010] P.T.S.R. 349 (the appeal to the Supreme Court in *Brent LBC v Risk Management Partners Ltd* [2011] UKSC 7, [2011] 2 A.C. 34 was confined to the claim for damages for breach of the Public Contracts Regulations 2006). Under the Local Democracy, Economic Development and Construction Act 2009 s.34, which is (still) not yet in force, a local authority is empowered to enter mutual insurance arrangements of the kind that gave rise to the litigation in the *Brent* case; the wide powers conferred by Localism Act 2011 s.1 (discussed below) may have made this specific provision redundant.

150 [2009] EWCA Civ 490 at [180].

151 The statutory section came into force on February 18, 2012 (Localism Act 2011 (Commencement No.3) Order 2012 (SI 2012/411) art.2).

152 Localism Act 2011 ss.2, 3 and 4 respectively. On the interpretation of s.4 see *R. (Durham Co Ltd) v Revenue and Customs Commissioners* [2016] UKUT 417 (TCC), [2017] S.T.C. 264 and *Peters v Haringey LBC* [2018] EWHC 192 (Admin).

153 See further, Layard [2012] Env. Law Rev. 134; Bowes and Stanton [2014] P.L. 392.

## (c) Proper Exercise of Powers

### General principle

*Replace paragraph with:*

There is extensive authority in support of the requirement that an authority's power to contract must have been exercised properly, in accordance with its public law obligations.[227] The same is true of any power to vary the contractual terms.[228] Thus, for instance, a decision to enter a contract must comply with any relevant procedural requirements,[229] and it must also be consistent with the general principles of public law governing the exercise of powers. These principles include the requirement to have regard only to relevant matters, the requirement not to exercise powers for a collateral purpose, and the requirement not to exercise powers irrationally. However, it must be noted that there is now also support (in dicta) for a narrower approach to this issue; under this narrower approach, a public authority's failure to exercise the power to enter a contract in accordance with its public law duties does not automatically result in the contract being ultra vires, but may require **11-034** an assessment of the nature of the breach of duty and of the state of knowledge of the other contracting party. This section first considers the wider approach (i.e. that a failure to exercise the power correctly makes the resulting contract void) before turning to the alternative approach.

227 *Hazell v Hammersmith and Fulham LBC* [1990] 2 Q.B. 697; *Crédit Suisse v Allerdale BC* [1995] 1 Lloyd's Rep. 315, [1997] Q.B. 306; *London & South Eastern Railway Ltd v British Transport Police Authority* [2009] EWHC 460 (Admin) at [47]–[48]. cf. the dicta in *Charles Terence Estates Ltd v Cornwall Council* [2012] EWCA Civ 1439, [2013] 1 W.L.R. 466, followed in *Pro-Vision Systems (UK) Ltd v United Lincolnshire Hospital NHS Trust* Unreported February 21, 2014 (Judge Waksman Q.C.) at [176].

228 *Wandsworth LBC v Winder* [1985] 1 A.C. 461.

229 e.g. *R. (Transport & General Workers Union) v Walsall MBC* [2001] EWHC 452 (Admin).

## Collateral purpose

*To the end of paragraph, after "was ultra vires.", add:*

11-036 By contrast, where a public body acknowledges that its powers to enter contracts do not extend to one preferred purpose, it may legitimately use such powers as it has to achieve the next best thing. For example, if a school wishing to provide transport for its students lacked the power to incur the capital expenditure of purchasing minibuses, it would not be ultra vires for the school to enter agreements to hire minibuses for the students as and when needed.[239a]

239a *School Facility Management Ltd v Governing Body of Christ the King College* [2020] EWHC 1118 (Comm) at [297].

## An alternative approach to the proper exercise of powers requirement?

*Replace paragraph with:*

11-038 Dicta in the Court of Appeal's decision in *Charles Terence Estates Ltd v Cornwall Council*[250] and in *School Facility Management Ltd v Governing Body of Christ the King College*[250a] may indicate that the courts are considering introducing a more flexible approach to situations where a public body has entered agreements pursuant to an improper exercise of its powers. In *Charles Terence Estates Ltd v Cornwall Council* Maurice Kay L.J. indicated that it depended on the circumstances whether such transactions were enforceable against the public body.[251] Etherton L.J. went further, stating that the validity of such transactions should be governed by the principle set out by Browne-Wilkinson J. in *Rolled Steel Products (Holdings) Ltd v British Steel Corp*[252] for determining the validity of transactions entered by companies.[253] Under that principle, the validity of transactions entered by a company in excess of its powers turns on whether the party with whom the transaction was entered "had notice that the transaction was in excess or abuse of the powers of the company". Both judges found support for their views in the dicta of Hobhouse L.J. in *Credit Suisse v Allerdale BC*[254]; and they both disapproved the dicta of Neill L.J. in the same case, which were to the effect that contracts entered into pursuant to an improper exercise of power were void.

250 [2012] EWCA Civ 1439, [2013] 1 W.L.R. 466. Followed in *Pro-Vision Systems (UK) Ltd v United Lincolnshire Hospital NHS Trust* Unreported February 21, 2014, Judge Waksman Q.C. at [176].

250a [2020] EWHC 1118 (Comm).

251 [2012] EWCA Civ 1439 at [37].

252 [1986] Ch. 246, 302–303 and 304 (discussed in detail at paras 10-020—10-026).

253 [2012] EWCA Civ 1439 at [48]–[49].

254 [1997] Q.B. 306

*Add new paragraphs:*

The Court of Appeal was not, unfortunately, referred to leading authorities (discussed in the preceding paragraphs), where the issue was directly in point, such as *Hinckley and Bosworth BC v Shaw*[255] and *London & South Eastern Railway Ltd v British Transport Police Authority*.[256] This criticism could not, however, be made of the decision of Foxton J. in *School Facility Management Ltd v Governing Body of Christ the King College*,[257] which is undoubtedly the most sophisticated and thorough judicial analysis of the issue yet undertaken. Foxton J. concluded that the law should distinguish between contracts of a kind which the body lacked statutory capacity to enter (and which were therefore void), and contracts of a kind which the body did have capacity to enter, but which had been entered into in a way that breached the authority's public law obligations. In this latter category, the contract would be void only if the authority's powers had been abused, and the other contracting party had notice of this abuse.[258] **11-038A**

[255] [2000] B.L.G.R. 9.

[256] [2009] EWHC 460 (Admin).

[257] [2020] EWHC 1118 (Comm).

[258] [2020] EWHC 1118 (Comm) at [159]–[162].

These dicta represent a very significant potential new direction of development. As Foxton J's judgment acknowledges, the new approach is not without its difficulties. It necessitates a fragmented approach to ultra vires, with different kinds of ultra vires acts being given diametrically opposed significance in private law. It also appears to apply only to situations in which a public authority is seeking to assert that its own acts have been ultra vires; while this might at first glance appear to be a justifiable restriction, it may well be a matter of pure chance which contracting party happens to be disadvantaged by the contractual performance and finds itself, therefore, taking the ultra vires point.[259] Earlier judges (including Neill L.J. and Hobhouse L.J. in the *Crédit Suisse* case[260]) had also been concerned by the opportunity for public authorities to use the ultra vires doctrine to disavow their own actions, and these concerns prompted legislation in the form of the Local Government (Contracts) Act 1997, which provided a certification mechanism for contracting parties to eliminate the problems of ultra vires.[260a] The Act was alert to the possibility that the manner in which a contract was entered by a public authority might make the transaction ultra vires, since in s.2(1) it describes the effect of certification as being that the contract takes effect "as if the local authority had power to enter into it (and had exercised that power properly in entering into it)". Although the contract in the *School Facility Management* case[260b] was not made with a local authority, so the 1997 Act procedure could not have been used, it is striking that a statutory mechanism existed which would have authorised precisely the kind of contract that the parties entered, but they chose not to use it.[260c] In any case, general assertions about the unfair application of ultra vires to contracting parties are far less persuasive now than they would have been prior to 1997. It should also be noted that, while the potential new approach takes inspiration from the approach to a company's powers set out in the *Rolled Steel* case, the ultra vires principle in its application to companies has now been abrogated by legislation[260d]; applying the *Rolled Steel* approach to public authorities would not, therefore, unify the law's treatment of companies and public authorities. **11-038B**

259 e.g. the "swaps" cases, such as *Westdeutsche Landesbank Girozentrale v Islington LBC* [1996] A.C. 669, where movements in currency markets dictated which party would wish to have the agreement declared void.

260 *Credit Suisse v Allerdale BC* [1997] Q.B. 306, see above, para.11-036.

260a See further paras 11-042 et seq.

260b *School Facility Management Ltd v Governing Body of Christ the King College* [2020] EWHC 1118 (Comm).

260c [2020] EWHC 1118 (Comm) at [28].

260d See para.10-027 above.

## 5. ESTOPPEL

### Estoppel and ultra vires

*Replace paragraph with:*

**11-048** Estoppel cannot prevent an act from being challenged on the ground of ultra vires.[336] For example, in *Rhyl Urban DC v Rhyl Amusements Ltd*[337] the Council had granted a succession of leases over Council land to the defendants in circumstances which would otherwise have estopped the Council from denying that it had the capacity to do so. However, it was said that "a plea of estoppel cannot prevail as an answer to a claim that something done by a statutory body is ultra vires",[338] and the supposed leases were held invalid. The underlying rationale for this rule is that "a party cannot by representation, any more than by other means, raise against himself an estoppel so as to create a state of things which he is legally disabled from creating".[338a] A similar rule, based on the same rationale, prevents the enforcement of a promise by a public authority that a contract it is entering is within its powers.[338b] By contrast, a promise by a third party that a public authority is acting within its powers when entering a contract is in principle enforceable. Where the third party is also a public authority, the promise will, it seems, only be enforceable if it would have been within the third party's powers to enter that contract.[338c]

336 *Fairtitle v Gilbert* (1787) 2 T.R. 169; *Minister of Agriculture and Fisheries v Hulkin* Unreported 1948, summarised in *Minister of Agriculture and Fisheries v Matthews* [1950] 1 K.B. 148, 153–154; *Minister of Agriculture and Fisheries v Matthews* [1950] 1 K.B. 148; *Rhyl Urban DC v Rhyl Amusements Ltd* [1959] 1 W.L.R. 465.

337 [1959] 1 W.L.R. 465.

338 *Rhyl Urban DC v Rhyl Amusements Ltd* [1959] 1 W.L.R. 465 at 474.

338a *Halsbury's Laws of England*, 4th edn Vol.16 para.1596, approved in *Janred Properties Ltd v Ente Nazionale Italiano Per Il Turismo (The Italian State Tourist Office)* Unreported July 14, 1983 CA; *School Facility Management Ltd v Governing Body of Christ the King College* [2020] EWHC 1118 (Comm) at [355]–[357].

338b *Eastbourne BC v Foster* [2002] I.C.R. 234 at [23]; *School Facility Management Ltd v Governing Body of Christ the King College* [2020] EWHC 1118 (Comm) at [358].

338c *School Facility Management Ltd v Governing Body of Christ the King College* [2020] EWHC 1118 (Comm) at [365].

## 6. PUBLIC PROCUREMENT

### (a) European Union Legislation

*Replace paragraph with:*

**11-052** Contracts made by the Crown, by public bodies and by the European Union are subject to fundamental principles of EU law enshrined in the Treaty of the European Union, such as freedom of movement of goods, freedom of establishment and freedom to provide services. Treaty provisions will remain part of domestic law after "IP completion day".[356a] The EU has also made special legislative provision to regulate the formation of such contracts in a series of Directives,[357] which have been implemented in the United Kingdom by statutory instruments.[358] The Directives make very detailed provision for every stage of the contracting process, and require public authorities to base the award of a contract on the "most economically advantageous tender".[359] As "EU-derived domestic legislation", these provisions will continue to have effect in domestic law on and after "IP completion day" (December 31, 2020).[359a]

[356a] European Union (Withdrawal) Act 2018 s.4, as amended. See further above, para.1-017.

[357] The current Directives are Directive 2014/24/EU of the European Parliament and of the Council of 26 February 2014 on public procurement and repealing Directive 2004/18/EC ([2014] O.J. L 94/65), Directive 2014/25/EU on procurement by entities operating in the water, energy, transport and postal services sectors and repealing Directive 2004/17/EC ([2014] O.J. L 94/243) and Directive 2007/66 amending Council Directives 89/665 and 92/13 with regard to improving the effectiveness of review procedures concerning the award of public contracts [2007] O.J. L335/31.

[358] Public Contracts Regulations 2015 (SI 2015/102) and Utilities Contracts Regulations 2016 (SI 2016/274).

[359] 2014/24/EU art.67; 2014/25/EU art.82.

[359a] See generally above paras 1-014 et seq.; for the treatment of "EU-derived domestic legislation" see in particular para.1-016B.

CHAPTER 12

# POLITICAL IMMUNITY AND INCAPACITY



## 1. FOREIGN STATES, SOVEREIGNS, AMBASSADORS AND INTERNATIONAL ORGANISATIONS

### Sovereign immunity and human rights

*Replace footnote 15 with:*

[15] [2006] UKHL 26, [2007] 1 A.C. 270. The European Court of Human Rights came to the same conclusion: *Jones v United Kingdom* [2014] 59 E.H.R.R. 1, applying the decision of the International Court of Justice in *Jurisdictional Immunities of the State (Germany v Italy: Greece intervening)*, February 3, 2012. cf. *Mahamdia v Algeria* (C-154/11) EU:C:2012:491, [2013] I.C.R. 1. See Seymour [2006] C.L.J. 479; Ranganathan [2015] C.L.J. 16. See *Belhaj v Straw* [2017] UKSC 3, [2017] 2 W.L.R. 456, [11(v)], [108]–[109] (Lord Mance), [258]–[268] (Lord Sumption); *Lysongo v Foreign and Commonwealth Office* [2018] EWHC 2955 (QB) at [34]–[35]. **12-003**

### State Immunity Act 1978

*Replace footnote 21 with:*

[21] The principle of immunity also precludes registration in England of a foreign judgment against a foreign state under the Administration of Justice Act 1920: see *AIC Ltd v Federal Government of Nigeria* [2003] EWHC 1357 (QB). As to Civil Jurisdiction and Judgments Act 1982 s.31, see *NML Capital Ltd v Argentina* [2011] UKSC 31, [2011] 2 A.C. 495; *Estate of Michael Heiser v Islamic Republic of Iran* [2019] EWHC 2074 (QB). See also *LR Avionics Technologies Ltd v Federal Republic of Nigeria* [2016] EWHC 1761 (Comm), [2016] 4 W.L.R. 120. **12-004**

*Replace paragraph with:*

**12-005** To the general principle of immunity there are several important and wide-ranging exceptions. The most important is that there is no immunity for a state's commercial transactions,[27] thus confirming the judicial developments confining the common law rule to acta iure imperii, though it may still be difficult to determine in any particular case the dividing line between commercial and governmental activity.[28] The funds in the bank account of a state's London embassy have been considered not to be used for commercial purposes.[29] If a state grants a lease of its premises to a privately owned company to which the state outsources consular activities such as the handling of passport and visa applications, the property is not being used for commercial purposes within the meaning of s.13(4) of the 1978 Act.[30] There is no immunity for contractual obligations (whether arising out of a commercial transaction or not) to be performed in the United Kingdom[31]; or in the case of contracts of employment made or to be performed in the United Kingdom[32]; or as to claims for death, personal injury or damage to property caused by misconduct in the United Kingdom[33]; or in proceedings relating to immovables in the United Kingdom[34] or to an interest in other property by way of succession, gift or bona vacantia[35]; or in the case of proceedings relating to various forms of intellectual property[36]; or the administration of estates or trusts, or insolvency, even though a state may claim an interest in the property[37]; or where a state is a member of a corporate or unincorporated body constituted under United Kingdom law or controlled from the United Kingdom[38]; or in relation to various tax claims[39]; or as to claims arising from use of ships for commercial purposes[40] (again confirming an important common law development); or, finally, where the state has submitted to the jurisdiction of the English courts.[41] Such immunity may not be relied on by persons in proceedings provided for under the International Criminal Court Act 2001 where that immunity arises by reason of a connection with a state party to the Statute of the International Criminal Court, done at Rome on July 17, 1998.[42]

[27] s.3(1)(a). In *NML Capital Ltd v Argentina* [2011] UKSC 31, [2011] 2 A.C. 495 it was held (by a majority) that proceedings to enforce a foreign judgment entered in respect of a commercial transaction are not, of themselves, proceedings relating to a commercial transaction: the same principle applies in respect of proceedings to register a foreign judgment against a foreign state under Administration of Justice Act 1920, *AIC Capital Partners v Federal Government of Nigeria* [2003] EWHC 1357 (QB), and to applications to enforce an arbitration award under Arbitration Act 1996 s.101, *Svenska Petroleum Exploration AB v Republic of Lithuania (No.2)* [2006] EWCA Civ 1529, [2006] Q.B. 886, applied in *Ministry of Trade of the Republic of Iraq v Tsavliris (International) Ltd* [2008] EWHC 612 (Comm), [2008] 2 Lloyd's Rep. 90. See further *ETI Euro Telecom International NV v Republic of Bolivia* [2008] EWCA Civ 880, [2008] 1 W.L.R. 665; *Continental Transfert Technique Ltd v Federal Government of Nigeria* [2009] EWHC 2898 (Comm); *Servaas Inc v Rafidain Bank* [2011] EWCA Civ 1256, [2012] 1 All E.R. (Comm) 527, affirmed [2012] UKSC 40, [2013] 1 A.C. 595; *La Generale des Carrieres et des Mines v FG Hemisphere Associates LLC* [2012] UKPC 27, [2013] 1 All E.R. 753; *Taurus Petroleum Ltd v State Oil Marketing Co of the Ministry of Oil, Iraq* [2015] EWCA Civ 835 at [39]–[48]; *Gold Reserve Inc v Bolivarian Republic of Venezuela* [2016] EWHC 153 (Comm), [2016] 1 W.L.R. 2829; *LR Avionics Technologies Ltd v Federal Republic of Nigeria* [2016] EWHC 1761 (Comm), [2016] 4 W.L.R. 120; cf. *Kensington International Ltd v Congo* [2005] EWHC 2684 (Comm), [2006] 2 B.C.L.C. 296.

[28] *I Congreso del Partido* [1983] 1 A.C. 244, where the House of Lords divided $3_2$ on this issue. Section 3(3) of the 1978 Act defines a "commercial transaction" as any contract and any guarantee or indemnity in respect of such a transaction or other financial obligation, or any other transaction or activity into which a state enters (apart from a contract of employment between a state and an individual) otherwise than in the exercise of sovereign authority. On this provision, see *Alcom Ltd v Republic of Colombia* [1984] A.C. 580; *Amalgamated Metal Trading Ltd v Department of Trade and Industry*, *The Times*, March 21, 1989; *Kuwait Airways Corp v Iraqi Airways Co* [1995] 1 W.L.R. 1147 (for further proceedings, see *Kuwait Airways Corp v Iraqi Airways Co (No.2)* [2001] 1 W.L.R. 430; *Kuwait Airways Corp v Iraqi Airways Co* [2003] EWHC 31 (Comm), [2003] 1 Lloyd's Rep. 448); *Central Bank of Yemen v Cardinal Finance Investment Corp* [2001] Lloyd's Rep. Bank. 1; *Svenska Petroleum Exploration AB v Government of the Republic of Lithuania (No.2)* [2006] EWCA Civ 1529, [2008] Q.B. 886; *Koo Golden East Mongolia v Bank of Nova Scotia* [2007] EWCA Civ 1529, [2008] Q.B. 717; *Orascom Telecom Holding SAE v Republic of Chad* [2008] EWHC 1841 (Comm), [2008] 2 Lloyd's Rep. 396; *Servaas Inc v Rafidain Bank* [2011] EWCA Civ 1256, [2012] 1 All E.R. (Comm) 527, affirmed [2012] UKSC 40, [2013] 1 A.C. 595; *NML Capital v Argentina* [2011] UKSC 31, [2011] 2 A.C. 495; *La Generale des Carrieres et des Mines v FG Hemisphere Associates LLC* [2012] UKPC 27, [2013] 1 All E.R. 753; see also *Littrell v Government of the United States (No.2)* [1995] 1 W.L.R. 82; *Holland v Lampen Wolfe* [2001] 1 W.L.R. 1573; *PT Garuda Indonesia Ltd v Australian Competition and Consumer Commission* [2011] FCAFC 52, (2011) 277 A.L.R. 67, affirmed [2012] HCA 33, (2012) 290 A.L.R. 681; *European Union v Syrian Arab Republic* [2018] EWHC 1712 (Comm), [30]. See Staker (1995) 66 B.Y.I.L. 496; Fox (1996) 112 L.Q.R. 186.

[29] *Alcom Ltd v Republic of Columbia* [1984] A.C. 580. See also *AIC Ltd v Federal Government of Nigeria* [2003] EWHC 1357 (QB); *Servaas Inc v Rafidain Bank*, above.

[30] *LR Avionics Technologies Ltd v Federal Republic of Nigeria* [2016] EWHC 1761 (Comm), [2016] 4 W.L.R. 120.

31 1978 Act s.3(1)(b), though note the limitation, s.3(2). See *J.H. Rayner (Mincing Lane) Ltd v Department of Trade and Industry* [1989] Ch. 72, 194–195, 222, 252, affirmed without reference to the point, [1990] 2 A.C. 418.

32 s.4. This section does not apply to proceedings concerning the employment of the members of a mission within the meaning of the Convention scheduled to the Diplomatic Privileges Act 1964 or of the members of a consular post within the meaning of the Convention scheduled to the State Immunity Act 1978 s.16(1)(a). See *Sengupta v Republic of India* [1983] I.C.R. 221; *United Arab Emirates v Abdelghafar* [1995] I.C.R. 65; *Arab Republic of Egypt v Gamal-Eldin* [1996] I.C.R. 13; *Ahmed v Government of the Kingdom of Saudi Arabia* [1996] I.C.R. 25; *Malaysian Industrial Development Authority v Jeyasingham* [1998] I.C.R. 307; *Government of the Kingdom of Saudi Arabia v Nasser* Unreported November 14, 2000, CA; Garnett (1997) 46 I.C.L.Q. 81; Garnett (2005) 54 I.C.L.Q. 705. And see *Fogarty v United Kingdom* (2002) 34 E.H.R.R. 302; *Al-Kadhimi v Government of Saudi Arabia* [2003] EWCA Civ 1689; *Aziz v Republic of Yemen* [2005] EWCA Civ 754, [2005] I.C.R. 1391; *Mauritius Tourism Promotion Authority v Wong Min* (UKEAT/0186/08/LA, November 24, 2008) (EAT); *United States of America v Nolan* [2009] I.R.L.R. 923; *Wokhuri v Kassam* [2012] EWHC 105 (Ch); *Abusabib v Taddese* [2013] I.C.R. 603; and see *Benkharbouche v Secretary of State for Foreign and Commonwealth Affairs* [2015] EWCA Civ 33, [2015] H.R.L.R. 3, [2017] UKSC 62, [2017] 3 W.L.R. 957; *Reyes v Al-Malki* [2017] UKSC 61, [2017] 3 W.L.R. 923; *Webster v United States of America* [2019] 10 WLUK 500 at [91]–[98]. See Sanger [2014] C.L.J. 1.

33 s.5; see *Military Affairs Office of The Embassy of the State of Kuwait v Caramba-Coker* (EAT/1054/02/RN, April 10, 2003); *Federal Republic of Nigeria v Ogbonna* [2012] 1 W.L.R. 139 (EAT); *Estate of Michael Heiser v Islamic Republic of Iran* [2019] EWHC 2074 (QB). cf. *Heiser v Iran* [2012] EWHC 2938 (QB).

34 As with proceedings for breach of covenants in a lease: *Intpro Properties (UK) Ltd v Sauvel* [1983] Q.B. 1019. cf. *Re B (A Child) (Care Proceedings: Diplomatic Immunity)* [2002] EWHC 1751 (Fam), [2003] Fam. 16.

35 1978 Act s.6. See *Palmer v Ingram* [2009] EWCA Civ 947.

36 s.7.

37 s.6(3). See *Re Rafidain Bank* [1992] B.C.L.C. 301.

38 s.8. See *Maclaine, Watson & Co Ltd v International Tin Council* [1989] Ch. 253, 282–283, affirmed on other grounds, [1990] 2 A.C. 418.

39 s.11. See Business Rate Supplements Act 2009 s.21(5).

40 s.10. See *Ministry of Trade of the Republic of Iraq v Tsavliris Salvage (International) Ltd* [2008] EWHC 612 (Comm), [2008] 2 Lloyd's Rep. 90.

41 s.2; see CPR r.6.44; see *A Co Ltd v Republic of X* [1990] 2 Lloyd's Rep. 520; *Kuwait Airways Corp v Iraqi Airways Co* [1995] 1 W.L.R. 1147 (for further proceedings, see *Kuwait Airways Corp v Iraqi Airways Co (No.2)* [2001] 1 W.L.R. 429; *Kuwait Airways Corp v Iraqi Airways Co* [2003] EWHC 31, (Comm), [2003] 1 Lloyd's Rep. 448); *Mills v Embassy of the United States of America* Unreported May 9, 2000, CA; *Sabah Shipyard (Pakistan) Ltd v The Islamic Republic of Pakistan* [2002] EWCA Civ 1643, [2003] 2 Lloyd's Rep. 571; *Servaas Inc v Rafidain Bank* [2011] EWCA Civ 1256, [2012] 1 All E.R. (Comm) 527, affirmed [2012] UKSC 40, [2013] 1 A.C. 595; *NML Capital Ltd v Argentina* [2011] UKSC 31, [2011] 2 A.C. 495; *European Union v Syrian Arab Republic* [2018] EWHC 1712 (Comm), [27]–[29]. On submission in arbitration proceedings, see s.9; *Svenska Petroleum Exploration AB v Government of the Republic of Lithuania* [2005] EWHC 9 (Comm), [2005] 1 Lloyd's Rep. 515; *Svenska Petroleum Exploration AB v Government of the Republic of Lithuania (No.2)* [2005] EWHC 2437 (Comm), [2006] 1 Lloyd's Rep. 181; affirmed [2006] EWCA Civ 1529, [2007] Q.B. 886; *Donegal International Ltd v Zambia* [2007] EWHC 197 (Comm), [2007] 1 Lloyd's Rep. 397; *Ministry of Trade of the Republic of Iraq v Tsavliris Salvage (International) Ltd* [2008] EWHC 612 (Comm), [2008] 2 Lloyd's Rep. 90; *London Steamship Owners Mutual Insurance Ltd v Spain* [2013] EWHC 3188 (Comm), [2014] 1 Lloyd's Rep. 309, affirmed [2015] EWCA Civ 333, [2015] 2 Lloyd's Rep. 33; *Gold Reserve Inc v Bolivarian Republic of Venezuela* [2016] EWHC 153 (Comm), [2016] 1 W.L.R. 2829; *LR Avionics Technologies Ltd v Federal Republic of Nigeria* [2016] EWHC 1761 (Comm), [2016] 4 W.L.R. 120; *London Steamship Owners Mutual Insurance Ltd v Spain* [2020] EWHC 1582 (Comm); *London Steamship Owners Mutual Insurance Ltd v Spain* [2020] EWHC 1920 (Comm).

42 International Criminal Court Act 2001 s.23(1). Where the person in question has an immunity by reason of a connection to a state which is not a party to the ICC Statute, proceedings may be taken against that person under the 2001 Act where the International Criminal Court has obtained a waiver of the immunity in relation to a request for the person's surrender: s.23(2)–(3).

*Replace footnote 43 with:*

43 ss.12–14; see *Alcom Ltd v Republic of Colombia* [1984] A.C. 580; *Westminster City Council v* **12-006**

*Government of the Islamic Republic of Iran* [1986] 1 W.L.R. 979; *Kuwait Airways Corp v Iraqi Airways Co* [1995] 1 W.L.R. 1147 (for further proceedings, see *Kuwait Airways Corp v Iraqi Airways Co (No.2)* [2001] 1 W.L.R. 429; *Kuwait Airways Corp v Iraqi Airways Co* [2003] EWHC 31, (Comm), [2003] 1 Lloyd's Rep. 448); *Crescent Oil and Shipping Services Ltd v Importang UEE* [1997] 3 All E.R. 428; *ABCI v De Banque Franco Tunisienne* [2003] EWCA Civ 205, [2003] 2 Lloyd's Rep. 146; *Wilhelm Finance Inc v Ente Administrador del Astillero Rio Santiago* [2009] EWHC 1074 (Comm), [2009] 1 C.L.C. 867; *NML Capital Ltd v Argentina* [2011] UKSC 31, [2011] 2 A.C. 495; *Mashate v Kaguta* [2011] EWHC 3111 (QB). And see *Soleh Boneh International Ltd v Government of the Republic of Uganda* [1993] 2 Lloyd's Rep. 208, 213; *Norsk Hydro ASA v State Property Fund of Ukraine* [2002] EWHC 2120 (Comm), [2009] Bus. L.R. 558; *Mid East Sales Ltd v United Engineering and Trading Co (PUT)* [2014] EWHC 1457 (Comm), [2014] 2 All E.R. (Comm) 623; *Embassy of Brazil v de Castro Cerqueira* [2014] 1 W.L.R. 3718 (EAT); *PCL v Y Regional Government of X* [2015] EWHC 68 (Comm), [2015] 1 Lloyd's Rep. 483; *Gold Reserve Inc v Bolivarian Republic of Venezuela* [2016] EWHC 153 (Comm), [2016] 1 W.L.R. 2829; *Certain Underwriters at Lloyd's London v Syrian Arab Republic* [2018] EWHC 385 (Comm). As to whether the service requirements of s.12 are mandatory or may be dispensed with, see *General Dynamics United Kingdom Ltd v The State of Libya* [2019] EWCA Civ 1110 at [57]–[62].

## Crown Acts of State

*Replace footnote 51 with:*

**12-007** [51] [2017] UKSC 1, [2017] A.C. 649 at [69]–[70] (Baroness Hale), [81] (Lord Sumption). See also *Alseran v Ministry of Defence* [2017] EWHC 3289 (QB), [38]–[39], [315]. In *Mohamed v Breish* [2020] EWCA Civ 637 the Court of Appeal explained the "one voice" principle (which is distinct from the Act of State doctrine), namely that where Her Majesty's Government has recognised the existence of a foreign state, or a person or body as the government of a foreign state, the English Court is bound to treat the state as a sovereign state, and the government as the government of a sovereign state, in its determination of disputes before it. The Court does so because the recognition of foreign states and governments is constitutionally part of the function of Her Majesty's Government as the executive branch of the state, and the Crown must speak with one voice in its executive and judicial functions in this aspect of international relations.

## Foreign Acts of State

*Replace paragraph with:*

**12-008** The principle of non-justiciability under the "act of state" doctrine may also extend to the acts of a foreign sovereign state performed on territory other than its own territory.[55] Indeed, there is now established a general principle that "the courts will not adjudicate upon the transactions of foreign sovereign states" (i.e. non-commercial transactions or matters of a private law character)[55a]—a principle which calls in such cases for "judicial restraint or abstention".[56] In *Belhaj v Straw*,[57] the Supreme Court analysed the Act of State doctrine in the context of its application to foreign sovereign nations and, in so doing, identified separate strands or rules of the doctrine: (1) a foreign state's legislation will normally be recognised and treated as valid, so far as it affects movable or immovable property within the foreign state's jurisdiction; (2) a domestic court will not normally question the validity of any sovereign act in respect of property within the foreign state's jurisdiction, at least in times of civil disorder; (3) a domestic court will treat as non-justiciable, meaning that it would abstain or refrain from adjudicating upon or questioning, certain categories of sovereign act by a foreign state abroad, even if they occur outside the foreign state's jurisdiction.[58] Further, the doctrine does not apply where there is no challenge to the validity or lawfulness of an act of a foreign state.[59] This principle does not, however, preclude an English court from ever taking cognisance of international law or from ever considering whether a violation of international law has occurred.[60] Thus, in appropriate circumstances, it is legitimate for an English court to have regard to the content of international law in deciding whether to recognise a foreign law on the grounds of public policy.[61] Further, the principle does not mean that the court must shut its eyes to a breach of an established principle of international law committed by one state against another when the breach is plain, since in such cases the standards being applied to adjudicate on the issues are clear and manageable and do not call for the exercise of judicial self-restraint.[62] Unlike sovereign immunity, the principle of non-justiciability under the "act of state" doctrine is not capable of being waived, because it is a matter going to the substantive jurisdiction of the Court.[63]

[55] *Belhaj v Straw* [2014] EWCA Civ 1394, [2015] 2 W.L.R. 1105 at [127]–[133], [2017] UKSC 3, [2017] 2 W.L.R. 456 at [165] (Lord Neuberger), [237] (Lord Sumption); *High Commissioner for Pakistan in the United Kingdom v Prince Mukkaram Jah* [2016] EWHC 1465 (Ch), [2016] W.T.L.R. 1763 at [84]–[87]. cf. *Yukos Capital Sarl v OJSC Rosneft Oil Co (No.2)* [2012] EWCA Civ 855, [2013] 3 W.L.R. 1329 at [66].

[55a] *High Commissioner for Pakistan v Prince Muffakham Jah* [2019] EWHC 2551 (Ch), [2020] Ch. 421 at [306]–[314].

[56] *Buttes Gas and Oil Co v Hammer (No.3)* [1982] A.C. 888, 931; and see *J.H. Rayner (Mincing Lane) Ltd v Department of Trade and Industry* [1990] 2 A.C. 418; *Arab Monetary Fund v Hashim (No.3)* [1991] 2 A.C. 114; *Kuwait Airways Corp v Iraqi Airways Co* [1995] 1 W.L.R. 1147 (for further proceedings, see *Kuwait Airways Corp v Iraqi Airways Co (No.2)* [2001] 1 W.L.R. 430; *Kuwait Airways Corp v Iraqi Airways Co* [2003] EWHC 31 (Comm), [2003] 1 Lloyd's Rep. 448); *Arab Monetary Fund v Hashim* [1993] 1 Lloyd's Rep. 543, 572, affirmed on this point [1996] 1 Lloyd's Rep. 589; *Philipp Brothers v Republic of Sierra Leone* [1995] 1 Lloyd's Rep. 289; *Westland Helicopters Ltd v Arab Organisation for Industrialisation* [1995] Q.B. 282; *R. v Home Secretary Ex p. Launder (No.2)* [1998] Q.B. 994; *R. v Home Secretary Ex p. Johnson* [1999] Q.B. 1174; *Azov Shipping Co v Baltic Shipping Co* [1999] 2 Lloyd's Rep. 159; *Skrine & Co v Euromoney Publications Plc* [2002] I.L.Pr. 281, affirmed on other grounds, [2001] EWCA Civ 1479, [2002] E.M.L.R. 278; *Kuwait Airways Corp v Iraqi Airways Co (Nos 4 and 5)* [2002] UKHL 19, [2002] 2 A.C. 883; *R. (on the application of Abassi) v Secretary of State for Foreign and Commonwealth Affairs* [2002] EWCA Civ 1598, [2003] U.K.H.R.R. 76; *Republic of Ecuador v Occidental Exploration and Production Co* [2005] EWCA Civ 116, [2006] Q.B. 70; *AY Bank Ltd v Bosnia and Herzegovina* [2006] EWHC 830 (Ch), [2006] 2 All E.R. (Comm) 463; *Tajik Aluminium Plant v Ermatov* [2006] EWHC 2374 (Comm). See also *R. v Christian* [2006] UKPC 47, [2007] 2 W.L.R. 120; *R. (on the application of Al Rawi) v Secretary of State for Foreign Affairs* [2006] EWHC 972 (Admin); *Mbasogo v Logo Ltd* [2006] EWCA Civ 1370, [2007] Q.B. 846; *Tasarruf Mevduati Sigorta Fonu v Demirel* [2006] EWHC 3354 (Ch), [2007] 1 Lloyd's Rep. 223; affirmed on other grounds [2007] EWCA Civ 799, [2007] 1 W.L.R. 2508; *Total E & P Soudan SA v Edmonds* [2007] EWCA Civ 50, [2007] C.P. Rep. 20; *Korea National Insurance Corp v Allianz Global Corporate and Speciality AG* [2008] EWCA Civ 1355, [2008] 2 C.L.C. 837; *Empresa Nacional de Telecommunicaciones SA v Deutsche Bank AG* [2009] EWHC 2570 (Comm), [2010] 1 All E.R. (Comm) 649; *Republic of Serbia v Imagesat International NV* [2009] EWHC 2853 (Comm), [2010] 1 Lloyd's Rep. 324; *Al Jedda v Secretary of State for Defence* [2010] EWCA Civ 758, [2011] 2 W.L.R. 225; *BTA Bank v Ablyazof* [2011] EWHC 202 (Comm); *Berezovsky v Abramovich* [2011] EWCA Civ 153, [2011] 1 C.L.C. 359; *Carey Group Plc v AIB Group (UK) Plc* [2011] EWHC 567 (Ch), [2011] 2 All E.R. (Comm) 461; *Masri v Consolidated Contractors International Co SAL* [2011] EWHC 1024 (Comm) at [243] et seq.; *Yukos Capital Sarl v OJSC Rosneft Oil Co* [2011] EWHC 1461 (Comm), [2011] 2 Lloyd's Rep. 443 (generally affirmed by the Court of Appeal, [2012] EWCA Civ 855, [2014] Q.B. 458); *Lucasfilm Ltd v Ainsworth* [2011] UKSC 39, [2012] 1 A.C. 208; *Rahmatullah v Secretary of State for Defence* [2012] UKSC 48, [2012] 3 W.L.R. 1087; *Altima Holdings and Investment Ltd v Kyrgyz Mobil Tel Ltd* [2011] UKPC 7, [2012] 1 W.L.R. 1804; *Yukos Capital Sarl v OJC Rosneft Oil Co (No.2)* [2012] EWCA Civ 855, [2013] 3 W.L.R. 1329; *Democratic Republic of the Congo v FG Hemisphere Associates LLC* [2011] HKFCA 747 (Hong Kong Final Court of Appeal); *Chugai Pharmaceutical Co Ltd v UCB Pharma SA* [2017] EWHC 1216 (Pat), [2017] Bus. L.R. 1455. See generally McGoldrick (2010) 59 I.C.L.Q. 981.

[57] [2017] UKSC 3, [2017] 2 W.L.R. 456.

[58] [2017] UKSC 3 at [11(iii)], [35]–[45] (Lord Mance), [120]–[124] (Lord Neuberger), [234] (Lord Sumption). It was doubted that there is a fourth rule that the doctrine may be invoked where a ruling would embarrass the United Kingdom in its international dealings: at [11(iv)] (Lord Mance), [148]–[149] (Lord Neuberger), [240]–[241] (Lord Sumption). See *Reliance Industries Ltd v Union of India* [2018] EWHC 822 (Comm), [2018] 1 Lloyd's Rep. 562 at [104]–[115]; *Ukraine v Law Debenture Trust Corp Plc* [2018] EWCA Civ 2026, [2019] 2 W.L.R. 655.

[59] *AAA v Unilever Plc* [2017] EWHC 371 (QB) at [35]–[62]; [2018] EWCA Civ 1532.

[60] *Kuwait Airways Corp v Iraqi Airways Co (Nos 4 and 5)* [2002] UKHL 19, [2002] 2 A.C. 883; *Republic of Ecuador v Occidental Exploration and Production Co* [2005] EWCA Civ 116; *AY Bank v Bosnia and Herzegovina* [2006] EWHC 830 (Comm), [2006] 2 All E.R. (Comm) 463; *Belhaj v Straw* [2014] EWCA Civ 1394, [2015] 2 W.L.R. 1105 at [54]–[55], [81]–[93], [2017] UKSC 3, [2017] 2 W.L.R. 456 at [11(v)], [85]–[107] (Lord Mance), [153]–[162] (Lord Neuberger), [249]–[280] (Lord Sumption); *Mohammed v Secretary of State for Defence* [2015] EWCA Civ 843. See also *Habib v Commonwealth of Australia* (2010) 183 F.C.R. 62 (Fed Ct Aust.); Collins (2002) 51 I.C.L.Q. 485.

[61] *Kuwait Airways Corp v Iraqi Airways Co (Nos 4 and 5)* [2002] UKHL 19; *Empresa Nacional de Telecommunicaciones SA v Deutsche Bank AG* [2009] EWHC 2579 (Comm), [2010] 1 All E.R. (Comm) 649; *Yukos Capital Sarl v OJSC Rosneft Oil Co* [2011] EWHC 1461 (Comm), [2011] 2 Lloyd's Rep. 443 (generally affirmed by the Court of Appeal, [2012] EWCA Civ 855, [2014] Q.B. 458). See also *Republic of Ecuador v Occidental Exploration and Production Co* [2005] EWCA Civ 116.

[62] *Kuwait Airways Corp v Iraqi Airways Co (Nos 4 and 5)* [2002] UKHL 19; *Belhaj v Straw* [2014] EWCA Civ 1394, [2015] 2 W.L.R. 1105 at [54]–[55], [81]–[93]; [2017] UKSC 3, [2017] 2 W.L.R. 456 at [11(v)], [85]–[107] (Lord Mance), [153]–[162] (Lord Neuberger), [249]–[280] (Lord Sumption); *Ukraine v Law Debenture Trust Corp Plc* [2018] EWCA Civ 2026, [2019] 2 W.L.R. 655 at [173]–[181].

[63] *R. v Bow Street Metropolitan Stipendiary Magistrate Ex p. Pinochet Ugarte (No.3)* [2000] 1 A.C. 61, 90; *High Commissioner for Pakistan in the United Kingdom v Prince Mukkaram Jah* [2016] EWHC 1465 (Ch), [2016] W.T.L.R. 1763 at [89]–[90]. However, it might be waived by an express and specific submission to arbitration: *Reliance Industries Ltd v Union of India* [2018] EWHC 822 (Comm), [2018] 1 Lloyd's Rep. 562 at [117]–[120], [128]–[131].

## Categories of persons entitled to diplomatic immunity

*Replace footnote 69 with:*

**12-011** [69] Diplomatic Privileges Act 1964 Sch.1 art.1. As a matter of customary international law and the common law, a receiving state is obliged to secure, for the duration of a special or ad hoc mission, personal inviolability and immunity from criminal jurisdiction for the members of the mission accepted as such by the receiving state: see *Khurts Bat v Investigating Judge of the German Federal Court* [2011] EWHC 2029 (Admin), [2013] Q.B. 349; *R. (on the application of the Freedom and Justice Party) v Secretary of State for Foreign and Commonwealth Affairs* [2016] EWHC 2010 (Admin) at [116]–[120]; [2018] EWCA Civ 1719, [2019] 2 W.L.R. 578, [136] (special mission).

## Diplomatic agents

*Replace paragraph with:*

**12-012** Diplomatic agents enjoy immunity from criminal, civil[70] and administrative jurisdiction and from execution, except in three cases: (a) a real action relating to private immovable property situated in the United Kingdom (unless the property is held for the purposes of the mission,[71] and this does not include a diplomatic agents private residence)[72]; (b) an action relating to succession in which the diplomatic agent is involved as executor, administrator or beneficiary as a private person; and (c) an action relating to any professional or commercial activity exercised by the diplomatic agent outside his official functions.[73] A like immunity is conferred on the members of the family of a diplomatic agent forming part of his household.[74] In *A Local Authority v AG*[74a] the Court held that there is no implied exception to diplomatic immunity, based on the Human Rights Act 1998 s.3, to protect children or vulnerable adults at risk within the diplomat's family forming part of his household. The Diplomatic Privileges Act 1964 applies only to permanent diplomatic missions; the status of special or ad hoc missions is a matter for the common law.[75]

[70] Including a divorce petition: *Shaw v Shaw* [1979] Fam. 62. For the position in relation to proceedings under the Child Abduction and Custody Act 1985, see *P v P (Diplomatic Immunity: Jurisdiction)* [1998] 1 F.L.R. 1026. See also *Abusabib v Taddese* [2013] I.C.R. 603 (employment claims).

[71] *Alcom Ltd v Republic of Colombia* [1984] A.C. 580.

[72] *Intpro Properties (UK) Ltd v Sauvel* [1983] Q.B. 1019, 1032–1033.

[73] Vienna Convention art.31. See *Wokuri v Kassam* [2012] EWHC 105 (Ch), [2013] Ch. 80; *Reyes v Al-Malki* [2017] UKSC 61, [2017] 3 W.L.R. 923. In *Basfar v Wong* [2020] 1 WLUK 330 the Employment Appeal Tribunal held that the law as to the meaning of "commercial activity" was represented by the Court of Appeal's decision in *Al-Malki v Reyes* [2015] EWCA Civ 32 and the decision of the minority of the Supreme Court which had approved the Court of Appeal's decision, even though the majority of the Supreme Court doubted the Court of Appeal's decision, but did not overrule it.

[74] Vienna Convention art.37(1).

[74a] *A Local Authority v AG* [2020] EWFC 18, [2020] 3 W.L.R. 133 at [29]–[39]. Though note *A Local Authority v AG (No. 2)* [2020] EWHC 1346 (Fam).

[75] *R. (on the application of the Freedom and Justice Party) v Secretary of State for Foreign and Commonwealth Affairs* [2016] EWHC 2010 (Admin); [2018] EWCA Civ 1719, [2019] 2 W.L.R. 578 at [12], [113]–[134], where it was held that the rule of customary international law was recognised and accepted as part of the common law.

## Diplomatic premises

*In line 7, after "or consular status.", add new footnote 79a:*

[79a] *Belfast City Council v Meifang* [2020] NICh 12 at [24]–[25]. **12-013**

## Certificate of entitlement

*Replace footnote 90 with:*

[90] Diplomatic Privileges Act 1964 s.4; and see *Engelke v Musmann* [1928] A.C. 433; *R. v Governor of Pentonville Prison Ex p. Teja* [1971] 2 Q.B. 274; *Khurts Bat v Investigating Judge of the German Federal Court* [2011] EWHC 2029 (Admin), [2013] Q.B. 349. cf. *Re P (Children Act: Diplomatic Immunity)* [1998] 1 F.L.R. 625, 626; *Apex Global Management Ltd v Fi Call Ltd* [2013] EWCA Civ 642, [2014] 1 W.L.R. 492; *Al Attiya v Al Thani* [2016] EWHC 212 (QB) at [37], [59], [83]; *R. (on the application of the Freedom and Justice Party) v Secretary of State for Foreign and Commonwealth Affairs* [2016] EWHC 2010 (Admin) at [174]; [2018] EWCA Civ 1719, [2019] 2 W.L.R. 578; *Mohamed v Breish* [2019] EWHC 306 (Comm). However, the entitlement to diplomatic immunity is dependent on the terms of the certificate: *A Local Authority v X* [2018] EWHC 874 (Fam) at [38]–[49]. **12-016**

## Consular immunity

*Replace paragraph with:*

**12-018** The regulation of consular immunity so far as foreign consuls and their staffs are concerned is governed by the Consular Relations Act 1968[96] giving effect to certain articles of the Vienna Convention on Consular Relations 1963. In the case of civil proceedings, consular officers, who are defined as "any person, including the head of a consular post, entrusted in that capacity with the exercise of consular functions",[97] and consular employees, who are any persons "employed in the administrative or technical service of a consular post",[98] shall not be amenable to the jurisdiction of the courts of this country in respect of acts performed in the exercise of consular functions.[98a] This immunity shall not apply, in the case of a contractual action, where such officer or employee did not contract expressly or impliedly as an agent of his sending state or in the case of an action by a third party for damage arising from an accident in the United Kingdom caused by a vessel, vehicle or aircraft.[99] Special provision is made for the fact that immunity from civil jurisdiction shall not be accorded to consular employees who carry on private gainful occupation in the United Kingdom.[100] The position of officers from the Commonwealth and the Republic of Ireland who perform duties substantially similar to those performed by consular officers from foreign countries is governed by the Consular Relations Act 1968[101] and Orders in Council made thereunder.

[96] As amended by the Diplomatic and Other Privileges Act 1971 and the Diplomatic and Consular Premises Act 1987.

[97] Consular Relations Act 1968 Sch.I art.1.

[98] Sch.I art.1.

[98a] *Belfast City Council v Meifang* [2020] NICh 12 at [27]–[36].

[99] Vienna Convention art.43.

[100] Vienna Convention art.57.

[101] s.12 as substituted by the Diplomatic and other Privileges Act 1971 s.4(1) and Sch.

## Submission to jurisdiction

*Replace paragraph with:*

12-022 The State Immunity Act 1978 now makes express provision for a state to submit to the jurisdiction of the court and thereby waive its state immunity, but such waiver does not exclude the assertion of absolute privilege[131] nor does submission to the adjudicative jurisdiction of the courts necessarily imply submission to the enforcement jurisdiction of the courts.[132] There are detailed rules as to what constitutes submission[133] but one of their main effects is to free the doctrine of waiver from its narrow common law limits. Submission may, under the Act, be by prior written agreement and is permitted after a dispute has arisen.[134] A state is also deemed to submit if it institutes the proceedings[135] or if it intervenes, or takes any step, in proceedings unless it does so in reasonable ignorance of facts entitling it to immunity and immunity is then claimed as soon as reasonably practicable.[136] A state may legally waive immunity by making a unilateral assurance with the intention that it should be bound according to the terms of the said assurance, even if the assurance is not given as the result of an international negotiation or in exchange for a quid pro quo or is not acknowledged by another state.[136a] However, intervention merely to claim immunity or to assert an interest in property in circumstances where the state would have been entitled to immunity in any proceedings brought against it does not constitute submission.[137] A contractual waiver of immunity, without any submission to the jurisdiction of the court, is not a submission for the purposes of the Act[138]; nor is submission to be deduced from a choice of law clause.[139] Submission extends to any appeal, but not to any counterclaim unless it arises out of the same legal relationship or facts as the claim.[140] The head of a state's diplomatic mission is deemed to have authority to submit on behalf of the state,[141] as is any person who entered into a contract on behalf of the state in respect of proceedings arising out of the contract.[142] Once submission to the jurisdiction is established, the waiver of state immunity is irrevocable.[143] Submission to the jurisdiction is not submission to execution, though such process may be issued with the written consent of the state.[144]

[131] *Fayed v Al Tajir* [1988] Q.B. 712.

[132] State Immunity Act 1978 s.13(2); *Alcom Ltd v Republic of Colombia* [1983] A.C. 580; *NML Capital Ltd v Argentina* [2011] UKSC 31, [2011] 2 A.C. 495; *Boru Hatlari Ile Petrol Tasima AS v Tepe Insaat Sanayii AS* [2018] UKPC 31. By s.13(2)(a), relief shall not be given against a State by way of injunction or order for specific performance or for the recovery of land or other property: *Belfast City Council v Meifang* [2020] NICh 12. Where a state has agreed in writing to submit a dispute which has arisen or which may arise, to arbitration, the state cannot then claim immunity as respects proceedings in the courts of the United Kingdom which relate to the arbitration, unless there is a contrary provision in the agreement or the arbitration agreement is between states: State Immunity Act 1978 s.9: see *Ministry of Trade of the Republic of Iraq v Tsavliris Salvage (International) Ltd* [2008] EWHC 612 (Comm), [2008] 2 Lloyd's Rep. 90. Section 9 extends to proceedings for permission to enforce an arbitration award under Arbitration Act 1996 s.101, but probably does not extend to enforcement of an award against property of a state: s.13(2)(b). See also *Svenska Petroleum Exploration AB v Government of the Republic of Lithuania (No.2)* [2005] EWHC 2437 (Comm), [2006] 1 Lloyd's Rep.181; affirmed [2006] EWCA Civ 1529, [2007] Q.B. 886; *Orascom Telecom Holding SAE v Republic of Chad* [2008] EWHC 1841 (Comm), [2008] 2 Lloyd's Rep. 396; *ETI Eurotelecom International NV v Republic of Bolivia* [2008] EWCA Civ 880, [2008] 1 W.L.R. 665; *Servaas Inc v Rafidain Bank* [2011] EWCA Civ 1256, [2012] 1 All E.R. (Comm) 527, affirmed [2012] UKSC 40, [2013] 1 A.C. 595 (but property of a state which originates in a commercial transaction is immune from execution if the state has chosen the property to be used for sovereign purposes rather than commercial purposes; see s.13(4) of the Act); *NML Capital Ltd v Argentina* [2011] UKSC 31, [2011] 2 A.C. 495; *The High Commissioner for Pakistan in the United Kingdom v National Westminster Bank Plc* [2015] EWHC 55 (Ch) at [72]–[76]; *Gold Reserve Inc v Bolivarian Republic of Venezuela* [2016] EWHC 153 (Comm), [2016] 1 W.L.R. 2829; *LR Avionics Technologies Ltd v Federal Republic of Nigeria* [2016] EWHC 1761 (Comm), [2016] 4 W.L.R. 120 at [20]–[23]. See also *PAO Tatneft v Ukraine* [2018] EWHC 1797 (Comm), [2018] 2 Lloyd's Rep. 403 at

[34]–[35], where it was held that the constraints under the Arbitration Act 1996 applicable to challenging an award do not apply in respect of a claim for immunity under the 1978 Act. See *Dicey, Morris and Collins on the Conflict of Laws*, 15th edn (2012), para.10-051.

[133] s.2. This section is a complete statement of the circumstances in which a state submits for the purposes of the Act: *Svenska Petroleum Exploration AB v Government of the Republic of Lithuania (No.2)* [2005] EWHC 2437 (Comm), [2006] 1 Lloyd's Rep. 181; affirmed [2006] EWCA Civ 1529, [2007] Q.B. 886; *NML Capital Ltd v Argentina* [2011] UKSC 31, [2011] 2 A.C. 495.

[134] s.2(2). See *A Co Ltd v Republic of X* [1990] 2 Lloyd's Rep. 520; *Ahmed v Government of the Kingdom of Saudi Arabia* [1996] I.C.R. 25 (meaning of "written agreement"); *Propend Finance Pty Ltd v Sing, The Times,* May 2, 1997; 111 Int. L.R. 611; *Mills v Embassy of the United States of America* Unreported May 9, 2000, CA; *Sabah Shipyard (Pakistan) Ltd v The Islamic Republic of Pakistan* [2002] EWCA Civ 1643, [2003] 2 Lloyd's Rep. 571; *Donegal International Ltd v Zambia* [2007] EWHC 197 (Comm), [2007] 1 Lloyd's Rep. 397; *Orascom Telecom Holding SAE v Republic of Chad* [2008] EWHC 1841 (Comm), [2008] 2 Lloyd's Rep. 396; *NML Capital Ltd v Argentina* [2011] UKSC 31, [2011] 2 A.C. 495; *London Steamship Owners Mutual Insurance Association Ltd v Spain* [2013] EWHC 3188 (Comm), [2014] 1 Lloyd's Rep. 309, affirmed [2015] EWCA Civ 333, [2015] 2 Lloyd's Rep. 33; and see *Thai-Liao Lignite (Thailand) Co Ltd v Laos* [2013] EWHC 2466 (Comm), [2013] 2 All E.R. (Comm) 883; *The High Commissioner for Pakistan in the United Kingdom v National Westminster Bank Plc* [2015] EWHC 55 (Ch) at [72]–[76]; *European Union v Syrian Arab Republic* [2018] EWHC 1712 (Comm), [27]–[29]; *Trafigura Pte Ltd v Government of the Republic of South Sudan* [2020] EWHC 2044 (Comm) at [24].

[135] s.2(3)(a).

[136] s.2(3)(b), (5). See *Kuwait Airways Corp v Iraqi Airways Co* [1995] 1 Lloyd's Rep. 25, CA, reversed, in part, on other grounds, [1995] 1 W.L.R. 1147, HL (for further proceedings, see *Kuwait Airways Corp v Iraqi Airways Co (No.2)* [2001] 1 W.L.R. 429; *Kuwait Airways Corp v Iraqi Airways Co* [2003] EWHC 31 (Comm), [2003] 1 Lloyd's Rep. 448); *London Branch of the Nigerian Universities Commission v Bastians* [1995] I.C.R. 358; *Arab Republic of Egypt v Gamal-Eldin* [1996] I.C.R. 13; *Malaysian Industrial Development Authority v Jeyasingham* [1998] I.C.R. 307; *Aziz v Republic of Yemen* [2005] EWCA Civ 745, [2005] I.C.R. 1391; *London Steamship Owners Mutual Insurance Ltd v Spain* [2020] EWHC 1582 (Comm).

[136a] *Re Al M (Assurances and Waiver)* [2020] EWHC 67 (Fam), [2020] 1 W.L.R. 1858 at [58].

[137] s.2(3), (4).

[138] *Svenska Petroleum Exploration AB v Republic of Lithuania (No.2)* [2005] EWHC 2437 (Comm), [2006] 1 Lloyd's Rep. 181; affirmed [2006] EWCA Civ 1529, [2007] Q.B. 886; *NML Capital Ltd v Argentina* [2011] UKSC 31, [2011] 2 A.C. 495.

[139] s.2(2).

[140] s.2(6). See *Propend Finance Pty Ltd v Sing, The Times,* May 2, 1997, 111 Int. L.R. 611; cf. *Sultan of Johore v Bendahar* [1952] A.C. 318 (appeal); *High Commissioner for India v Ghosh* [1960] 1 Q.B. 134 (counterclaim).

[141] s.2(7). See *Ahmed v Government of the Kingdom of Saudi Arabia* [1996] I.C.R. 25; *Arab Republic of Egypt v Gamal-Eldin* [1996] I.C.R. 13; *Propend Finance Pty Ltd v Sing, The Times,* May 2, 1997; 111 Int. L.R. 611; *Malaysian Industrial Development Authority v Jeyasingham* [1998] I.C.R. 307; cf. *Donegal International Ltd v Zambia* [2007] EWHC 197 (Comm), [2007] 1 Lloyd's Rep. 397 (authority of Minister). On the method of waiver or submission, see *Fayed v Al Tajir* [1988] Q.B. 712, 733, 736–737.

[142] s.2(7). See *Ahmed v Government of the Kingdom of Saudi Arabia* [1996] I.C.R. 25.

[143] *The High Commissioner for Pakistan in the United Kingdom v National Westminster Bank Plc* [2015] EWHC 55 (Ch) at [74].

[144] s.13(3); cf. *Re Suarez* [1917] 2 Ch. 131; *Duff Development Co v Government of Kelantan* [1923] 1 Ch. 385, [1924] A.C. 797, 810, 821, 830. See also *Mitchell v Ibrahim Al-Dahli* [2005] EWCA Civ 720 (undertaking by foreign state not to appeal costs order made against it does not imply waiver of immunity should enforcement of the costs order be sought).

## Waiver of diplomatic or consular immunity

*Replace footnote 145 with:*

[145] Sch.1 art.32. The diplomat cannot waive immunity, only the government of the sending state can: **12-023**
*A Local Authority v AG* [2020] EWFC 18, [2020] 3 W.L.R. 133 at [29].

CHAPTER 13

# EXPRESS TERMS

## 1. PROOF OF TERMS

### Proof of terms

*Replace footnote 5 with:*

13-002 [5] *Parker v South Eastern Ry* (1877) 2 C.P.D. 416, 421; *Howatson v Webb* [1908] 1 Ch. 1; *The Luna* [1920] P. 22; *L'Estrange v Graucob Ltd* [1934] 2 K.B. 394; *McCutcheon v David MacBrayne Ltd* [1964] 1 W.L.R. 125, 132–134; *Bahamas Oil Refining Co v Kristiansands Tank-rederie A/S* [1978] 1 Lloyd's Rep. 211; *Charlotte Thirty Ltd v Croker Ltd* (1990) 24 Con. L.R. 46; *Toll (FGCT) Pty Ltd v Alphapharm Pty Ltd* (2004) 211 A.L.R. 342; *Peekay Intermark Ltd v Australia and NZ Banking Group Ltd* [2006] EWCA Civ 386, [2006] 2 Lloyd's Rep. 511 at [43]; *One World (GB) Ltd v Elite Mobile Ltd* [2012] EWHC 3706 (QB) (although note the qualification expressed at [58] in relation to a possible exception to the rule where the term sought to be incorporated is onerous or unusual, on which see further *Dawson v Bell* [2016] EWCA Civ 96, [2016] B.C.L.C. 59 at [102]–[103]; *Yedina v Yedin* [2017] EWHC 3319 (Ch) at [268]); *Cargill International Trading Pte Ltd v Uttam Galva Steels Ltd* [2019] EWHC 476 (Comm) at [80] (although note the recognition at [89] of "exceptional cases in which the signing party was under undue pressure or had no real opportunity to read and consider the contract before signing"); *Higgins & Co Lawyers Ltd v Evans* [2019] EWHC 2809 (QB), [2020] 1 W.L.R. 141 at [73]. But see *Jaques v Lloyd D. George & Partners Ltd* [1968] 1 W.L.R. 625, 630; *Tilden Rent-a-Car Co v Clendenning* (1978) 83 D.L.R. (3d) 400; *Crocker v Sundance Northwest Resorts Ltd* (1988) 51 D.L.R. (4th) 321; *Ocean Chemical Transport Inc v Exnor Craggs Ltd* [2000] 1 Lloyd's Rep. 446, 454. See further Spencer [1978] C.L.J. 104; Macdonald [1999] C.L.J. 413, 420; Peden and Carter (2005) 21 J.C.L. 96 and below, para.13-015 n.70.

## (a) Contractual Undertakings and Representations

### Third parties

*Replace footnote 37 with:*

13-007 [37] [1951] 2 K.B. 854. See *Brown v Sheen & Richmond Car Sales Ltd* [1950] 1 All E.R. 1102; *Andrews v Hopkinson* [1957] 1 Q.B. 229; *Smith v Spurling Motor Bodies Ltd* (1961) 105 S.J. 967; *Yeoman Credit Ltd v Odgers* [1962] 1 W.L.R. 215; *Wells (Merstham) Ltd v Buckland Sand & Silica Ltd* [1965] 2 Q.B. 170. cf. *Drury v Victor Buckland Ltd* [1941] 1 All E.R. 269; *Independent Broadcasting Authority v EMI Electronics* (1980) 14 Build. L.R. 1; *Lambert v Lewis* [1982] A.C. 225; *Law Debenture Trust Corp v Ural Caspian Oil Corp Ltd* [1993] 1 W.L.R. 138 (reversed on other grounds, [1995] Ch. 152); *Fuji Seal Europe Ltd v Catalytic Combustion Corporation* [2005] EWHC 1659 (TCC), 102 Con L.R. 47; *Natixis SA v Marex Financial* [2019] EWHC 2549 (Comm) at [251]–[260].

## (b) Standard Form Contracts

### Course of dealing

*Replace paragraph with:*

13-011 Conditions will not necessarily be incorporated into a contract by reason of the fact that the parties have, on previous occasions, dealt with each other subject to those conditions.[54] But they may be incorporated by a "course of dealing" between the parties where each party has led the other reasonably to believe that he intended that their rights and liabilities should be ascertained by reference to the terms of a document which had been consistently used by them in previous transactions.[55] It should, however, be noted that a more relaxed approach is adopted in art.25 of the Regulation (EU) on Jurisdiction and the Recognition and Enforcement of Judgments in Civil and Commercial Matters[56] to the degree of *consensus* required for the incorporation of an exclusive jurisdiction clause.[57]

[54] *McCutcheon v David Macbrayne Ltd* [1964] 1 W.L.R. 125, HL (no consistent course of dealing); *Hollier v Rambler Motors (A.M.C.) Ltd* [1972] 2 Q.B. 71 (only three or four times in five years); *Capes (Hatherden) Ltd v Western Arable Services Ltd* [2009] EWHC 3065 (QB), [2010] 1 Lloyd's Rep. 477 (four contracts in same year with interval of five months between the last of them and the two contracts in question); *Transformers & Rectifiers Ltd v Needs Ltd* [2015] EWHC 269 (TCC), [2015] B.L.R. 336

(claimant failed to follow a consistent practice of enclosing its terms and conditions with every purchase order).

[55] *J. Spurling Ltd v Bradshaw* [1956] 1 W.L.R. 461, 467; *Cockerton v Naviera Aznar SA* [1960] 2 Lloyd's Rep. 450; *Henry Kendall & Sons v William Lillico & Sons Ltd* [1969] 2 A.C. 31, 90, 91, 104, 105, 130; *Transmotors Ltd v Robertson Buckley & Co Ltd* [1970] 1 Lloyd's Rep. 224; *Eastman Chemical International A.G. v N.M.T. Trading Ltd* [1972] 2 Lloyd's Rep. 25; *Gillespie Bros & Co Ltd v Roy Bowles Transport Ltd* [1973] Q.B. 400; *S.I.A.T. di del Ferro v Tradax Overseas SA* [1978] 2 Lloyd's Rep. 470 (affirmed [1980] 1 Lloyd's Rep. 53); *Lamport & Holt Lines Ltd v Coubro & Scrutton (M. & I.) Ltd* [1981] 2 Lloyd's Rep. 659 (affirmed [1982] 2 Lloyd's Rep. 42); *McCrone v Boots Farm Sales Ltd* 1981 S.L.T. 103; *George Mitchell (Chesterhall) Ltd v Finney Lock Seeds Ltd* [1983] Q.B. 284, 295 (affirmed [1983] 2 A.C. 803); *Johnson Matthey Bankers Ltd v State Trading Corp of India Ltd* [1984] 1 Lloyd's Rep. 427; *Circle Freight International Ltd v Medeast Gulf Exports Ltd* [1988] 2 Lloyd's Rep. 427; *Balmoral Group Ltd v Borealis UK Ltd* [2006] EWHC 1900 (Comm), [2006] 2 Lloyd's Rep. 629 at [362]–[366]; *Capes (Hatherden) Ltd v Western Arable Services Ltd* [2009] EWHC 3065 (QB), [2010] 1 Lloyd's Rep. 477 at [32]–[42]; *Hamad M Aldrees & Partners v Rotex Europe Ltd* [2019] EWHC 574 (TCC), 184 Con. L.R. 145 at [80]–[81]; cf. *Banque Paribas v Cargill International SA* [1992] 1 Lloyd's Rep. 96, 98; see Hoggett (1970) 33 M.L.R. 518. See also *Photolibrary Group Ltd v Burda Senator Verlag GmbH* [2008] EWHC 1343 (QB), [2008] 2 All E.R. (Comm) 881; *SKNL (UK) Ltd v Toll Global Forwarding* [2012] EWHC 4252 (Comm), [2013] 2 Lloyd's Rep. 115.

[56] Regulation 1215/2012 on jurisdiction and the recognition and enforcement of judgments in civil and commercial matters (recast) [2012] O.J. L351/1. The Regulation came into force on January 10, 2015 and recasts and replaces Regulation 44/2001 on jurisdiction and the recognition and enforcement of judgments in civil and commercial matters [2001] O.J. L12/1. The Regulation will, however, be revoked at the end of the implementation period: Civil Jurisdiction and Judgments (Amendment) (EU Exit) Regulations 2019 (SI 2019/479) at reg.89 (and for a similar revocation of Regulation 44/2001 see reg.84).

[57] See *The Tilly Russ (M.S.)* [1985] 1 Q.B. 931; *Mainschiffahrts-Genossenschaft eG v Les Gravières Rhénanes SARL* [1997] Q.B. 1; *SSQ Europe SA v Johann & Backes OHG* [2002] 1 Lloyd's Rep. 465; *Africa Express Line Ltd v Socofi SA* [2009] EWHC 3223 (Comm), [2010] 2 Lloyd's Rep. 181.

## Incorporation without express reference

*Replace footnote 58 with:*

[58] *British Crane Hire Corp Ltd v Ipswich Plant Hire Ltd* [1975] Q.B. 303; *Chevron International Oil Co Ltd v A/S Sea Team* [1983] 2 Lloyd's Rep. 356; *Laceys Footwear (Wholesale) Ltd v Bowler International Freight Ltd* [1997] 2 Lloyd's Rep. 369, 378; *Balmoral Group Ltd v Borealis UK Ltd* [2006] EWHC 1900 (Comm), [2006] 2 Lloyd's Rep. 629 at [357]; *Transformers & Rectifiers Ltd v Needs Ltd* [2015] EWHC 269 (TCC), [2015] B.L.R. 336 at [42]. cf. *Salsi v Jetspread Air Services Ltd* [1977] 2 Lloyd's Rep. 57; *Pancommerce SA v Veecheema BV* [1983] 2 Lloyd's Rep. 304, 305; *Neptune Orient Lines Ltd v J.V.C. (UK) Ltd* [1983] 2 Lloyd's Rep. 438; *Shipbuilders Ltd v Benson* [1992] 3 N.Z.L.R. 349; *Grogan v Robin Meredith Plant Hire* (1996) 15 Tr. L.R. 371; *Hamad M Aldrees & Partners v Rotex Europe Ltd* [2019] EWHC 574 (TCC), 184 Con. L.R. 145 at [167]–[181]. See also *Matrix Europe Ltd v Uniserve Holdings Ltd* [2008] EWHC 11 (QB), [2008] 1 C.L.C. 205 (BIFA terms applied even to unintentional delivery of goods). **13-012**

## Onerous or unusual terms

*Replace paragraph with:*

Although the party receiving the document knows it contains conditions, if the particular condition relied on is one which is a particularly onerous or unusual term, or is one which involves the abrogation of a right given by statute, the party tendering the document must show that it has been brought fairly and reasonably to the other's attention.[70] "Some clauses which I have seen", said Denning L.J.[71]: **13-015**

> "… would need to be printed in red ink on the face of the document with a red hand pointing to it before the notice could be held to be sufficient."

The words "onerous or unusual" are not terms of art[71a] and it has been observed that the authorities "do not always agree"[71b] on whether a particular term is "onerous or unusual".[71c] The hurdle which must be overcome has, however, been described as a "high hurdle".[71d] Terms which have been held to be "onerous or unusual" include broadly worded or "blanket" exclusion clauses[71e] and clauses which require a party to pay an excessive sum of money on the occurrence of a particular event.[71f] But not all exclusion or limitation clauses should be regarded as "onerous or unusual",[71g] nor is it the case that all terms which require the payment of potentially significant sums of money to the other party are "onerous or unusual".[71h] Much depends on the facts and circumstances of the case so that the court must "have full regard to the context and the respective bargaining positions of the parties".[71i] The guiding principle may be said to be that "the more outlandish the clause the greater the notice which the other party, if he is to be bound, must in all fairness be given".[71j] The requirement that the term has been brought "fairly and reasonably to the other's attention" is unlikely to be met in the case where the clause is "buried away in the middle of a raft of small print".[71k] The practical equivalent of a "red hand" may take the form of a "clear reference"[71l] to the term, such as using bold print to highlight the term, the use of capital letters or otherwise giving the clause a degree of prominence in the contract. A further alternative is expressly to draw the existence of the term to the attention of the other party. This additional requirement for "onerous or unusual" clauses applies to terms sought to be incorporated into the contract by notice. It does not apply to contracts which have been signed, although the case law has left open the possibility that in "exceptional" cases this requirement may apply to a contract which has been signed.[71m]

[70] *Parker v South Eastern Ry* (1877) 2 C.P.D. 416, 428; *Thornton v Shoe Lane Parking Ltd* [1971] 2 Q.B. 163; *Hollingworth v Southern Ferries Ltd* [1977] 2 Lloyd's Rep. 70; *Interfoto Picture Library Ltd v Stiletto Visual Programmes Ltd* [1989] Q.B. 433; *Dillon v Baltic Shipping Co* [1991] 2 Lloyd's Rep. 155; *A.E.G. (UK) Ltd v Logic Resource Ltd* [1996] C.L.C. 265; *Laceys Footwear v Bowler International Freight (Wholesale) Ltd* [1997] 2 Lloyd's Rep. 369, 384–385; *Ocean Chemical Transport Inc v Exnor Craggs Ltd* [2000] 1 Lloyd's Rep. 446, 451; *O'Brien v MGN Ltd* [2001] EWCA Civ 1279, [2002] C.L.C. 33; *Amiri Flight Authority v BAE Systems Plc* [2003] EWCA Civ 1447, [2003] 2 Lloyd's Rep. 767; *Kaye v NuSkin UK Ltd* [2009] EWHC 3509 (Ch), [2011] 1 Lloyd's Rep. 40; *Woodeson v Credit Suisse (UK) Ltd* [2018] EWCA Civ 1103; *Goodlife Foods Ltd v Hall Fire Protection Ltd* [2018] EWCA Civ 1371, [2018] B.L.R. 491 at [46]; *Bates v Post Office Ltd (No.3: Common Issues)* [2019] EWHC 606 (QB) at [959]–[1061].

[71] *J. Spurling Ltd v Bradshaw* [1956] 1 W.L.R. 461, 466.

[71a] *O'Brien v MGN Ltd* [2001] EWCA Civ 1279, [2002] C.L.C. 33 at [23].

[71b] *Goodlife Foods Ltd v Hall Fire Protection Ltd* [2018] EWCA Civ 1371, [2018] B.L.R. 491 at [33].

[71c] Further, they do not always agree as to the formulation of the test to be applied. In *Interfoto Picture Library Ltd v Stiletto Visual Programmes Ltd* [1989] Q.B. 433 the words used are "onerous or unusual" whereas in *Bates v Post Office Ltd (No.3: Common Issues)* [2019] EWHC 606 (QB) the test is more formulated in terms of whether the clause is "onerous and unusual". Thus it is not entirely clear whether it would suffice to demonstrate that the clause was "unusual" but not "onerous". However, it may be that the courts do not wish to get bogged down in a linguistic analysis of the different ways in which the test can be expressed (see *Bates* at [980]).

[71d] *Bates v Post Office Ltd (No.3: Common Issues)* [2019] EWHC 606 (QB) at [979]; *Higgins & Co Lawyers Ltd v Evans* [2019] EWHC 2809 (QB), [2020] 1 W.L.R. 141 at [73].

[71e] See, for example, *Thornton v Shoe Lane Parking Ltd* [1971] 2 Q.B. 163. See also *A.E.G. (UK) Ltd v Logic Resource Ltd* [1996] C.L.C. 265 where it was held that a term which required the purchaser to return defective goods at its own expense was both onerous and unreasonable.

[71f] See, for example, *Interfoto Picture Library Ltd v Stiletto Visual Programmes Ltd* [1989] Q.B. 433.

[71g] See, for example, *Shepherd Homes Ltd v Encia Remediation Ltd* [2007] EWHC 70 (TCC), [2007] B.L.R. 135; *Allen Fabrications Ltd v ASD Ltd* [2012] EWHC 2213 (TCC) at [57]–[64]; *Goodlife Foods Ltd v Hall Fire Protection Ltd* [2018] EWCA Civ 1371, [2018] B.L.R. 491 at [35]; *Natixis SA v Marex Financial* [2019] EWHC 2549 (Comm) at [490]–[502].

[71h] See, for example, *Photolibrary Group Ltd v Burda Senator Verlag GmbH* [2008] EWHC 1343 (QB), [2008] 2 All E.R. (Comm) 881 which should be contrasted in this respect with *Interfoto Picture Library Ltd v Stiletto Visual Programmes Ltd* [1989] Q.B. 433. There is also a line of cases concerned with arbitration clauses where the term has been held not to be onerous or unusual: *Stretford v Football As-*

*sociation Ltd* [2007] EWCA Civ 238, [2007] 2 Lloyd's Rep. 31; *Habas Sinai Ve Tibbi Gazlar Isthisal Endustri AS v Sometal SAL* [2010] EWHC 29 (Comm), [2010] 1 Lloyd's Rep. 661.

71i *Carewatch Care Services Ltd v Focus Caring Services Ltd* [2014] EWHC 2313 (Ch) at [84].

71j *Interfoto Picture Library Ltd v Stiletto Visual Programmes Ltd* [1989] Q.B. 433, 443. In *Goodlife Foods Ltd v Hall Fire Protection Ltd* [2018] EWCA Civ 1371, [2018] B.L.R. 491 at [101] Gross L.J. described the approach as the operation of a "sliding scale".

71k *Goodlife Foods Ltd v Hall Fire Protection Ltd* [2018] EWCA Civ 1371, [2018] B.L.R. 491 at [53].

71l *O'Brien v MGN Ltd* [2001] EWCA Civ 1279, [2002] C.L.C. 33 at [23].

71m Cases which appear to support the possibility that the requirement may apply to signed contracts include *Jaques v Lloyd D George & Partners Ltd* [1968] 1 W.L.R. 625, 630; *Ocean Chemical Transport Inc v Exnor Craggs Ltd* [2000] 1 Lloyd's Rep. 446, 454; *Amiri Flight Authority v BAE Systems Plc* [2003] EWCA Civ 1447, [2003] 2 Lloyd's Rep. 767 at [14]–[16]; *One World (GB) Ltd v Elite Mobile Ltd* [2012] EWHC 3706 (QB) at [52]–[58] and *Cargill International Trading Pte Ltd v Uttam Galva Steels Ltd* [2019] EWHC 476 (Comm) at [89]. But there is also authority which casts doubt on the existence of such an exception: *HIH Casualty and General Insurance Ltd v New Hampshire Insurance Co* [2001] EWCA Civ 735, [2001] 2 Lloyd's Rep. 161 at [209]; *Peekay Intermark Ltd v Australia and NZ Banking Group Ltd* [2006] EWCA Civ 386, [2006] 2 Lloyd's Rep. 511 at [43]; *Do-Buy 95 Ltd v National Westminster Bank Plc* [2010] EWHC 2862 (QB) at [91]; and *Bates v Post Office Ltd (No.3: Common Issues)* [2019] EWHC 606 (QB) at [1055(2)]. If there is such an exception it applies within very narrow limits (*Woodeson v Credit Suisse (UK) Ltd* [2018] EWCA Civ 1103 at [46]; *Higgins & Co Lawyers Ltd v Evans* [2019] EWHC 2809 (QB), [2020] 1 W.L.R. 141 at [75]–[79]) and it is unlikely to be invoked in the context of a contract between two commercial parties of roughly equal bargaining power. It is more likely to be invoked in the context of a consumer contract where the consumer had little or no time to read the document and was under pressure to sign it quickly (for a Canadian example in this category see *Tilden Rent-a-Car Co v Clendenning* (1978) 83 D.L.R. (3d) 400).

### Personal disability

*In line 3, after "inability to read", replace "our" with:*

the English 13-016

## 2. CLASSIFICATION OF TERMS

## (a) Conditions

### Conditions precedent

*To the end of paragraph, after "is not fulfilled.", add new footnote 121a:*

121a *O'Brien v TTT Moneycorp Ltd* [2019] EWHC 1491 (Comm) at [40]. 13-028

## (c) Intermediate Terms

### Instances of classification

*Replace footnote 157 with:*

157 *Grand China Logistics Holding (Group) Co Ltd v Spar Shipping AS* [2016] EWCA Civ 982, [2016] 2 Lloyd's Rep. 447 at [93]; *Ark Shipping Co LLC v Silverburn Shipping (IoM) Ltd* [2019] EWCA Civ 1161, [2019] 2 Lloyd's Rep. 603 at [81]. 13-035

### Classification of time stipulations

*Replace footnote 180 with:*

180 *Bunge Corp v Tradax Export SA* [1981] 1 W.L.R. 711, 716. It is in cases where there is an inter-dependence between the obligations of the parties that the term is most likely to be held to be a condition. Conversely, the absence of inter-dependence may be a factor relied upon by the court to support the conclusion that the term is intermediate: *Ark Shipping Co LLC v Silverburn Shipping (IoM) Ltd* [2019] EWCA Civ 1161, [2019] 2 Lloyd's Rep. 603 at [47]. 13-037

### Conclusion

*Replace footnote 207 with:*

13-040 [207] *Hongkong Fir Shipping Co Ltd v Kawasaki Kisen Kaisha Ltd* [1962] 2 Q.B. 26; *Cehave M.V. v Bremer Handelsgesellschaft mbH* [1976] Q.B. 44; *United Scientific Holdings Ltd v Burnley* [1978] A.C. 904, 928; *Bremer Handelsgesellschaft mbH v Vanden Avenne-Izegem PVBA* [1978] 2 Lloyd's Rep. 109, 113, 121, 128, 130; *Bunge Corp v Tradax Export SA* [1981] 1 W.L.R. 711, 715–716, 717, 719, 724; *Phibro Energy A.G. v Nissho Iwai Corp* [1990] 1 Lloyd's Rep. 38, 45, 58–59; *Grand China Logistics Holding (Group) Co Ltd v Spar Shipping AS* [2016] EWCA Civ 982, [2016] 2 Lloyd's Rep. 447 at [97], [99]; *Ark Shipping Co LLC v Silverburn Shipping (IoM) Ltd* [2019] EWCA Civ 1161, [2019] 2 Lloyd's Rep. 603 at [81]; *Duchy Farm Kennels Ltd v Steels* [2020] EWHC 1208 (QB), [2020] I.R.L.R. 632.

## 3. CONSTRUCTION OF TERMS

## (a) General Principles of Construction

### A summary of the applicable principles

*Replace footnote 236 with:*

13-047 [236] [2018] EWHC 163 (Comm), [2018] 1 Lloyd's Rep. 654 at [8]. Other helpful summaries of the approach adopted by the courts include *Greenhouse v Paysafe Financial Services Ltd* [2018] EWHC 3296 (Comm) at [11]; *Silverburn Shipping (IoM) Ltd v Ark Shipping Company LLC* [2019] EWHC 376 (Comm), [2019] 1 Lloyd's Rep. 554 at [25] and *Minera Las Bambas SA v Glencore Queensland Ltd* [2019] EWCA Civ 972 at [20].

## (c) The Matrix of Fact

### The "available background"

*Replace paragraph with:*

13-049 The courts will, in principle, look at all the circumstances surrounding the making of the contract and available to the parties (usually referred to as the "factual matrix" or "available background") which would assist in determining how the language of the document would have been understood by a reasonable person in their position. The range of materials on which the modern courts now draw is considerably wider as the ambit of the "factual matrix" has increased, permitting the court to draw upon a greater range of materials when seeking to put the words of the contract in their context and interpret them accordingly. The "available background" is limited to facts that were known or reasonably available to both (or all) of the parties to the contract; it does not suffice for this purpose to demonstrate that the facts were known only to one of the parties.[240] In determining what is "reasonably available" to both parties, the court should adopt a "restrained" approach given the "almost unlimited information and knowledge now available through the internet" and the fact that the parties are not subject to a duty to carry out investigations prior to entry into the contract.[240a] Rather, the question to be asked should focus on the knowledge a reasonable observer would have expected and believed both contracting parties to have had and each to have assumed the other to have had at the time of entry into the contract. It will not suffice to establish that the reasonable observer believed that the parties "might" have had such knowledge.[240b] But a court can take account of specialist or unusual knowledge which only parties entered into a contractual engagement of the sort in question might reasonably have been assumed to have had.[240c]

[240] *Arnold v Britton* [2015] UKSC 36, [2015] A.C. 1619 at [21]; *Kason Kek-Gardner Ltd v Process Components Ltd* [2017] EWCA Civ 2132 at [16]; *Spirit Energy Resources Ltd v Marathon Oil UK LLC* [2019] EWCA Civ 11 at [33].

[240a] *Lehman Brothers International (Europe) (In Administration) v Exotix Partners LLP* [2019] EWHC 2380 (Ch), [2020] 1 All E.R. (Comm) 635 at [110]; *Challinor v Juliet Bellis & Co* [2013] EWHC 347 (Ch) at [277].

[240b] *Challinor v Juliet Bellis & Co* [2013] EWHC 347 (Ch) at [279].

[240c] *Challinor v Juliet Bellis & Co* [2013] EWHC 347 (Ch) at [279]; *Hamid (t/a Hamid Properties) v Francis Bradshaw Partnership* [2013] EWCA Civ 470, [2013] B.L.R. 447 at [49].

## Public documents and standard form contracts

*Replace paragraph with:*

The "factual matrix" may weigh less heavily on the scales in the case of certain types of contract. One such example relates to "the interpretation of negotiable and registrable contracts or public documents".[248] Thus, the reasonable reader's background knowledge of a publicly registered document would include the fact that third parties might be expected to rely on the public information contained in the document but it would not ordinarily include matters which had not been included in the public document and remained private between the parties to the document.[249] In the case of a contract which is intended for standard use throughout a particular industry or market, the court is more likely to focus its attention on the background generally known to participants in the industry or the market and not on the background known to, or the understandings of, the individual parties to the particular transaction.[250] In such a case the standard form contract is not context-specific so that evidence of the particular factual background or matrix has a much more limited, if any, role to play. **13-051**

[248] *Cherry Tree Investments Ltd v Landmain Ltd* [2012] EWCA Civ 736, [2013] Ch. 305 at [124]. This point should not, however, be pushed too far given that otherwise there "is a modern tendency in the law to break down divisions in the rules on the interpretation of different kinds of document, both private and public, and to look for more general rules on how to ascertain the meaning of words": *Trump International Golf Club Scotland Ltd v Scottish Ministers* [2015] UKSC 74, [2016] 1 W.L.R. 85 at [33] and see to similar effect *Lambeth London Borough Council v Secretary of State for Housing, Communities and Local Government* [2019] UKSC 33, [2019] 1 W.L.R. 4317 at [16]–[19]. Thus there is no "bright line" to be drawn between public and private documents and the court must consider in each case the range of materials which it can permissibly draw upon when seeking to interpret the terms of the contract: *Pathway Finance Sarl v Defendants set out in Annex 1 to the Claim* [2020] EWHC 1191 (Ch) at [37].

[249] *Cherry Tree Investments Ltd v Landmain Ltd* [2012] EWCA Civ 736, [2013] Ch. 305 at [130].

[250] *AIB Group (UK) Ltd v Martin* [2001] UKHL 63, [2002] 1 W.L.R. 94 at [7]; *Lehman Brothers Special Financing Inc v National Power Corp* [2018] EWHC 487 (Comm), [2019] 1 All E.R. (Comm) 1027 at [36]–[40]; *Deutsche Trustee Co Ltd v Duchess VI Clo BV* [2019] EWHC 778 (Ch), [2019] 2 All E.R. (Comm) 530 at [31]; *Netherlands v Deutsche Bank AG* [2019] EWCA Civ 771 at [56]; *Lamesa Investments Ltd v Cynergy Bank Ltd* [2020] EWCA Civ 821 at [19]–[21].

## Pre-contractual negotiations

*Replace first paragraph with:*

Although the range of materials on which a court can draw when examining the "factual matrix" is broad, it is not without its limits. An important limit on the range of admissible materials is the parties' pre-contractual negotiations. While evidence of the facts about which the parties were negotiating is admissible to assist in the interpretation of the contract, in *Chartbrook Ltd v Persimmon Homes Ltd*[251] the House of Lords confirmed the well-established principle that the court is not entitled to look at what the parties said or did whilst the matter was in negotiation for the purposes of drawing inferences about what the contract means. The same principle **13-052** also applies to the admissibility of drafts or preliminary documents in aid of interpretation.[252] This does not exclude the use of such evidence to support a claim for rectification[253] or estoppel[254] or to establish that a fact which may be relevant as background was known to the parties.[255] However, as Lord Clarke pointed out in *Oceanbulk Shipping & Trading SA v TMT Asia Ltd*,[256] it may sometimes not be a straightforward task to distinguish between material which forms part of the pre-contractual negotiations which is part of the factual matrix and therefore admissible as an aid to interpretation[257] and material which is not part of the factual matrix and is not therefore admissible. In the former case the fact that the negotiations are "without prejudice" is immaterial.[258]

*Prenn v Simmonds*[259] Lord Wilberforce summed up the position as follows:

> "In my opinion, then, evidence of negotiations, or of the parties' intentions, and a fortiori of [the claimant's] intentions, ought not to be received, and evidence should be restricted to evidence of the factual background known to the parties at or before the date of the contract, including evidence of the 'genesis' and objectively the 'aim' of the transaction."

The phrase "'genesis' and ... the 'aim' of the transaction" has been held to be a "composite phrase" which enables the court to consider the circumstances which led to the execution of the contract in order to identify the purpose of the transaction and the construe the language used in the light of that purpose but which does not entitle a court to seek to rely on what was said during the course of pre-contractual negotiations for the purpose of drawing inferences about what the contract should be understood to mean.[259a]

[251] [2009] UKHL 38, [2009] 1 A.C. 1101. See *Inglis v Buttery* (1878) 3 App. Cas. 552, 558; *Leggott v Barrett* (1880) 15 Ch. D. 306, 311; *Millbourn v Lyons* [1914] 2 Ch. 231, 240; *Davis Contractors Ltd v Fareham U.D.C.* [1956] A.C. 696; *Prenn v Simmonds* [1971] 1 W.L.R. 1381, 1385; *Moschi v Lep Air Services Ltd* [1973] A.C. 331, 354; *L.G. Schuler A.G. v Wickman Machine Tools Ltd* [1974] A.C. 235; *Arrale v Costain Civil Engineering Ltd* [1976] 1 Lloyd's Rep. 98, 101, 103, 105; *The Raven* [1980] 2 Lloyd's Rep. 266, 270; *Sudatlantica Navegacion SA v Devamar Shipping Corp* [1985] 2 Lloyd's Rep. 271, 274; *Investors Compensation Scheme Ltd v West Bromwich Building Society* [1998] 1 W.L.R. 896, 913; *Aqua Design & Play International Ltd v Kier Regional Ltd* [2002] EWCA Civ 797, [2003] B.L.R. 111; *P&S Platt Ltd v Crouch* [2003] EWCA Civ 1110, [2004] 1 P. & C.R. 18; *NBTY Europe Ltd v Nutricia International BV* [2005] EWHC 734 (Comm), [2005] 2 Lloyd's Rep. 350 at [29]–[32]; *Absalom v TCRU Ltd* [2005] EWHC 1090 (Comm), [2005] 2 Lloyd's Rep. 735 at [25]; *Beazer Homes Ltd v Stroude* [2005] EWCA Civ 265, [2005] N.P.C. 45; *Dornoch Ltd v Mauritius Union Assurance Co Ltd* [2006] EWCA Civ 389, [2006] 2 Lloyd's Rep. 475 at [31]–[37]; *Nearfield Ltd v Lincoln Nominees Ltd* [2006] EWHC 2421 (Ch), [2007] 1 All E.R. (Comm) 441; *Pratt v Aigaion Insurance Co SA* [2008] EWCA Civ 1314, [2009] 1 Lloyd's Rep. 225 at [9]; *ING Lease (UK) Ltd v Harwood* [2007] EWHC 2292 (QB), [2008] Bus. L.R. 762; *Oceanbulk Shipping and Trading SA v TMT Asia Ltd* [2010] UKSC 44, [2011] 1 Lloyd's Rep. 96 at [46]; *Ted Baker Plc v AXA Insurance UK Plc* [2012] EWHC 1406 (Comm). But see *Canterbury Golf International Ltd v Yoshimoto* [2001] N.Z.L.R. 523, [2002] UKPC 40 at [25]; and the observations of Lord Nicholls in *Bank of Credit and Commerce International v Ali* [2001] UKHL 8, [2002] 1 A.C. 251 at [25], and in (2005) 121 L.Q.R. 577 at 582–588; *Proforce Recruit Ltd v Rugby Group Ltd* [2006] EWCA Civ 69 at [33]–[35]; McMeel (2003) 119 L.Q.R. 272. For the procedure to be adopted where evidence of pre-contractual negotiations is sought to be adduced, see *Anglo-Continental Educational Group (GB) Ltd v Capital Homes (Southern) Ltd* [2009] EWCA Civ 218, [2009] C.P. Rep. 30.

[252] *Inglis v Buttery* (1878) 3 App. Cas. 552; *National Bank of Australasia v Falkingham* [1902] A.C. 585, 591; *Youell v Bland Welch & Co Ltd* [1992] 2 Lloyd's Rep. 127. But an earlier contract may be looked at as part of the factual background for the purpose of interpreting a later contract, although this may be of limited utility where the later contract is intended to supersede the earlier one: *HIH Casualty and General Insurance Ltd v New Hampshire Insurance Co* [2001] EWCA Civ 735, [2001] 2 Lloyd's Rep. 161 at [83]; *Electrosteel Castings Ltd v Scan-Trans Shipping* [2002] EWHC 1993 (Comm), [2003] 1 Lloyd's Rep. 190 at [198]; *Egan v Static Control Components (Europe) Ltd* [2004] EWCA Civ 392, [2004] 2 Lloyd's Rep. 429 at [35]; *Multiplex Constructions (UK) Ltd v Cleveland Bridge (UK) Ltd (No.2)* [2007] EWHC 145 (TCC), (2007) 111 Con. L.R. 48 at [150]; *Medenta Finance Ltd v Hitachi Capital (UK) Plc* [2019] EWHC 516 (Comm) at [49]. cf. *Nearfield Ltd v Lincoln Nominees Ltd* [2006] EWHC 2421 (Ch) at [68]–[70].

[253] See above, para.3-057.

[254] See above, para.4-108. cf. *Ted Baker Plc v AXA Insurance UK Plc* [2012] EWHC 1406 (Comm) at [118].

[255] *Chartbrook Ltd v Persimmon Homes Ltd* [2009] UKHL 38, [2009] 1 A.C. 1101 at [42]; *Tartsinis v Navona Management Co* [2015] EWHC 57 (Comm) at [14]. For this purpose a fact known to both parties means "some objective part of the background matrix of fact other than a mere negotiating position taken by one of the parties, however vigorously expressed": *Northrop Grumman Missions Systems Europe Ltd v BAE Systems (Al Diriyah C4I) Ltd* [2015] EWCA Civ 844, [2015] B.L.R. 657 at [31].

[256] [2010] UKSC 44, [2011] 1 Lloyd's Rep. 96 at [39]. See to similar effect *Merthyr (South Wales) Ltd v Merthyr Tydfil County Borough Council* [2019] EWCA Civ 526 at [55].

[257] *Chartbrook Ltd v Persimmon Homes Ltd* [2009] UKHL 38, [2009] 1 A.C. 1101 at [45]; *Azimut-Benetti SpA v Healey* [2010] EWHC 2234 (Comm), [2010] T.C.L.R. 7; *Proteus Property Partners Ltd v South Africa Property Opportunities Plc* [2011] EWHC 768 (QB); *Oceanbulk Shipping & Trading SA v TMT Asia Ltd* [2010] UKSC 44, [2011] 1 Lloyd's Rep. 96; *Dean & Dean Solicitors v Dionissiou-Moussaoui* [2011] EWCA Civ 1331, [2012] 2 Costs L.O. 94.

[258] *Oceanbulk Shipping & Trading SA v TMT Asia Ltd* [2010] UKSC 44, [2011] 1 Lloyd's Rep. 96.

[259] [1971] 1 W.L.R. 1381.

[259a] *Merthyr (South Wales) Ltd v Merthyr Tydfil County Borough Council* [2019] EWCA Civ 526 at [53]–[54]; *NHS Commissioning Board v Vasant* [2019] EWCA Civ 1245, [2020] 1 All E.R. (Comm) 799 at [28].

## (d) The Meaning of the Language Used by the Parties

### Adoption of the ordinary meaning of words

*Replace paragraph with:*

The starting point in construing a contract is that words are to be given their ordinary and natural meaning. The interpretative exercise involves the court in identifying what the parties meant: **13-055**

> "... through the eyes of a reasonable reader, and, save perhaps in a very unusual case, that meaning is most obviously to be gleaned from the language of the provision."[279]

This is not necessarily the dictionary meaning of the word,[280] but that in which it is generally understood. The courts assume that the parties have used language in the way that reasonable persons ordinarily do. So terms are:

> "... to be understood in their plain, ordinary, and popular sense, unless they have generally in respect to the subject matter, as by the known usage of trade, or the like, acquired a peculiar sense distinct from the popular sense of the same words; or unless the context evidently points out that they must in the particular instance, and in order to effectuate the immediate intention of the parties to that contract, be understood in some other special and peculiar sense."[281]

[279] *Arnold v Britton* [2015] UKSC 36, [2015] A.C. 1619 at [17].

[280] An emphasis on the natural and ordinary meaning of the words used by the parties is not to be equated with "an unduly literal or semantic interpretation" (*Fomento de Construcciones y Contratas SA v Black Diamond Offshore Ltd* [2016] EWCA Civ 1141, [2017] 1 B.C.L.C. 196 at [12]) nor does it permit an over-literal interpretation of one provision without regard to the whole of the document, particularly in the case of complex documents which have been put into circulation in the market (*Metlife Seguros de Retiro SA v JP Morgan Chase Bank, National Association* [2016] EWCA Civ 1248). The normal or dictionary meaning of the words used may yield to their context (*Savills (UK) Ltd v Blacker* [2017] EWCA Civ 68 at [33]), although the balance to be struck between the natural and ordinary meaning of the words and their context is not always an easy one to strike.

[281] *Robertson v French* (1803) 4 East 130, 135. See also *Shore v Wilson* (1842) 9 Cl. & Fin. 355, 527; *Mallan v May* (1844) 13 M. & W. 511, 517; *Tielens v Hooper* (1850) 5 Ex. 830; *Grey v Pearson* (1857) 6 H.L. Cas. 61, 78, 106; *Beard v Moira Colliery Co* [1915] 1 Ch. 257, 268; *Royal Greek Government v Minister of Transport* [1949] 1 K.B. 525, 528; *Melanesian Mission Trust Board v Australian Mutual*

*Provident Society* [1997] 1 N.Z.L.R. 391, 394; *Charter Reinsurance Co Ltd v Fagan* [1997] A.C. 313, 384; *BP Exploration Operating Co Ltd v Kvaerner Oilfield Products Ltd* [2004] EWHC 999 (Comm), [2005] 1 Lloyd's Rep. 307 at [93]; *Thames Valley Power Ltd v Total Gas & Power Ltd* [2003] EWHC 2208 (Comm), [2006] 1 Lloyd's Rep. 441 at [25]; *Forrest v Glasser* [2006] EWCA Civ 1086, [2006] 2 Lloyd's Rep. 392 at [21]; *Pratt v Aigaion Insurance Co SA* [2008] EWCA Civ 1314, [2009] 1 Lloyd's Rep. 225 at [12]. Contrast *Staffordshire A.H.A. v South Staffordshire Waterworks Co* [1978] 1 W.L.R. 1387, 1394; *Charter Reinsurance Co Ltd v Fagan* [1997] A.C. 313, 391; *NHS Commissioning Board v Vasant* [2019] EWCA Civ 1245, [2020] 1 All E.R. (Comm) 799 at [42].

### Special meaning

*Replace footnote 290 with:*

13-058 [290] *Shore v Wilson* (1842) 9 Cl. & F. 355, 555; *Smith v Doe* (1821) 2 B. & B. 473, 550, 602; *Payne v Haine* (1847) 16 M. & W. 541; *Myers v Sarl* (1860) 3 E. & E. 306; *Perrin v Morgan* [1943] A.C. 399, 421; *Levermore v Jobey* [1956] 1 W.L.R. 697; *Sydall v Castings Ltd* [1967] 1 Q.B. 302; *NHS Commissioning Board v Vasant* [2019] EWCA Civ 1245, [2020] 1 All E.R. (Comm) 799 at [42]; cf. *Hospital for Sick Children v Walt Disney Productions Inc* [1968] Ch. 52; *Zeus Tradition Marine Ltd v Bell* [1999] 1 Lloyd's Rep. 703, 706. See below, para.13-131.

## (e) The Need to Have Regard to the Contract as a Whole

### Control by recitals

*Replace footnote 313 with:*

13-064 [313] *Leggott v Barrett* (1880) 15 Ch. D. 306, 311; *Re Moon Ex p. Dawes* (1886) 17 Q.B.D. 275, 286. See also *Young v Smith* (1865) L.R. 1 Eq. 180, 183; *Dawes v Tredwell* (1881) 18 Ch. D. 354, 358; *Foakes v Beer* (1884) 9 App. Cas. 605; *Australian Joint Stock Bank v Bailey* [1899] A.C. 396; *Royal Insurance Co Ltd v G. & S. Assured Investments Co Ltd* [1972] 1 Lloyd's Rep. 267, 274; *Rutter v Charles Sharpe & Co* [1979] 1 W.L.R. 1429, 1433; *Mr H TV Ltd v ITV2 Ltd* [2015] EWHC 2840 (Comm) at [38]; *Qatar National Bank Qpsc v The Owner of the Yacht Force India* [2020] EWHC 103 (Admlty) at [41].

### Alterations and deletions

*Replace paragraph with:*

13-067 As has been noted, evidence of prior negotiations is normally not admissible to construe a written contract and drafts will not be admitted either to alter the language of the contract or to help in its interpretation.[323] So, where an instrument appears to have been altered while the parties were negotiating, the court cannot look at it as it originally stood compared with the alterations which were made in it, to see whether those alterations will throw any light upon the question of interpretation.[324] However, when the parties use a printed form, and delete parts of it, there is some authority for the view that regard may be paid to what has been deleted as part of the surrounding circumstances in the light of which the meaning of the words which they chose to leave in is to be ascertained.[325] But there is weighty authority to the contrary.[326] In any event, it is doubtful whether the court can look at the words deleted except to resolve an ambiguity in the words retained.[327] The position may nevertheless be different where alterations are made to an already concluded agreement. In *Punjab National Bank v De Boinville*[328] Staughton L.J. said:

> "... if the parties to a concluded agreement subsequently agree in express terms that some words in it are to be replaced by others, one can have regard to all aspects of the subsequent agreement in construing the contract, including the deletions, even in a case which is not, or not wholly, concerned with a printed form."

Also where a one-off contract has been drafted by reference to a standard form contract which formed the basis for its drafting, the court can take into account the omission from the one-off contract of words that appear in the standard form contract in order to resolve an ambiguity in the former document.[329]

[323] See above, para.13-052.

[324] *Inglis v Buttery* (1878) 3 App. Cas. 552, 558, 569, 576; *Channel Islands Ferries Ltd v Sealink UK Ltd* [1987] 1 Lloyd's Rep. 559, 577 (affirmed [1988] 1 Lloyd's Rep. 323); *Health and Case Management Ltd v Physiotherapy Network Ltd* [2018] EWHC 869 (QB) at [7].

[325] *Baumwoll Manufactur von Scheibler v Gilchrest & Co* [1892] 1 Q.B. 253, 256; cf. [1893] A.C. 8, 15; *Gray v Carr* (1871) L.R. 6 Q.B. 522, 524, 529; *Stanton v Richardson* (1874) L.R. 9 C.P. 390; *Glynn v Margetson* [1893] A.C. 351, 357; *Caffin v Aldridge* [1895] 2 Q.B. 648, 650; *Santay & Co v Cox, McEllen & Co* (1921) 10 Ll.L. Rep. 459, 460; *Bailey Sons & Co v Ross, Smythe & Co* [1940] 3 All E.R. 60; *Louis Dreyfus et Cie v Parnaso Compania Naviera SA* [1959] 1 Q.B. 498; *London & Overseas Freighters Ltd v Timber Shipping Co SA* [1972] A.C. 1, 15; *Mottram Consultants Ltd v Bernard Sunley Ltd* [1975] 2 Lloyd's Rep. 197, 209; *Punjab National Bank v De Boinville* [1992] 1 W.L.R. 1138, 1148.

[326] *Ambatielos v Jurgens* [1923] A.C. 175, 185; *Sassoon v International Banking Corp* [1927] A.C. 711, 721; *City & Westminster Properties (1934) Ltd v Mudd* [1959] Ch. 129; *Finzel, Berry & Co v Eastcheap Dried Fruit Co* [1962] 1 Lloyd's Rep. 370, affirmed [1962] 2 Lloyd's Rep. 11; *Compania Naviera Termar SA v Tradax Export SA* [1965] 1 Lloyd's Rep. 198, 204; *Borthwick (Thomas) (Glasgow) Ltd v Bunge & Co Ltd* [1969] 1 Lloyd's Rep. 17; *Tradax Export v Volkswagenwerk* [1969] 2 Q.B. 599, 607; *Ben Shipping Co (Pte) Ltd v An-Board Bainne* [1986] 2 Lloyd's Rep. 285, 291; *Wates Construction (London) Ltd v Franthom Property Ltd* (1991) 7 Const. L.J. 243; *Rhodia Chirex Ltd v Laker Vent Engineering Ltd* [2003] EWCA Civ 1859, [2004] B.L.R. 75; *Mapani Copper Mines Plc v Millennium Underwriting Ltd* [2008] EWHC 1331 (Comm), [2009] Lloyd's Rep. I.R. 158.

[327] *Louis Dreyfus et Cie v Parnaso Cia. Naviera SA* [1959] 1 Q.B. 498, reversed on other grounds [1960] 2 Q.B. 49; *Mopani Copper Mines Plc v Millennium Underwriting Ltd* [2008] EWHC 1331 (Comm), [2008] All E.R. (Comm) 976 at [120]; *Bou-Simon v BGC Brokers LP* [2018] EWCA Civ 1525, [2019] 1 All E.R. (Comm) 955 at [28]–[29] and [36].

[328] [1992] 1 W.L.R. 1138, 1149. See also *Centrepoint Custodians Pty Ltd v Lidgerwood Investments Pty Ltd* [1990] V.R. 411; *Trasimex Holdings SA v Addax* BV [1997] 1 Lloyd's Rep. 610, 614; *HIH Casualty and General Insurance Ltd v New Hampshire Insurance Co* [2001] EWCA Civ 735, [2001] 2 Lloyd's Rep. 161 at [83], [84]; *KPMG v Network Rail Infrastructure Ltd* [2007] EWCA Civ 363, [2007] Bus. L.R. 1336; *Medenta Finance Ltd v Hitachi Capital (UK) Plc* [2019] EWHC 516 (Comm) at [49]. However, even in those cases where evidence of a deletion is admissible, the court is likely to exercise some caution when determining the assistance which it can derive from the deletion of certain words from a subsequent contract; *Mineralimportexport v Eastern Mediterranean Maritime Ltd ("The Golden Leader")* [1980] 2 Lloyd's Rep. 573, 575; *Health and Case Management Ltd v Physiotherapy Network Ltd* [2018] EWHC 869 (QB) at [71]–[73] and [78].

[329] *Team Services v Kier Management and Design* (1994) 63 B.L.R. 76.

## Inconsistent or repugnant clauses

*Replace paragraph with:*

Where the different parts of an instrument are inconsistent, effect must be given **13-070** to that part which is calculated to carry into effect the purpose of the contract as gathered from the instrument as a whole and the available background, and that part which would defeat it must be rejected.[333] The old rule was, in such a case, that the earlier clause was to be received and the later rejected[334]; but this rule was a mere rule of thumb, totally unscientific, and out of keeping with the modern construction of documents. When considering how to interpret a contract in the case of alleged inconsistency, the courts distinguish between a case where the contract makes provision for the possibility of inconsistency and the case where there is no such provision. In the latter case the contract documents should as far as possible be read as complementing each other and therefore as expressing the parties' intentions in a consistent and coherent manner.[335] However, matters are otherwise in the case where there is a term in the contract dealing with the possibility of inconsistency.[336] The parties may do this by including in their contract an order of precedence term which will determine how any conflict between the terms of the contract is to be resolved.[336a] In other cases the court should approach the interpretation of the contract without any pre-conceived assumptions and should neither strive to avoid nor to find an inconsistency but rather should approach the documents in a "cool and objective spirit to see whether there is inconsistency or not".[337] To be inconsistent a term must contradict another term or be in conflict with it, such that effect cannot fairly be given to both clauses.[338] A term may also be rejected if it is repugnant to the remainder of the contract.[339] However, an effort should be made to give effect to every clause in the agreement and not to reject a clause unless it is manifestly inconsistent with or repugnant to the rest of the agreement.[340] Thus, if there is a personal covenant and a proviso that the covenantor shall not be personally liable under the covenant, the proviso is inconsistent and void.[341] But if a clause merely limits or qualifies without destroying altogether the obligation created by another clause, the two are to be read together and effect is to be given to the contract as disclosed by the instrument as a whole.[342]

[333] *Walker v Giles* (1848) 6 C.B. 662, 702; *Love v Rowtor Steamship Co Ltd* [1916] 2 A.C. 527, 535; *Sabah Flour and Feedmills Sdn Bhd v Comfez Ltd* [1988] 2 Lloyd's Rep. 18; cf. *Taylor v Rive Droite Music Ltd* [2005] EWCA Civ 1300, [2006] E.M.L.R. 4.

[334] Shep.Touch. 88; *Doe d. Leicester v Biggs* (1809) 2 Taunt. 109, 113; *Forbes v Git* [1922] 1 A.C. 256, 259.

[335] *RWE Npower Renewables Ltd v JN Bentley Ltd* [2014] EWCA Civ 150.

[336] *Pagnan SpA v Tradax Ocean Transportation SA* [1987] 2 Lloyd's Rep. 342; *Alexander (as representative of the "Property 118 Action Group") v West Bromwich Mortgage Co Ltd* [2016] EWCA Civ 496, [2017] 1 All E.R. 942.

[336a] *Triple Point Technology Inc v PTT Public Co Ltd* [2019] EWCA Civ 230, [2019] 1 W.L.R. 3549 at [57].

[337] *Pagnan SpA v Tradax Ocean Transportation SA* [1987] 2 Lloyd's Rep. 342, 350; *Alexander (as representative of the "Property 118 Action Group") v West Bromwich Mortgage Co Ltd* [2016] EWCA Civ 496, [2017] 1 All E.R. 942.

[338] *Pagnan SpA v Tradax Ocean Transportation SA* [1987] 2 Lloyd's Rep. 342, 350; *Cobelfret Bulk Carriers NV v Swissmarine Services SA* [2009] EWHC 2883 (Comm), [2010] 1 Lloyd's Rep. 317 at [20]; *Public Company Rise v Nibulon SA* [2015] EWHC 684 (Comm); *Alexander (as representative of the "Property 118 Action Group") v West Bromwich Mortgage Co Ltd* [2016] EWCA Civ 496, [2017] 1 All E.R. 942; *Apache North Sea Ltd v Euroil Exploration Ltd* [2019] EWHC 3241 (Comm) at [14].

[339] *Adamastos Shipping Co Ltd v Anglo-Saxon Petroleum Co Ltd* [1959] A.C. 133; *Mercuria Energy Trading Pte Ltd v Citibank NA* [2015] EWHC 1481 (Comm), [2015] 1 C.L.C. 999 at [76].

[340] *Barton v Fitzgerald* (1812) 15 East 529, 541; *Bush v Watkins* (1851) 14 Beav. 425, 432; *Société Co-operative Suisse des Céréales et Matières Fourrageres v La Plata Cereal Co SA* (1947) 80 Ll.L. Rep. 530, 537; *Bremer Handelsgesellschaft mbH v J.H. Rayner & Co Ltd* [1979] 2 Lloyd's Rep. 216; *Sudatlantica Navegacion SA v Devamar Shipping Corp* [1985] 2 Lloyd's Rep. 271; *Pagnan SpA v Tradax Ocean Transportation SA* [1987] 2 Lloyd's Rep. 342, 349; *STX Pan Ocean Co Ltd v Ugland Bulk Transport AS* [2007] EWHC 1317 (Comm), [2008] 1 Lloyd's Rep. 86 at [18]; *RWE Npower Renewables Ltd v JN Bentley Ltd* [2014] EWCA Civ 150.

[341] *Furnivall v Coombes* (1843) 5 M. & G. 736. See also *Watling v Lewis* [1911] 1 Ch. 414; *Re Tewkesbury Gas Co* [1911] 2 Ch. 279 (affirmed [1912] 1 Ch. 1).

[342] Quoted with approval in *Yuchai Dongte Special Purpose Automobile Co Ltd v Suisse Credit Capital (2009) Ltd* [2018] EWHC 2580 (Comm), [2019] 1 Lloyd's Rep. 457 at [77]. See *Williams v Hathaway* (1877) 6 Ch. D. 544; *Forbes v Git* [1922] 1 A.C. 256, 259; *Walton (Grain & Shipping) Ltd v British Italian Trading Co Ltd* [1959] 1 Lloyd's Rep. 223, 227; *Pagnan SpA v Tradax Ocean Transportation SA* [1987] 2 Lloyd's Rep. 342, 351; *Alexander (as representative of the "Property 118 Action Group") v West Bromwich Mortgage Co Ltd* [2016] EWCA Civ 496, [2017] 1 All E.R. 942; *MT Højgaard A/S v E.ON Climate & Renewables UK Robin Rigg East Ltd* [2017] UKSC 59, [2017] B.L.R. 477. It is a question of construction for the court whether the multiple provisions which cover the same or similar territory are all effective to impose the several obligations that their terms suggest, or whether the effect of one or more provisions is to modify or exclude the apparent meaning of another provision of the contract: *125 OBS (Nominees1) v Lend Lease Construction (Europe) Ltd* [2017] EWHC 25 (TCC), 174 Con. L.R. 105 at [99].

## (f) The Significance of the Nature, Formality and Quality of the Drafting of the Contract

### Long term or "relational" contracts

*Replace paragraph with:*

There are no special rules of interpretation applicable to long-term or "relational"[351] contracts, although the courts may incline towards a more flexible approach which recognises the need for such contracts to be drafted in broad terms and be slow to conclude that the contract, or a term of the contract, is too vague to be enforced.[352] However, the courts may require the parties to such contracts to "adopt a reasonable approach in accordance with what is obviously the long-term purpose of the contract" and will not expect them to seek to take advantage of any "infelicities and oddities" in the drafting of the contract "in order to disrupt the project and maximise their own gain".[353] **13-074**

[351] The characteristics of a "relational" contract were set out in non-exhaustive terms by Fraser J. in *Bates v Post Office Ltd (No.3: Common Issues)* [2019] EWHC 606 (QB) at [725]–[726]. In broad terms a relational contract may be defined as a long-term contract which is very often co-operative in nature and which is characterised by a significant degree of flexibility.

[352] *Globe Motors Inc v TRW Lucas Varity Electric Steering Ltd* [2016] EWCA Civ 396, [2017] 1 All E.R. (Comm) 601 at [64]–[68]; *Teesside Gas Transportation Ltd v CATS North Sea Ltd* [2019] EWHC 1220 (Comm) at [38].

[353] *Amey Birmingham Highways Ltd v Birmingham City Council* [2018] EWCA Civ 264, [2018] B.L.R. 225 at [93].

## (g) Two Possible Meanings

### Saving the document

*Replace paragraph with:*

If the words used in an agreement are susceptible of two meanings, one of which would validate the instrument or the particular clause in the instrument, and the other render it void, ineffective or meaningless, the former sense is to be adopted. This principle is often expressed in the phrase *ut res magis valeat cum pereat*[358] and it applies where there is a "realistic" alternative construction of the words that are in dispute.[358a] Thus, if by a particular construction the agreement would be rendered ineffectual and the apparent object of the contract would be frustrated, but another construction, though in itself less appropriate looking to the words only, would produce a different effect, the latter interpretation is to be applied, if that is how the agreement would be understood by a reasonable person with a knowledge of the commercial purpose and background of the transaction.[359] So, where the words of a guarantee were capable of expressing either a past or a concurrent consideration, the court adopted the latter construction, because the former would render the instrument void.[360] If one construction makes the contract lawful and the other unlawful, the former is to be preferred. Thus a bond conditioned "to assign all offices" will be construed to apply to such offices as are by law assignable.[361] **13-078**

[358] *Verba ita sunt intelligenda ut res magis valeat cum pereat*: Bac. Max. 3; Noy. Max. 50. The judicial preference would now appear to be to consider the principle "without reference to its original formulation in Latin": *Egon Zehnder Ltd v Tillman* [2019] UKSC 32, [2020] A.C. 1543 at [38].

[358a] *Egon Zehnder Ltd v Tillman* [2019] UKSC 32, [2020] A.C. 1543 at [42]. The test does not require that the two interpretations be "equally plausible" but it is not so liberal that it is satisfied where there is "an element of ambiguity" to the term in dispute. It was held (at [42]) that to require "equal plausibility" was "to make unnecessary demands on the court and to set access to the principle too narrowly"

whereas "an element of ambiguity" was held to "countenance too great a departure from the otherwise probable meaning".

[359] *Solly v Forbes* (1820) 2 Brod. & Bing. 38, 48. See also Co.Litt. 42a; *Mills v Dunham* [1891] 1 Ch. 576, 590; *Lancashire CC v Municipal Mutual Insurance Ltd* [1996] 3 All E.R. 545, 553, 557; *Bank of Credit and Commerce International SA v Ali* [2001] UKHL 8, [2002] 1 A.C. 251, 269; *Multiplex Construction (UK) Ltd v Honeywell Control Systems Ltd* [2007] EWHC 447 (TCC), [2007] B.L.R. 195 at [57]–[58]; *Beckett Investment Management Group Ltd v Hall* [2007] EWCA Civ 613, [2007] I.C.R. 1539; *Pioneer Freight Futures Co Ltd v TMT Asia Ltd (No.2)* [2011] EWHC 1888 (Comm), [2011] 2 Lloyd's Rep. 565 at [574].

[360] *Haigh v Brooks* (1839) 10 A. & E. 309; *Goldshede v Swan* (1847) 1 Exch. 154; *Steele v Hoe* (1849) 14 Q.B. 431; *Broom v Batchelor* (1856) 1 H. & N. 255. See also *Rowell Leakey & Co v Scottish Provident Institution* [1927] 1 Ch. 55, 65 (insurance policy).

[361] *Harrington v Kloprogge* (1785) 2 B. & B. 678, note (a). See also *Fausset v Carpenter* (1831) 2 Dow. & Cl. 232; *Lewis v Davison* (1839) 4 M. & W. 654. The same principle applies to the performance of a contract: if a payment is made in performance of a contract partly legal and partly illegal it is presumed that it is made in performance of the legal part of the contract: *A. Smith & Son (Bognor Regis) Ltd v Walker* [1952] 2 Q.B. 319; *Cantor Art Services Ltd v Kenneth Bieber Photography Ltd* [1969] 1 W.L.R. 1226.

## (h) A Unitary and Iterative Approach

### Unitary

*Replace paragraph with:*

13-079 The interpretation or construction of a contract has been said to be:

> "… one unitary exercise in which the court must consider the language used and ascertain what a reasonable person, that is a person who has all the background knowledge which would reasonably have been available to the parties in the situation in which they were at the time of the contract, would have understood the parties to have meant."[362]

The principles which govern the construction of contracts are the same at law and in equity,[363] for simple contracts and for specialties.[364]

[362] *Rainy Sky SA v Kookmin Bank* [2011] UKSC 50, [2011] 1 W.L.R. 2900 at [21]. See also *Starlight Shipping Co v Allianz Marine and Aviation Versicherungs AG* [2014] EWHC 3068 (Comm), [2014] 2 Lloyd's Rep. 579 at [50]; *Arnold v Britton* [2015] UKSC 36, [2015] A.C. 1613 at [76]–[77]; *Wood v Capita Insurance Services Ltd* [2017] UKSC 24, [2017] A.C. 1173 at [11]; *Bluebon Ltd v Ageas (UK) Ltd* [2017] EWHC 3301 (Comm) at [30]; *Murray Holdings Ltd v Oscatello Investments Ltd* [2018] EWHC 162 (Ch) at [17] and [40]; *Pease v Henderson Administration Ltd* [2019] EWCA Civ 158 at [49]; *Lamesa Investments Ltd v Cynergy Bank Ltd* [2020] EWCA Civ 821 at [36]–[46].

[363] *Hotham v East India Co* (1787) Doug. 272, 277; *Eaton v Lyon* (1798) 3 Ves. Jr. 690, 692; *Re Terry and White's Contract* (1886) 32 Ch. D. 14, 21; *Bank of Credit and Commerce International SA v Ali* [2001] UKHL 8, [2002] 1 A.C. 251 at [25]; *Rainy Sky SA v Kookmin Bank* [2011] UKSC 50, [2011] 1 W.L.R. 2900 at [28]; *Starlight Shipping Co v Allianz Marine and Aviation Versicherungs AG* [2014] EWHC 3068 (Comm), [2014] 2 Lloyd's Rep. 579 at [50].

[364] *Seddon v Senate* (1810) 13 East 63, 74; *Total Transport Corp v Arcadia Petroleum Ltd* [1998] 1 Lloyd's Rep. 351, 362.

### Iterative

*Replace footnote 365 with:*

13-080 [365] *Wood v Capita Insurance Services Ltd* [2017] UKSC 24, [2017] A.C. 1173 at [12]. See also *Rainy Sky SA v Kookmin Bank* [2011] UKSC 50, [2011] 1 W.L.R. 2900 at [28]; *Napier Park European Credit Opportunities Fund Ltd v Harbourmaster Pro-Rata CLO 2 B V* [2014] EWCA Civ 984 at [31]–[32]; *BG Global Energy Ltd v Talisman Sinopec Energy UK Ltd* [2015] EWHC 110 (Comm) at [24]; *Arnold v Britton* [2015] UKSC 36, [2015] A.C. 1619 at [77]; *Europa Plus SCA SIF v Anthracite Investments (Ireland) Plc* [2016] EWHC 437 (Comm) at [29]; *AL Challis Ltd v British Gas Trading Ltd* [2017] EWCA Civ 1972 at [24]–[34]; *Khanty-Mansiysk Recoveries Ltd v Forsters LLP* [2018] EWCA Civ 89, [2018] P.N.L.R. 20 at [21]; *CCUK Finance Ltd v Barclays Bank Plc* [2018] EWHC 304 (Comm) at [26]; *Reliance Industries Ltd v Union of India* [2018] EWHC 822 (Comm), [2018] 1 Lloyd's Rep. 562 at [32];

*Deutsche Trustee Co Ltd v Duchess VI Clo BV* [2019] EWHC 778 (Ch), [2019] 2 All E.R. (Comm) 530 at [31] and *Pease v Henderson Administration Ltd* [2019] EWCA Civ 158 at [49]. See also Grabiner (2012) 128 L.Q.R. 41.

## (i) The Balancing Exercise and the Role of Business Common Sense

### Striking the balance

*Replace footnote 369 with:*

369 *Wood v Capita Insurance Services Ltd* [2017] UKSC 24, [2017] A.C. 1173 at [11]. For an example of this balancing process see *ACON Equity Management LLC v Apple Bodco Ltd* [2019] EWHC 2750 (Comm). **13-081**

### Grammatical errors

*Replace footnote 370 with:*

370 (1882) 8 App. Cas. 822. See also *Wills v Wright* (1677) 2 Mod. 285; *Waugh v Middleton* (1853) 8 Exch. 352, 356; *Vitol E&P Ltd v New Age (African Global Energy) Ltd* [2018] EWHC 1580 (Comm) at [28] ("punctuation may be misunderstood, erroneously used or overlooked"). But it does not follow from this that punctuation is irrelevant. So, for example, the use or absence of capital letters, may assume considerable significance in the case where capitalisation evidences that the term was used in its defined sense, whereas lack of capitalisation may suggest that the term has not been used in its defined sense: *Hopkinson v Towergate Financial (Group) Ltd* [2018] EWCA Civ 2744. **13-082**

### Absurdity, inconsistency, etc

*Replace paragraph with:*

A second situation, which can be closely related to the first, arises where the natural and ordinary meaning of the clause produces an absurd outcome or one which cannot be reconciled with the contract as a whole. In *Investors Compensation Scheme Ltd v West Bromwich Building Society*[375] Lord Hoffmann said[376]: **13-083**

> "The 'rule' that words should be given their 'natural and ordinary meaning' reflects the common sense proposition that we do not easily accept that people have made linguistic mistakes, particularly in formal documents. On the other hand, if one would nevertheless conclude from the background that something must have gone wrong with the language, the law does not require judges to attribute to the parties an intention which they plainly could not have had."

So, the principle that words must be construed in their ordinary sense is liable to be departed from where that meaning would involve an absurdity[377] or would create some inconsistency with the rest of the instrument.[378] It may also not be applied, as Lord Hoffmann indicates, where there has been an obvious linguistic mistake[379] or where, if the words were construed in their ordinary sense, they would lead to a very unreasonable result or impose upon the contractor a responsibility which it could not reasonably be supposed he meant to assume.[380] In *Wickman Machine Tools Sales Ltd v L.G. Schuler AG*[381] Lord Reid said:

> "The fact that a particular construction leads to a very unreasonable result must be a relevant consideration. The more unreasonable the result, the more unlikely it is that the parties can have intended it, and if they do intend it the more necessary it is that they shall make their intention abundantly clear."[382]

However, in *Chartbrook Ltd v Persimmon Homes Ltd*,[383] Lord Hoffmann cautioned that "it clearly requires a strong case to persuade the court that something must have gone wrong with the language" in order to justify a meaning which departs from the words actually used. Not only must it be clear that "something has gone wrong with the language", it must also be "clear what a reasonable person would have understood the parties to have meant"[384]: in other words, both the "problem" and the "solution" must be clear if the court is to give to the words a meaning other than that which they ordinarily bear. It is thus "only in exceptional cases" that commercial common sense can "drive the court to depart from the natural meaning of contractual provisions".[385] It is no part of the court's function to rewrite the contract for the parties so that, where the draftsman has not thought through the consequences of his own drafting, he will not be permitted to say that "something has gone wrong with the language" in order to save himself from the consequences of his own poor or inadequate drafting.[386] But in the case where from the language of the contract the court can discern that an event has occurred which was plainly not intended or contemplated by the parties and it is clear what the parties would have intended in the circumstances which have occurred, the court may give effect to that intention even if that intention is not consistent with the primary meaning of the words of the contract.[386a] It is, however, important to note the limits on the latter principle. The event must "plainly" not have been contemplated by the parties and it must also be "clear" what the parties would have intended in the circumstances which have occurred.[386b] The principle does not "extend to re-formulating or altering the parties' bargain".[386c]

375 [1998] 1 W.L.R. 896.

376 [1998] 1 W.L.R. 896, 913 (applied in *Sinochem International Oil (London) Co Ltd v Mobil Sales and Supply Group Corp* [2000] 1 Lloyd's Rep. 339, 344, 345, 346). cf. *Nippon Yusen Kubishika Kaisha v Golden Strait Corp* [2003] EWHC 16 (Comm), [2003] 2 Lloyd's Rep. 592 at [10], [14].

377 *Grey v Pearson* (1857) 6 H.L.C. 61, 106; *Abbott v Middleton* (1858) 7 H.L. Cas. 68, 114; *Thelluson v Rendlesham* (1859) 7 H.L. Cas. 429, 519; *Caledonian Ry v North British Ry* (1881) 6 App. Cas. 114, 130; *Ostfriesische Volksbank EG v Fortis Bank* [2010] EWHC 361 (Comm), [2010] 2 All E.R. (Comm) 921; cf. *Charter Reinsurance Co Ltd v Fagan* [1997] A.C. 313, 387; *Zeus Tradition Marine Ltd v Bell* [1999] 1 Lloyd's Rep. 703, 707; *BP Exploration Operating Co Ltd v Dolphin Drilling Ltd* [2009] EWHC 3119, [2010] 2 Lloyd's Rep. 192. An alternative remedy in such circumstances might be rectification, on which see above paras 3-057 et seq.

378 Words prima facie synonymous should be construed in the same sense throughout the instrument; *Re Birks* [1900] 1 Ch. 417, 418; *Yafai v Muthana* [2012] EWCA Civ 289, but there is no principle of general application to compel this: *Watson v Haggitt* [1928] A.C. 127.

379 *Static Control Components (Europe) Ltd v Egan* [2004] EWCA Civ 392, [2004] 2 Lloyd's Rep. 428; *BP Exploration Operation Co Ltd v Kvaerner Oilfield Products Ltd* [2004] EWHC 999 (Comm), [2005] 1 Lloyd's Rep. 307 at [95]; *Pratt v Aigaion Insurance Co SA* [2008] EWCA Civ 1314, [2009] 1 Lloyd's Rep. 225 at [9]; *Chartbrook Ltd v Persimmon Homes Ltd* [2009] UKHL 38, [2009] 1 A.C. 1101 at [14], [22]; *Westvilla Properties Ltd v Dow Properties Ltd* [2010] EWHC 30 (Ch), [2010] 2 P. & C.R. 19 at [20]; *W W Gear Construction Ltd v McGee Group Ltd* [2010] EWHC 140 (TCC), 131 Con. L.R. 63 at [12]; *ING Bank NV v Ros Roca SA* [2011] EWCA Civ 353, [2012] 1 W.L.R. 472 at [22]; *Caresse Navigation Ltd v Office Nationale de l'Electricité* [2013] EWHC 3081 (Comm), [2014] 1 Lloyd's Rep. 337 at [45]; cf. *Armitage v Staveley Industries Plc* [2004] EWHC 2320 (Comm), [2004] Pens. L.R. 385; *Canmer International Inc v UK Mutual Steamship Assurance Assn (Bermuda) Ltd* [2005] EWHC 1694 (Comm), [2005] 2 Lloyd's Rep. 479 at [24]–[29]; *Forrest v Glasser* [2006] EWCA Civ 1086, [2006] 2 Lloyd's Rep. 392 at [24]; *Royal Bank of Scotland Plc v Highland Financial Partners LP* [2010] EWCA Civ 809 at [11]; *Gessner Investments Ltd v Bombardier Inc* [2011] EWCA Civ 1118; *West v Ian Finlay & Associates* [2014] EWCA Civ 316, [2014] B.L.R. 324.

380 *Re Levy Ex p. Walton* (1881) 17 Ch. D. 746, 751; *Baumwoll Manufactur von Scheibler v Furness* [1893] A.C. 8, 15; *Dodd v Churton* [1897] 1 Q.B. 562, 566; *Miramar Maritime Corp v Holborn Oil Trading Ltd* [1984] A.C. 676, 682; *Antaios Compania Naviera SA v Salen Rederierna AB* [1985] A.C. 191, 200–201; *Harbinger UK Ltd v GE Information Services Ltd* [2000] 1 All E.R. (Comm) 166; *Kazakstan Wool Processors (Europe) Ltd v Nederlandsche Credietverzekering Maatschappij NV* [2000] 1 All E.R. (Comm) 708; *AET Inc Ltd v Arcadia Petroleum Ltd* [2009] EWHC 2337 (Comm), [2009] 2 Lloyd's Rep. 593 at [3]. Contrast *Jones v St John's College, Oxford* (1870) L.R. 6 Q.B. 115; *The Raven* [1980] 2 Lloyd's Rep. 266, 269; *Lakeport Navigation Co Panama SA v Anonima Petroli Italiana* [1982] 2 Lloyd's Rep. 205; *Pera Shipping Corp v Petroship SA* [1985] 2 Lloyd's Rep. 103, 107; *Eurico SpA v Phillipp Bros* [1987] 2 Lloyd's Rep. 215; *Benjamin Developments Ltd v Robt Jones (Pacific) Ltd* [1994]

3 N.Z.L.R. 189; *City Alliance Ltd v Oxford Forecasting Services Ltd* [2001] 1 All E.R. (Comm) 233; *Pratt v Aigaion Insurance Co SA* [2008] EWCA Civ 1314, [2009] 1 Lloyd's Rep. 225 at [23]; *Marine Trade SA v Pioneer Freight Futures Co Ltd BVI* [2009] EWHC 2656 (Comm), [2009] 2 Lloyd's Rep. 631 at [27]; *HHR Pascal BV v W2005 Puppet II BV* [2009] EWHC 2771 (Comm), [2010] 1 All E.R. (Comm) 399; *Global Coal Ltd v London Commodity Brokers* [2010] EWHC 1347 (Ch) at [71].

381 [1974] A.C. 235.

382 [1974] A.C. 235, 251. This dictum was cited with approval in *Wace v Pan Atlantic Group Ltd* [1981] 2 Lloyd's Rep. 339, 343; *Forsikringsaktieselskapet Vesta v J.N.E. Butcher Bain Dawes Ltd* [1989] 1 Lloyd's Rep. 331, 346; *Macedonia Maritime Co v Austin & Pickersgill Ltd* [1989] 2 Lloyd's Rep. 73, 81; *Niobe Maritime Corp v Tradax Ocean Transportation SA* [1995] 1 Lloyd's Rep. 579; *International Fina Services AG v Katrina Shipping Ltd* [1995] 2 Lloyd's Rep. 344, 350; *Charter Reinsurance Co Ltd v Fagan* [1997] A.C. 313, 355.

383 [2009] UKHL 38, [2009] 1 A.C. 1101 at [15]. See also *Enviroco Ltd v Farstad Supply A/S* [2009] EWCA Civ 1399, [2010] 2 Lloyd's Rep. 375 at [21].

384 *Chartbrook Ltd v Persimmon Homes Ltd* [2009] UKHL 38, [2009] 1 A.C. 1101 at [25]; *LSREF III Wight Ltd v Millvalley Ltd* [2016] EWHC 466 (Comm), 165 Con. L.R. 58; *Bouygues (UK) Ltd v Febrey Structures Ltd* [2016] EWHC 1333 (TCC); *BP Gas Marketing Ltd v La Societe Sonatrach* [2016] EWHC 2461 (Comm), 169 Con. L.R. 141 at [281]; *Murray Holdings Ltd v Oscatello Investments Ltd* [2018] EWHC 162 (Ch) at [58]–[61].

385 *Carillion Construction Ltd v Emcor Engineering Services Ltd* [2017] EWCA Civ 65, [2017] B.L.R. 203 at [46]; *Grove Developments Ltd v Balfour Beatty Regional Construction Ltd* [2016] EWCA Civ 990, [2017] 1 W.L.R. 1893 at [42]; *Arnold v Britton* [2015] UKSC 36, [2015] A.C. 1619 at [19]–[20]. For examples of such "exceptional" cases see *Sutton Housing Partnership Ltd v Rydon Maintenance Ltd* [2017] EWCA Civ 359 and *Monsolar IQ Ltd v Woden Park Ltd* [2020] EWHC 1407 (Ch).

386 *Prophet Plc v Huggett* [2014] EWCA Civ 1013, [2014] I.R.L.R. 797 (where a sentence in a restrictive covenant was held to be a "carefully drawn piece of legal prose" which reflected "exactly what the draftsman intended" but the draftsman had not thought through sufficiently the consequence of one of the restrictions which had been inserted into the clause: the Court of Appeal held that the employer had to live with the consequences of its own drafting). See also *Trillium (Prime) Property GP Ltd v Elmfield Road Ltd* [2018] EWCA Civ 1556 at [15]. In *Credit Suisse Asset Management LLC v Titan Europe 2006-1 Plc* [2016] EWCA Civ 1293 Arden L.J. at [28] referred to the fundamental principle of English law of party autonomy, from which it follows that the court will not rewrite the bargain that the parties have freely chosen to make (see also *BP Gas Marketing Ltd v La Societe Sonatrach* [2016] EWHC 2461 (Comm), 169 Con. L.R. 141 at [274]).

386a *Arnold v Britton* [2015] UKSC 36, [2015] A.C. 1619 at [22]; *Aberdeen City Council v Stewart Milne Group Ltd* [2011] UKSC 56, 2012 S.C.L.R. 114; *Netherlands v Deutsche Bank AG* [2019] EWCA Civ 771 at [51] and [62]; *Munich Re Capital Ltd v Ascot Corporate Name Ltd* [2019] EWHC 2768 (Comm). See also *Lloyds TSB Foundation for Scotland v Lloyd's Banking Group Plc* [2013] UKSC 3, [2013] 1 W.L.R. 366 and *Bromarin AB v IMD Investments Ltd* [1999] S.T.C. 301, 310.

386b *Astor Management AG v Atalaya Mining Plc* [2018] EWCA Civ 2407, [2019] 1 All E.R. (Comm) 885 at [40].

386c *W Nagel (a firm) v Pluczenik Diamond Co* [2018] EWCA Civ 2640, [2019] Bus. L.R. 692 at [34].

## Commercial common sense

*Replace paragraph with:*

The third situation is one in which the natural and ordinary meaning of the words used by the parties leads to a conclusion which is said by one of the parties to be a conclusion which is not commercially sensible and which cannot therefore have been intended by the parties. There is a significant body of authority in which the courts have attached substantial weight to the importance of giving to commercial documents a meaning which is commercially sensible. Thus it has been stated that commercial documents "must be construed in a business fashion"[387] and "there must be ascribed to the words a meaning that would make good commercial sense".[388] Indeed, in *The Antaios*[389] Lord Diplock said that[390]: **13-084**

> "... if detailed semantic and syntactical analysis of words in a commercial contract is going to lead to a conclusion that flouts business commonsense, it must yield to business commonsense."

Lord Diplock's dictum has been referred to many times.[391] It does not, however, mean that the court can rewrite the language used by the parties, where it is clear and unambiguous, in order to produce a more balanced, fair or "businesslike" result.[392] There is no overriding criterion of construction to the effect that an interpretation that makes more business common sense is to be preferred.[393] But if alternative interpretations are available, it will be necessary to consider the implications of each interpretation and which interpretation is most likely to give effect to the commercial purpose of the agreement.[394] In mercantile contracts, the words employed may also have acquired a special meaning,[395] and this may be a different meaning from their natural one.[396] Hence it is that mercantile contracts are to be construed according to the usage and custom of merchants,[397] provided that the custom is not inconsistent with the agreement.[398] When such contracts contain peculiar expressions which have in particular places or trades a known meaning attached to them, the meaning of these expressions is a question of fact, although the meaning of the contract still remains a question of law.[399] Further:

> "... the custom of trade, which is a matter of evidence, may be used to annex incidents to all written contracts, commercial or agricultural, and others, which do not by their terms exclude it, upon the presumption that the parties have contracted with reference to such usage, if it is applicable."[400]

[387] *Southland Frozen Meat and Produce Export Co Ltd v Nelson Brothers Ltd* [1898] A.C. 442, 444. See also *Glynn v Margetson & Co* [1893] A.C. 351, 359; *Menth & Co v Ropner & Co* [1913] 1 K.B. 27, 32; *Lake v Simmons* [1927] A.C. 487, 509; *Digby v General Accident Fire and Life Assurance Corp Ltd* [1940] 2 K.B. 226, 246; *Panamanian Oriental Steamship Corp v Wright* [1971] 1 Lloyd's Rep. 487, 492 ("a businesslike interpretation"); *Mannai Investment Co Ltd v Eagle Star Life Assurance Co Ltd* [1997] A.C. 749, 771 ("a commercially sensible construction"); *Handelsbanken Norwegian Branch of Svenska Handelsbanken AB (Publ.) v Dandridge* [2002] EWCA Civ 577, [2002] 2 Lloyd's Rep. 421 at [24] ("a businesslike interpretation in the context in which [the words] appear"); *Homburg Houtimport BV v Agrosin Private Ltd* [2003] UKHL 12, [2004] 1 A.C. 715 at [10] ("a business sense"); *Sirius International Insurance (Publ) v FAI General Insurance Ltd* [2004] UKHL 54, [2004] 1 W.L.R. 3251 at [19] ("a ... commercial approach").

[388] *Miramar Maritime Corp v Holborn Oil Trading Ltd* [1984] A.C. 676, 682; *International Fina Services AG v Katrina Shipping Ltd* [1995] 2 Lloyd's Rep. 344, 350; *Axa Reinsurance (UK) Plc v Field* [1996] 3 All E.R. 517, 526; *Society of Lloyd's v Robinson* [1999] 1 All E.R. (Comm) 545, 551.

[389] *Antaios Compania Naviera SA v Salen Rederierna AB* [1984] A.C. 191.

[390] *Antaios Compania Naviera SA v Salen Rederierna AB* [1985] A.C. 191, 201. See also *Shipping Corp of India Ltd v NBB Niederelke Schiffartsgesellschaft mbH & Co* [1991] 1 Lloyd's Rep. 77, 80; *Bankers Trust Co v State Bank of India* [1991] 2 Lloyd's Rep. 443, 456; *International Fina Services AG v Katrina Shipping Ltd* [1995] 2 Lloyd's Rep. 344, 350; *Charter Reinsurance Co Ltd v Fagan* [1997] A.C. 313, 355; but cf. 387; *Sinochem International Oil (London) Ltd v Mobil Sales and Supply Corp* [2001] 1 Lloyd's Rep. 339, 344; *Sirius International Insurance (Publ) v FAI General Insurance Ltd* [2004] UKHL 54, [2004] 1 W.L.R. 3251 at [19]; *Mora Shipping Inc v Axa Corporate Solutions Assurance SA* [2005] EWCA Civ 1069, [2005] 2 Lloyd's Rep. 769 at [32]; *Absalom v TCRU Ltd* [2005] EWHC 1090 (Comm), [2005] 2 Lloyd's Rep. 735 at [25].

[391] *Stocznia Gdynia SA v Gearbulk Holdings Ltd* [2008] EWHC 944 (Comm), [2008] 2 Lloyd's Rep. 202 at [26] (reversed on other grounds [2009] EWCA Civ 75, [2009] 1 Lloyd's Rep. 461); *Pratt v Aigaion Insurance Co SA* [2008] EWCA Civ 1314, [2009] 1 Lloyd's Rep. 225 at [9]; *Internet Broadcasting Corp Ltd v MAR LLC* [2009] EWHC 844 (Ch), [2009] 2 Lloyd's Rep. 295 at [27]; *Ostfriesische Volksbank EG v Fortis Bank* [2010] EWHC 361 (Comm), [2010] 2 All E.R. (Comm) 921; *Pink Floyd Music Ltd v EMI Records Ltd* [2010] EWCA Civ 1429, [2011] 1 W.L.R. 770; *Rainy Sky SA v Kookmin Bank* [2011] UKSC 50, [2011] 1 W.L.R. 2900; *E-Nik Ltd v Secretary of State for Communities and Local Government* [2012] EWHC 3027 (Comm), [2013] 2 All E.R. (Comm) 868 at [261].

[392] *Co-operative Wholesale Society Ltd v National Westminster Bank Plc* [1995] 1 E.G.L.R. 97, 98; *Skanska Rashleigh Weatherfoil Ltd v Somerfield Stores Ltd* [2006] EWCA Civ 1732, [2007] C.I.L.L. 2449; *Emeraldian Ltd Partnership v Wellmex Shipping Ltd* [2010] EWHC 1411 (Comm), [2010] 1 C.L.C. 993; *Gesner Investments Ltd v Bombardier Inc* [2010] EWHC 2643 (Comm), [2010] All E.R. (D) 234 (Comm) at [28]; *Rainy Sky SA v Kookmin Bank* [2011] UKSC 50, [2011] 1 W.L.R. 2900 at [23]; *Kudos Catering (UK) Ltd v Manchester Central Convention* [2012] EWHC 1192 (QB) at [40], [54]; *Greatship (India) Ltd v Oceanografia SA de CV* [2012] EWHC 3468 (Comm), [2013] 1 All E.R. (Comm)

1244 at [17]; *Ted Baker Plc v AXA Insurance UK Plc* [2012] EWHC 1406 (Comm), [2013] 1 All E.R. (Comm) 129 at [71]; *BMA Special Opportunity Hub Finance Ltd v African Minerals Finance Ltd* [2013] EWCA Civ 416 at [24]; *Fons Ltd v Corporal Ltd* [2014] EWCA Civ 304 at [16]; *Cottonex Anstalt v Patriot Spinning Mills Ltd* [2014] EWHC 236 (Comm), [2014] 1 Lloyd's Rep. 615 at [52]–[58]; *Soufflet Negoce SA v Fedcominvest Europe Sarl* [2014] EWHC 2405 (Comm), [2014] 2 Lloyd's Rep 537 at [27]; *Tartsinis v Navona Management Co* [2015] EWHC 57 (Comm) at [54]; *Arnold v Britton* [2015] UKSC 36, [2015] A.C. 1619 at [17]–[22]; *Credit Suisse Asset Management LLC v Titan Europe 2006-1 Plc* [2016] EWCA Civ 1293 at [28]; *Network Rail Infrastructure Ltd v ABC Electrification Ltd* [2019] EWHC (TCC) 1769, [2019] B.L.R. 522 at [39]; *Iraqi Civilians v Ministry of Defence* [2019] EWHC 3088 (QB).

393 *Soufflet Negoce SA v Fedcominvest Europe Sarl* [2014] EWHC 2405 (Comm), [2014] 2 Lloyd's Rep 537 at [27], applying *BMA Special Opportunity Hub Fund Ltd v African Minerals Finance Ltd* [2013] EWCA Civ 416 at [24].

394 *Rainy Sky SA v Kookmin Bank* [2011] UKSC 50, [2011] 1 W.L.R. 2900 at [30]. See also *Barclays Bank Plc v HHY Luxembourg SARL* [2010] EWCA Civ 1248, [2011] 1 B.C.L.C. 336 at [25], [26]; *Ener-G Holdings Plc v Hormell* [2011] EWHC 3290 (Comm) at [9]; *PT Thiess Contractors Indonesia v PT Kaltim Prima Coal* [2012] EWHC 690 (Comm); *Teal Assurance Co Ltd v WR Berkley Insurance (Europe) Ltd* [2013] UKSC 57, [2013] 2 All E.R. (Comm) 1009 at [29]–[31]; *Fons Ltd v Corporal Ltd* [2014] EWCA Civ 304 at [15]; *Teesside Gas Transportation Ltd v CATS North Sea Ltd* [2020] EWCA Civ 503.

395 See, e.g. *Care Shipping Corp v Itex Itagrani Export SA* [1993] Q.B. 1 ("sub-freights").

396 See, e.g. *Seacrystal Shipping Ltd v Bulk Transport Group Shipping Co Ltd* [1989] 1 Lloyd's Rep. 1, 6 ("whether in berth or not").

397 *Re Walkers, Winser & Hamm and Shaw, Son & Co* [1904] 2 K.B. 152; *Upjohn v Hitchens* [1918] 2 K.B. 48; see below, para.13-142.

398 *Gibbon v Young* (1818) 8 Taunt. 254; *Hayton v Irwin* (1879) 5 C.P.D. 130; *The Alhambra* (1881) 6 P.D. 68; *Re L. Sutro & Co and Heilbut, Symons & Co* [1917] 2 K.B. 348; *Westacott v Hahn* [1918] 1 K.B. 495; *Palgrave, Brown & Sons v S.S. Turid* [1922] 1 A.C. 397; *Ted Baker Plc v AXA Insurance UK Plc* [2012] EWHC 1406 (Comm); see below, para.13-138.

399 *Hutchinson v Bowker* (1839) 5 M. & W. 535; *Hill v Evans* (1862) 4 De G.F. & J. 288; see below, para.13-044.

400 *Gibson v Small* (1853) 4 H.L. Cas. 353, 397.

## Modifying

*Replace paragraph with:*

It has already been noted that the grammatical or ordinary sense of the words of a contract may be departed from if this would lead to some absurdity or inconsistency with the rest of the instrument or if there has been an obvious linguistic mistake.[416] It is also open to the court to correct a misnomer[417] or mistaken designation in a contract: *falsa demonstratio non nocet cum de corpore constat*.[418] So where the parties to a charterparty attached thereto a typed paramount clause which stated that: **13-092**

> "... this *bill of lading* shall have effect subject to the provisions of the Carriage by Sea Act of the United States ... which shall be deemed to be incorporated herein,"

it was held that the erroneous description of the charterparty as a bill of lading did not defeat the intention of the parties that the document should be subject to the Act.[419] However, the court will not be inclined to engage in a "verbal manipulation" of a designation in a contract if the actual words used make perfectly good sense without any modification.[420] An obvious mistake in a written instrument can be corrected as a matter of construction without obtaining a decree in an action for rectification[421] (by a process which has been referred to, not without criticism, as "corrective interpretation"[422]) but there must have been a clear mistake and it must be clear what correction ought to be made in order to cure the mistake.[423] Such a mistake may well emerge only upon consideration of the content of the instrument against the admissible background and correction of the mistake is then an aspect of the task of ascertaining what a reasonable person would have understood the parties to have meant.[424]

[416] See above, para.13-083.

[417] The law relating to misnomer was explored by Rix L.J. in *Dumford Trading AG v DAO Atlantrybflot* [2005] EWCA Civ 24, [2005] 1 Lloyd's Rep. 289, where this paragraph was cited (at [27]); but see below, para.13-134. See also *The Tutova* [2006] EWHC 2223 (Comm), [2007] 1 Lloyd's Rep. 104 at [10]; *Front Carriers Ltd v Atlantic and Orient Shipping Corp* [2007] EWHC 421 (Comm), [2007] 2 Lloyd's Rep. 131 at [44]; *Gastronome (UK) Ltd v Anglo Dutch Meals (UK) Ltd* [2006] EWCA Civ 1233, [2006] 2 Lloyd's Rep. 587 at [14]; *Liberty Mercian Ltd v Cuddy Civil Engineering Ltd* [2013] EWHC 2688 (TCC), [2014] 1 All E.R. (Comm) 761 at [81].

[418] *Llewellyn v Jersey* (1843) 11 M. & W. 183, 189; *Morrell v Fisher* (1849) 4 Ex. 591, 604; *Cowen v Truefitt Ltd* [1899] 2 Ch. 309; *Eastwood v Ashton* [1915] A.C. 900, 914; *Whittam v W.J. Daniel & Co Ltd* [1962] 1 Q.B. 271, 277; *F. Goldsmith (Sicklesmere) Ltd v Baxter* [1970] Ch. 85; *Modern Buildings Wales Ltd v Limmer and Trinidad Co Ltd* [1975] 1 W.L.R. 1281; *Nittan v Solent Steel Fabrication Ltd* [1981] 1 Lloyd's Rep. 633; *Lamport & Holt Lines Ltd v Coubro & Scrutton (M. & I.) Ltd* [1981] 2 Lloyd's Rep. 659 (affirmed [1982] 2 Lloyd's Rep. 42); *Mohammed bin Abdul Rahman Orri v Seawind Navigation Co SA* [1986] 1 Lloyd's Rep. 36; *Coral (UK) Ltd v Rechtman* [1996] 1 Lloyd's Rep. 235; *Gastronome (UK) Ltd v Anglo-Dutch Meats (UK) Ltd* [2006] EWCA Civ 1233, [2006] 2 Lloyd's Rep. 587. Contrast *Internaut Shipping GmbH v Fercometal SARL* [2003] EWCA Civ 812, [2003] 2 Lloyd's Rep. 430 (mistake beyond misnomer).

[419] *Adamastos Shipping Co Ltd v Anglo-Saxon Petroleum Co Ltd* [1959] A.C. 133. In the Court of Appeal, it had been held that the paramount clause was meaningless and to be rejected: [1957] 2 Q.B. 233.

[420] *Miramar Maritime Corp v Holborn Oil Trading Ltd* [1984] A.C. 676. But see *Mannai Investment Co Ltd v Eagle Star Life Assurance Ltd* [1997] A.C. 749.

[421] *East v Pantiles Plant Hire Ltd* [1982] 2 E.G.L.R. 111 at 112; *Holding & Barnes Plc v Hill House Hammond Ltd* [2001] EWCA Civ 1334 at [14]; *Lafarge (Aggregates) Ltd v London Borough of Newham* [2005] EWHC 1337 (Comm), [2005] 2 Lloyd's Rep. 577 at [25]; *Dalkia Utilities Services Plc v Celtech International Ltd* [2006] EWHC 63 (Comm), [2006] 1 Lloyd's Rep. 599 at [109]; *Littman v Aspen Oil Broking Ltd* [2005] EWCA Civ 1579, [2006] 2 P. & C.R. 2; *Monsolar IQ Ltd v Woden Park Ltd* [2020] EWHC 1407 (Ch); *Pathway Finance Sarl v Defendants set out in Annex 1 to the Claim* [2020] EWHC 1191 (Ch); *Ffrees Family Finance Ltd v U Holdings Ltd* [2020] EWHC 1911 (Ch). The relationship between interpretation and rectification has been variously described in the case law. In *Oceanbulk Shipping and Trading SA v TMT Asia Ltd* [2010] UKSC 44, [2011] 1 A.C. 662, Lord Clarke (at [45]) stated that the relationship between the two was "close", whereas Leggatt J. in *Tartsinis v Navona Management Co* [2015] EWHC 57 (Comm) at [13] described them as "very different exercises".

[422] *Cherry Tree Investments Ltd v Landmain Ltd* [2012] EWCA Civ 736, [2013] Ch. 305 at [62]; *Bouygues (UK) Ltd v Febrey Structures Ltd* [2016] EWHC 1333 (TCC); *LSREF III Wight Ltd v Millvalley Ltd* [2016] EWHC 466 (Comm); *Hayfin Opal Luxco 3 SARL v Windermere VII CMBS Plc* [2016] EWHC 782 (Ch); *Hopkinson v Towergate Financial (Group) Ltd* [2018] EWCA Civ 2744 at [44]. For criticism see Buxton [2010] C.L.J. 253.

[423] *East v Pantiles Plant Hire Ltd* [1982] 2 E.G.L.R. 11 at 112; *Chartbrook Ltd v Persimmon Homes Ltd* [2009] UKHL 38, [2009] 1 A.C. 1101 at [22]; *Pink Floyd Music Ltd v EMI Records Ltd* [2010] EWCA Civ 1429, [2011] 1 W.L.R. 770 at [21]; *ING Bank NV v Ros Roca* [2011] EWCA Civ 353, [2012] 1 W.L.R. 472 at [22]; *Liberty Mercian Ltd v Cuddy Civil Engineering Ltd* [2013] EWHC 2688 (TCC), [2014] 1 All E.R. (Comm) 761 at [81].

[424] *KPMG v Network Rail Infrastructure Ltd* [2007] EWCA Civ 363, [2007] Bus. L.R. 1336 at [44]–[50]; *Chartbrook Ltd v Persimmon Homes Ltd* [2009] UKHL 38, [2009] 1 A.C. 1101 at [22]–[23]; *ING Bank NV v Ros Roca* [2011] EWCA Civ 353, [2012] 1 W.L.R. 472 at [22]; *Liberty Mercian Ltd v Cuddy Civil Engineering Ltd* [2013] EWHC 2688 (TCC), [2014] 1 All E.R. (Comm) 761 at [81]; *McDonagh v Bank of Scotland Plc* [2018] EWHC 3262 (Ch) at [65] where it is noted that "to remove words from a written contract and then to interpret the contract without those words is a radical step".

## Rejecting

*Replace footnote 432 with:*

**13-094** [432] *Royal Greek Government v Minister of Transport* (1949) 83 Ll.L. Rep. 228, 235; *Chandris v Isbrandtsen-Moller Inc* [1951] 1 K.B. 385, 392; *Total Transport Corp v Arcadia Petroleum Ltd* [1998] 1 Lloyd's Rep. 351, 357; *Interactive E-Solutions JLT v O3B Africa Ltd* [2018] EWCA Civ 62, [2018] B.L.R. 167 at [24]; *Merthyr (South Wales) Ltd v Merthyr Tydfil County Borough Council* [2019] EWCA Civ 526 at [39].

## (j) Construction Against Grantor

### Construction against grantor

*Replace paragraph with:*

Another principle of construction is that a deed or other instrument shall be construed more strongly against the grantor or maker thereof.[435] This principle (or rule, as it has sometimes been described) is often misinterpreted. It is only to be applied to remove (and not to create) a doubt or ambiguity[436] and as a last resort where the issue cannot otherwise be resolved by the application of ordinary principles of construction.[437] Its application to negotiated contracts has also been doubted.[438] Nevertheless, despite certain doubts which have been cast upon it from time to time,[439] the principle has been cited as a rule of construction from Coke's time to the present day[440] (although the principle is now more often cited to the court than it is applied by the court[441]). For instance, Coke says,[442] "[i]t is a maxim in law that every man's grant shall be taken by construction of law most forcibly against himself"; and in 1949, Evershed M.R. said: **13-095**

> "We are presented with two alternative readings of this document and the reading which one should adopt is to be determined, among other things, by a consideration of the fact that the defendants put forward the document. They have put forward a clause which is by no means free from obscurity and have contended ... that it has a remarkably, if not an extravagantly, wide scope, and I think that the rule *contra proferentem* should be applied."[443]

[435] *Verba cartarum fortius accipiuntur contra proferentem* (Bac. Max. 3).

[436] *Borradaile v Hunter* (1843) 5 M. & G. 639; *Birrell v Dryer* (1884) 9 App. Cas. 345, 350; *Cornish v Accident Insurance Co* (1889) 23 Q.B.D. 453, 456; *London & Lancashire Insurance v Bolands Ltd* [1924] A.C. 836, 848; *Houghton v Trafalgar Insurance Co* [1954] 1 Q.B. 247; *Lakeport Navigation Co Panama SA v Anonima Petroli Italiana* [1982] 2 Lloyd's Rep. 205, 208; *Aqua Design & Play International Ltd v Kier Regional Ltd* [2002] EWCA Civ 797, [2003] B.L.R. 111; *Tektrol Ltd v International Insurance Co of Hanover Ltd* [2005] EWCA Civ 845, [2005] 2 Lloyd's Rep. 701 at [8]; *West v Ian Finlay & Associates (a firm)* [2014] EWCA Civ 316, [2014] B.L.R. 324; *Impact Funding Solutions Ltd v Barrington Support Services Ltd* [2016] UKSC 57, [2017] A.C. 73 at [6]; *Persimmon Homes Ltd v Ove Arup & Partners Ltd* [2017] EWCA Civ 373, [2017] P.N.L.R. 29 at [52]–[53]; *Haberdashers' Aske's Federation Trust Ltd v Lakehouse Contracts Ltd* [2018] EWHC 558 (TCC), [2018] Lloyd's Rep. I.R. 382 at [85].

[437] *Lindus v Melrose* (1858) 3 Hurl. & N. 177, 182; *Lakeport Navigation Company Panama SA v Anonima Petroli Italiana SpA* [1982] 2 Lloyd's Rep. 205, 208; *Sinochem International Oil (London) Co Ltd v Mobil Sales and Supply Corp* [2000] 1 Lloyd's Rep. 339 at [37]; *Direct Travel Insurance v McGeown* [2003] EWCA Civ 1606 at [13]; *Egan v Static Control Components (Europe) Ltd* [2004] EWCA Civ 392, [2004] 2 Lloyd's Rep. 429 at [37]; *Cattles Plc v Welcome Financial Services Ltd* [2010] EWCA Civ 599, [2010] 2 Lloyd's Rep. 514 at [43]; *AJ Building and Plastering Ltd v Turner* [2013] EWHC 484 (QB), [2013] Lloyd's Rep. I.R. 629 (see below, Vol.II, para.42-087, n.604); *Compania Sud Americana de Vapores SA v Hin-Pro International Logistics Ltd* [2015] EWCA Civ 401; *Hut Group Ltd v Nobahar-Cookson* [2016] EWCA Civ 128, [2016] C.L.C. 573 (although note the difference of view between Briggs L.J. (who at [12]–[21] invoked the *contra proferentem* rule) and Hallett L.J. and Moylan J. who did not (see paras [40] and [41]); *Carr v Thales Pension Trustees Ltd* [2020] EWHC 949 (Ch) at [60]–[61].

[438] *K/S Victoria Street v House of Fraser (Stores Management) Ltd* [2011] EWCA Civ 904, [2012] Ch. 497; *Compania Sud Americana de Vapores SA v Hin-Pro International Logistics Ltd* [2015] EWCA Civ 401, [2015] 2 Lloyd's Rep. 1 at [69]–[71]; *Transocean Drilling UK Ltd v Providence Resources Plc* [2016] EWCA Civ 372, [2016] 2 Lloyd's Rep. 51 at [20].

[439] *Taylor v St Helens Corp* (1877) 6 Ch. D. 264, 270, per Jessel M.R., but the cases on which he relies turned upon the construction of wills. In more modern times cases can be found in which doubts have been expressed about the significance of the rule for commercial contracts (see, for example, *K/S Victoria Street v House of Fraser (Stores Management) Ltd* [2011] EWCA Civ 904, [2012] Ch. 497 at [68] and *Nigeria v JP Morgan Chase Bank NA* [2019] EWHC 347 (Comm), [2019] 1 C.L.C. 207 at [34], where it is suggested that it is "unnecessary" to accept the continued existence of a contra proferentem rule

and that it can be replaced by the principle that "a party is unlikely to have agreed to give up a valuable right that it would otherwise have had without clear words").

[440] *Manchester College v Trafford* (1679) 2 Show. 31; *Johnson v Edgware, etc., Ry* (1866) 35 Beav. 480, 484; *Neill v Duke of Devonshire* (1882) 8 App. Cas. 135, 149; *Homburg Houtimport BV v Agrosin Private Ltd* [2003] UKHL 12, [2004] 1 A.C. 715 at [144]; *Dairy Containers Ltd v Tasman Orient Line CV (New Zealand)* [2004] UKPC 22, [2005] 1 W.L.R. 215 at [12]. The principle is now mandatory in respect of certain consumer contracts by reg.7 of the Unfair Terms in Consumer Contracts Regulations 1999 (SI 1999/2083) or, for contracts made on or after October 1, 2015, s.69 of the Consumer Rights Act 2015: see below, Vol.II, para.38-417.

[441] Perhaps for this reason Fraser J. in *Haberdashers' Aske's Federation Trust Ltd v Lakehouse Contracts Ltd* [2018] EWHC 558 (TCC), [2018] Lloyd's Rep. I.R. 382 at [85] stated that "there is precious little, if anything, of this doctrine remaining in commercial cases".

[442] Co.Litt. 36a, 183a, 183b.

[443] *John Lee & Son (Grantham) Ltd v Railway Executive* [1949] 2 All E.R. 581, 583.

## (k) Ejusdem Generis Principle

### No common category

*In line 2, after "can be restricted.", add new footnote 470a:*

13-101 [470a] *CFH Clearing Ltd v Merrill Lynch International* [2019] EWHC 963 (Comm) at [34].

## 4. ADMISSIBILITY OF EXTRINSIC EVIDENCE

## (a) The Parol Evidence Rule

### Whether document conclusive: the "parol evidence" rule

*Replace footnote 498 with:*

13-109 [498] *Evans v Roe* (1871–72) L.R. 7 C.P. 138; *Leggott v Barrett* (1880) 15 Ch. D. 306, 309, 311; *Henderson v Arthur* [1907] 1 K.B. 10; *Newman v Gatti* (1907) 24 T.L.R. 18; *Hitchings & Coulthurst Co v Northern Leather Co of America and Doushkess* [1914] 3 K.B. 907; *Hutton v Watling* [1948] Ch. 398; *Youell v Bland Welch & Co Ltd* [1992] 2 Lloyd's Rep. 127. But see *HIH Casualty and General Insurance Ltd v New Hampshire Insurance Co* [2001] EWCA Civ 735, [2001] 2 Lloyd's Rep. 161 at [83] and *Medenta Finance Ltd v Hitachi Capital (UK) Plc* [2019] EWHC 516 (Comm) at [49].

### Law Commission Report

*Replace footnote 513 with:*

13-112 [513] The Commission's Report was referred to with approval in *Wild v Civil Aviation Authority* Unreported September 25, 1987, CA and in *State Rail Authority of New South Wales v Heath Outdoor Pty Ltd* (1986) 7 N.S.W.L.R. 170, 192. See also *Yani Haryanto v E.D. & F. Man (Sugar) Ltd* [1986] 2 Lloyd's Rep. 44, 46; *Youell v Bland Welch & Co Ltd* [1992] 2 Lloyd's Rep. 127, 133, 140. Contrast the view expressed in Peel (ed.), *Treitel on The Law of Contract*, 15th edn (2020), para.6-021.

### "Entire agreement" clauses

*Replace footnote 550 with:*

13-117 [550] *Alman and Benson v Associated Newspapers Group Ltd* Unreported June 20, 1980; *Thomas Witter Ltd v T.B.P. Industries Ltd* [1996] 2 All E.R. 573; *Deepak Fertilisers and Petrochemicals Corp v ICI* [1999] 1 Lloyd's Rep. 387, 395; *South West Water Services Ltd v International Computers Ltd* [1999] B.L.R. 420, 424; *Government of Zanzibar v British Aerospace (Lancaster House) Ltd* [2000] 1 W.L.R. 2333, 2344; *Sabah Shipyard (Pakistan) Ltd v Govt of Pakistan* [2007] EWHC 2602 (Comm), [2008] 1 Lloyd's Rep. 240 at [130] (deceit); *Barclays Bank Plc v Unicredit Bank AG* [2014] EWCA Civ 302, [2014] 2 All E.R. (Comm) 115. The clause may in any event be ineffective under s.3 of the Misrepresentation Act 1967 (as amended by s.8 of the Unfair Contract Terms Act 1977) or under s.3(2)(b)(ii) of the 1977 Act; *First Tower Trustees Ltd v CDS (Superstores International) Ltd* [2018] EWCA Civ 1396, [2019] 1 W.L.R. 637. See also ss.11, 13 of the 1977 Act, and below, paras 15-070 n.423. Contrast *Trident Turboprop (Dublin) Ltd v First Flight Couriers Ltd* [2008] EWHC 1686

(Comm), [2008] 2 Lloyd's Rep. 581 at [42] (affirmed [2009] EWCA Civ 290, [2010] Q.B. 86). As to whether an entire agreement clause precludes a plea of estoppel by convention, see *Sere Holdings Ltd v Volkswagen Group UK Ltd* [2004] EWHC 1551 (Comm); *Dubai Islamic Bank v PSI Energy Holding Co* [2011] EWHC 2718 (Comm) at [83]; *Shoreline Housing Partnership Ltd v Mears Ltd* [2013] EWCA Civ 639, [2013] C.P. Rep. 39.

## (c) Evidence as to the True Nature of the Agreement

### True nature of the agreement

*Replace footnote 589 with:*

[589] *Steele v M'Kinlay* (1880) 5 App. Cas. 754, 778–779; *Macdonald v Whitfield* (1883) 8 App. Cas. 733, 745; *National Sales Corp Ltd v Bernardi* [1931] 2 K.B. 188; *McCall Bros Ltd v Hargreaves* [1932] 2 K.B. 423; *Yeoman Credit Ltd v Gregory* [1963] 1 W.L.R. 343; *Yuchai Dongte Special Purpose Automobile Co Ltd v Suisse Credit Capital (2009) Ltd* [2018] EWHC 2580 (Comm), [2019] 1 Lloyd's Rep. 457 at [28]; and see below, para.13-129. **13-126**

## (d) Evidence to Interpret or Explain the Written Agreement

### Special meaning of words

*Replace footnote 609 with:*

[609] *Shore v Wilson* (1842) 9 Cl. & Fin. 355, 511; *NHS Commissioning Board v Vasant* [2019] EWCA Civ 1245, [2020] 1 All E.R. (Comm) 799 at [42]. See also *L.G. Schuler A.G. v Wickman Machine Tools Sales Ltd* [1974] A.C. 235, 261 ("technical expressions"). **13-131**

CHAPTER 14

# IMPLIED TERMS



## 1. INTRODUCTION

### The relationship between interpretation and implication

*Replace paragraph with:*

The principles that traditionally govern the implication of terms differ from those which apply to the construction of express terms.[2] However, in *Att-Gen of Belize v Belize Telecom Ltd*[3] Lord Hoffmann challenged the validity of this difference in treatment on the ground that in both cases the court is seeking to establish what the contract would reasonably have been understood to mean having regard to the commercial purpose of the contract as a whole and the relevant available background of the transaction.[4] The extent to which the process of implication can be assimilated with the principles applicable to the interpretation of the express terms of a contract has since been the subject of some judicial comment[5] and academic controversy.[6] More recently the Supreme Court has sought to distance itself from the approach of Lord Hoffmann, with a majority describing his analysis in *Belize* as "a characteristically inspired discussion rather than authoritative guidance on the law of implied terms"[7] and it has subsequently been stated that it is "no longer" the case that the question whether a term ought to be implied into a contract is to be treated as an aspect of the interpretation of the contract.[8] Interpretation is concerned with "what is there"[9] and involves "deciding what the parties meant by what they did say",[10] whereas implication is concerned with "inserting what is not there"[11] and thus involves "deciding whether [the parties] would have said something they did not in fact say had the matter occurred to them".[12] Although the processes have been held to be different, the factors taken into account in the two processes are often the same in that both involve taking into account: **14-003**

> "the words used in the contract, the surrounding circumstances known or available to the parties at the time of the contract, commercial common sense and the reasonable reader or reasonable parties."[13]

The process of interpretation or construction generally precedes implication and has been described as "the precursor of implication"[14] so that, at least in "most cases", it is only after the process of interpreting or construing the express words of an agreement has been completed that the issue of whether a term is to be implied will be considered by the court.[15]

[2] See above, Ch.13.

[3] [2009] UKPC 10, [2009] 1 W.L.R. 1988 at [17]–[27]. For an earlier statement of Lord Hoffmann's views, expressed extrajudicially, see Lord Hoffmann (1997) 56 S.A.L.J. 656 and (1995) 29 *Law Teacher* 127.

[4] *Att-Gen of Belize v Belize Telecom Ltd* [2009] UKPC 10, [2009] 1 W.L.R. 1988 at [19]–[21].

[5] See, for example, *Stena Line Ltd v Merchant Navy Ratings Pension Fund Trustees Ltd* [2011] EWCA Civ 543, [2011] Pens. L.R. 22 at [36]; *Spencer v Secretary of State for Defence* [2012] EWHC 120 (Ch), [2012] 2 All E.R. (Comm) 480.

[6] See, for example, McLauchlan [2014] L.M.C.L.Q. 203; Courtney and Carter (2014) 31 J.C.L. 151; Hooley [2014] C.L.J. 315 at 327–334; Davies [2010] L.M.C.L.Q. 140; Kramer [2004] C.L.J. 384; G. McMeel, *McMeel on the Construction of Contracts: Interpretation, Implication and Rectification*, 3rd edn (2017), Ch.9.

[7] *Marks & Spencer Plc v BNP Paribas Securities Services Trust Co (Jersey) Ltd* [2015] UKSC 72, [2016] A.C. 742 at [31] per Lord Neuberger. Not all members of the Supreme Court are, however, of the same view. Thus in *Marks & Spencer* Lord Carnwath (at [74]) saw no sufficient reason to question the "continuing authority" of the judgment of Lord Hoffmann in *Belize* and the judgment of Lord Clarke (at [76]) is more equivocal, as is the judgment of Lord Mance in *Trump International Golf Club Scotland Ltd v Scottish Ministers* [2015] UKSC 74, [2016] 1 W.L.R. 85 at [42]–[44]. However, the judgment of Lord Neuberger represents the majority view, so that the authority of Lord Hoffmann's judgment has now been considerably diminished. See also *Utilise TDS Ltd v Davies* [2016] EWHC 2127 (Ch) at [52].

[8] *National Health Service Commissioning Board v Silovsky* [2017] EWCA Civ 1389, (2018) 159 B.M.L.R. 92 at [26]. See also *Parker v Roberts* [2019] EWCA Civ 121 at [88] ("We have been told in no uncertain terms by the Supreme Court that interpretation and implication are different"); *Law Debenture Trust Corp Plc v Ukraine* [2018] EWCA Civ 2026, [2019] Q.B. 1121 at [205]; *Sparks v Biden* [2017] EWHC 1994 (Ch) at [36].

[9] *Greenhouse v Paysafe Financial Services Ltd* [2018] EWHC 3296 (Comm) at [12].

[10] *Byron v Eastern Caribbean Amalgamated Bank* [2019] UKPC 16 at [22].

[11] *Greenhouse v Paysafe Financial Services Ltd* [2018] EWHC 3296 (Comm) at [12].

[12] *Byron v Eastern Caribbean Amalgamated Bank* [2019] UKPC 16 at [22]. It is at this point that the similarity between interpretation and implication is most apparent. As Hildyard J. observed in *Lehman Brothers International (Europe) (In Administration) v Exotix Partners LLP* [2019] EWHC 2380 (Ch), [2020] 1 All E.R. (Comm) 635 at [152] "the process of implication is at heart simply reading into the contract those terms which the parties are taken to have intended to include but failed or felt it unnecessary to make explicit".

[13] *Marks & Spencer Plc v BNP Paribas Securities Services Trust Co (Jersey) Ltd* [2015] UKSC 72, [2016] A.C. 742 at [27]; *Clin v Walter Lilly & Co Ltd* [2018] EWCA Civ 490, [2018] B.L.R. 321 at [25]; *Sparks v Biden* [2017] EWHC 1994 (Ch) at [36]; *Europa Plus SCA SIF v Anthracite Investments (Ireland) Plc* [2016] EWHC 437 (Comm) at [34]; *Byron v Eastern Caribbean Amalgamated Bank* [2019] UKPC 16 at [22]. The relationship between the two may be particularly close in the case where it is alleged that something has been omitted from the contract. As was noted by Snowden J. in *Hayfin Opal Luxco 3 SARL v Windermere VII CMBS Plc* [2016] EWHC 782 (Ch), [2018] 1 B.C.L.C. 118 at [68], the gap in such a case can be filled either by a process of corrective interpretation or by the implication of an appropriate term in the contract. But in either case it is important to note that the test applied by the court is a strict one, so that a court will not lightly correct the contract by supplying the alleged missing term, whether by corrective interpretation or by implication.

[14] *Trump International Golf Club Scotland Ltd v Scottish Ministers* [2015] UKSC 74, [2016] 1 W.L.R. 85 at [35] per Lord Hodge; *Bou-Simon v BGC Brokers LP* [2018] EWCA Civ 1525, [2019] 1 All E.R. (Comm) 955 at [13]; *Bates v Post Office Ltd (No.3: Common Issues)* [2019] EWHC 606 (QB) at [690].

[15] *Wells v Devani* [2019] UKSC 4, [2020] A.C. 129 at [28] and [59]; *Duval v 11-13 Randolph Crescent Ltd* [2020] UKSC 18, [2020] 2 W.L.R. 1157 at [26] and [51].

## 2. TERMS IMPLIED BY THE COURTS

### (a) The Development of the Law

#### Terms implied in fact: traditional principles

*Replace footnote 21 with:*

[21] *Marks & Spencer Plc v BNP Paribas Securities Services Trust Co (Jersey) Ltd* [2015] UKSC 72, [2016] A.C. 742 at [21]. It is important to note that the test is to be applied at the time of contracting and it is not appropriate for a court to seek to use the benefit of hindsight: *Bou-Simon v BGC Brokers LP* [2018] EWCA Civ 1525, [2019] 1 All E.R. (Comm) 955 at [12]. **14-006**

#### Necessity not reasonableness

*Replace paragraph with:*

The Supreme Court in *Marks & Spencer* affirmed that it is not enough to show that the term is a reasonable one for it to be implied into the contract.[47] Reasonableness may be a necessary requirement before a term will be implied[48] but it is not sufficient of itself to lead to the implication of a term into the contract.[49] Thus a term will not be implied into a detailed commercial contract merely because it appears fair or because the parties might have agreed to it had it been suggested to them.[50] Nor will a term be implied simply because it would improve the contract[51] or make the carrying out of it more convenient.[52] As it has been observed, "[t]he touchstone is always *necessity* and not merely *reasonableness*".[53] The test therefore remains one of necessity, albeit not "absolute necessity" but whether, without the term, the contract would lack commercial or practical coherence or whether it is necessary to imply the term "in order to make the contract work".[54] In short, in order to imply a term into an ordinary business contract, the term must be necessary to give business efficacy to the contract; it must be so obvious that it goes without saying; it must be capable of clear expression; and it must not contradict any express term of the contract.[55] Given the strict nature of the test established by the Supreme Court it is now no easy task to persuade a court to imply a term into a contract, particularly a written contract of some length which has been negotiated with the benefit of legal advice, and a number of cases can now be found in which the courts have applied the approach of the Supreme Court in *Marks & Spencer* and, on that basis, have declined to imply a term into the contract between the parties.[56] If the contract does not expressly provide for what is to happen when a particular event occurs or in a particular situation, the most usual inference to be drawn is that nothing is to happen and no term is to be implied.[57] **14-012**

[47] [2015] UKSC 72, [2016] A.C. 742 at [23]. See also *Rosenblatt (A Firm) v Man Oil Group SA* [2016] EWHC 1382 (QB) at [59]; *Bou-Simon v BGC Brokers LP* [2018] EWCA Civ 1525, [2019] 1 All E.R. (Comm) 955 at [12].

[48] *Young & Marten v McManus Childs Ltd* [1969] 1 A.C. 454, 465; *Liverpool CC v Irwin* [1977] A.C. 239, 262; *BP Refinery (Westenport) Pty Ltd v Shire of Hastings* (1977) 52 A.L.J.R. 20, 26, PC; *Inta Navigatiori v Ranch Investments Ltd* [2009] EWHC 1216 (Comm), [2010] 1 Lloyd's Rep. 74; *Fortis Bank SA/NV v Indian Overseas Bank* [2010] EWHC 84 (Comm), [2010] 2 Lloyd's Rep. 641 at [64]; *Cassa di Risparmio della Repubblica di San Marino SpA v Barclays Bank Ltd* [2011] EWHC 484 (Comm), [2011] 1 C.L.C. 701 at [544]; *Arash Shipping Enterprises Co Ltd v Groupama Transport* [2011] EWCA Civ 620, [2011] 2 Lloyd's Rep. 607 at [41].

[49] *Hamlyn & Co v Wood & Co* [1891] 2 Q.B. 488, 491; *Reigate v Union Manufacturing Co (Ramsbottom) Ltd* [1918] 1 K.B. 592, 598; *Re Comptoir Commercial Anversois v Power, Son and Co* [1920] 1 K.B. 868, 899; *George Trollope & Son v Martyn Bros* [1934] 2 K.B. 436, 443; *R. v Paddington and St Marylebone Rent Tribunal* [1947] K.B. 984, 990; *British Movietonews v London and District Cinemas Ltd* [1952] A.C. 166; *Bundar Property Holdings Ltd v J. S. Darwen (Successors) Ltd* [1968] 2 All E.R. 305; *Lupton v Potts* [1969] 1 W.L.R. 1749; *Trollope & Colls Ltd v N.W. Metropolitan Regional Hospital*

*Board* [1973] 1 W.L.R. 601; *Liverpool CC v Irwin* [1977] A.C. 239; *Duke of Westminster v Guild* [1985] Q.B. 688; *Holding and Management (Solitaire) Ltd v Ideal Homes Northwest Ltd* [2004] EWHC 2408 (TCC), [2004] Const. L.R. 114; *Friends Provident Life and Pensions Ltd v Sirius International Insurance Corp* [2005] EWCA Civ 601, [2005] 2 Lloyd's Rep. 517 at [32].

[50] [2015] UKSC 72, [2016] A.C. 742 at [21]; *CFH Clearing Ltd v Merrill Lynch International* [2019] EWHC 963 (Comm) at [52].

[51] *Trollope & Colls Ltd v N.W. Metropolitan Regional Hospital Board* [1973] 1 W.L.R. 601, 609; *Express Newspapers v Silverstone Circuits, The Independent,* June 16, 1989, CA; *Att-Gen of Belize v Belize Telecom Ltd* [2009] UKPC 10, [2009] 1 W.L.R. 1988 at [16].

[52] *Russell v Duke of Norfolk* [1949] 1 All E.R. 109.

[53] *Liverpool CC v Irwin* [1977] A.C. 239, 266; *BP Refinery (Westenport) Pty Ltd v Shire of Hastings* (1977) 52 A.L.J.R. 20, 26; *Harmony Shipping Co SA v Saudi Europe Line Ltd* [1980] 1 Lloyd's Rep. 44; *Tai Hing Cotton Mill Ltd v Liu Chong Hing Bank Ltd* [1986] A.C. 80, 104; *Scally v Southern Health and Social Services Board* [1992] 1 A.C. 294; *Bedfordshire CC v Fitzpatrick Contractors Ltd* (1998) 62 Const. L.R. 64, 71; *Mousaka Inc v Golden Seagull Maritime Inc* [2002] 1 Lloyd's Rep. 797, 802; *Meridian International Services Ltd v Richardson* [2008] EWCA Civ 609, [2008] Info. T.L.R. 139; *Brookfield Construction Ltd v Foster & Partners Ltd* [2009] EWHC 307 (TCC), [2009] B.L.R. 246; *Arla Foods UK Plc v Barnes* [2008] EWHC 2851 (Ch), [2009] 1 B.C.L.C. 699; *Mediterranean Salvage and Towage Ltd v Seamar Trading & Commerce Inc (The "Reborn")* [2009] EWCA Civ 531, [2009] 2 Lloyd's Rep. 639 at [15]–[18]; *IMT Shipping and Chartering GmbH v Chansung Shipping Co Ltd (The "Zenovia")* [2009] EWHC 739 (Comm), [2009] 2 Lloyd's Rep. 139 at [23]; *AET Inc Ltd v Arcadia Petroleum Ltd* [2009] EWHC 2337 (Comm), [2010] 1 Lloyd's Rep. 593 at [39]; *Fortis Bank SA/NV v Indian Overseas Bank* [2010] EWHC 84 (Comm), [2010] 2 Lloyd's Rep. 641 at [65]; *Strydom v Vendside Ltd* [2009] EWHC 2130 (QB); *Chantry Estates (South East) Ltd v Anderson* [2010] EWCA Civ 316, 130 Con. L.R. 11; *Re Agrimarche Ltd* [2010] EWHC 1655 (Ch), [2010] B.C.C. 775; *Dhamija v Sunningdale Joineries Ltd* [2010] EWHC 2396 (TCC), [2011] P.N.L.R. 9; *Cassa di Risparmio della Repubblica di San Marino SpA v Barclays Bank Ltd* [2011] EWHC 484 (Comm), [2011] 1 C.L.C. 701 at [544]; *Leander Construction Ltd v Mullaley & Co Ltd* [2011] EWHC 3449 (TCC), [2012] B.L.R. 152 at [41]; *NSB Ltd v Worldplay Ltd* [2012] EWHC 927 (Comm); *Consolidated Finance Ltd v McCluskey* [2012] EWCA Civ 1325, [2012] C.T.L.C. 133; *Euroption Strategic Fund Ltd v Skandinaviska Enskilda Banken AB* [2012] EWHC 584 (Comm), [2013] 1 B.C.L.C. 125; *Greatship (India) Ltd v Oceanografia SA de CV* [2012] EWHC 3468 (Comm), [2013] 1 All E.R. (Comm) 1244 at [41]; *Proton Energy Group SA v Orlen Lietuva* [2013] EWHC 2872 (Comm), [2014] 1 All E.R. (Comm) 972 at [43].

[54] *Marks & Spencer Plc v BNP Paribas Securities Services Trust Co (Jersey) Ltd* [2015] UKSC 72, [2016] A.C. 742 at [21] and [77]; *J N Hipwell & Son v Szurek* [2018] EWCA Civ 674 at [38]. Commercial coherence must be ascertained objectively and not simply from the perspective of one party. The fact that without the term the contract might potentially work to the disadvantage of one party in certain circumstances, in that it does not make a profit it might have made at other times, does not necessarily render the contract as a whole incoherent: *J Toomey Motors Ltd v Chevrolet UK Ltd* [2017] EWHC 276 (Comm) at [91]–[92]. The importance of "workability" was emphasised by Hildyard J. in *Lehman Brothers International (Europe) (In Administration) v Exotix Partners LLP* [2019] EWHC 2380 (Ch), [2020] 1 All E.R. (Comm) 635 at [171]–[172].

[55] *Hallman Holding Ltd v Webster* [2016] UKPC 3 at [14].

[56] See, for example, *Impact Funding Solutions Ltd v Barrington Support Services Ltd* [2016] UKSC 57, [2017] A.C. 73 at [31]–[32]; *BP Gas Marketing Ltd v La Societe Sonatrach* [2016] EWHC 2461 (Comm), 169 Con. L.R. 141 at [320]; *Teekay Tankers Ltd v STX Offshore & Shipbuilding Co Ltd* [2017] EWHC 253 (Comm), [2017] 1 Lloyd's Rep 387 at [190]; *J Toomey Motors Ltd v Chevrolet UK Ltd* [2017] EWHC 276 (Comm); *Gard Shipping AS v Clearlake Shipping Pte Ltd (The Zaliv Baikal)* [2017] EWHC 1091 (Comm), [2017] 2 All E.R. (Comm) 179 at [51]; *Co-operative Bank Plc v Hayes Freehold Ltd (in liquidation)* [2017] EWHC 1820 (Ch) at [99]; *Stevensdrake Ltd v Hunt* [2017] EWCA Civ 1173 at [50]; *Fraser Turner Ltd v PricewaterhouseCoopers LLP* [2018] EWHC 1743 (Ch) at [45]; *CFH Clearing Ltd v Merrill Lynch International* [2019] EWHC 963 (Comm) at [54]. Although it may now be more difficult to imply a term into a contract, cases can still be found in which the courts have been willing to make the implication: see, for example, *J N Hipwell & Son v Szurek* [2018] EWCA Civ 674 and *Sparks v Biden* [2107] EWHC 1994 (Ch).

[57] A proposition with which Lord Hoffmann expressed his agreement in *Att-Gen of Belize v Belize Telecom Ltd* [2009] UKPC 10, [2009] 1 W.L.R. 1988 at [17].

### Incomplete contract

*Replace paragraph with:*

**14-016** A further situation where a term may be implied is where the court is simply concerned to establish what the contract is, the parties not having themselves fully stated the terms: "[i]n this sense the court is searching for what must be implied".[68] There is no need for the court first to identify the existence of a contract before considering whether to imply a term into that contract: a term can be implied into what would otherwise be an incomplete agreement if it is necessary to do so in order to make the contract work as intended by the parties.[69] In *Liverpool City Council v Irwin*[70] the contract by which dwelling units in a council block were let to tenants consisted of "conditions of tenancy" which imposed obligations upon the tenants, but which were silent as to the contractual obligations of the landlord. The House of Lords implied an obligation on the part of the landlord to take reasonable care to keep the essential means of access and other communal facilities in reasonable repair. In *Sim v Rotherham Metropolitan BC*[71] the contracts under which secondary school teachers were employed were in general silent as to the extent of the teachers' obligations as teachers. The court implied an obligation on their part to cover for absent colleagues during non-teaching periods if requested to do so. And in *Scally v Southern Health and Social Services Board*[72] contracts of employment of public health service employees contained a term, derived from a collective agreement reached between representatives of the employers and of the employees, whereby a valuable pension benefit was conferred upon an employee contingent upon action being taken by him to avail himself of the benefit. An employee could not, in all the circumstances, reasonably be expected to be aware of the term unless it was drawn to his attention. The House of Lords implied an obligation on the employer to take reasonable steps to bring the term in question to the employee's attention so that he might be in a position to enjoy the benefit. In this type of case, the implication does not appear so much to depend on the intentions of the parties, but resembles more closely an implication of law,[73] since the term is implied as a "legal incident"[74] of a definable category of contract, though only where certain circumstances exist.

[68] *Liverpool City Council v Irwin* [1977] A.C. 239, 254.

[69] *Wells v Devani* [2019] UKSC 4, [2020] A.C. 129 at [30]–[35], distinguishing (at [31]) as an "unusual case" the decision of the Privy Council in *Scancarriers A/S v Aotearoa International Ltd* [1985] 2 Lloyd's Rep. 419 which was held (at [33]) not to stand for the "far-reaching proposition" that it is not possible to turn an incomplete bargain into a legally binding contract by adding expressly agreed terms and implied terms together.

[70] [1977] A.C. 239.

[71] [1987] Ch. 216. cf. *Bull v Nottinghamshire and City of Nottingham Fire and Rescue Authority* [2007] EWCA Civ 240, [2007] B.L.G.R. 439 (firefighters' contracts).

[72] [1992] 1 A.C. 294. cf. *University of Nottingham v Evett* [1999] 1 W.L.R. 594; *Crossley v Faithful & Gould Holdings Ltd* [2004] EWCA Civ 293, [2004] I.C.R. 1615; and see para.1-057, above; Vol.II, para.40-152.

[73] But it is still subject to the test of necessity; *Liverpool City Council v Irwin* [1977] A.C. 239, 254, 262, 266; *Scally v Southern Health and Social Services Board* [1992] 1 A.C. 294.

[74] *Liverpool City Council v Irwin* [1977] A.C. 239, 255, 270.

**Term must be formulated with sufficient precision**

*Replace footnote 76 with:*

[76] *Sparkes v Biden* [2017] EWHC 1994 (Ch) at [63]; *CFH Clearing Ltd v Merrill Lynch International* [2019] EWHC 963 (Comm) at [56]; *Marme Inversiones 2007 SL v Natwest Markets Plc* [2019] EWHC 366 (Comm) at [498]. **14-017**

## Implied term must not be inconsistent with an express term

*Replace paragraph with:*

**14-018** It is "a cardinal rule that no term can be implied into a contract if it contradicts an express term".[78] A contradiction, or inconsistency, can for this purpose take one of two forms: direct linguistic inconsistency or substantive inconsistency.[79] An inconsistency is linguistic where the wording of the proposed implied term contradicts or cannot be reconciled as a matter of language or grammar with one or more of the express terms of the contract. Substantive inconsistency is more difficult to define but it arises where the proposed implied term does not fit with the substance of the parties' rights and obligations under the express terms of the contract or their express allocation of the risk of the occurrence of a particular event. The fact that an implied term cannot be inconsistent with an express term of the contract lends support to the proposition that interpretation is "the precursor of implication",[80] and that the approach of the court should be "sequential"[81] rather than "iterative"[82] with the court first giving consideration to the express terms of the contract and, only when it has completed that task, should it turn to consider whether or not it is appropriate to imply a term into that contract. The implied term may, however, be "fashioned" to ensure that it is consistent with the express terms of the contract.[82a] Further, the fact that an express term "covers" a particular issue does not have the inevitable consequence that there can be no implied term where there is no inconsistency between the express term and the implied term, although in such a case "the existence of such an express term makes the co-existence of a further implied term on the same subject unlikely and especially so in a lengthy and carefully drafted document on which legal professionals have been advising".[82b]

[78] *Marks & Spencer Plc v BNP Paribas Securities Services Trust Co (Jersey) Ltd* [2015] UKSC 72, [2016] A.C. 742 at [28]. See also *BP Refinery (Westenport) Pty Ltd v Shire of Hastings* (1977) 52 A.J.L.R. 20, 26; *Duke of Westminster v Guild* [1985] Q.B. 688, 700; *Eurico Spa v Philipp Brothers* [1987] 2 Lloyd's Rep. 215, 219; *Gyllenhammar & Partners International Ltd v Sour Brodogradevna Industrija* [1989] 2 Lloyd's Rep. 403, 415; *Yorkshire Water Services Ltd v Sun Alliance & London Insurance Plc* [1997] 2 Lloyd's Rep. 21, 33; *Fast Ferries One SA v Ferries Australia Pty Ltd* [2000] 1 Lloyd's Rep. 534, 541; *Times Newspapers Ltd v George Weidenfeld & Nicolson Ltd* [2002] F.S.R. 29; *WX Investments Ltd v Begg* [2002] EWHC 925 (Ch), [2002] 1 W.L.R. 2849 at [28]; *Hadley Design Associates Ltd v Westminster CC* [2003] EWHC 1617 (TCC), [2004] T.C.L.R. 1; *Fairfax Gerrard Holdings Ltd v Capital Bank Plc* [2006] EWHC 3439 (Comm), [2007] 1 Lloyd's Rep. 171; *Wootton Trucks Ltd v Man ERF UK Ltd* [2006] EWCA Civ 1042, [2006] Eu. L.R. 1217; *Port of Tilbury (London) Ltd v Stora Enso Transport & Distribution Ltd* [2009] EWCA Civ 16, [2009] 1 Lloyd's Rep. 391 at [26]–[27]; *Lancore Services Ltd v Barclays Bank Plc* [2009] EWCA Civ 752, [2010] 1 All E.R. 763; *Dominion Corporate Trustees Ltd v Capmark Bank Europe Plc* [2011] EWCA Civ 380; *Southwark LBC v IBM UK Ltd* [2011] EWHC 549 (TCC), 135 Con, L.R. 136; *Carey Group Plc v AIB Group (UK) Plc* [2011] EWHC 567 (Ch), [2011] 2 All E.R. (Comm) 461; *Stevensdrake Ltd v Hunt* [2017] EWCA Civ 1173 at [49].

[79] *Irish Bank Resolution Corporation Ltd v Camden Markets Holding Corp* [2017] EWCA Civ 7, [2017] 2 All E.R. (Comm) 781 at [35].

[80] *Trump International Golf Club Scotland Ltd v Scottish Ministers* [2015] UKSC 74, [2016] 1 W.L.R. 85 at [35] per Lord Hodge.

[81] The approach adopted by Lord Neuberger in *Marks & Spencer Plc v BNP Paribas Securities Services Trust Co (Jersey) Ltd* [2015] UKSC 72, [2016] A.C. 742 at [28], albeit he did recognise that it may "conceivably be appropriate to reconsider the interpretation of the express term of a contract once one has decided whether to imply a term".

[82] The approach adopted by Lord Carnwath in *Marks & Spencer Plc v BNP Paribas Securities Services Trust Co (Jersey) Ltd* [2015] UKSC 72, [2016] A.C. 742 at [71]. In *Trump International Golf Club Scotland Ltd v Scottish Ministers* [2015] UKSC 74, [2016] 1 W.L.R. 85 at [43] Lord Mance observed that he "would not encourage advocates or courts to adopt too rigid or sequential an approach to the processes of consideration of the express terms and of consideration of the possibility of an implication.". Given that Lord Neuberger's judgment in *Marks & Spencer* is the majority judgment, the correct approach to take is therefore the "sequential" rather than the "iterative" approach, subject to Lord Neuberger's caveat noted in the previous footnote.

[82a] *Dymoke v Association for Dance Movement Psychotherapy UK Ltd* [2019] EWHC 94 (QB) at [60].

[82b] *Fraser Turner Ltd v PricewaterhouseCoopers LLP* [2018] EWHC 1743 (Ch) at [48], approved on appeal at [2019] EWCA Civ 1290 at [33].

## Entire agreement clauses and implied terms

*Replace paragraph with:*

An entire agreement clause does not generally affect or prevent the implication of a term as a matter of fact on the basis of necessity given that: **14-019**

> "... it cannot be supposed that the parties would have intended an entire agreement clause to cause the agreement to fail, and to prevent the court from saving it, if there is an available and appropriate means of doing so consistently with, and indeed to give effect to, what the Court finds must have been the true intention of the parties."[83]

A similar approach has been held to be applicable to a term implied in law, particularly where the nature of the implied term is to confer a valuable right on a contracting party.[83a] So, for example, an entire agreement clause should not be effective to exclude the operation of the implied term of trust and confidence in a contract of employment.[84] The reason for this is that an implied term is intrinsic to the agreement itself and so not caught by the terms of the entire agreement clause,[85] unless the clause uses express language the effect of which is specifically to exclude such implied terms.[86]

[83] *J N Hipwell & Son v Szurek* [2018] EWCA Civ 674 at [27]. See also *One Fish Co Ltd v Iceland Foods Ltd* [2017] EWHC 3366 (Comm) at [32]; *Kason Kek-Gardner Ltd v Process Components Ltd* [2017] EWCA Civ 2132 at [52]; *AXA Sun Life Services Plc v Campbell Martin Ltd* [2011] EWCA Civ 133, [2011] 2 Lloyd's Rep. 1 at [41]; *Exxonmobile Sales and Supply Corp v Texaco Ltd* [2003] EWHC 1964 (Comm), [2004] 1 All E.R. (Comm) 435 at [27]; *NHS Commissioning Board v Vasant* [2019] EWCA Civ 1245 at [51]; *Yoo Design Services Ltd v New Reality Pte Ltd* [2020] EWHC 1077 (Comm) at [82]–[85]; *Essex CC v UBB Waste (Essex) Ltd (No. 2)* [2020] EWHC 1581 (TCC) at [110]–[111]. However, the presence in the contract of an entire agreement clause may be regarded as a factor which counts against the implication of a term: *Sparks v Biden* [2017] EWHC 1994 (Ch) at [54].

[83a] *Nigeria v JP Morgan Chase Bank NA* [2019] EWHC 347 (Comm) at [37].

[84] On which see further para.14-027.

[85] *AXA Sun Life Services Plc v Campbell Martin Ltd* [2011] EWCA Civ 133, [2011] 2 Lloyd's Rep. 1 at [41].

[86] *AXA Sun Life Services Plc v Campbell Martin Ltd* [2011] EWCA Civ 133, [2011] 2 Lloyd's Rep. 1 at [41]. See also *Exxonmobile Sales and Supply Corp v Texaco Ltd (The Helene Knutsen)* [2003] EWHC 1964 (Comm), [2003] 2 Lloyd's Rep. 686 where an entire agreement clause which provided that the contract "contains the entire agreement of the parties ... and there is no other promise, representation, warranty, usage or course of dealing affecting it" was held to be effective to exclude an implied term based on custom or usage. In the case where the term is implied into the contract as a result of the intervention of Parliament, the relevant statute or statutory instrument may state in express terms that the implied term cannot be excluded, in which case there is no question of an entire agreement clause being capable of excluding such a term.

# (b) Illustrations

## Illustrations of cases where no term was implied

*To the end of paragraph, after "paid its commission[142]", add:*

; and into a contract of loan that the debtor pay interest to the creditor.[142a] **14-022**

[142a] *Al Jaber v Al Ibrahim* [2018] EWCA Civ 1690, [2019] 1 W.L.R. 885.

## Co-operation

*Replace footnote 144 with:*

14-023 [144] *Mackay v Dick* (1881) 6 App. Cas. 251, 263. See also *Hunt v Bishop* (1853) 8 Ex. 675; *Roberts v Bury Commissioners* (1870) L.R. 5 C.P. 310, 325; *Nelson v Dahl* (1879) 12 Ch. D. 568, 592 (affirmed (1881) 6 App. Cas. 38); *Sprague v Booth* [1909] A.C. 576, 580; *Kleinert v Abosso Gold Mining Co* (1913) 58 S.J. (PC) 45; *Harrison v Walker* [1919] 2 K.B. 453; *Colley v Overseas Exporters* [1921] 3 K.B. 302, 309; *Panamena Europa Navegacion v Frederick Leyland & Co Ltd* [1947] A.C. 428, 436; *Luxor (Eastbourne) Ltd v Cooper* [1941] A.C. 108, 118; *A. V. Pound & Co Ltd v M. W. Hardy & Co Inc* [1956] A.C. 588, 608, 611; *Sociedad Financiera de Bienes Raices v Agrimpex* [1961] A.C. 135; *Sunbeam Shipping Co Ltd v President of India* [1973] 1 Lloyd's Rep. 482, 486; *Schindler v Pigault* [1975] 1 C.L. 401; *Metro Meat Ltd v Fares Rural Co Pty Ltd* [1985] 2 Lloyd's Rep. 13, 14; *Merton LBC v Hugh Leach Ltd* (1985) 32 B.L.R. 51; *Kurt A. Becher GmbH & Co K.G. v Roplak Enterprises SA* [1991] 2 Lloyd's Rep. 23, 30, 34; *Davy Offshore Ltd v Emerald Field Contracting Ltd* (1991) 27 Con. L.R. 138; *Nissho Iwai Petroleum Inc v Cargill International SA* [1993] 1 Lloyd's Rep. 80, 84; *Scottish Power Plc v Kvaerner Construction (Regions) Ltd* 1999 S.L.T. 721; *Goodway v Zurich Insurance Co* [2004] EWHC 137, (2004) 96 Const. L.R. 49; *General Trading Co (Holdings) Ltd v Richmond Corp Ltd* [2008] EWHC 1479 (Comm), [2008] 2 Lloyd's Rep. 475 at [87]; *Hudson Bay Apparel Brands LLC v Umbro International Ltd* [2009] EWHC 2861 (Ch) at [119], [128], [136], [140]; *Yam Seng Pte Ltd v International Trade Corp Ltd* [2013] EWHC 111 (QB), [2013] 1 All E.R. (Comm) 1321 at [139]; *Swallowfalls Ltd v Monaco Yachtung & Technologies S.A.M.* [2014] EWCA Civ 186, [2014] 2 Lloyd's Rep. 50 at [32], [33]; *Ali v Petroleum Co of Trinidad and Tobago* [2017] UKPC 2, [2017] I.C.R. 531 at [8]; *Sanderson Ltd v Simtom Food Projects Ltd* [2019] EWHC 442 (TCC), [2019] B.L.R. 260 at [25]. See also below, para.24-033, Vol.II, para.37-075.

## Prevention of performance

*Replace paragraph with:*

14-024 By the same token:

> "... if a party enters into an arrangement which can only take effect by the continuance of a certain existing state of circumstances, there is an implied engagement on his part that he shall do nothing of his own motion to put an end to that state of circumstances under which alone the arrangement can become operative."[147]

Also where a binding contract is subject to a condition precedent,[148] a term may be implied that a party will not do an act which, if done, would prevent fulfilment of the condition.[149] But these implications are not inevitable[149a]: the alleged term may be unreasonably wide[150] or be displaced by an express term[151] or the nature of the contract may indicate otherwise.[152] A term may also be implied that a right, remedy or benefit expressly conferred upon one party to a contract or to which he may be entitled shall not be available if that party relies on his own breach of the contract to establish his claim.[153]

[147] *Stirling v Maitland* (1864) 5 B. & S. 840, 852. See also *Rhodes v Forwood* (1876) 1 App. Cas. 256, 272, 274; *Turner v Goldsmith* [1891] 1 Q.B. 544; *Ogdens Ltd v Nelson* [1905] A.C. 109; *Warren v Agdeshman* (1922) 38 T.L.R. 588; *C. French & Co Ltd v Leeston Shipping Co Ltd* [1922] 1 A.C. 451; *Southern Foundries (1926) Ltd v Shirlaw* [1940] A.C. 701; *William Cory & Son Ltd v City of London Corp* [1951] 2 K.B. 476, 484; *A. Hamson & Son (London) Ltd v S. Martin Johnson & Co Ltd* [1953] 1 Lloyd's Rep. 553; *Shindler v Northern Raincoat Ltd* [1960] 1 W.L.R. 1038; *The Unique Mariner (No.2)* [1979] 1 Lloyd's Rep. 37; *Merton LBC v Hugh Leach Ltd* (1985) 32 B.L.R. 51; *Martin-Smith v Williams* [1999] E.M.L.R. 571; *CEL Group Ltd v Nedloyd Lines UK Ltd* [2003] EWCA Civ 1716, [2004] 1 Lloyd's Rep. 381 at [11], [22] and [23]; *Yam Seng Pte Ltd v International Trade Corp Ltd* [2013] EWHC 111 (QB), [2013] 1 All E.R. (Comm) 1321 at [139]; *Duval v 11-13 Randolph Crescent Ltd* [2020] UKSC 18, [2020] 2 W.L.R. 1167 at [44]–[59]. See also Bateson [1960] J.B.L. 187; Burrows (1968) 31 M.L.R. 390; above, para.2-163; Vol.II, para.37-074.

[148] See above, para.13-028.

[149] *Holme v Guppy* (1838) 3 M. & W. 387, 389; *Inchbald v Western Neilgherry Coffee, etc., Co* (1864) 17 C.B. N.S. 733; *Roberts v Bury Improvements Commissioners* (1870) L.R. 5 C.P. 310, 316; *Mackay v Dick* (1881) 6 App. Cas. 251; *Dodd v Churton* [1897] 1 Q.B. 562, 566; *Barque Quilpué Ltd v Brown* [1904] 2 K.B. 264, 271; *Hickman & Co v Roberts* [1913] A.C. 229; *Trollope v Martyn* [1934] 2 K.B. 436; *Amalgamated Building Contractors Ltd v Waltham Holy Cross U.D.C.* [1952] 2 All E.R. 452, 455;

*Jebco Properties v Mastforce* [1992] N.P.C. 42; *Nissho Iwai Petroleum Co Inc v Cargill International SA* [1993] 1 Lloyd's Rep. 80; *Taylor v Rive Droite Music Ltd* [2005] EWCA Civ 1300, [2006] E.M.L.R. 4. See also below, para.24-033.

[149a] *Law Debenture Trust Corp Plc v Ukraine* [2018] EWCA Civ 2026, [2019] Q.B. 1121 at [207] (there is "no general rule" that a term will be implied prohibiting one party from "preventing" the performance of the other).

[150] *Philips Electronique Grand Public SA v British Sky Broadcasting Ltd* [1995] E.M.L.R. 472; *Times Newspapers Ltd v George Weidenfeld & Nicolson Ltd* [2002] F.S.R. 29.

[151] *Locke v Candy and Candy Ltd* [2010] EWCA Civ 1350, [2011] I.R.L.R. 163.

[152] *Aspdin v Austin* (1844) 5 Q.B. 671; *European, etc., Mail Co v Royal Mail Steam Packet Co* (1861) 30 L.J.C.P. 247; *Rhodes v Forwood* (1876) 1 App. Cas. 256; *Hamlyn v Wood* [1891] 2 Q.B. 488; *Luxor (Eastbourne) Ltd v Cooper* [1941] A.C. 108; *William Cory & Son Ltd v City of London Corp* [1951] 2 K.B. 476; *Farr v Admiralty* [1953] 1 W.L.R. 965; *Thompson v Asda-MFI Group Plc* [1988] Ch. 241; *Davy Offshore Ltd v Emerald Field Contracting Ltd* (1991) 27 Con. L.R. 138; *Philips Electronique Grand Public SA v British Sky Broadcasting Ltd* [1995] E.M.L.R. 477; *Multiplex Construction (UK) Ltd v Honeywell Control Systems Ltd* [2007] EWHC 447 (TCC), (2007) 111 Const. L.R. 78; see Vol.II, para.37-074.

[153] cf. *Richco International Ltd v Alfred C. Toepfer International GmbH* [1991] 1 Lloyd's Rep. 136, 144; *Bulk Shipping A.G. v Ipco Trading SA* [1992] 1 Lloyd's Rep. 39, 43; *Petroplus Marketing AG v Shell Trading International Ltd (The "Niviae")* [2009] EWHC 1024 (Comm), [2009] 2 Lloyd's Rep. 611 at [17].

### Implied restriction on contractual discretion

*Replace paragraph with:*

The courts have sought to ensure that contractual powers, particularly those relating to the exercise of a discretion, are not abused and they have done this by implying a term: **14-026**

> "... as to the manner in which such powers may be exercised, a term which may vary according to the terms of the contract and the context in which the decision-making power is given."[159]

The courts recognise that, in such cases, they are not the primary decision-makers and that their task is to review the decision that has been made by the contracting party.[160] The standard of review should be no higher than that developed in the context of the judicial review of administrative action and this may require not only that the contractual decision-maker exclude extraneous considerations from the decision-making process but that it should also be required to take into account those considerations which are obviously relevant to the decision in question.[161] Unless the court can imply a term that the outcome be objectively reasonable (for example a reasonable price or a reasonable term), the court will only imply a term that the decision-making process be lawful and rational in the public law sense, that the decision is made rationally (as well as in good faith) and consistently with its commercial purpose.[162] Thus a number of examples can be found of cases in which the courts have implied a term that the discretion should not be exercised dishonestly, for an improper purpose, capriciously, arbitrarily or in a way that no reasonable person, acting reasonably, would act.[163] The implied term has been described as a duty of rationality[164] but its precise scope may depend on the nature of the relationship between the parties[165] and, in a commercial context, may demand no more than that discretion be exercised "in pursuit of legitimate commercial aims".[166] The mere fact that a contracting party has a choice to exercise does not of itself attract the operation of the implied term.[167] So, for example, a term should not be implied where a contracting party has a decision to make in relation to the exercise of an absolute contractual right.[168] Similarly, the discretion conferred may be found, on its true construction, to be unqualified, in which case the court ought not to imply a term restraining the exercise of the right, given the rule that an implied term cannot contradict or be inconsistent with an express term of the contract.[169]

[159] *Braganza v BP Shipping Ltd* [2015] UKSC 17, [2015] 1 W.L.R. 1661 at [18].

[160] *Braganza v BP Shipping Ltd* [2015] UKSC 17, [2015] 1 W.L.R. 1661 at [19]; *Watson v Watchfinder.co.uk Ltd* [2017] EWHC 1275 (Comm), [2017] Bus. L.R. 1309 at [103].

[161] *Braganza v BP Shipping Ltd* [2015] UKSC 17, [2015] 1 W.L.R. 1661 at [28]–[29].

[162] *Braganza v BP Shipping Ltd* [2015] UKSC 17, [2015] 1 W.L.R. 1661 at [30].

[163] *British Telecommunications Plc v Telefónica O2 UK Ltd* [2014] UKSC 42, [2014] 4 All E.R. 907 at [37]; *Abu Dhabi National Tanker Co v Product Star Shipping Ltd* [1993] 1 Lloyd's Rep. 397, 404; *Paragon Finance Plc v Nash* [2001] EWCA Civ 1466, [2002] 1 W.L.R. 685 at [31]; *Gan Insurance Co Ltd v Tai Ping Insurance Co Ltd* [2001] EWCA Civ 1047, [2001] 2 All E.R. (Comm) 299 at [67]; *Socimer International Bank Ltd v Standard Bank London Ltd* [2008] EWCA Civ 116, [2008] 1 Lloyd's Rep. 538 at [60]–[69]; *Yam Seng Pte Ltd v International Trade Corp Ltd* [2013] EWHC 111 (QB), [2013] 1 All E.R. (Comm) 1321 at [145]; *Marex Financial Ltd v Creative Finance Ltd* [2013] EWHC 2155 (Comm), [2014] 1 All E.R. (Comm) 122 at [57], [89]; *Hockin v Royal Bank of Scotland* [2016] EWHC 925 (Ch) at [37]; *Monde Petroleum SA v WesternZagros Ltd* [2016] EWHC 1472 (Comm) at [242]–[276]; see above, para.1-059. cf. *Paragon Finance Plc v Pender* [2005] EWCA Civ 760, [2005] 1 W.L.R. 3412; *Everwarm Ltd v BN Rendering Ltd* [2019] EWHC 3060 (TCC), 187 Con. L.R. 240 at [123]; *UK Acorn Finance Ltd v Markel (UK) Ltd* [2020] EWHC 922 (Comm) at [63]. See also Vol.II, para.39-293 (interest rates); above, para.1-059, Vol.II, para.40-078 (bonuses). The cases in which a term of this nature has been implied are cases in which the contracting party had a choice to make among a range of options, taking into account the interests of both parties. Where, on the other hand, the discretion relates to the exercise of an absolute contractual right, there is no room for the implication of a term placing a limit on the exercise of that contractual right: *Mid Essex Hospital Services NHS Trust v Compass Group UK and Ireland Ltd* [2013] EWCA Civ 200, [2013] B.L.R. 265 at [83].

[164] *Faieta v ICAP Management Services Ltd* [2017] EWHC 2995 (QB), [2018] I.R.L.R. 227 at [21].

[165] *Braganza v BP Shipping Ltd* [2015] UKSC 17, [2015] 1 W.L.R. 1661 at [30] where the relationship between the parties was an employment relationship and it was acknowledged (at [32]) that an employment contract is "of a different character from an ordinary commercial contract".

[166] *Property Alliance Group Ltd v Royal Bank of Scotland Plc* [2018] EWCA Civ 355, [2018] 1 W.L.R. 3529 at [169].

[167] See also above, para.1-060.

[168] *Mid Essex Hospital Services NHS Trust v Compass Group UK and Ireland Ltd* [2013] EWCA Civ 200, [2013] B.L.R. 265 at [83]; *UBS AG v Rose Capital Ventures Ltd* [2018] EWHC 3137 (Ch) at [50]; *TAQA Bratini Ltd v Rockrose UKCS8 LLC* [2020] EWHC 58 (Comm); *Essex CC v UBB Waste (Essex) Ltd (No. 2)* [2020] EWHC 1581 (TCC) at [97]; *Cathay Pacific Airways Ltd v Lufthansa Technik AG* [2020] EWHC 1789 (Ch) at [183]. The question as to what amounts to a "discretion" for this purpose merits further examination: see, for example, *Brogden v Investec Bank Plc* [2016] EWCA Civ 1031, [2017] I.R.L.R. 90 at [20] where the Court of Appeal held that Leggatt J. had erred in concluding that the issue before the court was one that related to the exercise of a contractual discretion rather than the interpretation of the scope of a contractual right.

[169] See para.14-018 and *Reda Ltd v Flag* [2002] UKPC 38, [2002] I.R.L.R. 747 at [45]. However, a court may be slow to conclude that the express terms of the contract confer a power on a contracting party to exercise its discretion irrationally and so read the implied term into what might otherwise appear to be a very broadly worded term. So, for example, a clause which confers an "absolute discretion" on a contracting party may nevertheless be subject to the implied term: *Faieta v ICAP Management Services Ltd* [2017] EWHC 2995 (QB), [2018] I.R.L.R. 227. In this way a discretion which is stated to be "absolute" may not be quite as absolute as the party exercising the right may believe it to be.

## Implied term as to good faith

*Replace paragraph with:*

**14-028** English law has traditionally been hostile to the imposition of any general principle of good faith in the performance of contracts[174] but in *Yam Seng Pte Ltd v International Trade Corp Ltd*[175] Leggatt J. considered the arguments for (and against) the implication of such a duty. While the issue awaits definitive resolution, it would appear that the courts may now be willing to imply such a duty as a matter of law into a narrow category of contracts, such as "contracts between partners or others whose relationship is characterised as a fiduciary one"[176] or a "relational contract"[177] and to imply it as a matter of fact where the implication is necessary to give effect to the intention of the parties. However, the courts are likely to be slow to imply such a term as a matter of fact and are more likely to decline to do so either because it is inconsistent with or does not fit with the express terms of the contract[178] or because of the arm's-length nature of the relationship between the parties.[179] The willingness of the court to imply the term may also be linked to the substantive content of the term. The more demanding the term, the less willing the court may be to imply the term.[180] Conversely, if the term requires only that the parties act honestly and with integrity,[181] the court may be more willing to imply the term and, indeed, it may not be possible for the parties to exclude an obligation to act honestly.[182]

[174] See para.1-044, above.

[175] [2013] EWHC 111 (QB), [2013] 1 All E.R. (Comm) 1321 at [121]–[154]. Contrast *Mid Essex Hospital Services NHS Trust v Compass Group UK and Ireland Ltd* [2013] EWCA Civ 200, [2013] B.L.R. 265 at [105] and [150]; *TSG Building Services Plc v South Anglia Housing Ltd* [2013] EWHC 1151 (TCC), [2013] B.L.R. 484; *Hamsard 3147 Ltd v Boots UK Ltd* [2013] EWHC 3251 (Pat) at [85], [92]; and see above, paras 1-044, 1-058.

[176] *Yam Seng Pte Ltd v International Trade Corp Ltd* [2013] EWHC 111 (QB), [2013] 1 All E.R. (Comm) 1321 at [131].

[177] *Al Nehayan v Kent* [2018] EWHC 333 (Comm), [2018] 1 C.L.C. 216 at [167]–[174]; *Bates v Post Office Ltd (No.3: Common Issues)* [2019] EWHC 606 (QB) at [711] and [725]–[726]; *Essex CC v UBB Waste (Essex) Ltd (No.2)* [2020] EWHC 1581 (TCC) at [104]–[106]. A non-exhaustive list of the characteristics of a "relational" contract was set out by Fraser J. in *Bates v Post Office Ltd* at [725]. While these characteristics have been described as "helpful indicia" (*Essex CC v UBB Waste (Essex) Ltd (No.2)* [2020] EWHC 1581 (TCC) at [106]), there has also been doubt cast on the utility of this attempt to define a "relational" contract from which a good faith duty is then derived (see *UTB LLC v Sheffield United Ltd* [2019] EWHC 2322 (Ch) at [202]–[204]; *Russell v Cartwright* [2020] EWHC 41 (Ch) at [87] and *Cathay Pacific Airways Ltd v Lufthansa Technik AG* [2020] EWHC 1789 (Ch) at [216]). Rather than ask whether the contract is "relational" (on the basis of which a duty of good faith is then derived), the preferable approach would appear to be to examine all the facts and circumstances of the case, including the alleged "relational" nature of the contract, when answering the question whether a reasonable reader of the contract would consider an obligation of good faith to be so obvious as to go without saying or whether such an obligation is necessary for the proper working of the contract between the parties.

[178] *Carewatch Care Services Ltd v Focus Care Services Ltd* [2014] EWHC 2313 (Ch) at [109]; *Greenclose Ltd v National Westminster Bank Plc* [2014] EWHC 1156 (Ch); *Fujitsu Services Ltd v IBM United Kingdom Ltd* [2014] EWHC 752 (TCC); *TSG Building Services v South Anglia Housing Ltd* [2013] EWHC 1151 (TCC), [2013] B.L.R. 484; *Globe Motors Inc v TRW Lucas Varity Electric Steering Ltd* [2016] EWCA Civ 396, [2016] 1 C.L.C. 712 at [68]; *Teesside Gas Transportation Ltd v CATS North Sea Ltd* [2019] EWHC 1220 (Comm) at [38]; *Russell v Cartwright* [2020] EWHC 41 (Ch) at [89]; *Cathay Pacific Airways Ltd v Lufthansa Technik AG* [2020] EWHC 1789 (Ch) at [219] and [223]. Indeed, in an arm's length commercial relationship the courts will generally incline against the implication of a good faith term and will put the onus on the parties to include an express term to this effect if they wish to be bound by such a duty: *Chelsfield Advisers LLP v Qatari Diar Real Estate Investment Co* [2015] EWHC 1322 (Ch) at [80].

[179] *Hamsard 3147 Ltd v Boots UK Ltd* [2013] EWHC 3251 (Pat); *Portsmouth City Council v Ensign Highways Ltd* [2015] EWHC 1969 (TCC); *Myers v Kestrel Acquisitions Ltd* [2015] EWHC 916 (Ch).

[180] See, for example, *Hamsard 3147 Ltd v Boots UK Ltd* [2013] EWHC 3251 (Pat) at [86] where the term proposed was taken to require "a contracting party to subordinate its own commercial interests to those of the other contracting party". See also *Monde Petroleum SA v WesternZagros Ltd* [2016] EWHC 1472 (Comm), [2016] 2 Lloyd's Rep. 229 at [242]–[276].

[181] *D&G Cars v Essex Police Authority* [2015] EWHC 226 (QB), [2015] All E.R. (D) 85 (Mar) at [173]; *Apollo Window Blinds Ltd v McNeil* [2016] EWHC 2307 (QB); *T and L Sugars Ltd v Tate and Lyle Industries Ltd* [2015] EWHC 2696 (Comm) at [152] ("while it would be right to imply a term that the Defendant would act in good faith and honestly in carrying out the process envisaged in clauses 3.7.1 and 3.7.3, there is no proper basis for the implication of the very much more onerous term for which the Claimant argues"); *Wales (t/a Selective Investment Services) v CBRE Managed Services Ltd* [2020]

EWHC 16 (Comm) at [66]–[67] (where a term was implied that the parties would deal honestly with one another but not that they would deal with one another in good faith).

[182] *Yam Seng Pte Ltd v International Trade Corp Ltd* [2013] EWHC 111 (QB), [2013] 1 All E.R. (Comm) 1321 at [149].

## 3. TERMS IMPLIED BY CUSTOM AND USAGE

### When implied from usage or custom

*Replace footnote 206 with:*

**14-033** [206] *Yates v Pym* (1816) 6 Taunt. 446; *Daun v City of London Brewery Co* (1869) L.R. 8 Eq. 155, 161; *Nelson v Dahl* (1879) 12 Ch. D. 568, 575 (affirmed (1881) 6 App. Cas. 38); *Re Walkers, Winser & Hamm and Shaw, Son & Co* [1904] 2 K.B. 152; *Ropner v Stoate Hosegood & Co* (1905) 10 Com. Cas. 73; *Cunliffe-Owen v Teather and Greenwood* [1967] 1 W.L.R. 1421, 1438, 1439; *Constan Industries of Australia Pty Ltd v Norwich Winterthur Insurance (Aust.) Ltd* (1986) 160 C.L.R. 226; *Pryke v Gibbs Hartley Cooper Ltd* [1991] 1 Lloyd's Rep. 602, 615; *Danowski v Henry Moore Foundation, The Times,* March 19, 1996, CA; *Exxonmobil Sales and Supply Corp v Texaco Ltd* [2003] EWHC 1964 (Comm), [2003] 2 Lloyd's Rep. 686 at [21]; *Lehman Brothers International (Europe) (In Administration) v Exotix Partners LLP* [2019] EWHC 2380 (Ch), [2020] 1 All E.R. (Comm) 635 at [167].

CHAPTER 15

# EXEMPTION CLAUSES



## 1. IN GENERAL

### Types of exemption clause

*In line 7, after ""errors of description".", add new footnote 13a:*

[13a] cf. *European Film Bonds AS v Lotus Holdings LLC* [2020] EWHC 1115 (Ch) at [81], where the effect of two contract terms was held *not* to be an exclusion of liability as they rather provided a step in a procedural process which under the contract had the effect of removing an obligation on one of the parties to pay a sum. **15-003**

## 2. PRINCIPLES OF CONSTRUCTION

### General principles

*Replace footnote 49 with:*

[49] *The Starsin* [2004] 1 A.C. 715 at [144]; *Dairy Containers Ltd v Tasman Orient Line CV* [2004] UKPC 22, [2004] 2 All E.R. (Comm) 667 at [12]; *Nobahar-Cookson v Hut Group Ltd* [2016] EWCA Civ 128, [2016] 1 C.L.C. 573, esp. at [12]–[22] but cf. *Transocean Drilling UK Ltd v Providence Resources Plc* [2016] EWCA Civ 372, [2016] 2 All E.R. (Comm) 606 at [14] and [19] ("artificial approaches to **15-007**

construction" should not be applied to a contract by which the parties entered "mutual undertakings to accept the risk of consequential loss flowing from each other's breaches of contract"). And see Peel (ed.), *Treitel on The Law of Contract*, 15th edn (2020), para.7-010, Peel [2017] L.Q.R. 6; Tofaris [2019] L.M.C.L.Q. 270 and below, para.15-012.

## Clear and unambiguous expression

*Replace paragraph with:*

**15-008** The traditional rule is that exemption clauses must be expressed clearly and without ambiguity or they risk being ineffective.[50] In *J. Gordon Alison & Co Ltd v Wallsend Shipway and Engineering Co Ltd*,[51] a cylinder was sold by the defendants to the claimants "subject to our usual guarantee clauses". The clause relied on by the defendants "guaranteed" the purchaser against defects of material or workmanship for six months, but excluded liability for consequential damage. The question arose whether the guarantee clause was applicable to this particular contract, and the Court of Appeal held that it was not: "if a person was under a legal liability and wished to get rid of it he could only do so by using clear words".[52] Exemption clauses have therefore often been said to require strict construction, and the degree of strictness appropriate to their construction may properly depend upon the extent to which they involve departure from the implied obligations ordinarily accepted by the parties in entering into a contract of a particular kind[53] and whether the clause purports entirely to exclude an obligation or liability or merely to limit the compensation recoverable from the party in default.[54] Moreover, a majority of the Supreme Court has recently observed that this strict approach to exemption clauses properly so-called should also apply to terms:

> "... where they seek to prevent a liability from arising by removing, through a subsidiary provision, part of the benefit which it appears to have been the purpose of the contract to provide. The vice of a clause of that kind is that it can have a propensity to mislead, unless its language is sufficiently plain. All that said, words of exception may be simply a way of delineating the scope of the primary obligation."[55]

However, as earlier noted, it is clear that the normal principles of construction applicable to written contracts[56] apply equally to exemption clauses to ascertain what meaning the words bear.[57] This means that if the clause is expressed clearly and unambiguously, there is no justification for placing upon the language of the clause a strained and artificial meaning so as to avoid the exclusion or restriction of liability contained in it.[58] On the other hand, an exemption clause must be construed in the wider context of the contract as a whole, in a way which is consistent with business common sense and does not defeat the commercial object of the contract, and so as to give effect to the presumption that parties do not lightly abandon a remedy for breach of contract afforded them by the general law.[59] In an appropriate case, therefore, the existence of such a presumption does not prevent a court from finding, applying "all its tools of linguistic, contextual, purposive and common sense analysis", that the contract intended to deprive one of the parties of a right at law which he might otherwise have had.[60] As will be explained, more recently, for some judges this means that the traditional rule according to which exemption clauses should be construed *contra proferentem* has much less of a role to play at least as between two commercial contracting parties.[61]

[50] *Ailsa Craig Fishing Co Ltd v Malvern Fishing Co Ltd* [1983] 1 W.L.R. 964, 966, 970. See also *Gilbert-Ash (Northern) Ltd v Modern Engineering (Bristol) Ltd* [1974] A.C. 689, 717–718; *Photo Production Ltd v Securicor Transport Ltd* [1980] A.C. 827, 846, 850; *Bem Dis a Turk Ticaret S/A TR v International Agri Trade Co Ltd* [1999] 1 Lloyd's Rep. 729; *How Engineering Services Ltd v Lindner*

*Ceilings Floors Partitions Plc* (1999) 64 Const. L.R. 67, 79; *Cero Navigation Corp v Jean Lion & Cie* [2000] 1 Lloyd's Rep. 292, 297; *Stent Foundations Ltd v MJ Gleeson Group Plc* [2001] Build. L.R. 134; *Amiri Flight Authority v BAE Systems Plc* [2003] EWCA Civ 1447, [2003] 2 Lloyd's Rep. 767 at [25]; *Homburg Houtimport BV v Agrosin Private Ltd (The Starsin)* [2003] UKHL 12, [2004] 1 A.C. 715 at [144]; *Dairy Containers Ltd v Tasman Orient Line CV* [2004] UKPC 22, [2005] 1 W.L.R. 215 at [12]; *Stocznia Gdynia SA v Gearbulk Holdings Ltd* [2009] EWCA Civ 75, [2009] 1 Lloyd's Rep. 461 at [22]–[23]; *Seadrill Management Services Ltd v OAO Gazprom (The "Ekha")* [2010] EWHC 1530 (Comm), [2010] 1 Lloyd's Rep. 543 at [184], [217]–[218] (affirmed [2010] EWCA Civ 691). But see *Whitecap Leisure Ltd v John H Rundle Ltd* [2008] EWCA Civ 429, [2008] 2 Lloyd's Rep. 216 (imperfect clause enforced); *WW Gear Construction Ltd v McGee Group Ltd* [2010] EWHC 1460 (TCC), 131 Con. L.R. 63 and *Air Transworld Ltd v Bombardier Inc* [2012] EWHC 243 (Comm), [2012] 1 Lloyd's Rep. 349 (ordinary rules of construction apply); and cf. *Bahamas Oil Refining Co International Ltd v Owners of the Cape Bari Tankschiffahrts GmbH & Co KG* [2016] UKPC 20 at [31]–[40] (exclusion of limitation of liability arising by statute and international convention). But see *FG Wilson (Engineering) Ltd v John Holt & Co (Liverpool) Ltd* [2013] EWCA Civ 1232, [2014] 1 W.L.R. 2365 at [38], [59], [70] ("no set-off" clause need not be expressed in terms to qualify the payment obligation, though the decision was overruled on other grounds in *PST Energy 7 Shipping LLC v OW Bunker Malta Ltd* [2016] UKSC 23, [2016] 2 W.L.R. 1193 at [58]). On the special rules for the interpretation of contract terms (including exemption clauses) in consumer contracts see Vol.II, paras 38-347—38-351 (Unfair Terms in Consumer Contracts Regulations 1999 reg.7) and paras 38-414—38-417 (Consumer Rights Act 2015 s.69).

[51] (1927) 43 T.L.R. 323.

[52] (1927) 43 T.L.R. 323, 324.

[53] *Photo Production Ltd v Securicor Transport Ltd* [1980] A.C. 827, 850. See also *Suisse Atlantique Société d'Armement Maritime SA v NV Rotterdamsche Kolen Centrale* [1967] 1 A.C. 361, 482; *Whitecap Leisure Ltd v John H Rundle Ltd* [2008] EWCA Civ 429, [2008] 2 Lloyd's Rep. 16 at [20]; *Stocznia Gdynia SA v Gearbulk Holdings Ltd* [2009] EWCA Civ 75, [2009] 1 Lloyd's Rep. 461 at [23]; *Scottish Power UK Plc v BP Exploration Operating Co Ltd* [2016] EWCA Civ 1043 at [30].

[54] *Ailsa Craig Fishing Co Ltd v Malvern Fishing Co Ltd* [1983] 1 W.L.R. 964, 966, 970; *George Mitchell (Chesterhall) Ltd v Finney Lock Seeds Ltd* [1983] 2 A.C. 803, 814; *Whitecap Leisure Ltd v John H Rundle Ltd* [2008] EWCA Civ 429, [2008] 2 Lloyd's Rep. 216 at [20]–[22]; *McGee Group Ltd v Galliford Try Building Ltd* [2017] EWHC 87 (TCC), [2017] B.T.C. 19 at [22]–[25]. Contrast *Darlington Futures Ltd v Delco Australia Pty Ltd* (1987) 68 A.L.R. 385.

[55] *Impact Funding Solutions Ltd v Barrington Support Services Ltd (formerly Lawyers at Work Ltd)* [2016] UKSC 57, [2017] A.C. 73 at [35] per Lord Toulson (with whom Lord Mance, Lord Sumption and Lord Hodge agreed) (exclusion in contract of professional indemnity insurance). cf. Lord Hodge at [7] (with whom Lord Toulson, Lord Mance, and Lord Sumption agreed) who considered that the established strict construction of exemption clauses does not apply to "exclusion clauses" limiting the extent of cover in a contract of professional liability insurance.

[56] See above, para.13-041.

[57] *Sydney City Council v West* (1965) 114 C.L.R. 481; *Whitecap Leisure Ltd v John H Rundle Ltd* [2008] EWCA Civ 429, [2008] 2 Lloyd's Rep. 216 at [20]; *Air Transworld Ltd v Bombardier Inc* [2012] EWHC 243 (Comm), [2012] 1 Lloyd's Rep. 349 at [26]; *Motortrak Ltd v FCA Australia Pty Ltd* [2018] EWHC 990 (Comm) at [110]–[130].

[58] *Photo Production Ltd v Securicor Transport Ltd* [1980] A.C. 827, 846, 851; *George Mitchell (Chesterhall) Ltd v Finney Lock Seeds Ltd* [1983] 2 A.C. 803; *Darlington Futures Ltd v Delco Australia Pty Ltd* (1987) 68 A.L.R. 385; *Nobahar-Cookson v Hut Group Ltd* [2016] EWCA Civ 128, [2016] 1 C.L.C. 573 at [19].

[59] *Kudos Catering (UK) Ltd v Manchester Central Convention Complex Ltd* [2013] EWCA Civ 38 [2013] 2 Lloyd's Rep. 270 at [28]; *Transocean Drilling UK Ltd v Providence Resources Plc* [2014] EWHC 4260 (Comm), [2015] B.L.R. 190 at [39]; *First Tower Trustees Ltd v CDS (Superstores International) Ltd* [2018] EWCA Civ 1396, [2019] 1 W.L.R. 637 at [84]. Cf. paras 13-079 et seq.

[60] *Scottish Power UK Plc v BP Exploration Operating Co Ltd* [2016] EWCA Civ 1043 at [29] quoting Briggs L.J. in *Nobahar-Cookson v Hut Group Ltd* [2016] EWCA Civ 128, [2016] 1 C.L.C. 573 at [19].

[61] See below, para.15-012.

## Inconsistency with main purpose of contract

*Replace footnote 84 with:*

[84] *Transocean Drilling UK Ltd v Providence Resources Plc* [2016] EWCA Civ 372, [2016] 2 All E.R. (Comm) 606 at [27] per Moore-Bick L.J. (with whom McFarlane and Briggs L.JJ. agreed) referring to *Great North Eastern Railway Ltd v Avon Insurance Plc* [2001] EWCA Civ 780, [2001] 1 Lloyd's Rep. **15-010**

I.R. 793 (the relevant passages are at [31]). See also *Motortrak Ltd v FCA Australia Pty Ltd* [2018] EWHC 990 (Comm) at [126]–[130].

## Construction contra proferentem

*Replace paragraph with:*

**15-012** This traditional principle of construction embraces two differing, but closely related, principles.[95] First, as in the case of any other written document,[96] in situations of ambiguity the words of the document are to be construed more strongly against the party who made the document (the *proferens*) and who now seeks to rely on them. For example, in *John Lee (Grantham) Ltd v Ry Executive*[97] a railway warehouse was leased by the defendants to the claimants. A clause in the lease exempted the defendants from liability for:

> "... loss or damage (whether by act or neglect of the company or their servants or agents or not) which but for the tenancy hereby created would not have arisen."

Owing to a fire caused by the negligence of the defendants in allowing a spark to escape from a railway engine, goods in the warehouse were damaged. It was held that the words "which but for the tenancy hereby created would not have arisen" confined the exemption to liabilities created by the relationship of landlord and tenant. Although the clause was capable of a wider construction, it was ambiguous and would be construed more strongly against the defendants, the makers of the document. The second principle of construction is that, since a party seeking to rely upon an exemption clause bears the burden of proving that the case falls within its provisions,[98] any doubt or ambiguity will be resolved against him and in favour of the other party.[99] While this second principle has not been abandoned entirely by the courts, its significance in commercial contracts has been reduced. In *Nobahar-Cookson v Hut Group Ltd* a clause in a commercial contract provided that the sellers of a company would not be liable for any claim unless the buyer served notice of it within 20 business days "after becoming aware of the matter".[100] The Court of Appeal held that "there remains a principle that an ambiguity" in the meaning of such an exclusion clause:

> "... may have to be resolved by a preference for the narrower construction, if linguistic, contextual and purposive analysis do not disclose an answer to the question with sufficient clarity."[101]

The Court recognised that the phrase "after becoming aware of the matter" could have three possible meanings, but held that, given that the commercial purpose of the term was to prevent the buyer from keeping claims of which it was aware "up its sleeve", and assisted by the principle which it had stated, the phrase should be interpreted as referring to an awareness of a claim and not merely an awareness of facts which could give rise to a claim.[102] As regards *contra proferentem*, the Court of Appeal considered that:

> "This approach to exclusion clauses is not now regarded as a presumption, still less as a special rule justifying the giving of a strained meaning to a provision merely because it is an exclusion clause. Commercial parties are entitled to allocate between them the risks of something going wrong in their contractual relationship in any way they choose. Nor is it to be mechanistically applied wherever an ambiguity is identified in an exclusion clause. The court must still use all its tools of linguistic, purposive and common-sense analysis to discern what the clause really means."[103]

Rather, the principle is:

> "... essentially one of common sense; parties do not normally give up valuable rights without making it clear that they intend to do so."[104]

It will be seen, therefore, that this aspect of the construction *contra proferentem* is related to the approach of the courts which requires clear and unambiguous language effectively to exclude liability for breach.[105] Again, while accepting the existence of this aspect of the *contra proferentem* rule, in *Persimmon Homes Ltd v Ove Arup & Partners Ltd* the Court of Appeal observed that "[i]n relation to commercial contracts, negotiated between parties of equal bargaining power, that rule now has a very limited role,"[106] quoting Lord Neuberger M.R. in *K/S Victoria Street v House of Fraser (Stores Management) Ltd* to the effect that:

> "... 'rules' of interpretation such as contra proferentem are rarely decisive as to the meaning of any provisions in a commercial contract. The words used, commercial sense, and the documentary and factual context are, and should be, normally enough to determine the meaning of a contractual provision."[107]

So, while the rule may still be used to resolve "cases of genuine ambiguity", it should not be the court's starting point.[108] This therefore suggests that *contra proferentem* is relevant to the construction of ambiguous contract terms only *after* the courts have sought to resolve that ambiguity by reference to the general principles of construction according to which ambiguity may be resolved by reference to the matrix of fact within which the contract was made and to commercial common sense under the general approach to construction of contracts. By contrast, in the case of consumer contracts, the principle of interpretation *contra proferentem* has been given explicit legislative force as a result of the implementation of the Unfair Terms in Consumer Contracts Directive 1993,[109] first by the Unfair Terms in Consumer Contracts Regulations 1999 and then, as regards contracts made on or after October 1, 2015, by the Consumer Rights Act 2015. According to s.68(1) of the 2015 Act:

> "... [i]f a term in a consumer contract, or a consumer notice, could have different meanings, the meaning that is most favourable to the consumer is to prevail."

This law is discussed in Vol.II, Ch.38.[110]

[95] *Pera Shipping Corp v Petroship SA* [1984] 2 Lloyd's Rep. 363, 365; *Youell v Bland Welch & Co Ltd* [1992] 2 Lloyd's Rep. 127, 134; *Nobahar-Cookson v Hut Group Ltd* [2016] EWCA Civ 128, [2016] 1 C.L.C. 573 esp. at [14] and [16]; *Transocean Drilling UK Ltd v Providence Resources Plc* [2016] EWCA Civ 372, [2016] 2 All E.R. (Comm) 606 at [20] (*contra proferentem* has no role to play where the meaning of the words is clear or where a clause favours both parties equally); *Persimmon Homes Ltd v Ove Arup & Partners Ltd* [2017] EWCA Civ 373 at [52]–[53]; *Windsor-Clive v Rees* [2019] EWHC 1008 (Ch), [2019] 4 W.L.R. 74 at [44]–[60] (role of contra proferentem in reservations to landlord in a lease). See generally Peel in Burrows and Peel, *Contract Terms* (2007), Ch.4; Peel [2017] L.Q.R. 6; Barrett and Wilmot-Smith (2017) *Butterworths Journal of International Banking and Finance* Law 707; Tofaris [2019] L.M.C.L.Q. 270 at 282–284.

[96] This has been termed the "classic form" of the rule of construction *contra proferentem*: *Nobahar-Cookson v Hut Group Ltd* [2016] EWCA Civ 128, [2016] 1 C.L.C. 573 at [14] per Briggs L.J. and see above, para.13-086.

[97] [1949] 2 All E.R. 581. See also *Webster v Higgin* [1948] 2 All E.R. 127; *Houghton v Trafalgar Insurance Co Ltd* [1954] 1 Q.B. 247; *Billyack v Leyland Construction Co Ltd* [1968] 1 W.L.R. 471; *Adams v Richardson & Starling Ltd* [1969] 1 W.L.R. 1645, 1653; *Pera Shipping Corp v Petroship SA* [1985] 2 Lloyd's Rep. 103; *Whitecap Leisure Ltd v John H Rundle Ltd* [2008] EWCA Civ 429, [2008] 2 Lloyd's Rep. 216 at [22]; *Kingsway Hall Hotel Ltd v Red Sky IT (Hounslow) Ltd* [2010] EWHC 965 (TCC), (2010) 26 Const. L.J. 542.

98 See below, para.15-021.

99 This appears to be the sense in which the principle was referred to in *Photo Production Ltd v Securicor Transport Ltd* [1980] A.C. 827, 847; *Ailsa Craig Fishing Co Ltd v Malvern Fishing Co Ltd* [1983] 1 W.L.R. 964, 969, 970; *George Mitchell (Chesterhall) Ltd v Finney Lock Seeds Ltd* [1983] 2 A.C. 803, 814; *Homburg Houtimport BV v Agrosin Private Ltd* [2003] UKHL 12, [2004] 1 A.C. 71 at [144]; *Dairy Containers Ltd v Tasman Orient Line CV* [2004] UKPC 22, [2005] 1 W.L.R. 215 at [12].

100 [2016] EWCA Civ 128, [2016] 1 C.L.C. 573 at [5].

101 [2016] EWCA Civ 128 at [21] per Briggs L.J.

102 [2016] EWCA Civ 128 at [36] (with whom Hallett L.J. and Moylan J. agreed, though placing greater emphasis on the commercial sense of the resulting decision: [2016] EWCA Civ 128 at [40] and [41]).

103 *Nobahar-Cookson v Hut Group Ltd* [2016] EWCA Civ 128, [2016] 1 C.L.C. 573 at [19] per Briggs L.J.; followed in *European Film Bonds AS v Lotus Holdings LLC* [2020] EWHC 1115 (Ch) at [80]–[81], where it was also held that the term in question was not an exemption clause. See similarly *Persimmon Homes Ltd v Ove Arup & Partners Ltd* [2017] EWCA Civ 373 at [57] per Jackson L.J.

104 *Seadrill Management Services Ltd v OAO Gazprom* [2010] EWCA Civ 691, [2011] 1 All E.R. (Comm) 1077 at [29] per Moore-Bick L.J. quoted by Briggs L.J. in *Nobahar-Cookson v Hut Group Ltd* [2016] EWCA Civ 128 at [19]; *Federal Republic of Nigeria v JP Morgan Chase Bank N.A.* [2019] EWHC 347 (Comm) at [34].

105 Above, para.15-008.

106 *Persimmon Homes Ltd v Ove Arup & Partners Ltd* [2017] EWCA Civ 373 at [52] per Jackson L.J. (with whom Moylan and Beatson L.JJ. agreed). See similarly *Multiplex Construction Europe Ltd v Dunne* [2017] EWHC 3073 (TCC), [2018] B.L.R. 36 at [28]–[32] (in relation to contracts of guarantee); *Bates v Post Office Ltd (No.3: Common Issues)* [2019] EWHC 606 (QB) at [634]–[638] and see Vol.II, para.45-062.

107 [2011] EWCA Civ 904, [2012] Ch. 497 at [68], quoted at [2017] EWCA Civ 373 at [52].

108 *Taberna Europe CDO Plc v Selskabet AF 1* [2016] EWCA Civ 1261, [2017] Q.B. 633 at [23] per Moore-Bick L.J. See also *Transocean Drilling UK Ltd v Providence Resources Plc* [2016] EWCA Civ 372, [2016] 2 All E.R. (Comm) 606 at [20] and [28] (*contra proferentem* has no application to unambiguous clauses).

109 Directive 93/13/EEC of April 5, 1993 on unfair terms in consumer contracts, art.5.

110 For the 1999 Regulations reg.7 see Vol.II, paras 38-347—38-351; for the Consumer Rights Act 2015 s.69(1) see Vol.II, paras 38-414—38-417.

## Liability for negligence

*Replace footnote 120 with:*

15-013 120 [2017] EWCA Civ 373 at [56]. See also *Taberna Europe CDO II Plc v Selskabet AF1* [2016] EWCA Civ 1262, [2017] Q.B. 633 at [24] ("the law has moved on since [the decision in *Canada Steamship*]"); *Aprile SpA v Elin Maritime Ltd* [2019] EWHC 1001 (Comm) at [58]–[69]. See also Tofaris [2019] L.M.C.L.Q. 270 at 284–286.

## Words wide enough to cover negligence

*Replace footnote 137 with:*

15-014 137 *Austin v Manchester, Sheffield & Lincs Ry* (1852) 10 C.B. 454; *The Stella* [1900] P. 161; *Joseph Travers & Sons Ltd v Cooper* [1915] 1 K.B. 73; *Ashby v Tolhurst* [1937] 2 K.B. 242; *Harris Ltd v Continental Express Ltd*; *White v Blackmore* [1972] 2 Q.B. 651; *Stag Line Ltd v Tyne Shiprepair Group Ltd* [1984] 2 Lloyd's Rep. 211, 222; *Hunt & Winterbotham (West of England) Ltd v B.R.S. (Parcels) Ltd* [1962] 1 Q.B. 617 ("however sustained"). See also *Aprile SpA v Elin Maritime Ltd* [2019] EWHC 1001 (Comm) esp. at [69], noting that "words of exemption which are wider in effect than "howsoever caused" are difficult to imagine and, over the last 100 years, they have become "the classic phrase" whereby to exclude liability for negligence and unseaworthiness" (per Stephen Hofmeyr Q.C. sitting as a judge of the HC).

## Indemnity clauses

*Replace footnote 169 with:*

[169] See (effective indemnities): *A.E. Farr Ltd v Admiralty* [1953] 1 W.L.R. 965; *Swan Hunter and Wigham Richardson Ltd v France, Fenwick Tyne & Wear Co Ltd (The Albion)* [1953] 1 W.L.R. 1026; *James Archdale & Co Ltd v Comservices Ltd* [1954] 1 W.L.R. 459; *Harris Ltd v Continental Express Ltd* [1961] 1 Lloyd's Rep. 251; *Westcott v J.H. Jenner Plasterers and Bovis* [1962] 1 Lloyd's Rep. 309; *Spalding v Tarmac Civil Engineering Ltd* [1967] 1 W.L.R. 1508; *Gillespie Bros & Co Ltd v Roy Bowles Transport Ltd* [1973] 1 Q.B. 400; *Blake v Richards & Wallington Industries* (1974) 16 K.I.R. 151; *Comyn Ching & Co (London) v Oriental Tube Co* [1981] Com. L.R. 67; *Scottish Special Housing Association v Wimpey Construction UK Ltd* [1986] 1 W.L.R. 995; *Thompson v T. Lohan (Plant Hire) Ltd* [1987] 1 W.L.R. 649; *Hancock Shipping Co Ltd v Deacon & Trysail (Private) Ltd* [1991] 2 Lloyd's Rep. 550; *Nelson v Atlantic Power and Gas* (1995) S.L.T. 46; *Morris v Breaveglen Ltd* [1997] C.L.Y. 937; *Smedvig Ltd v Elf Exploration UK Plc* [1998] 2 Lloyd's Rep. 659; *Deepak Fertilisers and Petrochemicals Corp v ICI* [1999] 1 Lloyd's Rep. 387; *Great Eastern Shipping Co Ltd v Far East Chartering Ltd* [2011] EWHC 1372 (Comm), [2011] 2 Lloyd's Rep. 309 at [43]; *Greenwich Millennium Ltd v Essex Services Plc* [2014] EWCA Civ 960, [2014] 1 W.L.R. 3517 at [96]; *Capita (Banstead 2011) Ltd v RFIB Group Ltd* [2015] EWCA Civ 1310, [2016] 2 W.L.R. 1429; *Rabilizirov v A2 Dominion London Ltd* [2019] EWHC 186 (QB), [2019] T.C.L.R. 5 at [49]–[54]. Contrast (ineffective indemnities) *A.M.F. International Ltd v Magnet Bowling Ltd* [1968] 1 W.L.R. 1028; *Walters v Whessoe Ltd* [1968] 1 W.L.R. 1056; *British Crane Hire Corp Ltd v Ipswich Plant Hire Ltd* [1975] Q.B. 303; *C. Davis Metal Producers Ltd v Gilyott & Scott Ltd* [1975] 2 Lloyd's Rep. 422; *Smith v South Wales Switchgear Co Ltd* [1978] 1 W.L.R. 165; *Actis Co Ltd v Sankis S.S. Co Ltd* [1982] 1 Lloyd's Rep. 7; *Sonat Offshore SA v Amerada Hess Development Ltd* [1988] 1 Lloyd's Rep. 145; *Dorset CC v Southern Felt Roofing Co* (1990) 6 Const. L.J. 37; *Caledonia Ltd v Orbit Valve Co Europe* [1994] 1 W.L.R. 1515; *Glebe Island Terminals Pty Ltd v Continental Seagram Pty Ltd* [1994] 1 Lloyd's Rep. 213; *Shell Chemicals Ltd v P.&O. Roadtanks Ltd* [1995] 1 Lloyd's Rep. 297; *Stirling v Norwest* (1997) S.L.T. 974; *Hawkins v Northern Marine Management Ltd* 1998 S.L.T. 1107; *Stent Foundations Ltd v M.J. Gleeson Group Plc* [2001] B.L.R. 134; *Colour Quest Ltd v Total Downstream UK Plc* [2009] EWHC 540 (Comm), [2009] 2 Lloyd's Rep. 1 at [367]–[394]; *Seadrill Management Services Ltd v OAO Gazprom (The "Ekha")* [2010] 1 Lloyd's Rep. 543 at [217]–[218] (affirmed [2010] EWCA Civ 691); *Jose v MacSalvors Plant Hire Ltd* [2009] EWCA Civ 1329, [2010] T.C.L.R. 2. **15-018**

### 3. FUNDAMENTAL BREACH

## George Mitchell case

*Replace footnote 222 with:*

[222] [1983] 2 A.C. 803 at 813. See also *Radius Housing Association Ltd v JNP Architects* [2018] NIQB 57, [2018] P.N.L.R. 31 at [64]–[67] (lack of consent by employer to changes by architect does not prevent the latter from relying on a limitation clause, as this would be akin to holding that a fundamental breach prevented the contract breaker from relying on the contract). **15-026**

### 4. APPLICATION OF PRINCIPLES OF CONSTRUCTION TO PARTICULAR CONTRACTS

## Carriage of goods: deviation

*Replace footnote 253 with:*

[253] *Photo Production Ltd v Securicor Transport Ltd* [1980] A.C. 827, 845. In *Kenya Railways v Antares Pte Ltd* [1987] 1 Lloyd's Rep. 424, 430 and *State Trading Corp of India v M. Golodetz Ltd* [1989] 2 Lloyd's Rep. 277, 289, Lloyd L.J. stated that "they should now be assimilated into the ordinary law of contract", but this would be difficult to achieve while it remains the case that the protection of the clause goes in the absence of affirmation. See Baughen [1991] L.M.C.L.Q. 70. And see also *Daewoo Heavy Industries Ltd v Klipriver Shipping Ltd* [2003] EWCA Civ 451, [2003] 2 Lloyd's Rep. 1 and *Dera Commercial Estate v Derya Inc* [2018] EWHC 1273 (Comm), [2019] 1 All E.R. 1147 at [74]–[118] esp. at [107]–[108]. **15-032**

## Road and seaworthiness

*Replace footnote 261 with:*

[261] *Readhead v Midland Ry* (1869) L.R. 4 Q.B. 379; *J. Carter (Fine Worsteds) Ltd v Hanson Haulage (Leeds) Ltd* [1965] 2 Q.B. 495. However, where the consignor of goods is a consumer, then the contract **15-035**

of carriage may be treated as one for "services" so as to attract the statutory terms (and the controls on the exclusion of liability for their breach) in the Consumer Rights Act 2015 Pt 1 Ch.3, on which see Vol.II, paras 38-567 et seq.

## 6. LEGISLATIVE CONTROL OF EXEMPTION CLAUSES

## (a) Unfair Contract Terms Act 1977

### *(i) Overview*

#### The Unfair Contract Terms Act as enacted

*Replace footnote 379 with:*

15-062 [379] See Thompson, *Unfair Contract Terms Act 1977*; Rogers and Clarke, *The Unfair Contract Terms Act 1977*; Lawson, *Exclusion Clauses and Unfair Contract Terms*, 11th edn (2014); Peel (ed.), *Treitel on The Law of Contract*, 15th edn (2020), paras 7-039 et seq.; *Benjamin's Sale of Goods*, 9th edn (2014), paras 13-064 et seq.; Coote (1978) 41 M.L.R. 312; Adams (1978) 41 M.L.R. 703; Sealy [1978] C.L.J. 15; Reynolds [1978] L.M.C.L.Q. 201; Palmer and Yates [1981] C.L.J. 108; Adams and Brownsword (1988) 104 L.Q.R. 94; Peel (1993) 56 M.L.R. 98; Brown and Chandler (1993) 109 L.Q.R. 41; Adams (1994) 57 M.L.R. 960.

### *(ii) The Pattern of Control; Key Definitions*

#### Varieties of exemption clause

*Replace footnote 423 with:*

15-070 [423] *McGrath v Shah* (1989) 57 P. & C.R. 452; *Thomas Witter Ltd v TBP Industries Ltd* [1996] 2 All E.R. 573; *E.A. Grimstead & Son Ltd v McGarrigan* [1999] EWCA Civ 3029; *South West Water Services Ltd v International Computers Ltd* [1999] B.L.R. 420, 424; *Inntrepreneur Pub Co v East Crown Ltd* [2000] 2 Lloyd's Rep. 611, 614; *Watford Electronics Ltd v Sanderson CFL Ltd* [2001] EWCA Civ 317, [2001] Build. L.R. 143, 155; *SAM Business Systems Ltd v Hedley & Co* [2002] EWHC (TCC) 2733, [2003] 1 All E.R. (Comm) 465; *Trident Turboprop (Dublin) Ltd v First Flight Couriers Ltd* [2008] EWHC 1686 (Comm), [2008] 2 Lloyd's Rep. 581 at [42] (affirmed [2009] EWCA Civ 290, [2010] Q.B. 86); *AXA Sun Life Services Plc v Campbell Martin Ltd* [2011] EWCA Civ 133, [2011] 2 Lloyd's Rep. 1; *Crestsign Ltd v National Westminster Bank Plc* [2014] EWHC 3043 (Ch) at [112]–[119] (permission to appeal granted on other grounds: [2015] EWCA Civ 986); *Thornbridge Ltd v Barclays Bank Plc* [2015] EWHC 3430 (QB) at [97]–[111] (appeal dismissed by CA, Unreported January 9, 2018) (on "basis clauses" stipulating that defendants were not providing advice in relation to interest rate "swap agreements"); *Al-Hasawi v Nottingham Forest Football Club Ltd* [2018] EWHC 2884 (Ch). See also above paras 7-146 and 7-152—7-154. But cf. Vol.II, para.38-317.

#### The old law: "Dealing as consumer"

*Replace footnote 435 with:*

15-074 [435] See above, para.15-072. It has been held that employees do not "deal as consumer" as they are the providers of services: *Keen v Commerzbank AG* [2006] EWCA Civ 1536, [2007] I.R.L.R. 132 at [102] and see *Bates v Post Office Ltd (No.3: Common Issues)* [2019] EWHC 606 (QB) at [1072]–[1073].

### *(iii) The Controls Provided by the 1977 Act*

#### Liability arising in contract: the old law

*Replace footnote 478 with:*

15-084 [478] *African Export-Import Bank v Shebah Exploration and Production Co Ltd* [2017] EWCA Civ 845 at [25] per Longmore L.J. (with whom Henderson L.J. agreed), approving dicta in *McCrone v Boots Farm Sales* [1981] S.L.T. 103 at 105; *Hadley Design Associates v Westminster City Council* [2003] EWHC 1617 (TCC), [2004] T.C.L.R. 1 at [78]. See also *Bates v Post Office Ltd (No.3: Common Issues)* [2019] EWHC 606 (QB) at [1065]–[1075].

*Replace paragraph with:*

In cases falling within s.3, as against the party dealing as consumer or on the other's written standard terms of business, the other party cannot by reference to any contract term,[480] except in so far as the term satisfies the requirement of reasonableness, do either of two things: **15-085**

"(a) when himself in breach of contract, exclude or restrict any liability of his in respect of breach[[481]]; or

(b) claim to be entitled:

(i) to render a contractual performance substantially different from that which was reasonably expected of him[[482]]; or

(ii) in respect of the whole or part of his contractual obligations to render no performance at all.[483]

It would appear to be the intention of (b) that it should apply where there is no breach of contract at all, but where the obligation as to performance has been limited or qualified.[484] An example may be found in the case of a shipowner who agrees on written standard terms to provide a cruise to a travel agent for a party of tourists on a particular vessel on a particular route, but claims to be entitled to change the vessel by reference to a contract term.[485] A further example in a commercial contract might be that of a force majeure clause[486] by reference to which a seller of goods claims to be entitled to suspend or postpone delivery of the goods, or to deliver substitute goods, or to cancel the contract, upon the happening of events beyond his control. The argument could, however, be advanced[487] that the effect of clauses such as those mentioned is to define the scope of the obligation of the party seeking to rely on the clause with respect to performance: the contract must be read together with and subject to the clause.[488] The other party could not therefore reasonably expect that the party seeking to rely on the clause would render a contractual performance other than that as qualified by that clause, nor would there be any contractual obligation in respect of which the party seeking to rely on the clause would be claiming to render no performance at all. However, it is submitted that a sensible meaning can in most cases only be given to para.(b) if one assumes that the contractual performance and contractual obligation referred to is the performance required and the obligation imposed by the contract apart from the contract term relied on.[489] For this purpose, the contractual performance reasonably expected of a party may, in appropriate cases be determined by the content of representations made by that party in pre-contract negotiations.[490] On the other hand, where on its true construction a contract term provides for performance to a certain level by the party relying on the clause, the other party cannot claim that that very term entitles the party so relying to render a contractual performance substantially different from that which he reasonably expected. For example, in *Hodges v Aegis Defence Services (BVI) Ltd* a contractor providing security services in Iraq engaged the services of an individual and their contract contained a term under which the contractor agreed to take out insurance for a sum of $200,000 payable on that individual's death.[491] After the individual died during service, insurance monies were paid over a period in excess of that figure, but his widow (as principal nominee of the benefit of the insurance) claimed that the term required payment of $200,000 as a minimum lump sum and, secondly, that any term which gave the insured less than such a minimum lump sum fell within s.3(2)(b)(i) and was unreasonable.[492] However, Longmore L.J. (in the majority) held, first, that on its proper construction the term did not require such a lump sum and, secondly, that this meant that the contractor did not claim by reference to that term to be entitled to render a contractual performance substantially different from that which was expected of it under the contract.[493]

[480] Whether in the same or in another contract between the same parties. cf. 1977 Act s.10, below, para.15-128.

[481] See *Charlotte Thirty Ltd v Croker Ltd* (1990) 24 Con. L.R. 46; *St Alban's City and District Council v International Computers Ltd* [1996] 4 All E.R. 481.

[482] i.e. at the time the contract was made: *Shearson Lehman Hutton Inc v Maclaine Watson & Co Ltd* [1989] 2 Lloyd's Rep. 570, 612. See *Timeload Ltd v British Telecommunications Plc* [1995] E.M.L.R. 459.

[483] 1977 Act s.3(2)(a) and (b)."

[484] *Shearson Lehman Hutton Inc v Maclaine Watson & Co Ltd* [1989] 2 Lloyd's Rep. 570, 611–612; *AXA Sun Life Services Plc v Campbell Martin Ltd* [2011] EWCA Civ 133, [2011] 2 Lloyd's Rep. 1 at [50]. See also Law Commission, Scottish Law Commission, *Exemption Clauses* (1975) Law Com. No.69, Scot. Law Com. No.39, paras 143–146.

[485] cf. *Anglo-Continental Holidays Ltd v Typaldos Lines (London) Ltd* [1967] 2 Lloyd's Rep. 61, given by the Law Commissions in Law Com. No.69, Scot. Law Com. No.39, para.146 as an example of the sort of term which it intended should be included under its proposed controls which were similar to s.3(2)(b). cf. the special provisions controlling the variation of package holiday contracts by the Package Travel, Package Holidays and Package Tours Regulations 1992 (SI 1992/3288) (replaced as of July 1, 2018 by the Package Travel and Linked Travel Arrangements Regulations 2018 (SI 2018/634) on which see generally Vol.II, paras 38-137 et seq. and in particular paras 38-139 and 38-144).

[486] See below, paras 15-152 et seq.

[487] Treitel, *Frustration and Force Majeure*, 3rd edn (2014), para.12-022.

[488] See above, para.15-003.

[489] *Zockoll Group Ltd v Mercury Communications Ltd (No.2)* [1998] I.T.C.L.R. 104. See above, para.15-003.

[490] *SAM Business Systems Ltd v Hedley & Co* [2002] EWHC 2733 (TCC), [2003] 1 All E.R. (Comm) 465; *AXA Sun Life Services Plc v Campbell Martin Ltd* [2011] EWCA Civ 133, [2011] 2 Lloyd's Rep. 1 at [50].

[491] [2014] EWCA Civ 1449.

[492] [2014] EWCA Civ 1449 at [5] and [6].

[493] [2014] EWCA Civ 1449 at [52] (Longmore L.J). McCombe L.J. agreed with Longmore L.J. both as a matter of the construction of the term and its effectiveness, but as regards the latter on the ground that the term in question was reasonable under the 1977 Act: [2014] EWCA Civ 1449 at [33]–[34]. Vos L.J. dissented on the issue of construction and did not find it necessary to consider the effect of s.3(2)(b): [2014] EWCA Civ 1449 at [43]–[45]. Cf. *Everwarm Ltd v BN Rendering Ltd* [2019] EWHC 3060 (TCC), where a contract term entitled the employer of a building contractor to assess the value of work done and, therefore, what it owed and, where relevant, to recover the difference from what it had paid. It was held, first, that this assessment was subject to an implied term that it would not be undertaken in an arbitrary, capricious or irrational manner. It was further held that the express term (as properly construed in its contractual and statutory context and as so qualified) did not entitle the employer to render a performance substantially different from that which was reasonably expected of it as the "implied term and the combined system of notices and adjudication are sufficient controls to ensure that [the employer] cannot, unilaterally, carry out an Assessment and make a demand for payment which bears no relation to the value of the works undertaken by [the contractor]": at [158].

*Replace paragraph with:*

**15-086** Nevertheless it seems unlikely that a contract term entitling one party to terminate the contract in the event of a material breach by the other (e.g. failure to pay by the due date) would fall within paragraph (b), or, if it did so, would be adjudged not to satisfy the requirement of reasonableness.[494] Nor, it is submitted, would that provision extend to a contract term which entitled one party, not to alter the performance expected of himself, but to alter the performance required of the other party (e.g. a term by which a seller of goods is entitled to increase the price payable by the buyer to the price ruling at the date of delivery, or a term by which a person advancing a loan is entitled to vary the interest payable by the borrower on the loan).[495] Instead, "the contract term must be one which has an effect (indeed a substantial effect) on the contractual performance reasonably expected of the party who relies on the term. The key word is 'performance'."[496]

[494] But see *Timeload Ltd v British Telecommunications Plc* [1995] E.M.L.R. 459 (termination not limited to cases where there was a good reason) and below, para.15-105. cf. *Hadley Design Associates Ltd v Westminster CC* [2003] EWHC 1617 (TCC), [2004] T.C.L.R. 1 (one month's termination clause in architects' contract not unreasonable); *Bates v Post Office Ltd (No.3: Common Issues)* [2019] EWHC 606 (QB) at [1084] (termination clause fell within s.3(2)(b)(i) and (at [1107]) was found reasonable or not reasonable depending on its construction. On termination clauses generally see Whittaker in Burrows and Peel (eds) *Contract Terms* (2007), Ch.13 especially at pp.263–267.

[495] *Paragon Finance Plc v Nash* [2001] EWCA Civ 1466, [2002] 1 W.L.R. 685, at [76]–[77] (pet. dis. [2002] 1 W.L.R. 2303) approving the view of the law set out by the first two sentences of this paragraph in an earlier edition. But such a term in a consumer contract might be unfair and not binding on the consumer under the Unfair Terms in Consumer Contracts Regulations 1999, Vol.II, paras 38-220 et seq. or (as regards contracts made on or after October 1, 2015) the Consumer Rights Act 2015, on which see Vol.II, paras 38-365 et seq.

[496] *Paragon Finance Plc v Nash* [2001] EWCA Civ 1466 at [77] per Dyson L.J. The proper approach is therefore to identify "'the contractual performance' reasonably expected of [the party], in respect of which the contract term in question 'must have an effect (indeed a substantial effect)'": *Bates v Post Office Ltd (No.3: Common Issues)* [2019] EWHC 606 (QB) at [1081] (Fraser J.) and see further on applying this approach to a series of contract terms in contracts between the Post Office (PO) and sub-postmasters (SPMs) at [1082]–[1084], including terms under which the PO was entitled to change the character or the nature of its performance by unilateral variation of the terms upon which SPMs were appointed; terms which relate to the way in which the PO would be entitled to claim payment from, or reduce remuneration otherwise due to, the SPM for running the branch; and terms under which the PO could bring the appoint of the SPM to an end, such that the operation of the branch by the SPM who had been contracted for that purpose would come to an end.

## *(iv) Test of Reasonableness*

### Guidelines

*Replace paragraph with:*

The test of reasonableness set out by s.11(1) of the 1977 Act is a very broad one, but s.1(4) of the Act specifically provides that: **15-097**

> "In relation to any breach of duty or obligation, it is immaterial for any purpose of this Part of this Act whether the breach was inadvertent or intentional, or whether liability for it arises directly or vicariously."

This exclusion therefore clearly applies to the assessment of terms or notices under the test of reasonableness in s.11. More positively, s.11(2) of the Act refers to five guidelines laid down in Sch.2[547] and regard is to be had to these in determining whether a contract term satisfies the requirement of reasonableness.[548] The guidelines are only made expressly applicable for the purposes of s.6 (sale of goods and hire-purchase) and s.7 (other contracts for the supply of goods), but they are frequently regarded as being of general application.[549] The guidelines are:

(a) the strength of the bargaining positions of the parties relative to each other, taking account (among other things) alternative means by which the customer's requirements could have been met[550];
(b) whether the customer received an inducement to agree to the term, or in accepting it had an opportunity of entering into a similar contract with other persons, but without having to accept a similar term[551];
(c) whether the customer knew or ought reasonably to have known of the existence and extent of the term (having regard, among other things, to any custom of the trade and any course of dealing between the parties)[552];

(d) where the term excludes or restricts any relevant liability if some condition is not complied with, whether it was reasonable at the time of the contract to expect that compliance with that condition would be practicable[553];

(e) whether the goods were manufactured, processed or adapted to the special order of the customer.[554]

547 The guidelines are similar to those formerly set out in s.55(5) of the Sale of Goods Act 1893 as inserted by s.4 of the Supply of Goods (Implied Terms) Act 1973, and repealed on the enactment of the Sale of Goods Act 1979.

548 See Vol.II, paras 44-122 et seq.

549 *Flamar Interocean Ltd v Denmac Ltd* [1990] 1 Lloyd's Rep. 434, 438–439; *Stewart Gill Ltd v Horatio Myer & Co Ltd* [1992] Q.B. 600, 608. See also *Singer Co (UK) Ltd v Tees and Hartlepool Port Authority* [1988] 2 Lloyd's Rep. 164, 169; *St Alban's City and District Council v International Computers Ltd* [1995] F.S.R. 686 (affirmed [1996] 4 All E.R. 481); *Overseas Medical Supplies Ltd v Orient Transport Services Ltd* [1999] 2 Lloyd's Rep. 273, 277; *Pegler Ltd v Wang (UK) Ltd* [2000] B.L.R. 218; *Granville Oil and Chemicals Ltd v Davis Turner & Co Ltd* [2003] EWCA Civ 570, [2003] 2 Lloyd's Rep. 356 at [15]; *SAM Business Systems Ltd v Hedley & Co* [2002] EWHC (TCC) 2733, [2003] 1 All E.R. (Comm) 465 at [67]; *Balmoral Group Ltd v Borealis (UK) Ltd* [2006] EWHC 1900 (Comm), [2006] 2 Lloyd's Rep. 629; *Trustees of Ampleforth Abbey Trust v Turner and Townsend Management Ltd* [2012] EWHC 2137 (TCC), [2012] T.C.L.R. 8 at [199]; *Bates v Post Office Ltd (No.3: Common Issues)* [2019] EWHC 606 (QB) at [1089].

550 See *R.W. Green Ltd v Cade Bros Farms* [1978] 1 Lloyd's Rep. 602; *George Mitchell (Chesterhall) Ltd v Finney Lock Seeds Ltd* [1983] 2 A.C. 803; *Singer Co (UK) Ltd v Tees and Hartlepool Port Authority* [1988] 2 Lloyd's Rep. 164; *St Alban's City and District Council v International Computers Ltd* [1995] F.S.R. 686; *Schenkers Ltd v Overland Shoes Ltd* [1998] 1 Lloyd's Rep. 498; *Thames Tideway Properties Ltd v Serfaty & Partners* [1999] 2 Lloyd's Rep. 110; *Overseas Medical Supplies Ltd v Orient Transport Services Ltd* [1999] 2 Lloyd's Rep. 273; *British Fermentation Products Ltd v Compair Reavell Ltd* (1999) 66 Const. L.R. 1; *Watford Electronics Ltd v Sanderson CFL Ltd* [2001] EWCA Civ 317, [2001] Build. L.R. 143; *Granville Oil and Chemicals Ltd v Davis Turner & Co Ltd* [2003] EWCA Civ 57; *Frans Maas (UK) Ltd v Samsung Electronics (UK) Ltd* [2004] EWHC 1502 (Comm), [2004] 2 Lloyd's Rep. 251 at [159]; *Balmoral Group Ltd v Borealis UK Ltd* [2006] EWHC 1900 (Comm), [2006] 2 Lloyd's Rep. 629 at [407]–[409]; *Shepherd Homes Ltd v Encia Remediation Ltd* [2007] EWHC 70 (TCC), [2007] Build. L.R. 135; *Titan Steel Wheels Ltd v Royal Bank of Scotland Plc* [2010] EWHC 211 (Comm), [2010] 2 Lloyd's Rep. 92 at [105]; *AXA Sun Life Services Plc v Campbell Martin Ltd* [2011] EWCA Civ 133, [2011] 2 Lloyd's Rep. 1; *Southwark LBC v IBM UK Ltd* [2011] EWHC 549 (TCC), 135 Con. L.R. 136; *Rohlig UK Ltd v Rock Unique Ltd* [2011] EWCA Civ 18, [2011] 2 All E.R. (Comm) 1161; *Air Transworld Ltd v Bombardier Inc* [2012] EWHC 243 (Comm), [2012] 1 Lloyd's Rep. 349; *Avrora Fine Arts Investment Ltd v Christie, Manson & Woods Ltd* [2012] EWHC 2198 (Ch), [2012] P.N.L.R. 35 at [152]–[153]; *Allen Fabrications Ltd v ASD Ltd* [2012] EWHC 2213 (TCC) at [73]–[75]; *Elvanite Full Circle Ltd v AMEC Earth and Environmental (UK) Ltd* [2013] EWHC 1191 (TCC), 148 Con. L.R. 127 at [288] *Marex Financial Ltd v Creative Finance Ltd* [2013] EWHC 2155 (Comm), [2014] 1 All E.R. (Comm) 122 at [91], [92]; *West v Ian Finlay & Associates* [2014] EWCA Civ 316, [2014] B.L.R. 324. In *Denholm Fishselling Ltd v Anderson* (1991) S.L.T. (Sh. Ct.) 24, it was held that there was no preponderance of bargaining power where buyers might not be able to purchase except on similar standard conditions but nevertheless had a choice of suppliers but cf. *Thornbridge Ltd v Barclays Bank Plc* [2015] EWHC 3430 (QB) at [116] (appeal dismissed by CA, Unreported January 9, 2018) (equal bargaining power evidenced by party threatening to go elsewhere); *Polypearl Ltd v Building Research Establishment Ltd* Unreported July 28, 2016 (Mercantile Ct) at [105]; *Halsall v Champion Consulting Ltd* [2017] EWHC 1079 (QB), [2017] P.N.L.R. 32 at [297]; *Bates v Post Office Ltd (No.3: Common Issues)* [2019] EWHC 606 (QB) at [1097]–[1110]; *Natixis SA v Marex Financial* [2019] EWHC 2549 (Comm), [2019] 2 Lloyd's Rep. 431 at [525]–[526] (relative bargaining power of limited relevance where defendant performs a completely gratuitous service).

551 *R.W. Green Ltd v Cade Bros Farms* [1978] 1 Lloyd's Rep. 602; *George Mitchell (Chesterhall) Ltd v Finney Lock Seeds Ltd* [1983] 2 A.C. 803; *Singer Co (UK) Ltd v Tees and Hartlepool Port Authority* [1988] 2 Lloyd's Rep. 164; *Thames Tideway Properties Ltd v Serfaty & Partners* [1999] 2 Lloyd's Rep. 110; *Overseas Medical Supplies Ltd v Orient Transport Services Ltd* [1999] 2 Lloyd's Rep. 273; *Watford Electronics Ltd v Sanderson CFL Ltd* [2001] EWCA Civ 317; *Frans Maas (UK) Ltd v Samsung Electronics (UK) Ltd* [2004] EWHC 1502 at [410]; *Titan Steel Wheels Ltd v Royal Bank of Scotland Plc* [2010] EWHC 211 (Comm), [2010] 2 Lloyd's Rep. 92 at [105]; *AXA Sun Life Services Plc v Campbell Martin Ltd* [2011] EWCA Civ 133, [2011] 1 Lloyd's Rep. 1; *Southwark LBC v IBM UK Ltd* [2011] EWHC 549 (TCC), 135 Con. L.R. 136.

552 See *George Mitchell (Chesterhall) Ltd v Finney Lock Seeds Ltd* [1983] 2 A.C. 803; *Charlotte Thirty Ltd v Croker Ltd* (1990) 24 Con. L.R. 46; *AEG (UK) Ltd v Logic Resource Ltd* [1996] C.L.C. 625; *Thames Tideway Properties Ltd v Serfaty & Partners* [1999] 2 Lloyd's Rep. 110; *Overseas Medical Sup-*

*plies Ltd v Orient Transport Services Ltd* [1999] 2 Lloyd's Rep. 273; *British Fermentation Products Ltd v Compair Reavell Ltd* (1999) 66 Const. L.R. 1; *Watford Electronics Ltd v Sanderson CFL Ltd* [2001] EWCA Civ 317; *Britvic Soft Drinks Ltd v Messer UK Ltd* [2002] EWCA Civ 548, [2002] 2 Lloyd's Rep. 368; *Granville Oil and Chemicals Ltd v Davis Turner & Co Ltd* [2003] EWCA Civ 570; *Frans Maas (UK) Ltd v Samsung Electronics (UK) Ltd* [2004] EWHC 1502 at [411]; *Titan Steel Wheels Ltd v Royal Bank of Scotland Plc* [2010] EWHC 211 (Comm), [2010] 2 Lloyd's Rep. 92 at [106]; *AXA Sun Life Services Plc v Campbell Martin Ltd* [2011] EWCA Civ 133, [2011] 1 Lloyd's Rep. 1; *Rohlig UK Ltd v Rock Unique Ltd* [2011] EWCA Civ 18, [2011] 2 All E.R. (Comm) 1161; *Air Transworld Ltd v Bombardier Inc* [2012] EWHC 243 (Comm), [2012] 1 Lloyd's Rep. 349; *Avrora Fine Arts Investment Ltd v Christie, Manson & Woods Ltd* [2012] EWHC 2198 (Ch), [2012] P.N.L.R. 35 at [152]–[153]; *Allen Fabrications Ltd v ASD Ltd* [2012] EWHC 2213 (TCC) at [73]–[75]; *Elvanite Full Circle Ltd v AMEC Earth and Environmental (UK) Ltd* [2013] EWHC 1191 (TCC), 148 Con. L.R. 127 at [288] *Marex Financial Ltd v Creative Finance Ltd* [2013] EWHC 2155 (Comm), [2014] 1 All E.R. (Comm) 122 at [91], [92]; *West v Ian Finlay & Associates* [2014] EWCA Civ 316, [2014] B.L.R. 324 at [67]–[68]; *Barclays Bank Plc v Grant Thornton UK LLP* [2015] EWHC 320 (Comm) at [90]; *Polypearl Ltd v Building Research Establishment Ltd* Unreported July 28, 2016 (Mercantile Ct) at [105]; *Bates v Post Office Ltd (No.3: Common Issues)* [2019] EWHC 606 (QB) at [1092] (emphasising that this factor concerns what was known or ought to have been known of the existence and the *extent* of the term).

553 See *R.W. Green Ltd v Cade Bros Farms* [1978] 1 Lloyd's Rep. 602; *Stag Line Ltd v Tyne Ship Repair Group Ltd* [1984] 2 Lloyd's Rep. 211; *Rees-Hough Ltd v Redland Reinforced Plastics Ltd* (1985) 2 Con. L.R. 109; *Sargant v CIT (England) (t/a Citalia)* [1994] C.L.Y. 566; *Knight Machinery (Holdings) v Rennie* 1995 S.L.T. 166; *Granville Oil and Chemicals Ltd v Davis Turner & Co Ltd* [2003] EWCA Civ 570; *Elvanite Full Circle Ltd v AMEC Earth and Environmental (UK) Ltd* [2013] EWHC 1191 (TCC), 148 Con. L.R. 127 at [288]; *Commercial Management (Investments) Ltd v Mitchell Design & Construct Ltd* [2016] EWHC 76 (TCC) at [86]–[88].

554 It is uncertain whether the existence of this factor would operate against or in favour of the customer, but it is submitted that it should operate against the customer and in favour of the supplier. But see *Edmund Murray Ltd v BSP International Foundations Ltd* (1992) 33 Con. L.R. 1. cf. *British Fermentation Products Ltd v Compair Reavell Ltd* (1999) 66 Const. L.R. 1; *Watford Electronics Ltd v Sanderson CFL Ltd* [2001] EWCA Civ 317; *Air Transworld Ltd v Bombardier Inc* [2012] EWHC 243 (Comm), [2012] 1 Lloyd's Rep. 349 at [132]; *Allen Fabrications Ltd v ASD Ltd* [2012] EWHC 2213 (TCC) at [73]–[75].

### Limits on amount

*Replace paragraph with:*

Exemption clauses in contracts frequently limit the liability in damages of one party to a fixed or determinable sum. Section 11(4) provides: **15-099**

> "Where by reference to a contract term ... a person seeks to restrict liability to a specified sum of money, and the question arises (under this or any other Act) whether the term or notice satisfies the requirement of reasonableness, regard shall be had in particular (but without prejudice to subsection (2) above[556] in the case of contract terms) to—(a) the resources which he could expect to be available to him for the purpose of meeting the liability should it arise; and (b) how far it was open to him to cover himself by insurance."

This provision was clearly designed to provide some alleviation to the small business, and to professional persons, who may not have the resources available to meet unlimited liability or who may not be able to obtain insurance or who may be exposed to claims in excess of the sums for which insurance cover can be obtained.[557] But it might in some circumstances be construed to operate against those enterprises with such resources or which are able to insure.[558] It seems probable that the words "a specified sum of money" would embrace a determinable sum, e.g. the contract price. But it is more questionable whether (b) covers the situation where insurance cover can be obtained, but only on terms which are uneconomic in relation to the margin of profit achieved.[559]

556 See above, para.15-097.

557 The statement in the text was approved by *Goodlife Foods Ltd v Hall Fire Protection Ltd* [2017] EWHC 767 (TCC), [2017] B.L.R. 389 at [76] and [80]–[87] (affirmed [2018] EWCA Civ 1371, [2018] B.L.R. 491).

[558] The availability of insurance may be a relevant consideration in applying the test of reasonableness under s.11(1): see *George Mitchell (Chesterhall) Ltd v Finney Lock Seeds Ltd* [1983] 2 A.C. 803, 817 (below, para.15-103); *Rees-Hough Ltd v Redland Reinforced Plastics Ltd* (1985) 2 Con. L.R. 109; *Phillips Products Ltd v Hyland* [1987] 1 W.L.R. 659, 666–668; *Singer Co (UK) Ltd v Tees and Hartlepool Port Authority* [1988] 2 Lloyd's Rep. 164, 169; *Smith v Eric Bush* [1990] 1 A.C. 831, 858; *Overseas Medical Supplies Ltd v Orient Transport Services Ltd* [1990] 2 Lloyd's Rep. 273, 277; *Pegler Ltd v Wang* [2000] B.L.R. 218; *Frans Maas (UK) Ltd v Samsung Electronics (UK) Ltd* [2004] EWHC 1502 (Comm), [2004] 2 Lloyd's Rep. 251 at [159]; *Balmoral Group Ltd v Borealis UK Ltd* [2006] EWHC 1900 (Comm) at [415]–[416]. But the actual insurance position of the parties at the time is normally irrelevant: *Flamar Interocean Ltd v Denmac Ltd* [1990] 1 Lloyd's Rep. 434; cf. *St Alban's City and District Council v International Computers Ltd* [1995] F.S.R. 686 (affirmed [1996] 4 All E.R. 481); *Salvage Association v Cap Financial Services* [1995] F.S.R. 654; *SAM Business Systems Ltd v Hedley & Co* [2002] EWHC (TCC) 2733, [2003] 1 All E.R. (Comm) 465; *Shepherd Homes Ltd v Encia Remediation Ltd* [2007] EWHC 1710 (TCC), [2007] Build. L.R. 13; *Trustees of Ampleforth Abbey Trust v Turner and Townsend Management Ltd* [2012] EWHC 2137 (TCC), [2012] T.C.L.R. 8 at [201]; *Goodlife Foods Ltd v Hall Fire Protection Ltd* [2018] EWCA Civ 1371, [2018] B.L.R. 491 at [64]–[67]; [76]–[83].

[559] cf. *Smith v Eric Bush* [1990] 1 A.C. 831, 858 (cost); *Shepherd Homes Ltd v Encia Remediation Ltd* [2007] EWHC 70 (TCC), [2007] Build. L.R. 135.

## Reasonableness under Unfair Contract Terms Act 1977

*Replace footnote 576 with:*

15-104 [576] [1982] 1 W.L.R. 495. See also *Southwestern General Property Co Ltd v Marton* (1982) 263 E.G. 1090 and above, para.7-155; *Cleaver v Schyde Investments Ltd* [2011] EWCA Civ 929 (cl.7 of the *Standard Conditions of Sale*, 4th edn). cf. *Lloyd v Browning* [2013] EWCA Civ 1637, [2014] 1 P. & C.R. 11 at [33]–[36], [42] (cl.8 of *Standard Conditions of Sale*, 4th edn, held reasonable in context); *First Tower Trustees Ltd v CDS (Superstores International) Ltd* [2018] EWCA Civ 1396, [2019] 1 W.L.R. 637 at [68]–[76] and see above para.7-152 ("no-reliance" clauses).

*Replace footnote 617 with:*

15-111 [617] [2001] EWCA Civ 317, [2001] Build. L.R. 143 at [63]. See also *Salvage Association v CAP Financial Services* [1995] F.S.R. 654, 676; *E.A. Grimstead & Son Ltd v McGarrigan* [1999] EWCA Civ 3029 at [29]; *SAM Business Systems Ltd v Hedley & Co* [2002] EWHC 2733, [2003] 1 All E.R. (Comm) 465 at [63]; *Granville Oil and Chemicals Ltd v Davis Turner & Co Ltd* [2003] EWCA Civ 570, [2003] 2 Lloyd's Rep. 356 at [31]; *Frans Maas (UK) Ltd v Samsung Electronics (UK) Ltd* [2004] EWHC 1502 (Comm), [2004] 2 Lloyd's Rep. 251 at [158]; *JP Morgan Chase Bank v Springwell Navigation Corp* [2008] EWHC 1793 (Comm) at [604]; *Titan Steel Wheels Ltd v Royal Bank of Scotland Plc* [2010] EWHC 211 (Comm), [2010] 2 Lloyd's Rep. 92 at [100]; *Raiffeisen Zentralbank Osterreich AG v Royal Bank of Scotland Plc* [2010] EWHC 1392 (Comm), [2011] 1 Lloyd's Rep. 123 at [321]; *AXA Sun Life Services Plc v Campbell Martin Ltd* [2011] EWCA Civ 133, [2011] 2 Lloyd's Rep. 1; *Southwark LBC v IBM UK Ltd* [2011] EWHC 549 (TCC), 135 Con. L.R. 136; *Rohlig UK Ltd v Rock Unique Ltd* [2011] EWCA Civ 18, [2011] 2 All E.R. (Comm), 1161; *Camerata Property Inc v Credit Suisse Securities (Europe) Ltd* [2011] EWHC 479 (Comm), [2011] 2 B.C.L.C. 54; *Astrazeneca UK Ltd v Albermarle International Corp* [2011] EWHC 1574 (Comm), [2012] B.L.R. D1. cf. *Balmoral Group Ltd v Borealis UK Ltd* [2006] EWHC 1900 (Comm), [2006] 2 Lloyd's Rep. 629 at [404], [422]–[426]; *Avrora Fine Arts Investment Ltd v Christie, Manson & Woods Ltd* [2012] EWHC 2198 (Ch), [2012] P.N.L.R. 35 at [152]–[153]; *Elvanite Full Circle Ltd v AMEC Earth and Environmental (UK) Ltd* [2013] EWHC 1191 (TCC), 148 Con. L.R. 127 at [288]; *Marex Financial Ltd v Creative Finance Ltd* [2013] EWHC 2155 (Comm), [2014] 1 All E.R. (Comm) 122 at [91], [92]; *Natixis SA v Marex Financial* [2019] EWHC 2549 (Comm), [2019] 2 Lloyd's Rep. 431 at [522]–[534].

## Powers of the court

*Replace first paragraph with:*

15-112 Although the 1977 Act uses the words "except in so far as the term satisfies the requirement of reasonableness",[623] it is the term as a whole that has to be reasonable and not merely some part of it.[624] Thus if the term as a whole is unreasonable, a party cannot be heard to say that the part of the term on which he relies is reasonable.[625] However, where a single provision in a contract consists of several sub-clauses or sentences, it may be difficult to identify what is "the term" for the purposes of the Act.[626]

[623] Or, in ss.6(3), 7(3), "only in so far as".

[624] *Stewart Gill Ltd v Horatio Myer & Co Ltd* [1992] Q.B. 600, 608; *Lobster Group Ltd v Heidelberg*

*Graphic Equipment Ltd* [2009] EWHC 1919 (TCC) at [131]. cf. *R.W. Green Ltd v Cade Bros Farms* [1978] 1 Lloyd's Rep. 602; above, para.15-096.

[625] *Stewart Gill Ltd v Horatio Myer & Co Ltd* [1992] Q.B. 600, 607. But see *Skipskredittforeningen v Emperor Navigation* [1998] 1 Lloyd's Rep. 66, 75; *Bacardi-Martini Beverages Ltd v Thomas Hardy Packaging Ltd* [2002] EWCA Civ 549, [2002] 2 Lloyd's Rep. 379 at [26]; *J Murphy & Sons Ltd v Johnston Precast Ltd* [2008] EWHC 3024 (TCC); *Regus (UK) Ltd v Epcot Solutions Ltd* [2008] EWCA Civ 361, [2009] 1 All E.R. (Comm) 586 at [44]; *Goodlife Foods Ltd v Hall Fire Protection Ltd* [2017] EWHC 767 (TCC), [2017] B.L.R. 389 at [70] (affirmed [2018] EWCA Civ 1371, [2018] B.L.R. 491 without reference to this point).

[626] e.g. *Trolex Products Ltd v Merrol Fire Protection Engineers Ltd* Unreported November 20, 1991, CA, (contrasting views of Staughton and Nourse L.JJ. as to whether a clause should be treated as one or more "terms" for the purposes of the Act); *Goodlife Foods Ltd v Hall Fire Protection Ltd* [2017] EWHC 767 (TCC), [2017] B.L.R. 389 at [71] (though expressly obiter; affirmed [2018] EWCA Civ 1371, [2018] B.L.R. 491 without reference to this point).

*Replace footnote 629 with:*

[629] *Trolex Products Ltd v Merrol Fire Protection Engineers Ltd* Unreported November 20, 1991, CA, (under issue B(viii)), quoting with approval the view then tentatively expressed by the equivalent paragraph to para.15-114 in the 26th edition (1989) of the present work; *Goodlife Foods Ltd v Hall Fire Protection Ltd* [2017] EWHC 767 (TCC), [2017] B.L.R. 389 at [66]–[70] (affirmed [2018] EWCA Civ 1371, [2018] B.L.R. 491 without reference to this point distinguishing the issue of the "excision" of part of a term wholly ineffective under the 1977 Act and the issue considered in *Stewart Gill Ltd v Horatio Myer & Co Ltd* [1992] Q.B. 600 where it was held that a party had to show that the whole of a term was reasonable and not merely that part of a term on which it wished to rely). cf. Peel (ed.), *Treitel on The Law of Contract*, 15th edn (2020), para.7-075 arguing that the approach in *Trolex Products Ltd* is not easy to reconcile with *Thomas Witter Ltd v TBP Industries Ltd* [1996] 2 All E.R. 573, 598 which held unreasonable a contract term excluding liability for *any* pre-contractual misrepresentations on the ground that, on its proper construction, it includes a purported exclusion of liability for fraud: see *Thomas Witter Ltd v TBP Industries Ltd* [1996] 2 All E.R. 573, 598; *South West Water Services Ltd v International Computers Ltd* [1999] B.L.R. 420 and see above, para.7-155. **15-114**

*Add new paragraph:*

**Summary judgment** Under CPR r.24(2) a court may give summary judgment against a claimant or defendant on the whole of a claim or on a particular issue where they have no real prospect of success on it and where "there is no other compelling reason why the case or issue should be disposed of at a trial".[630a] It has been stated that "the issue of reasonableness is fact sensitive. Accordingly, particular caution is needed before concluding ... that the test of reasonableness is plainly satisfied" so that it is appropriate for a judge to grant summary judgment on the basis of a decision on the issue.[630b] **15-115A**

[630a] CPR r.24(2)(b). For general guidance on summary judgment see *Easyair Ltd (t/a Openair) v Opal Telecom Ltd* [2009] EWHC 339 (Ch) at [15] (Lewison J.), approved in *AC Ward & Sons Ltd v Catlin (Five) Ltd* [2009] EWCA Civ 1098, [2010] Lloyd's Rep. I.R. 301 at [24].

[630b] *Macquarie Internationale v Glencore* [2008] EWHC 1716 (Comm), [2008] 2 C.L.C. 223 at [84] per Walker J.; *Fine Lady Bakeries Ltd v EDF Energy Customers Ltd (formerly EDF Energy Customers Plc)* [2020] EWHC 87 (QB) at [41]–[45], [75]–[76] (judge below wrong to grant summary judgment on exclusion clauses challenged on the ground of their reasonableness, as issues of the relative bargaining position of the parties and the availability of insurance remained to be evidenced); *Lalji v Post Office Ltd* [2003] EWCA Civ 1873 at [17] per Brooke L.J.; cf. *Barclays Bank Plc v Grant Thornton UK LLP* [2015] EWHC 320 (Comm), [2015] 1 C.L.C. 180 at [55], where Cook J. recognised that reasonableness was a fact-sensitive issue but granted summary judgment on the issue (holding the exclusion clause reasonable at [89]–[91]) as he could "see no basis upon which any significant new factors could emerge at trial above and beyond what is currently known" and so he was therefore "in as good a position to resolve the matter now as any trial judge would be".

### (vi) *Incidental Matters*

**Anti-avoidance provisions**

*Replace footnote 684 with:*

15-128 [684] s.13; see above, para.15-069. See also Peel (ed.), *Treitel on The Law of Contract*, 15th edn (2020), para.7-076.

## (c) Other Legislation

**Carriage by road or rail**

*Replace footnote 697 with:*

15-133 [697] s.29 and see Vol.II, para.38-067. As from August 19, 2013, s.29 does not apply to anything governed by Regulation (EU) 181/2011 concerning the rights of passengers in bus and coach transport and amending Regulation (EC) No.2006/2004 [2011] O.J. L55/1, art.6 of which provides that the obligations which it contains cannot be excluded by the contract of transport. On IP completion day (on which see above, paras 1-014 et seq.), Regulation (EU) 181/2011 will form part of "retained EU law" as amended: Rights of Passengers in Bus and Coach Transport (Amendment etc.) (EU Exit) Regulations 2019 (SI 2019/141) reg.4 (reg.1(2)'s reference to the 2019 Regulations coming into force on "exit day" must be read as referring to IP completion day: European Union (Withdrawal Agreement) Act 2020 s.39(1), Sch.5 para.1). See also s.149 of the Road Traffic Act 1988 (agreements between user of motor vehicle and passenger, as amended by SI 2019/1047 reg.2, Sch.1 Pt 1 para.12 (in force November 1, 2019)) and, as regards passengers by rail, EC Regulation 1371/2007 [2007] O.J. L315/3 art.6 and the Rail Passengers' Rights and Obligations Regulations 2010 (SI 2010/1504). On IP completion day, Regulation (EC) 1371/2007 will form part of "retained EU law" as amended and the 2010 Regulations are also due to be amended: Rail Passengers' Rights and Obligations (Amendment) (EU Exit) Regulations 2018 (SI 2018/1165): (reg.1(2)'s reference to the 2018 Regulations coming into force on "exit day" must be read as referring to IP completion day: European Union (Withdrawal Agreement) Act 2020 s.39(1), Sch.5 para.1).

**Carriage by air**

*Replace paragraph with:*

15-135 The Warsaw Convention (as supplemented and amended) regulates the liability of a carrier by air in respect of the international carriage of goods, passengers and passengers' luggage. It is given statutory force by the Carriage by Air Act 1961, which was amended by the Carriage by Air (Supplementary Provisions) Act 1962 and by the Carriage by Air and Road Act 1979,[707] and applies with modifications to non-international carriage by the Carriage by Air Acts (Application of Provisions) Order 2004.[708] The Convention imposes certain liabilities on the carrier which cannot be excluded or limited by special contract; but, under its provisions, the carrier is prima facie relieved from liability in excess of certain stated pecuniary limits.

[707] See also SI 1998/1751, SI 1999/1312, SI 2002/263, SI 2004/1418, SI 2004/1899, SI 2004/1974, 2005/975, 2006/3303, 2009/3018; European Parliament and Council Regulations 889/2002, 261/2004, 875/2004. On IP completion day (on which see above, paras 1-014 et seq.), this body of law is due to be amended: see the Air Passenger Rights and Air Travel Organisers' Licensing (Amendment) (EU Exit) Regulations 2019 (SI 2019/278) (reg.1's reference to most of the provisions of the 2019 Regulations coming into force on "exit day" must be read as referring to IP completion day: European Union (Withdrawal Agreement) Act 2020 s.39(1), Sch.5 para.1). See Vol.II, paras 35-022—35-081.

[708] SI 2004/1899 as amended by SI 2019/278 Pt 3 reg.4. See also EC Regulation 889/2002. See Vol.II, para.35-018.

**Insurance**

*Replace footnote 709 with:*

15-136 [709] See Vol.II, para.42-124. See also s.149. Sections 148 and 149 were amended by SI 2019/1047 reg.1, Sch.I paras 11 and 12 (in force November 1, 2019).

### Solicitors

*Replace footnote 716 with:*

716 Solicitors Act 1974 ss.57(5), 61(2) (as amended). Where the agreement is a "consumer contract" within the meaning of the Consumer Rights Act 2015 Pt 2, its terms will in principle also be subject to the requirement of fairness set out in s.62 of that Act, see *Higgins & Co Lawyers Ltd v Evans* [2019] EWHC 2809 (QB), [2020] 1 W.L.R. 2809 at [101], on which see Vol.II, para.38-342 (note). **15-139**

### Finance

*Replace paragraph with:*

Any provision of the trust deed of an authorised unit trust scheme is void in so far as it would have the effect of exempting the manager or trustee from liability for any failure to exercise due care and diligence in a discharge of his functions in respect of the scheme.[718] Regulation 137 of the Payment Services Regulations 2017,[719] which implements in the UK the Second Payment Services Directive,[720] provides that: **15-140**

> "… a payment service provider may not agree with a payment service user that it will not comply with any provision of these Regulations unless—
>
> (a) such agreement is permitted by these Regulations, or
> (b) such agreement provides for terms which are more favourable to the payment service user than the relevant provisions of these Regulations."[721]

718 Financial Services and Markets Act 2000 s.253. "Authorised unit trust scheme" is defined in s.237.

719 SI 2017/752. The 2017 Regulations revoked with general effect from January 13, 2018 the substantive provisions of the earlier Payment Services Regulations 2009 (SI 2009/209) implementing the (first) Payment Services Directive, Directive 2007/64/EC of the European Parliament and the Council on payment services in the internal market [2007] O.J. L3319/1. On IP completion day (on which see above, paras 1-014 et seq.), the Payment Services Regulations are due to form part of "retained EU law" as amended by the Electronic Money, Payment Services and Payment Systems (Amendment and Transitional Provisions) (EU Exit) Regulations 2018 (SI 2018/1201) reg.3 and Sch.2 paras 23–73 which do not, however, amend reg.137 of the 2017 Regulations. See further Vol.II, paras 34-224 and 39-510.

720 (EU) 2015/2366 of the European Parliament and of the Council of 25 November 2015 on payment services in the internal market [2015] O.J. L337/35 ("Second Payment Services Directive").

721 Provisions in the 2017 Regulations allowing the exclusion of certain of their requirements include regs 40(7), 42(2)(b) and (c), 63(5) and 65(2) (none of which are due to be amended by SI 2018/1201).

### Mandatory character of much consumer protection legislation

*In line 5, after "EU directives which so require.", add new footnote 729a:*

729a On the UK's leaving the EU on "exit day" (as explained above, paras 1-014 et seq.) the UK legislation implementing the directives mentioned in this paragraph will form part of "retained EU law" subject to amendments which are noted at the particular paragraphs to which the reader is cross-referred in the following notes. **15-143**

## 8 FORCE MAJEURE CLAUSES

### Force majeure clauses

*Replace footnote 788 with:*

788 *B. & S. Contracts and Design Ltd v Victor Green Publications Ltd* [1984] I.C.R. 419. See also *Seadrill Ghana Operations Ltd v Tullow Ghana Ltd* [2018] EWHC 1640 (Comm), [2018] 2 Lloyd's Rep. 628 at [28], [82]–[98] and [131] (express term on both parties to "use their reasonable endeavours to mitigate, avoid, circumvent, or overcome the circumstances of force majeure"). **15-154**

## "Prevented" clauses

*Replace first paragraph with:*

**15-156** Where one party seeks to invoke the protection of a clause which states that he is to be relieved of liability if he is "prevented" from carrying out his obligations under the contract or is "unable" to do so, he must show that performance has become physically or legally impossible, and not merely more difficult or unprofitable.[799] It is not sufficient, for example in a contract of sale of goods, for the seller to show that his intended supplier is unable to supply the goods if he can obtain goods of the contract description from another supplier.[800] But the word "prevented" has always to be interpreted in the context of the particular contract. Thus where the intended method of performance is prohibited by government embargo, but a party is nevertheless able to perform in an alternative manner, it is a question of construction of the clause, and of fact, whether his performance has been effectively "prevented" by the embargo.[801] In particular, CIF sellers in a "circle" or "string" have in some cases been held entitled to rely on a clause of this nature when they or some shipper higher up the "string" were prevented by government embargo from shipping the goods, even though they could have attempted to purchase substitute goods afloat, on the ground that such an attempt would in the circumstances have been impractical and commercially unreasonable.[802] Once a party has discharged the burden of proving that performance has been prevented by the relevant event, he need not normally prove that he could have performed but for the occurrence of the event.[803] An independent state trading organisation may be able to establish that it has been prevented from delivering by "government intervention beyond its control" if an export embargo is imposed by its own government.[804] But, where it is alleged that performance has been prevented by refusal of a licence, the party required to obtain the licence may be obliged to show that he has made reasonable efforts to obtain the licence or that a licence would inevitably have been refused[805]; and, if an embargo is not absolute, but subject to certain exceptions, a seller may be obliged to show that he has no goods of the contract description available to him within the "loopholes" to which the embargo is subject.[806]

[799] *Blythe & Co v Richards Turpin & Co* (1916) 114 L.T. 753; *Tennants (Lancashire) Ltd v C.S. Wilson & Co Ltd* [1917] A.C. 495; *Re Comptoir Commercial Anversois and Power Son & Co* [1920] 1 K.B. 868; *Brauer & Co (G.B.) Ltd v James Clark (Brush Materials) Ltd* [1952] 2 All E.R. 497; *Ross T. Smyth & Co (Liverpool) Ltd v W.N. Lindsay Ltd* [1953] 2 Lloyd's Rep. 378; *Fairclough, Dodd & Jones Ltd v J.H. Vantol Ltd* [1957] 1 W.L.R. 136, 143, 144; *Tsakiroglou & Co v Noblee Thorl GmbH* [1962] A.C. 93; *Warinco A.G. v Fritz Mauthner* [1978] 1 Lloyd's Rep. 151; *Exportelisa SA v Giuseppe & Figli Soc. Coll.* [1978] 1 Lloyd's Rep. 433; *Huilerie l'Abeille v Société des Huileries du Niger* [1978] 2 Lloyd's Rep. 203; *Channel Islands Ferries Ltd v Sealink UK Ltd* [1988] 1 Lloyd's Rep. 323, 327; *Thames Valley Power Ltd v Total Gas & Power Ltd* [2005] EWHC 2208 (Comm), [2006] 1 Lloyd's Rep. 441 at [50]; *Tandrin Aviation Holdings Ltd v Aero Toy Store LLC* [2010] EWHC 40 (Comm), [2010] 2 Lloyd's Rep. 668 at [49]; *Dunavant Enterprises Inc v Olympia Spinning & Weaving Mills Ltd* [2011] EWHC 2028 (Comm), [2011] 2 Lloyd's Rep. 619 at [29], [32].

[800] *Joseph Pyke & Son (Liverpool) Ltd v Richard Cornelius & Co* [1955] 2 Lloyd's Rep. 747; *Fairclough Dodd & Jones Ltd v J. H. Vantol Ltd* [1957] 1 W.L.R. 136, 146; *Koninklijke Bunge v Cie Commerciale d'Importation* [1973] 2 Lloyd's Rep. 44; *P. J. van der Zijden Wildhandel NV v Tucker & Cross Ltd* [1975] 2 Lloyd's Rep. 240; *Exportelisa SA v Giuseppe & Figli Soc. Coll.* [1978] 1 Lloyd's Rep. 433; *Hoecheong Products Co Ltd v Cargill Hong Kong Ltd* [1995] 1 W.L.R. 404.

[801] *Tradax Export SA v André et Cie* [1976] 1 Lloyd's Rep. 416; *Warinco A.G. v Fritz Mauthner* [1978] 1 Lloyd's Rep. 151; *Bremer Handelsgesellschaft mbH v C. Mackprang Jr* [1979] 1 Lloyd's Rep. 221; *Avimex SA v Dewulf & Cie.* [1979] 2 Lloyd's Rep. 57; *André et Cie. SA v Etablissements Michel Blanc et Fils* [1979] 2 Lloyd's Rep. 427; *Bunge SA v Deutsche Conti Handelsgesellschaft mbH* [1979] 2 Lloyd's Rep. 455; *Continental Grain Export Corp v S.T.M. Grain* [1979] 2 Lloyd's Rep. 460; *Toepfer v Schwarze* [1980] 1 Lloyd's Rep. 385; *Bremer Handelsgesellschaft mbH v Westzucker GmbH* [1981] 1 Lloyd's Rep. 207; *Raiffeisen Hauptgenossenschaft v Louis Dreyfus & Co Ltd* [1981] 1 Lloyd's Rep.

345; *Bremer Handelsgesellschaft mbH v C. Mackprang Jr* [1981] 1 Lloyd's Rep. 292; *Cook Industries Inc v Meunerie Liegeois SA* [1981] 1 Lloyd's Rep. 359; *Tradax Export SA v Cook Industries Inc* [1982] 1 Lloyd's Rep. 385; *Bremer Handelsgesellschaft mbH v Raiffeisen Hauptgenossenschaft* [1982] 1 Lloyd's Rep. 599; *Bremer Handelsgesellschaft mbH v Continental Grain Co* [1983] 1 Lloyd's Rep. 269; *Bremer Handelsgesellschaft mbH v Bunge Corp* [1983] 1 Lloyd's Rep. 476; *Pancommerce SA v Veecheema BV* [1983] 2 Lloyd's Rep. 304; *Deutsche Conti-Handelsgesellschaft mbH v Bremer Handelsgesellschaft mbH* [1984] 1 Lloyd's Rep. 447; *Cook Industries v Tradax Export SA* [1985] 2 Lloyd's Rep. 454; *Bremer Handelsgesellschaft v Westzucker GmbH (No.3)* [1989] 1 Lloyd's Rep. 582. Cf. *Koninklijke Bunge v Compagnie Continentale d'Importation* [1973] 2 Lloyd's Rep. 44; *Tradax Export SA v Carapelli SpA* [1977] 2 Lloyd's Rep. 157; *Bremer Handelsgesellschaft mbH v Vanden Avenne-Izegem PVBA* [1978] 2 Lloyd's Rep. 109; *Sociedad Iberica de Molturacion SA v Tradax Export SA* [1978] 2 Lloyd's Rep. 545; *Bunge SA v Kruse* [1979] 1 Lloyd's Rep. 279 (affirmed [1980] 2 Lloyd's Rep. 142); *André et Cie SA v Tradax Export SA* [1983] 1 Lloyd's Rep. 254; *Bunge SA v Nidera BV* [2013] EWHC 84 (Comm), [2013] 1 Lloyd's Rep. 621 at [33], affirmed [2013] EWCA Civ 1628 at [22] (causal connection must be shown) (the application of the "prohibition clause" was not in issue before the SC [2015] UKSC 43, [2015] Bus. L.R. 987); *Seadrill Ghana Operations Ltd v Tullow Ghana Ltd* [2018] EWHC 1640 (Comm), [2018] 2 Lloyd's Rep. 628 at [70]–[80]. See McKendrick (ed.), *Force Majeure and Frustration of Contract*, 2nd edn (1995), Ch.15 (Bridge); Treitel, *Frustration and Force Majeure*, 3rd edn (2014), para.12-038.

[802] *Tradax Export SA v André et Cie* [1976] 1 Lloyd's Rep. 416, 423; *Bremer Handelsgesellschaft mbH v Vanden-Avenne Izegem PVBA* [1978] 2 Lloyd's Rep. 109, 115; *Continental Grain Export Corp v S.T.M. Grain* [1979] 2 Lloyd's Rep. 460, 473; *Cook Industries Inc v Tradax Export SA* [1983] 1 Lloyd's Rep. 327 (affirmed [1985] 2 Lloyd's Rep. 454). See *Benjamin's Sale of Goods*, 10th edn (2017) at para.18-393.

[803] *Bremer Handelsgesellschaft mbH v Vanden Avenne-Izegem PVBA* [1978] 2 Lloyd's Rep. 109, 114, 121; *Bremer Handelsgesellschaft mbH v C. Mackprang Jnr* [1980] 1 Lloyd's Rep. 210 (affirmed [1981] 1 Lloyd's Rep. 292); *Continental Grain Export Corp v S.T.M. Grain* [1979] 2 Lloyd's Rep. 460. cf. *Tradax Export SA v André et Cie* [1976] 1 Lloyd's Rep. 416; *Toepfer v Schwarze* [1977] 2 Lloyd's Rep. 380 (affirmed [1980] 1 Lloyd's Rep. 385); *André et Cie SA v Etablissements Michel Blanc et Fils* [1979] 2 Lloyd's Rep. 427. However, in *Classic Maritime Inc v Limbungan Makmur Sdn Bhd* [2019] EWCA Civ 1102 at [37]–[49], [91]–[92] and [95], the contract term in issue (called in the contract an "exceptions" clause) excluded liability for loss or damage "resulting from" a series of specified acts (including one applicable on the facts) which "directly affect the performance of either party". The CA held that on its proper construction this clause did not apply where the party claiming its benefit would not have performed its obligations even in the absence of the excepted event, distinguishing the effect of the contract term which was the subject of the decision of the HL in *Bremer Handelsgesellschaft mbH v Vanden Avenne-Izegem PVBA*, which was a "contractual frustration clause" in the sense of one which cancels the contract (or part of the contract) for the future without liability on either side (at [49]–[62], [92] and [95]).

[804] *C. Czarnikow Ltd v Centrala Handlu Zagranicznego Rolimpex* [1979] A.C. 351. cf. *Empresa Exportadora de Azucar v Industria Azucarera Nacional SA* [1983] 2 Lloyd's Rep. 171; *Mamidoil-Jetoil Greek Petroleum Co SA v Okta Crude Oil Refinery AD (No.2)* [2003] EWCA Civ 1031, [2003] 2 Lloyd's Rep. 635.

[805] *Re Anglo-Russian Merchant Traders and John Batt & Co (London) Ltd* [1917] 2 K.B. 679; *Brauer & Co (G.B.) Ltd v James Clarke (Brush Materials) Ltd* [1952] 2 All E.R. 497; *Malik Co v Central European Trading Agency Ltd* [1974] 2 Lloyd's Rep. 279; *Provimi Hellas A.E. v Warinco A.G.* [1978] 1 Lloyd's Rep. 67, 373; *Overseas Buyers Ltd v Granadex* [1980] 2 Lloyd's Rep. 608.

[806] *Tradax Export SA v André et Cie* [1976] 1 Lloyd's Rep. 416; *Bremer Handelsgesellschaft mbH v C. Mackprang Jr* [1979] 1 Lloyd's Rep. 221; *André et Cie SA v Etablissements Michel Blanc et Fils* [1979] 2 Lloyd's Rep. 427; *Avimex SA v Dewulf & Cie.* [1979] 2 Lloyd's Rep. 57; *Bunge SA v Deutsche Conti Handelsgesellschaft mbH* [1979] 2 Lloyd's Rep. 455; *Overseas Buyers Ltd v Granadex* [1980] 2 Lloyd's Rep. 608; *Raiffeisen Hauptgenossenschaft v Louis Dreyfus & Co Ltd* [1981] 1 Lloyd's Rep. 345; *Bremer Handelsgesellschaft mbH v Westzucker GmbH (No.2)* [1981] 2 Lloyd's Rep. 130; *Cook Industries Ltd v Tradax Export SA* [1985] 2 Lloyd's Rep. 454. cf. *Bremer Handelsgesellschaft mbH v Vanden Avenne-Izegem PVBA* [1978] 2 Lloyd's Rep. 109.

## Unfair Contract Terms Act 1977

*Replace footnote 869 with:*

[869] See *Shearson Lehman Hutton Inc v Maclaine Watson & Co Ltd* [1989] 2 Lloyd's Rep. 570, 612 and see, e.g. *Target Rich International Ltd v Forex Capital Markets Ltd* [2020] EWHC 1544 (Comm) at [131]–[134] (clause suspending obligations of the provider of a currency trading platform where there is an "exceptional market event" held reasonable). **15-167**

Chapter 16

# ILLEGALITY AND PUBLIC POLICY

## 1. INTRODUCTION

*Add new paragraph:*

16-003A **The principle of illegality as applied to contracts** Illegality can either be "statutory" or "common law" illegality. A recent illustration of the difference is the case of *Okedina v Chikale*.[18a] The court pointed out that statutory illegality arises where statute, expressly or by implication, renders the contract or a term of the contract unenforceable by one or other party.[18b]

> "The underlying principle is straightforward: if the legislation itself has provided that the contract is unenforceable in full and in the relevant respect, the court is bound to respect that provision. That being the rationale, the knowledge or culpability of the party who is prevented from recovering is irrelevant: it is a simple matter of obeying the statute."[18c]

Analysing the cases on statutory illegality as applied to contracts involves a degree of judicial discretion making the outcome unpredictable:

> "... [I]t does not necessarily follow from the fact that one party is prohibited from entering into a contract, and/or made subject to a penalty if they do so, that Parliament intended to 'prohibit' the contract itself in the relevant sense of rendering it unenforceable *by either party*. Whether that was the intention must depend on a consideration of all relevant factors including matters of public policy."[18d]

Common law illegality arises "where the formation, purpose or performance of the contract is illegal or contrary to public policy" and where it is appropriate to deny enforcement of the contract.[18e] In *Okedina* the claimant brought various claims of a contractual nature under a contract of employment. At the relevant time the claimant's visa had expired and she could no longer be legally employed because of a statutory prohibition rendering such employment illegal. The court gave a strongly purposive construction to the statutory provisions which the court referred to as the "blunt weapon of statutory illegality".[18f] The court considered that the relevant statutory prohibitions did not require the court to give it a construction that would have "the effect of depriving the innocent employee of all contractual remedies against the employer ...".[18g] As to common law illegality, the court considered that "[i]n his judgment in *Patel v Mirza* Lord Toulson was attempting to identify the broad principles underlying the illegality rule" and that there was no requirement for the court to consider "how the rule has been applied in the previous case law except where such an application is inconsistent with those principles".[18h] In other words, the application of the illegality doctrine is a purposive, principled doctrine. The defence of common law illegality was rejected because

> "the touchstone for the availability of [this defence is] that the employee has knowingly participated in the illegal performance of the contract ... so called 'knowledge plus participation'"[18i]

and the claimant did not know that her visa had not been extended.[18j]

[18a] [2019] EWCA Civ 1393, [2019] I.C.R. 1635 at [12].

[18b] [2019] EWCA Civ 1393 at [12].

[18c] [2019] EWCA Civ 1393 at [12].

[18d] [2019] EWCA Civ 1393 at [20].

[18e] [2019] EWCA Civ 1393 at [12]. The court held that *Patel v Mirza* [2016] UKSC 42, [2017] A.C. 467 had set out the approach to this form of illegality.

[18f] [2019] EWCA Civ 1393 at [49].

[18g] [2019] EWCA Civ 1393 at [49].

[18h] [2019] EWCA Civ 1393 at [62].

[18i] [2019] EWCA Civ 1393 at [13], referring to the judgment of Peter Gibson L.J. in *Hall v Woolston Hall Leisure Ltd* [2001] I.C.R. 99 at [31].

[18j] [2019] EWCA Civ 1393 at [14].

## 3. CONTRACTS INVOLVING THE COMMISSION OF A LEGAL WRONG

### (b) A Factors-Based Approach

#### *(i) The Treatment of Illegality Prior to the Factors-Based Approach*

**A more flexible approach pre Patel v Mirza**

*Replace paragraph with:*

A number of cases in the 1980s and 1990s had rejected the application of "rules of illegality" and had applied instead a general principle that the court would only refuse to assist the claimant where to do so would be "an affront to the public conscience".[86] This approach was rejected unanimously by the House of Lords in *Tinsley v Milligan*.[87] However, their Lordships disagreed as to what principle should apply in that case[88] and Lord Goff suggested that, if there was to be any change of approach it should only be attempted by legislation after a review by the Law Commission. A reference was duly made to the Law Commission, which published a series of consultation papers and reports. Initially the Law Commission's provisional proposals were that, where the formation, purpose or performance of a contract involves the commission of a legal wrong (other than a mere breach of **16-016** the contract in question), the court should be given a statutory discretion to decide whether or not illegality should operate as a defence to enforcement of the contract.[89] However, although there was considerable support for this approach, the Law Commission ultimately concluded that it should not recommend a statutory discretion except for claims under trusts. In a second consultation paper on illegality,[90] the Law Commission explained that this change of approach was partly because of the difficulty of drafting a statutory discretion that would be sufficiently certain and would not involve the courts in considering illegality in large numbers of cases where it would not arise under the common law rules, and partly because the Law Commission considered that, in dealing with of illegality, it was open to the courts to adopt a more flexible approach which took account of the policies underlying the doctrine.[91] The Law Commission stated:

> "We provisionally recommend that the courts should consider in each case whether the application of the illegality defence can be justified on the basis of the policies that underlie that defence. These include: (a) furthering the purpose of the rule which the illegal conduct has infringed; (b) consistency; (c) that the claimant should not profit from his or her own wrong; (d) deterrence; and (e) maintaining the integrity of the legal system. Against those policies must be weighed the legitimate expectation of the claimant that his or her legal rights will be protected."[92]

It distinguished this approach from the "public conscience test", which was "vague", because its suggested approach required the court to base their decision on the underlying policies.[93] The Law Commission confirmed this approach in its final Report, and it argued that since publication of its second consultation paper, Lord Hoffmann's observations in *Gray v Thames Trains Ltd*[94] had demonstrated that this "incremental change" was already taking place.[95] In *Henderson v Dorset Healthcare University NHS Foundation Trust*,[95a] where the facts were similar to those in *Gray v Thames Trains Ltd*,[95b] the court considered that the latter case remained binding on it[95c] and was not affected by *Patel v Mirza*.[95d]

86 See, for example *Euro-Diam Ltd v Bathurst* [1990] 1 Q.B. 1 and the decision of the Court of Appeal in *Tinsley v Milligan* [1992] Ch. 310.

87 [1994] 1 A.C. 340.

88 For the facts and decision, see below, para.16-221.

89 Law Commission, Consultation Paper No.154, *The Effect of Illegality on Contracts and Trusts*, para.9.4.

90 Law Commission, Consultative Report, Consultation Paper No.189, *The Illegality Defence* (2009); see paras 3.107–3.115.

91 Consultation Paper No.189, paras 3.136 (on enforcement of contract claims) and 4.42 (on restitution when a contract is unenforceable because of illegality).

92 Consultation Paper No.189, para.3.142.

93 Consultation Paper No.189, para.3.140.

94 [2009] 1 A.C. 1339 at [30].

95 *The Illegality Defence*, The Law Commission (Law Com No.320), para.3.38.

95a [2018] EWCA Civ 1841, [2018] 3 W.L.R. 1651.

95b [2009] 1 A.C. 1339.

95c [2018] EWCA Civ 1841 at [91].

95d [2017] A.C. 467. The court also considered that this was the case with respect to *Clunis v Camden and Islington Health Authority* [1998] Q.B. 978.

## (iii) The Adoption of a Factors-Based Approach

### A new approach—the current law

*Replace paragraph with:*

In *Patel v Mirza*[104] the Supreme Court fundamentally recast the doctrine of illegality in contract. The law remains that the court will not order performance or grant damages for breach of a contract if the claim should not be enforced because of illegality, but the question is to be decided on a "factors-based approach". However, the court will normally order restitution of any money or property transferred under it.[105] The result is that much of the previous law on judicial remedies with respect to illegal contracts is mainly of historical interest. In effect, in *Patel v Mirza* the Supreme Court, by a majority, has adopted the flexible approach advocated by the Law Commission. Lord Toulson (with whom Baroness Hale, Lord Kerr, Lord Wilson and Lord Hodge agreed; Lord Neuberger appears also to have supported Lord Toulson's approach[105a]) considered that the doctrine of illegality was: **16-018**

> "... not a matter which can be determined mechanistically. So how is the court to determine the matter if not by some mechanistic process? In answer to that question I would say that one cannot judge whether allowing a claim which is in some way tainted by illegality would be contrary to the public interest, because it would be harmful to the integrity of the legal system, without (a) considering the underlying purpose of the prohibition which has been transgressed, (b) considering conversely any other relevant public policies which may be rendered ineffective or less effective by denial of the claim, and (c) keeping in mind the possibility of overkill unless the law is applied with a due sense of proportionality. We are, after all, in the area of public policy. That trio of necessary considerations can be found in the case law."[106]

Lord Toulson added that the primary question was whether the "relief claimed should be granted" rather than "whether the contract should be regarded as tainted with illegality".[106a] A minority of the Justices of the Supreme Court (Lords Mance, Clarke and Sumption[106b]) disagreed with this approach. Lord Clarke, for example, considered that there was "no support in any of the authorities for this approach" and was contrary to *Hall v Herbert*[106c] and *Tinsley v Milligan*[106d] which had been cited by other members of the court.[106e] Subsequently, in *Mohammad Saeed v Mohammad Ibrahim*[106f] the court considered that in the light of *Patel v Mirza*:

> "... the question was whether consideration of the policy factors and of the nature and circumstances of the illegality should result, given the public interest in preserving the integrity of the justice system, in the denial of the relief claimed. Thus the focus was on whether relief should be granted rather than whether the contract was tainted by illegality."

This is undoubtedly an accurate reading of Lord Toulson's judgment.

[104] [2016] UKSC 42, [2017] A.C. 467; see also *Singularis Holdings Ltd v Daiwa Capital Markets Ltd* [2017] EWHC 257 (Ch) at [216]–[220].

[105] See paras 16-019 et seq.

[105a] See below, para.16-026.

[106] [2016] UKSC 42, [2017] A.C. 467 at [101].

[106a] [2016] UKSC 42 at [109].

[106b] The minority's approach is explained below, paras 16-027—16-029.

106c [1993] 2 S.C.R. 159.

106d [1994] 1 A.C. 340.

106e [2016] UKSC 42 at [219].

106f [2018] EWHC 1804 (Ch) at [89] (emphasis added). This is very much the approach of Lord Neuberger: see below para.16-031.

### *(iv) Rule-Based and Factors-Based Approaches Contrasted*

#### Countervailing policy

*Replace paragraph with:*

16-025 As indicated in Lord Toulson's summary in *Patel v Mirza* quoted earlier,[128] the court must "consider any other relevant public policy on which the denial of the claim may have an impact". In other words, it must take into account countervailing policy considerations. Thus in *Hounga v Allen* Lord Wilson had concluded that the countervailing policy considerations underlying the Race Relations Act outweighed the policy considerations in favour of applying the illegality defence.[129] Another example of countervailing policy reasons prevailing is provided by the Court of Appeal in *R. (on the application of Best) v Chief Land Registrar*.[130] There may be exceptional cases when even criminal acts should not attract the defence; and in particular the defence should not apply where the consequences of an illegal act are merely collateral to the claim.[131] In that case it was held that the importance of certainty of title was such when Parliament enacted that the occupation by the squatter constituted a criminal offence[132] it could not have intended the settled law of adverse possession to be upset, and the squatter could rely on adverse possession of possession of land to claim title to the land.[133] In *Stoffel & Co v Grondona*[133a] solicitors were sued for admitted professional negligence with respect to a conveyancing transaction which was part of a mortgage fraud of which they had no knowledge. The court, among other factors, considered it unlikely that the fight against mortgage fraud would be greatly assisted if "mortgagors involved in making false representations to mortgagees were unable to recover if their solicitors were negligent in failing to register the mortgagee's security".[133b] However, the illegality doctrine can be applied to thwart existing rights. In *Al-Dowaisan v Al-Salam*,[133c] a case involving an illegal tax fraud, it was held not to be a disproportionate response to deny the claimant a right to recover his property "[n]otwithstanding the interference with his rights of property under the first Protocol to the Convention on Human Rights, article 1 ...".[133d]

128 [2016] UKSC 42 at [120]; see above, para.16-024.

129 [2015] EWCA Civ 17, [2016] Q.B. 23 at [54].

130 [2015] EWCA Civ 17.

131 [2015] EWCA Civ 17 at [59] and [61].

132 Under Legal Aid, Sentencing and Punishment of Offenders Act 2012 s.144.

133 [2015] EWCA Civ 17 at [75]

133a [2018] EWCA Civ 2031.

133b [2018] EWCA Civ 2031 at [37].

133c [2019] EWHC 301 (Ch).

133d [2019] EWHC 301 (Ch) at [234].

### (v) The Restitutionary Basis of Recovery

**The minority approach: Lords Sumption and Mance**

*Replace paragraph with:*

As mentioned above, Lord Sumption considered that when a contract is unenforceable for illegality, the remedy of restitution should be available; it would not give effect to the illegal act but: **16-032**

> "... return the parties to the status quo ante where they should always have been ... This was Gloster L.J.'s main reason for upholding Mr Patel's right to recover the money."[191]

Lord Sumption gave the following hypothetical:

> "If I pay £10,000 to a hitman to kill my enemy, he should not kill my enemy and should not have £10,000. The fact that when it comes to the point he is unwilling or unable to kill my enemy does not give him any legal or moral entitlement to keep the £10,000. If he does kill him, the rational response is the same. He should be convicted of murder, but he should never have received the money for such a purpose and by the same token not be allowed to retain it."[191a]

This is rightly criticised by Burrows[191b] as being an inappropriate response to the extreme illegality involved and would entail that the party arranging the murder would gain what he wanted at no cost.

[191] [2016] UKSC 42 at [268]. Lord Sumption considered that a possible objection to this is that the court should not sully itself by being involved with the illegality as not being a "reputable foundation for the law of illegality": [2016] UKSC 42 at [268].

[191a] [2016] UKSC 42 at [254].

[191b] Burrows, "A New Dawn for the Law of Illegality" in Green and Bogg (eds), *Illegality after Patel v Mirza* (2018), Ch.2 at 33.

## (c) Application of the Factors-Based Approach

*Add new paragraph:*

**Application of new approach** The following paragraphs[201a] reflect "a rules-based approach" to illegality, as this was the basis on which the cases were decided. *Patel v Mirza*[201b] has adopted "a range of factors approach", but even if this had been applicable it is questionable whether the cases would have been differently decided. The Court of Appeal has said that there is no requirement for the court to consider "how the rule has been applied in the previous case law except where such an application is inconsistent with [the *Patel v Mirza*] principles".[201c] *Patel v Mirza* involved a restitutionary claim for repayment of money paid under an illegal contract involving the crime of insider dealing contrary to the Criminal Justice Act 1993 s.52. The analysis by Lord Toulson giving the judgment of the court involved a wide-ranging analysis of the law of contractual illegality and was not restricted to restitution and property claims. In *Singularis Holdings Ltd (In Liquidation) v Daiwa Capital Markets Europe Ltd*[201d] the court recognised that "*Patel v Mirza* was a restitution claim"[201e] but did not specifically confine its judgment to such claims[201f] and as a matter of principle there is little justification for so confining it. **16-033A**

[201a] That is paras 16-034–16-040.

[201b] [2016] UKSC 42, [2017] A.C. 461.

201c *Okedina v Chikale* [2019] EWCA Civ 1393 at [62].

201d [2019] UKSC 50, [2019] 3 W.L.R. 997 at [14].

201e [2019] UKSC 50 at [14].

201f The case involved illegality in providing false documents and breach of fiduciary obligations, see [2019] UKSC 50 at [16] and below, para.16-178.

## Illegality as to formation

*Replace paragraph with:*

**16-034** Contracts may be illegal when entered into because they cannot be performed in accordance with their terms without the commission of an illegal act. Thus the contract may involve a breach of the criminal law, statutory or otherwise, or alternatively it may be a statutory requirement that the parties to the transaction possess a licence and where they do not the contract will be illegal as formed. An example of a contract which was illegal as formed is provided by *Levy v Yates*,[204] a case concerned with the former statutory rule that no play could be lawfully acted within 20 miles of London without a royal licence, which might be given only in certain circumstances. In that case the contract, between a theatre owner and an impresario, was itself for the performance of a theatrical production prohibited by the statute. The contract was unenforceable since[205] "the agreement could not be carried into effect without a contravention of the law": the parties had contracted to do the very thing forbidden by the statute and the contract was therefore unenforceable. A contract which is illegal as to formation is "unenforceable" rather than "void" where void means "that the agreement was never made". The reason for this is that "property can pass under an illegal contract" and the court in certain circumstances will "enforce a contract which contains an element of illegality".[206] Although this results in an illegal contract having some legal consequences, this in no way constitutes enforcement.

204 (1838) 8 A. & E. 129; cf. *Dungate v Lee* [1959] 1 Ch. 545.

205 (1838) 8 A. & E. 129, 134. See also *Ewing v Osbaldiston* (1837) 2 My. & Cr. 53. Occasionally it will be difficult to classify a contract as being illegal as to formation as opposed to being illegal as performed: see *J. M. Allan (Merchandising) Ltd v Cloke* [1963] 2 Q.B. 340.

206 *Paros Plc v Wordlink Group Plc* [2012] EWHC 394 (Comm) at [80]. See para.16-218 ("Transfer of property under illegal transactions") and part 7 of this chapter ("Severance").

*Add new paragraph:*

**16-040A** **Role of appellate courts in illegality cases** In *Singularis Holdings Ltd (In Liquidation) v Daiwa Capital Markets Europe Ltd*[242a] the issue arose as to circumstances in which an appellate court should interfere with a first instance judgment applying the *Patel v Mirza*[242b] test. On appeal the court stated that with respect to this issue both parties had accepted that the court should only interfere "where the judge made an error of principle or reached a conclusion wholly outside the range of reasonable probabilities".[242c] A caveat was raised against this view in the Supreme Court, where Baroness Hale stated:

> "I should, however, record my reservations about the view expressed by the Court of Appeal as to the role of an appellate court in relation to the illegality defence: that an 'appellate court should only interfere if the first instance judge has proceeded on an erroneous legal basis, taken into account matters that were legally irrelevant' … Daiwa point out that applying the defence is 'not akin to the exercise of discretion' …[242d] and an appellate court is as well placed to evaluate the arguments as is the trial judge. It is not necessary to

resolve this in order to resolve this appeal and there are cases concerning the illegality defence pending in the Supreme Court where it should not be assumed that this court will endorse the approach of the Court of Appeal."[242e]

[242a] [2019] UKSC 50, [2019] 3 W.L.R. 997.

[242b] [2016] UKSC 42, [2017] A.C. 461.

[242c] [2018] 1 W.L.R. 2777 at [65].

[242d] Citing Lord Neuberger of Abbotsbury PSC in *Patel v Mirza* [2016] UKSC 42 at [175].

[242e] [2019] UKSC 50, [2019] 3 W.L.R. 997 at [21].

## 4. CONTRACTS CONTRARY TO PUBLIC POLICY THOUGH NOT INVOLVING A LEGAL WRONG

### (b) Objects Injurious to the Proper Working of Justice

#### *(iv) Maintenance and Champerty*

**Examples of justification**

*Replace footnote 450 with:*

[450] *Hill v Archbold* [1968] 1 Q.B. 686; *Bourne v Colodense Ltd* [1985] I.C.R. 291. Note that procedure has been introduced for the making of a group litigation order. This is designed to enable parties to bring a group action where their interests are sufficiently similar that a finding with respect to one of them or a set of them will be dispositive of the whole group action: RSC Pt 19 (Parties and Group Litigation). Part 19.6(1) refers to situations "(i) Where more than one person has the same interest in a claim ...". An example of such a claim is *Bates v Post Office Ltd (No.3: Common Issues)* [2019] EWHC 606 (QB) where, inter alia, a group of approximately 550 claimants who were sub-postmasters brought a group action against the Post Office. See also *Various Claimants v Barking Housing & Redbridge University Hospitals NHS Trust* Unreported May 21, 2014. 16-080

**Professional funders**

*Replace paragraph with:*

As the courts have pointed out there have been "major changes to the law and practice relating to the funding of litigation".[460] In *Singularis Holdings Ltd (In Official Liquidation) v Chapel Credit Opportunity Master Fund Ltd*[461] the court was told that litigation funding plays an important role in providing access to justice but that it is highly risky for funders, who often seek to protect themselves by asking for "outsize returns"; "it is not unusual (however undesirable this may be for all of the parties) for the funder to be entitled to the entirety of any award and for the claimant to be entitled to nothing".[462] Of course if the claimant is not successful the funder will lose all of its investment and if the recoveries are low there is a potential loss of a fraction of its investment.[462a] *Arkin v Borchard Lines Ltd*[462b] involved a litigation funder who provided funding for expert witnesses for a contingent fee of 25 per cent of the first £5 million in damages and 23 per cent thereafter. The professional funder took no part in the litigation and the agreement was non-champertous. The court held the agreement to be enforceable. The court considered that provided the agreement was non-champertous, if the funded party was unsuccessful the funder should be potentially liable for the costs of the opposing party up to the extent of the funding provided ("the *Arkin* cap"), whereas if the funder entered into a champertous agreement he would be "likely to render himself liable for the opposing party's costs without limit should the claim fail".[462c] The scope of the *Arkin* principle was developed in *Chapelgate Credit Opportunity Master Fund Ltd v Money*.[462d] In that case Snowden J. had declined to apply the *Arkin* cap; the funder 16-081 appealed unsuccessfully. There were a number of factors distinguishing the cases: (i) in *Arkin* the funder only funded part of the claimant's costs whereas all of the costs were funded by the funder in *Chapelgate*, (ii) in *Chapelgate* the funder stood to receive a return profit amounting to a multiple of what it spent and the court considered it "legitimate for a judge to attach importance to the funder's prospective gains as well as to its outlay ...",[462e] and (iii) the court was entitled to consider the extent to which "the *Arkin* cap would leave the respondents out of pocket".[462f] The Association of Litigation Funders of England and Wales have published a Code of Conduct of Litigation Funders.[462g]

[460] *Chapelgate Credit Opportunity Master Fund Ltd v Money* [2020] EWCA Civ 246 at [23].

[461] [2020] EWHC 1616 (Ch). In that case the funder was to be compensated by a share of the proceeds received by the claimant disregarding, inter alia, "any netting, set-off or other reduction including ... by reason of a counterclaim...". The question was whether a sum deducted because of contributory negligence of the claimant should be added to the recoverable proceeds when computing their value. The court held that they did not have to be added as the funding agreement did not by its terms so provide, it was a simple matter of construction of the agreement.

[462] [2020] EWHC 1616 (Ch) at [14]–[15].

[462a] [2020] EWHC 1616 (Ch) at [15].

[462b] [2005] EWCA Civ 655, [2005] 1 W.L.R. 3055 at [44]. See also *Singularis Holdings Ltd (In Official Liquidation v Chapel Credit Opportunity Master Fund Ltd* [2020] EWHC 1616 (Ch) at [14]–[16].

[462c] [2005] EWCA Civ 655 at [40].

[462d] [2020] EWCA Civ 246.

[462e] [2020] EWCA Civ 246 at [44].

[462f] [2020] EWCA Civ 246 at [44].

[462g] Jackson L.J., *Third Party Funding on Litigation Funding*, Sixth Lecture in the Civil Litigation Costs Review Implementation Programme, the Royal Courts of Justice, November 23, 2011 (the Code is attached to the lecture).

## (d) Contracts in Restraint of Trade

### *(i) Scope of the Doctrine*

#### Definition of restraint of trade

*Replace footnote 633 with:*

16-108 [633] [1968] A.C. 269, 298. At 298–299 Lord Reid said that one way of identifying whether a covenant was in restraint of trade was to identify the freedom that the covenantor would otherwise have was giving up. In *Quantum Advisory Ltd v Quantum Actuarial LLP* [2020] EWHC 1072 (Comm) at [64] HH Judge Keyser QC stated that although such "an approach can hardly suffice as a universal touchstone for the operation of the doctrine (cf. *Chitty on Contracts* at para 16-116 [below] for criticism) it seems to me, with respect, to have a proper place within the 'broad and flexible rule of reason'".

#### Criteria for application of doctrine

*Replace footnote 649 with:*

16-113 [649] See *Peninsula Securities Ltd v Dunnes Stores (Bangor) Ltd* [2018] NICA 7. An appeal to the Supreme Court has been heard but at July 31, 2020 judgment was still awaited.

*After point (8) paragraph, add new paragraph:*

16-118A (9) The courts have held that interchangability of products is not required for a finding that businesses are competitive and it "suffices if the products are 'similar' ... or 'sufficiently comparable'".[672a]

[672a] *Argus Media Ltd v Halim* [2019] EWHC 215 (QB) at [91].

## Time of application

*Replace footnote 673 with:*

[673] *Gledhow Autoparts Ltd v Delaney* [1965] 1 W.L.R. 1366, 1377; *Home Counties Dairies Ltd v Skilton* [1970] 1 W.L.R. 526, 533, 536; *Commercial Plastics Ltd v Vincent* [1965] 1 Q.B. 623, 644; *A. Schroeder Music Publishing Co Ltd v Macaulay* [1974] 1 W.L.R. 1308, 1309; *Watson v Prager* [1991] 1 W.L.R. 726, 738 ("The question of whether the ... agreement is unenforceable on restraint of trade grounds must be tested by reference to the state of affairs at the date of the agreement"); *Peninsula Securities Ltd v Dunnes Stores (Bangor) Ltd* [2018] NICA 7 (an appeal to the Supreme Court has been heard but at July 31, 2020 judgment was still awaited). **16-119**

## Interlocutory injunction

*Replace paragraph with:*

There are no special rules relating to the granting of an interlocutory injunction **16-134** in connection with covenants in restraint of trade.[750] This can give rise to problems particularly with respect to restraints in employment contracts. Since to be valid the restraint will inevitably be of limited duration, the granting of an interlocutory injunction may have the effect of disposing of the matter in that the delays associated with litigation will entail that a reasonable time will have expired by the time the matter comes on for trial on the merits. To deal with this, the courts have held that matters involving restraint of trade in employment contracts are "singularly appropriate for a speedy trial".[751] Where this is not possible, it is then proper for the judge to go on to consider the chances of the plaintiff succeeding in the action.[752] An example of where this was not practically possible is provided by the facts in *P14 Medical Ltd v Mahon*.[752a] In that case the claimant company sought an order of restraining the defendant from breaching restrictive covenants in his contract of employment and restraining him from disclosing any confidential information belonging to the claimant. The duration of the covenant was six months and it was estimated that, with a hearing involving disputed witness statements and the likely reservation of the judgment, five of the six months restriction period would have elapsed. On these facts the grant or refusal of the interlocutory injunction would have had the practical effect of putting an end to the litigation. In these circumstances the court was entitled to examine the merits of the case. After considering another range of matters the court granted the injunctive relief sought. The court had jurisdiction to grant an injunction on limited terms, for example, that an employee on "garden leave" may not accept employment with a named firm.[753] The court can also grant an injunction to "prevent the defendants from taking unfair advantage of the springboard which ... they must have built up by their misuse" of the confidential information.[754] This is referred to as "springboard" relief. Such relief is not confined to cases of abuse of confidential information and extends to former staff members taking unfair advantage or gaining an unfair start by serious breaches of their contract of employment.[755] The unfair advantage must still exist at the time the injunction is sought.[756]

[750] *Lawrence David Ltd v Ashton* [1991] 1 All E.R. 385 (it appears that the profession did consider that the *American Cyanamid* principles did not apply to restraint of trade covenants in employment contracts: 392).

[751] *Lawrence David Ltd v Ashton* [1991] 1 All E.R. 385, 395.

[752] *Lawrence David Ltd v Ashton* [1991] 1 All E.R. 385, 396; *Lansing Linde Ltd v Kerr* [1991] 1 All E.R. 418; *Business Seating (Reservations) Ltd v Broad* [1987] I.C.R. 729 (in both cases merits were considered and an interlocutory injunction refused); *Egon Zehnder Ltd v Tillman* [2017] EWHC 1278 (Ch), [2017] I.R.L.R. 828.

[752a] [2020] EWHC 1823 (QB).

[753] *Symbian Ltd v Christensen* [2001] I.R.L.R. 77; *SG&R Valuation Service Co LLC v Boudrais* [2008] EWHC 1340 (QB).

[754] *Roger Bullivant Ltd v Ellis* [1987] I.R.L.R. 491, 496.

[755] *UBS Wealth Management (UK) Ltd v Kestra Wealth LLP* [2008] EWHC 1974 (QB), [2008] I.R.L.R. 965 at [4].

[756] [2008] EWHC 1974 (QB) at [4].

### *(ii) Employer and Employee*

#### Relevant time

*To the start of paragraph, add:*

16-137 Where an employer seeks to enforce an employee's negative covenant, the starting point is "that the ordinary remedy is an injunction and proof of damage to the claimant is not required".[773a]

[773a] *Argus Media Ltd v Halim* [2019] EWHC 42 (QB) at [215].

#### Protection by general law and by covenant

*In line 26, page [1325], after "was the employer's client.[806]", add:*

16-139 As was stated by the court in the *Halim* decision[806a] "non-competition restrictions are commonly used, and upheld, in scenarios where lesser forms of restriction (such as confidentiality clauses or prohibitions on solicitation or dealing) would be inadequate or difficult to police".

[806a] *Argus Media Ltd v Halim* [2019] EWHC 42 (QB) at [124].

### *(iv) Partners*

#### Covenants on dissolution of partnership

*To the end of paragraph, after "that of the old firm.[920]", add:*

16-152 In *Ideal Standard International SA v Herbert*[920a] Sir Ross Cranston (sitting as a Judge of the High Court) considered that "[n]on-compete clauses for the vendor of a partnership will generally be enforced as reasonable and enforceable" and the court recognised the accepted position that such clauses will be more "strictly enforced than in the ordinary employee context".[920b]

[920a] [2018] EWHC 3326 (Comm), [2019] I.R.L.R. 431 at [28].

[920b] [2018] EWHC 3326 (Comm) at [27]. See above para.16-135.

### *(vi) Restraints on the Use of Land or Chattels*

#### Restraint contained in conveyance or lease

*Replace footnote 965 with:*

16-162 [965] [2018] NICA 7. The court also held that "a restrictive covenant enforced on a lease when *first* entering the lease would not be subject to the doctrine as the lease would not have contracted to give up some freedom which otherwise he could have had" (emphasis added) at [53]. An appeal to the Supreme Court has been heard but at July 31, 2020 judgment was still awaited.

## 6. Enforcement of Collateral, Proprietary and Restitutionary Rights

### (a) Attribution of Acts to a Company

*To the end of title, add new footnote 1091a:*

**The Stone & Rolls case**[1091a]

[1091a] But see para.16-203A for the Supreme Court's view that "*Stone & Rolls* can finally be laid to rest": *Singularis Holdings (In Liquidation) v Daiwa Capital Markets Europe Ltd* [2019] UKSC 50, [2019] 3 W.L.R. 997 at [34]. **16-202**

*Add new paragraph:*

**16-203A** **Attribution and the "one-man" company**[1108a] The issue of whether there was a special rule with respect to the doctrine of attribution in the context of the one-man company was addressed in *Singularis Holdings Ltd (In Liquidation) v Daiwa Capital Markets Europe Ltd.*[1108b] Singularis was a Cayman registered company. AS was its sole shareholder, a director, its chairman, president and treasurer. There were six directors who played a passive role the management of the company. It was argued that "Singularis was effectively a one-man company" and AS "its controlling mind and will ...".[1108c] Daiwa provided loan financing to Singularis to purchase shares. The shares were sold, the loan was repaid and Daiwa left holding a sum in excess of US$200 for Singularis. AS, who was authorised to do so, arranged for Singularis to instruct Daiwa to make various payments which the court found constituted a misappropriation of Singularis' funds. Before the lower courts a number of issues arose[1108d] but on appeal there were only two issues: (i) could the actions of AS be attributed to the company and (ii), if so attributable, was the claim defeated by the defence of illegality. On the facts in *Singularis v Daiwa* the court at first instance[1108e] had found that "Singularis was not a one-man company in the sense that the phrase was used in *Stone & Rolls*[1108f] and *Bilta*[1108g]".[1108h] However, even if it had been a one-man company the court considered "that there is no principle that in any proceedings where the company is suing a third party for breach of duty owed to it by that third party, the fraudulent conduct of a director is to be attributed to the company if it is a one-man".[1108i] Whether such conduct is attributable "is always to be found in consideration of the context and the purpose for which attribution is relevant".[1108j] With this as the "guiding principle" the court considered that "*Stone & Rolls* can finally be laid to rest".[1108k] The Supreme Court also agreed with the trial judge that even if AS's actions were attributable to the company, the company's claim should not fail because of illegality: to deny it would not enhance the purposes of the prohibitions of breach of fiduciary obligations and making false statements, would not be in the public interest and would be an unfair and disproportionate response.[1108l]

[1108a] "It has become the fashion to call companies of this class 'one-man companies'. This is a taking nickname but it does not help one much in the way of argument": per Lord Macnaghten in *Salomon v Salomon & Co Ltd* [1897] A.C. 22, 53.

[1108b] [2019] UKSC 50, [2019] 3 W.L.R. 997. Baroness Hale gave the judgment of the court.

[1108c] [2019] UKSC 50 at [26].

[1108d] [2019] UKSC 50 at [7]–[9].

[1108e] [2017] EWHC 257 (Ch), [2017] 1 B.C.L.C. 625.

[1108f] *Moore Stephens (a firm) v Stone & Rolls Ltd* [2009] UKHL 39, [2009] 1 A.C. 39; see above, para.16-202.

[1108g] *Jetivia SA v Bilta (UK) Ltd (reported sub nom. Bilta (UK) Ltd v Nazir (No.2))* [2015] UKSC 23, [2016] A.C. 1; see above, para.16-198.

[1108h] [2019] UKSC 50 at [33].

[1108i] [2019] UKSC 50 at [34].

[1108j] [2019] UKSC 50 at [34], citing *Bilta (UK) Ltd (In Liquidation) v Nazir (No.2)* [2015] UKSC 23, [2016] A.C. 1.

[1108k] [2019] UKSC 50 at [34].

[1108l] [2019] UKSC 50 at [16]–[21].

### (d) Recovery of Property Transferred for Illegal Purpose or Under Illegal Contracts

**Transfer of property under illegal transactions**

*In line 9, page [1371], after "of such a contract.[1215]", add:*

16-218 However, once property or an interest in property passes to an illegal transferee "he has all the remedies available to him as a valid holder of that property interest" and this "applies both in relation to the illegal transferor and to third parties".[1215a]

[1215a] *Stoffel & Co v Grondona* [2018] EWCA Civ 2031 at [33].

## 7. SEVERANCE

**General principles**

*Replace paragraph with:*

16-238 Prior to the Supreme Court decision in *Tilman v Egon Zehnder Ltd*[1317] there was great difficulty in reconciling authorities on the application of the doctrine of severance, but some order has now been given in the *Tilman* decision to the principles on which severance will be ordered. In *Tilman* the employee Ms Tilman entered into a non-competition covenant whereby she agreed that she would not "directly or indirectly engage or be concerned or interested in any business" carried on by her employer company or group company. The court was willing to sever the words "or interested" and thus validate the remainder of the contract.[1318] As regards severance in employment contracts Lord Wilson. delivering the judgment of the Supreme Court, considered that the "courts must continue to adopt a cautious approach to the severance of post-employment restraints".[1319] After an exhaustive review of the cases dealing with severance, the court considered it necessary to analyse three criteria for severance previously endorsed in *Beckett Investment Management Group Ltd v Hall*.[1320] It is proposed to deal with these principles in order.

[1317] [2019] UKSC 32, [2019] 3 W.L.R. 245.

[1318] [2019] UKSC 32 at [53] and [88].

[1319] [2019] UKSC 32 at [82].

[1320] [2007] EWCA Civ 613. The tests in *Beckett* are identical with those formulated in *Sadler v Imperial Life Assurance Co of Canada Ltd* [1988] I.R.L.R. 388, 392.

16-239 *Change title of paragraph:*

**The blue pencil test**

*Replace paragraph with:*

16-239 The first requirement for severance to operate is that "the unenforceable provision is capable of being removed without the necessity of adding or modifying the wording of what remains".[1321] As the court pointed out in *Tilman*, this "blue-pencil" test can work capriciously, as was pointed out by Bailhache J. in *Attwood v Lamont*[1322]:

> "a covenant 'not to carry on business in Birmingham or within 100 miles' may be severed so as to reduce the area to Birmingham, but a covenant 'not to carry on business within 100 miles of Birmingham' will not be severed so as to read 'will not carry on business in Birmingham'. The distinction seems to be artificial, but I think settled. "

Lord Wilson agreed: "the distinction is indeed settled".[1323]

[1321] [2019] UKSC 32 at [85].

[1322] [1920] 2 K.B. 146, 155 on appeal [1920] 3 K.B. 571.

[1323] [2019] UKSC 32 at [85].

*Replace paragraph with:*

**Remaining terms supported by adequate consideration** The second requirement for severance is that "the remaining terms continue to be supported by adequate consideration".[1324] The Supreme Court pointed out that where **16-240**

> "... it was the claimant employee who secured severance of the unreasonable obligations cast by the contract on himself,[1325] the court needed to satisfy itself ... that, were his unreasonable obligation to be removed, there would nevertheless remain consideration passing from him under the contract such as would support the obligation which he was seeking to enforce."[1326]

This was different from the usual situation where it is the employer who is seeking the severance. Where it is the employer who is seeking severance the employer "is in no way proposing to diminish the consideration passing from himself under the contract" which he seeks to enforce and therefore "in the usual situation the second requirement can be ignored".[1327]

[1324] [2019] UKSC 32 at [86].

[1325] As in *Sadler v Imperial Life Assurance Co of Canada Ltd* [1988] I.R.L.R. 388 and *Marshall v N.M. Financial Management Ltd* [1997] 1 W.L.R. 1527.

[1326] [2019] UKSC 32 at [86].

[1327] [2019] UKSC 32 at [86].

*Add new paragraph:*

**Impact of removal of unenforceable provision on character of contract** The third requirement for severance is that "the removal of the unenforceable provision does not so change the character of the contract that it becomes 'not the sort of contract that the parties entered into at all'".[1328] The court considered that this "crucial" criterion could not be equated with the requirements laid down by the majority of the Court of Appeal in the earlier case of *Atwood v Lamont*,[1329] that a covenant can be severed only if effect it is a combination of different covenants and that the part proposed to be removed is no more than trivial or technical, and held that the decision in the *Atwood* case should be overruled.[1330] The court considered that the third requirement: "... would be better expressed as being whether the removal of the covenant would not generate any major change in the overall effect of all the post-employment restraints in the contract. It is for the employer to **16-240A**

establish that its removal would not do so".[1331–1332]

[1328] [2019] UKSC 32 at [86].

[1329] [1920] 3 K.B. 571.

[1330] [2019] UKSC 32 at [91].

[1331–1332] [2019] UKSC 32 at [87].

**Severance and public policy**

*Replace first two sentences, "The second ... with public policy." with:*

**16-244** The court will not sever the bad from the good unless this accords with public policy.

## 8. Pleading and Practice

**16-246** *To the end of title, add new footnote 1360a:*

[1306a] On the proper role of appellate courts in cases where the range of factors' approach is applied, see above, para.16-040A.

CHAPTER 17

# JOINT OBLIGATIONS

## Joint Obligations

### Joinder of joint and several promisors

*Replace footnote 31 with:*

[31] *Cabell v Vaughan* (1669) 1 Saund. 291, n.4; Williams, *Joint Obligations* (1949), para.20; Peel (ed.), *Treitel on The Law of Contract*, 15th edn (2020), para.13-006. **17-011**

### Death of a joint contractor

*Replace footnote 33 with:*

[33] *White v Tyndall* (1888) 13 App. Cas. 263. Quaere whether this rule has been abolished by s.1(1) of the Law Reform (Miscellaneous Provisions) Act 1934: see Williams, *Joint Obligations*, at para.25; Peel (ed.), *Treitel on The Law of Contract*, 15th edn (2020), para.13-010. **17-012**

### Contribution between joint debtors

*Replace footnote 75 with:*

[75] *Deering v Earl of Winchelsea* (1787) 1 Cox 318; 2 Bos. & P. 270; *Hutton v Eyre* (1815) 6 Taunt. 289; *Coope v Twynam* (1823) Turn. & R. 426; *Pendelbury v Walker* (1841) 4 Y. & C. Ex. 424; *Boulter v Peplow* (1850) 9 C.B. 493; *Batard v Hawes* (1853) 2 E. & B. 287; see Williams, *Joint Obligations* (1949), Ch.9; Goff and Jones, *The Law of Unjust Enrichment*, 9th edn (2016), Ch.20; Burrows, *The Law of Restitution*, 3rd edn (2011), pp.458–460. **17-027**

### Contribution between persons liable in respect of the same damage

*Replace footnote 89 with:*

[89] The Act was based on the Report on Contribution of the Law Commission (Law Com. No.79, 1977); see generally Dugdale (1979) 42 M.L.R. 182; *Clerk & Lindsell on Torts*, 22nd edn (2018), paras 4-13—4-28. For private international law in relation to the 1978 Act, see *Roberts v Soldiers, Sailors, Airmen and Families Association* [2019] EWHC 1104 (QB), [2020] Q.B. 310. **17-029**

### Effect of judgment or compromise

*In line 4, after "this case only", replace "assuming that the factual basis of the claim can" with:*

if the party would have been liable assuming that the factual basis of the claim against him could **17-032**

CHAPTER 18

# THIRD PARTIES



## 2. THE COMMON LAW DOCTRINE

## (a) Parties to the Agreement

### Who are the parties?

*Replace footnote 21 with:*

[21] A highly specialised group of cases (beyond the scope of this book) concerns bills of lading issued in respect of goods shipped on a chartered ship: see *Carver on Bills of Lading*, 4th edn (2017), paras 4-032—4-062; *Homburg Houtimport BV v Agrosin Private Ltd (The Starsin)* [2003] UKHL 12, [2004] 1 A.C. 715. The general rule that a person who is named as the consignee in a contract of carriage contained in or evidenced by a bill of lading is not, merely by reason of being so named, "in a true sense an original party to the contract" (*Standard Chartered Bank v Dorchester LNG(2) Ltd (The Erin Schulte)* [2014] EWCA Civ 1382, [2015] 1 Lloyd's Rep. 97 at [16]); and the various qualifications of that rule, are likewise beyond the scope of this book. They are fully discussed in *Carver on Bills of Lading*, 4th edn (2017), paras 4-001—4-031. **18-004**

### Agency

*Replace footnote 80 with:*

18-014 [80] *Daly v General Steam Navigation Co Ltd (The Dragon)* [1979] 1 Lloyd's Rep. 257, 262; affirmed [1980] 2 Lloyd's Rep. 415; cf. *Wilson v Best Travel Ltd* [1993] 1 All E.R. 353, 355; *Bowerman v Association of British Travel Agents* [1995] 145 N.L.J. 1815 (holiday booked for pupil by her teacher); *Vitesse Yacht Charters SL v Spiers (The Deverne II)* (contract to charter a yacht for a holiday taken by two persons together held to have been made by one of them on behalf of both). For the question whether an f.o.b. seller (A) who ships goods on B's ship for transmission to the buyer (C) does so as principal or as agent for C, see *Carver on Bills of Lading*, 4th edn (2017), para.4-029.

## (c) Development of the Common Law Doctrine

### The doctrine established

*Replace footnote 108 with:*

18-021 [108] In *Scruttons Ltd v Midland Silicones Ltd* [1962] A.C. 446; above, para.15-050. The Court of Appeal had taken a similar view of the continued existence of the doctrine in *Green v Russell* [1959] 2 Q.B. 226. Parts of the passage from the *Pyrene* case at 426 referred to in the previous note are cited with approval in *AP Moeller-Maersk A/S v Sonaec Villas Cen Sad Fadoul* [2010] EWHC 355 (Comm), [2010] 2 All E. R. (Comm) 1159. It is there said at [45] that Devlin J. had, in the *Pyrene* case, "considered that the seller participated in the contract of affreightment [between buyer and carrier] so far as it affected him", and so was bound by a term in it limiting the carrier's liability even though he (the seller) was not a party to that contract. But the attention of the court in the *Moeller-Maersk* case was not drawn to Lord Simonds' statement in the *Scruttons* case, above at 471 that the *Pyrene* case could be "supported only on the facts of the case which may well have justified the implication of a contract between the parties" (i.e., between seller and carrier, so that there was privity of contract between them). For the "facts of the [*Pyrene*] case" that appear there to have justified such an implication, see *Carver on Bills of Lading*, 4th edn (2017), para.4-024.

## 3. SCOPE

### General

*Replace paragraph with:*

18-023 The common law doctrine of privity means, and means only, that a person cannot acquire rights, or be subjected to liabilities, *arising under* a contract to which he is not a party. For example, it means that, if A promises B to pay a sum of money to C, then C cannot sue A for that sum.[126] Similarly, if a contract between A and B contains a term purporting to exempt C from tortious liability to A, the doctrine of privity may prevent C from relying on that term in an action in tort brought against him by A.[127] But it does not follow that a contract between A and B cannot affect the legal rights of C indirectly. For example, in the situation just described, a clause in the contract between A and B can form the basis on which a separate collateral contract comes into existence between A and C, containing a promise by A to make the relevant terms of the contract between A and B available for the benefit of C[128]; such an agreement may also give rise to a bailment or sub-bailment between A and C by virtue of which C may be entitled to the benefit of, or be bound by, limitation or exemption clauses in the contract between A and B, even though the relationship between A and C is not contractual[129]; an agreement between A and B under which A accepts from B part payment of a debt owed by C to A in full settlement of that debt can benefit C by precluding A from suing C for the balance of the debt[130]; and a fortiori full performance by B of C's obligation to A can discharge that obligation. Conversely, a building contract between A and B may benefit C by defining his rights: e.g. by specifying the time at which payment becomes due to C under a subcontract between B and C for the execution of part of the work.[131] It is also possible for a contract between A and B to affect C adversely,[132] as in the bailment situation described above; other ways in which a contract between A and B may so affect C are more fully discussed later in this chapter.[133] In the following paragraphs, our concern is with a number of further situations in which a contract between A and B can operate to the advantage of C: in particular, with situations in which C may, where A has committed a breach of that contract, have a right of action against A in tort.

[126] *Tweddle v Atkinson* (1861) 1 B. & S. 393; above, para.18-021.

[127] *Scruttons Ltd v Midland Silicones Ltd* [1962] A.C. 446; paras 15-050, 18-021 above; but there may be a contract between A and C, as in *New Zealand Shipping Co Ltd v A.M. Satterthwaite & Co Ltd (The Eurymedon)* [1975] A.C. 154; *Port Jackson Stevedoring Pty Ltd v Salmond & Spraggon (Australia) Pty Ltd (The New York Star)* [1981] 1 W.L.R. 138; above, para.15-051. Contrast, in Canada, *London Drugs Ltd v Kuehne & Nagel International Ltd* [1992] 3 S.C.R. 299. And see *The Mahkutai* [1996] A.C. 650, where the actual decision is based, not on the doctrine of privity, but on the fact that an exclusive jurisdiction clause was not, as a matter of construction, one of the "exceptions, limitations, provisions, conditions and liberties" of the contract on which the third party sought to rely. Hence it was not necessary to decide whether the English courts should, in cases of this kind, adopt the Canadian view taken in the *London Drugs* case [1992] 3 S.C.R. 299, but Lord Goff at 665 in *The Mahkutai* left the point open.

[128] This is often the effect of so-called Himalaya Clause in bills of lading: see above *The Eurymedon* [1975] A.C. 154; *The New York Star* [1980] 1 W.L.R. 138; contrast *The Mahkutai* [1996] A.C. 650, where such a clause failed to protect C for the reason given in that note; and *Homburg Houtimport BV v Agrosin Private Ltd (The Starsin)* [2003] UKHL 12, [2004] 1 A.C. 715, at [34], [93], [147], [196] where the relevant term was invalid under art.III.8 of the Hague Rules; and see *The Starsin* at [155] for criticism of the expression "collateral contract" in this context. cf. *Whitsea Shipping and Trading Corp v El Paso Rio Clara Ltd (The Marielle Bolten)* [2009] EWHC 2552 (Comm), [2010] 1 Lloyd's Rep. 648 where the contract was referred to at [34] as "The Himalaya contract" and was not invalid under art.III.8 as (unlike the relevant contract in *The Starsin*) it was not a "contract of carriage" within that provision (above, para.15-134); and see generally the discussion of Himalaya Clauses in paras 15-051—15-052 above and in *Carver on Bills of Lading*, 4th edn (2017), paras 7-046—7-066.

[129] e.g. *Elder Dempster & Co v Paterson Zochonis & Co* [1924] A.C. 522; *Morris v C.W. Martin & Co* [1966] 1 Q.B. 716, 729; above, para.15-057; Vol.II, paras 33-026, 33-027; *Carver on Bills of Lading*, 4th edn (2017), paras 7-027—7-045; 7-093—7-110.

[130] *Hirachand Punamchand v Temple* [1911] 2 K.B. 330; above, para.4-128 (where the effect on such facts of the Contracts (Rights of Third Parties) Act 1999 is also discussed); cf. *Johnson v Davies* [1999] Ch. 117 at 130, and *Chelsea Building Society v Nash* [2010] EWCA Civ 1247, discussed above, footnotes to para.4-128. As a general rule, payment of a debt by a third party discharges the debt only if the payment is made with the intention of discharging the debt and with the debtor's authority: see *Crantrave Ltd v Lloyd's Bank Plc* [2000] Q.B. 917, where the first of these requirements was not satisfied. The inference that C authorised B to pay C's debt to A, or that C had ratified such a payment, so that the payment discharged the debt, may be drawn from the existence of a family relationship (such as that of a father and his children): see *Treasure & Son Ltd v Dawes* [2008] EWHC 2181 (TCC). The rule that payment of a debt by a person other than the debtor will discharge a debt only if the payment is made with the debtor's authority does not apply where the payment is made under legal compulsion: see *Electricity Supply Nominees Ltd v Thorn EMI Retailers Ltd* (1992) 63 P. & C.R. 143 at 148–149, per Fox L.J., applied in *Ibrahim v Barclays Bank Plc* [2012] EWCA Civ 640, [2012] 2 Lloyd's Rep. 13 at [46], [49]; this result follows even though the "compulsion" has arisen out of "a contractual obligation voluntarily assumed by the third party": at [49], in this case by a bank honouring its undertaking, given in a letter of credit, to pay the beneficiary the amount owed by the debtor; and see below para.29-105.

[131] *Co-operative Wholesale Society Ltd v Birse Construction Ltd* (1997) 84 B.L.R. 58.

[132] e.g. *West of England Shipowners Mutual Insurance Association (Luxembourg) v Cristal Ltd (The Glacier Bay)* [1996] 1 Lloyd's Rep. 370; *Banque Financière de la Cité v Parc (Battersea) Ltd* [1999] 1 A.C. 221.

[133] Below paras 18-140—18-153.

## (a) Liability in Negligence to Third Parties

### Duty of care may be owed to third party

*Replace footnote 135 with:*

18-024 [135] *Moukataff v B.O.A.C.* [1967] 1 Lloyd's Rep. 396; *Bart v B.W.I.A.* [1967] 1 Lloyd's Rep. 239 (where the claim failed as the sub-bailee's duty was limited to one to keep safely, and did not extend to transmission of the package); *Hispanica de Petroles SA v Vencedora Oceanica Navegacion SA (The Kapetan Markos NL) (No.2)* [1987] 2 Lloyd's Rep. 321. Such a sub-bailment may also operate to the disadvantage of C (the head bailor) in that he may be bound by an exemption or lien clause in the contract between A (the head bailee) and B (the sub-bailee): see *Morris v C.W. Martin Ltd* [1966] 1 Q.B. 716, 719; *K.H. Enterprise v Pioneer Container (The Pioneer Container)* [1994] 2 A.C. 324; *Spectra International Plc v Hayesoak Ltd* [1997] 1 Lloyd's Rep. 153; reversed on another ground [1998] 1 Lloyd's Rep. 162; *Sonicare International Ltd v EAFT Ltd* [1997] 2 Lloyd's Rep. 48; *T. Comedy (UK) Ltd v Easy Managed Transport Ltd* [2007] EWHC 611, [2007] 2 Lloyd's Rep. 397 at [64]. This application of the principle of sub-bailment results in the head bailor's being *bound* by terms in the contract between the head bailee and the sub-bailee. It must be distinguished from the situation in which the sub-bailee claims the *benefit* of a term in the contract between the head bailor and the head bailee, as in *Elder Dempster & Co v Paterson Zochonis & Co* [1924] A.C. 522: see *The Mahkutai* [1996] A.C. 650, 667–668, *Carver on Bills of Lading*, 4th edn (2017), paras 7-099, 7-100. No sub-bailment arises merely because a sub-agent has received the proceeds of the sale of the principal's property from the buyer: *Balsamo v Medici* [1984] 1 W.L.R. 951.

### Tort and contract liability distinguished

*In line 4, after "tort by C.", add new footnote 148a:*

18-026 [148a] However, if an exclusive jurisdiction clause governs the contractual dispute between A and B, that may also extend to a related action brought in tort by C against A: *Airbus SAS v Generali Italia SpA* [2019] EWCA Civ 805, [2019] 2 Lloyd's Rep. 59 at [77]–[84].

### Claimant having no title to thing damaged

*Replace footnote 206 with:*

18-036 [206] The benefit of the contract of carriage had not been transferred to C under Bills of Lading Act 1855 s.1 as the property in the goods had not passed to him. On the facts of *The Aliakmon* rights under the contract of carriage would now be transferred to C by virtue of the Carriage of Goods by Sea Act 1992 s.2: see *White v Jones* [1995] 2 A.C. 207, 265. But cases can still be imagined where this would not be the case: see *Carver on Bills of Lading*, 4th edn (2017), para.5-108.

## 4. CONTRACTS FOR THE BENEFIT OF THIRD PARTIES

## (a) Effects of a Contract for the Benefit of a Third Party

### *(i) Promisee's Remedies*

### Damages in respect of third party's loss: exceptions in general

*Replace paragraph with:*

18-054 Judicial awareness of the unsatisfactory results which can flow from the general rule stated in para.18-051 above and reaffirmed in the *Woodar* case[336] has led the courts to create a number of exceptions to that rule.[336a] For example substantial damages for breach of contract can be recovered by a trustee even though the loss is suffered by his cestui que trust[337]; by an agent even though the loss is suffered by his undisclosed principal[338]; by a local authority even though the loss is suffered by its inhabitants[339]; and by a shipper of goods for breach of his contract of carriage with the shipowner in respect of the loss of the goods, even though that loss is suffered by a person to whom the shipper has sold the goods and to whom the risk and property in them has passed but who has not himself acquired any rights under the contract of carriage against the ship-owner[340]: it will be convenient to refer to this last rule as "the *Albazero* exception", after the leading modern case in which it is recognised.[341] In all these exceptional cases, a person recovers substantial damages for breach of contract, even though the breach caused loss, not to him, but only to a third party.[342] A similar possibility is recognised in the law of tort which, like the law of contract, starts with the principle that the claimant can recover "no more and no less than he has lost".[343] But where a third party voluntarily renders services in caring for a claimant who has suffered personal injury as a result of a tort, the claimant can recover damages from the wrongdoer in respect of the value of those services; and the "central objective" of such an award has been described as "compensating the voluntary carer,"[344] for whom such damages must be held on trust by the claimant.[345] In substance, though not in form, the claimant in such a case recovers damages in respect of the loss which has been suffered by the third party in (for example) giving up his or her job so as to look after the injured claimant.

336 *Woodar Investment Development Ltd v Wimpey Construction UK Ltd* [1980] 1 W.L.R. 277, see above, paras 18-052 and 18-053.

336a Although as exceptions to the general rule they should perhaps be interpreted narrowly: *BV Nederlandse Industrie Van Eiprodukten v Rembrandt Entreprises Inc* [2019] EWCA Civ 596, [2019] 1 Lloyd's Rep. 491 at [75].

337 See, for example, below para.18-085. cf. *Pan Atlantic Insurance Co Ltd v Pine Top Insurance Co Ltd* [1988] 2 Lloyd's Rep. 505; below para.18-133; *Shell UK Ltd v Total UK Ltd* [2010] EWCA Civ 180, [2011] 1 Q.B. 86 (above, para.18-036) at [141], [144] can be explained on the ground either that the beneficial owner could itself sue (joining the legal owner to the action) for the loss it had suffered, or on the ground that "if formality is necessary ... [the legal owners] can recover the amount which [the beneficial owner (B)] has lost, but will hold the sums so recovered as trustees for" B (at [144]). According to *Rolls Royce Power Engineering Plc v Ricardo Consulting Engineers Ltd* [2003] EWHC 2871 (TCC), [2004] 2 All E.R. (Comm) 129 a contracting party cannot recover damages in respect of the third party's loss where the other contracting party did not, when the contract was made, know or have reason to know that the former party was contracting as trustee.

338 See *Siu Yin Kwan v Eastern Insurance Co Ltd* [1994] 2 A.C. 199, 207.

339 *St Albans C.C. v International Computers Ltd* [1996] 4 All E.R. 481.

340 *Dunlop v Lambert* (1839) 6 Cl. & F. 600, 626, 627 (as to which see *Alfred McAlpine Construction Ltd v Panatown Ltd* [2001] 1 A.C. 518 at 523 et seq.). cf. *Obestain Inc v National Mineral Development Corp Ltd (The Sanix Ace)* [1987] 1 Lloyd's Rep. 465. See also *Pegasus Management Holdings SCA v Ernst & Young* [2008] EWHC 2720 (Ch), [2009] P.N.L.R. 11 at [30] and *Fehn Schiffahrts GmbH & Co KG v Romani SPA* [2018] EWHC 1606 (Comm). The reasoning in *The Sanix Axe* was followed in *Titan Europe 2006-3 Plc v Colliers International UK Plc* [2015] EWCA Civ 1083, [2016] 1 All E.R. (Comm) 999 at [30] to enable an owner of property to recover damages in tort in respect of negligent valuation of property (in this case, choses in action) by virtue of his ownership of that property, even though that owner was not a party to the contract with the valuer; *Wibau Maschinenfabric Hartman SA v Mackinnon Mackenzie & Co (The Chanda)* [1989] 2 Lloyd's Rep. 494 (overruled on another point in *Daewoo Heavy Industries Ltd v Klipriver Shipping Ltd (The Kapitan Petko Voivoda)* [2003] EWCA Civ 451, [2003] 1 All E.R. (Comm) 801). The rule was recognised by the House of Lords in *Albacruz (Cargo Owners) v Albazero (Owners) (The Albazero)* [1977] A.C. 774, but held inapplicable as the buyer had acquired his own contractual rights against the shipowner under Bills of Lading Act 1855 s.1 (now repealed and replaced by Carriage of Goods by Sea Act 1992); Weir [1977] C.L.J. 24; *The Albazero* was distinguished in *Titan Europe 2006-3 Plc v Colliers International UK Plc* [2015] EWCA Civ 1083, [2016] 1 All E.R. (Comm) 999 at [32] on the ground that the loss in the latter case had been suffered by an owner in respect of property which he had retained while the claimant in the former case had, at the relevant time, parted with the property in question. In *Rolls Royce Power Engineering Plc v Ricardo Consulting Engineers Ltd* [2003] EWHC 2871 (TCC) the rule in *Dunlop v Lambert* (above) was said at [124] to apply only if, at the time of the contract, it was "in the actual contemplation of the parties that an identified third party or a third party who was a member of an identified class might suffer damage in the event of a breach of the contract." In the case of goods carried under a transferable bill of lading, this requirement will generally be satisfied since the transfer of such a bill must be within the carrier's contemplation. For discussion of another aspect of *Dunlop v Lambert*, above, see *Scottish & Newcastle International Ltd v Othon Ghalanos Ltd* [2008] UKHL 11, [2008] 1 Lloyd's Rep. 462 at [12], [39]–[40]. In the case of contracts to which the Carriage of Goods by Sea Act 1992 applies, a special statutory exception is created by s.2(4) of the Act to the general rule that a person can recover damages

only in respect of his own loss; for a full discussion of this subsection, see *Carver on Bills of Lading*, 4th edn (2017), paras 5-077—5-088. For the possible effects of arts 57 and 58 of the Rotterdam Rules (above, para.18-036) on s.2 of the 1992 Act, see below, para.18-117. These Rules contain no provision resembling s.2(4) of the 1992 Act.

[341] *The Albazero* [1977] A.C. 774.

[342] Exceptions to the general rule that a contracting party cannot recover damages in respect of loss suffered, not by himself, but by a third party (above, para.18-051) are further discussed by the Supreme Court in *Swynson Ltd v Lowick Rose LLP* [2017] UKSC 32, [2017] 2 W.L.R. 1161. Lord Neuberger in that case described some of these exceptions (in particular those discussed in paras 18-052—18-069 above) as "anomalous" (a word that perhaps carries a note of disapproval); and it is interesting to note that neither he nor any other member of the Supreme Court in that case made any reference to the judicial criticism of the general rule discussed in para.18-053 above, perhaps because these criticisms were not drawn to the attention of the Supreme Court in the *Swynson* case.

[343] *Hunt v Severs* [1994] 2 A.C. 350, 357.

[344] *Hunt v Severs* [1994] 2 A.C. 350, at 363.

[345] *Hughes v Lloyd* [2007] EWHC 3133 (Ch), [2008] W.T.L.R. 473; and see below, para.18-078. No such damages can be recovered where the voluntary carer is the tortfeasor: *Hunt v Severs* [1994] 2 A.C. 350; below para.18-078.

### The "broader ground": promisee's expense of curing the breach

*To the end of paragraph, after "in para.18-052 above.", add:*

**18-056** For the "broader ground" to apply, the claimant must also show that "at the time that the underlying contract was made, there was a common intention and/or a known object to benefit the third party or a class of persons to which the third party belonged".[354a]

[354a] *BV Nederlandse Industrie Van Eiprodukten v Rembrandt Entreprises Inc* [2019] EWCA Civ 596, [2019] 1 Lloyd's Rep. 491 at [73] (and see more generally the entire judgment of Coulson L.J.). However, Coulson L.J. also suggested, somewhat confusingly, that the broader ground is awarded in cases of "transferred loss", when the better view is that under the "broader ground" damages are awarded for the promisee's own loss.

### No transfer of affected property from promisee to third party

*Replace footnote 380 with:*

**18-058** [380] Quaere whether this extension will be applied in the carriage by sea context in which the exception originated: see *Carver on Bills of Lading*, 4th edn (2017), para.5-064.

## (b) Exceptions to the Doctrine

### *(ii) Contracts (Rights of Third Parties) Act 1999*

### Express provision

*Replace footnote 571 with:*

**18-092** [571] Above, para.15-052. For the effect of the 1999 Act on such clauses, see also *Carver on Bills of Lading*, 4th edn (2017), paras 7-075—7-080.

### Term purporting to confer benefit on third party

*Replace paragraph with:*

**18-093** Under subs.1(1)(b) of the 1999 Act, C may enforce a term of the contract if "the term purports to confer a benefit on him"[580]; but his right to do so in such a case is subject to s.1(2), by which C has no such right "if on a proper construction of the contract it appears that [A and B] did not intend the term to be enforceable by" C.[581] These will probably be the most significant provisions of the 1999 Act and their interpretation is likely to give rise to a number of difficulties. It seems that a "benefit" within s.1(1)(b) can include any performance due under the contract between A and B: thus it can include a payment of money, a transfer of property, or the rendering of a service; it can also (by virtue of s.1(6)) include the benefit of an exemption or limitation clause. The requirement that the term must "purport" to confer a benefit on C has been held to mean that it must have "the effect of conferring a benefit"[582] on him. If that is the position, there is no further requirement that benefiting the third party must be "the predominant purpose or intent behind the term".[583] But it is submitted that it must be *a* purpose of the parties, so that it would not suffice for C to show merely that he would happen to benefit from the performance of the term where A and B had no intention at all to confer that benefit on him.[584] The question whether A and B had any such intention would be one of construction.[585] If, for example, A were employed by B "to cut my hedge adjoining C's land", performance by A might benefit C, but the term would not "purport to confer a benefit" on C. The question of construction could be particularly hard to answer where A was a subcontractor employed by B to render services in relation to property owned by C.[586] Assuming that the *term* does purport to confer a benefit on C, it is then necessary to construe the *contract* as a whole to determine the nature and extent of C's right to enforce the term. This follows from s.1(4), under which:

> "... this section does not confer a right on [C] to enforce a term of a contract otherwise than subject to and in accordance with any other relevant terms of the contract."

This provision would, for example, apply if the term which C was seeking to enforce provided for the payment to him of £1,000, but another term of the contract provided that claims under the former term must be made within one year or that the claim must be made by arbitration (and not by litigation). On the other hand, it has been held that s.1(4) did not enable C to enforce an "adjudication" clause in the contract between A and B.[587] It was said that the "relevant rights" which C sought to enforce did not "engage the conditions within section 1(4) of the 1999 Act", though s.1(4) "would be engaged if there were an arbitration clause",[588] the reason for this distinction being that "[a]djudication, unlike arbitration, is not a mandatory alternative way in which a party has to enforce its rights. Adjudication is a voluntary method of dispute resolution in the sense that a party may, but is not obliged to, have a dispute temporarily resolved ...".[589] This reasoning gives rise to the problem that, while the phrase "conditions within section 1(4)" appears to reflect the Explanatory notes to the 1999 Act,[590] Section 1(4) itself does not use the word "conditions": it uses the less restrictive phrase "any other relevant term of the contract"; and while it may, with respect, be accepted that an adjudication clause does not, like an arbitration clause, impose a restrictive condition on the enforceability by C of rights under the contract, it is less clear why a clause of the former kind is not one of the "relevant terms of the contract"[591] within s.1(4).

[580] A term may purport to confer a benefit on C even though it is also for the benefit of B. This was held to be the position in *Cavanagh v Secretary of State for Work and Pensions* [2016] EWHC 1136 (QB), where a contract of employment contained a term by which the employer promised the employee to make specified deductions from the employee's pay and to pay these deductions to the employee's trade union. It was held that this term was enforceable against the employer by the union: the term purported to confer a benefit on the union even though it could also be said to benefit the employee.

[581] See *Royal Bank of Scotland v McCarthy* [2015] EWHC 3626 (QB), where an alternative ground for the decision (i.e. alternative to that stated in the footnote below) was that the fact that the third party had other remedies (than enforcement of the term in the contract between A and B) indicated that A and

B did not intend the term in the contract between them to be enforceable by C (at [143]), so that C's claim under the Contracts (Rights of Third Parties) Act failed by virtue of s.1(2) of that Act.

582 *Prudential Assurance Co Ltd v Ayres* [2007] EWHC 775 (Ch), [2007] 3 All E.R. 946 at [28], reversed [2008] EWCA Civ 52, [2008] 1 All E.R. 1266 on the different ground that the contract, on its true construction, purported, not to *benefit* C, but to *restrict* C's rights.

583 [2007] EWHC 775 at [28].

584 *Dolphin Maritime and Aviation Services Ltd v Sveriges Angfartygs Forening* [2009] EWHC 716 (Comm), [2009] 2 Lloyd's Rep. 123 (below, para.18-095) at [74] ("A contract does not purport to confer a benefit on a third party simply because the position of the third party will be improved if the contract is performed"); see too *Bates v Post Office Ltd (No.3)* [2019] EWHC 606 (QB) at [944]–[945]. Cf. *Petrologic Capital SA v Banque Cantonale de Geneve* [2012] EWHC 453 (Comm), where a letter of credit issued by A (a bank) to B (a seller of goods) contained a Swiss law and jurisdiction clause and it was held that this clause was not enforceable by C (the applicant for the letter of credit) as the clause was intended to govern the relation between A and B (at [53]) and as that contract did not purport to confer the benefit of the clause on C (at [54]).

585 *Nisshin Shipping Co Ltd v Cleaves & Co Ltd* [2003] EWHC 2602, [2004] 1 All E.R. (Comm) 481. Contrast *Re Lehman Brothers International (Europe)* [2012] EWHC 2997 (Ch), [2014] B.C.L.C. 294 where a contract between A and B created a charge in favour of B and provided that certain "associated companies" should be entitled to enforce that contract "where appropriate by virtue of" the 1999 Act (at [231]). Briggs J. described the question whether these words conferred rights of enforcement on such companies as one of "interpretation" (at [16]) and concluded that it would be "inappropriate" to interpret the contract as giving rise to "parallel enforcement at the instance of a potentially wide range of different creditors" as this interpretation would involve "an inherently un-businesslike concept" (at [236]). Even if, on its true construction, the term was intended by A and B to confer *some* benefit on C, a further question of construction could arise whether that benefit was the one claimed by C: see *Hurley Palmer Flatt Ltd v Barclays Bank Plc* [2014] EWHC 3042 (TCC), [2015] Bus. L.R. 106, where a contract between A and B for the provision of services by B was expressed to confer rights on C (a so-called "affiliate" of A) and also contained "adjudication provisions" which C sought to invoke. The actual decision was that the rights conferred on C were certain substantive rights or defences available to A, and not "procedure rights" such as those under the "adjudication provisions" (at [22]). See also *Royal Bank of Scotland v McCarthy* [2015] EWHC 3626 (QB) where the mere fact that a benefit to the third party was an "incidental effect" (at [137]) of the performance of the contract was held not to satisfy the requirement set out in s.1(1)(b) of the 1999 Act. The question whether the requirement stated in s.1(1)(b) of the Contracts (Rights of Third Parties) Act 1999 (i.e. whether the contract purported to confer a benefit on the third party) was one of the "construction" of the contract (at [123], [129]), and that the above requirement had not been satisfied. In support of this conclusion, the Court also relied on the sentence from the *Dolphin Maritime case* [2009] EWHC 716 (Comm), [2009] 2 Lloyd's Rep. 123 at [74], see above.

586 An analogous problem arose, apparently under Brazilian law, in *Petromec Inc v Petroleo Brasileiro SA Petrobas* [2004] EWHC 1180 (Comm), [2005] 1 Lloyd's Rep. 219 where A, a sub-bareboat charterer of an oil production platform, took out a policy of insurance with B relating to the platform. It was held that no claim on the policy could be brought in his own right by C, a sub-contractor engaged to do upgrading work on the platform, as A had not purported to insure for the benefit of C. In English law, similar reasoning could on such facts be applied to a claim brought under s.1(1)(b) of the 1999 Act. On appeal, the decision was affirmed without reference to the point of Brazilian law here discussed: [2005] EWCA Civ 891, [2006] 1 Lloyd's Rep. 121.

587 *Hurley Palmer Flatt Ltd v Barclays Bank Plc* [2014] EWHC 3042 (TCC), [2015] Bus. L.R. 106.

588 *Hurley Palmer Flatt Ltd v Barclays Bank Plc* [2014] EWHC 3042 (TCC), [2015] Bus. L.R. 106 at [26].

589 *Hurley Palmer Flatt Ltd v Barclays Bank Plc* [2014] EWHC 3042 (TCC), [2015] Bus. L.R. 106 at [28].

590 See *Hurley Palmer Flatt Ltd v Barclays Bank Plc* [2014] EWHC 3042 (TCC), [2015] Bus. L.R. 106 at [25].

591 There are other legal contexts in which "terms" has a wider import than "conditions": for example where the issue is whether certain charterparty terms have been incorporated into a bill of lading by a clause in the latter document: see *Carver on Bills of Lading*, 4th edn (2017), para.3-020.

## Third party to be "expressly" identified

*Replace paragraph with:*

**18-097** Under s.1(3) of the 1999 Act, it is a requirement of C's right to enforce A's promise that C must have been "*expressly* identified in the contract [between A and

B] by name, as a member of a class or as answering a particular description"[618]; and it follows from this requirement that C could not rely, for the purpose of s.1(1), on the argument that the contract referred to him by implication,[619] though the question whether the third party is "expressly" identified may itself raise a question of construction. In *Chudley v Clydesdale Bank Plc*,[620] Arck LLP opened an account described as "Arck LLP – Segregated Client Account" with the Bank, which was agreed to be linked to one particular investment scheme. The Bank agreed to hold the moneys in that account until a certain date, and only to allow withdrawals from the account if an unconditional undertaking was received from a named solicitor. Various investors paid into the scheme, which was later discovered to be fraudulent and Arck LLP entered liquidation. However, the Bank had released money from the account without obtaining the required undertaking, and the investors sought to bring a claim against the Bank as third parties to the contract between Arck LLP and the Bank. One issue was whether the investors were "expressly identified" under s.1(3). The Court of Appeal held that the contract should be interpreted as a whole, such that a reference to a "client account" was express identification of a class—clients of Arck LLP who were investing in that particular scheme.[620a] Flaux L.J. thought that the dictum of Waller L.J. in *Avraamides v Colwill*[620b] that the word "express" does not allow a "process of construction or implication" contains an error: the "or" should be replaced with "by".[620c] Construction by implication is impermissible, but the standard principles of interpretation can be employed in the usual way.[620d] It did not matter in the *Chudley* case that the investors did not know of the relevant contract at the time they made their investments: "it is not a requirement of the 1999 Act that a third party who is entitled to the benefit of a contract was aware of the contract at the time it was made or at any particular time thereafter".[620e]

618 Italics supplied.

619 See *Avraamides v Colwill* [2006] EWCA Civ 1533, [2007] B.L.R. 76 at [19], where on the transfer of B's business to A, A promised B to pay "any liabilities properly incurred by B." This was held not to amount to an express identification of one of B's former customers (even though A had also promised "to complete outstanding customer orders") since the "liabilities" to which it referred "would benefit third parties but of a large number of *unidentified* classes" (at [19], italics supplied). For identification of a third party "as a member of a class or as answering a particular description" within s.1(3), see *Crowson v HSBC Insurance Brokers Ltd* [2010] 1 Lloyd's Rep. I.R. 441 at [12] (directors of the company with which the contract had been made).

620 [2019] EWCA Civ 344, [2019] 2 All E.R. (Comm) 293.

620a [2019] EWCA Civ 344, [2019] 2 All E.R. (Comm) 293 at [78] (Flaux L.J.), [93] (Longmore L.J.).

620b [2006] EWCA Civ 1533, [2007] B.L.R. 76 at [19].

620c [2019] EWCA Civ 344, [2019] 2 All E.R. (Comm) 293 at [77].

620d See too *Laemthong International Lines Co Ltd v Artis (The Laemthong Glory) (No.2)* [2005] EWCA Civ 519, [2005] 1 Lloyd's Rep. 632 at [48].

620e [2019] EWCA Civ 344, [2019] 2 All E.R. (Comm) 293 at [80].

*Add new paragraphs:*

**18-097A** If, for example, the contracting parties had adopted a "private dictionary"[621] by which all references in their contract to "Jack" were to mean "Jack and Jill" then a term conferring a benefit on "Jack" would (at least probably) amount to an "express" identification of Jill, no less than of Jack. In the absence of such special circumstances, the question whether the naming of one person as a party can also be construed as an "express" reference to another person or persons can give rise to more difficulty. The point is illustrated by *The Alexandros T*,[622] where an agreement between named insurers (A) and the owners of a ship which had sunk (B) provided for the settlement of all claims by B against the "Underwriters".[623] This word was "construed an encompassing the servants or agents of insurers"[624] so as to satisfy, with regard to these persons, the requirements of s.1(1)(b) and s.1(2) of the 1999 Act.[625] It was further held (though with some hesitation[626]) that the servants or agents (C) were "expressly" identified within s.1(3) as "a class of third party intended to have a benefit conferred upon them by the settlement agreements,"[627] so that they were, by virtue of s.1(1), entitled to enforce terms of the agreement[628] between A and B by which claims against the "underwriters" had been "fully and finally settled". A similar problem of the identification of third party beneficiaries had arisen in the Canadian case of *London Drugs Ltd v Kuehne & Nagel International Ltd*[629] where the claimants had delivered valuable machinery to a warehousing company under a contract which limited the liability of "the warehouseman" to $40 per package. A majority of the Supreme Court of Canada held that the employees of the warehousing contractor were protected by this limitation of liability as "third party beneficiaries"[630] under a new (though restricted) exception to the doctrine of privity.[631] The question whether such an exception would be recognised in England remains, at the level of the Supreme Court, an open one; but the point of interest here is how the majority in the Supreme Court of Canada identified the employees as third party beneficiaries who were entitled to the benefit of the exception. The process of identification seems to have been one of implication: this appears from the statements that "the intention to extend the benefit of the ... clause to employees may be express or implied"[632] and that although the employees were not "express third party beneficiaries"[633] this fact did "not preclude a finding that they are *implied* third party beneficiaries".[634] It is clear from this reasoning that the employees were not expressly identified as third party beneficiaries, but that they were impliedly so identified; and if that reasoning were now followed in an English case arising from similar circumstances, then the question whether the employees had been "expressly" identified for the purpose of s.1(3) of the 1999 Act would have to be answered in the negative. That question does not, moreover, differ materially from the question whether, in *The Alexandros T* the servants or agents of the underwriters had, for the same purpose, been "expressly" identified by the word "underwriters"; and it is a matter of regret that, in *The Alexandros T*, the attention of Flaux J. was not drawn to the reasoning of the *London Drugs* case on the point here under discussion. Indeed, something resembling that reasoning appears to have been in Flaux J.'s mind when he said that his "initial reaction" was that the mere use of the word "underwriters" was "not sufficient for express identification":[635] but his ultimate conclusion was that because that word "encompass[ed] servants or agents" it "expressly identifies a class of persons intended to have a benefit conferred on them by the settlement agreements".[636] This language seems to refer back to an earlier part of the judgment in which it was held that "the requirements of section 1(1)(b) and (2)[637] are satisfied".[638] It is, however, with great respect, submitted that the learned judge's "initial reaction" is more consistent than his ultimate conclusion with the language and structure of s.1 of the 1999 Act. In particular, s.1(1)(b) (intention to benefit the third party) and s.1(3) (express identification) are separate and cumulative requirements,[639] so that reasoning which satisfies the first of these requirements cannot, of itself, satisfy the second.

**18-097B** The above paragraph was considered by the Court of Appeal in the *Chudley* case, discussed above.[639a] Flaux L.J. accepted that the requirements of s.1(1)(b) and s.1(3) are cumulative, but held that the same term could satisfy both requirements.[639b] Longmore L.J. commented that this was a clearer case than *The Alexandros T*, and although it was not necessary to decide whether that latter decision was correct, Longmore L.J. said: "I do not see how Flaux J. can be wrong to have concluded that the agents were to have the benefit of the contract and be entitled to sue upon it".[639c] That the *London Drugs* case used a process of implication does not mean that the same process would necessarily be required under the 1999 Act.

[621] See para.13-131 above.

[622] *Starlight Shipping Co v Allianz Versicherungs AG (The Alexandros T)* [2014] EWHC 3068 (Comm), [2014] 2 Lloyd's Rep. 579.

[623] For the text of the relevant parts of the agreements, see [2014] EWHC 3068 (Comm) at [7] (Clause 3) and [8] (Clause 2).

[624] [2014] EWHC 3068 (Comm) at [62], [88]. The process here is one of *construction* of the word "underwriters", not one of *implication* since the latter would not suffice for the purpose of s.1(3): *Avraamides v Colwill* [2006] EWCA Civ 1533, [2007] B.L.R. 76 at [19]. Lord Hoffmann's description in *Attorney General of Belize v Belize Telecom Ltd* [2009] UKPC 10, [2009] 1 W.L.R. 1988 of the process of implication as one of "the construction of the instrument as a whole" was extensively discussed by the Supreme Court in *Marks and Spencer Plc v BNP Paribas Security Services Trust Co (Jersey) Limited* [2015] UKSC 72, [2016] A.C. 742. Lord Neuberger (with whose judgment Lord Sumption and Lord Hodge agreed) there said (at [26]) that Lord Hoffmann's observation (quoted above) "could obscure the fact that construing the words used and implying additional words are different processes governed by different rules" and (at [31]) that they (i.e., those observations) should "henceforth be treated as a characteristically inspired discussion rather than authoritative guidance on the law of implied terms". For the same view, see also *Globe Motors Inc v Varity Electric Steering Ltd* [2016] EWCA Civ 396 [2017] 1 All E.R. (Comm) 601 at [58] and at [68], per Beatson L.J. following Lord Neuberger's statement, quoted above in this note, in the *Marks and Spencer* case. The majority view in the *Marks and Spencer* case was not there shared by Lord Carnwath (see at [74], while Lord Clarke said (at [76]) that both processes (i.e. construction and implication) could "properly be said to be 'part of the construction of the contract in a broad sense'." The judgments in the *Marks and Spencer* case on the present point are more fully discussed in, para.14-001 above. Even before the *Marks and Spencer* case (above) the scope of Lord Hoffmann's views in the *Belize* case had been narrowed by judicial statements to the effect that those views applied only to the implication of terms *in fact*, and not to the implication of terms *in law*: see *Société Générale, London Branch v Geys* [2012] UKSC [2013] 1 A.C. at [55] per Baroness Hale and *Yam Seng Ltd v International Trade Corporation Ltd* [2013] EWHC, [2013] 1 Lloyd's Rep. 526 at [131], [132], per Leggatt J.; for the difference between these two types of implied terms, see above, para.14-005.

[625] Above paras 18-093—18-095, following (at [86], [87]) *Laemthong International Lines Co Ltd v Artis (The Laemthong Glory) (No.2)* [2005] EWCA Civ 519, [2005] 1 Lloyd's Rep. 632.

[626] See [2014] EWHC 3068 (Comm) at [88], and below.

[627] [2014] EWHC 3068 (Comm) at [88].

[628] [2014] EWHC 3068 (Comm) at [88].

[629] [1992] 3 S.C.R. 299; more fully discussed in *Carver on Bills of Lading*, 4th edn (2017), paras 7-019—7-021.

[630] [1992] 3 S.C.R. 299 at 451.

[631] See above, para.18-022.

[632] [1992] 3 S.C.R. 299 at 449.

[633] [1992] 3 S.C.R. 299 at 451.

[634] [1992] 3 S.C.R. 299 at 451.

[635] [2014] EWHC 3068 (Comm) at [88].

[636] [2014] EWHC 3068 (Comm) at [88].

[637] For these requirements, see above, paras 18-093—18-095.

[638] [2014] EWHC 3068 (Comm) at [87].

[639] See the Explanatory notes to Clause 1 of the Bill appended to Law Com. No.242 ("*In addition* ... clause 1(3) requires that the third party be expressly identified ..."; italics supplied).

[639a] [2019] EWCA Civ 344, [2019] 2 All E.R. (Comm) 293.

[639b] [2019] EWCA Civ 344, [2019] 2 All E.R. (Comm) 293 at [79].

[639c] [2019] EWCA Civ 344, [2019] 2 All E.R. (Comm) 293 at [94].

### The first group of exceptions

*Replace footnote 691 with:*

18-117 [691] For details of this scheme, see *Carver on Bills of Lading*, 4th edn (2017), paras 5-012—5-110, 8-002—8-016, 8-036—8-060; the 1992 Act (unlike the 1999 Act) provides not only for the acquisition of rights by, but also for the imposition of liabilities on, third parties.

## *(iii) Other Statutory Exceptions*

### Fire insurance

*Replace footnote 776 with:*

18-134 [776] *Portavon Cinema Co v Price & Century Insurance Co* [1939] 4 All E.R. 601; *Mark Rowlands Ltd v Berni Inns Ltd* [1986] Q.B. 211; *Lonsdale & Thompson Ltd v Black Arrow Group Plc* [1993] Ch. 361; *Palliser Ltd v Fate Ltd (In Liquidation)* [2019] EWHC 43 (QB), [2019] Lloyd's Rep. I.R. 341.

## 5. ENFORCEMENT AGAINST THIRD PARTIES

### Exceptions to the doctrine of privity

*Replace footnote 803 with:*

18-140 [803] As under Carriage of Goods by Sea Act 1992 s.3, discussed in *Carver on Bills of Lading*, 4th edn (2017), paras 5-092—5-112.

### Scope of the rule

*Replace paragraph with:*

18-141 In cases governed by the general rule stated in para.18-139 above, a contract between A and B cannot impose a positive duty on C to render the performance specified in the contract; but the contract can impose legal restrictions on C's freedom of action in various other ways. For example, it may create a lien,[804] or a lease,[805] or an equitable interest, or give rise to a constructive trust affecting property,[806] and such interests can affect the rights of third parties who later acquire the property. Moreover, although a contract primarily creates rights and duties enforceable by the contracting parties against each other, it also incidentally imposes on third parties a duty not to induce one of the contracting parties to commit a breach of the contract. In the leading case of *Lumley v Gye*[807] it was held that a person who, knowing of a contract between two others, "maliciously", i.e. intentionally[808] induces one of them to commit a breach of it (e.g. by wrongfully refusing to perform it) is liable to the other for the tort of inducing a breach of the contract. In some later cases, this tort was described as one of "interference" by C with contractual rights which A had under a contract between A and B. This terminology was based on authorities[809] which had supported the "unified theory"[810] that tort liability for inducing a breach of contract was "a species of a more general tort of actionable interference with contractual rights,"[811] But this "unified theory" was rejected[812] by the House of Lords in *OBG Ltd v Allan*.[813] A sharp distinction was there drawn between two torts: that of inducing a breach of contract[814] and that of causing loss by unlawful means.[815] The details of this distinction are beyond the scope of a book on the law of contract. It suffices here to say that the former tort depends on C's having induced a breach by B,[816] while the latter does not[817]; that the former tort does not, while the latter does, depend on C's having used means (to induce the breach) which are "independently unlawful"[818]; and that the mental elements of the two torts differ in that the former requires no more than an intention to induce the breach by B while the latter requires an intention to cause loss to A.[819] If, for example, A's claim is based on the allegation that C has *prevented* B from performing his contract with A, but without B's having committed any *breach* of it, then C's liability (if any) is for the "unlawful means" tort and will arise only if the requirements of *that* tort are satisfied.[820] Our concern in this chapter is with the first of the two torts distinguished in the decision of the House of Lords in *OBG Ltd v Allen*,[821] i.e., with that of inducing a breach of contract.

[804] See *Faith v E.I.C.* (1821) 4 B. & Ald. 630; *Tappenden v Artus* [1964] 2 Q.B. 185; *Jare Trä AB v Convoys Ltd* [2003] EWHC 1488 (Comm), [2003] 2 Lloyd's Rep. 459. See also *T. Comedy (UK) Ltd v Easy Managed Transport Ltd* [2007] EWHC 611 (Comm), [2007] 2 All E.R. (Comm) 282 at [64] (third party bound by lien arising under contract of carriage by virtue of the doctrine of bailment on terms, referred to at para.18-139 above). Contrast *Chellaram & Sons Ltd v Butler's Warehousing and Distributing Ltd* [1978] 2 Lloyd's Rep. 412 (third party not bound by agreement purporting to confer on sub-bailee a lien more extensive than that which would, but for such agreement, arise at common law).

[805] As in *Ashburn Anstalt v Arnold* [1989] Ch. 1 (overruled on another ground in *Prudential Assurance Co Ltd v London Residuary Body* [1992] 2 A.C. 386).

[806] See *Ashburn Anstalt v Arnold* [1989] Ch. 1, where the mere fact that C had notice of an earlier contract between A and B was said at 25–26 to be insufficient to give rise to a constructive trust on C's acquisition of the land affected by that contract; and where Fox L.J. (delivering the judgment of the court) at 17 disapproved dicta in *Errington v Errington* [1952] 1 K.B. 290, to the effect that a contractual licence to occupy land granted by A to B gave rise to an equitable interest binding third parties; Hill (1988) 51 M.L.R. 226; Oakley [1988] C.L.J. 353. cf. also *Binions v Evans* [1972] Ch. 359; Smith [1973] C.L.J. 81; *Re Sharpe* [1980] 1 W.L.R. 219; *Pritchard v Briggs* [1980] Ch. 338 (option to purchase); *Lyus v Prowsa Developments* [1982] 1 W.L.R. 1044; *Lloyd v Dugdale* [2001] EWCA Civ 1754, [2001] 48 E.G.C.S. 129; contrast *Chaudhary v Yavus* [2011] EWCA Civ 1314, [2012] 2 All E.R. 418, where *Lyus v Prowsa Development* was described as a "very unusual" (at [61]) or "exceptional" (at [64]) case and distinguished on the ground that, in the *Chaudhary* case, there was "nothing in the contract to draw specific attention to [the third party's right]" (at [58]); and *Lloyd v Dugdale* was also distinguished on the ground that there was nothing in the contract in the *Chaudhary* case "to allow the court to conclude that by [that] contract the purchaser had undertaken to give effect to "the third party's interest" (at [59]).

[807] (1853) 2 El. & Bl. 216; for further proceedings, see 23 L.T. 66, 18 Jur. & 68 n., 23 L.J. Q.B. 116n.; Waddams (2001) 117 L.Q.R. 431.

[808] "Maliciously" in *Lumley v Gye* (1853) 2 El. & Bl. 216 meant no more than that "the defendant intended to procure a breach of contract": *OBG Ltd v Allan* [2007] UKHL 21, [2008] 1 A.C. 1 at [8]; cf. at [189], [191]. It follows that C must have actual knowledge, not only of the existence of the contract between A and B, but also of the term in it alleged to have been broken by B: *OBG Ltd v Allan* [2007] UKHL 21, [2008] 1 A.C. 1 at [39], [40]; though for this purpose C may be taken to have knowledge of a fact if he deliberately shuts his eyes to it: at [41]. For the requirement of knowledge of the contract and intention to procure its breach, see also *Unique Pub Properties Ltd v Beer Barrels Mineral Waters Ltd* [2004] EWCA Civ 586, [2005] 1 All E.R. (Comm) 181. The relevant intention will be negatived where C honestly and genuinely believed that B's relevant conduct would not amount to a breach: *OBG* case, above, at [68]–[70], [200]–[202]; this is true even where C's belief is based on a mistake of law: at [202]; *Meretz Investments NV v ACP Ltd* [2007] EWCA Civ 1303 at [114], [119], [124], [180]. In *Allen (t/a David Allen Chartered Accountants) v Dodd & Co Ltd* [2020] EWCA Civ 258, [2020] 2 W.L.R. 1070 at [27] Lewison L.J. said that "You must *actually realise* that the act you are procuring *will have* the effect of breaching the contract in question". C did not so realise when relying on legal advice that it was more probable than not that the contract would not be breached. It follows from the requirement of an intention to induce a breach that C is not liable for the tort if he acts carelessly: "Negligent interference is not actionable": *OBG* case above at [191]; *Miller v Bassey* [1994] EMLR 44 (where the defendant had been held liable without intending to induce the breach) is disapproved in the *OBG* case at [43], [166], [264]; and see at [202], citing *British Industrial Plastics Ltd v Ferguson* [1940] 1 All E.R. 479 in favour of the view that the requisite intention may be negatived by C's honest, if eccentric, belief that the conduct induced was not a breach. C is also not liable for this tort if he believed that he was entitled to act in a way that would prevent B from performing B's contract with A: *Meretz* case, above, at [124], [179]. Where the intention to induce B to break his contract with A is established, there is no further requirement that C must intend to cause loss: see below. To the extent that the contrary may be suggested in the *Meretz* case at [2], [127], the suggestions are, with respect, made per incuriam, and are inconsistent with, at [124], [179].

[809] e.g., *D.C. Thompson & Co v Deakin* [1952] Ch. 646: see *OBG Ltd v Allan* [2007] UKHL 21, [2008] 1 A.C. 1 at [26].

[810] *OBG Ltd v Allan* [2007] UKHL 21, [2008] 1 A.C. 1 before [26], at [27], [28], [264]; cf. [306], [320].

[811] *OBG Ltd v Allan* [2007] UKHL 21, [2008] 1 A.C. 1 at [27].

[812] See *OBG Ltd v Allan* [2007] UKHL 21, [2008] 1 A.C. 1 at [32]; cf. at [172], [173], [264].

[813] [2007] UKHL 21.

[814] At [3]–[5], [39]–[44], [168]–[172].

[815] At [6]–[8], [45]–[60], [141]–[163].

[816] cf. *Pan Oceanic Chartering Inc v UNIPEC UK Co Ltd* [2016] EWHC 2774 (Comm), [2017] 2 All E.R. (Comm) 196 at [253], concluding that under the law of New Jersey "breach of the contract interfered with is required for the tort of interfering with an existing contract".

[817] At [8].

[818] At [8]; cf. [32], [49], [51], [145], [148], [164].

[819] At [8], [47], [62], [141], [192]; for the mental element of the tort of inducing breach of contract, see above.

[820] See the *OBG* case [2007] UKHL 21 at [180], [189] ("there is no in-between hybrid tort of 'interfering with contractual relations'"). See too *Palmer Birch (A Partnership) v Lloyd* [2018] EWHC 2316 (TCC), [2018] 4 W.L.R. 164 at [161]–[164].

[821] See above. For the further distinction between the requirements of the tort of *causing loss* by unlawful means and that of *conspiracy* to cause loss by unlawful means, see the discussion of the *OBG* case in *Revenue and Customs Commissioners v Total Networks SL* [2008] UKHL 19, [2008] 2 All E.R. 143.

## Third party's liability in tort

*Replace footnote 849 with:*

**18-147** [849] *Sefton v Tophams* [1965] Ch. 1140, 1161, 1187; reversed without reference to this point [1967] A.C. 50. And see *Lictor Anstalt v MIR Steel UK Ltd* [2011] EWHC 3310 (Ch), [2012] 1 All E.R. (Comm) 592 at [53] ("persuasion [by C of B] is not required" in order to make C liable to A for inducing B to break his contract with A). For further proceedings in this case, in which C were held liable to A for knowingly procuring a breach of A's contract with B, see [2014] EWHC 3316 (Ch) at [260]. See too *Wolff v Trinity Logistics USA Inc* [2018] EWCA Civ 2765, [2019] 1 W.L.R. 3997 at [40]–[45].

## Third party's knowledge: the time factor

*Replace paragraph with:*

**18-151** So far, in discussing the third party liability in tort for inducing a breach of contract,[858] it has been assumed that C either knew or did not know of the contract between A and B. In the former situation, he could, but in the latter he could not, be liable for this tort.[859] There is also an intermediate situation, in which C at the time of his contract with B had no more than constructive notice of B's earlier contract with A, but then acquired actual knowledge of that contract before calling for (or receiving) performance of his own contract with B.[860] The question then arises whether, on such facts, C is liable to A for the tort of inducing a breach of the contract between A and B. That tort is subject to the defence of "justification",[861] which is certainly available to C where he had contracted with B *before* A had done so.[862] But the defence is a flexible one,[863] and the principle on which it is based appears to be equally applicable where C's contract with B was made *after* A's but in ignorance of it. The exercise by C of rights thus acquired in good faith against B should not, it is submitted, make C liable in tort to A.[864] Even in such a situation, however, C may be liable to A under the rules stated in para.18-144 above if the contract between A and B is *specifically* enforceable by A. Where the specific enforceability of this contract gives rise to an equitable interest, this interest can be asserted against C even though he had, when he contracted with B, only constructive notice of the contract. In such a case, the tort claim would be "of no value"[865] if, as has been submitted above, it arises only where C, when he contracted with B, had actual knowledge of A's rights; but it would equally be unnecessary,[866] since A could succeed against C on the different ground that the contract between A and

B was specifically enforceable by A and therefore conferred an equitable interest on A.

[858] Above, paras 18-141 et seq.

[859] Above, paras 18-141; 18-147.

[860] This was the position in *Swiss Bank Corp v Lloyds Bank Ltd* [1982] A.C. 584; see [1979] Ch. 548, 568–596 and below.

[861] See *OBG Ltd v Allan* [2007] UKHL 21, [2008] 1 A.C. 1 at [193]. For the defence of "justification" to the tort of inducing a breach of contract, see also *Royal Bank of Scotland Plc v McCarthy* [2015] EWHC 3626 (QB) at [107], [114], [115]. In that case, the tort claim was also rejected on the ground that there had been no "inducement" of any breach (at [105]). See too *Palmer Birch (A Partnership) v Lloyd* [2018] EWHC 2316 (TCC), [2018] 4 W.L.R. 164 at [175]–[182], [362].

[862] *Smithies v National Association of Operative Plasterers* [1909] 1 K.B. 310, 337; *Edwin Hill & Partners v First National Finance Corp Plc* [1989] 1 W.L.R. 225, 230; *Meretz Investments NV v ACP Ltd* [2007] EWCA Civ 1303 at [42], [142], [179]. For terms which may be imposed on C as a condition of obtaining relief against B, see *Guiness Peat Aviation (Belgium) N.V. v Hispania Lineas Aereas SA* [1992] 1 Lloyd's Rep. 190.

[863] *Glamorgan Coal Co v South Wales Miners' Federation* [1903] 2 K.B. 545, 574–575; cf. *Anton Durbeck GmbH v Den Norske Bank* [2005] EWHC 2497 (Comm), [2006] 1 Lloyd's Rep. 93, esp. at [68], [71]. In that case, A (a cargo-owner) contracted with B (a shipowner) for the carriage of goods which deteriorated and were lost when C (a bank) arrested and detained A's ship as security for a loan made by C to B before the contract of carriage between A and B had been made. It was held that C was not liable to A for the tort here under discussion.

[864] This was admitted in *Swiss Bank Corp v Lloyds Bank Ltd*, see [1979] Ch. 548, 569–573. Cf. *Zhu v Treasurer of New South Wales* [2004] HCA 56, (2004) 218 C.L.R. 530 at [108]–[171].

[865] *Swiss Bank Corp v Lloyds Bank Ltd* [1982] A.C. 584, 598, where it was held, on construction, that the contract did *not* impose an obligation to use the specific property for its performance and was *not* specifically enforceable: see below, para.27-018.

[866] [1982] A.C. 584, 598.

CHAPTER 19

# ASSIGNMENT



## 1. ASSIGNMENT

### Assignment under particular statutes

*Replace footnote 16 with:*

[16] Insolvency Act 1986 s.344; Companies Act 2006 ss.859A–859Q, replacing ss.860–861, 863, 866–867, 874; below, paras 19-061—19-067. | **19-003**

## (a) Statutory Assignments

### Written notice to the debtor

*Replace paragraph with:*

Under the statute notice in writing to the debtor is necessary. It is: **19-017**

> "... wrong to suppose that a separate document purposely prepared as a notice, and described as such, is necessary in order to satisfy the statute. The statute only requires that information relative to the assignment shall be conveyed to the debtor, and that it shall be conveyed in writing."[63]

Thus a written demand for payment sent by the assignee to the debtor has been held sufficient.[64] Beyond this, however, the statute has been strictly construed, and it has been held that the notice must be unconditional,[65] and that written notice must be given, even though the debtor cannot read.[66] So also it is essential that the notice be given to the debtor himself: thus, where an insured assigned the proceeds of a policy and notice was given to the broker through whom the proceeds were collected, it was held that the notice was insufficient.[67] The notice is apparently invalid if it purports to identify the assignment by giving its date and that date is a wrong date[68]; though there is nothing in the section which requires the assignment to be dated at all, and it has been held that a notice is valid though it wrongly states that another notice has already been given.[69] On the other hand, the statute does not prescribe any limit of time within which notice must be given,[70] nor does it lay down that the notice must be given by any particular person.[71] It may consequently be given after the death of either the assignor or the assignee.[72] Notice must be given before the assignee starts his action,[73] though failure to do this will not prevent the assignee from proceeding with his action on the footing that he is an equitable assignee.[74] In this event, however, the court may require the assignor to be made a party to the proceedings.[75]

[63] *Van Lynn Developments Ltd v Pelias Construction Co Ltd* [1969] 1 Q.B. 607, 615. See also *Denney, Gasquet and Metcalfe v Conklin* [1913] 3 K.B. 177; cf. *James Talcott Ltd v John Lewis & Co Ltd* [1940] 3 All E.R. 592 (equitable assignment); see also *Herkules Piling Ltd v Tilbury Construction Ltd* (1992) 61 Build. L.R. 107 (the disclosure to the debtor of a document of assignment on discovery in an action by the assignor held to be insufficient notice for a legal or equitable assignment).

[64] *Van Lynn Developments Ltd v Pelias Construction Co Ltd* [1969] 1 Q.B. 607. But cf. *Warner Bros Records Inc v Rollgreen Investments Ltd* [1976] Q.B. 430 (exercise of option).

[65] *The Balder London* [1980] 2 Lloyd's Rep. 489, 495.

[66] *Hockley and Papworth v Goldstein* (1920) 90 L.J. K.B. 111.

[67] *Amalgamated General Finance Co Ltd v C.E. Golding & Co Ltd* [1964] 2 Lloyd's Rep. 163; *Magee v U.D.C. Finance Ltd* [1983] N.Z.L.R. 438. But cf. the position of an equitable assignment, below, para.19-021 n.86.

[68] *Stanley v English Fibres Industries Ltd* (1899) 68 L.J. Q.B. 839; *W. F. Harrison & Co Ltd v Burke* [1956] 1 W.L.R. 419; criticised in (1956) 72 L.Q.R. 321 and explained in *Van Lynn Developments Ltd v Pelias Construction Co Ltd* [1969] 1 Q.B. 607 at 612. The *Harrison case* [1956] 1 W.L.R. 419, 421 contains a suggestion that a misstatement of the amount of the debt might also vitiate the notice as "the requirements of the Act must be strictly complied with" (Denning L.J.). But despite these dicta, it is possible that a notice which gives the wrong date or the wrong amount will now be effective if it reasonably conveyed to the debtor which debt was being assigned, cf. *Mannai Investment Co Ltd v Eagle Star Life Assurance Co Ltd* [1997] A.C. 749 (on which see above, paras 3-014 and 13-054). As Atkin J. said in *Denney, Gasquet, and Metcalfe v Conklin* [1913] 3 K.B. 177, 180, a notice of assignment is sufficient if it brings "to the notice of the debtor with reasonable certainty the fact that the deed does assign the debt due from the debtor so as to bind the debt in his hands and prevent him from paying the debt to the original creditor". Compare Smith and Leslie, *The Law of Assignment*, 3rd edn (2018), para.16.48 (incorrect statements may be treated as "surplusage").

[69] *Van Lynn Developments Ltd v Pelias Construction Ltd* [1969] 1 Q.B. 607; *Grey v Australian Motorists & General Insurance Co Pty Ltd* [1976] 1 N.S.W.L.R. 669 (date referred to but no date inserted).

[70] It has been held that a notice given before the assignment has taken place is not effective: *Williams v Atlantic Assurance Co Ltd* [1933] 1 K.B. 81, 106 and *WF Harrison Co Ltd v Burke* [1956] 1 W.L.R. 419, 421, 422, cited in Smith and Leslie, *The Law of Assignment*, 3rd edn (2018), para.16.43. Whether in this case it would suffice that it was clear to the debtor which debt was being assigned must be doubtful.

[71] *Bateman v Hunt* [1904] 2 K.B. 530, 538.

[72] *Walker v Bradford Old Bank* (1884) 12 Q.B.D. 511; *Bateman v Hunt* [1904] 2 K.B. 530; *Re Westerton* [1919] 2 Ch. 104.

[73] *Compania Colombiana de Seguros v Pacific Steam Navigation Co* [1965] 1 Q.B. 101, 128–129. It is arguable that this should no longer be the rule; and that instead a court could prevent any unfairness to defendants by exercising its discretion to disallow an application to amend the particulars of claim so as to add the assigned claim. Say, for example, a claimant is met by the defence that part (but not all) of what he is claiming is his company's, rather than his personal, claim. If he then takes a legal assignment from the company and gives written notice to the defendant, should he be able to apply for an amendment without bringing a fresh action? Or is the "rule" in the *Compania Colombiana* case a rigid one that would automatically mean that such an application would fail?

[74] *Weddell v Pearce & Major* [1988] Ch. 26, 42, in which Scott J. rejected the obiter dicta in the *Compania Colombiana* case [1956] 1 Q.B. 101 to the extent that Roskill J. had there said that there was no valid equitable assignment.

[75] Below, paras 19-039—19-042.

## (b) Equitable Assignments

### Notice

*Replace footnote 86 with:*

19-021 [86] *Jones v Farrell* (1857) 1 D. & J. 208; *Brice v Bannister* (1878) 3 Q.B.D. 569; *Deposit Protection Board v Dalia* [1994] 2 A.C. 367, CA (Simon Brown L.J. dissented, reasoning, with respect incorrectly, that even after notice the debtor remains liable to the equitable assignor: the question did not arise in the House of Lords, [1994] 2 A.C. 367, 391, which reversed the decision of the Court of Appeal in holding that, as a matter of statutory interpretation, only the original deposit maker, and not an assignee, was a "depositor" entitled to protection under s.58 of the Banking Act 1987); Peel (ed.), *Treitel on The Law of Contract*, 15th edn (2020), para.15-022. See also above para.19-018 n.77.

### Formalities for equitable assignments

*Replace paragraph with:*

19-026 An equitable assignment of a legal chose in action need not be in writing, nor in any particular form,[100] unless the contract giving rise to the right to be assigned so requires.[100a] On the other hand, an equitable assignment of an equitable chose in action must be in writing[101] if it is caught by s.53(1)(c) of the Law of Property Act 1925, which provides:

> "A disposition of an equitable interest or trust subsisting at the time of the disposition must be in writing signed by the person disposing of the same, or by his agent thereunto lawfully authorised in writing or by will."[102]

It has been held that the word "disposition" in this paragraph must be given a wide meaning, and that it is apt to cover a direction by the holder of an equitable interest to the trustee to hold the property on trust for a third party, whether or not this is strictly an assignment of the equitable interest.[103] A fortiori a direct assignment should do the same. The paragraph does not prevent the holder of a beneficial interest in a trust fund from himself making an oral declaration of trust, and so constituting himself trustee of his own beneficial interest, for this is neither an assignment nor a "disposition" of his own interest.[104] Nor (it seems) does the provision apply where a person assigns the legal title to a chose in action together with an option to acquire the beneficial interest, and the transferee subsequently exercises this option orally. For in this case the beneficial interest passes not by virtue of any assignment or disposition to the transferor, but by virtue of the exercise of the option.[105]

[100] *Brandt's Sons & Co v Dunlop Rubber Co* [1905] A.C. 454, 462; *Re Wale* [1956] 1 W.L.R. 1346, 1350; *Kijowski v New Capital Properties Ltd* (1990) 15 Con. L.R. 1, 8; *Allied Carpets Group Plc v MacFarlane* [2002] EWHC 1155, [2002] P.N.L.R. 38 at [32]–[33]; *Burridge v MPH Soccer Management Ltd* [2011] EWCA Civ 835. See, e.g. *Re Westerton* [1919] 2 Ch. 104 (bank deposit receipt); *Cotton v Heyl* [1930] 1 Ch. 510 (proprietary interest in invention); *Re Wheeler* [1938] Ch. 725 (money due under building contract); *Thomas v Harris* [1947] 1 All E.R. 444 (insurance policy); *Re Tout & Finch Ltd* [1954] 1 W.L.R. 178 (retention money under building contract); *Letts v IRC* [1957] 1 W.L.R. 201 (shares); cf. *Re Williams* [1917] 1 Ch. 1 (insurance policy); *James Talcott Ltd v John Lewis & Co Ltd* [1940] 3 All E.R. 592 (invoice); *Spellman v Spellman* [1961] 1 W.L.R. 921 (hire-purchase agreement); *E. Pfeiffer Weinkellerei-Weineinkauf GmbH v Arbuthnot Factors Ltd* [1988] 1 W.L.R. 150 (reservation of title clause); *Colonial Mutual General Insurance Co Ltd v A.N.Z. Banking Group (New Zealand) Ltd* [1995] 1 W.L.R. 1140 PC (insurance policy). It was held in *Phelps v Spon-Smith & Co* [2001] B.P.I.R. 326 that, although no formalities are required for an equitable assignment, three necessary requirements on the particular facts were: first, the intention to assign; secondly, clear identification of the chose which was

being assigned; and thirdly, some act by the assignor showing that he was passing the chose in action to the alleged assignee. None of these three was held to be satisfied. The third requirement (which Blackburne J., at [33], expressed as being "an outward expression by the assignor of his intention to make an immediate disposition of the subject matter of the assignment") was also held not to be made out in *Finlan v Eyton Morris Winfield* [2007] EWHC 914 (Ch), [2007] 4 All E.R. 143. Going the other way was *Coulter v Chief of Dorset Police* [2003] EWHC 3391 (Ch), [2004] 1 W.L.R. 1425 in which it was held that the benefit of a judgment (for costs) had been validly assigned in equity by a retiring chief constable to his successor. Patten J., at [16], said that there was: "... a sufficient outward manifestation of an intention that the successor office holder should obtain the benefits held on trust by a predecessor, for there to be an equitable assignment of the benefit of the judgment". On the question of whether the requirement of writing in the Copyright, Designs and Patents Act 1988 s.90(3) applies to an oral contract for the transmission of a legal interest in copyright, see *Western Front Ltd v Vestron Inc* [1987] F.S.R. 66, 76–78.

[100a] See below, para.19-045.

[101] Perhaps because of the difference in wording with Law of Property Act 1925 s.53(1)(b), which requires trusts of land to be *manifested and proved* by writing, it appears always to have been assumed that an oral disposition is void and not merely unenforceable.

[102] Quaere whether an equitable chose in action is necessarily an "equitable interest or trust". By s.53(2) it is expressly provided that the section does not affect the creation or operation of resulting, implied or constructive trusts, and in *Neville v Wilson* [1997] Ch. 144 the Court of Appeal held that an oral agreement to assign an equitable interest in shares constituted the promisor an implied or constructive trustee for the promisee, so that the requirement for writing contained in s.53(1)(c) was dispensed with by s.53(2). See further Hanbury and Martin, *Modern Equity*, 20th edn (2015), paras 3-004—3-016.

[103] *Grey v IRC* [1960] A.C. 1.

[104] *Grey v IRC* [1958] Ch. 690, 719; affirmed [1960] A.C. 1. Perhaps this should be regarded as a "subtrust": see (1958) 74 L.Q.R. 180, 182. But see Pettit, *Equity and the Law of Trusts*, 12th edn (2012), p.89; [1960] A.C. 1 at 16; above, para.19-022 n.89.

[105] This seems to follow from *William Cory & Son Ltd v IRC* [1965] A.C. 1088 though strictly speaking the decision is not inconsistent with the possibility that the exercise of the option to purchase in that case was invalidated by s.53(1)(c).

## Defective statutory assignments

*Replace paragraph with:*

**19-037** Difficult problems arise where a statutory assignment could have been used but the full requirements were not complied with. Where the defect is that no notice has been given to the debtor, it has been held that the assignment may be valid in equity without consideration, for the assignor has done all that he needed to do to transfer the chose, and notice can be given by the assignee.[135] Where the assignment was not made in writing, i.e. is oral, it will be void by statute if it ranks as a disposition of an equitable interest or trust.[136] If the subject-matter is a *legal* chose in action, it can still be argued that an assignor who has not made a statutory assignment has not done all that he can to transfer the chose; hence the transaction can at best be regarded as an agreement to assign and requires consideration. This view has been adopted in the High Court of Australia.[137] A counter-argument is, however, that before 1875 an assignee of a legal chose in action could not sue in his own name and only had a right to compel the assignor in accordance with the agreement to allow his name to be used and that this agreement required consideration; but that since 1875 the assignee can sue in his own name, joining the assignor if necessary as co-defendant, so that consideration is no longer necessary for any assignment. This argument may go too far[138] and may be based on an imperfect understanding of the old cases.[139] Those cases do not in fact indicate a settled view, and it may be that the better approach is that the question whether an oral transaction is an assignment or an agreement to assign is to be collected from its terms and not prejudged by the application of supposed rules.[140]

135 *Holt v Heatherfield Trust Ltd* [1942] 2 K.B. 1, above, para.19-034; *Magee v U.D.T. Finance Ltd* [1983] N.Z.L.R. 438. But as to options cf. *Warner Bros Records Inc v Rollgreen Ltd* [1976] Q.B. 430, above, para.19-005.

136 Above, para.19-026.

137 *Olsson v Dyson* (1969) 120 C.L.R. 365. See also *Anning v Anning* (1907) 4 C.L.R. 1049. Doubt was cast on some of the reasoning in *Olsson v Dyson* in *Corin v Patton* (1990) 169 C.L.R. 540 (Australia HC).

138 Peel (ed.), *Treitel on The Law of Contract*, 15th edn (2020), para.15-035.

139 See *Re Westerton* [1919] 2 Ch. 104; Peel (ed.), *Treitel on The Law of Contract*, 15th edn (2020), paras 15-027—15-036; below, paras 19-039—19-042.

140 See *German v Yates* (1915) 32 T.L.R. 52 (discussed (1955) 33 Can. Bar Rev. 284, 294–296).

## (c) Principles Applicable to Statutory and Equitable Assignments

### *(i) What Rights are Assignable*

*Change title of paragraph:*

**"No assignment clauses": the position at common law**[160]

160 See generally Allcock (1983) C.L.J. 328; Turner, "Legal assignment of rights of restricted assignability" [2008] L.M.C.L.Q. 306; Tolhurst and Carter, "Prohibitions on Assignment: A Choice to be Made" [2014] C.L.J. 405. **19-044**

*Replace paragraph with:*

In *Hendry v Chartsearch Ltd*[165] the majority of the Court of Appeal (Millett and Henry L.JJ., Evans L.J. preferring to leave the point open) held that, where there is a clause requiring consent, consent not to be unreasonably withheld,[166] it is fatal to the validity of the assignment that the debtor's consent was not sought; it is irrelevant that, on the facts, consent could not have been reasonably withheld. In *Sumitomo Mitsui Banking Corp Europe Ltd v Euler Hermes Europe SA (NV)*[166a] it was held that a clause permitting assignment only if the assignee confirmed to the debtor in writing its acceptance of the employer's repayment obligation pursuant to another clause of the contract prevented the assignee from obtaining rights against the debtor when that acceptance had not been given.[166b] **19-045**

165 *The Times*, September 16, 1998, CA.

166 See *British Gas Trading Ltd v Eastern Electricity Plc* Unreported December 18, 1996, CA, where it was held, upholding Colman J., *The Times*, November 29, 1996, that Eastern had unreasonably withheld its consent to an assignment.

166a [2019] EWHC 2250 (Comm), [2019] B.L.R. 561 at [37].

166b Unless there was a waiver of the requirement of writing, compare *MWB Business Exchange Centres Ltd v Rock Advertising Ltd* [2018] UKSC 24, [2018] 2 W.L.R. 1603: see [2019] EWHC 2250 (Comm) at [56]. On this aspect of the *MWB* case see below, para.22-045.

*Replace footnote 168 with:*

168 [1994] 1 A.C. 85, 108. See also *Hendry v Chartsearch Ltd*, *The Times*, September 16, 1998. In *Sumitomo Mitsui Banking Corp Europe Ltd v Euler Hermes Europe SA (NV)* [2019] EWHC 2250 (Comm), [2019] B.L.R. 561 at [35] it was accepted that failure to comply with the conditions imposed on assignment did not prevent the assignment being valid as between assignor and assignee. **19-046**

*Replace paragraph with:*

Moreover, it has been held that a covenant in a marriage settlement to settle after-acquired property could be enforced by the beneficiaries with respect to the proceeds of a life insurance policy that had been paid to the covenantor's executor, although the policy was expressed to be not assignable.[169] It has also been held that a purported assignment of a contract relating to the promotion and manage- **19-047** ment of boxing that was ineffective at law, because the contract prohibited assignment and involved personal services, was effective in equity as a declaration of trust of the benefit of the contract.[170] On the facts, this ensured that the parties' commercial intentions were effected. The distinction between a prohibited and therefore invalid assignment and a valid declaration of trust of the benefit of a contract was further analysed in *Barbados Trust Co Ltd v Bank of Zambia*.[171] A clause in a loan facility prevented assignment by the lender other than to a bank or financial institution unless the borrower (the Bank of Zambia) gave its prior written consent. There was an assignment to a bank (the Bank of America). That bank, without the borrower's consent, declared itself a trustee of its rights under the loan for the claimant, which was neither a bank nor a financial institution. The Court of Appeal (Waller L.J. dissenting) held that there had been no initially valid assignment to the Bank of America and, without that initially valid assignment, there could be no subsequent valid declaration of trust. However, had there been an initially valid assignment, the majority (Waller and Rix L.JJ., Hooper L.J. dissenting) thought that the Bank of America's declaration of trust would have been effective and that the beneficiary of the trust could have used the *Vandepitte* procedure[171a] to require the trustee to enforce the rights under the loan for the benefit of the beneficiary. The prohibition on assignment to a non-bank did not also prohibit a declaration of trust because a declaration of trust and an assignment are different and, as a matter of construction, the prohibition here did not extend to a declaration of trust.[172]

[169] *Re Turcan* (1888) 40 Ch. D. 5. See also *Re Griffin* [1899] 1 Ch. 408 and *Re Westerton* [1919] 2 Ch. 104, where it was held that bank deposits had been validly assigned though the deposit receipts were expressed to be not transferable in both cases; and *Spellman v Spellman* [1961] 1 W.L.R. 921, 925, per Danckwerts L.J.

[170] *Don King Productions Inc v Warren* [2000] Ch. 291: (it was also held that the benefit of the contract could be partnership property even though non-assignable). For criticism of the decision in *Don King*, making the argument that one cannot have a trust of, or charge over, unassignable rights, see Turner, "Charges of Unassignable Rights" (2004) 20 J.C.L. 97.

[171] [2007] EWCA Civ 148, [2007] 1 Lloyd's Rep. 495. See also *Co-operative Group Ltd v Birse Developments Ltd* [2014] EWHC 530 (TCC), [2014] B.L.R. 359.

[171a] "The trustee ... can take steps to enforce performance to the beneficiary by the other contracting party" and "if [the trustee] refuses to sue, the beneficiary can sue, joining the trustee as a defendant": *Vandepitte v Preferred Accident Insurance Corp* [1933] A.C. 70, 79.

[172] See the case-note on *Barbados Trust Co Ltd v Bank of Zambia* [2007] EWCA Civ 148, [2007] 1 Lloyd's Rep. 495 by M Smith, "Equitable Owners Enforcing Legal Rights?" (2008) 124 L.Q.R. 517 and also Smith and Leslie, *The Law of Assignment*, 3rd edn (2018) paras 25.46–25.52. The same authors point to another mechanism that can be used to avoid the effect of a prohibition, the "virtual assignment": see paras 18.22–18.24 and 25.53–25.54. See further Beale, Bridge, Gullifer and Lomnicka, *The Law of Security and Title-based Financing*, 3rd edn (2018), paras 7.80–7.90.

*Add new paragraph:*

19-047A **"No assignment clauses": legislative reform** The validity of "no-assignment clauses" at common law has been thought to be inconvenient, especially for small businesses, in the context of "receivables financing", where a business raises finance by selling debts owed to it by its customers to a financier. The financier may be content not to give notice of the assignment to the customer and to allow the business to continue to collect the debts as they fall due (often referred to as "non-notification" finance or "invoice discounting"). But in that scenario, where the ban on assignment is in practice irrelevant, the financier is running the risk of the business becoming insolvent. If, in contrast, the financier is only prepared to finance on a "notification" basis, so that it will receive payment from the debtor directly (often referred to as "factoring"), the ban on assignment is of central relevance and the financier may be unwilling to provide financing unless, for example, the customer can be persuaded to waive the no-assignment clause.[172a] It is for these reasons that there has been pressure for several years to reform the common law by invalidating some no assignment clauses. This led to s.1 of the Small Business, Enterprise and Employment Act 2015, which empowered the relevant Minister to make Regulations rendering ineffective some "no assignment" clauses, and the Business Contract Terms (Assignment of Receivables) Regulations 2018[172b] which have been made in exercise of that power. The Regulations apply to terms in contracts, entered into on or after December 31, 2018, which prohibit or restrict the assignment of receivables. Under reg.1, a receivable is a right to be paid under a contract for the supply of goods, services or intangible assets. Regulation 2(1) provides that a term has no effect to the extent that it prohibits or imposes a condition, or other restriction,[172c] on the assignment of a receivable arising under that contract or any other contract between the same parties. However, the Regulations apply only when the assignor (referred to as "the supplier") is not a large enterprise or a special purpose vehicle.[172d] Regulation 4 also excludes (presumably for specific policy reasons) various types of contract from the scope of reg.2(1). These include a contract for, or entered into in connection with, prescribed financial services; a contract which concerns any interest in land; a contract where one or more of the parties to the contract is acting for purposes which are outside a trade, business or profession; a contract where none of the parties to the contract has entered into it in the course of carrying on a business in the United Kingdom; contracts concerning national security; a contract which is entered into for the purposes of, or in connection with, the acquisition, disposal or transfer of an ownership interest in a firm, wherever it is incorporated or established, or of a business or undertaking or part of a business or undertaking, and which includes a statement to that effect; derivatives that are traded on markets; equipment leases; and various particular types of contracts involving petroleum licences, project finance and decommissioning and differences contracts under the Energy Acts 2008 and 2013 respectively.[172e]

[172a] The issues are explored in Beale, Gullifer and Paterson, "A case for interfering with freedom of contract? An empirically-informed study of bans on assignment" [2016] J.B.L. 203.

[172b] SI 2018/1254.

[172c] By reg.2(2), this includes confidentiality clauses that would prevent the financier from obtaining information necessary to determine the validity or value of the receivable, or the financier's ability to enforce it. The information that is treated as necessary is set out in reg.2(3).

[172d] By reg.3, reg.2(1) does not apply if the supplier (i.e. the person to whom the receivable is owed) is a "large enterprise" or a special purpose vehicle. Enterprises that are not treated as large include an individual, a partnership (other than an LLP or a limited partnership) or an unincorporated association, and companies (and there are equivalent provisions for LLPs) to which the small or the medium-sized companies regimes under Companies Act 2006 ss.381–384 and 465–467 applied at the date of their last-filed set of accounts. A special purpose vehicle is defined as a firm holding assets or financing commercial transactions which involve it incurring a liability under an agreement of £10 million or more.

[172e] For an account of the Regulations and the many exceptions see Beale, "The New Override of Bans on Assignment of Receivables" in Davies and Raczynska (eds), *Contents of Commercial Contracts: Terms Affecting Freedoms* (2020), Ch.7.

## Assignments savouring of maintenance

*In line 4, after "many important respects,", add new footnote 179a:*

[179a] e.g. to allow conditional fee arrangements, see above, para.16-085. **19-050**

## (ii) *Validity of Assignments against Assignor's Creditors and Successors in Title*

### Company liquidator or creditors

*Replace paragraph with:*

19-066 The position of a liquidator of a company which, prior to the commencement of the winding up, has assigned any of its rights is basically the same as that of a trustee in bankruptcy; that is, apart from assignments of future earnings, and from particular statutory provisions, a liquidator is bound by an assignment which would be binding on the company itself. But the statutory provisions relating to companies differ markedly from those relating to individual bankrupts in this particular respect. Apart from the general provisions relating to preferences, extortionate credit transactions, and transactions at an undervalue,[230] which are similar to those applying to individual bankrupts, the requirements of the Companies Act only apply to assignments by way of charge, normally but not necessarily a floating charge. By ss.859A–859Q of the Companies Act 2006, a company is required to register, inter alia, a charge on book debts, and failure to comply with the Act renders the charge void against a liquidator[231] or any creditor.[232] On the other hand, these sections, unlike s.344 of the Insolvency Act 1986, apply to any charge over many debts owed to the company,[232a] and not merely to a general charge or assignment. Further, failure to comply with the requirements of the Companies Act renders the charge void against any creditor of the company as well as against the liquidator.

[230] Insolvency Act 1986 ss.238–246. The provisions governing transactions defrauding creditors (ss.423–425 of the 1986 Act) are the same as those for individual bankrupts.

[231] See, e.g. *Orion Finance Ltd v Crown Financial Management Ltd* [1996] 2 B.C.L.C. 78, CA; *Orion Finance Ltd v Crown Financial Management Ltd (No.2)* [1996] 2 B.C.L.C. 382, CA. A liquidator includes, in certain circumstances, a person appointed in foreign proceedings in the nature of a winding-up: *NV Slavenburg's Bank v Intercontinental Natural Resources* [1980] 1 W.L.R. 1076, 1086–1087.

[232] On the meaning of creditor see Gough, *Company Charges*, 2nd edn (1998), pp.740–741; *Goode on Commercial Law*, edited by McKendrick, 5th edn (2016), para.24.51; *Re Ehrmann Bros Ltd* [1906] 2 Ch. 697.

[232a] Former s.860 of the Companies Act 2006 required registration of charges over specified types of property (e.g. book debts) and of any floating charge. Under s.859A any charge created by the company is registrable unless exempted by that section or other legislation, e.g. charges over money in bank accounts and some other forms of "financial collateral". For an account of the changes see Beale, Bridge, Gullifer, Lomnicka, *The Law of Security and Title-Based Financing*, 3rd edn (2018), paras 10.22–10.23.

*Replace footnote 233 with:*

19-067 [233] Companies Act 2006 ss.859A–859Q.

## (iii) *Priorities between Successive Assignees*

### Priorities

*Replace footnote 242 with:*

19-069 [242] *Dearle v Hall* (1823) 3 Russ. 1; see also *Lloyd v Banks* (1868) L.R. 3 Ch. App. 488; *Re Holmes* (1885) 29 Ch. D. 786; *Ward v Duncombe* [1893] A.C. 369; *Kelly v Selwyn* [1905] 2 Ch. 117; *Ellerman Lines Ltd v Lancaster Maritime Co Ltd* [1980] 2 Lloyd's Rep. 497; *The Attika Hope* [1988] 1 Lloyd's Rep. 439; *Compaq Computer Ltd v Abercorn Group Ltd* [1991] B.C.C. 484; *E. Pfeiffer Weinkellerei-Weineinkauf GmbH & Co v Arbuthnot Factors Ltd* [1988] 1 W.L.R. 150. The principle does not however apply in favour of a trustee in bankruptcy (*Re Anderson* [1911] 1 K.B. 896); a judgment creditor (*Scott v Lord Hastings* (1855) 4 Kay & J. 633); nor a volunteer (*Justice v Wynne* (1861) 12 Ir.Ch.Rep. 289). For further discussion of this difficult topic see *Snell's Equity*, 33rd edn (2014), paras 4.56–4.71-00;

Smith and Leslie, *The Law of Assignment*, 3rd edn (2018), paras 27.48–27.105; Beale, Bridge, Gullifer, Lomnicka, *The Law of Security and Title-Based Financing*, 3rd edn (2018), paras 14.09–14.20. See also Goode (1976) 92 L.Q.R. 554–559; Donaldson (1977) 93 L.Q.R. 324; Goode (1977) 93 L.Q.R. 487; McLauchlan (1980) 96 L.Q.R. 90; Oditah (1989) 9 O.J.L.S. 513; De Lacy [1999] Conv. 311.

### *(iv) Assignments "Subject to Equities"*

#### Assignments "subject to equities"

*Replace footnote 261 with:*

[261] *Geldof Metaalconstructie NV v Simon Carves Ltd* [2010] EWCA Civ 667, [2011] 1 Lloyd's Rep. 517. In *Wood v Commercial First Business Ltd (In Liquidation)* [2019] EWHC 2205 (Ch) (at [162]) it was held that claims for recovery of secret commissions on mortgages were not sufficiently connected to the mortgages to be available against assignees of the mortgages. **19-071**

*Add new paragraph:*

**Debtor's conduct may preclude reliance on defence** There is a separate question of whether the debtor's conduct may prevent it relying on a defence that it has against the assignor and that would otherwise be available also against the assignee, for example if the assignee made enquiries of the debtor before taking the assignment and the debtor gave the assignee misleading information, or if the debtor engaged in other inequitable conduct,[263a] or if the debtor is estopped.[263b] **19-071A**

[263a] *Mangles v Dixon* (1852) 3 H.L. Cas. 702 and *Athenaeum Life Assurance Society v Pooley* (1858) 3 De G. & J. 294, discussed in the *Bibby Factors* case [2015] EWCA Civ 1908 at [42]–[53]; see also *Property Links International Ltd v Coffee Republic* [2018] EWHC 3153 (Ch) at [35].

[263b] [2015] EWCA Civ 1908 at [54].

#### Claims for damages

*Replace footnote 266 with:*

[266] [1912] 1 K.B. 181. For criticism of this decision, see Peel (ed.), *Treitel on The Law of Contract*, 15th edn (2020), para.15-041. **19-072**

#### Successive assignments

*Replace footnote 272 with:*

[272] Peel (ed.), *Treitel on The Law of Contract*, 15th edn (2020), para.15-043. **19-074**

## 2. VICARIOUS PERFORMANCE

#### Vicarious performance

*Replace footnote 291 with:*

[291] *Stewart v Reavell's Garage* [1952] 2 Q.B. 545. This is to be distinguished from where the debtor's promise is not one to render the performance but merely to arrange for the services to be performed by another person (as the debtor's agent). In respect of the latter type of promise, the debtor's only obligation at common law is to exercise reasonable care and skill in selecting a competent person to perform. For this distinction (albeit that the promise in question was held to be of the former type) see *Wong Mee Wan v Kwan Kin Travel Services Ltd* [1996] 1 W.L.R. 38. See also Peel (ed.), *Treitel on The Law of Contract*, 15th edn (2020), para.17-013. **19-082**

## 4. ASSIGNMENT, NOVATION AND ACKNOWLEDGMENT

### Acknowledgment

*Replace footnote 317 with:*

19-091 [317] Peel (ed.), *Treitel on The Law of Contract*, 15th edn (2020), para.15-004.

*Replace footnote 322 with:*

19-092 [322] For the suggestion that the claimant in *Shamia v Joory* [1958] 1 Q.B. 448 might now have a right under the Contracts (Rights of Third Parties) Act 1999, see Peel (ed.), *Treitel on The Law of Contract*, 15th edn (2020), para.15-004.

CHAPTER 20

# DEATH AND BANKRUPTCY



## 1. DEATH

### When right of action arises

*In line 2, after "grant of probate.", add new footnote 7a:*

[7a] *Goodman v Goodman* [2014] Ch. 186; *Williams v Russell Price Farm Services Ltd* [2020] EWHC 1088 (Ch). **20-004**

CHAPTER 21

# PERFORMANCE



## 2. TIME OF PERFORMANCE

*Replace footnote 59 with:* 21-011

[59] Stoljar (1955) 71 L.Q.R. 527; Peel (ed.), *Treitel on The Law of Contract*, 15th edn (2020), paras 18-111—18-127; *Carter's Breach of Contract*, 2nd edn (2018), paras 5-38—5-69; J.E. Stannard, *Delay in the Performance of Contractual Obligations*, 2nd edn (2018), especially Chs 1–3; Andrews, Clarke, Tettenborn and Virgo, *Contractual Duties: Performance, Breach, Termination and Remedies*, 2nd edn (2017), Ch.11.

### Consequences of time being "of the essence"

*Replace footnote 106 with:*

[106] In the sense examined above, paras 13-025 et seq. In the case where the failure in timely performance is trivial, it is possible that the strictness of the rule may be tempered by the de minimis principle. However, to the extent that the de minimis rule has any application at all (which is doubtful), its role in commercial transactions is very narrow (*Lombard North Central Plc v European Skyjets Ltd (In Liquidation)* [2020] EWHC 679 (QB) at [44]–[45]). 21-015

### Form of relief: additional time to pay

*Replace footnote 116 with:*

[116] *Scandinavian Trading Tanker Co AB v Flota Petrolera Ecuatoriana* [1983] 2 A.C. 694; *Sport Internationaal Bussum BV v Inter-Footwear Ltd* [1984] 1 W.L.R. 776; *Vauxhall Motors Ltd v Manchester Ship Canal Co Ltd* [2019] UKSC 46, [2019] 3 W.L.R. 852. The jurisdiction is not, however, confined to proprietary or possessory rights in land but extends to proprietary or possessory rights arising under a commercial contract: *BICC Plc v Burndy Corp* [1985] Ch. 232. The scope of the jurisdiction, while clear in legal terms, has resulted in the drawing of distinctions which are difficult to defend in commercial terms (for example, the distinction between *Sport International Bussum* and *BICC v Burndy* is particularly difficult to defend). Although there have been criticisms of the scope of the jurisdiction, the courts continue to affirm that the jurisdiction does not extend to mere contractual rights and is confined 21-017

to the forfeiture of proprietary or possessory rights: *Cukurova Finance International Ltd v Alfa Telecom Turkey Ltd* [2013] UKPC 2, [2016] A.C. 923 at [94].

### Consequences of "time being made of essence"

*Replace footnote 119 with:*

21-018 [119] *Behzadi v Shaftesbury Hotels Ltd* [1992] Ch. 1, 12, 24; *Re Olympia & York Canary Wharf Ltd (No.2)* [1993] B.C.C. 159, 171–173; *Ocular Sciences Ltd v Aspect Vision Care Ltd* [1997] R.P.C. 289, 432–433; *Etzin v Reece* [2002] All E.R. (D) 405 (Jul); *Alegrow SA v Yayla Agro Gida San Ve Nak SA* [2020] EWHC 1845 (Comm) at [56]–[57].

## 3. PARTIAL PERFORMANCE OF AN ENTIRE OBLIGATION

21-028 *Replace footnote 179 with:*

[179] The law on "entire contracts" or, more accurately, entire obligations is reviewed in the Law Commission's Report (No.121 (1983)), paras 2.1–2.88 and Note of Dissent (pp.36–37). (This report is not to be implemented: see the 19th Annual Report of the Commission, para.2.11.) See also Peel (ed.), *Treitel on The Law of Contract*, 15th edn (2020), paras 17-031—17-048; Andrews, Clarke, Tettenborn and Virgo, *Contractual Duties: Performance, Breach, Termination and Remedies*, 2nd edn (2017), Ch.15, *Carter's Breach of Contract*, 2nd edn (2018), paras 6-84—6-93; Williams (1941) 57 L.Q.R. 373, 490. (The enactment of the Law Reform (Frustrated Contracts) Act 1943 (below, para.23-074) has rendered obsolete some of the common law discussed in this article.)

### Substantial performance

*Replace footnote 201 with:*

21-033 [201] Peel (ed.), *Treitel on The Law of Contract*, 15th edn (2020), para.17-040.

## 4. PAYMENT

## (a) In General

### Place of payment

*Replace footnote 327 with:*

21-056 [327] *Robey & Co v Snaefell Mining Co Ltd* (1887) 20 Q.B.D. 152; *The Eider* [1893] P. 119, 128; *Thompson v Palmer* [1893] 2 Q.B. 80; *Charles Duval & Co Ltd v Gans* [1904] 2 K.B. 685; *Fowler v Midland Electric Corp for Power Distribution Ltd* [1917] 1 Ch. 656; *Colt Technologies Services v SG Global Group SRL* [2020] EWHC 1417 (Ch) at [43]–[50]. The general rule applies to a tenant: *Haldane v Johnson* (1853) 8 Exch. 689; also where the creditor was out of England when the contract was made, but not where the creditor left England after the date: *Fessard v Mugnier* (1865) 18 C.B.(N.S.) 286. The presumption that the debtor must seek out the creditor at his place of business and pay him there is of long standing but it is readily displaced implicitly and not just expressly; in considering whether the presumption has been displaced the court can take account of modern ways of making commercial payment based on its daily experience: *Canyon Offshore Ltd v GDF Suez E&P Nederland BV* [2014] EWHC 3810 (Comm), [2015] Bus. L.R. 578 at [38]; *Lombard North Central plc v European Skyjets Ltd* [2020] EWHC 679 (QB) at [43].

## (b) Appropriation of Payments

### Rights to appropriate payments

*Replace footnote 357 with:*

21-061 [357] *Peters v Anderson* (1814) 5 Taunt. 596; *Simson v Ingham* (1823) 2 B. & C. 65; *Cory Bros & Co Ltd v Owners of Turkish S.S. "Mecca"* [1897] A.C. 286; *West Bromwich Building Society v Crammer* [2002] EWHC 2618 (Ch), [2003] B.P.I.R. 783; *Thomas v Ken Thomas Ltd* [2006] EWCA Civ 1504, [2007] Bus. L.R. 429 at [19]; *SAS Institute Inc v World Programming Ltd* [2019] EWHC 2496 (Comm) at [20]–[21].

## Debtor's right to appropriate

*Replace paragraph with:*

It is essential that an appropriation by the debtor should take the form of a communication, express or implied, to the creditor of the debtor's intention to appropriate the payment to a specified debt (or debts), so that the creditor may know that his rights of appropriation as creditor cannot arise.[358] It is not essential that the debtor should expressly specify at the time of the payment, which debt or account he intended the payment to be applied to. His intention may be collected from other circumstances showing that he intended at the time of the payment to appropriate it to a specific debt or account.[359] The intention of the debtor to make the appropriation must, however, be clearly established on an objective view of all the circumstances of the case as known to both parties.[359a] Thus, where at the date of the payment some of his debts are statute-barred and others are not, it will be inferred (in the absence of evidence to the contrary) that the debtor appropriated the payment to the debts that were not so barred.[360] **21-062**

[358] *Leeson v Leeson* [1936] 2 K.B. 156, 161; *Stepney Corp v Osofsky* [1937] 3 All E.R. 289; *Thomas v Ken Thomas Ltd* [2006] EWCA Civ 1504, [2007] Bus. L.R. 429 at [19].

[359] *Newmarch v Clay* (1811) 14 East 239, 244; *Shaw v Picton* (1825) 4 B. & C. 715; *Young v English* (1843) 7 Beav. 10; *Nash v Hodgson* (1855) 6 De G.M. & G. 474; *R. v Miskin Lower Justices* [1953] 1 Q.B. 533; *Khandanpour v Chambers* [2019] EWCA Civ 570 at [25].

[359a] *Khandanpour v Chambers* [2019] EWCA Civ 570 at [27]. The intention of the debtor may be express, implied or presumed (*SAS Institute Inc v World Programming Ltd* [2019] EWHC 2496 (Comm) at [55]) and it may, in a suitable case, relate to the appropriation of payments which are owed to the debtor by third parties.

[360] *Nash v Hodgson* (1855) 6 De G.M. & G. 474; cf. a balance owing on a current account: *Re Footman Bower & Co Ltd* [1961] Ch. 443 (and see below, para.21-068).

## Creditor's right to appropriate

*Replace paragraph with:*

Where the debtor has not exercised his option, and the right to appropriate has therefore devolved upon the creditor,[362] he may exercise it at any time "up to the very last moment"[363] or until something happens which makes it inequitable for him to exercise it.[364] The creditor's right is thus a "contingent" right which arises only in the event that the debtor does not make an appropriation.[364a] This being the case, the right of the creditor cannot logically occur earlier than the time of payment by the debtor, although it may be possible for a creditor to make a "contingent appropriation", that is to say, an appropriation which is only to operate in the event that the debtor fails to make an appropriation.[364b] The appropriation must be communicated in some form by the creditor to the debtor.[364c] This communication may take the form of an express notification given by the creditor to the debtor or it may take the form of the creditor dealing with the payment in a form that is visible to the debtor, as in the case where the creditor includes the payment in a running account between the parties.[364d] The appropriation may be made by a computer system which has been set up by the creditor as where, for example, a lender's computerised payment system appropriates payment by a debtor to the discharge of a particular debt.[365] What is "the very last moment" depends on the circumstances of each case. In one instance the creditor was held entitled, in the witness-box during the course of his action, to exercise his right to appropriate a payment by his debtor, as nothing had previously happened to determine his right of election.[366] The creditor need not make his election in express terms. He may declare it by bringing an **21-063** action or in any other way that makes his meaning and intention plain.[367] An entry in the creditor's books applying a payment to a particular debt does not constitute an election which will preclude the creditor from afterwards applying it to another debt, unless the entry has been communicated to the debtor.[368] Once, however, the election is made and communicated[369], it is irrevocable.[370]

[362] *Lowther v Heaver* (1889) 41 Ch. D. 248; *Potomek Construction Ltd v Zurich Securities Ltd* [2003] EWHC 2827 (Ch), [2004] 1 All E.R. (Comm) 672 at [69]. In the case of hire-purchase payments, see n.357, above.

[363] *Cory Bros & Co v Owners of Turkish S.S. "Mecca"* [1897] A.C. 286, 294.

[364] *Thomas v Ken Thomas Ltd* [2006] EWCA Civ 1504, [2007] Bus. L.R. 429 at [19].

[364a] *SAS Institute Inc v World Programming Ltd* [2019] EWHC 2496 (Comm) at [20]–[21]. The right of the creditor may also be excluded by the operation of a rule of law: see [2019] EWHC 2496 (Comm) at [27] and see also para.21-064, where it is noted that creditor may not appropriate to an illegal or irrecoverable demand.

[364b] *SAS Institute Inc v World Programming Ltd* [2019] EWHC 2496 (Comm) at [22].

[364c] *SAS Institute Inc v World Programming Ltd* [2019] EWHC 2496 (Comm) at [64]–[68].

[364d] *SAS Institute Inc v World Programming Ltd* [2019] EWHC 2496 (Comm) at [64].

[365] *Capital Home Loans Ltd v Countrywide Surveyors Ltd* [2011] 1 E.G.L.R. 153 at [72].

[366] *Seymour v Pickett* [1905] 1 K.B. 715. See also *Smith v Betty* [1903] 2 K.B. 317.

[367] *Cory Bros & Co Ltd v Owners of Turkish S.S. "Mecca"* [1897] A.C. 286, 294.

[368] *Simson v Ingham* (1823) 2 B. & C. 65; cf. *Deeley v Lloyds Bank Ltd* [1912] A.C. 756, 783, 784.

[369] The existence and extent of the creditor's obligation to communicate the appropriation requires further clarification. It may be that there is no obligation to communicate but only a requirement that there be some "overt act" by the creditor from which it can be sufficiently inferred that he has in fact made the election to appropriate (*Capital Home Loans Ltd v Countrywide Surveyors Ltd* [2011] 1 E.G.L.R. 153 at [86]) but, on the other hand, there are cases such as *Simson v Ingham* (1823) 2 B. & C. 65 which appear to suggest that there is an obligation to communicate imposed upon the creditor. If there is an obligation to communicate, a further question arises, namely to whom must the communication be made? Must it be to the debtor himself or can it be to any person who has in interest in how the payments were appropriated? In *Capital Home Loans Ltd v Countrywide Surveyors Ltd* H.H.J. Hazel Marshall Q.C. inclined (at [87]–[88]) to the latter view but that was a case in which the debtor had no obvious interest in the appropriation.

[370] *Smith v Betty* [1903] 2 K.B. 317; *Seymour v Pickett* [1905] 1 K.B. 715; *Albermarle Supply Co Ltd v Hind & Co* [1928] 1 K.B. 307.

## (d) Payment by Negotiable Instrument or Documentary Credit

### Alteration of instrument

*Replace footnote 450 with:*

**21-083** [450] *Alderson v Langdale* (1832) 3 B. & Ad. 660 (the alteration deprived the debtor of his remedy on the bill against the third party); cf. Bills of Exchange Act 1882 s.64. See also below, paras 25-020, 25-025; *Byles on Bills of Exchange and Cheques*, 30th edn (2020), paras 20-01—20-21.

CHAPTER 22

# DISCHARGE BY AGREEMENT



## 3. ACCORD AND SATISFACTION

### Compromise

*Replace footnote 44 with:*

[44] See Foskett, *The Law and Practice of Compromise*, 9th edn (2020). **22-013**

### Payment of part of a debt

*Replace footnote 64 with:*

[64] For the compromise of disputed claims, see above, paras 4-047—4-057. **22-016**

### Payment in different form, at earlier time, in different place

*Replace footnote 71 with:*

[71] *MWB Business Exchange Centres Ltd v Rock Advertising Ltd* [2016] EWCA Civ 553, [2017] Q.B. 604 (where the practical benefit obtained by the creditor landlord as a result of the rescheduling of the tenant's payment obligations under the licence was that the tenant would continue to occupy the property and it would not be left standing empty for some time at further loss to the landlord). On this case see further above, para.4-119. The Supreme Court found it unnecessary to deal with this issue when hearing an appeal from the decision of the Court of Appeal ([2018] UKSC 24, [2019] A.C. 119 at [18]). Lord Sumption in his brief consideration of the issue noted on the one hand that "practical expectation of benefit was the very thing which the House of Lords held not to be adequate consideration in *Foakes v Beer*" but, on the other hand, stated that *Foakes v Beer* "is probably ripe for re-examination". However the appeal in *MWB Business Exchange Centres* was held not to be an appropriate case for such a re-examination both because of the fact that "an enlarged panel of the court" had not been set up to hear the appeal and because the court's consideration of the issue would, in the event, have been no more than by way of obiter dictum. **22-017**

### Evidence of accord

*Replace footnote 81 with:*

22-022 [81] *Stour Valley Builders v Stuart, The Independent,* February 9, 1993, CA; cf. *Pereira v Inspirations East Ltd* (1992) C.A.T. 1048, discussed in more detail by Foskett, *The Law and Practice of Compromise*, 9th edn (2020), paras 3-33—3-44.

## 5. VARIATION

### Variation

*Replace footnote 130 with:*

22-032 [130] *Robinson v Page* (1826) 3 Russ. 114; *Goss v Lord Nugent* (1833) 5 B. & Ad. 58, 65; *Stead v Dawber* (1839) 10 A. & E. 57, 65; *Dodd v Churton* [1897] 1 Q.B. 562; *Fenner v Blake* [1900] 1 Q.B. 426; *Royal Exchange Assurance v Hope* [1928] Ch. 179; *Greenhouse v Paysafe Financial Services Ltd* [2018] EWHC 3296 (Comm) at [13]. See Dugdale and Yates (1976) 39 M.L.R. 680.

### Form of variation

*Replace footnote 135 with:*

22-033 [135] *Robinson v Page* (1826) 3 Russ. 114; *Stead v Dawber* (1839) 10 A. & E. 57; *Marshall v Lynn* (1840) 6 M. & W. 109; *Noble v Ward* (1867) L.R. 2 Ex. 135; *Sanderson v Graves* (1875) L.R. 10 Ex. 234; *Plevins v Downing* (1876) 1 C.P.D. 220; *British and Beningtons Ltd v N.W. Cachar Tea Co Ltd* [1923] A.C. 48; *United Dominions Trust (Jamaica) Ltd v Shoucair* [1969] 1 A.C. 340; *Richards v Creighton-Griffiths (Investments) Ltd* (1972) 225 E.G. 2104; *New Hart Builders Ltd v Brindley* [1975] Ch. 342; *McCausland v Duncan Lawrie Ltd* [1997] 1 W.L.R. 38; *Greenhouse v Paysafe Financial Services Ltd* [2018] EWHC 3296 (Comm) at [13].

### Effect of extra works

*Replace footnote 161 with:*

22-038 [161] *Macintosh v Midland Counties Ry* (1845) 14 M. & W. 548; *Legge v Horlock* (1848) 12 Q.B. 1015; *Jones v St John's College, Oxford* (1870) L.R. 6 Q.B. 115; *Tew v Newbold-on-Avon United District School Board* (1884) 1 Cab. & E. 260; *North Midland Building Ltd v Cyden Homes Ltd* [2018] EWCA Civ 1744, [2018] B.L.R. 565.

## 6. WAIVER

### Contracting out of waiver

*Replace paragraph with:*

22-045 It is not uncommon for contracting parties to seek by a term of their contract to exclude or restrict the operation of the doctrine of waiver. Thus a contract term may provide that in no event shall any delay, neglect or forbearance in enforcing any term of the contract be or be deemed a waiver of that term. Another frequently encountered term is one which provides that the contract can only be altered if the parties go through a prescribed formality (such as a written amendment, signed by both parties). Contracting parties are free to stipulate that a particular act, such as payment of a rental instalment under an equipment lease, should not be taken to waive a right to terminate for an earlier breach.[195] The freedom of contracting parties also extends to agreeing that any amendment to their contract must be made in writing and signed by both parties and the courts will give effect to such a clause.[196] English law therefore permits contracting parties to bind themselves as to the form of any variation to their contract and in this way to restrain their autonomy of action for the future.[197] There has been held to be no "conceptual inconsistency" between a general rule which enables contracts to be made informally and a specific rule that effect will be given to a contract term which requires that any variation be made in writing.[198] However, there may come a point where the actions of the parties in reliance upon the non-compliant oral variation are such that they will trigger the operation of an estoppel the effect of which will be to prevent a party from relying upon a contract term which lays down conditions for the formal validity of a variation. But the circumstances in which such an estoppel may operate largely remain to be defined.[198a] At a minimum there must be some words or conduct which unequivocally represents that the variation is valid notwithstanding its informality and "something more would be required for this purpose than the informal promise itself".[199]

195 *State Securities Plc v Initial Industry Ltd* [2004] EWHC 3482 (Ch), [2004] All E.R. (D) 317 (Jan) at [57]. For a clause to have this effect it may be necessary to state in express terms that payment should not be taken to waive a right to terminate for an earlier breach, because the courts are likely to be slow to infer such an intention where the clause is worded in general terms and refers merely to the "inaction [or] failure to exercise a right or delay": *Lombard North Central Plc v European Skyjets Ltd (In Liquidation)* [2020] EWHC 679 (QB) at [74].

196 *MWB Business Exchange Centres Ltd v Rock Advertising Ltd* [2018] UKSC 24, [2019] A.C. 119. The decision in *MWB* has been held to apply, by analogy, to no waiver clauses: *GPP Big Field LLP v Solar EPC Solutions SL (formerly Prosolia Siglio XXI)* [2018] EWHC 2866 (Comm), [203]. While a no waiver clause can itself be waived, the courts are likely to conclude that there has been such a waiver only where there is something that indicates that the waiver was to be effective notwithstanding the non-compliance with the no waiver clause: *Sumitomo Mistui Banking Corp Europe Ltd v Euler Hermes Europe SA (NV)* [2019] EWHC 2250 (Comm), [2019] B.L.R. 561 at [64].

197 *MWB Business Exchange Centres Ltd v Rock Advertising Ltd* [2018] UKSC 24, [2019] A.C. 119 at [11]; *NHS Commissioning Board v Vasant* [2019] EWCA Civ 1245, [2020] 1 All E.R. (Comm) 799 at [32].

198 *MWB Business Exchange Centres Ltd v Rock Advertising Ltd* [2018] UKSC 24, [2019] A.C. 119 at [15].

198a Although the courts have recognised the principle that estoppel has a role to play, they have not, as yet, identified the precise circumstances in which estoppel will operate: *Kabab-Ji SAL (Lebanon) v Kout Food Group (Kuwait)* [2020] EWCA Civ 6, [2020] 1 Lloyd's Rep 269 at [71]–[81]; *Great Dunmow Estates Ltd v Crest Nicholson Operations Ltd* [2019] EWCA Civ 1683, [2020] 2 All E.R. (Comm) 97 at [26]; *C Spencer Ltd v MW High Tech Projects UK Ltd* [2019] EWHC 2547 (TCC), [2019] B.L.R. 643 at [69].

199 *MWB Business Exchange Centres Ltd v Rock Advertising Ltd* [2018] UKSC 24, [2019] A.C. 119 at [16], citing the decision of the House of Lords in *Actionstrength Ltd v International Glass Engineering IN.GL.EN SpA* [2003] UKHL 17, [2003] 2 A.C. 541 at [9] and [51]. To similar effect see art.29(2) of the Vienna Convention on Contracts for the International Sale of Goods and art.2.1.18 of the UNIDROIT Principles of International Commercial Contracts, the former of which was considered by the Court of Appeal in *Kabab-Ji SAL (Lebanon) v Kout Food Group (Kuwait)* [2020] EWCA Civ 6, [2020] 1 Lloyd's Rep 269 at [74]–[77].

## Waiver of breach

*Replace paragraph with:*

One party may waive his right to terminate a contract consequent upon a repudiation of the contract by the other party.[203] It is, however, important to distinguish between the case in which a party waives his right to treat the contract as repudiated but does not abandon his right to claim damages for the loss suffered as a result of the breach[204] and the case where the innocent party waives not only his right to terminate performance of the contract but also his claim for damages for the breach.[205] The former is an example of waiver by election,[206] whereas the latter is more properly classified as a species of waiver by estoppel.[207] **22-047**

203 See below, para.24-007.

204 *Motor Oil Hellas (Corinth) Refineries SA v Shipping Corp of India* [1990] 1 Lloyd's Rep. 391, 397–398.

[205] This is sometimes known as "total waiver"; see Sale of Goods Act 1979 s.11(2); *Benjamin's Sale of Goods*, 10th edn (2017), paras 12-036—12-038; Peel (ed.), *Treitel on The Law of Contract*, 15th edn (2020), para.18-103 and below, para.24-007.

[206] See below, para.24-007.

[207] See below, para.24-007. There are important differences between the two types of waiver; see below, para.24-008 and Peel (ed.), *Treitel on The Law of Contract*, 15th edn (2020) at paras 18-089—18-104.

## 7. PROVISION FOR DISCHARGE IN THE CONTRACT ITSELF

### Express provision

*Replace footnote 213 with:*

**22-048** [213] See, e.g. *Stockloser v Johnson* [1954] 1 Q.B. 476; *Barton Thompson & Co Ltd v Stapling Machines Co* [1966] Ch. 499; *Shiloh Spinners Ltd v Harding* [1973] A.C. 691; *Starside Properties Ltd v Mustapha* [1974] 1 W.L.R. 816; *B.I.C.C. Plc v Burndy Corp* [1985] Ch. 232; *Transag Haulage Ltd v Leyland DAF Finance Plc* [1994] B.C.C. 356; *On Demand Information Plc v Michael Gerson (Finance) Plc* [2001] 1 W.L.R. 155; *Cukurova Finance International Ltd v Alfa Telecom Turkey Ltd* [2013] UKPC 2, [2016] A.C. 923; *Vauxhall Motors Ltd v Manchester Ship Canal Co Ltd* [2019] UKSC 46, [2019] 3 W.L.R. 852. Contrast *Galbraith v Mitchenall Estates Ltd* [1965] 2 Q.B. 473; *Mardorf Peach & Co Ltd v Attica Sea Carriers Corp of Liberia* [1977] A.C. 850; *Afovos Shipping Co SA v R. Pagnan and Filli* [1983] 1 W.L.R. 195; *Scandinavian Trading Tanker Co AB v Flota Petrolera Ecuatoriana* [1983] 2 A.C. 694; *Sport Internationaal Bussum BV v Inter-Footwear Ltd* [1984] 1 W.L.R. 776; *Union Eagle Ltd v Golden Achievement Ltd* [1997] A.C. 514; *Etzin v Reece* [2002] All E.R. (D) 405 (Jul); *More OG Romsdal Fylkesbatar AS v The Demise Charterers of the Ship "Jotunheim"* [2004] EWHC 671 (Comm), [2005] 1 Lloyd's Rep. 181; *Celestial Aviation Trading 71 Ltd v Paramount Airways Private Ltd* [2010] EWHC 185 (Comm), [2010] 1 C.L.C. 165.

CHAPTER 23

# DISCHARGE BY FRUSTRATION



## 1. INTRODUCTION

### Narrow scope

*Replace footnote 5 with:*

23-003

[5] *Pioneer Shipping Ltd v B.T.P. Tioxide Ltd (The Nema)* [1982] A.C. 724, 752; *Edwinton Commercial Corp v Tsavliris Russ (Worldwide Salvage & Towage) Ltd (The Sea Angel)* [2007] EWCA Civ 547, [2007] 2 Lloyd's Rep. 517 at [111]; *Gold Group Properties Ltd v BDW Trading Ltd* [2010] EWHC 323 (TCC), [2010] B.L.R. 235 at [68]; *Canary Wharf (BP4) T1 Ltd v European Medicines Agency* [2019] EWHC 335 (Ch) at [22]–[24]. See also *Lee Chee Wei v Tan Hor Peow Victor* [2007] SGCA 22, [2007] 3 S.L.R. 537 at [48].

## 2. THE TEST FOR FRUSTRATION

*Replace footnote 24 with:* 23-007

[24] See Treitel, *Frustration and Force Majeure*, 3rd edn (2010), paras 16-006—16-176; Peel (ed.), *Treitel on The Law of Contract*, 15th edn (2020), paras 19-123—19-133; J. Beatson, A. Burrows and J. Cartwright, *Anson's Law of Contract*, 31st edn (2020), pp.479–484; Cheshire, Fifoot and Furmston, *Law of Contract*, 17th edn (2017), pp.711–716; Andrews, Clarke, Tettenborn and Virgo, *Contractual Duties: Performance, Breach, Termination and Remedies*, 2nd edn (2017), Ch.16; Webber, *Effect of War on Contracts*, 2nd edn (1946), pp.404–478; McNair and Watts, *The Legal Effects of War*, 4th edn (1966),

pp.166 et seq., based on (1919) 35 L.Q.R. 84 and (1940) 56 L.Q.R. 173; Wade (1940) 56 L.Q.R. 519. For a comparison of different legal systems see E. Hondius and H.C. Grigoleit, *Unexpected Circumstances in European Contract Law* (2011).

### Introduction

*Replace footnote 28 with:*

23-007 [28] Citing *Hirji Mulji v Cheong Yue S.S. Co Ltd* [1926] A.C. 497, 510; *Joseph Constantine S.S. Line Ltd v Imperial Smelting Corp Ltd* [1942] A.C. 154, 183, 193; *National Carriers Ltd v Panalpina (Northern) Ltd* [1981] A.C. 675, 701. See also *Canary Wharf (BP4) T1 Ltd v European Medicines Agency* [2019] EWHC 335 (Ch) at [25].

### Objections to the implied term test

*Replace footnote 42 with:*

23-011 [42] [1981] A.C. 675, 687, 702, 717 (cf. at 693, 694). See also *Canary Wharf (BP4) T1 Ltd v European Medicines Agency* [2019] EWHC 335 (Ch) at [26(1)].

### Test of a radical change in the obligation

*Replace footnote 49 with:*

23-012 [49] *National Carriers Ltd v Panalpina (Northern) Ltd* [1981] A.C. 675; *Pioneer Shipping Ltd v B.T.P. Tioxide Ltd* [1982] A.C. 724; *Canary Wharf (BP4) T1 Ltd v European Medicines Agency* [2019] EWHC 335 (Ch) at [26(5)].

### Construction of the contract

*Replace footnote 59 with:*

23-014 [59] [1956] A.C. 696, 720–721, per Lord Reid; cf. 729, per Lord Radcliffe. In *Canary Wharf (BP4) T1 Ltd v European Medicines Agency* [2019] EWHC 335 (Ch) at [29] Marcus Smith J. emphasised that the interpretation of the contract is the "beginning" rather than the "end of the doctrine of frustration".

### Practical differences between the tests

*Replace footnote 76 with:*

23-018 [76] Peel (ed.), *Treitel on The Law of Contract*, 15th edn (2020), paras 19-123—19-133; Treitel, *Frustration and Force Majeure*, 3rd edn (2014), paras 16-013—16-017.

### A "multi-factorial" approach

*Replace footnote 78 with:*

23-019 [78] *Edwinton Commercial Corp v Tsavliris Russ (Worldwide Salvage & Towage) Ltd (The Sea Angel)* [2007] EWCA Civ 547, [2007] 2 Lloyd's Rep. 517 at [111]; *Melli Bank Plc v Holbud Ltd* [2013] EWHC 1506 (Comm), [2013] All E.R. (D) 165 (May) at [15]; *Bunge SA v Kyla Shipping Co Ltd* [2013] EWCA Civ 734, [2013] 2 Lloyd's Rep. 463 (affirming [2012] EWHC 3522 (Comm), [2013] 1 Lloyd's Rep. 565), where Longmore L.J. stated (at [7]) that the "tendency in the modern application of the law of frustration has been to move away from inflexible rules, such as cost versus value, to a multi-factorial approach". See also *Canary Wharf (BP4) T1 Ltd v European Medicines Agency* [2019] EWHC 335 (Ch) at [39]. The multi-factorial approach has also been approved by the Supreme Court of New Zealand in *Planet Kids Ltd v Auckland Council* [2013] NZSC 147, [2014] 1 N.Z.L.R. 149 at [62]. One consequence of the adoption of the multi-factorial approach may be to make it more difficult to strike out a claim that a contract has been frustrated, because of the need to have regard to the evidence as it relates to the various factors: see, for example, *Natixis v Famfa Oil* [2020] 2 WLUK 330.

## 3. ILLUSTRATIONS OF THE DOCTRINE

### (a) General

#### Methods of classifying the cases on frustration

*Replace paragraph with:*

Since the doctrine of frustration depends on the construction of the "obligation" created by the particular contract in the light of its own circumstances, reported decisions can be only a rough guide to the future application of the doctrine.[81] Nevertheless, the scope of the doctrine in practice must be gleaned from a study of the decisions in the law reports, although there is no "*numerus clausus*" or "limited class" of frustrating event.[81a] The cases may be classified by reference either to the different types of frustrating events (such as a change in the law or subsequent illegality,[82] outbreak of war,[83] cancellation of an expected event[84] or delay[85]), or by reference to particular categories of contracts where frustration has been invoked (such as personal contracts,[86] charterparties,[87] sale and carriage of goods,[88] building contracts,[89] leases,[90] and contracts for the sale of land[91]). The doctrine of executive necessity, according to which the Crown is unable to fetter by contractual undertakings the exercise in the future of its executive discretion, is discussed elsewhere in this Volume[92]; the discharge of contracts by the winding up of a company,[93] or by bankruptcy,[94] is also discussed elsewhere. **23-020**

[81] See above, para.23-014 n.60.

[81a] *Canary Wharf (BP4) T1 Ltd v European Medicines Agency* [2019] EWHC 335 (Ch) at [41].

[82] Below, paras 23-022 et seq.

[83] Below, para.23-030.

[84] Below, paras 23-033—23-034.

[85] Below, para.23-035.

[86] Below, paras 23-037—23-040.

[87] Below, paras 23-041—23-046.

[88] Below, paras 23-047—23-048.

[89] Below, paras 23-049—23-051.

[90] Below, paras 23-052—23-056.

[91] Below, para.23-057.

[92] See above, paras 11-007—11-009.

[93] See above, paras 10-047—10-051.

[94] See above, paras 20-032 et seq.

#### Illustrations of frustrating events

*Replace footnote 102 with:*

[102] *Davis Contractors Ltd v Fareham U.D.C.* [1956] A.C. 696, 729 (below, para.23-050); *National Carriers Ltd v Panalpina (Northern) Ltd* [1981] A.C. 675, 707; *Larrinaga & Co Ltd v Société Franco-Americaine des Phosphates de Médulla, Paris* (1923) 30 T.L.R. 316; *Hangkam Kwingtong Woo v Liu Lan Fong* [1951] A.C. 707; *Palmco Shipping Inc v Continental Ore Corp* [1970] 2 Lloyd's Rep. 21, 32 (a difference in expense between the expected and the actual performance is not sufficient to produce frustration); *United International Pictures v Cine Bes Filmcheck VE Yapimcilik AS* [2003] EWHC 798 (Comm), [2003] All E.R. (D) 278 (Apr) (abandonment of exchange rate mechanism held not to have frustrated a contract); *Tandrin Aviation Holdings Ltd v Aero Toy Store LLC* [2010] EWHC 40 (Comm), [2010] 2 Lloyd's Rep. 668 at [50]; *Gemcorp Commodities Trading SA v Zeefacto Oil & Gas Co* [2018] EWHC 3938 (Comm). See also the cases on Sale and Carriage of Goods cited below, paras 23-047—23-048. The proposition that an increase in expense is not, of itself, sufficient to produce frustration may **23-021**

not be absolute; see Beatson in Rose (ed.), *Consensus Ad Idem* (1996), Ch.6. On the question whether a term permitting determination upon notice may be implied into a long-term contract, see *Staffordshire A.H.A. v South Staffordshire Waterworks Co* [1978] 1 W.L.R. 1387; (pet. dis.) [1979] 1 W.L.R. 203, HL. cf. *Kirklees MBC v Yorks Woollen District Transport Co* [1978] 77 L.G.R. 448; *Watford BC v Watford Rural Parish Council* (1988) 86 L.G.R. 524; *Islwyn BC v Newport BC* (1994) 6 Admin. L.R. 386. On the judicial response to problems caused by a fall in the value of money, see Downes (1985) 101 L.Q.R. 98; also above para.21-074.

## (b) Common Types of Frustrating Events

### *(i) Subsequent Legal Changes and Supervening Illegality*

#### Subsequent legal changes

*Replace footnote 104 with:*

**23-022** [104] (1869) L.R. 4 Q.B. 180. See also *Islwyn BC v Newport BC* (1994) 6 Admin. L.R. 386; *Hildron Finance Ltd v Sunley Holdings Ltd* [2010] EWHC 1681 (Ch), [2010] 3 E.G.L.R. 1 and *Canary Wharf (BP4) T1 Ltd v European Medicines Agency* [2019] EWHC 335 (Ch) at [173]–[174] where it was noted by Marcus Smith J. that *Baily* might not be a true case of frustration because the entirety of the lease was not discharged. Rather, it was only the lessor who was discharged from his obligation not to build on the land. On this basis it was a case "where the supervening legal event rendered one particular covenant discharged, but the remaining obligations intact" (*Canary Wharf (BP4) T1 Ltd v European Medicines Agency* [2019] EWHC 335 (Ch) at [174]).

#### Changes affecting employment

*Replace footnote 106 with:*

**23-023** [106] [1934] A.C. 176. See also *Canary Wharf (BP4) T1 Ltd v European Medicines Agency* [2019] EWHC 335 (Ch) at [175].

#### Supervening illegality

*Replace footnote 109 with:*

**23-024** [109] McNair (1944) 60 L.Q.R. 160, 162–163; *Twentieth Century Fox Film Corporation v British Telecommunications Plc (No.2)* [2011] EWHC 2714 (Ch), [2012] 1 All E.R. 869 at [47]; *Canary Wharf (BP4) T1 Ltd v European Medicines Agency* [2019] EWHC 335 (Ch) at [41] and [170]. Supervening illegality may arise where the performance of the contract becomes unlawful for one party by reason of a supervening change in the law or as a result of a supervening change of circumstance which renders that which was previously lawful unlawful. Supervening illegality is probably included in the term "frustration" in the Law Reform (Frustrated Contracts) Act 1943 (below, paras 23-074 et seq.). Cases of supervening illegality may, however, raise issues which do not arise in other cases of frustration, in particular, the public interest in ensuring that the law is observed: see *Islamic Republic of Iran Shipping Lines v Steamship Mutual Underwriting Association (Bermuda) Ltd* [2010] EWHC 2661 (Comm), [2011] 1 Lloyd's Rep. 195 at [100].

#### Supervening illegality under a foreign law

*Replace paragraph with:*

**23-027** The validity and enforceability of a contract governed by English law is not as a general rule affected by the question whether the contract would be regarded as valid or whether its performance would be lawful according to the law of another country.[117] This rule is, however, the subject of exceptions. One such exception arises where a contract governed by English law as its applicable law is to be performed abroad, and that performance becomes illegal by the law of the place of performance (*lex loci solutionis*). In such a case, the contract will not, according to common law rules, be enforced in England.[118] The principle of frustration by supervening illegality operates where the change in the *lex loci solutionis* occurs after the formation of the contract but before its performance. For the principle to apply, performance must require the doing in a foreign country of something which the laws of that country make it illegal to do.[118a] Thus an English court declined to enforce a contract governed by English law for the payment in Spain of freight under a charterparty exceeding the maximum amount fixed, after the making of the contract, by Spanish law.[119] A party relying on frustration by the *lex loci solutionis* must generally show that the illegality covered the whole of the period within which performance was due; thus where a foreign export control regulation prohibited performance of a contract during only part of the contract period, the exporters were held liable for failure to perform during the time no prohibition existed.[120] But a contract governed by English law is not frustrated where the *lex loci solutionis*, without making performance illegal, merely excuses a party from performance in full.[121] Equally a contract governed by English law is not frustrated because the party liable to perform would, by his performance, contravene the law of the place of his residence, or of which he is a national (if that law is neither the applicable law nor the *lex loci solutionis*)[122] nor does it suffice that, according to the law of the place of performance, the act of performance is unlawful by the law of the country in which the act happens to be done.[123]

[117] *Dana Gas PJSC v Dana Gas Sukuk Ltd* [2017] EWHC 2928 (Comm), [2018] 1 Lloyd's Rep. 177 at [79]; *Dana Gas PJSC v Dana Gas Sukuk Ltd* [2018] EWHC 278 (Comm), [2018] 2 Lloyd's Rep. 16 at [29]; *Canary Wharf (BP4) T1 Ltd v European Medicines Agency* [2019] EWHC 335 (Ch) at [187].

[118] *Ralli Bros v Compania Naviera Sota y Aznar* [1920] 2 K.B. 287. For an illustration, see *The Nile Co for the Export of Agricultural Crops v H. & J.M. Bennett (Commodities) Ltd* [1986] 1 Lloyd's Rep. 555, 581–582 and see also *Lilly Icos LLC v 8PM Chemists Ltd* [2009] EWHC 1905 (Ch). While there is general acceptance of the proposition that the English courts will not enforce the contract in such a case, there is no unanimity in relation to the juridical basis for such a conclusion. Thus it has been argued that the basis is not to be found in frustration (see W. Day [2020] C.L.J. 64, esp. pp.84–86) but in a public policy rule favouring judicial abstention for reasons of comity. Authority can be found to support the proposition that *Ralli Bros* "turned on the doctrine of impossibility of performance in English law" (per Lord Collins of Mapesbury in *Ryder Industries Ltd v Chan Shui Woo* (2015) 18 HKCFA 85, [2016] 1 HKC 323 at [43]) but also that it is a rule the public policy underpinning of which is to be found in considerations of international comity (*Magdeev v Tsvetkov* [2020] EWHC 887 (Comm) at [297]–[341]).

[118a] The performance of the contract must necessarily involve an act which would be illegal according to the law of the place of performance: *Dell Emerging Markets (EMEA) Ltd v Systems Equipment Telecommunications Services SAL* [2018] EWHC 702 (Comm); *Cargill International Trading Pte v Uttam Galva Steels Ltd* [2019] EWHC 476 (Comm); *Colt Technology Services v SG Global Group SRL* [2020] EWHC 1417 (Ch).

[119] *Ralli Bros v Compania Naviera Sota y Aznar* [1920] 2 K.B. 287; cf. *AV Pound & Co Ltd v MW Hardy & Co Inc* [1956] A.C. 588 (refusal by foreign authorities to grant export licence for performance of an English contract). On a partial prohibition by the *lex loci solutionis*, see *Benjamin's Sale of Goods*, 10th edn (2017), paras 18-396—18-403.

[120] *Ross T Smyth & Co (Liverpool) Ltd v WN Lindsay (Leith) Ltd* [1953] 1 W.L.R. 1280. cf. *Walton (Grain and Shipping) Ltd v British Italian Trading Co Ltd* [1959] 1 Lloyd's Rep. 223.

[121] *Jacobs v Credit Lyonnais* (1884) 12 Q.B.D. 589 (the headnote of this case is misleading: see *Ralli Bros v Compania Naviera Sota y Aznar*, above, at 292, 297, 301); *Blackburn Bobbin Co Ltd v TW Allen & Sons Ltd* [1918] 2 K.B. 467.

[122] *Dicey, Morris and Collins on the Conflict of Laws*, 15th edn (2012), para.32-098; *Kleinwort Sons & Co v Ungarische Baumwolle Industrie Aktien-Gesellschaft* [1939] 2 K.B. 678 (the principle of this case is clearly approved by three members of the House of Lords in *Kahler v Midland Bank* [1950] A.C. 24); *Fox v Henderson Investment Fund Ltd* [1999] 2 Lloyd's Rep. 303, 306. See also *Canary Wharf (BP4) T1 Ltd v European Medicines Agency* [2019] EWHC 335 (Ch) at [187]–[189] where an underlease which was governed by English law was held not to be frustrated by any subsequent incapacity as a matter of EU law of the lessee.

[123] *Tamil Nadu Electricity Board v ST-CMA Electric Co Private Ltd* [2007] EWHC 1713 (Comm), [2008] 1 Lloyd's Rep. 93 at [47].

### (ii) Cancellation of an Expected Event

#### The "coronation cases": Krell v Henry

*Replace paragraph with:*

23-033 The cancellation of an expected event can, in exceptional circumstances, operate to frustrate a contract. That this is so can be demonstrated by reference to the "coronation cases", so-called because they arose out of actions brought in consequence of the postponement of the coronation processions in June 1902, owing to the illness of King Edward VII. These cases are important both because they show that the event which is alleged to have frustrated the contract need not result in the physical destruction of the subject matter of the contract, but may frustrate the "commercial purpose" of the contract and because they also illustrate the narrow confines within which the doctrine of frustration currently operates. The most prominent of these cases is *Krell v Henry*,[137] where the defendant agreed in writing to hire rooms in the plaintiff's flat in Pall Mall on June 26 and 27 in order to see the coronation processions which had been announced for those days. The written contract made no express reference to the processions, but it was clear from the circumstances that both parties regarded the viewing of the processions as the sole purpose of the hiring. When the processions were postponed, the defendant declined to pay the balance of the agreed rent, and the Court of Appeal upheld his refusal, on the ground that "the Coronation procession was the foundation of this contract and that the non-happening of it prevented the performance of the contract"[138] within the principle of *Taylor v Caldwell*.[139] The court also held that parol evidence was admissible to prove what was the subject matter of the contract.[140] Similarly, in *Chandler v Webster*[141] another contract to let rooms "to view the first Coronation procession" was held to be frustrated by the postponement; the same result occurred with contracts to take seats on a stand built in order to view the procession.[142]

[137] [1903] 2 K.B. 740. See Treitel, *Frustration and Force Majeure*, 3rd edn (2014), paras 7-006—7-014; McElroy & Williams (1941) 4 M.L.R. 241 and 5 M.L.R. 1. For extended judicial analysis of this line of cases see *Canary Wharf (BP4) T1 Ltd v European Medicines Agency* [2019] EWHC 335 (Ch) at [35]–[38] and [244]–[248].

[138] [1903] 2 K.B. 740, 751. The "point of the contract was the purchase and sale of a room with a view: the view never came to pass" (*Canary Wharf (BP4) T1 Ltd v European Medicines Agency* [2019] EWHC 335 (Ch) at [38]).

[139] (1863) 3 B. & S. 826 (above, para.23-005).

[140] [1903] 2 K.B. 740, 754.

[141] [1904] 1 K.B. 493. (That part of the case dealing with the legal consequences of frustration is no longer good law: see below, paras 23-072 et seq.)

[142] *Blakeley v Muller* [1903] 2 K.B. 760n. cf. *Clark v Lindsay* (1903) 88 L.T. 198; *Griffith v Brymer* (1903) 19 T.L.R. 434 (although this is a case of common mistake because the "impossibility" was antecedent).

#### Herne Bay Steamboat Co v Hutton

*Replace footnote 145 with:*

23-034 [145] For a judicial attempt at a reconciliation see the judgment of Marcus Smith J. in *Canary Wharf (BP4) T1 Ltd v European Medicines Agency* [2019] EWHC 335 (Ch) at [37]–[38]. See further the discussion of these cases in Peel (ed.), *Treitel on The Law of Contract*, 15th edn (2020), paras 19-042—19-044; Cheshire, Fifoot and Furmston, *Law of Contract*, 17th edn (2017), pp.717–718; McElroy & Williams (references in n.137, above).

## (c) Application of the Doctrine to Common Types of Contracts

### *(ii) Charterparties*

*Replace footnote 191 with:* **23-041**

[191] *Scrutton on Charterparties and Bills of Lading*, 24th edn (2020), art.21; Treitel, *Frustration and Force Majeure*, 3rd edn (2012), paras 5-052—5-055; see (in addition to the cases cited below) *Geipel v Smith* (1872) L.R. 7 Q.B. 404 (blockading of port); *Jackson v Union Marine Insurance Co Ltd* (1874) L.R. 10 C.P. 125 (stranding; above, para.23-006); *Dahl v Nelson, Donkin & Co* (1881) 6 App. Cas. 38 (dock authorities refused to admit ship because dock was full: held, charterer bound to permit unloading at alternative place mentioned in charterparty); *Lloyd Royal Belge SA v Stathatos* (1917) 34 T.L.R. 70 (ship detained by naval authorities for over two months); *Larrinaga & Co Ltd v Société Franco-Americaine des Phosphates de Médulla* (1923) 39 T.L.R. 316; *Hirji Mulji v Cheong Yue S.S. Co Ltd* [1926] A.C. 497 (requisitioning); *Court Line Ltd v Dant & Russell Inc* [1939] 3 All E.R. 314 (boom blocking river during war); *Joseph Constantine S.S. Line Ltd v Imperial Smelting Corp Ltd* [1942] A.C. 154 (explosion); *Blane S.S. Ltd v Minister of Transport* [1951] 2 K.B. 965 (stranding); *Atlantic Maritime Co Inc v Gibbon* [1954] 1 Q.B. 88 (marine insurance: restraint of princes clause); cf. *Hongkong Fir Shipping Co Ltd v Kawasaki Kisen Kaisha Ltd* [1962] 2 Q.B. 26 (delays caused by breakdowns and repairs where shipowners in breach); *Pioneer Shipping Ltd v B.T.P. Tioxide Ltd (The Nema)* [1982] A.C. 724 (long delay caused by strike at port of loading: see above, para.23-035); *Adelfamar SA v Silos E. Mangimi Martini SpA (The Adelfa)* [1988] 2 Lloyd's Rep. 466 (arrest of vessel by third party); *Bunge SA v Kyla Shipping Co Ltd* [2013] EWCA Civ 734, [2013] 2 Lloyd's Rep. 463 (affirming [2012] EWHC 3522 (Comm), [2013] 1 Lloyd's Rep. 565 (vessel suffered extensive damage when struck by another vessel when in port: contract held not to be frustrated). See also the cases cited above, para.23-035 n.151.

#### Examples not amounting to frustration

*Replace footnote 207 with:*

[207] Charterparties contain many express exceptions known as "excepted perils". See *Scrutton on Charterparties and Bills of Lading*, 24th edn (2020) at arts 122–135. For a case on the construction of an exceptions clause, see *Reardon Smith Line Ltd v Ministry of Agriculture* [1963] A.C. 691. **23-045**

### *(v) Leases and Tenancies*

#### Illustrations of events frustrating leases

*Replace paragraph with:*

Although there is no reported case in England in which a lease has been held to be frustrated, the reports do contain opinions on the types of situations in which the courts might so hold. The physical disappearance of the demised premises is the most obvious case: a convulsion of nature might "swallow up" the property, or bury it permanently under the sea[242]; or an upper floor flat might be totally destroyed by fire or earthquake.[243] Frustrating events not involving the physical disappearance of the land would include in the case of a building lease, subsequent legislation which permanently prohibited private building on the site[244]; or a fire which destroyed or seriously damaged the buildings on the demised premises.[245] More recently, in *Graves v Graves*,[246] although the Court of Appeal did not find it necessary to decide whether the agreement was frustrated, the same result was reached through the use of an implied term. A housing benefit office incorrectly told Mrs Graves that she could continue to receive housing benefit if she moved into a property owned by her ex-husband, despite the fact their daughter would be living with her. Receipt of this benefit was crucial to the agreement of both parties. The error was discovered several months after Mrs Graves had commenced a 12-month tenancy. It was held that, when it was clear that the housing benefit would not be received, the agreement was different in kind from that originally **23-053** contemplated. A term was thus implied that, if housing benefit was not payable, the tenancy would come to an end.[247]

[242] *Cricklewood Property and Investment Trusts Ltd v Leightons and Investment Trust Ltd* [1945] A.C. 221, 229; *National Carriers Ltd v Panalpina (Northern) Ltd* [1981] A.C. 675, 691, 700–701, 709. These examples were cited in *Holbeck Hall Hotel Ltd v Scarborough BC* (1998) 57 Con. L.R. 113, 152–153 where the judge was prepared to assume, without deciding the point, that an event of this nature would have operated to discharge the lease by frustration. See also *Canary Wharf (BP4) T1 Ltd v European Medicines Agency* [2019] EWHC 335 (Ch) at [194] where it was accepted that, at least in theory, a lease that continued to subsist as a property interest could nevertheless be frustrated. The focus of the court was upon the application of the doctrine of frustration to the underlease, not upon whether frustration could ever apply to a lease or an underlease.

[243] *National Carriers Ltd v Panalpina (Northern) Ltd* [1981] A.C. 675, 690. See Megarry and Wade, *The Law of Real Property*, 9th edn (2019), paras 17-102—17-105; *Woodfall's Law of Landlord and Tenant*, paras 11-041—11-042.

[244] *Cricklewood Property and Investment Trusts Ltd v Leightons and Investment Trust Ltd* [1945] A.C. 221, 229, 241. In *Rom Securities Ltd v Rogers (Holdings) Ltd* (1967) 205 E.G. 427, an agreement for a lease was frustrated by refusal of planning permission: see *National Carriers Ltd v Panalpina (Northern) Ltd* [1981] A.C. 675, 690, 694, 705 (where Lord Simon says that this was a case of frustration, although the judge dealt with it by implying a term), and 715. cf. the relevant American authorities: Corbin, *Contracts* (2001), Vol.14, paras 77.4–77.7; Williston, *Contracts*, 3rd edn (1978), Vol.18, para.1955. (In *Robertson v Wilson* (1958) 75 W.N. (N.S.W.) 503, a weekly tenancy was held to have been frustrated by the local authority's "closing order".)

[245] *National Carriers Ltd v Panalpina (Northern) Ltd* [1981] A.C. 675, 701, 713. (The consequences of fire would normally be covered by an express term in the lease.) On the earlier law dealing with the lessee's obligation to pay the rent even when the premises are destroyed, see McElroy and Williams (1941) 4 M.L.R. 241, 256–260. cf. *Taylor v Caldwell* (1863) 3 B. & S. 826 (a licence to use a hall: above para.23-005).

[246] [2007] EWCA Civ 660, [2007] 3 F.S.R. 26.

[247] [2007] EWCA Civ 660, [2007] 3 F.S.R. 26 at [40]–[42].

## 4. THE LIMITS OF FRUSTRATION

*Replace footnote 279 with:*

### Significance of a foreseen event[279]

23-059 [279] Treitel, *Frustration and Force Majeure*, 3rd edn (2014), Ch.13; Peel (ed.), *Treitel on The Law of Contract*, 15th edn (2020), paras 19-083—19-088; Hall (1984) 4 L.S. 300.

*Replace paragraph with:*

23-059 The parties to the contract may not have made express provision for the event which has occurred but they may have foreseen it happening. In such a case, the fact that the parties have foreseen the event but not made any provision for it in their contract will usually,[280] but not necessarily,[281] prevent the doctrine of frustration from applying when the event occurs. While an unforeseen event will not necessarily lead to the frustration of a contract,[282] a foreseen event will generally exclude the operation of the doctrine. The inference that a foreseen event is not a frustrating event is only a prima facie one and so can be excluded by evidence of contrary intention.[283] Thus, it is a question of construction of the contract whether the parties intended their silence to mean that the contract should continue to bind in that event,[284] or whether they intended the effect of the event, if it occurs, to be determined by any relevant legal rules.[285] The foreseeability of the event alleged to have frustrated the contract is relevant only in so far as it informs the parties' knowledge, expectations, assumptions and contemplations, in particular as to risk.[285a] If one party foresaw the risk, but the other did not, it will be difficult for the former to claim that the occurrence of the risk frustrates the contract.[286] On the other hand, a contract may be frustrated by supervening illegality, notwithstanding the fact that the war which has brought about the supervening illegality was foreseen.[287]

[280] *Tamplin S.S. Co Ltd v Anglo-Mexican Petroleum Co* [1916] 2 A.C. 397, 426; *Bank Line Ltd v Arthur Capel & Co* [1919] A.C. 435, 455, 462; *Gulnes (D/S A/S) v Imperial Chemical Industries Ltd* [1938] 1 All E.R. 24; *Davis Contractors Ltd v Fareham U.D.C.* [1956] A.C. 696, 731; *Paal Wilson & Co A/S v Partenreederei Hannah Blumenthal* [1983] 1 A.C. 854, 909; *McAlpine Humberoak Ltd v McDermott International Inc* (1992) 58 B.L.R. 1, 18; *Gold Group Properties Ltd v BDW Trading Ltd* [2010] EWHC 323 (TCC), [2010] B.L.R. 235 at [71]; *Flying Music Company Ltd v Theater Entertainment SA* [2017] EWHC 3192 (QB) at [63]–[68]; *Dayah v The Partners of Bushloe Street Surgery* [2020] EWHC 1375 (QB); Peel (ed.), *Treitel on The Law of Contract*, 15th edn (2020), paras 19-083—19-088.

[281] *Maritime National Fish Ltd v Ocean Trawlers Ltd* [1935] A.C. 524, 529; *Tatem Ltd v Gamboa* [1939] 1 K.B. 132 (above, para.23-044); *Jennings and Chapman Ltd v Woodman, Matthews & Co* [1952] 2 T.L.R. 409, 412; *Ocean Tramp Tankers Corp v V/O Sovfracht (The Eugenia)* [1964] 2 Q.B. 226, 239; *Nile Co for the Export of Agricultural Crops v H. & J.M. Bennett (Commodities) Ltd* [1986] 1 Lloyd's Rep. 555, 582; *Adelfamar SA v Silos E. Mangimi Martini SpA (The Adelfa)* [1988] 2 Lloyd's Rep. 466, 471.

[282] *Davis Contractors Ltd v Fareham U.D.C.* [1956] A.C. 696; *British Movietonews Ltd v London and District Cinemas Ltd* [1952] A.C. 166.

[283] *Edwinton Commercial Corp v Tsavliris Russ (Worldwide Salvage & Towage) Ltd (The Sea Angel)* [2007] EWCA Civ 547, [2007] 2 Lloyd's Rep. 517 at [103] (but cf. [127]).

[284] See, e.g. *Chandler Bros Ltd v Boswell* [1936] 3 All E.R. 179.

[285] For example, an intention that if the event were to happen, the parties would "leave the lawyers to sort it out": *Ocean Tramp Tankers Corp v V/O Sovfracht (The Eugenia)* [1964] 2 Q.B. 226, 239.

[285a] *Canary Wharf (BP4) T1 Ltd v European Medicines Agency* [2019] EWHC 335 (Ch) at [211].

[286] *Walton Harvey Ltd v Walter and Homfrays Ltd* [1931] 1 Ch. 274; *Edwinton Commercial Corp v Tsavliris Russ (Worldwide Salvage & Towage) Ltd (The Sea Angel)* [2007] EWCA Civ 547, [2007] 2 Lloyd's Rep. 517 at [83], approving [2006] EWHC 1713 (Comm), [2007] 1 Lloyd's Rep. 335 at [84]; Peel (ed.), *Treitel on The Law of Contract*, 15th edn (2020), para.19-083.

[287] *Ertel Bieber & Co v Rio Tinto Co Ltd* [1918] A.C. 260 (above, para.23-024).

## Event foreseeable but not foreseen

*Replace footnote 289 with:*

[289] The question is one of degree and so depends to a large extent on the facts and circumstances of the individual case. The courts have warned against the "over-refinement" of submissions on this issue and one can probably go no further than conclude that "the less that an event, in its type and its impact, is foreseeable, the more likely it is to be a factor which, depending on other factors in the case, may lead on to frustration": *Edwinton Commercial Corp v Tsavliris Russ (Worldwide Salvage & Towage) Ltd (The Sea Angel)* [2007] EWCA Civ 547, [2007] 2 Lloyd's Rep. 517 at [127]. This being the case, foreseeability has been described as a "slippery concept" that needs "careful handling" (*Canary Wharf (BP4) T1 Ltd v European Medicines Agency* [2019] EWHC 335 (Ch) at [213]). **23-060**

## Self-induced frustration

*Replace footnote 300 with:*

[300] *J. Lauritzen AS v Wijsmuller BV (The Super Servant Two)* [1989] 1 Lloyd's Rep. 148, 154. In *Canary Wharf (BP4) T1 Ltd v European Medicines Agency* [2019] EWHC 335 (Ch) at [206] Marcus Smith J. referred to self-induced frustration as "something of a misnomer" on the ground that it is "simply a reference to post-contractual events and actions which indicate that certain options – that might have ameliorated the frustrating event – have been closed off by the acts or omissions of the party claiming frustration". **23-061**

## The Super Servant Two

*Replace paragraph with:*

In the second case, *J. Lauritzen AS v Wijsmuller BV (The Super Servant Two)*,[303] the defendants agreed to transport the plaintiffs' rig using one or other of two barges, *Super Servant One* or *Super Servant Two*. The defendants later made an internal **23-063** decision to allocate the *Super Servant Two* to the performance of the contract with the plaintiffs but, before the time for performance of the contract, the *Super Servant Two* sank while transporting another rig in the Zaire River. The *Super Servant One* having been allocated to the performance of other concluded contracts, the defendants sought to argue that the sinking of the *Super Servant Two* had frustrated the contract between the parties. The Court of Appeal held that, whether or not the *Super Servant Two* sank as a result of negligence on the part of the defendants or their employees, the contract was not frustrated. If it sank as a result of negligence then, the court held, the contract was not frustrated because negligence did not constitute a supervening event.[304] Although the House of Lords in *Joseph Constantine S.S. Co v Imperial Smelting Corp Ltd*[305] left open the question whether "mere negligence" would justify a finding that frustration was self-induced,[306] subsequent cases have concluded that negligence does exclude a finding of frustration by asserting that a frustrating event must arise "without blame or fault on the side of the party seeking to rely on it".[307] "Fault" in this context is not confined to a breach of a duty of care owed to the plaintiffs: such an interpretation would have confined the law within "a legalistic strait-jacket" and distracted attention from the real question, which is:

> "... whether the frustrating event relied upon is truly an outside event or extraneous change of situation or whether it is an event which the party seeking to rely on it had the means and opportunity to prevent but nevertheless caused or permitted to come about."[308]

[303] [1990] 1 Lloyd's Rep. 1. See Peel (ed.), *Treitel on The Law of Contract*, 15th edn (2020), paras 19-093—19-095; McKendrick [1990] L.M.C.L.Q. 153.

[304] [1990] 1 Lloyd's Rep. 1, 10.

[305] [1942] A.C. 154.

[306] [1942] A.C. 154, 166–167, 179, 195, 202.

[307] *J. Lauritzen AS v Wijsmuller BV (The Super Servant Two)* [1990] 1 Lloyd's Rep. 1, 8.

[308] [1990] 1 Lloyd's Rep. 1, 10. See also *Canary Wharf (BP4) T1 Ltd v European Medicines Agency* [2019] EWHC 335 (Ch) at [44].

**Partial "frustration"**

*Replace footnote 322 with:*

23-066 [322] *Cricklewood Property and Investment Trust Ltd v Leightons Investment Trust Ltd* [1945] A.C. 221, 233–234; *John Lewis Properties Plc v Viscount Chelsea* [1993] 2 E.G.L.R. 77, 82. See above, para.23-052. See also the analysis of *Baily v De Crispigny* (1869) L.R. 4 Q.B. 180 (above para.23-022) adopted by Marcus Smith J. in *Canary Wharf (BP4) T1 Ltd v European Medicines Agency* [2019] EWHC 335 (Ch) at [173]–[174].

**Partial excuse at common law**

*Replace footnote 329 with:*

23-068 [329] See Peel (ed.), *Treitel on The Law of Contract*, 15th edn (2020), paras 17-059 and 19-052—19-053; *Benjamin's Sale of Goods*, 10th edn (2017), paras 18-401—18-402. See also *Poussard v Spiers and Pond* (1876) 1 Q.B.D. 410 where illness gave the plaintiff opera singer a temporary excuse for her non-performance of her contract with the defendants. The case has sometimes been viewed as an example of the operation of the doctrine of frustration but this explanation encounters the difficulty of explaining why the defendants had an option whether or not to rescind the contract. If the contract had indeed been frustrated it would have been discharged automatically, whereas, if the defendants had wished to hold the plaintiff to the terms of her contract, it seems clear that they could have done so: see further Treitel, *Frustration and Force Majeure*, 3rd edn (2014), para.5-061.

### Limits of partial excuse

*Replace footnote 334 with:*

[334] Peel (ed.), *Treitel on The Law of Contract*, 15th edn (2020), para.19-095. **23-069**

## 5. The Legal Consequences of Frustration

### Breaches before discharge

*Replace footnote 365 with:*

[365] Peel (ed.), *Treitel on The Law of Contract*, 15th edn (2020), para.19-115. **23-079**

### Burden of proof

*Replace footnote 384 with:*

[384] As was the case in *Davis and Primrose Ltd v Clyde Shipbuilding and Engineering Co Ltd* 1917 1 S.L.T. 297. See also Peel (ed.), *Treitel on The Law of Contract*, 15th edn (2020), paras 19-106–19-108 and for a slightly different argument to the same end see Williams, *The Law Reform (Frustrated Contracts) Act 1943* at p.39 who argues that expenses in s.1(2) means "expenses after deduction of gains resulting from those expenses". **23-082**

### Destruction of the end product

*Replace footnote 394 with:*

[394] See, e.g. Peel (ed.), *Treitel on The Law of Contract*, 15th edn (2020), para.19-113. **23-086**

### Contracts excluded from the Act

*Replace footnote 416 with:*

[416] This formulation of category (d) is an attempt to state the effect of a badly drafted provision of the Act, namely, s.2(5)(c) (as amended by the Sale of Goods Act 1979 s.63 and Sch.2 para.2). The provision appears to assume that the rules as to risk adequately cover the situation: see Vol.II, paras 44-189 et seq. Detailed arguments as to the effect of this involved provision may be found elsewhere, viz Williams (1942) 6 M.L.R. 46, 81–90; Cheshire, Fifoot and Furmston, *Law of Contract*, 17th edn (2017), pp.737–738; Peel (ed.), *Treitel on The Law of Contract*, 15th edn (2020), paras 19-120—19-122; C. Twigg-Flesner, R. Canavan and H. MacQueen (eds), Atiyah and Adams' Sale of Goods, 13th edn (2016), pp.290–293. Section 7 is discussed in more detail in Vol.II, paras 44-047—44-050. **23-096**

CHAPTER 24

# DISCHARGE BY BREACH



## 1. IN GENERAL

*Replace footnote 1 with:*

1 See Lord Devlin [1967] Camb. L.J. 192; Reynolds (1963) 79 L.Q.R. 534; Treitel (1967) 30 M.L.R. 139; Shea (1979) 42 M.L.R. 623; Beatson (1981) 97 L.Q.R. 389; Rose (1981) 34 C.L.P. 235; Carter (2012) 128 L.Q.R. 283; *Carter's Breach of Contract*, 2nd edn (2019); J.E. Stannard and D. Capper, *Termination for Breach of Contract* (2014).

### A middle ground

*Replace footnote 15 with:*

15 See Peel (ed.), *Treitel on The Law of Contract*, 15th edn (2020), paras 18-001—18-029 and also below, paras 24-037 and 24-038. **24-002**

### Affirmation

*Replace footnote 27 with:*

27 *Yukong Line Ltd of Korea v Rendsberg Investments Corp of Liberia* [1996] 2 Lloyd's Rep. 604, 608. Moore-Bick J. added that, in his view, the courts should generally be "slow" to accept that the innocent party has committed itself irrevocably to going on with the contract and then leave it to "the doctrine of estoppel" (below, para.24-006) to remedy any potential injustice which may arise in the case where the party in breach has relied upon a representation by the innocent party which suggests that the contract has been affirmed. See also *Internet Trading Clubs Ltd v Freeserve (Investments) Ltd Plc* [2001] All E.R. (D) 185 (Jun); *Jet2.com Ltd v SC Compania Nationala de Transporturi Aeriene Romane Tarom SA* [2012] EWHC 622 (QB), [2012] All E.R. (D) 218 (Mar) at [67]; *Ampurius Nu Homes Holdings Ltd v Telford Homes (Creekside) Ltd* [2012] EWHC 1820 (Ch), [2012] B.L.R. 387 at [123]; *Flanagan v Liontrust Investment Partners LLP* [2015] EWHC 2171 (Ch) and *Atlas Residential Solutions Management UK Ltd v Greengate SARL* [2020] EWHC 366 (Comm) at [110] at [216]. **24-003**

### Affirmation irrevocable

*Replace footnote 30 with:*

30 *Hain S.S. Co Ltd v Tate & Lyle Ltd* (1936) 41 Com. Cas. 350, 355; *Peyman v Lanjani* [1985] Ch. 457; *Motor Oil Hellas (Corinth) Refineries SA v Shipping Corp of India* [1990] 1 Lloyd's Rep. 391; *Yukong Line Ltd of Korea v Rendsberg Investments Corp of Liberia* [1996] 2 Lloyd's Rep. 604, 607; *Laing Management Ltd v Aegon Insurance Co (UK) Ltd* (1998) 86 Build. L.R. 70, 108. However, affirmation may not be irrevocable in the case of an anticipatory breach of contract. In the case of an anticipatory **24-004**

breach, it has been argued that the innocent party ought to be entitled to go back upon his affirmation unless there has been some change of position by the party in breach in reliance upon the affirmation which would be prejudiced by the change of mind by the innocent party (see Treitel (1998) 114 L.Q.R. 22 and Peel (ed.), *Treitel on The Law of Contract*, 15th edn (2020), paras 17-094 et seq., a view which gains some support in principle from Thomas J. in *Stocznia Gdanska SA v Latvian Shipping Co* [2001] 1 Lloyd's Rep. 537, 566 and from Rix L.J. on appeal to the Court of Appeal, [2002] EWCA Civ 889, [2002] 2 Lloyd's Rep. 436 at [97]–[99]).

## "Inchoate doctrine" of consistency

*Replace footnote 46 with:*

24-006 [46] *Glencore Grain Rotterdam BV v Lebanese Organisation for International Commerce* [1997] 4 All E.R. 514; *Alfred Street Properties Ltd v National Asset Management Agency* [2020] EWHC 397 (Comm) at [111].

## Effect of affirmation

*Replace footnote 73 with:*

24-010 [73] Goodhart (1962) 78 L.Q.R. 263; Furmston (1962) 25 M.L.R. 364; Scott [1962] Camb. L.J. 12. cf. Nienaber [1962] Camb. L.J. 213; Peel (ed.), *Treitel on The Law of Contract*, 15th edn (2020), paras 21-012—21-017 and, for a more general review of the case law, see Liu (2011) 74 M.L.R. 171.

## Effect if repudiation not accepted

*Replace footnote 81 with:*

24-011 [81] *Frost v Knight* (1871-72) L.R. 7 Ex. 111, 112; *Avery v Bowden* (1855) 5 E. & B. 714; (1856) 6 E. & B. 953 (below, para.24-025); *Heyman v Darwins Ltd* [1942] A.C. 356, 361; *Fercometal SARL v Mediterranean Shipping Co SA* [1989] A.C. 788; *Cantt Pak Ltd v Pak Southern China Property Investment Ltd* [2018] EWHC 2564 (Ch) (below, para.24-026).

*Replace footnote 91 with:*

24-012 [91] *Fercometal SARL v Mediterranean Shipping Co SA* [1989] A.C. 788, 805–806; *Cantt Pak Ltd v Pak Southern China Property Investment Ltd* [2018] EWHC 2564 (Ch) at [131]. Estoppel could also arise if the repudiating party represents that he will not exercise a right conferred on him by the contract. A wider role for estoppel was acknowledged by Brennan J. in *Foran v Wight* (1989) 168 C.L.R. 385, 421–422.

## Acceptance of repudiation

*Replace footnote 95 with:*

24-013 [95] *Vitol SA v Norelf Ltd* [1996] A.C. 800, 810–811; *Carter v Lifeplan Products Ltd* [2013] EWCA Civ 453 at [18]; *Stocznia Gdanska SA v Latvian Shipping Co* [2001] 1 Lloyd's Rep. 537, 563, 566. (Where the acceptance took the form of a notice to rescind which was in fact invalid. The important fact was held to be that the letter which constituted the acceptance unequivocally stated that the contractual obligations were at an end. The claimants had a right to terminate the contract and the fact that they did not set that ground out in the letter which constituted the acceptance was held to be irrelevant. The analysis of Thomas J. was upheld by the Court of Appeal but not without some hesitation: see [2002] EWCA Civ 889, [2002] 2 Lloyd's Rep. 436 at [88]–[92]. The safest course of action would have been for the innocent party expressly to have reserved its common law rights.) The latter case demonstrates that an invalid invocation of a right to terminate contractually, on account of a breach of contract, is capable of amounting to an acceptance of a repudiatory breach if it unequivocally demonstrates an intention to treat the contractual obligations as at an end as a result of the breach of contract. Given that the same conduct is capable of giving rise both to a contractual right to terminate and to a common law entitlement to accept a repudiatory breach, recourse to the former does not necessarily constitute an affirmation of the contract since in both cases the innocent party is electing to terminate the contract (see also *Gold Group Properties Ltd v BDW Trading Ltd* [2010] EWHC 1632 (TCC), [2010] All E.R. (D) 18 (Jul) at [110]). Matters are otherwise, however, in the case where a termination notice makes explicit reference only to a particular contractual clause. In such a case the notice might demonstrate that the giver of the notice was only relying upon the contractual clause and was not intending to accept the repudiation (*Shell Egypt West Manzala GmbH v Dana Gas Egypt Ltd* [2010] EWHC 465 (Comm), [2010] All E.R. (D) 156 (Mar) at [31]) but in each case it is necessary to pay careful attention to the terms of the notice that has been given and all the facts and circumstances of the case (*Vannin Capital PCC v RBOS Shareholders Action Group Ltd* [2018] EWHC 2821 (Ch) at [105]–[111]).

## No reason or bad reason given

*Replace footnote 108 with:*

[108] *Ridgway v Hungerford Market Co* (1835) 3 Ad. & El. 171, 177, 178, 180; *Baillie v Kell* (1838) 4 Bing. N.C. 638; *Boston Deep Sea Fishing and Ice Co v Ansell* (1888) 39 Ch. D. 339, 352, 364; *Taylor v Oakes Roncoroni Co* (1922) 127 L.T. 267, 269; *British & Beningtons Ltd v N.W. Cachar Tea Co* [1923] A.C. 48, 71; *Etablissements Chainbaux SARL v Harbormaster Ltd* [1955] 1 Lloyd's Rep. 303, 314; *Universal Cargo Carriers Corp v Citati* [1957] 2 Q.B. 401, 443–445; affirmed in part [1957] 1 W.L.R. 979, and reversed in part [1958] 2 Q.B. 254; *Denmark Productions Ltd v Boscobel Productions Ltd* [1969] 1 Q.B. 699, 722, 732; *The Mihalis Angelos* [1971] 1 Q.B. 164, 195, 200, 204; *Cyril Leonard & Co v Simo Securities Trust* [1972] 1 W.L.R. 80, 85, 87, 89; *Scandinavian Trading Co A/B v Zodiac Petroleum SA* [1981] 1 Lloyd's Rep. 81, 90; *State Trading Corp of India Ltd v M. Golodetz Ltd* [1988] 2 Lloyd's Rep. 182; *Sheffield v Conrad* (1988) 22 Con. L.R. 108; *South Caribbean Trading Ltd v Trafigura Beheer BV* [2004] EWHC 2676 (Comm), [2005] 1 Lloyd's Rep. 128 at [133]–[134]. The latter case demonstrates that there are limits to the willingness of the courts to speculate about the reaction of the innocent party to the breach of which he was unaware. In *Reinwood Ltd v L Brown & Sons Ltd* [2008] EWCA Civ 1090, [2009] B.L.R. 37 Lloyd L.J. observed (at [51]) that, although the principle is often used in relation to facts unknown to the party refusing at the time of its refusal, there "is no reason why it should not be used in relation to facts which were known to that party at that time. Waiver can apply to qualify that principle, but only in cases of, in effect, estoppel". Care must be also taken when applying the general rule to cases in which it is alleged that the repudiatory breach takes the form of a renunciation. In such a case an essential ingredient of the words or conduct amounting to a repudiation is that they are communicated to or otherwise known to the innocent party. If they are not, there cannot be a renunciation: *Seadrill Management Services Ltd v OAO Gazprom* [2009] EWHC 1530 (Comm), [2010] 1 Lloyd's Rep. 543 at [265]. However, the principle may not apply to an express term of a contract, such as an event of default clause, where the court may conclude, as a matter of interpretation of the clause, that a party is not entitled to rely on an event which is not set out in the notice itself: *Nakanishi Marine Co Ltd v Gora Shipping Ltd* [2012] EWHC 3383 (Comm) at [35(iii)] and *Lombard North Central Plc v European Skyjets Ltd (In Liquidation)* [2020] EWHC 679 (QB) at [62]–[68]. **24-014**

## Both parties in breach

*Replace footnote 121 with:*

[121] See generally Peel (ed.), *Treitel on The Law of Contract*, 15th edn (2020), para.18-109. **24-016**

## 2. RENUNCIATION

## Renunciation

*Replace footnote 124 with:*

[124] See also *Martin v Stout* [1925] A.C. 359; *Brinkibon Ltd v Stahag Stahl und Stahlwarenhandelgesellschaft mbH* [1980] 2 Lloyd's Rep. 556; affirmed [1983] 2 A.C. 34 (place of renunciation); *Grand China Logistics Holding (Group) Co Ltd v Spar Shipping AS* [2016] EWCA Civ 982, [2016] 2 Lloyd's Rep. 447 at [66]–[78]; *Teekay Tankers Ltd v STX Offshore & Shipbuilding Co Ltd* [2017] EWHC 253 (Comm), [2017] 1 Lloyd's Rep 387 at [217]. The question whether there has been a renunciation depends on what a reasonable person would understand from the conduct of the party alleged to have renounced the contract and all of the circumstances prevailing at the time of the termination, including the history of the transaction or relationship. Silence, being equivocal, will generally not amount to a renunciation (*Alegrow SA v Yayla Agro Gida San Ve Nak SA* [2020] EWHC 1845 (Comm) at [69]–[73]) but it may do so where the silence is held to "speak", that is to say, it does, in the circumstances, communicate an intention to renounce the contract (*Stocznia Gdanska SA v Latvian Shipping Co* [2002] EWCA Civ 889, [2002] 2 Lloyd's Rep. 436 at [96]). **24-018**

## 3. IMPOSSIBILITY CREATED BY ONE PARTY

## Anticipatory breach

*Replace paragraph with:*

Anticipatory breach of contract may be constituted by impossibility as well as by renunciation, and similar principles apply to both. So where a shipowner agreed to charter a ship upon her release from government service, but before the release **24-031** sold her to another person, it was held that he had put it out of his power to perform the agreement and the charterer was entitled to sue for damages forthwith. It was argued for the shipowner that he might have bought back the ship in time to fulfil the contract, but this was regarded as too speculative a possibility.[188] Also in *Universal Cargo Carriers Corp v Citati*,[189] where a charterer of a ship agreed to nominate a berth, to provide a cargo, and to finish loading, all before a certain day, and three days before this day had failed to do any of these things, it was held that the shipowner would be entitled to treat this default as an anticipatory breach of contract if it could prove that the charterer would not have been able to perform its obligations under the charterparty before the point in time at which the delay would have frustrated the commercial object of the venture. In this case it was held that it would not be sufficient for the innocent party to show that he had reasonable grounds for believing that the other party would be unable to perform at the appointed time; he would only be justified in treating himself as discharged if the other party was in fact unable to perform at that time: "[a]n anticipatory breach must be proved in fact and not in supposition".[190]

[188] *Omnium D'Enterprises v Sutherland* [1919] 1 K.B. 618; *Lovelock v Franklyn* (1846) 8 Q.B. 371; *Synge v Synge* [1894] 1 Q.B. 466; *Guy-Pell v Foster* [1930] 2 Ch. 169; cf. *Alfred C. Toepfer International GmbH v Itex Itagrani Export SA* [1993] 1 Lloyd's Rep. 360, 362.

[189] [1957] 2 Q.B. 401; affirmed in part [1957] 1 W.L.R. 979 and reversed in part [1958] 2 Q.B. 254. cf. *Hongkong Fir Shipping Co Ltd v Kawasaki Kisen Kaisha Ltd* [1962] 2 Q.B. 26; *Trade and Transport Inc v Iino Kaiun Kaisha Ltd* [1973] 1 W.L.R. 210; *F. C. Shepherd & Co Ltd v Jerrom* [1987] Q.B. 301, 323, 327–328; Peel (ed.), *Treitel on The Law of Contract*, 15th edn (2020), para.17-077.

[190] [1957] 2 Q.B. 401, 449–450; *Re Simoco Digital UK Ltd: Thunderbird Industries LLC v Simoco Digital UK Ltd* [2004] EWHC 209 (Ch), [2004] 1 B.C.L.C. 541 at [22]–[23]. But see *Embiricos v Sydney Reid & Co* [1914] 3 K.B. 45, 59 (frustration); *Hongkong Fir Shipping Co Ltd v Kawasaki Kisen Kaisha Ltd* [1962] 2 Q.B. 26, 57 (failure of performance); Peel (ed.), *Treitel on The Law of Contract*, 15th edn (2020), paras 17-090—17-091; Carter (1984) 47 M.L.R. 422. A party may not rely on the fact that performance is impossible insofar as that was the result of its own actions: *Barclays Bank Plc v Gatpaham Properties Ltd* [2008] EWHC 721 (Ch), [2008] All E.R. (D) 262 (Apr).

### No anticipation of express right to terminate

*Replace footnote 191 with:*

**24-032** [191] *Afovos Shipping Co SA v Pagnan & Filli* [1983] 1 W.L.R. 195. This, it is suggested, is the correct interpretation of Lord Diplock's statement (at 203) that the doctrine of anticipatory breach by conduct which disables a party to a contract from performing one of his primary obligations under the contract has no application to a breach of punctual payment of hire clause in a time charterparty of a ship. In so far as Lord Diplock suggested that the doctrine of anticipatory breach applies only to fundamental breaches, his reasoning cannot be supported: see Peel (ed.), *Treitel on The Law of Contract*, 15th edn (2020), para.17-087 and *Carter's Breach of Contract*, 2nd edn (2019), paras 4-40 and 7-38.

## 4. FAILURE OF PERFORMANCE

### Relation of the promises

*Replace footnote 201 with:*

**24-036** [201] Cited with approval in *Denmark Productions Ltd v Boscobel Productions Ltd* [1969] 1 Q.B. 699, 733. See also *Doherty v Fannigan Holdings Ltd* [2018] EWCA Civ 1615, [2018] 2 B.C.L.C. 623 at [22].

### Independent mutual promises

*Replace paragraph with:*

**24-037** In the exceptional case of independent mutual promises, each party has his remedy on the promise made in his favour without performing his part of the contract[203] and conversely neither party can claim to be discharged from liability on the contract by reason of the failure of the other to perform his part. Thus in *Fearon v Earl of Aylesford*,[204] an action on a separation deed, it was said that a husband would be bound to perform a covenant to pay money to a trustee for his wife, even though the wife might have broken a covenant in the same deed not to molest her husband. But the tendency of the courts is against construing contracts as containing two independent promises. So, in *General Billposting Co Ltd v Atkinson*,[205] it was held that a man who had been wrongfully dismissed from his employment was no longer bound by a restrictive covenant contained in his contract of employment as his employers by their action had repudiated the contract. The obligation to pay for shares has been held to be dependent on the transfer of the shares just as in the case of contract for the sale of land the vendor's obligation to convey and the purchaser's obligation to pay the purchase price are dependent obligations.[205a] Similarly it has been held that mutual covenants as to draining land by adjoining owners were dependent on each other and not independent promises.[206] On the other hand, it has long been established that a tenant's covenant to pay rent is independent of the landlord's covenant to repair the premises; the tenant is not discharged from his obligation to pay rent merely because his landlord is unwilling to fulfil his obligation.[207] Also in contracts of apprenticeship the covenants of the master and apprentice are normally independent of each other.[208]

[203] *Pordage v Cole* (1669) 1 Saund. 319, 320.

[204] (1884) 14 Q.B.D. 792, 800.

[205] [1909] A.C. 118. In *Rock Refrigeration Ltd v Jones* [1997] 1 All E.R. 1, 18–20 Phillips L.J. questioned the correctness of *General Billposting*, but the majority of the Court of Appeal were prepared to assume that it had been correctly decided. See further below, para.24-050 n.279.

[205a] *Doherty v Fannigan Holdings Ltd* [2018] EWCA Civ 1615, [2018] 2 B.C.L.C. 623, distinguished in *Mulville v Sandelson* [2019] EWHC 3287 (Ch) where the share transfer was held to be "essentially an ancillary obligation" (at [30]) and that the obligation to make payment under the settlement agreement was a "prior and unqualified obligation" which was therefore independent.

[206] *Kidner v Stimpson* (1918) 35 T.L.R. 63. See also *Sandelson v Mulville* [2019] EWHC 1620 (Ch).

[207] *Taylor v Webb* [1937] 2 K.B. 283 (but see *Regis Property Co Ltd v Dudley* [1959] A.C. 370). See also *Sandelson v Mulville* [2019] EWHC 1620 (Ch) at [24], noting the lack of an explanation for the rule and observing that it may be attributable either a "long-established rule" or to the fact that in the early authorities a rent covenant was not regarded as a condition precedent because it did not go to the "root" of the contract.

[208] *Winstone v Linn* (1823) 1 B. & C. 460; cf. *Ellen v Topp* (1851) 6 Exch. 424.

### Failure of performance: other situations

*Replace footnote 227 with:*

[227] [2014] EWCA Civ 436, 154 Con. L.R. 38 at [53]; *Green Deal Marketing Southern Ltd v Economy Energy Trading Ltd* [2019] EWHC 507 (Ch) at [125]. **24-041**

## 5. CONSEQUENCES OF DISCHARGE

### Obligations which survive discharge

*Replace footnote 279 with:*

[279] *Port Jackson Stevedoring Pty Ltd v Salmond and Spraggon (Australia) Pty Ltd* [1981] 1 W.L.R. 138, **24-050**
145. However, a restrictive covenant in a contract of employment will not generally survive where it is the employer who has repudiated the contract: *General Billposting Co Ltd v Atkinson* [1909] A.C. 118, above, para.16-132, although the correctness of this proposition was questioned by Phillips L.J. in *Rock Refrigeration Ltd v Jones* [1997] 1 All E.R. 1, 18–20 on the basis that "the law in relation to the discharge of contractual obligations by acceptance of a repudiation has been developed and clarified" since *General Billposting* was decided. The uncertainty was noted but not resolved by Lord Wilson in *Geys v Société*

*Générale, London Branch* [2012] UKSC 63, [2013] 1 A.C. 513 at [68] (and see also Lord Sumption at [141]). Although the subject of some doubt, the rule laid down in General Billposting continues to apply, in particular where it is the repudiator who is seeking to enforce the covenant against the innocent party (*Brown v Neon Management Services Ltd* [2018] EWHC 2137 (QB), [2019] I.R.L.R. 30 at [171]). The employer may, however, be able to protect his property and trade secrets on the basis that his rights of property will survive the termination of the contract as a result of the employee's acceptance of his repudiatory breach (*Rock Refrigeration Ltd v Jones* [1997] 1 All E.R. 1, 14 and (on rather wider grounds) 20). The underlying uncertainty in this area relates to the scope of the decision of the House of Lords in *General Billposting*, on which see Freedland (2003) 32 I.L.J. 48 and Dawson (2013) 129 L.Q.R. 508 (where *General Billposting* is examined in the light of recent Commonwealth case law).

CHAPTER 25

# OTHER MODES OF DISCHARGE



## 1. MERGER

### Merger of rights and liabilities

*Replace footnote 15 with:*

[15] See Megarry and Wade, *The Law of Real Property*, 9th edn (2019), paras 17-090—17-091. At common law merger was automatic; but by s.185 of the Law of Property Act 1925, the equitable rule now prevails; that merger depends upon the intention of the person who acquires the two estates. See *Capital and Counties Bank Ltd v Rhodes* [1903] 1 Ch. 631. **25-004**

### Debtor becomes creditor's personal representative

*Replace footnote 17 with:*

[17] *Wankford v Wankford* (1704) 1 Salk. 299; *Cheetham v Ward* (1797) 1 B. & P. 630; *Freakley v Fox* (1829) 9 B. & C. 130; *Re Applebee* [1891] 3 Ch. 422. See also *Jenkins v Jenkins* [1928] 2 K.B. 501 and *Williams, Mortimer and Sunnucks on Executors, Administrators and Probate*, 21st edn (2019), para.48-17, and above, para.17-023. **25-005**

### Creditor becomes debtor's personal representative

*Replace footnote 22 with:*

[22] *Bowring-Hanbury's Trustee v Bowring-Hanbury* [1943] Ch. 104. See generally *Williams, Mortimer and Sunnucks on Executors, Administrators and Probate*, 21st edn (2018), para.48-21; (1943) 59 L.Q.R. 117; (1943) 6 M.L.R. 233. **25-006**

### Merger by judgment recovered

*Replace footnote 29 with:*

[29] *Greathead v Bromley* (1798) 7 Term Rep. 455; *King v Hoare* (1844) 13 M. & W. 495; *Stewart v Todd* (1846) 9 Q.B. 759; *Re European Central Ry* (1876) 4 Ch. D. 33; *Kendall v Hamilton* (1879) 4 App. Cas. 504; *Aman v Southern Ry* [1926] 1 K.B. 59; *Virgin Atlantic Airways Ltd v Zodiac Seats UK Ltd* [2013] UKSC 46, [2014] A.C. 160 at [17]; *Moorjani v Durban Estates Ltd* [2019] EWHC 1229 (TCC). For the position in regard to judgment against one joint, or joint and several, debtor, see above, paras 17-015—17-017. For the effect of an arbitration award, see Vol.II, paras 32-145 et seq. **25-007**

## Damages "once for all"

*Replace footnote 32 with:*

25-008 [32] *Brunsden v Humphrey* (1884) 14 Q.B.D. 141, 147; *Darley Main Colliery Co v Mitchell* (1886) 11 App. Cas. 127, 132; *Conquer v Boot* [1928] 2 K.B. 336, 343; *Clark v Urquhart* [1930] A.C. 28, 54; *Virgin Atlantic Airways Ltd v Zodiac Seats UK Ltd* [2013] UKSC 46, [2014] A.C. 160 at [17] (a principle which "is not easily described as a species of estoppel"); *Moorjani v Durban Estates Ltd* [2019] EWHC 1229 (TCC). See also County Courts Act 1984 s.35. The general rule applies also to arbitrations.

## Estoppel by judgment

*Replace paragraph with:*

25-011 Estoppel by judgment, or estoppel *per rem judicatam*, is a rule of evidence[42] whereby a party is debarred from relitigating a cause of action which has been conclusively determined by the judgment of a court of competent jurisdiction in previous proceedings between the same parties or their privies, or an issue raised and determined in such proceedings which it was necessary[43] to determine for the purpose of those proceedings.[44] Estoppel *per rem judicatam* has two principal branches: cause of action estoppel and issue estoppel. Cause of action estoppel arises:

> "[W]here the cause of action in the later proceedings is identical to that in the earlier proceedings, the latter having been between the same parties or their privies and having involved the same subject matter. In such a case the bar is absolute in relation to all points decided unless fraud or collusion is alleged such as to justify setting aside the earlier judgment."[45]

On the other hand, issue estoppel arises:

> "[W]here a particular issue forming a necessary ingredient in a cause of action has been litigated and decided and in subsequent proceedings between the same parties involving a different cause of action to which the same issue is relevant one of the parties seeks to re-open that issue."[46]

Both estoppels are founded "upon the public interest in finality of litigation rather than the achievement of justice as between the individual litigants".[47]

[42] *Vervaeke v Smith* [1983] 1 A.C. 145; *Republic of India v India Steamship Co Ltd* [1993] A.C. 410, 422.

[43] *Kok Hoong v Leong Cheong Kweng Mines Ltd* [1964] A.C. 993; *Penn Texas Corp v Murat Anstalt (No.2)* [1964] 2 Q.B. 647; *Fidelitas Shipping Co Ltd v V/O Exportchleb* [1966] 1 Q.B. 630, 640; *Mills v Cooper* [1967] 2 Q.B. 459, 468; *Carl Zeiss Stiftung v Rayner & Keeler Ltd (No.3)* [1970] Ch. 506; *Helmville Ltd v Astilleros Espanoles SA* [1984] 2 Lloyd's Rep. 569; *In Re State of Norway's Application (No.2)* [1990] 1 A.C. 723, 743, 752; *In Re B. (Minors) (Care Proceedings: Issue Estoppel)* [1997] Fam. 117, 121–122.

[44] The subject is one of considerable difficulty and refinement: see R. Munday, *Cross and Tapper on Evidence*, 13th edn (2018), pp.88 et seq. For estoppel by a default judgment, see *Howlett v Tarte* (1861) 10 C.B.N.S. 813; *New Brunswick Ry Co v British and French Trust Corp Ltd* [1939] A.C. 1; *Kok Hoong v Leong Cheong Kweng Mines Ltd* [1964] A.C. 993. Neither dismissal for want of prosecution (*Pople v Evans* [1969] 2 Ch. 255) nor the withdrawal of proceedings (*Owens v Minoprio* [1942] 1 K.B. 193) is a foundation for res judicata.

[45] *Arnold v National Westminster Bank Plc* [1991] 2 A.C. 93, 104. See also *Virgin Atlantic Airways Ltd v Zodiac Seats UK Ltd* [2013] UKSC 46, [2014] A.C. 160 at [17].

[46] [1991] 2 A.C. 93, 105. See also *Virgin Atlantic Airways Ltd v Zodiac Seats UK Ltd* [2013] UKSC 46, [2014] A.C. 160 at [17].

[47] *Republic of India v India S.S. Co Ltd* [1993] A.C. 410, 415. See also *Duchess of Kingston's Case* (1776) 20 St. Tr. 619; *R. v Inhabitants of the Township of Hartington Middle Quarter* (1855) 4 El. & Bl. 780; *Flittens v Allfrey* (1874) L.R. 10 C.P. 29; *Hoystead v Commissioner of Taxation* [1926] A.C.

155, 170; *Fidelitas Shipping Co Ltd v V/O Exportchleb* [1966] 1 Q.B. 630, 640; *Thoday v Thoday* [1964] P. 181, 197–198; *Mills v Cooper* [1967] 2 Q.B. 459, 468; *Carl Zeiss Stiftung v Rayner & Keeler Ltd (No.2)* [1967] 1 A.C. 853, 916, 917; *Vervaeke v Smith* [1983] 1 A.C. 145; *Thrasyvoulou v Secretary of State for the Environment* [1990] 2 A.C. 273, 289; *Johnson v Gore Wood & Co (A Firm)* [2002] 2 A.C. 1, 30–31 and 59; R. Munday, *Cross and Tapper on Evidence*, 13th edn (2018), p.88.

## Requirements

*Replace footnote 55 with:*

[55] *Hoystead v Commissioner of Taxation* [1926] A.C. 155; *Marginson v Blackburn BC* [1939] 2 K.B. 426; *Bell v Holmes* [1956] 1 W.L.R. 1359; *Society of Medical Officers of Health v Hope* [1960] A.C. 551; *Randolph v Tuck* [1962] 1 Q.B. 175; *Wood v Luscombe* [1966] 1 Q.B. 69; *Re Mantey's Will Trusts (No.2)* [1976] 1 All E.R. 673. See also *Khan v Golechha International Ltd* [1980] 1 W.L.R. 1482; *Republic of India v India S.S. Co Ltd* [1993] A.C. 410; *Buehler AG v Chronos Richardson Ltd* [1998] 2 All E.R. 960 and R. Munday, *Cross and Tapper on Evidence*, 13th edn (2018), pp.98–100. In the case of issue estoppel, the decision on the issue must have been essential for the decision of the court and not merely collateral: see the cases cited in n.43, above. **25-012**

## Issues not raised previously

*Replace paragraph with:*

Both cause of action[56] and issue estoppel[57] may extend to issues which might have been put but were not raised and decided[58] in the earlier proceedings, although in special circumstances[59] the court may depart from this rule and permit the parties to raise such an issue. The court also has a power under rules of court and its inherent jurisdiction to stay or dismiss the action if a claimant seeks to raise in subsequent proceedings matters which were or should have been litigated in the earlier proceedings.[60] The courts will not, however, exercise their discretion in such a way as to deny to a claimant the right to bring "a genuine subject of litigation before the court".[61] The burden is therefore upon the defendant to establish that it is oppressive or an abuse of process for him to be subjected to the second action[62] and there will "rarely be a finding of abuse unless the latter proceeding involves what the court regards as unjust harassment of a party".[63] The question whether an action is an abuse of the court is "closely related"[64] to the question whether or not there is an estoppel *per rem judicatam* but it is not identical so that an action may be struck out on the ground that it is an abuse of the court where the plea of estoppel is not strictly made out.[65] Estoppel *per rem judicatam* may be raised as a defence,[66] but the more usual course is to apply to the court for an order that the statement of claim, or part thereof, be struck out and the action stayed or dismissed.[67] **25-013**

[56] *Arnold v National Westminster Bank Plc* [1991] 2 A.C. 93, 104, citing *Henderson v Henderson* (1843) 3 Hare 100, 114–115; *Hoystead v Commissioner of Taxation* [1926] A.C. 155, 170; *Yat Tung Investment Co Ltd v Dao Heng Bank Ltd* [1975] A.C. 581, 590.

[57] *Arnold v National Westminster Bank Plc* [1991] 2 A.C. 93, 106, citing *Fidelitas Shipping Co Ltd v V/O Exportchleb* [1966] 1 Q.B. 630, 642; *Brisbane City Council v Att-Gen for Queensland* [1979] A.C. 411, 425.

[58] The issue should have been decided as well as raised in the earlier proceedings: *Barrow v Bankside Agency Ltd* [1996] 1 W.L.R. 257 (plaintiff's claim not barred because it would not have been decided by the court in the earlier proceedings). A court can be expected to display a degree of caution before reaching the conclusion that the point in issue was decided by the earlier court. A court is likely to insist that the issue in question be "fundamental" to the substantive decision in the earlier case: *Gold Group Properties Ltd v BDW Trading Ltd* [2010] EWHC 1632 (TCC), [2010] All E.R. (D) 18 (Jul) at [86]. It is, however, important to emphasise that cause of action estoppel remains absolute in relation to all points which had to be and were decided in order to establish the existence or non-existence of a cause of action. The discretion to permit an issue to be raised in subsequent proceedings relates only to matters which were not decided but might have been raised in the earlier proceedings: *Virgin Atlantic Airways Ltd v Zodiac Seats UK Ltd* [2013] UKSC 46, [2014] A.C. 160 at [26].

[59] *Henderson v Henderson* (1843) 3 Hare 100, 115; *Yat Tung Investment Co Ltd v Dao Heng Bank Ltd* [1975] A.C. 581, 590; *Talbot v Berkshire CC* [1994] Q.B. 290, 298–300; *Barrow v Bankside Agency Ltd* [1996] 1 W.L.R. 257; *Republic of India v India S.S. Co Ltd (No.2)* [1998] A.C. 878, 897–898.

[60] *Henderson v Henderson* (1843) 3 Hare 100, 115; *Greenhalgh v Mallard* [1947] 2 All E.R. 255; *Fidelitas Shipping Co Ltd v V/O Exportchleb* [1966] 1 Q.B. 630, 640; *Yat Tung Investment Co Ltd v Dao Heng Bank Ltd* [1975] A.C. 581, 590; *L.E. Walwin & Partners Ltd v West Sussex CC* [1975] 3 All E.R. 604; *Brisbane City Council v Att-Gen for Queensland* [1979] A.C. 411, 425; *Green v Hampshire CC* [1979] I.C.R. 861, 865–866; *Vervaeke v Smith* [1983] 1 A.C. 145; *Dallal v Bank Mellat* [1986] Q.B. 441, 452; *The European Gateway* [1987] Q.B. 206, 212, 221; *S.C.F. Finance Co Ltd v Masri (No.3)* [1987] Q.B. 1028, 1049; *Talbot v Berkshire CC* [1994] Q.B. 290, 296; *Virgin Atlantic Airways Ltd v Zodiac Seats UK Ltd* [2013] UKSC 46, [2014] A.C. 160 at [17]; *Takhar v Gracefield Developments Ltd* [2019] UKSC 13, [2020] A.C. 450 at [62]. While the principle in *Henderson v Henderson* is concerned with the abuse of process, it is also a part of the law of res judicata (*Virgin Atlantic Airways* at [25]).

[61] *Johnson v Gore Wood & Co (A Firm)* [2002] 2 A.C. 1, 22. The speech of Lord Bingham contains a particularly valuable review of the authorities.

[62] *Johnson v Gore Wood & Co (A Firm)* [2002] 2 A.C. 1, 59–60. Note also the impact of art.6 of the European Convention on Human Rights on the reasoning of Lord Millett (59).

[63] *Johnson v Gore Wood & Co (A Firm)* [2002] 2 A.C. 1, 31; *Moorjani v Durban Estates Ltd* [2019] EWHC 1229 (TCC) at [17].

[64] *Dallal v Bank Mellat* [1988] Q.B. 441, 452. The closeness of the link can be seen in the fact that *Henderson v Henderson* (1843) 3 Hare 100 has been explained as an example of the extension of cause of action estoppel (*Arnold v National Westminster Bank Plc* [1991] 2 A.C. 93, 105) and of the exercise of the inherent jurisdiction of the court (*Yat Tung Investment Co Ltd v Dao Heng Bank Ltd* [1975] A.C. 581, 590). See to the same effect *Greenhalgh v Mallard* [1947] 2 All E.R. 255; *Hunter v Chief Constable of West Midlands* [1982] A.C. 529, 540; *The European Gateway* [1987] Q.B. 206, 212, 221; *S.C.F. Finance Co Ltd v Masri (No.3)* [1987] Q.B. 1028, 1049; and *Johnson v Gore Wood & Co (A Firm)* [2002] 2 A.C. 1, 31 ("separate and distinct" but having "much in common") and 59 (they are "all designed to serve the same purpose: to bring finality to litigation and avoid the oppression of subjecting a defendant unnecessarily to successive actions"); cf. *Barrow v Bankside Agency Ltd* [1996] 1 W.L.R. 257. In *Virgin Atlantic Airways Ltd v Zodiac Seats UK Ltd* [2013] UKSC 46, [2014] A.C. 160 at [17] Lord Sumption stated that "the more general procedural rule against abusive proceedings" may be regarded as underlying the principles of res judicata with the possible exception of the doctrine of merger. However, he also noted (at [25]) that res judicata and abuse of process are "juridically very different" with the former being a rule of substantive law, while the latter is "a concept which informs the exercise of the court's procedural powers". See also *Dickinson v UK Acorn Finance Ltd* [2015] EWCA Civ 1194, [2016] H.L.R. 17 at [20] ("the principles of abuse of process ... are quite different from the somewhat technical doctrines of cause of action estoppel and issue estoppel").

[65] *Yat Tung Investment Co Ltd v Dao Heng Bank Ltd* [1975] A.C. 581, 590; *Bragg v Oceanus Mutual Underwriting Association (Bermuda) Ltd* [1982] 2 Lloyd's Rep. 132, 137, 138–139; *J.H. Rayner (Mincing Lane) Ltd v Bank fur Gemeinwirtschaft AG* [1983] 1 Lloyd's Rep. 462, 469; *North West Water Ltd v Binnie & Partners* [1990] 3 All E.R. 547, 553; *House of Spring Gardens Ltd v Waite* [1991] 1 Q.B. 241, 254–255. The rule in *Henderson v Henderson* (1843) 3 Hare 100 has been held to apply where the first action concludes in a settlement, whereas the strict doctrine of res judicata would not apply in such a situation: *Johnson v Gore Wood & Co (A Firm)* [2002] 2 A.C. 1, 32–33 and 59.

[66] Although the CPR do not expressly require the defence to be specifically pleaded, it is advisable to continue to plead it specifically. The rules relating to the contents of the defence are set out in CPR Pt 16 r.16.5. See also *Morrison, Rose and Partners v Hillman* [1961] 2 Q.B. 266; *Lee v Citibank NA* [1981] H.K.L.R. 470 (irrelevancy of which proceedings were first commenced).

[67] *Carl Zeiss Stiftung v Rayner & Keeler Ltd (No.3)* [1970] Ch. 506.

## Ineffective judgments

*Replace footnote 73 with:*

**25-015** [73] *Duchess of Kingston's Case* (1776) 20 St. Tr. 573; *Girdlestone v Brighton Aquarium Co* (1879) 4 Ex. D. 107; *Abouloff v Oppenheimer & Co* (1882) 10 Q.B.D. 295; *Vadala v Lawes* (1890) 25 Q.B.D. 310; *Birch v Birch* [1902] P.130; *Nixon v Loundes* [1909] 2 Ir.Rep. 1; *Reg. v Humphreys* [1977] A.C. 1, 39. In the case where it can be demonstrated that a judgment has been obtained by fraud, and where no allegation of fraud had been made at the trial which led to that judgment, the party seeking to set aside that judgment is not required to show that the fraud could not with reasonable diligence have been discovered before judgment was obtained: *Takhar v Gracefield Developments Ltd* [2019] UKSC 13, [2020] A.C. 450 at [54]. In such a case the maxim that "fraud unravels all" trumps the interest in finality of judgments. Matters may, however, be different in the case where fraud was raised at the original trial and new evidence as to the existence of fraud is prayed in aid in order to advance a case for setting aside the judgment. In such a case, a court may have a discretion whether to admit the application to set aside the judgment ([2019] UKSC 13 at [55]). A similar discretion may exist where it can be demonstrated that a deliberate decision was taken not to investigate the possibility of fraud in advance of the first judgment (at [55]). However, the existence of a discretion in the latter two cases may be open to question: see Lord Sumption in *Takhar* [2019] UKSC 13 at [66]–[67].

## Foreign judgments in personam

*Replace paragraph with:*

At common law, a foreign judgment in personam which is final and conclusive[91] on the merits[92] will be entitled to recognition in England,[93] provided that it is given by a court having jurisdiction to give the judgment[94] and is not impeachable on grounds of fraud, public policy or breach of natural justice.[95] In the case of a judgment given by a court of a state party to the Brussels Convention on Jurisdiction and Enforcement of Judgments in Civil and Commercial Matters,[96] the Lugano Convention on Jurisdiction and Enforcement of Judgments in Civil and Commercial Matters[97] or the Regulation (EU) on Jurisdiction and the Recognition and Enforcement of Judgments in Civil and Commercial Matters[98] and which falls within the scope of either Convention or the Regulation, the judgment will (and must) be recognised in England.[99] Although certain exceptions are provided for in both Conventions and the Regulation,[100] these are very limited in nature and in particular an English court cannot ordinarily question the jurisdiction of the court by which the judgment was given.[101] Where the judgment is that of a court in another part of the United Kingdom, i.e. in Scotland or Northern Ireland, it would appear that such a judgment is entitled to recognition, and may be impeached, in accordance with the common law[102]; but the judgment cannot be refused recognition in England solely on the ground that, in relation to that judgment, the court which gave it was not a court of competent jurisdiction according to the rules of private international law in force in England.[103] **25-017**

[91] *Plummer v Woodburne* (1825) 4 B. & C. 625; *Scott v Pilkington* (1862) 2 B. & S. 11; *Nouvion v Freeman* (1889) 15 App. Cas. 1; *Beatty v Beatty* [1924] 1 K.B. 807; *Blohn v Desser* [1962] 2 Q.B. 116; *Colt Industries Inc v Sarlie (No.2)* [1966] 1 W.L.R. 1287; *Berliner Industriebank A.G. v Jost* [1971] 2 Q.B. 463; *Helmville Ltd v Astilleros Espanoles SA* [1984] 2 Lloyd's Rep. 569. cf. *Harrop v Harrop* [1920] 3 K.B. 386; *Re Macartney* [1921] 1 Ch. 522; *Westfal-Larson & Co A.S. v Ikerigi Compania Naviera SA* [1983] 1 Lloyd's Rep. 424. A foreign judgment may be final and conclusive even though it is subject to appeal or is under appeal; but cf. Administration of Justice Act 1920 s.9(2)(e); Foreign Judgments (Reciprocal Enforcement) Act 1933 ss.1(3), 5(1); *Joint Stock Company "Aeroflot-Russian Airlines" v Berezovsky* [2014] EWCA Civ 20, [2014] 1 C.L.C. 53 ("the English courts will not hold that a later foreign judgment infringes the finality principle when it interferes with a prior judgment if under the foreign law the prior judgment was not final and binding": at [29]).

[92] *Carl-Zeiss Stiftung v Rayner & Keeler Ltd (No.2)* [1967] 1 A.C. 853, 917, 925, 967 (estoppel *per rem judicatam*). In the context of issue estoppel, a decision "on the merits" may be procedural in nature: *D.S.V. Silo-und Verwaltungsgesellschaft mbH v Owners of the Sennar* [1985] 1 W.L.R. 490. cf. *Charm Maritime Inc v Kyriakou* [1987] 1 F.T.L.R. 265; *Harris v Quine* (1869) L.R. 4 Q.B. 653 (limitation); *Black-Clawson International Ltd v Papierworke-Aschaffenburg A.G.* [1975] A.C. 591 (limitation), but see now the Foreign Limitation Periods Act 1984 s.3.

[93] See *Dicey, Morris and Collins* at 14R-020. See also Administration of Justice Act 1920; Foreign Judgments (Reciprocal Enforcement) Act 1933; *Dicey, Morris and Collins* at 14R-173—14-196. Where there are two competing foreign judgments, each of which is pronounced by a court of competent jurisdiction and is final and not open to impeachment on any ground, then the general rule is that the earlier of them in time must be recognised and given effect to, to the exclusion of the latter, although there may be circumstances under which the party holding the earlier judgment may be estopped from relying on it: *Showlag v Mansour* [1995] 1 A.C. 431.

[94] i.e. according to the rules of English private international law: see *Dicey, Morris and Collins* at 14R-054—14-107. See also Administration of Justice Act 1920 s.9(2)(a), (b); Foreign Judgments (Reciprocal Enforcement) Act 1933 ss.4(1)(a)(ii), 2(a); Civil Jurisdiction and Judgments Act 1982 s.33 (as amended).

[95] See *Dicey, Morris and Collins* at 14R-137—14-172. By statute, an overseas judgment may also be

refused recognition if it is given in proceedings brought in breach of an agreement for settlement of a dispute: see Civil Jurisdiction and Judgments Act 1982 s.32 (as amended); *Tracomin SA v Sudan Oil Seeds Co Ltd (Nos 1 and 2)* [1983] 1 W.L.R. 1026; *Dicey, Morris and Collins* at 14R-097—14-100. See also Administration of Justice Act 1920 s.9(2)(c), (d), (f); Foreign Judgments (Reciprocal Enforcement) Act 1933 ss.4(1)(a)(iv), (v), 8(1), (2); *Owens Bank Ltd v Bracco* [1992] 2 A.C. 443; *House of Spring Gardens Ltd v Waite* [1991] 1 Q.B. 241; *Owens Bank Ltd v Etoile Commerciale SA* [1995] 1 W.L.R. 44.

[96] Brussels Convention (1968) together with the 1971 Protocol thereto, both as amended by the Convention on Accession (1978). See the Civil Jurisdiction and Judgments Act 1982 s.2(2) and Schs 1, 2, 3. See generally *Dicey, Morris and Collins*, at 14R-197—14-257. The Convention will, however, cease to be recognised and available in domestic law at the end of the implementation period (on which see above, paras 1-014 et seq.): Civil Jurisdiction and Judgments (Amendment) (EU Exit) Regulations 2019 (SI 2019/479) at reg.82.

[97] Lugano Convention (2007). This replaces the previous convention (1988) and took effect in the European Community and Norway on January 1, 2010 (see [2007] O.J. L339/3, given effect in the UK by the Civil Jurisdiction and Judgments Regulations 2009 (SI 2009/3131)). The Convention will, however, cease to be recognised and available in domestic law at the end of the implementation period: Civil Jurisdiction and Judgments (Amendment) (EU Exit) Regulations 2019 (SI 2019/479) at reg.82. The UK has submitted a formal application to rejoin the Lugano Convention as an individual member at the end of the implementation period but the outcome of that application, which will depend on assent being given by the current members, is presently unknown.

[98] Regulation 1215/2012 on jurisdiction and the recognition and enforcement of judgments in civil and commercial matters [2012] O.J. L351/1. The Regulation came into force on January 10, 2015 and recasts and replaces Regulation 44/2001 on jurisdiction and the recognition and enforcement of judgments in civil and commercial matters [2001] O.J. L.12/1. See the Civil Jurisdiction and Judgments Order 2001 (SI 2001/3929) art.3 and Schs 1, 2 (as amended by the Civil Jurisdiction and Judgments (Amendment) Regulations 2014 (SI 2014/2947)). The Regulation will, however, be revoked at the end of the implementation period: Civil Jurisdiction and Judgments (Amendment) (EU Exit) Regulations 2019 (SI 2019/479) at reg.89 (and for a similar revocation of Regulation 44/2001 see reg.84).

[99] The general duty to recognise the court judgment is to be found in arts 26, 29 and 30 of the Brussels Convention, arts 33, 36 and 37 of the Lugano Convention, and arts 36 and 37 of EU Regulation 1215/2012. The relationship between the two Conventions is regulated by art.64 of the Lugano Convention. The relationship between the Regulation and the two Conventions is regulated by arts 68 and 73 of the Regulation.

[100] Brussels Convention arts 27, 28, Lugano Convention arts 34, 35 and Regulation 1215/2012 arts 45, 46. An English court should not normally entertain a challenge to a Convention judgment in circumstances in which it would not permit a challenge to an English judgment: *Interdesco SA v Nullifire Ltd* [1992] 1 Lloyd's Rep. 180, 187–188.

[101] Brussels Convention art.28, Lugano Convention art.35 and Regulation 1215/2012 art.36.

[102] This would appear to be the effect of s.19 of the Civil Jurisdiction and Judgments Act 1982, since the section is negative in its wording. But see s.18 and Schs 6 and 7 (enforcement). See further Kirsty Hood, *Conflict of Laws Within the UK* (2007), paras 3.69 et seq.

[103] s.19(1), (2) (subject to s.19(3)). For definitions, see s.50.

## 2. ALTERATION OR CANCELLATION OF A WRITTEN INSTRUMENT

### Material alteration

*Replace footnote 110 with:*

**25-020** [110] *Pigot's Case* (1614) 11 Co. Rep. 26b (deed); *Master v Miller* (1791) 4 Term Rep. 320; *Croockewit v Fletcher* (1857) 1 Hurl. & N. 893; *Sellin v Price* (1867) L.R. 2 Ex. 189; *Grove Park Properties Ltd v Royal Bank of Scotland Plc* [2018] EWHC 3521 (Comm) at [13], and cases cited in n.137, below cf. *Hamelin v Bruck* (1846) 9 Q.B. 306; *Pattinson v Luckley* (1875) L.R. 10 Ex. 330. See generally *Norton on Deeds*, 2nd edn, p.34; Holmes (1897) 10 Harvard L.R. 457, 473; Williston (1904) 18 Harvard L.R. 105, 165 and for criticism of the rule see Rogers, *The End of Negotiable Instruments: Bringing Payment Systems Out of the Past* (2012), pp.102–110. For the effect of alteration on joint obligations, see above, para.17-022; for negotiable instruments, see below para.25-026 and Vol.II, para.34-140.

## The elements of the rule

*Replace paragraph with:*

The rule consists of two principal elements. First, the alteration must have been made deliberately. The promisor is therefore not discharged if the alteration is made by accident[115] or by mistake.[116] Not every amendment or note will amount to an "alteration".[117] Where, for example, the amendment is made in pencil, the court may infer that the amendment is not "an operative and final alteration"[118] but is merely an annotation or a suggestion.[119] Second, the alteration must have been material. The touchstone of materiality has been held to be whether or not: **25-022**

> "... there has been some alteration in the legal effect of the contract or instrument concerned simply in the sense of some alteration in the rights and obligations of the parties."[120]

In order to show that the alteration is material the:

> "... would-be avoider should be able to demonstrate that the alteration is one which, assuming the parties act in accordance with the other terms of the contract, is one which is potentially prejudicial[121] to his legal rights or obligations under the instrument."[122]

Whether or not the would-be avoider:

> "... might or might not have assented to the alteration prior to affixing his signature, had he been requested to do so, is not a matter for investigation by the court when applying the rule."[123]

[115] *Hong Kong and Shanghai Bank v Lo Lee Shi* [1928] A.C. 181; *Pickenham Romford Ltd (In Administration) v Deville* [2013] EWHC 2330 (Ch), [2014] 1 B.C.L.C. 380 at [24]; *Grove Park Properties Ltd v Royal Bank of Scotland Plc* [2018] EWHC 3521 (Comm) at [13].

[116] *Henfree v Bromley* (1805) 6 East 309; *Wilkinson v Johnson* (1824) 3 B. & C. 428; *Grove Park Properties Ltd v Royal Bank of Scotland Plc* [2018] EWHC 3521 (Comm) at [13].

[117] It may be necessary in certain cases to distinguish between an "alteration" to a document and an "appendage" to the contract. Thus the addition of an incorrect date after the document has been signed may amount to an "appendage" rather than an alteration: *Moussavi-Azad v Sky Properties Ltd* [2003] EWHC 2669 (QB), [2003] All E.R. (D) 38 (Dec) at [49]. This may be thought to introduce an unnecessary element of sophistry into the rule and that the better view is that such an addition is an "alteration" and the vital question then becomes whether that alteration is "material".

[118] *Co-operative Bank Plc v Tipper* [1996] 4 All E.R. 366, 372.

[119] [1996] 4 All E.R. 366.

[120] *Raiffeisen Zentralbank Österreich AG v Crossseas Shipping Ltd* [2000] 1 W.L.R. 1135, 1146.

[121] It is not necessary to show that prejudice has in fact occurred. The rule is a salutary one which is aimed at the prevention of fraud and so it suffices to establish that the prejudice is potential: *Raiffeisen Zentralbank Österreich AG v Crossseas Shipping Ltd* [2000] 1 W.L.R. 1135, 1148. However, there must be evidence from which a court can infer a potential prejudice: *Governor and Co of the Bank of Scotland v Henry Butcher & Co* [2003] EWCA Civ 67, [2003] 1 B.C.L.C. 575 at [73]–[74].

[122] *Raiffeisen Zentralbank Österreich AG v Crossseas Shipping Ltd* [2000] 1 W.L.R. 1135, 1148. The position may be otherwise where a bank note or negotiable instrument has been altered after its execution without the approval of the parties.

[123] *Raiffeisen Zentralbank Österreich AG v Crossseas Shipping Ltd* [2000] 1 W.L.R. 1135, 1150.

Chapter 26

# DAMAGES

## 1. THE NATURE OF DAMAGES FOR BREACH OF CONTRACT

### (a) General

#### Introduction

*Replace paragraph with:*

Subject to a number of controls,[1] the parties to a contract may themselves specify in their contract the remedy available to the innocent party following the other's breach.[2] In the absence of any such "tailor-made" clause on the remedy, the law on damages fills the gap with "default" provisions on the assessment of money compensation which apply to all types of contract.[3] Until *Att-Gen v Blake*,[4] the traditional view was that damages for a breach of contract committed by the defendant are a compensation to the claimant for the damage, loss or injury he has suffered through[5] that breach. The classic statement is that of Parke B in *Robinson v Harman*: **26-001**

> "The rule of the common law is, that where a party sustains a loss by reason of a breach of contract, he is, so far as money can do it, to be placed in the same situation, with respect to damages, as if the contract had been performed."[6]

In a recent case in the Supreme Court, it was emphasised that this remains the normal rule. Lord Reed (with whom the President, Lady Hale, and Lords Wilson and Carnwath agreed), said:

> "Damages for breach of contract are ... a substitute for performance. That is why they are generally regarded as an adequate remedy. The courts will not prevent self-interested breaches of contract where the interests of the innocent party can be adequately protected by an award of damages. Nor will the courts award damages designed to deprive the contract breaker of any profit he may have made as a consequence of his failure in performance. Their function is confined to enforcing either the primary obligation to perform, or the contract breaker's secondary obligation to pay damages as a substitute for performance ... The damages awarded cannot therefore be affected by whether the breach was deliberate or self-interested."[7]

Conversely, if the defendant has failed to perform, its willingness to perform if it could and the reasons for its failure are irrelevant unless the reasons mean that a protective clause (such as force majeure clause[7a]) applies or that the contract is discharged on the ground of frustration.[7b]

> "The compensatory principle which applies to the assessment of damages for breach of contract involves putting the innocent party in the position it would have been in if the contract had been performed ...
>
> There is no case, or at any rate none which was cited to us, in which the reason why a party is in breach of contract has been held to justify, let alone require, a different approach to the compensatory principle."[7c]

The claimant is, as far as money can do it and subject to the limitations referred to in the next paragraph, to be placed in the same position as if the contract had been performed.[8] This implies a "net loss" approach in which any gains made by the claimant as the result of the breach (e.g. savings made because he is relieved from performing his side of a contract which has been terminated for breach[9]; savings in taxation; benefits obtained from partial performance; or the salvage value of something left in his hands) must be set off against his losses arising from the breach (after he has taken reasonable steps to minimise those losses).[10] Where the claimant is to be compensated for loss of an income stream, a capital sum will be awarded with an appropriate discount for accelerated receipt.[11] In assessing damages for breach of contract, the court can take account of only the defendant's[12] strict, legal obligations: it cannot take account of:

> "... the expectations, however reasonable, of one contractor that the other will do something that he has assumed no legal obligation to do."[13]

Thus, if the contract-breaker had a choice of alternative methods of performance, damages will be assessed on the basis of his minimum legal obligation, viz on the alternative which would have been least onerous, or most beneficial to him.[14] If the claimant cannot establish an actual loss, he is entitled only to nominal damages.[15] Even where the claimant can prove his loss, damages are hardly ever a full recompense, since "it must be remembered that the rules as to damages can in the nature of things only be approximately just".[16]

[1] e.g. the law on penalties below, paras 26-190 et seq.; and statutory controls such as the Unfair Contract Terms Act 1977 (see above, Ch.15), the Unfair Terms in Consumer Contracts Regulations 1999 and the Consumer Rights Act 2015 (see below, Vol.II, Ch.38) and the Consumer Credit Act 1974 (as amended by the Consumer Credit Act 2006) (see below, Vol.II, paras 39-005 et seq.).

[2] For an example see *Scottish Power UK Plc v BP Exploration Operating Co Ltd* [2016] EWCA Civ 1043. There is a presumption that the parties do not intend to give up rights or claims which the general law gives them, and clear express words must be used in order to rebut this presumption: *Gilbert-Ash (Northern) Ltd v Modern Engineering (Bristol) Ltd* [1974] A.C. 689, 717–718 (Lord Diplock); but as the *Scottish Power* case shows, it is a matter of interpretation.

[3] Harris, Campbell and Halson, *Remedies in Contract and Tort*, 2nd edn (2002), pp.88–94.

[4] [2001] 1 A.C. 268 (see below, paras 26-046—26-065).

[5] For the necessary causal link between the breach and the loss, see below, para.26-066.

[6] *Robinson v Harman* (1848) 1 Ex. 850, 855; *Lock v Furze* (1865-66) L.R. 1 C.P. 441, 450–451, 453; *Livingstone v Rawyards Coal Co* (1880) 5 App. Cas. 25, 39; *Wertheim v Chicoutimi Pulp Co* [1911] A.C. 301, 307; *British Westinghouse Electric Co Ltd v Underground Electric Rys* [1912] A.C. 673, 689; *Watts & Co Ltd v Mitsui & Co Ltd* [1917] A.C. 227, 241; *Banco de Portugal v Waterlow & Sons Ltd* [1932] A.C. 452, 474; *Monarch S.S. Co Ltd v Karlshamns Oljefabriker (A/B)* [1949] A.C. 196, 220–221; *C. Czarnikow Ltd v Koufos* [1969] 1 A.C. 350, 414; *Johnson v Agnew* [1980] A.C. 367, 400.

[7] *Morris-Garner v One Step (Support) Ltd* [2018] UKSC 20, [2019] A.C. 649 at [35]. The reference to "primary" and "secondary obligations" refers to the explanation of the effect of a breach of contract given by Lord Diplock in *Photo Production Ltd v Securicor Transport Ltd* [1980] A.C. 827, 849, quoted above, para.24-049. Lord Reed noted that the rule that damages are only to compensate for loss is subject to an exception, namely a discretion to order an account of profits in exceptional circumstances where the other remedies are inadequate, in accordance with the House of Lords' decision in *Attorney General v Blake* [2001] 1 A.C. 268. For this and other exceptions see below, paras 26-047—26-065. For a fuller statement by Lord Reed of the principles see [2018] UKSC 20 at [95], quoted below, para.26-059.

[7a] See above, paras 15-152 et seq.

[7b] See above, Ch.23.

[7c] *Classic Maritime Inc v Limbungan Makmur Sdn Bhd* [2019] EWCA Civ 1102, [2019] 4 All E.R. 1145 at [66] and [84].

[8] For recent applications of this principle, see *Golden Strait Corp v Nippon Yusen Kubishika Kaisha* [2007] UKHL 12, [2007] 2 A.C. 353 at [9], [29], and [57] and *Bunge SA v Nidera BV* [2015] UKSC 43, [2015] 2 Lloyd's Rep. 469 at [76] (see below, para.26-082). If the victim of an anticipatory breach claims damages for non-performance, he must show that he would have been able to perform his obligations under the contract, otherwise he would be placed into a better position than if the party guilty of the repudiation had performed: *Flame SA v Glory Wealth Shipping Pte Ltd (The Glory Wealth)* [2013] EWHC 3153 (Comm), [2013] 2 Lloyd's Rep. 653, discussed by Peel (2015) 131 L.Q.R. 29 and McLauchlan [2015] J.B.L. 530. See also above, para.24-024.

[9] Thus a football club that has terminated a contract for improvements to its pitch before paying the price cannot recover the full price of employing a third party to carry out the work instead: *Gartell & Son v Yeovil Town Football & Athletic Club Ltd* [2016] EWCA Civ 62, [2016] B.L.R. 206.

[10] The language of "balancing" or "setting off" gains and losses is used by the House of Lords in the *British Westinghouse case* [1912] A.C. 673, 691, and in *Westwood v Secretary of State for Employment* [1985] A.C. 20, 44.

[11] *Zodiac Maritime Agencies Ltd v Fortescue Metals Group Ltd (The Kildare)* [2010] EWHC 903 (Comm), [2011] 2 Lloyd's Rep. 360 at [73]; *Mitsui Osk Lines Ltd v Salgaocar Mining Industries Private Ltd* [2015] EWHC 565 (Comm), [2015] 2 Lloyd's Rep. 518 at [56]–[58].

[12] It will on occasion take into account losses incurred by the claimant even though he was not legally obliged to incur them, e.g. payments made voluntarily to a third person injured as the result of the defendant's breach of contract. See below, para.26-036.

[13] *Lavarack v Woods of Colchester Ltd* [1967] 1 Q.B. 278, 294 (distinguished in a case of "unfair dismissal": *York Trailer Ltd v Sparkes* [1973] I.C.R. 518; cf. *Janciuk v Winerite Ltd* [1998] I.R.L.R. 63, and in *Horkulak v Cantor Fitzgerald International* [2004] EWCA Civ 1287, [2005] I.C.R. 402, which involved a discretionary bonus clause). Nor will the claimant be awarded damages for loss of remuneration under some hypothetical arrangement that the defendant might have made with the claimant but did not: *Lavarack v Woods of Colchester Ltd* [1967] 1 Q.B. 278, 297; *Faieta v ICAP Management Services Ltd* [2017] EWHC 2995 (QB) at [109]. Where an investor's portfolio was managed by the defendant firm, which failed to comply with its obligations to keep the portfolio within an agreed risk mandate and to operate "stop loss" provisions, the investor could not claim for a loss of increase in value that might have accrued to the portfolio had the firm acted properly and invested in accordance with certain benchmarks, as the firm was not obliged to manage the portfolio in such a way as to achieve particular returns on the investments or to obtain returns in accordance with the benchmarks: *Rocker v Full Circle Asset Management* [2017] EWHC 2999 (QB) at [310].

[14] See below, para.26-083.

[15] See below, para.26-010.

[16] *Rodocanachi v Milburn* (1886) 18 Q.B.D. 67, 78. See further below, para.26-018. But see Street at Ch.6, and cf. the use of actuarial calculations approved by the House of Lords in *Wells v Wells* [1999] 1 A.C. 345.

### Damages in lieu of specific performance or injunction

*Replace footnote 41 with:*

[41] *Morris-Garner v One Step (Support) Ltd* [2018] UKSC 20, [2019] A.C. 649 at [47], referring to *Jaggard v Sawyer* [1995] 1 W.L.R. 269, 290–291. **26-005**

## (h) Choice Between Methods of Assessment

### Court should chose most appropriate method of assessing loss

*Replace footnote 103 with:*

[103] *Morris-Garner v One Step (Support) Ltd* [2018] UKSC 20, [2019] A.C. 649 at [36], [37] and [96] (in the context of whether the claimant could elect to claim loss of 'negotiating damages': see below, paras 26-050 et seq.). **26-017**

## (i) Difficulty in the Assessment of Damages

### Difficulty of assessment

*Replace paragraph with:*

The fact that damages are difficult to assess does not disentitle the claimant to compensation for loss resulting from the defendant's breach of contract.[104] Where it is clear that the claimant has suffered substantial loss, but the evidence does not enable it to be precisely quantified, the court will assess damages as best it can on the available evidence.[105] The fact that the amount of that loss cannot be precisely ascertained does not deprive the claimant of a remedy.[106] The loss of profits suf- **26-018** fered by a claimant as the result of the defendant's breach of contract frequently depends on many speculative factors, but the courts will always attempt to assess the amount of the loss.[107] As was said in a recent fraud case:

> "Some claims for consequential loss are capable of being established with precision (for example, expenses incurred prior to the date of trial). Other forms of consequential loss are not capable of similarly precise calculation because they involve the attempted measurement of things which would or might have happened (or might not have happened) but for the defendant's wrongful conduct, as distinct from things which have happened. In such a situation the law does not require a claimant to perform the impossible, nor does it apply the balance of probability test to the measurement of the loss."[108]

If the exact loss cannot be determined, the court may have to use the nearest available measure. So if there is no market for the goods which the buyer has wrongly refused to accept, or no clear evidence of the market value, the price at which they were resold may be taken as the best evidence of their value.[109] When there is no direct evidence that of the value of services that should have been provided, damages may be calculated on the assumption that the services were worth a proportionate part of the contract price.[110] When the profit-earning capacity of a business sold was less than had been warranted by the seller and there was no evidence of either the business's actual value or the value it would have had if the warranty had been met, damages were assessed by working out the ratio between the price the buyer was willing to pay and the warranted earning capacity, and then applying that to the shortfall in earning capacity.[111]

[104] *Chaplin v Hicks* [1911] 2 K.B. 786 (below, para.26-079); *Simpson v L.N.W. Ry* (1876) 1 Q.B.D. 274.

[105] *Tai Hing Cotton Mill Ltd v Kamsing Knitting Factory* [1979] A.C. 91, 106; *Morris-Garner v One Step (Support) Ltd* [2018] UKSC 20; *Morris-Garner v One Step (Support) Ltd* [2018] UKSC 20 at [38], quoting this sentence in the 32nd edition.

[106] The preceding sentences were quoted with apparent approval in *Wemyss v Karim* [2016] EWCA Civ 27 at [43].

[107] See below, paras 26-146—26-149.

[108] *Parabola Investments Ltd v Browallia Cal Ltd* [2010] EWCA Civ 486, [2011] Q.B. 477 at [22], Toulson L.J. See also *Wellesley Partners LLP v Withers LLP* [2015] EWCA Civ 1146, [2016] Ch. 529 at [95]–[96]; *UBS AG (London Branch) v Kommunale Wasserwerke Leipzig GmbH* [2017] EWCA Civ 1567, [2017] 2 Lloyd's Rep. 621 at [284]; *Morris-Garner v One Step (Support) Ltd* [2018] UKSC 20, [2019] A.C. 649 at [37]. Where the claimant's proof has been made more difficult by the defendant's wrong, the principle in *Armory v Delamirie* (1722) 1 Str. 505 "raises an evidential (i.e. rebuttable) presumption in favour of the claimant which gives him the benefit of any relevant doubt. The practical effect of that is to give the claimant a fair wind in establishing the value of what he has lost": Jonathan Parker L.J. in *Browning v Brachers* [2005] EWCA Civ 753 at [210]; see also *Fearns v Anglo-Dutch Paint & Chemical Co Ltd* [2010] EWHC 1708 (Ch) at [70]; *Double G Communications Ltd v News Group International Ltd* [2011] EWHC 961 (QB) at [5]; *Yam Seng Pte Ltd v International Trade Corp Ltd* [2013] EWHC 111 (QB), [2013] 1 Lloyd's Rep. 526 at [189]; *Gul Bottlers (PVT) Ltd v Nichols Plc* [2014] EWHC 2173 (Comm) at [86]; *Morris-Garner v One Step (Support) Ltd* [2018] UKSC 20 at [38]. The principle applies where the defendant has suppressed or failed to produce evidence to which it has access, not when the evidence is simply incomplete or involves a measure of conjecture, see *Porton Capital Technology Funds v 3M UK Holdings Ltd* [2011] EWHC 2895 (Comm) at [244]; *University of Wales v London College of Business Ltd* [2016] EWHC 888 (QB) at [10].

[109] See below, para.44-379. Likewise, evidence of the actual earnings made by a ship may be used as evidence of the current rates in the charter market: *Glory Wealth Shipping Pte Ltd v North China Shipping Ltd (The North Prince)* [2010] EWHC 1692 (Comm), [2011] 1 All E.R. (Comm) 641, [16]–[19].

[110] See below, para.26-044.

[111] *Wemyss v Karim* [2016] EWCA Civ 27 at [49].

## (j) Appeals Against the Assessment of Damages

### Power of appellate court to reassess damages

*Replace footnote 116 with:*

[116] The appeal used to be by way of rehearing: CPR Sch.1: RSC Ord.59 r.3(1) which enabled the court to substitute its own view of the assessment of damages: *Flint v Lovell* [1935] 1 K.B. 354, 360; *Davies v Powell Duffryn Associated Collieries Ltd* [1942] A.C. 601, 616–617. Appeals are now normally limited reviews, CPR r.52.21, but CPR r.52.20 gives the Appeal Court all the powers of the lower court and power to alter its orders. The Court of Appeal is more willing to interfere with a judge's award than with a jury's award of damages: [1942] A.C. 601, 616; and if it reverses a decision for the defendant on the issue of liability, it will assess the damages itself: *Reaney v Co-operative Wholesale Society* [1932] W.N. 78; cf. the position in the Privy Council: *Ratnasingam v Kow Ah Dek* [1983] 1 W.L.R. 1235. **26-021**

## 2. COMPENSABLE HEADS OF LOSS

## (a) Expectation, Reliance and Restitution

### "Expectation" "reliance" and "restitution" interests

*Replace footnote 128 with:*

[128] See, e.g. below, paras 26-146—26-149. It is important to note that the expectation must derive from the contract that has been broken. So if a law firm negligently fails to warn a client against making a risky investment, the client may recover the money lost in the investment, and possibly damages for loss of other investment opportunities, see *Leggett v Giambrone Law LLP (In Liquidation)* [2020] EWHC 724 (QB) (below, para.26-079), but not the profit the client might have recovered had the investment been sound. Cf. *Esso Petroleum Ltd v Mardon* [1976] Q.B. 801, above, para.7-095. **26-022**

## (b) Expenditure Wasted as a Result of the Breach

### Reliance expenditure not directed at performance

*Replace paragraph with:*

Before the breach, or before it became apparent, the claimant may incur expenditure in reliance on the expected performance of the contract by the defendant where the expenditure was not incurred in or towards the performance of his own obligations; this is expenditure from which he expected to benefit, as part of the activity in which he was engaged, after he had received the benefit of the defendant's performance, but which the breach now renders futile. Subject to mitigation,[163] the claimant is entitled to damages to reimburse him for this expenditure, provided it was within the reasonable contemplation of the parties that it was not unlikely that the claimant would incur it in reliance on the contract, and that it would be wasted if the defendant committed the breach in question. (No test of reasonableness in incurring the expenditure has been imposed on the claimant, but if the expenditure was incurred unreasonably, it would not satisfy the remoteness test.) So where the buyer of goods had them repaired before he had to give them up to a third party (because it later emerged that the seller had no title to them), he recovered the cost of the repairs which was wasted from his point of view.[164] Other illustrations of the recovery of wasted expenditure are the cost of painting a machine before it was found to be defective[165]; the cost of transporting goods to a sub-buyer before they were examined and rejected[166]; and the cost of equipping a salvage expedition to a tanker which the buyer had been promised was on the "Jourmand Reef", when in fact neither the tanker nor the reef existed.[167] **26-030**

[163] See below, para.26-087. The claimant's damages will be calculated on the basis that he took reasonable steps to realise the salvage value of anything left on his hands after the breach.

[164] *Mason v Burningham* [1949] 2 K.B. 545. See also *Steam Herring Fleet Ltd v V.S. Richards & Co Ltd* (1901) 17 T.L.R. 731 (expenses in preparing for a voyage; delay in delivering ship). See also *Saint Line Ltd v Richardsons, Westgarth & Co Ltd* [1940] 2 K.B. 99, 105.

[165] *Cullinane v British "Rema" Manufacturing Co Ltd* [1954] 1 Q.B. 292. See also *Richard Holden Ltd v Bostock & Co Ltd* (1902) 18 T.L.R. 317 (beer wasted when ingredient found to be contaminated); *New York Laser Clinic Ltd v Naturastudios Ltd* [2019] EWHC 2892 (QB) (though the claimant opted to claim for loss of profit rather than reliance expenditure only).

[166] *Molling & Co v Dean & Son Ltd* (1901) 18 T.L.R. 217.

[167] *McRae v Commonwealth Disposals Commission* (1950) 84 C.L.R. 377 (see above, para. 26-029). The High Court of Australia dismissed a claim for loss of profit as speculative.

## Claims for both profit and reliance loss

*Replace footnote 179 with:*

26-032 [179] This paragraph in the 32nd edition was cited and applied in *A v B* [2018] EWHC 2325 (Comm), [2019] 1 Lloyd's Rep. 385 at [89]. See also *TC Industrial Plant Pty Ltd v Robert's (Queensland) Pty Ltd* [1964] A.L.R. 1083; Stoljar [1975] 91 L.Q.R. 68. In *Hydraulic Engineering Co Ltd v McHaffie Goslett & Co* (1878) 4 Q.B.D. 670, both wasted expenses and profits were awarded, but it is not clear whether the latter were *net* profits. See also *Saint Line Ltd v Richardsons, Westgarth & Co Ltd* [1940] 2 K.B. 99 which accepted a claim involving both. The distinction between gross and net profits is recognised in *C.C.C. Films (London) Ltd v Impact Quadrant Films Ltd* [1985] Q.B. 16, 32.

## Damages assessed on a "no transaction" basis

*Replace paragraph with:*

26-034 In a limited number of situations, where the claimant claims that he would not have entered into a particular transaction but for the defendant's negligent advice (or failure to advise), his damages have been assessed at the amount needed to restore him to the position he would have been in if he had never entered the transaction.[183] So in *Hayes v Dodd*[184] a solicitor negligently advised the plaintiff that he had a right of way to give access to the leasehold property he proposed to acquire as a site for his business. There was no legally enforceable vehicular right of way and the business failed through the lack of adequate access. Damages were assessed on the "no transaction" basis, viz all the wasted expenditure incurred by the plaintiff (the initial cost of the lease and goodwill, rent, rates, insurance, bank interest and other expenses wasted until the time he reasonably gave up the business) *less* the amounts recovered by the plaintiff through selling the lease and his plant (the mitigation rules applied). In *South Australia Asset Management Corp v York Montague Ltd*[185] the question was whether a valuer who is employed by a potential secured lender and who negligently overvalues the property offered as security is liable not only for the difference between the negligent valuation of the property and its actual value at the time but for the whole loss suffered by the claimant if the property market falls so that the security becomes even less adequate. The Court of Appeal[186] distinguished between "no transaction" cases, in which the transaction would not have proceeded but for the defendant's negligence, and "successful transaction" cases in which it would have proceeded but possibly on different terms or for a different amount: once it was proved that the lender would not have made the particular loan but for the valuer's negligence, the valuer was liable for the entire loss flowing from the transaction so far as it was foreseeable. The House of Lords[187] disagreed, holding that the distinction between "no transaction" and "successful transaction" cases should be abandoned. Lord Hoffmann, with whose reasons the other Members of the Judicial Committee agreed, said that the starting point must be the scope of the defendant's duty and the kind of loss for which the claimant is entitled to compensation.[188] The principle:

> "... is that a person under a duty to take reasonable care to provide information on which someone else will decide upon a course of action is, if negligent, not generally regarded as responsible for all the consequences of that course of action. He is responsible only for the consequences of the information being wrong. A duty of care which imposes upon the informant responsibility for losses which would have occurred even if the information which he gave had been correct is not in my view fair and reasonable as between the parties. It is therefore inappropriate either as an implied term of a contract or as a tortious duty arising from the relationship between them. The principle thus stated distinguishes between a duty to *provide information* for the purpose of enabling someone else to decide upon a course of action and a duty to *advise* someone as to what course of action he should take. If the duty is to advise whether or not a course of action should be taken, the adviser must take reasonable care to consider all the potential consequences of that course of action. If he is negligent, he will therefore be responsible for all the foreseeable loss which is a consequence of that course of action having been taken. If his duty is only to supply information, he must take reasonable care to ensure that the information is correct and, if he is negligent, will be responsible for all the foreseeable consequences of the information being wrong."[189]

This has become known as the SAAMCo principle. In *Hughes-Holland v BPE Solicitors*[190] the Supreme Court confirmed where the defendant's duty was to advise on the transaction as a whole, the claimant is in principle entitled to recover its full loss from entering the transaction; whereas where the duty was only to provide information on which the claimant was to base its decision, even if the information was critical to the claimant's decision, the defendant may be liable for the financial consequences of its being wrong but not for the financial consequences of the claimant entering into the transaction so far as these are greater. Lord Sumption, with whose judgment the President and other Justices agreed, said:

> "In cases falling within Lord Hoffmann's 'advice' category, it is left to the adviser to consider what matters should be taken into account in deciding whether to enter into the transaction. His duty is to consider all relevant matters and not only specific factors in the decision. If one of those matters is negligently ignored or misjudged, and this proves to be critical to the decision, the client will in principle be entitled to recover all loss flowing from the transaction which he should have protected his client against. The House of Lords might have said of the 'advice' cases that the client was entitled to the losses flowing from the transaction if they were not just attributable to risks within the scope of the adviser's duty but to risks which had been negligently assessed by the adviser.
>
> By comparison, in the 'information' category, a professional adviser contributes a limited part of the material on which his client will rely in deciding whether to enter into a prospective transaction, but the process of identifying the other relevant considerations and the overall assessment of the commercial merits of the transaction are exclusively matters for the client (or possibly his other advisers). In such a case, as Lord Hoffmann explained in [*Nykredit Mortgage Bank Plc v Edward Erdman Group Ltd (No.2)*[191]], the defendant's legal responsibility does not extend to the decision itself. It follows that even if the material which the defendant supplied is known to be critical to the decision to enter into the transaction, he is liable only for the financial consequences of its being wrong and not for the financial consequences of the claimant entering into the transaction so far as these are greater. Otherwise the defendant would become the underwriter of the financial fortunes of the whole transaction by virtue of having assumed a duty of care in relation to just one element of someone else's decision."[192]

So the first basis applied where a broker negligently advised the claimant to enter a transaction; he was held liable for all the losses suffered by the claimant from that entry.[193] In contrast, if the defendant's duty was only to give information on a particular aspect of the proposed transaction or, as has occurred in a number of conveyancing cases, to report to a lender on title or similar matters, the claimant should not recover the whole of the loss suffered through entering the transaction that turned out to be bad for other reasons.[194] Thus if the defendant's duty was to advise the client on whether to enter another transaction or arrangement, because of the defendant's breach of contract the claimant entered that other transaction when it would not otherwise have done so, and the transaction turned out badly for other reasons, the claimant may be able to recover its wasted expenditure in full.[195] However, the claimant's loss must still have been within the contemplation of the parties[196]; and again[197] the claimant is not put into a better position than he would have been in if the contract had been performed properly. Thus a claimant will not recover if the project would not have been viable and the claimant would have lost its investment even without the defendant's breach.[198] It is clearly established that when the defendant fraudulently induced the claimant to enter into a transaction, even if it is not an "advice" case, damages may also be assessed on the "no transaction" basis.[199] In fraud cases, neither the normal remoteness test nor the principle that the claimant must not be put into a better position than if the contract had been performed applies.[200]

183 *Aneco Reinsurance Underwriting Ltd v Johnson & Higgins Ltd* [2001] UKHL 51, [2001] 2 All E.R. (Comm) 929, HL (advice to enter the transaction, as distinct from the provision of specific information).

184 [1990] 2 All E.R. 815, CA.

185 [1997] A.C. 191 (below, para.26-180).

186 sub nom. *Banque Bruxelles Lambert SA v Eagle Star Insurance Co Ltd* [1995] Q.B. 375.

187 [1997] A.C. 191.

188 [1997] A.C. 191, 211.

189 [1997] A.C. 191, 214. *Hayes v James & Charles Dodd (A Firm)* [1990] 2 All E.R. 815, CA and *County Personnel (Employment Agency) Ltd v Alan R Pulver and Co* [1987] 1 W.L.R. 916, CA were seemingly approved on the basis of the mitigation or "extrication" principle ("a reasonable attempt to cope with the consequences of the defendant's breach of duty") see [1997] A.C. 191, 219, though in *Hayes v James & Charles Dodd* the damages went beyond "extrication" and covered *all* the plaintiff's wasted expenditure from the beginning of the transaction.

190 [2017] UKSC 21, [2018] A.C. 599, noted by Thomson (2017) 76 C.L.J. 473.

191 [1997] 1 W.L.R. 1627, HL.

192 *Hughes-Holland v BPE Solicitors* [2017] UKSC 21 at [40]–[41].

193 *Aneco Reinsurance Underwriting Ltd v Johnson & Higgins Ltd* [2001] 2 All E.R. (Comm) 929, HL, as explained in *Hughes-Holland v BPE Solicitors* [2017] UKSC 21 at [43]–[44].

194 See [2017] UKSC 21 at [47]–[52], disapproving the reasoning in the *Steggles Palmer* and *Colin Bishop* cases (two of the cases brought by the *Bristol and West Building Society*, and reported in [1997] 4 All E.R. 582), and also the application of the *Steggles Palmer* case by the Court of Appeal in *Portman Building Society v Bevan Ashford* [2000] P.N.L.R. 344. In *Manchester Building Society v Grant Thornton UK LLP* [2019] EWCA Civ 40, [2019] 1 W.L.R. 4610 at [54]–[63], accountants had given negligent information about the permissible accounting treatment of swaps. The Court of Appeal applied the paragraphs from Lord Sumption's judgment quoted above and held that the case was not an "advice" case but an "information" case, so the defendant was liable only for the consequences of its information on accounting being wrong. As the claimant had not proved that the losses it had incurred would not have been suffered had the information been correct, the claim must fail (at [98]).

195 The burden of proving the extent of the defendant's duty is on the claimant: [2017] UKSC 21 at [53].

196 It is thought that if the defendant has undertaken such a duty to advise, then the loss will not be one for which the defendant could not reasonably be assumed to be taking responsibility: cf. below, paras 26-137 et seq.

[197] cf. para.26-031.

[198] As in *Hughes-Holland v BPE Solicitors* [2017] UKSC 21, see at [11], [19].

[199] *Smith New Court Securities Ltd v Scrimgeour Vickers (Asset Management) Ltd* [1997] A.C. 254; see paras 7-061—7-065.

[200] See paras 7-057—7-059.

## (c) Expenditure and Other Types of Loss Caused by the Breach

### Incidental losses

*Replace paragraph with:*

Subject to the rules on causation and remoteness and to the test of acting reasonably,[201] the claimant may recover as damages reasonable costs[202] he incurred in mitigating the loss caused by the breach or in otherwise dealing with the consequences of breach.[203] This expenditure does not fit readily into any of the three categories of "restitution", "reliance" or "expectation" loss. It is sometimes termed "incidental" loss.[204] So where the defendant delayed delivery of a crane sold to the plaintiff whom he knew to be an importer of timber, the plaintiff recovered the extra cost of man-handling timber at his wharf.[205] Other illustrations are the recovery of the cost of substitute performance by a third party[206]; the recovery of storage charges after the defendant refused to accept goods[207]; the recovery of the reasonable cost of rebuilding,[208] repairing or replacing[209] property of the claimant damaged or destroyed through the defendant's breach of contract; the recovery of medical or rehabilitation expenses when the breach causes physical injury to the claimant[210]; extra freight and insurance costs arising from late delivery of goods.[211] Unlike in the case of reliance expenditure, there is no question of this category being subject to a ceiling on recovery being fixed by the expected profitability of the contract or activity.[212] **26-035**

[201] The cost of "reasonable" action may be recovered even if it later appears that some other action would have been better: *Gebruder Metelmann GmbH v NBR (London) Ltd* [1984] 1 Lloyd's Rep. 614, 634.

[202] See below, para.26-112.

[203] *Richard Holden Ltd v Bostock & Co Ltd* (1902) 18 T.L.R. 317 (cost of sending notices to customers to minimise loss of business); *Heskell v Continental Express Ltd* [1950] 1 All E.R. 1033, 1046 (cost of trying to trace goods). On claims for interest charges incurred, see below, paras 26-277 et seq. On mitigation, see below, para.26-087.

[204] e.g. American Law Institute, *Restatement of Contracts 2nd* (1981), § 347.

[205] *John M. Henderson & Co Ltd v Montague L. Meyer Ltd* (1941) 46 Com. Cas. 209, 219–220. See also on the costs caused by delay, *Borries v Hutchinson* (1865) 19 C.B.(N.S.) 445 (extra freight and insurance); *Watson v Gray* (1900) 16 T.L.R. 308 (increased building costs).

[206] Below, para.26-039. However, this may be regarded as an alternative way to assess the expectation interest.

[207] *Harlow & Jones Ltd v Panex (International) Ltd* [1967] 2 Lloyd's Rep. 509 (there was no available market). See also *S.S. Ardennes (Cargo Owners) v S.S. Ardennes (Owners)* [1951] 1 K.B. 55 (increased import duty payable).

[208] *Harbutt's "Plasticine" Ltd v Wayne Tank and Pump Co Ltd* [1970] 1 Q.B. 447. See also *Smith v Johnson* (1899) 15 T.L.R. 179 (mortar supplied by a builder was below standard; it was used for building a wall which the local authority later condemned as unsafe; the owner recovered from the builder the cost of pulling it down and of rebuilding). See also *Calabar Properties Ltd v Stitcher* [1984] 1 W.L.R. 287 (cost of alternative accommodation during repairs to flat occupied by tenant).

[209] *Bacon v Cooper (Metals) Ltd* [1982] 1 All E.R. 397.

[210] The decision in *Grant v Australian Knitting Mills Ltd* [1936] A.C. 85 supports the view that damages for personal injury caused by breach of contract should be assessed on a similar basis to that used in tort. Conversely, the legal policy that prevents a claimant in tort recovering the cost of bringing up a

healthy child (see *McFarlane v Tayside Health Board* [2000] 2 A.C. 59, HL (Sc) and *Rees v Darlington Memorial Hospital NHS Trust* [2004] 1 A.C. 309, HL (E)) applies equally to claims in contract: *B v IVF Hammersmith Ltd* [2018] EWCA Civ 2803, [2020] Q.B. 93 (see above, para.1-198B).

[211] *Borries v Hutchinson* (1865) 18 C.B.(N.S.) 445.

[212] See above, paras 26-027, 26-031.

## 3. MEASURES OF COMPENSATION

### (b) Substitute Performance (Cost of Completion or Repairs)

#### Damages for the cost of completion, reinstatement or repairs

*Replace paragraph with:*

**26-039** In appropriate circumstances,[225] damages may be assessed on the basis of what it will cost the claimant to obtain performance (or completion of performance) of the contractual undertaking by a third party.[226] Where the contract was one to transfer goods to the claimant, it is assumed that the claimant will obtain performance by purchasing goods which conform to the contractual requirements, and damages will be assessed as the difference between the cost (if reasonable) of the substitute purchase and the price fixed in the original contract (the rules of mitigation apply). In other situations, the damages are assessed as the difference between the market value of the defendant's performance in its defective or incomplete state, and the market value of the performance if it had been properly completed.[227] In a contract to perform services or for work and materials it will be assumed that the claimant will have the incomplete or defective performance completed or corrected and the damages will be assessed by the cost of getting this done; however, in *Ruxley Electronics and Construction Ltd v Forsyth* the House of Lords held that if the claimant will not have the work done or it would be unreasonable to do so, the damages will again be measured by the difference in value, which may be less than the cost of having the work done. The claimant is entitled to the reasonable cost of having the remedial work done if, in all the circumstances, it is (or was) reasonable for him to insist on having the work done.[228] Factors which are relevant to the issue of reasonableness include:

- (i) the claimant has actually had the work done[229]; or
- (ii) he undertakes to have it done[230] (but such an undertaking will not, on its own, make it reasonable for the claimant to have it done[231]); or
- (iii) he shows a "sufficient intention" to have the work done if he receives damages on this basis[232]: the claimant's subjective intention is relevant.[233]

[225] In contrast, in tort cases in which a property has been damaged through the defendant's negligence, the true measure of the claimant's loss is the diminution in the value of the property, which should be pleaded as general damage; the cost of repairs is no more than evidence of the diminution in value and mitigation is not relevant: that loss cannot be mitigated by having the property repaired at a lower cost: *Coles v Hetherton* [2013] EWCA Civ 1704, [2014] 1 W.L.R. 60 at [28]–[29] and [31] (referring to Admiralty cases such as *The Kingsway* [1918] P. 344 and also *Dimond v Lovell* [2002] 1 A.C. 384).

[226] The advantages of this remedy are reviewed by Harris, Campbell and Halson, *Remedies in Contract and Tort*, 2nd edn (2002), pp.210–216.

[227] *Tito v Waddell (No.2) (The Ocean Island case)* [1977] Ch. 106. In appropriate circumstances, damages may be awarded for loss of amenity, even the loss of a personal, subjective value in obtaining the benefit of performance. Such a measure will fall between the cost of reinstatement and the diminution in market value.

[228] [1996] A.C. 344 (see the comment by Poole (1996) 59 M.L.R. 272; and Coote [1997] C.L.J. 537); *Harbutt's "Plasticine" Ltd v Wayne Tank and Pump Co* [1970] 1 Q.B. 447, 473. On the question of the reasonableness of substitute performance in building contracts, see *East Ham Corp v Bernard Sunley*

& *Sons Ltd* [1966] A.C. 406 (repairs carried out promptly when defect discovered); *Radford v De Froberville* [1971] 1 W.L.R. 1262 (commented on by Wallace in (1980) 96 L.Q.R. 101, 341); *Bevan Investments Ltd v Blackhall and Struthers (No.2)* [1973] 2 N.Z.L.R. 45; [1978] 2 N.Z.L.R. 97; *G.W. Atkins Ltd v Scott* (1980) 7 Const. L.J. 215, CA. See generally Rowan (2017) 76 C.L.J. 616. In *Freeborn v De Almeida Marcal (t/a Dan Marcal Architects)* [2019] EWHC 454 (TCC) breach of contract by an architect resulted in the cinema room required being completely different to what had been promised. The defects could not be rectified at reasonable cost. The claimants' decision to demolish it and not to rebuild was reasonable and they recovered their wasted expenditure and the cost of demolition, plus damages for loss of amenity (see below, para.26-157).

229 *Jones v Herxheimer* [1950] 2 K.B. 106.

230 The *Ocean Island* case [1977] Ch. 106, 333.

231 *Ruxley Electronics and Construction Ltd v Forsyth* [1996] A.C. 344, 373.

232 The *Ocean Island* case [1977] Ch. 106, 333; *Radford v De Froberville* [1971] 1 W.L.R. 1262, 1269–1270; cf. the tort case of *Dodd Properties Ltd v Canterbury City Council* [1980] 1 W.L.R. 433.

233 The *Ruxley Electronics* case [1996] A.C. 344, 359, 372–373. The principles are summarised in *Harrison v Shepherd Homes Ltd* [2011] EWHC 1811 (TCC), (2011) 27 Const. L.J. 709 at [263] (Ramsey J.) (affirmed [2012] EWCA Civ 904). In *Endurance Corporate Capital Ltd v Sartex Quilts and Textiles Ltd* [2020] EWCA Civ 308 it was held that the claimant's intention to reinstate the property normally need not be "fixed and settled". Leggatt L.J. said that where the feature of the property that it would be expensive to reinstate is of value only to the claimant, the claimant's intention is relevant as evidence of whether the feature does indeed have that value, and also it may be unreasonable to require the defendant to pay the cost of restoring the feature if the claimant does not in fact intend to do so: at [63].

## (c) Claimant's Original Purpose Fulfilled Despite Breach

### Sale of goods cases

*Replace paragraph with:*

Where the contract was for the sale of goods for which a market price can be established, the traditional answer has been that the claimant is entitled to the difference in value between what should have been delivered and what was delivered, even if he has been able to use the goods for their intended purpose without any loss.[240] Thus if the buyer bought the goods to resell, and had agreed a sub-sale before the defect was known, the traditional answer has been to say that the buyer is entitled to the difference in value even if the sub-buyer has paid the full agreed price despite the defect. Thus the Sale of Goods Act 1979 s.53 provides for damages where the seller delivers defective goods which the buyer does not, or is unable, to reject, and provides: **26-043**

> "(3) In the case of breach of warranty of quality such loss is prima facie the difference between the value of the goods at the time of delivery to the buyer and the value they would have had if they had fulfilled the warranty."

In *Att-Gen v Blake* Lord Nicholls said:

> "If a shop keeper supplies inferior and cheaper goods than those ordered and paid for, he has to refund the difference in price. That would be the outcome of a claim for damages for breach of contract. That would be so irrespective of whether the goods in fact served the intended purpose."[241]

In *Slater v Hoyle and Smith Ltd*[242] it was held by the Court of Appeal that where the seller delivered defective goods, but the buyer was nevertheless able to perform a sub-contract by delivering the goods to his sub-buyer, the buyer's damages against the seller should not be reduced by taking this into account; the buyer was entitled to rely on the normal measure of damages under s.53(3) viz the difference between (a) the market price, at the time and place of delivery, of goods up to the contractual quality; and (b) the market price, at the time and place of delivery of the goods actually delivered.[243] However, in *Kwei Tek Chao v British Traders and Shippers Ltd* Devlin J. said[244]:

> "[I]t may very well be that in the case of string contracts, if the seller knows that the merchant is not buying merely for re-sale generally, but upon a string contract where he will re-sell those specific goods and where he could only honour his contract by delivering those goods and no others, the measure of loss of profit on re-sale is the right measure."

In that case the question was whether the plaintiffs could recover greater damages than the difference between the contract price and the market price, for loss of profit on a sub-sale; it was held that the parties did not contemplate a sub-sale of the specific goods, so that the loss of profit on the sub-sale was too remote. But in *Biggin & Co Ltd v Permanite Ltd*[245] Devlin J. had said

> "Damages which arise under the so-called 'second rule' in *Hadley v. Baxendale*[246] ... are sometimes referred to as if they were an increased sum which the plaintiff could obtain if he could show 'special circumstances,' or as if the rule embodied a measure of damage specially beneficial to the plaintiff which he could invoke if he fulfilled the necessary conditions. It is, no doubt, true that it generally operates in favour of a plaintiff rather than against him, but I think that it is capable of doing either ..."

> "If ... a sub-sale is within the contemplation of the parties, I think that the damages must be assessed by reference to it, whether the plaintiff likes it or not. Suppose that the only fault in the compound was its incompatibility with bitumen felt, the chance that it might produce bad results would certainly reduce its market value before use. But if it is the plaintiff's liability to the ultimate user that is contemplated as the measure of damage and if in fact it is used without injurious results so that no such liability arises, the plaintiff could not claim the difference in market value, and say that the sub-sale must be disregarded."

These dicta have been relied on by the Court of Appeal to hold, first, that where any loss on the sub-sale was less than difference between the contract price and the market price, the correct measure was the loss on the sub-sale; and secondly, that this applies not only when the claimant was obliged to supply the specific goods under the sub-sale but also if it was contemplated that the claimant would do so though not obliged to. In *Bence Graphics International Ltd v Fasson UK Ltd*[247] the seller knew that the buyer would sell on to others (after manufacturing the goods into another product); the Court of Appeal (by a majority) held that the parties contemplated that the measure of damages for defects in the goods should be the extent of the buyer's liability (if any) to those others resulting from the defect. The decision in *Slater*'s case was doubted, on the ground that s.53(3) laid down only a prima facie rule, which should not be applied if "at the time of making their contract the parties were aware of facts which indicated to both that the loss would not be the difference between the value of the goods delivered and the market value"[248]; it would give the buyer "more than his true loss".[249] The *Bence* case has been the subject of trenchant criticism on the grounds that remoteness is relevant only to claims for consequential loss, not to the difference in value between the goods delivered and the goods as they should have been; and that the effect of the sub-sale should be taken into account only when the buyer was legally obliged to supply the same specific goods under the sub-sale, in which case it is arguable that if the buyer received the full sub-sale price, it suffered no loss at all.[250] Nonetheless, in *Euro-Asian Oil SA (formerly Euro-Asian Oil AG) v Credit Suisse AG*[251] the Court of Appeal approved the trial judge's decision to limit the claimant's to the loss on the sub-sale, rather than the higher difference between the contract price and the market price at the date for delivery, even though the buyer could have fulfilled the sub-sale using other goods, on the ground that the parties contemplated a sub-sale. It is submitted that these cases should not be followed. At most the fact that the buyer has sold the goods on at less than the market price, or has passed them to the sub-buyer without complaint, should be taken into account only when the buyer was obliged to pass on the specific goods to the sub-buyer, and not when it was merely contemplated that it might do so. But in the light of the development described in the next paragraph, it is not clear that the result of the sub-sale should result in the buyer recovering less than the difference between the contract price and the market price at the date of delivery, even in the case where the buyer is obliged to supply the self-same goods under the sub-sale.

[240] This situation must be distinguished from the case in which the claimant has been able to mitigate its loss by subsequent action that reduced or eliminated it: see para.26-103. Most of the cases cited in that paragraph concern the recovery of loss beyond the value of the promised performance itself, but it is thought that mitigation may also reduce the claim below the difference in value between the promised performance and the performance in fact rendered. For example, if the buyer has the goods repaired so that they conform to the contract for less than the difference in value, the buyer will recover only the cost of repair not the difference in value between the goods as they should have been and as they were delivered.

[241] [2001] 1 A.C. 268 at 286; see also *Morris-Garner v One Step (Support) Ltd* [2018] UKSC 20, [2019] A.C. 649 at [80].

[242] [1920] 2 K.B. 11.

[243] The buyers were not obliged to deliver to the sub-buyer the goods which they bought from the original seller, and in fact some of the goods which they delivered to the sub-buyer came from a different source. It is submitted that the decision in this case is to be preferred to the reasoning of the Privy Council in the analogous case of *Wertheim v Chicoutimi Pulp Co* [1911] A.C. 301 (late delivery), which is criticised below, see para.26-179 and Vol.II, para.44-407, and in *Benjamin's Sale of Goods*, 10th edn (2017) at para.17-039. However, in *Bence Graphics International Ltd v Fasson UK Ltd* [1998] Q.B. 87 at 103–105, Auld L.J. cast doubt on *Slater v Hoyle Smith Ltd* and approved the decision in *Wertheim*'s case and Vol.II, para.44-413).

[244] [1954] 2 Q.B. 459, 489–490.

[245] [1951] 1 K.B. 422, 435–436. See also *C. Czarnikow Ltd v Koufos* [1969] 1 A.C. 350, 416 (Lord Pearce).

[246] (1854) 9 Ex. 341; see below, para.26-119.

[247] [1998] Q.B. 87. See also *Louis Dreyfus Trading Ltd v Reliance Trading Ltd* [2004] EWHC 525 (Comm), [2004] 2 Lloyd's Rep. 243 (parties contemplated sale of the same goods to the sub-buyer under a specific contract); *Choil Trading SA v Sahara Energy Resources Ltd* [2010] EWHC 374 (Comm) at [124]–[130].

[248] [1998] Q.B. 87 at 101 and 102.

[249] [1998] Q.B. 87 at 102 (see Vol.II, para.44-413).

[250] See Treitel (1997) 113 L.Q.R. 188 and Peel (ed.), *Treitel on The Law of Contract*, 15th edn (2020), para.20-054. See also *Benjamin's Sale of Goods*, 10th edn (2017) at paras 17-057 and 17-082. Contrast *McGregor on Damages*, 20th edn (2017), paras 25-068—25-069.

[251] [2018] EWCA Civ 1720, [2019] 1 Lloyd's Rep. 444.

## Shortcomings in contracts for services

*Replace footnote 254 with:*

[254] *Morris-Garner v One Step (Support) Ltd* [2018] UKSC 20, [2019] A.C. 649 at [80]. Lord Reed remarked that it "is not excluded by the principle in *Robinson v Harman* (above, para.26-001), but is an example of its application". Earlier he had said that "... damages for breach of contract ... are a substitute for the end-result of performance, not for the economic end-result of performance" (at [40]). **26-044**

## 4. MEASURES THAT ARE NOT CLEARLY COMPENSATORY

### (a) Introduction

**Measure that go beyond compensation**

*Replace footnote 271 with:*

26-047 [271] *The Solholt* [1983] 1 Lloyd's Rep. 605, 608. See also *Morris-Garner v One Step (Support) Ltd* [2018] UKSC 20, [2019] A.C. 649 at [35], quoted above, para.26-001.

### (b) Exemplary Damages

**Wider meaning of "exemplary damages"**

*In line 10, page [1826], after "any breach of contract.[286] However, in", replace "special" with:*

26-049 some

### (c) "Negotiating Damages"

**Introduction**

*Replace footnote 291 with:*

26-050 [291] [2018] UKSC 20, [2019] A.C. 649 at [3]. Sometimes Lord Reed uses this phrase to encompass both damages under Lord Cairn's Act and "user damages": e.g. at [24]. The case is noted by Burrows (2018) 134 L.Q.R. 515, Davies [2018] L.M.C.L.Q. 433 and Bartscherer (2019) 82 M.L.R. 367.

**The extension suggested by Att-Gen v Blake**

*Replace paragraph with:*

26-052 The damages in the *Wrotham Park* case were awarded under Lord Cairns' Act.[301] Subsequently the House of Lords said that the assessment of damages was governed by the same principles whether the damages were awarded under the Act or at common law,[302] which might suggest that damages awarded on a similar basis are available in breach of contract cases generally. Subsequently the *Wrotham Park* decision was doubted in two decisions of the Court of Appeal,[303] but it was approved (obiter) by the House of Lords in *Att-Gen v Blake*.[304] In that case Lord Nicholls seemed to regard the *Wrotham Park* case as a breach of contract case,[305] and suggested that negotiating damages are not restricted to the invasion of a property interest or to Lord Cairns' Act cases:

> "In a suitable case damages for breach of contract may be measured by the benefit gained by the wrong-doer from the breach. The defendant must make a reasonable payment in respect of the benefit he has gained."[306]

*Wrotham Park* damages were awarded or discussed in a number of cases after *Att-Gen v Blake*.[307] Many of the cases involved either infringements of intellectual property rights or breach of confidence, but the courts sometimes appeared willing to make an award on the "hypothetical bargain" basis where there had been only a breach of contract and not an infringement of property rights or breach of confidence, if there were special circumstances to justify it. Thus in *Experience Hendrix LLC v PPX Enterprises Inc*[308] the Court of Appeal awarded damages based on a share of the defendant's profit where the defendant had broken a settlement agreement under which the defendant had agreed not to release further recordings from master tapes that were the defendant's property, even though the claimants could not show that this caused it any loss. The Court of Appeal used some of the factors relevant to the granting of an account of profits[309] as relevant to their discretion to grant *Wrotham Park* damages. The court took into account the fact that the defendant "did do the very thing it had contracted not to do"[310]; that the defendant "knew that it was doing something which it had contracted not to do"[311]; that it was a "deliberate breach",[312] a "flagrant contravention" of the defendant's obligation.[313] However, the Court held that the circumstances need not be exceptional in the way required if an account of profits is to be ordered.[314] In another case it was held that where the defendant has failed to provide the services promised but the claimant cannot show a consequential loss, if damages cannot be awarded on the simple difference in value between the services promised and those provided,[315] an award on the hypothetical bargain basis could be made instead.[316] In the *Morris-Garner* case the Court of Appeal held that *Wrotham Park* damages may be awarded when it will be very difficult to prove the loss that has been caused by the breach; the question is whether an award would be a just response.[317] However the decision was reversed by the Supreme Court,[318] which held that at common law, as opposed to under Lord Cairns' Act, negotiating damages may not be awarded in claims for breach of contract that do not involve the infringement of a proprietary interest or the like,[319] even if the breach was deliberate or the loss was hard to assess.[320] After the Supreme Court's decision it is clear that in the case of infringement of the claimant's property right and when damages are awarded in lieu of specific performance or an injunction, the claimant may be awarded damages based on the "use value" of the property concerned or the amount that the claimant could reasonably have demanded as the price for allowing the defendant to act as he did.[321] Despite the suggestions in *Blake*'s case and some subsequent decisions, this measure of loss is not applicable in other cases of breach of contract.

301 Senior Courts Act 1981 s.50 (formerly Lord Cairns' Act).

302 *Johnson v Agnew* [1980] A.C. 367, 400.

303 *Surrey CC v Bredero Homes Ltd* [1993] 1 W.L.R. 1361; *Jaggard v Sawyer* [1995] 1 W.L.R. 269. The cases subsequent to Wrotham Park are exhaustively analysed in *WWF-World Wide Fund for Nature v World Wrestling Federation Entertainment Inc* [2007] EWCA Civ 286, [2008] 1 W.L.R. 445.

304 [2001] 1 A.C. 268. See below, paras 29-170 et seq.

305 In *Pell Frischmann Engineering Ltd v Bow Valley Iran Ltd* [2009] UKPC 45, [2010] B.L.R. 73 at [48] Lord Walker remarked: "The breach of a restrictive covenant is also generally regarded as the invasion of a property right ... since a restrictive covenant is akin to a negative easement. (It is therefore a little surprising that Lord Nicholls in *Blake* ... referred to *Wrotham Park* as a 'solitary beacon' concerned with breach of contract; that case was concerned with the breach of a restrictive covenant to which neither the plaintiff nor the defendant was a party; but the decision of the House of Lords in *Blake* decisively covers what their Lordships have referred to as a non-proprietary breach of contract.)".

306 [2001] 1 A.C. 268, 283–284.

307 In addition to the cases cited in the text, see *Lunn Poly Ltd v Liverpool & Lancashire Properties Ltd* (2006) 25 E.G. 210; *Field Common Ltd v Elmbridge BC* [2008] EWHC 2079 (Ch), [2009] 1 P. & C.R. 1 and *Devenish Nutrition v Sanofi-Aventis* [2008] EWCA Civ 1086, [2009] 3 All E.R. 27.

308 [2003] EWCA Civ 323 at [44], [58].

309 Below, para.26-063.

310 [2003] EWCA Civ 323 at [36].

311 [2003] EWCA Civ 323 at [36].

312 [2003] EWCA Civ 323 at [58].

313 [2003] EWCA Civ 323 at [54].

314 [2003] EWCA Civ 323 at [24]–[25].

315 See above, para.26-041.

[316] *Giedo van der Garde BV v Force India Formula One Team Ltd* [2010] EWHC 2373 (QB).

[317] [2016] EWCA Civ 180, [2017] Q.B. 1 at [122] and [145]–[146], rejecting the holding in *Abbar v Saudi Economic & Development Co (SEDCO) Real Estate Ltd* [2013] EWHC 1414 (Ch) at [225] that "the inability to demonstrate identifiable financial loss of the conventional sort is a pre-condition to the award of such damages". The Court of Appeal decision was noted by Davies [2017] L.M.C.L.Q. 201. In *Marathon Asset Management LLP v Seddon* [2017] EWHC 300 (Comm) Leggatt J. said (at [217]) he did not find it easy to discern the principle on which the award for breach of obligations not to compete had been made in the *One Step* case. The fact that the claimant's loss would be difficult to prove or quantify might be a good reason for granting an injunction rather than leaving the claimant to seek damages, but it is not a principled reason for awarding a sum of money which does not depend on whether the claimant has suffered any loss at all. Awarding a gain-based remedy can only be a just response where compensatory damages are an inherently inadequate remedy because they would not represent adequate redress for the wrong done to the claimant even where any loss caused by the defendant's wrong can be fully identified and reversed (at [214]–[215]).

[318] [2018] UKSC 20, [2019] A.C. 649.

[319] See above, para.26-051 and below, para.26-058.

[320] At [97]. The Singapore Court of Appeal has taken a different approach, holding that *Wrotham Park* damages are available only if (1) neither specific relief not common law damages are available (i.e. the damages would be nominal; (2) there has been a breach of a negative covenant; and (3) the case is "not one where it would be irrational or totally unrealistic to expect the parties to bargain for the release of the relevant covenant, even on a hypothetical basis": *Turf Club Auto Emporium Pte Ltd v Yeo Boong Hua* [2018] SGCA 44 at [217].

[321] See also *Pell Frischmann Engineering Ltd v Bow Valley Iran Ltd* [2009] UKPC 45, [2010] B.L.R. 73 at [48].

## Compensatory basis

*Replace paragraph with:*

**26-053** Perhaps the "use value" damages awarded in tort and property infringement cases are not clearly compensatory, and it has sometimes been stated that the damages awarded in the *Wrotham Park* case[322] were on a restitutionary basis.[323] In earlier editions of this work such damages were referred to as "partial disgorgement" of the "wrongful" profits made through the breach.[324] However, in the later *WWF* case[325] the award was held to be a form of compensatory damages. It is now clear that both "use value" or "user" damages and kind of damages awarded in the *Wrotham Park* case are to be regarded as a form of compensation. In *Morris-Garner v One Step (Support) Ltd*, Lord Reed, referring to cases involving claims in tort and cases of the infringement of property rights, said:

> "In these cases, the courts have treated user damages as providing compensation for loss, albeit not loss of a conventional kind. Where property is damaged, the loss suffered can be measured in terms of the cost of repair or the diminution in value, and damages can be assessed accordingly. Where on the other hand an unlawful use is made of property, and the right to control such use is a valuable asset, the owner suffers a loss of a different kind, which calls for a different method of assessing damages. In such circumstances, the person who makes wrongful use of the property prevents the owner from exercising his right to obtain the economic value of the use in question, and should therefore compensate him for the consequent loss. Put shortly, he takes something for nothing, for which the owner was entitled to require payment."[326]

Similarly, the measure used in awards in lieu of an injunction under Lord Cairns' Act reflect:

> "... the fact that the refusal of an injunction had the effect of depriving the claimant of an asset which had an economic value."[327]

[322] [1974] 1 W.L.R. 798.

[323] See the judgment of Steyn L.J. in *Surrey CC v Bredero Homes Ltd* [1993] 1 W.L.R. 1361, 1369 and the discussion in *McGregor on Damages*, 20th edn (2017), para.14-048. See also below, para.29-162.

[324] In *Experience Hendrix LLC v PPX Enterprises Inc* [2003] EWCA Civ 323, [2003] E.M.L.R. 25, [2003] F.S.R. 46 at [16] such damages were explained on a restitutionary, not a compensatory, basis.

[325] *WWF-World Wide Fund for Nature v World Wrestling Federation Entertainment Inc* [2007] EWCA Civ 286, [2008] 1 W.L.R. 445. It was necessary for the court to examine the *Wrotham Park* basis for assessing damages in order to reach its decision, which was based on the claimant's abuse of process in seeking such damages after inviting the judge below to decide whether to order an account of profits on the basis that there would be no claim for *Wrotham Park* damages: at [74].

[326] *Morris-Garner v One Step (Support) Ltd* [2018] UKSC 20 at [30]; see below, para.26-058. See similarly Stevens, *Torts and Rights* (2007), 59–61; Barnett [2009] R.L.R. 79, 81 and work cited there. See also Andrews, Clarke, Tettenborn and Virgo, *Contractual Duties: Performance, Breach, Termination and Remedies*, 2nd edn (2017), paras 26-023—26-024.

[327] [2018] UKSC 20, [2019] A.C. 649 at [63]. Burrows, *Remedies for Torts, Breach of Contract and Equitable Wrongs*, 4th edn (2019), p.328, comments that the Supreme Court's rejection of a restitutionary analysis is "disappointing" but that there are "plausible arguments" to justify a compensatory analysis.

## Terminology: "negotiating damages"

*Replace footnote 332 with:*

[332] [2018] UKSC 20, [2019] A.C. 649 at [3]. Sometimes Lord Reed uses this phrase to encompass both damages under Lord Cairn's Act and "user damages": e.g. at [24]. **26-054**

## Damages in lieu of specific performance or injunction

*Replace footnote 335 with:*

[335] [2018] UKSC 20, [2019] A.C. 649. **26-055**

## Court to adopt most appropriate method

*Replace footnote 339 with:*

[339] [2018] UKSC 20, [2019] A.C. 649 at [63]. **26-056**

## Assessing hypothetical bargain damages

*Replace footnote 351 with:*

[351] [2018] UKSC 20, [2019] A.C. 649 at [159]. **26-057**

## "User" damages in tort and for invasion of property interest

*Replace footnote 360 with:*

[360] [2018] UKSC 20, [2019] A.C. 649. **26-058**

## Damages at common law where no infringement of property

*Replace paragraph with:*

As explained earlier, where there has been no infringement of the claimant's **26-059** property right,[363a] and the damages are not being awarded under Lord Cairns' Act in lieu of specific performance or an injunction, "negotiating damages" may not be awarded. Lord Reed set out his conclusions on damages where the damages are awarded at common law, rather than under Lord Cairns' Act, and there has been no infringement of a property right or the like, as follows[364]:

"[…]

(6) Common law damages for breach of contract are intended to compensate the claimant for loss or damage resulting from the non-performance of the obligation in question. They are therefore normally based on the difference between the effect of performance and non-performance upon the claimant's situation.

(7) Where damages are sought at common law for breach of contract, it is for the claimant to establish that a loss has been incurred, in the sense that he is in a less favourable situation, either economically or in some other respect, than he would have been in if the contract had been performed.
(8) Where the breach of a contractual obligation has caused the claimant to suffer economic loss, that loss should be measured or estimated as accurately and reliably as the nature of the case permits. The law is tolerant of imprecision where the loss is incapable of precise measurement, and there are also a variety of legal principles which can assist the claimant in cases where there is a paucity of evidence.
(9) Where the claimant's interest in the performance of a contract is purely economic, and he cannot establish that any economic loss has resulted from its breach, the normal inference is that he has not suffered any loss. In that event, he cannot be awarded more than nominal damages.
(10) [...]
(11) Common law damages for breach of contract cannot be awarded merely for the purpose of depriving the defendant of profits made as a result of the breach, other than in exceptional circumstances, following *Attorney General v Blake*.
(12) Common law damages for breach of contract are not a matter of discretion. They are claimed as of right, and they are awarded or refused on the basis of legal principle."

Lord Reed did not altogether rule out consideration of the price the claimant might have obtained for releasing the defendant from its obligations, but it should only be used as evidence of the claimant's loss. He said:

> "It is not easy to see how, in circumstances other than [where the breach results in the loss of a valuable asset created or protected by the right which was infringed[365]], a hypothetical release fee might be the measure of the claimant's loss. It would be going too far, however, to say that it is only in those circumstances that evidence of a hypothetical release fee can be relevant to the assessment of damages. If, for example, in other circumstances, the parties had been negotiating the release of an obligation prior to its breach, the valuations which the parties had placed on the release fee, adjusted if need be to reflect any changes in circumstances, might be relevant to support, or to undermine, a subsequent quantification of the losses claimed to have resulted from the breach. It would be a matter for the judge to decide whether, in the particular circumstances, evidence of a hypothetical release fee was relevant and, if so, what weight to place upon it. However, the hypothetical release fee would not itself be a quantification of the loss caused by a breach of contract, other than [where the breach results in the loss of a valuable asset created or protected by the right which was infringed]."[366]

On the facts of the *Morris-Garner* case, the defendants had made wrongful use of confidential information and broken non-solicitation covenants.[367] However, the claimant's only interest in the defendants' performance of their obligations under the covenants was commercial, and the substance of its case was that it suffered financial loss as a result of the defendants' breach of contract. The judge had ordered a hearing on quantum which should proceed but not, as the judge had ordered, on the basis of an assessment of the amount which would notionally have been agreed between the parties, acting reasonably, as the price for releasing the defendants from their obligations. The claimant did not have a right to elect how the damages should be assessed.[368] The judge should measure, as accurately as he could on the available evidence, the financial loss which the claimant had actually sustained. Any evidence led in respect of a hypothetical release fee was for the judge to consider but the fee is not itself the measure of the claimant's loss.[369]

[363a] The Singapore Court of Appeal has rejected the restriction to cases in which the contractual right

breached is an economically valuable asset: *Turf Club Auto Emporium Pte Ltd v Yeo Boong Hua* [2018] SGCA 44 at [278].

364 [2018] UKSC 20, [2019] A.C. 649 at [95].

365 Lord Reed does not mention here cases where the damages are awarded under Lord Cairns' Act, but then also a hypothetical release fee may be relevant; see above, para.26-055.

366 [2018] UKSC 20 at [94].

367 On this point see further below, para.26-060.

368 [2018] UKSC 20 at [96].

369 [2018] UKSC 20 at [100].

## What amounts to an infringement property rights

*Replace paragraph with:*

The majority in *Morris-Garner v One Step (Support) Ltd*[370] accepted that negotiating damages are an appropriate way to compensate a claimant when the breach of contract concerned has deprived the claimant of the use of its property, or has interfered with a property right. The *Wrotham Park* case was one such case: the complaint was not based on breach of contract but on breach of a restrictive covenant. Lord Reed said in his conclusions: **26-060**

> "(10) Negotiating damages can be awarded for breach of contract where the loss suffered by the claimant is appropriately measured by reference to the economic value of the right which has been breached, considered as an asset. That may be the position where the breach of contract results in the loss of a valuable asset created or protected by the right which was infringed. The rationale is that the claimant has in substance been deprived of a valuable asset, and his loss can therefore be measured by determining the economic value of the right in question, considered as an asset. The defendant has taken something for nothing, for which the claimant was entitled to require payment."

The majority said that this applied to patent infringement and breaches of other intellectual property rights; and that it might be appropriate to treat disclosures of confidential information in the same way where the confidentiality of the information had an independent value.[371] This had been the basis on which negotiated damages had been awarded in both *Pell Frischmann Engineering Ltd v Bow Valley Iran Ltd*[372] and *Vercoe v Rutland Fund Management Ltd*[373]: "In effect, the court awarded damages based on the commercial value of the information which the defendants misused."[374] However, confidential information does not always have a separate commercial value; on the facts of the *One-Step* case, the trial judge had not given a separate award for breach of the confidentiality provisions, seemingly because the harm it would cause:

> "... would be reflected in an award in respect of the breach of the non-compete and non-solicit covenants. No appeal has been taken against these aspects of his decision."[375]

Lord Reed said:

> "... what is important is that the contractual right is of such a kind that its breach can result in an identifiable loss equivalent to the economic value of the right, considered as an asset, even in the absence of any pecuniary losses which are measurable in the ordinary way. That is something which is true of some contractual rights, such as a right to control the use of land, intellectual property or confidential information, but by no means of all. For example, the breach of a non-compete obligation may cause the claimant to suffer pecuniary loss resulting from the wrongful competition, such as a loss of profits and goodwill,

which is measurable by conventional means, but in the absence of such loss, it is difficult to see how there could be any other loss."[376]

It is, with respect, hard to see when a right that information be kept confidential will have an economic value, "considered as an asset", and when not. A possible explanation is that the information will be treated as having an economic value when it would have been valuable to a third party. For example, the information that was misused in the *Vercoe* case was about a business opportunity that the claimants could have exploited, had the defendants not misused the information to exploit it themselves. In the *Morris-Garner* case the information was market research. This might have an independent value, but the trial judge had not treated it as having any and the issue was not appealed. But the explanation suggested is hard to fit with the decision in the *Pell Frischmann* case. The confidential information in that case was about exploiting an oilfield owned by a third party in whose eyes the claimants had become persona non grata, making it hard to see that the information could be used in a partnership between the claimant and anyone else; Lord Walker said that the rights were now only of "negative nuisance value". Yet the Privy Council held that damages on the *Wrotham Park* basis should be awarded. This is hard to reconcile with Lord Reed's explanation.

[370] [2018] UKSC 20, [2019] A.C. 649.

[371] Lord Sumption, while agreeing with the result reached by the majority, took a different approach on this point. He viewed infringement of patent rights and breaches of confidentiality agreements as not falling within the "infringement of property rights" rule but as breaches of contract. In a patent infringement case:

> "A patentee may exploit his legal monopoly in either or both of two ways, (i) by manufacturing and selling the patented article or (ii) by licensing others to do so. In case (i), the measure of damages is the profits which he has lost by the diversion of sales to the infringer ... This is the same as the ordinary measure of damages for breach of a non-compete agreement. In case (ii), the measure of damages is the royalty which the infringer would have had to pay if he had obtained the licence which would have been available ..."

In such cases, including simple breach of contract cases, the court should award damages to compensate the claimant for any loss it had suffered, and "the notional price of a release may nonetheless be relevant, not as an alternative measure of damages but as an evidential technique for estimating what the claimant can reasonably be supposed to have lost" (at [106]). Lord Carnwath, who agreed with the majority but also gave a separate judgment, went to some lengths to explain the difference between Lord Sumption's approach and the majority's. Lord Sumption's judgment is analysed by Bartscherer (2019) 82 M.L.R. 367, 372–376. The Singapore Court of Appeal has rejected the restriction to cases in which the contractual right breached is an economically valuable asset: *Turf Club Auto Emporium Pte Ltd v Yeo Boong Hua* [2018] SGCA 44 at [278]. See also Burrows, *Remedies for Torts, Breach of Contract and Equitable Wrongs*, 4th edn (2019), pp.329–323.

[372] [2009] UKPC 45, [2010] B.L.R. 73 at [46].

[373] [2010] EWHC 424 (Ch) at [292].

[374] [2018] UKSC 20 at [83]–[84].

[375] [2018] UKSC 20 at [17]. Possibly the confidential information—contact details of previous customers—would be of value only to the defendants, who might be expected to have some influence over previous customers, and not to a third person.

[376] At [93]. In *Priyanka Shipping Ltd v Glory Bulk Carriers Pte Ltd* [2019] EWHC 2804 (Comm), [2019] 1 W.L.R. 6677 it was held that the seller of a ship that the buyer undertook to use only for the purposes of demolition had no proprietary or financial interest in the vessel, and the buyer's use of the vessel for trading, though in breach of contract, did not involve the buyer taking or using something in which the seller had an interest, a valuable asset, for which the seller was entitled to require payment (at [196]).

**Negotiating damages and other loss**

*Replace footnote 377 with:*

26-061 [377] [2018] UKSC 20, [2019] A.C. 649. The Court of Appeal [2016] EWCA Civ 180, [2017] Q.B. 1 at

[122] and [145]–[146], had rejected the holding in *Abbar v Saudi Economic & Development Co (SEDCO) Real Estate Ltd* [2013] EWHC 1414 (Ch) at [225] that "the inability to demonstrate identifiable financial loss of the conventional sort is a pre-condition to the award of such damages".

## (d) Account of Profits

### Account of profits for breach of contract

*Replace paragraph with:*

In *Att-Gen v Blake*[385] the traitor Blake had written and published a book in breach of the confidentiality agreement made by him when he entered the Secret Intelligence Service.[386] The House of Lords gave the claimant the "exceptional" remedy of an account of the profits made by the defendant as a result of the breach. Their Lordships avoided any definition of "exceptional" circumstances which would justify an account of profits as the remedy for breach of contract. **26-063**

> "Normally the remedies of damages, specific performance and injunction, coupled with the characterisation of some contractual obligations as fiduciary, will provide an adequate response to a breach of contract. It will be only in exceptional cases, where those remedies are inadequate, that any question of accounting for profits will arise.[387] No fixed rules can be prescribed. The court will have regard to all the circumstances, including the subject matter of the contract, the purpose of the contractual provision which has been breached, the circumstances in which the breach occurred, the consequences of the breach and the circumstances in which relief is being sought. A useful general guide, although not exhaustive, is whether the plaintiff had a legitimate interest in preventing the defendant's profit-making activity and, hence, in depriving him of his profit.
>
> It would be difficult, and unwise, to attempt to be more specific ..."[388]

It appears that no one factor is crucial. But judges have given some factors which may be relevant to their decision:

(a) The moral character of the defendant's conduct in breaching, e.g. was it "deliberate and cynical"; did it involve "doing exactly what one promised not to do"? In *Blake*, Lord Nicholls said that none of the following facts "would be, by itself, a good reason for ordering an account of profits":

> "... the fact that the breach was cynical and deliberate; the fact that the breach enabled the defendant to enter into a more profitable contract elsewhere; and the fact that by entering into a new and more profitable contract the defendant put it out of his power to perform his contract with the plaintiff."[389]

But his words imply that these lacks might contribute to the cumulative weight in favour of the remedy. Other relevant factors in *Blake* were that the breach of contract involved committing a criminal offence[390]; and that he committed repeated breaches.[391] In *Hendrix*[392] an account of profits was not awarded on the particular facts[393] but it was recognised that such a remedy was possible in a commercial case[394] and in granting "negotiating damages" the Court of Appeal took into account the fact that the defendant "did do the very thing it had contracted not to do"[395]; that the defendant "knew that it was doing something which it had contracted not to do"[396]; and that it was a "deliberate breach",[397] a "flagrant contravention" of the defendant's obligation.[398] But prior to *Hendrix* courts did not treat moral considerations as relevant in commercial transactions.

(b) The question whether the claimant "had a legitimate interest in preventing the defendant's profit-making activity".[399] In *Blake*, the Crown's interest in protecting the Secret Service's information met this test but in *Experience Hendrix*, a case between commercial parties, such a legitimate interest was found because on orthodox rules the claimant would be confined to nominal damages—the claimant could not adequately prove any loss, or could prove only minor loss.[400]

(c) The analogy with fiduciary obligations. Before the *Blake* decision it was clear that an account of profits could be awarded for breach of a fiduciary obligation: although Blake was not a fiduciary, their Lordships said that his obligation was "closely akin to a fiduciary obligation".[401] In effect, Blake extended the previous category of fiduciaries by creating a quasi-fiduciary out of a contractual obligation. In *Experience Hendrix* it was said that an account of profits was not justified on the facts because the defendant's situation was not analogous with a fiduciary's duty: "there is no direct analogy between [the defendant's] position and that of a fiduciary."[402] The concept that contractual obligations may give rise to remedies previously given only to genuine fiduciaries is unsatisfactory because it is uncertain and so unpredictable in its application.

In *Morris-Garner v One Step (Support) Ltd*[403] the Supreme Court confirmed that an account of profit may be ordered, but only in exceptional cases.[404] Lord Reed[405] gave a brief summary of what Lord Nicholls had said but no further indication of when a case would be treated as exceptional.

385 [2001] 1 A.C. 268. See also below, paras 29-159 et seq.

386 Though subsequently it has been questioned whether he had in fact given a contractual undertaking: see Simpson (2009) 125 L.Q.R. 433.

387 Although Scott [2007] L.M.C.L.Q. 465, 468 treats both the remedy given in the *Wrotham Park* case and in *Blake*'s case as compensatory, these words show that the remedy in *Blake*'s case is not one of damages; and a compensatory analysis must now be doubted.

388 [2001] 1 A.C. 268, 285 (per Lord Nicholls).

389 [2001] 1 A.C. 268, 286 E–F.

390 [2001] 1 A.C. 268, 286 G–H.

391 [2001] 1 A.C. 268, 286 G. Repetition of breaches was an important factor in the *Niad* case [2001] All E.R. (D) 324.

392 *Experience Hendrix LLC v PPX Enterprises Inc* [2003] EWCA Civ 323, [2003] E.M.L.R. 25, [2003] F.S.R. 46.

393 The situation was not sufficiently exceptional for an account of all profits. See above, para.29-052.

394 An account of profits in a commercial case was granted at first instance in *Esso Petroleum Co Ltd v Niad Ltd* [2001] All E.R. (D) 324, see below para.26-065.

395 [2003] EWCA Civ 323 at [36].

396 [2003] EWCA Civ 323 at [36].

397 [2003] EWCA Civ 323 at [58].

398 [2003] EWCA Civ 323 at [54].

399 *Att-Gen v Blake* [2001] 1 A.C. 268, 285.

400 *Experience Hendrix* [2003] EWCA Civ 323 at [58].

401 *Att-Gen v Blake* [2001] 1 A.C. 268, 287 F–G.

402 *Experience Hendrix* [2003] EWCA Civ 323 at [37].

403 [2018] UKSC 20, [2019] A.C. 649 at [159].

404 [2018] UKSC 20 at [95(11)]. The Supreme Court of Canada has taken the same view: *Atlantic Lottery Corp Inc v Babstock* 2020 SCC 19 at [53]. At [55]–[58] Brown J. offers some observations as to when a claimant may have a legitimate interest in the defendant's profit-making activities such as to justify an account of profits. See also *Turf Club Auto Emporium Pte Ltd v Yeo Boong Hua* [2018] SGCA 44 at [255].

[405] [2018] UKSC 20 at [64].

## 5. Causation and Contributory Negligence

### (a) Causation

#### Requirement of a causal connection

*Replace footnote 419 with:*

[419] The loss must have been caused by the breach itself, since "damages for breach of contract may ... [not] be awarded ... for loss caused by the manner of the breach": per Lord Steyn in *Malik v Bank of Credit and Commerce International SA* [1998] A.C. 20, 51 (citing *Addis v Gramophone Co* [1909] A.C. 488). For a case in which an employee's breach of a contractual duty of confidence did not cause a disgruntled customer to sue the employer, as the customer had commenced her action before the breach, see *Colville v Seventy Thirty Ltd* [2019] EWHC 880 (QB). **26-066**

#### Duty to prevent third party's act

*Replace footnote 428 with:*

[428] *London Joint Stock Bank Ltd v Macmillan* [1918] A.C. 777. See also *De la Bere v Pearson* [1908] 1 K.B. 280; *Stansbie v Troman* [1948] 2 K.B. 48; *Marshall v Rubypoint Ltd* [1997] 25 E.G. 142; cf. *Cobb v G.W. Ry* [1894] A.C. 419. Deliberate conduct will not break the chain of causation if that was the very thing that the defendant ought to have prevented: *Reeves v Commissioner of Police of the Metropolis* [2000] 1 A.C. 360, 367, cited by Evans-Lombe J. in *Barings Plc v Coopers & Lybrand (No.7)* [2003] EWHC 1319 (Ch) at [742]. However, this applies to the occurrence and not necessarily to the consequences: *Assetco Plc v Grant Thornton UK LLP* [2019] EWHC 150 (Comm), [2019] Bus. L.R. 2291 at [989]. **26-069**

*Replace paragraph with:*

In *Weld-Blundell v Stephens*,[431] the defendant, in breach of his contract, negligently left a libellous letter (written by the plaintiff) where it was read by a third party, who was likely to, and did, communicate its contents to the persons libelled; the latter recovered damages for libel from the plaintiff, who thereupon sued the defendant. The House of Lords, by a bare majority, held that the plaintiff could recover only nominal damages for the defendant's breach of contract, and not the damages and costs paid in the libel action. There appear to have been two reasons: the plaintiff was liable in any event, and though in general terms, disclosure by a third party was foreseeable, it was a "new and independent" cause.[432] Much seems to depend on the court's assessment of the facts; it is submitted that a party may be liable when his breach and a foreseeable breach of duty by a third party, even a deliberate breach, have combined to cause the loss.[433] **26-070**

[431] [1920] A.C. 956 (some intervening act was foreseeable: see at 974, 987, 991. But see Peel (ed.), *Treitel on The Law of Contract*, 15th edn (2020), para.20-103.

[432] *Weld-Blundell v Stephens* [1920] A.C. 956, 986.

[433] See Peel (ed.), *Treitel on The Law of Contract*, 15th edn (2020), para.20-103; *Clerk & Lindsell on Torts*, 22nd edn (2017), paras 2-107 et seq.

#### Intervening act or omission of the claimant

*Replace paragraph with:*

There may be a break in the chain of causation where the claimant, following the defendant's breach of contract, has suffered loss through his own voluntary act or omission even though the loss was not of a kind that was unforeseeable, so that it was not too remote.[433a] In *Quinn v Burch Bros (Builders) Ltd*[434] the defendants could have foreseen that their failure (in breach of contract) to supply the plaintiff, an independent contractor, with adequate equipment might result in an accident if he **26-071** used unsuitable equipment. When this actually happened so that the plaintiff was injured, the Court of Appeal held that it was the voluntary choice of the plaintiff following the breach of contract which *caused* the accident; the breach of contract did not cause it but merely gave the plaintiff the opportunity to injure himself by his choice to use the unsuitable equipment, despite his appreciation of the risk involved.[435] Similarly, where a buyer engaged a third party to repair the defect in a machine supplied by the seller, but the buyer then failed to inspect the repairs before using the machine, the Court of Appeal held[436] that the cause of the subsequent explosion was the negligence of the buyer in using the machine without inspecting it to see whether the defect had been adequately repaired.[437] However:

> "... it is difficult to conceive that anything less than unreasonable conduct on the part of the claimant would be capable of breaking the chain of causation;"

merely unreasonable conduct on a claimant's part will not necessarily do so, whereas reckless conduct often will.[438] A highly relevant factor is whether the claimant knew of the defendant's breach; he need not have "exact knowledge of the legal niceties" or even "actual knowledge that a breach of contract has occurred—otherwise there would be a premium on ignorance" but:

> "... the more the claimant has actual knowledge of the breach, of the dangerousness of the situation which has thus arisen and of the need to take appropriate remedial measures, the greater the likelihood that the chain of causation will be broken."[439]

[433a] *Clay v TUI UK Ltd* [2018] EWCA Civ 1177, [2018] 4 All E.R. 672 at [25], referring to *Simmons v British Steel Plc* [2004] UKHL 20, 2004 S.C. (H.L.) 94 at [67].

[434] [1966] 2 Q.B. 370 (followed in *Sole v W. J. Hallt Ltd* [1973] Q.B. 574 but it is submitted that this decision is unsatisfactory on this point); see also *O'Connor v B. D. Kirby & Co* [1972] 1 Q.B. 90.

[435] cf. *Galoo v Bright Grahame Murray* [1994] 1 W.L.R. 1360 (above, para.26-066). cf. also *Young v Purdy* [1997] P.N.L.R. 130; *Clay v TUI UK Ltd* [2018] EWCA Civ 1177. An analogous situation is dealt with in *Lambert v Lewis* [1982] A.C. 225 (below, para.26-095; Vol.II, para.44-417). This decision indicates that a buyer who negligently fails to discover a defect in the goods may not be able to recover from the seller for breach of his implied undertakings as to the quality of the goods: see Hervey (1981) 44 M.L.R. 575.

[436] *Beoco Ltd v Alfa Laval Co Ltd* [1995] Q.B. 137. Compare the outcome in *Borealis AB v Geogas Trading SA* [2010] EWHC 2789 (Comm), [2011] 1 Lloyd's Rep. 482, where the buyers had no reason to suspect the contamination which caused the damage that occurred.

[437] Although the seller was liable for the cost of repairing the original defect, and for the loss of the buyer's profit while the original repairs were made, the seller was not liable for the cost of repairing the explosion damage, nor for the further loss of production after the explosion. The need for further repairs to remedy the original defect had been overtaken by the need for more extensive repairs due to the explosion, and the buyer could not recover damages for the loss of production during the notional period which would have been necessary for further repairs even if there had been no explosion.

[438] *Borealis AB v Geogas Trading SA* [2010] EWHC 2789 (Comm), [2011] 1 Lloyd's Rep. 482 at [42]–[47]. The *Borealis* case was applied in *Flanagan v Greenbanks Ltd* [2013] EWCA Civ 1702, 151 Con. L.R. 98. See also *Clay v TUI UK Ltd* [2018] EWCA Civ 1177 (highly unreasonable conduct broke chain of causation). Even deliberate conduct will not break the chain of causation if that was the very thing that the defendant ought to have prevented: See above, para.26-069.

[439] [2010] EWHC 2789 (Comm) at [46], referring to *Lambert v Lewis* [1982] A.C. 225, 276–277 and *Schering Agrochemicals Ltd v Resibel NVSA* Unreported November 26, 1992.

## A fact-specific issue

*Replace footnote 444 with:*

26-073 [444] *Borealis AB v Geogas Trading SA* [2010] EWHC 2789 (Comm), [2011] 1 Lloyd's Rep. 482 at [47], citing a dictum by Evans-Lombe J. in *Barings Plc v Coopers & Lybrand (No.7)* [2003] EWHC 1319 (Ch) at [838].

## The claimant's lost opportunities: hypothetical consequences

*Replace paragraph with:*

The claimant may claim that, in the absence of the defendant's breach of contract, he might have obtained a benefit or avoided a loss[454]: this consequence was not certain to follow proper performance of the contract but the breach deprived the claimant of the opportunity to benefit from it. The question usually arises when the defendant has failed to do something, but it could arise where his performance had been inadequate or deficient in some way.[455] The law distinguishes three situations: where the hypothetical consequence involves the hypothesis of the claimant's act, where it involves that of a third person[456] and where it involves the occurrence of a contingency outside the control of either party to the contract. It seems, however, that the second and third cases are treated in the same way. **26-077**

[454] The question whether a past event occurred must be decided on the balance of probabilities—once the claimant proves that it was more likely than not to have occurred, the court treats it as a definite fact: *Davies v Taylor* [1974] A.C. 207, 213 (a tort case); it does "not raise any question of what might have been the situation in a hypothetical state of facts": *Hotson v East Berkshire A.H.A.* [1987] A.C. 750, 785; *Allied Maples Group Ltd v Simmons and Simmons* [1995] 1 W.L.R. 1602, 1610 (Stuart-Smith L.J.); and so "chances" are not legally relevant. See Reece (1996) 59 M.L.R. 188.

[455] Where the defendant's negligence has allegedly led to the claimant losing an opportunity to pursue a claim in litigation or in commercial negotiation, the defendant may bear an evidential burden to prove that there is no causal link between the negligence and the loss: see *Mount v Barker Austin* [1998] P.N.L.R. 493, 510, applied in *Harding Homes (East Street) Ltd v Bircham Dyson Bell* [2015] EWHC 3329 (Ch) at [34].

[456] A case may depend on what both the claimant and a third party would have done: e.g. *John (t/a Quantum Digital) v Lucasfilm Ltd LLC* [2018] EWHC 624 (QB) at [91]–[93].

## A hypothetical action of the claimant

*In line 3, after "acted in a certain way.", add new footnote 456a:*

[456a] The same will apply if the question is the action of a third party who is the agent of or closely associated with the claimant: *Veitch v Avery* [2007] EWCA Civ 711, [2008] P.N.L.R. 7 at [26] (father and son); *Connaught Income Fund, Series 1 (In Liquidation) v Hewetts Solicitors* [2016] EWHC 2286 (Ch) at [226]–[228]; *Assetco Plc v Grant Thornton UK LLP* [2019] EWHC 150 (Comm), [2019] Bus. L.R. 2291 at [455]. **26-078**

## A hypothetical action of a third party

*Replace paragraph with:*

This situation arises where a particular contingency depends on whether a third party would have acted in a certain way.[459] Where the claimant claims that, in the absence of the breach of contract by the defendant, a third party would have acted in a particular way, so as to benefit the claimant, he need not prove that hypothetical action on the balance of probabilities. Provided that the claimant can prove[460] that in the absence of the breach there was a "real" or "substantial" (not a speculative) chance of the third party's action,[461] and the loss of chance is not too remote,[462] the court must assess the chance of that action resulting (usually as a percentage) and then discount the claimant's damages for his loss by reference to that percentage.[463] In the leading case of *Chaplin v Hicks*[464] the defendant, by a breach of contract in conducting a contest, deprived the plaintiff, one of 50 finalists, of the opportunity to compete for one of the 12 prizes. Although there could be no precision in calculating the value of her lost chance, she was entitled to substantial damages. Similarly, where the breach of contract caused the claimant to lose his chance of success in litigation, the question is what chance the claimant would have had of a favourable outcome. So where the client's claim became statute-barred **26-079** because his solicitor failed to bring proceedings within time, the measure of the client's damages recovered from the solicitor was the expected proceeds of the original claim[465]: what he might have recovered in the original claim must be discounted by reference to his chances of success in recovering it.[466] "The more the contingencies, the lower the value of the chance or opportunity of which the plaintiff was deprived."[467] Where one contingency may depend on another, the chance should be evaluated as a percentage of a percentage.[468]

[459] This issue could arise in a case where it was also relevant to decide how the claimant himself would have acted: the *Allied Maples* case [1995] 1 W.L.R. 1602. Loss of profits will always depend on many speculative factors, such as third parties continuing to deal with the claimant: this paragraph, however, deals with the loss of a specific opportunity.

[460] On the balance of probabilities: *North Sea Energy Holdings NV v Petroleum Authority of Thailand* [1999] 1 All E.R. (Comm) 173, 187, CA (no substantial chance shown). A case is not one of loss of chance merely because the court has to evaluate what someone would have done had the contract not been broken: *Law Debenture Trust Corp Plc v Elektrim SA* [2010] EWCA Civ 1142 at [45]–[46].

[461] *John (t/a Quantum Digital) v Lucasfilm Ltd LLC* [2018] EWHC 624 (QB) at [93]. The principle does not apply if there is no chance that the third party would have acted so as to benefit the claimant: *Ocean Outdoor UK Ltd v Hammersmith and Fulham LBC* [2019] EWCA Civ 1642, [2020] 2 All E.R. 966 at [91].

[462] As in *Wright v Lewis Silkin LLP* [2016] EWCA Civ 1308, [2017] P.N.L.R. 16 at [62]–[66]. On remoteness see below, paras 26-117 et seq. In *Leggett v Giambrone Law LLP (In Liquidation)* [2020] EWHC 724 (QB) it was held that, had the claimants been advised properly, they would have pursued other investment opportunities, and there was a 75 per cent chance that they would have secured them; as they were known to be looking for such opportunities, the loss was not too remote nor was an implied assumption of responsibility (see below, paras 26-137 et seq.) inappropriate (at [49]). Accordingly they were entitled to 75 per cent of the rent they could have obtained from an alternative property development.

[463] *Allied Maples* [1995] 1 W.L.R. 1602, CA: a claim in tort, but the facts also amounted to a breach of contract. The case was considered in *Bank of Credit and Commerce International SA v Ali (No.3)* [2002] EWCA 82, [2002] 3 All E.R. 750 (loss of the chance of employment)). See also *Maden v Clifford Coppock & Carter (A Firm)* [2004] EWCA Civ 1037, [2005] 2 All E.R. 43 (80 per cent chance of obtaining a particular level of damages in an out-of-court settlement); *Wellesley Partners LLP v Withers LLP* [2015] EWCA Civ 1146, [2016] Ch. 529 (distinguishing, at [96]–[98], the different exercise of assessing or quantifying the loss once the loss of chance has been established; on assessment, see below, para.26-080A and also above, para.26-018); *Commodities Research Unit International (Holdings) Ltd v King and Wood Mallesons LLP* [2016] EWHC 727 (QB), [2016] P.N.L.R. 29; *McGill v Sports and Entertainment Media Group* [2016] EWCA Civ 1063, [2017] 1 W.L.R. 989; *Assetco Plc v Grant Thornton UK LLP* [2019] EWHC 150 (Comm), [2019] Bus. L.R. 2291 at [387]–[388]. The chance of the third party's action can be considerably less than 50 per cent. It had been suggested that if the claimant can show that on the balance of probabilities the third party would have acted in a particular way that would have benefited the claimant, the claimant's damages should not be discounted: see the tentative view of Gross L.J. in *AerCap Partners 1 Ltd v Avia Asset Management AB* [2010] EWHC 2431 (Comm), [2010] 2 C.L.C. 578 at [76] ("The rationale of the loss of a chance doctrine is to permit recovery to a claimant who, by reason of uncertainty, would otherwise be unable to prove causation to the standard of a balance of probabilities; it is not to deny full recovery to a claimant who successfully meets that burden. Underlying the loss of a chance doctrine, are, as it seems to me considerations of policy and good sense. But where a claimant can establish causation on a balance of probabilities, such considerations do not oblige the court and the parties nonetheless to evaluate the chances involved"). But this was doubted in *Wellesley Partners LLP v Withers LLP* [2015] EWCA Civ 1146, [2016] Ch. 529 at [108]; and in *Assetco Plc v Grant Thornton UK LLP* [2019] EWHC 150 (Comm) at [405]–[406] and [414]. It was held that whatever the probability of the third party acting in a particular way, the chances of the third party so acting should be taken into account in the assessment of the loss, though the likelihood may be so high that no deduction will be made at the quantification stage (at [416]); for an example see *Dickinson v Jones Alexander & Co* [1993] 2 F.L.R. 521. The fact that the third party has given evidence may make it easier for the court to assess the chance but it is still the percentage chance that is to be assessed: [2019] EWHC 150 (Comm) at [460]. Where the claim is for the loss of a chance to sell property to a third party, the court must consider the price that the third party might have offered as well as the chance of the resale: *Dennard v PricewaterhouseCoopers LLP* [2010] EWHC 812 (Ch) at [200].

[464] [1911] 2 K.B. 786, CA. (This case, and *Kitchen v Royal Air Force Association* [1958] 1 W.L.R. 563 were cited by the House of Lords in *Hotson v East Berkshire A.H.A.* [1987] A.C. 750, 782, 792–793 (a tort case).)

[465] *Kitchen v Royal Air Force Association* [1958] 1 W.L.R. 563, 575–576; *Cook v Swinfen* [1967] 1 W.L.R. 457; *Malyon v Lawrence, Messer & Co* [1968] 2 Lloyd's Rep. 539.

466 cf. *Yeoman's Executrix v Ferries* (1967) S.L.T. 332 (the value of an "out-of-court" settlement of the plaintiff's claim).

467 *Hall v Meyrick* [1957] 2 Q.B. 455, 471 (reversed by the Court of Appeal on other grounds).

468 *Ministry of Defence v Wheeler* [1998] 1 All E.R. 790, CA. Where the claimant had different chances of success on different issues in litigation but they are affected by the same considerations, it is not appropriate to multiply the chances together; an overall view should be taken: *Hanif v Middleweeks* [2000] Lloyd's Rep. P.N. 920, CA. Similarly, where there are multiple contingencies that are not independent, the court should make an overall assessment rather than simply multiplying the percentage chances of each one: *Tom Hoskins Plc v EMW Law* [2010] EWHC 479 (Ch), [2010] E.C.C. 20 at [133]–[134]; *Harding Homes (East Street) Ltd v Bircham Dyson Bell* [2015] EWHC 3329 (Ch) at [42]. This also applies if the contingencies overlap, whereas if they are wholly independent, a mathematical "percentage of a percentage" approach should be applied: *Assetco Plc v Grant Thornton UK LLP* [2019] EWHC 150 (Comm) at [448]–[449].

*Add new paragraph:*

**Quantification of loss distinguished from loss of chance** Where the claimant would have been able to make a substitute contract that was not dependent on how a particular third party would have acted, the loss of chance doctrine does not apply. Thus if the claimant would have made another contract in a relevant market, there is no place for a discount to reflect the chance that a substitute contract would not have been made.[471a] If the court finds that the claimant would have traded profitably, the issue is not one of causation but of quantifying the loss,[471b] and the court must make the best assessment it can of the profit that would have been made.[471c] **26-080A**

471a *Owners of the Front Ace v Owners of the Vicky 1 (The Vicky 1)* [2008] EWCA Civ 101, [2008] 2 Lloyd's Rep. 45 at [72]; applied in *A v B* [2018] EWHC 2325 (Comm), [2019] 1 Lloyd's Rep. 385 at [99]–[100].

471b *Vasiliou v Hajigeorgiou* [2010] EWCA Civ 1475 at [21]–[25] and [44].

471c *Parabola Investments Ltd v Browallia Cal Ltd* [2010] EWCA Civ 486, [2011] Q.B. 477 at [23], Toulson L.J. (a fraud case).

### Contingency has occurred by time of trial

*Replace paragraph with:*

If the contingency has actually occurred before the time of assessment, the damages should be assessed on the basis of the actual facts as then known, despite the fact that the contingency occurred only after the breach of contract. So in *The Golden Victory*,[472] where a charterparty to be performed over seven years contained a war clause, the House of Lords assessed damages for the charterer's repudiation on the basis that war had actually broken out before the time when damages were assessed so that the charterparty would have been brought to an end at that time. In *Bunge SA v Nidera BV*[473] the Supreme Court held that the principle applies to a sale contract for a single delivery as much as to a contract for performance over a period of time. Both cases involved an anticipatory repudiation, and the question was whether the events that occurred after the repudiation had been accepted would have affected the innocent party's right to performance. In each case, the party that had repudiated would have cancelled the contract under its clauses.[473a] **26-082**

472 *Golden Strait Corp v Nippon Yusen Kubishika Kaisha, The Golden Victory* [2007] UKHL 12, [2007] 2 A.C. 353; applied in *Tele2 International Card Co SA v Kub 2 Technology Ltd* [2009] EWCA Civ 9. It has been held that when assessing damages for breach of contract by reference to the value of a company or other property at the date of breach, whose value depends upon a future contingency, account can be taken of what is subsequently known about the outcome of the contingency as a result of events subsequent to the valuation date, but only where that is necessary in order to give effect to the compensatory principle and where to do so would not cut across the contractual allocation of risk: *(UK) Ltd v Kwik-Fit (GB) Ltd* [2014] EWHC 2178 (QB) at [35]–[38] (but for a contrary suggestion, see *OMV Petrom SA v Glencore International AG* [2016] EWCA Civ 778, [2016] 2 Lloyd's Rep. 432 at [56]); *Hut Group Ltd v Nobahar-Cookson* [2014] EWHC 3842 (QB) at [184] (purchaser of shares bore risk of fall and

chance of rise in value, so when shares not as warranted, difference in value should be calculated at time of breach and subsequent increase in value of shares should not be taken into account: at [218]). The decision in *The Golden Victory* has been controversial; see e.g. Mustill (2008) 124 L.Q.R. 569; Reynolds (2008) 38 H.K.L.J. 333; and McLauchlan, in D. Saidov and R. Cunnington (eds), *Contract Damages: Domestic and International Perspectives* (2008) 349; Carter and Peden (2008) 24 J.C.L. 145; Harder [2009] J.B.L. 679; Stevens, in Neyers, Bronaugh and Pitel (eds), *Exploring Contract Law* (2009) 171.

[473] [2015] UKSC 43, [2015] 2 Lloyd's Rep. 469 especially at [22] and [87]. Dicta by Lord Scott in *The Golden Victory* ([2007] UKHL 12 at [34]–[35]), which had led Hamblen J. to doubt whether the approach used in that case applies to a sale contract for a single delivery (see [2013] EWHC 84 (Comm), [2013] 1 Lloyd's Rep. 621 at [55]) were taken to have been referring to the simple case of repudiation by non-delivery or non-acceptance: [2015] UKSC 43 at [87]; *Bunge SA v Nidera BV* is noted by Carter and Tolhurst (2016) 132 L.Q.R. 1, Yip and Goh [2016] J.B.L. 335.

[473a] Contrast *Classic Maritime Inc v Limbungan Makmur Sdn Bhd* [2019] EWCA Civ 1102, [2019] 4 All E.R. 1145 (above, para.26-001), in which the party that had failed to perform was not protected by a force majeure clause and was liable to put the claimant into the position it would have been in had the defendant performed: see esp. at [80].

## 6. MITIGATION OF DAMAGE

### (a) The Principles of Mitigation

26-087 *To the end of title, add new footnote 496a:*

[496a] For discussion of the mitigation rule and its relationship to causation see Courtney (2019) 42 M.U.L.R. 406.

#### Mitigation

*Replace footnote 497 with:*

26-087 [497] For a recent judicial summary of the principles of mitigation, see *Thai Airways International Public Co Ltd v KI Holdings Co Ltd* [2015] EWHC 1250 (Comm), [2015] 1 C.L.C. 765 at [31]–[38] during which Leggatt J. remarked that the three rules are all aspects of the principle of causation (see at [33]). See also *Bunge SA v Nidera BV* [2015] UKSC 43, [2015] 2 Lloyd's Rep. 469 at [81] (Lord Toulson).

#### Avoidable loss

*Replace footnote 500 with:*

26-089 [500] *Darbishire v Warran* [1963] 1 W.L.R. 1067, 1075; *The Solholt* [1983] 1 Lloyd's Rep. 605, 608, CA: *Copley v Lawn* [2009] EWCA Civ 580, [2010] Bus. L.R. 83 at [29]–[30]. For a recent example, see *IG Index Ltd v Ehrentreu* [2015] EWHC 3390 (QB), quoting this passage in the 31st edition (at [120]) (affirmed [2018] EWCA Civ 79). Only the claimant's net gain from his mitigating effort will be deducted—he may set off against his substitute profits or earnings the reasonable expenses incurred in obtaining them: *Westwood v Secretary of State for Employment* [1985] A.C. 20, 44. See further below, para.26-103.

#### "Reasonable steps"

*Replace paragraph with:*

26-090 The question as to what it was reasonable for a person to do in mitigation of damage is not a question of law but one of fact in the circumstances of each particular case.[506] A business claimant is not "under any obligation to do anything other than in the ordinary course of business"[507]; the standard is not a high one, since the defendant is a wrongdoer:

> "The law is satisfied if the party placed in a difficult situation by reason of the breach of a duty owed to him has acted reasonably in the adoption of remedial measures, and he will not be held disentitled to recover the cost of such measures merely because the party in breach can suggest that other measures less burdensome to him might have been taken."[508]

Questions about the reasonableness of the claimant's steps to mitigate his loss have arisen in cases (discussed elsewhere[509]) where the defendant has failed to complete the contractual work (e.g. building or repair work) and the claimant claims damages for the cost of substitute performance by a third party. But the claimant need not take risks with his money[510] in attempting to mitigate, nor need he take a step which might endanger his own commercial reputation, e.g. by enforcing subcontracts.[511] The claimant is under no duty, even under an indemnity from the defendant, to embark on a complicated and difficult piece of litigation against a third party,[512] nor is the claimant required to sacrifice any of his property or rights in order to mitigate the loss.[513] It has been suggested[514] that the claimant's duty to mitigate does not require him to guard against the effects of inflation per se, i.e. it does not apply to the risk of pure price increases which may lead to "inflationary increases in damages" after the date of the breach of contract.[515] Nor does a claimant who has been forced to mitigate by making short-term arrangements in a spot market have to keep checking whether a market for longer alternatives has since become available.[516]

506 *Payzu Ltd v Saunders* [1919] 2 K.B. 581, 588, 589; *Gul Bottlers (PVT) Ltd v Nichols Plc* [2014] EWHC 2173 (Comm) at [22]. Nonetheless it requires an objective analysis that may involve more than just fact-finding, so an appellate court may interfere if the trier of fact has clearly gone wrong: *LSREF III Wight Ltd v Gateley LLP* [2016] EWCA Civ 359, [2016] P.N.L.R. 21 at [39].

507 *Dunkirk Colliery Co v Lever* (1878) 9 Ch. D. 20, 25 (approved by Lord Haldane in *British Westinghouse Electric Co Ltd v Underground Electric Rys* [1912] A.C. 673, 689). For a recent application of this principle see *Pacific Interlink Sdn Bhd v Owner of the Asia Star (The Asia Star)* [2009] SGHC 91, [2009] 2 Lloyd's Rep. 387. The test of whether the claimant took reasonable steps is whether what they did was objectively reasonable for someone in that position: *Deutsche Bank AG v Total Global Steel Ltd* [2012] EWHC 1201 (Comm) at [159]. The claimant may have to take an obvious step even if it is not part of its ordinary business: *LSREF III Wight Ltd v Gateley LLP* [2016] EWCA Civ 359, [2016] P.N.L.R. 21 (lender on security of lease should have pursued lessor's offer to remove clause providing for forfeiture on lessee-borrower's insolvency).

508 *Banco de Portugal v Waterlow* [1932] A.C. 452, 506. See also *Moore v DER Ltd* [1971] 1 W.L.R. 1476, 1479; *Borealis AB v Geogas Trading SA* [2010] EWHC 2789 (Comm), [2011] 1 Lloyd's Rep. 482 at [50] and [137].

509 See above, para.26-039 and the cases cited in the footnotes to that paragraph. See also *Farley v Skinner* [2001] UKHL 49, [2002] 2 A.C. 732: it may be reasonable for a house purchaser not to sell and move out when he discovers a breach of contract affecting his use and enjoyment.

510 *Jewelowski v Propp* [1944] K.B. 510; *Lesters Leather & Skin Co v Home and Overseas Brokers* (1948) 64 T.L.R. 569. The duty of the buyer to purchase substitute goods if the seller defaults (below, para.26-098, and Vol.II, para.44-388) will, of course, involve the buyer in expenditure, but the buyer will normally have available the money with which he intended to pay for the seller's goods. The impecuniosity of the claimant is discussed below, paras 26-091—26-094.

511 *Finlay & Co v N. v Kwik Hoo Tong H.M.* [1929] 1 K.B. 400; *Banco de Portugal v Waterlow* [1932] A.C. 452 (which also, at 471, supports the proposition that the claimant need not act so as to injure innocent persons); *Anglo-African Shipping Co of New York Inc v J. Mortner Ltd* [1962] 1 Lloyd's Rep. 81, 94 (on appeal, [1962] 1 Lloyd's Rep. 610); *London and South of England Building Society v Stone* [1983] 1 W.L.R. 1242.

512 *Pilkington v Wood* [1953] Ch. 770; *Natixis SA v Marex Financial* [2019] EWHC 2549 (Comm), [2019] 2 Lloyd's Rep. 431 at [549]. cf. simple litigation: *Walker v Geo H. Medlicott & Son* [1999] 1 All E.R. 685 at 697 (a tort case).

513 *Elliott Steam Tug Co v Shipping Controller* [1922] 1 K.B. 127, 140–141. cf. *Weir (Andrew) & Co v Dobell & Co* [1916] 1 K.B. 722. A claimant is not required as a matter of law to take any steps to sue parties who, in addition to the defendant, are liable to the claimant for the same loss: though sometimes treated as an aspect of mitigation, this is best regarded as a separate rule: see *Natixis SA v Marex Financial* [2019] EWHC 2549 (Comm), [2019] 2 Lloyd's Rep. 431 at [544]–[547], citing *McGregor on Damages*, 20th edn, para.9-094 and following *Haugesund Kommune v Depfa ACS Bank* [2010] EWCA Civ 579, [2012] Q.B. 549.

514 Libling and Feldman (1979) 95 L.Q.R. 270, 282. See also *Radford v De Froberville* [1977] 1 W.L.R. 1262, 1287; and Wallace (1980) 96 L.Q.R. 101, 341.

515 See below, para.26-096 on the relevant date for the assessment of damages.

516 *Zodiac Maritime Agencies Ltd v Fortescue Metals Group Ltd* [2010] EWHC 903 (Comm), [2011]

2 Lloyd's Rep. 360 at [65]; followed in *Glory Wealth Shipping Pte Ltd v Korea Line Corp (The Wren)* [2011] EWHC 1819 (Comm), [2011] 2 Lloyd's Rep. 370 (owners not entitled to have damages assessed on market basis at later date from which the market revived; the revived market is relevant to mitigation but does not itself give the measure of damages: at [30]–[32]).

## (c) Timing of Mitigation and the Assessment of Damages

### The time for mitigating action

*Replace footnote 541 with:*

26-095 [541] *East Ham Corp v Bernard Sunley & Sons Ltd* [1966] A.C. 406; *Van den Hurck v R. Martens & Co Ltd* [1920] 1 K.B. 850 (see Vol.II, para.44-413). One judge has held that the mitigation rules do not apply until the plaintiff knows of the breach: *Youell v Bland Welch & Co Ltd (The "Superhulls Cover" case)* [1990] 2 Lloyd's Rep. 431, 461–462; but another judge has applied the rules when the plaintiff should have known of the breach: *Toepfer v Warinco* [1978] 2 Lloyd's Rep. 569, 578. cf. Peel (ed.), *Treitel on The Law of Contract*, 15th edn (2020), para.20-077.

## (d) Offers by the Defendant

26-101 *To the end of title, add new footnote 579a:*

[579a] See Courtney (2020) 136 L.Q.R. 245.

## (e) Savings to be Taken into Account

### Benefit arising from decision to sell property required in order to perform contract

*In line 20, page [1866], after "There was not a sufficient causal link", add new footnote 618a:*

26-107 [618a] In other words, there must be "legal causation" as well as factual, "but for" causation: *Assetco Plc v Grant Thornton UK LLP* [2019] EWHC 150 (Comm), [2019] Bus. L.R. 2291 at [1057].

*In line 1, after "may prove controversial.", add new footnote 621a:*

26-108 [621a] See also Burrows, *Remedies for Torts, Breach of Contract and Equitable Wrongs*, 4th edn (2019), pp.151–152.

### Act by third party

*Replace footnote 625 with:*

26-109 [625] *Swynson Ltd v Lowick Rose LLP (In Liquidation) (formerly Hurst Morrison Thomson LLP)* [2017] UKSC 32, [2018] A.C. 313 at [13], [47]–[49], [97] and [99].

## (f) Expenses of Mitigation

### Recovery of loss or expense suffered while attempting to mitigate

*Replace footnote 633 with:*

26-112 [633] The rule has no application to the cost of actions carried out by a third party, not at the claimant's request, even though they may reduce the claimant's loss: *Swynson Ltd v Lowick Rose LLP (In Liquidation) (formerly Hurst Morrison Thomson LLP)* [2017] UKSC 32, [2018] A.C. 313 at [13], [46] and [97]; see above, para.26-109.

# 7. Remoteness of Damage and Assumption of Responsibility

## (b) Remoteness

### The Heron II

*In line 19, after "result of a breach of contract'"[697]", add new sub-paragraph:*

26-125 Likewise, in *Attorney General of the Virgin Islands v Global Water Associates*

*Ltd*[697a] Lord Hodge, delivering the advice of the Privy Council, said that

> "... what was reasonably contemplated depends upon the knowledge which the parties possessed at that time or, in any event, which the party, who later commits the breach, then possessed. ... [T]he test to be applied is an objective one. One asks what the defendant must be taken to have had in his or her contemplation rather than only what he or she actually contemplated. In other words, one assumes that the defendant at the time the contract was made had thought about the consequences of its breach."

697a [2020] UKPC 18 at [33]–[34].

## The degree of probability

*Replace paragraph with:*

What was in the contemplation of reasonable men obviously depends on the relevant degree of likelihood[713] that a particular kind of loss may occur, and this issue was extensively discussed in *The Heron II*.[714] Lord Reid used: **26-128**

> "... the words 'not unlikely' as denoting a degree of probability considerably less than an even chance but nevertheless not very unusual and easily foreseeable."[715]

Although Lord Morris thought it unnecessary to choose any one phrase[716] he used "not unlikely to occur",[717] with "liable to result" as an alternative[718]; Lord Hodson accepted the latter phrase.[719] Both Lords Pearce[720] and Upjohn[721] adopted the words "a real danger" or "a serious possibility"[722] which were the phrases used in the House of Lords in 1991.[723] (Four of their Lordships in *The Heron II* agreed that the colloquialism "on the cards" should not be used.[724]) The Privy Council has now adopted the "serious possibility" test.[724a] What was made clear in *The Heron II* is that in contract cases it is not sufficient that the loss was "reasonably foreseeable", at least if this refers to the low probability that will satisfy the remoteness test in tort cases.[725] The contractual test requires a higher degree of probability than the test for remoteness in tort.[726] One reason for this may be that the remoteness rule in contract aims to encourage the parties to exchange information about unusual losses that might flow from breach. As Lord Reid said in *The Heron II*:

> "The modern rule in tort is quite different and it imposes a much wider liability. The defendant will be liable for any type of damage which is reasonably foreseeable as liable to happen even in the most unusual case, unless the risk is so small that a reasonable man would in the whole circumstances feel justified in neglecting it; and there is good reason for the difference. In contract, if one party wishes to protect himself against a risk which to the other party would appear unusual, he can direct the other party's attention to it before the contract is made, and I need not stop to consider in what circumstances the other party will then be held to have accepted responsibility in that event. In tort, however, there is no opportunity for the injured party to protect himself in that way, and the tortfeasor cannot reasonably complain if he has to pay for some very unusual but nevertheless foreseeable damage which results from his wrongdoing."

In tort cases, in contrast, the rule aims to protect the defendant from liability for events of very low probability.[727]

713 *Southern Portland Cement Ltd v Cooper* [1974] A.C. 623, 640.

714 [1969] 1 A.C. 350. For how the rules apply to late delivery by carriers, see below, para.26-148.

715 [1969] 1 A.C. 350, 383. (See also his statements at 388: "a very substantial degree of probability".)

716 [1969] 1 A.C. 350, 397, 399.

717 [1969] 1 A.C. 350, 406.

[718] [1969] 1 A.C. 350, 406. "Liable to result" was also one of the phrases accepted in the *Victoria Laundry Case* [1949] 2 K.B. 528, 540.

[719] [1969] 1 A.C. 350, 410–411. (Lord Reid, at 389, rejected this phrase.)

[720] [1969] 1 A.C. 350, 415.

[721] [1969] 1 A.C. 350, 425.

[722] These words were rejected by Lord Reid (at 390), who also rejected "foreseeable as a real possibility" (at 385). *Victoria Laundry* [1949] 2 K.B. 528, 540, also accepted "a real danger" or "a serious possibility". (The latter phrase was used by the Court of Appeal in *H. Parsons (Livestock) Ltd v Uttley, Ingham & Co Ltd* [1978] Q.B. 791, 802, 805, 807.)

[723] *Bank of Nova Scotia v Hellenic Mutual War Risks Association (Bermuda) Ltd* [1992] 1 A.C. 233, 267.

[724] [1969] 1 A.C. 350, 390, 399, 415, 425. (It was yet another phrase used in *Victoria Laundry* [1949] 2 K.B. 528, 540.)

[724a] *Attorney General of the Virgin Islands v Global Water Associates Ltd* [2020] UKPC 18 at [32], citing also (at [29]) Burrows, *A Restatement of the English Law of Contract* (2016), p.20.

[725] [1969] 1 A.C. 350, 385, 411, 425.

[726] See Harris, Campbell and Halson, *Remedies in Contract and Tort*, 2nd edn (2002) at pp.331–333.

[727] See Bishop (1983) 12 JLS 241.

### Concurrent liability

*Replace footnote 732 with:*

26-129 [732] See A Burrows, "Limitations on Compensation" in Burrows and Peel, *Commercial Remedies* (2003), pp.27, 35; *McGregor on Damages*, 20th edn (2017), para.22-009; Peel (ed.), *Treitel on The Law of Contract*, 14th edn (2015), para.20-112; see now 15th edn (2020), para.20-133.

### Loss of a kind that is "not unusual"

*Replace footnote 754 with:*

26-132 [754] cf. Peel (ed.), *Treitel on The Law of Contract*, 15th edn (2020), para.20-127 ("it appeared that there was no basis, so far as remoteness is concerned, for imposing any further limit as to its recoverability").

## (c) Assumption of Responsibility

### Assumption of responsibility

*Replace footnote 781 with:*

26-137 [781] "Where a loss is identified as occurring in the ordinary course of things, there is no basis, as far as remoteness is concerned, for imposing any further limit to its recovery": Peel (ed.), *Treitel on The Law of Contract*, 12th edn (2007), para.20-087, 15th edn (2020), paras 20-119 and 20-127. See also Burrows, *Remedies for Torts, Breach of Contract and Equitable Wrongs*, 4th edn (2019), pp.97–98 (but noting that this position may have to qualified).

### Factors negating an assumption of responsibility

*In line 20, after "kind of understanding.", add new footnote 820a:*

26-143 [820a] In *Attorney General of the Virgin Islands v Global Water Associates Ltd* [2020] UKPC 18 at [26] Lord Hodge said that the Board was "not concerned ... with ... questions of market understanding" addressed in *The Achilleas*.

### Evaluation

*Replace footnote 828 with:*

26-144 [828] In *Sylvia Shipping Co Ltd v Progress Bulk Carriers Ltd* [2010] EWHC 542 (Comm), [2010] 2 Lloyd's Rep. 81 Hamblen J. held that assumption of responsibility would be relevant only in exceptional cases and quoted the last 19 lines of this paragraph in the 31st edition with apparent approval. On the facts (loss of a sub-charter when the owners were late in delivering the vessel) the loss was not "unquantifiable, unpredictable, uncontrollable or disproportionate" (at [73]). See also *Supershield Ltd v Siemens Building Technologies FE Ltd* [2010] EWCA Civ 7, [2010] 1 Lloyd's Rep. 349 ("*Hadley v Baxendale* remains a standard rule but ... there may be cases where the court, on examining the contract and the commercial background, decides that the standard approach would not reflect the expectation or intention reasonably to be imputed to the parties" (at [43])). See also *Borealis AB v Geogas Trading SA* [2010] EWHC 2789 (Comm), [2011] 1 Lloyd's Rep. 482 at [48]; *Pindell Ltd v AirAsia Berhad (formerly AirAsia SDN BHD)* [2010] EWHC 2516 (Comm) at [84]; *Saipol SA v Inerco Trade SA* [2014] EWHC 2211 (Comm), [2015] 1 Lloyd's Rep. 26 at [17]. (In the *AirAsia Berhad* case Tomlinson J. would have been prepared to find that was not was not a type of loss for which the lessees assumed responsibility ([2010] EWHC 2516 (Comm) at [87]); but the ground for his decision was that it was not sufficiently likely that a 20-year-old aircraft would be sold on terms that gave such a short window for delivery for the lessees to be liable for loss of the sale (at [86])) In *John Grimes Partnership Ltd v Gubbins* [2013] EWCA Civ 37, [2013] B.L.R. 126 at [24], Sir David Keene said that he agreed with Toulson L.J's statement in *Supershield* quoted above but would put it in different words: "If there is no express term dealing with what types of losses a party is accepting potential liability for if he breaks the contract, then the law in effect implies a term to determine the answer. Normally, there is an implied term accepting responsibility for the types of losses which can reasonably be foreseen at the time of contract to be not unlikely to result if the contract is broken. But if there is evidence in a particular case that the nature of the contract and the commercial background, or indeed other relevant special circumstances, render that implied assumption of responsibility inappropriate for a type of loss, then the contract-breaker escapes liability." Burrows, *Remedies for Torts, Breach of Contract and Equitable Wrongs*, 4th edn (2019), pp.103–105, takes the view that generally the risk of loss should be allocated to the party in breach if that party could have contemplated the type of loss that occurred as a serious possibility, and disagrees with the outcome in *The Achilleas*; but argues that there may be cases in which the mere fact that the defendant was told of the risk should not suffice for it to be fair and reasonable to make the defendant liable, for example if a taxi driver is told that delay may cause the customer to lose a profitable contract. Factors such as whether there was an adjustment to the price, disproportion between the price and the loss and the extent to which the parties could be expected to be insured are relevant.

## (d) Illustrations of Remoteness and Responsibility: Loss of Profits

### Seller's liability for loss of profits

*Replace footnote 836 with:*

[836] If the defendant had been told of the special contracts, and should have realised, as a reasonable man, that he was undertaking responsibility for the loss of higher-than-usual profits in the case of breach, he would have been able to demand a higher price, or to cover himself with an exemption. **26-146**

## 8. PARTICULAR RESTRICTIONS ON RECOVERY OF DAMAGES

## (a) Non-pecuniary Losses

### Loss of amenity

*Replace footnote 880 with:*

[880] Lord Mustill cited the article by Harris, Ogus and Phillips (1979) 95 L.Q.R. 581 (which was also cited in *Farley v Skinner* [1994] 1 W.L.R. 650 at [21]). The *Ruxley Electronics* decision [1996] A.C. 344 decision is discussed in *Att-Gen v Blake* [2001] 1 A.C. 268, 298 (a dissenting speech). At 282, in Lord Nicholl's speech (approved by the majority) he said that: "The law recognises that a party to a contract may have an interest in performance which is not readily measurable in terms of money". See also *Morris-Garner v One Step (Support) Ltd* [2018] UKSC 20, [2019] A.C. 649 at [39]–[40]. **26-156**

*Replace footnote 883 with:*

[883] In earlier cases, in the absence of such specificity, damages have been refused for distress caused by reliance on a survey about the condition of a house: *Watts v Morrow* [1991] 1 W.L.R. 1421, CA; or for breach of a covenant for quiet enjoyment in a tenancy agreement: *Branchett v Beaney* [1992] 3 All E.R. 910, CA. However, damages may be awarded for "mental suffering" directly related to physical inconvenience and discomfort caused by breach of contract: *Watts v Morrow* [1991] 1 W.L.R. 1421, 1440–1445 (see above, para.26-153). In *Farley v Skinner* Lord Scott, with whom Lord Browne-Wilkinson agreed, appears to suggest that whenever a party has not been provided with a contractual benefit to which he was entitled, he is entitled to compensation even if the breach has caused no other loss (at [106]). This has been relied on to suggest that if a party to a compromise agreement breaches it **26-157**

by making disparaging comments about the other, the other may recover a modest amount even if she suffered no financial loss: *Halcyon House Ltd v Baines* [2014] EWHC 2216 (QB) at [256]–[257]. In *Freeborn v De Almeida Marcal (t/a Dan Marcal Architects)* [2019] EWHC 454 (TCC) homeowners were awarded £5,000 general damages when an architect's breach of contract prevented them from having a function room and private cinema in which to entertain their friends (at [158]).

### Loss of reputation

*Replace footnote 900 with:*

**26-159** [900] *Gomes v Higher Level Care Ltd* [2018] EWCA Civ 418, [2018] 2 All E.R. 740. In the light of *Dunnachie v Kingston upon Hull City Council* [2004] UKHL 36, [2005] 1 A.C. 226 the Court of Appeal doubted the correctness of a number of cases awarding such damages in other types of case (*Brassington v Cauldon Wholesale Ltd* [1978] I.C.R. 405, right under Employment Protection Act 1975 s.53 not to have action short of dismissal taken against a person because of membership of an independent trade union; *Cleveland Ambulance NHS Trust v Blane* [1997] ICR 851, right under Trade Union and Labour Relations (Consolidation) Act 1992 s.146 not to have action short of dismissal taken against a person for taking part in the activities of an independent trade union; *London Borough of Hackney v Adams* [2003] I.R.L.R. 402, discrimination on ground of trade union activity) but left the question open ([2018] EWCA Civ 418 at [66]).

## 9. ILLUSTRATIONS OF THE ASSESSMENT OF DAMAGES

## (b) Sale of Goods

### Resale at below market price

*Replace footnote 930 with:*

**26-166** [930] See above, para.26-043; and Peel (ed.), *Treitel on The Law of Contract*, 15th edn (2020), para.20-051.

### Delay in delivery

*Replace footnote 943 with:*

**26-169** [943] See Peel (ed.), *Treitel on The Law of Contract*, 15th edn (2020), para.20-052.

### Delivery of defective goods

*Replace paragraph with:*

**26-170** If the goods delivered are defective but buyer accepts them, the damages will prima facie be the difference between the value the goods should have had and their actual value.[945] If there is no available market in which the buyer can obtain a substitute,[946] it may be reasonable for the buyer to have the goods repaired and the cost of doing so will be recoverable.[947] Where the goods were bought for resale, the fact that the buyer loses a profitable resale will be relevant only if the buyer was not able to mitigate his loss and the further loss was not too remote.[948] Conversely, it has been held that the buyer's damages should not be reduced because he has succeeded in reselling the defective goods at more than the market price for goods in that condition.[949] However, in *Bence Graphics International Ltd v Fasson UK Ltd*[950] the Court of Appeal held that the buyer's position under a sub-sale should be taken into account. The seller knew that the buyer would sell on to others (after manufacturing the goods into another product); the Court held that the parties contemplated that the measure of damages for defects in the goods should be the extent of the buyer's liability (if any) to those others resulting from the defect; other loss was too remote. The decision in *Slater's* case was doubted, on the ground that s.53(3) laid down only a prima facie rule, which should not be applied if the parties contemplated a different loss or if it would give the buyer "more than his true loss".[951] It is submitted that the buyers should have recovered the difference in value. First, remoteness is not relevant when the claim is simply for the difference in value between what was contracted for and what was delivered. As submitted earlier, the sub-sale is relevant only if the buyer was bound to deliver the same specific goods under the sub-sale. If the buyer was not so obliged, it might have fulfilled the sub-sale by purchasing and processing other goods, or have used other goods from stock and then have re-sold the contract goods at the current price; in either case the buyer should be entitled to the difference between the contract price and market price.[952] The fact that they were able to pass on the defective goods without incurring liability again seems to be their own good fortune.[953] Moreover, it can again be argued that even when the sub-sale requires delivery of the same goods, the buyer should always be entitled to the difference between the contract price and the market price, by analogy to the decisions on failures to provide services which do not result in any further loss to the claimant.[954] The *Bence* case seems to be a further example of the court concentrating on the end-result rather than the buyer's performance interest.[955] It is true that in cases in which the buyer has reached a reasonable settlement with the sub-buyer, who has retained the goods, the amount paid under the settlement has been treated as the most that the buyer can recover, even if the settlement was at an undervalue, but the point seems to have been assumed rather than argued.[956]

[945] Sale of Goods Act 1979 s.53: see below, Vol.II, para.44-411.

[946] If the buyer cannot obtain an exact substitute, an issue of "betterment" may arise: see above, para.26-105.

[947] See above, para.26-039.

[948] For example, if the seller knew that the buyer would re-sell the self-same goods: cf. *Re R and H Hall Ltd and WH Pim (Junior) Co's Arbitration* [1928] All E.R. Rep. 763, above, para.26-165.

[949] *Slater v Hoyle Smith Ltd* [1920] 2 K.B. 11.

[950] [1998] Q.B. 87. cf. *Louis Dreyfus Trading Ltd v Reliance Trading Ltd* [2004] EWHC 525 (Comm), [2004] 2 Lloyd's Rep. 243 (parties contemplated sale of the same goods to the sub-buyer under a specific contract); *Choil Trading SA v Sahara Energy Resources Ltd* [2010] EWHC 374 (Comm) at [124]–[139]. In the *Bence* case Auld L.J. cast doubt on *Slater v Hoyle Smith Ltd* and approved the decision in *Wertheim*'s case, see above, para.26-169 and Vol.II, para.44-413).

[951] [1998] Q.B. 87 at 102 (see below, Vol.II, paras 44-413—44-415).

[952] See above, para.26-043; and Peel (ed.), *Treitel on The Law of Contract*, 15th edn (2020), para.20-051.

[953] See the powerful criticism of Treitel (1997) 113 L.Q.R. 188, and Peel (ed.), *Treitel on The Law of Contract*, 15th edn (2020), para.20-054. In *OMV Petrom SA v Glencore International AG* [2016] EWCA Civ 778, [2016] 2 Lloyd's Rep. 432 Christopher Clarke L.J. seemed to think that the *Bence Graphics* case could not stand with *Slater v Hoyle Smith Ltd*, but left the matter open (at [45]–[46]).

[954] See above, para.26-043.

[955] See above, paras 26-042—26-046.

[956] *Biggin v Permanite* [1951] 2 K.B. 314; *Fluor v Shanghai Zhenhua Heavy Industry Co Ltd* [2018] EWHC 1 (TCC) at [465].

## (d) Contracts Concerning Land

### Valuer-surveyor's report to a purchaser

*Replace footnote 992 with:*

[992] *Watts v Morrow* [1991] 1 W.L.R. 1421, CA, following *Phillips v Ward* [1956] 1 W.L.R. 471, and *Perry v Sidney Phillips & Son* [1982] 1 W.L.R. 1297; though the rule is not invariable, see *County Personnel (Employment Agency) Ltd v Alan R Pulver and Co* [1987] 1 W.L.R. 916, 925–926 (e.g. when evidence on difference in value is inadequate: see *Moore v National Westminster Bank* [2018] EWHC **26-178**

1805 (TCC), 179 Con. L.R. 226 at [22]). See also *Gardner v Marsh & Parsons* [1997] 1 W.L.R. 489 (the fact that five years after the purchase the landlord, a third party, remedied the defect at his expense was held to be too remote to be taken into account in assessing the purchaser's damages against a surveyor); *Moore v National Westminster Bank* [2018] EWHC 1805 (TCC). (In these cases the courts refused to assess damages at the cost of repairs; see above, paras 26-039 et seq.; but the cost of repair may be taken as the best evidence of the difference in value, see *Moore v National Westminster Bank* [2018] EWHC 1805 (TCC).) In *Watts v Morrow*, the court left open the question as to *when* the market value should be ascertained: [1991] 1 W.L.R. 1421, 1437–1438. In *Dent v Davis Blank Furniss* [2001] Lloyd's Rep. P.N. 534 where a solicitor failed to advise the purchaser that part of the property was registered as common land, the judge applied the diminution in value test, not at the time of purchase but at the later date when the purchaser succeeded in partially mitigating his loss.

## The "SAAMCo" rule

*Replace paragraph with:*

**26-180** In the *South Australia* case[999] the House of Lords imposed a limit[1000] on the extent of damages payable by a valuer who negligently over-values the intended security and the security turns out to be inadequate through a combination of this and a fall in the value of the property. The lender's "ultimate loss" (viz the difference between: (i) the capital of the actual loan; and (ii) the net proceeds of realising the security, plus any repayments by the borrower) is caused by, and is not too remote a consequence of, the negligence[1001] but the lender's damages for his capital loss may not exceed the extent of the initial deficiency in the supposed value of the security, viz the difference between the amount of the defendant's negligent over-valuation and what would have been a proper[1002] valuation at the time of the loan.[1003] Within this limit, however, the lender may recover his ultimate loss of capital even though it is due to a fall in the market value of the security since the loan was made.[1004] In addition to his claim for loss of capital, the lender may claim: (1) his reasonable expenses of realising the security; and (2) interest (see next paragraph).

[999] *South Australia Asset Management Corp v York Montague Ltd* [1997] A.C. 191 (also known as the *B.B.L.* or *Banque Bruxelles* case). Lord Hoffmann, who gave the only speech, dealt almost exclusively with the scope of the valuer's limited duty of care under the tort of negligence, but he also said that the same result would follow from an implied term in the contract: at 211, 212. The High Court of Australia has not followed the *South Australia* case: *Kenny Good Pty Ltd v MGICA (1992) Ltd* [2000] Lloyd's Rep. P.N. 25.

[1000] See however the "advice cases" recognised by the House of Lords in the *South Australia* case [1997] A.C. 191 and discussed by the Supreme Court in *Hughes-Holland v BPE Solicitors* [2017] UKSC 21, [2018] A.C. 599, above, para.26-034.

[1001] *Nykredit Mortgage Bank Plc v Edward Erdman Group Ltd (No.2)* [1997] 1 W.L.R. 1627, HL, 1631, 1638. The *Nykredit* case and *Platform Home Loans Ltd v Oyston Shipways Ltd* [2000] 2 A.C. 190, explain the decision in the *South Australia* case [1997] A.C. 191. Although the lender may suffer a form of loss when it makes the loan, it will normally be appropriate to calculate the lender's loss at the date of trial when the amount of loss may have crystallised: *Nykredit* case [1997] 1 W.L.R. 1627, 1633; *LSREF III Wight Ltd v Gateley LLP* [2016] EWCA Civ 359, [2016] P.N.L.R. 21 at [33].

[1002] See below, para.26-183.

[1003] The "amount of the loss … [is] limited to the extent of the overvaluation": the *Nykredit* case [1997] 1 W.L.R. 1627, 1632. The limitation on damages laid down in the *South Australia* case covers both categories previously recognised by *Swingcastle Ltd v Alastair Gibson* [1991] 2 A.C. 223, viz where, given a proper report, the lender: (1) would have lent nothing at all on the proposed security; and (2) would have lent a smaller sum. On the relevance of a mortgage indemnity guarantee policy for the benefit of the lender, see *Arab Bank Plc v John D. Wood Commercial Ltd* [2000] 1 W.L.R. 857, CA.

[1004] As in *South Australia Asset Management Corp v York Montague Ltd* [1997] A.C. 191 itself: see *Hughes-Holland v BPE Solicitors* [2017] UKSC 21, [2018] A.C. 599 at [45]–[46], where Lord Sumption defends the SAAMCo limit as "a tool for giving effect to the distinction between (i) loss flowing from the fact that as a result of the defendant's negligence the information was wrong and (ii) loss flowing from the decision to enter into the transaction at all", even if it may be "mathematically imprecise".

## (e) Contracts Affecting Running of Business

**26-184** *Replace footnote 1012 with:*

[1012] The alternative measures mentioned in this section in the 32nd edition were referred to with apparent approval by Lord Reed in *Morris-Garner v One Step (Support) Ltd* [2018] UKSC 20, [2019] A.C. 649 at [37].

### Management costs

*Replace footnote 1015 with:*

1015 [2007] EWCA Civ 3, [2007] Bus. L.R. 726 at [86]. See also *Al Rawas v Pegasus Energy Ltd* [2008] EWHC 617 (QB), [2009] 1 All E.R, 346, especially at [22]–[23]; *4Eng Ltd v Harper* [2008] EWHC 915 (Ch), [2009] Ch. 91 at [40]; *Borealis AB v Geogas Trading SA* [2010] EWHC 2789 (Comm), [2011] 1 Lloyd's Rep. 482 at [147]; *Azzurri Communications Ltd v International Telecommunications Equipment Ltd* [2013] EWPCC 17 at [86]–[88]; *Mental Health Care (UK) Ltd v Edward Lupen Healthcare (UK) Ltd* [2019] EWHC 1 (Ch) at [146]–[151]; *DBE Energy Ltd v Biogas Products Ltd* [2020] EWHC 1232 (TCC) at [194]. **26-185**

## (g) Sale of Shares

### Shares

*To the end of paragraph, after "the market rises.[1041]", add:*

Where a warranty is given as to the shares sold and the warranty is broken, the prima facie measure of damages is the difference between the value of the shares on the assumption that the warranty was true and the actual value.[1041a] **26-189**

1041a *Lion Nathan Ltd v CC Bottlers Ltd* [1996] 1 W.L.R. 1438 (PC), 1441; *Ageas (UK) Ltd v Kwik-Fit (GB) Ltd* [2014] Bus. L.R. 1338 at [14]; *Hut Group Ltd v Nobahar-Cookson* [2014] EWHC 3842 (QB) at [180] (appeal on another point dismissed [2016] EWCA Civ 128); *Oversea-Chinese Banking Corp Ltd v Ing Bank NV* [2019] EWHC 676 (Comm) at [33]–[40].

# 10. Liquidated Damages, Deposits and Forfeiture of Sums Paid

## (a) Liquidated Damages or Penalty

### Introduction

*Replace footnote 1045 with:*

1045 [2015] UKSC 67, [2016] A.C. 1172, noted by Conte (2016) 132 L.Q.R. 382 and Morgan [2016] C.L.J. 11; see also Day [2016] J.B.L. 115 and 251; Summers [2016] L.M.C.L.Q. 95; Day, "Disproportionate Penalties in Commercial Contracts", in Davies and Raczynska (eds), *Contents of Commercial Contracts* (2020), 211. In what follows the decisions will frequently be referred to as "*Cavendish Square*" and "*ParkingEye*". **26-190**

### "Underliquidated damages"

*Replace footnote 1061 with:*

1061 See Peel (ed.), *Treitel on The Law of Contract*, 15th edn (2020), paras 7-044 and 20-165. **26-193**

### A question of law

*Replace footnote 1081 with:*

1081 *Sainter v Ferguson* (1849) 7 C.B. 716, 727; *Cargill International Trading Pte Ltd v Uttam Galva Steels Ltd* [2019] EWHC 476 (Comm) at [37]. **26-196**

## (b) Genuine Pre-estimate of the Likely Loss

### Pre-estimate of damage

*Replace footnote 1108 with:*

1108 *MSC Mediterranean Shipping Co SA v Cottonex Anstalt* [2015] EWHC 283 (Comm) at [70]–[71], **26-202** referring to dicta in *Abrahams v Performing Rights Society Ltd* [1995] I.C.R. 1028, 1040–1041. However, in a contract in which the liquidated damages were only payable while the contract remained on foot, the innocent party was not entitled to ignore a repudiation and keep the contract alive so as to be able to continue to claim liquidated damages, as they would have no legitimate interest is doing so: at [94]–[105]. The Court of Appeal [2016] EWCA Civ 789, [2016] 2 Lloyd's Rep. 494 agreed (at [43]) though it decided the case on other grounds: see above, para.26-116.

### Single sum payable upon different breaches

*Replace footnote 1128 with:*

**26-205** [1128] *Wallis v Smith* (1882) 21 Ch. D. 243; *Pye v British Automobile Commercial Syndicate Ltd* [1906] 1 K.B. 425; *Dunlop Pneumatic Tyre Co Ltd v New Garage and Motor Co Ltd* [1915] A.C. 79; *Philips Hong Kong Ltd v Att-Gen of Hong Kong* (1993) 61 B.L.R. 41, 62–63 (Privy Council refers to: "... the error of assuming that, because in some hypothetical situation the loss suffered will be less than the sum quantified in accordance with the liquidated damage provision, that provision must be a penalty"). This suggests that the validity of a clause should be judged by its normal operation: Peel (ed.), *Treitel on The Law of Contract*, 14th edn (2015), para.20-131. (This issue is not discussed in the 15th edn (2020).)

### Graduated damages

*Replace footnote 1143 with:*

**26-207** [1143] *Clydebank Engineering Co v Don Jose Ramos Yzquierdo y Castaneda* [1905] A.C. 6; *Philips Hong Kong Ltd v Att-Gen of Hong Kong* (1993) 61 B.L.R. 41, 60, PC; *Alfred McAlpine Capital Projects Ltd v Tilebox Ltd* [2005] Build. L. R. 271 (TCC). See also *Law v Redditch Local Board* [1892] 1 Q.B. 127; *Cellulose Acetate Silk Co Ltd v Widnes Foundry (1925) Ltd* [1933] A.C. 20 (below, para.26-243). The party entitled to the benefit of a liquidated damages clause in the event of failure to complete on time cannot take advantage of it if the delay is partly due to his own fault: *Peak Construction (Liverpool) Ltd v McKinney Foundations Ltd* (1971) 69 L.G.R. 1, 11, 16, unless the contract provides otherwise: see *North Midland Building Ltd v Cyden Homes Ltd* [2018] EWCA Civ 1744, [2018] B.L.R. 565 and below, Vol.II, para.37-121. On the effect of termination of the contract on liquidated damages for delay that have accrued before the date of termination, see below, Vol.II, para.37-123A. Demurrage under a charterparty is a case of graduated liquidated damages: *President of India v Lips Maritime Corp* [1988] A.C. 395, 422–423.

## (c) Commercially Justified But Not a Deterrent

### "Commercial justifications" and "legitimate interests"

*Replace paragraph with:*

**26-210** It seems likely that the "commercial justifications" given in the cases referred to in this section and listed by Christopher Clarke L.J. in the passage cited in the previous paragraph, would also constitute legitimate interests[1162] within the meaning of the Supreme Court's new test.[1163] If that is correct, there is no further need to refer to "commercial justification" as a test of whether an agreed damages or similar clause is valid or a penalty.

[1162] *Cargill International Trading Pte Ltd v Uttam Galva Steels Ltd* [2019] EWHC 476 (Comm) (clause setting default rate of interest) at [44], referring to this paragraph. On what constitutes a legitimate interest see below, paras 26-214 et seq.

[1163] In *Cavendish Square* and *ParkingEye* Lord Hodge said that the broader approach adopted in this group of cases "involves a correct analysis of the law" ( [2015] UKSC 67 at [225]; see also at [246]).

## (d) Deterrence to Protect a Legitimate Interest

*To the end of title, add new footnote1190a:*

### "Legitimate interest"[1190a]

**26-214** [1190a] Rowan (2019) 78 C.L.J. 148.

*Replace footnote 1193 with:*

**26-214** [1193] This test was applied in *Hayfin Opal Luxco 3 SARL, Hayfin Topaz 3 SCA v Windermere VII CMBS*

*Plc* [2016] EWHC 782 (Ch), [2018] B.C.L.C. 118 at [142] and in *BHL v Leumi Abl Ltd* [2017] EWHC 1871 (QB), [2017] 2 Lloyd's Rep. 237 at [44]. In *First Personnel Services Ltd v Halfords Ltd* [2016] EWHC 3220 (Ch) no evidence was given to justify a rate of interest on late payment far above both the usual commercial rate and what was payable under the Late Payment of Commercial Debts (Interest) Act 1998; it was not justified by the creditor's interest in securing punctual payment having regard to its own liability to pay employees (at [163]).

## Difficulty of proving loss

*Replace paragraph with:*

Lords Neuberger and Sumption referred to a legitimate interest in obtaining performance rather than merely damages[1196]; and, in support of their argument that in fashioning the rules on remedies the law takes into account legitimate interests, referred to the rule that specific performance may be available (subject to other constraints) if the innocent party has "a legitimate interest extending beyond pecuniary compensation for the breach".[1197] In each of the cases before the court, it seems that damages would not be adequate compensation, nor be adequate as a deterrent to breach, as it would be hard to prove what loss, if any, flowed from any particular breach.[1198] The same was true in the case of in *Dunlop Pneumatic Tyre Co Ltd v New Garage and Motor Co Ltd*,[1199] in which a payment of £5 per tyre sold at below the list price was upheld. **26-215**

[1196] [2015] UKSC 67 at [28]. In *Vivienne Westwood Ltd v Conduit Street Development Ltd* [2017] EWHC 350 (Ch), [2017] L. & T.R. 23 Timothy Fancourt Q.C., sitting as a Deputy Judge of the High Court, said the test is whether the claimant has a legitimate interest beyond pecuniary compensation for any loss caused by the particular breach, so as to justify the secondary obligation (at [49]). The interest must in in performance of the tenant's obligations, not merely in being able to claim the higher rent that became payable in the event of the tenant failing to comply with one of its obligations (at [52]). On the facts, the term that required the tenant, in the event of any non-trivial breach of its obligations, to pay a substantially higher rent was out of all proportion to the lessor's interest in having the tenant perform every one of its obligations rather than pay compensation for any breaches (at [63]), especially as the increased rent was payable in addition to damages for any loss caused by the breach. The increased rent was payable with retroactive effect from the start of the lease, but even if it had been purely prospective it would have been a penalty (at [65]).

[1197] [2015] UKSC 67 at [30]. If the court has jurisdiction to make an order of specific performance or to grant an injunction but refuses to do so, under Lord Cairns' Act the court may make an award of "negotiating damages", which though compensatory in nature go beyond the conventional measures of compensation that are available at common law: see *Morris-Garner v One Step (Support) Ltd* [2018] UKSC 20, [2019] A.C. 649, discussed above, paras 26-050 et seq. This too supports the notion that the claimant may have a legitimate interest in deterrence when conventional damages would not be an adequate remedy.

[1198] cf. para.27-018 (difficulty in quantifying damages may mean damages inadequate).

[1199] [1915] A.C. 79. In *Signia Wealth Ltd v Vector Trustees Ltd* [2018] EWHC 1040 (Ch) it was held that provisions of an employment contract applying different valuations to the shares of "good leavers" and "bad leavers" were not disproportionate to the employer's legitimate interests in ensuring that shares remain with those directly involved with the company and in incentivising employees to stay: at [653(7)].

## Insolvency risk

*Add new paragraph:*

The argument that a clause requiring payment of more than a genuine pre-estimate of the loss would still be valid if it was "commercially justified" was first accepted in a case in which a clause in a loan agreement imposed a higher rate of interest on default.[1211a] The commercial justification is that a borrower in default is a greater credit risk and "money is more expensive for a less good credit risk than for a good credit risk".[1211b] Such clauses are now valid under the "legitimate interest" test,[1211c] provided that the default rate is not extravagant or unconscionable compared to the legitimate interest.[1211d] **26-219A**

[1211a] *Lordsvale Finance Plc v Bank of Zambia* [1996] Q.B. 752, 762–764; see above, para.26-209.

1211b [1996] Q.B. 752, 763; *Holyoake v Candy* [2017] EWHC 3397 (Ch) at [486]; *Cargill International Trading Pte Ltd v Uttam Galva Steels Ltd* [2019] EWHC 476 (Comm) at [50].

1211c See above, para.26-210. On the rates that have been upheld, see below, para.26-285.

1211d See below, paras 26-226 et seq.

## Continuing performance after a repudiation

*Replace footnote 1223 with:*

**26-221** 1223 *Isabella Shipowner SA v Shagang Shipping Co Ltd (The Aquafaith)* [2012] EWHC 1077 (Comm), [2012] 2 Lloyd's Rep. 61 at [44]. In *Attica Sea Carriers Corp v Ferrostaal Poseidon Bulk Reederei GmbH (The Puerto Buitrago)* [1976] 1 Lloyd's Rep. 250 the innocent party has been held to have no legitimate interest in claiming the hire of a chartered ship until it was returned fully repaired, when the vessel was beyond economic repair; and in *MSC Mediterranean Shipping Co SA v Cottonex Anstalt* [2016] EWCA Civ 789, [2016] 2 Lloyd's Rep. 494 the court said there would be no legitimate interest in claiming the demurrage in respect of containers that were being detained by a third party with no end in sight, so that the contractual venture had become frustrated (at [43]): see above, para.26-116.

## Conclusion on legitimate interest

*Replace paragraph with:*

**26-225** It is submitted that a claimant will have a sufficient legitimate interest in obtaining performance rather than damages to justify an agreed damages clause that is intended to deter breach, rather than as a pre-estimate of loss, in the following situations:

- if the claimant would face serious difficulties in proving what loss, if any, flowed from the breach[1241];
- if the claimant would face serious difficulties in detecting whether there has been a breach[1242];
- if damages will not be an adequate remedy because, if the defendant fails to perform, the claimant will not be able to obtain substitute goods, other property or services (irrespective of the fact that specific performance of the contract might not be available for other reasons)[1243];
- if loss will be suffered by a third party rather than by, or in addition to, the claimant[1244];
- if having to claim damages from the defendant would put the claimant's solvency at risk[1245];
- if the defendant's default means that the claimant faces a greater risk in future[1245a];
- if even though neither the claimant nor a third party will suffer any loss through the defendant's breach, the claimant has an exceptional interest in ensuring that defendant performs such that the court would award an account of profits, as in *Att-Gen v Blake*[1246]; or
- more generally, if deterrence is an essential element of a lawful scheme.[1247]

In contrast, the claimant does not have a legitimate interest in obtaining more than damages, or agreed damages that are substantially more than a genuine pre-estimate of the likely loss, merely because the claimant would have to incur time and expense in arranging a substitute transaction, or simply would prefer performance to claiming damages[1248]; nor because the late payment fee will benefit the cashflow of the claimant's business[1248a]; nor because the claimant hopes to secure a large share of any profit the defendant might make through breaking the contract, when damages would otherwise be an adequate remedy.[1249]

1241 See above, para.26-215.

1242 See above, para.26-216.

[1243] See above, para.26-217.

[1244] See above, para.26-218.

[1245] See above, para.26-219.

[1245a] See above, para.26-219A.

[1246] See above, para.26-224.

[1247] As in the *ParkingEye* case, see above, para.26-213.

[1248] See above, para.26-220.

[1248a] *R. v Whatcott* [2019] EWCA Crim 1889 at [38].

[1249] See above, para.26-223.

### "Not extravagant or unconscionable"

*In line 5, after "the legitimate interest.", add new footnote 1249a:*

[1249a] For examples of default rates of interest that were held (before the SC decision in *Cavendish Square*) to be commercially justified or (after it) not extravagant or unconscionable compared to the claimant's legitimate interest, see *Cargill International Trading Pte Ltd v Uttam Galva Steels Ltd* [2019] EWHC 476 (Comm) at [70]. **26-226**

### "Not ... unconscionable"

*Replace footnote 1265 with:*

[1265] In *ZCCM Investments Holdings Plc v Konkola Copper Mines Plc* [2017] EWHC 3288 (Comm) Lionel Percy Q.C. (sitting as a judge of the High Court) said (at [33]) that he was required to look not only at the legitimate interests of the claimant but also "at the circumstances in which the contract came to be concluded, including matters such as the relative bargaining power of the parties and whether [the defendant] had legal advice at the time the contract was concluded". See also *Signia Wealth Ltd v Vector Trustees Ltd* [2018] EWHC 1040 (Ch) at [653(3)] ("The court should be careful, in a commercial case, where the contract has been negotiated without suggestion of oppression, when applying the doctrine"); *European Film Bonds AS v Lotus Holdings LLC* [2020] EWHC 1115 (Ch) (at [167]) (clauses "part of a series of complex agreements, drawn up by sophisticated businessmen with experience of the film industry, and with the benefit of legal advice. It is commonplace that contracts such as these will have deadlines and those deadlines may have serious consequences. That does not make them penal and render them unenforceable."). **26-229**

## (e) Scope of the Law of Penalties

### Sums payable on and other consequences of breach

*Replace footnote 1269 with:*

[1269] *White and Carter (Councils) Ltd v McGregor* [1962] A.C. 413 (above, para.26-114). However, in a contract in which the liquidated damages were only payable while the contract remained on foot, the innocent party was not entitled to ignore a repudiation and keep the contract alive so as to be able to continue to claim liquidated damages, as they would have no legitimate interest is doing so: *MSC Mediterranean Shipping Co SA v Cottonex Anstalt* [2015] EWHC 283 (Comm) at [94]–[105]; the Court of Appeal [2016] EWCA Civ 789, [2016] 2 Lloyd's Rep. 494 agreed that there was no legitimate interest in continuing to perform but because the contractual venture had been frustrated: see above, para.26-116. The contrast between a debt and liquidated damages is drawn by the House of Lords in *President of India v Lips Maritime Corp* [1988] A.C. 395, 422–423, 424. **26-230**

## *(i) Types of Clause Within the Penalty Doctrine*

### Types of clause within the penalty rules

*Replace paragraph with:*

In *Cavendish Square Holding BV v Makdessi*[1273] the Supreme Court held that the penalty clause rules apply not only to agreed damages clauses but also to provisions that would result in a party who breaks the contract[1273a] from receiving (or "forfeiting"[1274]) a sum to which it would otherwise be entitled,[1275] and also to provi- **26-231** sions that require a party in breach to transfer property to the other party at less than its full value.[1276] The Supreme Court also stated that the penalty rules also apply to deposits and possibly to other types of forfeiture clause; these will be considered in a separate section.[1277]

[1273] [2015] UKSC 67, [2016] A.C. 1172.

[1273a] In *European Film Bonds AS v Lotus Holdings LLC* [2020] EWHC 1115 (Ch) at [159]–[163] it was argued that the penalty doctrine may also apply when the consequence of a breach is visited on a third party, but the point does not seem to have been decided, see at [167].

[1274] Lord Hodge includes clauses allowing the innocent party to withhold payments otherwise due to the party in breach within the phrase "forfeiture of sums due": [2015] UKSC 67 at [226]. He seemed to envisage that such a clause might fall within both the penalty rules and the doctrine of relief against forfeiture; but it should be noted that the latter is confined to cases involving the loss of a proprietary or possessory interest, see below, para.26-254.

[1275] See [2015] UKSC 67 at [170] (Lord Mance), [226]–[227] (Lord Hodge); Lord Toulson agreed with the relevant passages of both their judgments (at [292]). Lords Neuberger and Sumption (with whom Lord Carnwath agreed) were prepared to assume this without deciding it (at [73]); they considered that cl.5.1 of the agreement in the *Cavendish Square* case was part of the parties' primary obligations and therefore altogether outside the penalty rules: see below, para.26-239. However, Lord Clarke preferred to leave this question open; he must therefore have held that the penalty rules do apply to clauses of this type. In *Gilbert Ash (Northern) Ltd v Modern Engineering (Bristol) Ltd* [1974] A.C. 689 the House of Lords had considered a clause entitling the contractor to "suspend or withhold" the payment of money due to the subcontractor on any breach of contract. It had been conceded that the clause fell within the doctrine, but a majority of the House of Lords appeared to consider that the concession was correct: see [2015] UKSC 67 at [70], [154] and [226].

[1276] See at [170] and [183] (Lord Mance); [230] and [280] (Lord Hodge). On this point Lord Clarke (at [291]) agreed with Lord Hodge and Lord Toulson (at [292]) with both Lord Mance and Lord Hodge.

[1277] See below, paras 26-245 et seq.

### *(ii) Events Other Than Breach*

**Sum payable on event other than breach**

*Replace footnote 1306 with:*

26-234 [1306] Applied in *Holyoake v Candy* [2017] EWHC 3397 (Ch) at [468]–[488]; *Nosworthy v Instinctif Partners Ltd* Unreported February 28, 2019, EAT at [71]; and *ICICI Bank UK Plc v Assam Oil Co Ltd* [2019] EWHC 750 (Comm) at [32]. If the sum is payable on one of several events, some of which are breaches and others are not, the penalty rule will apply if the event that in fact triggered the payment was a breach, but not otherwise, nor if, as on the facts of the case, it was a breach of a different contract by another party: *Edgeworth Capital (Luxembourg) Sarl v Ramblas Investments BV* [2015] EWHC 150 (Comm) at [60], [69]; the Court of Appeal confirmed that the penalty rule did not apply, [2016] EWCA Civ 412 at [7]. The death or bankruptcy of a party might be another event, not constituting a breach, upon which money is to be paid. cf. *Mount v Oldham Corp* [1973] Q.B. 309 (claim for a term's school fees in lieu of notice withdrawing a pupil). In *Signia Wealth Ltd v Vector Trustees Ltd* [2018] EWHC 1040 (Ch) it was held that provisions of an employment contract applying different valuations to the shares of "good leavers" and "bad leavers" were not within the doctrine just because whether the employee had broken the contract was one factor in determining whether a leaver was good or bad: at [653(5)].

**Sums payable on exercise of an option under the contract**

*Replace footnote 1307 with:*

26-235 [1307] *Fratelli Moretti SpA v Nidera Handelscompagnie BV* [1981] 2 Lloyd's Rep. 47, 53; for another example see *BHL v Leumi Abl Ltd* [2017] EWHC 1871 (QB), [2017] 2 Lloyd's Rep. 237 at [44].

### *(iii) "Primary Obligations"*

**Primary obligations**

*Replace paragraph with:*

26-239 In *Cavendish Square Holding BV v Makdessi*[1318] Lords Neuberger and Sumption (with whom Lord Carnwath agreed) held that the clauses which provided that the seller of the business, if he was in breach of the non-competition covenants, would not receive the outstanding instalments of the price, and would require him to transfer further shares to the buyers at a much reduced value, were not subject to the penalty rules at all. Even if they were triggered by the seller's breach, clause 5.1 bore no relation to damages; it represented the reduced price that the buyer was prepared to pay for the business if it could not count on the loyalty of the seller, and so formed part of the "primary obligations" of the parties.[1319] The analysis of clause 5.6 was essentially similar: it represented the reduced price that the purchaser was prepared to pay when it could not count on the loyalty of Makdessi.[1320] The law places controls over only the parties' secondary obligations, not their primary obligations,[1321] and both clauses belong among the primary obligations, even if the occasion of their operation was a breach of contract.[1322] In any event, both clauses were justified by the same legitimate interest in matching the price to the value that the seller was providing.[1323] Unlike an agreed damages clause, if the clauses did not stand there is no scale by which the court could make an award. The other members of the Supreme Court either decided the case on the ground that the clauses came within the penalty rules but did not amount to penalties, or preferred to leave the matter open.[1324] With respect, it is unclear how a payment (or other obligation that is within the doctrine[1325]) that is "triggered" by a breach of contract by the defendant but which is a primary obligation is to is to be distinguished from an agreed damages clause. The fact that the clause is in the form of a price reduction seems to emphasise form over substance; and while it is true that ex ante there is no alternative scale by which the court could fix appropriate prices, when an agreed damages clause is held to be unenforceable the court makes an ex post assessment of the actual loss suffered by the claimant. It seems that a court could equally assess damages in terms of the reduction in value in the shares caused by a breach by the seller of a non-competition covenant, and the valuation could include an element for the risk that the seller who had been disloyal once may be disloyal again.

1318 [2015] UKSC 67, [2016] A.C. 1172.

1319 [2015] UKSC 67 at [74]–[75]. Compare *Vivienne Westwood Ltd v Conduit Street Development Ltd* [2017] EWHC 350 (Ch), in which an increased rent became payable in the event of any breach of its obligations by the tenant: the court held that the increased rent was a secondary obligation that was capable of being a penalty (at [49]). In contrast, in *Re SHB Realisations Ltd (formerly BHS Ltd) (In Liquidation)* [2018] EWHC 402 (Ch), [2018] Bus. L.R. 1173 at [37]–[38], it was held that a clause in a CVA under which the company would pay a reduced rent but if the agreement were terminated because the company failed to make the payments due, the full rent would become payable once more, was held not to be a penalty.

1320 [2015] UKSC 67 at [81].

1321 [2015] UKSC 67 at [14] and [32].

1322 [2015] UKSC 67 at [83].

1323 [2015] UKSC 67 at [82].

1324 Lord Mance said that cl.5.1 had the effect of revising the price payable for the shares but he clearly considered the clause to be subject to the penalty doctrine: see [2015] UKSC 67 at [181]; similarly, though cl.5.6 had the effect of reshaping of the parties' primary relationship (at [183]), it was valid because it was neither exorbitant or unconscionable (at [185]). Lord Hodge agreed that there were "strong arguments" for regarding each clause as primary obligations to which the doctrine does not apply: at [270] and [280]; but he decided the validity of cl 5.1 by applying the penalty doctrine, and held that cl.5.6 was a secondary obligation, adding that "if all such clauses were treated as primary obligations, there would be considerable scope for abuse". Lord Toulson agreed with the relevant parts of both Lord Mance's and Lord Hodge's judgments. Lord Clarke agreed with Lord Hodge rather than with Lords Neuberger and Sumption on these points: at [291]. Some initial uncertainty seems to have been caused by the circulation of a draft version of the judgments in which Lord Clarke's reservations were not included. This suggested that a majority had considered the relevant clauses to be outside the scope of the penalty rules. In *European Film Bonds AS v Lotus Holdings LLC* [2020] EWHC 1115 (Ch) Andrew

Hochhauser Q.C., sitting as a Deputy Judge of the High Court, said (at [167]) that there was "a strong argument" that a clause providing for "deemed acceptance" of a film if the customer "failed" to return it by a stated date did not engage the penalty doctrine but was "part of an expedited delivery procedure"; but in any event the clause was not extravagant, exorbitant or unconscionable (see above, para.26-226).

1325 See above, para.26-231.

## (f) Effect of Clause if a Penalty

### Can damages exceed the sum fixed in penal clause?

*Replace footnote 1345 with:*

26-243 1345 In *Cellulose Acetate Silk Co Ltd v Widnes Foundry (1925) Ltd* [1933] A.C. 20, 26, the House left "... open the question whether, where a penalty is plainly less in amount than the prospective damages, there is any legal objection to suing on it or, in a suitable case, ignoring it and suing for damages". cf. dicta to the effect that the penalty fixes the maximum recoverable: *Wilbeam v Ashton* (1807) 1 Camp. 77; *Elphinstone v Monkland Iron & Coal Co* (1886) L.R. 11 App. Cas. 332, 346; *Elsley v J.G. Collins Insurance Agencies Ltd* (1978) 83 D.L.R. (3d) 1, 14–16; *W. & J. Investments Ltd v Bunting* [1984] 1 N.S.W.L.R. 331, 335–336. See also Hudson (1974) 90 L.Q.R. 31; Gordon (1974) 90 L.Q.R. 296; Hudson (1975) 91 L.Q.R. 25; Barton (1976) 92 L.Q.R. 20; Hudson (1985) 101 L.Q.R. 480; Peel (ed.), *Treitel on The Law of Contract*, 15th edn (2020), para.20-165.

## (h) Deposits and Forfeiture

### *(ii) Forfeiture of Sums Paid*

### Relief against forfeiture of proprietary or possessory interests

*Replace footnote 1404 with:*

26-254 1404 *Sport Internationaal Bussum BV v Inter-Footwear Ltd* [1984] 1 W.L.R. 776 (followed in *Crittall Windows Ltd v Stormseal (UPVC) Window Systems Ltd* [1991] R.P.C. 265). But it is not a purely contractual right where a hirer is entitled to indefinite possession of chattels so long as he makes hire payments: hence relief against forfeiture is available: *On Demand Information Plc v Michael Gerson (Finance) Plc* [2002] UKHL 13, [2003] 1 A.C. 368 at [29]. In *Vauxhall Motors Ltd (formerly General Motors UK Ltd) v Manchester Ship Canal Co Ltd* [2019] UKSC 46, [2019] 3 W.L.R. 852 (affirming [2018] EWCA Civ 1100, [2019] Ch. 331) relief was given in respect of a possessory right over land, enabling the licensee to discharge surface water into a canal. Lord Briggs J.S.C., giving the majority judgment, noted (at [33]) that in *Celestial Aviation Trading 71 Ltd v Paramount Airways Private Ltd* [2010] EWHC 185 (Comm), [2011] 1 Lloyd's Rep. 9 Hamblen J. had held that relief could not be given where the possessory rights (under operating leases of aircraft) were of limited duration, which suggests that for relief to be available, possessory rights in goods might have to last for the economic life of chattels. Lord Briggs pointed out that possessory rights in land may well qualify for relief though not perpetual, and that in *The Scaptrade* [1983] 2 A.C. 694, 700 Lord Diplock had suggested that relief can be given in the case of charterparties by demise, so "even in relation to chattels a rule that the possessory right should be indefinite may go too far" (at [51]).

## 12. INTEREST

## (b) Damages for Loss of Interest at Common Law

### Loss of interest compensable if pleaded and proved

*Replace footnote 1518 with:*

26-275 1518 [2007] UKHL 34 at [16]–[17], [94]. [100], [132] and [154]. (Lord Mance rejected the invitation to revisit the common law rule.) In a fraud case, compound interest was refused when the claimants had merely pleaded that they had suffered loss and damage, without any allegation of the use to which the monies paid away as a result of the fraud would have been put had there been no fraud, or allegation of losses the claimants had suffered in addition to having paid away the principal sums: *JSC BTA Bank v Ablyazov* [2013] EWHC 867 (Comm). The court awarded simple interest under its statutory discretion: see below, para.26-281. It has been held that "general evidence" that the claimant suffered loss from the delay will suffice: *Equitas Ltd v Walsham Bros & Co Ltd* [2013] EWHC 3264 (Comm) at [123], [2014]

Lloyd's Rep. I.R. 398; *Sainsbury's Supermarkets Ltd v Mastercard Inc* [2016] CAT 11 at [521]. In *Peacock v Imagine Property Developments Ltd* [2018] EWHC 1113 (TCC) a party had not been able to show that the delay in payment had prevented even the chance of it entering specific transactions. However, it was known that the party depended on payments from one part of a project to fund the next, so damages for "being kept out of the money", based on the cost of borrowing to an entity with the same characteristics, were not too remote and should be awarded (see at [150]).

## (d) Statutory Rights to Interest

### Interest on commercial debts

*Replace footnote 1525 with:*

[1525] s.3(1), Late Payment of Commercial Debts (Interest) Act 1998. A claim for unliquidated damages is not within the Act, at least in the absence of some mechanism in the contract that has the effect of converting the claim into part of the contract price: *National Museums and Galleries on Merseyside Board of Trustees v AEW Architects and Designers Ltd* [2013] EWHC 3025 (TCC) at [7]–[8]; *Mailbox (Birmingham) Ltd v Galliford Try Construction Ltd* [2017] EWHC 67 (TCC), [2017] B.L.R. 180 at [56]. Rather, the court has discretion to award interest under s.35A of the Senior Courts Act 1981, see para.26-281. The Act does not apply to "NHS contracts", which under National Health Service Act 2006 s.9(5) "do not give rise to contractual rights or liabilities": *SSP Health Ltd v NHS Litigation Authority* [2019] EWHC 3291 (Admin) (appeal outstanding). **26-277**

## (e) Statutory Discretion to Award Interest

### Statutory power to award interest

*Replace footnote 1555 with:*

[1555] *Wentworth v Wiltshire CC* [1993] 2 All E.R. 256, 269 (also at 263) (not a contract case). Section 3 of the 1934 Act explicitly excluded "the giving of interest upon interest": see *Bushwell Properties Ltd v Vortex Properties Ltd* [1975] 1 W.L.R. 1649 ("the court is not to award interest on such part of the sum claimed as represents contractual interest": at 1660). (The decision was reversed on another point: [1976] 1 W.L.R. 591.) The Law Commission has recommended that the courts be given power to award compound interest: see *Pre-Judgment Interest on Debts and Damages* (Law Com. No.287, 2004).) (Both the Canadian and Australian courts have allowed compound interest: see McInnes 118 (2002) L.Q.R. 516.) In equity, compound interest has been awarded for profits made through breach of a fiduciary duty: *Wallersteiner v Moir (No.2)* [1975] Q.B. 373. In *Westdeutsche Landesbank Girozentrale v Islington LBC* [1996] A.C. 669, the House of Lords held that in equity compound interest may be awarded only in cases of fraud or against a trustee (or other person in a fiduciary position) in respect of profits improperly made by him. See also *Mathew v T.M. Sutton Ltd* [1994] 1 W.L.R. 1455, 1463; *Glenn v Watson* [2018] EWHC 2483 (Ch). **26-281**

### Rates of interest

*Replace paragraph with:*

The court is empowered to award interest "at different rates in respect of different periods".[1590] In business[1591] contexts, the rate of interest should reflect the current commercial rate.[1592] The approach of the Commercial Court is to award interest at a rate which broadly represents the rate at which the successful party would have had to borrow the amount recovered over the period in question.[1593] The Court of Appeal has upheld the practice of the Commercial Court to award interest at a borrower's rate of 1 per cent above the base rate prevailing from time to time,[1594] but this is only a presumption which can be displaced if its application would be unfair to either party.[1595] The Court of Appeal has recognised that the borrowing costs of small businesses are often higher than for first class borrowers for whom 1 per cent above base rate is appropriate: interest on damages at 3 per cent above base rate was awarded,[1596] where the claim is made by an employee the appropriate rate is the cost of unsecured borrowing by individuals.[1597] **26-285**

[1590] 1981 Act s.35A(6); s.69(5) of the 1984 Act. Delay by the claimant in progressing his claim may be reflected in a reduced rate of interest for the overall period (instead of depriving him of all interest for the period of the delay): *Derby Resources A.G. v Blue Corinth Marine Co Ltd (No.2)* [1998] 2 Lloyd's Rep. 425.

[1591] Compare a case where the claimant was a charity: *Hackney Empire Ltd v Aviva Insurance UK Ltd* [2013] EWHC 2212 (TCC), 149 Con. L.R. 213. In cases where one party is a private person, the Court of Appeal is reluctant to interfere with the judge's discretion in fixing the rate of interest: *Watts v Morrow* [1991] 1 W.L.R. 1421, 1443–1444, 1446. See also *West v Ian Finlay & Associates* [2014] EWCA Civ 316 at [75]; and for recognition that there may be cases in which the investment rate may be more appropriate than the borrowing rate, and also a third type of case which does not fall into either category, see *Attrill v Dresdner Kleinwort* [2013] EWCA Civ 394 at [30]–[35] and *Reinhard v Ondra* [2015] EWHC 2943 (Ch) (a case of the third type; award of 3 per cent over base rate; followed in *Zagora Management Ltd v Zurich Insurance Plc (No.2)* [2019] EWHC 205 (TCC), 182 Con. L.R. 240).

[1592] cf. *The Mecca* [1968] P. 665, 672.

[1593] *Cremer v General Carriers SA* [1974] 1 W.L.R. 341, 355–358. See *JSC BTA Bank v Ablyazov* [2013] EWHC 867 (Comm) (a fraud case) at [20] et seq. The court should not look at the special position of the claimant and should consider the rate at which claimants in general could borrow, but should take into account that larger concerns can often borrow at lower rates than smaller ones: *Tate & Lyle Food and Distribution v Greater London Council* [1982] 1 W.L.R. 149, 154 (Forbes J.'s decision on damages and interest was not appealed); *Fiona Trust v Privalov* [2011] EWHC 664 (Comm) at [13]–[16]; *Carrasco v Johnson* [2018] EWCA Civ 87 at [17]; *Assetco Plc v Grant Thornton UK LLP* [2019] EWHC 592 (Comm), [2019] Bus. L.R. 2291 at [10]–[14].

[1594] *Polish S.S. Co v Atlantic Maritime Co* [1985] Q.B. 41, 67 (followed in *Metal Box Co Ltd v Currys Ltd* [1988] 1 W.L.R. 175, 182–183 (insurers subrogated to a claim in tort for loss of chattels)). See *National Westminster Bank Plc v Rabobank Nederland* [2007] EWHC 1742 (Comm), [2007] All E.R. (D) 477 (Oct). (Base rate replaces the minimum lending rates previously used: see *Cia Banca de Panama SA v George Wimpey & Co Ltd* [1980] 1 Lloyd's Rep. 598, 615–617; *Shearson Lehman Hutton Inc v Maclaine Watson & Co Ltd* [1990] 3 All E.R. 723, 732–733.) "The London Interbank Offered Rate (LIBOR) has very much come to the fore as an appropriate interest rate to award [though] it has tended to have been utilised by agreement of the parties rather than by adjudication of the court": *McGregor on Damages*, 20th edn (2017), para.19-155, cited in *Fiona Trust v Privalov* [2011] EWHC 664 (Comm) at [18].

[1595] The *Shearson Lehman* case [1990] 3 All E.R. 723, 733. It is not relevant that the claimant was cash rich and might not have had to borrow to fund the deficit: *SABIC UK Petrochemicals Ltd v Punj Lloyd Ltd* [2013] EWHC 3202 (TCC) at [10]. However, evidence is admissible as to the rate at which persons with the general attributes of the claimant could have borrowed the money: *Tate & Lyle Food and Distribution Ltd v G.L.C.* [1982] 1 W.L.R. 149, 154–155.

[1596] *Jaura v Ahmed* [2002] EWCA Civ 210, [2002] 4 C.L. 130.

[1597] *Attrill v Dresdner Kleinwort Ltd, Commerzbank AG* [2012] EWHC 1468 (QB) at [5].

*Replace footnote 1603 with:*

**26-286** [1603] CPR r.36.5(4).

### Debt or damages in foreign currency

*Replace paragraph with:*

**26-287** When the debt or damages are calculated in a foreign currency the court may order that the interest rate applicable to the debt shall be such rate as the court thinks fit.[1603a] It has been said that, the rate of interest should be the commercial borrowing rate in that currency in the relevant country.[1604]

[1603a] Administration of Justice Act 1970 s.44A (added by Private International Law (Miscellaneous Provisions) Act 1995 s.1(1)). For judgments in the county court, see County Courts Act 1984 s.74(5A) (inserted by Private International Law (Miscellaneous Provisions) Act 1995 s.2). See further below, paras 30-295—30-305.

[1604] *Miliangos v George Frank (Textiles) (No.2)* [1977] Q.B. 489, 497; *Helmsing Schiffahrts v Malta Drydocks Corp* [1977] 2 Lloyd's Rep. 444, 449. In *Novoship (UK) Ltd v Mikhaylyuk* [2014] EWCA Civ 908, [2015] Q.B. 499 at [128]–[138] it was held that s.44A is based on the "compensatory principle": see *ACLBDD Holdings Ltd v Staechelin* [2018] EWHC 428 (Ch) at [5].

CHAPTER 27

# ACTION FOR AN AGREED SUM, SPECIFIC PERFORMANCE AND INJUNCTION



## 3. SPECIFIC PERFORMANCE

## (a) Introduction

### Meaning of "specific performance"

*To the end of paragraph, after "the present chapter.", add:*

Nevertheless, specific performance may be awarded in respect of money payment "where an action in damages or debt would not properly vindicate the claimant's right".[83a] **27-013**

[83a] *Avonwick Holdings Ltd v Azitio Holdings Ltd* [2020] EWHC 1844 (Comm) at [1039] citing Virgo et al, *Contractual Duties: Performance, Breach, Termination and Remedies*, 2nd edn (2019) at paras 27-036 and 27-038 and *Snell's Equity* at para 17-011. Examples include: promises to pay annuities and pensions, agreements to pay money where the payment is intended to provide a vital injection of cash into a joint venture, where the contract is to pay a third party, so that the damages recoverable by the contracting party would be merely nominal, or where the contract is to make periodical payments, requiring a multiplicity of actions at law to enforce payment. Specific performance is routinely awarded to vendors of real property where the effect is the simple payment of money, see below para.27-017. But see the case above at [1040], where specific performance was denied because the payment obligation based on a contractual calculation was not one "which it is contemplated will be performed by a third party. It is a calculation which, if necessary, the Court could perform". Therefore the "ordinary remedy" ("an action in damages or debt") would not be inadequate.

### Contract specifically enforceable in part only

*Replace footnote 88 with:*

27-014 [88] *Rainbow Estates Ltd v Tokenhold Ltd* [1999] Ch. 64, 72–73; *Odessa Tramways Co v Mendel* (1878) 8 Ch. D. 235 (where contract is severable, specific performance of each part can be separately ordered); *Internet Trading Club Ltd v Freeserve Investments Ltd* [2001] E.B.L.R. 142 at [30] (where specific performance of an unseverable part was refused); *Zinc Cobham 1 Ltd (In Administration) v Adda Hotels* [2018] EWHC 1025 (Ch), [2018] L. & T.R. 36 at [48] (where the court could not grant specific performance of the principal trading obligations in the contract, and so, "by parity of reasoning", could not grant specific performance of ancillary parts of the contract that related to the mode of trading).

## (b) The "Adequacy" of Damages

### Appropriateness of the remedy

*Replace paragraph with:*

27-015 The historical foundation of the equitable jurisdiction to order specific performance of a contract is that the claimant cannot obtain a sufficient remedy by the common law judgment for damages.[90] Hence the traditional view was that specific performance would not be ordered where damages were an "adequate" remedy.[91] Typically, this would be the case where the claimant could readily make a substitute contract for a performance that is equivalent to that promised by the defendant: the claimant would then be adequately compensated by damages based on the difference between the cost (or market price) of the substitute, and the contract price. Indeed, an award of specific performance in such a case could conflict with the mitigation requirement and may be considered to be oppressive to the defendant.[92] In *Co-operative Insurance Society Ltd v Argyll Stores (Holdings) Ltd*[93] Lord Hoffmann expressed the concern that in some circumstances an award of specific performance may allow "the plaintiff to enrich himself at the defendant's expense" by negotiating an excessive price for releasing the defendant from performance; one that exceeds the value of performance to the plaintiff and approaches the cost of performance to the defendant.[94] Some of the early authorities[95] approach this problem by asking whether damages would *in fact* adequately compensate the claimant. At a later stage in the development of the subject, the courts tended rather to ask whether damages were *likely* to be an adequate remedy for breach of the *type* of contract before the court.[96] Later again, the courts have asked whether specific performance was the most *appropriate* remedy in the circumstances of each case[97] and whether specific performance will "do more perfect and complete justice than an award of damages".[98] The point was well put in a case in which an interim injunction was sought:

> "The standard question … , 'Are damages an adequate remedy?' might perhaps, in the light of the authorities in recent years, be rewritten: 'Is it just, in all the circumstances, that a plaintiff should be confined to his remedy in damages?'"[99]

More recently, the Supreme Court has stated: "the minimum condition for an order of specific performance is that the innocent party should have a legitimate interest extending beyond pecuniary compensation for the breach".[99a] In applying this test, courts will compare the cost incurred by compliance with an order with the likely loss suffered should the order not be given.[99b]

[90] *Harnett v Yielding* (1805) 2 Sch. & Lef. 549, 553.

[91] *Co-operative Insurance Society Ltd v Argyll Stores (Holdings) Ltd* [1998] A.C. 1, 11; *Bankers Trust Co v P.T. Jakarta International Hotels Development* [1999] 1 Lloyd's Rep. 910 at 911. See also *Lawrence*

*v Fen Tigers Ltd* [2014] UKSC 13, [2014] 2 All E.R. 622 at [158]; *Ashworth v Royal National Theatre* [2014] EWHC 1176 (QB) at [31], see n.245.

92 See *Re Schwabacher* (1908) 98 L.T. 127 and other authorities cited in para.27-011, n.75. For oppression in cases of specific relief by way of injunction, see also below, para.27-081.

93 [1998] A.C. 1.

94 [1998] A.C. 1 at [15].

95 e.g. *Adderley v Dixon* (1824) 1 S. & S. 607, 610.

96 e.g. *Cohen v Roche* [1927] 1 K.B. 169.

97 *Beswick v Beswick* [1968] A.C. 58, 88, 90–91, 102; cf. *Coulls v Bagot's Executor and Trustee Co* [1967] A.L.R. 385, 412.

98 *Tito v Waddell (No.2)* [1977] Ch. 106, 322; *Rainbow Estates Ltd v Tokenhold Ltd* [1999] Ch. 64 at 72–73.

99 *Evans Marshall & Co Ltd v Bertola SA* [1973] 1 W.L.R. 349, 379 (and see the subsequent proceedings: [1975] 2 Lloyd's Rep. 373); *Araci v Fallon* [2011] EWCA Civ 668 at [42], where the reference to "Chapter 27" of the 30th edition of this book seems to be to its para.27-015 (still so numbered in the present edition); cf. in a different but analogous context *Miliangos v George Frank (Textiles) Ltd* [1976] A.C. 443.

99a *Cavendish Square Holding EV v Makdessi* [2015] UKSC 67, [2016] A.C. 1172 at [30]; applied in *Zinc Cobham 1 Ltd (In Administration) v Adda Hotels* [2018] EWHC 1025 (Ch), [2018] L. & T.R. 36 at [48]; and see *UTB LLC v Sheffield United Ltd* [2019] EWHC 2322 (Ch) at [495] (ownership of a famous Premier League football club "confers all kinds of non-financial benefits that ... [the claimants] find attractive and rewarding irrespective of financial gain or loss").

99b *Zinc Cobham 1 Ltd (In Administration) v Adda Hotels* [2018] EWHC 1025 (Ch) at [48]. The appellant landlord sought to enforce a covenant to keep a hotel property up to certain "operating standards". The court found that the remedial work sought by the order would add little value to the property, but would cost the respondent tenants £100 million to carry out. An order would be "inequitable" (at [48]).

## Difficulty of quantifying damages

*In line 8, after "reason, specific performance", replace "can be" with:*

has been 27-018

*To the end of paragraph, after "bill of lading.[113]", add:*

On the other hand, Lord Reed[113a] recently stated that the law has long recognised and dealt with difficulties in assessing damages.[113b] Such difficulties did not justify the abandonment of any attempt to measure loss and resort to the benefit gained by the wrongdoer as an alternative basis for an award of contractual damages. Nor, it seems, would it, of itself, satisfy the necessary minimum condition of "a legitimate interest beyond pecuniary compensation" required for an award of specific performance.[113c]

113a *Morris-Garner v One Step (Support) Ltd* [2018] UKSC 20, [2019] A.C. 649 at [73].

113b See further above, para.26-018.

113c *Zinc Cobham 1 Ltd (In Administration) v Adda Hotels* [2018] EWHC 1025 (Ch), [2018] L.& T.R. 36 at [48].

## Damages nominal, not recoverable, or excluded

*Replace footnote 120 with:*

120 *AB v CD* [2014] EWCA Civ 229, [2014] 3 All E.R. 667 at [25]–[27], following Mance L.J. in *Bath and North East Somerset DC v Mowlem Plc* [2004] EWCA Civ 115, [2004] B.L.R. 153, especially at [15]. The existence of such a term was one factor to be taken into account in answering the question put (in the passage quoted in para.27-015) by Sachs L.J. in *Evans Marshall & Co Ltd v Bertola SA* [1973] 1 W.L.R. 349 at 379, viz whether it was "just in all the circumstances that a [claimant] should be confined to his remedy in damages": *AB v CD* [2014] EWCA Civ 229 at [32]. *SDI Retail Services Ltd v Rangers Football Club Ltd* [2018] EWHC 2772 (Comm) at [60] (damages were not an adequate remedy due to the "cap on damages and the exclusion of consequential losses"). The same principle applies to a claim 27-019

for an interim injunction: *McAfee Ireland Ltd v DSG Retail Ltd* [2019] 8 WLUK 10 at [16] (QBD Commercial Court).

## Availability of substitute

*Replace footnote 129 with:*

**27-020** [129] *Duncuft v Albrecht* (1841) 12 Sim. 189; *Cheale v Kenward* (1858) 3 De G. & J. 27; *Langen & Wind Ltd v Bell* [1972] Ch. 685; *Jobson v Johnson* [1989] 1 W.L.R. 1026; cf. *Pao On v Lau Yiu Long* [1980] A.C. 614, where this point was conceded; *Harvela Investments Ltd v Royal Trust Co of Canada (C.I.) Ltd* [1986] A.C. 207 (shares not available in the market and giving a controlling interest in the company); *Grant v Cigman* [1996] 2 B.C.L.C. 24; *Pena v Dale* [2003] EWHC 1065, [2004] B.C.L.C. 508 at [135] ( purchase of shares in a private company specifically enforced); *Watson v Watchfinder.co.uk Ltd* [2017] EWHC 1275 (Comm); *Patel v Iqbal* [2020] EWHC 1174 (Ch) at [45] (purchase of shares in a private unquoted company in respect of which there is no readily available market). The question of the availability of a substitute arose in a different context in *Araci v Fallon* [2011] EWCA Civ 68 (below, para.27-079), where the "difficulty of obtaining a substitute jockey" (at [57]) was not (as it is in the authorities considered in the present paragraph (27-020)) that of the other party to the contract (the claimant) but that of a third party, and *this* difficulty was no bar to the grant of an injunction to restrain the jockey's breach. The claimant *had* obtained a substitute jockey, though one who, unlike the defendant, had "not previously ridden" the horse in question (at [20]).

## Sale of goods: "unique" goods

*Replace footnote 133 with:*

**27-022** [133] *Pusey v Pusey* (1684) 1 Vern. 273; *Somerset v Cookson* (1735) 3 P. Wms. 390; *Lowther v Lowther* (1806) 13 Ves. Jr. 95; a slightly wider view may have been taken by *Falcke v Gray* (1859) 3 Drew. 651, 658. And see *Gregor Fisken Ltd v Carl* [2020] EWHC 1385 (Comm) at [187] (specific performance ordered for the delivery of the original gearbox of a rare Ferrari).

## Non-delivery of "specific or ascertained goods"

*Replace footnote 140 with:*

**27-023** [140] It was the fear of giving the buyer priority over secured creditors that was the main reason why specific performance was refused in *Re Wait* [1927] 1 Ch. 606: see especially 640. The buyer's problems in that case arose from the general rule, laid down by Sale of Goods Act 1979 s.16, that property under a contract of sale cannot pass in goods which are unascertained: see *Re Goldcorp Exchange Ltd* [1995] 1 A.C. 74. And see *VTB Commodities Trading DAC v JSC Antipinsky Refinery* [2020] EWHC 72 (Comm), [2020] 1 W.L.R. 1227 at [77] ("the rationale for refusing specific performance of contracts for the sale of future unascertained goods goes beyond the fact that damages will usually be an adequate remedy ... The granting of such a remedy effectively turns a contractual claim into a quasi-proprietary right in respect of goods which have not been allocated to the contract and may have been sold to a third party"). Contrast *Re Stapylton Fletcher* [1994] 1 W.L.R. 1181, where the goods were segregated from the seller's own stock after sale. The buyer's interests are now in turn protected by a statutory exception to the general rule in s.16: see s.20A, discussed in para.27-024 below after n.72. Insolvency of the defendant is not a ground for refusing specific performance where the remedy is normally available as a matter of course: *Amec Properties v Planning Research and Systems* [1992] 1 E.G.L.R. 70.

## Specific enforcement of contracts not within section 52

*Replace footnote 160 with:*

**27-025** [160] This possibility was doubted in *Re London Wine Co (Shippers)* [1986] P.C.C. 121, 149; but in that case it was not necessary to reach a conclusion on the specific enforceability of a contract for the delivery of goods which were not "specific or ascertained" since on the facts damages were clearly an adequate remedy: cf. above, para.27-020. In *VTB Commodities Trading DAC v JSC Antipinsky Refinery* [2020] EWHC 72 (Comm), [2020] 1 W.L.R. 1227 at [78] Phillips L.J. held that s.52 and the *Sky Petroleum* decision gave rise to a strong presumption that specific performance will be limited to cases of specific or ascertained goods.

## (c) Contracts Not Specifically Enforceable: Services and Constant Supervision

### Constant supervision and continuous duties

*Replace paragraph with:*

The court will not specifically enforce a contract under which one party is bound by continuous duties, the due performance of which might require constant supervision by the court.[293] In *Ryan v Mutual Tontine Association*[294] the lease of a service flat gave the tenant the right to the services of a porter who was to be "constantly in attendance". Specific enforcement of this right was refused on the ground that it would have required "that constant superintendence by the court, which the court in such cases has always declined to give".[295] For the same reason the courts have refused specifically to enforce a tenant's undertaking to cultivate a farm in a particular manner[296]; the obligations of a railway company to operate signals and to provide engine power[297]; a contract to keep an airfield in operation[298]; a contract to keep a shop open[299]; the obligations of a shipowner under a voyage charterparty[300]; a contract to deliver goods by instalments[301]; one which "would require an unacceptable degree of supervision [of the seller's performance] in a foreign land"[302]; and a long-term contract to supply catering services to a convention centre which would require "daily and detailed co-operation" between the parties[303]; and a contract requiring the tenant of a hotel to operate it in a certain way and conforming to certain standards.[303a] The difficulty of supervision is also one ground that has been given for the refusal of the courts in some cases specifically to enforce contracts to do building work[304] or to keep buildings in repair.[305] But in such cases specific performance is sometimes ordered and no practical difficulty seems to have arisen in enforcing such orders.[306] This suggests that the "difficulty" of supervision has been somewhat exaggerated; and various devices at the court's disposal can be deployed to overcome it. The court can, for example, appoint a receiver to perform the acts specified in the order,[307] or appoint an expert to act as officer of the court for the purpose, or it can authorise the claimant to appoint a person to act as agent of the defendant for the purpose of performing those acts.[308] In *Sparks v Biden*[309] the Court ordered specific performance of a term implied into the option agreement to the effect that the buyer was under an obligation to market and sell each house constructed as part of the development "within a reasonable time" of the option having been exercised and the planning permission having been obtained. The Court would "adjourn the working out of that order to the Master". Where the acts to be done under the contract are not to be done by the defendant personally, the court can order him simply to enter into a contract to procure those acts to be done. From this point of view, *Ryan v Mutual Tontine Association*[310] may be contrasted with *Posner v Scott-Lewis*[311] where the lessor of a block of luxury flats covenanted, so far as lay in his power, to employ a resident porter to perform a number of specified tasks. It was held that the covenant was specifically enforceable in the sense that the lessor could be ordered to appoint a resident porter for the performance of those tasks. 27-042

[293] This principle plainly does not apply to continuous obligations to pay money, e.g. under an agreement to pay an annuity, for it is well settled that such an agreement can be specifically enforced: above, para.27-018.

[294] [1893] 1 Ch. 116.

[295] [1893] 1 Ch. 116 at 123. In *Vertex Data Science Ltd v Powergen Retail Ltd* [2006] EWHC 1340 (Comm), [2006] 2 Lloyd's Rep. 591 at [42] the principle was, unusually, applied because the services to be supplied *by the claimant* would require constant supervision. For this case, see also above, para.27-040.

[296] *Rayner v Stone* (1762) 2 Eden 128; *Phipps v Jackson* (1887) 56 L.J. Ch. 550; cf. *Hill v Barclay* (1810) 16 Ves. Jr. 402 (tenant's covenant to repair); contrast *Jeune v Queens Cross Properties Ltd* [1974] Ch. 97 (landlord's covenant to repair); *Barrett v Lounava (1982) Ltd* [1990] 1 Q.B. 348 (landlord's implied covenant to repair); *Blue Manchester Ltd v North West Ground Rents Ltd* [2019] EWHC 142 (TCC), 182 Con. L.R. 59 (landlord's covenant to repair).

[297] *Powell Duffryn Steam Coal Co v Taff Vale Ry* (1874) L.R. 9 Ch. App. 331; *Blackett v Bates* (1865) L.R. 1 Ch. App. 117.

[298] *Dowty Boulton Paul Ltd v Wolverhampton Corp* [1971] 1 W.L.R. 204; for later proceedings in this case, see [1973] Ch. 94.

[299] *Braddon Towers Ltd v International Stores Ltd* [1987] E.G.L.R. 209 (decided in 1959); *Co-operative Insurance Society Ltd v Argyll Stores (Holdings) Ltd* [1998] A.C. 1, below, para.27-043.

[300] *De Mattos v Gibson* (1859) 4 De G. & J. 276. The view expressed in *Scandinavian Tanker Co AB v Flota Petrolera Ecuatoriana (The Scaptrade)* [1983] 2 A.C. 694, 700–701, that a time charter cannot be specifically enforced against the shipowner, is best explained on the ground that such enforcement would require too much supervision.

[301] *Dominion Coal Co v Dominion Iron & Steel Co* [1909] A.C. 293. But see above, para.27-025 at n.159. In *Thames Valley Power Ltd v Total Gas and Power Ltd* [2005] EWHC 2208, [2006] 1 Lloyd's Rep. 441 (above, para.27-026) the court declared that a buyer was "entitled to damages and an order by way of specific performance" of the suppliers' obligation under a long term contract for the supply of gas. At the time of the order, the contract had nearly five years to run but no reference was made to any difficulty of supervision, perhaps because the suppliers had indicated their willingness to continue the supply if the decision on the issue of liability went against them (at [58]).

[302] *TTK LIG Ltd* [2011] EWCA Civ 1170, [2012] 1 All E.R. (Comm) 429 at [95].

[303] *Kudos Catering (UK) Ltd v Manchester Convention Complex Ltd* [2013] EWCA Civ 38, [2013] 2 Lloyd's Rep. 270 at [17]. The point arose in the context of the construction of an exemption clause and was made in support of the argument that the construction relied on by the recipient of the services would render the agreement "devoid of contractual content since there [was] no sanction for non-performance" (at [19]) by that party.

[303a] *Zinc Cobham 1 Ltd (In Administration) v Adda Hotels* [2018] EWHC 1025 (Ch), [2018] L. & T.R. 36. The difficulties in supervision meant that "the only enforcement mechanism would be contempt of court", which the court declared "wholly inappropriate" (at [15]).

[304] Below, para.27-044.

[305] *Flint v Brandon* (1803) 8 Ves. Jr. 159; *Wheatley v Westminster Brymbo Coal Co* (1869) L.R. 9 Eq. 538; but see *Jeune v Queens Cross Properties Ltd*, above, n.296.

[306] See *Storer v G.W. Ry* (1842) 2 Y. & C. Ch. 48 (agreement to construct and "for ever thereafter to maintain one neat archway": specific performance decreed); *Kennard v Cory Bros* [1922] 2 Ch. 1 (mandatory injunction to keep a drain open); *Rainbow Estates Ltd v Tokenhold Ltd* [1999] Ch. 64.

[307] cf. *Gibbs v David* (1870) L.R. 20 Eq. 373 (receiver appointed in a rescission action to run a mine).

[308] cf. Law of Property Act 1925 s.101; Insolvency Act 1986 s.44 (as amended by Insolvency Act 1994 s.2).

[309] [2017] EWHC 1994 (Ch) at [67].

[310] Above at n.294.

[311] [1987] Ch. 25; Jones [1987] C.L.J. 21.

## Building contracts: specific enforcement against builder

*In line 10, after "(i) the work is precisely defined", add new footnote 322a:*

27-044 [322a] See *Blue Manchester Ltd v North West Ground Rents Ltd* [2019] EWHC 142 (TCC), 182 Con. L.R. 59 (an order that a landlord repair loose glass panels on a hotel façade could be drawn with sufficient certainty and particularity).

## (d) Impossibility, In-Utility, Unfairness and Vagueness

### Severe hardship to defendant

*Replace paragraph with:*

Specific performance may be refused on the ground that the order will cause severe hardship to the defendant. Thus, in *Denne v Light*[340] the court refused to order specific performance, against the buyer, of a contract to purchase farming land wholly surrounded by land which belonged to others and over which the buyer would have no right of way. Specific performance may also be refused where the cost of performance to the defendant is wholly out of proportion to the benefit which performance will confer on the claimant[341]; and where the defendant can put himself into a position to perform only by taking legal proceedings against a third party (especially if the outcome of such proceedings is in doubt.)[342] Severe hardship may be a ground for refusing specific performance even though it results from circumstances which arise after the conclusion of the contract, which affect the person of the defendant rather than the subject matter of the contract, and for which the claimant is in no way responsible. For example, in *Patel v Ali*[343] a purchaser's claim for specific performance of a contract for the sale of a house was rejected after a four-year delay (for which neither party was responsible), the vendor's circumstances having during this time changed disastrously as a result of her husband's bankruptcy and of an illness which had left her disabled. On the other hand, "mere pecuniary difficulties" would "afford no excuse".[344] Thus the purchaser of a house will not be denied specific performance merely because the vendor finds it difficult, on a rising market, to acquire alternative accommodation with the proceeds of the sale,[345] and even where the death of the vendor's husband resulted in the vendor's inability to work from anxiety and depression.[346] Nor will specific enforcement be refused merely because compliance with the order exposes the defendant to the risk of a strike by his employees,[347] or the loss of its entire interest in a joint venture.[348] Likewise, specific performance was not denied when the claimant exercised an option to purchase shares in a football club for a fixed price simply because the value of the shares had increased due to the club being promoted to the Premier League.[348a] **27-048**

[340] (1857) 8 D.M. & G. 774; cf. *Wedgewood v Adams* (1843) 6 Beav. 600. See also *Sullivan v Henderson* [1973] 1 W.L.R. 333, above, para.27-020, n.130; *Jaggard v Sawyer* [1995] 1 W.L.R. 269 (injunction); *Insurance Co v Lloyd's Syndicate* [1995] 1 Lloyd's Rep. 273, 276 (injunction).

[341] *Tito v Waddell (No.2)* [1977] Ch. 106, 326; *Morris v Redland Bricks Ltd* [1970] A.C. 652; *Zinc Cobham 1 Ltd (In Administration) v Adda Hotels* [2018] EWHC 1025 (Ch), [2018] L. & T.R. 36 (where the court refused to grant an order which would require the defendant to carry out works estimated at £100 million (equating to more than four times the defendant's annual rent of £26 million), and which far exceed the claimant's likely loss; this "has an air of unreality and fictionality", at [48]).

[342] *Wroth v Tyler* [1974] Ch. 30 (where an additional ground for refusing specific performance was that the third party against whom the proceedings would have to be taken was the defendant's wife, so that the proceedings would tend to split up the family); cf. *Watts v Spence* [1976] Ch. 165, 173.

[343] [1984] Ch. 238.

[344] [1984] Ch. 238 at 288; cf. *Francis v Cowcliffe* (1977) 33 P. & C.R. 368.

[345] *Mountford v Scott* [1975] Ch. 258; cf. *Easton v Brown* [1981] 3 All E.R. 278.

[346] *Shah v Greening* [2016] EWHC 548 (Ch).

[347] *Howard E. Perry & Co v British Railways Board* [1980] 1 W.L.R. 1375.

[348] *Man UK Properties Ltd v Falcon Investments Ltd* [2015] EWHC 1324 (Ch).

[348a] *UTB LLC v Sheffield United Ltd* [2019] EWHC 2322 (Ch) at [497].

### Conduct of the claimant

*Replace paragraph with:*

27-053 "The conduct of the party applying for [specific] relief is always an important element for consideration".[372] However, a "claimant for specific performance of a contract is not disqualified from equitable relief merely because it has done wrong to the defendant. It must be something wrong that relates to the contract that the claimant seeks to enforce, such that it would be against conscience for the court to grant the particular relief sought".[372a] Thus specific performance may be refused if the claimant fails to perform a promise which he made in order to induce the defendant to enter into the contract, but which is neither binding contractually, nor (because it relates to the future) operative as a misrepresentation.[373] Specific performance may also be refused if the claimant's main object in seeking this form of relief is to avoid a set-off that could have been raised against a claim by him for damages.[374] A similar view may be taken where the claimant has made misrepresentation but the right to rescind for that misrepresentation has been lost. But if the right has been lost by reason of the defendant's affirmation of the contract,[375] he will not be allowed to rely on the misrepresentation as a defence to specific performance since he in turn would be guilty of "unconscionable inconsistency in conduct"[376] in seeking, after affirmation, to invoke the misrepresentation for this purpose. But his conduct would not be open to such criticism where the right to rescind had been lost by *impossibility of restitution* arising otherwise than from the defendant's conduct.[377] Hence, in a case of this kind the misrepresentation, though no longer a ground for rescission, could be relied on as a defence to the equitable remedy of specific performance.[378]

[372] *Lamare v Dixon* (1873) L.R. 6 H.L. 414, 413; *Chappell v Times Newspapers Ltd* [1975] 1 W.L.R. 482; *Wilton Group v Abrams* [1990] B.C.C. 310, 317 ("commercially disreputable" agreement). And see above, para.27-050.

[372a] *UTB LLC v Sheffield United Ltd* [2019] EWHC 2322 (Ch) at [506].

[373] *Lamare v Dixon* (1873) L.R. 6 H.L. 414. And see *Volumatic Ltd v Ideas for Life Ltd* [2019] EWHC 2273 (IPEC) at [65], [68] and [71], where specific performance would have been denied, had the court found a contract, due to misrepresentation, breach and laches.

[374] *Handley Page Ltd v Commissioners of Customs and Excise* [1970] 2 Lloyd's Rep. 459.

[375] Above, paras 7-133—7-138.

[376] *Geest Plc v Fyffes Plc* [1999] 1 All E.R. (Comm) 672, 694.

[377] Above, paras 7-119 et seq.

[378] *Geest Plc v Fyffes Plc* [1999] 1 All E.R. (Comm) 672 at 694. And see below, para 27-043.

### Vagueness

*Replace paragraph with:*

27-060 An agreement may be so vague that it cannot be enforced at all, even by an action for damages.[399] But although an agreement is definite enough to be enforced in some form of legal proceedings, it may still be too vague to be enforced specifically.[400] For example, specific performance has been refused of a contract to publish an article as to the exact text of which the parties disagreed,[401] and of a contract requiring the occupiers of hotels to trade in accordance with certain standards, parts of which were not specific enough to make an order for specific performance.[401a] The reason for refusing specific performance in these cases appears to be that the court would find it difficult or impossible to state in its order precisely what the defendant was bound to do in obedience to the order; and precision is essential since failure to comply with the court's order may lead to attachment for contempt.[402] However, if an obligation can be performed in a number of different ways:

> "... [i]t is open to the court, in order to give its order specificity and effectiveness, to spell out what performance is required in the particular circumstances of the case."

Moreover, it is appropriate in such cases "to include a liberty to apply, so that the parties can, if it becomes necessary, come back for further directions".[403] In *Sparks v Biden*[404] the Court ordered specific performance of a term implied into the option agreement to the effect that the buyer was under an obligation to market and sell each house constructed as part of the development "within a reasonable time" of the option having been exercised and the planning permission having been obtained. The Court would "adjourn the working out of that order to the Master". Where the contract confers a power on one party to consent to the other party's exercise of an option conferred by the contract, the court may specifically enforce an implied duty not to exercise the power unreasonably, capriciously or arbitrarily.[405] An agreement is also not too vague to be specifically enforced merely because it is expressed to be subject to such amendments as may reasonably be required by one (or by either) party.[406]

[399] Above, para.2-148, *Waring & Gillow v Thompson* (1912) 29 T.L.R. 154.

[400] *Collins v Plumb* (1810) 16 Ves. Jr. 454 as explained in *Catt v Tourle* (1869) L.R. 4 Ch. App. 654, 658; *Wilson v Northampton & Banbury Junction Railway Co* (1874) 9 Ch. App. 279, as explained in *Tito v Waddell (No.2)* [1977] Ch. 106, 322–323; cf. *Vertex Data Science Ltd v Powergen Retail Ltd* [2006] EWHC 1340 (Comm), [2006] 2 Lloyd's Rep. 591 (above, para.27-039, n.295) at [46]. For recognition of the above possibility in a case in which the actual claim was one for damages, see *Durham Tees Valley Airport Ltd v Bmibaby Ltd* [2010] EWCA Civ 485, [2011] 1 Lloyd's Rep. 68 at [90]; for this case, see above, para.2-152. The agreement in this case might not have been specifically enforceable *against* the claimant as such an order would require "constant supervision" (see above, para.27-042 at n.298). Similar reasoning might apply to a claim for specific performance by the claimant; such a claim could also give rise to a problem of mutuality of remedy (see below, para.27-063). And see *Co-operative Insurance Society Ltd v Argyll Stores (Holdings) Ltd* [1988] A.C. 1, 13, and at 14: "The fact that the terms of a contractual obligation are sufficiently definite to escape being void for uncertainty, or to found a claim for damages, or to permit compliance to be made a condition of relief against forfeiture, does not necessarily mean that they will be sufficiently precise to be capable of being specifically enforced." See further, *118 Data Resource Ltd v IDS Data Services Ltd* [2014] EWHC 3629 at [23]–[30], where specific performance on a summary judgment was denied in respect of a clause allowing the claimant to enter the defendant's offices to ensure compliance with the agreement, because there was no mechanism to ensure that the defendant only searched for material relating to the agreement and not for other commercially sensitive information; and it was unclear what the claimant could do if it found a breach.

[401] *Joseph v National Magazine Co* [1959] Ch. 14; cf. *Slater v Raw*, *The Times*, October 15, 1977.

[401a] *Zinc Cobham 1 Ltd (In Administration) v Adda Hotels* [2018] EWHC 1025 (Ch), [2018] L. & T.R. 36 at [47]–[48].

[402] cf. *Lawrence David Ltd v Ashton* [1989] I.C.R. 123, 132; *Lock International Plc v Beswick* [1989] 1 W.L.R. 1268.

[403] *Alfa Finance Holdings AD v Quarzwerke GmbH* [2015] EWHC 243 at [8]–[9].

[404] [2017] EWHC 1994 (Ch) at [67].

[405] *Watson v Watchfinder.co.uk Ltd* [2017] EWHC 1275 (Comm) at [101], [102].

[406] *Sweet & Maxwell Ltd v Universal News Services Ltd* [1964] 2 Q.B. 699; *Alpenstow Ltd v Regalian Properties Plc* [1985] 1 W.L.R. 721. See also *AAA v CCC* [2020] EWCA Civ 846, where the defendant unsuccessfully argued that both the injunctive relief ordered at trial and the contractual provisions on which it was based (involving covenants not to make any adverse or derogatory comment about the claimant, its directors or employees or to do anything which might bring any of them into disrepute) were too uncertain.

## (e) Human Rights and Public Interest

### Human rights and public interest

*Replace footnote 414 with:*

27-062 [414] [2014] EWHC 1176 (QB) at [27]; see *Pertemps Medical Group Ltd v Ladak* [2020] EWHC 163 (QB) at [37], in the context of an interim injunction, below para.27-079A.

## 4. Injunction

### Negative contracts

*Replace paragraph with:*

27-077 Where a contract is negative in nature, or contains an express negative stipulation, breach of it may be restrained by injunction.[513] In such cases an injunction is normally granted as a matter of course, so that the fact that "damages would be an adequate remedy ... is not generally a relevant consideration where the injunction restrains the breach of a negative covenant".[514] But as the remedy is an equitable one, it is in principle a discretionary remedy and it may be refused on the ground that its award would cause such "particular hardship"[515] to the defendant as to be oppressive to him.[516] Moreover, "[i]n determining whether ... an injunction should be refused in the exercise of the court's discretion, the consequences of the grant or the refusal of an injunction for both parties will be relevant, and that may include consideration of whether damages would be a sufficient and appropriate remedy for the claimant".[516a] A prohibitory injunction to restrain future breaches would not be "oppressive" merely because observance of the contract was burdensome to the defendant[517] or because its breach would cause little or no prejudice to the claimant,[518] for, in deciding whether to restrain breach of a negative stipulation, the court is not normally concerned with "the balance of convenience or inconvenience".[519] The question is whether granting a prohibitory injunction would be "so prejudicial to the defendant and cause him such hardship that it would be unconscionable".[519a] If the defendant has already broken his contract (e.g. by fencing land that he promised to leave open) he may be ordered by a *mandatory* injunction actually to undo the breach. Such an order *is* subject to a "balance of convenience" test, and may, accordingly, be refused if the prejudice suffered by the defendant in having to restore the original position heavily outweighs the advantage that will be derived from such restoration by the claimant.[520] In determining whether the "balance of convenience" test should apply, courts should look at the substance of the injunction, rather than the formal distinction between prohibitory and mandatory injunctions.[520a] In determining whether to grant a mandatory injunction, the court will take into account the adequacy of damages,[520b] and the nature of the breach. Thus where the defendant had in breach of a restrictive covenant erected a building so as to block the claimant's sea view, a mandatory injunction was granted as the breach had been committed deliberately, with full knowledge of the claimant's rights, and as damages would not have been an adequate remedy.[521] Where the defendant had, in breach of an intellectual property licensing agreement, entered a contract with a third party without giving the licensee the opportunity to match the third party's offer, a mandatory injunction was given in respect of the contract with the third party: the defendant was required to inform the third party it would not perform, not to perform and not to assist the third party to perform. Damages might be inadequate given the contractual cap on damages and an exclusion of consequential losses; the defendant and the third party had entered the agreement fully aware that the claimant would object to it; and the grant would not be out of all proportion to the requirements of the case, nor would the order operate with extreme (or any) harshness on the defendant.[522]

[513] *Martin v Nutkin* (1724) 2 P. Wms. 266. An injunction cannot be granted to restrain a party to a contract from doing acts which have, because the contract has been brought to an end, ceased to be breaches of the contract: see *Medina Housing Association v Case* [2002] EWCA Civ 2001, [2003] 1 All E.R. 1084. It is, of course, possible for a negative stipulation to continue to apply after positive obligations of performance have come to an end, whether by notice or by lapse of time, as in the restraint of trade cases discussed in para.27-086, below.

[514] *Araci v Fallon* [2011] EWCA Civ 668 at [70], per Elias L.J. citing para.27-060 of the 30th edition of this book (para.27-077 in the present edition) with apparent approval. Since in that case damages were *not* an adequate remedy (above para.27-019 n.117 and below, para.27-067) it can be argued that the point made in the dictum cited in the text above did not strictly arise. Contrast *Tye v House* (1998) 76 P. & C.R. 188 where adequacy of damages was held to be relevant in refusing to award an injunction against the seller's breach of an exclusivity agreement in respect of land because the exclusivity did not require the vendor to sell to the prospective purchaser, only to compensate the latter's wasted expenses.

[515] *Insurance Co v Lloyd's Syndicate* [1995] 1 Lloyd's Rep. 272, 276 (where there was no such hardship). cf. above, para.27-036 (severe hardship).

[516] See below, para.27-081.

[516a] *Priyanka Shipping Ltd v Glory Bulk Carriers Pte Ltd* [2019] EWHC 2804 (Comm), [2019] 1 W.L.R. 6677 at [97].

[517] cf. above, para.27-048.

[518] *Kemp v Sober* (1851) 1 Sim.(N.S.) 517; *Tipping v Eckersley* (1855) 2 K. & J. 264; *Marco Productions Ltd v Pagola* [1945] K.B. 111; *Hollis & Co v Stocks* [2000] I.R.L.R. 712.

[519] *Doherty v Allman* (1878) 3 App. Cas. 709, 720; cf. *Warner Bros Pictures Inc v Nelson* [1937] 1 K.B. 209, 217; *Wakeham v Wood* (1982) 43 P. & C.R. 40; *Att-Gen v Barker* [1990] 3 All E.R. 257, 262.

[519a] *Insurance Co v Lloyd's Syndicate* [1995] 1 Lloyd's Rep 272, 277; *SDI Retail Services Ltd v Rangers Football Club Ltd* [2018] EWHC 2772 (Comm) at [58]–[60].

[520] *Sharp v Harrison* [1922] 1 Ch. 502; *Shepherd Homes Ltd v Sandham* [1971] Ch. 340; for subsequent proceedings, see [1971] 1 W.L.R. 1062; *Films Rover International Ltd v Cannon Film Sales* [1987] 1 W.L.R. 670 (for further proceedings, see [1989] 1 W.L.R. 912); *Sutton Housing Trust v Lawrence* (1987) 19 H.L.R. 520 (mandatory and prohibitory injunction); *Reed v Madon* [1989] Ch. 408; *SDI Retail Services Ltd v Rangers Football Club Ltd* [2018] EWHC 2772 (Comm) at [50]; *Land Rover Group Ltd v UPF (UK) Ltd* [2002] EWHC 3183 (QB), [2003] B.C.L.C. 122 at [60], where the "balance of convenience" test was applicable also on the principle stated in para.27-078 below as the injunction was an interim one. For another such case, see *Landmark Brickworks Ltd v Sutcliffe* [2011] EWHC 1239 (QB), [2011] I.R.L.R. 976 at [80], [86]–[88].

[520a] *SDI Retail Services Ltd v Rangers Football Club Ltd* [2018] EWHC 2772 (Comm) at [50].

[520b] See *QBE Management Services (UK) Ltd v Dymoke* [2012] EWHC 80 (QB), [2012] I.R.L.R. 458 where the injunction was designed to deprive the defendant of any commercial advantage gained by him as a result of his breaches of duties of fidelity arising under his contract of employment with the claimant. Thus, the effect of the injunction resembled a mandatory injunction, since that effect was to restore the parties to the position in which they were before the breaches had been committed. Hence one reason given for granting the injunction was that "damages would not be an adequate remedy" (at [280]). And see *Eircom UK Ltd v Department for Finance* [2018] NIQB 75; *SDI Retail Services Ltd v Rangers Football Club Ltd* [2018] EWHC 2772 (Comm) at [50].

[521] *Wakeham v Wood* (1982) 43 P. & C.R. 40; *HKRUK II (CHC) Ltd v Heaney* [2010] EWHC 2245 (Ch), [2010] 3 E.G.L.R. 15 (mandatory injunction to restrain wrongful interference with right to light); cf. *Mortimer v Bailey* [2004] EWCA Civ 1514, [2005] 2 P. & C.R. 9 (where the main issue was whether there had been undue delay in applying for a mandatory injunction to pull down an extension built in breach of covenant).

[522] *SDI Retail Services Ltd v Rangers Football Club Ltd* [2018] EWHC 2772 (Comm). The defendant had entered into a contract with a third party, in breach of its obligations to the claimant. The court reasoned that the terms of the contract made it clear that both parties were fully aware that the claimant would object to it (at [59]).

## Interim injunctions

*Replace paragraph with:*

**27-078** Applications for interim injunctions are likewise, in general,[523] subject (inter alia) to the "balance of convenience" test.[524] One application of the balance of convenience test is to cases where the injunction is sought for such a period that to grant it would amount in substance to a final resolution of the dispute between the parties. The court will, in considering such a claim for interim relief, take into account the likelihood of the claimant's success at the eventual trial.[525] The court can also take into account the financial prejudice which is likely to be suffered either by the claimant if the injunction is refused,[526] or by the defendant if it is granted,[527] and if at the trial the dispute were to be resolved in that party's favour. An award of damages to that party might then be an "inadequate" remedy for reasons discussed earlier in this Chapter[528]: e.g. because there was an appreciable risk of the other party's not being able to pay the amount of the award. In one case[529] the inadequacy of damages was the reason for the grant of an interim injunction to prevent the local authority from giving effect to notices of redundancy issued to certain employees. Damages may also be inadequate where the infringement of the interest that a party is trying to protect by way of an injunction is a person's privacy or reputation,[530] or where the claimant may be deprived of their shareholding.[530a] On the other hand, the public interest[531] or damage to the defendant's reputation[532] may outweigh the potential damage to the claimant. In one case,[532a] the court held that damages would be an inadequate remedy for either party, should it succeed at trial: for the claimant because it would suffer a substantial adverse effect on its reputation that would be difficult to quantify, and for the defendant should it succeed at trial because it would suffer non-financial losses. The court held that the balance of convenience lay in favour of the defendant, the London Underground, because of the strong public interest in allowing it to proceed to introduce new trains. In one case, the court was unable to reach a conclusion on the balance of convenience and refused an injunction since "the least irremediable prejudice would result from preserving the status quo".[532b]

[523] i.e. subject to the exception discussed at para.27-079 below. The "balance of convenience" test may also be excluded by the "statutory context" in which the interim injunction is sought: see *London Underground Ltd v Associated Society of Locomotive Engineers and Firemen* [2011] EWHC 3506 (QB), [2012] I.R.L.R. 196 at [13], where that context was provided by ss.219 and 221 of the Trade Union and Labour Relations (Consolidation) Act 1992.

[524] *Texaco Ltd v Mulberry Filling Station Ltd* [1972] 1 W.L.R. 814; *Evans Marshall & Co v Bertola* [1973] 1 W.L.R. 349; *Clifford Davis Management Ltd v W.E.A. Records Ltd* [1975] 1 W.L.R. 61; *Mike Trading & Transport Ltd v R. Pagnan & Fratelli* [1980] 2 Lloyd's Rep. 546; *Locobail International Finance v Agroexport (The Sea Hawk)* [1986] 1 W.L.R. 657; *Kerr v Morris* [1987] Ch. 90, 112; *Films Rover International v Cannon Film Sales Ltd* [1987] 1 W.L.R. 670, for further proceedings see [1989] 1 W.L.R. 912; *Evening Standard Co Ltd v Henderson* [1987] I.C.R. 588; *Provident Financial Group Ltd v Hayward* [1989] I.C.R. 160; *Lock International Plc v Beswick* [1989] 1 W.L.R. 1268; *Channel Tunnel Group v Balfour Beatty Construction Ltd* [1993] A.C. 334; *GFI Group Inc v Eaglestone*, [1994] I.R.L.R. 119; *Series 5 Software v Clarke* [1996] 1 All E.R. 853; *Tate & Lyle Industries v Cia. Usina Bulhoes* [1997] 1 Lloyd's Rep. 355; *Townsend Group Ltd v Cobb* [2004] EWHC 3432, *The Times*, December 1, 2004; *Ericsson AB v EADS Defence and Security Systems* [2009] EWHC 2598 (TCC) at [29]–[33]; *Lauffer v Barking, Havering and Redbridge University Hospitals NHS Trust* [2009] EWHC 2360 (QB) at [46]–[54]; *Serco Ltd v National Union of Rail, Maritime and Transport Workers* [2011] EWCA Civ 226, [2011] 3 All E.R. 913 at [10]. For the principles governing such injunctions, see generally *American Cyanamid Co v Ethicon Ltd* [1975] A.C. 396; *Fellowes v Fisher* [1976] Q.B. 122 and *Lawrence David Ltd v Ashton* [1989] I.C.R. 123 (holding these principles to be applicable in restraint of trade cases); *Martin & Co (UK) Ltd v Cedra Ltd* [2015] EWHC 1036 (Ch) at [63]–[64]; *AB v CD* [2014] EWHC 1 (QB) at [41], [2014] EWCA Civ 229, [2014] 3 All E.R. 667 at [6] (the appeal was allowed for the reason discussed in para.27-019, n.120); *Ashworth v Royal National Theatre* [2014] EWHC

1176 (QB) at [33]; *SDI Retail Services Ltd v King* [2018] EWHC 1697 (Comm) at [6]–[16]; *McAfee Ireland Ltd v DSG Retail Ltd* [2019] 8 WLUK 10 (QBD Commercial Court) at [14]–[16].

525 *Cambridge Nutrition Ltd v BBC* [1990] 3 All E.R. 523; *Lansing Linde Ltd v Kerr* [1991] 1 W.L.R. 251, 258–259; *Imutran v Uncaged Campaigns Ltd* [2001] 2 All E.R. 385; *Associated Foreign Exchange Ltd v International Foreign Exchange Ltd* [2010] EWHC 1178 (Ch), [2010] I.R.L.R. 694 (interim injunction to enforce non-solicitation covenant against employee refused as the likely outcome of the trial was that the covenant would be held unenforceable); *Pertemps Medical Group Ltd v Ladak* [2020] EWHC 163 (QB) at [42]–[53] (interim injunction granted because the claimant was likely to attain injunctive relief at trial); *P14 Medical Ltd v Mahon* [2020] EWHC 1823 (QB) at [123] (interim injunction granted primarily because of the claimant's likelihood of success at trial).

526 *Themehelp Ltd v West* [1996] Q.B. 84, doubted on another point in *Group Josi Re v Walbrook Ins. Co Ltd* [1996] 1 W.L.R. 1152, 1162; *British Airways Plc v Unite the Union* [2009] EWHC 3541 (QB), [2010] I.R.L.R. 423 at [83] (balance of convenience in favour of injunction against strike over Christmas period as this was "fundamentally more damaging" than one called "at any other time of the year"). The interim injunction was discharged on another ground in further proceedings: [2010] EWCA Civ 669, [2010] I.C.R. 1316. See also *Medina Dairy Ltd v Nampak Plastics Europe Ltd* [2020] 2 WLUK 70 at [36] (interim injunction granted because the cessation of supply of would curtail the claimant's ability to fulfil its obligations to its customers); *Re R-Squared Holdco Ltd* [2020] EWHC 23 (Ch) at [65]–[67] (interim injunction granted because the consequences of refusing may have been irreversible).

527 *Cambridge Nutrition Ltd v B.B.C.* [1990] 3 All E.R. 523; *P. I. International Ltd v Llewellyn* [2005] EWHC 407, [2005] U.K.C.L.R. 530; *Eircom UK Ltd v Department for Finance* [2018] NIQB 75.

528 Above, para.27-019 at n.123. See e.g. *Martin & Co (UK) Ltd v Cedra Ltd* [2015] EWHC 1036 (Ch) at [52]–[62]; *Blade Motor Group Ltd v Reynolds & Reynolds Ltd* [2018] EWHC 497 (Ch).

529 *Taylor v Birmingham City Council* [2017] EWHC 2576 (QB).

530 *PJS v News Group Newspapers Ltd* [2016] UKSC 26 at [43]; *Kent Community Health NHS Foundation Trust v NHS Swale Clinical Commissioning Group* [2016] EWHC 1393 (TCC) at [15]. See *Bombardier Transportation UK Ltd v London Underground Ltd* [2018] EWHC 2926 (TCC), [2019] B.L.R. 83, in the context of an order to lift the suspension of a contract entered into by a public body. The court stated that "there must be cogent evidence showing that the loss of reputation alleged would lead to financial losses that would be significant and irrecoverable as damages or very difficult to quantify fairly" (at [58]). The fact that the contracts lost by the claimant were of high value, prestigious, and of global interest meant that damages were not an adequate remedy for the claimant in the case. And see *Circle Nottingham Ltd v NHS Rushcliffe Clinical Commissioning Group* [2019] EWHC 1315 (TCC) at [45], where the court rejected an argument based on reputational damage because any such damage will be "largely swept away" upon success at trial.

530a *Re R-Squared Holdco Ltd* [2020] EWHC 23 (Ch) at [65]–[67].

531 See *R. (on the application of Ideal Carehomes (Number One Ltd)) v Care Quality Commission* [2018] EWHC 886 (Admin)). The court refused to order an interim injunction to restrain the regulator from publishing its inspection report into the claimant's care home. The public interest in the publication of the report and the need to inform the public clearly outweighed the potential damage to the claimant's business and reputation. And see *Kent Community Health NHS Foundation Trust v NHS Swale Clinical Commissioning Group* [2016] EWHC 1393 (TCC) on what is meant by the adequacy of damages for a not-for-profit organisation and on the role of the public interest in assessing the balance of convenience; and *Allfiled UK Ltd v Eltis* [2015] EWHC 1300 (Ch) on the effect of the claimant's delay. See *Eircom UK Ltd v Department for Finance* [2018] NIQB 75.

532 See *Rashid v Oil Companies International Marine Forum* [2018] EWHC 659 (QB), where the court refused an interim injunction to reinstate the claimant's ship inspection accreditation because, should the withdrawal of accreditation after a disciplinary process be found lawful, the defendant's reputation would be damaged by permitting the claimant to undertake inspections.

532a *Bombardier Transportation UK Ltd v London Underground Ltd* [2018] EWHC 2926 (TCC), [2019] B.L.R. 83. See also *P14 Medical Ltd v Mahon* [2020] EWHC 1823 (QB) at [118]–[120].

532b *Circle Nottingham Ltd v NHS Rushcliffe Clinical Commissioning Group* [2019] EWHC 1315 (TCC) at [92].

*Add new paragraph:*

**Interim injunctions and right to free speech** Where an interim injunction may interfere with a party's right of freedom of expression, the Human Rights Act 1998 s.12(3) stipulates that "No such relief is to be granted so as to restrain publication before trial unless the court is satisfied that the applicant is likely to establish that publication should not be allowed". In contrast to the *American Cyanamid*[539a] test 27-079A that requires the claimant to establish a "real prospect of success", s.12 "requires the court to apply an enhanced merits test",[539b] in the sense that "courts will be exceedingly slow to make interim restraint orders where the applicant has not satisfied the court he will probably ('more likely than not') succeed at the trial".[539c] But courts may have to depart from this general approach and require a lesser degree of likelihood where, for example, the potential adverse consequences of disclosure are particularly grave, where a short-lived injunction is necessary to enable the court to hear and give proper consideration to an application for interim relief pending the trial or any relevant appeal,[539d] where the defendant acts in bad faith,[539e] or where the parties have freely and expressly[539f] agreed on the restriction to free speech,[539g] especially where both parties were legally advised.[539h] The express agreement exception is explained by the important public interest of encouraging parties to litigation to settle their disputes with confidence that the court would be likely to enforce the terms of their settlement.[539i] Thus, in granting an interim injunction against a defendant who breached a settlement agreement not to make any adverse or derogatory comments about the claimant, its directors or employees, or do anything that would bring it into disrepute,[539j] Pepperall J. said:

> "the court should accord particular weight to the fact that this action is brought to enforce obligations contained in a settlement agreement that was freely entered into, involved the payment of a six-figure sum in full and final settlement of all disputes arising from the employment and in respect of which Mr Ladak [the defendant] had the benefit of independent legal advice."[539k]

[539a] *American Cyanamid Co v Ethicon Ltd* [1975] A.C. 396.

[539b] *Pertemps Medical Group Ltd v Ladak* [2020] EWHC 163 (QB) at [37] ("the usual *American Cyanamid* test is modified and no relief can be granted merely on satisfying the court that there is a serious issue to be tried").

[539c] *Cream Holdings Ltd v Banerjee* [2014] UKHL 44 at [22]; *ABC v Telegraph Media Group Ltd* [2018] EWCA Civ 2329 at [51]; *Taher v Cumberland* [2019] EWHC 524 (QB) at [110].

[539d] *Cream Holdings Ltd v Banerjee* [2014] UKHL 44 at [22]; *ABC v Telegraph Media Group Ltd* [2018] EWCA Civ 2329 at [16].

[539e] *Taher v Cumberland* [2019] EWHC 524 (QB) at [106], [112]–[113].

[539f] *ABC v Telegraph Media Group Ltd* [2018] EWCA Civ 2329 at [22], quoting *HRH the Prince of Wales v Associated Newspapers Ltd* [2006] EWCA Civ 1776, where "there is an express contractual obligation of confidence which may have been broken, it is 'arguable' that the express duty carries more weight 'than a duty of confidentiality that is not buttressed by express agreement', but the extent to which is does so 'will depend upon the facts of the individual case'"; *Pertemps Medical Group Ltd v Ladak* [2020] EWHC 163 (QB) at [41].

[539g] *Warren v Random House Group Ltd* [2008] EWCA Civ 834 at [22]; *Mionis v Democratic Press SA* [2017] EWCA Civ 1194 at [87].

[539h] *Mionis v Democratic Press SA* [2017] EWCA Civ 1194 at [67]; *Taher v Cumberland* [2019] EWHC 524 (QB) at [106].

[539i] *Mionis v Democratic Press SA* [2017] EWCA Civ 1194 at [67], [104]; *ABC v Telegraph Media Group Ltd* [2018] EWCA Civ 2329 at [24]–[25], [41], [60], [64].

[539j] *Pertemps Medical Group Ltd v Ladak* [2020] EWHC 163 (QB).

[539k] *Pertemps Medical Group Ltd v Ladak* [2020] EWHC 163 (QB) at [41].

## Oppression

*Replace paragraph with:*

**27-081** We shall see later in this chapter[541] that the court has power by statute to award damages in lieu of specific performance or injunction. That power is likely to be exercised if the injury to the claimant is small, if it can readily be estimated in money, if compensation in money would adequately compensate the claimant and if the grant of an injunction would be oppressive to the defendant.[542] These conditions were satisfied, and an injunction was accordingly refused, in *Jaggard v Sawyer*,[543] where the defendants had built a house on land which could be reached only by committing a breach of covenant and a trespass against neighbouring house-owners, including the plaintiff. An injunction restraining such access would have rendered the new house "landlocked and incapable of beneficial ownership"[544]; and this would have been oppressive as the defendants had acted "openly and in good faith"[545] and not "in blatant disregard of the plaintiff's rights"[546] in building the house. The test is, again, one of *oppression*,[547] rather than one of *balance of convenience*: if the plaintiff had sought interlocutory relief *before* the house had been built, she "would almost certainly have obtained it".[548]

541 See below, para.27-095.

542 See the tort case of *Shelfer v City of London Electric Light Co* [1895] 1 Ch. 287, 322–333, held to be applicable by analogy in *Vestergaard Frandsen A/S v Bestnet Europe Ltd* [2009] EWHC 1456 (Ch), [2010] F.S.R. 2 at [41] to a claim for misuse of confidential information. See also the "noise nuisance" tort case of *Lawrence v Fen Tigers Ltd* [2014] UKSC 13, [2014] 2 All E.R. 623 where the four requirements (based on the judgment of A.L. Smith L.J. in *Shelfer v City of London Electric Light Co* [1895] 1 Ch. 287 at p.322–323) were reviewed by the Supreme Court. Lord Neuberger, P. said that the approach to the problem should be "more flexible" (at [119]) than that stated in the *Shelfer* case (above). Lords Sumption and Clarke (while expressing their agreement with Lord Neuberger: see at [154], [169]), went so far as to say that the *Shelfer* case was "out of date" at [161], [171], though this view may be at least in part restricted to "the special treatment of nuisance" (at [160]) in this context; while Lords Mance at [165] and Carnwath at [247] would, while agreeing generally with Lord Neuberger's "nuanced approach" (at [165]; cf. at [247]) in such a context attach particular importance to "the right to enjoy one's home without disturbance". The requirements stated in the text above do not apply where it is the *wrongdoer* who claims that specific relief is the more appropriate remedy since in such a case the grant of the injunction cannot be oppressive to him: *Marcic v Thames Water Utilities (No.2)* [2001] 4 All E.R. 326 reversed on another ground [2003] UKHL 66, [2004] 2 A.C. 42. All four of the requirements stated in the text above must be satisfied by the party claiming that an award of damages would be a more appropriate remedy than specific enforcement: see *HKRUK II (CHC) Ltd v Heaney* [2010] EWHC 2245 (Ch), [2010] E.G.L.R. 15 (below, n.546) at [63], where the requirement that the damages must be "small" was not satisfied (at [81]). In that case, the *wrongdoer* was, unusually, the claimant, the action being one for a declaration as to the wrongdoer's rights. It does not follow from the reasoning of the case that a claim *by the injured party* for damages in lieu of an injunction would likewise have failed. In the text above, "defendant" refers to the more usual situation in which it is the wrongdoer who is the defendant. And see *Priyanka Shipping Ltd v Glory Bulk Carriers Pte Ltd* [2019] EWHC 2804 (Comm), [2019] 1 W.L.R. 6677 at [124] (not unconscionable or oppressive to grant an interim injunction simply because the defendant made a bad bargain).

543 [1995] 1 W.L.R. 269.

544 [1995] 1 W.L.R. 269 at 288.

545 [1995] 1 W.L.R. 269 at 289; cf. *Priyanka Shipping Ltd v Glory Bulk Carriers Pte Ltd* [2019] EWHC 2804 (Comm) at [122], where the deliberate nature of the breaches was a factor in granting the interim injunction.

546 [1995] 1 W.L.R. 269 at 283. cf. the *HKRUK II* case, above n.542, where a mandatory injunction was granted against a developer who had continued with building work knowing that it would result in actionable interference with a neighbour's right to light; and where compensation would have amounted to a considerable sum. In the circumstances, it would have been wrong to compel the injured party to accept monetary (as opposed to specific) relief (at [83]–[85]).

547 cf. above, para. 27-077.

548 [1995] 1 W.L.R. 269 at 289, cf. 283. See also the similar case of *Gafford v Graham* (1998) 76 P. & C.R. D18; and the tort case of *Regan v Paul Properties Ltd* [2006] EWCA Civ 1391, [2007] Ch. 135 where the claimant had begun to protest five months before interference with his right to light by the defendant became imminent and was granted injunctive relief. Contrast the further tort case of *Watson v Croft Promosport Ltd* [2009] EWCA Civ 15, [2009] 3 All E.R. 249, where an injunction against noise nuisance was granted as the wrong had caused substantial injury to the claimant, the injunction would not be oppressive to the defendants and there were no exceptional circumstances to justify the refusal of injunctive relief.

## Restraint of trade

*Replace paragraph with:*

**27-086** Another type of contract containing a negative promise, which is often enforced by injunction, is that which restrains an employee or the vendor of a business from competition with the employer or purchaser.[572] Such terms are invalid at common law unless they are reasonable.[573] While the cases discussed in para.27-084 above assumed that the term is valid and turn on the question of whether an injunction would indirectly compel specific performance of the positive obligations of the contract, it is arguable that the purpose of the negative stipulation in *Lumley v Wagner*[574] was to restrain competition, as it might have been physically possible for the defendant to sing at Drury Lane for two nights a week and to sing elsewhere on other nights. Yet the judgment does not discuss the question whether the contract was invalid for restraint of trade. It used to be thought that the two lines of cases could be distinguished on the ground that the restraint cases concerned the validity of covenants which took effect *after* employment; while the *Lumley v Wagner* line of cases concerned the remedy for breaches of covenants operating *during* employment. There may be considerable force in this view where the term of the engagement is fairly short (as it was in *Lumley v Wagner*), since in such a case the negative stipulation is likely to be reasonable, and therefore valid under the rules relating to restraint of trade, by reason of its limited duration. But there are other situations in which the distinction between covenants operating after and those operating during employment may be hard to draw or not obviously relevant in the particular context, especially where a service contract is a long-term one or gives the employer a series of options to renew it,[575] or where long periods of notice have to be given to terminate the contract.[576] Stipulations which operate during employment (no less than those which operate thereafter) can therefore sometimes have their validity tested under the restraint of trade doctrine[577]; but even where their *validity* is not subject to these tests, the *remedy* of injunction is likely to be granted only where these tests are satisfied.[578] The employer will be allowed to enforce such a stipulation by injunction only if this remedy will not put the sort of pressure on the employee that was discussed in para.27-084 above.[579] It is further submitted that, even where a covenant in restraint of trade takes effect after the period of service, and is valid, it may be appropriate not to enforce it by *injunction* (but only by an action for damages) if the grant of an injunction would leave the employee with no other reasonable means of making a living to comply with the covenant. In such a case, the grant of an injunction might well be regarded as oppressive and refused on that ground, and the employer be left to his remedy in damages.[580] Moreover, an injunction to enforce a valid restraint of trade may be denied if the claimant's delay has induced the defendant's detrimental reliance.[581] A short delay (even of two months) may make it inequitable to grant an injunction where it was deliberately timed to caused avoidable loss to third parties.[582]

[572] See above, paras 16-106 et seq.

[573] See above, para.16-123. See *Tillman v Egon Zehnder Ltd* [2017] EWCA Civ 1054 at [35]; Longmore L.J. held that: "the law which avoids contracts in unreasonable restraint of trade is based on the wide public policy of promoting competition and protecting employees from too readily abandoning the exercise of their right reasonably to compete after termination"; *Argus Media Ltd v Halim* [2019] EWHC 42 (QB), [2019] I.R.L.R. 442 at [226] (a term restricting the use of confidential information was not enforced through the grant of an injunction, as it was considered too wide and broadly worded); and *Monex Europe Ltd v Pothecary* [2019] EWHC 1714 (QB) at [57]–[59] (a term precluding former employees from working for a competitor company was not a reasonable restraint of trade as it was not necessary to protect the employer's business interests); *P14 Medical Ltd v Mahon* [2020] EWHC 1823

(QB) (interim injunction granted because claimant likely to establish at trial that the non-competition, non-solicitation and non-supply clauses were not unreasonable restraints of trade as the restraints were only for six months and the defendant was a very senior former employee).

574 (1852) 1 De G.M. & G. 604; above para.27-082. In *Araci v Fallon* [2011] EWCA Civ 688 (above, para.27-079, n.534) it was said at [56] to be common ground that, in that case, "restraint of trade [was] not a relevant consideration: see *Warner Brothers Pictures Ltd v Nelson* [1937] 1 K.B. 209" (below, para.27-087). The agreement in the *Araci* case (see at [11]–[14]) did not give rise to a relationship of employer and employee.

575 See the terms of the contracts in *Warner Bros v Nelson* [1937] 1 K.B. 209 and cf. *Eastham v Newcastle United Football Club Ltd* [1964] Ch. 413.

576 e.g. in cases of "garden leave". See *Symbian Ltd v Christensen* [2001] I.R.L.R. 77, assuming that the restraint of trade doctrine can apply to such cases.

577 *Young v Timmins* (1831) 1 Cr. & J. 331 as explained in *Esso Petroleum Co Ltd v Harper's Garage (Stourport) Ltd* [1968] A.C. 269, 328–329; *A. Schroeder Music Publishing Co Ltd v Macaulay* [1974] 1 W.L.R. 1308; *Clifford Davis Management Ltd v W.E.A. Record Ltd* [1975] 1 W.L.R. 61; above, para.16-148.

578 *William Hill Organisation Ltd v Tucker* [1998] I.R.L.R. 313; *Symbian Ltd v Christensen* [2001] I.R.L.R. 77 at [52].

579 See above para.27-084 at nn.564 and 565, and *Delaney v Staples* [1992] 1 A.C. 687, 692–693. *Argus Media Ltd v Halim* [2019] EWHC 42 (QB) at [220], [222] and [226]. Freedman J. (at [222]) stated that the hardship faced by the employee did not make the grant of an injunction unconscionable, as the employee had "brought this hardship on himself by his conduct". Notably, the employee had his "eyes open as regards to at least the possibility that his activities amount to a breach of [the restrictive covenants]" (at [220]), and had given misleading information to the defendant employer.

580 cf. above, para.27-081.

581 *Lindsay Petroleum Co v Hurd* (1874) L.R. 5 P.C. 221 and *Fisher v Brooker* [2009] UKHL 41, [2009] 1 W.L.R. 1764.

582 *Legends Live Ltd v Harrison* [2016] EWHC 1938 (QB) at [90]–[110] (claimant's delay of two months meant the defendant had become an integral part of a competing show and an injunction would affect the livelihoods of other performers).

## 5. DAMAGES AND SPECIFIC PERFORMANCE OR INJUNCTION

### Statutory power to award damages in lieu of specific performance or injunction

*In line 8, after "of those remedies.", add new footnote 626a:*

626a In *UTB LLC v Sheffield United Ltd* [2019] EWHC 2322 (Ch) at [492], it was noted that damages in lieu of specific performance could be awarded even where damages are not expressly claimed ("it is hard to imagine circumstances in which it would be equitable to exercise a discretion to refuse specific performance and leave the claimant with no remedy"). **27-095**

### Assessment of damages

*Replace footnote 645 with:*

645 [1980] A.C. 367 at 401; above, para.26-096; and see *UTB LLC v Sheffield United Ltd* [2019] EWHC 2322 (Ch) at [493], where damages in lieu (had they been awarded) would have been assessed at the date of judgment; cf. *Suleman v Shahsavari* [1988] 1 W.L.R. 1181. **27-097**

### "Negotiating damages"

*In line 3, after "matter of discretion,", delete "but".* **27-098**

CHAPTER 28

# LIMITATION OF ACTIONS



*Replace footnote 1 with:*

1 See generally McGee, *Limitation of Actions*, 8th edn (2018); Di Mambro, *Law of Limitation* (looseleaf 2008); Law Commission Report, *Limitation of Actions* (Law Com. No.270, 2001). For conflict of laws in relation to limitation of actions, see below, paras 30-272—30-273.

## 1. PERIODS OF LIMITATION

### Specialties

*Replace paragraph with:*

By s.8 of the 1980 Act, no action upon a specialty can be brought after the expiration of 12 years from the date when the cause of action accrued[14]: but this does not affect any action for which a shorter period of limitation is prescribed by any other provision of the Act.[15] The words "action upon a specialty" refer to any action to enforce an obligation created or secured by an instrument which is executed as a deed[16] or is an action under a statute.[17] However, the period of limitation prescribed by the Act to recover arrears of rent[18] or arrears of interest on a mortgage[19] is six years even if the lease or mortgage is by deed. **28-003**

14 s.8(1).

15 s.8(2).

16 This includes an action for damages as well as for a debt: *Aiken v Stewart Wrightson Members' Agency Ltd* [1995] 1 W.L.R. 1281. If the formalities required of a deed under s.1 of the Law of Property (Miscellaneous Provisions) Act 1989 are complied with, the deed is a specialty even if it has not been sealed: *Liberty Partnership Ltd v Tancred* [2018] EWHC 2707 (Comm), [2019] Q.B. 903. See, gener-

ally, *Matadeen v Caribbean Insurance Co Ltd* [2002] UKPC 69, [2003] 1 W.L.R. 670. The execution of a document under seal is itself not sufficient to make it "clear on its face" that it is intended to be a deed and therefore a specialty: see above, para.1-132. Also in *Re Compania de Electricidad de la Provincia de Buenos Aires Ltd* [1980] Ch. 146, it was held that an action to enforce an obligation which was merely acknowledged or evidenced by a sealed instrument was not an "action upon a specialty".

17 *Collin v Duke of Westminster* [1985] Q.B. 581; *Rahman v Sterling Credit Ltd* [2001] 1 W.L.R. 496. But if s.9 applies ("an action to recover any sum recoverable by virtue of any enactment") the limitation period is six years not twelve: see *Re Farmizer (Products) Ltd* [1997] 1 B.C.L.C. 589. The *Rahman* case was distinguished in *Patel v Patel* [2009] EWHC 3264 (QB), [2010] 1 All E.R. (Comm) 864, where it was held that a cause of action for relief under ss.140A–140D of the Consumer Credit Act 1974 (claiming that there is an "unfair relationship") is a continuing one so that the limitation period under s.8 does not expire 12 years after the contract is made. In *Hill v Spread Trustee Co Ltd* [2006] EWCA Civ 542, [2007] 1 W.L.R. 2404 it was held that a claim, under s.423 of the Insolvency Act 1986, by a trustee in bankruptcy for the avoidance of a transaction is subject to a six-year limitation period under s.9 (statute) or the 12-year limitation period under s.8 (specialty). On the facts, it did not matter which of these two was applied. The cause of action ran from the date when the bankruptcy order was made. In another case on s.423 brought by a creditor, s.8, and not s.9, was held to be applicable because the initial remedy sought was a challenge to the validity of a property transfer rather than to recover a sum of money; and the cause of action was held to accrue when the creditor became a victim which was when he became "capable of being prejudiced" by the transfer: *Giles v Rhind* [2007] EWHC 687 (Ch), affirmed [2008] EWCA Civ 118.

18 s.19. See also *Romain v Scuba TV Ltd* [1997] Q.B. 887 (action against guarantor of lessee).

19 s.20(5). See also *Re Compania de Electricidad de la Provincia de Buenos Aires Ltd* [1980] Ch. 146 (arrears of interest on bond). But where the mortgagor is seeking to redeem or the mortgagee is accounting to the mortgagor for the surplus, more than six years' interest may be retained by the mortgagee: *Edmunds v Waugh* (1866) L.R. 1 Eq. 48; *Holmes v Cowcher* [1970] 1 W.L.R. 834; *Ezekiel v Orakpo* [1997] 1 W.L.R. 340. The limitation period for an action to recover a principal sum of money secured by a mortgage or the proceeds of the sale of land is 12 years from the date on which the right to receive the money accrued: s.20(1). See, generally on s.20, *Bristol & West Plc v Bartlett* [2002] EWCA Civ 1181, [2003] 1 W.L.R. 284; *Scottish Equitable Plc v Thompson* [2003] EWCA Civ 225, [2003] H.L.R. 48; *West Bromwich Building Society v Wilkinson* [2005] UKHL 44, [2005] 1 W.L.R. 2303; *Gotham v Doodes* [2006] EWCA Civ 1080, [2007] 1 W.L.R. 86; *Yorkshire Bank Finance Ltd v Mulhall* [2008] EWCA Civ 1156, [2009] 2 All E.R. (Comm) 164.

### Personal injuries and death

*Replace paragraph with:*

**28-006** In the case of any action for breach of duty existing by virtue of a contract where the damages claimed by the claimant consist of or include damages for personal injuries to the claimant or any other person, neither the period applicable to simple contracts[29] nor that applicable to specialties[30] applies, but the limitation period is three years from: (a) the date on which the cause of action accrued; or (b) the date of the claimant's knowledge (if later) of certain facts relevant to his right of action against the defendant.[31] "Personal injuries" includes any disease and any impairment of a person's mental or physical condition.[32] But it has been held that an action against insurance brokers for damages for breach of duty (in failing to arrange insurance so that the claimant is unable to recover against his insurers for personal injury) is not within s.11 because the damages claimed do not include damages in respect of personal injuries.[33] And a claim under the Third Party (Rights Against Insurers) Act 2010 is not a claim for damages in respect of personal injuries because it is a claim for an indemnity once a claim for damages has been quantified.[34]

29 s.11(2).

30 ss.8(2), 11(2).

31 ss.11, 14. See *Clerk & Lindsell on Torts*, 22nd edn (2018), paras 32-36—32-69.

32 s.38(1).

33 *Ackbar v C.F. Green & Co Ltd* [1975] Q.B. 582. cf. *Howe v David Brown Tractors (Retail) Ltd* [1991] 4 All E.R. 30, CA; *Bennett v Greenland Houchen & Co* [1998] P.N.L.R. 458, CA.

[34] *Burns v Shuttlehurst Ltd* [1999] 1 W.L.R. 1449 (the Act in question in this case was the Third Party (Rights Against Insurers) Act 1930 but that statute has since been repealed by the 2010 Act).

## Breach of trust or fiduciary duty

*Replace paragraph with:*

Actions for breach of trust and breach of fiduciary duty are distinct from actions for breach of contract; and commonly such actions are brought outside a contractual context. Nevertheless, where one contracting party owes fiduciary duties to the other, an action for breach of fiduciary duty may be brought. It may therefore be thought helpful here to refer, albeit very briefly, to the law on limitation of actions for these equitable causes of action. As regards breach of trust, the crucial section of the Limitation Act 1980 is the complex s.21. The basic regime of that section is that there is a six-year limitation period, running from the date when the right of action accrued, for a breach of trust[85] (or, as laid down in *Williams v Central Bank of Nigeria*,[86] for the equitable wrong of dishonest assistance or knowing receipt) but that actions for fraudulent breach of trust to which the trustee was a party or privy to, or to recover from the trustee trust property or its proceeds are excluded and have no statutory limitation period.[87] As regards a breach of fiduciary duty outside s.21, the courts tend to apply a six-year limitation period by analogy under s.36(1) of the Limitation Act 1980.[88] **28-019**

[85] s.21(3).

[86] [2014] UKSC 10, [2014] 2 W.L.R. 355.

[87] s.21(1). See *Tito v Waddell (No.2)* [1977] Ch. 106, 247–249, *Armitage v Nurse* [1998] Ch. 241, *Gwembe Valley Development Co Ltd v Koshy* [2003] EWCA Civ 1048, *Re Loftus* [2006] EWCA Civ 1124, [2007] 1 W.L.R. 1124, *Statek Corp v Alford* [2008] EWHC 32 (Ch), [2008] B.C.C. 266. The application of s.21(1) to a company director has been the subject of several decisions. It is clear that s.21(1)(a) applies to directors (because they are trustees in relation to the company's property); but it appears that, while s.21(1)(b) applies to actions to recover the company's property or proceeds, it does not apply to a claim, for example, for secret profits made by the director: *First Subsea Ltd v Balltec Ltd* [2017] EWCA Civ 186, [2018] Ch. 25; *Burnden Holdings (UK) Ltd v Fielding* [2018] UKSC 14, [2018] A.C. 857. Cf. *Gwembe Valley Development Co Ltd v Koshy* [2003] EWCA Civ 1048, [2004] 1 B.C.L.C. 131. In *Re Loftus*, it was further held that where the Limitation Act 1980 lays down that there is no limitation period prescribed by the Act (as, e.g. under s.21(1) for fraudulent breach of trust or to recover trust property), that does not preclude the operation of laches and acquiescence. See below, para.28-140.

[88] *Soar v Ashwell* [1893] 2 Q.B. 390, 393, *Taylor v Davies* [1920] A.C. 636, 652, *Paragon Finance Plc v Thakerar & Co* [1999] 1 All E.R. 400, *Coulthard v Disco Mix Club Ltd* [2000] 1 W.L.R. 707, *Cia de Seguros Imperio v Heath (REBX) Ltd* [2001] 1 W.L.R. 112, *Harrison (Properties) Ltd v Harrison* [2001] EWCA Civ 1467, [2002] 1 B.C.L.C. 162, *Gwembe Valley Development Co Ltd v Koshy* [2003] EWCA Civ 1048. cf. *James v Williams* [2000] Ch. 1. See below, para.28-136.

## Carriage by sea

*Replace footnote 100 with:*

[100] Athens Convention 1974 art.16. See *Gold Shipping Navigation Co SA v Lulu Maritime Ltd* [2009] EWHC 1365 (Admlty), [2010] 2 All E.R. (Comm) 64 (which also clarified that the two-year period extends to counterclaims). In *Feest v South West Strategic Health Authority* [2015] EWCA Civ 708, [2016] Q.B. 503 it was held that the two-year limitation period under the Athens Convention does not bar a claim by an alleged tortfeasor for contribution against the carrier, under the Civil Liability (Contribution) Act 1978, in respect of personal injury to a passenger. Article 16(3) extends the two-year period, up to a long-stop of three years, where there is domestic legislation providing for "suspension" or "interruption" of the limitation period: this provision was held to include the domestic law's postponement of the limitation period for disability (by reason of age) in the Scottish case of *Warner v Scapa Flow Charters* [2018] UKSC 52, [2018] 1 W.L.R. 4974. **28-023**

### Carriage by air

*Replace footnote 107 with:*

28-024 [107] *Dawson v Thomson Airways Ltd* [2014] EWCA Civ 845, [2015] 1 W.L.R. 883; see below, Vol.II, para.35-051.

## 2. ACCRUAL OF THE CAUSE OF ACTION

### Concurrent liability in tort

*To the end of paragraph, after "diminution in value of an asset.", add new footnote 153a:*

28-034 [153a] Lord Walker (at [41]) distinguishes the case in which damage may be expected but has not occurred from the common case in which the claimant has suffered damage even though it is not possible to assess the amount until some future event has occurred: see *Holt v Holley and Steer Solicitors* [2020] EWCA Civ 851 (cause of action accrued when, through alleged negligence, client lost practical opportunity to present evidence).

### Successive and continuing breaches

*Replace footnote 159 with:*

28-035 [159] *Spoor v Green* (1874) L.R. 9 Ex. 99, 111. For examples, see *Equitas Ltd v Walsh Bros & Co Ltd* [2013] EWHC 3264 (Comm) (duty to remit funds: see at [59]–[71]); *2 Entertain Video Ltd v Sony DADC Europe Ltd* [2020] EWHC 972 (TCC) (duty to take precautions and keep goods in safe place: see at [252]–[254]). There was held to be no continuing obligation to deliver goods of the correct quality, so that there was a simple breach at the time of delivery, in *VAI Industries (UK) Ltd v Bostock & Bramley* [2003] EWCA Civ 1069, [2003] B.L.R. 359.

### Money lent

*Replace footnote 165 with:*

28-036 [165] See, generally, *Boot v Boot* [1996] 2 F.C.R. 713; *Goldsmith v Chittell* [2016] EWHC 630 (Ch). Analogously to s.6, where there is a failure to pay sums owing under a consumer credit agreement which, under the Consumer Credit Act 1974, requires a default notice, time under s.5 of the 1980 Act does not begin to run until the debtor has failed to comply with the default notice: *PRA Group (UK) Ltd v Doyle* [2019] EWCA Civ 12, [2019] 1 W.L.R. 3783.

*Replace footnote 179 with:*

### Negotiable instruments[179]

28-041 [179] See *Byles on Bills of Exchange and Cheques*, 20th edn (2020), Ch.29; *Chalmers and Guest on Bills of Exchange and Cheques*, 18th edn (2017), paras 7-056—7-060.

### Building contracts

*In line 4, after "practical or substantial completion),", add new footnote 230a:*

28-054 [230a] See, e.g. *Swansea Stadium Management Co Ltd v Swansea City and County Council* [2018] EWHC 2192 (TCC), [2019] P.N.L.R. 4.

*Add new paragraph:*

28-058A **Unfair credit relationships** It was held in *Patel v Patel*[240a] that the cause of action under the provisions on unfair relationships under the Consumer Credit Act 1974 s.140A is a continuing one accruing from day to day until the relationship ends.[240b] That case involved post-contractual behaviour but a claim for the return of secret commissions has been also been held to accrue only when the unfair relationship was ended by the court's order setting aside the transaction.[240c]

240a [2009] EWHC 3264 (QB), see Vol.II, para.39-222.

240b Hence, it accrues at the date of trial in the case of an extant relationship and otherwise at the date when the relationship ended. See below, Vol.II, para.38-228.

240c *Wood v Commercial First Business Ltd (In Liquidation)* [2019] EWHC 2205 (Ch) at [184].

## 5. EXTENSION OF THE PERIOD

## (b) Fraud, Concealment or Mistake

### Fraud

*In line 4, after "diligence have discovered it.", add new footnote 315a:*

315a The requirements of "discovery" and "reasonable diligence" are considered in detail in *Granville Technology Group Ltd (In Liquidation) v Infineon Technologies AG* [2020] EWHC 415 (Comm) at [24]–[56] and *Boyse International (Ltd) v Natwest Markets Plc* [2020] EWHC 1264 (Ch). **28-084**

### Concealment

*Replace footnote 319 with:*

319 s.32(2). In *Giles v Rhind* [2008] EWCA Civ 118 it was held that a claim for the avoidance of a transaction under s.423 of the Insolvency Act 1986 involves an allegation of a "breach of duty" within s.32(2) of the 1980 Act; "breach of duty" in that subsection should not be narrowly construed as applying only to, for example, a tort, breach of contract, or breach of an equitable duty to the claimant. This interpretation of breach of duty was followed in *Canada Square Operations Ltd v Potter* [2020] EWHC 672 (QB) (appeal outstanding), where s.32(2) was held to apply when a lender made a deliberate decision not to disclose a secret commission on PPI, which rendered the relationship unfair within the meaning of Consumer Credit Act 1974 s.140A. See below, Vol.II, para.39-228. **28-085**

## (d) Agreement of the Parties

### Pleading the statute

*Replace paragraph with:*

A party is not bound to rely on limitation as a defence if he does not wish to do so. In general, the court will not raise the point *suo officio* even if it appears from the face of the pleading that the relevant period of limitation has expired.[419] A defendant who wishes to rely on limitation must, in his defence, give details of the expiry of any relevant limitation period relied on.[420] Even where the effect of the statute is to extinguish the claimant's title to land[421] or goods,[422] it would not be sufficient simply to deny that title[423] and the statute should be specifically pleaded.[424] Where it is clear that there is a defence of limitation, the defendant can apply to strike out a statute-barred claim on the ground that the statement of case discloses no reasonable grounds for bringing the claim or that the statement of case is an abuse of the court's process.[425] **28-108**

419 But the court will take the point on behalf of a person under a disability: *Re E.G.* [1914] 1 Ch. 927.

420 CPR PD 16 para. 13.1.

421 Limitation Act 1980 s.17.

422 s.3(2); see Vol.II, para.44-234.

423 See also CPR r.16.5.

424 Contrast Franks, *Limitation of Actions* (1959), p.265.

425 CPR r.3.4(2)(a) and (b). See *Ronex Properties Ltd v John Laing Construction Ltd* [1983] Q.B. 398, 405–406; *Leicester Wholesale Fruit Market Ltd v Grundy* [1990] 1 W.L.R. 107.

### Negotiations

*Replace footnote 442 with:*

28-112 [442] See CPR rr.3.1(2)(f), 26.4. For the effect on limitation of a "standstill agreement", see *Russell v Stone* [2017] EWHC 1555 (TCC), [2018] 1 All ER (Comm) 839.

## 7. COMMENCEMENT OF PROCEEDINGS

### Legal proceedings

*Replace footnote 463 with:*

28-117 [463] CPR PD 7A, para.5.1; *Barnes v St Helens MBC* [2006] EWCA Civ 1372, [2007] 1 W.L.R. 879. On the relevance of the non-payment of the correct court fee to the commencement of proceedings for limitation purposes, see *Page v Hewetts Solicitors* [2012] EWCA Civ 805; *Bhatti v Ashgar* [2016] EWHC 1049 (QB); *Glenluce Fishing Co Ltd v Watermota Ltd* [2016] EWHC 1807 (TCC). For commencement of arbitration proceedings, see Vol.II, para.32-081.

### Defence, set-off and counterclaim

*Replace paragraph with:*

28-124 A further difficulty which arises is that it is a matter of considerable refinement whether a particular cross-claim is to be treated as a defence or as a set-off/counterclaim.[496] Lord Denning M.R. further put forward the view, in obiter dicta, that the word "set-off" (in what is now s.35(3) of the 1980 Act) means only a legal set-off and does not apply to an equitable set-off.[497] On this view, if a cross-claim arises out of the same transaction as the claim, or out of a transaction that is so closely related to the claim that it would be manifestly unjust to allow the claim without taking into account the cross-claim,[498] it is to be treated as time-barred only in equity.[499–503]

[496] See *Mondel v Steel* (1841) 8 M. & W. 858; *Henriksens Rederi A/S v T.H.Z. Rolimpex* [1974] Q.B. 233; *Aries Tanker Corp v Total Transport Ltd* [1977] 1 W.L.R. 185; *Axel Johnson Petroleum v MG Mineral Group AG, The Jo Lind* [1992] 2 All E.R. 163; *ICICI Bank UK Plc v Assam Oil Co Ltd* [2019] EWHC 750 (Comm) at [45].

[497] *Henriksens Rederi A/S v T.H.Z. Rolimpex* [1974] Q.B. 233, 246. But see Cairns and Roskill L.JJ. at 254, 264. Lord Denning's view was agreed with by Hobhouse J. in *Kleinwort Benson Ltd v Sandwell BC* (1993) 91 L.G.R. 323, 386, [1994] 4 All E.R. 890, 945.

[498] See, e.g. *Morgan & Son v S. Martin Johnson & Co* [1949] 1 K.B. 107; *Hanak v Green* [1958] 2 Q.B. 9; *Federal Commerce & Navigation Co Ltd v Molena Alpha Inc* [1978] Q.B. 974; affirmed [1979] A.C. 757; *The Raven* [1980] 2 Lloyd's Rep. 266; *British Anzani (Felixstowe) Ltd v International Marine Management (UK) Ltd* [1980] Q.B. 137; *Fuller v Happy Shopper Markets Ltd* [2001] 2 Lloyd's Rep. 49; *Geldof Metaalconstructie NV v Simon Carves Ltd* [2010] EWCA Civ 667.

[499–503] s.36(2); *Filross Securities Ltd v Midgeley* (1998) 43 E.G. 134. Contrast *Aries Tanker Corp v Total Transport Ltd* [1977] 1 W.L.R. 185 (Hague Rules) and, e.g. Carriage of Goods by Road Act 1965 Sch. art.32(4); *Impex Transport Aktieselskabet v AG Thames Holdings Ltd* [1981] 1 W.L.R. 1547; *Casillo Grani v Napier Shipping Co* [1984] 2 Lloyd's Rep. 481.

## 9. LIMITATION IN EQUITY

### Introductory

*Replace footnote 547 with:*

28-135 [547] s.36(1). This also applies to s.7 (arbitration awards), s.9 (statutory claims) and s.24 (actions on judgments). In *Wood v Commercial First Business Ltd (In Liquidation)* [2019] EWHC 2205 (Ch) (appeal outstanding) it was held that a claim to recover a secret commission, to the extent that it is properly classified as a claim for money had and received, was barred by Limitation Act 1980 s.5, and to the extent that it was to be characterised as a claim for equitable compensation, it was barred by analogy under s.36: at [178].

## The statute applied by analogy

*Replace paragraph with:*

The statute may be applied to equitable relief by analogy.[550] In *P&O Nedlloyd BV v Arab Metals Co, The UB Tiger*[551] it was held, in an excellent judgment by Moore-Bick L.J., that the usual contractual limitation period of six years does not apply by analogy under s.36(1) to a claim for specific performance.[552] This is because, first, there is no directly equivalent remedy at common law to specific performance and, secondly, specific performance does not even require there to be an existing breach of contract.[553] Laches can, however, apply. The view was also expressed that even if, contrary to the court's view, there were a statutory limitation period applicable to specific performance, laches within that period, provided comprising more than mere delay, could still apply to bar the relief.[554] What about an injunction to prevent a breach of contract? There appears to be no case in which the statutory limitation period has been applied by analogy to an injunction and, in the light of the reasoning in *P & O Nedlloyd BV v Arab Metals Co, The UB Tiger* (and especially Moore-Bick L.J's first reason above), it seems unlikely that the statutory six-year limitation period will be applied by analogy. If that is correct, then laches alone—and not a statutory limitation period—applies to a claim for an injunction to prevent a breach of contract. If limitation periods do not apply by analogy to specific performance or injunctions, are there any examples, in the law of contract,[555] of a statutory limitation period applying to equitable relief by analogy? It would appear that one example is (equitable) rescission of a contract so that equitable rescission of a contract appears to be barred if the delay exceeds six years.[556] But, in such a case, even if the statute is applied by analogy, a claim for rescission may be barred, short of the statutory period, on account of acquiescence, affirmation, or laches at least if the laches comprises more than mere delay.[557] **28-136**

[550] s.36(1). For an example see *Wood v Commercial First Business Ltd (In Liquidation)* [2019] EWHC 2205 (Ch) (appeal outstanding), above, para.28-135.

[551] [2006] EWCA Civ 1717, [2007] 1 W.L.R. 2288.

[552] See also *Williams v Greatrex* [1957] 1 W.L.R. 31. cf. Beatson, "Limitation Periods and Specific Performance" in Lomnicka and Morse (eds), *Contemporary Issues in Commercial Law* (1997), pp.9–23.

[553] As shown in *Hasham v Zenab* [1960] A.C. 316.

[554] See below, para.28-140.

[555] There are clear examples outside the law of contract. For example, the six-year limitation period has been applied by analogy to monetary claims (e.g. equitable compensation) for breach of fiduciary duty; see above, para.28-018. In *Kleinwort Benson Ltd v Sandwell BC* [1994] 4 All E.R. 890, 943, Hobhouse J. noted that it was common ground between the parties that, in so far as s.5 of the 1980 Act applied to an action for money had and received, the same limitation period by reason of s.36 would apply to the equitable remedy (after tracing) sought by the bank.

[556] *Molloy v Mutual Reserve Life Insurance Co* (1906) 94 L.T. 756; *Oelkers v Ellis* [1914] 2 K.B. 139; *Armstrong v Jackson* [1917] 2 K.B. 822. But in *Wood v Commercial First Business Ltd (In Liquidation)* [2019] EWHC 2205 (Ch) (appeal outstanding) it was held that though a claim to recover a secret commission, to the extent that it was to be characterised as a claim for equitable compensation, was barred (at [178]), the right to rescind was not: s.36, "on a simple analysis of the wording", "can have no impact" (at [180]–[181]; seemingly the point was conceded). Why rescission was not barred by analogy is not clear.

[557] See below, para.28-145.

CHAPTER 29

# RESTITUTION



*Replace footnote 1 with:*

[1] For a full treatment of the subject matter of this chapter, see: Burrows, *The Law of Restitution*, 3rd edn (2011); Virgo, *The Principles of the Law of Restitution*, 3rd edn (2015); Goff and Jones, *The Law of Unjust Enrichment*, 9th edn (2016). See also Beatson, *The Use and Abuse of Unjust Enrichment* (1991); Birks, *An Introduction to the Law of Restitution* (1985); Birks, *Unjust Enrichment*, 2nd edn (2005); Maddaugh and McCamus, *The Law of Restitution*, 2nd edn (2004); McInnes, *The Canadian Law of Unjust Enrichment and Restitution* (2014); Mason, Carter and Tolhurst *Restitution Law in Australia*,

3rd edn (2016); Palmer, *The Law of Restitution* (1978) (four Vols); *The American Law Institute's Restatement of the Law Third, Restitution and Unjust Enrichment* (2011); Tang, *Principles of the Law of Restitution in Singapore* (2019).

## 1. INTRODUCTION

## (c) The Theoretical Basis of the Law of Restitution

### The principle of unjust enrichment

*Replace paragraph with:*

**29-011** The American Law Institute's *Restatement of the Law Third, Restitution and Unjust Enrichment* states that "a person who is unjustly enriched at the expense of another is subject to liability in restitution."[51] The House of Lords in *Lipkin Gorman v Karpnale Ltd* held that the concept of unjust enrichment lies at the heart of, and is the principle underlying, the individual instances in which the law gives a right of recovery in restitution.[52] However, despite the strong support of several judges including Lords Wright,[53] Atkin,[54] Denning,[55] Pearce[56] and Goff[57] and numerous academic writers, the precise shape of English law has been formed against a background of scepticism,[58] which continues in some quarters because of particular concerns about the lack of a clear normative justification for the imposition of liability where the defendant has been unjustly enriched.[58a]

[51] (2011) art.1. See Mitchell and Swadling (eds) *The Restatement Third: Restitution and Unjust Enrichment: Critical and Comparative Essays* (2013).

[52] [1991] 2 A.C. 548, 559, 578. See also *Woolwich Equitable B.S. v IRC* [1993] A.C. 70, especially 196–197 (Lord Browne-Wilkinson); *Westdeutsche Landesbank Girozentrale v Islington LBC* [1996] A.C. 669, especially 710 (Lord Browne-Wilkinson) (see also at 688 (Lord Goff), 718 (Lord Browne-Wilkinson), 720 (Lord Woolf), 738 (Lord Lloyd)); *Kleinwort Benson Ltd v Lincoln CC* [1999] 2 A.C. 349; *Deutsche Morgan Grenfell Group Plc v IRC* [2006] UKHL 49, [2007] 1 A.C. 558; *Sempra Metals Ltd v I.R.C.* [2007] UKHL 34, [2008] 1 A.C. 561; *Cobbe v Yeoman's Row Management Ltd* [2008] UKHL 55, [2008] 1 W.L.R. 1752; *Test Claimants in the Group Litigation v HMRC* [2012] UKSC 19, [2012] 2 A.C. 337; *Pitt v Holt* [2013] UKSC 26, [2013] 2 A.C. 108; *Benedetti v Sawiris* [2013] UKSC 50, [2014] A.C. 938; *Bank of Cyprus UK Ltd v Menelaou* [2015] UKSC 66, [2016] A.C. 176; *Patel v Mirza* [2016] UKSC 42, [2017] A.C. 467. These built on *Fibrosa Spolka Akcyjna v Fairbairn Lawson Combe Barbour* [1943] A.C. 32, especially Lord Wright at 61 (quoted at para.29-001, above).

[53] *Brook's Wharf and Bull Wharf Ltd v Goodman Bros* [1937] 1 K.B. 534, 545; *Fibrosa Spolka Akcyjna v Fairbairn Lawson Combe Barbour Ltd* [1943] A.C. 32, 61–64; Lord Wright (1938) 6 Camb. L.J. 305 (reprinted in his *Legal Essays and Addresses*, pp.1–33).

[54] *United Australia Ltd v Barclays Bank Ltd* [1941] A.C. 1, 27–29.

[55] *Nelson v Larholt* [1948] 1 K.B. 339, 343; *Larner v LCC* [1949] 2 K.B. 683; *Kiriri Cotton Co Ltd v Dewani* [1960] A.C. 192, 204–205; (1949) 65 L.Q.R. 37; *Hussey v Palmer* [1972] 1 W.L.R. 1286.

[56] *Att-Gen v Nissan* [1970] A.C. 179, 228 (approving Winn L.J.'s dicta in [1968] 1 Q.B. 286, 352).

[57] As well as *Lipkin Gorman v Karpnale Ltd* [1991] 2 A.C. 548 and *Woolwich Equitable B.S. v IRC* [1993] A.C. 70, see *B.P. (Exploration) Co (Libya) Ltd v Hunt (No.2)* [1979] 1 W.L.R. 788, 799 (Robert Goff J.); affirmed [1981] 1 W.L.R. 232, CA; [1983] 2 A.C. 352, HL; *British Steel Corp v Cleveland Bridge and Engineering Co Ltd* [1984] 1 All E.R. 504, 511 (Robert Goff J.); *Whittaker v Campbell* [1984] Q.B. 318, 327 (Robert Goff L.J.); *R. v Tower Hamlets LBC Ex p. Chetnik Developments Ltd* [1988] A.C. 858, 882 (Lord Goff).

[58] *Orakpo v Manson Investments Ltd* [1978] A.C. 95, 104 (Lord Diplock). See also *Bossevain v Weil* [1950] A.C. 327, 341 (Lord Radcliffe); *Reading v Att-Gen* [1951] A.C. 507, 513 (Lord Porter); *Ministry of Health v Simpson* [1951] A.C. 251, 275 (Lord Simonds); *Morris v Tarrant* [1971] 2 Q.B. 143, 160–162 (Lane J.); *Stoke on Trent CC v Wass* [1988] 1 W.L.R. 1406; *Guinness Plc v Saunders* [1990] 2 A.C. 663, 689 (Lord Templeman); Holdsworth (1939) 55 L.Q.R. 37 (cf. Winfield at p.161); Landon (1937) 53 L.Q.R. 302; Gutteridge (1934) 5 C.L.J. 204, 223–229; Radcliffe (1938) 54 L.Q.R. 24.

[58a] Watts (2016) C.L.P. 289; Stevens (2018) 134 L.Q.R. 574; Smith, "Restitution: A New Start" in Devonshire and Havelock (eds), *The Impact of Equity and Restitution in Commerce* (2018) p.91. Cf. Burrows (2019) 78 C.L.J. 521; Letelier (2020) 136 L.Q.R. 121.

## The state of the unjust enrichment principle

*Replace paragraph with:*

In conclusion, the modern cases show an increasing tendency to cut through technicality to perceive and define the underlying principle of unjust enrichment.[73–74] English law has joined US jurisdictions,[75] Australian law,[76] Canadian law,[77] Scots law,[78] French law,[79] Roman-Dutch law,[80] and Singapore law,[81] in accepting the principle of unjust enrichment. In *Uren v First National Home Finance Ltd*[82] it was held that English law does not yet recognise a free-standing claim of unjust enrichment such that the claimant can simply plead an enrichment which is unjust. Rather, the claimant needs to establish either that the claim falls within one of the recognised grounds of restitution or within a new ground which is a justifiable extension from the established grounds. In *F J Chalke Ltd v Commissioners for Her Majesty's Revenue and Customs*[83] Henderson J. recognised that a number of different causes of action exist within the unjust enrichment principle, each with their own requirements, such as the cause of action for tax unlawfully demanded,[84] and that for the recovery of money paid under a mistake of law.[85] In *Investment Trust Companies v Revenue and Customs Commissioners*[86] Lord Reed recognised that law of unjust enrichment is founded on the principle of corrective justice and that its purpose is to "correct normatively defective transfers of value" typically by restoring the parties to their pre-transfer positions; with "normative" referring to a defect recognised by the law of unjust enrichment. **29-015**

[73–74] *Woolwich Equitable B.S. v IRC* [1993] A.C. 70, 166 (Lord Goff).

[75] e.g. *Restatement of the Law Third, Restitution and Unjust Enrichment* art.1 and comment (b); Dawson, *Unjust Enrichment* (1951); Palmer, *The Law of Restitution* (1978) (four volumes).

[76] *Pavey and Matthews Pty Ltd v Paul* (1987) 69 A.L.R. 57. For a significant attack on the validity of the principle in Australia, see Gummow J. in *Roxborough v Rothmans of Pall Mall Australia Ltd* (2002) 76 A.L.J.R. 203, HC of Australia, but cf. Beatson and Virgo (2002) 118 L.Q.R. 352. See also *Farah Constructions Pty Ltd v Say-Dee Pty Ltd* [2007] HCA 2; *Matthew Lumbers v W. Cook Builders Pty Ltd* [2008] HCA 27; *Bofinger v Kingsway Group Ltd* [2009] HCA 44 at [86] In *Australian Financial Services and Leasing Pty Ltd v Hills Industries Ltd* [2014] HCA 14, [78] the plurality recognised that "the concept of unjust enrichment is not the basis of restitutionary relief in Australian law". Rather, the "enquiry is conducted by reference to equitable principles", namely whether the retention of monies paid to the defendant can be considered to be unconscionable. The difficulty with this approach relates to the identification of when the defendant's retention can be considered to be unconscionable. The plurality recognised that 'conscience' does not involve the judge's subjective evaluation of the justice of the case, and purported to identify equitable principles to assess what conscience demands. But the only indication as to what these principles are involved reference to "a construct of standards and values" or, as Chief Justice French recognised, at [16], a legal standard "informing guiding criteria for particular classes of case". But there was no attempt to identify what these standards, values or criteria might be. In *Mann v Paterson Constructions Pty Ltd* [2019] HCA 32 at [199], the plurality recognised unjust enrichment as a "unifying legal concept" whilst not being an all-embracing theory of restitutionary rights and remedies, and considered, at [212], that the English and Australian approaches to the law of restitution were not as far apart as once thought.

[77] *Deglman v Guaranty Trust Co of Canada* [1954] S.C.R. 725; *Pettkuss v Becker* [1980] 2 S.C.R. 834; *Rawluk v Rawluk* [1990] 1 S.C.R. 70; *Garland v Consumer's Gas Distributors Inc* [2004] 1 S.C.R. 629; *Pacific National Investments Ltd v Corp of the City of Victoria* (2004) S.C.C. 75.

[78] *Morgan Guaranty Trust Co of N.Y. v Lothian R.C.* (1995) S.C. 151, 229; *Shilliday v Smith* (1998) S.L.T. 976, 978.

[79] Gutteridge and David (1934) 5 Camb. L.J. 204.

[80] e.g. *Hussenabai Hassanally v Mohamed Muheeth Mohamed Cassim* [1960] A.C. 592; *Willis Faber Enthoven Ltd v Receiver of Revenue* (1992) (4) S.A. 202.

[81] *Wee Chiaw Sek Anna v Ng Li-Ann Genevieve* [2013] SGCA 36. Also in Malaysia: *Dream Property v Atlas Housing* [2015] 2 M.L.J. 441.

[82] [2005] EWHC 2529 (Ch).

[83] [2009] EWHC 952 (Ch), [2009] S.T.C. 2027 at [127]; *Claimants in the FII Group Litigation v Commissioners for HM Revenue and Customs (No.2)* [2014] EWHC 4302 (Ch), [2015] S.T.I 49 at [248] (Henderson J.). See also *Deutsche Morgan Grenfell Group Plc v IRC* [2006] UKHL 49, [2007] 1 A.C. 558 at [17] (Lord Hoffmann).

[84] See below, para.29-090.

[85] See below, para.29-047.

[86] [2017] UKSC 29, [2018] A.C. 275 at [42]–[43].

**Different claims within the law of restitution**

*Replace paragraph with:*

**29-016** An alternative theory of restitution assumes that the award of restitutionary remedies is not confined to situations where the defendant has been unjustly enriched. The Privy Council in *Skandinaviska Enskilda Banken AB v Conway*[86a] recognised that the unjust enrichment model may not readily accommodate all situations where a personal claim lies for restitution and unjust enrichment should not become a Procrustean bed, requiring all claims for restitution to be forced into it. Restitutionary remedies can be considered to be available by reference to three distinct principles. The first of these is the unjust enrichment principle itself. Secondly, such remedies may also be awarded where the defendant has benefited from the commission of some form of wrongdoing, such as certain torts,[87] equitable wrongs[88] and, exceptionally, for breach of contract.[89] In such cases the cause of action is founded on the wrong rather than unjust enrichment. Thirdly, restitution may also be awarded where the defendant has interfered with property in which the claimant has a legal or equitable proprietary interest. In such claims the underlying cause of action is the vindication of the claimant's property rights rather than unjust enrichment.[90] This latter principle remains controversial, with a number of jurists preferring to explain restitutionary claims to substitute property as founded on unjust enrichment.[91] How the claim is characterised matters as regards what needs to be proved to establish the claim and the application of defences.

[86a] [2019] UKPC 36, [2019] 3 W.L.R. 493 at [80].

[87] See below, para.29-147.

[88] See below, para.29-163.

[89] See below, para.29-158.

[90] *Foskett v McKeown* [2001] 1 A.C. 102, 109 (Lord Browne-Wilkinson). See also 115 (Lord Hoffmann), 118 (Lord Hope) and 129 (Lord Millett); *Armstrong DLW GmbH v Winnington Networks Ltd* [2012] EWHC 10 (Ch), [2013] Ch. 156. However, in *Bank of Cyprus UK Ltd v Menelaou* [2015] UKSC 66, [2016] A.C. 176 a majority of the Supreme Court recognised that the proprietary remedy of subrogation could be awarded to reverse the defendant's unjust enrichment. See Watterson (2016) 75 C.L.J. 209, Salmons (2017) 76 C.L.J. 399 and Gregson (2020) 136 L.Q.R. 481. See further below, para.29-166.

[91] See especially Birks [2001] C.L.P. 231; Burrows (2001) 117 L.Q.R. 412; Goff and Jones; cf. Lord Millett in Burrows and Rodgers (eds), *Mapping the Law: Essays in Honour of Peter Birks* (2006) p.265. See also *Handayo v Tjong Very Sumito* [2013] SGCA 44, where the Singapore Court of Appeal considered that such claims might be founded on unjust enrichment, but, having rejected want of authority as a ground of restitution, failed to identify an alternative ground of restitution.

## 2. UNJUST ENRICHMENT

### (a) The Content of the Unjust Enrichment Principle

#### The elements of unjust enrichment

*To the paragraph, after "on the commission of a wrong.[93]", add:*

The remedy to reverse an unjust enrichment is monetary.[93a] 29-017

[93a] *Lehman Brothers International (Europe) v Exotix Partners LLP* [2019] EWHC 2380 (Ch), [2020] 1 All E.R. (Comm) 635 at [176] (Hildyard J.).

#### Defences and denials

*Replace paragraph with:*

29-018 The claimant bears the burden of proving the elements of the unjust enrichment claim, namely that the defendant has been enriched at the claimant's expense and that one of the recognised grounds of restitution apply.[104] Once this has been established, the burden shifts to the defendant, either to deny that an element of the cause of action has been established or to identify a reason why the defendant should not be liable or why the liability should be reduced by pleading a defence. So, for example, if the defendant argues that there was a legal basis for the receipt of an enrichment, such as a valid gift, this is properly characterised as a denial of the claim, because the claimant bears the burden of proving that there was no legal basis for the enrichment.[105] This will also be established where the benefit was conferred pursuant to a valid Common Law, equitable or statutory obligation owed by the claimant to the defendant,[106] or was conferred pursuant to a court order which has not been set aside,[106a] or was conferred by the claimant while performing an obligation owed to a third party.[107] This proved significant in *MacDonald Dickens and Macklin v Costello*[108] where the claimant had provided a service to a company and was held to be unable to sue the defendants in unjust enrichment for the value of the service, even though the defendants were the sole directors and shareholders of the company. This was because the award of a restitutionary remedy would undermine the contractual arrangement between the claimant and the company, even though there was no such contract between the claimant and the defendants. In *Barton v Gwynn-Jones*[108a] the Court of Appeal held that the rule in *Costello* only applied to the express allocation of risk or obligation arising from a contract.[108b] Consequently in that case, where a company had agreed to pay the claimant £1.2 million if the claimant introduced a purchaser who bought the company's property for £6.5 million and the person introduced by the claimant bought the property for £6 million, it was held that the claimant had no claim under the contract, but could bring a restitutionary claim for the reasonable value of the services provided. This was because the contract was interpreted as not excluding the claim in unjust enrichment; it would have been different if the contract stated that the liability to pay the money arose if and only if the property was sold for £6.5 million. This is dubious since, by allowing the unjust enrichment claim, the court interfered with the bargain made by the parties. It was incorrect to conclude that a claim in unjust enrichment would only undermine a subsisting contract if it contradicted its express terms. The terms have to be considered as a whole and ought to be determinative of the transaction in question. The claim in *Costello* did not fail because there was an express term in the contract which precluded the claimant from bringing the claim in unjust enrichment. Rather, it was because the contract between the claimant and the company remained on foot, leaving no room for a claim in unjust enrichment. Likewise, in *Barton* the contract continued to govern and there should have been no claim in unjust enrichment.

The claim for restitution will also be denied where the benefit was transferred by the defendant in submission to an honest claim, under process of law or a compromise of a disputed claim.[109] The claim will also be denied where the claimant is considered to have acted "voluntarily" or "officiously".[110] If, however, the defendant argues that his position has changed after the enrichment has been received, this is a defence, which the defendant bears the burden of proving, because the change of position is only considered to be relevant after the cause of action has been established.[111] Other defences include where the claimant is estopped from establishing the claim,[112] or where public policy precludes restitution.[113]

[104] *Banque Financière de la Cité v Parc (Battersea) Ltd* [1991] 1 A.C. 221, 227 (Lord Steyn). See Goudkamp and Mitchell, "Denials and Defences in the Law of Unjust Enrichment", in Mitchell and Swadling (eds), *The Restatement Third: Restitution and Unjust Enrichment: Critical and Comparative Essays* (2013), Ch.6.

[105] *Kleinwort Benson Ltd v Lincoln CC* [1999] 2 AC 349, 408 (Lord Hope). See also *Fairfield Sentry Ltd v Migani* [2014] UKPC 9, [18] (Lord Sumption).

[106] *Brittain v Rossiter* (1879) 11 Q.B.D. 123, 127; *Gilbert & Partners v Knight* [1968] 2 All E.R. 248, 250 (Harman L.J.); *Pan Ocean Shipping Ltd v Creditcorp Ltd* [1994] 1 W.L.R. 161, 164, 165 (Lord Goff); *Portman B.S. v Hayman Taylor Neck* [1998] 4 All E.R. 202; *Berezovsky v Edmiston* [2010] EWHC 1883 (Comm) at [70] (Field J.) (where payment for services is provided for under a contract, the claimant is precluded from claiming a quantum meruit for the reasonable value of the services); *ICICI Bank UK Plc v Assam Oil Co Ltd* [2019] EWHC 750 (Comm) at [38] (Andrew Burrows Q.C.); *Murkenbeck and Marshall v Vinyl Factory Ltd* [2019] EWHC 3225 (TCC) at [83] (Adam Constable Q.C.); *Alfred Street Properties Ltd v National Asset Management Agency* [2020] EWHC 397 (Comm) at [117] (Phillips L.J.). Where a claim in unjust enrichment has already crystallised, the parties may enter into a contract to provide for restitution which will then prevail over the unjust enrichment claim. That contract may itself be terminated, in which case the original unjust enrichment claim will continue to operate, save if the contract is interpreted as extinguishing the unjust enrichment claim: *Newland Shipping and Forwarding Ltd v Toba Trading FZC* [2014] EWHC 661 (Comm) at [92] (Leggatt L.J.). In *Universal Advance Technology Ltd v Lloyds Bank Plc* [2016] EWCA Civ 933 a claim in debt in respect of goods supplied failed because the goods had not been supplied and, consequently, if the claim had succeeded the claimant would have become unjustly enriched at the expense of the defendant. See also *Lowick Rose LLP v Swynson Ltd* [2017] UKSC 32, [2018] A.C. 313 at [119] (Lord Neuberger).

[106a] *Gibbs v Lakeside Developments Ltd* [2018] EWCA Civ 2874, [2019] 4 W.L.R. 6. See also *De Medina v Grove* (1846) 10 Q.B. 152.

[107] *Brown & Davies Ltd v Galbraith* [1972] 1 W.L.R. 997; *Pan Ocean Shipping Ltd v Creditcorp Ltd* [1994] 1 W.L.R. 161, 166, 170–171; *Esso Petroleum v Hall Russell & Co* [1989] A.C. 643; *Matthew Lumbers v W. Cook Builders Pty Ltd* [2008] HCA 27. See Getzler (2009) L.Q.R. 196; Goymour (2008) C.L.J. 469.

[108] [2011] EWCA Civ 930, [2012] Q.B. 244; see Davies (2012) C.L.J. 37. See also *McGill v Sports and Entertainment Media Group* [2014] EWHC 3000 (QB) at [156] (Judge Waksman Q.C.); *Erith Holdings Ltd v Murphy* [2017] EWHC 1364 (TCC), [102] (O'Farrell J.); *Wales v CBRE Managed Services Ltd* [2020] EWHC 16 (Comm), [137] (H.H.J. Halliwell).

[108a] [2019] EWCA Civ 1999. See Day and Virgo (2020) 136 L.Q.R. 349.

[108b] [2019] EWCA Civ 1999 at [31] (Asplin L.J.).

[109] See below, paras 29-042, 29-197.

[110] See *Falke v Scottish Imperial Insurance Co* (1886) 34 Ch. D. 234, 248 (Bowen L.J.); *Ruabon S.S. Co v The London Assurance* [1990] A.C. 6, 10; *Walsh v Singh* [2009] EWHC 3219 (Ch), [2010] 1 F.L.R. 1658 at [65] (Judge Purle Q.C.) (quantum meruit not available where provision of services made voluntarily and not in the expectation of reward but in the expectation of a long-term relationship); *MacDonald Dickens and Mackin v Costello* [2011] EWCA Civ 930, [2012] Q.B. 244 at [21] (Etherton L.J.). See also *Owen v Tate* [1976] Q.B. 402; below, paras 29-115—29-118; Hope (1929) Cornell L.Q. 25; Wade (1966) Vanderbilt L.R. 1183; Evans, [1998] R.L.R. 1, 8. cf. *G.N. Ry v Swaffield* (1874) L.R. 9 Ex. 132; *Matheson v Smiley* [1932] 2 D.L.R. 787; *Cobbe v Yeoman's Row Management Ltd* [2008] UKHL 55, [2008] 1 W.L.R. 1752; Wilmot-Smith (2011) 127 L.Q.R. 610.

[111] See below, para.29-186.

[112] See below, para.29-183.

[113] See below, paras 29-042, 29-080, 29-202. See also *R. Leslie Ltd v Sheill* [1914] 3 K.B. 607; *Boissevain v Weil* [1950] A.C. 327; *Haugesund Kommune v Depfa ACS Bank* [2010] EWCA Civ 579, [2012] Q.B. 549.

## (b) Enrichment

### The nature of the enrichment

*Replace paragraph with:*

29-019 Enrichment may take the form of a positive addition to the recipient's wealth, such as by the receipt of money,[115] or a negative one, for instance where an inevitable expense has been saved. The most common example of the second type of benefit is the discharge of an obligation owed by the defendant, whether by the claimant paying his creditor[116] or abating a nuisance[117] or the claimant performing some other service[118] for which the defendant is primarily responsible. An enrichment has also been held to include where the claimant has forgone a valid claim against the defendant, such as a claim for compensation for unfair dismissal.[119] In *Bank of Cyprus UK Ltd v Menelaou*[120] the Supreme Court recognised that the transfer of freehold property without a charge, when the property should have been subject to a valid charge, constituted an enrichment to the extent of the amount with which the property should have been charged. In *Lowick Rose LLP v Swynson Ltd*[121] Lord Mance recognised that an enrichment included the reduction of a loss which would otherwise have been recoverable by a claim for damages for breach of contract or breach of a duty. In assessing whether the defendant has been enriched by the receipt of money it is also necessary to have regard to any consequent liabilities which might negate the enrichment. So, for example, in *Jeremy D Stone Consultants Ltd v National Westminster Bank Plc*[122] it was recognised that a bank was not enriched by a payment to it for the account of a customer, even though the bank became beneficially entitled to the money, because the increase in the bank's assets was matched by an immediate balancing liability in the form of the debt which it owed to its customer. In such circumstances the claimant should sue the customer rather than the bank. A trustee who obtains legal title to an asset as a principal will be considered to be enriched even though the trustee has no beneficial interest in the asset.[122a] An agent will not, however, be enriched by the receipt of payments made to them for the account of their principal,[122b] although the preferable view is that this should only be the case once the money has been transferred to the principal.[122c] Where there have been payments between the claimant and the defendant, the net amount will constitute the relevant enrichment.[123]

[115] *Kelly v Solari* (1841) 9 M. & W. 54 (below, para.29-035); *Brook's Wharf and Bull Wharf Ltd v Goodman Bros* [1937] 1 K.B. 534 (below, para.29-108); *Sixteenth Ocean GmbH and Co KG v Société Générale* [2018] EWHC 1731 (Comm).

[116] *Exall v Partridge* (1799) 8 T.R. 208 (below, para.29-109). See also *National Bank of Egypt International Ltd v Oman Housing Bank SAOC* [2002] EWHC 1760 (Comm), [2003] 1 All E.R. (Comm) 246. See also *Richards v Worcestershire County Council* [2017] EWCA Civ 1998 (discharge of defendant's statutory liabilities).

[117] *Gebhardt v Saunders* [1892] 2 Q.B. 452 (below, para.29-113).

[118] Below, para.29-113.

[119] *Gibb v Maidstone and Tunbridge Wells NHS Trust* [2010] EWCA Civ 678 at [30] (Laws L.J.).

[120] [2015] UKSC 66, [2016] A.C. 176.

[121] [2017] UKSC 32, [2018] A.C. 313 at [57]. See also Lord Neuberger at [113].

[122] [2013] EWHC 208 (Ch).

[122a] *Skandinaviska Enskilda Banken AB v Conway* [2019] UKPC 36, [2019] 3 W.L.R. 493. See also *King v Stewart* (1892) 66 L.T. 339.

[122b] *Skandinaviska Enskilda Banken AB v Conway* [2019] UKPC 36, [2019] 3 W.L.R. 493.

[122c] As occurred in *Challinor v Juliet Bellis and Co* [2015] EWCA Civ 59. Alternatively, where the money has been transferred to the principal the agent might be considered to have a defence, rather than not being treated as enriched. See below para.29-195.

[123] In *Skandinaviska Enskilda Banken AB (Publ), Singapore Branch v Asia Pacific Breweries (Singapore) Pte Ltd* [2011] SGCA 22, [2011] 3 S.L.R. 540. this was called "the running account method" of valuing an enrichment. See also *Investment Trust Companies v Revenue and Customs Commissioners* [2017] UKSC 29, [2018] A.C. 275 at [30] (Lord Reed).

## Non-monetary benefits

*Replace paragraph with:*

**29-020** Establishing a restitutionary claim in respect of non-money benefits is more difficult than claims relating to money in part, due to the fact that:

> "... by their very nature services cannot be restored: nor in many cases can goods be restored, for example where they have been consumed or transferred to another."[124]

Furthermore, even where the benefit takes the form of an increase in the value of the defendant's property, the increase can only be realised by forcing a sale.[125] In the case of the rendering of services as opposed to the payment of money, "the identity and value of the resulting benefit to the recipient may be debatable".[126] Many, but not all, cases involving the rendering of services are anyway capable of analysis as a genuine implied contract,[127] thus not engaging the law of restitution. Where a genuine contract cannot be implied a claim in unjust enrichment may lie. Services may take many forms and while some result in an accretion to the defendant's wealth, for instance by improving his property, other "pure" services do not. An unjust enrichment claim might still be available even as regards "pure" services if they can be regarded as beneficial, which will typically be established if the defendant, knowing that they were to be paid for,[127a] had requested[127b] them, freely accepted them[128] or acquiesced in them.[129] The unjust enrichment cases involving free acceptance or acquiescence do not depend upon the service adding to the defendant's wealth; the service per se is treated as a benefit.[130] Thus, restitution has been awarded in respect of plans prepared in anticipation of the conclusion of a contract by a developer but rendered useless when the landowner decided not to proceed,[131] and in respect of work done by a person on his own property at the request of prospective tenants when negotiations for a lease broke down.[132] Restitution will not be awarded if the dealing between the parties shows that the risk is to be borne by the party rendering the services.[133]

[124] *B.P. Exploration Co (Libya) Ltd v Hunt (No.2)* [1979] 1 W.L.R. 783, 799, affirmed by the House of Lords [1983] 2 A.C. 352.

[125] In *Greenwood v Bennett* [1973] 1 Q.B. 195 (below, para.29-055) a sale had, in fact, taken place.

[126] *B.P. Exploration Co (Libya) Ltd v Hunt (No.2)* [1979] 1 W.L.R. 783, 799 (Robert Goff J.); affirmed by the Court of Appeal [1981] 1 W.L.R. 232 and by the House of Lords [1983] 2 A.C. 352. See also Burrows at pp.46–61; Virgo at pp.75–77; Jones (1977) 93 L.Q.R. 273; Barker (2001) 54 C.L.P. 255.

[127] *RTS Flexible Systems Ltd v Molkerei Alios Müller GmbH* [2010] UKSC 14, [2010] 1 W.L.R. 753. Below, para.29-071.

[127a] See *Moorgate Capital (Corporate Finance) Ltd v Sun European Partners LLP* [2020] EWHC 593 (Comm), where the provision of a service was not considered to be beneficial.

[127b] *Dowman Imports Ltd v 2 Toobz Ltd* [2020] EWHC 291 (Comm) at [36] (H.H.J. Russen Q.C.).

[128] See Burrows at pp.56–59; Goff and Jones at paras 4-43—4-50; Virgo at pp.85–90. In *Rowe v Vale of White Horse D.C.* [2003] EWHC 388 (Admin), [2003] 1 Lloyd's Rep. 418, 421 (Lightman J.) free acceptance was recognised, obiter, as relevant to establish both an enrichment and a ground of restitution where home-owners had received sewerage services without charge. Free acceptance was not established on the facts because there had been no acquiescence by the defendant in the supply of services for a consideration. See also *McDonald v Coys of Kensington* [2004] EWCA Civ 47, [2004] 1 W.L.R. 2775 (free acceptance could be established on the facts) at [32] (Mance L.J.); *Chief Constable of the Greater Manchester Police v Wigan Athletic AFC Ltd* [2008] EWCA Civ 1449, [2009] 1 W.L.R. 1580 (policing of football matches at a higher level than requested, no free acceptance because the club was unable to reject these additional services alone). In *Wee Chiaw Sek Anna v Ng Li-Ann Genevieve* [2013] SGCA 36 the Singapore Court of Appeal, at [108], noted the controversy about recognising free acceptance as a ground of restitution, because unjust enrichment is claimant-focused and does not focus on the fault of the defendant.

[129] *Ellis v Hamlen* (1810) 3 Taunt 52, 53; *Nemes v Ata Chaglayan* Unreported October 11, 1982, CA; *Marston Construction Co Ltd v Kigass Ltd* [1989] 46 B.L.R. 109. cf. *Bookmakers Afternoon Greyhound Services Ltd v Wilfred Gilbert Staffordshire Ltd* [1994] F.S.R. 723, 742–744.

[130] *William Lacey (Hounslow) Ltd v Davis* [1957] 1 W.L.R. 932; *Brewer Street Investments Ltd v Barclay Woollen Co* [1954] 1 Q.B. 428, 433–434 (Somervell L.J.), 438 (Denning L.J.); *British Steel Corp v Cleveland Bridge and Engineering Co Ltd* [1984] 1 All E.R. 504. cf. *Sumpter v Hedges* [1898] 1 Q.B. 673; *Wiluszynski v Tower Hamlets LBC* [1989] I.C.R. 493; *Dowman Imports Ltd v 2 Toobz Ltd* [2020] EWHC 291 (Comm) at [35] (H.H.J. Russen Q.C.). Below, paras 29-071 et seq.

[131] *William Lacey (Hounslow) Ltd v Davis* [1957] 1 W.L.R. 932; *Sabemo v N. Sydney M.C.* [1977] 2 N.S.W.L.R. 880; *Marston Construction Co Ltd v Kigass Ltd* [1989] 46 B.L.R. 109; *Countrywide Communications Ltd v ICL Pathway Ltd* [2000] C.L.C. 324; *Bridgewater v Griffiths* [2000] 1 W.L.R. 524; *Cobbe v Yeoman's Row Management Ltd* [2008] UKHL 55, [2008] 1 W.L.R. 1752 (services in obtaining grant of planning permission).

[132] *Brewer St Investments Ltd v Barclays Woollen Co Ltd* [1954] 1 Q.B. 428.

[133] *Regalian Properties Plc v London Dockland Development Corp* [1995] 1 W.L.R. 212. See also *Bookmakers Afternoon Greyhound Services Ltd v Wilfred Gilbert Staffordshire Ltd* [1994] F.S.R. 723; *Matthew Lumbers v W. Cook Builders Pty Ltd* [2008] HCA 27; *MacDonald Dickens and Macklin v Costello* [2011] EWCA Civ 930, [2012] Q.B. 244; *Dowman Imports Ltd v 2 Toobz Ltd* [2020] EWHC 291 (Comm) at [42] (H.H.J. Russen Q.C.).

## Use value of money

*Replace paragraph with:*

In *Sempra Metals (formerly Metallgesellschaft Ltd) Ltd v IRC*[140] the House of Lords held that a taxpayer which had paid tax earlier than it was legally required to do could establish that the Revenue had been unjustly enriched, with the enrichment consisting of the Revenue's opportunity to use the money until the tax was properly due (so-called "use" or "opportunity" value of money). This enrichment was valued with reference to compound interest which the defendant would have had to pay to borrow an equivalent amount of money to that which had been received from the taxpayer and which, for the Revenue, was a rate which was lower than the commercial rate. Such a claim for the use value of money, which was subsequently considered to involve a freestanding cause of action[141] distinct from a claim to recover the value of the money received, would be available in respect of any unjust enrichment claim where money had been paid which was not due to the defendant. This aspect of the decision in *Sempra Metals* was, however, overruled by the Supreme Court in *Prudential Assurance Co Ltd v HMRC*[142] on the ground that a claim for the use value of money was inconsistent with the analysis of unjust enrichment claims adopted by the Supreme Court in *Investment Trust Companies v Revenue and Customs Commissioners*,[143] namely that the defendant's enrichment involves a transfer of value which must be directly obtained at the expense of the claimant, who must have incurred a loss as a result of providing the benefit. As the Supreme Court recognised in *Prudential Assurance*, where the claimant mistakenly pays £1,000 to the defendant which is repaid by the defend- 29-023 ant a month later, the fact that the defendant has had an opportunity to use that money for a month has not involved an additional and distinct transfer of value from the claimant to the defendant. It follows that a distinct claim for the use value of money is no longer available.

140 [2007] UKHL 34, [2008] 1 A.C. 561. See *Kowalishin v Roberts* [2015] EWHC 1333 (Ch); *Littlewoods Ltd v HM Revenue and Customs Commissioners* [2017] UKSC 70, [2018] A.C. 869.

141 *Littlewoods Ltd v HM Revenue and Customs Commissioners* [2017] UKSC 70, [2018] A.C. 869, [28] (Lords Reed and Hodge).

142 [2018] UKSC 39, [2019] A.C. 929. See Wilmot-Smith (2019) 135 L.Q.R. 195, Georgiou [2019] L.M.C.L.Q. 38 and Day (2019) 78 C.L.J. 24.

143 [2017] UKSC 29, [2018] A.C. 313. See below, paras 29-028 and 29-029.

*In line 27, after "unjust enrichment. In", italicise case name "Sempra Metals":*

**29-023** *Sempra Metals*

## Valuing enrichment

*Replace paragraph with:*

**29-024** In *Benedetti v Sawiris*[145] the Supreme Court clarified the law on valuing an enrichment. Value is to be ascertained at the time when the enrichment was received and without regard to subsequent profit accruing.[146] The starting point for the valuation exercise is to identify the objective market value of the benefit. A significant distinction is to be drawn between the "ordinary market value" and the "objective value of the benefit". The former is the price which would have been agreed in the market in the absence of some unusual characteristic of the purchaser, whereas the latter is the value of the benefit to the reasonable person in the position of the defendant. Usually both values will be the same, and will simply involve an assessment of what it would have cost a reasonable person to acquire the goods or services elsewhere in the market. The objective value of the benefit may be higher or lower than the ordinary market value by virtue of the defendant's position, where the defendant's position would have been taken into account by the market. This includes, for example, the defendant's buying power which enables him to negotiate a low price, his credit rating and the defendant's age, gender, occupation and state of health. This objective value may be reduced but not increased by reference to the defendant's own personal preferences and idiosyncratic views as to the value of the enrichment. It follows that subjective devaluation is recognised and subjective over-valuation is not recognised, although Lord Clarke, with whom Lords Kerr and Wilson agreed, did reserve the possibility of recognising subjective over-valuation in exceptional circumstances; he did not indicate what those circumstances might be. The defendant bears the burden of proving subjective devaluation. Subjective devaluation will not be possible where the enrichment was freely accepted.[147]

145 [2013] UKSC 50, [2014] A.C. 938. See also *MacInnes v Gross* [2017] EWHC 46 (QB) at [162]–[166] (Coulson J.).

146 *Wright v Rowland* [2017] EWHC 2478 (Comm) at [86] (Christopher Butcher Q.C.).

147 *ACLBDD Holdings Ltd v Staechelin* [2018] EWHC 44 (Ch) at [159] (Morgan J.).

## (d) The Grounds of Restitution

### The rationales of the grounds of restitution

*Replace footnote 183 with:*

183 See, for example, *Rowe v Vale of White Horse DC* [2003] EWHC 388 (Admin), [2003] 1 Lloyd's L.R. 418 where free acceptance was recognised as a ground of restitution, albeit not established on the facts, where services were provided in circumstances where the defendant had not rejected them when there was an opportunity to do so and the defendant, as a reasonable person, should have known that the claimant expected to be paid for the services. See also *Sharab v Prince Al-Waleed Bin Talal Bin Abdul-Aziz Al-Saud* [2012] EWHC 1798 (Ch), [2012] 2 C.L.C. 612 at [68]; *Diamandis v Wills* [2015] EWHC 312 (Ch) at [82] (Stephen Morris Q.C.); *Barton v Gwynn-Jones* [2018] EWHC 2426 (Ch) at [185] (Pearce J.) (although this was expressly not adopted by the Court of Appeal: [2019] EWCA Civ 1999 at [38] (Asplin L.J.)). **29-031**

## (e) Mistake

### Definition of mistake

*Replace footnote 197 with:*

197 See *Leslie v Farrar Construction Ltd* [2015] EWHC 58 (TCC), [255] (Judge Stephen Davies). See *Lehman Brothers International (Europe) Ltd v Exotix Partners LLP* [2019] EWHC 2380 (Ch), [2020] 1 All E.R. (Comm) 635 at [200] (Hildyard J.) for an example of an incorrect tacit assumption. **29-034**

### Doubt as to the liability to pay

*Replace footnote 231 with:*

231 [2006] UKHL 49, [2007] 1 A.C. 558 at [27]. Lord Hoffmann considered that this should be determined by an objective test. This has subsequently been analysed as not representing the law, but as constituting instead a suggestion as to how the law might develop: *BP Oil International Ltd v Target Shipping Ltd* [2012] EWHC 1590 (Comm), [2012] 2 Lloyd's Rep. 245 at [245] (Andrew Smith J.). Lord Hoffmann's judgment was, however, commended by Lord Walker in *Pitt v Holt* [2013] UKSC 26, [2013] 2 A.C. 108 at [114]. **29-038**

### Payments made for good consideration

*Replace paragraph with:*

Money paid in discharge of a genuine legal obligation cannot be recovered merely because the payer was induced to fulfil his legal obligation by a mistake. In *Fairfield Sentry Ltd v Migani*[244] Lord Sumption recognised that a mistaken payment cannot be recovered "to the extent [it] discharges a contractual debt of the payee".[244a] But he went on to recognise that, "[s]o far as the payment exceeds the debt properly due, then the payer is in principle entitled to recover the excess". In that case restitution was not awarded where the claimant was contractually bound to make the payments which it sought to recover. As Lord Hope recognised in *Kleinwort Benson Ltd v Lincoln CC*, "The payee cannot be said to have been unjustly enriched if he was entitled to receive the sum paid to him".[245] For example,[246] where the claimant paid money due under a contract to agents of a foreign government in ignorance of the fact that a revolution had broken out which subsequently led to the downfall of the government, it was not recoverable even though the claimant would not have made the payment had he known what was happening[247]: **29-041**

> "... the money was paid, not under a mistake of fact as to the existence of an obligation; it was paid in pursuance of an obligation which in fact existed"[248]

and was effective to discharge that obligation. Where, however, the claimant paid money under a contract to agents of the other party in ignorance of the fact that the contract had already been repudiated by the other party, it was held that the payment was recoverable because it did not discharge any legal obligation.[249] *Aiken v Short*,[250] which was the basis for the view that only "liability" mistakes sufficed to permit repayment, is in fact an example of failure to recover a payment which was effective to discharge a debt. The plaintiff bankers paid a sum of money to the defendant in discharge of a debt owed by one Carter to the defendant which was secured by a mortgage on property which supposedly belonged to Carter. The plaintiffs purchased the property from Carter subject to the defendant's interest on the understanding that they would pay off Carter's debt to the defendant. The plaintiffs paid the defendant because they believed that they were getting rid of the encumbrance on their title and, when it transpired that Carter did not in fact own the property, they claimed to recover the sum as having been paid under a mistake of fact. The Court of Exchequer held that the money was irrecoverable. The payment was authorised by Carter[251] and was effective to discharge the debt; the defendant therefore gave good consideration for the payment.[252] The operation of this rule is also illustrated by cases in which a bank mistakenly pays a third party who presents a cheque drawn upon it by a customer. The question whether the bank may recover the payment depends on whether the payment was with or without mandate.[253] Thus, where the bank pays, having overlooked notice of the customer's death or his instructions countermanding the cheque, the bank will be able to recover the payment.[254] Because it has paid without mandate the bank cannot debit the customer's account and the payment does not discharge the customer's debt to the payee. Where, however, the bank mistakenly thinks the customer has sufficient funds or overdraft facilities to meet the cheque, the payment will be irrecoverable.[255] The payment is within the bank's mandate, the bank is therefore entitled to have recourse to the customer and the payment does discharge the customer's debt to the payee.

[244] [2014] UKPC 9 at [18].

[244a] This should be interpreted as referring to a contractual debt owed to the payee: *ICICI Bank UK Plc v Assam Oil Co Ltd* [2019] EWHC 750 (Comm) at [38] (Andrew Burrows Q.C.).

[245] [1999] 2 A.C. 349, 408. In *Alfred Street Properties Ltd v National Asset Management Agency* [2020] EWHC 397 (Comm) at [117], Phillips L.J. confirmed that the bar only applied where the defendant had a right to receive payment.

[246] *Kerrison v Glyn, Mills, Currie & Co* (1910) 15 Com. Cas. 241, 247–248; reversed on the facts (1911) 81 L.J. K.B. 465; 17 Com. Cas. 41; *Steam Saw Mills Co Ltd v Baring Bros & Co Ltd* [1922] 1 Ch. 244, 251, 254; *British American Continental Bank v British Bank for Foreign Trade* [1926] 1 K.B. 328, 336–337, 341, 344.

[247] *Steam Saw Mills Co Ltd v Baring Bros & Co Ltd* [1922] Ch. 244.

[248] [1922] Ch. 244, 254.

[249] *British American Continental Bank v British Bank for Foreign Trade* [1926] 1 K.B. 328; *Commonwealth of Australia v McCormack* (1982) 69 F.L.R. 9 (overpayment of sum due under lease paid having forgotten about previous part payment, recovered).

[250] (1856) 1 H. & N. 210.

[251] (1856) 1 H. & N. 210, 214, 215. This was said to be a "crucial" fact in the case: *Barclays Bank Ltd v W.J. Simms, Son and Cooke (Southern) Ltd* [1980] Q.B. 677, 687 (Robert Goff J.).

[252] cf. *Customs and Excise Commissioners v National Westminster Bank Plc* [2002] EWHC 2204 (Ch), [2003] 1 All E.R. (Comm) 327: unsolicited payment to a creditor's bank account would not discharge a debt unless it was accepted as doing such.

[253] *Barclays Bank Ltd v W.J. Simms, Son and Cooke (Southern) Ltd* [1980] Q.B. 677, 699–700 (Robert Goff J.).

254 [1980] Q.B. 677. This would appear to be the case whether or not the customer's account was adequate to meet the cheque; Vol.II, para.34-130.

255 *Pollard v Bank of England* (1871) L.R. 6 Q.B. 623; *Barclays Bank Ltd v W.J. Simms, Son and Cooke (Southern) Ltd* [1980] Q.B. 677, 699–700; *Lloyds Bank Plc v Independent Insurance Co Ltd* [2000] Q.B. 110.

## Mistaken voluntary dispositions

*Replace paragraph with:*

There is an equitable jurisdiction to rescind voluntary dispositions which have been made by mistake. The operation of this equitable jurisdiction is more restrictive than the Common Law regime for the recovery of mistaken payments. The nature of this equitable jurisdiction was examined by the Supreme Court in *Pitt v Holt*.[328] There are three interlinked elements: (i) the donor was mistaken at the time of the disposition[329]; (ii) the mistake was sufficiently serious, but it need not be fundamental in the manner which is required to set aside a contract; and (iii) the assertion of the donee's rights would be objectively unjust or unconscionable, rendering the mistake of sufficient gravity to rescind the disposition. On the facts of that case it was held that a mistake as to the tax consequences of a disposition was sufficiently serious to trigger the equitable jurisdiction to rescind the disposition for mistake, although probably it is only in exceptional cases that such mistakes will render the disposition voidable. Rescission of a voluntary disposition for mistake may operate differently to rescission of a contract since for a voluntary disposition it is necessary to ensure that the effect of rescission is not unjust, unfair or unconscionable.[329a] Consequently, full restitution may not be required, it being sufficient that the parties are restored substantially to their original position.[329b] Where a settlor or trustee has conferred a benefit on the donees in a tax-efficient manner as contemplated by statute, this will be characterised as legitimate such that it would be unconscionable not to rescind the disposition for mistake.[330] Although the jurisdiction to rescind voluntary deeds of dispositions for mistake is equitable, the principles identified by the Supreme Court have been considered to be applicable at Common Law to limit claims for restitution of gifts transferred by mistake even though there was no underlying deed to rescind.[331] **29-052**

328 [2013] UKSC 26, [2013] A.C. 108. See Davies and Virgo [2013] R.L.R. 73. See also *Kennedy v Kennedy* [2014] EWHC 4129 (Ch); *Wright v National Westminster Bank Plc* [2014] EWHC 3158 (Ch); *Freedman v Freedman* [2015] EWHC 1457 (Ch), [2015] W.T.L.R. 1187; *Van der Merwe v Goldman* [2016] EWHC 790 (Ch), [2016] 4 W.L.R. 71; *Bainbridge v Bainbridge* [2016] EWHC 898 (Ch), [2016] W.T.L.R. 943. In *Co-operative Bank Plc v Hayes Freehold Ltd* [2017] EWHC 1820 (Ch) at [130] Carr J. recognised that the jurisdiction to rescind did not apply where the transaction was neither a gift nor a voluntary disposition. In that case a deed of release from a landlord's covenants was not characterised as a voluntary disposition because in return an underlease was surrendered and so consideration was provided.

329 In *Wright v National Westminster Bank Plc* [2014] EWHC 3158 (Ch) at [11], Norris J. confirmed that there was no need to establish that the mistake was induced by misrepresentation or fraud.

329a *Rogge v Rogge* [2019] EWHC 1949 (Ch).

329b *Rogge v Rogge* [2019] EWHC 1949 (Ch).

330 *Kennedy v Kennedy* [2014] EWHC 4129 (Ch), [2015] W.T.L.R. 837, [39] (Etherton C). In *Gresh v RBC Trust Co (Guernsey) Ltd* (2016) 18 I.T.E.L.R. 753 the Royal Court of Guernsey held that a request by a member of a pension fund to be paid a lump sum distribution in the mistaken belief that it was not subject to tax, did not constitute an equitable mistake because there was nothing which rendered the retention of the distribution unconscionable as between the member and the pension fund.

331 *Pagel v Farman* [2013] EWHC 2210 (Comm); *Spaul v Spaul* [2014] EWCA Civ 679 at [52] (Rimer L.J.). See further Dodds [2016] R.L.R. 129.

## (f) Failure of Basis

### Illustrations of total failure of basis

*Replace footnote 364 with:*

29-059 [364] *Bostock v Jardine* (1865) 3 H. & C. 700. See also *Rostam Agrochemical Co Ltd v GAT Microencapsulation GmbH* [2018] EWHC 2765 (Comm) (payment transferred in expectation of a commercial collaboration agreement being made which was not forthcoming); *Quinn Infrastructure Services Ltd v Sullivan* [2019] EWHC 2863 (Comm) (money paid conditional on being used to pay licence fees which subsequently did not need to be paid).

### Recovery of deposits

*Replace footnote 436 with:*

29-068 [436] *Howe v Smith* (1884) 27 Ch. D. 89, 97–98; *Simpson Marine (Sea) Pte Ltd v Jiarawaran* [2019] SGCA 7, [2019] 2 Lloyd's Rep. 196. But see the proposals of the *Law Com. Working Paper No.61* (1975), paras 49–67.

### Quantum meruit to fix remuneration

*Replace footnote 450 with:*

29-071 [450] e.g. *Way v Latilla* [1937] 3 All E.R. 759, HL; *William Lacey (Hounslow) Ltd v Davis* [1957] 1 W.L.R. 932; *British Steel Corp v Cleveland Bridge & Engineering Co Ltd* [1984] 1 All E.R. 504; *Debenham, Tewson & Chinnocks v Rimington* [1990] 34 E.G. 55. See Ball (1983) 99 L.Q.R. 572; McKendrick (1988) 8 O.J.L.S. 197. See also *Lagos v Grunwaldt* [1910] 1 K.B. 41, 48; *Robins v Power* (1858) 4 C.B.(N.S.) 778. cf. *Re Richmond Gate Property Co Ltd* [1965] 1 W.L.R. 335. If the person at whose request the work is done subsequently promises a definite sum as remuneration, the so-called rule in *Lampleigh v Braithwaite* (1615) Hob. 105 may apply: see above, para.4-030. See also *Benedetti v Sawiris* [2013] UKSC 50, [2014] A.C. 938 where Lord Clarke recognised, at [9], that where there is a contract between the parties the court may imply a term to pay reasonable remuneration. This has sometimes been called a claim in quantum meruit. The focus is on the intention of the parties objectively ascertained. Where there is no contract, the quantum meruit operates within the law of unjust enrichment, and the focus is on the benefit to the defendant. See also *ACLBDD Holdings Ltd v Staechelin* [2018] EWHC 44 (Ch).

### Quantum meruit for work done where the contract is terminated by breach

*Replace footnote 469 with:*

29-072 [469] Burrows at pp.346–347; Virgo at p.311. This has been recognised in Australia: *Mann v Paterson Constructions Pty Ltd* [2019] HCA 32. Although in *Cobbe v Yeoman's Row Management Ltd* [2008] UKHL 55, [2008] 1 W.L.R. 1752 the House of Lords recognised a claim for quantum meruit in respect of work done in anticipation of a contract being made, which was distinct from a separate claim apparently founded on total failure of basis, which was itself apparently distinct from a claim in unjust enrichment; it is unclear what the difference between the three claims is. See also *Butler-Creagh v Hersham* [2011] EWHC 2525 (QB) at [129] (Eady J.). In the same way that partial failure of basis should be a sufficient ground of restitution for claims for restitution for money (see para.29-067, above), so too partial failure of basis should be sufficient to ground claims for the reasonable value of services.

### Quantum meruit and contractual remedies

*Replace paragraph with:*

29-073 In *Taylor v Motability Finance Ltd*[473] a distinction was drawn between claims involving goods and services and claims involving money, with the assumption being that the ground of total failure of basis only applied to the latter claim. In that case the defendant had terminated an employment contract with the claimant. The claimant argued that this constituted a repudiatory breach so that a restitutionary remedy could be awarded outside of the contract for the work done grounded on total failure of basis. This argument was rejected because the claimant had fully performed the contract by providing services to the defendant and so, although the primary obligation to perform had been revoked, the contractual regime subsisted in terms of the secondary obligation to pay damages for breach. It appears from this decision that, where a claimant has paid money to the defendant and has received nothing in return, the contractual regime no longer applies once the contract has been discharged, so that a restitutionary claim will lie.[474] Where, however, goods or services are provided by the claimant who has substantially performed the contract, the contractual regime still governs the award of remedies despite the repudiation of the contract.[475] This distinction was approved in *Howes Percival LLP v Page*[476] where it was held that, where a solicitor had a conditional right to receive payment for services if litigation was successful, once the defendant had committed a repudiatory breach of the contract there was no right to obtain a quantum meruit for the services provided by the solicitor, but only damages for the breach of contract. This would be particularly significant where the defendant was likely to lose the litigation, for then the solicitor would not have suffered any loss. It was recognised that a similar result would be achieved if a contract with an estate agent was breached, where the conditions necessary for the payment of commission to the estate agent had not been met. The creation of such a distinction dependent on the nature of the enrichment received by the defendant is difficult to defend. In *Elek v Bar-Tur*[477] David Donaldson Q.C. reluctantly accepted that a claimant who has provided services pursuant to a contract which has been repudiated following breach by the defendant, can bring a restitutionary claim to recover the value of the services. However, following *Taylor v Motability Finance*,[478] he recognised that this only applies where the claimant has been unable to complete his contractual performance and as a result the defendant's counter-performance is not yet due. Where, however, the claimant has fully performed and is entitled to payment under the contract, the claimant cannot bring a claim for unjust enrichment. Such an approach has been endorsed by the High Court of Australia. In *Mann v Paterson Constructions Pty Ltd*[479] it was recognised that where a contract was terminated by a builder for a repudiatory breach by a landowner, the builder was confined to suing for breach of contract in respect of services provided for which a contractual right to be paid had accrued, because there was no failure of basis.[480] Where, however, services had been provided for which no contractual right to be paid had accrued, the builder could seek a quantum meruit for the reasonable value of the service provided.

473 [2004] EWHC 2619 (Comm).

474 [2004] EWHC 2619 (Comm) at [25] (Cooke J.).

475 [2004] EWHC 2619 (Comm).

476 [2013] EWHC 4104 (Ch).

477 [2013] EWHC 207 (Ch), [2013] 2 E.G.L.R. 159.

478 [2004] EWHC 2619 (Comm).

479 [2019] HCA 32. See Wilmot-Smith (2020) 136 L.Q.R. 196.

480 [2019] HCA 32 at [169] (Nettle, Gordon and Edelman JJ.).

**Relevance of the contract price**

*Replace paragraph with:*

Although it might be thought wrong to allow the innocent party to "reverse" the contractual allocation of risks[486] and difficult to value the benefit without regard to the contract price,[487] it has also been argued that the contract price was agreed in the context of a contemplated complete performance and that this would not neces- **29-075** sarily have been agreed for part performance.[488] The presence of economies of scale may mean that it does not follow that a person who agrees to pave 10 miles of road for a specified price would have agreed to pave 10 yards at a prorated price.[489] Furthermore, to allow a party in breach to reduce the award by reference to the contract price in effect awards him "a portion of his anticipated profit on the contract despite the fact that he was the contract breaker".[490] Finally, the contrast with claims for the recovery of money paid under contracts on the ground that there has been a total failure of basis should be noted. In those cases the objection that recovery might reverse the contractual allocation of risks does not appear to have been taken.[491] An alternative to prorating the contract price is to limit the quantum meruit to the total contract price. This has been justified on the ground that it fully protects the claimant's expectations but avoids giving him a "windfall".[492] However, it does so by awarding the person who has committed a repudiatory breach which has led to the contract being discharged[493] a portion of his contractual expectations, and has the consequence of producing disequilibrium between the position of a claimant who has done a small proportion of the work, where the contract price limit would in fact rarely apply, and the position of one who has done the bulk of the work, where the limit would be more likely to apply.[494] In *Mann v Paterson Constructions Pty Ltd*[495] the High Court of Australia recognised that, where it was possible to bring a claim for a quantum meruit for services provided pursuant to a contract which had been terminated for a repudiatory breach, usually the value of the services should not exceed the contract price, because the contract (although discharged) should inform the content of the defendant's obligation to make restitution where the failed basis upon which the service was provided was the performer's right to complete the performance and earn the price according to the contract terms. It was recognised, however, that exceptionally it might be appropriate to value the service above the contract price.[496–498]

486 Burrows at pp.349–350 would restrict the quantum meruit to a proration of the contract price unless there is incontrovertible benefit.

487 *Burchall v Gowrie & Blockhouse Collieries* [1910] A.C. 614; *B.P. Exploration Co (Libya) Ltd v Hunt (No.2)* [1979] 1 W.L.R. 783, 822, 825 (Robert Goff J.). See also *Law Com. Working Paper No.65* (1975), paras 26–32 for other difficulties of valuation. See further Law Com. No.121, paras 2.50—2.57. In *ERDC Group Ltd v Brunel University* [2006] EWHC 687 (TCC) quantum meruit was assessed with reference to the contract price where the claim arose for work done after the expiry of a letter of appointment which had provided a contractual basis for the previous work. See also *Anchor 2020 Ltd v Midas Construction Ltd* [2019] EWHC 435 (TCC), [157] (Waksman J.).

488 Palmer (1959) 20 Ohio State L.J. 264; *The Law of Restitution* (1978), Vol.I, pp.404–406.

489 *The Law of Restitution* (1978), Vol.I, pp.404–406. This example is taken from the facts of *Kehoe v Rutherford* (1893) 27 A. 912 in which only a proportionate part of the price was recovered.

490 Palmer at p.401. See also *Prickett v Badger* (1856) 1 C.B.(N.S.) 296, 306.

491 Above, para.29-059.

492 Goff and Jones at paras 3-47—3-51.

493 On discharge, see above, Chs 22–24.

494 Beatson at pp.14–15. In the road example, if the contract price was £1 million, and the market price was £2 million, the limit would only affect a claimant who had completed more than half the work.

495 [2019] HCA 32 at [215] (Nettle, Gordon and Edelman JJ.)

496–498 Such as in *Boomer v Muir* (1933) 24 P. 2d 570. In *MacInnes v Gross* [2017] EWHC 46 (QB) Coulson J. recognised (at [166]) that an agreement as to remuneration for services may unusually be the best evidence of the objective market value of the services provided, but usually other objective evidence would be required, such as expert evidence. See also *Wright v Rowland* [2017] EWHC 2478 (Comm) at [86] (Christopher Butcher Q.C.).

## Additional remuneration

*Replace paragraph with:*

Despite the existence of a valid contract between the parties, a claim for quantum meruit may lie where the services provided are over and above those for which the parties contracted.[498a] Consequently, a claim for quantum meruit may allow recovery of a reasonable sum as additional remuneration for extra work performed by a building contractor, where, although the contract permitted the owner to order extra work, the amount of extra work actually ordered was so great as to go beyond the scope of the contract and entitle the builder to claim that he should not be limited to the maximum profit fixed by the contract.[499] The same principle has been applied to a contract of employment, where, in lieu of an increase of salary, the employer promised to pay a bonus on the net trading profits of the business, but the method of assessing the bonus was never agreed.[500] In another case[501] the claimant was requested by the defendant to do some additional work as a property consultant outside of the scope of the contract between them, for which no remuneration was fixed under the contract. It was held that the defendant was liable to pay the claimant for this work, with the award determined on a quantum meruit basis. **29-076**

[498a] Considered in *Diamandis v Willis* [2015] EWHC 312 (Ch) at [84] (Stephen Morris Q.C.).

[499] *Sir Lindsay Parkinson & Co Ltd v Commissioners of Works* [1949] 2 K.B. 632. cf. *Gilbert & Partners v Knight* [1968] 2 All E.R. 248.

[500] *Powell v Braun* [1954] 1 W.L.R. 401. But cf. Vol.II, para.40-079.

[501] *Cooke v Hopper* [2012] EWCA Civ 175.

## Anticipated contracts

*Replace paragraph with:*

The remedy of quantum meruit may extend to services performed in anticipation that negotiations will lead to the conclusion of a contract, provided that the services were requested or acquiesced in by the recipient,[502] or can be considered to be incontrovertibly beneficial.[503] It has been said that, in this context, quantum meruit is not truly restitutionary, since it is only "an incident in assessing the amount due under an ordinary contract where the amount is blank".[504] It is, however, difficult to accept this in the case of services rendered in anticipation that a contract would be entered into later[505] and, in such a case, a quantum meruit is not subject to contractual defences such as a claim for late delivery.[506] In *British Steel Corp v Cleveland Bridge & Engineering Co Ltd*[507] Robert Goff J. said that the obligation imposed in such cases sounds in restitution and not in contract, and the typical ground of restitution will be total failure of consideration.[508] In *MSM Consulting Ltd v United Republic of Tanzania*[509] Clarke J. identified various principles relating to quantum meruit claims arising from work done in anticipation of a contract which did not materialise, including that it is not possible to claim for the cost of bidding for the contract; a remedy will not be available where the claimant knowingly[509a] took the risk of being reimbursed only if a contract was concluded[509b]; and the court might impose an obligation on the defendant who has received a benefit if they have behaved unconscionably in declining to pay for it.[510] **29-077**

[502] *William Lacey (Hounslow) Ltd v Davis* [1957] 1 W.L.R. 932; *Peter Lind & Co Ltd v Mersey Docks and Harbour Board* [1972] 2 Lloyd's Rep. 234; *Sabemo v N. Sydney Municipal Council* [1977] 2 N.S.W.L.R. 880; *Marston Construction Co Ltd v Kigass Ltd* [1989] 46 B.L.R. 109; *Regalian Properties Plc v London Dockland Development Corp* [1995] 1 W.L.R. 212; *Countrywide Communications Ltd v ICL Pathway Ltd* [2000] C.L.C. 324; *Cobbe v Yeoman's Row Management Ltd* [2008] UKHL 55, [2008] 1 W.L.R. 1752; *MSM Consulting Ltd v United Republic of Tanzania* [2009] EWHC 121 (QB);

*Killen v Horseworld Ltd* [2011] EWHC 1600 (QB); *Dowman Imports Ltd v 2 Toobz Ltd* [2020] EWHC 291 (Comm). cf. *Brewer Street Investments Ltd v Barclays Woollen Co Ltd* [1954] 1 Q.B. 428.

[503] See para.29-021, above.

[504] Winfield, *Quasi-Contracts* (1952), p.53.

[505] *William Lacey (Hounslow) Ltd v Davis* [1957] 1 W.L.R. 932, 939; *Brewer Street Investments Ltd v Barclays Woollen Co Ltd* [1954] 1 Q.B. 428, 435–436. See also Goff and Jones at Ch.16.

[506] *British Steel Corp v Cleveland Bridge & Engineering Co Ltd* [1984] 1 All E.R. 504.

[507] [1984] 1 All E.R. 504, 511; *Countrywide Communications Ltd v ICL Pathway Ltd* [2000] C.L.C. 324.

[508] *Benedetti v Sawiris* [2013] UKSC 50, [2014] AC 938 at [86] (Lord Reed) and [175] (Lord Neuberger); *Valencia v Llupar* [2012] EWCA Civ 396, [51] (Mummery L.J.).

[509] [2009] EWHC 121 (QB) at [171]. See also *Lissack v Manhattan Loft Corp Ltd* [2013] EWHC 128 (Ch) at [86] (Roth J.); *Elek v Bar-Tur* [2013] EWHC 207 (Ch), [2013] 2 E.G.L.R. 159 (no restitution where the claimant had received the expected counter-performance from the defendant but then renounced it); *Benedetti v Sawiris* [2013] UKSC 50, [2014] A.C. 938. See generally Havelock [2011] R.L.R. 72.

[509a] *Dowman Imports Ltd v 2 Toobz Ltd* [2020] EWHC 291 (Comm) at [42] (H.H.J. Russen Q.C.).

[509b] See, for example, *Moorgate Capital (Corporate Finance) Ltd v Sun European Partners LLP* [2020] EWHC 593 (Comm) at [140] (Peter MacDonald Eggers Q.C.).

[510] See also *Whittle Movers Ltd v Hollywood Express Ltd* [2009] EWCA Civ 1189 at [22] (Waller L.J.) (and see Davies (2010) 126 L.Q.R. 175); *Tahar Benourad v Compass Group Plc* [2010] EWHC 1882 (QB) at [106] (Beatson J.) (quantum meruit awarded primarily because the defendant had requested the claimant to provide the service); *Killen v Horseworld Ltd* [2011] EWHC 1600 (QB) (where Cox J. inappropriately described, at [66], quantum meruit as a cause of action); *AMP Advisory and Management Partners v Air Force India Formula One Team* [2019] EWHC 2426 (Comm); *Dowman Imports Ltd v 2 Toobz Ltd* [2020] EWHC 291 (Comm) at [51] (H.H.J. Russen Q.C.) (it would be unconscionable for the defendant to change the rules of the game by moving the goalposts at which the claimant was aiming). See Wilmot-Smith (2011) 127 L.Q.R. 610 (no role for risk-taking reasoning when determining liability; this can be dealt with instead through the construction of the relevant condition for the work).

## Valuing the quantum meruit

*Replace paragraph with:*

**29-078** In *Benedetti v Sawiris*[511] the Supreme Court considered fundamental principles relating to the valuation of the quantum meruit. In that case the claimant had facilitated an investment in a company. The claimant sought to recover remuneration for the services he had provided. It was held that the value of the services should be assessed by reference to their market value without reference to a later compromise offer made by the defendant because it was not possible to award more than the objective value of the enrichment, although a lesser sum might be awarded if the defendant valued the enrichment below the market value. In determining the objective market value of an enrichment it was appropriate to have regard to the defendant's position, such as his buying power to negotiate a lower price or his credit rating. This is relevant to the objective value of the enrichment since it is the type of circumstance which would be taken into account by the market in determining the value of the enrichment. Defects in the service provided should be taken into account when valuing the quantum meruit.[511a]

[511] [2013] UKSC 50, [2014] A.C. 938. See also *Aclbdd Holdings Ltd v Staechelin* [2018] EWHC 44 (Ch) at [169] (Morgan J.); *AMP Advisory and Management Partners v Air Force India Formula One Team* [2019] EWHC 2426 (Comm) at [201] (Moulder J.).

[511a] *Anchor 2020 Ltd v Midas Construction Ltd* [2019] EWHC 435 (TCC) at [157] (Waksman J.).

### Money paid under illegal contracts

*Replace footnote 541 with:*

541 [2016] UKSC 42 at [101]. Cf. *Ochroid Trading Ltd v Chua Siok Lui* [2018] SGCA 5 where the Court of Appeal in Singapore adopted a more restrictive approach to the award of restitution where the claim was tainted by illegality. **29-083**

## (g) Ultra vires Receipts by the Revenue and Public Authorities

### Scope of right

*Replace paragraph with:*

The *Woolwich* principle is applicable when money has been paid to a public authority as a result of a mistake of law.[582] In *Deutsche Morgan Grenfell Group Plc v IRC*[583] the House of Lords recognised that, if statutory provisions for recovery of taxes are not available,[584] claims for restitution of tax paid by mistake can be founded at common law either on the *Woolwich* principle or on the ground of mistake of law and the claimant can choose the preferable ground.[585] The practical consequence of this decision is that the claimant can choose to rely on the extended limitation period under s.32(1)(c) of the Limitation Act 1980 which applies to claims involving mistake and for which time does not begin to run until the mistake could reasonably have been discovered.[586] The *Woolwich* principle extends to cases in which the public authority has made no demand for payment, for example where an ultra vires tax is paid in reasonable anticipation of a demand.[587] Although Lord Goff and Lord Slynn in *Woolwich* expressly reserved the question of whether the principle extends to cases in which the tax or other levy has been wrongfully exacted for reasons other than that the demand was ultra vires, for example because the authority has misconstrued the relevant statute or regulation,[588] such misconstruction is likely to be ultra vires[589] and will anyway constitute a mistake of law. In *Investment Trust Companies (In Liquidation) v Revenue and Customs Commissioners*[590] it was held that the *Woolwich* principle is only available to those claimants who were themselves directly liable for the payment of overpaid tax, because such claimants were subject to the coercive powers of the state. The claimants in that case, who were contractually liable to third parties for the payments which were then transferred to the Revenue, could bring a claim grounded on mistake instead.[591] The *Woolwich* principle has been held not to apply where a landlord, who had received overpayments of housing benefits, repaid them to the local authority, although a defect in the notice meant that the council could not in fact have enforced the recovery of the money.[592] Although the council's demand was defective, it was not backed by coercive powers and it would have been open to the council to go through the process correctly and make a second regular and valid demand.[593] Whilst it is clear that the *Woolwich* principle extends beyond taxation to licence fees[594] it is not yet clear whether it extends to unauthorised charges for the provision of services by statutory utilities, hitherto dealt with under the *colore officii* principle.[595] While explicit guidance was not given on the range of bodies subject to the principle, it is submitted that it should apply to public bodies whose authority to charge is subject to and limited by public law principles, and to other bodies whose authority to charge is solely the product of statute, and thus limited.[596] Although the *Woolwich* claim is based on the ultra vires nature of the receipt, it appears that it is not a precondition to recovery that this be established in judicial review proceedings.[597] The right of recovery is a private law right, albeit one aris- **29-091** ing from the background of public law.[598] When licence fees were paid pursuant to Regulations which were subsequently quashed as being unlawful, it was not appropriate to consider what fee the public authority would have charged if lawful regulations had been made; the principle of legality applies and the public authority is required to make restitution of what it had unlawfully received.[598a]

[582] [1993] A.C. 70, 177, 205.

[583] [2006] UKHL 49, [2007] 1 A.C. 558. See Virgo [2007] B.T.R. 27.

[584] See below, para.29-092.

[585] See also *Test Claimants in the Franked Investment Income (FII) Group Litigation* [2012] UKSC 19, [2012] AC 337; *Investment Trust Companies (in liquidation) v HMRC* [2013] EWHC 665 (Ch) at [51] (Henderson J.).

[586] See above, para.28-089. In *Test Claimants in the Franked Investment Income (FII) Group Litigation v Commissioners for Her Majesty's Revenue and Customs* [2012] UKSC 19, [2012] 2 A.C. 337 the Supreme Court held that, to fall within the section, the mistake had to be an essential element of the cause of action and not just a causal reason for the overpayment, so the extended limitation period will not be available to claims founded on the *Woolwich* principle. Where the unlawfulness of the tax has been determined by the CJEU it has been held that time will begin to run once that court declared the payment of the tax to be unlawful: *Test Claimants in the FII Group Litigation v HMRC* [2014] EWHC 4302 (Ch) [2015] S.T.I. 49 [465] (Henderson J.). Where, however, the unlawfulness of the tax has been declared by the domestic courts, if this was determined by the Supreme Court, time will only begin to run from that point, even if the unlawfulness of the tax has been established at first instance, since finality would only be achieved with the decision of the final court of appeal, and even though the claimant had brought proceedings for restitution earlier: *Test Claimants in the FII Group Litigation v HMRC* [2014] EWHC 4302 [2015] S.T.I. 49 at [461]. But note Beswick [2019] L.M.C.L.Q. 112, who argues that a mistake should be considered to be discoverable once a claimant has issued proceedings raising a mistake. The application of this extended limitation period was abrogated by statute as regards claims for recovery of taxes: Finance Act 2004 s.320 and Finance Act 2007 s.107. The latter provisions have been held to infringe EU law as regards its application to the restitution of taxes paid in breach of EU law: *Test Claimants in the FII Group Litigation v IRC* (C-362/12) EU:C:2013:834, [2014] 2 C.M.L.R. 33, as regards the former provision; *Test Claimants in the Franked Investment Income (FII) Group Litigation v Commissioners for HM Revenue and Customs* [2012] UKSC 19, [2012] 2 A.C. 337, as regards the latter provision. See further *Jazztel Plc v Revenue and Customs Commissioners* [2017] EWHC 677 (Ch), [2017] 1 W.L.R. 3869 at [100(vi)] where the former provision was disapplied for the recovery of overpaid taxes where the right had accrued before the statute came into force, but this right was only discovered subsequently: so called "hidden retrospectivity".

[587] *Test Claimants in the Franked Investment Income (FII) Group Litigation v Commissioners for Her Majesty's Revenue and Customs* [2012] UKSC 19, [2012] 2 A.C. 337. Noted Virgo and Goymour (2012) C.L.J. 488.

[588] [1993] A.C. 70, 177 (Lord Goff), 205 (Lord Slynn).

[589] *Re Racal Communications Ltd* [1981] A.C. 374.

[590] [2013] EWHC 665 (Ch), [2013] S.T.I. 1490.

[591] See further para.29-028, above, for analysis of the Supreme Courts' decision in the case.

[592] *Norwich City Council v Stringer* (2001) 33 H.L.R. 15.

[593] In *Ipswich Town Football Club Co Ltd v Chief Constable of Suffolk* [2017] EWHC 375 (QB) the *Woolwich* principle applied even though the demand for payment was not backed by legal compulsion, save that the defendant, the police, had an economic power through monopoly to compel payment. Compulsion was considered (at [73]) to be a trait of a *Woolwich* claim but was not a requisite part of the test.

[594] *Hemming v Westminster City Council* [2013] EWCA Civ 591.

[595] *Steele v Williams* (1853) 8 Ex Ch. 625; *Hooper v Exeter Corp* (1887) 56 L.J. Q.B. 457; *Queens of the River S.S. Co Ltd v Conservators of the River Thames* (1899) 15 T.L.R. 474 (harbour dues and pier charges); *South of Scotland Electricity Board v British Oxygen Co Ltd* [1959] 1 W.L.R. 587 (electricity charges). See below, paras 29-100—29-102; *Att-Gen v Wilts United Dairies Ltd* (1921) 37 T.L.R. 884; *R. v Brocklebank Ltd* [1925] 1 K.B. 52; *Mason v New South Wales* (1959) 102 C.L.R. 108. In *Ipswich Town Football Club Co Ltd v Chief Constable of Suffolk* [2017] EWHC 375 (QB) the *Woolwich* principle was applied to recover payments for services provided by the police, for which payment was not lawfully due, even though the charges could not be characterised as fiscal.

[596] [1993] A.C. 70, 79, 138 (Glidewell and Butler-Sloss L.JJ.); *AEM (Avon) Ltd v Bristol City Council* [1999] L.G.R. 93. See Beatson (1993) 109 L.Q.R. 401, 406–418. cf. *Green v Portsmouth Stadium Ltd*

[1953] 2 Q.B. 190 (where the principle would not apply because, but for the statute, there would have been no limit on the amount the defendant would have been able to charge). See *Waikato Regional Airport Ltd v The Att-Gen (on behalf of the Director General of Agriculture and Forestry)* [2003] UKPC 50, [2004] 3 N.Z.L.R. 1, where the *Woolwich* principle was extended to the recovery of governmental levies, and *Hemming v Westminster City Council* [2013] EWCA Civ 591, where it was applied to that part of licence fees paid to run sex shops which was unlawfully demanded.

597 [1993] A.C. 70, 200 (Lord Slynn) and see Lord Goff's suggestion (at 174) that the right of recovery might need to be limited by strict time limits which implies that the three-month time limit for judicial review proceedings does not apply. In *Woolwich* there had been judicial review proceedings: *R. v IRC Ex p. Woolwich Equitable Building Society* [1990] 1 W.L.R. 1400, and see [1993] A.C. 70, 169 (Lord Goff).

598 See *Lonrho Plc v Tebbit* [1992] 4 All E.R. 280, 288; *Roy v Kensington and Chelsea and Westminster F.P.C.* [1992] 1 A.C. 624. It is now possible to obtain a restitutionary remedy in an application for judicial review: CPR r.54.3(2). Such proceedings are subject to a three-month limitation period. It is possible to seek restitution without prior judicial review proceedings and so avoid this shorter limitation period (*British Steel v Customs and Excise Commissioners* [1997] 2 All E.R. 366) although this has been criticised as an abuse of process: *NEC Semi-Conductors v IRC* [2006] EWCA Civ 25, [2006] S.T.C. 606 at [97] (Sedley L.J.); *Jones v Powys Local Health Board* [2008] EWHC 2562 (Admin). The validity of the non-judicial review route to obtain restitution from a public authority remains unclear after the decisions of the House of Lords in *Deutsche Morgan Grenfell Group Plc v IRC* [2006] UKHL 49, [2007] 1 A.C. 558 and *Sempra Metals Ltd v IRC* [2007] UKHL 34, [2008] 1 A.C. 561, although the recognition that the claimant taxpayer could rely on the ground of mistake of law to gain the benefit of the extended limitation period under the Limitation Act 1980 might suggest that there is no intrinsic objection to using the non-judicial review procedure. In *Hemming v Westminster City Council* [2013] EWCA Civ 591 Beatson L.J. at [138] endorsed the private law nature of the right to restitution such that the time limit for judicial review claims does not apply to claims for restitution against public bodies. In *Richards v Worcestershire County Council* [2017] EWCA Civ 1998 the claimant was allowed to pursue a private law claim for restitution arising from the claimant discharging the defendant's statutory obligations, even though this raised questions as to whether the defendant had performed public law duties. Simple interest can be awarded, under Senior Courts Act 1981 s.35A, in respect of such claims: *R. (Kemp) v Denbighshire Local Health Board* [2006] EWHC 181 (Admin), [2007] 1 W.L.R. 639. See generally Walpole [2018] R.L.R. 42.

598a *Vodafone Ltd v The Office of Communications* [2020] EWCA Civ 183, [2020] 2 W.L.R. 1108.

## Statutory provisions

*Replace paragraph with:*

The restitutionary right is, in the context of taxation, limited by statutory provisions for the recovery of overpayments. The broadest is the right to recover any payment of VAT that is not due[599]; the narrowest is the more discretionary remedy in s.33 of the Taxes Management Act 1970 for the recovery of overpaid income tax and capital gains tax[600] by reason of an error or mistake in a tax return as is "reasonable and just".[601] There is no right of recovery where the error reflected "the practice generally prevailing" when the return was made. Where, moreover, a statutory appeal mechanism is applicable to the facts, the payee will be required to seek its remedy through the statutory framework.[602] **29-092**

599 Value Added Tax Act 1994 s.80 as amended by the Finance (No.2) Act 2005. See Virgo [1998] B.T.R. 582. Where the statutory scheme for the recovery of overpaid VAT applies, it is exclusive and excludes common law claims for restitution founded on mistake or the *Woolwich* principle: *Littlewoods Ltd v Commissioners for Her Majesty's Revenue and Customs* [2017] UKSC 70, [2018] A.C. 869. When restitution of overpaid VAT is awarded, interest is calculated on a simple rather than compounded basis: *Littlewoods Ltd v HMRC* [2017] UKSC 70, [2018] A.C. 869. See Williams (2018) 77 C.L.J. 468.

600 Claims for recovery which fall under this provision cannot be brought at common law: *Monro v H.M. Revenue and Customs* [2008] EWCA Civ 306, [2009] Ch. 69. See also *R. (on the application of Child Poverty Action Group) v Secretary of State for Work and Pensions* [2010] UKSC 54, [2011] 2 A.C. 15 where the statutory scheme for the recovery of overpaid social security benefits under s.71 of the Social Security Administration Act 1992 was held to exclude the common law claim to restitution. The statutory scheme only applies where a payment of a benefit has been made as a result of an erroneous award arising from misrepresentation or non-disclosure and does not extend to the recovery of payments made as a result of a mistake in assessing the award. Where, however, an unauthorised payment has been made in excess of the amount awarded this can be recovered on the ground of mistake.

[601] See also Inheritance Tax Act 1984 s.241; Council Tax (Administration and Enforcement) Regulations 1992 (SI 1992/613); Income and Corporation Taxes Act 1988 s.790 (corporation tax on dividend income: see *Claimants in Class 8 of the CFC and Dividend Group Litigation v Revenue and Customs Commissioners* [2019] EWHC 338 (Ch), [2019] 1 W.L.R. 5097).

[602] *Woolwich Equitable Building Society v IRC* [1993] A.C. 70, 168–170 (Lord Goff).

### Defences

*Replace footnote 614 with:*

**29-093** [614] As amended by the Finance (No.2) Act 2005 s.3. See *Baines and Ernst Ltd v Revenue and Customs Commissioners* [2006] EWCA Civ 1040; *Weber's Wine World Handels GmbH v Abgabenberufungskommission Wien* (C-147/01) EU:C:2003:533; [2005] All E.R. (EC) 224; *British Association of Leisure Parks, Piers and Attractions Ltd v Revenue and Customs Commissioners* [2011] UKFTT 622 (TC); *Anglian Water Services Ltd v Revenue and Customs Commissioners* [2018] UKUT 431 (TCC). In *Marks and Spencer Plc v Her Majesty's Commissioners of Customs and Excise* [2009] UKHL 8, [2009] 1 All E.R. 939 the House of Lords, following a decision of the ECJ (Case 309/06 *Marks and Spencer Plc v Commissioners of Customs and Excise*), did not apply the defence in respect of a claim for the recovery of overpaid VAT which was incompatible with EU law, on the ground that its application would have been discriminatory. In *Investment Trust Companies v Revenue and Customs Commissioners* [2017] UKSC 29, [2018] A.C. 275 at [81] Lord Reed characterised this as a statutory defence of passing on.

## (h) Compulsion

### Unlawful or illegitimate compulsion

*Replace paragraph with:*

**29-095** The question of what amounts to unlawful or illegitimate compulsion will depend on the circumstances of the particular case. Although the reported cases deal mainly with issues of duress of goods[622] and extortion *colore officii*,[623] duress of the person is included[624] and other forms of pressure on the person who pays, including economic duress, will be recognised.[625] As a general rule, to constitute duress the pressure must be exerted by a threat to commit an unlawful act,[626] but it has been recognised that a lawful threat can be illegitimate, particularly where it was coupled with prior unlawful conduct,[627] save where the person making the threat believed in good faith that they were entitled to make the threat.[627a] Although, in the absence of legislative guidance,[628] distinguishing legitimate from illegitimate demands is likely to be controversial, the courts may be assisted by drawing on cases of conspiracy where no unlawful means are used,[629] and by having regard to usual trade practice. The coercive force[630] of the compulsion will depend on its immediacy,[631] on the ability of the payer to obtain legal advice or legal protection before making the payment,[632] and, in some circumstances, on the availability of an effective alternative remedy or course of action open to the payer.[633] It was sometimes said that economic duress had to coerce the claimant's will so as to vitiate his consent,[634] but this approach has been criticised and the better view is to ask whether, where pressure has been applied, that pressure went beyond what the law considers legitimate.[635] If the payment amounts to a genuine compromise of a disputed claim honestly made by the payee,[636] or the payment is made in the course of or under threat of legal proceedings,[637] or the transaction is affirmed,[638] it cannot be recovered. Similarly, if the claimant cannot offer the defendant counter-restitution.[639]

[622] Below, para.29-097.

[623] Below, para.29-100.

[624] Below, para.29-096.

[625] e.g. threats of duress to goods will suffice: *Maskell v Horner* [1915] 3 K.B. 106 (see below, para.29-097), as will threats to commit other torts: *Universe Tankships Inc of Monrovia v International Transport Workers Federation* [1983] 1 A.C. 366. Threats to commit a breach of contract can amount to duress, and a payment in excess of the contract price which is made as the result of a coercive threat by the payee to commit a breach of his contractual obligations unless the excess payment is made, may be recovered in a restitutionary claim: see *Pao On v Lau Yiu Long* [1980] A.C. 614; *North Ocean Shipping Co Ltd v Hyundai Construction Co Ltd* [1979] Q.B. 705; *B. & S. Contracts and Design Ltd v Victor Green Publications Ltd* [1984] I.C.R. 419; *The Alev* [1989] 1 Lloyd's Rep. 138; *Atlas Express Ltd v Kafco (Importers and Distributors) Ltd* [1989] Q.B. 833; *C.T.N. Cash and Carry Ltd v Gallagher Ltd* [1994] 4 All E.R. 714 and the Australian cases of *Nixon v Furphy* (1925) 25 S.R. (N.S.W.) 151 and *Sundell & Sons v Emm Yannoulatos (Overseas) Pty Ltd* (1956) 56 S.R. (N.S.W.) 323; cf. *Crescendo Management Pty Ltd v Westpac Banking Corp* (1988) 19 N.S.W.L.R. 40. On economic duress see above, para.8-015; *D. & C. Builders Ltd v Rees* [1966] 2 Q.B. 617 (above, paras 4-134, 8-020).

[626] See *R. v Att-Gen for England and Wales* [2002] UKPC 22.

[627] *Times Travel (UK) Ltd v Pakistan International Airlines Corp* [2019] EWCA Civ 828. See also *Borelli v Ting* [2010] UKPC 21; *Progress Bulk Carriers Ltd v Tube City IMS LCC* [2012] EWHC 273 (Comm), [2012] 1 Lloyd's Rep 501 (Comm) at [42] (Cooke J.); *Universe Tankships Inc of Monrovia v International Transport Workers Federation* [1983] 1 A.C. 366, 384 (Lord Diplock), 401(Lord Scarman); *Dimskal S.S. Co Ltd v ITWF* [1992] 2 A.C. 152; *R v Attorney-General for England and Wales* [2003] UKPC 22 at [113]; *Thorne v Motor Trade Association* [1937] A.C. 797; *Norreys v Zeffert* [1939] 2 All E.R. 186; Burrows at pp.277–282; Goff and Jones at para.10-12. cf. *C.T.N. Cash and Carry Ltd v Gallagher Ltd* [1994] 4 All E.R. 714; *Leyland Daf Ltd v Automotive Products Plc* [1994] 1 B.C.L.R. 244; *Royal Boskalis Westminster NV v Mountain* [1999] Q.B. 674, 730–731.

[627a] *Times Travel (UK) Ltd v Pakistan International Airlines Corp* [2019] EWCA Civ 828.

[628] Such as the Trade Union legislation in the *Universe Tankships* case [1983] 1 A.C. 366, although the threat there was to commit a tort.

[629] *Crofter Hand-Woven Harris Tweed Ltd v Veitch* [1942] A.C. 435; *Sorrell v Smith* [1925] A.C. 700, 712.

[630] *Skeate v Beale* (1841) 11 Ad. & E. 983, 990 ("the fear ... does not deprive anyone of his free agency who possesses that ordinary degree of firmness which the law requires all to exert"). But see *Barton v Armstrong* [1976] A.C. 104.

[631] *Maskell v Horner* [1915] 3 K.B. 106, 118 (Lord Reading C.J.) ("under the compulsion of urgent and pressing necessity"). cf. *Twyford v Manchester Corp* [1946] Ch. 236, and *Somes v British Empire Shipping Co* (1860) 8 H.L. Cas. 338.

[632] *Maskell v Horner* [1915] 3 K.B. 106, 120. See below, para.29-097.

[633] The presence of an alternative remedy has been said to be irrelevant in cases involving detention of the payer's property (*Astley v Reynolds* (1731) 2 Str. 915, below, para.29-098; *Kanhaya Lal v National Bank of India* (1913) 29 T.L.R. 314, 315. cf. *Ashmole v Wainwright* (1842) 2 Q.B. 837, 845) but would appear to be relevant where there is no such detention (*Knibbs v Hall* (1794) Peake 276; *Twyford v Manchester Corp* [1946] Ch. 236, 241–242; *Pao On v Lau Yiu Long* [1980] A.C. 614, 635; *B. & S. Contracts and Design Ltd v Victor Green Publications Ltd* [1984] I.C.R. 419; *The Alev* [1989] 1 Lloyd's Rep. 138, 146–147; *Hennessy v Craigmyle & Co* [1986] I.C.R. 461. cf. *North Ocean Shipping v Hyundai Construction Co Ltd* [1979] Q.B. 705, 715, 719.

[634] *The Siboen and The Sibotre* [1976] 1 Lloyd's Rep. 293, 336; *North Ocean Shipping v Hyundai Construction Co Ltd* [1979] Q.B. 705, 717, 719; *Pao On v Lau Yiu Long* [1980] A.C. 614, 635.

[635] *Universe Tankships Inc of Monrovia v I.T.W.F.* [1983] 1 A.C. 366, 384, 400; *B. & S. Contracts and Design Ltd v Victor Green Publications Ltd* [1984] I.C.R. 419, 426–428; *Dimskal S.S. Co Ltd v I.T.W.F.* [1992] 2 A.C. 152, 165–166.

[636] *Atlee v Backhouse* (1838) 3 M. & W. 633; *Wakefield v Newbon* (1844) 6 Q.B. 276, 281; *Callisher v Bischoffsheim* (1870) L.R. 5 Q.B. 449; *Miles v New Zealand Alford Estate Co* (1885) 32 Q.B.D. 266, 291; *The Siboen and the Sibotre* [1976] 1 Lloyd's Rep. 293, 334. See above, paras 4-053—4-054.

[637] See below, para.29-104.

[638] *North Ocean Shipping Co Ltd v Hyundai Construction Co Ltd* [1979] Q.B. 705, 720–721; *B. & S. Contracts and Design Ltd v Victor Green Publications Ltd* [1984] I.C.R. 419, 428.

[639] See *Halpern v Halpern (Nos 1 and 2)* [2007] EWCA Civ 291, [2008] Q.B. 195.

## Duress of the person

*Replace paragraph with:*

Duress of the person[640] entitles a party to a contract to avoid it[641]; consequently, **29-096** restitution of benefits conferred under the voidable contract will be ordered by the court, following rescission by the innocent party. Even if there has been no contract, benefits conferred on the defendant as the result of duress by him may be recoverable from him by a claim in restitution.[642] The duress will usually amount to a tort and recovery can also be founded on the principles governing restitution for wrongdoing considered below.[643]

[640] Above, para.8-012.

[641] Above, paras 8-056—8-058.

[642] *Singh v Redford* [2018] EWHC 2390 (Ch).

[643] Below, paras 29-147 et seq.

## 3. Restitution for Wrongs

### (a) General Principles

**Disgorgement for wrongs**

*Replace footnote 850 with:*

29-145 [850] Smith (1992) 71 Can. B.R. 672, 696. See also Edelman, *Gain-Based Damages: Contract, Tort, Equity and Intellectual Property* (2002); *Murad v Al-Saraj* [2005] EWCA Civ 1235, [2005] W.T.L.R. 1573 at [108] (Jonathan Parker L.J.); *Atlantic Lottery Corp Inc v Babstock* 2020 SCC 19 at [23] (Brown J.).

**Nature of the obligation to make restitution**

*Replace footnote 858 with:*

29-146 [858] *Macmillan Inc v Bishopsgate Investment Trust Plc (No.3)* [1995] 1 W.L.R. 978, 988 (Millett J.); *Atlantic Lottery Corp Inc v Babstock* 2020 SCC 19 at [23] (Brown J.).

### (b) Tort

**"Waiver of tort"**

*Replace paragraph with:*

29-147 If a person commits a tort and in so doing enriches himself by taking or using the property of another, the latter may, if certain conditions are satisfied, recover the value of that which has been wrongfully taken or used instead of suing for damages for the injury done. The remedies of compensation and restitution are not concurrent and the claimant is compelled to elect which he will pursue.[863] If he elects to seek restitution, he is sometimes said to "waive the tort".[864] Historically, there were a number of advantages of suing for restitution rather than damages,[865] e.g. avoidance of special pleading and of immunity from suit in tort,[866] a different period of limitation, the ability to prove for the claim in the tortfeasor's bankruptcy[867] and circumvention of the rule preventing survival of an action in tort against the estate of a tortfeasor. Some advantages may, however, continue today, such as the avoidance of the necessity to prove the actual loss suffered by the claimant (e.g. the exact value of goods lost through conversion) by claiming instead the sum received by the defendant.[868] Furthermore it may be possible to recover more than the loss sustained by claiming any profit made by the defendant which is attributable to the tort.[869] These last two advantages may, however, be less important than they were in view of the relevance of the defendant's gain in assessing compensatory damages in certain actions in tort.[870]

[863] On election, see below, para.29-153.

[864] This follows Keener, *A Treatise on the Law of Quasi-Contracts* (1893), p.159. The principle is fully discussed by the House of Lords in *United Australia Ltd v Barclays Bank Ltd* [1941] A.C. 1. The doctrine of "waiver of tort" was rejected by the Supreme Court of Canada in *Atlantic Lottery Corp Inc v Babstock* 2020 SCC 19, as being a misnomer and apt to cause confusion. Crucially, the tort is not waived but constitutes the cause of action; waiver of tort is not a cause of action in its own right.

[865] Winfield, *Province of the Law of Tort* (1931), pp.143–146.

[866] e.g. the Crown's immunity before the Crown Proceedings Act 1947. See Williams, *Crown Proceedings* (1948), pp.11–13.

[867] See Law Reform (Miscellaneous Provisions) Act 1934 which was applied in *Chesworth v Farrar* [1967] 1 Q.B. 407. For the present position see, Insolvency Act 1986 s.382 and Insolvency Rules 1986 (SI 1986/1925) rr.13.1, 13.12.

[868] *King v Leith* (1787) 2 Term Rep. 141, 145; *Parker v Norton* (1796) 6 T.R. 695, 700; *Feltham v Terry* (1772) Lofft. 207, 208. This sum may exceed what could be recovered by claiming damages for loss suffered: *Bavins and Sims v London and South Western Bank Ltd* [1900] 1 Q.B. 270. See Marshall Evans (1966) 82 L.Q.R. 167–169.

[869] See below, para.29-152.

[870] See below, paras 29-151—29-152.

### Torts which may give rise to a restitutionary claim

*Replace footnote 882 with:*

[882] *Lightly v Clouston* (1808) 1 Taunt. 112; *Foster v Stewart* (1814) 3 M. & S. 191 (see the discussion of these cases in Winfield, *Quasi-Contracts* (1952), pp.98–99); *Blizzard Entertainments SAS v Bossland GmbH* [2019] EWHC 1665 (Ch). **29-148**

## (c) Breach of Contract

### Account of profits

*Replace paragraph with:*

It was held *in Att-Gen v Blake*[949] that, in an exceptional case, where compensatory damages, specific enforcement and injunctions are inadequate remedies for a breach of contract or are not available, the court can require the defendant to account to the claimant for benefits received from a breach of contract, even where the breach does not involve the use of or interference with the claimant's property: **29-159**

> "The law recognises that a party to a contract may have an interest in performance which is not readily measurable in terms of money. On breach the innocent party suffers a loss. He fails to obtain the benefit promised by the other party to the contract. To him the loss may be as important as financially measurable loss, or more so. An award of damages, assessed by reference to financial loss, will not recompense him properly. For him a financially assessed measure of damages is inadequate."[950]

In determining whether to order an account of profits, the court will have regard to all the circumstances, including the subject matter of the contract, the purpose of the contractual provision which has been breached, the circumstances in which the breach occurred, the consequences of the breach and the circumstances in which relief is being sought. Lord Nicholls of Birkenhead (with whom Lord Goff and Lord Browne-Wilkinson agreed) stated that:

> "... a useful general guide, although not exhaustive, is whether the plaintiff had a legitimate interest in preventing the defendant's profit-making activities and, hence, in depriving him of his profit."[951]

The Crown was held to have such an interest in preventing a former member of the intelligence services who had undertaken not to divulge any official information gained as a result of his employment from profiting from breaches of the undertaking in an autobiography. He was therefore not entitled to receive the royalties which had been held by his publishers.

949 [2001] 1 A.C. 268. Disgorgement for breach of contract has also been recognised as an exceptional remedy in Canada: *Atlantic Lottery Corp Inc v Babstock* 2020 SCC 19.

950 *Att-Gen v Blake* [2001] 1 A.C. 268, 282 (Lord Nicholls). See also above, para.26-063. Lord Hobhouse dissented on the ground (at 298) that an account of profits, a remedy based on property rights, should not be given where the necessary property rights are absent. cf. *Hospitality Group Pty Ltd v Australian Rugby Football Union Ltd* [2001] FCA 1040 (in Australia loss recoverable for breach of contract is limited to compensation); Campbell and Harris (2002) 22 L.S. 308; Campbell (2002) 65 M.L.R. 256.

951 [2001] 1 A.C. 268, 285. See also Lord Steyn at 292 (defendant's position closely analogous to that of a fiduciary); *Atlantic Lottery Corp Inc v Babstock* 2020 SCC 19 at [53] (Brown J.).

### Negotiating damages

*Replace footnote 973 with:*

**29-162** 973 [2018] UKSC 20, [2018] 2 W.L.R. 1353; Burrows (2018) 134 L.Q.R. 515; Day [2018] R.L.R. 60; Bartscherer (2019) M.L.R. 367. See also *Turf Club Auto Emporium Pty Ltd v Yeo Boong Hua* [2018] SGCA 44, although the conditions for the award of such damages in Singapore are different; Yip and See (2019) 135 L.Q.R. 36.

## (d) Equitable Wrongdoing

### Types of equitable wrongdoing

*Replace paragraph with:*

**29-163** Restitutionary remedies are available for a number of equitable wrongs, including actions for breach of fiduciary duty[974] and breach of confidence.[975] A fiduciary who has profited from his breach of duty will be liable to account for all the profits made, even if they would have been made had the defendant not breached his fiduciary duty.[976] A fiduciary who has received contractually agreed remuneration will not be liable to account for that profit despite a breach of fiduciary duty, since the remuneration was not an unauthorised benefit,[976a] save if the breach of fiduciary duty is characterised as serious by going to the root of the contract, such as where the breach arose from the start of the contract.[976b] Forfeiture of remuneration is not restitutionary but operates to punish the fiduciary for a serious breach of duty.[976c]

974 *Regal (Hastings) Ltd v Gulliver* [1967] 2 A.C. 134n; *Boardman v Phipps* [1967] 2 A.C. 46; *Crown Dilmun, Dilmun Investments Ltd v Nicholas Sutton, Fulham River* [2004] EWHC 52 (Ch), [2004] 1 B.C.L.C. 468; *Re Quarter Master UK Ltd* Unreported July 15, 2004 (Paul Morgan Q.C.); *Murad v Al-Saraj* [2005] EWCA Civ 1235, [2005] W.T.L.R. 1573. See generally Conaglen, *Fiduciary Loyalty* (2010).

975 *Peter Pan Manufacturing Corp v Corsets Silhouette Ltd* [1964] 1 W.L.R. 96; *Att-Gen v Guardian Newspapers Ltd (No.2)* [1990] 1 A.C. 109. See also Jones (1970) 86 L.Q.R. 463. In *LAC Minerals Ltd v International Cornoa Resources Ltd* (1989) 61 D.L.R. (4th) 14 profits were held on constructive trust. As to whether the remedy of account of profits or reasonable damages for release of an obligation of confidence should be awarded, see *Vercoe v Rutland Fund Management Ltd* [2010] EWHC 424 (Ch) at [340]–[343] (Sales J.); *Force India Formula One Team Ltd v 1 Malaysia Racing Team Sdn Bhd* [2012] EWHC 616 (Ch); *Walsh v Shanahan* [2013] EWCA Civ 411 at [63] (Rimer L.J.) (a matter of judicial discretion).

976 *Murad v Al-Saraj* [2005] EWCA Civ 1235, [2005] W.T.L.R. 1573. See also *Novoship (UK) Ltd v Nikitin* [2014] EWCA Civ 908, [2015] Q.B. 499 at [96] (Longmore L.J.). Whether a fiduciary will be liable to account for a profit made from his position is not dependent on whether the principal had been damaged or benefited from the breach of duty: *Akita Holdings Ltd v Honourable Attorney-General of*

*the Turks and Caicos Islands* [2017] UKPC 7, [2017] A.C. 590; *Parr v Keystone Healthcare Ltd* [2019] EWCA Civ 1246, [2019] 4 W.L.R. 99.

[976a] *HPOR Servicos De Concultoria Ltda v Dryships Inc* [2018] EWHC 3451 (Comm), [2019] 1 Lloyd's Rep. 260.

[976b] *Imageview Management Ltd v Jackson* [2009] EWCA Civ 63, [2009] 2 All E.R. 666; *HPOR Servicos De Concultoria Ltda v Dryships Inc* [2018] EWHC 3451 (Comm), [2019] 1 Lloyd's Rep. 260.

[976c] *HPOR Servicos De Concultoria Ltda v Dryships Inc* [2018] EWHC 3451 (Comm), [2019] 1 Lloyd's Rep. 260 at [110] and [114] (Cockerill J.).

### Receipt of a bribe, secret profit or commission

*Replace footnote 984 with:*

[984] [2014] UKSC 45, [2015] A.C. 250. See also *Crown Prosecution Service v Aquila Advisory Ltd* [2019] EWCA Civ 588. **29-164**

## 4. Proprietary Restitutionary Claims

## (a) Establishing Proprietary Rights

### Defendant's acquiescence in improvements to his land

*Replace footnote 1021 with:*

[1021] *Inwards v Baker* [1965] 2 Q.B. 29; *Chalmers v Pardoe* [1963] 1 W.L.R. 677; *Ward v Kirkland* [1966] 1 W.L.R. 601, 626–632; *Lee-Parker v Izzet* [1972] 1 W.L.R. 775, 780–781. cf. *E.R. Ives Investment Ltd v High* [1967] 2 Q.B. 379; *Siew Soon Wah v Yong Tong Hong* [1973] A.C. 836; *Dodsworth v Dodsworth* [1973] E.G. 233; *Crabb v Arun DC* [1976] Ch. 179 (one landowner encouraged the adjoining owner to act to his prejudice in the belief he would be given a right of way); *Jones v Jones* [1977] 1 W.L.R. 438; *Pascoe v Turner* [1979] 1 W.L.R. 431; *Grant v Edwards* [1986] Ch. 638; *Gillett v Holt* [2001] Ch. 210; *Cobbe v Yeoman's Row Management Ltd* [2008] UKHL 55, [2008] 1 W.L.R. 1752; *Thorner v Majors* [2009] UKHL 18, [2009] 1 W.L.R. 776. For earlier authorities, see *Dillwyn v Llewelyn* (1862) 4 De G.F. & J. 517; *Ramsden v Dyson* (1866) L.R. 1 H.L. 129; *Willmot v Barber* (1880) 15 Ch. D. 96; *Plimmer v Mayor of Wellington* (1884) 9 App. Cas. 699. See also Allan (1963) 79 L.Q.R. 238; *Van den Berg v Giles* [1979] 2 N.Z.L.R. 111. cf. above, paras 4-141 et seq. **29-169**

## (b) Following and Tracing

### Withdrawals from a mixed fund in a bank account

*Replace footnote 1070 with:*

[1070] *Barlow Clowes (International) Ltd v Vaughan* [1992] 4 All E.R. 22, 42, 44. Where, however, it can be shown that money in which a beneficiary has an interest has been withdrawn from an account and money in which a different beneficiary has an interest is subsequently deposited to the account, the "lowest intermediate balance" rule will apply such that the claim of the first beneficiary will be rateably reduced: *James Roscoe (Bolton) Ltd v Winder* [1915] 1 Ch. 62; *Caron v Jahani* [2020] NSWCA 117. **29-175**

## (c) Proprietary Restitutionary Claims

### Subrogation

*Replace footnote 1101 with:*

[1101] *Bank of Cyprus UK Ltd v Menelaou* [2015] UKSC 66, [2016] A.C. 176; *Lowick Rose LLP v Swynson Ltd* [2017] UKSC 32, [2018] A.C. 313. See also *Banque Financière de la Cité SA v Parc (Battersea) Ltd* [1999] 1 A.C. 221, where the claimant sought a personal remedy against a third party by means of subrogation; *Cheltenham & Gloucester Plc v Appleyard* [2004] EWCA Civ 291; *Anfield (UK) Ltd v Bank of Scotland* [2010] EWHC 2374 (Ch), [2011] 1 W.L.R. 2414 at [10] (Proudman J.); *Sandher v Pearson* [2013] EWCA Civ 1822; *Re Beppler & Jacobson Ltd* [2016] EWHC 20 (Ch) at [122] (Hildyard J.). In *Niru Battery Manufacturing Co v Milestone Trading Ltd (No.2)* [2004] EWCA Civ 487, [2004] 2 All E.R. (Comm) 289, the remedy of subrogation was ordered to prevent the defendant's unjust enrichment arising from the discharge of a liability owed by the defendant. It is unclear, however, why this **29-180** remedy was sought or obtained since the claimant had a direct restitutionary claim to recover the value of the benefit obtained by the defendant and did not need to step into the shoes of any other party to bring such a claim. The High Court of Australia rejected unjust enrichment as the doctrinal foundation of subrogation in Australia: *Bofinger v Kingsway Group Ltd* [2009] H.C.A. 44; Ridge (2010) 126 L.Q.R. 188. In *Prudential Assurance Co Ltd v Revenue and Customs Commissioners* [2018] UKSC 39, [2019] A.C. 929 at [68] the Supreme Court recognised that the award of subrogation might be based on a different principle to that of unjust enrichment. See generally Gregson (2020) 136 L.Q.R. 481.

## Personal restitutionary remedies

*Replace paragraph with:*

**29-181** Where the defendant has received property in which the claimant had an equitable proprietary interest, but the defendant no longer has that property or its traceable substitute, the claimant may sue the defendant in the action for unconscionable receipt.[1135] The remedy which is awarded, namely the value of the property received, will be restitutionary. Alternatively, the defendant may be liable for dishonestly assisting a breach of trust or fiduciary duty,[1136] but the remedy will typically be compensatory since it is usually assessed with reference to the claimant's loss rather than the defendant's gain.[1137] It has, however, been recognised that it will be possible to award an account of profits where the defendant who assisted or encouraged a breach of trust or fiduciary duty profited from the assistance or encouragement.[1138] It has also been recognised that a defendant will be liable to account for the value of property transferred in breach of fiduciary duty even though the defendant did not obtain the profits personally, at least where the property was transferred to a third party at the direction of the defendant who retained control of the property once received by the third party.[1139] Similarly, where the defendant has received property in which the claimant has a legal proprietary interest, but the defendant has not retained that property or its traceable substitute, the claimant can recover the value of the property[1140] or, as regards a personal claim to vindicate legal proprietary rights in a chose in action or other intangible property, in an action for the value of the property.[1141]

[1135] *Bank of Credit and Commerce International (Overseas) Ltd v Akindele* [2001] Ch. 437; *Papamichael v National Westminster Bank* [2003] 1 Lloyd's Rep. 341, 375: requiring proof of actual knowledge of the circumstances of the misapplication. cf. *Farah Construction Pty Ltd v Say-Dee Pty Ltd* [2007] HCA 22; Ridge and Dietrich (2008) 124 L.Q.R. 26. See also *Criterion Properties Plc v Stratford UK Properties LLC* [2003] 1 W.L.R. 2108 (need to have regard to the defendant's actions and knowledge in the context of the commercial relationship as a whole to determine whether the test of unconscionability was satisfied; the House of Lords concluded that the case was not concerned with the question of unconscionability but whether directors had authority to sign an agreement: [2004] UKHL 28, [2004] 1 W.L.R. 1846). On the interpretation of the test of unconscionability see also *Crown Dilmun, Dilmun Investments Ltd v Nicholas Sutton, Fulham River* [2004] EWHC 52 (Ch), [2004] 1 B.C.L.C. 468 at [200] (Peter Smith J.); *It's a Wrap (UK) Ltd v Gula* [2006] EWCA Civ 544, [2006] B.C.C. 626; *Armstrong DLW GmbH v Winnington Networks Ltd* [2012] EWHC 10 (Ch), [2013] Ch. 156 at [132] (same test as for bad faith for change of position: see below, para.29-191). A person who receives property in their capacity as an agent will not be liable for unconscionable receipt: *Uzinterimpex JSC v Standard Bank Plc* [2008] EWCA Civ 819. The remedy is not proprietary because it involves only a personal liability to account or to compensate and so has nothing to do with the constructive trust: *Williams v Central Bank of Nigeria* [2014] UKSC 10, [2014] A.C. 1189; *Watson v Kea Investments Ltd* [2019] EWCA Civ 1759, [2019] 4 W.L.R. 145 at [40] (McCombe L.J.) (liable to account as if a formal trustee and in default). In *Fistar v Riverwood Legion and Community Club Ltd* [2016] NSWCA 81 the New South Wales Court of Appeal recognised that a strict liability claim in unjust enrichment for money had and received relating to stolen money lay even though the claimant alternatively had a claim in unconscionable receipt which required proof of fault.

[1136] *Royal Brunei Airlines Sdn Bhd v Tan* [1995] 2 A.C. 378 (objective test of dishonesty: at 389 (Lord Nicholls)); *Twinsectra Ltd v Yardley* [2002] UKHL 12, [2002] 2 A.C. 164 (knowledge of circumstances of dishonesty required: at [20] (Lord Hoffmann) and at [35] (Lord Hutton)). Now see *Barlow Clowes International Ltd v Eurotrust International Ltd* [2005] UKPC 37, [2006] 1 W.L.R. 1476 (objective test of dishonesty). See also *Abou-Rahmah v Abacha* [2006] EWCA Civ 1492, [2007] 1 Lloyd's Rep. 115

and Virgo [2007] C.L.J. 22; *Starglade Properties Ltd v Nash* [2010] EWCA Civ 1314 at [32]; *Fiona Trust & Holding Corp v Privalov* [2010] EWHC 3199 (Comm) at [1437] (Andrew Smith J.).

1137 *Sinclair Investment Holdings SA v Versailles Trade Finance Ltd* [2007] EWHC 915 (Ch), [2007] 2 All E.R. (Comm) 993 at [101] (Rimer J.).

1138 *Ultraframe (UK) Ltd v Fielding* [2005] EWHC 1638 (Ch) at [1600] (Lewison J.); *Fiona Trust & Holding Corp v Privalov* [2010] EWHC 3199 (Comm) at [66] (Andrew Smith J.); *Novoship (UK) Ltd v Nikitin* [2014] EWCA Civ 908, [2015] Q.B. 499 (but only where the assistance was a real or effective cause of the profits). Cf. *Ancient Order of Foresters in Victoria Friendly Society Ltd v Lifeplan Australia Friendly Society* [2018] HCA 43, where the but for test of causation was adopted by the High Court of Australia and the defendant was held liable to account for its entire profit arising from a joint venture.

1139 *Fiona Trust & Holding Corp v Privalov* [2010] EWHC 3199 (Comm) [2010] EWHC 3199 (Comm) at [1540] (Andrew Smith J.). cf. *Ultraframe (UK) Ltd v Fielding* [2005] EWHC 1638 (Ch) at [1600] (Lewison J.).

1140 *Lipkin Gorman (A Firm) v Karpnale Ltd* [1991] 2 A.C. 548. Although the House of Lords analysed this claim with reference to the unjust enrichment principle, following the decision of the same court in *Foskett v McKeown* [2001] A.C. 102, it is better analysed with reference to the vindication of property rights principle. See Virgo in Getzler (ed.), *Rationalizing Property, Equity and Trusts: Essays in Honour of Edward Burn* (2003), p.104; *OEM Plc v Schneider* [2005] EWHC 1072 (Ch). This analysis was approved by Stephen Morris Q.C. in *Armstrong DLW GmbH v Winnington Networks Ltd* [2012] EWHC 10 (Ch), [2013] Ch. 156 at [75].

1141 *Armstrong DLW GmbH v Winnington Networks Ltd* [2012] EWHC 10 (Ch), [2013] Ch. 156 at [88] (Stephen Morris Q.C.). A claim in conversion is not available in respect of intangible property. cf. *OBG Ltd v Allan* [2007] UKHL 21, [2008] 1 A.C. 1.

## 5. DEFENCES

## (b) Change of Position

### Change of position as a separate defence

*Replace paragraph with:*

In *Lipkin Gorman v Karpnale Ltd*[1174] the House of Lords recognised a broad defence of change of position. This was said to be: **29-186**

> "... available to a person whose position has so changed that it would be inequitable in all the circumstances to require him to make restitution, or alternatively to make restitution in full."[1175]

The defence is said to be one of the general principles of the law of restitution[1176] and, even before the decision of the House of Lords, its supposed existence was used as a justification for widening the scope of recovery for mistake.[1177] Change of position is a wider defence than estoppel because it does not depend on breach of duty or misrepresentation by the payee. In one respect, however, it is narrower than estoppel in not recognising expenditure on everyday expenses.[1178] The broad formulation was explicitly chosen by the House of Lords to allow for the development of the defence on a case by case basis.[1179] In *Commerzbank AG v Gareth Price-Jones*[1180] Mummery L.J. recognised that "the decided cases steer a cautious course, aiming to avoid the dangers of a diffuse discretion and the restrictions of rigid rules". Munby J. stated that the defence was "intended to be a broadly stated concept of practical justice" and that "technicality and black letter law are to be avoided".[1181] Where the basis of a claim is the unjust enrichment of the defendant then in principle the defence should be based on the extent of the defendant's enrichment and should apply to the extent that the enrichment has been erased.[1182] In the context of mistake, as the ground of recovery is wide and does not bar recovery by a negligent payer,[1183] it is particularly important to accept a broad defence. Moreover, although the evidential burden is on the defendant to establish the defence, it has been said that the court should beware of applying too strict a standard because it may be unrealistic to expect a defendant to produce conclusive evidence of a change of position, given that when he changed his position he can have had no expectation that he might thereafter have to prove that he did so and the reason why he did so.[1184] It appears that the defence will not apply where the restitutionary claim is founded on the vindication of the claimant's property rights rather than unjust enrichment, at least where the claimant seeks a proprietary remedy.[1185] The defence will also not be available to restitutionary claims brought by a liquidator to recover payments characterised as voidable preferences by statute, because the common law gives priority to the operation of the statutory scheme of distribution for the benefit of the creditors as a class over the detrimental impact which recovery might have upon the creditor against whom the claim for restitution is made.[1185a]

[1174] [1991] 2 A.C. 548.

[1175] *Lipkin Gorman v Karpnale Ltd* [1991] 2 A.C. 548, 580 (Lord Goff). See also at 558 and 568. This case departed from the previous position on which see e.g. *Durrant v Ecclesiastical Commissioners* (1880) 6 Q.B.D. 234; *Larner v L.C.C.* [1949] 2 K.B. 683, 688–689; *Baylis v Bishop of London* [1913] Ch. 127; *Re Diplock* [1948] Ch. 465, 476; affirmed sub nom. *Minister of Health v Simpson* [1951] A.C. 251, 276. See also New Zealand Judicature Amendment Act 1958 s.94B.

[1176] *R. v Tower Hamlets LBC Ex p. Chetnik Developments Ltd* [1988] A.C. 858. However, in *Skandinaviska Enskilda Banken AB v Conway* [2019] UKPC 36, [2019] 3 W.L.R. 493 at [95] the Privy Council noted that the defence was not necessarily available in all cases of restitution.

[1177] *Barclays Bank Ltd v W. & J. Simms, Son and Cooke (Southern) Ltd* [1980] Q.B. 677, above, para.29-036; *Rover International Ltd v Cannon Film Sales Ltd (No.3)* [1989] 1 W.L.R. 912; *Midland Bank Plc v Brown Shipley & Co Ltd* [1991] 2 All E.R. 690, 701–702; *Rural Municipality of Storthoaks v Mobil Oil Canada Ltd* [1975] 55 D.L.R. (3d) 1; *David Securities Pty Ltd v Commonwealth of Australia* [1992] 66 A.L.J.R. 768. See also *Scottish Equitable Plc v Derby* [2001] 3 All E.R. 818. cf. Birks and Swadling [1999] All E.R. 319–320. See further McInnes (2002) 118 L.Q.R. 209.

[1178] *Lipkin Gorman v Karpnale* [1991] 2 A.C. 548, 559–560, 580 (Lord Goff); *National Westminster Bank Plc v Somer* [2002] 1 All E.R. 198, 213 (Potter L.J.); *Barros Mattos Jnr v McDaniels Ltd* [2004] EWHC 1188 (Ch), [2005] 1 W.L.R. 247 at [16] (Laddie J.).

[1179] See, e.g. *Dextra Bank & Trust Co Ltd v Bank of Jamaica* [2002] 1 All E.R. (Comm) 193, PC.

[1180] [2003] EWCA Civ 1663, [2004] 1 P. & C.R. DG15 at [32].

[1181] *Commerzbank AG v Gareth Prices-Jones* [2003] EWCA Civ 1663 at [48]. See also *Scottish Equitable Plc v Derby* [2001] EWCA Civ 369, [2001] 3 All E.R. 818 at [26], [34] (Robert Walker L.J.); *Niru Battery Manufacturing Co v Milestone Trading Ltd* [2002] EWHC (Comm) 1425, [2002] 2 All E.R. (Comm) 705, 743 (Moore-Bick J.).

[1182] So the defence is not available where money received is used to discharge a debt, since the defendant will remain enriched by the discharge of the debt: *Scottish Equitable Plc v Derby* [2001] EWCA Civ 369, [2001] 3 All E.R. 818 at [35] (Robert Walker L.J.); *National Bank of Egypt International Ltd v Oman Housing Bank SAOC* [2002] EWHC 1760 (Comm), [2003] 1 All E.R. (Comm) 246; *Wards Solicitors v Hendawi* [2018] EWHC 1907 (Ch) at [31] (even if the substitute creditor would not give the defendant debtor such an easy time, this being one of the "vicissitudes of life") (H.H.J. Paul Matthews).

[1183] See above, para.29-039.

[1184] *Phillip Collins Ltd v Davis and Satterfield* [2000] 3 All E.R. 808. See also *Scottish Equitable Plc v Derby* [2001] EWCA Civ 369, [2001] 3 All E.R. 818; *National Westminster Bank Plc v Somer* [2001] EWCA Civ 970, [2002] 1 All E.R. 198, 215 (Potter L.J.).

[1185] *Foskett v McKeown* [2001] 1 A.C. 102, 129 (Lord Millett); *Papamichael v National Westminster Bank* [2003] 1 Lloyd's Rep. 341, 376 (Judge Chambers Q.C.); *Armstrong DLW GmbH v Winnington Networks Ltd* [2012] EWHC 10 (Ch), [2013] Ch. 156, [99]–[103] (Stephen Morris Q.C.); *Test Claimants in the FII Group Litigation v HMRC (No.2)* [2014] EWHC 4302 (Ch), [2015] S.T.I. 49 at [348] (Henderson J.). See above, para.29-174.

[1185a] *Skandinaviska Enskilda Banken AB v Conway* [2019] UKPC 36, [2019] 3 W.L.R. 493.

## Key requirements of change position

*Replace list with:*

(1) There must be a causative link between the receipt of the benefit by the defendant and his or her change of position, so that, but for the receipt of the benefit,[1186] the defendant's position would not have changed, either because the defendant no longer has the benefit received[1186a] or because the defendant, in reliance on the receipt of the benefit, has changed his position in some other way. **29-187**

(2) The defendant's position must have changed in circumstances which make it inequitable for him or her to make restitution to the claimant. Specific principles can be identified to assist in the determination of what is equitable for these purposes.

[1186] *Test Claimants in the FII Group Litigation v HMRC (No 2)* [2014] EWHC 4302 (Ch), [2015] S.T.I. 49 at [343] (Henderson J.); *Wards Solicitors v Hendawi* [2018] EWHC 1907 (Ch) at [33] (H.H.J. Paul Matthews). See also *Dexia Crediop SpA v Comune di Prato* [2016] EWHC 2824 (Comm) at [75], where it followed from the recognition of the but-for test of causation that the defence would not be applicable if the defendant would have incurred the expenditure in the ordinary course of events.

[1186a] So that detrimental reliance need not be established: *Wards Solicitors v Hendawi* [2018] EWHC 1907 (Ch) at [33] (H.H.J. Matthews).

## Illustrations of change of position

*Replace paragraph with:*

The mere fact of having spent money or delivered property does not suffice to establish the defence.[1187] The paradigm case of change of position is where the payee has detrimentally relied on a payment made to him which he has received in good faith.[1188] For instance, where the recipient of a mistaken payment, acting in good faith, pays the money or part of it to charity or makes a purchase which he would not have made but for the payment, it is unjust to require him to make restitution to the extent that he has so changed his position.[1189] Thus, on the facts of *Lipkin Gorman v Karpnale Ltd*, where a person who had stolen money used it to gamble, the gaming club was not required to repay the entire amount gambled but only their net winnings from the thief.[1190] In these cases the loss ought to lie where it falls, on the payer who has initiated the loss-causing event, at least where neither party is at fault. But if the payee has used the money to cover expenses which would have been incurred even if he had never received the payment in question, the defence will not be established.[1191] If the defendant has incurred expense in repaying money to the claimant, such as bank fee, this can constitute a relevant change of position.[1191a] In *Australian Financial Services and Leasing Pty Ltd v Hills Industries Ltd*[1192] the High Court of Australia recognised that the defence was available where the defendant had relied on the receipt of money and suffered an irreversible detriment, which was established in that case where the defendant had decided not to pursue claims against the claimant following the receipt of a mistaken payment. Irreversible detriment by itself is not, however, sufficient to establish the defence, since it must also be shown, at least in England and Wales, that but for the receipt of the enrichment the detriment would not have occurred.[1193] With regard to situations where the recipient has altered his position in "anticipatory reliance" on a payment, the Privy Council[1194] has held, obiter, that the defence of change of position is in principle available and confined cases of reliance on void contracts, where the defence failed, to their exceptional facts[1195]; this was subsequently applied by the High Court.[1196] The defence is founded on a principle of justice designed to protect **29-188** the defendant from a claim to restitution in respect of a benefit received by him in circumstances in which it would be inequitable to pursue that claim, or to pursue it in full. Since an unjust enrichment claim can only be established if the expected payment has in any event been received by the defendant, giving effect to "anticipatory reliance" in that context will indeed operate to protect the security of an actual receipt.[1197] The change of position must, on the evidence, be referable in some way to the payment of the money.[1198] It has been suggested that payment of redemption proceeds without the protection of an effective indemnity could constitute a relevant change of position.[1198a]

[1187] *Rover International Ltd v Cannon Films Sales Ltd (No.3)* [1989] 1 W.L.R. 912. See also *United Overseas Bank v Jiwani* [1976] 1 W.L.R. 964, 968–969.

[1188] This is the only interpretation of the test in Australia: *David Securities Commonwealth Bank of Australia* (1992) 175 C.L.R. 353, 385; *State Bank of New South Wales Ltd v Swiss Bank Corp* (1995) 39 N.S.W.L.R. 350, 356–7; *Citigroup v National* [2012] NSWCA 381, 82 NSWLR 391 at [5]–[6] (Bathurst C.J., Allsop P. and Meagher J.A.) at [64]–[65] (Barrett J.A.); *Australian Financial Services and Leasing Pty Ltd v Hills Industries Ltd* [2014] HCA 14, [25] (French C.J.), [81], [88] (Hayne, Crennan, Kiefel, Bell and Keane JJ.).

[1189] *Lipkin Gorman v Karpnale* [1991] 2 A.C. 548, 559 (Lord Bridge), 579 (Lord Goff). Where the item purchased has a second-hand value there is unjust enrichment to the extent of the second-hand value of that item, but where, for example, the money is spent on a holiday which leaves no by-product, the enrichment is erased by the change of position.

[1190] *Lipkin Gorman v Karpnale* [1991] 2 A.C. 548, 559, 579–580 (Lord Goff). For the reason why the provision of gaming services was not regarded as good consideration see above, para.29-080.

[1191] *R.B.C. Dominion Securities Inc v Dawson* [1994] 111 D.L.R. (4th) 230.

[1191a] *Wards Solicitors v Hendawi* [2018] EWHC 1907 (Ch) at [36] (H.H.J. Paul Matthews).

[1192] [2014] HCA 14.

[1193] *Test Claimants in the FII Group Litigation v HMRC (No.2)* [2014] EWHC 4302 (Ch), [2015] S.T.I. 49 at [354] (Henderson J.).

[1194] *Dextra Bank & Trust Co Ltd v Bank of Jamaica* [2002] 1 All E.R. (Comm) 193 at [39]. The Court of Appeal expressly recognised that an anticipatory change of position is a good defence in *Commerzbank AG v Gareth Price-Jones* [2003] EWCA Civ 1663, [2004] 1 P. & C.R. DG15 at [38] (Mummery L.J.) and [64] (Munby J.).

[1195] *South Tyneside MBC v Svenska International Plc* [1995] 1 All E.R. 545; *Barber v N.W.S. Bank* [1996] 1 W.L.R. 641; *State Bank of N.S.W. Ltd v Swiss Bank Corp* [1997] 6 Bank. L.R. 34. Nolan in Birks (ed.), *Laundering and Tracing* (1995), Ch.6.

[1196] *Charles Terence Estates Ltd v Cornwall County Council* [2011] EWHC 2542 (QB), [2012] 1 P. & C.R. 2 at [98] (Cranston J.). See also *Skandinaviska Enskilda Banken AB (Publ), Singapore Branch v Asia Pacific Breweries (Singapore) Pte Ltd* [2011] SGCA 22, [2011] 3 S.L.R. 540.

[1197] *Dextra Bank & Trust Co Ltd v Bank of Jamaica* [2002] 1 All E.R. (Comm) 193 at [39]. In *Jeremy D Stone Consultants Ltd v National Westminster Bank* [2013] EWHC 208 (Ch) Sales J. (at [251]) recognised that commission of a strict liability regulatory failure was insufficiently grave to debar a defendant from relying on the defence.

[1198] *Phillip Collins Ltd v Davis and Satterfield* [2000] 3 All E.R. 808. See also *Scottish Equitable Plc v Derby* [2001] EWCA Civ 369, [2001] 3 All E.R. 818.

[1198a] *Skandinaviska Enskilda Banken AB v Conway* [2019] UKPC 36, [2019] 3 W.L.R. 493 at [119].

### Link between receipt and specific expenditure unnecessary

*Replace footnote 1206 with:*

**29-189** [1206] *Mistakes of Law and Ultra Vires Public Authority Receipts and Payments* (Cm.2731) (Law Com. No.227, 1994), para.2.21; Burrows at p.529; Virgo at pp.683–686. cf. Birks [1991] L.M.C.L.Q. 473; Birks, *Restitution—The Future* (1991), pp.141–143. In *Skandinaviska Enskilda Banken AB v Conway* [2019] UKPC 36, [2019] 3 W.L.R. 493 at [120] it was recognised that the change of position need not be voluntary.

### Non-pecuniary change of position

*Replace footnote 1207 with:*

**29-190** [1207] [2003] EWCA Civ 1663, [2004] 1 P. & C.R. DG15 at [39], [40], [43] (Mummery L.J.) and [59]

(Munby J.). In *Alfred Street Properties Ltd v National Asset Management Agency* [2020] EWHC 397 (Comm) at [120], Phillips L.J. recognised that the loss of an opportunity to set-off monies against a debt could constitute a change of position.

## Bad faith

*Replace footnote 1210 with:*

[1210] See, in the context of the action for dishonest assistance in a breach of trust, *Group Seven Ltd v Notable Services Ltd* [2019] EWCA Civ 614, [2020] Ch. 129 (objective test of dishonesty in the light of the facts known by the defendant, following the criminal law definition of dishonesty in *Ivey v Genting Casinos (UK) Ltd* [2017] UKSC 67, [2018] A.C. 391). **29-191**

CHAPTER 30

# CONFLICT OF LAWS



## 1. PRELIMINARY CONSIDERATIONS

*Change title of paragraph:* **30-005**

**United Kingdom's exit from the EU ("Brexit")**

*Replace paragraph with:*

As noted above,[11] the future legal relationship of the UK to the EU remains to be determined. In the absence of any arrangements which include the UK remaining bound by EU law, the impact on conflict of laws is potentially very significant. Key European private international law instruments, notably the Brussels I Regulation (recast) (which governs jurisdiction in European cases) and the Rome II **30-005**

Regulation (which governs choice of law in non-contractual cases) would cease to have effect. Most significantly for the purposes of this chapter, the Rome I Regulation, which applies to all contracts entered into on or after December 17, 2009, and whose rules form the main subject matter of this chapter, would no longer be directly effective EU law. The UK ceased being a Member State of the European Union on January 31, 2020 ("exit day"). However, under the terms of the UK EU Withdrawal Agreement (ratified and implemented into national law by the European Union (Withdrawal Agreement) Act 2020) there is an "implementation period" during which although the UK is no longer a Member State of the EU, it remains subject to EU rules, including the Rome I Regulation. Unless extended, the implementation period ("IP") will end on December 31, 2020. If no other agreement is made by "IP completion day", the Rome I Regulation will become part of retained EU law.[12]

[11] See above, paras 1-014—1-018.

[12] See above, para.1-015A. From an early stage after the referendum, the UK Government has made it clear that the Rome I and Rome II Regulations will form part of retained EU law. On March 29, 2019, the government enacted the Law Applicable to Contractual Obligations and Non-Contractual Obligations (Amendment etc.) (EU Exit) Regulations 2019 (SI 2019/834) (under powers granted by the European Union (Withdrawal) Act 2018 s.8). This Regulation will incorporate the provisions of the Rome I and Rome II Regulations into domestic law with only minor or consequential amendments necessary to prevent, remedy or mitigate any failure of retained EU law to operate effectively or any other deficiency of retained EU law, arising from the withdrawal of the UK from the EU.

## 3. THE ROME I REGULATION

**30-018** *Replace footnote 96 with:*

[96] See for discussion, *Dicey, Morris and Collins*, 15th edn (2012), Chs 32 and 33; Fentiman, *International Commercial Litigation*, 2nd edn (2015), Chs 4–6; Plender and Wilderspin, *The Private International Law of Obligations*, 5th edn (2020), Chs 4–15; Cheshire, North and Fawcett, *Private International Law*, 15th edn (2017), Ch.19; Merrett, *Employment Contracts in Private International Law* (2011); Tang, *Electronic Consumer Contracts in the Conflict of Laws* (2009); Hill, *Cross-Border Consumer Contracts* (2008); Leible and Ferrari (eds), *The Rome I Regulation: the Law Applicable to Contractual Obligations in Europe* (2009); McParland, *The Rome I Regulation on the Law Applicable to Contractual Obligations* (2015); Magnus and Mankowski, *Rome I Regulation—Commentary* (2017); Bonomi (2008) 10 Yb. P.I.L. 165; Lein (2008) 10 Yb. P.I.L. 177; Asensio (2008) 10 Yb. P.I.L. 199; Ancel (2008) 10 Yb. P.I.L. 221; Guiterrez (2008) 10 Yb. P.I.L. 233; Garcimartin Alferez (2008) 10 Yb. P.I.L. 245; Heiss (2008) 10 Yb. P.I.L. 261; Bonomi (2008) 10 Yb. P.I.L. 285; Merrett (2009) 5 J.Priv. Int. L. 49; Merkin (2009) 5 J.Priv. Int. L. 69; Ferrari, 2009 Rev. Crit. d.i.p. 459; Crawford, 2010 S.L.T. 17; Kenfack, 2009 *Clunet* 3; Francq, 2009 *Clunet*, 41; Haftel, 2010 *Clunet* 761; Spagnolo (2010) 6 J. Priv. Int. L. 417; Scott [2010] L.M.C.L.Q. 640; Yuksel (2011) 7 J. Priv. Int. L. 149; Boonk [2011] L.M.C.L.Q. 227; Mankowski [2017] J. Priv. Int. L. 231. On IP completion day (on which see above para.30-005 and paras 1-014 et seq.) the provisions of the Rome I Regulation will become part of retained EU law. The substance of the rules will remain the same but there are consequential amendments in order for the rules to work effectively as UK domestic law after exit day. These rules and amendments are implemented in the Law Applicable to Contractual Obligations and Non-Contractual Obligations (Amendment etc.) (EU Exit) Regulations 2019 (SI 2019/834).

### (a) In General

#### History and purpose

*Replace paragraph with:*

**30-018** In 1980 the then Member States of the European Community concluded a Convention on the Law Applicable to Contractual Obligations. This Convention (which is known as the Rome Convention) was ratified by the United Kingdom in 1991 and was implemented in United Kingdom law in the Contracts (Applicable Law) Act 1990.[98] The provisions of the 1990 Act which give the force of law in the United Kingdom to the Rome Convention,[99] entered into force on April 1, 1991.[100]

Consequently the rules of the Convention will apply to contracts falling within its scope which are entered into after that date[101] but before December 17, 2009, the date on which the Rome I Regulation entered into force.[102] As mentioned above, the rules of the Convention are not covered in this edition; readers are referred to the previous edition, see above, para.30-003. Schedule 3 to the Act sets out the text of the Brussels Protocol which enables questions concerning the interpretation of the Rome Convention to be referred to the Court of Justice of the European Union (hereafter the "European Court").[103] Although the United Kingdom ratified the Brussels Protocol on implementing the Convention, delay in ratification by Belgium[104] meant that it did not enter into force internationally until August 1, 2004 and was eventually implemented in United Kingdom law on March 1, 2005.[105]

[98] Contracts (Applicable Law) Act 1990 s.2(1). The English text of the Convention is set out in Sch.1 to the Act "for ease of reference": s.2(4). Each language text is, however, equally authentic: Rome Convention art.33. For the French, German, Italian and Dutch texts, see Kaye at pp.478–505. The Rome Convention was seen as a way of buttressing the work done, originally, in the Brussels Convention on jurisdiction and the enforcement of judgments in civil and commercial matters 1968, designed to establish uniform rules for the international jurisdiction of courts amongst the Member States: [1978] O.J. L304/77, replaced as from March 1, 2002 for all Member States except Denmark, by Regulation 44/2001 on jurisdiction and the recognition and enforcement of judgments in civil and commercial matters [2001] O.J. L12/1 (the Brussels I Regulation) and see SI 2001/3929. The latter Regulation applies to Denmark by virtue of a parallel agreement, [2006] O.J. L120/22, with effect from July 1, 2007: SI 2007/1655. Regulation 44/2001 is amended by Commission Regulation (EC) 280/2009 of April 6, 2009, amending Annexes I, II, III and IV: [2009] O.J. L93/13. Regulation 44/2001 has itself been replaced by Regulation 1215/2012 on jurisdiction and the recognition and enforcement of judgments in civil and commercial matters (recast) [2012] O.J. L351/1 (the Brussels I Regulation recast) which applies from January 10, 2015. The provisions of the Brussels I Regulation recast rest on the EU legal principle of mutual recognition and accordingly depend of reciprocity. UK regulations have been made (which would come into force on IP completion day) which would revoke the Brussels I Regulation recast, and would make significant consequential amendment to the UK primary legislation (notably the Civil Jurisdiction and Judgments Act 1982) and UK secondary legislation (see above para.30-005 and para.1-016B). On links between the Brussels I, Rome I and Rome II Regulations, see Crawford and Carruthers (2014) 63 I.C.L.Q. 1.

[99] Note the power to make reservations to arts 7(1) and 10(1)(e) in art.22 of the Convention. The UK has exercised this power so that arts 7(1) and 10(1)(e) do not have the force of law in the United Kingdom: Contracts (Applicable Law) Act 1990 s.2(2). See below, paras 30-092, 30-252.

[100] SI 1991/707.

[101] Rome Convention art.17, which provides that the Convention shall apply in a contracting state to contracts made after the date on which it has entered into force with respect to that State. Accordingly, contracts entered into *on or before* April 1, 1991, which will be rare, given the passage of time, will be governed by common law choice of law rules (as to which see above, paras 30-006 et seq.).

[102] Rome I Regulation arts 28, 29. On IP completion day (on which see above para.30-005 and paras 1-014 et seq.) the provisions of the Rome I Regulation will become part of retained EU law. The UK will also cease to participate in the Rome Convention, requiring amendments to the Contracts (Applicable Law) Act 1990, which incorporated the Convention into domestic law, in order to preserve the substantive rules of the Convention so that they will continue to apply to contracts entered into between April 1, 1991 and December 16, 2009). These rules and amendments are implemented in the Law Applicable to Contractual Obligations and Non-Contractual Obligations (Amendment etc.) (EU Exit) Regulations 2019 (SI 2019/834).

[103] Sch.2 to the Act contains the text of the Luxembourg Convention providing for accession to the Rome Convention by Greece. Sch.3A to the Act contains the text of the Funchal Convention providing for the accession to the Rome Convention by Spain and Portugal (see SI 1994/1900) which entered into force for the United Kingdom on December 1, 1997. Sch.3B to the Act contains the text of the 1996 Convention providing for the accession to the Rome Convention of Austria, Finland and Sweden (see SI 2000/1825), which came into force on January 1, 2001. A consolidated version of the text of the Rome Convention can be found in [1998] O.J. C27/34.

[104] Belgium finally ratified the Protocol on May 5, 2004.

[105] SI 2004/3448. A Convention was signed on April 14, 2005 providing for the accession of the Czech Republic, Estonia, Cyprus, Latvia, Lithuania, Hungary, Malta, Poland, Slovenia and the Slovak Republic to the Rome Convention and the Brussels Protocol, but this is not yet in force. For the Recommendation for a Council Decision concerning the accession of Bulgaria and Romania, see COM(2007) 217 final. A consolidated version of the Convention and the Protocol is printed in [2005] O.J. C334/11.

*Replace footnote 106 with:*

30-019 [106] Treaty of Amsterdam art.65. See [1997] O.J. C340/1. For the history, see Plender and Wilderspin, *The European Private International Law of Obligations*, 5th edn (2020), Ch.4.

### Interpretation: the European Court

*Replace footnote 126 with:*

30-022 [126] See *Intercontainer Interfrigo SC (ICF) v Balkenende Oosthuizen BV* (C-133/08) EU:C:2009:617, [2010] Q.B. 411; *Koelzsch v État du Grand-Duché du Luxembourg* (C-29/10) [2012] Q.B. 210; *Voogsgeerd v Navimer SA* (C-384/10) EU:C:2011:842, [2012] I.L.Pr. 16; *Schlecker v Meilitta* (C-64/12) EU:C:2013:551; *United Antwerp Maritime Agencies (Unamar) NV v Navigation Maritime Bulgare* (C-184/12) EU:C:2013:663, [2014] 1 Lloyd's Rep. 161; *Haeger & Schmidt GmbH v MMA IARD* (C-305/13) EU:C:2014:2320, [2015] Q.B. 319 and on the *Regulation ERGO Insurance SE v If P&C Insurance AS* (Joined cases C-359/14 and C-475/14) EU:C:2016:40; *Verein für Konsumenteninformation v Amazon EU Sarl* (C-191/15) EU:C:2016:612. On the interpretation of UK legislation whose source is EU law after IP completion day, see above para.1-017B.

### Meaning of "contractual obligations"

*Replace footnote 176 with:*

30-037 [176] *Raiffeisen Zentralbank Osterreich AG v Five Star General Trading LLC* [2001] EWCA Civ 68; *Base Metal Trading Ltd v Shamurin* [2004] EWCA Civ 1316, [2005] 1 W.L.R. 1157; see also *Atlantic Telecom GmbH, Noter* (2004) S.L.T. 1031. See *Dicey, Morris and Collins*, para.32-023; Kaye, pp.97–98. See, for example, in the context of an "implied in law" obligation *Pan Oceanic Chartering Inc v UNIPEC UK Co Ltd* [2016] EWHC 2774 (Comm) and, in the context of a claim made under the French tourism code, *Committeri v Club Mediterranee SA* [2018] EWCA Civ 1889, where the contract was "indispensable" to the claim.

## (b) Exclusions

### Matrimonial property regimes, etc.

*Replace footnote 214 with:*

30-049 [214] See Proposal for Council Regulations for matrimonial property regimes and registered partnerships COM(2011) 126 final; COM(2011) 127 final. Following the failure to reach a political agreement on these proposals, on March 2, 2016, the European Commission adopted a proposal for a Council decision authorising enhanced cooperation in the area of jurisdiction, applicable law and the recognition and enforcement of decisions on the property regimes of international couples, covering both matters of matrimonial property regimes and the property consequences of registered partnerships (COM(2016) 108 final). The Commission also published proposals for two new Regulations, a Council Regulation on jurisdiction, applicable law and the recognition and enforcement of decisions in matters of matrimonial property regimes (COM(2016) 106 final) and a proposal for a Council Regulation on jurisdiction, applicable law and the recognition and enforcement of decisions in matters of the property consequences of registered partnerships (COM(2016) 107 final). Council Regulation 2016/1103 of June 24, 2016 ([2016] O.J. L183/1) applies in Member States which participate in advanced cooperation from January 29, 2019 in the context of matrimonial property and the property consequences of registered partners.

### Arbitration agreements and agreements on the choice of court

*Replace footnote 232 with:*

30-051 [232] In practice it may be that the law applicable to the contractual aspects of the arbitration agreement will normally be the same as that which governs the contract of which it forms part: *Dicey, Morris and*

*Collins*, para.32-021. In *BCY v BCZ* [2016] S.G.H.C. 249, [2016] 2 Lloyd's Rep 583, the High Court of Singapore applied such a presumption. In *Enka Insaat ve Sanayi AS v OOO Insurance Co Chubb* [2020] EWCA Civ 574 the Court of Appeal considered the relative importance of the law governing the underlying contract and the curial law, holding that the law of the underlying contract was likely to be outweighed by the curial law unless it was by express choice.

## Questions governed by the law of companies, etc.

*Replace footnote 241 with:*

[241] Giuliano-Lagarde Report, p.12. The exclusion relates to matters concerning the structural aspects of companies. The mere fact that there is a link between a contract and such questions was not sufficient (*Verein für Konsumenteninformation v TVP Treuhand* (C-272/18) EU:C:2019:827). **30-053**

## Power of agent to bind principal, etc.

*Replace footnote 247 with:*

[247] Giuliano-Lagarde Report, p.13. For discussion, see *Dicey, Morris and Collins*, paras 33-405—33-425. Application of the common law rules on this matter may be affected by the Directive on Self-employed Commercial Agents [1986] O.J. L382/17 implemented in England and Wales and Scotland by the Commercial Agents (Council Directive) Regulations 1993 (SI 1993/3053), as amended by SI 1993/3173 and SI 1998/2868, and in Northern Ireland by the Commercial Agents (Council Directive) Regulations (Northern Ireland) 1993 (SI 1993/483). The Regulations govern the relations between commercial agents and their principals and apply in respect of the activities of commercial agents in Great Britain (reg.1(2)). It is specifically provided that regs 3–22, which deal with the mutual rights and obligations of agent and principal, remuneration of the agent, the conclusion and termination of the agency contract and miscellaneous matters such as service of notices, do not apply where the parties have agreed that the agency contract is to be governed by the law of another Member State (reg.1(3)(a)). Conversely, regs 3–22 will apply where the law of another Member State, corresponding to the Regulations, enables the parties to agree that the agency contract is to be governed by the law of a different Member State and the parties have agreed that it is to be governed by English law (reg.1(3)(b)). For consideration of some of the conflict of laws problems which arise in the context of the Directive and the Regulations, see *Ingmar GB Ltd v Eaton Leonard Technologies Inc* (C-381/98) EU:C:2000:605, [2000] E.C.R. I-9305, discussed by Verhagen (2002) 51 I.C.L.Q. 135; *Accentuate Ltd v ASIGRA Inc* [2009] EWHC 2655 (QB), [2009] 2 Lloyd's Rep. 599; *United Antwerp Maritime Agencies (Unamar) NV v Navigation Maritime Bulgare* (C-184/12) EU:C:2013:663, [2014] 1 Lloyd's Rep. 161; *Fern Computer Consultancy Ltd v Intergraph Cadworx & Analysis Solutions Inc* [2014] EWHC 2908 (Ch). For further discussion, see Vol.II, para.31-017; *Bowstead and Reynolds on Agency*, 21st edn (2018), Ch.11; *Dicey, Morris and Collins*, paras 33-416—33-425. On the interpretation of the compensation provisions of the Regulations, see *Lonsdale v Howard & Hallam Ltd* [2007] UKHL 32, [2007] 1 W.L.R. 2055, Vol.II, para.31-149. As the Regulations are national law they will remain in force after IP completion day. However, they originate from an EU Directive and may be subject to amendment or repeal in the longer term. **30-054**

## Trusts

*Replace footnote 253 with:*

[253] For choice of law rules in trusts, see *Dicey, Morris and Collins* at Ch.29. See *Tod v Barton* [2002] EWHC 264 (Ch), [2002] W.T.L.R. 469; *Chellaram v Chellaram (No.2)* [2002] EWHC 632 (Ch), [2002] 3 All E.R. 17; *Saad Investment Co Ltd (In Liquidation) v Samba Financial Group* [2020] EWHC 853 (Ch). **30-055**

# (c) Habitual Residence

## Branch, agency, etc.

*Replace footnote 278 with:*

[278] Under the Rome Convention, application of the presumption would point to the law of the characteristic performer's principal place of business unless *under the terms of the contract* performance must be effected through a place of business other than the principal place of business. There was some controversy in the case law as to whether it must be a term of the contract that performance was to be effected through the relevant branch: *Ennstone Building Products Ltd v Stanger Ltd* [2002] EWCA Civ 916, [2002] 1 W.L.R. 3059. cf. *Iran Continental Shelf Oil Co v IRI International Corp* [2002] EWCA Civ 1024, [2004] 2 C.L.C. 696; *Trafigura Beheer BV v Kookmin Bank Co* [2005] EWHC 2350 (Comm); **30-062**

[2006] EWHC 1450 (Comm), [2006] 2 Lloyd's Rep. 455 and *GDE LLC v Anglia Autoflow Ltd* [2020] EWHC 105 (Comm). cf. Rome II Regulation art.23(1), second paragraph.

## (d) Freedom of Choice

### Introduction

*Replace footnote 292 with:*

30-066 [292] See *Dicey, Morris and Collins*, 15th edn (2012), paras 32-040 et seq.; Plender and Wilderspin, *The European Private International Law of Obligations*, 5th edn (2020), Ch.6; Cheshire, North and Fawcett, *Private International Law*, 15th edn (2017), pp.706 et seq.; Fentiman, *International Commercial Litigation*, 2nd edn (2015), pp.196 et seq.; Heiss in Leible and Ferrari (eds) *The Rome I Regulation: the Law Applicable to Contractual Obligations in Europe* (2009), p.1.

### "Clearly demonstrated"

*Replace footnote 312 with:*

30-072 [312] There is no Recital in the Regulation which indicates that this is the intention. cf. *Dicey, Morris and Collins*, 15th edn (2012), p.1809, n.217 (no significance in change of language in Rome I which was intended to bring the English and German text into line with the French text of the Rome Convention). The same view was expressed in *Lawlor v Sandvik Mining and Construction Mobile Crushers & Screens Ltd* [2013] EWCA Civ 365 at [3], relying on this authority and in *GDE LLC v Anglia Autoflow Ltd* [2020] EWHC 105 (Comm). And see *Caresse Navigation Ltd v Office National De L'Electricite* [2013] EWHC 3081 (Comm), [2014] 1 Lloyd's Rep. 337.

### Relevant factors

*Replace footnote 320 with:*

30-073 [320] *Marubeni Hong Kong and South China Ltd v Mongolian Government* [2002] 2 All E.R. (Comm) 873. cf. *Burrows v Jamaica Private Power Co Ltd* [2002] 1 All E.R. (Comm) 374; *Samcrete Egypt Engineers and Contractors SAE v Land Rover Exports Ltd* [2001] EWCA Civ 2019, [2002] C.L.C. 533 (deletion of English jurisdiction and choice of law clause from draft contract indicates that parties had made no choice as to the governing law). In *The Komninos S.* [1991] 1 Lloyd's Rep. 370, the jurisdiction clause referred to "British" courts. This was construed as choice of English courts and English law ("[w]hatever the constitutional niceties, it seems to me altogether far-fetched, in truth a lawyer's point, to suppose that the parties can have intended to embrace the Courts of British dependencies overseas" and "scarcely less far-fetched to suppose that the parties can have meant or intended to embrace" the courts of Scotland or Northern Ireland: 374, per Bingham L.J.). In *GDE LLC v Anglia Autoflow Ltd* [2020] EWHC 105 (Comm) neither party had turned their mind to the question of governing law such that the existence of an English jurisdiction clause did not support any mutual choice of English law.

### Limitations on choice

*Replace footnote 365 with:*

30-081 [365] Plender and Wilderspin, 5th edn (2020), paras 6-062 et seq.; Cheshire, North and Fawcett, pp.711 et seq.; Bonomi (2008) 10 Y.B.I.L. 285.

### Mandatory rules of English law

*Replace footnote 394 with:*

30-087 [394] See *Primetrade AG v Ythan Ltd* [2005] EWHC 2399 (Comm), [2006] 1 All E.R. 367 at [14]–[15] (Carriage of Goods by Sea Act 1992 is not mandatory and only applies if the law applicable to the contract is English law); *Roberts (A Child) v Soldiers, Sailors, Airmen and Families Association* [2020] EWCA Civ 926 (Civil Liability (Contribution) Act 1978 is mandatory and applies to all proceedings for contribution brought in England and Wales); Cheshire, North and Fawcett, pp.747–749.

### Overriding mandatory provisions: law of the forum

*Replace footnote 407 with:*

[407] See *Ingmar GB Ltd v Eaton Leonard Technologies Inc* (C-381/98) EU:C:2000:605, [2000] E.C.R. I-9305; *Fern Computer Consultancy Ltd v Intergraph Cadworx & Analysis Solutions Inc* [2014] EWHC 2908 (Ch); *Office of Fair Trading v Lloyds TSB Bank Plc* [2007] UKHL 48, [2008] 1 A.C. 316; *Duarte v Black & Decker Corp* [2007] EWHC 2720 (QB). cf. *Boissevain v Weil* [1949] 1 K.B. 482; *Corocraft Ltd v Pan American Airways Inc* [1969] 1 Q.B. 616; *The Hollandia* [1982] Q.B. 872 (affirmed [1983] 1 A.C. 565); *English v Donnelly* (1958) S.C. 494, not followed in *Hong Kong Shanghai (Shipping) Ltd v The Cavalry* [1987] H.K.L.R. 287; *Chiron Corp v Organon Teknika (No.2)* [1993] F.S.R. 567; *Kaye's Leasing Corp Pty Ltd v Fletcher* (1964) 116 C.L.R. 124; *Att-Gen's Reference No.1 of 1987* (1987) 47 S.A.S.R. 152; *DR Insurance Co v Central National Insurance Co* [1996] 1 Lloyd's Rep. 74. See also *Akai Pty Ltd v The People's Insurance Co Ltd* (1996) 188 C.L.R. 418; cf. *Akai Pty Ltd v People's Insurance Co Ltd* [1998] 1 Lloyd's Rep. 80. And see *Duncan v Motherwell Bridge and Engineering Co Ltd* (1952) S.C. 131. In *KMG International NV v Chen* [2019] EWHC 2389 (Comm) (a case decided under the Rome II Regulation) the court held that the rule against reflective loss was not an overriding mandatory provision. **30-091**

## (e) Applicable Law in the Absence of Choice

### Background

*Replace footnote 416 with:*

[416] See the 32nd edition of this book (2015), paras 30-070—30-091. In *GDE LLC v Anglia Autoflow Ltd* [2020] EWHC 105 (Comm) this default provision in art.4(1) was applied where the presumption could not be applied because the agent who was the characteristic performer of the contract was not yet in existence at the time the contract was entered into. **30-095**

### Principles

*Replace footnote 426 with:*

[426] See, e.g. *Samcrete Egypt Engineers and Contractors SAE v Land Rover Exports Ltd* [2001] EWCA Civ 2019, [2002] C.L.C. 533. See generally Plender and Wilderspin, 5th edn (2020), Ch.7; Cheshire, North and Fawcett, pp.724 et seq.; Fentiman, *International Commercial Litigation* 2nd edn (2015), pp.207 et seq.; Magnus in Leible and Ferrari (eds) *The Rome I Regulation: the Law Applicable to Contractual Obligations in Europe* (2009), p.51; Ferrari, 2009 Rev. Crit. d.i.p. 459. **30-098**

### Rights in rem

*Replace footnote 448 with:*

[448] *Dicey, Morris and Collins*, paras 33-233, 33-244—33-247; Plender and Wilderspin, 5th edn (2020), para.7-062; see Timeshare Act 1992, as amended by Timeshare Regulations 1997 (SI 1997/1081) which implement in the United Kingdom EU Directive 94/97 [1994] O.J. L280/83 on the protection of purchasers in respect of certain aspects of contracts relating to the purchase of the right to use immovable properties on a timeshare basis. See also on timeshares, Directive 2008/122/EC of the European Parliament and of the Council of January 14, 2009 on the protection of consumers in respect of certain aspects of timeshare, long-term holiday product, resale and exchange contracts [2009] O.J. L33/10, implemented in the UK by SI 2010/2960, as amended by SI 2011/1065 and repealing and replacing Timeshare Act 1992. Where the timeshare property is situated in a contracting state to the Brussels or Lugano Conventions on Jurisdiction and the Enforcement of Judgments in Civil and Commercial Matters, other than the United Kingdom, an English court may have no jurisdiction over a claim for misrepresentation or breach of contract brought by a timeshare purchaser against a timeshare owner since the claim may be one the object of which is a tenancy of immovable property, and such claims are subject to the exclusive jurisdiction of the situs of the immovable according to art.16(1) of each Convention: see *Klein v Rhodos Management Ltd* (C-73/04) EU:C:2005:607, [2005] E.C.R. I-8667. Where however the timeshare purchaser has financed the purchase with money lent by a bank, art.16(1) does not impose this jurisdictional bar on a claim against the bank pursuant to the provisions of ss.56(2) and 75 of the Consumer Credit Act 1974 ("connected lender" liability, discussed in Vol.II, paras 39-303—39-305); *Jarrett v Barclays Bank* [1999] Q.B. 1, overruling *Lynch v Halifax Building Society and Royal Bank of Scotland Plc* [1995] C.C.L.R. 42; and see *Office of Fair Trading v Lloyds TSB Bank Plc* [2007] UKHL 48, [2008] 1 A.C. 316. The position would appear to be the same under Council Regulation 44/2001 art.22(1) and Council Regulation 1215/2012 art.24(1). **30-104**

### Contract outside art.4(1)

*Replace footnote 462 with:*

30-110 [462] *Albon v Naza Motor Trading Sdn Bhd* [2007] EWHC 9 (Ch), [2007] 1 W.L.R. 2489; *Lawlor v Sandvik Mining and Construction Mobile Crushers and Screens Ltd* [2013] EWCA Civ 365; *Kent v Paterson-Brown* [2018] EWHC 2008 (Ch); Giuliano-Lagarde Report, p.209; *Dicey, Morris and Collins*, para.33-410. Such contracts may be consumer contracts: see below, paras 30-148 et seq.

### Displacement of the presumption under the Rome Convention

*Replace footnote 504 with:*

30-117 [504] *Societe Nouvelle des Papeteries de l'Aa v BV Machinefabriek BOA* (1992) N.J. 750. See on this case *Struycken* [1996] LMCLQ 18; Plender and Wilderspin, 5th edn (2020), paras 7-024—7-025. And see *Caledonia Subsea Ltd v Microperi Srl* (2002) S.L.T. 1022.

### Letters of credit and guarantees

*Replace footnote 527 with:*

30-120 [527] *Bank of Baroda v Vysya Bank Ltd* [1994] 2 Lloyd's Rep. 87; cf. *Offshore International SA v Banco Central SA* [1977] 1 W.L.R. 399. See also *PT Pan Indonesia Bank Ltd Tbk v Marconi Communications International Ltd* [2005] EWCA Civ 422; *Governor & Co of the Bank of Ireland v State Bank of India* [2011] NIQB 22. In *Taurus Petroleum Ltd v State Oil Marketing Co of the Ministry of Oil, Iraq* [2017] UKSC 64, the Supreme Court applied English law to the obligations of the issuing bank in relation to both the beneficiary and the nominated bank. England was the place of the branch of the issuing bank rather than the nominated bank. However, there was no detailed analysis of the Rome I Regulation in this context. For a critical analysis of this decision see R. Gwynne [2018] L.M.C.L.Q. 450.

## (f) Contracts of Carriage

30-126 *Replace footnote 536 with:*

[536] *Dicey, Morris and Collins*, 15th edn (2012), paras 33R-071 et seq., 33R-091 et seq.; Plender and Wilderspin, 5th edn (2020), Ch.8; Nielsen in Leible and Ferrari (eds), *The Rome I Regulation: the Law Applicable to Contractual Obligations in Europe* (2009), p.99; Kenfack, 2009 Clunet 3; Okoli [2015] L.M.C.L.Q. 512.

### Meaning of contract for carriage of goods

*Replace footnote 551 with:*

30-130 [551] Giuliano-Lagarde Report, p.21; *Scrutton on Charterparties*, 24th edn (2019), paras 1.013 et seq. Art.4(2) will apply to such charters: *Dicey, Morris and Collins*, para.33-266; *Martrade Shipping & Transport GmbH v United Enterprise Corp* [2014] EWHC 1884 (Comm), [2014] 2 Lloyd's Rep. 198.

## (g) Consumer Contracts

### Background

*Replace paragraph with:*

30-148 Article 5 of the Rome Convention made particular provision for "certain consumer contracts".[581] Generally, such contracts (which were somewhat narrowly defined and from the category of which certain types of contract were excluded) were governed by the law chosen by the parties subject to the limitation that a choice of law could not have the effect of depriving the consumer of the protection of the mandatory rules of the law of the country in which the consumer had his habitual residence in certain (narrowly defined) situations.[582] In the absence of choice, the contract was governed by the law of the consumer's habitual residence if one of the situations where a choice of law would be controlled by reference to mandatory rules was present, but in other cases the applicable law in the absence of choice was governed by the general rule in art.4 of the Convention.[583] The rules were particularly difficult to apply to contracts concluded "on-line" and the provisions supplied a somewhat limited degree of protection to consumers. Article 6 of the Regulation makes fresh provision for consumer contracts endeavouring to take account, amongst other things, of the effect of electronic commerce on consumer transactions and the need for increased levels of consumer protection.[584]

[581] See the 32nd edition of this book (2015), paras 30-091—30-122; *Dicey, Morris and Collins*, 14th edn (2006), paras 33-002—33-054; Hill, *Cross-Border Consumer Contracts* (2008); Tang, *Electronic Consumer Contracts in the Conflict of Laws* (2009); Plender and Wilderspin, 5th edn (2020), Ch.9; Kaye, *The New Private International Law of Contract of the European Community* (1993), pp.203–220; Basedow in Meeusen, Pertegas and Straetmans (eds), *The Enforcement of International Contracts in the European Union* (2004), pp.269–288; Straetmans in Meeusen, Pertegas and Straetmans (eds), *The Enforcement of International Contracts in the European Union* (2004), pp.295–322; Morse in Lomnicka and Morse (eds), *Contemporary Issues in Commercial Law* (1997), pp.117–135; Hartley in North (ed.), *Contract Conflicts* (1982), Ch.6; Morse (1992) 41 I.C.L.Q. 1. Gillies (2007) 3 J. Priv. Int. L. 89; Tang (2007) 3 J. Priv. Int. L. 113; Gillies (2008) 16 *International Journal of Law and Information Technology* 242.

[582] Rome Convention art.5(2).

[583] Rome Convention art.5(3).

[584] See Recitals 23 and 24 to the Regulation. See generally, *Dicey, Morris and Collins*, 15th edn (2012), paras 33R-125 et seq.; Plender and Wilderspin, 5th edn (2020), Ch.9; Tang, *Electronic Consumer Contracts in the Conflict of Laws* (2009); Hill, *Cross-Border Consumer Contracts* (2008), especially Ch.12; Gillies (2008) 16 *International Journal of Law and Information Technology* 242; Garcimartin Alferez (2009) 5 J. Priv. Int. L. 85. And see Proposal for a Regulation of the European Parliament and of the Council on a Common European Sales Law, COM(2011) 635 final. This proposal was withdrawn on December 16, 2014: COM(2014) 910 final.

## Contract for the supply of services

*Replace footnote 591 with:*

[591] Rome I art.6(4)(a). This is in similar terms to the Rome Convention art.5(4)(b) considered in *Verein für Konsumenteninfomation v TVP Treuhand* (C-272/18) EU:C:2019:827. As to the meaning of habitual residence, see above, paras 30-060 et seq. **30-151**

## Contract of carriage

*Replace paragraph with:*

Secondly, art.6. does not apply to: **30-152**

> "… a contract of carriage other than a contract relating to package travel within the meaning of Council Directive 90/314/EEC of June 13, 1990 on package travel, package holidays and package tours."[594]

Unless, therefore, the contract of carriage relates to package travel, art.6 will not apply and the law applicable to the contract of carriage will be determined in accordance with art.5 of the Regulation.[595] Broadly speaking, a contract relates to package travel if it is a contract which, for an inclusive price, provides for a combination of travel and accommodation.[596] This exclusion generally reflects the position under the Rome Convention.[597]

[594] Directive 90/314 on package travel [1990] O.J. L158/59 art.6(4)(b). The Directive is implemented in the United Kingdom by the Package Travel, Package Holidays and Package Tours Regulations 1992 (SI 1992/3288). A new Package Travel Directive (2015/2302/EU) entered into force on December 31, 2015 and is implemented by the Package Travel and Linked Travel Arrangements Regulations 2018 (SI 2018/634), which came into force on July 1, 2018. In Germany it has been held that a timeshare contract

is not a contract the object of which is a supply of services for the purposes of Rome Convention art.5(1): BGH NJW 1997, 1697; Knöfel (1998) I.C.L.Q. 439, 443.

595 Above, paras 30-126 et seq.

596 cf. Rome Convention art.5(4)(b) and (5). See *Pammer v Reederei Schlüter GmbH & Co KG* (C-585/08) EU:C:2010:740 and *Pammer v Hotel Alpenhof* (C-144/09) EU:C:2010:740, [2010] E.C.R. I-12527; applied in *Cole v IVI Madrid SL* [2019] 9 WLUK 373.

597 Rome Convention art.5(4) and (5).

### Contract between consumer and professional

*Replace footnote 614 with:*

**30-157** 614 See Recitals 7 and 24 to the Rome Regulation. On the differences between the two rules see *Petruchová v FIBO Group Holdings Ltd* (C-208/18) EU:C:2019:825.

## (h) Insurance Contracts

*Replace footnote 680 with:*

### Structure of art.7[680]

**30-171** 680 *Dicey, Morris and Collins*, 15th edn (2012), paras 33R-183 et seq.; Plender and Wilderspin, 5th edn (2020), Ch.10; Heiss (2008) 10 Yb. P.I.L. 261; Merrett (2009) 5 J. Priv. Int. L. 49; Merkin (2009) 5 J. Priv. Int. L. 69; Gruber in Leible and Ferrari (eds), *The Rome I Regulation: the Law Applicable to Contractual Obligations in Europe* (2009), p.129.

## (i) Individual Employment Contracts

**30-195** *Replace footnote 729 with:*

729 *Dicey, Morris and Collins*, 15th edn (2012), paras 33R-248 et seq.; *Schleker v Boedeker* (C-64/12) EU:C:2013:551, [2014] Q.B. 320; Merrett, *Employment Contracts in Private International Law* (2011); Plender and Wilderspin, 5th edn (2020), Ch.11; Mankowski in Leible and Ferrari (eds), *The Rome I Regulation: the Law Applicable to Contracts in Europe* (2009), p.171; Barnard (2009) I.L.J. 122; Scott [2010] L.M.C.L.Q. 640; Merrett (2010) I.L.J. 355; Merrett (2015) I.L.J. 53. And see generally *Koelzsch v État du Grand Duché de Luxembourg* (C-29/10) EU:C:2011:151, [2012] Q.B. 210; *Voogsgeerd v Navimer SA* (C-384/10) EU:C:2011:842, [2012] I.L.Pr. 16, interpreting equivalent but not identical provisions of the Rome Convention art.6.

*Replace footnote 738 with:*

### Individual employment contracts[738]

**30-197** 738 Merrett, *Employment Contracts in Private International Law* (2011); Plender and Wilderspin, *The European Private International Law of Obligations*, 5th edn (2020), Ch.11; *Dicey, Morris and Collins on the Conflict of Laws*, 14th edn (2006), paras 33-059—33-102; Lasok and Stone, *Conflict of Laws in the European Community* (1987), pp.384–385; Kaye, *The New Private International Law of Contract of the European Community* (1993), pp.224–238; Polak in Meeusen, Pertegas and Straetmans (eds), *The Enforcement of International Contracts in the European Union* (2004), pp.323–342; Morse in North (ed.), *Contract Conflicts* (1982), Ch.7; Gillies (2010) 41 I.L.J. 355; Scott [2010] L.M.C.L.Q. 640; Barnard [2009] 38 I.L.J. 122; Hoey and McArdie [2008] Jur. Rev. 291; Cavalier and Upex (2006) 55 I.C.L.Q. 587; Morse (1992) 41 I.C.L.Q. 1; Smith and Cromack (1993) 22 I.L.J. 1. In 1976 the European Commission published a proposal for a Regulation concerning conflict of laws in employment relationships: see COM(175) 653 final, discussed by Hepple in Lipstein (ed.), *Harmonisation of Private International Law by the EEC* (1978), p.390; Forde (1979) *Legal Issues of European Integration* 85. Had this proposal not been withdrawn in 1981 ([1981] O.J. C307/3) and reached fruition it would have taken precedence over art.6 pursuant to art.20 of the Rome Convention. See also Directive 96/71 concerning the posting of workers in the framework of the provision of services [1997] O.J. L18/1. This Directive has not been formally implemented in the United Kingdom by specific regulations, but it has been said that the repeal of the Employment Rights Act 1996 s.196 by the Employment Relations Act 1999 s.32(3) (below, para.30-204 n.767) has facilitated implementation of the Directive by extending rights which are derived from European Union legislation (and also, normally, English employment law) to workers who are "temporarily" working in Great Britain: see *Hansard*, HC Vol.336, col.32. This Directive takes precedence over the Rome Convention, pursuant to art.20. See on the *Directive Mazzoleni and Inter Surveillance Assistance SARL* (C-165/98) EU:C:2001:162, [2001] E.C.R. I-2189;

*Finalarte Sociedade de Construcao* (C-49/98, C-50/98, C-52/98–C-54/98 and C-68/98, C-71/98) EU:C:2001:564, [2001] E.C.R. I-7831; *Portugaia Construcoes Ltd* (C-164/99) EU:C:2002:40, [2002] E.C.R. I-787; *Ruffert v Land Nidersachen* (C-346/06) EU:C:2008:189, [2008] 2 C.M.L.R. 39; *Svenska Staten v Holmqvist* (C-310/07) EU:C:2008:573, [2009] I.C.R. 675. See generally *Koelzsch v Ëtat du Grand-Duché de Luxembourg* (C-29/10) EU:C:2011:151, [2012] Q.B. 210; *Voogsgeerd v Navimer SA* (C-384/10) EU:C:2011:842, [2012] I.L.Pr. 16; *Schlecker v Boedeker* (C-64/12) EU:C:2013:551, [2014] Q.B. 320; Smith and Villiers (1996) Jur. Rev. 167.

*Replace footnote 742 with:*

[742] See Merrett, Ch.3; Plender and Wilderspin, 5th edn (2020), paras 11-007 et seq.; *Dicey, Morris and Collins*, paras 33-063—33-066. **30-197**

## Meaning of employment contract

*Replace paragraph with:*

The meaning of employment contract in the Rome Regulation should correspond, so far as possible, with the meaning given to the expression in the context of the Judgments Regulation recast.[745] What the particular meaning will turn out to be may depend on the circumstances of the case but the following considerations may form the broad contours of an autonomous meaning.[746] The first criterion identifying a contract of employment is the provision of services by one party over a period of time for which remuneration is paid; the second criterion is the existence of control and direction over the provision of the services by the counterparty and a relationship of subordination; and the third criterion is the integration to some extent of the provider of services within the organisational framework of the counterparty.[747] These criteria are not, however, "hard edged" criteria which can be mechanistically applied, since there may, for example, be degrees of control and degrees of integration within the relevant organisational framework. And in applying these broad criteria regard must be had, particularly, to the terms of the contract.[748] **30-198**

[745] Judgments Regulation recast art.20. See Recital 7 to the Rome 1 Regulation. And see cases cited in preceding note.

[746] *WPP Holdings Italy Srl v Benatti* [2007] EWCA Civ 263 at [46].

[747] Each of these three criteria was referred to by the European Court in *Holterman Ferho Exploitatie BV v Spies von Büllesheim* (C-47/14) EU:C:2015:574, [2015] I.L.Pr. 44 when considering the meaning of employment contract under the Judgments Regulation. In *Bosworth v Arcadia Petroleum Ltd* (C-603/17) EU:C:2019:310, [2019] I.L.Pr. 22 the CJEU concluded that the contracts of company directors were not contracts of employment because the required degree of subordination was not present.

[748] *WPP Holdings Italy Srl v Benatti* [2007] EWCA Civ 263 at [47].

## Territorial limitations

*In line 2, page [2362], after "other rights contained in the Act.", add new footnote 767a:*

[767a] See, in the context of the whistleblowing provisions in s.47B, *Foreign and Commonwealth Office v Bamieh* [2019] EWCA Civ 803. **30-204**

## Contract and tort

*Replace footnote 788 with:*

[788] Above, para.30-041. cf. Plender and Wilderspin, 5th edn (2020), paras 2-054 et seq.; Merrett, pp.188 et seq. **30-212**

## (j) Voluntary Assignment and Contractual Subrogation

### Background

*Replace footnote 794 with:*

30-213 [794] Rome I art.27(2), above, para.30-027, below para.30-217. See Consultation Paper, paras 85–87. cf. the original Proposal of the Commission art.13. For discussion of this difficult topic, see *Dicey, Morris and Collins*, 15th edn (2012), paras 24-050 et seq.; Plender and Wilderspin, 5th edn (2020), paras 13-001–13-018; Flessner and Verhagen, *Assignment in European Private International Law* (2006); Fentiman, *International Commercial Litigation* 2nd edn (2015), pp.233 et seq.; Garcimartin-Alferez in Leible and Ferrari (eds), *The Rome I Regulation: the Law Applicable to Contractual Obligations in Europe* (2009); Perkins [2008] *Financial Markets Law Review* 238; Bridge (2009) 125 L.Q.R. 671; Verhagen and Van Dongen (2010) 6 J. Priv. Int. L. 1; Hartley (2011) 60 I.C.L.Q. 29; Mollman [2011] L.M.C.L.Q. 262; Goode [2015] L.M.C.L.Q. 289. On the application of Rome I to intellectual property rights, see Torremans (2008) 4 J. Priv. Int. L. 397.

### Priorities

*Replace paragraph with:*

30-217 In the discussion of art.12(2) of the Rome Convention in the earlier edition of this work it was tentatively suggested that the question of priorities between competing assignments of the same debt could fall within art.12(2) and could thus be governed by the law governing the right to which the assignment related.[805] This question being part of the broader controversy as to whether art.12 of the Convention was applicable to the proprietary as well as the contractual effects of an assignment.[806] In *Raiffeisen Zentralbank Osterreich AG v Five Star General Trading LLC*.[807] A bank had taken an assignment of a policy of marine insurance, issued by French insurers but governed by English law, from a shipowner, as part of an arrangement whereby the bank lent money to the shipowner to assist in the purchase of a ship. The ship was lost and the bank sought to recover the insurance moneys from the insurers in proceedings to which the shipowner and cargo owner were parties, by invoking the assignment. The bank argued, on the basis of art.12(2) of the Rome Convention, that English law determined whether the assignment could be so invoked since English law governed the policy and was thus the law governing the right to which the assignment related, which under art.12(2) was the law which determined the conditions under which the assignment could be invoked against the debtor. Since the bank had given notice of the assignment to the insurers in accordance with English law, there was, argued the bank, no impediment to its claim. The cargo owners (who had obtained attachment orders in France of the insurance and proceeds) argued that art.12(2) of the Rome Convention had no application since the claim by the bank was proprietary in nature and the Convention only applied to contractual obligations.[808] The relevant applicable law was thus the *lex situs* of the right assigned[809] which in the instant case was French law and under French law the bank could not invoke the assignment against the insurers because it had not complied with a requirement of French law whereby notice of the assignment had to be given through a French bailiff. The Court of Appeal, adopting a broad interpretation of "contract", took the view that, for the purposes of the Rome Convention, the issue could legitimately be treated as a contractual one.[810] More particularly, art.12(2) "manifests the clear intention to embrace the issue and to state the appropriate law by which it must be determined".[811] Reinforcing the propositions set out in the previous paragraph, the court went on to say that by virtue of art.12(2):

> "... the contract giving rise to the obligation governs not merely its assignability, but also 'the relationship between the assignee and the debtor' and 'the conditions under which the assignment can be invoked against the debtor', as well as 'any question whether the debtor's obligations have been discharged."[812]

The provision:

> "... on its face ... treats as matters within its scope, and expressly provides for, issues both as to whether the debtor owes moneys to and must pay the assignee (their 'relationship') and under what 'conditions', e.g. as regards the giving of notice."[813]

Although the question was not considered by the Court of Appeal, it was submitted in the earlier edition of this work[814] that the thrust of the decision would make it seem likely that the law governing the right assigned will also, pursuant to art.12(2), decide questions of priorities as between competing voluntary assignments of that right. This conclusion must now be regarded as not following under the Regulation. First, the Commission's original Proposal contained a rule providing that whether the assignment or subrogation could be relied upon against third parties should be governed by the law of the assignor's or the author of the subrogation's habitual residence[815] which might suggest that priorities were not covered by art.12(2). Secondly, the proposed rule provoked so much criticism that it was eliminated during the negotiations[816] and the Consultation Paper expresses the view that the question of priorities is for national law.[817] Thirdly, under the review clause the Commission was required to produce a report on the question of the effectiveness of an assignment or subrogation of a claim against third parties and the priority of the assigned or subrogated claim over a right of another person "the report to be accompanied, if appropriate, by a proposal to amend" the Regulation.[818] This again suggests that these questions are not covered by the present text of art.14(2). Finally, on March 12, 2018, in accordance with this requirement, the Commission published a proposed Regulation on the law applicable to the third-party effects of assignments of claims.[819] Under this proposal, the third-party or proprietary effects of an assignment (which includes the rights of an assignee to assert his legal title over a claim assigned to him towards other assignees or beneficiaries) (art.2(e)) is in general governed by the law of the country in which the assignor has its habitual residence at the material time (art.4(1)). The issue was finally resolved by the European Court in *BNP Paribas, Luxembourg v TeamBank Nürnberg*,[819a] the court holding that art.14 did not designate the law applicable to the third party effects of the assignment of the claim by the same creditor to successive assignees. Unless and until the proposed Regulation is implemented the question will be governed by the common law where there is no clear answer to what law will be applied.[819b]

[805] See 32nd edition, para.30-293. This was probably the common law rule: *Dicey, Morris and Collins*, para.24-054; Cheshire, North and Fawcett, pp.1288–1289; *Le Feuvre v Sullivan* (1855) 10 Moo. P.C. 1; *Kelly v Selwyn* [1905] 2 Ch. 117; cf. *Republica de Guatemala v Nunez* [1927] 1 K.B. 669, 695 (obiter in favour of lex fori); McKendrick, *Goode on Commercial Law*, 5th edn (2016), paras 37-86—37-87; Rogerson, *Collier's Conflict of Laws*, 4th edn (2013), p404 (*lex situs* of debt).

[806] *Dicey, Morris and Collins*, para.24-064 takes the view that proprietary effects are included. Contrast Goode, 5th edn (2016), paras 37-86—37-87 and Moshinsky (1992) 109 L.Q.R. 591, who take the view that they are not. See, generally, Plender and Wilderspin, 5th edn (2020), Ch.13.

[807] [2001] EWCA Civ 68, [2001] Q.B. 825. For comment, see Plender and Wilderspin, 5th edn (2020), paras 13-033 et seq.; Stevens in Bridge and Stevens (eds), *Cross-Border Security and Insolvency* (2001), pp.213–216; Stevens and Struycken (2002) 118 L.Q.R. 15; Briggs [2001] 72 B.Y.B.I.L. 461.

[808] See above, para.30-037.

[809] Relying, inter alia, on Goode, *Commercial Law*, 2nd edn (1995), pp.1129–1130.

[810] [2001] EWCA Civ 68, [2001] Q.B. 825 at [34]–[43].

[811] [2001] EWCA Civ 68 at [43].

[812] [2001] EWCA Civ 68.

[813] [2001] EWCA Civ 68. The court referred to two decisions of the German Supreme Court to similar effect: see *Raiffeisen* [2001] EWCA Civ 68 at [49]–[50]; see also von Bar (1989) 53 RabelsZ 462. The court also referred to a decision of the Dutch Hoge Raad, discussed by Struycken [1998] L.M.C.L.Q. 345 and Koppenol-Laforce (1998) N.I.L.R. 129: see [2001] EWCA Civ 68, [2001] Q.B. 825 at [51]–[52].

[814] 32nd edition, para.30-293. *Dicey, Morris and Collins*, para.24-062.

[815] Proposal art.14(3).

[816] Consultation Paper, paras 85, 86.

[817] Consultation Paper, para.85.

[818] Rome I art.27(2). See also, Consultation Paper, para.87.

[819] COM(2018) 96 final.

[819a] C-548/18, EU:C:2019:848.

[819b] The lex situs of the debt (although this is not easily determined in the case of intangible property), the place of residence of the debtor or the law of the underlying debt are all possible candidates. See further Plender and Wilderspin, *The European Private International Law of Obligations*, 5th edn (2020), para.13-044, suggesting that the pragmatic approach might be to adopt the solution in art.14(2).

## (k) Legal Subrogation

### Background

*Replace paragraph with:*

**30-218** Article 13 of the Rome Convention contained provisions expressed to apply to "[s]ubrogation".[820] However, in this context "subrogation" bears a limited meaning: art.13 was concerned only with cases where a creditor has a claim in *contract* against the debtor and a third person "has a duty to satisfy the creditor, or has in fact satisfied the creditor in discharge of that duty".[821] Thus the provision extends to a contract of guarantee where the guarantor has paid the creditor and is thus subrogated to the latter's rights against the debtor,[822] but not to subrogation by operation of law when the debt to be paid originates in a tort (e.g. where the insurer succeeds to the insured's right of action against the tortfeasor).[823] The principal rule was contained in art.13(1) while art.13(2) applied the same rule where several persons were subject to the same contractual claim and one of them had satisfied the debtor. Article 15 of the Regulation is expressed to apply to "[l]egal subrogation" and reproduces, with a minor linguistic change of no substantive effect, the text of art.13(1) of the Convention.[824] Article 16 of the Regulation, headed "[m]ultiple liability" deals with cases where a creditor has a claim against several debtors who are liable for the same claim and one of them has already satisfied the claim in whole or in part, i.e. the situation dealt with in art.13(2) of the Convention. Article 16 is dealt with below.[825]

[820] See *Dicey, Morris and Collins*, para.32-211; Plender and Wilderspin, 5th edn (2020), paras 13-042 et seq.; Takahashi, *Claims for Contribution and Reimbursement in an International Context* (2000), pp.78–82; Kaye, *The New Private International Law of Contract of the European Community* (1993), pp.327–330; Morse (1992) 2 Ybk. Eur. L. 107, 158.

[821] Rome Convention art.13(1).

[822] Giuliano-Lagarde Report, p.35.

[823] Giuliano-Lagarde Report, p.35; *West Tankers Inc v RAS Riunione Adriatica di Sicurta SpA* [2005] EWHC 454 (Comm), [2005] 1 C.L.C. 347 and C-185/07 EU:C:2009:69, [2009] E.C.R. I-663, [2009] 1 A.C. 1138; and see Third Parties (Rights Against Insurers) Act 2010 s.18.

[824] See Plender and Wilderspin, 5th edn (2020), paras 13-047–13-049; *Dicey, Morris and Collins*, 15th edn (2012), para.32-163. Art.15 is discussed in *ERGO Insurance SE v If P&C Insurance AS* (Joined Cases C-359/14 and C-475/14) EU:C:2016:40.

[825] Below, paras 30-221 et seq.

## (l) Multiple Liability

### Principle

*Replace footnote 833 with:*

[833] See Plender and Wilderspin, 5th edn (2020), paras 13-050–13-052; *Dicey, Morris and Collins*, 15th edn (2012), para.32-163. **30-221**

### Right of recourse

*Replace footnote 834 with:*

[834] cf. art.13(2) of the Rome Convention. However, in *Roberts (A Child) v Soldiers, Sailors, Airmen and Families Association* [2020] EWCA Civ 926, the Civil Liability (Contribution) Act 1978 was held to have mandatory or overriding effect and accordingly to apply to all proceedings for contribution brought in England and Wales regardless of the otherwise applicable law. **30-222**

## (m) Set-off

*Replace footnote 835 with:* **30-224**

[835] Plender and Wilderspin, 5th edn (2020), paras 13-053–13-057; Hellner in Leible and Ferrari (eds), *The Rome I Regulation: the Law Applicable to Contractual Obligations in Europe* (2009), p.251; *Dicey, Morris and Collins*, 15th edn (2012), para.32-160.

## 4. SCOPE OF THE APPLICABLE LAW

## (a) Material Validity of the Contract

*Replace footnote 849 with:* **30-229**

[849] *Dicey, Morris and Collins*, 15th edn (2012), paras 32R-082 et seq.; Plender and Wilderspin, *The European Private International Law of Obligations*, 5th edn (2020), paras 14-059–14-069; Cheshire, North and Fawcett, *Private International Law*, 15th edn (2017), pp.755–758; Kaye, *The New Private International Law of Contract of the European Community* (1993), pp.269–279.

### Formation of the contract

*To the end of paragraph, after "is commercially unreasonable.", add new footnote 867a:*

[867a] In *Seniority Shipping Corporation SA v City Seed Crusting Industries Ltd, m.v. "Joker"* [2019] EWHC 3541 (Comm) art.10(2) was not applicable as the application of the putative proper law was eminently reasonable and in accordance with ordinary expectations of international trade. **30-231**

## (b) Formal Validity of the Contract

*Replace footnote 876 with:* **30-235**

[876] *Dicey, Morris and Collins*, 15th edn (2012), paras 32R-127 et seq.; Cheshire, North and Fawcett, pp.758–761; Plender and Wilderspin, 5th edn (2020), paras 14-070–14-076; Kaye, *The New Private International Law of Contract of the European Community* (1993), pp.281–295; Lagarde in North (ed.), *Contract Conflicts* (1982), pp.51–54.

## (c) Capacity

### Introduction

*To the end of paragraph, after "common law rules.", add new footnote 920a:*

30-248 [920a] In *Ukraine v Law Debenture Trust Corp Plc* [2018] EWCA Civ 2026, the Court of Appeal held that the capacity of a foreign state to contract flows from its recognition and personality as a state and was not analogous to the capacity of either a natural person or a foreign company.

### Corporations

*Replace footnote 926 with:*

30-250 [926] *Risdon Iron and Locomotive Works Ltd v Furniss* [1906] 1 K.B. 49, 56–57; *Banque Internationale de Commerce de Petrograd v Goukassow* [1923] 2 K.B. 682, 690–691; *Janred Properties Ltd v ENIT* [1989] 2 All E.R. 444; *J.H. Rayner (Mincing Lane) Ltd v Department of Trade and Industry* [1990] 2 A.C. 418; *Sierra Leone Telecommunications Co Ltd v Barclays Bank Plc* [1998] 2 All E.R. 821; *Merrill Lynch Capital Services Inc v Municipality of Piraeus* [1997] C.L.C. 1214; *Azov Shipping Co v Baltic Shipping Co* [1999] 2 Lloyd's Rep. 159; *Grupo Torras SA v Al-Sabah* [1999] C.L.C. 1469, reversed in part on other grounds, [2001] C.L.C. 221; *Continental Enterprises Ltd v Shandong Zucheng Foreign Trade Group Co* [2005] EWHC 92 (Comm); *Laemthong International Lines Co Ltd v Artis (No.3)* [2005] EWHC 1595 (Comm). See also *Marubeni Hong Kong and South China Ltd v Government of Mongolia* [2004] EWHC 472 (Comm), [2004] 2 Lloyd's Rep. 198, affirmed on other grounds, [2005] EWCA Civ 395, [2005] 1 W.L.R. 2497; Foreign Corporations Act 1991 s.1; Overseas Companies (Execution of Documents and Registration of Charges) Regulations 2009 (SI 2009/1917), inserting modified versions of Companies Act 2006 ss.43–48 and 51, in respect of the execution of documents by overseas companies. See also *Integral Petroleum SA v SCU-Finaz AB* [2015] EWCA Civ 144 (a rule of Swiss law requiring the acts of a company to be authorised by two signatories applied as the law of incorporation). In *Canary Wharf v European Medicines Authority* [2019] EWHC 335 (Ch) questions of capacity of the EMA were governed by EU law as the law of its place of incorporation.

## (d) Particular Issues

30-251 *Replace footnote 935 with:*

[935] See *Dicey, Morris and Collins*, 15th edn (2012), paras 32R-140 et seq.; Cheshire, North and Fawcett, *Private International Law*, 15th edn (2017), pp.764–772; Plender and Wilderspin, 5th edn (2020), Ch.14; Kaye, *The New Private International Law of Contract of the European Community* (1993), pp.297–310; Lagarde in North (ed.), *Contract Conflicts* (1982), p.49, at pp.54–57.

## (f) Illegality and Public Policy

### Act illegal under law of country where to be performed

*Replace footnote 1074 with:*

30-284 [1074] *Kahler v Midland Bank Ltd* [1950] A.C. 24, 48; *Société Co-operative Suisse des Cereales, etc. v Plata Cereal Co SA* (1947) 80 Ll. L. Rep. 530, 543–544: *Walton (Grain and Shipping) Ltd v British Italian Trading Co* [1959] 1 Lloyd's Rep. 223, 236; *Bangladesh Export Import Co Ltd v Sucden Kerry SA* [1995] 2 Lloyd's Rep. 1, 5; *Ispahani v Bank Melli Iran* [1998] Lloyd's Rep. Bank. 133; see also *Society of Lloyd's v Fraser* [1998] C.L.C. 1630, 1652; *Fox v Henderson Investment Fund Ltd* [1999] 2 Lloyd's Rep. 303; *Royal Boskalis Westminster NV v Mountain* [1999] Q.B. 674, 733–734; *Tekron Resources Ltd v Guinea Investment Co Ltd* [2004] EWHC 2577 (QB), [2004] 2 Lloyd's Rep. 26; *Continental Enterprises Ltd v Shandong Zucheng Foreign Trade Group Co* [2005] EWHC 92 (Comm); *Marlwood Commercial Inc v Kozeny* [2006] EWHC 872 (Comm); *Lilly Icos LLC v 8PM Chemists Ltd* [2009] EWHC 1905 (Ch), [2010] F.S.R. 95 at [260]–[266]; *Dicey, Morris and Collins*, 15th edn (2012), paras 32-094 et seq.; Cheshire, North and Fawcett, pp.769–772; F.A. Mann (1937) 18 B.Y.I.L. 97, 107–113; Morris (1953) 6 Vand. L. Rev. 510; Reynolds (1992) 108 L.Q.R. 553. In *Ryder Industries Ltd v Chan Shui Woo* (2015) 18 HKCFAR 544 [42]–[43] Lord Collins endorsed the view that the decision in *Ralli Bros* turned on the doctrine of impossibility of performance in English law. This statement was approved in *Magdeev v Tsvestkov* [2020] EWHC 887 (Comm) although the *Ralli Bros* principle did not apply on the facts of the case because performance of the dominant part of the contract was not illegal.

## Ralli Bros and The Rome Convention

*Replace footnote 1077 with:*

1077 Contracts (Applicable Law) Act 1990 s.2(2) and Sch.1 art.22 and see, for example, *Wallis Trading Inc v Air Tanzania* [2020] EWHC 339 (Comm). See on the status of the *Ralli Bros* rule in the Convention context, *Dicey, Morris and Collins*, paras 32-148—32-151; Reynolds, above. **30-285**

## Relevant country

*Replace footnote 1093 with:*

1093 *Greece v Nikiforidis* (C-135/15) EU:C:2016:774, [2017] I.C.R. 147 at [49]. In *Canary Wharf v European Medicines Authority* [2019] EWHC 335 (Ch) illegality under the law of the place of incorporation of a company was irrelevant. **30-288**

## Illegality under other foreign law

*Replace paragraph with:*

Illegality under any foreign law, be it the law of one party's nationality,[1099] or of a country where performance may, but need not, take place,[1100] or of the place of contracting[1101] does not per se affect the enforceability of the contract either at common law or, because of the United Kingdom's reservation to art.7(1) of the Convention,[1102] under the provisions of the Rome Convention. Article 9(3) of the Rome I Regulation, likewise, does not allow illegality by the law of a party's nationality or the law of the place of contracting to affect the validity of the contract per se, but it does open up the possibility of application of the law of the place of performance where the obligations arising out of the contract have been, but do not have to be, performed in a particular country.[1103] **30-291**

1099 *Kleinwort Sons & Co v Ungarische Baumwolle Industrie AG* [1939] 2 K.B. 678; *Kahler v Midland Bank Ltd* [1950] A.C. 24, 48; *Toprak Mahsulleri Ofisi v Finagrain Compagnie Commerciale Agricole et Financière SA* [1979] 2 Lloyd's Rep. 98; or, for a company, the place of incorporation: *Canary Wharf v European Medicines Authority* [2019] EWHC 335 (Ch).

1100 *Kahler v Midland Bank Ltd* [1950] A.C. 24, 36, 39, 48. And see *Zivnostenska Banka v Frankman* [1950] A.C. 57, 79; *Regazzoni v K.C. Sethia Ltd* [1956] 2 Q.B. 490, 514, 523; *Nile Co for the Export of Agricultural Crops v Bennett (Commodities) Ltd* [1986] 1 Lloyd's Rep. 555, 581. See also *Fox v Henderson Investment Fund Ltd* [1999] 2 Lloyd's Rep. 303.

1101 *Vita Foods Products Inc v Unus Shipping Co Ltd* [1939] A.C. 277, 297–300. See F.A. Mann (1937) 18 B.Y.I.L. 97, 107–113. cf. *The Torni* [1932] P. 78; *Re Missouri S.S. Co Ltd* (1889) 42 Ch. D. 321, 336; *The Hollandia* [1983] 1 A.C. 565, 576.

1102 See *Wallis Trading Inc v Air Tanzania* [2020] EWHC 339 (Comm) and above, para.30-286.

1103 Rome I art.9(3), above, para.30-286.

## Examples of public policy

*Replace paragraph with:*

Since the application of the doctrine of public policy must depend very much on the circumstances of individual cases, it is not possible to categorise the situations justifying its invocation with any precision. However, in the past, English courts have refused to enforce champertous contracts,[1111] contracts in restraint of trade,[1112] contracts involving trading with the enemy,[1113] and contracts involving collusive arrangements for a divorce.[1114] The principle will also apply where the parties make the contract with the intention that its performance should involve the commission in a foreign and friendly country of an act which would violate that country's **30-293** laws.[1115] These cases of initial illegality may also now potentially come within art.9(3), discussed in para.30-288 above. It has also been held that public policy is infringed where the contract, or circumstances in which it was made, render it incompatible with English ideas of justice and morality.[1116] Thus a contract governed by (and valid by) its foreign applicable law may be held unenforceable in England because it was entered into as a result of coercion.[1117] And where a contract governed by English law involved a transaction, to be performed abroad, which was contrary to a head of English public policy based on general principles of morality, the same public policy applying in the country of performance, the contract was similarly unenforceable.[1118]

1111 *Grell v Levy* (1864) 16 C.B.(N.S.) 73; cf. *Trendtex Trading Corp v Crédit Suisse* [1982] A.C. 679; *Camdex International Ltd v Bank of Zambia* [1998] Q.B. 22; *Fraser v Buckle* [1996] 1 I.R. 1. Although champerty has ceased to be a crime or a tort in England, Criminal Law Act 1967 s.14, it will render a contract illegal.

1112 *Rousillon v Rousillon* (1880) 14 Ch. D. 351, which should be restricted to restraint of trade affecting trade in England. And see *Duarte v Black and Decker Corp* [2007] EWHC 2720 (QB), [2008] 1 All E.R. (Comm) 401, above, para.30-093.

1113 *Robson v Premier Oil and Pipe Line Co* [1915] 2 Ch. 124, 136; *Dynamit A/G v Rio Tinto Co Ltd* [1918] A.C. 260.

1114 *Hope v Hope* (1857) 8 De G.M. & G. 731.

1115 *Regazzoni v K.C. Sethia Ltd* [1958] A.C. 301. And see *De Wutz v Hendricks* (1824) 2 Bing. 314; *Foster v Driscoll* [1929] 1 K.B. 470; *British Nylon Spinners v I.C.I. Ltd* [1955] Ch. 37, 52; *Euro-Diam Ltd v Bathurst* [1990] 1 Q.B. 1; *Royal Boskalis Westminster NV v Mountain* [1999] Q.B. 674; *Ispahani v Bank Melli Iran* [1998] Lloyd's Rep. Bank. 133; *Soleimany v Soleimany* [1999] Q.B. 785 (arbitration award based on such a contract unenforceable in England); *Westacre Investments Inc v Jugoimport-SDPR Holding Co Ltd* [1999] Q.B. 740, affirmed [2000] Q.B. 288 (public policy of sustaining international arbitration awards outweighed public policy of discouraging international commercial corruption); see also *Society of Lloyd's v Fraser* [1998] C.L.C. 1630, 1652; *Fox v Henderson Investment Fund Ltd* [1999] 2 Lloyd's Rep. 303. This rule applies, in all probability, to cases where a contract is governed by a foreign law as well as to cases where it is governed by English law (as was the case in *Regazzoni v K.C. Sethia Ltd*): see *Royal Boskalis Westminster NV v Mountain* [1999] Q.B. 674, 692, 703, 734–736; cf. *Ispahani v Bank Melli Iran*. It also applies where the object of the contract is to break the penal or revenue laws of a foreign country (*Regazzoni v K.C. Sethia Ltd; Re Emery's Investment Trusts* [1959] Ch. 410; *Euro-Diam Ltd v Bathurst; Soleimany v Soleimany*) or foreign exchange control legislation (*Kahler v Midland Bank Ltd* [1950] A.C. 24, 27; *Zivnostenska Banka v Frankman* [1950] A.C. 57, 72; *Re Helbert Wagg & Co Ltd's Claim* [1956] Ch. 323, 349, 351; *Re Lord Cable* [1977] 1 W.L.R. 7, 24; *Ispahani v Bank Melli Iran*, above). An English court will not *enforce* the penal or revenue or other public laws of a foreign country: see *Camdex International Ltd v Bank of Zambia* [1997] C.L.C. 714; *Dicey, Morris and Collins*, 15th edn (2012), paras 5-020 et seq. See also *Barros Mattos Junior v MacDaniels Ltd* [2004] EWHC 1188 (Ch), [2005] 1 W.L.R. 247; *Marlwood Commercial Inc v Kozeny* [2006] EWHC 872 (Comm); *Islamic Republic of Iran v Barakat Galleries Ltd* [2007] EWCA Civ 1374, [2008] 1 All E.R. 1177. As to exchange control in the conflict of laws, see *Dicey, Morris and Collins*, 15th edn (2012), paras 37R-061 et seq. On the way in which foreign laws are to be treated for the purposes of applying the rules of English law founded on ex turpi causa non oritur actio see *Dicey, Morris and Collins*, para.32-012. The principle will not apply where the illegal intent related to only a small incident of an otherwise lawful venture (as was the case in *Magdeev v Tsvetkov* [2020] EWHC 887 (Comm)). In *KMG International NV v Chen* [2019] EWHC 2389 (Comm) (a case decision under the Rome II Regulation) the court held that the rule allowing a claim governed by Dutch law which might contravene the English rule against reflective loss would not contravene public policy.

1116 *Kaufman v Gerson* [1904] 1 K.B. 591; *Royal Boskalis Westminster NV v Mountain* [1999] Q.B. 674. See also *Robinson v Bland* (1706) 2 Burr. 1077, 1084; *Re Missouri S.S. Co* (1889) 42 Ch. D. 321, 336. A contract to oust the jurisdiction of a foreign court (unlike one to oust the jurisdiction of the English court) is not contrary to public policy: cf. *Addison v Brown* [1954] 1 W.L.R. 779.

1117 *Royal Boskalis Westminster NV v Mountain* [1999] Q.B. 674; *Kaufman v Gerson* [1904] 1 K.B. 591. In the former case it was stated, at 689, 729, that the degree of coercion exercised in the particular case is relevant, and whether the degree of coercion exercised in the latter case would be regarded as sufficient today was questionable. In *Dimskal Shipping Co SA v International Transport Workers Federation* [1992] 2 A.C. 152, 158 it was held that whether a contract was void or voidable for duress depended on the law applicable to the contract, which was English law. However, if the law applicable to the contract is a foreign law and that law would regard the contract as valid despite the presence of duress of an unconscionable degree, the English court will refuse to enforce the contract on the grounds of public policy as happened in *Royal Boskalis Westminster NV v Mountain*, where a contract governed and valid by Iraqi law was procured by threats to use personnel as part of the "human shield" in the course of the Iraq-Kuwait conflict. In *Kaufman v Gerson*, a wife was held to have acted under duress by agreeing to pay sums to her husband's employer under a contract governed and valid by French law, on terms that the employer would refrain from bringing a criminal prosecution against the husband for misappropriation of the employer's funds, hardly duress of the same order. In *Ukraine v Law Debenture Trust Corp Plc* [2018] EWCA Civ 2026 the Court of Appeal applied public policy to disapply the act of state doctrine in order to assess an allegation of duress against Russia.

1118 *Lemenda Trading Co Ltd v African Middle East Petroleum Co Ltd* [1988] Q.B. 448. See also *Tekron Resources Ltd v Guinea Investment Co Ltd* [2003] EWHC 2577 (QB), [2004] 2 Lloyd's Rep. 26; *Marlwood Commercial Inc v Kozeny* [2006] EWHC 872 (Comm); *Donegal International Ltd v Zambia* [2007] EWHC 197 (Comm), [2007] 1 Lloyd's Rep. 397; *R v V* [2008] EWHC 1531 (Comm), [2009] 1 Lloyd's Rep. 97.

## (g) Foreign Currency Obligations

### Currency of damages

*Replace footnote 1142 with:*

1142 *Services Europe Atlantique Sud v Stockholms Rederaktiebolag Svea* [1979] A.C. 685. See *Bain v Field* (1920) 5 Ll.L. Rep. 16; *Ottoman Bank v Chakarian (No.1)* [1930] A.C. 277; *Kraut AG v Albany Fabrics Ltd* [1977] Q.B. 182; *Société Francaise Bunge SA v Belcan NV* [1985] 3 All E.R. 378; *Metaalhandel J.A. Magnus BV v Ardfields Transport Ltd* [1988] 1 Lloyd's Rep. 197; *The Texaco Melbourne* [1994] 1 Lloyd's Rep. 473 (loss felt in Ghanaian cedis and measured in that currency despite fall in rate of exchange from 2.75 cedis to dollar at date of breach to 375 at date of judgment; criticised by Knott [1994] L.M.C.L.Q. 311); *Virani Ltd v Manuel Revert Y Cia SA* [2003] EWCA Civ 1651, [2004] 2 Lloyd's Rep. 14. See also *B.P. Exploration Co (Libya) Ltd v Hunt (No.2)* [1981] 1 W.L.R. 232 (affirmed [1983] 2 A.C. 352 (restitutionary award under Law Reform (Frustrated Contracts) Act 1943)). In *Cathay Pacific Airlines Ltd v Lufthansa Technick AG* [2019] EWHC 715 (Ch) the court applied this principle in holding that there was nothing to prevent it from making an order for costs in a foreign currency. 30-299

CHAPTER 31

# AGENCY

## 1. AGENCY IN GENERAL

### Scope of this chapter

*Replace paragraph with:*

**31-001** Despite the fact that this chapter appears in Vol.II of the present work, which is entitled "Specific Contracts", agency is a much wider topic than a specific named contract. At common law the word "agency" can be said to represent a body of general rules under which one person, the agent, has the power to change the legal relations of another, the principal.[2] It is sometimes indeed said that prima facie what a person can do himself he can do by an agent; but this is not always so.[3] The main areas in which this power is analysed are the law of contract, where an agent may have power to bind and entitle his principal by contract and by acts connected with the performance of a contract, and the law of property, where he may have power to receive property for his principal or make a valid disposition of his principal's property; and these are dealt with in this chapter. Similar reasoning may appear in other areas (e.g. torts, evidence); but the doctrines of agency are not always so well worked out beyond the main spheres of their operation, and the context in which the reasoning is used and the extent of its use may therefore require careful consideration in each case. Agency reasoning may also be deployed in contexts far from the original paradigm. In such cases the use of the paradigm is often incomplete, but the general reasoning is usually recognisable.[4] The central doctrines which have been developed stress the generality of the agent's power to bind and entitle his principal, while himself dropping out of the transaction and incurring neither rights nor liabilities, though sometimes the agent may himself be liable and entitled in addition.[5] These may be said to concern the external aspect of agency. There are also certain typical rules concerning the rights and liabilities of principal and agent inter se. These usually, but not always, involve contractual relations between principal and agent, which can sometimes be appropriately called a contract of agency but are more likely to operate as special rules against the background of some other contract, such as a contract of employment or of hire of services. In particular, they deal with the agent's duties (normally of reasonable care), impose fiduciary duties on the agent,[6] and regulate his rights to remuneration (typically by commission) and to indemnity.[7] These, which alone fit the idea of agency as a specific contract, are usually said to concern the internal aspect of agency.

[2] *Restatement, Third, Agency*, paras 1.01, 2.01 (action that has "legal consequences for the principal").

[3] The power to act by an agent is sometimes expressly recognised by statute: e.g. Bills of Exchange Act 1882 ss.22–26, 91; Limitation Act 1939 s.24 (now s.30 of the Limitation Act 1980) (see *Wright v Pepin* [1954] 1 W.L.R. 635; *Re Transplanters (Holding Co) Ltd* [1958] 1 W.L.R. 822). The power of trustees to delegate to others is regulated by Trustee Delegation Act 1999; Trustee Act 2000 ss.11–23. As to rights to conduct litigation for another see *Gregory v Turner* [2003] EWCA Civ 183, [2003] 1 W.L.R. 1149; as to verification of documents for another by affidavit see *Clauss v Pir* [1988] Ch. 267. Where a statute is silent, the normal implication is that, in the absence of other indications, the basic rule permitting acts by an agent applies: see *R. v Kent Justices* (1873) L.R. 8 Q.B. 305; *Re Whitley Partners Ltd* (1886) 32 Ch. D. 337; *R. v Assessment Committee of St Mary Abbot's, Kensington* [1891] 1 Q.B. 378; *LCC v Agricultural Food Products Ltd* [1955] 2 Q.B. 218; *McRae v Coulton* (1986) 7 N.S.W.L.R. 644 (containing illuminating discussion as to forms of signature); *General Legal Council (on the application of Whitter) v Frankson* [2006] UKPC 42, [2006] 1 W.L.R. 2803. The Statute of Frauds Amendment Act 1828

s.6 (as to which, see Vol.I, para.7-043) has been held to require personal signature, which has caused difficulties as to signature by agents of companies: see *Hirst v West Riding Union Banking Co* [1901] 2 K.B. 560; *UBAF Ltd v European American Banking Corp (The Pacific Colocotronis)* [1984] Q.B. 713 (noted [1984] J.B.L. 248); and see *McRae v Coulton*, above. A signature may be in electronic form: *Lindsay v O'Loughnane* [2010] EWHC 529 (QB) at [95]; in the context of the Statute of Frauds and guarantees: *Golden Ocean Group Ltd v Salgaocar Mining Industries Pvt Ltd* [2011] EWHC 56 (Comm), [2011] 1 W.L.R. 2575 at [95] (discussing different possible meanings of "electronic signature"); on appeal [2012] EWCA Civ 265, [2012] 1 Lloyd's Rep. 542 at [31] et seq. See also *Ramsay v Love* [2015] EWHC 65 (Ch) (writing machine operated by person with general authority).

[4] For example, in the context of liquidators and receivers: see Tan and Wee, Ch.8 in *Agency Law in Commercial Practice*, Busch, Macgregor and Watts (eds) (2016); *Menon v Pask* [2019] EWHC 2611 (Ch), [2020] Ch. 66. For consideration of the identifying features of agency reasoning see *UBS AG v Kommunale Wasserwerke Leipzig GmbH* [2017] EWCA Civ 1567, [2017] 2 Lloyd's Rep. 621 at [79] et seq.; *Zedra Trust Co (Jersey) Ltd v Hut Group Ltd* [2019] EWHC 2191 (Comm); *National Bank of Kazakhstan v Bank of New York Mellon SA/London Branch* [2020] EWHC 916 (Comm) at [54]. For an extreme use of the analogy see, e.g. *The Global Santosh* [2016] UKSC 20, [2016] 1 W.L.R. 1853, where it is used to allocate responsibility among subcontractors in the unloading of ships.

[5] See below, paras 31-083, 31-084.

[6] In *UBS AG v Kommunale Wasserwerke Leipzig GmbH* [2017] EWCA Civ 1567, [2017] 2 Lloyd's Rep. 621 at [92] it is said by the majority of the Court of Appeal that "there are no doubt many forms of non-fiduciary agency". Except as regards agency in a very loose sense, this, with respect, may be doubted. See however further discussion by Marcus Smith J. in *Pengelly v Business Mortgage Finance 4 Plc* [2020] EWHC 2002 (Ch).

[7] See below, paras 31-136 et seq. *Restatement, Third*, adds a requirement of control by the principal: see para.1.01. It is submitted in *Bowstead and Reynolds on Agency*, 21st edn (2018) at para.1-018 that this is of limited significance; but it is alluded to by Hamblen L.J. in *London Borough of Haringey v Ahmed* [2017] EWCA Civ 1861, [2018] 1 P.&C.R. DG12 at [28].

### Incomplete agency: canvassing agents

*Replace footnote 12 with:*

[12] Below, paras 31-118 et seq.; *Premium Real Estate Ltd v Stevens* [2009] 2 N.Z.L.R. 384 (real estate agent); *McWilliam v Norton Finance (UK) Ltd* [2015] EWCA Civ 186, [2015] 1 All E.R. (Comm) 1026 (credit broker); *Tigris International BV v China Southern Airlines Co Ltd* [2014] EWCA Civ 1649; *Pengelly v Business Mortgage Finance 4 Plc* [2020] EWHC 2002 (Ch) (mortgage broker). **31-002**

### Use of the terms "agent", "agency"

*Replace footnote 20 with:*

[20] See, e.g. *Wong Mee Wan v Kwan Kin Travel Services Ltd* [1996] 1 W.L.R. 38 (tour operator held principal and so liable for negligence of sub-contractor); *Titshall Ltd v Qwerty Travel Ltd* [2011] EWCA Civ 1569; cf. *Shepperd v Crystal Holidays Ltd* [1997] C.L. 500 (holiday company agent to make contract with skiing instructor); *IRC v SecretHotels2 Ltd* [2014] UKSC 16, [2014] 2 All E.R. 685 (intermediary making hotel bookings: context, VAT). Such contracts are now controlled by the Package Travel and Linked Travel Arrangements Regulations 2018 (SI 2018/634). See Vol.I, para.14-051. **31-005**

## 2. EXAMPLES OF TYPES OF AGENT

*Replace footnote 65 with:*

### Real estate agents[65]

[65] See above, para.31-002; below, paras 31-115, 31-140 et seq. The qualifications and activities of estate agents are affected by the Estate Agents Act 1979. See also Consumers, Estate Agents and Redress Act 2007 Pt 3, as amended; Consumer Protection from Unfair Trading Regulations 2008 (SI 2008/1277); Conway, "Regulation of Estate Agents", House of Commons Briefing Paper No.CPB 6900, April 18, 2019. **31-012**

*Replace footnote 75 with:*

[75] e.g. *Regier v Campbell-Stuart* [1939] Ch. 766; *Premium Real Estate Ltd v Stevens* [2009] 2 N.Z.L.R. 384; see below, paras 31-118 et seq. **31-012**

### Partners

*Replace footnote 83 with:*

31-014 [83] But a "limited partner" has no power to bind his firm: Limited Partnership Act 1907 s.6 (though a member of a limited liability partnership has: Limited Liability Partnerships Act 2000 s.6); and joint adventurers are not necessarily partners with power to bind each other: *Heaps v Dobson* (1863) 15 C.B.(N.S.) 460; cf. *United Dominions Corp Ltd v Brian Pty Ltd* (1985) 157 C.L.R. 1. The last 11 words of s.5 are notoriously ambiguous: see Montrose (1939) 17 Can. Bar Rev. 700–701; Thomas (1971) 6 Victoria U. of Wellington L.R. 1.

## 3. COMMERCIAL AGENTS

### Commercial agents

*Replace paragraph with:*

31-017 An EC Directive, the most conspicuous effect of which is to confer special rights for certain agents, designated "commercial agents", in the event of termination of authority[96] has fairly recently been brought into effect in Great Britain by regulation,[97] and although the notion is unfamiliar in Great Britain,[98] cases in which agents have argued that they are entitled to the benefit of the regulations are now appearing. They "govern the relations between commercial agents and their principals".[99] "Commercial agent" is defined as "a self-employed intermediary[100] who has continuing authority[101] to negotiate[102] the sale or purchase of goods[103] on behalf of another person (the "principal"), or to negotiate and conclude the sale or purchase of goods on behalf of and in the name of[104] that principal".[105] There are specific exceptions for officers of companies or associations, partners, insolvency practitioners,[106] gratuitous agents, agents operating on commodity exchanges or in commodity markets,[107] the Crown Agents,[108] and persons whose activities as commercial agents are to be considered secondary.[109] This latter must be assessed by reference to the particular arrangement rather than the general balance of the agent's activities.[110]

[96] Commercial Agents Directive 86/153 [1986] O.J. L382/17.

[97] By the Commercial Agents (Council Directive) Regulations 1993 (SI 1993/3053) as amended by SI 1993/3173 and SI 1998/2868; Northern Ireland is covered by the Commercial Agents (Council Directive) Regulations (Northern Ireland) 1993 (SI 1993/483), effective from January 14, 1994. There is a full discussion in *Bowstead and Reynolds on Agency*, 21st edn (2018), Ch.11. For specialised works see Saintier and Scholes, *Commercial Agents and the Law* (2005); Randolph and Davey, *The European Law of Commercial Agency*, 3rd edn (2010); Singleton, *Commercial Agency Agreements: Law and Practice*, 4th edn (2015).

[98] A useful analysis of the functions of a commercial agent is given by A.G. Trstenjak in *Wood Floor Solutions Andreas Domberger GmbH v Silva Trade SA* (C-19/09) EU:C:2010:137, [2010] I.L.Pr. 21 at AG53 et seq.

[99] Commercial Agents Regulations reg.1(2). In *Wood Floor Solutions Andreas Domberger GmbH v Silva Trade SA* (C-19/09) EU:C:2010:137, [2010] 1 W.L.R. 900 the CJEU treated such a contract as one for the provision of services for the purposes of Council Regulation 44/2001 on jurisdiction and the enforcement of judgments. (This report does not include the opinion of A.G. Trstenjak, above.)

[100] Such agency is not confined to natural persons: *Bell Electric Ltd v Aweco Appliance Systems GmbH & Co* [2002] EWHC 872, [2002] Eu. L.R. 443. The intermediary may have several principals: *Rossetti Marketing Ltd v Diamond Sofa Co Ltd* [2011] EWHC 2482 (QB), [2011] E.C.C. 28; point not referred to on appeal [2012] EWCA Civ 1021, [2013] 1 All E.R. (Comm) 308.

[101] The word "authority" could be taken to exclude some agents whose functions were purely canvassing (above, para.31-002), i.e. introducing business in some limited way. But in many cases there is an appointment of an agent whose main or even sole function is to introduce business over a period, and several cases accept such persons as coming within the definition: e.g. the cases cited below, n.102 and *Fern Computer Consultancy Ltd v Intergraph Cadworx & Analysis Solutions Inc* [2014] EWHC 2908 (Ch), [2014] Bus. L.R. 1397. Authority may be "continuing" if there is authority to conclude a single

contract plus authority to negotiate extensions: *Poseidon Chartering BV v Marianne Zeeschip VO* (C-3/04) EU:C:2006:176, [2006] 2 Lloyd's Rep. 105. The nature and scope of an agent's retainer is to be judged by reference to his contract but at the time relief is determined: *W Nagel v Pluczenik Diamond Co NV* [2017] EWHC 1750 (Comm), [2017] 2 Lloyd's Rep. 215 at [33]–[34]; affirmed without reference to this point [2018] EWCA Civ 2640, [2019] 1 Lloyd's Rep. 36.

102 "Negotiate" does not require that the agent have authority to agree terms: *PJ Pipe & Valve Co Ltd v Audco India Ltd* [2005] EWHC 1904 (QB), [2006] Eu. L.R. 368; *Nigel Fryer Joinery Services Ltd v Ian Firth Hardware Ltd* [2008] 2 Lloyd's Rep. 1080; *Invicta UK v International Brands Ltd* [2013] EWHC 1564 (QB), [2013] E.C.C. 30; *W Nagel v Pluczenik Diamond Co NV* [2017] EWHC 1750 (Comm), [2017] 2 Lloyd's Rep. 215 ("foster relationship of trust and promote goodwill"); affirmed without reference to this point [2018] EWCA Civ 2640, [2019] 1 Lloyd's Rep. 36. In *Green Deal Marketing Southern Ltd v Economy Energy Trading Ltd* [2019] EWHC 507 (Ch), [2019] 2 All E.R. (Comm) 191 a person whose task was to persuade customers to switch supplier was held a commercial agent. The activities may be carried out on the principal's premises, and the agent may perform other functions also: *Zako SPRL v Sanidel SA* (C-452/17) [2019] Bus. L.R. 343.

103 As to which see *Tamarind International Ltd v Eastern Natural Gas (Retail) Ltd* [2000] Eu. L.R. 708 (gas); *Green Deal Marketing Southern Ltd v Economy Energy Trading Ltd* [2019] EWHC 507 (Ch), [2019] 2 All E.R. (Comm) 191 (gas and electricity). In *Computer Associates UK Ltd v Software Incubator Ltd* [2018] EWCA Civ 518 it is decided that computer software supplied as a download does not rank as "goods" for the purposes of the regulation. Whether a licence to use it would rank as a sale is therefore not decided, though the question had been considered (on the basis that "goods" were involved) in *Fern Computer Consultancy Ltd v Intergraph Cadworx & Analysis Solutions Inc* [2014] EWHC 2908 (Ch), [2014] Bus. L.R. 1397. The question of software supplied on a disk, on which there is sale of goods authority, is not determined. See further *Benjamin's Sale of Goods*, 10th edn (2017), para.1-086. Questions on the *Computer Associates* case were referred to the CJEU in March 2019.

104 This would appear to include situations where the principal is unidentified: see below, para.31-089. But it does not include indirect agents (*commissionnaires*, above, para.31-004): *Mavrona & Sia OE v Delta Etaireia Symettochon AE* (C-85/03) EU:C:2004:83, [2004] O.J. C94/17; or in general agents who contract in their own name, which would cover agents for undisclosed principals: *Sagal v Atelier Bunz GmbH* [2009] EWCA Civ 700, [2009] 2 Lloyd's Rep. 303.

105 Commercial Agents Regulations reg.2(1). A national law requiring such agents to register cannot prevent the application of the Directive: *Bellone v Yokohama SpA* (C-215/97) EU:C:1998:189, [1998] E.C.R. I-2191.

106 As defined in s.388 of the Insolvency Act 1986 (as amended).

107 As to which see *W Nagel v Pluczenik Diamond Co NV* [2018] EWCA Civ 2640, [2019] 1 Lloyd's Rep. 36 (diamond market).

108 Commercial Agents Regulations reg.2(1), (2).

109 Commercial Agents Regulations reg.2(3). This provision is then defined specifically for the UK by a (rather unsatisfactory) Schedule. The vires of this part of the regulations was unsuccessfully challenged in *Crane v Sky In-Home Services Ltd* [2007] EWHC 66 (Ch), [2007] 2 All E.R. (Comm) 599.

110 See *AMB Imballaggi Plastics SRL v Pacflex Ltd* [1999] 2 All E.R. (Comm) 249, 254; *Tamarind International Ltd v Eastern Natural Gas (Retail) Ltd* [2000] Eu. L.R. 708; *Edwards v International Connection (UK) Ltd* [2006] EWCA Civ 662; *Crane v Sky In-Home Services Ltd* [2007] EWHC 66 (Ch), [2007] 2 All E.R. (Comm) 599 (extended discussion). UK courts, interpreting the extremely obscure definition contained in the Schedule to the regulations (described as "an almost impenetrable piece of drafting" in *AMB Imballaggi v Pacflex Ltd* [1999] 2 All E.R. (Comm) 249, 254), have used the restriction to impose quite strict limits on when the regulations apply, seeking to confine them to what may be called "goodwill-generating" functions even when some other agency function is more prominent. See *Gailey v Environmental Waste Controls* 2004 Scot SC 300 (OH), [2004] Eu.L.R.423; *McAdam v Boxpak Ltd* [2006] CSIH 9, 2006 S.L.T. 217. See a careful discussion of the genesis of the provision by Saintier [2012] J.B.L. 128; *Bowstead and Reynolds on Agency*, 21st edn (2018), paras 11-020 et seq. On a smaller scale, an argument, based on *Crane v Sky In-Home*, above, that where software is sold linked to hardware, the hardware constitutes the goods and the software is only secondary was rejected in *Fern Computer Consultancy Ltd v Intergraph Cadworx & Analysis Solutions Inc* [2014] EWHC 2908 (Ch), [2014] Bus. L.R. 1397. But where the main function was excluded because in a commodity market, a lesser function was also excluded as secondary in *W Nagel v Pluczenik Diamond Co NV* [2017] EWHC 1750 (Comm), [2017] 2 Lloyd's Rep. 215.

## 4. Creation of Agency

### (a) Express Agreement

#### Powers of attorney

*Replace paragraph with:*

**31-025** A power of attorney is a formal granting of authority by one person to another to act on the first person's behalf, usually in situations of illness or absence, though sometimes for commercial purposes.[144] By virtue of the Powers of Attorney Act 1971 s.1,[145] an instrument creating a power of attorney must be executed as a deed[146] by the donor of the power.[147] The use of a prescribed form is also required for a Lasting Power of Attorney under the Mental Capacity Act 2005.[148]

[144] See Aldridge, *Powers of Attorney*, 11th edn (2016); Dal Pont, *Powers of Attorney*, 3rd edn (LexisNexis: Australia, 2019).

[145] As amended principally by the Law of Property (Miscellaneous Provisions) Act 1989 s.4 and Sch.1 and the Regulatory Reform (Execution of Deeds and Documents Order 2005 (SI 2005/1906). The statute does not define "power of attorney", though it gives a specimen form for one.

[146] As to the requisites of a deed (e.g. as to witnesses) see Law of Property (Miscellaneous Provisions) Act 1989 s.1. An imperfect power of attorney may rank as an informal authorisation in writing: *Rose v Rose* (1986) 7 N.S.W.L.R. 679.

[147] The Act also makes provision for proof of powers of attorney (s.3), and provides a form of general power of attorney (s.10 and Sch.1). The donee may normally execute any instrument, sign or do any act in his own name: s.7 (as amended by the Law of Property (Miscellaneous Provisions) Act 1989 s.4 and Sch.1); as to which see *Clauss v Pir* [1988] Ch. 267; *Yu Hing Tong Ltd v Fung Hing Chiu Cyril* [2016] 5 H.K.L.R.D. 567.

[148] Mental Capacity Act 2005 s.9 and Sch.1. See below, paras 31-168, 31-172.

### (c) Ratification

#### General rule

*In penultimate line, after "party claims ratification", replace "against" with:*

**31-027** by

#### Who can ratify

*Replace footnote 169 with:*

**31-029** [169] cf. *AM Satterthwaite Ltd v New Zealand Shipping Co Ltd (The Eurymedon)* [1975] A.C. 154; and see *Haberdasher Aske's Federation Trust Ltd v Lewisham LBC* [2018] EWHC 558 (TCC), [2018] B.L.R. 511.

#### Knowledge of circumstances

*Replace footnote 177 with:*

**31-030** [177] This is suggested in *ING Re (UK) Ltd v R&V Versicherung AG* [2006] EWHC 1544 (Comm), [2006] 2 All E.R. (Comm) 870 at [155]–[156], though the reliance was in fact held unjustified. See also *Taheri v Vitek* [2014] NSWCA 209 at [135].

#### Limits on ratification

*Replace paragraph with:*

**31-034** It is plain that there must be some limits on the applicability of ratification, which is a sensible and practical idea in many situations, but could give rise to obviously unfair results in others. There has been little agreement, however, on what technique is to be used for this purpose. In the famous case of *Bird v Brown*[192] it was held that stoppage *in transitu* could not be ratified after the *transitus* had ended. This can be explained on the basis that to allow ratification would have been to divest a property interest, that of the consignee; or more generally that it would allow a time limit to be extended by ratification. The notion that a property interest cannot be divested by a ratification must certainly, if confined to the strict sense of property rights and their validity against third parties,[193] be correct, and may explain this case and another holding that the unauthorised exercise of an option (by the solicitor of the person entitled) could not be ratified after the expiry of the relevant period.[194] But the *contractual* aspect of the second situation can be considered separately, and in general a time limit rule is too narrow to provide a solution. There are in fact other situations where it is thought that ratification should be permitted even though the effect is to extend a time limit. It has been held that ratification of an act which if authorised would have prevented the limitation period from running is effective though it takes place after the expiry of the period.[195] It has been said that ratification must be within a reasonable time "which cannot extend after the time at which the contract is to commence".[196] But although it has been suggested that such a reasonable time rule should be the main control[197] there are numerous dicta against the existence of such a rule.[198] The question is elaborately discussed in two fairly recent decisions, one not allowing ratification,[199] the other permitting it.[200] What emerges from them is that the matter can only be solved by a general principle, of which even the property cases are perhaps to be treated as examples, that ratification is not effective where to allow it would be unfairly prejudicial to the other party.[201] On this basis, a ratification on which the ratifier does not rely against the third party might, in some circumstances, be effective against the ratifier.

192 (1850) 4 Ex. 786. See *The Borvigilant* [2003] EWCA Civ 935, [2003] 2 Lloyd's Rep. 520 at [79] et seq.

193 And hence not taking in notions operating only between the parties such as an accrued cause of action (see *The Borvigilant*, above at [89]) or an accrued defence (see *Smith v Henniker-Major & Co* [2002] EWCA Civ 762, [2003] Ch. 182 at [71]).

194 *Dibbins v Dibbins* [1996] 2 Ch. 348. See also *Re Construction Forestry Mining and Energy Union* (1994) 181 C.L.R. 539, 545 (act must be valid and effective when done); *Aldford House Freehold Ltd v Grosvenor (Mayfair) Estate* [2018] EWHC 3430 (Ch), [2019] 1 W.L.R. 1489 (invalid notice under Leasehold Reform, Housing and Urban Development Act 1993 not ratifiable).

195 *Presentaciones Musicales SA v Secunda* [1994] Ch. 271 (issue of writ). The matter is considered in *Causwell v General Legal Council* [2019] UKPC 9 (ratification of disciplinary proceedings, affirming the significance of construction of any relevant statute, and stating that in the absence of contrary intention ordinary principles permit rather than prevent ratification).

196 *Metropolitan Asylums Board v Kingham & Sons* (1890) 9 T.L.R. 217, 218, per Fry L.J.

197 C.-H. Tan (2001) 117 L.Q.R. 626.

198 See *Celthene Pty Ltd v WJK Hauliers Ltd* [1981] 1 N.S.W.L.R. 606, 615; *Bedford Ins Co Ltd v Instituto de Resseguros do Brasil* [1985] Q.B. 966, 986–987.

199 *Smith v Henniker-Major & Co* [2002] EWCA Civ 762, [2003] Ch. 182 (no ratification of deed of assignment three years after execution).

200 *The Borvigilant* [2003] EWCA Civ 935, [2003] 2 Lloyd's Rep. 520 (ratification by sub-contractor of clause conferring immunity from liability in tort).

201 See *Smith v Henniker-Major & Co*, above, at [71]; *The Borvigilant*, above, at [70], [78], [79], [88]; *Restatement, Third, Agency*, para.4.05.

## (f) Delegation

### Effect of delegation

*Replace footnote 263 with:*

31-042 [263] *Powell & Thomas v Evan Jones & Co* [1905] 1 K.B. 11; *Markel International Insurance Co Ltd v Surety Guarantee Consultants Ltd* [2008] EWHC 1135 (Comm), [2009] Lloyd's Rep. I.R. 77; cf. *FM Capital Partners Ltd v Marino* [2018] EWHC 2905 (Comm) at [95] et seq.

## 5. AUTHORITY

### Express and implied authority

*Replace footnote 276 with:*

31-044 [276] See *Lysaght v Falk Bros & Co Ltd* (1905) 2 C.L.R. 421, 430, 439; *Tobin v Broadbent* (1947) 75 C.L.R. 378 (power of attorney); *Heinl v Jyske Bank (Gibraltar) Ltd* [1999] Lloyd's Rep. Bank. 511, 521; *Hopkins v TL Dallas Group Ltd* [2004] EWHC 1379, [2005] 1 B.C.L.C. 543 at [89]; also *Criterion Properties Plc v Stratford UK Properties LLC* [2004] UKHL 28, [2004] 1 W.L.R. 1846; Watts [2017] J.B.L. 269 (explaining or rebutting dicta and arguments to the contrary); *Bowstead and Reynolds on Agency*, 21st edn (2018), art.23. Cf. *Taheri v Vitek* [2014] NSWCA 209 at [105] et seq. (power of attorney legislation). As to authority to act illegally, see *Bowstead and Reynolds on Agency*, 21st edn (2018), para.2-025.

### Express authority: construction of documents

*Replace footnote 282 with:*

31-045 [282] *Bryant v Banque du Peuple* [1893] A.C. 170, 177; *Jonmenjoy Coondoo v Watson* (1884) 9 App. Cas. 561; *Re Dowson & Jenkins' Contract* [1904] 2 Ch. 219. And see *Jacobs v Morris* [1902] 1 Ch. 816; *Danby v Coutts & Co* (1885) 29 Ch. D. 500; *Reckitt v Barnett, Pembroke & Slater* [1929] A.C. 176. But if the power of attorney fails for lack of formality the strict interpretation rule no longer applies: *Katara Hospitality v Guez* [2018] EWHC 3063 (Comm).

*Replace footnote 289 with:*

### Usual authority[289]

31-047 [289] See further as to this term *Bowstead and Reynolds on Agency*, 21st edn (2018), para.3-005. The notion is discussed in *Ukraine v Law Debenture Trust Corp Plc* [2018] EWCA Civ 2026, [2019] Q.B. 1121. See also as to directors *East Asia Co Ltd v PT Satria Tirtatama Energindo* [2019] UKPC 30, [2020] 2 All E.R. 2940.

## 6. PRINCIPAL'S RELATIONS WITH THIRD PARTIES

## (a) General Rule

### General rule: identified and unidentified principal

*Replace paragraph with:*

31-054 The general rule in contract is that a principal is bound by, and entitled to the benefit of, the contract of his agent made on his behalf within the scope of such agent's actual authority, express or implied. This conclusion, though a standard one, obviously only follows where the agent acted as such and not on his own account. It is not always clear on the facts when this is so. If the agent acts specifically, whether orally or in writing, on behalf of a principal whom he identifies,[318] then the conclusion will normally follow. If the principal is unidentified (e.g. "bought for our principals"), it may be necessary to prove who the principal was and that the agent intended to act for him.[319] Where the agent has the same or similar instructions from different principals there may be a further problem.[320]

[318] This would include a principal described but not named, e.g. the heirs of property, whoever they may be: *Lyell v Kennedy* (1899) 14 App. Cas. 437.

[319] See *Teheran-Europe Co Ltd v ST Belton (Tractors) Co Ltd* [1969] 2 Q.B. 545, 555–556. See (but in the context of insurance of construction projects) *National Oilwell (UK) Ltd v Davy Offshore Ltd* [1993] 2 Lloyd's Rep. 582, 596–597, per Colman J. This passage from the *National Oilwell* case, in the context of construction insurance, was doubted by Leggatt J. in the context of undisclosed principal (below, para.31-064) in *Magellan Spirit ApS v Vitol SA* [2016] EWHC 454 (Comm), [2016] 2 Lloyd's Rep. 1 at [19], apparently on the basis that objective criteria should be applied to the ascertainment of a principal. It was accepted in a different context in *Sackville UK Property Select II (GP) No.1 Ltd v Robertson Taylor Insurance Brokers Ltd* [2018] EWHC 122 (Ch), [2018] 1 P. & C.R. DG24 at [46] (on the question of on whose behalf a notice under a lease was served), and the dicta of Colman J. were explained in another construction insurance case, *Haberdasher Aske's Federation Trust Ltd v Lewisham LBC* [2018] EWHC 558 (TCC), [2018] B.L.R.511 at [39], [42]–[43], [50], [52] and in the context of chartering in *Americas Bulk Transport (Liberia) v Cosco Bulk Carrier Ltd (China)* [2020] EWHC 147 (Comm) at [23]. Obviously, where objective evidence is available, for example in a contract between principal and agent, as often in construction cases, an objective ascertainment of intention is obviously much easier to require. In an agency context it is doubtful whether this will always be practicable.

[320] See e.g. *Scott and Horton v Godfrey* [1901] 2 K.B. 726 (practice on the London Stock Exchange as it operated at the time: see in particular the arguments of counsel). See in general Reynolds, in Busch and McGregor (eds), *Agency Law and Commercial Practice* (2015), Ch.3.

*Add new paragraphs:*

**Agent not stated to be such** If a person who might be an agent is simply named without more in a contract (which in such circumstances is more likely to be in writing) the first assumption may be that he is in fact acting as a party to the contract and will be the party liable and entitled on it.[321] It is possible however that he may nevertheless, despite lack of indication in a written contract, be acting not as principal but only as agent: and it may be argued that the contractual matrix surrounding his dealings with the third party gave the third party reason to know that he dealt only as agent for another person, who can be identified.[322] Even if the parol evidence rule[323] were applied to the document, evidence may be given as to the capacity in which the parties acted. Clear evidence would be required of the understanding of the parties and of the identity of the principal for whom the agent was acting. But where the document is clear, the proposition that external evidence can be deployed may not be beyond argument.[323a] **31-054A**

[321] See *Magellan Spirit ApS v Vitol SA* [2016] EWHC 454 (Comm), [2016] 2 Lloyd's Rep. 1, [28]. See also *Cooke v Wilson* (1856) 1 C.B. (N.S.) 153, 162 per Cresswell J.: "Prima facie, when a man signs a contract in his own name, he is a contracting party; and there must be something very strong upon the face of the instrument to prevent the liability attaching to him".

[322] e.g. *Filatona Trading Ltd v Navigator Equities Ltd* [2020] EWCA Civ 109 (where the principal's name did not appear in the controlling provisions of the written contract). The full contractual matrix is exhaustively analysed by Teare J. at first instance: [2019] EWHC 173 (Comm). Both judgments make use of material on the undisclosed principal situation, which is not strictly relevant. See also *Humfrey v Dale* (1857) 7 E. & B. 266, 275 (aff'd (1858) E.B. & E. 1004); *Internaut Shipping GmbH v Fercometal SARL* [2003] EWCA Civ 812, [2003] 2 Lloyd's Rep. 430 at [56]; *Hamid v Francis Bradshaw Partnership* [2013] EWCA Civ 470, [2013] B.L.R. 447, [50]–[57]; *Aspen Underwriting Ltd v Kairos Shipping Co Ltd* [2018] EWCA Civ 2590, [2019] 1 Lloyd's Rep. 221 (point not in issue on appeal [2020] UKSC 110); *Turks Shipyard Ltd v Owners of the Vessel November* [2020] EWHC 661 (Admlty); *IVY Technology Ltd v Martin* [2020] EWHC 94 (Comm); *Restatement, Third, Agency*, para.6.01 at p.9.

[323] As to which see above, Vol.I, paras 13-109 et seq.

[323a] See *Taylor v Rhino Overseas Inc* [2020] EWCA Civ 353 at [46] et seq. per Arnold L.J., citing dicta of Jackson L.J. in *Hamid v Francis Bradshaw Partnership*, above, described as a "more relaxed approach", but contrasting dicta of Blair J. in *Barbudev v Eurocom Cable Management Bulgaria Eood* [2011] EWHC 1560, [2011] 2 All ER (Comm) 951 at [114]. The dicta of Jackson L.J. are followed in *Gregor Fisken Ltd v Carl* [2020] EWHC 1385 (Comm) and *Maftoon v Sayed* [2020] EWHC 1801 (TCC).

31-054B **Undisclosed principal—a different situation** The situation described above should not be confused with a true undisclosed principal situation. The latter occurs where a party undoubtedly makes a contract as principal, but in doing so is in fact authorised by a further principal the existence or relevance of whom he does not disclose. In such a case, unless the contract is one by its terms expressly or impliedly confined to the parties, the undisclosed principal is liable and entitled on the contract in addition to (or perhaps alternatively to) the agent. In such a case proof that the agent had actual authority and intended to act for the principal, and that the contract does not expressly impliedly exclude the undisclosed principal's right to sue or his liability to be sued, will be crucial. This unusual and specialised doctrine of the undisclosed principal and the limits on it are considered below.[323b]

[323b] See paras 31-063 et seq.

31-054C In recent cases it has been said that there should be a reservation for the situations, referred to above, where the name of the principal is established by extrinsic evidence supplementing or displacing a name in a (usually written) contract, who is thereby established as acting as agent, to the effect that such an interpretation does not apply where the terms of the contract "unequivocally and exhaustively" identify the parties to it, or some similar phrase.[323c] This is plainly connected with the rule excluding the intervention of an undisclosed principal referred to above,[323d] though the formulation is stricter and directed towards identity of original parties, and hence more relevant in disclosed principal situations. The two situations are certainly analytically different. In the undisclosed principal situation there is by definition a contract with the agent, and the question is whether its terms are inconsistent with the intervention of another person as principal, bearing in mind that the first or original principal, who turns out to be an agent, is certainly still liable and entitled on the contract. In the disclosed and identified principal situation referred to above, the evidence establishes who the principal is, and (usually) that the agent is not liable: the question is whether there is any clause[323e] or other feature of the contractual matrix which makes such an interpretation not possible.[323f] This has been said to raise a heavy burden to prove.[323g]

[323c] These words appear in the judgment of Teare J. at 1st instance in *Aspen Underwriting Ltd v Kairos Shipping Co Ltd* [2017] EWHC 1904 (Comm) at [42] (for subsequent stages see above, n.322). See the *Filatona* case, above, [2020] EWCA Civ 109 at [62] et seq. and [100] et seq.

[323d] See the *Filatona* case at first instance, [2019] EWHC 173 where Teare J. suggests, at [64], that substantially the same principle should apply for cases involving disclosed principals.

[323e] Examples of appropriate clauses are given in the *Filatona* case at [90]. But "entire agreement" clauses, though highly relevant, are not necessarily efficacious to exclude disclosed or undisclosed principals: see *Kaefer Aislamientos SA de CV v AMS Drilling Mexico SA de CV* [2019] EWCA Civ 10, [2019] 1 W.L.R. 3514 at [113].

[323f] For a clear explanation of this difference see the judgment of Males L.J. in the *Filatona* case, [2020] EWCA Civ 109 at [121].

[323g] See the *Filatona* case in the Court of Appeal [2020] EWCA Civ 109 at [126]; at first instance [2019] EWHC 173 (Comm) at [294].

31-054D A well-known dictum of Diplock L.J., referred to as "the beneficial assumption in commercial cases",[323h] alludes to unidentified and undisclosed principals in a way which suggests that in neither case will limits on the contracting parties be easy to establish; but it does not cover identified principal situations.[323i]

> "Where an agent has such actual authority and enters into a contract with another party intending to do so on behalf of his principal, *it matters not whether he discloses to the*

*other party the identity of his principal, or even that he is contracting on behalf of a principal at all*, if the other party is willing or leads the agent to believe that he is willing to treat as a party to the contract anyone on whose behalf the agent may have been authorised to contract. *In the case of an ordinary commercial contract such willingness of the other party may be assumed* by the agent unless either the other party manifests his unwillingness or there are other circumstances which should lead the agent to realise that the other party was not so willing."[323j]

Though it is often said that the agent "drops out" of an authorised transaction, there are in fact circumstances in which he is liable as well as his principal. These matters are considered below.[323k]

[323h] By Lord Lloyd of Berwick in *Siu Yin Kwan v Eastern Assurance Co Ltd* [1994] 2 A.C. 199, 209, PC.

[323i] As Males L.J. points out in the *Filatona* case, above, that there is no need to rely on such a presumption in the disclosed and identified principal situation, where the facts are known.

[323j] *Teheran-Europe Co Ltd v S.T. Belton (Tractors) Ltd* [1968] 2 Q.B. 545, 555 (italics supplied).

[323k] See paras 31-084 et seq.

## (b) Apparent Authority

### Apparent authority

*Replace paragraph with:*

Where a person by words or conduct represents to a third party that another has authority to act on his behalf, he may be bound by the acts of that other as if he had in fact authorised them.[328] This doctrine, called the doctrine of apparent or ostensible authority,[329] applies to cases where a person allows another who is not his agent at all to appear as his agent,[330] to cases where a principal allows his agent to appear to have more authority than he actually has,[331] to cases where a principal makes reservations in his agent's authority that limit the authority which such agent would normally have, but fails to indicate this to third parties,[332] and to cases where a principal allows it to appear that an agent has authority when such authority has in fact been reduced or terminated.[333] The doctrine is said to be an application of the estoppel principle,[334] but it is a somewhat weak one, the normal rules being leniently applied, particularly in the contractual context as regards reliance on the representation.[335] What is clear, however, is that, as in most legal systems, the liability ultimately springs from the conduct of the principal rather than the position of the third party.[336] The words "represent", and "representation", though regularly used in this context (and below), probably carry too specific connotations.[337] The rules as traditionally stated may however be divided as follows. **31-056**

(i) A representation must be made by words or conduct. But though such representation may be express, it may also be implied from acts of a quite general nature, e.g. putting the agent in a position carrying with it a usual authority.[338] Such a representation may arise from a course of dealing (especially one involving regular ratification), though it has been said that authority will not readily be inferred from this.[339]

(ii) The representation must be made by the principal, or someone authorised in accordance with the law of agency to act for him.[340] A representation by the agent as to his authority cannot of itself create apparent authority.[341] But the conduct of the principal may make it more reasonable for the agent's representation as to facts upon which his authority depends to be relied on[342]; and in a well-known decision the principal was held bound on the basis that the agent, known to have limited authority to contract, nevertheless had authority to communicate the principal's approval to the transaction in question.[343] The facts of the case were somewhat marginal, in that the communication of assent was said to be implicit in an actual contractual offer. But it has recently been affirmed that there are common situations, particularly in organisations, where a subordinate has no authority, actual or apparent, to perform an act, but may have actual or apparent authority to report the decisions of a superior or group of superiors in respect of which action has been or will be taken.[344]

(iii) On general principles the representation must be of fact and not of law.[345] But propositions as to mistake of law may now need reconsideration in view of the decision of the House of Lords in *Kleinwort Benson Ltd v Lincoln CC*.[346]

(iv) The third party must act on the representation.[347] If he does not know of any representation, express or implied, but deals with the agent as a principal, it is obvious that he cannot rely on the doctrine.[348] But the requirement that there must be a representation which is relied on is not interpreted strictly. Thus though a person cannot be held out as agent to the world,[349] the representation need not be to a specific person: it has been said that "the holding out must be to the particular individual who says he relied on it, or under such circumstances of publicity as to justify the inference that he knew of it and acted upon it".[350] Sometimes negligent conduct is relied on as constituting a holding out: this is principally so in the case of property transactions, to which indeed the passage quoted above refers. In that context it has sometimes been said that there must be a duty of care towards the third party, but here again it appears that such a duty can be owed to quite a wide class of persons.[351] It does not seem that the third party's reliance need have been to his detriment: although it is clear that if he did not rely on the representation at all,[352] or ignored a clear opportunity of ascertaining the agent's authority,[353] or was put on inquiry by the facts of the transaction,[354] he cannot hold the principal liable, it is probably sufficient reliance merely to enter into a transaction on the faith of the representation.[355]

(v) The doctrine applies though the agent effects a forgery,[356] if the act in the course of which the forgery occurred was within his apparent authority and the third party was unaware of the forgery.[357] The same is true where the agent is fraudulent, or acts illegally in some other way.[358]

(vi) The doctrine, being based on estoppel, does not of itself entitle a principal to sue on the contract[359]: but he will normally be able to ratify right up to the moment of trial.

(vii) The authority will be that which the agent reasonably appeared to have to the third party, taking into account the manifestations of the principal, the implied authority normally applicable in the circumstances or to a person in the agent's position, or both.[360] It has often been said that there is no constructive notice in commercial transactions and there is quite extensively argued recent authority[361] that the third party can rely on an appearance of authority unless its belief that there was authority was "dishonest or irrational", which would include turning a blind eye. But though there is also authority that "nothing short of bad faith will do"[362] such an approach may go too far in protecting third parties, and does not accord with all the existing authority cited here.[363] The position as previously understood is restored by a recent Privy Council case which considers the dicta cited and recognises that a claimant cannot rely on apparent authority "if it failed to make the inquiries that a reasonable person would have made in all the circumstances in order to verify that [the agent] had authority".[363a]

[328] *Pickering v Busk* (1812) 15 East 38; *Pickard v Sears* (1837) 6 A. & E. 469; *Freeman v Cooke* (1848) 2 Exch. 654; *Smith v M'Guire* (1858) 3 Hurl. & N. 554; *Pole v Leask* (1863) 33 L.J. Ch. 155, 162; *Freeman & Lockyer v Buckhurst Park Properties (Mangal) Ltd* [1964] 2 Q.B. 480, 503 (the leading definition); *Hely-Hutchinson v Brayhead Ltd* [1968] 1 Q.B. 549.

[329] But often referred to in nineteenth-century cases as implied authority.

[330] e.g. *Barrett v Deere* (1828) Moo. & M. 200; *F. Mildner & Sons v Noble* [1956] C.L.Y. 32; *Povey v Taylor* (1966) 116 New L.J. 1656. Such cases are rare. Much useful American material is referred to in *Hoddesdon v Koos Bros* 135 A. 2d 702 (1957) (bogus shop salesman).

[331] e.g. *Todd v Robinson* (1825) Ry. & M. 217. A possible modern example is *Pacific Carriers Ltd v BNP Paribas* (2004) 215 C.L.R. 451.

[332] e.g. *Montaignac v Shitta* (1890) 15 App. Cas. 357; *Manchester Trust v Furness* [1895] 2 Q.B. 539; *Waugh v HB Clifford & Sons Ltd* [1982] Ch. 374.

[333] e.g. *Summers v Solomon* (1857) 7 E. & B. 879; *Drew v Nunn* (1879) 4 Q.B.D. 661; *Rockland Industries Inc v Amerada Minerals Corp* [1980] 2 S.C.R. 2; (1980) 108 D.L.R. (3d) 513; *AMB Generali Holding AG v SEB Trygg Liv Holding Aktiebolaget* [2005] EWCA Civ 1237, [2006] 1 Lloyd's Rep. 318 at [37]; below, para.31-169.

[334] *Freeman & Lockyer v Buckhurst Park Properties (Mangal) Ltd* [1964] 2 Q.B. 480, 503; *Rama Corp v Proved Tin & General Investments* [1952] 2 Q.B. 147, 149–150; *Pole v Leask* (1863) 33 L.J. Ch. 155, 162. The initial burden of proof is on the person alleging authority: *PEC Asia Ltd v Golden Rice Co Ltd* [2014] EWHC 1583 (Comm). See Tan Cheng Han (2020) 136 L.Q.R. 315.

[335] "Each form of estoppel has its own elements, although some are common. The similarities warrant their recognition as a form of estoppel but the differences make each a distinct form with its own history and requirements": Handley, *Estoppel by Conduct and Election*, 2nd edn (2016), p.30.

[336] See Watts [2015] L.M.C.L.Q. 36, 39. For a recent example see *Fielden v Christie-Miller* [2015] EWHC 87 (Ch), [2015] 2 P. & C.R. DG5.

[337] *Restatement, Third, Agency* uses the better word "manifestation": paras 1.03, 2.03.

[338] *Freeman & Lockyer v Buckhurst Park Properties (Mangal) Ltd*, above, at 503 (managing director); *Panorama Developments (Guildford) Ltd v Fidelis Furnishing Fabrics Ltd* [1971] 2 Q.B. 711 (company secretary); *Waugh v HB Clifford & Sons Ltd* [1982] Ch. 374 (solicitor); *Egyptian Intl Foreign Trade Co v Soplex Wholesale Supplies Ltd (The Raffaella)* [1985] 2 Lloyd's Rep. 36 (documentary credits manager); *Shearson Lehman Bros Inc v Maclaine, Watson & Co Ltd (No.2)* [1988] 1 W.L.R. 16, 28; *Pharmed Medicare Private Ltd v Univar Ltd* [2002] EWCA Civ 1569, [2003] 1 All E.R. (Comm) 321. As to usual authority see, above, para.31-047. For the view that deeds constitute an exception to the need for a representation by the principal on the basis of the indoor management rule, see Watts (2002) 2 O.U.C.L.J. 93.

[339] See *PEC Asia Ltd v Golden Rice Co Ltd* [2014] EWHC 1583 (Comm), citing *Slingsby v District Bank Ltd* [1932] 1 K.B. 544, 566; but cf. Watts [2015] L.M.C.L.Q. 36, 57–60. See also *MVV Environment Devonport Ltd v NTO Shipping GmbH & Co KG* [2020] EWHC 1371 (Comm) (no apparent authority to name a party as shipper on bills of lading to be derived from failure to object over a period).

[340] *Freeman & Lockyer v Buckhurst Park Properties (Mangal) Ltd*, above, at 506; *British Bank of the Middle East v Sun Life Assurance Co of Canada (UK) Ltd* [1983] 2 Lloyd's Rep. 9, HL (no authority to answer queries as to authority of another agent); cf. *Canadian Laboratory Supplies Ltd v Engelhard Industries of Canada Ltd* [1979] 2 S.C.R. 787; (1979) 97 D.L.R. (3d) 1: *ING Re (UK) Ltd v R & V Versicherungs AG* [2006] EWHC (Comm) 1544, [2006] 2 All E.R. (Comm) 870; *PEC Asia Ltd v Golden Rice Co Ltd* [2014] EWHC 1583 (Comm) at [623]. In *Crabtree-Vickers Pty Ltd v Australian Direct Mail Advertising and Addressing Co Pty Ltd* (1975) 133 C.L.R. 72 it was held that an agent with apparent authority cannot by his conduct give rise to apparent authority in a sub-agent. Sed quaere: see below, para.31-060, n.377.

[341] *Freeman & Lockyer v Buckhurst Park Properties (Mangal) Ltd* [1964] 2 Q.B. 480 at 505; *Att-Gen for Ceylon v Silva* [1953] A.C. 461, 479; *Armagas Ltd v Mundogas SA (The Ocean Frost)* [1986] A.C. 717; *Savill v Chase Holdings (Wellington) Ltd* [1989] 1 N.Z.L.R. 257.

[342] *Colonial Bank v Cady and Williams* (1890) 15 App. Cas. 267, 273; and see *Canadian Laboratory*

*Supplies Ltd v Englehard Industries of Canada Ltd*, above. An example is where an agent has usual authority to conduct a particular item of business: see *Egyptian Intl Foreign Trade Co v Soplex Wholesale Supplies Ltd (The Raffaella)*, above (documentary credits manager); *United Bank of Kuwait Ltd v Hammoud* [1988] 1 W.L.R. 1051 (solicitor); *Gurtner v Beaton* [1993] 2 Lloyd's Rep. 369 (aviation manager); but cf. *Hirst v Etherington* [1999] Lloyd's Rep. P.N. 938 (solicitor).

343 *First Energy (UK) Ltd v Hungarian Intl Bank Ltd* [1993] 2 Lloyd's Rep. 194, an important case. But cf. *Armagas Ltd v Mundogas SA (The Ocean Frost)* [1986] A.C. 717; and *Hirst v Etherington*, above, in each of which there was little beyond an avowal by the agent that he had or had obtained authority.

344 *Kelly v Fraser* [2012] UKPC 25, [2013] 1 A.C. 450 (Vice-President of company responsible for Employee Benefits Division reporting decision of and action taken for Trustees of Pension Fund). See also *Stavrinides v Bank of Cyprus Public Co Ltd* [2019] EWHC 1328 (Ch). The *First Energy* case is perceptively considered at some length, but not favoured, by the Court of Appeal of Singapore in *Skandinaviska Enskilda Banken SA v Asia Pacific Breweries (Singapore) Pte Ltd* [2011] 3 S.L.R. 540. See also Watts [2015] L.M.C.L.Q. 36, 40 et seq.

345 See *Chapleo v Brunswick PBBS* (1881) 6 Q.B.D. 696.

346 [1999] 2 A.C. 349. See above, Vol.I, paras 29-044 et seq.

347 *Freeman & Lockyer v Buckhurst Park Properties (Mangal) Ltd*, above, at 503; *Nationwide BS v Lewis* [1998] Ch. 482 (partnership).

348 *Freeman & Lockyer v Buckhurst Park Properties (Mangal) Ltd*, above, at 503; *Underwood v Bank of Liverpool* [1924] 1 K.B. 775; *Farquharson Bros & Co v King & Co* [1902] A.C. 325.

349 *Dickinson v Valpy* (1829) 10 B. & C. 128, 140.

350 *Farquharson Bros & Co v King & Co*, above, at 341, per Lord Lindley (quoting Parke B.).

351 *Swan v North British Australasian Co* (1863) 2 H. & C. 175, 182; *Mercantile Bank of India v Central Bank of India Ltd* [1938] A.C. 287; *Mercantile Credit Co Ltd v Hamblin* [1965] 2 Q.B. 242, 271; *Moorgate Mercantile Co Ltd v Twitchings* [1977] A.C. 890 and see below, para.31-076.

352 *Swan v North British Australasian Co*, above; *Mac Fisheries Ltd v Harrison* (1924) 53 L.J. K.B. 811.

353 *Jacobs v Morris* [1902] 1 Ch. 816 (power of attorney); *Australian Bank of Commerce v Perel* [1926] A.C. 737. A fortiori if he knew or must be taken to have known of the lack of authority: *Morris v Kanssen* [1946] A.C. 459.

354 See (vii) below.

355 cf. *Silver v Ocean SS Co* [1930] 1 K.B. 416; *PEC Asia Ltd v Golden Rice Co Ltd* [2014] EWHC 1583 (Comm) at [73]. Where there is no obligation to be enforced the requirement may be even looser: see *Shearson Lehman Bros Inc v Maclaine, Watson & Co Ltd (No.2)* [1988] 1 W.L.R. 16, 29, HL. But cf. *Nationwide BS v Lewis* [1998] Ch. 482, where in the context of s.14 of the Partnership Act 1890 it was held that reliance on a holding-out as partner must be affirmatively proved.

356 *Uxbridge Permanent Benefit Building Society v Pickard* [1939] 2 K.B. 248; assuming always that he is purporting to act as agent. But a *counterfeit* signature or seal is simply a nullity and involves of itself no representation that the forger purports to act as agent: see *Northside Development Pty Ltd v Registrar-General* (1990) 170 C.L.R. 146 especially at 199–200.

357 See *Ruben v Great Fingall Consolidated* [1906] A.C. 439 where this was not so.

358 *Navarro v Moregrand* [1951] 2 T.L.R. 674; cf. *Barker v Levinson* [1951] 1 K.B. 342.

359 *Restatement, Third, Agency* allows the principal to sue: see para.2.03 and Reporter's Notes, p.136, citing *Equitable Variable Life Assurance Co v Wood* 362 S.E.2d 741 (Va., 1987). But the reasoning is unconvincing.

360 See above, paras 31-046 et seq. as to implied authority; and for examples *Waugh v HB Clifford & Sons Ltd* [1982] Ch. 374; *United Bank of Kuwait Ltd v Hammoud* [1988] 1 W.L.R. 1051; *Hirst v Etherington* [1999] Lloyd's Rep. P.N. 938 (solicitors); *Egyptian Intl Foreign Trade Co v Soplex Wholesale Supplies Ltd (The Raffaella)* [1985] 2 Lloyd's Rep. 36 (documentary credits manager); *Gurtner v Beaton* [1993] 2 Lloyd's Rep. 369 (aviation manager). Where evidence as to what is usual in the particular occupation is relied on, this may be prejudicial to a third party who did not know of the practice, as in the harsh case of *British Bank of the Middle East v Sun Life Assurance Co of Canada (UK) Ltd* [1983] 2 Lloyd's Rep. 9, HL (levels of manager within company); cf. however *Cleveland Mfg Co Ltd v Muslim Commercial Bank Ltd* [1981] 2 Lloyd's Rep. 646.

361 In the judgment of Lord Neuberger in the Hong Kong Court of Final Appeal in *Thanakhorn Kasikorn Thai Chamchat v Akai Holdings Ltd* (2010) 13 H.K.C.F.A.R. 479 at [51].

362 *Lexi Holdings v Pannone & Partners* [2009] EWHC 2590 (Ch) at [61] et seq., per Briggs J. The Hong Kong case was followed by the Court of Appeal in *Quinn v CC Automotive Group Ltd* [2010] EWCA Civ 1412, [2011] 2 All E.R. (Comm) 584, where it is said that the reasonableness of the third party's belief was "neither here nor there"; see also *Newcastle International Airport Ltd v Eversheds LLP*

[2012] EWHC 2648 (Ch), [2013] P.N.L.R. 5; *Acute Property Developments Ltd v Apostolou* [2013] EWHC 200 (Ch), [2013] Bus. L.R. D22; *LNOC Ltd v Watford Association Football Club Ltd* [2013] EWHC 3615 (Comm).

363 See *Bowstead and Reynolds on Agency*, 21st edn (2018), art.73: Watts [2015] L.M.C.L.Q. 36. In particular it does not accord well with recent discussion in the context, admittedly different, of the inquiries to be made by bona fide purchaser in an equitable but commercial (banking) context: see *Papadimitriou v Crédit Agricole Corp* [2015] UKPC 13, [2015] 1 W.L.R. 4265; see also *Gray v Smith* [2013] EWHC 4136 (Comm), [2014] 2 All E.R. (Comm) 359.

363a *East Asia Co Ltd v PT Satria Tirtatama Energindo* [2019] UKPC 30, [2020] 2 All E.R. 294 at [93].

## "True" estoppel

*Replace footnote 364 with:*

364 e.g. *Spiro v Lintern* [1973] 1 W.L.R.1002; *Worboys v Carter* [1987] 2 E.G.L.R. 1. For another example see *Geniki Investments International Ltd v Ellis Stockbrokers Ltd* [2008] EWHC 549 (QB), [2008] 1 B.C.L.C. 662. See also *City Bank of Sydney v McLaughlin* (1909) 9 C.L.R. 615, 625. The idea that this estoppel is different from that generally applicable in connection with apparent authority is rejected by the Singapore Court of Appeal in *The Bunga Melati 5* [2015] 2 S.L.R. 114. See also Tan Cheng Han (2020) 136 L.Q.R. 315. **31-057**

## Agents of companies

*Replace footnote 367 with:*

367 See also Vol.I, paras 10-020 et seq.; *Gower's Principles of Modern Company Law*, 10th edn (2016), Ch.7. **31-058**

## Apparent authority of Crown agents

*Replace footnote 388 with:*

388 As to constitutional limitations on the agent of a foreign state see *Donegal International Ltd v Republic of Zambia* [2007] EWHC 197 (Comm), [2007] 1 Lloyd's Rep. 397; *Law Debenture Trust Corp Plc v Ukraine* [2018] EWCA Civ 2026, [2019] Q.B. 1121. **31-062**

# (c) Undisclosed Principal

## Doctrine of the undisclosed principal

*Replace footnote 391 with:*

391 *Duke of Norfolk v Worthy* (1808) 1 Camp. 337; *Browning v Provincial Insurance Co of Canada* (1873) L.R. 5 P.C. 263, 272; *Siu Yin Kwan v Eastern Insurance Co Ltd* [1994] 2 A.C. 199, giving (at 376) a useful statement of the rules. The doctrine was applied to a breach under s.14(5) of the Sale of Goods Act 1979 in *Boyter v Thomson* [1995] 2 A.C. 628; see Brown (1996) 112 L.Q.R. 49. It has been invoked quite often in recent years, though not always with full understanding. Some of the cases concern not contractual rights and duties, but jurisdiction: see, e.g. *Magellan Spirit ApS v Vitol SA* [2016] EWHC 454 (Comm), [2016] 2 Lloyd's Rep. 1 and *Kaefer Aislamientos SA de CV v AMS Drilling Mexico SA de CV* [2019] EWCA Civ 10, [2019] 1 W.L.R. 3514. **31-063**

## Meaning of "undisclosed principal"

*Replace paragraph with:*

The cases do not define the term, but it seems to mean in general a principal who **31-065** is not known by the third party to be connected with the particular transaction. On general principle, principal and agent must have consented to the existence of an agency relationship. It seems clear also that in entering into the contract, the agent must intend to do so on the principal's behalf.[414] Thus the mere fact that a company is operated by an individual for his own benefit does not make him the undisclosed principal of that company in a particular transaction.[415] But there are difficulties in going beyond this.[416] Two possibilities present themselves. One is that the undisclosed principal must be a person who has authorised the agent to bring him into contractual privity with the third party, but whose connection with the transaction is not disclosed, whether by his own wish or by the wish of the agent. The second is that an undisclosed principal is anyone who uses the services of another on an agency basis, viz the agent is remunerated by commission and undertakes only to use best endeavours, but nevertheless expects the agent to deal on his own account (sometimes called by some civil lawyers "indirect representation").[417] There is authority for both meanings. The first seems clearly correct.[418] Those legal systems which identify a category of indirect representation usually permit or require the involvement of the principal, at any rate as claimant in some circumstances (usually insolvency of the agent), and writers familiar with such systems sometimes, but not entirely correctly, treat the common law undisclosed principal doctrine as a different approach to the same problem.[419]

[414] *Siu Yin Kwan v Eastern Insurance Co Ltd* [1994] 2 A.C. 199, 207, above, para.31-064; and as to proof of intention see further above, para.31-054.

[415] *Yukong Lines Ltd v Rendsburg Investments Corp (The Rialto) (No.2)* [1998] 1 Lloyd's Rep. 322, considered in *Magellan Spirit ApS v Vitol SA* [2016] EWHC 454 (Comm), [2016] 2 Lloyd's Rep. 1 at [28]; and see *Atlas Maritime Co SA v Avalon Maritime Ltd (The Coral Rose)* [1991] 1 Lloyd's Rep. 563. For other attempts to fix the liability on the individual behind the company by means of agency reasoning see *The Swan* [1968] 1 Lloyd's Rep. 5 (liable concurrently in contract), below, para.31-084; *Williams v Natural Life Health Foods Ltd* [1998] 1 W.L.R. 830 (on the facts, director did not undertake duty); *Salim v Ingham Enterprises Pty Ltd* (1998) 55 N.S.W.L.R. 7 (director of company held the real principal); *Peterson Farms Inc v C & M Farming Ltd* [2004] EWHC 121 (Comm), [2004] 1 Lloyd's Rep. 603 (company not agent for others in group); below, para.31-075.

[416] See dicta in *Teheran-Europe Co Ltd v ST Belton (Tractors) Ltd* [1968] 2 Q.B. 545, 552, 561; *Bowstead and Reynolds on Agency*, 21st edn (2018), para.8-073.

[417] See above, para.31-004.

[418] See *Magellan Spirit ApS v Vitol SA* [2016] EWHC 454 (Comm), [2016] 2 Lloyd's Rep. 1 at [29] et seq., where the issue of the authorisation required of the principal arises directly, and careful attention is given to the requirements where there is no express agreement. See also *National Bank of Kazakhstan v Bank of New York Mellon NV* [2020] EWHC 916 (Comm) at [49] et seq.

[419] See Kortmann and Kortmann, Ch.6 in *Agency Law in Practice*, Busch and Macgregor (eds) (2016).

## Exclusion of undisclosed principals

*Replace paragraph with:*

**31-066** Where an agent makes a contract in writing in his own name, parol evidence is generally admissible to show that another person was the real principal, so that that principal can sue, for, as stated above, its effect is to add a party rather than to vary the contract.[420] But an undisclosed principal cannot intervene where such intervention would be inconsistent with the terms of the contract itself.[421] Sometimes such exclusion is an express term of the contract[422]; thus when an agent contracts for a named principal, no other principal can intervene.[423] But sometimes the exclusion is derived from words in the contract descriptive of the agent: thus it has been held, in the context of the parol evidence rule, that no intervention is permissible where the agent is described as "owner"[424] or "proprietor",[425] though a different solution has been reached in similar, more recent cases.[426] It seems that not too much should be derived from the use of particular words: the question is whether on the full interpretation of the situation, personality is a term of the contract.[427] The normal assumption has been said to be that in the case of ordinary commercial contracts the third party is willing to deal with anyone by whom the counterparty was authorised.[428]

[420] *Fred Drughorn Ltd v Rederiaktiebolaget Transatlantic* [1919] A.C. 203.

[421] See *Teheran-Europe Co Ltd v ST Belton (Tractors) Ltd* [1968] 2 Q.B. 545, 552.

[422] *UK Mutual Steamship Association v Nevill* (1887) 19 Q.B.D. 110.

[423] See *Phillips v Duke of Bucks* (1683) 1 Vern. 227; *J.H. Rayner (Mincing Lane) Ltd v Department of Trade and Industry* [1990] 2 A.C. 418, 516; *Foster v Action Aviation Ltd* [2014] EWCA Civ 1368.

[424] *Humble v Hunter* (1848) 12 Q.B. 310. See also *Davis v Capel* [1959] N.Z.L.R. 825.

[425] *Formby v Formby* (1910) 102 L.T. 116 (though the point was not actually decided); *Fawcett v Star Car Sales Ltd* [1960] N.Z.L.R. 406; *JH Rayner (Mincing Lane) Ltd v Department of Trade and Industry* [1989] Ch. 72, 190–191 ("as principals").

[426] *Fred Drughorn Ltd v Rederiaktiebolaget Transatlantic* [1919] A.C. 203 ("charterer"); *Killick & Co v Price & Co* (1896) 12 T.L.R. 263; *Danziger v Thompson* [1944] K.B. 654; *Hanstown Properties Ltd v Green* (1977) 246 E.G. 917, CA ("tenant"); *Epps v Rothnie* [1945] K.B. 562 ("landlord"); *O/Y Wasa SS Co v Newspaper Pulp & Wood Exports* (1949) 82 Ll.L. Rep. 936 ("disponent owner": authorities reviewed); *Finzel Berry & Co v Eastcheap Dried Fruit Co* [1962] 1 Lloyd's Rep. 370, 375; affirmed [1962] 2 Lloyd's Rep. 11; *Murphy v Rae* [1967] N.Z.L.R. 103; *Asty Maritime Co Ltd v Rocco Giuseppe & Figli (The Astyanax)* [1985] 2 Lloyd's Rep. 109.

[427] McLauchlan, *The Parol Evidence Rule* (Wellington, NZ, 1976), Ch.13.

[428] *Teheran-Europe Co Ltd v ST Belton (Tractors) Ltd* [1968] 2 Q.B. 545, 555, quoted above, para.31-054; applied in *Novasen SA v Alimenta SA* [2011] EWHC 49 (Comm), [2011] 1 Lloyd's Rep. 390 (commodity sale). For a case where this did not apply see *Rolls Royce Power Engineering Plc v Ricardo Consulting Engineers Ltd* [2003] EWHC 2871, [2004] 2 All E.R. (Comm) 129. An undisclosed principal was held to be excluded by the wording of an insurance contract in *Talbot Underwriting Ltd v Nausch, Hogan & Murray Inc (The Jascon 5)* [2006] EWCA Civ 889, [2006] 2 Lloyd's Rep. 195. Contrast *Ferryways NV v Associated British Ports* [2008] EWHC 225 (Comm), [2008] 1 Lloyd's Rep. 639, where intervention on an employment contract was permitted; *White v Baycorp Advantage Business Information Services Ltd* (2006) 200 F.L.R. 125 (rental agreement and assignment); *Diamond Stud Ltd v New Zealand Bloodstock Finance Ltd* [2010] NZCA 423 (terms of auction did not exclude undisclosed principal).

*Replace paragraph with:*

**31-067** There may nevertheless be other situations where the personality of the agent is so important that no one else can intervene; but the true applicable rule for such situations is still uncertain. Thus in *Said v Butt*[429] it was held that an undisclosed principal (a theatre critic) could not intervene and take the benefit of a contract for admission to a theatre on a first night; but the judgment is reasoned on the assumption that the contract is between the principal and the third party, which is probably not so. There are dicta suggesting simply that an undisclosed principal cannot intervene where the personality of the agent is relevant,[430] but one of the cases can be explained on the grounds that an undisclosed principal intervenes subject to defences available against the agent, and the other on the grounds that only the agent to whom it was made could rescind for misrepresentation. It was suggested[431] that there was a rule that the undisclosed principal cannot intervene where the benefit of the contract is unassignable or its burden cannot be vicariously performed.[432] It is clear that if the burden of the contract cannot be performed vicariously the undisclosed principal cannot intervene on the performer's side to enforce it, since his intervention would itself be a breach of the contract.[433] But the assignment analogy has been rejected by the Privy Council in a case concerning a policy of liability insurance, which was unassignable, but where in the circumstances the identity of the employer insured was admitted to be a matter of indifference to the insurer.[434] It seems therefore that the basic exclusionary rule must be no more than the general proposition, that the undisclosed principal cannot intervene where the terms of the contract, express or implied, exclude his right to sue and his liability to be sued.[435] This gives limited guidance, but from extended discussion in recent cases it appears that the whole contractual matrix is to be taken into consideration, and the "beneficial assumption" of Diplock L.J. quoted in para.31-054 above borne in mind.[435a] If the agent represents that he does not act for a, or for a particular, principal, and this is incorrect, this is a misrepresentation: the third party has a defence to an action on the contract and may take proceedings to rescind it.[436] But mere non-disclosure that the agent acts for a principal does not of itself amount to misrepresentation.[437]

[429] [1920] 3 K.B. 497 (the action brought was actually for inducement of breach of contract). See also *Smith v Wheatcroft* (1878) 9 Ch. D. 223, discussed by Goodhart and Hamson, below, n.431 at 344.

[430] *Greer v Downs Supply Co* [1927] 2 K.B. 28; *Collins v Associated Greyhound Racecourses Ltd* [1930] 1 Ch. 1.

[431] Goodhart and Hamson (1932) 4 C.L.J. 320. There was some support in *Dyster v Randall & Sons* [1926] Ch. 932, where an undisclosed principal was held entitled to enforce a contract where he knew that the third party would not have sold to him, and one of the reasons given was that the benefit of the contract could have been assigned. See also *Nash v Dix* (1898) 78 L.T. 445, where the "agent" was held to have bought for resale to his principal. See also above para.31-063.

[432] See Vol.I, paras 19-055 et seq., 19-082 et seq.

[433] Goodhart and Hamson (1932) 4 C.L.J. 320 at 341.

[434] *Siu Yin Kwan v Eastern Insurance Co*, above, at 207: see above, para.31-064. A number of recent cases have cited reasoning as to exclusion of undisclosed principals in connection with disclosed principals, or in situations where it is not clear which is involved. Some have used a test which asks whether the terms of a contract "unequivocally and exhaustively" identify the parties to it: see above, para.31-054. This reference to identity is more relevant to disclosed principals and of itself too narrow a rule for undisclosed principals.

[435] *Siu Yin Kwan v Eastern Insurance Co Ltd*, above, at 207.

[435a] See *Aspen Underwriting Ltd v Credit Europe Bank NV* [2018] EWCA Civ 2590, [2019] 1 Lloyd's Rep. 221 at [49] et seq. (on appeal, [2020] UKSC 11); *Kaefer Aislamientos SA de CV v AMS Drilling Mexico SA de CV* [2019] EWCA Civ 10, [2019] 1 W.L.R. 354 at [109] et seq. (stating that an "entire agreement" clause is "cogent indication" that an undisclosed principal was not acted for, but not conclusive). See further above, para.31-054.

[436] *Archer v Stone* (1898) 79 L.T. 34.

[437] *Dyster v Randall* [1926] Ch. 932.

## (d) Principals and Third Parties: Further Rules

### Deeds, bills, notes and cheques

*Replace paragraph with:*

**31-068** There are exceptions to the general rules in the case of deeds, bills, notes and cheques. No one can sue or be sued on any deed inter partes unless he is described as a party thereto and the deed is executed in his name.[438] But when the agent is a trustee of his rights for his principal, the principal may enforce his rights under the deed in the name of the agent, joining the agent as co-plaintiff or as co-defendant.[439] And by virtue of the Powers of Attorney Act 1971 s.7(1),[440] if the donee of a power of attorney is an individual, he may, if he thinks fit, execute any instrument with his own signature, and do any other thing in his own name by the authority of the donor of the power. This would include the execution of a deed, provided the required procedures are observed.[441] It would seem, however, that the principal should be mentioned in the deed, and that the section does not permit intervention by an undisclosed principal.[442] As regards bills, notes and cheques, no one can be liable on any such instrument unless his signature is upon it,[443] and no one can be liable as acceptor of a bill except the person on whom it was drawn,[444] except where it is accepted for honour. But signature of a principal's name by an authorised agent suffices in these cases.[445]

[438] *Schack v Anthony* (1813) 1 M. & S. 573; *Berkeley v Hardy* (1826) 3 B. & C. 355. But the principal may be able to sue by virtue of s.56 of the Law of Property Act 1925 if the deed purports to grant something to him: see *Beswick v Beswick* [1968] A.C. 58. And if the deed is not inter partes, he can sue if he is a covenantee: see *Cooker v Child* (1673) 2 Lev. 74; *Sunderland Marine Insurance Co v Kearney* (1851) 16 Q.B. 925. For the view that properly executed deeds bind the principal even if they are not authorised see Watts (2002) 2 O.U.C.L.J. 93.

[439] *Harmer v Armstrong* [1934] Ch. 65.

[440] Superseding Law of Property Act 1925 s.123(1); and as modified by s.1(8) of and Sch.1 to the Law of Property (Miscellaneous Provisions) Act 1989; Regulatory Reform (Execution of Deeds and Documents) Order 2005 (SI 2005/1906).

[441] As to sealing see above, para.31-025.

[442] See *Harmer v Armstrong*, above, where it was assumed that such intervention was not in general possible.

[443] Bills of Exchange Act 1882 s.23, 89.

[444] s.17(1); *Polhill v Walter* (1832) 3 B. & Ad. 114; *Steele v M'Kinlay* (1880) 5 App. Cas. 754.

[445] s.91(1).

## Effect of judgment against agent

*Replace paragraph with:*

Where the agent, having made a contract in such terms that he is personally liable,[458] has been sued on it to judgment, it appears that no action is maintainable against the principal on the same contract. This rule is said to be based on the notion that there cannot be two judgments on the same debt,[459–460] though it is open to criticism as being an unnecessary extension of the rules for joint debts, which have in any case in this respect been altered by statute.[461] It has most recently been justified on the basis of the liability of principal and agent being alternative.[461a] It certainly applies where the principal is undisclosed[462]; but it seems that it may apply also where he is disclosed, though the authority and rationale here are distinctly less compelling.[463] The rule has been applied though the first judgment was a summary one under Ord.14 of the then Rules of the Supreme Court,[464] or a default judgment,[465] or in an action in which principal and agent were sued jointly,[466] or was obtained for part only of the amount claimed,[467] or was wholly unsatisfied.[468] It has been applied notwithstanding that judgment was set aside by consent,[469] but not where it was set aside on the merits.[470] But it cannot, of course, apply where there are completely separate causes of action.[471] And even if it is in general correct, it is difficult to justify in the case of summary or default judgments, where the interpretation of the facts may in effect be settled by accidents of how litigation arises, and an undefended judgment against a party who is in fact not liable at all (and perhaps cannot pay either) could bar an action against the party who is liable. Two fairly recent Commonwealth cases refuse to accept the doctrine in such a situation.[472] **31-070**

[458] i.e. when his principal is undisclosed and in certain other circumstances, as to which see below, paras 31-084 et seq.

[459–460] See *Kendall v Hamilton* (1879) 4 App. Cas. 504, 515; *Moore v Flanagan* [1920] 1 K.B. 919, 926.

[461] Civil Liability Contribution Act 1978 s.3. But the obtaining of such a judgment might still rank as an election: below, para.31-071.

[461a] *Taylor v Van Dutch Marine Holding Ltd* [2019] EWHC 1951 (Ch), [2019] Bus. L.R. 2610 (containing a useful survey of the topic) (point not decided on appeal sub nom. *Taylor v Rhino Overseas Inc* [2020] EWCA Civ 353).

[462] *Priestly v Fernie* (1865) 3 H. & C. 977; *Kendall v Hamilton* (1879) 4 App. Cas. 504 at 514–515; *Marginson v Ian Potter & Co* (1976) 136 C.L.R. 161, 169.

[463] See *Morel Bros & Co Ltd v Earl of Westmorland* [1904] A.C. 11; *Sullivan v Sullivan* [1912] 2 I.R. 116, 127–128; *Moore v Flanagan*, above; *RMKRM (A Firm) v MRMVL (A Firm)* [1926] A.C. 761; *Debenham's Ltd v Perkins* (1925) 133 L.T. 252, 254; *Barrington v Lee* [1972] 1 Q.B. 326 (all cases of disclosed but unidentified principals).

[464] *Morel Bros & Co Ltd v Earl of Westmorland*, above.

[465] *Cross & Co v Mattews and Wallace* (1904) 91 L.T. 500; *Taylor v Van Dutch Marine Holdings Ltd* [2019] EWHC 1951 (Ch).

[466] *Moore v Flanagan* [1920] 1 K.B. 919.

[467] *French v Howie* [1906] 2 K.B. 674.

[468] *Kendall v Hamilton* (1879) 4 App. Cas. 504, 514; *London General Omnibus Co Ltd v Pope* (1922) 38 T.L.R. 270.

[469] *Hammond v Schofield* [1891] 1 Q.B. 453; and see *Cross & Co v Matthews and Wallace* (1904) 91 L.T. 500; *Cyril Lord (Carpet Sales) v Browne* (1966) 111 S.J. 51; cf. *Longman v Hill* (1891) 7 T.L.R. 639.

[470] *Hammond v Schofield*, above; *Partington v Hawthorne* (1888) 55 J.P. 807; *Goodey v Garriock* [1972] 2 Lloyd's Rep. 369; *Petersen v Moloney* (1951) 84 C.L.R. 91.

[471] See *Debenham's Ltd v Perkins* (1933) 125 L.T. 252 (two sales); *BO Morris Ltd v Perrott and Bolton* [1945] 1 All E.R. 567 (cheque). See also *Isaacs v Salbstein* [1916] 2 K.B. 139 (first party sued not liable). See below, para.31-084.

[472] *LC Fowler & Sons v St Stephen's College Board of Governors* [1991] 3 N.Z.L.R. 304; *Lang Transport Ltd v Plus Factor International Trucking Ltd* (1997) 143 D.L.R.(4th) 672.

## Election

*Replace paragraph with:*

**31-071** Where principal and agent are both liable, it is further said that the third party may lose his right to sue one by an unequivocal election to sue the other[473]; this is again because the two rights are said to be inconsistent.[474] This doctrine is even more open to question than that regarding judgment[475]: it is difficult to see any reason for it (though an *estoppel* would be a different matter). The vast majority of cases invoke it only to hold that there has been no election. Those suggesting that there has been election in cases of undisclosed principals[476] can be explained on the basis of estoppel, whereby the third party induced the principal to settle with the agent[477]: those cited for the proposition in connection with disclosed principals can be explained as cases on formation of contract, dealing with the question "With whom was the contract made"?[478] If election does apply here, however, on general grounds before a party can be held to have elected he must have had knowledge of the facts[479]: but once the facts are discovered he must make his election within a reasonable time, at least if principal or agent would be prejudiced by the delay.[480] The question whether an election has been made is one of fact to be decided in all the circumstances of the case.[481] Debiting one party may[482] or may not[483] constitute such election. The institution of legal proceedings against one party provides a prima facie case of election,[484] but is not conclusive evidence: nor is filing a winding-up[485] petition and obtaining an order, nor proving in one party's bankruptcy,[486] nor obtaining leave to sign judgment against one party,[487] nor appointing an arbitrator.[488]

[473] *Clarkson Booker v Andjel* [1964] 2 Q.B. 775; *Calder v Dobell* (1871) L.R. 6 C.P. 486, 499; *Curtis v Williamson* (1874) L.R. 10 Q.B. 57; dicta in *Chestertons v Barone* [1987] 1 E.G.L.R. 15; *Playboy Club London Ltd v Banca Nazionale del Lavoro* [2018] UKSC 43, [2018] 1 W.L.R. 4041 at [12].

[474] Citing *Scarf v Jardine* (1882) 7 App. Cas. 345, 360; *Clarkson Booker v Andjel*, above, at 794.

[475] See *Bowstead and Reynolds on Agency*, 21st edn (2018), art.82. In the United States "election" is used to cover both aspects of the doctrine, and leading cases (rightly) reject the notion: e.g. *Grinder v Bryans Road Building and Supply Co*, 423 1 2d 453 Ct App Md 1981 ("the foregoing reasoning is unassailable on any other ground than its lack of strict adherence to the precedents"). Election as a basis is rejected in *Taylor v Van Dutch Marine Holding Ltd* [2019] EWHC 1951 (Ch) (point not dealt with on appeal sub nom. *Taylor v Rhino Overseas Inc* [2020] EWCA Civ 253); though it is accepted in *IVY Technology Ltd v Martin* [2020] EWHC 94 (Comm).

[476] *MacClure v Schemeil* (1871) 20 W.R. 168; *Smethurst v Mitchell* (1859) 1 E. & E. 622.

[477] See below, para.31-072.

[478] See *Addison v Gandassequi* (1812) 4 Taunt. 574; *Paterson v Gandasequi* (1812) 15 East 62; *Thomson v Davenport* (1829) 9 B. & C. 78. For recent examples see *Pendleton v Westwater* [2001] EWCA Civ 1841 and *Balgobin v South West Regional Health Authority* [2012] UKPC 11, [2013] 1 A.C. 582, both

holding default judgments not to constitute election in such situations. Both cases, especially the first, contain dicta ascribing a limited role to election.

479 *Dunn v Newton* (1884) Cab. & El. 278; *Clarkson Booker v Andjel* [1964] 2 Q.B. 775, 792.

480 *Smethurst v Mitchell* (1859) 1 E. & E. 622; but see explanation of this case in *Davison v Donaldson* (1882) 9 Q.B. 623, 628.

481 *Calder v Dobell* (1871) L.R. 6 C.P. 486; *Clarkson Booker v Andjel*, above, at 792.

482 *Addison v Gandassequi* (1812) 4 Taunt. 574 (but see explanation of this case above).

483 *Thomson v Davenport* (1829) 9 B. & C. 78; *Eastman v Harry* (1875) 33 L.T. 800.

484 *Clarkson Booker v Andjel* [1964] 2 Q.B. 775; *Cyril Lord (Carpet Sales) v Browne* (1966) 111 S.J. 51; *Chestertons Ltd v Barone* [1987] 1 E.G.L.R. 15; cf. *Blake v Melrose* [1950] N.Z.L.R. 781 (third-party notice). In *Taylor v Van Dutch Marine Holdings Ltd* [2019] EWHC 1951 (Ch) it was said, obiter, that making and serving an application for asset seizure in Monaco would have constituted election had it been relevant.

485 *Con-Stan Industries of Australia Pty Ltd v Norwich Winterthur Insurance (Australia) Ltd* (1986) 160 C.L.R. 226.

486 *Curtis v Williamson* (1874) L.R. 10 Q.B. 57. But cf. *Fell v Parkin* (1882) 52 L.J. Q.B. 99; *MacClure v Schemeil* (1871) 20 W.R. 168.

487 *C Christopher (Hove) Ltd v Williams* [1936] 3 All E.R. 68.

488 *Pyxis Special Shipping Co Ltd v Dritsas & Kaglis Bros Ltd (The Scaplake)* [1978] 2 Lloyd's Rep. 380.

## (e) Agent Bribed

### Effect of bribery of agent

*Replace paragraph with:*

> "For the purposes of the civil law a bribe means the payment of a secret commission, which only means (i) that the person making the payment makes it to the agent of the other person with whom he is dealing; (ii) that he makes it to that person knowing that that person is acting as the agent of the other person with whom he is dealing; (iii) that he fails to disclose to the other person with whom he is dealing that he has made that payment to the person whom he knows to be the other person's agent."[496] **31-073**

Once the bribe is established it is conclusively presumed against the donor of the bribe that his motive was corrupt and against the agent that he was affected and influenced by the payment.[497] Practices permitting undisclosed commissions will not be upheld.[498] It is not necessary that the bribe induce a contract.[499] A principal whose agent has accepted a secret commission is therefore not obliged to prove that the agent's mind was actually influenced by the receipt of the commission.[500] The third party is regarded as a party to the breach of duty where he knows that he is depriving the principal of the disinterested advice of the agent, or is wilfully blind to that,[501] and the principal may rescind a transaction entered into with him[502]; and when the principal has repudiated a contract on an insufficient ground he may subsequently justify the repudiation on the ground of the bribe, even though ignorant of it at the time of repudiation.[503] If he rescinds, he is not required to account for the bribe, which he may recover from the agent or retain and treat as a gift to himself.[504] Besides his right to rescind, a principal whose agent has been bribed may recover from the third party the amount of the bribe in an action said to lie in money had and received[505]; or he may sue the third party in tort[506] for loss suffered.[507] Only the entry of judgment on one or the other cause of action will constitute a final election between the two.[508] He may likewise sue the agent on the same two causes of action, subject again to election.[509] But he may not obtain double recovery in such proceedings, and if he sues both, satisfaction of judgment against one will bar an action against the other except for any excess.[510] Where the loss suffered is less than the amount of the bribe, the (restitutionary) action in money had and received will obviously be preferable.

[496] *Industries & General Mortgage Co v Lewis* [1949] 2 All E.R. 573, 575, per Slade J.; followed in *Taylor v Walker* [1958] 1 Lloyd's Rep. 490. An excellent and more recent exposition of the rules is to be found in the first instance judgment of Christopher Clarke J. in *Novoship (UK) Ltd v Michayluk* [2012] EWHC 3586 (Comm) at [108]–[109] (partly reversed [2014] EWCA Civ 908, [2015] Q.B. 499); see also *Wood v Commercial First Business Ltd* [2019] EWHC 2205 (Ch), [2020] C.T.L.C. 1. It may sometimes be appropriate to disclose the actual amount of the commission: see Scrutton L.J. in *Fullwood v Hurley* [1928] 1 K.B. 498; *Hurstanger Ltd v Wilson* [2007] EWCA Civ 299, [2007] 1 W.L.R. 2351; cf. *Medsted Associates Ltd v Canaccord Genuity Wealth (International) Ltd* [2019] EWCA Civ 83, [2019] 2 All E.R. 959. For bribery by an agent of the third party, see *Armagas Ltd v Mundogas SA (The Ocean Frost)* [1986] A.C. 717, 743–745, 755, CA. The first instance decision also contains discussion of the effect of a bribe paid, agreed or adopted after the conclusion of the contract: see [1985] 1 Lloyd's Rep. 1, 18–22. Where the bribed agent acted in some respects for both parties the question will be whether in paying the bribe the agent was acting within the scope of its agency for the party seeing to enforce the contract: *UBS v Kommunale Wasserwerke Leipzig GmbH* [2014] EWHC 3615 (Comm) at [615] et seq. (point not dealt with on appeal [2017] EWCA Civ 1567). In the case of a company, disclosure to one director is insufficient: *Ross River Ltd v Cambridge City Football Club* [2007] EWHC 2115 (Ch), [2008] 1 All E.R. 1004. See also Vol.I, para.29-164; Berg [2001] L.M.C.L.Q. 27 (a valuable article). Bribery can be a criminal offence under the Bribery Act 2010.

[497] *Industries and General Mortgage Co v Lewis*, above; *Hovenden v Milhoff* (1900) 83 L.T. 41; *Harrington v Victoria Graving Dock Co* (1878) 3 Q.B.D. 549.

[498] *Fullwood v Hurley* [1928] 1 K.B. 498.

[499] *Petrotrade Inc v Smith* [2000] 1 Lloyd's Rep. 486.

[500] *Shipway v Broadwood* [1899] 1 Q.B. 369; *Smith v Sorby* (1875) 3 Q.B.D. 552n.

[501] *Tigris International NV v China Southern Airlines Co Ltd* [2014] EWCA Civ 1649 at [79]; *Pengelly v Business Mortgage Finance 4 Plc* [2020] EWHC 2002 (Ch).

[502] *Panama & South Pacific Telegraph Co v India Rubber, etc. Co* (1875) L.R. 10 Ch. App. 515, 526; *Re a Debtor* [1927] 2 Ch. 367, 376–377; *Taylor v Walker* [1958] 1 Lloyd's Rep. 490, 509–513; *North & South Trust Co v Berkeley* [1971] 1 W.L.R. 470, 485. But not a transaction entered into before the bribery: *Ross River Ltd v Cambridge City Football Club* [2007] EWHC 2115 (Ch), [2008] 1 All E.R. 1004.

[503] *Alexander v Webber* [1922] 1 K.B. 642; *Boston Deep Sea Fishing & Ice Co v Ansell* (1888) 39 Ch. D. 339.

[504] *Logicrose Ltd v Southend United Football Club* [1988] 1 W.L.R. 1256.

[505] The action is in personam but is difficult to justify in terms of restitution since the third party pays rather than receives the bribe. For discussion see *Bowstead and Reynolds on Agency*, 21st edn (2018), para.8-223; and see below. Compare the action against the agent: below, para.31-132.

[506] Said to be not deceit but a "special form of fraud": see *ING Re (UK) Ltd v R & V Versicherungs AG* [2006] EWHC (Comm) 1344, [2006] 2 All E.R. (Comm) 870 at [19].

[507] *Mahesan v Malaysia Government Officers' Co-operative Housing Society Ltd* [1979] A.C. 374, explaining *Hovenden & Sons v Millhoff* (1900) 83 L.T. 41; *Arab Monetary Fund v Hashim* [1996] 1 Lloyd's Rep. 589. Both causes of action are difficult to classify, and it is therefore possible that the leading case of *Mahesan*, a Privy Council decision, may at some time need reconsideration.

[508] *Mahesan v Malaysia Government Officers' Co-operative Housing Society Ltd*, above, applying *United Australia Ltd v Barclays Bank Ltd* [1941] A.C. 1.

[509] *Mahesan v Malaysia Government Officers' Co-operative Housing Society Ltd*, above, para.31-043.

[510] *Mahesan v Malaysia Government Officers' Co-operative Housing Society Ltd*, above, at 382–383, applying *United Australia Ltd v Barclays Bank Ltd*, above. But see Tettenborn (1979) 95 L.Q.R. 68; Needham (1979) 95 L.Q.R. 536.

## (f) Agent's Torts

### Agent's torts

*Replace paragraph with:*

**31-075** A principal is liable for the torts of his agent in accordance with the normal principles of vicarious liability in tort. Thus he is liable for the acts of an employee agent acting in the course of his employment, and also where the agent is an independent contractor in the (uncertain) circumstances in which the duty is held non-delegable.[518] The criteria for connection with the employer have however over recent years been the subject of considerable relaxation in connection with physical assault[519] and persons whose positions can be regarded as analogous to those of employees.[520] From the point of view of agency law, the significant question is whether in view of this relaxation the agency-based notion of authority has any longer a role to play in determining tort liability for representations, which constitute an area in which it might still be expected to do so. In *Armagas Ltd v Mundogas SA (The Ocean Frost)*[521] it was held by the House of Lords that a principal was not liable for the deceit of an employee agent where the agent was acting outside his actual and apparent authority, and that in such circumstances the contractual agency rules applied rather than the tortious vicarious liability rules, which might have imposed liability. This is still the case in England.[521a] More recently however the current looser vicarious liability criteria have been applied to make a bank liable for a misrepresentation by a junior employee that was not actually or apparently authorised, and it was said that the reasoning in *The Ocean Frost* was confined to deceit.[522] It is difficult to see why a principal should be more readily liable for his agent's negligent misrepresentation than for his fraud, and a significant Privy Council case in which a principal was held not liable for the unauthorised act of an agent[523] was not cited. It has fairly recently been clarified that liability for misrepresentations is based on an assumption of responsibility,[524] with the result that a company director who did not assume responsibility for a negligently prepared report was held not liable, though the company was. It follows from this that an agent who is actually or apparently authorised but does not assume personal responsibility can create an assumption of responsibility by his principal.

> "Just as an agent can contract on behalf of another without assuming personal liability, so an agent can assume responsibility on behalf of another for the purposes of the *Hedley Byrne* rule without assuming personal responsibility."[525]

Thus a vendor of land has been held liable, where appropriate reliance could be established, for non-fraudulent misrepresentations by his estate agent,[526] or by his solicitor.[527] This indicates a rule whereby the principal of a *non-employee agent* will in appropriate cases be liable on a misrepresentation made by his agent within actual or apparent authority,[528] and there seems no reason why the same reasoning should not apply in respect of this tort to employee agents.[529] There are also a few cases holding a principal liable for wrongful statements of an independent contractor not involving representations, and hence not using any notion of authority, on reasoning which nevertheless appears to connect to their status as an agent but not to any idea of non-delegable duty.[530] Unless they can be limited to statements, they are presumably to be explained as examples, possibly unusual, justified by some more general notion of vicarious liability, going beyond employment and outside the sphere of representation, in respect of matters undertaken in order to achieve the principal's objectives.[531]

518 This category has been rationalised and to some extent expanded of late: see *Woodland v Essex CC* [2013] UKSC 66, [2014] A.C. 357. See *Clerk & Lindsell on Torts*, 22nd edn (2018), Ch.6. For discussion of a recent case in the Singapore Court of Appeal comparing the two techniques see David Tan (2018) 134 L.Q.R. 193.

519 *Lister v Hesley Hall Ltd* [2001] UKHL 22, [2001] 1 A.C. 215 (warden of school boarding house);

for a more recent example see *Mohamud v Wm Morrison Supermarkets Plc* [2016] UKSC 11, [2016] A.C. 677 (supermarket petrol station attendant assaulting customer).

[520] e.g. *Dubai Aluminium Co Ltd v Salaam* [2002] UKHL 48, [2002] 2 A.C. 366 (partner: dishonest assistance in breach of trust) (see esp. at [23]–[36], [123]–[131]); *Various Claimants v Institute of Brothers of the Christian Schools* [2012] UKSC 56, [2013] 2 A.C. 1 (monks involved in education); *Cox v Ministry of Justice* [2016] UKSC 10, [2016] A.C. 660 (prisoner working in prison kitchen); *Barclays Bank Plc v Various Claimants* [2020] UKSC 13, [2020] 2 W.L.R. 960. See *Clerk and Lindsell on Torts*, 22nd edn (2018), paras 6-27 et seq.

[521] [1986] A.C. 717.

[521a] It is assumed in *Winter v Hockley Mint Ltd* [2018] EWCA Civ 2480, [2019] 1 W.L.R. 1617. The possibility of applying the "close connection" test to the acts of an agent is considered in *Frederick v Positive Solutions (Financial Services) Plc* [2018] EWCA Civ 431, but it was held that the test was not in any case satisfied because the agent had been engaged in a recognisably independent business.

[522] *So v HSBC Bank Plc* [2009] EWCA Civ 296, [2009] 1 C.L.C. 503. See Watts (2012) 128 L.Q.R. 260; [2015] L.M.C.L.Q. 36.

[523] *Kooragang Investments Pty v Richardson & Wrench Ltd* [1982] A.C. 462 (valuation by employee using letterhead to person to whom he had been prohibited from giving valuations).

[524] *Williams v Natural Life Health Foods Ltd* [1998] 1 W.L.R. 830.

[525] *Standard Chartered Bank v Pakistan National Shipping Corp (No.2)* [2002] UKHL 43, [2003] 1 A.C. 959 at [21] per Lord Hoffmann; see also *Williams v Natural Life Health Foods Ltd*, above, at 838; *Steel v NRAM Ltd* [2018] UKSC 13, [2018] W.L.R. 1190 at [24] ("this concept remains the foundation of the liability" per Lord Wilson of Culworth).

[526] *Richards v Norris Smith Real Estate Ltd* [1977] 1 N.Z.L.R. 152.

[527] *Cemp Properties (UK) Ltd v Dentsply Research and Development Corp* [1989] 2 E.G.L.R. 196 (Misrepresentation Act 1967 s.2(1)). See further *Steel v NRAM Ltd* [2018] UKSC 13 and below, para.31-111.

[528] See a useful discussion in *Ong Hang Ling v American International Assurance Co Ltd* [2018] 5 S.L.R. 549 at [207] et seq.

[529] The question is instructively discussed by Flaux L.J. in *Frederick v Positive Solutions (Financial Services) Ltd* [2018] EWCA Civ 431, where however it was not necessary to reach a conclusion as the case was plainly one where the person concerned did no more than provide the opportunity for unauthorised wrongdoing by another, as in the *Kooragang* case above.

[530] See *Colonial Mutual Life Assurance Society Ltd v Producers' and Citizens' Cooperative Assurance Co Ltd* (1931) 46 C.L.R. 41, where an Australian company was held liable for defamation of another company by its independent agent while seeking business for it—though surely a fringe case: contrast *Colonial Mutual Life Assurance Society v Macdonald* [1931] A.D. 412 (same company in South Africa not liable for negligent driving of representative while on business). However, the Australian case is in effect accepted in connection with defamation on Twitter (in the context of elections) in *Monir v Wood* [2018] EWHC 3525 (QB). For a simpler example see *Gordon v Selico Co Ltd* [1986] 1 E.G.L.R. 71 (estate agent). For a wider rationale see Atiyah, *Vicarious Liability in the Law of Torts* (1967), Chs 9 and 10.

[531] See *Sweeney v Boylan Nominees Ltd* (2006) 226 C.L.R. 161 at [14] et seq. (equipment leasing company not liable for negligence of independent contractor used by it for repair services).

## (g) Disposition of Property through Agent

### Cases where the agent has some authority

*Replace footnote 544 with:*

31-078 [544] *Wishart v Credit & Mercantile Plc* [2015] EWCA Civ 655, [2015] 2 P. & C.R. 15 at [52] per Sales L.J. In this case the person concerned abstained entirely from involvement in the mechanics of purchase of land, thus leaving documents in the hands of a person acting on his behalf.

## 7. AGENT'S RELATIONS WITH THIRD PARTIES

## (a) On the Main Contract

### Unidentified principal

*Replace footnote 614 with:*

[614] There may be problems in identifying the principal, which may turn on the agent's intention. See above, para.31-054. **31-089**

### Deeds

*Replace footnote 621 with:*

[621] *Appleton v Binks* (1804) 5 East 148; *Hancock v Hodgson* (1827) 12 Moore 504; *Chapman v Smith* [1907] 2 Ch. 97; *Plant Engineers (Sales) Ltd v Davis* (1969) 113 S.J. 484. It is not clear whether these cases are affected by s.7(1) of the Powers of Attorney Act 1971, as amended (replacing Law of Property Act 1925 s.123) under which an agent having a power of attorney may execute a deed with his own signature and seal. **31-090**

### Where principal is company not yet in existence

*Replace footnote 653 with:*

[653] *Rover International Ltd v Cannon Film Sales Ltd* [1987] B.C.L.C. 540; decision varied on other grounds [1989] 1 W.L.R. 912. See in general Gower's Principles of Modern Company Law, 10th edn (2016), paras 5-25 et seq. **31-098**

## (c) Breach of Warranty of Authority

### Implied representation of authority

*Replace footnote 673 with:*

[673] *Nelson v Nelson* [1997] 1 W.L.R. 233; *AMB Generali Holding AG v SEB Trygg Liv Holding AB* [2005] EWCA Civ 1237, [2006] W.L.R. 276. See also *Knight Frank LLP v Du Haney* [2011] EWCA Civ 404; *Bronze Monkey LLC v Simmons & Simmons LLP* [2017] EWHC 3097 (Comm), [2018] P.N.L.R. 14. **31-101**

### Description of principal

*Replace footnote 679 with:*

[679] *P&P Property Ltd v Owen White and Catlin LLP* [2018] EWCA Civ 1082, [2018] P.N.L.R. 29; Reynolds (2018) 134 L.Q.R. 511. **31-103**

## (e) Tort

### Agent's liability in tort

*Replace footnote 728 with:*

[728] *Welsh Development Agency v Export Finance Ltd* [1992] B.C.L.C. 148; cf. *The Leon* [1991] 2 Lloyd's Rep. 611, 623–625. See also *PT Sandipala Arthaputra v STMicroelectronics Asia Pacific Pte Ltd* [2018] 1 S.L.R. 818; *Bumi Armada Offshore Holdings Ltd v Tozzi SrL* [2019] 1 S.L.R. 10 (controlling shareholder of parent company not liable for breach by subsidiary); Koh (2020) 136 L.Q.R. 30. **31-111**

## 8. OBLIGATIONS OF PRINCIPAL AND AGENT INTER SE

## (a) Duties of Agents

### *(ii) Common Law: Exercise of Care and Skill*

#### Disclosure of misdoing

*Replace paragraph with:*

**31-116** It is usually said that a failure by the agent to disclose his own misdoings is not in itself a breach of contract,[752] so that an employee negotiating for severance is not bound, in the absence of fraud, to disclose such breaches of duty as would have given the employer the opportunity of dismissing him.[753] But it has been held that an employee may sometimes be under a duty to disclose breaches of duty by *other* employees[754] and also that outside the above context a director, as a fiduciary owing a duty of loyalty, may come under a duty to disclose his own breaches that have ongoing relevance to the principal's business[755]: it may be that a senior employee would also.[756]

[752] *Healey v Société Anonyme Francaise Rubastic* [1917] 1 K.B. 946; *University of Nottingham v Fishel* [2000] I.C.R. 1462.

[753] *Bell v Lever Bros Ltd* [1932] A.C. 161, 228.

[754] *Sybron Corp v Rochem Ltd* [1984] Ch. 112.

[755] *Item Software (UK) Ltd v Fassihi* [2004] EWCA Civ 1244, [2005] 2 B.C.L.C. 91 (not followed in Australia in *P & V Industries Pty Ltd v Porto* [2006] VSC 131 and said in *Stupples v Stupples & Co (High Wycombe) Ltd* [2012] EWHC 1226 (Ch), [2013] 1 B.C.L.C. 729 at [59] to concern directors).

[756] This depends to some extent on whether the duty is fiduciary or specific to directors and perhaps certain employees. See *Bowstead and Reynolds on Agency*, 21st edn (2018), para.6-054; Berg (2005) 121 L.Q.R. 213; Flannigan [2006] Bus. L.Rev. 258 (Canada); Ho and Lee [2007] C.L.J. 348; Watts (2007) 123 L.Q.R. 21.

### *(iii) Equity: Fiduciary Duties and Duties of Loyalty*

**31-118** *Replace footnote 760 with:*

[760] See in general Goff and Jones, *Law of Restitution*, 7th edn (2007), Ch.33 (not in later editions); Finn, *Fiduciary Obligations* (1977, republ. 2016), Pt II; *Snell's Equity*, 34th edn (2020), Ch.7; *Bowstead and Reynolds on Agency*, 21st edn (2018), arts 43–51. The fiduciary duties of directors are now prescribed by statute: see Companies Act 2006 Pt 10 Ch.2.

#### Fiduciary duties and duties of loyalty

*Replace paragraph with:*

**31-118** An agent, where he undertakes to act for another in circumstances giving rise to a relationship of trust and confidence, owes fiduciary duties derived from Equity to prefer his principal's interests to his own.[761] Although there are dicta which might appear to indicate that the fiduciary duties are based entirely on the contract between principal and agent[762] it is fairly well established that they are separate[763] (though not without overlap) and to some extent counterbalance the stricter rules on implication of contract terms at common law. In any case, not all agents act under a contract.[764] These duties are sometimes subsumed into the wider phrase "duties of loyalty", some of which are positive duties, though taking in the two basic fiduciary duties imposed by equity and discussed below, that of avoiding conflicts of interest and that of not profiting from position, which are themselves negative only and thus can be said to be prophylactic in operation.[765] Breach of these duties generally entails deliberate, not negligent acts.[766] But the two basic duties referred to above and explained below operate strictly, without proof of intentional wrongdoing, or even fault.

[761] Not all intermediaries acting for others come within this phrase. For examples where there was no relevant duty see *Halton International Inc (Holdings) SARL v Guernroy Ltd* [2005] EWHC 1968 (Ch), [2006] 1 B.C.L.C. 78 (power of attorney to vote shares); affirmed [2006] EWCA Civ 801, [2006] W.T.L.R. 1241; *John Youngs Insurance Services Ltd v Aviva Insurance Service UK Ltd* [2011] EWHC 1515 (TCC) (claims handling and building repair services: agency services fiduciary but not other services in same contract); *CH Offshore Ltd v Internaves Cobsorcio Naviero SA* [2020] EWHC 1710 (Comm) (intermediate brokers). Where the Commercial Agents Regulations (above, para.31-017) apply the agent must act "dutifully and in good faith": reg.3(1). The duty is unexcludable: reg.5. Arguments on the basis of good faith were rejected in *Smith v Reliance Water Controls Ltd* [2003] Eu. L.R. 874 and *Monk v Largo Foods Ltd* [2016] EWHC 1837 (Comm) (on the power to terminate). There may be criminal liability under the Fraud Act 2006, especially s.4: see discussion in *Cavell USA Inc v Seaton Insurance Co* [2009] EWCA Civ 1363, [2009] 2 C.L.C. 991 at [25].

[762] *Kelly v Cooper* [1993] A.C. 205, 213–214; and see *Clark Boyce v Mouat* [1994] 1 A.C. 428, 437.

[763] *Re Goldcorp Exchange Ltd* [1995] 1 A.C. 74, 98.

[764] Above, para.31-117; and see *Conway v Ratiu* [2005] EWCA Civ 1302, [2006] 1 All E.R. 571.

[765] This is the basis of a distinctive approach by Conaglen, *Fiduciary Loyalty* (2010); see also Flannigan (2006) 122 L.Q.R. 449. But for a different view see Heydon (2014) 20 *Trusts and Trustees* 1006. Analysis on the basis of positive duties is supported by the law concerning trustees and that concerning directors and sometimes even senior employees; and it has the advantage of taking in certain duties, which can be described as relating to a "fraud on a power", which require fiduciaries undoubtedly acting within their authority nevertheless to take into account the interests of their principals in certain ways: see *Bowstead and Reynolds on Agency*, 21st edn (2018), para.8-220; Lord Sales (2020) 136 L.Q.R. 384.

[766] *Bristol & West BS v Mothew* [1998] Ch. 1, 19.

*Replace footnote 767 with:*

[767] *New Zealand Netherlands Society "Oranje" Inc v Kuys* [1973] 1 W.L.R. 1126, 1130 per Lord Wilberforce. For an example where a person who acted as a go-between in a property transaction was held not to owe fiduciary duties see *Prince Eze v Conway* [2019] EWCA Civ 88. **31-119**

**Conflict of interest**

*Replace paragraph with:*

A general principle,[769] is that as a fiduciary, an agent must not, without first obtaining the informed consent of his principal, put himself in a position where his duty to his principal conflicts[770] or may conflict[771] with his own interests or the interests of another principal.[772] An injunction may often be obtained against an agent who is or may be in such a position.[773] Any benefit or gain made in circumstances where a conflict or significant possibility of conflict existed must be accounted for to the principal.[774] A principal who has full knowledge of the facts may however assent to the agent's acts[775]; and sometimes his instructions may be so specific as to leave the agent with no discretion, and hence to exclude this rule.[776] **31-121**

[769] See *Lewin on Trusts*, 20th edn (2020), Ch.45; *Bowstead and Reynolds on Agency*, 21st edn (2018), art.44; *Chan v Zacharia* (1984) 154 C.L.R. 178, 198–199. Cf. *Pilmer v Duke Group Ltd* (2001) 207 C.L.R. 165, 199.

[770] See below; and generally *Re Cape Breton Co* (1885) 29 Ch. D. 795, 811; affirmed on other grounds sub nom. *Cavendish-Bentinck v Fenn* (1887) 12 App. Cas. 652; *Aberdeen Ry v Blaikie Bros* (1854) 1 Macq. 461; *Bray v Ford* [1896] A.C. 44; *Phipps v Boardman* [1967] 2 A.C. 46; *Industrial Development Consultants Ltd v Cooley* [1972] 1 W.L.R. 443; *Canadian Aero Services Ltd v O'Malley* [1974] S.C.R. 592, (1973) 40 D.L.R. (3d) 371; cf. *Peso Silver Mines Ltd v Cropper* [1966] S.C.R. 673, (1966) 58 D.L.R. (2d) 1. And see Estate Agents Act 1979 s.21.

[771] See *Anglo-African Merchants Ltd v Bayley* [1970] 1 Q.B. 311; *North & South Trust Co v Berkeley* [1971] 1 W.L.R. 470; *Farrington v Rowe McBride & Partners* [1985] 1 N.Z.L.R. 83; *Clark Boyce v Mouat* [1994] 1 A.C. 428. Requirements of disclosure are imposed on estate agents by the Estate Agents (Provision of Information) Regulations 1991 (SI 1991/859) reg.2. See also Estate Agents (Undesirable Practices) (No.2) Order 1991 (SI 1991/1032); Consumer Protection from Unfair Trading Regulations 2008 (SI 2008/1277). Exemptions are made by s.70 of the Enterprise and Regulatory Reform Act 2013. See also Consumer Rights Act 2015 ss.83 et seq. (letting agents).

[772] cf. above, para.31-040 (no actual incapacity); see also below, para.31-125.

[773] The majority of the cases concern confidential information possessed by accountants and solicitors: see *Prince Jefri Bolkiah v KPMG* [1999] 2 A.C. 222; below, para.31-122, n.781.

[774] See below, para.31-130; *Chan v Zacharia* (1984) 154 C.L.R. 178, 198–199; *Imageview Management Ltd v Jack* [2009] EWCA Civ 63, [2009] 1 Lloyd's Rep. 436 (a strong application of the rule; see Watts (2009) 125 L.Q.R. 369 and below, para.31-161). The case is followed in *Rahme v Smith & Williamson Trust Corp Ltd* [2009] EWHC 911 (Ch). As to account of profits, see below, para.31-130.

[775] *Cavendish-Bentinck v Fenn* (1887) 12 App. Cas. 652; *Queensland Mines Ltd v Hudson* (1978) 52 A.L.J.R. 399, PC. But the knowledge must be full: see *Hurstanger Ltd v Wilson* [2007] EWCA Civ 299, [2007] 1 W.L.R. 235; cf. *Medsted Associates Ltd v Canaccord Genuity Wealth (International) Ltd* [2019] EWCA Civ 83, [2019] 2 All E.R. 959 (no duty to disclose actual amount of commission received); *Pengelly v Business Mortgage Finance 4 Plc* [2020] EWHC 2002 (Ch).

[776] See *Dalgety & Co Ltd v Gray* (1919) 26 C.L.R. 249, 256, PC (loan to principal); *RH Deacon & Co Ltd v Varga* (1972) 30 D.L.R. (3d) 653; affirmed (1973) 41 D.L.R. (3d) 767 (stockbroker); *Volkers v Midland Doherty Ltd* (1985) 17 D.L.R. (4th) 343.

*Replace footnote 793 with:*

### Self-dealing[793]

31-124 [793] See *Bowstead and Reynolds on Agency*, 21st edn (2018), art.45; Conaglen, *Fiduciary Loyalty* (2010), pp.126–128; Goff and Jones, *Law of Unjust Enrichment*, 9th edn (2016), paras 8-175 et seq. This is referred to separately in *Bristol & West B.S. v Mothew* [1998] Ch. 1, 19.

## *(iv) Remedies*

### Equity: injunction and rescission

*Replace footnote 826 with:*

31-128 [826] See *Snell's Equity*, 34th edn (2020), paras 7-053 et seq.

31-129 *Change title of paragraph:*

### Equity: duty to account and restoration of the trust estate

*Replace paragraph with:*

31-129 Equity provides much of the reasoning in this area, substantive as well as remedial, and must be invoked when a claim is in respect of one of the equitable duties and is not simply a common law claim for breach of contract or negligence.[827] The remedy to which general reference is usually made is that of a duty to account, though some of the technical terminology within this is more relevant to the procedure accompanying the taking of an account against a trustee, and the modern approach is to look more to substantive general principles.[828] To the extent that an agent is in possession or control of the principal's money or funds as trustee and misapplies them, equity will both require the agent personally to restore the trust fund and will also give proprietary remedies to the extent that the moneys or their traceable substitutes are identifiable in the agent's or a third party's hands, subject to applicable defences that the third party may have.[829] Where such remedies are applicable, there would be consequences as regards limitation, for by virtue of s.21(1)(b) of the Limitation Act 1980 its provisions do not apply to actions by a beneficiary to recover trust property. Such reasoning when deployed in a commercial context may be used to facilitate attempts to avoid the consequences of, for example, a fall in property values. Although it seems that the normal rules for accounting by trustees do not in all circumstances call for the restitution of the entire trust fund,[830] recent English decisions concerning fact situations of this sort have invoked rules of equitable compensation to facilitate making an award for no more than the amount perceived as having been lost by reason of the trustee's actions, using some general notion of "but for" causation to assist in the process.[831] It is not clear that the somewhat ill-defined category of equitable compensation needed to be enlarged in this way to provide a way of dealing with inadmissible claims. There must also certainly be situations where an agent who holds as trustee, for example a solicitor in conveyancing matters whose power to pay out a fund is specifically limited, could be rightly made liable for wrongful disposal of the trust estate.[832]

[827] See *Bowstead and Reynolds on Agency*, 21st edn (2018), at paras 6-040 to 6-044; and Millett (1998) 114 L.Q.R. 214.

[828] See *Libertarian Investments v Hall* [2013] 16 H.K.C.F.A.R. 681 at [97]–[99], [166]–[172].

[829] See *Re Dawson* [1966] 2 N.S.W.L.R. 211; *Youyang Pty Ltd v Minter Ellison Morris Fletcher* (2003) 212 C.L.R. 484 (see Elliott and Edelman (2003) 119 L.Q.R. 545); *Bairstow v Queen's Moat House Plc* [2001] EWCA Civ 712, [2001] B.C.L.C. 531; *Lloyd's TSB Bank Plc v Markandan & Uddin* [2012] EWCA Civ 65, [2012] 2 All E.R. 884.

[830] See Lord Millett in *Libertarian Investments v Hall*, n.828 above, at [166]–[172]; (1998) 114 L.Q.R. 214, 227; *Lewin on Trusts*, 20th edn (2020), paras 41-001 et seq.

[831] *Target Holdings Ltd v Redferns* [1996] A.C. 421; *AIB Group (UK) Plc v Mark Redler & Co Solicitors* [2014] UKSC 58, [2015] A.C. 1503; Lee (2015) J. Eq. 94; but cf. Ho (2015) 131 L.Q.R. 213; Gummow (2015) 45 Aust. Bar Rev. 5; Millett [2015] *UK Supreme Court Yearbook* 193; Turner [2015] C.L.J. 188; Davies (2015) 78 M.L.R. 681. Cf. *Auden McKenzie (Pharma Division) v Patel* [2019] EWCA Civ 2291, [2020] B.C.C. 316; and see Ho and Nolan (2020) 136 L.Q.R. 402, 412–417. Profits made are accessory to the trust estate: e.g. Tang Ying Loi v Tang Ying Yip (2017) 20 H.K.C.F.A.R. 53 (fiduciary "borrowed" trust fund).

[832] As in *Various Claimants v Giambrone & Law* [2017] EWCA Civ 1193, [2018] P.N.L.R. 2, where however common law damages are also considered. On this case see Ho and Nolan (2020) 134 L.Q.R. 402, 415–417.

## Account of profits and proprietary remedies

*Replace footnote 833 with:*

[833] See, e.g. *Regal (Hastings) Ltd v Gulliver* [1942] 1 All E.R. 378, [1967] 2 A.C. 134n.; *Phipps v Boardman* [1967] 2 A.C. 46. For a recent discussion of account of profits see *Parr v Keystone Healthcare Ltd* [2019] EWCA Civ 1246, [2019] 4 W.L.R. 99. **31-130**

*Replace footnote 839:*

## Equitable compensation[839]

[839] See *Bowstead and Reynolds on Agency*, 21st edn (2018), para.6-043. The nature of equitable compensation is considered in *Interactive Technology Corp Ltd v Ferster* [2018] EWCA Civ 1594, [2018] 2 P.&C.R. DS22; cf. above, para.31-129 as to restoration of the trust estate. **31-131**

*Replace paragraph with:*

The acceptance of a general notion of equitable compensation is a fairly recent development, at any rate in England and Wales.[840] The phrase refers to a monetary award for loss caused by breach of fiduciary duty,[841] and is to be distinguished from "equitable damages", a phrase that can be used of an award of damages in lieu of specific performance under Lord Cairns' Act, which used to be regarded by some as the only occasion in which a court of Equity could give monetary judgments. Equitable compensation is plainly an appropriate remedy where an agent acts disloyally[842] or acts in breach of trust.[843] It is less clear whether a mere conflict of interest will support equitable compensation, unless the claimant can establish that had the conflict been disclosed the principal would not have made the decision that caused the loss.[844] The conflict of interest may, however, help to support an allegation that the agent has acted in breach of his (contractual or tortious) duties of care.[845] Where equitable compensation is awarded, the common law principles for the assessment of damages and contributory negligence are in principle not **31-131** relevant.[846] In general, questions of causation are more likely to be relevant in some form than matters of contemplation, foreseeability and scope of duty.[847] But where the duty broken is simply one of exercising care, the duty, even if historically remediable in equity as well as common law, is not a fiduciary one and common law principles apply.[848] This whole problem often arises in connection with the multiple functions of professionals such as solicitors and accountants, who are primarily persons offering services on a commercial basis (for example, they have no duty to tell their clients that another person offering the same services would charge less), but may perform many functions in respect of which they are fiduciaries, often because of information known by or available to them, and if solicitors, may also hold property on trust, though frequently only for a short time and in support or implementation of a transaction for which their services are utilised. They may sometimes have agency powers, for example to make contracts or settle cases on behalf of their principals,[849] and their knowledge may sometimes be attributed to their principals. This conjunction of roles may require very careful analysis within legal categories, bearing in mind that a reasonable external observer might regard many of the disputes litigated as simply concerning inadequate performance by a solicitor of his contractual duties. A similar breakdown of functions can be applied to company directors.[849a]

840 Trustees have always been liable for causing loss to the beneficiaries. The wider right now accepted is often traced back to *Nocton v Ashburton* [1914] A.C. 932, a case in which the reasoning is not completely clear.

841 See *Libertarian Investments Ltd v Hall* (2013) 16 H.K.C.F.A.R. 681 at [84] et seq., per Ribeiro P.J.; [166] et seq. per Lord Millett N.P.J.; *Interactive Technology Corp Ltd v Ferster* [2018] EWCA Civ 1594.

842 See, e.g. *Také Ltd v BSM Marketing Ltd* [2009] EWCA Civ 45 (agent for furniture); *Premium Real Estate Ltd v Stevens* [2009] 2 N.Z.L.R. 384 (estate agent).

843 See *Bairstow v Queen's Moat House Plc* [2001] EWCA Civ 712, [2001] 2 B.C.L.C. 531.

844 See *Gwembe Valley Development Co Ltd v Koshy (No.3)* [2003] EWCA Civ 1048, [2004] 1 B.C.L.C. 131 at [159] (held account of profits appropriate).

845 See *Hilton v Barker Booth & Eastwood* [2005] UKHL 8, [2005] 1 W.L.R. 567 (conflict of interest between two principals, where damages on a common law basis appear to be envisaged).

846 See *Canson Enterprises Ltd v Boughton & Co* [1991] 4 S.C.R. 534, (1997) 85 D.L.R. (4th) 129.

847 See *Swindle v Harrison* [1997] 4 All E.R. 705; *Gwembe Valley Development Co Ltd v Koshy* [2003] EWCA Civ 1048, [2004] 1 B.C.L.C. 131.

848 *Bristol & West BS v Mothew* [1998] Ch. 1 (oversight in conveyancing); and see *Bank of New Zealand v New Zealand Guardian Trust Co Ltd* [1999] 1 N.Z.L.R. 664. Contra, Heydon (2014) 20 *Trusts and Trustees* 1006.

849 See above, paras 31-013, 31-083.

849a See Kershaw (2020) 136 L.Q.R. 454.

### *(vi) Agent Holding Money for Principal*

**Trustee or debtor?**

*Replace footnote 859 with:*

31-133 859 See *Burdick v Garrick* (1870) L.R. 5 Ch. App. 233; *Kirkham v Peel* (1880) 43 L.T. 171; 44 L.T. 195; *Henry v Hammond* [1913] 2 K.B. 515; *Neste Oy v Lloyds Bank Plc* [1983] 2 Lloyd's Rep. 658 (ship's agents) (disapproved in respect of one transaction in respect of which a constructive trust was found, in *Angove's Pty Ltd v Bailey* [2016] UKSC 47, [2016] 1 W.L.R. 3179); *Kingscroft Insurance Co Ltd v HS Weavers (Underwriting) Agencies Ltd* [1993] 1 Lloyd's Rep. 187; *Canadian Pacific Air Lines Ltd v Canadian Imperial Bank of Commerce* (1987) 42 D.L.R. (4th) 375; *Stephens Travel Service Intl Pty Ltd v Qantas Airways Ltd* (1988) 13 N.S.W.L.R. 331 (travel agent). An agent may of course hold under a *Quistclose* trust: see *Lewin on Trusts*, 20th edn (2020), paras 9-040 et seq.

### Interest

*Replace footnote 863 with:*

[863] See *Lewin on Trusts*, 20th edn (2020), para.41-094. 31-134

## (b) Rights of Agents

### *(i) Remuneration*

### Right to remuneration

*Replace footnote 872 with:*

[872] The Estate Agents Act 1979 s.18, requires the agent to give the client certain information as to "prospective liabilities", largely defined in terms of "remuneration", before entering into a contract under which he will "engage in estate agency work": otherwise the contract is not enforceable without the leave of the court (which may be granted subject to conditions). If however the contract is unilateral, viz formed on the introduction of a purchaser, it would seem that such a situation will not strictly arise. Further prescription as to information which must be supplied is made in the Estate Agents (Provision of Information) Regulations 1991 (SI 1991/859). It is considered in *Great Eastern Group Ltd v Digby* [2011] EWCA Civ 1120, where a majority of the Court of Appeal takes the view that "remuneration" includes damages for breach of a sole agency contract. 31-137

### Claims on a restitutionary quantum meruit

*Replace footnote 882 with:*

[882] *Benedetti v Sawiris* [2013] UKSC 50, [2014] A.C. 938. See Vol.I, paras 29-080 et seq.; *Bowstead and Reynolds on Agency*, 21st edn (2018), para.7-009; Goff and Jones, *Law of Unjust Enrichment*, 9th edn (2016), Ch.17. See also *MSM Consulting Ltd v United Republic of Tanzania* [2009] EWHC 121 (QB), 123 Con. L.R. 154; below, para.31-148. 31-138

### Commission

*Replace paragraph with:*

The remuneration of the agent typically, but not always,[883] takes the form of a commission, being a percentage of the value of the transaction the agent is to bring about for the principal. In such cases the agent does not become entitled to his commission until the event has occurred upon which his entitlement arises. What this event is must normally be ascertained from the terms of the agency contract. In most cases where the agent is engaged to find a third party to enter into a contract with his principal there will be little difficulty because the event will occur when the principal and the third party enter into the contract which the agent was engaged to bring about. The agent's task is then successfully completed.[883a] 31-139

[883] For a case (in the context of the Commercial Agents Regulations) where an agent was remunerated by markup see *Mercantile International Group Plc v Chuan Soon Huat Industrial Group Plc* [2002] EWCA Civ 288, [2002] 1 All E.R. (Comm) 788.

[883a] In *Wells v Devani* [2019] UKSC 4, [2020] A.C. 129 it was agreed that commission would be paid on a property transaction at 2 per cent, but there was no reference to the time at which it became due. It was held, rejecting an argument that there was no complete agreement, that it was to be assumed as intended to be payable on completion, which had occurred.

### Estate agents[884]

*Replace footnote 889 with:*

[889] *Dennis Reed Ltd v Goody* [1950] 2 K.B. 277, 284, per Denning L.J. See also *Wells v Devani* [2019] UKSC 4, [2020] A.C. 129, above, para.31-139. 31-140

### Agent must be effective cause of transaction

*Replace footnote 936 with:*

31-147 [936] *Homesearch (Thames & Chilterns) Ltd v Cowham* [2008] EWCA Civ 26, [2008] 1 W.L.R. 909; *Silvercloud Financial Solutions Ltd v High Street Solicitors Ltd* [2020] EWHC 878 (Comm).

### Termination of contract: common law

*Replace paragraph with:*

31-151 Where any contract between principal and agent is unilateral the principal may be able to terminate it, i.e. revoke his offer, before the agent has earned commission,[965] except in those cases where a collateral contract not to revoke is appropriate.[966] Where the contract is bilateral, however, the termination may be a breach of contract, rendering the principal liable for accrued commission, or in damages for loss of the prospect of earning commission.[966a] Whether notice is required to terminate a continuing agency contract of indefinite duration depends also on its express or implied terms. No term will necessarily be implied to prevent either party terminating summarily, but such an implication may be made if it is appropriate, which it usually will be. This may be so where the contract is analogous to a contract of employment, or where the agent undertakes to use his best endeavours to carry out his principal's business, or has expended capital sums to carry out his duties. In such cases, for example, a term may be implied that either party must give the other reasonable notice of termination.[967] Such a contract can, of course, also be determined by the principal in consequence of the agent's repudiatory breach.[968] But if it is the principal whose breach is repudiatory, the agent likewise can accept the breach and determine the contract.[969] The question of termination of *contract* is not the same as that of termination of *authority*, which is dealt with below.[970]

[965] *Motion v Michaud* (1892) 8 T.L.R. 447; *Joynson v Hunt & Son* (1905) 93 L.T. 470; *Levy v Goldhill* [1917] 2 Ch. 297.

[966] The dictum of (Reginald) Goff L.J. in *Daulia Ltd v Four Millbank Nominees Ltd* [1978] Ch. 231, 239 is surely too wide.

[966a] For a recent example see *W Nagel v Pluczenik Diamond Co NV* [2018] EWCA Civ 2640, [2019] 1 Lloyd's Rep. 36.

[967] *Bauman v Hulton Press Ltd* [1952] 2 All E.R. 1121; *Martin-Baker Aircraft Co Ltd v Murison* [1955] 2 Q.B. 556; *Decro-Wall International SA v Practitioners in Marketing Ltd* [1971] 1 W.L.R. 361, 376–377; *Crawford Fitting Co v Sydney Valve and Fittings Pty Ltd* (1988) 14 N.S.W.L.R. 438; cited in *Alpha Lettings Ltd v Neptune Research and Development Ltd* [2003] EWCA Civ 704; *Paper Reclaim Ltd v Aoteasoa International Ltd* [2007] 3 N.Z.L.R. 169. Reasonableness is judged at the time of termination: *Turner v Ogilvy & Mather (NZ) Ltd* [1996] 1 N.Z.L.R. 641, 646. See Carnegie (1969) 85 L.Q.R. 392; Vol.I, para.14-029.

[968] See below, para.31-161; Vol.I, Ch.24.

[969] e.g. *Decro-Wall International SA v Practitioners in Marketing Ltd*, above (where the agent (actually a distributor) was also granted an injunction: see also *Evans Marshall & Co Ltd v Bertola SA* [1973] 1 W.L.R. 349).

[970] Below, para.31-166.

### Calculation of compensation

*Replace footnote 1022 with:*

31-155 [1022] [2006] EWCA 63, [2006] 1 W.L.R. 1281 at [29], per Moore-Bick L.J. Cases considering calculation of compensation since *Lonsdale* include *McQuillan v McCormick* [2010] EWHC 1112 (QB), [2011] E.C.C. 18 (jewellery); *Invicta UK Ltd v International Brands Ltd* [2013] EWCA Civ 1564 (QB), [2013] E.C.C. 30 (wine for supermarkets); *Alan Ramsay Sales & Marketing Ltd v Typhoo Tea Ltd* [2016] EWHC 486 (Comm), [2016] 4 W.L.R. 59 (food sector); *Monk v Largo Foods Ltd* [2016] EWHC 1837 (Comm) (consultant to food manufacturer) and *W Nagel v Pluczenik Diamond Co NV* [2018] EWCA Civ 2640, [2019] 1 Lloyd's Rep. 36 (diamond broker).

### Loss of commission at common law by default or misconduct

*Replace paragraph with:*

Where the agent commits a breach of his obligations, it may obviously sometimes be the case that thereby he does not perform the act or acts entitling him to remuneration, which he therefore cannot claim.[1046] However, a more serious breach may be regarded as going to the root of the contract and hence repudiatory, or creating a total failure of consideration. In such a case the agent's services may be terminated, damages may be due, and no further commission will be payable, and commission already received recoverable, beyond anything already earned.[1047] In a recent case, however, *Imageview Management Ltd v Jack*,[1048] an agent acting on commission who had secured employment for a professional footballer also acted for the relevant club to procure an immigration permit for his client and charged the club a fee for doing so. The Court of Appeal held that there was a breach of fiduciary duty, and in consequence the commission was forfeit: no more commission need be paid and the footballer was entitled to repayment of the commission already paid.[1049] The sum paid for the permit was treated as a secret profit and to be paid to the agent without any allowance for the value of work done.[1050] The only exception that appears to be envisaged to such a forfeiture was one of "harmless collaterality".[1051] The decision as to the secret profit is less controversial, but as regards the greater forfeiture this is a harsh case and it is not clear that there is satisfactory authority in equity or common law for the notion of forfeiture in this context. Had there been a total failure of consideration as regards the agent's performance, the money paid would be refundable and no more money due. But the principal services required had here been uncontroversially performed and it is equally not clear that a non-dishonest breach of fiduciary obligation, as this seems to have been, should be treated under general contract law as of itself creating such a failure or as justifying forfeiture. The previous cases use various different lines of reasoning[1052] and cannot be said to be clear except in strong hostility to breach of fiduciary duty.[1053] The *Imageview* case has since been both followed[1054] and distinguished.[1055] It is possible that the introduction of the notion of forfeiture in this area may at some time require reconsideration. Apart from this, the principal can waive the breach,[1056] but waiver will not be implied merely from the principal's accepting the benefit of the transaction negotiated,[1057] or suing the agent for a bribe received.[1058] Where the breach does not go to the whole of the agent's obligation, he may be able to recover commission[1059]; and where the breach is in respect of a severable transaction he may be able to recover commission for services not affected by the breach.[1060] **31-161**

[1046] e.g. *Salomons v Pender* (1865) 3 Hurl. & C. 639 (also involving an element of self-dealing).

[1047] e.g. *Boston Deep Sea Fishing & Ice Co v Ansell* (1888) 39 Ch. D. 339. See also *Macnamara v Martin* (1908) 7 C.L.T. 699 (conduct contrary to fiduciary duties after commission earned).

[1048] [2009] EWCA Civ 63, [2009] Bus. L.R. 1034: see Watts (2009) 125 L.Q.R. 369; Oram [2010] L.M.C.L.Q. 95.

[1049] See at [51].

[1050] See at [59].

[1051] See at [30].

[1052] The strongest for the result obtained are *Andrews v Ramsay & Co* [1903] 2 K.B. 635 and *Rhodes v Macalister* (1923) 29 Com. Cas. 19.

[1053] See the brief but trenchant judgment of Mummery L.J. at [64].

[1054] *Rahme v Smith & Williamson* [2009] EWHC 911 (Ch); *Stupples v Stupples & Co (High Wycombe) Ltd* [2012] EWHC 1226 (Ch), [2013] 1 B.C.L.C. 729; *Avrahami v Biran* [2013] EWHC 1776 (Ch);

*Hosking v Marathon Asset Management LLP* [2016] EWHC 2418 (Ch), [2017] Ch. 157 (forfeiture of share in partnership profits); *HPOR Servicos de Concultoria Ltda v Dryships Inc* [2018] EWHC 3451 (Comm), [2019] 2 All E.R. (Comm) 168. See also *Premium Real Estate Ltd v Stevens* [2009] 2 N.Z.L.R. 384, decided very shortly after the *Imageview* case.

[1055] *Accidia Foundation v Simon C. Dickinson Ltd* [2010] EWHC 3058 (Ch); *Bank of Ireland v Jaffery* [2012] EWHC 1377 (Ch); *Wright Hassall LLP v Horton Jr* [2015] EWHC 3716 (QB); *Gamatronic (UK) Ltd v Hamilton* [2016] EWHC 2225 (QB). A more lenient view is taken in *Staechelin v ACLBDD Holdings Ltd* [2019] EWCA Civ 817, [2019] 3 All E.R. 429 (no forfeiture of commission for non-dishonest failure to pass on information about earlier offer).

[1056] *Harrods Ltd v Lemon* [1931] 2 K.B. 157; *Thornton Hall & Partners v Wembley Electrical Appliances Ltd* [1947] 2 All E.R. 630.

[1057] *Salomons v Pender* (1865) 3 H. & C. 639; *Rhodes v Macalister* (1923) 29 Com. Cas. 19.

[1058] *Andrews v Ramsay* [1903] 2 K.B. 635.

[1059] *Keppel v Wheeler* [1927] 1 K.B. 577; and see *Robinson Scammell & Co v Ansell* [1985] 2 E.G.L.R. 41 (bona fide mistake); *Eric V Stansfield (A Firm) v South East Nursing Home Services Ltd* [1986] 1 E.G.L.R. 29; *The Peppy* [1997] 2 Lloyd's Rep. 722, 728–729.

[1060] *Hippisley v Knee Brothers* [1905] 1 K.B. 1; *Nitedals Taendstikfabrik v Bruster* [1906] 2 Ch. 671; *Stupples v Stupples & Co (High Wycombe) Ltd* [2012] EWHC 1226 (Ch), [2013] 1 B.C.L.C. 729 (commission still earned on work for another client). But cf. *Headway Construction Co Ltd v Downham* (1974) 233 E.G. 675.

### *(ii) Indemnity at Common Law*

#### Indemnity of agent

*Replace footnote 1065 with:*

31-162 [1065] This may be more limited: see *Brook's Wharf v Goodman* [1937] 1 K.B. 534. But the duty to indemnify is sometimes stated in very general terms: see *Dugdale v Lovering* (1875) L.R. 10 C.P. 196; *Sheffield Corp v Barclay* [1905] A.C. 392; *Secretary of State v Bank of India* [1938] 2 All E.R. 797; *Owen v Tate* [1976] Q.B. 402; *Yeung Kai Yung v Hong Kong and Shanghai Banking Corp* [1981] A.C. 787; cf. *Naviera Mogor SA v Soc Metallurgique de Normandie (The Nogar Marin)* [1988] 1 Lloyd's Rep. 412; Vol.I, paras 29-119 et seq.; Goff and Jones, *Law of Unjust Enrichment*, 9th edn (2016), paras 19-16 et seq.

### 9. Termination of Authority

#### Powers of attorney

*Replace footnote 1120 with:*

31-168 [1120] The common law does not require that the power be expressed to be irrevocable, and the circumstances here prescribed for which is must be given form a creative exercise on the common law position. The words are however taken by Lord Sumption in *Angove's Pty Ltd v Bailey* [2016] UKSC 17, [2016] 1 W.L.R. 3179 as reflecting that position: see above, para.31-167.

#### Enduring powers of attorney

*Replace footnote 1131 with:*

31-171 [1131] See *Cretney and Lush on Lasting and Enduring Powers of Attorney*, 8th edn (2017) and as to the purposes of the legislation Law Com. No.122 (1983). A case on the wording as applied to successive enduring powers is *Re J* [2009] EWHC 436 (Ch), [2009] 2 All E.R. 1051.

#### Lasting powers of attorney

*Replace first paragraph with:*

31-172 The above type of Power of Attorney has now been superseded by a new type of instrument, the Lasting Power of Attorney, provided by the Mental Capacity Act 2005,[1133] the relevant parts of which became effective on October 1, 2007.[1134] This is a wider type of power, under which the donee, or different donees, can be given authority to act in respect of the donor's personal welfare as well as his or her property and affairs,[1135] though limited powers can of course be conferred in either respect. Such powers require two separate documents, one for each power, in prescribed form.[1136] The Act begins with elaborate "principles" regarding what constitutes mental incapacity,[1137] and what constitutes the "best interests" of the incapacitated person.[1138] Even without such a document, a person may sometimes be justified in acting reasonably in the interests of another in respect of care or treatment,[1139] and may in other circumstances be entitled to pledge that other's credit, use that other's money and obtain reimbursement.[1140] These powers are not dissimilar from the more limited authority applicable in cases of agency of necessity and are referred to also under that head.[1141] Lasting Powers of Attorney require a "certificate of capacity" that the donor acts voluntarily and understands the purpose of the document.[1142] The power is invalid until registered,[1143] but registration can be effected before the onset of incapacity. It is revocable both before and after registration provided the donor has capacity to do so.[1144] The court may control the exercise of the power,[1145] or appoint a "deputy" to take decisions for the incapacitated person.[1146] The Court of Protection is reconstituted by the Act as part of the reforms. There are provisions protecting the donee and bona fide third parties where no power was created or the power has been revoked.[1147] Regulations supplement the provisions of Schs 1 and 4 to the Act regarding registration and revocation of powers of the new, and also of the former, types.[1148] The Act is supported by a Code of Practice issued by the Lord Chancellor.[1149]

1133 ss.9–29; stemming from recommendations contained in Law Com No.231 (1995). Certain modifications largely connected with deprivation of liberty are made by the Mental Health Act 2007.

1134 SI 2007/1897. Some parts of the Act had already been brought into effect on April 1 by SI 2007/563. See in general Bartlett, *Blackstone's Guide to the Mental Capacity Act 2005*, 2nd edn (2008); Bryant (2007) No.84, Trusts and Estates Law & Tax Jo 5; Hopkins and Nichols (2006) 150 S.J. 632 (drawing attention to difficulties).

1135 ss.9, 11, 12.

1136 Lasting Powers of Attorney, Enduring Powers of Attorney and Public Guardian Regulations 2007 (SI 2007/1253) cl.5 (as amended) (setting out forms for use).

1137 ss.1–3.

1138 s.4 (specifying criteria for establishing reasonable belief).

1139 ss.5, 6.

1140 s.8 (the person lacking capacity is liable for necessaries supplied by virtue of s.7).

1141 See above, annotation to para.31-037.

1142 Sch.1 cl.2(1)(e).

1143 s.9(2)(b).

1144 s.13(1) (2). Bankruptcy of the donor need not always constitute revocation: see s.13(3) (4).

1145 ss.22–23.

1146 s.16.

1147 s.14, in terms similar to s.9 of the Enduring Powers of Attorney Act 1985 and similarly modifying s.5 of the Powers of Attorney Act 1971.

1148 See Lasting Powers of Attorney, Enduring Powers of Attorney and Public Guardian Regulations 2007 (SI 2007/1253) (as amended).

1149 In accordance with ss.42 and 43 of the Act, and published by TSO.

Chapter 32

# ARBITRATION



## 1. Statutory Regulation

### Scope of application of the Act: seat of arbitration in England

*Replace footnote 19 with:*

[19] Arbitration Act 1996 s.3. See DAC Report paras 26, 27; *ABB Lummus Global Ltd v Keppel Fels Ltd* [1999] 2 Lloyd's Rep. 24 (LCIA rules); *Dubai Islamic Bank PJSC v Paymentech Merchant Services Inc* [2001] 1 Lloyd's Rep. 65, 74; *Arab National Bank v El Abdali*, above; and *Braes of Doune Wind Farm (Scotland) Ltd v Alfred McAlpine Business Services Ltd*, above (relevant circumstances); Petrodulos [2002] L.M.C.L.Q. 66. See also *Tonkstar Ltd v American Home Assurance Co* [2006] EWHC 1234 (Comm), [2005] 1 Lloyd's Rep. I.R. 32 (which court is to determine seat); *Process and Industrial Developments Ltd v Nigeria* [2019] EWHC 2241 (Comm), [2019] 2 Lloyd's Rep. 361 at [42]–[53]. **32-007**

## 2. The Arbitration Agreement

### Definition of "arbitration agreement" and arbitrability

*Replace footnote 82 with:*

[82] But see *O'Callaghan v Coral Racing Ltd* [1998] C.L.Y. 854 (gaming contract); *Accentuate Ltd v Asigra Inc* [2009] EWHC 2655 (QB), [2009] 2 Lloyd's Rep. 599 at [62]–[89] (mandatory provisions of EU law); *Clyde & Co LPP v Bates van Winkelhof* [2011] I.R.L.R. 467 (sex discrimination in employment). See also *Interprods Ltd v De la Rue International Ltd* [2014] EWHC 68 (Comm), [2014] 1 Lloyd's Rep. 540; *London Steam Ship Owners Mutual Insurance Association Ltd v Spain (No.2)* [2013] EWHC 3188 (Comm), [2014] 1 Lloyd's Rep. 309 (allegations of criminality) and *Re Vocam Europe Ltd* [1998] B.C.C. 396; *Exeter City Association Football Club v Football Conference Ltd* [2004] EWHC 31 (Ch), [2004] 1 W.L.R. 2910; *Fulham Football Club (1987) Ltd v Richards* [2011] EWCA Civ 855, [2012] 1 All E.R. 414 (statutory rights of a member of a company); *Watson v Hemingway Design Ltd* [2020] I.C.R. 1063 at [56]–[61] (arbitration agreement void by the Employment Rights Act 1996 s.203 and the Equality Act 2010 s.144); *Bridgehouse (Bradford No. 2) Ltd v BAE Systems Plc* [2020] EWCA **32-020**

Civ 759 at [55]–[65] (arbitrability of applications for relief under the Companies Act 2006 s.1028(3)). The arbitral tribunal may decide the issue: *Azov Shipping Co v Baltic Shipping Co* [1999] 2 Lloyd's Rep. 159, 178; *Republic of Serbia v Image Sat International* [2009] EWHC 2583 (Comm), [2010] 1 Lloyd's Rep. 324 at [114], [123]. Arbitrability and who should determine it is discussed by various authors in (1996) 12 *Arbitration International*, Issues 2 and 3.

### Separability of arbitration agreement

*To the end of paragraph, after "clause is contained.[127]", add:*

32-028 However, the concept of separability does not preclude the arbitration agreement being construed with the remainder of the matrix agreement as a whole, especially where that is the parties' intention.[127a]

[127a] *Kabab-Ji Sal (Lebanon) v Kout Food Group (Kuwait)* [2020] EWCA Civ 6, [2020] 1 Lloyd's Rep. 269 at [66].

*Replace footnote 130 with:*

32-029 [130] *Paul Smith Ltd v H & S International Holdings Inc* [1991] 2 Lloyd's Rep. 127; *Tri MG Intra Asia Airlines v Norse Air Charter Ltd* [2009] SGHC 13, [2009] 1 Lloyd's Rep. 258. Courts exercising their supervisory role under the 1996 Act do so as a branch of the state, not as a mere extension of the consensual arbitration process: *Minister of Finance v International Petroleum Investment Co* [2019] EWCA Civ 2080, [2020] Bus. L.R. 45 at [44], [54]. See also *Enka Insaat Ve Sanayi AS v OOO "Insurance Co Chubb"* [2020] EWCA Civ 574, [2020] 3 All E.R. 577 at [42]–[56].

### Scope of the arbitration agreement

*Replace footnote 135 with:*

32-030 [135] *Re Hohenzollern Act für Locomotivbahn and the City of London Contract Corp* (1886) 54 L.T. 596. In *Nori Holdings Ltd v Public Joint-Stock Co Bank Otkritie Financial Corp* [2018] EWHC 1343 (Comm), [2018] 2 Lloyd's Rep. 80 at [60], the Court held that an arbitration agreement in respect of "any dispute or disagreement" does not imply a limitation to the effect that the agreement did not extend to a claim in insolvency proceedings to avoid a transaction as being a transaction at an undervalue.

### Companies

*Replace footnote 166 with:*

32-038 [166] *Morris v Harris* [1927] A.C. 252; *Baytur SA v Finagro Holdings SA* [1992] 1 Lloyd's Rep. 134; *Chung v Silver Dry Bulk Co Ltd* [2019] EWHC 1147 (Comm). cf. *Eurosteel Ltd v Stinnes AG* [2000] 1 All E.R. (Comm) 964 (assignment before dissolution).

## 3. STAY OF LEGAL PROCEEDINGS

### Foreign proceedings outside the EU

*Replace footnote 217 with:*

32-053 [217] *Pena Copper Mines Ltd v Rio Tinto Co Ltd* (1912) 105 L.T. 846; *Gorthon Invest AB v Ford Motor Co Ltd* [1976] 2 Lloyd's Rep. 720; *Marazura Navegacion SA v Oceanus Mutual Underwriting Association* [1977] 1 Lloyd's Rep. 283; *Tracomin SA v Sudan Oil Seeds Co Ltd (No.2)* [1983] 1 W.L.R. 1026; *Sokana Industries Co Inc v Freyre & Co Inc* [1994] 2 Lloyd's Rep. 57; *Aggeliki Charis Compania Maritima SA v Pagnan SpA* [1995] 1 Lloyd's Rep. 87; *Schiffahrtsgesellschaft Detlev von Appen GmbH v Voest Alpine Intertrading GmbH* [1997] 1 Lloyd's Rep. 179; *Shell International Petroleum Co v Coral Oil Co Ltd* [1999] 1 Lloyd's Rep. 72; *Bankers Trust Co Ltd v PT Jakarta International Hotels and Development* [1999] 1 Lloyd's Rep. 910; *XL Insurance Ltd v Owens Corning* [2002] 2 Lloyd's Rep. 500; *The Epsilon Rosa (No.2)* [2002] EWHC 2033 (Comm), [2002] 2 Lloyd's Rep. 701; affirmed [2003] EWCA Civ 509, [2003] 2 Lloyd's Rep. 509; *Through Transport Mutual Insurance Association (Eurasia) Ltd v New India Assurance Co Ltd* [2004] EWCA Civ 1598, [2005] 1 Lloyd's Rep. 67; *Atlanska Plovibda v Consignaciones Asturianas SA* [2004] EWHC 1273 (Comm), [2004] 2 Lloyd's Rep. 109 at [25]; *Starlight Shipping Co v Tai Ping Insurance Co Ltd* [2007] EWHC 1893 (Comm), [2008] 1 Lloyd's Rep. 330; *Shashoua v Sharma* [2009] EWHC 957 (Comm), [2009] 2 Lloyd's Rep. 376; *Midgulf International Ltd v Groupe Chimiche Tunisien* [2010] EWCA Civ 66, [2010] 2 Lloyd's Rep. 543; *AES Ust-Kamenogorsk Hydropower Plant LLP v Ust-Kamenogorsk Hydropower Plant JSC* [2013] UKSC 35, [2013] 1 W.L.R. 1889; *REC Wafer Norway AS v Moser Baer Photo Voltaic Ltd* [2010] EWHC 2581

(Comm), [2011] 1 Lloyd's Rep. 410; *Tryggingarfelagio Foroyar P/F v CPT Empresas Maritimas SA* [2011] EWHC 589 (Admlty); *STX Pan Ocean Co Ltd v Woori Bank* [2012] EWHC 981 (Comm); *Joint Stock Asset Management Co Ingosstrakh-Investments v BNP Paribas SA* [2012] EWCA Civ 644, [2012] 1 Lloyd's Rep. 649; *Caresse Navigation Ltd v Zurich Assurances Maroc (The Channel Ranger)* [2014] EWCA Civ 1366, [2015] 1 Lloyd's Rep. 256; *Golden Endurance Shipping SA v RMA Watanya SA* [2014] EWHC 3917 (Comm), [2015] 1 Lloyd's Rep. 266. See also *Ecom Agroindustrial Corp Ltd v Mosharaf Composite Textile Mill Ltd* [2013] EWHC 1276 (Comm), [2013] 2 All E.R. (Comm) 983 (mandatory injunction); *Michael Wilson & Partners Ltd v Emmott* [2018] EWCA Civ 51, [2018] 1 Lloyd's Rep. 299; *Nori Holdings Ltd v Public Joint-Stock Co Bank Otkritie Financial Corp* [2018] EWHC 1343 (Comm), [2018] 2 Lloyd's Rep. 80. cf. *Louis Dreyfus Commodities Kenya Ltd v Bolster Shipping Co Ltd* [2010] EWHC 1732 (Comm), [2011] 1 Lloyd's Rep. 455; *Dicey, Morris and Collins on the Conflict of Laws*, 15th edn, para.16-088; Dunning (2008) 74 *Arbitration* 254, 259. For the test to be applied by an English court when invited to grant an anti-suit injunction, see *Donohue v Armco* [2001] UKHL 64, [2002] 1 Lloyd's Rep. 425; *Turner v Grovit* [2001] UKHL 654, [2002] 1 W.L.R. 107 at [22]–[29]; *Malhotra v Malhotra* [2012] EWHC 3020 (Comm), [2013] 1 Lloyd's Rep. 285; *AES Ust-Kamenogorsk Hydropower Plant LLP v Ust-Kamenogorsk Hydropower Plant JSC* [2013] UKSC 35, [2013] 1 W.L.R. 1889; *Enka Insaat Ve Sanayi AS v OOO "Insurance Co Chubb"* [2020] EWCA Civ 574, [2020] 3 All E.R. 577 at [42]–[56].

## The Revised Brussels Regulation

*In line 17, after "1215/2012 of the European Parliament and the Council", add new footnote 231a:*

[231a] The Regulation will not apply to proceedings of which the English Court is first seised after December 31, 2020: see European Union (Withdrawal Agreement) Act 2018 ss.1B, 2; Civil Jurisdiction and Judgments (Amendment) (EU Exit) Regulations 2019 (SI 2019/479) regs 82, 92–93; European Union (Withdrawal Agreement) Act 2020 ss.2, 39. The UK has submitted a formal application to re-join the Lugano Convention as an individual member at the end of the implementation period but the outcome of that application, which will depend on assent being given by the current members, is presently unknown. **32-055**

## Stay of legal proceedings

*Replace footnote 253 with:*

[253] *Lombard North Central Plc v GATX Corp* [2012] EWHC 1067 (Comm), [2012] 1 Lloyd's Rep. 662. cf. *Sheffield United Football Club v West Ham United Football Club Plc* [2008] EWHC 2855 (Comm), [2009] 1 Lloyd's Rep. 167 (application for anti-suit injunction not such a matter). In *Sodzawiczny v Ruhan* [2018] EWHC 1908 (Comm), [43], it was held that a "matter" was any issue which is capable of constituting a dispute or difference which may fall within the scope of an arbitration agreement. **32-064**

### 4. COMMENCEMENT OF ARBITRAL PROCEEDINGS

## Power of court to extend time for beginning arbitral proceedings

*Replace second paragraph with:*

It is to be noted that subs.3(a) places no limit on the circumstances referred to and that all the circumstances in which the application for an extension arises are potentially relevant,[306] provided that they caused or at least significantly contributed to the failure to observe the time bar.[307] But the court can have regard only to such circumstances as were "outside the reasonable contemplation of the parties when they agreed the provision in question" and this may involve consideration of the relevant transaction, of ordinary practices within that type of transaction and with the reasonable expectation of parties involved in such a transaction.[308] It has also been said that the circumstances must be such that, if they had been drawn to the attention of the parties when they agreed the provision, they would at the very least have contemplated that the time-bar might not apply.[309] The fact that a party failed to read or comprehend the time limitation clause in the contract, or the fact that a party made a mistake as to the operation of the clause both in regard to making a **32-076** claim and appointing an arbitrator, has been held not to be something which was outside the reasonable contemplation of the parties.[310] The ground set out in subs.3(b) would appear to require at least that the failure to comply with the time bar is attributable to the conduct of the party relying on the clause.[311]

[306] *Vosnoc Ltd v Trans Global Projects Ltd* [1998] 1 W.L.R. 101, 112. See also *Haven Insurance Co Ltd v EUI Ltd* [2018] EWCA Civ 2494, [2019] Lloyd's Rep. I.R. 128 at [46]–[48].

[307] *Monella v Pizza Express (Restaurants) Ltd* [2003] EWHC 2966 (Ch), [2004] 12 E.G. 172.

[308] *Cathiship SA v Allanasons Ltd* [1998] 2 Lloyd's Rep. 511.

[309] *Harbour & General Works Ltd v Environmental Agency* [2000] 1 W.L.R 950, 960; *Korbetis v Transgrain Shipping BV* [2005] EWHC 1345 (QB); *SOS Corporacion Alimentaria SA v Inerco Trade SA* [2010] EWHC 162 (Comm), [2010] 2 Lloyd's Rep. 345 at [54]; *Fimbank plc v KCH Shipping Co Ltd* [2020] EWHC 1765 (Comm) at [77]–[83].

[310] *Harbour & General Works Ltd v Environmental Agency*, above. *Grimaldi Compãgnía di Navigazione Spa v Sekihyo Lines Ltd* [1999] 1 W.L.R. 708; *Fox & Widley v Guram* [1998] 3 E.G. 142; *Harbour & General Works Ltd v Environmental Agency*; *Thyssen Inc v Calypso Shipping Corp SA* [2002] 2 Lloyd's Rep. 243, 248; *Monella v Pizza Express (Restaurants) Ltd* [2003] EWHC 299 (Ch), [2004] E.G. 172; *SOS Corporacion Alimentaire SA V Inerco Trade SA* [2010] EWHC 162 (Comm), [2010] 2 Lloyd's Rep. 345 (extension refused). cf. *Vosnoc Ltd v Trans Global Projects Ltd* [1998] 1 W.L.R. 101; *Union Trans-Pacific Co Ltd v Orient Shipping Rotterdam BV* [2002] EWHC 1451 (Comm) (extension granted). See (2009) 75 *Arbitration* (4) 481, 483.

[311] *Fox & Widley v Guram*, above; *Grimaldi Compãgnía di Navigazione Spa v Sekihyo Lines Ltd*, above, at 725; *Cathiship SA v Allanasons Ltd* [1998] 2 Lloyd's Rep. 511 at 522; *Harbour & General Works Ltd v Environmental Agency* [2002] 1 Lloyd's Rep. 65, 72, [2000] I W.L.R. 950; *Thyssen Inc v Calypso Shipping Corp SA*, above, at 248; *Lantic Sugar Ltd v Baffin Investments Ltd* [2009] EWHC 3325 (Comm), [2010] 2 Lloyd's Rep. 141; *William McIlroy Swindon Ltd v Quinn Insurance Ltd* [2010] EWHC 2448 (TCC), [2011] B.L.R. 136 at [104], [108]; *Anglian Water Services Ltd v Laing O'Rourke Utilities Ltd* [2010] EWHC 1529 (TCC), [2011] 1 All E.R. (Comm) 1143; *Expofrut SA v Melville Services Inc* [2015] EWHC 1950 (Comm), [2015] 2 C.L.C. 218 at [12]–[14]; *National Bank of Fujairah v Times Trading Corp* [2020] EWHC 1983 (Comm) at [28]–[32].

## 5. THE ARBITRAL TRIBUNAL

### Removal of arbitrator

*Replace footnote 386 with:*

32-096 [386] *Save and Prosper Pensions Ltd v Homebase Ltd* [2002] L. & T.R. 11 (arbitrator's firm instructed in substantial property matter by associated company of one of the parties); *Sphere Drake Insurance v American Reliable Insurance Company* [2004] EWHC 796 (Comm) (arbitrator involved as consultant to certain key players in the market at centre of dispute); *ASM Shipping Ltd of India v TTMI Ltd of England* [2005] EWHC 2238 (Comm), [2006] 1 Lloyd's Rep. 375, [2006] EWCA Civ 1341, [2007] 1 Lloyd's Rep. 136 (arbitrator instructed as counsel in previous case against one of the parties); *Sierra Fishing Co Ltd v Mohamed* [2015] EWHC 140 (Comm), [2015] 1 Lloyd's Rep. 514 (arbitrator's business connections, involvement in negotiations and drafting of agreement, conduct of reference). cf. (where application to remove failed) *Andrews (t/a BA Constructers) v Bradshaw* [2000] B.L.R. 6 (irritation on part of arbitrator and receiving payment of fee from one party where the other refused to pay); *Laker Airways Inc v FLS Aerospace Ltd* [2000] 1 W.L.R. 113 (arbitrator in same chambers as barrister representing one of parties, but see *Smith v Kvaerner Cementation Foundations Ltd* [2006] EWCA Civ 242, [2007] 1 W.L.R. 370 at [171]); *Rustal Trading Ltd v Gill & Duffus SA* [2000] 2 Lloyd's Rep. 14 (arbitrator involved in earlier dispute with party's consultant); *AT & T Corp v Saudi Arabian Cable Co* [2000] 1 Lloyd's Rep. 22, [2000] 2 Lloyd's Rep. 127, CA (arbitrator was non-executive director of rival bidder for project); *ASM Shipping Ltd v Harris* [2007] EWHC 1513 (Comm), [2008] 1 Lloyd's Rep. 61 (two arbitrators remain after recusal of third for alleged bias); *Goel v Amega Ltd* [2010] EWHC 2454 (Comm) (case management issues); *A v B* [2011] EWHC 2345 (Comm), [2011] 2 Lloyd's Rep. 591 (barrister arbitrator involved in case for solicitors for party); *Interprods Ltd v De La Rue International Ltd* [2014] EWHC 68 (Comm) (arbitrator after appointment was appointed arbitrator in two other cases where one party represented by solicitors for claimant: s.68(2)(a) application failed); *Cofely Ltd v Bingham* [2016] EWHC 240 (Comm), [2016] 2 All E.R. (Comm) 129 at [98]–[116] (arbitrator removed on the ground of apparent bias where 18 per cent of his appointments and 25 per cent of his arbitrator/adjudicator income over the previous three years had come from cases involving the defendant as a party or as a claims consultant and where the Chartered Institute of Arbitrators acceptance of nomination form calls for disclosure of "any involvement, however remote, with either party over the last five years"); *W Ltd v M Sdn Bhd* [2016] EWHC 422 (Comm), [2016] 1 Lloyd's Rep. 552 at [27]–[44] (the IBA

Guidelines 2014 are of assistance to the Court, but they are not a statement of English law; the Court noted some "weaknesses" in the IBA Guidelines 2014); *Halliburton v Chubb Bermuda Insurance Ltd* [2018] EWCA Civ 817, [2018] 1 W.L.R. 3361 (arbitrator had accepted appointments in a number of references concerning the same or overlapping subject matter with only one common party). For the test to be applied in cases of alleged bias, see *Dimes v Proprietors of Grand Junction Canal* (1852) 3 H.L Cas. 759; *R. v Spencer* [1987] A.C. 128; *R. v Gough* [1993] A.C. 646; *R. v Bow Street Magistrate Ex. P Pinochet Ugarte (No.2)* [2002] 1 A.C. 119; *Laker Airways Inc v FLS Aerospace Ltd*, above; *Locobail (UK) Ltd v Bayfield Property Ltd* [2000] Q.B. 451; *AT & T Corp v Saudi Arabian Cable Co* above; *Re Medicaments and Related Classes of Goods (No.2)* [2001] 1 W.L.R. 700; *Porter v Magill* [2001] UKHL 67, [2002] 2 A.C. 357 at [103]; *ASM Shipping Ltd of India v TTMI Ltd of England*, above, at [39]; *Cofely Ltd v Bingham* [2016] EWHC 240 (Comm), [2016] 2 All E.R. (Comm) 129 at [72]; *H v L* [2017] EWHC 137 (Comm), [2017] 1 Lloyd's Rep. 553 at [16]. As to the relevance of non-disclosure of the circumstances which might give rise to doubts as to an arbitrator's impartiality, see *Dadoun v Biton* [2019] EWHC 3441 (Ch) at [37]–[40]; *PAO Tatneft v Ukraine* [2019] EWHC 3740 (Ch) at [82]–[100]. See IBA Guidelines on conflicts of interest in International Arbitration 2014; Chartered Institute of Arbitrators: Code of Professional and Ethical Conduct (2009); AAA/ABA Code of Ethics for Arbitrators in Commercial Disputes (2004 revision); Chung (2011) 77 *Arbitration* 167; Park (2011) 27 *Arbitration International* 473. As to the validity of a rule in the Arbitrators' Code of Conduct of the International Cotton Association, see *Aldcroft v International Cotton Association Ltd* [2017] EWHC 642 (Comm), [2017] 1 Lloyd's Rep. 635.

## 6. JURISDICTION OF THE ARBITRAL TRIBUNAL

### Tribunal can rule on its own jurisdiction

*Replace footnote 420 with:*

[420] s.30(1). See the Chartered Institute of Arbitrators: Guidelines for Arbitrators dealing with Jurisdictional Problems (2011) 77 *Arbitration* 220; *Vee Networks Ltd v Econet Wireless International Ltd* [2004] EWHC 2909 (Comm), [2005] 1 Lloyd's Rep. 192 at [22]; *UR Power GmbH v Kuok Oils and Grains Pte Ltd* [2009] EWHC 1940 (Comm), [2009] 2 Lloyd's Rep. 495; *Dallah Real Estate & Tourism Co v Ministry of Religious Affairs of the Government of Pakistan* [2010] UKSC 46, [2011] 1 A.C. 763 at [25], [79], [93]–[95]; *Assaubayer v Michael Wilson and Partners Ltd* [2014] EWHC 821 (QB). But see the cases cited above, para.32-068, n.273 (court may nevertheless be the first to decide). In *C v D1* [2015] EWHC 2126 (Comm) at [135] the Court said that s.30 is likely to contain an exhaustive definition of jurisdictional matters. In *Cockett Marine Oil DMCC v ING Bank NV* [2019] EWHC 1533 (Comm) at [53], [59], the Court held that an issue whether an assignee could claim the benefit of an arbitration agreement was an issue as to whether there was a valid arbitration agreement. **32-101**

## 7. THE ARBITRAL PROCEEDINGS

### Conduct of the reference

*Replace paragraph with:*

Section 33 of the 1996 Act sets out the general duty of the arbitral tribunal in the conduct of the reference. The tribunal is to act fairly and impartially as between the parties, giving each party a reasonable opportunity of putting his case and dealing with that of his opponent,[447] and is to adopt procedures suitable to the circumstances of the particular case, avoiding unnecessary delay or expense, so as to provide a fair means for the resolution of the matters falling to be determined.[448] Whether the means provided are reasonable and whether the procedures are fair are to be objectively determined, but they are not unduly demanding standards. A procedure may be fair even if it is not perfect.[448a] The tribunal must comply with this general duty in conducting the arbitral proceedings, in its decisions on matters of procedure and evidence and in the exercise of all other powers conferred upon it.[449] This is a mandatory provision.[450] Subject to the overriding requirements of fairness, impartiality and even-handedness, it is intended to encourage the tribunal to adapt its procedures to suit the particular case and not slavishly to follow court or other set procedures if these are inappropriate.[451] **32-106**

[447] s.33(1)(a). In *Reliance Industries Ltd v Union of India* [2018] EWHC 822 (Comm), [2018] 1 Lloyd's Rep. 562 at [25] it was held that the requirement in the UNCITRAL Rules, art.15(1), that each party should have a "full" opportunity of presenting its case, rather than a "reasonable" opportunity as required by s.33(1)(a), did not impose a higher burden on the arbitral tribunal. It was observed that the different wording was introduced in s.33(1)(a) by the DAC (para.165) because the word "full" might have reflected a difference in timing.

[448] s.33(1)(b); *SCM Financial Overseas Ltd v Raga Establishment Ltd* [2018] EWHC 1008 (Comm), [2018] 2 Lloyd's Rep. 99 at [60].

[448a] *SCM Financial Overseas Ltd v Raga Establishment Ltd* [2018] EWHC 1008 (Comm), [2018] 2 Lloyd's Rep. 99 at [58].

[449] s.33(2).

[450] s.4(1) and Sch.1.

[451] DAC Report para.151; *Margulead v Exide Technologies* [2004] EWHC 1019 (Comm), [2005] 1 Lloyd's Rep. 324 (claimant not allowed last word).

## Want of prosecution

*Replace footnote 509 with:*

**32-119** [509] *TAG Wealth Management v West* [2008] EWHC 1466 (Comm), [2008] 2 Lloyd's Rep. 699. However, if the parties have contracted for a shorter limitation period, the arbitral tribunal can exercise this power before the expiry of the limitation period under the Limitation Act 1980: *Dera Commercial Estate v Derya Inc* [2018] EWHC 1673 (Comm), [2019] 1 Lloyd's Rep. 57, [63]–[73].

## 8. Powers of the Court

### Court powers in support of arbitral proceedings

*Replace footnote 532 with:*

**32-123** [532] s.43(3), i.e. England and Wales, or (as the case may be) Northern Ireland. However, the arbitration need not have its seat in England and Wales; it is sufficient if the witness is present in England and the tribunal conducts the examination while in England or by video-link whilst abroad: *A v C* [2020] EWHC 258 (Comm), [2020] Bus. L.R. 426 at [29]–[30]; rev'd on other grounds [2020] EWCA Civ 409.

*Replace paragraph with:*

**32-124** Section 44 of the Act also confers upon the court, unless otherwise agreed between the parties,[533] the same powers on certain matters in relation to arbitral proceedings as it has in relation to legal proceedings.[534] These are: the taking and preservation of evidence, making orders in relation to property, the sale of any goods, and the granting of an interim injunction or the appointment of a receiver.[535] However, these powers may only be used when the tribunal or arbitral institution is unable to act or to act effectively.[536] This limitation is entirely consistent with one of the aims of the Act, which is to restrict the power of the court to intervene in the arbitral process. Exercise of the power should not usurp the function of the arbitrators.[537] If the case is one of urgency, the court may, on the application of a party or proposed party to the arbitral proceedings, make such orders as it considers necessary for the purpose of preserving evidence or assets,[538] for instance, it may make a search order or grant a freezing injunction.[539] It may also grant an anti-suit injunction[540] as the right to have disputes referred to arbitration is an "asset".[541] But if the case is not one of urgency or if the order sought is not necessary for the purpose of preserving evidence or assets,[542] then the court can act only upon an application of a party to the arbitral proceedings made with the permission of the tribunal or the agreement in writing of the other parties.[543] Similarly, if the court has made an urgent order but the matter ceases to be urgent, the court does not retain jurisdiction to deal with the continuation or variation of the order unless the tribunal or the parties have agreed that the court may so act.[543a] It has been held that orders under s.44 cannot be made against non-parties to the arbitration agreement,[544] save that the court can order the taking of evidence from witnesses who are not parties to the arbitration agreement pursuant to s.44(2)(a).[544a]

[533] The arbitration clause may, on its true construction, exclude the power of the court to grant ancillary relief (*Mantovani v Carapelli* [1980] 1 Lloyd's Rep. 375), though such a construction will be rare: see *The Lisboa* [1980] 2 Lloyd's Rep. 546; *Petronin SA v Sechav Marine Ltd* [1995] 1 Lloyd's Rep. 603, 613; *Ultisol Transport Contractors Ltd v Bouygues Offshore SA (No.1)* [1996] 2 Lloyd's Rep. 140, 144, reversed on other grounds [1998] 2 Lloyd's Rep. 461; *Re Qs Estate* [1999] 1 Lloyd's Rep. 931; *SAB Miller Africa BV v East African Breweries Ltd* [2009] EWCA Civ 1564, [2010] 2 Lloyd's Rep. 422 at [8]. But see *B v S* [2011] EWHC 691, [2011] 2 Lloyd's Rep. 18 (FOSFA conditions).

[534] s.44(1). *Hiscox Underwriting Ltd v Dickson Manchester & Co Ltd* [2004] EWHC 479, [2004] 2 Lloyd's Rep. 438 (interim order for disclosure); *Assimina Maritime Ltd v Pakistan Shipping Corp* [2004] EWHC 3005 (Comm), [2005] 1 Lloyd's Rep. 525 (no power to order disclosure by non-party but power to order preservation of documents by non-party); *Lauritzencool AB v Lady Navigation Inc* [2005] EWCA Civ 579, [2005] 2 Lloyd's Rep. 63 (interim injunction restraining activity outside the contract pending arbitration); *Cetelem SA v Roust Holdings Ltd* [2005] EWCA Civ 618, [2005] 2 Lloyd's Rep. 494 (injunction to deliver contractual documentation before arbitration commenced); *SAB Miller Africa BV v East African Breweries Ltd* [2009] EWCA Civ 1564, [2010] 2 Lloyd's Rep. 442 (injunction to restrain breach of contract pending establishment of tribunal). See also s.44(6) Sch.2 para.4 (exercise of power by judge–arbitrator) and CPR Pt 62PD 62. The permission of the court is required for any appeal under s.44: s.44(7) (but see below, para.32-185); *SAB Miller Africa BV v East African Breweries Ltd* [2009] EWCA Civ 1564, [2010] 2 Lloyd's Rep. 422.

[535] s.44(2). See Thomas (1997) 13 *Arbitration International* 105. cf. *Tsakos Shipping & Trading SA v Orizon Tanker Co Ltd* [1998] C.L.C. 1003 (order for inspection and tests set aside); *Commerce and Industry Co of Canada v Certain Underwriters of Lloyd's of London* [2002] 1 W.L.R. 1323 (application for examination of witnesses to provide depositions in New York arbitration refused); *Econet Wireless Ltd v Vee Networks Ltd* [2006] EWHC 1568 (Comm), [2006] 2 Lloyd's Rep. 428 (application for injunction to restrain sale of shares refused); *Permasteelisa Japan KK v Bouyguesstroi* [2007] EWHC 3508 (TCC) (application for injunction to restrain calls on performance bonds refused); *Travelers Insurance Co Ltd v Countrywide Surveyors Ltd* [2010] EWHC 2455 (TCC), [2011] 1 All E.R. (Comm) 631 (order for pre-action disclosure refused); *Silver Dry Bulk Co Ltd v Homer Hulbert Maritime Co Ltd* [2017] EWHC 44 (Comm), [2017] 1 Lloyd's Rep. 154 at [47]–[53] (order for letters of request to a foreign court refused); *Dainford Navigation Inc v PDVSA Petroleo SA* [2017] EWHC 2150 (Comm), [2017] 2 Lloyd's Rep 409 (order for sale of goods the subject of the proceedings). For the power of the court under s.37 of the Senior Courts Act 1981 to intervene outside the 1996 Act, see *Hiscox Underwriting Ltd v Dickson Manchester & Co*, above; *Cetelem SA v Roust Holdings Ltd*, above, at [74]; *Weissfisch v Julius* [2006] EWCA Civ 218, [2006] 1 Lloyd's Rep. 716 at [33]; *Elektrim SA v Vivendi Universal SA (No.2)* [2007] EWHC 571 (Comm), [2007] 2 Lloyd's Rep. 8; *Starlight Shipping Co v Tai Ping Insurance Co Ltd* [2007] EWHC 1893 (Comm), [2008] 1 Lloyd's Rep. 230; *Republic of Kazakhstan v Istil Group Inc (No.2)* [2007] EWHC 2729 (Comm), [2008] 1 Lloyd's Rep. 382; *Sheffield United Football Club Ltd v West Ham United Football Club Plc* [2008] EWHC 2855 (Comm), [2009] 1 Lloyd's Rep. 167 at [31]–[32]; *British Telecommunications Plc v SAE Group Inc* [2009] EWHC 252 (TCC), [2009] B.L.R. 231 (CPR Pt 8); *SAB Miller Africa BV v East African Breweries Ltd* [2009] EWCA Civ 1564, [2010] 2 Lloyd's Rep. 422; *REC Wafer Norway AS v Moser Baer Photo Voltaic Ltd* [2010] EWHC 2581 (Comm), [2011] 1 Lloyd's Rep. 410; *Enercon GmbH v Enercon (India) Ltd* [2012] EWHC 689 (Comm), [2012] 1 Lloyd's Rep. 519 at [68]; *AES Ust-Kamenogorsk Hydropower Plant LLP v Ust-Kamenogorsk Hydropower Plant JSC* [2013] UKSC 35, [2013] 1 W.L.R. 1889 at [48]; *Barnwell Enterprises Ltd v ECP Africa FII Investments LLC* [2013] EWHC 2517 (Comm), [2014] 1 Lloyd's Rep. 171. See also in relation to s.33(2) of the 1981 Act: *Travelers Insurance Co Ltd v Countrywide Surveyors Ltd* [2010] EWHC 2455 (TCC), [2011] 1 All E.R. (Comm) 631; *Mi-Space (UK) Ltd v Lend Lease Construction (EMEA) Ltd* [2013] EWHC 2001 (TCC), [2013] B.L.R. 600. For the power of the court under s.25(3) of the Civil Jurisdiction and Judgments Act 1982 and the restraints imposed by the ICSID Convention and sovereign immunity, see *ETI Euro Telecom International NV v Republic of Bolivia* [2008] EWCA Civ 800, [2008] 2 Lloyd's Rep. 421.

[536] s.44(5); *Pacific Maritime Asia Ltd v Holystone Overseas Ltd* [2007] EWHC 2319 (Comm), [2008] 1 Lloyd's Rep. 371 (arbitrator's order would not be sufficiently effective); *Hiscox Underwriting Ltd v Dickson Manchester & Co Ltd*, above (arbitrator newly appointed and unfamiliar with case and so, in effect, unable to act). Contrast *Econet Wireless Ltd v Vee Networks Ltd*, above (England not appropriate forum); *Patley Wood Farm LLP v Brake and Brake* [2014] EWHC 4192 (Ch) (arbitrator's directions not workable). See also *Sheffield United Football Club Ltd v West Ham United Football Club Ltd*, above (actions likely to be taken by parties would lead to an identical impasse).

[537] *ZIM Integrated Shipping Services Ltd v European Containers ICS* [2013] EWHC 3581 (Comm).

[538] s.44(3); *Cetelem SA v Roust Holdings Ltd*, above; *National Insurance and Guarantee Group Ltd v*

*M Young Legal Services Ltd* [2004] EWHC 2972 (QB), [2005] 2 Lloyd's Rep. 46; *Starlight Shipping Co v Tai Ping Insurance Co Ltd*, above; *Pacific Maritime Asia Ltd v Holystone Overseas Ltd*, above; *Sheffield United Football Club Ltd v West Ham United Football Club Ltd*, above; *BNP Paribas SA v Open Joint Stock Company Russian Machines* [2011] EWHC 308 (Comm), [2012] 1 Lloyd's Rep. 61 (even against non-party); *Euroil Ltd v Cameroon Offshore Petroleum SARL* [2014] EWHC 52 (Comm); *Schillings International LLP v Scott* [2019] EWHC 1335 (Ch) (no urgency). See also *Telenor East Holdings II AS v Altumo Holdings and Investments Ltd* [2011] EWHC 735 (Comm) (on meaning of "necessary" in s.44(3)). Unless there is an existing or intended arbitration there is no "party or proposed party": *AES Ust-Kamenogorsk Hydropower Plant LLP v Ust-Kamenogorsk Hydropower Plant JSC* [2010] EWHC 772 (Comm), [2010] 2 Lloyd's Rep. 493 at [20] (affirmed [2011] EWCA Civ 647).

[539] *Re Q's Estate* [1999] 1 Lloyd's Rep. 931; *Cogentra AG v Sixteen Thirteen Marine SA* [2008] EWHC 1615 (Comm), [2008] 2 Lloyd's Rep. 602; *Emmott v Michael Wilson & Partners Ltd (No.2)* [2009] EWHC 1 (Comm), [2009] 1 Lloyd's Rep. 233 at [83].

[540] See para.32-053, above.

[541] *Cetelem SA v Roust Holdings Ltd*, above, at [57]; *Starlight Shipping Co v Tai Ping Insurance Co Ltd*, above at [21]; *Sheffield United Football Club Ltd v West Ham United Football Club Ltd*, above at [32]; *BNP Paribas SA v Open Joint Stock Company Russian Machines*, above.

[542] *Cetelem SA v Roust Holdings Ltd*, above, at [47]; *Mobil Cerro Negro Ltd v Petroleos Venezuela SA* [2008] EWHC 532, [2008] 1 Lloyd's Rep. 684; *Travelers Insurance Co Ltd v Countrywide Surveyors Ltd* [2010] EWHC 2455 (TCC), [2011] 1 All E.R. (Comm) 631. In *Cetelem SA v Roust Holdings Ltd*, above, it was stated that a contractual right or chose in action was an "asset" (at [57], [62]); *Euroil Ltd v Cameroon Offshore Petroleum SARL* [2014] EWHC 52 (Comm). But discretion to make an order is more likely to be exercised where the asset is a conventional asset: *ZIM Integrated Shipping Serves Ltd v European Containers ICS* [2013] EWHC 3581 (Com); *Euroil Ltd v Cameroon Offshore Petroleum SARL*, above, at [18]–[20].

[543] s.44(4); *Petroleum Investigation Co Ltd v Kantupan Holdings Co Ltd* [2002] 1 All E.R. (Comm) 124; *Assimina Maritime Ltd v Pakistan Shipping Corp*, above.

[543a] *VTB Commodities Trading DAC v JSC Antipinksy Refinery* [2020] EWHC 72 (Comm), [2020] 1 W.L.R. 1227 at [36]–[39], [44].

[544] *DTEK Trading SA v Morozov* [2017] EWHC 94 (Comm), [2017] 1 Lloyd's Rep. 126; *Trans-Oil International SA v Savoy Trading LLP* [2020] EWHC 57 (Comm) at [35]–[45]; *A v C* [2020] EWHC 258 (Comm), [2020] Bus. L.R. 426 at [34]; [2020] EWCA Civ 409 at [54]–[55].

[544a] *A v C* [2020] EWCA Civ 409 at [35]–[47], [58]–[74].

*Replace footnote 545 with:*

**32-125** [545] s.2(3); *Mobil Cerro Negro Ltd v Petroleos Venezuela SA* [2008] EWHC 532, [2008] 1 Lloyd's Rep. 684 (but see s.43(3): *A v C* [2020] EWHC 258 (Comm), [2020] Bus. L.R. 426 at [29]–[30]; rev'd on other grounds [2020] EWCA Civ 409). cf. *Channel Tunnel Group Ltd v Balfour Beatty Construction Ltd* [1993] A.C. 334; *Econet Wireless Ltd v Vee Networks Ltd*, above. The court has power to order "provisional, including protective measures" under art.35 of Regulation (EU) 1215/2012 (Brussels *bis*) even though the courts of another contracting state have jurisdiction as to the substance of the matter. cf. *Van Uden Maritime BV v Kommanditgesellschaft in Firma Decoline* (C-391/95) EU:C:1998:543; [1999] Q.B. 1225, ECJ.

## Anti-arbitration injunction

*Replace footnote 561 with:*

**32-130** [561] *Zaporozhyve Production Society v Ashly Ltd* [2002] EWHC 1410 (Comm); *Arab National Bank v El-Abdali* [2004] EWHC 238 (Comm), [2005] 1 Lloyd's Rep. 541; *Weissfisch v Julius* [2006] EWCA Civ 218, [2006] 1 Lloyd's Rep. 716; *Intermet FZCO v Ansol Ltd* [2007] EWHC 226 (Comm); Elektrim SA v Vivendi Universal SA (No.2) [2007] EWHC 571 (Comm), [2007] 2 Lloyd's Rep. 8; *Albon v Naza Motor Trading Sdn Berhad (No.4)* [2007] EWCA Civ 1124, [2008] 1 Lloyd's Rep. 1; *Republic of Kazakhstan v Istil Group Inc (No.2)* [2007] EWHC 2729 (Comm), [2008] 1 Lloyd's Rep. 382; *Excalibur Ventures LLC v Texas Keystone Inc* [2011] EWHC 1624 (Comm), [2011] 2 Lloyd's Rep. 289; *Golden Ocean Group Ltd v Humpuss Intermodal Transportasi TBK Ltd* [2013] EWHC 1240 (Comm), [2013] 2 All E.R. (Comm) 1025; Dunning (2008) 74 *Arbitration* 254. See also *British Telecommunications Plc v SAE Group Inc* [2009] EWHC 252 (TCC), [2009] B.L.R. 231 (declaration). The court has power to injunct arbitral proceedings taking place in another Member State of the European Union: *Claxton Engineering Services Ltd v TXM Olaj-es Gazkutato KFT* [2010] EWHC 345 (Comm), [2011] 1 Lloyd's Rep. 510 (but see [2011] EWCA Civ 410); Seriki (2013) 16 Int. A.L.R. 2, 43. As to the Court's exceptional power to restrain by injunction a foreign-seated arbitration outside the EU, see *Sabbagh v Khoury* [2019] EWCA Civ 1219.

## 9. THE AWARD

### Remedies

*Replace footnote 594 with:*

594 s.48(5)(b): CPR Pt 24 24PD-001. See *Tilia Sonera Ab v Hilcourt (Docklands) Ltd* [2003] EWHC 3540 (Ch); *McCaughan v Belwood Homes Ltd* [2011] Arb. L.R. 53 (N.I.); Gemmell (2010) 76 *Arbitration* 467; *Sterling v Rand* [2019] EWHC 1034 (Ch). **32-135**

## 11. POWERS OF THE COURT IN RELATION TO THE AWARD

### Challenging the award: serious irregularity

*Replace footnote 719 with:*

719 s.68(1). See CPR Pt 62. The claim form must identify exactly what constitutes the alleged irregularity: *Orascom TMT Investments Sarl v Veon Ltd* [2018] EWHC 985 (Comm) at [2]; *T v V & W* [2018] EWHC 1492 (Comm) at [5]. It is unlikely that the Court's power under s.68 extends to removing an arbitral tribunal; that power is reserved under s.24: *RJ v HB* [2018] EWHC 2833 (Comm), [2018] 2 Lloyd's Rep. 613 at [15]–[16]. **32-162**

*Replace paragraph with:*

For "serious irregularity" to have occurred there must, first, have been an irregularity of one or more of the following kinds[723]: **32-163**

- (a) failure by the tribunal to comply with s.33 of the Act (general duty of the tribunal)[724];
- (b) the tribunal exceeding its powers (otherwise than by exceeding its substantive jurisdiction: see s.67)[725];
- (c) failure of the tribunal to conduct the proceedings in accordance with the procedure agreed by the parties[726];
- (d) failure by the tribunal to deal with all the issues that were put to it[727];
- (e) any arbitral or other institution or person vested by the parties with powers relating to the proceedings or the award exceeding its powers;
- (f) uncertainty or ambiguity as to the effect of the award[728];
- (g) the award being obtained by fraud or the award or the way in which it was procured being contrary to public policy[729];
- (h) failure to comply with the requirements as to the form of the award[730]; or
- (i) any irregularity in the conduct of the proceedings or in the award which is admitted by the tribunal or by any arbitral or other institution or person vested by the parties with powers in relation to the proceedings or the award.[731]

It will be noted that the list of irregularities is a closed one. Some of the listed elements nevertheless have their origins in the previous law relating to misconduct, "procedural mishaps" and mistakes admitted by the arbitrator.[732] However, the award cannot be challenged on the ground that the tribunal has come to an erroneous decision, whether of fact or law, and whether or not its findings of fact are supported by evidence.[733] In a two-tier arbitration, under which there is a right of appeal to an appeal board and the appeal board's award supersedes that of the first tier arbitrator, it is submitted that the award cannot be challenged on the ground of any irregularity in the conduct of the first tier proceedings if no irregularity is alleged in respect of the appeal.[734]

723 s.68(2).

724 *Weldon Plant Hire Ltd v Commission for the New Towns* [2000] B.L.R. 496; *Pacol Ltd v Joint Stock*

*Co Rossakhar* [2000] 1 Lloyd's Rep. 109; *Rustal Trading Ltd v Gill & Duffus SA* [2000] 1 Lloyd's Rep. 14; *Sanghi Polyesters (India) v International Investor (KCFC) (Kuwait)* [2000] 1 Lloyd's Rep. 480; *Groundshire v VHE Construction* [2001] Build. L.R. 395; *RC Pillar & Sons v Edwards* [2001] C.I.L.L. 1799; *Aoot Kalmneft v Glencore International AG* [2002] 1 Lloyd's Rep. 128; *Al Hadha Trading Co v Tradigrain SA* [2002] 2 Lloyd's Rep. 512, 523–524; *Checkpoint Ltd v Strathclyde Pension Fund* [2003] EWCA Civ 84, [2003] E.G. 214; *Bulfracht (Cyprus) Ltd v Boneset Shipping Co Ltd* [2002] EWHC 2292 (Comm), [2002] 2 Lloyd's Rep. 681; *Warborough Investments Ltd v S Robinson & Sons (Holdings) Ltd* [2003] EWCA 751, [2003] 2 E.G.L.R. 149; *Minermet SpA Milan v Luckyfield Shipping Corp SA* [2004] EWHC 729 (Comm), [2004] 2 Lloyd's Rep. 348; *Westland Helicopters Ltd v Sheikh Salah al-Hejailan (No.1)* [2004] EWHC 1625 (Comm), [2004] 2 Lloyd's Rep. 523; *Tame Shipping Ltd v Easy Navigation Ltd* [2004] EWHC 1862 (Comm), [2004] 2 Lloyd's Rep. 626; *Newfield Construction Ltd v Tomlinson* [2004] EWHC 3051 (TCC), (2004) 97 Const. L.R. 98; *Alphapoint Shipping Ltd v Rotem Amfert Negev* [2004] EWHC 2232 (Comm), [2005] 1 Lloyd's Rep. 23; *Vee Networks Ltd v Econet Wireless International Ltd* [2004] EWHC 2909 (Comm), [2005] 1 Lloyd's Rep. 192; *Margulead Ltd v Exide Technologies* [2004] EWHC 1019 (Comm), [2005] 1 Lloyd's Rep. 324; *Home of Homes Ltd v Hammersmith & Fulham LBC* [2003] EWHC 807, (2003) 92 Const. L.R. 48; *Ronly Holdings Ltd v JSC Zestafoni G Nicoladze Ferroalloy Plant* [2004] EWHC 1354 (Comm), [2004] 1 C.L.C. 1168; *Omnibridge Consulting Ltd v Clearsprings Management Ltd* [2004] EWHC 2276 (Comm); *St George's Investment Co Ltd v Gemini Consulting Ltd* [2004] EWHC 2358 (Ch); *Bottiglieri di Navigazione SpA v Cosco Qingdao Ocean Shipping Co* [2005] EWHC 244 (Comm), [2005] 2 Lloyd's Rep. 1; *ASM Shipping Ltd of India v TTMI Ltd of England* [2005] EWHC 2238 (Comm), [2006] 1 Lloyd's Rep. 375, [2006] EWCA Civ 1341, [2007] 1 Lloyd's Rep. 136; *Bernuth Lines Ltd v High Seas Shipping Ltd* [2005] EWHC 3020 (Comm), [2006] 1 Lloyd's Rep. 536 at [53]; *Claire & Co Ltd v Thames Water Utilities Ltd* [2005] EWHC 1022 (TCC), [2005] Build. L.R. 366; *Cameroon Airlines v Transnet Ltd* [2004] EWHC 1829 (Comm), [2006] T.C.L.R. 1; *ABB AG v Hochtief Airport GmbH* [2006] EWHC 388 (Comm), [2006] 2 Lloyd's Rep. 1; *Norbrook Laboratories Ltd v Tank* [2006] EWHC 1055 (Comm), [2006] 2 Lloyd's Rep. 485; *Sumukan Ltd v Commonwealth Secretariat (No.2)* [2007] EWHC 188 (Comm), [2007] 1 Lloyd's Rep. 370 (reversed [2007] EWCA Civ); *HBC Hamburg Bulk Carriers GmbH & Co KG v Tangshan Haixing Shipping Co Ltd* [2006] EWHC 3250 (Comm), [2007] 2 Lloyd's Rep. 222; *OAO Northern Shipping Co v Remolcadores de Marin SL* [2007] EWHC 1821 (Comm), [2007] 2 Lloyd's Rep. 302; *JD Wetherspoon Plc v Jay Mar Estates* [2007] EWHC 856 (TCC), [2007] Build. L.R. 285; *Bandwith Shipping Corp v Intaari* [2007] EWCA Civ 998, [2008] 1 Lloyd's Rep. 7; *Stern Settlement Trustees v Levy* [2007] EWHC 1187 (TCC), (2007) 113 Const. L.R. 92; *TAG Wealth Management v West* [2008] EWHC 1466 (Comm), [2008] 2 Lloyd's Rep. 699; *Thomas O'Donoghue v Enterprise Inns Plc* [2008] EWHC 815 (Comm); *F Ltd v M Ltd* [2009] EWHC 275 (TCC), [2009] 2 Lloyd's Rep. 537 (irrelevance of dissenting arbitrator's opinion); *Van der Giessen de-Noord Shipbuilding Division BV v Imtech Marine & Offshore BV* [2008] EWHC 2904 (Comm), [2009] 1 Lloyd's Rep. 273; *UR Power GmbH v Kuok Oils and Grains Pte Ltd* [2009] EWHC 1940 (Comm), [2009] 2 Lloyd's Rep. 495; *Compania Sud-Americana de Vapores SA v Nippon Yusen Kaisha* [2009] EWHC 1880 (Comm), [2010] 1 Lloyd's Rep. 436; *Double K Oil Products 1996 Ltd v Neste Oil OYJ* [2009] EWHC 3380 (Comm), [2010] 1 Lloyd's Rep. 141; *Michael Wilson & Partners Ltd v Emmott* [2011] EWHC 1441 (Comm); *Milan Nigeria Ltd v Angeliki B Maritime Co* [2011] EWHC 892 (Comm); *Ispat Industries Ltd v Western Bulk Pte Ltd* [2011] EWHC 93 (Comm); *AK Kablo Imalat San Ve Tic AS v Intamex SA* [2011] EWHC 2970 (Comm); *Microperi SrL v Shipowners Mutual P&I Association* [2011] EWHC 2686 (Comm); *EDF Man Sugar Ltd v Belmont Shipping Ltd* [2011] EWHC 2992 (Comm), [2012] 1 Lloyd's Rep. 206; *Abuja International Hotels Inc v Meridien SAS* [2012] EWHC 87 (Comm), [2012] 1 Lloyd's Rep. 461; *Petrochemical Industries Co (KSC) v Dow Chemical Co* [2012] EWHC 2739 (Comm), [2012] 2 Lloyd's Rep. 691; *Terna Bahrain Holding Co WLL v Al Shamsi* [2012] EWHC 3283 (Comm), [2013] 1 All E.R. (Comm) 580 at [85]; *Bulk Ship Union SA v Clipper Bulk Shipping Ltd* [2012] EWHC 2595 (Comm), [2012] 2 Lloyd's Rep. 533 at [11]–[18]; *Flame SA v Glory Wealth Shipping Pte Ltd* [2013] EWHC 3153 (Comm), [2013] 2 Lloyd's Rep. 653 at [101]–[107]; *Interprods Ltd v De La Rue International Ltd* [2014] EWHC 68 (Comm) at [18] (see above, para.32-096); *Secretary of State for Defence v Turner Estate Solutions Ltd* [2014] EWHC 244 (TCC); *Brockton Capital LLP v Atlantic-Pacific Capital Inc* [2014] EWHC 1459 (Comm), [2014] 2 Lloyd's Rep. 475; *Lorand Shipping Ltd v Davof Trading (Africa) BV* [2014] EWHC 3521 (Comm), [2015] 1 Lloyd's Rep. 67; *BV Scheepswerf Damen Gorinchem v Marine Institute* [2015] EWHC 1810 (Comm), [2015] 2 Lloyd's Rep. 351; *W Ltd v M Sdn Bhd* [2016] EWHC 422 (Comm), [2016] 1 Lloyd's Rep. 552; *Obrascon Huarte Lain SA v Qatar Foundation for Education, Science and Community Development* [2019] EWHC 2539 (Comm), [2019] 2 Lloyd's Rep. 559 at [45]. On the use by the arbitrator of his own knowledge and experience, see above, para.32-096, n.388.

725 cf. *Equatorial Traders Ltd v Louis Dreyfus Trading Ltd* [2002] 2 Lloyd's Rep. 638; *Westland Helicopters Ltd v Sheikh Salah al-Hejailan*, above; *Newfield Construction Ltd v Tomlinson*, above; *Republic of Ecuador v Occidental Exploration & Production Co (No.2)* [2006] EWHC 345 (Comm), [2006] 1 Lloyd's Rep. 773; *ABB AG v Hochtief Airport GmbH*, above; *Gulf Import & Export Co v Bunge SA* [2007] EWHC 2667 (Comm), [2008] 1 Lloyd's Rep. 316 at [20]; *CNH Global NV v PGN Logistics Ltd* [2009] EWHC 977 (Comm), [2009] 1 C.L.C. 807; *Abuja International Hotels Inc v Meridien SAS* [2012] EWHC 87 (Comm), [2012] 1 Lloyd's Rep. 461; *New Age Alzarooni 2 Ltd v Range Energy Natural Resources Inc* [2014] EWHC 4358 (Comm). In *Lesotho Highlands Development Authority v Impregilo SpA* [2005] UKHL 43, [2006] 1 A.C. 221, the House of Lords held that a mere error of law by the arbitrators did not amount to an excess of power under s.68(2)(b), but at [29] Lord Steyn gave

some examples of such an excess of power. See also *B v A* [2010] EWHC 1626 (Comm), [2010] 2 Lloyd's Rep. 681 (error in application of chosen law); *C v D1* [2015] EWHC 2126 (Comm) at [136]–[147]; *Essar Oilfield Services Ltd v Norscot Rig Management Pvt Ltd* [2016] EWHC 2361 (Comm), [2016] 2 Lloyd's Rep. 481 at [41]–[47]; *PT Transportasi Gas Indonesia v ConocoPhillips (Grissik) Ltd* [2016] EWHC 2834 (Comm), [2016] 2 Lloyd's Rep. 600 at [53]–[56].

726 *Westland Helicopters v Sheikh Salah al-Hejailan*, above; *Newfield Construction Ltd v Tomlinson*, above; *Michael Wilson & Partners Ltd v Emmott* [2011] EWHC 1441 (Comm). In *Pakistan v Broadsheet LLC* [2019] EWHC 1832 (Comm) the Court held that inadequate reasons for the award were not a serious irregularity under s.68(2)(c).

727 *Weldon Plant Hire Ltd v Commission for the New Towns* [2000] B.L.R. 496; *Ascot Commodities NV v Olam International Ltd* [2001] EWHC 520 (Comm), [2002] C.L.C. 277; *Hussman (Europe) Ltd v Al Ameen Development & Trade Co* [2002] 2 Lloyd's Rep. 83; *Petroships Pte Ltd v Petec Trading and Investment Corp* [2001] 2 Lloyd's Rep. 348, 351, 355, 357; *Checkpoint Ltd v Strathclyde Pension Fund* [2003] EWCA Civ 84; *Torch Offshore LLS v Cable Shipping Inc* [2004] EWHC 787 (Comm), [2004] 2 Lloyd's Rep. 446; *Tame Shipping Ltd v Easy Navigation Ltd*, above; *Alphapoint Shipping Ltd v Rolem Amfert Negev Ltd*, above; *Margulead Ltd v Exide Technologies*, above; *World Trade Corp v C Czarnikow Sugar Ltd* [2004] EWHC 2332 (Comm), [2005] 1 Lloyd's Rep. 422; *Marklands Ltd v Virgin Retail Ltd* [2003] EWHC 3428, [2004] 27 E.G. 130; *Fidelity Management SA v Myriad International Holdings BV* [2005] EWHC 1193 (Comm), [2005] 2 Lloyd's Rep. 508; *Benaim (UK) Ltd v Davies Middleton & Davies Ltd (No.2)* [2005] EWHC 1370 (TCC), (2005) 102 Const. L.R. 1; *Protech Projects Constructions Pty Ltd v Al-Kharafi & Sons* [2005] EWHC 2165 (Comm), [2005] 2 Lloyd's Rep. 779; *Sinclair v Woods of Winchester Ltd* [2005] EWHC 1631, (2005) 102 Const. L.R. 127; *ABB AG v Hochtief Airport GmbH*, above; *London Underground Ltd v Citylink Telecommunications Ltd* [2007] EWHC 1749 (TCC), [2007] Build. L.R. 391 at [41]; *TAG Wealth Management v West* [2008] EWHC 1466, [2008] 2 Lloyd's Rep. 699; *Van der Giessen de-Noord Shipbuilding Division BV v Imtech Marine & Offshore BV* [2008] EWHC 2904 (Comm), [2009] 1 Lloyd's Rep. 273 at [8]–[15]; *Metropolitan Property Realizations Ltd v Atmore Investments Ltd* [2008] EWHC 2925 (Ch) (criticised by Dundas (2009) 75 *Arbitration* 284); *Pace Shipping Co Ltd v Churchgate (Nigeria) Ltd* [2009] EWHC 1975 (Comm), [2010] 1 Lloyd's Rep. 183; *Double K Oil Products 1996 v Neste Oil OYJ* [2009] EWHC 3380 (Comm), [2010] 1 Lloyd's Rep. 141; *Shaw v MFP Foundation & Pilings Ltd* [2010] EWHC 1839 (TCC); *Buyuk Camlica Shipping Trading and Industry Co Inc v Progress Bulk Carriers Ltd* [2010] EWHC 442 (Comm), [2011] Bus. L.R. D99; *Michael Wilson & Partners Ltd v Emmott* [2011] EWHC 1441 (Comm); *Ispat Industries Ltd v Western Bulk Pte Ltd* [2011] EWHC 93 (Comm); *Soeximex SAS v Agrocorp International Pte Ltd* [2011] EWHC 2743 (Comm), [2012] 1 Lloyd's Rep. 52; *Latvian Shipping Co v Russian People's Insurance Co* [2012] EWHC 1412 (Comm); *Transition Feeds LLP v Itochu Europe LLP* [2013] EWHC 3629 (Comm); *Secretary of State for the Home Department v Raytheon Systems Ltd* [2014] EWHC 4375 (TCC) at [33]. A mere failure to set out in the award the tribunal's reasoning in relation to all the arguments advanced in the arbitration will not suffice: *Margulead Ltd v Exide Technologies*, above, at [29]–[35]; *Fidelity Management SA v Myriad International Holdings BV* [2005] EWHC 1193 (Comm), [2005] 2 Lloyd's Rep. 508 at [7]–[10]. In *Petrochemical Industries Co (KSC) v Dow Chemical Co* [2012] EWHC 2739 (Comm), [2012] 2 Lloyd's Rep. 691 at [16]–[21] Andrew Smith J. considered the distinction between "issues" on the one hand and "arguments", "points", "lines of reasoning" and "steps in an argument" on the other. See also *Atkins Ltd v Secretary of State for Transport* [2013] EWHC 139 (TCC), [2013] B.L.R. 193; *Primera Maritime (Hellas) Ltd v Jiangsu Eastern Heavy Industry Co Ltd* [2013] EWHC 3066 (Comm), [2014] 1 All E.R. (Comm) 813 at [8]; *Transition Feeds LLP v Itochu Europe Plc* [2013] EWHC 3629 (Comm) at [18]; *BV Scheepswerf Damen Gorinchem v Marine Institute* [2015] EWHC 1810 (Comm); *PT Transportasi Gas Indonesia v ConocoPhillips (Grissik) Ltd* [2016] EWHC 2834 (Comm), [2016] 2 Lloyd's Rep. 600 at [57]–[64]; *A v B* [2017] EWHC 596 (Comm), [2017] 2 Lloyd's Rep. 1 at [35]–[39].

728 *Gbangbola v Smith & Sherriff Ltd* [1998] 3 All E.R. 730. *Benaim (UK) Ltd v Davies Middleton & Davies Ltd (No.2)*, above; *Pace Shipping Co Ltd v Churchgate (Nigeria) Ltd* [2009] EWHC 1975 (Comm), [2010] 1 Lloyd's Rep. 183; *Xstrata Coal Queensland Pty Ltd v Benxi Iron & Steel (Group) International Economic & Trading Co Ltd* [2020] EWHC 324, [2020] Bus. L.R. 954.

729 *Cuflet Chartering v Carousel Shipping Co Ltd* [2001] 1 Lloyd's Rep. 707; *Profilati Italia Srl v Painewebber Inc* [2001] 1 Lloyd's Rep. 715; *Thyssen Canada Ltd v Mariana Maritime SA* [2005] EWHC 219 (Comm), [2005] 1 Lloyd's Rep. 640; *Protech Projects Construction Pty Ltd v Al-Kharafi & Sons*, above; *Elektrim SA v Vivendi Universal SA* [2007] EWHC 11 (Comm), [2007] 1 Lloyd's Rep. 693, especially at [75]–[87]; *DDT Trucks of North America Ltd v DDT Holdings Ltd* [2007] EWHC 1542 (Comm), [2007] 2 Lloyd's Rep. 213 at [22]–[23]; *Colliers International Property Consultants v Colliers Jordan Lee Jafaar Sd Bhd* [2008] EWHC 1524 (Comm), [2008] 2 Lloyd's Rep. 368; *R v V* [2008] EWHC 1531 (Comm), [2009] 1 Lloyd's Rep. 97; *Michael Wilson & Partners Ltd v Emmott* [2011] EWHC 1441 (Comm); *Nestor Maritime SA v Sea Anchor Shipping Co Ltd* [2012] EWHC 996 (Comm); *Stockman Interhold SA v Arricano Real Estate Plc* [2017] EWHC 2909 (Comm), [2018] 1 Lloyd's Rep. 135 at [168]–[169]. In *Double K Oil Products 1996 Ltd v Neste Oil OYJ* [2009] EWHC 3380 (Comm), [2010] 1 Lloyd's Rep. 141, Blair J. stated that the court had to be satisfied that some form of reprehensible or unconscionable conduct had contributed in a substantial way to the obtaining of the award (allegation in the case was fraud in the production of evidence). See also *Chantiers de*

*L'Atlantique SA v Gaztransport & Technigaz SAS* [2011] EWHC 3383 (Comm) at [53]–[62]; *Celtic Bioenergy Ltd v Knowles* [2017] EWHC 472 (TCC), [2017] 1 Lloyd's Rep. 495 (fraud in a party's deliberate failure to draw the tribunal's attention to relevant correspondence). In *Alexander Brothers Ltd v Alstom Transport SA* [2020] EWHC 1584 (Comm) at [104]–[105] the Court held that where the arbitration tribunal has jurisdiction to determine the relevant issue of illegality and has determined that there was no illegality on the facts, there is very nearly no scope for this Court to re-open the issue of illegality, save in exceptional circumstances, when dealing with a public policy objection to recognition or enforcement. As to relevance of the public policy of a foreign state, see *PT Transportasi Gas Indonesia v ConocoPhillips (Grissik) Ltd* [2016] EWHC 2834 (Comm), [2016] 2 Lloyd's Rep. 600 at [66]–[72].

730 *Al Hadha Trading Co v Tradigrain SA* [2002] 2 Lloyd's Rep. 512, 521; *Benaim (UK) Ltd v Davies Middleton & Davies Ltd*, above. In *Pakistan v Broadsheet LLC* [2019] EWHC 1832 (Comm) the Court held that inadequate reasons for the award were not a serious irregularity under s.68(2)(h).

731 *Gannet Shipping Ltd v Eastrade Commodities Inc* [2002] 1 Lloyd's Rep. 713, 717–718. An admission by a member of the tribunal who is in the minority or who dissents would not be sufficient for this purpose: *A v B* [2017] EWHC 596 (Comm), [2017] 2 Lloyd's Rep. 1 at [53]–[56].

732 See the 27th edition of this book, Vol.I, paras 15-040—15-042.

733 *Lindner Ceilings Floors Partitions Plc v How Engineering Services Ltd* [2001] Build. L.R. 90; *Arduina Holdings BV v Celtic Resource Holdings Plc* [2006] EWHC 3155 (Comm); *Schwebel v Schwebel* [2010] EWHC 3280 (TCC), [2011] 2 All E.R. (Comm) 1048; *Flame SA v Glory Wealth Shipping Pte Ltd* [2013] EWHC 3153 (Comm), [2013] 2 Lloyd's Rep. 653; *Atkins Ltd v Secretary of State for Transport* [2013] EWHC 139 (TCC), [2013] B.L.R. 193; *Sonatrach v Statoil Natural Gas LLC* [2014] EWHC 875 (Comm), [2014] 2 Lloyd's Rep. 252 at [11]; *New Age Alzarooni 2 Ltd v Range Energy Natural Resources Inc* [2014] EWHC 4358 (Comm) at [13]; *Secretary of State for the Home Department v Raytheon Systems Ltd* [2014] EWHC 4375 (TCC) at [33]; *R v K* [2020] EWHC 841 (Fam) at [60]. See also *World Trade Corp v C Czarnikow Sugar Ltd* [2004] EWHC 2322 (Comm), [2005] 1 Lloyd's Rep. 422 (weight of evidence); *Lesotho Highlands Development Authority v Impregilo SpA* [2005] UKHL 43, [2006] 1 A.C. 221 at [28]. But it may be that a failure by the tribunal to take account of or consider evidence (as opposed to an alleged failure to evaluate the evidence correctly) could come within ss.33(2), 68(2)(a). *Arduina Holdings BV v Celtic Resources Holdings Plc* [2006] EWHC 3155 (comm) at [46]; *Schwebel v Schwebel* [2010] EWHC 3280 (TCC) at [27]; *Petrochemical Industries Co (KSC) v Dow Chemical Co* [2012] EWHC 2739 (Comm), [2012] 2 Lloyd's Rep. 691 at [36]; *Brockton Capital LLP v Atlantic-Pacific Capital Inc* [2014] EWHC 1459 (Comm), [2014] 2 Lloyd's Rep. 275. In *Elektrim SA v Vivendi Universal SA* [2007] EWHC 11 (Comm), [2007] 1 Lloyd's Rep. 693 at [75]–[76] Aikens J. said that the previous law was no longer applicable which gave to the court a power to remit the award where fresh evidence came to light after the award was made; cf. *BSG Resources Ltd v Vale SA* [2019] EWHC 3347 (Comm) at [19]; Gee (2006) 22 *Arbitration International* 337, 366.

734 *Costa v British Indian Trading Co Ltd* [1963] 1 Q.B. 201.

*Replace footnote 737 with:*

**32-164** 737 *Vee Networks Ltd v Econet Wireless International Ltd* [2004] EWHC 2909 (Comm), [2005] 1 Lloyd's Rep. 192 at [88]–[90]; *SCM Financial Overseas Ltd v Raga Establishment Ltd* [2018] EWHC 1008 (Comm), [2018] 2 Lloyd's Rep. 99 at [62]–[64].

*Replace footnote 749 with:*

**32-167** 749 See (on s.22 of the Arbitration Act 1950) *Fletamentos Maritimos SA v Effjohn International BV (No.2)* [1997] 2 Lloyd's Rep. 302; *ZCCM Investments Holdings Plc v Kansanshi Holdings Plc* [2019] EWHC 1285 (Comm), [2019] 2 Lloyd's Rep. 29 (decision on a procedural issue).

## Appeal on point of law

*Replace footnote 773 with:*

**32-170** 773 s.69(7). As to the width of the Court's powers under s.69(7), see *Martin v Harris* [2019] EWHC 2735 (Ch), [2020] Bus. L.R. 122 at [27]–[32]. cf. *Loon Navigation Corp v Sinochem International Petroleum (Bahamas) Co Ltd* [2002] EWHC 2812, [2003] 1 All E.R. (Comm) 405; *Vrinera Marine Co Ltd v Eastern Rich Operations Inc* [2004] EWHC 1752 (Comm), [2004] 2 Lloyd's Rep. 465 at [15]. There is no reason why the judge who granted permission to appeal on a point of law cannot hear the substantive appeal: *L v A* [2016] EWHC 1789 (Comm) at [4]–[8].

## Challenge or appeal: restrictions and time limits

*Replace paragraph with:*

**32-176** An application or appeal may not be brought if the applicant or appellant has not first exhausted any available process of appeal or review and any available recourse under s.57 (correction of award or additional award).[793] Any application or appeal must be brought within 28 days of the date of the award or, if there has been any arbitral process of appeal or review, of the date when the applicant or appellant was notified of the result of that process.[794] This period may be extended by the court in accordance with rules of the court[795] (though the criteria applicable to applications for such an extension may differ from those applicable under the CPR).[796]

[793] s.70(2); CPR Pt 62, PD 62.11; *Groundshire v VHE Construction* [2001] Build. L.R. 395; *Al Hadha Trading Co v Tradigrain SA* [2002] 2 Lloyd's Rep. 512; *Torch Offshore LLC v Cable Shipping Inc* [2004] EWHC 787 (Comm), [2004] 2 Lloyd's Rep. 446; *Sinclair v Woods of Winchester Ltd* [2005] EWHC 1631 (QB), (2005) 102 Const. L.R. 127; *Bulk Ship Union SA v Clipper Bulk Shipping Ltd* [2012] EWHC 2595 (Comm), [2012] 2 Lloyd's Rep. 533 at [31]–[32]; cf. *Gbangbola v Smith & Sherriff Ltd* [1998] 3 All E.R. 730; *World Trade Corp v C Czarnikow Sugar Ltd* [2004] EWHC 2332 (Comm), [2005] 1 Lloyd's Rep. 422; *Ases Havacilik Servis ve Destek Hizmetleri AS v Delkor UK Ltd* [2012] EWHC 3518 (Comm), [2013] 1 Lloyd's Rep. 254 at [19]–[24]; *A Ltd v B Ltd* [2014] EWHC 1870 (Comm). See above, para.32-143 and *Buyuk Camlica Shipping Trading and Industry Co Inc v Progress Bulk Carriers Ltd* [2010] EWHC 442 (Comm), [2011] Bus. L.R. D99.

[794] s.70(3); *Westland Helicopters Ltd v Sheikh Salah al-Hejailan (No.1)* [2004] EWHC 1625 (Comm), [2004] 2 Lloyd's Rep. 523; *Thyssen Canada Ltd v Mariana Maritime SA* [2005] EWHC 219 (Comm), [2005] 1 Lloyd's Rep. 640; *Sinclair v Woods of Winchester Ltd*, above; *UR Power GmbH v Kuok Oils and Grains Pte Ltd* [2009] EWHC 1940 (Comm), [2009] 2 Lloyd's Rep. 495 at [58] and *PEC Ltd v Asia Golden Rice Ltd* [2012] EWHC 846 (Comm), [2013] 1 Lloyd's Rep. 82 (two-tier arbitration). It is a moot point whether the extended time for appeal under s.70(2)(a) or applies to an application under s.57 as well: see *Surefire Systems Ltd v Guardian ECL Ltd* [2005] EWHC 1860 (TCC), [2005] B.L.R. 534; *Price v Carter* [2010] EWHC 1451 (TCC). In *Essar Oilfield Services Ltd v Norscot Rig Management Pvt Ltd* [2016] EWHC 2361 (Comm), [2016] 2 Lloyd's Rep. 481 at [90]–[93] the Court held that if the award is corrected pursuant to s.57, the 28-day time period runs from the date of the corrected award, provided that the application to correct is material to the issue being raised by the application to the Court. An application is material if it is necessary to enable the party to know whether he has grounds to challenge the award or not. If a material application to correct the award is refused, time starts running from the date of the decision that there would be no correction: *Xstrata Coal Queensland Pty Ltd v Benxi Iron & Steel (Group) International Economic & Trading Co Ltd* [2020] EWHC 324 (Comm), [2020] Bus. L.R. 954 at [36]–[42]. See also *K v S* [2015] EWHC 1945 (Comm), [2015] 2 Lloyd's Rep. 363; *Daewoo Shipbuilding & Marine Engineering Co Ltd v Songa Offshore Equinox Ltd* [2018] EWHC 538 (Comm), [2018] 1 Lloyd's Rep. 443 at [52]–[65]. An application or appeal may also be struck out for want of prosecution: *Huyton SA v Jakil Spa* [1999] 2 Lloyd's Rep. 83.

[795] s.80(5), CPR rr.3.1, 3.9; *Dubai Islamic Bank PJSC v Paymentech Merchant Services Inc* [2001] 1 Lloyd's Rep. 65, 75; *Aoot Kalmneft v Glencore International AG* [2002] 1 Lloyd's Rep. 128, 134; *Peoples Insurance Co of China v Vysanthi Shipping Co Ltd* [2003] EWHC 1655 (Comm), [2003] 2 Lloyd's Rep. 616; *Thyssen Canada Ltd v Mariana Maritime SA*, above; *Sinclair v Woods of Winchester Ltd*, above; *Elektrim SA v Vivendi Universal SA* [2007] EWHC 11 (Comm), [2007] 1 Lloyd's Rep. 693 at [72]; *PEC Ltd v Asia Golden Rice Ltd* [2012] EWHC 846 (Comm), [2013] 1 Lloyd's Rep. 82; *Terna Bahrain Holding Co WLL v Al Shamsi* [2012] EWHC 3283 (Comm), [2013] 1 All E.R. (Comm) 580; *London Steam Ship Owners Mutual Insurance Association Ltd v Spain (The Prestige)* [2013] EWHC 2840 (Comm), [2014] 1 All E.R. (Comm) 300.

[796] In *Aoot Kalmneft v Glencore International AG*, above, Colman J. (at 137) set out six considerations which, in his judgment, were likely to be material to the exercise by the court of its power to extend time (applied in *Nagusina Naviera v Allied Maritime Inc* [2002] EWCA Civ 1147, [2003] 2 C.L.C. 1; *Gold Coast Ltd v Naval Gijon SA* [2006] EWHC 1044 (Comm), [2006] 2 Lloyd's Rep. 400 (s.79 application); *DDT Trucks of North America Ltd v DDT Holdings Ltd* [2007] EWHC 1542 (Comm), [2007] 2 Lloyd's Rep. 213); *Colliers International Property Consultants v Colliers Jordan Lee Jafaar Sdn Bhd* [2008] EWHC 1524 (Comm), [2008] 2 Lloyd's Rep. 396; *L Brown & Sons Ltd v Crosby Homes (North West) Ltd* [2008] EWHC 817 (TCC), [2008] Build. L.R. 366; *ASM Shipping Ltd of India v TTMI Ltd of England* [2009] 1 Lloyd's Rep. 293n; *UR Power GmbH v Kuok Oils and Grains Pte Ltd* [2009] EWHC 1940 (Comm), [2009] 2 Lloyd's Rep. 495 at [62], [63]; *Broda Agro Trade (Cyprus) Ltd v Alfred C Toepfer International Ltd* [2010] EWCA Civ 1100, [2011] 1 Lloyd's Rep. 243; *Chantiers de L'Atlantique SA v Gaztransport & Technigaz SAS* [2011] EWHC 3383 (Comm) at [63]; *Nestor Maritime SA v Sea Anchor Shipping Co Ltd* [2012] EWHC 996 (Comm); *PEC Ltd v Asia Golden Rice Ltd* [2012] EWHC 846 (Comm), [2013] 1 Lloyd's Rep. 82 at [21]; *Terna Bahrain Holding Co WLL v Al Shamsi* [2012] EWHC 3283 (Comm), [2013] 1 All E.R. (Comm) 580 at [27]–[34]; *London Steam Ship Owners Mutual Insurance Association Ltd v Spain (The Prestige)* [2013] EWHC 2840 (Comm), [2014] 1 All E.R. (Comm) 300; *K v S* [2015] EWHC 1945 (Comm); *Daewoo Shipbuilding & Marine Engineering Co Ltd v Songa Offshore Equinox Ltd* [2018] EWHC 538 (Comm), [2018] 1 Lloyd's Rep. 443 at [70]–[77]; *State A v Party B* [2019] EWHC 799 (Comm), [2019] 1 Lloyd's Rep. 569; Dundas (2012) 78 *Arbitration* (3) 293. In *S v A* [2016] EWHC 846 (Comm), [2016] 1 Lloyd's Rep. 604 at [26], the Court applied the test laid down in *Terna Bahrain Holding Company WLL v Al Shamsi*, because it was common ground that

it should do so, but questioned whether such a test should continue to apply in light of the Court's more recent decision in *Denton v TH White Ltd* [2014] EWCA Civ 906, [2014] 1 W.L.R. 3926.

## Enforcement of awards

*Replace footnote 835 with:*

32-186 [835] *Soleimany v Soleimany* [1999] Q.B. 785 (illegality). cf. *R v V* [2008] EWHC 1531 (Comm), [2009] 1 Lloyd's Rep. 97; *Process and Industrial Developments Ltd v Nigeria* [2019] EWHC 2241 (Comm), [2019] 2 Lloyd's Rep. 361 at [102]. See s.81(1)(c).

## Foreign awards

*Replace paragraph with:*

32-190 A foreign award may be enforced in England against a party to the arbitration agreement and to the arbitration leading to the award[855a] in a number of ways. First, it may likewise be enforced under s.66 of the Act or by action.[856] Secondly, an award made,[857] in pursuance of an arbitration agreement, in the territory of a state[858] which is a party to the New York Convention on the Recognition and Enforcement of Foreign Arbitral Awards (1958) may, by permission of the court, be enforced in the same manner as a judgment or order of the court to the same effect by virtue of s.101 of the 1996 Act.[859] Thirdly, except insofar as an award is a New York Convention award, by virtue of Pt II of the Arbitration Act 1950 a foreign award is enforceable in the same manner as an English award if it is made in pursuance of an arbitration agreement to which the Geneva Protocol (1923) applies,[860] and which is made between persons of whom one is subject to the jurisdiction of a state party to the Geneva Convention for the Execution of Foreign Arbitral Awards (1927),[861] and the award is made in such a state.[862] Fourthly, an arbitration award made in a Commonwealth country to which Pt II of the Administration of Justice Act 1920 or Pt I of the Foreign Judgments (Reciprocal Enforcement) Act 1933 has been extended[863] can be enforced in the same manner as a judgment of a court in that place, i.e. by registration under those Acts, provided that it has become enforceable in the same manner as a judgment given by a court in that country.[864] Fifthly, various other statutes permit the enforcement of certain awards upon registration.[865] The conditions for enforcement and the grounds on which enforcement of a foreign award may be refused must be ascertained by reference to the particular statute,[866] but neither at common law nor under the statutes concerned can the merits of the arbitrator's decision be impugned.

[855a] *Kabab-Ji Sal (Lebanon) v Kout Food Group (Kuwait)* [2020] EWCA Civ 6, [2020] 1 Lloyd's Rep. 269 at [81].

[856] See ss.2(2)(b), 104 and *Dicey, Morris and Collins on the Conflict of Laws*, 15th edn, para.16-099.

[857] An award is to be treated as made at the seat of the arbitration (see above, para.32-140) regardless of where it was signed, despatched or delivered to any of the parties: s.100(2)(b).

[858] For a list of contracting states, see *http://www.newyorkconvention.org* and *http://www.uncitral.org*.

[859] See ss.66(4), 100–104 and *Government of the State of Kuwait v Sir Frederick Snow and Partners* [1984] A.C. 426; *Agromet Motoimport v Maulden Engineering (Beds) Ltd* [1985] 1 W.L.R. 762; *Bank Mellat v GAA Development and Construction Co* [1988] 2 Lloyd's Rep. 44. cf. *Deutsche Schachtbau- und Tiefbohrgesellschaft mbH v R'as al-Khaimah National Oil Co* [1990] 1 A.C. 295; *Soleh Boneh International Ltd v Government of Uganda* [1993] 2 Lloyd's Rep. 208; *Minmetals German GmbH v Ferco Steel Ltd* [1999] 1 All E.R. Comm. 315; *Norsk Hydro ASA v The State Property Fund of Ukraine* [2002] EWHC 2120 (Comm); *Dicey, Morris and Collins on the Conflict of Laws*, 15th edn, para.16-128; CPR r.62.18. In *Pencil Hill Ltd v US Citta Di Palermo SpA*, Unreported, January 19, 2016 at [30], the Court said that there is a strong leaning towards the enforcement of foreign arbitral awards and the circumstances in which the English Court may refuse enforcement are narrow. In this case, the Court allowed the enforcement of an award which included a penalty. For procedure, see *Lombard Knight v Rainstorm Pictures Inc* [2014] EWCA Civ 356, [2014] 2 Lloyd's Rep. 74. The court retains jurisdic-

tion in relation to challenge to or appeal from an award (ss.67–69) if the seat of arbitration is in England (or, as the case may be Northern Ireland): s.2(1) and *Hiscox v Outhwaite* [1992] 1 A.C. 562. A judgment entered in terms of the award under s.101(3) carries interest under s.17 of the Judgments Act 1838; *Gater Assets Ltd v Nak Naftogaz Ukrainiy (No.3)* [2008] EWHC 1108 (Comm), [2008] 2 Lloyd's Rep. 295; *Sonatrach v Statoil Natural Gas LLC* [2014] EWHC 875 (Comm), [2014] 2 Lloyd's Rep. 252.

860 Arbitration Act 1950 Sch.1.

861 Arbitration Act 1950 Sch.2.

862 Arbitration Act 1996 ss.66(4), 99; *Dicey, Morris and Collins on the Conflict of Laws*, 15th edn, para.16-100; CPR Pt 62; DAC Report para.346.

863 For a list of such countries, see *http://www.lexisnexis.com/uk/lexispsl/disputeresolution/home*.

864 Administration of Justice Act 1920 s.12(1); Foreign Judgments (Reciprocal Enforcement) Act 1933 s.10A (added by Civil Jurisdiction and Judgments Act 1982 Sch.10 para.4); *Dicey, Morris and Collins on the Conflict of Law*, 15th edn, para.16-161; CPR r.62.20. See also *LR Avionics Technologies Ltd v Federal Republic of Nigeria* [2016] EWHC 1761 (Comm), [2016] 4 W.L.R. 120 at [24]–[27].

865 Arbitration (International Investment Disputes) Act 1966 ss.1, 2; Multilateral Investment Guarantee Agency Act 1988 s.4; Carriage of Goods by Road Act 1965 ss.4(1), 7(1) and Sch.; Arbitration Act 1996 s.66(4) and Sch.3 paras 21, 24, 49; *Dicey, Morris and Collins on the Conflict of Laws*, 15th edn, paras 16-161, 16-172; CPR r.62.21.

866 For the closed list of cases in which recognition or enforcement of a New York Convention award may be refused, see s.103 of the 1996 Act and *Rosseel NV v Oriental Shipping (UK) Ltd* [1991] 2 Lloyd's Rep. 625; *China Agrebusiness Development Corp v Balli Trading* [1998] 2 Lloyd's Rep. 76; *Soinco Saci v Novokuznetsk Aluminium Plant* [1998] 2 Lloyd's Rep. 337; *Westacre Investments Ltd v Jugoimport-SPDR Holding Co Ltd* [2000] Q.B. 288; *Soleimany v Soleimany* [1999] Q.B. 785; *Minmetals German GmbH v Ferco Steel Ltd* [1999] 1 All E.R. (Comm) 315; *Omnium de Traitement SA v Hilmarton Ltd* [1999] 2 Lloyd's Rep. 222; *Eco Swiss China Time Ltd v Benetton International NV* [1999] 2 All E.R. (Comm) 44, ECJ; *Irvani v Irvani* [2000] 1 Lloyd's Rep. 412; *ABCI v Banque Franco-Tunisienne* [2002] 1 Lloyd's Rep. 511, 538; *Dardana Ltd v Yukos Oil Co* [2002] EWCA Civ 543, [2002] 2 Lloyd's Rep. 326; *Reeves v One World Challenge LLC* [2005] NZCA 314; *Svenska Petroleum Exploration AB v Government of the Republic of Lithuania* [2005] EWHC 9 (Comm), [2005] 1 Lloyd's Rep. 515; *Ipco (Nigeria) Ltd v Nigerian National Petroleum Ltd* [2005] EWHC 726 (Comm), [2005] 2 Lloyd's Rep. 326; *Kanoria v Guinness* [2006] EWCA Civ 222, [2006] 1 Lloyd's Rep. 701; *Tamil Nadu Electricity Board v ST-CMS Electric Co Private Ltd* [2007] EWHC 1713 (Comm), [2008] 1 Lloyd's Rep. 93; *Gater Assets Ltd v NAK Naftogaz Ukrainiy (No.2)* [2008] EWHC 237 (Comm), [2008] 1 Lloyd's Rep. 479; *AC Ward & Sons Ltd v Catlin (Five) Ltd* [2009] EWCA Civ 1098; *Dallah Real Estate & Tourism Co v Ministry of Religious Affairs of the Government of Pakistan* [2010] UKSC 46, [2011] 1 A.C. 763; *Norsk Hydro ASA v State Property Fund of Ukraine* [2002] EWHC 2120 (Admin), [2009] Bus. L.R. 558; *Nigerian National Petroleum Corp v IPCO (Nigeria) Ltd (No.2)* [2008] EWCA Civ 1157, [2009] 1 Lloyd's Rep. 89 (enforcement in part); *HJ Heinz Co Ltd v EFL Inc* [2010] EWHC 1203 (Comm), [2010] 2 Lloyd's Rep. 727; *Yukos Capital SARL v OJSC Rosneft Oil Co* [2012] EWCA Civ 855, [2013] 1 All E.R. 223; *Honeywell International Middle East Ltd v Meydan Group LLC* [2014] EWHC 1344 (TCC), [2014] 2 Lloyd's Rep. 133; *Diag Human SE v Czech Republic* [2014] EWHC 1639 (Comm), [2014] 2 Lloyd's Rep. 283; *IPCO (Nigeria) Ltd v Nigerian National Petroleum Corp* [2015] EWCA Civ 1144, [2016] 1 Lloyd's Rep. 5, [2015] EWCA Civ 1145, [2016] 1 Lloyd's Rep. 36; *Lombard Knight v Rainstorm Pictures Inc* [2014] EWCA Civ 356, [2014] 2 Lloyd's Rep. 74; *Travis Coal Restructured Holdings LLC v Essar Global Fund Ltd* [2014] EWHC 2510 (Comm), [2014] 2 Lloyd's Rep. 414; *Malicorp Ltd v Egypt* [2015] EWHC 361 (Comm), [2015] 1 Lloyd's Rep. 423; *Stati v Republic of Kazakhstan* [2017] EWHC 1348 (Comm), [2017] 2 Lloyd's Rep. 201; *RBRG Trading (UK) Ltd v Sinocore International Co Ltd* [2017] EWHC 251 (Comm), [2017] 2 Lloyd's Rep. 375; [2018] EWCA Civ 838. In *Carpatsky Petroleum Corp v PJSC Ukrnafta* [2020] EWHC 769 (Comm), [2020] Bus. L.R. 1284 at [122]–[126] the Court held that if substantially the same complaint as to the procedural fairness or irregularity of the arbitration, which is presented to this court as a reason for non-enforcement under the 1996 Act s.103(2), has been made and decided upon by the supervisory court, then that should be regarded as precluding the point being raised again, unless it can be plainly perceived that it would cause injustice to recognise an issue estoppel (or an abuse of process) in the circumstances; the same consideration may well apply to the same objection having been determined by another enforcing court. But the court has power under s.103(5) to adjourn the decision on enforcement and to order security: see *Soleh Boneh International Ltd v Government of Uganda* [1993] 2 Lloyd's Rep. 208; *Dardana Ltd v Yukos Oil Co*, above; *Apis AS v Fantazia Kereskedelmi* [2001] 1 All E.R. (Comm) 348; *Ipco (Nigeria) Ltd v Nigerian National Petroleum Ltd*, above; *Gater Assets Ltd v NAK Naftogaz Ukrainiy* [2007] EWHC 697 (Comm), [2007] 1 Lloyd's Rep. 522; *Nigerian National Petroleum Corp v IPCO (Nigeria) Ltd (No.2)*, above; *Dowans Holding SA v Tanzania Electric Supply Co Ltd* [2011] EWHC 1957 (Comm), [2011] 2 Lloyd's Rep. 474; *IPCO (Nigeria) Ltd v Nigerian National Petroleum Corp* [2015] EWCA Civ 1144, [2016] 1 Lloyd's Rep. 5, [2015] EWCA Civ 1145, [2016] 1 Lloyd's Rep. 36; *Travis Coal Restructured Holdings LLC v Essar Global Fund Ltd* [2014] EWHC 2510 (Comm), [2014] 2 Lloyd's Rep. 414; *National Joint Stock Company Naftogaz of Ukraine v Public Joint Stock Company Gazprom*

[2019] EWHC 658 (Comm), [2019] 2 Lloyd's Rep. 20; *J (Lebanon) v K (Kuwait)* [2019] EWHC 899 (Comm); *PAO Tatneft v Ukraine* [2019] EWHC 3740 (Ch) at [82]. In *IPCO (Nigeria) Ltd v Nigerian National Petroleum Corp* [2017] UKSC 16, [2017] 1 W.L.R. 970 the Supreme Court held that there was nothing in s.103(2) or (3) which provided that an enforcing court could make the decision of an issue raised under that subsection conditional on the provision of security in respect of the award (unlike s.103(5)).

*Replace footnote 869 with:*

32-192 [869] *Svenska Petroleum Exploration AB v Government of the Republic of Lithuania (No.2)* [2006] EWCA Civ 1529, [2007] Q.B. 886; *Norsk Hydro ASA v State Property Fund of Ukraine* [2002] EWHC 2120 (Admin), [2009] Bus. L.R. 558; *London Steam Ship Owners Mutual Insurance Association Ltd v Spain (No.2)* [2015] EWCA Civ 333, [2015] 2 Lloyd's Rep. 33; *Taurus Petroleum Ltd v State Oil Marketing Company of the Ministry of Oil, Republic of Iraq* [2013] EWHC 3494 (Comm), [2014] 1 All E.R. (Comm) 942; *Gold Reserve Inc v Bolivarian Republic of Venezuela* [2016] EWHC 153 (Comm), [2016] 1 W.L.R. 2829; *LR Avionics Technologies Ltd v Federal Republic of Nigeria* [2016] EWHC 1761 (Comm), [2016] 4 W.L.R. 120; *London Steamship Owners Mutual Insurance Ltd v Spain* [2020] EWHC 1582 (Comm). This is a distinct question from that of immunity from execution: see *Dicey, Morris and Collins on the Conflict of Laws*, 15th edn, para.10-014. See above para.12-021.

## 12. MISCELLANEOUS

### Immunity of arbitrators and arbitral institutions, etc

*Replace footnote 904 with:*

32-202 [904] s.29(3). See *C Ltd v D* [2020] EWHC 1283 (Comm). But see s.25; above, para.32-097.

CHAPTER 33

# BAILMENT



## 1. IN GENERAL

### Bailment and tort

*Replace paragraph with:*

The demise of the consent theory of bailment may herald a move towards the law of tort and the eventual absorption of bailment into the mainstream of the law of tort. It is suggested that this is an unlikely development. Although liability in tort and in bailment may overlap[27] the two sources of liability are in fact independent and the "common law liabilities of a bailee ... appear both independent of, and significantly different from, those that would apply under the general law of tort".[28] The clearest example of this is the fact that the burden of proof in a negligence case rests upon the claimant, whereas in a bailment case the burden of proof is upon the bailee to show that he has discharged his duties.[29] Although liability in tort and in bailment are conceptually distinct, the failure of parliamentary draftsmen to **33-004** recognise a distinct head of liability based on breach of bailment has meant that, in some contexts, the courts have construed a reference to "tort" as including a reference to "breach of bailment".[30] On the other hand, claims by a bailor against his bailee which are based on breach of bailment (e.g. breach of his common law duty of care)[31] may not fall within the overall category of "wrongful interference with goods" defined in s.1 of the Torts (Interference with Goods) Act 1977.[32] Each case turns on the construction of the particular statute and, while in some cases the courts have strained for instrumental reasons to encompass a bailment action within the fold of tort, the cases cannot be used to construct a more general argument in support of the assimilation of bailment to tort. They are authority only in relation to the particular statute under consideration.

[27] See below, paras 33-010—33-014.

[28] Palmer at para.1-047. For example, in the case of a gratuitous bailment, it does not follow from the fact that the bailment is not contractual that the liability of the bailee must lie in tort. The liability of the bailee is best seen as being sui generis: *Yearworth v North Bristol NHS Trust* [2009] EWCA Civ 37, [2010] Q.B. 1 at [48].

[29] See, e.g. *British Road Services Ltd v Arthur V Crutchley & Co Ltd* [1968] 1 All E.R. 811, 822 and *Volcafe Ltd v Cia Sud Americana de Vapores SA (trading as CSAV)* [2018] UKSC 61, [2019] A.C. 358 at [8]–[9]. Further examples of the differences between an action in bailment and an action in tort are provided by Palmer at paras 1-048—1-071.

[30] *American Express Co v British Airways Board* [1983] 1 W.L.R. 701 (s.29(1) of the Post Office Act 1969 which provided that "no proceedings in tort shall lie against the Post Office ..." in respect of loss or damage to mail): cf. *Chesworth v Farrar* [1967] 1 Q.B. 407 (see below, para.33-007, n.38).

[31] See below, paras 33-032, 33-049. See also below, para.33-026 (text at n.127).

[32] See Palmer (1978) 41 M.L.R. 629. cf. *Harold Stephen & Co Ltd v Post Office* [1977] 1 W.L.R. 1172, 1177–1178, 1179–1180. A claim arising from a contractual bailment has been held not to fall within the definition of "wrongful interference" in the Act and a similar conclusion may be reached in the case of contractual claims where concurrent liability exists in contract and tort or bailment: *Scipion Active Trading Fund v Vallis Group Ltd* [2020] EWHC 1451 (Comm) at [107]–[108].

## 2. POSSESSION AND RELATED MATTERS

### The obligation to return the goods

*Replace footnote 53 with:*

**33-010** [53] *British Crane Hire Corp Ltd v Ipswich Plant Hire Ltd* [1975] Q.B. 303, 311, 313; *Scipion Active Trading Fund v Vallis Group Ltd* [2020] EWHC 1451 (Comm) at [93]. (See also below, para.33-064.) On the termination of a bailment see below, para.33-014. cf. the cases on the termination of the hiring under a hire-purchase agreement, see below, paras 39-330—39-338; see also Vol.I, para.16-219. On the measure of damages in conversion (which now includes former cases of detinue: see below, this paragraph), see *Rosenthal v Alderton & Sons Ltd* [1946] K.B. 374; *Sachs v Miklos* [1948] 2 K.B. 23; *Munro v Willmott* [1949] 1 K.B. 295; *Strand Electric and Engineering Co Ltd v Brisford Entertainments Ltd* [1952] 2 Q.B. 246; *General and Finance Facilities Ltd v Cooks Cars (Romford) Ltd* [1963] 1 W.L.R. 644; *Hillesden Securities Ltd v Ryjak Ltd* [1983] 1 W.L.R. 959. See *McGregor on Damages*, 20th edn (2017), Ch.38; *Clerk & Lindsell on Torts*, 22nd edn (2017), paras 17-93 et seq.; and see for damages in similar hire-purchase cases, below, paras 39-341, 39-426.

### Jus tertii

*Replace footnote 86 with:*

**33-016** [86] *Scipion Active Trading Fund v Vallis Group Ltd* [2020] EWHC 1451 (Comm) at [102]–[113]. One interpretation of the section might be that it covers a situation where the bailor *could* have sued for wrongful interference, e.g. where there was overlapping liability in tort or in contract. But liability in contract could arise in circumstances in which no tort had been committed: Palmer at para.4-062.

### The bailee's claim against a third party

*Replace footnote 111 with:*

[111] *The Winkfield* [1902] P. 42; *Scipion Active Trading Fund v Vallis Group Ltd* [2020] EWHC 1451 (Comm). See also *Rooth v Wilson* (1817) 1 B. & Ald. 59 (gratuitous bailee); *Swaffer v Mulcahy* [1934] 1 K.B. 608 (replevin by bailee). **33-024**

## 3. GRATUITOUS BAILMENT

## (a) Deposit

### Deposits with bankers

*Replace footnote 172 with:*

[172] *Re United Service Co* (1870) L.R. 6 Ch. App. 212. See below, paras 34-438—34-440; and Paget's *Law of Banking*, 15th edn (2018), para.7.2. **33-035**

## 4. BAILMENTS FOR VALUABLE CONSIDERATION

## (b) Custody for Reward

### *(i) In General*

### Custody for reward

*Replace paragraph with:*

Where goods are delivered to a bailee to be taken care of by him in return for remuneration to be paid by the bailor, the contract is one of custody for reward.[252] Possession of the chattel must be transferred to the bailee.[253] By s.13 of the Supply of Goods and Services Act 1982[254] (covering bailments where the bailee acts in the course of a business), s.49(1) of the Consumer Rights Act 2015 (covering bailments between a trader and a consumer, where the contract is made on or after October 1, 2015[255]) and by the common law (applicable to other cases) the bailee must take reasonable care of the chattel, according to the circumstances of the particular case.[256] Thus, the bailee must take reasonable care to see that the place[257] where the chattel is kept is fit for the purpose of custody.[258] But there is no authority "to hold that a depositor of goods for safe custody, who, by himself or his servants, has had an opportunity of observing certain defects in the storehouse, must be taken to have agreed that any risk of injury to his goods which might possibly be occasioned by these defects should be borne by him, and not by his paid bailee ... the duty is incumbent on the latter, in the due fulfilment of his contract, of considering whether his premises can be safely used for the storage of [the goods bailed], and, if they cannot, to take immediate steps for placing the goods in a position of safety".[259] The bailee must also take reasonable care to protect the chattel against any imminent danger[260]; this may include a duty to take reasonable precautions against arson or vandalism by third parties.[261] He must take all proper measures to protect the bailor's interests when the chattel is stolen[262] or when claims adverse to the bailor are made to the chattel.[263] The bailee is not, however, an insurer and he will not be liable (apart from a special obligation undertaken in the contract)[264] where the loss or damage occurred without negligence on his part.[265] **33-049**

[252] In deposit (above, para.33-032) there is no reciprocal advantage enjoyed by the bailee. As to custody "for reward" where there is no special payment for the custody, see below, para.33-057.

[253] cf. *Ashby v Tolhurst* [1937] 2 K.B. 242; *Tinsley v Dudley* [1951] 2 K.B. 18. (See below, para.33-061.)

[254] See above, paras 33-044 and 33-046.

[255] See below, para.38-571.

[256] *Houghland v RR Low (Luxury Coaches) Ltd* [1962] 1 Q.B. 694; *Morris v CW Martin & Sons Ltd* [1966] 1 Q.B. 716, 726. (The older formulation of the standard was that the custodian for reward must exercise the care and diligence exercised by a careful man in the custody of his own chattels of a similar kind: see *Coggs v Bernard* (1703) 2 Ld. Raym. 909, 916; *Dean v Keate* (1811) 3 Camp. 4; Jones at pp.86, 87.) It is not a defence that the bailee treated the chattel with the same care as he treated his own chattels: *Re United Service Co* (1870) L.R. 6 Ch. App. 212.

[257] The bailee must also take care that any equipment used in connection with the chattel (e.g. tackle) is adequate for the purpose: *Thomas v Day* (1803) 4 Esp. 262.

[258] *Searle v Laverick* (1874) L.R. 9 Q.B. 122; *Brabant & Co v King* [1895] A.C. 632; *Turner v Stallibrass* [1898] 1 Q.B. 56; *Martin v LCC* [1947] K.B. 628. But the bailee's duty is reduced if the bailor directs where the goods are to be placed: *Harper v Jones* (1879) 4 V.L.R. (L) 536.

[259] *Brabant & Co v King*, above, at 641 (on the facts the goods bailed were explosive goods).

[260] *Brabant & Co v King*, above, at 641 (flood).

[261] *Lockspeiser Aircraft Ltd v Brooklands Aircraft Co Ltd* [1990] C.L.Y. 250 (examined in detail by Palmer at para.14-032); *2 Entertain Video Ltd v Sony DADC Europe Ltd* [2020] EWHC 972 (TCC). But the duty is only one to take reasonable care: *Sutcliffe v Chief Constable of West Yorkshire* [1996] R.T.R. 86; *Rana v Tears of Sutton Bridge* [2015] EWHC 2597 (QB).

[262] *Coldman v Hill* [1919] 1 K.B. 443.

[263] *Ranson v Platt* [1911] 2 K.B. 291. See above, para.33-015.

[264] A contractual obligation upon the bailee to insure the goods may justify the implication of an implied term making the bailee fully liable for loss of, or damage to, the goods: Roberts (1973) 124 New L.J. 849. On an undertaking to insure, see *Lockspeiser Aircraft Ltd v Brooklands Aircraft Co Ltd*, above.

[265] *Searle v Laverick* (1874) L.R. 9 Q.B. 122; *Chapman v GW Ry* (1880) 5 Q.B.D. 278; *Fagan v Green and Edwards Ltd* [1926] 1 K.B. 102; *Volcafe Ltd v Cia Sud Americana de Vapores SA* [2018] UKSC 61, [2019] A.C. 358 at [8]. The position is different where the bailee delivers the chattel to an unauthorised person: see below, para.33-052. It is not, however, necessary in order to avoid liability for a bailee to show what caused the loss: the bailee must show either that he took reasonable care of the goods or that his failure to do so did not contribute to the damage: *Coopers Payen Ltd v Southampton Container Terminal Ltd* [2003] EWCA Civ 1223, [2004] 1 Lloyd's Rep. 331 at [28].

## The onus of proof and the scope of the duty

*Replace footnote 267 with:*

**33-050** [267] *Brook's Wharf and Bull Wharf Ltd v Goodman Bros* [1937] 1 K.B. 534, 538–539; *Gutter v Tait* (1947) 177 L.T. 1; *Houghland v RR Low (Luxury Coaches) Ltd* [1962] 1 Q.B. 694; *Global Dress Co Ltd v WH Boase & Co Ltd* [1966] 2 Lloyd's Rep. 72; *Transmotors Ltd v Robertson, Buckley & Co Ltd* [1970] 1 Lloyd's Rep. 224; *Port Swettenham Authority v TW Wu and Co (M) Sdn Bhd* [1979] A.C. 580, 590; *Volcafe Ltd v Cia Sud Americana de Vapores SA* [2018] UKSC 61, [2019] A.C. 358 at [9]. See also above, paras 33-012, 33-032 (deposit); see below, para.33-064, 33-079 (hire), 35-059, 36-018 (carriage). cf. *Phipps v New Claridge's Hotel Ltd* (1905) 22 T.L.R. 49.

### *(ii) Illustrations of Custody for Reward*

## Agisters

*Replace footnote 323 with:*

**33-059** [323] *Jackson v Cummins* (1839) 5 M. & W. 342; *Re Southern Livestock Producers Ltd* [1964] 1 W.L.R. 24; *Bell and Bell v Clare* (1989) 23 F.C.R. 274; *Shieanov v Sarner International Ltd* [2020] EWHC 1214 (QB) at [62]–[64]. See also *Ward v Fielden* [1985] C.L.Y. 2000 (racehorse trainer has no lien over horses being trained).

## (d) Work and Labour

### Lien of the worker

*Replace paragraph with:*

Where a worker is to be paid[545] for work done on a chattel bailed to him[546] he has at common law, after completion of the work,[547] a lien[548] on the chattel for the remuneration due to him[549]; hence he may refuse to return the chattel until he is paid.[550] An express or implied term of the contract, especially one relating to credit, may, however, exclude such a lien.[551] The lien covers the sum due for materials supplied and work performed on the chattel,[552] but not charges for warehousing or storage, even during the period of the lien.[553] There is no lien at common law for the maintenance of the chattel in its original condition without improvement.[554] The lien is lost by waiver[555] or by the worker relinquishing possession of the chattel,[556] but the mere taking of security for the debt does not discharge the lien, unless it is inconsistent with the existence of the lien.[557] **33-093**

[545] The statements of the rule assume that the lien arises although a precise price may not have been fixed beforehand: e.g. *Scarfe v Morgan* (1838) 4 M. & W. 270, 283.

[546] The worker must have possession of the chattel: *Forth v Simpson* (1849) 13 Q.B. 680; *James Bibby Ltd v Woods and Howard* [1949] 2 K.B. 449, 453. Further, his work must be "on" the chattel and not simply "with" the chattel: *Shieanov v Sarner International Ltd* [2020] EWHC 1214 (QB) at [54]–[80].

[547] If the bailor countermands his order for the work before it is completed, the worker has a lien for the work actually done: *Lilley v Barnsley* (1844) 1 C. & K. 344, 346.

[548] A lien does not entitle the worker to exercise any remedy of self-help, e.g. by removing engine parts so as to disable a ship from moving: *The "Gregos"* [1985] 2 Lloyd's Rep. 347, 361–362. (The worker is simply entitled to retain the chattel in his possession.) A lien cannot be exercised if the worker fails to give the bailor proper details of the work done: *Thaper v Singh* [1987] F.L.R. 369 (accountant).

[549] Where the remuneration has not been agreed, but the worker claims an unreasonably high amount, the bailor who pays under protest may have a claim in restitution to recover the excess over a reasonable charge: see above, para.33-048; Vol.I, paras 29-098—29-103.

[550] Story at para.440; *Franklin v Hosier* (1821) 4 B. & Ald. 341; *Scarfe v Morgan* (1838) 4 M. & W. 270 (lien on mare for services of stallion); *Steadman v Hockley* (1846) 15 M. & W. 553, 556–557. cf. *R. v Wade* (1869) 11 Cox C.C. 549; *Woodworth v Conroy* [1976] 1 Q.B. 884 (accountants have a lien over the books of account, files and papers delivered to them in the course of their professional work); and the lien of an agent, see above, para.31-164.

[551] *Raitt v Mitchell* (1815) 4 Camp. 146 (custom excluding lien); *Chase v Westmore* (1816) 5 M. & S. 180, 186; *Scarfe v Morgan*, above, at 283; *Forth v Simpson* (1849) 13 Q.B. 680. See also the references in nn.558, 559, below.

[552] On a general lien, see Paton at pp.345–347.

[553] *Somes v British Empire Shipping Co Ltd* (1860) 8 H.L. Cas. 338 (distinguished by the House of Lords in *China Pacific SA v Food Corp of India* [1982] A.C. 939, 962–963 (owner benefited from the expenditure, which was made *before* he demanded redelivery of the goods: gratuitous bailment following salvage)). The principle laid down in *Somes* has since been restrictively interpreted (see *Metall Market OOO v Vitorio Shipping Co Ltd (The "Lehmann Timber")* [2013] EWCA Civ 650, [2014] Q.B. 760 at [70]) and it would now appear to stand for the proposition that the common law remedy of an artificer's lien does not attach to it, or contain within it, a right of claim to the expenses of enforcing it or exercising it and that there is no lien for such expenses unless the contract provides for one (at [90]). In any event, the principle in *Somes* is unlikely to apply outside the context of an artificer's lien, given that it has been stated to be of "doubtful status outside that context" (at [122]). See also *Hartley v Hitchcock* (1816) 1 Stark. 408.

[554] *Jackson v Cummins* (1839) 5 M. & W. 342 (mere agistment of an animal: see above, para.33-059; cf. charges for training an animal: *Bevan v Waters* (1828) Mood. & M. 235; *Forth v Simpson* (1849) 13 Q.B. 680); *Hatton v Car Maintenance Co Ltd* [1915] 1 Ch. 621; *Shieanov v Sarner International Ltd* [2020] EWHC 1214 (QB) at [54]–[80]. cf. *Steadman v Hockley* (1846) 15 M. & W. 553, 556.

[555] *White v Gainer* (1824) 2 Bing. 23.

[556] *Hartley v Hitchcock* (1816) 1 Stark. 408; *Jacobs v Latour* (1828) 5 Bing. 130; *Legg v Evans* (1840) 6 M. & W. 36, 42; *Pennington v Reliance Motor Works Ltd* [1923] 1 K.B. 127; *Hatton v Car Maintenance Co Ltd*, above. cf. *Albemarle Supply Co Ltd v Hind & Co* [1928] 1 K.B. 307 (lien continued despite temporary loss of possession); *Caldwell v Sumpters* [1972] Ch. 478 (solicitor's lien over documents not lost when they were sent to the client's present solicitors with the request to hold them to the order of the sender).

[557] *Angus v McLachlan* (1883) 23 Ch. D. 330. cf. *Ex p. Willoughby* (1881) 16 Ch. D. 604.

## (e) Innkeepers

### Defences: negligence of the guest

*Replace footnote 685 with:*

33-112 [685] *Cashill v Wright*, above; *Gee, Walker & Slater Ltd v Friary Hotel (Derby) Ltd* (1949) 66 T.L.R. (Pt 1) 59. cf. R. Munday, *Cross and Tapper on Evidence*, 13th edn (2018), p.130, n.56 (discussing *Medawar v Grand Hotel Co* [1891] 2 Q.B. 11).

## (f) Pledge

### *(i) Pledge at Common Law*

### Other powers of the pledgee

*Replace footnote 812 with:*

33-133 [812] *Chabbra Corp Pte Ltd v Jag Shakti (Owners)* [1986] A.C. 337 (following *Swire v Leach* (1865) 18 C.B.(N.S.) 479; and *The Winkfield* [1902] P. 42); *Scipion Active Trading Fund v Vallis Group Ltd* [2020] EWHC 1451 (Comm) at [74]–[79]. See above, para.33-024, n.113.

CHAPTER 34

# BILLS OF EXCHANGE AND BANKING

## 1. NEGOTIABLE INSTRUMENTS

## (b) Bills of Exchange

### *(iii) The Consideration for a Bill*

#### Need to move from promisee

*Replace footnote 223 with:*

34-061 [223] *Oliver v Davis* [1949] 2 K.B. 727; *Hasan v Willson* [1977] 1 Lloyd's Rep. 431; *MK International Development Co Ltd v Housing Bank* [1991] 1 Bank. L.R. 74; *Lomax Leisure Ltd v Miller* [2008] 1 B.C.L.C. 262, [47]–[50]; *Confezioni v Rozenthal* [2011] EWHC 4105 (QB) at [19]–[27]. See generally, *Chalmers and Guest on Bills of Exchange and Cheques*, 18th edn (2017), paras 4-023 et seq.; *Byles on Bills of Exchange and Cheques*, 30th edn (2020), paras 19-011 et seq.

### *(iv) Transfer of Bills*

#### Rights of holder: generally

*Replace footnote 321 with:*

34-092 [321] *Byles on Bills of Exchange and Cheques*, 30th edn (2020), paras 18-013 et seq.; Crawford, *Payment, Clearing and Settlement in Canada* (2002), Vol.II, pp.986 et seq.; Cowen & Gering, *Law of Negotiable Instruments in South Africa*, 5th edn, pp.103–109 et seq. The distinction is not fully worked out in decided cases, but see *Watson v Russell* (1864) 5 B. & S. 968; 34 L.J. Q.B. 93 (suggesting that the drawer and the drawee of a cheque are not always immediate parties). See also *Oscar Harris, Son & Co v Vallarman & Co* [1940] 1 All E.R. 185, CA; *Bank Lenmi Le-Israel v Coniplan (UK) Ltd* Unreported July 31, 1987; *Solo Industries UK Ltd v Canara Bank* [2001] 2 Lloyd's Rep. 578 at [39], CA; *GMAC Commercial Finance Ltd v Mint Apparel Ltd* [2010] EWHC 2452 (Comm) at [26]. For a detailed discussion, see *Chalmers and Guest on Bills of Exchange and Cheques*, 18th edn (2017), paras 4-005 et seq.

## Rights of mere holder

*Replace paragraph with:*

Section 38(1) prescribes that a holder (or "mere holder") has the right to bring an action on the bill in his own name,[329] but does not indicate what type of defence is available against him. From a comparison of the language of this subsection with s.38(2) it emerges that, as against an action by a mere holder, the defendant is entitled to raise defences stemming from a defect in title of prior parties and at least some personal defences available against them. This view derives support from old authorities which, in view of the absence of explicit regulation of the question in the Act, remain good law. Thus, it has been held that absence of consideration[330] and total failure of consideration[331] are valid defences against a mere holder. Partial failure of consideration is a valid defence where a liquidated amount is involved,[332] but cannot be raised where the amount involved is an unascertained or unliquidated demand.[333] Thus, an acceptor does not have a valid defence to an action on the bill where arbitration proceedings are brought by him against the payee in respect of the underlying contract of sale. Neither can the claim involved be raised by way of a set-off or a counterclaim.[334] A fortiori, a right against a previous party which has no direct bearing on the bill or on the transaction related to it, such as an independent right of set-off, cannot be raised as a defence to the holder's action on the bill.[335] **34-094**

[329] An action to enforce a negotiable instrument may be brought under Pt 24 of the CPR (previously under RSC Ord.14) under which the claimant applies for summary judgment. As to when leave to defend will be granted, see *Byles on Bills of Exchange and Cheques*, 30th edn (2020), paras 26-013 et seq.; and *James Lamont & Co Ltd v Hyland* [1950] 1 K.B. 585; *Brown Shipley & Co Ltd v Alicia Hosiery Ltd* [1966] 1 Lloyd's Rep. 668; *Barclays Bank Ltd v Aschaffenburger Zellstoffwerke AG* [1967] 1 Lloyd's Rep. 387 (below, para.34-102); *All Trades Distributors Ltd v Agencies Kaufman Ltd* (1969) 113 S.J. 995; *Saga of Bond Street Ltd v Avalon Promotions Ltd* [1972] 2 Q.B. 325; *Cebora SNC v SIP (Industrial Products) Ltd* [1976] 1 Lloyd's Rep. 271; *Montebianco Industrie Tessili SpA v Carlyle Mills (London) Ltd* [1981] 1 Lloyd's Rep. 509. Although these cases were decided under RSC Ord.14, they are likely to remain good law (*Safa Ltd v Banque du Caire* [2000] 2 Lloyd's Rep. 600, 605–606, Waller L.J.). See, e.g. *Solo Industries UK Ltd v Canara Bank* [2001] 2 Lloyd's Rep. 578 at [22]–[28]; *Isovel Contracts Ltd (in administration) v ABB Building Technologies Ltd* [2002] 1 B.C.L.C. 390 at [15]–[22]; *Banque Saudi Fransi v Lear Siegler Services Inc* [2007] 2 Lloyd's Rep. 47 at [14]–[16]; *Enka Insaat Ve Sanayi AS v Banca Populare Dell'Alto Adige SpA* [2009] EWHC 2410 (Comm) at [19]–[25]; *National Infrastructure Development Co Ltd v Banco Santander SA* [2017] EWCA Civ 27 at [20]–[24].

[330] *Forman v Wright* (1851) 11 C.B. 481, 492–494; cf. *Easton v Pratchett* (1835) 1 Cr. M. & R. 798, 808–809; *Milnes v Dawson* (1850) 5 Exch. 948, 950–951. Note that s.28(2) does not confer on a mere holder the right to enforce a bill against an accommodation party. As regards the authority of cases decided before the passing of the Act, see above, para.34-006.

[331] See para.34-098, below, showing this defence as available even against a holder for value.

[332] *Forman v Wright*, above; *Agra and Masterman's Bank v Leighton* (1866) L.R. 2 Ex. 56, 64, 65 (supply of ascertained portion of goods instead of delivery of quantity ordered); *Thoni GmbH v RTP Equipment Ltd* [1979] 2 Lloyd's Rep. 282.

[333] *Day v Nix* (1824) 9 Moo. C.P. 159; 2 L.J. (O.S.) C.P. 133; *Sully v Frean* (1854) 10 Ex. 535; *Warwick v Nairn* (1855) 10 Exch. 762 (alleged inferiority of quality of goods).

[334] *Nova (Jersey) Knit Ltd v Kammgarn Spinnerei GmbH* [1977] 1 W.L.R. 713, where the majority of the House of Lords further refused to grant a stay based on the arbitration agreement respecting the underlying contract. But much turns on the construction of the arbitration agreement: as to which, see *Fiona Trust & Holding Corp v Privalov* [2007] UKHL 40, [2008] 1 Lloyd's Rep. 254. See also *Piallo GmbH v Yafriro International Pte Ltd* [2013] SGHC 260, disapproved of by Sing CA in *Cassa di Risparmio di Parma e Piacenza SpA v Rals International Pte Ltd* [2016] SGCA 53. In *Uttam Galva Steels Ltd v Gunvor Singapore Pte Ltd* [2018] EWHC 1098 (Comm), where there was a challenge to the arbitrator's jurisdiction, Picken J. held, at [57], "that there is no rule of English law that an arbitration clause cannot extend to a claim under a bill of exchange, certainly anyway as between the immediate parties to the underlying sale contract and in circumstances where those parties remain the parties to the bill of exchange" (adding, at [61]–[62], that the reasoning of the Sing CA in the *Rals* case was flawed, having been overly influenced by the fact that the claimants in that case were (third party) indorsees of the relevant promissory notes). *Uttam* is noted by LK Ho (2018) 134 L.Q.R. 548. By

contrast, in *China Export & Credit Insurance Corp v Emerald Energy Resources Ltd* [2018] EWHC 1503 (Comm), application for stay of English proceedings, commenced under non-exclusive jurisdiction clause in promissory note, was refused despite arbitration clause in underlying contract.

335 *Burrough v Moss* (1830) 10 B. & C. 558, 563; *Whitehead v Walker* (1842) 10 M. & W. 696; *Oulds v Harrison* (1854) 10 Exch. 572, 578–579; *Re Overend, Gurney & Co Ex p. Swan* (1868) L.R. 6 Eq. 344, 359–360. cf. *Re European Bank Ex p. Oriental Commercial Bank* (1870) L.R. 5 Ch. App. 358. But an agreement made at the time the bill is executed, which contemplates a future set-off, may be an equity affecting the bill: *Holmes v Kidd* (1858) 3 H. & N. 891.

## *(vii) Discharge of Bill*

### Claims for repayment by drawee or acceptor

*Replace footnote 430 with:*

**34-125** 430 *Buller v Harrison* (1777) 2 Cowp. 565, 568; *Pollard v Bank of England* (1871) L.R. 6 Q.B. 623, 631; *Bank of Montreal v The King* (1906) 11 O.L.R. 595 (affirmed 38 S.C.R. 258 (1907) Can); *Gowers v Lloyds and National Provincial Bank* [1938] 1 All E.R. 766, 773; *National Westminster Bank Ltd v Barclays Bank International Ltd* [1975] Q.B. 654. This doctrine, originally protecting an agent who has changed his position by paying the money received to his principal, has been restated as a general defence to an action in restitution in *Lipkin Gorman v Karpnale Ltd* [1991] 2 A.C. 548. However, this is probably wrong as the defence of an agent who has paid money over to his principal is best regarded as a separate defence with its own rules (*Portman Building Society v Hamlyn Taylor Neck (a firm)* [1998] 4 All E.R. 202 at 207, per Millett L.J.; *Jones v Churcher* [2009] EWHC 722 (QB), [2009] 2 Lloyd's Rep. 94 at [77]–[78]; *Jeremy D Stone Consultants Ltd v National Westminster Bank Plc* [2013] EWHC 208 (Ch) at [244]). But note that the agent can be sued as long as the proceeds remain in his hands; the agent cannot defeat such an action by asserting a lien or right of set-off over the proceeds: *Kleinwort, Sons & Co v Dunlop Rubber Co* (1907) 97 L.T. 263; *Kerrison v Glyn, Mills Currie & Co* (1911) 81 L.J. K.B. 465; *RE Jones Ltd v Waring and Gillow Ltd* [1926] A.C. 670. The payment over defence is not available to a trustee who is not acting as an agent: *Skandinaviska Enskilda Banken AB v Conway* [2019] UKPC 36 at [82]–[93]. See further, E Bant, "Payment over and change of position: lessons from agency law" [2007] L.M.C.L.Q. 225.

### Attempt to reconcile

*Replace footnote 446 with:*

**34-129** 446 [1980] Q.B. 677 at 695. For a recent example of Goff J.'s exception (2)(a), see *Leslie v Farrar Construction Ltd* [2016] EWCA Civ 1041 at [51]–[56]. For a recent reference to exception (2)(b), see *ICICI Bank UK Plc v Assam Oil Co Ltd* [2019] EWHC 750 (Comm) at [38].

### Assessment

*Replace footnote 459 with:*

**34-134** 459 Important recent cases on the availability of the change of position defence include: *Philip Collins Ltd v Davis* [2000] 3 All E.R. 808; *Scottish Equitable Plc v Derby* [2001] EWCA Civ 369, [2001] 2 All E.R. (Comm) 274; and *Crédit Suisse (Monaco) SA v Attar* [2004] EWHC 374 (Comm) (on the need for a causal connection between the mistaken receipt and the change of position); *Dextra Bank & Trust Co Ltd v Bank of Jamaica* [2002] 1 All E.R. (Comm) 193; and *Commerzbank AG v Gareth Price-Jones* [2003] EWCA Civ 1663 (on anticipatory change of position); *Niru Battery Manufacturing Co v Milestone Trading Ltd* [2002] EWHC 1425 (Comm), [2002] 2 All E.R. (Comm) 705, 741; approved [2003] EWCA Civ 1446, [2004] 4 All E.R. (Comm) 193 (on what constitutes "bad faith"); *Barros Mattos Junior v MacDaniels Ltd* [2004] EWHC 1188 (Ch), [2004] 3 All E.R. 299 (on change of position which constituted an illegal action); *Campden Hill Ltd v Chakrani* [2005] EWHC 911 (Ch) (on retention of benefit acquired as result of change of position); *Abou-Rahmah v Abacha* [2006] EWCA Civ 492, [2007] 1 Lloyd's Rep. 115 (on defendant's conduct at time of change of position); *Test Claimants in the FII Group Litigation v Commissioners for Revenue and Customs* [2008] EWHC 2893 (Ch), [2009] S.T.C. 254 at [320], [337] (wrongdoer bar to the defence of change of position); *Jones v Churcher* [2009] EWHC 722 (QB), [2009] 2 Lloyd's Rep. 94 (when good faith requires inquiry to be made before disposing of the mistaken payment); *Haugesund Kommune v Depfa ACS Bank* [2010] EWCA Civ 579, [2012] 2 W.L.R. 199 (recipient of payment made under void contract of loan took risk that money would have to be repaid); *Jeremy D Stone Consultants Ltd v National Westminster Bank Plc* [2013] EWHC 208 (Ch) (on whether defence barred by bank's alleged failure to monitor its relationship with customer, contrary to the Money Laundering Regulations 2007 reg.8(1), and its alleged failure to report criminal activity, contrary to the Proceeds of Crime Act 2002 s.330); *Bellis (a firm) v Challinor* [2015] EWCA Civ 59 at

[115]–[120] (in circumstances failure to make diligent enquiry before disposing of mistaken payment did not constitute commercially unacceptable conduct); *T & L Sugars Ltd v Tate & Lyle Industries Ltd* [2015] EWHC 2696 (Comm) at [137] (on anticipatory reliance); *Dexia Crediop SpA v Comune di Prato* [2016] EWHC 2824 (Comm) at [75] (on need for "but for" causal connection between the receipt and any change of position)—but see also [2017] EWCA Civ 428, where the Court of Appeal reversed an earlier, related judgment on a key conflict of law issue in this case, and also held (at [213]) that there was no basis for restitutionary claims by either party; *Skandinaviska Enskilda Banken AB v Conway* [2019] UKPC 36 at [94]–[117] (no change of position defence to unjust enrichment claim following voidable preference). In *BMP Global Distribution Inc v Bank of Nova Scotia* [2009] 1 S.C.R. 504, [62]–[65], the Supreme Court of Canada held that (1) the general of change of position defence applies to mistaken payments made on forged cheques; and (2) neither the collecting bank nor the payee changed their position merely by allowing the proceeds of a cheque to be credited to the payee's account. For detailed coverage, see E. Bant, *The Change of Position Defence* (2009). See generally, Vol.I, paras 29-186 et seq.

## (c) Cheques

### *(i) General Provisions*

#### Cheque truncation

*Replace footnote 513 with:*

[513] Described by Bingham J. in *Barclays Bank v Bank of England* [1985] 1 All E.R. 385 at 387. However, since November 2007 the payee of a UK cheque has been entitled to interest (if the account bears interest) or credit, if overdrawn, on the proceeds after a maximum of two days from deposit of the cheque, to withdraw the proceeds after a maximum of four days and to know the fate of the cheque after a maximum of six days (known as "T+2–4–6"). This means that after six working days funds credited to his account cannot be reclaimed, e.g. if there are insufficient funds in the drawer's account. In *Re Crown Holdings (London) Ltd (In Liquidation)* [2019] EWHC 3302 (Ch) a reference in a court order to a cheque being "received as cleared funds" was interpreted to mean "T+2", i.e. when the bank account of the drawee was credited with the proceeds of the cheque, as that was when interest would accrue and countermand was no longer possible. The speed of the cheque clearing process will be increased with full implementation of the UK's new image-based cheque clearing system expected in the summer of 2018. Cleared funds will be available at the latest by midnight of the working day following deposit (Cheque & Credit Clearing Company, *Cheque Imaging Explained*, October 30, 2017, pp.2–3). See further, para.34-153. **34-152**

### *(iii) Travellers' Cheques*

#### Loss of uncountersigned cheque

*Replace footnote 583 with:*

[583] For contracts made before October 1, 2015, the applicability of the Unfair Contract Terms Act 1977 and the Unfair Terms in Consumer Contracts Regulations 1999 (SI 1999/2083), will need to be considered in relation to any provision in the contract between issuer and the traveller. For such contracts made on or after October 1, 2015, Pt 2 of the Consumer Rights Act 2015 amends the Unfair Terms in Consumer Contracts Act 1977 so that it no longer applies to "consumer contracts" or "consumer notices" as defined by the new Act, and revokes and replaces the Unfair Terms in Consumer Contracts Regulations 1999. For detailed analysis of the impact of the 2015 Act on the 1977 Act and 1999 Regulations, see below, Ch.38. See also Brexit paragraphs in Vol.I, Ch.1, especially para.1-016B. **34-175**

## (d) Promissory Notes

#### Delivery

*In line 2, after "delivery to the payee or bearer.", add new footnote 599a:*

[599a] For when a banknote (a promissory note payable to the bearer on demand) is "issued" for the purpose of VAT legislation and the VAT treatment applicable to the issue of banknotes, see *Clydesdale Bank Plc v Revenue and Customs Commissioners* [2019] UKFTT 419 (TC) at [87]–[92]. **34-183**

## 2. Aspects of Banking Law

*Add new paragraphs:*

34-214A **Corporate Insolvency and Governance Act 2020** The Corporate Insolvency and Governance Act 2020 ("the Act") entered into force on June 26, 2020. The Act passed through Parliament very quickly in order to bring about changes that were thought necessary to support struggling businesses as they deal with the economic effects of Covid-19. However, it should be noted that many of the changes are permanent and not merely temporary. The Act represents the most significant reform of insolvency law in the UK in recent years.

There are three permanent reforms set out in the Act: a moratorium, a ban on the operation of termination provisions (or so called ipso facto clauses) and the introduction of a new pre-insolvency rescue and reorganisation procedure. Temporary reforms include a relaxation of the wrongful trading regime and the suspension of statutory demands and winding-up petitions where financial difficulties are attributable to the Covid-19 pandemic.[658a] What follows is an overview of the new moratorium and restrictions on ipso facto clauses, together with a summary of the exemptions available to banks (and certain types of financial service companies) and parties to certain financial services-related contracts.

[658a] The temporary measures relating to wrongful trading, statutory demands and winding-up petitions covered the period from 1 March 2020 to 30 September 2020. The duration of *some* temporary measures has since been extended by the Corporate Insolvency and Governance (Coronavirus) (Extension of the Relevant Period) Regulations 2020 (SI 2020/1031), e.g. those relating to the use of statutory demands and winding-up petitions were extended to 31 December 2020. The temporary provision relating to the suspension of liability for wrongful trading was not extended and automatically expired on 30 September 2020. The Corporate Insolvency and Governance (Coronavirus) (Early Termination of Certain Temporary Provisions) Regulations 2020 (SI 2020/1033), mean that as from 1 October 2020 any company seeking a Pt A1 moratorium (under the Insolvency Act 1986), or extension of a Pt A1 moratorium, will need to be likely to be rescued as a going concern as a result, even taking into account financial distress caused by the coronavirus.

34-214B **Moratorium** The Act inserts a new Pt A1 into the Insolvency Act 1986 which provides for a new insolvency process whereby directors of insolvent companies, or companies that are likely to become insolvent, can obtain a moratorium period for an initial period of 20 business days, with the ability to extend for a period of 20 business days without consent, and with the possibility for further extensions of up to one year or more.[658b] The moratorium period provides the directors with the opportunity to explore options for the rescue or restructuring of the company. The moratorium is overseen by an insolvency practitioner acting as a "monitor", although the directors remain in control of the company, subject to certain constraints. Subject to certain key exceptions,[658c] the company will not have to pay debts falling due prior to the moratorium (i.e. it will be given a "payment holiday"), but will have to pay debts falling due during the moratorium.[658d] For the duration of the moratorium period, the moratorium prevents the enforcement of security (subject to exceptions, including security over financial collateral), the commencement of insolvency proceedings or other legal proceedings against the company, and the forfeiture of a lease.[658e] The moratorium is similar in its effect to that which is available in an administration of a company, although the new process also prevents the crystallisation of a floating charge (subject to exceptions, including a floating charge that is a security financial collateral arrangement).[658f]

[658b] Where a company is an English company that is not subject to a winding-up petition, the directors of the company can obtain a moratorium by filing relevant documents with the court. Where an overseas company (or an English company that is subject to a winding-up petition) wishes to obtain a moratorium, it must make an application to the court. For a short period (until September 30, 2020), an English company that is subject to a winding-up petition may still obtain a moratorium by the filing of documents and without the need to apply to the court.

[658c] See para.34-214D below.

[658d] Insolvency Act 1986 ("IA 1986") s.A18.

[658e] IA 1986 ss.A20–A21. The court may give permission to creditors to enforce legal rights and take proceedings, provided an application for permission may not be made for the purpose of enforcing a pre-moratorium debt for which the company has a payment holiday.

[658f] IA 1986 s.A22.

**Ipso facto clauses** The Act inserts a new s.233B into the Insolvency Act 1986 which prohibits the termination of any contract for the supply of goods and services to a company, or doing "any other thing" in respect of that contract, by reason of the company entering into an "insolvency procedure", which includes a moratorium under the new moratorium process.[658g] The reference to "any other thing" is extremely broad and would affect provisions such as the right to charge default interest, accelerate and any other contractual consequence. The new s.233B is intended to address the typical practice of suppliers threatening to terminate unless their pre-insolvency arrears are paid and the terms of the continued supply are made more favourable. Subject to certain key exceptions,[658h] the supplier will be forced to continue to supply the debtor on the same terms and will not be guaranteed payment of arrears, with the supplier being able to terminate only if the company or relevant office holder consents or the court is satisfied that the continuation of the contract would cause the supplier hardship and grants permission for the termination.[658i] It remains possible to terminate on non-insolvency grounds (e.g. non-payment) where the default occurs following the commencement of the insolvency procedure, but not where the default occurs prior to the commencement of such procedure and the counterparty did not exercise the right to terminate before the insolvency procedure commended, when a counterparty would require company or office holder consent, or a hardship order from the court before it could terminate the contract.[658j] 34-214C

[658g] However, where the counterparty enters into a scheme of arrangement under the Companies Act 2006 Pt 26, ipso facto clauses remain enforceable.

[658h] See para.34-214D below.

[658i] IA 1986 s.233B(3), (5).

[658j] IA 1986 s.233B(4), (5).

**Exclusions** The impact of the moratorium, and the ipso facto clause provisions, on banks is limited. First, the moratorium is available to all companies except excluded entities. The Act contains a long list of excluded entities, which includes deposit-taking banks, investment banks and investment firms, insurers, payment and e-money institutions and certain market infrastructure bodies.[658k] Secondly, whilst the company will not be obliged to pay most pre-moratorium debts during the moratorium, the payment holiday does not apply to debts or liabilities arising under a contract or other instrument involving financial services.[658l] These include (inter alia) financial contracts (loans, financial leases, guarantees or commitments, commodities contracts, securities contracts), securitisation transactions, derivatives and 34-214D spot contracts, capital market investments, market contracts.[658m] This exclusion is particularly beneficial to lenders, for it means that all payments of interest and principal falling due under a loan agreement must be paid whether or not they fall due pre- or post-moratorium and, if they are not paid, the monitor is required to bring the moratorium to an end. However, for the duration of the moratorium, lenders will be prevented from (i) enforcing security, (ii) filing for insolvency proceedings, (iii) crystallising a floating charge, or (iv) commencing any legal proceedings.[658n]

Similarly, excluded entities, which again includes deposit-taking banks, investment banks and investment firms, insurers, payment and e-money institutions and certain market infrastructure bodies, are excluded from the ipso facto clause provisions where they themselves are in distress or where they are a supplier to a business in distress.[658o] For other types of entity that do not fall within the list of excluded entities (including, e.g. hedge funds), the question will be whether there is an exclusion for the particular contract. Financial contracts (including loan agreements, financial leasing, swap agreements and derivatives and capital markets arrangements)[658p] are excluded from the ipso facto clause provisions and can continue to be terminated or varied on the grounds of insolvency.[658q] There is also an exception for any set-off or netting arrangement. This means that lenders will be permitted to draw-stop facilities, accelerate loans, charge default interest, exercise contractual rights of set-off and otherwise exercise their contractual rights associated with an event of default under the facility.[658r]

658k IA 1986 Sch.ZA1.

658l IA 1986 s.A18(3).

658m IA 1986 Sch.ZA2.

658n See para.34-214B.

658o IA 1986 Sch.4ZZA Pt 2. The list of excluded entities for the purposes of ipso facto clause provisions is similar to, but not identical with, the list of excluded entities (set out in IA 1986 Sch.ZA1) for the purposes of the new moratorium.

658p IA 1986 Sch.4ZZA Pt 3.

658q IA 1986 s.233B(10).

658r But see the letter "Covid-19: IFRS 9, capital requirements and loan covenants", dated March 26, 2020, from Sam Woods of the Prudential Regulation Authority to the CEOs of UK banks, which sets out guidance regarding the treatment of borrowers who breach covenants owing to Covid-19 (*https://www.bankofengland.co.uk/-/media/boe/files/prudential-regulation/letter/2020/covid-19-ifrs-9-capital-requirements-and-loan-covenants.pdf?la=en&hash=77F4E1D06F713D2104067EC6642FE95EF2935EBD*). Lenders are expected to treat breaches of covenant arising from Covid-19 "differently" and "consider waiving" those breaches. Lenders are expected to waive those breaches in good faith without imposing new unrelated charges or conditions.

## (a) Bank Regulation

### *(i) Overview*

#### Financial Services Act 2012

*Replace footnote 661 with:*

34-216 661 The process of reform has been wide ranging. This has been achieved through primary legislation, supported by a raft of statutory instruments. Three legislative developments stand out. First, the Banking Act 2009 established (a) a permanent special resolution regime, which gave the Treasury, Bank of England and FSA (now PRA/FCA) "stabilisation options" for dealing with banks that get into financial difficulties; (b) a new bank insolvency procedure to facilitate the orderly winding up of a failed bank;

and (c) a new bank administration procedure for use where there has been a partial transfer of business from a failing bank. Secondly, the Financial Services (Banking Reform) Act 2013 introduced a retail ringfence for banks; primary loss-absorbing capacity for systemically important banks; a preference for certain depositors on insolvency; a "bail-in" tool as a new stabilisation option available to the Bank of England where a bank is failing; a new framework for the oversight of individuals within banks, including a new criminal offence aimed at senior managers whose reckless decisions cause a bank to fail; a new payment systems regulator and a special administration regime for operators of systemically important inter-bank payment systems and securities settlement systems in the event of insolvency. Thirdly, the Treasury published various statutory instruments to implement the Bank Recovery and Resolution Directive 2014/59/EU of 15 May 2014, which establishes a common framework across the EU for the recovery and resolution of failing credit institutions and investment firms (the main piece of legislation implementing the Directive is the Bank Recovery and Resolution Order 2014 (SI 2014/3329)). See also Brexit paragraphs in Vol.I, Ch.1, and Bank Recovery and Resolution and Miscellaneous Provisions (Amendment) EU Exit) Regulations 2018 (SI 2018/1394).

## Banking Conduct of Business Sourcebook (BCOBS)

*Replace footnote 675 with:*

[675] See paras 34-222—34-223A below. **34-219**

*Replace footnote 689 with:*

[689] See, e.g. *Parmar v Barclays Bank Plc* [2018] EWHC 1027 (Ch) (unsuccessful swap mis-selling claim). The definition of a "private person" is to be found in FSMA 2000 (Rights of Action) Regulations 2001 (SI 2001/2256), as amended. The courts have interpreted the definition broadly so that a company carrying on business of any kind, irrespective of whether this related to financial services, is not a "private person" for these purposes. See *Titan Steel Wheels Ltd v Royal Bank of Scotland Plc* [2010] EWHC 211 (Comm), [2010] 2 Lloyd's Rep. 92 at [68]–[70]; *Camerata Property Inc v Credit Suisse Securities (Europe) Ltd* [2012] EWHC 7 (Comm), [2012] 1 C.L.C. 234 at [89]–[98]; *Bailey v Barclays Bank Plc* [2014] EWHC 2882 (QB) at [44]; *Thornbridge Ltd v Barclays Bank Plc* [2015] EWHC 3430 (QB) at [138]–[141] (appeal dismissed, Unreported January 9, 2018); *Sivagnanam v Barclays Bank Plc* [2015] EWHC 3985 (Comm) at [8]–[21]; *Target Rich International Ltd v Forex Capital Markets Ltd* [2020] EWHC 1544 (Ch) at [61]–[82]. A claim by a private person under s.138D(2) of the FSMA 2000 may be assigned: *Connaught Income Fund Series 1 v Capital Financial Management Ltd* [2014] EWHC 3619 (Comm), [2015] 1 All E.R. (Comm) 751 at [45]–[46]. Exceptions to right of action under s.138D(2) are found in subss.(3) and (5). **34-221**

## The Standards of Lending Practice

*Add new paragraph:*

A revised version of the Standards of Lending Practice for Business Customers will come into operation on November 1, 2019 ("the 2019 Standards"). The 2019 Standards apply to lending to business customers with a consolidated turnover of up to £25 million. In terms of application of the 2019 Standards a distinction is made between (a) businesses with an annual turnover of no more than £6.5 million and which do not have a complex ownership structure (the 2019 Standards will apply in their entirety), and (b) businesses with a turnover greater than £6.5 million (for some business customers the relevant section of the 2019 Standards may apply in its entirety, whilst for others only particular elements will apply, although firms must adhere in full to the section on governance and oversight). The 2019 Standards apply to products offered for business lending purposes: overdraft, loan, credit card, commercial mortgage and chargecard products. The 2019 Standards do not apply to trade loans or invoice financing. A separate set of Standards continue to apply to asset finance products. In August 2020, the text of the Standards of Lending Practice for Business Customer (and the related Information for Practitioners) was revised so as to apply to products offered under the government's Bounce Bank Loan Scheme and the Coronavirus Business Interruption Loans Scheme. **34-223A**

### Payment Services Regulations 2017

*Replace footnote 691 with:*

34-224 [691] SI 2017/752, as amended. On the effects of Brexit see Vol.I, paras 1-014 et seq.; and Financial Services and Markets Act 2000 (Amendment) (EU Exit) Regulations 2019 (SI 2019/632); Financial Services (Electronic Money, Payment Services and Miscellaneous Amendments) (EU Exit) Regulations 2019 (SI 2019/1212).

*To the end of paragraph, after "payment services providers.[712]", add:*

34-226 This extension has encouraged the development of Open Banking whereby bank customers can open up their banking data and accounts to trusted third parties allowing for increased innovation, greater competition and customer choice, as well as increased financial inclusion.[712a]

[712a] See also the Competition and Markets Authority's Retail Banking Market Investigation Order 2017. On Open Banking generally, see J Black, "Open banking: an emerging technology grows to maturity" [2019] P.L.C. 19; J Black, "In Open Banking's brave new world could using a third party to initiate payments weaken consumer protection?" [2019] J.I.B.F.L. 25.

## *(ii) The Regulation of Deposit-taking*

*To the end of title, add new footnote 716a:*

### Financial Services and Markets Act 2000[716a]

34-230 [716a] On the effects of Brexit see Vol.I, paras 1-014 et seq.; and Financial Services and Markets Act 2000 (Amendment) (EU Exit) Regulations 2019, (SI 2019/632), Financial Services (Miscellaneous) (Amendment) (EU Exit) Regulations 2019 (SI 2019/710) and EEA Passport Rights (Amendment etc, and Transitional Provisions) (EU Exit) Regulations 2018 (SI 2018/1149), which are some of the many pieces of secondary legislation that amend the FSMA 2000 in the face of Brexit.

### Financial Services Compensation Scheme

*Replace footnote 751 with:*

34-241 [751] See the Deposit Guarantee Scheme Regulations 2015 (SI 2015/486), which implement in part Directive 2014/49/EU of the European Parliament and of the Council of 16th April 2014 on deposit guarantee schemes (recast) repealing Directive 94/19/EC of 30th May 1994 on deposit-guarantee schemes. On the effects of Brexit see Vol.I, paras 1-014 et seq. and Deposit Guarantee Scheme and Miscellaneous Provisions (Amendments) (EU Exit) Regulations 2018 (SI 2018/1285).

## *(iii) EU Harmonisation Measures*

### EU single market in banking

*Replace footnote 755 with:*

34-242 [755] Regulation (EU) 575/2013 of the European Parliament and of the Council on prudential requirements for credit institutions and investment firms. On the effects of Brexit see Vol.I, paras 1-014 et seq. and Capital Requirements (Amendment) (EU Exit) Regulations 2019 (SI 2019/1232) and Capital Requirements (Amendment) (EU Exit) Regulations 2018 (SI 2018/1401).

### Single European passport

*Replace footnote 757 with:*

34-243 [757] s.31(1)(b) and Sch.3. See also the Financial Services and Markets Act 2000 (EEA Passport Rights) Regulations 2001 (SI 2001/2511). On the effects of Brexit see Vol.I, paras 1-014 et seq. and EEA Passport Rights (Amendment, etc, and Transitional Provisions) (EU Exit) Regulations 2018 (SI 2018/1149).

### Single payment market

*Replace footnote 761 with:*

[761] SI 2017/752, as amended. On the effects of Brexit see Vol.I, paras 1-014 et seq. and Financial Services and Markets Act 2000 (Amendment) (EU Exit) Regulations 2019 (SI 2019/632) and Financial Services (Electronic Money, Payment Services and Miscellaneous Amendments) (EU Exit) Regulations 2019 (SI 2019/1212). **34-245**

## (b) The Relationship of Banker and Customer

### *(i) Definition of a Bank*

### Who is a banker: common law definition

*Replace footnote 770 with:*

[770] *United Dominions Trust Ltd v Kirkwood*, above, approving the definition of banking business in Paget, *Law of Banking*, 9th edn, pp.5–7 (currently 15th edn (2018), para.4.2). **34-247**

### *(ii) Definition of a Customer*

### Account in nominee's name

*Replace footnote 783 with:*

[783] EU Member States had to implement the Fourth Money Laundering Directive 2015/849/EU by June 26, 2017. The UK did this through the Money Laundering, Terrorist Financing and Transfer of Funds (Information on the Payer) Regulations 2017 (SI 2017/692), which replace the Money Laundering Regulations 2007 (SI 2007/2157) and the Transfer of Funds (Information on the Payer) Regulations 2007 (SI 2007/3298). The Fifth Money Laundering Directive 2018/843/EU had to be implemented in EU Member States by January 10, 2020, and this was done in the UK through the Money Laundering and Terrorist Financing (Amendment) Regulations 2019 (SI 2019/1511), which amended SI 2017/692. The Sanctions and Anti-Money Laundering Act 2018 enables the government to make regulations for the detection, investigation and prevention of money laundering or terrorist financing. **34-253**

### *(iii) Nature of the Banker–Customer Relationship*

### Nature of relationship

*Replace footnote 785 with:*

[785] *Foley v Hill* (1848) 2 H.L. Cas. 28; *Joachimson v Swiss Bank Corp* [1921] 3 K.B. 110; *Rowlandson v National Westminster Bank Ltd* [1978] 1 W.L.R. 798, 803–804; *Financial Services Authority v Anderson* [2010] EWHC 599 (Ch) at [44]; *First City Monument Bank Plc v Zumax Nigeria Ltd* [2019] EWCA Civ 294 at [25], [36], [74]–[75], [80]. **34-254**

*Add new paragraph:*

In an attempt to impose contractual duties of good faith upon their banks, certain customers have unsuccessfully argued that the bank-customer relationship is underpinned by an overarching "relational contract" or "customer contract" into which such a duty could be implied.[786a] The argument is unlikely to succeed where, as is usually the case, the bank provides services to its customers through a series of written standard form contracts. An ordinary loan agreement is not a "relational" contract of any kind, and the lender is not placed under an implied duty to act honestly and in good faith.[786b] **34-254A**

[786a] *Portland Stone Firms Ltd v Barclays Bank Plc* [2018] EWHC 2341 (QB); *Standish v Royal Bank of Scotland Plc* [2018] EWHC 1829 (Ch); *Broomhead v National Westminster Bank Plc* [2018] EWHC 1574 (Ch).

786b *Morley v Royal Bank of Scotland Plc* [2020] EWHC 88 (Ch) at [159], Kerr J., adding (at [160]) that the lender's decision to call in the loan was a contractual right and not a contractual discretion (cf. the lender's power to obtain a revaluation of the charged assets, and to charge a default interest rate, which were said to be contractual discretions which had to be exercised for purposes rationally connected to the lender's commercial purposes, and so as not to vex the borrower maliciously, as set out in *Property Alliance Group Ltd v RBS Plc* [2018] EWCA Civ 355 at [169]). See also *UBS AG v Rose Capital Ventures Ltd* [2018] EWHC 3137 (Ch) at [56].

## *(iv) Fiduciary Relationship and Duty of Care*

### The general rule

*Replace footnote 787 with:*

34-255 787 *Governor and Company of the Bank of Scotland v A Ltd* [2001] EWCA Civ 52, [2001] Lloyd's Rep. Bank. 73 at [25]; *JP Morgan Chase Bank v Springwell Navigation Corp* [2008] EWHC 1186 (Comm) at [573] (affirmed [2010] EWCA Civ 1221, [2010] 2 C.L.C. 705); *Forsta Ap-Fonden v Bank of New York Mellon SA* [2013] EWHC 3127 (Comm) at [173]; *Barclays Bank Plc v Svizera Holdings BV* [2014] EWHC 1020 (Comm) at [8]; *Bailey v Barclays Bank Plc* [2014] EWHC 2882 (QB) at [87]–[90]; *WW Property Investments Ltd v National Westminster Bank Plc* [2016] EWCA Civ 1142 at [57]; *Rehman v Santander UK Plc* [2018] EWHC 748 (QB) at [43]; *First City Monument Bank Plc v Zumax Nigeria Ltd* [2019] EWCA Civ 294 at [25], [36], [80]. The fact that the bank holds third party security to cover the customer's indebtedness does not convert the banker-customer relationship into a fiduciary one: *Kotonou v National Westminster Bank Plc* [2010] EWHC 1659 (Ch), [2011] 1 All E.R. (Comm) 1164 (held bank as lender owes no duty to borrower to call on third party security before it lapsed). Neither does a lender owe an equitable duty to act in good faith on a debt restructuring of its borrower merely because it holds security by way of mortgage when it does not exercise, or threaten to exercise, its powers under that security: *Standish v Royal Bank of Scotland Plc* [2018] EWHC 1829 (Ch) at [48]–[49]. A mortgagee's equitable duty of good faith is narrow in scope and does not restrict the lender's discretion to call in an uncommitted loan that was repayable on demand, so long as the lender enforces its security for the proper purpose of satisfying the debt: *UBS AG v Rose Capital Ventures Ltd* [2018] EWHC 3137 (Ch) at [34]–[38] (also holding at [52]–[56] that neither as a matter of construction nor as an implied term of the mortgage contract was the lender under a duty to exercise its discretion to call in the loan in a manner which was not arbitrary, capricious, perverse and/or irrational: see also *Morley v Royal Bank of Scotland Plc* [2020] EWHC 88 (Ch) at [159]–[160]). But some activities of a multifunctional bank may give rise to fiduciary duties, e.g. acting as custodian of its customer's securities (*JP Morgan Chase Bank v Springwell Navigation Corp* [2008] EWHC 1186 (Comm) at [573] (affirmed [2010] EWCA Civ 1221, [2010] 2 C.L.C. 705); *Forsta Ap-Fonden v Bank of New York Mellon SA* [2013] EWHC 3127 (Comm) at [173]). Even then, the fact the bank is a fiduciary in some respects does not mean that it is a fiduciary in all respects (*Forsta Ap-Fonden v Bank of New York Mellon SA*, above, at [174]; *Saltri III v MD Mezzanine SA SICAR* [2012] EWHC 3025 (Comm), [2013] 1 All E.R. (Comm) 661 at [123]). For detailed coverage, see E.P. Ellinger, E. Lomnicka and C.V.M. Hare, *Ellinger's Modern Banking Law*, 5th edn (2011), Ch.5, s.4.

### Limitations of general principle defined

*Replace paragraph with:*

34-258 It is clear from the cases considered in the foregoing paragraphs that banks are held to be subject to fiduciary duties or special duties of care only in exceptional cases. Basically, such a duty arises where the bank has assumed liability or has held itself out in a manner that justifies its imposition.[794] A duty of care is more readily invoked if the bank has derived some benefit, be it direct or indirect, from the transaction involved or if it placed itself in a situation which led to a conflict of interests between the customer and itself.[795] Cases of this sort are, of course, rare. In its ordinary dealings, the bank need not be unduly suspicious and cannot, for instance, be expected to initiate enquiries about the motive behind a payment instruction given to it by the customer's duly authorised agent unless there are some very clear indications that ought to alert the bank about the agent's fraudulent design.[796] Usually, all that is to be expected of a bank is the exercise of reasonable care in the discharge of its duties to customers. In determining whether a bank has acted negligently, regard must be had to all relevant circumstances as well as to standard banking practice. This principle emerges most clearly from an earlier authority, *Schioler v Westminster Bank Ltd*.[797] The plaintiff, a Danish national domiciled in Denmark but resident in the United Kingdom, maintained an account with the Guernsey branch of the defendant bank. Dividends due to the plaintiff from a Malaysian company were usually remitted by it for credit of this account in sterling, an arrangement under which the plaintiff was not liable to taxation in the United Kingdom. On one occasion, however, the dividend was remitted by a voucher expressed in foreign currency. In the absence of facilities in Guernsey for the negotiation of foreign currency drafts, the dividend voucher was forwarded by the Guernsey branch for collection to the bank's head office in England. The plaintiff, thereupon, became subject to payment of United Kingdom income tax, which was duly deducted by the bank. The plaintiff's action in breach of contract was dismissed by Mocatta J., who held that the bank had not acted negligently in failing to ask for specific instructions when the dividend was received in foreign currency. As the bank had acted in accordance with established banking practice, it was not in breach of a duty of care.

[794] For such an exceptional case, see *Verity and Spindler v Lloyds Bank Plc* [1995] C.L.C. 1557 (bank manager assumed the role of borrowers' financial adviser); cf. *Murphy v HSBC Bank Plc* [2004] EWHC 467 (Ch) (bank assumed no responsibility to borrowers who had own solicitors and accountants to advise them).

[795] *Barclays Bank Plc v Quincecare Ltd* [1992] 4 All E.R. 363 at 375–376 (the duty arises as an implied term of the banker-customer contract and a concurrent tortious duty). Under the *Quincecare* duty, as it is known, a bank must refrain from executing an order to make a payment where it knows it to be dishonestly given, or shuts its eyes to the obvious fact of the dishonesty, or acts recklessly in failing to make such enquires as an honest and reasonable man would make, or is "put on enquiry" by having reasonable grounds for believing that the order is an attempt to misappropriate funds: *Singularis Holdings Ltd (In Liquidation) v Daiwa Capital Markets Europe Ltd* [2020] UKSC 50 at [1]. The question of what a bank should do when it is put on inquiry that a payment instruction ought not to be executed will vary according to the particular facts of the case, and may include making inquiries of its customer (but subject to any duty of confidentiality the bank may separately owe to the person giving the payment instruction, or the fact that money laundering legislation requires a suspicious activity report to be made to the National Crime Agency, when a bank is prohibited from raising the matter with the customer): *JP Morgan Chase Bank NA v Federal Republic of Nigeria* [2019] EWCA Civ 1641 at [20]–[22]. In most cases, the bank will be required to do something more than simply deciding not to comply with a payment instruction ([2019] EWCA Civ 1641 at [21]). The duty may be excluded by the terms of the banking contract ([2019] EWCA Civ 1641 at [40]). The *Quincecare* duty extends beyond banks to include payment service providers that hold assets on behalf of their customers and follow payment instructions: *Hamblin v World First Ltd* [2020] 6 WLUK 314.

[796] As in *Singularis Holdings Ltd (in liquidation) v Daiwa Capital Markets Europe Ltd* [2017] EWHC 257 (Ch), affirmed on other grounds [2018] EWCA Civ 84. There was no appeal on the judge's finding of the *Quincecare* duty of care (above), or breach of that duty, although Vos C. stressed (at [98]) that "it will be a rare situation for a bank to be put on inquiry; there is a high threshold" and that the instant case was "an unusual one, the circumstances of which are unlikely often to arise". Dismissing the defendant bank's appeal ( [2019] UKSC 50), the Supreme Court held that the fraudulent misappropriation of funds out of a corporate customer's account by one of its directors, who was the company's Chairman and sole shareholder, was not to be attributed to the company so as to afford the bank a defence (based on illegality, lack of causation or by an equal and opposite claim against the company in deceit) to the company's claim for breach of the bank's *Quincecare* duty of care: the purpose of the duty was to protect the company from the misconduct of its trusted agent, and to attribute the fraud of that person to the company would be to denude the the duty of any value in cases where it was needed most (Baroness Hale at [35]). See further above, Vol.I, para.16-203A. For an argument that the *Quincecare* duty, based on a negligence standard, is misconceived, and that the correct default standard is one of dishonesty, see P. Watts, "The *Quincecare* duty: misconceived and misdelivered" [2020] J.B.L. 403.

[797] [1970] 2 Q.B. 719.

## Everyday transactions

*Replace footnote 802 with:*

34-259 [802] As regards liability owed to third parties, arising in the context of an ordinary banking transaction, see: *TE Potterton Ltd v Northern Bank Ltd* [1993] 1 I.R. 413 (paying bank owes payee of cheque a duty to act carefully and honestly when advising payee of its reasons for dishonour of cheque); *Chapman v Barclays Bank Plc* [1997] Bank. L.R. 315, CA (bank owes no duty of care to third party who had financial interest in the borrower's affairs); *Wells v First National Commercial Bank* [1998] P.N.L.R. 552, CA (bank instructed to make funds transfer to named beneficiary owes no duty of care to that beneficiary and will not be liable to him if it fails to execute the instruction); *Abou-Rahmah v Abacha* [2005] EWHC 2662 (QB), [2006] 1 All E.R. (Comm) 247; affirmed. [2006] EWCA Civ 1492, [2007] 1 Lloyd's Rep. 115, but with no appeal on this issue (receiving bank does not owe a duty of care to the payer of funds, who is not its customer and to whom it has undertaken no special responsibility, to pay money received only to the beneficiary identified in the payer's instructions or, in the case of discrepancies, to clarify the identity of the beneficiary with the payer); *Customs and Excise Commissioners v Barclays Bank Plc* [2006] UKHL 28 [2007] 1 A.C. 181 (bank notified by a third party of freezing injunction granted to the third party against one of the bank's customers affecting an account held by the customer with the bank, owes no duty to the third party to take reasonable care to comply with the terms of the injunction); *Riyad Bank v Ahli United Bank (UK) Plc* [2006] EWCA Civ 780, [2006] 2 Lloyd's Rep. 292 (where there is a contractual chain, the normal position is that the chain should not be bypassed by a claim in tort, but a duty of care may exist where discussions and representations are made directly to the party who suffers loss); *So v HSBC Bank Plc* [2009] EWCA Civ 296, [2009] 1 C.L.C. 503 (bank owes duty of care to third party when representing that it had accepted and intended to carry out its customer's instructions); *Chudley v Clydesdale Bank Plc (t/a Yorkshire Bank)* [2017] EWHC 2177 (Comm) at [248]–[250] (no sufficient proximity between bank and third party to establish duty of care on which to base claim that bank negligent in putting a "dangerous document" into circulation), but on appeal [2019] EWCA Civ 344 held that third party could rely on Contracts (Rights of Third Parties) Act 1999 to assert own contractual rights against bank). Somewhat exceptionally, a bank arranging a capital market transaction was recently held liable for breach of a duty of care owed to third party bondholders: see *Golden Belt 1 Sukuk Company v BNP Paribas* [2017] EWHC 3182 (Comm) (bank arranging Sukuk—Islamic bond—issue owed tortious duty of care to bondholders to ensure promissory note that supported issuer's liability was properly executed).

## Effect of contractual documents on duty of care

*Replace first paragraph with:*

34-260 Where a bank provides specialist banking services to financially sophisticated customers under the terms of contractual documentation drafted by specialist lawyers, the court will be slow to find a duty of care in tort going beyond the rights and obligations carefully set out in those documents.[803] There are a number of cases which illustrate that contractual terms, such as those which deny that advice has been given and/or relied upon, may prevent the coming into existence of any duty of care to advise.[804] The prevailing view has been that where these terms define the basis upon which the parties act, they do not constitute exclusion clauses falling within the ambit of the Unfair Contract Terms Act 1977 or s.3 of the Misrepresentation Act 1967,[805] although such a term may constitute an unfair term when found in a "consumer contract" within the meaning of the Consumer Rights Act 2015.[806]

[803] *IFE Fund SA v Goldman Sachs International* [2006] EWHC 2887 (Comm), [2007] 1 Lloyd's Rep. 264 at [63], per Toulson J.; affirmed [2007] EWCA Civ 811, [2007] 2 Lloyd's Rep. 449 (syndicated loan); applied in *Maple Leaf Macro Volatility Master Fund v Rouvroy* [2009] EWHC 257 (Comm), [2009] 1 Lloyd's Rep. 475 at [369]. See also *Barclays Bank Plc v Svizera Holdings BV* [2014] EWHC 1020 (Comm) at [68]–[70] (applying the opinion of Lord Hodge in *Grant Estates Ltd v Royal Bank of Scotland Plc* [2012] CSOH 133 at [73] as to when a tortious duty of care to advise would arise in the case of a bank or other financial institution). But contrast *Sumitomo Bank Ltd v Banque Bruxelles Lambert SA* [1997] 1 Lloyd's Rep. 487, where Langley J. held that provisions as to the arranging bank's duties, rights and exonerations under the syndicated loan agreement did not prevent, and were not inconsistent with, a general duty of care being owed to syndicate members. See also *Golden Belt 1 Sukuk Company v BNP Paribas* [2017] EWHC 3182 (Comm), where standard disclaimers in Offering Circular did not prevent bank arranging Sukuk—Islamic bond—issue being held in breach of tortious duty of care to bondholders to ensure promissory note that supported issuer's liability was properly executed. The contractual documents may also regulate the existence and extent of a fiduciary relationship, especially where the parties are both substantial financial institutions dealing on an arm's length basis

(*Forsta Ap-Fonden v Bank of New York Mellon SA* [2013] EWHC 3127 (Comm) at [177]–[178]; *Saltri III v MD Mezzanine SA SICAR* [2012] EWHC 3025 (Comm) at [123(f)]; *CFH Clearing Ltd v Merrill Lynch International* [2019] EWHC 963 (Comm) at [78]–[83], where also held that bank engaged in arm's length foreign exchange transactions was under no duty to take reasonable care to ensure the transactions were correctly priced to reflect market practice).

804 *Springwell Navigation Corp v JP Morgan Chase Bank* [2008] EWHC 1186 (Comm), affirmed [2010] EWCA Civ 1221, [2010] 2 C.L.C. 705; *IFE Fund SA v Goldman Sachs International* [2007] EWCA Civ 811, [2007] 2 Lloyd's Rep. 449; *Peekay Intermark v Australia & New Zealand Banking Group* [2006] EWCA Civ 386, [2006] 2 Lloyd's Rep. 511; *Valse Holdings v Merrill Lynch International Bank* [2004] EWHC 2471 (Comm); *Bankers Trust International Plc v PT Dharmala Sakti Sejahtera* [1996] C.L.C. 518; *Credit Suisse International v Stichting Vestia Groep* [2014] EWHC 3103 (Comm) at [113]–[114]. See also *Titan Steel Wheels Ltd v Royal Bank of Scotland Plc* [2010] EWHC 211 (Comm), [2010] 2 Lloyd's Rep. 92 (held contract terms gave rise to contractual estoppel or, alternatively, negatived the existence of a duty of care); *Raiffeisen Zentralbank Österreich AG v Royal Bank of Scotland Plc* [2010] EWHC 1392 (Comm), [2011] 1 Lloyd's Rep. 123 (held no representation/no responsibility provisions in Information Memorandum gave rise to contractual estoppel). The decision of the Court of Appeal in *Springwell Navigation Corp v JP Morgan Chase Bank* [2010] EWCA Civ 1221, [2010] 2 C.L.C. 705, is important because it upholds the doctrine of contractual estoppel, applying the approach taken by the Court of Appeal (possibly obiter) in *Peekay Intermark Ltd v ANZ Banking Group*, above. Followed in *Cassa di Risparmio della Repubblica di San Marino SpA v Barclays Bank Ltd* [2011] EWHC 484 (Comm), [2011] 1 C.L.C. 701 at [492]–[508]; *Standard Chartered Bank v Ceylon Petroleum Corp* [2011] EWHC 1785 (Comm) at [526]–[534], affirmed on different ground [2012] EWCA Civ 1049; *Barclays Bank Plc v Svizera Holdings BV* [2014] EWHC 1020 (Comm) at [58]–[63], [71]; *Crestsign Ltd v National Westminster Bank Plc* [2014] EWHC 3043 (Ch) at [119]; *Credit Suisse International v Stichting Vestia Groep* [2014] EWHC 3103 (Comm) at [307]–[308] (contractual estoppel applied to agreement about a state of affairs in the future) and [309]–[310] (questioning whether contractual estoppel is really a form of estoppel at all); *Thornbridge Ltd v Barclays Bank Plc* [2015] EWHC 3430 (QB) at [111] (appeal dismissed, Unreported January 9, 2018); *Marz Ltd v Bank of Scotland Plc* [2017] EWHC 3618 (Ch) at [240]–[275]; *Wallis Trading Inc v Air Tanzania Co Ltd* [2020] EWHC 339 (Comm) at [79]–[81]. The principle of contractual estoppel is now "firmly established" at Court of Appeal level: see *First Tower Trustees Ltd v CDS (Superstores International) Ltd* [2018] EWCA Civ 1396 at [47]–[48], [91]–[95]. But note that contract terms may not assist a bank when relied upon in a different context from the one in which they were intended to apply (*Camerata Property Inc v Credit Suisse Securities (Europe) Ltd* [2011] EWHC 479 (Comm), [2011] 2 B.C.L.C. 54 at [184]: for related proceedings, see [2012] EWHC 7 (Comm) and [2013] EWHC 29 (Comm)) or where the terms are limited in their scope (*UBS AG (London Branch) v Kommunale Wasserwerke Leipzig GmbH* [2014] EWHC 3615 (Comm) at [773]–[784]), and that a "disclaimer" cannot create a contractual estoppel when it is not part of the contract (*Taberna Europe CDO II Plc v Selskabet AF1.September 2008 (In Bankruptcy)* [2015] EWHC 871 (Comm) at [120]; reversed on appeal [2016] EWCA Civ 1262, where Court of Appeal held at [19]–[20] that a non-contractual "duty-negating" clause fell outside s.3 of the Misrepresentation Act 1967 because it was found in the very document that was said to contain the misrepresentation). See also *Sofer v Swissindependent Trustees SA* [2019] EWHC 2071 (Ch) at [139]–[140], rev'd [2020] EWCA Civ 699. For criticism of recent trend towards "documentary fundamentalism", see G. McMeel [2011] L.M.C.L.Q. 185. In the *Springwell* case [2008] EWHC 1186 (Comm) at [431]ff, Gloster J. held that an investment bank owed no general advisory duty to a sophisticated investor who was aware of the risks he was running. Her decision on this point was not challenged on appeal; however, the Court of Appeal (above, at [123]) accepted Gloster J.'s tentative conclusion (above, at [108]) that there might be a "low level duty of care" on the part of a salesman not to make any negligent misstatements and to use reasonable care not to recommend a highly risky investment without pointing out that it was such. However, the courts have tended to reject claims based on the existence of an advisory duty of care in the context of selling financial investments, e.g., most recently, *Property Alliance Group Ltd v Royal Bank of Scotland Plc* [2018] EWCA Civ 355; *London Executive Aviation Ltd v Royal Bank of Scotland Plc* [2018] EWHC 74 (Ch); *Marz Ltd v Bank of Scotland Plc* [2017] EWHC 3618 (Ch); *Finch v Lloyds TSB Bank Plc* [2016] EWHC 1236 (QB) at [52]–[58]; *Thornbridge Ltd v Barclays Bank Plc* [2015] EWHC 3430 (QB) at [96] (appeal dismissed, Unreported January 9, 2018); cf. *Rubenstein v HSBC Bank Plc* [2011] EWHC 2304 (QB), [2011] 2 C.L.C. 459 at [70], where there was a one-to-one enquiry about a specific investment transaction: reversed in part (on causation) [2012] EWCA Civ 1184, [2013] 1 All E.R. (Comm) 915. For brief discussion of statutory regulatory regime governing the sale of financial products by banks, see para.34-434 below.

805 *IFE Fund SA v Goldman Sachs International* [2006] EWHC 2887 (Comm), [2007] 1 Lloyd's Rep. 264 at [70]–[71], per Toulson J., affirmed [2007] EWCA Civ 811, [2007] 2 Lloyd's Rep. 449 at [28]; *Springwell Navigation Corp v JP Morgan Chase Bank* [2008] EWHC 1186 (Comm) at [671], affirmed [2010] EWCA Civ 1221, [2010] 2 C.L.C. 705; *Titan Steel Wheels Ltd v Royal Bank of Scotland Plc* [2010] EWHC 211 (Comm), [2010] 2 Lloyd's Rep. 92 at [98]; *Raiffeisen Zentralbank Österreich AG v Royal Bank of Scotland Plc* [2010] EWHC 1392 (Comm), [2011] 1 Lloyd's Rep. 123 at [316]–[317]; *Marz Ltd v Bank of Scotland Plc* [2017] EWHC 3618 (Ch) at [240]–[275], distinguishing *First Tower Trustees Ltd v CDS (Superstores International) Ltd* [2017] 4 W.L.R. 73 at [31]–[32]. In *Springwell*, the

Court of Appeal held (at [181]–[182]) that "no representation" and "non-reliance" provisions of the relevant contract were caught by s.3 of the Misrepresentation Act 1967 because they were "an attempt retrospectively to alter the character and effect of what had gone before and so in substance an attempt to exclude or restrict liability" (citing Christopher Clarke J. in *Raiffeisen*, above, at [315], who also said, at [314], that "the key question ... is whether the clause attempts to rewrite history or parts company with reality"). Nevertheless, the Court of Appeal held that the terms were reasonable when taken in context and in the light of the fact that the principal behind Springwell was a sophisticated investor in emerging market investments who was conscious of the risks involved. cf. *Thornbridge Ltd v Barclays Bank Plc* [2015] EWHC 3430 (QB) at [105] (appeal dismissed, Unreported January 9, 2018), where H.H.J. Moulder, sitting as a judge of the High Court, said "the test is not whether the clause attempts to rewrite history or parts company with reality. The first step is to determine as a matter of construction whether the terms define the basis upon which the parties were transacting business or whether they were clauses inserted as a means of evading liability"; *Sears v Minco Plc* [2016] EWHC 433 (Ch) at [74]–[84] (see criticism of the reasoning in these cases in *First Tower Trustees Ltd v CDS (Superstores International) Ltd* [2018] EWCA Civ 1396 at [66], [110]). For a non-exhaustive list of factors that may be taken into account when determining whether a "basis clause" or an "exclusion clause" for the purposes of the Unfair Contract Terms Act 1977 or s.3 of the Misrepresentation Act 1967, see *Carney v NM Rothschild & Sons Ltd* [2018] EWHC 958 (Comm) at [94] (at [97]–[100] the court also considered the effect of "basis clauses" in the context of the "unfair relationship" provisions in ss.140A and 140B of the Consumer Credit Act 1974). It should be noted that different, more stringent, rules apply in the case of fraud: see Vol.I, para.15-150.

[806] Consumer Rights Act 2015 (CRA 2015) Pt 2. Note also CRA 2015 s.50(1), which effectively makes anything that is said or written to a consumer about the bank, or the service provided by the bank, a term of any contract to supply the service as between bank and consumer if relied upon by the consumer: s.50(2) allows the bank to qualify any pre-contractual representations, but only if it does so on the "same occasion" or if it represents a "change to [what was said or written] that has been expressly agreed between the consumer and the trader". See further, para.38-572 below.

## Money laundering

*Replace footnote 814 with:*

**34-261** [814] Hence the Court of Appeal reversed Hamblen J.'s decision to give summary judgment to the bank on the customer's claim for damages for alleged loss suffered as a result of the bank's breach of duty in failing to carry out his payment instructions. Delivering judgment at the trial of the action (see [2012] EWHC 1283 (QB)), Supperstone J. dismissed the customer's claim, holding that (1) there was an implied term in the banking contract that permitted the bank, because it suspected money laundering, to delay the execution of the customer's payment instructions until it received consent under POCA (at [45], [236]); (2) there was no duty on the bank to provide the customer with information in relation to the delay and that, in any event, there was an implied term in the banking contract that permitted the bank to refuse to provide that information where doing so might contravene its duties under POCA (at [169], [171]–[172], [238]). For related proceedings, see [2011] EWCA Civ 1154 (on disclosure of the names of employees who had reported their suspicions); [2011] EWCA Civ 1669 (on amendment to allege bad faith on the part of bank employees). See also *Lonsdale v National Westminster Bank plc* [2018] EWHC 1843 (QB) at [54]–[66], where the judge refused to strike out and/or summarily dismiss the claimant customer's claim that the defendant bank acted in breach of contract by freezing his accounts. The judge stressed (at [64]) that whether or not the bank had a genuine suspicion was a primary fact, which the customer had put in issue, that required to be proved by evidence that would be tested at trial. The judge also refused to strike out and/or summarily dismiss the customer's claims against the bank (a) for breach of his rights under the Data Protection Act 1998 to see personal data held by the bank, and (b) for defamation (stating, at [131]–[134], that absolute privilege for defamatory words should not be extended to cover reports to the National Crime Agency (NCA), but that a bank which reports suspicious activity to the NCA would have the benefit of qualified privilege).

### *(v) Banks and Undue Influence*

## O'Brien guidelines in practice

*Replace footnote 834 with:*

**34-268** [834] *Royal Bank of Scotland Plc v Etridge (No.2)* [2001] UKHL 44, [2002] 2 A.C. 773 at [51]. This probably goes further than contemplated in *Barclays Bank Plc v O'Brien* [1994] 1 A.C. 180, since Lord Browne-Wilkinson considered (at 197) that it would only be the exceptional case in which the bank should not only advise the surety to obtain independent legal advice but should insist that she do so. See also the *Standards of Lending Practice for Personal Customers 2017* (para.34-222 above) at p.7 (Account maintenance and servicing), point 8, and p.11 (Customer vulnerability), the *Standards of Lend-*

*ing Practice for Business Customers 2017*(para.34-223) at pp.6–7 (Product sale), points 13 and 14, pp.9–10 (Product execution), point 6; and pp.14–15 (Vulnerability), and the *Standards of Lending Practice for Business Customers 2019* (para.34-223A) at pp.7–8 (Product sale), points 13 and 14, pp.10–11 (Product execution), point 7; and pp.18–19 (Vulnerability).

## Nature of the transaction

*Replace footnote 848 with:*

848 At [49]. See *Mahon v FBN Bank (UK) Ltd* [2011] EWHC 1432 (Ch), [2011] B.P.I.R. 1029 (bank still put on inquiry despite wife being sole shareholder and company secretary); *Syndicate Bank v Dansingani* [2019] EWHC 3439 (Ch) (bank put on inquiry despite husband and wife being directors and shareholders of debtor company); cf. *National Westminster Bank Plc v Alfano* [2012] EWHC 1020 (QB) at [54] (guarantors were directors or senior managers of debtor company). For loan made to family partnership, see *O'Neill v Ulster Bank Ltd* [2015] NICA 64, [2016] B.P.I.R. 126 at [17] (arguable that situation analogous to where wife stands surety for loan made to company in which she is a shareholder). **34-272**

## Reasonable steps that a bank should take

*Replace footnote 852 with:*

852 This includes the case where the certificate is given by a legal executive, provided that the advice was independent and was given with the authority of the legal executive's principal: *Barclays Bank Plc v Coleman* [2001] Q.B. 20 at [78], affirmed [2001] UKHL 44, [2002] 2 A.C. 773 at [292]. The mere fact that the wife has seen a solicitor is not enough without confirmation that he has given her independent advice: *Lloyds TSB Bank Plc v Holdgate* [2002] EWCA Civ 1543, [2003] H.L.R. 25; *First National Bank Plc v Achampong* [2003] EWCA Civ 487, [2004] 1 F.C.R. 18; cf. *Gov and Co of the Bank of Scotland v Hill* [2002] EWCA Civ 1081, [2002] 29 E.G.C.S. 152. See also *UCB Corporate Services Ltd v Williams* [2002] EWCA Civ 555, [2002] 3 F.C.R. 448 (bank did not even know wife had seen a solicitor); *Syndicate Bank v Dansingani* [2019] EWHC 3439 (Ch) (wife's confirmation to bank that implications of guarantee were known to her, and that she did not need legal advice, was merely an example of husband's assertion of dominance and control over her financial affairs). **34-273**

## Future transactions

*Replace footnote 859 with:*

859 See also the *Standards of Lending Practice for Personal Customers* (para.34-222 above) at p.7 (Account maintenance and servicing), point 8, and the *Standards of Lending Practice for Business Customers 2017* (para.34-223 above) at pp.9–10 (Product execution), point 6, and the *Standards of Lending Practice for Business Customers 2019* (para.34-223A) at pp.10–11 (Product execution), point 7. **34-274**

## Rescission

*Replace footnote 868 with:*

868 Subject to the usual bars, including that restitutio in integrum is impossible (but it need not be precise); there has been affirmation or delay (*First National Bank Plc v Walker* [2001] 1 F.C.R. 21, CA); there has been intervention of a bona fide purchaser for value without notice (*CIBC Mortgages Plc v Pitt* [1994] 1 A.C. 200). See generally, Vol.I, para.8-103. If the property subject to the security is jointly owned by a husband and wife then, even though the security may not be enforceable against the wife, it may be against the husband, and so the court may still order the property to be sold, under the Trusts of Land and Appointment of Trustees Act 1996 s.14, in order to realise the husband's share: see *First National Bank Plc v Achampong* [2003] EWCA Civ 487, [2004] 1 F.C.R. 18 (noted by Thompson [2003] Conv. 314). See also *Edwards v Lloyds TSB* [2004] EWHC 1745 (Ch); *Santander UK Plc v Fletcher* [2018] EWHC 2778 (Ch). **34-277**

### *(vi) Banks as Constructive Trustees*

## Dishonest assistance

*Replace footnote 903 with:*

903 *Sinclair Investment Holdings SA v Versailles Trade Finance Ltd* [2007] EWHC 915 (Ch), [2007] 2 All E.R. (Comm) 993 at [120]–[125], where Rimer J. stressed that the remedy was personal and not **34-284**

proprietary. Sometimes an account of profits will be awarded against an accessory who profits from the assistance: see *Novoship (UK) Ltd v Mikhaylyuk* [2014] EWCA Civ 908, [2015] Q.B. 499, requiring a sufficiently direct causal connection between the accessory's gain and the dishonest assistance (noted by P. Davies (2015) 131 L.Q.R. 173; P. Devonshire [2015] C.L.J. 222); cf. *Akita Holdings Ltd v AG of Turks and Caicos Islands* [2017] UKPC 7, [2017] A.C. 590 and *Lifeplan Australia Friendly Society Ltd v Ancient Order of Foresters in Victoria Friendly Society Ltd* [2017] FCAFC 74, (2017) 250 F.C.R. 1 for approaches conflicting with *Novoship* (noted by P.G. Turner [2018] C.L.J. 255), and also *Ancient Order of Foresters in Victoria Friendly Society Ltd v Lifeplan Australia Friendly Society Ltd* [2018] HCA 43, (2018) 360 A.L.R. 1, HC of Aust (noted by A.B. Douglas (2019) 135 L.Q.R. 214). For further discussion of the remedies available against a dishonest assister, see S.B. Elliott and C. Mitchell (2004) 67 M.L.R. 16; S. Baughen [2007] L.M.C.L.Q. 545, 556–558; P. Ridge (2008) 124 L.Q.R. 445.

**Requirements for accessory liability**

*Replace footnote 904 with:*

**34-285** [904] As summarised by Cresswell J. in *Bankgesellschaft Berlin AG v Makris* Unreported January 22, 1999. See also summary in *FM Capital Partners Ltd v Marino* [2018] EWHC 1768 (Comm) at [82]–[85]; and in *Magner v Royal Bank of Scotland International Ltd* [2020] UKPC 5 at [10].

*(iii) Accessory or assister*

*Replace paragraph with:*

**34-289** The person upon whom liability is to be imposed must as a matter of fact have been accessory or assisted in the misfeasance or breach of trust. What is sufficient for "assistance" is "simply conduct which in fact assists the fiduciary to commit the act which constitutes the breach of trust or fiduciary duty".[914a] In many cases banks will not find it easy to avoid the charge that they were accessory to or assisted in a breach of trust, especially one that involves the fraudulent misapplication of trust funds. The provision of banking services to persons behaving in a fraudulent or improper manner often exposes a bank to potential liability under this head. The misapplied trust funds will usually be held in bank accounts and moved between bank accounts. The banks that hold those accounts, as well as any other bank involved as an intermediary in the funds transfer process, run the risk of being accused of providing assistance to the dishonest fiduciary. For example, payment by a bank on the instructions of fraudulent directors of a company of moneys of the company to another person may be such assistance.[915] More worrying still, at least from the bank's point of view, is that the mere provision of advisory services to the fiduciary can be deemed "assistance" where there is a sufficient causative link between that advice and the breach of trust,[916] even though the bank itself never comes into contact with the misapplied funds.[917] It is because the "assistance" net can be cast so widely that attention has focused so crucially on the level of mental intent required the person giving assistance for him to be held liable under this head of constructive trusteeship. Banks and other financial institutions involved in millions of money transmission activities on a daily basis, and so particularly vulnerable to the charge of "assistance", have always argued that the level of mental intent should be high.

[914a] *Madoff Securities International v Raven* [2013] EWHC 3147 (Comm) at [351].

[915] See, e.g. *Selangor United Rubber Estates Ltd v Cradock (No.3)* [1968] 1 W.L.R. 1555; *Karak v Rubber Co Ltd v Burden (No.2)* [1972] 1 W.L.R. 602.

[916] See *Brown v Bennett* [1999] B.C.C. 525 at 533.

[917] In *Casio Computer Co Ltd v Sayo* [2001] EWCA Civ 661 at [15], the Court of Appeal held that loss caused by the breach of fiduciary duty is recoverable from the accessory without the need to show a *precise* causal link between the assistance and the loss. See also *Group Seven Ltd v Notable Services LLP* [2019] EWCA Civ 614 at [110]: "On authority, the matter must be approached in two stages. It must be shown that the conduct in fact assisted the breach of trust, and that the loss directly resulted from

the breach of trust. The test at the first stage is that the assistance given must be more than minimal ... The test at the second stage is that the loss in fact resulted from the breach of trust ... What must be shown is that the conduct assisted the breach of trust and that but for the breach of trust the loss would not have occurred". In *Bilta (UK) Ltd v Natwest Markets Plc* [2020] EWHC 546 (Ch) at [162]–[174] (an unusual case, applying *Alpha Sim v CAZ Distribution Services* [2014] EWHC 207 (Ch)), it was held that the assistance of the defendant banks was through purchases by its traders of carbon credits from an intermediary that had purchased the credits from the claimant companies whose directors had acted in breach of fiduciary duty.

### *(iv) Dishonesty*

*Replace footnote 922 with:*

[922] At 389. Recklessness is not equivalent to dishonesty but it can be a sign of dishonesty: see Lord Nicholls at 389–391, as interpreted by Lewison L.J. in *Clydesdale Bank Plc v Workman* [2016] EWCA Civ 73, [2016] P.N.L.R. 18 at [48]–[53]. Lord Nicholls said that "[c]arelessness is not dishonesty" (above). See also *Ivey v Genting Casinos (UK) Ltd* [2017] UKSC 67, [2017] 3 W.L.R. 1212 at [62]; *Singularis Holdings Ltd (In Liquidation) v Daiwa Capital Markets Europe Ltd* [2017] EWHC 257 (Ch) at [147], affirmed on other grounds [2018] EWCA Civ 84 and [2019] UKSC 50. **34-291**

*Replace paragraph with:*

Lord Nicholls expressly referred to an "objective standard" of dishonesty. But he also spoke of honesty having "a strong subjective element" and that, for the most part, "dishonesty is to be equated with a conscious impropriety". This left room for doubt and uncertainty as to the precise test to be adopted when assessing whether or not an accessory has been dishonest.[923] However, the "now clearly established"[924] test of dishonesty was explained in *Barlow Clowes International Ltd v Eurotrust International Ltd* by Lord Hoffmann as follows[925]: **34-292**

> "Although a dishonest state of mind is a subjective mental state, the standard by which the law determines whether it is dishonest is objective. If by ordinary standards a defendant's mental state would be characterised as dishonest, it is irrelevant that the defendant judges by different standards. Their Lordships held this to be a correct state of the law and their Lordships agree."

In *Ivy v Genting Casinos (UK) Ltd*,[926] where the Supreme Court (obiter) adopted a unified test of dishonesty in both criminal and civil law, Lord Hughes acknowledged that the test of dishonesty was as set out by Lord Nicholls in *Royal Brunei Airlines Sdn Bhd v Tan*, and by Lord Hoffmann in *Barlow Clowes*, and continued:

> "When dishonesty is in question the fact-finding tribunal must first ascertain (subjectively) the actual state of the individual's knowledge or belief as to the facts. The reasonableness or otherwise of his belief is a matter of evidence (often in practice determinative) going to whether he held the belief, but it is not an additional requirement that his belief must be reasonable; the question is whether it is genuinely held. When once his actual state of mind as to knowledge or belief as to facts is established, the question whether his conduct was honest or dishonest is to be determined by the fact-finder by applying the (objective) standards of ordinary decent people. There is no requirement that the defendant must appreciate that what he has done is, by those standards, dishonest."

In *Barlow Clowes*,[926a] the Privy Council observed that it was sufficient for the defendant to have entertained a "clear suspicion" that monies were being misappropriated from the company, and then to have made a decision not to ask questions about the transactions he was assisting. It did not matter that the defendant did not know that the monies that were being paid away were held on trust or even what a trust meant, or that he did not know the precise involvement of the fraudsters. It was enough for liability that the defendant suspected that the relevant individuals had no right to use the company's money for speculative investments of their own, and yet he chose not to inquire.

[923] In *Twinsectra Ltd v Yardley* [2002] UKHL 12, [2002] 2 A.C. 164 a majority of the House of Lords held that a "combined test" of dishonesty was to be applied in a case of dishonest assistance; in other words, before there could be a finding of dishonesty it must be established that the defendant's conduct was dishonest by the ordinary standards of reasonable and honest people (the objective element) and that he himself realised that by those standards his conduct was dishonest (the subjective element).

[924] *Ivey v Genting Casinos (UK) Ltd* [2017] UKSC 67, [2017] 3 W.L.R. 1212 at [62], per Lord Hughes (obiter).

[925] [2005] UKPC 37, [2006] 1 W.L.R. 1476 at [10]. Lord Hoffmann was also a party to the *Twinsectra* decision (above). The objective test was also approved in *Abou-Rahman v Abacha* [2006] EWCA Civ 1492, [2007] 1 Lloyd's Rep. 115 at [59] (Arden L.J.); *Starglade Properties Ltd v Nash* [2010] EWCA Civ 1314 at [32] (Morritt C.); *Magner v Royal Bank of Scotland International Ltd* [2020] UKPC 5 at [10]. Note Gloster L.J.'s dissent in *UBS AG (London Branch) v Kommunale Wasserwrke Leipzig GmbH* [2017] EWCA Civ 1567 at [347] on ground that it was "impractical and unreal to introduce into commercial transactions the moral standards of the vicarage": Lord Briggs and Hamblen L.J. (the majority) held at [113] that "[w]here a party to an intended transaction deals with the other party's agent secretly and behind his back, and dishonestly assists that agent to abuse his fiduciary duties to the other party so as to bring that transaction about, then the first party's conscience may be affected not merely by the particular form of abuse by the agent of which it actually knew, but also by any other abuse [in this case, a bribe] which the agent chose to employ to bring about the transaction with the first party".

[926] [2017] UKSC 67, [2017] 3 W.L.R. 1212 at [74]. The *Ivey* test was adopted by the Court of Appeal in *Group Seven Ltd v Notable Services LLP* [2019] EWCA Civ 614, [56]–[60], a dishonest assistance case where knowledge, in this context, was confined to actual and blind-eye knowledge for the purpose of the subjective first stage of the test (the imputation of blind-eye knowledge requires there to be (i) the existence of a suspicion, grounded on specific facts, that certain other facts may exist, and (ii) a conscious decision to refrain from taking any steps to confirm their existence): the existence of mere suspicions falling short of blind-eye knowledge, and the weight (if any) to be attributed to them, were matters to be taken into account at the objective second stage of the test. Obiter, the Court of Appeal (at [103]) took the provisional view that the simplicity of the two stage *Ivey* test for dishonesty should not be complicated by the introduction, as a matter of law, of a "minimum content of knowledge" requirement. Other cases where the *Ivey* test has been applied to dishonest assistance claims include *Bilta (UK) Ltd v Natwest Markets Plc* [2020] EWHC 546 (Ch) at [160]; *Payroller Ltd (In Liquidation) v Little Panda Consultants Ltd* [2020] EWHC 391 (QB) at [66]; *Iranian Offshore Engineering & Construction Co v Dean Investment Holdings SA* [2019] EWHC 472 (Comm) at [153]; *FM Capital Partners Ltd v Marino* [2018] EWHC 1768 (Comm) at [82] (and see [2019] EWHC 725 (Comm) for issues arising from the taking of an account in relation to equitable compensation for dishonest assistance in this case); *Carr v Formation Group Plc* [2018] EWHC 3116 (Ch) at [20]–[28] (expert evidence of market practice not admissible in relation to objective standard as to dishonesty); *Autogas (Europe) Ltd v Ochocki* [2018] EWHC 2345 (Ch) at [13]–[14]. In *Magner v Royal Bank of Scotland International Ltd* [2020] UKPC 5 at [11], Lord Hodge stated that the Solicitors Act 1974 s.85 "does not release a bank or building society from liability for the dishonest assistance of the misappropriation by a solicitor of his clients' funds. But it discloses an intention by Parliament that, as a general rule, a banker is entitled to act upon the solicitor's instructions relating to a client account without inquiring into the propriety of those instructions". Lord Hodge added that "[t]he banker does not owe duties to the solicitor's clients as a trustee of their funds".

[926a] [2005] UKPC 37, [2006] 1 W.L.R. 1476 at [28]. See also *Bilta (UK) Ltd v Natwest Markets Plc* [2020] EWHC 546 (Ch) at [236]–[237]; *Payroller Ltd (In Liquidation) v Little Panda Consultants Ltd* [2020] EWHC 391 (QB) at [66]–[69] ("[i]t is sufficient that he knew or at least turned a blind eye to the fact that the funds being received ... involved a breach of fiduciary duty on the part of the directors").

## Knowing receipt

*Replace footnote 928 with:*

**34-293** [928] *Arthur v Att-Gen of the Turks and Caicos Islands* [2012] UKPC 30 at [37]. But for the purpose of claiming a contribution from another wrongdoer under the Civil Liability (Contribution) Act 1978, the remedy for knowing receipt is deemed to be "compensatory": see *Charter Plc v City Index Ltd* [2007] EWCA Civ 1382, [2008] 2 W.L.R. 950 at [32]. Whether the liabilities of knowing assistants and knowing recipients are distinct or whether knowing assistance and knowing receipt establish one overarching liability to account is uncertain: contrast *Novoship (UK) Ltd v Mikhaylyuk* [2014] EWCA Civ 908, [2015] Q.B. 499 with *Akita Holdings Ltd v AG of Turks and Caicos Islands* [2017] UKPC 7, [2017] A.C. 590 and *Lifeplan Australia Friendly Society Ltd v Ancient Order of Foresters in Victoria Friendly Society Ltd* [2017] FCAFC 74, (2017) 250 F.C.R. 1 (and see P.G. Turner [2018] C.L.J. 255), and also with

*Ancient Order of Foresters in Victoria Friendly Society Ltd v Lifeplan Australia Friendly Society Ltd* [2018] HCA 43, (2018) 360 ALR 1, HC of Aust (noted by A.B. Douglas (2019) 135 L.Q.R. 214).

## Requirements of recipient liability

*Replace footnote 929 with:*

929 [1994] 2 All E.R. 685 at 700. See also *Iranian Offshore Engineering & Construction Co v Dean Investment Holdings SA* [2019] EWHC 472 (Comm) at [175]. On the requirement that the disposal of the assets must be in breach of duty, see *Brown v Bennett* [1999] B.C.L.C. 649, 655, as interpreted by Nugee J. (obiter) in *Courtwood Holdings SA v Woodley Properties Ltd* [2018] EWHC 2163 (Ch) at [190] ("it is a prerequisite of a claim in knowing receipt that the disposition to the recipient is 'in breach of trust', that is that the disposition is itself a breach of trust (or breach of fiduciary duty)". On the question of tracing, the court may decide that funds held in the defendant's bank account were the traceable proceeds of funds originally held by the claimant, notwithstanding that the claimant cannot prove every stage in the process by which the funds were ultimately transferred to the defendant, see *Relfo Ltd (In Liquidation) v Varsani* [2014] EWCA Civ 360, especially at [56]–[68] (noted by S. Watterson [2014] C.L.J. 496). **34-294**

## Unconscionability as the test of liability

*Replace footnote 943 with:*

943 [2001] Ch. 437; the *Akindele* test of "unconscionability" has been endorsed by the Court of Appeal in the following cases: *Criterion Properties Plc v Stratford UK Properties Ltd* [2002] EWCA Civ 1883, [2003] 1 W.L.R. 2108 at [20]–[39] (affirmed on different grounds: [2004] UKHL 28, [2004] 1 W.L.R. 1846); *Charter Plc v City Index Ltd* [2007] EWCA Civ 1382, [2008] Ch. 313 at [8]; *Uzinterimpex JSC v Standard Bank Plc* [2008] EWCA Civ 819, [2008] 2 Lloyd's Rep. 456 at [37]–[46]; and, following agreement of the parties, by the Privy Council in *Arthur v Att-Gen of the Turks and Caicos Islands* [2012] UKPC 30 at [33]–[36] (stressing the difference between proprietary and personal remedies). See also *Brent LBC v Davies* [2018] EWHC 2214 (Ch) at [558]–[563]. **34-302**

*Replace footnote 949 with:*

949 In *Papamichael v National Westminster Bank Plc* [2003] EWHC 164 (Comm), [2003] 1 Lloyd's Rep. 341 at [247], Judge Chambers Q.C. treated actual knowledge as a necessary condition for liability. In *Crown Dilmun v Sutton* [2004] EWHC 52 (Ch), [2004] 1 B.C.L.C. 468 at [200], Peter Smith J., reluctantly applying the Court of Appeal decision in *Criterion Properties*, held that "attribution of knowledge is not enough. It must be unconscionable for the ... defendant to retain the benefit". In *Starglade Properties Ltd v Nash* Unreported January 26, 2010, N. Strauss Q.C. (sitting as a deputy judge of the High Court) said, at [57], that unconscionability provides "a flexible test, which requires the court to consider what is right, taking into account the nature and extent of the defendant's knowledge and all the circumstances relating to the receipt. Actual knowledge which could put a reasonable man on enquiry, coupled with a failure to enquire, may suffice ...". (Although the Court of Appeal reversed the deputy judge's decision on the claim based on dishonest assistance (see para.34-296 above), there was no appeal against his decision on the knowing receipt claim: see [2010] EWCA Civ 1314 at [6].) In *Law Society of England and Wales v Habitable Concepts Ltd* [2010] EWHC 1449 (Ch), Norris J. held, at [16], that "[t]he unexplained nature of the bank credit and its sheer scale would call for enquiry to be made by anyone who wished to deal with the credit with a clear conscience". In *Armstrong DLW GmbH v Winnington Networks Ltd* [2012] EWHC 10 (Ch), S. Morris Q.C. (sitting as a deputy judge of the High Court) said, at [132], that, in a commercial context, *Baden* types (1) to (3) knowledge on the part of a defendant renders receipt of trust property unconscionable (adding that it is not necessary to show that the defendant realised that the transaction was "obviously" or "probably" in breach of trust or fraudulent; the possibility of impropriety or the claimant's interest is sufficient); and that *Baden* types (4) and (5) knowledge also renders receipt "unconscionable" but only if, on the facts actually known to the defendant, a reasonable person would either have appreciated that the transfer was probably in breach of trust or would have made inquiries or sought advice which would have revealed the probability of the breach of trust. In *Crédit Agricole Corp and Investment Bank v Papadimitriou* [2015] UKPC 13 at [20], where the (different) issue was whether the appellant bank was a bona fide purchaser of assets without constructive notice of an existing proprietary interest in them, the Privy Council stated that "[t]he bank must make inquiries if there is a serious possibility of a third party having such a right or, put in another way, if the facts known to the bank would give a reasonable banker in the position of the particular banker serious cause to question the propriety of the transaction". Note Lord Sumption's (at [33]) statement that "[w]hether a person claims to be a bona fide purchaser of assets without notice of a prior interest in them, or disputes a claim to make him accountable as a constructive trustee on the footing of a knowing receipt, the question what constitutes constructive notice or knowledge is the same". See also *Thanakharn Kasikorn Thai Chamkat (Mahachon) v Akai Holdings Ltd* (2010) H.K.C.F.A.R. 479 at [135], where Lord Neuberger, delivering the judgment of the Hong Kong Court of Final Appeal, said that the test of **34-303**

"unconscionability" for knowing receipt was "effectively identical" to that of "irrationality" for determining whether a defaulting agent has apparent authority, and that "equity would follow the law" absent special circumstances (explained and criticised by R. Lee and L. Ho in (2012) 75 M.L.R. 91: for a return to the orthodox "unreasonableness" test as to when a third party is put on inquiry in a case of apparent authority, see *East Asia Co Ltd v PT Satria Tirtatama Energindo* [2012] UKPC 30). In *Relfo Ltd (In Liquidation) v Varsani* [2012] EWHC 2168 (Ch) at [79]–[80] (affirmed [2014] EWCA Civ 360), Sales J. said "one needs to be a little careful in using this formulation" (i.e. unconscionability), and preferred to speak in terms of the "relevant knowledge" identified by Millett J. in *Agip (Africa) Ltd v Jackson* [1990] 1 Ch. 265, 291F–G, when referring to the first of the two main types of knowing receipt (see para.34-295 above). In *Arthur v Att-Gen of the Turks and Caicos Islands* [2012] UKPC 30 at [40], Sir Terence Etherton, delivering the advice of the Privy Council, said "Knowing receipt in the *Akindele* sense is ... not merely absence of notice but unconscionable conduct amounting to equitable fraud. It is a classic example of lack of *bona fides*". In *Payroller Ltd (In Liquidation) v Little Panda Consultants Ltd* [2020] EWHC 391 (QB) at [81], Freedman J. said "[i]t is not necessary for the defendant to know all the facts associated with the wrong and it is sufficient that he knew enough of the facts surrounding the misapplication of the property to make it unconscionable for him to retain the benefit of the receipt".

## *(vii) Duty of Secrecy*

### Duty of secrecy

*Replace paragraph with:*

34-306 The relationship of banker and customer is of a confidential nature and, as a general rule, the banker is under a duty of secrecy. The leading English case is *Tournier v National Provincial Bank*, where Atkin L.J.[958] observed that this duty applies not only to information derived by the banker from the account, but extends also to information obtained from other sources, if the occasion upon which the information is obtained arises out of the banking relationship of the bank and its customer. It does not, however, preclude the bank from referring to or disclosing information which the enquirer can readily obtain from another source, such as a caution in bankruptcy proceedings and, presumably, a caveat.[959] Generally, though, the bank's duty of confidentiality does not terminate on the closing of the account and, presumably, survives the death of the customer. In *Tournier's* case the Court of Appeal indicated, further, that the banker may disclose such information in the following cases[960]:

(a) when there is compulsion by law, e.g. when the banker is obliged to give evidence in legal proceedings[961];
(b) when public interest calls for disclosure, e.g. when during war time the customer's activities disclose dealings with the enemy[962]; and
(c) when the disclosure is necessary in the banker's own interest, e.g. when, in order to claim repayment of an overdraft, he has to disclose that the customer's account is overdrawn.[963]

Finally, *Tournier's* case indicates that the banker is entitled to give information when expressly or impliedly authorised so to do by the customer.[964] There is an established trade practice that banks provide each other with credit references relating to their customers. In the past banks justified this practice on the ground that their customers gave their implied consent to it. However, in *Turner v Royal Bank of Scotland Plc*,[965] a case where the customer had a personal account with the bank, the Court of Appeal held that this practice was not sufficiently "notorious" (i.e. known to the bank's customers) to make it an implied term of the banker–customer contract.[966] The Court of Appeal ignored the fact that the customer also held a business account at the bank, and so it is unclear whether *Turner* applies to business customers.[967]

958 [1924] 1 K.B. 461, 485, and see Bankes L.J. at 474. In *Tournier* the bank's duty of confidentiality

was held to be an implied term of the bank–customer contract; alternatively, it may arise from an express assurance of confidentiality by the bank (see, e.g. *Primary Group (UK) Ltd v Royal Bank of Scotland Plc* [2014] EWHC 1082 (Ch), where "negotiating damages" awarded, applying the now preferred nomenclature of *Morris-Garner v One Step (Support) Ltd* [2018] UKSC 20 at [3]), or out of an equitable obligation of confidence (see, e.g. *CF Partners (UK) LLP v Barclays Bank Plc* [2014] EWHC 3049 (Ch), where "negotiating damages" awarded). When dealing with information which would, in any event, attract confidentiality at common law, and there exists also an express obligation of confidentiality, the better view is that some greater weight should be given to that obligation of confidentiality: *Saab v Dangate Consulting Ltd* [2019] EWHC 1558 (Comm) at [151] (dealing with the defence of public interest disclosure). For case law relating to the prohibition of disclosure to other companies in the same group, see *Bank of Tokyo v Karoon* [1987] A.C. 45n, CA, 53–54; *Bhogal v Punjab National Bank* [1988] 2 All E.R. 296, 305, CA. See the *Standards of Lending Practice for Personal Customers* (para.34-222 above) at pp.7 (Account maintenance and servicing: "Firms will maintain the security of customers' data but may share information about the day-to-day running of a customer's account(s), including positive data, with credit reference agencies where the firm has agreed to follow the principles of reciprocity. [CONC 5]"), and for the same guidance with regard to business customers, see the Standards of Lending Practice for Business Customers 2017 (para.34-223 above) at pp.9–10 (Product execution), point 5 and the *Standards of Lending Practice for Business Customers 2019* (para.34-223A) at pp.10–11 (Product execution), point 6. See also the *Lending Code*, revised 2nd edn (2014), para.[15] (customer's personal information to be treated as private and confidential).

959 *Christofi v Barclays Bank Plc* [1998] 1 W.L.R. 1245; affirmed [2000] 1 W.L.R. 937.

960 "Where the case is within one of the qualifications to the duty of confidence, the duty, *ex hypothesi*, does not exist": *El Jawhary v Bank of Credit and Commerce International SA* [1993] B.C.L.C. 396 at 400, per Nicholls V.-C. See also *Barclays Bank Plc v Taylor* [1989] 1 W.L.R. 1066 at 1074, per Lord Donaldson M.R.

961 Consider, e.g. the banker's duty of making payment to sequestrators and of disclosing to them the state of the customer's account: *Bucknell v Bucknell* [1969] 1 W.L.R. 1204; *Eckman v Midland Bank Ltd* [1973] Q.B. 519. For another instance of legal compulsion, see, e.g. the Income Tax Act 2007 s.771. See also the Bankers Books Evidence Act 1879 s.7, and the analysis in *Williams v Summerfield* [1972] 2 Q.B. 512; and in *R. v Marlborough St Metropolitan Stipendiary Magistrate Ex p. Simpson* [1980] Crim. L.R. 305; Police and Criminal Evidence Act 1984 s.9; the Companies Act 1985 ss.434(2), 452(1A); Insolvency Act 1986 ss.236, 366; Financial Services and Markets Act 2000 Pt XI. Note that disclosure of such information by way of a discovery will be ordered, as a matter of justice, in respect of proceedings in which the bank's customer is sued in fraud by a third party: *A v C* [1980] 2 All E.R. 347; *Bankers Trust Co v Shapira* [1980] 3 All E.R. 353; *C v S* [1999] Lloyd's Rep. Bank. 26 (giving important guidance to banks served with a disclosure order and also concerned with prosecution for "tipping off": two "tipping off" offences are now to be found in the Proceeds of Crime Act 2002 s.333A, with the separate offence of prejudicing an investigation in s.342; see also *Bank of Scotland v A Ltd* [2001] EWCA Civ 52, [2001] 1 W.L.R. 751; *Tayeb v HSBC Bank Plc* [2004] EWHC 1529 (QB), [2004] 4 All E.R. 1024). And note that where the bank is compelled to disclose, it is not under a duty to oppose the orders or to notify the customer: *Barclays Bank v Taylor* [1989] 1 W.L.R. 1066, CA. A bank is likewise not in breach of its duty of confidentiality where it produces documents as ordered in a subpoena duces tecum (now called a "witness summons" under the Civil Procedure Rules 1998): *Robertson v Canadian Imperial Bank of Commerce* [1994] 1 W.L.R. 824, PC.

Legislation to combat money laundering and the financing of terrorist activities is particularly draconian. A bank commits an offence if it fails to disclose to the National Crime Agency its knowledge or suspicion, or that it has reasonable grounds for knowledge or suspicion, that a customer is engaged in money laundering or terrorist offences (Proceeds of Crime Act 2002 s.330; Terrorism Act 2000 s.21A, as inserted by the Anti-terrorism, Crime and Security Act 2001 Sch.2 Pt 3). The threshold for suspicion is low: the bank only has to consider that there is a more than fanciful possibility that the relevant facts exist (*K Ltd v National Westminster Bank Plc* [2006] EWCA Civ 1039, [2007] 1 W.L.R. 311 at [16], applied in *Shah v HSBC Private Bank (UK) Ltd* [2009] EWHC 79 (QB), [2009] 1 Lloyd's Rep. 328 at [45], reversed [2010] EWCA Civ 31, [2011] 1 All E.R. (Comm) 67, but *K Ltd* applied at [21], and also applied by Supperstone J. at the trial of the action: [2012] EWHC 1283 (QB) at [67]–[69])). Subjectively, the bank may itself know or suspect the customer is engaged in money laundering or terrorist offences but, even if it does not, it may objectively have reasonable grounds for such knowledge or suspicion. Such disclosure is a "protected disclosure", i.e. it "is not to be taken to breach any restriction on the disclosure of information (however arising)" (Proceeds of Crime Act 2002 s.337(1); Terrorism Act 2000 s.21B(1), as inserted). In general terms, a customer who opens an account at a bank in the UK must be taken to have accepted and be entitled to assume that the bank will act in accordance with applicable anti-money laundering and terrorism legislation (*Tayeb v HSBC Bank Plc* [2004] EWHC 1529 (Comm), [2004] 4 All E.R. 1024 at [57], per Colman J.).

A bank (the paying bank) may be granted a *Norwich Pharmacal* order against another bank (the beneficiary's bank) compelling it to disclose information in relation to the identity of certain of its customers who were beneficiaries of electronic payments made as a result of the paying bank's own mistakes, e.g. making a duplicate payment, selection of an incorrect mandate or insertion of an incorrect account number, see *Santander UK Plc v National Westminster Bank Plc* [2014] EWHC 2626 (Ch);

*Santander UK Plc v Royal Bank of Scotland Plc* [2015] EWHC 2560 (Ch) at [11]–[17], but with criticism of the ruling in *Santander UK Plc v National Westminster Bank Plc*, above, that a claim in unjust enrichment was a wrong capable of justifying a *Norwich Pharmacal* order (noted by M. Campbell [2016] L.M.C.L.Q. 42).

962 For recent cases recognising the existence of an independent ground of disclosure under this qualification, see *Price Waterhouse v BCCI Holdings (Luxembourg) SA* [1992] B.C.L.C. 583; *Douglas v Pindling* [1996] A.C. 890, PC; *Pharaon v Bank of Credit and Commerce International SA (In Liquidation)* [1998] 4 All E.R. 455. For earlier tentative (and obiter) recognition, see *Libyan Arab Foreign Bank v Bankers Trust Co* [1989] Q.B. 728, 771, per Staughton J. See also *Rodaro v Royal Bank of Canada*, 59 O.R. (3d) 74 (2002), Ont CA, noted by Ogilvie (2004) 19 B.F.L.R. 103.

963 See *Kaupthing Singer & Friedlander Ltd v Coomber* [2011] EWHC 3589 (Ch) at [52], [56]; *Deutsche Bank (Suisse) SA v Khan* [2013] EWHC 482 (Comm) at [384]–[393]. See also *Sunderland v Barclays Bank Ltd* (1938) 5 L.D.A.B. 163; *Nam Tai Electronics Inc v Price- waterhouseCoopers* [2008] 1 H.K.C. 427 at [49], [53], [54] HKCFA. See also *Primary Group (UK) Ltd v Royal Bank of Scotland Plc* [2014] EWHC 1082 (Ch) at [192], where disclosure was held not to be "reasonably necessary" for the bank's own protection. The "interests of the bank exception" probably needs to be reassessed in the light of developments in the law of confidence, misuse of private information and data protection (as to which, see R. Spearman [2012] J.I.B.F.L. 78).

964 It has been suggested that where such consent has been given not freely but under compulsion, for instance, by a foreign court, the bank ought to refuse to make disclosure: *Re ABC* [1985] F.L.R. 159 Cayman Islands. But see R. Cranston, E. Avgouleas, K. van Zwieten, C. Hare and T. van Sante, *Principles of Banking Law*, 3rd edn (2018), 266. For examples where legislation allows disclosure but only with customer consent, see the Small and Medium Sized Business (Credit Information) Regulations 2015 (SI 2015/1945) regs 3(2), 6(1)(b); the Small and Medium Sized Business (Finance Platforms) Regulations 2015 (SI 2015/1946) regs 3(4), 6(3)(b).

965 [1992] 2 All E.R. (Comm) 664.

966 *Turner* dealt with banking practice between 1986 and 1989, and therefore predates the 1994 revision of the *Banking Code* (for personal customers) which made banker's references subject to the express consent of the customer concerned. A similar requirement was contained in the *Business Banking Code* (for business customers) first published in 2002. Both Codes were replaced in November 2009 by a new Banking and Payment Services (BPS) conduct regime (see above, para.34-219). See now the Standards of Lending Practice for consumer customers and also for business customers (paras 34-222—34-223A above); none of which make direct reference to the practice of giving banker's references, although both the 2017 and the 2019 versions of the *Standards of Lending Practice for Business Customers* state that "[f]irms should ensure that the customer's consent is sought prior to sharing any business or personal details with a third party or an alternative source of finance" (Product information, point 4). A bank has been held to owe a duty of care to its customer when providing information to credit reference agencies in relation to that customer, and to owe a duty of care to the customer's spouse where she was a joint holder of the same account and a co-director of the family business which largely depended on her husband's credit (but "almost certainly" not in the ordinary case): *Gatt v Barclays Bank Plc* [2013] EWHC 2 (QB) at [35], where held that bank was not liable to spouse in contract (she was also a customer of the bank), negligence or defamation where it sent computerised information about her husband to credit reference agencies stating that an account, which was a joint account with her, was "delinquent" because the overdraft exceeded the agreed limit. See also *Boyo v Lloyds Bank Plc* [2019] EWHC 2279 (QB) at [53]–[57] for availability of bank's defence of qualified privilege to customer's defamation action, and at [65]–[67] for bank's duty of care, when providing information to credit reference agencies. For the duty imposed on designated banks to provide information about their small and medium-sized business customers to designated credit reference agencies (CRAs), and the duty on designated CRAs to provide credit information about small and medium-sized businesses to finance providers, see the Small and Medium Sized Business (Credit Information) Regulations 2015 (SI 2015/1945).

967 E.P. Ellinger, E. Lomnicka and C.V.M. Hare, *Ellinger's Modern Banking Law*, 5th edn (2011), pp.195–197.

## Extraterritorial orders

*Replace footnote 973 with:*

**34-309** 973 *R. v Grossman* (1981) 73 Cr. App. R. 302; *MacKinnon v Donaldson, Lufkin & Jenrette Securities Corp* [1986] Ch. 482. See also *Société Eram Shipping Co Ltd v Compagnie Internationale de Navigacion* [2003] UKHL 30, [2003] 3 W.L.R. 21 at [22]–[23] and [67], HL (similar principles expressed when court refuses to grant third party debt order over credit balance in foreign bank account). cf. *Masri v Consolidated Contractors International Co SAL (No.2)* [2008] EWCA Civ 303, [32]–[35], per Lawrence Collins L.J., but see also *Masri v Consolidated Contractors International Co SAL (No.4)* [2008] EWCA Civ 876, [15]–[16], [80], [2009] UKHL 43, [19], [26]; *Bilta (UK) Ltd v Nazir (No.2)* [2015] UKSC 23, [2016] A.C. 1 at [212]; *R. (on the application of KBR Inc) v Director of the Serious Fraud Office* [2018] EWHC 2368 (Admin) at [25]–[29]. Interestingly, in *Credit Suisse Trust Ltd v Intesa Sanpaolo SpA*

[2014] EWHC 1447 (Ch), the English High Court granted *Norwich Pharmacal* relief to the victim of fraud by ordering the London branches of two Italian banks to provide information about a customer, despite the fact that the banking activity took place in Italy and all the information sought was held in Italy: the only link to the UK was that the banks had branches in London. In *Bank Mellat v HM Treasury* [2019] EWCA Civ 449, the judge was held to have properly exercised her discretion to order disclosure (subject to confidentiality restrictions) by an Iranian bank of unredacted documents said to contain confidential customer information which would constitute a breach of Iranian criminal law. In *Byers v Samba Financial Group* [2020] EWHC 853 (Ch), Fancourt J. balanced the actual risk of prosecution in the foreign state triggered by an English disclosure order against the importance of the disclosure to conducting a fair trial (applying the test set out in *Bank Mellat* at [63]), and found (at [107]) that the balancing exercise favoured the ordering of disclosure.

### *(viii) Termination of Relationship*

#### Termination of relationship by consent

*Replace footnote 978 with:*

978 As to what constitutes a reasonable period of notice, see *Prosperity Ltd v Lloyds Bank Ltd* (1923) 39 T.L.R. 372 (refusing to grant a mandatory injunction ordering the bank to reopen the account). See also *National Commercial Bank of Jamaica Ltd v Olint Corp Ltd*, above, at [16]–[21], where application for injunction also refused on grounds that, where customer disputes closure of his account, damages will usually be an adequate remedy. cf. *N v S* [2015] EWHC 3248 (Comm) at [12]–[13], reversed [2017] EWCA Civ 253: at trial—*N v Royal Bank of Scotland Plc* [2019] EWHC 1770 (Comm) at [92]–[95]—it was held that the bank had considered, rationally and in good faith (and, if required, reasonably), that there had been "exceptional circumstances" for closing its customer's accounts without notice (as the bank was contractually entitled to do under its account terms). **34-310**

## (c) The Current Account

### *(i) Rights and Duties of the Banker*

#### Nature of relationship

*Replace paragraph with:*

The relationship between the banker and a customer who has opened a current account is that of debtor and creditor.[980] The debt is, however, payable only on demand at the branch in which the account is kept.[981] Thus, it is not the banker's duty to seek his creditor, the customer, and repay the debt. The banker is under an obligation to honour cheques of the customer, provided an adequate credit balance is available.[982] When drawing a cheque the customer, acting as principal, authorises his banker—his agent—to make payment.[983] A relationship of principal and agent is, accordingly, superimposed on the basic relationship of creditor and debtor. In carrying out instructions given to the bank by its customer—the principal—it must exercise reasonable care and skill.[984] Its main duty, though, is to adhere strictly to the terms of its mandate.[985] **34-311**

980 *Foley v Hill* (1848) 2 H.L. Cas. 28; *Joachimson v Swiss Bank Corp* [1921] 3 K.B. 110. A bank opening a current account must satisfy certain "customer due diligence" requirements contained in the Money Laundering, Terrorist Financing and Transfer of Funds (Information on the Payer) Regulations 2017 (SI 2017/692) Pts 3–4, implementing the Fourth Money Laundering Directive 2015/849/EU (the Fifth Money Laundering Directive 2015/849/EU was implemented in the UK through the Money Laundering and Terrorist Financing (Amendment) Regulations 2019 (SI 2019/1511), which amended SI 2017/692). It must also normally satisfy the requirements of the Banking Conduct of Business Sourcebook (BCOBS) and the Payment Services Regulations 2017 (SI 2017/752), as amended. For details, see E.P. Ellinger, E. Lomnicka and C.V.M. Hare, *Ellinger's Modern Banking Law*, 5th edn (2011), Ch.7, s.2.

981 *Joachimson v Swiss Bank Corp*, above; *Arab Bank Ltd v Barclays Bank DCO* [1954] A.C. 495. The rule that repayment must be demanded at the branch of the bank that holds the account is ripe for review in the light of modern technology and business practices when customers can now access their accounts remotely, via cash machines and through debit cards, and where some banks operate over the internet and through telephone banking services with no branches at all. The courts in one overseas

jurisdiction seem prepared to jettison the rule (*Damayanti Kantilal Doshi v Indian Bank* [1999] 4 S.L.R. 1, 11, Sing CA).

982 *Joachimson v Swiss Bank Corp*, above; *Bank of New South Wales v Laing* [1954] A.C. 135, 154; *Barclays Bank Ltd v WJ Simms Ltd* [1980] 1 Q.B. 692, 699; *Sierra Leone Telecommunication Co Ltd v Barclays Bank Plc* [1998] 2 All E.R. 821, 827; *Re Spectrum Plus Ltd* [2005] 2 A.C. 680 at [59].

983 *London Joint Stock Bank v Macmillan* [1918] A.C. 777; *Westminster Bank v Hilton* (1926) 43 T.L.R. 124. This remains the case even where the account is overdrawn: *Coutts & Co v Stock* [2000] 1 W.L.R. 906 at 909, Lightman J., endorsed by the Court of Appeal (obiter) in *Hollicourt (Contracts) Ltd v Bank of Ireland* [2001] 2 W.L.R. 290 at 296, 300.

984 *Astro Amo Compania Naviera SA v Elf Union SA (The Zographia M)* [1976] 2 Lloyd's Rep. 382, 393; *Barclays Bank Plc v Quincecare Ltd* [1992] 4 All E.R. 363, 376.

985 Conflict can exist between the bank's duty to honour the mandate and its duty to exercise reasonable care and skill in and about the execution of the mandate, e.g. where an agent authorised to draw on his principal's bank account does so for his own benefit or for an unauthorised purpose: see *Lipkin Gorman (a firm) v Karpnale Ltd* [1989] 1 W.L.R. 1340, CA, varied on another point: [1991] 2 A.C. 548; *Barclays Bank Plc v Quincecare Ltd* [1992] 4 All E.R. 363; *Verjee v CIBC Bank & Trust Co (Channel Islands) Ltd* [2001] Lloyd's Rep. Bank. 279; *JP Morgan Chase Bank NA v Federal Republic of Nigeria* [2019] EWCA Civ 1641; *Singularis Holdings Ltd (In Liquidation) v Daiwa Capital Markets Europe Ltd* [2017] EWHC 257 (Ch), affirmed [2018] EWCA Civ 84 and [2019] UKSC 50.

## Overdrafts

*Replace footnote 1002 with:*

**34-315** 1002 *Emerald Meats (London) Ltd v AIB Group (UK) Ltd* [2002] EWCA Civ 460 at [12]; *Lloyds Bank Plc v Voller* [2000] 2 All E.R. (Comm) 978 at 982, CA; *Barclays Bank Ltd v WJ Simms, Son & Cooke (Southern) Ltd* [1980] Q.B. 677 at 699. The Supreme Court has held that bank charges levied on personal current account customers in respect of unauthorised overdrafts constitute part of the price or remuneration for the banking services provided and, in so far as the terms giving rise to the charges are in plain intelligible language, no assessment of the fairness of those terms, under the Unfair Terms in Consumer Contracts Regulations 1999, may relate to their adequacy as against the services provided: see *Office of Fair Trading v Abbey National Plc* [2009] UKSC 6, [2010] 1 A.C. 696 (but contrast European Court of Justice's strict interpretation of art.4(2) exception in underlying EC Directive 1993/13/EEC: *Kásler v OTP Jelzálogbank Zrt* (C-26/13) EU:C:2014:282; *Jean-Claude Van Hove v CNP Assurances SA* (C-96/14) EU:C:2015:262; *Andriciuc v Banca Românească SA* (C-186/16) EU:C:2017:703). Note that, in response to the Supreme Court's decision in *OFT v Abbey National Plc*, the Consumer Rights Act 2015 s.64(2), introduces an additional requirement for the application of the exclusion from the test of unfairness of terms relating to the main subject matter of the contract or the price/quality ratio: the term must be both transparent (expressed in plain and intelligible language and, in the case of a written term, legible: subs.(3)) and (which is new) prominent (brought to the consumer's attention in such a way that an average consumer would be aware of the term: subss.(4)–(5)), and not a term listed in Pt 1 of Sch.2 of the 2015 Act (subs.(6)) Pt 2 of the 2015 Act replaced the 1999 Regulations for contracts made on or after October 1, 2015 (see below, Ch.38)). Andrew Smith J. held at first instance in *Abbey National* that such bank charges could not be characterised as penalties because they were levied other than upon a breach of contract: [2008] EWHC 875 (Comm), [2008] 2 All E.R. (Comm) 625. When reviewing the penalty clause jurisdiction in *Cavendish Square Holding BV v Makdessi* [2015] UKSC 67, [2016] A.C. 1172, the Supreme Court (at [40]–[43]) declined to follow the approach taken in Australia and retained the requirement that the penalty doctrine is only triggered by breach. The different approaches to the breach requirement in the two jurisdictions has been confirmed by the High Court of Australia in *Paciocco v ANZ Banking Group Ltd* [2016] HCA 28 at [7]–[10] and [119]–[127], and see also *Andrews v Australia and New Zealand Banking Group Ltd* [2012] HCA 30, (2012) 290 A.L.R. 595. For whether overdraft charges can be challenged as part of an "unfair credit relationship" under Consumer Credit Act 1974 ss.140A–D, see D. Cook, A. Ibrahim and A. Khan [2011] J.I.B.F.L. 212, and the expanding case law on these provisions, including *Plevin v Paragon Personal Finance Ltd* [2014] UKSC 61, [2014] 1 W.L.R. 4222 (the leading case); *Nelmes v Nram Plc* [2016] EWCA Civ 491; *McMullon v Secure the Bridge Ltd* [2015] EWCA Civ 884; *Barclays Bank Plc v McMillan* [2015] EWHC 1596 (Comm); *Deutsche Bank (Suisse) SA v Khan* [2013] EWHC 482 (Comm) (providing a helpful, non-exhaustive list of potentially relevant factors); *Carney v NM Rothschild & Sons Ltd* [2018] EWHC 958 (Comm); *Broomhead v National Westminster Bank Plc* [2018] EWHC 1574 (Ch); *Greenlands Trading Ltd v Pontearso* [2019] EWHC 278 (Ch); *Pilgrim Rock Ltd v Iwaniuk* [2019] EWHC 203 (Ch); *Wood v Commercial First Business Ltd* [2019] EWHC 2205 (Ch); *Promontoria (Henrico) Ltd v Samra* [2019] EWHC 2327 (Ch); *Canada Square Operations Ltd v Potter* [2020] EWHC 672 (QB).

## Combining accounts

*Replace footnote 1006 with:*

**34-316** 1006 *Garnett v M'Kewan*, above, does not regard the right of combination as subject to notice; *National*

*Westminster Bank Ltd v Halesowen Presswork and Assemblies Ltd* [1972] A.C. 785, 807, 810, 820 treats the question as still open but contains strong dicta suggesting that notice, even though with immediate effect, is required. For retail customers, the bank's right of set-off (or combination) is now regulated by the FCA's *Banking Conduct of Business Sourcebook* (BCOBS), which imposes certain information requirements pre-contract (BCOBS 4.1.4AG(2)(a)(i),(ii)), pre-use of set-off rights (BCOBS 4.1.4AG(2)(b)(i),(ii)) and post-use of set-off rights (BCOBS 4.1.4AG(2)(c)). BCOBS also imposes limits on the use of set-off rights against retail customers: see BCOBS 5.1.3AG(1),(2)(a) (customer must be left with a "subsistence balance"); BCOBS 5.1.3AG(2)(b)(i),(ii) (no set-off of personal debts against ring-fenced or earmarked funds) and BCOBS 5.1.3BG(1),(2) (refund is usual remedy unless not fair to do so). Neither the *Standards of Lending Practice for Personal Customers* nor the Standards of Lending Practice for Business Customers 2017 and 2019 (paras 34-222—34-223A above) have detailed provisions about the use of the right of set off.

## Effect of agreement

*To the end of paragraph, after "as equitable owner.[1015]", add:*

A bank may have a common law right of combination of accounts maintained within the jurisdiction but in different currencies due to express agreement or the way the parties conducted themselves during the course of their banking relationship.[1015a] **34-317**

[1015a] *Syndicate Bank v Dansingani* [2019] EWHC 3439 (Ch) at [295]–[298].

## Proceeds of Crime Act 2002

*Replace paragraph with:*

A bank must freeze an account where it knows or suspects that the account contains the proceeds of crime.[1034] In practice, the bank cannot give an explanation to its customer for fear of committing a "tipping-off" offence,[1035] unless the relevant authorities (the National Crime Agency (NCA))[1036] consent or the court so directs.[1037] The bank does not act in breach of contract by refusing to honour its customer's payment instructions where it is suspicious that the money in the account is criminal property.[1038] The bank must report its knowledge or suspicion to NCA.[1039] If, after an initial period of seven days to investigate the matter, NCA refuses to give the bank consent to deal with the suspect account, it remains frozen for a further period of 31 days.[1040] At any stage the bank, or any other person affected by the freezing of the account, may ask NCA to look at the matter again.[1041] At the end of the 31 day moratorium, NCA must apply to the court for an order to prohibit further dealing with the funds in the account.[1042] Unless such an order has been made, the bank is now bound to act in accordance with its customer's instructions. **34-321**

[1034] *Squirrell Ltd v National Westminster Bank Plc* [2005] EWHC 664 (Ch), [2006] 1 W.L.R. 637, considering s.328 of the Proceeds of Crime Act 2002 which creates an offence of facilitating the acquisition, retention, use or control of criminal property. The Money Laundering, Terrorist Financing and Transfer of Funds (Information on the Payer) Regulations 2017 (SI 2017/692), which replace the Money Laundering Regulations 2007 (SI 2007/ 2157), and the Transfer of Funds (Information on the Payer) Regulations 2007 (SI 2007/3298), do not change the principal offences under the POCA 2002, nor the regime for reporting money laundering suspicions.

[1035] s.333A ("tipping-off" offences). See also s.342 (offence of prejudicing an investigation).

[1036] The NCA replaced the Serious Organised Crime Agency in 2013.

[1037] *Bank of Scotland v A Ltd* [2001] EWCA Civ 52, [2001] 1 W.L.R. 751; *Amalgamated Metal Trading Ltd v City of London Police Financial Investigation Unit* [2003] EWHC 703 (Comm), [2003] 1 W.L.R. 2711. But see also *National Crime Agency v N* [2017] EWCA Civ 253 at [71], where Hamblen L.J. said that *Bank of Scotland v A*, a tipping-off case, had to be "considered with caution and cannot be regarded as providing general guidance" in the context of the statutory consent regime contained in POCA 2002.

[1038] *K Ltd v National Westminster Bank Plc* [2006] EWCA Civ 1039, [2007] 1 W.L.R. 311, where it was held that the bank does not have to adduce evidence to support any such suspicion or even show that there were reasonable grounds for the suspicion. But in *Shah v HSBC Private Bank (UK) Ltd* [2010] EWCA Civ 31, [2011] 1 All E.R. 67, the Court of Appeal held that where a customer brings non-summary proceedings against his bank claiming damages to compensate for loss caused to him because of the bank's failure to carry out his payment instructions, and the bank relies on its suspicion that the requested transfer involved funds which were criminal property, there was no reason why the bank should not be required at trial to prove that it had the relevant suspicion: at the trial the High Court held that HSBC did in fact have a genuine suspicion that the funds were criminal property, see [2012] EWHC 1283 (QB). See also *Lonsdale v National Westminster Bank Plc* [2018] EWHC 1843 (QB) at [54]–[66], where the judge refused to strike out and/or summarily dismiss the claimant customer's claim that the defendant bank acted in breach of contract by freezing his accounts. The judge stressed (at [64]) that whether or not the bank had a genuine suspicion was a primary fact, which the customer had put in issue, that required to be proved by evidence that would be tested at trial. The judge also refused to strike out and/or summarily dismiss the customer's claims against the bank (a) for breach of his rights under the Data Protection Act 1998 to see personal data held by the bank, and (b) for defamation (stating, at [131]–[134], that absolute privilege for defamatory words should not be extended to cover reports to the NCA, but that a bank which reports suspicious activity to the NCA would have the benefit of qualified privilege).

1039 Proceeds of Crime Act 2002 s.330(2)(a) and (b) extend the reporting requirement to where the bank has reasonable grounds for knowledge or suspicion that another person is engaged in money laundering. The report constitutes an "authorised disclosure" under s.338 of the 2002 Act, amended by the Serious Crime Act 2015 from June 1, 2015 to include a new subs.(4A), which provides that "when an authorised disclosure is made in good faith, no civil liability arises in respect of the disclosure on the part of the person by or on whose behalf it is made".

1040 s.335. The court has recently been given power to extend the moratorium period up to 186 days through amendments to Pt 7 of the 2002 Act, introduced by the Criminal Finances Act 2017 s.10 (in force on October 31, 2017).

1041 *R. (on the application of UMBS Online Ltd) v Serious Organised Crime Agency* [2007] EWCA Civ 406. In *National Crime Agency v N* [2017] EWCA Civ 253 at [59]–[64], the Court of Appeal held that the court had jurisdiction to override the compulsory statutory consent procedure under POCA 2002 by granting interim relief, but stated that, as the balance of convenience is likely to lie in favour of the public interest in the prevention of money laundering in most cases, such intervention was likely to be exceptional.

1042 s.41.

## *(ii) Termination of Duty to Pay*

### Winding up

*Replace paragraph with:*

**34-327** The bank has to exercise extreme caution where a customer, who is a body corporate, is being wound up. By s.127 of the Insolvency Act 1986, in a winding-up of a company by the court, any disposition of the company's property made after the commencement of the winding-up is, unless the court orders otherwise, void. According to s.129 of the 1986 Act, the winding-up of a company by the court is deemed to commence at the time of the presentation of the petition for winding-up (or, if the company was already in voluntary liquidation, at the time when the resolution for voluntary winding-up was passed). Section 127 does not specify the appropriate remedy of the company's liquidator when the disposition is avoided but the Court of Appeal indicated in *Hollicourt (Contracts) Ltd v Bank of Ireland* that the right of recovery is restitutionary.[1057] Problems for the bank arise if, due to oversight or to its ignorance of the pending petition, the bank allows payments to be made into and out of the company's account. Until recently, all payments into and out of a company's bank account were considered to be dispositions of the company's property and void.[1058] That view has turned out to be too sweeping. Payments into an account in credit have been held not to constitute dispositions of the company's property as the amount standing to the credit of the customer's account is increased.[1059] Payments into an overdrawn account do constitute dispositions of the company's property and are void under s.127 unless validated by the court.[1060] Payments made out of a company's bank account, whether the account is in credit or overdrawn, have been held not to constitute a disposition of the company's property to the bank, which merely acts as the company's agent in making a disposition in favour of the third party.[1061] In any event, a bank is well advised to ask the company for a validation order under s.127 before allowing it to continue to operate the account as notice of the winding-up petition terminates the bank's authority to honour its customer's cheques.[1062–1063]

[1057] [2001] Ch. 555, CA. A change of position defence may defeat the restitutionary claim, although this will depend on the circumstances of the particular case, and the issues raised by the application of that defence are different to those raised by a request for a validation order: see *Re Tain Construction Ltd* [2003] B.P.I.R. 1188. See also *Rose v AIB Group (UK) Plc* [2003] 1 W.L.R. 2791 at [41]–[43]; *Re D'Eye* [2016] B.P.I.R. 883 at [55]; *Clark v Meerson* [2018] B.P.I.R. 661 at [47]; *Officeserve Technologies Ltd v Annabel's (Berkeley Square) Ltd* [2018] EWHC 2168 (Ch) at [41]; *Re MKG Convenience Ltd (in liquidation), Abdulali v NISA Retail Ltd* [2019] EWHC 1383 (Ch) at [67]–[70]. But there is doubt as to whether a change of position defence is available against a restitutionary claim following avoidance under s.127 due to obiter observations of Privy Council in *Skandinaviska Enskilda Banken AB v Conway* [2019] UKPC 36 at [114]–[117] (where issue was whether change of position defence available to restitutionary claim following voidable preference).

[1058] *Re Gray's Inn Construction Ltd* [1980] 1 W.L.R. 711, CA.

[1059] *Re Barn Crown Ltd* [1994] 4 All E.R. 42, criticised in K van Zwieten (ed.), *Goode on Principles of Corporate Insolvency Law*, 5th edn (2018), para.13-125.

[1060] *Re Gray's Inn Construction Ltd*, above; *Re Tain Construction Ltd* [2003] B.P.I.R. 1188.

[1061] *Hollicourt (Contracts) Ltd v Bank of Ireland*, above, CA, endorsing the ruling of Lightman J. in *Coutts & Co v Stock* [2000] 1 W.L.R. 906. But in *Officeserve Technologies Ltd (In Liquidation) v Anthony-Mike* [2017] EWHC 1920 (Ch), H.H.J. Paul Matthews, sitting as Judge of the High Court, stated obiter (at [88]) that whilst he agreed with Lightman J. that there is no disposition of the company's property to the bank on the facts of *Coutts & Co v Stock*, where the account was overdrawn, he considered that there is a disposition caught by s.127 where the account is in credit because the bank's liability to the company has been reduced. The judge (at [88]) preferred the reasoning of Blackburne J. at first instance in *Hollicourt (Contracts) Ltd v Bank of Ireland* [2000] 1 W.L.R. 895, although he did not refer to the Court of Appeal's reasoning when reversing Blackburne J. on appeal at [2001] Ch. 555, and (at [97]) relied on dicta of Lord Neuberger in *Akers v Samba Financial Group* [2017] UKSC 6, [2017] A.C. 424 at [74] to the effect that the giving up of contractual rights by a company would be a "disposition" within s.127.

[1062–1063] *Pettit v Novakovic* [2007] B.P.I.R. 1643 at [7]. Presentation of the petition does not *automatically* terminate the bank's mandate: *Hollicourt (Contracts) Ltd v Bank of Ireland*, above. The principles that govern the validation of a disposition, either prospectively or retrospectively, are set out in *Re Gray's Inn Construction Ltd* [1980] 1 W.L.R. 711, CA; and in *Denney v John Hudson & Co Ltd* [1992] B.C.L.C. 901; see also *Wilson v 375 Live Ltd* [2015] EWHC 870 (Ch). *Re Gray's Inn Construction Ltd* was explained and amplified by the Court of Appeal in *Express Electrical Distributors Ltd v Beavis* [2016] EWCA Civ 765, [2016] 1 W.L.R. 4783, where Sales L.J. (at [56]) said validation would ordinarily only be granted "if there is some special circumstance which shows that the disposition in question will be (in a prospective application case) or has been (in a retrospective application case) for the benefit of the general body of unsecured creditors, such that it is appropriate to disapply the usual pari passu principle". Sales L.J.'s approach to validation orders was recently applied in *Re MKG Convenience Ltd (In Liquidation), Abdulali v NISA Retail Ltd* [2019] EWHC 1383 (Ch) at [47].

## Bankruptcy

*Replace footnote 1066 with:*

[1066] *Paget's Law of Banking*, 15th edn (2018), para.21.9. **34-328**

## Third party debt orders

*Replace paragraph with:*

**34-329** Service of a third party debt order (formerly called a "garnishee order") relieves the banker of his obligation to pay his customer's cheques or other payment instruction, until the order is discharged, regardless of the respective amounts of the balance and the judgment debt.[1067] In many interim third party debt orders, however, a named sum is now expressed as the limit attachable, in which case it is the practice of bankers to earmark such specified amount together with an additional sum to cover estimated costs and to allow the customer to operate on the remaining balance. An interim third party debt order citing a solicitor as a judgment debtor will attach the balance on the solicitor's "clients" account.[1068] A third party debt order attaches foreign currency balances maintained with a bank in the United Kingdom,[1069] but not with a foreign branch unless by the law applicable in that place an English order would be recognised as discharging the liability of the third party to the judgment debtor.[1070] The procedural rules relating to third party debt orders are to be found in Pt 72 of the Civil Procedure Rules 1998[1071] where reference is made to a third party debt order being made in respect of "any debt due or accruing due to the judgment debtor from a third party".[1072] The essential condition for the effectiveness of a third party debt order is that there should be a subsisting debt owed to the judgment debtor[1073]; execution cannot be levied against a debt if the judgment debtor has parted with his interest in it.[1074] Doubts as to whether money standing to the credit of a customer in a current account could be deemed "due or accruing" were resolved in *Joachimson v Swiss Bank Corp*.[1075] Ordinarily a demand is necessary before moneys so credited strictly fall due, but the Court of Appeal held that service of a garnishee summons operated as a demand.[1076] Compliance with a final third party debt order discharges the bank's indebtedness to its own customer, but there is no discharge if the bank pays in reliance on only an interim order.[1077]

1067 *Rogers v Whiteley* [1892] A.C. 118. See also *Edmunds v Edmunds* [1904] p.362. For a detailed analysis including the question of priorities, see E.P. Ellinger, E. Lomnicka and C.V.M. Hare, *Ellinger's Modern Banking Law*, 5th edn (2011), pp.459–470, and 477 for similarities and differences between a freezing injunction (which also relieves a bank of its duty to honour its customer's mandate) and an interim third party debt order. For the nature of the duty of disclosure in an application for an interim third party debt order, and how it differs from disclosure in the case of freezing orders, see *State Bank of India v Mallya* [2019] EWHC 995 (QB) at [9]–[11]; *BCS Corporate Acceptances Ltd v Terry* [2018] EWHC 2349 (QB) at [70]–[78]; *Merchant International Co Ltd v Natsionalna Aktsionerna Kompaniia Naftogaz Ukrainy* [2014] EWHC 391 (Comm) at [68]–[71].

1068 *Plunkett v Barclays Bank* [1936] 2 K.B. 107, but the order is unlikely to be made final where the account is a trust account.

1069 *Choice Investments Ltd v Jeromnimon (Midland Bank Garnishee)* [1981] Q.B. 149; *Camdex International Ltd v Bank of Zambia (No.3)* (1997) 6 Bank. L.R. 44, CA.

1070 *Société Eram Shipping Co Ltd v Compagnie Internationale de Navigation* [2003] UKHL 30, [2004] 1 A.C. 260; *Kuwait Oil Tanker Co SAK v Qabazard* [2003] UKHL 31, [2004] 1 A.C. 300. The situs of the debt is vitally important. In *Taurus Petroleum Ltd v State Oil Marketing Company of the Ministry of Oil, Republic of Iraq* [2017] UKSC 64 at [31]–[32], [60], [72], [83], [124]–[125], the Supreme Court held (unanimously), overturning *Power Curber International Ltd v National Bank of Kuwait* [1981] 2 Lloyd's Rep. 394 on the point, that the general rule that the situs of a debt is the debtor's residence (i.e. the place where the debt is recoverable) applies to letters of credit: for a credit issued by the London branch of an overseas bank, when the credit incorporated UCP 600 (art.3 of which provides that "[b]ranches of a bank in different countries are to be considered as separate banks"), the situs of the debt due under the credit was London, thereby making the debt susceptible to a third party debt order made by an English court. For a review of the authorities on locating the situs of a debt, and a summary of the principles emerging therefrom (including displacement of the general rule that the debt is properly recoverable or enforceable in the place of residence, or domicile, of the debtor), see *Hardy Exploration and Production (India) Inc v India* [2018] EWHC 1916 (Comm) at [53]–[82].

1071 Pt 72 of the Civil Procedure Rules 1998 came into effect on March 25, 2002, replacing RSC Ord.49.

1072 In *Alawiye v Mahamood* [2005] EWHC 277 (Ch), [2006] 3 All E.R. 668, Lindsay J. held that, in the absence of any contrary indication, the court could and should accept, as sufficient for the purposes of an interim third party debt order under CPR r.72.4, evidence in which the judgment creditor was able to say no more than that the judgment debtor had previously had an account with the third party bank and that it had previously been in credit. Lindsay J. also stated (obiter) that the fact that the account had previously been overdrawn did not of itself preclude there being a debt to the judgment debtor from the third party, at least where there is nothing to indicate that, overall, the bank is not a debtor to the judgment debtor.

1073 An order can only be made when the debt is owed solely to the judgment debtor: *Taurus Petroleum Ltd v State Oil Marketing Company of the Ministry of Oil, Republic of Iraq* [2017] UKSC 64 at [24], citing Field J. at first instance [2013] EWHC 3494 (Comm), [2014] 1 Lloyd's Rep. 432 at [13]. See also *National Bank of Kazakhstan v Bank of New York Mellon SA/NV* [2020] EWHC 916 (Comm) at [92] and [104] (where, for purposes of Belgian garnishment order, English court had to decide whether debt was payable by London branch of defendant bank to Republic of Kazakhstan or National Bank of Kazakhstan).

1074 *Taurus Petroleum Ltd v State Oil Marketing Company of the Ministry of Oil, Republic of Iraq* [2017] UKSC 64 at [68]. See also *Merchant International Co Ltd v Natsionalna Aktsionerna Kompaniia Naftogaz Ukrainy* [2014] EWCA Civ 1603; *Rekstin v Severo Sibirsko Gosudarstvennoe Aksionernoe Obschestvo Koseverputj and the Bank for Russian Trade Ltd* [1933] 1 K.B. 47; *Re General Horticultural Co* (1886) 32 Ch. D. 512, 515 (which, according to Lord Clarke in *Taurus*, above, at [45]–[46], does not establish any independent principle of "honest dealing", but merely reaffirms that a judgment creditor cannot by means of a third party debt order levy execution on property that does not belong to the judgment debtor); *Hardy Exploration and Production (India) Inc v India* [2018] EWHC 1916 (Comm) at [120] (there must be an existing obligation in respect of the debt at the date of the making or service of the Interim Third Party Debt Order: there is no existing obligation where a contingency or condition precedent has not yet been satisfied at the relevant date).

1075 [1921] 3 K.B. 110, 131.

1076 By contrast, no debt is "due or accruing due" when loan repayable on 30 days' written notice, which was held to be a condition precedent to an obligation to repay the sums loaned, unless and until notice served, *Michael Wilson & Partners Ltd v Sinclair* [2020] EWHC 1249 (Comm) at [22]–[33]. As regards the right of the bank served with a third party debt order to deduct its expenses from the amount attached, see *Gerry Webb Transport v Brenner* [1985] C.L. 152.

1077 *Crantrave Ltd v Lloyds TSB Bank Plc* [2000] Q.B. 917, CA. Where there is a prior equitable charge or flawed asset arrangement over the account, the court will not make a third party debt order final: *Fraser v Oystertec Plc* [2004] EWHC 1582 (Ch), [2005] B.P.I.R. 381.

### *(iv) Special Types of Current Accounts*

#### Survivorship

*Replace footnote 1153 with:*

1153 J. Odgers (ed.), *Paget's Law of Banking*, 15th edn (2018), [5.21]. **34-355**

#### Trust accounts

*In line 11, after "improper purposes he is not liable.", add new footnote 1166a:*

1166a However, in *Chudley v Clydesdale Bank Plc* [2019] EWCA Civ 344 at [77]–[80] a customer's instruction to its bank to set up an account for client monies was held to give rise to a contract enforceable by the clients under the Contracts (Rights of Third Parties) Act 1999. See above, Vol.I, para.18-097. **34-359**

## (d) Discount and Collection

#### Instances of negligence

*Replace footnote 1205 with:*

1205 See the Money Laundering, Terrorist Financing and Transfer of Funds (Information on the Payer) Regulations 2017 (SI 2017/692), implementing the Fourth Money Laundering Directive 2015/849/EU. The Fifth Money Laundering Directive 2018/843/EU had to be implemented in EU Member States by 10 January 2020, and this was done in the UK through the Money Laundering and Terrorist Financing (Amendment) Regulations 2019 (SI 2019/1511), which amended SI 2017/692. The Sanctions and Anti-Money Laundering Act 2018 enables the government to make regulations for the detection, investigation and prevention of money laundering or terrorist financing. **34-366**

## (e) The Giro System and Electronic Transfer of Funds

#### Transfer of value

*Replace paragraph with:*

A giro operation does not involve the transfer of property, simply the adjust- **34-379** ment of separate property rights (i.e. choses in action) of the payer and the payee against their own banks.[1243] It is, therefore, something of a misnomer to speak of the "transfer" of funds as there is no actual transfer of coins and bank notes from the payer to the payee.[1244] Moreover, there is no assignment of any debt that may be owed to the payer by his own bank.[1245] As Staughton J. observed in *Libyan Arab Foreign Bank v Bankers Trust Co*[1246]:

> "'Transfer' may be a somewhat misleading word, since the original obligation is not assigned (notwithstanding dicta in one American case which speaks of assignment)[1247]; a new obligation by a new debtor is created."

Transfer of *value*, rather than the transfer of funds, is probably a more accurate description of the giro process.

[1243] *R. v Preddy* [1996] A.C. 815, 834, HL; *First City Monument Bank Plc v Zumax Nigeria Ltd* [2019] EWCA Civ 294 at [27], [76].

[1244] See *Foskett v McKeown* [2001] 1 A.C. 102, 128, per Lord Millett: "No money passes from paying bank to receiving bank or through the clearing system (where the money flows may be in the opposite direction) there is simply a series of credits and debits which are causally and transactionally linked". See also *Customs and Excise Commissioners v FDR Ltd* [2000] S.T.C. 672 at [37]; and *Dovey v Bank of New Zealand* [2000] 3 N.Z.L.R. 641, 648 NZCA; *European Bank Ltd v Citibank Ltd* [2004] NSWCA 76 at [57]–[62]; *Darkinjung Pty Ltd v Darkinjung Local Aboriginal Land Council* [2006] NSWSC 1217 at [13]; *Scottish Exhibition Centre Ltd v Commissioners for Revenue and Customs* [2008] S.T.C. 967 at [19], Ct of Sess. IH; *First City Monument Bank Plc v Zumax Nigeria Ltd* [2019] EWCA Civ 294 at [27], [73]–[85].

[1245] *R. v Preddy*, above (credit transfer); *Mercedes-Benz Finance Ltd v Clydesdale Bank Plc* [1997] C.L.C. 81, Ct of Sess. OH (debit transfer).

[1246] [1989] Q.B. 728, 750.

[1247] Presumably, Staughton J. was referring to *Delbrueck & Co v Manufacturers Hanover Trust Co*, 609 F. 2d. 1047 at 1051 (1979) (see below, para.34-426).

**Statutory controls**

*Replace footnote 1290 with:*

34-401 [1290] SI 2017/752, as amended. See also, para.34-224 above. On the effects of Brexit see Vol.I, paras 1-014 et seq., Financial Services and Markets Act 2000 (Amendment) (EU Exit) Regulations 2019 (SI 2019/632) and Financial Services (Electronic Money, Payment Services and Miscellaneous Amendments) (EU Exit) Regulations 2019 (SI 2019/1212).

**Payment Services Regulations 2017**

*To the end of list item "(3)", add:*

34-402 This extension has encouraged the development of Open Banking whereby bank customers can open up their banking data and accounts to trusted third parties, allowing for increased innovation, greater competition and customer choice, as well as increased financial inclusion.[1310a]

[1310a] See also the Competition and Markets Authority's Retail Banking Market Investigation Order 2017. On Open Banking generally, see J Black, "Open banking: an emerging technology grows to maturity" [2019] P.L.C. 19; J Black, "In Open Banking's brave new world could using a third party to initiate payments weaken consumer protection?" [2019] J.I.B.F.L. 25.

**Non-execution or defective execution**

*Replace footnote 1323 with:*

34-406 [1323] PSRs 2017 reg.91(2) (PSRs 2009 reg.75(2)), but note that reg.91 only applies where a payment order is initiated *directly* by the payer (PSRs 2017 reg.91(1)): for non-execution or defective execution of a payment order initiated by the payer through a payment initiation service, see PSRs 2017 reg.93, which includes, in reg.93(2), (4), a requirement that a payment initiation service provider, on request, must immediately compensate an account servicing payment service provider for losses incurred or sums paid as a result of the refund to the payer. The general rule is that the payer's bank must ensure that the amount of the payment transaction is credited to the account of the payee's bank by the end of the business day following receipt of the payment order (PSRs 2017 reg.86(1); PSRs 2009 reg.70(1)); but subject to exceptions in the case of payment instructions initiated by way of a paper payment order, and certain payment transactions (e.g. not in euros or sterling) executed wholly within the EEA (PSRs 2017 reg.86(2), (3); PSRs 2009 reg.70(3), (4)). See also *Tidal Energy Ltd v Bank of Scotland Plc* [2013] EWHC 2780 (QB), [2013] 2 Lloyd's Rep. 605 at [22] (affirmed [2014] EWCA Civ 1107 without reference to this point), where H.H.J. Havelock-Allan Q.C. said (obiter) that if PSRs 2009 reg.75 had applied to the transfer (it did not because the PSRs had been expressly excluded by the bank's terms and conditions), the unique identifier given by the payer would have been incorrect because there was a mismatch between the payee's name, on the one hand, and the account number and sort code, on the other, in which case reg.74(2) would have applied. PSRs 2009 reg.74(2) provides: "Where the unique identifier provided by the payment service user is incorrect, the payment service provider is not liable under regulation 75 or 76 for non-execution or defective execution of the payment transaction, but the payment service provider—(a) must make reasonable efforts to recover the funds involved in the payment transaction; and (b) may, if agreed in the framework contract, charge the payment service user for any such recovery". See also *Technoservice Int Srl v Poste Italiane SpA* (C-245/18) EU:C:2019:242, where the European Court of Justice held that the limitation of liability provided for in the Payment Services Directive 2007/64 art.74(2) applies to both the payer's and the payee's payment service provider. For equivalent provision to PSRs 2009 reg.74(2), see PSRs 2017 reg.90(2). For what constitutes "reasonable efforts" on the part of both the payer's and the payee's payment service provider, see R. Leow, "Recovering mistaken payments before the financial ombudsman" [2019] L.M.C.L.Q. 215, 226–230. It is anticipated that a Confirmation of Payee system will be introduced into the UK in 2020 in order to deal with authorised push payment (APP) fraud (the system will not cover direct debits). When setting up a new payment, a payment service provider will be able to check the name of the payee identified in the payment instruction against the actual name of the payee of the account identified in the payment instruction: see Payment Systems Regulator, Confirmation of Payee (Consultation Paper CP 19/4, May 2019). In the case of APP fraud, the payer has a claim in restitution against a payee who has received the funds with knowledge of the fraud (on the basis of *Westdeutsche Landesbank Girozentrale v Islington LBC* [1996] A.C. 669, 709 et seq.: see above, para.34-136). The payer is likely to be able to obtain a freezing injunction, and even a declaratory order for return of the funds, against such a payee (*World Proteins KFT v Mateen* [2019] EWHC 2030 (QB) and [2019] EWHC 1146 (QB)). The payer might be entitled to bring a derivative action on behalf of the payee company used as a vehicle for fraud, against the bank or payment service provider holding the payee's account, where the payee holds the transferred funds as trustee for the payer and commits a breach of trust or in other exceptional circumstances, including fraud: *Hamblin v World First Ltd* [2020] 6 WLUK 314.

## Position of the paying banker at common law

*Replace footnote 1350 with:*

[1350] See *Tidal Energy Ltd v Bank of Scotland Plc* [2014] EWCA Civ 1107, [2014] 2 Lloyd's Rep. 549, where the Court of Appeal, by a majority, construing a CHAPS transfer order in accordance with banking practice, held that a CHAPS transfer was within mandate when the payment was made to an account matching the sort code and account number—but not the name of the payee/beneficiary customer—provided by the payer. For casenotes, see G. McMeel [2015] L.M.C.L.Q. 1; T.K.C. Ng (2015) 131 L.Q.R. 202; S. Booysen [2018] J.I.B.F.L. 405. For the new Confirmation of Payee system, see above, para.34-406. An attempt by the bank to draft its terms and conditions of use of online facilities widely so as to impose liability on a consumer customer for unauthorised debits to his account, regardless of the circumstances, is likely to be held to be "unfair" under the Unfair Terms in Consumer Contracts Regulations 1999 or, for contracts made on or after October 1, 2015, Pt 2 of the Consumer Rights Act 2015 (which revokes and replaces the 1999 Regulations): see *Spreadex Ltd v Cochrane* [2012] EWHC 1290 (Comm) (consumer opened spread betting account via bookmaker's website). **34-408**

## Position of the payee's bank under the Payment Services Regulations 2017

*Replace footnote 1376 with:*

[1376] PSRs 2017 reg.90(2); PSRs 2009 reg.74(2). See above, para.34-406. In *Tecnoservice Int Srl v Poste Italiane SpA* (C-245/18) EU:C:2019:24, the European Court of Justice held that the limitation of liability provided for in the Payment Services Directive 2007/64 art.74(2) applies to both the payer's and the payee's payment service provider. This includes the situation where, as in *Tecnoservice* itself, an incorrect unique identifier is provided by the payer together with the correct name of the intended recipient of the transfer. For the new Confirmation of Payee system (which will not cover direct debits), see above, para.34-406. **34-412**

### Position of recipient (payee's) banker at common law

*In line 2, after "agent is indisputable", add new footnote 1378a:*

34-413 [1378a] But the recipient (payee's) bank does not hold funds received from the payer's bank on trust for the payee; it is merely under a personal obligation to credit the payee's account: *First City Monument Bank Plc v Zumax Nigeria Ltd* [2019] EWCA Civ 294 at [32]–[37], [47], [80]–[82] (international funds transfer received by correspondent bank and credited to account of payee's bank).

### Relationship between transferor and recipient (payee's) banker

*Replace paragraph with:*

34-417 The recipient (payee's) bank does not owe a duty of care to a non-customer transferor of a giro transfer to pay money received only to the recipient identified in the transferor's instructions, or to clarify any discrepancies in those instructions as to the recipient's identity with the transferor.[1382]

[1382] *Abou-Rahman v Abacha* [2005] EWHC 2662 (QB), [2006] 1 All E.R. (Comm) 247, where Treacy J. refused to follow *Royal Bank of Canada v Stangl*, 32 A.C.W.S. (3d) 17 (1992), a Canadian decision to the opposite effect. The Court of Appeal affirmed Treacy J.'s decision but there was no appeal on this issue: [2006] EWCA Civ 1492, [2007] 1 Lloyd's Rep. 115. See R. Leow, "Recovering mistaken payments before the financial ombudsman" [2019] L.M.C.L.Q. 215, 230–234 (on liability of receiving/payee's bank in unjust enrichment).

### Position of correspondent (intermediary) bank at common law

*Replace paragraph with:*

34-419 Where there is no correspondent banking relationship between the paying bank and the payee's bank (i.e. the banks do not hold accounts with each other), the paying bank effects the transfer by giving an appropriate instruction to a correspondent (or intermediary) bank.[1390] A bank may use a correspondent bank, in particular, to service transactions originating in a foreign country in which it does not have a physical presence.[1390a] An international funds transfer will require the services of at least one correspondent bank unless the payer's bank and the payee's bank are themselves correspondents (i.e. hold accounts with each other).[1390b] In English law there is, of course, no privity of contract between such a "correspondent bank" and the paying bank's customer. This principle, which is based on cases establishing that there is no privity of contract between the principal and his agent's sub-agents,[1391] has been applied to international money transfers in *Royal Products Ltd v Midland Bank Ltd*.[1392] The same authority further shows that the paying bank may be liable for its correspondent's negligence or default. In this case, a Maltese merchant, who maintained a current account with the defendant bank, instructed it to transfer an amount of £13,000 to the credit of his account with the B Bank in Malta. The N Bank in Malta, which was instructed by the defendant bank to effect the necessary transfer, executed it despite the fact that strong rumours about the B Bank's imminent collapse were circulating at the relevant time. The merchant claimed that the N Bank, with which he had his other account in Malta and with which he had accordingly a relationship of customer and banker, ought to have warned him about the position. He sought to hold the defendant bank responsible for the default and negligence alleged. Dismissing the action, Webster J. held that, on the facts, no negligence was attributable to the N Bank. But his Lordship observed that the paying bank owed its customer, the payer, a duty of care and skill in selecting its correspondent and added that, in the absence of a clause to the contrary, the paying bank could be vicariously liable for the negligence and default of its correspondent.[1393] It is, however, important to note that most modern banking forms include a clause under which a correspondent is engaged at the customer's risk and expense. As the paying bank is not in a position to exercise any control over its correspondent, such a clause appears reasonable.

[1390] Where an intermediary bank incurs liability as a result of carrying out the instructions of the payer's bank, it will usually be entitled to an indemnity or contribution from the payer's bank: *Hon Soc of the Middle Temple v Lloyds Bank Plc* [1999] 1 All E.R. (Comm) 193.

[1390a] *First City Monument Bank Plc v Zumax Nigeria Ltd* [2019] EWCA Civ 294 at [26].

[1390b] *First City Monument Bank Plc v Zumax Nigeria Ltd* [2019] EWCA Civ 294 at [26] (held that an international funds transfer received by a correspondent bank, and credited to an account of the payee's bank, was not held by the payee's bank on trust for the intended payee; the payee's bank was under a personal obligation to credit the account of the payee).

[1391] *Calico Printers' Association Ltd v Barclays Bank Ltd*, above. Note that the converse is true in other legal systems, such as in the United States: *Evra Corp v Swiss Bank Corp*, 522 F. Supp. 820 (1981) (reversed on another point 673 F. 2d 1982 (1982)): see also Uniform Commercial Code s.4A-305. A problem of conflict of laws arises therefore in certain cases involving international money transfers. And see Vroegop [1990] L.M.C.L.Q. 540, especially 550 et seq. Where a collecting bank collects an instrument for a remitting bank, there is no privity of contract between the collecting bank and the customer of the remitting bank either at common law or under the Uniform Rules for Collections, 1995 revision (URC 522): *Grosvenor Casinos Ltd v National Bank of Abu Dhabi* [2008] EWHC 511 (Comm), [2008] 2 All E.R. (Comm) 112 at [157], Flaux J., distinguishing *Bastone & Firminger Ltd v Nasima Enterprises (Nigeria) Ltd* [1996] C.L.C. 1902 at 1908, Rix J., who thought the URC point arguable. See further, H. Bennett (2008) 124 L.Q.R. 532.

[1392] [1981] 2 Lloyd's Rep. 194, 198.

[1393] This view derives support from the House of Lord's decision in *Equitable Trust Co of New York Ltd v Dawson Partners* (1927) 27 Ll.L. Rep. 49.

*Add new paragraph:*

**Payment accompanied by incorrect destination account details** *The Laconia* and *The Chikuma* concerned the moment at which hire transferred to shipowners' banks could be said to have been paid to the shipowners themselves within the meaning of the hire payment clause in the relevant charterparty. In both cases the transfer had been accompanied by the correct account details. The position would be different where the transfer was accompanied by incorrect destination account details. In *K v A*,[1414a] a sale contract on GAFTA terms provided that payment was to be "100% net cash within two banking days to the seller's bank" on presentation of an invoice. The seller emailed an invoice with its correct bank account details to an intermediary broker which, according to the broker's email account records, the broker forwarded to the buyer.[1414b] However, a fraudster intercepted the email and changed the account details to a different account held at a different branch of the same bank. The buyer sent payment to the (incorrect) bank account specified on the invoice it received. Popplewell J. made several pertinent observations on the law relating to payment by funds transfer.[1414c] First, he noted that "[a]n obligation to pay in cash, against the background of modern banking practice, permits any commercially recognised method of transferring funds, providing it is equivalent to cash, that is to say that it gives the payee the unconditional and unfettered right to the immediate use of the funds".[1414d] Secondly, he held that the contract in this case clearly contemplated that in order to enable the buyer to pay the price "in cash" the seller would not only notify the identity and branch of their bank, which was not identified in the contract itself, but would nominate the destination account details which the buyer would need in order to be able to make a payment which was equivalent to cash. Thirdly, he held that it was "obviously right" that the payment obligation was not fulfilled unless transfer instructions from the buyer were accompanied by the destination account details notified by the seller, because without such details there could be no question of a transfer which was equivalent to net cash. The contractual obligation of the buyer was to make payment to the 34-430A seller's bank for the account of the seller, in the sense that it had to be accompanied by the account details which the seller had notified. Therefore, much turned on whether the broker, which had received the correct account details from the seller, acted as agent for the buyer for this purpose under GAFTA terms. The judge remitted the point back to the GAFTA Board of Appeal for decision.

1414a [2019] EWHC 1118 (Comm).

1414b The buyer denied receiving the email with the correct account details.

1414c At [26]–[29].

1414d Applying *The Brimnes* [1973] 1 W.L.R. 386, 400, per Brandon J., endorsed by the Court of Appeal [1975] Q.B. 929, 948, 963.

## (g) Giving Information on Financial Transactions

### Scope

*Replace footnote 1423 with:*

34-434 1423 The position at common law is considered in the paragraphs below. However, there is also a regulatory regime that controls the way a bank provides investment advice and sells investment products contained in the Financial Services and Markets Act 2000 and the Financial Conduct Authority's (FCA) Conduct of Business Sourcebook (COBS) (prior to April 1, 2013, the Financial Services Authority was the relevant regulatory body). Specific obligations on a bank turn on the type of customer with which it is dealing, and banks are required to categorise their clients as retail clients, professional clients and eligible counterparties. Breach of FCA conduct of business rules is actionable, as if it were an actionable breach of statutory duty, by a "private person" suffering loss (FSMA 2000 s.138D: prior to April 1, 2013, this was found in s.150 of the 2000 Act). For definition of a "private person", see para.34-221 above. For recent decisions on categorisation of clients, see *Maple Leaf Macro Volatility Master Fund v Rouvroy* [2009] EWHC 257 (Comm), [2009] 1 Lloyd's Rep. 475; *Wilson v MV Global UK Ltd* [2011] EWHC 138 (QB); *Bank Leumi (UK) Plc v Wachner* [2011] EWHC 656 (Comm); and see also J. Ahern [2011] J.I.B.F.L. 556. Recent decisions on what constitutes investment advice include *Rubenstein v HSBC Bank Plc* [2011] EWHC 2304 (QB), [2011] 2 C.L.C. 459, reversed in part [2012] EWCA Civ 1184, [2013] 1 All E.R. (Comm) 915; *Zaki v Credit Suisse (UK) Ltd* [2011] EWHC 2422 (Comm), [2011] 2 C.L.C. 523, affirmed [2013] EWCA Civ 14, [2013] 1 B.C.L.C. 640; *City Index Ltd v Balducci* [2011] EWHC 2562 (Ch), [2012] 1 B.C.L.C. 317; *Al Salaiman v Credit Suisse Securities (Europe) Ltd* [2013] EWHC 400 (Comm); *Thornbridge Ltd v Barclays Bank Plc* [2015] EWHC 3430 (QB); *Parmar v Barclays Bank Plc* [2018] EWHC 1027 (Ch); *London Executive Aviation Ltd v Royal Bank of Scotland Plc* [2018] EWHC 74 (Ch) (criticised by R. Edwards [2018] J.I.B.F.L. 606). No claim for breach of statutory duty is available for breaches of FSMA 2000 which are not specifically defined in the Act as giving rise to a claim for breach of statutory duty (*Hall v Cable and Wireless Plc* [2009] EWHC 1793 (Comm), [2011] B.C.C. 543 at 548–549); there is no common law duty of care to comply with the FSMA 2000 regulatory regime (*Brown v InnovatorOne Plc* [2012] EWHC 1321 (Comm) at [1276]). In *Green & Rowley v Royal Bank of Scotland Plc* [2013] EWCA Civ 1197, [2013] 2 C.L.C. 634 the Court of Appeal held that the existence of a statutory means of enforcement of the (then current) conduct of business rules under FSMA 2000 s.150 (now under s.138D), meant that no separate co-extensive common law duty of care arose and there could be no claim for breach of those rules other than under s.150. The case was highly fact sensitive (which is something that the courts often stress: see, e.g. *London Executive Aviation Ltd v Royal Bank of Scotland Plc* [2018] EWHC 74 (Ch) at [160]). The bank had not undertaken an advisory duty. As Tomlinson L.J. said (at [23]): "*Absent that feature*, there is neither justification nor need for the imposition of a common law duty independent of but co-extensive with the remedy provided by statute" (emphasis added). *Green & Rowley* was distinguished in *Crestsign Ltd v National Westminster Bank Plc* [2014] EWHC 3043 (Ch) at [146]–[147], where the Deputy High Court Judge resisted "the fallacious reasoning that because common law duties and COBS duties are not coterminous, and because [the claimant] is excluded from the class of persons able to sue for breach of COBS duties, the banks can owe no common law duty which happens to overlap with a COBS duty". In *CGL Group Ltd v Royal Bank of Scotland* [2017] EWCA Civ 1073 at [103], the Court of Appeal held that banks do not owe a duty of care in tort to customers when carrying out a regulatory review of potential swaps mis-selling cases which was required as a result of agreement between the FCA and various banks. In *Elite Property Holdings Ltd v Barclays Bank Plc* [2018] EWCA Civ 1688 at [59]–[65], the Court of Appeal held that a bank does not owe a contractual duty to its customer as to its conduct of a FCA review, absent some clear expression of intention by the bank to assume a contractual obligation. In *Flex-E-Vouchers Ltd v Royal Bank of Scotland* [2016] EWHC 2604 (QB) at [53] and [67], it was held that there was no implied term in a swap sale contract that the bank would comply with the requirements of the FSA/FCA's Handbook, including when it conducted a regulatory review. Similarly, in *Target Rich International Ltd v Forex Capital Markets Ltd* [2020] EWHC 1544 (Ch) at [88]–[104] it was held that COBS rules were not incorporated into a foreign exchange trading contract either expressly or by implication of fact or law, and no duty of care arose in tort to comply with COBS rules.

## Advising on investments

*Replace paragraph with:*

In general a bank is not under a legal obligation to provide advice, but if it gives advice then it must do so using reasonable care and skill.[1424] In *Woods v Martins Bank*[1425] it was held that giving advice on financial matters to customers or potential customers is a banking business and that the banker owes his customer a duty to act with reasonable care and skill in giving such advice. The duty will be contractual where the claimant can prove a contract under which the defendant bank has agreed to provide a service including the provision of advice,[1426] otherwise the claimant must establish a tortious duty to advise, and such a duty will arise only in exceptional circumstances.[1427] Its breach would, for example, give rise to an action in damages where, in a transaction between the bank and the customer, the customer has pursued to his detriment a course of action in reliance on a negligent statement made by the bank.[1428] In view of the decision of the House of Lords in *Hedley Byrne & Co v Heller & Partners*[1429] and the later decision of the Privy Council in *Royal Bank Trust Co (Trinidad) Ltd v Pampellone*[1430] it is clear that a bank owes a similar duty of care where it agrees to advise a person who is neither an actual nor a potential customer. The latter authority, though, shows that the scope of the duty owed depends largely on the circumstances of the enquiry and, further, on the information the bank agrees to provide. In *Pampellone's* case the majority of the Judicial Committee held that, where the advice furnished by the bank to the enquirer was confined to his being supplied with a consultant's report on the subject of the enquiry, the bank could not be regarded as warranting or endorsing this advice and was not under a duty to suggest to the customer that reports of the type furnished could not be regarded as conclusive.[1431] An issue may arise as to whether advice was given or information merely provided.[1432] The *Hedley Byrne* duty to take care not to misstate is much narrower than the advisory duty where it was to be expected that relevant professional standards (e.g. FCA conduct of business rules) would form part of the assessment as to whether it had been broken.[1433] It has even been suggested there may be what has been described as a "mezzanine" duty or intermediate duty, occupying the middle ground between a full duty to advise on the one hand, and a limited duty not to mislead on the other, whereby the bank that chooses to explain the nature and effect of a proposed transaction owes a duty to do so fully, accurately and properly.[1434] However, in *Property Alliance Group Ltd v Royal Bank of Scotland Plc*,[1435] the Court of Appeal made clear that this was not the correct approach: 34-435

> "The expression 'mezzanine' duty or intermediate duty, first coined in *Crestsign*, is best avoided. It appears to reflect the notion that there is a continuous spectrum of duty, stretching from not misleading, at one end, to full advice, at the other end. Rather, concentration should be on the responsibility assumed in the particular factual context as regards the particular transaction or relationship in issue."

[1424] *Finch v Lloyds TSB Bank Plc* [2016] EWHC 1236 (QB) at [52].

[1425] [1959] 1 Q.B. 55, especially at 70–72, distinguishing *Banbury v Bank of Montreal* [1918] A.C. 626. See also *Bank of Montreal v Young*, 60 D.L.R. (2d) 220 (1966). cf. *Mutual Life and Citizens' Assurance Co v Evatt* [1971] A.C. 793.

[1426] Supply of Goods and Services Act 1982 s.13; Consumer Rights Act 2015 s.49. cf. *Marz Ltd v Bank of Scotland Plc* [2017] EWHC 3618 (Ch) (express contractual duties of advice specified in bank's terms and conditions negated by express term of ISDA Master Agreement which prevailed as a comprehensive and specifically applicable set of contractual terms relating to swap transaction); *Worthing v Lloyds Bank Plc* [2015] EWHC 2836 (QB) (no strict contractual obligation to correct original investment advice).

1427 *Finch v Lloyds TSB Bank Plc* [2016] EWHC 1236 (QB) at [47]–[59] (borrower's claim that lender owed a contractual or tortious duty to advise it about a potentially onerous clause in a loan agreement failed because there was no contract whereby the lender was to provide advice and there was nothing exceptional about the relationship to justify the imposition of a tortious duty to advise, especially where borrower represented by professional advisers and giving of advice might have been contrary to lender's best interests). As to bank being under no duty in tort to disclose its internal risk assessments and estimates of break costs of swaps contracts, see *Property Alliance Group Ltd v Royal Bank of Scotland Plc* [2018] EWCA Civ 355 at [56]; *Marz Ltd v Bank of Scotland Plc* [2017] EWHC 3618 (Ch) at [332]; *London Executive Aviation Ltd v Royal Bank of Scotland Plc* [2018] EWHC 74 (Ch) at [244]–[254]; *Parmar v Barclays Bank Plc* [2018] EWHC 1027 (Ch) at [208]–[209], [215]–[217]; and also *Deslauriers v Guardian Asset Management Ltd* [2017] UKPC 34 at [22] (lender under no duty to advise borrower about internal policies or external influences, regulatory or otherwise, which affect decision to reject application for additional loan). A lender is under no duty in tort to advise borrower on the suitability of a mortgage (*Mason v Godiva Mortgages Ltd* [2018] EWHC 3227 (QB) at [32]–[37], where also held that there was no implied term importing such a duty because it would be inconsistent with express terms of mortgage contract). Lenders were held to be under no contractual or tortious duty to advise on the suitability of investments made with borrowed funds in tax avoidance schemes, nor were they vicariously liable for any breach of duty by the independent financial adviser who had acted for the borrowers, when the schemes did not work as intended: *Barness v Ingenious Media Ltd* [2019] EWHC 3299 (Ch). As regards the weight given to a bank's promotional materials, see *James v Barclays Bank Plc* (1995) 4 Bank. L.R. 131; cf. *Finch v Lloyds TSB Bank Plc*, above, at [58].

1428 *Esso Petroleum Co Ltd v Mardon* [1976] Q.B. 801; *Box v Midland Bank Ltd* [1979] 2 Lloyd's Rep. 391, which shows also that a bank is liable for a branch manager's negligent statement; note that judgment was reversed on the question of costs: [1981] 1 Lloyd's Rep. 434. See also *Verity and Spindler v Lloyds Bank Plc* [1995] C.L.C. 1557.

1429 [1964] A.C. 465. For a fuller account, see Vol.I, paras 7-091 et seq.

1430 [1987] 1 Lloyd's Rep. 218. See also *Federal Savings Credit Union Ltd v Hessian*, 98 D.L.R. (3d) 488 (1979).

1431 When a person passes on information supplied by another, the question whether he is adopting that information as his own or making some representation about it is a question of interpretation depending on the facts (*Webster v Liddington* [2014] EWCA Civ 560, [2014] P.N.L.R. 26 at [36], and setting out a non-exhaustive list of possible scenarios at [46]). The test for determining which scenario applies is an objective one (*IFE Fund SA v Goldman Sachs International* [2006] EWHC 2887 (Comm), [2007] 1 Lloyd's Rep. 264 at [50], per Toulson J., affirmed [2007] EWCA Civ 811, [2007] 2 Lloyd's Rep. 449). Generally, bank does not make representation about accuracy or reliability of valuation or competence of third party valuer simply by passing on valuation report commissioned for bank's own internal purposes to intended borrower or guarantor (*Rehman v Santander UK Plc* [2018] EWHC 748 (Ch) at [37]). See above, Vol.I, para.7-012.

1432 Although we have recently been reminded by Lord Sumption that the labels of advice and information are "neither distinct nor mutually exclusive categories": *Hughes-Holland v BPE Solicitors* [2017] UKSC 21, [2017] 2 W.L.R. 1029 at [39]. See also *Lloyds Bank Plc v McBains Cooper Consulting Ltd* [2018] EWCA Civ 452 at [33]. But the descriptive inaccuracy of the labels used does not undermine the fact that there is a clear and important distinction between an "advice" case and an "information" case with regard to the scope of the duty undertaken and, therefore, the measure of liability: *Manchester Building Society v Grant Thornton UK LLP* [2019] EWCA Civ 40 at [54]–[59].

1433 *Green & Rowley v Royal Bank of Scotland Plc* [2012] EWHC 3661 (QB) at [82], affirmed [2013] EWCA Civ 1197, [2013] 2 C.L.C. 634, and see, especially, [18] and [23], per Tomlinson L.J.; *Rubenstein v HSBC Bank Plc* [2011] EWHC 2304 (QB), [2011] 2 C.L.C. 459 at [87], reversed in part [2012] EWCA Civ 1184, [2013] 1 All E.R. (Comm) 915; *Shore v Sedgwick Financial Services Ltd* [2007] EWHC 2509 (Admin), [2008] P.N.L.R. 10 at [161]; *Seymour v Ockwell* [2005] P.N.L.R. 758 at 784; *Loosemore v Financial Concepts* [2001] Lloyd's Rep. P.N. 235 at 241; *Anderson v Openwork Ltd* [2015] EW Misc B14 (Slough County Court) at [13], [22]–[25]; *O'Hare v Coutts & Co* [2016] EWHC 2224 (QB) at [206]–[208], where Kerr J. adopted the test in *Montgomery v Lanarkshire Health Board* [2015] A.C. 1430, a medical negligence case, to define the standard of care to be applied in the explanation of risk as part of the provision of investment advice, and considered that compliance with COBS rules "is ordinarily enough to comply with a common law duty to inform, forming part of the duty to exercise reasonable skill and care; while breach of them will ordinarily also amount to a breach of that common law duty" (see also *Thomas v Triodos Bank NV* [2017] EWHC 314 (QB) at [89] for application of the test of materiality in the *Montgomery* case); *London Executive Aviation Ltd v Royal Bank of Scotland Plc* [2018] EWHC 74 (Ch) at [237]. See also *Grant Estates Ltd (In Liquidation) v Royal Bank of Scotland Plc* [2012] CSOH 133 at [79]. *Green & Rowley* was distinguished in *Crestsign Ltd v National Westminster Bank Plc* [2014] EWHC 3043 (Ch) at [147] on the ground that in *Green & Rowley* the court was concerned with whether a duty was owed at common law co-terminous with the (then current) COBS rules.

1434 *Crestsign Ltd v National Westminster Bank Plc* [2014] EWHC 3043 (Ch) at [142]–[146], relying on *Bankers Trust International Plc v PT Dharmala Sakti Sejahtera* [1996] C.L.C. 518, 533D–E. See also *Wani LLP v Royal Bank of Scotland Plc* [2015] EWHC 1181 (Ch) at [34]–[36], [48]; *Thomas v Triodos Bank NV* [2017] EWHC 314 (QB) at [81]. But contrast the doubts as to the existence of such an intermediate duty expressed by the judge in *Thornbridge Ltd v Barclays Bank Plc* [2015] EWHC 3430 (QB) at [118]–[131] (appeal dismissed, Unreported January 9, 2018); and the restrictive interpretation of *Crestsign* adopted by Asplin J. in *Property Alliance Group Ltd v Royal Bank of Scotland Plc* [2016] EWHC 3342 (Ch) at [195]–[196] (on appeal, see main text below), which was endorsed in *Marz Ltd v Bank of Scotland Plc* [2017] EWHC 3618 (Ch) at [237] and in *London Executive Aviation Ltd v Royal Bank of Scotland Plc* [2018] EWHC 74 (Ch) at [236].

1435 [2018] EWCA Civ 355 at [67].

## (h) The Banker as Bailee

### Degree of care

*Replace footnote 1449 with:*

1449 The causes of action against the bank may include breach of contract, tort, breach of duty as bailee and liability for conversion (as to which, see *Schwarzschild v Harrods Ltd* [2008] EWHC 521 (QB)). See, e.g. *Scipion Active Trading Fund v Vallis Group Ltd* [2020] EWHC 1451 (Comm) at [86]–[114] (contractual bailment governed by English law gave bailor right to possession of bailed goods and claim to substantial damages for breach of contract of bailment by bailee). **34-438**

## (i) Bankers' Commercial Credits

### *(i) The UCP*

### Main changes in the 2007 revision

*Replace footnote 1470 with:*

1470 The UCP may be modified or excluded in specified respects by the terms of the credit (*Taurus Petroleum Ltd v State Oil Company of the Ministry of Oil, Republic of Iraq* [2017] UKSC 64 at [61]), although art.1 of UCP 600 provides that such modification or exclusion must be express. The question is one of ordinary contractual construction (*Yuchai Dongte Special Purpose Automobile Co Ltd v Suisse Credit Capital (2009) Ltd* [2018] EWHC 2580 (Comm) at [76]). **34-446**

### Construction of the UCP

*Replace paragraph with:*

English courts regard the provisions of the UCP as standard contractual terms which must be incorporated into the credit and construed according to normal principles governing the construction of commercial contracts. The modern approach to the construction of commercial contracts is contextual,[1475] although the courts tend to take a more literal approach to the construction of standard form contracts that reflect market practice or upon which third parties are likely to rely.[1476] This is reflected in the way the Supreme Court recently approached the construction of letters of credit in *Taurus Petroleum Ltd v State Oil Company of the Ministry of Oil, Republic of Iraq*,[1477] where emphasis was placed upon the language of the credits, construed in their contractual context, and not upon extraneous circumstances. Nevertheless, when construing provisions of the UCP, the courts "seek to give effect to the international consequences underlying the UCP".[1478] In *Fortis Bank SA/NV v Indian Overseas Bank*, Thomas L.J. said that the UCP was to be construed: **34-448**

"... in accordance with its underlying aims and purposes reflecting international practice and the expectations of international bankers and international traders so that it underpins the operation of letters of credit in international trade. A literal and national approach must be avoided."[1479]

The English courts have been willing to imply a term into the UCP,[1480] although Thomas L.J., without reaching a concluded view on the subject, has cautioned that, given its international status, "there would be real difficulties in using a rule of national law as to the implication of terms (if distinct from a method of construction) to write an obligation into the UCP".[1481]

[1475] See Vol.I, paras 13-041 et seq.

[1476] See Vol.I, para.13-051.

[1477] [2017] UKSC 64 at [8], [73]. The High Court of Australia adopted a similar approach to the construction of a performance bond in *Simic v New South Wales Land & Housing Corporation* [2016] HCA 47 at [8]–[11], [31], [77]–[101]. In *Yuchai Dongte Special Purpose Automobile Co Ltd v Suisse Credit Capital (2009) Ltd* [2018] EWHC 2580 (Comm) at [49] a Deputy High Court Judge stated that "extrinsic evidence can be relevant to a letter of credit ... I do not accept that a letter of credit is akin to a negotiable or quasi-negotiable document. However, having said that, where the issue is as to the parties to the contract, and one party has, effectively, via the use of a particular form [in this case, a SWIFT MT700 message], indicated that it is the issuer, then there is a need for caution about the evidence that one should look at. Quite clearly, there is the need to be satisfied that the relevant material goes to the question of the identification of the parties to the contract; and the further need to be satisfied that that material was known, or at the least, available to both parties".

[1478] *Glencore International AG v Bank of China* [1996] 1 Lloyd's Rep. 135, 148, per Sir Thomas Bingham M.R.

[1479] [2011] EWCA Civ 58, [2011] 2 Lloyd's Rep. 33 at [29]. See also *Tecnicas Reunidas Saudia for Services and Contracting Co Ltd v Korea Development Bank* [2020] EWHC 968 (TCC) at [47]–[48], [56] (construction of URDG 758). Opinions of the ICC Commission on Banking Technique and Practice and DOCDEX decisions provide evidence as to international banking practice: see *Benjamin's Sale of Goods*, 10th edn (2017), para.23-007.

[1480] *Seaconsar (Far East) Ltd v Bank Markazi Jomhouri Islami Iran* [1999] 1 Lloyd's Rep. 36, 39. See also *Bankers Trust Co v State Bank of India* [1991] 1 Lloyd's Rep. 587, 599, reversed on grounds of interpretation: [1991] 2 Lloyd's Rep. 443. In the context of performance bonds, the courts have consistently emphasised that it will be rare for a term to be implied into such a contract, see below, para.34-523.

[1481] *Fortis Bank SA/NV v Indian Overseas Bank* [2011] EWCA Civ 58, [2011] 2 Lloyd's Rep. 33 at [55]; cited with evident approval by Blair J. in *Deutsche Bank AG, London v CIMB Bank Berhad* [2017] EWHC 1264 (Comm) at [37].

### Discrepant documents, waiver and notice

*Replace footnote 1489 with:*

**34-452** [1489] *Kydon Compania Naviera v National Westminster Bank Ltd* [1981] 1 Lloyd's Rep. 68, 79. See also *Benjamin's Sale of Goods*, 10th edn (2017), para.23-222; *Paget's Law of Banking*, 15th edn (2018), para.37.19.

## *(v) The Relationship of Banker and Seller*

### The autonomy of an irrevocable credit

*Replace footnote 1596 with:*

**34-502** [1596] For a possible further exception, see below, para.34-509. For the tendency to construe a bank's irrevocable undertaking, such a cumbersomely phrased performance bond, as autonomous, see *Siporex Trade SA v Banque Indosuez* [1986] 2 Lloyd's Rep. 146. In *Wuhan Guoyu Logistics Group Co v Emporiki Bank of Greece SA* [2012] EWCA Civ 1629, [2013] 1 All E.R. (Comm) 1191, Longmore L.J. (with the agreement of Rimer and Tomlinson L.JJ.) tried to find some consistency of approach when deciding whether a document was a suretyship guarantee or an autonomous "on demand" guarantee. He said (at [25]) that "while everything must in the end depend on the words actually used by the parties, there is nevertheless a presumption that, if certain elements are present in the document, the document will be construed in one way or the other". He cited and approved (at [26]) of the analysis in *Paget's*

*Law of Banking*, 11th edn (1996), and now contained in almost identical words in the 15th edition (2018), para.35.8, which provides that: "where an instrument (i) relates to an underlying transaction between the parties in different jurisdictions, (ii) is issued by a bank, (iii) contains an undertaking to pay 'on demand' (with or without the words 'first' and/or 'written'); and (iv) does not contain clauses excluding or limiting the defences available to a guarantor, it will almost always be construed as a demand guarantee." It should be noted, however, that the Court of Appeal held that the instrument in this case was an "on demand" guarantee despite the fact that the fourth element of the presumption was absent. The same result followed in *Spliethoff's Bevrachtingskantoor BV v Bank of China Ltd* [2015] EWHC 999 (Comm) at [71] and [81], *Caterpillar Motoren GmbH and Co KG v Mutual Benefits Assurance Co* [2015] EWHC 2304 (Comm) at [21] and [27]; *South Lanarkshire Council v Aviva Insurance Ltd* [2016] CSOH 83 at [26] (Outer House of Court of Session) and *Bitumen Invest AS v Richmond Mercantile Ltd FZC* [2016] EWHC 2957 (Comm) at [31]. The presumption that an instrument gives rise to independent, primary liability seems to apply "[w]here … the granter is a bank or other financial institution whose business includes the granting of financial instruments for a fee", e.g. an insurance company: *South Lanarkshire Council v Aviva Insurance Ltd*, above, at [25], per Lord Doherty, citing *Meritz Fire & Marine Insurance Co Ltd v Jan de Nul NV* [2010] EWHC 3362 (Comm), [2011] 1 All E.R. (Comm) 1049 at [65]–[66], per Beatson J.; *Caterpillar Motoren GmbH & Co KG v Mutual Benefits Assurance Co*, above, at [20], per Teare J.; *Spliethoff's Bevrachtingskantoor BV v Bank of China Ltd*, above, at [83], per Carr J. See also *Wuhan Guoyu Logistics Group Co Ltd v Emporiki Bank of Greece SA* [2013] EWCA Civ 1679, [2014] 1 Lloyd's Rep. 273, where it was held that money paid by bank to beneficiary under the "on demand" guarantee was not held in trust for bank when, between beneficiary making demand in good faith and payment being made to beneficiary, it had been conclusively determined by a final arbitration award that the event which triggered demand had not in fact fallen due. In *Marubeni Hong Kong & South China Ltd v The Government of Mongolia* [2005] EWCA Civ 395, [2005] 2 All E.R. (Comm) 289 at [28], Carnwath L.J. said that cases where documents are issued by banks which are "described as, or assumed to be, performance bonds … provide no useful analogy for interpreting a document which was not issued by a bank and which contains no overt indication of an intention to create a performance bond or anything analogous to it". But the presumption that an instrument issued by a non-bank party does not give rise to independent primary liability may be rebutted by the clear language of the instrument itself, as in *IIG Capital LLC v Van Der Merwe* [2008] EWCA Civ 542, [2008] 2 Lloyd's Rep. 187; *Meritz Fire & Marine Insurance Co Ltd v Jan de Nul NV*, above, affirmed [2011] EWCA Civ 827, [2011] 2 Lloyd's Rep. 379; *ABM Amro Commercial Financed Plc v McGinn* [2014] EWHC 1674 (Comm); *Caterpillar Motoren GmbH and Co KG v Mutual Benefits Assurance Co*, above; *Bitumen Invest AS v Richmond Mercantile Ltd FZC*, above; *Ultrabulk AS v Jagatramka* [2017] EWHC 2792 (Comm); *Multiplex Construction Europe Ltd v Dunne* [2017] EWHC 3073 (TCC). For cases where the presumption was not rebutted, see *Vossloh Aktiengesellschaft v Alpha Trains (UK) Ltd* [2010] EWHC 2443 (Ch), [2011] 2 All E.R. (Comm) 307; *Carey Value Added SL v Grupo Urvasco SA* [2010] EWHC 1905 (Comm), [2011] 2 All E.R. (Comm) 140; *North Shore Ventures Ltd v Anstead Holdings Inc* [2011] EWCA Civ 230, [2011] 3 W.L.R. 628; *Autoridad del Canal de Panama v Sacyr SA* [2017] EWHC 2228 (Comm); *Shanghai Shipyard Co Ltd v Reignwood International Investment (Group) Co Ltd* [2020] EWHC 803 (Comm). In *Rubicon Vantage International Pte Ltd v Krisenergy Ltd* [2019] EWHC 2012 (Comm) at [18] it was recently held that (a) the *Marubeni* presumption deals with whether a particular instrument should be construed as imposing autonomous obligations, or merely as a see-to-it guarantee, and that the *Marubeni* presumption is spent once that question has been answered; (b) there is no presumption that an on-demand obligation itself should be construed narrowly rather than broadly merely because it is a non-bank that has agreed to such obligations; and (c) the scope of an on-demand obligation should be construed according to normal principles of contract construction, free from any antecedent presumption as to what meaning it is likely to have, or as towards a wide or narrow construction.

## Rejection notice

*Replace footnote 1644 with:*

[1644] *Kydon Compania Naviera SA v National Westminster Bank Ltd (The Lena)* [1981] 1 Lloyd's Rep. 68, 79. See also *Benjamin's Sale of Goods*, 10th edn (2017), para.23-222; *Paget's Law of Banking*, 15th edn (2018), para.37.19. **34-512**

### *(vi) The Relationship of Issuing and Correspondent Bankers*

## Principal and agent

*To the end of paragraph, after "request and expense.", add:*

The correspondent bank also acts as agent of the issuing bank when examining and accepting or rejecting the tendered documents, so that where the correspondent bank accepts discrepant documents, as between the issuing bank and the beneficiary of the credit, its acceptance will bind the issuing bank, its principal.[1675a] **34-520**

[1675a] *Yuchai Dongte Special Purpose Automobile Co Ltd v Suisse Credit Capital (2009) Ltd* [2018] EWHC 2580 (Comm) at [80]–[82].

## *(vii) The Tender of Documents*

### Construction of terms of credit

*Replace footnote 1681 with:*

34-523 [1681] (1922) 13 Ll.L. Rep. 21, 24. But note that when the terms of the credit are construed, it is important to read it as a whole: *Elder Dempster Lines Ltd v Ionic Shipping Agency Inc* [1968] 1 Lloyd's Rep. 529, 535–536; see also *Kreditbank Antwerp v Midland Bank Plc* [1998] Lloyd's Rep. Bank. 173; affirmed [1999] Lloyd's Rep. Bank 219, where the trial judge said that where a credit was ambiguous any doubts should be resolved so as to give the transaction efficacy; but his words are not supported by the Court of Appeal. Whether the strict compliance rule applies to performance bonds and demand guarantees has been the subject of some uncertainty: but see *IE Contractors Ltd v Lloyds Bank Plc* [1990] 2 Lloyd's Rep. 496 at 500–501, per Staughton L.J. ("[i]t is a question of construction of the bond"), applied in *Sea-Cargo Skips AS v State Bank of India* [2013] EWHC 177 (Comm), [2013] 2 Lloyd's Rep. 477 at [30], *Lukoil Mid-East Ltd v Barclays Bank Plc* [2016] EWHC 166 (TCC) at [17]; *South Lanarkshire Council v Coface SA* [2016] CSIH 15 at [12]; *MUR Joint Ventures BV v Compagnie Monegasque de Banque* [2016] EWHC 3107 (Comm) at [26]–[28]; *Sumitomo Mitsui Banking Corp Europe Ltd v Euler Hermes Europe SA* [2019] EWHC 2250 (Comm) at [71]. See also *Simic v New South Wales Land and Housing Corp* [2016] HCA 47 at [6], where French C.J., sitting in the High Court of Australia, stated: "Two complementary principles apply to letters of credit and performance bonds alike—the principle of strict compliance and the principle of autonomy or independence."

### Regularity of documents

*To the end of paragraph, after "of the credit).", add new footnote 1702a:*

34-528 [1702a] The 21-day period specified in art.14(c) can be truncated or extended, or made to run from a different date, by the terms of the credit: see, e.g. *Euro-Asian Oil SA v Credit Suisse AG* [2018] EWCA Civ 1720, [2019] 1 Lloyd's Rep. 444 ("documents presented more than 21 days from bill of lading date but within documentary credit validity period acceptable").

### Invoices and certificates

*Replace footnote 1737 with:*

34-541 [1737] UCP 600 art.14(h), provides that non-documentary conditions are to be ignored. See also J. Zhang, "Disregarding non-documentary conditions in letters of credit: Is it as easy as it appears to be?" [2018] L.M.C.L.Q. 527. As regards the nature of a certificate of inspection, see *Commercial Banking Co of Sydney v Jalsard Pty Ltd* [1973] A.C. 279; note that the bank is not liable for the genuineness of a certificate: *Gian Singh & Co Ltd v Bank de L'Indochine* [1974] 1 Lloyd's Rep. 56; affirmed [1974] 2 Lloyd's Rep. 1. As regards the conformity of a certificate, see *Astro Exito Navegacion SA v Chase Manhattan Bank NA* [1986] 1 Lloyd's Rep. 455. As regards false certificates presented without the tenderor's knowledge of fraud, see *Montrod Ltd v Grundkotter Fleischvertriebs GmbH* [2001] All E.R. (Comm) 368; affirmed [2001] EWCA Civ 1954, [2002] 1 W.L.R. 1975.

## (j) The Banker's Lien

### Extent of lien

*Replace footnote 1748 with:*

34-546 [1748] *Paget's Law of Banking*, 14th edn (2014), para.14.11 (the example no longer appears in the 15th edition).

CHAPTER 35

# CARRIAGE BY AIR



## 2. THE INTERNATIONAL CONVENTIONS

### The Montreal Convention 1999

*Replace paragraph with:*

**35-006** The Montreal Convention overhauls the whole "Warsaw system" covering the full range of issues dealt with in the earlier instruments, including liability for passengers, baggage, cargo and delay, and incorporates the effect of the Guadalajara Convention.[19] It clarifies the exclusivity of the Convention rules and provides that punitive, exemplary or other non-compensatory damages are not to be recoverable.[20] By July 31, 2020 it had 137 States Parties and so is the Convention most often applicable to international carriage by air. In its provisions as to jurisdiction, the Convention adds a "fifth jurisdiction" for passenger claims. It makes new and more modern provision as to passenger documentation. For damages not exceeding a prescribed amount for each passenger, the carrier is not able to exclude or limit its liability. The carrier is not liable for such damages to the extent that they exceed the prescribed amount if the carrier proves that (a) such damage was not due to the negligence or other wrongful act or omission of the carrier or its servants or agents; or (b) such damage was solely due to the negligence or other wrongful act or omission of a third party. The prescribed amount was 100,000 SDRs in the original text of the Convention; it was raised with effect from December 30, 2009 to 113,100 SDRs and with effect from December 28, 2019 to 128,821 SDRs.[21] As to baggage, the Convention provides that the carrier must deliver to the passenger a baggage identification tag for each piece of checked baggage; the "baggage check" of the earlier instruments in the Warsaw system disappears. The cargo provisions are based, with minor improvements, upon those in Montreal Protocol No.4. Effect is given to the Convention in English law by the Carriage by Air Acts (Implementation of the Montreal Convention 1999) Order 2002.[22]

[19] For a pessimistic assessment of its treatment in national courts, see Tompkins (2014) 39 A.S.L. 203.

[20] See *O'Carroll v Ryanair*, 2009 S.C.L.R. 125.

[21] The decision to raise the amount was in the form of a decision of the ICAO Council under art.24 of the Convention.

[22] SI 2002/263, which came into force on June 28, 2004.

## 3. SCOPE AND APPLICATION OF THE CONVENTIONS

### Conventions provide exclusive cause of action

*To the end of paragraph, after "of the Convention.", add:*

35-013 A decision of the High Court of Australia has held that the Convention rules apply not just to claims by passengers (or the representatives of deceased passengers) but also to claims under Australian common law by family members of passengers for negligently caused psychiatric harm following the death of a passenger.[49a]

[49a] *Parkes Shire Council v South West Helicopters Pty Ltd* [2019] HCA 14.

### Jurisdiction

*Replace footnote 56 with:*

35-016 [56] Questions of procedure are governed by the *lex fori*, the law of the court seised of the case: Carriage by Air Acts (Application of Provisions) Order 2004 (SI 2004/1899) Sch.2 art.28(2); Carriage by Air Act 1961 Sch.1 art.28(2); Sch.1A as inserted by SI 1999/1312 art.28(2); Sch.1B as inserted by SI 2002/263 art.33(4). The English court would, therefore, determine whether a particular case falls under its jurisdiction, as opposed to that of a court in Scotland or Northern Ireland. See the Scottish decision to this effect: *Abnett v British Airways Plc*, 1995 S.C.L.R. 654. Although the matter remains controversial, the CJEU held in *Guaitoli v easyJet Airline Co Ltd* (C-213/18) [2019] 4 W.L.R. 160 that art.33(1) governed not only the allocation of jurisdiction as between the States party to the Convention, but also the allocation of territorial jurisdiction as between the courts of each of those States.

## 4. EUROPEAN LEGISLATION: "THE MONTREAL REGULATION"

35-018 *Change title of paragraph:*

### Council Regulation 2027/97 and European Parliament and Council Regulation 889/2002

*Replace paragraph with:*

35-018 The European Union first legislated on carriage by air in Council Regulation 2027/97 of October 9, 1997 on air carrier liability in the event of accidents.[76] This was limited to passenger liability but anticipated a number of features of the Montreal Convention 1999. Regulation 2027/97 was radically amended, and in effect replaced, by European Parliament and Council Regulation 889/2002 of May 13, 2002[77] to align it fully with the Montreal Convention 1999 and to extend it to cover baggage liability.[78] The amending Regulation applied from June 28, 2004, the date on which the Montreal Convention entered into force for the European Union. The necessary changes to the law of the United Kingdom were made by the Air Carrier Liability Regulations 2004[79] and the Air Carrier Liability (No.2) Regulations 2004.[80] The Convention provisions which would otherwise be applicable do not apply to EU carriers to the extent that the amended Regulation has the force of law[81]; an EU carrier is one holding an air operating certificate issued by the authorities of a Member State. Pre-requisites for the issue of a licence include the carrier having a principal place of business in the Member State and that nationals of a Member State own or effectively control the carrier. The EU Regulation implements the relevant provisions of the Montreal Convention in respect of the carriage of passengers and their baggage and lays down certain supplementary provisions, and also extends the application of these provisions to carriage by air within a single Member State. The liability of an EU air carrier in respect of passengers and their baggage is declared to be governed by all provisions of the Montreal Convention relevant to such liability,[82] including its limitation provisions.[83] The Regulation obliges Member States to apply the Montreal Convention in cases where they are under a treaty obligation to apply some other instrument in the Warsaw system, and it may prove to be open to challenge in this respect. The Regulation also deals with the supplementary sum which, in accordance with art.22(2) of the Montreal Convention, may be demanded by a Union air carrier when a passenger makes a special declaration of interest in delivery of their baggage at destination. This sum is to be based on a tariff, to be made available to passengers on request, which is related to the additional costs involved in transporting and insuring the baggage concerned over and above those for baggage valued at or below the liability limit.[84]

[76] For text see [1997] O.J. L285/1.

[77] For text see [2002] O.J. L140. See also the application of the amended Regulation by the Agreement on the European Economic Area 1992 as adjusted by the Brussels Protocol 1993 and the amendments made by Decisions of the EEA Joint Committee.

[78] The effect is that the Montreal Convention becomes part of the EU legal order: *Wallentin-Hermann v Alitalia-Linee Aeree Italiane SpA* (C-549/07) EU:C:2008:771, [2008] E.C.R. I-11061; *Stott v Thomas Cook Tour Operators Ltd* [2012] EWCA Civ 66 at [28]; *Air Baltic Corp AS v Lietuvos Respublikos specialiųjų tyrimų tarnyba* (C-429/14) EU:C:2016:88, [2016] 1 Lloyd's Rep. 407 at [23].

[79] SI 2004/1418, amended with effect from IP completion day (on which see Vol.I, paras 1-014 et seq.) by the Air Passenger Rights and Air Travel Organisers' Licensing (Amendment) (EU Exit) Regulations 2019 (SI 2019/278).

[80] SI 2004/1974. With effect from IP completion day, Regulation 2027/97, as amended by the Air Passenger Rights and Air Travel Organisers' Licensing (Amendment) (EU Exit) Regulations 2019 (SI 2019/278), applies only to UK air carriers. A UK air carrier is one with a valid operating licence granted by the Civil Aviation Authority. This amendment makes no change in the obligations of a UK air carrier under the Regulation.

[81] Carriage by Air Act 1961 s.1(2) as substituted by the Carriage by Acts (Implementation of the Montreal Convention 1999) Order 2002 (SI 2002/263) art.2(2); Carriage by Air Acts (Application of Provisions) Order 2004 (SI 2004/1899) art.3(2).

[82] Regulation 2027/97 art.3(1) as substituted by Regulation 889/2002 art.1(4). For the effect of the Regulation on non-international carriage, see below, para.35-082.

[83] *Bogiatzi v Deutscher Luftpool* (C-301/08) EU:C:2009:649, [2010] 1 All E.R. (Comm) 555 (a case under Regulation 2027/97 and the Warsaw Convention, but of wider application).

[84] Regulation 2027/97 art.3a as inserted by Regulation 889/2002 art.1(5).

## Advance payments

*Replace paragraph with:*

The amended Regulation 2027/97 makes provision in respect of advance or interim payments. The minimum advance in the event of death is the equivalent of 16,000 SDRs per passenger, and an advance payment is declared not to be returnable, except in the cases prescribed in art.20 of the Montreal Convention or where **35-019** the person who received the advance payment was not the person entitled to compensation.[85]

[85] Regulation 2027/97 art.5 as substituted by Regulation 889/2002 art.1(7).

### Conditions of carriage

*Replace paragraph with:*

35-020 The amended Regulation 2027/97 also deals with the provision of information to passengers.[86] All air carriers must, when selling carriage by air in the Union, ensure that a summary of the main provisions governing liability for passengers and their baggage, including deadlines for filing an action for compensation and the possibility of making a special declaration for baggage, is made available to passengers at all points of sale including sale by telephone and via the internet.[86a] In order to comply with this requirement, Union air carriers (but not other air carriers) must use a notice set out in the Annex to the Regulation.[86b] In addition, all air carriers must in respect of carriage by air provided or purchased in the EU, provide each passenger with a written indication of the applicable limit for that flight on the carrier's liability in respect of death or injury, if such a limit exists; the applicable limit for that flight on the carrier's liability in respect of destruction, loss of or damage to baggage, and a warning that baggage greater in value than this figure should be brought to the airline's attention at check-in or fully insured by the passenger prior to travel; and the applicable limit for that flight on the carrier's liability for damage occasioned by delay.[86c] Failure to comply with the requirements of art.3a or art.6 of the amended Regulation is made an offence by the Air Carrier Liability Regulations 2004.[87]

[86] Regulation 2027/97 art.6 as substituted by Regulation 889/2002 art.1(8).

[86a] Regulation 2027/97 art.6(1) as substituted by Regulation 889/2002 art.1(8). As amended with effect from IP completion day by the Air Passenger Rights and Air Travel Organisers' Licensing (Amendment) (EU Exit) Regulations 2019 (SI 2019/278), this will apply when carriage is sold within the United Kingdom (and in the case of non-UK carriers only in relation to carriage to, from or within the United Kingdom).

[86b] Regulation 2027/97 art.6(1) as substituted by Regulation 889/2002 art.1(8). As amended with effect from IP completion day by the Air Passenger Rights and Air Travel Organisers' Licensing (Amendment) (EU Exit) Regulations 2019 (SI 2019/278), this will apply to UK air carriers and to non-UK carriers in relation to carriage to, from or within the United Kingdom.

[86c] Regulation 2027/97 art.6(2) as substituted by Regulation 889/2002 art.1(8). As amended with effect from IP completion day by the Air Passenger Rights and Air Travel Organisers' Licensing (Amendment) (EU Exit) Regulations 2019 (SI 2019/278), this will apply to in respect of carriage by air provided or purchased in the United Kingdom, and in the case of carriage performed by non-UK air carriers, only in relation to carriage to, from or within the United Kingdom.

[87] SI 2004/1418, as amended with effect from IP completion day by the Air Passenger Rights and Air Travel Organisers' Licensing (Amendment) (EU Exit) Regulations 2019 (SI 2019/278).

### Insurance requirements

*Replace paragraph with:*

35-021 The amended Regulation 2027/97 requires a Union air carrier to be insured up to a level that is adequate to ensure that all persons entitled to compensation receive the full amount to which they are entitled in accordance with the Regulation.[88] European Parliament and Council Regulation 785/2004 of April 21, 2004 on insurance requirements for air carriers and air operators,[89] which came into force on May 1, 2005, requires all air carriers and aircraft operators flying within, into, out of, or over the territory of a Member State to have specified levels of insurance cover in respect of their aviation-specific liability in respect of passengers (death and personal injury caused by accidents), for loss or destruction of or damage to baggage and cargo, and to third parties (death, personal injury and damage to property caused by accidents).[90] The insured risks must cover acts of war, terrorism, hijacking, acts of sabotage, unlawful seizure of aircraft and civil commotion. Insurance in respect of the carriage of mails is excluded.[91] In the United Kingdom, an air carrier or aircraft operator (other than a carrier or operator regulated by another Member State) who fails to comply with these requirements commits an offence.[92] The United Kingdom regulations require passenger liability insurance in the case of non-commercial operations by aircraft with a maximum take-off mass of 2,700 kg or less of at least 100,000 SDRs per passenger,[93] and designate the Civil Aviation Authority as the competent authority for the purposes of Regulation 785/2004.[94]

[88] Regulation 2027/97 art.3(2) as substituted by Regulation 889/2002 art.1(4). This provision is revoked with effect from IP completion day (on which see Vol.I, paras 1-014 et seq.), by the Air Passenger Rights and Air Travel Organisers' Licensing (Amendment) (EU Exit) Regulations 2019 (SI 2019/278).

[89] For text see [2004] O.J. L188.

[90] Regulation 785/2004 art.4(1). The levels of cover were raised by Commission Regulation 285/2010 [2010] O.J. L87. The provisions as to the minimum level of insurance in respect of passengers, baggage and cargo do not apply with respect to flights over the territory of the Member States carried out by non-Community air carriers and by aircraft operators using aircraft registered outside the Community which do not involve a landing on, or take-off from, such territory. With effect from IP completion day, Regulation 785/2004, as amended by the Civil Aviation (Insurance) (Amendment) (EU Exit) Regulations 2018 (SI 2018/1363) and the Civil Aviation (Insurance) (Amendment) (EU Exit) Regulations 2020 (SI 2020/692), will apply to all air carriers and to all aircraft operators flying within, into, out of, or over the territory of the United Kingdom. The provisions as to the minimum level of insurance in respect of passengers, baggage and cargo will not apply with respect to flights over the territory of the United Kingdom carried out by non-UK air carriers and by aircraft operators using aircraft registered outside the United Kingdom which do not involve a landing on, or take-off from, the territory of the United Kingdom.

[91] Regulation 785/2004 art.1(2). There are insurance requirements in this context, to be found in Council Regulation 2407/92 art.7 and the law of the various parts of the United Kingdom.

[92] Civil Aviation (Insurance) Regulations 2005 (SI 2005/1089) reg.5.

[93] Civil Aviation (Insurance) Regulations 2005 reg.4 (amended with effect from IP completion day by the Civil Aviation (Insurance) (Amendment) (EU Exit) Regulations 2018 (SI 2018/1363) to revoke reg.4(2) (no offence if aircraft registered and operator licensed in an EU Member State other than the UK); for penalties see reg.12.

[94] Civil Aviation (Insurance) Regulations 2005 reg.3. With effect from IP completion day, reg.3, as amended by the Civil Aviation (Insurance) (Amendment) (EU Exit) Regulations 2018 (SI 2018/1363) will specify that the CAA is the competent authority for the purposes of Regulation 785/2004 art.5. The Secretary of State is exceptionally the competent authority in cases where a permit is required under arts 113 or 115 of the Air Navigation Order 2016 (SI 2016/765) in respect of certain aircraft registered outside the United Kingdom.

## 5. LIABILITY OF THE CARRIER

### (a) Passengers: Death or Injury

#### Information for passengers

*Replace paragraph with:*

An air carriage contractor (a carrier concluding a contract of carriage, a tour **35-026** operator or ticket seller) must inform the passenger at the time of reservation of the identity of the operating air carrier or carriers, and notify the passenger if there is any change in the operating carrier.[114] There are further requirements as to the publication of air fares which must show separately any taxes, airport charges, and other charges, surcharges or fees such as those related to security or fuel that have been added to the basic fare. Optional price supplements must be communicated in a clear, transparent and unambiguous way at the start of any booking process and their acceptance by the customer must be on an "opt in" basis.[115]

[114] European Parliament and Council Regulation 2111/2005 art.11. Failure to comply is made an offence by the Civil Aviation (Provision of Information to Passengers) Regulations 2006 (SI 2006/3303).

[115] European Parliament and Council Regulation 1008/2008 of 24 September 2008 on common rules for the operation of air services in the Community (re-titled with effect from IP completion day (on which see Vol.I, paras 1-014 et seq.) by the Operation of Air Services (Amendments etc) (EU Exit) Regulations 2018 (2018/1392) to refer to "common rules for the operation of air services in the United Kingdom"), art.23(1); *Air Berlin Plc & Co Luftverkehrs KG v Bundesverband der Verbraucherzentralen und Verbraucherverbande - Verbraucherzentrale Bundesverband eV* (C-290/16) EU:C:2017:523. For enforcement in the UK, see Pt 2 of the Operation of Air Services in the Community (Pricing etc.) Regulations 2013 (SI 2013/486) (regs 6 to 27 inclusive are revoked by the Consumer Protection (Enforcement) (Amendment etc.) Regulations 2020 (SI 2020/484)); Enterprise Act 2002 s.212 for which the Operation of Air Services in the Community (Pricing etc.) Regulations 2013 (SI 2013/486) are listed for enforcement purposes: Consumer Protection (Enforcement) (Amendment etc.) Regulations 2020 (SI 2020/484) reg.4 and Sch.

## "Accident"

*Replace paragraph with:*

**35-029** The term "accident" is not defined for the purposes of the conventions. A statutory definition, for the purposes of accident investigation, defines "accident" as including "any fortuitous or unexpected event by which the safety of an aircraft or any person is threatened".[125] The United States Supreme Court has held that an "accident" must be an unexpected or unusual event or happening that is external to the passenger: it is not sufficient that the plaintiff suffers injury as a result of his or her own internal reaction to the usual, normal and expected operation of the aircraft.[126] It is clear that an aircraft crash, or a hijack, will constitute an accident, but so may less dramatic incidents such as extreme cases of turbulence, and incidents during flight such as the spillage of scalding hot drinks[126a] or the service of infected food. A United States decision held that sexual molestation by a fellow passenger was an "accident"[127]: the characteristics of air travel made the plaintiff vulnerable. The Court of Appeal followed that decision but questioned the need to establish that an accident had to be a characteristic of air travel[128] (and the CJEU later held that the concept of "accident" did not depend on the presence of a hazard typically associated with aviation)[128a]; that the assault was an accident was confirmed in the House of Lords.[129] It is not an accident when a passenger becomes ill during a normal flight; it has been held that the occurrence of deep vein thrombosis, and a failure to warn of the risk of its occurrence, cannot be an accident,[130] but where a passenger who later died had been refused a change of seat to avoid the cigarette smoke to which he was allergic, this was held to be an unusual event external to the passenger and so an "accident".[131] There is a range of judicial views on the question whether an omission may amount to an accident (and whether a distinction can properly be drawn between act and omission in this context).[132] Some United States courts have taken into account normal industry practice, seeing a departure from such practice as necessarily constituting an "unusual and unexpected event". The better view is that a court must always ask whether there was an "unexpected or unusual event"; some departures from an industry standard might be "accidents" in that sense but others not.[133] Discussion of a departure from industry practice is appropriate for liability based on negligence, which is not relevant under the Montreal Convention.

[125] Civil Aviation Act 1982 s.75(4).

[126] *Air France v Saks*, 105 S.Ct. 1338 (1985) cf. *Chaudhari v British Airways Plc*, *The Times*, May 7, 1997, CA (passenger with paralysis of the left side of his body could not claim that a fall on board the aircraft occurring as he tried to stand was an "accident"); *Barclay v British Airways Plc* [2008] EWCA Civ 1419, [2009] 1 All E.R. 871 (passenger's slip on standard feature of passenger cabin, a plastic strip covering the seat fix tracking, not an "accident"); *Labbadia v Alitalia (Societa Aerea Italiana SpA)* [2019] EWHC 2103 (Admin), [2019] 2 Lloyd's Rep. 273 (slip on compacted snow on disembarkation stairs without any canopy held an "accident"); *Ford v Malaysian Airline Systems Berhad* [2013] EWCA Civ 1163, [2014] 1 Lloyd's Rep. 301 (passenger unable to urinate during flight due to a medical condition, so "internal" to the passenger; diuretic administered by a doctor also on board; later tests suggested that treatment inappropriate; held not an "unusual" event for the purposes of art.17).

[126a] As in *GN v ZU* (C-532/18) [2020] 1 Lloyd's Rep. 124.

[127] *Wallace v Korean Air*, 214 F. 3d 293 (2000), 2nd Cir.

[128] *Morris v KLM Royal Dutch Airlines* [2001] EWCA Civ 790, [2001] 3 All E.R. 126.

[128a] *GN v ZU* (C-532/18) [2020] 1 Lloyd's Rep. 124.

[129] See *Morris v KLM Royal Dutch Airlines*, above; *King v Bristow Helicopters Ltd* [2002] UKHL 7, [2002] 2 A.C. 628.

[130] *Re Deep Vein Thrombosis and Air Travel Group Litigation* [2005] UKHL 72, [2006] 1 A.C. 495. For a full discussion, see Shawcross and Beaumont, at Vol.1, paras VII[691] et seq.

[131] *Olympic Airways v Husain*, 124 S.Ct. 1221 (2004).

[132] *Olympic Airways v Husain*, 124 S.Ct. 1221 (2004); *Povey v Qantas Airways Ltd* [2005] HCA 33, (2005) 216 A.L.R. 427; *Deep Vein Thrombosis and Air Travel Group Litigation* [2003] EWCA Civ 1005, [2004] Q.B. 234, per Lord Phillips of Worth Matravers M.R. and the same case on appeal, [2005] UKHL 72, [2006] 1 A.C. 495, per Lord Mance.

[133] The view taken in *Blansett v Continental Airlines Inc* 379 F 3d 177 (2004), 5th Cir.

## Defences available to the carrier: "all necessary measures"

*Replace footnote 139 with:*

[139] 100,000 SDRs in the original text of the Convention, raised by decisions of the ICAO Council with effect from December 30, 2009 to 113,100 SDRs and with effect from December 28, 2019 to 128,821 SDRs. **35-031**

## Upper financial limit of liability

*Replace footnote 153 with:*

[153] 100,000 SDRs in the original text of the Convention, raised by decisions of the ICAO Council with effect from December 30, 2009 to 113,100 SDRs and with effect from December 28, 2019 to 128,821 SDRs. **35-033**

## Contracting carriers and "actual" carriers

*Replace footnote 197 with:*

[197] European Parliament and Council Regulation 2111/2005 of December 14, 2005 on the establishment of a Community list of air carriers subject to an operating ban within the Community and on informing air transport passengers of the identity of the operating air carrier and repealing Article 9 of Directive 2004/36 arts 10–13. With effect from IP completion day (on which see Vol.I, paras 1-014 et seq.), the title of Regulation 2111/2005 will be amended by the Aviation Safety (Amendment, etc) (EU Exit) Regulations 2019 (SI 2019/645) to refer to "the establishment of a United Kingdom list of air carriers subject to an operating ban within the United Kingdom", regs 10 and 12 will be amended to limit their application to circumstances with a specified link to the United Kingdom, and reg.13 will be revoked. **35-045**

### Disabled persons and persons with reduced mobility

*Replace paragraph with:*

**35-048** European Parliament and Council Regulation 1107/2006 concerning the rights of disabled persons and persons with reduced mobility when travelling by air applies in respect of both disabled persons and persons with reduced mobility, defined as: "any person whose mobility when using transport is reduced due to any physical disability (sensory or locomotor, permanent or temporary, intellectual disability or impairment, or any other cause of disability, or age, and whose situation needs appropriate attention and the adaptation to his or her particular needs of the service made available to all passengers)",[201] thus including the blind, the old and also those with a temporary injury.[202] In the United Kingdom enforcement of Regulation 1107/2006 is by means of a civil procedure which replaced the earlier criminal offences.[203] Regulation 1107/2006 applies to persons using or intending to use commercial passenger air services departing from, transiting through or arriving at an airport in an EU Member State; and departing from an airport in a third country to an airport in an EU Member State, if the operating carrier is a Union air carrier (but only with regard to the provisions on prevention of refusal of carriage and assistance by air carriers).[204]

[201] Regulation 1107/2006 art.2(a).

[202] It applies with effect from July 26, 2007 with regard to the provisions on refusal of carriage, and with effect from July 26, 2008 with regard to the other provisions: Regulation 1107/2006 art.18.

[203] Civil Aviation (Access to Air Travel for Disabled Persons and Persons with Reduced Mobility) Regulations 2014 (SI 2014/2833) reg.4 as amended by SI 2016/729 (which designates the CAA and dispute resolution bodies); regs 5 to 23 are revoked by the Consumer Protection (Enforcement) (Amendment etc.) Regulations 2020 (SI 2020/484). See Enterprise Act 2002 s.212 for which 2014 Regulations are listed for enforcement purposes: Consumer Protection (Enforcement) (Amendment etc.) Regulations 2020 (SI 2020/484) reg.4 and Sch.

[204] Regulation 1107/2006 art.1(2) and (3). See Viegas, (2013) 38 A.S.L. 47. With effect from IP completion day (on which see Vol.I, paras 1-014 et seq.), Regulation 1107/2006, as amended by the Air Passenger Rights and Air Travel Organisers' Licensing (Amendment) (EU Exit) Regulations 2019 (SI 2019/278) will apply to disabled persons and persons with reduced mobility, using or intending to use commercial passenger air services on departure from, on transit through, or on arrival at an airport, when the airport is situated in the territory of the United Kingdom; and to passengers departing from an airport situated in a country other than the United Kingdom to an airport situated in (a) the United Kingdom, if the operating carrier is a Community air carrier or a UK air carrier; or (b) the territory of an EU Member State, if the operating carrier is a UK air carrier: reg.1(2) and (3) as so amended. A UK air carrier is one with a valid operating licence granted by the CAA: reg.2(m).

## (b) Passengers: Denied Boarding, Cancellation and Long Delay

### Regulation 261/2004

*Replace paragraph with:*

**35-049** Under European Parliament and Council Regulation 261/2004,[212] compensation is payable and other assistance is to be provided to passengers denied boarding or subjected to cancellation of or long delay to their journey. This takes the form of standardised and immediate assistance in contrast to the individualised damage for delay under the Montreal Convention 1999.[213] It follows that Regulation 261/2004 does not operate to limit the liability of the carrier for delay under the Montreal (or Warsaw) Convention, and that the Montreal Convention does not preclude the payment of compensation under the Regulation.[214] Regulation 261/2004 applies to passengers departing from an airport in the EU, and to passengers departing from an airport in a third country on a flight operated by a Community carrier to an airport in an EU state, unless they received benefits or compensation and were given assistance in that third country.[215] Where connecting flights are concerned, the Regulation applies when the first leg is operated from an EU airport and this causes a connecting flight to be missed, even if the resulting denied boarding is on the second leg operated by a non-Community carrier and wholly outside the EU.[216]

[212] European Parliament and Council Regulation 261/2004 of February 11, 2004 establishing common rules on compensation and assistance to passengers in the event of denied boarding and of cancellation or of long delay in flights. Airlines must ensure that a clearly legible and visible notice containing prescribed wording as to the Regulation's provisions is displayed to passengers at check-in, and must provide passengers affected by denied boarding, cancellation or delay with a notice setting out the rules for compensation and assistance: art.14. For commentary on many aspects of the Regulation, see Bobek and Prassl (eds), *Air Passenger Rights: Ten Years On* (2016).

[213] *R. (on application of International Air Transport Association) v Department for Transport* (C-344/04) EU:C:2006:10, [2006] E.C.R. I-403.

[214] *Gahan v Emirates* [2017] EWCA Civ 1530 at [31]ff.; *Guaitoli v easyJet Airline Co Ltd* (C-213/18) [2019] 4 W.L.R. 160.

[215] Regulation 261/2004 art.3(1). See *Emirates Airlines Direktion für Deutschland v Schenkel* (C-173/07) EU:C:2008:400, [2008] E.C.R. I-5237. With effect from IP completion day (on which see Vol.I, paras 1-014 et seq.), Regulation 261/2004, as amended by the Air Passenger Rights and Air Travel Organisers' Licensing (Amendment) (EU Exit) Regulations 2019 (SI 2019/278), will apply to passengers departing from an airport located in the United Kingdom, and to passengers departing from an airport located in a country other than the United Kingdom to an airport situated in (a) the United Kingdom if the operating air carrier of the flight concerned is a Community carrier or a UK air carrier; or (b) the territory of an EU Member State if the operating air carrier of the flight concerned is a UK air carrier, unless the passengers received benefits or compensation and were given assistance in that other country: art.3(1) as so amended. A UK air carrier is one with a valid operating licence granted by the CAA: reg.2(m).

[216] *Gahan v Emirates* [2017] EWCA Civ 1530 (effectively overruling *Sanghvi v Cathay Pacific Airways* [2011] EWHC 1684 (Ch), [2012] 1 Lloyd's Rep 46). A proposed revision of Regulation 261/2004 would secure the result reached in *Gahan*: see COM (2013) 130 final.

*In second paragraph, after "published departure time)", add new footnote 216a:*

[216a] A number of French decisions (e.g. *A v Air France* (Cour de cassation, October 10, 2019) require the passenger to prove arrival at check-in at the required time; in some but not all cases production of a boarding pass has been held sufficient. The CJEU has held that that passengers who hold a confirmed reservation on a flight, and have taken that flight, must be considered to have properly satisfied the requirement to present themselves for check-in; production of a boarding card is not required: LC v easyJet Airline Co Ltd (C-756/18) [2019] 2 Lloyd's Rep. 591. **35-049**

*After second paragraph, add new paragraphs:*

The CAA is designated under the Civil Aviation (Denied Boarding, Compensation and Assistance) Regulations 2005 for the purposes of Regulation 261/2004 art.16(1) as responsible for the enforcement of the Regulation.[219a] Where appropriate, it must take the measures necessary to ensure that the rights of passengers are respected. Each passenger may complain to the CAA of either of the dispute resolution bodies designated for the purposes of art.16(2) of the Regulation about an alleged infringement of the Regulation.[219b] **35-049**

An operating air carrier is guilty of an offence if, in the United Kingdom or elsewhere, it fails to comply with an obligation imposed on it by arts 4, 5, 6, 10, 11 or 14 in respect of a passenger whose flight is either from (a) an airport in the United Kingdom, or (b) a country which is not an EEA state to such an airport.[219c]

[219a] Civil Aviation (Denied Boarding, Compensation and Assistance) Regulations 2005 (SI 2005/975) reg.5(1).

[219b] Civil Aviation (Denied Boarding, Compensation and Assistance) Regulations 2005 (SI 2005/975) reg.5(2) as substituted by the Civil Aviation (Denied Boarding, Compensation and Assistance and Ac-

cess to Air Travel for Disabled Persons and Persons with Reduced Mobility) (Amendment) Regulations 2016 (SI 2016/729).

219c Civil Aviation (Denied Boarding, Compensation and Assistance) Regulations 2005 (SI 2005/975) reg.3 as amended by the Air Passenger Rights and Air Travel Organisers' Licensing (Amendment) (EU Exit) Regulations 2019 (SI 2019/278). With effect from IP completion day (on which see Vol.I, paras 1-014 et seq.), an operating air carrier is guilty of an offence if, in the United Kingdom or elsewhere, it fails to comply with an obligation imposed on it by arts 4, 5, 6, 10, 11 or 14: reg.3 as further amended by the Air Passenger Rights and Air Travel Organisers' Licensing (Amendment) (EU Exit) Regulations 2019 (SI 2019/278).

## Jurisdiction

*Replace paragraph with:*

**35-050** Regulation 261/2004 does not contain any provisions regarding jurisdiction. It was confirmed by the European Court in *Rehder v Air Baltic Corp*[220] that the relevant jurisdictional rules are those in the Brussels I Regulation (recast).[221] For the purposes of art.7 of the Brussels I Regulation (recast) the place of departure and the place of destination may both be considered as places in which the services of an airline were to be supplied.[222] In the case of connecting flights, where the claim is based on long delay in arrival at the destination, the place of performance of such a flight is the place of arrival of the second leg, as one of the main places of provision of services under a contract for carriage by air.[223] Where the operating carrier is not also the contracting carrier, the matter is nonetheless, despite the absence of a contract between the carrier and the operating carrier, "a matter relating to a contract" for the purposes of art.7(1)(a) of the Brussels I Regulation (recast).[224]

220 C-204/08, EU:C:2009:439, [2009] E.C.R. I-6073. See to the same effect *ZX v Ryanair DAC* (C-464/18) [2019] 1 Lloyd's Rep. 537, [2019] I.L.Pr. 31.

221 European Parliament and Council Regulation 1215/2012 of December 12, 2012 on jurisdiction and the recognition and enforcement of judgments in civil and commercial matters (or its predecessor Regulation 44/2001).

222 *Rehder v Air Baltic Corp* (C-204/08) EU:C:2009:439, [2009] E.C.R. I-6073; *flightright GmbH v Iberia LAE SA* (C-606/19) [2020] 1 Lloyd's Rep. 534 (place of departure of first leg of connecting flight even though claim related to cancellation of the final leg and against the air carrier for that leg).

223 *flightright GmbH v Air Nostrum Líneas Aéreas del Mediterráneo SA* and *Barkan v Air Nostrum Lineas Aereas del Mediterraneo SA* (Joined Cases C-274/16 and C-448/16) EU:C:2018:160.

224 *flightright GmbH v Air Nostrum Líneas Aéreas del Mediterráneo SA* and *Barkan v Air Nostrum Lineas Aereas del Mediterraneo SA* (Joined Cases C-274/16 and C-448/16) EU:C:2018:160 (decided under the original Brussels I Regulation 44/2001); *Králová v Primera Air Scandinavia A/S* (C-215/18).

*Add new paragraph:*

**35-050A** **Which carrier is liable?** Liability under Regulation 261/2004 is always that of the operating carrier. "Operating carrier" is defined to mean "an air carrier that performs or intends to perform a flight under a contract with a passenger or on behalf of another person, legal or natural, having a contract with that passenger".[225] In the usual case, the relevant carrier will be that which operated the flight on which the delay or denied boarding occurred but the position is less straightforward where there are connecting flights booked as part of a single journey. It is not uncommon for a delay on the first of two flights (not necessarily in itself sufficient to attract the Regulation) causes a passenger to arrive too late for a connecting flight and therefore to be denied boarding. The Court of Appeal in *Gahan v Emirates*, in which both flights were by the same carrier, held the carrier liable on such facts: the first leg was operated from an EU airport and it was immaterial that the denied boarding was on the second leg operated by a non-Community carrier and wholly outside the EU.[225a]

An extraordinary decision of the Court of Justice of the EU strains the meaning of "operating carrier" beyond any reasonable interpretation. In *CS v Ceske aerolinie as*,[225b] a delay occurred on the second leg, causing the passenger to arrive at the destination more than three hours late. The defendant, a Community carrier, performed the first leg departing from an EU airport. It was clearly the "operating carrier" in respect of that flight. It did not perform the flight on which the delay occurred but the court held that as, for some purposes, flights with one or more connections that are the subject of a single reservation must be regarded as a single unit, it was also the case that, in the context of such flights, "an operating air carrier that has operated the first flight cannot take refuge behind a claim that the performance of a subsequent flight operated by another air carrier was imperfect". The defendant was therefore liable for the delay. The court also relied on art.3(5) of the Regulation, which provides that where an operating air carrier which has no contract with the passenger performs obligations under the Regulation, it is to be regarded as doing so on behalf of the person having a contract with that passenger. Without any full analysis the court held that it followed that where, in the context of connecting flights consisting of two flights that were the subject of a single reservation, the second flight is performed under a code-share agreement by an operating air carrier other than the operating air carrier that entered into the contract of carriage with the passengers concerned and that performed the first flight, the latter carrier remains subject to contractual obligations to the passengers, even in relation to the performance of the second flight. It is far from clear how a code-share agreement can be relevant to liability to the passenger, especially as EU law recognises the importance to the passenger of knowing which airline is the actual operator.[225c]

[225] Regulation 261/2004 art.2(b).

[225a] *Gahan v Emirates* [2017] EWCA Civ 1530.

[225b] C-502/18, EU:C:2019:604.

[225c] See para.35-026.

## Denied boarding

*After first paragraph, add new paragraph:*

An incident of denied boarding must be considered in context. Compensation was held not to be payable to a passenger who had a single reservation for connecting flights and that reservation was amended against the passenger's will, so that the passenger was denied boarding on the first planned flight but was given a seat on a later flight which allowed the passenger to board the second planned flight and to reach the final destination at the arrival time originally scheduled.[231a] **35-052**

[231a] *OI v Air Nostrum Lineas Aereas del Mediterraneo SA* (C-191/19).

## The remedies: compensation

*Replace paragraph with:*

Where compensation is prescribed as a remedy under Regulation 261/2004, for denied boarding,[251] cancellation,[252] and under the *Sturgeon* rule as to long delay in arrival at destination,[253] the level of compensation payable depends upon the length of the flight, namely (a) €250 for flights of 1,500 km or less; (b) €400 for intra-EC flights of more than 1,500 km and other flights between 1,500 and 3,500 km; and **35-057**

(c) €600 for all other flights, the distance being calculated to the last destination at which the denial of boarding or cancellation will delay the passenger's arrival.[254] "Distance" relates, in the case of air routes with connecting flights, only to the distance calculated between the first point of departure and the final destination on the basis of the "great circle" method, regardless of the distance actually flown.[255] The amount of mandatory compensation is halved when the airline offers re-routing to final destination on a flight which arrives not later than two, three or four hours respectively later than the original scheduled arrival time.[256] Article 12 of the Regulation provides that the compensation provided for by art.7 is "without prejudice to a passenger's rights to further compensation", although the compensation granted under art.7 may be deducted from such compensation. This allows a national court to award compensation for damage, including non-material damage, under the Montreal Convention or under the applicable domestic law of a Member State arising from breach of a contract of carriage by air. It may not serve as a legal basis for a claim for compensation of the expenses a passenger incurred because of the failure of that carrier to fulfil its obligations to assist and provide care under art. 8 and art.9 of Regulation 261/2004 in case of delay or cancellation of a flight.[257]

[251] Regulation 261/2004 art.4; see para.35-052.

[252] Regulation 261/2004 art.5(1); see para.35-053.

[253] See para.35-055.

[254] Regulation 261/2004 art.7(1). With effect from IP completion day (on which see Vol.I, paras 1-014 et seq.), the compensation will be (a) £220 for all flights of 1,500 kilometres or less; (b) £350 for all flights between 1,500 and 3,500 kilometres; (c) £520 for all other flights: Regulation 261/2004 art.7(1) as amended by the Air Passenger Rights and Air Travel Organisers' Licensing (Amendment) (EU Exit) Regulations 2019 (SI 2019/278).

[255] *Bossen v Brussels Airlines SA/NV* (C-559/16) EU:C:2017:644.

[256] Regulation 261/2004 art.7(2). See *Sanghvi v Cathay Pacific Airways* [2011] EWHC 1684 (Ch), [2012] 1 Lloyd's Rep 46 at [27]–[28].

[257] *Sousa Rodríguez v Air France* (C-83/10) EU:C:2011:652, [2012] 1 C.M.L.R. 40; *McDonagh v Ryanair* (C-12/11) EU:C:2013:43 [2013] 2 C.M.L.R. 32; *Graham v Thomas Cook Group UK Ltd* [2012] EWCA Civ 1355. Compensation is payable even if the flight in question is part of a package covered by the Package Travel Directive: *Králová v Primera Air Scandinavia A/S* (C-215/18).

### Compensation not payable in extraordinary circumstances

*Replace first paragraph with:*

**35-058** If the cancellation or delay of more than three hours in arrival at destination is caused by extraordinary circumstances, which could not have been avoided even if all reasonable measures had been taken, the carrier is not obliged to pay the standardised compensation provided for in art.7 of the Regulation; the burden of proof is on the carrier.[258] Two recitals address this issue: Recital (14) lists as situations that might constitute extraordinary circumstances:

> "... cases of political instability, meteorological conditions incompatible with the operation of the flight concerned, security risks, unexpected flight safety shortcomings and strikes that affect the operation of an operating air carrier."

Recital (15) deals specifically with the impact of an air traffic management decision.[259] In *Wallentin-Hermann v Alitalia Linee Aeree Italiane SpA*,[260] the European Court noted that "extraordinary circumstances" was not defined in the text of the Regulation, and that as art.5(3) derogated from the principle of compensation it had to be interpreted strictly. The carrier must prove that the cancellation is caused by extraordinary circumstances which could not have been avoided even if all reasonable measures had been taken: the carrier must establish that, even if it had deployed all its resources in terms of staff or equipment and the financial means at its disposal, it would clearly not have been able—unless it had made intolerable sacrifices in the light of the capacities of its undertaking at the relevant time—to prevent the extraordinary circumstances with which it was confronted from leading to the cancellation of the flight.[261] The examples given in Recital (14) did not themselves constitute extraordinary circumstances, but they might produce such circumstances.

[258] Regulation 261/2004 art.5(3). The National Enforcement Bodies under the Regulation produced in April 2013 a list of events they considered "extraordinary circumstances"; it has no legal force.

[259] *Blanche v easyJet Airline Co Ltd* [2019] EWCA Civ 69.

[260] C-549/07, EU:C:2008:771 (which applies in cases falling within Recital (14), but not in an art.15 case: *Blanche v easyJet Airline Co Ltd* [2019] EWCA Civ 69).

[261] *Wallentin-Hermann v Alitalia Linee Aeree Italiane SpA* (C-549/07) EU:C:2008:771; *Egltis v Latvijas Republikas Ekonomickas ministrija* (C-294/10) EU:C:2011:303, [2011] 3 C.M.L.R. 40. See *Dunbar v easyJet Airline Co Ltd*, 2015 GWD 36-570, Sh Ct (North Strathclyde, Paisley).

*Replace second paragraph with:*

A technical problem caused by failure to maintain an aircraft is to be regarded as inherent in the normal exercise of an air carrier's activity, and not as amounting to "extraordinary circumstances".[262] The same is true even of unexpected problems, not attributable to poor maintenance, given the very complex operating systems of aircraft.[263] A collision with mobile boarding stairs has been held to be an event inherent in the normal exercise of the activity of the air carrier and consequently, cannot be considered as an extraordinary circumstance.[264] The same result has been reached in cases concerning bird strikes,[265] "wildcat" strike action by aircrew in response to airline announcement of re-structuring plans,[266] damage to an aircraft tyre caused by a foreign object on the runway,[266a] closure of the runway owing to a fuel spillage,[266b] lightning hitting the aircraft during take-off,[267] or lightning damage to an aircraft intended for use.[267a] The spread of volcanic ash from an eruption of the Icelandic volcano Eyjafjallajökull in 2010 did amount to "extraordinary circumstances"[268]; so did the closure of the runway at Treviso airport owing to a fuel spillage.[268a] At least in certain circumstances, the sudden illness of the pilot may amount to "extraordinary circumstances".[269] So may the behaviour of an unruly passenger that forces the pilot to divert to another airport to disembark the passenger.[269a] An operating carrier may be able to rely on extraordinary circumstances affecting a previous flight by the same aircraft when they cause they cause the cancellation or long delay complained of.[269b] **35-058**

[262] *Wallentin-Hermann v Alitalia Linee Aeree Italiane SpA* (C-549/07) EU:C:2008:771; *Jet2.com Ltd v Huzar* [2014] EWCA Civ 791, [2014] 4 All E.R. 581; *A v Finnair Oyj* (C-832/18) (failure to replace defective component despite spare part in stock).

[263] *Van der Lans v Koninklijke Luchtvaartmaatschappij NV* (C-257/14) EU:C:2015:618. cf. *Bland v Thomas Cook Airlines Ltd* Unreported January 21, 2016, Manchester Cty Ct (aircraft tyre damaged by foreign object on runway: extraordinary circumstance).

[264] *Siewert v Condor Flugdienst GmbH* (C-394/14) EU:C:2014:2377.

[265] *Pesková v Travel Service as* (C-315/15) EU:C:2017:342, [2017] Bus. L.R. 1134.

[266] *Krüsemann v TUIfly GmbH* (C-195/17; joined with many others) EU:C:2018:258, [2018] Bus. L.R. 1191; see Kucko (2019) 44 A.S.L. 321. See *Ryanair DAC v Commissioner for Civil Aviation* [2020] IEC 54 (strike not extraordinary circumstance, whether or not "wild-cat".

[266a] *Germanwings GmbH v Pauels* (C-501/17) EU:C:2019.288.

[266b] *Moens v Ryanair Ltd* (C-159/18) EU:C:2018:1040.

[267] *Monarch Airlines Ltd v Evans and Lee* Unreported January 14, 2016, Luton Cty Ct.

[267a] See *X v easyJet* (French cour de cassation, September 12, 2018).

[268] *Marshall v Iberia Lineas Aereas de España SA* Unreported December 13, 2010, Mayor's and City of London Ct (reversed but not on this point, H.H.J. Birtles, 2011, Unreported); *Williams v KLM Royal Dutch Airlines* Unreported 2011, Taunton Cty Ct; *Rosen v EasyJet Airline Co Ltd* Unreported December 15, 2011, Croydon County Ct. However the volcanic eruption did not excuse the carrier from providing the remedies other than compensation: *McDonagh v Ryanair* (C-12/11) EU:C:2013:43, [2013] 2 C.M.L.R. 32.

[268a] *Moens v Ryanair Ltd* (C-159/18) EU:C:2018:1040.

[269] *Marchbank-Smith v Virgin Atlantic Airways Ltd* Unreported January 14, 2015, Manchester Cty Ct; cf. *D v Air India* (Cour de cassation, February 5, 2020).

[269a] *LE v Transport Aéreos Portugueses SA* (C-74/19). It is difficult to support the reasoning in *Bass v easyJet Airline Co Ltd* Unreported October 24, 2019 Luton Cty Ct) where the diversion of a flight due to passenger illness was held not to amount to "extraordinary circumstances" as illness was inherent in the carrying of passengers by air, a risk that the air carrier was aware of and had to be prepared for.

[269b] *LE v Transport Aéreos Portugueses SA* (C-74/19).

## The remedies: reimbursement or re-routing, care

*Replace paragraph with:*

**35-059** The remedy of reimbursement or re-routing under art.8 of Regulation 261/2004 obliges the airline to offer the passenger the choice between (a) reimbursement of the full ticket cost[269c] for the part or parts of the journey not made, and for the part or parts already made if the flight is no longer serving any purpose in relation to the passenger's original travel plan, together with, when relevant, a return flight to the first point of departure at the earliest opportunity[269d]; and (b) re-routing under comparable transport conditions[270] to final destination at the earliest opportunity or, at the passenger's choice, at a later date.[271] In a number of cases the question has arisen whether a passenger whose flight has been seriously delayed at departure and who chooses the option to be reimbursed for the ticket price by the airline is still entitled to compensation under art.7 of the Regulation. Although the Regulation seems to be sufficiently clear in this matter concerning cancelations in art.5 (the answer would be affirmative), the Regulation lacks a clear provision on this matter for delays. Breach of art.8 does not give rise to a civil action for damages,[272] but is a matter for administrative enforcement, the Civil Aviation Authority being responsible for enforcement in the United Kingdom.[273]

[269c] The full cost includes any commission paid by the passenger to an intermediary, unless the commission was fixed without the airline's knowledge: *Harms v Vueling Airlines SA* (C-601/17) EU:C:2018:702, [2018] Bus. L.R. 2298.

[269d] Reimbursement is excluded where the passenger is entitled to claim under the Package Travel Directive from the tour organiser: Regulation 261/2004 art.8(2); *HQs v Aegean Airlines SA* (C-163/18) EU:C:2019:585, [2019] Bus. L.R. 2032.

[270] See *Marshall v Iberia Lineas Aereas de España SA* Unreported 2011 (H.H.J. Birtles) (putting on a wait list not comparable to a confirmed flight).

[271] *LE v Transport Aéreos Portugueses SA* (C-74/19) (re-routing to arrive a day late not a reasonable measure); *Hendy v Iberian Lineas de España SA* Unreported March 21, 2011, Oxford County Ct; *Rozen v EasyJet Airline Co Ltd* Unreported December 15, 2011, Croydon County Ct.

[272] *Graham v Thomas Cook Group UK Ltd* [2012] EWCA Civ 1355.

[273] Civil Aviation (Denied Boarding, Compensation and Assistance) Regulations 2005 (SI 2005/975) reg.5(1). Dispute resolution bodies are specified in reg.5(2) as substituted by SI 2016/729.

## (c) Baggage

### Liability for damage, destruction or loss

*Replace paragraph with:*

In cases governed by the Warsaw Convention 1929, the liability of the carrier in respect of registered baggage is limited to a sum of 250 francs per kilogramme[290] of the lost or damaged package,[291] and liability in respect of objects of which the passenger takes charge himself is limited to 5,000 francs per passenger.[292] In cases governed by the Warsaw-Hague text, the limits remain as in the 1929 Convention.[293] Under the Warsaw-Hague text, however, when the loss, damage or delay of a part of the registered baggage, or of an object contained therein, affects the value of other packages covered by the same baggage check, the total weight of such package or packages must also be taken into consideration in determining the limit of liability.[294] The limits in the 1929 Convention and the Warsaw-Hague text as amended by Montreal Additional Protocols 1975 No.1 and No.2 respectively, and in cases under the MP4 Convention, are 17 SDRs per kilogramme for registered baggage, and 332 SDRs per passenger for unregistered baggage.[295] Under the Montreal Convention 1999 (and the rules of that Convention as applied to Union air carriers under EU law) the liability of the carrier in the case of destruction, loss, damage, or delay to checked or unchecked baggage was limited in the original text of the Convention to 1,000 SDRs for each passenger.[296] This limit was raised with effect from December 30, 2009 to 1,131 SDRs for each passenger and from December 28, 2019 to 1,288 SDRs for each passenger.[297] The Convention limits apply per passenger; this means that it is not correct to apply the limit separately to claims in respect of material and non-material damage,[298] but that if a single piece of baggage contains property belonging to two or more passengers, each may recover the actual loss up to the convention maximum, and it is immaterial that there is only one baggage check.[299] The sums specified in the Convention are maximum sums, but a claimant must establish the actual loss in accordance with the normal rules of evidence.[300] In all cases, the carrier's liability in respect of registered or checked baggage may be increased if the passenger makes, at the time when the package was handed over to the carrier, a special declaration of the value at delivery and pays a supplementary sum if the case so requires. In that case, the carrier will be liable to pay a sum not exceeding the declared sum, unless it proves that the sum is greater than the actual value to the passenger at delivery.[301] **35-063**

[290] Carriage by Air Acts (Application of Provisions) Order 2004 (SI 2004/1899) Sch.2 art.22(2).

[291] cf. the cargo case of *Data Card Corp v Air Express International Corp* [1984] 1 W.L.R. 198.

[292] Carriage by Air Acts (Application of Provisions) Order 2004 (SI 2004/1899) Sch.2 art.22(3).

[293] Carriage by Air Act 1961 Sch.1 art.22(2) (3) (which, as amended by the Carriage by Air and Road Act 1979 s.4, actually contains the limits as amended by Montreal Additional Protocol No.2 of 1975); *Bland v British Airways Board* [1981] 1 Lloyd's Rep. 289, CA; *Collins v British Airways Board* [1982] Q.B. 734, CA.

[294] Carriage by Air Act 1961 Sch.1 art.22(2)(b). cf. the cargo case of *Allied Implants Technology Ltd v Lufthansa Cargo AG* [2000] 2 Lloyd's Rep. 46.

[295] Carriage by Air Acts (Application of Provisions) Order 2004 (SI 2004/1899) Sch.3 art.22(2), (3); Carriage by Air Act 1961 Sch.1 art.22(2), (3) (as amended by the Carriage by Air and Road Act 1979 s.4); Sch.1A as inserted by SI 1999/1312 art.22(2)(a), (3).

[296] Carriage by Air Act 1961 Sch.1B as inserted by SI 2002/263 art.22(2) (applied to European Union air carriers by Council Regulation 2027/97 art.3.1 as substituted by Parliament and Council Regulation 889/2002).

297 By decisions of the ICAO Council under art.24 of the Convention.

298 *Walz v Clickair SA* (C-63/09) EU:C:2010:251, [2011] 1 All E.R. (Comm) 1037.

299 Bundesgerichtshof, March 15, 2011, XZR 99/10.

300 *SL v Vueling Airlines SA* (C-86/19).

301 Carriage by Air Acts (Application of Provisions) Order 2004 (SI 2004/1899) Sch.2 art.22(2); Carriage by Air Act 1961 Sch.1 art.22(2)(a); Sch.1A as inserted by SI 1999/1312 art.22(2)(a); Sch.1B as inserted by SI 2002/263 art.22(2).

## (d) Cargo

### Upper financial limit of liability

*Replace paragraph with:*

**35-071** In cases governed by the Warsaw Convention 1929, the liability of the carrier in respect of cargo is limited to a sum of 250 francs per kilogramme of the lost or damaged package.[332] In cases governed by the Warsaw-Hague text, the limits remain as in the 1929 Convention.[333] Under the Warsaw-Hague text, however, when the loss, damage or delay of a part of the cargo, or of an object contained therein, affects the value of other packages covered by the same air waybill, the total weight of such package or packages must also be taken into consideration in determining the limit of liability.[334] The limits in the 1929 Convention and the Warsaw-Hague text as amended by Montreal Additional Protocol 1975 No.1 and No.2 respectively, and in cases under the MP4 Convention are 17 SDRs per kilogramme.[335] The same limit was set in the original text of the Montreal Convention 1999 but the limit was raised with effect from December 30, 2009 to 19 SDRs per kilogramme and with effect from December 28, 2019 to 22 SDRs per kilogramme.[336] In all cases, the carrier's liability may be increased if the consignor makes, at the time when the package was handed over to the carrier, a special declaration of the value at delivery and pays a supplementary sum if the case so requires. In that case, the carrier will be liable to pay a sum not exceeding the declared sum, unless it proves that the sum is greater than the actual value to the consignor at delivery.[337]

332 Carriage by Air Acts (Application of Provisions) Order 2004 (SI 2004/1899) Sch.2 art.22(2); *Data Card Corp v Air Express International Corp* [1984] 1 W.L.R. 198.

333 Carriage by Air Act 1961 Sch.1 art.22(2) (which, as amended by the Carriage by Air and Road Act 1979 s.4, actually contains the limits as amended by Montreal Additional Protocol No.2 of 1975).

334 Carriage by Air Act 1961 Sch.1 art.22(2)(b); *Allied Implants Technology Ltd v Lufthansa Cargo AG* [2000] 2 Lloyd's Rep. 46.

335 Carriage by Air Acts (Application of Provisions) Order 2004 (SI 2004/1899) Sch.3 art.22(2); Carriage by Air Act 1961 Sch.1 art.22(2), (3) (as amended by the Carriage by Air and Road Act 1979 s.4); Sch.1A as inserted by SI 1999/1312 art.22(2)(a); Sch.1B as inserted by SI 2002/263 art.22(2).

336 By decisions of the ICAO Council under art.24 of the Convention.

337 Carriage by Air Acts (Application of Provisions) Order 2004 (SI 2004/1899) Sch.2 art.22(2); Carriage by Air Act 1961 Sch.1 art.22(2)(a); Sch.1A as inserted by SI 1999/1312 art.22(2)(a); Sch.1B as inserted by SI 2002/263 art.22(2).

### Who can sue the carrier?

**35-078** *In line 9, after "the applicable Convention[365]", delete ":".*

## (e) Delay to Passengers, Baggage or Cargo

### Liability for delay

*Replace footnote 383 with:*

383 See Shawcross and Beaumont, on Air Law, para.VII[1003.1] and the very full judgment in *Chaing v Air Canada* Unreported January 22, 2016, Kingston-upon-Thames Cty Ct. 35-080

### Upper limit of liability

*Replace paragraph with:*

In cases governed by the Warsaw Convention 1929, the liability of the carrier for delay is limited to a sum of 125,000 francs per passenger; 250 francs per kilogramme in the case of registered baggage or cargo; and 5,000 francs per passenger in respect of objects of which the passenger takes charge.[384] In cases governed by the Warsaw-Hague text, the passenger limit is raised to 250,000 francs,[385] but the other limits are unchanged. The Warsaw-Hague figures are restated in Montreal Protocol No.2 of 1975 as 16,600 SDRs, 17 SDRs per kilogramme, and 332 SDRs per passenger,[386] and these limits were retained in the MP4 Convention.[387] The limit of the carrier's liability under the original text of the Montreal Convention 1999 was set in the carriage of passengers at 4,150 SDRs per passenger, in the carriage of baggage at 1,000 SDRs per passenger, and 17 SDRs per kilogramme of cargo[388]; the limits were raised to 4,694 SDRs, 1,131 SDRs and 19 SDRs with effect from December 30, 2009; and to 5,346 SDRs, 1,288 SDRs and 22 SDRs with effect from December 28, 2019.[389] 35-081

384 Carriage by Air Acts (Application of Provisions) Order 2004 (SI 2004/1899) Sch.2 art.22.

385 Carriage by Air Act 1961 Sch.1 art.22 as originally enacted.

386 Carriage by Air Act 1961 Sch.1 art.22 as amended by the Carriage by Air and Road Act 1979 s.4(1).

387 Carriage by Air Act 1961 Sch.1A as inserted by SI 1999/1312 art.22.

388 Carriage by Air Act 1961 Sch.1B as inserted by SI 2002/263 art.22.

389 By decisions of the ICAO Council under art.24 of the Convention.

## 6. NON-INTERNATIONAL CARRIAGE

### Applicable rules

*Replace paragraph with:*

The Conventions treated above regulate only international carriage. Carriage which is not international carriage as defined in any of the Conventions falls outside the Convention system. The applicable law is to be found in two sources. Union air carriers engaged in the carriage of persons or baggage are subject to Council Regulation 2027/97 as amended byEuropean Parliament and Council Regulation 889/2002,[390] which applies the provisions of the Montreal Convention 1999 to national as well as international carriage. However, Regulation 2027/97 applies only to "air carriers" defined by art.2(1)(a) to mean air transport undertakings with valid operating licences, and to "Community air carriers" defined by art.2(1)(b) to mean air carriers with valid operating licences granted by a Member State[390a]; so, carriage within a single Member State to view a property from the air by a carrier not required to have a valid operating licence is not to be within the Regulation or (as it was not international carriage) the Montreal Convention.[391] The liability of other 35-082 air carriers, and EU air carriers engaged in the carriage of cargo, is governed by Sch.1 to the Carriage by Air Acts (Application of Provisions) Order 2004,[392] which applies a modified version of the Montreal Convention 1999. Subject to the Regulation, the 2004 Order applies to all carriage by air other than carriage to which the Warsaw-Hague text, the MP4 Convention or the Montreal Convention 1999 applies, and Sch.1 applies to carriage which is not international carriage as defined in Schs 2 or 3 (applying the original Warsaw Convention and that Convention as amended by Montreal Additional Protocol No.1 of 1975).[393] To avoid giving too extensive a scope to the predecessor provisions, for it was arguable that the provisions of the United Kingdom Order applied to internal carriage in other countries, the House of Lords held that their application is limited to (a) carriage in which the places of departure and destination and any agreed stopping places are all within the United Kingdom or other British territory; and (b) non-convention carriage involving a place of departure or destination or an agreed stopping place in a foreign state and a place of departure or destination or an agreed stopping place in the United Kingdom or other British territory.[394]

[390] See above, paras 35-018 et seq.

[390a] With effect from IP completion day (on which see Vol.I, paras 1-014 et seq.), Regulation 2027/97, as amended by the Air Passenger Rights and Air Travel Organisers' Licensing (Amendment) (EU Exit) Regulations 2019 (SI 2019/278), applies only to UK air carriers. A UK air carrier is one with a valid operating licence granted by the Civil Aviation Authority: Regulation 2027/97 as so amended, art.2(b).

[391] *Prüller-Frey v Brodnig* (C-240/14) EU:C:2015:567, [2015] 1 W.L.R. 5031.

[392] SI 2004/1899 art.3. With effect from IP completion day, Regulation 2027/97 art.3, as amended by the Air Passenger Rights and Air Travel Organisers' Licensing (Amendment) (EU Exit) Regulations 2019 (SI 2019/278) will apply Sch.1 of the Order to non-UK carriers and to UK carriers engaged in the carriage of cargo.

[393] Carriage by Air Acts (Application of Provisions) Order 2004 (SI 2004/1899) arts 3(1) and 4.

[394] *Holmes v Bangladesh Biman Corp* [1989] A.C. 1112.

CHAPTER 36

# CARRIAGE BY LAND



## 2. INTERNAL CARRIAGE

### (a) Goods

#### *(i) Common and Private Carriers*

**The near extinction of the common carrier**

*To the end of paragraph, after "as a common carrier.[58]", add:*

In *Volcafe Ltd v Cia Sud Americana de Vapores SA*,[58a] the Supreme Court said that:

"... although the position of common carriers is commonly referred to by way of background in the case law, as it was in the judgments below, it is no longer a useful paradigm for the common law liability of a shipowner. Common carriers have for many years been an almost extinct category. For all practical legal purposes, the common law liability of a carrier, unless modified by contract, is the same as that of bailees for reward generally."

[58a] *Volcafe Ltd v Cia Sud Americana de Vapores SA* [2018] UKSC 61, [2019] A.C. 358 at [8].

## (b) Passengers

### Exceptions to the general limitations on carriers' contracting out of liability

*Replace footnote 372 with:*

**36-064** [372] Athens Convention art.3. As to the effect of the time limitation in art.16, see *Higham v Stena Sealink Ltd* [1996] 1 W.L.R. 1107; *South West Strategic Health Authority v Bay Island Voyages* [2015] EWCA Civ 708, [2016] Q.B. 503; *Warner v Scapa Flow Charters* [2018] UKSC 52, [2018] 1 W.L.R. 4974.

# 3. International Carriage

## (a) Introduction

### Modification to COTIF: the Vilnius Protocol

*Replace footnote 447 with:*

**36-081** [447] The Carriage of Dangerous Goods and Use of Transportable Pressure Equipment Regulations 2009 (SI 2009/1348, as amended by SI 2011/1885) implement RID. A new Appendix C (RID) has been formulated to take the place of the 2011 RID, with effect from January 1, 2019, although there does not yet appear to be implementing legislation in the United Kingdom. See above para.36-035.

## (b) Goods by Rail

### Application of CIM

*Replace paragraph with:*

**36-086** CIM applies to every contract of carriage of goods by rail for reward when the place of taking over of the goods and the place designated for delivery are situated in two different Member States, irrespective of the place of business and the nationality of the parties to the contract of carriage.[464] It follows that CIM will apply even though the carriage is performed through the territory of a non-Member State[465] and that CIM will not apply if the place of taking over and the place of delivery are in the same state even though the carriage is performed through the territory of another state. CIM will also apply to contracts of carriage of goods by rail where only one of the place of taking over or place of delivery are in a Member State provided the parties to the contract agree that CIM will apply.[466] CIM will further apply where the international carriage is the subject of a single contract which contract includes carriage by road or internal inland waterway as a supplement to the trans-frontier carriage by rail or carriage by sea or trans-frontier inland waterway if the latter services are listed in accordance with art.24 of COTIF.[467] However, CIM will not apply where the carriage is performed between stations situated on the territory of neighbouring states, when the infrastructure of the stations is managed by one or more infrastructure managers subject only to one of those states.[468] Any stipulation in the contract of carriage which, directly or indirectly, derogates from CIM shall be null and void, but such nullity shall not operate to nullify the other provisions of the contract.[469]

[464] CIM art.1(1).

[465] *Azienda Autonoma Ferrovie dello Stato v La Pace* (1976) 11 E.T.L. 137, Corte di Cassazione Civile, Italy; *Anon.*, Gerechtshof Den Haag, April 30, 2019 (2019) 55 E.T.L. 71.

[466] CIM art.1(2). See *Anon.*, Gerechtshof Den Haag, April 30, 2019 (2019) 55 E.T.L. 71.

[467] CIM art.1(3), (4). See *Anon.* (2013) 49 E.T.L. 228, BGH. As to rail-road traffic, see also CMR art.2(1) and para.36-119 below.

[468] CIM art.1(6).

[469] CIM art.5.

### Interpretation of the Convention

*To the end of paragraph, after "interpretation of CIM.", add new footnote 469a:*

[469a] See *Anon.*, Gerechtshof Den Haag, April 30, 2019 (2019) 55 E.T.L. 71. **36-087**

### Successive and substitute carriers

*Replace footnote 523 with:*

[523] CIM art.45(1). Article 45 does not preclude there being joint and several liability on the part of the carrier and sub-carrier: *Anon.*, Gerechtshof Den Haag, April 30, 2019 (2019) 55 E.T.L. 71. **36-096**

## (d) Goods by Road

### Consignment note

*Replace footnote 647 with:*

[647] Sch. art.8(1). As to the meaning of "apparent condition", see *Stef Transport Rennes v D&M Fraser* [2018] EWHC 2756 (Comm) at [31]. The carrier is not obliged to check the manner in which the goods were loaded (assuming that the carrier did not load the goods): *Generali Transports Assurances ea v Kuhne & Nagel ea* (2002) 37 E.T.L. 511. The apparent condition of goods includes the pre-cooling of the goods which are to be carried by refrigerated transport: *Anon.*, Oberlandesgericht Zweibrücken, March 12, 2019 (2019) 54 E.T.L. 449. **36-122**

### Loss, damage and delay

*Replace paragraph with:*

The carrier is liable for loss (total or partial), damage and delay in delivery in substantially the same circumstances as he is under CIM.[684] The general assertion of a carrier's liability in art.17(1) of CMR thus broadly corresponds to the position of a carrier in English law, quite apart from the Convention.[684a] Nonetheless art.17(1) does not exclude the carrier's liability for non-performance or for loss of or damage or delay to something other than the consigned goods, provided, of course, that this has not resulted from loss of or damage or delay to the consigned goods, in which case CMR does limit or exclude liability.[685] The loss or damage must occur between the time at which the carrier takes over the goods and the time of delivery.[686] The goods appear to be taken over by the carrier for the purposes of this provision when they pass from the control of the sender to that of the carrier, irrespective of when the carriage begins. "Delivery" similarly is marked by the goods leaving the carrier's control and passing into the control of the consignee.[687] The passing of control is a question of fact in the individual case. The terms "loss" and "damage" are used in an ordinary sense.[687a] Consequently even very serious damage to goods falls to be assessed for compensation purposes as damage under **36-126** art.25 of the Convention rather than being regarded as "constructive total loss" embraced by art.23.[688] Delay occurs when the goods have not been delivered within the agreed time limit[689] or, if none has been agreed, within a reasonable time.[690] If goods have not been delivered within 30 days of the agreed time limit or, if none, within 60 days of the carrier taking over the goods, this is conclusive evidence of loss.[691] The effect of these provisions is to make the limitation period in art.32(1)(b)[692] (which applies in cases of total loss) apply in cases where goods are damaged but not delivered.[693]

[684] Sch. art.17(1); see above, para.36-093. Art.17(1) does not in any event exhaust the carrier's liabilities: see also art.7(3) (above, para.36-123) and art.21 (failure of carrier to collect "cash on delivery" charge from consignee). Other liabilities may arise under national law. See, generally, Clarke at Ch.5; *Anon.*, Rechtbank te Rotterdam, March 30, 2016, (2016) 52 E.T.L. 101.

[684a] Where the sender's loss would have been caused in any event even if the carrier fails in its duty, see *Anon.*, Oberlandesgericht Frankfurt am Main, September 11, 2019 (2019) 55 E.T.L. 33.

[685] *Shell Chemicals UK Ltd v P & O Roadtanks Ltd* [1993] 1 Lloyd's Rep. 114, 116; affirmed on other grounds: [1995] 1 Lloyd's Rep. 297 (driver mistakenly collected a tank of detergent instead of contractual consignment of particular liquid chemical); *NV De Dijcker/NV Sonatra* (2007) 42 E.T.L. 427, Hof van Beroep te Antwerpen. See also *Anon.* (1993) 28 E.T.L. 917, where it was held that a claim based on inaccurate information provided by the carrier as to the location and expected arrival time of his vehicle was a claim under national law and not under the Convention. The Court of Appeal has confirmed that the CMR regime is inapplicable to personal injury suffered in the course of carriage: *Noble v RH Group Ltd* Unreported February 5, 1993. In *Tiense Suikerraffinaderij ea* (2014) 49 E.T.L. 337, the Hof van Cassatie van België held that other types of loss are governed by national law. See also *Dalesi v VC Europe BV* (2016) 52 E.T.L. 567, Gerechtshof Arnheim-Leeuwarden.

[686] As to the meaning of "taking over the goods", see *NV De Dijcker/NV Sonatra* (2007) 42 E.T.L. 427, Hof van Beroep te Antwerpen.

[687] Sch. art.15(1) provides that where circumstances prevent delivery of the goods after their arrival at the place designated for delivery, the carrier shall ask the sender for instructions. Where art.15(1) applies, there is no delivery within art.32(a) and consequently no limitation period begins to run: *Moto Vespa SA v MAT (Britannia Express) Ltd* [1979] 1 Lloyd's Rep. 175, 180. cf. *Castrol Industries Belgium nv v De Rijke Vloeistoffentransport bv* (1999) 35 E.T.L. 544, Antwerp. See Clarke, *International Carriage of Goods by Road: CMR*, 6th edn (2014), para.37. Where there has been online payment fraud, delivery takes place when the goods are handed over to the person instructed by the sender, even if that person's identity is feigned: *Anon.*, Oberlandesgericht Koblenz, May 9, 2019 (2019) 55 E.T.L. 26.

[687a] *Stef Transport Rennes v D&M Fraser* [2018] EWHC 2756 (Comm) at [32].

[688] *William Tatton and Co Ltd v Ferrymasters Ltd* [1974] 1 Lloyd's Rep. 203, 206; *Worldwide Carriers Ltd v Ardtran International Ltd* [1983] 1 Lloyd's Rep. 61, 63–64. When a carrier has to return damaged goods for repairs, such return carriage is covered by the original contract which has not been executed by reason of the non-delivery of the goods at their destination: *SA Soffritti Milan v Usines Balteau* (1977) 12 E.T.L. 881, Court of Appeal, Brussels.

[689] This time limit will be binding, provided that it has been agreed, even if it has not been included in the consignment note: *Anon.* (1994) 29 E.T.L. 97, BGH; cf. art.6(2)(f). This is not surprising, given art.5.

[690] Sch. art.19. This article emphasises the need for diligence in the making up of complete loads when partial loads are taken. The provisions in the Convention regarding compensation for delay presuppose performance (albeit late) of the contract by the carrier. They do not apply when the carrier has not performed the contract of carriage at all: *Gondrand SA v Agrati* [1978] L.M.C.L.Q. 518, Court of Appeal, Milan.

[691] Sch. art.20(1). cf. *Anon.* (2001) 37 E.T.L. 353, BGH. See Clarke at paras 56, 58.

[692] See below, para.36-143.

[693] *Worldwide Carriers Ltd v Ardtran International Ltd* [1983] 1 Lloyd's Rep. 61, 65; *ICI Plc v MAT Transport Ltd* [1987] 1 Lloyd's Rep. 354, 360. cf. *Royal Insurance Cie v Transport R Marcel* (1978) 13 E.T.L. 742, Tribunal de Commerce, Paris.

## The carrier's exemptions from liability: art.17(2)

*Replace footnote 698 with:*

698 Frozen meat carried on a refrigerated trailer has been held not to have any relevant inherent vice within the meaning of art.17(2): *Ulster-Swift Ltd v Taunton Meat Haulage Ltd* [1975] 2 Lloyd's Rep. 502, 505–506: affirmed [1977] 1 Lloyd's Rep. 346, 351–352 CA. cf. *Centrocoop Export-Import SA v Brit European Transport Ltd* [1984] 2 Lloyd's Rep. 618. See further *Stef Transport Rennes v D&M Fraser* [2018] EWHC 2756 (Comm) at [33]. **36-127**

## The carrier's exemptions from liability: art.17(4)

*Replace paragraph with:*

**36-128** The second type of excepted risks, embraced by art.17(4), covers loss or damage arising from the special risks inherent in one or more of the following circumstances: (a) carriage in open, unsheeted vehicles when their use has been expressly agreed and specified in the consignment note; (b) absence or inadequacy of packing of goods liable to wastage or damage if not properly packed[706]; (c) handling, loading, stowage or unloading of the goods by the sender, the consignee, or persons acting on their behalf[707]; (d) the nature of certain kinds of goods which particularly exposes them to total or partial loss or to damage, especially through breakage, rust, decay,[708] desiccation, leakage, normal wastage, or the action of moth or vermin; (e) insufficient or inadequate marks or numbers on packages; and (f) the carriage of livestock.[709] If the carrier establishes that the loss or damage could be attributed to one or more of these excepted risks, this is rebuttably presumed, provided that in (a) above there has not been an abnormal shortage or a loss of any package.[710] If a claimant rebuts, within the meaning of the second sentence of art.18(2), the presumption under the first sentence of that paragraph that loss or damage could be attributed to an excepted risk, the carrier is then liable for loss or damage under art.17(1). To disprove the presumption the standard of proof is that of the balance of probabilities.[711] The carrier under CMR art.18(4) is not entitled to the exemption granted by art.17(4)(d) above where he performs the carriage in a specially equipped vehicle, unless he proves that all steps incumbent on him in the circumstances with regard to the choice, maintenance and use of the equipment were taken.[712] Under art.18(5) the carrier, when carrying livestock, must show that he took all steps normally incumbent on him in the circumstances, despite the exemption in art.17(4)(f). There should be a reduction in the carrier's liability to the extent that the loss or damage was contributed to matters falling within one or more of the exemptions.[713]

706 This exemption was construed strictly in *Tetroc Ltd v Cross-Con (International) Ltd* [1981] 1 Lloyd's Rep. 192. cf. *Anon.*, App. Paris 19.10.93 (1993) B.T. 792. See also *Aquascutum Ltd v Europa Freight Corp* Unreported November 20, 1985; *Anon.*, Oberster Gerichtshof Österreich, April 27, 2016, (2016) 51 E.T.L. 560.

707 Whilst many decisions of Continental courts on the interpretation of art.17(4)(c) have been reported, these courts have differed widely in their approach. There has been a tendency to introduce legal concepts drawn from the particular municipal law. Some decisions suggest that the sender is always responsible for loading and stowage. Others make the carrier responsible and suggest that he has been guilty of a wrongful act and neglect if he has not checked loading and stowage, unless the parties agree contractually otherwise (*Anon.*, Oberster Gerichtshof Österreich, July 6, 2016, (2016) 51 E.T.L. 565), carried out by the sender. See, e.g. *Anon.*, Bundesgerichtshof, March 19, 2015, (2016) 51 E.T.L. 99. See Wijffels (1976) 11 E.T.L. 208, 211–229, for an analysis of Continental decisions interpreting art.17(4)(c) in 12 different ways. Whilst CMR does not expressly provide that unloading must be performed by the carrier, the carrier has been held responsible for unloading in the absence of stipulations to the contrary or exemptions resulting from the nature of the goods: *PVBA Wanman and Zorn v Transport Internationaux L'Essor Maritime Français* (1976) 11 E.T.L. 231, Hof van Beroep, Ghent. If the carrier notices during the carriage that the goods have been packed defectively within the meaning of

art.17(4)(b) he must take all steps to avoid damage to the goods. Failure to do so will result in liability for any damage being apportioned between the carrier and the sender: *Anon.* (1976) 11 E.T.L. 261, Oberlandesgericht, Saarbrucken. A carrier who undertakes to unload goods is liable for the whole operation even if that carrier is a successive carrier: *Anon.* (1993) 28 E.T.L. 286, Hof Brussel. He should refuse to unload if in his view it is likely to prove dangerous. Alternatively, he should at least enter reservations: *SA Polysar France v Booy Clean Belgium* (1977) 12 E.T.L. 293, Commercial Court, Antwerp. Art.8 requires the carrier to check the condition of the goods and their packaging. Further, it has been held that art.17(4)(c) does not exonerate a carrier from checking the stowage of the goods performed by the sender. If the carrier performs the carriage, notwithstanding obvious inadequacies or defects in the stowage, the carrier will be liable for the resultant damage: *Anon.* (1993) 28 E.T.L. 618, Cass.; *GIE La Réunion Européene v SA Warin* (1995) 30 E.T.L. 688, Cass. However, it may be that the carrier is under no obligation to check the loading or stowage of the goods, if adequately performed by one who is accustomed to such operations (i.e. a specialist): *Anon.* (1993) 28 E.T.L. 768, Rechtbank van Koophandel te Antwerpen. See *Cigna Insurance Co of Europe v Intercargo NV* (1999) 34 E.T.L. 264. On the other hand, in *Anon.* (2007) 42 E.T.L. 766, Bundesgerichtshof, it was held that the carrier's liability would be reduced pursuant to art.17(5) where the carrier stowed the goods but subject to the sender's supervision.

708 The carrier was relieved of liability under this head in *Centrocoop Export-Import SA v Brit European Transport Ltd* [1984] 2 Lloyd's Rep. 618. As to the breadth of this defence, see *W Donald & Son (Wholesale Meat Contractors) Ltd v Continental Freeze Ltd*, 1984 S.L.T. 182; *Anon.* (2013) 49 E.T.L. 213, Oberster Gerichtshof Österreich.

709 See art.18(5) and *Hans Johan Kosta v Samson Transport Co A/S* (1997) 32 E.T.L. 230, Denmark.

710 Sch. art.18(2), (3). Where a sender of dangerous goods has not informed the carrier of the nature of the danger and the necessary precautions and where this information has not been entered in the consignment note, the sender or the consignee has the burden of proving that the carrier knew the nature of the danger: art.22(1). The phrase "*could be attributed to*" means that the carrier need only prove that one or more of the excluded matters relied upon could plausibly have caused the damage, not that on a balance of probabilities the excluded matter did cause the damage: *Exportadora Valle de Colina SA v AP Moller-Maersk A/S* [2010] EWHC 3224 (Comm) at [24]–[26]; *Stef Transport Rennes v D&M Fraser* [2018] EWHC 2756 (Comm) at [34]. cf. *Hijka BV v Vermeulen* [1978] L.M.C.L.Q. 650 DC, Utrecht; *GIE Law Réunion Européene v SA Warin* (1995) 30 E.T.L. 688, Cass. See also *Hans Johan Kosta v Samson Transport Co A/S* (1997) 32 E.T.L. 230, Denmark. The carrier need not have entered reservations in the consignment note: *van Asten bvba v Mercator nv* (1999) 35 E.T.L. 386, Hof Cass., Belgium.

711 *Ulster-Swift Ltd v Taunton Meat Haulage Ltd* [1977] 1 Lloyd's Rep. 346, 352; *Exportadora Valle de Colina SA v AP Moller-Maersk A/S* [2010] EWHC 3224 (Comm) at [24]–[26].

712 When the court is considering whether or not a carrier has proved that he took all steps incumbent on him in the circumstances pursuant to art.18(4), the court can take into account not only the evidence adduced by the carrier as to the steps taken but also evidence as to the soundness or otherwise of the goods at the time of loading. Where the goods have admittedly deteriorated during the period of transport, the court is entitled to hold that the carrier has failed to discharge the burden of proof on him under art.18(4) if, on all the evidence, it was more likely than not that he had failed to take some unidentified step incumbent on him: *Ulster-Swift Ltd v Taunton Meat Haulage Ltd* [1977] 1 Lloyd's Rep. 346, 353. The court considered that this interpretation of art.18(4) was consistent with the view that in English law a claimant need not prove what was the precise, specific event by reason of which his goods were lost whilst in the custody of the carrier: cf. *Houghland v RR Low (Luxury Coaches) Ltd* [1962] 1 Q.B. 694. The court found that the carrier had discharged this burden of proof under art.18(4) in *Centrocoop Export-Import SA v Brit European Transport Ltd* [1984] 2 Lloyd's Rep. 618. See also *Anon.*, Oberlandesgericht Zweibrücken, March 12, 2019 (2019) 54 E.T.L. 449.

713 Sch. art.17(5); *Anon.* (2007) 42 E.T.L. 766, Bundesgerichtshof.

## Upper financial limits of liability and measure of damages

*Replace paragraph with:*

**36-130** Where a carrier is held liable for loss of the goods, the value of the goods is calculated for compensation purposes as being their value at the place and time at which they were accepted for carriage.[722] The value is fixed according to the commodity exchange price, or, failing that, the current market price, or, failing both, the normal value of goods of the same kind and quality.[723] The carrier's liability for loss of the goods is limited to 8.33 units of account per kilogramme of gross weight short,[724] unless the sender declared in the consignment note a higher value[725] or a special interest in delivery[726] against an agreed surcharge. The carrier must also refund the carriage charges, customs duties and other charges incurred in respect of the carriage.[727] The expression "the carriage" in this context is restricted to the carriage covered by the contract and does not embrace, for example, the return carriage charges and storage costs of goods damaged during the period of carriage covered by the contract.[728] The carriage charges, customs duties and other charges are refunded in full in the case of damage amounting to total destruction but only in proportion to the damage sustained in the event of damage not amounting to total destruction.[729] The carrier's liability for delay is limited to the carriage charges.[730] His liability for damage is the amount by which the goods have diminished in value, but may not exceed the amount payable in respect of loss.[731] The carrier is also liable to the sender for compensation for an amount representing the "cash on delivery" charge,[732] in the event that the carrier fails to collect that charge.[733] The court has power at any stage of the proceedings to make such order as appears to be just and equitable if the carrier's liability is limited, and may have regard to other proceedings which have been, or are likely to be, commenced in the United Kingdom or elsewhere.[734]

[722] Sch. art.23(1). See, generally, Clarke at Ch.8. CMR only provides compensation for loss of, or damage to, the goods carried. A claim for compensation for damage done, e.g. to the sender's or the consignee's tanks, cannot be brought within CMR: *English and American Insurance Co Ltd v Transport Nagels* (1977) 12 E.T.L. 420, Commercial Court, Antwerp. In *NV Valkeniersnatie v NV International Services and Freightforwarding* (2006) 41 E.T.L. 272, Hof van Beroep te Antwerpen, it was held that where a carrier was instructed to take out 100 per cent insurance, but failed so to do, he could not rely on the limits set out in art.23.

[723] Sch. art.23(2). Such exchange, market or normal value is a reference to the standard rate for the goods and ignores the peculiar situation of the goods in question: *Anon.* (1993) 28 E.T.L. 740, BGH. The current market price has been held not to include, e.g. any excise duty payable on the product sold in a home market: *James Buchanan and Co Ltd v Babco Forwarding and Shipping (UK) Ltd* [1977] Q.B. 208 CA; unanimously affirmed on this point: [1978] A.C. 141. Contra, *Anon.* (1994) 29 E.T.L. 360, Supreme Court of Denmark.

[724] Sch. art.23(3) as amended by the Carriage by Air and Road Act 1979 s.4(2). See *Topdanmark Forsikring A/S v DSV Road A/S* (2016) 51 E.T.L. 93, Supreme Court of Denmark; *Anon.* (2018) 53 E.T.L. 453, Bundesgerichtshof; *Anon.* (2018) 54 E.T.L. 218, Oberster Gerichtshof Österreich. This section gave effect as part of English law, with effect from December 18, 1980, to a Protocol to CMR which entered into force on that date: see above, para.36-118. Prior to that time the unit used in the Convention was the gold franc: this franc had the same meaning as in the rail Conventions CIM, CIV and the Additional Convention CAV, which Conventions were abrogated when the new rail Convention COTIF entered into force on May 1, 1985: see above, paras 36-079—36-081. The Protocol which effected the changeover to units of account also added a new paragraph to CMR which became art.23(7) and which provided that the unit of account in the Convention was to be the Special Drawing Right (SDR) as defined by the International Monetary Fund ("IMF"). The amount specified in art.23(3) is to be converted into the national currency of the State of the court seised of the case on the basis of the value of that currency on the date of the judgment or the date agreed upon by the parties. When, however, the amounts on which compensation under the Convention is based are not expressed in the currency of the country in which payment is claimed, conversion shall be at the rate of exchange applicable on the day and at the place of payment of compensation: 1965 Act Sch. art.27(2).

[725] Sch. art.24.

[726] Sch. art.26.

[727] Sch. art.23(4). The expression "other charges incurred in respect of the carriage" was construed by reference to the French text ("*les autres frais encourus a l'occasion du transport*") as meaning "any other expenses which the owner of the goods has to pay as a result of the carriage of the goods": *James Buchanan & Co Ltd v Babco Forwarding and Shipping (UK) Ltd* [1977] Q.B. 208 at 224, per Lawton L.J.: affirmed by the House of Lords [1978] A.C. 141. Lord Wilberforce (at 154) agreed that the English and French versions of art.23(4) are equally broad and loosely-drafted. They should, in his Lordship's opinion, be interpreted broadly so as to cover charges arising in the course of the removal from the failure of the carrier to carry in accordance with the contract of carriage. Viscount Dilhorne (at 158) construed the words "in respect of" as meaning "in consequence of" or "arising out of" in this context. See Clarke, *International Carriage of Goods by Road: CMR*, 6th edn (2014), para.98; *Anon.* (2004) 39 E.T.L. 93,

Bundesgerichtshof. A survey fee incurred as part of the cost of realising the damaged value of goods falls within art.23(4): *ICI Plc v MAT Transport Ltd* [1987] 1 Lloyd's Rep. 354, 362; as do premiums for the insurance of the goods carried: *M Bardiger Ltd v Halberg Spedition Aps* Unreported, October 26, 1990. As to charges and duties due to the non-reconciliation of documents after the theft of goods during transport see, *Philip Morris Holland BV v Transportgroep Van der Graaf BV* (2006) 41 E.T.L. 804, Hoge Raad der Nederlanden. However, the cost of cleaning or destruction of the goods does not fall within art.23(4): *PB v O en A* (1999) 35 E.T.L. 566, Ghent. The plaintiff will be entitled to a refund under art.23(4) where the carrier is guilty of wilful misconduct, although the limitation "no further damages shall be payable" will not, in that event, apply: *Lacey's Footwear (Wholesale) Ltd v Bowler International Freight Ltd* [1997] 2 Lloyd's Rep. 369. See also *Transport Van Laer NV v Comexas Benelux NV* (2002) 37 E.T.L. 475; *Sandeman Coprimar SA v Transitos y Transportes Integrales SA* [2003] EWCA Civ 113, [2003] 2 W.L.R. 1496; *Philip Morris Products SA v Smidl SRO* Unreported, November 17, 2017; *Anon.*, Gerechtshof 'S-Hertogenbosch, April 30, 2019 (2019) 54 E.T.L. 540.

[728] *William Tatton Co Ltd v Ferrymasters Ltd* [1974] 1 Lloyd's Rep. 203. However in *James Buchanan & Co Ltd v Babco Forwarding and Shipping (UK) Ltd*, above, [1977] Q.B. 208 at 215, the Court of Appeal (per Lord Denning M.R.) expressed the opinion that, in light of their broader interpretation of the Convention, return carriage charges and storage costs should be allowed. See also *Thermo Engineers Ltd v Ferrymasters Ltd* [1981] 1 W.L.R. 1470, 1478.

[729] *William Tatton and Co Ltd v Ferrymasters Ltd* [1974] 1 Lloyd's Rep. 203.

[730] Sch. art.23(5). The compensation which may be awarded pursuant to this provision need not be the carriage charges themselves; the compensation is limited in quantum to the amount of those charges. The provision refers to "damage" resulting from delay. It is suggested that this is a reference to any financial deprivation suffered by the claimant, rather than to physical damage sustained by the goods: *Anon.* (1993) 28 E.T.L. 740, BGH. The claimant may recover both damages sustained directly or losses incurred as a result of his liability to another party: *Anon.* (1994) 29 E.T.L. 97, BGH. If goods are lost as a result of delay, it has been held that the limitation provisions under art.23(1)–(4) on the one hand and under art.23(5) on the other hand may be aggregated (*Deniz-Er v NV Soncotra* (2007) 42 E.T.L. 275, Hof van Beroep te Gent). This decision is to be doubted; see Clarke, *International Carriage of Goods by Road: CMR*, 6th edn (2014), para.59.

[731] Sch. art.25. See generally, *William Tatton and Co Ltd v Ferrymasters Ltd* [1974] 1 Lloyd's Rep. 203.

[732] Which should have been entered on the face of the consignment note (art.6(2)(c)). Given art.4, it is unlikely that the failure to enter the COD charge on the consignment note will deprive any contractual requirement that the charge be collected against delivery to the consignee of its force.

[733] Sch. art.21. In *Eastern Kayam Carpets Ltd v Eastern United Freight Ltd* Unreported December 6, 1983, the court held that such a charge was not limited to freight and could extend to the price of the goods. The charge to be collected by the carrier could be in cash or in the form of a draft (*Anon.* (1970) 5 E.T.L. 670, Arrond. Breda). If the carrier is ordered to deliver the goods against receipt of a certified cheque, this order must be obeyed with all reasonable care to ensure that the carrier receives a certified cheque: *Anon.* (1994) 29 E.T.L. 464, Hof van Cassatie van België; cf. *Eastern Kayam Carpets Ltd v Eastern United Freight Ltd*, above; *Anon.* (1996) 31 E.T.L. 404, BGH. The COD charge would not include any document which did not represent payment of the charge (*Eastern Kayam Carpets Ltd v Eastern United Freight Ltd*, above). See also *Coveretex v Dendertrans Int* (1997) 32 E.T.L. 602.

[734] s.3.

## Wilful misconduct: an exception to limitation

*In line 3, after "damage was caused by his wilful misconduct,", add new footnote 735a:*

**36-131** [735a] As to the requirement of a causal connection, see *Anon.* (2017) 53 E.T.L. 297, Cour de Cassation de France.

## Reservations at delivery and extinction of claims

*Replace footnote 790 with:*

**36-143** [790] Sch. art.30(2). See *Anon.* (2018) 53 E.T.L. 180, Rechtbank Zeeland-West-Brabant.

## Limitation of actions

*In line 2, after "three years in the case of wilful misconduct.", add new footnote 797a:*

[797a] As to the three-year limitation period in the case of wilful misconduct, see *Anon.* (2018) 53 E.T.L. 308, Hanseatisches Oberlandesgerichts Hamburg; *Anon.* (2018) 53 E.T.L. 460, Gerechtshof 'S-Hertogenbosch. **36-144**

## Jurisdiction

*Replace paragraph with:*

Article 31(1) prescribes those states in which legal proceedings may be brought in connection with any contract of carriage to which the CMR Convention applies, in addition to the state agreed between the parties,[814] namely the state of the residence of the defendant, the state where the goods are taken over by the carrier, the place designated for delivery of the goods or the state which has been agreed by the parties.[815] This is intended to provide a self-contained code for the allocation of jurisdiction,[816] so that Regulation (EU) 1215/2012[817] or any other jurisdiction regulation[817a] is inapplicable insofar as the same rule is provided for in both conventions, provided that the applicable rule in CMR is highly predictable, facilitates the sound administration of justice, enables the risk of concurrent proceedings to be minimised, and is construed harmoniously with the objectives of the Regulation, ensuring the free movement of judgments in the European Union.[818] In the event of more than one set of proceedings being commenced in more than one state, art.31(2) provides that the later action will not be entertained if it concerns the same parties and is brought on the same grounds.[819] The claimant may bring proceedings against the first carrier, the last carrier or the carrier who was performing that part of the carriage where the relevant loss, damage or delay has occurred.[820] When the defendant carrier seeks recourse against other carriers concerned in the carriage, such action is governed by art.39(2), which is more restrictive than art.31(1). Such recourse must (not may, as suggested by the provision itself) be brought in the state of residence of one of those carriers.[821] Article 39(2) is concerned only with actions among carriers and not claims by cargo interests (whose claims are governed by art.31).[822] It appears not to be open to the carriers to agree an alternative forum for the determination of the carrier's recourse claim, except possibly arbitration.[823] **36-146**

[814] *Catlin Insurance Co (UK) v Gasia* (2013) 49 E.T.L. 222, Rechtbank van Koophandel te Antwerpen.

[815] A carrier who did not agree to a particular jurisdiction, and had no notice of a particular jurisdiction agreement, would not be bound by that agreement: *British American Tobacco Switzerland SA v Exel Europe Ltd* [2012] EWHC 694 (Comm), [2012] 2 Lloyd's Rep. 1 at [46]–[51], [2015] UKSC 65, [2016] A.C. 262 at [26]. Accordingly, a successive carrier cannot be sued in proceedings brought against the primary carrier pursuant to a jurisdiction agreement between the claimant and the primary carrier, if the successive carrier did not agree to that clause and if the jurisdiction agreement is not in the consignment note, subject to the other heads of jurisdiction in CMR: *British American Tobacco Switzerland SA v Exel Europe Ltd* [2015] UKSC 65, [2016] A.C. 262. In *Anon.* (2002) 37 E.T.L. 80, BGH, it was held that art.31 extends to extra-contractual claims. See also *Anon.*, Oberster Gerichtshof Österreich, February 25, 2015, (2015) 50 E.T.L. 700. Art.31(1) does not lay down any formal requirements for any jurisdiction agreement between the parties (cf. art.23 of EC Regulation 44/2001). Whether the factual requirement of an "agreement" on jurisdiction will be construed in the manner adopted by the European Court of Justice in the context of art.23 of EC Regulation 44/2001 is unclear. In *LSG-RA Leutner GmbH v BVBA Ideal Transport* (2006) 41 E.T.L. 570, the Hof van Beroep te Gent held that the parties are free to choose a jurisdiction without stating it in the waybill and that the agreement was to be adjudged by reference to national law; see, however, (2007) 42 E.T.L. 401, Hof van Cassatie van Belgie. There is much to be said in favour of a consistent approach, given the difficulties posed by multi-modal transport

involving carriage by road (which in isolation would be governed by CMR) and by sea (which in isolation would require jurisdiction agreements to comply with art.23 of the Brussels I Regulation).

[816] *Arctic Electronics (UK) Ltd v McGregor Sea and Air Services* [1985] 2 Lloyd's Rep. 510, 514. Art.31 gives the plaintiff the option to choose the forum, so that the forum should not be able to exercise any otherwise available power to decline jurisdiction: cf. *Milor Srl v British Airways Plc* [1996] 3 All E.R. 537; *Deaville v Aeroflot Russian International Airlines* [1997] 2 Lloyd's Rep. 67, 72 (Warsaw Convention art.28). In *Ideal Transport v LSG-RA Leutner GmbH* (2007) 42 E.T.L. 401, the Hof van Cassatie van Belgie held that the choice offered by art.31 was cumulative and a contractual choice of forum did not necessarily prevail.

[817] Council Regulation 1215/2012 art.71. This Regulation applies to proceedings instituted on or after January 10, 2015: Civil Jurisdiction and Judgments (Amended) Regulations 2014 (SI 2014/2947) reg.1. See *Harrison & Son Ltd v RT Steward Transport Ltd* (1993) 28 E.T.L. 747; *British American Tobacco Switzerland SA v Exel Europe Ltd* [2015] UKSC 65, [2016] A.C. 262; *Nickel & Goeldner Spedition GmbH v "Kintra" UAB* (C-157/13) EU:C:2014:2145, [2015] Q.B. 96 (CJEU). However, note the ECJ's decision in *Réunion Européenne SA v Spliethoff's Bevrachtingskantoor BV* [1999] C.L.C. 282, which concerned multi-modal carriage by sea and then land, and the application of the Brussels Convention. See *Anon.*, Oberster Gerichtshof Österreich (2003) 38 E.T.L. 656, 658, 661; *DFDS Transport A/S v Dieter Mehrholz Internationale Transporte* (2004) 39 E.T.L. 74, Supreme Court of Denmark; *Royal & Sun Alliance Insurance Plc v MK Digital Fze (Cyprus) Ltd* [2005] EWHC 1408 (Comm), [2005] 2 Lloyd's Rep. 679 at [55]–[69]; reversed on other grounds [2006] EWCA Civ 629, [2006] 2 Lloyd's Rep. 110; *Zurich Insurance Plc v Abnormal Load Services (International) Ltd* (C-88/17) [2018] 4 W.L.R. 155. Regulation (EU) 1215/2012 applies until December 31, 2020: European Union (Withdrawal) Act 2018 s.2; the Civil Jurisdiction and Judgments (Amendment) (EU Exit) Regulations 2019 (SI 479/2019) regs 92–93; European Union (Withdrawal Agreement) Act 2020 s.2.

[817a] *BA van Velthaven v Containerships CSG Rotterdam BV* (2019) 55 E.T.L. 41.

[818] *TNT Express Nederland BV v AXA Versicherung AG* (C-533/08) EU:C:2010:243, [2011] R.T.R. 11. In the same case, the ECJ held that it did not have jurisdiction to interpret art.31 of CMR. See *British American Tobacco Switzerland SA v Exel Europe Ltd* [2015] UKSC 65, [2016] A.C. 262 at [48]–[58]. See also *Nipponkoa Insurance Co (Europe) Ltd v Inter-Zuid Transport BV* (C-452/12) EU:C:2013:858, (2013) 49 E.T.L. 165, ECJ, where it was held that art.31 must be interpreted in a manner which ensures conditions which are no less favourable than the objectives under the Regulation.

[819] *Andrea Merzario Ltd v Internationale Spedition Leitner Gesellschaft mbH* [2001] EWCA Civ 61, [2001] 1 Lloyd's Rep. 490. cf. the French text of the CMR Convention: "*pour la même cause*". Arts 21 and 22 of the Brussels Convention have been held to remain applicable, because CMR does not regulate the matters of *lis alibi pendens*: *Frans Maas Logistics (UK) Ltd v CDR Trucking BV* [1999] 2 Lloyd's Rep. 179; *Royal & Sun Alliance Insurance Plc v MK Digital Fze (Cyprus) Ltd* [2005] EWHC 1408 (Comm), [2005] 2 Lloyd's Rep. 679 at [55]–[69]; reversed on other grounds [2006] EWCA Civ 629, [2006] 2 Lloyd's Rep. 110. This question was identified but not resolved in *Harrison & Son Ltd v RT Steward Transport Ltd* (1993) 28 E.T.L. 747. cf. *Deaville v Aeroflot Russian International Airlines* [1997] 2 Lloyd's Rep. 67, 71 (Warsaw Convention). See Council Regulation 44/2001 arts 27 and 28. In *Anon.* (2006) 41 E.T.L. 561, the Oberster Gerichtshof Österreich held that lis pendens must be assumed under art.31 where the respective claims are for negative declaratory relief and affirmative relief (contra *Anon.* (2004) E.T.L. 255, BGH; *Anon.* (2004) E.T.L. 264, BGH.

[820] Sch. art.36. However, art.36 is not a provision stipulating in which jurisdiction proceedings by cargo claimants may be brought; that is a matter for art.31. See *British American Tobacco Switzerland SA v Exel Europe Ltd* [2015] UKSC 65, [2016] A.C. 262 at [19]–[20], [34]–[47], [67], [69].

[821] See above, paras 36-140—36-141. *Harrison & Son Ltd v RT Steward Transport Ltd* (1993) 28 E.T.L. 747; *Cummins Engine Co Ltd v Davis Freight Forwarding (Hull) Ltd* [1981] 2 Lloyd's Rep. 402, 408–409; contra, *Arctic Electronics (UK) Ltd v McGregor Sea and Air Services* [1985] 2 Lloyd's Rep. 510, adopting the view of Eveleigh L.J. in *Cummins Engine Co Ltd v Davis Freight Forwarding (Hull) Ltd* [1981] 2 Lloyd's Rep. 402, 409. In *Blue Water Shipping A/S v Melship Eesti OÜ* (2000) 35 E.T.L. 772, the Supreme Court of Denmark held that art.39 referred to the residence of the defendant successive carrier and not the claimant successive carrier. cf. art.40.

[822] *British American Tobacco Switzerland SA v Exel Europe Ltd* [2015] UKSC 65, [2016] A.C. 262 at [36]–[37], [62], [68].

[823] Sch. art.33, which gives force to an arbitration clause in the contract of carriage, will bind the parties to the contract of carriage. Such parties are identified in s.14(2)(c) of the 1965 Act.

## No contracting out

*Replace footnote 827 with:*

[827] Sch. art.41(1). A carrier's general conditions of contract can never relieve him of his liability if such conditions derogate from CMR: *SA Chemin de Fer Industriel Groups v Geszait* (1978) 13 E.T.L. 285, Commercial Court, Brussels; *Datec Electronic Holdings Ltd v United Parcels Service Ltd* [2005] EWCA Civ 1418, [2006] 1 Lloyd's Rep. 279 at [24]; *Air & Road OVT SrL v Zurich* (2018) 53 E.T.L. 469, Rechtbank Zeeland-West-Brabant. **36-148**

Chapter 37

# CONSTRUCTION CONTRACTS

## 1. THE NATURE OF CONSTRUCTION CONTRACTS

### (a) Definitions

#### Application of Housing Grants, Construction and Regeneration Act 1996

*Replace footnote 16 with:*

**37-006** [16] s.104(5). For a consideration of the principles that apply to such "hybrid" contracts, see *Equitix Ltd v Bester Generation UK Ltd* [2018] EWHC 177 (TCC), [2018] B.L.R. 281 per Coulson J. at [19]–[23].

### (f) PFI Contracts

#### Example of PFI project

*Replace footnote 98 with:*

**37-041** [98] *Biffa Waste Services v Maschinenfabrik Ernst Hese GmbH* [2008] EWHC 6 (TCC), [2008] B.L.R. 155; see also *Amey Birmingham Highways Ltd v Birmingham City Council* [2018] EWCA Civ 264, [2018] B.L.R. 225.

## 2. FORMATION OF CONTRACT

### (b) Contract/No Contract

#### Concluded agreement

*Replace paragraph with:*

Construction contracts are often the product of lengthy negotiation over a range of issues such as scope of work, price, time for completion, specification and performance criteria. It will be a question of importance and often one of some complexity to decide at what point (if at all) in the negotiations the parties reached a concluded agreement. Some important guidelines are set out in *Trollope & Colls v Atomic Power Constructions*[128] and *Pagnan v Feed Products*[129] which can be summarised in the following propositions[130]: **37-049**

- (i) in order to determine whether a contract has been concluded in the course of negotiations, one must look to the negotiations as a whole[131];
- (ii) there must be an intention by both parties, continuing up to the date of the supposed contract, to make a contract;
- (iii) at the date of the supposed contract, the parties must have been of one mind on all the terms which they then regarded as being required in order that a contract should come into existence;
- (iv) the terms on which the parties were of one mind must not omit any term which, even though the parties did not realise it, was in fact essential to be agreed if the contract was to be commercially workable;
- (v) in relation to the agreement of further terms the parties must intend that agreement would become binding forthwith, even though there were terms still to be agreed;
- (vi) there must be some manifestation which indicated with sufficient clarity the acceptance by the offeree of the offer as then made to him, such acceptance complying with any stipulation in the offer itself as to the manner of acceptance.

[128] [1963] 1 W.L.R. 333.

[129] [1987] 2 Lloyd's Rep. 601, 619, per Lloyd L.J. The principles set out by Lloyd L.J. were expressly referred to in *Mitsui Babcock Energy v John Brown Engineering* (1996) 51 Con. L.R. 129, 166–167. See also *Birse Construction Ltd v St David Ltd* [1999] B.L.R. 194 and *Anchor 2020 Ltd v Midas Construction Ltd* [2019] EWHC 435 (TCC), 184 Con. L.R. 215.

[130] See *RTS Flexible Systems Ltd v Molkeri Alois Muller GmbH & Co* [2010] UKSC 14, [2010] 1 W.L.R. 753 at [48]–[49] where the Supreme Court held that these same principles applied whether one was considering a contract concluded in correspondence or by oral communications and conduct. See also *Iliffe & Iliffe v Feltham Construction Ltd* [2014] EWHC 2125 (TCC), per Stuart-Smith J. at [79]–[82] for a summary of the relevant principles in a construction context. In *Hamid v Francis Bradshaw Partnership* [2013] EWCA Civ 470, [2013] B.L.R. 447, the Court of Appeal found that where an issue arises as to the identity of a party referred to in a written contract extrinsic evidence is admissible to assist in the resolution of that issue and that, if an objective analysis shows that a party has been misdescribed in the document, the court may correct that error as a matter of construction, not rectification; however, in *Liberty Mercian Ltd v Cuddy Civil Engineering Ltd* [2013] EWHC 2688 (TCC), [2014] B.L.R. 179, it was held that in order to identify the true parties to a written contract the principle of misnomer may only apply to replace the identified contracting party with another entity in circumstances there was a clear mistake on the face of the instrument when it is read by reference to its relevant background or context and where it is clear what correction should be made. See also *Arcadis Consulting (UK) Ltd v Hyder Consulting (UK) Ltd* [2018] EWCA Civ 2222, 181 Con. L.R. 1 for a further consideration by the Court of Appeal of acceptance of a counter-offer in full by the conduct of a contractor in performing building works.

[131] See also, *Hussey v Horne-Payne* (1879) L.R. 4 App. Cas. 311; *Port Sudan Cotton v Chettiar* [1977] 2 Lloyd's Rep. 5, 10; *Bushwall Properties v Vortex* [1976] 1 W.L.R. 591, 603; *British Steel Corp v Cleveland Bridge* [1984] 1 All E.R. 504, 509; *Pagnan v Granaria* [1986] 2 Lloyd's Rep. 547, 548; *VHE*

*Construction v Alfred McAlpine Construction* (1997) C.I.L.L. 1253, 1254; *Global Asset Capital Inc v Aabar Block SARL* [2017] EWCA Civ 37, [2017] 4 W.L.R. 163.

### 3. Contract Terms

## (a) General Principles Apply

### Application of principles

*In line 31, after "latter yield a fairly clear conclusion.", add:*

37-065 In *Hancock v Promontoria Ltd* it was held that on a question of construction of a contractual document, the document ordinarily had to be placed before the court as a whole, although sometimes it might be obvious that parts could properly be omitted—but a clear explanation had to be provided of the nature and extent of the omissions, and the reasons for them.[186a]

[186a] [2020] EWCA Civ 907, [2020] 4 W.L.R. 100 at [74].

## (c) Implied Terms

### General principles

*Replace footnote 200 with:*

37-072 [200] *The Moorcock* (1889) 14 P.D. 64, 68, CA; *Reigate v Union Manufacturing Co* [1918] 1 K.B. 592, 605, CA. In *Clin v Walter Lilly & Co Ltd v Clin* [2018] EWCA Civ 490 it was held that in order to make a Design Portion JCT Contract work effectively there was an implied term to the effect that the employer, who had the responsibility for obtaining planning permission, should take due diligence to obtain the same, and that this obligation included a requirement to provide in good time to the local authority the information that its planning officers require and are lawfully entitled to expect in order to grant the necessary consents. For the application of this finding in the context of the planning consent requirement in dispute, see *Walter Lilly & Co Ltd v Clin* [2019] EWHC 945 (TCC), 184 Con. L.R. 34.

### Co-operation

*To the end of paragraph, after "the implication of terms generally.", add:*

37-075 In the context of a PFI contract it was held in *Essex County Council v UBB Waste Ltd* that a duty of good faith and co-operation could be implied in a contract for the construction of a mechanical biological waste treatment facility in the event that the contract could properly be described as a relational contract, where a high degree of communication, co-operation and mutual trust and confidence was required.[224a]

[224a] [2020] EWHC 1581 (TCC) at [100]–[116], applying *Yam Seng Pte Ltd v International Trade Corp Ltd* [2013] EWHC 111 (QB) and *Al Nehayan v Kent* [2018] EWHC 333 (Comm). Cf. above, Vol.I, paras 1-058 and 1-058A.

## (d) Statutes Relevant to Construction

### Defective Premises Act 1972

*To the end of list add new (vii):*

37-083 (vii) a person will only fall within the scope of s.1(1) if they "[take] on work for or in connection with" the provision of a dwelling. This includes the builder who carries out the work and any professionals who positively contribute to the construction by carrying out design work. It does not include persons whose role is a solely negative one of seeing that no work is done which contravenes the building regulations and therefore approved inspectors are generally excluded from s.1(1).[256a]

[256a] *Lessees and Management Co of Herons Court v Heronslea Ltd* [2019] EWCA Civ 1423, [2019] 1 W.L.R. 5849 at [40].

### Unfair Contract Terms Act 1977

*Replace footnote 261 with:*

[261] See *Commercial Management (Investments) Ltd v Mitchell Design & Construct Ltd* [2016] EWHC 76 (TCC), 164 Con L.R. 139. **37-084**

## (e) Tort in Construction

### Overview

*In line 4, after "encountered in the construction context.", add new footnote 291a:*

[291a] See *Palmer Birch v Lloyd* [2018] EWHC 2316 (TCC), [2018] 4 W.L.R. 164 for a successful claim in the economic torts of inducing a breach of contract and unlawful conspiracy against two individuals who stood behind a company that agreed to pay a contractor for certain work under a building contract. **37-092**

### Tort and contract

*Replace footnote 306 with:*

[306] [2015] EWCA Civ 1146, [2016] 2 W.L.R. 1351. **37-094**

4. PARTICULAR FEATURES

## (c) Completion, Maintenance and Performance

### Completion

*Replace paragraph with:*

Standard form contracts will usually be found to stipulate the degree of completion required to bring the construction period to an end. This may be referred to as "*practical*" completion[402] or "*substantial*" completion which may also be subject to passing any final testing or commissioning prescribed by the contract.[403] There may also be provisions entitling the contractor to achieve completion notwithstanding outstanding work.[404] In the absence of qualifying provisions, the work must be sensibly finished even though subject to defects or uncompleted details for which allowance is made.[405] The achievement of completion is unaffected by the subsequent manifestation of defects that were latent at the date of completion,[406] although such defects will entitle the owner to an abatement of, or set-off against, the contract price or any instalment payable upon completion.[407] Practical completion is often easier to recognise than define. It means completion free from patent defects other than ones to be ignored as trifling, but the mere fact that a defect was irremediable does not necessarily mean that the works are not practically complete.[407a] **37-112**

[402] JCT 2011, cl.2.30.

[403] ICC Form cl.48(1). See also *University of Warwick v Balfour Beatty Group Ltd* [2018] EWHC 3230 (TCC), 182 Con. L.R. 158 for a consideration of the meaning of practical completion in the context of an amended JCT Design and Build form of contract.

[404] ICC Form cl.49(1).

[405] *Hoenig v Isaacs* [1952] 2 All E.R. 176; *Bolton v Mahadeva* [1972] 1 W.L.R. 1009.

[406] *Jarvis v Westminster CC* [1970] 1 W.L.R. 637.

[407] *Gilbert-Ash v Modern Engineering* [1974] A.C. 689, HL.

[407a] *Mears Ltd v Costplan Services Ltd* [2019] EWCA Civ 502, [2019] 4 W.L.R. 55.

### (d) Extension of Time and Liquidated Damages

*Add new paragraph:*

37-123A **Liquidated damages after termination of contract** Liquidated damages are commonly assessed by applying an agreed weekly rate to the period between the contractual completion date (as extended by any extension of time provision) and the actual date that the works are completed. If the contract is terminated before the contract works are completed, then liquidated damages will cease to accrue upon termination, and, depending upon the wording of the liquidated damages and termination provisions, the right to accrued liquidated damages will also commonly be lost.[449a]

[449a] *Triple Point Technology Inc v PTT Public Co Ltd* [2019] EWCA Civ 230, [2019] 1 W.L.R. 3549.

### (e) Bonds and Guarantees

**Categories of bond**

*Replace footnote 461 with:*

37-127 [461] *Trade Indemnity Co Ltd v Workington Harbour and Dock Board* [1937] A.C. 1, 17; *Tins' Industrial Co Ltd v Kono Insurance Ltd* [1987] 3 H.K.C. 71, 77; *Trafalgar House Construction (Regions) Ltd v General Surety and Guarantee Co Ltd* [1996] A.C. 199; *Paddington Churches Housing Association v Technical and General Guarantee* [1999] B.L.R. 244; *Yuanda Co Ltd v Multiplex Construction* [2020] EWHC 468 (TCC), 189 Con L.R. 26.

## 5. PAYMENT

### (b) Interim Payment Under the Housing Grants, Construction and Regeneration Act 1996

**Payment under the Housing Grants, Construction and Regeneration Act 1996**

*To the end of paragraph, after list, add:*

37-145 Where the terms of the contract do not comply with the requirements of the 1996 Act, the relevant terms of the Scheme for Construction Contract are implied to the extent necessary to achieve compliance with the Act.[519a]

[519a] 1996 Act s.110(3). See also *Bennett (Construction) Ltd v CIMC MBS Ltd* [2019] EWCA Civ 1515, [2019] 4 W.L.R. 155 at [54].

**Payment notices**

*Replace footnote 524 with:*

37-148 [524] *S&T (UK) Ltd v Grove Developments Ltd* [2018] EWCA Civ 2448, [2019] B.L.R. 1 at [55].

**Payment notices in default**

*Replace footnote 527 with:*

37-149 [527] *S&T (UK) Ltd v Grove Developments Ltd* [2018] EWCA Civ 2448, [2019] B.L.R. 1 at [55].

### Pay less notices

*Replace footnote 532 with:*

532 *S&T (UK) Ltd v Grove Developments Ltd* [2018] EWCA Civ 2448, [2019] B.L.R. 1 at [55]. **37-150**

### Effect of failure to serve a pay less notice

*Replace second paragraph with:*

The amount which the employer has to pay as a result of having failed to serve the requisite notices may well exceed the true value of the works as calculated pursuant to the contractual valuation mechanism. This is an inevitable risk of the statutory regime and does not provide any defence to the employer. The employer can recover any overpayment which it might make in such circumstances by utilising the contractual dispute resolution processes to obtain a determination of the true value of the work and a consequent determination as to any amount that must be repaid as a result. Such a claim can be brought at any time after the employer has paid the full amount stated as due in the relevant payment notice.[537–540] **37-151**

537–540 *S&T (UK) Ltd v Grove Developments Ltd* [2018] EWCA Civ 2448, [2019] B.L.R. 1 at [107].

## 10. Disputes

## (e) Adjudication

*Add new paragraph:*

**37-263A** **Excluded operations and hybrid contracts** Section 105(2) of the Housing Grants, Construction and Regeneration Act 1996 excludes a variety of matters from the scope of the Act which would otherwise have been classed as construction operations, particularly in the energy and natural resources sectors. Where construction work falls within the excluded operations defined in s.105(2) of the Act does not apply, with the result that the adjudication terms of the Act are not implied.

A particular problem is caused by contracts for the carrying out of work that falls partly within the scope of the Act and partly outside the scope of the Act. These are described as hybrid contracts[859a] and in such instances, the Act applies to those works falling within the scope of the Act, but not the excluded works.[859b] In the context of adjudication this leads to a particular difficulty because a party seeking to claim more money in relation to a disputed interim payment will only be entitled to adjudicate on those parts of the work falling within the Act. However, the exact boundaries of the excluded operations in s.105(2) of the Act are not easy to identify and any error by the referring party is liable to deprive the adjudicator of jurisdiction.[859c] As such, it can be very difficult for a referring party to formulate a valid referral in such instances and litigation may be a preferable route.[859d]

859a *C Spencer Ltd v MW High Tech Projects UK Ltd* [2020] EWCA Civ 331 at [2].

859b Housing Grants, Construction and Regeneration Act 1996 s.104(5).

859c *Severfield (UK) Ltd v Duro Felguera UK Ltd* [2015] EWHC 2975 (TCC) at [14].

859d See *C Spencer Ltd v MW High Tech Projects UK Ltd* [2020] EWCA Civ 331 at [56]–[57], where the Court expressed sympathy for the referring party's situation in such a case, but confirmed that the onus was on the referring party only to refer matters falling within the scope of the Act.

*Add new paragraph:*

**37-268A** **Adjudication and insolvent parties** Adjudicators' decisions may not be enforced where one party is insolvent, either in the technical sense of being in liquidation or in the factual sense of being unable to pay their debts as they fall due. Where the successful party is in liquidation, the Court will ordinarily stay enforcement of any sum awarded by the adjudicator[896a] but the Court will generally not stop an adjudication commenced by an insolvent party by issuing an injunction.[896b] Where a successful party is not in liquidation but would probably be unable to repay an adjudicator's award if subsequently reversed by litigation or arbitration proceedings, a stay may be available depending on the facts.[896c] Where the losing party is impecunious, the decision will generally be enforced, but it cannot be used to wind up the losing party if the latter has an arguable cross-claim.[896d]

[896a] *Wimbledon Construction Co 2000 Ltd v Vago* [2005] EWHC 1086 (TCC), [2005] B.L.R. 374, approved in *Gosvenor London Ltd v Aygun Aluminium UK Ltd* [2018] EWCA Civ 2695, [2019] B.L.R. 99. However, it may be possible for an insolvent company to enforce an award if it can provide sufficient security in respect of any future order for repayment of the sum awarded and any costs of the enforcement action and subsequent final determination proceedings. See *Meadowside Building Developments Ltd (In Liquidation) v 12-18 Hill Street Management Co Ltd* [2019] EWHC 2651 (TCC), 186 Con. L.R. 148 at [87].

[896b] *Bresco Electrical Services Ltd (In Liquidation) v Michael J Lonsdale (Electrical) Ltd* [2020] UKSC 25, [2020] Bus. L.R. 1140.

[896c] The principles upon which such a stay will be available are those set out in *Wimbledon Construction Co 2000 Ltd v Vago* [2005] EWHC 1086 (TCC), [2005] B.L.R. 374 at [26] as extended by *Gosvenor London Ltd v Aygun Aluminium UK Ltd* [2018] EWCA Civ 2695, [2019] B.L.R. 99.

[896d] *Shaw v MFP Foundations & Piling Ltd* [2010] EWHC 9 (Ch), [2010] 2 B.C.L.C. 85. If there is no cross-claim, it may be sufficient that the adjudicator's decision is disputed in good faith. This question was left open in *Shaw*.

CHAPTER 38

# CONSUMER CONTRACTS

## 1. INTRODUCTION

### The importance of European law

*Replace paragraph with:*

However, from the late 1980s EEC (later EC and now EU) law has become increasingly important as a source of legislative protection for consumer contractors, typically by way of directive and therefore requiring implementation by the UK into national law, whether by statute or, as has been more usual, by secondary legislation under the European Communities Act 1972.[17] Some of these legislative instruments have required national rules governing consumer contracts which are concluded in particular ways (as in the case of "doorstep selling"[18] and "distance contracts"[19]); some have required rules governing aspects of particular types of **38-003** contracts (as in the case of contracts for the sale of goods,[20] timeshare contracts,[21] package travel contracts,[22] consumer credit[23] and passenger transport[24]); and perhaps the most prominent example, the Unfair Terms in Consumer Contracts Directive 1993, which subjected most contract terms which have not been "individually negotiated" in *all* consumer contracts to a test of unfairness.[25] At this earlier stage in its development, EU contract law generally required only "minimum harmonisation", that is to say, the European legislation required only minimum rights or protections for the consumer, thereby allowing Member States to enact national laws which are more protective of consumers than the EU law required.[26] However, at the beginning of the present century, the European Commission started a wide-ranging review of EC/EU legislation in the area of contract law, with particular reference to consumer law,[27] and this had a number of consequences for EU (and therefore UK) consumer contract law. First, the Commission has sought (and to an extent achieved) the reform and consolidation of existing directives so as to provide greater consistency between them, this being noticeable particularly in the Consumer Rights Directive 2011,[28] which, inter alia, consolidated the information duties required by the directives concerning "doorstep selling" (later "off-premises contracting")[29] and "distance contracts",[30] though it did not consolidate the requirements contained in directives on guarantees in contracts for the sale of goods[31] nor on unfair contract terms[32] as had earlier been proposed.[33] Other earlier consumer contract directives have also been subject to reform and consolidation, for example, on timeshare contracts[34] and package travel contracts.[35] Secondly, the Commission has sought to move directives in the area of consumer protection from requiring "minimum harmonisation" to requiring "full harmonisation", that is to say, the European legislation sets rights or protections for the consumer for which Member States must provide but which they must not exceed in the interests of greater protection for the consumer.[36] Thirdly, and related to this, by the Unfair Commercial Practices Directive 2005 the European legislator enacted an important general and "fully harmonised" framework for the regulation of unfair commercial practices business-to-consumer.[37] While the 2005 Directive is expressly stated as being "without prejudice to contract law and, in particular, to the rules on the validity, formation or effect of a contract"[38] and the UK's first implementation reflected this scope,[39] in 2014 the UK legislator nonetheless chose to give some "contract law" effects to certain aspects of the 2005 Directive's requirements, thereby creating new rights to redress for consumers against their trader contracting partners.[40] Fourthly, the EU has itself put in place, and also required Member States to put in place, various enforcement mechanisms for the protection of consumers.[40a] Fifthly, the EU legislator brought earlier European Conventions on jurisdiction and the recognition and enforcement of judgments (the "Brussels Convention")[41] and on the law applicable to contractual obligations (the "Rome Convention")[42] directly within the fold of EU law by enacting regulations to replace them.[43] These regulations set uniform rules of private international law governing applicable law for "contractual obligations" and jurisdiction, recognition and the enforcement of judgments in "matters relating to a contract"[44] as well as special rules for, for example, consumers in these contexts.[45] The present significance of these private international law rules governing consumer contracts is that the European Court of Justice has interpreted the concepts which they use (notably, "consumer"), and this case-law may be helpful in the interpretation of the same or similar concepts in the EU substantive law legislation governing consumer contracts.[46]

[17] European Communities Act 1972 s.2(2). On the impact of the UK's leaving the EU, see below, para.38-004 and more generally Vol.I, paras 1-014 et seq.

[18] Directive 85/577/EEC to protect the consumer in respect of contracts negotiated away from business premises [1985] O.J. L372/31 implemented in UK law by the Consumer Protection (Cancellation of Contracts Concluded Away from Business Premises) Regulations 1987 (SI 1987/2117), which were replaced by the Cancellation of Contracts made in a Consumer's Home or Place of Work, etc. Regulations 2008 (SI 2008/1816). The current law is contained in the Consumer Contracts (Information, Cancellation and Additional Charges) Regulations 2013 (SI 2013/3134) ("2013 Regulations") on which see below, paras 37-059 et seq.

[19] Directive 97/7/EC on the protection of consumers in respect of distance contracts [1997] O.J. L144/19 implemented in UK law by the Consumer Protection (Distance Selling) Regulations 2000 (SI 2000/2334) (the current law is contained in the 2013 Regulations, on which see below paras 38-061 et seq.); Directive 2002/65/EC concerning the distance marketing of consumer financial services [2002] O.J. L271/16 art.3(2) implemented principally by the Financial Services (Distance Marketing) Regulations 2004 (SI 2004/2095) on which see below, para.38-136.

[20] Directive 99/44/EC on certain aspects of the sale of consumer goods and associated guarantees [1999] O.J. L171/7 ("Consumer Sales Directive", "1999 Directive") (due to be repealed by Directive (EU) 2019/770 of the European Parliament and of the Council of 20 May 2019 [2019] O.J. L136/28) and see below, paras 38-433 and 38-436.

[21] Directive 94/47/EC on the protection of purchasers in respect of certain aspects of contracts relating to the purchase of the right to use immovable properties on a timeshare basis [1994] O.J. L280/83 and see for the current legislation below, paras 38-148—38-154.

[22] Directive 90/314/EEC on package travel, package holidays and package tours [1990] O.J. L158/59; [1994] O.J. L280/83, repealed and replaced by Directive (EU) 2015/2302 on package travel and linked travel arrangements [2015] O.J. L326/1. See below, paras 38-137—38-147.

[23] Directive 87/102/EEC on consumer credit [1987] O.J. L42/48 repealed and replaced by Directive 2008/48/EC on credit agreements for consumers [2008] O.J. L133/66.

[24] e.g. Regulation (EC) 261/2004 establishing common rules on compensation and assistance to passengers in the event of denied boarding and of cancellation or long delay of flights [2004] O.J. L46/1.

[25] Directive 93/13/EEC [1993] O.J. L95/29 ("1993 Directive"), below, para.38-218.

[26] See, notably, Directive 93/13/EEC of April 5, 1993 on unfair terms in consumer contracts, art.8 and see below, para.38-022.

[27] See Communication from the Commission to the Council and the European Parliament on European Contract Law COM(2001) 398 final; Communication from the Commission to the European Parliament and the Council, *A more coherent European Contract Law, An Action Plan* COM(2003) 68 final; European Contract Law and the revision of the acquis: the way forward COM(2004) 651 final; EU Commission, *Green Paper from the Commission on policy option for progress towards a European Contract Law for consumers and businesses* COM(2010) 348 final.

[28] Directive 2011/83/EU on consumer rights [2011] O.J. L304/64 ("Consumer Rights Directive" or "2011 Directive"), below, para.38-060.

[29] Directive 85/577/EEC to protect the consumer in respect of contracts negotiated away from business premises [1985] O.J. L372/31.

[30] Directive 97/7/EC on the protection of consumers in respect of distance contracts [1997] O.J. L144/19. The Consumer Rights Directive did not, however, include elements from the Directive 2002/65/EC concerning the distance marketing of consumer financial services [2002] O.J. L271/16.

[31] Directive 99/44/EC on certain aspects of the sale of consumer goods and associated guarantees [1999] O.J. L171/7 (the "Consumer Sales Directive").

[32] Directive 93/13/EEC of April 5, 1993 on unfair terms in consumer contracts [1993] O.J. L95/29 ("Unfair Terms in Consumer Contracts Directive" or "1993 Directive").

[33] Proposal for a Directive of the European Parliament and of the Council on Consumer Rights of 8 October 2008 COM(2008) 614/3 final, Chs IV and V.

[34] Directive 2008/122/EC on the protection of consumers in respect of certain aspects of timeshare, long-term holiday product, resale and exchange contracts [2009] O.J. L33/30 repealing and replacing Directive 94/47/EC on the protection of purchasers in respect of certain aspects of contracts relating to the

purchase of the right to use immovable properties on a timeshare basis [1994] O.J. L280/83; Directive 2008/48/EC on credit agreements for consumers [2008] O.J. L133/66.

[35] Directive (EU) 2015/2302 on package travel and linked travel arrangements [2015] O.J. L326/1 revoking and replacing Directive 90/314/EEC on package travel, package holidays and package tours.

[36] e.g. Directive 2011/83/EU on consumer rights art.4; Directive 2008/48/EC on credit agreements for consumers recital 9, though as the following recitals explain, the directive leaves a good deal of competence in Member States as regards matters outside its carefully delineated scope; Directive (EU) 2015/2302 on package travel and linked travel arrangements [2015] O.J. L326/1 art.4 (full harmonisation with exceptions). See also Directive (EU) 2019/771 of the European Parliament and of the Council of 20 May 2019 on certain aspects concerning contracts for the sale of goods, etc. [2019] O.J. L136/28 art.4 (which repeals the earlier "minimum harmonization" Consumer Sales Directive 1999) and Directive (EU) 2019/770 of the European Parliament and of the Council of 20 May 2019 on certain aspects concerning contracts for the supply of digital content and digital services [2019] O.J. L136/1 art.4 (both of these directives are due to be implemented in the laws of Member States by July 1, 2021, although at the time of writing it appears likely that the UK will leave the EU before this date: see Vol.I, paras 1-014 et seq. and below, para.38-004).

[37] Directive 2005/29/EC concerning unfair business-to-consumer commercial practices [2005] O.J. L149/22 ("Unfair Commercial Practices Directive" or "2005 Directive") especially art.4. The Directive excludes certain areas from "full harmonisation", notably, art.3(9) (financial services) and see generally below, paras 38-159 et seq.

[38] Directive 2005/29/EC art.3(2), on which see Whittaker in Weatherill and Bernitz (eds), *The Regulation of Unfair Commercial Practices under EC Directive 2005/29, New Rules and New Techniques* (2007), Ch.8.

[39] The Consumer Protection from Unfair Trading Regulations 2008 (SI 2008/1277) ("2008 Regulations") reg.29 (as enacted) provided explicitly that "an agreement shall not be void or unenforceable by reason only of a breach of these regulations" but said no more as to the wider lack of effect of the Regulations on the "law of contract", apparently on the basis that they set out the consequences of the new controls and did not need to set out other non-consequences.

[40] Consumer Protection (Amendment) Regulations 2014 (SI 2014/870) inserting, notably, new Pt 4A Consumers' Rights to Redress in Consumer Protection from Unfair Trading Regulations 2008 (SI 2008/1277). See further, below paras 38-172 et seq. However, at the EU level, this position will change on the coming into force of Directive (EU) 2019/2161 of the European Parliament and of the Council of 27 November 2019 ... as regards the better enforcement and modernisation of Union consumer protection rules [2019] O.J. L328/7 art.3(5) (inserting a new art.11a in the 2005 Directive) which requires the introduction of redress for consumers harmed by unfair commercial practices: see further below, para.38-175A. The 2019 Directive must be implemented on November 28, 2021 (i.e. after IP completion day) and as a result the UK is not required to do so: cf. above, para.38-004.

[40a] Some of these enforcement mechanisms are required by the directives which affect contract law directly, as is notably the case with the Unfair Terms in Consumer Contracts Directive 1993 art.7, on which see below, paras 38-353 et seq. However, more general enforcement of EU consumer protection is provided for by Directive 2009/22/EC on injunctions for the protection of consumers' interests [2009] O.J. L110/30 and Regulation (EU) 2017/2394 of the European Parliament and of the Council of 12 December 2017 on cooperation between national authorities responsible for the enforcement of consumer protection laws and repealing Regulation (EC) 2006/2004 [2017] O.J. L345/1 on which see below, paras 38-133–38-133A.

[41] Convention on Jurisdiction and the Enforcement of Judgments in Civil and Commercial Matters 1968.

[42] Rome Convention on the Law Applicable to Contractual Obligations 1980.

[43] Regulation (EC) 593/2008 on the law applicable to contractual obligations ("Rome I") [2008] O.J. L177/6; Regulation (EC) 864/2007 applicable to non-contractual obligations ("Rome II Regulation") [2007] O.J. L199/40 (some of whose provisions bear an important relationship with contract, notably art.12 "*culpa in contrahendo*"); Council Regulation 44/2001 on jurisdiction and the recognition and enforcement of judgments in civil and commercial matters [2001] O.J. L12/1 ("Brussels I Regulation") first replaced the Brussels Convention and then was itself replaced as from January 10, 2015 by Regulation (EU) 1215/2012 of 12 December 2012 on jurisdiction and the recognition and enforcement of judgments in civil and commercial matters (recast) ("the Brussels Ibis Regulation"). The status of these European private international law instruments is set to change on the UK's exit from the EU: see Vol.I, para.1-016C.

[44] Brussels Ibis Regulation art.7(1); Rome I Regulation generally.

45 Brussels Ibis Regulation arts 17–19; Rome I Regulation art.6.

46 See below para.38-016.

*Change title of paragraph:*

**Impact of the UK's leaving the EU on consumer contract law**[47]

47 See generally Vol.I, paras 1-014 et seq. 38-004

*Replace paragraph with:*

38-004 On January 24, 2020 the UK Government concluded a Withdrawal Agreement with the EU under which the UK left the EU at 11.00pm on January 31, 2020 ("exit day"),[48] but it was further agreed that there would be a transition period running from exit day until 11pm on December 31, 2020[49] under which EU law would still apply in the UK (with certain exceptions).[50] The principal legislation governing the withdrawal of the UK from the EU is contained in the European Union (Withdrawal) Act 2018 ("2018 Act") as amended by the European Union (Withdrawal Agreement) Act 2020 ("2020 Act"), which refers to the transition period as the "implementation period" ("IP") and the date on which it expires as "IP completion day".[50a] On IP completion day the 2018 Act in principle preserves the EU legislative acquis as part of UK law ("retained EU law") including almost all of the law governing consumer contracts and consumer protection legislation.[50b] Moreover, this means that the EU-derived legislation which is brought across to form part of UK domestic law as "retained EU law" after the end of the IP refers to that legislation which is operative immediately before the end of the IP (IP completion day) rather than immediately before exit day.[50c] On the other hand, this also means that in principle directly applicable EU law coming into force *after* IP completion day will not form part of "retained EU law"; nor as presently provided is the UK under any obligation to implement any EU Directive which requires Member States to adopt measures to implement it after IP completion day.[50d] In the course of 2018 and 2019 a considerable body of subordinate legislation was made under the 2018 Act as enacted for this purpose, and in the context of contracts these instruments have in common that their operative provisions were generally expressed as due to come into force on "exit day".[50e] As earlier noted, the definition of "exit day" was finalised as January 31, 2020, but the text of these earlier subordinate instruments has not been changed. Instead, the 2020 Act states that any subordinate legislation made under the 2018 Act or any other enactment "which provides, by reference to exit day (however expressed), for all or part of that or any other subordinate legislation to come into force immediately before exit day, on exit day or at any time after exit day is to be read instead as providing for the subordinate legislation or (as the case may be) the part to come into force immediately before IP completion day, on IP completion day or (as the case may be) at the time concerned after IP completion day".[50f] Subordinate legislation made under the 2018 Act after EU exit day is sometimes expressed directly as coming into force by reference to IP completion day.[50g] As is explained in Vol.I of the present work,[50h] a number of issues relating to impact of EU law after IP completion day have been settled by the 2018 and 2020 Acts, notably, the status of past and future decisions of the Court of Justice of the EU for the interpretation of EU legislation implemented in UK law.[50i] However, until IP completion day, EU law has been preserved in the UK despite its having left the EU[50j] and this chapter therefore remains written on this basis thereby treating EU law and UK legislation implementing EU law as though the UK were still a Member State. However, it will note, where relevant and practicable, the principal particular changes to UK law presently foreseen to take effect on IP completion day by the relevant amending regulations made under the 2018 Act.[50k] It should be borne in mind, however, that these may themselves be changed, in particular if the subject-matter of the legislation forms part of any agreement between the UK and the EU regarding their future relationship.

[48] Agreement on the Withdrawal of the United Kingdom of Great Britain and Northern Ireland from the European Union and the European Atomic Energy Community (January 24, 2020) (the "Withdrawal Agreement 2020") art.185.

[49] Under the Withdrawal Agreement 2020 art.132, this period may be extended for one or two years if agreed by a "Joint Committee" by July 1, 2020, but as a matter of UK law, s.15A of the European Union (Withdrawal) Act 2018 as inserted by s.33 of the European Union (Withdrawal Agreement) Act 2020 prohibits UK ministers agreeing such an extension.

[50] Withdrawal Agreement 2020 art.127.

[50a] 2018 Act s.1A(6) (as inserted by the 2020 Act s.1) referring for "IP completion day" to s.39(1)–(5) of the 2020 Act and see note above in this paragraph on the restraints on the postponement of this date.

[50b] See Vol.I, paras 1-016–1-016C.

[50c] CMA, *UK exit from the EU, Guidance on the functions of the CMA under the Withdrawal Agreement* (CMA113, January 28, 2020), para.2.19.

[50d] This follows from the Withdrawal Agreement itself, as art.127(3) states that the EU law which generally applies to the UK during the transition "shall produce in respect of and in the United Kingdom the same legal effects as those which it produces within the Union and its Member States". This applies, for example, to Directive (EU) 2019/771 of the European Parliament and of the Council of 20 May 2019 on certain aspects concerning contracts for the sale of goods, etc [2019] O.J. L136/28 art.24 of which requires its implementation by July 1, 2021 (on which see below, para.38-436) and to Directive (EU) 2019/2161 of the European Parliament and of the Council of 27 November 2019 ... as regards the better enforcement and modernisation of Union consumer protection rules [2019] O.J. L328/7 art.7 of which requires its implementation by November 28, 2021.

[50e] Where appropriate, the amending secondary legislation provides that relevant provisions leave unaffected contracts entered into before "exit day." For example, the Consumer Protection (Amendment etc.) (EU Exit) Regulations 2018 (SI 2018/1326) reg.1(3) provides that most of its Parts come into effect on "exit day" (which must be read to refer to IP completion day: 2020 Act s.39(1), Sch.5 para.1). Regulation 11 of the 2018 Regulations later provides that "nothing in regulation 3 [which amends the Consumer Rights Act 2015] or regulation 6(2) [which amends the Consumer Protection from Unfair Trading Regulations 2008] applies to a contract entered into before exit day" (the reference to "exit day" is due to be replaced by "IP completion day"; Consumer Protection (Enforcement) (Amendment etc.) (EU Exit) Regulations 2020 (Draft) Pt 3 reg.4(8)). On these amendments see below, paras 38-365 (note) and 38-165 (note) respectively.

[50f] 2020 Act s.39(1), Sch.5 para.1. Schedule 5 makes further provision regarding, in particular, exceptions to be made to this general position.

[50g] e.g. the Draft Alternative Dispute Resolution for Consumer Disputes (Extension of Time Limits for Legal Proceedings) (Amendment etc.) (EU Exit) Regulations 2020 reg.1(2) providing that the Regulations generally come into force on "IP completion day".

[50h] Vol.I, paras 1-017–1-017B.

[50i] Vol.I, para.1-017B.

[50j] Above, paras 1-016–1-016C.

[50k] Above, para.1-016.

## Earlier approaches to UK implementation of European directives

*Replace paragraphs with:*

38-005 For a long time UK implementation of the various European directives governing consumer contracts was often effected in a piecemeal way. Indeed, in many instances, directives were implemented by standalone statutory instrument, thereby creating new and distinct bodies of legislative controls; this can be seen in the context of package travel, package tours and package holidays,[51] doorstep selling[52] and distance contracts.[53] In the case of the Unfair Terms in Consumer Contracts Directive 1993, the resulting standalone statutory instrument created a set of legislative rules which overlapped considerably with, but formally were entirely separate from, the existing domestic legislation in the area, the Unfair Contract Terms Act 1977. In the context of unfair contract terms, the resulting complexity attracted a good deal of criticism, and, in turn, a recommendation from the Law Commissions that the legislation should be recast into a single enactment.[54] In the case of other directives, the UK legislature sought to integrate their requirements within existing legislative frameworks. In the case of timeshare contracts, this was easily achieved as these had already been the subject of regulation by UK statute.[55] However, in other cases, the process was more difficult, a particularly striking example being found in the legislative implementation of the Consumer Sales Directive of 1999, which was effected in English law principally by the insertion of a new Pt 5A into the Sale of Goods Act 1979.[56] This amendment created a series of dedicated rights for consumer buyers in respect of the "contractual non-conformity" of the goods in addition to (and in an awkward relationship with) the classic rights of rejection of the goods, restitution of the price and damages for breach of the implied statutory conditions governing satisfactory quality and fitness for purpose also foreseen by the Sale of Goods Act.[57] Here, therefore, implementation of the European directive lead to very considerable substantive complexity and, to an extent, overlap, even though it was effected by change to existing wider legislation.

[51] Package Travel and Linked Travel Arrangements Regulations 2018 (SI 2018/634) revoking and replacing Package Travel, Package Holidays and Package Tours Regulations 1992 (SI 1992/3288) on which see below, paras 38-137—38-147.

[52] Consumer Protection (Cancellation of Contracts Concluded Away from Business Premises) Regulations 1987 (SI 1987/2117) later replaced by the Cancellation of Contracts made in a Consumer's Home or Place of Work, etc. Regulations 2008 (SI 2008/1816). As will be explained, the latter have been revoked and replaced by the Consumer Contracts (Information, Cancellation and Additional Charges) Regulations 2013 (SI 2013/3134): below, paras 38-061 et seq.

[53] Consumer Protection (Distance Selling) Regulations 2000 (SI 2000/2334) which have been revoked and replaced by the Consumer Contracts (Information, Cancellation and Additional Charges) Regulations 2013 (SI 2013/3134) (below, paras 37-061 et seq.); Financial Services (Distance Marketing) Regulations 2004 (SI 2004/2095) (below, para.38-136).

[54] Law Commission, Scottish Law Commission, *Unfair Terms in Contracts* (Law Com. No.292, Scot Law Com. No.199, 2005).

[55] Timeshare Act 1992, which preceded the Directive 94/47/EC on the protection of purchasers in respect of certain aspects of contracts relating to the purchase of the right to use immovable properties on a timeshare basis. The 1994 Directive was implemented by amendment of the Timeshare Act 1992 by regulation: Timeshare Regulations 1997 (SI 1997/1081). Subsequently, the UK's treatment of timeshare and related contracts has been made by the Timeshare, Holiday Products, Resale and Exchange Contracts Regulations 2010 (SI 2010/2960) on which see below, paras 38-148—38-154.

[56] On this implementation, see below, paras 38-439 et seq.

[57] s.14.

### Major reforms to UK consumer contract legislation: (i) the Consumer Rights Act 2015

*At the start of the paragraph, replace "Recent" with:*
More recent | **38-006**

### (ii) Consumer Contracts (Information, Cancellation and Additional Charges) Regulations 2013

*In line 9, after "though they also", replace "create" with:*

38-007 created

### The relationship between "contract law" and prohibitions or preventive measures

*Replace footnote 79 with:*

38-010 [79] Directive 2005/29 art.3(2), recital 9. cf. Consumer Rights Directive 2011 art.3(5) below, paras 38-063—38-065. However, this position will change at the EU level on the coming into force of Directive (EU) 2019/2161 of the European Parliament and of the Council of 27 November 2019 ... as regards the better enforcement and modernisation of Union consumer protection rules [2019] O.J. L328/7, art.3(5) of which inserts a new art.11a in the 2005 Directive which requires the introduction of redress for consumers harmed by unfair commercial practices: see further below, para.38-175A.

### Changes in the law

*Replace paragraph with:*

38-012 The preceding paragraphs make clear that there has been very considerable change in the legislation governing consumer contracts in the course of the present decade. In general, this chapter will set out the law as it is in force at the time of writing,[82] with some reference to the earlier law where this is helpful to understand its development. However, in the case of the regulation of unfair contract terms and the special rules and remedies applicable to contracts for the sale of goods and related contracts, hire and contracts for the supply of services and (where the earlier law remains applicable to contracts entered into before October 1, 2015, when the relevant provisions in the Consumer Rights Act 2015 came into force)[83] this chapter will discuss first the old law (together with the important interpretation given to it both by the European Court of Justice and by English courts) and then the new law, highlighting similarities and differences with the earlier position.[84] It will also note any amendments of legislation which are due to come into force on IP completion day when the UK's departure from the EU comes into full effect.[85]

[82] i.e. July 31, 2020.

[83] Consumer Rights Act 2015 (Commencement No.3, Transitional Provisions, Savings and Consequential Amendments) Order 2015 (SI 2015/1630) art.3(a)–(c) (with the exceptions and qualifications made by arts 4 and 6 as amended by SI 2016/484 art.2(3)); see further below, paras 38-216, 38-366 and 38-437).

[84] See below, paras 38-220—38-364, 38-365—38-426 and 38-432 et seq. respectively.

[85] On this see above, para.38-004 and Vol.I, paras 1-014 et seq.

## 2. The Relationship of EU and UK Consumer Contract Law

### (a) The Continuing Interpretative Significance of EU Directives

*To the end of title, add new footnote 94a:*

### Significance of EU source of English consumer contract law for its interpretation[94a]

38-014 [94a] However, see above, Vol.I, para.1-017B on the changing significance of the case law of and principles laid down by the CJEU for "retained EU law", this significance differing as between those laid down before and on or after IP completion day. As there noted, the principle of conforming interpretation provides an important example of a "retained general principle of EU law": European Union (Withdrawal) Act 2018 s.6(7).

*Replace footnote 95 with:*

[95] For the main European decisions see *Von Colson and Kammann v Land Nordrhein-Westfalen* (C-14/83) EU:C:1984:153 [1984] E.C.R. 1891, *Marleasing SA v La Comercial Internacionale de Alimentacion SA* (C-106/89) EU:C:1990:395, [1990] E.C.R. I-4135, *Pfeiffer v Deutsches Rotes Kreuz, Kreisverband Waldshut eV* (C-397–403/01) EU:C:2004:584, [2004] E.C.R. I-8835, *Schulte v Deutsche Bausparkasse Badenia AG* (C-350/03) EU:C:2005:637, [2005] E.C.R. I-9215 at para.71 and see Prechal, *Directives in EC Law*, 2nd edn (2005), Ch.8; Craig and De Búrca, *EU Law*, 6th edn (2015), pp.209 et seq. For the UK see in particular *Robertson v Swift* [2014] UKSC 50, [2014] 1 W.L.R. 3438 at [20]–[23] approving the summary of the impact of this principle by Sir Andrew Morritt, C. at *Vodafone 2 v Commissioners for Her Majesty's Revenue and Customers* [2010] Ch. 77 at [37]; *United States of America v Nolan* [2015] UKSC 63, [2016] A.C. 463 where Lord Mance (with whom Lord Neuberger of Abbotsbury, Baroness Hale of Richmond and Lord Reed agreed) at [14] described the principle of conforming interpretation as "a cardinal principle of European Union and domestic law". On the changed status of decisions of the CJEU after the UK's exit from the EU, see Vol.I, para.1-017. **38-014**

## "Autonomous" and national interpretations

*Replace footnote 102 with:*

[102] *Ekro BV Vee- en Vleeshandel v Produktschap voor Vee en Vlees* (C-327/82) EU:C:1984:11; [1984] E.C.R. 00107 para.11; *UsedSoft GmbH v Oracle International Corp* (C-128/11) EU:C:2012:407 para.39 and see similarly *Infopaq International* (C-5/08) EU:C:2009:465, [2009] E.C.R. I-6569 para.27; *Stichting ter Exploitatie van Naburige Rechten (SENA) v Nederlandse Omroep Stichting (NOS)* (C-245/00) EU:C:2003:68, [2003] E.C.R. I-1251 para.23; *BKK Mobil Oil Körperschaft des öffentlichen Rechts v Zentrale zur Bekämpfung unlauteren Wettbewerbs eV* (C-59/12) EU:C:2013:634, October 3, 2013 para.25. On the position after IP completion day, see above, para.38-004 and Vol.I, paras 1-014 et seq. and esp. para.1-017B. **38-015**

## Interpretative approach of Court of Justice

*Replace footnote 117 with:*

[117] e.g. *Asociación de Consumidores Independientes de Castilla y León v Anuntis Segundamano España SL* (C-413/12) EU:C:2013:800; *Walbusch Walter Busch GmbH & Co KG v Zentrale zur Bekämpfung unlauteren Wettbewerbs Frankfurt am Main eV* (C-430/17) EU:C:2019:47 of January 23, 2019 at paras 34 and 42 (balancing art.38 (requiring a high level of consumer protection) and arts 11 (freedom of expression and information) and 16 (freedom to conduct business); *Bundesverband der Verbraucherzentralen und Verbraucherverbände - Verbraucherzentrale Bundesverband eV v Amazon EU Sàrl* (C-649/17) EU:C:2019:576 of July 10, 2019 esp. at para.44. **38-016**

*To the end of title, add new footnote 124a:*

## Approach of English courts[124a]

[124a] On the changing significance of the case law of and general principles laid down by the CJEU for the interpretation of "retained EU law" by UK courts, see Vol.I, para.1-017B. **38-018**

*Replace footnote 127 with:*

[127] e.g. *Robertson v Swift* [2014] UKSC 50, [2014] 1 W.L.R. 3238 at [23]–[24], [27]–[28]; *ParkingEye Ltd v Beavis* [2015] UKSC 67, [2015] 3 W.L.R. 1373 at [105]–[106], [208] and [308] (although the learned Justices of the SC differed as to the proper application of the CJEU's case-law): see below, paras 38-275—38-277. **38-018**

## The duty of national courts to intervene of their own motion to protect EU consumer rights

*Replace paragraph with:*

In a series of cases starting with *Océano Grupo Editorial*, the European Court of Justice has held that national courts have both a power and a duty to raise of their own motion the question of the unfairness of a term in a consumer contract falling within the Unfair Terms in Consumer Contracts Directive,[128] as long as the national **38-019** court "has available to it the legal and factual elements necessary for that task".[129] This position is justified by the Court by the need to ensure that the consumer enjoys effective protection in view of the real risk that he is unaware of his rights or encounters difficulties in enforcing them.[130] This line of cases appeared at first to be distinct from the Court's general case-law governing the question whether a national court must raise an issue of EU law of its own motion under *Van Schijndel*,[131] according to which national procedural rules on this question must not be less favourable than those governing similar domestic actions nor render virtually impossible or excessively difficult the exercise of rights conferred by EU law.[132] Moreover, in *Rampion*[133] the Court of Justice extended this special judicial protection for consumers, holding that a national court must have the power to raise the rights of the consumer under the Consumer Credit Directive 1986[134] of its own motion, given that that directive's purpose was to ensure the creation of a common consumer credit market and the protection of consumers.[135] On the other hand, in *Martín Martín* the Court held that a national court of appeal may, of its own motion, declare void a contract which infringes the Doorstep Selling Directive's provisions on consumer protection,[136] even though the issue had not been raised at first instance,[137] but in doing so it preferred to follow its approach in *Van Schijndel*, seeing this limitation on the power of national courts as "justified by the principle that, in a civil suit, it is for the parties to take the initiative, and that, as a result, the court is able to act of its own motion only in exceptional cases where the public interest requires intervention".[138] According to the Court, the Doorstep Selling Directive 1985 seeks to redress the imbalance and, therefore, disadvantage with which consumers, as "weaker parties" are faced with in the circumstances of doorstep selling by providing them with a right of cancellation, notice of which the business must give to them.[139] This notice of the consumer's rights "plays a central role in the overall scheme of the directive ... for the exercise of that right and, therefore, for the effectiveness of consumer protection sought by the Community legislature"[140]: positive intervention allows the national court to "compensate for the imbalance between the consumer and the trader" in the context.[141] More recently, this approach has been adopted by the Court in the context of the Unfair Contract Terms Directive itself[142] as well as to the availability of different rights for the consumer in respect of non-conformity of goods bought under the Consumer Sales Directive 1999.[143]

[128] *Océano Grupo Editorial SA v Murciano Quintero* (C-240/98 to C-244/98) EU:C:2000:346, [2000] E.C.R. I-4941; *Mostaza Claro v Centro Móvil Milenium SL* (C-168/05) EU:C:2006:675, [2006] E.C.R. I-10421. On this case-law see below, paras 38-331—38-335. For a general discussion of these questions see Whittaker in Leczykiewicz and Weatherill (eds) *The Involvement of EU Law in Private Relationships* (2013) Ch.6.

[129] *Pannon GSM Zrt v Erzsébet Sustikné Györfi* (C-243/08) EU:C:2009:350, [2009] E.C.R. I-4713 at para.32; *Bucura v SC Bancpost SA* (C-348/14) EU:C:2015:447, July 9, 201 para.44. See also below, para.38-020 on the circumstances in which a national court has a duty to request further information in support of its protection of consumers. On the possibility that a Member State may incur liability for a court's failure to protect a consumer's EU law rights see *Tomášová v Republic of Slovenská* (C-168/15) EU:C:2016:602 July 28 2016, below, para.38-331.

[130] *Océano Grupo Editorial SA v Murciano Quintero* (C-240/98 to C-244/98) EU:C:2000:346 at para.26.

[131] *Van Schijndel v Stichting Pensioenfonds voor Fysiotherapeuten* (C-430/93 and C-431/93) EU:C:1995:441, [1995] E.C.R. I-4705 ("*Van Schijndel* (C-430/93 and C-431/93)"); *Peterbroeck, Van Campenhout & Cie SCS v Belgium* (C-312/93) EU:C:1995:437; [1995] E.C.R. I-4599; *Heemskerk BV and Firma Schaap v Productschap Vee en Vlees* (C-455/06) EU:C:2008:650, [2008] E.C.R. I-08763.

[132] *Van Schijndel* (C-430/93 and C-431/93) at para.17.

[133] *Rampion v Franfinance SA* (C-429/05) EU:C:2007:575, [2007] E.C.R. I-8017 ("*Rampion* (C-429/05)").

[134] Directive 87/102/EEC [1987] O.J. L42/48.

[135] *Rampion* (C-429/05) at para.59; *Radlinger v Finway a.s.* (C-377/14) EU:C:2016:283, April 21, 2016 at paras 62–74 (information duties) and see below, para.38-068.

[136] Directive 85/577/EEC. The Directive itself requires only that the consumer be given a right of cancellation of the contract, but the Court held that a national court was entitled to declare a contract void in these circumstances: first, because the Directive allows national authorities a discretion in determining the consequences which follow the infringement in question; and second, because the Directive puts in place only a minimum level of harmonisation: *Martín Martín v EDP Editores SL* (C-227/08) EU:C:2009:792, [2009] E.C.R. I-11939, paras 32–33. On this directive generally and its replacement by the Consumer Rights Directive 2011 see below, paras 38-059—38-060.

[137] *Martín Martín v EDP Editores SL* (C-227/08) EU:C:2009:792, [2009] E.C.R. I-11939, para.18.

[138] C-227/08 para.20.

[139] C-227/08 paras 21–26.

[140] C-227/08 para.27.

[141] C-227/08 para.28.

[142] *Banif Plus Bank Zrt v Csipai* (C-472/11) EU:C:2013:88; [2013] W.L.R. (D) 76 at para.27; *Asturcom Telecommunicaciones SL v Rodriquez Nogueira* (C-40/08) EU:C:2009:615, [2009] E.C.R. I-9579, below, para.38-333. Cf. *Bankia SA v Merino* (C-109/17) EU:C:2018:735 of September 19, 2018 at paras 33–34 and 49 (national court has no *duty* to raise the existence of an unfair commercial practice of its own motion even where it is allegedly related to the existence of an unfair term in a consumer contract, in part because the finding of an unfair commercial practice has no direct impact on the validity of the contract or its terms, on the latter see below, para.38-026). In *Salvoni v Fiermonte* (C-347/18) EU:C:2019:661 the CJEU refused to extend the approach in its case-law on the 1993 Directive to the context of the recognition of judgments, holding that a national court requested to issue a certificate under Regulation (EU) 1215/2012 of December 12, 2012 on jurisdiction and the recognition and enforcement of judgments in civil and commercial matters (recast) (the Brussels Ibis Regulation) [2012] O.J. L351/1 art.53 in respect of a judgment which has acquired the force of *res judicata* is *precluded* from considering of its own motion whether there has been breach of the special rules on jurisdiction for consumers in that Regulation so as to inform the consumer of this and thereby allow the latter to rely on the remedy in art.45 which permits refusal of recognition on this ground: art.45(1)(e)(i).

[143] Directive 1999/44/EEC; *Duarte Hueros v Autociba SSA and Automóviles Citroen España SA* (C-32/12) EU:C:2013:637, [2014] 1 C.M.L.R. 53 especially at paras 31–43 (in the context of a national rule denying a court the power recognise the consumer's right to reduction of the price on the ground of non-conformity where the consumer had claimed unsuccessfully rescission of the contract). cf. *Radlinger v Finway a.s.* (C-377/14) EU:C:2016:283, April 21, 2016 at paras 62–74 where the CJEU recognised an obligation on the national court to consider whether the information duties of the trader under the Consumer Credit Directive 2008 had been complied with simply by reference to the need to ensure the protection of the consumer and to its earlier case-law.

## A wider duty to request information from parties?

*Replace paragraph with:*

In *Faber v Autobedrijf Hazet Ochten BV*[144] the Court of Justice of the EU considered whether a national court has a duty to consider of its own motion whether a party to a contract subject to a dispute was a "consumer" so as to attract the application of national legislation implementing the Consumer Sales Directive 1999. In doing so, the Court followed its own general approach under *Van Schijndel*, so as to subject any national procedural rules to the principles of equivalence and effectiveness.[145] According to the Court: **38-020**

> "In that regard, it is, in principle, for the national court, for the purpose of identifying the legal rules applicable to a dispute which has been brought before it, to assign a legal classification to the facts and acts on which the parties rely in support of their claims. That legal classification is a prerequisite in a case in which, like that in the main proceedings, the guarantee or warranty in respect of the goods sold, on which the applicant is relying, may be governed by different rules depending on the purchaser's status. Such a classifica-

> tion does not, in itself, imply that the court is, of its own motion, exercising a discretion, but merely that it is establishing and ascertaining whether there is a statutory condition which determines the applicable legal rule."[146]

This view reflects a general approach in many continental national procedural laws according to which it is the role of a civil court to classify the facts and transactions ("acts"[147]) on which parties base their claims following the principle *iura novit curia* ("the court knows the law"), but it contrasts sharply with the approach of the common law generally (and English law in particular) where in principle it is for the parties to characterise in legal terms the basis of their claims.[148] Following *Van Schijndel*, the Court of Justice did not treat the court's duty here to be one governed merely by national law to be applied in the EU law context by way of application of the principle of equivalence,[149] but rather one which may need to reflect the principle of effectiveness:

> "... the principle of effectiveness requires a national court before which a dispute relating to a contract which may be covered by that directive has been brought to determine whether the purchaser may be classified as a consumer, even if the purchaser has not expressly claimed to have that status, as soon as that court has at its disposal the matters of law and of fact that are necessary for that purpose *or may have them at its disposal simply by making a request for clarification*."[150]

To decide otherwise would be "tantamount to making the consumer subject to the obligation to carry out a full classification of his situation himself, failing which he would lose the rights which the EU legislature intended to confer on him" by the 1999 Directive.[151] Moreover, in *Lintner* in the context of the Unfair Contract Terms Directive, the Court of Justice required that, where a national court has serious doubts from the case before it as to the fair nature of particular terms which are related to the subject matter of the dispute even if they are not invoked by the consumer, but it cannot *determine* the issue of fairness it must "take, if necessary of its own motion, investigative measures in order to complete that case file, by asking the parties, in observance of the principle of *audi alteram partem*, to provide it with the clarifications or documents necessary for that purpose".[152] As will be seen, from the point of view of English law the radical aspect of these cases is the requirement that, where a national court cannot on the facts as otherwise available to it determine whether a case before it falls within the scope of national legislation implementing an EU consumer protection directive or allow it to decide an issue relevant to the consumer's rights, then it may be required as a matter of EU law to request a party to clarify the factual position so as to be able to do so.

144 C-497/13 EU:C:2015:357, June 4, 2015 ("*Faber* (C-497/13)").

145 *Van Schijndel v Stichting Pensioenfonds voor Fysiotherapeuten* (C-430/93 and C-431/93) EU:C:1995:441, [1995] E.C.R. I-4705 above, para.38-019.

146 *Faber* (C-497/13) at para.38.

147 cf. the French version of para.38, which refers to "*faits et actes*".

148 See generally Whittaker in Leczykiewicz and Weatherill (eds), *The Involvement of EU Law in Private Relationships* (2013) Ch.6.

149 *Faber* (C-497/13) at para.39.

150 *Faber* (C-497/13) at para.46 (emphasis added). cf. the more cautious approach of A.G. Sharpston, advising that the national court should not have a duty to go beyond the ambit of the dispute as defined by the parties and not, therefore, where the legal and factual elements are neither already part of the file nor are obtainable in accordance with *national* procedural law: Opinion in *Faber* (C-497/13) of November 27, 2014, especially at paras 70–73.

[151] *Faber* (C-497/13) at para.44. For this purpose, the Court held that it is irrelevant whether or not a consumer is assisted by a lawyer: *Faber* (C-497/13) at para.47.

[152] *Lintner v UniCredit Bank Hungary Zrt.* (C-511/17) EU:C:2020:188. This approach to the role of a national court is reminiscent of the position of German civil courts: see Whittaker in Leczykiewicz and Weatherill (eds), *The Involvement of EU Law in Private Relationships* (2013) Ch.6, pp.98–101 referring to *Zivilprozessordnung*, para.139.

## Significance for English law

*Replace paragraph with:*

In the context of the regulation of unfair contract terms, the significance of the case-law following *Océano Grupo Editorial*[153] has long been recognised and this was given legislative expression in the UK by the Consumer Rights Act 2015 which provides that, in proceedings before a court which relate to a term of a consumer contract[154]: **38-021**

> "The court must consider whether the term is fair even if none of the parties to the proceedings has raised that issue or indicated that it intends to raise it"[155]

provided that:

> "... the court considers that it has before it sufficient legal and factual material to enable it to consider the fairness of the term."[156]

Outside this context, the UK legislation (primary and secondary) which implements EU consumer contract directives does not refer to any power or duty in courts to raise the issue of any rights which the consumer may have under EU law of their own motion. However, given the case-law in *Rampion*,[157] *Martín Martín*,[158] *Faber v Autobedrijf Hazet Ochten BV*[159] and *Lintner*,[159a] it is clear that a court in England and Wales may have a duty to raise of its own motion the issue of whether a party to proceedings is a "consumer" and, if so, what rights he or she may enjoy under the legislation implementing EU consumer contract law subject principally to the condition that the right is important for the effectiveness of the particular consumer protection which is foreseen by the EU directive; and a court may even be required to request a party to clarify the facts to do so.

[153] *Océano Grupo Editorial SA v Murciano Quintero* (C-240/98 to C-244/98) EU:C:2000:346, [2000] E.C.R. I-4941.

[154] Consumer Rights Act 2015 s.71(1) and see below, para.38-392 in particular on the question whether restricting the court's duty to the situation where "proceedings before a court *relate to* a term of a consumer contract" is compatible with the case-law of the CJEU.

[155] Consumer Rights Act 2015 s.71(2).

[156] Consumer Rights Act 2015 s.71(3).

[157] *Rampion v Franfinance SA* (C-429/05) EU:C:2007:575, [2007] E.C.R. I-8017.

[158] Directive 85/577/EEC; *Martín Martín v EDP Editores SL* (C-227/08) EU:C:2009:792, [2009] E.C.R. I-11939 paras 32–33.

[159] C-497/13 EU:C:2015:357, above, para.38-020.

[159a] *Lintner v UniCredit Bank Hungary Zrt.* (C-511/17) EU:C:2020:188, above, para.38-020.

## (b) The Intensity of Harmonisation Required by EU Legislation

### Examples of "minimum harmonisation" directives

*Replace footnote 169 with:*

38-024 [169] Cf. Directive (EU) 2019/771 of the European Parliament and of the Council of 20 May 2019 on certain aspects concerning contracts for the sale of goods, etc. [2019] O.J. L136/28 [2019] O.J. L136/28, which repeals and replaces Directive 99/44/EC and which requires full harmonisation (art.4) although with exceptions, recognising notably "the freedom of Member States to allow consumers to choose a specific remedy, if the lack of conformity of the goods becomes apparent within a period after delivery, not exceeding 30 days" (art.3(7)). The 2019 Directive must be implemented by January 1, 2022 (art.24) and so after IP completion day, and this means that the UK will not be under any obligation to implement it unless its doing so forms part of any agreement it concludes as to the future relationship with the EU: see Vol.I, para.1-015A. The 2019 Directive is noted further below, para.38-436.

### Examples of "full harmonisation" and "partial full harmonisation": Unfair Commercial Practices Directive 2005

*In line 20, after "appear to fall within its scope.", add new footnote 182a:*

38-026 [182a] However, Directive (EU) 2019/2161 of the European Parliament and of the Council of 27 November 2019 ... as regards the better enforcement and modernisation of Union consumer protection rules [2019] O.J. L328/7 art.3(5) (inserting a new art.11a in the 2005 Directive) requires the introduction of redress for consumers harmed by unfair commercial practices, but as the 2019 Directive must be implemented on November 28, 2021 (i.e. after IP completion day) the UK is not required to do so: see below, para.38-175A.

### Consumer Rights Directive 2011

*Replace footnote 193 with:*

38-028 [193] Directive 2011/83/EU Ch.IV ("Other consumer rights"). Directive (EU) 2019/2161 of the European Parliament and of the Council of 27 November 2019 ... as regards the better enforcement and modernisation of Union consumer protection rules [2019] O.J. L328/7 art.4 makes a number of amendments to the 2011 Directive, but as the 2019 Directive must be implemented on November 28, 2021 (i.e. after IP completion day) the UK is not required to do so: cf. above, para.38-004. Article 4 of the 2011 Directive (quoted in the text following this note) is not due to be amended by the 2019 Directive.

## 3. DEFINITIONS OF CONSUMER CONTRACT

## (b) "Consumer"

### Background

*Replace paragraph with:*

38-030 Although until recently the approach of English law to the definition of the person to be protected by its consumer protection legislation was particular and contextual, three broad approaches could be identified.[200] First, the Consumer Credit Act 1974 applied (and still applies) its principal controls to "consumer credit agreements", defined as agreements between an individual (the "debtor") and any other person (the "creditor") by which the creditor provides the debtor with credit of any amount.[201] Secondly, the Unfair Contract Terms Act 1977 protected persons "dealing as consumer" against exemption clauses and indemnity clauses.[202] Thirdly, a number of particular statutes and statutory instruments implementing EU directives protected "consumers" defined in a near-standard form of words derived from their parent directives, as in the case of the Doorstep Selling Regulations 1987[203] and the Unfair Terms in Consumer Contracts Regulations 1999.[204] Of these three approaches, the Consumer Credit Act's definition of the ambit of its controls by reference to the person provided with credit remains distinct and special for its purposes, the established domestic approach being subject to a further layer of complexity by the restricted scope of controls required by the Consumer Credit Directive 2008.[205] This law is discussed in Ch.39 of the present work.[206] By contrast, since 2012 UK legislation has sought to bring a considerable degree of consistency to the definition of the "protected party" (the consumer) in its consumer contract protection law, these changes being inspired in part by the concern to provide a consistent approach to the interpretative gloss given to "consumer" at the EU level by the Consumer Rights Directive 2011.[207]

[200] cf. above, para.38-002.

[201] Consumer Credit Act 1974 s.8(1) (as amended) and see below, para.39-016.

[202] On this law (abrogated by the Consumer Rights Act 2015) see Vol.I, Ch.15 and especially paras 15-073—15-079.

[203] Consumer Protection (Cancellation of Contracts Concluded Away from Business Premises) Regulations 1987 (SI 1987/2117) reg.2(1) ("Doorstep Selling Regulations 1987") ("'consumer' means a person, other than a body corporate, who, in making a contract to which these Regulations apply, is acting for purposes which can be regarded as outside his business") and cf. Directive 85/577/EEC art.2 ("'consumer' means a natural person who, in transactions covered by this Directive, is acting for purposes which can be regarded as outside his trade or profession").

[204] SI 1999/2083 reg.3(1) ("'consumer' means any natural person who, in contracts covered by these Regulations, is acting for purposes which are outside his trade, business or profession") and cf. Directive 93/13/EEC art.2(b) ("'consumer' means any natural person who, in contracts covered by this Directive, is acting for purposes which are outside his trade, business or profession").

[205] Directive 2008/48/EC concerning credit agreements for consumers [2008] O.J. L133/66, replacing Directive 87/102/EEC concerning consumer credit O.J. L42/48.

[206] See below, para.39-011.

[207] Consumer Rights Directive 2011 recital 17; art.2(1) and see below, paras 38-036, 38-041.

### "Natural persons"

*Replace paragraph with:*

This standard definition restricts consumers to "natural persons"[210] and therefore, unlike a person "dealing as consumer" under the Unfair Contract Terms Act as enacted, a company cannot rely on UK regulations implementing a directive containing this definition, even if it acts "for purposes which are outside [its] business",[211] unless the implementing legislation (or other UK legislation) extends the scope of its controls to persons contracting in this way.[212] The Court of Justice of the EU has ruled that an association of natural persons (such as a "commonhold association" of real property) which is considered by national law to be a "legal subject" which is neither a natural nor a legal entity, cannot be considered to be a "consumer" within the meaning of the Unfair Contract Terms Directive as it is not a "natural person", though this does not prevent a national court from interpreting its implementing legislation as extending to such an association, as the Directive requires only minimum harmonisation.[213] **38-033**

[210] *Cape Snc v Idealservice Srl* (C-541/99 and C-542/99) EU:C:2001:625, [2001] E.C.R. I-09049.

[211] *Cape Snc v Idealservice Srl* (C-541/99 and C-542/99) EU:C:2001:625; 1999 Regulations reg.3(1). On "dealing as consumer" under the 1977 Act (before it was amended by the Consumer Rights Act 2015) see Vol.I, paras 15-073—15-079.

[212] For English law, the 1999 Regulations were extended to consumer arbitration agreements defining "consumer" for this purpose as legal as well as natural persons: Arbitration Act 1996 s.90; *Heifer International Inc v Christiansen* [2007] EWHC 3015 (TCC), [2008] All E.R. (D) 120 (Jan) and see

below, para.38-225. This extension remains in place under the Consumer Rights Act 2015, below, para.38-412.

213 *Condominio di Milano, via Meda v Eurothermo SpA* (C-329/19) EU:C:2020:263 at paras 25–38 distinguishing (at para.30) the position in its earlier judgment in *EVN Bulgaria lofikatsia Sofia v Dimitrov* (Joined Cases C-708/17 and C-725/17) EU:C:2019:1049 at para.59 where a contract for the supply of energy to a building held in commonhold was held to be a "consumer contract" within the meaning of the Consumer Rights Directive 2011 on the basis that the contracts there had been concluded with the "unit holders" rather than with the commonhold association through its administrator. Cf. the decision of the French First Chamber of the *Cour de cassation* of June 4, 2014, [2014] Bull. civ.1 no.102, [2014] E.C.C. 30 which held that a co-ownership association (a *syndicat de copropriétaires*) which is treated as having legal personality by French law could not count as a "consumer" for the purposes of French legislation implementing Directive 93/13/EEC art.7 both on the ground of its possessing legal personality and on the ground that such an association (even though formed by private individuals) has as its object an economic activity in the upkeep and management of the property and therefore was not "*non-professionnel*" (non-business).

## European case-law

*Replace paragraph with:*

**38-034** More generally, the Court of Justice of the EU has made clear that it will take an autonomous definition of the concept of "consumer" for the purposes of the EU secondary legislative instruments which use this term.[214] In this respect, the Court of Justice is likely to take into account the purpose of this body of legislation, which it sees as being protective of consumers, while still acknowledging that the need for harmonisation is justified by the requirements of the internal market.[215] So, for example, the Court has explained in relation to the Unfair Terms in Consumer Contracts Directive that:

> "... the system of protection established by Directive 93/13 is based on the idea that the consumer is in a weak position vis-à-vis the trader as regards both his bargaining power and his level of knowledge, which leads to the consumer agreeing to terms drawn up in advance by the trader without being able to influence the content of those terms."[216]

However, the Court has taken a fairly restrictive view of "consumer" for these purposes,[217] particularly when contrasted with the expansive view taken by English law for the purposes of the Unfair Contract Terms Act, where it has been held that a business which makes a contract of a kind which does not form a regular part of its business may "deal as consumer".[218] So, for example, in *Di Pinto*[219] the question arose whether a trader could ever be a "consumer" for the purposes of the Doorstep Selling Directive, which used the standard defining language for "consumer" earlier noted.[220] The European Court held that:

> "... the criterion for the application of protection lies in the connection between the transactions which are the subject of the canvassing and the professional activity of the trader: the latter may claim that the directive is applicable only if the transaction in respect of which he is canvassed lies outside his trade or profession. Article 2, which is drafted in general terms, does not make it possible, with regard to acts performed in the context of such a trade or profession, to draw a distinction between normal acts and those which are exceptional in nature."[221]

The Court added that:

> "Acts which are preparatory to the sale of a business, such as the conclusion of a contract for the publication of an advertisement in a periodical, are connected with the professional activity of the trader although such acts may bring the running of the business to an end, they are managerial acts performed for the purpose of satisfying requirements *other than the family or personal requirements of the trader.*"[222]

The last italicised phrase could be seen as suggesting that a person does not act as a consumer unless contracting for their "family or personal needs". In *Benincasa v Dentalkit*[223] the European Court considered the concept of consumer for the purposes of art.13 of the Brussels Convention,[224] upholding its previous view that this referred to "private final consumer" in this context[225]:

> "Consequently, only contracts concluded for the purpose of satisfying an individual's own needs in terms of private consumption come under the provisions designed to protect the consumer as the party deemed to be the weaker party economically."[226]

The Court of Justice has held that, in order to determine whether a person was acting as a consumer for the purposes of the Directive on unfair terms in consumer contracts, a national court should take into account:

> "... all the circumstances of the case, particularly the nature of the goods or service covered by the contract in question, capable of showing the purpose for which those goods or that service is being acquired."[227]

This was seen as a "functional criterion".[228] However, the concept of "consumer" is:

> "... objective in nature and is distinct from the concrete knowledge the person in question may have, or from the information that person actually has."[229]

As a result, while lawyers may constitute "traders" in their contracts with their own clients,[230] they may, even if they are technically knowledgeable, nonetheless act as consumers in other transactions as they may be weaker parties compared to the traders with whom they deal.[231] For example, in *Bachman* a transport company (of which A was director) concluded a contract of loan with a finance company, B, the loan being guaranteed by A's mother, C, and secured on her home. When the company was faced with insolvency, D (A's brother) concluded a contract of novation of the original loan contract with B under which he undertook to pay back the loan over a period at interest.[232] Subsequently, D sought to establish that he had entered this contract of novation as a consumer and was therefore entitled to challenge some of its terms as unfair under national legislation implementing the 1993 Directive. The Court of Justice of the EU held that a physical person in D's position could be a consumer if the national court found that he acted for private purposes (notably, to save his mother from the imminent enforcement of the guarantee of the original loan) rather than for business or professional purposes or in "manifest connection" with a role in the (insolvent) transport company.[233] Finally, in *Petruchovà* the Court of Justice considered the circumstances in which an individual who had concluded a "framework contract" with a broker to enable her to make transactions on the international FOREX (foreign exchange) market can count as a "consumer" for the purposes of the special consumer jurisdiction provided by art.17 of the Brussels Regulation.[233a] The Court of Justice reaffirmed that the concept of "consumer" has to be interpreted restrictively for this particular purpose and that the question whether a person is a consumer has to be decided "by referring to the position of that person in a given contract, in relation to the nature and purpose of the contract, and not to the subjective situation of that person".[233b] In the context, the individual was a University student working part-time and there was nothing in the court file which suggested that she concluded the contract as part of a professional activity.[233c] Moreover, in deciding whether such a person was actually acting "outside and independently of any professional activity", a national court should *not* take into account factors such as the value of the transactions carried out under contracts such as framework contracts, the extent of the risks of financial loss associated with the conclusion of such contracts, that person's possible knowledge or expertise in the field of financial instruments or their active conduct in connection with such transactions.[233d]

[214] e.g. *Cape Snc v Idealservice Srl* (C-541/99) EU:C:2001:625, [2001] E.C.R. I-09049 paras 16–17 (Unfair Terms in Consumer Contracts Directive); *France v Di Pinto* (361/89) EU:C:1991:118, [1991] E.C.R. I-1189 (Doorstep Selling Directive). The CJEU has assumed that the irregular position of a person travelling by rail without a ticket (and refusing to buy a ticket when asked) can be a "consumer" for the purposes of the 1993 Directive: *Nationale Maatschappij der Belgische Spoorwegen (NMBS) v Kanyeba, Nijs. Dedroog* (C-349 to C-351/18) EU:C:2019:936 at paras 55 et seq. on which see below, paras 38-020 and 38-332A.

[215] This is typically required by the competence on which the directives have been made, this being art.114 TFEU (formerly art.95 EC).

[216] *Pereničovà v SOS finance, spol. sro* (C-453/10) EU:C:2012:144, [2012] 2 C.M.L.R. 28 para.27 repeating similar formulations in earlier judgments from *Mostaza Claro v Centro Móvil Milenium SL* (C-168/05) EU:C:2006:675, [2006] E.C.R. I-10421 (which used "seller or supplier" rather than "trader"). See similarly *BKK Mobil Oil Körperschaft des öffentlichen Rechts v Zentrale zur Bekämpfung unlauteren Wettbewerbs eV* (C-59/12) EU:C:2013:634, October 3, 2013 para.35 in the context of the Unfair Commercial Practices Directive 2005. It is partly on this ground that a "consumer" does not lose this capacity on the completed performance of the contract: *SC Raiffeisen Bank SA v JB* (C-698/18 and C-699) EU:C:2020:537, paras 73–74.

[217] Reich (1995) 4 *European Review of Private Law* 285, 292–293.

[218] Unfair Contract Terms Act 1977 s.12; *R. & B. Customs Brokers Co Ltd v United Dominions Trust Ltd* [1988] 1 W.L.R. 321: on which see Vol.I, para.15-074.

[219] *France v Di Pinto* (361/89) EU:C:1991:118, [1991] E.C.R. I-1189.

[220] Directive 85/577 to protect the consumer in respect of contracts negotiated away from business premises [1985] O.J. L372/31 art.2 (repealed and replaced by Directive 2011/83/EU on consumer rights [2011] O.J. L304/64).

[221] EU:C:1991:118, [1991] E.C.R. I-1189 at [15].

[222] EU:C:1991:118, [1991] E.C.R. I-1189 at [16] (emphasis added).

[223] C-269/95 EU:C:1997:337, [1997] E.C.R. I-3767.

[224] Brussels Convention on Jurisdiction and the Enforcement of Foreign Judgments in Civil and Commercial Matters of September 27, 1968 replaced by Council Regulation 44/2001 on jurisdiction and the recognition and enforcement of judgments in civil and commercial matters [2001] O.J. L12/1, which was itself replaced as from January 10, 2015 by Regulation (EU) 1215/2012 of 12 December 2012 on jurisdiction and the recognition and enforcement of judgments in civil and commercial matters (recast) ("the Brussels Ibis Regulation").

[225] EU:C:1997:337, [1997] E.C.R. I-3767 at para.15; *Shearson Lehman Hutton* (C-89/91) EU:C:1993:15, [1993] E.C.R. I-139 at paras 20 and 22.

[226] EU:C:1997:337, [1997] E.C.R. I-3767 at [17].

[227] *Costea v SC Volksbank România SA* (C-110/14) EU:C:2015:538, April 23, 2015 at para.23.

[228] *Tarcău v Banca Comercială Intesa Sanpaolo România SA* (C-74/15) EU:C:2015:772, Order of CJEU November 19, 2015 at para.27.

[229] *Costea v SC Volksbank România SA* (C-110/14) EU:C:2015:538, April 23, 2015 at para.21. See similarly, *Tarcău v Banca Comercială Intesa Sanpaolo România SA* (C-74/15) EU:C:2015:772, Order of CJEU November 19, 2015 para.27 on which see below, paras 38-226 and 45-156. See also *Petruchová v FIBO Group Holdings Ltd* (C-208/18) EU:C:2019:825, above, para.38-034.

[230] *Šiba v Devėnas* (C-537/13) EU:C:2015:14, January 15, 2015 [2015] Bus. L.R. 291 paras 23 and 24.

[231] *Costea v SC Volksbank România SA* (C-110/14) EU:C:2015:538, April 23, 2015 at paras 20–27. See also *Pouvin and Dijoux v Électricité de France (EDF)* (C-590/17) EU:C:2019:232 of March 21, 2019 at para.28, referring to this "broad definition" which therefore allows the protection granted by the 1993 Directive to all natural persons finding themselves in the weaker position as regards their bargaining power or level of knowledge. The CJEU held that an employee could be a "consumer" in relation to a

financial service provided by his employer (a loan for the purchase of property used for private purposes): C-590/17 at paras 29–32.

[232] *Bachman v FAER IFN SA* (C-535/16) EU:C:2017:321 (Order of the Court of April 27, 2017, available in French).

[233] See similarly *Dumitraş v BRD Groupe Société Générale* (C-534/15) EU:C:2016:700, Order of the CJEU of September 14, 2016 at paras 38-29 (absence of "functional links" between guarantor and company debtor (such as being a director or holding non-negligible shares) could justify national court in finding that the guarantor was a consumer).

[233a] *Petruchová v FIBO Group Holdings Ltd* (C-208/18) EU:C:2019:825 ("*Petruchovà* (C-208/18)").

[233b] *Petruchovà* (C-208/18) at para.41 referring to *Schrems v Facebook Ireland Ltd* (C-498/16) EU:C:2018:37, para.29 on which see further below, para.38-037.

[233c] *Petruchovà* (C-208/18) at para.46.

[233d] *Petruchovà* (C-208/18) at para.59, following the advice of A.G. Tanchev who (at paras 58–63) had expressly preferred the approach of the HC in *Standard Bank London Ltd v Apostolakis (No.1)* [2000] I.L. Pr. 766 to that taken in *AMT Futures Ltd v Mazillier, Dr Meier & Dr Guntner Rechtsanwaltsgesellschaft mbH*, on which see below, para.38-040. The CJEU followed its decision in *Petruchovà* (C-208/18) in *AU v Reliantco Investments Ltd* (C-500/18) EU:C:2020:264.

## The Consumer Rights Directive and its possible wider influence

*Replace paragraph with:*

On the other hand, while the Consumer Rights Directive of 2011 (which principally repealed and replaced the earlier Doorstep Selling Directive and Distance Contracts Directive[238]) uses an almost identical form of words to define consumer as is used by the EU standard definition as earlier identified,[239] recital 17 states that: **38-036**

> "... in the case of dual purpose contracts, where the contract is concluded for purposes partly within and partly outside the person's trade and the trade purpose is so limited as not to be predominant in the overall context of the contract, that person should also be considered as a consumer."

While rather awkwardly phrased, this recital therefore includes a person as a "consumer" where they act mainly for non-trade purposes and it therefore reflects a more extensive view of the understanding of "consumer" by the EU legislature than was taken by the Court of Justice in the context of the Brussels Convention in *Gruber v Bay Wa AG*,[240] where any business purpose other than one which is "so limited as to be negligible" deprives a person of their status as consumer.[241] The Consumer Rights Directive seeks to achieve this by indicating the proper interpretation to be taken to the standard form of words defining consumer and, owing to the significance of the recitals to a directive for the interpretation of its text,[242] this gloss on "consumer" therefore clearly governs the definition in the Consumer Rights Directive itself; and this directive did make an insertion into the 1993 Directive, though not one of substantive significance.[243] Moreover, this gloss may well have a wider significance as it could encourage the Court of Justice to hold that "consumer" can include persons *mainly* acting outside their trade or profession for the purposes of other substantive law directives in the consumer *acquis*, distinguishing its more restrictive approach in *Gruber* on the basis that it concerned the special (and therefore exceptional) provisions in the Brussels Convention governing international jurisdiction.[244] This way of thinking was, indeed, adopted by Advocate General Crux Villalón in *Costea v SC Volksbank România SA*.[245] On the other hand, the recent Directive on sale of goods to consumers (which will repeal and replace the Consumer Sales Directive 1999) retains the standard definition of "consumer"[245a] but its preamble provides in respect of this definition that:

"Member States should also remain free to determine in the case of dual purpose contracts, where the contract is concluded for purposes that are partly within and partly outside the person's trade, and where the trade purpose is so limited as not to be predominant in the overall context of the contract, whether, and under which conditions, that person should also be considered a consumer."[245b]

Given this contrast with the Consumer Rights Directive 2011, the position would appear to be that there is no single approach in EU legislation to the question whether a natural person contracting a "dual purpose contract" counts as a consumer.

[238] Below, para.38-060.

[239] "'Consumer' means any natural person who, in contracts covered by this Directive, is acting for purposes which are outside his trade, business, craft or profession". The main difference is the additional reference to "craft": cf. above, para.38-032.

[240] C-464/01 EU:C:2005:32, [2005] E.C.R. I-439 ("*Gruber* (C-464/01)").

[241] Above, para.38-035.

[242] Above, para.38-016.

[243] The 2011 Directive art.32 inserts a new art.8a in the 1993 Directive which requires Member States to inform the EU Commission of any exercises of their power to extend the protection for consumers by way of art.8. See also Directive 2013/11/EU of May 21, 2013 on ADR for consumer disputes [2013] O.J. L165/63 art.4(1)(a) of which defines "consumer" in the standard way, but its recital 18 then glosses this definition in an almost identical way as 2011 Directive recital 17. A similar pattern is found in Directive 2014/17/EU of February 4, 2014 on credit agreements for consumers relating to immovable property [2014] O.J. L60/34 (the "Mortgage Credit Directive") recital 12 and art.4(1), referring to the definition of "consumer" in Directive 2008/48/EC of April 23, 2008 on credit agreements for consumers [2008] O.J. L133/66 art.3(1). This supports the view that the Court of Justice should hold that this gloss is to be applied more generally to definitions of "consumer" in the EU consumer protection *acquis*, unless the context otherwise requires.

[244] Above, para.38-035.

[245] (C-110/14) EU:C:2015:538, April 23, 2015 especially at paras 35–47. The CJEU in its judgment of September 3, 2015 did not address this issue. In *Heriot-Watt University v Schlamp* [2020] SC EDIN 15 (February 24, 2020), the Sherriff Ct (Lothian and Borders) adopted the position in A.G. Villalón's Opinion in *Costea* and therefore held for the purposes of the Brussels Ibis Regulation art.17 that a contracting party "must be regarded as a consumer if the trade or professional purpose is not predominant". No reference was made to the decision of the CJEU in *Schrems* (C-498/16) discussed in para.38-037.

[245a] Directive (EU) 2019/771 of the European Parliament and of the Council of 20 May 2019 on certain aspects concerning contracts for the sale of goods, etc [2019] O.J. L136/28 art.2(2).

[245b] Directive (EU) 2019/771 recital 22. Identical provision is made by Directive (EU) 2019/770 of the European Parliament and of the Council of 20 May 2019 [2019] O.J. L136/1 on certain aspects concerning contracts for the supply of digital content and digital services recital 17 and art.2(6). On these directives, see below, para.38-436.

*Replace paragraph with:*

**38-037** Most recently in *Schrems v Facebook Ireland Ltd* the Court of Justice again considered the issue of a contract with mixed purposes for the purposes of the special international jurisdiction for consumers provided by arts 15 and 16 of the Brussels Regulation, though in a very different context from its earlier decision in *Gruber*.[246] In *Schrems*, the applicant for various declarations had been a user of the social network Facebook for some years, initially for his own personal purposes (such as exchanging photographs and chatting), but he later opened a "Facebook page" so as to report to internet users on his legal proceedings against Facebook Ireland, his lectures, media appearances, etc. and to publicise his books in relation to alleged infringements of data protection. He founded an association which seeks to uphold the fundamental right to data protection and had assigned to him, by more than 25,000 people worldwide, claims to be brought in the proceedings from which a reference was made to the Court of Justice. In terms of its interpretation of "consumer" for these purposes, the Court of Justice in *Schrems* recognised that, while the concepts in the Brussels Regulation had to be interpreted:

> "... independently, by reference principally to the general scheme and objectives of that regulation ... account must, in order to ensure compliance with the objectives pursued by the legislature of the European Union in the sphere of consumer contracts, and the consistency of EU law, also be taken of the definition of 'consumer' in other rules of EU law."[247]

One issue before the Court of Justice was the proper approach to a case where an individual acted partly outside his trade or profession and party within it.[248] In this respect, the Court expressly followed its earlier decision in *Gruber* to the effect that the link between an individual and his trader or profession must be:

> "... so slight as to be marginal and, therefore, had only a negligible role in the context of the supply in respect of which the contract was concluded, considered in its entirety."[249]

As regards the particular case before it, the Court considered that where digital social network services are used over a long time, changes in their use are relevant to the user's status as (or as not) "consumer". The Court added that:

> "... [t]his interpretation implies, in particular that a user of such services may, in bringing an action, rely on his status as a consumer only if the predominantly[250] non-professional use of those services, for which the applicant initially concluded a contract, has not subsequently become predominantly professional."[251]

With respect, use of a criterion of "predominance" of one purpose over another differs significantly from the approach in *Gruber* where any non-negligible business or professional purpose rules out a person's being a consumer; instead this approach is that adopted by the Consumer Rights Directive as earlier explained.[252] The Court of Justice's position in *Schrems* on the understanding of "consumer" in relation to mixed purpose contracts is equivocal, although it appears to be moving towards including as a "consumer" a person who acts predominantly for non-business purposes. In the particular circumstances of *Schrems* itself, the Court considered that neither the actual expertise of the applicant which he might have acquired in the field covered by Facebook's services[253] nor his various activities (publishing, lecturing, etc.) undertaken for the purposes of representing the rights and interests of service users (including as to personal data) could deprive him of the status of "consumer", not least as the contrary interpretation would disregard the objective set out in art.169(1) TFEU of promoting the right of consumers to organise themselves in order to safeguard their interests.[254] Here, therefore, wider EU law principle was used to guide the application of the concept of "consumer".

[246] C-498/16 EU:C:2018:37, January 25, 2018 ("*Schrems* (C-498/16)").

[247] *Schrems* (C-498/16) at para.28 referring to its observations in *Vapenik v Thurner* (C-508/12) EU:C:2013:790, December 5, 2013 which concerned Regulation (EC) No.805/2004 of the European Parliament and of the Council of 21 April 2004 creating a European Enforcement Order for uncontested claims [2004] O.J. L143/15.

[248] The CJEU also held that where consumers assign their claims to another individual, the latter cannot rely on the special provisions in the Brussels Regulation provided for "consumers" as regards those assigned claims, as art.16(1) assumes that the action being brought is by the consumer against the other party to the contract: *Schrems* (C-498/16) at paras 42–49.

[249] *Schrems* (C-498/16) at para.32, citing *Gruber* (C-464/01) at para.39. The CJEU in *Schrems* (C-498/17) at para.30 had earlier stated apparently more strictly that "only contracts concluded outside and independently of any trade or professional activity or purpose, *solely* for the purpose of satisfying an individual's own needs in terms of private consumption, are covered by the special rules laid down by the regulation to protect the consumer as the party deemed to be the weaker party" (emphasis added). However, in *Milivojević v Raiffeisenbank St Stefan-Jagerberg-Wolfsberg eGen* (C-630/17) EU:C:2019:123 at para.91, the CJEU repeated the formula in *Schrems* quoted in the text clearly seeing it as representing its earlier decision. In *Weco Project ApS v Loro Piana* [2020] EWHC 2150 (Comm) at [48] the HC held (obiter) that the relevant test of "consumer" under the Brussels Ibis Regulation was contained in the CJEU's decisions in *Schrems* and *Milivojević* as set out in the text and on the facts that the wealthy individual who had concluded a contract to arrange the carriage of a luxury sailing yacht with a freight forwarder from the Caribbean to the Mediterranean *was not* a "consumer" as the yacht was to be used for significant business purposes as well as personal leisure: at [75]–[76]. However, the HC further held that the individual *was* a "consumer" under the test in the Consumer Rights Act 2015 Pt 2: at [107] as "the purpose of the transport was mainly for non-business purposes, even though the business use could not be said to be negligible".

[250] The original here and later in the paragraph states "predominately".

[251] *Schrems* (C-498/16) at para.38.

[252] Above, para.38-036.

[253] Citing *Costea v SC Volksbank România SA* (C-110/14) EU:C:2015:538, above, paras 38-034 and 38-252.

[254] *Schrems* (C-498/16) at paras 39–40. The CJEU in *Petruchovà* (C-208/18) EU:C:2019:825 followed its earlier approach in *Schrems* on the interpretation of "consumer" for the purposes of the Brussels Regulation art.17, though not in the particular context of a contract for mixed purposes: see above, para.38-034.

## United Kingdom case-law on earlier definition

*Replace paragraph with:*

**38-040** However, in *Maple Leaf Macro Volatility Master Fund v Rouvroy*[264] Andrew Smith J. questioned the conclusion of Longmore J. as regards the status as consumer of the defendants in the *Apostolakis* case, which he saw as concerning the question whether the dealing of the defendants there was of a nature that they were to be regarded as carrying on a trade. Andrew Smith J. distinguished the case before him, which instead concerned the question whether an agreement made by directors of (and major shareholders in) a company for funding of a securities transaction to regain control of that company was so connected with their business activities as not to be regarded as outside their trade. He held that it was not to be so regarded, so that the directors did not qualify as "consumers" either for the purposes of art.15 of the Brussels I Regulation or of the Unfair Terms in Consumer Contracts Regulations 1999.[265] In commenting on the contrast between the *Apostolakis* and *Rouvroy* decisions, the High Court in *AMT Futures Ltd v Mazillier, Dr Meier & Dr Guntner Rechtsanwaltsgesellschaft mbH* considered that the dividing line between investors who count as "consumers" and those who do not "is likely to be heavily dependent on the circumstances of each individual and the nature and pattern of investment".[265a]

However, this UK case-law should be read in the light of the decision of the Court of Justice of the EU in *Petruchová* earlier noted,[265b] where that Court held (in the context of a framework contract concluded by an individual with a broker to enable her to engage in the FOREX market) that the issue whether such a person was a "consumer" for the purposes of the Brussels Regulation turned on whether she was acting "outside and independently of any professional activity", and that for this purpose a national court should *not* take into account factors such as the value of the transactions carried out under contracts such as framework contracts, the extent of the risks of financial loss associated with the conclusion of such contracts, that person's possible knowledge or expertise in the field of financial instruments or their active conduct in connection with such transactions.[265c] In doing so, the Court of Justice approved the position adopted by its Advocate General, who had expressly preferred the approach of the High Court in *Standard Bank London Ltd v Apostolakis (No.1)*[265d] to that taken in *AMT Futures Ltd v Mazillier, Dr Meier & Dr Guntner Rechtsanwaltsgesellschaft mbH*.[265e]

In *Prostar Management Ltd v Twaddle*,[266] a professional footballer claimed that he acted as "consumer" for the purposes of the 1999 Regulations in relation to his receipt of services under a management agreement for the promotion of his career, profile and sponsorship. The Glasgow and Strathkelvin Sheriff Court had regard to the decisions of the European Court in *Di Pinto*[267] and *Benincasa*[268] and rejected this claim, holding that being a footballer was the defender's "trade or profession" and that the contract in question could not be regarded as being outside it.[269] In *Overy v Paypal (Europe) Ltd*[270] the High Court, having reviewed the European case-law on the proper understanding of "consumer" including the Court of Justice's decision in *Gruber*,[271] held that the claimant, a professional photographer who opened a "business account" with an online provider of electronic payment services and who used it partly for the purposes of his photography business and partly to sell his house by means of an online competition, did not count as a "consumer" so as to be protected by the 1999 Regulations: first, while the competition was "not an adventure in the nature of trade", he also intended to use it for his photography business and "that purpose could not reasonably be regarded as one which was insignificant or negligible"[272]; and, secondly, by the nature of the application which he made online and the information which the claimant provided in so doing, "he clearly conducted himself in such a way as to lead to the obvious conclusion that he was acting in his trade or professional capacity".[273] Finally, in *Ashfaq v International Insurance Co of Hannover Plc* the Court of Appeal applied the approach of the High Court in *Overy v Paypal (Europe) Ltd* to the context of an individual who had concluded a contract of insurance on a house which he let to tenants as part of a letting business.[274] In these circumstances, the individual did not contract as a "consumer" within the meaning of the 1999 Regulations, not least as the contract was in the form of a business insurance.[275] These decisions,[275a] it should be noted, were all made before the Court of Justice had given judgment in *Schrems v Facebook Ireland Ltd*.[276]

[264] [2009] EWHC 257 (Comm), [2009] 1 Lloyd's Rep. 475.

[265] [2009] EWHC 257 (Comm) at [209] and [270]. The Brussels Convention on jurisdiction and the enforcement of judgements in civil and commercial matters 1968 art.13 was replaced by Regulation (EU) 1215/2012 of 12 December 2012 on jurisdiction and the recognition and enforcement of judgments in civil and commercial matters (recast) ("the Brussels Ibis Regulation") art.17.

[265a] [2014] EWHC 1085 (Comm), [2015] 2 W.L.R. 187 at [58]. This issue was not discussed on appeal to the CA or the SC: [2015] EWCA Civ 143, [2015] Q.B. 699; [2017] UKSC 13, [2017] 2 W.L.R. 853. In *Ang v Reliantco Investments Ltd* [2019] EWHC 879 (Comm), [2019] 3 W.L.R. 161 at [23]–[70] esp. at [63] and [65], the HC considered that the making of investments by a private individual of her personal surplus wealth in the hope of generating good returns does not generally count as business activity and expressly approved the view just noted of the HC in *AMT Futures Ltd*, though adding that the spread, regularity and value of investment activity cannot determine the issue as this would replace the non-business purpose test in the Regulation.

[265b] Above, para.38-034.

[265c] *Petruchová* (C-208/18) EU:C:2019:825, above, para.38-034 at para.59.

[265d] [2000] I.L. Pr. 766, above.

[265e] Opinion of A.G. Tanchev in *Petruchová* (C-208/18) EU:C:2019:825; CJEU judgment of October 3, 2019 paras 58 and 59.

[266] [2003] S.L.T. (Sh. Ct.) 11.

[267] *France v Di Pinto* EU:C:1991:118, [1991] E.C.R. I-1189.

[268] C-269/95 EU:C:1997:337, [1997] E.C.R. I-3767.

[269] [2003] S.L.T. (Sh. Ct.) 11 at [12]–[14].

[270] [2012] EWHC 2659 (QB), [2013] Bus. L.R. Digest D1.

[271] C-464/01 EU:C:2005:32, above, paras 38-034—38-035.

[272] [2012] EWHC 2659 (QB) at [174]–[175] per Judge Hegarty Q.C. and cf. *Gruber v Bay Wa AG* (C-464/01) EU:C:2005:32, [2005] E.C.R. I-439 at para.54 discussed above, para.38-035.

[273] [2012] EWHC 2659 (QB) at [176] per Judge Hegarty Q.C. and cf. *Gruber v Bay Wa AG* (C-464/01) EU:C:2005:32, [2005] E.C.R. I-439 at para.54 discussed above, para.38-035.

[274] [2017] EWCA Civ 357, [2017] H.L.R. 29.

[275] [2017] EWCA Civ 357 at [45]–[57]. cf. *Chesterton Global Ltd v Finney* Unreported April 30, 2010, Lambeth County Ct where an individual who leased a "buy-to-let" property was held to have done so as a "consumer".

[275a] For further decisions see *Barclays Bank Plc v Kufner* [2008] EWHC 2319 (Comm), [2009] 1 All E.R. (Comm) 1 at [31] (person entering guarantee contract to acquire (through an offshore company) the component parts of a ship chartering business not a "consumer"); *Heifer International Inc v Christiansen* [2007] EWHC 3015 (TCC), [2008] All E.R. (D) 120 (Jan) at [243]–[250] (offshore company set up to purchase a residential property for its beneficial owners acted "for purposes outside [its] trade, business, or profession" when it entered contracts for the purchase and renovation of the property in question); *Wilson v MF Global UK Ltd* [2011] EWHC 138 (QB) at [129]–[131] (claimant trading through defendant in volatile financial market apparently held not a "consumer"); *Turner & Co (GB) Ltd v Abi* [2010] EWHC 2078 (QB), [2011] 1 C.M.L.R. 17 at [42] (shareholder director of a business commissioning an agent to sell the business not acting as a "consumer" but for the purposes of that business); *Office of Fair Trading v Foxtons Ltd* [2009] EWHC 1681 (Ch), [2009] 29 E.G. 98 (C.S.) at [28] (owners of property seeking to lease it acted as "consumers" in entering a letting agency contract with an estate agent, although other "professional" or "commercial" landlords would not); *RTA (Business Consultants) Ltd v Bracewell* [2015] EWHC 630 (QB), [2015] Bus. L.R. 800 at [51]–[60] (person contracting with estate agent for the sale of his business not a "consumer" for the purposes of the Cancellation of Contracts made in a Consumer's Home or Place of Work, etc. Regulations 2008 (SI 2008/1816)); *R. (on the application of Bluefin Insurance Services Ltd) v Financial Ombudsman Service Ltd* [2014] EWHC 3413 (Admin), [2015] Bus. L.R. 656 at [121]–[128] (director of company taking out a Directors and Officers Insurance Policy was not a "consumer" for the purposes of the Financial Ombudsman Service's jurisdiction (which was defined by reference, inter alia, to the definition of "consumer" in the 1993 Directive) as the insurance concerned his liability for acts in the course of his trade, business, or profession); *Kinloch v Coral Racing Ltd* [2017] CSOH 43, 2017 S.L.R. 856 at [158]–[159] (claimant held to be a professional gambler and therefore not a "consumer" for the purpose of the 1999 Regulations). cf. *Evans v Cherry Tree Finance Ltd* Unreported April 13, 2007, Ch D (concession that if any purposes for which the claimant contracted were outside his trade or business, then he was a consumer as defined by the regulations).

[276] Above, para.38-037.

**38-041** *Change title of paragraph:*

### The UK standard legislative definition of "consumer"

*In line 3, after "to be protected.", add new footnote 276a:*

**38-042** [276a] See, e.g. *Weco Project ApS v Loro Piana* [2020] EWHC 2150 (Comm) at [75]–[76], [107] where it was held that an individual who contracted to arrange the carriage of a luxury sailing yacht with a freight forwarder did so as a "consumer" within the meaning of Pt 2 of the 2015 Act, even though he was not a "consumer" for the purposes of the special jurisdiction provisions in the Brussels Ibis Regulation as "the purpose of the transport was mainly for non-business purposes, even though the business use could not be said to be negligible". Cf. above, para.33-037 (note).

### The "average consumer"

*Replace paragraph with:*

**38-044** EU legislation and case-law has been seen as reflecting various "standards" by which consumers' behaviour or understanding should be viewed: "confident" or sophisticated consumers; "average" consumers; and "vulnerable" consumers.[294]

However, of these approaches, the dominant one in the Court of Justice is the standard of the "average consumer" who is "reasonably well informed and reasonably observant and circumspect", a standard well established by it in the context of legislation on misleading advertising and the marketing of particular products.[295] This standard is not, however, a uniform one and this was reflected in the way in which the concept of "average consumer" was described and used by the Unfair Commercial Practices Directive 2005.[296] As earlier noted, the 2005 Directive creates a fully harmonised "general framework" for preventive measures of consumer protection though it is "without prejudice to contract law".[297] For this purpose, the 2005 Directive distinguishes between: (i) the average consumer; (ii) the average member of the group where a commercial practice is directed to a particular group of consumers; and (iii) the average member of a clearly identifiable group of consumers who are particularly vulnerable to the practice or the underlying product because of their mental or physical infirmity, age or credulity in a way which the trader could reasonably be expected to foresee.[298] Given this background, the "average consumer" is therefore a necessary element in the UK's legislation on unfair commercial practices, which, as earlier noted, has been extended to create certain rights to redress for consumers against traders.[299]

[294] See further Weatherill in Weatherill and Bernitz (eds), *The Regulation of Unfair Commercial Practices under EC Directive 2005/29* (2007), Ch.7.

[295] The case-law in question can be seen in *Pippig Augenoptik GmbH & Co KG v Hartlauer Handelsgesellschaft mbH* (C-44/01) EU:C:2003:205, [2003] E.C.R. I-3095 at [55]; *De Landtsheer Emmanuel SA v Comite Interprofessionnel du Vin du Champagne* (381/05) [2007] Bus. L.R. 1484; *Lidl Belgium GmbH & Co KG v Etablissementen Franz Colruyt NV* (356/04) [2007] Bus. L.R. 492 at [78] (misleading advertising); *Gut Springenheide GmbH and Rudolf Trusky v Oberkreisdrektor des Kreises Steinfurt-Amft fur Lebensmitteluberwachung* (C-210/96) EU:C:1998:369, [1998] E.C.R. I-4657 (marketing standards for eggs); *Estée Lauder Cosmetics GmbH & Co OHG v Lancaster Group GmbH* (C-220/98) EU:C:2000:8, [2000] E.C.R. I-0117 (marketing of cosmetics); *Mundipharma v Office for Harmonisation in the Internal Market (Trade Marks and Designs)–Altana Pharma (RESPICUR)* (T-256/04) EU:T:2007:46, [2007] E.C.R. II-449 (trademarks); *Tifosi Optics Inc v Office for Harmonisation in the Internal Market (Trade Marks and Designs) (OHIM)* (T-531/12) EU:T:2014:855 (trade marks). See also the recent discussion of "average consumer" in *OFT v Purely Creative* [2011] EWHC 106 (Ch), [2011] E.C.C. 20 at [73]–[74]; *Secretary of State for Business, Innovation and Skills v PLT Antimarketing Ltd* [2015] EWCA Civ 76, [2015] C.T.L.C.8 at [30]–[31] for the purposes of the 2008 Regulations.

[296] Directive 2005/29/EC concerning unfair business-to-consumer commercial practices [2005] O.J. L149/22, recitals 18 and 19; arts 5(2)(b) and (3), 6(1) and (2), 7(1) and (2), and 8. This directive is implemented in UK law by the Consumer Protection from Unfair Trading Regulations 2008 (SI 2008/1277), on which see below, paras 38-157 et seq.

[297] Directive 2005/29 art.3(2), below, para.38-157 but cf. paras 38-172 et seq.

[298] These distinctions are drawn from 2005 Directive art.5(2) and 5(3), below, para.38-169.

[299] Above, para.38-003 and see below, paras 38-172 et seq.

## Other legislative contexts

*Replace footnote 306 with:*

[306] Consumer Rights Directive 2011 art.5(1), 6(1) and 7(1) ("plain, intelligible language"); Consumer Contracts (Information, Cancellation and Additional Charges) Regulations 2013 (SI 2013/3134) regs 9(1), 10(1) and 13(1). See also *Verbraucherzentrale Berlin v Unimatic Vertriebs GmbH* (C-485/17) EU:C:2018:642 of August 7, 2018 where the CJEU referred to the understanding of the "average consumer" for the purposes of the definition of "business premises" under art.2(9) of the 2011 Directive, on which see below, para.38-081. **38-046**

### Consumers as the supplier of goods or services?

*Replace paragraph with:*

38-047 Typically, a "consumer" is a person who receives goods or services from a trader,[308] but the standard definition of consumer (both in EU law and in recent UK legislation[309]) is not explicitly restricted in this way, since an individual who acts for purposes that are (wholly or mainly[310]) outside his or her trade, business, craft or profession may equally *supply* goods or services to a trader, for example, in the case of a person who sells their second-hand car to a dealer or a person who guarantees a relative's debts to a bank. Moreover, in the case of consumer contract law derived from EU law, its declared purpose of the protection of consumers as the weaker or less informed party[311] may apply equally to an individual who *supplies* goods or services to a trader as to one who receives them. It is submitted, however, that the question whether such an individual is included within the various legislative schemes of protection in EU or UK law cannot be given a general answer, but must instead be considered in the context of each scheme, for while some legislation is clear on the question, other legislation is more open to argument. For example, the Unfair Commercial Practices Directive 2005 states that it applies to "unfair *business-to-consumer* commercial practices",[312] defined as:

> "... act, omission, course of conduct or representation, commercial communication including advertising and marketing, by a trader, directly connected with the promotion, sale or supply of a product to consumers."[313]

The general test of an unfair commercial practice also suggests that it applies only to commercial practices in relation to "products" supplied *to* a consumer[314] and the European Commission has expressed the view that the 2005 Directive does not apply to "consumer-to-business relations".[315] On the other hand, the main examples of unfair commercial practices in the 2005 Directive (misleading statements, misleading omissions and aggressive behaviour) are not worded in a way which suggests such a restriction.[316] Moreover, the 2005 Directive is concerned with commercial *practices* business-to-consumer, both from the point of view of fairness of competition between traders and of the protection of "consumers",[317] and unfair commercial practices can take place where an individual supplies goods or services to a trader on the basis of, for example, a misleading statement, omission or aggressive practice. But if the Commission's view is correct, then the Consumer Protection from Unfair Trading Regulations 2008 go further than the 2005 Directive requires, as they define "commercial practice" as any act, etc. "by a trader, which is directly connected with the promotion, sale or supply of a product *to or from* consumers".[318] This extension also applies to the rights to redress for consumers against traders created by amendment in 2014 of the 2008 Regulations.[319] By contrast, the Consumer Rights Act 2015 Pt 1 states explicitly that its provisions governing "goods contracts" apply only to "contracts for a trader to supply goods *to a consumer*"[320]: this restriction makes sense, of course, given that these provisions create rights for *buyers*.[321] And while the wording of the Unfair Terms in Consumer Contracts Directive 1993 (formerly implemented in UK law by the Unfair Terms in Consumer Contracts Regulations 1999 and now by the Consumer Rights Act 2015)[322] is not completely clear, the Court of Justice has held that there is no requirement that the "consumer" be the recipient of goods or services and so the Directive may apply to a contract under which a natural person acting other than in the course of business guarantees a loan made by a creditor to a commercial company.[323]

[308] cf. "dealing as consumer" under the Unfair Contract Terms Act 1977 before this concept was abolished by the Consumer Rights Act 2015. Under the 1977 Act, a person might "deal as consumer" in supplying goods or services to a person contracting in the course of business: Peel (ed.), *Treitel on The Law of Contract*, 14th edn (2015), para.7-054; Vol.I, para.15-074.

[309] Above, paras 38-036, 38-041.

[310] On this point, see above, para.38-036.

[311] See above, para.38-034.

[312] Directive 2005/29/EC concerning unfair business-to-consumer commercial practices [2005] O.J. L149/22 art.1.

[313] Directive 2005/29/EC art.2(d).

[314] Directive 2005/29/EC art.5, especially 5(2)(b).

[315] First Report from the Commission to the European Parliament, the Council and the European Economic and Social Committee on the application of Directive 2005/29/EC, etc. accompanying Communication Com (2013) 138 final, p.10.

[316] Directive 2005/29/EC arts 6–8.

[317] Directive 2005/29/EC recitals 1–5.

[318] SI 2008/1277 reg.2(1). It is submitted that this extension of the scheme of the 2005 Directive is compatible with its general requirement of "full harmonisation" as, on the narrower view taken by the Commission, consumer-to-business commercial practices fall outside the 2005 Directive's scope and therefore beyond the force of this requirement: cf. above, para.38-025.

[319] SI 2008/1277 reg.27A(2)(b) referring to "consumer to business contract" (though restricted to sale of goods) and see below, para.38-177.

[320] Consumer Rights Act 2015 s.3(1). See similarly s.33(1) ("contract for a trader to supply digital content to a consumer") and s.48(1) ("contract for a trader to supply a service to a consumer"): below, paras 38-465 et seq.

[321] The main exception to this is 2015 Act s.51's provision regarding the imposition of a reasonable price on the consumer under "services contracts": below, para.38-578.

[322] See below, paras 38-211 et seq.

[323] *Tarcău v Banca Comercială Intesa Sanpaolo România SA* (C-74/15) Order of CJEU November 19, 2015, on which see below, para.38-226 and para.45-156. In *Harvey v Dunbar Assets Plc* [2017] EWCA Civ 60, [2017] Bus. L.R. 784 at [69]–[70] the CA was prepared to assume from this decision (without deciding) that an individual who guarantees a company debt *can* be a consumer, provided that he is not connected to the company and has been acting outside his business, trader or profession, though it held that the individual before them was held not to satisfy those conditions.

*Change title of paragraph:* **38-049**

## UK legislation

*Replace paragraph with:*

More recent UK consumer protection legislation differs in relation to the issue of burden of proof as to "consumer". For example, the legislation governing consumer insurance contracts sets no express burden of proof on this issue.[332] This is also the case as regards the Consumer Contracts (Information, Cancellation and Additional Charges) Regulations 2013, which, inter alia, imposes duties of information on traders and provides consumers with rights of cancellation in certain circumstances,[333] and the Consumer Protection from Unfair Trading Regulations 2008, both as regards its provisions prohibiting unfair commercial practices and its new provisions creating rights to redress for consumer in respect of certain such practices.[334] The reason for this lack of express provision as to burden of proof in **38-049** these sets of regulations is that they implement EU directives which require "full harmonisation" and such a rule could be seen as extending the protection for consumers within their respective scopes.[335] In contrast, the Consumer Rights Act 2015 provides that:

> "A trader claiming that an individual was not acting for purposes wholly or mainly outside the individual's trade, business, craft or profession must prove it."[336]

This burden of proof applies for the purposes of Pt 1 of the Act (which provides rules governing contracts between a trader and a consumer for the trader to supply goods, digital content or services) and of Pt 2 of the Act (which provides rules governing unfair contract terms). Some of these rules are new and original (not being drawn from EU law),[337] but the majority are drawn either from earlier domestic UK legislation[338] or from EU directives requiring only minimum harmonisation.[339] The main exception to this pattern is found in the 2015 Act's provisions governing the delivery of and passing of risk in goods in contracts to supply goods[340] which implement provisions in the Consumer Rights Directive 2011 which requires (generally and in these cases) "full harmonisation".[341] In these situations, it is therefore possible that the 2015 Act fails properly to implement this Directive in that, to this extent, it goes beyond its requirements within its scope.

[332] Consumer Insurance (Disclosure and Representations) Act 2012 s.1 defining "consumer insurance contract" and adopted by Insurance Act 2015 s.1.

[333] Consumer Contracts (Information, Cancellation and Additional Charges) Regulations 2013 (SI 2013/3134) reg.4 "consumer".

[334] Consumer Protection from Unfair Trading Regulations 2008 (SI 2008/1277) reg.2(1) "consumer" as amended by Consumer Protection (Amendment) Regulations 2014 (SI 2014/870).

[335] The 2008 Regulations (SI 2008/1277) implement the Unfair Commercial Practices Directive 2005 on whose "full harmonisation" see below, para.38-159; the 2013 Regulations (SI 2013/3134) implement the Consumer Rights Directive 2011 on whose "full harmonisation" see below, para.38-062.

[336] Consumer Rights Act 2015 s.2(4).

[337] e.g. Consumer Rights Act 2015 ss.33–47 (contracts to supply digital content).

[338] Unfair Contract Terms Act 1977; Sale of Goods Act 1979; Supply of Goods and Services Act 1982.

[339] Directive 93/13/EEC art.8; Directive 99/44/EEC art.8, above, paras 38-022—38-024.

[340] 2015 Act s.28–29.

[341] Consumer Rights Directive 2011/83/EEC arts 18 and 20. As will be explained, the 2015 Act also implements the Directive 2011 art.6(5) to the extent to which it gives contractual force to the information required of and given by traders to consumers under those Regulations: 2015 Act ss.11(4)–(6), 12; 36(3)–(4); and 50(3), below, paras 38-499—38-500, 38-548—38-549 and 38-575 respectively.

## (c) The Other Party to Consumer Contracts—"Traders"

### Background

*Replace paragraph with:*

38-050 The fact that one of the parties to a contract has concluded it in the course of a business has long been significant in English contract law, the best-known example being the restriction of the statutory implication of terms as to quality and fitness for purpose of goods sold to sellers so acting.[342] Whether a person does or does not contract "in the course of a business" is also relevant under the Unfair Contract Terms Act 1977, many of whose controls are restricted to exemption clauses governing "business liability",[343] and some of whose controls were for the benefit of persons "dealing as consumer", an element of whose definition contained a requirement that the other party does have to make the contract in the course of a business.[344] While the Consumer Rights Act 2015 abolished the category of persons "dealing as consumer"[345] and repealed and reformed some of the "business liabilities" contained in the Sale of Goods Act 1979, the notion of a party contracting "in the course of a business" remains significant in some non-consumer contracts, as discussed elsewhere in the present work.[346] For present purposes, modern legislation governing consumer contracts (both EU and UK) defines the non-consumer party to a consumer contract by reference, broadly speaking, to that person's acting in the course of a business, but the precise wording used has differed considerably depending on the context.

[342] Sale of Goods Act 1893 s.14(2) (which required that the goods are of a description which it is in the course of the seller's business to supply); Sale of Goods Act 1979 s.14(2) and (3) (sale of goods in the course of a business).

[343] Unfair Contract Terms Act 1977 s.1(3) (as amended).

[344] Unfair Contract Terms Act 1977 s.12(1)(b). As earlier noted, the Consumer Rights Act 2015 s.75, Sch.4 para.11 deletes the notion of "dealing as consumer" from the 1977 Act: see below, paras 38-372 and see Vol.I, paras 15-073—15-079.

[345] Consumer Rights Act 2015 s.75, Sch.4 para.11 and see below, paras 38-372.

[346] e.g. Sale of Goods Act 1979 s.14 (amended by the 2015 Act s.60, Sch.1 para.13); Supply of Goods and Services Act 1982 s.4 (as amended by the 2015 Act s.60, Sch.1 para.40), s.13. See below, para.44-096.

## EU legislation

*Replace paragraph with:*

Unlike the relatively consistent approach to the definition of "consumer" in EU consumer protection legislation,[347] EU directives have used a wide variety of terms and definitions to describe the party to a consumer contract other than the consumer depending on the particular subject matter of that legislation. So, for example, the Unfair Terms in Consumer Contracts Directive refers to the "seller or supplier" of goods and services, meaning: **38-051**

> "... any natural or legal person who, in contracts covered by this Directive, is acting for purposes relating to his trade, business or profession, whether publicly owned or privately owned."[348]

The term "seller or supplier" is not, however, reflected in some other language versions of the 1993 Directive, which instead refer to a "professional" or "tradesman", defined in a similar manner.[349] Other directives refer to the trader party to a consumer contract by reference to the type of contract in question, as in the case of a "seller" under the Consumer Sales Directive 1999 which principally concerns contracts for the sale of goods, and who is then defined in a similar way to the 1993 Directive except that it omits the reference to public or private ownership.[350] The UK's implementation of these directives reflected this diversity of terminology and of definition.[351] However, the Unfair Commercial Practices Directive 2005 may be seen as marking the beginning of a more consistent approach in this respect, providing that:

> "... 'trader' means any natural or legal person who, in commercial practices covered by this Directive, is acting for purposes relating to his trade, business, craft or profession and anyone acting in the name of or on behalf of a trader."[352]

This general form of words was taken up by the Consumer Rights Directive 2011, which provides that:

> "... 'trader' means any natural or legal person, *irrespective of whether privately or publicly owned*, who is acting, including through any other person acting in his name or on his behalf, for purposes relating to his trade, business, craft or profession in relation to contracts covered by this Directive."[353]

It will be seen, though, that while "trader" is used in both cases, there remains no textual consistency in relation to the question whether the trader is public or private (in activity or ownership) and whether the trader acts personally or through an agent.

[347] Above, para.38-032.

[348] Directive 93/13/EEC art.2(c). The French version of this provision refers to "business activity, whether public or private" ("*activité professionnelle, qu'elle soit publique or privée*").

[349] The non-consumer party to the contract is termed *professionnel* in the French and *Gewerbetreibender* in the German versions of Directive 93/13/EEC art.2(c).

[350] Directive 99/44/EEC art.1(2)(c). Cf. the definition of "seller" used by Directive (EU) 2019/771 on certain aspects concerning contracts for the sale of goods [etc.] of the European Parliament and of the Council of 20 May 2019 [2019] O.J. L136/28 (which will repeal and replace the 1999 Directive) art.2(3), which includes reference to "any natural person or any legal person, irrespective of whether privately or publicly owned". For similar treatments to the 1999 Directive, see theTimeshare Directive 94/47 art.2 ("vendor") and Package Travel Directive 90/314/EEC art.2(2) and (3) ("organizer" and "retailer"), though this approach was amended by Directive (EU) 2015/2302 on package travel and linked travel arrangements [2015] O.J. L326/1, which revokes and replaces the 1990 Directive. Art.3 of the 2015 Directive defines "organiser" and "retailer" as categories of "trader", which is itself defined and which extends to persons facilitating a "linked travel arrangement": see below, paras 38-142 et seq. The directives differ also as to whether they mention that the business party acts through an agent: cf. the Doorstep Selling Directive 85/577/EEC art.2 ("anyone acting in the name or on behalf of a trader") and the Unfair Terms in Consumer Contracts Directive 93/13/EEC art.2(c) which makes no such reference.

[351] The 1999 Directive was first implemented in English law by amendment of the Supply of Goods (Implied Terms) Act 1973, the Sale of Goods Act 1979 and the Supply of Goods and Services Act 1982 (as explained below, paras 38-439 et seq.), all of which define the trader party to the contract as "seller", "bailor" or "supplier" as the case may be.

[352] Directive 2005/29/EC art.2(b).

[353] Directive 2011/83/EU art.2(2) (emphasis added) and see also recital 16.

### BKK Mobil Oil and Šiba v Devėnas

*In last line, page [897], after "the Directive's application.[367]", add:*

38-053 It has later been confirmed that this is the case whether or not the would-be trader is acting for profit.[367a]

[367a] *Karel de Grote-Hogeschool Katholieke Hogeschool Antwerpen VZW v Kuijpers* (C-147/16) EU:C:2018:320, May 17, 2018 at paras 44–60 (not-for-profit independent educational institution subsidised mostly by public funds can be a "seller or supplier" in relation to a contract by which the student agrees to repay sums due in respect of registration fees and a study trip, though the CJEU apparently distinguished such a contract from the provision of the education itself on the basis that it is not a "service" within the meaning of TFEU art.57). See also *Pouvin and Dijoux v Electricite de France (EDF)* (C-590/17) EU:C:2019:232 of March 21, 2019 at paras 35–38.

### A regular part of his business?

*In line 8, after "to its business", replace "or" with:*

38-054 nor

## EU law

*Replace paragraph with:*

This then raises the question as to the likely view of the Court of Justice as to the need for regularity in contracting for a trader to act in the course of a business for the purposes of EU consumer protection legislation. This may, of course, be influenced by the particular wording or context of the directive in question, but the Court of Justice of the EU would resolve the question by reference to its purposes in the light of general EU principle. In this respect, EU legislation in this context is intended to create protection for consumers as "weaker" and less well-informed parties throughout the European Union and by this means increase consumer confidence and thus the facilitation of the establishment of the internal market.[374] In this respect, a consumer may often not be aware or be able to become aware of the nature of the business of a supplier of goods or services and, therefore, whether or not the contract which he intends to conclude does or does not form a regular part of its business. In terms of authority, as has been seen, the Court of Justice in *BKK Mobil Oil* did not require a trader's act to fall "within the framework of a regular profit-making activity" as had its Advocate General.[375] Moreover, in *Pouvin and Dijoux v Electricite de France (EDF)*, the Court of Justice held that an employer whose main activity consists of supplying energy and not in offering financial instruments, may still be a "seller or supplier" in relation to a contract of loan which it concluded with its employee and his spouse as "that employer has technical information and expertise, and human and material resources that a natural person, namely the other party to the contract, is not deemed to have".[376] For the Court of Justice, the concept of "seller or supplier" for the purposes of the 1993 Directive is "objective in nature and does not depend on whether the professional decides to act in the context of its main activity or a secondary and ancillary one".[377] **38-055**

Finally, in *Kamenova* the question arose as to the circumstances in which a natural person simultaneously who offers to sell new and second-hand goods through a website may be classified as a "trader" for the purposes of the Unfair Commercial Practices Directive or the Consumer Rights Directive.[378] The Court of Justice held that this depends on whether the person acts "for purposes relating to his trade, business or profession", a question which requires a "case-by-case approach".[379] For this purpose, the Court set out a non-exhaustive list of criteria relevant to the particular context: whether the platform was organised and set up for profit; whether the seller had technical information and expertise relating to the products offered for sale not necessarily possessed by the consumer; whether the seller had a legal status enabling her to engage in commercial activities and the extent to which the online sale was connected to the seller's commercial or professional activity[379a]; whether the seller was subject to VAT; whether the seller, acting on behalf of a particular trader or on her own behalf or through another person acting in her name and on her behalf, received remuneration or an incentive (as in the case of "influencers"); whether the seller purchased new or second-hand goods in order to resell them, so as to make it a regular, frequent and/or simultaneous activity when compared to her usual commercial or business activity; whether the goods for sale were all of the same type or value, and, in particular, whether the offer was concentrated on a small number of goods.[379b] The Court explained that compliance with one or more of these criteria (such as selling with the view to profit) does not, in itself, mean that the online seller is a "trader".[379c]

[374] e.g. 1993 Directive recitals 5, 6 and 10. On the role of EU consumer law as protecting the consumer as weaker party and less well-informed party see further *Pereničovà v SOS finance, spol. sro* (C-453/10) EU:C:2012:144, [2012] 2 C.M.L.R. 28 para.27.

[375] *BKK Mobil Oil* (C-59/12) and cf. A.G. Bott's Opinion at para.42 quoted more fully above, para.38-053.

[376] C-590/17, EU:C:2019:232 of March 21, 2019 at para.40.

[377] C-590/17, EU:C:2019:232 of March 21, 2019 at para.41.

[378] *Komisiaza zashtita na potrebeitelite v Kamenova* (C-105/17) EU:C:2018:80 ("*Kamenova* (C-105/17)") at para.24.

[379] *Kamenova* (C-105/17) at paras 36–37.

[379a] In some national laws, "commercial activities" (translating "*actes de commerce*") are defined by law and may be restricted to persons enjoying the status to do so.

[379b] *Kamenova* (C-105/17) at paras 37–38 following the Opinion of A.G. Szpunar at paras 50–51.

[379c] *Kamenova* (C-105/17) at paras 39–40.

## 4. INFORMATION REQUIREMENTS AND CONSUMERS' RIGHTS OF CANCELLATION

### (a) Introduction

*To the end of title, add new footnote 413a:*

**The Consumer Rights Directive 2011**[413a]

**38-060** [413a] The 2011 Directive is subject to considerable amendment by Directive (EU) 2019/2161 of the European Parliament and of the Council of 27 November 2019 ... as regards the better enforcement and modernisation of Union consumer protection rules [2019] O.J. L328/7 art.4, including requiring new definitions of "sales contract" and "service contract", additional specific information requirements for contracts concluded on online marketplaces and making more elaborate provision on penalties. However, as the 2019 Directive must be implemented by Member States on November 28, 2021 (i.e. after IP completion day) the UK is not required to implement these changes unless it agrees to do so under an agreement with the EU as to their future relationship: see above, para.38-004 and Vol.I, paras 1-014 et seq. The future changes at the EU level will, however, be noted in the footnotes to the following paragraphs for reference.

*Replace paragraph with:*

**38-060** The main provisions of the 2011 directive are concerned with the reformulation of the information requirements and rights of cancellation for door-step selling (renamed "off-premises contracting") and distance contracts generally (but not distance contracts related to financial services[414]), but the directive also introduced new information requirements in traders to consumers in contracts which are neither off-premises contracts nor distance contracts, and requires certain other measures for the protection of consumers in relation to contracts (for example, in relation to the imposition of "additional payments").[415] After implementation of the 2011 Directive in UK law by the Consumer Contracts (Information, Cancellation and Additional Charges) Regulations 2013 (the "2013 Regulations"),[416] these regulations contain the general and most important information and cancellation provisions governing consumer contracts. However, there are other, special provisions governing particular categories of contract: "distance contracts" for the supply of financial services,[417] timeshare,[418] package travel[419] and contracts concluded by electronic means.[420] There are also information requirements imposed on traders in relation to alternative dispute resolution (ADR).[421] This section will focus on the 2013 Regulations, but its final paragraphs will outline the legislation governing these special categories.[422]

[414] These remain governed by Directive 2002/65/EC.

415 Consumer Rights Directive 2011 Ch.IV "Other Consumer Rights". On the 2011 Directive generally see European Commission, *DG Justice Guidance Document concerning Directive 2011/83/EU*, etc. (June 2014) ("DG Justice Guidance Document on 2011 Directive") available at *http://ec.europa.eu/justice/consumer-marketing/files/crd_guidance_en.pdf*. See also European Commission, *Report from the Commission to the European Parliament and the Council on the application of Directive 2011/83/EU*, COM(2017) 259 final (with accompanying Commission Staff Working Document SWD (2017) 169 final). In *Bundesverband der Verbraucherzentralen und Verbraucherverbände - Verbraucherzentrale Bundesverband eV v Amazon EU Sàrl* (C-649/17) EU:C:2019:576 of July 10, 2019 esp. at para.44, the CJEU observed that, where an information requirement in the Directive was not clear, in determining its proper interpretation it was necessary to "ensure the right balance between a high level of consumer protection and the competitiveness of undertakings, as stated in recital 4 [of the Directive] while respecting the undertaking's freedom to conduct a business, as set out in Article 16 of the Charter [of Fundamental Rights]".

416 SI 2013/3134.

417 Financial Services (Distance Marketing) Regulations 2004 (SI 2004/2095) below, para.38-136.

418 Timeshare, Holiday Products, Resale and Exchange Contracts Regulations 2010 (SI 2010/2960) below, paras 38-148—38-154

419 The Package Travel and Linked Travel Arrangements Regulations 2018 (SI 2018/634) revoking and replacing the Package Travel, Package Holidays and Package Tours Regulations 1992 (SI 1992/3288); see below, paras 38-137—38-147.

420 Electronic Commerce (EC Directive) Regulations 2002 (SI 2002/2013) reg.9, below, para.38-156. There are two further situations foreseen by the Consumer Rights Act 2015 in which traders must provide information to consumers and others. First, ss.83–88 impose a duty on letting agents to publicise their fees, though the enforcement measures provided by s.87 of the Act do not affect the validity of any contract made. Secondly, ss.90–95 (as amended by the Digital Economy Act 2017 s.105 as from April 6, 2018) impose on persons who resell tickets for a recreational, sporting or cultural event in the UK through a secondary ticketing facility a number of information duties (e.g. as to the ticket, the venue, etc.), prohibit the original seller from cancelling resold tickets or blacklisting persons reselling (in both cases subject to conditions), but again the enforcement measures provided by s.93 do not affect the validity of any contract made.

421 Directive 2013/11/EU of May 31, 2013 on alternative dispute resolution for consumer disputes [2013] O.J. L165/63, below, para.38-155.

422 See below, paras 38-135 et seq.

## Consumer Contracts (Information, Cancellation and Additional Charges) Regulations 2013

*Replace paragraph with:*

The UK implemented most (though not all) of the requirements of the Consumer Rights Directive by the Consumer Contracts (Information, Cancellation and Additional Charges) Regulations 2013 (the "2013 Regulations").[423] The 2013 Regulations therefore revoked and replaced earlier UK regulations implementing the directives which the 2011 Directive itself replaced, the Cancellation of Contracts made in a Consumer's Home or Place of Work, etc. Regulations 2008[424] and the Consumer Protection (Distance Selling) Regulations 2000.[425] This section will principally explain the provisions of the 2013 Regulations governing information and cancellation,[426] and will note the special rules governing, for example, timeshare contracts,[427] but will leave until later in this chapter the UK's legislation implementing the Consumer Rights Directive's requirements other than those relating to information and cancellation.[428] As yet there is little case-law on either the 2011 Directive or the 2013 Regulations, but, where still relevant, reference will be made to European and English case-law on the directives and regulations which they respectively replaced. **38-061**

423 SI 2013/3134 (in force June 13, 2014). (These regulations are subject to very minor amendment as of the UK's leaving the EU ("exit day"): Consumer Protection (Amendment etc.) (EU Exit) Regulations 2018 (SI 2018/1326) reg.8. On the definition of "exit day" see above, para.38-004 and Vol.I, para.1-016.) The Consumer Rights Act 2015 ss.11(4) and (5), 12 (goods contracts), s.36(3) and (4), 37 (digital

content contracts) and s.50 (services contracts) give effect to the Consumer Rights Directive 2011 art.6(5)'s requirement that information provided by traders as required by the 2011 Directive (in relation to off-premises and distance contracts) forms part of the contract: see below, paras 38-105, 38-499—38-500, 38-548—38-549 and 38-575. The Consumer Rights (Payment Surcharges) Regulations 2012 (SI 2012/3110) (as amended by the Payment Services Regulations 2017 (SI 2017/752)) give effect to the Consumer Rights Directive 2011 art.19 on which see below, para.38-428.

424 SI 2008/1816, itself replacing Consumer Protection (Cancellation of Contracts Concluded away from Business Premises) Regulations 1987 (SI 1987/2117) implementing the Directive 85/577/EEC. The 2008 Regulations (SI 2008/1816) therefore do not apply to contracts entered into on or after June 13, 2014, being the date of coming into force of the 2013 Regulations: 2013 Regulations reg.2(b).

425 SI 2000/2334 implementing Directive 97/7/EC. The 2000 Regulations (SI 2000/2334) therefore do not apply to contracts entered into on or after June 13, 2014, being the date of coming into force of the 2013 Regulations: 2013 Regulations reg.2(a).

426 They also note the earlier provisions governing information and cancellation in the Financial Services (Distance Marketing) Regulations 2004 (SI 2004/2095) which implemented the Distance Contracts for Financial Services Directive 2002 [2002] O.J. L271/16. On these regulations see below, para.38-136.

427 See below, paras 38-148 et seq.

428 The Consumer Rights Directive's provisions (arts 18 and 20) on delivery of goods and the passing of risk in "sales contracts" were implemented in UK law first by the 2013 Regulations regs 42 and 43, but were reimplemented by the Consumer Rights Act 2015 ss.28 and 29. The Consumer Rights Directive's provisions on fees for the use of means of payment (art.19) were implemented by the Consumer Rights (Payment Surcharges) Regulations 2012 (SI 2012/3110) (on which see below, para.38-428) and its provision on "communication by telephone", "additional payments" and inertia selling (arts 21, 22 and 27 respectively) were implemented by the 2013 Regulations regs 41, 40 and 39 respectively (on which see below, paras 38-430—38-431).

### Autonomous interpretations and "national general contract law"

*Replace footnote 436 with:*

**38-063** 436 cf. above, para.38-015. Presumably, however, this allocation of contract issues left unregulated by the 2011 Directive to national contract law would be subject to the general principles of EU law, notably, the principle of effectiveness. cf. for this purpose, the approach of the CJEU to the principle of the autonomy of national procedural law, above, paras 38-019—38-020.

### Contract law issues regulated by the 2011 Directive

*Replace footnote 441 with:*

**38-064** 441 Consumer Rights Directive 2011 recital 60; art.27. This change was effected in UK law by insertion of the Consumer Protection from Unfair Trading Regulations 2008 (SI 2008/1277) reg.27M by the 2013 Regulations reg.39 (as itself renumbered by SI 2014/870).

## (b) Contracts Covered by the 2013 Regulations

### All consumer contracts

*Replace paragraph with:*

**38-069** Article 3(1) of the 2011 Directive as enacted states that:

> "This Directive shall apply, under the conditions and to the extent set out in its provisions, to any contract concluded between a trader and a consumer. It shall also apply to contracts for the supply of water, gas, electricity or district heating, including by public providers, to the extent that these commodities are provided on a contractual basis."[462a]

As a result, and although it is nowhere stated explicitly, the 2013 Regulations also apply in principle to *all types of consumer contract*, defined by reference to their parties, although some provisions have a more restricted ambit.[463] For this purpose, the 2013 Regulations use the standard definition of "trader" and of "consumer" adopted by recent UK consumer law:

> "... 'consumer' means an individual acting for purposes that are wholly or mainly outside the individual's trade, business, craft or profession."[464]

> "... 'trader' means a person acting for purposes relating to that person's trade, business, craft or profession, whether acting personally or through another person acting in the trader's name or on the trader's behalf."[465]

> "... 'business' includes the activities of any government department or local or public authority."[466]

The background to these definitions and their likely significance have already been discussed.[467]

462a This provision is amended by Directive (EU) 2019/2161 of the European Parliament and of the Council of 27 November 2019 ... as regards the better enforcement and modernisation of Union consumer protection rules [2019] O.J. L328/7 art.4(2)(a) so as to restrict the first sentence to contracts "where the consumer pays or undertakes to pay the price" and it is supplemented by new provision (art.11a of the 2011 Directive) concerning the supply to the consumer of digital content not supplied on a tangible medium or of a digital service. On the significance of the 2019 Directive for UK law, see above, para.38-060 (note to heading).

463 cf. below para.38-079 on the question whether the 2011 Directive (and therefore the 2013 Regulations) apply (at least sometimes) to contracts consumer-to-business as well as business-to-consumer.

464 2013 Regulations reg.4 "consumer".

465 2013 Regulations reg.4 "trader".

466 2013 Regulations reg.5 "business".

467 Above, paras 38-030—38-049, 38-050—38-058 respectively.

**Distinctions according to the subject matter of the contract**

*Replace paragraph with:*

The 2011 Directive which the 2013 Regulations implement distinguishes *four* categories of contract according to their subject matter: (i) sales contracts, (ii) services contracts, (iii) contracts for the supply of digital content not on a tangible medium,[473] and (iv) contracts for the supply of water, gas or electricity where they are not put up for sale in a limited volume or set quantity, or district heating.[474] However, this four-fold classification is not followed entirely by the 2013 Regulations, which instead include within "service contracts" the contracts falling within the Directive's category (iv).[475] As a result, the 2013 Regulations distinguish between three distinct categories of consumer contract defined according to their subject matter and, at times, regulate them specially: "sales contracts", "service contracts" and "contracts for the supply of digital content not on a tangible medium".[476] While it is nowhere clearly stated by the Regulations, it would seem clear from the requirements of the 2011 Directive, that the provisions in the Regulations which impose requirements on traders in respect of information apply to all these three types of contract, even though some of the elements of their definitions appear to be restricted to sales and services contracts.[477] As will be seen, though, some of the rules governing consumer contracts apply only to sales contracts, service contracts,[478] or contracts for the supply of digital content not on a tangible medium,[479] and this three-fold distinction is particularly clear in the rules governing the commencement of the "normal period" for cancellation in off-premises and distance contracts,[480] and in the way in which some particular information require- **38-072** ments are described.[481] As will be seen, this three-fold distinction according to the subject matter of consumer contracts is also reflected in the Consumer Rights Act 2015, though it is treated there differently.[482]

[473] As the 2011 Directive recital 19 states: "[i]f digital content is supplied on a tangible medium, such as a CD or a DVD, it should be considered as goods within the meaning of this Directive". cf. *Software Incubator Ltd v Computer Associates UK Ltd* [2018] EWCA Civ 518, [2018] 2 All E.R. (Comm) 398 (contract for the supply of software does not constitute a "sale of goods" for the purposes of the Commercial Agents (Council Directive) Regulations 1993 (SI 1993/3053)).

[474] This is made clear by recital 19, which states that the latter two types of contract "should be classified, for the purpose of this Directive, neither as sales contracts nor as service contracts". This is then followed through by its definitions of "goods", "sales contract" and "service contract" in art.2(3), (5) and (6) respectively. The definitions in the 2011 Directive are due to be amended by Directive (EU) 2019/2161 of the European Parliament and of the Council of 27 November 2019 ... as regards the better enforcement and modernisation of Union consumer protection rules [2019] O.J. L328/7 ("Directive (EU) 2019/2161") art.4(1). However, as the 2019 Directive must be implemented by Member States on November 28, 2021 (i.e. after IP completion day) the UK is not required to implement these changes unless it agrees to do so under an agreement with the EU as to their future relationship: see above, para.38-004.

[475] 2013 Regulations reg.5 "service". This treatment in the 2013 Regulations is compatible with the 2011 Directive's requirements as it applies the same rules to supplies of water, gas or electricity where they are not put up for sale in a limited volume, etc. as to services: arts 5(2), 7(3), 8(8), 9(2)(a) and (c), 14(4)(a) and 17(2).

[476] "Tangible medium" is not explicitly defined by the Directive nor by the Regulations, but reg.5 defines "goods" as "any tangible moveable items, but that includes water, gas and electricity if and only if they are put up for sale in a limited volume or a set quantity".

[477] See notably, element (d) of the definition of "off-premises contract" in reg.5 which refers to the trader's intended "selling goods or services to the consumer"; and the requirement in the definition of "distance contract" also in reg.5 that the contract should be concluded under "an organised distance sales or service-provision scheme": for these, see below, paras 38-081—38-085, 38-086—38-089.

[478] For "sales contract" see reg.12(4)(a); reg.28(3) (below, para.38-112); reg.30(3)–(6) (below, para.38-117); reg.34(5) and (9) (below, para.38-114) and reg.35(1) (below, para.38-128); for "service contract" see reg.30(2)(a) (below, para.38-073) and reg.36(2) (below, para.38-074).

[479] 2013 Regulations reg.12(5), 16(3), 30(2)(b) and 37.

[480] 2013 Regulations reg.30 (below, para.38-117).

[481] 2013 Regulations Sch.1 paras (a), (c), (e); Sch.2 paras (a), (f), (j), the references to "digital content" being added by SI 2014/870 reg.9(3) and (4).

[482] Consumer Rights Act 2015 Pt 1 Ch.2 (goods contracts); Ch.3 (digital content contracts, though the exclusion from this category of digital content contracts supplied on a tangible medium is inherent in the definition of "goods contracts" and these contracts require a price, below, para.38-541) and Ch.4 ("services contracts"). In particular, the 2015 Act does not distinguish sharply as regards the different types of contract under which digital content is supplied, but rather allows its categories of contract (and therefore their regulation) to overlap (either with "goods contracts" or "services contracts") as its subject matter requires. See below, paras 38-484, 38-504 and 38-543.

### "Sales contract" and "service contract"

*Replace paragraph with:*

38-073 The 2013 Regulations define "sales contract" as:

> "... a contract under which a trader transfers or agrees to transfer the ownership of goods to a consumer and the consumer pays or agrees to pay the price, including any contract that has both goods and services as its object."[483]

"Goods" for these purposes are defined as:

"… any tangible moveable items, but that includes water, gas and electricity if and only if they are put up for sale in a limited volume or set quantity".[484]

"Service contract" is defined as:

"… a contract, other than a sales contract, under which a trader supplies or agrees to supply a service to a consumer and the consumer pays or agrees to pay the price."[485]

And "service" is stated as including:

"(a) the supply of water, gas or electricity if they are not put up for sale in a limited volume or a set quantity, and
(b) the supply of district heating."[486]

483 2013 Regulations reg.5 "sales contract" reflecting closely 2011 Directive art.2(5). The definition in the 2011 Directive is to be amended by Directive (EU) 2019/2161 art.4(1)(c) (on this directive generally see above, para.38-060 (note)). cf. Consumer Rights Act 2015 s.5, below, para.38-486—38-488.

484 2013 Regulations reg.5 "goods"; 2011 Directive art.2(3). The definition in the 2011 Directive is to be amended by Directive (EU) 2019/2161 art.4(1)(a) (on this directive generally see above, para.38-060 (note)).

485 2013 Regulations reg.5 "service contract"; 2011 Directive art.2(6). The definition in the 2011 Directive is to be amended by Directive (EU) 2019/2161 art.4(1)(a) (on this directive generally see above, para.38-060 (note)). cf. Consumer Rights Act 2015 s.48, below, para.38-568.

486 2013 Regulations reg.5 "service", picking up the explanation in 2011 Directive recital 25 of its own use of "service" in the definition of "service contract" in art.2(6). Recital 25 continues by noting that "district heating refers to the supply of heat, inter alia, in the form of steam or hot water, from a central source of production through a transmission and distribution system to multiple buildings, for the purpose of heating". From the point of view of legislative drafting, the inclusion of these types of contract within "service contract" allows the Regulations to state the relevant cancellation period in a single provision (2013 Regulations reg.30(2)(a), on which see below, para.38-117) whereas the 2011 Directive makes specific provision for them which is identical to service contracts as more generally understood: Directive 2011/83/EU arts 9(2)(a) and (c). cf. the different treatment of "services contracts" under the Consumer Rights Act 2015 s.48, below, para.38-568.

## Contracts for the supply of digital content

*Replace paragraph with:*

"Digital content" is defined by the 2013 Regulations as "data which are produced and supplied in digital form".[489] As recital 19 to the 2011 Directive explains: **38-075**

"Digital content means data which are produced and supplied in digital form, such as computer programs, applications, games, music, videos or texts, irrespective of whether they are accessed through downloading or streaming, from a tangible medium or through any other means."[490]

However, neither the 2013 Regulations nor the 2011 Directive define contracts for the supply of digital content even though they regulate them specially,[491] but recital 19 explains that:

"If digital content is supplied on a tangible medium, such as a CD or a DVD, it should be considered as goods within the meaning of this Directive."

This fits with the definitions of "sales contracts" in both the Directive and the Regulations as the tangible medium would constitute "goods" ("tangible moveable item") and the digital content would form an element of those goods.[492] On the other hand, "contracts for digital content which is not supplied on a tangible medium" would not fall within the definition of sales contracts nor are they specifically included within service contracts, unlike contracts for the supply of water, gas or electricity where they are not put up for sale in a limited volume or set quantity, or district heating.[493] Reflecting this view, the 2013 Regulations make special provision governing this category of contract as regards the consumer's loss of the right to cancel if he or she has consented to the beginning of performance.[494] Moreover, in the view of the European Commission, the distinction drawn by recital 19 of the 2011 Directive between digital content supplied under a sales contract or services contract and digital content supplied in non-tangible digital form means that contracts for online digital content are subject to the Directive even if they do not involve the payment of a price by the consumer, as there is no requirement as to contracts for the supply of digital content in digital form equivalent to the requirement of payment of a price as regards sales and service contracts.[495] As the Commission acknowledges, this view leads not merely to a considerable expansion of the scope of the application of the Directive, but it also leads to the drawing of difficult lines as to the application of the Directive in relation to the free supply of digital content (i.e. without payment of a price), but the Commission argues that the Directive should not apply to online digital content provided by means of broadcasting of information on the internet "without the express conclusion of a contract" nor "in itself" to access to a website or a download from a website. In this respect, it may be that the Court of Justice would consider it necessary to find an autonomous definition of contract for this purpose, but it could hold that the definition of a "contract" should instead fall under art.3(5)'s general allocation of issues not governed by the Directive to "national general contract law" as earlier explained.[496] Moreover, there remains a difficult line between the supply of free digital content online (which, according to the Commission, is covered by the Directive) and free online services, such as cloud storage or webmail, where the main contractual obligation of the trader is not to provide digital content but rather a service allowing the creation, processing, storing or sharing of data that is produced by a consumer.[497] Such free online services are clearly not covered by the 2011 Directive (nor by the 2013 Regulations) since "service contracts" are defined contracts for the supply of a service to the consumer in return for a price.[498] In this respect, the position under the Consumer Rights Act 2015 differs. The 2015 Act identifies a distinct legislative category of "a contract for the supply of digital content" for the purposes of its own provisions in Ch.3 of Pt 1, being "a contract for a trader to supply digital content to a consumer" where "it is supplied for a price paid by the consumer" or where:

> "... it is supplied free with goods or services or other digital content for which the consumer pays a price, and ... it is not generally available to consumers unless they have paid a price for it or for goods or services or other digital content,"[499]

where "price" is specially defined so as to include "the consumer using, by way of payment, any facility for which money has been paid".[500] This leaves contracts for the supply of digital content for some consideration other than for a price as so understood outside the provisions of Ch.3, but they may well fall within the scope of Ch.4's provisions on "services contracts" which (unlike the 2013 Regulations) are *not* defined so as to require the payment of a *price* by the consumer.[501] And of course, where the digital content is supplied on a tangible medium (such as on a CD) which can count as "an item that includes digital content", then Ch.1's provisions on "goods contracts" may apply.[502]

[489] 2013 Regulations reg.5 "digital content"; 2011 Directive art.2(11). This definition is adopted by the Consumer Rights Act 2015 s.2(9), below, para.38-540.

490 2011 Directive recital 19, first sentence.

491 2013 Regulations reg.12(5) (below, para.38-101); reg.16(3) (below, para.38-101); reg.30(2) and 30(6) (below, para.38-117); reg.37 (below, para.38-128). cf. Consumer Rights Act 2015 s.33 which defines "contract to supply digital content" for the purpose of Ch.3 of the Act specially for its purposes: below, para.38-541. The position is set to change at the EU level once the amendments to the 2011 Directive provided by Directive (EU) 2019/2161 art.4 take effect. As recital 30 to Directive (EU) 2019/2161 explains, it aligns the definitions of digital content and digital services in the 2011 Directive with those contained in the new Directive (EU) 2019/770 of the European Parliament and of the Council on certain aspects concerning contracts for the supply of digital content and digital services and "[d]igital content covered by Directive (EU) 2019/770 covers a single act of supply, a series of individual acts of supply, or continuous supply over a period of time". However, neither of these recent EU directives require implementation before IP completion day: on Directive 2019/2161 see above, para.38-060 (note); on Directive (EU) 2019/770 generally see below, para.38-486.

492 On which see above, para.38-073.

493 See above, para.38-073.

494 2013 Regulations reg.37; 2011 Directive art.14(4)(b).

495 *DG Justice Guidance Document on 2011 Directive*, para.12.1. See also EU Commission, *Report from the Commission to the European Parliament and the Council on the application of Directive 2011/83/EU* (etc.) COM(2017) 259 final, para.5 noting that "some interested parties consider that the application of the [2011 Directive] to 'free' digital content is not absolutely clear". This is reflected in the treatment of "digital content contracts other than for a price paid by the consumer" in 2013 Regulations regs 9(3), 10(5) and 13(6), below, para.38-105. Directive (EU) 2019/2161 art.4(2) will change this position at the EU level by inserting a new art.3(1a) into the 2011 Directive so that it applies "where the trader supplies or undertakes to supply digital content which is not supplied on a tangible medium or a digital service to the consumer and the consumer provides or undertakes to provide personal data to the trader, except where the personal data provided by the consumer are exclusively processed by the trader for the purpose of supplying the digital content which is not supplied on a tangible medium or digital service in accordance with this Directive or for allowing the trader to comply with legal requirements to which the trader is subject, and the trader does not process those data for any other purpose": on the 2019 Directive, see above, paras 38-060 (note) and 38-069 (note).

496 Above, paras 38-063—38-067 and 38-070.

497 EU Commission, *Report from the Commission to the European Parliament and the Council on the application of Directive 2011/83/EU* (etc.) COM(2017) 259 final, para.5 (arguing that the 2011 Directive should be amended so as to include such free online digital services).

498 2011 Directive art.2(6); 2013 Regulations reg.5, above, para.38-073.

499 2015 Act s.33(1) and (2), and see below, paras 38-541—38-542.

500 2015 Act s.33(3), below, para.38-541.

501 2015 Act s.48, below, para.38-568; cf. 2013 Regulations reg.5 "service contract", above, para.38-073.

502 See below, para.38-487 and esp. in relation to 2015 Act s.16, below, para.38-504.

## Exclusions from the scope of the 2013 Regulations

*Replace paragraph with:*

The 2013 Regulations exclude from their general scope a number of types of contracts and of contracts concluded in certain ways,[503] as well as excluding certain types of contracts from their provisions requiring traders to give consumers information,[504] and from their provisions governing the consumer's right of cancellation.[505] In terms of exclusions from their general scope, reg.6 provides that the 2013 Regulations do not apply to gambling contracts[506]; contracts for services of a banking, credit, insurance, personal pension, investment or payment nature[507]; contracts for the creation of immovable property or of rights in immovable property[508]; contracts for rental of accommodation for residential purposes[509]; contracts for the construction of new buildings or the construction of substantially new buildings by the conversion of existing buildings[510]; contracts for the supply of foodstuffs, beverages or other goods intended for current consumption in the household and which are supplied by a trader on frequent and regular rounds to the **38-076** consumer's home, residence or workplace[511]; package travel within the scope of the Package Travel Directive 2015[512]; and timeshare and related contracts within the scope of the Timeshare Directive.[513] Moreover, the 2013 Regulations do not apply to contracts concluded by means of automatic vending machines or automated commercial premises[514]; contracts concluded with a telecommunications operator through a public telephone for the use of the telephone[515]; contracts concluded for the use of one single connection, by telephone, internet or fax, established by a consumer[516]; or to contracts under which goods are sold by way of execution or otherwise by authority of law.[517]

503 2013 Regulations reg.6.

504 2013 Regulations reg.7(2)–(4), below, para.38-077. The information requirements for off-premises contracts are also excluded as regards repair or maintenance contracts" as defined: 2013 Regulations reg.11.

505 2013 Regulations regs 27(2)–(3), 28 on which see below, paras 38-112.

506 2013 Regulations reg.6(1)(a) which explains this category.

507 2013 Regulations reg.6(1)(b); 2011 Directive arts 2(12) and 3(3)(d). There are two exceptions for the case of the effect of cancellation or withdrawal on "ancillary contracts" (reg.38(4)) and "additional payments" (reg.40(3), discussed below, para.38-430): 2013 Regulations reg.6(3). In the case of off-premises contracts, this exclusion marks a significant difference from the 2008 Regulations (SI 2008/1816) which applied to contracts of consumer credit with certain exclusions: regs 5 and 6. In the case of "distance contracts" (but not off-premises contracts), duties of information and rights of cancellation are provided by the Financial Services (Distance Marketing) Regulations 2004 (SI 2004/2095) reg.2(1) of which defines "financial service" identically to the excluded contracts in reg.6(1)(b) of the 2013 Regulations: SI 2004/2095 implementing Directive 2002/65/EC concerning the distance marketing of consumer financial services, on which see below, para.38-136.

508 2013 Regulations reg.6(1)(c), implementing 2011 Directive art.3(3)(e). In *Travel Vac SL v Antelm Sanchis* (C-423/97) EU:C:1999:197, [1999] E.C.R. I-2195 at para.25 the ECJ held that the Doorstep Selling Directive 1985 could apply to a contract of timeshare despite an exclusion of contracts relating to immovable property (art.3(2)(a)) identical to the one provided by the 2011 Directive art.3(3)(e) as long as the contract "concerns the provision of separate services of a value higher than that of the right to use the property". However, in *Schulte v Deutsche Bausparkasse Badenia AG* (C-350/03) EU:C:2005:637, [2005] E.C.R. I-9215 paras 77–80 the ECJ held that this did not mean that the 1985 Directive could apply to a separate contract of sale of immovable property even though it formed part of a single economic unit in which service elements predominated. This point is now resolved in its specific context by 2011 Directive art.3(3)(h) (implemented in UK law by 2013 Regulations reg.6(1)(h)) which excludes from its scope contracts falling under the Timeshare Directive 2008/122/EC. Similarly, in *Friz GmbH v von der Heyden* (C-215/08) EU:C:2010:186, [2010] E.C.R. I-02947 the ECJ held that Directive 85/577 could apply to a contract under which the consumer entered a "real property fund by means of the acquisition of holdings in a partnership in exchange for a capital investment" despite its exclusion of contracts concerning rights to immovable property, but such a contract is likely to fall within the exclusion of "contracts for services of a banking, credit, insurance, personal pension, investment or payment nature" in the 2011 Directive art.3(3)(d) as explained by art.2(12) (implemented by the 2013 Regulations reg.6(1)(b)).

509 2013 Regulations reg.6(1)(d).

510 2013 Regulations reg.6(1)(e). The CJEU has held that a contract under which an architect agrees merely to draw up plans for a house for an individual consumer does not fall within this exception: *NK v MS* (C-208/19) EU:C:2020:382 at para.48.

511 2013 Regulations reg.6(1)(f).

512 2013 Regulations reg.6(1)(g), referring to "package travel contracts" within the scope of Directive (EU) 2015/2302 on package travel and linked travel arrangements [2015] O.J. L326/1, which repealed and replaced Directive 90/314/EEC on package travel, package holidays and package tours. (On IP completion day (on which see above, para.38-004 and Vol.I, paras 1-014 et seq.), this reference will be replaced by one to the Package Travel and Linked Travel Arrangements Regulations 2018: Consumer Protection (Amendment etc.) (EU Exit) Regulations 2018 (SI 2018/1326) reg.8(3)(a).) The exclusion in reg.6(1)(f) therefore does not apply to "linked travel arrangements" which are not excluded from the scope of the 2011 Directive: 2015 Directive art.3(2), (3) and (5) and art.27(2) (amending the 2011 Directive art.3(3)). See below, paras 38-137—38-141. While art.12(5) of the 2015 Directive provides that, as regards off-premises contracts, Member States may provide in their national laws that the traveller has the right to withdraw from a package travel contract within a period of 14 days *without giving any*

*reason*, unlike the general position provided for termination by travellers under the 2015 Directive, the UK government decided not to make provision to this effect in the Package Travel and Linked Travel Arrangements Regulations 2018: see Department of Business, Energy & Industrial Strategy, *Updating Consumer Protection in the Package Travel Sector, Government Response* (April 2018), paras 79 and 84.

[513] Directive 2008/122/EC on the protection of consumers in respect of certain aspects of timeshare, long-term holiday product, resale and exchange contracts ("Timeshare Directive 2009"); 2013 Regulations reg.6(1)(h). On IP completion day (on which see above, para.38-004 and Vol.I, paras 1-014 et seq.), this reference will be replaced by one to the Timeshare, Holiday Products, Resale and Exchange Contracts Regulations 2010: Consumer Protection (Amendment etc.) (EU Exit) Regulations 2018 (SI 2018/1326) reg.8(3)(b). On the Timeshare Directive 2009 and the 2010 Regulations see below, paras 38-148—38-154.

[514] 2013 Regulations reg.6(2)(a).

[515] 2013 Regulations reg.6(2)(b).

[516] 2013 Regulations reg.6(2)(c).

[517] 2013 Regulations reg.6(2)(d).

## Contracts for passenger transport services

*To the end of paragraph, after "exception of the right of cancellation."[528], add:*

Moreover, even if the notion of a "contract for passenger transport services"[528a] **38-078** in the part-exclusion from the scope of the 2011 Directive generally follows the interpretation earlier given to "contracts for the provision of transport services" by the Court in relation to the Distance Contracts Directive, it does not cover a contract whose object is to entitle the consumer to a price reduction when passenger transport contracts are subsequently concluded (for example, a "rail card").[528b]

[528a] 2011 Directive art.3(3)(k).

[528b] *Verbraucherzentrale Berlin eV v DB Vertrieb GmbH* (C-583/18) EU:C:2020:199 at paras 29–39.

### *(i) "Off-Premises Contracts"*

## "Off-premises contracts"

*Replace footnote 538 with:*

[538] Consumer Rights Directive 2011 recital 22 explains that "[b]usiness premises should include **38-081** premises in whatever form (such as shops, stalls or lorries) which service as a permanent or usual place of business for the trader. Market stalls and fair stands should be treated as business premises if they fulfil this condition. Retail premises where the trader carries out his activity on a seasonal basis, for instance during the tourist season at a ski or beach resort, should be considered as business premises as the trader carries out his activity in those premises on a usual basis. Spaces accessible to the public, such as streets, shopping malls, beaches, sports facilities and public transport, which the trader uses on an exceptional basis for his business activities as well as private homes or workplaces should not be regarded as business premises. The business premises of a person acting in the name or on behalf of the trader as defined in this Directive should be considered as business premises within the meaning of this Directive". In *Verbraucherzentrale Berlin eV v Unimatic Vertriebs GmbH* (C-485/17) EU:C:2018:642 of August 7, 2018 the CJEU held that the relevant protections for the consumer in the 2011 Directive do not apply where the consumer is on the trader's "business premises" because there "the consumer can be expect to be solicited by the trader so that, should the case arise, he could not properly claim subsequently that he was surprised by the offer made by the trader" (at para.34). For this reason, inter alia, the CJEU held that "the expression 'on a usual basis' … must be understood as referring to the fact that the activity at issue being carried out on the premises is a normal activity" (at para.39). Therefore, a national court considering whether a stand at a trade fair for a few days was "business premises" must have regard to "the actual appearance of that stand in the eyes of the public and, more specifically, whether, in the eyes of the average consumer, it is presented as a place where the trader occupying it carries out his activities, including seasonal activities, on a usual basis, with the result that such a consumer may reasonably expect, by visiting it, to be solicited by the trader" (at para.43).

### (ii) *Distance Contracts*

**"A contract concluded ... under an organised distance sales or service-provision scheme"**

*In line 10, after "through secure pages,", add new footnote 563a:*

38-087 [563a] cf. the guidance provided by A.G. Sharpston on the related concept of a "organised distance sales scheme" in art.2(a) of Directive 2002/65/EC concerning the distance marketing of consumer financial services [2002] O.J. L271/16, concluding that "if the system has been conceived so that everything can take place at distance, there is an organised distance service-provision scheme": Opinion (C-639/18) at para.65 and see also at paras 63–68.

## (c) Information Requirements

### (ii) *Off-Premises Contracts and Distance Contracts*

**The information required**

*Replace paragraph with:*

38-098 Schedule 2 to the 2013 Regulations[609] lists the information so required:

"(a) the main characteristics of the goods, services or digital content,[610] to the extent appropriate to the medium of communication and to the goods, services or digital content[611];

(b) the identity of the trader (such as the trader's trading name);

(c) the geographical address at which the trader is established and, where available,[611a] the trader's telephone number, fax number and e-mail address, to enable the consumer to contact the trader quickly and communicate efficiently[611b];

(d) where the trader is acting on behalf of another trader, the geographical address and identity of that other trader;

(e) if different from the address provided in accordance with paragraph (c), the geographical address of the place of business of the trader, and, where the trader acts on behalf of another trader, the geographical address of the place of business of that other trader, where the consumer can address any complaints;

(f) the total price of the goods, services or digital content inclusive of taxes, or where the nature of the goods, services or digital content is such that the price cannot reasonably be calculated in advance, the manner in which the price is to be calculated;

(g) where applicable, all additional delivery charges and any other costs or, where those charges cannot reasonably be calculated in advance, the fact that such additional charges may be payable;

(h) in the case of a contract of indeterminate duration or a contract containing a subscription, the total costs per billing period or (where such contracts are charged at a fixed rate) the total monthly costs;

(i) the cost of using the means of distance communication for the conclusion of the contract where that cost is calculated other than at the basic rate;

(j) the arrangements for payment, delivery, performance, and the time by which the trader undertakes to deliver the goods, to perform the services or to supply the digital content;

(k) where applicable, the trader's complaint handling policy;

(l) where a right to cancel exists, the conditions, time limit and procedures for exercising that right in accordance with regulations 27 to 38;

(m) where applicable, that the consumer will have to bear the cost of returning the goods in case of cancellation and, for distance contracts, if the goods, by their nature, cannot normally be returned by post, the cost of returning the goods;

(n) that, if the consumer exercises the right to cancel after having made a request in accordance with regulation 36(1), the consumer is to be liable to pay costs in accordance with regulation 36(4);

(o) where under regulation 28, 36 or 37 there is no right to cancel or the right to cancel may be lost, the information that the consumer will not benefit from a right to cancel, or the circumstances under which the consumer loses the right to cancel;

(p) in the case of a sales contract, a reminder that the trader is under a legal duty to supply goods that are in conformity with the contract;

(q) where applicable, the existence and the conditions of after-sale customer assistance, after-sales services and commercial guarantees;

(r) the existence of relevant codes of conduct, as defined in regulation 5(3)(b) of the Consumer Protection from Unfair Trading Regulations 2008, and how copies of them can be obtained, where applicable;

(s) the duration of the contract, where applicable, or, if the contract is of indeterminate duration or is to be extended automatically, the conditions for terminating the contract;

(t) where applicable, the minimum duration of the consumer's obligations under the contract;

(u) where applicable, the existence and the conditions of deposits or other financial guarantees to be paid or provided by the consumer at the request of the trader;

(v) where applicable, the functionality,[612] including applicable technical protection measures, of digital content[613];

(w) where applicable, any relevant compatibility of digital content with hardware and software that the trader is aware of or can reasonably be expected to have been aware of[614];

(x) where applicable, the possibility of having recourse to an out-of-court complaint and redress mechanism, to which the trader is subject, and the methods for having access to it.[615]

The information relating to the consumer's cancellation right in paras (l), (m) and (n) above may be provided by means of the "model instructions on cancellation" set out by the Regulations, and if the trader uses this model correctly filled in, this is to be treated as compliance with those requirements.[616] The Regulations also provide that, if a right to cancel exists, the trader must give (or, in the case of distance contracts, make available to) the consumer a cancellation form which they set out.[617] In the case of off-premises contracts, the information and any cancellation form must be given on paper or, if the consumer agrees, on another durable medium and must be legible[618]; for distance contracts, it must be legible in so far as the information is provided on a durable medium.[619] In the case of distance contracts, the 2013 Regulations qualify the general rules as to the provision of information where they are concluded through a means of distance communication which allows limited space or time to display the information.[620]

[609] As amended by SI 2014/870 and implementing 2011 Directive art.6. Article 6 is subject to amendment by Directive (EU) 2019/2161 of the European Parliament and of the Council of 27 November 2019 ... as regards the better enforcement and modernisation of Union consumer protection rules [2019] O.J. L328/7 art.4(4), whose art.4(5) inserts a new art.6(a) into the 2011 Directive setting out additional specific information requirements for distance contracts concluded on online marketplaces. However, the 2019 Directive must be implemented by November 28, 2021 (i.e. after IP completion day) and as a result the UK is not required to do so: cf. above, paras 38-060 (note) and on IP completion day more generally above, para.38-004.

[610] "Digital content" means "data which are produced and supplied in digital form": 2013 Regulations reg.5 "digital content".

[611] On the special significance of this requirement under the Consumer Rights Act 2015 s.11(4) (goods contracts) and s.36(3) (digital content contracts), see below, paras 38-499 and 38-548 respectively.

[611a] On this see *EIS GmbH v TO* (C-266/19) EU:C:2020:384.

[611b] On this requirement see *Bundesverband der Verbraucherzentralen und Verbraucherverbände - Verbraucherzentrale Bundesverband eV v Amazon EU Sàrl* (C-649/17) EU:C:2019:576 of July 10, 2019 (although the main point in issue was a qualification on the information requirement in art.6(1)(c) of the 2011 Directive which was not retained by the 2013 Regulations).

[612] 2013 Regulations reg.5 provides that "'functionality' in relation to digital content includes region coding, restrictions incorporated for the purposes of digital rights management, and other technical restrictions".

[613] On the particular significance of this category of information under the Consumer Rights Act 2015 s.36(3), see below, para.38-548.

[614] On the particular significance of this category of information under the Consumer Rights Act 2015 s.36(3), see below, para.38-548.

[615] 2013 Regulations Sch.2, which notes that in the case of a public auction (as defined by reg.5 "public auction" and explained by the 2011 Directive recital 24) the information listed in paras (b) to (e) may be replaced with the equivalent details for the auctioneer."

[616] 2013 Regulations reg.10(3) (off-premises contracts); reg.13(3) (distance contracts), referring to the "Model instructions for cancellation" in Sch.3 Pt A.

[617] 2013 Regulations reg.10(1)(b) (off-premises contracts); reg.13(1)(b) (distance contracts); Sch.3 Pt B.

[618] 2013 Regulations reg.10(2). Regulations 10 (3), (4), and (6) makes further incidental provision as to these requirements. Regulation 11 makes special provision for the provision of information in connection with repair or maintenance contracts. "Durable medium" is defined by reg.5 as: "paper or email, or any other medium that—(a) allows information to be addressed personally to the recipient, (b) enables the recipient to store the information in a way accessible for future reference for a period that is long enough for the purposes of the information, and (c) allows the unchanged reproduction of the information stored". On "durable medium" see *Content Services Ltd v Bundesarbeitskammer* (C-49/11) July 5, 2012 paras 39–50 in the context of the Distance Contracts Directive 1997: "a durable medium must ensure that the consumer, in a similar way to paper form, is in possession of the [relevant] information ... to enable him to exercise his rights where necessary": (C-49/11) at para.42.

[619] 2013 Regulations reg.13(2).

[620] 2013 Regulations reg.13(4) implementing Consumer Rights Directive art.8(4) as explained by the CJEU in *Walbusch Walter Busch GmbH & Co KG v Zentrale zur Bekämpfung unlauteren Wettbewerbs Frankfurt am Main eV* (C-430/17) EU:C:2019:47 of January 23, 2019, paras 37–47. Directive (EU) 2019/2161 art.4(7)(a) will replace art.8(4): on the 2019 Directive see above, para.38-060 (note).

## Distance contracts concluded by electronic means

*Replace footnote 621 with:*

38-099 [621] 2013 Regulations reg.14. See also Directive (EU) 2019/2161 art.4(5) inserting a new art.6(a) into the 2011 Directive setting out additional specific information requirements for distance contracts concluded on online marketplaces on which see above, para.38-098 (note).

### *(iii) On-Premises Contracts*

## The information required

*Replace footnote 635 with:*

38-103 [635] As amended by SI 2014/870 and implementing 2011 Directive art.5. Article 5 is subject to amendment by Directive (EU) 2019/2161 art.4(3), but the 2019 Directive must be implemented by November 28, 2021 (i.e. after IP completion day) and as a result the UK is not required to do so: cf. above, paras 38-060 (note) and on IP completion day more generally above, para.38-004.

## *(iv) The Effects of the Information Requirements*

### General

*To the end paragraph, after "the 2013 Regulations.", add new footnote 645a:*

645a However, the significance of decisions of the CJEU will change on IP completion day, see above, para.38-004 and Vol.I, para.1-017B. **38-104**

### Misleading omissions

*Replace footnote 670 with:*

670 This reflects accurately the Unfair Commercial Practices Directive 2005 art.7(5), which refers to a "non-exhaustive list" in its Annex II, and the latter includes Directive 97/7/EC on distance contracts, arts 4 and 5 of which were the predecessor provisions to the information requirements now contained in the Consumer Rights Directive 2011 arts 6 and 7 which are implemented in UK law by the 2013 Regulations regs 13 and 14. For the "complementary nature" of information obligations under specific EU legislation and the provision in art.7(5) of the 2005 Directive (implemented by reg.6(3)(b) of the 2008 Regulations), see *Abcur AB v Apoteket Farmaci, Apoteket AB and Apoteket Farmaci AB* (C-544/13 and C-545/13) July 16 2015 at paras 78–82 (medicinal products for human use). For discussion of the significance of "misleading omission" under reg.6(3)(a) of the 2008 Regulations see *Secretary of State for Business, Innovation and Skills v PLT Antimarketing Ltd* [2015] EWCA Civ 76, [2015] C.T.L.C.8 at [30]–[31] where the Court of Appeal identified the "critical question" as being "whether the average consumer can be said to need to obtain that information from the trader in question, rather than obtain it (for example) by shopping around, and finding out for himself whether something better, or cheaper, is on offer": *Secretary of State for Business, Innovation and Skills v PLT Antimarketing Ltd* at [31] per Briggs L.J. (with whom Ryder and Richards L.JJ. agreed) later referring to this as "the "needs" test": *Secretary of State for Business, Innovation and Skills v PLT Antimarketing Ltd* at [40]. cf. the approach of the CJEU to art.6 of the 2005 Directive's requirements as regards "misleading actions" in *Nemzeti Fogyasztóvédelmi Hatóság v UPC Magyarország Kft* (C-388/13) of April 18, 2015 at paras 53–54 (where a trader provides erroneous information to the consumer, the fact that the consumer could himself have obtained the correct information is irrelevant). Where information is *not* required by relevant EU legislation, then its omission cannot be *deemed* to be material by way of application of art.7(5) of the 2005 Directive (which is implemented in UK law by reg.6(3)(b) of the 2008 Regulations): *Dyson Ltd v BSH Home Appliances NV* (C-632/16) EU:C:2018:599 of July 25, 2018 at paras 42–45. **38-110**

### Misleading actions

*Replace footnote 678 with:*

678 2008 Regulations reg.5(2)(a) and (b). In *Abcur AB v Apoteket Farmaci, Apoteket AB and Apoteket Farmaci AB* (C-544/13 and C-545/13) July 16 2015 the CJEU held that art.3(4) of the 2005 Directive "applies only in so far as there are no specific EU law provisions regulating specific aspects of unfair commercial practices, such as information requirements and rules on the way the information is presented to the consumer" in relation to medical products for human use (at para.79) and that, where the specific provisions conflict with the provisions in the 2005 Directive, the former "take precedence and apply to those specific aspects of unfair commercial practices" (at para.81), but in the result, this allowed advertising practices relating to such medical products to fall within the scope of the 2005 Directive "provided that the conditions for the application of that directive are satisfied" (at para.83). Moreover, the CJEU has explained that "the term 'conflict' [in art.3(4)] refers to the relationship between the provisions in question which goes beyond a mere disparity or simple difference, showing a divergence which cannot be overcome by a unifying formula enabling both situations to exist alongside each other without the need to bring them to an end": *Autorità Garante della Concorrenza e del Mercato v Wind Tre SpA and Vodafone Italia SpA* (Joined Cases C-54/17 and C-55/17) EU:C:2018:710 of September 13, 2018 at para.60. For an example of the application of art.3(4) see *Citroën Commerce GmbH v Zentralvereinigung des Kraftfahrzeuggewerbes zur Aufrechterhaltung lauteren Wettbewerbs eV (ZLW)* (C-476/14) July 7, 2016 at paras 44–46 where the CJEU held that the provision in the 2005 Directive regarding the materiality of certain information in invitations to purchase for the purposes of misleading omissions (which included "the price inclusive of taxes" (art.7(4)(c))) could not apply to the case before them "as the aspect relating to the selling price referred to in an advertisement", as that issue was governed by Directive 98/6/EC on consumer protection in the indication of the prices of products offered to customers [1998] O.J. L80/27 art.3(1)'s provision on "selling price": the 1998 Directive governed this "specific aspect" within the meaning of art.3(4) of the 2005 Directive, which therefore "cannot apply as regards that aspect" (C-476/14 judgment at para.45). See also *Dyson Ltd v BSH Home Appliances NV* (C-632/16) EU:C:2018:59; of July 25, 2018 at paras 32–41 (EU legislation required a "uniform energy label" for vacuum cleaners and the effect of art.3(4) of the 2005 Directive meant that **38-111**

the omission of certain information not required by this label therefore could not constitute a "misleading omission" within the meaning of art.7 of that Directive).

## (d) The Consumer's Right of Cancellation or Withdrawal

### *(i) The Situations in Which the Right Arises and its Duration*

**The contracts affected**

*Replace paragraph with:*

**38-112** Part 3 of the 2013 Regulations creates rights of cancellation for consumers, and regulates the effect of their exercise and of the withdrawal of an offer by a consumer, in respect of off-premises and distance contracts but not on-premises contracts.[682] Part 3 excludes the same types of contracts from the application of these provisions as they exclude from Pt 2's information requirements,[683] in addition to those types of contracts or contracts made in particular circumstances which are excluded entirely from the scope of the 2013 Regulations.[684] Part 3 also excludes from its scope contracts for the supply of goods or services of certain types or supplied in certain circumstances, for example, for the supply of goods made to the consumer's specifications or are clearly personalised,[685] wine bought *en primeur*,[686] newspapers, periodicals or magazines supplied other than under a subscription,[687] contracts for the supply of accommodation, transport of goods, vehicle rental services, catering or services relating to leisure activities, if the contract provides for a specific date or period of performance[688] and contracts concluded at a public auction.[689] Moreover, the rights conferred by Pt 3 cease to be available to the consumer in the case of contracts for the supply of sealed goods which are not suitable for return due to health protection or hygiene reasons, if they become unsealed after delivery; contracts for the supply of sealed audio or sealed video recordings or sealed computer software, if the goods become unsealed after delivery; and any sales contract, if the goods become mixed inseparably (according to their nature) with other items after delivery.[690]

[682] 2013 Regulations reg.27(1) (referring to Pt 3). For the definition of these contracts see above, paras 38-081 (off-premises contract); 38-086 (distance contract) and 38-090 (on-premises contract).

[683] 2013 Regulation reg.27(2)–(4) and cf. reg.7(2)–(5) whose contents are noted above, para.38-077. The only qualification on this position is that contracts for passenger transport services are wholly excluded from Pt 3 of the 2013 Regulations, whereas their exclusion from Pt 2 finds an exception in the case of distance contracts concluded by electronic means: see above, para.38-078.

[684] Above, para.38-076.

[685] 2013 Regulations reg.28(1)(b). A contract under which an architect agrees merely to draw up plans for a house for an individual consumer does not fall within this exception, even though the plans themselves are "goods" and are "made to the consumer's specification or clearly personalised" (as set out by art.16(c) of the 2011 Directive) as this is secondary compared to the main subject-matter of the contract which is the supply of an intellectual service ("*une prestation intellectuelle*"), though it could count as a "service contract" so as fall within the exception to the right of cancellation in art.16(a) (implemented by 2013 Regulations reg.36(2) on which see below, para.38-115) where such a contract is fully performed (and subject to other conditions): *NK v MS* (C-208/19) EU:C:2020:382 at paras 58–65 (available in French).

[686] 2013 Regulations reg.28(1)(d) as explained by 2011 Directive recital 49.

[687] 2013 Regulations reg.28(1)(f).

[688] 2013 Regulations reg.28(1)(h).

[689] 2013 Regulations reg.28(1)(g); "public auction" is defined by reg.5 "public auction". The full list is contained in 2013 Regulations reg.28.

[690] 2013 Regulations reg.28(3). Following its general approach to exceptions from rules of consumer

protection (above, para.38-085), the CJEU has held that these exclusions must be interpreted strictly: *slewo - schlafen leben wohnen GmbH v Ledowski* (C-681/17) EU:C:2019:255 of March 27, 2019 at para.34. In that case, the CJEU held that the exception of "contracts for the supply of sealed goods which are not suitable for return due to health protection or hygiene reasons" applies "only if, after the packaging has been unsealed, the goods contained therein are definitively no longer in a saleable condition due to genuine health protection or hygiene reasons, because the very nature of the goods makes it impossible or excessively difficult, for the trader to take the necessary measures allowing for resale without affecting either of those requirements": C-681/17 at para.40. As a result, a mattress covered with a protective film which the consumer has removed cannot fall within this exception any more than does a garment, which may also come in contact with the human body when it is tried on by a consumer. For this purpose, the CJEU clearly envisaged that the goods would still be "saleable" for this purpose even if they had to be cleaned and sold second-hand: C-681/17 at paras 41–48.

## Supply of services or digital content in cancellation period

*Replace footnote 703 with:*

[703] 2013 Regulations reg.36(2) and see the example foreseen by the CJEU in *NK v MS* (C-208/19) EU:C:2020:382 at paras 58–65, above, para.38-112 (note). This restriction on the availability of the right of cancellation does not apply to contracts for the supply of water, gas, electricity or district heating (on which see above, para.38-073). For the consequences of a consumer's exercise of a right to cancel falling outside this restriction where services are supplied during the cancellation period; see 2013 Regulations reg.36(3)–(6), below, paras 38-128—38-130. **38-115**

## The cancellation period

*Replace footnote 710 with:*

[710] Directive 2011/83/EU art.9. Directive (EU) 2019/2161 art.4(8) will insert a new art.9a into the 2011 Directive allowing Member States (subject to certain conditions) to extend the withdrawal period to 30 days for contracts concluded in the context of unsolicited visits by a trader to a consumer's home or excursions organised by a trader with the aim or effect of promoting or selling products to consumers: on the 2019 Directive see above, para.38-060 (note). **38-116**

## Cancellation period extended for breach of information requirement

*Replace footnote 731 with:*

[731] Directive 2011/83/EU recital 43. The uniform nature of this period stems from the Directive's general requirement of "full harmonisation" in art.4, see above, para.38-062. See, however, the possibility for Member States to extend the period to 30 days in some circumstances provided by Directive 2019/2161 art.4(8): above, para.38-116 (note). **38-118**

## No effective waiver of right by consumer

*Replace footnote 741 with:*

[741] Above, para.38-014 and on the continuing significance of this "principle of conforming interpretation" after IP completion day see above, para.38-004 and Vol.I, para.1-017B. **38-120**

### *(ii) The Effects of Cancellation or Withdrawal*

## Supply of services or digital content in cancellation period

*In line 2, after "a tangible medium.", add new footnote 785a:*

[785a] At the EU level, there will be a further special treatment as Directive 2019/2161 art.4 (11)(a) will insert a new art.14(2a) into the 2011 Directive providing that "in the event of withdrawal from the contract, the consumer shall refrain from using the digital content or digital service and from making it available to third parties". On this Directive generally see above, para.38-060 (note). **38-130**

### (e) Enforcement

*Change title of paragraph:* **38-133**

## "Enforcement orders" under the Enterprise Act 2002 Part 8

*Replace paragraph with:*

**38-133** Under Pt 8 of the Enterprise Act 2002, the CMA (replacing the OFT)[809] and other persons or bodies termed "enforcers", may apply to the court for an "enforcement order" against a person to stop breaking legislation enacted for the benefit of consumers.[810] The 2002 Act distinguishes for this purpose between "domestic infringements"[811] (which are concerned with enforcement of national protections by UK-based enforcers) and "Community infringements" (for which cross-border enforcement was created and which also covers domestic action by UK enforcers in respect of breaches of specified UK laws implementing the Directives specified by the Consumer Injunctions Directive).[812] A number of the directives and their UK implementing legislation which are the subject of this chapter are included for the purposes of "Community infringements" and these include, for present purposes, the Consumer Rights Directive 2011[813] and the 2013 Regulations.[814] The Consumer Rights Act 2015 amended Pt 8 so as to provide new powers to allow a court to require a person against whom an "enforcement order" is made to take "enhanced consumer measures",[814a] and to these were added in 2020 a power to make an "online interface order" so as to give effect to a requirement of the EU Consumer Protection Cooperation ("CPC") Regulation 2017.[814b] As will be explained, on the UK's exit from the EU coming into full effect on IP completion day (set at the time of writing at December 31, 2020), there are also due to be significant amendments to the Pt 8 scheme, including the replacement of "Community infringements" with "Schedule 13 infringements".[814c]

Under Pt 8, "enforcers"[814d] are divided into "general enforcers",[815] which include the CMA and local weights and measures authorities in Great Britain; "designated enforcers", which are any public or private body in the United Kingdom which the Secretary of State designates as a person or body one of whose purposes is the protection of the collective interests of consumers and which include the Civil Aviation Authority, the Information Commissioner and the Rail Regulator[816]; "Community enforcers", which are qualified entities listed for this purpose by the EU, the list including a number of public and private bodies (notably, consumers' associations)[817]; and "CPC enforcers", which are bodies or persons designated by the Secretary of State under the EU Regulation on consumer protection co-operation,[818] these including the CMA, local weights and measures authorities and certain other public bodies and persons.[819] The inclusion of "Community enforcers" within the class of those entitled to apply for enforcement orders reflects the policy of the EU to promote cross-border policing under its own consumer protection legislation.[820] The designation of "CPC enforcers" seeks to give effect to a policy of encouraging and facilitating co-operation between European national authorities in the enforcement of consumer protection.[821] Where a domestic or a Community infringement (including therefore an infringement of the requirements of the 2013 Regulations) harms the collective interest of consumers,[822] an "enforcer" can apply to the court for an enforcement order, but only after engaging in appropriate consultation with the person against whom the order would be made and, if the enforcer is not the CMA, after the enforcer has given notice to the CMA of the enforcer's intention to apply for the enforcement order, and the appropriate minimum period has elapsed.[823] Where a court finds that an infringement has been committed or is likely to be committed by the defendant to proceedings brought under these provisions, it may make an enforcement order, notably, to prevent the defendant from continuing the relevant conduct.[824]

[809] As from April 1, 2014, the OFT was abolished and its functions under the 1999 Regulations taken over by the Competition and Markets Authority ("CMA"): Enterprise and Regulatory Reform Act 2013 (Competition) (Consequential, Transitional and Saving Provisions) (No.2) Order 2014 (SI 2014/549) Sch.1 para.26; Public Bodies (The Office of Fair Trading Transfer of Consumer Advice Scheme Function and Modification of Enforcement Functions) Order 2013 (SI 2013/783) art.10.

[810] The Enterprise Act 2002 Pt 8 came into force on June 20, 2003: The Enterprise Act 2002 (Commencement No.3, Transitional and Transitory Provisions and Savings) Order 2003 (SI 2003/1397) art.2. It replaced the Fair Trading Act 1973 Pt III and the Stop Now Orders (EC Directive) Regulations 2001 (SI 2001/1422). Its provisions concerning "Community infringements" implement into UK law Directive 2009/22/EC on injunctions for the protection of consumers' interests [2009] O.J. L110/30. It has been held that the conduct of a person taking place *before* the coming into force of Pt 8 of the Enterprise Act 2002 can form the basis of granting an order under it: *Office of Fair Trading v MB Designs (Scotland) Ltd* [2005] S.L.T. 691 at [23], OH of the Ct of Sess., where Pt 8 is discussed more generally. The powers contained in the Enterprise Act 2002 were extended (in particular) by the Enterprise Act 2002 (Amendment) Regulations 2006 (SI 2006/3363) implementing arts 4(6) and 13(4) of the Regulation 2006/2004 on co-operation between national authorities responsible for the enforcement of consumer protection laws (the Regulation on consumer protection co-operation), as amended by Directive 2005/29/EC. The Consumer Rights Act 2015 s.79 Sch.7 changed the powers contained in Pt 8 of the 2002 Act, as noted in the present and following paragraphs, in relation to conduct which occurs, or which is likely to occur, after its commencement: 2015 Act s.79(2). This section (together with the other provisions in Pts 1 and 2 of the Act) came into force on October 1, 2015: see below, para.38-366. For general guidance on the use of the Pt 8 powers by the CMA see CMA, *Consumer Protection: enforcement guidance* (CMA58, August 17, 2016), available at *https://assets.publishing.service.gov.uk/government/uploads/system/uploads/attachment_data/file/546521/cma58-consumer-protection-enforcement-guidance.pdf.*

[811] Enterprise Act 2002 s.211 (which was amended on the coming into force of s.75 and Sch.7 of the 2015 Act).

[812] Enterprise Act 2002 s.212; OFT, *Enforcement of consumer protection legislation, Guidance on Pt 8 of the Enterprise Act* (2003), para.3.15. The first consumer injunctions directive (98/27/EC) of 1998 was revoked and replaced by the Directive 2009/22/EC on injunctions for the protection of consumers' interests (2009) O.J. L 110/1 whose list in Annex I of relevant directives is much amended.

[813] Enterprise Act 2002 ss.210 and 212, Sch.13 Pt 1 para.9F. The list in Sch.13 also includes the Package Travel Directive 2015 ("Directive (EU) 2015/2302") (Sch.13 Pt 1 para.4; see below, para.38-137—38-138); the Unfair Terms in Consumer Contracts Directive 93/13 (Sch.13 Pt 1 para.5; see below, para.38-218); the Consumer Sales Directive 1999/44/EC (Sch.13 Pt 1 para.8; see below, para.38-433) and the Unfair Commercial Practices Directive 2005/29/EC (Sch.13 Pt 1 para.9C; see below, para.38-159); and art.62 of Directive 2015/2366/EU of the European Parliament and of the Council of November 25, 2015 on payment services in the internal market (Sch.13 Pt 1 para.16: see below, para.38-428). The powers of a court in relation to "enforcement orders" are contained in s.217 of the 2002 Act and with the coming into force of the Consumer Rights Act 2015 are extended so as to allow a court to require a person against whom an order is made to take "enhanced consumer measures": see below, para.38-134.

[814] Enterprise Act 2002 (Part 8 EU Infringements) Order 2014 (2014/2908) art.4, Sch.

[814a] Enterprise Act 2002 s.217(10A) as inserted by the Consumer Rights Act 2015 s.79, Sch.7 para.7, on which see below, para.38-134.

[814b] Regulation (EU) 2017/2394 of the European Parliament and of the Council of 12 December 2017 on cooperation between national authorities responsible for the enforcement of consumer protection laws and repealing Regulation (EC) 2006/2004 [2017] O.J. L345/1. To ensure the effective operation of the 2017 Regulation in the UK, the Consumer Protection (Enforcement) (Amendment etc.) Regulations 2020 (SI 2020/484) were made (in force June 2, 2020), and these amended, inter alia, the 2002 Act, on which see below, paras 38-133A and 38-133B.

[814c] On IP completion day see above, para.38-004 and Vol.I, paras 1-014 et seq. and on this change see below, para.38-133A.

[814d] On IP completion day (on which generally see above, para.38-004 and Vol.I, paras 1-014 et seq.) the categories of "enforcers" are to be amended as noted below, para.38-133A.

[815] Enterprise Act 2002 s.213(1).

[816] Enterprise Act 2002 s.213(2)–(4); the Enterprise Act 2002 (Part 8 Designated Enforcers: Criteria for Designation, Designation of Public Bodies as Designated and Transitional Provisions) Order 2003 (SI 2003/1399) art.5, Sch.1.

[817] Enterprise Act 2002 s.213(5); Directive 2009/22/EC on injunctions for the protection of consum-

ers' interests. The list of qualified bodies is listed by the EU Commission and published in the Official Journal.

[818] The "CPC Regulation" in the 2002 Act referred first to Regulation (EU) 2006/2004 on co-operation between national authorities responsible for the enforcement of consumer protection laws [2004] O.J. L364/1. However, Regulation (EU) 2006/2004 was repealed and replaced with effect from January 17, 2020 by Regulation (EU) 2017/2394 of the European Parliament and of the Council of 12 December 2017 on cooperation between national authorities responsible for the enforcement of consumer protection laws and repealing Regulation (EC) 2006/2004 [2017] O.J. L345/1 and from June 2, 2020 references to the "CPC Regulation" in the 2002 Act refer to the 2017 Regulation: Consumer Protection (Enforcement) (Amendment etc.) Regulations 2020 (SI 2020/484) reg.2(14) substituting a new s.235A in the 2002 Act. As the CMA has explained, the 2017 Regulation "preserves the main features of the 2006 CPR Regulation, but strengthens the cooperation mechanisms and provides for a wider range of investigation and enforcement powers for national authorities": CMA, *UK exit from the EU, Guidance on the functions of the CMA under the Withdrawal Agreement* (CMA113, January 28, 2020), para.5.10. In order to ensure the effective operation of the 2017 Regulation in the UK, the Consumer Protection (Enforcement) (Amendment etc.) Regulations 2020 (SI 2020/484) were made (in force June 2, 2020), amending, inter alia, the 2002 Act Pt 8 in certain respects. The principal innovation of these amendments was to give the CMA new powers enabling them to facilitate the removal of online content from or restrict access to websites by applying to a court for an "online interface order" (on which see below, para.38-133B), to amend the list of Directives and Regulations in Sch.13 of the Act and to amend the provisions as to "enhanced consumer measures" (on which see below, para.38-134): see SI 2020/484 reg.2. On the position after IP completion day, see below, para.38-133A.

[819] Enterprise Act 2002 s.213(5A).

[820] Directive 2009/22/EC recitals 4–8.

[821] Regulation 2006/2004 recitals.

[822] Enterprise Act 2002 ss.211(1)(c), 212(1). On the requirement of "harming the collective interest of consumers" see *Office of Fair Trading v MB Designs (Scotland) Ltd* [2005] S.L.T. 691 at [23], [1], [13]–[16].

[823] Enterprise Act 2002 s.214(1) as replaced by Public Bodies (the Office of Fair Trading Transfer of Consumer Advice Scheme Function and Modification of Enforcement Functions) Order 2013 (SI 2013/783) art.9(2) and amended by Enterprise and Regulatory Reform Act 2013 (Competition) (Consequential, Transitional and Saving Provisions) Order 2014 (SI 2014/892) Sch.1 para.7.

[824] 2002 Act ss.217–218 (as amended). Section 219 of the 2002 Act provides a power in enforcers to accept an undertaking from a person who has engaged, is engaging or who is likely to engage in conduct constituting an infringement in specified circumstances. The question whether proceedings under Pt 8 of the 2002 Act should be brought under Pt 7 or Pt 8 of the CPR will depend on whether they involve a "substantial dispute of fact": *Competition and Markets Authority v Care UK Health and Social Care Holdings Ltd* [2019] EWHC 2828 (Ch) at [31]–[35].

*Add new paragraphs:*

38-133A **Amendments to Part 8 of the 2002 Act on IP completion day** As outlined in the previous paragraph, the scheme of control set out in Pt 8 of the 2002 Act distinguishes between "domestic infringements" and "Community infringements" and sets out a series of categories of enforcers which includes "Community enforcers" and "CPC enforcers". However, on the full coming into effect of the UK's leaving the EU on IP completion day (which is currently defined as December 31, 2020 at 11.00pm[824a]), this scheme is due to be subject to significant change,[824b] reflecting in particular the fact that European cross-border enforcement of EU consumer protection legislation will no longer apply (unless the UK and the EU agree that it should as part of their future relationship). First, the category of "Community infringement" is replaced with one of "Schedule 13 infringement" and the existing lists of EU legislation (and UK legislation implementing EU legislation) giving rise to Community infringements are replaced with a substituted Sch.13 to the 2002 Act.[824c] Accordingly, a "Schedule 13 infringement" is defined as "an act or omission which contravenes a listed enactment and which harms the collective interest of consumers", it being provided that "[a]n enactment is a listed enactment if it is specified in Schedule 13 or to the extent that it is so specified".[824d] Secondly, while the Act's recognition of "general enforcers" and "designated enforcers" remains,[824e] its inclusion of "Community enforcers" is deleted as is its reference to the Secretary of State designating persons under the CPC Regulation,[824f] there being substituted instead a list of "Schedule 13 enforcers".[824g] As this scheme foresees, the content of Sch.13 of the 2002 Act is therefore replaced with a list of enactments which can give rise to "Schedule 13 infringements", these consisting of 27 UK legislative instruments, both primary and secondary and whether or not they implemented EU legislation,[824h] and two EU regulations "retained" after the UK's exit from the EU by the European Union (Withdrawal) Act 2018,[824i] notably, the Denied Boarding Regulation.[824j] The UK legislation contained in Sch.13 includes the Consumer Contracts (Information, Cancellation and Additional Charges) Regulations 2013 (SI 2013/3134), as well as the Consumer Protection from Unfair Trading Regulations 2008 (SI 2008/1277) and many provisions in Pts 1 and 2 of the Consumer Rights Act 2015.[824k] Overall, therefore, the CMA has advised that, after IP completion day, "businesses based in the UK or elsewhere that trade with UK consumers must comply with UK consumer protection laws" and that, although it will seek "to continue to develop relationships and work with all our international counterparts", "the exact nature of consumer protection law enforcement cooperation to be agreed with the EU as part of the Future Relationship is not known".[824l]

[824a] European Union (Withdrawal) Act 2018 s.1A(6) (as inserted by European Union (Withdrawal Agreement) Act 2020 s.1, referring for "IP completion day" to s.39(1)–(5) of the 2020 Act. On the UK's exit from the EU and IP completion day see above, para.38-004 and Vol.I, paras 1-014 et seq.

[824b] These changes are contained in the Consumer Protection (Enforcement) (Amendment etc.) (EU Exit) Regulations 2019 (SI 2019/203) ("SI 2019/203"), which come into force on IP completion day (the reference in reg.1 to "exit day" must be read as referring to "IP completion day" European Union (Withdrawal Agreement) Act 2020 s.39(1), Sch.5 para.1) and see above, para.38-004 and Vol.I, paras 1-014 et seq.). The SI 2019/203 regs 9 and 10 make transitional provisions.

[824c] As a result, the orders specifying the relevant UK and EU laws are to be revoked: SI 2019/203 reg.7 specifying the following orders: SI 2003/1374; SI 2005/2418; SI 2006/3372; SI 2014/2908; SI 2015/1628. Transitional provision is also made by SI 2019/203 for Community infringements or suspected Community infringements occurring before exit day: regs 9 and 10. SI 2019/203 comes into force on IP completion day as reg.1's reference to the Regulations coming into force on "exit day" must be read as referring to IP completion day: European Union (Withdrawal Agreement) Act 2020 s.39(1), Sch.5 para.1.

[824d] Enterprise Act 2002 s.212 as amended by SI 2019/203 reg.3(3), referring to the s.212(6A) and (6B) as inserted by SI 2019/203 reg.3(2)(b).

[824e] Enterprise Act 2002 s.213(1)–(4).

[824f] Regulation (EU) 2017/2394 of the European Parliament and of the Council of 12 December 2017 on cooperation between national authorities responsible for the enforcement of consumer protection laws and repealing Regulation (EC) 2006/2004 [2017] O.J. L345/1: 2002 Act s.235A (as substituted by the Consumer Protection (Enforcement) (Amendment etc.) Regulations 2020 (SI 2020/484) reg.2(14)).

[824g] Enterprise Act 2002 s.213(5), deleted by SI 2019/203 reg.3(4)(a); s.213(5A), amended by SI 2019/203 reg.3(4)(b); s.213(10) and (11), deleted by SI 2019/203 reg.3(4)(c). Other references in the Act to Community infringement, Community enforcer and CPC infringement are also replaced accordingly or the relevant provision deleted: SI 2019/203 reg.3(5)–(19).

[824h] SI 2019/203 reg.3(20), referring to the Schedule to these regulations. Some of these UK regulations are themselves revoked except as regards contracts made before their date of revocation, as in the case of the Unfair Terms in Consumer Contracts Regulations 1999 (SI 1999/2083): SI 2019/203 Sch. para.1, inserting new Sch.13 para.9 to the 2002 Act. Others remain fully in force: e.g. the Consumer Protection from Unfair Trading Regulations 2008 (SI 2008/1277): SI 2019/203 Sch. para.1, inserting new 2002 Act Sch.13 para.19.

[824i] 2018 Act s.3(1) and (2), on which see above, para.38-004 and Vol.I, paras 1-014 et seq.

[824j] SI 2019/203 Sch. para.1 referring to Regulation (EC) 261/2004 Otherwise, Sch.13 para.28 (as substituted by SI 2019/203 Sch. para.1) refers to art.10(4) of Regulation (EU) 2015/751 of the European Parliament and of the Council of 29 April 2015 on interchange fees for card-based payment transactions.

[824k] SI 2019/203 Sch. para.1, inserting new 2002 Act Sch.13 paras 25, 19 and 27 respectively.

[824l] CMA, *UK exit from the EU, Guidance on the functions of the CMA under the Withdrawal Agreement* (CMA113, January 28, 2020), paras 5.19–5.21.

38-133B **"Online interface orders"** In 2020, Pt 8 of the 2002 Act was amended so as to introduce a power in the CMA to apply to the High Court or County Court for an "online interface order" or an "interim online interface order"[824m] and so give effect to provisions of the replacement CPC Regulation 2017,[824n] which explains that:

> "In the digital environment in particular, the competent authorities should be able to stop infringements covered by this Regulation quickly and effectively … In cases where there is a risk of serious harm to the collective interests of consumers, the competent authorities should be able to adopt interim measures in accordance with national law, including the removal of content from an online interface or ordering the explicit display of a warning to consumers when they access an online interface."[824o]

Reflecting the Regulation,[824p] an "online interface" is defined by the 2002 Act (as amended) as "any software, including a website, part of a website or an application, that is operated by or on behalf of a trader, and which serves to give consumers access to the trader's goods and services".[824q] The Act provides that, on the application of the CMA, the court may make an "online interface order"

> "if it finds that
>
> (a) there has been or is likely to be a Community infringement,[824r]
> (b) there are no other available means of bringing about the cessation or prohibition of the infringement which, by themselves, would be wholly effective, and
> (c) it is necessary to make the order to avoid the risk of serious harm to the collective interests of consumers."[824s]

Such an order

> "must direct the person against whom it is made to do, or to co-operate with another person so that other person may do, one or more of the following—
>
> (a) remove content from or modify content on an online interface;
> (b) disable or restrict access to an online interface;
> (c) display a warning to consumers accessing an online interface;
> (d) delete a fully qualified domain name and take any steps necessary to facilitate the registration of that domain name by the CMA."[824t]

Provision is also made for "interim" online interface orders subject to certain conditions including that "it is expedient to bring about the cessation or prohibition of the Community infringement immediately".[824u]

[824m] See Enterprise Act 2002 esp. s.218ZA–218ZD (as inserted by SI 2020/484 reg.2(5)) (in force June 2, 2020: reg.1(2)).

[824n] Regulation (EU) 2017/2394 of the European Parliament and of the Council of 12 December 2017 on cooperation between national authorities responsible for the enforcement of consumer protection laws and repealing Regulation (EC) 2006/2004 [2017] O.J. L345/1 esp. reg.9(4). The 2017 Regulation applied on January 17, 2020, i.e. while the UK was still a Member State of the EU.

[824o] Regulation (EU) 2017/2394 recital 14.

[824p] Regulation (EU) 2017/2394 art.3(15).

824q 2002 Act s.218ZD(1) (as inserted by SI 2020/484 reg.2(5)).

824r On IP completion day, the reference to "Community infringements" will be replaced by "Schedule 13 infringements" as noted above, para.38-133A.

824s 2002 Act s.218ZB(1) (as inserted by SI 2020/484 reg.2(5)).

824t 2002 Act s.218ZB(2) (as inserted by SI 2020/484 reg.2(5)).

824u 2002 Act s.218ZC(1) (as inserted by SI 2020/484 reg.2(5)).

*To the end of title, add new footnote 824v:*

**"Enhanced consumer measures"[824v]**

824v The law in this paragraph is amended on IP completion day by the Consumer Protection (Enforcement) (Amendment etc.) Regulations (SI 2019/203) reg.3 as noted above, para.38-133A. **38-134**

*Replace paragraph with:*

The Consumer Rights Act 2015[825] amended the Enterprise Act 2002 Pt 8 so as to extend a court's power to make an "enforcement order" under the 2002 Act so as to require a person against whom the order is made to take "enhanced consumer measures".[826] The provisions were then amended in 2020 so as to give effect to provisions of the Consumer Cooperation Regulation 2017.[826a] There are three categories of enhanced consumer measures: the "redress category", the "compliance category", and the "choice category".[827] Each of these categories of measure is defined by the legislation.[828] Measures in the "redress category" are: **38-134**

"(a) measures offering compensation or other redress to consumers—
  (i) who have suffered loss as a result of the conduct which has given rise to the enforcement order or undertaking,[828a] or
  (ii) where that conduct constitutes a Community infringement,[828b] who have been affected in any other way by that conduct,
(b) where the conduct which has given rise to the enforcement order or undertaking relates to a contract, measures offering consumers falling within paragraph (a)(i) or (ii) the option to terminate (but not vary) that contract
(c) where consumers cannot be identified, or falling within paragraph (a)(i) or (ii) cannot be identified without disproportionate cost to the subject of the enforcement order or undertaking, measures intended to be in the collective interests of consumers."[829]

It will be seen that this power allows a court to order a trader to offer compensation to consumers who have suffered loss as a result of an infringement of a legislative provision for their protection or the option of terminating any contract to which that infringement relates. However, this power is subject both to the conditions of the availability of an enforcement order under Pt 8 generally (and in particular that an infringement harms the *collective* interests of consumers[830]) and to a general requirement that such enhanced consumer measures may be ordered only as the court considers to be just and reasonable[831] and to a series of particular conditions set by the Act for this purpose.[832]

825 The relevant provisions came into force on October 1, 2015: 2015 Act s.79 and Sch.7; Consumer Rights Act 2015 (Commencement No. 3, Transitional Provisions, Savings and Consequential Amendments) Order 2015 (SI 2015/1630) art.3(e) and (i). The amendments to the provisions made by the Consumer Protection (Enforcement) (Amendment etc.) Regulations 2020 (SI 2020/484) ("SI 2020/484") came into force on June 2, 2020 (reg.1(2)).

826 2002 Act s.217(10A) as inserted by Sch.7 para.6. The power also extends the court's power in relation to taking undertakings: 2002 Act s.217(10B).

826a Consumer Protection (Enforcement) (Amendment etc.) Regulations 2020 (SI 2020/484) reg.2 (in force on June 2, 2020) and see Regulation (EU) 2017/2394 of the European Parliament and of the

Council of 12 December 2017 on cooperation between national authorities responsible for the enforcement of consumer protection laws and repealing Regulation (EC) 2006/2004 [2017] O.J. L345/1 esp. art.9(4).

[827] See 2002 Act s.219A(2)–(5) as inserted by 2015 Act s.79, Sch.7 para.8.

[828] 2002 Act s.219A(1) as inserted by 2015 Act s.79, Sch.7 para.8.

[828a] e.g. a claim by the CMA that the trader defendant should repay "administration fees" paid under allegedly unfair contract terms: *Competition and Markets Authority v Care UK Health and Social Care Holdings Ltd.* [2019] EWHC 2828 (Ch) (which concerned whether the proceedings were properly brought under CPR Pt 7 or Pt 8).

[828b] On IP completion day, the reference to "Community Infringement" will be replaced by a reference to "Schedule 13 Infringement" as explained above, para.38-133A.

[829] 2002 Act s.219A(2) as inserted by 2015 Act s.79, Sch.7 para.8 and as amended by SI 2020/484 reg.2(9) (in force June 2, 2020).

[830] 2002 Act ss.211(1) and 212(2), above, para.38-133.

[831] 2002 Act s.219B(1) as inserted by 2015 Act s.79, Sch.7 para.8.

[832] 2002 Act s.219B and 219C as inserted by 2015 Act s.79, Sch.7 para.8 and as amended by SI 2020/484 reg.2(1). Similar conditions are imposed on the taking of undertakings by an enforcer: 2002 Act ss.219(5ZA) and (5ZB), 219A and 219B as inserted by 2015 Act s.79, Sch.7 paras 7 and 8.

## (f) Special Rules for Financial Services Contracts, Timeshare Contracts, Package Travel Contracts, Contracts Concluded by Electronic Means and ADR

### *(i) Introduction*

#### Special rules governing particular contracts in EU law

*To the end of paragraph, after "recipient is a consumer.[841]", add:*

38-135 Each of these sets of rules derived from EU law are due to be affected on IP completion day when the UK's leaving the EU comes into full effect and the changes involved will be noted in the following paragraphs.[841a]

[841a] On the UK's leaving the EU generally and the significance of IP completion day see above, para.38-004 and Vol.I, paras 1-014 et seq.

### *(ii) The Distance Marketing of Financial Services*

#### Summary

*Replace paragraph with:*

38-136 As earlier noted, contracts for the provision of financial services are excluded from the scope of the 2013 Regulations,[842] but the earlier Financial Services (Distance Marketing) Regulations 2004[843] make very broadly similar provision for distance contracts for the provision of financial services[844] as the 2013 Regulations make in relation to other contracts. So, a "distance contract" under the 2004 Regulations is defined as:

> "... any contract concerning one or more financial services concluded between a supplier and a consumer under an organised distance sales or service-provision scheme run by the supplier or by an intermediary, who, for the purpose of that contract, makes exclusive use of one or more means of distance communication up to and including the time at which the contract is concluded."[845]

The 2004 Regulations impose information requirements on the supplier of the service which are similar to those under the 2013 Regulations though tailored to suit the subject matter of the contracts, and this information is to be provided "in a clear and comprehensible manner appropriate to the means of distance communication used".[846] However, certain categories of financial service contracts are excluded from these pre-contractual requirements[847] and the 2004 Regulations also exclude more generally from their principal provisions governing information duties and the consumer's right to cancel some contracts for and supplies of financial services where equivalent provision is made by other regimes, notably, contracts and supplies made by a supplier who is an "authorised person, the making or performance of which constitutes or is part of a regulated activity carried on by him" within the meaning of the Financial Services and Markets Act 2000[848] and those made by suppliers established in another State within the EEA where the law of that State regulates the contract or supply in accordance with the 2002 Directive.[849] The 2002 Regulations' provisions on cancellation by the consumer are also similar to those under the 2013 Regulations (though they make a series of detailed exceptions to the availability of the consumer's right to cancel[850]) and so provide that the consumer may cancel within a period of 14 days from the conclusion of the contract, unless the supplier has failed to provide information as they require, in which case the period is 14 days after the day of supply of that information.[851] The effect of an exercise of the right to cancel is that the notice of cancellation terminates the contract at the time when it is given,[852] with a consequential refund of monies paid by the consumer subject to a charge made by the supplier in respect of a "service actually provided by the supplier in accordance with the contract".[853] Equally, the consumer must refund any sums or return any property transferred to him or her under the contract.[854] The 2004 Regulations specify that any contract term which is inconsistent with their application is void[855] and that they will apply notwithstanding any choice of applicable law of a State which is not an EEA State if the contract or supply has a close connection with the territory of an EEA State.[856] The 2004 Regulations entrust their enforcement to the Financial Conduct Authority,[857] the Competition and Markets Authority and local weights and measure authorities, depending on the nature of the alleged breach,[858] and this enforcement may include an application for an injunction.[859]

[842] 2013 Regulations reg.6(1)(b), above, para.38-076.

[843] SI 2004/2095, implementing Directive 2002/65/EC concerning the distance marketing of consumer financial services [2002] O.J. L271/16 ("2002 Directive"), cf. above, para.38-027. On IP completion day (on which see above, para.38-004 and Vol.I, paras 1-014 et seq.), the 2004 Regulations (arts 2, 4, 7, 8, 16 and Sch.1) are due to be amended in particular so as to address issues arising in relation to distance contracts for financial services made by suppliers in the EEA and consumers in the UK and in relation to financial services supplied by such suppliers to consumers in the UK: see Financial Services (Distance Marketing) (Amendment and Savings Provisions) (EU Exit) Regulations 2019 (SI 2019/574) (art.1(3)'s reference to Pt 3's amendments coming into force on "exit day" must be read as referring to "IP completion day": European Union (Withdrawal Agreement) Act 2020 s.39(1), Sch.5 para.1) and see above, para.38-004 and Vol.I, paras 1-014 et seq.). See in particular reg.4 as so amended, noted below.

[844] "Financial service" means any service of a banking, credit, insurance, personal pension, investment or payment nature: 2004 Regulations reg.2(1).

[845] 2004 Regulations reg.2(1) "distance contract". In *KH v Sparkasse Sudholstein* (C-639/18) EU:C:2020:477 at paras 25–34 the CJEU held that an agreement for a new interest rate amending an existing loan agreement with a fixed interest rate without either extending the term of the loan or altering its amount and doing so under a term in the existing loan agreement which provided for the agreement of such an amendment or, failing such agreement, for the application of a variable rate of interest does not count as a "contract concerning financial services" as it came within the qualification in art.1(2) of the 2002 Directive (implemented by the 2004 Regulations reg.5(1)) governing "an initial service agreement followed by successive operations or a series of separate operations of the same nature performed over time". In doing so, the CJEU held (at para.27) that "the characteristic obligation of [a credit agreement] is the actual granting of the sum loaned, while the borrower's obligation to repay that

sum is merely a consequence of the performance of the service by the lender", relying on *Kareda v Benko* (C-249/16) EU:C:2017:472 at para.41 to this effect in the context of the Regulation (EU) 1215/2012 art.7(1) (the Brussels I Regulation).

846 2004 Regulations reg.7 especially reg.7(2) and Sch.1. A restricted range of information is required where a financial services distance contract is also a contract for payment services to which the Payment Services Regulations 2017 apply: reg.7(1A) and reg.8(1A) as amended by the Payment Services Regulations 2017 (SI 2017/752) (in force generally January 13, 2018).

847 2004 Regulations reg.7(6) and (7) (consumer credit agreements and authorised non-business overdraft agreements).

848 2004 Regulations reg.4(2) referring to regs 7–11, 15 (with the qualifications made by reg.4(5)). Regulation 4(3) disapplies the 2004 Regulations regs 7 and 8 (i.e. the main information requirements) as regards contracts made by a supplier who is an "appointed representative" within the meaning of s.39(2) of the Financial Services Markets Act 2000, where the making or performance of that contract constitutes or is part of a regulated activity within the meaning of s.22 of the 2000 Act (apart from an "exempt regulated activity" within the meaning of s.325(2) of that Act) carried on by the supplier, with similar exclusions as regards supplies by such persons as regards reg.15 (which concerns unsolicited services). Regulation 4(4) makes the same exclusions as regards contracts or supplies where the supplier is bound, etc. by "rules of a designated professional body which are equivalent to those regulations" and the making or performance of that contract or the supply constitutes or is part of an exempt regulated activity carried on by the supplier. Regulation 6(3) and (4) make certain saving provisions in respect of these exclusions.

849 2004 Regulations reg.4(1) referring to regs 7–14, 15. See further reg.4 more generally. On IP completion day (on which see above, para.38-004 and Vol.I, paras 1-014 et seq.), reg.4(1) and (6) are amended and new regs 4(1A)–4(1C) inserted: see Financial Services (Distance Marketing) (Amendment and Savings Provisions) (EU Exit) Regulations 2019 (SI 2019/574) reg.6. As a result, regs 7–11 do not apply in relation to any contract made between an EEA supplier contracting from an establishment in an EEA State and a consumer in the UK unless the EEA supplier is a payments supplier, a relevant EEA alternative investment fund manager ("AIFM"), or the operator, trustee or depositary of a relevant recognised scheme; regs 12 and 13 do not apply to such a contract unless the EEA supplier is an authorised person, or a payments supplier; and reg.15 does not apply in relation to any supply of financial services by an EEA supplier from an establishment in an EEA State to a consumer in the UK unless the EEA supplier is a payments supplier, a relevant EEA AIFM, or the operator, trustee or depositary of a relevant recognised scheme; reg.4(1C) defines "payments supplier" and AIFM for these purposes and reg.4(6) (as amended) defines "operator", "trustee", "depositary" and "relevant recognised scheme".

850 2004 Regulations reg.11, e.g. contract where the price of that service depends on fluctuations of the money market outside the supplier's control.

851 2004 Regulations regs 9 and 10.

852 2004 Regulations reg.9(2).

853 2004 Regulations reg.13, especially reg.13(3) and (6).

854 2004 Regulations reg.13(11) and (12).

855 2004 Regulations reg.16(1) reflecting 2002 Directive art.12(1).

856 2004 Regulations reg.16(3) reflecting 2002 Directive art.12(2). To this extent, the general rules in the Rome I Regulation are therefore qualified: Regulation (EC) 593/2008 on the law applicable to contractual obligations ("Rome I Regulation") on which see Vol.I, paras 30-018 et seq. On IP completion day (on which see above, para.38-004 and Vol.I, paras 1-014 et seq.) reg.16(3) is to be amended so as to provide that the 2004 Regulations apply despite any contract term which applies or purports to apply the law of a country other than the UK, if the contract or supply has a close connection with the UK or any part of the UK: see Financial Services (Distance Marketing) (Amendment and Savings Provisions) (EU Exit) Regulations 2019 (SI 2019/574) reg.9.

857 2004 Regulations reg.17.

858 2004 Regulations reg.17.

859 2004 Regulations reg.19. Further enforcement provisions are set out in regs 20–23.

### *(ii) Package Travel, Package Holidays, Package Tours and Linked Travel Arrangements*

#### Introduction

*Replace paragraph with:*

The Package Travel Directive 1990[860] (the "1990 Directive") made a series of "minimum harmonisation" requirements for the protection of consumers[861] and was implemented into UK law by the Package Travel, Package Holidays and Package Tours Regulations 1992[862] ("1992 Regulations"). However, the 1990 Directive was repealed and replaced by Directive (EU) 2015/2302 on package travel and linked travel arrangements,[863] and its new requirements are made on the general basis of "full harmonisation" of the laws of Member States.[864] In the case of the UK, the Package Travel and Linked Travel Arrangements Regulations 2018 were issued by the government (the "2018 Regulations") on May 24, 2018[865] and came into force generally on July 1, 2018 as required by the Directive.[866] The following paragraphs therefore continue to discuss the 1992 Regulations (implementing the 1990 Directive) but will then outline the provisions of the 2018 Regulations (which are themselves subject to amendment on IP completion day when the UK's leaving the EU comes into full effect).[866a] **38-137**

[860] Directive 90/314/EEC of 13 June 1990 on package travel, package holidays and package tours: [1990] O.J. L158/59.

[861] 1990 Directive art.8. On the nature of "minimum harmonisation" see above, para.38-022.

[862] SI 1992/3288.

[863] [2015] O.J. L326/1 ("2015 Directive"). Repeal of the 1990 Directive is with effect from July 1, 2018: 2015 Directive art.29.

[864] 2015 Directive art.4.

[865] The Package Travel and Linked Travel Arrangements Regulations 2018 (SI 2018/634).

[866] 2018 Regulations reg.1. See also the documents available at *https://www.gov.uk/government/consultations/updating-consumer-protection-in-the-package-travel-sector*, including Department of Business, Energy & Industrial Strategy, *Updating Consumer Protection in the Package Travel Sector, Government Response* (April 2018).

[866a] Below, para.38-142.

### (aa) Package Travel, Package Holidays and Package Tours Regulations 1992

*Replace footnote 867 with:*

#### Scope of the 1992 Regulations[867]

[867] As noted above, para.38-137, on the coming into force of the 2018 Regulations implementing the Package Travel Directive 2015, the 1992 Regulations (and their amending regulations) were revoked, but they continue to apply to contracts concluded before the commencement date of the new regulation, i.e. July 1, 2018: 2018 Regulations reg.37. **38-138**

#### Information, withdrawal and cancellation

*Replace footnote 880 with:*

[880] 1992 Regulations reg.13(1)–(2). Where the consumer has a right to reimbursement under the 1992 Regulations, he cannot claim reimbursement of the cost of his air ticket which forms part of this package under Regulation (EC) 261/2004 of February 11, 2004 establishing common rules on compensation and assistance to passengers in the event of denied boarding and of cancellation or of long delays in flights (reg.8(2) of which refers explicitly to the right to reimbursement arising under the 1990 Direc- **38-139**

tive), but he can claim compensation: *HQ v Aegean Airlines* (C-163/18) EU:C:2019:585 para.31; *Králová v Primera Air Scandinavia* (C-215/18) EU:C:2020:235 at paras 33–38: and on the 2004 Regulation generally see above, paras 35-049 et seq. The 2015 Directive is not referred to by art.8(2) of the 2004 Regulation and itself states (art.14(5)) that "any right to compensation or price reduction under this Directive shall not affect the rights of travellers under Regulation (EC) No 261/2004"; this is reflected in the 2018 Regulations reg.16(7) on which see below, para.38-146 (note).

## Liability for proper performance of the contract

*Replace paragraph with:*

38-140 The 1992 Regulations also make the organiser and retailer of a package:

> "... liable to the consumer for the proper performance of the obligations under the contract, irrespective of whether such obligations are to be performed by that other party or by other suppliers of services."[883]

The organiser and retailer are liable for "any damage caused" to the consumer as a result of the improper performance of the contract,[884] unless it is due neither to their own fault or to that of another supplier of services[885] because it is attributable to the consumer, or to other specified circumstances.[886] For this purpose, damages in respect of "damage" suffered by the consumer may include compensation for personal injuries and, following the position established at common law, physical discomfort and mental distress, including for disappointment and loss of enjoyment.[887] The Regulations provide that liability on this basis cannot be excluded in respect of personal injury or death, but liability for a term of the contract may limit the amount of compensation in respect of other damage unless the limitation is unreasonable.[888]

[883] 1992 Regulations reg.15(1). The contract must oblige the consumer to communicate to the supplier of the services concerned or to the organiser or retailer any failure in the services at the place where they are supplied: 1992 Regulations reg.15(9).

[884] "Improper performance" depends on the terms of the contract and in the absence of an assumption of an absolute obligation on the part of the supplier of the service, reasonable care will be required: *Hone v Going Places Ltd* [2001] EWCA Civ 947 at [15]–[16]; applied in *Evans v Kosmar Villa Holidays Plc* [2007] EWCA Civ 1003, [2008] 1 W.L.R. 297 at [21] and see *Committeri v Club Mediterranee SA* [2018] EWCA Civ 1889, [2019] I.L. Pr. 19 at [46], where it was held that liability arising from (French) national law implementing the 1990 Directive and therefore arising in respect of "the proper performance of the obligations arising from the contract" is contractual rather than non-contractual for the purposes of the EU private law instruments on applicable law, i.e. Regulation 593/2008 on the law applicable to contractual obligations ("Rome I") [2008] O.J. L177/6 (on which see Vol.I, paras 30-019 et seq.) and Regulation 864/2007 of the European Parliament and of the Council law applicable to non-contractual obligations ("Rome II Regulation") [2007] O.J. L199/40. See also *X v Kuoni Travel Ltd* [2018] EWCA Civ 938, [2018] 1 W.L.R. 3777 at [33]–[37] (express term accepting responsibility if "holiday arrangement" "is not of a reasonable standard", but act of electrician employee in guiding consumer through hotel grounds and sexually assaulting her was not part of the "holiday arrangements" and see further the following note).

[885] It has been held that the reasonable care of the service supplier must be judged by the standards of the place where the service is provided: *Lougheed v On the Beach Ltd* [2014] EWCA Civ 1538 at [16] applying *Wilson v Best Travel Ltd* [1993] 1 All E.R. 353 (which was decided at common law). In *X v Kuoni Travel Ltd* [2018] EWCA Civ 938 at [38], [40]–[48] a majority of the CA said obiter that an electrician employee of a hotel (which *was* a supplier of the service to the consumer) was not himself a "supplier" of a service within the meaning of reg.15(2) of the 1992 Regulations so as to allow the possible application of the defences to liability there contained nor within an express term accepting responsibility for holiday arrangements. The SC has referred questions on the proper interpretation of art.5(2) of the 1990 Directive (which reg.15(2) implements) to the CJEU regarding whether, in such a context, the defence in art.5(2) (second part of third alinea) can apply and, if so, by which criteria and on the application of "supplier of services" in such a context: [2019] UKSC 37 at [22] and [23] and (C-578/19) (reference for a preliminary ruling made July 30, 2019).

[886] 1992 Regulations reg.15(2) implementing 1990 Directive art.5(2).

[887] See *Milner v Carnival Plc* [2010] EWCA Civ 389, [2010] P.I.Q.R. Q3. For the common law position see *Jarvis v Swann Tours Ltd* [1973] Q.B.233; *Jackson v Horizon Holidays* [1975] 1 W.L.R. 1468

and see Vol.I, para.26-155. In *Leitner v Tui Deustchland GmbH & Co KG* (C-168/00) EU:C:2002:163, [2002] E.C.R. I-2631 the ECJ held that "damage" under the Package Travel Directive 1990 includes loss of enjoyment and therefore national laws must allow recovery for this type of loss in their national legislation implementing the Directive.

[888] 1992 Regulations reg.15(4)–(5). The contract may also provide for compensation to be limited in accordance with international conventions which govern the relevant services forming part of the package: reg.15(3).

### Enforcement

*Replace footnote 889 with:*

[889] Enterprise Act 2002 ss.210(6)(b) and (7), 212; Sch.13 Pt 1 para.4 (before July 1, 2018); Enterprise Act 2002 (Part 8 Community Infringements Specified UK Laws) Order 2003 (SI 2003/1374) Sch.1 para.3. On IP completion day, "Community infringements" are to be replaced by "Schedule 13 infringements" and the 1992 Regulations are to be included within the substituted Sch.13 of the 2002 Act to the extent to which the latter remain in force: Consumer Protection (Enforcement) (Amendment etc.) (EU Exit) Regulations 2019 (SI 2019/203) reg.3(20) and Sch. para.1 inserting new 2002 Act Sch.13 para.8. On this change more generally see above, para.38-133A. **38-141**

## (bb) Package Travel and Linked Travel Arrangements Regulations 2018

### Package Travel Directive 2015 and the 2018 Regulations

*Replace paragraph with:*

As earlier noted, the 1990 Directive was repealed and replaced by Directive (EU) 2015/2302 on package travel and linked travel arrangements.[892] A principal aim of this new directive was to adapt the protection for consumers in relation to package travel earlier required by the 1990 Directive in the light of major changes in the market, notably, as a result of the increasing importance of the internet as a medium through which travel services are made available.[893] As earlier noted, the UK government issued regulations for the implementation of the 2015 Directive in UK law, the Package Travel and Linked Travel Arrangements Regulations 2018 (the "2018 Regulations") which revoked the 1992 Regulations and which came into force generally on July 1, 2018,[894] applying to contracts made on or after that date.[895] The following paragraphs will outline the most significant of their features for the purposes of contract law, noting relevant amendments to be made on IP completion day when the UK's leaving the EU comes into full effect.[895a] **38-142**

[892] [2015] O.J. L326/1 ("2015 Directive"). Repeal of the 1990 Directive is with effect from July 1, 2018: 2015 Directive art.29.

[893] 2015 Directive recital 2.

[894] 2018 Regulations reg.1(2) (with the exception there noted).

[895] 2018 Regulations reg.1(2); reg.37(2) (preserving the 1992 Regulations in relation to contracts concluded under them before July 1, 2018).

[895a] On this see generally above, para.38-004 and Vol.I, paras 1-014 et seq. The amendments to the 2018 Regulations are made by the Package Travel and Linked Travel Arrangements (Amendment etc.) (EU Exit) Regulations 2018 (SI 2018/1367) (the reference in reg.1(1) to "exit day" must be read as referring to "IP completion day": European Union (Withdrawal Agreement) Act 2020 s.39(1), Sch.5 para.1). These amendments do not apply to a package travel contract nor a linked travel arrangement concluded before exit day: SI 2018/1367 reg.1(2) (the reference to "exit day" is due to be replaced with "IP completion day": Consumer Protection (Enforcement) (Amendment etc.) (EU Exit) Regulations 2020 (Draft) Pt 3 reg.5).

### Scope of the Regulations

*Replace footnote 901 with:*

[901] 2018 Regulations reg.2(1) "travel service"; cf. 2015 Directive art.3(1). On IP completion day (on **38-143**

which see above, para.38-004), the legislative definitions of "other motor vehicles" and "motorcycles" is to be changed so as to refer to UK regulations rather than to EU directives: SI 2018/1367 reg.3(a)(ii).

### Responsibility for the performance of the package

*Replace footnote 926 with:*

38-146 [926] 2018 Regulations reg.16(3) and (4); cf. 2015 Directive art.14(3) and above, para.38-340 under the 1992 Regulations. The 2018 Regulations reg.16(7) provides that any right to compensation or price reduction under these Regulations does not affect the rights of travellers under listed EU passenger rights legislation (defined in reg.2(1) and including Regulation (EC) 261/2004 on denied boarding) and the international conventions.

### Effectiveness of traveller's protection and enforcement

*Replace paragraph with:*

38-147 Part 5 of the 2018 Regulations makes provision for the effectiveness of the protection of travellers from the insolvency of the organisers of package travel and linked travel arrangements.[927] The Regulations make it an offence in an organiser or retailer of a package, or a facilitator of a linked travel arrangement, to fail in their respective duties of information and, in the case of the former, in respect of the content of the package travel contract, and in respect of certain failures as regards the traveller's insolvency protection.[928] The Regulations specify that local weights and measures authorities and the Civil Aviation Authority are the enforcement authorities for these purposes.[929] In addition, the Regulations substitute the 2015 Directive for the 1990 Directive in the list of instruments which may give rise to a "Community infringement" and so apply Pt 8 of the Enterprise Act 2002 for their purposes; and they substitute the 2018 Regulations as the regulations specified as the UK law giving effect to the 2015 Directive for these purposes.[930] Finally, the Regulations render any waiver or contractual arrangement purporting to restrict the application of the Regulations not binding on the traveller.[931]

[927] cf. 2015 Directive arts 17 to 18, and 19(1). 2018 Regulations regs 19–23 and 26–27 are subject to minor amendment on IP completion day by SI 2018/1367 regs 5–11.

[928] As regards package travel, see 2018 Regulations regs 5(5) (information); reg.7(12) (failure in respect of the content of the contract, etc.), and regs 19(9) and 25 (insolvency requirements); as regards linked travel arrangements, see reg.26(10) (information and insolvency requirements). See further regs 32–34 (due diligence defence, liability of persons other than the principal offender, and prosecution time limit).

[929] 2018 Regulations reg.31 (in Northern Ireland, the enforcement authority is the Department for the Economy in Northern Ireland).

[930] 2018 Regulations reg.38(3) referring to 2002 Act Sch.13 Pt 1 para.4; reg.38(7) amending the Enterprise Act 2002 (Part 8 Community Infringements Specified UK Laws) Order 2003 (SI 2003/1374) Sch.1. On IP completion day, "Community infringements" are to be replaced by "Schedule 13 infringements" and the 2018 Regulations are to be included for this purpose within the substituted Sch.13 of the 2002 Act to the extent to which the latter remain in force: Consumer Protection (Enforcement) (Amendment etc.) (EU Exit) Regulations 2019 (SI 2019/203) reg.3(20) and Sch. para.1 inserting new 2002 Act Sch.13 para.28. On this change more generally see above, para.38-133A.

[931] 2018 Regulations reg.30(2) and (3).

## *(iii) Timeshare and Related Contracts*

### Timeshare and related contracts

*Replace footnote 932 with:*

38-148 [932] SI 2010/2960. These regulations will be amended on IP completion day (on which see above, para.38-004 and Vol.I, paras 1-014 et seq.): Timeshare, Holiday Products, Resale and Exchange Contracts (Amendment etc.) (EU Exit) Regulations 2018 (SI 2018/1397) (the reference in reg.1 to "exit day" must be read as referring to "IP completion day": European Union (Withdrawal Agreement) Act 2020 s.39(1), Sch.5 para.1). The amendments (when in force) will not apply to contracts entered into before "exit day": reg.3 (the reference to "exit day" is due to be replaced with "IP completion day": Consumer Protection (Enforcement) (Amendment etc.) (EU Exit) Regulations 2020 (Draft) Pt 3 reg.6(2)). Where relevant, the effects of these amending regulations will be summarised in the notes to the following paragraphs.

## Information requirements

*Replace footnote 952 with:*

952 2010 Regulations reg.12(6)–(7). On IP completion day (on which see above, para.38-004 and Vol.I, paras 1-014 et seq.) reg.12(7) will be deleted and reg.12(6) amended by the Timeshare, Holiday Products, Resale and Exchange Contracts (Amendment etc.) (EU Exit) Regulations 2018 (SI 2018/1397) reg.2(3) so that reg.12(6) would require the information to be provided in English and to permit it, in addition, to be provided in another language. The 2018 Regulations reg.2(5)–(8) will make further amendments of the Standard Information Forms in Schs 1–4. On these amending regulations see above, para.38-149. **38-150**

## Formalities

*Replace footnote 962 with:*

962 2010 Regulations reg.17. On IP completion day, reg.17 will be much amended by the Timeshare, Holiday Products, Resale and Exchange Contracts (Amendment etc.) (EU Exit) Regulations 2018 (SI 2018/1397) reg.2(4) so as to require the information to be provided in English and to permit it to be provided in another language. On these amending regulations see above, para.38-149. **38-151**

## Exclusion by agreement or choice of law

*Replace paragraph with:*

The 2010 Regulations provide that a term of a "regulated contract"[980] is void to the extent that it purports to allow the consumer to waive the rights conferred on them by these Regulations.[981] Article 12 of the 2009 Directive makes overt provision for its application "in international cases", but in the scheme of the 2010 Regulations these special controls on choice of applicable law are given effect by reg.5's provisions specifying the "holiday accommodation contracts" to which the Regulations apply.[982] The background to this special provision is that under the Rome I Regulation, the contracts falling within the scope of the 2009 Directive[983] may fall under art.3's general provisions allowing choice of law and art.6's special provisions governing consumer contracts[984] or, where they do not, art.4's default provisions governing contracts even where (as in the case of timeshare contracts) they concern rights in rem in immovable property and tenancies.[985] In very broad terms, the 2009 Directive[986] (and so also the 2010 Regulations) seek to give consumers additional protection to that provided by the Rome I Regulation[987] so as to prevent the avoidance of their controls by choice of applicable law, in a similar way to the anti-avoidance provisions in the Unfair Terms in Consumer Contracts Directive 1993[988] and the Consumer Sales Directive 1999.[989] As a result, reg.5 provides that the 2010 Regulations apply to a "holiday accommodation contract"[990] in any one of three circumstances. First, where the contract is to any extent governed by the law of the United Kingdom, or of a part of the United Kingdom.[991] Secondly, where the contract is to any extent governed by the law of a country other than an EEA State, but the relevant accommodation[992] is in immovable property situated in an EEA State, and "the parties to the contract are to any extent subject to the jurisdiction of a court in the United Kingdom in relation to the contract".[993] And thirdly, where the contract is to any extent governed by the law of a country other than an EEA State, is not directly related to immovable property, and the trader carries on commercial or professional activities in the United Kingdom or **38-153** by any means directs such activities to the United Kingdom and the contract falls within the scope of those activities.[994] Finally, it would appear that an express choice of law clause in a contract falling within the scope of the 2010 Regulations may be assessed for its fairness under the general controls on unfair contract terms implementing the Unfair Terms in Consumer Contracts Directive 1993, i.e. the Consumer Rights Act 2015 Pt 2 (and formerly the Unfair Terms in Consumer Contracts Regulations 1999).[995]

[980] Above, para.38-149.

[981] 2010 Regulations reg.19.

[982] 2010 Regulations reg.5; "holiday accommodation contracts" are defined by reg.4. These two elements, together with the provisions in reg.6 excluding certain arrangements, are then put together for the definition of "regulated contract" by reg.3, as explained above, para.38-149.

[983] Regulation (EC) 593/2008 on the law applicable to contractual obligations ("Rome I Regulation") reg.6(4)(b) refers to the repealed Timeshare Directive 1994, but the 2009 Directive art.18 requires this reference to be construed as referring to the 2009 Directive.

[984] Rome I Regulation art.6(4)(b).

[985] Rome I Regulation art.4(1)(c) and (d) on which see Dicey, Morris and Collins, *The Conflict of Laws*, 15th edn (2012), Vol.II, paras 33-044, 33-047—33-048. On these provisions of the Rome I Regulation generally see Vol.I, para.30-103.

[986] 2009 Directive art.12(2).

[987] 2009 Directive recital 17.

[988] 1993 Directive art.6(2) below, paras 38-352 and 38-418.

[989] 1999 Directive art.7(2) below, para.38-533.

[990] Defined by 2010 Regulations regs 4 and 7–10, above, para.38-149.

[991] 2010 Regulations reg.5(1) and (2).

[992] Defined as "(i) the accommodation which is the subject of the contract, or (ii) in a case where a pool of accommodation is the subject of the contract, some or all of the accommodation in that pool": 2010 Regulations reg.5(5)(a).

[993] 2010 Regulations reg.5(1), (3) and (5)(b). On IP completion day (on which see above, para.38-004 and Vol.I, paras 1-014 et seq.) reg.5(3)(b) will be amended by the Timeshare, Holiday Products, Resale and Exchange Contracts (Amendment etc.) (EU Exit) Regulations 2018 (SI 2018/1397) reg.2(2) so as replace "an EEA State" with "the United Kingdom". On these amending regulations see above, para.38-149.

[994] 2010 Regulations reg.5(1), (4) and (5)(b). Reg.5(5)(b) is due to be amended by the Timeshare, Holiday Products, Resale and Exchange Contracts (Amendment etc.) (EU Exit) Regulations 2018 (SI 2018/1397) reg.2(2) so as replace "an EEA State" with "the United Kingdom". On these amending regulations see above, para.38-149.

[995] cf. *Verein für Konsumenteninformation v Amazon EU Sàrl* (C-191/15) July 28, 2016, see below, para.38-321.

## Enforcement

*Replace footnote 1001 with:*

38-154 [1001] Enterprise Act 2002 (Part 8 Community Infringements Specified UK Laws) Order 2003 (SI 2003/1374) Sch.1 para.1. On IP completion day (on which see above, para.38-004 and Vol.I, paras 1-014 et seq.), "Community infringements" will be replaced by "Schedule 13 infringements" and the 2010 Regulations are to be included within the substituted Sch.13 of the 2002 Act for this purpose: Consumer Protection (Enforcement) (Amendment etc.) (EU Exit) Regulations 2019 (SI 2019/203) reg.3(20) and Sch. para.1 inserting new 2002 Act Sch.13 para.22. On this change more generally see above, para.38-133A.

### *(iv) Trader's Information Duties in Relation to ADR*

**EU law and ADR**

*Replace paragraph with:*

EU legislation has provided for the establishment of a European online dispute resolution (ODR) platform[1004] and has required Member States to ensure that ADR is available for consumer disputes by the "ADR Directive",[1005] although the legislation does not make ADR mandatory.[1006] The European ODR platform was established by the EU Commission and is available to allow consumers and traders in the EU and the EFTA states to resolve disputes relating to the online purchase of goods and services without going to court,[1007] although it will cease to be available to traders and consumers in the UK on IP completion day when the UK's leaving the EU comes into full effect.[1007a] As part of the wider scheme, the ADR Directive requires Member States to impose on traders a duty to inform consumers as to the availability of ADR.[1008] Following the scope of the Directive as a whole, this requirement applies to domestic and cross-border disputes[1009] relating to contractual obligations stemming from sales contracts or service contracts[1010] between traders and consumers, where the consumer claims against the trader.[1011] Implementing this requirement in the UK, the Alternative Dispute Resolution for Consumer Disputes (Competent Authorities and Information) Regulations 2015 (the "2015 Regulations") distinguish between two situations.[1012] First, where a trader is obliged to use ADR services provided by an ADR entity or EU listed body[1013] under an enactment, the rules of a trade association to which the trader belongs, or a term of a contract, the trader must provide the name and website address of the ADR entity or EU listed body on its website, if it has one and in the "general terms and conditions of sales or service contracts between the trader and a consumer where they exist".[1014] Secondly, where a trader has exhausted its internal complaint handling procedure when considering a complaint from a consumer relating to a sales contract or a service contract: **38-155**

"... the trader must inform the consumer, on a durable medium:

(a) that the trader cannot settle the complaint with the consumer;
(b) of the name and website address of an ADR entity or EU listed body which would be competent to deal with the complaint, should the consumer wish to use alternative dispute resolution; and
(c) whether the trader is obliged, or prepared, to submit to an alternative dispute resolution procedure operated by that ADR entity or EU listed body."[1015]

These requirements apply in addition to any information requirements applicable to traders regarding out-of-court redress procedures contained in any other enactment.[1016] The 2015 Regulations make similar provision as to the provision of information by online traders and online marketplaces to consumers regarding the ODR platform.[1017] In addition to these information requirements, the ADR Directive makes other requirements in relation to consumer contracts which are implemented by the 2015 Regulations, including that Member States must ensure that an agreement between a consumer and a trader to submit complaints to an ADR entity is not binding on the consumer if it was concluded before the dispute has materialised and if it has the effect of depriving the consumer of his right to bring an action before the courts for the settlement of the dispute.[1018]

[1004] Regulation (EU) 524/2013 of 21 May 2013 on online dispute resolution for consumer disputes

(Regulation on consumer ODR) [2013] O.J. L165/1. On IP completion day (on which see generally above, para.38-004 and Vol.1, paras 1-014 et seq.), this regulation is to be revoked: Consumer Protection (Amendment etc.) (EU Exit) Regulations 2018 (SI 2018/1326) reg.10 (reg.1(3)'s reference to reg.10's coming into force on "exit day" must be read as referring to IP completion day: European Union (Withdrawal Agreement) Act 2020 s.39(1), Sch.5 para.1).

1005 Directive 2013/11/EU of 21 May 2013 on alternative dispute resolution for consumer disputes [2013] O.J. L165/63.

1006 ADR Directive art.1 referring to the availability of ADR procedures to consumers "on a voluntary basis", though adding that the Directive is without prejudice to national legislation making participation in such procedures mandatory provided that such legislation does not prevent the parties from exercising their right of access to the judicial system: see further *Menini and Rampanelli v Banco Populare Societa Cooperativa* (C-75/16) of June 14, 2017 at paras 45 et seq.

1007 See *https://ec.europa.eu/consumers/odr/main/?event=main.home.show.*

1007a As a result, traders and consumers in the UK will no longer be able to use the Online Dispute Resolution platform from January 1, 2021: Department for Business, Energy & Industrial Strategy Guidance, *Consumer Rights and Business: Changes from 1 January 2021, https://www.gov.uk/guidance/consumer-rights-and-business-changes-from-1-january-2021.* For IP completion day, see above, para.38-004 and Vol.I, paras 1-014 et seq.

1008 ADR Directive art.13.

1009 ADR Directive art.2(1).

1010 "Sales contracts" and "services contracts" are defined by the ADR Directive art.4(1)(c) and (d) (as implemented by the 2015 Regulations reg.5). Recital 16 explains that this means that the Directive applies to disputes between traders and consumers "in all economic sectors, other than the exempted sectors" and includes "disputes arising from the sale or provision of digital content for remuneration".

1011 ADR Directive recital 16; art.2 (with exclusions there made), especially art.2(2)(g).

1012 Alternative Dispute Resolution for Consumer Disputes (Competent Authorities and Information) Regulations 2015 (SI 2015/542) reg.19 (as amended by the Alternative Dispute Resolution for Consumer Disputes (Amendment) Regulations 2015 (SI 2015/1392)) (the amendment came into force on July 9, 2015 but could not take effect until the commencement of SI 2015/542 reg.19 on October 1, 2015). On IP completion day (on which see generally above, para.38-004 and Vol.I, paras 1-014 et seq.), the 2015 Regulations are due to be amended by the Consumer Protection (Amendment etc.) (EU Exit) Regulations 2018 (SI 2018/1326) reg.9. The following notes will refer to amendments made by reg.9 where relevant to the present discussion.

1013 2015 Regulations (as amended by SI 2015/1392) reg.4 provides that an "ADR entity" means a person whose name appears on a list maintained by the Secretary of State or other person specified by the Regulations (reg.5 referring to Sch.1 Pt 1 col.1; Pt 2) as satisfying a list of requirements: reg.9(4), 10 and Sch.3. An "EU listed body" means a person, other than an ADR entity, whose name appears on a list referred to in the ADR Directive art.20(2): 2015 Regulations reg.5. On IP completion day (on which see above, para.38-004 and Vol.I, paras 1-014 et seq.), the reference to EU listed bodies will be deleted: Consumer Protection (Amendment etc.) (EU Exit) Regulations 2018 (SI 2018/1326) reg.9(3)(b).

1014 2015 Regulations reg.19(1). On IP completion day (on which see above, para.38-004 and Vol.I, paras 1-014 et seq.), the references in reg.19 to "EU listed body" will be deleted: Consumer Protection (Amendment etc.) (EU Exit) Regulations 2018 (SI 2018/1326) reg.9(14).

1015 2015 Regulations reg.19(2). On IP completion day (on which see above, para.38-004 and Vol.I, paras 1-014 et seq.), the references in reg.19 to EU listed bodies will be deleted: Consumer Protection (Amendment etc.) (EU Exit) Regulations 2018 (SI 2018/1326) reg.9(14).

1016 2015 Regulations reg.19(3).

1017 2015 Regulations reg.19A (as amended by SI 2015/1392) (in force January 9, 2016). For the European ODR platform, see above in this paragraph. On IP completion day (on which see above, para.38-004 and Vol.I, paras 1-014 et seq.), reg.19A will be deleted in keeping with the revocation of the ODR Regulation itself: Consumer Protection (Amendment etc.) (EU Exit) Regulations 2018 (SI 2018/1326) regs 9(15) and 10.

1018 ADR Directive art.10(1); 2015 Regulations reg.14B (inserted by SI 2015/1392 reg.2(8)) (in force on July 9, 2015). On IP completion day (on which see above, para.38-004 and Vol.I, paras 1-014 et seq.), reg.14B will be amended so as to omit the words "cross-border dispute or" in each place they occur and thereby restrict its scope to "domestic disputes" as defined by reg.5 of the 2015 Regulations: Consumer Protection (Amendment etc.) (EU Exit) Regulations 2018 (SI 2018/1326) reg.9(10).

## (v) *Contracts Concluded by Electronic Means*

### Summary

*Replace paragraph with:*

The Electronic Commerce (EC Directive) Regulations 2002 (the "Electronic Commerce Regulations 2002")[1018a] reg.9 (implementing art.10 of the Electronic Commerce Directive 2000[1019]) imposes a duty on providers of information society services, such as selling goods online,[1020] to provide information on specified matters before the conclusion of contract to be concluded by electronic means.[1021] The matters on which information must be provided "in a clear, comprehensible and unambiguous manner" relate to the different technical steps to follow to conclude the contract, whether or not the concluded contract will be filed by the service provider and whether it will be accessible, the technical means for identifying and correcting input errors prior to the placing of an order, and the languages offered for the conclusion of the contract[1022]; the provider must make available[1023] any terms and conditions applicable to the contract to recipients in a way which allows them to store and reproduce them[1024]; and it must also indicate any relevant code of conduct to which it subscribes and how they may be accessed.[1025] The provider must acknowledge receipt of any order without undue delay and by electronic means and must make available[1026] the technical means which allow the identification and correction of input errors.[1027] With the exception of the duty to make terms and conditions available, these duties do not apply to "contracts concluded exclusively by exchange of electronic mail or by equivalent individual communications".[1028] Moreover, while the duties apply for the benefit of all "recipients" of the service, they may be excluded by agreement only where the parties are not consumers.[1029] The Electronic Commerce Regulations 2002 provide that the duties which they impose on service providers in this respect[1030] shall be enforceable by the recipient of the service in the tort of breach of statutory duty[1031] and that, in the case of a failure in the service provider to make available means of allowing a person to identify and correct input elements, a person may rescind any contract made, unless a court orders otherwise on the former's application.[1032] Apart from the last provision, the service provider's failures to perform these duties are not stated as affecting the validity of any contract made, but as a "Community infringement" they may attract enforcement measures under Pt 8 of the Enterprise Act 2002.[1033] **38-156**

[1018a] SI 2002/2013. On IP completion day (on which generally see above, para.38-004 and Vol.I, paras 1-014 et seq.), the 2002 Regulations will be amended: Electronic Commerce (Amendment etc.) (EU Exit) Regulations 2019 (SI 2019/87) reg.3 (reg.1's reference to the 2019 Regulations coming into force on "exit day" must be read as referring to IP completion day: European Union (Withdrawal Agreement) Act 2020 s.39(1), Sch.5 para.1). The amendments to the 2002 Regulations affect some of the definitions in regs 2, 4–6, 10 and Sch. para.4 but do not affect regs 9, 11, 13 and 15 of the 2002 Regulations whose effect is noted in this paragraph. They do not change the definitions in reg.2(1) of "service provider" and "information society services", but they do change the definition of "established service provider" as noted below.

[1019] Directive 2000/31/EC on certain legal aspects of information society services, in particular electronic commerce, in the Internal Market ("Directive on electronic commerce") [2000] O.J. L178/17.

[1020] Electronic Commerce Regulations 2002 (SI 2002/2013) reg.2(1) defines "service provider" as "any person providing an information society service" and explains "information society services" by reference to the 2000 Directive art.2(a) (which itself refers to Directive 98/34/EC laying down a procedure for the provision of technical standards and regulations [1998] O.J. L204/37 art.1(2)) and recital 17's explanation that it covers "any service normally provided for remuneration, at a distance, by means of electronic equipment for the processing (including digital compression) and storage of data, and at the individual request of a recipient of a service", though recital 18 further explains, inter alia, that "[i]nformation society services span a wide range of economic activities which take place on-line" and "are not solely restricted to services giving rise to on-line contracting but also, in so far as they represent an economic activity, extend to services which are not remunerated by those who receive them, such as those offering on-line information or commercial communications, or those providing tools allowing for search, access and retrieval of data". On this see *Criminal Proceedings against Vanderborght* (C-339/15) of May 4, 2017 at paras 37 to 50 (advertising relating to dentistry services by means of a website created by a member of a regulated profession constitutes a commercial communication which is part of an information society service or which constitutes such a service for the purposes of art.8 of the 2000 Directive). After IP completion day (on which see above, para.38-004 and Vol.I, paras 1-014 et seq.), the definitions of "service provider" and "information society services" remain intact, but the definition of an "established service provider" is amended: 2002 Regulations reg.2(1) as amended by SI 2019/87 reg.3(2)(b).

[1021] SI 2002/2013 reg.9. Regulations 6–8 impose other requirements on society service providers: to make available general information (such as the name of the provider, geographical address, etc.) in a form which is "easily, directly and permanently accessible"; to ensure the clarity of commercial communications provided; and to ensure that unsolicited commercial communications sent by electronic mail are clearly and unambiguously identifiable as such as soon as it is received.

[1022] Electronic Commerce Regulations 2002 reg.9(1).

[1023] On this concept cf. above, para.38-091.

[1024] Electronic Commerce Regulations 2002 reg.9(3). This requirement may be enforced by court order: reg.14.

[1025] Electronic Commerce Regulations 2002 reg.9(2).

[1026] On this concept cf. above, para.38-091.

[1027] Electronic Commerce Regulations 2002 reg.11(1) and (2).

[1028] Electronic Commerce Regulations 2002 reg.9(4) and 11(3).

[1029] Electronic Commerce Regulations 2002 reg.9(1) and (2), and 11(1).

[1030] i.e. under Electronic Commerce Regulations 2002 regs 6–8, 9(1) and 11(1)(a).

[1031] Electronic Commerce Regulations 2002 reg.13.

[1032] Electronic Commerce Regulations 2002 reg.15 referring to the duty in reg.11(1)(b).

[1033] Enterprise Act 2002 s.210(6) and 212; Sch.13 Pt 1 para.9; Enterprise Act 2002 (Part 8 Community Infringements Specified UK Laws) Order 2003 (SI 2003/1374) Sch.1 para.1 (2002 Regulations regs 6, 7, 8, 9 and 11 as "specified UK laws"). On these enforcement powers see above, paras 38-133—38-134. On IP completion day (on which see above, para.38-004 and Vol.I, paras 1-014 et seq.), "Community infringements" are to be replaced by "Schedule 13 infringements" and the Electronic Commerce Regulations 2002 regs 6–9 and 11 are included within the substituted Sch.13 of the 2002 Act for this purpose: Consumer Protection (Enforcement) (Amendment etc.) (EU Exit) Regulations 2019 (SI 2019/203) reg.3(20) and Sch. para.1 inserting new 2002 Act Sch.13 para.11. On this change more generally see above, para.38-133A.

## 5. UNFAIR COMMERCIAL PRACTICES AND THE CONSUMER'S RIGHTS TO REDRESS

## (a) Introduction

### Legislative history

*Replace footnote 1034 with:*

38-157 [1034] SI 2008/1277. In the following the "2008 Regulations" refers to SI 2008/1277 as amended principally by SI 2014/870 in contrast to the "2008 Regulations (as issued)", which refers to the 2008 Regulations before their amendment in 2014. On IP completion day (on which see above, para.38-004 and Vol.I, paras 1-014 et seq.), the 2008 Regulations will be subject to minor amendments which will be noted where relevant: Consumer Protection (Amendment etc.) (EU Exit) Regulations 2018 (SI 2018/1326) reg.6.

## (b) The Unfair Commercial Practices Directive 2005

### General

*Replace footnote 1041 with:*

1041 [2005] O.J. L149/22. Directive (EU) 2019/2161 of the European Parliament and of the Council of 27 November 2019 ... as regards the better enforcement and modernisation of Union consumer protection rules [2019] O.J. L328/7 ("Directive (EU) 2019/2161") art.3 makes significant amendment to the 2005 Directive, but the 2019 Directive must be implemented on November 28, 2021 (i.e. after IP completion day) and as a result the UK is not required to do so (see above, para.38-004 and Vol.I, paras 1-014 et seq.), though it is possible that the UK may nevertheless adopt some of the changes required by the 2019 Directive either under an agreement between the UK and the EU as to their future relationship or simply on their merits. The most significant amendments to the 2005 Directive made by the 2019 Directive (by arts 3(5) and (6)) concern redress (new 2005 Directive art.11a and see below, para.38-175A) and penalties (replacement art.13 of the 2005 Directive). The 2019 Directive arts 3(3) and 3(4) amend 2005 Directive art.6 (misleading actions) and art.7 (misleading omissions), and art.3(7) adds further examples of "commercial practices which are in all cases considered unfair" in Annex I to the 2005 Directive. On the 2005 Directive as enacted see in particular the essays in Collins (ed.) *The Forthcoming EC Directive on Unfair Commercial Practices, Contract, Consumer and Competition Law Implications* (2004) and in Weatherill and Bernitz (eds), *The Regulation of Unfair Commercial Practices under EC Directive 2005/29, New Rules and New Techniques* (2007). **38-159**

### Scope of the 2005 Directive

*Replace paragraph with:*

**38-160** For present purposes, there are two important aspects of the scope of the Directive. First, it applies to "unfair business-to-consumer commercial practices ... before, during and after a commercial transaction in relation to a product".[1045] As noted by the Court of Justice of the EU, the Directive gives a "particularly wide definition"[1046] to "business-to-consumer commercial practices" for this purpose, as this refers to:

> "... any act, omission, course of conduct or representation, commercial communication including advertising and marketing, by a trader directly connected with the promotion, sale or supply of a product to consumers."[1047]

A "product" is also understood very broadly, as it means "any goods or service including immovable property, rights and obligations".[1048] Overall, therefore, a good deal of what traders do in relation to the conclusion and performance of contracts with consumers falls within the scope of the 2005 Directive. On the other hand, secondly, the 2005 Directive provides that it is "without prejudice to contract law and, in particular, to the rules on the validity, formation or effect of a contract".[1049] As a result, the national, as well as EU,[1050] legal rules of "contract law" are not affected by the 2005 Directive and this means, in particular, that national contract laws are protected from the potential impact of the Directive's full harmonisation. For this purpose, the reference "in particular" to the rules on the validity, formation or effect of a contract strongly suggest that "contract law" refers to rules governing the relative rights and obligations of parties to a contract.[1051] On the other hand, this also means that Member States are free in principle to give "contract law" significance to some or all of the prohibitions of unfair commercial practices as the Directive understands them.[1051a]

1045 2005 Directive art.3(1).

1046 *Total Belgium & Galatea* (C-261/07 and C-299/07) EU:C:2009:244 at [49].

1047 2005 Directive art.2(d). A "commercial practice" is an activity which is "commercial" in nature, i.e. it originates with a "trader" (on which see above, paras 38-050—38-058 and esp. at para.38-055) and constitutes "an act, omission, course of conduct or commercial communication 'directly connected with the promotion, sale or supply of a product to consumers'": *RLvS Verlagsgesellschaft mbH v Stuttgarter Wochenblatt GmbH* (C-391/12) EU:C:2013:669 of October 17, 2013 para.37; *Komisiaza zashtita na potrebeitelite v Kamenova* (C-105/17) EU:C:2018:808 of October 4, 2018 at para.42. The CJEU has explained that "although commercial practices are closely linked to a commercial transaction involving a product, they are nevertheless not confused with the product which is the subject of that transaction": *Openbarr Ministerie v Kirschstein* (C-393/17) EU:C:2019:563 of July 4, 2019 at para.42. A "commercial practice" covers "any measure taken in relation not only to the conclusion of a contract but also to its performance, and in particular the measures taken in order to obtain payment for the product": *UAB "Gelvora" v Valstybinė vartotoų teisių apsaugos tarnyba* (C-357/16) of July 20, 2017 at para.21. The CJEU further held that where the claims assigned to a debt collection agency originated in the supply of a service (the provision of credit at interest), its debt recovery activities may be regarded as a "product" within the meaning of art.2(c) of the 2005 Directive and may constitute an unfair "commercial practice" as the measures which it adopts are liable to influence the consumer's decision in respect of payment of the product: C-357/16 at paras 21–25. For this purpose, the fact that the existence of the debt was confirmed by a court decision and that that decision was passed for enforcement to a bailiff is without consequence: C-357/16 at para.31. By contrast, in *Openbarr Ministerie v Kirschstein* (C-393/17) of July 4, 2019 at paras 45–46, the CJEU held that a national rule (there legislation criminalising the award of degrees of bachelor or master etc. without the required authorisation) which aims to determine the operator who is authorised to provide a service in a commercial transaction without directly regulating the practices which the operator may use to promote or dispose of the sales of that service does not relate to a commercial practice in direct connection with the provision of that service within the meaning of art.2(d) of the 2005 Directive: *Openbarr Ministerie v Kirschstein* (C-393/17) at paras 45–46.

[1048] 2005 Directive art.2(c). On the CJEU's interpretation of "product" to include practices in which a debt collection agency engages to recover the debt, see *UAB "Gelvora" v Valstybinė vartotoų teisių apsaugos tarnyba* (C-357/16) of July 20, 2017 noted in the previous note. Cf. the amended definition of "product" to be introduced at the EU level by Directive (EU) 2019/2161 art.3(1)(a) as "any good or service including immovable property, *digital service and digital content*, as well as rights and obligations" (emphasis added)). On the 2019 Directive, see above, para.38-159 (note).

[1049] Directive 2005/29/EC art.3(2), on which see Whittaker in Weatherill and Bernitz (eds), *The Regulation of Unfair Commercial Practices under EC Directive 2005/29, New Rules and New Techniques* (2007), Ch.8. Art.3(3), (7)–(10) of the 2005 Directive contains further matters in respect of which the Directive is "without prejudice", for example, "any conditions of establishment or of authorisation regimes, or to the deontological codes of conduct or other specific rules governing regulated professions in order to uphold high standards of integrity on the part of the professional", on which see *Criminal Proceedings against Vanderborght* (C-339/15) of May 4, 2017 at paras 26–30.

[1050] 2005 Directive recital 9.

[1051] Whittaker, in Weatherill and Bernitz (eds), *The Regulation of Unfair Commercial Practices under EC Directive 2005/29, New Rules and New Techniques* (2007) and cf. above, para.38-063 for a similar understanding of "contract law" for the purposes of the Consumer Rights Directive 2011 art.3(5).

[1051a] It should be noted, however, that Directive (EU) 2019/2161 art.3(5) imposes a new requirement to create rights for redress for consumers in respect of unfair commercial practices: see below, para.38-175A. On the 2019 Directive, see above, para.38-159 (note).

## A transitional period for "minimum harmonisation" legislation

*Replace paragraph with:*

**38-162** On the other hand, art.3(5) of the 2005 Directive protected from the force of its "full harmonisation" national legal prohibitions of business-to-consumer commercial practices which were "more restrictive or prescriptive" than the 2005 Directive and which implemented the requirements of EU "minimum harmonisation" legislation, but only where this was already provided by national law for the protection of consumers at the time of the coming into force of the 2005 Directive and only for a transitional period of six years, ending on June 11, 2013.[1056] This means, therefore, that, after this date, national legal provisions which prohibit the use or recommendation for use of unfair terms *beyond* the requirements of minimum harmonisation directives *without* an evaluation of the fairness of that "commercial practice" within the meaning of the 2005 Directive are inconsistent with the 2005 Directive; in particular, national law is not entitled to add to the list of commercial practices provided by Annex 1 of the 2005 Directive which "shall in all circumstances be regarded as unfair".[1057] As will be seen in relation to the regulation of unfair contract terms under the Consumer Rights Act 2015, the relationship which the 2005 Directive envisages between its own fully harmonised requirements and other more particular, minimum harmonisation directives can cause problems for national implementing measures which go beyond the controls which these directives require.[1058]

[1056] 2005 Directive art.3(5); *European Commission v Belgium* (C-421/12) of July 10, 2014 at [73]. This permission was subject to a condition that the measures were "essential to ensure that consumers are adequately protected against unfair commercial practices and must be proportionate to the attainment of this objective". This transitional period was not extended as was foreseen as possible by the 2005 Directive art.3(5), third sentence: EU Commission, First Report on the application of Directive 2005/29/EC of the European Parliament and of the Council of 11 May 2005 concerning unfair business-to-consumer commercial practices in the internal market, etc. COM(2013) 139 final, para.2.4 (stating that no such extension should be made). Reflecting their transitional character, Directive (EU) 2019/2161 art.3(2) revokes art.3(5) and (6) of the 2005 Directive and replaces them with provision allowing Member States to adopt "provisions to protect the legitimate interests of consumers with regard to aggressive or misleading marketing or selling practices in the context of unsolicited visits by a trader to a consumer's home or excursions organised by a trader with the aim or effect of promoting or selling products to consumers". On the 2019 Directive, see above, para.38-159 (note).

[1057] 2005 Directive art.5(5), recital 17; *Zentral sur Bekämpfung unlauteren Weebewerbs eV v Plus Warenhandelsgessellschaft mbH* (C-304/08) EU:C:2010:12, [2010] E.C.R. I-00217 at [45]; *Wamo BVBA v JBC NV* (C-288/10) EU:C:2011:443, [2011] E.C.R. I-5835 at [37]. Four additional examples of commercial practices unfair in all circumstances are added to the list in Annex I of the 2005 Directive by Directive (EU) 2019/2161 art.3(7), but as the 2019 Directive requires implementation by November 28, 2021 (i.e. after IP completion day), the UK is not required to do so unless this is agreed by the UK and EU as part of their future relationship: see above, para.38-159 (note) and on IP completion day above, para.38-004 and Vol.I, paras 1-014 et seq.

[1058] Below, paras 38-421—38-426.

### Enforcement

*Replace paragraph with:*

38-164 Following its broad declaration that "unfair commercial practices shall be prohibited",[1066] the 2005 Directive requires Member States to put in place "adequate and effective means" to enforce compliance with its provisions and to lay down penalties for the infringement of national provisions implementing its requirements.[1067] Moreover, the 2005 Directive adds itself to the list of legislation which attract the cross-border injunctive relief under the Consumer Injunctions Directive and the Regulation on Consumer Protection Co-operation.[1068]

[1066] 2005 Directive art.5(1).

[1067] 2005 Directive arts 11 and 13.

[1068] 2005 Directive art.16; Directive 98/27 on injunctions for the protection of consumers' interests [1998] O.J. L166/51 (itself repealed and replaced by Directive 2009/22/EC on injunctions for the protection of consumers' interests [2009] O.J. L110/30); Regulation (EC) 2006/2004 on cooperation between national authorities responsible for the enforcement of the consumer protection law [2004] O.J. L364/1. Regulation (EC) 2006/2004 was repealed and replaced with effect from January 17, 2020 by Regulation (EU) 2017/2394 of the European Parliament and of the Council of 12 December 2017 on cooperation between national authorities responsible for the enforcement of consumer protection laws and repealing Regulation (EC) No 2006/2004 O.J. L345/1. The significance of this addition is explained below, para.38-171. On the 2017 Regulation itself, see above, paras 38-133 et seq.

## (c) The General Scheme of the 2008 Regulations

*To the end of title, add new footnote 1068a:* 38-165

[1068a] The 2008 Regulations reg.27A(5)(b) and Sch.1 paras 8 and 23 are subject to minor amendment on IP completion day (on which see above, para.38-004 and Vol.I, paras 1-014 et seq.) by the Consumer

Protection (Amendment etc.) (EU Exit) Regulations 2018 (SI 2018/1326) reg.6 as noted where relevant in the notes to the following paragraphs.

## Faithful implementation of the 2005 Directive

*Replace footnote 1069 with:*

38-165 [1069] 2008 Regulations regs 3–7. The main definitional provisions are contained in reg.2. On the amendment of the 2005 Directive by Directive (EU) 2019/2161 art.3, see above, para.38-159 (note).

## "Commercial practice"

*Replace footnote 1076 with:*

38-166 [1076] The definition of "commercial practice" in reg.2(1) combines the definition of "business-to-consumer commercial practices" in art.2(d) of the 2005 Directive, with art.3(1)'s definition of the scope of the Directive, with the clarification that there is no need for a commercial transaction to have been made. In *Warwickshire CC v Halfords Autocentres Ltd* [2018] EWHC 3007 (Admin), [2019] 1 W.L.R. 3597 at [35]–[41] it was held that the requirement that an act, omission etc. be "directed connected with the promotion, sale or supply of a product to consumers" does not mean that a trader's action triggered by a test-purchase made by a trading standards officer could not be a "commercial practice" even though the *actual* transaction was not made with a "consumer" for the purposes of a prosecution of that trader under reg.9 for a "misleading action" within the meaning of reg.5.

## "Commercial practice" and isolated events

*Replace footnote 1097 with:*

38-167 [1097] [2013] EWCA Crim 818, above. In *Warwickshire CC v Halfords Autocentres Ltd* [2018] EWHC 3007 (Admin), it was accepted that the 2005 Directive (and therefore the 2008 Regulations) covers both isolated acts and repeated behaviour, referring both to *UPC Magyarország* (C-388/13) and *R. v X. Ltd* [2013] EWCA Crim 818 at [22] (quoted above) where Lewison L.J. accepted that a commercial practice can be derived from a single incident. On the changing significance on IP completion day of decisions of the CJEU for the interpretation of UK legislation derived from EU law by English courts, see Vol.I, para.1-017B.

## Other definitions

*Replace footnote 1099 with:*

38-168 [1099] 2008 Regulations reg.2(1) "product", which also makes special provision for this purpose for cases where a trader demands payment from a consumer in full or partial settlement of C's liabilities, where the "product" is to be treated as that full or partial settlement: 2008 Regulations reg.2(1A) and (1B). As will be explained, there are restrictions on the definition of "product" for the purposes of the consumer's rights to civil redress: 2008 Regulations regs 27C and 27D, below, para.38-176. The definition of "product" in the 2005 Directive is found in art.2(b) (though it will be amended by Directive 2019/2161 art.3(1)(a) as noted above, para.38-160 (note)).

## "Average consumer"

*Replace footnote 1112 with:*

38-169 [1112] And see *Criminal Proceedings against Canal Digital Denmark A/S* (C-611/14) at para.39. See also *R. (on the application of Cityfibre Ltd) v Advertising Standards Authority* [2019] EWHC 950 (Admin), esp. at [101]–[114].

## Criminal offences

*Replace paragraph with:*

38-170 Part 3 of the 2008 Regulations creates a series of criminal offences in traders where they knowingly or recklessly engage in a commercial practice which fails the general test of unfairness,[1113] where the practice constitutes a misleading action,[1114] a misleading omission[1115] or an aggressive commercial practice,[1116] or where it consists of a commercial practice prohibited in all circumstances.[1117] These crimes may, on summary conviction, lead to a fine not exceeding the statutory maximum, or, on conviction on indictment, to a fine or imprisonment for a term not exceeding two years or both.[1118] In principle, a person convicted of an offence under the Regulations may be ordered to pay compensation to the victim (the consumer),[1119] but this power has been interpreted as requiring evidence of loss and has in general been little used.[1120] The 2008 Regulations make further provision incidental to the creation of these offences,[1121] including for a defence of due diligence.[1122]

1113 2008 Regulations reg.8 (subject to the conditions there specified).

1114 2008 Regulations reg.9 referring to reg.5, but excluding the case foreseen by reg.5(3)(b). See *Warwickshire CC v Halfords Autocentres Ltd* [2018] EWHC 3007 (Admin), [2019] 1 W.L.R. 3597 on prosecutions after a test-purchase by a trading standards officer, above, para.38-166.

1115 2008 Regulations reg.10 referring to reg.6.

1116 2008 Regulations reg.11 referring to reg.7.

1117 2008 Regulations reg.12 referring to Sch.1, but excluding for these purposes the commercial practices foreseen by Sch.1 paras 11 ("advertorial") and 28 (including in an advertisement a direct exhortation to children to buy advertised products or persuade their parents or other adults to buy advertised products for them).

1118 2008 Regulations reg.13. Until March 12, 2015 the maximum fine available on summary conviction was £5,000 (level 5 on the standard scale), but on that date this was changed to an unlimited fine by the Legal Aid, Sentencing and Punishment of Offenders Act 2012 s.85.

1119 Powers of Criminal Courts (Sentencing) Act 2000 s.130(4). Section 130 and other relevant provisions of the 2000 Act are due to be repealed and replaced by the Sentencing Bill 2019-21 (HL Bill 105) Sch.28 para.1 (Lords' Second Reading, June 25, 2020). The main replacement provisions are contained in the 2019-21 Bill cll.133–135.

1120 Law Commission, Scottish Law Commission, *Consumer Redress for Misleading and Aggressive Practices* (2012) Law Com No.332; Scot Law Com No.226, Cm 8323 para.2.44, 2.46.

1121 2008 Regulations reg.14 (time limit for prosecution); reg.15 (offences committed by bodies of persons); reg.16 (offence due to the default of another person); reg.17 (due diligence defence); reg.18 (innocent publication of advertisement defence).

1122 2008 Regulations reg.17.

## Enforcement by authorities

*Replace paragraph with:*

Apart from these criminal offences, the 2008 Regulations are buttressed by two systems of enforcement of their prohibition of unfair commercial practices.[1122a] First, Pt 4 of the Regulations sets out a special scheme of enforcement, under which every weights and measures authority has a duty to enforce the regulations, and the CMA has a power to do so,[1123] in both cases taking into account the desirability of encouraging control of unfair commercial practices by such established means as it considers appropriate in all the circumstances.[1124] These enforcement authorities have the power to make test purchases and powers of entry and investigation.[1125] Secondly, the 2008 Regulations amended the Enterprise Act 2002 so as to include the 2005 Directive in the list of directives and regulations which give rise to a "Community infringement" and also to designate the 2008 Regulations as the specified UK law so as to apply Pt 8 of the 2002 Act for their purposes.[1126] As a result, where an infringement of the prohibition against unfair commercial practices by a trader harms the collective interest of consumers,[1127] an "enforcer" can apply to the court for an enforcement order, subject to the conditions set out earlier.[1128] The 2008 Regulations also provide that, where an enforcer has brought an application for an enforcement order under Pt 8 of the 2002 Act against a trader in respect of a **38-171** contravention of the requirements of the 2005 Directive, the court has a power to require that trader to provide evidence as to the accuracy of any factual claim made as part of a commercial practice by that trader.[1129] Where the trader fails to do so or fails to do so adequately, "the court may consider that the factual claim is inaccurate".[1130]

[1122a] Directive (EU) 2019/2161 art.3(6) replaces the 2005 Directive's brief art.13 on penalties with a more elaborate set of requirements, but as the 2019 Directive has to be implemented on November 28, 2021 (i.e. after IP completion day), the UK will not be required to do so unless as part of a wider agreement with the EU as to their future relationship: see above, para.38-004 and Vol.I, paras 1-014 et seq. On the other hand, in 2018 the then UK government announced its intention of introducing legislation to give civil courts the power to impose financial penalties for breaches of consumer law of up to 10 per cent of a firm's worldwide turnover which would broadly reflect a requirement in art.13(3) of the 2005 Directive as so amended: Department of Business, Energy & Industrial Strategy, *Modernising Markets, Consumer Green Paper* (April 2018), para.165.

[1123] 2008 Regulations reg.19(1) and (1A). In Northern Ireland, this duty is owed by Department of Enterprise, Trade and Investment in Northern Ireland. The duty to enforce does not extend to the consumer's rights to redress in Pt 4A of the Regulations: reg.19(1).

[1124] 2008 Regulations reg.19(4).

[1125] These powers were earlier contained in the 2008 Regulations regs 20–25, but as from October 1, 2015 (SI 2015/1630 art.3(h)) these provisions were revoked and replaced by more general provision in the Consumer Rights Act 2015 s.77, Sch.5 (para.10 of which refers to the enforcement of the 2008 Regulations reg.19(1) and (1A). Consumer Rights Act 2015 (Commencement No.3, Transitional Provisions, Savings and Consequential Amendments) Order 2015 (SI 2015/1630) art.5, Sch.2 para.115 subject to transitional provisions set out in art.8).

[1126] 2008 Regulations reg.26; Enterprise Act 2002 Sch.13 para.9C; Enterprise Act 2002 (Part 8 Community Infringements Specified UK Laws) Order 2003 (SI 2003/1374) Sch.1 para.1 as inserted by 2008 Regulations Sch.2 Pt 2 para.100. On IP completion day (on which see above, para.38-004 and Vol.I, paras 1-014 et seq.), "Community infringements" are to be replaced by "Schedule 13 infringements" and the 2008 Regulations are to be included within the substituted Sch.13 of the 2002 Act for this purpose: Consumer Protection (Enforcement) (Amendment etc.) (EU Exit) Regulations 2019 (SI 2019/203) reg.3(20) and Sch. para.1 inserting new 2002 Act Sch.13 para.19. On this change more generally see above, para.38-133A.

[1127] Enterprise Act 2002 ss.211(1)(c), 212(1). See above, para.38-133.

[1128] Enterprise Act 2002 ss.214–218 (as amended) and see above, paras 38-133—38-134.

[1129] Enterprise Act 2002 s.218A(1) and (2) as inserted by 2008 Regulations reg.27.

[1130] Enterprise Act 2002 s.218A(3) as inserted by 2008 Regulations reg.27.

## (d) The Rights to Civil Redress for Consumers

### *(i) Introduction*

#### No duty on court to raise issue of consumer's rights to redress

*In line 8, after "consumers), that Directive", replace "does" with:*

38-174 as enacted did

*Add new paragraph:*

38-175A **Rights to civil redress to be required by EU law** As was earlier noted, the 2005 Directive prohibited unfair commercial practices but it did not require Member States to create rights to civil redress for the consumers (or others) affected by them.[1153a] However, this position is set to change at the EU level on the coming into force of Directive (EU) 2019/2161 for the better enforcement and modernisation of Union consumer protection rules,[1153b] which requires the introduction of civil redress for consumers harmed by unfair commercial practices; this redress must include "compensation for damage suffered by the consumer and, where relevant, a price reduction or the termination of the contract" and it is further provided that these "remedies shall be without prejudice to the application of other remedies available to consumers under Union or national law".[1153c] Member States nevertheless retain a considerable discretion as to the availability and nature of these remedies as the new provision states that "Member States may determine the conditions for the application and effects of those remedies" and they "may take into account, where appropriate, the gravity and nature of the unfair commercial practice, the damage suffered by the consumer and other relevant circumstances".[1153d] However, the 2019 Directive must be implemented on November 28, 2021 (i.e. after IP completion day[1153e]) and as a result the UK is not required to implement its requirements unless it agrees to do so as part of any agreement with the EU as to their future relationship. If this were the case, or if the UK legislature were to choose to follow the new EU provision, it would require changes to the UK scheme of civil redress put in place by the (amended) 2008 Regulations as set out in the following paragraphs. In particular, while the UK scheme is restricted to two forms of unfair commercial practices (misleading actions and aggressive commercial practices[1153f]), the new EU requirement applies to all unfair commercial practices, thereby including misleading omissions, and practices unfair under the general test contained in the 2005 Directive.[1153g] Moreover, as just noted, the new EU provision requires that the remedies for consumers in respect of unfair commercial practices "shall be without prejudice to the application of other remedies available to consumers under Union or national law".[1153h] While under current UK law in general a consumer may claim under another a rule of law even though he has a "right to redress" under Pt 4A of the 2008 Regulations, this is not true of a claim for damages under s.2(1) of the Misrepresentation Act 1967.[1153i] It may be, therefore, that the amendment of the 2005 Directive may suggest to the UK legislator that it should change this position so as in particular to allow a consumer to opt freely between claiming damages under Pt 4A of the 2008 Regulations and under s.2(1) of the 1967 Act, subject only to the rule that the consumer may not recover double compensation.[1153j]

[1153a] Above, para.38-160.

[1153b] Directive (EU) 2019/2161 of the European Parliament and of the Council of 27 November 2019 ... as regards the better enforcement and modernisation of Union consumer protection rules [2019] O.J. L328/7 ("Directive (EU) 2019/2161") on which more generally see above, para.38-159 (note).

[1153c] Directive (EU) 2019/2161 art.3(5) (inserting a new art.11a in the 2005 Directive).

[1153d] 2005 Directive art.11a(1) as inserted by Directive (EU) 2019/2161 art.3(5).

[1153e] This is set at December 31, 2020: above, para.38-004 and see generally Vol.I, paras 1-014 et seq.

[1153f] Below, paras 38-176 et seq.

[1153g] 2005 Directive art.3(2) and (3) (the general test) and art.7 (misleading omissions).

[1153h] Directive (EU) 2019/2161 art.3(5) inserting new art.11a(1) in the 2005 Directive.

[1153i] Misrepresentation Act 1967 s.2(4) on which see below, para.38-208.

[1153j] 2008 Regulations reg.27L(2), below, para.38-204.

## *(ii) General Conditions for the Availability of the Rights to Redress*

### Introduction

*In line 8, after "action or aggressive", add:*

**38-176** commercial

### First condition: contract or payment

*In line 9, after "rather than with "contract law".", add new footnote 1161a:*

**38-177** [1161a] Above, para.38-160.

### False or deceptive information

*In line 6, after "information is factually correct", add new footnote 1177a:*

**38-180** [1177a] The requirement that the misleading action "deceives or is likely to deceive the average consumer" does not mean that a misleading action inherently requires dishonesty on the part of the trader as the requirement "concerns the *deceptive nature* of that practice vis-à-vis that average consumer": *Competition and Markets Authority v Care UK Health and Social Care Holdings Ltd* [2019] EWHC 2828 (Ch) at [29] (per Ms Kelyn Bacon QC). As no allegation of dishonesty was in issue, the CMA's enforcement proceedings under Pt 8 of the Enterprise Act 2002 did not for this reason have to be brought under CPR Pt 7, though this would be necessary where they involve "a substantial dispute of fact".

### The special cases

*Replace footnote 1191 with:*

**38-182** [1191] 2005 Directive art.6(2). Directive 2019/2161 art.3(3) will amend art.6(2) of the 2005 Directive so as to add a further special case, i.e. where a commercial practice involves "any marketing of a good, in one Member State, as being identical to a good marketed in other Member States, while that good has significantly different composition or characteristics, unless justified by legitimate and objective factors". However, as the 2019 Directive requires implementation on November 28, 2021 (i.e. after IP completion day), the UK is not in principle required to implement the change: on Directive 2019/2161 see above, para.38-159 (note).

### Misleading omissions

*In line 1, after "Regulation 6 of the 2008 Regulations", add new footnote 1210a:*

**38-185** [1210a] Regulation 6 implemented art.7 of the 2005 Directive which is due to be amended significantly by Directive 2019/2161 art.3(4), but as the 2019 Directive requires implementation on November 28, 2021 (i.e. after IP completion day, on which see above, para.38-004 and Vol.I, paras 1-014 et seq.), the UK is not in principle required to implement these changes: on Directive 2019/2161 see above, para.38-159 (note).

**38-186** *Change title of paragraph:*

### Aggressive commercial practice

*Replace paragraph with:*

**38-186** Regulation 7(1) provides:

> "(1) A commercial practice is aggressive if, in its factual context, taking account of all of its features and circumstances—
> (a) it significantly impairs or is likely significantly to impair the average consumer's freedom of choice or conduct in relation to the product concerned through the use of harassment, coercion or undue influence; and
> (b) it thereby causes or is likely to cause him to take a transactional decision he would not have taken otherwise."

"Consumer", "average consumer", "product" and "transactional decision" are defined in the same way as they are for the purposes of the rights to redress for consumers in respect of misleading actions.[1224] Regulation 7(2) then explains that:

> "(2) In determining whether a commercial practice uses harassment, coercion or undue influence account shall be taken of—
> (a) its timing, location, nature or persistence;
> (b) the use of threatening or abusive language or behaviour;
> (c) the exploitation by the trader of any specific misfortune or circumstance of such gravity as to impair the consumer's judgment, of which the trader is aware, to influence the consumer's decision with regard to the product;
> (d) any onerous or disproportionate non-contractual barrier imposed by the trader where a consumer wishes to exercise rights under the contract, including rights to terminate a contract or to switch to another product or another trader; and
> (e) any threat to take any action which cannot legally be taken."

For these purposes, "coercion" includes the use of physical force[1225] and "undue influence" means:

> "... exploiting a position of power in relation to the consumer so as to apply pressure, even without using or threatening to use physical force, in a way which significantly limits the consumer's ability to make an informed decision."[1226]

The Court of Justice of the EU has explained that:

> "... undue influence is not necessarily impermissible influence but influence which, without prejudice to its lawfulness, actively entails, through the application of a certain degree of pressure, the forced conditioning of the consumer's will."[1226a]

For the Court of Justice, therefore, both the particular concept of undue influence and the concept of aggressive commercial practice more generally are concerned with the freedom of choice of the consumer.[1226b] While this was seen by the Court as related to the importance to the consumer of information relating to the contract (as the reference to an "informed decision" in the definition of undue influence suggests), it acknowledged that the mere fact that the consumer has not had access to information sufficient to guarantee his free choice does not, in itself, constitute an aggressive commercial practice.[1226c] Therefore, where a trader concludes or amends contracts for the supply of telecommunication services by delivering its standard-form contract by courier with the courier waiting for the consumer's decision without the latter having time to study it in advance or at the time, this does not constitute an aggressive commercial practice in the absence of "additional practices" whose effect is to put pressure on the consumer and so significantly impair his freedom of choice.[1226d] Such "additional practices" could consist of "the courier insisting on the need to sign the contract" as "such an attitude is liable to make that consumer feel uncomfortable and thus to confuse his thinking in relation to the transactional decision to be taken", as would be the case where he is told that a later conclusion of the contract would be possible only on less favourable conditions or on the payment of contractual penalties.[1226e]

[1224] 2008 Regulations reg.2(1) "consumer"; reg.2(2)–(6) "average consumer"; reg.27B(2) "transactional decision": see above, paras 38-168, 38-169 and 38-183 respectively. Regulation 2(1) defines "product" generally (see above, para.38-168), but this definition is then qualified by regs 27C–27D for the purposes of the rights to redress provided by Pt 4A as explained below, para.38-176.

[1225] 2008 Regulations reg.7(3)(a).

[1226] 2008 Regulations reg.7(3)(b).

[1226a] *Prezes Urzędu Ochrony Konkurencji i Konsumentów v Orange Polska SA* (C-628/17) EU:C:2019:480 of June 12, 2019 at para.33.

[1226b] *Prezes Urzędu Ochrony Konkurencji i Konsumentów v Orange Polska SA* (C-628/17) EU:C:2019:480 at paras 33–34. On "aggressive commercial practices" and the CJEU's earlier case-law see Caronna (2018) 43 E.L.Rev. 880.

[1226c] *Prezes Urzędu Ochrony Konkurencji i Konsumentów v Orange Polska SA* (C-628/17) EU:C:2019:480 at para.43.

[1226d] *Prezes Urzędu Ochrony Konkurencji i Konsumentów v Orange Polska SA* (C-628/17) EU:C:2019:480 at paras 44–45.

[1226e] *Prezes Urzędu Ochrony Konkurencji i Konsumentów v Orange Polska SA* (C-628/17) EU:C:2019:480 at paras 47–48.

## Prohibited practice by a "producer"

*In penultimate line, after "manufacturer, EEA importer", add new footnote 1235a:*

**38-188** [1235a] On IP completion day (on which see above, para.38-004 and Vol.I paras 1-014 et seq.), reg.27A(5)(b) is to be amended so as to refer to an importer into the UK rather than into the EEA: SI 2018/1326 reg.6(2).

### *(iii) The Three Rights to Redress*

## The right to unwind the contract: consumer to business contracts

*Replace footnote 1281 with:*

**38-194** [1281] The phrase "treat the contract as at an end" seems to be used here in a different sense from its use in the Consumer Rights Act 2015. Under the Act, it is assumed that a consumer may enjoy "a right to treat the contract as at an end" for breach of an express term and for this purpose "treating a contract as at an end means treating it as repudiated": Consumer Rights Act 2015 s.19(11)(e) and 19(13) (goods contracts); s.54(7)(f) (services contracts), that is, what is often called termination for breach of contract, which is coupled with a right to damages for breach of contract. The 2015 Act s.20(4) also sees its special consumer rights to reject goods as involving the treating of the contract as at an end and may be accompanied with damages: 2015 Act ss.19(3), (4), (10) and (11)(a): see below, paras 38-513—38-523 and (on the general law) Vol.I, paras 24-001 et seq. It cannot be intended that a consumer who unwinds a consumer to business contract entered into as the result of a prohibited practice by a trader should recover damages for breach of contract; the consumer's right to damages is governed by reg.27J, see below, paras 38-198—38-203.

## Measure of recovery for financial loss

*In line 2, page [1009], after "transferred).[1312] And if", replace "the right to unwind or right to rescind is, or is no longer" with:*

**38-199** neither the right to unwind nor the right to rescind are, or are no longer

## General relationship of "rights to redress" and claims under the wider law

*Replace footnote 1327 with:*

**38-204** [1327] Powers of Criminal Courts (Sentencing) Act 2000 s.130(4). While the making of an order "is not part of the sentence of the court strictly speaking", there is an "important relationship between the sentence of the court and the desirability or otherwise of making one": *R. v Brogan* [1975] 1 All E.R. 879, 881, 880 per Scarman J. Section 130 and other relevant provisions of the 2000 Act are due to be repealed and replaced by the Sentencing Bill 2019-21 (HL Bill 105) Sch.28 para.1 (Lords' Second Reading, June 25, 2020). The main replacement provisions are contained in the 2019-21 Bill cll.133–135.

### Damages for fraud

*In the penultimate line, after "the Regulations is", add:*
reasonable | 38-206

### Misrepresentation Act 1967 s.2 disapplied

*In line 19, after "loss was not", add:*
reasonably | 38-208

## 6. The Control of Unfair Contract Terms

## (a) Introduction

### Legislative control of the fairness of contract terms

*Replace paragraph with:*

By contrast, the impact of legislation on the fairness of contract terms has been very considerable and particularly so in the case of consumer contracts. Sometimes this control has been effected by the creation of rights or obligations on the parties to particular types of contracts which are not susceptible of contrary exclusion by agreement, notably as regards contracts of consumer credit,[1368] tenancy[1369] and employment.[1370] Other than this regulation of particular types of contract, before 1995 the most important restriction on the effectiveness of contract terms was the Unfair Contract Terms Act 1977, which subjected exemption and limitation clauses (and certain related clauses) both as regards persons "dealing as consumer"[1372] and commercial parties to considerable restrictions.[1373] While this Act also imposed a requirement of reasonableness on the effectiveness of indemnity clauses in consumer contracts,[1373] until the UK was required to implement the Unfair Terms in Consumer Contracts Directive 1993 (the "1993 Directive"),[1374] English law contained no system of control on the basis of fairness applicable to all or most other types of contract term. The 1993 Directive requires Member States to put in place two types of control. First, very broadly, it requires that terms in all types of consumer contracts that have not been "individually negotiated" are binding on consumers only if they are "fair",[1375] with the important exception of terms which define the main subject matter of the contract and as regards the price/quality ratio, provided that they are plain and intelligible (the "core exclusion")[1376]; it also requires more generally that written terms be plain and intelligible.[1377] Secondly, the 1993 Directive requires Member States to put in place adequate and effective means to prevent the continued use of unfair terms in consumer contracts.[1378] The 1993 Directive requires only "minimum harmonisation" and so in principle allows Member States to retain or adopt more protective measures for consumers in national laws within its scope.[1379] 38-212

[1368] See Consumer Credit Act 1974, and para.39-100.

[1369] e.g. Landlord and Tenant Act 1985 s.8 (applicable since March 20, 2019 only to Wales); s.9A(4) (applicable to England from March 20, 2019) (terms as to fitness for human habitation to be "implied, notwithstanding any stipulation to the contrary").

[1370] See paras 40-219 et seq.

[1372] The protections were provided for persons "dealing as consumer": Unfair Contract Terms Act 1977 ss.3–7, 12, Vol.I paras 15-073—15-079.

[1373] See above, Vol.I, para.15-062.

1373 Unfair Contract Terms Act 1977 s.4 and see above, Vol.I, paras 15-088—15-090.

1374 Directive 93/13/EEC on unfair terms in consumer contracts [1993] O.J. L95/21 ("1993 Directive") and see below, paras 38-218— 38-219.

1375 1993 Directive arts 3, 4(1) and 6, below, paras 38-241 et seq.

1376 1993 Directive art.4(2), on which see below, paras 38-245 et seq.; 38-394 et seq. Terms which reflect legislation or the common law are also excluded from the scope of the Directive as a whole: 1993 Directive art.1(2), below, paras 38-233—38-240 and 38-388.

1377 1993 Directive art.5 and see below, paras 38-347 et seq. and 38-414—38-417.

1378 1993 Directive art.7.

1379 1993 Directive art.8. On "minimum harmonisation" and its significance see above, paras 38-022—38-023. For the difficulties caused by the relationship of the 1993 Directive and the Unfair Commercial Practices Directive 2005, see below, paras 38-421—38-426.

## Consumer Rights Act 2015

*Replace paragraph with:*

**38-215** The Consumer Rights Act 2015[1389] ("the 2015 Act" or "the Act") reflects the view of the Law Commissions and the UK government that UK consumer law (and especially consumer contract law) was unnecessarily complex, at times inconsistent (especially in relation to the two sets of legislative provisions governing unfair contract terms[1390]) and scattered in an unhelpful way across a series of legislative enactments, some primary legislation and some secondary, some implementing EU legislation and some purely domestic.[1391] However, the 2015 Act did not follow the Law Commissions' earlier strategy of placing the controls on unfair contract terms in a single Act and, to a considerable extent, a single framework,[1392] but instead divided the control of unfair terms sharply between terms found in consumer contracts (regulated by the 2015 Act, principally in Pt 2) and terms (principally exemption clauses[1393]) in other contracts (regulated by the Unfair Contract Terms Act 1977). Moreover, the 2015 Act was also concerned to provide new, dedicated rules for consumer rights in respect of goods, digital content and services (Pt 1 of the Act), and as a result deleted provisions specifically governing consumer contracts from other more general legislation, notably, the Sale of Goods Act 1979, and disapplied many other of the provisions of those Acts as regards "consumer contracts".[1394] The 2015 Act also introduced significant reforms to the law governing the enforcement of consumer protection laws, domestic and EU, with amendments, inter alia, of Pt 8 of the Enterprise Act 2002 so as to create a new possibility for courts to order "enhanced consumer measures" to individuals affected by breach of a consumer protection measure.[1395] These changes affected the powers of regulators in respect of the prevention of unfair contract terms. In summary, the 2015 Act's strategy in relation to unfair contract terms had four aspects[1396]: first, it re-implemented the Directive on unfair terms in consumer contracts, following closely the Directive's general approach, but modifying some of its rules in a way more protective of consumers; secondly, it amended the Unfair Contract Terms Act 1977 so as no longer to apply to terms in "consumer contracts" or "consumer notices" as defined by the new Act; thirdly, it provided that the trader's liability arising from breach of new statutory terms in "goods contracts", "digital content contracts" and "services contracts" governing the quality, fitness for purpose, etc. of their subject matter do not bind the consumer[1397]; and, fourthly, the 2015 Act extended the enforcement measures (injunctions against, and undertakings, by traders[1398]) which it put in place for the control of unfair terms reflecting the Directive to contract terms rendered not binding on consumers under its provisions more generally, as well as to "consumer notices" also rendered not binding on consumers under the Act.[1399]

[1389] The Consumer Rights Act 2015 was accompanied by a set of *Explanatory Notes* prepared by the Department for Business, Innovation and Skills ("*Explanatory Notes* 2015"). See also Conway, *Consumer Rights Act, Briefing Paper* (House of Commons Library, SN 6588, October 1, 2015). On IP completion day (on which see generally, above, para.38-004 and Vol.I, paras 1-014 et seq.) the Consumer Rights Act 2015 is due to be amended and these amendments will be noted where relevant in the following paragraphs: see 2015 Act s.32 (below, para.38-533), s.59 (below, para.38-497), s.73 (below, para.38-388) and s.74 (below, para.38-418) (amendments to be made by the Consumer Protection (Amendment etc.) (EU Exit) Regulations 2018 (SI 2018/1326) reg.3) (reg.1's reference to the 2018 Regulations coming into force on "exit day" must be read as referring to IP completion day: European Union (Withdrawal Agreement) Act 2020 s.39(1), Sch.5 para.1). The 2015 Act Sch.5 (Investigatory Powers etc.) (below, para.38-420) is to be amended on IP completion day by the Consumer Protection (Enforcement) (Amendment etc.) (EU Exit) Regulations 2019 (SI 2019/203) reg.4 (reg.1's reference to the 2019 Regulations coming into force on "exit day" must be read as referring to IP completion day: European Union (Withdrawal Agreement) Act 2020 s.39(1), Sch.5 para.1). The Consumer Rights Act 2015 (Enforcement) (Amendment) Order 2019 (SI 2019/1074) arts 2 and 3 (in force July 23, 2019)) made minor amendments to Schs 3 and 5 of the 2015 Act.

[1390] Unfair Contract Terms Act 1977; Unfair Terms in Consumer Contracts Regulations 1999.

[1391] *Explanatory Notes* 2015, paras 5–9. Law Commission, Scottish Law Commission, Unfair Terms in Consumer Contracts (2005) Law Com No.292, Scot Law Com No.199 ("Law Com. Unfair Terms (2005)"; Law Commission, Scottish Law Commission, *Unfair Terms in Consumer Contracts: Advice to the Department for Business, Innovation and Skills* (March 2013) ("Law Com. Advice (2013)"); BIS, *Enhancing Consumer Confidence by Clarifying Consumer Law* (July 2012) ("BIS, Clarifying Consumer Law"). See also BIS, *Enhancing Consumer Confidence through Effective Enforcement, Consultation on consolidating and modernising consumer law enforcement powers* (March 2012).

[1392] Above, para.38-214.

[1393] Unfair Contract Terms Act 1977 as amended by the 2015 Act applies only to exemption clauses and other clauses falling within s.3(2)(b) of the 1977 Act: see Vol.I, paras 15-080 et seq.

[1394] See generally below, paras 38-465 et seq.

[1395] Consumer Rights Act 2015 s.79; Sch.7 above, para.38-134.

[1396] See below, paras 38-370—38-374.

[1397] Below, paras 38-465 et seq. (with the qualifications there noted).

[1398] These are detailed in 2015 Act Sch.4, on which see below, para.38-420.

[1399] 2015 Act ss.31(7), 47(5), 57(7), 70 and Sch.3, on which see below, para.38-374. In addition, the provisions in Pt 2 of the 2015 Act which implemented the 1993 Directive were designated as a specified UK law for the purposes of s.212 of the Enterprise Act 2002 ("Community infringements"), and acts or omissions in respect of any provision in Pt 2 of the 2015 Act are specified as possible "domestic infringements" for the purposes of s.211 of the Enterprise Act 2002. On IP completion day, "Community infringements" are to be replaced by "Schedule 13 infringements" and relevant provisions of the 2015 Act are included within the substituted Sch.13 of the 2002 Act for this purpose: Consumer Protection (Enforcement) (Amendment etc.) (EU Exit) Regulations 2019 (SI 2019/203) reg.3(20) and Sch. para.1 inserting new 2002 Act Sch.13 para.27. On this change more generally see above, para.38-133A. For more general discussion of these powers see below, paras 38-420—38-426.

## (b) The Directive on Unfair Terms in Consumer Contracts

### Introduction

*Replace paragraph with:*

On April 5, 1993 the EC Council enacted a directive on Unfair Terms in Consumer Contracts ("the Directive").[1406] It was made under art.95 of the EC Treaty (now art.114 TFEU), which empowered the European legislator to issue directives for the approximation of provisions laid down by laws, regulations or administrative action which have as their object the establishment and functioning of the common market, making particular mention of proposals in the field of consumer protection which must "take as a base a high level of protection".[1407] The preamble to the Directive makes clear that its purposes are: (i) to reduce distor- **38-218** tions in competition between sellers of goods[1408] and suppliers of services caused by differences in rules governing terms in consumer contracts; (ii) to create effective uniform legal protection for consumers from the imposition of unfair contract terms,[1409] especially (but not exclusively) where this concerns transactions with suppliers in Member States other than their own[1410]; and (iii) to enhance the awareness of consumers as to the rules of law which govern consumer contracts in Member States other than their own, for otherwise they may be deterred from entering direct transactions with suppliers in other Member States.[1411] The Directive requires only minimum requirements for the control of fairness and transparency of terms in consumer contracts, it being expressly acknowledged that Member States are free to retain or to introduce systems of control which are more protective of consumers.[1412] This means, inter alia, that decisions of courts of other Member States concerning the interpretation of their legislation implementing the Directive have to be treated with considerable care, as their interpretation may be of national legislation which (lawfully) goes further than the Directive requires.[1413] The Directive is to be amended by the insertion of new provision governing penalties for the infringement of national provisions implementing it.[1413a] However, the Directive which provides for this amendment must be implemented on November 28, 2021,[1413b] i.e. after IP completion day, and as a result the UK is not bound to do so unless this forms part of an agreement with the EU governing their future relationship.[1413c]

[1406] Directive 93/13 on unfair terms in consumer contracts [1993] O.J. L95/21 ("1993 Directive"). The 1993 Directive art.10(1) provides that the national provisions implementing the Directive "shall be applicable to all contracts concluded after 31 December 1994" and therefore do not apply to contracts concluded before that date: *SC Raiffeisen Bank SA v JB* (C-698/18 and C-699/18) EU:C:2020:537, para.42. For discussion of the Directive or the Unfair Terms in Consumer Contracts Regulations, see Dean (1993) 56 M.L.R. 581; Collins (1994) 14 O.J.L.S. 229; Macdonald (1994) J.B.L. 441; Hondius (1994) 7 *Journal of Contract Law* 34; Willett (1994) Con. L.J. 114; Beale in Beatson and Friedmann (eds), *Good Faith and Fault in Contract Law* (1995), Ch.9; Bright and Bright (1995) 111 L.Q.R. 655; Weatherill (1995) 3 *European Review of Private Law* 307, especially 316 et seq. cf. Joerges at 175; Collins at 353; de Moor at 257; Weatherill, *E.C. Consumer Law and Policy* (2005), pp.115 et seq.; Howells and Wilhelmsson, *E.C. Consumer Law* (1997), pp.88 et seq.; Beatson, *Anson's Law of Contract*, 28th edn (2002), pp.200–203, 300 et seq.; Macdonald [1999] C.L.J. 413; Whittaker (2000) 116 L.Q.R. 95; Bright (2000) 20 L.S. 331; Whittaker (2004) *ZEuP* 75; Whittaker (2010) 73 M.L.R. 106. The EU Commission has issued a notice, *Guidance on the interpretation and application of Council Directive 93/13/EEC of 5 April 1993 on unfair contract terms in consumer contracts* (July 22, 2019) C(2019) 5325 final ("Commission guidance C(2019) 5325 final") which seeks to summarise the caselaw of the CJEU on the directive.

[1407] EC Treaty art.95(3) (now art.114(3) TFEU).

[1408] But see discussion, below, paras 38-222 et seq.

[1409] Directive 1993 recital 9.

[1410] This is clear from recital 2's use of the phrase "*notably*, when [sellers or suppliers] sell or supply in other Member States" (emphasis added) and in recital 7 ("both at home and throughout the internal market"). See also *Sziber v ERSTE Bank Hungary Zrt* (C-483/16) EU:C:2018:367 paras 56–59.

[1411] Directive 1993 recital 5.

[1412] Directive 1993 art.8 and see *Caja de Ahorros y Monte de Piedad de Madrid v Asociación de Usuarios de Servicios Bancarios (Ausbanc)* (C-484/08) EU:C:2010:309, [2010] 3 C.M.L.R. 43 (in relation to art.4(2) of the Directive, on which see above, para.38-022), *Pereničovà v SOS finance, spol. sro* (C-453/10) EU:C:2012:144, [2012] 2 C.M.L.R. 28 paras 34–36 (in relation to art.6(1) in fine of the Directive). The Proposal for a Directive on Consumer Rights of October 8, 2008 COM(2008) 614/3 final art.4 (full harmonisation) sought to change this position as regards the 1993 Directive, but the relevant provisions (arts 30–39 of the Proposal) were not present in the Directive as enacted: Directive 2011/83/EU on consumer rights [2011] O.J. L304/64.

[1413] e.g. the decision of the French Cour de Cassation in Civ.(1) March 15, 2005, Bulletin civil I No.135 which held that the French legislation protecting *consommateurs ou non-professionnels* against unfair contract terms could apply for the protection of a corporation as included within the term *non-professionnel* as long as it acted outside its business, even though both the Directive itself and the ECJ make clear that "consumer" refers only to human persons: 1993 Directive art.2(b) and above, para.38-032.

[1413a] Directive (EU) 2019/2161 of the European Parliament and of the Council of 27 November 2019 ... as regards the better enforcement and modernisation of Union consumer protection rules [2019] O.J. L328/7 art.1 inserting new art.8b into the 1993 Directive.

[1413b] Directive (EU) 2019/2161 art.7(1).

[1413c] See above, para.38-004 and Vol.I, para.1-015A.

## Significance of the Directive for English law

*Replace paragraph with:*

While the UK was a Member State of the EU, UK courts were under a duty to interpret the provisions of the 2015 Act seeking to implement the 1993 Directive "as far as possible" in a way so as to give proper effect to the UK's obligations under the Directive as interpreted by the Court of Justice of the EU[1414] and, as noted in Vol.I, Ch.1 of the present work, during the transition period until IP completion day (set as December 31, 2020), the status of case law of the Court of Justice for the interpretation of UK implementing legislation remains the same.[1415] However, after IP completion day, the status of its case law changes. Case law and principles already laid down by the Court of Justice (including the principle of conforming interpretation) will in principle still bind UK courts, except for the Supreme Court and other courts designated by regulation; whereas case law and principles laid down by that court after IP completion day will not bind any UK court, though a court may have regard to them.[1416] This being the case, existing case law and principles already laid down by the Court of Justice of the EU on the 1993 Directive[1417] remain important for the interpretation of the relevant provisions of the 2015 Act. This case law has explained the Court of Justice's own interpretative role relative to the roles of national courts,[1417a] has ruled on the proper interpretation of concepts used by the 1993 Directive or provided guidance on their application by national courts,[1417b] has set a duty in national courts to raise the issue of the unfairness of a term in a consumer contract of their own motion,[1417c] and has explained the relationship between the test of unfairness of contract terms under the 1993 Directive and the test of unfairness of commercial practices under the Unfair Commercial Practices Directive 2005.[1417d] However, it should further be noted that in certain respects[1417e] the 2015 Act is more protective of consumers than was required by the 1993 Directive and, where this is the case, the interpretation of the provisions of the Directive itself by the Court of Justice may not be appropriate to the interpretation of the provisions of the 2015 Act. **38-219**

[1414] See above, para.38-014.

[1415] Vol.I, para.1-015A and see also above, para.38-004. On the effect of the UK leaving the EU more generally see Vol.I, paras 1-014 et seq.

[1416] Vol.I, para.1-017B.

[1417] For an overview of the CJEU's case-law on the 1993 Directive see EU Commission, Guidance on the interpretation and application of Council Directive 93/13/EEC of 5 April 1993 on unfair contract terms in consumer contracts (July 22, 2019) C(2019) 5325 final.

[1417a] *Freiburger Kommunalbauten GmbH Baugesellschaft & Co KG v Hofstetter* (C-237/02) [2004] 2 C.M.L.R. 13; *Nemzeti Fogyasztóvédelmi Hatóság v Invitel Távközlési Zrt.* (C-472/10) EU:C:2012:242 at [21]–[22]; *Aziz v Caixa d'Estalvis de Catalunya, Tarragona i Manresa* (C-415/11) EU:C:2013:164 at [66]–[67]; *RWE Vertrieb AG v Verbraucherzentrale Nordrhein-Westfalen eV* (C-92/11) EU:C:2013:180 at [48]–[54]; *Constructora Principado SA v Menéndez Álvarez* (C-226/12) EU:C:2014:10 at [20]–

[25]; *Sebestyén v Kovári* (C-342/13) EU:C:2014:1857 at [25]–[35]. On this case law see below, para.38-329.

1417b See notably, in relation to art.4(2) of the 1993 Directive: *Kásler v OTP Jelzálogbank Zrt.* (C-26/13) EU:C:2014:282 at [37]; *Matei v SC Volksbank România SA* (C-143/13) EU:C:2015:127 and *Van Hove v CNP Assurances SA* (C-96/14) EU:C:2015:262, in relation to art.4(2) of the 1993 Directive. For guidance on the application of the test of unfairness in art.3 of the 1993 Directive see *Nemzeti Fogyasztóvédelmi Hatóság v Invitel Távközlési Zrt.* (C-472/10) EU:C:2012:242 at [26]–[28]; *Aziz v Caixa d'Estalvis de Catalunya, Tarragona i Manresa* (C-415/11) EU:C:2013:164 at [68]–[69], [73]–[74]; *Constructora Principado SA v Menéndez Álvarez* (C-226/12) EU:C:2014:10 at [21]–[29]. See below, paras 38-249 et seq.

1417c See, notably, *Océano Grupo Editorial SA v Murciano Quintero* (C-240/98 to C-244/98) [2000] E.C.R. I-4941; *Mostaza Claro v Centro Movil Milenium SL* (C-168/05) [2006] E.C.R. I-10421: see below, paras 38-331–38-332A. The 2015 Act seeks to give legislative recognition to this case law in s.71 "Duty of court to consider fairness of term" on which see below, para.38-392.

1417d Directive 2005/29 concerning unfair business-to-consumer commercial practices in the internal market [2005] O.J. L149/22 and see notably, *Pereničovà v SOS finance, spol. sro* (C-453/10) below, para.38-278.

1417e See below, paras 38-379—38-382.

## (c) The Old Law: the Unfair Terms in Consumer Contracts Regulations 1999

### *(i) The Types of Contracts Governed by the 1999 Regulations*

**All types of consumer contracts**

*Replace paragraph with:*

**38-222** The 1999 Regulations (following the English version of the 1993 Directive) provide that they apply in relation to "unfair terms in contracts concluded between a seller or supplier and a consumer",[1424] but they define "seller or supplier" without reference to the types of contracts involved.[1425] Moreover, the terminology of sale and supply is not used at the same points in the Directive in a number of its other language versions, which instead use words translatable as "trader" (such as the French, *professionnel*) instead of "seller and supplier" and recital 10 of the Directive explains that its rules "should apply to *all* contracts concluded between sellers or suppliers and consumers".[1426] The general view of commentators has long been that the 1993 Directive applies to all types of consumer contracts defined by reference only to the status of their parties: the "seller and supplier" and the "consumer"[1427] and this was put beyond doubt by the Court of Justice in *Brusse v Jahani BV*,[1428] *Šiba v Devėnas*,[1429] and *Tarcău*.[1430] In *Brusse v Jahani BV* the Court of Justice considered a question on the proper interpretation of the definition of "seller or supplier" in the context of Dutch law, given that, like the English version, the Dutch version of the Directive uses "seller" to describe the business party to the contract.[1431] Having reviewed the various language versions of the Directive, the Court noted that, whatever the terminology used in the different versions, they all defined the business party in the same way (as reflected in the definition in the 1999 Regulations reg.3(1)) and that therefore:

> "... beyond the term used to designate the other party to the contract with the consumer, the legislature's intention was not to restrict the scope of the directive solely to contracts concluded between a seller and a consumer."[1432]

Noting the reference in recital 10 to "all contracts" concluded between sellers and suppliers and consumers,[1433] the Court concluded that:

"... it is therefore by reference to the capacity of the contracting parties, according to whether or not they are acting for purposes relating to their trade, business or profession that the directive defines the contracts to which it applies."[1434]

This view of the scope of the Directive reflects the purpose of the Directive in the protection of consumers as "weaker parties" as regards both their bargaining power and their level of knowledge.[1435] As a result, the Court held that a contract of residential tenancy concluded between a landlord acting for purposes relating to his trade, business or profession and a tenant acting for purposes which do not relate to his trade, business or profession fell within the scope of the Directive.[1436] In *Šiba v Devėnas*,[1437] the Court of Justice followed its earlier view in *Brusse* and therefore held that contracts for the supply of legal services fell within the scope of the Directive, even though the lawyer supplying those services exercised a "liberal profession" (which is distinguished from a business in the laws of some Member States).[1438] And in *Tarcău v Banca Comercială Intesa Sanpaolo România SA*, the Court of Justice followed this earlier case-law and therefore held that the 1993 Directive could apply to a contract of guarantee undertaken by a natural person acting other than in the course of business under which he or she guaranteed the obligations of a debtor company to a commercial lender.[1439] According to the Court of Justice:

"... [t]he purpose of the contract is ... subject to the exceptions listed in the recital 10 of the Directive ... , irrelevant in determining the scope of the directive."[1440]

As a result, the Directive (and therefore the 1999 Regulations) do not restrict the categories of contract to which they apply in the sense of the types of subject matter with which they are concerned; the contracts to which they apply are defined exclusively by reference to the status of the two parties: "seller and supplier" and "consumer".[1441] On the other hand, in *Šiba v Devėnas* the Court held that the nature of the subject matter of the contract would be relevant to the assessment of the fairness of its terms.[1442]

1424 1999 Regulations reg.4(1); 1993 Directive art.1. The 1994 Regulations reg.3(1) and Sch.1 paras (a)–(d) were expressed as not applying to contracts relating to employment, contracts relating to succession rights, any contract relating to rights under family law and any contract relating to the incorporation and organisation of companies or partnerships. This reflected 1993 Directive recital 10, as noted below in this paragraph.

1425 1999 Regulations reg.3(1), "seller or supplier".

1426 (Emphasis added): "*que ces règles doivent s'appliquer à tout contrat conclu entre un professionnel et un consommateur*". Similar formulations are found in the Italian, Spanish and German versions of the Directive; 1993 Directive art.2.

1427 On the 1993 Directive see Tenreiro (1993) 7 *Contrats-Concurrence-Consommation* 1; Trochu (1993) D.S. Chron 315, 317; Weatherill, *EU Consumer Law and Policy* (2005) p.117; Calais-Auloy and Steinmetz, *Droit de la consommation*, 7th edn (2006), para.179 (although referring to the French legislation implementing the Directive). The arguments in favour of this position have been rehearsed in successive editions of the present work, Vol.I, Ch.15 since its 27th edition.

1428 C-488/11 EU:C:2013:341, May 30, 2013.

1429 C-537/13 EU:C:2015:14, January 15, 2015 [2015] Bus. L.R. 81 ("*Šiba v Devėnas* (C-537/13)"). See also *Karel de Grote–Hogeschool Katholieke Hogeschool Antwerpen VZW v Kuijpers* (C-147/16) of May 17, 2018 at paras 53–54; *Pouvin and Dijoux v Électricité de France (EDF)* (C-590/17) EU:C:2019:232 of March 21, 2019 at para.19.

1430 *Tarcău v Banca Comercială Intesa Sanpaolo România SA* (C-74/15) Order of CJEU November 19, 2015 ("*Tarcău* (C-74/15)").

1431 C-488/11 EU:C:2013:341, paras 25–27 ("*verkoper*").

[1432] *Brusse v Jahani BV* (C-488/11) EU:C:2013:341 ("*Brusse* (C-488/11)"), para.28. On the definition in the Regulations see below, para.38-224.

[1433] 1993 Directive recital 10 notes that, "as a result" of its application to "all contracts concluded between sellers or suppliers and consumers", it does *not* apply to "contracts relating to employment, contracts relating to succession rights, contracts relating to rights under family law and contracts relating to the incorporation and organization of companies and partnership agreements". Generally, these exclusions (which were reflected in the text of the 1994 Regulations reg.3(1), Sch.1) are straightforward given that the parties to these types of contract would not qualify as "seller or supplier" and "consumer" within the meaning of the 1993 Directive, but the position of contracts relating to employment is less straightforward. For this purpose, the CJEU has recently held that where an employee concludes a contract, *other than the employment contract*, with his employer, this does not prevent the employee counting as a "consumer" and his or her employer counting as a "seller or supplier" within the meaning of the 1993 Directive: *Pouvin and Dijoux v Électricité de France (EDF)* (C-590/17) EU:C:2019:232 of March 21, 2019 at paras 29–43. As a result, a contract of loan by an employer to its employee for the purpose of the purchase of a property for the employee's private purposes can be a "consumer contract" even though the main activity of the employer is not the provision of finance: C-590/17. However, the CJEU also recognised the existence of "the exclusion of employment contracts from the scope of [the 1993 Directive]", holding that such a loan contract is not excluded on this ground as it "does not regulate an employment relationship or employment conditions and, consequently, cannot be classified as an "employment contract": C-590/17 at para.32. This strongly suggests that contracts of employment or contracts which otherwise regulate an employment relationship or employment conditions cannot themselves be a "consumer contract" under the 1993 Directive. As a result, where a private individual (the employer) acting outside their trade or profession concludes a contract of employment with a person (the employee) acting in the course of their trade or profession, (e.g. a private individual employing a nanny for his or her children), this contract would not be a "consumer contract" within the meaning of the 1993 Directive, even though otherwise such an employer could be seen as a "consumer" and the employee the "seller or supplier" of those services.

[1434] *Brusse* (C-488/11) para.30.

[1435] *Brusse* (C-488/11) para.31.

[1436] *Brusse* (C-488/11) para.34.

[1437] *Šiba v Devėnas* (C-537/13) January 15, 2015.

[1438] *Šiba v Devėnas* (C-537/13) at paras 17, 20–24.

[1439] *Tarcău v Banca Comercială Intesa Sanpaolo România SA* C-74/15 Order of CJEU November 19, 2015 ("*Tarcău* (C-74/15)") (an "order" is made by the CJEU where it considers that the question for a preliminary ruling admits of no reasonable doubt). See similarly *Bucura v SC Bancpost SA* (C-348/14) EU:C:2015:447, July 9, 201 (available in French) paras 35–38 (1993 Directive may apply where the alleged "consumer" contracted as "co-debtor" to a person concluding a contract of consumer credit); *Dumitraş v BRD Groupe Société Générale* (C-534/15) Order of the CJEU of September 14, 2016 (contract of guarantee by individual in context of group of companies); *Bachman v FAER IFN SA* (C-535/16) (Order of the Court of April 27, 2017, available in French) (contract of novation under which individual undertook obligations arising under earlier commercial contract of loan). See also *Air Berlin Plc & Co Luftverkehrs KG v Bundesverband der Verbraucherzentralen und Verbraucherverbande - Verbrachcrzentrale Bundesverband eV* (C-290/16) of July 6, 2017 at para.44, holding that the 1993 Directive is a "general directive for consumer protection, intended to apply to all sectors of economic activity" and therefore national legislation implementing the 1993 Directive could apply to the contracts of air transport falling within the scope of Regulation (EC) 1008/2008 of the European Parliament and of the Council on common rules for the operation of air services in the Community in the absence of express provision in that Regulation to the contrary (which there is not).

[1440] *Tarcău* (C-74/15) at para.22. On the status of these "exceptions" see below, para.38-222, in relation to the 1993 Directive recital 10.

[1441] See below, paras 38-224—38-227 on the definitions of these terms.

[1442] 1993 Directive art.4(1); C-537/13 at paras 33–35, below, para.38-284.

## Further examples

*Replace paragraph with:*

**38-223** The Directive's Annex setting out an indicative list of terms which may be unfair (appearing in Sch.2 to the 1999 Regulations) assumes that it applies to non-physical property, including transactions in transferable securities, financial instruments and to the purchase or sale of foreign currency, traveller's cheques or international money orders denominated in foreign currency.[1443] This being so, contracts of assignment or of the licensing of contractual rights (for example, a right to use computer software) are also included within the ambit of the Regulations. The Directive applies to contracts of settlement by which a trader and consumer agree to waive rights or claims they may have arising under an earlier contract for the supply of goods or services.[1443a] And English courts have held or assumed that the Regulations apply to a wide variety of types of consumer contract, notably, contracts of residential tenancy[1444]; contracts for the supply of a newly-built house,[1445] contracts for the provision of financial services,[1446] contracts of membership of a gymnasium,[1447] and the contract under which a person enjoys free parking for a limited period.[1448]

1443 1999 Regulations Sch.2 para.2(c). On the role of this Schedule more generally, see below, paras 38-299 et seq.

1443a *XZ v Ibercaja Banco SA* (C-452/18) EU:C:2020:536 para.59 and see below, paras 38-260A, 38-262C and 38-339A.

1444 *London Borough of Newham v Khatun* [2004] EWCA Civ 55, [2005] Q.B. 37 and see *Peabody Trust Governors v Reeve* [2008] EWHC 1432 (Ch) at [30], [2009] L. & T.R. 6; *Shaftsbury House (Developments) Ltd v Lee* [2010] EWHC 1484 (Ch) at [54], *Rochdale BC v Dixon* [2011] EWCA Civ 1173, [2012] H.L.R. 6.

1445 *Zealander v Laing Homes Ltd* (2000) 2 T.C.L.R. 724. The CJEU has assumed that the 1993 Directive applies to contracts for the purchase of immovable property by a consumer from a builder: *Constructora Principado SA v Menéndez Álvarez* (C-226/12) EU:C:2014:10, January 16, 2014.

1446 *Director General of Fair Trading v First National Bank* [2001] UKHL 52, [2002] 1 A.C. 481 (below, para.38-246); *Abbey National Plc v Office of Fair Trading* [2009] UKSC 6, [2010] 1 A.C. 696 (the "Bank Charges" case) (below, paras 38-247—38-248). The 1993 Directive recital 19 assumes that contracts of insurance may fall within its scope. As will be seen, contracts of loan to a consumer secured by mortgage on property have formed a significant part of the CJEU's case-law: below, para.38-270.

1447 *Office of Fair Trading v Ashbourne Management Services Ltd* [2011] EWHC 1237 (Ch), [2011] E.C.C. 31.

1448 *ParkingEye Ltd v Beavis* [2015] UKSC 67, [2016] A.C. 1172, below, paras 38-275—38-277.

### "Sellers or suppliers"

*Replace footnote 1449 with:*

1449 cf. 1994 Regulations reg.2 "sellers", "suppliers" and "business". Commission guidance C(2019) 5325 final pp.7–8. **38-224**

### "Consumer"

*Replace footnote 1460 with:*

1460 1993 Directive art.2(b). See also Commission guidance C(2019) 5325 final pp.7–8. **38-225**

### An autonomous view of "contract"?

*To the end of paragraph, after "consumer protection within the EU.", add:*

And, while the EU Commission in its recent guidance on the proper interpretation of the 1993 Directive, did not explicitly take a view on this general question, it did note that some decisions of the CJEU have accepted the application of the directive where the consumer has not provided *monetary consideration* for goods or services, as in the case of guarantees for a loan taken out by another party.[1483a] **38-229**

1483a Commission guidance C(2019) 5325 final, pp.9–10, e.g. *Tarcău* (C-74/15), above, para.38-222.

*Replace paragraph with:*

If the Court of Justice were to take such an autonomous view of contract, it is **38-230** likely that it would do so on the basis of an agreement between the parties or an agreement intended to have legal effects.[1484] If the Court of Justice were to do so, this would sometimes require an English court to classify as contractual for the purposes of the Directive a transaction which in English law is considered non-contractual.[1485] Three examples may be given. First, the laws of most of the Member States contain no requirement conceptually equivalent to English law's doctrine of consideration.[1486] This raises the possibility of including within the ambit of the Directive the terms on which professional services are provided gratuitously. Secondly, the relationship between the beneficiary of a trust and the trustee may sometimes be considered "contractual" for the purposes of the Directive (and therefore the Regulations), even though it is not in the general English law.[1487] Thirdly, some provisions of public services, such as water and electricity, may be held to be "contractual" for the purposes of the Regulations even though they are non-contractual under general English law.[1488] In this respect, the European Commission has drawn attention to its statement in the Council's minutes in connection with the adoption of the common position concerning art.2 of the Directive on the notion of the contract which "points out that the notion of contract also includes transactions involving supplies of goods or services in a regulatory framework".[1489] Moreover, in *Schulz & Egbringhoff*,[1490] in the context of the exclusion from the 1993 Directive of contract terms required by legislation,[1491] Advocate General Wahl distinguished between contracts under which electricity or gas was supplied under contracts by suppliers under a legal "universal service obligation" some of whose terms were set by legislation, which he referred to as "contracts, which are governed by national legislation, [which] do not fall within the sphere of freedom of contract"[1492] and those made in the absence of such an obligation under "special contracts" which are "concluded on the basis of freedom of contract".[1493] This approach therefore distinguishes between two categories of *contract*, those which are closely regulated by law (both as regards an obligation to conclude the contract in the supply and some of its terms) and those not so regulated, and thereby assumes that the fact of such regulation does not preclude the transaction from being classed as a contract for the purposes of the 1993 Directive.[1494] On the other hand, where terms of a consumer contract are required by law in this way in principle they fall within the exclusion from the scope of the 1993 Directive as being terms which reflect "mandatory statutory or regulatory provisions" unless a Member State has not included this exclusion in its implementing legislation.[1495]

1484 Whittaker (2000) 116 L.Q.R. 95. See, notably, the definition of "contract" for the purposes of the Amended proposal for a Directive of the European Parliament and of the Council on certain aspects concerning contracts for the online and other distance sales of goods COM(2017) 637 final art.2(g) to the effect that "'contract' means an agreement intended to give rise to obligations or other legal effects", thereby adopting the definition in the proposed Common European Sales Law art.2 in Proposal for a Regulation on a Common European Sales Law COM(2011) 635 final (proposal withdrawn by the Commission in December 2014), on which see above, Vol.I paras 1-013 and 1-025. In this respect, recital 17 to the Amended Proposal claims that its definition reflects "the common traditions of all Member States". See *KH v Sparkasse Sudholstein* (C-639/18) EU:C:2020:206 at paras 45–51, where A.G. Sharpston advised that the notion of a "contract concerning financial services" in art.2(a) of Directive 2002/65 concerning the distance marketing of consumer financial services [2002] O.J. L271/16 should be given an autonomous interpretation and that for this purpose "a key element for a 'contract' to exist within the meaning of Article 2(a) is that there should be an agreement between the parties, that is to say a meeting of minds" (para.51) (the decision of the CJEU of June 18, 2020 did not express a view on this issue, though it did not accept its A.G.'s advice on the question whether the amending agreement was a "contract concerning financial services"): see above, para.38-136 (note). But cf. below in relation to *Nationale Maatschappij der Belgische Spoorwegen (NMBS) v Kanyeba, Nijs. Dedroog* (C-349 to C-351/18) EU:C:2019:936.

[1485] On the other hand, some legal relationships which involve elements of agreement in one or both parties may nevertheless be properly characterised as "non-contractual" in English law owing to the nature or extent of their regulation: e.g. the relationship between a student on the Bar Professional Training Course and the Bar Council: *R. (on the application of Prescott) v General Council of the Bar* [2015] EWHC 1919 (Admin) at [79].

[1486] There was no more than a superficial conceptual similarity between the former French law doctrine of *la cause* and the doctrine of consideration and there is no similarity in terms of their respective overall functions: see Whittaker, in Bell, Boyron and Whittaker, *Principles of French Law*, 2nd edn (2008), pp.321–322; H. Kötz and A. Flessner, *European Contract Law* (trans. Weir, 1997), Vol.I, pp.54 et seq. In 2016, the notion of *la cause* was deleted from the French *Code civil* on the wider reform of French contract law by *Ordonnance* No.2016/131 of February 10, 2016.

[1487] cf. *Gray v Taylor* [1998] 1 W.L.R. 1093 in which the Court of Appeal held that a person occupying an almshouse under a charitable trust was not a tenant.

[1488] For the non-contractual nature of the supply of electricity and water to domestic consumers (even though they pay), see the Electricity Act 1989 ss.16, 22 and *Norweb v Dixon* [1995] 1 W.L.R. 636 and the Water Industry Act 1991 ss.53–56 and *Read v Croydon Corp* [1938] 4 All E.R. 631. cf. the position in relation to gas under the Gas Act 1995 ss.7 and 8 amending Gas Act 1986 ss.7 and 8.

[1489] European Commission, *Report on Directive 93/13/EEC on unfair terms in consumer contracts*, COM(2000) final, p.15.

[1490] A.G. Opinion, *Schulz v Technische Werke Schussental GmbH und Co KG, Egbringhoff v Stadwerke Ahaus GmbH* (C-359 and C-400/11) of May 8, 2014. The CJEU's decision of October 23, 2014 did not reflect on the differences between the two categories of contract.

[1491] 1993 Directive art.1(2), below, paras 38-233—38-240.

[1492] A.G. Opinion, C-359 and C-400/11 at para.34.

[1493] A.G. Opinion, C-359 and C-400/11 at para.38 (as in the earlier decision of the CJEU in *RWE Vertrieb AG v Verbraucherzentrale Nordrhein-Westfalen eV* (C-92/11) EU:C:2013:180, March 21, 2013, below, para.38-234. cf. *Roundlistic Ltd v Jones* [2016] UKUT 325 (LC) at [100], where it was held that a lease of residential premises granted by a landlord to its tenant was a contract concluded between those parties, despite the fact that it was concluded within the context of the obligation on the landlord to grant a new lease pursuant to the Leasehold Reform, Housing and Urban Development Act 1993: this issue was not appealed and the CA assumed that such a lease was a "contract" for the purposes of the 1999 Regulations: [2018] EWCA Civ 2284, [2019] H.L.R. 17, though it was further held that these terms of the new lease were excluded from the scope of the 1999 Regulations on the basis that they reflected "mandatory statutory provisions" within the meaning of reg.4(2), on which see below, para.38-238.

[1494] For the A.G., therefore, the terms of the contracts before the Court (which did not reflect freedom of contract) fell within the special provisions on the transparency of contract terms in the relevant Energy Directives and not the 1993 Directive: C-359 and C-400/11 at para.47.

[1495] 1993 Directive art.1(2). The omission of the exclusion is permitted by its requirement of "minimum harmonization" under art.8 of the Directive. On this exclusion and its implementation in UK law, see below, paras 38-233—38-240.

*After first paragraph, add new paragraph:*

However, recently in *Kanyeba*[1495a] the question arose as to whether the concept of "contract" should be understood autonomously for the purposes of the 1993 Directive in a national context where the exclusion contained in art.1(2) of the Directive had not been implemented.[1495b] There, three people (the "consumers"[1495c]) had travelled on Belgian trains without buying a ticket and had, moreover, refused to "regularize" their position by buying tickets onboard when asked to or by paying further sums (which increased over time) when invited to, all as provided by the national conditions governing carriage by rail. When these accumulated sums were claimed by the railway company from the travellers, the latter argued that they were payable under a contract and that the "terms" on which they were based were therefore open to challenge on the ground of their unfairness under national legislation implementing the 1993 Directive; the railway company countered that the travellers were not carried under a contract at all and that the sums with which they were charged arose from the regulations governing rail transport.[1495d] It was not clear 38-230 as a matter of (Belgian) national law whether the legal basis of the national conditions of carriage was contractual or regulatory nor whether or not the relationship between the traveller without a valid ticket was contractual.[1495e] In this context, Advocate General Pitruzella advised the Court that the EU regulation on rail passengers' rights and obligations (which governed "contracts of transport"[1495f]) and the 1993 Directive merely presuppose the existence of a contract between traveller and carrier; they do not determine "when a legal relationship may be classified as a contract of carriage or the time at which a contract of carriage can be deemed to be concluded", and this means that "it is entirely within the discretion of the Member States to classify the nature of the legal relationship which is created" in the situations in question.[1495g] However, the Court of Justice disagreed. It held, first, that according to the wording of the EU regulation on rail passengers' rights and obligations "the word 'contract' is generally understood to designate an agreement by consensus intended to produce legal effects"[1495h] and that "by allowing free access to its train and, on the other hand, by boarding that train with an intention to travel, both the rail undertaking and the passenger demonstrate their agreement to enter into a contractual relationship".[1495i] Moreover, the legal context and objectives of the EU Regulation (and its relationship to the COTIF[1495j]) show that a person travelling without a ticket does so under a "contract of transport" since, in particular, otherwise the carrier could not rely on the national conditions of transport against such travellers and the latter could be deprived of their rights under the EU Regulation.[1495k] On the other hand, in the Court's view, this position is without prejudice to the validity of the contract or to the consequences of its non-performance in this situation, which are not governed by the EU Regulation and therefore belong to national law.[1495l] Given this decision on the EU Regulation, the Court of Justice considered it unnecessary to decide whether the Directive on unfair terms in consumer contracts applies to the relationship governing such a traveller, but it did consider the question whether art.6 of the Directive prevented a national court from modifying the amount stipulated by a penalty clause in a consumer contract[1495m] on the express premise that the term did not fall outside the scope of the Directive owing to the exclusion in art.1(2) (i.e. as reflecting legislative provisions)[1495n]: this strongly suggests that it assumed that the relationship between the parties more generally fell within the scope of the Directive as a "consumer contract". While, therefore, the Court of Justice did not decide that the Directive requires an autonomous interpretation to the concept of "contract" for its purposes, it did not follow its Advocate General's view that it did not.

[1495a] *Nationale Maatschappij der Belgische Spoorwegen (NMBS) v Kanyeba, Nijs. Dedroog* (C-349 to C-351/18), ("*Kanyeba* (C-349 to C-351/18)"), Opinion of A.G. Pitruzella, June 11, 2019; Judgment of the CJEU, November 7, 2019.

[1495b] Opinion of A.G. Pitruzella, para.57.

[1495c] *Kanyeba* (C-349 to C-351/18), CJEU, para.22.

[1495d] It was noted that Belgian law had not incorporated into its implementation of the 1993 Directive, the exclusion of terms reflecting mandatory statutory or regulatory provisions provided by art.1(2): *Kanyeba* (C-349 to C-351/18) A.G. Opinion, para.57. This meant that, if the legal relationship between the traveller and the carrier were held to be contractual, its "terms" would fall to be assessed for their fairness even if required by regulations governing rail transport.

[1495e] *Kanyeba* (C-349 to C-351/18), CJEU, para.23.

[1495f] Regulation (EC) 1371/2007 of the European Parliament and of the Council of 23 October 2007 on rail passengers' rights and obligations [2007] O.J. L315/14.

[1495g] *Kanyeba* (C-349 to C-351/18), Opinion of June 11, 2019, paras 38–40 and see also at paras 41, 49–50.

1495h *Kanyeba* (C-349 to C-351/18), CJEU, para.36. Cf. *KH v Sparkasse Sudholstein* (C-639/18) EU:C:2020:206 at paras 45–51 A.G. Sharpston advising (in the context of art.2(a) of Directive 2002/65 concerning the distance marketing of consumer financial services [2002] O.J. L271/16) that "a key element for a 'contract' to exist within the meaning of Article 2(a) is that there should be an agreement between the parties, that is to say a meeting of minds" (para.51). The decision of the CJEU of June 18, 2020 did not express a view on this issue, though it did not accept its A.G.'s advice on the question whether the amending agreement was a "contract concerning financial services": see above, para.38-136 (note).

1495i *Kanyeba* (C-349 to C-351/18), CJEU, para.37.

1495j EU Regulation Annex I setting out Appendix A of the Convention concerning International Carriage by Rail (COTIF) of 9 May 1980 and in particular art.9; on COTIF generally see above, paras 36-100 et seq.

1495k *Kanyeba* (C-349 to C-351/18), CJEU, paras 37–53.

1495l *Kanyeba* (C-349 to C-351/18), CJEU, para.52.

1495m *Kanyeba* (C-349 to C-351/18), CJEU, paras 55 et seq.

1495n The CJEU did so on the basis that the question whether a clause actually fell within art.1(2) was a question for the national court in the light of its own guidance on the proper interpretation of that provision (on which see below, para.38-234), but, as its A.G. had noted, the national law of the referring court (Belgian law) had not included the exclusion in art.1(2) in its national implementing legislation: Opinion of A.G. Pitruzella para.57.

### *(ii) Contract Terms Excluded from the 1999 Regulations*

## General

*Replace footnote 1507 with:*

1507 1999 Regulations reg.4(1); 1993 Directive arts 2(a), 3(1). In *Kiss v Kiss* (C-621/17) A.G. Hogan in his Opinion of May 15, 2019, para.50 n.17 took the view that "term" for the purposes of the 1993 Directive "must be understood in a substantial and not in a formal sense, i.e. referring to a specific right or obligation laid down in a contract and not to a particular paragraph of the contract. As a result a clause may contain several terms and a term may take the form of several clauses". (These points were not discussed by the CJEU in its decision of October 3, 2019; EU:C:2019:820.) The particular context for A.G. Hogan's view was the proper approach to the exclusion in art.4(2) of the Directive (on which see below, paras 38-245 et seq.), but it could also affect a court's approach to art.6's stipulation that "unfair terms" are not binding on the consumer (on which see below, para.38-341). **38-232**

*At end of title, add new footnote 1517a:*

## Case-law of the CJEU[1517a]

1517a It should be noted that the significance of case-law of the CJEU for English courts changes on IP completion day: above, para.38-004 and Vol.I, para.1-017B. **38-234**

*Replace paragraph with:*

**38-234** In *RWE Vertrieb AG v Verbraucherzentrale Nordrhein-Westfalen eV*,[1518] the Court of Justice of the EU clarified the interpretation of the exclusion of terms provided by art.1(2) of the 1993 Directive.[1519] In that case, the German law governing the supply of natural gas to consumers distinguished between supplies by gas suppliers under "standard tariff contracts", where the supplier was under a legal obligation to conclude contracts with consumers, and "special contracts", where they were not. German legislation set the general terms and conditions of supply of the standard tariff contracts, but did not do so for the special contracts. However, the wording of the standard conditions of the *special* contracts concluded by the supplier in the main proceedings corresponded to those required for the tariff contracts by the legislation, and in this sense, they "reflected" those legal provisions. The issue before the Court was whether the contract terms in the special contracts of supply of natural gas to consumers fell under the controls of unfairness in the German legislation implementing the 1993 Directive or whether they fell instead within the exclusion in that legislation foreseen by art.1(2) of that Directive. Referring to recital 13 of the Directive, the Court of Justice considered that this exclusion is justified by the fact that "it may legitimately be supposed that the national legislature struck a balance between all the rights and obligations of the parties to certain contracts",[1520] and held that this reasoning does not apply to the situation where a consumer contract merely reproduces a rule of national law applicable to *another* category of contracts to which the national legislation in question does not apply:

> "... [a]n intention of the parties to extend the application of those rules to a different contract cannot be equated to the establishment by the national legislature of a balance between all the rights and obligations of the parties to the contract."[1521]

The Court of Justice concluded, therefore, that the Directive applies to terms such as those in the "special contracts" of supply of gas to consumers before it.[1522] The Court therefore held that art.1(2) does not apply to contract terms in a legislative scheme where the scheme does not apply to the contract in question,[1523] but it assumed that the exclusion found in art.1(2) *does* apply to terms in a contract which copy out legislative or other legal rules which would otherwise apply to that contract, even where those legislative rules do not themselves *require* to be so expressed in the contract, as art.1(2)

> "... extends to terms which reflect provisions of national law that apply between the parties to the contract independently of their choice or those that apply by default in the absence of other arrangements established by the parties."[1524]

In *Kušionová*[1525] the Court of Justice followed its earlier approach to art.1(2) in *RWE Vertrieb AG*, noting that this exclusion should be interpreted strictly[1526] and that it is for the national court to determine whether a particular contract term falls within this test.[1526a] On the other hand, the Court of Justice in *RWE Vertrieb AG* did not consider directly the question whether art.1(2)'s exclusion applies to contract terms which are not directly determined by national legislation but which are approved or otherwise regulated under a legislative scheme or to contract terms which are varied under a lawful exercise of a statutory power in the seller or supplier.[1527] A significant example of the former would be where the terms of supply of a public service are drawn up by the (commercial) supplier of that service, but then subjected either to a requirement of approval by an administrative body or to a structure of review by a "watchdog" institution. If this approval or review were undertaken under "legislative or regulatory provisions" the latter could be said to "determine indirectly" the content of the contracts, as foreseen by recital 13 of the Directive. On the other hand, the Court of Justice could instead distinguish between those provisions which *determine* and those which *provide for approval* of the terms on which services are provided, only the former being within the terms of art.1(2). This distinction could be supported by the clearly restrictive approach of the Court of Justice to the exclusion in art.1(2) in *RWE Vertrieb AG*, following its general approach to exclusions from schemes for the protection of consumers[1528] and also to the expressions of this restrictive approach in recent case-law of the Court of Justice in the context of consumer credit.[1528a]

[1518] *RWE Vertrieb AG v Verbraucherzentrale Nordrhein-Westfalen eV* (C-92/11) EU:C:2013:180, March 31, 2013 ("*RWE Vertrieb AG* (C-92/11)"). See further on the case-law of the CJEU: Commission guidance C(2019) 5325 final, pp.11–13.

[1519] *RWE Vertrieb AG* (C-92/11).

[1520] *RWE Vertrieb AG* (C-92/11) at para.29. As the CJEU has further explained, the purpose of the exclusion in art.1(2) of the Directive is therefore to preserve the balance struck by the national legislature: *Woonhaven Antwerpen BV CVBA v Berkani and Hajji* (C-446/17) EU:C:2017:954, Order of CJEU of December 7, 2017 at paras 25–26 (available in French) where it was held that the exclusion does not apply to mandatory provisions governing judicial powers of assessment of the unfair character of a contract term: at para.27. See further *Banco Santander v Demba, Cortés v Banco de Sabadell SA* (C-96/16 and C-94/17) EU:C:2018:643 at paras 43–45; *Profi Credit Polska SA z siedziba w Bielsku- Bialej v QJ* (C-84/19, C-222/19 and C-252/19) EU:C:2020:259 of September 3, 2020 at para.63 (contract term imposing a charge on the consumer which conforms to a legislative maximum does not fall within art.1(2)). On the other hand, the CJEU has held that the exclusion in art.1(2) can apply to contract terms reflecting mandatory provisions of national law inserted by the legislature *after* the conclusion of the contract; *OTP Bank Nyrt v Ilyés and Kiss* (C-51/17) EU:C:2018:750 of September 20, 2018 at para.70.

[1521] *RWE Vertrieb AG* (C-92/11) at para.29.

[1522] *RWE Vertrieb AG* (C-92/11) at para.38.

[1523] cf. *Peabody Trust Governors v Reeve* [2008] EWHC 1432 (Ch), [2009] L. & T.R. 6 at [40]–[62], where it was said that a variation clause which successfully incorporated the power of variation provided by s.103 in a tenancy contract to which that provision did *not* apply would be unfair within the meaning of the 1999 Regulations.

[1524] *RWE Vertrieb AG* (C-92/11) para.26; *Kušionová v SMART Capital a.s.* (C-34/13) of September 10, 2014 para.79; *Andriciuc v Banca Românească* (C-186/16) of September 20, 2017 at paras 27–31; *NG, OH v SC Banca Transilvania SA* (C-81/19) EU:C:2020:532 at para.25.

[1525] *Kušionová v SMART Capital a.s.* (C-34/13) of September 10, 2014.

[1526] *Kušionová v SMART Capital a.s.* (C-34/13) para.77.

[1526a] See also *NG, OH v SC Banca Transilvania SA* (C-81/19) EU:C:2020:532 at paras 24 and 28.

[1527] cf. Unfair Contract Terms Act 1977 s.29(2) contract term to be taken as satisfying the requirement of reasonableness "if it is incorporated or approved by, or incorporated pursuant to a decision or ruling of, a competent authority acting in the exercise of any statutory jurisdiction or function and is not a term in a contract to which the competent authority is itself a party": Vol.I, para.15-124.

[1528] C-92/11 EU:C:2013:180. Cf. *Aqua Med sp.z o.o. v Skora* (C-266/18) EU:C:2019:28 of April 3, 2019 at paras 35–37 (contract term which gave jurisdiction "to the court which has jurisdiction under the relevant provisions" does not fall within art.1(2) as it "does not, strictly speaking, reflect a specific national provision, since the national provisions ... provide for a set of rules governing the arrangements for determining jurisdiction, and the seller or supplier can choose whichever is the most favourable to him").

[1528a] A term of a contract of consumer credit to purchase a residence which fixes a variable interest rate by reference to one of the official reference indices provided by national legislation for this purpose does not fall within the exclusion in art.1(2) as the legislation in question did not require the index to be used, but merely fixed the conditions for its use by credit institutions: *Gómez del Moral Guasch v Bankia SA* (C-125/18) EU:C:2020:138, para.37. Moreover, where national legislation fixes a maximum for the cost of credit apart from interest, a term in a contract of consumer credit which provides a method for the calculation of this cost without taking into account the costs actually incurred does not itself "reflect" that legislation so as to be excluded from the scope of control of the 1993 Directive under art.1(2): such national legislation does not determine the rights and obligations of the contracting parties, but merely restricts their freedom to fix the cost of credit apart from interest, and therefore leaves it open to a national court to assess the fairness of their doing so in the contract even if this is below the legislative maximum: *Mikrokasa SA w Gdyni v XO* (C-779/18) of March 26, 2020 at paras 56–57 (available in French).

## Statutory obligation to grant contract on same terms

*Replace paragraph with:*

In *Jones v Roundlistic Ltd*,[1542] a new lease had been granted to a tenant by her landlord under its obligation imposed by the Leasehold Reform, Housing and Urban Development Act 1993.[1543] The Upper Tribunal (Lands Chamber) noted that the terms upon which the landlord was obliged to grant the new lease were provided by the Act and that, while there was scope for some alternations in the terms, the Act's starting-point was that the new lease was to be on the same terms as the existing lease subject to certain limited modifications.[1544] In these circumstances, the Up- **38-238** per Tribunal concluded that the 1999 Regulations did not apply to the terms of the new lease on the basis that they fell within the exclusion in reg.4(2) as "mandatory statutory provisions".[1545] The 33rd edition of this work as first published criticised this decision on the basis that it extended the scope of application of reg.4(2) beyond the likely interpretation by the Court of Justice of the EU of art.1(2) of the 1993 Directive which reg.4(2) implements[1546]: art.1(2) is to be strictly construed[1547] and there is a difference between contract terms required by legislation itself (where "it may legitimately be supposed that the national legislature struck a balance between all the rights and obligations of the parties to certain contracts"[1548]) and contract terms which reflect an earlier contract between the parties whose content has not been the object of any legislative consideration or imposition. A majority of the Court of Appeal disagreed with the view of the Upper Tribunal on this issue, holding that on a natural reading reg.4(2) covers only cases where the content of terms is prescribed by legislation and that, decisively, the policy underlying art.1(2) of the 1993 Directive reflects the fact that the "legislator/regulator must be taken to have given proper weight to consumer protection when prescribing a term to be included in the contract".[1548a] This policy would clearly not apply where, as here, the legislation said nothing about the substance of the terms to be incorporated into the new lease, the court expressly approving the view taken by the 33rd edition.[1548b]

1542 [2016] UKUT 325 (LC); [2018] EWCA Civ 2284, [2019] 1 W.L.R. 4461.

1543 i.e. ss.43, 56 and 57.

1544 [2016] UKUT 325 (LC) at [101].

1545 [2016] UKUT 325 (LC) at [101]. It had been held that the new lease was a "contract" for the purposes of the 1999 Regulations despite its compulsory elements: see above, para.38-230.

1546 See notably *RWE Vertrieb AG* (C-92/11), above, para.38-234.

1547 *Kušionová v SMART Capital a.s.* (C-34/13) of September 10, 2014 para.77

1548 *RWE Vertrieb AG* (C-92/11) at para.29. See also the explanation of the exclusion in art.1(2) in recital 13 of the 1993 Directive that "the statutory or regulatory provisions of the Member States which directly or indirectly determine the terms of consumer contracts are presumed not to contain unfair terms".

1548a [2018] EWCA Civ 2284, [2019] H.L.R. 17 at [40] per Underhill L.J. (with whom Singh L.J. agreed at [50], Sir Andrew McFarlane P. dissenting at [33]–[34]). However, the CA (Underhill and Singh L.JJ.) affirmed the decision below on the basis that the contract term in question was not unfair: even if it caused a significant imbalance in the rights and obligations of the consumer, this was not "contrary to good faith": [2018] EWCA Civ 2284 at [48] and below, para.38-275.

1548b [2018] EWCA Civ 2284 at [40] and [41] per Underhill L.J.

### *(iii) The Requirement of Fairness*

### (aa) The Exclusion of Terms Which Have Been "Individually Negotiated"

**In general**

*Replace footnote 1562 with:*

38-242 1562 1999 Regulations reg.5(1); 1993 Directive art.3; *Engilbertsson v Íslandsbanki hf* (E-25/13) (EFTA Court) of August 28, 2014 at paras 125–126; *OTP Bank Nyrt v Ilyés and Kiss* (C-51/17) EU:C:2018:750 of September 20, 2018 at paras 46–49 (contract terms later amended by legislation are not "individually negotiated"). On the Consumer Rights Act 2015 see below, para.38-389.

## "Individual negotiation"

*Replace paragraph with:*

Moreover, reg.5(2) of the 1999 Regulations weight the issue of individual negotiation firmly in favour of the consumer, providing that: 38-243

> "... a term shall always be regarded as not having been individually negotiated where it has been drafted in advance and the consumer has therefore not been able to influence the substance of the term."

The Regulations place the burden of proof as to the issue of individual negotiation on the person who claims that a term has been so negotiated.[1567] In *UK Housing Alliance Ltd v Francis*[1568] the Court of Appeal held that the mere fact that a consumer had instructed solicitors in relation to the conclusion of the contract and that these had the opportunity of considering and therefore of influencing the allegedly unfair terms did not mean that any individual term had been individually negotiated: the supplier must prove that the relevant term was individually negotiated and reg.5(2) "imposes an absolute prohibition on a finding of individual negotiation if there has not been an ability to influence the substance of a term", and "it does not follow from the existence of the ability to influence the substance of a term that the term has, in fact, been individually negotiated".[1569] Finally, the Regulations also provide that:

> "Notwithstanding that a specific term or certain aspects of it in a contract has been individually negotiated, these Regulations shall apply to the rest of a contract if an overall assessment of it indicates that it is a pre-formulated standard contract."[1570]

Thus, the presence of an individually negotiated term in a consumer contract does not necessarily exclude the application of the Regulations to the rest of the contract. This means that, for example, the general terms of a standard form contract of consumer sale whose delivery date for the goods, price or other particular aspect of the contract has been "individually negotiated" will not escape the requirement of fairness altogether.

1567 1999 Regulations reg.5(4). In *XZ v Ibercaja Banco SA* (C-452/18) EU:C:2020:536, paras 33–35 the CJEU considered that a contract term drafted in advance which intended to amend a potentially unfair term in a previous contract concluded between the same parties, or to deal with the consequences of the other term being unfair, is likely to be held not to have been individually negotiated, but a national court must still verify whether the consumer was able to influence the substance of the new term, taking into account, in particular, whether or not the new term reflected a general policy of the trader and the fact that the trader did not provide the consumer with a copy of the new contract and did not allow her to become familiar with its terms: paras 36 and 37. On the other hand, the fact that the consumer made a handwritten statement that she had understood the potentially unfair term in the previous contract is not enough to allow a court to conclude that the second contract was individually negotiated and that the consumer was able to influence the substance of the term: at para.38.

1568 [2010] EWCA Civ 117, [2010] Bus. L.R. 1034. cf. *Khurana v Webster Construction Ltd* [2015] EWHC 758 (TCC) at [52] (a term presented by a party in a letter as an offer for consideration and possible acceptance by the other where there is no evidence that it had been drafted prior to the production of the letter in question was not "drafted in advance").

1569 [2010] EWCA Civ 117 at [19], per Longmore L.J. (applied by *Harrison v Shepherd Homes Ltd* [2011] EWHC 1811 (TCC), [103]–[105]). See also the discussion in *XZ v Ibercaja Banco SA* (C-452/18) EU:C:2020:536 paras 32–39 noted above in this paragraph.

1570 1999 Regulations reg.5(3).

## (bb) The "Core Exclusion"

### The "core exclusion" in the 1999 Regulations

*Replace final sentence with:*

**38-245** Until IP completion day, English courts are bound to follow this case-law of the Court of Justice in their decisions on reg.6(2) of the Regulations as it implements art.4(2) of the Directive without amendment.[1583]

[1583] European Communities Act 1972 s.3(1), but see *Casehub Ltd v Wolf Cola Ltd* [2017] EWHC 1169 (Ch), [2017] 5 Costs L.R. 835, noted below, para.38-264. On the changing significance of case law of the CJEU for English courts on IP completion day see above, para.38-004 and Vol.I, para.1-017B. Under the "minimum harmonisation" clause in the 1993 Directive art.8 UK law is entitled to narrow the core exclusion which it provides in the interests of more extensive consumer protection and this has apparently been effected by the Consumer Rights Act 2015 s.64, below, paras 38-394—38-403.

### European case-law

*Replace paragraph with:*

**38-249** Since the decision of the Supreme Court in *OFT v Abbey National Plc*, the Court of Justice of the EU has considered the exclusion contained in art.4(2) of the 1993 Directive on a number of occasions.[1607] This European case-law takes a very different view of the interpretation of art.4(2) from that adopted by the Supreme Court in *OFT v Abbey National Plc* and provides significant guidance on its application which must be used by English courts.[1608] Of these cases, the most important are *Kásler*, *Matei*, *Van Hove* and *Andriciuc*.[1609] It should be noted, however, that the significance of case-law of the Court of Justice for English courts changes on IP completion day and in particular the Supreme Court will no longer be bound to follow the case law of the Court of Justice.[1609a]

[1607] See, in particular, *Caja de Ahorros y Monte de Piedad de Madrid v Asociación de Usuarios de Servicios Bancarios (Ausbanc)* (C-484/08) EU:C:2010:309, June 3, 2010 [2010] 3 C.M.L.R. 43; *Pohotovosť s.r.o. v Korčkovska* (C-76/10) of November 16, 2010 (available only in French); *Nemzeti Fogyasztóvédelmi Hatóság v Invitel Távközlési Zrt* (C-472/10) EU:C:2012:242, April 26, 2012 ("*Invitel* (C-472/10)"); *Kásler v OTP Jelzálogbank Zrt* (C-26/13) EU:C:2014:282, April 30, 2014 ("*Kásler* (C-26/13)"); and *Matei v SC Volksbank România SA* (C-143/13) EU:C:2015:127, February 26, 2015 ("*Matei* (C-143/13)"); *Van Hove v CNP Assurances SA* (C-96/14) EU:C:2015:262, April 26, 2015 ("*Van Hove* (C-96/14)"); *Bucura v SC Bancpost SA* (C-348/14) EU:C:2015:447, July 9, 2015; and *Andriciuc v Banca Românească* (C-186/16) of September 20, 2017 ("*Andriciuc* (C-186/16)").

[1608] For this reason, it is submitted that the reasoning of English courts which have applied the interpretation of art.4(2) of the 1993 Directive by the SC in *OFT v Abbey National Plc* or otherwise without reference to the recent case-law of the CJEU as described in the text should not be relied on or should be relied on only in the light of the case-law of the CJEU: for these earlier decisions see *Office of Fair Trading v Ashbourne Management Services Ltd* [2011] EWHC 1237 (Ch), [2011] E.C.C. 31 (terms which set a minimum duration for gym membership of one year with either no or only a very limited possibility of cancellation without liability fell within the main subject matter of the contract but remained reviewable for fairness on other grounds); *Foxtons Ltd v O'Reardon* [2011] EWHC 2946 (QB) (term in exclusive estate agency contract for sale of property provided that agent's fee was payable on exchange of contracts fell within reg.6(2)(a) as it defined the main subject matter of the contract). cf. *Financial Services Authority v Asset L.I. Inc (t/a Asset Land Investment Inc)* [2013] EWHC 178 (Ch) at [132] (terms in contracts for the sale of land under a collective investment scheme which described services undertaken by the seller held not to relate to the *main* subject matter of the contract, which was the sale and purchase of land). On appeal, the Court of Appeal considered that the issue of the unfairness of the terms was unnecessary for the issues before the court, but it would have agreed with the court below: [2014] EWCA Civ 435, [2015] 1 All E.R. 1 at [96]–[99]. cf. the view of the HC in *Casehub Ltd v Wolf Cola Ltd* [2017] EWHC 1169 (Ch), [2017] 5 Costs L.R. 835 noted below, para.38-264, that it was bound to follow the decision of the SC in *Abbey National Plc* rather than the guidance of the CJEU.

[1609] Below, paras 38-250 et seq. See also Commission guidance C(2019) 5325 final, pp.23–25.

[1609a] See above, para.38-004 and Vol.I, para.1-017B.

## Matei

*To the end of paragraph, after "return by the creditor.", add:*

In this way, the Court of Justice appears to require a distinct service to be identified to constitute consideration for the "risk charge" (an "actual service which could constitute consideration for that charge"). In the absence of such a counter-part for the charge, the question of its adequacy (and therefore the second limb of the exclusion in art.4(2)) "does not arise".[1642a] **38-257**

[1642a] *Matei* (C-143/13) para.70. Cf. the very different interpretation given to *Matei* by A.G. Hogan in *Kiss v Kiss* (C-621/17) EU:C:2019:411 Opinion of May 15, 2019 at paras 35–38. There, a contract of consumer credit included two terms under which a "disbursement commission" (a fixed sum of about €250) and a "management charge" of 2.4 per cent per annum were payable by the consumer borrower. Even though the contract did not specify the services for which this charge was made, A.G. Hogan advised that the term providing for the management charge could fall within the second limb of art.4(2) of the 1993 Directive on the basis that the charge formed "one element of the price to be paid" in return for the loan: "a single service may give rise to several price clauses" without taking the clauses outside the exclusion, and the "a clause may contain several terms and a term may take the form of several clauses: C-143/13 at para.50. However, he further advised that the terms were not in "plain intelligible writing": C-143/13, para.44 and see below, para.38-262. (The CJEU in its decision of October 3, 2019 EU:C:2019:820 did not address this issue, but focussed on the nature and significance of the requirement of transparency). In *Profi Credit Polska SA z siedziba w Bielsku- Bialej v QJ* (C-84/19, C-222/19 and C-252/19) EU:C:2020:259 A.G. Hogan in his Opinion of April 2, 2020, paras 49–60 took a similar view of art.4(2) as he had in *Kiss v Kiss*, but this view was not followed by the CJEU in its judgment of September 3, 2020 at paras 81 and 86 as it stated that the application of the second limb of the exception in art.4(2) of the Directive did not apply to the contract terms in question as they did not specify the services to which the charges which they imposed referred; the terms were also likely to have failed the requirement of transparency.

## Andriciuc

*Replace paragraph with:*

The decision of the Court of Justice in *Andriciuc v Banca Românească* (C-186/16) provides a good example of a case where it clearly considered that the contract term in question fell *within* the exclusion provided by art.4(2).[1651] In that case, the consumers, resident in Romania and with incomes in Romanian currency, had contracted loans from a bank under which they had to make monthly repayments in the same foreign currency (Swiss francs) as that in which the contracts had been concluded, with the consequence that the risk in fluctuations as between the Romanian currency and the Swiss franc was borne entirely by the consumers. The consumers sought to challenge the fairness of the terms providing for the loan to be repaid in the same currency in which it was made, but the question arose whether those terms fell within the exclusion in Romanian legislation implementing art.4(2) of the Directive. Having referred to its own case-law in *Kásler*, *Matei* and *Van Hove*,[1652] the Court of Justice concluded that "a number of elements in the documents before the Court" indicate that the relevant terms are covered by the notion of "main subject matter of the contract" within the meaning of the first limb of art.4(2).[1653] The Court observed: **38-260**

> "In that connection, it must be observed that, under a loan agreement, the lender undertakes, in particular, to make available to the borrower a certain sum of money and the latter undertakes, in particular, to repay that sum, usually with interest, on the scheduled payment dates. Therefore, the essential obligations of such a contract relate to a sum of money which must be determined by the stipulated currency in which it is paid and repaid. Thus, as the Advocate General observed…, the fact that a loan must be repaid in a certain currency relates, in principle, not to an ancillary repayment arrangement, but to very nature of the debtor's obligation, thereby constituting an essential element of a loan agreement."[1654]

In this respect, the Court of Justice distinguished the situation before it from *Kásler* on the basis that, although the loans there were denominated in foreign currency, they had to be repaid in the national currency according to the selling rate of the exchange applied by the bank, whereas in *Andriciuc* the loans had to be repaid in the same foreign currency as that in which they were issued.[1655] As a result, the Court of Justice was clear that the term setting the repayment in Swiss francs fell within the exclusion of art.4(2), subject to the proviso that it was drafted in plain intelligible language.[1656]

[1651] *Andriciuc v Banca Românească* (C-186/16) of September 20, 2017 ("*Andriciuc* (C-186/16)").

[1652] Above, paras 38-250—38-259.

[1653] *Andriciuc* (C-186/16) at paras 27–31.

[1654] *Andriciuc* (C-186/16) para.38 referring to the Opinion of A.G. Wahl, paras 46 et seq. See also *CY v Caixabank SA* (C-224/19, C-259/19) EU:C:2020:578 at paras 62–64.

[1655] *Andriciuc* (C-186/16) at para.40.

[1656] *Andriciuc* (C-186/16) at para.41. On its decision on the proviso, see below, para.38-262.

*Add new paragraph:*

38-260A **Ibercaja Banco SA** In *XZ v Ibercaja Banco SA*[1656a] a trader and a consumer had concluded a contract of consumer credit secured by a mortgage with a variable rate of interest (the first contract) and then had concluded a contract (the second contract, termed a "novation agreement") under which they agreed to amend the lower limit on the variable rate (contained in its "floor clause") and also to a mutual waiver of any claim arising from the first contract, including therefore in particular any claim by the consumer that the terms of the first contract were unfair and not binding on him or her.[1656b] The Court of Justice was asked by a Spanish court to rule on the validity of the *second* contract under the 1993 Directive. According to Advocate General Saugmandsgaard Øe, the "non-binding" effect of the 1993 Directive on any term in the *first* consumer contract does not in principle render such a second contract invalid,[1656c] and the Court of Justice appeared to agree as it instead considered the fairness of the terms of the *second* contract under the Directive,[1656d] in particular as regards the provision of information enabling the consumer to understand the legal consequences for themselves.[1656e] In this case, however, the Court noted that the consumer's agreement to waive their rights was capable of forming the "main subject-matter of the contract" within the meaning of art.4(2) of the Directive so as to fall outside the requirement of fairness[1656f]: as Advocate General Saugmandsgaard Øe had observed, it is "the very essence" of a settlement to contain a clause concerning the waiver of all rights, actions or claims relative to the dispute.[1656g] However, the Court of Justice focused its own guidance on the proviso to art.4(2) that the terms are in plain intelligible language, a proviso which is explained in the following paragraphs.[1656h]

[1656a] C-452/18, Opinion of A.G. Saugmandsgaard Øe of January 20, 2020 (available in French) ("C-452/18, A.G. Opinion"); decision of the CJEU (C-452/18) of July 9, 2020 EU:C:2020:536 ("*Ibercaja Banco SA* (C-452/18)").

[1656b] As noted below, para.38-343, national case-law had found *some* floor clauses unfair under national legislation implementing the 1993 Directive.

[1656c] C-452/18, A.G. Opinion paras 34 and 35. See below, para.38-339A where the conditions for this position are noted.

[1656d] *Ibercaja Banco SA* (C-452/18) paras 59–61.

[1656e] *Ibercaja Banco SA* (C-452/18) at para.77.

1656f *Ibercaja Banco SA* (C-452/18) at para.68. On the exclusion in art.4(2) (the first limb) and this proviso see above, paras 38-245 et seq.

1656g C-452/18, A.G. Opinion para.73 applying the approach to the first limb of art.4(2) adopted by the CJEU in *Kásler v OTP Jelzálogbank Zrt* (C-26/13) EU:C:2014:282 paras 49 and 50, above, para.38-251.

1656h See, in particular, below, para.38-262C.

## The condition that the "terms are in plain intelligible language"

*Replace paragraph with:*

The exclusions from the assessment of unfairness contained in art.4(2) of the Directive and reflected in reg.6(2) of the 1999 Regulations are subject to the condition that the relevant terms are expressed in plain and intelligible language: where they are not the terms are for this reason subject to the test of unfairness.[1658] The Court of Justice has made clear both the importance and the demanding character of this condition.[1658a] First, in *Pohotovost' sro v Korckovskà*[1659] the Court of Justice held that the omission of the APR (which, together with other "essential terms of the contract"[1660] was required by the Consumer Credit Directive of 1987[1661]) from a term of a contract of consumer credit which concerned the cost of the loan could be seen by a national court as having a decisive impact on the question whether that term was "in plain intelligible language", and, if it was so held, the term failed the condition for the application of art.4(2) and fell to be assessed for its fairness under art.3 of the Directive.[1662] This decision has considerable implications given the breadth of scope of application and the extent of information requirements imposed by the law (and EU law in particular) in relation to consumer contracts.[1663] Secondly, in *Kásler* the Court of Justice explained more generally the significance of the condition that the "terms are in plain intelligible language", holding that it has the same scope as the requirement of plain intelligible writing in art.5 of the 1993 Directive,[1664] and that the latter includes a requirement that the consumer should actually be given an opportunity of examining all the terms of the contract.[1665] The Court then noted that it had previously held in the context of art.5 that pre-contractual information on the terms of the contract and the consequences of concluding it is of "fundamental importance for a consumer" as it provides the basis on which "he decides whether he wishes to be bound by the terms previously drawn up by the seller or supplier".[1666] For this reason, "the requirement of transparency" of contract terms in the 1993 Directive (including in art.4(2)) cannot be "reduced merely to their being formally and grammatically intelligible", but must be understood in a broad sense given that the Directive is based on the idea that the consumer is in a position of weakness compared to the trader "in particular as regards his level of knowledge".[1667] As a result, the requirement of transparency requires that the "consumer is in a position to evaluate, on the basis of clear, intelligible criteria, the economic consequences for him which derive from" the term in question; the reasons for the trader using the term and its relationship with other contractual terms should be clear and intelligible.[1668] In the context of the terms before it, which concerned the application of different exchange rates to different aspects of the contract of consumer credit,[1669] the national referring court must therefore: 38-261

"... determine whether, having regard to all the relevant information, including the promotional material and information provided by the lender in the negotiation of the loan agreement, the *average consumer, who is reasonably well informed and reasonably observant and circumspect*, would not only be aware of the difference, generally observed on the securities market, between the selling rate of exchange and the buying rate of exchange of a foreign currency, but also be able to assess the potentially significant economic consequences for him resulting from the application of the selling rate of exchange for the calculation of the repayments for which he would ultimately be liable and, therefore, the total cost of the sum borrowed."[1670]

It will be seen therefore, that the Court of Justice requires national courts to consider as a condition for the application of the exclusion in art.4(2) not merely whether a term is formally or grammatically clear but also whether (in its context) it allows the average consumer to understand its practical significance for himself.[1671]

1658 For examples in the English courts see *Bankers Insurance Co Ltd v South* [2003] P.I.Q.R. P.28 at [24] (exclusion in travel insurance held "plain and intelligible"); *Financial Services Authority v Asset L.I. Inc (t/a Asset Land Investment Inc)* [2013] EWHC 178 (Ch), [2013] 2 B.C.L.C. 480 at [132] (terms in contracts for the sale of land under a collective investment scheme which described services undertaken by seller held not to be in "plain, intelligible" language and so reviewable for unfairness even if they otherwise fell within the exclusion of reg.6(2) of the 1999 Regulations). On appeal, the Court of Appeal considered that the issue of the unfairness of the terms was unnecessary for the issues before the court, but it would have agreed with the court below: [2014] EWCA Civ 435, [2015] 1 All E.R. 1 at [96]–[99].

1658a See also Commission guidance C(2019) 5325 final pp.26–31.

1659 C-76/10 of November 16, 2010 (available only in French). The decision was an "order" (*ordonnance*) made under art.104(3) of the Rules of Procedure of the Court of Justice, according to which a "question referred to the Court for a preliminary ruling is identical to a question on which the Court has already ruled, or where the answer to such a question may be clearly deduced from existing case-law, the Court may, after hearing the Advocate General, at any time give its decision by reasoned order in which reference is made to its previous judgment or to the relevant case-law".

1660 Directive 87/102 on consumer credit [1987] O.J. L42/48 art.4(3).

1661 Directive 87/102 on consumer credit [1987] O.J. L42/48 art.4(2)(a).

1662 C-76/10 para.72, citing *Caja de Madrid* (C-484/08) para.32 and see similarly *EPS KSI Slovensko s.r.o. v Danko* (C-448/17) EU:C:2018:745 of September 20, 2018 (credit agreement's use of a mathematical formula for the calculation of the APR without the information necessary to make that calculation is equivalent to a simple failure to provide the APR). The CJEU in *Pohotovost' sro* further held that the national court could find that the term was unfair as a result of the omission of the APR: C-76/10 at para.73.

1663 See above, paras 38-059 et seq., especially in respect of "on-premises contracts", off-premises contracts and distance contracts.

1664 *Kásler* (C-26/13) at para.69. On art.5 see below paras 38-347 et seq. (1999 Regulations reg.7) and paras 38-414—38-417 (Consumer Rights Act 2015 s.68).

1665 *Kásler* (C-26/13) at para.67 referring to 1993 Directive recital 12.

1666 *Kásler* (C-26/13) at para.70 referring to *RWE Vertrieb AG v Verbraucherzentrale Nordrhein-Westfalen eV* (C-92/11) EU:C:2013:180, March 21, 2013 at para.44, below, para.38-350.

1667 *Kásler* (C-26/13) at paras 71–72.

1668 *Kásler* (C-26/13) at para.75.

1669 Above, para.38-254.

1670 *Kásler* (C-26/13) at para.74 (emphasis added).

1671 The CJEU has held that the plainness and intelligibility of a term must be assessed "by referring, at the time of conclusion of the contract, to all the circumstances attending the conclusion of the contract and to all the other terms of the contract, even though some of those terms have been declared or presumed to be unfair and annulled at a later time by the national legislature": *OTP Bank Nyrt v Ilyés and Kiss* (C-51/17) EU:C:2018:750 of September 20, 2018 at paras 79–80, drawing on the terms of art.4(1) of the 1993 Directive which itself refers to the assessment of the unfairness of a contract term. On the wider significance of the "average consumer" in EU law see above, paras 38-044—38-046. The CJEU has held that the requirement of transparency must be assessed by the court in its context and that this is incompatible with national case law which holds that a particular contract term in itself satisfies this requirement: *CY v Caixabank SA* (C-224/19, C-259/19) EU:C:2020:578 at para.69.

*Replace paragraph with:*

For this purpose, *Van Hove* provides an example of how very demanding the requirement of transparency can be. There, a contract of insurance contained a term which restricted cover for the consumer to the situation where he suffered from "total incapacity for work" where "after 90 consecutive days' interruption of activity following an accident or illness ... he finds himself unable to take up any activity, paid or otherwise".[1672] The French court had considered that while "plain and precise", this term is capable of being understood in various ways, including that it does not rule out payment other than where the consumer is not fit to carry on any activity whatsoever[1673] so that it cannot be ruled out that, even though grammatically intelligible, "the scope of that term was not understood by the consumer".[1674] The notion of "activity, paid or otherwise" is, in the view of the Court of Justice, "extremely broad and vague"; moreover, the consumer may not necessarily have been aware of the difference between the concept of "total incapacity for work" under the contract and "partial permanent incapacity" within the meaning of French social security law.[1675] It was, therefore, for the national court to assess all the information available to the consumer as well as the contract itself, in deciding whether an average consumer would have understood this difference and its potentially significant economic consequences.[1676] Moreover, the fact that the insurance contract was related to loan contracts could also be relevant as: **38-262**

> "... [t]he consumer cannot be required ... to have the same vigilance regarding the extent of the risks covered by that insurance contract as he would if he had concluded that contract and the loan contracts separately."[1677]

It will be seen that, in this way, the understanding of the average consumer of the significance of a contract term is crucial to the application of the exclusion in art.4(2), though it is relevant to the condition of transparency rather than to the identification of the terms subject to the exclusion.[1678] A similarly demanding approach was taken in *Andriciuc*, which concerned a term requiring repayment of a loan in a foreign currency where the loan was itself issued in that same currency.[1679] The Court of Justice noted that, in deciding whether the contract:

> "... puts the consumer in a position to evaluate, on the basis of clear, intelligible criteria, the economic consequences for him which derive from [the contract]",[1680]

a national court should refer to all relevant facts, "including the promotional material and information provided by the lender in the negotiation of the loan agreement" with the view to ascertaining whether:

> "... all the information likely to have a bearing on the extent of his commitment have [sic] been communicated to the consumer, enabling him to estimate in particular the total cost of his loan."[1681]

In this respect, the Court of Justice noted the Recommendation of the European Systematic Risk Board on lending in foreign currencies to the effect that financial institutions:

> "... must provide borrowers with adequate information to enable them to take well-informed and prudent decisions and should at least encompass the impact on instalments of a severe depreciation of the legal tender of the Member State in which a borrower is domiciled and of an increase of the foreign interest rate."[1682]

As a result, in the case of such a contract, the consumer/borrower must be clearly informed that he is being exposed to a certain foreign exchange risk which may become difficult to bear if there is a fall in value of the currency in which he receives his income and the lender must set out the possible variations in exchange rate and the risks in taking out a loan in a foreign currency.[1683] In this respect, of particular interest is the Court of Justice's use of a European recommendation to help determine the content of the information to be supplied by a trader if it is to satisfy the requirement that a term is in plain, intelligible writing.

[1672] *Van Hove v CNP Assurances SA* (C-96/14) of April 23, 2015, on which see above, para.38-259.

[1673] *Van Hove* (C-96/14) para.42.

[1674] *Van Hove* (C-96/14) para.43.

[1675] *Van Hove* (C-96/14) paras 45–46.

[1676] *Van Hove* (C-96/14) para.47.

[1677] *Van Hove* (C-96/14) para.48. As will be seen, the Consumer Rights Act 2015 follows this approach in its provision implementing art.4(2) of the Directive by expressly referring to the "average consumer" for the purpose of its condition that the term be prominent as well as transparent: see 2015 Act s.64(2)–(5) below, paras 38-395—38-401.

[1678] cf. the approach of the Court of Appeal in *OFT v Abbey National Plc* (reversed by the SC in the same case) which adopted the viewpoint of an average consumer to distinguish between those contract terms which set the "price or remuneration" and other terms, as suggested by earlier editions of the present Work: [2009] EWCA Civ 116, [2009] 2 W.L.R. 1286 at [72] referring to the present work (30th edn, 2008) Vol.I para.15-058, reversed [2009] UKSC 6, [2010] 1 A.C. 696 at [113]. On the decision of the SC, see above, paras 38-247—38-248.

[1679] *Andriciuc v Banca Românească* (C-186/16) of September 20, 2017 ("*Andriciuc* (C-186/16)") above, para.38-260. See similarly *OTP Bank Nyrt v Ilyes and Kiss* (C-51/17) EU:C:2018:750 of September 20, 2018 at paras 71–78; *GT v JS* (C-38/17) EU:C:2019:461 of June 5, 2019 paras 33–36.

[1680] *Andriciuc* (C-186/16) at para.45.

[1681] *Andriciuc* (C-186/16) at paras 46–47.

[1682] *Andriciuc* (C-186/16) at para.49 referring to Recommendation ESRB/2011/1 of September 21, 2011 on lending in foreign currencies, [2011] O.J. C342/1, Recommendation A—Risk awareness of borrowers, para.1 [2011] O.J. C342/1.

[1683] *Andriciuc* (C-186/16) at para.50.

*Add new paragraphs:*

**38-262A** In *Gómez del Moral Guasch*, the Court of Justice of the EU gave further guidance as to the application of the transparency requirement in the context of a contract of consumer credit with a variable rate of interest.[1683a] There, a term of the contract of consumer credit set the interest rate by reference to one of the official reference indices provided by national legislation for this purpose, though the one selected was both less usual and more costly to the consumer than others so provided.[1683b] In the view of the Court of Justice, the transparency requirement means that:

> "an average consumer, who is reasonably well-informed and reasonably observant and circumspect, is in a position to understand the specific functioning of the method used for calculating that rate and thus evaluate, on the basis of clear, intelligible criteria, the potentially significant economic consequences of such a term on his or her financial obligations."[1683c]

While it is for the national court to assess whether this is the case, including by reference to the promotional material and information provided by the lender before contract,[1683d] it should determine whether "*all the information* likely to have a bearing on the extent of his or her commitment have been communicated to the consumer, enabling the consumer to estimate in particular the total cost of the loan."[1683e]

However, for this purpose, in the circumstances it was relevant that the essential information relating to way in which the index rate was determined was "easily accessible to anyone intending to take out a mortgage loan" in the relevant national legislation and was capable of enabling the reasonably observant and circumspect consumer to understand how the index was calculated.[1683f] It was also relevant that credit institutions at the time were required by national law to provide consumers with data relating to the fluctuations of the index rate in question during the preceding two years as well as with its most recent available value and this would give the consumer "an objective indication as to the economic consequences arising from the application of such an index" and provide "a useful point of comparison between the calculation of the variable interest rate based on the [the particular index rate] and other formulas for calculating interest rates".[1683g] This guidance illustrates how demanding the transparency requirement can be in a context such as consumer credit, but it also illustrates that in assessing whether or not it has been satisfied on the facts a national court should consider all the sources of information available to the "average consumer" and not just information provided or to be provided by the trader.[1683h]

1683a *Gómez del Moral Guasch v Bankia SA* (C-125/18) EU:C:2020:138 para.37 ("*Gómez del Moral Guasch v Bankia SA* (C-125/18)".

1683b The rate in question was the average rate of mortgage loans granted by the Spanish savings banks ("IRPH" of Spanish savings banks) whereas 90 per cent of mortgage loans taken out in Spain instead referred to the Euro Interbank Offered Rate ("the Euribor index"): *Gómez del Moral Guasch v Bankia SA* (C-125/18) at para.22.

1683c *Gómez del Moral Guasch v Bankia SA* (C-125/18) at para.51.

1683d *Gómez del Moral Guasch v Bankia SA* (C-125/18) at para.52.

1683e *Gómez del Moral Guasch v Bankia SA* (C-125/18) at para.52 (emphasis added).

1683f *Gómez del Moral Guasch v Bankia SA* (C-125/18) at para.53.

1683g *Gómez del Moral Guasch v Bankia SA* (C-125/18) at para.54.

1683h See also *XZ v Ibercaja Banco SA* (C-452/18) EU:C:2020:536 at paras 44–56 where the CJEU followed its approach in *Gómez del Moral Guasch v Bankia SA* but accepted (at para.52) that where a bank lends money on a variable interest rate with a "floor clause", it "cannot ... be required to provide precise information regarding the financial consequences of variations in the interest rate during the course of the contract, since those variations depend on unforeseeable future events that are outwith the seller or supplier's control".

**Transparency as regards the trader's services** On the other hand, the Court of Justice has interpreted the requirement of transparency in a less demanding way in the case of the information which the consumer is to receive about the services to be provided by the trader. In *Kiss v Kiss*, a contract of consumer credit included two terms under which a "disbursement commission" (a fixed sum of about €250) and a "management charge" of 2.4 per cent per annum were payable by the consumer in addition to the interest itself in circumstances where it was not clear what services the trader provided in respect of either the commission or the management charge.[1683i] The Court of Justice was asked to consider whether this meant that these terms were not "plain and intelligible" within the meaning of arts 4(2) and 5 and, if so, whether they were unfair.[1683j] In the case of the management charge, the Court found that the consumer was in a position to understand "the potentially significant economic consequences for him" of the term as required by the Court's earlier case- 38-262B law,[1683k] but in the case of the commission charge the national court should consider whether the contract set out transparently the reasons justifying the remuneration corresponding to that charge.[1683l] On the other hand, the Court of Justice held that its case-law did *not* require the lender to specify in the contract the nature of all the services supplied in return for the charges imposed by one or more of the contract terms, though it is important that the nature of the services actually provided can be reasonably understood or deduced from the contract as a whole and that the consumer must be in a position to check that there is no overlap between the different costs or between the services which they remunerate.[1683m]

[1683i] C-621/17, EU:C:2019:820 (French version used) ("*Kiss v Kiss* (C-621/17)").

[1683j] The CJEU did not think it necessary to consider the issue discussed by A.G. Hogan (Opinion at paras 35–38) as to whether the lack of a service in return for a particular sum payable under the contract affected whether the second limb of the exclusion in art.4(2) applied: see above, para.38-257(note).

[1683k] *Kásler* (C-26/13) para.75, above, para.38-261; *Van Hove* (C-96/14) para.47; *Andriciuc* (C-186/16) paras 45–47, above, para.38-262.

[1683l] *Kiss v Kiss* (C-621/17) para.40 following *Matei* (C-143/13) para.77.

[1683m] *Kiss v Kiss* (C-621/17) para.40.

38-262C **Transparency in settlement contracts** As earlier noted, in *XZ v Ibercaja Banco SA* the Court of Justice held that a clause in a settlement agreement between a bank and a consumer under which the parties waive any rights or claims relating to an earlier consumer credit contract may fall within the first limb of the exclusion contained in art.4(2) of the 1993 Directive (on the basis that the clause relates to the definition of the main subject matter of the settlement contract), but only if it satisfies the requirement of transparency.[1683n] In this respect, the national court considered that the bank had not provided the consumer with sufficient information as to the unfairness of the term in the earlier contract nor of their rights to recover money as "unduly paid" if that term were held unfair and not binding.[1683o] However, in this respect, the Court of Justice noted that the unfairness of a term must be assessed as of the time of the conclusion of the contract:

> "taking account of all the circumstances which could have been known to that seller or supplier at that time, and which were such as to affect the future performance of that contract, since a contractual term may give rise to an imbalance between the parties which manifests itself only during the performance of the contract."[1683p]

In this respect, while the unfairness of the term (a "floor clause") in the consumer credit contract which was the subject of settlement had been established by the national supreme court at the relevant time, that decision had been prospective and it was only later that that supreme court had accepted that art.6 of the Directive precluded such temporal limitation.[1683q] At the time of the conclusion of the second contract, therefore, the unfairness of the floor clause was *foreseeable* by the bank, but it was not certain as it had not been so established between the contracting parties; nor was it apparent that the law as it stood at that time meant that the bank knew that the unfairness of the term would have given the consumer a right to full reimbursement of sums paid.[1683r] The national court should therefore assess "the level of certainty which existed at the time of conclusion of the novation agreement as regards the unfairness of the initial 'floor' term" in order to determine what information the requirement of transparency required of the bank in presenting the term under which the consumer waived his or her rights arising from the consumer credit contract.[1683s] However, the Court of Justice then ruled that the term in the second contract under which the consumer waived her rights arising from the earlier credit contract "may be regarded as 'unfair', particularly where the consumer was not provided with the relevant information enabling him or her to understand the legal consequences for him or her", the Court referring to the example in the "indicative list" of terms whose object or effect is "excluding or hindering the consumer's right to take legal action or exercise any other legal remedy".[1683t] In this way, a failure in transparency of a term can both disapply the exclusion in art.4(2) and contribute to a finding of unfairness under art.3(1).

[1683n] *XZ v Ibercaja Banco SA* (C-452/18) EU:C:2020:536 ("*Ibercaja Banco SA* (C-452/18)") at para.68, on which see above, para.38-260A. The CJEU held that consumers could not waive their rights to challenge the fairness of the terms in any future dispute: *Ibercaja Banco SA* (C-452/18) paras 75–77 and see below para.38-339A.

[1683o] *Ibercaja Banco SA* (C-452/18) para.69.

[1683p] *Ibercaja Banco SA* (C-452/18) para.70.

[1683q] *Ibercaja Banco SA* (C-452/18) para.71.

[1683r] *Ibercaja Banco SA* (C-452/18) paras 72 and 73.

[1683s] *Ibercaja Banco SA* (C-452/18) para.74.

[1683t] *Ibercaja Banco SA* (C-452/18) para.75 (first indent), On the example in para.1(q) see below, para.38-301.

**OFT v Abbey National Plc viewed in the light of the European case-law**

*To the end of paragraph, after "matter of authority.[1694]", add:*

However, it should be noted that after IP completion day, the Supreme Court (in particular) will no longer be bound to follow existing case law of the Court of Justice.[1694a] **38-264**

[1694a] Above, para.38-219 and on IP completion day see above, para.38-004 and Vol.I, paras 1-014 et seq.

## (cc) The Composite Test of Unfairness

**The test in the Regulations**

*Replace footnote 1700 with:*

[1700] 1993 Directive arts 3 and 4(1). For a recent general discussion of the case-law of the CJEU on this test see Commission guidance C(2019) 5325 final, pp.20 et seq. **38-265**

**The basic test**

*Replace paragraph with:*

The basic test of unfairness of a term is that: **38-266**

> "... contrary to the requirement of good faith it causes a significant imbalance in the parties' rights and obligations under the contract, to the detriment of the consumer."

The significance of this test gave rise to considerable comment,[1702] and for some its use of the notion of good faith introduced into English law a new and somewhat alien concept. In this respect, it is helpful to bear in mind the origins of the reference to good faith, this flowing from its use in the German legislation which significantly influenced the Directive.[1703] In turn, this German legislation can be seen as the legislative recognition of existing judicial controls on unfair contract terms, this law-making being justified by the Civil Code's general provision requiring good faith of parties to contracts[1704]: "good faith" in this context can be seen as little more than a convenient legal pigeon-hole in which to have placed within the structure of the Civil Code judicial developments which took into account a range of considerations deemed appropriate to the control in hand.[1705] For this reason, it could be thought that the reference to "good faith" in the Directive is no more than a bow in the direction of these origins. Indeed, such a very limited significance to the phrase "contrary to the requirement of good faith" has been adopted by some French writers[1706] and this was reflected in its omission from France's implementing legislation.[1707] For a French lawyer it is unnecessary for two reasons: first, because the French Civil Code already makes a general requirement of the performance of contracts in good faith[1708] (an argument of no significance for English law), but, secondly, because a business supplier could not be considered to remain in good faith if he were to seek to enjoy the disproportionate advantages set out in the contract concluded with the consumer.[1709] From this perspective, the requirement that the term "causes a significant imbalance in the parties' rights and obligations under the contract to the detriment of the consumer" is sufficient in itself.[1709a]

[1702] Collins at 229; Beale, Ch.9 pp.242 et seq.; Weatherill (1995) 3 *European Review of Private Law* 307; Howells and Willhemson at p.88, pp.96 et seq.; Beatson pp.200–203, 300 et seq., pp.291 et seq.; Bright in Burrows and Peel, *Contract Terms* (2007), Ch.9.

[1703] i.e. *Gesetz zur Regelung des Rechts der Allgemeinen Geschäftsbedingungen* ("Standard Contract Terms Act") of 1976, translated in part by Dannemann in Markesinis, Lorenz and Dannemann, at pp.908 et seq. (The German Standard Contracts Act 1976 itself was abrogated and replaced by a revised BGB para.307(1).) The first draft of the Directive was much closer to the German legislation, applying to commercial as well as to consumer contracts. Apart from the German law, the laws of some other Member States law had used the notion of good faith in their control of unfair contract terms, for example, Spanish law: Paisant, *Recueil Dalloz Sirey*, 1995 Chronique p.99, p.100.

[1704] BGB para.242 and see Zimmermann, *The New German Law of Obligations* (2005), pp.173–178.

[1705] Zimmermann and Whittaker, *Good Faith in European Contract Law* (2000), Ch.1. It is noteworthy that the German Standard Terms Act of 1976 did not attempt to explain the requirement of good faith by reference to the already elaborate case-law based on para.242 BGB, but instead listed the clauses which are either necessarily void or are void if they fail a test of "reasonableness": see Standard Contract Terms Act 1976 paras 9–11.

[1706] See Larroumet, *Droit Civil, Les obligations Le contrat*, 5th edn (2003), Tome 3, p.422; Paisant, at p.100.

[1707] *Loi* 95/96 of February 1, 1995, now art.L.132-1 al. 1 Code de la consommation (as amended) Again, this reflects French legislative and judicial tradition which preferred to use the notion of the abuse of rights (hence, "*clauses abusives*") rather than the (admittedly closely related) notion of good faith.

[1708] In the case of the Code civil as first enacted in 1804, good faith was expressed only as applying to the performance of contracts (art.1134 al. 3 C.civ.), but after reform to French contract law in 2016, art.1104 requires that contracts are "negotiated, formed and performed in good faith".

[1709] Paisant at p.100.

[1709a] Cf. *Tóth v ERSTE Bank Hungary Zrt.* (C-34/18) (Opinion of 29 March, 2019) paras 55–62 esp. at para.58 where A.G. Hogan took the view (which he accepted was not reflected in the case-law of the CJEU) that the phrase "contrary to the requirement of good faith" is not distinct from the overall criterion of "significant imbalance", but is instead "essentially descriptive of the state of affairs" where there is a significant imbalance (a point not addressed by the CJEU in its decision of September 19, 2019). See similarly *Kiss v Kiss* (C-621/17) Opinion of A.G. Hogan of May 15, 2019 at para.66, although the CJEU in its decision of October 19, 2019 paras 49 and 50 did not follow its A.G.'s view. While noting A.G. Hogan's view, the EU Commission has preferred to see the reference to good faith and the test of significant imbalance as "closely linked": Commission guidance C(2019) 5325 final, p.32.

**Aziz and Menéndez Álvarez**

*Replace paragraph with:*

**38-270** In *Aziz* the Court of Justice explained the test of "significant imbalance" and the proper approach to the condition that this imbalance must arise "contrary to the requirement of good faith" in a reference from a Spanish court asking for guidance as to whether three terms in a contract of loan secured by a mortgage of residential property to be repaid over 33 years were unfair within the meaning of the Directive.[1717] First, as the Court had previously explained, "the system of protection introduced by the directive is based on the idea that the consumer is in a weaker position vis-à-vis the seller or supplier, as regards both his bargaining power and his level of knowledge" and the Directive's provision that unfair terms are not binding on the consumer "aims to replace the formal balance which the contract establishes between the rights and obligations of the parties with an effective balance which re-establishes equality between them".[1718] The Court then held that:

> "... in order to ascertain whether a term causes a 'significant imbalance' in the parties' rights and obligations arising under the contract, to the detriment of the consumer, it must in particular be considered what rules of national law would apply in the absence of an agreement by the parties in that regard. Such a comparative analysis will enable the national court to evaluate whether and, as the case may be, to what extent, the contract places the consumer in a legal situation less favourable than that provided for by the national law in force. To that end, an assessment should also be carried out of the legal situation of that consumer having regard to the means at his disposal, under national legislation, to prevent continued use of unfair terms."[1719]

The Court continued:

> "With regard to the question of the circumstances in which such an imbalance arises 'contrary to the requirement of good faith', having regard to the sixteenth recital in the preamble to the directive ... the national court must assess for those purposes whether the seller or supplier, dealing fairly and equitably with the consumer, could reasonably assume that the consumer would have agreed to such a term in individual contract negotiations."[1720]

The Court of Justice therefore requires national courts to make a hypothetical judgment as to what the *seller or supplier* could *reasonably assume* as to the agreement of the consumer, an approach which links the judicial control of the fairness of contract terms to the condition that the terms in question were not "individually negotiated",[1721] seeing the court's control as a substitute for the consumer's own decision-making. For this purpose, Advocate General Kokott, to whose Opinion the Court had referred with approval, added that:

> "In this connection, it is important inter alia whether such contractual terms are common, that is to say they are used regularly in legal relations in similar contracts, or are surprising, whether there is an objective reason for the term and whether, despite the shift in the contractual balance in favour of the user of the term in relation to the substance of the term in question, the consumer is not left without protection."[1722]

The Court of Justice, by way of "guidance" to the national court, then explained the proper question for it to consider in relation to an acceleration clause in a contract of loan under which the lender would have been entitled to call in the totality of the loan on expiry of the 33 years where the consumer borrower failed to pay any of the principal or the interest on the loan.[1723] Where a borrower under a long-term loan defaulted over a "limited specific period", the national court should:

> "... assess in particular ... whether the right of the [lender] to call in the totality of the loan is conditional upon the non-compliance by the consumer with an obligation which

> is of essential importance in the context of the contractual relationship in question, whether that right is provided for in cases in which such non-compliance is sufficiently serious in the light of the term and amount of the loan, whether that right derogates from the relevant applicable rules and whether national law provides for adequate and effective means enabling the consumer subject to such a term to remedy the effects of the loan being called in."[1724]

So, while the Court did indeed refer to the position under the national law applicable in the absence of the relevant term, it first took a view as to the proper position in respect of the operation of such a clause, that is, that the obligation is "of essential importance" and/or the consumer's non-compliance "is sufficiently serious". Here, therefore, the Court of Justice requires the national court to compare the position under the contract term and the position which *should* be the case given what it considers to be these proper considerations. The Court of Justice, following its Advocate General's advice, also found the "indicative list" in the Annex to the Directive (and found in the 1999 Regulations Sch.2) particularly helpful in setting out the considerations the national court should take into account.[1725]

[1717] *Aziz* (C-415/11).

[1718] *Aziz* (C-415/11) at paras 44–45, referring to *Banco Español de Crédito, SA v Calderón Camino* (C-618/10) EU:C:2012:349, June 14, 2012 at paras 39–40.

[1719] *Aziz* (C-415/11) at para.68. Cf. *Kiss v Kiss* (C-621/17) EU:C:2019:820 (French version used) at para.55 where the contract terms provided for charges on the consumer which were recognised by national law with the result that the CJEU doubted whether they put the consumer in a less favourable position than national law itself.

[1720] *Aziz* (C-415/11) at para.69. The approach in *Aziz* was followed closely in the order of the CJEU in *Sebestyén v Kővári* (C-342/13) EU:C:2014:1857, April 3, 2014 at paras 27–28; *Kiss v Kiss* (C-621/17) EU:C:2019:820 at para.50.

[1721] 1993 Directive art.3, especially 3(2), above, paras 38-242—38-244.

[1722] *Aziz* (C-415/11) Opinion of A.G. Kokott, at para.75.

[1723] See also below, para.38-307 (default interest clause).

[1724] *Aziz* (C-415/11) at para.73.

[1725] *Aziz* (C-415/11) at para.74 and see below, paras 38-299 et seq.

*Replace footnote 1758 with:*

**ParkingEye Ltd v Beavis**[1758]

38-275 [1758] [2015] UKSC 67, [2015] 3 W.L.R. 1373.

*Replace footnote 1767 with:*

38-275 [1767] [2015] UKSC 67 at [106]; A.G. Kokott's Opinion in *Aziz* (C-415/11) at para.75 quoted above, para.38-270. In *Roundlistic v Jones* [2018] EWCA Civ 2284, [2019] 1 W.L.R. 4461 at [47]–[49], [50], the Court of Appeal applied the approach to the test of unfairness and, in particular, the requirement of good faith taken by the CJEU in *Aziz* and adopted by the SC in *ParkingEye Ltd*. The CA therefore approved the decision below holding that a term of a new lease granted pursuant to the landlord's obligation under the Leasehold Reform, Housing and Urban Development Act 1993 and therefore replicating a term in an earlier lease not subject to the 1999 Regulations, was not "contrary to the requirement of good faith". While it was arguable that the fact that the terms were replicated itself militated against a finding of unfairness, for the CA the important point was that "the processes of the 1993 Act gave the lessee the opportunity not only to seek to renegotiate any terms which had become unfair as a result of developments since they were first agreed but to have the question whether such a term should be included determined by a tribunal"; moreover, both parties benefited from legal advice. In these circumstances, the lessor/trader was entitled reasonably to assume that the lessee/consumer would have agreed to such a term in individual contract negotiations: [2018] EWCA Civ 2284 at [48] per Underhill L.J. (with whom Singh L.J. agreed).

*Replace footnote 1773 with:*

1773 [2015] UKSC 67 at [208], having noted (at [202]–[203]), the 1999 Regulations reg.6(1) and the 1993 Directive recital 16 to this effect. Cf. the summary of the approach in *Aziz* by the EU Commission that the CJEU "finds it *particularly relevant* to consider whether the seller or supplier could reasonably assume that the consumer would have agreed to the term in individual negotiations": Commission guidance C(2019) 5325 final p.32 (emphasis added). **38-276**

## Comments

*Replace paragraph with:*

The Supreme Court in *ParkingEye Ltd* took care to follow and apply the guidance of the Court of Justice of the EU on the interpretation and application of the test of unfairness in the 1993 Directive.[1779a] In this respect, however, while the hypothetical test used by the Court of Justice in *Aziz* to explain the significance of the requirement of good faith was expressed in general terms, it is submitted that it should not be taken as the touchstone of that requirement. Instead, Lord Mance's interpretation of the hypothetical test as *relevant* to the assessment of good faith but not conclusive of it is to be preferred, not least as recital 16 of the Directive itself explains the significance of good faith by reference to a series of other matters and without reference to the hypothetical test.[1780] Moreover, the hypothetical test is itself open to criticism. First, on the basis that it requires a court to take a view as to the assumptions of a reasonable trader in the position of the actual trader (what he would have assumed) and of a reasonable consumer in the position of the actual consumer (what he would have decided). Such fictitious tests tend to shift the focus of the court away from the level of the substantive imbalance caused to the consumer by the term in issue and the wider interests of the parties and others with which the test of unfairness should be concerned. Secondly, on the basis that the hypothetical test assumes that the fundamental problem with the terms of consumer contracts is that they are not individually negotiated and that on this ground the consumer's freedom of contract is undermined, rather than that consumers are to be protected because they are "weaker parties" as regards both their bargaining power and their level of knowledge.[1781] Moreover, Lord Mance's interpretation of the Court of Justice's guidance also avoids the difficulty otherwise found in relation to the new law under the Consumer Rights Act 2015 whose controls on unfair contract terms are not restricted to terms which are not individually negotiated, as it would make little sense to apply the hypothetical test to a term which had in fact been individually negotiated.[1782] In terms of the application of the hypothetical test on the facts of *ParkingEye Ltd*, with respect, the view of the majority of the Supreme Court that the terms in *ParkingEye Ltd* were not unfair as a matter of consumer law coupled with its reformulation of the common law governing penalty clauses[1783] is likely to give rise to concern that traders can effectively impose on consumers the payment of sums for breaches of contract even where the level of the sums is unrelated to any loss actually suffered by those traders.[1783a] **38-277**

1779a It should be noted that the significance of case-law of the CJEU for English courts changes on IP completion day: above, para.38-004 and Vol.I, para.1-017B.

1780 Above, para.38-267.

1781 See above, para.38-270.

1782 See below, para.38-389.

1783 See Vol.I, paras 26-190 et seq.

1783a In the particular context of *ParkingEye*, Parliament has enacted the Parking (Code of Practice) Act 2019 (operative provisions not in force at the time of writing). The Act requires the Secretary of State to prepare a code of practice about the operation and management of private parking facilities, which would contain guidance that promotes good practice in their operation and management and about appeals about parking charges: Parking (Code of Practice) Act 2019 s.1. The Act does not directly affect the binding character of contract terms providing for parking charges as s.5(1) provides that "[a] failure on the part of any person to act in accordance with any provision of the parking code does not of itself make that person liable to any legal proceedings…", but the operator of a parking facility which breaches the code may be precluded from obtaining the details of a car owner from the DVLA and so prevented from enforcing a parking charge; s.5(2). Moreover, the parking code will be admissible in any legal proceedings (s.5(5)) and could be seen as relevant to the fairness of any term of a consumer parking contract.

### "Unfairness" under the 1993 Directive and "unfair commercial practices"

*Replace footnote 1797 with:*

**38-278** [1797] *Pereničovà* (C-453/10) para.46. *Bankia SA v Merino* (C-109/17) of September 19, 2018 at paras 48–50. In *Bankia SA* esp. at paras 33–34 and para.49 the CJEU held that a national court has no *duty* to raise the existence of an unfair commercial practice of its own motion even where it is allegedly related to the existence of an unfair term in a consumer contract, though it may do so.

### Potential for unfairness

*Replace footnote 1804 with:*

**38-281** [1804] *Andriciuc v Banca Românească* (C-186/16) of September 20, 2017 para.54 referring to *Bucura v SC Bancpost SA* (C-348/14) EU:C:2015:447, July 9, 2015 para.48; *GT v JS* (C-38/17) EU:C:2019:461 of June 5, 2019 at paras 40–41.

### The significance of imbalance

*Replace footnote 1812 with:*

**38-282** [1812] [2012] EWHC 1290 (Comm) at [14]–[16] (absence of consideration) and see below, para.38-304 (note). cf. *Roundlistic Ltd v Jones* [2016] UKUT 325 (LC) at [103] where the Upper Tribunal (Lands Chamber) had held that the fact that the terms of a new long lease (subject to the 1999 Regulations) granted on the same terms as a lease for which it was substituted (which had 80 years remaining and which was not subject to the 1999 Regulations) meant that a term of the new lease could not be said to "cause" a significant imbalance in the rights and obligations of the contracting parties: "[i]f there was a significant imbalance it already existed". However, the CA disagreed on the basis that it was the term of the *new* lease which was the subject of the litigation and therefore the claim of unfairness: *Jones v Roundlistic Ltd* [2018] EWCA Civ 2284, [2019] 1 W.L.R. 4461 at [35], [42] and [50]. See also *Abbott v RCI Europe* [2016] EWHC 2602 (Ch) at [45]–[47] (term of a contract under which consumers "deposited" their own timeshare rights with a company so as to enable them to exchange those rights for access to other properties held fair as creating no significant imbalance given the fetters imposed by law on the company's exercise of its discretion under the term and the power in the consumers to cancel the contract without penalty).

### "The nature of the goods or services"

*Replace paragraph with:*

**38-284** In certain types of case, the nature of the goods or services could argue for the fairness of a term which in other contexts would clearly be unfair. So, for example, in *Bryen & Langley Ltd v Boston*[1817] it was considered material to the issue of fairness of a term that the transaction before the court was not of a "normal 'consumer' type, like buying a television set", but, for the individual or individuals concerned, a major project such as the costly construction of a building which would be undertaken only with the benefit of appropriate professional advice. A second example may be found in the context of clauses allowing the forfeiture of a purchaser's deposit in contracts of sale of land. Here, at first sight the loss of ten per cent of the purchase price if the purchaser withdraws from the contract suggests that such a clause is unfair, but it may not be given the need of the seller to cover transaction costs and also to be indemnified for likely loss of profit on the transaction. Indeed, a term allowing a person (the alleged consumer) who had agreed to participate in a world voyage by clipper to cancel the contract at a charge of 75 per cent of the price was held to be fair as not disproportionate in the context since that person's commitment to the venture was important.[1818] It may be under this heading that a court could properly consider the impact of (good) industry practice in relation to the type of contract in question in assessing a term's fairness. For example, *Higgins & Co Lawyers Ltd v Evans* concerned a clause in a conditional fee agreement which provided that the contract came to an end automatically on the death of the claimant for personal injuries, and that, where the solicitors chose not to continue the proceedings on behalf of the estate, the latter would be liable for their "basic charges".[1818a] The High Court held that the clause was fair, inter alia, because it was clear and transparent and expressed in simple language, was common to many conditional fee agreements (and indeed reflected the relevant Law Society's model Conditions) and serves a "fair and transparent purpose" in that the "calculus of risk in a personal injury action fundamentally changes when a claimant dies".[1818b]

[1817] [2004] EWHC 2450 (TCC), 98 Con. L.R. 82 at [45]; [2005] EWCA Civ 973, [2005] All E.R. (D) 507 (Jul) (appeal allowed on other grounds).

[1818] *Boyde v Clipper Ventures Plc* 2013 S.C.L.R. 313, 2013 G.W.D. 12-243.

[1818a] [2019] EWHC 2809 (QB), [2020] 1 W.L.R. 2809 at [101]–[103] (decided under s.62 of the Consumer Rights Act 2015, on which see below, paras 38-389 et seq.).

[1818b] [2019] EWHC 2809 (QB) at [101], per Saini J.

## "All the circumstances attending the conclusion of the contract"

*Replace footnote 1826 with:*

[1826] The common law approach appears, by contrast, to distinguish between the general law of notice, where the unusual or onerous nature of a contract term is relevant to the degree of notice required (*Interfoto Picture Library Ltd v Stiletto Visual Programmes Ltd* [1989] Q.B. 433) and the rule governing signed documents, where it is not: *L'Estrange v F Graucob* [1934] 2 K.B. 394. See Peel (ed.), *Treitel on The Law of Contract*, 15th edn (2020), paras 6-004—6-006. **38-285**

*Replace footnote 1829 with:*

[1829] *Nemzeti Fogyasztóvédelmi Hatóság v Invitel Távközlési Zrt.* (C-472/10) EU:C:2012:242, [26]–[28], below, para.38-314; *RWE Vertrieb AG v Verbraucherzentrale Nordrhein-Westfalen eV* (C-92/11) EU:C:2013:180, March 21, 2013 at [44], below, para.38-315; *Constructora Principado SA v Menéndez Álvarez* (C-226/12) EU:C:2014:10, January 16, 2014 at para.26; *Kiss v Kiss* (C-621/17) EU:C:2019:820 (French version used) at para.49. In his Opinion in *Kiss v Kiss* of May 15, 2019, para.60 A.G. Hogan had advised the CJEU that "[i]t is only when, as interpreted by reference to the special interpretative rule contained in Art.5 [that is, interpretation most in favour of the consumer], the contractual term still creates an imbalance to the detriment of the consumer that it might be considered as unfair"; this specific point was not addressed by the CJEU itself. **38-285**

## Lack of plainness or intelligibility sufficient?

*Replace paragraph with:*

**38-286** What is more open to contention is whether a lack of plainness or intelligibility (often referred to as transparency) can render a term unfair within the meaning of the Regulations without more.[1834] The key hurdle to allowing it to do so is the first element of the composite test of unfairness, viz that the term must cause "a significant imbalance in the parties' rights and obligations arising under the contract, to the detriment of the consumer".[1835] Clearly, a case can be imagined where a term (while not plain and intelligible) does not attempt to create such an imbalance (notably, where any imbalance is to the *benefit* of the consumer) and so would not be rendered unfair by the Regulations; but in this situation it is difficult to see why the consumer would wish to argue that such a term was "not binding" on him (though a body entrusted with a policing role in relation to unfair contract terms may nevertheless wish to intervene).[1836] However, where a contract term either seeks to bind a consumer to a particular duty or seeks to create rights which do not benefit him (notably, as compared to his existing rights or the rights of the seller or supplier under the contract more widely), a court could find that such an "imbalance" in the rights and obligations of the parties was "significant" merely on the ground that the consumer was not able to appreciate its extent: as the Director General of Fair Trading observed:

> "... it would clearly be difficult to maintain that unintelligible or ambiguous terms were *not* unfair if they had some potential for detriment to the consumer."[1837]

The final step in this direction (noted without comment by the European Commission) is that courts in some Member States have held that a failure in the requirement of transparency itself constitutes "unfairness" within the meaning of the Directive.[1838] However, this equating of the two requirements contained in the Directive does not accord with the way in which they are set out in the Directive as distinct both in their content and even more in their effects.[1839] Indeed, if a mere failure in transparency would lead without more to a failure in fairness this would render the distinctive treatment of the requirement of transparency entirely otiose. For this reason, the Law Commissions' view that "non-transparent terms" are not automatically unfair, though the lack of transparency is an important factor in the evaluation of their fairness[1840] is to be supported.[1841] As Advocate General Hogan has recently put it, art.5 of the Directive (which contains the requirement of plain intelligible language) "does not constitute an alternative test of unfairness".[1841a]

[1834] cf. Study Group on a European Civil Code and Research Group on EC Private Law (Acquis Group), *Principles, Definitions and Model Rules of European Private Law*, Interim Outline edn (2008), *Draft Common Frame of Reference* art.II.-9:402(2) which provides that "[i]n a contract between a business and a consumer a term which has been supplied by the business in breach of the duty of transparency ... may on that ground alone be considered unfair". No similar provision was contained in the Proposal for a Regulation for a Common European Sales Law COM(2011) 635 final, Annex I, arts 79–83 CESL.

[1835] 1999 Regulations reg.5(1), above, para.38-266 and see Bright in Burrows and Peel, *Contract Terms* (2007), p.172 at 184–186.

[1836] On this see below, paras 38-353 et seq.

[1837] OFT, *Unfair Contract Terms*, Bulletin No.2 (September 1996), p.8.

[1838] EC Commission, Report on the Implementation of Directive 93/13/EEC on unfair terms in consumer contracts COM(2000) 248 final, p.18.

[1839] Below, paras 38-339—38-351.

[1840] Law Com., Scottish Law Com., *Unfair Terms in Consumer Contracts: Advice to the Department for Business, Innovation and Skills* (March 2013), para.S.34; para.6.60.

[1841] See also Commission guidance C(2019) 5325 final pp.37–39. Cf. *Verein für Konsumenteninformation v Amazon EU Sàrl* (C-191/15) July 28, 2016 at para.68 where, as will be seen below, para.38-321, the CJEU came close to saying that an express choice of law clause in a consumer contract *will* be unfair if the trader does not explain that its effect is limited by the restrictions imposed by art.6(2) of the Rome I Regulation on the law applicable to contractual obligations, on the basis that this means that the term fails the requirement of plain intelligible language.

[1841a] *Tóth v ERSTE Bank Hungary Zrt* (C-34/18) (Opinion of March 29, 2019) para.86 (a point not discussed by the CJEU in its decision of September 19, 2019); *Kiss v Kiss* (C-621/17) Opinion of A.G. Hogan of May 15, 2019, para.60 (the point not being discussed by the CJEU in its judgment of October 3, 2019); *Profi Credit Polska SA z siedziba w Bielsku- Bialej v QJ* (C-84/19, C-222/19 and C-252/19) Opinion of A.G. Hogan of April 2, 2020, para.112 (a point not discussed by the CJEU in its decision of September 3, 2020).

## (dd) The "Indicative List" of Terms

### Introduction

*Replace paragraph with:*

Following the list in the Annex to the 1993 Directive exactly, Sch.2 of the 1999 Regulations contains an identical "indicative and non-exhaustive list of the terms which may be regarded as unfair".[1883] This list has been termed a "grey list",[1884] for the terms which it contains are not necessarily to be held unfair (a "black list"),[1884a] but this terminology may be misleading as inclusion within the list does not formally give rise to any presumption that a term will be unfair.[1885] On the other hand, the Court of Justice has emphasised the list's importance, observing that: **38-299**

> "If the content of the annex [to the Directive] does not suffice in itself to establish automatically the unfair nature of a contested term, it is nevertheless an essential element on which the competent court may base its assessment as to the unfair nature of that term."[1886]

Given its merely illustrative nature, it may appear odd that the second part of Sch.2 purports to restrict the scope of particular examples of terms found in the first part, but this reinforces the importance which was attached by the drafters of the Directive to the illustrative list.[1887] Even so, it needs to be emphasised that a type of term included on the list may be held by a court to be fair in the circumstances before it. Moreover, as earlier explained, the appearance of a contract term on the list has a second significance, for where it does so it will be held to fall outside the "core exclusion" set by art.4(2) of the Directive and provided by reg.6(2) of the 1999 Regulations.[1888] It is clear that a particular contract term may fall within more than one of the examples in the list.[1888a]

[1883] 1999 Regulations reg.5(5), Sch.2 para.1; 1993 Directive, Annex. For the role of the list of terms under the Consumer Rights Act 2015 see below, para.38-391.

[1884] *Matei v SC Volksbank România SA* (C-143/13) EU:C:2015:127, February 26, 2015 para.60.

[1884a] A Member State may declare the terms on the list (or other terms) to be unfair in all circumstances as the Directive requires only minimum harmonisation: 1993 Directive art.8 and see *Tóth v ERSTE Bank Hungary Zrt.* (C-34/18) EU:C:2019:764 para.47. On "minimum harmonization" see above, paras 38-022 and 38-212.

[1885] cf. the position under the Proposal for a Regulation on a Common European Sales Law COM(2011) 635 final, Annex I art.84 CESL (a list of "contract terms which are always unfair") and art.85 CESL (a list of "contract terms which are presumed to be unfair"). On the proposal, see Vol.I, para.1-013.

[1886] *Nemzeti Fogyasztóvédelmi Hatóság v Invitel Távközlési Zrt* (C-472/10) EU:C:2012:242, April 26, 2012 para.26, and see below para.38-314; *Sebestyén v Kővári* (C-342/13) EU:C:2014:1857, April 3, 2014 at para.32; *Tóth v ERSTE Bank Hungary Zrt.* (C-34/18) EU:C:2019:764 at para.45.

[1887] 1999 Regulations Sch.2 para.2. The ECJ has held that national legislation implementing the 1993 Directive need not itself include the list in the Directive's Annex. However: "Inasmuch as [it] is of indicative and illustrative value, it constitutes a source of information both for the national authorities responsible for applying the implementing measures and for individuals affected by those measures", and so its "form and method of implementation [must] offer a sufficient guarantee that the public can obtain knowledge of it". The Court held that the European Commission had failed to show that this requirement was not satisfied where (in Sweden) the Annex had been included in the *travaux préparatoires* of the implementing legislation and where these constitute an important aid to legislative interpretation: *Commission v Sweden* (C-478/99) EU:C:2002:281, [2002] E.C.R. I-04147.

[1888] Above, para.38-253.

[1888a] See *SC Topaz Development SRL v Juncu* (C-211/17) Order of October 24, 2019, where a combined termination and penalty clause in a contract of sale of a building was seen as falling within three of the

examples of terms in the 1993 Directive's indicative list in its Annex (paras 1(d), (e) and (f)), on which see below, para.38-305.

### Exclusion or limitation clauses

*Replace paragraph with:*

38-301 Terms which have the object or effect of:

"(a) excluding or limiting the legal liability of a seller or supplier in the event of the death of a consumer or personal injury to the latter resulting from an act or omission of that seller or supplier;

(b) inappropriately excluding or limiting the legal rights of the consumer vis-à-vis the seller or supplier or another party in the event of total or partial non-performance or inadequate performance by the seller or supplier of any of the contractual obligations, including the option of offsetting a debt owed to the seller or supplier against any claim which the consumer may have against him;

...

(q) excluding or hindering the consumer's right to take legal action or exercise any other legal remedy, particularly by requiring the consumer to take disputes exclusively to arbitration not covered by legal provisions, unduly restricting the evidence available to him or imposing on him a burden of proof which, according to the applicable law, should lie with another party to the contract."

Many of the terms within these examples would be classed as exemption clauses within the meaning of the Unfair Contract Terms Act 1977,[1889] or would come within the broader category of contract term falling within s.3(2) of that Act,[1890] but, as earlier noted, the ambit of the controls in the 1977 Act is sometimes narrower than the ambit of the Regulations.[1891] So, for example, a clause in a contract for the purchase of new homes by which the builders/sellers alleged that they were not liable for any failure to carry out the design of the works with proper skill and care was held unfair within the meaning of the 1999 Regulations, even though the purchasers were legally advised.[1892] Moreover, the Regulations are not restrained by any such limiting definitions as are found in the 1977 Act, and, as the OFT has put it:

> "If a term achieves the same effect as an unfair exemption clause, it will be unfair whatever its form or mechanism. This applies, for instance, to terms which 'deem' things to be the case, or get consumers to declare that they are—whether they really are or not—with the aim of ensuring no liability arises in the first place."[1893]

An example of a term which requires a declaration may be found in the case of a contract for the provision of medical services under which the consumer/patient declares that he knows medical facts which could only be known with any certainty by experts.[1894] The High Court has found (in circumstances described as unusual) a "withholding notice clause" in the JCT Minor Works standard contract by which the consumer/employer's right of set off can be exercised only if the appropriate notice has been served in time to the building contractor to be unfair within the meaning of the Regulations.[1895] Moreover, the OFT interpreted the impact of clauses which limit the consumer's right to offset a debt broadly. So, in its view:

> "There is no objection to terms which state the consumer's normal legal obligation to pay promptly and in full what is properly owing—that is, the full price, on satisfactory completion of the contract. But suspicion falls on terms which say, or clearly imply, that the consumer must in all cases complete his payment of the whole contract price, without any deduction, as soon as the supplier chooses to regard his side of the bargain as finished.

> They are likely to be seen as excluding the right of set-off even if they do not actually mention that right."[1896]

And in *Aziz*[1897] the Court of Justice of the EU saw para.1(q) of the Annex to the Directive[1898] as relevant to the fairness of a term under which a lender under a long-term contract of loan secured by a mortgage of residential premises was able unilaterally to determine the amount of debt unpaid, this having considerable procedural advantages under the national procedural law applicable. In these circumstances, the national court

> "... must in particular assess whether and, if appropriate, to what extent, the term in question derogates from the rules applicable in the absence of agreement between the parties, so as to make it more difficult for the consumer, given the procedural means at his disposal, to take legal action and exercise rights of the defence."[1899]

On the other hand, it has been held that a term in the standard contract between an airline and its passengers which required the latter to submit any claims for compensation for delay or cancellation of their flights under the Denied Boarding Regulation[1899a] directly to the airline and to allow it 28 days to respond directly to them rather than via a third party (such as a solicitor or a claims management firm) has been held not unfair within the meaning of the 1993 Directive.[1899b] The contract made clear that the airline was willing to deal with a third party engaged by a customer, but only if the customer had first attempted to deal directly with them and had either received no response within 28 days or had been unsuccessful. In these circumstances, the contract term requiring claims to be directed to the airline did not cause a significant imbalance in the parties' rights and obligations, as it set out a "straightforward procedure for initiating a flight disruption claim against [the airline] that is reasonable in scope", and the passenger was not "excluded or hindered" in a material sense from her right to take legal action or exercise any other legal remedy to which she was entitled under the Regulation.[1899c]

1889 s.13 and see above, Vol.I, para.15-069.

1890 See above, Vol.I, paras 15-070, 15-084—15-086

1891 Above, para.38-231.

1892 *Harrison v Shepherd Ltd* [2011] EWHC 1811 (TCC) at [111]–[113]; affirmed on other grounds [2012] EWCA Civ 904.

1893 OFT, Unfair Contract Terms Guidance OFT311 (2008), para.1.5. See also CMA, *Consumer law compliance review: cloud storage, Findings report* (May 27, 2016), above, para.38-221 (note), paras 5.59–5.66 (on exclusions or limitations of liability in contract for the provision of "cloud computing" services).

1894 OFT, Unfair Contract Terms Guidance OFT311, Annex A, p.8.

1895 *Domsalla v Dyason* [2007] EWHC 1174 (TCC), at [94]–[97]. cf. *West v Ian Finlay and Associates* [2014] EWCA Civ 316, [2014] B.L.R. 324 ("net contribution clause" whose effect was to limit the liability of an architect to its own reasonable responsibility for the loss or damage suffered by its employer not unfair in the circumstances): see above, para.38-273.

1896 *Unfair Contract Terms Guidance* OFT311 (2008), para.2.5.3. The CJEU has confirmed that a contract term which merely states that the consumer must perform all his own obligations even if he considers that the trader has not performed all of its own does not fall within para.1(q) of the Annex to the Directive as long as it does not affect the legal position of the consumer under national law: *Tóth v ERSTE Bank Hungary Zrt.* (C-34/18) EU:C:2019:764 at para.60.

1897 *Aziz v Caixa d'Estalvis de Catalunya, Tarragona i Manresa* (C-415/11) of March 14, 2013.

1898 Implemented in UK law by the 1999 Regulations Sch.2 para.1(q).

1899 *Aziz* (C-415/11) at para.75. The CJEU has also seen Annex para.1(q) as relevant to the fairness of a term of a contract under which the consumer waives his or her rights against the trader arising under an earlier contract between them: *XZ v Ibercaja Banco SA* (C-452/18) EU:C:2020:536 at para.77 and see above, para.38-262C.

[1899a] Regulation (EC) 261/2004 of February 11, 2004 establishing common rules on compensation and assistance to passengers in the event of denied boarding and of cancellation or of long delays in flights, on which see above, paras 35-049 et seq.

[1899b] *Bott & Co Solicitors v Ryanair DAC* [2018] EWHC 534 (Ch), [2018] 3 Costs L.O. 375.

[1899c] [2018] EWHC 534 (Ch) at [134]–[139]. It was further held that the term was not inconsistent with Regulation (EC) 261/2004 art.15's prohibition of the exclusion or waiver of an airline's obligations to passengers: [2018] EWHC 534 (Ch) at [130]–[131]. The CA upheld the latter decision, finding it unnecessary to decide further issues (apparently including the issue of the fairness of the term within the meaning of the 1993 Directive): [2019] EWCA Civ 143, [2019] 1 W.L.R. 3375 at [71]–[75].

## Arbitration and adjudication clauses

*Replace footnote 1903 with:*

38-302 [1903] Arbitration Act 1996 ss.89, 90; Unfair Arbitration Agreements (Specified Amount) Order 1999 (SI 1999/2167) (in force January 1, 2000). These provisions are amended by the Consumer Rights Act 2015, which revoked and replaced the 1999 Regulations: below, para.38-412. Under Directive 2013/11/EU on alternative dispute resolution for consumer disputes [2013] O.J. L165/63 (the "ADR Directive") art.10 Member States must ensure that an agreement between a consumer and a trader to submit complaints to an ADR entity (as defined by art.4(1)(h)) is not binding on the consumer if it was concluded before the dispute has materialised and if it has the effect of depriving the consumer of his right to bring an action before the courts for the settlement of the dispute and that in ADR procedures which aim at resolving the dispute by imposing a solution the solution imposed may be binding on the parties only if they were informed of its binding nature in advance and specifically accepted this. This requirement is implemented in UK law by the Alternative Dispute Resolution for Consumer Disputes (Competent Authorities and Information) Regulations 2015 (SI 2015/542) reg.14B (as inserted by SI 2015/1392 reg.2(8)) (in force on July 9, 2015) and see further above, para.38-155 (including the changes taking effect on IP completion day).

## Choice of jurisdiction clauses

*Replace footnote 1917 with:*

38-303 [1917] [2001] Lloyd's Rep. Bank 240, 250. It had previously been held that these contracts were "consumer contracts" for the purposes of the 1999 Regulations: *Standard Bank London Ltd v Apostolakis (No.1)* [2000] I.L. Pr. 766 and see above, para.38-039. See also *Weco Project ApS v Loro Piana* [2020] EWHC 2150 (Comm) at [108]–[110] (where the HC found a choice of international jurisdiction clause was not unfair within the meaning of s.62 of the 2015 Act and therefore did not need to consider, in particular, the argument that this control did not apply as it was incompatible with the scheme of the Brussels Ibis Regulation.

## Unbalanced forfeiture clauses

*Replace paragraph with:*

38-305 Terms which have the object or effect of:

"(d) … permitting the seller or supplier to retain sums paid by the consumer where the latter decides not to conclude or perform the contract, without providing for the consumer to receive compensation of an equivalent amount from the seller or supplier where the latter is the party cancelling the contract."

The type of terms described in this paragraph include terms under which either a part-payment or deposit paid by a consumer may be forfeited and proved to be a significant object of the OFT's work. In this respect, important factors in the fairness of such a term are the proportion between the sum to be forfeited and any loss to be suffered by the seller or supplier by the consumer's cancellation[1922] and, as para.(d) mentions, the existence of any counter-balancing provision in the contract for the benefit of the consumer. In *SC Topaz Development SRL v Juncu*[1922a] the Court of Justice considered para.(d) of the Annex to the 1993 Directive (implemented in UK law by para.(d) quoted above[1922b]) in the context of a term in a contract to sell a building by a trader to a consumer which allowed the trader unilaterally to terminate the contract for delay in payment of any sum owing for longer than five working days, to keep any monies already paid by the consumer and to recover a penalty of 30 per cent of the contract price without prejudice to any damages. In the Court's view, such a term appears to fall within para.(d)[1922c] as it allows the seller not to perform the contract and to retain sums paid and a penalty without allowing the consumer to terminate for the trader's non-performance with an equivalent level of compensation for the consumer.[1922d]

1922 OFT, *Unfair contract terms guidance* (2008) OFT311 (above, para.38-221 (note)), para.6.2.

1922a C-211/17, Order of October 24, 2019 (available in French).

1922b i.e. 1999 Regulations Sch.2 para.1(d).

1922c 1993 Directive Annex para.1(d).

1922d C-211/17, Order of October 24, 2019 paras 55–57. The term also fell within the Annex para.1(e) (penalty clauses) on which see below, paras 38-306–38-308) and para.1(f) (cancellation clauses) on which see below, para.38-308.

## Penalty clauses

*Replace paragraph with:*

Terms which have the object or effect of: **38-306**

> "(e) requiring any consumer who fails to fulfil his obligation to pay a disproportionately high sum in compensation".

The type of term described in this paragraph bears a considerable similarity to the common law understanding of a "penalty clause", since the disproportionately high nature of a sum to be paid on breach argues in favour of it being a penalty.[1923] Clearly, though, clauses which are penal in their potential effect may be subjected to the test of fairness under the Regulations, whether or not they count as penalties in the common law sense.[1924] So, for example, it has been held that a clause which requires a consumer to pay interest at 8 per cent over the Bank of England current base rate on sums due to the business under the contract 30 days after the issue of an account is unfair within the meaning of the 1999 Regulations, even though it constituted a genuine pre-estimate of damage likely to be suffered by the claimant in the event of non-payment and therefore not a penalty clause under the then accepted approach at common law,[1925] this decision on the unfairness of the term resting principally on the grounds that the term was unusual and not balanced by a similar term governing unpaid monies such as damages which may fall due *to* the consumer.[1926] In *Office of Fair Trading v Ashbourne Management Services Ltd*,[1927] one standard form consumer contract for gym club membership of a year's duration with monthly payments by the consumer contained an express term allowing the business to terminate on the ground of the consumer's breach where the term was not a technical condition and the breach did not require to be repudiatory. Where the term further provided that the consumer was liable for all sums which *would have fallen due* if the contract had not been terminated early on the ground of breach, it was held to be both a penalty at common law and unfair.[1928] By contrast, in another standard form contract for gym membership before the court, a plain and intelligible term allowed termination only for repudiatory breach, and its requirement for accelerated payment of sums which would have fallen due (subject to a discount for this acceleration) was held to be neither a penalty at common law nor unfair within the meaning of the Regulations.[1929]

1923 See *Cavendish Square Holding BV v Makdessi, ParkingEye Ltd v Beavis* [2015] UKSC 67, [2015] 3 W.L.R. 1373, discussed Vol.I, paras 26-190 et seq. The decision of the SC in *ParkingEye Ltd* in relation to the 1999 Regulations is noted below, para.38-307 and also above, paras 38-275—38-277.

[1924] cf. Vol.I, paras 26-190 et seq. In *Kindlance v Murphy* Unreported December 12, 1997, NI Ch D an "interest acceleration clause" in a contract of mortgage was held unfair within the meaning of the 1994 Regulations. For an example of the upholding as fair of a clause requiring a consumer to pay a sum on his own termination of the contract, see *Gosling v Burrard-Lucas* [1999] 1 C.L. 197. For a further decision on allegedly penalty-like terms in financial services contracts see *Evans v Cherry Tree Finance Ltd* Unreported April 13, 2007, Ch D (early redemption clause with six-month deferment unfair in the circumstances).

[1925] *Munkenbeck & Marshall v Harold* [2005] EWHC 356 (TCC), [2005] All E.R. (D) 227. The common law position was recast by the SC in *Cavendish Square Holding BV v Makdessi, ParkingEye Ltd v Beavis* [2015] UKSC 67, [2015] 3 W.L.R. 1373, discussed Vol.I, paras 26-190 et seq.

[1926] [2005] EWHC 356 (TCC) at [12] and [15].

[1927] [2011] EWHC 1237 (Ch), [2011] E.C.C. 32.

[1928] [2011] EWHC 1237 (Ch) at [188]–[190] referring to *Financings Ltd v Baldock* [1963] 2 Q.B. 104. See similarly *SC Topaz Development SRL v Juncu* (C-211/17) Order of October 24, 2019 (available in French), para.59 and above, para.38-305.

[1929] [2011] EWHC 1237 (Ch) at [207] referring to *Lombard North Central Plc v Butterworth* [1987] Q.B. 527.

## Cancellation clauses

*In line 7, after "party to "dissolve"", add new footnote 1936a:*

**38-308** [1936a] The CJEU has held, however, that Annex para.1(f) of the 1993 Directive (implemented by the 1999 Regulations Sch.1 para.1(f), quoted in the text) can apply to a clause allowing the trader to terminate for a (minor) contractual non-performance by the consumer, and this suggests a different understanding of the word "dissolve" as it appears to include termination for breach rather than referring merely to termination at the choice of the trader without such a ground: see *SC Topaz Development SRL v Juncu (C-211/17)* Order of October 24, 2019 (available in French), paras 60–61 and above, para.38-305. Cf. *Higgins & Co Lawyers Ltd v Evans* [2019] EWHC 2809 (QB), [2020] 1 W.L.R. 2809 at [101] where it was held that the equivalent paragraph in the Consumer Rights Act 2015 (Sch.2 Pt 1 para.7) was not relevant to a contract term whose effect was to terminate the contract automatically on the death of one of its parties.

## Variation clauses

*Replace footnote 1953 with:*

**38-312** [1953] 1999 Regulations Sch.2 para.2 states that: "(b) Paragraph 1(j) is without hindrance to terms under which a supplier of financial services reserves the right to alter the rate of interest payable by the consumer or due to the latter, or the amount of other charges for financial services without notice where there is a valid reason, provided that the supplier is required to inform the other contracting party or parties thereof at the earliest opportunity and that the latter are free to dissolve the contract immediately; ... (c) Paragraphs 1(g), (j) and (l) do not apply to: transactions in transferable securities, financial instruments and other products or services where the price is linked to fluctuations in a stock exchange quotation or index or a financial market rate that the seller or supplier does not control; contracts for the purchase or sale of foreign currency, traveller's cheques or international money orders denominated in foreign currency; (d) Paragraph 1(l) is without hindrance to price indexation clauses, where lawful, provided that the method by which prices vary is explicitly described." For an example of guidance on the application of the Directive to a price indexation clause see *Engilbertsson v Íslandsbanki hf* (E-25/13) of August 28, 2014 (EFTA Court) at paras 97–98, 141–146 (emphasising the importance of the clarity and quality of information provided to the consumer about such a clause). For general guidance by the Financial Conduct Authority on variation clauses in the context of consumer contracts for the provision of financial services see FG18/7: Fairness of variation terms in financial services consumer contracts under the Consumer Rights Act 2015 (December 19, 2018).

## Choice of law clauses

*Replace paragraph with:*

**38-321** In *Verein fur Konsumenteninformation v Amazon EU Sarl*, the Court of Justice considered the relationship between the fairness under the 1993 Directive of a standard choice of law clause in a consumer contract and the rules governing choice of applicable law in the Rome I Regulation[1996] in the context of term of an online trader's standard contract which designated the law of Luxembourg (which was the place of the trader's "seat") as "applicable to the exclusion of the United Nations Convention on the international sale of goods".[1997] The Court noted that arts 3(1) and 6(1) of the Rome I Regulation recognise that in principle the parties to a consumer contract may choose the law applicable to it, but that art.6(2) adds that, subject to certain conditions, any such choice of law does not "have the result of depriving the consumer of the protection afforded to him by provisions that cannot be derogated from by agreement" under the law of his habitual residence[1998] and this may include national law rules implementing the 1993 Directive even where they ensure a higher level of protection for the consumer than the Directive requires.[1999] The Court of Justice of the EU therefore considered the proper approach to a national court's consideration of the fairness of such a express choice of law under the 1993 Directive, whose starting point should be the position under the Rome I Regulation, and that therefore:

> "... a pre-formulated term on the choice of the applicable law designating the law of the Member State in which the seller or supplier is established is unfair only in so far as it displays certain specific characteristics inherent in its wording or context which cause a significant imbalance in the rights and obligations of the parties."[2000]

For this purpose, the unfairness of a such a term may result from its failure to conform to the requirement of plain and intelligible language by the trader in failing to inform the consumer that the effects of such a term are qualified by the mandatory statutory provisions of the consumer's place of residence provided for his protection.[2001] If the national court finds that the trader has failed to do so and "so leads the consumer into error by giving him the impression that only the law of [the Member State chosen] applies to the contract", then the choice of law clause would itself be an unfair term.[2002]

[1996] C-191/15 July 28, 2016 ("*Amazon EU Sàrl* (C-191/15)"), on which see Ruhl (2018) 55 CML Rev. 201. See similarly *Verein fur Konsumenteninformation v TVP Treuhand- und Verwaltungsgesellschaft fur Publikumsfonds mbH & Co KG* (C-272/18) EU:C:2019:827 at paras 58–60.

[1997] C-191/15 July 28, 2016 ("*Amazon EU Sàrl* (C-191/15)").

[1998] Regulation (EC) 593/2008 on the law applicable to contractual obligations ("Rome I") [2008] O.J. L177/6.

[1999] *Amazon EU Sàrl* (C-191/15) at para.59 (noting art.8 of the Directive).

[2000] *Amazon EU Sàrl* (C-191/15) at para.67.

[2001] *Amazon EU Sàrl* (C-191/15) at paras 69–70. In *Verein fur Konsumenteninformation v TVP Treuhand- und Verwaltungsgesellschaft fur Publikumsfonds mbH & Co KG* (C-272/18) EU:C:2019:827 at paras 58 and 59, the CJEU held that this approach is "not limited to a specific form for the conclusion of contracts, namely, inter alia, by electronic means, and are of a general nature".

[2002] *Amazon EU Sàrl* (C-191/15) at para.71.

## Other potentially unfair terms

*Replace paragraph with:*

The guidance of the OFT (adopted by the CMA[2003]) contains a number of types **38-322**
of terms found in consumer contracts which it considers are likely to be considered to be unfair within the meaning of the Regulations.[2004] These include terms which allow the supplier to impose unfair financial burdens, such as a right to demand payment of unspecified amounts by way of security deposit,[2005] put on the consumer the onus to judge technical matters in which the supplier is expert but in which the consumer is not (for example, placing on a consumer the determination whether a driveway was ready for resurfacing with tarmacadam)[2006]; terms where the appar-

ent supplier of the service states in small print that he acts only as agent for another person (for example, in the provision of a holiday cottage)[2007]; and "unfair enforcement clauses", for example, a term which grants to a seller of goods a right to enter the consumer's home and repossess the goods in certain circumstances without recourse to the court.[2008] And the CMA has taken action to stop online gambling firms using unfair contract terms under which the firms could confiscate money from players' accounts on the ground that they had not logged in for a certain amount of time.[2008a]

[2003] Above, para.38-221 (note).

[2004] OFT, *Unfair contract terms guidance* (2008) OFT311 para.18.

[2005] OFT, *Unfair contract terms guidance* (2008) OFT311 para.18.1.2.

[2006] OFT, *Unfair Contract Terms*, Bulletin No.3 (March 1997), p.24.

[2007] OFT, *Unfair Contract Terms*, Bulletin No.3, p.28.

[2008] OFT, *Unfair contract terms guidance* (2008) OFT311 para.18.3.3. As has been seen, a person travelling under a package travel contract may transfer the benefit of that contract, subject to a certain conditions: see the Package Travel and Linked Travel Arrangements Regulations 2018 reg.9 replacing the Package Travel, Package Holidays and Package Tours Regulations 1992 reg.10 (transfer of bookings), above, paras 38-144 and 38-139 respectively.

[2008a] CMA Press Release (August 29, 2018) (action taken under Consumer Rights Act 2015 Pt 2): see *https://www.gov.uk/government/news/online-gambling-firms-remove-restrictions-on-cash-withdrawals.*

*Replace paragraph with:*

**38-323** Apart from these examples, an important type of term which may be thought of as vulnerable under the Regulations is one which allows the seller or supplier to terminate the contract on a minor breach by the consumer, whether this stems from a very slight breach of a significant term or the breach of a very minor term of the contract (notably, where the contract classes the terms in question as "conditions" as opposed to warranties).[2009] The Law Commission has suggested that terms in contracts of sale of goods which delay the formation of the contract until dispatch of the goods may be unfair as they "potentially create an imbalance between retailer and consumer, as the consumer is obliged to pay money to the retailer without the retailer being under a contractual obligation to deliver the goods" and prevents the application of the rules on the transfer of ownership in the goods.[2009a] Other types of clauses which may be thought to be potentially unfair are those which restrict a consumer's legal or equitable rights, such as in relation to discharge of a guarantee on variation of the contract or negligence in relation to the security[2010]; a term which permits the supplier to pass on information about the consumer more freely or widely than would otherwise be allowed under the Data Protection Act.[2011] Moreover, it has been held that a contract term which provides that the consumer must indemnify the business in respect of its legal or other costs in any action or proceedings and pay it a reasonable sum in respect of time spent in connection with such an action or proceedings was unfair within the meaning of the 1999 Regulations, even though the court saw the force of the argument that such a term could protect the business against unfair treatment by the customer who could use the business's unrecoverable costs to negotiate a discount on the unpaid contract price: the term remained unbalanced by any similar provision for the benefit of the consumer.[2012] Terms under which an estate agent charged commission on the renewal of a lease by the tenant and on the sale of the property to the tenant have been held unfair, although the court was careful to state that its decision did not mean that all renewal commission clauses were unfair since the clauses in question were capable of operating onerously and not enough had been done to draw them to the attention of the consumer.[2013] On the other hand, it has been held that a term in a sale and leaseback contract under which the tenant/consumer loses the right to the final part of the purchase price (constituting a third of the total figure) on termination of the lease by the landlord under the tenancy agreement (where this final part would otherwise have been be payable on expiry of ten years or the giving up of the tenancy by the tenant) was not unfair within the meaning of the Regulations on the ground that the term did not create a significant imbalance in the rights and obligation of the parties to the detriment of the consumer and was not contrary to the requirement of good faith.[2014] According to Longmore L.J., while it is possible to conceive of circumstances where such a term might create such an imbalance:

> "… especially if the original contract price was below the market price and the rental market (or perhaps the sale market) was buoyant at the time of the possession … the matter has to be judged at the time when the contract is made and it would be equally possible to envisage a stagnant market in which the landlord would find it difficult to re-let the property or even re-sell it. In those circumstances the retention of what is less than one third of the price does not cause any imbalance let alone a significant one".[2015]

And it has been held that a term in a loan agreement under which the lender was entitled to recover the legal and other costs of enforcing its terms and recovering the money did not cause any significant imbalance in the parties' rights and obligations to the detriment of the consumer and was not unfair.[2016] Finally, it was held that a claimant who had contracted for the provision of a family burial plot in an area of a cemetery providing for Muslim burials on the express basis (in the face of the Covid-19 pandemic) that there would be two-tier burials until further notice and that the upper tier would not be reserved for the family of the deceased in the lower tier had no arguable case that this term was unfair within the meaning of the s.62 of the 2015 Act.[2016a]

[2009] See Vol.I, paras 13-019 et seq. and Whittaker in Burrows and Peel, *Contract Terms* (2007), 255, 262–263. See also *SC Topaz Development SRL v Juncu* (C-211/17) Order of October 24, 2019 (available in French), paras 60–61 referring to the 1993 Directive Annex para.1(f), above, para.38-308 (note).

[2009a] Law Com. Consultation Paper No.246, *Consumer sales contracts: transfer of ownership: a consultation paper* (July 27, 2020), para.4.26.

[2010] This example depends on the wider interpretation being given to "consumer contract" as explained above, para.38-226. (Such a term would not come within Sch.2 para.1(b) of the 1999 Regulations as it would not relate to a right in respect of the other party's inadequate *performance*.)

[2011] OFT, *Unfair contract terms guidance* (2008) OFT311 Annex I, p.122.

[2012] *Munkenbeck & Marshall v Harold* [2005] EWHC 356 (TCC), [2005] All E.R. (D) 227 at [12]–[15].

[2013] *Office of Fair Trading v Foxtons Ltd* [2009] EWHC 1681 (Ch), [2009] 29 E.G. 98 (C.S.) at [91]–[95], [101], [103]–[106]. The decision on unfairness of the renewal commission clauses was taken after the court had held that they did not fall within the exclusion of reg.6(2) on the ground that they were not "plain and intelligible" (at [70], [74]), even if they formed part of the "core bargain".

[2014] *UK Housing Alliance (North West) Ltd v Francis* [2010] EWCA Civ 117, [2010] Bus. L.R. 1034, especially at [27]–[29]. cf. *Solitaire Property Management Co Ltd v Holden* [2012] UKUT 86 (LC) at [34] (term under which landlord holds funds supplied by tenant in case of "temporary deficiency" in moneys available to meet service charge expenses found fair).

[2015] [2010] EWCA Civ 117 at [27].

[2016] *Shaw v Nine Regions Ltd* [2009] EWHC 3553 (QB). See also *Higgins & Co Lawyers Ltd v Evans* [2019] EWHC 2809 (QB), [2020] 1 W.L.R. 2809 at [101] (clause in a conditional fee agreement terminating the contract on the death of the claimant and imposing a liability to pay "basic charges" in the latter's estate held fair), on which see above, para.38-284.

[2016a] *Meghjee v BW Foundation* [2020] 6 WLUK 214.

### (ee) The Timeframe for Assessment of the Fairness of a Term

**Assessment as between the parties: "the conclusion of the contract"**

*In line 6, after "contract concluded earlier.", add new footnote 2029a:*

38-326 2029a Cf. *XZ v Ibercaja Banco SA* (C-452/18) EU:C:2020:536 above, para.38-262C (a term of a contract amending a term of an earlier consumer credit contract between the parties could itself be assessed for their fairness as of the time of the conclusion of the *later* contract).

### (ff) The Relative Roles of the Court of Justice of the EU, National Courts and the Parties

*To the end of title, add new footnote 2038a:*

**The relative roles of the Court of Justice of the EU and national courts in relation to the issue of fairness**[2038a]

38-329 2038a On IP completion day when the UK's leaving the EU comes into full effect (on which see Vol.I, paras 1-014 et seq. and esp. para.1-016) it will cease to be possible for a UK court or tribunal to refer any matter to the Court of Justice of the EU: 2018 Act s.6(1).

**Judicial discretion and domestic appeals**

*Replace footnote 2052 with:*

38-330 2052 Peel (ed.), *Treitel on The Law of Contract*, 15th edn (2020), para.7-068 and see Vol.I, para.15-101.

**The power and duty of national courts to intervene of their own initiative**

*Replace paragraph with:*

38-331 In *Océano Grupo Editorial SA v Murciano Quintero*,[2055] which concerned proceedings brought by suppliers against consumers, the European Court of Justice held that, at least where a term in a consumer contract was clearly unfair within the meaning of the Directive, the national court is entitled to raise the issue of fairness of its own initiative, this being necessary to ensure that the consumer enjoys effective protection in view of the real risk that he is unaware of his rights or encounters difficulties in enforcing them.[2056] In the particular circumstances of the case, the term in question was a choice of local jurisdiction within Spain which chose the court of the place of establishment of the seller or supplier: here, the Spanish court was entitled to refuse jurisdiction on the basis that the clause was unfair within the meaning of the Directive. While in *Océano Grupo Editorial SA*[2057] the Court of Justice was careful to express its view in terms of a *power* in national courts to intervene of their own initiative,[2058] in *Mostaza Claro v Centro Móvil Milenium SL*[2059] the Court of Justice went further, holding that national courts have a duty to intervene of their own initiative in order to ensure that the protection promised by the Directive is effectively ensured for consumers. In that case, the Court ruled that a national court faced with a claim by a consumer for annulment of an arbitral award against her must annul the award if it considers that the arbitration clause on the basis of which the arbitration took place was invalid as an unfair term in a consumer contract within the meaning of the Directive, even though the consumer had not raised the issue of invalidity in the course of the arbitral proceedings and would normally be prevented from raising the issue by a subsequent action for annulment of the award as a matter of national procedural law. According to the Court:

> "The nature and importance of the public interest underlying the protection which the

> Directive confers on consumers justify ... the national court *being required to assess of its own motion* whether a contractual term is unfair, compensating in this way for the imbalance which exists between the consumer and the seller or supplier."[2060]

In *Pannon GSM Zrt v Erzsébet Sustikné Győrfi*[2061] the Court of Justice confirmed that a national court bears an *obligation* to examine of its own motion the issue of the possible fairness of a contract term within the meaning of the Directive, but it restricted this obligation to the situation "where it has available to it the legal and factual elements necessary for that task".[2062] This qualification, whose language echoes the formulation used by the Court in *Freiburger Kommunalbautern*[2063] to describe the role of national courts in assessing the fairness of terms under art.3 of the Directive, recognises that in some situations a national court will not be in a position to come to a view as to the fairness of a term in the circumstances, possibly in part owing to the absence of consumer's own representations or evidence adduced for this purpose. Moreover, the Court of Justice added that:

> "In carrying out that obligation, the national court is not ... required under the Directive to exclude the possibility that the term in question may be applicable, if the consumer, after having been informed of it by that court, does not intend to assert its unfair or non-binding status."[2064]

So, a national court's obligation to assess the fairness of a contract term does not mean that it should refuse to apply the term where the consumer itself wishes it, a position which fits entirely with art.6(1)'s provision that an unfair term will "not be binding on the consumer".[2065] Indeed, where a national court, having raised the issue of its own motion, considers that a term in a consumer contract in proceedings before it is unfair within the meaning of the Directive, it must as a general rule inform the parties to the dispute of that fact and invite them to set out their views on the matter by way of application of the principle of *audi alteram partem* found in art.47 of the Charter of Fundamental Rights of the European Union.[2066] As will be seen, under the new law governing the control of unfair terms in consumer contracts under the Consumer Rights Act 2015, legislative provision is made to give explicit effect to this case-law of the Court of Justice.[2067]

2055 C-240/98 to C-244/98 EU:C:2000:346, [2000] E.C.R. I-4941.

2056 EU:C:2000:346, [2000] E.C.R. I-4941 at [26].

2057 See also *Cofidis SA v Fredout* (C-473/00) EU:C:2002:705, [2002] E.C.R. I-10875.

2058 Whittaker (2001) 117 L.Q.R. 215, 217–218 (arguing for recognition of such a duty).

2059 C-168/05 EU:C:2006:675, [2006] E.C.R. I-10421.

2060 C-168/05 EU:C:2006:675, at [38] (emphasis added).

2061 C-243/08 EU:C:2009:350, [2009] E.C.R. I-4713.

2062 C-243/08 at [32] and see *Bucura v SC Bancpost SA* (C-348/14) EU:C:2015:447, July 9, 201 para.44. In *Tomášová v Republic of Slovenská* (C-168/15) EU:C:2016:602 July 28, 2016 at paras 33–34 (available only in French), the CJEU held that only on its decision in *Pannon* had it made clear that national courts have an *obligation* to consider the fairness of terms in consumer contracts and that therefore before the date of this decision a national court could not be said to have committed a sufficiently serious breach of EU law by its failure to do so for the purpose of state liability under the *Francovich* principle (on which see Craig and de Búrca, *EU Law*, 6th edn (2015) pp.251 et seq.).

2063 *Kommunalbauten GmbH Baugesellschaft & Co KG v Hofstetter* (C-237/02) EU:C:2004:209, [2004] 2 C.M.L.R. 13 at [21] and [22] and see above, para.38-329.

2064 C-243/08 EU:C:2009:350, at [33] and see similarly at [35]. See also *Lintner v UniCredit Bank Hungary Zrt.* (C-511/17) EU:C:2020:188, para.33.

2065 1993 Directive art.6(1), below, para.38-339.

2066 *Banif Plus Bank Zrt v Csipai* (C-472/11) EU:C:2013:88; [2013] W.L.R. (D) 76 at [29]; *Brusse v*

*Jahani BV* (C-488/11) EU:C:2013:341, May 30, 2013 at para.52; *Lintner v UniCredit Bank Hungary Zrt.* (C-511/17) EU:C:2020:188, para.43.

2067 See 2015 Act s.71 and below, para.38-392.

## "National procedural autonomy" and its limits

*Replace footnote 2068 with:*

38-332 2068 C-137/08 EU:C:2010:659 at [45] (although the national court's question had earlier (para.[25]) been expressed in permissive rather than mandatory terms). On the CJEU's case-law in this area see also Commission guidance C(2019) 5325 final pp.50 et seq.

*Add new paragraph:*

38-332A However, in *Lintner v UniCredit Bank Hungary Zrt.*[2075a] the Court of Justice clarified its position on the duties of national courts in relation to the assessment of the fairness of the terms of a consumer contract. In that case a consumer complained of the unfairness of a clause in a consumer credit contract under which the lender reserved to itself a power to vary the terms of the contract, but the national court was uncertain as to whether its duty to consider the fairness of the terms of the contract extended to *all* the contract's terms or only the one in dispute. In this respect, the Court of Justice held, first, that, where a national court has available to it the legal and factual elements it needs, the duty to consider the fairness of a contract term of its own motion extends to "those contractual terms which are connected to the subject matter of the dispute" as defined by the parties in their pleadings even if they are not challenged by the consumer's claim, but it does not extend to *all* the terms of the contract.[2075b] Moreover, secondly, in cases where from "the elements of law and fact in the file" before it, a national court has serious doubts as to the unfair nature of particular terms which are related to the subject matter of the dispute but which are *not* invoked by the consumer but the court is not able to make "definitive assessments in that regard" then it must "take, if necessary of its own motion, investigative measures in order to complete that case file, by asking the parties, in observance of the principle of *audi alteram partem*, to provide it with the clarifications or documents necessary for that purpose".[2075c]

2075a C-511/17, EU:C:2020:188 ("*Lintner* (C-511/17)").

2075b *Lintner* (C-511/17) at para.34. Where national legislation permits a lender stipulating in the contract of consumer credit that the borrower should issue a blank promissory note for the purpose of securing the debt and the lender/payee later completes the note and claims the sums under it, the national court must consider whether both the terms of the promisor note agreement and the underlying term requiring it in the credit contract are fair within the meaning of the 1993 Directive: *Profi Credit Polska SA v Włostowska* (C-419/18 and C-483/18) EU:C:2019:930 at para.60.

2075c *Lintner* (C-511/17) at para.37. The CJEU further noted that where this was the case the national court must give the parties an opportunity to "set out their views" and to give the consumer the opportunity not to assert the unfair or non-binding status of the term: paras 42–43.

*Replace paragraph with:*

38-333 Behind this case-law of the Court of Justice is an implicit recognition of the principle that national courts "know the law" (this principle being known widely under the Latin tag "*iura novit curia*") and specifically that they therefore are on notice as to the ambit of the protection required by the Directive so as to enable them—and indeed to require them—to intervene of their own initiative; it also assumes a more interventionist role for the court in the gathering of evidence than is traditional in English law.[2076] On the other hand, the laws of civil procedure differ very considerably between Member States in terms of the relative roles of the courts and the parties to litigation in the identification of the facts on the basis of which they claim and their characterisation in legal terms, and this realisation forms one reason for the Court's acceptance of what is sometimes termed the "principle of the procedural autonomy of the Member States".[2077] However, while this principle provides the starting point for the Court of Justice, it then subjects national rules in question to the double test of the principle of effectiveness and the principle of equivalence.[2078] So, for example, in *Asturcom Telecommunicaciones SL v Rodriquez Nogueira*[2079] the Court of Justice of the EU considered whether a national court seized with a claim to enforce an arbitral award against a consumer where the arbitrators acted under an arbitration clause in a consumer contract can and/or must consider the unfairness of that arbitration clause within the meaning of the 1993 Directive, even where the consumer was neither present in the arbitration proceedings nor applied to the appropriate court for the annulment of the arbitrators' decision (as she was entitled under the applicable national law). The Court of Justice took as its starting point "the principle of res judicata":

> "... [i]n the absence of Community legislation in this area, the rules implementing the principle of res judicata are a matter for the national legal order, in accordance with the principle of the procedural autonomy of the Member States. However, those rules must not be less favourable than those governing similar domestic actions (principle of equivalence); nor may they be framed in such a way as to make it in practice impossible or excessively difficult to exercise the rights conferred by Community law (principle of effectiveness)."[2080]

Applying this to the particular circumstances:

> "... the need to comply with the principle of effectiveness cannot be stretched so far as to mean that, in circumstances such as those in the main proceedings, a national court is required not only to compensate for a procedural omission on the part of a consumer who is unaware of his rights, as in the case which gave rise to the judgment in *Mostaza Claro*[2081] but also to make up fully for the total inertia on the part of the consumer concerned who, like the defendant in the main proceedings, neither participated in the main proceeding nor brought an action for annulment of the arbitration award, which therefore became final."[2082]

As regards the principle of equivalence, the Court of Justice held that:

> "... the conditions imposed by domestic law under which the courts and tribunals may apply a rule of Community law of their own motion must not be less favourable than those governing the application by those bodies of their own motion of rules of domestic law of the same ranking."[2083]

Given that art.6(1) of the 1993 Directive (which holds unfair terms "not binding on the consumer") is a mandatory rule, where a national court seized with an action for enforcement of a final arbitral award would, under domestic rules of procedure, assess of its own motion whether an arbitration clause was in conflict with domestic rules of this character, then it would be obliged to do so for the purposes of the 1993 Directive, as long as it has available the legal and factual elements necessary for this task.[2084] In this way, the Court of Justice sought to balance the policy of protection of the consumer pursued by the 1993 Directive and the policy of promoting the finality of decision-making (even of private arbitral decisions), and, at a more general level, to balance the demands of EU legal principle (or principles) and the so-called principle of the "autonomy" (and therefore integrity of approach) of national procedural laws. By doing so, in this context to an extent the Court has drawn back from its apparently greater willingness to intervene in (and override) national approaches to the relative roles of national courts and the parties to civil litigation previously revealed in *Océano Grupo Editoriale*[2085] and *Mostaza Claro*.[2086]

On the other hand, more recently in *Faber* in the context of the Consumer Sales Directive 1999, the Court of Justice showed a greater willingness to use the principle of effectiveness to override national procedural law, notably so as to require a national court to request parties to clarify the facts which they put forward so as to enable it to determine whether or not national law implementing EU consumer protection legislation is applicable[2087]; and in *Lintner*, the Court required the national court to take "investigative measures in order to complete that case file".[2087a] In the context of the law governing unfair terms in consumer contracts under the Consumer Rights Act 2015, it is a question whether an UK court could interpret that Act's legislative recognition of the court's duty to consider whether a term is fair "even if none of the parties to the proceedings has raised that issue or indicated that it intends to raise it"[2087b] given that the duty is subject to an explicit condition (reflecting the case-law of the Court of Justice at the time) that the court "has before it sufficient legal and factual material to enable it to consider the fairness of the term".[2087c]

2076 Whittaker (2001) 117 L.Q.R. 215; Whittaker in Leczykiewicz and Weatherill (eds), *The Involvement of EU Law in Private Relationships* (2013) Ch.6. See also above, para.38-020 discussing *Faber v Autobedrijf Hazet Ochten BV* (C-497/13) EU:C:2015:357, June 4, 2015.

2077 *Cofidis SA v Fredout* (C-473/00) EU:C:2002:705 at para.28; *Asturcom Telecomunicaiones SL v Rodriguez Nogueira* (C-40/08) EU:C:2009:615, [2009] E.C.R. I-9579 at para.38.

2078 See generally Craig and de Búrca, *EU Law, Text, Cases and Materials*, 6th edn (2015), pp.239 et seq.

2079 C-40/08 EU:C:2009:615, [2009] E.C.R. I-9579. See also *Banco Español de Crédito, SA v Calderón Camino* (C-618/10) EU:C:2012:349, June 14, 2012. This case concerned, inter alia, the question whether, under a national order for payment procedure a national court must consider the fairness of the terms of a consumer contract on which the basis of which payment is claimed, the term in question being a term fixing the interest rate for late payment. The CJEU distinguished *Pannon* (C-243/08) EU:C:2009:350, above para.38-331 and *Pénzügyi* (C-137/08) EU:C:2010:659, above, para.38-332 on the basis that the case before it concerned the national court's responsibilities in the context of an order for payment procedure before the consumer lodged an objection, holding that the national procedure before it breached the principle of effectiveness as it completely prevented the national court from assessing the fairness of a term relating to late payments in a contract of consumer credit: C-618/10 EU:C:2012:349, at paras 45, 49–57. See similarly *Finanmadrid EFC SA v Albán Zambrano* (C-49/14) EU:C:2016:98, February 18, 2016; *Profi Credit Polska SA w Bielsku Bialej v Wawrzosek* (C-176/17) EU:C:2018:711 (national order for payment procedure based on promissory note) and *Bondora* (C-453/18) EU:C:2019:921 A.G. Sharpston of October 31, 2019 (duty to raise issue of fairness of term applies to the European order for payment procedure under Regulation (EC) 1896/2006 of the European Parliament and of the Council of 12 December 2006 creating a European order for payment procedure [2006] O.J. L399/1. See also *Aziz v Caixa d'Estalvis de Catalunya, Tarragona i Manresa* (C-415/11) EU:C:2013:164, March 14, 2013 at paras 50, 59–64; *Sánchez Morcillo v Banco Bilbao Vizcaya Argentaria SA* (C-169/14) EU:C:2014:2099, July 17, 2014; *Banco Santander SA v Sánchez López* (C-598/15) EU:C:2017:945, December 7, 2017 (all three concerning Spanish procedures for the enforcement of mortgages); *Jőrös v Aegon Magyarország Hitel Zrt* (C-397/11) EU:C:2013:340, May 30, 201 at paras 29–38 and *Brusse v Jahani BV* (C-488/11) EU:C:2013:341, May 30, 2013 paras 42–46 (both concerning national rules and the role of *appellate* courts in circumstances where the unfairness of term had not been raised at first instance); *Baczó v Raiffeisen Bank Zrt* (C-567/13) EU:C:2015:88, February 12, 2015 (national rules governing competent national court to hear consumer claims); *ERSTE Bank Hungary Zrt v Sugár* (C-32/14) EU:C:2015:637, October 1, 2015 (effectiveness of the protection of consumers in context of national law governing notaries); *BBVA SA v Peñalva López* (C-8/14) EU:C:2015:731, October 29, 2015 (time-limit for relying on unfairness of terms specified by transitional legislation); *Radlinger v Finway a.s.* (C-377/14) EU:C:2016:283, April 21, 2016 at paras 51–59 (court's duty applies to insolvency proceedings).

2080 C-40/08 EU:C:2009:615 at para.38.

2081 C-168/05 EU:C:2006:675, [2006] E.C.R. I-10421.

2082 C-40/08 EU:C:2009:615 at para.47.

2083 C-40/08 EU:C:2009:615 at para.49.

2084 C-40/08 EU:C:2009:615, paras 50–55. In English law under the Arbitration Act 1996 a person subject to an arbitral award may bring proceedings challenging the substantive jurisdiction of that award, whether or not he participated in the arbitral proceedings, but he must normally do so within certain time-limits and subject to certain restrictions: see above, paras 32-157—32-161. Where a person alleged to be a party to arbitral proceedings took no part in them, that person may challenge the arbitral award on the ground that there was no valid arbitral agreement by bringing court proceedings for a declaration or injunction or other appropriate relief, or he may challenge the award on the ground of the arbitral tribunal's lack of substantive jurisdiction: Arbitration Act 1996 ss.72(1)(a) and 67(1)(a) respectively. And where the other party seeks to enforce any such arbitral award by permission of the court, this permission will not be granted where the person against whom it is sought to be enforced shows that the tribunal lacked substantive jurisdiction to make the award, though any such an objection to jurisdiction must be made timeously: Arbitration Act s.73(2), below para.32-186. It is submitted that this national system of challenges to the jurisdiction of an arbitral award (including one grounded on the "non-binding" nature of an arbitration clause unfair within the meaning of the 1993 Directive) would satisfy the principle of effectiveness as explained by the European Court in the *Asturcom Telecommunicaciones SL* case. Moreover, for the purposes of this system of challenges, no distinction is to be made by an English court (whether in proceedings challenging the award or in considering defences to an application to enforce an award) as between a challenge on the ground of the non-binding nature of the arbitration agreement under the 1993 Directive and on any other legal ground which challenges the validity of the arbitration agreement and, in this way, the principle of equivalence is also satisfied.

[2085] C-240/98 to C-244/98 EU:C:2000:346, [2000] E.C.R. I-4941.

[2086] C-168/05 EU:C:2006:675, [2006] E.C.R. I-10421.

[2087] *Faber v Autobedrijf Hazet Ochten BV* (C-497/13) EU:C:2015:357, June 4, 2015 on which see above, para.38-020. cf. A.G. Kokott's view that, where relevant to the fairness of a term of a consumer contract under the Unfair Terms in Consumer Contracts Directive 1993, a national court has an obligation to raise the unfairness of any *commercial practice* within the meaning of the Unfair Commercial Practices Directive 2005: *Margarit Panicello v Hernández Martínez* (C-503/15) EU:C:2017:126, A.G. Opinion of September 15, 2016 at [127]–[128]. The CJEU (judgment of February 16, 2017) did not comment on these issues.

[2087a] *Lintner v UniCredit Bank Hungary Zrt.* (C-511/17) EU:C:2020:188 at para.37. The CJEU further noted that where this was the case the national court must give the parties an opportunity to "set out their views" and to give the consumer the opportunity not to assert the unfair or non-binding status of the term: paras 42–43.

[2087b] Consumer Rights Act 2015 s.71(2).

[2087c] Consumer Rights Act 2015 s.71(3) and see below, para.38-392.

### "Neutral" assessment of fairness

*In line 19, after "to its attention by the parties.", add new footnote 2109a:*

[2109a] However, after IP completion day (on which see above, para.38-004 and Vol.I, paras 1-014 et seq.) UK courts would no longer be the same position as the significance of case law of the CJEU will change: see Vol.I, para.1-017B. **38-337**

## (gg) The Effects of a Finding That a Term is Unfair

### "Not binding on the consumer"

*To the end of quotation, after "the unfair terms.", add new footnote 2115a:*

[2115a] See also Commission guidance C(2019) 5325 final pp.41–50 summarising the case-law of the CJEU. **38-339**

*Add new paragraph:*

**The "non-binding" character of unfair terms and "waiver" agreements** In *XZ v Ibercaja Banco SA*[2121a] the question arose as the validity of a contract (called a "novation agreement") concluded between parties to an earlier contract of consumer credit under which the parties amended a term in the credit contract setting the lower limit of the variable interest rate (a "floor clause"), confirmed that that contract was valid and waived any rights or claims relating to it. Subsequently, the consumer contested the fairness of the floor clause in the credit contract and claimed, inter alia, that the second contract was a nullity as a result of the floor clause in the credit contract being "not binding on the consumer" under art.6(1) of **38-339A**

the 1993 Directive. In this respect, the Court of Justice held, first, that while art.6(1) renders an unfair contract term not binding on the consumer, the consumer's "right to effective consumer protection includes the option to waive the exercise of one's rights"[2121b] as long as the consumer's agreement was "free and informed".[2121c] In the view of the Court, the position of settlement agreements was analogous, with the result that:

> "a consumer may waive the right to rely on the unfairness of a contractual term in the context of a novation agreement, whereby the consumer waives the effects that would result from that term being declared to be unfair, provided that that waiver is the result of free and informed consent."[2121d]

In this way, art.6(1) does not itself render not binding a later settlement agreement under which the consumer waives his right or claims under an earlier consumer contract, but it will do so where that waiver was not "free and informed".[2121e] Moreover, the terms of such a consumer contract may in principle themselves be assessed for their fairness,[2121f] in particular as regards information enabling him or her to understand the legal consequences for him or her.[2121g] On the other hand, the Court of Justice added that:

> "a consumer may not legitimately waive, *for the future*, the legal protection and the rights that he or she derives from Directive 93/13. By definition, he or she cannot appreciate the consequences of agreeing to such a term as regards disputes which may arise in the future."[2121h]

This stems from the mandatory nature of art.6(1) of the Directive.[2121i]

[2121a] *XZ v Ibercaja Banco SA* (C-452/18) EU:C:2020:536 ("*Ibercaja Banco SA* (C-452/18)").

[2121b] *Ibercaja Banco SA* (C-452/18) at para.25 citing *Sales Sinués v Caixabank SA, Drame Ba v Catalunja Caixa SA* (Joined Cases C-381/14 and C-385/14) EU:C:2016:909 para.25. See also *Pannon GSM Zrt v Erzsébet Sustikné Győrfi* (C-243/08) EU:C:2009:350, [2009] E.C.R. I-4713, above, paras 38-331 and 38-339.

[2121c] *Ibercaja Banco SA* (C-452/18) at paras 25 and 27 referring to *Banif Plus Bank Zrt v Csipai* (C-472/11) EU:C:2013:88; [2013] W.L.R. (D) 76 at para.35. In this respect, A.G. Saugmandsgaard Øe of January 20, 2020 (available in French), para.54 appeared to assume that the "free" character of the consumer's consent is to be determined by national contract law rules (e.g. in English law the law of duress or undue influence), a question not addressed by the CJEU.

[2121d] *Ibercaja Banco SA* (C-452/18) at para.28.

[2121e] *Ibercaja Banco SA* (C-452/18) at para.30.

[2121f] *Ibercaja Banco SA* (C-452/18) at para.59.

[2121g] *Ibercaja Banco SA* (C-452/18) at para.77 (summarising earlier paragraphs). On the possibility of such a term falling within the exclusion in art.4(2) of the Directive see above, para.38-262C.

[2121h] *Ibercaja Banco SA* (C-452/18) at para.75 (emphasis added).

[2121i] *Ibercaja Banco SA* (C-452/18) at para.76.

### "The contract shall continue to bind the parties upon those terms if it is capable of continuing in existence without the unfair terms"

*Replace paragraph with:*

**38-341** The Court of Justice of the EU has held that the purpose of the 1993 Directive:

> "... consists in restoring the balance between the parties while in principle preserving the validity of the contract as a whole, not in abolishing all contracts containing unfair terms ... As regards the criteria for assessing whether a contract can indeed continue to exist without the unfair terms, it must be noted that both the wording of article 6(1) ... and the requirements concerning the legal certainty of economic activities plead in favour of an

> objective approach in interpreting that provision, so that ... the situation of one of the parties to the contract, in this case the consumer, cannot be regarded as the decisive criterion determining the fate of the contract."[2124]

As a result, under the Directive itself, a national court cannot base its decision on the continuance of the contract solely on a possible advantage for the consumer of its annulment,[2125] although it may do so if national law so provides owing to the minimum nature of the harmonisation required by art.8 of the Directive.[2126] By contrast, the Court of Justice has held that a national provision which empowers a national court to *replace* unfair terms with a modified (and fair) term is not compatible with art.6(1) of the Directive.[2127] On the other hand, as art.6(1) expressly provides, "the contract shall continue to bind the parties upon those terms if it is capable of continuing in existence without the unfair terms". As a result, the Court of Justice has held where a term in a contract of consumer credit fixing default interest has been held unfair and so not binding on the consumer, the national court may nevertheless impose interest under another term of the contract imposing "ordinary interest" not itself held unfair and so still binding on the consumer.[2127a]

Moreover, a national court is not precluded "in accordance with the principles of the law of contract, from deleting an unfair term and substituting for it a supplementary provision of national law" (i.e. a national legal rule applicable to the issue governed by the term in the absence of other or contrary agreement[2128]) where this would enable "real balance between the rights and obligations of the parties to be restored" and where otherwise the invalidity of the unfair term would require the court to annul the contract in its entirety with disadvantageous consequences to the consumer.[2129] A key example could be found in the case of a term relating to the main subject matter of the contract which fails the condition set by art.4(2) that it must be "plain and intelligible" and which is found to be unfair and so not binding on the consumer[2130]; if a supplementary rule allows a court to govern the issue of the main subject matter, then reliance on it could rescue the contract from overall invalidity.[2131] For example, where the unfairness (and therefore invalidity) of a term setting a variable interest rate in a contract of consumer credit by reference to a particular index would otherwise lead to the nullity of contract as a whole, the Court of Justice considered that a national court could replace that invalid term by setting the interest rate by reference to another legislative index applicable in the absence of agreement: this was justified in the interests of the consumer as annulment of the whole contract would be likely to lead to the immediate repayment of the capital by the consumer.[2131a] Another possible example in English law may be found in the position as regards the price in a contract for the sale of goods. If a term setting the price of the goods falls outside the exclusion in reg.6(2) of the 1999 Regulations and is found to be unfair and not binding on the consumer, it could be argued that the court could substitute a "reasonable price" for the price fixed under that contract term by way of s.8 of the Sale of Goods Act 1979, for in this situation the price could be said not to have been "fixed by the contract", left by the contract to be fixed in a manner agreed by the contract or have been determined by the course of dealing between the parties as foreseen by that section.[2132] On the other hand, it could be countered that, where a contract term fixing the price has been found unfair and "not binding" on the consumer, it nevertheless cannot be said that there is no price "fixed by the contract" so as to allow the application of s.8(3).[2133]

2124 *Pereničovà v SOS finance, spol. sro* (C-453/10) EU:C:2012:144, [2012] 2 C.M.L.R. 28 ("*Pereničovà* (C-453/10)") paras 31–32; *Jőrös v Aegon Magyarország Hitel Zrt* (C-397/11) EU:C:2013:340, May 30, 201 at paras 44–48.

[2125] *Pereničovà* (C-453/10) para.33. The question whether a contract can continue to exist without the unfair term is to be determined as a matter of national contract law, subject to the requirement (noted in the text) that the situation of one of the parties to the contract cannot be regarded as the decisive criterion: *Dziubak v Raiffeisen Bank International AG* (C-260/18) EU:C:2019:819 at para.40.

[2126] *Pereničovà* (C-453/10) at paras 34–35.

[2127] *Banco Español de Crédito, SA v Calderón Camino* (C-618/10) EU:C:2012:349, June 14, 2012, paras 69–73. See also *Brusse v Jahani BV* (C-488/11) EU:C:2013:341, May 30, 2013 at paras 54–60; *Kásler v OTP Jelzálogbank Zrt* (C-26/13) EU:C:2014:282, April 30, 2014 ("*Kásler* (C-26/13)") at paras 76–79; *Unicaja Banco, SA v Hidalgo Rueda* (C-482/13, C-484/13, C-485/12 and C-487/13) EU:C:2015:21, January 21, 2015 at paras 28–32; *Abanca Corporación Bancaria SA v Salamanca Santos, Bankia SA v Rodríquez Ramírez* (C-70/17 and C-179/17) EU:C:2019:250, March 26, 2019 at paras 54–55; *Gómez del Moral Guasch v Bankia SA* (C-125/18) EU:C:2020:138, para.59.

[2127a] *Banco Santander v Demba, Cortés v Banco de Sabadell SA* (C-96/16 and C-94/17) EU:C:2018:643 at paras 73–79 where it was explained that this result also follows where "the default interest rate is fixed in the form of an increase in the ordinary interest rate by a certain number of percentage points. In the latter case, as the unfair term consists in that increase, Directive 93/13 requires solely that that increase be annulled": at para.77. In this way, the CJEU appeared implicitly to accept the "blue-pencilling" of a single contract term, in effect deleting its unfair element or elements while retaining its other, not unfair elements. Cf. however, *Abanca Corporación Bancaria SA v Salamanca Santos, Bankia SA v Rodríquez Ramírez* (C-70/17 and C-179/17) EU:C:2019:250 March 26, 2019 at para.55 where the CJEU held that the deletion of part of a contract term (so as to remove its unfair character) would constitute a revision of the term by altering its substance and was not permitted. See further Commission guidance C(2019) 5325 final pp.44–46. A.G. Hogan has expressed the view that "the notion of 'term' used by the 1993 Directive must be understood in a substantial and not in a formal sense for the purposes of art.4(2): *Kiss v Kiss* (C-621/17) Opinion of A.G. Hogan of May 15, 2019, para.50 (issue not addressed by the CJEU in its decision of October 3, 2019) and above, para.38-232.

[2128] In English law, in principle such a supplementary rule may be fixed by statute (as in the case of rules governing contracts of sale of goods under the Sale of Goods Act 1979) or at common law, whether expressed in terms of a general legal position (such as the law governing termination for repudiatory breach) or by way of implied term. However, the CJEU has cast indirect doubt on whether recourse could be had to the common law for this purpose as it has ruled out reference to "national [legislative] provisions of a general nature which provide that the effects expressed in a legal transaction are to be supplemented, inter alia, by the effects arising from the principle of equity or from established customs" on the basis that these provisions have not been subject to "a specific assessment by the legislature with a view to establishing that balance" between the rights and obligations of the parties: *Dziubak v Raiffeisen Bank International AG* (C-260/18) EU:C:2019:819 at paras 59–62. While it could be argued that in a common law system the proper balance of the parties' rights and obligations can be fixed equally properly and specifically by the common law as by the legislature (so addressing one point of the CJEU's concern), it remains true that this balance is not fixed by the legislature.

[2129] *Kásler* (C-26/13) at paras 82–84; *Unicaja Banco, SA v Hidalgo Rueda* (C-482/13, C-484/13, C-485/12 and C-487/13) EU:C:2015:21, January 21, 2015 at para.33; *Abanca Corporación Bancaria SA v Salamanca Santos, Bankia SA v Rodríquez Ramírez* (C-70/17 and C-179/17) EU:C:2019:250 March 26, 2019 at paras 56–64. See also Commission guidance C(2019) 5325 final pp.46–49. The unfavourable consequences to the consumer of annulment should be assessed in relation to the circumstances existing or foreseeable at the time when the dispute arose, rather than when the contract was concluded and the consumer may object to being protected by the upholding of the contract in this way: *Dziubak v Raiffeisen Bank International AG* (C-260/18) EU:C:2019:819 at paras 50 and 55. Where the contract cannot be upheld by replacing the unfair contract term, a national court is not entitled instead to uphold the original unfair term itself unless the consumer gives his "free and informed consent" to this effect: at paras 63–68.

[2130] See above, paras 38-261, 38-262.

[2131] *Kásler* (C-26/13) at paras 81–83. This possible effect of the non-binding nature of a term which defines the main subject-matter of the contract was recognised by the CJEU in *Dunai v ERSTE Bank Hungary Zrt* (C-118/17) EU:C:2019:207 of March 14, 2019 at para.52, noting that the question whether it is legally possible for the contract as a whole to survive is a matter for the national court. However, the CJEU held that the Directive precludes national legislation which substitutes a legislative term for an unfair term and thereby prevents the national court from holding that the contract as a whole cannot continue to exist without that unfair term where the continuation of the contract is contrary to the interests of the consumer: C-118/17 at paras 52–56.

[2131a] *Gómez del Moral Guasch v Bankia SA* (C-125/18) EU:C:2020:138 at paras 60–67.

[2132] Sale of Goods Act 1979 s.8(1) and (2) and see below, paras 44-051—44-052.

[2133] Peel (ed.), *Treitel on The Law of Contract*, 15th edn (2020), para.7-126. cf. Bridge, *The Sale of Goods*, 3rd edn (2014), para.9.44 who notes (without referring to s.8(3) of the 1979 Act) that in these circumstances the absence of a power in the court to rewrite the contract means that the contract cannot continue and so must be unwound. Similar issues would arise in relation to price terms found unfair and not binding in contracts for the provision of services in relation to the Supply of Goods and Services Act 1982 s.15.

## No application of national "supplementary rules" more generally

*Replace paragraph with:*

As has been noted above, the Court of Justice of the EU allows a national court to apply a national supplementary rule (that is, one applicable in the absence of other or contrary agreement[2134]) to govern an issue regulated by a contract term found unfair and therefore not binding on the consumer, where otherwise the contract would fail to the prejudice of the consumer, subject to the condition that such an application would enable a "real balance between the rights and obligations of the parties to be restored".[2135] However, the Court of Justice has emphasised that this acceptance of the application of national rules in substitution for a contract term held unfair is limited to these particular circumstances.[2136] In *Banco Bilbao Vizcaya Argentaria SA* the strictness of this position for the trader was confirmed by the Court in considering whether a Spanish court could apply its general rules governing interest on late payments of debts provided by the Spanish Civil Code for the situation where no contract term setting a rate of interest has been fixed instead of an express term in a consumer contract of loan setting default interest found unfair under national legislation implementing the 1993 Directive.[2137] In its Order,[2138] the Court held that the effect of art.6(1) of the Directive is that: **38-342**

> "... national courts are bound solely to exclude the application of the unfair contract term so that it produces no binding effects on the consumer, without their being empowered to revise its content. Indeed, the contract must in principle subsist without any modification other than the suppression of the unfair contract terms to the extent to which such a survival of the contract is legally possible under the rules of national law."[2139]

As a result, where a court declares a penalty clause in a consumer contract to be unfair, art.6(1) "cannot be interpreted as allowing the national court ... to reduce the amount of the penalty imposed on the consumer instead of excluding entirely the application of the clause"[2140]; such a power of revision would "contribute to the elimination of the deterrent effect exercised on traders by the pure and simple non-application of such unfair contract terms as regards consumers", to the extent to which traders would be tempted to use them knowing that, if they were later invalidated, they could still look to the court to protect the interest with which the term was concerned.[2141] Moreover, in the case of a penalty clause such as the default interest clause before it, its annulment would not have any negative consequences for the consumer as the amounts which he or she would have to pay would necessarily be less.[2142] This decision has some potentially radical consequences in the context of English law. First, in the particular context of *Banco Bilbao Vizcaya Argentaria SA*, where a term in a consumer contract imposing a contractual rate interest for late payment of any sum owed by the consumer is held unfair and not binding on the consumer under the 1999 Regulations, a court could not award the trader actual interest losses caused by this late payment even if pleaded and proved as is generally possible at common law,[2143] nor, apparently, could a court exercise a statutory discretion to impose interest in respect of any such late payment.[2144] Secondly, the approach of the Court of Justice to "supplementary provisions of national law" is not restricted to the context of late payments of sums of money, and has been applied, for example, to a penalty stipulated for travel by rail in the absence of a ticket.[2144a] For example, where a term in a consumer contract imposes on the consumer liability to pay a sum of money on breach of contract is held unfair and not binding on the consumer under the 1999 Regulations,[2145] the trader would *not* be entitled to recover damages for any loss actually caused by the consumer's breach under the general common law, as here the common law rules on damages must be viewed as "supplementary rules" which would substitute for the (unfair) term in the consumer contract. Such an effect of a finding of unfairness of a contract term under the 1999 Regulations contrasts strikingly with the effect of a finding that a term is a penalty clause at common law, as such a finding does not prevent the injured party from recovering damages at common law against the party in breach in respect of proven and legally recoverable losses.[2146] It is difficult to foresee, however, how far the approach of the Court of Justice in *Bilbao Vizcaya Argentaria SA* should be taken. For example, if a term in a consumer contract providing a power of termination in the trader for breach of contract by the consumer in certain circumstances were found unfair under the 1999 Regulations, it could be argued that such a finding prevents the trader from relying on the general common law of repudiatory breach so as to terminate the contract in respect of the circumstances foreseen by the term in question. Certainly, such a result would have a strong deterrent effect on traders including unfair termination clauses, and thus contribute to the effectiveness of the protection of consumers. However, even if this were the case, it is submitted that such a result should not prevent the trader from terminating the contract on the grounds of breach by the consumer on grounds not foreseen by the unfair contract term, whether under a fair (and therefore binding) express term or at common law.[2146a] Finally, the degree of uncertainty as to the limits of the approach of the Court of Justice in Bilbao Vizcaya Argentaria SA has been increased by its very recent decision in *CY v Caixabank SA*.[2146b] In this case the Court of Justice held, inter alia, that where a contract term which places all the costs of setting up and discharging a mortgage executed in relation to a loan on the consumer is held unfair, a national court *may* still allow these costs (or part of these costs) to rest with the consumer if national law would anyway so provide.[2146c] In so deciding, the Court did not refer to its earlier case-law discussed in the previous paragraphs starting with *Kásler* which has rejected the application of national supplementary law instead of an unfair contract term except where this would enable a "real balance between the rights and obligations of the parties to be restored" and where otherwise the invalidity of the unfair term would require the court to annul the contract in its entirety with disadvantageous consequences to the consumer.[2146d] Nor did it address the concern of this earlier case-law that allowing a trader to rely on national legal provisions against a consumer instead of a term held unfair would undermine the deterrent effect of the Directive. In these circumstances, the lasting status of the decision must remain in doubt.

[2134] The French expression used is "*une disposition de droit national à caractère supplétif*". This invokes the classic civil law distinction between legal provisions applying subject to other or contrary agreement (*les lois supplétives de volonté* or *ius dispositivum*) and legal provisions applying irrespective of the parties' agreement (*les lois impératives* or *ius cogens*).

[2135] *Kásler v OTP Jelzálogbank Zrt* (C-26/13) EU:C:2014:282, April 30, 2014 at paras 82–84; *Unicaja Banco SA v Hidalgo Rueda* (C-482/13, C-484/13, C-485/12 and C-487/13) EU:C:2015:21, January 21, 2015 ("*Unicaja Banco, SA* (C-482/13, etc.)") at para.33.

[2136] *Unicaja Banco SA* (C-482/13, etc.) at para.33.

[2137] *Banco Bilbao Vizcaya Argentaria SA v Quintano Ujeta* (C-602/13) EU:C:2015:397, Order of June 11, 2015 (available only in French) ("*Bilbao Vizcaya Argentaria SA* (C-602/13)"). The CJEU followed this ruling closely in very similar circumstances in *Banco Grupo Cajatres SA v Manjón Pinilla* (C-90/14) EU:C:2015:465, July 8, 2015 at paras 33–38.

2138 The fact that the CJEU decided in the form of an Order rather than a judgment reflects its view that its response to the national court's question could clearly be deduced from its existing case-law: *Bilbao Vizcaya Argentaria SA* (C-602/13), para.29 referring to art.99 of the Court's own rules of procedure.

2139 *Bilbao Vizcaya Argentaria SA* (C-602/13) at para.33. The translations from the French text of the CJEU's Order here and in the remainder of this paragraph are the editor's.

2140 *Bilbao Vizcaya Argentaria SA* (C-602/13) at para.34.

2141 *Bilbao Vizcaya Argentaria SA* (C-602/13) at para.36.

2142 *Bilbao Vizcaya Argentaria SA* (C-602/13) at para.39. The CJEU accepted that this lack of negative effect would be "subject to verification by the referring court". Cf. the position as regards the application of an interest rate set by another term of the contract instead of by the (unfair) term setting a default interest rate: *Banco Santander SA v Demba, Cortés v Banco de Sabadell SA* (C-96/16 and C-94/17) EU:C:2018:643 at paras 74–77, above, para.38-341 note. Cf. also Commission guidance C(2019) 5325 final p.49.

2143 cf. Vol.I paras 26-273—26-275 explaining the general common law position.

2144 See Vol.I, paras 26-281—26-286, referring notably to the Senior Courts Act 1981 s.35A.

2144a *Nationale Maatschappij der Belgische Spoorwegen (NMBS) v Kanyeba, Nijs. Dedroog* (C-349 to C-351/18) EU:C:2019:936 paras 65–74 (where the CJEU left open the possibility of the traveller being liable under national *extra-contractual* liability rules). On the question whether such a person travels under a "consumer contract" see above, para.38-230.

2145 Such a contract term is foreseen as one which "may be regarded as unfair" by the 1999 Regulations reg.5(5); Sch.2 para.1(e), see above, paras 38-306—38-307. An example may be found in *Munkenbeck & Marshall v Harold* [2005] EWHC 356 (TCC), [2005] All E.R. (D) 227, above, para.38-306.

2146 *McGregor on Damages*, 20th edn (2017), paras 15-026—15-027; and see *Cavendish Square Holding BV v Makdessi, ParkingEye Ltd v Beavis* [2015] UKSC 67, [2015] 3 W.L.R. 1373 at [9].

2146a Cf. *Higgins & Co Lawyers Ltd v Evans* [2019] EWHC 2809 (QB), [2020] 1 W.L.R. 2809 at [101] at point (vi) where a term in a conditional fee agreement automatically terminating the contract on the death of the claimant for personal injuries and imposing payment on the latter's estate of the solicitor's "basic charges" (which would have to be reasonable by way of application of the Solicitors Act 1974 s.70) was *not* unfair in part on the ground that, if the clause were unfair and non-binding, the rest of the contract would remain in force and the estate would therefore come under an obligation to pay reasonable fees.

2146b C-224/19, C-259/19 EU:C:2020:578 (available in French).

2146c C-224/19, C-259/19 at paras 54 and 55.

2146d *Kásler v OTP Jelzálogbank Zrt.* (C-26/13) EU:C:2014:282 at paras 82–84 and see above, para.38-341 for further references.

## Restitution of money paid by the consumer

*Replace footnote 2155 with:*

2155 *Gutiérrez Naranjo* (Joined Cases C-154/15, C-307/15 and C-308/15) at para.73. On the other hand, where a contract term which places all the costs of setting up and discharging a mortgage executed in relation to a loan on the consumer is held unfair, a national court *may* still allow these costs (or part of these costs) to rest with the consumer if national law would anyway so provide: *CY v Caixabank SA* (C-224/19, C-259/19) EU:C:2020:578 of 16 July 2020 at para.55. **38-343**

*Replace paragraph with:*

The particular issues presented to the Court of Justice in *Gutiérrez Naranjo* are not directly relevant to the interpretation and application of the 1999 Regulations (nor indeed their successor provisions in the Consumer Rights Act Pt 2[2156]) by English courts. However, *Gutiérrez Naranjo* makes clear that EU law requires in principle that a consumer who has paid money under a contract term found unfair has a right to recovery of that money, as in the case of penalty clause, an unfair price variation clause or an unintelligible[2157] and unfair clause setting the price itself. However, the exact legal nature of this recovery and its incidents (for example, as regards any limitation period applicable or possibly even any defence of change of position by the seller or supplier or contributory fault in the consumer[2157a]) could **38-344** still be thought to be a matter for national (and therefore English) law, as being "detailed rules" governing the effect of the non-bindingness of the term in question, subject to the qualification that the practical effect of the nature and incidents of the recovery must not prejudice the effectiveness of the consumer's protection.[2158] In terms of the classification of such a claim as a matter of the English law of restitution, it could be thought that recovery of money paid by a consumer could be placed on the ground of the failure of basis on which it had been paid (traditionally called failure of consideration)[2159] or possibly on the ground of a mistake of law.[2160]

2156 Below, paras 38-365 et seq.

2157 This further requirement stems from the proviso to the "core exclusion" from the test of unfairness: see above, para.38-261, 38-262.

2157a According to the EU Commission, Commission guidance C(2019) 5325 final p.50, "only provisions related to legal certainty, in particular res judicata and reasonably limitation periods, may limit such restitutionary effect", referring to *Gutiérrez Naranjo* (Joined Cases C-154/15, C-307/15 and C-308/15) at paras 67–69.

2158 *Gutiérrez Naranjo* (Joined Cases C-154/15, C-307/15 and C-308/15) at paras 66 and 69. On limitation of actions see *SC Raiffeisen Bank SA v JB* (C-698/18 and C-699/18) EU:C:2020:537 paras 63–67, 75–76 (a limitation period of three years for claims of restitution of sums paid under an unfair contract term is in principle "reasonable" and so consistent with the principle of effectiveness, but not where the period starts to run from the time of completed performance of the contract as it is likely to have expired before the consumer is aware of the possible unfairness of the contract's terms; the principle of equivalence has also to be observed); similarly, *CY v Caixabank SA* (C-224/19 C-259/19) EU:C:2020:578 paras 85–92. cf. *Cofidis CA v Fredout* (C-473/00) EU:C:2002:705, [2002] E.C.R. I-10875 (national limitation period held unable to prevent court intervening as regards the fairness of a contract term) and *Hamilton v Volksbank Filder eG* (C-412/06) EU:C:2008:215, [2008] E.C.R. I-2383 especially A.G. Maduro's Opinion at para.24 ("The existence of a general principle of limitation should therefore be recognised, while leaving the Member States the necessary discretion to implement it in their respective legal systems").

2159 See Vol.I, paras 29-057 et seq.

2160 *Chesterton Global Ltd v Finney* Unreported April 30, 2010, Lambeth County Ct; *Re Welcome Financial Services Ltd* [2015] EWHC 815 (Ch) at [106] and see generally on this ground of recovery Vol.I, paras 29-033—29-058.

### Terms "not binding" on consumer and third parties

*Replace footnote 2168 with:*

38-345 2168 cf. the position in *Roundlistic Ltd v Jones* [2018] EWCA Civ 2284, [2019] 1 W.L.R. 4461 where, however, these points were not raised: on this case, see above, para.38-230. See also *Casehub Ltd v Wolf Cola Ltd* [2017] EWHC 1169 (Ch), [2017] 5 Costs L.R. 835 at [25]–[31] (assignment by consumers of their restitutionary claims under the 1999 Regulations to claimant company held valid) and see further below, para.38-400.

## *(iv) The Requirement of Plain and Intelligible Language*

*To the end of title, add new footnote 2181a:*

### Broad approach to the requirement of transparency in the CJEU[2181a]

38-350 2181a It should be noted that the significance of case-law of the CJEU for English courts changes on IP completion day: above, para.38-004 and Vol.I, para.1-017B.

*Replace footnote 2186 with:*

38-350 2186 *RWE Vertrieb AG* (C-92/11) at para.44. In *Verein für Konsumenteninformation v Amazon EU Sàrl* (C-191/15) EU:C:2016:612, July 28, 2016 above, para.38-321, the CJEU identified the unfairness of a choice of foreign law clause in its failure to conform to the requirement of plain and intelligible language by the trader in failing to inform the consumer that the effects of such a term are qualified by the mandatory statutory provisions of the consumer's place of residence provided for his protection. However, in *Tóth v ERSTE Bank Hungary Zrt.* (C-34/18) EU:C:2019:764 at paras 68–69, the CJEU refused to see this case-law as justifying the existence of a duty in a trader to alert consumers to relevant national general procedural provisions governing burden of proof nor to their interpretation by the courts as this would go further than could reasonably be expected of the trader under the requirement of transparency; and later in *Profi Credit Polska SA z siedziba w Bielsku- Bialej v QJ* (C-84/19, C-222/19 and C-252/19) EU:C:2020:259 Opinion of April 2, 2020 at para.96, A.G. Hogan argued (in the context of a consumer credit contract) that a failure in a trader to specify the tasks it must perform or the costs which it must bear to provide the service should not be seen as a lack of "plain, intelligible language" within the meaning of art.4(2). In his view, "[i]t is only if the financial consequences of the contract, considered as a whole or as to the subject matter of the contract, are not clear from the contract, in particular due to the existence of an excessive number of price clauses, that such clauses can be considered as not fulfilling that condition". The CJEU in its judgment of September 3, 2020 at para.75 took a rather more demanding view of the requirement of transparency holding that while "the seller or supplier is not obliged to specify the nature of each service provided in return for the costs imposed on the consumer under the terms of the contract, ... it is important that the nature of the services actually provided can be reasonably understood or inferred from the contract considered as a whole. In addition, the consumer must be able to ascertain that there is no overlap between those various costs or the services for which those costs are paid".

### The effects of failure to comply with the requirement of transparency

*To the end of paragraph, after "test of unfairness.2193", add:*

Finally, a finding that a contract term fails the requirement for transparency is relevant to the assessment of that term's fairness.[2193a] **38-351**

[2193a] See above, para.38-286.

## *(vi) The Prevention of Unfair Terms*

### Use or recommendation for use of contract terms as a "commercial practice"

*Replace footnote 2276 with:*

[2276] Above, para.38-170. Moreover, where a trader knows that the contract term on the basis of which he claims payment is unenforceable in law and acts dishonestly in doing so, he may be convicted of fraud under the general criminal law: *R. v Whatcott* [2019] EWCA Crim 1889. **38-364**

## (d) The New Law: The Consumer Rights Act 2015

## *(i) Introduction and Overview*

### Background

*Replace footnote 2283 with:*

[2283] The Act is accompanied by a set of Explanatory Notes prepared by the Department for Business, Innovation and Skills ("*Explanatory Notes* 2015"). On IP completion day (on which see generally, above, para.38-004 and Vol.I, paras 1-014 et seq.) the 2015 Act is due to be amended and these amendments will be noted where relevant in the following paragraphs: see 2015 Act s.32 (below, para.38-533), s.59 (below, para.38-497), s.73 (below, para.38-388) and s.74 (below, para.38-418) (amendments to be made by the Consumer Protection (Amendment etc.) (EU Exit) Regulations 2018 (SI 2018/1326) reg.3) (reg.1's reference to the 2018 Regulations coming into force on "exit day" must be read as referring to IP completion day: European Union (Withdrawal Agreement) Act 2020 s.39(1), Sch.5 para.1). The 2015 Act Sch.5 (Investigatory Powers etc.) (below, para.38-420) is to be amended on IP completion day by the Consumer Protection (Enforcement) (Amendment etc.) (EU Exit) Regulations 2019 (SI 2019/203) reg.4 (reg.1's reference to the 2019 Regulations coming into force on "exit day" must be read as referring to IP completion day: European Union (Withdrawal Agreement) Act 2020 s.39(1), Sch.5 para.1). The Consumer Rights Act 2015 (Enforcement) (Amendment) Order 2019 (SI 2019/1074) arts 2 and 3 (in force July 23, 2019)) made minor amendments to Schs 3 and 5 of the 2015 Act. **38-365**

### The strategies of the 2015 Act in relation to contract terms

*Replace footnote 2319 with:*

[2319] 2015 Act s.70; Sch.3. In addition, the relevant provisions of the 2015 Act are specified as the UK law which gives effect to the 1993 Directive for the purposes of Pt 8 of the Enterprise Act 2002: Enterprise Act 2002 (Part 8 Community Infringements Specified UK Laws) Order 2003/1374 Sch.1 **38-374**

(referring to the 2015 Act ss.2, 61–64, 67–70, 72 to 74; Schs 2 and 3 and Sch.5 Pt 3) as amended by the Enterprise Act 2002 (Part 8 Community Infringements and Specified Laws) (Amendment) Order 2015 (SI 2015/1628) art.2. Moreover, acts or omissions in respect of any provision in Pts 1 and 2 of the 2015 Act are specified as possible "domestic infringements" for the purposes of s.212 of the Enterprise Act 2002: Enterprise Act 2002 (Part 8 Domestic Infringements) Order 2015 (SI 2015/1727) art.2. On the compatibility of the latter with EU law, see below, paras 38-421—38-426. On IP completion day (on which see above, para.38-004 and Vol.I, paras 1-014 et seq.), "Community infringements" are to be replaced by "Schedule 13 infringements" and the relevant provisions of the 2015 Act are to be included within the substituted Sch.13 of the 2002 Act for this purpose: Consumer Protection (Enforcement) (Amendment etc.) (EU Exit) Regulations 2019 (SI 2019/203) reg.3(20) and Sch. para.1 inserting new 2002 Act Sch.13 para.27. On this change more generally see above, para.38-133A.

### *(ii) The Relationship of the Consumer Rights Act to EU Law*

#### Interpretation of provisions in the 2015 Act implementing the 1993 Directive

*Replace paragraph with:*

38-376 As earlier explained,[2327] the Court of Justice has held that the concepts and expressions used by the provisions of the 1993 Directive must normally be given an "autonomous" European interpretation[2328] and this means that, following the principle of the "indirect effect" of directives (sometimes known as the principle of conforming interpretation of national legislation implementing EU directives), English courts are under a duty to interpret the provisions of the 2015 Act seeking to implement the 1993 Directive "as far as possible" in a way so as to give proper effect to the UK's obligations under the Directive.[2329] As a result, the decisions of the Court of Justice on the 1993 Directive which have explained its own interpretative role relative to the roles of national courts,[2330] which have ruled on the proper interpretation of concepts used by the 1993 Directive or have provided guidance on their application by national courts,[2331] have explained the duty of national courts to raise the issue of the unfairness of a term in a consumer contract of their own motion,[2332] and the relationship between the test of unfairness of contract terms under the 1993 Directive and the unfairness of commercial practices under the Unfair Commercial Practices Directive 2005[2333] are relevant equally to the UK's reimplementation of that Directive by the 2015 Act as they are under the 1999 Regulations. This continuing relevance also holds good as regards case-law of the Court of Justice on other European legislative instruments on which it may draw in any future interpretation of the Directive's concepts, as in its case-law on the concept of "consumer".[2334] However, this last example raises a different issue, as the 2015 Act defines "consumer" in a way which may be broader in one respect than the interpretation of the Court of Justice to "consumer"[2335]; and this raises the question whether UK law is entitled as a matter of EU law to extend its legislative controls on unfair terms drawn from the 1993 Directive beyond those required by that Directive. On the coming into full effect of the UK's leaving the EU on IP completion day, the existing case law of the Court of Justice on the 1993 Directive and the wider consumer *acquis* more generally remains relevant to the interpretation of the provisions of the 2015 Act which implement the Directive, but its significance changes as it will no longer bind the Supreme Court (nor other courts as designated by regulation); and case-law of the Court of Justice laid down on or after IP completion day *may* merely be taken into consideration by a UK court.[2335a]

[2327] See above, para.38-015.

[2328] *Kásler v OTP Jelzálogbank Zrt* (C-26/13) EU:C:2014:282, April 30, 2014 at [37].

[2329] Above, para.38-017.

2330 Above, para.38-329.

2331 See above, paras 38-250—38-262, 38-270—38-271 and 38-314—38-315.

2332 See, notably, *Océano Grupo Editorial SA v Murciano Quintero* (C-240/98 to C-244/98) EU:C:2000:346, [2000] E.C.R. I–4941; *Mostaza Claro v Centro Móvil Milenium SL* (C-168/05) EU:C:2006:675, [2006] E.C.R. I-10421 on which above, paras 38-331—38-332. The 2015 Act seeks to give legislative recognition to this case-law in s.71 "Duty of court to consider fairness of term" on which see below, para.38-392.

2333 Directive 2005/29 concerning unfair business-to-consumer commercial practices in the internal market [2005] O.J. L149/22 ("2005 Directive") and see above, para.38-278 and, notably, *Pereničovà v SOS finance, spol. sro* (C-453/10) EU:C:2012:144.

2334 Above, paras 38-034—38-035.

2335 2015 Act s.2(3) (applicable to Pt 1, and applied to Pt 2 by s.76(2)) and see below para.38-384.

2335a See European Union (Withdrawal) Act 2018 s.6 (as amended or to be amended by the European Union (Withdrawal Agreement) Act 2020 s.26) on which see Vol.I, para.1-017B.

**English law before the Consumer Rights Act 2015**

*Replace footnote 2348 with:*

2348 Enterprise Act 2002 s.212 (as amended) and see above, para.38-361. On the UK's leaving the EU on "exit day", "Community infringements" are to be replaced by "Schedule 13 infringements" and the 2008 Regulations and the 1999 Regulations (to the extent that they remain in force) are included within the substituted Sch.13 of the 2002 Act for this purpose: Consumer Protection (Enforcement) (Amendment etc.) (EU Exit) Regulations 2019 (SI 2019/203) reg.3(20) and Sch. para.1 inserting new 2002 Act Sch.13 paras 19 and 9. On this change more generally see above, para.38-133A. **38-378**

## *(iii) Scope of Controls on Contract Terms and Notices in Pt 2 of the Consumer Rights Act*

**"Consumer"**

*In line 15, after "were repealed by the", add:*

2015 **38-384**

**Terms or notices reflecting "mandatory statutory or regulatory provisions" or international conventions**

*Replace footnote 2399 with:*

2399 2015 Act s.73(1). On IP completion day (on which see generally above, para.38-004 and Vol.I, paras 1-014 et seq.), the words "or the EU" are to be deleted: Consumer Protection (Amendment etc.) (EU Exit) Regulations 2018 (SI 2018/1326) reg.3(4) (reg.1(3)'s reference to reg.3(4)'s coming into force on "exit day" must be read as referring to IP completion day: European Union (Withdrawal Agreement) Act 2020 s.39(1), Sch.5 para.1). **38-388**

## *(iv) Contract Terms and Notices Not Binding on the Consumer Where Assessed as Unfair*

### (aa) Terms of Consumer Contracts

**Duty of court in relation to the issue of fairness**

*Replace paragraph with:*

The 2015 Act sought to give explicit effect to the case-law of the Court of Justice of the EU as regards the duty of national courts to consider the fairness of a term in a consumer contract within the scope of the controls set out by the 1993 Directive.[2424] This followed the recommendation of the Law Commissions, which considered that such a statement would be helpful to bring this obligation to the at- **38-392** tention of the courts and, especially, the lower courts.[2425] Section 71 of the Act therefore provides that:

> "(1) Subsection (2) applies to proceedings before a court which relate to a term of a consumer contract.
> (2) The court must consider whether the term is fair even if none of the parties to the proceedings has raised that issue or indicated that it intends to raise it.
> (3) But subsection (2) does not apply unless the court considers that it has before it sufficient legal and factual material to enable it to consider the fairness of the term."

The qualification on the ambit of the duty made by s.71(3) reflects closely the qualification put on the national court's duty by the Court of Justice of the EU in *Pannon*[2426] but, as has been seen, the case-law of the Court of Justice has moved on since *Pannon* and in *Lintner* it required a national court which doubted the fairness of a term in a consumer contract but did not have the legal and factual materials to determine the issue, to "take, if necessary of its own motion, investigative measures in order to complete that case file, by asking the parties, in observance of the principle of *audi alteram partem*, to provide it with the clarifications or documents necessary for that purpose".[2427] As a matter of EU law, a UK court would be under a duty to interpret s.71 if possible so as to conform to this interpretation of the law,[2427a] but it may be doubted whether the clear words of s.71 can be so interpreted. Moreover, after the end of the "implementation period" on IP completion day, while in principle UK courts will remain under the duty of conforming interpretation of "retained EU" (which would include the UK implementation of the 1993 Directive in the 2015 Act),[2427b] certain UK courts (including the Supreme Court) would have the power to decide *not* to follow the case-law of the Court of Justice.[2427c] Such a decision could be appropriate as regards the interpretation of the extent of courts' duties adopted in Lintner on the basis in part that it is incompatible with the clear words of the 2015 Act and in part that the role for civil courts which this decision requires does not reflect fundamental principles of English civil procedure by which it is for the parties to adduce evidence of facts rather than for the court to require them to do so.

Secondly, the 2015 Act s.71(1) restricts the court's duty to consider the fairness of a term to the situation where "proceedings before a court *relate to* a term of a consumer contract"[2428] and this, together with the wording of s.71(2), suggests that the duty to consider the fairness of a contract term arises only where the proceedings before the court *relate to the term which is to be so considered for its fairness*.[2429] While similar wording has sometimes been used by the Court of Justice of the EU,[2430] it is submitted that such an interpretation of s.71 would risk imposing on English courts a more limited duty than is foreseen by recent case-law of the Court of Justice. For, under that case-law, a national court before which proceedings are brought relating to a consumer contract is under a duty to assess of its own motion "those contractual terms which are connected to the subject matter of the dispute" as defined by the parties in their pleadings even if those terms are not challenged by the consumer's claim.[2431] Again, it would be a question whether, following the principle of conforming interpretation, a UK court could interpret s.71 so as to conform to this case-law in the Court of Justice.[2432]

Finally, it should be noted that, on its terms (which are restricted to considering the *fairness* of a term) and reflecting the case-law of the Court of Justice (which also concerns the assessment of the fairness of terms under the 1993 Directive) which forms its background, the duty in a court under s.71 appears not to apply to cases where the controls on a term of a consumer contract would lead to its ineffectiveness *without* any assessment of its fairness. Paradoxically, therefore, a court would appear not to be under a duty to consider and hold ineffective a contract term excluding liability for death and personal injury "barred" by s.65[2433] nor contract terms which are ineffective to exclude or restrict liability for breach of the statutory terms in Pt 1 of the 2015 Act without any consideration of their fairness.[2433a]

[2424] See, notably, *Mostaza Claro v Centro Móvil Milenium SL* (C-168/05) EU:C:2006:675, [2006] E.C.R. I-10421; *Pannon GSM Zrt v Erzsébet Sustikné Györfi* (C-243/08) EU:C:2009:350, [2009] E.C.R. I-4713 and on this case-law and its progeny, above, paras 38-019—38-021, 38-331—38-335.

[2425] Law Com. Advice (2013), para.7.90.

[2426] *Pannon GSM Zrt v Erzsébet Sustikné Györfi* (C-243/08) EU:C:2009:350, [2009] E.C.R. I-4713 at [32], above, para.38-331. For an example of a UK court considering that it did *not* have sufficient material for this purpose see *Allner v Peters & May Group Ltd* [2019] EWHC 3258 (Comm) at [29].

[2427] *Lintner v UniCredit Bank Hungary Zrt* (C-511/17) EU:C:2020:188 at para.37 and see above, paras 38-020 and 38-332A.

[2427a] Above, para.38-014.

[2427b] This follows from the retention after the completion of the "implementation period" (IP) of "retained general principles of EU law" which generally means those laid down by the CJEU before IP completion day, presently set as December 31, 2020 at 11.00pm see generally above, para.38-004 and Vol.I, paras 1-014 et seq.

[2427c] European Union Withdrawal Act 2018 s.6(4) and (5) (with amendments and insertions made or to be made under the European Union (Withdrawal Agreement) Act 2020 s.26. See Vol.I, para.1-017B.

[2428] 2015 Act s.71(1) (emphasis added).

[2429] cf. the observation in the *Explanatory Notes* 2015 para.341 in relation to s.71 that "the courts would only have to look at the term or terms in question, not the entire contract; this reflects the principle in Case C-137/08 *VB Pénzügyi v Schneider* in 2010".

[2430] Notably, *VB Pénzügyi Lizing Zrt v Schneider* (C-137/08) EU:C:2010:659, [2010] E.C.R. I-847 at para.49 referring to the duty of the court to decide whether "a contractual term *which is the subject of the dispute* before it falls within the scope of the Directive" (emphasis added).

[2431] *Lintner v UniCredit Bank Hungary Zrt.* (C-511/17) EU:C:2020:188 at para.34.

[2432] The same qualification applies as to the status of decisions of the CJEU after IP completion day as is earlier noted in the text: and see Vol.I, para.1-017B.

[2433] See below, para.38-409.

[2433a] See below, para.38-531 (goods contracts); para.38-564 (digital content contracts); and para.38-586 (services contracts).

## Burden of proof as to fairness of a contract term

*Replace paragraph with:*

Unlike the position under the Unfair Contract Terms Act 1977 as regards the **38-393**
reasonableness of contract terms,[2434] neither the 1993 Directive nor the 1999 Regulations set an express burden of proof as to the fairness or unfairness of terms. As earlier explained,[2435] while the position is not clear, the Court of Justice is most likely to take the view that the issue of fairness of terms under the 1993 Directive is not itself one appropriate to the allocation of a burden of proof, but instead for a "neutral assessment" of the term, although any facts on which the trader or consumer relies for this purpose would be subject to the normal rules of burden of proof established by national law.[2436] As a result, the Law Commissions considered that no provision should be made as to the burden of proof as to fairness of a term the new legislation, beyond the statement as to the duty of courts to raise the issue of fairness of their own motion,[2437] since "[t]o put the burden of proof on the consumer, even if it was just to prove a prima facie case, may not fit with the requirements of the EU law".[2438] Following this view, the Consumer Rights Act 2015 does not provide for the allocation of a burden of proof as to the fairness of

terms, except to the extent to which it imposes a duty in courts to consider the issue of fairness of their own motion.[2439] This therefore leaves the issue of burden of proof as to fairness in the same state as under the 1999 Regulations. However, if the Court of Justice were to rule on the issue of burden of proof after IP completion day,[2439a] a UK court would not have to follow this ruling, though it may have regard to it.[2439b]

[2434] s.11(5) (reasonableness).

[2435] See paras 38-335—38-337.

[2436] See para.38-337.

[2437] Above, para.38-392.

[2438] Law Com. Advice (2013), para.7.91.

[2439] 2015 Act s.71, above, para.38-392.

[2439a] On which see above, para.38-004 and Vol.I, paras 1-014 et seq.

[2439b] European Union (Withdrawal) Act 2018 s.6(1)(a) and (2) (as amended by the European Union (Withdrawal Agreement) Act 2020 s.26(1)(a)) and see Vol.I, para.1-017B.

### Comments; relationship to recent case-law of the CJEU

*Replace footnote 2486 with:*

38-399 [2486] *Matei* (C-143/13) at para.70 and see above, para.38-257 where, however, the very different interpretation given to *Matei* by A.G. Hogan in *Kiss v Kiss* (C-621/17) EU:C:2019:41 Opinion of May 15, 2019 at paras 35–38 is also noted.

*Replace paragraph with:*

38-400 In this respect, in *Casehub Ltd v Wolf Cola Ltd* the High Court rejected the invitation of the claimant (to whom consumers had assigned their claims[2488]) that it should not follow the Supreme Court's decision in *Abbey National Plc* in relation to the exclusion in s.64 of the 2015 Act on the basis that it was inconsistent with the later decisions of the CJEU in *Kásler* and *Matei*, on the grounds that it was bound by the Supreme Court's decision and that it was "far from clear that the CJEU cases ... have the effect for which [the claimant] contends".[2489] In *Casehub*, the consumers (and other customers) had contracted with the defendant for the internet storage of data by way of "cloud computing". Under their contracts, the defendant charged its customers a £20 monthly subscription fee for a fixed term of 12 months; if a customer terminated its agreement within the minimum term, a cancellation fee was payable calculated as a lump sum equivalent to the total remaining monthly charges less a 10 per cent discount said to reflect the fact that the customer was paying early. Due to system problems, a number of the defendant's customers did not receive their log-in information to access the service and they therefore terminated their contracts within the first month, being then charged a £196 cancellation fee. The claimant contended that the cancellation fee provisions in the consumer contracts were unlawful as unfair under s.62 of the 2015 Act and that therefore the consumers were not liable to pay the fees and could recover fees already paid. However, the High Court rejected this claim, holding that the cancellation fees provisions in the contracts came within the exclusion provided by s.64 of the Act. The assessment of the fairness of these terms would involve "the assessment ... of the appropriateness of the price payable under the contract" under s.64(1)(b), since, while the cancellation fee does not comprise the price payable under the contract, it was a monetary obligation on the customer which formed part of that price in accordance with the approach of the Supreme Court in *Abbey National Plc* to contracts providing for a package of ways of charging for a package of services.[2490]

With respect, however, it is doubtful whether the High Court's approach to the authority of the Supreme Court's decision was correct given the requirement in s.3(1) of the European Communities Act 1972 that questions of the meaning of EU law (here, art.4(2) of the 1993 Directive) must be determined in accordance with "the principles laid down by and any relevant decision of the European Court" and given that the High Court did not explain how the European case-law did not have the effect contended for in relation to the Supreme Court's decision. Moreover, the inclusion within the exclusion in s.64(1)(b) of a term under which a fee is charged on "cancellation" of the contract by the consumer did not take into account the presence in Sch.2 Pt 1 of the 2015 Act (which lists terms which may be regarded as unfair) of:

> "... [a] term which has the object or effect of requiring that, where the consumer decides not to conclude or perform the contract, the consumer must pay the trader a disproportionately high sum in compensation or for services which have not been supplied."

It is more than arguable that the cancellation fee term in the cloud computing contract in *Casehub* fell within this example of a term in that it required the consumers to pay "a disproportionately high sum in compensation or for services which [were] not supplied"; and under s.64(6) of the Act (following case-law of the Court of Justice), s.64 "does not apply to a term of a contract listed in Part 1 of Schedule 2".[2491] Finally, however, it should be noted that the significance of existing as well as future decisions of the Court of Justice will change on IP completion day, with the effect, in particular, that the Supreme Court will be free not to follow earlier case law of or general principles laid down by the European Court.[2491a]

[2488] The HC held that these assignments of the consumers' restitutionary claims against the defendant were valid and not unenforceable on the ground of maintenance and champerty: [2017] EWHC 1169 (Ch), [2017] 5 Costs L.R. 835 at [25]–[31].

[2489] [2017] EWHC 1169 (Ch), [2017] 5 Costs L.R. 835 at [53]–[54].

[2490] [2017] EWHC 1169 (Ch) at [49]–[56] referring in particular to [2009] UKSC 6 at [42] (Lord Walker) and [78] (Lord Phillips), on which see above, paras 38-247—38-248.

[2491] Above, para.38-398.

[2491a] European Union (Withdrawal) Act 2018 s.6(1)(a) and (2) (as amended by the European Union (Withdrawal Agreement) Act 2020 s.26(1)(a)) and see Vol.I, para.1-017B.

## (bb) Certain Types of Term of "Secondary Contracts"

### **Extending the controls of Pt 2 to certain types of term in "secondary contracts"**

*Replace paragraph with:*

Section 72 of the Consumer Rights Act 2015 Act applies the rules of Pt 2 to "a term of a contract ('the secondary contract')" that "reduces the rights or remedies or increases the obligations of a person under another contract ('the main contract')",[2498] "that would apply to the term if it were in the main contract".[2499] For these purposes, it does not matter "whether the parties to the secondary contract are the same as the parties to the main contract" or "whether the secondary contract is a consumer contract".[2500] On the other hand, these rules do not apply "if the secondary contract is a settlement of a claim arising under the main contract".[2501] This provision has no counterpart in the 1999 Regulations (or the 1993 Directive), but is related to s.10 of the Unfair Contract Terms Act 1977, which provides that: 38-402

> "A person is not bound by any contract term prejudicing or taking away rights of his which

> arise under, or in connection with the performance of, another contract, so far as those rights extend to the enforcement of another's liability which [Part I of the Act] prevents that other from excluding or restricting."

The purpose of this anti-avoidance provision has been said to prevent a person (a) from enforcing against another person (B) a clause in a contract between them (the "secondary contract") which provides that B is not to sue a third person (C) under a contract between B and C and which would have been ineffective under the 1977 Act if it had been contained in the contract between B and C (the "main contract").[2502] It therefore applies, for example, to the case where a term in a direct contract between a manufacturer of goods and a person purports to affect the rights of that person as buyer under the Sale of Goods Act 1979 against the retailer from whom he or she purchases the goods[2503] or to the case where a supplier (B) contracts to supply a customer (C) with a product under a contract (the main contract) containing no exemption clause, but the customer (C) also enters a servicing contract with A (the secondary contract) under which C is precluded from exercising his rights against B under the main contract.[2504] While the scope of s.10 has been described as "enigmatic",[2505] it has been held not to apply to the compromise or waiver of an existing contractual claim such as the release by a person of rights which have accrued to him as the result of the breach of another contract to which he is party[2506] nor to the case where the parties to the main contract and the secondary contract are the same.[2507]

[2498] 2015 Act s.72(1).

[2499] 2015 Act s.72(2).

[2500] 2015 Act s.72(3).

[2501] 2015 Act s.72(4).

[2502] Peel (ed.), *Treitel on The Law of Contract*, 15th edn (2020), para.7-076. This lack of enforceability could result either directly from a provision of the Act (e.g. s.2(1), s.6(2)) or from a finding of "unreasonableness" of such a term (e.g. s.2(2) or s.6(3) as assessed under s.11).

[2503] See Vol.I, para.15-128.

[2504] *Tudor Grange Holdings Ltd v Citibank N.A.* [1992] Ch. 53 at [66].

[2505] Vol.I, para.15-128.

[2506] *Tudor Grange Holdings Ltd v Citibank N.A.* [1992] Ch. 53; Vol.I, para.15-128.

[2507] *Tudor Grange Holdings Ltd v Citibank N.A.* [1992] Ch. 53 at [66]; Peel (ed.), *Treitel on The Law of Contract*, 15th edn (2020), paras 7-076—7-077.

### *(vi) The Requirement for Transparency*

**Effects of failure to fulfil requirement for transparency**

*In line Replace paragraph with:*

**38-417** First, s.69(1) of the 2015 Act provides:

> "If a term in a consumer contract, or a consumer notice, could have different meanings, the meaning that is most favourable to the consumer is to prevail."

This seeks to implement the requirement in art.5 of the 1993 Directive (earlier implemented in reg.7(2) of the 1999 Regulations), with the difference that this rule of interpretation is not restricted to the interpretation of *written* terms (as is reg.7(2)[2563]) and that it extends to "consumer notices". This rule reflects the traditional approach at common law under construction *contra proferentem*[2564] except that it specifies that where a term could have different meanings, it is the *most* favourable to the consumer which is to be adopted. Secondly, the 2015 Act provides that the enforcement measures provided for regulators for the enforcement of the law of unfair terms applies to the enforcement of the requirement of transparency of terms and notices as it does to the requirement of fairness,[2565] a position which was not stated in the 1999 Regulations.[2566] Following the 1993 Directive (and the 1999 Regulations), the 2015 Act provides that the special rule of construction does not apply for the purposes of proceedings for an injunction under this enforcement regime.[2567]

2563 The position under the 1993 Directive in this respect is not entirely clear. The first sentence of art.5 (which requires plain, intelligible writing), is restricted expressly to "contracts where all or certain terms offered to the consumer are in writing"; while the second sentence ("[w]here there is doubt about the meaning of a term, the interpretation most favourable to the consumer shall prevail") is not so restricted, it could be thought that its scope remains restricted by what has been stated in the first sentence.

2564 See Vol.I, para.15-012.

2565 2015 Act s.70(1) referring to "the enforcement of this Part", i.e. Pt 2.

2566 For argument that these measures did extend to the requirement of transparency, see above, para.38-355; Law Com. Advice (2013), paras 6.60–6.63.

2567 2015 Act s.69(2); 1993 Directive art.5; 1999 Regulations reg.7(2).

### *(vii) Prevention of Avoidance by Choice of Law*

**Special rule governing choice of law of non-Member State**

*Replace paragraph with:*

As required by the 1993 Directive for contracts within its scope[2568] (and following the 1999 Regulations, though using a different wording),[2569] s.74 of the Consumer Rights Act 2015 provides that, where a consumer contract has a close connection with the UK, a choice of law of a country or territory other than an EEA State[2570] as the contract's applicable law does not affect the application of Pt 2's provisions governing unfair contract terms.[2571] This special rule required by the 1993 Directive[2572] differs from the general position provided by the Rome I Regulation,[2573] to which the Act helpfully cross-refers to indicate to the reader the rules applicable in the absence of a choice of the law of a country or territory other than an EEA.[2574] Article 6(1) of the Rome I Regulation provides the law of the consumer's habitual residence as the applicable law governing consumer contracts in the absence of agreement otherwise: **38-418**

> "... provided that the professional:
>
> (a) pursues his commercial or professional activities in the country where the consumer has his habitual residence, or
>
> (b) by any means, directs such activities to that country or to several countries including that country,
>
> and the contract falls within the scope of such activities."[2574a]

Furthermore, where these same conditions are satisfied, art.6(2) of the Rome I Regulation provides that any agreement in the consumer contract on applicable law may not:

> "... have the result of depriving the consumer of the protection afforded to him by provisions that cannot be derogated from by agreement by virtue of the law which, in the absence of choice, would have been applicable on the basis of paragraph 1."

If these conditions are *not* satisfied, then the rules governing the law applicable to the consumer contract fall under the general scheme governing contracts in the Rome I Regulation.[2575] It seems clear that the special provision governing agreements on applicable law in the 1993 Directive takes precedence over the general scheme set out in the Rome I Regulation (which makes uniform provision governing the law applicable to contractual obligations) and is best seen as constituting a special "overriding mandatory provision" in the sense of art.9 of that Regulation.[2576] It is to be noted that, to the extent to which the Act extends the definition of "consumer contract" beyond the definition taken by the Court of Justice for the purposes of the 1993 Directive,[2577] the 2015 Act also extends the application of this special rule governing choice of law.[2578] Such an extension of the applicable law rule may be reconciled with the uniform character of the rules set out for contractual obligations generally by the Rome I Regulation,[2579] but only to the extent to which it gives effect to "overriding mandatory rules" of the UK as part of the law of the forum or of the law of place of performance of the contract's obligations.[2580] The 2015 Act makes no provision equivalent to the exclusion of "international supply contracts" nor the rules governing *English* choice of law clauses as are found in the Unfair Contract Terms Act.[2581] It should be noted, however, that the Court of Justice of the EU has held that where a consumer contract contains a choice of law clause which designates the law of another Member State, that term may itself be an unfair term within the meaning of the 1993 Directive.[2582]

[2568] 1993 Directive art.6(2).

[2569] 1999 Regulations reg.9 on which see above, para.38-352.

[2570] The EEA States comprise the EU Member States plus Iceland, Liechtenstein and Norway. The 1993 Directive forms part of the EU law which these latter States have agreed to apply: Agreement on the European Economic Area (updated version to April 12, 2014) art.72; Annex XIX para.7(a). On IP completion day (on which see above, para.38-004 and Vol.I, paras 1-014 et seq.), the reference to "an EEA State" is to be replaced by "the United Kingdom or any part of the United Kingdom": Consumer Protection (Amendment etc.) (EU Exit) Regulations 2018 (SI 2018/1326) reg.3(5)(b) (the reference to "exit day" in reg.1(3) to the 2018 Regulations governing their coming into force must be read as referring to IP completion day: European Union (Withdrawal Agreement) Act 2020 s.39(1), Sch.5 para.1). This change is subject to transitional provision: SI 2018/1326 reg.11.

[2571] It is to be noted that the restriction of s.74's special rule to the application of Pt 2, means that it does not apply so as specially to protect the rules rendering terms not binding on consumers under Pt 1 of the Act, i.e. those rules governing the exclusion or restriction of liability arising from Pt 1 provisions by 2015 Act ss.31, 47 and 57. cf. similar provision in 2015 Act s.32 in respect of "contracts to supply goods" under Pt 1 Ch.2 of the Act, reflecting the Consumer Sales Directive 1999 art.7(2), below, para.38-533.

[2572] 1993 Directive art.6(2).

[2573] Regulation (EC) 593/2008 of the European Parliament and of the Council of 17 June 2008 on the law applicable to contractual obligations ("Rome I") [2008] O.J. L177/6 on which generally see Vol.I, paras 30-019 et seq.; Dicey, Morris and Collins, *The Conflict of Laws*, 15th edn (2012), Vol.II, paras 33-126 et seq. and, in relation to the 1993 Directive art.6(2), paras 33-168—33-173.

[2574] 2015 Act s.74(2) and see the note above in this paragraph concerning the replacement on IP completion day of the reference to "an EEA State" by "the United Kingdom or any part of the United Kingdom": SI 2018/1326 reg.3(5)(b).

[2574a] On IP completion day (on which see above, para.38-004 and Vol.I, paras 1-014 et seq.) the Rome I Regulation will form part of "retained EU law" with amendments: Law Applicable to Contractual Obligations and Non-Contractual Obligations (Amendment etc.) (EU Exit) Regulations 2019 (SI 2019/834) reg.10 (the reference in reg.1 to the Regulations coming into force on "exit day" must be read as referring to IP completion day: European Union (Withdrawal Agreement) Act 2020 s.26(1), Sch.5 para.1). The 2019 Regulations reg.10(6) makes only technical amendment to art.6(4) of the Rome I Regulation as retained.

[2575] Rome I Regulation, notably, arts 3 and 4 on which see Vol.I, paras 30-066—30-125.

2576 Rome I Regulation arts 9 and 23 (on which generally see Vol.I, paras 30-024 and 30-211 et seq.); Plender and Wilderspin, *The European Private International Law of Obligations*, 3rd edn (2009), paras 9-092—9-093.

2577 See above, paras 38-035—38-036 (especially in relation to the definition of "consumer" in 2015 Act s.2(3) as an individual acting "wholly *or mainly* outside that individual's trade", etc.).

2578 s.74(1) *in fine* provides that "this *Part* [i.e. Pt 2] applies despite that choice".

2579 See especially Rome I Regulation Ch.2 "Uniform Rules".

2580 Rome I art.9. In the absence of such a specially extended applicable law rule, the substantive controls in the 2015 Act on unfair contract terms which are *not* required by the 1993 Directive could be given effect despite a choice of law other than of UK law as legal provisions which cannot be derogated from by agreement under (and subject to the conditions of) Rome I Regulation arts 3(3) and 6(2), on which see Vol.I, paras 30-082 and 30-148 et seq.

2581 Unfair Contract Terms Act ss.26 and 27 on which see Vol.I paras 15-122 and 15-125 respectively. As regards ss.26 and 27(1), this reflects the earlier recommendations of the Law Commissions for consumer contracts (made in relation to the Rome Convention on the law applicable to contractual obligations 1980, which preceded the Rome I Regulation): Law Commission and Scottish Law Commission *Unfair Terms in Contracts* (2005) Pt 7, especially paras 7.6 and 7.9; their recommendations as regards s.27(2) were more nuanced, but are not reflected directly in the 2015 Act, except to the extent to which s.74 applies its rule on choice of law so as to protect the controls on unfair contract terms in Pt 2 of the Act other than those required by the 1993 Directive.

2582 *Verein für Konsumenteninformation v Amazon EU Sàrl* (C-191/15) EU:C:2016:612, July 28, 2016, above, para.38-321.

## *(viii) Enforcement*

### Enforcement measures under the Consumer Rights Act 2015

*Replace paragraph with:*

**38-420** The approach of the 2015 Act to the enforcement of the controls which it requires for unfair terms and notices reflects this earlier law, but extends the special scheme (earlier set out by the 1999 Regulations and now set out by Sch.3 of the Act) to the Act's controls on terms generally[2590] as well as providing that the investigatory powers needed for these purposes are the same as for the enforcement of consumer protection legislation more widely.[2591] Under Sch.3 of the Act, the CMA and other "regulators"[2592] (who are the same as the "qualifying bodies" foreseen by the 1999 Regulations[2593]) possess a power to apply for an injunction against a person if it thinks that the person is "using, or proposing or recommending the use of, a term or notice" in the following circumstances[2594]: where a term or notice purports to exclude or restrict liability imposed by Pt 1 (for example, in respect of the satisfactory quality of goods supplied) or business liability for death or personal injury resulting from negligence[2595]; where a term or notice is unfair within the meaning of Pt 2 "to any extent"[2596]; and where a term or notice fails the requirement of transparency.[2597] Schedule 3 also provides regulators with powers to consider complaints about a term or notice in the same circumstances,[2598] and to accept an undertaking from a person against whom it has applied, or thinks it is entitled to apply for an injunction.[2599] Courts may grant an injunction on such conditions, and against such respondents to the proceedings, as it thinks appropriate.[2600] The powers in regulators are therefore wider in their scope of application than those contained in the 1999 Regulations in three principal ways: first, they apply to those provisions in the 2015 Act which reflect provisions in the 1977 Act and which render terms not binding on consumers without any assessment of their fairness[2601]; secondly, they apply to terms assessed as unfair under the general test even where (owing to the extended character of the scope of this test) they would not fall to be assessed under the 1999 Regulations (or the 1993 Directive)[2602]; and, thirdly, they apply to "consumer notices" in the same way as they apply to contract terms.[2603] In addition, the 2015 Act does not affect the possibility of enforcement measures being taken under Pt 8 of the Enterprise Act 2002 in respect of "Community infringements" which harm the collective interests of consumers and these include acts or omissions which contravene the 1993 Directive[2604] or which contravene laws of an EEA State (including the UK) which give effect to that Directive and which "provide additional permitted protections" beyond its minimum requirements, if "such additional protection is permitted by that Directive".[2605] For this purpose, the relevant provisions in Pt 2 of the 2015 Act which implement the 1993 Directive have been designated as a specified UK law for the purposes of s.212 of the 2002 Act[2606] and in addition, acts or omissions in respect of any provision in Pt 2 of the 2015 Act are specified as possible "domestic infringements" for the purposes of s.211 of the Enterprise Act 2002.[2607] Furthermore, the 2015 Act enhanced the consumer measures which are available under Pt 8 of the Enterprise Act so as to include, for example, measures offering compensation or other redress to consumers who have suffered loss as a result of the conduct which has given rise to the enforcement order.[2608] Thirdly, although not mentioned by the 2015 Act, in principle the use or recommendation for use of an unfair term or notice by a trader in its commercial practices with consumers can constitute an "unfair commercial practice" within the meaning of the Consumer Protection from Unfair Trading Regulations 2008.[2609]

[2590] 2015 Act ss.31(7), 47(5), 57(7) and 70(1).

[2591] 2015 Act s.70(2), applying the investigatory powers in Sch.5 (which replace the special provisions on investigatory powers in the 1999 Regulations reg.13): see especially s.77 and Sch.5 paras 2(d), 6 ("unfair contract terms enforcer"), and 13(7) and (8). On the temporal application of these powers, see above, para.38-366 (note), where the qualifications on this general position are noted. On the UK's leaving the EU on "exit day" (on which see above, para.38-004 and Vol.I, paras 1-014 et seq.) Sch.5 is due to be amended so as to replace references to "Community infringement" with "Schedule 13 infringement" and "EU enforcer" with "Schedule 13 enforcer": reg.4. This harmonises the provisions in the 2015 Act Sch.5 with the changes to be made to the Enterprise Act 2002 Pt 8, on which see above, para.38-133A.

[2592] The 2015 Act replaces the expression "qualifying body" used by the 1999 Regulations and instead refers to all those empowered to enforce its provisions governing unfair contract terms (including the CMA) as "regulators": 2015 Act Sch.3 para.8(1).

[2593] See above, para.38-360; 2015 Act Sch.3 para.8(1), though para.8(2) allows the Secretary of State to amend this list (the Director General of Electrical Supply of Northern Ireland and the Director General of Gas for Northern Ireland were replaced by the Northern Ireland Authority for Utility Regulation).

[2594] 2015 Act Sch.3 para.3(1).

[2595] 2015 Act Sch.3 para.3(2) referring to ss.31, 47, 57 and 65(1) of the Act and see above, para.38-409 and below, paras 38-531, 38-564 and 38-586.

[2596] 2015 Act Sch.3 para.3(3). This includes both terms or notices assessed as unfair under s.62 and terms deemed to be unfair under s.63(6) or the Arbitration Act 1996 s.91, on which see above, paras 38-389 et seq. and 38-412.

[2597] 2015 Act Sch.3 para.3(5) and see s.68, above, paras 38-414—38-416. The application of the enforcement measures to this requirement is therefore made explicit by the Act, though it was not under the 1999 Regulations and see above, para.38-355.

[2598] 2015 Act Sch.3 para.2 (reflecting 1999 Regulations reg.10).

[2599] 2015 Act Sch.3 para.6(1).

[2600] 2015 Act Sch.3 para.5(1). This broadly reflects 1999 Regulations reg.12(3) and (4).

[2601] 2015 Act Sch.3 para.3(2), above, paras 38-409—38-410, 38-412.

[2602] The scope of the test of unfairness is widened in the following ways: the definition of "consumer" is extended by s.2(3) and 76(2), above, para.38-384; the subjection of terms which have been individually negotiated to the test of unfairness by s.62, above, para.38-389; the exclusion from the assessment of fairness of terms which specify the main subject matter of the contract, etc. in s.64 is subjected to an additional condition of "prominence", above, paras 38-398—38-400. The 2015 Act does not expressly apply the Sch.3 enforcement regime to its controls on the effectiveness of certain terms on choice of applicable law as set out in s.74, as the latter is not expressed as rendering such terms unfair or otherwise not binding on consumers so as to fall within one of the categories in Sch.3 para.(2), (3) or (5) as required by para.3(1)(b), but art.6(2) of the 1993 Directive requires Member States to "take the necessary measures to ensure that the consumer does not lose the protection granted" by it and so such an effect could possibly be achieved by way of "conforming interpretation" as explained above, para.38-418.

[2603] 2015 Act ss.62(2), (6) and (7), 65 and 68; Sch.3 para.3(3) and (5).

[2604] Enterprise Act 2002 s.212(1)(a). On IP completion day, "Community infringements" are to be replaced by "Schedule 13 infringements" and the relevant provisions of the 2015 Act are to be included within the substituted Sch.13 of the 2002 Act for this purpose: Consumer Protection (Enforcement) (Amendment etc.) (EU Exit) Regulations 2019 (SI 2019/203) reg.3(20) and Sch. para.1 inserting new 2002 Act Sch.13 para.27. On this change more generally see above, para.38-133A.

[2605] Enterprise Act 2002 s.212(1)(b) and (2). On the impact of the full coming into effect of the UK leaving the EU on IP completion day see previous note.

[2606] Enterprise Act 2002 s.212(3) (to be replaced on IP completion day: SI 2019/203 reg.3(2)); Enterprise Act 2002 (Part 8 Community Infringements Specified UK Laws) Order 2003 art.3, Sch., as amended by the Enterprise Act 2002 (Part 8 Community Infringements and Specified UK Laws) (Amendment) Order 2015 (SI 2015/1628) art.2(2)(a), listing 2015 Act ss.2, 61–64, 67–70, 72–74, Schs 2 and 3 and Sch.5 Pt 3.

[2607] Enterprise Act 2002 s.211(2); Enterprise Act 2002 (Part 8 Domestic Infringements) Order 2015 (SI 2015/1727) art.2.

[2608] Consumer Rights Act 2015 s.79, Sch.7 inserting new s.219A in the Enterprise Act 2002. The example is found in s.219A(2)(a): see above, para.38-134.

[2609] Below, paras 38-362—38-363.

## The impact of "full harmonisation" under the Unfair Commercial Practices Directive 2005

*In the penultimate line, after "the (now expired", add:*

and to be deleted[2617a] **38-422**

[2617a] Directive (EU) 2019/2161 of the European Parliament and of the Council of 27 November 2019 ... as regards the better enforcement and modernisation of Union consumer protection rules [2019] O.J. L328/7 art.3(2) will revoke art.3(5) and (6) of the 2005 Directive as noted above, para.38-162 (note).

## Conclusion

*Replace footnote 2635 with:*

[2635] See above, para.38-014 and cf. Vol.I, para.1-017B. **38-426**

*Add new paragraph:*

**38-426A** **The possible impact of the UK's exit from the EU on this discussion** The position outlined above may be set to change on the full coming into force of the UK's leaving the EU on IP completion day (December 31, 2020).[2640a] Subject to the terms of any agreement between the UK and the EU as to their future relationship, after this date in principle the UK would no longer be bound by EU law obligations, including those arising from the fully harmonising nature of the 2005 Directive. However, the European Union (Withdrawal) Act 2018 retains much of the EU law *acquis* in UK law and the prospective amendment of the 2008 Regulations (which implemented the 2005 Directive) which will take effect on IP completion day[2640b] and their inclusion within Schedule 13 of the Enterprise Act 2002 for the purposes of the new category of "Schedule 13 Infringements"[2640c] indicates that the 2008

Regulations will be retained after the UK has left the EU. In this respect, the 2018 Act provides that, after IP completion day, the principle of supremacy applies "so far as relevant to the interpretation, disapplication or quashing of any enactment or rule of law passed or made before IP completion day".[2640d] Moreover, the 2018 Act provides that "retained EU law"[2640e] is in principle to be interpreted "in accordance with any retained case law and any retained general principles of EU law,[2640f] and, having regard (among other things) to the limits, immediately before exit day, of EU competences"[2640g] , although "the Supreme Court is not bound by any retained EU case law"[2640h] and explains that "[i]n deciding whether to depart from any retained EU case law, the Supreme Court ... must apply the same test as it would apply in deciding whether to depart from its own case law".[2640i] The Court of Justice of the EU has made clear that the 2005 Directive requires full harmonisation within its scope,[2640j] but it has not ruled on the specific question of the compatibility with this requirement of national enforcement measures relating to extensions of protections required for consumers by other EU directives (such as the Unfair Contract Terms Directive). It may be that this degree of uncertainty as to the impact of the 2005 Directive (and therefore the 2008 Regulations) could allow a UK court to hold that the enforcement measures in the 2015 Act are not incompatible with "retained EU law" even where they go beyond the protections for consumers required by the 1993 Directive.

2640a On this see above, para.38-004 and Vol.I, paras 1-014 et seq.

2640b Consumer Protection (Amendment etc.) (EU Exit) Regulations 2018 (SI 2018/1326) reg.6 (the reference in reg.1(3) of the 2018 Regulations to the coming into force of reg.6 on "exit day" must be read as referring to IP completion day: European Union (Withdrawal Agreement) Act 2020 s.39(1), Sch.5 para.1).

2640c Consumer Protection (Enforcement) (Amendment etc.) (EU Exit) Regulations 2019 (SI 2019/203) reg.3(20), Sch. para.1 inserting new 2002 Act Sch.13 para.19 (the reference in reg.1 of the 2019 Regulations to their coming into force on "exit day" must be read as referring to IP completion day: European Union (Withdrawal Agreement) Act 2020 s.39(1), Sch.5 para.1).

2640d 2018 Act s.5 (1) and (2) (as prospectively amended by the 2020 Act and coming into force on a day to be appointed: 2018 Act s.25(4)). See Vol.I, para.1-017A.

2640e 2018 Act s.6(7) and see Vol.I, para.1-016.

2640f Defined in terms of temporal origin by s.6(7) of the 2018 Act as those which are made or laid down immediately before exit day: s.6(7) "retained EU case law" and "retained general principles of EU law". See also 2018 Act Sch.1 paras 2 and 3.

2640g 2018 Act s.6(3).

2640h 2018 Act s.6(4)(a). See further Vol.I, para.1-017B where the possibility of this ability not to follow existing case law of the CJEU being extended by regulation to other courts is noted.

2640i 2018 Act s.6(5).

2640j Above, para.38-159.

## (e) Special Rules Governing Consumer Payments

### Payment surcharges: the controls

*Replace paragraph with:*

38-428 The Consumer Rights (Payment Surcharges) Regulations 2012 as made[2646] implemented art.19 of the Consumer Rights Directive and reg.4 therefore provides that a trader must not charge consumers in respect of the use of a given means of payment fees that exceed the cost borne by the trader for the use of that means (such as an administration, booking or handling fee),[2647] where the payment is made for the purposes of a sales contract, a service contract or a contract for the supply of water, gas, electricity, district heating or digital content.[2648] Regulation 4's prohibition does not refer to any particular method of payment (such as a credit or debit card) and therefore applies to any means of payment that a trader decides to accept, including cash, cheques, prepaid cards, charge cards, etc. and this means that any new methods of paying will also be subject to this prohibition as the technology relating to payments develops.[2649] This law applies to contracts entered into on or after April 6, 2013.[2650] However, this protection for consumers was supplemented by a wide prohibition on payment surcharges[2651] on the amendment of the Consumer Rights (Payment Surcharges) Regulations 2012 by the Payment Services Regulations 2017,[2652] implementing a requirement imposed by the Second Payment Services Directive 2015.[2653] Under the 2015 Directive, a payee, such as a retailer, "shall not request charges for the use of payment instruments" where their interchange fees are capped under the Interchange Fees Regulation 2015,[2654] and this includes the majority of consumer debit and credit cards.[2655] However, the UK's implementation of this aspect of the 2015 Directive went further than this requirement, as the Directive permits where a Member State considers that this is needed to encourage competition and promote the use of efficient payment instruments.[2656] As a result, under reg.6A(1) of the 2012 Regulations (as inserted by the 2017 Regulations), "a payee[2657] must not charge a payer[2658] any fee in respect of payment by means of a payment instrument" as long as it is not a commercial card or other payment instrument,[2659] whether or not it is a card-based payment instrument within the meaning of the Interchange Fees Regulation 2015; nor must a payee charge in respect of a payment service (such as a direct debit) in euro.[2660] As a result (and subject to territorial limitations[2661]), reg.6A(1) imposes a ban on surcharging applicable to all non-commercial retail payment instruments.[2662] According to the Explanatory Memorandum to the 2017 Regulations,

> "... this is intended to level the playing field across all non-commercial retail payment instruments and create a clearer picture for consumers in which they know the full price of the product/service they are purchasing upfront and are confident that there will be no additional charges when they come to pay using a particular payment instrument."[2663]

Where reg.6A(1) does not apply owing in particular to the method of payment used (and subject to its own conditions), reg.4 still prohibits traders from charging consumers more than the direct cost borne by them for use of the relevant means of payment.[2664] Finally, reg.6A(2) imposes the latter type of control in respect of most payments between businesses made with commercial payment instruments.[2665]

[2646] SI 2012/3110 ("2012 Regulations") (and as amended by the 2013 Regulations (SI 2013/3134)). On IP completion day (on which see above, para.38-004 and Vol.I, paras 1-014 et seq.) the 2012 Regulations will form part of "retained EU law" with relatively minor amendments as noted where relevant in the following notes: Consumer Protection (Amendment etc.) (EU Exit) Regulations 2018 (SI 2018/1326) reg.7 (reg.1(3)'s reference to reg.7's coming into force on "exit day" must be read as referring to IP completion day: European Union (Withdrawal Agreement) Act 2020 s.39(1), Sch.5 para.1).

[2647] 2012 Regulations reg.4. "Trader" and "consumer" are defined by reg.2 in the new standard UK definitions described above, paras 38-050—38-058 (especially at 38-057) and 38-030—38-049 (especially at 38-041) respectively. For explanation of what can properly be charged by a trader as the "cost" for use see *DG Justice Guidance Document on 2011 Directive*, para.9.3.

[2648] 2012 Regulations reg.5(1). The definitions of these various categories of contract provided by reg.3 of the 2012 Regulations is mirrored by those found in the 2013 Regulations reg.5, on which see above, paras 38-073—38-075. Regulation 5(1) and (2) of the 2012 Regulations exclude from the rule against excessive charges a series of "excluded contracts" as allowed by the 2011 Directive, notably including contracts for financial services contracts, this list following the exclusions in 2013 Regulations reg.6, with the addition of contracts for social services and health services (as explained by reg.5(2)(a) and (b) (the latter of which is amended on IP completion day (on which see above, para.38-004 and Vol.I, paras 1-014 et seq.) by the Consumer Protection (Amendment etc.) (EU Exit) Regulations 2018 (SI 2018/1326) reg.7(2) (reg.1(3)'s reference to reg.7's coming into force on "exit day" must be read as referring to IP completion day: European Union (Withdrawal Agreement) Act 2020 s.39(1), Sch.5 para.1). Regulation 6 of the 2012 Regulations provides a temporary exemption from the prohibition in reg.4 where the trader's business is an existing micro-business or a new business as explained in their Schedule.

[2649] Department of Business, Energy & Industrial Strategy, *The Consumer Rights (Payment Surcharges) Regulations 2012, Guidance* (June 2018), para.8.5.

[2650] 2012 Regulations reg.1(1) and (2). Reg.6 provides for a temporary exemption from the requirements of reg.4 for micro-businesses and new business as defined by the Sch. to the Regulations.

[2651] 2012 Regulations reg.6A. The new rules contained in reg.6A apply to charges made on or after January 13, 2018, except for charges under contracts entered into before July 18, 2017 (the date on which the 2017 Regulations were made): 2012 Regulations reg.1(3) as inserted by the 2017 Regulations Sch.8 (as regards the temporal effect on contracts of reg.6A); 2017 Regulations reg.1(6) (in relation to the prohibition on charging in reg.6A).

[2652] SI 2017/752 ("2017 Regulations") reg.156; Sch.8 Pt 3 para.12. The 2017 Regulations are due to be amended on IP completion day (on which generally see above, para.38-004 and Vol.I, paras 1-014 et seq.) but these amendments apply only marginally to the provisions discussed here: Electronic Money, Payment Services and Payment Systems (Amendment and Transitional Provisions) (EU Exit) Regulations 2018 (SI 2018/1201) Sch.2 Pt 2 (reg.1(3)'s reference to these provisions coming into force on "exit day" must be read as referring to IP completion day: European Union (Withdrawal Agreement) Act 2020 s.39(1), Sch.5 para.1).

[2653] Directive (EU) 2015/2366 of the European Parliament and of the Council of 25 November 2015 on payment services in the internal market [2015] O.J. L337/35 ("2015 Directive"), art.62(3)–(4).

[2654] Regulation (EU) 2015/251 of the European Parliament and of the Council of 29 April 2015 on interchange fees for card-based payment transactions [2015] O.J. L123/1 ("Interchange Fees Regulation 2015"). On IP completion day (on which generally see above, para.38-004 and Vol.I, paras 1-014 et seq.) the Interchange Fees Regulation 2015 (which will generally form part of "retained EU law") is due to be amended: Interchange Fee (Amendment) (EU Exit) Regulations 2019 (SI 2019/284) ("SI 2019/284") Pt 3 (reg.1(2)'s reference to the Regulations coming into force on "exit day" must be read as referring to IP completion day: European Union (Withdrawal Agreement) Act 2020 s.39(1), Sch.5 para.1). These amendments restrict the scope of the retained Regulation to the UK rather than the EU.

[2655] Explanatory Memorandum to the 2017 Regulations, para.7.16.

[2656] 2015 Directive art.62(5).

[2657] A "payee" for the purposes of reg.6A is defined in reg.3 of the 2012 Regulations (as inserted) by reference to reg.2(1) of the 2017 Regulations as "a person who is the intended recipient of funds which have been the subject of a payment transaction". Unlike reg.4, therefore, reg.6A is not restricted to payments made to traders.

[2658] Under reg.3 of the 2012 Regulations (as inserted and referring to reg.2(1) of the 2017 Regulations) "... 'payer' means—(a) a person who holds a payment account and initiates, or consents to the initiation of, a payment order from that payment account; or (b) where there is no payment account, a person who gives a payment order".

[2659] 2012 Regulations reg.6A(1)(a)(ii) and (b)(ii). "Commercial card" is defined by art.2(6) of the Interchange Fees Regulation 2015 (not due to be amended by SI 2019/284) as "any card-based payment instrument issued to undertakings or public sector entities or self-employed natural persons which is limited in use for business expenses where the payments made with such cards are charged directly to the account of the undertaking or public sector entity or self-employed natural person".

[2660] "Payment service" is defined by reg.3 of the 2012 Regulations (as amended) by reference to the 2017 Regulations reg.2(1), which itself refers to a list in its Sch.1 (due to be amended on IP completion day (on which generally see above, para.38-004 and Vol.I, paras 1-014 et seq.) by SI 2018/1201 Sch.2 Pt 2 para.69).

[2661] These are contained in the 2012 Regulations reg.6B which currently refers to the location in "an EEA State" of the payment service provider of the payer or the payment service provider of the payee. On IP completion day, these references to "an EEA State" are to be replaced by references to "the United Kingdom": Consumer Protection (Amendment etc.) (EU Exit) Regulations 2018 (SI 2018/1326) reg.7(3) (reg.1(3)'s reference to reg.7(3)'s coming into force on "exit day" must be read as referring to IP completion day: European Union (Withdrawal Agreement) Act 2020 s.39(1), Sch.5 para.1). On IP completion day see generally above, para.38-004 and Vol.I, paras 1-014 et seq.

[2662] Explanatory Memorandum to the 2017 Regulations para.7.16.

[2663] Explanatory Memorandum to the 2017 Regulations para.7.16.

[2664] See above, in this paragraph.

[2665] This is the effect of reg.6A(2)'s use of the very general terms "payer" and "payee" as earlier noted.

### Payment surcharges: enforcement

*Replace footnote 2668 with:*

[2668] Enterprise Act 2002 (Part 8 EU Infringements) Order 2014 (SI 2014/2908) art.3 and Sch. The Consumer Rights Directive 2011 and art.62(3) (second sentence), (4) and (5) of the Payment Services Directive 2015 are listed in the 2002 Act Sch.13 paras 9F and 16 respectively. On IP completion day (on which generally see above, para.38-004 and Vol.I, paras 1-014 et seq.), "Community infringements" are to be replaced by "Schedule 13 infringements" and the 2012 Regulations regs 4 and 6A–10 are to be included within the substituted Sch.13 of the 2002 Act for this purpose: Consumer Protection (Enforcement) (Amendment etc.) (EU Exit) Regulations 2019 (SI 2019/203) reg.3(20) and Sch. para.1 inserting new 2002 Act Sch.13 para.24 (reg.1's reference to the Regulations coming into force on "exit day" must be read as referring to IP completion day: European Union (Withdrawal Agreement) Act 2020 s.39(1), Sch.5 para.1). On this change more generally see above, para.38-133A. **38-429**

### Helpline charges over basic rate

*In line 5, after "the basic rate.", add new footnote 2676a:*

[2676a] This prohibition applies regardless of the type of telephone number by which the consumer customer can contact the trader and therefore applies equally to a speed dial number at a rate higher than the basic rate even if the trader also provides another telephone number at the basic rate and therefore the consumer can be said to have chosen to use the higher rate number: *Starman v Tarbijakaitseamet* (C-332/17) EU:C:2018:721 of September 13, 2018 at paras 30–33. **38-431**

## 7. CONTRACTS FOR THE SUPPLY OF GOODS, DIGITAL CONTENT OR SERVICES

## (a) Introduction

### Consumer Sales Directive 1999

*Replace paragraph with:*

However, this established pattern of treatment was changed on implementation **38-433**
of the Consumer Sales Directive of 1999.[2688] The main purpose of this directive is to require uniform rules governing certain aspects of contracts of sale of goods by sellers acting in the course of a business to consumer buyers[2689] on the basis of "minimum harmonisation",[2690] but its scope extends also to "contracts for the supply of goods to be manufactured and produced".[2691] The Directive has three main requirements to be given effect in national laws. First, it requires that "the seller must deliver goods to the consumer which are in conformity with the contract of sale", and then presumes "conformity" (rebuttably[2691a]) in a series of circumstances similar to those with which the English lawyer is familiar from the statutory implied terms inss.13 to 15 of the Sale of Goods Act 1979, i.e. that the goods comply with their description, are fit for any purpose made known by the consumer to the seller and accepted by him, are "fit for the purposes for which goods of the same type are normally used" and "show the quality and performance which are normal in goods of the same type and which the consumer can reasonably expect",[2692] as well as generally being in "conformity with the contract of sale", i.e. any express contract terms.[2693] However, some aspects of the 1999 Directive's requirement of conform-

ity were new to English law at the time, notably, the specified relevance to the quality which a consumer can reasonably expect of goods of "public statements on the specific characteristics of the goods made about them by the seller, the producer or his representative".[2694] Secondly, the Directive requires a series of rights for consumer buyers in respect of the "contractual non-conformity" of the goods: at a first level, a right to repair or replacement of the goods[2695]; and, if these remedies are unavailable or fail,[2696] a right to "an appropriate reduction in the price"[2697] and a right to "rescission" of the contract as long as the non-conformity of the goods is not minor.[2698] The Directive also makes incidental provision for these rights of conformity, notably as regards proof of non-conformity[2699] and the limitation period for the rights which it requires for consumers.[2700] Thirdly, the Directive requires that "guarantees" by sellers or producers to consumers[2701] shall be binding.[2702]

[2688] Directive 1999/44/EC on certain aspects of the sale of consumer goods and associated guarantees [1999] O.J. L171/12 ("Consumer Sales Directive" or "1999 Directive"). As noted below, para.38-436 the EU has enacted the Directive (EU) 2019/771 on certain aspects concerning contracts for the sale of goods [etc.] of the European Parliament and of the Council of 20 May 2019 [2019] O.J. L136/28 which repeals and replaces the 1999 Directive.

[2689] 1999 Directive art.1(2)(a) "consumer"; (b) "consumer goods"; and (c) "seller".

[2690] 1999 Directive art.8.

[2691] 1999 Directive art.1(4) deeming these to be "contracts of sale" for the purposes of the Directive.

[2691a] 1999 Directive recital 8.

[2692] 1999 Directive art.2(1), 2(2)(c) and (d). The formulations of these requirements are elaborated further in the Directive.

[2693] 1999 Directive art.2(1), recital 7.

[2694] 1999 Directive art.2(2)(d) and (4).

[2695] 1999 Directive art.3(3). On art.3 see *Quelle AG v Bundersverband des Versbraucherzentralen und Verbraucherverbande* (C-404/06) [2008] E.C.R. I-2685 (art.3 does not permit national law to impose liability on consumer buyer for compensation for use of non-conforming goods replaced); *Gebr. Weber GmbH v Wittmer, Putz v Medianess Electronics GmbH* (C-65/09 and C-87/09) [2011] 3 C.M.L.R. 27 (on which see below, para.38-517); *Fülla v Toolport GmbH* (C-52/18) EU:C:2019:447 (on which see below, para.38-517 (note)).

[2696] On the specific requirements in this respect as implemented in UK law, see below, paras 38-451—38-517 and 38-518.

[2697] 1999 Directive art.3(5).

[2698] 1999 Directive art.3(5) and (6).

[2699] 1999 Directive art.5(3).

[2700] 1999 Directive art.5(1) and (2).

[2701] Defined in 1999 Directive art.1(2)(e).

[2702] 1999 Directive art.6.

**38-436** *Change title of paragraph:*

**EU directives on distance contracts for the sale of goods and on contracts for the supply of digital content**

*Replace paragraph with:*

**38-436** In May 2019, the EU enacted new directives governing contracts of sale of goods and contracts for the supply of digital content: the Directive on aspects of the law governing sales of goods[2723] repeals the Consumer Sales Directive 1999[2724] (which was implemented in UK law by Ch.2 of Pt 1 of the 2015 Act[2725]) and the Directive on certain aspects concerning contracts for the supply of digital content and digital services,[2726] (which is original to EU law, though its subject-matter overlaps with that of Ch.3 of Pt 1 of the 2015 Act[2727]). Both Directives require "full harmonisation"[2728] (unlike the earlier Consumer Sales Directive 1999[2728a]) and must be implemented by Member States by July 1, 2021 so as to apply from January 1, 2022, the 1999 Directive being repealed on the latter date.[2728b] This implementation deadline is therefore beyond IP completion day (set as December 31, 2020, when the UK's leaving the EU comes into full effect) and, as a result, the UK is under no obligation to implement these directives, unless this forms part of any agreement made between the UK and the EU as to their future relationship.[2728c]

[2723] Directive (EU) 2019/771 of the European Parliament and of the Council of 20 May 2019 on certain aspects concerning contracts for the sale of goods, etc. [2019] O.J. L136/28 ("Directive (EU) 2019/771").

[2724] Directive (EU) 2019/771 art.23.

[2725] On this law see below, paras 38-485 et seq.

[2726] Directive (EU) 2019/770 of the European Parliament and of the Council of 20 May 2019 [2019] O.J. L136/1 ("Directive (EU) 2019/770"). On this directive see Sein and Spindler (2019) 15 E.R.C.L. 257.

[2727] On this law, see below, paras 38-535—38-566.

[2728] Directive (EU) 2019/771 art.4; Directive (EU) 2019/770 art.4.

[2728a] 1999 Directive art.8 and see above, para.38-433.

[2728b] Directive (EU) 2019/771 (sale of goods) arts 23 and 24, it being provided (art.24(2)) that the provisions of the 2019 Directive "shall not apply to *contracts concluded* before 1 January 2022" (emphasis added). Directive (EU) 2019/770 (supply of digital content) art.24, it being provided (art.24(2)) that its provisions "shall apply to *the supply* of digital content or digital services which occurs from 1 January 2022 with the exception of Articles 19 [which concerns the modification of digital content] and 20 [which concerns the trader's right to redress] of this Directive which shall only apply to *contracts concluded* from that date" (emphasis added).

[2728c] See above, para.38-004 and Vol.I, paras 1-014 et seq.

## (b) The Old Law: Special Rules for Buyers and Hirers in Consumer Cases

### *(iii) Special Remedies for Buyers Dealing as Consumers*

#### Right is that of buyer

*Replace footnote 2772 with:*

[2772] In *Gebr Weber GmbH v Wittmer* (C-65/09 and C-87/09) EU:C:2011:396, [2011] E.C.R. I-05257 at para.55, the CJEU held that, under the 1999 Directive, a seller must pay for the installation of the goods replacing defective goods correctly installed where this is necessary for their replacement. However, the CJEU appeared to suggest that considerations of proportionality could lead to the reduction of the sum payable, which might in turn lead to availability of the remedies of reduction of price and rescission. It is not easy to see any warrant for such a progression in the Regulations. The ECJ earlier held that national legislation permitting the seller to invoice the buyer for use of the goods, where they are replaced after a period, is contrary to the requirement that repair or replacement are "free of charge" (words not appearing in the UK Regulations): *Quelle AG v Verbraucherzentralen und Verbraucherverbande* (C-404/06) EU:C:2008:231, [2008] E.C.R. I-2685. See also *Fülla v Toolport GmbH (C-52/18)* (C-52/18) EU:C:2019:447, below, para.38-517 (note). 38-448

#### Discretion as to appropriate remedy

*Replace footnote 2792 with:*

[2792] Similar provision is made by the Supply of Goods and Services Act 1982 s.11R(3)–(4) for contracts for the transfer of goods as understood by that Act. See further below, para.38-522 in relation to the 38-455 compatibility of such a discretion (as now provided by the Consumer Rights Act 2015 s.58) with the Consumer Sales Directive as interpreted by the CJEU.

## (c) The New Law: Consumer Rights in Respect of Goods Contracts, Digital Content Contracts and Services Contracts

### The law recast by the 2015 Act: "goods contracts", "digital content contracts" and "services contracts"

*In line 2, after "earlier, Pt 1 of the 2015 Act", add new footnote 2830a:*

38-465 [2830a] On IP completion day (on which see generally, above, para.38-004 and Vol.I, paras 1-014 et seq.), the 2015 Act will be amended as noted above, para.38-215 (note). In the case of Pt 1 of the Act, these amendments concern only s.32 (discussed below, para.26-111) and s.59's definition of "'producer' in relation to goods or digital content" which will be defined so as to include their "importer into the United Kingdom" rather than their "importer into the European Economic Area" (amendments to be made by the Consumer Protection (Amendment etc.) (EU Exit) Regulations 2018 (SI 2018/1326) reg.3(3) (reg.1(3)'s reference to reg.3's coming into force on "exit day" must be read as referring to IP completion day: European Union (Withdrawal Agreement) Act 2020 s.39(1), Sch.5 para.1). The 2018 Regulations reg.11 provides that "nothing in regulation 3 [which amends the 2015 Act] ... applies to a contract entered into before exit day" (the reference to "exit day" is due to be replaced by "IP completion day"; Consumer Protection (Enforcement) (Amendment etc.) (EU Exit) Regulations 2020 (Draft) Pt 3 reg.4(8)). On this see below, para.38-497.

### Other aims

*In line 8, after "themselves have echoes of both.", add new footnote 2841a:*

38-468 [2841a] However, see Directive (EU) 2019/770 of the European Parliament and of the Council of 20 May 2019 on certain aspects concerning contracts for the supply of digital content and digital services [2019] O.J. L136/1 on which see above, para.38-436.

### Issues still regulated by the Sale of Goods Act 1979

*Replace footnote 2867 with:*

38-473 [2867] 2015 Act s.4; 1979 Act ss.16–19, 20A–20B, below, paras 44-130—44-188. As noted below, para.38-477 the Law Commission has consulted on the amendment of the 2015 Act so as to provide dedicated rules on the transfer of ownership for consumer sales: see Law Com. Consultation Paper No.246, *Consumer sales contracts: transfer of ownership: a consultation paper* (July 27, 2020).

### Interpretation of 2015 Act Pt 1

*Replace paragraph with:*

38-477 Many concepts used by the 2015 Act are defined by it.[2884] For example, the 2015 Act provides that contracts to supply goods are treated as including a term that "the trader must have the right to sell or transfer the goods at the time when ownership of the goods is to be transferred",[2885] and defines "ownership" for this purpose,[2886] though it then refers its reader to the 1979 Act "for the time when ownership of goods is transferred" in relation to contracts of sale.[2887] Other concepts used by the 2015 Act are left undefined by it. It is submitted that the proper interpretation of these concepts depends on whether the provision in which they appear reflects EU legislation. Where it does (even in cases where the Act goes beyond what that legislation requires), then its interpretation may require an autonomous European interpretation.[2888] Where, on the other hand, the concept does not reflect EU legislation or has not received and would not receive such an autonomous interpretation, then its interpretation would be subject to the normal rules governing the interpretation of UK statutes. In the case of concepts known to the common law or previously (or more generally) used by domestic statutes, in principle reference should be made to their interpretation under this wider English law. However, where a particular concept is used in provisions which reflect EU law and in other provisions which do not (but reflect domestic legislation) difficulty may arise. So, for example, "possession" is used by the Act in its definition of "hire of goods" (which does not reflect EU law),[2889] but it is also used in the Act's provisions governing the passing of risk[2890] and, by reference, on the delivery of goods,[2891] both of which reflect provisions in the Consumer Rights Directive 2011.[2892]

[2884] See notably, 2015 Act ss.2, 3–8, 33, 48 and 59.

[2885] 2015 Act s.17 provides exceptions for contracts for the hire of goods (s.17(1)(a)) and where circumstances show or imply that the trader intended to transfer only a more limited title (s.17(1) and (4)–(7).

[2886] 2015 Act s.4(1) "the general property in goods, not merely a special property".

[2887] 2015 Act s.4(2) referring to 1979 Act ss.16–20B. The Law Commission has consulted on the amendment of the 2015 Act so as to provide dedicated rules on the transfer of ownership for consumer sales, in particular so as to protect consumers who have paid in advance for goods and then seller becomes insolvent: see Law Com. Consultation Paper No.246, *Consumer sales contracts: transfer of ownership: a consultation paper* (July 27, 2020). See also the Law Commission's earlier report: *Consumer Prepayments on Retailer Insolvency* (2016) Law Com. No.368.

[2888] Above, para.38-015. See also above, para.38-004 and Vol.I, para.1-017B on the changing significance of European case law for English courts after IP completion day.

[2889] 2015 Act s.6.

[2890] 2015 Act s.29 referring to "physical possession".

[2891] 2015 Act s.28; "delivery" is defined by s.59(1) as the "voluntary transfer of possession from one person to another".

[2892] 2011 Directive arts 18 and 20 (both referring to "physical possession"). See further, below, paras 38-526 and 38-527.

## *(ii) "Goods Contracts"*

### (aa) The Four Types of "Goods Contracts"

**"Sales contracts"**

*Replace paragraph with:*

The 2015 Act provides that: **38-486**

> "A contract is a sales contract if under it—
> (a) the trader transfers or agrees to transfer ownership of goods to the consumer, and
> (b) the consumer pays or agrees to pay the price."[2929]

Apart from the substitution of "ownership of goods" for "the property in goods", this definition follows closely the definition of "contract of sale of goods" in the 1979 Act,[2930] and this substitution makes no substantive difference given that the 2015 Act defines "ownership" as "the general property in goods, not merely a special property".[2931]

[2929] 2015 Act s.5(1). cf. *Software Incubator Ltd v Computer Associates UK Ltd* [2018] EWCA Civ 518, [2018] 2 All E.R. (Comm) 398 (permission to appeal to SC granted) where it was held that a contract for the supply of software does not constitute a "sale of goods" for the purposes of the Commercial Agents (Council Directive) Regulations 1993 (SI 1993/3053).

[2930] 1979 Act s.2(1) below, paras 44-020 et seq.

[2931] 2015 Act s.4(1) and cf. 1979 Act s.61(1) defining "property" as "general property in goods, and not merely a special property", on which see below, para.44-015. In the *PST Energy 7 Shipping LLC v OW Bunker Malta (The Res Cogitans)* [2016] UKSC 23, [2016] 2 W.L.R.1193 the SC held (in a commercial context) that a contract providing for possession of goods to be given, coupled with a legal entitlement to sue or consumer them before the property in them is transferred upon payment is not a contract of sale of goods within the meaning of the Sale of Goods Act 1979 (see below, para.44-020). On the significance of this decision for the definition of "sales contract" for the purposes of the 2015 Act, see *Benjamin's Sale of Goods*, 11th edn (2020), paras 14-068—14-071.

## (bb) The Statutory Terms and "Goods Conforming to a Contract"

### Goods to be of satisfactory quality

*Replace footnote 2998 with:*

**38-497** [2998] 2015 Act s.59(1) defines "producer in relation to goods or digital content" as the manufacturer, the importer into the European Economic Area, or any person who purports to be a producer by placing the person's name, trade mark or other distinctive sign on the goods or using it in connection with the digital content", a definition deriving from the 1999 Directive art.1(2)(d). On IP completion day (on which see above, para.38-004 and Vol.I, paras 1-014 et seq.), the "United Kingdom" will be substituted for the "European Economic Area" in this definition: Consumer Protection (Amendment etc.) (EU Exit) Regulations 2018 (SI 2018/1326) reg.3(3) (reg.1(3)'s reference to reg.3's coming into force on "exit day" must be read as referring to IP completion day: European Union (Withdrawal Agreement) Act 2020 s.39(1), Sch.5 para.1). The 2018 Regulations reg.11 provides that "nothing in regulation 3 [which amends the 2015 Act] ... applies to a contract entered into before exit day".

### Goods to be as described

*In line 7, after "of implementation of the Consumer Rights Directive 2011", add new footnote 3106a:*

**38-499** [3016a] On the amendment of the Consumer Rights Directive by Directive (EU) 2019/2161 of the European Parliament and of the Council of 27 November 2019 ... as regards the better enforcement and modernisation of Union consumer protection rules [2019] O.J. L328/7 art.4, see above, para.38-060 (note).

## (cc) The Scheme of Remedies for the Consumer

### The right to reject: general provisions

*Replace footnote 3105 with:*

**38-513** [3105] cf. Vol.I, para.24-035 (the injured party treating the contract as discharged on the ground of total or partial failure to perform) and Peel (ed.), *Treitel on The Law of Contract*, 15th edn (2020), para.18-001 referring to "termination for breach" and discussing the varied terminology used for this purpose by the common law.

### Right to repair or replacement

*Replace footnote 3126 with:*

**38-517** [3126] 1999 Directive art.3(3)–(4) on which see *Quelle AG v Bundersverband des Versbraucherzentralen und Verbraucherverbande* (C-404/06) [2008] E.C.R. I-2685 and *Gebr Weber GmbH v Wittmer, Putz v Medianess Electronics GmbH* (C-65/09 and C-87/09) [2011] 3 C.M.L.R. 27 at [50]–[62] (the requirement that the repair or replacement should be "free of charge" extends to the cost of removing goods not in conformity and installation where this is necessary for the goods replacement). In *Fülla v Toolport GmbH* (C-52/18) EU:C:2019:447 paras 32 and 33 the CJEU interpreted art.3 as requiring that "any repair or replacement must be made free of charge, within a reasonable time and without significant inconvenience to the consumer" and this meant that "the place where goods not in conformity are to be made available to the seller to be repaired or replaced must be appropriate for ensuring that they are brought into conformity in compliance with that triple requirement". In the case of a distance contract, this place depends on the specific circumstances of each individual case, taking into account the nature of the goods and the purpose for which the consumer required them: paras 40–45. However, where the goods need to be transported to the seller's place of business, the seller does not have to pay the cost of such transport in advance unless the burden of doing so would deter the consumer from asserting his rights: at para.56. On the implementation of art.3 by the 2002 Regulations see above, paras 38-447—38-449.

## Right to price reduction or final right to reject

*Replace paragraph with:*

38-518 These rights reflect the second level of remedies required by the 1999 Directive and formerly implemented in UK law by the 2002 Regulations.[3135] Under the right to a price reduction, the consumer may require the trader to reduce or extinguish[3136] the price[3137] which the consumer is required to pay under the contract, and/or to receive a refund from the trader for anything already paid by the consumer above the reduced amount.[3138] In this respect, neither the 1999 Directive nor the Act explain the precise purpose of a price reduction (beyond referring to reduction by an "appropriate amount"[3139]), but it would seem that (following its origins in the civil law[3140]) in general the reduction should reflect the difference in value between what was received by the consumer compared to what he should have received if the goods had conformed to the contract.[3141] Section 24(5) of the Act further provides, however, that:

> "A consumer who has the right to a price reduction and the final right to reject may only exercise one (not both), and may only do so in one of these situations—
> (a) after one repair or one replacement, the goods do not conform to the contract;
> (b) because of section 23(3) the consumer can require neither repair nor replacement of the goods; or
> (c) the consumer has required the trader to repair or replace the goods, but the trader is in breach of the requirement of section 23(2)(a) to do so within a reasonable time and without significant inconvenience to the consumer."[3142]

For the purposes of subs.(5)(a) there has been a repair or replacement if the consumer has requested or agreed to repair or replacement of the goods (whether in relation to one fault or more than one), and the trader has delivered goods to the consumer, or made goods available[3143] to the consumer, in response to the request or agreement.[3144]

3135 1999 Directive art.3(5)–(6). On implementation by the 2002 Regulations see above, paras 38-451—38-454.

3136 This is the effect of s.24(2)'s provision that: "[t]he amount of the reduction may, where appropriate, be the full amount of the price or whatever the consumer is required to transfer". From the fact that the Act does not allow a right of rejection in respect of digital content (see below, para.38-561), it would appear that the drafters of the Act took the view that there can be no right to reject where the consumer has nothing physical to hand back. Where the consumer is in this position as regards a "goods contract", a consumer could recover a 100 per cent reduction in price.

3137 "Price reduction" may also apply to anything else the consumer is required to transfer under the contract: s.24(1) and (2). However, where this is the case, the right to a price reduction does not apply where what the consumer is (before the reduction) required to transfer under the contract (whether or not already transferred) cannot be divided up so as to enable the trader to receive or retain only the reduced amount, or if anything transferred which cannot be the subject of substitution cannot be given back in its original state: s.24(4) referring to s.20(12) in this respect.

3138 2015 Act s.24(1). Section 24(3) provides that s.20(10)–(17) applies to the consumer's right to receive a refund as outlined above, para.38-514.

3139 1999 Directive art.3(2) and (5) ("appropriate reduction"); 2015 Act s.24(1)(a) (reduction by an "appropriate amount").

3140 In Roman law, the *actio quanti minoris* in sale reflected, e.g., in art.1644 of the French Code civil. cf. the "right to a discount" under the 2008 Regulations, above, paras 38-196—38-197.

3141 cf. *Principles, Definitions and Model Rules of European Private Law, Draft Common Frame of Reference* (DCFR) prepared by the Study Group for a European Civil Code and the Research Group on EC Private Law (Acquis Group) (2010) art.III.-3:601 Right to reduce price. See also Directive (EU) 2019/771 (which is to repeal and replace the Consumer Sales Directive 1999, above, para.38-436), art.15 of which provides that "[t]he reduction of price shall be proportionate to the decrease in the value of the goods which were received by the consumer compared to the value the goods would have if they were in conformity". See further below, para.38-582 in relation to 2015 Act s.56 (price reduction in relation to services contracts).

3142 On these requirements see above, para.38-517. In *Fülla v Toolport GmbH* (C-52/18) EU:C:2019:447 at para.66 the CJEU held that in the case of a distance contract, the obligation on the seller to repair or replace the goods within a reasonable time is not satisfied "if the seller does not take any appropriate steps ... to inspect the goods not in conformity, including the obligation to inform the consumer, within a reasonable time, of the place where the goods not in conformity are to be made available to him to be brought into conformity". The County Court at Nottingham has held that a requirement made by a consumer to repair a car by the car dealer can satisfy the condition set by s.24(5), even though the car was sold by the dealer's associated finance house (the "trader" for this purpose), as long as the dealer acted on behalf of the finance house in relation to handling defects in the cars sold: *Gordon v Volkswagen Financial Services (UK) Ltd (t/a Audi Finance)* Unreported April 30, 2019 esp. at [28]–[34].

3143 For these purposes goods that the trader arranges to repair at the consumer's premises are made available when the trader indicates that the repairs are finished: 2015 Act s.24(7).

3144 2015 Act s.24(6).

## Discretion as to appropriate remedy

*Replace paragraph with:*

**38-521** The 2015 Act s.58 provides that in any proceedings in which one of the special remedies provided for consumers by Ch.2[3155] is sought, the court enjoys two additional powers.[3156] First, on the application of the consumer, the court may make an order requiring specific performance by the trader of any obligation imposed on the trader in respect of repair or replacement of the goods.[3157] For this purpose, an order of specific performance would not seek to enforce the primary obligations of the contract, whether based on an express, implied or statutory term; instead, specific performance would seek to enforce the trader's secondary obligation (arising on breach of the obligations arising on breach of the relevant statutory term) to repair or replace the goods, and thereby protect the consumer's right to *corrective* performance.[3158] Secondly, where a consumer claims the right to repair or replacement or the right to a price reduction or the final right to reject (termed the "relevant remedies" by s.58), but the court decides that the provisions governing these rights "have the effect that exercise of another of these rights is appropriate", "the court may proceed as if the consumer had exercised that other right".[3159] The court may make an order under s.58 unconditionally or on such terms and conditions as to damages, payment of the price and otherwise as it thinks just.[3160] Finally, on their terms, the court's powers under s.58 do not extend to the "other remedies" for consumers as this is understood by the Act and as explained below.[3161]

3155 2015 Act s.58(1), referring to s.19(3) and (4) and therefore to the legal grounds of the consumer's rights in respect of the statutory terms as to quality, fitness for purpose, etc. under the special rules governing conformity of the goods or for breach of requirements that are stated in the contract as there provided: above, para.38-493. The powers of the court in s.58 therefore do not extend to proceedings brought in respect of the costs incurred by the consumer under s.19(5) in relation to breach of the statutory terms under s.12, nor to the right of rejection foreseen by s.19(6) as regards breach of the statutory term as to the trader's right to supply under s.17. Moreover, while the remedies for consumers foreseen by s.19(3) and (4) are the short-term right to reject, the right to repair or replacement and the right to a price reduction or the final right to reject, s.58's provisions affect only the latter 4 of these remedies. Section 58 makes similar provision in respect of the special rights which Chs 3 and 4 of Pt 1 of the Act create in respect of digital contents contracts and services contracts, on which see below, paras 38-560 and 38-583 respectively.

3156 As explained above, para.38-455, these powers in the court were earlier provided by the Sale and Supply of Goods to Consumers Regulations 2002 (SI 2002/3045) on the first implementation of the Consumer Sales Directive 1999, even though they were not foreseen by that Directive.

3157 2015 Act s.58(2) referring to s.23 of the Act, above, para.38-517.

3158 Whittaker (2017) 133 L.Q.R. 47 at 61–63 and see above, para.38-517.

3159 2015 Act s.58(4) and (5). The "relevant remedies" are defined by s.58(8)(a), referring to ss.23 and 24. For this purpose, if the consumer has claimed to exercise the final right to reject, the court may order that any reimbursement to the consumer is reduced by a deduction for use, to take account of the use the consumer has had of the goods in the period since they were delivered to the extent provided by s.24(9) and (10): 2015 Act s.58(5) and (6).

3160 2015 Act s.58(7).

3161 Below, para.38-323.

## The court's discretions in relation to sales contracts

*Replace paragraph with:*

In the case of contracts for the *sale* of goods ("sales contracts"), the consumer's right to repair or replacement of goods in the 2015 Act reflects requirements of the Consumer Sales Directive 1999 and therefore during the transition period between the UK leaving the EU on January 31, 2020 and IP completion day (set at December 31, 2020[3161a]) the provisions of the Act relating to them must, in accordance with the principle of conforming interpretation, be interpreted with this in mind and in the light of the principle of effectiveness, here, of the consumer's protection.[3162] For this purpose, in *Weber and Putz* the Court of Justice of the EU assumed that the consumer's specific rights (i.e. repair or replacement) under the Directive were enforceable in kind against the seller, holding that national law must not allow replacement to be refused by a trader on the ground of disproportionality with regard to the value of the goods as conforming and the significance of the non-conformity, even though in the circumstances this meant that the trader had to bear the costs of the removal of goods installed by the consumer and the reinstallation of the replacement goods.[3163] This suggests that an English court should not refuse specific performance in support of the consumer's right to repair or replacement of goods sold on the ground that damages would be an adequate remedy, as this would to this extent replace the consumer's "European rights" with damages and so render them ineffective; it also suggests that the court should not take into account other traditional elements governing the availability of specific performance stemming from its equitable nature on the basis that the Directive itself provides only two circumstances (impossibility and disproportionality compared to the other specific remedy) where the trader is entitled to refuse to repair or replace.[3164] Finally, following the decision in *Weber and Putz* itself, in the case of "sales contracts", the court's powers to substitute another "appropriate right" under s.58 is incompatible with the 1999 Directive in that it allows a court to refuse a right to repair or replacement in circumstances other than those which are foreseen by art.3 of the Directive. However, on IP completion day, the proper approach to interpretation of the provisions of the 2015 Act which implement EU legislation (and here the 1999 Directive) changes.[3164a] For this purpose, while the decision of the Court of Justice in *Weber and Putz* would already form part of "retained EU case law" and the principle of conforming interpretation and the principle of effectiveness constitute "retained general principles of EU law" before IP completion day so as in principle to bind UK courts (except the Supreme Court and other courts specified by regulation),[3164b] it could be argued that the explicit terms of s.58 as to the substitu- **38-522** tion of remedy are not susceptible to interpretation so as to conform to the approach of the Court of Justice of the 1999 Directive. Merely as a matter of EU law, the principle of conforming interpretation does not require national courts to interpret their legislation where this is not possible given the words used (that is, interpretation "*contra legem*"),[3164c] but even after IP completion day UK courts may still be required to "disapply" national legislation under the (retained) principle of supremacy.[3164d]

[3161a] On this see above, para.38-004 and Vol.I, paras 1-014 et seq.

[3162] See Whittaker (2017) 133 L.Q.R. 47 at 63–66. On the Consumer Sales Directive 1999 generally, see above, para.38-433. On "sales contracts" see above, paras 38-486—38-488.

[3163] *Gebr Weber GmbH v Wittmer, Putz v Medianess Electronics GmbH* (C-65/09 and C-87/09) EU:C:2011:396, [2011] 3 C.M.L.R. 27 at paras 63–78.

[3164] 1999 Directive art.3(3), reflected in 2015 Act s.23(3)–(4) and see above, para.38-517.

[3164a] See Vol.I, paras 1-015A and 1-017B.

[3164b] European Union (Withdrawal) Act 2018 s.6(3)–(5D) (as amended by the European Union (Withdrawal Agreement) Act 2020 and see Vol.I, para.1-017B.

[3164c] *Association de médiation sociale v Union locale des syndicats CGT* (C-176/12) EU:C:2014:2 at para.39; *Kásler v OTP Jelzálogbank Zrt* (C-26/13) EU:C:2014:282 at para.65.

[3164d] See Vol.I, paras 1-017A and 1-017B.

## (dd) Other Rules About Goods Contracts

### Delivery of goods in sales contracts

*Replace footnote 3216 with:*

38-526 [3216] 2011 Directive art.4, above, para.38-062. A possible way out of this problem would be to hold that "cancelling the order" refers to a right to cancel an off-premises contract or distance contract under the 2013 Regulations (in which the content of s.28 was earlier contained), but the context of the provision in s.28 does not suggest that this is so: see SI 2013/3134 reg.42(10)–(11) and above, paras 38-112 et seq. For the position as regards the principle of supremacy and the principle of conforming interpretation after IP completion day see Vol.I, paras 1-017A and 1-017B.

### Goods under guarantee

*Replace paragraph with:*

38-528 Section 30 of the 2015 Act implements art.6 of the Consumer Sales Directive 1999,[3227a] thereby replacing its earlier implementation by the Sale and Supply of Goods to Consumers Regulations 2002[3228] and while the drafting differs between the two, the substance remains the same. Accordingly, s.30 applies where there is a contract to supply goods,[3229] and there is a guarantee in relation to the goods. A "guarantee" for these purposes is:

> "... an undertaking to the consumer given without extra charge by a person acting in the course of the person's business (the "guarantor"[3230]) that, if the goods do not meet the specifications set out in the guarantee statement or in any associated advertising—
>
> (a) the consumer will be reimbursed for the price paid for the goods, or
> (b) the goods will be repaired, replaced or handled in any way."[3231]

The Act provides that the guarantee "takes effect, at the time the goods are delivered, as a contractual obligation owed by the guarantor" under the conditions set out in the guarantee statement and in any associated advertising.[3232] The guarantor must ensure that the guarantee sets out in plain and intelligible language[3233] the contents of the guarantee and the essential particulars for making claims under the guarantee and that it states that the consumer has statutory rights in relation to the goods and that those rights are not affected by the guarantee.[3234] Section 30 makes further detailed provision as to the contents and availability to the consumer of the guarantee.[3235]

[3227a] The 1999 Directive is to be repealed and replaced by Directive (EU) 2019/771 of the European Parliament and of the Council of 20 May 2019 on certain aspects concerning contracts for the sale of goods, etc [2019] O.J. L136/28 on which see above, para.38-436.

[3228] SI 2002/3045 reg.15, above, para.38-462.

[3229] 2015 Act s.30(1) and see 2015 Act s.3(1) and (2), above, para.38-485.

[3230] There is no definition of "guarantor" in the 2015 Act except the designation in s.30(2), with the result that any person who gives a guarantee as is described there (whether the trader party to the goods contract, the producer of the goods or any other person) can be a "guarantor" subject to the condition that they act in the course of their business. On the definition of "business" for this purpose see 2015 Act s.2(7) and above, para.38-482 as explained by paras 38-052—38-055.

[3231] 2015 Act s.30(2).

[3232] 2015 Act s.30(3). This would mean that any failure in respect of the undertakings in the guarantee would give rise to the normal remedies for breach of contract (and notably damages) provided under the general law: on damages see Vol.I, Ch.26.

[3233] As the 2015 Act s.30 implements art.6 of the 1999 Directive, it is submitted that the interpretation of this requirement should follow the approach taken by the CJEU for the purposes of the Unfair Terms in Consumer Contracts Directive 1993 arts 4(2) and 5, as explained above, paras 38-261, 38-262 and 38-350.

[3234] 2015 Act s.30(4). Where the goods are offered within the territory of the United Kingdom, the guarantee must be written in English: 2015 Act s.30(4)(c).

[3235] These contents must include the name and address of the guarantor and the duration and territorial scope of the guarantee. The guarantor and any other person who offers to supply to consumers the goods which are the subject of the guarantee must, on request by the consumer, make the guarantee available to the consumer within a reasonable time, in writing and in a form accessible to the consumer: 2015 Act s.30(5)–(7).

### Enforcement of the duties on guarantors and other traders by s.30

*Replace footnote 3242 with:*

[3242] Enterprise Act 2002 s.212; Sch.13 Pt 1 para.8; s.30 of the 2015 Act is designated as a "specified law" for the purposes of s.212 (Enterprise Act 2002 (Part 8 EU Infringements) Order 2014 (SI 2014/2908) art.4 and Sch.) and may be the basis of a "domestic infringement" under s.211 of the 2002 Act (Enterprise Act 2002 (Part 8 Domestic Infringements) Order 2015 (SI 2015/1727) art.2) and see above paras 38-133—38-134. On IP completion day (on which see above, para.38-004 and Vol.I, paras 1-014 et seq.), "Community infringements" are to be replaced by "Schedule 13 infringements" and s.30 of the 2015 Act is to be included within the substituted Sch.13 of the 2002 Act for this purpose: Consumer Protection (Enforcement) (Amendment etc.) (EU Exit) Regulations 2019 (SI 2019/203) reg.3(20) and Sch. para.1 inserting new 2002 Act Sch.13 para.27. On this change more generally see above, para.38-133A. **38-530**

## (ee) Exclusion of Liability and Choice of Law

### Enforcement of provisions on exclusion of trader's liabilities

*Replace footnote 3255 with:*

[3255] The difficulty arises from the fact that the controls on exclusion clauses governing liability under s.31 of the 2015 Act go beyond the scope of the controls required by the Consumer Sales Directive 1999 (whose controls on the exclusion of liability in art.7(1) apply only to contracts for the sale of goods within its definition in art.1) and, where this is the case, beyond the intensity of the controls required by Unfair Terms in Consumer Contracts Directive 1993 (in that they invalidate such clauses in all **38-532** circumstances rather than subjecting them to the test of unfairness) and that enforcement measures in respect of the "commercial practice" of use of such exemption clauses would therefore fall foul of the "full harmonisation" of the Unfair Commercial Practices Directive 2005. For an explanation of this difficulty see above, paras 38-421— 38-426A. The difficulty does not exist as regards the controls on the exclusion of liability under ss.11(4) and (5), 12, 28 and 29 of the 2015 Act which are required by the Consumer Rights Directive 2011 art.25.

## Special rule governing choice of law

*Replace paragraph with:*

**38-533** As required by the Consumer Sales Directive 1999 as regards those contracts of sale of goods falling within its scope,[3256] s.32 makes special provision for choice of law for "sales contracts".[3257] Accordingly, s.32 provides that where the law of a country or territory other than an EEA State is chosen by the parties to be applicable to a sales contract, but the sales contract has a close connection with the United Kingdom, Ch.2 applies despite that choice.[3258] In this way, s.32 makes very similar provision to s.74 of the 2015 Act for the purposes of Pt 2's controls on unfair terms, in this case following the Unfair Terms in Consumer Contract Directive's own special provision on choice of law.[3259] However, reflecting the fact that some of the provisions in Ch.2 reflect the Consumer Rights Directive 2011 rather than the Consumer Sales Directive 1999, and that the 2011 Directive makes no special provision for choice of law, s.32 excludes from its special provision those sections of Ch.2 which reflect the 2011 Directive.[3260] For the cases where these exclusions apply, the Rome I Regulation on the law applicable to contractual obligations applies instead.[3261]

[3256] 1999 Directive art.7(2). The relevant provisions of the 1999 Directive apply to contracts for the sale of goods and deem contracts for the supply of consumer goods to be manufactured and produced to be included in this category for this purpose: art.1(2)(b) "consumer goods", (c) "seller" and art.1(4)) above, paras 38-486—38-488.

[3257] Defined by s.5.

[3258] 2015 Act s.32(1). On IP completion day (on which see above, para.38-004 and Vol.I, paras 1-014 et seq.), the reference to "an EEA State" in s.32(1)(a) is to be replaced by "the United Kingdom or any part of the United Kingdom": Consumer Protection (Amendment etc.) (EU Exit) Regulations 2018 (SI 2018/1326) reg.3(5)(b) (the reference in reg.1(3) to reg.3's coming into force on "exit day" must be read as referring to IP completion day: European Union (Withdrawal Agreement) Act 2020 s.39(1), Sch.5 para.1). Transitional provision is made by the 2018 Regulations reg.11.

[3259] 1993 Directive art.6(2). For discussion of s.74 of the Act, art.6(2) of the 1993 Directive and their relationship to the general provisions governing applicable law in Regulation (EC) 593/2008 on the law applicable to contractual obligations ("Rome I Regulation") see above, para.38-418.

[3260] 2015 Act s.32(2). The relevant provisions are 2015 Act ss.11(4) and (5) and 12 (implementing the 2011 Directive's provisions governing information requirements, on which see above, paras 38-105, 38-499—38-500); s.28 (delivery, on which see above, para.38-526); s.29 (passing of risk, on which see above, para.38-527) and s.31(1)(d), (j) and (k) (which concern the exclusion of liability under ss.12, 28 and 29, on which see above, para.38-531). On the 2011 Directive and its amendment at the EU level, see above, para.38-060.

[3261] 2015 Act s.32(3) referring to Regulation (EC) 593/2008 on the law applicable to contractual obligations ("Rome I Regulation") on which generally see Vol.I, paras 30-019 et seq. The application of these rules may lead to the application of English law under the Act even though the contract is governed generally by the law of another EU Member State, as in the case where art.6 of the Rome I Regulation applies. On IP completion day (on which see above, para.38-004 and Vol.I, paras 1-014 et seq.), the words in s.32(3) "or the law ... is chosen" are to be deleted: Consumer Protection (Amendment etc.) (EU Exit) Regulations 2018 (SI 2018/1326) reg.3(5)(b) (the reference in reg.1(3) to reg.3's coming into force on "exit day" must be read as referring to IP completion day: European Union (Withdrawal Agreement) Act 2020 s.39(1), Sch.5 para.1). Transitional provision is made by the 2018 Regulations reg.11.

### Enforcement of Pt 1 more generally

*Replace paragraph with:*

As earlier explained, enforcement authorities enjoy considerable powers under Pt 8 of the Enterprise Act 2002 to enforce designated UK legislation and EU legislation.[3262] As has been seen, many (though not all) of the provisions of Ch.2 of the 2015 Act reflect requirements of the Consumer Sales Directive 1999 or the Consumer Rights Directive 2011, and any breach of these requirements would constitute "Community infringements" within the meaning of Pt 8 of the 2002 Act.[3263] The relevant provisions in Ch.2 of the 2015 Act which implement the 1999 Directive or the 2011 Directive or which "provide additional permitted protections" have therefore been designated as specified UK laws for the purposes of s.212 of the 2002 Act.[3264] In addition, acts or omissions in respect of any provision in Pt 1 of the 2015 Act are specified as possible "domestic infringements" for the purposes of s.211 of the Enterprise Act 2002.[3265] **38-534**

3262 Above, paras 38-133—38-134.

3263 Enterprise Act 2002 s.212; Sch.13 Pt 1 paras 8 and 9F lists these directives for this purpose. On IP completion day (on which see above, para.38-004 and Vol.I, paras 1-014 et seq.), "Community infringements" are to be replaced by "Schedule 13 infringements" and the relevant provisions of the 2015 Act are included within the substituted Sch.13 of the 2002 Act for this purpose: Consumer Protection (Enforcement) (Amendment etc.) (EU Exit) Regulations 2019 (SI 2019/203) reg.3(20) and Sch. para.1 inserting new 2002 Act Sch.13 para.27 (reg.1's reference to the 2019 Regulations coming into force on "exit day" must be read as referring to IP completion day: European Union (Withdrawal Agreement) Act 2020 s.39(1), Sch.5 para.1). The provisions in Pt 1 of the 2015 Act in question are: ss.2, 3, 5, 9–15, 19, 23, 24, 28–32, 36(3) and (4), 37, 38, 42, 50, 54, 58 and 59. On this change more generally see above, para.38-133A.

3264 Enterprise Act 2002 s.212(3); Enterprise Act 2002 (Part 8 Community Infringements Specified UK Laws) Order 2003 (SI 2003/1374) art.3; Sch., as amended by the Enterprise Act 2002 (Part 8 Community Infringements and Specified UK Laws) (Amendment) Order 2015 (SI 2015/1628) art.2(2)(b) listing 2015 Act ss.2, 3, 9–11, 13–15, 19, 23, 24, 30–32, 58 and 59 (1999 Directive); art.3(2) listing 2015 Act ss.5, 11(4)–(6), 12, 19, 28, 29, 36(3)–(4), 37, 38, 42, 50 and 54 (2011 Directive). See also the preceding note on the impact of coming into full effect of the UK's leaving the EU on IP completion day.

3265 Enterprise Act 2002 s.211(2); Enterprise Act 2002 (Part 8 Domestic Infringements) Order 2015 (SI 2015/1727) art.2.

## *(iv) Digital Content Contracts*

### Introduction

*Replace paragraph with:*

Chapter 3 of Pt 1 of the 2015 Act makes original provision governing important aspects of "digital content contracts", which it defines for these purposes.[3266] Under earlier law, it was by no means clear whether a person who "buys" digital content does so under a contract of sale of goods, a contract for services or something else.[3267] As a result, consumers who purchase digital content were unclear as to what rights they might have, how they should seek to enforce those rights against the trader and whether these rights were subject to exclusion by agreement. The 2015 Act sought therefore to create a "new category of digital content in consumer law with a bespoke set of rights and remedies appropriate to the unique nature of digital content".[3268] In doing so, however, the 2015 Act drew on earlier legislation in a number of important ways, adapting earlier provisions to suit the new context as well as supplementing them so as to provide for the distinctive features of the modern supply of digital content to consumers. **38-535**

3266 cf. the Directive (EU) 2019/770 of the European Parliament and of the Council of 20 May 2019 on certain aspects concerning contracts for the supply of digital content and digital services [2019] O.J. L136/1 on which see above, para.38-436.

3267 *Explanatory Notes* 2015 para.169 referring to Bradgate, "*Consumer rights in digital products: A research report prepared for the UK Department for Business, Innovation and Skills*", Institute for Commercial Law Studies, Sheffield and BIS, available at: *http://www.bis.gov.uk/assets/biscore/consumer-issues/docs/c/10-1125-consumer-rights-in-digital-products*. cf. *Software Incubator Ltd v Computer Associates UK Ltd* [2018] EWCA Civ 518, [2018] 2 All E.R. (Comm) 398 where it was held that a contract for the supply of software does not constitute a "sale of goods" for the purposes of the Commercial Agents (Council Directive) Regulations 1993 (SI 1993/3053).

3268 *Explanatory Notes* 2015, para.172.

*Replace footnote 3270 with:*

**38-536** 3270 Consumer Rights Directive 2011 art.2(11). This definition will remain the same on the amendment of the 2011 Directive by Directive 2019/2161 art.4(1)(e), cross-referring to the definition in Directive (EU) 2019/770 art.2(2). On these directives see above, para.38-060 (note) and para.38-436 respectively.

## (bb) The Statutory Terms

### Digital content to be of satisfactory quality

*Replace paragraph with:*

**38-546** The 2015 Act s.34 makes almost identical provision as to the satisfactory quality of digital content supplied under a "digital content contract"[3321] as s.9 of the Act makes in relation to the satisfactory quality of goods supplied under a "goods contract",[3322] itself being familiar from earlier statutory provisions, notably governing sale of goods.[3323] Section 34 provides that:

"(1) Every contract to supply digital content is to be treated as including a term that the quality of the digital content is satisfactory.

(2) The quality of digital content is satisfactory if it meets the standard that a reasonable person would consider satisfactory, taking account of—

- (a) any description of the digital content,
- (b) the price mentioned in section 33(1) or (2)(b) (if relevant), and
- (c) all the other relevant circumstances (see subsection (5)).

(3) The quality of digital content includes its state and condition; and the following aspects (among others) are in appropriate cases aspects of the quality of digital content—

- (a) fitness for all the purposes for which digital content of that kind is usually supplied;
- (b) freedom from minor defects;
- (c) safety;
- (d) durability.

(4) The term mentioned in subsection (1) does not cover anything which makes the quality of the digital content unsatisfactory—

- (a) which is specifically drawn to the consumer's attention before the contract is made,
- (b) where the consumer examines the digital content before the contract is made, which that examination ought to reveal, or
- (c) where the consumer examines a trial version before the contract is made, which would have been apparent on a reasonable examination of the trial version.

(5) The relevant circumstances mentioned in subsection (2)(c) include any public statement about the specific characteristics of the digital content made by the trader, the producer or any representative of the trader or the producer. [3323a]

(6) That includes, in particular, any public statement made in advertising or labelling.

(7) But a public statement is not a relevant circumstance for the purposes of subsection (2)(c) if the trader shows that—
- (a) when the contract was made, the trader was not, and could not reasonably have been, aware of the statement,
- (b) before the contract was made, the statement had been publicly withdrawn or, to the extent that it contained anything which was incorrect or misleading, it had been publicly corrected, or
- (c) the consumer's decision to contract for the digital content could not have been influenced by the statement.

(8) In a contract to supply digital content a term about the quality of the digital content may be treated as included as a matter of custom."

Apart from replacement of the references to "goods" with references to "digital content", s.34 omits s.9's reference to "appearance and finish"[3324] as a possible aspect of the quality of digital content (for obvious reasons). Secondly, s.34(4)(c) replaces s.9's provision for the case of a contract to supply goods by sample (to the effect that the statutory term does not cover anything which would have been apparent on a reasonable examination of the sample[3325]), with provision for the case where the consumer examines a "trial version" before the contract is made, to the effect that the statutory term does not cover anything which would have been apparent on a reasonable examination of the trial version. It is to be noted that s.34(5)–(7) also makes public statements relevant to the standard that a reasonable person would consider satisfactory in s.9(5)–(7) which reflects a requirement of the Consumer Sales Directive, even though the Directive itself does not apply to digital content contracts.[3326] In order to achieve a harmonious interpretation between these provisions of the Act in s.9 and s.34, a court would need therefore to follow whatever interpretation were taken by the Court of Justice to the Directive's provisions underlying s.9.[3326a] In terms of the significance of "satisfactory quality" in the context of digital content contracts, according to the Act's *Explanatory Notes*:

> "... a reasonable person's expectations as to quality are likely to vary according to the nature of the content and some aspects of quality set out in subsection (3) may not be relevant in particular cases. So for example a reasonable person might expect a simple music file to be free from minor defects so that a track which failed to play to the end would not be of satisfactory quality. However, it is the norm to encounter some bugs in a complex game or piece of software on release so a reasonable person might not expect that type of digital content to be free from minor defects. Consequently the application of the quality aspect 'freedom from minor defects' to digital content will depend on reasonable expectations as to quality."[3327]

Under s.42 of the Act breach of the statutory term in s.34 gives rise in the consumer to the right to repair or replacement and the right to a price reduction, and may also give rise to other remedies under the general law.[3328]

[3321] On this category see 2015 Act s.33(1), (2) and (7) and above, paras 38-540—38-541. On the 1979 Act s.14, see below, paras 44-095 et seq.

[3322] 2015 Act s.9, above, para.38-497.

[3323] 1979 Act s.14(2).

[3323a] 2015 Act s.59(1) defines "producer in relation to goods or digital content" as the manufacturer, the importer into the European Economic Area, or any person who purports to be a producer by placing the person's name, trade mark or other distinctive sign on the goods or using it in connection with the digital content", a definition deriving from the 1999 Directive art.1(2)(d). On IP completion day (on which see above, para.38-004 and Vol.I, paras 1-014 et seq.), the "United Kingdom" will be substituted for the "European Economic Area" in this definition: Consumer Protection (Amendment etc.) (EU Exit)

Regulations 2018 (SI 2018/1326) reg.3(3) (reg.1(3)'s reference to reg.3's coming into force on "exit day" must be read as referring to IP completion day: European Union (Withdrawal Agreement) Act 2020 s.39(1), Sch.5 para.1).

[3324] 2015 Act s.9(3)(b).

[3325] 2015 Act s.9(4)(c).

[3326] 1999 Directive art.1(2)(b) "consumer goods". The provision governing public statements is found in art.2(2)(d) and (4). On these provisions see above, para.38-497.

[3326a] The statement in the text must be read subject to the change in significance of the case law of CJEU on IP completion day as noted in Vol.1, para.1-017B.

[3327] *Explanatory Notes* 2015 para.179.

[3328] 2015 Act s.42(1) and (2) on the operation of which, see above, para.38-544. On the consumer's rights and remedies see below, paras 38-557 et seq.

## (cc) The Scheme of Remedies for the Consumer

### No right to reject digital content for breach of the statutory terms

*Replace footnote 3423 with:*

38-561 [3423] See Vol.I, Ch.24 and especially para.24-052 and see also paras 29-057—29-067 (referring to "failure of basis"). The *possibility* of such a right of termination of the contract is allowed by the fact that the provisions in s.42(6)–(8) governing "other remedies" and preventing the consumer from treating the contract as at an end are restricted to breach of the statutory terms in ss.34–37 and 41(1) of the 2015 Act. The approach of Directive (EU) 2019/770 of the European Parliament and of the Council of 20 May 2019 on certain aspects concerning contracts for the supply of digital content and digital services [2019] O.J. L136/1 (on which see above, para.38-436) differs here, as arts 14(6), 15–17 provide for the circumstances in which a consumer may terminate a contract for the supply of digital content or a digital service and also for the consequences of such a termination.

## (ee) Exclusion of Liability and Enforcement

### Enforcement

*Replace footnote 3449 with:*

38-566 [3449] Enterprise Act 2002 s.212(3); Enterprise Act 2002 (Part 8 EU Infringements) Order 2014 (SI 2014/2908) art.4; Sch. (as amended by the Enterprise Act 2002 (Part 8 Community Infringements and Specified UK Laws) (Amendment) Order 2015 (SI 2015/1628) art.3(2)) listing, inter alia, 2015 Act ss.36(3)–(4), 37, 38 and 42. On IP completion day (on which see above, para.38-004 and Vol.I, paras 1-014 et seq.), "Community infringements" are to be replaced by "Schedule 13 infringements" and ss.36(3) and (4), 37, 38 and 42 of the 2015 Act are to be included within the substituted Sch.13 of the 2002 Act for this purpose: Consumer Protection (Enforcement) (Amendment etc.) (EU Exit) Regulations 2019 (SI 2019/203) reg.3(20) and Sch. para.1 inserting new 2002 Act Sch.13 para.27 (reg.1's reference to the 2019 Regulations coming into force on "exit day" must be read as referring to IP completion day: European Union (Withdrawal Agreement) Act 2020 s.39(1), Sch.5 para.1). On this change more generally see above, para.38-133A.

## *(v) Services Contracts*

## (bb) The Statutory Terms

### Things "said or written" by the trader irrespective of a duty to do so

*Replace paragraph with:*

38-574 As noted earlier, the impact of s.50(1) is qualified and this is effected by s.50(2), according to which:

> "Anything taken into account by the consumer as mentioned in subsection (1)(a) or (b) is subject to—

(a) anything that qualified it and was said or written to the consumer by the trader on the same occasion, and
(b) any change to it that has been expressly agreed between the consumer and the trader (before entering into the contract or later)."

So, the impact of s.50(1) may be qualified either by what the trader says or writes at the time ("on the same occasion"[3482a]) or by any change agreed between the consumer, whether before entering the contract or at some later date.[3483] Despite these qualifications, it will be seen that the 2015 Act gives contractual force to pre-contractual statements in a range of situations where it would not be clearly the case under the general law of "warranty".[3484]

[3482a] It would seem for this reason that neither a later qualification even if made before the contract was concluded nor a qualification contained in an express term of the contract itself if made other than "on the same occasion" would fall within s.50(2)'s provision: cf. for this purpose the facts of *Allner v Peters & May Group Ltd* [2019] EWHC 3258 (Comm) where (allegedly) a statement was made in writing before contract that a yacht would be delivered before a certain date and the contract contained an express term making clear that no commitment was made to delivery dates: see below, para.38-586.

[3483] In principle, such a term in a consumer contract which effected such a change could itself be an unfair term and so not binding on the consumer under s.62 of the 2015 Act, on which see above, paras 38-389 et seq. For an example of the claimed application of s.50(1), see *Allner v Peters & May Group Ltd* [2019] EWHC 3258 (Comm) and below, para.38-586.

[3484] See Vol.I paras 7-004, 13-003—13-005.

## (cc) The Scheme of Remedies for the Consumer

### Discretion as to appropriate remedy

*In line 12, after "and otherwise as it thinks just.[3525]", add:*

It should be noted that, on their terms, the court's powers under s.58 do not extend to the consumer's "other remedies" as this is understood by the Act and as explained below.[3525a] **38-583**

[3525a] Below, para.38-584.

## (dd) Exclusion of Liability

### Exclusion of liability for breach of the statutory terms

*After the first paragraph, add new paragraph:*

An illustration of the relationship between breach of the statutory term in s.50(1) and the controls on the exclusion of liability in s.57 may be found in *Allner v Peters & May Group Ltd*.[3544a] There (on the facts as alleged) the defendant had contracted to arrange for the transport of the claimant's yacht from Genoa to the Caribbean, and the defendant had stated prior to the conclusion of the contract that the yacht would definitely arrive in time for Christmas. The contract contained express provision which made clear that delivery dates were not ones to which the defendant was committing itself and requiring any claim to be brought within nine months.[3544b] The yacht did not arrive in time and the claimant relied on s.50(1) of the 2015 Act on the basis that the defendant's pre-contractual comments bound them and overrode the defendant's terms and conditions, including the clause imposing the nine month time-limit.[3544c] The claimant relied on the controls on the exclusion of liability under s.57 of the Act, arguing that the clause sought to "exclude liability" arising for breach of the term in s.50(1).[3544d] The High Court concluded that there was a tri- **38-586** able issue arising, in particular, from the claimant's argument as to the effect of s.57 on the defendant's time-limit clause.[3544e]

[3544a] [2019] EWHC 3258 (Comm).

[3544b] [2019] EWHC 3258 (Comm) at [12] and [16].

[3544c] [2019] EWHC 3258 (Comm) at [12]–[13].

[3544d] [2019] EWHC 3258 (Comm) at [34].

[3544e] [2019] EWHC 3258 (Comm) at [38]–[47]. For this purpose, the parties and the court proceeded on the basis that the relevant controls were to be found in s.57(3) of the 2015 Act, although, with respect, given that the claimant based his case on breach of the term in s.50(1) of the Act, the relevant control was to be found in s.57(2) of the Act. On these provisions, see above in the text of this paragraph.

## (ee) Enforcement

### Enforcement of provisions on exclusion of trader's liabilities

*Replace paragraph with:*

**38-587** As earlier explained in relation to the 2015 Act's treatment of unfair contract terms more generally, the Act applies the enforcement measures provided for the control of unfair contract terms under Pt 2 (and derived from the 1993 Directive[3545]) to its controls of contract terms in Pt 1 of the Act.[3546] Secondly, the provisions in Ch.4 of the 2015 Act which implement the Consumer Rights Directive 2011 or which "provide additional permitted protections"[3547] (notably, the provisions in s.50 giving contractual effect to certain categories of information provided by the trader to the consumer) have been designated as specified UK laws for the purposes of s.212 of the Enterprise Act 2002 Act so as to attract enforcement orders in relation to "Community infringements".[3548] And, thirdly, acts or omissions in respect of any provision in Pt 1 of the 2015 Act are specified as possible "domestic infringements" for the purposes of s.211 of the Enterprise Act 2002.

[3545] 1993 Directive art.7.

[3546] 2015 Act s.57(7) referring to Sch.3. See above, paras 38-419 et seq.

[3547] Enterprise Act 2002 s.212(1)(b).

[3548] Enterprise Act 2002 s.212(3); Enterprise Act 2002 (Part 8 Community Infringements Specified UK Laws) Order 2003 art.3. The Consumer Rights Directive 2011 is also listed for this purpose in the 2002 Act Sch.13 para.9F. On IP completion day (on which see above, para.38-004 and Vol.I, paras 1-014 et seq.), "Community infringements" are to be replaced by "Schedule 13 infringements" and ss.59 and 54 of the 2015 Act are to be included within the substituted Sch.13 of the 2002 Act for this purpose: Consumer Protection (Enforcement) (Amendment etc.) (EU Exit) Regulations 2019 (SI 2019/203) reg.3(20) and Sch. para.1 inserting new 2002 Act Sch.13 para.27 (reg.1's reference to the 2019 Regulations coming into force on "exit day" must be read as referring to IP completion day: European Union (Withdrawal Agreement) Act 2020 s.39(1), Sch.5 para.1). On this change more generally see above, para.38-133A.

CHAPTER 39

# CREDIT AND SECURITY

## 1. THE REGULATION OF CONSUMER CREDIT

*Replace footnote 1 with:*

[1] See Guest and Lloyd, *Encyclopedia of Consumer Credit Law* (1975, looseleaf); Goode, *Consumer Credit: Law and Practice* (looseleaf); Goode, *Consumer Credit Law* (1989); Harding, *Consumer Credit and Consumer Hire* (1995); Philpott et al, *The Law of Consumer Credit and Hire* (2009); Rosenthal, *Consumer Credit Law and Practice – A Guide*, 5th edn (2018).

### Changes since 1974

*To the end of paragraph, after "the FSMA 2000.", add new footnote 6a:*

**39-002** [6a] But see para.39-004, below, for possible changes to these "retained provisions".

### The future of consumer credit regulation

*Replace paragraph with:*

**39-004** A five-year review of consumer credit regulation has been undertaken by the FCA[13] and it may be that, in response, the Treasury will replace the dual FSMA 2000 and 1974 Act regime by a single FSMA 2000 regime (although it may be that those parts of the 1974 Act that cannot be replicated in the FCA rulebook CONC (for example, those imposing sanctions, the unfair relationship[14] and the connected lender liability[15] provisions) will remain in the 1974 Act).

[13] See the FCA's *Review of retained provisions of the Consumer Credit Act: Final Report* (presented to Parliament March 2019). For previous documents, see *Call for Input: Review of retained provisions of the Consumer Credit Act*, February 2016 and *The Interim Report*, August 2018.

[14] CCA 1974 ss.140A–140C; see below, paras 39-212 et seq.

[15] CCA 1974 ss.75 and 75A; see below, paras 39-303—39-305.

### Banks and investment firms authorised in other EEA states

*Replace paragraph with:*

**39-012** The implementation of the EU's Banking Directive[50] and Markets in Financial Instruments Directive[51] was affected by legislative provisions contained in or made under the Financial Services and Markets Act 2000.[52] The philosophy underlying the Directives is that of "home state control", i.e. the authorisation and regulation of the institutions concerned are matters for the home state, with the host state having only a limited regulatory role. As a result of these provisions, the control exercisable by virtue of the Consumer Credit Act 1974 and the Financial Services and Markets Act 2000 is presently reduced in the case of (broadly) an institution established in an EEA state ("home state") other than the United Kingdom that is authorised to carry on the relevant activity by its home state regulator.[53] Such a firm is presently entitled to establish a branch or provide services in another EEA state (the entitlement is sometimes referred to as "the single market passport") in accordance with the EU Treaty as applied in the EEA and subject to the conditions of the relevant single market directive.[54] If it seeks to exercise its passport rights in the United Kingdom it will presently qualify for authorisation by satisfying certain formal conditions such as informing the Financial Conduct Authority (FCA) of its intentions and being informed of the rules that apply to the conduct of its activities in the United Kingdom.[55] In particular, such a firm that qualifies for authorisation is presently ordinarily exempted from the need to apply for FCA authorisation.[56] The precise impact of "Brexit" on the operation of the "single market passport" is presently uncertain.[56a]

[50] Directive 2013/36/EU (and related texts), so-called "CRR/CRD IV", replacing Directive 2006/48, replacing Directive 2000/12, which in turn replaced the Second Banking Coordination Directive 89/646.

[51] "MiFID" (Directive 2004/39), replacing the Investment Services Directive (ISD), Directive 93/22, was itself replaced by "MiFID II" (Directive 2014/65/EU) and "MiFIR" (Regulation EU No.600/2014) in January 2017.

[52] FSMA 2000 ss.31(1)(b), 37 and Sch.3, as amended.

[53] FSMA 2000 Sch.3 Pt I para.5.

[54] FSMA 2000 Sch.3 Pt I para.7.

[55] FSMA 2000 Sch.3 Pt I paras 12–15.

[56] FSMA 2000 Sch.3 Pt I para.15(3).

[56a] But see the Consumer Credit (Amendment) (EU Exit) Regulations 2018 (SI 2018/1038) (whereby in, inter alia, ss.98A and 157, on the "exit day", "a retained EU obligation" will be substituted for "an EU obligation"), and the Financial Services and Markets Act 2000 (Amendment) (EU Exit) Regulations 2019 (SI 2019/632) (miscellaneous amendments, noted where relevant).

## Other EU Directives

*Replace paragraph with:*

Other EU Directives have had an impact on the statutory regulatory regime, in particular, the Electronic Commerce Directive 2000,[61] the Distance Marketing of Consumer Financial Services Directive 2002,[62] the Unfair Commercial Practices Directive 2005,[63] the Revised Payment Services Directive 2015 ("PSD2")[64] and the Consumer Rights Directive 2011.[65] The Mortgage Credit Directive 2014[66] resulted in further significant changes to the statutory regime, in particular the transfer of second charge residential mortgage regulation to the Financial Services and Markets Act 2000 regime. English law, as altered by the implementation of these directives, is not expected to be substantially amended as a result of Brexit, at least in the near future.[67] **39-014**

[61] Directive 2003/31, implemented, as far as consumer credit is concerned, primarily by the Consumer Credit Act 1974 (Electronic Communications) Order 2004 (SI 2004/3236) made under the Electronic Communications Act 2000.

[62] Directive 2002/65, implemented by the Financial Services (Distance Marketing) Regulations 2004 (SI 2004/2095), see below, para.39-126.

[63] Directive 2005/29, implemented by the Consumer Protection from Unfair Trading Regulations 2008 (SI 2008/1277), as amended by the Consumer Protection (Amendment) Regulations 2014 (SI 2014/870) in relation to contracts entered into on or after October 1, 2014. See, generally, above, paras 38-157 et seq.

[64] Replacing the old Payment Services Directive 2007, Directive 2007/64/EC. PSD2 has been implemented, as far as consumer credit is concerned, primarily by the Payment Services Regulations 2017 (SI 2017/752). Overlap with the 1974 Act is, to some extent, avoided: see, in particular regs 41 and 64. See further, paras 34-224 and 39-510 et seq.

[65] Directive 2011/83/EU. The Government implemented that part of the Directive that amended previous Directives conferring cancellation rights in certain sales on consumers, by the Consumer Contracts (Information, Cancellation and Additional Charges) Regulations 2013 (SI 2013/3134), an order under the European Communities Act 1972. See further below, para.39-125. See now the Consumer Rights Act 2015 (for contracts made on or after October 1, 2015) which updates and clarifies the law on goods and services and unfair contract terms, considered further above in paras 38-365 et seq.

[66] See above, para.39-003.

[67] See above, Vol.I, paras 1-016 et seq. But see the Consumer Credit (Amendment) (EU Exit) Regulations 2018 (SI 2018/1038) (whereby in, inter alia, CCA 1974 ss.98A and 157, on the "exit day", "a retained EU obligation" will be substituted for "an EU obligation"), and the Financial Services and Markets Act 2000 (Amendment) (EU Exit) Regulations 2019 (SI 2019/632) (miscellaneous amendments, noted where relevant).

## (a) Terminology

### "[Consumer] credit agreement"

*Replace paragraph with:*

**39-016** The 1974 Act defines a "consumer credit agreement" as an agreement[72] between an individual ("the debtor") and any other person ("the creditor") by which the creditor provides[73] the debtor with credit[74] of any amount.[75] The expression "individual" is stated to include a partnership consisting of two or three persons not all of whom are bodies corporate and any other unincorporated body not consisting entirely of bodies corporate.[76] Hence an agreement for the provision of credit where the debtor is a body corporate will not be a "consumer credit agreement".[77] But if the debtor is an unincorporated body, such as a society or club, or is a sole trader or partnership of three or fewer persons, there can be a "consumer credit agreement" notwithstanding that the debtor carries on a business and that the credit is advanced for business purposes.[78] The definition of "credit agreement" (omitting the term "consumer") in the RAO is almost identical, with the use of the terms "borrower" and "lender" instead of "debtor" and "creditor".[79] Therefore the application of the regulatory regime is generally determined by the status of the debtor/borrower and not by the purpose of the advance, subject to two qualifications in relation to "business" credit.[80] First, as noted below,[81] "business" agreements for over £25,000 are exempt from regulation. Second, as a result of the implementation of the Consumer Credit Directive[82] (which does not apply to "business" credit) the regulatory regime is less onerous in a number of respects in relation to regulated "business" credit agreements, although creditors may choose to opt into the "Directive" formal requirements for regulated credit agreements.[83]

[72] For the Act to apply there must be an "agreement", and not merely, e.g. an offer or letter of intent or proposal (see Vol.I, Ch.2). There may, however, be difficulty in ascertaining whether there is an agreement for a line of credit or whether the actual credit agreement is made in pursuance of the line of credit or both.

[73] i.e. agrees to provide: see CCA 1974 Sch.2 Example 21 and *National Westminster Bank Plc v Story* [1999] C.C.L.R. 70, CA.

[74] See below, para.39-019.

[75] CCA 1974 s.8(1). Section 8 was amended (i) (from April 6, 2008) by the Consumer Credit Act 2006 ss.2(1) and 5; (ii) (from October 31, 2008) by SI 2008/2826; (iii) (from April 1, 2014) by SI 2013/1881 and (iv) (from February 28, 2014) by SI 2014/436 (s.8(1) does not apply to a "green deal plan", because CCA 1974 s.189B applies instead (see below, para.39-257)); (v) (from 21 March 2016, in implementation of the Mortgage Credit Directive) by SI 2015/910; (vi) (from immediately after the amendment noted in (v) above) by SI 2016/392; (vii) (from December 31, 2020) by SI 2019/632. See the almost identical definition in RAO art.60LB(3). As noted above (para.39-005), originally the Act imposed a financial limit.

[76] CCA 1974 s.189(1), as amended (from April 6, 2007) by the Consumer Credit Act 2006 s.1. See CCA 1974 Sch.2 Pt II Examples 19, 24. See the almost identical definition of "relevant recipient of credit" in RAO art.60L.

[77] Except under CCA 1974 s.185(5), as amended by the Consumer Credit Act 2006 s.5(8), where such a body corporate contracts jointly with an individual. See *Bank of Ireland (UK) Plc v McLaughlin* [2014] NIQB 104 (corporate debtor not within CCA 1974).

[78] See CCA 1974 Sch.2 Pt II Examples 7, 15, 19.

[79] RAO art.60B(3) (for the definition of "relevant recipient of credit", see RAO art.60L).

[80] Moreover, the application of the financial promotion provisions in CONC 3 do not apply to prospective *business* debtors: CONC 3.1.6R(1) (as was the case with the now repealed 2004 Advertising Regulations), see below, para.39-067.

[81] RAO art.60C(3)–(7) (previously CCA 1974 s.16B), below para.39-046.

[82] See above, para.39-011.

[83] See below, para.39-080.

## "Regulated" consumer credit agreement

*Replace footnote 86 with:*

[86] s.8(3), cross-referring to the definition in the RAO Ch.14A. But (as a result of the implementation of the Mortgage Credit Directive (see above, para.39-003) on March 21, 2016) there is the further qualification that, for the agreement to be a "regulated credit agreement" for the purposes of the CCA 1974, the agreement must *not* be for the acquisition or retention of property rights in land or a building (see amendment to s.8(3) in SI 2015/910 art.3 and Sch.1 para.2(2)). Note, from December 31, 2020, as a result of Brexit, the amendments made to s.8(3) and the addition of s.8(3A) (to remove references to the Directive) by the Financial Services and Markets Act 2000 (Amendment) (EU Exit) Regulations 2019 (SI 2019/632) reg.194. **39-017**

## "Credit"

*Replace paragraph with:*

The expression "credit" is not defined in the 1974 Act or the RAO,[95] but is stated in both instruments to include "a cash loan, and any form of financial accommodation".[96] These words embrace all types of loan (e.g. moneylenders' loans, bank and building society loans, overdrafts, pawnbrokers' loans, advances on mortgage, etc.), the sale of goods on instalment credit terms (e.g. credit sales, conditional sales, budget accounts, option accounts, subscription accounts, etc.), the supply of services on credit, check trading, credit cards and charge cards[97] and debit cards.[98] In fact, any agreement for, say, the supply of goods or services where "credit" is extended (in the sense of the grant of a contractual right to defer the payment of a debt, whether the payment is to be made in one amount or by instalments)[99] will be a consumer credit agreement if the debtor is an individual. In many commercial agreements, payment is to be made in arrear; such agreements can therefore be consumer credit agreements (if the debtor is not a body corporate or large partnership), although they may be "exempt agreements"[100] and hence will not necessarily be regulated agreements. It has been held that arrangements for the instalment payment of a settlement sum, scheduled to a Tomlin Order, does not constitute "credit" on the basis, inter alia, that the deferral of payment was a "normal incident of a wider transaction not involving the lending of money".[100a] **39-019**

[95] The essence of credit is the contractual right to defer payment of an existing debt, or to incur a debt and defer its payment: *R. v Mitchell* [1955] 1 W.L.R. 1125; *R. v Garlick* (1958) 42 Cr. App. R. 141; *Grant v Watton (Inspector of Taxes)* [1999] S.T.C. 330, 345; *Dimond v Lovell* [2000] 1 Q.B. 261; affirmed [2002] 1 A.C. 384. For the problems which arise, see Guest and Lloyd *Encyclopedia of Consumer Credit Law* (1975, looseleaf) at para.2-010; and Goode, *Consumer Credit: Law and Practice*, Pt C, Ch.24. See also *Santander UK Plc v Harrison* [2013] EWHC 199 (QB), [2013] C.C.L.R. 4: the capitalisation of arrears (by adding them to the outstanding capital balance and increasing the monthly repayments correspondingly) whilst being the provision of "credit" was not the provision of a "cash loan" (for the purposes of SI 2008/831 art.4(1) which uses the term "cash loan", see below, para.39-148).

[96] CCA 1974 s.9(1); RAO art.60L (and see art.61(3)(c) in relation to mortgages). See CCA 1974 Sch.2 Pt II Examples 16, 19, 21. This wide definition of "credit" is also adopted in numerous other statutory provisions, e.g. the Consumer Protection (Distance Selling) Regulations 2000 (SI 2000/2334) reg.3(1); the Financial Services (Distance Marketing) Regulations 2004 (SI 2004/2095) reg.2(1).

[97] See CCA 1974 Sch.2 Pt II Example 16.

[98] But see below, para.39-488.

[99] See *Storlink UK v Thomas* [1996] C.L.Y. 1225, Cty Ct; *Dimond v Lovell* [2000] 1 Q.B. 261, affirmed [2002] 1 A.C. 384. Contrast *Legal and General Assurance Soc v Cooper* [1994] C.L.Y. 2656, Cty Ct (advance of monies against future commission did not constitute the provision of "credit"); *Tilby v Perfect Pizza Ltd* (2002) N.L.J. 397, [2003] C.C.L.R. 9 (ATE insurance premium payable only when risk arose did not involve "credit"); *Nejad v City Index Ltd* [2000] C.C.L.R. 7 (so-called "credit allocation" in betting context not "credit" as indebtedness would not necessarily arise); *McMillan Williams v Range* [2004] EWCA 294, [2004] 1 W.L.R. 1858 (no "credit" where unclear at the outset if indebtedness would arise); *Maple Leaf Macro Volatility Master Fund v Rouvroy* [2009] EWHC 257, [2009] C.C.L.R. 9 (no "credit" in funding agreement where no certainty that obligations to pay under the agreement would arise); *OFT v Ashbourne Management Services Ltd* [2011] EWHC 1237 (Ch) (monthly payment for gym membership did not give rise to "credit"); *Burrell v Helical (Bramshott Place) Ltd* [2015] EWHC 3727 (Ch) (no deferment of any obligation to pay hence no "credit").

[100] By virtue of the RAO art.60F (previously CCA 1974 s.16(5) and the Exempt Agreements Order (SI 1989/869) art.3, made thereunder) the following (inter alia) are "exempt agreements" (see below, paras 39-038 et seq.): (i) certain "borrower-lender-supplier" agreements (see below, para.39-030) for fixed-sum credit (see below, para.39-026) where the number of payments to be made by the borrower does not exceed 12 (previously four) if those payments are required to be made within a period of 12 months (or less) beginning with the date of the agreement and (ii) certain "borrower-lender-supplier" agreements (see below, para.39-030) for running-account credit (see below, para.39-024) where the number of payments to be made by the borrower in repayment of the whole credit per period of not more than three months does not exceed one. In both cases (as a result of the Consumer Credit Directive (see above, para.39-011)) there must be no charge for the credit. Further, by virtue of the RAO art.60G, certain "borrower-lender" agreements (see below, para.39-033) at low rates of charge are exempt.

[100a] *CFL Finance Ltd v Bass* [2019] EWHC 1839 (Ch), approved by Marcus Smith J. in *Gertner v CFL Finance Ltd* [2020] EWHC 1241 (Ch). Cf. *Holyoake v Candy* [2017] EWHC 3397 (Ch) (which concerned the settlement of credit agreements).

### The Consumer Credit Directive: "credit exceeding £60,260"

*Replace footnote 114 with:*

**39-022** [114] When the Mortgage Credit Directive (see above, para.39-003) was implemented on March 21, 2016, so-called "residential renovation agreements" (as defined in CCA 1974 s.189(1) to mean, essentially, unsecured loans to renovate residential property) above this threshold became subject to the "new" (consumer credit) directive regime: see amendments made by SI 2015/910 art.3 and Sch.1 paras 3, 11, 13, 14. See also the amendments made by (a) SI 2016/392 and (b) (after Brexit, removing the reference to the Directive) SI 2019/632.

### Exempt land mortgages

*Replace paragraph with:*

**39-039** There are essentially three main types of exempt agreements where the credit is secured on land.[218] The first[219] is a credit agreement that is a "regulated mortgage contract" (or "regulated home purchase plan"), both as defined in the RAO.[220] The effect of this exemption is to remove from the control of the 1974 Act[221] the majority of land mortgages (as well as "regulated home purchase plans") where the borrower is an individual, the loan is secured by a mortgage on land in the EEA and at least 40 per cent of that land is used as a dwelling house by the borrower or his family. The reason for this exemption from the Consumer Credit Act 1974 regime is that such agreements are regulated under the Financial Services and Markets Act 2000. Secondly,[222] certain types of credit agreements[223] secured by a land mortgage[224] where the lender is either a local authority or a lender specified by the FCA in its rules and falling within various categories,[225] also constitute exempt agreements. The list of institutions that may be so "specified" (and hence whose land mortgages of a specified description may be "exempt agreements") includes banks, building societies, insurers, friendly societies, organisations of employers or workers, charities and land improvement companies.[226] The third main type of exempt land mortgage[227] is a consumer credit agreement secured by a land mortgage of a dwelling where the lender is a housing authority.[228]

[218] See also (i) below, para.39-040 and (ii) the exemption for "borrower-lender-supplier" agreements secured on land and financing the purchase of land where the number of payments is 12 (previously four) or less in RAO art.60F(4), referred to below in para.39-041.

[219] RAO art.60C(2). When the Mortgage Credit Directive (see above, para.39-003) was implemented on March 21, 2016 this exemption was extended to all (not just first charge) residential mortgages: see amendment to art.60C(2) in SI 2015/910 art.3 and Sch.1 para.4(13) and the amendment to the definition of "regulated mortgage contract" in art.61 by SI 2015/910 art.3 and Sch.1 para.4(21).

[220] RAO arts 61(3) (as amended by SI 2015/910 art.3 and Sch.1 para.4(21)) and 63F (added by the Financial Services and Markets Act 2000 (Regulated Activities) (Amendment No.2) Order 2006 (SI 2006/2383)), respectively. This exemption was previously in CCA 1974 s.16(6C)–(6E), added on October 31, 2004 by the Financial Services and Markets Act 2000 (Regulated Activities) Order 2001 (SI 2001/544) art.90(2) and amended (to add the reference to "regulated home purchase plan") on April 6, 2007 by the Financial Services and Markets Act 2000 (Regulated Activities) (Amendment No.2) Order 2006 (SI 2006/2383) art.25(2). This category now (since the implementation on March 21, 2016 of the Mortgage Credit Directive (see above, para.39-003): see below, para.39-531) covers most residential mortgages.

[221] As noted above, para.39-038, whilst the "unfair relationship" provisions in CCA 1974 ss.140A–140C generally apply to "exempt agreements", those provisions do not apply to these two categories of exempt agreements (see s.140A(5)). However CCA 1974 s.126 (as substituted by 2013/1881 art.20(38), as amended by SI 2014/506) applies to preclude enforcement of a land mortgage securing a "regulated mortgage contract" (but not a "home purchase plan") without a court order: s.126(1)(b).

[222] RAO art.60E(1)–(4). This exemption was previously in CCA 1974 s.16(1), (2), as amended. Note that since March 21, 2016 this exemption does not apply in so far as it is not permitted by the Mortgage Credit Directive (see above, para.39-003): see new RAO art.60HA, added by SI 2015/910 art.3 and Sch.1 para.4(19) and amended by SI 2019/632.

[223] A "relevant credit agreement relating to the purchase of land" as precisely defined in RAO art.60E(7) (and see art.60E(8)–(10)).

[224] "legal or equitable mortgage secured on land" as defined in RAO art.60L(1).

[225] Those specified in RAO art.60E(3). Under the old CCA 1974 provisions, the institutions (and the relevant agreements) were specified by the Exempt Agreements Order 1989 (SI 1989/869) (as extensively amended).

[226] The list also includes bodies corporate "named or specifically referred to in any public general Act" and bodies corporate "named or specifically referred to in an order" made under "a relevant housing provision" (as defined in RAO art.60E(7)).

[227] RAO art.60E(5). Note that since March 21, 2016 this exemption does not apply in so far as it is not permitted by the Mortgage Credit Directive (see above, para.39-003): see new RAO art.60HA added by SI 2015/910 art.3 and Sch.1 para.4(19) and amended by SI 2019/632.

[228] "Housing authority" is defined in RAO art.60E(7). This exemption was previously in CCA 1974 s.16(6A), (6B) inserted by the Housing and Planning Act 1986 s.22.

## "Investment mortgages" exemption

*Replace footnote 231 with:*

[231] RAO art.60D (previously CCA 1974 s.16C, added on October 1, 2008 by the Legislative Reform (Consumer Credit) Order 2008 (SI 2008/2826), as amended by the Financial Services and Markets Act 2000 (Amendment) (EU Exit) Regulations 2019 (SI 2019/632); see the transitional provisions (ensuring that the financial limit was not removed for these agreements until the exemption came into force) in SI 2008/831 art.3(1) and Sch.2). As is the case in all other exempted land mortgages (except for those exempted by RAO art.60C(2)), the "unfair relationship" provisions in ss.140A–140C (see below, paras 39-212 et seq.) apply. And CCA 1974 s.126 also applies to art.60D mortgages: CCA 1974 s.126(2). **39-040**

### Exempt credit agreements: number of payments

*Replace footnote 243 with:*

**39-041** [243] RAO art.60F(4). Note that since March 21, 2016 this exemption does not apply in so far as it is not permitted by the Mortgage Credit Directive (see above, para.39-003): see new RAO art.60HA, added by SI 2015/910 art.3 and Sch.1 para.4(19) and amended by SI 2019/632. There are also special exemptions for the financing of insurance premium exemptions in RAO art.60F(5) and (6).

### Exempt credit agreements: low-cost of credit

*Replace footnote 245 with:*

**39-042** [245] RAO art.60G. It essentially re-enacts, *but with some changes*, (the now revoked) Consumer Credit (Exempt Agreements) Order 1989 (SI 1989/869) art.4, made under (the now repealed) CCA 1974 s.16(5)(b). Art.4 was substantially amended as a result of the implementation of the Consumer Credit Directive (above, para.39-011). Note the amendments made to art.60G when (i) the Mortgage Credit Directive (see above, para.39-003) was implemented on March 21, 2016 (to render it compatible with the Directive) by SI 2015/910 art.3 and Sch.1 para.4(17) and (ii) Brexit occurred, by SI 2019/632.

### Exempt credit agreements: other categories

*Replace footnote 248 with:*

**39-043** [248] RAO art.60C(8), as amended by the Financial Services and Markets Act 2000 (Amendment) (EU Exit) Regulations 2019 (SI 2019/632). It essentially re-enacts, *but with some changes*, (the now revoked) Consumer Credit (Exempt Agreements) Order 1989 (SI 1989/869) art.5, made under (the now repealed) CCA 1974 s.16(5)(c). Some ordinary foreign trade transactions would otherwise be caught.

### High net worth (HNW) "opt-out" exemption

*Replace paragraph with:*

**39-045** There is an exemption for certain credit and consumer hire agreements made with "high net worth" (HNW) borrowers or hirers.[252] Four conditions need to be satisfied: (a) the borrower or hirer must be an "individual"[253]; (b) the agreement itself must include a prescribed signed "declaration"[254] that the borrower or hirer agrees to forgo the "protection and remedies" applicable to regulated agreements[255]; (c) a "statement of high net worth",[256] must have been made[257] in relation to the borrower or hirer; and (d) this statement of high net worth must have been made during the year ending with the date of the agreement. However, as this exemption is incompatible with the Consumer Credit Directive,[258] it is only available for agreements outside the scope of the Directive: credit agreements secured on land,[259] agreements where credit in excess of £60,260 is provided[260] and hire agreements.

[252] RAO art.60H (credit) (as amended by the Financial Services and Markets Act 2000 (Amendment) (EU Exit) Regulations 2019 (SI 2019/632)) and art.60Q (hire) (previously CCA 1974 s.16A, added by the Consumer Credit Act 2006 s.3). The exemption mirrors the one for "certified sophisticated investors" in relation to financial promotion under the Financial Services and Markets Act 2000 (Financial Promotion) Order 2005 (SI 2005/1529) art.50.

[253] i.e. a natural person and not a partnership or unincorporated association (or corporation, although these cannot make regulated agreements anyway). See above, para.39-016.

[254] Complying with the relevant FCA rules (see the *FCA Handbook*, CONC App 1.4.6) (previously the (now repealed) Consumer Credit (Exempt Agreements) Order 2007 (SI 2007/1168) art.3 and Sch.1).

[255] Although (see above, para.39-038) the "unfair relationship" provisions in ss.140A–140C (below, paras 39-212 et seq.) apply and the declaration must say so.

[256] Again complying with the relevant FCA rules (see *FCA Handbook*, CONC App 1.4.6) (previously the (now repealed) Consumer Credit (Exempt Agreements) Order 2007 (SI 2007/1168) art.5 and Sch.2).

[257] It must be made by a person of a description "specified" by the FCA rules (and hence not by the borrower or hirer themselves) and must state that, in that person's opinion, the borrower or hirer either has

an income or has net assets above a certain (specified by the rules) amount (presently net annual income after tax of above £150,000) or net assets (which are defined to exclude the primary residence and pension rights) of at least £500,000. A copy of this statement must be provided to the lender or owner before the agreement is made.

258 See above, para.39-011.

259 To render it compatible with the Mortgage Credit Directive (see above, para.39-003) art.60H was amended when that Directive was implemented on March 21, 2016: see (i) new RAO art.60HA, added by SI 2015/910 art.3 and Sch.1 para.4(19) and (ii) amendment made by SI 2015/910 art.3 and Sch.1 para.4(18). See also the "Brexit" amendment in the Financial Services and Markets Act 2000 (Amendment) (EU Exit) Regulations 2019 (SI 2019/632).

260 See RAO art.60H(b) (and above, para.3-022). But when the Mortgage Credit Directive (see above, para.39-003) was implemented on March 21, 2016, the credit exceeding £60,260 could not be for the purpose of (a) the renovation of residential property or (b) acquiring or retaining property rights in land or buildings: see amendments to art.60H in SI 2015/910 art.3 and Sch.1 para.4(18). But agreements within (b) are in any event outside the 1974 regime: see amendment to s.8(3) in SI 2015/910 art.3 and Sch.1 para.2(2)).

## "Business purpose" exemption

*Replace footnote 262 with:*

262 RAO art.60C(3)–(7) (credit) and RAO art.60O (hire) (previously CCA 1974 s.16B, added by the Consumer Credit Act 2006 s.4). As noted above, paras 39-016 and 39-035, in general, "business" credit and hire is within the scope of the regulatory regime. The old CCA 1974 provision was unsuccessfully invoked in *Bassano v Alfred Toft, Peter Biddulph, Peter Biddulph Ltd, Borro Loan Ltd, Borro Loan 2 Ltd* [2014] EWHC 377 (QB), [2014] C.C.L.R. 8. See also, on RAO art.60C(3)–(7), *Newmafruit Farms Ltd v Pither* [2016] EWHC 2205 (QB), [2017] C.C.L.R. 8 and *Brooker v Advanced Industrial Technology Corp Ltd* [2019] EWHC 3160 (Ch). See also the new art.60C(4A)–(4C) added by the Financial Services and Markets Act 2000 (Regulated Activities) (Coronavirus) (Amendment) Order 2020 (SI 2020/480), exempting business loans of £25,000 or less under the coronavirus Bounce Back Loan Scheme ("the BBLS") operated by the British Business Bank Plc. 39-046

## "Non-commercial agreement"

*Replace footnote 289 with:*

289 CCA 1974 s.189(1). The CCA 1974 does not make provision in s.171 as to the onus of proof, but it would seem that the burden lies on the person alleging the agreement to be a non-commercial agreement. In *Khodari v Tamimi* [2009] EWCA Civ 1109, [2010] C.C.L.R. 3 a series of large loans over six years in a private context by a banker "to foster the relationship with an important client" at gambling clubs were held not to have been made "in the course of business" and hence to be "non-commercial" loans. For another example of a non-commercial agreement, see *Bassano v Alfred Toft, Peter Biddulph, Peter Biddulph Ltd, Borro Loan Ltd, Borro Loan 2 Ltd* [2014] EWHC 377 (QB), [2014] C.C.L.R. 8. See also *Woolsey v Payne* [2015] EWHC 968 (Ch) and *GML International v Harfield* [2020] EWHC 909 (QB). 39-049

## "Multiple agreement"

*Replace paragraph with:*

Section 18 of the 1974 Act,[289a] which is primarily an anti-avoidance provision,[290] defines the expression "multiple agreement". Of all the sections in the Act it is this section which has given rise in practice to the greatest difficulty of interpretation.[291] Subsections (1), (2) and (3) appear to envisage four situations. First, where the terms of the agreement are such as to place a *part* of it within one category of agreement mentioned in the Act and another *part* of it within a category not so mentioned (for example, a "save and loan" agreement where the loan part is a consumer credit agreement and the savings part falls outside the Act).[292] Secondly, where the terms of the agreement are such as to place a *part* of it within one category of agreement mentioned in the Act, and another *part* of it within a different category of agreement so mentioned.[293] Thirdly, where the terms of the agreement are such as to place a *part* of it within two or more categories of agreement 39-050 mentioned in the Act, the other part or parts falling outside the Act, or within one category, or likewise within two or more categories.[294] Fourthly, where the agreement is a "single" or *unitary* agreement, not in parts, and the terms of the agreement are such as to place it within two or more categories of agreement mentioned in the Act.[295] In all four situations, there is a "multiple agreement". But where *part* of an agreement falls within the first three situations mentioned above, that part is to be treated for the purposes of the Act as a *separate agreement*, and the Act applies to it accordingly.[296] However, in the fourth situation, the agreement is to be treated as an agreement in each of the categories in question, and the Act applies to it accordingly,[297] but it is not split into separate agreements.[298]

[289a] The FCA's *Review of retained provisions of the Consumer Credit Act: Final Report* (see para.39-004, n.14, above) states (see Annex 5, para.39) that s.18 should be retained in legislation, as an FCA rule could not replicate its provisions. However, it is noted that "it could benefit from simplification and clarification, particularly in relation to its scope and effect". The Review also notes that the impact of s.18 will be reduced in so far as information requirements and other CCA provisions are repealed and replaced by FCA rules in CONC.

[290] See Auld L.J. in *National Westminster Bank Plc v Story* [1999] C.C.L.R. 70, CA. See also the FCA's *Review of retained provisions of the Consumer Credit Act: Final Report* (see para.39-004, n.14, above). Annex 5, para.34 thereof notes that the rationale for s.18 is twofold: (a) anti-avoidance: to ensure that the CCA is not avoided by artificially combining distinct agreements in order the exceed the regulatory limit of £25,000 for business lending (see above, para.39-046) and (b) to determine how multiple agreements are to be treated (especially documented): the agreement must comply with the statutory requirements for *each* category and not merely those that apply to the predominant category.

[291] See Guest and Lloyd, *Encyclopedia of Consumer Credit Law* (1975, looseleaf) at para.2-019; Goode, *Consumer Credit: Law and Practice* (looseleaf), Pt C, paras 25.101 et seq. The reform of s.18 was considered in the review that lead to the Consumer Credit Act 2006 (see the DTI Consultation Document, *Tackling loan sharks—and more!* (July 2002)) but as the impact of s.18 was diminished both by the repeal of s.127(3)–(4) and the removal of the financial limit, no proposals for reform were forthcoming. The Home Credit Market Investigation Order 2007 (made by the Competition Commission under the Enterprise Act 2002 ss.161 and 164 and amended in 2011) art.9 is in almost identical terms to s.18. For appellate case-law see *National Westminster Bank Plc v Story* [1999] C.C.L.R. 70 and *Southern Pacific Mortgage Ltd v Heath* [2010] EWCA Civ 1135, [2010] C.C.L.R. 4 (followed by Horner J in *Swift Advances Plc v Scott* [2018] NICh 28). See also: *National Home Loans Corp Plc v Hannah* [1997] C.C.L.R. 7, Cty Ct; *Wilson v First County Trust Ltd (No.1)* [2003] C.C.L.R. 1; *Ocwen v Coxall* [2004] C.C.L.R. 7; *London North Securities Ltd v Meadows* [2005] EWCA Civ 956, [2005] C.C.L.R. 7. For cases where s.18 was held inapplicable, see *Dimond v Lovell* [2002] 1 A.C. 384; *Burdis v Livsey* [2002] EWCA Civ 510, [2003] Q.B. 36; *Goshawk Dedicated (No.2) Ltd v Bank of Scotland* [2005] EWHC 2908 (Ch), [2006] C.C.L.R. 1.

[292] CCA 1974 s.18(1)(a) and Sch.2 Example 18. But see s.18(6) (exemption for furnished lettings). cf. *National Home Loans Corp Plc v Hannah* [1997] C.C.L.R. 7, Cty Ct.

[293] CCA 1974 s.18(1)(a) and Sch.2 Example 16 (but Example 16, in suggesting that an agreement could fall within both s.18(1)(a) and 18(1)(b), was regarded as erroneous by Lloyd L.J. in *Southern Pacific Mortgage Ltd v Heath* [2009] EWCA Civ 1135).

[294] CCA 1974 s.18(1)(b).

[295] CCA 1974 s.18(1)(b). For an example, see *Southern Pacific Mortgage Ltd v Heath* [2010] EWCA Civ 1135, [2010] C.C.L.R. 4: (obiter) credit card agreements and (ratio) the loan agreement in that case, were "single" (or unitary) agreement within s.18(1)(b).

[296] CCA 1974 s.18(2). Where part of an agreement falls within the third situation, the agreement (i.e. the separate agreement constituted by subs.(2)) is also to be treated as an agreement in each of the categories in question, and the Act applies to it accordingly (s.18(3)). See also s.18(4) (construction and apportionment).

[297] CCA 1974 s.18(3).

[298] The opening words of subs.(2) make it clear that the subsection is applicable only where *part* of an agreement falls within subs.(1) and see *Southern Pacific Mortgage Ltd v Heath* [2010] EWCA Civ 1135, [2010] C.C.L.R. 4.

## (b) Authorisation of Credit and Hire Businesses

### Activities requiring FCA authorisation

*Replace footnote 381 with:*

[381] But note the exemptions for land mortgages, see above, para.39-038; below, para.39-529. Residential mortgages within RAO art.61 (so-called "regulated mortgage contracts") are not "regulated agreements" (see RAO art.60C(2)) and hence not "regulated agreements" for the purpose of the CCA 1974 regime; but they are regulated (as "regulated mortgage contracts") under the parallel FSMA 2000 regime. See below, para.39-529. **39-061**

### Authorisation and regulatory control

*Replace paragraph with:*

Authorisation under the FSMA 2000 brings with it all the regulatory control that the FCA may exercise under that Act over "authorised persons". Hence, as well as having to satisfy the conditions for obtaining and then maintaining "authorisation",[387] authorised persons are subject to the *FCA Handbook*, which has a special "Module" of rules[388] and guidance devoted to consumer credit: the CONC Module.[389] Moreover, the FCA has power to ban products[390] and control high-cost short-term lending.[391] Authorised persons are also subject to high level "Principles for Business",[391a] such as Principle 6 whereby "a firm must pay due regard to the interests of its customers and treat them fairly" (the so-called "TCF Principle"). Whilst a breach of a "rule" is generally actionable by "private persons" (as defined) suffering loss,[391b] breach of a Principle does not give rise to the same right. However the offending firm may be disciplined for breach of a Principle and the FCA may require it to pay compensation to parties who have been harmed. The FCA has extensive powers of monitoring "authorised persons"[392] and a wide variety of disciplinary powers ranging from varying, suspending or withdrawing authorisation[393] to the imposition of penalties[394] and requiring remedial action.[395] The FCA's disciplinary powers are subject to an appeal to the Upper Tribunal.[396] However, an authorised person that breaches the FCA rulebook is not subject to any criminal penalty[397] and their agreements are generally not impeachable on that ground alone.[398] Finally, the Financial Ombudsman Scheme ("FOS")[399] applies to disputes between authorised persons and their customers. FOS makes its determinations on the basis of what is "fair and reasonable" and it takes into account whether the firm has complied with the Principles,[400] and if it did not do so may order it to pay compensation to the consumer. **39-063**

[387] See FSMA 2000 Pt 4A. Note especially s.55B ("threshold conditions") and also the "control of business transfers" powers in FSMA 2000 Pt VII. On "threshold conditions" see *Lewis Alexander Ltd v FCA* [2019] UKUT 49 (TCC).

[388] Breach is generally actionable by "private persons" (as defined) suffering loss: FSMA 2000 s.138D, as noted below.

[389] For the FCA's rule-making powers, see FSMA 2000 Pt 9A.

[390] FSMA 2000 s.137D.

[391] FSMA 2000 s.137C. See further below, para.39-292.

[391a] See the "PRIN" Module of the FCA Handbook.

[391b] FSMA 2000 s.138D.

[392] See its far-reaching powers to obtain information in FSMA 2000 Pt XI.

[393] See FSMA 2000 ss.55J (variation or cancellation) and s.206A (suspension). Note also its power to impose requirements under ss.55L, 55N, 55O and prohibitions and restrictions under FSMA 2000 s.55P.

[394] See FSMA 2000 s.206. The FCA may also publicly censure: FSMA 2000 s.205.

[395] See FSMA 2000 s.384. The FCA may also apply to court for injunctions (s.380) or restitution orders (s.382).

[396] See FSMA 2000 s.55Z4 (for powers under Pt 4A) and ss.208(4), 384(6) (for other sanctions).

[397] See FSMA 2000 s.138E(1).

[398] See FSMA 2000 s.138E(2)—but there is an exception (s.138E(3)) for the special high cost credit rules under s.137C and the product intervention rules under s.137D.

[399] See FSMA 2000 Pt XVI.

[400] *R. (on the application of British Bankers Association) v Financial Services Authority* [2011] EWHC 999 (Admin). Its determinations may be at variance with the strict legal position: *R. (on the application of Heather Moor & Edgecomb Ltd) v Financial Ombudsman Service* [2008] EWCA Civ 642.

### Trading whilst unauthorised

*Replace footnote 402 with:*

**39-064** [402] FSMA 2000 s.23(1) and see *R. v Gopee* [2019] EWCA Crim 601 (appeals against convictions for undertaking an unlawful money lending business). Unlicensed trading was also a criminal offence under (the now repealed) CCA 1974 ss.39(1), 167 and Sch.1. See *R. v Linegar* [2009] EWCA Crim 648 (sentencing appeal).

### Trading "through" unauthorised persons

*Replace footnote 407 with:*

**39-065** [407] FSMA 2000 ss.27, 28A. See *Chickombe v FCA* [2018] UKUT 258 (TCC) concerning a Tribunal appeal under FSMA 2000 s.28B(3) in relation to agreements financing timeshare accommodation that had been brokered by an unauthorised broker and considered for enforcement under FSMA 2000 s.28A. This introduces a degree of "self-policing" into the authorisation regime. In other, non "credit-related activities", an application needs to be made to the *court* to uphold the agreements: s.28.

### FCA determinations to enforce agreements

*Replace footnote 409 with:*

**39-066** [409] FSMA 2000 s.28B. See *Chickombe v FCA* [2018] UKUT 258 (TCC).

## (c) Seeking Business

### Canvassing

*Replace footnote 429 with:*

**39-068** [429] CCA 1974 s.49. A Determination has been made by the Director General of Fair Trading under s.49(3) (the FCA now being the responsible authority), with respect to the exclusion of current accounts from s.49(1), (2). See Guest and Lloyd, *Encyclopedia of Consumer Credit Law* (1975, looseleaf) at para.4-4800. See also ss.153, 154 (below, para.39-252) and the FCA's guidance on ss.48 and 49 in CONC 3.10.3(3)–(7). The FCA's *Review of retained provisions of the Consumer Credit Act: Final Report* (see para.39-004, n.13, above) states (see Annex 7, para.64) that the FCA was not aware of any instance where the offences in this section had been prosecuted. However, whilst stating (para.7.97) that "the criminal offences in the CCA may no longer be necessary" it also notes (para.7.103) that "there may be arguments in favour of keeping the current offences in respect of canvassing ... this merits further consideration". For additional obligations imposed on such lenders, see the Home Credit Market Investigation Order 2007, as amended in 2011, made by the Competition Commission under the Enterprise Act 2002 ss.161, 164.

### Circulars to minors

*Replace paragraph with:*

**39-069** It is also an offence[430] for a person, with a view to financial gain, to send to a minor a document[430a] inviting him to borrow money, obtain goods on credit or hire, obtain services on credit, or apply for information or advice on borrowing money or otherwise obtaining credit, or hiring goods.[431]

[430] CCA 1974 s.167 and Sch.1.

[430a] It would seem that this term would cover emails and SMS texts but not telephone calls.

[431] CCA 1974 s.50. cf. *Alliance and Leicester Building Society v Leicestershire CC, The Times,* March 15, 1993. The FCA's *Review of retained provisions of the Consumer Credit Act: Final Report* (see para.39-004, n.13, above) states (see Annex 7, para.69) that the FCA was not aware of any instance where the offences under s.50 had been prosecuted. (However, see *Alliance and Leicester Building Society v Leicestershire CC,* noted above.) Moreover, nor was it "aware of evidence of the deliberate targeting of minors" (para.67). However, whilst stating (para.7.97) that "the criminal offences in the CCA may no longer be necessary" it also notes (para.7.103) that "there may be arguments in favour of keeping the current offences in respect of ... circulars to minors ... this merits further consideration". For a (now repealed) exemption from s.50 with respect to student loans, see the Education (Student Loans) Act 1990 Sch.2 para.3(A) (as amended).

## (d) Antecedent Negotiations

### "Antecedent negotiations"

*In line 1, after "by s.56(1)", add new footnote 435a:*

[435a] The FCA's *Review of retained provisions of the Consumer Credit Act: Final Report* (see para.39-004, n.13, above) states (see Annex 5, para.30) the FCA's view that s.56 should be retained in legislation as FCA rules could not replicate its provisions (especially subs.(2) if the deemed agent is not an authorised person). **39-071**

*Replace paragraph with:*

The first category of antecedent negotiations mentioned above is self-explanatory, and it is clear that it will embrace negotiations conducted by an employee or an agent of the creditor or owner. The second category covers negotiations conducted by, for example, a dealer in relation to goods to be sold by the dealer[443] to a financier and which are to be the subject of a hire-purchase, conditional sale or credit sale agreement between the financier and the debtor (the usual "tripartite" transaction). It is to be noted that this category relates only to negotiations in relation to *goods* and to the goods sold or proposed to be sold by the dealer to the financier.[444] The third category refers, for instance, to negotiations conducted by a supplier of goods or services who supplies them for money advanced by a financier to the debtor as a restricted-use loan[445] under pre-existing arrangements between the financier and the supplier. **39-072**

[443] See *Black Horse Ltd v Langford* [2007] EWHC 907, [2007] C.C.L.R. 5: s.56(1)(b) did not apply to a dealer who (although having the status of a "credit broker") sold the goods to an intermediary who then sold to the creditor in that the dealer was not the "credit broker" who sold the goods to the creditor. But note (i) the Law Commissions' Joint Report: *Consumer Redress for Misleading and Aggressive Practices* (March 2012), Cm.8323, Recommendation 51, recommending that s.56 should be "clarified" to cover dealers acting through intermediaries and (ii) the FCA's *Review of retained provisions of the Consumer Credit Act: Final Report* (see para.39-004, n.13, above), para.5.28, which notes the Law Commissions' recommendation and states that "it is unclear whether the legislation intended to make a distinction depending on whether a dealer sells goods directly to the creditor or via an intermediary".

[444] But see *UDT v Whitfield and First National Securities* [1987] C.C.L.R. 60, Cty Ct; and *Forthright Finance Ltd v Ingate* [1997] 4 All E.R. 99, CA (finance house held liable for dealer's failure to fulfil his undertaking to the debtor to discharge the outstanding balance on a vehicle traded-in by the debtor as part of a transaction to take a new vehicle on hire-purchase). Contrast *Powell v Lloyd's Bowmaker Ltd*, 1996 S.L.T. (Sh Ct) 117. In *Van Gordon v VWFS (UK) Ltd (t/a Audi Finance)* Unreported April 30, 2019, Nottingham Cty Ct, it was held that s.56(4) does not apply to subsequent negotiations concerning the repair of the goods (although, on the facts, the dealer was held to be the agent of the creditor at common law).

[445] See above, para.39-027; below, para.39-302. See *Scotland v British Credit Trust Ltd* [2014] EWCA Civ 790 (main loan, but not loan for PPI, was "restricted-use") (and see below).

### Negotiator as agent

*Replace footnote 450 with:*

39-075 [450] CCA 1974 s.56(2). See also below, para.39-302. Unlike CCA 1974 s.75(2), below, para.39-303, no express right of indemnity is conferred on the creditor against the negotiator but a right to contribution would arise under Civil Liability (Contribution) Act 1978 (confirmed obiter in *Scotland v British Credit Trust Ltd* [2014] EWCA Civ 790). For the relevance of s.56 in attributing activities of others to the creditor in the context of the "unfair relationship" provisions (below, para.39-222) see *Plevin v Paragon Personal Finance Ltd* [2013] EWCA Civ 1658 (point not considered on appeal [2014] UKSC 61) and *Scotland v British Credit Trust Ltd* [2014] EWCA Civ 790 (s.56(2) rendered activities of "negotiator" relevant). And see *Van Gordon v VWFS (UK) Ltd (t/a Audi Finance)* Unreported April 30, 2019, Nottingham Cty Ct (dealer not statutory agent (although was agent, on the facts, at common law) in relation to subsequent negotiations about repair of goods) and *Premium Credit Ltd v Primary Care Management Solutions Ltd* [2018] EWHC 3083 (Comm) (had the agreement been regulated and hence s.56(1)(c) applied, designated "agent" of borrower would have been deemed statutory agent of creditor).

## (e) The Agreement

### Pre-contract disclosure

*Replace paragraph with:*

39-076 Regulations may be made under s.55 of the 1974 Act,[456] requiring specified information to be disclosed in the prescribed manner to the debtor or hirer before a regulated agreement is made.[457] In *Madison CF UK (t/a 118118 Money) v Various Defendants*,[457a] Hildyard J. opined that "the purpose … is to enable customers to compare credit offerings across different providers by the provision of information in a standard format". Failure to comply with the regulations made under s.55 renders the agreement enforceable against the debtor or hirer on an order of the court only.[458] In consequence of the implementation of the Consumer Credit Directive[459] there are now two sets of "Disclosure" regulations in relation to regulated credit (but not hire) agreements: the Consumer Credit (Disclosure of Information) Regulations 2004[460] and (in implementation of the Directive) the Consumer Credit (Disclosure of Information) Regulations 2010.[461] The 2004 Regulations now only apply to agreements outside the scope of the Directive, unless the creditor is able to and has opted into the "Directive" regime.[462] Hence the 2004 Regulations (as well as still applying to regulated hire agreements) only apply to: (a) credit agreements secured on land (except to those to which s.58,[463] applies); (b) agreements for credit in excess of £60,260[464]; (c) "business" credit agreements; and (d) "small" debtor-creditor-supplier agreements for restricted use.[465] The 2010 "Directive" Regulations essentially apply to other regulated credit agreements. They require the pre-contract information to be provided in the exact format set out in the Standard European Consumer Credit Information (SECCI) sheet at Annex 1 of the Directive, reproduced in Sch.1 to the 2010 Regulations. Although the requirements in the two sets of regulation are similar, there are some significant differences.[465a]

[456] s.55 does not apply to the types of agreement listed in CCA 1974 s.74(1)(a) (non-commercial agreement, see above, para.39-049), in s.74(1)(b) ("authorised business overdraft agreements") and in s.82(4) (variation). And note the further exclusions, in relation to each set of regulations mentioned in the text.

[457] See CCA 1974 s.189B(3), Sch.2A: in s.55, references to "debtor" in relation to "green deal plans" (as defined in CCA 1974 s.189(1), see below, para.39-257) are to be read as references to the "improver", as defined in CCA 1974 s.189B(6). Note also CCA 1974 s.55C (copy of draft credit agreement available on request), below, para.39-079.

[457a] [2018] EWHC 2786 (Ch), [7].

[458] CCA 1974 s.55(2), as substituted by SI 2010/1010 reg.16. This only applies to the 2004 Regulations (see text) as only these are made under s.55. The 2010 Regulations (see text) are made under the European Communities Act 1972.

[459] See above, para.39-011.

[460] SI 2004/1481.

[461] SI 2010/1013, as amended by SI 2010/1969 regs 31–40 and SI 2011/11 reg.8.

[462] See SI 2004/1483 reg.2, as amended by SI 2010/1010 reg.75 and SI 2010/1969 reg.24. Opt-in is not possible for hire agreements. The Regulations also exclude (a) agreements within CCA 1974 s.58 (as an "advance copy" is provided under that section, see below, para.39-535) and (b) "distance contracts", as defined in the Financial Services (Distance Marketing) Regulations 2004 SI 2004/2095 (as (usually, if the contract is made with a "consumer") those regulations will apply, see below, para.39-126).

[463] See previous note, above and (for s.58) below, para.39-535.

[464] When the Mortgage Credit Directive (see above, para.39-003) was implemented on March 21, 2016, they now also apply to so-called "residential renovation agreements" (as defined in CCA 1974 s.189(1) to mean, essentially, unsecured loans to renovate residential property) above this threshold: see amendments made by SI 2015/910 art.3 and Sch.1 paras 11, 13.

[465] See above, para.39-048.

[465a] e.g. the 2004 Regulations do not prescribe any particular format or the order of presentation of the information or the form of wording. In the 2010 Regulations there is a "lighter" disclosure regime for arranged overdrafts and there are different requirements for distance and telephone contracts. The FCA's *Review of retained provisions of the Consumer Credit Act: Final Report* (see para.39-004, n.13, above) states at para.6.31 that the obligation to provide information in s.55 could be replaced by a corresponding FCA rule but that breach of such a rule would not carry the same sanction and hence the existing sanction should be retained in legislation.

## Assessment of creditworthiness

*Replace footnote 472 with:*

[472] See above, para.39-011. See *Schyns v Belfius Banque SA* (C-58/18) (on the Consumer Credit Directive's art.5(6) obligation to explain pre-contractual information and the extent to which it requires a credit assessment of the debtor). See also *OPR-Finance SRO v GK* (C-679/18) EU:C:2020:167 (CJEU case on the appropriate approach to assessing remediation for breach by a creditor of the duty to assess creditworthiness). **39-078**

## Copy of draft agreement

*Replace footnote 480 with:*

[480] Added on February 1, 2011 by SI 2010/1010 reg.6 (not repealed and replaced by rules in FCA Handbook, CONC). See CCA 1974 s.189B(3), Sch.2A: in CCA 1974 s.55C, references to "debtor" in relation to "green deal plans" (as defined in CCA 1974 s.189(1), see below, para.39-257) are to be read as references to the "improver"/"first bill payer", as defined in CCA 1974 s.189B(6). The FCA's *Review of retained provisions of the Consumer Credit Act: Final Report* (see para.39-004, n.14, above) states (see para.5.26 and Annex 5, para.13) that s.55C could be repealed and replaced by an FCA rule imposing a corresponding obligation, without adversely affecting the appropriate degree of consumer protection. The sanction for breach of an FCA rule (private a right of action for damages under FSMA 2000 s.138D) would be equivalent to the breach of statutory duty action under s.55C(3). However the FCA adds (see para.6.26 and Annex 5, para.14) that repeal and replacement by an FCA rule, should other related provisions remain in the CCA (for example ss.77–78, 79, below, para.39-128 et seq.), would result in an undue fragmentation of the regime and so such a step should be considered in that wider context. **39-079**

## Form and content of agreement: general

*To the end of paragraph, after "regulated credit agreements.", add:*

There are significant differences between the requirements of the two sets of regulations as to content, format (the 1983 Regulations prescribe various "sub-headings" and preclude interspersion of information) and forms of wording.[493a] **39-080**

[493a] The FCA's *Review of retained provisions of the Consumer Credit Act: Final Report* (see para.39-004, n.13, above) states (see para.6.31) that the obligation to provide information in s.60 could be replaced by a corresponding FCA rule but that breach of such an FCA rule would not carry the same sanction and hence the existing sanction should be retained in legislation. Moreover the Review states

that "there may be merit ... in aligning the requirements (subject to the CCD compliance) and providing firms with additional flexibility along the lines of the 2010 regulations" (see para.6.39).

*Replace footnote 505 with:*

## Signing of agreement[505]

39-083 [505] The Consumer Credit Directive (see above, para.39-011) does not require a signature but is without prejudice to national rules as to the validity of agreements. Hence, the CCA 1974 requirement for a signature has been retained. For a discussion of electronic contracting, see Philpott, "E-Commerce and Consumer Credit" (2001) 3 J.I.F.M. 131; and Guest and Lloyd, *Encyclopedia of Consumer Credit Law* (1975, looseleaf) at para.2-062. See also *Golden Ocean Group Ltd v Salgaocar Mining Industries PVT Ltd* [2012] 2 All E.R. (Comm) 978 at 932 (name typed in an email is a signature); *Bassano v Alfred Toft, Peter Biddulph, Peter Biddulph Ltd, Borro Loan Ltd, Borro Loan 2 Ltd* [2014] EWHC 377 (QB), [2014] C.C.L.R. 8 (clicking "I accept" which generated a PDF document with the debtor's typed name, fulfilled the "signature" requirement in CCA 1974 s.61(1)). The FCA's *Review of retained provisions of the Consumer Credit Act: Final Report* (see para.39-004, n.13, above) states (see para.5.23) that s.61 should be retained in legislation. However the Review does consider whether the signature requirement might be modified (see Annex 6, paras 146–162) and notes that the statutory obligation in s.61 could be replaced by a corresponding FCA rule but that breach of such a FCA rule would not carry the same sanction and hence the existing sanction should be retained in legislation. See also Annex 6 paras 158–162 containing some discussion of the problems with electronic signatures.

## Supply of copies: two regimes:

*Replace footnote 525 with:*

39-085 [525] Added on February 1, 2011 by SI 2010/1010 reg.8. See also CCA 1974 s.61B, added by SI 2010/1010 reg.9: special copy requirements for overdrafts. The FCA's *Review of retained provisions of the Consumer Credit Act: Final Report* (see para.39-004, n.13, above) states (see para.6.31) that the obligation in s.61A could be replaced by a corresponding FCA rule but that breach of such an FCA rule would not carry the same sanction and hence the existing sanction should be retained in legislation.

*To the end of title, add new footnote 536a:*

## Supply of copies: "old" ss.62–63 regime[536a]

39-088 [536a] The FCA's *Review of retained provisions of the Consumer Credit Act: Final Report* (see para.39-004, n.13, above) states (see para.6.31) that the obligations in ss.62 and 63 could be replaced by a corresponding FCA rule but that breach of such an FCA rule would not carry the same sanction and hence the existing sanction should be retained in legislation.

*To the end of title, add new footnote 558a:*

## Supply of copies: "Directive" s.61A regime[558a]

39-092 [558a] For the potential impact of the FCA's *Review of retained provisions of the Consumer Credit Act: Final Report* (see para.39-004, n.13, above), see para.39-085, above.

*Replace footnote 562 with:*

39-092 [562] CCA 1974 s.61B, added on February 1, 2011 by SI 2010/1010 reg.9. The FCA's *Review of retained provisions of the Consumer Credit Act: Final Report* (see para.39-004, n.13, above) states (see para.6.31) that the obligation in s.61B could be replaced by a corresponding FCA rule but that breach of such an FCA rule would not carry the same sanction and hence the existing sanction should be retained in legislation.

## Failure to comply

*Replace footnote 571 with:*

39-094 [571] CCA 1974 s.127(1); below, para.39-200. For refusals to enforce, see *PB Leasing Ltd v Patel and Patel (t/a Plankhouse Stores)* [1995] C.C.L.R. 82; *Smerdon v Ellis* [1997] C.L.Y. 960; *Re Dixon-Vincent* [1997] C.L.Y. 958; *Rendle v Hicks* [1998] C.L.Y 2504; *Barons Finance Ltd & Reddy Corp Ltd v Makanju* [2013] EWHC 153 (QB), [2013] C.C.L.R. 3; *Consolidated Finance Ltd v Collins* [2013] EWCA Civ 475. And see below as to the "irredeemably unenforceable" case-law. For enforcement orders made, see *National Guardian Mortgage Corp v Wilkes* [1993] C.C.L.R. 1 (but interest rate reduced);

*Rank Xerox v Hepple* [1993] C.C.L.R. 1 (but reduction of amount payable); *Hatfield v Hiscock* [1996] C.C.L.R. 68; *London North Securities Ltd v Meadows* [2005] EWCA Civ 956 (but PPP not payable); *Wilson v Hurstanger Ltd* [2007] EWCA Civ 299 (but some sums not payable). Note *Wells v Devani* [2019] UKSC 4, a case on the Estate Agents Act 1979 s.18(6), which is almost identical in terms to CCA 1974 s.127.

## (f) Withdrawal and Cancellation

*Replace footnote 589 with:* 39-095

[589] See Guest and Lloyd, *Encyclopedia of Consumer Credit Law* (1975, looseleaf), paras 2-058, 2-068—2-075; and Goode, *Consumer Credit: Law and Practice* (looseleaf), Pt C, Ch.31. The FCA's *Review of retained provisions of the Consumer Credit Act: Final Report* (see para.39-004, n.14, above) states (see Annex 5, paras 148–149) that the cancellation provisions should be retained in legislation because their repeal would adversely affect the appropriate degree of consumer protection. In particular, although the FCA has rule-making power to make cancellation rules (FSMA 2000 s.137B(3)), such rules could not replicate the full effect of s.66A (especially, subss.(7)(b) and (11)). However, the view is also expressed that "having two separate regimes for withdrawal [s.66A] and cancellation [ss.67–73] could potentially cause confusion ... because of the differences in the requirements and obligations under the two regimes'. Hence, the FCA continues: "there is a case to consider aligning the requirements (subject to EU law while it applies)" and this would "provide an opportunity to review the scope and application of the provisions".

### Agreement not to withdraw

*Replace footnote 609 with:*

[609] But see the exceptions in CCA 1974 ss.74(1) (see below, para.39-103) and 82(4) (variations). Under CCA 1974 s.59(2) and SI 1983/1552, certain types of agreement are excluded from s.59(1), namely, agreements to enter into prospective hire agreements and agreements to enter into prospective restricted-use agreements for fixed-sum credit, in both cases the goods being used for business purposes. See also *Lakin v Exe Haulage Ltd* [2006] C.L.Y. 705, Cty Ct: s.59 inapplicable to exempt agreement. The FCA's *Review of retained provisions of the Consumer Credit Act: Final Report* (see para.39-004, n.13, above) states (see Annex 5, para.23) that s.59 should be retained in legislation as an FCA rule could not replicate its provisions. 39-100

### 14-day "right of withdrawal"

*Replace footnote 610 with:*

[610] See above, para.39-011. See *JC v Kreissparkasse Saarlouis* (C-66/19) EU:C:2020:242 (CJEU case on when the 14-day right of withdrawal period under the CCD (and hence s.66A) begins to run). 39-101

*To the end of title, add new footnote 766a:*

### Package Travel and Linked Travel Arrangements Regulations 2018[766a]

[766a] These were amended by the Package Travel and Linked Travel Arrangements (Amendment) (EU Exit) Regulations 2018 (SI 2018/1367) as a result of Brexit, in exercise of the powers in the European Union (Withdrawal) Act 2018 s.8(1). 39-124

*Replace paragraph with:*

These regulations[767] confer upon a "traveller"[767a] under a "package travel contract", on payment of "an appropriate and justifiable termination fee" a right to terminate the contract at any time before the start of the package. But in the event of "unavoidable and extraordinary circumstances"[767b] at the place of destination or its immediate vicinity, which significantly affect (a) the performance of the package, or (b) the carriage of passengers to the destination, the traveller may terminate the contract before the start of the package without paying any termination fee and in such a case the traveller is entitled to a full refund of any payments made for the package (but not additional compensation). The definition of "traveller" in the regulations is not in any way linked to the conceptual framework of the 1974 Act and there is no exception in a case where an associated credit agreement is subject 39-124 to the right of withdrawal under s.66A of the 1974 Act or is a "cancellable" agreement under s.67 of the 1974 Act.

[767] SI 2018/634 (implementing Council Directive 2015/2302). See above, paras 38-132 et seq. See also Guest and Lloyd, *Encyclopedia of Consumer Credit Law* (1975, looseleaf) at para.2-068.

[767a] Defined in reg.2 as an "individual who is seeking to conclude a contract or is entitled to travel on the basis of a contract concluded" within the regulations.

[767b] As defined in reg.2, see previous note.

### Consumer Contracts (Information, Cancellation and Additional Charges) Regulations 2013

*Replace footnote 769 with:*

**39-125** [769] SI 2013/3134. For a fuller consideration, see above, paras 38-112 et seq. For case-law on the predecessor Cancellation of Contracts made in a Consumer's Home or Place of Work, etc. Regulations 2008 (SI 2008/1816), see *W v Veolia Environmental Services (UK) Plc* [2011] EWHC 2020 (hire contract unenforceable under those regulations as signed at home without the requisite notice); *Salat v Barutis* [2013] EWCA Civ 1499 (lack of cancellation notice in motorcycle hire agreement); *Allproperty Claims v Tang* [2015] EWHC 2198 (lack of notification of cancellation right rendered agreement unenforceable) and *RTA (Business Consultants) Ltd v Bracewell* [2015] EWHC 630 (QB) (meaning of "consumer").

## (g) Supply of Information

### Information to debtor under fixed-sum credit agreement on request

*Replace paragraph with:*

**39-128** Section 77 of the 1974 Act requires[793] the creditor under a regulated agreement for fixed-sum credit[794] (other than a non-commercial agreement[795]) to give[796] the debtor, on request, a copy of the executed agreement (if any)[797] and of any other document referred to in it,[798] together with a statement of the account between them.[799] In order to be valid the request must be in writing, and a fee of £1 must be paid.[800] The statement must be signed by or on behalf of the creditor and must show (according to the information to which it is practicable for him to refer):

(a) the total sum paid under the agreement by the debtor;
(b) the total sum which has become payable under the agreement by the debtor but remains unpaid, and the various amounts comprised in that total sum, with the date on which each became due; and
(c) the total sum which is to become payable under the agreement by the debtor and the various amounts comprised in that total sum, with the date or mode of determining the date, when each becomes due.[801]

If the creditor fails to comply within 12 working days[802] after receiving a request, he is not entitled, while the default continues, to enforce the agreement.[803]

[793] CCA 1974 s.77(1), except where relieved under s.77(2), below, or s.77(3) (no sums payable and repeated requests).

[794] Defined in CCA 1974 ss.10(1)(b), 189(1); above, para.39-026.

[795] Defined in CCA 1974 s.189(1); above, para.39-049. See CCA 1974 s.77(5).

[796] Defined in CCA 1974 s.189(1) (as amended by SI 2004/3236 art.2(2)) to mean "deliver or send by appropriate method".

[797] See above, para.39-084. See also CCA 1974 s.180.

[798] See above, para.39-090.

[799] See *NRAM Plc v McAdam & Hartley* [2015] EWCA Civ 751, reversing [2014] EWHC 4174 (Comm): (obiter) s.77 does not apply to non-regulated agreements that are documented as regulated

agreements. See also CCA 1974 s.189B(3), Sch.2A: in CCA 1974 s.77, references to "debtor" in relation to "green deal plans" (as defined in CCA 1974 s.189(1), see below, para.39-257) are to be read as references to the "current bill payer"/"previous bill payer" (as defined in CCA 1974 s.189B(6)). Note s.77A (para.39-129, below) which requires the creditor *automatically* to provide a statement of account annually. The FCA's *Review of retained provisions of the Consumer Credit Act: Final Report* (see para.39-004, n.13, above) states (see para.6.31) that the obligation to provide information in s.77 could be replaced by a corresponding FCA rule but that breach of such an FCA rule would not carry the same sanction and hence the existing sanction should be retained in legislation.

800 CCA 1974 s.77(1). The amount was raised from 15p to 50p by SI 1983/1571 and to £1 by SI 1998/997. See *Carey v HSBC Bank Plc* [2009] EWHC 3417 (QB) (on the similar CCA 1974 s.78 copy (below, para.39-132) requirement). See also the Guidance in the *FCA Handbook* CONC 13.

801 CCA 1974 s.77(1). But see s.77(2) (modification where creditor possesses insufficient information to comply with (c)). See also CCA 1974 s.172 (statement binding, below, para.39-138), and SI 1983/1557 reg.7. See also CCA 1974 s.86E(3) (if a "default sum" (see CCA 1974 s.187A and below, para.39-135) is payable, the statement may incorporate the notice of default sum required by s.86E) and CCA 1974 s.130A(5) (if post-judgment interest is payable, the statement may incorporate the notice required under s.130A(5)).

802 Prescribed by SI 1983/1569.

803 CCA 1974 s.77(4)(a). The court presently has no discretion to order enforcement (although this may change as a result of the implementation of the FCA's *Review of retained provisions of the Consumer Credit Act: Final Report* (see para.39-004, n.13, above), see para.39-129. See *McGuffick v Royal Bank of Scotland Plc* [2009] EWHC 2386, [2010] C.C.L.R. 2, on the meaning of "enforcement" (does not cover reporting default to credit reference agency) and for confirmation that the creditor's contractual rights are merely *unenforceable*, not extinguished. Section 77(4)(b) (an offence was committed after one month) was repealed by the Consumer Protection from Unfair Trading Regulations 2008 (SI 2008/1277) reg.30(1) and Sch.2 para.19.

## Annual information to debtor under fixed-sum credit agreement

*Replace footnote 804 with:*

804 Inserted by the Consumer Credit Act 2006 s.6 from October 1, 2008 (see SI 2007/3300 art.3(3)) but applicable to agreements whenever made. New subss.(1A)–(1E) were substituted and amendments to subss.(5) and (7) made on October 1, 2008 by SI 2008/2826. See also the new subs.(9) (inapplicable to unauthorised overdrawing on current account) inserted by SI 2010/1010 reg.23. See CCA 1974 s.189B(3), Sch.2A: in CCA 1974 s.77A, references to "debtor" in relation to "green deal plans" (as defined in CCA 1974 s.189(1), see below, para.39-257) are to be read as references to the "current bill payer" (as defined in CCA 1974 s.189B(6)). Note s.77 (para.39-128, above), which enables the debtor to request a statement of the account (together with a copy of the executed agreement etc.). The FCA's *Review of retained provisions of the Consumer Credit Act: Final Report* (see para.39-004, n.13, above) states (see para.6.31) that the obligation to provide information in s.77A could be replaced by a corresponding FCA rule but that breach of such an FCA rule would not carry the same sanction and hence the existing sanction should be retained in legislation. Moreover (see paras 7.91–7.92) it was suggested that the court be given power (similar to that in CCA 1974 s.127, see para.39-200, below) "to mitigate the risk of disproportionate outcomes". **39-129**

## Statement of account to debtor under fixed-sum credit agreement on request

*Replace footnote 816 with:*

816 Added on February 1, 2011 by SI 2010/1010 reg.26. The FCA's *Review of retained provisions of the Consumer Credit Act: Final Report* (see para.39-004, n.13, above) states (see para.5.24) that s.77B could be repealed and replaced by an FCA rule imposing a corresponding obligation without adversely affecting the appropriate degree of consumer protection. The sanction for breach of an FCA rule (private a right of action for damages under FSMA 2000 s.138D) would be equivalent to the breach of statutory duty action under s.77B(8). However the Review adds (see para.6.26) that repeal and replacement by an FCA rule, should other related provisions remain in the CCA 1974 (for example ss.77–79, below, para.39-128 et seq.), would result in undue fragmentation of the regime and so such a step should be considered in that wider context. **39-130**

## Notices of sums in arrears (NOSIAs): fixed-sum credit agreements

*Replace footnote 827 with:*

827 Added by the Consumer Credit Act 2006 s.9 and coming into force on October 1, 2008 (see SI 2007/ **39-131**

3300) but see the transitional provisions in the 2006 Act Sch.3 para.6. Section 86B was amended by SI 2008/2826 and to provide for "green deal plans" (see CCA 1974 s.189B) by the Energy Act 2011 and SI 2014/436. The FCA's *Review of retained provisions of the Consumer Credit Act: Final Report* (see para.39-004, n.13, above) states (see para.6.31) that the obligation to provide information in s.86B could be replaced by a corresponding FCA rule but that breach of such an FCA rule would not carry the same sanction and hence the existing sanction should be retained in legislation.

## Information to debtor under running-account credit agreement on request

*Replace footnote 839 with:*

39-132 [839] It was amended by SI 2006/1508 and to provide for "green deal plans" (as defined in CCA 1974 s.189(1), see below, para.39-257) by the Energy Act 2011. See (i) *McGuffick v Royal Bank of Scotland Plc* [2009] EWHC 2386 (Comm), [2010] C.C.L.R. 2, above, para.39-128 (on the similar provision in CCA 1974 s.77) (ii) *Carey v HSBC Bank Plc* [2009] EWHC 3417 (QB) and *Phoenix Recoveries (UK) Ltd v Kotecha* [2011] EWCA Civ 105 (on the copy requirement under CCA 1974 s.78). See also FCA's Guidance in its Handbook CONC 13, replacing (in part) the OFT's *Guidance on ss.77, 78 and 79 of the Consumer Credit Act 1974* (OFT 1272 Oct 2010). The FCA's *Review of retained provisions of the Consumer Credit Act: Final Report* (see para.39-004, n.13, above) states (see para.6.31) that the obligation to provide information in s.78 could be replaced by a corresponding FCA rule but that breach of such an FCA rule would not carry the same sanction and hence the existing sanction should be retained in legislation.

39-133 *Change title of paragraph:*

## Automatic periodic information to debtor under running-account credit agreement

## Notices of sums in arrears (NOSIAs): running-account credit agreements

*Replace paragraph with:*

39-134 Further information needs to be given to a debtor under a regulated agreement for running-account credit[857] (other than a non-commercial[858] or small[859] agreement) if they fall in arrears. Section 86C[860] requires the creditor to give,[861] in the form and with the contents prescribed,[862] a "notice of sums in arrears" (a so-called "NOSIA") after the debtor becomes two payments in arrears.[863] This notice must be given at a time no later than the next periodic statement under s.78(4)[864] and may be incorporated in it.[865] The provisions of s.86C are otherwise similar to those of s.86B. The notice must be free of charge[866] and accompanied by[867] the "arrears information sheet" drafted by the FCA.[868] The debtor may make an application to court for a time order but only after giving a counter-notice (a "notice of intent") with a proposal for payment.[869] The creditor is not entitled during the period of non-compliance to enforce the agreement[870] and the debtor is not liable to pay any interest that relates to that period or any "default sum" that is incurred or becomes payable during that period.[871]

[857] Defined in CCA 1974 ss.10(1)(a), 189(1); above, para.39-024.

[858] Defined in CCA 1974 s.189(1); above, para.39-049. See CCA 1974 s.86C(7)(b).

[859] CCA 1974 s.17, above, para.39-048. See CCA 1974 s.86C(7)(b).

[860] Added to the CCA 1974 by the Consumer Credit Act 2006 s.10 and coming into force on October 1, 2008 (see SI 2007/3300) but see the transitional provisions in the 2006 Act Sch.3 para.7. Section 86C was amended by SI 2008/2826. The FCA's *Review of retained provisions of the Consumer Credit Act: Final Report* (see para.39-004, n.13, above) states (see para.6.31) that the obligation to provide information in s.86C could be replaced by a corresponding FCA rule but that breach of such an FCA rule would not carry the same sanction and hence the existing sanction should be retained in legislation.

[861] Defined in CCA 1974 s.189(1) (as amended by SI 2004/3236 art.2(2)) to mean "deliver or send by appropriate method".

[862] CCA 1974 s.86C(6) and see the Consumer Credit (Information Requirements and Duration of

Licences and Charges) Regulations 2007 (SI 2007/1167) regs 24–26 and Sch.3. See also s.86E(3) (if a "default sum" (see s.187A and below, para.39-135) is payable, the notice may incorporate the notice of default sum required by s.86E) and s.130A(5) (if post-judgment interest is payable, the notice may incorporate the notice required under s.130A(5)). Section 172 (statements binding, below, para.39-143) does *not* apply to s.86C notices.

[863] CCA 1974 s.86C(1), (2). Hence a debtor who repeatedly misses every second payment will not receive a NOSIA.

[864] See above, para.39-133.

[865] CCA 1974 s.86C(4).

[866] CCA 1974 s.86C(5). cf. statements under ss.77, 78, 79.

[867] CCA 1974 s.86C(3).

[868] CCA 1974 s.86A(1), (2) (added by the Consumer Credit Act 2006 s.8) requires the FCA to prepare and publish by General Notice such a sheet. It is available on the FCA website.

[869] CCA 1974 s.129(1)(ba), see below, para.39-202.

[870] CCA 1974 s.86D(2), (3), added by the Consumer Credit Act 2006 s.11.

[871] CCA 1974 s.86D(4), added by the Consumer Credit Act 2006 s.11. For "default sums", see below, para.39-135.

## Notice of default sum

*Replace footnote 873 with:*

[873] Added to the CCA 1974 by the Consumer Credit Act 2006 s.12 and coming into force on October 1, 2008 (see SI 2007/3300) but see the transitional provisions in the 2006 Act Sch.3 para.8 (applicable to agreements whenever made but only to default sums payable after October 1, 2008). See also CCA 1974 s.189B(3), Sch.2A: in s.86E, references to "debtor" in relation to "green deal plans" (as defined in s.189(1), see below, para.39-257) are to be read as references to the "current bill payer"/"previous bill payer" (as defined in s.189B(6)). The FCA's *Review of retained provisions of the Consumer Credit Act: Final Report* (see para.39-004, n.13, above) states (see para.6.31) that the obligation to provide information in s.86E could be replaced by a corresponding FCA rule but that breach of such an FCA rule would not carry the same sanction and hence the existing sanction should be retained in legislation. **39-135**

## Default sums: other provisions

*Replace footnote 887 with:*

[887] CCA 1974 s.86F(2). And see s.86E(4), above at para.39-135. See CCA 1974 s.189B(3), Sch.2A: in s.86F, references to "debtor" in relation to "green deal plans" (as defined in s.189(1), see below, para.39-257) are to be read as references to the "current bill payer"/"previous bill payer" (as defined in s.189B(6)). The FCA's *Review of retained provisions of the Consumer Credit Act: Final Report* (see para.39-004, n.13, above) states (see Annex 5, para.108) that s.86F should be retained in legislation as repeal would adversely affect the appropriate degree of consumer protection. Whilst an FCA rule could impose corresponding obligations, it could not automatically render void or invalid a term providing for compound interest on default sums; a challenge to such a term would require the debtor to take the initiative. **39-136**

## Information as to whereabouts of goods

*Replace footnote 911 with:*

[911] CCA 1974 ss.80(2), 167 and Sch.1. Although many of the criminal offences imposed by the CCA 1974 for breaches of notice requirements were repealed by the Consumer Protection from Unfair Trading Regulations 2008 (SI 2008/1277) reg.30(1) and Sch.2, this one (which exceptionally imposes criminal liability on the debtor or hirer) has been retained. See the FCA's *Review of retained provisions of the Consumer Credit Act: Final Report* (see para.39-004, n.13, above) which states (see para.7-97) that the FCA's general view is that "the criminal offences in the CCA may no longer be necessary". **39-140**

## Information as to settlement figure

*Replace footnote 917 with:*

[917] CCA 1974 s.97(1) (as amended by SI 2010/1010 reg.33). The prescribed form and particulars are **39-141**

set out in the Consumer Credit (Settlement Information) Regulations 1983 (SI 1983/1564, as amended by SI 2004/1483 and SI 2004/3236). The settlement figure has to take account of the contractual or statutory rebate on early settlement: see s.95 (below, para.39-158) and SI 2004/1483, as amended by SI 2004/2619; *Home Insulation v Wadsley* [1988] 10 C.L.Y. 419. See also s.172 (statements binding, below, para.39-143); and *Lombard North Central Plc v Stobart, The Times,* March 2, 1990, CA (estoppel of creditor at common law). See *NRAM Plc v McAdam & Hartley* [2015] EWCA Civ 751, reversing [2014] EWHC 4174 (Comm): (obiter) s.97 does not apply to non-regulated agreements that are documented as regulated agreements. See also CCA 1974 s.189B(3), Sch.2A: in s.97, references to "debtor" in relation to "green deal plans" (as defined in CCA 1974 s.189(1), see para.39-257) are to be read as references to the "improver"/"current bill payer" (as defined in CCA 1974 s.189B(6)). There is a similar obligation under CCA s.97A to provide a settlement figure after part-payment (see especially s.97A(2)(h), below, para.39-160). See the FCA's *Review of retained provisions of the Consumer Credit Act: Final Report* (see para.39-004, n.13, above) which notes (see para.6.31) that the obligation to provide a settlement statement in s.97 could be replaced by a corresponding FCA rule but that breach of such an FCA rule would not carry the same sanction and hence the existing sanction should be retained in legislation.

### Termination statement

*In line 1, after "Section 103", add new footnote 918a:*

39-142 [918a] See the FCA's *Review of retained provisions of the Consumer Credit Act: Final Report* (see para.39-004, n.13, above) which notes (see Annex 5, para.180) that s.103 could be replaced by an FCA rule (although s.172(2), para.39-143, below, would no longer apply) without adversely affecting the appropriate degree of consumer protection, especially as the sanction for breach of an FCA rule (action under FSMA 2000 s.138D) is similar to the breach of statutory duty sanction for breach of s.103.

## (h) Variation of Agreements

39-145 *Replace footnote 937 with:*

[937] See generally, Guest and Lloyd, *Encyclopedia of Consumer Credit Law* (1975, looseleaf), para.2-083; and Goode, *Consumer Credit: Law and Practice*, Pt C, Ch.35. See also the FCA's *Final Guidance: Fairness of variation terms in financial services consumer contracts under the Consumer Rights Act 2015* (FG18/7), December 2018.

*Replace footnote 946 with:*

### Unilateral variation under a power in agreement: the general rule[946]

39-146 [946] The more complex notice provisions imposed by the Payment Services Regulations 2017 (SI 2017/752) reg.50 in relation to agreements within their scope (as to which, see generally, above, paras 34-224 et seq.), has been disapplied in relation to CCA 1974-regulated agreements: see SI 2017/752 reg.41(2). The FCA's *Review of retained provisions of the Consumer Credit Act: Final Report* (see para.39-004, n.14, above) states (see Annex 5, para.71) that s.82(1) should be retained in legislation as repeal would adversely affect the appropriate degree of consumer protection. Whilst an FCA rule could impose equivalent obligations on creditors, it could not provide for equivalent consequences (in particular automatic invalidity); challenges to unfair variation terms under the Consumer Rights Act 2015 require applications to court by the debtor. However (see para.6.30) the Review notes that the information requirements in secondary legislation could be replaced by FCA rules.

### Mutual variation by subsequent agreement: "modifying agreement"

*Replace footnote 962 with:*

39-148 [962] See SI 2008/831 art.4: the removal of the financial limit by the Consumer Credit Act 2006 s.2(1) (see above, para.39-005) has no effect for the purposes of the application of s.82(2) where no fresh credit in the form of a "cash loan" is provided or where an *exempt* agreement varies or supplements an existing agreement. The former provision sought to ensure that the removal of the financial limit did not have the unintended consequence of bringing agreements that were originally exempt from regulation, into regulation as a result of a variation that did not increase the cash available. See *Santander UK Plc v Harrison* [2013] EWHC 199 (QB), [2013] C.C.L.R. 4 (noted above at para.39-019): SI 2008/831 art.4 inapplicable as, although new "credit" was provided, it was not in the form of a "cash loan". The FCA's *Review of retained provisions of the Consumer Credit Act: Final Report* (see para.39-004, n.13, above) states (see Annex 5, para.80-81) that s.82(2) should be retained in legislation as repeal would adversely affect the appropriate degree of consumer protection in so far as an FCA rule could not replicate the unenforceability sanction for non-compliant modifying agreements. On the other hand (see paras 6.31

and 6.43) it is stated that the obligation to provide information in s.82(2)–(6B) could be replaced by a corresponding FCA rule but that breach of such an FCA rule would not carry the same sanction and hence the existing sanction should be retained in legislation. The Review also suggests that the information requirements associated with modifying agreements should be repealed and replaced by FCA rules and that "there is a case to consider whether it would be possible to clarify and simplify the provisions whilst achieving the policy objectives".

## (i) Appropriation of Payments and Early Settlement

### Early settlement

*Replace footnote 1004 with:*

[1004] CCA 1974 s.94(1). See also CCA 1974 s.94(2) (notice may embody the exercise by the debtor of any option to purchase goods conferred by the agreement, etc.) and CCA 1974 s.97 (right to settlement statement, above, para.39-141). See CCA 1974 s.189B(3), Sch.2A: in s.94, references to "debtor" in relation to "green deal plans" (as defined in CCA 1974 s.189(1), see below, para.39-257) are to be read as references to the "improver"/"current bill payer" (as defined in CCA 1974 s.189B(6)). The FCA's *Review of retained provisions of the Consumer Credit Act: Final Report* (see para.39-004, n.13, above) states (see Annex 5, para.161) that the early settlement provisions should be retained in legislation as an FCA rule could not replicate elements of their provisions and hence repeal would adversely affect the appropriate degree of consumer protection. However, the suggestion is made to align the full and partial repayment provisions, to simplify aspects and to review the information provisions. **39-157**

## (j) Restrictions on Enforcement or Termination of Agreement

*Add new paragraph:*

**Covid-19: Temporary measures to alleviate repayment difficulties** The FCA has used its rule-making and guidance powers over authorised persons[1039a] to require creditors to take various steps to help customers experiencing short-term cash flow problems due to the Covid-19 pandemic.[1039b] These temporary measures apply to most forms of consumer credit, for example, personal loans,[1039c] high-cost short-term ("payday") loans,[1039d] credit cards,[1039e] overdrafts,[1039f] motor finance,[1039g] hire-purchase, leasing and pawn broking.[1039h] In particular the debtor may apply for a three month[1039i] "payment freeze"[1039j] (although interest will still accrue, except in the case of high-cost short-term loans) without prejudicing their credit rating. Special provision is also made for mortgages[1039k] (and insurance[1039l]). These temporary measures have not been seamlessly integrated into the consumer credit regime which itself has debtor-protection measures for debtors in financial trouble. For example, the FCA rules impose general obligations on creditors to exercise forbearance when debtors are in difficulties.[1039m] Moreover the provisions in the CCA that require warning notices to be given to debtors in various situations still apply.[1039n] **39-163A**

[1039a] See above, para.39-063. Principle for Business 6 ("TCF") is particularly relevant here. The measures are only to be applied if not prejudicial to the debtor.

[1039b] There is a useful summary at: *https://www.fca.org.uk/consumers/coronavirus-information-personal-loans-credit-cards-overdrafts*. For proposed more general "breathing space" measures for debtors in difficulties, see the draft Debt Respite Scheme (Breathing Space Moratorium and Mental Health Crisis Moratorium) (England and Wales) Regulations 2020.

[1039c] *https://www.fca.org.uk/publications/finalised-guidance/personal-loans-and-coronavirus-updated-temporary-guidance-firms.*

[1039d] *https://www.fca.org.uk/publications/finalised-guidance/high-cost-short-term-credit-agreements-and-coronavirus-updated-temporary-guidance-firms.*

[1039e] *https://www.fca.org.uk/publications/finalised-guidance/credit-cards-including-retail-revolving-credit-and-coronavirus-updated-temporary-guidance-firms.*

[1039f] *https://www.fca.org.uk/publications/finalised-guidance/overdrafts-and-coronavirus-updated-temporary-guidance-firms*. Customers are entitled £500 interest-free arranged overdraft for three months.

[1039g] *https://www.fca.org.uk/publications/finalised-guidance/motor-finance-agreements-and-coronavirus-updated-temporary-guidance-firms?utm_source=Expert+advice&utm_campaign=56161c44c4-EMAIL_CAMPAIGN_2020_07_16_03_19&utm_medium=email&utm_term=0_19bd99be06-56161c44c4-284331937&mc_cid=56161c44c4&mc_eid=26317a130b-and-coronavirus-updated-temporary-guidance-firms?utm_source=Expert+advice&utm_campaign=56161c44c4-EMAIL_CAMPAIGN_2020_07_16_03_19&utm_medium=email&utm_term=0_19bd99be06-56161c44c4-284331937&mc_cid=56161c44c4&mc_eid=26317a130b.*

[1039h] *https://www.fca.org.uk/publications/finalised-guidance/rent-own-buy-now-pay-later-and-pawnbroking-agreements-and-coronavirus-updated-temporary-guidance.*

[1039i] Presently extendable to six months.

[1039j] And if security is provided it cannot be enforced.

[1039k] *https://www.fca.org.uk/consumers/mortgages-coronavirus-consumers.*

[1039l] *https://www.fca.org.uk/consumers/insurance-and-coronavirus.*

[1039m] See the FCA Handbook (a) CONC Module, especially CONC 7 and (b) (in relation to regulated mortgages) MCOB Module, especially MCOB 13. See also the Standards of Lending Practice (financial difficulties sections), above, para.39-013.

[1039n] See below, paras 39-164 et seq. The "NOSIAs" (below, paras 39-131 and 39-124) are particularly confusing to debtors subject to the payment freeze.

## Enforcement notice (non-default cases)

*In line 5, after "give notice before taking certain action.", add new footnote 1039o:*

39-164 [1039o] The FCA's *Review of retained provisions of the Consumer Credit Act: Final Report* (see para.39-004, n.13, above) states (see Annex 5, para.88) that s.76 (together with ss.87 and 98) should be retained in legislation as repeal would adversely affect the appropriate degree of consumer protection in giving to consumer a chance to take action to preclude enforcement. Whilst an FCA rule could impose corresponding obligations on creditors, it could not reproduce the consequences of non-compliance. However, the Review notes that there would be scope to improve the associated information requirements. However, it states that "there may be an argument for extending the 7-day period", although it notes that this will mean that creditors would have to wait longer to enforce the agreement: see Annex 6, paras 197–200. Finally (see para.6.30) it notes that the information requirements in secondary legislation could be replaced by FCA rules.

## Default notice

*Replace paragraph with:*

39-166 Section 87(1)[1049a] of the 1974 Act requires the service[1050] of a "default notice" on the debtor or hirer before the creditor or owner can be entitled, by reason of any *breach* by the debtor or hirer of a regulated agreement:

(a) to terminate the agreement[1051];
(b) to demand earlier payment of any sum[1052];
(c) to recover possession of any goods or land;
(d) to treat any right conferred on the debtor or hirer by the agreement as restricted or deferred[1053]; or
(e) to enforce any security.[1054]

It has been held that a default notice is not required before a default is reported to a credit reference agency as such reporting, in not being an "enforcement" of the agreement,[1054a] does not fall within s.87(1).[1054b] Express exemption has been granted from the need to serve a default notice to non-commercial agreements[1055] where no security[1056] is provided.[1057] In *PRA Group (UK) Ltd v Doyle*,[1057a] it was held that the service of a default notice under s.87 was not merely a procedural requirement but (in combination with the terms of the agreement in that case) qualified a creditor's substantive right. It followed that the cause of action only arose on service of a default notice and that limitation started to run from the date of the default notice.

[1049a] The FCA's *Review of retained provisions of the Consumer Credit Act: Final Report* (see para.39-

004, n.14, above) states (see Annex 5, para.94) that ss.87–89 should be retained in legislation as their provisions cannot be replicated by an FCA rule and hence repeal would adversely affect the appropriate degree of consumer protection. However (see para.6.30) the Review notes that the information requirements in secondary legislation could be replaced by FCA rules.

1050 Defined in CCA 1974 ss.176, 189(1). See *Lombard North Central v Power-Hines* [1995] C.C.L.R. 24, Cty Ct (notice posted but never received validly served). See also the notice requirements under the Pre-Action Protocol on Debt Claims ("Debt PAP"), in force October 1, 2017.

1051 For termination in non-breach cases, see CCA 1974 s.98; below, para.39-172. See also CCA 1974 s.98A(3): termination in non-breach cases of certain "open-ended" consumer credit agreements, below para.39-173.

1052 e.g. under an "acceleration clause" in the agreement.

1053 See s.87(2): this does not prevent the creditor from treating the right to draw upon any credit as restricted or deferred, and taking such steps as may be necessary to make the restriction or deferment effective. See also s.87(5) (added on February 10, 2011 by SI 2010/1010 reg.37): s.87(1)(d) inapplicable to certain "open-ended" agreements (i.e. credit agreements of no fixed duration) as the specific requirements as to notice in such cases is in CCA 1974 s.98A(4), see below para.39-173.

1054 s.87(1). See CCA 1974 s.189B(3), Sch.2A: in s.87, references to "debtor" in relation to "green deal plans" (as defined in CCA 1974 s.189(1), see below, para.39-257) are to be read as references to the "current bill payer"/"previous bill payer" (as defined in CCA 1974 s.189B(6)). The doing of an act whereby a floating charge becomes fixed is not an enforcement of a security (see CCA 1974 s.185(5) (as amended by the Consumer Credit Act 2006 s.5(8))) and the Agricultural Credits Act 1928): s.87(3). See also CCA 1974 s.111 (service on surety) below, para.39-174.

1054a Following *McGuffick v Royal Bank of Scotland Plc* [2009] EWHC 2386 (Comm), see para.39-128, above.

1054b *Boyo v Lloyds Bank Plc* [2019] EWHC 2279 (QB).

1055 Defined in CCA 1974 s.189(1); see above, para.39-049.

1056 Defined in CCA 1974 s.189(1); see below, para.39-180.

1057 s.87(4); SI 1983/1561 reg.2(9). See also CCA 1974 s.130(3).

1057a [2019] EWCA Civ 12. But see the view of Bowden in [2019] J.B.L. 407 that s.87 is merely a procedural requirement and that this decision is per incuriam. Note also *PRA Group (UK) Ltd v Segal* Unreported December 19, 2017 (Norwich Cty Ct): the fact that no compliant default notice was sent rendered the relationship "unfair" for the purposes of CCA 1974 s.140A (see below, para.39-212 et seq.).

## Notice of termination (non-default cases)

*Replace footnote 1080 with:*

1080 Hence s.98 does not apply once the term of the agreement has expired: *Evans v Finance-U-Ltd* [2013] EWCA Civ 869. The FCA's *Review of retained provisions of the Consumer Credit Act: Final Report* (see para.39-004, n.13, above) states (see Annex 5, para.88) that s.98 (together with ss.76 and 87) should be retained in legislation as repeal would adversely affect the appropriate degree of consumer protection in giving to consumer a chance to take action to preclude termination. Whilst an FCA rule could impose corresponding obligations on creditors, it could not reproduce the consequences of non-compliance. However, the Review notes that there would be scope to improve the associated information requirements. Moreover, it states that "there may be an argument for extending the 7-day period", although it notes that this will mean that creditors would have to wait longer to terminate the agreement: see Annex 6, paras 197–200. Finally (see para.6.30) it notes that the information requirements in secondary legislation could be replaced by FCA rules. **39-172**

## Termination etc. of open-end consumer credit agreements

*Replace paragraph with:*

In consequence of the implementation of the Consumer Credit Directive[1089] a new s.98A[1089a] has been added[1090] to the 1974 Act governing the termination of regulated credit agreements that are "open-ended" (that is, of indefinite duration). However, it does not apply to overdrafts or to agreements secured on land (mortgages are outside the scope of the Directive).[1091] First,[1092] it enables a *debtor* by notice and free of charge, to terminate such an agreement at any time. The agreement may provide for a period of notice but this must not exceed one month. Moreover, the creditor **39-173** may require the notice of termination to be in writing, otherwise it may take any form. But this provision does not affect any right that the debtor has to terminate an agreement for breach of contract in the usual way.[1093] Second,[1094] it limits the exercise of any contractual right that the *creditor* has to terminate such an agreement in that the termination must be effected by notice in writing and may not take effect for two months, or such longer period as the agreement may provide. But again, this does not affect any right that the creditor has to terminate an agreement for breach of contract.[1095] Third,[1096] special provision is made governing the termination or suspension of the debtor's right to draw on credit (whether prompted by the debtor's breach of contract or not, although in the former case the usual default notice provision does not apply[1097]). Generally, the creditor must serve a notice in writing, with objectively justified reasons, on the debtor before the termination or suspension takes effect or, if that is "not practicable", immediately afterwards.

[1089] See above, para.39-011.

[1089a] The FCA's *Review of retained provisions of the Consumer Credit Act: Final Report* (see para.39-004, n.13, above) states (see Annex 5, para.166) that s.98A should be retained in legislation as an FCA rule could not replicate a statutory right to terminate and hence repeal would adversely affect the appropriate degree of consumer protection.

[1090] With effect from February 1, 2011 by SI 2010/1010 reg.38.

[1091] CCA 1974 s.98A(8).

[1092] CCA 1974 s.98A(1).

[1093] CCA 1974 s.98A(7).

[1094] CCA 1974 s.98A(3). Note that CCA 1974 s.129 (time orders, see below, para.39-202) does not apply in relation to a s.98A(3) notice (cf. CCA 1974 ss.76, 87 and 98 notices).

[1095] CCA 1974 s.98A(7). But note that generally a default notice must then be served under CCA 1974 s.87, see above, para.39-166.

[1096] CCA 1974 s.98A(4)–(6). Where the Payment Services Regulations 2017 (SI 2017/752) apply (see generally, above, paras 34-224 et seq.), the provisions in reg.71(2)–(5) as to stopping the use of a "payment instrument" are disapplied in cases covered by s.98A(4)–(6): see SI 2017/752 reg.64(2). See the Consumer Credit (Amendment) (EU Exit) Regulations 2018 (SI 2018/1038) reg.2(2): in s.98A(5)(a), on the "exit day", "a retained EU obligation" will be substituted for "an EU obligation".

[1097] See CCA 1974 s.87(5), added by SI 2010/1010 reg.37.

## Copy of notices to "surety"

*Replace footnote 1102 with:*

39-174 [1102] CCA 1974 s.111(1). For the definition of "surety", see below, para.39-183. Perhaps because of an oversight, s.111 has not been amended to apply also to a s.98A(3) or (4)(b) creditor's notice (see above, para.39-173) or the various "NOSIAs" under ss.86B and 86C (see above, paras 39-131 and 39-134).

## Death of debtor or hirer

*Replace footnote 1104 with:*

39-175 [1104] See CCA 1974 s.189B(3), Sch.2A: in s.86, references to "debtor" in relation to "green deal plans" (as defined in CCA 1974 s.189(1), see below, para.39-257) are to be read as references to the "current bill payer"/"previous bill payer" (as defined in CCA 1974 s.189B(6)). See also s.185(4) (death of one of two or more hirers or debtors). The FCA's *Review of retained provisions of the Consumer Credit Act: Final Report* (see para.39-004, n.13, above) states (see Annex 5, para.94) that s.86 could not be replaced by an FCA rule with corresponding effect and hence should be retained in legislation as repeal would adversely affect the appropriate degree of consumer protection in "safeguarding the customer's family from distress and from unfairness and hardship".

*Replace footnote 1111 with:*

## Increase of interest rate on default[1111]

1111 For interest payable on default sums see CCA 1974 s.86F, above, para.39-136 and for interest on judgment debts, see CCA 1974 s.130A, below, para.39-206. See also CCA 1974 s.78A (notification of change of interest, above, para.39-147). The FCA's *Review of retained provisions of the Consumer Credit Act: Final Report* (see para.39-004, n.13, above) states (see Annex 5, para.108) that s.93 should be retained in legislation as repeal would adversely affect the appropriate degree of consumer protection. Whilst an FCA rule could impose corresponding obligations on creditors, it could not automatically render void or invalid a term providing for increased default interest and any challenge to such a term would require the debtor to take the initiative. **39-177**

*Replace paragraph with:*

Whilst default interest is generally unobjectionable at common law,[1111a] s.93 of the 1974 Act prevents a debtor under a regulated consumer credit agreement from being obliged to pay interest on sums which, in breach of the agreement, are unpaid by him at a rate exceeding the rate payable on the principal apart from any default.[1112] And where the charge made for credit is not technically interest but, e.g. a finance charge, then that rate of charge is likewise not to be increased on default.[1113] But the section does not prevent interest being charged on interest due but unpaid at a rate not exceeding the rate payable on the principal apart from any default.[1114] Nor, it is submitted, does the section[1114a] prevent a creditor (e.g. a bank) stipulating two rates of interest, one for "authorised" overdrafts and the other for overdrafts which are unauthorised. *Carrasco v Johnson*[1114b] established that any provision for default interest caught by s.93 is wholly void, not just void as to any difference between the term and default rates.[1114c] **39-177**

1111a Unless it is a "penalty": see below, para.39-204. See *Greenlands Trading Ltd v Pontearso* [2019] EWHC 278 (Ch), in which Nugee J. (sitting on an appeal from the county court) upheld a decision that a secured six month bridging loan (not a regulated agreement) with a £1,995 "default administration fee" and 3 per cent per month default interest fee rate to be paid on default, was unfair under the unfair relationship provisions (CCA 1974 ss.140A–140C, see below, paras 39-212 et seq.) but only to the extent of the default administration fee, as the default interest rate was regarded as "industry standard". But see *Banco Santander v Demba and Cortes v Banco de Sabadell* (Joined Cases C-96/16 and C-94/17) on the application of Unfair Contract Terms Directive (and hence Consumer Rights Act 2015 Pt 2) to terms charging default interest.

1112 i.e. "where the total charge for credit includes an item in respect of interest, at a rate exceeding that rate of interest": s.93(a). See *McMullon v Secure the Bridge Ltd* [2015] EWCA Civ 884 (so-called "fee" was clearly "interest"). A similar (but not identical) provision was contained in s.7 of the Moneylenders Act 1927 (see *Mutual Loan Fund Association v Sanderson* [1937] 1 All E.R. 380). This section causes particular difficulty in the case of "interest free" credit, see Guest and Lloyd, *Encyclopedia of Consumer Credit Law* (1975, looseleaf), para.2-094. See CCA 1974 s.189B(3), Sch.2A: in s.93, references to "debtor" in relation to "green deal plans" (as defined in CCA 1974 s.189(1), see below, para.39-257) are to be read as references to the "current bill payer"/"previous bill payer" (as defined in CCA 1974 s.189B(6)).

1113 s.93(b). In this case, items included in the total charge for credit by virtue of rules made by the FCA under RAO art.60M(2)(d) ("linked transactions" see above, paras 39-055 et seq.) are to be disregarded.

1114 For the positions at common law, see below, paras 39-285 et seq. Similarly a provision that "on the debtor making default in payment of any instalment, the *whole amount* of principal and interest remaining unpaid shall forthwith become due and payable" would not appear to contravene s.93 since "the whole amount of principal and interest" are not sums which are unpaid in breach of the agreement and thus the interest may be increased on them by virtue of the provision. But see CCA 1974 s.95(1) (rebate on early settlement, above para.39-158). As to whether a clause providing for accelerated payment of principal and interest is a penalty, see below, para.39-272, and *Wadham Stringer Finance Ltd v Meaney* [1981] 1 W.L.R. 39. The provision for a rebate in CCA 1974 s.95 (see above, para.39-158) may prevent it being penal: *Forward Trust Plc v Robinson* [1987] C.C.L.R. 10, Cty Ct.

1114a But the FCA has outlawed the charging of higher "unauthorised overdraft" interest rates: see *High-Cost Credit Review: Overdraft policy* PS19/16 (June 2019).

1114b [2018] EWCA Civ 87.

1114c Although in that case the creditor did eventually get the contractual rate, as the court ordered interest (pre-judgment) at the contractual rate under the County Courts Act 1984 (and after judgment at the rate prescribed by the County Courts (Interest on Judgment Debts) Order 1991 (SI 1991/1184)—which was 8 per cent).

### Contracting out forbidden

*Replace footnote 1116 with:*

39-179 [1116] CCA 1974 s.173(1), (2). The FCA's *Review of retained provisions of the Consumer Credit Act: Final Report* (see para.39-004, n.13, above) states (see Annex 5, para.46) that s.173 should be retained in legislation in respect of those CCA provisions that remain in the CCA or other legislation as an FCA rule could not replicate its provisions and hence repeal would adversely affect the appropriate degree of consumer protection.

## (k) Security

### Enforcement of security

*In line 1, after "Section 113", add new footnote 1150a:*

39-190 [1150a] The FCA's *Review of retained provisions of the Consumer Credit Act: Final Report* (see para.39-004, n.13, above) states (see Annex 5, para.113) that s.113 should be retained in legislation as an FCA rule could not reproduce its effect and hence repeal would adversely affect the appropriate degree of consumer protection in that it (together with other "security" provisions) is "an effective anti-avoidance mechanism ... support[ing] the other components of the regime for securities".

### Security rendered invalid

*In line 1, after "Section 106", add new footnote 1155a:*

39-192 [1155a] The FCA's *Review of retained provisions of the Consumer Credit Act: Final Report* (see para.39-004, n.13, above) states (see Annex 5, para.113) that s.106 should be retained in legislation as an FCA rule could not reproduce its effect and hence repeal would adversely affect the appropriate degree of consumer protection in that it (together with other "security" provisions) is "an effective anti-avoidance mechanism ... support[ing] the other components of the regime for securities".

### Pledges

*In line 1, after "Sections 114 to 122", add new footnote 1173a:*

39-194 [1173a] The FCA's *Review of retained provisions of the Consumer Credit Act: Final Report* (see para.39-004, n.13, above) states (see Annex 5, paras 131–132) that "there would be benefit in modernising [the CCA pawn-broking] provisions to ensure they are fit for purpose and reflect modern forms of communication". The view is further expressed that FCA rules could achieve similar results (with debtors' rights being reformulated as creditors' conduct obligations) except in a few cases (see esp. ss.117, 120 and 121) and hence that such provisions should be retained in legislation as repeal would adversely affect the appropriate degree of consumer protection. However "there are arguments for keeping all of sections 116 to 121 in legislation to avoid undue fragmentation of the regulatory regime". Moreover (see para.7-97) the FCA's view is that "the criminal offences in the CCA may no longer be necessary" and this would apply to ss.114(2) and 119.

## (l) Judicial Control

### Enforcement orders in cases of infringement

*Replace footnote 1215 with:*

39-200 [1215] See CCA 1974 s.189B(3), Sch.2A: in s.127, references to "debtor" in relation to "green deal plans" (as defined in CCA 1974 s.189(1), see below, para.39-257) are to be read as references to the "improver"/"current bill payer"/"previous bill payer" (as defined in CCA 1974 s.189B(6)). See *Wells v Devani* [2019] UKSC 4, a case on the Estate Agents Act 1979 s.18(6), which is almost identical in terms to CCA 1974 s.127.

### Time orders

*Replace footnote 1235 with:*

39-202 [1235] See CCA 1974 s.189B(3), Sch.2A: in s.129, references to "debtor" in relation to "green deal plans" (as defined in CCA 1974 s.189(1), see below, para.39-257) are to be read as references to the "current bill payer"/"previous bill payer" (as defined in CCA 1974 s.189B(6)). For the content on an application for a time order, see CPR Pt 7 r.97PD–0037.3; CCR Ord.49 r.4(5). CPR Pt 7PD 7B 3.1; Pt 55PD 55, 7.1; Form N440. See *Jenkins v Cedar Holdings Ltd* [1988] C.C.L.R. 34, Cty Ct: time order made by Registrar was a final and not interlocutory order (so any appeal subject to (now) CPR Sch.2 CCR Ord.37 r.6). See CCA 1974 s.129(3) in relation to Scotland. The FCA's *Review of retained provisions of the Consumer Credit Act: Final Report* (see para.39-004, n.13, above) states (see Annex 5, para.191) that ss.129–133, 136 should be retained in legislation on the grounds that their repeal would adversely affect the appropriate degree of consumer protection, in particular for vulnerable consumers in financial difficulties. However the Review adds that "there may be merit in reviewing the triggers for a time order application and the associated procedures".

## Interest payable on judgment debts

*Replace paragraph with:*

Section 130A[1266] of the 1974 Act imposes notification requirements in relation to post-judgment interest[1267] arising by virtue of a term in a regulated agreement, as it is not always obvious to judgment debtors that such interest is still payable.[1268] (The section does not apply in relation to post-judgment interest required to be paid under certain statutory provisions.[1269]) The section provides that a creditor or owner under a regulated agreement (other than a "non-commercial"[1270] or "small"[1271] agreement)[1272] cannot recover such interest on a judgment debt until he gives[1273] the debtor or hirer, free of charge,[1274] notice in the prescribed form[1275] after judgment and continues to give such a notice at intervals of not more than six months. Interest can only start running on the day the first notice is given[1276] and ceases to run if the requisite subsequent notice is not given within the six-month period, although it resumes running the day after notice is given.[1277] **39-206**

1266 Inserted by the Consumer Credit Act 2006 s.17 on October 1, 2008 (SI 2007/3300) and applicable to agreements whenever made but only as regards judgments debts arising after commencement (see the 2006 Act Sch.3 para.13). See CCA 1974 s.189B(3), Sch.2A: in s.130A, references to "debtor" in relation to "green deal plans" (as defined in CCA 1974 s.189(1), see below, para.39-257) are to be read as references to the "current bill payer"/"previous bill payer" (as defined in CCA 1974 s.189B(6)). The FCA's *Review of retained provisions of the Consumer Credit Act: Final Report* (see para.39-004, n.13, above) states (see Annex 5, para.108) that s.130A should be retained in legislation as repeal would adversely affect the appropriate degree of consumer protection. Whilst an FCA rule could impose corresponding obligations on creditors, it could not automatically render void or invalid a term providing for post-judgment interest and a challenge to such a term would require the debtor to take the initiative.

1267 CCA 1974 s.130A(9) defines this as interest calculated by reference to the period after the giving of the judgment under which the judgment debt is payable.

1268 See *Director General of Fair Trading v First National Bank Plc* [2001] UKHL 52, [2002] 1 A.C. 481: such a term, although it took the debtor by surprise, held not to be "unfair" under the Unfair Terms in Consumer Contract Regulations 1999 (SI 1999/2083), above paras 38-246 et seq. As noted above at para.38-220, those regulations are replaced, for contracts made on or after October 1, 2015, by provisions in the Consumer Rights Act 2015 Pt 2.

1269 viz (a) the AJ (Scotland) Act 1972 s.4; (b) the Judgements Enforcement (NI) Order 1981; and (c) County Courts Act 1984 s.74. The County Court (Interest on Judgments Debts) Order 1991 (SI 1991/1184) (L.12) (made under County Courts Act 1984 s.74) provides that interest shall not be payable under that Order where the relevant judgment debt relates to a CCA 1974-regulated agreement. Hence the inclusion of terms allowing interest to be charged after a court judgment in such agreements, at issue in the *First National Bank Plc* case.

1270 Defined in CCA 1974 s.189(1), see above, para.39-049.

1271 Defined in CCA 1974 s.17, see above, para.39-048.

1272 CCA 1974 s.130A(8). And see the further limitation as to interest awarded under statute, noted above.

1273 Defined in CCA 1974 s.189(1) (as amended by SI 2004/3236 art.2(2)) to mean "deliver or send by appropriate method".

1274 CCA 1974 s.130A(4).

1275 CCA 1974 s.130A(6) and see the Consumer Credit (Information Requirements and Duration of

Licences and Charges) Regulations 2007 (SI 2007/1167) regs 34–35 and Sch.5 (as amended by SI 2008/1751). The notice may be incorporated in a statement (e.g. a statement under CCA 1974 ss.77–78) or other notice (e.g. under CCA 1974 s.86B, 86C or 87) given under the Act: CCA 1974 s.130A(5).

1276 CCA 1974 s.130A(2).

1277 CCA 1974 s.130A(3).

## (m) Unfair Relationships

39-212 *Replace footnote 1300 with:*

1300 See Guest and Lloyd, *Encyclopedia of Consumer Credit Law* (1975, looseleaf), paras 2-141A—2-141D; and Goode, *Consumer Credit: Law and Practice*, Pt C, Ch.47; Brown [2009] L.M.C.L.Q. 90; Lomnicka [2012] J.B.L. 713; Brown (2016) 36(2) L.S. 230–257. The FCA's *Review of retained provisions of the Consumer Credit Act: Final Report* (see para.39-004, n.14, above) states (see Annex 5, para.205) that ss.140A–140C should be retained in legislation as they could not be replaced by FCA rules without adversely affecting the appropriate degree of consumer protection. Moreover the FCA stated that it did not consider it necessary to provide guidance on the meaning of "unfairness" in these provisions (although previously the OFT had done so, see below, para.39-212).

### Extortionate credit bargains

*Replace paragraph with:*

39-212 The Consumer Credit Act 1974[1301] originally contained provisions[1302] enabling the court to reopen a credit agreement if it found that the credit bargain was "extortionate".[1303] The threshold for intervention (that payments were "grossly exorbitant" or the bargain otherwise "grossly" contravened fair dealing) was very high[1304] and hence very few challenges on this basis were successful.[1305] The Consumer Credit Act 2006 repealed and replaced these provisions[1306] with new ss.140A–140D.[1307] The new provisions essentially lower the threshold to one of a relationship between the creditor and the debtor (taking into account both the credit agreement and "any related agreement") that is "unfair to the debtor".[1308] Such a claim succeeded in the Supreme Court in the context of the sale of PPI in *Plevin v Paragon Personal Finance Ltd.*[1309]

1301 See also (on the existing equitable jurisdiction of the Chancery Division in relation to mortgages) *Cityland and Property (Holdings) Ltd v Dabrah* [1968] Ch. 166.

1302 See the similar provision in the Insolvency Act 1986 s.343 for the reopening of credit transactions of an individual who is adjudged bankrupt. See also Insolvency Act 1986 s.244 (winding-up of companies).

1303 ss.137–140 came into force on May 16, 1977, SI 1977/325 (c.11). See 29th edn of this work, paras 39-191 and Bentley and Howells [1989] Conv. 234. The OFT reviewed ss.137–140 in *Unjust Credit Transactions* (1991) and recommended the widening of the operation of the sections by the substitution of "unjust credit transaction" for "extortionate credit bargain", but this was never implemented and has been overtaken by the introduction of the new "unfair relationship" provisions.

1304 *Broadwick Financial Services v Spencer* [2002] EWCA Civ 35, [2002] 1 All E.R. (Comm) 446 at [80]. See also *First National Securities Ltd v Bertrand* [1980] C.C.L.R. 1, Cty Ct; *A Ketley Ltd v Scott* [1981] I.C.R. 241; *Wills v Wood* (1984) 128 S.J. 222, CA; *Davies v Directloans Ltd* [1986] 1 W.L.R. 823.

1305 In *Woodstead Finance v Petrou, The Times,* January 23, 1986, the Court of Appeal did not disturb a mortgage at an APR of 42.5 per cent p.a. as this rate was normal for short-term loans. And see *A Ketley Ltd v Scott* [1981] I.C.R. 241; and *Davies v Directloans Ltd* [1986] 1 W.L.R. 823, where interest rates of 48 per cent and 21.7 per cent (APR), on agreements that were secured by a land mortgage, were upheld. Contrast, however, *Barcabe v Edwards* [1983] C.C.L.R. 11, Cty Ct, interest of 100 per cent p.a. (APR 319 per cent) on unsecured loan reduced to 40 per cent p.a.; *Devogate v Jarvis* Unreported 1987, Cty Ct, interest of APR 39 per cent reduced to 30 per cent where loan was well secured; *Shahabinia v Gyachi* Unreported 1988 interest rates on non-commercial loans of 104 per cent, 78 per cent and 156 per cent reduced to 15 per cent; *Prestonwell Ltd v Capon* Unreported 1988, Cty Ct, interest rate of 42 per cent flat reduced by half, the risk being low; *Castle Phillips & Co v Wilkinson* [1992] C.C.L.R. 83, Cty Ct interest rate of 4 per cent per month (interest being deducted from the loan) on secured "bridging" loan reduced to 20 per cent p.a.; *Batooneh v Asombang* [2003] EWHC 2111 (QB) (interest rate of

100 per cent on informal commercial loan reduced to 25 per cent); *County Leasing Ltd v East* [2007] EWHC 2907 (reopening of business loan of over £370,000).

1306 Consumer Credit Act 2006 ss.19–22 on April 6, 2007 (SI 2007/123). The new provisions essentially apply to agreements *whenever made*, as long as they have not been paid off (become "completed agreements") by April 6, 2008 (see the (complex) transitional provisions in the 2006 Act Sch.3 para.1(2) (definition of "completed agreement") and para.14). On the application of the transitional provisions, see *Soulsby and Soulsby v FirstPlus Financial Group Plc* Unreported March 5, 2010, QBD, Leeds & District Registry Mercantile Court (old provisions applied) and *Barnes v Black Horse Ltd* [2011] EWHC 1416 (QB) (new provisions applied, see below, para.39-214).

1307 s.140D (Advice and information from OFT) was repealed on April 1, 2014, by SI 2013/1881 art.20(4), when consumer credit regulation was transferred to the FCA (see above, para.39-002) as the FCA has general power to issue guidance under the Financial Services and Markets Act 2000 s.139A. But the FCA stated in its *Review of retained provisions of the Consumer Credit Act: Final Report* (see para.39-004, n.14, above) that it did not consider it necessary to provide guidance on the meaning of "unfairness" in these provisions.

1308 See further, below, para.39-217—39-222.

1309 [2014] UKSC 61 (see further below, para.39-222) and see *Scotland v British Credit Trust Ltd* [2014] EWCA Civ 790. For previous cases where the claim was successful, see: *Patel v Patel* [2009] EWHC 3264 ("exorbitant" interest and lack of transparency in loans between friends); *Morrison v Betterpace Ltd (t/a Log Book Loans)* Unreported September 1, 2009, Lowestoft Cty Ct (APR of 485.25 of refinancing loan reduced to APR of 343.4 per cent charged on previous loan); *MBNA Europe Ltd v Thorius*, Newcastle Cty Ct [2010] E.C.C. 8 (sale of PPI); *Barons Finance Ltd v Olubisi* Unreported April 26, 2010, Mayor's & City of London Ct (vulnerable consumer "exploited")); *Nelmes v NRAM Plc* [2016] EWCA Civ 491 (in business context, payment by the lender of a "procurement fee" (being half the arrangement fee charged by the lender to the borrower) to the borrower's broker deprived the borrower of the disinterested advice of his broker and hence rendered the credit relationship "unfair"; lender accountable to borrower for all the undisclosed "procurement fee" plus interest from the date of payment); *Townson v FCE Bank Plc (t/a Ford Credit)* Unreported June 23, 2016, Birmingham Cty Ct ("unfair relationship" found where PPI (of which the debtor was unaware and by implication did not want) was sold by car dealer to a debtor under a hire-purchase agreement). For successful post-*Plevin* cases, see *Doran v Paragon Personal Finance Ltd* Unreported June 28, 2018 (Manchester Cty Ct); *Goldhill Finance Ltd v Berry* Unreported October 26, 2018 (London Cty Ct) (exercise of common law right to possession after stay of execution of warrant of possession); *Pilgrim Rock v Iwanuik* [2019] EWHC 203 (Ch) (rate of interest compounded quarterly rising to 9 per cent in the event of default, where the creditor had done nothing to enforce its rights for four years while interest was accruing at the escalated default rate); *Greenlands Trading Ltd v Pontearso* [2019] EWHC 278 (Ch) (as to "default administration fee"); *Wood v Commercial First Business Ltd* [2019] EWHC 2205 (Ch) (undisclosed commission deprived the debtor of the disinterested advice of the broker). For cases where the claim was unsuccessful, see: *Khodari v Tamimi* [2009] EWCA Civ 1109, [2010] C.C.L.R. 3 ("very large" 10 per cent charge for short-term loans to wealthy compulsive gambler, where credit risk was high and "defendant wanted these loans and could well afford to repay them"); *Maple Leaf Macro Volatility Master Fund v Rouvroy* [2009] EWHC 257, [2009] C.C.L.R. 9 ((obiter) funding agreement to assist acquisition of control of company); *McGuffick v RBS Plc* [2009] EWHC 2386 (reporting to credit reference agencies whilst agreement was "temporarily unenforceable" due to breach of CCA 1974 s.77); *Carey v HSBC Bank Plc* [2009] EWHC 3417 (QB) (breach of CCA 1974 s.78); *Shaw v Nine Regions Ltd* [2009] EWHC 3514 ("log book" loan with high interest rate of 119 per cent per annum); *Black Horse Ltd v Speak* [2010] EWHC 1866 (QB); *Consolidated Finance Ltd v Hunter* [2010] B.P.I.R. 1322 (loan at market rate for similar short-term bridging loans); *Paragon Mortgages Ltd v McEwan-Peters* [2011] EWHC 2491 (Comm); *Rahman v HSBC Bank Plc* [2012] EWHC 11 (Ch); *Deutsche Bank (Suisse) SA v Khan* [2013] EWHC 482 (Comm), noted at [2013] C.C.L.R. 5; *Chubb v Dean* [2013] EWHC 1282 (Ch); *Conlon v Black Horse Ltd* [2013] EWCA Civ 1658, [2014] C.C.L.R. 4; *Gardner v Clydesdale Bank Ltd* [2013] EWHC 4356 (Ch); *Link Financial Ltd v North Wilson* [2014] EWHC 252 (Ch), [2014] C.C.L.R. 6; *Scotland v British Credit Trust Ltd* [2014] EWCA Civ 790 (mis-selling of PPI); *Graves v Capital Home Loans* [2014] EWCA Civ 1297 (buy-to-let loan); *McMullon v Secure the Bridge Ltd* [2015] EWCA Civ 884 (bridging loan); *Barclays Bank Plc v McMillan* [2015] EWHC 1596 (Comm) (loan to finance US law firm's partner's capital subscription on usual terms); *Bluestone Mortgages Ltd v Momoh* [2015] EW Misc B4 (CC) (refusal of permission to appeal the decision of the county court that failure to notify in advance that mortgagee would invoke usual clause in buy-to-let mortgage permitting him to pay outstanding lease charges if mortgagor failed to do so, did not give rise to an unfair relationship); *Commercial First Business Ltd v Pickup* [2017] C.T.L.C. 1, [2017] C.C.L.R. 15 (although only the fact (and not the amount) of commission was disclosed by the brokers, the debtors were experienced property investors and knew all the relevant facts (*Deutsche Bank (Suisse) SA v Khan* applied)); *Clydesdale Bank Plc v Gough (t/a JC Gough & Sons)* [2017] EWHC 2230 (Ch) (in business lending context where debtor and guarantor had independent legal advice, no unfairness found in the way the lender had exercised or enforced its rights against both); *Santander UK Plc v Wells* [2017] EWHC 2413 (Ch) (claimant had delayed too long in making claim); *Ulster Bank Ltd v Esmaili* [2017] NICh 14; (no unfairness found in business lending context where debtor was experienced property developer); *Holyoake v Candy* [2017] EWHC 3397 (Ch) (permission to appeal refused by Court of Appeal: [2018] C.C.L.R. 8) (Nugee J. rejected an "unfairness" claim in business lending context, applying *Deutsche Bank (Suisse) SA v Khan*, above, where both debtor and creditor were property developers); *Carney v NM Rothschild and Sons Ltd* [2018] EWHC 958 (Comm); (no "unfairness" where the debtors received independent advice and the loan agreement made it clear (via "basis" clauses) that the creditor was not providing advice); *Hodell v Clydesdale Bank Plc* [2018] EWHC 1009 (QB) (no "unfair relationship" in commercial lending to experienced property development partnership); *Greenlands Trading Ltd v Pontearso* [2019] EWHC 278 (Ch) (as to "industry standard" default interest); *Broomhead v National Westminster Bank Plc* [2018] EWHC 1574 (Ch); *Praetura Asset Finance Ltd v Wood* [2019] EWHC 2231 (Comm) (brief dismissal of unfair relationship allegation in the context of a large business loan); *Promontoria (Henrico) Ltd v Samra* [2019] EWHC 2327 (Ch) (refusal to find an unfair relationship in a secured business loan).

## Wide application of "unfair relationship" provisions

*Replace paragraph with:*

**39-213** It is important to note four points concerning the application of the "unfair relationship" provisions. First, the scope of the provisions is wide in generally extending to all consumer credit agreements with individuals[1310] and hence they apply irrespective of the size of the loan or purpose of the credit.[1311] The provisions apply not only to regulated credit agreements but also to most "exempt agreements",[1312] as well as "non-commercial agreements"[1313] (and even, in theory, "small agreements"[1314]). They do not, however, apply to an agreement that is an exempt agreement by virtue of being a regulated land mortgage or home purchase plan.[1315]

[1310] "Credit agreement" for these purposes is defined in CCA 1974 s.140C(1) to mean (essentially) a consumer credit agreement (see above, para.39-016). Hence corporate debtors are not covered: *Bank of Ireland (UK) Plc v McLaughlin* [2016] NICA 33, [2017] C.C.L.R. 5 (refusal of appeal from the lower court ([2014] N.I.Q.B. 104) that a guarantor of a corporate debtor could not invoke the unfair relationship provisions); *Newmafruit Farms Ltd v Pither* [2016] EWHC 2205 (QB), [2017] C.C.L.R. 8 (corporate debtor could not invoke the unfair relationship provisions). Moreover, s.140C(2) defines "debtor" and "creditor" for these purpose to cover assignees, in the same way as does CCA 1974 s.189(1) in relation to consumer credit agreements. See the definition of "credit" in CCA 1974 s.9(1): above, para.39-019. The power to reopen does not apply to hiring agreements, but see CCA 1974 s.132 (above, para.33-090). Nor does it apply to a sale and leaseback transaction: *Lavin v Johnson* [2002] EWCA Civ 1138 (not "credit", for the purposes of the previous extortionate credit bargain provisions). See also *Maple Leaf Macro Volatility Master Fund v Rouvroy* [2009] EWHC 257 (funding agreement did not provide "credit"). See s.140C(5)–(6) (adaptation of language). And see CCA 1974 s.189C(1)(a): a "green deal consumer credit agreement" (as defined in CCA 1974 s.189B(8) to mean a green deal plan (as defined in CCA 1974 s.189(1), see below, para.39-257) that is to be treated as a consumer credit agreement for the purpose of this Act by virtue of CCA 1974 s.189B(1) is to be treated as credit agreement for the purposes of s.140A and 140B. And note CCA 1974 s.189B(3), Sch.2A: in s.140A, references to "debtor" in relation to "green deal plans" are to be read as references to the "improver"/"current bill payer"/"previous bill payer" (as defined in CCA 1974 s.189B(6)).

[1311] *Patel v Patel* [2009] EWHC 3264: business loan (albeit between family members) of £200,000 re-opened. And note the "buy-to-let" loans considered (but not re-opened) in *Paragon Mortgages Ltd v McEwan-Peters* [2011] EWHC 2491 (Comm); *Graves v Capital Home Loans Ltd* [2014] EWCA Civ 1297; *Bluestone Mortgages Ltd v Momoh* [2015] EW Misc B4 (CC) and *Nelmes v NRAM Plc* [2016] EWCA Civ 491. See also *Holyoake v Candy* [2017] EWHC 3397 (Ch) (business loan of £12 million—but no "unfairness") and *Pilgrim Rock v Iwanuik* [2019] EWHC 203 (Ch) (commercial loan between co-venturers (albeit to an individual) where interest was compounded quarterly and rose to higher default rate, where creditor had done nothing to enforce its rights for four years while interest was accruing at the escalated default rate). But it is generally more difficult to challenge business credit: see the cases cited in para.39-212, above, especially *Deutsche Bank (Suisse) SA v Khan* [2013] EWHC 482 (Comm).

[1312] For exempt agreements, see above, paras 39-038 et seq. There are two exceptions: see below.

[1313] Defined in CCA 1974 s.189(1); above, para.39-049; *Khodari v Tamimi* [2009] EWCA Civ 1109.

[1314] CCA 1974 s.17; above, para.39-048.

[1315] i.e. exempt under RAO art.60C(2) (see above, para.39-039): s.140A(5). See *AIB v Donnelly* [2015] NI Master 13 (Master Hardstaff) (confirmation that unfair relationship provisions do not apply to FSMA 2000 regulated mortgage contracts). Hence when the Mortgage Credit Directive (see above, para.39-003) was implemented on March 21, 2016 and most second charge residential mortgages became "'regulated mortgage contracts" under the 2000 Act regime, this protection was lost for such residential mortgages.

## Discretion

*Replace paragraph with:*

Finally, even if the relationship is found to be "unfair to the debtor", the court has a residual discretion whether or not to reopen the credit agreement.[1326] The court might refuse to do so if, for example, the debtor unduly delayed in seeking relief[1327] or the debtor failed to disclose his true financial position[1328] or the debtor obtained the credit by false representations[1329] or if the debtor, who was not naïve or unsophisticated, did not complain either at the time or when giving evidence in hindsight.[1329a] **39-216**

[1326] *Holyoake v Candy* [2017] EWHC 3397 (Ch); *Santander UK Plc v Wells* [2017] EWHC 2413 (Ch) (claimant had delayed too long, without an excuse, in making claim).

[1327] This would apply especially to a "spent" agreement: see para.39-215 (and, for decisions on "spent" agreements under the old "extortionate credit bargain" provisions, see *First National Securities Ltd v Bertrand* [1980] C.C.L.R. 1, Cty Ct; and *Davies v Directloans Ltd* [1986] 1 W.L.R. 823). See now: *Santander UK Plc v Wells* [2017] EWHC 2413 (Ch) (claimant had delayed too long in making claim).

[1328] *A Ketley Ltd v Scott* [1981] I.C.R. 241 (a decision under the old "extortionate credit bargain" provisions).

[1329] *A Ketley Ltd v Scott*, above (inflated valuation of security given); for further refusals under the old "extortionate credit bargain" provisions, see *First National Securities Ltd v Bertrand* Unreported 1978, Cty Ct; *Premier Finance Co Ltd v Gravesande* [1983] C.C.L.R. 1, Cty Ct. But in *Link Financial Ltd v North Wilson* [2014] EWHC 252 (Ch), [2014] C.C.L.R. 6, misrepresentations by the debtor did not, on the facts, preclude a finding that the relationship was "unfair".

[1329a] *Greenlands Trading Ltd v Pontearso* [2019] EWHC 278 (Ch) per Nugee J., obiter. However Nugee J. added that the question of whether a relationship was unfair was a matter for the court and that the views of the borrower, in particular whether they regarded the relationship as unfair, were generally irrelevant.

## When relationship is "unfair to the debtor"

*Replace second paragraph with:*

Determining whether one or more of the three factors in s.140A(1) give rise to an "unfair" relationship, s.140A(2) requires the court to "have regard to all matters it thinks relevant", the subsection making it clear that these may include matters "relating to" the debtor and to the creditor (or an "associate" or "former associate" of the creditor[1335]). This general wording is a departure from the old "extortionate credit bargain" provisions; they listed various "factors" in relation to the debtor and creditor that the court was obliged to have regard to.[1336] It seems clear that this reference to "matters relating to" the debtor or creditor is intended to preserve the relevance of those previously listed factors.[1337] Moreover, it was held in *Pilgrim Rock v Iwanuik*[1337a] that the behaviour of a person who was neither an agent[1337b] nor an associate[1337c] of the creditor might still be relevant under s.140A(2), even though his actions could not otherwise[1337d] be attributed to the creditor. It was said that "by reason of the language of [subs.(2)], the court's enquiry was not limited to matters legally attributable to the creditor" and hence background information as to the person who controlled the corporate creditors (in particular that this person and the debtor were joint venturers and friends and not dealing at arm's length) was relevant under s.140A(2). **39-217**

[1335] See previous note.

[1336] The (repealed) s.138(2)(b), (3)–(5), As well as these factors, the court had to have regard to "interest rates prevailing" at the time of contracting and "any other relevant considerations": (repealed) s.138(2)(a), (b).

[1337] The (repealed) s.138(3) listed (as factors applicable in relation to the debtor) the debtor's age, experience, business capacity and state of health, and the degree to which he was under financial pressure, and the nature of that pressure. Although there was no specific requirement that these subjective factors should have been known to the creditor, nor that a particular factor should have influenced the terms of the credit bargain, the courts implied such requirements: *Coldunell Ltd v Gallon* [1986] 1 Q.B. 1184, CA and see *Deutsche Bank (Suisse) SA v Khan* [2013] EWHC 482 (Comm), noted at [2013] C.C.L.R. 5, where Hamblen J. adopted a similar approach. The (repealed) s.138(4) listed (as factors applicable in relation to the creditor) the degree of risk accepted by him (having regard to the value of any security provided), his relationship to the debtor and whether a "colourable cash price" was quoted for any goods or services included in the credit bargain.

[1337a] [2019] EWHC 203 (Ch).

[1337b] And hence potentially relevant under subs.(1)(c) ("on behalf of"), see below.

[1337c] See subs.(3), considered above.

[1337d] Under subs.(1)(c) nor subs.(3), see two previous notes.

## Post-contracting behaviour

*Replace paragraph with:*

**39-218** Factors (b) and (c) in s.140A(1)[1338] are novel in that they relate to the creditor's post-contracting behaviour.[1339] Other statutory provisions, for example the Unfair Contract Terms Act 1977[1340] and the Consumer Rights Act 2015 Pt 2[1341] are more limited in focusing on the contractual terms *at the time of contracting*.[1342]

[1338] See below, paras 39-221 and 39-222.

[1339] CCA 1974 s.140A(1)(c) also covers pre-contracting behaviour: see below, para.39-222.

[1340] See above, Vol.I, paras 15-062 et seq.

[1341] Replacing (for contracts made on or after October 1, 2015) the Unfair Terms in Consumer Contracts Regulations 1999 (SI 1999/2083), see above, paras 38-221 et seq.

[1342] As did the (now repealed) "extortionate credit bargain" provisions themselves.

## "Terms of the agreement or any related agreement"

*Replace paragraph with:*

**39-219** The first factor[1343] that can render the relationship "unfair to the debtor" is the actual terms of the credit agreement or any "related agreement".[1344] It should be noted that, unlike the position under the Consumer Rights Act 2015 Pt 2,[1345] the question is not whether the *terms themselves* are "unfair", but whether the *terms render the relationship* "unfair to the debtor". Usually, the most relevant terms are likely to be those concerning the charge for credit (especially interest).[1346] However, other terms, for example those requiring the payment of excessive early redemption fees[1347] may, at least if considered in the context of other terms of the credit agreement, be held to render the relationship "unfair to the debtor".[1348] Moreover, the terms of "any related agreement"[1349] are also relevant, for example those in linked transactions that might impose obligations on a debtor[1350] to a third party. Hence in *Link Financial Ltd v North Wilson*[1351] the credit relationship was held to be "unfair" because of the "draconian effect" of a term in the timeshare agreement that was financed by the credit agreement.[1352]

[1343] CCA 1974 s.140A(1)(a).

[1344] Defined in s.140C(4), see above, para.39-214.

[1345] Replacing (for contracts made on or after October 1, 2015) the Unfair Terms in Consumer Contract Regulations 1999 (SI 1999/2083), see above, paras 38-221 et seq. For the application of the predecessor regulations to a mortgage, see *Falco Finance Ltd v Gough* [1999] C.C.L.R. 16, Cty Ct.

[1346] See below, para.39-220.

[1347] Early redemption payments under *regulated* agreements are controlled by the Act (see above, para.39-158) and it is a moot point whether those protections will, in effect, be extended to non-regulated agreements on the basis that any other approach would be "unfair to the debtor".

1348 For case-law under the old "extortionate credit bargain" provisions (which required "grossly exorbitant" payments), see *Grangewood Securities Ltd v Ellis* Unreported November 9, 2000, Milton Keynes Cty Ct. But see *Broadwick Financial Services v Spencer* [2002] EWCA Civ 35, [2002] 1 All E.R. (Comm) 446 [61]–[78].

1349 Defined in s.140C(4), see above, para.39-214.

1350 Or his relative.

1351 [2014] EWHC 252 (Ch), [2014] C.C.L.R. 6.

1352 A "related agreement" within s.140C(4)(b): a linked transaction under s.19(1)(b).

## Charge for credit

*Replace paragraph with:*

It is clear that the charge for credit, although normally a "core term" under the Consumer Rights Act 2015[1353] and hence generally not open to challenge under that Act, is very relevant in determining if the relationship is "unfair to the debtor" under the "unfair relationship" provisions.[1354] The previous "extortionate credit bargain" provisions explicitly required the court to have regard to the "interest rates prevailing at the time [the agreement] was made".[1355] The case-law under the "unfair relationship" provisions has so far generally followed[1356] the previous approach under the old "extortionate credit bargain" provisions of judging interest rates against the market rate for that type of loan.[1357] Thus rates charged by banks, building societies and finance houses are of little relevance where money has been borrowed from a moneylender in circumstances that or for a purpose for which such institutions would not have lent money. Further, in relation to the (now repealed) Moneylenders Act, it had been said that "the rate of interest might in certain circumstances be of itself a fallacious test as to whether the transaction was harsh and unconscionable. In many circumstances one shilling interest for a week on £1, or five shillings interest on £1 for a short period, though an enormous rate of interest ought not to be set aside".[1358] However, whilst under the old extortionate credit bargain provisions a subsequent rise or fall in interest rates was irrelevant,[1359] this may now be a relevant "matter",[1360] especially as the third factor[1361] refers to inaction (for example, not lowering interest rates) by the creditor after the making of the agreement. **39-220**

1353 See above, paras 38-363 et seq.

1354 For successful "interest rate" challenges see: *Patel v Patel* [2009] EWHC 3264 (inter alia, "exorbitant" interest) and some county court decisions (*Morrison v Betterpace Ltd (t/a Log Book Loans)* Unreported September 1, 2009, Lowestoft Cty Ct (APR of 485.25 of refinancing loan reduced to APR of 343.4 per cent charged on previous loan) and *Barons Finance Ltd v Olubisi* Unreported April 26, 2010 Mayor's & City of London Court (vulnerable consumer "exploited")); *Pilgrim Rock v Iwanuik* [2019] EWHC 203 (Ch) (secured loan in the context of a joint venture, where the rate of interest was 6 per cent compounded quarterly rising to 9 per cent on default (and where the creditor had done nothing to enforce its rights for four years while interest was accruing at the escalated default rate)). For unsuccessful challenges see *Khodari v Tamimi* [2009] EWCA Civ 1109, [2010] C.C.L.R. 3 ("very large" 10 per cent charge for short-term loans); *Shaw v Nine Regions Ltd* [2009] EWHC 3514 (APR 341 per cent and interest rate of 119 per cent p.a.); *Consolidated Finance Ltd v Hunter* [2010] B.P.I.R. 1322 (loan at market rate for similar short-term bridging loans); *Chubb v Dean* [2013] EWHC 1282 (Ch) (charges ((i) interest of 1.85 per cent per month compounded monthly and (ii) a 1.25 per cent per month "facility fee") "even in combination" merely represented a "stiff commercial bargain"; an unfair relationship would have required a "very much higher interest rate"); *Holyoake v Candy* [2017] EWHC 3397 (Ch) ("steep" fees, with no explanation of how they had been calculated or whether they were in line with industry norms, for extending credit agreement did not render business credit "unfair"); *Greenlands Trading Ltd v Pontearso* [2019] EWHC 278 (Ch) (default interest rate upheld as "industry standard").

1355 (The repealed) s.138(2)(a).

1356 Implicitly; the case-law under the new provisions has made no reference to the old "extortionate credit bargain" case-law. See the cases cited above (but see *Holyoake v Candy* [2017] EWHC 3397 (Ch) which referred to *A Ketley Ltd v Scott* [1981] I.C.R. 241) and see *Greenlands Trading Ltd v Pontearso*

[2019] EWHC 278 (Ch), noted in next note. For the old case-law on interest rates, see *A Ketley Ltd v Scott* [1981] I.C.R. 241; *Davies v Directloans Ltd* [1986] 1 W.L.R. 823; *Woodstead Finance v Petrou, The Times,* January 23, 1986, CA; *Broadwick Financial Services Ltd v Spencer* [2002] EWCA Civ 35, [2002] 1 All E.R. (Comm) 446.

1357 The OFT's Guidance under (the now repealed) CCA 1974 s.140D (*Unfair Relationships: Enforcement action under Part 8 of the Enterprise Act 2002* (OFT 854Rev), May 2008, revised August 2011) also accepted that this should be the approach, para.3.21, even requiring the cost to be "much higher" than market rates for an "unfair relationship" to arise. And see *Greenlands Trading Ltd v Pontearso* [2019] EWHC 278 (Ch), where Nugee J. did not disturb a default interest rate as it was "industry standard".

1358 *Blair v Buckworth* (1908) 24 T.L.R. 474, 476.

1359 The wording was: "prevailing at the time [the agreement] was made". See *Paragon Finance Plc v Nash* [2001] EWCA Civ 1466, [2002] 1 W.L.R. 685; *Broadwick Financial Services v Spencer* [2002] EWCA Civ 35, [2002] 1 All E.R. (Comm) 446; *Paragon Finance Plc v Pender* [2005] EWCA Civ 760, [2005] C.C.L.R. 5.

1360 CCA 1974 s.140A(2). See *Patel v Patel* [2009] EWHC 3264 (QB).

1361 CCA 1974 s.140A(1)(c), see below, para.39-222.

## Exercise or enforcement of rights by creditor

*Replace paragraph with:*

**39-221** The second factor[1362] that can render a relationship "unfair to the debtor" is "the way in which the creditor has exercised or enforced any of his rights" under either the credit agreement itself of "any related agreement".[1363] Although it is the exercise or enforcement of the *creditor's* rights that are material (and not, for example, the rights of third parties to any "related agreements"), the court must have regard[1364] to activities by or on behalf of an "associate"[1365] or "former associate" of the creditor.[1366] Requiring the court to evaluate how a creditor exercises or enforces his contractual rights is a further novel feature of these provisions. In the business context, the courts have so far not found that the enforcement by creditors of agreements on default have given rise to "unfair relationships",[1367] although there are dicta that "arbitrary" or "exploitative" enforcement could do so.[1368] Similarly, in so far as it was held that the reporting of arrears to a credit reference agency was not an "enforcement" of a temporarily unenforceable agreement (due to a breach of s.77[1369]) it was further held that this did not give rise to an "unfair relationship".[1370] However, in the consumer context there are various regulatory standards requiring creditors to exercise forbearance and consideration towards borrowers experiencing difficulty[1371] and it is likely these will inform decisions on whether enforcement in those contexts has rendered a relationship "unfair". In *Re London Scottish Finance (In Administration)*[1372] it was held that in the case of "irredeemably"[1373] unenforceable credit agreements, the sending of letters demanding payment of arrears and stating that failure could result in the loss of the debtors' home (which was untrue) gave rise to an "unfair relationship" if this threat was a (not necessarily the only) cause of the debtors' decision to pay. But demanding payment in the case of an unenforceable (but potentially enforceable under s.127) agreement did not.[1374]

1362 CCA 1974 s.140A(1)(b).

1363 Defined in CCA 1974 s.140C(4), see above, para.39-214.

1364 "except to the extent that it is not appropriate to do so".

1365 Defined in CCA 1974 s.184.

1366 CCA 1974 s.140A(3).

1367 *Bluestone Mortgages Ltd v Faith Momoh* [2015] EW Misc B4 (CC) (refusal of permission to appeal the decision of the county court that failure to notify in advance that mortgagee would invoke usual clause in buy-to-let mortgage permitting him to pay outstanding lease charges if mortgagor failed to do so, did not give rise to an unfair relationship); *Clydesdale Bank Plc v R Gough t/t JC Gough & Sons and Anne Michelle Gough* [2017] EWHC 2230 (Ch) (where debtor and guarantor had independent legal advice, no unfairness found in the way the lender had exercised or enforced its rights against both); *Holyoake v Candy* [2017] EWHC 3397 (Ch); *Broomhead v National Westminster Bank Plc* [2018] EWHC 1574 (Ch).

1368 *Maple Leaf Macro Volatility Master Fund v Rouvroy* [2009] EWHC 257 (Comm); *Paragon Mortgages Ltd v McEwan-Peters* [2011] EWHC 2491 (Comm); *Rahman v HSBC Bank Plc* [2012] EWHC 11 (Ch); *Deutsche Bank (Suisse) SA v Khan* [2013] EWHC 482 (Comm), noted at [2013] C.C.L.R. 5; *Graves v Capital Home Loans* [2014] EWCA Civ 1297. See also *Goldhill Finance Ltd v Berry* Unreported October 26, 2018 (London Cty Ct): unfair relationship arose where creditor sought to exercise his common law right to possession of debtor's property after the court had stayed execution of a warrant of possession.

1369 See above, para.39-128.

1370 *McGuffick v RBS Plc* [2009] EWHC 2386 (Comm).

1371 See the *FCA Handbook* (a) CONC Module, especially CONC 7 and (b) (in relation to regulated mortgages) *MCOB Module*, especially MCOB 13. See also the Standards of Lending Practice (financial difficulties sections), above, para.39-013.

1372 [2013] EWHC 4047 (Ch).

1373 By virtue of the now repealed CCA 1974 s.127(3), see above, para.39-094.

1374 *McGuffick v RBS Plc* [2009] EWHC 2386 (Comm) (above) followed. See also *PRA Group (UK) Ltd v Segal* Unreported December 19, 2017 (Norwich Cty Ct): it was legitimate to ring, send text messages and write to the debtor to try and obtain payment as these were legitimate debt collection tools that did not make the relationship unfair. However the fact that a non-compliant default notice was sent (see CCA 1974 s.87, above paras 39-166 et seq.) rendered the relationship unfair.

## Any other action by creditor

*Replace paragraph with:*

The third factor[1375] that can render a relationship "unfair to the debtor" is any other[1376] action or inaction[1377] by, or on behalf of,[1378] the creditor either before or after the making of the credit agreement or "any related agreement".[1379] Again,[1380] the court must have regard[1381] to activities by or on behalf of an "associate"[1382] or "former associate" of the creditor[1383] but not the activities of third parties to any "related agreements" (unless they are agents or associates).[1383a] This third factor covers pre-contracting behaviour such as (mis)statements[1384] made by the creditor, his agents or "associates" before the credit agreement (or "related" agreement) as well as their post-contracting behaviour. Initially, the courts were generally reluctant to undermine well-established principles of common law[1385] or to augment existing regulatory regimes by imposing novel duties on creditors whether at the time of contracting or thereafter.[1386] However, in *Plevin v Paragon Personal Finance Ltd*[1387] the sale of (expensive[1388]) PPI (payment protection insurance) in circumstances where neither the large amount nor existence of the commission received by the creditor[1389] was revealed to the debtor, was held by the Supreme Court to give rise to an "unfair relationship" despite the sale having been effected in accordance with the relevant regulatory regime.[1390] Moreover, on the special facts of *Patel v Patel*,[1391] the omission to reduce the interest rate (when the bank base rate reduced) and to provide any elementary periodic documentary evidence of the debtor's (rising) indebtedness over a long period of time (together with an initial "extortionate" interest rate) gave rise to an "unfair relationship". An expansive approach to the jurisdiction was also adopted in *Scotland v British Credit Trust Ltd*.[1392] The limitation period for a claim in misrepresentation had expired but, citing *Patel*,[1393] the Court of Appeal did not regard this as precluding a finding that those misrepresentations rendered the credit relationship "unfair".[1394] 39-222

1375 CCA 1974 s.140A(1)(c).

1376 i.e. other that the exercise or enforcement of rights by the creditor, referred to in CCA 1974 s.140A(1)(b), see above, para.39-221.

1377 "any other thing done (or not done)". In *Pilgrim Rock v Iwanuik* [2019] EWHC 203 (Ch) a relationship was found to be unfair where (inter alia) a creditor had done nothing to enforce its rights for four years while interest was accruing at an escalated default rate. See also *PRA Group (UK) Ltd v Doyle* [2019] EWCA Civ 12 where the first instance judge held that the unfair relationship provisions would prevent the creditor delaying unduly in enforcing his rights so as to prolong the limitation period (see above, para.39-166), but Etherton M.R. did not consider it "necessary or appropriate ... to speculate" on whether this was the case.

1378 It was confirmed in *Plevin v Paragon Personal Finance Ltd* [2014] UKSC 61 (reversing [2013] EWCA Civ 1658 (followed in *Scotland v British Credit Trust Ltd* [2014] EWCA Civ 790)) that these words required an agency relationship and should not be construed more broadly. It would also seem (although this issue was not determined by the Supreme Court) that (if applicable) the "deemed agency" in CCA 1974 s.56(2) (see, above, para.39-075 and below, para.39-302) could also render a creditor liable under s.140A(1)(c) for the acts of a "negotiator" (and see *Scotland v British Credit Trust Ltd* [2014] EWCA Civ 790)).

1379 Defined in CCA 1974 s.140C(4), see above, para.39-214.

1380 See the similar position under CCA 1974 s.140A(1)(b), above, para.39-221.

1381 "except to the extent that it is not appropriate to do so".

1382 Defined in CCA 1974 s.184.

1383 CCA 1974 s.140A(3).

1383a But see *Pilgrim Rock v Iwanuik* [2019] EWHC 203 (Ch), above, para.39-217 (behaviour of a person who was neither an agent nor an associate of the creditor might still be relevant under s.140A(2)).

1384 For cases under the Moneylenders Acts jurisdiction reopening loans on this basis, see *Victorian Daylesford Syndicate Ltd v Dott* [1905] 2 Ch. 624; *Carringtons Ltd v Smith* [1906] 1 K.B. 79; and (debtor improperly induced to borrow) *Lewis v Mills* (1914) 30 T.L.R. 438. See also (debtor's vulnerability known to creditor): *Bonnard v Dott* (1906) 21 T.L.R. 491; *Part v Bond* (1906) 22 T.L.R. 253; *Blair v Buckworth* (1908) 24 T.L.R. 474; and (debtor did not understand terms): *Levene v Greenwood* (1904) 20 T.L.R. 389; *Carringtons Ltd v Smith*, above; *Levene v Titchener* (1907) 23 T.L.R. 508; *Harris v Clarson* (1910) 27 T.L.R. 30; *Stirling v Rose* (1913) 30 T.L.R. 67. See *Deutsche Bank (Suisse) SA v Khan* [2013] EWHC 482 (Comm), noted at [2013] C.C.L.R. 5 (misrepresentations alleged but not proved).

1385 Such as (i) the law on misrepresentation (see Neuberger L.J. in *Harrison v Black Horse Ltd* [2011] EWCA Civ 1128 at [30]–[31], criticising the "open-ended approach" of the judge in *Yates v Nemo Personal Finance* Unreported May 14, 2010, Manchester Cty Ct; (ii) promissory estoppel (see *Paragon Mortgages Ltd v McEwan-Peters* [2011] EWHC 2491 (Comm)); (iii) fiduciary law, breaches of statutory duty and negligence (see *Harrison v Black Horse Ltd* [2010] EWHC 3152 (QB)). But see *Barnes v Black Horse Ltd* [2011] EWHC 1416 (QB), per H.H.J. Waksman Q.C.: "it is not inconceivable that matters that may not be sufficient to generate duties of a fiduciary or tortious nature, or breaches thereof", may be relevant in the unfair relationship context.

1386 See Lomnicka [2012] J.B.L. 713 at 727 and Lomnicka, "The impact of rule-making by financial services regulators on the common law: the lessons of PPI", in Gullifer and Vogenauer (eds) *English and European Perspectives on Contract and Commercial Law: Essays in Honour of Hugh Beale* (2014), Ch.4. See the views of H.H.J. Waksman Q.C. in *Carey v HSBC Bank Plc* [2009] EWHC 3417 (QB) (refusal to give the "more dramatic remedy" available under the "unfair relationship" provisions when a more limited sanction (temporary unenforceability) was available under the CCA 1974) and in *Carney v NM Rothschild and Sons Ltd* [2018] EWHC 958 (Comm); (although it did not matter that the limitation period for the common law claims for bad advice and misrepresentation had expired, "the same elements as are required by the [common law] cause of action should be shown when such matters are raised as constituting an unfair relationship"). But note *Scotland v British Credit Trust Ltd* [2014] EWCA Civ 790 per Kitchen L.J. (the fact that there was an alternative (albeit time-barred) claim under CCA 1974 s.75 (see below, para.39-303) did not preclude application of s.140A).

1387 [2014] UKSC 61.

1388 The premium (for a £60,000 loan) was £10,200 for five years; equivalent standalone cover would only have cost £2,083.84.

1389 87 per cent of the premium, paid by the insurer, an associated company of the creditor. The FCA has intervened in relation to PPI (see FCA PS 17/3: Payment protection insurance complaints: Feedback on CP16/20 and final rules and guidance (March 2017)) and has set a single 50 per cent commission "tipping point" (with undisclosed profit-share (as defined) being treated in the same way as undisclosed commission) at which it states that firms should presume, for the purposes of handling PPI complaints and making recompense (the excess over 50 per cent together with interest), that the failure to disclose commission gives rise to an unfair relationship under s.140A.

1390 In the "ICOB" (now ICOBS) Module of the FCA Handbook, issued by the FSA under statutory powers (FSMA 2000 s.138 replaced by new s.137A) after the requisite rigorous consultation which considered at length, and decided against, requiring positive disclosure of the fact and amount of commissions. In the Court of Appeal in *Harrison v Black Horse Ltd* [2011] EWCA Civ 1128, at [58] (overruled by the Supreme Court) Neuberger M.R. had stated that the "touchstone must ... be the standard imposed by the regulatory authorities ... not resort to a visceral instinct that the relevant conduct is beyond the pale".

1391 [2009] EWHC 3264 (QB). A family elder was advanced a loan of £200,000 in 1992 for his small retail businesses by his younger, but commercially much more sophisticated, former protégé at the "exorbitant" rate of 20 per cent per annum compounded monthly when the bank rate was 7 per cent. With very few repayments demanded, the indebtedness had grown to over £1m.

1392 [2014] EWCA Civ 790.

1393 See also below, para.39-228.

1394 This was so even when the creditor's right of recourse against the misrepresentor (whether statutory (under s.75(2), see below, para.39-303) or common law/contractual (in relation to a s.56 agency claim, see above, para.39-075)) was also time-barred. See also *Carney v NM Rothschild and Sons Ltd* [2018] EWHC 958 (Comm); (unfair relationship claim available even when the limitation period for the common law claims for bad advice and misrepresentation had expired).

## Nature of relief[1410]

*Replace paragraph with:*

In reopening the agreement, the court may,[1411] make one or more of the seven types of order listed in s.140B(1) of the 1974 Act, viz: **39-225**

(a) require the creditor, or any associate[1412] or former associate of his, to repay the whole or part of any sum paid by the debtor or surety[1413] by virtue of the agreement or any related agreement,[1414] whether paid to the creditor or to any other person[1415];
(b) require the creditor, or any associate[1416] or former associate of his, to do or not to do (or to cease doing) anything specified in the order in connection with the agreement or any related agreement[1417];
(c) reduce or discharge any sum payable by the debtor or surety[1418] by virtue of the agreement or any related agreement[1419];
(d) direct the return to a surety[1420] of any property provided by him for the purposes of the security[1421];
(e) otherwise set aside the whole or part of any duty imposed on the debtor or a surety[1422] by virtue of the agreement or any related agreement[1423];
(f) alter the terms of the agreement or any related agreement[1424];
(g) direct accounts to be taken[1425] between any persons.[1426]

1411 See above, para.39-216, as to the court's discretion.

1412 Defined in CCA 1974 s.184.

1413 Defined in CCA 1974 s.189(1), see above, para.39-183.

1414 See above, para.39-214.

1415 CCA 1974 s.140B(1)(a), previously CCA 1974 s.139(2)(c), with the addition of the power to make an order against an associate or former associate as well as the creditor. And see s.140B(3), noted below. For orders to repay premiums of mis-sold PPI policies see *Scotland v British Credit Trust Ltd* [2014] EWCA Civ 790 and *Plevin v Paragon Personal Finance Ltd* [2016] C.C.L.R. 5, March 2, 2015, Manchester Cty Ct (the sequel to *Plevin v Paragon Personal Finance Ltd* [2014] UKSC 61), where the amount of commission received by the PPI seller was, on the facts, regarded as the appropriate remediation. In *Nelmes v NRAM Plc* [2016] EWCA Civ 491 the court ordered the repayment of a secret commission paid by the lender to the borrower's broker, plus interest. In *Swift Advances Plc v Scott* [2019] NICh 16 (where an unfair relationship was found in a PPI mis-selling case given (i) the PPI term was half the period of the loan and (ii) a substantial undisclosed commission was paid to the broker) the relief granted was that the borrowers had no obligation to pay the PPI premium or any interest thereon). But see above, para.39-222: the FCA has suggested that the recompense when complaints are settled by firms should be the excess over 50 per cent of the premium together with interest.

1416 Defined in CCA 1974 s.184.

1417 See above, para.39-214. CCA 1974 s.140B(1)(b). There was no corresponding provision in the (now repealed) CCA 1974 s.139(2). See *Link Financial Ltd v North Wilson* [2014] EWHC 252 (Ch) (order that no further sum was payable under the credit agreement); *Scotland v British Credit Trust Ltd* [2014] EWCA Civ 790 (debtor not liable to repay the loan so far as it related to a mis-sold PPI policy).

1418 Defined in CCA 1974 s.189(1), see above, para.39-183.

1419 CCA 1974 s.140B(1)(c). See above, para.39-214. There was no corresponding provision in the (now repealed) CCA 1974 s.139(2). See *Patel v Patel* [2009] EWHC 3264 (QB): reduction of amount contractually due by ordering the debtor to repay the amount initially advanced, with such repayments as the debtor had made being regarded as satisfying any entitlement to interest. In *Greenlands Trading Ltd v Pontearso* [2019] EWHC 278 (Ch) Nugee J. upheld, on appeal, the decision to discharge the liability to pay a "default administration fee" of £1,998 (where default interest was also payable but left undisturbed). See also s.140B(3), noted below.

1420 Defined in CCA 1974 s.189(1), see above, para.39-183.

1421 CCA 1974 s.140B(1)(d), previously CCA 1974 s.139(2)(d).

1422 Defined in CCA 1974 s.189(1), see above, para.39-183.

1423 CCA 1974 s.140B(1)(e), previously s.139(2)(e). See above, para.39-214. See *Pye v Ambrose* [1994] C.L.Y. 594, [1994] N.P.C. 53: jurisdiction in s.139(2)(e) confined to relieving the debtor from payment of a sum of money and did not extend to relieving him from an obligation to convey property.

1424 CCA 1974 s.140B(1)(f), previously s.139(2)(e). See above, para.39-214. In *Pilgrim Rock v Iwanuik* [2019] EWHC 203 (Ch) Fancourt J. upheld on appeal, the decision to vary the terms of the loan agreement to reduce the rate of interest, to provide for compounding annually rather than quarterly and to lengthen the term thereby limiting the period for which default interest could be charged.

1425 Or in Scotland, an accounting to be made.

1426 CCA 1974 s.140B(1)(g), previously s.139(2)(a).

### Compromise of claim

*Replace footnote 1432 with:*

**39-226A** 1432 See [2018] C.C.L.R. 8. See also *CFL Finance Ltd v Bass* [2019] EWHC 1839 (Ch) (compromise upheld and not found to be an "unfair relationship").

### Retrospective effect and limitation

*Replace paragraph with:*

**39-228** The court's powers are not limited to agreements made after the entry into force of the "unfair relationship" provisions but, subject to transitional provisions, extend to agreements and transactions made before that date.[1438] The limitation period for actions under the old "extortionate credit bargain" provisions caused controversy and similar issues arise under the new provisions. First, it seems[1439] that a debtor who invokes the provisions is making a "claim for relief" for the purposes of the Limitation Act 1980 and, hence, that claim (even if raised by way of defence[1440]) is subject to the appropriate limitation period. However, in *Canada Square Operations Ltd v Potter*[1440a] the unfair relationship provisions were held to confer a statutory "right of action" (in that case for non-disclosure of PPI commission giving rise to an unfair relationship) and hence resulted in the creditor committing a "breach of duty" under the Limitation Act 1980 s.32(2).[1440b] Hence the primary limitation period for recovery of the deliberately undisclosed and hence unrecovered balance of commission was disapplied under Limitation Act 1980 s.32(1)(b). Second, in principle, the limitation period for an action under the new provisions is 12 years under s.8(1) of the Limitation Act 1980 since the claim is a claim on a specialty.[1441] But in relation to a claim for repayment (as opposed, for example, to a claim for relief from future liability), s.9(1) of the 1980 Act prescribes a limitation period of six years for "an action to recover any sum recoverable by virtue of any enactment".[1442] The limitation period will run from the date on which the cause of action accrued. It was held in *Patel v Patel*[1443] that the cause of action under the new provisions is a continuing one accruing from day to day until the relationship ends.[1444] This is in contrast to the position under the old extortionate credit bargain provisions where, after much controversy, it was assumed[1445] that the cause of action accrued at the date of the agreement. *Patel* concerned the post-contracting behaviour (and omissions) of the creditor and it may be that if the allegations relate only to the terms and/or the pre-contracting behaviour of the debtor, then the date of the agreement is a more appropriate date from which the limitation period should run. In any event, if the provisions are invoked by way of legal set-off or counterclaim, such a claim is deemed to have been commenced on the date of the original action.[1446]

If an unfair relationship claim is successful, this may result, in effect, in the extension of the normal limitation period that would normally apply to the relevant concurrent common law claim.[1446a] But, in exercise of its discretion under these statutory provisions,[1446b] the court may, in any event, reject a delayed claim.[1446c]

1438 See *Patel v Patel* [2009] EWHC 3264 (agreement made in 1992). The (complex) transitional provisions are in Consumer Credit Act 2006 Sch.3 paras 14–16. See above, para.39-212.

1439 It was so held (in relation to the old provisions) in *Nolan v Wright* [2009] EWHC 305, [2009] C.C.L.R. 8.

1440 In *Nolan v Wright* [2009] EWHC 305 (Ch), [2009] C.C.L.R. 8 the view that the limitation period would not apply if the debtor raised the provisions by way of defence to reduce the amount claimed (put forward by Dobson (1998) 142 S.J. 274, and see, in another context, *Henriksens A/S v Rolimpex* [1974] 1 Q.B. 233, CA, especially 245G, above, para.28-123) was rejected. But see note referring to Limitation Act 1980 s.35(1)(b), below.

1440a [2020] EWHC 672 (QB).

1440b That term was interpreted widely (following *Giles v Rhind* [2008] EWCA Civ 118) so as to cover a "legal wrongdoing of any kind, giving rise to a right of action" and not in the more narrow sense of a breach of duty in the contractual, tortious, equitable or fiduciary sense.

1441 Which covers an obligation imposed by statute: *Collin v Duke of Westminster* [1985] Q.B. 581. See (on the old provisions) *Nolan v Wright* [2009] EWHC 305, [2009] C.C.L.R. 8, relying on dicta in *Rahman v Sterling Credit Ltd* [2001] 1 W.L.R. 498, CA.

1442 *Rahman v Sterling Credit Ltd* [2001] 1 W.L.R. 496, CA. See *Doran v Paragon Personal Finance Ltd* Unreported June 28, 2018 (Manchester Cty Ct): *Plevin v Paragon Personal Finance Ltd* [2014] UKSC 61 applied to claim for PPI premium plus interest although claim was made 13 years after the credit and PPI agreements were made but less than five years after loan was repaid.

1443 [2009] EWHC 3264 (QB), see above, para.39-222.

1444 Hence, it accrues at the date of trial in the case of an extant relationship and otherwise at the date when the relationship ended. *Patel* was applied in (i) *Doran v Paragon Personal Finance Ltd* [2018] 6 WLUK 518 (Manchester Cty Ct, June 28, 2018) (a claim made more than 13 years after the agreement was made but less than five years after the loan was repaid was successful as it fell within the six-year limitation period); (ii) *Wood v Commercial First Business Ltd* [2019] EWHC 2205 (Ch) (time would only begin to run for limitation purposes when the credit relationship ended, which in that case was on the coming into effect of an order rescinding the mortgage). But *Rahman v Sterling Credit Ltd* [2000] EWCA Civ 222, [2001] 1 W.L.R. 496 was not considered: see note to *Wood* at [2020] C.C.L.R. 4.

1445 In *Nolan v Wright* [2009] EWHC 305 (Ch), [2009] C.C.L.R. 8 (relying on dicta in *Rahman v Sterling Credit Ltd* [2001] 1 W.L.R. 496, CA). It was so held in *First National Bank Plc v Ann* [1997] C.L.Y. 963, Cty Ct.

1446 Limitation Act 1980 s.35(1)(b)—although the court has a discretion to order that it be dealt with as a separate action (CPR Pt 20 r.9(1), made under Limitation Act 1980 s.35), in which case the limitation period will start when that cause of action accrued (see *Ernst and Young v Butte Mining Plc* [1997] 1 W.L.R. 1485).

1446a See *Scotland v British Credit Trust Ltd* [2014] EWCA Civ 790 (limitation period for a claim in misrepresentation had expired but, citing *Patel*, the Court of Appeal did not regard this as precluding a finding that those misrepresentations rendered the credit relationship "unfair". This was so even though the creditor's right of recourse against the misrepresentor (whether statutory (under CCA 1974 s.75(2)) or common law/contractual (in relation to a CCA 1974 s.56 claim)) was also time barred). See also *Carney v NM Rothschild and Sons Ltd* [2018] EWHC 958 (Comm) (limitation period had expired for the common law bad advice and misrepresentation claims and yet unfair relationship provisions were considered potentially applicable).

1446b See para.39-216, above.

1446c *Santander UK Plc v Wells* [2017] EWHC 2413 (Ch) (claimant had delayed too long in making claim, having had plenty of opportunity to make it earlier but having "chosen or neglected not to so and [having] given no adequate explanation therefor").

## (n) Ancillary Credit Businesses

### Credit broking: exclusions

*Replace footnote 1464 with:*

39-233 1464 See (i) RAO art.36(2): activity within RAO art.36H (operating an electronic system in relation to lending, see below, para.39-256); (ii) RAO art.36D (activities within RAO arts 60B(1) and 60L(1): entering into agreements as lender or owner respectively, see above, para.39-061); (iii) RAO art.36E (activities in relation to regulated mortgages and home purchase plans—but note the new version of art.36E inserted on March 21, 2016, by SI 2015/910 art.3 and Sch.1 para.4(7), when the Mortgage Credit Directive (see above, para.39-003) was implemented. Note also the addition of art.36FA (registered social landlord exemption) by SI 2019/1067.

### Canvassing certain ancillary credit services off trade premises

*In line 1, after "Section 154", add new footnote 1543a:*

39-252 1543a The FCA's *Review of retained provisions of the Consumer Credit Act: Final Report* (see para.39-004, n.13, above) states (see para.7-97) that "the criminal offences in the CCA may no longer be necessary", but it also notes (para.7.103) that "there may be arguments in favour of keeping the current offences in respect of canvassing ... this merits further consideration".

### Right to recover brokerage fees

*Replace whole paragraph with:*

39-253 Section 155 of the 1974 Act confers a right in certain circumstances to recover from the credit-broker brokerage fees paid in advance in the event that an introduction by a credit-broker does not bear fruit within six months.[1549] The section applies[1550] where an individual has sought an introduction for a purpose that would have been fulfilled by his entry into (a) a regulated agreement or (b) an agreement for credit secured on land (in the case of an individual desiring to obtain credit to finance the acquisition or provision of a dwelling) or (c) an exempt agreement[1551] or (d) an agreement which is not a regulated credit agreement or a regulated consumer hire agreement but which would be such an agreement if the law applicable to the agreement were the law of a part of the United Kingdom. However, it does not apply[1552] where the credit-broker is an authorised person (or appointed representative) and the fee relates to a regulated mortgage[1553] or home purchase plan (i.e. the activity is excluded from the definition of "credit broking" by art.36E of the RAO[1554]).

When s.155 applies, the excess over £5[1555] of a fee or commission for his services charged by a credit-broker to an individual ceases to be payable or, as the case may be, is recoverable by the individual if the introduction does not result in his entering into a "relevant agreement" (for whatever reason) within the six months following the introduction.[1556] For this purpose, an agreement is a "relevant agreement" in relation to an individual if it is the *type* of agreement sought by that individual.[1557]

1549 For a fuller discussion, see Guest and Lloyd, *Encyclopedia of Consumer Credit Law* (1975, looseleaf), para.2-156 and see the guidance in *FCA Handbook*, CONC 2.5.9 and CONC 6.8.3 (more limited than the now revoked OFT's Guidance: *Credit brokers and intermediaries: OFT guidance for brokers, intermediaries and the consumer credit and hire businesses which employ or use their services* (OFT 1288, November 2011), especially Ch.6). There are particular difficulties in deciding what is a "fee or commission" (e.g. sums charged by brokers for "packaging agents") for these purposes. And note s.173 (contracting out not possible). Apart from s.155 there may be rights to recovery at common law (for example on the grounds that the basis for the payment has totally failed, see above paras 29-057 et seq.). T he FCA's *Review of retained provisions of the Consumer Credit Act: Final Report* (see para.39-004, n.14, above) states (see Annex 5, para.9) that s.155 could be repealed and replaced by an FCA rule imposing a corresponding obligation on creditors without adversely affecting the appropriate degree of consumer protection. This would have the advantage of (i) bringing it together with existing FCA CONC provisions on credit broker fees (noted in n.1588, below) and (ii) providing an opportunity to consider some of the suggestions for reform noted in the Review (see Ch.5, paras 5.56–5.58).

1550 See CCA 1974 s.155(2).

1551 See above, paras 39-038 et seq.

1552 See CCA 1974 s.155(2A).

1553 See below, para.39-529.

1554 See above, para.39-233.

1555 The amount was raised from £1 to £3 by SI 1983/1571 and to £5 by SI 1998/997.

1556 CCA 1974 s.155(1). The six-month limit was set before faster, digital communications became common. See also CCA 1974 ss.70(7), 181. If, after making a "relevant agreement", the debtor exercises his right to withdraw (under CCA 1974 s.66A, see above, para.39-101) or cancel (CCA 1974 s.67, see above, para.39-102), it seems s.155 applies as the agreement is (in statutory terms) "treated as if it had never having been entered into".

1557 CCA 1974 s.155(3). The OFT Guidance (see above) stated that the credit-broker's licence was at risk if he did not inform the debtor of (a) the amount of the fee before undertaking the credit brokerage services and (b) the debtor's right under s.155. For similar obligations, see now the *FCA Handbook*, CONC 4.4.2R(2) and (4) and, in relation to (b), see para.39-255, below.

### Right to recover other payments

*To the end of paragraph, after "over to a third party", add:*

The onus is on the individual to request the refund; there is no requirement that the broker pro-actively make the refund (for example where no introduction is made or no relevant agreement will be entered into). 39-254

## (o) Operating an Electronic System in Relation to Lending

### Operating an electronic system in relation to lending

*Replace footnote 1571 with:*

1571 See, in relation to ordinary lending, above, para.39-063. For special P2P regulatory provisions, see *FCA Handbook*, CONC 3.7A (financial promotion); CONC 4.3 (pre-contractual requirements); CONC 5.5 (creditworthiness assessment); CONC 7.17–7.19 (NOSIAs etc.); CONC 11.2 (cancellation). But borrowers are not protected by the Financial Services Compensation Scheme. See the new rules announced by the FCA's Policy Statement PS 19/14 (June 2019). 39-256

## 2. LOANS AND INTEREST

## (a) Loans of Money

### Proof of loan

*Replace footnote 1608 with:*

1608 *Seldon v Davidson* [1968] 1 W.L.R. 1083; *Chapman v Jaume* [2012] EWCA Civ 476. This approach has not been accepted in Australia (see e.g. *Alexiadis v Zirpiadis* (2013) 302 A.L.R. 148) but has been followed in New Zealand (*Re Matthews* [1993] 2 N.Z.L.R. 91). 39-264

### Time for repayment

*Replace footnote 1624 with:*

1624 *Brighty v Norton* (1862) 3 B. & S. 312; *Toms v Wilson* (1862) 4 B. & S. 442, 453; *Moore v Shelley* 39-267

(1883) 8 App. Cas. 285, 293; *R.A. Cripps & Son Ltd v Wickenden* [1973] 1 W.L.R. 944; *Bank of Baroda v Panessar*, above. See also *UBS AG v Rose Capital Ventures Ltd* [2018] EWHC 3137 (Ch), applying *Braganza v BP Shipping Ltd* [2015] UKSC 17 (no implication of any limitations on the express right of a creditor, in an on-demand five year loan, to demand full payment at its "absolute discretion" after three months' notice). But see the Consumer Rights Act 2015 Sch.2 para.8, replacing (for contracts made on or after October 1, 2015) the Unfair Terms in Consumer Contracts Regulations 1999 (SI 1999/2083) Sch.2 para.1(g) above, para.38-309.

### Term loans

*In line 8, after "event at the end of the term.", add new footnote 624a:*

**39-268** [1624a] See *UBS AG v Rose Capital Ventures Ltd* [2018] EWHC 3137 (Ch), previous footnote.

### Acceleration clauses

*Replace footnote 1645 with:*

**39-272** [1645] *The Angelic Star* [1988] 1 Lloyd's Rep. 122, followed in *ZCCM Investments Holdings Plc v Konkola Copper Mines Plc* [2017] EWHC 3288 (Comm) and *Holyoake v Candy* [2017] EWHC 3397 (Ch) at 466.

### Defective notice

*Replace footnote 1650 with:*

**39-274** [1650] *Concord Trust v Law Debenture Trust Corp Plc* [2005] UKHL 27, [2005] 1 W.L.R. 1592 at [30]–[45]. See also, on inaccurate default notices, *Lombard North Central Plc v European Skyjets Ltd (In Liquidation)* [2020] EWHC 679 (QB) at [46].

### Pari passu and negative pledge clauses

*Replace footnote 1680 with:*

**39-279** [1680] In particular, the issue will turn on whether the chargor has ostensible authority to deal with the collateral. See *English & Scottish Mercantile Investment Co Ltd v Brunton* [1892] 2 Q.B. 700, 707 and above, Ch.31, esp. para.31-056.

## (b) Interest

### Rates of interest

*Replace paragraph with:*

**39-292** Since the Usury Laws Repeal Act 1854 there was, until recently (apart from the discretionary power of the court to alter interest rates conferred by the "unfair relationship" provisions in the Consumer Credit Act 1974[1729] and by the Insolvency Act 1986[1730]) no specific statutory control over the rate of interest that may be agreed by the parties to a transaction.[1731] But in response to the rise of the "pay-day lending" industry, the Financial Conduct Authority was initially given the power to control the cost of credit and various other terms in certain credit agreements[1732] and now has an *obligation* to make rules controlling the cost of "high-cost short-term credit" (as defined).[1733] The FCA has also imposed a price cap on certain "rent-to-own" agreements.[1734]

[1729] ss.140A–140C, see above, paras 39-212 et seq. See, for example, *Pilgrim Rock v Iwanuik* [2019] EWHC 203 (Ch), in which Fancourt J. upheld on appeal the decision to vary the terms of the loan agreement to reduce the rate of interest, to provide for compounding annually rather than quarterly and to lengthen the term thereby limiting the period for which default interest could be charged.

[1730] ss.244 and 343.

[1731] However, there is power under the Credit Unions Act 1979 s.11(5) to limit the interest that can be charged by credit unions: see the Credit Unions (Maximum Interest Rate on Loans) Order 2013 (SI 2013/2589) (3 per cent per month).

[1732] Financial Services and Markets Act 2000 s.137C (added by the Financial Services Act 2012 s.24).

[1733] Financial Services and Markets Act 2000 s.137C, as amended by the Financial Services (Banking Reform) Act 2013 s.131(1). The rules are in the CONC Module of the FCA Handbook: see CONC 5A.

[1734] i.e. conditional sale (below, paras 39-439 et seq.) or hire-purchase (below, paras 39-356 et seq.) agreements for "household goods" (as defined): see the FCA's document: *Rent-to-own price cap – feedback on CP18/35 and final rules*, PS19/6 (March 2019). The provisions are in the FCA's Handbook, CONC 5B. The sanction (see CONC 5B.6.1) is that charges in excess of the cap are unenforceable.

## Variation of interest rate

*Replace paragraph with:*

The rate of interest stipulated in a loan agreement may be either a fixed rate or a rate that automatically varies, for example, in accordance with movements in a base rate or inter-bank rate or by reference to an index or some other factor specified in the agreement. But some loan agreements provide that the lender has the power to vary the interest rate unilaterally at his discretion.[1735] Such a provision is not unlawful as such at common law, but very clear words are required to achieve that result.[1736] The power is, however, even at common law not completely unfettered. In *Paragon Finance Plc v Nash*[1737] the Court of Appeal held that the unilateral power of a mortgagee to set the rate of interest from time-to-time was subject to an implied term that the discretion to vary rates should not be exercised dishonestly, for an improper purpose, capriciously, arbitrarily or in a way in which no reasonable lender, acting reasonably, would do, although on the facts it was held that there was no real prospect of the defendant borrower proving a breach of this implied term at trial.[1738] Some further protection is afforded to a borrower who is a consumer[1739] by Sch.2 to the Consumer Rights Act 2015 Pt 2[1740] which contains an indicative and non-exhaustive list[1741] of the terms which may be regarded as unfair. It includes terms "enabling the trader to alter the terms of the contract unilaterally without a valid reason which is specified in the contract",[1742] although this is expressly stated not to include[1743]: 39-293

> "… a term by which a supplier of financial services reserves the right to alter the rate of interest payable by or due to the consumer, or the amount of other charges for financial services without notice where there is a valid reason, if (a) the supplier is required to inform the consumer of the alteration at the earliest opportunity, and (b) the consumer is free to dissolve the contract immediately."

How a creditor exercises its powers of variation may also render a credit relationship "unfair" under the "unfair relationship" provisions of the Consumer Credit Act 1974[1744] and hence enable the court to exercise its wide powers to reopen a credit agreement under those provisions. In addition, now that consumer credit is regulated by the Financial Conduct Authority under the Financial Services and Markets Act 2000,[1745] the wide regulatory powers under that Act may be used to control the exercise of such a power.[1746] Moreover, consumers are also protected by various statutory notification requirements[1747] as regards interest rate variations, and the Standards of Lending Practice[1748] also stipulate for the provision by banks and building societies of information as to changes in interest rates.

[1735] Subject to any statutory notification requirements noted below.

[1736] *Lombard Tricity Finance Ltd v Paton* [1989] 1 All E.R. 918. Applied in *Amberley UK Ltd v West Sussex CC* [2011] EWCA Civ 11 (power to raise care home fees) and *Daniels v Lloyds Bank Plc* [2018] EWHC 660 (Comm) (bank's power to vary the terms of an executive director's long term incentive plan). But contrast *Alexander v West Bromwich Mortgage Co Ltd* [2016] EWCA Civ 496 (power to vary interest inconsistent with mortgage offered as "tracker mortgage").

[1737] [2001] EWCA Civ 1466, [2000] 1 W.L.R. 685 (pet. dis. [2002] 1 W.L.R. 2263) followed in

*Broadwick Financial Services Ltd v Spencer* [2002] EWCA Civ 35, [2002] 1 All E.R. (Comm) 446 and applied (in context of raising fees and costs) in *Addison v Esso Petroleum Co Ltd* [2003] EWHC 1730 (Comm) (affirmed, on a different point, [2004] EWCA Civ 1470).

1738 And see *Sterling Credit Ltd v Rahman (No.2)* [2002] EWHC 3008 (Ch), [2003] C.C.L.R. 13 (no implied obligation to *reduce* interest rate); *Paragon Finance Plc v Plender* [2005] EWCA Civ 760, [2005] C.C.L.R. 5 (lender increased rates due to adverse financial circumstances).

1739 But in a commercial context see *Myers v Kestrel Acquisitions Ltd (Kestrel)* [2015] EWHC 916 (Ch) (no implied duty to vary in good faith).

1740 Replacing (for contracts made on or after October 1, 2015) the Unfair Terms in Consumer Contracts Regulations 1999 (SI 1999/2083), as amended; above paras 38-221 et seq. See the decisions of the CJEU on this aspect of the Unfair Contract Terms Directive 1993, in particular the Grand Chamber ruling in *Gómez del Moral Guasch v Bankia SA (C-125/18)* (C-125/18) EU:C:2020:138.

1741 s.63, replacing (for contracts made on or after October 1, 2015) the Unfair Terms in Consumer Contracts Regulations 1999 (SI 1999/2083) reg.5(5). See the FCA's *Final Guidance: Fairness of variation terms in financial services consumer contracts under the Consumer Rights Act 2015* (FG18/7), December 2018.

1742 Consumer Rights Act 2015 Sch.2 para.11 (and see also para.12), replacing, with minor changes in wording (for contracts made on or after October 1, 2015) the Unfair Terms in Consumer Contracts Regulations 1999 (SI 1999/2083) Sch.2 para.1(j) and see also SI 1999/2083 Sch.2 para.1(k), above, paras 38-312 et seq.

1743 Consumer Rights Act 2015 Sch.2 paras 22 (and see also para.23), replacing, with minor changes in wording (for contracts made on or after October 1, 2015) the Unfair Terms in Consumer Contracts Regulations 1999 (SI 1999/2083) Sch.2 para.2(b). See Guest and Lloyd, *Encyclopedia of Consumer Credit Law* (1975, looseleaf), para.2-083.

1744 See above, paras 39-212 et seq.

1745 See above, para.39-002. Note in particular Principle for Business 6 (as amplified in the *FCA Handbook* CONC Module) which states that a firm "must pay due regard to the interests of its customers and treat them fairly".

1746 Via disciplinary powers, see above, para.39-063. See also, in relation to "regulated mortgage contracts", the FCA's discussion paper, DP14/2: *Variation Terms: Assessing the Fairness of Changes to Mortgage Contracts* (July 2014) and its consultation paper: GC18/2: *Fairness of variation terms in financial services consumer contracts under the Consumer Rights Act 2015* (May 2018).

1747 Consumer Credit Act 1974 s.82(1) (above, para.39-146) and the *FCA Handbook*, CONC 4.7 (replacing the repealed Consumer Credit Act 1974 s.78A (above, para.39-147) (notice required in the case of regulated agreements); Payment Services Regulations 2017 (SI 2017/752) (above, paras 34-224 et seq.) (notice required in the case of certain "payment services contracts").

1748 See above, para.39-013.

## Default interest

*Replace paragraph with:*

**39-294** A contractual provision for payment of a higher rate of interest after a default in payment by the borrower is open to attack as a penalty.[1749] But a clause that provides for interest to increase on default will not be held to give rise to a penalty if the increase is not retrospective but only prospective from the date of default, if the dominant contractual purpose of the clause is not to deter default, and if the increase is modest and commercially justifiable by reason of the increased credit risk represented by a debtor in default.[1750] It is submitted that the old practice of banks to charge a certain rate of interest on "authorised" overdrafts (incurred by prior arrangement with the bank), and a higher rate on "unauthorised" overdrafts (incurred without prior arrangement or in excess of the authorised overdraft limit), would not have been held to impose a penalty.[1751] However, where the borrower is a consumer, a provision for payment of a higher rate of interest on default is open to challenge as being "unfair", and so not binding on the consumer, under the Consumer Rights Act 2015 Pt 2.[1752] Moreover, the "unfair relationship" provisions of the Consumer Credit Act 1974 may apply to enable the court to reopen the agreement.[1753]

[1749] *Astley v Weldon* (1801) 2 B. & P. 346, 353; *Wallis v Smith* (1882) 21 Ch. D. 243; *Dunlop Pneumatic Tyre Co Ltd v New Garage and Motor Co Ltd* [1915] A.C. 79, 86; *Cavendish Square Holdings BV v Makdessi* [2015] UKSC 67, see above, paras 26-190 et seq. See also Consumer Credit Act 1974 s.93 (above, para.39-177) and s.86F (above, para.39-136: interest on default sum can only be simple). A reduction in the rate of interest in the event of prompt payment will not make the unreduced interest penal: *Astley v Weldon*, above, at 353; *Herbert v Salisbury and Yeovil Railway Co* (1866) L.R. 2 Eq. 221; *Wallingford v Mutual Society* (1880) 5 App. Cas. 685, 702. See also *Euro London Appointments Ltd v Claessens International Ltd* [2006] EWCA Civ 385, [2006] 2 Lloyd's Rep. 436.

[1750] *Lordsvale Finance Plc v Bank of Zambia* [1996] Q.B. 752 (approved in *Cavendish Square Holdings BV v Makdessi* [2015] UKSC 67 at [26]–[28], [146]–[148], [222] and [239]–[241]); *Lancore Services Ltd v Barclays Bank Plc* [2008] EWHC 1264 (Ch); *Deutsche Bank (Suisse) SA v Khan* [2013] EWHC 482 (Comm), noted at [2013] C.C.L.R. 5; *Holyoake v Candy* [2017] EWHC 3397 (Ch); *Lombard North Central Plc v European Skyjets Ltd (In Liquidation)* [2020] EWHC 679 (QB). Contrast *Jeancharm Ltd v Barnet Football Club Ltd* [2003] EWCA Civ 58, [2003] 92 Const. L.R. 26 (default interest of 5 per cent per week held penal). For default interest being held penal, on the basis that "the size of the uplift [was] in its nature a punishment for or deterrent to breach, rather than an ordinary commercial re-rating to reflect a change in risk (or administration cost)" see also *Hong Leuong Finance Ltd v Tan Gin Huay* [1999] 2 S.L.R. 153; *Beil v Mansell (No. 2)* (2006) 2 Qd. R. 499 and *Elberg v Fraval* [2012] VSC 342, all cited in *Cavendish Square Holdings BV v Makdessi* [2015] UKSC 67 at [147]–[148].

[1751] See also above, para.39-177. But this practice is outlawed from April 6. 2020: see the FCA's Overdraft Policy Statement PS 19/16 (June 2019).

[1752] Replacing, with minor changes in wording, (for contracts made on or after October 1, 2015) the Unfair Terms in Consumer Contracts Regulations 1999, see above, paras 38-221 et seq. and for a case under those regulations: *Falco Finance Ltd v Gough* (1999) 149 N.L.J. 7.

[1753] See below, para.39-301. But an "industry standard" default rate was not disturbed in *Greenlands Trading Ltd v Pontearso* [2019] EWHC 278 (Ch). Cf. *Pilgrim Rock v Iwanuik* [2019] EWHC 203 (Ch).

**Interest payable by statute**

*Replace footnote 1763 with:*

[1763] s.328(4), (5), as amended by the Banks and Building Societies (Priorities on Insolvency) Order 2018 (SI 2018/1244). Cf. s.322(2). **39-296**

## (c) Effect of Consumer Credit Regulation

**Overdrafts**

*Replace paragraph with:*

Special dispensation was originally provided for most overdrafts from the documentation and cancellation provisions in Pt V of the Consumer Credit Act 1974. However, the implementation of the Consumer Credit Directive,[1782] which itself contains special provisions for overdrafts, has resulted in complex modifications (which depend on the type of overdraft) of Pt V in relation to overdrafts.[1783] In particular, there is now an obligation to supply a copy of an overdraft agreement.[1784] Moreover, non-business overdrafts are subject to (special) pre-contract disclosure obligations[1785] and to the new (general) duty to assess creditworthiness.[1786] There are also special information provisions regarding the consequences of "overrunning" (i.e. overdrawing without a pre-arranged overdraft or exceeding a pre-arranged overdraft limit).[1787] The remainder of the 1974 Act generally continues to apply, for example, the provisions of the Act relating to the variation of agreements,[1788] the service of enforcement,[1789] default[1790] or termination[1791] notices (and other requisite notices during the course of the agreement),[1792] security,[1793] the form of guarantees and indemnities given in respect of the overdraft,[1794] and in particular the exclusive jurisdiction of the county court over actions brought by the creditor to enforce the overdraft agreement or any security relating to it.[1795] However, the FCA has made special provision for overdrafts in its Handbook.[1795a] **39-300**

[1782] See above, para.39-011.

[1783] See s.74 as amended by SI 2010/1010 reg.17.

[1784] s.61B, added on February 1, 2011 by SI 2010/1010 reg.9, as amended by SI 2010/1969 reg.7. The FCA's *Review of retained provisions of the Consumer Credit Act: Final Report* (see para.39-004, n.13, above) states (see para.6.31) that the obligation in s.61B could be replaced by a corresponding FCA rule but that breach of such an FCA rule would not carry the same sanction and hence the existing sanction should be retained in legislation.

[1785] See above, para.39-076.

[1786] See above, para.39-078.

[1787] *FCA Handbook*, CONC 4.7 and CONC 6.3.3–6.3.4 (replacing the repealed Consumer Credit Act 1974 Pt VA (ss.74A and 74B), added on February 1, 2011 by SI 2010/1010 regs 21 and 22 (as amended by 2010/1969 regs 9 and 10)), noted above at para.39-127.

[1788] s.82(1); above, para.39-145. But note, in relation to overdrafts, the new s.82(1B)–(1E) (added on February 1, 2011 by SI 2010/1010 reg.28) and the new s.78A(4), the combined effect of which is that only *increases* in charges and interest rate need be notified.

[1789] s.76; above, para.39-164.

[1790] s.87; above, para.39-166.

[1791] s.98; above, para.39-172. But note that s.98A (above, para.39-173) dealing with the termination of agreements of indefinite duration, does not apply to overdrafts: s.98A(8).

[1792] s.78 (above, para.39-132), s.86C (above, para.39-134) and s.86E (above, para.39-135).

[1793] s.113; above, para.39-190.

[1794] SI 1983/1556; above, para.39-184.

[1795] s.141(1); above, para.39-199.

[1795a] See its Overdrafts Policy Statement, PS 19/16 (June 2019) outlawing various practices such as higher interest rates for "unauthorised" overdrafts and various fees.

## Unfair relationships

*Replace paragraph with:*

**39-301** The provisions of the Consumer Credit Act 1974 relating to "unfair relationships" apply to loans to individuals[1796] and they have been invoked in a number of cases concerning loans.[1797] Many cases have concerned business loans and in that context the challenge has almost always been unsuccessful.[1798]

[1796] ss.140A–140C, above, paras 39-212 et seq.

[1797] *Plevin v Paragon Personal Finance Ltd* [2014] UKSC 61 (sale of PPI with loan rendered relationship "unfair" on facts); *Patel v Patel* [2009] EWHC 3264 (QB) ("exorbitant" interest "unfair"); cf. *Khodari v Tamimi* [2009] EWCA Civ 1109, [2010] C.C.L.R. 3 ("very large" 10 per cent charge for short-term loans to wealthy compulsive gambler, where credit risk was high and "defendant wanted these loans and could well afford to repay them", not "unfair relationship"); *Consolidated Finance Ltd v Hunter* [2010] B.P.I.R. 1322 (loan at market rate for similar short-term bridging loans not "unfair"); *Carey v HSBC Bank Plc* [2009] EWHC 3417 (QB); *Black Horse Ltd v Speak* [2010] EWHC 1866 (QB); *Link Financial Ltd v North Wilson* [2014] EWHC 252 (Ch), [2014] C.C.L.R. 6; *McMullon v Secure the Bridge Ltd* [2015] EWCA Civ 884. And see cases in next footnote.

[1798] *Paragon Mortgages Ltd v McEwan-Peters* [2011] EWHC 2491 (Comm) (buy to let); *Holyoake & Hotblack Holdings Ltd v Nicholas Candy, Christian Candy, CPC Group Ltd* [2017] EWHC 3397 (Ch). See especially the business bank loan cases: *Rahman v HSBC Bank Plc* [2012] EWHC 11 (Ch); *Deutsche Bank (Suisse) SA v Khan* [2013] EWHC 482 (Comm), noted at [2013] C.C.L.R. 5 and cited in many subsequent "business" cases; *Chubb v Dean* [2013] EWHC 1282 (Ch); *Gardner v Clydesdale Bank Ltd* [2013] EWHC 4356 (Ch); *Barclays Bank Plc v McMillan* [2015] EWHC 1596 (Comm); *Clydesdale Bank Plc v R Gough t/t JC Gough & Sons and Anne Michelle Gough* [2017] EWHC 2230 (Ch); *Santander UK Plc v Clive Roger Wells & Graham Mervyn Wells* [2017] EWHC 2413 (Ch); *Ulster Bank Ltd v Esmaili* [2017] NICh 14; *Holyoake v Candy* [2017] EWHC 3397 (Ch) (permission to appeal refused by Court of Appeal: [2018] C.C.L.R. 8); *Carney v NM Rothschild and Sons Ltd* [2018] EWHC 958 (Comm); *Hodell v Clydesdale Bank Plc* [2018] EWHC 1009 (QB); *Broomhead v National Westminster Bank Plc* [2018] EWHC 1574 (Ch); *Greenlands Trading Ltd v Pontearso* [2019] EWHC 278 (Ch); *Wood v Commercial First Business Ltd* [2019] EWHC 2205 (Ch); *Praetura Asset Finance Ltd v Wood* [2019] EWHC 2231 (Comm); *Promontoria (Henrico) Ltd v Samra* [2019] EWHC 2327

(Ch). But see *Pilgrim Rock v Iwanuik* [2019] EWHC 203 (Ch) (commercial loan between co-venturer friends found to be "unfair").

## "Connected lender liability": Misrepresentation or breach by supplier

*Replace footnote 1807 with:*

1807 For problems arising under s.75, see Guest and Lloyd, *Encyclopedia of Consumer Credit Law* (1975, looseleaf), para.2-076; Hare [2008] L.M.C.L.Q. 338; Bisping [2011] J.B.L. 457. See also *Rampion v Franfinance SA* (C-429/05) EU:C:2007:575, [2008] C.M.L.R. 8, ECJ (scope of art.11(2) of Consumer Credit Directive (87/102), implemented in the UK by s.75). The Law Commissions' Joint Paper: *Consumer Redress for Misleading and Aggressive Practices* Cm.8323 (March 2012), para.7.139 proposed that a "misleading practice" should qualify as a "misrepresentation" under s.75 but, although originally included in the draft of SI 2014/870, this did not appear in the enacted version. The FCA's *Review of retained provisions of the Consumer Credit Act: Final Report* (see para.39-004, n.13, above) states (see Annex 5, para.61) that s.75 (and s.75A, below, para.39-305) should be retained in legislation as an FCA rule could not replicate its provisions and hence repeal would adversely affect the appropriate degree of consumer protection. However, various problems with s.75 are noted (see the *Review*, Ch.5, para.5.34) and it is suggested that they be considered and that the scope of s.75 be clarified. **39-303**

## Additional "connected lender liability"

*Replace paragraph with:*

A new s.75A was added[1822] to the Consumer Credit Act 1974 in implementation of the Consumer Credit Directive,[1823] which contains additional provisions on creditor liability. The liability is generally[1824] narrower in scope than that imposed by s.75. First, s.75A does not apply to credit agreements outside the scope of the Directive.[1825] Second, it only applies in the case of so-called "linked credit agreements" (a "Directive" concept), defined[1826] to mean regulated consumer credit agreements that: (i) "exclusively" finance an agreement for the supply of specific goods or service[1826a]; and (ii) where either: (a) the creditor uses the services of the supplier in connection with the preparation or making of the credit agreement, or (b) the specific goods or services are "explicitly specified" in the credit agreement. The section provides that if the debtor under such a "linked credit agreement" has a claim against the supplier in respect of a breach of contract (only), the debtor may pursue that claim against the creditor but only where, essentially, the debtor is unable to obtain satisfaction from the supplier. Thus the section only provides for so-called "second in line" liability on the part of the creditor. Third, the section does not apply if the cash value of the goods or services is £30,000 or less.[1827] Hence, it will apply (to situations otherwise within its scope), where s.75 is unavailable because the cash price exceeds that sum and s.75 will apply (to situations otherwise within its scope) where the cash price is £30,000 or less (as long as it is above £100). **39-305**

1822 On February 1, 2011 by 2010/1010 reg.25 (as amended by SI 2010/1969 reg.11). See CCA 1974 s.189B(3), Sch.2A: in s.75A, references to "debtor" in relation to "green deal plans" (as defined in CCA 1974 s.189(1), see above, para.39-257) are to be read as references to the "improver" (as defined in CCA 1974 s.189B(6)). See the recommendation in the FCA's *Review of retained provisions of the Consumer Credit Act: Final Report* (see para.39-004, n.13, above) at Annex 5, para.61 that s.75A (and s.75, above, para.39-303) should be retained in legislation as an FCA rule could not replicate its provisions and hence repeal would adversely affect the appropriate degree of consumer protection.

1823 See above, para.39-011. See especially art.15.2 (and 15.3) of the Directive.

1824 But see below: it (unlike s.75) applies where the cash price is over £30,000.

1825 s.75A(6)(b)–(c) and (7), viz: (i) credit in excess of £60,260, (ii) "business" credit and (iii) agreements secured on land. Since the Mortgage Credit Directive (see above, para.39-003) was implemented on March 21, 2016, exemption (i) no longer applies to so-called "residential renovation agreements" (as defined in CCA 1974 s.189(1) to mean, essentially, unsecured loans to renovate residential property) above this threshold: see amendment to s.75A in SI 2015/910 art.3 and Sch.1 para.2(7).

1826 In s.75A(5).

[1826a] Hence s.75A (unlike s.75) does not apply to payments by credit card.

[1827] s.75A(6)(a).

## 3. HIRE-PURCHASE AGREEMENTS

### (b) At Common Law

#### Title to goods

*Replace footnote 1874 with:*

39-316 [1874] Supply of Goods (Implied Terms) Act 1973 s.8(1)(b), considered in *Caithness Flagstone Ltd v Ballyvesey Holdings Ltd* [2020] SAC (Civ) 1; see also below, para.44-078. Corresponding terms are "treated as included" in consumer contracts made on or after October 1, 2015 under Consumer Rights Act 2015 s.17(2)), with the extended statutory rights available in such cases (Consumer Rights Act 2015 ss.19–27 and above, paras 38-512 et seq.).

### (c) Effect of Consumer Credit Regulation

#### Definition

*To the end of paragraph, after "any other specified event.[2035]", add:*

39-356 A new term was introduced in April 2019 for the purposes of imposing a price cap[2035a]: a "rent-to-own" agreement, which means a hire-purchase (or conditional sale[2035b]) agreement in relation to "household goods".[2035c]

[2035a] See the FCA's document: *Rent-to-own price cap – feedback on CP18/35 and final rules*, PS19/6 (March 2019). The provisions are in the FCA's Handbook, CONC 5B. The sanction (see CONC 5B.6.1) is that charges in excess of the cap are unenforceable.

[2035b] See below, para.39-439.

[2035c] As defined in CONC 5B. See, passim, that Module of the FCA Handbook.

#### Unfair relationships

*Replace footnote 2046 with:*

39-359 [2046] ss.140A–140C, above, paras 39-212 et seq. And note the price cap imposed in relation to "household goods", noted above, para.39-356.

#### Application of the regulatory regime

*To the end of paragraph, after "(and conditional sale) agreements.[2049]", add:*

39-360 Moreover, the FCA has imposed a price cap on hire-purchase (and conditional sale[2049a]) agreements in relation to "household goods".[2049b]

[2049a] Below, para.39-439.

[2049b] See above, para.39-356 and the FCA Handbook, CONC 5B.

#### Protected goods

*Replace footnote 2053 with:*

39-361 [2053] CCA 1974 s.90(7). The FCA's *Review of retained provisions of the Consumer Credit Act: Final Report* (see para.39-004, n.13, above) states (see Annex 5, para.100) that ss.90–92 should be retained in legislation as repeal would adversely affect the appropriate degree of consumer protection.

#### Consequences of contravention

*Replace footnote 2067 with:*

39-365 [2067] CCA 1974 s.91. See also CCA 1974 s.142(2) (declaration) and *Capital Finance Co Ltd v Bray* [1964] 1 W.L.R. 323. In the summary of the judgment submitted to the court in *Grace v Black Horse*

*Ltd* [2014] EWCA Civ 1413, [46] the s.91 sanction was described as "draconian", but the FCA's *Review of the retained provisions of the Consumer Credit Act: Final Report* (see para.39-004, n.13, above) expressed the view that s.91 "promotes appropriate emphasis on compliance with the key provisions in relation to protected goods".

## Entry on premises

*Replace footnote 2075 with:*

2075 CCA 1974 s.92(1). See CPR Pt 7PD 7B. The FCA's *Review of the retained provisions of the Consumer Credit Act: Final Report* (see para.39-004, n.13, above) states (see Annex 5, para.100) that s.92 should be retained in legislation as repeal would adversely affect the appropriate degree of consumer protection as an FCA rule could not make corresponding provision. **39-366**

## Debtor's right to terminate agreement

*Replace footnote 2082 with:*

2082 CCA 1974 s.99(1). cf. *Wadham Stringer Finance Ltd v Meaney* [1981] 1 W.L.R. 39 (acceleration clause in conditional sale agreement). Despite calls for its abolition, it was decided, after consultation, to retain the VTR, see: *A Consultation on Voluntary Termination of Hire Purchase and Conditional Sale Agreements under the Consumer Credit Act 1974*, DTI, Sept 2004 and OFT 761. Note also the FCA's *Review of the retained provisions of the Consumer Credit Act: Final Report* (see para.39-004, n.13, above) which states (see Annex 5, para.166) that ss.99–100 should be retained in legislation as an FCA rule could not replicate their effects. However the view was expressed that "there may be merit in a review of the provisions, and how they operate, taking into account changes in the market and the relevant products". **39-367**

# (d) Defective Goods

## Warranties and representations by dealers

*Replace footnote 2124 with:*

2124 *North Central Wagon and Finance Co Ltd v White and Powell* [1955] C.L.Y. 1204; *Campbell Discount Co Ltd v Gall* [1961] 1 Q.B. 431; *Yeoman Credit Ltd v Apps* [1962] 2 Q.B. 508; *Branwhite v Worcester Works Finance Ltd* [1969] 1 A.C. 552; *Williams (JD) & Co v McCauley Parsons and Jones* [1994] C.C.L.R. 78; *Woodchester Equipment (Leasing) Ltd v British Association of Canned and Preserved Foods Importers and Distributors Ltd* [1995] C.L.Y. 2459; *PB Leasing Ltd v Patel* [1995] C.C.L.R. 82; *Lombard North Central Plc v Gate* [1998] C.C.L.R. 51, Cty Ct; *Brewer v Mann* [2012] EWCA Civ 246. See Guest (1963) 79 L.Q.R. 33; Hughes (1964) 27 M.L.R. 395. Contrast *Purnell Secretarial Services Ltd v Lease Management Services Ltd* [1994] C.C.L.R. 127 and *Van Gordon v Volkswagen Financial Services (UK) Ltd (t/a Audi Finance)* Unreported April 30, 2019 (Nottingham Cty Ct) (on facts, supplier was agent at common law). **39-380**

*Replace footnote 2133 with:*

2133 CCA 1974 s.56(2). But it was held in *Van Gordon v VWFS (UK) Ltd (t/a Audi Finance)* Unreported April 30, 2019 (Nottingham Cty Ct) that s.56 does not apply to subsequent negotiations concerning the repair of the goods (although on the facts the dealer was held to be the agent of the creditor at common law). **39-381**

## Implied terms

*Replace footnote 2140 with:*

2140 See Vol.I, para.15-093; below, para.44-117. For an exclusion clause (between business people) effectively excluding s.10(2) of the 1973 Act (see below, para.39-384) see *Caithness Flagstone Ltd v Ballyvesey Holdings Ltd* [2020] SAC (Civ) 1. **39-382**

## Remedies for breach

*Replace footnote 2169 with:*

2169 See *Yeoman Credit v Odgers Vospers Motor House (Plymouth) (Third Party)* [1962] 1 W.L.R. 215, CA; *Brewer v Mann* [2012] EWCA Civ 246 (obiter, breach of s.9(1)); *Van Gordon v Volkswagen Financial Services (UK) Ltd (t/a Audi Finance)* Unreported April 30, 2019 (Nottingham Cty Ct) (breach of s.9). **39-387**

### Measure of damages

*Replace footnote 2182 with:*

39-389 [2182] *Charterhouse Credit Co Ltd v Tolly* [1963] 2 Q.B. 683; *Garside v Black Horse Ltd* [2010] EWHC 190 (QB); *Brewer v Mann* [2012] EWCA Civ 246; *Van Gordon v Volkswagen Financial Services (UK) Ltd (t/a Audi Finance)* Unreported April 30, 2019 (Nottingham Cty Ct) (damages for breach of s.9).

## (e) Rights and Liabilities of Third Parties

### *(vi) Insolvency*

### Bankruptcy of hirer

*Replace paragraph with:*

39-428 The estate of a bankrupt hirer, including the benefit of any hire-purchase contract,[2317] vests in the trustee in bankruptcy immediately on his appointment taking effect or, in the case of the official receiver, on his becoming trustee, with the owner having the right to prove for any liability arising under the contract.[2318] Most hire-purchase agreements, however, provide that, if a bankruptcy order is made against the hirer or the hirer petitions for his own bankruptcy, then either the hire-purchase agreement and the hiring are forthwith and automatically to come to an end[2319] or the owner is entitled to terminate the agreement. Once the agreement so terminates, it would seem that the hirer will have no interest in the goods or in the agreement which could pass to his trustee in bankruptcy.[2320]

[2317] See Insolvency Act 1986 s.283. The *rights* under a hire-purchase agreement, being choses in action, do not fall within the exemption (from vesting) for a "tool of the trade" (even though the subject matter of the agreement could be such "tool"): see *Dragan Mikki v William Duncan* [2016] EWCA Civ 1312.

[2318] Insolvency Act 1986 s.306.

[2319] This is not permissible where the agreement is a regulated agreement under the Consumer Credit Act 1974: see CCA 1974 s.98(1), above, para.39-172.

[2320] *Crawcour v Salter* (1881) 18 Ch. D. 30; *McEntire v Crossley Bros Ltd* [1895] A.C. 457; *Re Apex Supply Co Ltd* [1942] Ch. 108. See *Dragan Mikki v William Duncan* [2016] EWCA Civ 1312 at [20]. Contrast *Re Piggin, Dicker v Lombank* (1962) 112 L.J. 424.

### Winding-up or receivership of hirer

*To the end of paragraph, after "receiver is appointed.[2325]", add:*

39-431 However, in order to give company debtors a "breathing space" in times of temporary financial difficulty, amendments made by the Corporate Insolvency and Governance Act 2020 enable the directors to apply to court for a moratorium, similar to that which operates in the case of an administration,[2325a] so that (inter alia) the permission of the court is needed in order to repossess goods under any hire-purchase agreement.

[2325a] See below, para.39-433. The relevant provisions are in the new Pt A1 of the Insolvency Act 1986, inserted by the 2020 Act. See generally Insolvency Act 1986 Pt A1 Ch.4 and esp. s.A21(1)(d) (effect on hire-purchase).

## 4. CONDITIONAL SALE AGREEMENTS

### Definition

*To the end of paragraph, after "as well as goods.", add:*

39-442 A new term was introduced in April 2019 for the purposes of imposing a price cap[2360a]: a "rent-to-own" agreement, which means a conditional sale (or hire purchase[2360b]) agreement in relation to "household goods".[2360c]

[2360a] See the FCA's document: *Rent-to-own price cap – feedback on CP18/35 and final rules*, PS19/6 (March 2019). The provisions are in the FCA's Handbook, CONC 5B. The sanction (see CONC 5B.6.1) is that charges in excess of the cap are unenforceable.

[2360b] See above, para.39-356.

[2360c] As defined in CONC 5B. See, passim, that Module of the FCA Handbook.

## Unfair relationships

*Replace footnote 2373 with:*

[2373] CCA 1974 ss.140A–140C, paras 39-212 et seq. And note the price cap imposed in relation to "household goods" agreements, noted above, para.39-442. **39-447**

## 6. CREDIT AND OTHER PAYMENT CARDS, AND CHECKS

## Credit cards

*Replace footnote 2448 with:*

[2448] On four-party cards, see *Office of Fair Trading v Lloyds TSB Bank Plc* [2007] UKHL 48. See also *Bank of Scotland v Truman* [2005] EWHC 583, [2005] C.C.L.R. 3 (a "five-party" arrangement). **39-473**

## The consumer credit regulatory regime

### *(i) Credit card agreements*

*Replace paragraph with:*

**39-486** A three-party or four-party credit card agreement will likewise normally be for running-account credit.[2478] Insofar as the card may be used to obtain goods or services, it will be a debtor-creditor-supplier agreement[2479] for restricted-use credit.[2480] The issuer of the card, as creditor, will be liable, under s.75 of the Consumer Credit Act 1974,[2481] jointly and severally with the supplier in respect of any claim that the debtor may have in respect of a misrepresentation or breach of contract in relation to the transaction financed by the agreement, i.e. the supply of the goods or services. Insofar as the card may be used to obtain cash, the agreement is probably a debtor-creditor[2482] agreement for unrestricted-use credit.[2483]

[2478] See above, para.39-024.

[2479] See above, para.39-030. It will be a category 12(b) agreement, see above, para.39-031. *Office of Fair Trading v Lloyds TSB Bank Plc* [2006] EWCA Civ 268 (affirmed, on another point: [2007] UKHL 48) confirmed that there were the requisite "arrangements" in a four-party credit card transaction. And see *Bank of Scotland v Truman* [2005] EWHC 583, [2005] C.C.L.R. 3 (still "arrangements" between a fifth party with agency relationship with party to four-party credit card). It remains a moot point whether suppliers who use "master merchants" to process payments through the card schemes have requisite "arrangements" with the relevant credit card issuer or whether s.187(3) would apply to deny this.

[2480] See above, para.39-027.

[2481] See above, para.39-303 (subject, in particular, to the £100 minimum cash price referred to in that section). And it was held that the protection applies even where card (issued under a "United Kingdom credit agreement") finances a "foreign transaction": *Office of Fair Trading v Lloyds TSB Bank Plc* [2007] UKHL 48. CCA 1974 s.75A (see above, para.39-305) does not apply.

[2482] See above, para.39-033.

[2483] See above, para.39-029.

## Acceptance of credit-token

*Replace footnote 2543 with:*

[2543] CCA 1974 s.66(2). The burden of proof is on the creditor: CCA 1974 s.171(4)(a). The FCA's *Review* **39-502** *of retained provisions of the Consumer Credit Act: Final Report* (see para.39-004, n.13, above) states (see Annex 5, para.124) that s.66 (together with ss.83 and 84, below, para.39-503) should be retained in legislation in respect of CCA-regulated credit facilities that do not involve the provision of "payment services" within the Payment Services Regulations 2017 (PSRs) (SI 2017/752) Pt 7, so that s.66 should continue to apply where a credit token is not a "payment instrument" within the PSRs. Otherwise the FCA's view is that "the overall protection is broadly comparable" under the CCA and the PSRs and hence that the advantages of a more unified regime suggest that the CCA provisions be replaced with the PSRs where a CCA-regulated agreement is also an agreement for payment services.

*Replace footnote 2545 with:*

### Misuse of credit-token[2545]

39-503 [2545] Compare the position in relation to the misuse of "payment instruments" under the Payment Services Regulations 2017 (SI 2017/752), noted below, paras 39-512—39-515. The FCA's *Review of retained provisions of the Consumer Credit Act: Final Report* (see para.39-004, n.13, above) states (see Annex 5, para.124) that ss.83 and 84 (together with s.66, above, para.39-502) should be retained in legislation in respect of CCA-regulated credit facilities that do not involve the provision of "payment services" within the PSRs Pt 7, so that those sections will continue to apply where a credit token is not a "payment instrument" within the PSRs. Otherwise the FCA's view is that "the overall protection is broadly comparable" under the CCA and the PSRs and hence that the advantages of a more unified regime suggest that the CCA provisions be replaced with the PSRs where a CCA-regulated agreement is also an agreement for payment services.

### Issue of new credit-tokens

*Replace footnote 2570 with:*

39-509 [2570] CCA 1974 s.85(1). See also SI 1983/1557 reg.8. The FCA's *Review of retained provisions of the Consumer Credit Act: Final Report* (see para.39-004, n.13, above) contains (see Annex 5, para.124) some discussion of s.85 setting out options for its amendment, especially as customers can require/obtain a copy of the agreement under ss.77–79 (above, paras 39-127 et seq.): see Review Annex 6, paras 193–196. The Review states (see para.6.31) that the obligation to provide information in s.85 could be replaced by a corresponding FCA rule but that breach of such a FCA rule would not carry the same sanction and hence the existing sanction should be retained in legislation.

*To the end of title, add new footnote 2580a:*

### Relationship with consumer credit regulatory regime[2580a]

39-511 [2580a] The FCA's *Review of retained provisions of the Consumer Credit Act: Final Report* (see para.39-004, n.13, above) states (see Annex 5, para.124) that CCA 1974 ss.66, 83 and 84 (above, paras 39-502, 39-503) should be retained in legislation in respect of CCA-regulated credit facilities that do not involve the provision of "payment services" within the PSRs Pt 7, so that those sections will continue to apply where a credit token is not a "payment instrument" within the PSRs. Otherwise the FCA's view is that "the overall protection is broadly comparable" under the CCA and the PSRs and hence that the advantages of a more unified regime suggest that the CCA provisions be replaced with the PSRs where a CCA-regulated agreement is also an agreement for payment services.

### Comparison with consumer credit Act regulatory regime

*Replace footnote 2601 with:*

39-514 [2601] See above, para.39-503. See para.39-511, above where it is noted that FCA's *Review of retained provisions of the Consumer Credit Act: Final Report* (see para.39-004, n.13, above) notes that "the overall protection is broadly comparable" under the CCA and the PSRs and hence that the advantages of a more unified regime suggest that the CCA provisions be replaced with the PSRs where a CCA-regulated agreement is also an agreement for payment services.

## 8. MORTGAGES OF LAND

### Consumer credit regulation

*Replace paragraph with:*

39-529 The Consumer Credit Act 1974 (CCA 1974) can apply to an agreement notwithstanding that it is secured by a mortgage or charge on land or relates to an advance for the purchase of land.[2664] But certain land mortgage transactions are "exempt agreements" under the regime.[2665] Most importantly[2666] most residential mortgages[2667] and so-called "regulated home purchase plans",[2668] are "exempt agreements" for the purposes of the regime because they are regulated under a special regime established under the Financial Services and Market Act 2000 (FSMA 2000). Hence there are presently two statutory regimes for the regulation of land mortgages, both now administered by the Financial Conduct Authority.[2669] Other categories of "exempt" land mortgages are considered above.[2670] Moreover, land mortgages may take advantage of the more general exemptions for "high net worth" debtors[2671] and for credit agreements entered into for the debtor's business purposes.[2672] Although otherwise not covered by the CCA 1974 regime, such exempt agreements (apart from those regulated under the FSMA 2000 regime[2673]) are nevertheless not excepted from the "unfair relationship" provisions.[2674]

2664 See Guest and Lloyd, *Encyclopedia of Consumer Credit Law* (1975, looseleaf), paras 2-059, 2-061, 2-066, 2-068, 2-127; Goode, *Consumer Credit: Law and Practice*, Pt C, Ch.38.

2665 See above, paras 39-038 et seq.

2666 See above, para.39-039. The relevant provision is now in the Regulated Activities Order 2001 (SI 2001/544) ("RAO") art.60C(2).

2667 i.e. "regulated mortgage contracts" within the RAO art.61 as amended by SI 2001/3544 art.8 and SI 2006/2383 art.17.

2668 Within the RAO art.63F(3)(a) as added (on April 6, 2007) by SI 2006/2383 art.18.

2669 Since the transfer of consumer credit regulation from the OFT to the FCA: see above, para.39-002. It may be that in the future the regime originating in the CCA 1974 will be "folded into" the more recent FSMA 2000 regime and the decision will be taken to disapply the CCA 1974 and CONC to all new secured lending on land.

2670 para.39-039. There is also a special exemption for so-called "investment mortgages": RAO art.60D, see above, para.39-046.

2671 See above, para.39-045. The relevant provision is in the RAO art.60H, as amended on March 21, 2016, when the Mortgage Credit Directive (see above, para.39-003) was implemented so as to ensure that the exemption is compatible with it: SI 2015/910 art.3 and Sch.1 para.4(18). And note the amendment made by the Financial Services and Markets Act 2000 (Amendment) (EU Exit) Regulations 2019 (SI 2019/632).

2672 See above, para.39-047. The relevant provision is in the RAO art.60C(3)–(7) Moreover, second charge business loans are not "regulated mortgage contracts": see new RAO art.61A(1)(c), added by SI 2015/910 art.3 and Sch.1 para.4(22) and amended by SI 2019/632.

2673 See CCA 1974 s.140A(5). Hence when the Mortgage Credit Directive (see above, para.39-003 and below para.39-428) was implemented on March 21, 2016 and second charge residential loans become regulated under FSMA 2000, they lost the protection of those provisions.

2674 See above, paras 39-212 et seq. For the application of those provisions to land mortgages, see *Consolidated Finance Ltd v Hunter* [2010] B.P.I.R. 1322, Macclesfield Cty Ct; *Paragon Mortgages Ltd v McEwan-Peters* [2011] EWHC 2491 (Comm); *Goldhill Finance Ltd v Berry* [2018] 10 WLUK 480, London Cty Ct; *Promontoria (Henrico) Ltd v Samra* [2019] EWHC 2327 (Ch). See also McMurtry, "Consumer Credit Act mortgages: unfair terms, time orders and judicial discretion" [2010] J.B.L. 107.

## The Mortgage Credit Directive

*Replace footnote 2685 with:*

2685 See the amendment to be made to RAO art.61(3) by SI 2015/910 art.3 and Sch.1 para.4(21). But note the exclusions in the new RAO art.61A, added by SI 2015/910 art.3 and Sch.1 para.4(22) and amended by SI 2019/632. **39-531**

*Replace footnote 2708 with:*

## Special "pause" provisions[2708]

2708 For the problems associated with these provisions, see Guest and Lloyd, *Encyclopedia of Consumer* **39-535**

*Credit Law* (1975, looseleaf), paras 2-059, 2-062. The FCA's *Review of retained provisions of the Consumer Credit Act: Final Report* (see para.39-004, n.13, above) states (see Annex 5, para.21) that s.58 should be retained in legislation as an FCA rule could not replicate its provisions as to the consequences of non-compliance and hence repeal would adversely affect the appropriate degree of consumer protection. However, this will not be necessary if the decision is taken to disapply the CCA and CONC to all new secured lending on land.

## Enforcement

*Replace footnote 2725 with:*

**39-537** [2725] As substituted on March 30, 2014 by Financial Services and Markets Act 2000 (Consumer Credit) (Miscellaneous Provisions) (No.2) Order 2014 (SI 2014/506) art.5(4). The FCA's *Review of retained provisions of the Consumer Credit Act: Final Report* (see para.39-004, n.13, above) states (see Annex 5, para.208) that s.126 should be retained in legislation as it could not be replicated by an FCA rule and hence repeal would adversely affect the appropriate degree of consumer protection.

Chapter 40

# EMPLOYMENT

## 1. INTRODUCTION

### Legal consequences of a contract of employment

*Replace footnote 27 with:*

40-006 [27] Atiyah at pp.327 et seq. But some relationships other than that of employment may also invoke vicarious liability in tort, e.g. *Ormrod v Crosville Motor Services Ltd* [1953] 1 W.L.R. 1120; cf. *Att-Gen for New South Wales v Perpetual Trustee Co Ltd* [1955] A.C. 457. The scope of vicarious liability on the borderlines of employment has been subject to extensive litigation at the highest appellate levels in recent years. See *Various Claimants v Institute of the Brothers of the Christian Schools* [2012] UKSC 56, [2013] A.C. 1; *Woodland v Swimming Teachers Association* [2013] UKSC 66, [2014] A.C. 537; *Cox v Ministry of Justice* [2016] UKSC 10, [2016] A.C. 660; *Armes v Nottinghamshire CC* [2017] UKSC 60, [2018] A.C. 355; and *Barclays Bank Plc v Various Claimants* [2020] UKSC 13, [2020] 2 W.L.R. 960, where the Supreme Court declined the suggestion that employers' vicarious liability could be systemically aligned with the statutory concept of the "worker".

### Classification for particular purposes

*Replace footnote 48 with:*

40-008 [48] [1995] I.R.L.R. 493. Comparison should now be made with the decision in *R. (on the application of Health and Safety Executive) v Pola* [2009] EWCA Crim 655, where the Court of Appeal limited the application of the requirement of continuing mutuality of obligation, confirming that in this particular interpretative context there was no requirement of a continuing or overarching obligation between the periods when the workers in question were at work. Cf. the approach of the European Court of Justice in the context of the Lugano Convention 2007, where senior directors with significant influence over their own contractual arrangements were held not to be employed under contracts of service: *Bosworth v Arcadia Petroleum Ltd* (C-603/17) EU:C:2019:310.

### The contract of service or personally to execute any work or labour: "workers" and "persons employed"

*Replace paragraph with:*

40-009 In the area of employment legislation, there is one major type of variant upon the contract "of employment" or "service" which is very extensively used and requires distinct consideration. This variant adds to the basic concept of the contract of employment by including any other contract personally to execute any work or labour. This addition brings in some contracts between employers and independent contractors, i.e. some contracts which are not contracts of employment. The conditions for this extension outside the contract of employment are that the contract shall be for personal performance by the worker[49] and probably that it shall be for work alone rather than for work and materials. The extended formula probably includes some labour-only sub-contractors who would be held not to have contracts of employment.[50] Where this kind of formula is used, it is sometimes coupled with the terminology of "workman" or "worker" to distinguish it from the simple concept of "employee", but, as the ensuing examples show, there is a lack of consistency in this respect:

(1) The provisions, formerly contained in the Industrial Courts Act 1919, for courts of inquiry into industrial disputes, apply in relation to trade disputes defined with reference to "workers" which includes both contracts of employment and any other contract whereby the worker undertakes to do or to perform personally any work or services for another party to the contract who is not a professional client of his.[51] The provisions made by the Employment Relations Act 1999 concerning the recognition of trade unions by employers apply in relation to the same category of "workers".[52]

(2) Employment Rights Act 1996 Pt II (which deals with protection of workers in relation to the payment of wages, and replaces the Truck Acts 1831–1940) applies to "workers", the worker being defined as an individual who has entered into or works under a contract of service or apprenticeship or any other contract whereby the individual undertakes to do or perform personally any work or services for another party to the contract whose status is not by virtue of the contract that of a client or customer of any profession or business undertaking carried on by the individual.[53] The same formula has been used to identify the scope of a number of major pieces of recent employment legislation, such as the National Minimum Wage Act 1998,[54] the Working Time Regulations 1998,[55] and the Part-time Workers (Prevention of Less Favourable Treatment) Regulations 2000.[56] The Supreme Court, in its decision in *Pimlico Plumbers v Smith*, found that a self-employed plumber was a worker for the purposes of these provisions, emphasising in particular that a limited substitution right in the worker's contract could not defeat a personal service obligation so as to disqualify the claimant from being regarded as a "worker" (or, likewise, from being regarded as an "employee" in "employment" for the purposes of employment equality legislation).[57]

(3) In a recent string of cases arising from intermittent work arrangements in the so-called "on-demand" or "gig economy", the employment tribunals and employment appeal tribunals,[57a] as well as the Court of Appeal,[57b] have generally taken the view that individuals were employed as workers. For a notably different outcome, albeit in the context of trade union recognition, see the CAC's decision in *Independent Workers' Union of Great Britain v RooFoods Ltd (t/a Deliveroo)*.[57c]

(4) The Equality Act 2010 applies its various provisions concerning employment equality to persons in "employment", defined as "employment under a contract of service or apprenticeship or a contract personally to execute any work or labour".[58] In its decision in *Jivraj v Hashwani*,[59] the Supreme Court has adopted a narrow construction of the concept of "employment under a contract personally to execute any work or labour" as that concept is used in the various kinds of employment discrimination legislation detailed under this head of this paragraph, holding that it is in effect limited to work taking place under the direction of the employer.

(5) The Trade Union and Labour Relations (Consolidation) Act 1992 defines "trade disputes" and "trade unions" in terms of "workers" and defines "workers" as in example (2) above.[60]

(6) The concept of "worker"—defined as in example (4) above—is invoked in relation to the duty of employers to disclose information to the representatives of workers for the purposes of collective bargaining.[61]

49 See *Ingram v Barnes* (1857) 7 E. & B. 115; *Broadbent v Crisp* [1974] I.C.R. 248. In *Mirror Group*

*Newspapers Ltd v Gunning* [1986] I.C.R. 145 the Court of Appeal held that the expression referred to a contract the dominant purpose of which was the execution of personal work or labour. See *Wright v Redrow Homes (North West) Ltd* [2004] EWCA Civ 469, [2004] I.C.R. 1126 where the contracts of independent individual bricklaying contractors were construed as intended to require them to work "personally" so as to constitute them as "workers"; compare para.40-022.

50 *Stuart v Evans* (1883) 49 L.T. 138; and see below, para.40-026.

51 Trade Union and Labour Relations (Consolidation) Act 1992 ss.215, 218.

52 See Trade Union and Labour Relations (Consolidation) Act 1992 Sch.A1 para.165, referring to s.296(a) and (b).

53 Employment Rights Act 1996 s.230(3). A relatively inclusive approach to the construction of the category of "workers" was taken by the Employment Appeal Tribunal in *James v Redcats (Brands) Ltd* [2007] I.C.R. 1006. Compare the similarly inclusive approach to the category of "worker" taken by the Court of Appeal in *Hospital Medical Group Ltd v Westwood* [2012] EWCA Civ 1005, [2013] I.C.R. 415 which concerned a doctor engaged on a self-employed basis to carry out cosmetic surgical procedures, and contrast *Suhail v Barking, Havering & Redbridge NHS Trust* Unreported June 11, 2015, EAT.

54 ss.1(2), 54(3). Many of the statutory formulations of categories of "workers" expressly include those working under contracts of apprenticeship. In *Edmonds v Lawson* [2000] I.C.R. 567, it was held that, on the particular facts, a pupil barrister did not have a contract of apprenticeship and hence was not a "worker" within the meaning of s.54 of the National Minimum Wage Act 1998.

55 SI 1998/1833 regs 3(2), 2(1). In *Byrne Brothers (Formwork) Ltd v Baird* [2002] I.R.L.R. 96, the Employment Appeal Tribunal held that building trade workers working as self-employed labour-only sub-contractors qualified as "workers" within the meaning of the Working Time Regulations 1998 (in which the term is defined in the same way as under s.230(6) of the Employment Rights Act 1996) although they clearly were not employed under contracts of employment and had some power to provide a substitute to carry out their work. Compare para.40-022. Compare *Cotswold Developments Construction Ltd v Williams* [2006] I.R.L.R. 181, which confirms the role of mutuality of obligation in deciding whether the contractual relationship of "worker" and employer exists in a given case. Compare also in this respect *Community Dental Centres Ltd v Sultan-Darmon* [2010] UKEAT/0532/09/1208, [2010] I.R.L.R. 1024 where the Employment Appeal Tribunal held that there was insufficient mutuality of obligation to support the conclusion that there was a contractual relation of "worker" and employer. Compare now also *Conroy v Scottish Football Association Ltd* [2014] UKEATS 0024/13/JW.

56 SI 2000/1551 regs 3(1), 2, 1(2). See below, para.40-156.

57 [2018] UKSC 29. The general approach was applied in *Addison Lee Ltd v Lange* [2019] I.C.R. 637, EAT.

57a *Aslam v Uber BV* [2018] I.R.L.R. 97, EAT; *Addison Lee Ltd v Gascoigne* [2018] I.C.R. 1826, EAT.

57b [2018] EWCA Civ 2748 (Underhill LJ. dissenting). The Supreme Court heard Uber's appeal in July 2020.

57c [2018] I.R.L.R. 84 (CAC) (not workers for purposes of either s.296 of the Trade Union and Labour Relations (Consolidation) Act 1992, or s.230(3)(b) of the Employment Rights Act 1996). Moreover, the union's subsequent judicial review application which had received permission to proceed in part was subsequently rejected in *R. (on the application of Independent Workers Union of Great Britain) v Central Arbitration Committee* [2018] EWHC 3342 (Admin). In the same context, see now also the decision regard foster carers: *National Union of Professional Foster Carers (NUPFC) v Certification Officer* [2020] I.C.R. 607.

58 s.83(2). See *Mingeley v Pennock and Ivory* [2004] EWCA Civ 328, [2004] I.C.R. 727, where the relationship between a taxi-driver and the organisation coordinating his work was held not to amount to a contract personally to execute any work or labour. It was expressly recognised in *Quinnen v Hovells* [1984] I.C.R. 525 that this category may include self-employed persons who comply with its requirements. See also *Mirror Group Newspapers Ltd v Gunning* [1986] I.C.R. 145. In *Tanna v Post Office* [1981] I.C.R. 374 it was held that full effect must be given to the word "personally", so that the case was not covered of a sub-postmaster who was responsible for seeing that the work of the Post Office was carried out either by himself or by staff chosen by him. In *Sheehan v Post Office Counters Ltd* [1999] I.C.R. 734, the Employment Appeal Tribunal confirmed the "dominant purpose of personal performance" test as propounded in *Mirror Group Newspapers Ltd v Gunning* [1986] I.C.R. 145, and applied it to hold, much as in *Tanna v Post Office* [1981] I.C.R. 374, that a sub-postmaster was not employed under "a contract personally to do any work". This view of the situation of those persons was confirmed in *Wolstenholme v Post Office Ltd* [2003] I.R.L.R. 546. Comparison should now be made with the decision in *Muschett v HM Prison Service* [2010] EWCA Civ 25, [2010] I.R.L.R. 451, where the Court of Appeal held that there was no contractual obligation between the agency worker and the Prison Service as the end-user of his services such as was necessary to establish a "contract personally to execute any work or labour". In *Burton v Higham* [2003] I.R.L.R. 257 it was held that temporary agency workers came within this definition although not within the definition of "employees" having contracts of employment. See *South East Sheffield Citizens Advice Bureau v Grayson* [2004] I.R.L.R. 353, EAT,

where an unpaid volunteer worker was held to fall outside this definition; and the Court of Appeal similarly so decided in *X v Mid-Sussex Citizens Advice Bureau* [2011] EWCA Civ 28. The Supreme Court, [2012] UKSC 59, [2013] 1 All E.R. 1038 confirmed the decision of the Court of Appeal, holding that unpaid volunteer workers were outside the scope of disability discrimination protection afforded by Directive 2000/78/EC. cf. also now *Unite the Union v Nailard* [2016] I.R.L.R. 906.

[59] [2011] UKSC 40, [2011] 1 W.L.R. 1872. This continues to cast some doubt, which it will require further litigation to resolve, on the standing and relevance of the authorities cited in the preceding footnote. In *Halawi v WDFG UK Ltd (t/a World Duty Free)* [2014] EWCA Civ 1387, [2015] I.R.L.R. 50, Arden L.J. expressed concern at the resulting exclusionary effects of this approach; though cf. also *Windle v Secretary of State for Justice* [2016] EWCA Civ 459, [2016] I.R.L.R. 628. In the case of personal service companies, another avenue for recourse could be found in *EAD Solicitors LLP v Abrams* [2015] I.R.L.R. 978, EAT.

[60] ss.1, 218(1), 244(1), 296(1). Compare *Smith v Carillion (JM) Ltd* [2015] EWCA Civ 209, [2015] I.R.L.R. 467.

[61] Trade Union and Labour Relations (Consolidation) Act 1992 s.181.

## 2. THE FACTORS IDENTIFYING A CONTRACT OF EMPLOYMENT

### Special cases: (2) agency workers

*Replace paragraph with:*

Where, as now happens in an increasingly wide range of occupations, employment is obtained via an employment agency, radically divergent analyses of the legal relationships may occur. The worker may be held to have contracted with the agency and not with the client under whose control he or she is placed.[177] In other cases, the worker may be held to have contracted with the client and merely to have received an introduction from the agency.[178] On either view, it has then to be decided whether the worker is an employee. It has been suggested that in the case where the worker is under contract with the agency, there is a sui generis type of contract for the provision of services to a third party.[179] It has also been held[180] that where temporaries on the books of an employment agency were under no obligation to accept bookings offered by the employers, who in turn had no obligation to find work for their temporaries, the relationship between the employers and the temporaries lacked the elements of continuity and care associated with the contract of employment. Some labour-only sub-contracting arrangements are comparable to employment via an agency,[181] and both systems can raise problems insofar as they can involve the avoidance of the ordinary legal consequences of employment under contracts of employment.[182] The case law is rather fluctuating on the question whether and when an agency worker has a contract of employment either with the agency or with its client business to which the agency sends the worker. The prevailing trend seemed to have been set by the assertion in the leading case of *McMeechan v Secretary of State for Employment*[183] that there is no rule of law against there being a contract of employment either with the agency or with the client business. However, the Court of Appeal in *Dacas v Brook Street Bureau (UK) Ltd*, held that the temporary agency worker was not an "employee" of the agency, though she might be an employee of the end-user of her services.[184] The approach in the *Dacas* case was applied to similar effect in *Bunce v Postworth Ltd (t/a Skyblue)*.[185] There was at one stage in recent years a readiness to discern an "implied contract of employment" arising between the worker and the client business arising out of an assignment or series of assignments over a long period of time.[186] However, the Court of Appeal ruled in *James v Greenwich BC*[187] that such a contract can be implied only where it is "necessary" to do so,[188] their view being that if this represented a lacuna in the law determining the rights of agency workers, it could be filled only by legislation. The fact that an individual has a contract of employ- 40-027 ment with one employer does not preclude their being a worker in the extended agency work sense under s.43K of the Employment Rights Act 1996.[189] The conduct of the business of employment agencies is regulated by the Employment Agencies Act 1973,[190] and by regulations made thereunder.[191] The conditions of employment of agency workers are further regulated by the Agency Workers Regulations 2010.[192] The main effect of these Regulations is to provide a right on the part of agency workers, after a qualifying period of 12 weeks' employment, to the same basic terms and conditions of employment[192a] as those which they would have been accorded if they had been recruited directly by the hirer of their services from the temporary work agency.[193]

[177] *O'Sullivan v Thompson-Coon* (1973) 14 K.I.R. 108.

[178] *Alderton v Richard Burgon Associates (Manpower) Ltd* [1974] Crim. L.R. 318.

[179] *Construction Industry Training Board v Labour Force Ltd* [1970] 3 All E.R. 220, 225F (Cooke J.). cf. *Ironmonger v Movefield Ltd* [1988] I.R.L.R. 461.

[180] *Wickens v Champion Employment* [1984] I.C.R. 365, 371D.

[181] cf. *Construction Industry Training Board v Labour Force Ltd* [1970] 3 All E.R. 220.

[182] See above, paras 40-025—40-026.

[183] [1997] I.C.R. 549.

[184] *Dacas v Brook Street Bureau (UK) Ltd* [2004] EWCA Civ 217, [2004] I.R.L.R. 358.

[185] [2005] EWCA Civ 490, [2005] I.R.L.R. 557; compare the decision of the Court of Appeal in *Consistent Group Ltd v Kalwak* [2008] EWCA Civ 430, [2008] I.R.L.R. 505.

[186] *Franks v Reuters Ltd* [2003] I.R.L.R. 423; contrast the earlier *Hewlett Packard Ltd v O'Murphy* [2002] I.R.L.R. 4.

[187] [2008] EWCA Civ 35, [2008] I.R.L.R. 302. Comparison should now be made with the decision in *Muschett v HM Prison Service* [2010] EWCA Civ 25, [2010] I.R.L.R. 451, where the Court of Appeal held that there was no contractual obligation between the agency worker and the Prison Service as the end-user of his services such as was necessary to establish a "contract personally to execute any work or labour". (It would follow that there was no contract of employment between them.) Compare also *RSA Consulting Ltd v Evans* [2010] EWCA Civ 866, where the Court of Appeal held that the assessment of whether it was necessary to imply a "worker's" contract between the claimant and an intermediary agency must not be limited to documentary evidence alone and must extend to consideration of the actual relationship between the parties; a further exploration of that position is to be found in the decision of the Court of Appeal in *Evans v Parasol Ltd* [2010] EWCA Civ 866, [2011] I.C.R. 37. The negative tendency against finding a contract of employment between the agency worker and the end-user was further manifested in *Alstom Transport v Tilson* [2010] EWCA Civ 1308.

[188] The test being that laid down by Bingham L.J. in *The Aramis* [1989] 1 Lloyd's Rep. 213 at 224. Compare now also *Smith v Carillion (JM) Ltd* [2015] EWCA Civ 209, [2015] I.R.L.R. 467.

[189] *Day v Lewisham and Greenwich NHS Trust* [2017] EWCA Civ 329, [2017] I.R.L.R. 623; see also *McTigue v University Hospital Bristol NHS Foundation Trust* [2016] I.R.L.R. 742, EAT.

[190] As amended by Employment Protection Act 1975 s.114 and Sch.13, which transfer the licensing of private employment agencies from local authorities to the Secretary of State for Employment; and further amended by s.31 of and Sch.7 to the Employment Relations Act 1999.

[191] A series of regulations were revised and replaced by the Conduct of Employment Agencies and Employment Businesses Regulations 2003 (SI 2003/3319). Those have since been amended by the Conduct of Employment Agencies and Employment Businesses (Amendment) Regulations 2007 (SI 2007/3575) and by the Conduct of Employment Agencies and Employment Businesses (Amendment) Regulations 2010 (SI 2010/1782) with effect from October 1, 2010. See now also the Conduct of Employment Agencies and Employment Businesses (Amendment) Regulations 2016 (SI 2016/510).

[192] SI 2010/93, in force from October 1, 2010, implementing the EU Temporary Agency Work Directive 2008/104/EC, [2008] O.J. L327/9. (SI 2010/93 was amended by SI 2011/1941 to correct drafting errors.)

[192a] This does not, however, extend to an entitlement to the same number of hours: *Kocur v Angard Staffing Solutions Ltd* [2019] EWCA Civ 1185.

[193] reg.5, subject to reg.7 which specifies the qualifying period. Compare, however, *Moran v Ideal Cleaning Services Ltd* [2014] 2 C.M.L.R. 37, EAT: permanent secondees from an agency not within

scope of Agency Workers Regulations 2010. In *Coles v Ministry of Defence* [2015] I.R.L.R. 872, EAT the confinement of the equal treatment obligation to basic working and employment conditions was emphasised in the context of recruitment to jobs. For a detailed discussion of less favourable treatment, see *Kocur v Angard Staffing Solutions Ltd* [2018] I.R.L.R. 388, EAT. For the apportionment of liability to compensation as between the agency and the end-user of the worker's services in respect, for example, of pay inequality between women and men, see *London Underground v Amissah* [2019] EWCA Civ 125.

## Special cases: (3) office-holders

*Replace paragraph with:*

There is authority to the effect that the fact that a person is the holder of a public ecclesiastical or tenured office does not ipso facto prevent that person from being classified as working under a contract of employment.[194] Those authorities show that the holding of office neither requires nor excludes the conclusion that the holder is an employee, but simply leaves that question to be decided according to the normal criteria.[195] Similarly, in the context of the civil service, "appointment" of a worker may refer either to office holding or to contractual employment.[196] In *Gilham v Ministry of Justice*, the Court of Appeal found that judges were office holders, and therefore excluded from statutory whistleblower protection.[197] This was overturned on appeal to the Supreme Court, where it was held that s.230(3)(b) was to interpreted as including judicial office holders in its material scope.[197a] There is a further, and again quite distinct, question as to whether a contract of employment contains: **40-028**

> "... elements of a public character which would enable the court to extend to the employee the protection flowing from the right to be heard enjoyed by the holders of an office."[198]

Such a "right to be heard" may exist in conjunction with a contract of employment[199] or in the absence of a contract of employment[200]; its presence or absence is in no way conclusive of whether or not the legal relationship takes the form of a contract of employment.

[194] *102 Social Club v Bickerton* [1977] I.C.R. 911; *Barthorpe v Exeter Diocesan Board of Finance* [1979] I.C.R. 900. It was also so held by the Employment Appeal Tribunal in *Johnson v Ryan* [2000] I.C.R. 236, where it was decided that the holding of the statutory office of rent officer was not inconsistent with employee status.

[195] The older cases concerning ecclesiastical office-holders, particularly *Re National Insurance Act 1911—Re Employment of Church of England Curates* [1912] 2 Ch. 563 were doubted in the *Barthorpe* case so far as they suggested an inconsistency between employment and office—see [1979] I.C.R. at 903G–906D, per Slynn J.; though that suggestion had appeared to be reinstated, so far as ecclesiastical office is concerned, by a dictum in *President of the Methodist Conference v Parfitt* [1984] I.C.R. 176, 184H (Dillon L.J.), and when *Re National Insurance Act 1911*, above, was approved and applied, so far as it held that a curate in the Church of England is not employed under a contract of employment, in *Diocese of Southwark v Coker* [1998] I.C.R. 140. However, authority in favour of the approach taken in the *Barthorpe* case, and against the approach taken in the *Parfitt* case, is provided by the decision of the House of Lords in *Percy v Church of Scotland Board of National Mission* [2005] UKHL 73, [2006] 2 A.C. 28, followed in *New Testament Church of God v Stewart* [2007] I.R.L.R. 178, EAT (upheld by CA on its special facts, [2007] EWCA Civ 1004, [2008] I.C.R. 282) and in *President of the Methodist Conference v Preston* [2011] EWCA Civ 1581; taken cumulatively, these decisions effectively negate any presumptions against intention to create legal relations or against the existence of mutuality of obligation in the construction of the relationships between ministers of religion and their churches; see also *JGE v Trustees of Portsmouth Roman Catholic Diocesan Trust* [2012] EWCA Civ 938 in which a Roman Catholic priest was held to have been in a relationship sufficiently "akin to employment" to constitute a basis for imposing vicarious liability. In *President of the Methodist Conference v Preston* [2013] UKSC 29, [2013] 2 A.C. 163, however, the Supreme Court, reversing the above-cited decision of the Court of Appeal, held that the relationship between a Methodist minister and the Methodist Church did not, by reason of the particular way in which that relationship had been constituted, take the legal form of a contract of employment, rather consisting of the holding of an office under the constitutional provisions of that Church. Though compare Lady Hale's dissenting opinion, and now also *Sharpe v Worcester Diocesan Board of Finance Ltd* [2015] EWCA Civ 399, [2015] I.R.L.R. 663. See further Ecclesiastical Offices (Terms of Service) Measure 2009 (No.1), as amended.

[196] *Secretary of State for Justice v Betts* [2017] I.R.L.R. 804, EAT.

[197] [2017] EWCA Civ 2220, [2018] I.R.L.R. 315.

[197a] [2019] UKSC 44, [2019] 1 W.L.R. 5905.

[198] *102 Social Club v Bickerton* [1977] I.C.R. 911, 917F, per Phillips J.

[199] cf. *Malloch v Aberdeen Corp* [1971] 1 W.L.R. 1578, 1595, per Lord Wilberforce; see below, para.40-192.

[200] cf. *Ridge v Baldwin* [1964] A.C. 40, 65, per Lord Reid.

### Special cases: (5) employee shareholders

*To the end of paragraph, after "next legislative opportunity".[208]", add:*

40-030 It has been held that employees who have already entered into an employee shareholder agreement need an explicit agreement to regain their statutory rights.[208a]

[208a] *Barrasso v New Look Retailers Ltd* [2020] I.C.R. 448.

## 3. FORMATION OF THE CONTRACT

### Effect of illegality on statutory rights

*Replace footnote 244 with:*

40-037 [244] *Hounga v Allen* [2014] UKSC 47, [2014] 1 W.L.R. 2889. See now also *Patel v Mirza* [2016] UKSC 42, [2017] A.C. 467; and *Okedina v Chikale* [2019] EWCA Civ 1393.

### Form: written particulars

*In line 7, after "than two months", add new footnote 288a:*

40-040 [288a] This obligation applies irrespective of whether the contract is flexible as to whether its duration will exceed the two-month period: *Stefanko v Maritime Hotel Ltd (In Voluntary Liquidation)* [2019] I.R.L.R. 322, EAT.

## 5. RIGHTS AND DUTIES UNDER AND ASSOCIATED WITH A CONTRACT OF EMPLOYMENT

## (a) Duties of the Employee

### Duty of fidelity

*Replace footnote 401 with:*

40-062 [401] *Robb v Green* [1895] 2 Q.B. 315; *Wessex Dairies Ltd v Smith* [1935] 2 K.B. 80; *Hivac Ltd v Park Royal Scientific Instruments Ltd* [1946] Ch. 169; *Sanders v Parry* [1967] 1 W.L.R. 753. See also *Morison v Moat* (1851) 9 Hare 241. It was confirmed in *Lonmar Global Risks Ltd v West* [2010] EWHC 2878 (QB), [2011] I.R.L.R. 138, reiterating the view previously taken in *University of Nottingham v Fishel* [2000] I.C.R. 1462, that the duty of loyalty or good faith is not without more to be equated with a fiduciary obligation; compare the discussion of the "duty to account" in para.40-069. Compare also *Threlfall v ECD Insight Ltd* [2012] EWHC 3543 (QB), [2013] I.R.L.R. 185 where Lang J. reinforces the proposition that a senior employee with a duty of fidelity as to act in good faith vis-à-vis the employer is nevertheless not thereby necessarily or ordinarily under a fiduciary obligation to that employer. The contrast between the duty of fidelity owed by an employee and the fiduciary duty owed by a company director had also been emphasised by the Court of Appeal in *Ranson v Customer Systems Plc* [2012] EWCA Civ 841, [2012] I.R.L.R. 769 and had also been invoked by the Court of Appeal in *Caterpillar Logistics Services (UK) Ltd v Huesca de Crean* [2012] EWCA Civ 156, [2012] 3 All E.R. 129 as a factor in refusing to the employer of barring-out relief against a former employee. Cf. now *Human Kind Charity v Gittens* [2019] 10 WLUK 813, EAT.

## (b) Duties of the Employer

### (i) Remuneration

### The national minimum wage

*Replace footnote 541 with:*

541 *Whittlestone v BJP Home Support Ltd* [2014] I.C.R. 275, EAT; cf. *Esparon (t/a Middle West Residential Care Home) v Slavikovska* [2014] I.R.L.R. 598, EAT. Different considerations may apply where the worker's home was her place of work: *Shannon v Rampersad (t/a Clifton House Residential Home)* [2015] I.R.L.R. 982, EAT, or in connection with on-call time and sleep-in shifts: *Royal Mencap Society v Tomlison-Blake* [2018] EWCA Civ 1641, [2018] I.R.L.R. 932. **40-080**

### Holiday Pay under the Working Time Regulations and Directive

*Replace paragraph with:*

The Working Time Regulations,[550] as described more fully in a later paragraph,[551] now confer an important general entitlement to a minimum period of paid holiday. In *Lock v British Gas Trading Ltd* (C-539/12),[552] the CJEU held that the Working Time Directive required that holiday pay not be limited to basic salary where commission was part of the employee's remuneration. This approach to "normal remuneration" was essentially followed in *Dudley MBC v Willetts*,[553] when the Employment Appeal Tribunal held that voluntary overtime pay could be included for purposes of holiday pay calculation. In *Harpur Trust v Brazel*, the Court of Appeal held that in the case of part-time workers, holiday pay entitlement was not to be pro-rated by reference to the fact that a worker had not worked for the entire year.[553a] Moreover, in *King v Sash Window Workshop Ltd*, it was held that EU law prohibits national provisions or practices that prevent a worker from carrying over or accumulating, until the termination of the employment relationship, paid annual leave rights not exercised in respect of several consecutive reference periods because the employer refused to remunerate that leave.[554] **40-082**

550 SI 1998/1833 in force from October 1, 1998. See reg.13 as amended by the Working Time (Amendment) Regulations 2001 (SI 2001/3256).

551 See below, para.40-112.

552 [2014] 3 C.M.L.R. 53, [2014] I.C.R. 813. For the domestic follow-up, see *Lock v British Gas Trading Ltd* [2016] EWCA Civ 983, [2016] I.R.L.R. 946.

553 [2017] I.R.L.R. 870, EAT.

553a [2019] EWCA Civ 1402.

554 C-214/16 EU:C:2017:914 (CJEU), [2018] 2 C.M.L.R. 10.

### Payment during absence due to sickness: the position at common law

*Replace paragraph with:*

The position at common law is that the right of the employee to claim salary or wages during his or her absence from work on account of illness or injury depends entirely on the terms of his or her contract. Particulars of terms relating to incapacity for work due to sickness or injury, including any provisions for sick pay, must be issued to the employee under the Contracts of Employment legislation.[560] There are provisions under that legislation requiring the employer to allow sick pay where absence due to sickness occurs during a statutory period of notice.[561] A large proportion of contracts of employment now include some form of scheme for payment during absence due to sickness. If no express term deals with the matter, the court must attempt to infer an implied term from all the relevant circumstances. In older **40-084** authorities, the following considerations have been thought relevant in determining such an implied term:

(1) If it is known to the parties that, in practice, the particular employer does not pay wages during illness to employees engaged in a capacity similar to that of the one in question,[562] it is an implied term of the contract that no wages are payable during the employee's illness.[563] On the other hand, if it is known to both parties that wages are usually paid during illness it will be an implied term of the contract that the employee shall be entitled to his wages throughout the period of his employment despite any absence due to illness.[564]

(2) If the employee receives sick pay out of a fund to which both the employer and the employees contribute, the employee is not entitled to wages while he or she receives benefits from the fund.[565] On the other hand, the receipt of social security sickness benefits does not of itself prevent the employee from claiming wages during the time he or she is in receipt of those benefits.[566]

(3) When the employee is paid by time, e.g. by the hour, and is not paid for any time in which he or she does not work, the employee will not normally be entitled to wages in respect of periods of absence through illness.[567] Similarly an employee paid by piecework (without any provision for guaranteed remuneration) is not entitled to wages if, through illness, he or she is unable to work.[568]

(4) Contracts of employment have been said to be of two kinds, one in which the consideration for the wages is actual work, and the other in which it is readiness and willingness to work, if of ability to do so.[569] It has been thought that in the former case, wages are not payable during the employee's illness, whilst in the latter case they are.[570] In *Beveridge v KLM UK Ltd*[571] it was ruled that an employee who offers her services to an employer is entitled, at common law, to be paid unless a specific condition of the contract regulates otherwise. However, that pronouncement has to be related to the specific context in which an employee claimed to be fit and certified to return to work, while the employers required their own medical adviser to confirm.

(5) It has been held that where there is a contractual obligation to pay sick pay, but no agreed term as to its duration, a term should be implied which is reasonable having regard to the normal practice in the industry.[572]

(6) It should be noted that the existence of an express sick pay scheme may result in an implied term restricting the employer's power to terminate the contract during the absence of the employee due to sickness.[573]

[560] Employment Rights Act 1996 s.1(4)(d)(ii).

[561] Employment Rights Act 1996 s.88(1).

[562] e.g. where there was a notice in the place of employment that half-pay up to a total of 21 days a year would be paid *as a matter of grace* during illness: *Petrie v Mac Fisheries Ltd* [1940] 1 K.B. 258; or where the employee had been ill on several previous occasions and had not asked for nor been paid any wages: *O'Grady v Saper Ltd* [1940] 2 K.B. 469.

[563] *Petrie v Mac Fisheries* [1940] 1 K.B. 258; *O'Grady v Saper Ltd* [1940] 2 K.B. 469.

[564] *K v Raschen* (1878) 38 L.T. 38.

[565] *Niblett v Midland Ry* (1907) 23 T.L.R. 240.

[566] cf. *Marrison v Bell* [1939] 2 K.B. 187.

[567] *Hancock v BSA Tools Ltd* [1939] 4 All E.R. 538.

568 See *Browning v Crumlin Valley Collieries* [1926] 1 K.B. 522.

569 *Petrie v Mac Fisheries Ltd* [1940] 1 K.B. 258; *O'Grady v M Saper Ltd* [1940] 2 K.B. 469; *Hancock v BSA Tools Ltd* [1939] 4 All E.R. 538. See also Lord Denning (1939) 55 L.Q.R. 353.

570 *Cuckson v Stones* (1859) 1 E. & E. 248; *Warren v Whittingham* (1902) 18 T.L.R. 508; *Marrison v Bell* [1939] 2 K.B. 187. The headnote is inaccurate: *O'Grady v Saper Ltd* [1940] 2 K.B. 469, 473.

571 [2000] I.R.L.R. 765.

572 *Howman & Son v Blyth* [1983] I.C.R. 416.

573 Compare *Aspden v Webbs Poultry & Meat Group (Holdings) Ltd* [1996] I.R.L.R. 521. (As to the effect on such a scheme of the termination of the insurance policy which supports it, compare *Bainbridge v Circuit Foil (UK) Ltd* [1997] I.C.R. 541). See also, in the disability context, *Awan v ICTS UK Ltd* [2019] I.C.R. 696.

## Payment during disciplinary suspension

*Replace footnote 653 with:*

653 *Wallwork v Fielding* [1922] 2 K.B. 66. However, in *North West Anglia NHS Foundation Trust v Gregg* [2019] EWCA Civ 387 it was held that, in the case of *interim* suspension pending or during disciplinary proceedings where the contract did not address the question of payment, the default position should be that the suspension should not attract the deduction of pay. **40-093**

## General restrictions on deductions made, or payments received, by employers

*Replace footnote 716 with:*

716 Employment Rights Act 1996 s.13(1). See *Agarwal v Cardiff University; Tyne and Wear Passenger Transport Executive (t/a Nexus) v Anderson* [2018] EWCA Civ 2084, [2019] I.C.R 433. **40-099**

### *(ii) Other Duties*

## The Working Time Regulations

*Replace paragraph with:*

Important controls upon working time, required by the EC Working Time Directive[826] and the Young Workers Directive,[827] were introduced by the Working Time Regulations 1998,[828] which have been the subject of various subsequent amending Regulations.[829] The main provisions of these Regulations are, in brief summary, as follows. The Regulations apply to "workers"; the original restriction to those above the minimum school leaving age was revoked in 2003.[830] "Workers" are so defined as not to be confined to those with contracts of employment, though so as to exclude the genuinely self-employed.[831] "Working time" is to be interpreted widely and purposively, including for example travel from a worker's place of residence to customer premises,[832] the attendance of meetings as a trade union or health and safety representative,[833] or when a worker is logged into a gig economy platform and under an obligation to accept tasks if offered.[833a] **40-112**

The Regulations set a working time limit of an average of 48 hours per week, with a standard averaging period of 17 weeks which may be extended to up to 52 weeks by a collective agreement between employer(s) and trade union(s), or by a "workforce agreement" between employers and elected workforce representatives, or, in the case of employers of no more than 20 workers, which the workers sign individually.[834] Workers may agree in writing as individuals to disapply the weekly working hours limit.[835] Provision is made for remedies,[835a] and to protect workers from suffering detriment (such as a denial of promotion or of training opportunities) because they refuse to agree to disapply the limits.[836] There are also measures by which night workers are subject to a working time limit of an average of 8 hours in each 24 hour period, and by which night workers whose work involves special hazard or heavy physical or mental strain are subject to an 8 hour limit for each 24 hour period.[837] Stricter limits upon maximum working time and night work are set for young workers.[838] There are also measures relating to rest breaks and rest periods, whereby workers are entitled to one day off each week and young workers are entitled to two days off each week,[839] whereby workers are entitled to 11 hours consecutive rest per day and young workers are entitled to 12 hours consecutive rest per day,[840] and whereby workers are entitled to a rest break of at least 20 minutes in a working day of longer than 6 hours, and young workers are entitled to a rest break of at least 30 minutes in a working day of longer than 4.5 hours.[841] It is incumbent on the employer proactively to ensure that working arrangements allow for workers to take their due rest breaks.[842] Certain of those provisions are subject to exceptions in respect of collective or "workforce" agreements.[843] The Regulations also confer upon workers within their scope, an entitlement to four weeks paid annual leave.[844] There is provision for the enforcement of the limits on weekly working time and night work by the health and safety enforcing authorities,[845] and for workers to assert in claims or complaints to employment tribunals, their entitlements, such as to rest periods and breaks and paid annual leave, and their rights to be protected from detriment, such as for refusing to agree to disapply limits on working time.[846] The Court of Justice has given a wide interpretation to these provisions: in *Ville de Nivelles v Matzak*, for example, it was held that even standby time spent at home could count as "working time".[847]

[826] Directive 2003/88.

[827] Directive 94/33.

[828] SI 1998/1833, in force from October 1, 1998.

[829] The Working Time Regulations 1999 (SI 1999/3372), the Working Time (Amendment) Regulations 2001 (SI 2001/3256), the Working Time (Amendment) Regulations 2002 (SI 2002/3128), and the Working Time (Amendment) Regulations 2003 (SI 2003/1684). See also now the Working Time (Amendment) Regulations 2006 (SI 2006/99) and, in relation to agricultural workers, the Working Time (Amendment) (England) Regulations 2013 (SI 2013/2228).

[830] SI 1998/1833 reg.26 was revoked by SI 2003/1684 reg.9.

[831] See regs 3, 36; and see above, para.40-009.

[832] *Federacion de Servicios Privados del sindicato Comisiones obreras (CC OO) v Tyco Integrated Security SL* (C-266/14) EU:C:2015:578, [2016] 1 C.M.L.R. 22.

[833] *Edwards v Encirc Ltd* [2015] I.R.L.R. 528, EAT.

[833a] *Addison Lee Ltd v Lange* [2019] I.C.R. 637, EAT.

[834] See reg.23 and Sch.1. It was, however, held in *Barber v RJB Mining (UK) Ltd* [1999] I.C.R. 679, QBD that where an employer seeks to require workers to work longer hours than the maximum hours applicable to them under the Regulations, and they are unwilling to agree to do so, they may be granted a declaration that the employer's attempt so to require them to exceed the statutory maximum violates an obligation which has become part of their contract of employment.

[835] See reg.5.

[835a] See reg.30. Compensation was held not to extend to injury to feelings in *Santos Gomes v Higher Level Card Ltd* [2018] EWCA Civ 418, [2018] I.C.R. 1571.

[836] See reg.31.

[837] See reg.6.

[838] See new regs 5A, 6A, inserted by the Working Time (Amendment) Regulations 2002 (SI 2002/3128).

[839] See reg.11.

[840] See reg.10.

[841] See reg.12. Whether rest pursuant to reg.24(a) is "equivalent" to the 20-minute break is a question of fact to be determined by the Employment Tribunal: *Network Rail Infrastructure Ltd v Crawford* [2019] EWCA Civ 269, [2019] 2 All E.R. 1095.

[842] *Grange v Abellio London Ltd* [2017] I.R.L.R. 108, EAT.

[843] See reg.23. Compare, as to collective agreements, *Prison Service v Bewley* [2004] I.C.R. 422, EAT.

[844] See reg.13 as amended by the Working Time (Amendment) Regulations 2001 (SI 2001/3256). For details, see above, para 40-081.

[845] See reg.28.

[846] See regs 30–32.

[847] C-518/15 EU:C:2018:82.

## The rights of the employee in relation to trade union membership and activities

*Replace paragraph with:*

Under the provisions of ss.146 to 151 of the Trade Union and Labour Relations (Consolidation) Act 1992 as subsequently amended,[860] a worker[861] has a right not to be subjected to any detriment as an individual by any act, or any deliberate failure to act,[862] by his employer if the act or failure takes place for the purpose of preventing or deterring him from becoming a member of an independent trade union, or penalising him for doing so,[863] or from taking part in the activities of an independent trade union at any appropriate time, or penalising him for doing so,[864] or compelling him to be or become a member of any trade union or of a particular trade union or of one of a number of particular trade unions.[865] The Employment Relations Act 2004 established new or enhanced rights for workers not to be offered inducements relating to trade union membership and collective bargaining, and extended their rights not to suffer detrimental action in circumstances relating to trade union membership.[866] **40-115**

[860] The most important amendments were made by s.13 of the Trade Union Reform and Employment Rights Act 1993, by s.2 of and Sch.2 to the Employment Relations Act 1999, and also by ss.29–32 of the Employment Relations Act 2004, inserting the new ss.145A–145B of the Trade Union and Labour Relations (Consolidation) Act 1992. As to the latter, see now *Kostal UK Ltd v Dunkley* [2019] EWCA Civ 1009.

[861] Excluded classes of employees are: share fishermen—s.284, work outside Great Britain—s.285. Crown employees are included—s.273. The Employment Act 2004 s.31 amended ss.146–151 of the 1992 Act to extend, to workers who are not employees, the existing protections of employees against detrimental action by their employer for being, or not being, a member of a trade union or for taking part in the activities of their union.

[862] The effects of deliberate omission, as well as of positive action, are now included, reversing by statute the decision of the House of Lords on this point in *Associated Newspapers Ltd v Wilson; Associated British Ports Ltd v Palmer* [1995] I.C.R. 406.

[863] s.146(1)(a). See *Jet2.Com Ltd v Denby* [2018] I.C.R. 597, EAT. Compare, in relation to unfair dismissal, see below, para.40-229.

[864] s.146(1)(b). See *Robb v Leon Motor Services Ltd* [1978] I.C.R. 506, EAT: and *Marley Tile Co v Shaw* [1980] I.C.R. 72. See also now *Department of Transport v Gallacher* [1994] I.C.R. 967.

[865] s.146(1)(c).

[866] ss.29–32 of the 2004 Act make a series of additions and amendments to ss.146–151 of the Trade Union and Labour Relations (Consolidation) Act 1992; s.29 of the 2004 Act inserts new ss.145A–F into the 1992 Act.

## Equality clauses in contracts of employment (1) gender equality

*Replace footnote 902 with:*

[902] See s.79(1)–(4). See *British Coal Corp v Smith* [1996] I.C.R. 515, HL. Compare *Allonby v Ac-* **40-126**

*cringtion & Rossendale College* (C-256/01) EU:C:2004:18, [2004] I.R.L.R. 224, ECJ, as to the construction of the "same employment" concept in accordance with art.141(1) of the EC Treaty. Compare also *DEFRA v Robertson* [2005] EWCA Civ 138, [2005] I.C.R. 750, expounding the notion of attributability of differences between terms and conditions of employment to a "single source" which had been articulated by the ECJ in *Lawrence v Regent Office Care Ltd* (C-320/00) EU:C:2002:498, [2002] E.C.R. I-7325. See further *North v Dumfries and Galloway Council* [2013] UKSC 45, [2013] 4 All E.R. 413, and *ASDA Stores Ltd v Brierley* [2019] EWCA Civ 44, [2019] 2 C.M.L.R. 18.

## Disability discrimination during the period of employment

*Replace footnote 942 with:*

40-135 [942] ss.6, 12–14, 20 (duty to make adjustments), 39 subject to s.83(11) and Sch.9 Pt 1 (occupational requirements). The provisions are extended to discrimination occurring after the employment relationship has come to an end where the discrimination arises out of and is closely connected to the relationship in question—s.108. Provision for complaint to an employment tribunal is made by s.120(1), and for the awarding of remedies by s.124. Compare also *Hainsworth v Ministry of Defence* [2014] EWCA Civ 763, [2014] I.R.L.R. 728 (employer's reasonable adjustment duty did not extend to an employee's association with a disabled person), and *Abertawe Bro Morgannwg University Local Health Board v Morgan* [2018] EWCA Civ 640, [2018] I.C.R. 1194.

## Rights in connection with parenthood and family responsibility

*(4) Paternity leave*

*To the end of paragraph, after "case of adoption.", add new footnote 967a:*

40-144 [967a] For a challenge under the Equality Act 2010 to the shared parental leave regime, see *Ali v Capita Customer Management Ltd* [2019] EWCA Civ 900.

## References and testimonials

*Replace footnote 988 with:*

40-147 [988] *Cox v Sun Alliance Life Ltd* [2001] I.R.L.R. 448. Compare *Hincks v Sense Network Ltd* [2018] EWHC 533 (QB), [2018] I.R.L.R. 614.

## Extensions of the implied obligation of trust and confidence

*Replace footnote 1025 with:*

40-152 [1025] *Gogay v Hertfordshire CC* [2000] I.R.L.R. 703. Cf. now *Lambeth LBC v Agoreyo* [2019] EWCA Civ 322, where the Court of Appeal reinstated the County Court's finding that the employer had "reasonable and proper cause" to suspend a teacher pending further disciplinary investigation.

## Further applications and extensions of the implied obligation of trust and confidence

*Replace footnote 1030 with:*

40-153 [1030] [2006] EWCA Civ 1536, [2007] I.C.R. 623. Compare also now *Khatri v Cooperatieve Centrale Raiffeisen-Boerenleenbank BA* [2010] EWCA Civ 397, where the requirement of rational exercise of discretions with regard to the awarding of bonuses was reaffirmed, and *Patural v DB Services (UK) Ltd* [2015] EWHC 3659 (QB), [2016] I.R.L.R. 286. See now also *Faieta v ICAP Management Services Ltd* [2017] EWHC 2995 (QB), [2018] I.R.L.R. 227.

## The limits of the implied obligation of trust and confidence

*Replace footnote 1036 with:*

40-154 [1036] [2004] UKHL 35, [2005] 1 A.C. 503. The implied term imports an obligation not deliberately to mislead an employee as to reasons for dismissal: *Rawlinson v Brightside Group Ltd* [2018] I.R.L.R. 180, EAT.

## Disclosures of information in the public interest

*Replace footnote 1052 with:*

1052 Employment Rights Act 1996 s.47B as inserted by s.2 of the 1998 Act. See *Timis v Osipov* [2018] EWCA Civ 2321, [2019] I.C.R. 655. **40-155**

## Duties to avoid less favourable treatment of part-time work and fixed-term work

*Replace first paragraph with:*

Two important measures have been taken in response to EC Directives, conferring (to the extent defined) upon those working under certain specific types of employment contract or arrangement a right to equality of treatment with those employed under the corresponding "standard" type of employment contract or arrangement. The Part-time Workers (Prevention of Less Favourable Treatment) Regulations 2000,[1057] implementing Council Directive 97/81 on part-time work,[1058] require part-time workers[1059] not to be treated less favourably than full-time workers of the same employer who work under the same type[1060] of employment contract,[1061] on the ground of being a part-time worker, unless there is objective justification for that less favourable treatment.[1062] A part-time worker may complain to an employment tribunal of the violation of that right.[1063] **40-156**

1057 SI 2000/1551, in force from July 1, 2000. See also now the Part-time Workers (Prevention of Less Favourable Treatment) Regulations 2001 (SI 2001/1107), in force from May 1, 2001, and the Part-time Workers (Prevention of Less Favourable Treatment) Regulations 2002 (SI 2002/2035), in force from October 1, 2002, which make further consequential provisions.

1058 Directive 97/81 as extended to the UK by Directive 98/23.

1059 As defined in reg.1(2), similarly as in Employment Rights Act 1996 s.230(3). Compare *Christie v Department for Constitutional Affairs* [2007] I.C.R. 1553, EAT, where it was held that a part-time tribunal chairman came within the Regulations. In *O'Brien v Department of Constitutional Affairs* [2008] EWCA Civ 1448, [2009] I.R.L.R. 294 the Court of Appeal held that part-time judicial office holders are not "workers" for the purpose of these Regulations; however, in *O'Brien v Ministry of Justice* (C-393/10) EU:C:2012:110 the ECJ suggested that this decision was non-compliant with the Directive. In *O'Brien v Department of Constitutional Affairs* [2013] UKSC 6, [2013] 1 W.L.R. 522 the Supreme Court duly held that the decision of the ECJ did require a recognition that the part-time Recorder was entitled to be regarded as a "worker" for the purposes of the 2000 Regulations. *O'Brien* was distinguished in *Gilham v Ministry of Justice* [2017] I.R.L.R. 23, EAT, where a narrower interpretation was favoured in the context of purely domestic employment rights. The Court of Appeal dismissed a further appeal in the latter case, [2017] EWCA Civ 2220, [2018] I.R.L.R. 315.

1060 See reg.2. See for the judicial construction of this Regulation, and the clarification of the notion of comparable workers which it articulates, *Mathews v Kent and Medway Towns Fire Authority* [2006] UKHL 8, [2006] I.C.R. 365, and cf. now also *Roddis v Sheffield Hallam University* [2018] I.R.L.R. 706, EAT, and *British Airways Plc v Pinaud* [2018] EWCA Civ 2427, [2019] I.C.R. 487.

1061 SI 2000/1551.

1062 See reg.5(2).

1063 See regs 5(2), 8.

*After first paragraph, add new paragraph:*

The provisions have been subject of intensive litigation with regard to judicial office holders. In *Christie v Department for Constitutional Affairs*,[1063a] it was held that a part-time tribunal chairman came within the Regulations. More generally, in *O'Brien v Department of Constitutional Affairs* the Court of Appeal held that part-time judicial office holders are not "workers" for the purpose of these Regulations[1063b]; however, in *O'Brien v Ministry of Justice* the CJEU suggested that this decision was non-compliant with the Directive.[1063c] In *O'Brien v Department of Constitutional Affairs* the Supreme Court duly held that the decision of the CJEU **40-156** did require a recognition that the part-time Recorder was entitled to be regarded as a "worker" for the purposes of the 2000 Regulations.[1063d] *O'Brien* was distinguished in *Gilham v Ministry of Justice*,[1063e] where a narrower interpretation was favoured in the context of purely domestic employment rights. The Court of Appeal dismissed a further appeal in the latter case.[1063f]

[1063a] [2007] I.C.R. 1553, EAT.

[1063b] [2008] EWCA Civ 1448, [2009] I.R.L.R. 294.

[1063c] C-393/10, EU:C:2012:110.

[1063d] [2013] UKSC 6, [2013] 1 W.L.R. 522.

[1063e] [2017] I.R.L.R. 23, EAT.

[1063f] [2017] EWCA Civ 2220, [2018] I.R.L.R. 315. Cf. with regard to limitations periods and the judicial pension scheme, *Miller v Ministry of Justice* [2019] UKSC 60.

## 6. TERMINATION OF THE CONTRACT

### (e) Assignment, Winding-up and Changes in the Employing Enterprise

#### Transfer of employment: (2) the effect of the TUPE Regulations

*Replace footnote 1247 with:*

**40-180** [1247] SI 2006/246 reg.4(4), subject to reg.9 which is more permissive towards variations of contract where transferors are subject to insolvency proceedings. See *Kavanagh v Crystal Palace FC 2000 Ltd* [2013] EWCA Civ 1410, [2014] 1 All E.R. 1033, and *Manchester College v Hazel* [2014] EWCA Civ 72, [2014] I.R.L.R. 392. For an illustration of how a transfer can be the sole or principal reason, even where other factors are in play, see *Hare Wines Ltd v Kaur* [2019] EWCA Civ 216.

### (h) Constructive Dismissal

#### Termination as the result of constructive dismissal

*Replace paragraph with:*

**40-194** For the purposes of the various legislative provisions concerning dismissal, such as the unfair dismissal legislation and the redundancy payments legislation, "dismissal" includes the case where the employee terminates the contract of employment with or without notice in circumstances such that he or she is entitled to terminate it without notice by reason of the employer's conduct.[1349] Where these conditions are fulfilled, the employee's resignation is treated as a constructive dismissal by the employer, provided that the employer's conduct is the main operative cause of the resignation.[1350] In *Western Excavating (ECC) Ltd v Sharp*,[1351] it was decided that the test for constructive dismissal as so defined was a contractual one, namely whether the employer's conduct amounted to a fundamental breach or repudiation of the contract of employment. This decision has resulted not only in considerable development of case law on the generally implied duties of the employer such as the duty to preserve trust and confidence[1352] but also in extensive discussion in the case law of what constitutes repudiation on the part of the employer. This frequently involves an inquiry into the implied terms of the particular contract concerning geographical mobility[1353] or into the question of when the employer repudiates the contract by altering the terms and conditions of employment.[1354] It would seem that the question of whether there has been a repudiation by the employer should be viewed as a mixed question of law and fact with the result that a finding by an employment tribunal about repudiation or fundamental breach of an implied term should be disturbed on appeal only where there was no basis of evidence properly to support such a finding.[1355] It would also seem that the notion that a party to a contract does not repudiate it by pursuing a bona fide but mistaken view of its effect[1356] can have only a very limited application in disputes between employer and employee over terms and conditions of employment.[1357] There is no constructive dismissal if the employee affirms the contract after and despite the employer's repudiation.[1358] But delay in accepting the repudiation, and even continuing to work and accept remuneration are not in themselves conclusive of affirmation on the employee's part; there must be a consideration of the whole of the circumstances including factors such as whether the employee acted under protest or not.[1359] It was held by the Employment Appeal Tribunal in *Morrow v Safeway Stores Ltd*[1360] that conduct on the part of the employer which was sufficiently undermining of trust and confidence to amount to a breach of the implied obligation of trust and confidence was as such repudiatory of the contract of employment and so entitled the employee to resign and claim to have been constructively dismissed. In *Waltham Forest LBC v Omilaju (No.2)*[1360a] it was held that the final act or "last straw" in a series of actions which cumulatively amounted to constructive dismissal need not itself be a breach of contract or unreasonable; but it had to be more than very trivial and had to be capable of contributing, however slightly, to a breach of the implied obligation as to mutual trust and confidence.[1360b] It was held by the Court of Appeal in *Rossiter v Pendragon Plc*[1361] that the test for constructive dismissal in relation to changes of terms and conditions associated with the transfer of an undertaking involved the same requirement of a repudiatory breach of contract as in other situations, this requirement being neither negated nor reduced by the TUPE Regulations.[1362] As has been explained and explored in an earlier paragraph,[1363] the decision of the House of Lords in the leading case of *Johnson v Unisys Ltd*,[1364] that the implied obligation as to trust and confidence does not apply to limit the employer's power of dismissal, has left a difficult question as to when that implied obligation is applicable to conduct on the part of the employer which would, if the obligation applies to it, amount to constructive dismissal. In *Edwards v Chesterfield Royal Hospital NHS Trust*[1365] the Supreme Court confirmed the demarcation of the "*Johnson* exclusion" which had emerged from the *Eastwood* case,[1366] whereby that exclusion applies in respect of "steps on the part of the employer leading to dismissal" unless the loss complained of as resulting from those steps "precedes and is independent of the dismissal process".[1367] According to this demarcation, the mere fact that a step taken by the employer might in itself amount to a *constructive* dismissal, even if it is eventually followed by a distinct act of dismissal on the part of the employer, does not in and of itself place that step within the "*Johnson* exclusion"—so that, for example, the suspension of an employee may still on its facts be held to be in breach of the implied obligation of mutual trust and confidence and may give rise to liability as a contractually wrongful constructive dismissal not caught by the "*Johnson* exclusion".[1368]

1349 Employment Rights Act 1996 ss.95(1)(c), 136(1)(c); see below, paras 40-220—40-221, 40-250.

1350 cf. *Jones v Sirl & Son (Furnishers) Ltd* [1997] I.R.L.R. 493.

1351 [1978] I.C.R. 221. The decision was applied and reaffirmed in *Bournemouth University Higher Education Corp v Buckland* [2010] EWCA Civ 121, [2010] I.R.L.R. 445, where the Court of Appeal rejected the argument that a "band of reasonable responses" test should apply, and moreover rejected the argument that there was any doctrine of cure of fundamental breach which was special to employment law.

1352 See above, para.40-151. Compare now, on the question of breach of the implied term of trust and confidence arising out of the transfer of an undertaking, *Sita (GB) Ltd v Burton* [1998] I.C.R. 17. See also now *Glendale Managed Services v Graham* [2003] I.R.L.R. 465.

1353 See *Little v Charterhouse Magna Ltd* [1980] I.R.L.R. 19; *Jones v Associated Tunnelling Ltd* [1981] I.R.L.R. 477.

1354 See, e.g. *Ford v Millthorn Toleman Ltd* [1980] I.R.L.R. 30; *Millbrook Furnishing Ltd v McIntosh* [1981] I.R.L.R. 309; *Pedersen v Camden LBC* [1981] I.C.R. 674n. For attempted imposition of a variation in terms, coupled with the threat of dismissal if variation rejected, as constructive dismissal, see *Greenaway Harrison Ltd v Wiles* [1994] I.R.L.R. 380.

1355 See *Pedersen v Camden LBC* [1981] I.C.R. 674n.; *Millbrook Furnishing Ltd v McIntosh* [1981] I.R.L.R. 309; *Woods v WM Car Services Ltd* [1981] I.C.R. 666. There is, however, authority for the view that the question is one of law for the appellate tribunal—*Walker v Josiah Wedgwood Sons Ltd* [1978] I.C.R. 744, 750E–H, or that if the question is a mixed one, that nonetheless gives the appellate tribunal primary control over the issue—cf. *O'Brien v Associated Fire Alarms Ltd* [1968] 1 W.L.R. 1916.

1356 *Sweet & Maxwell Ltd v Universal News Services Ltd* [1964] 3 All E.R. 30; *Woodar Investments v Wimpey Construction Ltd* [1980] 1 All E.R. 571.

1357 *Financial Techniques Ltd v Hughes* [1981] I.R.L.R. 32, paras 28, 29, per Templeman L.J.; doubting *Frank Wright Ltd v Punch* [1980] I.R.L.R. 217; *Millbrook Furnishing Ltd v McIntosh* [1981] I.R.L.R. 309.

1358 *Western Excavating (ECC) Ltd v Sharp* [1978] I.C.R. 221, 226; *Bashir v Brillo Manufacturing Co* [1979] I.R.L.R. 295; *Cox Toner International Ltd v Crook* [1981] I.C.R. 823; *Brown v Neon Management Services Ltd* [2018] EWHC 2137 (QB), [2019] I.R.L.R. 30.

1359 *Bashir v Brillo Manufacturing Co* [1979] I.R.L.R. 295, at paras 15–19; *Cox Toner International Ltd v Crook* [1981] I.C.R. 823, 829C–H. See also *Chindove v Morrisons Supermarket Plc* [2014] UKEAT 0043/14/BA.

1360 [2002] I.R.L.R. 9.

1360a [2004] EWCA Civ 1493, [2005] I.R.L.R. 35.

1360b Compare also *Bunning v GT Bunning & Sons Ltd* [2005] EWCA Civ 104, in which the judgment of Wall L.J. adds further support to the notion of the "last straw" as articulated in the *Omilaju* case; compare also *GAB Robins (UK) Ltd v Triggs* [2008] EWCA Civ 17, [2008] I.R.L.R. 317. Cf. also *Kaur v Leeds Teaching Hospitals NHS Trust* [2018] EWCA Civ 978, [2018] 4 All E.R. 238.

1361 [2002] I.C.R. 1063, CA.

1362 Compare above, para.40-180, from which it will be seen that reg.4(9) of the 2006 TUPE Regulations apparently provides an alternative statutory form of constructive dismissal in such circumstances.

1363 See above, para.40-154.

1364 [2001] I.C.R. 480. In *Kerry Foods Ltd v Lynch* [2005] I.R.L.R. 681, the doctrine in *Johnson v Unisys Ltd* received an important application or extension, in that it was held that where an employing enterprise sought to impose a six-day week on an employee working a five-day week, its conduct amounted not to a repudiatory breach of the obligation as to mutual trust and confidence, but rather to a giving of lawful notice to terminate the contract of employment coupled with an offer of re-engagement on different terms.

1365 [2011] UKSC 58.

1366 *Eastwood v Magnox Electric Plc, McCabe v Cornwall CC* [2004] UKHL 35, [2005] 1 A.C. 503.

1367 Lord Dyson in *Edwards* at [51] quoting from Lord Nicholls in *Eastwood* at [29]. Lord Dyson continued: "In other words 'the court must decide whether earlier events do or do not form part of the dismissal process'" quoting from Lord Steyn in *Eastwood* at [39].

1368 Hence the possibility that "an employer may be better off dismissing an employee than suspending him", an outcome regarded as "unsatisfactory and anomalous" but "the inevitable consequence of the interrelation between the common law and statute": Lord Dyson in *Edwards* at [51] quoting from Lord Nicholls in *Eastwood* at [15] and [30] to [33].

## 7. Remedies, and Rights Incidental to the Termination of Employment

### (c) Protection of the Employee's Accrued Rights in the Employer's Insolvency

#### Recourse to the National Insurance Fund on insolvency of employer

*Replace footnote 1419 with:*

1419 Employment Rights Act 1996 s.184(1). For an application in the context of TUPE, see *Graysons Restaurants Ltd v Jones* [2019] EWCA Civ 725, [2019] All E.R. 688. 40-200

### (f) Employment Tribunal Jurisdiction

#### Jurisdiction of employment tribunals in relation to contracts of employment

*Replace footnote 1519 with:*

1519 Employment Tribunals Act 1996 (as renamed by the Employment Rights (Dispute Resolution) Act 1998) s.3(2)(a). Cf. *ONI v Unison Trade Union* [2018] I.C.R. 1111, EAT. 40-213

## 8. Unfair and Discriminatory Dismissal

### (a) Unfair Dismissal

#### *(i) General Considerations*

#### Employments covered, employments specifically excluded

*Replace footnote 1545 with:*

1545 Employment Rights Act 1996 s.94, taken in conjunction with s.230(1) of Employment Rights Act 1996 (definition of "employee"). See above, paras 40-010—40-025, for definition of the contract of employment. As to the implicit exclusion of employees working abroad, see now *Lawson v Serco Ltd* [2006] UKHL 3, [2006] I.C.R. 250, in which the House of Lords allowed the appeals of certain claimants in a group of joined appeals, remitting their cases to the employment tribunal for rehearing, and further explicated the territorial scope of the right not be unfairly dismissed. Compare now *Dhunna v Creditsights Ltd* [2014] EWCA Civ 1238, [2014] I.C.R. 105, and *British Council v Jeffery* [2018] EWCA Civ 2253, [2019] I.C.R. 929. 40-216

#### *(ii) Dismissal and Effective Date of Termination*

#### The effective date of termination

*Replace second paragraph with:*

For certain above-mentioned purposes for which the definition applies, namely that of the initial qualifying period and that of the calculation of basic award of compensation, the effective date of termination is postponed[1597] to the date when a duly given statutory minimum period of notice[1598] would have expired. The application of the above statutory definition to termination by payment in lieu of notice depends upon the view taken of the juridical nature of a payment in lieu of notice, a matter considered in an earlier paragraph.[1599] Where a dismissal is expressed in a notice or letter, it has been held that the termination does not take effect until the employee has read that notice or letter or had a reasonable opportunity to do so.[1600] Where an employee is suspended without pay pending a domestic appeal against dismissal, it has been held that where the appeal is unsuccessful, the effective date 40-223 of termination is that of the original dismissal.[1601] If, however, the employee is contractually entitled to remuneration during such suspension, the effective date of termination is postponed until notification of the rejection of the appeal.[1602] Where an employer wrongfully repudiates the contract of employment by wrongful dismissal, it has been held that even if the elective theory whereby wrongful repudiation requires acceptance to terminate the contract is applicable,[1603] the effective date of termination for statutory purposes is nevertheless the date of the summary dismissal rather than the later date on which notice duly given on that date would have expired[1604] (subject only to the statutory extension for the statutory minimum period of notice).[1605]

[1597] Employment Rights Act 1996 s.97(2)–(5). See *Dhami v Top Spot Night Club* [1977] I.R.L.R. 231.

[1598] See above, para.40-164; *Fox Maintenance Ltd v Jackson* [1978] I.C.R. 110. In *Harper v Virgin Net Ltd* [2004] EWCA Civ 271, [2004] I.R.L.R. 390 it was held that the legislation did not bring about a further postponement of the effective date of termination to the later date at which a contractual notice period, longer than the statutory minimum notice period, would have expired. See also *Lancaster & Duke Ltd v Wileman* [2019] I.C.R 125, EAT.

[1599] See above, para.40-182.

[1600] *Brown v Southall & Knight* [1980] I.C.R. 617. The decision was followed, and its doctrine was re-vindicated and elaborated, by the Court of Appeal and by the Supreme Court in *Gisda Cyf v Barratt* [2009] EWCA Civ 648, [2010] UKSC 41. See now also *Sandle v Adecco UK Ltd* [2016] I.R.L.R. 941, EAT and especially *Newcastle upon Tyne Hospitals NHS Foundation Trust v Haywood* [2018] UKSC 22, [2018] 1 W.L.R. 2073.

[1601] *Sainsbury Ltd v Savage* [1981] I.C.R. 1.

[1602] *Drage v Governors of Greenford High School* [2000] I.R.L.R. 314.

[1603] See above, para.40-193.

[1604] *Robert Cort & Son Ltd v Charman* [1981] I.C.R. 816; compare also *BMK Ltd v Logue* [1993] I.C.R. 601. In *Lambert v Croydon College* [1999] I.C.R. 409, the Employment Appeal Tribunal held that a compromise agreement (see above, para.40-174) for early retirement on grounds of ill-health could validly fix the effective date of termination of employment for statutory purposes, even though it fixed it at a date earlier than that on which the agreement was made.

[1605] See above, para.40-169.

### *(iii) Unfairness*

#### **Substantial reasons for dismissal**

*Replace paragraph with:*

**40-225** It is provided[1617] that at the first stage[1618] of the determination whether a dismissal was fair or unfair, it is for the employer to show what was the reason or principal reason for the dismissal,[1619] and that it was a reason falling within a statutory list[1620] of substantial reasons justifying dismissal.[1621] The list is as follows:

(1) Reasons related to the capability[1622] or qualifications[1623] of the employee for performing work of the kind which he or she was employed to do.[1624] This may include supervening ill-health incapacitating the employee from carrying out his or her former work.[1625]
(2) Reasons related to the conduct of the employee.[1626] These need *not* necessarily be reasons going to the lengths of justifying summary dismissal for misconduct at common law.[1627]
(3) Redundancy of the employee.[1628] This is defined by reference to the definition of the term used in the redundancy payments legislation.[1629]
(4) Contravention of a statutory duty if the employment is continued.[1630] This covers cases such as that where an employee employed as a driver is disqualified from driving or driving a particular type of vehicle by order of

a court.

(5) Dismissal of an employee engaged expressly as a statutory replacement employee in order to make it possible for the replaced employee to resume his or her original work.[1631]

(6) Any other substantial reason of a kind such as to justify the dismissal of an employee holding the position which that employee held.[1632] This is a residual catch-all category leaving the whole issue ultimately within the discretion of the tribunals and courts. That discretion has not been limited by decided cases; there is no reason to suppose, for instance, that this category need be construed ejusdem generis with the other, specific, categories.[1633]

Special considerations apply to dismissals taking place because of the transfer of an undertaking within the meaning of the Transfer of Undertakings (Protection of Employment) Regulations. With effect from April 6, 2006, the existing Transfer of Undertakings (Protection of Employment) Regulations were revised and replaced by the Transfer of Undertakings (Protection of Employment) Regulations 2006.[1634] The new Regulations contain provisions which clarify the circumstances under which it is unfair for employers to dismiss employees for reasons connected with a relevant transfer.[1635]

1617 Employment Rights Act 1996 s.98.

1618 See above, para.40-224.

1619 Employment Rights Act 1996 s.98(1)(a). In *Royal Mail Ltd v Jhuti* [2019] UKSC 55, the Supreme Court held that the Employment Tribunal was under a duty to ascertain and act on the true reason for dismissal, rather than the proffered reason which was not the genuine one.

1620 Employment Rights Act 1996 s.98(2), subject to s.98(2A) with regard to retirement, as to which see below, para.40-226.

1621 Employment Rights Act 1996 s.98(1)(b).

1622 Defined by s.98(3)(a) Employment Rights Act 1996; compare *Abernethy v Mott, Hay & Anderson* [1974] I.C.R. 323; *Turner v Wadham Stringer Ltd* [1974] I.C.R. 277; *Blackman v Post Office* [1974] I.C.R. 151; *Kraft Foods Ltd v Fox* [1978] I.C.R. 311; *Miller v Executors of JC Graham* [1978] I.R.L.R. 309; *Bristol-Meyers Co Ltd v Matlock* [1978] 13 I.T.R. 158; *Sutton & Gates v Boxall* [1979] I.C.R. 67, EAT.

1623 Defined by s.98(3)(b) of Employment Rights Act 1996.

1624 Employment Rights Act 1996 s.98(2)(a).

1625 cf. *Merseyside and North Wales Electricity Board v Taylor* [1975] I.C.R. 185. See *Patterson v Messrs Bracketts* [1977] I.R.L.R. 137; *Spencer v Paragon Wallpapers Ltd* [1976] I.R.L.R. 373; *Liverpool AHA v Edwards* [1977] I.R.L.R. 471; *Finch v Betabake (Anglia) Ltd* [1977] I.R.L.R. 470; *Williamson v Alcan (UK) Ltd* [1978] I.C.R. 104; *Post Office v Jones* [1977] I.R.L.R. 422; *East Lindsey DC v Daubney* [1977] I.R.L.R. 181.

1626 Employment Rights Act 1996 s.98(2)(b). See, among the earlier leading authorities, *Morrish v Henlys (Folkestone) Ltd* [1973] I.C.R. 482; *Wallace v Guy Ltd* [1973] I.C.R. 119; *St Anne's Board Mill Co Ltd v Brien* [1973] I.C.R. 444; *Shipside (Ruthin) Ltd v TGWU* [1973] I.C.R. 503; *Hilti (Great Britain) Ltd v Windridge* [1974] I.C.R. 352; *Atkin v Enfield Group Hospital Management Committee* [1975] I.R.L.R. 217; *Conway v Matthew Wright & Nephew Ltd* [1977] I.R.L.R. 89; *Singh v London County Bus Services* [1976] I.R.L.R. 176; *Trust Houses Forte Ltd v Murphy* [1977] I.R.L.R. 186; *Torr v British Railways Board* [1977] I.C.R. 785; *Redbridge LBC v Fishman* [1978] I.C.R. 569; *Horrigan v Lewisham LBC* [1978] I.C.R. 15; *West Yorkshire MDC v Platts* [1978] I.C.R. 33; *Mansard Precision Engineering Co Ltd v Taylor* [1978] I.C.R. 828; *Nottinghamshire CC v Bowley* [1978] I.R.L.R. 252; *Johnson Matthey Metals Ltd v Harding* [1978] I.R.L.R. 248; *Tesco Stores Ltd v Heap* [1978] 13 I.T.R. 17; *Boychuk v H. & J. Symons Holdings Ltd* [1977] I.R.L.R. 395; *Coward v John Menzies (Holdings) Ltd* [1977] I.R.L.R. 428; *British Labour Pump Co Ltd v Byrne* [1979] I.C.R. 347; *Monie v Coral Racing* [1981] I.C.R. 109, CA; *Weddell & Co Ltd v Tepper* [1980] I.C.R. 286, CA; *British Home Stores Ltd v Burchell* [1980] I.C.R. 303, EAT; *UCATT v Brain* [1981] I.C.R. 542, CA; *Whitbread & Co Plc v Mills* (1988) I.R.L.R. 501; *Reilly v Sandwell MBC* [2018] UKSC 16, [2018] I.C.R. 705.

1627 See above, paras 40-226 et seq.

[1628] Employment Rights Act 1996 s.98(2)(c)—see below, paras 40-231—40-252.

[1629] Employment Rights Act 1996 s.235(3).

[1630] Employment Rights Act 1996 s.98(2)(d).

[1631] Employment Rights Act 1996 s.106(2)–(3) (replacement of employee suspended from work on medical grounds—see above, para.40-087—or on maternity grounds or absent by reason of pregnancy or confinement).

[1632] Employment Rights Act 1996 s.98(1)(b).

[1633] cf. *RS Components Ltd v Irwin* [1973] I.C.R. 535; *Hollister v National Farmers Union* [1979] I.C.R. 542.

[1634] SI 2006/246. See above, para.40-180.

[1635] See reg.7.

## Retirement and unfair dismissal

*Replace paragraph with:*

**40-226** Among the very significant new legal incidents which the Employment Equality (Age) Regulations 2006[1636] attached to the notion of "retirement"[1637] was a special regime for "retirement" within the law of unfair dismissal. This special regime was created by introducing new provisions into the Employment Rights Act 1996; it was known as the "default retirement age" regime because it authorised employers, on certain specified conditions, to maintain a mandatory retirement age for their employees which by default would be that of 65. These provisions were repealed by the Employment Equality (Repeal of Retirement Age Provisions) Regulations 2011,[1638] and the effect of that repeal, when coupled with the abolition of the previously existing age limits on claims for unfair dismissal which had accompanied the introduction of that special regime, is to expose the imposition of retirement upon an employee by an employer to the general law of unfair dismissal at whatever age it takes place. There is some official indication that employers may be able to maintain their own "employer-justified retirement age" regimes[1639]; the scope of this facility has begun to be effectively tested in litigation.[1640]

[1636] SI 2006/1031.

[1637] As to which see also paras 40-039, 40-125.

[1638] SI 2011/1069 which took full effect on October 1, 2011.

[1639] ACAS *Working without the default retirement age-guidance for employers* (March 2011).

[1640] Compare, however, *Seldon v Clarkson Wright and Jakes* [2010] UKSC 16 from which some incidental guidance may be derived. The maintaining of a retirement age of 65 was subsequently held to have been proportionate on the facts: *Seldon v Clarkson Wright & Jakes* [2014] I.R.L.R. 748, EAT. See also *Pitcher v Chancellor, Masters and Scholars of the University of Oxford and Saint John the Baptist College in the University of Oxford* Unreported May 16, 2019 (ET 3323858/2016); and on the linked question of pension entitlements, compare *Lord Chancellor v McCloud; Secretary of State for the Home Department v Sargeant* [2018] EWCA Civ 2844, [2019] I.R.L.R. 477.

## Cases on "reasonableness"

*Replace footnote 1651 with:*

**40-228** [1651] *West Midland Co-operative Society Ltd v Tipton* [1986] I.C.R. 192. See, in relation to a contractual right of appeal, *Patel v Folkestone Nursing Home Ltd* [2018] EWCA Civ 1689, [2018] I.R.L.R. 924, and more generally, *Afzal v East London Pizza Ltd (t/a Dominos Pizza)* [2018] I.C.R. 1652, EAT.

## Dismissal by reason of trade union membership, non-membership or activity

*Replace footnote 1659 with:*

**40-229** [1659] s.152(1)(b). See, for the scope of trade union activities, *Morris v Metrolink RATP Dev Ltd* [2018]

EWCA Civ 1358, [2018] I.R.L.R. 853. "Appropriate time" is defined by s.152(2). See *Chant v Aquaboats Ltd* [1978] I.C.R. 643; *City of Birmingham DC v Beyer* [1977] I.R.L.R. 211; *Marley Tile Co Ltd v Shaw* [1980] I.C.R. 72, CA.

### *(iv) Remedies*

#### Enforcement of orders for reinstatement or re-engagement

*In penultimate line, after "remedy of compensation", add new footnote 1743a:*

1743a For an illustration of the additional award under the Employment Rights Act 1996 s.117, see *R. (on the application of Mackenzie) v University of Cambridge* [2019] EWCA Civ 1060, [2019] 4 All E.R. 289. 40-240

## (b) Discriminatory and Victimising Dismissals

#### Dismissals unlawful under the Equality Act 2010

*Replace paragraph with:*

Under the relevant provisions of the Equality Act 2010, the dismissal of an employee by an employer is unlawful if it is discriminatory[1801] in the defined sense that it involves direct[1802] or indirect[1803] discrimination by reference to one or a combination of[1804] a specified set of "protected characteristics"[1805] consisting of age,[1806] disability,[1807] gender reassignment,[1808] marriage or civil partnership,[1809] pregnancy and maternity,[1810] race,[1811] religion or belief,[1812] sex,[1813] and sexual orientation.[1814] Under further provisions of the same Act, the dismissal of an employee by an employer is also unlawful if it constitutes victimisation[1815] in the defined sense that it takes place because the employee does a "protected act", or because the employer believes that the employee has done or may do such an act,[1816] defined as consisting of, inter alia, the bringing of proceedings under the Act or the taking of steps in connection with such proceedings, or otherwise the alleging of contravention of the Act.[1817] A dismissal[1818] which is unlawful under the provisions of the Act may be the subject of a complaint to an employment tribunal[1819] which, if it upholds the complaint, may make an order declaring the rights of the parties,[1820] an order for the payment of compensation,[1821] formerly but no longer limited in the same way as compensation for unfair dismissal, or a recommendation that a particular course of action be taken by the respondent,[1822] presumably including a recommendation for reinstatement or re-engagement.[1823] There are provisions to prevent double compensation under this Act and the unfair dismissal provisions in respect of the same dismissal.[1824] The definition of discrimination rendered unlawful by this Act, and the scope of and exceptions to its employment provisions have been considered in earlier paragraphs[1825] in relation to unlawful discrimination occurring during the period of employment. 40-247

1801 s.39(2)(c).

1802 s.13.

1803 s.19.

1804 s.14.

1805 s.4.

1806 s.5; as to which it should specially be noted that it is provided that dismissal because of age is not discriminatory if the employer shows that it is a proportionate means of achieving a legitimate aim: s.13(2). Such an Employer Justified Retirement Age ("EJRA") policy was held to give rise to a lawful ground for dismissal in *Pitcher v Chancellor, Masters and Scholars of the University of Oxford and Saint John the Baptist College in the University of Oxford* Unreported May 16, 2019 (ET 3323858/2016).

1807 s.6.

1808 ss.7, 16.

1809 s.8.

1810 s.18.

1811 s.9.

1812 s.10. In *Gray v Mulberry Co (Design) Ltd* [2019] EWCA Civ 1720 the notion of "philosophical belief" was held not to extend to a strongly held view about entitlement to copyright.

1813 s.11.

1814 s.12.

1815 s.39(4)(c) referring to s.27.

1816 s.27(1).

1817 s.27(2)–(5).

1818 The term "dismissal" is not defined in the Act; compare the case law definition of that term under the unfair dismissal provisions—see above, paras 40-220—40-221.

1819 s.120.

1820 s.124(2)(a).

1821 s.124(2)(b).

1822 s.124(2)(c).

1823 Compare above, paras 40-238—40-239.

1824 Employment Rights Act 1996 s.126. See above, para.40-241.

1825 Above, paras 40-128—40-134.

## 9. REDUNDANCY PAYMENTS AND PROCEDURE

## (b) Redundancy Procedure

### Introduction

*Replace paragraph with:*

**40-259** Part IV Ch.II of the Trade Union and Labour Relations (Consolidation) Act 1992 imposes procedural requirements upon employers in the handling of redundancies. The procedural obligations are of two types:

(a) the obligation to consult with representatives of recognised trade unions or of employees; and
(b) the obligation to give advance warning of certain redundancies to the Secretary of State.

These provisions, described in the next two paragraphs, represent an intention to give effect to the European Union Directive on the Approximation of the Laws of the Member States relating to Collective Redundancies.[1910] They were further amended by the Trade Union Reform and Employment Rights Act 1993 and give effect to an amending Directive of 1992.[1911]

1910 Council Directive 75/129.

1911 s.34, implementing Council Directive 92/56.

### Consultation with the representatives of recognised trade unions or of employees

*Replace footnote 1914 with:*

**40-260** 1914 s.188(1). The restriction to "at one establishment" had been placed in doubt by *USDAW v Ethel*

*Austin Ltd (In Administration)* [2014] EWCA Civ 142, [2014] 2 C.M.L.R. 45, but was subsequently confirmed by the CJEU in *USDAW v Ethel Austin Ltd* (C-80/14) EU:C:2015:291, [2015] 3 C.M.L.R. 32. A seagoing vessel was held to be an "establishment" in *Seahorse Maritime Ltd v Nautilus International* [2018] EWCA Civ 2789, [2019] I.R.L.R. 286.

## Notification of proposed redundancies to the Secretary of State

*Replace footnote 1934 with:*

[1934] That is to say, currently, the Department of Business, Energy, and Industrial Strategy. **40-263**

CHAPTER 42

# INSURANCE



## 1. THE NATURE OF INSURANCE

### Indemnity insurance

*Replace footnote 18 with:*

[18] *Ventouris v Mountain (The Italia Express)* [1992] 2 Lloyd's Rep. 281; *Sprung v Royal Insurance (UK) Ltd* [1999] Lloyd's Rep. I.R. 111; *Griffiths v Liberty Syndicate 4472* [2020] EWHC 948 (TCC). cf. *Callaghan v Dominion Insurance Co Ltd* [1997] 2 Lloyd's Rep. 541. This characterisation of an indemnity has been adhered to of late in deference to precedent, and has been criticised in that it restricts the scope of recoverable damages: Clarke, *The Law of Insurance Contracts* (looseleaf), para.30-9B1; Campbell [2000] L.M.C.L.Q. 42. See also *Pride Valley Foods Ltd v Independent Insurance Co Ltd* [1999] Lloyd's Rep. I.R. 120. See the Law Commission's Consultation Paper: *Insurance Contract Law: Post Contract* 42-003

*Duties and other Issues* (LCCP No.201, December 2011). See below, para.42-105. In the award of interest against an insurer, the Court will generally allow interest to run, not from the date of the loss, but from the date by which the insurer should have considered the validity of the claim, taking into account the nature of the loss, the way the claim was presented and the circumstances which required investigation: *Quorum A/S v Schramm (No.2)* [2002] 2 All E.R. (Comm) 179.

## 3. THE EVENT INSURED AGAINST

### Event insured against

*Replace footnote 139 with:*

42-018 [139] The word "event" here refers to the "peril" insured against. In many policies, the word "event" may be used to refer to the originating cause of the peril. This, however, is not necessarily so, being a matter of construction of the contract. As to the meaning of the words "event", "occurrence", "cause" and "claim", see *Kuwait Airways Corp v Kuwait Insurance Co SAK* [1996] 1 Lloyd's Rep. 664, 686, QB, [1997] 2 Lloyd's Rep. 687, CA, [1999] 1 Lloyd's Rep. 803, HL. *Caudle v Sharp* [1995] L.R.L.R. 433; *Cox v Bankside Members' Agency Ltd* [1996] 1 Lloyd's Rep. 26; *Axa Reinsurance (UK) Plc v Field* [1996] 1 W.L.R. 1026; *Municipal Mutual Insurance Ltd v Sea Insurance Co* [1998] C.L.C. 957; *Brown v GIO Insurance Ltd* [1998] Lloyd's Rep. I.R. 201; *Roberts Irving & Burns v Stone* [1998] Lloyd's Rep. I.R. 258; *Spire Healthcare Ltd v Royal & Sun Alliance Insurance Plc* [2016] EWHC 3278 (Comm), [2017] Lloyd's Rep. I.R. 118, [2018] EWCA Civ 317, [2018] Lloyd's Rep. I.R. 425. In *Simmonds v Gammell* [2016] EWHC 2515 (Comm), [2016] 2 Lloyd's Rep. 631 at [22]–[27], Sir Jeremy Cooke confirmed that in identifying an aggregating "event", it should be appropriate to the aggregating function, it should be a common factor which could properly be described as an event, and it should be causative of the losses claimed under the policy, which need not be proximate, but must not be too remote. Such words often define the application of monetary limits or excess or deductible clauses and must be construed having regard to the policy as a whole and applied having regard to the degree of unity of time, cause and location: *Mann v Lexington Insurance Co* [2001] 1 Lloyd's Rep. 1. See also *Aioi Nissay Dowa Insurance Co Ltd v Heraldglen Ltd* [2013] EWHC 154 (Comm), [2013] 2 All E.R. 231, where it was held that losses arising on a reinsurance contract in respect of liabilities incurred by reason of the attacks on the World Trade Center in September 2001 arose out of two events, not one. The words "related series of acts or omissions" have been interpreted to embrace several losses having a common causal relationship, meaning that the acts or events together resulted in each of the claims; the fact that claims might have the same underlying cause and were of a very similar nature was not sufficient to constitute a "related series" in *Lloyd's TSB General Insurance Holdings v Lloyds Bank Group Insurance Co Ltd* [2003] UKHL 48, [2003] Lloyd's Rep. I.R. 623 at [27]–[29], [51]. See also *AIG Europe Ltd v Woodman* [2017] UKSC 18, [2017] 1 W.L.R. 1168. Cf. *Bank of Queensland Ltd v AIG Australia Ltd* [2019] NSWCA 190, [2019] Lloyd's Rep. I.R. 639 (NSWCA).

### (a) The Nature of the Event

### Uncertainty

*In line 4, after "wear and tear,", add new footnote 141a:*

42-020 [141a] The policy may contain exclusions against specific types of wear and tear, e.g. corrosion, condensation, and if so it may be interpreted as excluding only that corrosion or condensation which would arise in any event: *Manchikalapati v Zurich Insurance Plc* [2019] EWCA Civ 2163, [2020] Lloyd's Rep. I.R. 77 at [175].

## 4. UTMOST GOOD FAITH AND FAIR PRESENTATION OF THE RISK

### (a) The Common Law

### The duty to disclose material circumstances

*Replace footnote 236 with:*

42-034 [236] *Pan Atlantic Insurance Co Ltd v Pine Top Insurance Co Ltd* [1995] 1 A.C. 501 (rejecting the "decisive influence" test of materiality, but holding that an insurer cannot rely upon a material non-disclosure (or misrepresentation) as a ground for avoiding the contract if the non-disclosure (or misrepresentation) did not actually *induce* the making of the contract), as interpreted by the Court of Appeal in *St Paul Fire & Marine Insurance Co (UK) Ltd v McConnell Dowell Constructors Ltd* [1996]

1 All E.R. 96. On this basis, a circumstance can be "material" even if it actually *decreases* the risk, but this does not mean that such a circumstance would have to be disclosed because, in the absence of inquiry, Marine Insurance Act 1906 s.18(3)(a) specifically exempts the assured from having to disclose any circumstance which diminishes the risk: see *St Paul Fire & Marine Insurance Co (UK) Ltd v McConnell Dowell Constructors Ltd*, above, at 107. As to the relationship between the concepts of materiality and risk, see *Niramax Group Ltd v Zurich Insurance Plc* [2020] EWHC 535 (Comm) at [148]–[158].

### Inducement

*In line 10, after "on those terms", add new footnote 297a:*

[297a] *Niramax Group Ltd v Zurich Insurance Plc* [2020] EWHC 535 (Comm). **42-041**

### Modification of the duty by contract

*Replace footnote 334 with:*

[334] *HIH Casualty and General Insurance Ltd v Chase Manhattan Bank* [2003] UKHL 6, [2003] 2 Lloyd's Rep. 61; *Seashell of Lisson Grove Ltd v Aviva Insurance Ltd* [2011] EWHC 1761 (Comm). As to the effect of innocent non-disclosure clauses, see *Arab Bank Plc v Zurich Insurance Company* [1999] 1 Lloyd's Rep. 262; *Kumar v AGF Insurance Ltd* [1999] 1 W.L.R 1747; *UK Acorn Finance Ltd v Markel (UK) Ltd* [2020] EWHC 922 (Comm). **42-044**

## (c) Insurance Act 2015

### Exceptions to the duty of disclosure

*Replace footnote 375 with:*

[375] 2015 Act s.3(5). See *Young v Royal and Sun Alliance Plc* [2019] CSOH 32, [2019] Lloyd's Rep. I.R. 482; affirmed [2020] CSIH 25, 2020 S.L.T. 597. **42-054**

### The insurer's remedies for unfair presentation of the risk

*Replace footnote 396 with:*

[396] 2015 Act s.8(2) and Sch.1 para.5. See Davey [2019] L.M.C.L.Q. 360. **42-057**

## (d) Post-contractual Duty of Utmost Good Faith

### The post-contractual duty of utmost good faith: the common law

*Replace paragraph with:*

**42-061** The preceding discussion has concentrated on the duty of full disclosure which exists up to the time of the making of the insurance contract. There are, however, other aspects of the duty. For example, there is a "post-contractual" duty of disclosure in cases where the insurance contract is to be amended or renewed; in reality, in such cases, the pre-contractual duty of disclosure revives so that the insurer may exercise his underwriting judgment afresh with the benefit of material information.[410] In other contexts, concerning the insurance contract's performance, the courts have held that there is a duty not to be fraudulent, but no wider duty.[411] Obviously, there is a duty not to present fraudulent claims, although the precise nature and ambit of this duty is presently uncertain; in particular, it is unclear whether it properly falls within the wider duty of utmost good faith. The duty not to make fraudulent claims, which at the least is recognised as a sui generis common law duty, is considered separately in the context of claims in general.[412] In addition, the parties should not perform the insurance contract, in contexts other than claims, fraudulently: for example, where the assured provides information to the insurer during the course of the risk. It may be that the doctrine of utmost good faith has a wider role to play, such as where a liability insurer or a reinsurer assumes a contractual right to act on behalf of the assured or reassured respectively,[413] or possibly influencing the construction to be given to the terms of an insurance contract.[414] There may be circumstances where, having regard to the duty of utmost good faith, the insurer will assume a duty to warn the assured that it is not complying with the relevant terms of the insurance contract in respect of claims.[415]

[410] For a survey of the post-contractual duty of disclosure, see *K/S Merc-Scandia XXXXII v Lloyd's Underwriters* [2001] EWCA Civ 1275, [2001] 2 Lloyd's Rep. 563. It is now established that there is no general duty of disclosure in respect of claims: *Royal Boskalis Westminster NV v Mountain* [1997] L.R.L.R. 523; reversed on other grounds by the Court of Appeal: [1999] Q.B. 674; *Manifest Shipping & Co Ltd v Uni-Polaris Shipping Co Ltd (The Star Sea)* [2001] UKHL 1, [2001] 2 W.L.R. 170. As to the scope of the post-contractual duty, see further *Equitas Insurance Ltd v Municipal Mutual Insurance Ltd* [2019] EWCA Civ 718, [2019] Lloyd's Rep. I.R. 359 at [104].

[411] *Manifest Shipping & Co Ltd v Uni-Polaris Shipping Co Ltd (The Star Sea)* [2001] UKHL 1, [2001] 2 W.L.R. 170; *K/S Merc-Scandia XXXXII v Lloyd's Underwriters* [2001] EWCA Civ 1275, [2001] 2 Lloyd's Rep. 563; *Agapitos v Agnew (The Aegeon)* [2002] EWCA Civ 247, [2002] 2 Lloyd's Rep. 42. Cf. where a settlement agreement was procured by the insurer's non-fraudulent misrepresentation: *Dodds v Southern Response Earthquake Services Ltd* [2019] NZHC 2016, [2020] Lloyd's Rep. I.R. 129 (NZHC).

[412] See below, para.42-098.

[413] *Cox v Bankside Members' Agency Ltd* [1995] 2 Lloyd's Rep. 437, 471–472; cf. *Gan Insurance Co Ltd v Tai Ping Insurance Co Ltd (No 2 and 3)* [2001] 1 Lloyd's Rep. I.R. 667 at [68], [76].

[414] *Harrower v Hutchinson* (1870) LR 5 Q.B. 584, 592.

[415] *Ted Baker Plc v Axa Insurance UK Plc* [2017] EWCA Civ 4097, [2017] Lloyd's Rep. I.R. 682 at [69]–[90].

## 6. THE CONTRACT OF INSURANCE

### The slip

*Replace footnote 460 with:*

42-069 [460] *Thompson v Adams* (1889) 23 Q.B.D. 361; *Grover v Mathews* [1910] 15 Com. Cas. 249; *Re Yager and Guardian* (1912) 108 L.T. 38; *Eagle Star Insurance v Spratt* [1971] 2 Lloyd's Rep. 116; *The Zephyr* [1984] 1 Lloyd's Rep. 58. For the position where a policy wording differs from slip, see *HIH Casualty and General Insurance Ltd v New Hampshire Insurance Co* [2001] EWCA Civ 735, [2001] 2 All E.R. (Comm) 39 at [81]–[95], where the Court of Appeal held that there was no rule of law that the policy was conclusive evidence of the insurance contract. Identifying the terms and meaning of the contract depended on a process of construction and analysis of the relationship between the slip and the policy and determining the parties' intention (cf. *Youell v Bland Welch & Co Ltd* [1992] 2 Lloyd's Rep. 127). See *New Hampshire Insurance Co v MGN Ltd* [1997] L.R.L.R. 24, 32–34, 53–54; *Generali Italia SpA v Pelagic Fisheries Corp* [2020] EWHC 1228 (Comm) at [85].

### Construction of insurance contracts

*Replace paragraph with:*

42-077 Insurance contracts are subject to the same approach to contractual construction as other contracts, namely that the words of the contract will be interpreted to divine their contextual meaning consistently with the sense and purpose of the policy, even if that is at odds with the literal meaning of the contract.[522] The commercial purpose of the insurance contract, however, should not be lightly invoked to undermine the importance of the contractual language which the parties have chosen to embody their agreement.[523] Therefore, where a word is used in an insurance policy which has a technical, legal connotation, the court will not necessarily infer that the parties intended that meaning and will inquire into the ordinary, commercial meaning to be ascribed to the word.[524] On the other hand, if an insurance term has a settled judicially accepted meaning, the courts are loathe to apply a different interpretation.[525] Similarly, the Court will assume that the parties intended to use words which had a special or peculiar meaning in the particular market or trade in that sense.[526] If the insurance contract is based on a standard form of contract to which the parties have added special clauses, greater weight will be given to the special provisions, and, in the event of conflict or inconsistency between the general and special provisions, the latter will prevail.[527] There is one rule of construction applicable to ordinary contracts which applies with particular force in the context of insurance contracts, namely that *verba chartarum fortius accipiuntur contra proferentem*: i.e. where the contractual provision is ambiguous, the provision will be construed against the person who drafts or puts forward the provision, which in many (but not all) cases will be the insurer.[528] The construction of contractual terms "against the insurer" is not limited to cases where the insurer has produced the wording. If the insurer seeks to rely on a provision, such as a condition precedent or warranty, so as to extinguish or reduce his basic obligations, the court will resist such a construction unless the contractual terms are especially clear.[529] Having regard to the decision of the Supreme Court in *Impact Funding Solutions Ltd v Barrington Support Services Ltd*,[530] the fact that a provision in an insurance contract is expressed as an exception or exclusion does not necessarily mean that it should be approached with a pre-disposition to construe it narrowly or restrictively, at least insofar as it delineates the scope of the insurer's primary obligation of indemnity, as opposed to excluding a liability or a remedy where the primary obligation would otherwise have rendered the insurer liable.

[522] *Sirius International Insurance Co (Publ) v FAI General Insurance Ltd* [2004] UKHL 54, [2004] 1 W.L.R. 3251 at [18]–[19]; *Blackburn Rovers Football & Athletic Club Plc v Avon Insurance Plc* [2005] EWCA Civ 423, [2005] Lloyd's Rep. I.R. 447 at [9]. In *AXA Corporate Solutions SA v National Westminster Bank Plc* [2010] EWHC 1915 (Comm), [2011] Lloyd's Rep. I.R. 438, the Court construed the term "*Terrorism exclusion (wording to be agreed)*" to operate as an exclusion and did not require a further clause to be identified. See *Manchikalapati v Zurich Insurance Plc* [2019] EWCA Civ 2163, [2020] Lloyd's Rep. I.R. 77 at [68].

[523] *Spire Healthcare Ltd v Royal & Sun Alliance Insurance Plc* [2016] EWHC 3278 (Comm), [2017] Lloyd's Rep. I.R. 118 at [11], [2018] EWCA Civ 317, [2018] Lloyd's Rep. I.R. 425.

[524] *Wooldridge v Canelhas Comercio Importacao e Exportacao Ltda* [2004] EWCA Civ 984, [2005] 1 All E.R. (Comm) 43 ("robbery"); cf. *Dobson v General Accident Fire & Life Assurance Corp Plc* [1990] 1 Q.B. 274 ("theft").

[525] See, e.g. *Ramco (UK) Ltd v International Insurance Co of Hannover Ltd* [2004] EWCA Civ 675, [2004] 2 Lloyd's Rep. 595 at [32]; *AIG Europe (Ireland) Ltd v Faraday Capital Ltd* [2006] EWHC 2707, [2007] Lloyd's Rep. I.R. 267 at [24]; reversed on other grounds [2007] EWCA Civ 1208, [2008] Lloyd's Rep. I.R. 454.

[526] *Gard Marine v Tunnicliffe* [2011] EWHC 1658 (Comm), [2012] Lloyd's Rep. I.R. 1.

[527] *Milton Furniture Ltd v Brit Insurance Ltd* [2015] EWCA Civ 671, [2016] Lloyd's Rep. I.R. 192 at [24].

[528] *Tektrol Ltd v International Insurance Co of Hanover Ltd* [2005] EWCA Civ 845, [2005] 1 All E.R. (Comm) 132.

[529] *Tektrol Ltd v International Insurance Co of Hanover Ltd* [2005] EWCA Civ 845, [2005] 1 All E.R. (Comm) 132; *Royal & Sun Alliance Insurance Plc v Dornoch Ltd* [2005] EWCA Civ 238, [2005] 1 All E.R. (Comm) 590; *Blackburn Rovers Football & Athletic Club Plc v Avon Insurance Plc* [2005] EWCA Civ 423, [2005] Lloyd's Rep. I.R. 447 at [9].

[530] [2016] UKSC 57, [2017] A.C. 73 at [35]. See also *Crowden v QBE Insurance (Europe) Ltd* [2017] EWHC 2597 (Comm), [2018] Lloyd's Rep. I.R. 83; *Manchikalapati v Zurich Insurance Plc* [2019] EWCA Civ 2163, [2020] Lloyd's Rep. I.R. 77 at [46]–[48].

## 7. THE TERMS OF THE INSURANCE CONTRACT

### Waiver

*Replace footnote 591 with:*

42-086 [591] *Brownsville Holdings Ltd v Adamjee Insurance Co Ltd (The Milasan)* [2002] 2 Lloyd's Rep. 458, 467; *HIH Casualty and General Insurance Ltd v Axa Corporate Solutions* [2002] Lloyd's Rep. I.R. 325; affirmed [2002] EWCA Civ 1253, [2003] Lloyd's Rep. I.R. 1; *Kosmar Villa Holidays Plc v Trustees of Syndicate 1243* [2008] EWCA Civ 147, [2008] Lloyd's Rep. I.R. 489; *Argo Systems FZE v Liberty Insurance Pte Ltd* [2011] EWCA Civ 1572, [2012] 1 Lloyd's Rep. 129; *UK Acorn Finance Ltd v Markel (UK) Ltd* [2020] EWHC 922 (Comm) at [50]; cf. *Bhopal v Sphere Drake Insurance Plc* [2002] Lloyd's Rep. I.R. 413. See also Soyer [2002] L.M.C.L.Q. 199, 208–209.

## 9. CLAIMS

### Notice of loss

*Replace footnote 650 with:*

42-093 [650] *Williams v Lancashire and Yorkshire Accident* (1902) 51 W.R. 222. In *Zurich Insurance Plc v Maccaferri Ltd* [2016] EWCA Civ 1302, [2017] Lloyd's Rep. I.R. 200 at [31]–[32], the Court of Appeal held that "'Immediately' itself does not mean instantaneously but 'with all reasonable speed considering the circumstances of the case'". As to the impact of prejudice in determining what is a reasonable time, see *Shinedean Ltd v Alldown Demolition (London) Ltd* [2006] EWCA Civ 939, [2006] Lloyd's Rep. I.R. 846. For a recent decision on the meaning of "as soon as practicable", see *HLB Kidsons v Lloyd's Underwriters* [2007] EWHC 1951 (Comm), [2008] Lloyd's Rep. I.R. 237 at [60], [2008] EWCA Civ 1206, [2009] 1 Lloyd's Rep. 8. In *Denso Manufacturing UK Ltd v Great Lakes Reinsurance (UK) Plc* [2017] EWHC 391 (Comm), [2017] Lloyd's Rep. I.R. 240 at [55]–[56], the Court considered the meaning of "as soon as" and "without delay" in a different context. See also *Towergate Financial (Group) Ltd v Hopkinson* [2020] EWHC 984 (Comm) ("as soon as possible").

### Jurisdiction

*Replace paragraph with:*

42-096 Where a dispute arises between the insurer and the assured, the country in which suit may or must be brought will be determined in accordance with: (i) Regulation (EU) 1215/2012 of the European Parliament and Council which applies in respect of EU Member States and proceedings instituted on or after January 15, 2015[664]; (ii) EC Council Regulation 44/2001 (Brussels I Regulation) which applies in respect of the EU Member States and proceedings instituted before January 15, 2015[665]; (iii) the Civil Jurisdiction and Judgments Act 1991, which applies to the Contracting States to the Lugano Convention[666]; or (iv) in all other cases, in accordance with the non-Regulation and non-Convention rules in each Member or Contracting State.[667] This regime continues to apply until December 31, 2020.[667a] Articles 10 to 16 of Regulation 1215/2012 determine where suit may be brought where the defendant insurer or assured is domiciled in a Member State.[667b] These provisions generally allow the assured to sue the insurer in a Member State where the insurer or the assured is domiciled, or where the insurer is a co-insurer in a Member State where the leading insurer is sued.[668] Where the insurance contract insures immovable property or liability, the insurer may additionally be sued in the Member State where the harmful event occurred[669]; in the case of liability insurance, the insurer may also be sued in the Member State by being joined in the proceedings by which the assured is sued by a third party.[670] By contrast, Regulation 1215/2012 requires the insurer to sue the assured only in the Member State where the assured is domiciled.[671] A third party, such as a person to whom the assured is liable, may sue the insurer in the Member States where the insurer or the assured is domiciled in the Member State where the harmful event occurred or as a co-defendant in proceedings instituted by the third party against the assured.[672] The insurance contract may provide that any dispute under the contract be submitted to the courts of a particular country. By arts 15(5) and 16,[673] such agreements will be enforced in respect of marine and aviation policies and insurance contracts in respect of "large risks",[674] provided that there has been a consensual agreement to the jurisdiction and that the formal requirements are satisfied.[675] Jurisdiction agreements in other types of policy will be enforced in the more limited circumstances set out in art.13.[676] Reinsurance contracts are not governed by arts 8 to 14, but are treated as normal commercial contracts and are dealt with under the general provisions of the Regulation.[677]

664 Civil Jurisdiction and Judgments (Amendment) Regulations 2014 (SI 2014/2947) reg.1.

665 By the Civil Jurisdiction and Judgments Order 2001 (SI 2001/3929), the Regulation entered into force on March 1, 2002. Prior to this date, the Civil Jurisdiction and Judgments Act 1982, incorporating the Brussels Convention on Jurisdiction and the Enforcement of Judgments in Civil and Commercial Matters 1968, as amended, and the Civil Jurisdiction and Judgments Act 1991 applied.

666 See the Civil Jurisdiction and Judgments Act 1991, as amended by the Civil Jurisdiction and Judgments Order 2001 (SI 2001/3929). A new Lugano Convention was signed on October 30, 2007, designed to harmonise the rules applicable under the Lugano Convention and Regulation 44/2001: see the Civil Jurisdiction and Judgments Regulations 2009 (SI 2009/3131).

667 In England and Wales, such rules are found in CPR r.6.37 and Practice Direction 6B.

667a European Union (Withdrawal) Act 2018 ss.1B, 2; the Civil Jurisdiction and Judgments (Amendment) (EU Exit) Regulations 2019 (SI 2019/479) regs 82, 92–93; European Union (Withdrawal Agreement) Act 2020 ss.2, 39. The UK has submitted a formal application to re-join the Lugano Convention as an individual member at the end of the implementation period but the outcome of that application, which will depend on assent being given by the current members, is presently unknown.

667b See recently *Aspen Underwriting Ltd v Credit Europe Bank NV* [2020] UKSC 11, [2020] Lloyd's Rep. I.R. 274.

668 Regulation 1215/2012 art.11. See *New Hampshire Insurance Co v Strabag Bau AG* [1992] 1 Lloyd's Rep. 361; *Tradigrain SA v SIAT SpA* [2002] EWHC 106 (Comm), [2002] 2 Lloyd's Rep. 553. See also arts 8 to 11 of the 2007 Lugano Convention.

669 Regulation 1215/2012 art.12.

670 Regulation 1215/2012 art.13(1).

671 Regulation 1215/2012 art.14(1). Under art.14(1) of the Regulation (art.12 of the 2007 Convention), the insurer must sue the assured in the state of domicile of the assured, whether or not the insurer is domiciled in a Member State: *Jordan Grand Prix Ltd v Baltic Insurance Group* [1999] 1 All E.R. 289. As to the scope of art.12, see also *National Justice Compania Naviera SA v Prudential Assurance Co Ltd (The Ikarian Reefer) (No.2)* [2000] 1 W.L.R. 603.

672 Regulation 1215/2012 arts 11–13. See *FBTO Schadeverzekeringen NV v Odenbreit* (Case 463/06) [2008] Lloyd's Rep. I.R. 354; *Mapfre Mutualidad Compania de Seguros y Reaseguros SA v Keefe* [2015] EWCA Civ 598.

673 Lugano Convention 2007 arts 13(5) and 14. See *Charman v WOC Offshore BV* [1993] 1 Lloyd's Rep. 378, [1993] 2 Lloyd's Rep. 551; *Tradigrain SA v SIAT SpA* [2002] EWHC (Comm) 106, [2002] 2 Lloyd's Rep. 553.

674 "Large risks" are defined in Directive 2009/138/EC of the European Parliament and Council.

675 See art.23 of the Regulation (art.23 of the 2007 Convention). See *AIG Europe (UK) Ltd v Anonymous Greek Insurance Co of General Insurances (The Ethniki)* [2000] Lloyd's Rep. I.R. 343. As an example of a case where the Court has had to decide whether the parties have chosen a particular jurisdiction from a variety listed in the open cover, see *Tradigrain SA v SIAT SpA* [2002] EWHC (Comm) 106, [2002] 2 Lloyd's Rep. 553.

676 2007 Convention art.13.

677 *Fisher v Unione Italiana de Riassicurazione SpA* [1999] Lloyd's Rep. I.R. 215; *Agnew v Lansförsäkringsbølagens AB* [2000] 1 All E.R. 737; *AIG Europe (UK) Ltd v Anonymous Greek Insur-*

*ance Co of General Insurances (The Ethniki)* [2000] Lloyd's Rep. I.R. 343; *Group Josi Reinsurance Co SA v Universal General Insurance Co* (C-412/98) EU:C:2000:399, [2001] Lloyd's Rep. I.R. 483.

### Remedy for fraudulent claims: the common law

*Replace footnote 708 with:*

42-099 [708] *Joseph Fielding Properties (Blackpool) Ltd v Aviva Insurance Ltd* [2010] EWHC 2192 (QB), [2011] Lloyd's Rep. I.R. 238 at [88]–[99]. In the event of a fraudulent claim, the insurer may also have a remedy for deceit. In *AXA Insurance UK Plc v Financial Claims Solutions Ltd* [2018] EWCA Civ 1330, [2019] R.T.R. 1, the Court of Appeal allowed an insurer to recover exemplary damages by reason of a fraudulent claim.

### The amount recoverable

*Replace paragraph with:*

42-105 A claim under a contract of insurance which is a contract of indemnity is a claim for unliquidated damages even, it seems, when the contract is a valued one.[746] The amount recoverable, or the "measure of indemnity", will depend on the nature (and terms) of the insurance contract. Losses under contingency policies and insurances against financial loss or liability will be readily calculated. As regards property policies, for the purposes of measuring the indemnity under the policy, there are two types of losses, namely a total loss and a partial loss. A total loss generally refers to the irretrievable deprivation of possession of the property (e.g. theft or confiscation) or to the physical destruction of the property.[747] In the realm of marine insurance, there is an additional category of total loss, namely a "constructive total loss", which applies commercial considerations to establishing the existence of a total loss.[748] A partial loss is any loss other than a total loss. A partial loss is often measured by reference to a depreciation in value or the cost of reinstatement or repair.[749] The measure of damages in the case of valued contracts[750] raises few difficulties. If there is a total loss the assured recovers the agreed value, and if there is a partial loss the assured recovers a proportion (which reflects the depreciation in the actual value) of the agreed value or, where appropriate, the cost of repair or reinstatement.[751] The measure of indemnity under the unvalued contracts is the value[752] at the date[753] and place[754] of the loss, and, if available, the market value will prima facie be the amount recoverable, but otherwise the cost of restoration may provide the basis for the indemnity,[755] and this latter basis is usually used for cases of partial loss.[756] In marine insurance rules have been worked out to make an adjustment for "new for old"[757] but there are no settled rules for this in non-marine insurance.[758] The policy may contain a policy limit, often referred to as the "the sum insured". This does not represent the sum which the assured will receive in the event of a loss. The assured will recover the amount of his loss, subject to the ceiling imposed by the limit.[759] However, subject to the terms of the policy, it will be presumed that the policy limit will apply to each of successive losses under the policy and not to the aggregate of those losses, even if the aggregate exceeds the policy limit.[760] It may be that the policy will provide that the limit will apply to aggregated losses.[761] In such cases, where the assured has a number of claims to be presented under the policy, the assured, not the insurer, has the right to determine the sequence in which the claims are presented against the insurer.[762] Where two or more assureds, or third parties deriving title to sue, present claims under the one policy and there is insufficient cover to indemnify all the claimants, the available cover shall respond to each claim in the order it is established under the policy[763] and if each of the claims are established at the same time, the claims must be satisfied on a pro rata basis.[764]

[746] *Jabbour v Custodian of Israeli Absentee Property* [1954] 1 W.L.R. 139. Accordingly, the assured may not recover as damages any losses occasioned as a result of the insurer's failure to pay other than that which was to be indemnified under the policy: *Ventouris v Mountain (The Italia Express)* [1992] 2 Lloyd's Rep. 281; *Sprung v Royal Insurance (UK) Ltd* [1999] Lloyd's Rep. I.R. 111; *Callaghan v Dominion Insurance Co Ltd* [1997] 2 Lloyd's Rep. 541; contra *Grant v Co-operative Insurance Society Ltd* (1983) 134 N.L.J. 81; *Transthene Packaging Co Ltd v Royal Insurance (UK) Ltd* [1996] L.R.L.R. 32, 41. The assured's entitlement to damages may be different if the insurer is in breach of other obligations under the insurance contract: *Transthene Packaging Co Ltd v Royal Insurance (UK) Ltd*, above; cf. *Sprung v Royal Insurance (UK) Ltd*, above; *Tonkin v UK Insurance Ltd* [2006] EWHC 1120 (TCC), [2007] Lloyd's Rep. I.R. 283 at [34]–[39]. Upon the entry into force of ss.13A and 16A of the Insurance Act 2015 on May 4, 2017, the assured is entitled to recover damages for the late payment of a claim under an insurance contract in breach of a term implied by s.13A requiring the insurer to pay insurance claims within a reasonable time. In non-consumer insurance contracts, it is open to the parties to agree to a modification of this implied term to the insurer's benefit subject to the restrictions imposed by s.16A of the 2015 Act and the transparency requirements of the Insurance Act 2015. See below, para.42-112.

[747] *Scott v Copenhagen Reinsurance Co (UK) Ltd* [2003] EWCA Civ 688, [2003] Lloyd's Rep. I.R. 752 at [22], [34]–[40]. The fact that there is a "mere chance" of recovery of the property does not mean that there has been no loss: at [40].

[748] Marine Insurance Act 1906 s.60. The doctrine of constructive total loss does not apply to non-marine insurance: *Moore v Evans* [1917] 1 K.B. 458; *Scott v Copenhagen Reinsurance Co (UK) Ltd* [2003] EWCA Civ 688, [2003] Lloyd's Rep. I.R. 752.

[749] *Prattley Enterprises Ltd v Vero Insurance New Zealand Ltd* [2016] NZSC 158, [2017] Lloyd's Rep. I.R. 175 at [38]–[43].

[750] The policy may be in part a valued policy and in part an unvalued policy: *Grimaldi Ltd v Sullivan* [1997] C.L.C. 64.

[751] *Elcock v Thomson* [1949] 2 K.B. 755; *Kusel v Atkin* [1997] 2 Lloyd's Rep. 749. As to the relationship between depreciation in value and the reasonable cost of repair, see *Coles v Hetherton* [2012] EWHC 1599 (Comm), [2013] Lloyd's Rep. I.R. 9 at [31].

[752] This value does not include loss of profits or other consequential losses unless specifically insured: see above, para.42-027.

[753] *Hercules Insurance v Hunter* (1835) 14 S. 147, Ct of Sess.; *Chapman v Pole* (1870) 22 L.T. 306; *Re Wilson and Scottish Insurance* [1920] 2 Ch. 28; *Leppard v Excess Insurance Co Ltd* [1979] 2 Lloyd's Rep. 91; *Tonkin v UK Insurance Ltd* [2006] EWHC 1120 (TCC), [2007] Lloyd's Rep. I.R. 283 at [20]–[25].

[754] *Rice v Baxendale* (1861) 7 H. & N. 96, 101.

[755] *Westminster Fire v Glasgow Provident* (1888) 13 App. Cas. 699, 713; *Exchange Theatre Ltd v Iron Trades Mutual Insurance Co* [1983] 1 Lloyd's Rep. 674, 688–689; affirmed [1984] 1 Lloyd's Rep. 149. cf. *Anderson v Commercial Union*, 1998 S.L.T. 826, where it was held that whilst the insurer was bound to indemnify the assured against the costs of repair, he was not obliged (absent a clause) to indemnify the assured *as and when* such costs were incurred. In *Great Lakes Reinsurance (UK) SE v Western Trading Ltd* [2016] EWCA Civ 1003, [2016] Lloyd's Rep. I.R. 643 at [40], the Court of Appeal held that where real property is destroyed the measure of indemnity to which the insured is entitled will depend on: (i) the terms of the policy; (ii) the interest of the insured in, or its obligations in respect of, the property insured; and (iii) the facts of the case including, in particular, the intention of the insured at the time of the loss. If the insured has a limited interest in the property it will be material to consider whether the subject matter of the insurance is the whole interest in the property insured and not solely that of the insured himself and, if it is the whole interest, whether the insured is accountable to others for any sum received in excess of his interest. At [67]–[75], the Court held that where no reinstatement costs had yet been incurred, whether or not the cost of reinstatement was the correct measure of indemnity depended on whether the insured had a fixed, settled and genuine intention to reinstate. However, see also *Manchikalapati v Zurich Insurance Plc* [2019] EWCA Civ 2163, [2020] Lloyd's Rep. I.R. 77 at [86]–[89], [96]–[110]; *Endurance Corporate Capital Ltd v Sartex Quilts & Textiles Ltd* [2020] EWCA Civ 308 at [60]–[73]. See also *Prattley Enterprises Ltd v Vero Insurance New Zealand Ltd* [2016] NZSC 158, [2017] Lloyd's Rep. I.R. 175 at [38]–[43].

[756] *Scottish Amicable v Northern Assurance* (1883) 11 R. 287, Ct of Sess., 295; *Pleasurama v Sun Alliance* [1979] 1 Lloyd's Rep. 389, 393. However, the position may vary depending on the practicability of doing the repairs and the genuineness of the assured's intentions to undertake them or to sell: *Glad Tidings v Wellington Fire Insurance Co*, 46 D.L.R. (2d.) 475 (1964); *Reynolds v Phoenix Assurance Co* [1978] 2 Lloyd's Rep. 440; *Leppard v Excess Insurance Co Ltd* [1979] 2 Lloyd's Rep. 91; *Sartex Quilts*

*and Textiles Ltd v Endurance Corporate Capital Ltd* [2019] EWHC 1103 (Comm); [2020] EWCA Civ 308. See also *Gleniffer Finance Corp v Bamar Wood and Products* [1978] 2 Lloyd's Rep. 49.

757 See Marine Insurance Act 1906 s.69(1). As to claims for partial losses under the Marine Insurance Act 1906 ss.69 and 77; see *Manifest Shipping & Co Ltd v Uni-Polaris Insurance Co Ltd (The Star Sea)* [1995] 1 Lloyd's Rep. 651, 664–666, [1997] 1 Lloyd's Rep. 360; affirmed [2001] UKHL 1, [2001] 2 W.L.R. 170; *Kusel v Atkin* [1997] 2 Lloyd's Rep. 749.

758 *Prattley Enterprises Ltd v Vero Insurance New Zealand Ltd* [2016] NZSC 158, [2017] Lloyd's Rep. I.R. 175 at [38]–[43]. cf. *Vance v Forster* (1841) Ir. Circ. Rep. 47; *Castellain v Preston* (1883) 11 Q.B.D. 380, 400.

759 *Leppard v Excess Insurance Co Ltd* [1979] 2 Lloyd's Rep. 91, 95. See also *Kyzuna Investments Ltd v Ocean Marine Mutual Insurance Association (Europe)* [2000] 1 Lloyd's Rep. 505, where it was held that the words "sum insured" did not represent the insured value for the purposes of Marine Insurance Act 1906 s.27(2). The principles applicable to determining whether a policy of marine insurance is a valued or unvalued policy are generally applicable to non-marine insurance policies: *Quorum A/S v Schramm* [2002] 1 Lloyd's Rep. 249; *Thor Navigation Inc v Ingosstrakh Insurance Co Ltd* [2005] EWHC 19 (Comm), [2005] 1 Lloyd's Rep. 547.

760 *South Staffordshire Tramways Co Ltd v Sickness & Accident Assurance Association Ltd* [1891] 1 Q.B. 402; *Re Law Car and General Insurance Corp Ltd* [1913] 2 Ch. 103, 118. See also Marine Insurance Act 1906 s.77. In *Ridgecrest NZ Ltd v IAG New Zealand Ltd* [2014] NZSC 117, [2015] Lloyd's Rep. I.R. 34 at [48]–[52] the New Zealand Supreme Court held that the doctrine of merger (by which the assured is not entitled to recover an indemnity for unrepaired damage amounting to a partial loss where it is followed by a total loss) did not apply, as a matter of law, to non-marine insurance.

761 Where there is a danger of the policy limit being exhausted, it is important to be able to identify to what event, peril or cause the limit will apply: *Kuwait Airways Corp v Kuwait Insurance Co SAK* [1996] 1 Lloyd's Rep. 664, 686; affirmed [1997] 2 Lloyd's Rep. 687, [1999] 1 Lloyd's Rep. 803; *Caudle v Sharp* [1995] L.R.L.R. 433; *Cox v Bankside Members' Agency Ltd* [1996] 1 Lloyd's Rep. 26; *Axa Reinsurance (UK) Plc v Field* [1996] 1 W.L.R. 1026; *Mann v Lexington Insurance Co* [2001] 1 Lloyd's Rep. 1; *Standard Life Assurance Ltd v Oak Dedicated Ltd* [2008] EWHC 222 (Comm), [2008] Lloyd's Rep. I.R. 552 ("and/or claimant"); *Aioi Nissay Dowa Insurance Co Ltd v Heraldglen Ltd* [2013] EWHC 154 (Comm), [2013] 2 All E.R. 231.

762 *Cox v Deeny* [1996] L.R.L.R. 288, 298–299.

763 *Cox v Bankside Members' Agency Ltd* [1995] 2 Lloyd's Rep. 437.

764 *Cox v Deeny* [1996] L.R.L.R. 288, 299.

## Reinstatement

*To the end of paragraph, after "provide an indemnity.[795]", add:*

42-111 If the policy allows for reinstatement as the basis of indemnity, it does not necessarily follow (depending on the policy wording) that the assured must undertake the reinstatement (or any remedial work) before becoming entitled to an indemnity measured by reference to the cost of such reinstatement (or remedial work).[795a]

795a *Manchikalapati v Zurich Insurance Plc* [2019] EWCA Civ 2163, [2020] Lloyd's Rep. I.R. 77 at [86]–[89], [96]–[110]; *Endurance Corporate Capital Ltd v Sartex Quilts & Textiles Ltd* [2020] EWCA Civ 308 at [60]–[73].

# 10. THE RIGHTS OF THE INSURER UPON PAYMENT

*Replace footnote 813 with:*

## Subrogation[813]

42-115 813 For a useful monograph on the doctrine, see Mitchell and Watterson, *Subrogation—Law and Practice* (2007), Ch.10. Subrogation applies to contracts of indemnity generally: see *AXA SA v Genworth Financial International Holdings Inc* [2019] EWHC 3376 (Comm), [2020] 1 Lloyd's Rep. 229.

## Subrogation: rights of action

*Replace footnote 827 with:*

[827] *Castellain v Preston* (1883) 11 Q.B.D. 380, 388. See also Marine Insurance Act 1906 s.79. See further the Mercantile Law Amendment Act 1856. Subrogation applies where the indemnified person and the person possessed of the right of action against a third party is the same person or entity: *AXA SA v Genworth Financial International Holdings Inc* [2019] EWHC 3376 (Comm), [2020] 1 Lloyd's Rep. 229 at [153]. **42-116**

## Contribution

*Replace footnote 857 with:*

[857] *Weddell v Road Transport & General Insurance Co Ltd* [1932] 2 K.B. 563. The position is more complex where one policy contains an "other insurance" exclusion and the other policy contains a rateable proportion clause: *National Farmers Union Mutual Insurance Society Ltd v HSBC Insurance (UK) Ltd* [2010] EWHC 773 (Comm), [2011] Lloyd's Rep. I.R. 86. See further *Allianz Australia Insurance Ltd v Lloyd's Underwriters* [2019] NSWCA 271, [2020] Lloyd's Rep. I.R. 203 (NSWCA). See above, para.42-108. **42-118**

### 11. SPECIFIC TYPES OF INSURANCE CONTRACT

### (a) Liability Insurance

## General characteristics

*Replace paragraph with:*

**42-120** Under contracts of liability insurance, the insurer undertakes to indemnify the assured against legal liability to third persons. Proof of liability is usually a condition precedent to the assured's right to recover, but proof of payment to the third party is not required in the absence of a stipulation to that effect.[861] Detailed provisions usually give the insurer the right to contest or to compromise the assured's liability,[862] since otherwise the insurer cannot use his ordinary rights of subrogation without first paying the assured the full amount of his estimated loss.[863] The terms of the policy usually indemnify the assured against the costs of his defence.[864] Often liability insurance excludes contractual as opposed to tortious liability, and it may be that even where both exist in respect of the same damage to the same person, the insurer is protected.[865] However, if a policy covers an assured against all sums which he may become liable at law to pay as damages, the natural and ordinary meaning of "liable at law" includes contractual liability.[866] "Liability" for these purposes exists when it has been established by judgment, award or agreement.[867] The establishment of loss by a judgment or settlement does not automatically establish the existence or basis of such legal liability; it is still open to the insurer to challenge that there was an actual legal liability, in which case it is for the assured to prove that there was such an actual legal liability.[868] The actual cause of the liability must be established in order to determine whether the liability falls within the insured perils of the policy; the manner in which the claim is brought against the assured is not determinative.[869] Liability policies place much importance on notification provisions, by which the assured will inform the insurer either of a claim or a circumstance which might give rise to a claim. The purpose of such provisions is to give the insurer the opportunity to investigate the claim or require the assured to defend the claim. It also serves as a mechanism to attach the policy under which notice was given to a claim arising subsequently to the expiry of the policy.[870]

[861] *Johnston v Salvage Association* (1887) 19 Q.B.D. 458, 460; *Lancashire Insurance v IRC* [1899] 1 Q.B. 353, 359; *Brice v Wackerbarth* [1974] 2 Lloyd's Rep. 274.

[862] As to the effect of clauses requiring the insurer's consent to any settlement of the assured's liability and/or prohibiting admissions of liability, see *Gan Insurance Co Ltd v Tai Ping Insurance Co Ltd* [2001] EWCA Civ 1042, [2001] Lloyd's Rep. I.R. 291; *Beazley Underwriting Ltd v Al Ahleia Insurance Co* [2013] EWHC 677 (Comm), [2013] Lloyd's Rep. I.R. 561.

[863] See above, para.42-116.

[864] See, e.g. *Forney v Dominion Insurance Co Ltd* [1969] 1 W.L.R. 928. As to cases where defence costs are incurred in respect of both an insured liability and a non-insured liability, see *New Zealand Forest Products Ltd v New Zealand Insurance Co Ltd* [1997] 1 W.L.R. 1237; *John Wyeth & Brothers Ltd v Cigna Insurance Co of Europe SA/NV* [2001] EWCA Civ 175, [2001] Lloyd's Rep. I.R. 420, 454. In the absence of a contractual provision providing such cover, there is no entitlement to defence costs under a liability insurance policy: *Astrazeneca Insurance Co Ltd v XL Insurance (Bermuda) Ltd* [2013] EWCA Civ 1660, [2014] Lloyd's Rep. I.R. 509. Defence costs cover is itself not an instance of liability insurance: *The Cultural Foundation v Beazley Furlonge Ltd* [2018] EWHC 1083 (Comm); contra *Tarbuck v Avon Insurance* [2002] Lloyd's Rep. I.R. 393, 395, which was commented on obiter in *In Re OT Computers* [2004] EWCA Civ 653, [2004] Lloyd's Rep. I.R. 669, [17]–[22].

[865] See *Dominion Bridge Co v Toronto General*, 32 D.L.R. (2d) 374 (1962). See also *Foundation of Canada Engineering Corp Ltd v Canadian Indemnity Co* [1977] 2 W.W.R. 75 Can. In *Cape Distribution Ltd v Cape Intermediate Holdings Plc* [2016] EWHC 1786 (QB), [2017] Lloyd's Rep. I.R. 1, at [161]–[163] the Court held that the contractual liability exclusion applied only to claims which could be made only in contract.

[866] *Aswan Engineering Establishment Co Ltd v Iron Trades Mutual Insurance Co Ltd* [1989] 1 Lloyd's Rep. 289. cf. *Smit Tak Offshore Services v Youell* [1992] 1 Lloyd's Rep. 154; *Tesco Stores Ltd v Constable* [2007] EWHC 2088 (Comm), [2008] Lloyd's Rep. I.R. 302, [26], [30]–[31], [2008] EWCA Civ 362, [2008] Lloyd's Rep. I.R. 636 (where it was held that a public liability policy did not cover contractual liability); *MJ Gleeson Group Plc v Axa Corporate Solutions Assurance SA* [2013] Lloyd's Rep. I.R. 677. If the policy insures against the assured's legal liability to pay "as damages" to third parties, this suggests that compensation must be payable by reason of the assured's wrongdoing: *Bartoline Ltd v Royal & Sun Alliance Insurance Plc* [2007] Lloyd's Rep. I.R. 423; and a claim for restitution may not be covered: *Peninsular and Oriental Steam Navigation Co v Youell* [1997] 2 Lloyd's Rep. 136, 141. Certain types of liability policies may be subject to certain restrictions if not prohibition. As regards "directors and officers" liability insurance, see Companies Act 2006 ss.232–234.

[867] *Post Office v Norwich Union Fire Insurance Society* [1967] 2 Q.B. 363; *Bradley v Eagle Star* [1989] 1 Lloyd's Rep. 465; *Yorkshire Water v Sun Alliance & London Insurance Ltd* [1997] 2 Lloyd's Rep. 21. In *Lumbermens Mutual Casualty Co v Bovis Lend Lease Ltd* [2004] EWHC 2197 (Comm), [2005] Lloyd's Rep. 74, the court held that a liability will not be established by a settlement agreement where that settlement agreement does not identify the specific cost of discharging the liability in question. Accordingly, where under a global settlement agreement, the assured agreed to receive, not pay, a single sum in settlement of all claims and counterclaims, the assured's liability for the counterclaims was held not to have been established and extrinsic evidence could not be adduced for that purpose. This proposition is questionable. The decision in *Lumbermens* was subjected to a disapproving critique in *Enterprise Oil Ltd v Strand Insurance Co Ltd* [2006] EWHC 58 (Comm), [2006] 1 Lloyd's Rep. 500 at [150]–[175]; *AIG Europe (Ireland) Ltd v Faraday Capital Ltd* [2006] EWHC 2707, [2007] Lloyd's Rep. I.R. 267 at [69]–[71]; reversed on other grounds [2007] EWCA Civ 1208, [2008] Lloyd's Rep. I.R. 454. If the assured settles a claim made against him, it may be open to the insurer to defend the claim under the policy on the ground that there had been no legal liability: *Peninsular and Oriental Steam Navigation Co v Youell* [1997] 2 Lloyd's Rep. 136; *Beazley Underwriting Ltd v Travelers Companies Inc* [2011] EWHC 1520 (Comm), [2012] Lloyd's Rep. I.R. 78; cf. *Commercial Union Assurance Co Plc v NRG Victory Reinsurance Ltd* [1998] 2 All E.R. 434 (reinsurance).

[868] *Astrazeneca Insurance Co Ltd v XL Insurance (Bermuda) Ltd* [2013] EWHC 349 (Comm), [2013] Lloyd's Rep. I.R. 290 at [38]–[39], [96]; affirmed [2013] EWCA Civ 1660, [2014] Lloyd's Rep. I.R. 509.

[869] *West Wake Price & Co v Ching* [1957] 1 W.L.R. 45; *Thornton Springer v NEM Insurance Co Ltd* [2000] 1 All E.R. (Comm) 486. This is so, even if the policy uses the word "alleging" in order to describe the insured peril (*MDIS Ltd v Swinbank* [1999] Lloyd's Rep. I.R. 516), although it will always be a question of construction. As to the effect of a judgment obtained by a claimant against the assured, see *Omega Proteins Ltd v Aspen Insurance UK Ltd* [2010] EWHC 2280 (Comm), [2011] Lloyd's Rep. I.R. 183; cf. *London Borough of Redbridge v Municipal Mutual Insurance Ltd* [2001] Lloyd's Rep. I.R. 545, 550–551; cf. *Cheltenham & Gloucester Plc v Sun Alliance and London Insurance Plc* Unreported May 30, 2001, Inner House, Ct of Sess.; cf. *Sun Life Assurance Co of Canada v Lincoln National Life Insurance Co* [2004] EWCA Civ 1660, [2005] 1 Lloyd's Rep. 606. As to the operation of an insolvency exclusion by reference to a "claim", see *AIG Australia Ltd v Kaboko Mining Ltd* [2019] FCAFC 96, [2019] Lloyd's Rep. I.R. 575 (Full Fed. Ct of Australia).

[870] *HLB Kidsons v Lloyd's Underwriters* [2007] EWHC 1951 (Comm), [2008] Lloyd's Rep. I.R. 237 at [22]–[23], [2008] EWCA Civ 1206, [2009] 1 Lloyd's Rep. 8. See also *Euro Pools Plc v Royal & Sun Alliance Insurance Plc* [2019] EWCA Civ 808.

## (b) Motor Insurance

### Road Traffic Act 1988

*Replace paragraph with:*

**42-124** The Road Traffic Act 1988[894] requires persons who control[895] the use[896] of motor vehicles[896a] on the road or other public place[897] to maintain insurance[898] against liability for death or injury to third parties (including passengers[899] in the vehicle) arising out of such use[900] and also against the liability (imposed by the Act)[901] to pay for emergency medical treatment for injuries (including fatal injuries) arising out of such use. With effect from December 31, 1988, insurance against liability for damage to the property of a third party has also been compulsory.[902] The Act does not require the personal liability of everyone using the vehicle to be covered so long as the insurance covers the use by the person in question[903]: thus an insurance by an employer which covers his liability for use by his employees is sufficient,[904] though if the insurance specifies the persons or classes of persons who are covered, such persons are given a statutory right to seek indemnity from the insurer, although not strictly parties to the contract of insurance.[905] The Act does not require insurance, inter alia, against contractual liability, against liability for death or injury sustained by persons in the employment of a person insured in accordance with the foregoing requirements, where the injury arises out of and in the course of that employment, or against damage to the vehicle insured; or cover in excess of £1,000,000 in respect of property damage arising out of any one accident.[906] An insurance is ineffective for the purposes of the Act unless a certificate of insurance in prescribed form is delivered by the insurer to the assured.[907] Failure to insure in accordance with the statutory requirements not only constitutes a criminal offence[908] but also a breach of a statutory duty which may give rise to liability in damages to persons thereby prejudiced.[909] On July 19, 2018, the Automated and Electric Vehicles Act 2018 received Royal Assent. By s.2(1) of that Act, an insurer is liable for any damage (meaning death, personal injury and, subject to exceptions, property damage) sustained by an insured person or any other person which has been caused by an automated vehicle when driving itself on a road or other public place in Great Britain. By s.2(4), unless there has been an unauthorised software alteration or a failure to update software, the insurer's liability for such damage cannot be excluded or limited by a term of the insurance policy or in any other way. This Act has not yet entered into force.

[894] Replacing the Road Traffic Act 1972, as amended by (inter alia) the Motor Vehicle (Compulsory Insurance) (No.2) Regulations 1973 (SI 1973/2143); SI 1974/791 (extending compulsory motor-vehicle insurance to cover liabilities arising out of use in other European Community countries); and the Motor Vehicles (Compulsory Insurance) Regulations 1987 (SI 1987/2171) (extending compulsory insurance to cover liability for damage to the property of a third party); and the Motor Vehicles (Compulsory Insurance) Regulations 1992 (SI 1992/3036) (ensuring that cover extends to the entire Community and affords cover no less than the law required than by the relevant Member States). The 1973, 1987 and 1992 Regulations each seek to implement EC Directives 72/166, 85/5 and 90/232. The 1988 Act came into force (subject to the transitory provisions in Sch.5 to the Road Traffic (Consequential Provisions) Act 1988) on May 15, 1989: see Road Traffic Act 1988 s.197.

[895] See *Monk v Warbey* [1935] 1 K.B. 75, 80; *Lloyd v Singleton* [1953] 1 Q.B. 357; *Kelly v Cornhill Insurance* [1964] 1 Lloyd's Rep. 1; *Newbury v Davis* [1974] R.T.R. 367.

[896] "Use" connotes control, management or operation: *Brown v Roberts* [1965] 1 Q.B. 1; and has been held to include the owner of a parked vehicle which owing to its condition could only be moved and not driven: *Elliott v Grey* [1960] 1 Q.B. 367; but there is no use if the vehicle is completely immovable: *Thomas v Hooper* [1986] R.T.R. 1. In *R&S Pilling v UK Insurance Ltd* [2019] UKSC 16, [2019] 2 W.L.R. 1015, the Supreme Court held that the repair of a car, which the owner was driving but due to disrepair could not be lawfully and safely driven, and which the owner wished to effect as soon as possible in order to be able to drive the car lawfully and safely, did not amount to "use" of the car. See also: *Leathley v Tatton* [1980] R.T.R. 21; *B (A Minor) v Knight* [1981] R.T.R. 136; *Stinton v Stinton* [1995] R.T.R. 167; *Hatton v Hall* [1997] R.T.R. 212. In *O'Mahoney v Joliffe* [1999] Lloyd's Rep. I.R. 321, the Court of Appeal held that a pillion passenger on a motorcycle who had agreed on a joint venture to go for a drive was a "user" within the meaning of the 1972 Uninsured Drivers Agreement (see below, para.42-126) and that "user" had the same meaning under the 1988 Act. See *Vnuk v Zavarovalnica Triglav dd* (C-162/13) EU:C:2014:2146, [2015] Lloyd's Rep. I.R. 142. In *Sahin v Havard* [2016] EWCA Civ 1202, [2017] 1 W.L.R. 1853 at [20], the Court of Appeal held that permitting the use of a vehicle is not the same as using the vehicle such that the liability of someone who permits another to use a vehicle without an insurance policy is not a liability which is itself required to be insured under s.145 and is not therefore a liability which an insurer is obliged to satisfy under s.151.

[896a] As to the meaning of "vehicle", see *Advantage Insurance Co Ltd v Stoodley* [2018] EWHC 2135 (QB), [2019] R.T.R. 7.

[897] s.192(1); *Lister v Romford Ice and Cold Storage Co* [1957] A.C. 555. The House of Lords held that a car park was not a "road": *Clarke v General Accident Fire and Life Assurance Corp Plc* [1998] 1 W.L.R. 1647. The legislation was amended to extend to "other public place" by the Motor Vehicles (Compulsory Insurance) Regulations 2000 (SI 2000/726). See further *R&S Pilling v UK Insurance Ltd* [2019] UKSC 16, [2019] 2 W.L.R. 1015.

[898] See ss.144 and 146 for alternative schemes for deposits and securities and for the classes of persons exempted from the provisions of the Act.

[899] See *Farrell v Whitty* (C-356/05) EU:C:2007:229, [2007] Lloyd's Rep. I.R. 525; *Drozdovs v Baltikums AAS* (C-277/12) EU:C:2013:685, [2014] R.T.R. 14; *Haasová v Petrik (Note)* (C-22/12) EU:C:2013:692, [2014] R.T.R. 15.

[900] In *Dunthorne v Bentley* [1996] R.T.R. 428, the Court of Appeal held that the plaintiff's injuries were caused by the defendant who, having run out of petrol had left her car to seek assistance, ran in front of the plaintiff's car, and that the injuries arose out of the defendant's use of her vehicle. In *Dodson v Peter H Dodson Insurance Services* [2001] 1 W.L.R. 1012, a motor insurance policy was construed as continuing to provide an indemnity against the driver's liabilities even though the principal vehicle which had been insured under the policy had been sold. cf. *Slater v Buckinghamshire CC* [2004] Lloyd's Rep. I.R. 432. In *AXN v Worboys* [2012] EWHC 1730 (QB), [2013] Lloyd's Rep. I.R. 207 the Court held that the liability of an insured taxi driver who administered poison and carried out sexual assaults on his passengers did not arise out of the use of a motor vehicle on the road or other public place, because such acts broke the chain of causation.

[901] See ss.157 and 158.

[902] Road Traffic Act 1988 s.145(3)(a).

[903] *Ellis v Hinds* [1947] K.B. 475; see also *Baugh v Crago* [1976] 1 Lloyd's Rep. 563. Nor does it require cover in respect of liability to a person driving the vehicle: *Cooper v MIB* [1985] Q.B. 575.

[904] See n.872, above.

[905] s.148(7); *Tattersal v Drysdale* [1935] 2 K.B. 174; *Austin v Zurich* [1945] 1 K.B. 250, 255.

[906] Road Traffic Act 1988 s.145(4), as amended by the Motor Vehicles (Compulsory Insurance) Regulations 2007 (SI 2007/1426). As to the boundary between the Employers Liability (Compulsory Insurance) Act 1969 and the Road Traffic Act 1988 s.145(4A), see *AXA Insurance UK Plc v Norwich Union Insurance Ltd* [2007] EWHC 1046 (Comm), [2008] Lloyd's Rep. I.R. 122.

[907] s.147.

[908] s.143(2). The offence is an absolute one: *Baugh v Crago* [1976] 1 Lloyd's Rep. 563.

[909] *Monk v Warbey* [1935] 1 K.B. 75; *Martin v Dean* [1971] 2 Q.B. 208. In *Norman v Aziz* [2000] Lloyd's Rep. I.R. 52, a civil right to damages for breach of s.143(1)(b) of the 1988 Act was held to exist in favour of a victim against the owner of a vehicle who allowed an uninsured driver to use that vehicle; the existence of the Motor Insurers Bureau uninsured drivers agreement (see below, para.42-125) and the relevant EC Directive had no effect on this cause of action. The defendant to a claim for damages for personal injury is not entitled to counterclaim for a breach of this statutory duty for purely economic losses in connection with the defendant's liability to the claimant, as opposed to the defendant's own injuries: *Bretton v Hancock* [2005] EWCA Civ 404, [2005] Lloyd's Rep. I.R. 454 at [42]–[50].

## Rights of third parties

*Replace paragraph with:*

The Act entitles the third party to make a direct claim upon the insurer upon obtaining judgment against the person insured,[910] so long as notice[911] of the bringing of proceedings has been given to the insurer before or within seven days after their commencement and there has been no stay of execution pending an appeal.[912] In order that the third party may make a direct claim against the insurer, the assured's liability to the third party must be covered by the terms of the policy.[913] This right is not available, however, if before the event giving rise to the death, injury or damage the insurance was cancelled (and the certificate dealt with in accordance with the Act)[914] or if the insurer in an action commenced before or within three months[915] of the commencement of the action by this third party has obtained a declaration that he is entitled (apart from any provision in the insurance) to avoid the insurance for non-disclosure or misrepresentation.[916] In addition to the foregoing, the Act renders ineffective any provisions of the insurance restricting the cover by reference to such matters as the characteristics of the vehicle or the driver,[917] though the insurer can recover from the person insured any payments made to third parties which but for the provision he would not have been obliged to make. Similarly provisions relieving the insurer by reason of some act or omission after the event giving rise to a claim under the insurance are ineffective[918] as are other rights to avoid or cancel the insurance unless falling within the qualifications to the rights of the third party outlined above.[919] Finally, it should be noted that the Act also renders ineffective any prior agreement or understanding between the user of a vehicle and a passenger whereby the liability of the user is restricted or excluded or the enforcement of such liability is made subject to conditions.[920] European Council Directives[921] require Member States to ensure that insurance coverage exists for civil liability for personal injuries and property damage arising as a result of the use of motor vehicles. The intention of the Directives is to ensure that the victims of motor accidents are able to prosecute and establish their claims in comparable ways in each Member State.[922] By the European Communities (Rights against Insurers) Regulations 2002,[923] where a person has a cause of action in tort against a person insured under a policy complying with s.145 of the Road Traffic Act 1988 arising out of an accident involving the insured vehicle,[923a] the claimant may, without prejudice to his right against the insured person, issue proceedings directly against the insurer immediately and the insurer shall be liable to the claimant to the extent that he is liable to the insured person. **42-125**

[910] Proceedings cannot be pursued against an "unknown" or "unnamed" driver if it is conceptually not possible to serve, and therefore, bring the proceedings to the attention of, the defendant: *Cameron v Liverpool Victoria Insurance Co Ltd* [2019] UKSC 6, [2019] 1 W.L.R. 1471.

[911] As to the requirements of the notice to be given, see *Wylie v Wake* [2001] P.I.Q.R. P13.

[912] ss.151–152. With effect from December 31, 1988, an insurer is bound, subject to certain exceptions, to satisfy a judgment obtained even against a person not insured by the policy if it relates to a liability required to be covered: see Road Traffic Act 1988 s.151(2)(b). In *Churchill Insurance Co Ltd v Fitzgerald* [2012] EWCA Civ 1166, [2013] Lloyd's Rep. I.R. 137 the Court of Appeal considered s.151(8) of the Road Traffic Act 1988, by which the insurer is entitled to recover the amount of the judgment from the assured who caused or permitted the use of the vehicle which gave rise to the liability.

[913] s.151(2)(a). In *EUI Ltd v Bristol Alliance Ltd Partnership* [2012] EWCA Civ 1267, [2013] Lloyd's Rep. I.R. 351 the Court of Appeal held that the third party could not recover from the motor insurer in circumstances where the damage to property to which the third party's claim related arose by reason of the assured's deliberate act, which was expressly excluded from cover under the motor policy. See also

*Stych v Dibble* [2012] EWHC 1606 (QB), [2013] Lloyd's Rep. I.R. 80; *AXN v Worboys* [2012] EWHC 1730 (QB), [2013] Lloyd's Rep. I.R. 207.

[914] s.152(1)(c).

[915] If the insurer starts proceedings after the proceedings by the third party have been started, then to take advantage of this provision, he must give the claimant in the action by the third party notice specifying the non-disclosure or misrepresentation relied upon and (if required) make such claimant a party to his action: s.152(2); *Cross v British Oak Insurance Co Ltd* [1938] 2 K.B. 167; *Zurich v Morrison* [1942] 2 K.B. 53.

[916] s.152(2), as amended by the Insurance Act 2015 s.21(4). In *Colley v Shuker* [2019] EWHC 781 (QB) the Court considered that s.152(2) is incompatible with EU jurisprudence, in particular EU Directive 2009/103/EC.

[917] s.148.

[918] s.148.

[919] s.152. cf. *Matadeen v Caribbean Insurance Co Ltd* [2002] UKPC 69, [2003] 1 W.L.R. 670.

[920] s.149.

[921] Directives 72/166, 84/5, 88/357, 90/232, 2000/26 and 2005/14.

[922] *Criminal Proceedings against Ruiz Bernáldez* (C-129/94) EU:C:1996:143, [1996] All E.R. (EC) 741.

[923] SI 2002/3061.

[923a] In *Carroll v Taylor* [2020] EWHC 153 (QB), [2020] Lloyd's Rep. I.R. 216, the claimant suffered injuries 40 minutes after being left by a taxi driver, who had accepted the claimant's passage but had stolen the claimant's debit card and PIN; it was held that the claimant's injuries had not arisen out of the use of the taxi on a road.

## Third parties and uninsured drivers

*In line 1, after "Insurers' Bureau (MIB)", add new footnote 923b:*

**42-126** [923b] In *Motor Insurers' Bureau v Lewis* [2019] EWCA Civ 909; [2019] Lloyd's Rep. I.R. 390, the Court of Appeal held that the MIB was a direct emanation of the State and that Council Directive EU Directive 2009/103/EC had direct effect against the MIB.

Chapter 43

# RESTRICTIVE AGREEMENTS AND COMPETITION



## 1. Introduction

### Scope and plan of the chapter

*In the ante-penultimate line, after "and Markets Authority", add:*
("CMA") | **43-001**

*Add new paragraphs:*

**Implications of the United Kingdom's exit from the European Union ("Brexit")** **43-001A** The legal implications of the United Kingdom's exit from the EU ("Brexit") are dealt with in Vol.I of this work.[1a] As described there, the United Kingdom left the EU from 11pm on January 31, 2020 ("exit day"),[1b] although under the terms of the Withdrawal Agreement concluded between the United Kingdom and the EU, EU law will continue to apply in the United Kingdom until the end of a transition period (referred to in the European Union (Withdrawal) Act 2018 as an "implementation period"[1c]) that will expire at 11.00pm on December 31, 2020 ("IP completion day").[1d] Therefore, until IP completion day, EU competition law, including arts 101 and 102 of the Treaty on the Functioning of the European Union

("TFEU") and Regulation 1/2003, will continue to be applicable in and to the UK, and shall be interpreted and applied, as if the UK were still an EU member[1e]; and s.60 of the Competition Act 1998 (which requires that the provisions of that Act "be dealt with in a manner that is consistent" with EU competition law[1f]) remains in force. The CMA has published guidance on its functions during the implementation period.[1g]

[1a] Vol.I, paras 1-104—1-018.

[1b] Vol.I, para.1-015A.

[1c] European Union (Withdrawal) Act 2018 s.1A(6), as inserted by the European Union (Withdrawal Agreement) Act 2020 s.1. See Vol.I, para.1-015A.

[1d] Vol.I, para.1-015A.

[1e] Agreement on the Withdrawal of the United Kingdom of Great Britain and Northern Ireland from the European Union and the European Atomic Energy Community (January 24, 2020) (the "Withdrawal Agreement 2020"), arts 126 (Transition Period) and 127 (Scope of the transition).

[1f] See below, paras 43-140—43-142.

[1g] CMA, *UK exit from the EU, Guidance on the functions of the CMA under the Withdrawal Agreement* (CMA113).

**43-001B** The situation at the end of the implementation period is presently uncertain and will depend on the terms of any agreement reached between the United Kingdom and the EU on their future relationship. In the absence of any agreement, which at the time of writing is a distinct possibility, it is likely that the legislation adopted in 2019 for such a scenario (known as a "no deal Brexit") will come into effect; this includes a statutory instrument, the Competition (Amendment etc.) (EU Exit) Regulations 2019,[1h] which were due to come into effect on "exit day". This statutory instrument is also likely to come into force even in the event of an agreement being concluded. This Chapter sets out the position following "IP completion day" under these Regulations, although it is likely that these Regulations will require amendment to reflect the continued application of EU law in the UK during the implementation period.

[1h] SI 2019/93.

**43-001C** In such a scenario, arts 101 and 102 will cease to have effect in the United Kingdom with effect from IP completion day.[1i] At this point, Regulation 1/2003 will be revoked[1j]; the CMA (and other regulators) and national courts will no longer have jurisdiction to apply arts 101 and 102[1k]; and s.60 will be repealed[1l] and replaced by a new s.60A that will apply to courts, the CMA and regulatory authorities when applying the Competition Act 1998.[1m] EU block exemption regulations will continue to apply under s.10 of the Competition Act 1998, as "retained exemptions".[1n] All Commission decisions adopted before IP completion day will remain binding on and in the UK, enforceable by the Commission and subject to review by the EU courts.[1o] The Commission will also remain competent in respect of any administrative procedures opened by it under Regulation 1/2003 into suspected infringements of arts 101 and/or 102 concerning natural or legal persons residing or established in the United Kingdom or compliance with EU competition law in the UK[1p] and any final decision adopted before this date or later in any proceedings initiated before this date shall be binding on and in the United Kingdom,[1q] enforceable by the Commission[1r] and reviewable exclusively by the EU courts.[1s] The Commission will, similarly, remain competent to review any mergers notified to it under the EU Merger Regulation before this date.[1t]

[1i] Competition (Amendment etc.) (EU Exit) Regulations 2019 (SI 2019/93) reg.62. Accordingly, arts 101, 102 and 106(1) and (2) TFEU (and arts 53, 54 and 57 of the EEA Agreement) will cease to apply in the United Kingdom from this date. See below, para.43-001D.

[1j] Competition (Amendment etc.) (EU Exit) Regulations 2019 (SI 2019/93) reg.63(a) and Sch.3 para.1(f). See below, para.43-001D.

[1k] Competition (Amendment etc.) (EU Exit) Regulations 2019 (SI 2019/93) reg.64 and Sch.4 paras 4–6. See below, paras 43-065, 43-066 and 43-072. The CMA (and other regulators) and national courts will continue to apply equivalent provisions of the Competition Act 1998, i.e. the Chapter I and II prohibitions, which are considered below: see below, paras 43-081 et seq. (in relation to the Ch.I prohibition) and 43-117 et seq. (in relation to the Ch.II prohibition).

[1l] Competition (Amendment etc.) (EU Exit) Regulations 2019 (SI 2019/93) reg.22. See below, para.43-143.

[1m] Competition (Amendment etc.) (EU Exit) Regulations 2019 (SI 2019/93) reg.23. See below, paras 43-143—43 143B.

[1n] Competition (Amendment etc.) (EU Exit) Regulations 2019 (SI 2019/93) reg.3(5). See below, para.43-114.

[1o] Withdrawal Agreement 2020 art.95.

[1p] Withdrawal Agreement 2020 art.92(1) and (2)(b).

[1q] Withdrawal Agreement 2020 art.95(1).

[1r] Withdrawal Agreement 2020 art.95(2).

[1s] Withdrawal Agreement 2020 art.95(3).

[1t] Withdrawal Agreement 2020 art.92(1) and (2)(c). Any final decision adopted before this date in such proceedings shall be binding on and in the United Kingdom (art.95(1)) and the Commission may enforce any commitments given to it before this date or in proceedings initiated before this date (art.95(2)). All such decisions shall be reviewed exclusively by the EU courts (art.95(3)).

Although arts 101 and 102 will cease to apply in the United Kingdom from IP completion day, all existing rights, powers, liabilities, obligations, restrictions, remedies and procedures under them as at that date will continue to apply as provisions of domestic law,[1u] such that agreements entered into before that day that infringe art.101(1) and are not exempt under art.101(3) are void and unenforceable (under art.101(2))[1v] and affected parties remain entitled to damages for losses caused by an infringement of arts 101 and/or 102,[1w] including in respect of infringements found by a Commission decision adopted before that day or after it in accordance with arts 92 and 95 of the Withdrawal Agreement 2020. Accordingly, claims (or a defence to a claim) before a court or tribunal relating to pre-IP completion day infringements of arts 101 and/or 102 (or of arts 53 and/or 54 of the EEA Agreement) may continue or be brought after IP completion day.[1x] **43-001D**

[1u] European Union (Withdrawal) Act 2018 ss.1A(1)–(3) and 4(1) and Competition (Amendment etc.) (EU Exit) Regulations 2019 (SI 2019/93) reg.62. See below, para.43-007.

[1v] Competition (Amendment etc.) (EU Exit) Regulations 2019 (SI 2019/93) reg.62.

[1w] Competition (Amendment etc.) (EU Exit) Regulations 2019 (SI 2019/93) regs 62 and 64 and Sch.4 para.14. See below, para.43-066.

[1x] Competition (Amendment etc.) (EU Exit) Regulations 2019 (SI 2019/93) reg.64 and Sch.4 para.14.

## Council Regulation 1/2003

*Replace paragraph with:*

The way in which arts 101 and 102 TFEU[2] are applied in practice was fundamentally changed as a result of the application of Regulation 1/2003 from May 1, 2004.[3] The European Commission has since 1962 been the principal institution charged with the enforcement of the competition provisions of the TFEU as a **43-002** result of powers conferred upon it by Council Regulation 17.[4] That Regulation provided for the notification of agreements to the Commission which had exclusive competence to grant an "individual exemption" under art.101(3) to an agreement that infringed art.101(1). However, it became increasingly clear that a centralised system of enforcement was no longer appropriate for the effective application of the competition rules, especially with the enlargement of the European Union to 25 Member States on May 1, 2004 (and subsequently to 28). Regulation 1/2003, which also applies from May 1, 2004, introduced significant changes to the enforcement of arts 101 and 102. The system of notification of agreements for individual exemption was abolished and in its place art.101, in its entirety, and art.102 are directly applicable without prior decision of the Commission. The Commission shares the competence to apply arts 101 and 102 with national competition authorities and national courts.[5]

[2] Arts 101 and 102 TFEU were previously arts 85 and 86 of the European Economic Community Treaty and subsequently arts 81 and 82 of the European Community Treaty. Much of the relevant case law and literature, of course, refers to the articles by their former numbers; however, the text below will always refer to the current ones.

[3] [2003] O.J. L1/1.

[4] [1962] O.J. 204/62, [1962] O.J.Sp.Ed. 87.

[5] See below, paras 43-065—43-076.

### Relationship between the EU competition rules and the provisions of domestic law

*Replace paragraph with:*

**43-003** One of the main principles behind the reforms leading to the enactment of the Competition Act 1998 in the UK was the desire to harmonise domestic law with the EU competition rules in order to reduce the costs incurred by the business community in complying with the previous domestic regime, which was formulated in very different terms from arts 101 and 102. The extent to which the provisions of the Competition Act must be interpreted consistently with EU law is considered below at paras 43-140 and 43-142. Many agreements which fall within art.101 TFEU will also infringe the Ch.I prohibition in the 1998 Act; similarly conduct which is unlawful under art.102 TFEU will also fall within the Ch.II prohibition. There may, however, be a small number of cases where, notwithstanding the modelling of the Ch.I and II prohibitions upon arts 101 and 102, different outcomes would be achieved under the EU and the domestic rules. With effect from May 1, 2004, art.3 of Regulation 1/2003 determines the relationship between the EU competition rules and the provisions of domestic competition law. Where national competition authorities and national courts apply national competition law to agreements and conduct that may affect trade between Member States, they must also apply arts 101 and 102.[6] If an agreement affects trade between Member States but does not fall within art.101(1) or satisfies the conditions in art.101(3), it is not possible to apply stricter domestic competition law to it.[7] However, where conduct affects trade between Member States but does not infringe art.102, Member States are not precluded from imposing stricter national competition laws or sanctions on such conduct.[8] It is also possible for a Member State to apply stricter national rules, both in relation to agreements and to conduct, where those rules predominantly pursue an objective different from that pursued by arts 101 and 102 TFEU.[9] It is expected that arts 101 and 102 TFEU and Regulation 1/2003 will cease to have effect in the United Kingdom from IP completion day.[10]

[6] Regulation 1/2003 art.3(1).

[7] Regulation 1/2003 art.3(2).

[8] Regulation 1/2003 art.3(3).

[9] Regulation 1/2003 art.3(3).

[10] See above, paras 43-001B and 43-001C.

## 2. COMPETITION RULES UNDER THE TFEU

### (a) In General

#### Purpose of this section

*Replace paragraph with:*

The purpose of this section is to give a brief outline of the rules on competition law under the TFEU insofar as they may affect contractual rights and obligations. **43-004** Specialised works should be consulted for a fuller treatment.[11] It is expected that arts 101 and 102 will cease to have effect in the UK from IP completion day, although rights, liabilities and obligations existing at that date will continue to be enforceable under UK law.[11a]

[11] e.g. Bailey and John (eds.), *Bellamy and Child, European Union Law of Competition*, 8th edn (2018). For comparative treatment of EU and UK competition law see Whish and Bailey, *Competition Law*, 9th edn (2018).

[11a] See above, paras 43-001B—43-001D and below, para.43-007.

#### Direct effect

*To the end of paragraph, add:*

It is expected that arts 101 and 102 will cease to have effect in the United **43-007** Kingdom from IP completion day.[20a] However, all existing rights, powers, liabilities, obligations, restrictions, remedies and procedures under arts 101 and 102 that existed as of exit day will continue to be recognised, available, enforced, allowed and followed after the end of implementation period contained in the Withdrawal Agreement 2020.[20b] This also applies to rights etc. under arts 101 and 102 that accrue during the implementation period in accordance with the Withdrawal Agreement 2020.[20c] Therefore, arts 101 and 102 will remain enforceable in relation to agreements entered into or conduct committed before the IP completion day, including a right to damages for losses caused by an infringement of these provisions committed before IP completion day. In accordance with arts 92 and 95 of the Withdrawal Agreement 2020, this applies in respect of infringements found by a Commission decision adopted both before that day and after it. Accordingly, claims (or a defence to a claim) before a court or tribunal relating to pre-IP completion day infringements of arts 101 and/or 102 (or of arts 53 and/or 54 of the EEA Agreement) may continue or be brought after IP completion day.[20d] Any rights, etc. derived from arts 101 and 102 will, however, cease to be recognised and available in domestic law (and to be enforced, allowed and followed) from IP completion day in respect of infringements of EU competition law committed after that date.[20e]

[20a] See above, paras 43-001B and 43-001C.

[20b] European Union (Withdrawal) Act 2018 s.4(1) and Competition (Amendment etc.) (EU Exit) Regulations 2019 (SI 2019/93) reg.62.

[20c] European Union (Withdrawal) Act 2018 s.1A(1)–(3), inserted by the European Union (Withdrawal) Act 2020 s.1.

[20d] Competition (Amendment etc.) (EU Exit) Regulations 2019 (SI 2019/93) reg.64 and Sch.4 para.14.

[20e] Competition (Amendment etc.) (EU Exit) Regulations 2019 (SI 2019/93) reg.62.

### Principal sources of law

*Replace paragraph with:*

43-008 Apart from the relevant provisions of the Treaty, there is a considerable body of secondary legislation, in particular the block exemptions[21] promulgated by the EU institutions.[22] The European Commission, which, together with the national competition authorities and national courts, is responsible for the enforcement of the competition law provisions of the Treaty, also publishes official notices and announcements giving guidance on matters of interpretation.[23] In addition to this legislation there are the decisions of the European Commission concerning particular agreements and conduct, and the jurisprudence of the General Court (formerly the Court of First Instance of the European Communities) and the European Court of Justice.[24]

[21] See below, paras 43-033—43-034.

[22] For a description of the EU institutions and of the different forms of secondary legislation see Hartley, *The Foundations of European Union Law*, 8th edn (2014).

[23] The relevant legislation, notices, etc. can be found in *Butterworths Competition Law Handbook*, 25th edn (2019). The European Commission also issues an *Annual Report on Competition Policy*, available on its website: *https://ec.europa.eu/competition/publications/annual_report/index.html*.

[24] The General Court was established in 1988 and hears appeals from Commission decisions in, inter alia, competition cases. Appeals from the General Court on points of law are made to the Court of Justice. Decisions of these courts are binding on the English courts: European Communities Act 1972 s.3(1) (as amended by the European Communities (Amendment) Act 1986). For the effect of "Brexit" on the binding nature of judgments of the General Court and the Court of Justice, see below, para.43-009.

### Supremacy of EU law

*To the end of paragraph, add:*

43-009 In *Sainsbury's Supermarkets Ltd v Visa Europe Services LLC, Mastercard Inc* the Supreme Court held that it was bound to follow the judgment of the Court of Justice in *MasterCard Inc v Commission*[29a] that multilateral interchange fees set by Mastercard had an appreciable effect on competition and thus infringed art.101(1), as the factual basis of the Court of Justice's judgment and the cases before it, concerning fees set by both Mastercard and Visa, were materially indistinguishable.[29b]

[29a] *MasterCard Inc v European Commission* (C-382/12P) EU:C:2014:14.

[29b] *Sainsbury's Supermarkets Ltd v Visa Europe Services LLC, Mastercard Inc* [2020] UKSC 24 at [92]–[94].

*Add new paragraph:*

43-009A The supremacy of EU law will continue to apply on or after exit day so far as relevant to the interpretation, disapplication or quashing of any enactment or rule of law passed or made before exit day.[29c] It does not apply to any enactment or rule of law passed or made on or after exit day.[29d] A court or tribunal is not bound by any principles laid down, or any decisions made, on or after IP completion day by the EU courts,[29e] but may have regard to anything done on or after this day by the EU courts, another EU entity (such as the European Commission) or the EU so far as it is relevant to any matter before it.[29f]

[29c] European Union (Withdrawal) Act 2018 s.5(2).

[29d] European Union (Withdrawal) Act 2018 s.5(1).

[29e] European Union (Withdrawal) Act 2018 s.6(1).

[29f] European Union (Withdrawal) Act 2018 s.6(2).

### European Economic Area

*Replace paragraph with:*

The European Economic Area, first established in 1994, now comprises all the 28 states of the European Union and the EFTA states other than Switzerland (namely Iceland, Norway and Liechtenstein). The aim of the EEA Agreement is, inter alia, to ensure the uniform application of competition law throughout the EEA, and to this end art.53(1), (2) and (3) of the EEA Agreement in effect reproduces art.101(1), (2) and (3) TFEU and art.54 of the EEA Agreement reproduces art.102 TFEU. Other provisions of the EEA Agreement contain procedural and substantive rules which mirror the existing EU secondary legislation in the competition field. The EEA Agreement also provides for the establishment of the EFTA Surveillance Authority which has similar powers to the Commission and is subject to review by the EFTA Court of Justice. Article 56 of the EEA Agreement provides complex rules for the allocation of jurisdiction between the Commission and the EFTA Surveillance Authority in competition cases depending on the effect that the conduct under scrutiny has on trade between the EU and EFTA. A full analysis of the scope of the EEA Agreement is beyond the scope of this work[30] but practitioners should bear in mind the possible application of EU competition law to contracts affecting the above-named territories. As a result of the United Kingdom having left the European Union, it also withdrew from the EEA Agreement with effect from 11.00pm on January 31, 2020, subject to a transitional period that will expire at 11.00pm on December 31, 2020.[30a] **43-010**

[30] For discussion of the EEA rules see Bailey and John (eds), *Bellamy and Child, European Union Law of Competition*, 8th edn (2018), paras 1.077—1.087.

[30a] Withdrawal Agreement 2020 arts 126 and 129. Although the UK and the three EFTA States that are party to the EEA Agreement concluded a Separation Agreement on January 28, 2020, this does not contain provisions on competition law that are equivalent to the Withdrawal Agreement 2020 arts 92 and 95.

## (b) Article 101(1)

### Undertaking

*Replace paragraph with:*

A "functional" approach must be taken to the meaning of the term "undertaking": a legal entity may be acting as an undertaking when performing some functions but not when performing others.[32] The term "undertaking" is a wide one covering almost any legal or natural person engaged in an economic activity, regardless of its legal status and the way in which it is financed.[33] It is capable of covering public and private companies, partnerships, trade associations,[34] individuals,[35] professionals,[36] sole traders[37] and religious organisations.[37a] An undertaking need not be a profit-making body.[38] Employees are not undertakings[39]; in *Becu*[40] the Court of **43-013**

Justice confirmed that employees are incorporated into the economic unit of the undertaking they work for and so are not themselves undertakings within the meaning of EU competition law. A commercial agent is capable of acting as an undertaking, though an agreement between a principal and a "genuine" commercial agent will normally fall outside art.101(1).[41] So far as Member States[42] are concerned, a distinction must be drawn between the situation where the State acts in the exercise of its powers as a public authority or carries on non-economic activities (in relation to which it is not to be treated as an undertaking)[43] and where it is engaged in economic activities of an industrial or commercial nature (in relation to which it is covered by art.101).[44]

[32] See, e.g. *SELEX Sistemi Integrati SpA v Commission* EU:C:2009:191, [2009] E.C.R. I-2207.

[33] *Höfner & Elser v Macrotron* EU:C:1991:161, [1991] E.C.R. I-1979; *Enichem v Commission* EU:T:1991:74, [1991] E.C.R. II-1623, para.235; *Commission v Italy* EU:C:1998:303, [1998] E.C.R. I-3851 where the Court added that any activity consisting in offering goods or services on a given market is an economic activity.

[34] *Luttikhuis v Coberco* EU:C:1995:434, [1995] E.C.R. I-4515 (dairy cooperative); *Dansk Pelsdyravlerforening v Commission* EU:T:1992:79, [1992] E.C.R. II-1931 (fur traders association). A body can be both an undertaking and an association of undertakings: *Frubo v Commission* EU:C:1975:61, [1975] E.C.R. 563.

[35] See, e.g. *RAI v UNITEL* [1978] O.J. L157/39 (opera singer).

[36] See, e.g. *Wouters v Algemene Raad van de Nederlandse Orde van Advocaten* EU:C:2002:98, [2002] E.C.R. I-1577, paras 45–49.

[37] *CNSD* [1993] O.J. L203/27 (customs agents); *COAPI* [1995] O.J. L122/37 (industrial property agents).

[37a] *Congregacion de Escuelas Pias Provincia Betania v Ayuntamiento de Getafe* (C-74/16) EU:C:2017:496 (Catholic Church an undertaking in respect of education services for which it charged a fee).

[38] *Van Landewyck v Commission* EU:C:1980:248, [1980] E.C.R. 3125, para.88.

[39] *Suiker Unie v Commission* EU:C:1975:174, [1975] E.C.R. 1663, 2007, para.539.

[40] EU:C:1999:419, [1999] E.C.R. I-5665.

[41] *Suiker Unie*, above, paras 538–540. See below, para.43-059.

[42] *Diego Calì & Figli v Servici ecologici Porto di Genova* EU:C:1997:160, [1997] E.C.R. I-1547.

[43] See, e.g. *SAT Eurocontrol v Commission* EU:C:1994:7, [1994] E.C.R. I-43 (body set up under international law to levy air traffic control charges not an undertaking); *Poucet* EU:C:1993:63, [1993] E.C.R. I-637 (body administering state sickness benefit not an undertaking); *Diego Calì & Figli*, above (body providing harbour pollution control services not an undertaking); *FENIN v Commission* EU:C:2006:453, [2006] E.C.R. I-6295 (organisations responsible for operation of the Spanish health service not undertakings).

[44] See, e.g. *IAZ v Commission* EU:C:1983:310, [1983] E.C.R. 3369 (water supply companies).

**43-020** *Change title of paragraph:*

**Creation of an internal market**

*In line 2, after "the creation of", replace "a single" with:*

**43-020** an internal

**The test to be applied**

*Replace paragraph with:*

**43-021** The test for determining whether conduct has as its object or effect[68] the prevention, restriction or distortion of competition has been laid down in a number of leading cases, in particular in *Société Technique Minière*[69]; *Delimitis v Henninger Bräu*[70]; *Wouters*[71]; and *Cartes Bancaires*[72]; *Generics*[72a] and *Budapest Bank.*[72b] In

*Budapest Bank*, the Court of Justice confirmed that, although if an agreement has an anti-competitive object there is no requirement to examine its effects on competition, a court or competition authority may nevertheless do so and the same anti-competitive conduct may be regarded as having as both its object and its effect the restriction of competition.[72c] Generally speaking, the first step is to determine the object of the agreement. If it is not clear that the object is to restrict competition, one must then analyse the effect of the agreement within its legal and economic context; that is, assess the way in which competition would occur in the absence of the agreement and consider how this is likely to have been affected by the operation of the agreement. Among the many relevant factors for working out whether an agreement has a restrictive effect are the nature and quantity of the products covered by the agreement, the position and importance of the parties in the market for the products concerned, the isolated nature of the agreement or, alternatively, whether it forms part of a network of similar agreements.[73] Other material factors include the existence of any intellectual property rights and the number and size of competing undertakings.

68 The terms "object" or "effect" are disjunctive rather than cumulative, so that the existence of either is sufficient: see *Technique Minière*, below.

69 *Société Technique Minière v Maschinenbau Ulm* EU:C:1966:38, [1966] E.C.R. 235.

70 *Delimitis v Henninger Bräu* EU:C:1991:91, [1991] E.C.R. I-935. For an analysis of the application of art.101 to a distribution agreement covering non-EEA states see *Javico International v Yves Saint Laurent Parfums* EU:C:1998:173, [1998] E.C.R. I-1983.

71 *J.C.J. Wouters v Algemene Raad van de Nederlandse Orde van Advocaten* (C-309/99) EU:C:2002:98, [2002] E.C.R. I-1577.

72 *Groupement des cartes bancaires (CB) v European Commission* (C-67/13) EU:C 2014:2204.

72a *Generics (UK) Ltd v Competition and Markets Authority* (C-307/18) EU:C:2020:52.

72b *Gazdasági Versenyhivatal v Budapest Bank Nyrt* (C-228/18) EU:C:2020:265.

72c *Gazdasági Versenyhivatal v Budapest Bank Nyrt* (C-228/18) EU:C:2020:265 at [40]–[44].

73 The *Delimitis* case restated the law on the relevance of the existence of a network of agreements; cf. the earlier case of *Brasserie De Haecht v Wilkin* EU:C:1967:54, [1967] E.C.R. 407.

## The "object" of the agreement

*To the end of paragraph, add:*

In *Generics (UK) Ltd v Competition and Markets Authority*, the Court of Justice confirmed that the concept of a "restriction of competition by object" must be interpreted strictly and can be applied only to agreements that, taking account of their provisions, objectives and legal and economic context (i.e. the nature of the goods or services affected, as well as the conditions for the functioning and structure of the market in question), have "a sufficient degree of harm to competition" such that it is not necessary to assess their effects as by their very nature they are harmful to the proper functioning of normal competition,[78a] including by disguising or being equivalent to a market-sharing or market-exclusion agreement.[78b] An agreement that, by its terms, restricts normal competition between actual or potential competitors and has no explanation other than the parties' commercial interest not to engage in competition will infringe art.101(1) by object.[78c] The Court of Justice confirmed this approach in *Budapest Bank*,[78d] such that an agreement that indirectly fixes purchase or selling prices may be regarded as restricting competition by object by "neutralising" one aspect of competition.[78e] The Court also held, however, that although there is not an exhaustive list of agreements that are to be regarded as restricting competition by object, there must be "sufficiently reliable and robust **43-022** experience" of an agreement's nature, purpose and potential to affect competition for it to be found, by its very nature, to be harmful to the proper functioning of competition for a restriction of competition by object to be found[78f]; this may also be established if there are "strong indications" of a negative effect on prices.[78g] Where this is not the case, an in-depth examination of its effects on competition is required.[78h]

[78a] *Generics (UK) Ltd v Competition and Markets Authority* (C-307/18) EU:C:2020:52 at [67]–[68].

[78b] *Generics (UK) Ltd v Competition and Markets Authority* (C-307/18) EU:C:2020:52 at [76]–[77]. See also *Gazdasági Versenyhivatal v Budapest Bank Nyrt* (C-228/18) EU:C:2020:265 at [33]–[40] and [51].

[78c] *Generics (UK) Ltd v Competition and Markets Authority* (C-307/18) EU:C:2020:52 at [81]–[82] and [87].

[78d] *Gazdasági Versenyhivatal v Budapest Bank Nyrt* (C-228/18) EU:C:2020:265 at [62]–[63].

[78e] *Gazdasági Versenyhivatal v Budapest Bank Nyrt* (C-228/18) EU:C:2020:265 at [33]–[40] and [51]–[56].

[78f] *Gazdasági Versenyhivatal v Budapest Bank Nyrt* (C-228/18) EU:C:2020:265 at [76].

[78g] *Gazdasági Versenyhivatal v Budapest Bank Nyrt* (C-228/18) EU:C:2020:265 at [82]–[83].

[78h] *Gazdasági Versenyhivatal v Budapest Bank Nyrt* (C-228/18) EU:C:2020:265 at [77]–[79].

## (c) Article 101(3)

### Agreements likely to satisfy article 101(3)

*Replace paragraph with:*

**43-032** All four criteria must be satisfied in order for art.101(3) to be applicable.[105] Agreements that restrict competition by object may be more difficult to justify under art.101(3) than agreements that restrict competition by effect.[105a] The Commission has published Guidelines on the application of art.81(3) of the Treaty (art.101(3) TFEU).[106] Since May 1, 2004 Regulation 1/2003 abolished the system of notification of agreements to the Commission for individual exemption under art.101(3) and the exclusive competence of the Commission to make decisions under that provision in individual cases; instead the parties to agreements and their advisers are expected to assess the application of art.101(3) themselves. The burden of proof of demonstrating that the four criteria of art.101(3) are satisfied falls on the party which is in breach of art.101(3) and is seeking exemption under art.101(3). It must do so on the balance of probabilities and requires an empirical assessment to be made of the likely negative effects of an agreement on competition and consumers (i.e. anti-competitive effects), and any efficiencies and other benefits resulting from the restriction (i.e. pro-competitive effects); this in turn requires the party seeking to rely on art.101(3) to produce detailed, cogent and convincing arguments and evidence.[106a] In *Sainsbury's Supermarkets Ltd v Visa Europe Services LLC, Mastercard Inc* the Supreme Court held that the requirement that consumers receive a "fair share" of the benefits means that art.101(3) is not satisfied where an agreement causes disadvantages to consumers on one market but has benefits for consumers on another market, unless the two groups of consumers are the same.[106b]

[105] See, e.g. *Métropole Télévision SA v Commission* EU:T:1996:99, [1996] E.C.R. II-649.

[105a] *Gazdasági Versenyhivatal v Budapest Bank Nyrt* (C-228/18) EU:C:2020:265 at [41].

[106] [2004] O.J. C101/97.

[106a] *Sainsbury's Supermarkets Ltd v Visa Europe Services LLC, Mastercard Inc* [2020] UKSC 24 at [116]–[137].

[106b] *Sainsbury's Supermarkets Ltd v Visa Europe Services LLC, Mastercard Inc* at [144] and [170]–[174].

### Block exemptions

*Replace footnote 108 with:*

[108] Note that if the agreement falls within an EU block exemption it will automatically enjoy parallel exemption from the Ch.I prohibition in UK competition law by virtue of the Competition Act 1998 s.10: see below, para.43-114. From IP completion day, a parallel exemption under s.10 will be known as a "retained exemption": see below, para.43-114. **43-033**

### Block exemptions currently in force

*Replace footnote 109 with:*

[109] The texts of the block exemptions, as amended, and the Commission Notices giving guidance on the interpretation of certain regulations, are printed in *Butterworths Competition Law Handbook*, 25th edn (2019). They are also available on the Commission's website, at *https://ec.europa.eu/competition/antitrust/legislation/legislation.html.* **43-034**

## (d) Application of Art.101 to Specific Agreements

### Typical horizontal agreements

*Replace list with:*

(i) *Price fixing* Since price is the main instrument of competition, art.101(1)(a) expressly prohibits agreements which "directly or indirectly fix purchase or selling prices or any other trading conditions". There have been many cases in which horizontal price-fixing agreements have been condemned and in which very substantial fines have been imposed. Price fixing in any form is caught, including, for example, agreements on the level of discounts, prior consultation on price lists, agreements on recommended prices, maximum prices and collective resale price maintenance. Price fixing in the services sector is unlawful as well as in the goods sector. Buyers' cartels can be caught as well as those of sellers.[117] **43-035**

(ii) *Market sharing* Prominent among agreements which fall within art.101(1)(b) and (c) are horizontal agreements between competitors to refrain from supplying into each other's markets. Such agreements frustrate the aims of the TFEU since they often divide up supplies along the lines of national boundaries and thus directly inhibit the free movement of goods and the creation of the internal market.[118] Market sharing can be achieved by the sharing of customers as well as by allocating geographic areas to the parties. A further kind of agreement likely to infringe art.101(1) occurs where manufacturers allocate to each other quotas for the production or supply of products to the market of each participant. Article 101(1) may also be infringed where one manufacturer grants exclusive selling rights to a competitor in respect of a particular territory. A market sharing arrangement confined to the territory of one Member State may still infringe art.101(1) since it is liable to affect the patterns of imports and exports that might otherwise take place.

(iii) *Exchange of information* Whether the exchange of information restricts competition within the meaning of art.101(1) depends inter alia on the nature of the information exchanged and the structure of the market to which the information agreement relates.[119] The exchange of information among competitors is likely to infringe art.101(1) if that information would normally be regarded as a business secret. Information about prices and other trading conditions is usually regarded as commercially sensitive and confidential. There is no objection to the collection by a trade association of statistical information giving an aggregate picture of the output and sales of the industry provided that individual company figures cannot be identified, or provided the information is sufficiently historical that it is unlikely to affect future behaviour.

(iv) *Collusive tendering* The practice of collusive tendering whereby firms agree amongst themselves to collaborate over their response to invitations to tender infringes art.101(1) and may attract large fines.[120]

(v) *Joint selling or purchasing* Joint selling or purchasing agreements may fall within art.101(1) where the parties agree the price they are prepared to charge or to pay or where they agree to buy or sell wholly or mainly through a joint operation such as a subsidiary company or other trade association they have established for this purpose. The Commission has published guidance on the applicability of art.101 to those kinds of benign horizontal agreements which often generate beneficial effects on competition; these include joint purchasing or production, research and development and standardisation agreements.[121]

(vi) *Pay-for-delay agreements* An agreement between the owner of a patent and a manufacturer of generic drugs contemplating entry into the market upon expiry of the patent, whereby the patent owner makes a payment to the generic producer not to enter the market, may amount to an agreement that restricts competition by object.[122] In *Generics (UK) Ltd v Competition and Markets Authority* the Court of Justice held that a settlement agreement between the owner of a process patent for an active ingredient and generic manufacturers who are preparing to enter the market with generic versions of the same medicinal product and who dispute the validity of that patent and/or that their own product infringes that process patent, whereby the generic manufacturers undertakes not to enter the market and not to pursue revocation of the patent in return for payments by the patent owner, constitutes a restriction of competition by object.[122a]

[117] For detailed analysis of horizontal price-fixing agreements see Bailey and John (eds), *Bellamy and Child, European Union Law of Competition*, 8th edn (2018), paras 5.041–5.065; Whish and Bailey, *Competition Law*, 9th edn (2018), pp.530–541.

[118] For detailed analysis of horizontal market-sharing agreements see Bailey and John (eds), *Bellamy and Child, European Union Law of Competition*, 8th edn (2018), paras 5.071–5.091; Whish and Bailey, *Competition Law*, 9th edn, pp.541–544.

[119] For detailed analysis of the exchange of information see Whish and Bailey, *Competition Law*, 9th edn (2018), pp.551–559.

[120] For detailed analysis of collusive tendering agreements see Whish and Bailey, *Competition Law*, 9th edn (2018), pp.547–549.

[121] Commission's Guidelines on Horizontal Cooperation Agreements [2010] O.J. C11/1.

[122] See, e.g. *Lundbeck*, Commission decision of June 19, 2013, upheld on appeal *H. Lundbeck A/S v Commission* (T-472/13) EU:T:2016:449, [2016] 5 C.M.L.R. 18; further appeal pending in *H. Lundbeck A/S and Lundbeck Ltd v Commission* (C-561/16P): see Opinion of AG Kokott, EU:C:2020:428, advising that the appeal be dismissed; *Servier/Perindopril*, Commission decision of July 9, 2014, finding that such patent settlement agreements constitute a restriction of competition by object upheld on appeal *Servier SAS v Commission* (T-691/14) EU:T:2018:922; further appeal pending in *Servier SAS* (C-201/19P).

[122a] *Generics (UK) Ltd v Competition and Markets Authority* (C-307/18) EU:C:2020:52. Where the pat-

ent owner holds a dominant position for medicines containing the active ingredient, it will also infringe art.102 by excluding potential competition from generic manufactures that would otherwise have entered the market.

### Joint ventures

*Replace footnote 125 with:*

[125] e.g. Bailey and John (eds), *Bellamy and Child, European Union Law of Competition*, 8th edn (2018), Ch.6; Whish and Bailey, *Competition Law*, 9th edn (2018), Ch.15. **43-036**

### Mergers

*Replace paragraph with:*

Article 101(1) does not apply to the acquisition of control of one company by another and mergers are governed by a separate legal regime under the EU Merger Regulation, Council Regulation 139/2004[126] and the subsidiary legislation and Commission Notices issued in implementation of the Merger Regulation. Some joint ventures fall to be considered under the Merger Regulation, if they are "full function", that is if they have all the necessary resources in terms of funding, staff and assets to carry out the functions normally carried out by undertakings operating on the same market.[127] Again, reference should be made to specialist works for an analysis of this complex area of the law.[128] As a result of the United Kingdom leaving the European Union, the Merger Regulation will cease to apply to and in the UK from IP completion day (11.00pm on December 31, 2020),[128a] although the Commission remains competent to review any merger notified to it before that date[128b] and to enforce commitments given to it by merging parties.[128c] **43-037**

[126] [2004] O.J. L24/1.

[127] See *Commission Consolidated Jurisdictional Notice*, July 10, 2007.

[128] See, e.g. Levy and Cook, *European Merger Control Law: a Guide to the Merger Regulation* (2003); Bailey and John (eds), *Bellamy and Child, European Union Law of Competition*, 8th edn (2018), Ch.8; Whish and Bailey, *Competition Law*, 9th edn (2018), Ch.21.

[128a] Competition (Amendment etc.) (EU Exit) Regulations 2019 (SI 2019/93) reg.63 and Sch.3 para.1(g).

[128b] Withdrawal Agreement 2020 art.92(1), (2) and (3)(c).

[128c] Withdrawal Agreement 2020 art.95(1) and (2).

### Application of article 101(1) to vertical agreements

*In line 9, after "integration of the", replace "single" with:*

internal **43-038**

### Intellectual property licences

*Replace footnote 157 with:*

[157] See e.g. Bailey and John (eds), *Bellamy and Child, European Community Law of Competition*, 8th edn (2018), Ch.9; Whish and Bailey, *Competition Law*, 9th edn (2018), Ch.19. **43-054**

*Change title of paragraph:* **43-056**

### Technology transfer agreements

## (e) Article 102

### Contractual clauses as infringements of article 102

*To the end of paragraph, add:*

Article 102 will cease to apply to and in the United Kingdom from IP comple- **43-061** tion day (11.00pm on December 31, 2020), although the Commission remains competent to continue any administrative procedure into a suspected infringement of art.102 that has been initiated before that date[174a] and to enforce commitments given or remedies imposed in any decision adopted either before that date or in procedures that continue after that date.[174b]

[174a] Withdrawal Agreement 2020 art.92(1), (2) and (3)(b). See above, para.43-001C.

[174b] Withdrawal Agreement 2020 art.95(1) and (2).

**Dominant undertakings**

*Replace paragraph with:*

**43-062** A detailed description of the test for ascertaining whether an undertaking enjoys a dominant position is beyond the scope of this work.[175] Broadly speaking, one must first identify the product sector and the geographical area in which the undertaking being scrutinised competes[176] and then calculate the market share of that market supplied by the undertaking and the number and size of its competitors.[177] Many other factors are relevant in determining dominance, in particular the ownership of intellectual property rights and the existence of any other barriers to new entry to the market by potential competitors. Dominance of itself is not a contravention of the Treaty, but dominant undertakings have a "special responsibility" not to engage in any conduct which will hinder the maintenance of such competition that still takes place in the market.[178] This responsibility becomes greater, and as a corollary a finding of abuse becomes more likely, the weaker the competitive constraints facing the dominant undertaking in a market are. However, in *Irish Sugar v Commission*[179] the General Court stated that the fact that an undertaking is in a dominant position cannot deprive it of its entitlement to protect its own commercial interests when they are attacked, although such behaviour cannot be allowed if its purpose is to strengthen the dominant position and thereby abuse it. Articles 101 and 102 are not mutually exclusive and conduct which falls within art.101 may also be an abuse.[180]

[175] See, e.g. Bailey and John (eds), *Bellamy and Child, European Union Law of Competition*, 8th edn (2018), Ch.10; Whish and Bailey, *Competition Law*, 9th edn (2018), pp.25–46 and pp.187–196. Note also that the European Commission has published "Guidance on the Commission's enforcement priorities in applying Article [102 TFEU] to abusive exclusionary conduct by dominant undertakings", [2010] O.J. C45/7. This document is not a formal set of guidelines describing the law of art.102 TFEU; however, it does provide useful insights into the way in which the Commission regards particular types of behaviour under art.102, and indicates the circumstances in which it might be inclined to open proceedings in relation to possibly abusive behaviour.

[176] The leading cases on definition of the relevant market include *United Brands v Commission* EU:C:1978:22, [1978] E.C.R. 207; *Hoffmann-La Roche v Commission* EU:C:1979:36, [1979] E.C.R. 461; *Michelin v Commission* EU:C:1983:313, [1983] E.C.R. 3461; *Hilti v Commission* EU:T:1991:70, [1991] E.C.R. II-315.

[177] A broad rule of thumb is that a market share of over 40 per cent sustained over a number of years may be an indication of dominance; there has only been one finding of dominance below 40 per cent, in *Virgin/British Airways* [2000] O.J. L30/1, where the Commission considered British Airways held a dominant position with a market share of 39.7 per cent in the market for the procurement of air travel agency services (the decision was upheld on appeal to the General Court in *British Airways v Commission* EU:T:2003:343, [2003] E.C.R. II-5917 and on appeal to the Court of Justice in *British Airways v Commission* EU:C:2007:166, [2007] E.C.R. I-2331).

[178] *Michelin v Commission* EU:C:1983:313, [1983] E.C.R. 3461, 3511.

[179] EU:T:1999:246, [1999] E.C.R. II-2969.

[180] On the relationship between arts 101 and 102 see, e.g. *Ahmed Saeed* EU:C:1989:140, [1989] E.C.R. 803; *Tetra Pak I* EU:T:1990:41, [1990] E.C.R. II-309.

**Examples of abusive contractual provisions**

*To the end of paragraph, add:*

(iv) *Pay for delay agreements* Pay for delay agreements, whereby a patent owner enters into an agreement with a generic manufacturer to settle litigation in which the validity of the patent is challenged, in return for a payment to the generic manufacturer not to enter the market and not to pursue revocation of the patent may infringe art.101: see para.43-035, above. Where the patent owner holds a dominant position for the medicine protected by the patent, it will also infringe art.102 by excluding potential competition from generic manufactures that would otherwise have entered the market.[187a] **43-063**

[187a] *Generics (UK) Ltd v Competition and Markets Authority* (C-307/18) EU:C:2020:52.

## (f) Enforcement at the National Level

**Direct applicability of articles 101 and 102**

*To the end of paragraph, add:*

Regulation 1/2003 will be revoked and cease to apply in the United Kingdom from IP completion day (11.00pm on December 31, 2020)[191a] and the CMA will cease to have the power to apply arts 101 and 102 from that date, including in relation to investigations commenced before that date.[191b] Claims (or a defence to a claim) before a court or tribunal relating to pre-IP completion day infringements of arts 101 and/or 102 (or of arts 53 and/or 54 of the EEA Agreement) may continue or be brought after IP completion day.[191c] **43-065**

[191a] Competition (Amendment etc.) (EU Exit) Regulations 2019 (SI 2019/93) reg.63 and Sch.3 para.1(f). See above, para.43-001C.

[191b] Competition (Amendment etc.) (EU Exit) Regulations 2019 (SI 2019/93) reg.64 and Sch.4 paras 4–6.

[191c] Competition (Amendment etc.) (EU Exit) Regulations 2019 (SI 2019/93) reg.64 and Sch.4 para.14.

**Role of the national courts**

*To the end of paragraph, add:*

Articles 101 and 102 will cease to have direct effect in the United Kingdom from IP completion day, although they will remain applicable to agreements and conduct entered into before that day, such that an agreement that infringes art.101 is unenforceable and a person who has suffered loss as a result of an infringement of arts 101 and/or 102 will retain a right to obtain damages in respect of such loss.[191d] Accordingly, claims (or a defence to a claim) before a court or tribunal relating to pre-IP completion day infringements of arts 101 and/or 102 (or of arts 53 and/or 54 of the EEA Agreement) may continue or be brought after IP completion day.[191e] **43-066**

[191d] See above, para.43-001D.

[191e] Competition (Amendment etc.) (EU Exit) Regulations 2019 (SI 2019/93) reg.64 and Sch.4 para.14.

**Effect of Regulation 1/2003**

*In line 4, after "agreement or conduct", replace "have" with:*

has **43-067**

## Severance of void terms

*Replace paragraph with:*

43-068 Although art.101(2) provides that the prohibited *agreement* is void, the Court of Justice has held that it is in fact only the restrictive clauses in the agreement which are invalidated by art.101(2).[194] If those clauses can be severed from the agreement in accordance with the test usually applied under domestic law, the remainder of the agreement may be enforced.[195] However, in *English Welsh & Scottish Railway Ltd v E.ON Plc* the High Court held that directions by the Office of Rail Regulation, which has concurrent powers with the CMA to enforce the competition rules in the UK, that various terms of a coal carriage agreement between the parties were unlawful and should be removed altered the contract so fundamentally that it became void and unenforceable in its entirety.[196] In *Calor Gas Ltd v Express Fuels (Scotland) Ltd* the Outer House of the Court of Session in Scotland reached the conclusion that an exclusive dealing agreement was unenforceable by the supplier, Calor Gas, as it infringed art.101.[197] In *Robert Andrew Jones v Ricoh UK Ltd*[198] the Chancery Division of the High Court concluded that cl.7 of a Confidentiality Agreement was void and unenforceable as it was contrary to art.101(1) TFEU; the High Court subsequently held that cl.7 was severable from the remainder of the agreement which remained enforceable.[199] In *Martin Retail Group Ltd v Crawley Borough Council*[200] the Central London County Court held that a Proposed User clause in a letting scheme of retail premises was void and unenforceable under the Competition Act 1998 s.2(4).

194 *Société de Vente de Ciments et Bétons v Kerpen & Kerpen* EU:C:1983:374, [1983] E.C.R. 4173, 4184.

195 See *Richard Cound Ltd v BMW (GB) Ltd* [1997] Eu.L.R. 277, CA; applied in, e.g. *Benford Ltd v Cameron Equipment* [1997] Eu.L.R. 334, Merc Ct; *Parks v Esso Petroleum* [1999] 1 C.M.L.R. 455. See also *Byrne v Inntrepreneur Beer Supply Co Ltd* [1999] Eu.L.R. 834. For the English law of severance see Vol.I, paras 16-236 et seq.

196 [2007] EWHC 599 (Comm), [2007] U.K.C.L.R. 1653.

197 [2008] CSOH 13.

198 [2010] EWHC 1743 (Ch).

199 *Robert Andrew Jones v IOS (RUK) Ltd and Ricoh UK Ltd* [2012] EWHC 348 (Ch) at [44].

200 [2014] L. & T.R. 17.

## Breaches of arts 101 or 102 as a cause of action

*To the end of paragraph, add:*

43-070 As a result of the UK's withdrawal from the European Union, this right of action will not apply to any infringement of arts 101 or 102 committed after IP completion day (11.00pm on December 31, 2020), but will apply to any infringement committed before this date, even if the claim is brought after this date.[206a] These Regulations will continue to have effect after IP completion day, as "EU-derived domestic legislation".[206b]

206a See above, para.43-001D.

206b See Vol.I, paras 1-016B and 1-017B.

## Causes of action in English law

*Replace footnote 210 with:*

43-071 210 *Gibbs Mew Plc v Gemmell* [1998] Eu.L.R. 588; *Passmore v Morland* [1999] 1 C.M.L.R. 1129; *Parks v Esso Petroleum* [1999] 1 C.M.L.R. 455 and the cases cited therein.

### Role of national competition authorities

*Replace paragraph with:*

Under the regime introduced by Regulation 1/2003 national competition authorities share the competence to apply arts 101 and 102 alongside the national courts and the European Commission. National competition authorities have the power to make decisions bringing an infringement to an end, to order interim measures, to accept commitments from the parties in lieu of an adverse decision and to decide that there are no grounds for action on their part. The Regulation contains a number of provisions which are intended to promote cooperation between the Commission and the national competition authorities; a network of competition authorities, the "European Competition Network", has been established which will facilitate the handling of cases between the competition authorities in Europe.[211a] The Commission has published a Notice on Cooperation within the Network of Competition Authorities.[212] Following the UK's withdrawal from the EU, the CMA (and other regulators) will no longer have the power to apply arts 101 and 102 from IP completion day (11.00pm on December 31, 2020), including in respect of investigations that it has commenced before that date, which it may not continue after this date.[212a] Where an investigation has both a "domestic element" and an "EU element", as the CMA (or other regulator) is investigating a suspected infringement of both UK and EU competition law, the part of the investigation before this date will be treated, after this date, as being done for the domestic element of the investigation.[212b] **43-072**

[211a] With the United Kingdom's withdrawal from the European Union on January 31, 2020, the CMA has ceased to be a member of the European Competition Network, but will participate—by invitation—in cases involving the United Kingdom until the end of the transitional period provided for in art.126 of the Withdrawal Agreement 2020: art.128(5).

[212] [2004] O.J. C101/43.

[212a] Competition (Amendment etc.) (EU Exit) Regulations 2019 (SI 2019/93) reg.64 and Sch.4 para.5.

[212b] Competition (Amendment etc.) (EU Exit) Regulations 2019 (SI 2019/93) reg.64 and Sch.4 para.6.

## (g) Enforcement at the EU Level

### Commission investigations and adverse decisions

*To the end of paragraph, add:*

The Commission will continue to be competent to investigate any suspected infringement of arts 101 and/or 102 relating to competition in the United Kingdom where its investigation is initiated before the end of the implementation period.[215a] Any decision addressed to the United Kingdom or to natural and legal persons residing or established in the United Kingdom adopted by the Commission before the end of the implementation period foreseen by the Withdrawal Agreement 2020 (i.e. on or before December 31, 2020[215b]) or after the end of this period where its investigation was initiated before the end of this period is binding on and in the United Kingdom.[215c] Such decisions will be enforced by the Commission[215d] and shall be reviewed exclusively by the EU courts.[215e] **43-074**

[215a] Withdrawal Agreement 2020 art.92(1) and (2)(b).

[215b] Withdrawal Agreement 2020 art.126.

[215c] Withdrawal Agreement 2020 art.95(1).

[215d] Withdrawal Agreement 2020 art.95(2).

[215e] Withdrawal Agreement 2020 art.95(3).

## 3. UNITED KINGDOM COMPETITION LAW

### (a) Introduction

#### Reform of the law

*Replace final sentence with:*

43-077 The withdrawal by the United Kingdom from the European Union will to lead to a number of changes to the domestic competition law of the United Kingdom from IP completion day,[227] although no significant changes to either the substantive law or to the CMA's investigation procedures are presently foreseen.

[227] See below, paras 43-097, 43-102, 43-114, 43-131, 43-136 and 43-143—43-143B. For a general overview of the effect of "Brexit" on competition law in the UK, see above, paras 43-001A—43-001D. For a general note on "Brexit", see Vol.I, paras 1-014 et seq.

#### Part I of the Competition Act 1998

*Replace footnote 230 with:*

43-079 [230] All the materials referred to in the text are listed in Whish and Bailey, *Competition Law*, 9th edn (2018), pp.345–346; the guidelines are available at *https://www.gov.uk/topic/competition/competition-act-cartels*.

#### Section 60: the "governing principles" clause

*To the end of paragraph, add:*

43-080 Section 60 is discussed at paras 43-140—43-142 below. With effect from IP completion day (11.00pm on December 31, 2020), s.60 will be repealed and replaced by a new s.60A.[230a]

[230a] See below, paras 43-143, 43-143A and 43-143B.

### (b) The Ch.I Prohibition: Agreements

#### Effect on trade within the United Kingdom

*To the end of paragraph, after "the Ch.I prohibition.", add new footnote 237a:*

43-084 [237a] As a result of the United Kingdom's withdrawal from the EU, art.101 remains applicable to such agreements until IP completion day (11.00pm on December 31, 2020), but not thereafter: see above, para.43-001C.

#### "Undertakings"

*Replace paragraph with:*

43-085 This expression will be interpreted as it has been in EU law: reference should be made to para.43-013, above. The Competition Appeal Tribunal handed down an important judgment on the meaning of the term "undertaking" in *BetterCare Group Ltd v Director General of Fair Trading*.[238] The Tribunal concluded that a Northern Irish Health Trust, when procuring facilities for the provision of residential and nursing care to elderly people, was acting as an undertaking and therefore fell within the ambit of the Competition Act 1998. It is possible that this case might have been decided differently if it had been heard after the judgment of the Court of Justice in *FENIN v Commission*.[239] In *Achilles Information Ltd v Network Rail Infrastructure Ltd* the Tribunal held that the regulation of access to railway network infrastructure (including to ensure safety) was an essential part of, and indissociable from, Network Rail's economic activity of the operation of railway infrastructure, such that schemes regulating access fell within the scope of the Ch.I prohibition.[239a] In *Strident Publishing Ltd v Creative Scotland* the Tribunal held that Creative Scotland, the principal public-sector arts-funding body in Scotland, was not an undertaking, as the awarding of grants for the publishing of books was not an economic activity, as the making of grants to support creative activity for public benefit was the function of a public authority carried out under a statutory power, which Creative Scotland undertook with no financial gain or return obtained or expected, such that it was not an activity that would be done by a private body on a commercial basis.[239b] The CMA has found that self-employed doctors providing private healthcare services were each an undertaking.[239c]

[238] [2002] C.A.T. 7, [2002] Comp. A.R. 299.

[239] See above, para.43-013 n.43.

[239a] *Achilles Information Ltd v Network Rail Infrastructure Ltd* [2019] C.A.T. 20 at [100]–[103]; appeal dismissed on this point in *Network Rail Infrastructure Ltd v Achilles Information Ltd* [2020] EWCA Civ 323 at [54]–[60], rejecting Network Rail's submission that it was acting in a non-economic regulatory function.

[239b] *Strident Publishing Ltd v Creative Scotland* [2020] C.A.T. 11 at [42]–[52].

[239c] CMA, Case 50782-1, *Privately funded ophthalmology services*, CMA decision of July 1, 2020.

## Agreements, decisions and concerted practices

*Replace paragraph with:*

These expressions are an exact replica of the provisions in art.101(1) TFEU: **43-086**
reference should be made to paras 43-015—43-018 above, as to their meaning in EU law, and to paras 43-140—43-142 (before IP completion day) and paras 43-143—43-143B (after IP completion day) below, on the extent to which the competition authorities in the UK will be obliged and/or able to follow the jurisprudence of the Courts of the European Union and the decisional practice of the European Commission in interpreting these expressions. In its decision in *Hasbro UK Ltd, Argos Ltd and Littlewoods Ltd* the OFT (the predecessor of the CMA) found that a single, overall agreement and/or concerted practice existed between Hasbro, a toy manufacturer, and two of its retailers, Argos and Littlewoods, to fix the resale prices of various toys; this decision was upheld on appeal to the Competition Appeal Tribunal[240] and to the Court of Appeal.[241] An important judgment of the Competition Appeal Tribunal, exploring the application of the concept of a concerted practice to the practice of collusive tendering, is *Apex Asphalt and Paving Co Ltd v OFT*, which concluded that the OFT's finding that there had been an infringement of the Ch.I prohibition was correct.[242] Section 2(5) and (6) of the Act provide that, unless the context otherwise requires, any reference in the Act to an agreement includes a reference to a decision and/or concerted practice. In *Achilles Information Ltd v Network Rail Infrastructure Ltd* the Tribunal held that schemes by which Network Rail authorised third parties to access its railway network infrastructure were agreements or concerted practices, even though the terms of those schemes were imposed by Network Rail and were not freely negotiated: by participating in the schemes, the third parties acquiesced in their provisions.[242a]

[240] *Argos Ltd v OFT* [2004] C.A.T. 24, [2005] Comp. A.R. 588.

[241] *Argos Ltd v OFT* [2006] EWCA Civ 1318, [2006] U.K.C.L.R. 1135; see similarly the so-called *Football Shirt* case, *JJB Sports Plc v OFT*, which is also the subject of the Court of Appeal judgment in [2006] EWCA Civ 1318.

[242] [2005] C.A.T. 4, [2005] Comp. A.R. 507; see similarly *Makers UK Ltd v OFT* [2007] C.A.T. 11, [2007] Comp A.R. 699.

[242a] *Achilles Information Ltd v Network Rail Infrastructure Ltd* [2019] C.A.T. 20 at [99]; appeal dismissed on this point in *Network Rail Infrastructure Ltd v Achilles Information Ltd* [2020] EWCA Civ 323 at [64]–[67], rejecting Network Rail's argument that the sole supplier requirement was imposed unilaterally by it and therefore did not constitute an agreement.

## Object or effect of preventing, restricting or distorting competition

*To the end of paragraph, add:*

43-087 Even where an agreement has the object or effect of preventing, restricting or distorting competition, it will not infringe the Ch.I prohibition if it is objectively necessary for an agreement to be workable or to achieve its effect.[243a] The burden of demonstrating an objective justification falls on the party seeking to rely on the restriction; in *Achilles Information Ltd v Network Rail Infrastructure Ltd* the Tribunal held that Network Rail had failed to discharge this burden, as it could not demonstrate that requiring undertakings seeking access to its railway network infrastructure to use a single supplier of quality assurance services nominated by it was essential to ensure safety on the railway network, as there were ways in which safety could be assured with more than one supplier of supplier assurance services.[243b] In *Ping Europe Ltd v Competition and Markets Authority* the Court of Appeal held that an internet sales policy implemented by a manufacturer of golf clubs prohibiting authorised dealers from selling clubs on their websites caused a sufficient degree of harm to competition to be classified as an object restriction.[243c]

[243a] *Achilles Information Ltd v Network Rail Infrastructure Ltd* [2019] C.A.T. 20 at [155], citing *MasterCard Inc v Commission* (C-382/12P) EU:C:2014:2201 at [89]–[91].

[243b] *Achilles Information Ltd v Network Rail Infrastructure Ltd* [2019] C.A.T. 20 at [226]–[255].

[243c] *Ping Europe Ltd v Competition and Markets Authority* [2020] EWCA Civ 13, upholding the Tribunal's judgment in *Ping Europe Ltd v Competition and Markets Authority* [2018] C.A.T. 13.

## Establishing an effect on competition

*Replace paragraph with:*

43-088 Where an agreement does not have the object of restricting competition it is necessary to examine, within its legal and economic context, whether it might have the effect of doing so. In *The Racecourse Association v OFT* the Competition Appeal Tribunal concluded that the OFT had failed to establish that the collective selling of the rights to broadcast horse-racing events had an anti-competitive effect[244]; and in *P&S Amusements Ltd v Valley House Leisure Ltd* the High Court considered that there was no possibility of establishing that a beer tie in a lease of a public house in Blackpool could do so.[245] In *Achilles Information Ltd v Network Rail Infrastructure Ltd* the Tribunal found that although schemes regulating access to Network Rail's railway infrastructure, which required suppliers to use a single supplier of quality assurance services nominated by Network Rail, did not have the object of restricting competition, they did have the effect of doing so, as their effect was to prevent market entry and reserve the market for such services to the exclusive supplier nominated by Network Rail.[245a]

[244] [2005] C.A.T. 29, [2005] Comp. A.R. 99.

[245] [2006] EWHC 1510 (Ch), [2006] U.K.C.L.R. 867.

[245a] *Achilles Information Ltd v Network Rail Infrastructure Ltd* [2019] C.A.T. 20 at [107]–[120] (finding no restriction of competition by object) and [141]–[154] (finding an appreciable restriction of competition by effect); appeal dismissed on this point in *Network Rail Infrastructure Ltd v Achilles Information Ltd* [2020] EWCA Civ 323 at [93]–[101].

## Section 2(4): voidness

*In line 5, after "exemption under s.10", add:*

43-091 (or, after IP completion day, a "retained exemption"[249a])

[249a] See below, para.43-114.

## Severance

*Replace footnote 255 with:*

[255] See below, paras 43-140—43-143. Section 60 will be repealed and replaced with a new s.60A after IP completion day: see below, paras 43-143—43-143B. **43-092**

## Void or illegal?

*Replace footnote 257 with:*

[257] See Mitchell, Mitchell and Watterson (eds), *Goff and Jones: The Law of Restitution*, 9th edn (2016), Ch.25. **43-093**

## Schedule 1: mergers and concentrations

*In line 7, after "investigation of mergers.", add new footnote 260a:*

[260a] See above, para.43-001C on the impact of Brexit on the application of the EU Merger Regulation in the UK during the implementation period under the Withdrawal Agreement 2020 and para.43-037 following IP completion day. **43-095**

*Change title of paragraph:* **43-097**

## Schedule 1 Pt II: EU merger

*To the end of paragraph, add:*

Part II will cease to apply with effect from IP completion day.[265a] **43-097**

[265a] Competition (Amendment etc.) (EU Exit) Regulations 2019 (SI 2019/93) reg.28.

## Schedule 3 para.3: EEA regulated markets

*To the end of paragraph, add:*

This exclusion will be repealed from IP completion day.[272a] **43-102**

[272a] Competition (Amendment etc.) (EU Exit) Regulations 2019 (SI 2019/93) reg.29(2).

## Schedule 3 para.5: compliance with legal requirements

*Replace footnote 274 with:*

[274] "Legal requirement" is defined in para.5(3). With effect from IP completion day, para.5(3) will be amended to remove para.5(3)(b) and (c), which excluded from the Chs I and II prohibitions agreements made to comply with legal requirements imposed by or under EU law, the EEA Agreement or the law of another Member State: Competition (Amendment etc.) (EU Exit) Regulations 2019 (SI 2019/93) reg.29(3). **43-104**

## Schedule 3 para.7: public policy

*To the end of paragraph, add:*

During the Covid-19 pandemic in 2020, the Secretary of State made regulations under s.71(3) and Sch.3 para.7 to exclude, on public policy grounds, from the Ch.I prohibition certain agreements concerning the supply of groceries,[276a] health services in England[276b] and Wales,[276c] ferry services to the Isle of Wight,[276d] and milk and other dairy products.[276e] Although each Order permitted certain collaboration between competitors, none permitted price-fixing or the sharing of information on prices or costs. To benefit from the exclusion an agreement must be notified to the Secretary of State, who maintains a public register of notified agreements.[276f] **43-106**

[276a] Competition Act 1998 (Groceries) (Coronavirus) (Public Policy Exclusion) Order 2020 (SI 2020/369).

[276b] Competition Act 1998 (Health Services for Patients in England) (Coronavirus) (Public Policy Exclusion) Order 2020 (SI 2020/368).

[276c] Competition Act 1998 (Health Services for Patients in Wales) (Coronavirus) (Public Policy Exclusion) Order 2020 (SI 2020/435).

[276d] Competition Act 1998 (Solent Maritime Crossings) (Coronavirus) (Public Policy Exclusion) Order 2020 (SI 2020/370).

[276e] Competition Act 1998 (Dairy Produce) (Coronavirus) (Public Policy Exclusion) Order 2020 (SI 2020/481). This Order expired on August 1, 2020.

[276f] The public register is available at: *https://www.gov.uk/guidance/competition-law-exclusion-orders-relating-to-coronavirus-covid-19?utm_source=ddbcdc56-e883-45e8-aeaa-60fbe2472312&utm_medium=email&utm_campaign=govuk-notifications&utm_content=immediate*.

### Schedule 3 para.8: coal and steel

*In the penultimate line, after "effect when the", add:*

**43-107** European Coal and Steel Community Treaty

### Schedule 4: professional rules

*In line 6, after "the “governing principles”", add:*

**43-109** in

### Section 9: exemption criteria

*Replace paragraph with:*

**43-111** The criteria for exemption under domestic law are set out in s.9. The wording is similar to, though not identical to, art.101(3). Unlike art.101(3), s.9 expressly applies to improvements in the production or distribution of goods *and* services. Section 9 provides as follows:

> “This section applies to any agreement which—
> (a) contributes to—
> (i) improving production or distribution, or
> (ii) promoting technical or economic progress,
> while allowing consumers a fair share of the resulting benefit; and
> (b) does not—
> (i) impose on the undertakings concerned restrictions which are not indispensable to the attainment of those objectives; or
> (ii) afford the undertakings concerned the possibility of eliminating competition in respect of a substantial part of the products in question.”

In applying s.9(1) the CMA will have regard to the European Commission’s Guidelines on the Application of art.101(3) TFEU.[284] In *Achilles Information Ltd v Network Rail Infrastructure Ltd* a scheme requiring undertakings seeking access to Network Rail’s railway infrastructure to use exclusively a supplier of supplier assurance services specified by it did not satisfy the conditions for exemption under s.9, as any claimed safety benefits of the scheme were not linked to the sole-supplier requirement (but would be attained in any effective and efficient regime of supplier assurance) and any economic benefits to Network Rail (in the form of lower administrative costs) of having a sole supplier were limited, such that the agreement did not have benefits for the purposes of s.9(a).[284a]

[284] See the CMA's Guideline *Agreements and Concerted Practices*, OFT 401 para.5.5.

[284a] *Achilles Information Ltd v Network Rail Infrastructure Ltd* [2019] C.A.T. 20 at [260]–[275]. The Tribunal also held that the two conditions in s.9(b)(i) and (ii) were not satisfied: at [277]–[279]. An appeal on this point was dismissed in *Network Rail Infrastructure Ltd v Achilles Information Ltd* [2020] EWCA Civ 323 at [119]–[124].

## Sections 6–8: block exemption

*In line 4, after "s.10 on "parallel exemptions"", add:*

(or, from IP completion day, "retained exemptions"[284b]), **43-113**

[284b] See below, para.43-114.

## Section 10: parallel exemption

*Replace paragraph with:*

Section 10 provides for "parallel exemption". This is a device whereby an agreement that benefits from an EU individual or block exemption, or which would so benefit if the agreement were to affect trade between Member States, automatically is also exempted from the Ch.I prohibition. The same benefits are available for exemptions obtained under the EEA Agreement.[288] A controversial aspect of s.10 is that it states that the CMA has power, in certain circumstances, to impose conditions or obligations subject to which a parallel exemption is to take effect, to vary it in other ways, or even cancel it.[289] However, art.3(2) of Regulation 1/2003 provides that it would be unlawful, as a matter of EU law, for the CMA to impose stricter terms on an agreement that is permitted under art.101.[290] Following the United Kingdom's withdrawal from the EU, from IP completion day (11.00pm on December 31, 2020) "parallel exemptions" will be referred to as "retained exemptions" and an EU block exemption regulation will be referred to as a "retained block exemption regulation".[290a] The Secretary of State will have a power to amend a retained block exemption regulation and the CMA may recommend the Secretary of State to do so.[290b] The Competition (Amendment etc.) (EU Exit) Regulations 2019 make a number of amendments to the retained block exemption regulations, from IP completion day.[290c] **43-114**

[288] s.10(11).

[289] s.10(5)–(8).

[290] See above, para.43-067; see also Whish and Bailey, *Competition Law*, 9th edn (2018), pp.75–79.

[290a] Competition Act 1998 s.10 as amended by the Competition (Amendment etc.) (EU Exit) Regulations 2019 (SI 2019/93) reg.3. The following EU block exemption regulations will continue to have effect in domestic law as retained exemptions until their expiry date, under s.10(11), as inserted by those Regulations:

(a) Council Regulation (EC) 169/2009 applying rules of competition to transport by rail, road and inland waterway;
(b) Commission Regulation (EC) 906/2009 on the application of Article 81(3) of the Treaty to certain categories of agreements, decisions and concerted practices between liner shipping companies (consortia);
(c) Commission Regulation (EU) 330/2010 on the application of Article 101(3) of the Treaty on the Functioning of the European Union to categories of vertical agreements and concerted practices;
(d) Commission Regulation (EU) 461/2010 on the application of Article 101(3) of the Treaty on the Functioning of the European Union to categories of vertical agreements and concerted practices in the motor vehicle sector;
(e) Commission Regulation (EU) 1217/2010 on the application of Article 101(3) of the Treaty on the Functioning of the European Union to certain categories of research and development agreements;
(f) Commission Regulation (EU) 1218/2010 on the application of Article 101(3) of the Treaty on the Functioning of the European Union to certain categories of specialisation agreements;

(g) Commission Regulation (EU) 316/2014 on the application of Article 101(3) of the Treaty on the Functioning of the European Union to categories of technology transfer agreements.

290b Competition Act 1998 s.10A, as inserted by the Competition (Amendment etc.) (EU Exit) Regulations 2019 (SI 2019/93) reg.4.

290c SI 2019/93 reg.63 and Sch.3 paras 3 (transport by rail, road and inland waterway), 4 (liner shipping consortia), 5 (vertical agreements), 6 (motor vehicle distribution), 7 (research and development agreements), 8 (specialisation agreements) and 9 (technology transfer agreements).

## (c) The Ch.II Prohibition: Abuse of a Dominant Position

### Format of the Ch.II prohibition

*To the end of paragraph, add:*

43-117 An agreement that infringes the Ch.I prohibition may also infringe the Ch.II prohibition if entered into by a dominant undertaking. In *Achilles Information Ltd v Network Rail Infrastructure Ltd* a requirement by Network Rail that undertakings seeking access to its railway network infrastructure use only a provider of supplier assurance services nominated by it was found by the Competition Appeal Tribunal to infringe the Ch.I prohibition[292a] and (on the assumption that Network Rail was dominant) prima facie also infringed the Ch.II prohibition as it had a significant foreclosure effect on the supply of supplier assurance services in the Great Britain railway sector and the sole supplier requirement was not objectively justified.[292b]

292a See above, paras 43-085—43-088.

292b *Achilles Information Ltd v Network Rail Infrastructure Ltd* [2019] C.A.T. 20 at [292]–[314]; appeal dismissed on this point in *Network Rail Infrastructure Ltd v Achilles Information Ltd* [2020] EWCA Civ 323 at [127]–[151].

### Abuse of a dominant position

*To the end of paragraph, after "the Ch.II prohibition.", add new footnote 299a:*

43-122 299a On the duty of UK courts, tribunals and competition authorities to have regard to the jurisprudence of the EU courts and the European Commission's decisions in applying the Ch.II prohibition, see below, paras 43-140—43-142 (before IP completion day) and 43-143—43-143B (after IP completion day).

## (d) Market Investigations

### Determination of a reference

*To the end of paragraph, add:*

43-129 The CMA also has the power to require the amendment of existing agreements or to restrict a party's ability to enter into new agreements, where it considers that this is necessary to remedy the adverse effect on competition identified by it. In June 2019, following a market investigation into the supply of investment consultancy and fiduciary management services, the CMA adopted an Order that, in some circumstances, prevented pension scheme trustees from entering into contracts for the supply of such services or increasing the assets under management by an existing supplier unless they have first carried out a competitive tendering exercise.[311a]

311a Investment Consultancy and Fiduciary Management Market Investigation Order 2019.

## (e) Investigation and Enforcement

### Power to investigate

*To the end of paragraph, add:*

43-131 As a result of the United Kingdom's withdrawal from the EU, the CMA will, from IP completion day, no longer have the power to investigate suspected infringements of arts 101 and 102 and it must not continue any investigation that it was conducting under these provisions immediately before this day.[316a]

[316a] See above, para.43-072.

### Company director disqualification

*Replace paragraph with:*

The Company Directors Disqualification Act 1986 provides for the possibility of company directors being disqualified from office for a period of up to 15 years where they knew, or ought to have known, that their company has transgressed EU or UK competition law.[338] The CMA has published guidance on the situations in which it will apply to court for a disqualification order.[339] In *Competition and Markets Authority v Martin*[339a] a former director of an estate agent was disqualified for seven years for being aware of his employees' participation in a price-fixing cartel and failing to take steps to prevent or end his company's involvement in the cartel. A disqualified director may receive permission from the court to continue acting as a director of a specific company where there is a need for him to continue acting as a director of that company and the public will remain protected against a repetition of the director's misconduct.[339b] **43-136**

[338] Company Directors Disqualification Act 1986 ss.9A–9E (inserted by Enterprise Act 2002 s.204). With effect from IP completion day (see above, paras 43-001A—43-001D), a company's infringement of arts 101 and/or 102 TFEU will cease to be grounds for a director's disqualification: Competition (Amendment etc.) (EU Exit) Regulations 2019 (SI 2019/93) reg.60 and Sch.1 para.1.

[339] CMA, *Guidance on Competition Disqualification Orders* (CMA102).

[339a] [2020] EWHC 1751 (Ch).

[339b] Company Directors Disqualification Act 1986 s.17. See *Stamatis v Competition and Markets Authority* [2019] EWHC 3318 (Ch).

### Third party actions

*To the end of paragraph, add:*

In *BritNed v ABB* the Court of Appeal confirmed that the correct and only measure for damages for an infringement of UK or EU competition law is compensatory, to reflect the claimant's losses caused by the infringement; there is no basis for either punitive damages or a restitutionary remedy; thus, in a claim for losses caused by a cartel, the claimant may recover the difference between the (cartelised) price paid and the price that would have been charged absent the cartel.[341a] **43-137**

[341a] *BritNed Development Ltd v ABB AB and ABB Ltd* [2019] EWCA Civ 1840.

## (f) The Competition and Markets Authority

### The Competition and Markets Authority

*In line 5, after "Office of Fair", replace "trading" with:*

Trading **43-138**

## (g) The Competition Appeal Tribunal

### The Competition Appeal Tribunal

*Replace paragraph with:*

The Competition Appeal Tribunal was created by the Enterprise Act, is headed **43-139** by a President, and is seised of appeals from decisions of the CMA and the sectoral regulators under the Competition Act; claims for damages following decisions finding an infringement of either the UK or EU competition law provisions; and applications for judicial review of decisions of the CMA and the Secretary of State in market investigation references. The Competition Appeal Tribunal Rules 2015[343] set out the procedure to be followed in appeals to the Tribunal and apply from October 1, 2015. Appeals may be made by the subjects of such decisions[344] and by third parties.[345] Appeals on points of law may be made with leave from the Competition Appeal Tribunal to the Court of Appeal.[346] It is also now possible for the Competition Appeal Tribunal to hear so-called "standalone" actions for an injunction and/or damages as a result of changes introduced with effect from October 1, 2015; that is to say it can now hear cases where there has been no prior decision by a competition authority in the UK or the EU.

[343] SI 2015/1648.

[344] s.46.

[345] s.47.

[346] s.49.

## (h) Miscellaneous

### Section 60(1)

*In line 17, after "protection of the", replace "single" with:*

43-141 internal

### Section 60 and Brexit

*Replace paragraph with:*

43-143 Section 60 will be repealed from IP completion day (11.00pm on December 31, 2020)[353] and replaced by a new s.60A.[354] Section 60A provides as follows:

> **"Certain principles etc to be considered or applied from exit day**
>
> **60A**—(1) This section applies when one of the following persons determines a question arising under this Part in relation to competition within the United Kingdom—
>
> (a) a court or tribunal;
> (b) the CMA;
> (c) a person acting on behalf of the CMA in connection with a matter arising under this Part.
>
> (2) The person must act (so far as is compatible with the provisions of this Part) with a view to securing that there is no inconsistency between—
>
> (a) the principles that it applies, and the decision that it reaches, in determining the question, and
> (b) the principles laid down by the Treaty on the Functioning of the European Union and the European Court before exit day, and any relevant decision made by that Court before exit day, so far as applicable immediately before exit day in determining any corresponding question arising in EU law,
>
> subject to subsections (4) to (7).
>
> (3) The person must, in addition, have regard to any relevant decision or statement of the European Commission made before exit day and not withdrawn."

[353] Competition (Amendment etc.) (EU Exit) Regulations 2019 (SI 2019/93) reg.22.

[354] Competition (Amendment etc.) (EU Exit) Regulations 2019 (SI 2019/93) reg.23.

*After the first paragraph, add new paragraphs:*

The intention behind s.60A is that, in applying the provisions of the Competition Act, in particular the Ch.I and II prohibitions, the courts, the Competition Appeal Tribunal, the CMA and sector regulators with power to apply these prohibitions should apply them in a manner that is consistent with the treatment of corresponding provision of arts 101 and 102 before exit day (i.e. December 31, 2020[355]) in accordance with the EU court's jurisprudence and the European Commission's decisional practice and guidance as at that date. They will not be obliged to follow EU court judgments or Commission decisions or guidance made on or after that date. However, in practice, it is expected that, whilst not bound to do so, courts, tribunals and the CMA and other regulatory authorities will have regard to judgments of the EU courts and Commission decisions and guidance, if relevant to any matter before them.[356] A "decision of the European Court or the European Commission" includes a decision on the interpretation of a provision of EU law and on the civil liability of an undertaking for harm caused by its infringement of EU law.[357] **43-143A**

355 It is expected that the definition of "exit day" will be amended to reflect the provisions of the Withdrawal Agreement 2020.

356 Cf. European Union (Withdrawal) Act 2018 s.6(1) and (2), in relation to the interpretation of retained EU law.

357 Competition Act 1998 s.60A(9).

The duty in s.60A(2) is subject to a number of exceptions. First, it does not apply to any principle of EU law and any relevant decision of the EU courts made before exit day if the principle or decision is excluded from United Kingdom law on or after exit day, other than if a principle or decision is excluded only by virtue of an exclusion or revocation in the Competition (Amendment etc.) (EU Exit) Regulations 2019.[358] Secondly, principles of EU law are to be taken in account as they had effect in EU law immediately before exit day, without regard to the effect of principles laid down and decisions made by the EU courts on or after exit day.[359] Thirdly, and importantly, it does not apply where the court, tribunal or CMA or other regulatory authority considers it appropriate not to do so in the light of one or more of the following: **43-143B**

- (a) differences between the Ch.I and II prohibitions and arts 101 and 102 immediately before exit day;
- (b) differences between markets in the United Kingdom and markets in the European Union;
- (c) developments in forms of economic activity since the time when the principle of EU law or the EU court or European Commission was laid down or made;
- (d) generally accepted principles of competition analysis or the generally accepted application of such principles;
- (e) a principle laid down, or decision made, by the EU Court on or after exit day; and
- (f) the particular circumstances under consideration.[360]

There is, therefore, considerable scope for the United Kingdom courts, the Competition Appeal Tribunal and the CMA and sector regulators to disregard principles of EU law applicable to arts 101 and 102 when applying the Ch.I and II prohibitions. This could, over time, lead to considerable divergence between United Kingdom and EU competition law, although where principles of EU competition law itself develop over time, they may (as permitted by s.60A(7)(e)) decide to follow the later, post-exit day jurisprudence of the EU courts.

358 Competition Act 1998 s.60A(4) and (5).

359 Competition Act 1998 s.60A(8).

360 Competition Act 1998 s.60A(7).

CHAPTER 44

# SALE OF GOODS

## 1. In General

## (a) Introduction

### First implementation of 1999 Directive: amendment of existing legislation

*Replace footnote 37 with:*

44-007 [37] A new Directive of 2019 (Directive (EU) 2019/771) governing certain aspects of the law governing consumer contracts for the sale of goods (and repealing the Consumer Sales Directive 1999) is not due to be implemented until July 1, 2021, i.e. after IP completion day, as to which see Vol.I, paras 1-014 et seq. See the discussion of the "old law" above, paras 38-438—38-464.

### The Consumer Rights Act 2015

*Replace footnote 45 with:*

44-009 [45] 2011 Directive art.6(5), above para.38-500, 2015 Act ss.11(4)–(6), 12 (goods contracts); above para.38-549; s.36(3)–(4) and 37 (digital content contracts); above para.38-572, ss.50(3)–(4) (services contracts). The 2011 Directive is subject to considerable amendment by Directive (EU) 2019/2161. However, as the 2019 Directive must be implemented by Member States on November 28, 2021 (i.e. after IP completion day) the UK is not required to implement these changes unless it agrees to do so under an agreement with the EU as to their future relationship: see Vol.I, paras 1-014 et seq.

### Vienna Convention of 1980

*Replace footnote 78 with:*

[78] See COM(2011) 635 (final) of 11.10.2011. Following a positive opinion from the Legal Affairs (JURI) Committee (Memo/13/792) on February 26, 2014 the proposal received strong backing from the European Parliament (Memo 14/137). However, on December 16, 2014 the EU Commission presented its Work Programme for 2015 to the European Parliament and the existing proposal for a Common European Sales Law was listed as item 60 in the Annex of withdrawn proposals (Com (2014) 910 final). The reason given for the withdrawal was: "Modify proposal in order to fully unleash the potential of e-commerce in the Digital Single Market". In its Digital Single Market Strategy published on May 6, 2015 (Com (2015) 192 final) the Commission referred to the need to modernise and simplify consumer rules for online and digital purchases, but the Digital Single Market agenda also covers a wide range of other issues and the likely substance and form of any new proposal in relation to sales remains very unclear. In December 2015, the Commission proposed a directive on contracts for online and other distance sales of goods (the Online Sale of Goods Directive COM(2015) 635 final). This would partly replace the existing Consumer Sales Directive with regard to distance sales (both online and offline). The proposed Online Sale of Goods Directive is part of the Digital Single Market Strategy and comes alongside several other proposed legal instruments, notably in connection with digital content supply and the portability of digital content. On May 25, 2016 the Commission published an e-commerce package (COM(2016) 320 final) aimed at three particular aspects of ecommerce: unjustified geo-blocking, transparency of parcel delivery prices and enforcement of consumer rights. On October 31, 2017, the Commission published an amended proposal (COM(2017) 637) which would repeal the Consumer Sales Directive 1999 and create a set of rules common to all consumer sales, both online and offline and including face-to-face sales. Directive 2019/770 on aspects concerning contracts for the supply of digital content and digital services and Directive 2019/771 on aspects concerning contracts for the sale of goods were published in the official journal on May 22, 2019 and must be transposed into national law by July 1, 2021 with entry into force on January 1, 2022. As these Directives must be implemented after IP completion day the UK is not required to implement them unless it agrees to do so under an agreement with the EU as to their future relationship: see Vol.I, paras 1-014 et seq. and above, paras 38-024 et seq. **44-014**

## 2. Formation of the Contract

## (a) Contract of Sale

### Sale and agreement to sell

*Replace footnote 102 with:*

[102] It is not, of course, essential that any immediate right to possession should be passed by the contract: see *Watts v Seymour* [1967] 2 Q.B. 647. But the title passed must be absolute and not merely possessory: see *Rowland v Divall* [1923] 2 K.B. 500; and the transfer of property must be the essence of the contract: see *PST Energy 7 Shipping LLC v OW Bunker Malta Ltd (The Res Cogitans)* [2016] UKSC 23. The Supreme Court, upholding the decision of the Court of Appeal ([2015] EWCA Civ 1058; see L. Shmilovits [2016] L.M.C.L.Q. 20 and A. Tettenborn [2016] L.M.C.L.Q. 24 and, in relation to the decision of the Supreme Court, L. Gullifer [2017] L.Q.R 244 and D. Saidov [2019] J.B.L. 1), held that a contract for the supply of fuel bunkers, which contained a retention of title clause and permitted the purchasing vessel owners to consume the bunkers during the credit period, was not a contract for the sale of goods within the meaning of s.2(1). See below, para.44-174. **44-020**

## (b) Capacity of Parties

### Capacity of parties

*Replace footnote 168 with:*

[168] But in *Roberts v Gray* [1913] 1 K.B. 520 a minor was held liable on an executory contract for education. cf. also Treitel, *The Law of Contract*, 15th edn (2020), para.12-004; Goff and Jones, *The Law of Unjust Enrichment*, 9th edn (2016), para.24-018 (liability is contractual). **44-033**

## 3. TERMS OF THE CONTRACT

### (a) Conditions, Warranties, Misrepresentations and Puffs

#### Unfair commercial practices

*Replace footnote 268 with:*

44-062 [268] See above, paras 38-172 et seq. On IP completion day (on which see generally Vol.I, paras 1-014 et seq.), the 2008 Regulations will be subject to minor amendment: Consumer Protection (Amendment etc.) (EU Exit) Regulations 2018 (SI 2018/1326) reg.6.

### (b) Implied Terms

#### *(ii) Implied Term as to Correspondence with Description*

#### Sale by sample and description

*Replace footnote 410 with:*

44-092 [410] e.g. *Toepfer v Continental Grain Co* [1974] 1 Lloyd's Rep. 11; *Gill & Duffus SA v Berger & Co Inc* [1984] A.C. 382, 393–394; cf. *NV Bunge v Cie Naga d'Importation et d'Exportation SA (The Bow Cedar)* [1980] 2 Lloyd's Rep. 601; *Cauwenberghe & Fils SA v Tropical Product Sales SA* [1986] 1 Lloyd's Rep. 535; *Septo Trading Inc v Tintrade Ltd* [2020] EWHC 1795 (Comm).

#### *(iii) Implied Terms about Quality and Fitness for Purpose*

#### Guidelines

*Replace footnote 442 with:*

44-100 [442] This is supported by *Jewson Ltd v Boyhan* [2003] EWCA Civ 1030, [2004] 1 Lloyd's Rep. 505 (boilers yielding low home energy ratings and reducing attractiveness of newly converted flats: satisfactory—see at [67] et seq.), cited in *Balmoral Group Ltd v Borealis (UK) Ltd* [2006] EWHC 1900 (Comm), [2006] 2 Lloyd's Rep. 629 at [140]. Compare *Bajaj Healthcare Ltd v Fine Organics Ltd* [2019] EWHC 2316 (Ch), where there was an express term that goods had to be of similar quality to earlier instalments, the presence of a contaminant meant that they were not of satisfactory quality even though the contaminant would not have been detected by the tests specified in the contract.

#### Reasonably fit for purpose

*Replace footnote 485 with:*

44-109 [485] *Slater v Finning Ltd* [1997] A.C. 473 (engine for boat). See also *Griffiths v Peter Conway Ltd* [1939] 1 All E.R. 685 (skin sensitive to tweed): *Ingham v Emes* [1955] 2 Q.B. 366 (hair dye); *Crozier v A & P Canada Inc* (2010) 329 D.L.R. (4th) 565 (peanut butter: claimant had long history of Crohn's disease). cf. *BSS Group Plc v Makers (UK) Ltd* [2011] EWCA Civ 809 (the fact that the plumbing equipment supplied was not compatible was not due to some unknown idiosyncrasy of the buyer). In *DBE Energy Ltd v Biogas Products Ltd* [2020] EWHC 1232 (TCC) a plant was not fit for purpose where the seller had also been found to be responsible for the design of the facility.

#### *(v) Pre-contractual Information to Consumers*

#### Pre-contractual information to be included as term of consumer contract

*Replace footnote 512 with:*

44-116 [512] 2011/83/EU of October 15, 2011. The 2011 Directive is subject to considerable amendment by Directive (EU) 2019/2161 of the European Parliament and of the Council of 27 November 2019 as regards the better enforcement and modernisation of Union consumer protection rules [2019] O.J. L328/7 art.4, including requiring new definitions of "sales contract" and "service contract", additional specific information requirements for contracts concluded on online marketplaces and making more elaborate provision on penalties. However, as the 2019 Directive must be implemented by Member States on November 28, 2021 (i.e. after IP completion day) the UK is not required to implement these changes unless it agrees to do so under an agreement with the EU as to their future relationship: see Vol.I, paras 1-014 et seq.

## (c) Stipulations as to Time

### Late delivery in consumer contracts for goods

*Replace footnote 606 with:*

[606] Directive 2011/83/EU of October 25, 2011. The 2011 Directive is subject to considerable amendment by Directive (EU) 2019/2161 of the European Parliament and of the Council of 27 November 2019. However, as the 2019 Directive must be implemented by Member States on November 28, 2021 (i.e. after IP completion day) the UK is not required to implement these changes unless it agrees to do so under an agreement with the EU as to their future relationship: see Vol.I, paras 1-014 et seq. **44-129**

4. EFFECTS OF THE CONTRACT

## (a) Transfer of Property as between Seller and Buyer

### Undivided shares in goods forming part of a bulk

*Replace footnote 695 with:*

[695] See also the other reasons set out in the Report of the English and Scottish Law Commission *Sale of Goods Forming Part of a Bulk* (Law Com. No.215 and Scot. Law Com. No.145) (1993). See generally M. Bridge [2019] L.M.C.L.Q. 57. **44-160**

*Replace footnote 730 with:*

### "Romalpa" clauses: retention of title[730]

[730] See Parris, *Retention of Title on Sale of Goods* (1982); Parris, *Effective Reservation of Title Clauses* (1986); Dickson, *Retention of Title Clauses* (1987); McCormack, *Reservation of Title*, 2nd edn (1995); Davies, *Effective Retention of Title* (1991); Wheeler, *Retention of Title Clauses: Impact and Implications* (1991); *Benjamin's Sale of Goods*, 10th edn (2017), paras 5-143 et seq.; Palmer and McKendrick, *Interests in Goods*, 2nd edn (1998), Ch.28. The periodical literature is voluminous. For the problems involved regarding conflict of laws see *Benjamin's Sale of Goods*, 10th edn (2017), at para.26-151. **44-173**

### Right to consume before property has passed

*Replace footnote 744 with:*

[744] [2016] UKSC 23, [2016] 2 W.L.R. 1193, [2016] 1 Lloyd's Rep. 589. For a critical review of this decision see L. Gullifer [2017] L.Q.R 244. The Court of Appeal in *Wood v TUI Travel Plc (t/a First Choice)* [2017] EWCA Civ 11, [2017] 1 Lloyd's Rep 322 held that *PST Energy 7 Shipping LLC* was not authority for the proposition that there was no intention that property in any food or drink served by a hotel to guests would pass to them. The conclusion in *PST Energy 7 Shipping LLC* depended upon the relationship between a retention of title clause and the liberty to consume fuel in which property had not already passed and was accordingly distinguishable. See also *Gregor Fisken v Carl* [2020] EWHC 1385 (Comm), rejecting an argument based on *PST Energy* and holding that the contract in question was a contract for the sale of goods. **44-174**

## (b) When the Risk Passes

### Passing of the risk

*Replace footnote 829 with:*

[829] This section does not apply to consumer contracts for the sale of goods which fall within Ch.2 of Pt 1 of the Consumer Rights Act 2015. In consumer contracts for the sale of goods the 2015 Act provides special rules for the passing of risk, see above para.38-527. Special rules concerning the passing of risk **44-189**

were required by the Consumer Rights Directive 2011. These rules were initially implemented in reg.43 of the Consumer Contracts (Information, Cancellation and Additional Charges) Regulations 2013. These rules are now repeated in the Consumer Rights Act 2015. See above, para.38-527. The 2011 Directive is subject to considerable amendment by Directive (EU) 2019/2161 of the European Parliament and of the Council of 27 November 2019. However, as the 2019 Directive must be implemented by Member States on November 28, 2021 (i.e. after IP completion day) the UK is not required to implement these changes unless it agrees to do so under an agreement with the EU as to their future relationship: see Vol.I, paras 1-014 et seq.

## 5. PERFORMANCE OF THE CONTRACT

## (b) Rules Governing Delivery

### *(iv) Expenses in Connection with Delivery*

#### Expenses of delivery

*Replace footnote 1062 with:*

**44-256** [1062] cf. *Neill v Whitworth* (1866) L.R. 1 CP 684; *Playford v Mercer* (1870) 22 L.T. 41; *Acme Wood Flooring Co v Sutherland Innes Co* (1904) 9 Com. Cas. 170; *White v Williams* [1912] A.C. 814; *Gregor Fisken Ltd v Carl* [2020] EWHC 1385 (Comm).

## 6. REMEDIES OF THE SELLER

## (a) Rights of Unpaid Seller against the Goods

### *(ii) Stoppage in Transit*

#### Other provisions as to transit

*Replace footnote 1451 with:*

**44-334** [1451] *Berndtson v Strang* (1868) L.R. 3 Ch. App. 588. In a charter by demise (a type of "lease" of a ship: see *Scrutton on Charterparties and Bills of Lading*, 24th edn (2019), para.1.013 et seq.) the charterer is in possession of the ship and the master is his employee.

## (c) Action for Damages

#### An available market

*Replace footnote 1679 with:*

**44-368** [1679] *Marshall Co v Nicoll Son*, 1919 S.C. 244, 253; affirmed 1919 S.C.(H.L.) 129; *Thompson Ltd v Robinson (Gunmakers) Ltd* [1955] Ch. 177, 187. There is no "available market" for a unique article like a second-hand car: *Lazenby Garages Ltd v Wright* [1976] 1 W.L.R. 459, CA; nor is such a market likely in a "command economy": *Derby Resources AG v Blue Corinth Marine Co Ltd (The Athenian Harmony)* [1998] 2 Lloyd's Rep. 410, 416. In *Air Studios (Lyndhurst) Ltd v Lombard North Central Plc* [2012] EWHC 3162 (QB), [2013] 1 Lloyd's Rep. 63, a case of non-delivery by a seller, it was said that there may be a market for used goods even if the precise model or brand sold was not available: "the availability of equivalent second-hand goods capable of performing the same functions in much the same way would constitute an available market for 'the goods in question'. A buyer of such equivalent goods would be in the same financial position as if the contract had been performed" (at [93]). In *Hughes v Pendragon Sabre Ltd (t/a Porsche Centre Bolton)* [2016] EWCA Civ 18 a rare new limited edition Porsche was sufficiently specialised for there to be insufficient activity to evidence a market. In *Septo Trading Inc v Tintrade Ltd* [2020] EWHC 1795 (Comm), although no evidence had been adduced of actual sales, there was held to be an available market in off-spec oil given that the market for fuel oil was large and diverse.

## 7. REMEDIES OF THE BUYER

### (c) Damages for Defective Quality

#### (i) Diminution in Value

**Breach of warranty**

*Replace footnote 1966 with:*

1966 This subsection is in terms of *Hadley v Baxendale* (1854) 9 Exch. 341 (see Vol.I, para.26-119); *H Parsons (Livestock) Ltd v Uttley Ingham Co Ltd* [1978] Q.B. 791, 800, 807. Consequential damages can be claimed under s.53(2) if they arise directly and naturally from the breach: *Saipol SA v Inerco Trade SA* [2014] EWHC 2211 (Comm). In *MacAlpine Grant ILCO Ltd v AFR Refridgeration Ltd* [2020] EWHC 106 (QB) the natural consequences of breach when a refrigeration unit failed included the damage to expensive drugs which were spoiled as a result. In addition, special damages may be claimed under s.54 (see below, para.44-416—44-435). **44-411**

**Buyer performing sub-contract despite seller's breach**

*Replace paragraph with:*

It was held by the Court of Appeal in *Slater v Hoyle and Smith Ltd*[1995] that where **44-415** the seller delivers defective goods, but the buyer is nevertheless able to perform a sub-contract by delivering the goods to his sub-buyer, the buyer's damages against the seller should not be reduced by taking this into account; the buyer is entitled to rely on the normal measure of damages under s.53(3) viz the difference between (a) the market price, at the time and place of delivery, of goods up to the contractual quality; and (b) the market price, at the time and place of delivery, of the goods actually delivered.[1996] However, the authority of *Slater v Hoyle and Smith Ltd* has been severely undermined by the decision of the Court of Appeal in *Bence Graphics International Ltd v Fasson UK Ltd*.[1997] The seller knew that the buyer would sell on to others (after manufacturing the goods into another product); the Court of Appeal held that the parties contemplated that the measure of damages for defects in the goods should be the extent of the buyer's liability (if any) to those others resulting from the defect. In *Bence's* case the decision in *Slater's* case was doubted, on the ground that s.53(3) laid down only a prima facie rule, which should not be applied if it would give the buyer "more than his true loss".[1998] The *Bence* case has been the subject of trenchant criticism on the grounds that remoteness is relevant only to claims for consequential loss, not to the difference in value between the goods delivered and the goods as they should have been; and that the effect of the sub-sale should be taken into account only when the buyer was legally obliged to supply the same specific goods under the sub-sale, in which case it is arguable that if the buyer received the full sub-sale price, it suffered no loss at all.[1999] Nonetheless, in *Euro-Asian Oil SA (formerly Euro-Asian Oil AG) v Credit Suisse AG*[2000] the Court of Appeal approved the trial judge's decision to limit the claimant's to the loss on the sub-sale, rather than the higher difference between the contract price and the market price at the date for delivery, even though the buyer could have fulfilled the sub-sale using other goods, on the ground that the parties contemplated a sub-sale. It is submitted that these cases should not be followed and that the buyers should have recovered the difference in value. First, remoteness is not relevant when the claim is simply for the difference in value between what was contracted for and what was delivered. The sub-sale is relevant only if the buyer was bound to deliver the same specific goods under the sub-sale. If the buyer was not so obliged, it might have fulfilled the sub-sale by purchasing and processing other goods, or have used other goods from stock and then have re-sold the contract goods at the current price; in either case the buyer should be entitled to the difference between the contract price and market price.[2001] The fact that they were able to pass on the defective goods without incurring liability again seems to be their own good fortune.[2002] Moreover, it can be argued that even when the sub-sale requires delivery of the same goods, the buyer should always be entitled to the difference between the contract price and the market price, by analogy to the decisions on failures to provide services which do not result in any further loss to the claimant.[2003] The *Bence* case seems to be a further example of the court concentrating on the end-result rather than the buyer's performance interest.[2004] It is true that in cases in which the buyer has reached a reasonable settlement with the sub-buyer, who has retained the goods, the amount paid under the settlement has been treated as the most that the buyer can recover, even if the settlement was at an undervalue, but the point seems to have been assumed rather than argued.[2005]

[1995] [1920] 2 K.B. 11.

[1996] The buyers were not obliged to deliver to the sub-buyer the goods which they bought from the original seller, and in fact some of the goods which they delivered to the sub-buyer came from a different source. It is submitted that the decision in this case is to be preferred to the reasoning of the Privy Council in the analogous case of *Wertheim v Chicoutimi Pulp Co* [1918] A.C. 301 (late delivery), which is criticised see above, para.44-408 n.1947, and in Benjamin at paras 17-039, 17-057—17-058. However, in *Bence Graphics International Ltd v Fasson UK Ltd* [1998] Q.B. 87 at 103–105, Auld L.J. approved the decision in *Wertheim's* case (see below (this paragraph) and see above, paras26-043, 26-166 and 26-170).

[1997] [1998] Q.B. 87. See *Louis Dreyfus Trading Ltd v Reliance Trading Ltd* [2004] EWHC 525 (Comm), [2004] 2 Lloyd's Rep. 243 (parties contemplated sale of the same goods to the sub-buyer under a specific contract); *Choil Trading SA v Sahara Energy Resources Ltd* [2010] EWHC 374 (Comm) at [124]–[139].

[1998] [1998] Q.B. 87 at 102 (see above, para.44-413). The *Bence Graphics* case was distinguished in *Bear Stearns Bank Plc v Forum Global Equity Ltd* [2007] EWHC 1576 (Comm) (a case involving shares rather than goods) on the grounds that in the *Bear Stearns* case the parties had not contemplated that the buyers would resell precisely the same shares (at [204]–[207]); and that it was a case of non-delivery rather than of delivery of defective goods (at [208]).

[1999] See Treitel (1997) 113 L.Q.R. 188 and Peel (ed.), *Treitel on The Law of Contract*, 15th edn (2020), para.20-051. See also *Benjamin's Sale of Goods*, 10th edn (2017), paras 17-057—17-082. Contrast *McGregor on Damages*, 20th edn (2017), paras 25-068—25-069.

[2000] [2018] EWCA Civ 1720, [2019] 1 Lloyd's Rep 444.

[2001] See above, para.26-043; and Peel (ed.), *Treitel on The Law of Contract*, 15th edn (2020), para.20-051.

[2002] See the powerful criticism of Treitel (1997) 113 L.Q.R. 188, and Peel (ed.), *Treitel on The Law of Contract*, 15th edn (2020), para.20-054. In *OMV Petrom SA v Glencore International AG* [2016] EWCA Civ 778, [2016] 2 Lloyd's Rep. 432 Christopher Clarke L.J. seemed to think that the *Bence Graphics* case could not stand with *Slater v Hoyle Smith Ltd*, but left the matter open (at [45]–[46]).

[2003] See above, para.26-043.

[2004] See above, paras 26–042—26–046.

[2005] *Biggin v Permanite* [1951] 2 K.B. 314; *Fluor v Shanghai Zhenhua Heavy Industry Co Ltd* [2018] EWHC 1 (TCC) at [465].

### (ii) Losses other than Diminution in Value

#### Physical injury to the buyer

*Replace footnote 2057 with:*

2057 *Grant v Australian Knitting Mills Ltd* [1936] A.C. 85. See also *Wren v Holt* [1903] 1 K.B. 610; *Geddling v Marsh* [1920] 1 K.B. 668; *Morelli v Fitch Gibbons* [1928] 2 K.B. 636; *Andrews v Hopkinson* [1957] 1 Q.B. 229; *Godley v Perry* [1960] 1 W.L.R. 9. (The damages may include the normal heads of damages in the assessment in tort for personal injuries or death: [1960] 1 W.L.R. 9 at 13.) Special rules apply to the award of interest on such damages: see Vol.I, para.26-281. Cf. *Busby v Berkshire Bed Co Ltd* [2018] EWHC 2976 (QB) where the unusual circumstances of the accident meant that personal injury as a result of a defective bed could not have been reasonably foreseen and could not have been in anyone's prior contemplation. **44-427**

## (d) Other Remedies of the Buyer

#### Specific performance

*Replace footnote 2134 with:*

2134 Details must be sought in standard works on equity: Fry, *Specific Performance of Contracts*, 6th edn, especially pp.36–41; McGhee (ed) *Snell's Equity*, 34th edn (2019), Ch.17; *Ashburner's Principles of Equity*, 2nd edn, pp.382–408. See also Vol.I, Ch.27. **44-440**

#### Specific or ascertained goods

*Replace footnote 2143 with:*

2143 See also *Re London Wine Co (Shippers)* [1986] P.C.C. 121 and *VTB Commodities Trading DAC v JSC Antipinsky Refinery* [2020] EWHC 72 (Comm). On the facts of *Re Wait* an order of specific performance would have given the buyer priority over the general creditors in the seller's bankruptcy. **44-441**

#### Discretion of the court

*Replace footnote 2156 with:*

2156 e.g. *Snell's Equity*, 34th edn (2019), paras 17-039, 17-045; Vol.I, paras 27-050, 27-053. **44-444**

#### Injunction

*Replace footnote 2164 with:*

2164 Sharpe, *Injunctions and Specific Performance*, 5th edn; Kerr, *Injunctions*, 6th edn, pp.409 et seq.; *Ashburner's Principles of Equity*, 2nd edn, pp.384–387; *Snell's Equity*, 34th edn (2019), Ch.18; Spry, *The Principles of Equitable Remedies*, 9th edn (2013), Chs 4 and 5; *Doherty v Allman* (1878) 3 App. Cas. 709, 719–721. See also Vol.I, paras 27-077 et seq. **44-445**

## 8. Consumer Protection Act 1987

*Replace footnote 2190 with:* **44-449**

2190 See Miller, *Product Liability and Safety Encyclopaedia* (1979–date), Div. V; Miller and Goldberg, *Product Liability* (2004); Stapleton, *Product Liability* (1994); Whittaker, *Liability for Products* (2005); *Benjamin's Sale of Goods*, 10th edn (2017), paras 14-227 et seq. The Act is subject to relatively minor amendments on IP completion day by the Product Safety and Metrology etc. (Amendment etc.) (EU Exit) Regulations 2019 (SI 2019/696) reg.6 and Sch.3, see Vol.I, paras 1-014 et seq.

## CHAPTER 45

# SURETYSHIP



## 1. IN GENERAL

### Guarantees and indemnities: the distinction itself

*Replace paragraph with:*

**45-008** The distinction between the two contracts is, in brief, that in a contract of guarantee the surety assumes a secondary liability to answer for the debtor who remains primarily liable; whereas in a contract of indemnity the surety assumes a primary liability, either alone or jointly with the principal debtor.[28] Whether a contract falls into one class or the other, and whether the normal incidents of a contract of that class are modified, are ordinary questions of construction.[29] In this respect, while the presence or absence of the language of "guarantee" in the document is not conclusive, outside the context of documents issued by banks,[30] the absence of language appropriate to provide for the creditor "the additional security of a demand bond" creates a strong presumption in favour of a merely secondary liability.[31] Moreover:

> "... with the parties free to agree whatever terms they choose, there is in this field of law a spectrum of contractual possibilities ranging from the classic contract of guarantee, properly so called, at the one end, where liability of the guarantor is exclusively secondary and will be discharged if, for example, there is any material variation to the underlying contract between principal and creditor, to the performance or demand bond (or demand guarantee)[32] at the other end, where liability in the giver of the bond may be triggered by mere demand and without proof of default by the principal (and indeed where it may be apparent that the principal is not in default)."[33]

However, as has been explained, the nature of the relationship between the creditor and the surety may differ from the nature of the relationship between the debtor and the surety. It is therefore possible that even where the relationship between the surety and the creditor is that of a contract of indemnity, the debtor may still be primarily liable as between himself and the surety.[34] Thus although a contract of indemnity cannot itself *be* a contract of suretyship, the party liable under such a contract may be a surety as against the debtor and it is common and convenient to speak of him as such, even though he has assumed a primary liability towards the creditor. On the other hand, it is of course perfectly possible to have a contract of indemnity in which there is no suretyship at all, because, for example, the party liable under the indemnity has not contracted at the request of another debtor. Thus a dealer who agrees by a "recourse agreement" to indemnify a finance company against any loss under a hire-purchase transaction is not a surety either against the creditor or against the debtor. And even where, as between two debtors, one is primarily liable and the other only secondarily liable, there is not necessarily a contract of suretyship. For instance, where a tenant assigns his interest under a lease and the assignee covenants to indemnify the assignor against liability for breach of covenants in the lease, the assignee is, as between himself and the assignor, primarily liable, but there is no contract of suretyship between them.[35] And similarly, where property is sold subject to a mortgage, the mortgagor is not surety for the purchaser.[36]

[28] This sentence was quoted by the Court of Appeal with apparent approval in *Marubeni Hong Kong and South China Ltd v The Mongolian Government* [2005] EWCA Civ 395, [2005] 1 W.L.R. 2497 at [20]. See also *Vossloh Aktiengesellschaft v Alpha Trains (UK) Ltd* [2010] EWHC 2443 (Ch), [2010] All E.R. (D) 86 (Oct) at [23]–[25]; *Slade v Abbhi* [2018] EWHC 2039 (Comm) at [92]–[94] affirmed sub nom. *Abbhi v Slade* [2019] EWCA Civ 2175, [2019] Costs L.R. 2039.

[29] *Moschi v Lep Air Services Ltd* [1973] A.C. 331; *Associated British Ports v Ferryways NV* [2009] EWCA Civ 189, [2009] 1 Lloyd's Rep. 595; *Multiplex Construction Europe Ltd v Dunne* [2017] EWHC 3073 (TCC), [2018] B.L.R. 36.

[30] See below, para.45-009 (performance guarantees).

[31] *Marubeni Hong Kong and South China Ltd v The Mongolian Government* [2005] EWCA Civ 395, [2005] 1 W.L.R. 2497 at [30].

[32] On which see below, para.45-009.

[33] *Vossloh Aktiengesellschaft v Alpha Trains (UK) Ltd* [2010] EWHC 2443 (Ch), [2010] All E.R. (D) 86 (Oct) at [34], per Sir William Blackburne. See also *Catalyst Business Finance Ltd v Very Tangy Television Ltd* [2018] EWHC 1669 (QB) at [30] ("hybrid document in which some of the obligations are primary and some secondary").

[34] But the "common form" provision stating that the guarantor is liable as a principal debtor does not convert every guarantee into an indemnity: *General Produce Co v United Bank Ltd* [1979] 2 Lloyd's Rep. 255.

[35] *Baynton v Morgan* (1888) 22 Q.B.D. 74 and see *Allied London Investments Ltd v Hambro Life Assurance Ltd* (1983) 269 E.G. 41; and *Selous Street Properties Ltd v Oronel Fabrics Ltd* (1984) 270 E.G. 643 and 743. On the effect of the Landlord and Tenant (Covenants) Act 1995 on tenant's covenants on assignment see below, paras 45-015—45-017.

[36] *Re Errington* [1894] 1 Q.B. 11.

## Performance guarantees

*Replace paragraph with:*

A number of cases have involved discussion of the nature of "performance guarantees" which are, in essence, exceptionally stringent contracts of indemnity.[38] They are contractual undertakings, normally granted by banks, to pay or repay, a specified sum in the event of any default in performance by the principal debtor of some other contract with a third party, the creditor. Sometimes the bank's liability arises on mere demand by the creditor, notwithstanding that it may appear on the evidence that the principal debtor is not in any way in default, or even that the creditor himself is in default under the principal contract.[39] Such guarantees are sometimes called "first demand guarantees"[40] or "demand bonds".[41] It has been held that performance guarantees of this nature are analogous to a bank's letter of credit, and that the bank's liability is of a primary nature which is unaffected by allegations that the creditor is in breach of the main contract between him and the principal debtor.[42] The question whether a particular instrument (such as a "refund guarantee") takes the form of an independent performance bond (or stand-by letter of credit) or a true "see to it" guarantee is one of construction of the instrument in its factual and contractual context having regard to its commercial purpose.[43] While there may be a number of indications in an instrument which argue in favour of it being a "true guarantee" or, conversely, an "on-demand bond", 45-009

> "... [w]here an instrument (i) relates to an underlying transaction between the parties in different jurisdictions, (ii) is issued by a bank, (iii) contains an undertaking to pay 'on demand' (with or without the words 'first' and/or 'written') and (iv) does not contain clauses excluding or limiting the defences available to a guarantor, it will almost always be construed as a demand guarantee."[44]

On the other hand, there is a "strong presumption" that a "guarantee" concluded other than by a bank is not a demand or independent performance bond,[45] although this presumption may be rebutted.[46] In the event of fraud the court may be able to intervene to protect the surety; but the court has refused to imply a term to the effect that the beneficiary of such a guarantee will give notice of a claim only if there is reasonable cause.[47] Clear evidence is needed that the beneficiary's demand is fraudulent to the knowledge of the bank if the bank is to be restrained from paying under such a guarantee or bond, but this does not mean that all possible explanations other than fraud must be totally ruled out. It means that fraud must be the "only realistic inference".[48]

[38] *Edward Owen Engineering Ltd v Barclays Bank International Ltd* [1978] Q.B. 159; *RD Harbottle (Mercantile) Ltd v National Westminster Bank Ltd* [1978] Q.B. 146; *Howe Richardson Scale Co Ltd v Polimex-Cekop* [1978] 1 Lloyd's Rep. 161; *Bolivinter Oil SA v Chase Manhattan Bank NA* [1984] 1 W.L.R. 392; *Attaleia Marine Co Ltd v Bimeh Iran (Iran Insurance Co) (The Zeus)* [1993] 2 Lloyd's Rep. 497. cf. *Trafalgar House Construction (Regions) Ltd v General Surety & Guarantee Co Ltd* [1996] 1 A.C. 199; *Frans Maas (UK) Ltd v Habib Bank AG Zurich* [2001] Lloyd's Rep. Bank 14; *Solo Industries UK Ltd v Canara Bank* [2001] EWCA Civ 1059, [2001] 1 W.L.R. 1800; *Banque Saudi Fransi v Lear*

*Siegler Services Inc* [2005] EWHC 2395, [2006] 1 Lloyd's Rep. 273; *Wuhan Guoyu Logistics Group Co Ltd v Emporiki Bank of Greece SA* [2012] EWCA Civ 1629, [2012] 2 C.L.C. 986.

39 See cases cited in previous note; cf. *General Surety & Guarantee Co Ltd v Francis Parker Ltd* (1977) 6 Build. L.R. 16. This does not mean, though, that a bank must always pay when asked: "a Bank is not obliged to accept without investigation a demand which is ambiguous, or potentially misleading": *Frans Maas (UK) Ltd v Habib Bank AG Zurich*, above, at [27].

40 See further on the nature and variety of such guarantees, *Benjamin's Sale of Goods*, 10th edn (2017), Ch.24 especially at paras 24-003—24-006, contrasting "orthodox guarantees" and "autonomous guarantees". *Benjamin's Sale of Goods*, paras 24-007—24-010 explains the various international uniform rules which may be incorporated into an "autonomous guarantee", notably the I.C.C. Uniform Rules on Demand Guarantees (URDG 458) whose revised version URDG 758 applies, subject to contrary intention, to any guarantee incorporating the URDG issued on or after July 1, 2010. For an example of the application of the URDG 458 see *Meritz Fire & Marine Insurance Co Ltd v Jan de Nul NV* [2011] EWCA Civ 827, [2011] 2 Lloyd's Rep. 379.

41 *Marubeni Hong Kong and South China Ltd v The Mongolian Government* [2005] EWCA Civ 395, [2005] 1 W.L.R. 2497 at [30].

42 See cases cited above, second note in the present paragraph. As to bankers' letters of credit, see above, paras 34-441 et seq.

43 *Gold Coast Ltd v Caja de Ahorros del Mediterraneo* [2002] 1 Lloyd's Rep. 617, 620; *Marubeni Hong Kong and South China Ltd v The Mongolian Government* [2005] EWCA Civ 395, [2005] 1 W.L.R. 2497 at [28].

44 *Paget's Law of Banking*, 11th edn (1996), quoted with approval by the Court of Appeal in *Caja de Ahorros v Gold Coast Ltd* [2002] 1 Lloyd's Rep. 617 at [16]; *Wuhan Guoyu Logistics Group Co Ltd v Emporiki Bank of Greece SA* [2012] EWCA Civ 1629, [2012] 2 C.L.C. 986 at [26]–[27]; *Caja de Ahorros v Gold Coast Ltd* [2001] EWCA Civ 1806, [2002] 1 Lloyd's Rep. 617 at [16]; *Caterpillar Motoren GmbH & Co KG v Mutual Benefits Assurance Co* [2015] EWHC 2304 (Comm), [2015] 2 Lloyd's Rep. 261 at [13]–[15], [19]–[22] and [25]–[27]; *Spliethoff's Bevrachtingskantoor BV v Bank of China Ltd* [2015] EWHC 999 (Comm), [2015] 2 Lloyd's Rep. 123 at [69]–[85]; *Autoridad del Canal de Panama v Sacyr SA* [2017] EWHC 2228 (Comm), [2017] 2 Lloyd's Rep. 351 at [81]–[103]; *Shanghai Shipyard Co Ltd v Reignwood International Investment (Group) Co Ltd* [2020] EWHC 803 (Comm) at [29]–[36] (appeal pending). But where a contract contains a clause as is mentioned in (iv) of "Paget's presumption" (quoted in the text) this may be explicable as inserted so as to put beyond doubt that the rule applicable to true guarantees does not apply: [2015] EWHC 2304 (Comm) at [21], referring to *Caja de Ahorros v Gold Coast Ltd del Mediterraneo* [2001] EWCA Civ 1806, [2002] 1 Lloyd's Rep. 617 at [25]. The passage quoted in the text appears in almost identical words in *Paget's Law of Banking*, 14th edn (2014), para.34.8.

45 *Marubeni Hong Kong and South China Ltd v The Mongolian Government* [2005] EWCA Civ 395, [2005] 1 W.L.R. 2497 at [30]; *IIG Capital LLC v Van Der Merwe* [2008] EWCA Civ 542, [2008] 2 Lloyd's Rep. 187 at [8]; cf. *Caterpillar Motoren GmbH & Co KG v Mutual Benefits Assurance Co* [2015] EWHC 2304 (Comm), [2015] 2 Lloyd's Rep. 261 at [20] (no material distinction between bank and other financial institution, such as an insurance company engaged in the business of providing bonds to its customers).

46 *IIG Capital LLC v Van Der Merwe* [2008] EWCA Civ 542, [2008] EWCA Civ 542 at [33], per Waller L.J. (with whom Lawrence Collins and Rimer L.JJ. agreed). cf. *Carey Value Added SL v Grupo Urvasco SA* [2010] EWHC 1905 (Comm), [2011] 2 All E.R. (Comm) 140 at [38]–[43]; *Vossloh Aktiengesellschaft v Alpha Trains (UK) Ltd* [2010] EWHC 2443 (Ch), [2010] All E.R. (D) 86 (Oct) at [53]; *North Shore Ventures Ltd v Anstead Holdings Inc* [2011] EWCA Civ 230, [2011] 2 Lloyd's Rep. 45 at [46]–[47]; *Ultrabulk A/S v Jagatramka* [2017] EWHC 2792 (Comm), [2018] 1 Lloyd's Rep. 384 at [16]; *Shanghai Shipyard Co Ltd v Reignwood International Investment (Group) Co Ltd* [2020] EWHC 803 (Comm) at [31]–[36] (appeal pending). Where the principal contract is in the nature of a financing transaction (even though in the form of a sale and demise charter with a "deed of guarantee" as part of it), any presumption generally applicable to non-banking cases will more readily give way to language to the contrary: *Bitumen Invest AS v Richmond Mercantile Ltd FZC* [2016] EWHC 2957 (Comm), [2017] 1 Lloyd's Rep. 219 at [17] (where the fact that the trigger for payment was the issue of a demand for an amount certified by the beneficiary of the guarantee provided the key feature in finding it to be an "on demand guarantee" ([2016] EWHC 2957 (Comm) esp. at [21]–[26])). Where the instrument is made outside the banking context (as in the case of an undertaking by a parent company of the principal debtor), and it imposes (even to an extent) autonomous liabilities, the presumption in *Marubeni Hong Kong and South China Ltd* referred to in the text is not likely to assist in determining the extent of the obligation undertaken and the latter should be decided by considering the words used free of any presumption: *Rubicon Vantage International Pte Ltd v Krisenenergy Ltd* [2019] EWHC 2012 (Comm) at [18].

47 *State Trading Corp of India Ltd v ED & F Man (Sugar) Ltd* [1981] Com. L.R. 235.

[48] *United Trading Corp SA v Allied Arab Bank Ltd* [1985] 2 Lloyd's Rep. 554; *TTI Team Telecom International Ltd v Hutchison 3G UK Ltd* [2003] EWHC 762, [2003] 1 All E.R. (Comm) 914 at [29] et seq.; *Korea Industry Co v Andoll* [1990] 2 Lloyd's Rep. 183, CA Sing. cf. *Themehelp Ltd v West* [1995] 3 W.L.R. 751 which concerned a claim by the principal debtor for an injunction to restrain the beneficiary of the bond from serving notice under the guarantee.

### Assignment by creditor of benefit of contract guaranteed

*To the end of paragraph, after "concerns the land".", add new footnote 72a:*

[72a] As "tenancy" is defined by the Landlord and Tenant (Covenants) Act 1995 s.28(1) as including an agreement for a tenancy, "assignment" (which is defined as including "equitable assignment") extends the Act's reach to an assignment which is not yet effective in law, such as a specifically enforceable agreement to assign or an unregistered or formally defective assignment: *Sackville UK Property Select II (GP) No.1 Ltd v Roberson Taylor Insurance Brokers Ltd* [2018] EWHC 122 (Ch), [2018] L. & T.R. 22 at [32], where it was, however, held that the party whose assignment had not been registered was not the "tenant" within the meaning of the lease (and so not able to exercise a contractual right of termination) as not being a "successor in title" of the assignor: [2018] EWHC 122 (Ch) at [33]–[34]. **45-014**

## 2. Formation of the Contract

## (b) Consideration

### General

*Replace footnote 117 with:*

[117] *Pau On v Lau Liu Long* [1980] A.C. 614, 629; *Longulf Trading (UK) Ltd v Niyazi Onen Gida Sanayi AS* [2019] EWHC 1573 (Comm) at [11]–[12] and see Vol.I, para.4-031. The passage in the text from "More difficulty" to the end was quoted with apparent approval by the court in *Longulf Trading (UK) Ltd v Niyazi Onen Gida Sanayi AS* [2019] EWHC 1573 (Comm) at [11]. **45-022**

## (c) Grounds of Vitiation of the Contract

### Non-disclosure

*Replace paragraph with:*

However, further light was cast on the creditor's duty of disclosure by *North Shore Ventures Ltd v Anstead Holdings Inc*,[197] where the Court of Appeal reviewed earlier authorities.[198] The court concluded that the instrument before it was: **45-038**

> "... not a contract uberrimae fidei but a loan guarantee. The authorities are clear that in such a case the duty of disclosure does not go further than the limit set by Lord Campbell in *Hamilton v Watson* and by Lord Scott of Foscote in *Royal Bank of Scotland Plc v Etridge (No. 2)*.[199] Accordingly there is no duty to disclose facts or matters which are not unusual features of the contractual relationship between the creditor and the debtor, or between the creditor and other creditors of the debtor."[200]

The Court of Appeal therefore held the contract of guarantee binding on the surety, even though the creditor had failed to disclose that the principal debtors were being investigated for embezzlement and that their bank accounts had been frozen as these were not "unusual features of the contractual relationship between the creditor and the debtor".[201] Although it was not therefore necessary for its decision, the Court of Appeal also expressed the view that where a duty of disclosure does arise the creditor is not absolved from it because he reasonably believes that the surety knows of it already: "[i]f the belief of the creditor turns out to be not well founded then ... he should suffer the consequences not the surety".[202] On the other hand, in *Deutsche Bank AG v Unitech Global Ltd* the Court of Appeal held that where the contract provided that the guarantor owed "an obligation to indemnify [the creditor] if any amount is not recoverable on the basis of a guarantee 'for any reason'", then these "wide words" would encompass irrecoverability by reason of non-disclosure and so allow recovery under this true indemnity provision.[202a] It has indeed been held that the limited duty of disclosure applicable to contracts of guarantee does not apply to contracts of indemnity.[202b]

[197] [2011] EWCA Civ 230, [2012] Ch. 31.

[198] Notably, *Hamilton v Watson* (1845) 12 Cl. & Fin. 109; *National Provincial Bank v Glanusk* [1913] 3 K.B. 335; *Smith v Bank of Scotland* 1997 S.C. (H.L.) 111, especially at 118; *London General Omnibus Company Ltd v Holloway* [1912] 1 K.B. 72; *Royal Bank of Scotland Plc v Etridge (No.2)* [2001] UKHL 44, [2002] 3 W.L.R. 102.

[199] [2001] UKHL 44 at [188], above, para.45-037.

[200] [2011] EWCA Civ 230 at [31], per Sir Andrew Morritt C. (with whom Smith L.J. agreed); *Deutsche Bank AG v Unitech Global Ltd* [2013] EWHC 2793 (Comm), [2014] 2 All E.R. (Comm) 268 at [47], [49]–[51] (affirmed on other grounds [2016] EWCA Civ 119, [2016] 1 W.L.R. 3598 though see at [19]); *Barclays Bank Plc v Borkhatria* [2018] EWHC 1326 (Comm) at [19]–[23]. In *Borkhatria*, it was said that while in principle the limited duty of disclosure does not continue after the execution of the guarantee, it is arguable that it revives in relation to variations of the guarantee and also in relation to requests to the guarantor to consent to variations to the contract between the creditor and debtor which would otherwise have discharged the guarantee: [2018] EWHC 1326 (Comm) at [32]–[37].

[201] [2011] EWCA Civ 230 at [32]. The CA did not express a view on the question whether a suitably drafted term of the guarantee could exclude the effect of an otherwise operative non-disclosure on the validity of the contract of guarantee: [2011] EWCA Civ 230.

[202] [2011] EWCA Civ 230 at [37], per Sir Andrew Morritt C.

[202a] [2016] EWCA Civ 119, [2016] 1 W.L.R. 3598 at [20] applied by *Barclays Bank Plc v Borkhatria* [2018] EWHC 1326 (Comm) at [41]–[46].

[202b] *GPP Big Field LLP v Solar EPC Solutions SL* [2018] EWHC 2866 (Comm) at [127]–[130], [143] and [148] (Richard Salter Q.C. sitting as a Deputy Judge of the HC) referring (at [128]) to "long-standing and authoritative dicta" in support of this view (*Duncan Fox & Co v North & South Wales Bank* (1880) 6 App. Cas. 1 at 10–11 (Lord Selbourne L.C.)), to *Deutsche Bank AG v Unitech Global Ltd* [2016] EWCA Civ 119 (which proceeded on the basis that the duty does not apply to contracts of indemnity), and considering that the limited duty of disclosure for guarantors is "in modern conditions ... anomalous and difficulty to justify". It was further held that any such a duty of disclosure had not been breached: [2018] EWHC 2866 (Comm) at [153] and [156].

## 3. FORMALITIES

### A question of construction

*Replace paragraph with:*

**45-046** According to Lord Diplock in *Moschi v Lep Air Services Ltd*, in distinguishing between guarantees and indemnities, "every case must depend upon the true construction of the actual words in which the promise is expressed".[237] However, it has been said that:

> "The fact that the parties have used the word 'guarantee' is not itself conclusive, but in doubtful cases it may provide some guide, especially if the word is repeated a number of times in the document ... Another guide is whether the creditor's rights against the principal debtor and against the guarantor, or indemnifier, are co-extensive. If the person liable under the contract may be liable for a greater amount than the principal debtor, the contract is probably one of indemnity."[238]

On the other hand, it has been held that the absence of usual provisions included in contracts of guarantee (for example, to permit variation of the obligations or giving of time without discharge of the surety) is "at best neutral" in construing a promise as a guarantee or an indemnity.[239] In common with the general position, this process of construction should bear in mind the factual matrix in which the words were used by the parties.[240]

[237] [1973] A.C. 331, 349. See also *Vossloh Aktiengesellschaft v Alpha Trains (UK) Ltd* [2010] EWHC 2443 (Ch), [2010] All E.R. (D) 86 (Oct) at [19]–[27]; *Multiplex Construction Europe Ltd v Dunne* [2017] EWHC 3073 (TCC), [2018] B.L.R. 36 at [40]–[42] (referring to the significance of the commercial purpose of the provision contained in a wider transaction); *GPP Big Field LLP v Solar EPC Solutions SL* [2018] EWHC 2866 (Comm) at [122]–[126]. In *Abbhi v Slade* [2019] EWCA Civ 2175, [2019] Costs L.R. 2039 at [44], it was observed that in determining whether a contract created a primary or a secondary liability, while the circumstances of the case and the terms of the contract are ones of fact, the question "whether or not a contract on those terms is or is not a contract of guarantee is an issue of legal classification and thus a question of law" (per Flaux L.J., with whom King and David Richards L.JJ. agreed).

[238] *Clement v Clement* (1996) 71 P. & C.R. D19, CA, per Warner J., quoted with approval by Peter Gibson L.J. in the CA. See also *Dennis v Revenue and Customs Commissioners* [2018] UKFTT 735 (TC), [2019] S.F.T.D. 593 at [31]–[34], [44]–[46], where a clause in a shareholders' agreement was held not to constitute a "guarantee" of a loan for the purposes of s.253(4) of the Taxation of Chargeable Gains Act 1992 on the ground that the principle of co-extensiveness was not satisfied, it being added that in the circumstances there was also no meaningful right of subrogation, this being a normal incident of a contract of guarantee).

[239] *Associated British Ports v Ferryways NV* [2008] EWHC 1265 (Comm), [2008] 2 Lloyd's Rep. 353 at [61], per Field J., quoted with approval by Maurice Kay L.J. (with whom Sir Anthony Clarke M.R. and Jacob L.J. agreed) [2009] EWCA Civ 189, [2009] 1 Lloyd's Rep. 595 at [12].

[240] *Clement v Clement*, above and see below, paras 45-064 et seq. and Vol.I, paras 13-041 et seq.

**Examples**

*Replace paragraph with:*

Given that s.4 applies only where there is some person other than the surety who is primarily liable, it does not apply where there has never been any party liable other than the defendant.[241] So, if A orders goods and instructs them to be delivered to B, and the intention of the parties is that A alone is to be liable for the price, this does not fall within the section.[242] This is not indeed a contract of suretyship at all but a mere contract for the sale of the goods to A. But if the intention of the parties is that the recipient of the goods is to be primarily liable, and the other party is only to be liable if the recipient does not pay, this is a contract of guarantee within the section.[243] Similarly, the section does not apply where there was originally another party liable to the creditor but his liability has been discharged. So if A agrees to pay B a debt owed to B by C, and B agrees to discharge C, this is a novation and not within the section.[244] A is not agreeing to meet C's liability, for that liability has gone; he is agreeing to meet a new liability which is his alone, and the section does not apply.[245] The same is true where C owes a debt to B and B agrees to discharge C in return for a new joint obligation undertaken by A and C together; A is not undertaking to answer for C's old debt (for that has gone) but for the new joint debt on which he is primarily liable.[246] It has also been held that a promise by A to B that A will pay to C a debt due from B to C is not within the section; if the promise were made by A to C it would be a promise to answer for the debt "of another", but where the promise is made to B himself, it is a promise to answer for the promisee's own debt and not for the debt "of another".[247] So also a promise by a principal debtor to indemnify another if he will act as surety for him is not within the section for the debtor is undertaking to answer for his own debt or default and not for that "of another".[248] A further example may be found in the situation where A agrees with C that he will put B in funds to pay B's liabilities to C, as in the case where A agrees to fund B's litigation costs to be incurred by C (B's solicitor) in circumstances where it was clear that B was not able to pay them himself.[248a] This contract was interpreted as an agreement by A to pay C for his legal services "in any event"[248b] 45-047 and independently of any default by B: A's liability was therefore primary rather than secondary and fell outside the statute.[248c] Moreover, quite apart from the use of words of indemnification, a clause according to which the promisor agrees to be "bound by any acknowledgment or admission by the [first debtor] and by any judgment" in favour of the creditor against the first debtor clearly indicates the imposition of a primary liability; and a "conclusive evidence" provision in the same clause demonstrates that the liability of the promisor is not dependent upon any conclusive determination of the first debtor's liability to the creditor, and this provides "a compelling indication that the [promisor's] liability under the deed of indemnity is primary rather than secondary".[249] Finally, there may be a third possibility beyond the distinction between a guarantee and an indemnity, that is, that an alleged guarantor or surety has not taken on any personal obligation (primary or secondary) but has merely acted as an agent for a third party primarily liable, by doing no more than, for example, communicating what that third party is itself to do to satisfy the primary liability, as in the case where a company director says that he will see to it that the company performs a given task, which is not necessarily to be construed as that director taking any obligation on himself personally.[250]

241 *Lakeman v Mountstephen* (1874) L.R. 7 H.L. 17.

242 *Birkmyr v Darnell* (1705) 1 Salk. 27.

243 *Simpson v Penton* (1834) 2 Cr. & M. 430.

244 As to novation, see Vol.I, para.19-087.

245 *Goodman v Chase* (1818) 1 B. & Ald. 297; *Butcher v Steuart* (1843) 11 M. & W. 857.

246 *Ex p. Lane* (1846) 1 De G. 300.

247 *Eastwood v Kenyon* (1840) 11 A. & E. 438; *Guild & Co v Conrad* [1894] 2 Q.B. 885, discussed and followed by *Abbhi v Slade* [2019] EWCA Civ 2175, [2019] Costs L.R. 2039 at [44]–[49].

248 *Thomas v Cook* (1828) 8 B. & C. 728.

248a *Abbhi v Slade* [2019] EWCA Civ 2175, [2019] Costs L.R. 2039 at [45].

248b [2019] EWCA Civ 2175 at [46]. The CA later noted that, under the oral agreement, A's obligation to put B in funds arose *before* any liability in B arose to C and was therefore not coterminous with B's: at [50]. On the rule of construction that prima facie a surety's obligations are co-extensive with those of the principal debtor, see below, para.45-070.

248c [2019] EWCA Civ 2175 at [49], applying the analysis of the CA in *Guild & Co v Conrad* [1894] 2 Q.B. 885. The CA considered that it made no difference that A's obligation was to put B in funds to pay C rather than to pay C directly: at [50].

249 *ABM AMRO Commercial Finance Plc v McGinn* [2014] EWHC 1674 (Comm), [2014] 2 Lloyd's Rep. 333 at [36], per Flaux J., followed by *Catalyst Business Finance Ltd v Very Tangy Television Ltd* [2018] EWHC 1669 (QB) at [41]–[47].

250 *MyBarrister Ltd v Hewetson* [2017] EWHC 2624 (Ch), [2018] Bus. L.R. 752 at [62]–[63].

## Note or memorandum

*Replace paragraph with:*

**45-055** In order to satisfy the Statute the document which is relied on as a note or memorandum of the agreement must itself acknowledge or recognise the existence of a contract and this cannot be the case where it is expressed as "subject to contract".[272] It must also contain a statement of its material terms.[273] On the other hand, it has been held that:

> "... where ... there is an offer in writing made by the party to be bound which contains the essential terms of what is offered *and* the party to be bound accepts that his offer has been accepted unconditionally, albeit orally, there is a sufficient note or memorandum to satisfy section 4."[274]

It is sometimes possible for two documents to be read together so as to find a note or memorandum satisfying the section, but in order for this to be done it is necessary that the document containing the defendant's signature should contain some reference, express or implied, to the other document which it is sought to read with the first[275]; and any memorandum or note "must not only state the terms of the contract but also contain an acknowledgment or recognition by the signatory to the document that a contract had been entered into".[275a]

[272] *Carlton Communications Plc v Football League* [2002] EWHC 1650 at [78] applying *Tiverton Ltd v Wearwell Ltd* [1975] Ch. 146 (Law of Property Act 1925 s.40); *Motemtronic Ltd v Autocar Equipment Ltd* Unreported June 20, 1996, CA, transcript No.656 of 1996, per Aldous L.J.; *Fairstate Ltd v General Enterprise & Management Ltd* [2010] EWHC 3072 (QB), [2010] All E.R. (D) 301 (Nov) at [58] and [88] (identification of principal debtor and duration of guarantee both material).

[273] [2002] EWHC 1650 at [79] and cf. above, para.45-052 (note) referring to the possibility of permitting a claimant to waive a material term omitted from a memorandum where it is solely for his benefit and not of a major importance.

[274] *J Pereira Fernandes SA v Mehta* [2006] EWHC 813 (Ch) at [16], [2006] 2 All E.R. 881, per Judge Pelling Q.C.

[275] *Timmins v Morland Street Property Ltd* [1958] Ch. 110 (a case on s.40 of the Law of Property Act 1925); *Golden Ocean Group Ltd v Salgaocar Mining Industries Pvt Ltd* [2012] EWCA Civ 265, [2012] Lloyd's Rep. 542 at [24].

[275a] *Golden Ocean Group Ltd v Salgaocar Mining Industries Pvt Ltd* [2012] EWCA Civ 265 at [24] per Tomlinson L.J., so interpreting *Timmins v Morland Street Property Ltd* [1958] Ch. 110 at 116; *Slade v Abbhi* [2018] EWHC 2039 (Comm) at [110]–[112]; affirmed on other grounds sub nom. *Abbhi v Slade* [2019] EWCA Civ 2175, [2019] Costs L.R. 2039.

*Replace footnote 277 with:*

**Signature to agreement or memorandum**[277]

[277] cf. the position under s.2 of the Law of Property (Miscellaneous Provisions) Act 1989, on which see Vol.I, paras 5-037–5-037D. **45-057**

*Replace paragraph with:*

The note or memorandum of the guarantee must be "signed by the party to be charged" or by his agent.[278] It is not necessary that it should be signed by the other party to the transaction.[279] Nor for this purpose need it be a "signature" in the popular sense for it suffices if the defendant's name is written or printed by himself or even by an agent[280]; and it may appear anywhere in the document so long as it is intended to authenticate the whole document.[281] Where the defendant wrote and signed a guarantee which contained a mistake, and on the mistake being discovered, he wrote a memorandum across the original guarantee correcting the mistake, but did not sign it afresh, it was held that his original signature was a signature of the whole and satisfied the section.[282] And where the director of a company agreed orally to guarantee the company's liabilities and signed a contract on behalf of the company, but omitted to sign a guarantee form in the same document, it being orally agreed that his one signature should be sufficient to deal also with his personal capacity, it was held that the requirements of the statute had been satisfied.[283] Moreover, as has been indicated, where an agent has orally agreed to a personal guarantee, but signs a document which includes such a guarantee only on behalf of his principal, he is bound personally: "[t]he question is not what is the intention of the person signing the memorandum, but is one of fact, viz is there a note or memorandum of the promise signed by the party to be charged?".[284] On the other hand, it has been held that where an alleged guarantee was contained in an email sent with the would-be guarantor's authority, the automatic insertion of an email address in the message by an internet service provider did not constitute a signature **45-057** by its writer within the meaning of s.4 as it did not represent any intention to authenticate the message by the writer.[285] However, the court accepted that:

> "... if a party or a party's agent sending an e-mail types his or her or his or her principal's name to the extent required or permitted by existing case law in the body of an e-mail, then ... that would be sufficient signature of the purposes of section 4 [of the Statute of Frauds]."[286]

[278] Where the original signed guarantee document cannot be found, signature may be established by other evidence: *Bank of Scotland v Mazamal Hussain* [2011] EWHC 1934 (QB) at [42]–[44]; *Mitsui OSK Lines Ltd v Salgaocar Mining Ltd* [2015] EWHC 565 (Comm) at [41].

[279] *Laythoarp v Bryant* (1836) 2 Bing. N.C. 735.

[280] *Leeman v Stocks* [1951] Ch. 941. And see Vol.I, para.5-008 on the status of "electronic signatures" for this purpose.

[281] *Caton v Caton* (1867) L.R. 2 H.L. 127.

[282] *Bluck v Gompertz* (1852) 7 Ex. 862.

[283] *VSH Ltd v BKS Air Transport Ltd* [1964] 1 Lloyd's Rep. 460.

[284] *Re Hoyle* [1893] 1 Ch. 84, 100, per Smith L.J., quoted with approval by Lord Brandon in *Elpis Maritime Co Ltd v Marti Chartering Co Ltd (The Maria D)* [1992] 1 A.C. 21 at 32–33; *Golden Ocean Group Ltd v Salgaocar Mining Industries Pvt Ltd* [2012] EWCA Civ 265, [2012] 1 Lloyd's Rep. 542 at [37].

[285] *J Pereira Fernandes SA v Mehta* [2006] EWHC 813 (Ch), [2006] 2 All E.R. 881 at [25]–[30], per Judge Pelling Q.C.

[286] *J Pereira Fernandes SA v Mehta*, above, at [31]. See also *WS Tankship II BV v Kwangju Bank Ltd* [2011] EWHC 3103 (Comm), [2012] C.I.L.L. 3155 at [155] (bank causing its name to appear in header of "SWIFT message" is sufficient signature). It was common ground before (and accepted by) the CA that an electronic signature is sufficient and that a first name, initials or perhaps a nickname will suffice, as long as it was done in a manner which indicates that it is intended to authenticate the document: *Golden Ocean Group Ltd v Salgaocar Mining Industries Pvt Ltd* [2012] EWCA Civ 265, [2012] 1 Lloyd's Rep. 542 at [32]. These cases are discussed by the Law Commission, *Electronic execution of documents*, Consultation Paper No.237 (August 21, 2018) paras 3.59–370 and see also Law Commission, *Electronic execution of documents*, Law Com. No.386 (September 3, 2019), paras 3.25–3.26.

## 4. CONSTRUCTION OF THE CONTRACT

### Liability under a guarantee and entitlement to petition in bankruptcy

*Replace footnote 376 with:*

**45-073** [376] [2011] EWCA Civ 1286 at [67]. Cf. *Davies v Revelan Estates (Wigston) Ltd* [2019] EWHC 1766 (Ch), [2019] B.P.I.R. 1102 at [22]–[24] where the contract was held to be one of indemnity giving rise to a claim only in damages and therefore for an unliquidated sum.

### Conditions precedent to liability of surety

*Replace footnote 414 with:*

**45-081** [414] *Re Brown's Estate* [1893] 2 Ch. 300; *Bradford Old Bank Ltd v Sutcliffe* [1918] 2 K.B. 833; *Bank of Adelaide v Lorden* (1970) 127 C.L.R. 185; *General Surety & Guarantee Co Ltd v Francis Parker Ltd* (1977) 6 Build. L.R. 18; *Duchess Theatre Co v Lord* [1993] N.P.C. 163; *Hampton v Minns* [2002] 1 W.L.R. 1; *Barclays Bank Plc v Price* [2018] EWHC 2719 (Comm) at [20]. Where the surety's obligation is primary rather than secondary (as with a true guarantee), a requirement of payment on demand will not import a contingency, so that the cause of action accrues when the debt falls due rather than only on demand, but this does not apply where payment is promised within a period after demand: *Re Brown's Estate* [1893] 2 Ch. 300; *M & S Fashions Ltd v Bank of Credit and Commerce International SA* [1993] Ch. 425, 435–436, 447; *Levin v Tannenbaum* [2013] EWHC 4457 (Ch) at [25]–[37].

## 6. DISCHARGE OF SURETY

### (c) Discharge of Surety through Variation of Contract between Debtor and Creditor

#### Binding agreement

*Replace footnote 544 with:*

544 *Overend Gurney & Co Ltd v Oriental Financial Corp Ltd* (1874) L.R. 7 H.L. 348. Cf. *GPP Big Field LLP v Solar EPC Solutions SL* [2018] EWHC 2866 (Comm) at [165]–[166]. **45-108**

#### Agreement to allow variation or giving of time

*Replace footnote 558 with:*

558 [2005] EWCA Civ 630 at [14]; applied in *Maxted v Investic Bank Plc* [2017] EWHC 1997 (Ch) at [16]–[19]. See further Salter (2017) 8 J.I.B.F.L. 459. See also *Wittmann (UK) Ltd v Willdav Engineering SA* [2007] EWCA Civ 824, [2007] B.L.R. 509 at [20]–[22], where it was also said that any consent to the variation made by the surety must be communicated to the creditor: [2007] EWCA Civ 824 at [27] (Moore-Bick L.J.) and see *GPP Big Field LLP v Solar EPC Solutions SL* [2018] EWHC 2866 (Comm) at [173]. **45-112**

*Add new paragraph:*

**Contracts of indemnity** In *GPP Big Field LLP v Solar EPC Solutions SL* it was held, if obiter,[562a] by the High Court that the "overwhelming preponderance of view" in the cases and textbooks cited to it is that the rule in *Holme v Brunskill*[562b] applies only to true contracts of guarantee and does not apply to contracts of indemnity.[562c] There are, in the view of the High Court, "sound reasons of policy" to support this conclusion and for not extending the rule beyond the situations established by authority.[562d] The rule **45-112A**

> "unduly favours the guarantor, in that it discharges the guarantor completely upon the occurrence of any variation which is not 'obviously insubstantial' or clearly for the benefit of the guarantor.[562e] It represents a trap for the unwary creditor. Yet it is plainly not regarded as a fundamental right of the guarantor, since the law (subject to any relevant statutory control of unfair terms) permits the creditor to contract out of it by the terms of the guarantee."[562f]

Not extending the rule in *Holme v Brunskill* to contracts of indemnity properly so-called, "therefore promotes legal certainty".[562g]

562a The HC also held that there was no agreement to vary the contract between the principal debtor and the creditor on the facts: *GPP Big Field LLP v Solar EPC Solutions SL* [2018] EWHC 2866 (Comm) at [169]–[170].

562b (1878) 3 Q.B.D. 495 at 505 and see above, para.45-105.

562c *GPP Big Field LLP v Solar EPC Solutions SL* [2018] EWHC 2866 (Comm) at [131]–[142], [145]–[147] esp. at [145] referring to O'Donovan and Phillips, *The Modern Contract of Guarantee*, 3rd English edn by Courtney and Phillips (2016) para.7-070 (which considers the position not clearly settled), and relying in particular on dicta in *Associated British Ports v Ferryways NV* [2009] EWCA Civ 189, [2009] 1 Lloyd's Rep. 595 at [1], *Vossloh Aktiengesellschaft v Alpha Trains (UK) Ltd* [2010] EWHC 2443 (Ch), [2010] All E.R. (D) 86 (Oct) at [26], [27] and *ABM AMRO Commercial Finance Plc v McGinn* [2014] EWHC 1674 (Comm), [2014] 2 Lloyd's Rep. 333 at [37]. See also *The Law of Guarantees*, 7th edn (2015), para.9-025 stating that "the rule in *Holme v Brunskill* applies to guarantees properly so called, and not to demand guarantees, which impose autonomous liability on the guarantor which is independent of the underlying contract" and referring to *WS Tankship II BV v Kwangju Bank Ltd* [2011] EWHC 3103 (Comm), [2012] C.I.L.L. 3155 at [143] and [144].

562d *GPP Big Field LLP v Solar EPC Solutions SL* [2018] EWHC 2866 (Comm) at [146].

[562e] See above, para.45-104.

[562f] [2018] EWHC 2866 (Comm) at [147], per Richard Salter Q.C. sitting as a Deputy Judge of the HC.

[562g] [2018] EWHC 2866 (Comm) at [147], per Richard Salter Q.C.

## (d) Discharge of Surety on Other Grounds

### Neglect of creditor in relation to securities

*Replace footnote 596 with:*

45-120 [596] *The Mutual Loan Association v Sudlow* (1858) 5 C.B.(N.S.) 449; *Strange v Fooks* (1863) 4 Giff. 408; *Wulff v Jay* (1872) L.R. 7 Q.B. 756; *General Mediterranean Holding SA SPF v Qucomhaps Holdings Ltd* [2018] EWCA Civ 2416 at [18]–[26].

### Creditor free to decide whether to realise security

*Replace footnote 608 with:*

45-121 [608] *China and South Sea Bank Ltd v Tan Soon Gin* [1990] 1 A.C. 536, 545 and see *White v Davenham Trust Ltd* [2011] EWCA Civ 747, [2011] Bus. L.R. 1443 at [38]; *Close Brothers Ltd v AIS (Marine) 2 Ltd* [2019] 1 Lloyd's Rep. 510 at [12].

### Implied term

*Replace footnote 619 with:*

45-122 [619] On the general approach to the implication of terms, see Vol.I, Ch.14. See also *General Mediterranean Holding SA.SPF (aka General Mediterranean Holding SA) v Qucomhaps Holdings Ltd* [2017] EWHC 1409 (QB) (no implied term in principal contract that creditor should take a particular step in foreign court proceedings to protect security) (the CA's decision was concerned only with allegations of breach of duties in equity rather than on the basis of breach of implied terms: *General Mediterranean Holding SA SPF v Qucomhaps Holdings Ltd* [2018] EWCA Civ 2416 at [16]).

### Statutory demands under Insolvency Act against guarantor

*Replace footnote 626 with:*

45-123 [626] [2011] EWCA Civ 747, [2011] Bus. L.R. 1443; applied in *Inbakumar v United Trust Bank Ltd* [2012] EWHC 845 (Ch), [2012] B.P.I.R. 758. In *Promontoria (Chestnut) Ltd v Bell* [2019] EWHC 1581 (Ch) esp. at [40]–[50], it was held that security provided by guarantors for the indebtedness of a principal debtor is "security" within the meaning of r.6.5(4)(c) for the purposes of statutory demands against those guarantors themselves.

## 8. LEGISLATIVE PROTECTION OF SURETIES

## (c) Unfair Contract Terms Act 1977

### Exclusion of surety's rights to be discharged

*Replace footnote 791 with:*

45-154 [791] Unfair Contract Terms Act 1977 s.3(1). It would appear that if such a clause failed the reasonableness test, it could nevertheless still be effective to prevent the surety from being discharged from his liability, as the effect of s.3 is to prevent the creditor from "excluding or restricting any liability of his in respect of breach … except in so far as … the contract term satisfies the requirement of reasonableness". cf. Peel (ed.), *Treitel on The Law of Contract*, 15th edn (2020), para.7-069.

## (d) Unfair Terms in Consumer Contracts

### Application of these controls to contracts of suretyship

*In line 4, after "no definitive answer until" replace "the recent Order of the Court of Justice of the EU" with:*

the Order of the Court of Justice of the EU **45-156**